DRAMA AND PERFORMANCE
An Anthology

Gary Vena
Manhattan College

Andrea Nouryeh
St. Lawrence University

HarperCollinsCollegePublishers

DEDICATION

For Terrence, Anita, and our theatre students.

Cover Photo: Chekhov's ''The Seagull,'' directed by Tsunetoshi Hirowatari, of the Tokyo Engeki Ensemble. Photograph by Shin Takaiwa. Courtesy of Tokyo Engeki Ensemble and photographer.

Acquisitions Editor: Lisa Moore
Manufacturing Manager: Willie Lane

For permission to use copyrighted material, grateful acknowledgment is made to the copyright holders on p. 1204, which are hereby made part of this copyright page.

Drama & Performance

Library of Congress Cataloging-in-Publication Data

Drama and performance : an anthology / [edited by] Gary Vena & Andrea
    Nouryeh,
        p. cm.

    Inclues bibliographical references and index.
    ISBN 0–673–98201–7 (alk. paper)
    1. Drama—Collections.   I. Vena, Gary, 1942– .   II. Nouryeh,
    Andrea.
    PN6112.D69   1995
    808.82–dc20
                                                                                95–45334
                                                                                CIP

95 96 97 98 9 8 7 6 5 4 3 2 1

CONTENTS

PREFACE

"Life can only be understood backwards, but it must be lived forwards," wrote Søren Kierkegaard. His words tell us something about time's ironic courtship with human destiny. Traditionally, the fields of theatre history and dramatic literature have reflected this linear progression, which has enabled us to study each period or style as a response to or reaction against the conventions or styles that have preceded it. Our anthology is arranged accordingly. The plays, presented in the order of their initial stage productions, invite thoughtful comparisons with those of their own time and place or with others created before or after in the span of more than two thousand years.

While our approach is linear, the plays need not be read in chronological order. Viewed as a blueprint for performance, each assesses human conflicts by portraying the encounters of characters who represent ideas, supernatural forces, legendary heroes, and living beings from every class of society. Viewed as literature, each play displays a similar concern for structure, language, and meaning.

But why *Drama and Performance?* Why not "drama *as* performance" or "drama *in* performance?" The reasons are clear. First we have approached the dramatic script as a work of literary art whose structure differs considerably from other genres and must be evaluated accordingly. Next we have paid homage to the strength of that work *in performance,* even if its production history has been problematical. Thus we emphasize the indelible relationship between the shelf life of any serious work and its rightful place on the stage. The playwright's achievement in each of these works remains as vital on the printed page as it does in performance. Václav Havel pays tribute to this dynamism in his March 27, 1994, message for World Theatre Day, by claiming that "theatre is better suited than any other medium to reveal, in genuinely compelling and challenging ways, not only the dark forces that are dragging the world down, but also everything bright and luminous, in which its hopes are contained."

Any play, no matter how effectively it resonates on the printed page, must stretch beyond its literary boundaries to achieve its fullest dimension in live performance. Unlike other works of fiction whose rich rewards can be privately shared with the reader, drama demands the collaboration of numerous agents. Often guided by a stage director, with the assistance of set, lighting, and costume designers, the story comes to life. The aims of drama, however, are best served in a communal or public setting in which the audience deciphers the text through the wide assortment of verbal and nonverbal clues provided through the actors' interpretation of their roles. Perhaps this remarkable transformation from script to spectacle prompted Sam Shepard to remark, "I always liked the idea that plays happened in three dimensions, that here was something that came to life in space."

Each drama in this anthology represents a distinct historical period, dramatic style, or artistic movement; each ennobles the expanding story of humankind; and each weaves a thematic tapestry of other times, places, and people in whom we recognize ourselves. While these plays—both full-length and one-act—must finally speak for themselves, the reception of each is guided by a carefully focused preface that (1) assesses the play and playwright within a specific historical, political, or social context; (2) highlights the play against the author's wider contribution to world drama; (3) synopsizes the story of the play; (4) analyzes structure and language; and (5) discusses performance history. Following each play, we have also provided a guide for critical reading by means of study questions and recommendations of additional readings and video materials of the plays in performance to enhance our knowledge and appreciation. Unless otherwise cited, quoted lines contained in each preface are extracted from the corresponding play.

Another dimension of this text will also enlighten our readers: the inclusion of an accompanying reflection on the play—often the words of artists who have been directly associated with these works in performance—to provide a firsthand point of view. Although their words are the result of extensive interviewing, the question/answer format has been eliminated to give their responses an uninterrupted flow. In other cases, carefully chosen theatre reviews and photographs provide important documentation that should prove equally helpful. For the reader's convenience, we have boldfaced unfamiliar terms throughout the text; definitions of these terms can be found in the glossary.

INTRODUCTION

Drama holds a unique place in the world of literature. Derived from Greek and Latin words that stress "doing" or "performing," drama is meant to be more than language on a page. Although plays tell stories like novels and other works of fiction, an altogether different process takes place using stage directions and dialogue to describe the environment or the characters who inhabit it. Even when theatrical conventions have called for an empty stage, as was the case in the Elizabethan drama, the words of the characters painted pictures for the audience. The plays of Shakespeare, like poetry, were meant to be heard more than seen. This is the reason Hamlet suggests that he will "hear a play tomorrow," confirming that it is the language which is primary. But Hamlet also knows that hearing the play is not enough. It will be the impact of the words accompanied by the dumb show that will "catch the conscience of the King." Throughout Western drama, successful playwrights have always known that their words needed to be enacted as well as spoken in order for the story to come alive. The dialogue, the stage directions, and the cast lists are intended to serve live performances. So while other literary works reach their potential as works of art in the act of reading, either silently or aloud, dramas seem incomplete without the spectacle of production.

To comprehend the world of the play, we must acknowledge this relationship between the printed page and the theatrical event. Why, then, should one read dramatic literature at all? We recognize the importance of witnessing firsthand the duality of a playtext as a work of literature *and* as the "score" for a production, yet plays in live performance are often inaccessible. Although we can appreciate dramatic scripts in film or video productions, few plays are ever recorded. Those that are, often undergo significant alteration to serve the medium. Our encounter with the world's dramatic literature, therefore, is through the script, as we discover for ourselves what twentieth-century director/set designer Robert Edmond Jones meant when he wrote that "the loveliest and most poignant of all stage pictures are those that are seen in the mind's eye."

How do we prepare ourselves to read plays and derive the insights and pleasures they offer us? Considerably more is demanded of our imaginations than in most other forms of literature. We must see and understand what is explicitly said and done, as well as be alerted to what is implied and left unspoken. We need to be able to determine where the action is taking place, which characters are present even if they are not speaking, and what is happening from moment to moment. We must become familiar with how dramatic scripts work in setting the stage, developing the characters, and advancing the story. In essence, our role as readers is two-sided: that of spectator and director, capable of visualizing the play as if we were witnessing it or creating it on stage. Understanding the components of the drama makes this task less daunting.

From the very outset, the dramatist gives us clues about the world of the play. The title is often a key. The initial stage directions or a character's first words set the scene. Perhaps a cast list prompts our curiosity about who is going to be important. These primary ingredients set the play into motion. As the story takes shape, characters interacting in space hold our attention moment by moment. Certain characters may know less than we do because they have been offstage, while others, although silent, may have witnessed or heard the same scene as we have. Stage directions help us determine who is entering or leaving the action. Awareness of who is onstage and who is not will give us insight into how the scene will affect the characters' attitudes or responses later in the play.

Most plays move forward through the resolution of **conflicts** that develop between characters. These conflicts create tension and become the catalysts for further physical or psychological action. Often characters' speech patterns and points of view, other characters' responses to them, and descriptions about them before they arrive on the scene predispose us to empathize with them or judge them harshly. Intrigued with what motivates their behavior, we anticipate how their conflicts will be resolved. Our investment in the outcome and the release of tension that may result ensures that we remain caught up in the story.

Playwrights usually create three-dimensional characters who are distinct individuals and seem to represent people who react to the outside world as we do. Whether they stand at the center of the drama—the **protagonist** (the hero) or **antagonist** (his or her opponent)—or whether they stand at the periphery or somewhere in between, we get to know them as if we were meeting them for the first time. We notice their physical characteristics as well as their manner of speech. We notice their social characteristics and listen for their moral convictions and values. Regardless of what they say, the explosive articulation of one character is no less eloquent or revealing than the well-timed silences of another. As in real life, however, we are best able to assess them by observing their actions: what they do when faced with dilemmas is just as relevant as what they say.

Although we will be moved to draw conclusions about such characters in relation to our own choices and behaviors, we must avoid psychoanalyzing them as if they were real people. In spite of their three-dimensionality, most characters are created to serve particular functions in the story and elicit either our sympathy or disdain. In addition to the protagonist and the antagonist around whom the narrative centers, there is often a **confidant(e)** who listens to the principal characters and advises them, a **raisonneur** who articulates the playwright's point of view, and a **foil** who, by exhibiting contrasting personality traits, may be used to set off another character who is in similar circumstances. In fact, the playwright may create characters who are **stereotypes** or may represent ideas. They usually conform to our expectations and are easily recognizable since they take on the physical and personality traits that we usually associate with that type. These characters are two-dimensional or flat, having more in common with cartoon figures than real people. Their interactions take on the flavor of a contest of ideas rather than of a conflict between people.

No matter what kinds of characters are introduced to us, questions will arise. What do these characters want? Why do they want it? Does anything stand in their way? What is their plan of action? How far are they willing to go to get what they want? The internal and external struggles facing them are the basic building blocks of the dramatic story.

Drama is revealed in time. When the action employs *real* or clock time, it continues without interruption for the same one- or two-hour period required for the play to be completed. Most plays use *psychological* time, however, telescoping actions that would take hours, days, or even years. They depict the crucial or pivotal moments from the characters' lives to represent their journeys toward selfhood. How these stories unfold (the format) is determined by their **plot** structures.

Plays that adhere to a beginning-middle-end design are linear and usually center on one character. The time needed for the protagonist to attain what he or she wants or come to some realization about the foolhardiness of this pursuit is broken up into consecutive units of stage time, usually **scenes,** which mirror the multiple places or obstacles that the character encounters along the way. One or more scenes may comprise an **act,** while there may be anywhere from two to five acts in a full-length play. In some plays, there are several lines of development: various **subplots** that focus on minor characters serve as commentaries or **analogous actions** to the main plot, which revolves around the protagonist.

Exposition establishes the background or circumstances in which we encounter our characters. We learn rather quickly about the setting in terms of historical time and social conditions, the place of action, and the occasion that has brought them together. A **prologue** serves this purpose in *The Trojan Women* and *Doctor Faustus*. In *The Sea Gull* and *Ghosts,* a character returns after a long absence and asks questions. An opening conversation reveals pertinent information about the world of the play prior to the action in *Phèdre* and *Life Is a Dream*. Then something happens to change things and set the story into motion, what is known as the *point of attack*.

While the protagonist moves to achieve his or her objective, complications mount as conflicts remain unresolved. An unexpected event or an intruder becomes the catalyst for change, and struggle inevitably ensues. This clash of wills results from the need to return an unbalanced world to equilibrium. The tensions that arise from this turmoil fill out the play's center and arouse our interest as we anticipate solutions. The action culminates in a crisis, or turning point, that forces the protagonist to make a decision. In the final moments, the **denouement,** we feel the impact of this choice and witness some restoration of order, whether tragic or comic, to the world of the play.

This model does not illustrate the nonlinear structures of many plays written in the twentieth century. Some of these may be episodic, in which scenes are connected formally rather than determined by the ones that precede them; some may be structured thematically, that is, scenes are held together by a common idea; some may be circular, in which the ongoing action takes us back to the beginning. There is no cause-and-effect relationship in the action and often no resolution. Instead, the events of the play are ordered by the exploration of an idea, an exploration of characters or the situation in which they find themselves. The focal point is the ensemble rather than the protagonist. *Play, Double Gothic,* and *Still Life* are representative.

Narratives are not always apparent in plays with nonlinear plots. As the opposing points of view of the characters are revealed, as formal patterns in the dialogue and the actions are perceived, as the connections between characters emerge, we are inclined to construct our personal version of the story. In spite of the fact that no clear storyline exists, these plays engage us no less than traditional ones by creating tension that needs to find release.

Our comprehension of what the play is about (the content) usually grows from the outcome of the action and its consequences for the characters. Its **themes** are often implied, derived from the characters' relationships, discourse, and behaviors rather than explicitly stated. In Greek drama, for example, the **chorus** comments on the action to enlighten the audience about fate and the nature of the human condition. In medieval drama, the use of symbols and **allegory** offer lessons for living righteously. Throughout plays from the Renaissance, stage characters express their struggles with forces beyond their control. Their **monologues** and **soliloquies** call attention to our own limitations as human beings. In the move toward realism, drama has tackled every conceivable social, political, and psychological thread in the fabric of our lives. Its themes have even explored ''the art of making art,'' as Stephen Sondheim has described it.

Language in the form of dialogue nourishes the playwright's craft. The spoken lines illuminate the characters' motives and behaviors. Vocabulary, dialectical patterns, and colloquialisms easily establish social status. Rhythms of speech determined by the interplay of articulation and pause reveal personality and convey the rational thoughts and irrational emotions of the speakers. These displays of language elucidate the alliances and conflicts depicted on stage. Whether verse or prose, words control character development and themes.

With an awareness of all the elements that make up drama, the playreader is now prepared to assume the role of spectator. Try to read the play in one sitting, letting it unfold on a stage in your mind's eye from start to finish. Try to visualize the characters as performers on this stage in order to experience the play as if you were attending a live performance. Since you cannot integrate all the components of the play on the first reading, return to selected passages, this time reading them aloud to hear the words and discover the nuances of stage language, specifically how the characters react to each other. An advantage to reading the plays with others is that you will experience the drama as part of a shared, public, and communal event.

In your role as director of this imaginary performance, you can interact with the script in a variety of ways: you are free to read back and forth across the storyline, to follow a single character through the action, to take the time to ponder specific lines and speeches, and to immerse yourself in the different interpretations available to you. Once you are prepared to analyze themes, character development, conflict and resolutions, and language, you will also be equipped to fashion your own production out of the script. It is your choice to determine what the play will look like and what themes will be emphasized.

As long as your choices are rooted in the playwright's words, the options are endless. You might design a realistic **set** with appropriate furniture and doors or construct an environment with platforms and scaffolds. Your next challenge is to **block** the actions of characters as they speak their lines. Sensitive to the attitudes that color their words and elicit replies, you will be able to hear exactly how you would want these lines to be spoken. Once you have sorted out these elements, your most challenging task involves the artistic arrangement of these components, as they emerge in your playreading imagination, into an integrated stage picture.

The final aspect of your directorial assignment is to acquaint yourself with the theatrical conventions of the time in which the play was written and to investigate the historical and cultural contexts to which the playwright was responding. This will enable you to envision the elements of the stage picture that the playwright had in mind. You will also understand how the play's ideas reflected on the society in which the playwright lived. Such knowledge will allow you to grapple with themes and characters removed from their original contexts and used to comment on the contemporary world. Furthermore, your appreciation of theatrical productions from other countries or those that stray from the playwright's time period to address a contemporary audience will be greatly enriched.

As you read the works in this anthology, we hope that you will be challenged as well as entertained. We believe that the literature of the drama is vital. More than stories told through dialogue and stage directions, plays are records of moments in history. They vividly capture how people have thought and acted throughout the world for over two thousand years. We share Shakespeare's belief that theatre is a metaphor for life, that ''all the world's a stage, and all the men and women merely players.'' It is our conviction, therefore, that these plays will not only present you with insight into eras and places that are unfamiliar to you but, more importantly, they will lead you to make new discoveries about yourselves.

ACKNOWLEDGMENTS

We extend our heartfelt thanks to artists who granted us interviews and whose experiences have personally enlightened the performance dimensions of this anthology: Claude Beauclair, Joyce Ebert, Eldon Elder, George Ferencz, Crystal Field, Rolf Fjelde, Wynn Handman, Tsunetoshi Hirowatari, Michael Kahn, Woo Ok Kim, Barry Kyle, Paula Laurence, Abbey Lincoln, Barbara Martinez-Jittner, Elizabeth McGovern, Timothy Near, Edward Parone, Carey Perloff, Stephen Porter, John Rubinstein, Madeleine Sherwood, David Warrilow, and Jiri Zizka.

No less thankful are we to those who helped us acquire their work: Linda Asher, Lionel Casson, Frank Chin, Edwin Honig, Tina Howe, Donald Keene, Walter Kerr, Michael Kirby, Emily Mann, William Packard, Henry Salerno, and Luis Valdez.

We acknowledge the valuable suggestions made by John Scarry during the early stages of this work, and we are deeply indebted to Louis Rachow whose warm and generous assistance never wavered.

Contributors appeared at every turn and their help is gratefully recognized: Katlin Bencsath, Br. Francis Bowers, F. S. C., Jarka Burian, Thomas Butson, Debbie Briley, Jean Chothia, Patrick Dawson, Sr. Gloria Degnan, S. C., Phillip Esparza, Linda Faigao-Hall, Deborah Fehr, Br. Thomas Ferguson, F. S. C., Christopher Fitz-Simon, Donald Fowle, Andres Gutierrez, Lynn Hall, James V. Hatch, Nancy Hereford, Holly Hill, Mariko Hori, Barbara Jeppesen, Denis Johnston, Joanne Klein, Robert Kramer, Marlo LaCorte, Giorgos Lazanis, Samuel Leiter, Theodore Mann, Don Marinelli, Susan McCosker, Jennifer McMaster, Claudia Menza, Kati Mitchell, Phyllis Moberley, Françoise Mojeret, Lucinda Morrison, Mary Ann O'Donnell, Frances Oliver, Tom Olsson, Carole Puccino, Elizabeth Ramirez, Gus Santisteban, Nicola Scadding, David Schaff, Sawaka Shiga, Sidney Sondergard, Donald Tanguay, Candice Turner-Smith, Patricia Taylor, Nevart Wanger, and Donald and Janet Waters.

We are also thankful for the suggestions made by reviewers of this text throughout various stages of development: Judith Barlow, State University of New York at Albany; Gilbert Bloom, Ball State University; Roger Ellis, Grand Valley State University; and Robert Hansen, University of North Carolina at Greensboro.

Finally, we thank our family and friends who were always there to listen and encourage us: Sheila Beritz, Pamela Cavallo, Barbara Eberhardt, Annette Fiechter, John Frick, Tom Mikotowicz, Christopher Nouryeh, Stephen Vallillo, Lucy Vena, and Richard Vena.

G.V. & A.J.N.

THE TROJAN WOMEN
EURIPIDES (486–406 B.C.)

Every great play, serious or comic, every valid theory of dramatic art owes its existence directly or indirectly to Greek tragedy. Remove Euripides, and the modern theatre ceases to exist.

—DONALD CLIVE STUART

Joyce Ebert as Andromache in *The Trojan Women,* presented by the Circle-in-the-Square in 1963, under the direction of Michael Cacoyannis. *Photo used with permission from the Estate of Bert Andrews.*

Ground plan of a typical Greek theatre.

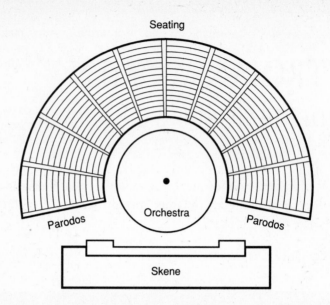

APPROACHING CLASSICAL TRAGEDY

Dare any playreader approach the art of Greek tragedy by assessing the work of one of its less conventional practitioners? Euripides might justify our attempt. While time has quietly vindicated his literary eccentricities, the events of human history have repeatedly confirmed the timelessness of his characters and themes. The youngest of three Greek tragic poets, headed by Aeschylus (525–456 B.C.) and Sophocles (496–406 B.C.), Euripides created a dramatic art which satisfied the formalized stage conventions of the religious festivals that paid homage to Dionysus, the time-honored god of wine and revelry, and the spiritual patron of drama. His male actors wore tragic masks, headdress, and long robes; his poetic dialogue was interspersed with choral songs and monologues spoken by individual actors or by a chorus that numbered from twelve to fifty members; and performances of his plays called for exaggerated voices and gestures declaimed under the daylit Grecian sky.

Unlike Aeschylus and Sophocles whose plays investigated the fatal interplay between human and divine orders, Euripides reshaped such grandeur and spectacle to focus on the internal human experience and, in later works, introduced comic elements to touch the mind and heart of the spectator. Questioning traditional Athenian values, his plays were deemed dangerous and judged inferior to the elaborate structure and style of the plays of Aeschylus and Sophocles. Yet their innovative psychological examinations of character and socio-political issues, which contrasted sharply with the drama of his day, have prompted a much needed re-evaluation. Furthermore, their emphasis on human dilemmas constitute Euripides' strongest legacy to the art of drama in our own time.

The works of all three tragedians had flourished for over a century before the Greek philosopher Aristotle (384–322 B.C.) devised his *Poetics,* in which he systematically ana-lyzed the components of literature, notably the drama, and established a dynamic set of criteria for judging Western literary art. His observations focused on selected dramas per-formed before thousands of citizens who sat in the horseshoe-like space of the Temple of Dionysus to watch the actors in the circular **orchestra** below.

What these playgoers saw and heard were the gestures and voices of vigorously rehearsed actors, quite noticeably set apart from the chorus, who moved through a series of connected actions toward some unexpected fate. The central actor was cast as the **pro-tagonist,** the heroic figure who was challenged by a second actor, the **antagonist,** whose arguments blocked his or her desired goal. During these dramatized conflicts, peaks of emotion swelled and subsided, sweeping over the awestricken crowd, signaling the rising and falling actions or **complication** of the drama. Aristotle observed how the playwright built toward one particular moment—the highest point in the action or **climax**—where the fate of the protagonist took a negative turn.

Plot was the word Aristotle used to describe this "arrangement of the incidents," which he regarded as "the first principle, and, as it were, the soul of a tragedy: Character holds the second place."[1] Regarding the events within this plot, Aristotle suggested that "the change [in the protagonist's] fortune should not be from bad to good, but, reversely, from good to bad."[2] The unraveling or **denouement,** which "extend[ed] from the beginning of the change to the end," brought closure to the action.[3] In the end, exaltation had sprung from the protagonist's tragic fate to uplift the spectators, an outcome known as **katharsis,** "through pity and fear effecting the proper purgation of these emotions."[4]

Aristotle insisted that characters speak in a "language embellished, I mean language into which rhythm, 'harmony,' and song enter [and] that some parts are rendered through the medium of verse alone, others again with the aid of song."[5] While it is impossible to determine if he approved of Euripides' handling of the quantitative parts into which the tragedy itself was divided, namely the "Prologue, Episode, Exodos, Choric song, this last being divided into Parodos and Stasimon," it is apparent that the manner in which Euripides handled the Chorus did not please him.[6] "It should be an integral part of the whole, and share in the action, in the manner not of Euripides but of Sophocles," he exclaimed. Showing a preference for the Sophoclean style, in which the Chorus was effectively portrayed "as one of the actors,"[7] he criticized Euripides for progressively detaching the Chorus from the main action.

Among other interesting suggestions, Aristotle warned younger playwrights to avoid "a multiplicity of plots" as practiced by certain poets "who have dramatized the whole story of the Fall of Troy, instead of selecting portions, like Euripides."[8] While he took Euripides to task for certain stylistic choices, Aristotle nevertheless singled him out as a playwright who knew how to maneuver his characters' fortunes and who "follow[ed] this principle in his plays, many of which end[ed] unhappily [and made him] the most tragic of the poets."[9] Perhaps his most revealing judgment still speaks to us in the present tense: that "Sophocles drew men as they ought to be; Euripides, as they are."[10]

MAJOR WORKS

Euripides wrote about ninety plays of which eighteen have survived. Dates of earlier works vary among scholars and, of these, only *Cyclops* (442 B.C.) survives. Burlesquing the story of Odysseus and the Cyclops as told by Homer, this is his one extant satyr play and the only extant example of this form. Other plays include *Alcestis* (438 B.C.), *Medea* (431 B.C.), *Hippolytus* (428 B.C.), *Andromache* (c. 426 B.C.), *Hecuba* (424 B.C.), *The Children of Heracles, Heracles, The Suppliants,* and *Ion* (all probably written between 417 and 415 B.C.), *The Phoenician Women* (415 B.C.), *Electra* (413 B.C.), *Helen* (412 B.C.), *Iphigenia Among the Taurians* (c. 412 B.C.), *Orestes* (408 B.C.), *The Bacchants* (c. 406 B.C.), and the unfinished *Iphigenia in Aulis* (c. 406 B.C.). Their rich themes have included revenge, the eternal love triangle and the destructive forces of sexual lust, the victimization of women, the power of passion over reason, and the growth of human character through suffering.

The Trojan Women (415 B.C.) is the third play of Euripides' only known trilogy, with *Alexander* and *Palamedes,* the first two plays of the trilogy, lost. Standing alone, the play offers qualitative insights into the art of Greek tragedy. Its effortless display of emotional realism, a cast of characters who symbolize the different faces of women, and a firm moral purpose assure its position on world stages today.

THE ACTION

Helen, wife of Menelaus of Sparta, had fled her home with Paris, a Prince of Troy. Accompanied by Agamemnon, Menelaus set sail for Troy to retrieve his wife and capture Troy as punishment for Paris' deed. Laying siege to the city, they were unsuccessful in capturing the city for ten long years, during which time Hector was killed by Achilles, and Paris was slaughtered. Troy remained undefeated until Odysseus devised a giant wooden horse armed with Greek soldiers, which the Trojans dragged inside the walls of their city. When enemy soldiers emerged from it, King Priam of Troy was murdered and the city was captured. It is precisely at this point that Euripides begins his play.

What follows is a devastating dirge in which the widowed Queen Hecuba confronts what remains of her family: daughter Cassandra, daughter-in-law Andromache, and the latter's son, Astyanax. Held captive by the enemy, now headed by the boastful Helen, the women vividly describe the events that have brought them to their respective tragic ends. In the background, a chorus of Trojan women similarly bemoans the fate that has befallen them and the uncertain future that lies ahead.

STRUCTURE AND LANGUAGE

The Trojan Women is a character-centered play, whose realistic language triumphs over its low-keyed action, its cast of royal survivors awakening to the devastation of their homeland, Troy, ''slowly burning, as yet more smoke than flame.'' These women and children would best have been destroyed, suggests Euripides who, in dramatizing this holocaust's aftermath, has assembled five legendary characters to protest imperialism and the immorality of war. So universal is their dirge and so realistic its outpouring, that a contemporary audience might easily juxtapose their conventional ''tragic masks'' with the faces of survivors from Hiroshima, My Lai, or Bosnia.

Historically speaking, Euripides' plaintive outcry against war serves as the play's most salient and eloquent feature. It was the playwright's personal response to his countrymen's destruction of the island of Melos for wishing to preserve its neutrality in the Peloponnesian War (431–404 B.C.). When this position offended Athens, Athenian forces slaughtered the men and enslaved the women and children. Bordering on political tract, the play was destined to lose the popular support of the Athenian audience it attacked.

Perhaps the radical Euripides felt that his chief artistic aim was to dramatize emotional situations that would give audiences a perspective on Athenian policy from the point of view of those being victimized. The play's theme of protest was developed through the use of a fairly static, linear arrangement of impassioned monologues, mostly by women, interrupted by short verbal interactions. In an ironic twist, he was further inspired to employ the characters and events of Homeric legend to make the lesson more palatable to his countrymen. Moreover, he chose to depict the defeated Trojans as the play's protagonists, hoping to demonstrate what the Greek victory had meant in human terms.

While Euripides is credited with a variety of styles that characterize his reputation as an innovator and modernist, his conventional use of quantitative movements, or measured verse segments, fulfills the requisites of Greek tragedy. These are the *prologue, parodos, episode, stasimon,* and *exodos,* designed to balance the dramatic action in much the same way that divisions of scenes and acts function in later Western drama. These movements follow the opening arguments spoken by two gods who introduce the play's struggle between Greek victors and Trojan survivors. The first to appear is Athena, daughter of Zeus and patroness of Athens, who confronts Poseidon, god of the sea and defender of Troy, now proudly boasting how he ''built the towers of stone/ around this town of Troy.''

Responding at once to the destruction at hand and wishing to "put enmity aside," Athena agrees to make her "Trojan foes rejoice,/ and give the Greeks a bitter homecoming" by asking her father "to strike [their] ships with fire" on their return to Athens.

When both gods exit, daybreak reveals the ramparts of Troy where Hecuba, the aged queen and widow of Priam, lifts her prostrate body slowly from the ground to express her unfathomable grief:

> Oh, I'll rock myself this way, that way,
> to the sound of weeping, the song of tears,
> dropping down forever.
> The song no feet will dance to ever,
> for the wretched, the ruined.

The words of Athena and Poseidon as well as Hecuba's tone-setting lamentation constitute the **prologue** of the play and prompt the heartrending procession that follows.

Entering in two halves, one consisting of older women, the other of younger, the Chorus joins Hecuba to commiserate with her loss of family and home. "In the tent we were weeping, too,/ for we are slaves," intones one of the women, whose words betray their loss of freedom. Described alternatingly as "first woman," "another woman," "a woman," and "the other," they establish themselves in this translation as single characters who speak or chant, for heightened emotional effect, before they collectively form the Chorus and intone their choral ode in unison. Their official entrance forms the **parodos.**

Talthybius, a Greek messenger and enemy of Troy, fetches Hecuba's daughter Cassandra, who sings a cynical bridal song with ecstatic emotion. Bearing the "hymen" or torch, emblematic both of marriage and death, this holy virgin has been reduced to madness by Troy's destruction and the deaths of her father and brothers. Now she must render her prized virginity to the enemy Agamemnon:

> O Mother, crown my triumph with a wreath.
> Be glad, for I am married to a king.
> Send me to him, and if I shrink away,
> drive me with violence.

Prophesying the murder of Agamemnon in words that must be shielded from the enemy— "I shall kill him, Mother, lay his house as low as he laid ours"—her exit concludes **episode** I and indicates a change of action.

The choral response, or **stasimon** I, rekindles the story of the Greek invasion, quite familiar to Euripides' audience, by highlighting the bloody details:

> A four-wheeled cart brought the horse to the gates,
> brought ruin to me,
>   captured, enslaved me.
> Gold was the rein and the bridle,
> deadly the arms within,
> and they clashed loud to heaven as the threshold was
>   passed.

The pain experienced personally by each woman is magnified by the collective voice of the community as represented by the Chorus. Each individual tragedy is symbolic of the consequences of Athenian treachery.

Episode II introduces Andromache, the widow of Hecuba's most heroic son Hector. She is accompanied by the young Astyanax, Hector's child. Hector's murderer, Achilles, now claims Andromache as booty and demands the boy's death. The noble Andromache screams at enemy soldiers as they tear him from her arms:

> O Greeks, you have found out ways to torture
> that are not Greek.
> A little child, all innocent of wrong—
> You wish to kill him.

Her plea to preserve Astyanax, in whose youthful hands the future of Troy was held, is echoed in a choral ode, stasimon II, that recounts the legend of Troy's founding and survival of past wars.

The final entrance, or episode III, belongs to the infamous Helen, Paris' mistress, for whom the war was reputedly fought. She now blames Hecuba, mother of Paris, for giving birth to an adulterous son who thought "he should lead the Trojans/ to victory and lay all Greece to ruins." But Helen is startled by the pronouncements of her husband Menelaus, who tells her in Hecuba's presence that:

> Death is near.
> Men there are waiting for you. In their hands are stones.
> Die—a small price for the Greeks' long suffering.
> You shall not any more dishonor me.

Their final encounter unravels the string of tightly wrought confrontations and unsettled conclusions which Euripides has woven with unrelenting force.

Meanwhile the Chorus openly grieves at having to leave its homeland in stasimon III, and Hecuba anticipates her fate as prize to Odysseus. *The Trojan Women* closes with a memorable **exodos** in which Talthybius hands over the slaughtered Astyanax to Hecuba for burial as the sobbing women bid farewell to each other. Adhering to a classical formula, Euripides has created a realistic image of a city and its people in ruins.

A powerful note of dramatic irony still hovers over the proceedings, however, as the audience recalls Poseidon's deadly promise "to stir the sea,/ the wide Aegean" when the last Greek ship has departed. The fulfillment of this promise would no doubt have won the playwright's approval. Brandishing his pacifism in a society that showed a healthy appetite for war, Euripides was able to fashion his art for political ends in a world where nations still reverted to war to prove their superiority.

ABOUT THE TRANSLATION

Edith Hamilton's claim that *The Trojan Women* "is the most modern in feeling of all Greek tragedies" guides her approach to producing a faithful English translation that has worked successfully in contemporary performance.[11] Her arrangement of Euripides' poetic lines or versification implores us to investigate the dramatic possibilities of characters who must convey, in a few short breaths, unfathomable horror and loss. There is no fixed meter, nor are lines the same length; rhyme is avoided, just as it was by the Greek tragedians.

Hamilton's translation honors the musicality of Euripides' achievement by employing those same rhetorical devices the playwright used to hold his audience. The aria-like lamentations of Hecuba initially elicit our sympathy, as we slowly comprehend Cassandra's outrage, however distancing her madness is. We are further seduced by the anguish over loyalty to her dead husband of Andromache, who represents the ideal wife and mother, despite Hecuba's insistence that obedience to the enemy will protect Hector's son and heir. A second duet between Andromache and Talthybius announces that Astyanax must die, forcing us to confront the play's anti-war message. Arguments build to a climax when Hecuba puts Helen on trial and accuses Menelaus, the symbol of Athens, of going to war for so specious a reason as male pride. Echoing the playwright's range of expression from the most intimate monologue to fullest choral declamation, Hamilton has produced a poignant and persuasive text. Our respect for her translation finally centers around realistic characters who prompt important questions about gender representation and language in a play that was written by a man, filled with women, and performed by men.

THE TROJAN WOMEN-IN-PERFORMANCE

The burning landscape of Troy, as depicted in Homer's *Iliad* (c. eighth century B.C.), has inspired countless artists through the centuries, with Euripides' tragedy often infusing the spirit of these works. On the dramatic stage, for example, the psychology and ethics of love and war, prompted by scenic Troy, formed the thematic core of Shakespeare's *Troilus and Cressida* (1609) and French poet and tragedian Jean Racine's *Andromaque* (1667). This fascination with the Trojan incident also inspired two musical achievements in nineteenth-century France: Jacques Offenbach's pungent operetta, *La Belle Hélène* (1864), and Hector Berlioz' epic opera, *Les Troyennes* (1890). On the modern continental stage, Euripides' characters anticipated the invasion of the Greeks in Jean Giraudoux's pacifist play, *La Guerre de Troie N'Aura Pas Lieu,* translated into English as *Tiger at the Gates* (1935).

The Trojan Women has promulgated messages of protest in wartime and provided strong actors with challenging roles. English-language productions have shown us Hecuba in portrayals by May Whitty and Flora Robson and America's Eva LeGallienne and Mildred Dunnock. Three international directors have interpreted Euripides' script and uncovered their own private visions of the art of ancient tragedy in the contemporary world. With stirring and memorable results, their landmark productions have bridged the play's rich psychological portraits and timely themes to a world rife with imperialism, wars, and the threat of nuclear extinction.

Michael Cacoyannis directed the play for the Festival of Two Worlds at Spoleto, Italy, in July 1963 and in a production that opened in New York on 23 December of that same year. But he never dreamed that the New York engagement would last more than six hundred performances and establish a record for one of our oldest surviving dramas. Using the 1937 English translation by Edith Hamilton, whose compact and hard language he thought ''very near the original in spirit,'' Greek-born Cacoyannis took a straightforward, almost reverential view of character and action that matched the unadorned, classical design of the play. His direction also satisfied the mournful demeanor of American audiences who had recently experienced the assassination of President John F. Kennedy. Moreover, the production fortuitously accompanied America's further immersion into its longest and bloodiest entanglement away from home, the Vietnam War, in which a total of 489 Americans had already been killed or wounded by the end of 1963.

Cacoyannis intentionally preserved the small theatre space of Off-Broadway's Circle-in-the-Square and avoided the stereotypical furnishings usually afforded classical revivals: vertical columns, elaborate period costuming, and pseudo-archaic gestures. Instead he utilized the long rectangular playing area at the front of the auditorium, then introduced a broad flight of steps leading to an elevated rampart, behind which a white luminous screen served as backdrop. This effectively silhouetted the characters in half-light to full and emphasized a chorus of nine women whom he directed to move with mild, sustained choreography. All of the performers wore modified Greek costumes to suggest, rather than recreate, the time and place of the action. ''This play was given by a playwright with burning conviction for a living audience,'' explained Cacoyannis, ''and we want to present it to another living audience today.''[12] He eliminated Athena from the prologue and amplified a pre-recorded voice of Poseidon to introduce the argument and set the scene. This alteration proved practical and artistically feasible, as it directed audience attention to Hecuba, who became the first stage character to appear. It also established her pivotal function, since she remained on stage through most of the performance.

Mad Cassandra, dressed in mourning black, appeared with torch in hand, weaving crookedly across the rectangular space with wild hair streaming across her gazing eyes. The seductive, brazen Helen approached Menelaus and lifted the veil from her face at the precise moment she asked, ''Am I to live or not?'' Then there was Andromache, whose separation from her son was no easy sight to behold as she stumbled toward the child and wrapped her cloak around him, then flung him with a cry across the stage, hoping to lose herself amid the chorus of women positioned like columns of stone.

A musical score by Jean Prodromides heightened the ominous mood, as the chorus broke into full chant during the play's exodos. Animated by Cacoyannis' uncluttered direction, Euripides' intermissionless dirge, which lasted one and three-quarter hours, had touched the audience.

The consequences of America's involvement in Vietnam had generated bitter repercussions. Compounded by national issues of sexual equality and civil rights, which were resounding globally as well, the aftermath of the war prompted political performances that were outspoken statements of dissatisfaction with American society. Furthermore, the international theatre scene was generating a surge of artistic exploration and experimentation, out of which numerous radical stylists were emerging. One of these was Andrei Serban.

The Rumanian-born director mounted a three-part marathon of Greek tragedy requiring two separate evenings of performance, titled *Fragments of a Trilogy*. Premiering at the La Mama Theatre Annex in 1974, *The Trojan Women* constituted one part of his ''epic opera.'' Unlike Cacoyannis, Serban deconstructed the play's mythological components to reveal its symbolic subtext.

Serban's imagery evoked the terror, eroticism, lamentation, hatred, and fear found in Euripides' drama. He further explored the power of ancient languages to touch the multicultural background of his audience. Resorting to the original Greek and other languages, he incorporated a variety of grunts, whispers, groans, shouts, shrieks, laments, and incantations from the actors until cognitive meaning became absorbed by the colorations of oral speech: words as *sounds* rather than *signs*. Elizabeth Swados' musical direction, which incorporated bells, gongs, strings, and drums, allowed the new language spoken by the actors to achieve a powerful rhythm and harmony. Finally he transformed the performance area into an environmental space inhabited simultaneously by actors and spectators. ''When Helen of Troy is wheeled in, in a tumbrel,'' observed one critic, ''the audience quite naturally becomes a crowd of Trojans watching her humiliation.''[13]

Serban's stage pictures remained stark and vivid: Cassandra was led off like an animal with a rope around its neck; Andromache knelt on a ramp and washed her son's body, surrounded by spectators; while in a final tableau the enchained women sat stoically on stage and held boat-ribs to suggest the ship that carried them into exile. The critics unanimously agreed that Serban's eclectic **mise-en-scène** had been ''successful in rekindling the ancient tragic fires.''[14] The universal resonance of his theatrical vision was confirmed when *Fragments of a Trilogy* was restaged for the Ninth Iran Festival of the Arts at Shiraz, among the towering ruins of Persepolis.

Tadashi Suzuki, who adapted, designed, and directed *The Trojan Women* in 1974 for the Suzuki Company of Toga, interpreted Euripides' play as a political response to Japanese atrocities. He reset the action in a ruined Tokyo cemetery just after World War II, where a nameless old woman, who has survived the destruction of family and home, relives her tragedy as she unpacks the remnants of her household from a small bundle.

Incorporating Kabuki percussive music and acrobatic movements, the production honored the formal design of Noh drama as the old woman recalled the events that had brought her to this place. (See Preface to *Sekidera Komachi,* p. 152.) Performed without intermission, the one-hundred-minute-long production inhabited a dark stage hung with cloud-like drapes, accommodating a small chorus of seven old men who scuttled across the stage like crabs and often froze into formalized dramatic poses. The woman's trance-like journey back in time conjured forth the spirits of Hecuba and Cassandra, whom she became.

Suzuki's production purposely showcased the acting versatility of Kayoko Shiraishi, who impersonated three principal characters: the old woman, Hecuba, and Cassandra. By letting her black kimono fall back to reveal a white one, Shiraishi transformed herself from grieving queen to mad priestess in a voice that "scrapes, roars and scorches like a human blow-torch. As Hecuba, her rasping accusations have such inexorability, this female cry suggests the voice of the conscience of mankind in contemplating the holocaust."[15] Returning to the present, where the old woman dies after refusing shelter from a flower-seller, Suzuki introduced a contemporary song, heard in the background, concerning the futility of a woman's grief. The action is finalized by a traditional Jizo (Buddhist God), who wanders through the debris and symbolizes the indifference of the gods to Japan's suffering.

REFLECTIONS ON THE TROJAN WOMEN

Joyce Ebert portrayed Andromache at the Circle-in-the-Square in New York under the direction of Michael Cacoyannis. She received both the Obie and Clarence Derwent Awards for her performance.

In 1963, just after John Kennedy was assassinated, I went into a production of [Pirandello's] *Six Characters in Search of an Author,* under William Ball's direction. At that same time, Michael Cacoyannis was looking for *another* Andromache, since the actress he recently cast in the role had quit for whatever reason. The saga of casting Andromache was insane and I believe that three actresses had quit before I joined rehearsals about two weeks before the first preview. [Producer] Ted Mann brought Cacoyannis to see *Six Characters* and he decided I could do it. So I came down and read for him and got the part.

Michael was and is a marvelous director, but an authoritarian one. Part of this authoritarian style was to demonstrate the role through personal line readings, which is something I knew how to deal with. I was not asked to imitate him, but rather to get the meaning of what he was trying to convey in his voice. My part was scored like an opera aria, although I was not present during the first few weeks of rehearsal to know if this was how he handled the other actors. Mildred Dunnock was playing Hecuba. Her diction was perfect. While her voice was not a big one, it was light and very musical. Carrie Nye was Cassandra. Her vocal qualities were unusual, so effective for Hecuba's mad daughter. Jane White as Helen had a strong voice that was exactly right for the irony of her situation. Then there was our wonderful chorus. Michael's direction was difficult, but I knew how to take it.

Andromache is a wonderful part for a young, mature woman to play. It's one of the few classical Greek roles in which the action happens on stage: the direct action of having her child taken away from her. Michael's vision of the part was inspired, so rehearsing it began to get more and more exciting. There was a point at which the messenger tells me that my child must die. And there's a moment in which I try to push the boy back up into my womb, that's how tightly I hugged him to protect him. Then I encircled the playing area and ended with an earth cry that started from the center of my body, a kind of primal scream.

Rehearsals went well, despite nervous headaches and arm rashes that I attributed to Michael because it was really very difficult to mesh my own emotions with the form he had given me. He actually gave me the form, which is why I was able to handle this part

Continued

throughout the play's long run. Having the form, I could supply different emotions at different times to keep it fresh. As we approached our first preview, I just knew things were good. By opening night, Michael was backstage, still demonstrating certain reminders to squeeze that last tear from me in my scenes on stage. It was a splendid opening and, after all the exciting reviews were in, the problem for all of us concerned was to keep the performance fresh for the rest of the run, a great challenge for me since I played the role for about a year.

We received extraordinary reactions from our audiences as well. Shortly after we opened, in this scene where I finally push my son away from me, a woman in the audience sobbed audibly, "Oh, no! no!, Oh, no!" Till this day I can still hear her husband comforting her with the words, "It's only a play! It's only a play!" That's the kind of impact the scene had.

The Trojan Women was a play that created much strife among its cast members. Michael had choreographed the chorus to movements of chest-beating and ground-pounding, all of which prompted some not so peaceful repercussions among these wonderful chorus members who rehearsed tirelessly to meet his expectations.

Michael was acquainted with the play from earlier productions in his own country, as well as a production he directed at the Spoleto Festival [in Italy] just prior to ours. He knew exactly what he wanted and made just a few minor adjustments with Edith Hamilton's beautiful translation which was so alive, unlike the stilted translations of so many Greek plays. Michael was so caught up with directing us, I sometimes thought he could play any of these characters himself. That's how well he knew what he wanted from us.

I had studied singing before I decided to act. So I saw what he was trying to get from our line readings. It was not a matter of sustaining syllables in legato fashion, although it was possible to approach my dialogue this way, but more a matter of highs and lows and, most importantly, rhythm: the voice can go higher in some of Andromache's more lyrical passages and lower in some of her more dramatic ones. Fast, slow, then fast and slow together. Euripides has scored his play to accommodate these changes. Those tremendous speeches must be approached as musical arias, like a singer who must supply his own emotions to the form. As an actor, I could use any one of a number of things, provided I stay within the form. And that is what carried me through the run of the play. There's no use doing it like a ham actor, repeating the same things all the time, emptily. You have to fill it. If you cannot fill it on certain nights, then you must rely on the form to carry you through.

I had performed in a number of Shakespeare's plays but, unlike most classical plays, *The Trojan Women* was more primal, more of an essence of things; it dug down into basic emotions, and these emotions had to be big on stage. There was not much room for subtlety. When I entered rehearsals, for example, I could not figure out what the relationship was between Hecuba and Andromache. Then it finally struck: who mourned Hector the most? That was the issue, I thought. So there grew this relationship between mother and daughter-in-law, which is not an easy relationship to begin with. Of course Hector was a great man and hero who died in his efforts to save his country. But during rehearsals I often wondered why certain things were being said about him, till I gradually focused on this special and difficult relationship with Hecuba. Michael never talked about it, nor did I feel any need to discuss it with Miss Dunnock. The relationship just fell into place and worked so well in performance.

My child being taken from me was a strong action to deal with as I had lost a child of my own a couple of years before—through miscarriage. So I instinctively used these stronger personal emotions for Andromache's bigger moments. Then there was the recent assassination of Kennedy, a sudden and tragic event that made me feel that Andromache had much in common with Jackie Kennedy, through her personal loss of husband and the country's loss of its leader. Of course, such timing was purely coincidental. Years later I did a reading of Andromache's big speech for an anniversary of the holocaust and, even though it concerned the destruction of Troy, it was very apropos to what had occurred in the concentration camps and proved quite effective. Then there's the more recent crisis with Iraq, which shows that mankind still has not gotten past what is depicted in *Trojan Women.* We don't ever seem to learn.

I thought of myself as mother and wife when I walked on the stage, although the one thing I have left is my son Astyanax. While Euripides shows us different kinds of womanhood to express his anti-war sentiment, I represented the younger version of mother and wife whose losses serve to contrast with Hecuba's.

I shook in my boots before I went on, thinking about all of the critics who sat in the audience. I was determined not to be intimidated by anybody. That seemed to get my juices going. The evening worked like magic and Cacoyannis was thrilled. The farewell to my child—I still remember parts of that as being unique. It's instilling in the boy a courage as well as saying good-bye. It's like feeling defenseless and naked, with nothing to hide behind. There was a lot of anger and destruction in the play, which placed the performers at the end of their emotional tethers and, quite understandably, affected the performance. We were all being sent into slavery. And the fact that we did it in one act had a cumulative power which affected all of us on stage. Years later I saw a wonderful production in Greece. Andromache entered in a cart, rather than walking on, as I did. It still sent the same chills down my spine.

Notes

1. Walter Jackson Bate, ed., CRITICISM: THE MAJOR TEXTS *(New York: Harcourt, Brace & World, 1952), 23.*
2. *Ibid., 27.*
3. *Ibid., 30.*
4. *Ibid.*
5. *Ibid., 22.*
6. *Ibid., 26.*
7. *Ibid., 31.*
8. *Ibid.*
9. *Ibid., 27.*
10. *Ibid., 37.*
11. *Edith Hamilton, trans.,* THREE GREEK PLAYS *(New York: W. W. Norton, 1937), 16.*
12. *"Michael Cacoyannis Talks About* The Trojan Women," THE NEW YORK TIMES, *22 Dec. 1963.*
13. *"Fragments of a Trilogy,"* SATURDAY REVIEW, *8 Feb. 1975, p. 41.*
14. *Gerald Rabkin,* SOHO WEEKLY, *1 Jan. 1976.*
15. *John Barber,* DAILY TELEGRAPH, *11 Nov. 1985.*

THE TROJAN WOMEN

EURIPIDES

TRANSLATED BY EDITH HAMILTON

CHARACTERS

Poseidon

Athena

Hecuba

Cassandra

Andromache

Helen

Talthybius

Menelaus

Astyanax

Chorus of Women

*(The scene is a space of waste ground except for a few huts
to right and left, where the women selected for the Greek
leaders are housed. Far in the background Troy, the wall in
ruins, is slowly burning, as yet more smoke than flame. In
front a woman with white hair lies on the ground. It is just
before dawn. A tall dim figure is seen, back of the woman.)*

POSEIDON.

    I am the sea god. I have come
up from the salt sea depths of the Aegean,
from where the sea nymphs' footsteps fall,
weaving the lovely measures of the dance.
For since that day I built the towers of stone   **5**
around this town of Troy, Apollo with me,
—and straight we raised them, true by line and
    plummet—
good will for them has never left my heart,
my Trojans and their city.
City? Smoke only—all is gone,   **10**
perished beneath Greek spears.
A horse was fashioned, big with arms.
Parnassus was the workman's home,
in Phocia, and his name Epeius.
The skill he had Athena gave him.   **15**
He sent it through the walls—it carried death.
The wooden horse, so men will call it always,
which held and hid those spears.
A desert now where groves were. Blood drips down
from the gods' shrines. Beside his hearth   **20**
Priam lies dead upon the altar steps
of Zeus, the hearth's protector.
While to the Greek ships pass the Trojan treasure,
gold, gold in masses, armor, clothing,
stripped from the dead.   **25**
The Greeks who long since brought war to the town,
—ten times the seed was sown before Troy fell—
wait now for a fair wind for home,
the joyful sight of wife and child again.
Myself defeated by the Argive goddess   **30**
Hera and by Athena, both in league together—
I too must take my leave of glorious Troy,
forsake my altars. When a town is turned
into a desert, things divine fall sick.
Not one to do them honor.   **35**
Scamander's stream is loud with lamentation,
so many captive women weeping.
Their masters drew lots for them. Some will go
to Arcady and some to Thessaly.
Some to the lords of Athens, Theseus' sons.   **40**
Huts here hold others spared the lot, but chosen
for the great captains.
With them, like them a captive of the spear,
the Spartan woman, Helen.
But if a man would look on misery,   **45**
it is here to see—Hecuba lies there
before the gates. She weeps.
Many tears for many griefs.
And one still hidden from her.
But now upon Achilles' grave her daughter   **50**
was killed—Polyxena. So patiently she died.
Gone is her husband, gone her sons, all dead.
One daughter whom the Lord Apollo loved,
yet spared her wild virginity, Cassandra,

Agamemnon, in the dark, will force upon
   his bed.   55
No thought for what was holy and was God's.
O city happy once, farewell.
O shining towers, crumbling now
beneath Athena's hand, the child of God,
or you would still stand firm on deep
   foundations.   60

(*As he turns to go the goddess* PALLAS ATHENA *enters.*)

ATHENA.
   Am I allowed to speak to one who is
   my father's nearest kinsman,
   a god among gods honored, powerful?
   If I put enmity aside, will he?
POSEIDON.
   He will, most high Athena. We are kin,   65
   old comrades too, and these have magic power.
ATHENA.
   Thanks for your gentleness. What I would say
   touches us both, great king.
POSEIDON.
   A message from the gods? A word from Zeus?
   Some spirit, surely?   70
ATHENA.
   No, but for Troy's sake, where we stand, I seek
   your power to join my own with it.
POSEIDON.
   What? Now—at last? Has that long hatred left you?
   Pity—when all is ashes—burned to ashes?
ATHENA.
   The point first, please. Will you make common
     cause   75
   with me? What I wish done will you wish, too?
POSEIDON.
   Gladly. But what you wish I first must know.
   You come to me for Troy's sake or for Greece?
ATHENA.
   I wish to make my Trojan foes rejoice,
   and give the Greeks a bitter home-coming.   80
POSEIDON.
   The way you change! Here—there—then back again.
   Now hate, now love—no limit ever.
ATHENA.
   You know how I was outraged and my temple.
POSEIDON.
   Oh that—when Ajax dragged Cassandra out?
ATHENA.
   And not one Greek to punish him—not one to blame
     him.   85
POSEIDON.
   Even though your power ruined Troy for them.
ATHENA.
   Therefore with you I mean to hurt them.

POSEIDON.
   Ready for all you wish. But—hurt them? How?
ATHENA.
   Give them affliction for their coming home.
POSEIDON.
   Held here, you mean? Or out on the salt
     sea?   90
ATHENA.
   Whenever the ships sail.
   Zeus shall send rain, unending rain, and sleet,
   and darkness blown from heaven.
   He will give me—he has promised—his thunderbolt,
   to strike the ships with fire. They shall burn.   95
   Your part, to make your sea-roads roar—
   wild waves and whirlwinds,
   while dead men choke the winding bay.
   So Greeks shall learn to reverence my house
   and dread all gods.   100
POSEIDON.
   These things shall be. No need of many words
   to grant a favor. I will stir the sea,
   the wide Aegean. Shores and reefs and cliffs
   will hold dead men, bodies of many dead.
   Off to Olympus with you now, and get   105
   those fiery arrows from the hand of Zeus.
   Then when a fair wind sends the Greeks to sea,
   watch the ships sail.

(*Exit* ATHENA.)

   Oh, fools, the men who lay a city waste,
   giving to desolation temples, tombs,   110
   the sanctuaries of the dead—so soon
   to die themselves.

(*Exit* POSEIDON.)
(*The two gods have been talking before daylight, but now
the day begins to dawn and the woman lying on the ground
in front moves. She is* HECUBA, *the aged queen of Troy.*)

HECUBA.
   Up from the ground—O weary head, O breaking
     neck.
   This is no longer Troy. And we are not
   the lords of Troy.   115
   Endure. The ways of fate are the ways of the wind.
   Drift with the stream—drift with fate.
   No use to turn the prow to breast the waves.
   Let the boat go as it chances.
   Sorrow, my sorrow.   120
   What sorrow is there that is not mine,
   grief to weep for.
   Country lost and children and husband.
   Glory of all my house brought low.
   All was nothing—nothing, always.   125

Keep silent? Speak?
Weep then? Why? For what?

(She begins to get up.)

Oh, this aching body—this bed—
it is very hard. My back pressed to it—
Oh, my side, my brow, my temples.   130
Up! Quick, quick. I must move.
Oh, I'll rock myself this way, that way,
to the sound of weeping, the song of tears,
dropping down forever.
The song no feet will dance to ever,   135
for the wretched, the ruined.
O ships, O prows, swift oars,
out from the fair Greek bays and harbors,
over the dark shining sea,
you found your way to our holy city,   140
and the fearful music of war was heard,
the war song sung to flute and pipe,
as you cast on the shore your cables,
ropes the Nile dwellers twisted and coiled,
and you swung, oh, my grief, in Troy's
        waters.   145
What did you come for? A woman?
A thing of loathing, of shame,
to husband, to brother, to home.
She slew Priam, the king,
father of fifty sons,   150
she wrecked me upon
the reef of destruction.
Who am I that I wait*
here at a Greek king's door?
A slave that men drive on,   155
an old gray woman that has no home.
Shaven head brought low in dishonor.
O wives of the bronze-armored men who fought,
and maidens, sorrowing maidens,
plighted to shame,   160
see—only smoke left where was Troy.
Let us weep for her.
As a mother bird cries to her feathered brood,
so will I cry.
Once another song I sang   165
when I leaned on Priam's scepter,
and the beat of dancing feet
marked the music's measure.
Up to the gods
the song of Troy rose at my signal.   170

(The door of one of the huts opens and a woman steals out, then another, and another.)

*This is the way Professor Murray translates the line and the one following. The translation is so simple and beautiful, I cannot bear to give it up for a poorer one of my own.

FIRST WOMAN.
    Your cry, O Hecuba—oh, such a cry—
    What does it mean? There in the tent
    we heard you call so piteously,
    and through our hearts flashed fear.
    In the tent we were weeping, too,   175
    for we are slaves.
HECUBA.
    Look, child, there where the Greek ships lie—
ANOTHER WOMAN.
    They are moving. The men hold oars.
ANOTHER.
    O God, what will they do? Carry me off
    over the sea in a ship far from home?   180
HECUBA.
    You ask and I know nothing,
    but I think ruin is here.
ANOTHER WOMAN.
    Oh, we are wretched. We shall hear the summons.
    Women of Troy, go forth from your home,
    for the Greeks set sail.   185
HECUBA.
    But not Cassandra, oh, not her.
    She is mad—she has been driven mad. Leave her
        within.
    Not shamed before the Greeks—not that grief too.
    I have enough.
        O Troy, unhappy Troy, you are gone   190
    and we, the unhappy, leave you,
    we who are living and we who are dead.

(More women now come out from a second hut.)

A WOMAN.
    Out of the Greek king's tent
    trembling I come, O Queen,
    to hear my fate from you.   195
    Not death—They would not think of death
    for a poor woman.
ANOTHER.
    The sailors—they are standing on the prow.
    Already they are running out the oars.
ANOTHER (*she comes out of a third hut and several follow
    her*).
    It is so early—but a terror woke me.   200
        My heart beats so.
ANOTHER.
    Has a herald come from the Greek camp?
    Whose slave shall I be? I—bear that?
HECUBA.
    Wait for the lot drawing. It is near.
ANOTHER.
    Argos shall it be, or Phthia?   205
        or an island of the sea?
        A Greek soldier lead me there,
    far, far from Troy?

HECUBA.

    And I a slave—to whom—where—how?

    You old gray woman, patient to endure,   **210**

    you bee without a sting,

    only an image of what was alive.

      or the ghost of one dead.

    I watch a master's door?

      I nurse his children?   **215**

      Once I was queen in Troy.

ONE WOMAN TO ANOTHER.

    Poor thing. What are your tears

    to the shame before you?

THE OTHER.

    The shuttle will still pass through my hands,

    but the loom will not be in Troy.   **220**

ANOTHER.

    My dead sons. I would look at them once more.

    Never again.

ANOTHER.

      Worse to come.

    A Greek's bed—and I—

ANOTHER.

    A night like that? Oh, never—   **225**

      oh, no—not that for me.

ANOTHER.

    I see myself a water carrier,

    dipping my pitcher in the great Pierian spring.

ANOTHER.

      The land of Theseus, Athens, it is known

    to be a happy place. I wish I could go there.   **230**

ANOTHER.

    But not to the Eurotas, hateful river,

    where Helen lived. Not there, to be a slave

    to Menelaus who sacked Troy.

ANOTHER.

    Oh, look. A man from the Greek army—

    a herald. Something strange has happened,   **235**

    he comes so fast. To tell us—what?

    What will he say? Only Greek slaves are here,

    waiting for orders.

(*Enter* TALTHYBIUS *with soldiers.*)

TALTHYBIUS.

    You know me, Hecuba. I have often come

    with messages to Troy from the Greek camp.   **240**

    Talthybius—these many years you've known me.

    I bring you news.

HECUBA.

    It has come, women of Troy. Once we only feared it.

TALTHYBIUS.

    The lots are drawn, if that is what you feared.

HECUBA.

    Who—where? Thessaly? Phthia? Thebes?   **245**

TALTHYBIUS.

    A different man takes each. You're not to go

      together.

HECUBA.

    Then which takes which? Has any one good fortune?

TALTHYBIUS.

    I know, but ask about each one, not all at once.

HECUBA.

    My daughter, who—who drew her?

      Tell me—   **250**

    Cassandra. She has had so much to bear.

TALTHYBIUS.

    King Agamemnon chose her out from all.

HECUBA.

    Oh! but—of course—to serve his Spartan wife?

TALTHYBIUS.

    No, no—but for the king's own bed at night.

HECUBA.

    Oh, never. She is God's, a virgin, always.   **255**

    That was God's gift to her for all her life.

TALTHYBIUS.

    He loved her for that same strange purity.*

HECUBA.

    Throw away, daughter, the keys of the temple.

    Take off the wreath and the sacred stole.

TALTHYBIUS.

    Well, now—a king's bed is not so bad.   **260**

HECUBA.

    My other child you took from me just now?

TALTHYBIUS (*speaking with constraint*).

    Polyxena, you mean? Or someone else?

HECUBA.

    Her. Who drew her?

TALTHYBIUS.

    They told her off to watch Achilles' tomb.

HECUBA.

    To watch a tomb? My daughter?   **265**

    That a Greek custom?

    What strange ritual is that, my friend?

TALTHYBIUS (*speaking fast and trying to put her off*).

    Just think of her as happy—all well with her.

HECUBA.

    Those words—Why do you speak like that?

    She is alive?   **270**

TALTHYBIUS (*determined not to tell her*).

    What happened was—well, she is free from trouble.

HECUBA (*wearily giving the riddle up*).

    Then Hector's wife—my Hector, wise in war—

    Where does she go, poor thing—Andromache?

---

*This line, too, is Professor Murray's, and retained here for the
reason given earlier.

TALTHYBIUS.
Achilles' son took her. He chose her out.
HECUBA.
And I, old gray head, whose slave am I,   275
creeping along with my crutch?
TALTHYBIUS.
Slave of the king of Ithaca, Odysseus.
HECUBA.
Beat, beat my shorn head! Tear, tear my cheek!
His slave—vile lying man. I have come to this—
There is nothing good he does not hurt—a lawless
    beast.   280
He twists and turns, this way and that, and back
    again.
A double tongue, as false in hate as false in love.
Pity me, women of Troy,
I have gone. I am lost—oh, wretched.
An evil fate fell on me,   285
a lot the hardest of all.
A WOMAN.
You know what lies before you, Queen, but I—
What man among the Greeks owns me?
TALTHYBIUS (to the soldiers).
Off with you. Bring Cassandra here. Be quick,
you fellows. We must give her to the
    chief,   290
into his very hand. And then these here
to all the other generals. But what's that—
that flash of light inside there?

(Light shines through the crevices of one of the huts.)

Set fire to the huts—is that their plan,
these Trojan women? Burn themselves
    to death   295
rather than sail to Greece. Choosing to die instead.
How savagely these days the yoke bears down
on necks so lately free.
Open there, open the door. (Aside.) As well for them
    perhaps,
but for the Greeks—they'd put the blame
    on me.   300
HECUBA.
No, no, there is nothing burning. It is my daughter,
Cassandra. She is mad.

(CASSANDRA enters from the hut dressed like a priestess, a
wreath in her hair, a torch in her hand. She does not seem
to see anyone.)

CASSANDRA.
Lift it high—in my hand—light to bring.
    I praise him. I bear a flame.
    With my torch I touch to fire   305
    this holy place.
    Hymen, O Hymen.

Blessed the bridegroom,
    blessed am I
to lie with a king in a king's bed in Argos.   310
    Hymen, O Hymen.
Mother, you weep
tears for my father dead,
mourning for the beloved
    country lost.   315
I for my bridal here
lift up the fire's flame
to the dawn, to the splendor,
to you, O Hymen.
Queen of night,   320
give your starlight
to a virgin bed,
as of old you did.
Fly, dancing feet.
Up with the dance.   325
    Oh, joy, oh, joy!
Dance for my father dead,
    most blest to die.
Oh, holy dance!
Apollo—you?   330
Lead on then.
There in the laurel grove
I served your altar.
    Dance, Mother, come.
    Keep step with me.   335
Dear feet with my feet
    tracing the measure
    this way and that.
Sing to the Marriage god,
oh, joyful song.   340
Sing for the bride, too,
joyously all.
Maidens of Troy,
dressed in your best,
honor my marriage.   345
Honor too him
whose bed fate drives me to share.
A WOMAN.
Hold her fast, Queen, poor frenzied girl.
She might rush straight to the Greek camp.
HECUBA.
O fire, fire, when men make marriages   350
you light the torch, but this flame flashing here
is for grief only. Child, such great hopes once I had.
I never thought that to your bridal bed
Greek spears would drive you.
Give me your torch. You do not hold it straight,   355
you move so wildly. Your sufferings, my child,
have never taught you wisdom.
You never change. Here! someone take the torch
into the hut. This marriage needs no songs,

but only tears.   360
CASSANDRA.
   O Mother, crown my triumph with a wreath.
Be glad, for I am married to a king.
Send me to him, and if I shrink away,
drive me with violence. If Apollo lives,
my marriage shall be bloodier than Helen's.   365
Agamemnon, the great, the glorious lord of Greece—
I shall kill him, Mother, lay his house as low
as he laid ours, make him pay for all
he made my father suffer, brothers, and—
But no. I must not speak of that—that axe   370
which on my neck—on others' too—
nor of that murder of a mother.
All, all because he married me and so
pulled his own house down.
But I will show you. This town now, yes,
   Mother,   375
is happier than the Greeks. I know that I am mad,
but Mother, dearest, now, for this one time
I do not rave.
One woman they came hunting, and one love,
Helen, and men by tens of thousands died.   380
Their king, so wise, to get what most he hated
destroyed what most he loved,
his joy at home, his daughter, killing her
for a brother's sake, to get him back a woman
who had fled because she wished—not forced
   to go.   385
And when they came to the banks of the Scamander
those thousands died. And why?
No man had moved their landmarks
or laid siege to their high-walled towns.
But those whom war took never saw their
   children.   390
No wife with gentle hands shrouded them for their
   grave.
They lie in a strange land. And in their homes
are sorrows, too, the very same.
Lonely women who died, old men who waited
for sons that never came—no son left to them   395
to make the offering at their graves.
That was the glorious victory they won.
But we—we Trojans died to save our people,
no glory greater. All those the spear slew,
friends bore them home and wrapped them in their
   shroud   400
with dutiful hands. The earth of their own land
covered them. The rest, through the long days they
   fought,
had wife and child at hand, not like the Greeks,
whose joys were far away.
And Hector's pain—your Hector. Mother, hear
   me.   405
This is the truth: he died, the best, a hero.

Because the Greeks came, he died thus.
Had they stayed home, we never would have known
   him.
This truth stands firm: the wise will fly from war.
But if war comes, to die well is to win   410
the victor's crown.
The only shame is not to die like that.
So, Mother, do not pity Troy,
or me upon my bridal bed.
TALTHYBIUS (*has been held awestruck through all this, but
can bear no more*).
   Now if Apollo had not made you mad   415
I would have paid you for those evil words,
bad omens, and my general sailing soon.

(*Grumbles to himself.*)

   The great, who seem so wise, have no more sense
than those who rank as nothing.
Our king, the first in Greece, bows down   420
before this mad girl, loves her, chooses her
out of them all. Well, I am a poor man,
but I'd not go to bed with her.

(*Turns to* CASSANDRA.)

   Now you—you know your mind is not quite right.
So all you said against Greece and for Troy,   425
I never heard—the wind blew it away.
Come with me to the ship now.

(*Aside.*)

   A grand match for our general, she is.

(*To* HECUBA, *gently.*)

   And you, do follow quietly when Odysseus' men
   come.
His wife's a good, wise woman, so they say.   430
CASSANDRA (*seeming to see* TALTHYBIUS *for the first time
and looking him over haughtily*).
   A strange sort of slave, surely.
Heralds such men are called,
hated by all, for they are tyrants' tools.
You say my mother goes to serve Odysseus?

(*She turns away and speaks to herself.*)

   But where then is Apollo's word, made clear   435
to me, that death will find her here?
And—no, that shame I will not speak of.
Odysseus! wretched—but he does not know.
   Soon all these sorrows, mine and Troy's, will
   seem
compared to his like golden hours.   440
Ten years behind him here, ten years before him.
Then only, all alone, will he come home,

and there find untold trouble has come first.
But his cares—why let fly one word at him?
Come, let us hasten to my marriage.   445
We two shall rest, the bridegroom and the bride,
within the house of death.
O Greek king, with your dreams of grandeur yet to
    come,
vile as you are, so shall your end be,
in darkness—all light gone.   450
And me—a cleft in the hills,
washed by winter rains,
his tomb near by.
There—dead—cast out—naked—
and wild beasts seeking food—   455
It is I there—I myself—Apollo's servant.
O flowers of the God I love, mysterious wreaths,
away. I have forgotten temple festival,
I have forgotten joy.
Off. I tear them from my neck.   460
Swift winds will carry them
up to you, O God of truth.
My flesh still clean, I give them back to you.
Where is the ship? How do I go on board?
Spread the sail—the wind comes swift.   465
Those who bring vengeance—three are they,
And one of them goes with you on the sea.
Mother, my Mother, do not weep. Farewell,
dear City. Brothers, in Troy's earth laid, my father,
a little time and I am with you.   470
You dead, I shall come to you a victor.
Those ruined by my hand who ruined us.

(*She goes out with* TALTHYBIUS *and the soldiers.* HECUBA,
motionless for a moment, falls.)

A WOMAN.
    The Queen! See—see—she is falling.
    Oh, help! She cannot speak.
    Miserable slaves, will you leave her on the
        ground,   475
    old as she is. Up—lift her up.
HECUBA.
    Let me be. Kindness not wanted is unkindness.
    I cannot stand. Too much is on me.
    Anguish here and long since and to come—
    O God—Do I call to you? You did not help.   480
    But there is something that cries out for God
    when trouble comes.
    Oh, I will think of good days gone,
    days to make a song of,
    crowning my sorrow by remembering.   485
    We were kings and a king I married.
    Sons I bore him, many sons.
    That means little—but fine, brave lads.
    They were the best in all Troy.

No woman, Trojan, Greek, or stranger,   490
had sons like mine to be proud of.
I saw them fall beneath Greek spears.
My hair I shore at the grave of the dead.
Their father—I did not learn from others
that I must weep for him—these eyes beheld
    him.   495
I, my own self, saw him fall murdered
upon the altar, when his town was lost.
My daughters, maidens reared to marry kings,
are torn from me. For the Greeks I reared them.
All gone—no hope that I shall look upon   500
their faces any more, or they on mine.
And now the end—no more can lie beyond—
an old gray slave woman I go to Greece.
The tasks they know for my age hardest, mine.
The door to shut and open, bowing low   505
—I who bore Hector—meal to grind; upon
the ground lay this old body down that once
slept in a royal bed; torn rags around me,
torn flesh beneath.
And all this misery and all to come   510
because a man desired a woman.
Daughter, who knew God's mystery and joy,
what strange chance lost you your virginity?
And you, Polyxena—where are you gone?
No son, no daughter, left to help my need,   515
and I had many, many—
Why lift me up? What hope is there to hold to?
    This slave that once went delicately in Troy,
take her and cast her on her bed of clay,
rocks for her pillow, there to fall and die,   520
wasted with tears. Count no one happy,
however fortunate, before he dies.

CHORUS.
    Sing me, O Muse, a song for Troy,
    a strange song sung to tears,
    a music for the grave.   525
    O lips, sound forth a melody
        for Troy.

    A four-wheeled cart brought the horse to the gates,
    brought ruin to me,
        captured, enslaved me.   530
    Gold was the rein and the bridle,
    deadly the arms within,
    and they clashed loud to heaven as the threshold was
        passed.
    High on Troy's rock the people cried,
    "Rest at last, trouble ended.   535
    Bring the carven image in.
    Bear it to Athena,
    fit gift for the child of God."

Who of the young but hurried forth?
Who of the old would stay at home?   540
With song and rejoicing they brought death in,
treachery and destruction.

All that were in Troy,
hastening to the gate,
drew that smooth-planed horse of wood   545
carven from a mountain pine,
where the Greeks were hiding,
where was Troy's destruction,
gave it to the goddess,
gift for her, the virgin,   550
driver of the steeds that never die.

With ropes of twisted flax,
as a ship's dark hull is drawn to land,
they brought it to her temple of stone,
to her floor that soon would run with blood,   555
    to Pallas Athena.

    On their toil and their joy
the dark of evening fell,
but the lutes of Egypt still rang out
    to the songs of Troy.   560

And girls with feet light as air
dancing, sang happy songs.
The houses blazed with light
through the dark splendor,
    and sleep was not.   565

A GIRL.
    I was among the dancers.
    I was singing to the maiden of Zeus,
    the goddess of the hills.
    A shout rang out in the town,
    a cry of blood through the houses,   570
    and a frightened child caught his mother's skirt
    and hid himself in her cloak.
    Then War came forth from his hiding place—
    Athena, the virgin, devised it.
    Around the altars they slaughtered us.   575
    Within on their beds lay headless men,
    young men cut down in their prime.
    This was the triumph-crown of Greece.
    We shall bear children for her to rear,
    grief and shame to our country.   580

(*A chariot approaches, loaded with spoils. In it sits a woman and a child.*)

A WOMAN.
    Look, Hecuba, it is Andromache.
    See, in the Greek car yonder.

Her breast heaves with her sobs and yet
the baby sleeps there, dear Astyanax,
    the son of Hector.   585
ANOTHER.
    Most sorrowful of women, where do you go?
    Beside you the bronze armor that was Hector's,
    the spoil of the Greek spear, stripped from the dead.
    Will Achilles' son use it to deck his temples?
ANDROMACHE.
    I go where my Greek masters take me.   590
HECUBA.
    Oh, our sorrow—our sorrow.
ANDROMACHE.
    Why should you weep? This sorrow is mine.
HECUBA.
    O God—
ANDROMACHE.
    What has come to me is mine.
HECUBA.
    My children—   595
ANDROMACHE.
        Once we lived, not now.
HECUBA.
        Gone—gone—happiness—Troy—
ANDROMACHE.
    And you bear it.
HECUBA.
    Sons, noble sons, all lost.
ANDROMACHE.
    Oh, sorrow is here.   600
HECUBA.
    For me—for me.
ANDROMACHE.
    For the city, in its shroud of smoke.
    Come to me, O my husband.
HECUBA.
    What you cry to lies in the grave.
    My son, wretched woman, mine.   605
ANDROMACHE.
    Defend me—me, your wife.
HECUBA.
    My son, my eldest son,
    whom I bore to Priam,
    whom the Greeks used shamefully,
    come to me, lead me to death.   610
ANDROMACHE.
    Death—oh, how deep a desire.
HECUBA.
    Such is our pain—
ANDROMACHE.
    For a city that has fallen, fallen.

HECUBA.
    For anguish heaped upon anguish.
ANDROMACHE.
    For the anger of God against Paris,   615
    your son, who fled from death,
    who laid Troy's towers low
        to win an evil love.
    Dead men—bodies—blood—
    vultures hovering—   620
    Oh, Athena the goddess is there, be sure,
    and the slave's yoke is laid upon Troy.
HECUBA.
    O country, desolate, empty.
ANDROMACHE.
    My tears fall for you.
HECUBA.
    Look and see the end—   625
ANDROMACHE.
    Of the house where I bore my children.
HECUBA.
    O children, your mother has lost her city,
    and you—you have left her alone.
    Only grief is mine and mourning.
    Tears and more tears, falling, falling.   630
    The dead—they have forgotten their pain.
    They weep no more.
A WOMAN (*aside to another*).
    Tears are sweet in bitter grief,
    and sorrow's song is lamentation.
ANDROMACHE.
    Mother of him whose spear of old brought
        death   635
    to Greeks unnumbered, you see what is here.
HECUBA.
    I see God's hand that casts the mighty down
    and sets on high the lowly.
ANDROMACHE.
    Driven like cattle captured in a raid,
    my child and I—the free changed to a slave.   640
    Oh, changed indeed.
HECUBA.
    It is fearful to be helpless. Men just now
    have taken Cassandra—forced her from me.
ANDROMACHE.
    And still more for you—more than that—
HECUBA.
    Number my sorrows, will you? Measure them?   645
    One comes—the next one rivals it.
ANDROMACHE.
    Polyxena lies dead upon Achilles' tomb,
    a gift to a corpse, to a lifeless thing.
HECUBA.
    My sorrow! That is what Talthybius meant—
    I could not read his riddle. Oh, too plain.   650

ANDROMACHE.
    I saw her there and left the chariot
    and covered her dead body with my cloak,
    and beat my breast.
HECUBA.
    Murdered—my child. Oh, wickedly!
    Again I cry to you. Oh, cruelly slain!   655
ANDROMACHE.
    She has died her death, and happier by far
    dying than I alive.
HECUBA.
    Life cannot be what death is, child.
    Death is empty—life has hope.
ANDROMACHE.
    Mother, O Mother, hear a truer word.   660
    Now let me bring joy to your heart.
    I say to die is only not to be,
    and rather death than life with bitter grief.
    They have no pain, they do not feel their wrongs.
    But the happy who has come to wretchedness,   665
    his soul is a lost wanderer,
    the old joys that were once, left far behind.
    She is dead, your daughter—to her the same
    as if she never had been born.
    She does not know the wickedness that killed
        her.   670
    While I—I aimed my shaft at good repute.
    I gained full measure—then missed happiness.
    For all that is called virtuous in a woman
    I strove for and I won in Hector's house.
    Always, because we women, whether right or
        wrong,   675
    are spoken ill of
    unless we stay within our homes, my longing
    I set aside and kept the house.
    Light talk, glib women's words,
    could never gain an entrance there.   680
    My own thoughts were enough for me,
    best of all teachers to me in my home.
    Silence, a tranquil eye, I brought my husband,
    knew well in what I should rule him,
    and when give him obedience.   685
    And this report of me came to the Greeks
    for my destruction. When they captured me
    Achilles' son would have me.
    I shall be a slave to those who murdered—
    O Hector, my beloved—shall I thrust him aside,   690
    open my heart to the man that comes to me,
    and be a traitor to the dead?
    And yet to shrink in loathing from him
    and make my masters hate me—
    One night, men say, one night in a man's bed   695
    will make a woman tame—
    Oh, shame! A woman throw her husband off

and in a new bed love another—
Why, a young colt will not run in the yoke
with any but her mate—not a dumb beast   700
that has no reason, of a lower nature.
O Hector, my beloved, you were all to me,
wise, noble, mighty, in wealth, in manhood, both.
No man had touched me when you took me,
took me from out my father's home   705
and yoked a girl fast to you.
And you are dead, and I, with other plunder,
am sent by sea to Greece. A slave's yoke there.
Your dead Polyxena you weep for,
what does she know of pain like mine?   710
The living must have hope. Not I, not any more.
I will not lie to my own heart. No good will ever
    come.
But oh, to think it would be sweet.

A WOMAN.
We stand at the same point of pain. You mourn your
    ruin,
and in your words I hear my own calamity.   715

HECUBA.
Those ships—I never have set foot on one,
but I have heard of them, seen pictures of them.
I know that when a storm comes which they think
they can ride out, the sailors do their best,
one by the sail, another at the helm,   720
and others bailing.
But if great ocean's raging overwhelms them,
they yield to fate.
They give themselves up to the racing waves.
So in my many sorrows I am dumb.   725
I yield, I cannot speak.
The great wave from God has conquered me.
But, O dear child, let Hector be,
and let be what has come to him.
Your tears will never call him back.   730
Give honor now to him who is your master.
Your sweet ways—use them to allure him.
So doing you will give cheer to your friends.
Perhaps this child, my own child's son,
you may rear to manhood and great aid for
    Troy,   735
and if ever you should have more children,
they might build her again. Troy once more be a
    city!
Oh—one thought leads another on.
But why again that servant of the Greeks?
I see him coming. Some new plan is here.   740

(*Enter* TALTHYBIUS *with soldiers. He is troubled and advances hesitatingly.*)

TALTHYBIUS.
Wife of the noblest man that was in Troy,
O wife of Hector, do not hate me.
Against my will I come to tell you.
The people and the kings have all resolved—

ANDROMACHE.
What is it? Evil follows words like those.   745

TALTHYBIUS.
This child they order—Oh, how can I say it—

ANDROMACHE.
Not that he does not go with me to the same
    master—

TALTHYBIUS.
No man in Greece shall ever be his master.

ANDROMACHE.
But—leave him here—all that is left of Troy?

TALTHYBIUS.
I don't know how to tell you. What is bad,   750
words can't make better—

ANDROMACHE.
I feel you kind. But you have not good news.

TALTHYBIUS.
Your child must die. There, now you know
the whole, bad as it is.

ANDROMACHE.
Oh, I have heard an evil worse   755
than a slave in her master's bed.

TALTHYBIUS.
It was Odysseus had his way. He spoke
to all the Greeks.

ANDROMACHE.
O God. There is no measure to my pain.

TALTHYBIUS.
He said a hero's son must not grow up—   760

ANDROMACHE.
God, on his own sons may that counsel fall.

TALTHYBIUS.
—but from the towering wall of Troy be thrown.
Now, now—let it be done—that's wiser.
Don't cling so to him. Bear your pain
the way a brave woman suffers.   765
You have no strength—don't look to any help.
There's no help for you anywhere. Think—think.
The city gone—your husband too. And you
a captive and alone, one woman—how
can you do battle with us? For your own good   770
I would not have you try, and draw
hatred down on you and be shamed.
Oh, hush—never a curse upon the Greeks.
If you say words that make the army angry
the child will have no burial, and without pity— 775
Silence now. Bear your fate as best you can.

So then you need not leave him dead without a
   grave,
and you will find the Greeks more kind.

ANDROMACHE.

Go die, my best beloved, my own, my treasure,
in cruel hands, leaving your mother comfortless. **780**
Your father was too noble. That is why
they kill you. He could save others,
he could not save you for his nobleness.
My bed, my bridal—all for misery—
when long ago I came to Hector's halls **785**
to bear my son—oh, not for Greeks to slay,
but for a ruler over teeming Asia.
Weeping, my little one? There, there.
You cannot know what waits for you.
Why hold me with your hands so fast, cling so
   fast to me? **790**
You little bird, flying to hide beneath my wings.
And Hector will not come—he will not come,
up from the tomb, great spear in hand, to save you.
Not one of all his kin, of all the Trojan might.
How will it be? Falling down—down—oh,
   horrible. **795**
And his neck—his breath—all broken.
And none to pity. You little thing,
curled in my arms, you dearest to your mother,
how sweet the fragrance of you.
All nothing then—this breast from where **800**
your baby mouth drew milk, my travail too,
my cares, when I grew wasted watching you.
Kiss me—Never again. Come, closer, closer.
Your mother who bore you—put your arms around
   my neck.
Now kiss me, lips to lips. **805**
O Greeks, you have found out ways to torture
that are not Greek.
A little child, all innocent of wrong—
you wish to kill him.
O Helen, evil growth, that was sown by
   Tyndareus, **810**
you are no child of Zeus, as people say.
Many the fathers you were born of,
Madness, Hatred, Red Death, whatever poison
the earth brings forth—no child of Zeus,
but Greece's curse and all the world's. **815**
God curse you, with those beautiful eyes
that brought to shame and ruin
Troy's far-famed plains.
Quick! take him—seize him—cast him down—
if so you will. Feast on his flesh. **820**
God has destroyed me, and I cannot—
I cannot save my child from death.
Oh hide my head for shame and fling me
into the ship.

(*She falls, then struggles to her knees.*)

My fair bridal—I am coming— **825**
Oh, I have lost my child, my own.

A WOMAN.

O wretched Troy, tens of thousands lost
for a woman's sake, a hateful marriage bed.

TALTHYBIUS (*drawing the child away*).

Come, boy, let go. Unclasp those loving hands,
poor mother. **830**
Come now, up, up, to the very height,
where the towers of your fathers crown the wall,
and where it is decreed that you must die.

(*To the soldiers.*)

Take him away.
A herald who must bring such orders **835**
should be a man who feels no pity,
and no shame either—not like me.

HECUBA.

Child, son of my poor son, whose toil was all in
   vain,
we are robbed, your mother and I, oh, cruelly—
robbed of your life. How bear it? **840**
What can I do for you, poor piteous child?
Beat my head, my breast—all I can give you.
Troy lost, now you—all lost.
The cup is full. Why wait? For what?
Hasten on—swiftly on to death. **845**

(*The soldiers, who have waited while* HECUBA *speaks, go out with the child and* TALTHYBIUS. *One of them takes* ANDROMACHE *to the chariot and drives off with her.*)

CHORUS.

The waves make a ring around Salamis.
The bees are loud in the island.
King Telamon built him a dwelling.
It fronted the holy hills,
where first the gray gleaming olive **850**
Athena showed to men,
the glory of shining Athens,
her crown from the sky.
He joined himself to the bowman,
the son of Alcmena, for valorous deeds. **855**
Troy, Troy he laid waste, my city,
long ago when he went forth from Greece.

*When Troy was destroyed the first time, the reason was that the Trojan king had promised two immortal horses to Hercules ("the son of Alcmena") but did not give them to him. Hercules in revenge ruined the city. The son of this king was Ganymede, cupbearer to Zeus.

When he led forth from Greece the bravest
in his wrath for the steeds* withheld,
and by fair-flowing Simois stayed his oar   860
that had brought him over the sea.
Cables there made the ship fast.
In his hand was the bow that never missed.
It brought the king to his death.
Walls of stone that Phoebus had built   865
he wrecked with the red breath of fire.
He wasted the plain of Troy.
Twice her walls have fallen. Twice
a blood-stained spear struck her down,
    laid her in ruin.

In vain, O you who move   870
with delicate feet where the wine-cups are gold,
son of that old dead king,
who fill with wine the cup Zeus holds,
service most fair—
she who gave you birth is afire.   875
The shores of the sea are wailing for her.
As a bird cries over her young,
women weep for husbands, for children,
for the old, too, who gave them birth.
Your dewy baths are gone,   880
and the race-course where you ran.
Yet your young face keeps the beauty of peace
in joy, by the throne of Zeus.
While Priam's land
lies ruined by Greek spearsmen.   885

Love, O Love,
once you came to the halls of Troy,
and your song rose up to the dwellers in heaven.
How did you then exalt Troy high,
binding her fast to the gods, by a union—   890
No—I will not speak blame of Zeus.
But the light of white-winged Dawn, dear to men,
is deadly over the land this day,
shining on fallen towers.
And yet Dawn keeps in her bridal bower   895
her children's father, a son of Troy.
Her chariot bore him away to the sky.
It was gold, and four stars drew it.
Hope was high then for our town.
But the magic that brought her the love of
    the gods   900
has gone from Troy.

(*As the song ends* MENELAUS *enters with a bodyguard of
soldiers.*)

MENELAUS.
    How bright the sunlight is today—
    this day, when I shall get into my power

Helen, my wife. For I am Menelaus,
the man of many wrongs.   905
I came to Troy and brought with me my army,
not for that woman's sake, as people say,
but for the man who from my house,
and he a guest there, stole away my wife.
Ah, well, with God's help he has paid the price,   910
he and his country, fallen beneath Greek spears.
I am come to get her—wretch—I cannot speak her
    name
who was my wife once.
In a hut here, where they house the captives,
she is numbered with the other Trojan women.   915
The men who fought and toiled to win her back,
have given her to me—to kill, or else,
if it pleases me, to take her back to Argos.
And it has seemed to me her death in Troy
is not the way. I will take her overseas,   920
with swift oars speeding on the ship,
and there in Greece give her to those to kill
whose dearest died because of her.

(*To his men.*)

    Attention! Forward to the huts.
    Seize her and drag her out by that long blood-
        drenched hair—   925

(*Stops suddenly and controls himself.*)

    And when fair winds come, home with her to
        Greece.

(*Soldiers begin to force the door of one of the huts.*)

HECUBA (*comes slowly forward*).
    O thou who dost uphold the world,
    whose throne is high above the world,
    thou, past our seeking hard to find, who art thou?
    God, or Necessity of what must be,   930
    or Reason of our reason?
    Whate'er thou art, I pray to thee,
    seeing the silent road by which
    all mortal things are led by thee to justice.
MENELAUS.
    What have we here? A queer prayer that.   935
HECUBA (*she comes still nearer to him and he recognizes
    her*).
    Kill her, Menelaus? You will? Oh, blessings on you!
    But—shun her, do not look at her.
    Desire for her will seize you, conquer you.
    For through men's eyes she gets them in her power.
    She ruins them and ruins cities too.   940
    Fire comes from her to burn homes,
    magic for death. I know her—so do you,
    and all these who have suffered.

(HELEN *enters from the hut. The soldiers do not touch her.*
She is very gentle and undisturbed.)

HELEN (*with sweet, injured dignity, angry at all*). *Not*
 Menelaus, these things might well make a woman
  fear.
 Your men with violence have driven me from my
  room,   945
 have laid their hands upon me.
 Of course I know—almost I know—you hate me,
 but yet I ask you, what is your decision,
 yours and the Greeks? Am I to live or not?

MENELAUS.
 Nothing more clear. Unanimous, in fact.   950
 Not one who did not vote you should be given me,
 whom you have wronged, to kill you.

HELEN.
 Am I allowed to speak against the charge?
 To show you if I die that I shall die
 most wronged and innocent?   955

MENELAUS.
 I have come to kill you, not to argue with you.

HECUBA.
 Oh, hear her. She must never die unheard.
 Then, Menelaus, let me answer her.
 The evil that she did in Troy, you do not know.
 But I will tell the story. She will die.   960
 She never can escape.

MENELAUS.
 That means delay. Still—if she wants to speak,
 she can. I grant her this because of what you say,
 not for her sake. She can be sure of that.

HELEN.
 And perhaps, no matter if you think I speak   965
 the truth or not, you will not talk to me,
 since you believe I am your enemy.
 Still, I will try to answer what I think
 you would say if you spoke your mind,
 and my wrongs shall be heard as well as yours.   970
 First: who began these evils? She, the day
 when she gave birth to Paris. Who next was guilty?
 The old king who decreed the child should live,
 and ruined Troy and me—Paris, the hateful,
 the firebrand.   975
 What happened then? Listen and learn.
 This Paris—he was made the judge for three,
 all yoked together in a quarrel—goddesses.
 Athena promised he should lead the Trojans
 to victory and lay all Greece in ruins.   980
 And Hera said if he thought her the fairest
 she would make him lord of Europe and of Asia.

But Aphrodite—well, she praised my beauty—
astonishing, she said—and promised him
that she would give me to him if he judged   985
that she was loveliest. Then, see what happened.
She won, and so my bridal brought all Greece
great good. No strangers rule you,
no foreign spears, no tyrant.
Oh, it was well for Greece, but not for me,   990
sold for my beauty and reproached besides
when I deserved a crown.
But—to the point. Is that what you are thinking?
Why did I go—steal from your house in secret?
That man, Paris, or any name you like to call   995
 him,
his mother's curse—oh, when he came to me
a mighty goddess walked beside him.
And you, poor fool, you spread your sails for Crete,
left Sparta—left him in your house.
Ah well—Not you, but my own self I ask,   1000
what was there in my heart that I went with him,
a strange man, and forgot my home and country?
Not I, but Aphrodite. Punish her,
be mightier than Zeus who rules
the other gods, but is her slave.   1005
She is my absolution—
One thing with seeming justice you might say.
When Paris died and went down to the grave,
and when no god cared who was in my bed,
I should have left his house—gone to the
  Greeks.   1010
Just what I tried to do—oh, many times.
I have witnesses—the men who kept the gates,
the watchmen on the walls. Not once, but often
they found me swinging from a parapet,
a rope around this body, stealthily   1015
feeling my way down.
The Trojans then no longer wanted me,
but the man who next took me—and by force—
would never let me go.
My husband, must I die, and at your hands?   1020
You think that right? Is that your justice?
I was forced—by violence. I lived a life
that had no joy, no triumph. In bitterness
I lived a slave.
Do you wish to set yourself above the gods?   1025
Oh, stupid, senseless wish!

A WOMAN.
 O Queen, defend your children and your country.
 Her soft persuasive words are deadly.
 She speaks so fair and is so vile.
 A fearful thing.   1030

HECUBA.

> Her goddesses will fight on my side while
> I show her for the liar that she is.
> Not Hera, not virgin Athena, do I think
> would ever stoop to folly great enough
> to sell their cities. Hera sell her Argos,   **1035**
> Athena Athens, to be the Trojan's slave!
> playing like silly children there on Ida,
> and each one in her insolence demanding
> the prize for beauty. Beauty—why was Hera
> so hot for it? That she might get herself   **1040**
> a better mate than Zeus?
> Athena—who so fled from marriage that she begged
> one gift from Zeus, virginity.
> But she would have the prize, you say. And why?
> To help her hunt some god to marry her?   **1045**
> Never make gods out fools to whitewash your own
>   evil.
> No one with sense will listen to you.
> And Aphrodite, did you say—who would not laugh?
> —must take my son to Menelaus' house?
> Why? Could she not stay quietly in heaven   **1050**
> and send you on—and all your town—to Troy?
> My son was beautiful exceedingly.
> You saw him—your own desire was enough.
> No need of any goddess.
> Men's follies—they are Aphrodite.   **1055**
> She rose up from the sea-foam; where the froth
> and foam of life are, there she is.
> It was my son. You saw him in his Eastern dress
> all bright with gold, and you were mad with love.
> Such little things had filled your mind in
>   Argos,   **1060**
> busied with this and that.
> Once free of Sparta and in Troy where gold,
> you thought, flowed like a river, you would spend
> and spend, until your spendthrift hand
> had drowned the town.   **1065**
> Your luxuries, your insolent excesses,
> Menelaus' halls had grown too small for them.
> Enough of that. By force you say he took you?
> You cried out? Where? No one in Sparta heard you.
> Young Castor was there and his brother too,   **1070**
> not yet among the stars.
> And when you came to Troy and on your track the
>   Greeks,
> and death and agony in battle,
> if they would tell you, "Greece has won today,"
> you would praise this man here, Menelaus,   **1075**
> to vex my son, who feared him as a rival.
> Then Troy had victories, and Menelaus
> was nothing to you.
> Looking to the successful side—oh yes,
> you always followed there.   **1080**

> There was no right or wrong side in your eyes.
> And now you talk of ropes—letting your body down
> in secret from the wall, longing to go.
> Who found you so?
> Was there a noose around your neck?   **1085**
> A sharp knife in your hand? Such ways
> as any honest woman would have found,
> who loved the husband she had lost?
> Often and often I would tell you, Go,
> my daughter. My sons will find them other
>   wives.   **1090**
> I will help you. I will send you past the lines
> to the Greek ships. Oh, end this war
> between our foes and us. But this was bitter to you.
> In Paris' house you had your insolent way.
> You liked to see the Eastern men fall at your
>   feet.   **1095**
> These were great things to you.
> Look at the dress you wear, your ornaments.
> Is that the way to meet your husband?
> You should not dare to breathe the same air with him.
> Oh, men should spit upon you.   **1100**
> Humbly, in rags, trembling and shivering,
> with shaven head—so you should come,
> with shame at last, instead of shamelessness,
> for all the wickedness you did.
> King, one word more and I am done.   **1105**
> Give Greece a crown, be worthy of yourself.
> Kill her. So shall the law stand for all women,
> that she who plays false to her husband's bed,
> shall die.

A WOMAN.

> O son of an ancient house, O King, now show   **1110**
> that you are worthy of your fathers.
> The Greeks called you a woman, shamed you
> with that reproach. Be strong. Be noble. Punish her.

MENELAUS (*impatiently*).

> I see it all as you do. We agree.
> She left my house because she wanted to—   **1115**
> went to a stranger's bed. Her talk of Aphrodite—
> big words, no more. (*Turns to* HELEN.) Go. Death is
>   near.
> Men there are waiting for you. In their hands are
>   stones.
> Die—a small price for the Greeks' long suffering.
> You shall not any more dishonor me.   **1120**

HELEN (*kneeling and clinging to him*).

> No! No! Upon my knees—see, I am praying to you.
> It was the gods, not me. Oh, do not kill me.
> Forgive.

HECUBA.

> The men she murdered. Think of those
> who fought beside you—of their children too.   **1125**
> Never betray them. Hear that prayer.

MENELAUS (*roughly*).
>   Enough, old woman. She is nothing to me.
>   Men, take her to the ships and keep her safe
>   until she sails.

HECUBA.
>   But not with you! She must not set foot on your
>   ship.   **1130**

MENELAUS (*bitterly*).
>   And why? Her weight too heavy for it?

HECUBA.
>   A lover once, a lover always.

MENELAUS (*pauses a moment to think*).
>   Not so when what he loved has gone.
>   But it shall be as you would have it.
>   Not on the same ship with me. The advice is
>   good.   **1135**
>   And when she gets to Argos she shall die
>   a death hard as her heart.
>   So in the end she will become a teacher,
>   teach women chastity—no easy thing,
>   but yet her utter ruin will strike terror   **1140**
>   into their silly hearts,
>   even women worse than she.

CHORUS.
>   And so your temple in Ilium,
>   your altar of frankincense,
>   are given to the Greek,   **1145**
>   the flame from the honey, the corn and the oil,
>   the smoke from the myrrh floating upward,
>   the holy citadel.
>   And Ida, the mountain where the ivy grows,
>   and rivers from the snows rush through the
>   glens,   **1150**
>   and the boundary wall of the world
>   where the first sunlight falls,
>   the blessed home of the dawn.
>
>   The sacrifice is gone, and the glad call
>   of dancers, and the prayers at evening to
>   the gods   **1155**
>   that last the whole night long.
>   Gone too the golden images,
>   and the twelve Moons, to Trojans holy.
>   Do you care, do you care, do you heed these things,
>   O God, from your throne in high heaven?   **1160**
>   My city is perishing,
>   ending in fire and onrushing flame.

A WOMAN.
>   O dear one, O my husband,
>   you are dead, and you wander
>   unburied, uncared for, while over-seas   **1165**
>   the ships shall carry me,
>   swift-winged ships darting onward,
>   on to the land the riders love,

>   Argos, where the towers of stone
>   built by giants reach the sky.   **1170**

ANOTHER.
>   Children, our children.
>   At the gate they are crying, crying,
>   calling to us with tears,
>   Mother, I am all alone.
>   They are driving me away   **1175**
>   to a black ship, and I cannot see you.

ANOTHER.
>   Where, oh where? To holy Salamis,
>   with swift oars dipping?
>   Or to the crest of Corinth,
>   the city of two seas,   **1180**
>   where the gates King Pelops built
>   for his dwelling stand?

ANOTHER.
>   Oh, if only, far out to sea,
>   the crashing thunder of God
>   would fall down, down on Menelaus' ship,   **1185**
>   crashing down upon her oars,
>   the Aegean's wild-fire light.
>   He it was drove me from Troy.
>   He is driving me in tears
>   over to Greece to slavery.   **1190**

ANOTHER.
>   And Helen, too, with her mirrors of gold,
>   looking and wondering at herself,
>   as pleased as a girl.
>   May she never come to the land of her fathers,
>   never see the hearth of her home,   **1195**
>   her city, the temple with brazen doors
>   of goddess Athena.
>   Oh, evil marriage that brought
>   shame to Greece, the great,
>   and to the waters of Simois   **1200**
>   sorrow and suffering.

(TALTHYBIUS *approaches with a few soldiers. He is carrying the dead child.*)

ANOTHER WOMAN.
>   Before new sufferings are grown old
>   come other new.
>   Look, unhappy wives of Troy,
>   the dead Astyanax.   **1205**
>   They threw him from the tower as one might pitch a
>   ball.
>   Oh, bitter killing.
>   And now they have him there.

TALTHYBIUS (*he gives the body into* HECUBA'S *arms*).
>   One ship is waiting, Hecuba, to take aboard
>   the last of all the spoil Achilles' son was given,   **1210**
>   and bear it with the measured beat of oars
>   to Thessaly's high headlands.

The chief himself has sailed because of news
he heard, his father's father
driven from his land by his own son.   1215
So, more for haste even than before,
he went and with him went Andromache.
She drew tears from me there upon the ship
mourning her country, speaking to Hector's grave,
begging a burial for her child, your Hector's
    son,   1220
who thrown down from the tower lost his life.
And this bronze-fronted shield, the dread of many a
    Greek,
which Hector used in battle,
that it should never, so she prayed,
hang in strange halls, her grief before her eyes,   1225
nor in that bridal chamber where she must be a wife,
Andromache, this dead boy's mother.
She begged that he might lie upon it in his grave,
instead of cedar wood or vault of stone.
And in your arms she told me I must lay him,   1230
for you to cover the body, if you still
have anything, a cloak left—
And to put flowers on him if you could,
since she has gone. Her master's haste
kept her from burying her child.   1235
So now, whenever you have laid him out,
we'll heap the earth above him, then
up with the sails!
Do all as quickly as you can. One trouble
I saved you. When we passed Scamander's
    stream   1240
I let the water run on him and washed his wounds.
I am off to dig his grave now, break up the hard
    earth.
Working together, you and I,
will hurry to the goal, oars swift for home.

HECUBA.
    Set the shield down—the great round shield of
        Hector.   1245
    I wish I need not look at it.

(TALTHYBIUS *goes out with the soldiers.*)

You Greeks, your spears are sharp but not your wits.
You feared a child. You murdered him.
Strange murder. You were frightened, then? You
    thought
he might build up our ruined Troy? And yet   1250
when Hector fought and thousands at his side,
we fell beneath you. Now, when all is lost,
the city captured and the Trojans dead,
a little child like this made you afraid.
The fear that comes when reason goes away—   1255
Myself, I do not wish to share it.

(*She dismisses the Greeks and their ways.*)

Beloved, what a death has come to you.
If you had fallen fighting for the city,
if you had known strong youth and love
and godlike power, if we could think   1260
you had known happiness—if there is
happiness anywhere—
But now—you saw and knew, but with your soul
you did not know, and what was in your house
you could not use.   1265
Poor little one. How savagely our ancient walls,
Apollo's towers, have torn away the curls
your mother's fingers wound and where she pressed
her kisses—here where the broken bone grins
    white—
Oh no—I cannot—   1270
Dear hands, the same dear shape your father's had,
how loosely now you fall. And dear proud lips
forever closed. False words you spoke to me
when you would jump into my bed, call me sweet
    names
and tell me, Grandmother, when you are dead,   1275
I'll cut off a great lock of hair and lead my soldiers
    all
to ride out past your tomb.
Not you, but I, old, homeless, childless,
must lay you in your grave, so young,
so miserably dead.   1280
Dear God. How you would run to greet me.
And I would nurse you in my arms, and oh,
so sweet to watch you sleep. All gone.
What could a poet carve upon your tomb?
"A child lies here whom the Greeks feared
    and slew."   1285
Ah, Greece should boast of that.
Child, they have taken all that was your father's,
but one thing, for your burying, you shall have,
the bronze-barred shield.
It kept safe Hector's mighty arm, but now   1290
it has lost its master.
The grip of his own hand has marked it—dear to me
    then—
His sweat has stained the rim. Often and often
in battle it rolled down from brows and beard
while Hector held the shield close.   1295
Come, bring such covering for the pitiful dead body
as we still have. God has not left us much
to make a show with. Everything I have
I give you, child.
    O men, secure when once good fortune
        comes—   1300
fools, fools. Fortune's ways—
here now, there now. She springs

away—back—and away, an idiot's dance.
No one is ever always fortunate.

(*The women have come in with coverings and garlands.*)

A WOMAN.
    Here, for your hands, they bring you clothing for the
        dead.   **1305**
    got from the spoils of Troy.
HECUBA (*shrouding the body and putting garlands beside it*).
    Oh, not because you conquered when the horses
        raced,
    or with the bow outdid your comrades,
    your father's mother lays these wreaths beside you,
    and of all that was yours, gives you this
        covering.   **1310**
    A woman whom God hates has robbed you,
    taken your life, when she had taken your treasure
    and ruined all your house.
A WOMAN.
    Oh, my heart! As if you touched it—touched it.
    Oh, this was once our prince, great in the city.   **1315**
HECUBA.
    So on your wedding day I would have dressed you,
    the highest princess of the East your bride.
    Now on your body I must lay the raiment,
    all that is left of the splendor that was Troy's.
    And the dear shield of Hector, glorious in
        battle,   **1320**
    mother of ten thousand triumphs won,
    it too shall have its wreath of honor,
    undying it will lie beside the dead.
    More honorable by far than all the armor
    Odysseus won, the wicked and the wise.   **1325**
A WOMAN.
    You, O child, our bitter sorrow,
    earth will now receive.
    Mourn, O Mother.
HECUBA.
    Mourn, indeed.
A WOMAN.
    Weeping for all the dead.   **1330**
HECUBA.
    Bitter tears.
A WOMAN.
    Your sorrows that can never be forgotten.

(*The funeral rite is now begun,* HECUBA *symbolically healing
the wounds.*)

HECUBA.
    I heal your wounds; with linen I bind them.
    Ah, in words only, not in truth—
    a poor physician.   **1335**
    But soon among the dead your father
    will care for you.

A WOMAN.
    Beat, beat your head.
    Lift your hands and let them fall,
    moving in measure.   **1340**
HECUBA.
    O Women. Dearest—
A WOMAN.
    Oh, speak to us. Your cry—what does it mean?
HECUBA.
    Only this the gods would have,
    pain for me and pain for Troy,
    those they hated bitterly.   **1345**
    Vain, vain, the bulls we slew.
    And yet—had God not bowed us down,
    not laid us low in dust,
    none would have sung of us or told our wrongs
    in stories men will listen to forever.   **1350**
    Go: lay our dead in his poor grave,
    with these last gifts of death given to him.
    I think those that are gone care little
    how they are buried. It is we, the living,
    our vanity.   **1355**

(*Women lift the shield with the body on it and carry it out.*)

A WOMAN.
    Poor mother—her high hopes were stayed on you
    and they are broken.
    They called you happy at your birth,
    a good man's son.
    Your death was miserable exceedingly.   **1360**
ANOTHER.
    Oh, see, see—
    On the crested height of Troy
    fiery hands. They are flinging torches.
    Can it be
    some new evil?   **1365**
    Something still unknown?
TALTHYBIUS (*stops as he enters and speaks off stage*).
    Captains, attention. You have been given charge
    to burn this city. Do not let your torches sleep.
    Hurry the fire on.
    When once the town is level with the ground   **1370**
    then off for home and glad goodbye to Troy.
    And you, you Women—I will arrange for you
    as well, one speech for everything—
    whenever a loud trumpet-call is sounded,
    go to the Greek ships, to embark.   **1375**
    Old woman, I am sorriest for you,
    follow. Odysseus' men are here to get you.
    He drew you—you must leave here as his slave.
HECUBA.
    The end then. Well—the height of sorrow, I stand
        there. Troy is burning—I am going.   **1380**
    But—hurry, old feet, if you can,

a little nearer—here, where I can see
my poor town, say goodbye to her.
You were so proud a city, in all the East
the proudest. Soon your name the whole world
   knew,   1385
will be taken from you. They are burning you
and leading us away, their slaves.
O God— What makes me say that word?
The gods— I prayed, they never listened.
Quick, into the fire— Troy, I will die with you. 1390
Death then—oh, beautiful.

TALTHYBIUS.
   Out of your head, poor thing, with all you've suffered.
   Lead her away— Hold her, don't be too gentle.
   She must be taken to Odysseus.
   Give her into his hands. She is his—   1395
   (*Shakes his head.*)
   his prize.

(*It grows darker.*)

A WOMAN.
   Ancient of days, our country's Lord,
   Father, who made us,
   You see your children's sufferings.
   Have we deserved them?   1400

ANOTHER.
   He sees—but Troy has perished, the great city.
   No city now, never again.

ANOTHER.
   Oh, terrible!
   The fire lights the whole town up.
   The inside rooms are burning.   1405
   The citadel—it is all flame now.

ANOTHER.
   Troy is vanishing.
   War first ruined her.
   And what was left is rushing up in smoke,
   the glorious houses fallen.   1410
   First the spear and then the fire.

HECUBA (*she stands up and seems to be calling to someone
   far away*).
   Children, hear, your mother is calling.

A WOMAN (*gently*).
   They are dead, those you are speaking to.

HECUBA.
   My knees are stiff, but I must kneel.
   Now, strike the ground with both my hands— 1415

A WOMAN.
   I too, I kneel upon the ground.
   I call to mine down there.
   Husband, poor husband.

HECUBA.
   They are driving us like cattle—taking us away.

A WOMAN.
   Pain, all pain.   1420

ANOTHER.
   To a slave's house, from my country.

HECUBA.
   Priam, Priam, you are dead,
   and not a friend to bury you.
   The evil that has found me—
   do you know?   1425

A WOMAN.
   No. Death has darkened his eyes.
   He was good and the wicked killed him.

HECUBA.
   O dwellings of the gods and O dear city,
   the spear came first and now
   only the red flame lives there.   1430

A WOMAN.
   Fall and be forgotten. Earth is kind.

ANOTHER.
   The dust is rising, spreading out like a great wing of
     smoke.
   I cannot see my house.

ANOTHER.
   The name has vanished from the land,
   and we are gone, one here, one there.   1435
   And Troy is gone forever.

(*A great crash is heard.*)

HECUBA.
   Did you hear? Did you know—

A WOMAN.
   The fall of Troy—

ANOTHER.
   Earthquake and flood and the city's end—

HECUBA.
   Trembling body—old weak limbs,   1440
   you must carry me on to the new day of slavery.

(*A trumpet sounds.*)

A WOMAN.
   Farewell, dear city.
   Farewell, my country, where once my children lived.
   On to the ships—
   There below, the Greek ships wait.   1445

(*The trumpet sounds again and the women pass out.*)

FOCUS QUESTIONS

1. How does the Prologue, spoken by Poseidon and Athena, serve the play?
2. Assess Euripides' handling of the Chorus. Has he preserved or destroyed its function as one character?
3. Develop separate character sketches of Talthybius and Menelaus and describe their roles in relation to the women in the play.
4. How do the different verse formats of Cassandra's first and second monologues reflect their respective content?
5. Develop a character sketch of Helen based on her reputation in history as well as the playwright's portrait.
6. In a short essay, discuss the different faces of women depicted in the play.
7. Describe how Euripides condemns Athens in its dealings with the allies.

OTHER ACTIVITIES

1. Prepare a dramatic reading of Hecuba's opening soliloquy and discuss its emotional impact.
2. Block Andromache's farewell to Astyanax by describing the stage movements of the characters who participate in this scene. Notice the stage directions Euripides has already built into Andromache's words: for example, "Put your arms around my neck./ Now kiss me, lips to lips."
3. View the 1971 Cacoyannis film version of *The Trojan Women* and discuss the effectiveness of the play's transference to the screen.

BIBLIOGRAPHY

Arnott, Peter D. *Public and Performance in the Greek Theatre*. New York: Routledge, 1989.

Barlow, Shirley Ann. *The Imagery of Euripides: A Study in the Dramatic Use of Pictorial Language*. London: Methuen, 1971.

Burian, Peter, ed. *Directions in Euripidean Criticism: A Collection of Essays*. Durham, NC: Duke University Press, 1985.

Burnett, Anne. *Catastrophe Survived: Euripides' Plays of Mixed Reversal*. Oxford: Clarendon Press, 1971.

Cropp, Martin, and Gordon Fick. *Resolutions and Chronology in Euripides: The Fragmentary Tragedies*. London: Institute of Classical Studies, 1985.

Diggle, James. *Studies on the Text of Euripides*. New York: Oxford University Press, 1981.

Foley, Helene P. *Ritual Irony: Poetry and Sacrifice in Euripides*. Ithaca, NY: Cornell University Press, 1985.

Gregory, Justina. *Euripides and the Instruction of the Athenians*. Ann Arbor: University of Michigan, 1991.

Micheline, Ann. *Euripides and the Tragic Tradition*. Madison: University of Wisconsin Press, 1987.

Murray, Gilbert. *Euripides and His Age*. Oxford, 1946. Reprint Westport, CT: Greenwood Press, 1979.

Norwood, Gilbert. *Essays on Euripidean Drama*. New York: Cambridge University Press, 1954.

Powell, Anton, ed. *Euripides, Women and Sexuality*. New York: Routledge, 1990.

Scodel, Ruth. *The Trojan Trilogy of Euripides*. Gottingen: Vandenhoeck & Ruprecht, 1979.

Vellacott, Philip. *Ironic Drama: A Study of Euripides' Method and Meaning.* London and New York: Cambridge University Press, 1975.

Vince, Ronald. *Ancient and Medieval Theatre: A Historiographical Handbook.* Westport, CT: Greenwood Press, 1984.

Whitman, Cedric Hubbell. *Euripides and the Full Circle of Myth.* Cambridge: Harvard University Press, 1974.

RECOMMENDED VIDEOTAPES AND RECORDINGS

Euripides' Life and Times: The Trojan Women. VHS. 38 min. Distributed by Insight Media, New York. Features professionally acted scenes from the play.

The Trojan Women. VHS. 105 min. 1971. MCA Distributing Corp. In English. Edith Hamilton, trans. Michael Cacoyannis, director. Starring Katherine Hepburn, Vanessa Redgrave, Genevieve Bujold, Irene Papas.

The Trojan Women. Sound cassette. 36 min. 1973. Kenneth Cavendar. Everett/Edwards, World Literature Cassette Curriculum.

THE BIRDS
ARISTOPHANES (C. 450–C. 385 B.C.)

Birds is the longest extant comedy, to modern taste one of the most imaginative and stylish, and on any reckoning one of the most spectacular.

—K. J. DOVER

Pithetaerus and Euelpides surrounded by the Chorus in *The Birds,* presented by the Greek Art Theatre in 1959, under the direction of Karolos Koun. *Photo: Dimis Argyropoulos.*

APPROACHING CLASSICAL COMEDY

The face of classical Greek drama wears two masks: one tragic, the other comic. Although comedy was officially recognized at the City Dionysia after the birth of tragedy, both origins can be traced to the same religious festivals that honored Dionysus, god of wine and fertility. Entering the performance space and wearing an oversized mask that covered his entire head and rested on his shoulders, the comic actor—unlike his tragic counterpart—padded his belly and buttocks and flaunted an exaggerated phallus to symbolize the source of Dionysian power. But more importantly, his purpose was to elicit laughter from the spectator.

In contrast with his detailed description of tragedy, Aristotle's investigation of comedy is more succinct, yet no less illuminating. Observing how comedy imitates ''characters of a lower type'' in contrast with tragedy's loftier figures, he saw the actor's comic mask as ''ugly and distorted'' but with no implication of pain.[1] Perhaps his description warrants an understanding of the classical Greek concept of beauty, which denoted harmonious integration or wholeness. Hence its opposite, or lack of integration, was considered incongruous or ugly—the right stuff for comedy. We are caught by surprise when a sudden pratfall rudely interrupts the poised demeanor of an actor on stage, and we laugh at his ridiculousness. Presuming he has not hurt himself, for his action is merely imitative or make-believe, we confront an important aspect of comedy's grimacing mask in the comic actor's deliberate fall from grace, his unexpected shift from order to disorder, from wholeness to disintegration.

In Plato's *Symposium,* Socrates tells his two listeners, one of whom is the comic playwright Aristophanes, that ''the man who knew how to write a comedy could also write a tragedy, and that a skillful tragic writer was capable of being also a comic writer''—an intimidating notion for any playwright who chooses one form over the other, as Aristophanes certainly did.[2] Plato's remark is important: it reminds us that the rituals from which tragedy and comedy developed were serious means for purifying the community of its ills. While tragedy reflected on the myths and legends of the past as a way of solidifying a sense of collective identity and responsibility, comedy stemmed from the need to identify human foibles and eccentricities as a way of maintaining a balanced society and pointing out the need for change. Comedic obscenity, clowning, irreverence, and satire were antidotes as crucial to Greek audiences as the tragic katharsis. Its joyful renewal and celebration of a happy ending were as vital as tragedy's fear and suffering.

If an essential component of classical tragedy was retrospection, in which the playwright reflected on the heroes and legends that shaped Athens' destiny, the targets of **Old Comedy** were topical: the ammunition was political satire or ridicule. No wonder Aristophanes, the only playwright of this genre whose works survive, was able to burlesque the major personalities and events of his day in sharply etched scenes that won instant audience approval. In short, his comedy provided imaginative opportunities for tackling a variety of issues, including a direct political address to the spectators—the **parabasis**—which interrupted the action.

The fact that more than fifty Athenian comic writers competed with Aristophanes during his lifetime shows how popular and diverse the tradition was. Except for eleven of the forty comedies Aristophanes wrote, we are left with no comic models against which to measure his achievement. Thus our practical model for Old Comedy, also known as Aristophanic Comedy, must rest on the works of the playwright who lends his name to the form.

MAJOR WORKS

Three of Aristophanes' plays, *Acharnians* (425 B.C.), *Peace* (421 B.C.), and *Lysistrata* (411 B.C.), deal directly with the effects of the long-running Peloponnesian turmoil. In one of his more enduring works, *Lysistrata,* written when his country had already invested twenty-one years in the war, the playwright creates an Athenian protagonist who valiantly persuades her countrywomen, including those wives from other warring districts, to deny sexual intercourse to their husbands until the men agree to end the war. Aristophanes' innovative premise, with its colorful characters, explicit language, and smartly executed comic turns, not only makes strong anti-war sentiment palatable to the audience, but also strikes a blow for universal feminism. As an alternative solution in *Peace,* the hero flies to Mount Olympus to retrieve the goddess Peace.

Turning serious emotional confrontations over to the tragedians, Aristophanes seeks laughter everywhere: *Knights* (424 B.C.) depicts the conflict between a master and his slaves and, through the clever use of comic allegory, parallels domestic and political hierarchies in Athenian society; in *Clouds* (423 B.C.), the great Socrates, whose latest philosophical teachings are the talk of Athens, hangs from the air to protect himself from the earth's force, which threatens to drain his intellect; *Wasps* (422 B.C.) satirizes the Athenian's passion for jury duty and the unruly organization of the court system; and in two later works, *Women at the Thesmophoria* (411 B.C.) and *Frogs* (405 B.C.), Euripides becomes a popular literary target when, in the former, the women of Athens accuse him of misogyny, a reputation the tragedian partly owed to Aristophanes; while, in the latter, his unconventional style of tragedy is mercilessly assaulted.

When the Peloponnesian War had ended in 404 B.C., Aristophanes and his younger contemporary comic writers turned away from political commentary to focus on contemporary domestic issues. This was a phase of comedy in which the political satire and *parabasis* of Old Comedy were dropped, and the role and size of the chorus were reduced. Aristophanes' *Ecclesiazusae* (392–391 B.C.) and *Plutus* (388 B.C.) are the only complete examples of this transitional form, which became known as **Middle Comedy.** His plays, whether they exemplify Old or Middle Comedy, revel in the present moment and, as *The Birds* (414 B.C.) so lavishly demonstrates, in the contemplation of humanity's future as well.

THE ACTION

Escaping Athens, the only society they know, Pithetaerus (loyal friend) and Euelpides (eternal optimist) have climbed to an elevated peak where Epops, King of the Birds, now rules. Formerly a man, but changed by Apollo into a bird, Epops has flown all over the world, and they hope he has discovered a city ''more pleasant to live in'' than Athens. Dismayed that Epops has no answer for them, Pithetaerus conceives a plan that will allow the birds to seize all the power of the universe and rule over mankind and the gods. Excited by this prospect, Epops summons his airy kingdom for further consultation with these two featherless intruders.

Pithetaerus and Euelpides return to the action as converts to the flock, awkwardly sporting their own sets of wings. The play's comic solution follows a series of rapid-fire encounters with charlatans and quacks, all from earth and full of the same evil schemes from which our protagonists originally fled; and a smoky, slapstick truce with Prometheus and consorts who, at Pithetaerus' suggestion, might be willing to roast certain ''politically unreliable'' fowl for dinner.

STRUCTURE AND LANGUAGE

The Birds took second prize at the drama festival held at the Theatre of Dionysus in 414 B.C. Its unconventional and fantastic premise suggests that human beings will become superior to the immortal gods by founding a better world, with assistance from the bird kingdom. The play is surprisingly ambitious in design. Typical features include the familiar prologue (the appearance of Pithetaerus and Euelpides) in which the Happy Idea of creating a Utopia in the clouds is presented; the *parodos* (entrance of the bird chorus); and an uncomplicated **agon** (debate) conveniently patterned on crisis versus solution, in which the birds, who support or oppose Epops' plan, argue its merits. As part of the unearthly resolution, Pithetaerus wins the hand of a goddess, captured by the **komos** or marriage celebration, symbolizing the union of earth and heaven. Revealing Aristophanes at the peak of his artistry, *The Birds* epitomizes the victory of the actor's comic mask over his tragic one.

The comedy luxuriates in Aristotle's demand for thought, language, character, plot, spectacle, and music. Its two protagonists easily embody Aristotle's call for lower types: in this case, two desperate Athenians who seek refuge on a mountaintop high above their urban woes. They also represent the Western drama's first comic team, a veritable odd couple, whose misadventures lead them into the heart of the comic conflict. ''The city's infested,'' cries Euelpides. ''That's why we left.'' Hearing this familiar complaint echoed early in the play, the audience joyfully anticipates the crazy antics of two comic surrogates who find the courage to assert themselves in behalf of a Utopia of which even the gods would be jealous.

Now it may not be wise to reflect too seriously on the preposterous events that occur in *The Birds,* for the playwright's primary aim is laughter. But it is the kind of laughter that bears a hard edge and is rarely escapist. Therefore it is difficult to ignore the comedy's underlying political allegory, wherein Aristophanes' cry for universal harmony or his warnings against environmental pollution and a corrupt legal system are eloquently voiced. Indeed these larger issues still provoke our modern sensibilities and transcend the historical event that supposedly prompted Aristophanes to compose his fantasy, the Sicilian Expedition of 415 B.C., an occurrence that would have given Athens control over the entire Mediterranean empire had it succeeded.

Fortunately, no serious theorizing can diminish the poetry, pageantry, and hilarious comedy that embellish the action. As for the eponymous birds, they prove to be less active in advancing the outcome of the play than in providing colorful atmosphere with their violent threats to our heroes from earth. Thus in militaristic fashion, twenty-four actors—the size of the chorus in Greek comedy—descend from different corners of the sky to express their anger. Upon learning that their leader has been consorting with the enemy below, they exclaim:

> We are cheated and betrayed, we have suffered shame and wrong!
> Our comrade and our King, who has fed with us so long,
> Has broken every oath, and his holy plighted troth,
> And the old social customs of our clan!

Pleading for his life in a formal Aristophanic argument that counterpoints the chorus's sharp metrical pronouncements, Pithetaerus proves how feathered creatures once ruled the universe. He even proposes an architectural design for their new city, to be called Cloud Cuckoo-land, nestled ''twixt the Earth and the Sky,/ Encircling it all with a brick-builded wall/ Like Babylon's, solid and high.''

Encouraged by Pithetaerus, who consults briefly with Euelpides, the birds tighten formation to address the audience in this temporary suspension of the dramatic action known as the *parabasis*. Voicing the playwright's warning to all human beings ''who are dimly existing below'' but who repeatedly dare to overstep their own mortality by honoring false gods, the birds assert their superiority in this first *parabasis* with a resounding crescendo: ''Truly to be clad in feathers is the very best of things!'' At his own expense, Aristophanes tackles the critics in a second *parabasis*, by letting his outspoken chorus describe the messy aerial revenge they will wreak upon them ''should the reviews [of his play] be bad tomorrow.''

Allowing two sides of a question to be argued in the presence of the audience, an important structural feature of *The Birds,* Aristophanes is asking us to assess the serious issues underlying his satire. But no matter how formulaic his devices seem to us today, their overall design embraces the same demands of character, action, and theme achieved by tragedy. Above all, the tightly knitted comic actions, which are unified by time and place, carry his initial premise to a logical and festive conclusion.

Yet something unsettling still lurks at the bottom of his laugh-filled agenda. Perhaps it is the remote implication that Cloud Cuckoo-land can exist only in the minds of its two comic heroes and that, for better or worse, they will never be free of their earthly woes. While this is never spelled out, it is humorously suggested by visitors from below: a poet, realtor, lawyer, and tax inspector, each of whom has heard about the brand new city and has come to investigate. Representing the more undesirable features of any bureaucratic system, these nuisances offer unwanted advice for a price, including that of a local Athenian prophet who also arrives at the scene to warn them that ''the signs are all very unfavorable.''

Rounded up and dragged out of sight, the playwright's trusty targets are personified and satirized in one fell swoop, while their respective causes—art, the environment, politics, the economy, and religion—are lambasted once and for all. The prophet's negative note resounds in our ears. But those of us wishing to contemplate Aristophanes' dream for humankind, including its radiant and soaring possibilities, will be guided by our laughter until it is time to awaken.

ABOUT THE TRANSLATION

Walter Kerr has addressed important textual and production matters in this version, which has made it a popular choice among contemporary stage directors. Amalgamating several reputable translations and recasting their lines in a colloquial vein, the results swing effortlessly between prose and verse. The verbal humor has been sharpened by the elimination of textual obscurities; the visual humor has been enhanced by richly detailed stage directions. For in spite of their urgent appeal to Athenian audiences, the topical references that constituted the backbone and contributed to the popularity of Aristophanes' plays have discouraged contemporary producers from staging them. *The Birds,* however, is surprisingly free of these allusions.

Capturing both the energy and style of musical comedy, a format that has much in common with the sung verse of Aristophanes' original text, Kerr's version pays homage to the ancient comic master. For this reason musicalization has often provided the most viable key to reviving his comedies. The plots thrive naturally on tuneful embellishment and show-stopping incidents and provide easy correlations to choral song and dance, all popular ingredients in the theatre for which he wrote.

Furthermore, no convention has been omitted, including the playwright's use of theatrical reference, in which the actor momentarily steps out of character to call attention to his performance. When Pithetaerus doubts the chorus's willingness to work harmoniously with him, their leader boldly exclaims: ''And if I break my word (glancing directly out front), may the audience speak unkindly of me in the lobby.'' Except for a conventional act break that has been inserted after the second and shorter *parabasis,* Kerr's embellishments remain loyal to the original.

THE BIRDS-IN-PERFORMANCE

When the German poet and dramatist, Johann Wolfgang von Goethe, pursued the ideals of classicism through his staging of the ancient Greek drama, his agenda included a lavish production of Aristophanes' *Birds*. The year was 1780, when Goethe was thirty-one years old and no mere apprentice to literary taste, although his greatest artistic endeavors were still ahead of him. If his initial immersion into the Greek experience failed to generate an immediate revival of interest in Aristophanes on page or stage, it nevertheless called attention to the important fact that several of Aristophanes' comedies could fit comfortably into the growing international repertory that was receiving enthusiastic support from German-speaking audiences.

In 1909, the Austrian director Max Reinhardt ushered Aristophanes into the twentieth century with a production of *Lysistrata* that proved so successful that it toured extensively throughout Europe before and after World War I. In fact, Reinhardt's steadfast involvement with classical Greek plays generated further impact, since his former students, including several from Greece, eventually reflected their master's influence in their own productions of the classical drama.

What is more interesting is the circular journey that ensued: the Greek drama eventually found its way back to the country that inspired its birth, although now it was performed in modern Greek. Yet a wave of controversy prevailed as late as 1959, when Karolos Koun, the founder and principal director of the Art Theatre (Theatro Technis), directed a production of *The Birds* that the Athenian government quickly banned because of its sacrilegious overtones. Nevertheless, Koun's production received the Theatre des Nations' first prize in 1962 and was performed for the World Theatre Season in London in 1964. Bernard Levin voiced unanimous critical praise when the play opened at the Aldwych:

> Mr. Koun's production is total theatre, if the phrase has any meaning: song, mime, dance, masks, slapstick, symbolism, all are pressed into service in his endlessly inventive staging. The use of the chorus in particular shows infinite imagination; its members swirl about the stage with hardly a moment's stillness, yet there is no feeling of fussiness, still less of repetition. The whole thing is a marvelous spectacle, and a thoroughly fitting revival of a great work.[3]

Under Koun's influence, *The Birds* has remained a great favorite at Epidaurus. Elsewhere on the continent, the National Theatre of Prague produced *The Birds* in 1934, using a totally abstract constructivist set.

Under the artistic direction of an Irishman named Terence Gray, whose interest in producing Greek drama was both eccentric and exemplary, the comedy reached England in 1883 and became a popular favorite at the Cambridge Festival Theatre between 1926 and 1933. The play first surfaced in North America in academic surroundings, however. William Randolph Hearst financed the transformation of a natural amphitheatre at the University of California at Berkeley in 1904, built to reflect the Epidaurean design, where *The Birds* was presented in Greek. The play's popularity grew over the following decades as countless English-speaking productions on American college and university campuses attracted younger audiences. Even the renowned Federal Theatre Project produced the comedy in New York City in 1938 for a limited run.

In the latter half of the twentieth century, the comedy has been musicalized in a variety of professional productions. Notable is the jazz version produced by the Actors Workshop of San Francisco under the direction of Herbert Blau, during the 1963–1964 season. This one-hundredth production for the company had music composed and arranged by Dave Van Kriedt, a former member of both the Dave Brubeck Quartet and the Stan Kenton Band. In 1971, a musical version based on Kerr's arrangement was presented at the Cleveland Playhouse under Joseph Garry's direction.

A highly touted American production of the play was given in a sedate, tree-lined American city whose only connection with Greek culture was that it took its name from the Greek general Demetrius Ypsilanti, who bravely fought the Turks in 1827. Although the ultimate dream of building a permanent Greek theatre in the city park of Ypsilanti, Michigan, never materialized, a temporary theatre was constructed in the ballpark of Eastern Michigan University during the two weeks between the end of the university's baseball season and the opening performance on June 29, 1966.

Under the artistic direction of Alexis Solomos, *The Birds* was produced in rotating repertory with Aeschylus' *Oresteia,* each giving forty performances. A notable feature of the engagement was its celebrity casting: the legendary actor-comedian Bert Lahr appeared as Pithetaerus, while the renowned classical actress Judith Anderson portrayed Clytemnestra in the Aeschylean trilogy. The casting of Lahr was indeed fortuitous, not only for his power to attract a large summer audience to a renovated stadium that was presenting two Greek plays, but also that *The Birds* was "the happy occasion for Bert Lahr to fashion one of his uniquely funny performances."[4] The ambitious event won the plaudits of audiences and critics alike, despite the fact that fund-raising efforts failed and the requisite amount of money to construct a permanent Greek theatre was never forthcoming.

Ypsilanti's dream for an artistically successful first season was realized on numerous production levels. The list of professional practitioners executing the plays was headed by production-designer Eldon Elder, whose work was already familiar to Broadway and regional theatre audiences. In addition to designing the sets for both Ypsilanti productions, as well as costuming *The Birds,* his most challenging assignment had begun one year earlier with his designs for the Greek Festival Stage.

REFLECTIONS ON THE BIRDS

Eldon Elder designed the sets and costumes for Aristophanes'
The Birds *at the Ypsilanti Greek Theatre.*

It is quite a difficult challenge to realize any classical theatre tradition in a contemporary setting. To begin with, there is a large historical gap. But it can be done if we tap into the right sources. Fortunately Alexis Solomos, the director, had a strong impact by knowing exactly what he wanted, especially in constructing a Greek theatre along the lines of a third-century B.C. original. That set the form for me at once.

Our orchestra was a full circle—no part was cut off by the **proscenion.** We constructed a staircase that linked the circular orchestra with the proscenion, although I widened this staircase, which was traditionally quite narrow to allow the actors greater access between both playing areas. I also adapted a flexible backdrop for this play and *The Oresteia,* so that we could change quickly from one play to the other merely by removing these panels of branches, or woven thicket, that were attached to stanchions or posts across the back of the proscenion in *The Birds.* A different set of panels could be put up very quickly for *The Oresteia,* so that we could play in rotating repertory. The change-overs were easily handled from one performance to the other.

Of course there was justification for this in our own speculations about a third-century Greek theatre: that there were wooden posts to separate the panels or screens, the so-called triangular *periaktoi,* that would revolve to give a different backdrop from one play

Continued

to another in the same theatre. Alex had served as director of the National Theatre of Greece for many years and had directed frequently at Epidaurus. He strongly believed that if we were going to do Greek plays, then we should adhere to the established stage configurations. That is why our repertory summer worked surprisingly well in the playing field, surrounded by a stadium seating capacity that was close to fifteen hundred and was increased slightly by special box seats that lined the front sections of the bleachers. Of course the stadium was nowhere near the scale of an open-air theatre like the one at Epidaurus. But it was quite effective nevertheless.

It was also his suggestion that there might be some parallel between the ceremonial dress of the American Indian and the costumes of the Bird Chorus. That opened the possibility for me to work with turkey feathers and other rich plumage used by the American Indians. We really scouted the territory looking for feather merchants both in Michigan and New York. So the chorus's wings, half-masks, and elaborately feathered head-pieces had a kind of inspiration in the American Indian. I did some research. At one point, I even considered purchasing some headpieces that were available on the market, but decided they were too specific. I did not want them to trigger the wrong set of symbols and responses. So we really just took our inspiration from the Indian headdress, bought feathers by the pound, and made our own.

The feathers were easy to work with and the headdresses created no problems, except that they tickled the actors' necks. The male birds wore rich turkey-feather plumage, while the females wore spike-eared wig attachments. They were always in half-mask, with contrasting beak and cutout eyes. I designed the wings to detach from the sleeves of the body-stocking, the basic costume. There was a string of feathers down each arm, scaled smaller and smaller from the actor's shoulders as they reached his wrists. I also fastened long feathers at the lower back, to create the effect of a lengthy tail.

Against this massive bird chorus, the earthling Euelpides wore an outfit of sharp vertical stripes (he was a tall, skinny actor), enhanced with plumage soon after he was officially received into the Kingdom of the Birds, to contrast with Pithetaerus' horizontal stripes (he was short and wide). The feathers were very colorful and the color schemes were coordinated. To differentiate the male and female choristers, the males wore lighter-colored body stockings with dye-painted designs on their chests. The actors had no difficulty handling their costumes, although the choristers did a great deal of movement to suggest flying and waving. Their noise effects even contributed to the live music.

There was a costume workshop in Ypsilanti where the principal work was done. Body stockings for the chorus were not stock items and had to be made by a company in New York that specialized in custom-made articles. As I remember, the special dye-painting for the male birds was part of that process. So the work was divided between both New York and Ypsilanti. The director and actors were happy with the different aspects of physical production, including the costumes I designed. Even Bert Lahr (Pithetaerus) was happy with his costumes, which was very important. Bert, famous as the Cowardly Lion in *The Wizard of Oz,* was a terrible worrier as many comics are—worried about every little prop, every piece of stage business, and every piece of costume. But in the end, once we established mutual trust and respect, he was very easy to work with.

Even though we took a very historical position in relation to the stage itself—the shape of the stage, its entrances and exits, the placement of chorus and things like that— still Alex was very free in his blocking, since we had no way of knowing what the play originally looked like. Having decided to hire an actor like Bert Lahr, who would prove wonderfully outrageous in the part, Alex gave him the go-ahead to invent business and lines. Both actor and director justified this by saying that Aristophanes allowed improvisations and line insertions, and whether he did or not, it seemed probable. I like to think that Bert was a direct link to the kind of classic comedian who originally did these plays. When he read the play, he admitted he knew nothing about classical literature. But he liked the play and saw its comic possibilities and what he could do with them. Furthermore, even if our director had not originally intended to build the play around him, Bert was an artist of such magnitude and force that he would have shaped it as he shaped everything he worked in.

Bert's biggest problem was his voice: it did not project and was all gravel—surely one of his greatest qualities as a comic actor, but severely challenged in this open-air setting. I guess the most serious problem we ultimately faced was how to project it in so large a space. So we constructed a grid of suspended microphones. This accounted for some acoustical problems as several critics noticed, since there were bound to be playing areas that were not covered. Bert was finally fitted with a remote chest mike.

Since the physical backgrounds of both plays were quite different, so was the lighting. *The Birds* required generalized lighting, in contrast with *The Oresteia,* which was full of highlights, shadows, and specific area lighting. What connected the two productions more than anything else was the configuration of the stage, which could not change and did not change in the classical theatre either. Only the background of the stage changed, as well as the lighting and the kind and color of the costumes. Ideas went back and forth to Greece, where Alex lived. He arrived from Greece with just enough time to cast and rehearse. Therefore most of the intensive design work on each production was already completed before he arrived.

The Birds was full of props: the musical instruments, the slapstick, and the pig-bladder—all of these came out of classical reference and research. Then I would create either contemporary variations on them or attempt a kind of "authentic" reproduction. For example, a throne designed for Pithetaerus was really a plywood cutout with a vague suggestion, distorted somewhat, of the classical look.

Behind the woven thicket were some loft-ladders that the chorus of birds could climb, crossing each other in two directions so they could reach the upper level. Then there was a huge rock at the center of the stage, fastened to the upright stanchions. There was an opening in the center, which was always mandatory for center-stage entrances, with the thickets stretching out to the sides. While the director blocked his actors at all parts of the stage, a great deal of the action was directed to take place in the orchestra, perhaps more than actually took place there in classical times.

While I have never considered myself a scholar in this area, I never believed that there was a complete separation—as some scholars claim—between the proscenion and the orchestra. It just does not make sense that the actors would have been stuck up on the

Continued

proscenion, particularly in the comedies. In both our productions, actors worked all areas of the stage. For example, we placed a series of stone blocks around the perimeter of the orchestra circle, where we often positioned our Bird Chorus. This gave the other characters a reason to come down into this space—the center of the circle—and play to the birds, to speak to them, to make them the link between the audience and the principal actors.

Our production contained several wonderful stage effects: one allowed the goddess Iris—performed by Ruby Dee—to descend on a crane, not unlike the effect of a "deus ex machina." In order to fly her in, we used a modern crane that was positioned behind the stage house: the kind of machinery that is used for construction, for building skyscrapers, that can lift and swing forward. So the actress was lifted up, while the arm of the crane was tilted forward to project her over the top of the scenery, which was close to thirty feet high. Attached to a single wire that was connected to this crane, she was deposited right in the middle of the orchestra circle. The audiences loved it! Another effect occurred at the play's triumphal conclusion, a kind of wedding march. Pithetaerus and his bride made a grand entrance on a chariot pulled by the bird chorus through the *parodos,* a feature of every Greek theatre. The effect was quite spectacular, including the headdresses worn by the bride and groom: cone-shaped structures that were more than two feet high, decorated with fluttering feathers.

Maybe some day we will find the right means and the right venue to propel a Greek theatre revival into an annual festival. It may have to incorporate non-Greek plays to support itself, as certain Shakespeare festivals around the world have needed to do. I have always enjoyed working with classical plays. When they are well done, there is nothing more rewarding for the actors or the audience. The problem is that American artists have limited experience in acting, directing, or designing productions of these plays. As outrageous as the Ypsilanti performance was, Bert Lahr certainly had this special comic gift to justify such an elaborate undertaking. But most of all, this production in which he starred was still making all the political and social comments Aristophanes had intended.

Notes

1. *Walter Jackson Bate, ed.,* CRITICISM: THE MAJOR TEXTS *(New York: Harcourt, Brace & World, 1952), 22.*
2. *Plato,* THE SYMPOSIUM, *W. Hamilton, trans., (Baltimore: Penguin Books, 1951), 113.*
3. *Bernard Levin,* DAILY MAIL, *14 May 1964.*
4. *Henry Hewes,* SATURDAY REVIEW, *16 July 1966.*

THE BIRDS
ARISTOPHANES
ARRANGED FOR THE STAGE BY WALTER KERR

CHARACTERS

A Full-Length Play for a Flexible Cast

Pithetaerus the Footloose, *a crappel*
Euelpides the Footsore, *a fearling*
Trochilus, *the Butler Bird*
Epops, *King of the Birds*
Procne the Nightingale, *wife to Epops*
Leader of the Chorus

Priest-Bird
Poet
Prophet
Real Estate Man
Inspector
Lawyer
First Messenger
Second Messenger

Iris the Swift, *a small-time Goddess*
Herald
Prompter, *offstage voice*
Prometheus
Hercules
Barbarian God
Neptune
Chorus of Birds

TIME: About 414 B.C.
PLACE: A rugged mountain-top, some distance from Athens.

THE SETTING: Limitless sky in the background. The rock formations should afford six or seven varied entrances, at different heights, with stair-like formations to connect the acting levels. At one side a little bridge between two pinnacles. A high point of the stage at DR[1] is so arranged as to be useful to Pithetaerus as a sort of pulpit.

Various gnarled and barren trees, especially on the upper reaches of the stage, including one tree which is practical for a perch and may occasionally be used by one of the Birds.

At DL, there is a gap in the rock formation which seems to lead downward and which is used for any ascent from the earth.

In a crevice somewhere upstage is concealed Procne's nest, if possible behind a movable scrim which is identical with the other rock surfaces when not lighted from within.

[1]C = center stage. Hereafter, other references to areas of the stage are indicated by the following letters: L = left; R = right; UR = upstage right; UC = upstage center; UL = upstage left; DL = downstage left; DC = downstage center; and DR = downstage right.

ACT ONE

SCENE: PITHETAERUS *and* EUELPIDES *appear DL, as though climbing from the earth below.* PITHETAERUS *carries a crow in his arms,* EUELPIDES, *a jay. Both are exhausted from the long climb. Before they can relax, however, Euelpides' jay begins pecking its head vigorously toward C.*

EUELPIDES (*listening to his jay*). Straight ahead, you say? To the tree over there? (*The jay nods excitedly and* EUEL-PIDES *starts C. As* PITHETAERUS *follows him, his own crow begins wagging its head violently in another direction.*)

PITHETAERUS. Oh, this damn pigeon! (*To the bird.*) What do you say now? Go two miles back? (PITHETAERUS *howls with disgust and collapses on a rock, near L.* EUEL-PIDES *comes to him, shaking his finger at the crow.*)

EUELPIDES. Listen, bird. You're supposed to be   5
guiding us. But all we do is go backwards and sideways.
We haven't got that kind of time. (*The crow bites his
shaking finger and he leaps away, nursing it.*)

PITHETAERUS. To think that I—a mature man!—should
travel a hundred miles with a bird giving me directions!
(*His crow sets up a violent jerking and* EUELPIDES *comes
in warily to listen.*)

EUELPIDES (*interpreting*). He says it isn't far as the   10
crow flies. (PITHETAERUS *looks at the crow in disgust,
begins slapping its head vigorously; the crow bites him.*
EUELPIDES, *surveying the rocky terrain.*) Personally, I'm
worn down to my toenails.

PITHETAERUS.   If I only knew where we were—

EUELPIDES (*wistfully*). Suppose we could ever find   15
our way home again?

PITHETAERUS.   No.

EUELPIDES.   Oh, dear.

PITHETAERUS (*sudden renewal of determination*). And if I
could I wouldn't want to!   20

EUELPIDES.   Oh, dear.

PITHETAERUS (*on his feet again, looking around*). I wonder
what road this is.

EUELPIDES.   Oh, dear. (*Helpfully.*) It's the Oh Dear Road.
(PITHETAERUS *swats him one, he dodges; he then takes
it out on his jay, swatting the bird as he continues.*)
A lot of good you are! (*Calling to* PITHETAERUS,   25
who is wandering about the stage.) I told you we couldn't
trust that bird-seller. Telling us these fellows would just
naturally lead us to the King of the Birds! (*Sits down, C,
despondently.*) I don't think they ever heard of the King
of the Birds. And if they did, I'll bet they're dis-   30
loyal. (*Jay opens his mouth.*) Don't open your face like
that! You look anything but attractive. (*Jay's head begins
jutting toward R.*) Where? Where? Over there? (*His eyes
glued to the jay, he quickly rises and moves in the indicated direction.*) All right. All right. I'm going. Keep
showing me. (*He walks smack into a wall of rock,   35
rebounds, turns on the jay.*) That's rock! Oh, you knew
that! That's what you had in mind! (*Begins to throttle his
jay.* PITHETAERUS, *who has been wandering UC, peering
off at the highest point of the rocks with his back to us,
now seems to be engaged in some excitement with his
bird.*) Find something? What's your bird doing?

PITHETAERUS (*in a rage*). Biting my damn fingers off!

EUELPIDES.   Any road up there?   40

PITHETAERUS.   Nothing. No road anywhere.

EUELPIDES.   Oh, dear. I haven't got a nerve left. I've used
up every single nerve trying to go to the birds, and now
they're all gone. (*He shudders violently.*) See? (*Turns to
the audience, comes down toward them.*) I suppose   45
you wonder what we're doing here? I wonder, too.
(*Keeping up a direct conversation with the audience, he
now goes to L where they have entered, and hauls over a
couple of heavy sacks filled with equipment. He drags*

*these across stage, with great effort, and deposits them
at extreme DR, meanwhile continuing the conversation.*)
You probably think we're crazy. We are. We come of very
good families. Legitimate. We were very respected people
back home. Athens. Very fine city. You probably think
we were thrown out. (*Shakes his head.*) Just got up   50
and left. Walked out. Still walking. We don't hate Athens.
Fine city. Rich, too. Everybody equal. Every man has absolute freedom to pay taxes. Every man has a constitutional right to ruin himself. (*These are read as though
they were virtues; now his face falls.*) Of course,   55
the town's full of lawyers. Always suing everybody. Government men, too. And inspectors. Always inspectors!
(PITHETAERUS *has momentarily abandoned his search
above to listen to these last remarks; now he adds his own
complaints, coming down to* EUELPIDES *and sitting down
while* EUELPIDES *continues doing all the work.*)

PITHETAERUS.   Tell 'em about the real estate. Tell 'em
about the long-haired poets!

EUELPIDES.   He's right. The city's infested. A lot of   60
prophets, too. Always predicting what's going to happen
the day after tomorrow. Very wearing.

PITHETAERUS.   Bores, bores, bores!

EUELPIDES.   That's why we left.

PITHETAERUS.   Get away from the bores, get a little   65
peace!

EUELPIDES.   That's why we're looking for the King of the
Birds. (*His work finished, coming down to the audience
again.*) If *anybody* should know of a nice quiet place
where a couple of men could settle—with no   70
bores—it should be the King of the Birds. Birds get
around. (PITHETAERUS *suddenly jumps up, attending to
his crow.*)

PITHETAERUS.   My bird's doing something!

EUELPIDES.   I'll bet I know what.

PITHETAERUS (*excited, moving anxiously wherever the bird
indicates, but never more than a few steps in any one
direction*). No . . . no, watch!   75

EUELPIDES (*indifferently and sadly, to the audience, playing
against Pithetaerus' excitement*). So we started off with
a stewpot, a knife and fork—a few myrtle berries—and,
now you know.

PITHETAERUS.   Here! Look!

EUELPIDES (*to his jay, laconically*). Has that other   80
bird really got anything? (*The jay shakes its head slowly,
with contempt.*)

PITHETAERUS.   It's behaving like there were other birds
around somewhere! (*Now Euelpides' bird becomes
agitated.*)

EUELPIDES.   Mine's doing it, too! Where? Where? (*He
runs agitatedly wherever his bird indicates, so that both
PITHETAERUS and EUELPIDES are scurrying hither and
thither independently. Suddenly they cross each other unexpectedly, so that EUELPIDES gives a little scream of*

fright, then calms down as he sees it is PITHETAERUS.)
Oh, it's you.   **85**

PITHETAERUS.   Yes, dammit, it's me! Look for some birds!

EUELPIDES.   Maybe we could scare them up if we made
some noise.

PITHETAERUS (*indicating rock RC*). That's right. Here . . .
kick your leg against that rock.   **90**

EUELPIDES (*responds automatically, about to do it, then considers*). Wouldn't it be louder if we used your head?

PITHETAERUS (*roaring*). Kick your leg against that rock!

EUELPIDES (*resignedly*). All right. (*Braces himself and does
it; lets out a great series of yowls.*)

PITHETAERUS (*listening to the yowls with approval*). That's
fine. That ought to do it. (*Motioning* EUELPIDES *to*   **95**
join him.) Ready, now. They'll be coming.

(*Together they move warily, expectantly, among the rocks
UR. Coming on from UL, we see* TROCHILUS, *the Butler Bird,
entering matter-of-factly, nose in air. He turns around a rock
unexpectedly and comes face to face with* PITHETAERUS *and*
EUELPIDES. *ALL leap into the air in terror of each other,
screaming and chattering, and dive for hiding places.* PITHETAERUS *and* EUELPIDES *hide in the rock formation at R,*
TROCHILUS *high on the rock formation at L.*)

EUELPIDES.   Mercy have Apollo. I mean, Apollo have
mercy. (*His teeth chatter.*)

PITHETAERUS (*peeping over a ledge, trembling*). What a
beak!   **100**

TROCHILUS (*waveringly, from his hiding place*). Men! Bird-catchers!

PITHETAERUS (*trying to get up nerve, his voice faltering*).
H-ho there! D-d-don't be frightened of us!

TROCHILUS (*adopting the same bravura, calling across*).
F-f-frightened of you? F-f-frightened of men? (*Bats his
wings at them.*) Y-y-you're done for!   **105**

EUELPIDES (*helpfully*). Oh . . . we're not men! (*To himself.*)
No. Never say that.

TROCHILUS (*relaxing*). You're not? What are you, then?

EUELPIDES (*indicating* PITHETAERUS). Well, I don't know
about him, but I'm a bird. An African bird. The   **110**
. . . the Fearling.

TROCHILUS.   Never heard of him. (*Becoming braver, taking command.*) And what kind of a bird is that bird?
Huh?

PITHETAERUS (*half-rising from behind ledge*). Why,   **115**
I'm a . . . (*Pauses to consider, then with some self-disgust.*) . . . a Crapple, if you must know.

EUELPIDES.   One of the yellow-bellied school.

PITHETAERUS (*regaining confidence*). Now, see here.
You're a bit of a fright yourself. What are you?   **120**

TROCHILUS (*coming down the rock, manservant style*). I am
a butler bird. Butler to Epops, King of the Birds.

EUELPIDES (*excited*). He's our man! (*Trochilus' head whips
around, alert.*) I mean, bird.

TROCHILUS.   Choose your language.   **125**

PITHETAERUS (*tentatively coming down from the rock formation*). Would you . . . do us the kindness to call your
master?

TROCHILUS.   I'm sorry. He has just fallen asleep after a
dainty supper of berries, and a few choice grubs. I picked
the grubs myself.   **130**

EUELPIDES (*relaxed now, assuming an air*). Wake him up.
Tell him we're here.

TROCHILUS.   He will be angry.

PITHETAERUS (*taking a deep breath*). We'll risk it.

TROCHILUS.   Very well. (*Starts to go; L above,*   **135**
pauses to check.) The Fearling, and the . . .

PITHETAERUS (*obligingly*). Crapple.

TROCHILUS.   Crapple. I think I understand. (TROCHILUS
goes, UL. PITHETAERUS *and* EUELPIDES *follow him a step
or two, completely off the rock formation; then* PITHETAERUS *turns on* EUELPIDES *and kicks him to DR.*)

PITHETAERUS.   You mouse! You flyspeck! What were you
so frightened about? You were so frightened you   **140**
made me frightened. What was the matter with you?

EUELPIDES.   I was frightened.

PITHETAERUS.   Where's your jay? You were so frightened,
you big coward, you let your jay go!

EUELPIDES.   Where's your crow?   **145**

PITHETAERUS (*realizing he no longer has his crow*). I gave
him his freedom.

EUELPIDES.   That was decent of you.

(*There is a sudden loud whirr and* EPOPS *rises to the top of
a rock at the highest stage point, UC.* PITHETAERUS *and
EUELPIDES realize that something has happened. Slowly they
turn to face* EPOPS, *above. When they have finally turned full
face to him, they collapse in a trembling heap together, and
scurry on hands and knees for the shelter of a DR rock.*)

EPOPS (*in a great voice*). Who wants me?

EUELPIDES (*terrified, trying to laugh it off*). I can't   **150**
imagine. (*To* PITHETAERUS.) Did you see anybody?

EPOPS.   Does someone dare to laugh at the King of the
Birds?

EUELPIDES.   No . . . no . . . just a little giddy . . .
(*Shoving* PITHETAERUS, *as though to start him running
out of this place.*) Giddyap. (PITHETAERUS   **155**
collapses into Euelpides' arms; EUELPIDES *is struggling
to hold him up during the ensuing conversation.*)

EPOPS.   You must know, strangers, that I once was a man.

EUELPIDES (*looking down at* PITHETAERUS). We all were.

EPOPS.   Born of woman, married to a wife, I was unfaithful
to my dear Procne. Now I am changed by Apollo into a
bird, and Procne is the nightingale, and I am   **160**
faithful at last.

EUELPIDES (*to the audience*). We're certainly getting the exposition out.

EPOPS.   Who are you?

EUELPIDES.   Mortals. Haven't had any affairs with   165
nightingales.

EPOPS.   From what country?

EUELPIDES.   The land of democracy, where everyone is
equal.

EPOPS (*suddenly suspicious*). You're not govern-   170
ment men?

EUELPIDES.   Anti-government men.

EPOPS (*relaxing, moving gracefully across bridge at L so
that he can see them better from across the stage*). The-
y're getting around to that, are they?

EUELPIDES.   Not fast enough. That's why we came.

EPOPS.   Why have you come? (PITHETAERUS, *in*   175
Euelpides' arms, begins to stir.)

PITHETAERUS.   What? What?

EUELPIDES.   He wants to know why we came.

PITHETAERUS.   Tell him.

EUELPIDES.   If you can lie down somewhere else, I will.
(*Drops* PITHETAERUS *with a thud and goes to C, speaking
up to* EPOPS *on the bridge at mid-L.* PITHETAERUS *crawls
to a small rock and sits down.*) We came to see   180
you.

EPOPS.   Why me?

EUELPIDES (*taking on graces and airs, in the manner of a
rather florid ambassador*). Because formerly you were a
man, as we are. Formerly you had debts, as we do. And
formerly you did not want to pay them, as we   185
don't. Furthermore, now that you're a bird, you must have
flown everywhere. And while you were flying all over the
world, you must have seen—somewhere—some little
town, where a man can sit back, stretch out, drop a berry
into his mouth . . . (*Pantomimes what he de-*   190
scribes.)

PITHETAERUS (*chiming in*). . . . and not be bothered with
bores!

EPOPS.   Are you looking for a city greater than your own?

EUELPIDES.   No, not a greater one. Just one more pleasant
to live in.   195

PITHETAERUS (*nodding*). No bores.

EPOPS.   What sort of city would please you?

EUELPIDES.   I'll tell you. A city where the following would
be the most important business transacted: Some friend
would come banging on your door at a reasonable   200
hour in the morning, and say: (*Dramatizing, in a harsh
voice.*) "Get up! Get your wife and children! Get over to
my house. Sit down at my table and eat till you bust. And
if you don't, I'll be mad at you!" I have something like
that in mind.   205

EPOPS.   I see. Sort of . . . roughing it?

EUELPIDES.   Yes.

EPOPS (*to* PITHETAERUS). And you?

PITHETAERUS.   My tastes are similar.

EPOPS.   I see. As a matter of fact, there is a city like   210
that. It's on the Red Sea.

PITHETAERUS (*rising, asserting himself now*). No, no! No
sea ports. Let a ship dock, and there'll be a process server
on it. Someplace remote. Uninhabited. Inaccessible. (*Has
been envisioning such a place as he speaks; suddenly
there is a gleam in his eye.*) Wait a minute. Now,   215
wait a minute!

EUELPIDES (*resignedly*). You have an idea.

PITHETAERUS.   Yes!

EUELPIDES.   The last idea you had was using birds for
guides. I hate to bring it up.   220

PITHETAERUS (*excited*). No, listen, now. Listen! (*Grabs
EUELPIDES by the shoulders and sits him down between
himself and EPOPS, who moves slightly down on his rock
perch.*)

EUELPIDES.   It isn't as though I had a choice. (*To the audience.*) You do. You can go home anytime.

PITHETAERUS (*striding around, his eyes ablaze as he works
out his plan*). Sh-h-h-h!

EUELPIDES (*relaying it unnecessarily to the audience*).
Sh-h-h-h!   225

PITHETAERUS (*ready to talk now, becoming momentously
confidential with EPOPS*). Tell me. What is it like to live
with the birds themselves?

EPOPS.   What?

PITHETAERUS.   You ought to know. What's the life like?

EPOPS (*rising and moving on the bridge as he considers*).
Why, it's not a bad sort of life. Of course, you   230
have no money.

EUELPIDES.   I'm as good as a bird now. (PITHETAERUS
kicks him.)

EPOPS.   And, naturally, you have none of the problems that
go with money.

EUELPIDES.   That's logical. (PITHETAERUS *kicks*   235
him.)

EPOPS.   The food is nice. White sesame, myrtle, poppies,
mint—

EUELPIDES.   Worms. (PITHETAERUS *about to kick him,
EUELPIDES quickly walks, without making himself erect,
from one rock to another.*)

PITHETAERUS (*grandiosely*). I am beginning to conceive a
great plan. (*To* EPOPS, *moving up the rocks at R*   240
toward him.) All you have to do is take my advice.

EPOPS.   Take your advice? How?

PITHETAERUS (*after a significant pause*). Found a city!

EPOPS.   A city for birds? What kind of city could we have?

PITHETAERUS (*dragging* EPOPS *to high point UC*).
Oh, come on, come on! Don't be a fool. Here.   245
Look down. (EPOPS *bends over the high point and looks
down, then waits for* PITHETAERUS *to say something
more; he doesn't.*)

EPOPS.   I'm looking.

PITHETAERUS.   Now look up.

EPOPS (*repeats business*). I'm looking.

PITHETAERUS.   Turn your head around. (EPOPS   250
does, twisting his head.) Well! What do you find?

EPOPS.   That my neck is getting stiff.

PITHETAERUS.   No, no! What do you *see*?

EPOPS.   The same old clouds and sky.

PITHETAERUS (*as though it were quite simple*). That's it! The land of the birds!   255

EPOPS.   I knew that.

EUELPIDES (*still below, indifferent*). *I* knew that. He gets excited about nothing.

PITHETAERUS.   But you can turn it into a city!

EPOPS (*incredulous*). A city in the air?   260

PITHETAERUS.   Surround it with walls and fortify it!

EUELPIDES (*to audience*). He's going to surround space.

EPOPS.   What for?

PITHETAERUS.   To seize all the power of the universe . . . for yourself. For the birds. (*Offhand.*) And, of   265 course, we'll have a little share in it, too. (*The salesman again.*) You can reign over mankind as you now do over grasshoppers! You can rule the gods!

EPOPS.   How?

PITHETAERUS.   By starving them into submission.   270

EPOPS.   I don't follow you.

EUELPIDES.   You're not the first.

PITHETAERUS.   Now listen! When men are on their last legs, when they're desperate . . . what is the only thing that can help them?   275

EPOPS.   The gods.

PITHETAERUS.   And how do they get the gods to help them?

EPOPS (*including a small altar-like rock DL of C*). By offering sacrifice. They put a goat or an ox in the sacrificial fire.   280

PITHETAERUS (*moving downstage with* EPOPS *and dramatizing what he says*). And the smoke rises up through the air until it reaches the heavens. The gods notice it, and come to the rescue. Is that right? (EPOPS *nods.*) Listen carefully. In the practical business affairs of Earth, suppose I am a man living in this country. (*Marks*   285 *out an area on the ground with his foot;* EUELPIDES *jumps up and puts his foot in the area, helpfully.*) But I want to go to that country over there on business. (*Indicates an area some distance toward R.*) Between the two countries is a middle country which I must pass through. (EUELPIDES *starts to travel toward the second area through middle area, but* PITHETAERUS *stops him midway.*) Now, when I want to pass through it,   290 what do I have to do?

EPOPS.   Pay tribute.

PITHETAERUS.   Precisely! (EUELPIDES *reaches for his purse, but it is empty; shrugs, goes away and sits down, L.*) Now here is all that smoke going through *your* country for nothing. But if you build a wall and fortify it,   295 you can demand that men acknowledge you as rulers of the universe and pay you a tribute. Otherwise, *you don't let the smoke through!* (*He pauses for* EPOPS *and*

EUELPIDES *to grasp and admire this notion.*) In addition, with no smoke coming up, the gods starve to   300 death. You rule the universe!

EPOPS (*his imagination fired, darting about the stage*). By snares! By networks! By cages! That's the cleverest idea I've ever heard. I've been wanting to get back at that Apollo. (*Faces them.*) If I can get the approval of   305 the other birds, I'll do it.

PITHETAERUS.   Will you explain the matter to them?

EPOPS.   No, *you* will. You're a splendid talker.

EUELPIDES.   Splendid.

PITHETAERUS.   How will you get them all together?   310

EPOPS.   No trouble at all. I shall awaken dear Procne, my nightingale. Once they hear our voices, they will come to us hot on the wing!

PITHETAERUS.   Then hurry, my dear fellow, hurry. Wake up Procne!   315

(*Begin* MUSIC. EPOPS *waves them aside as he goes to the nest in the rocks.* PITHETAERUS *and* EUELPIDES *scurry DL of C and conceal themselves, watching.* EPOPS *makes several birdlike sounds and the nest door slowly opens, or unfolds.* PROCNE *is discovered asleep. Slowly she wakes. Moving from the nest, she dances drowsily, waking herself, as* EPOPS *speaks softly.*)

EPOPS.

Chase off drowsy sleep, my mate!
Shake off thy slumbers, and clear and strong
Let loose thy flood of glorious song.
With the liquid note of thy tawny throat
Through the leafy curls of the woodbine
sweet   320
Send thy pure sound to the heavenly seat
Of Phoebus, lord of the golden lair,
Who lists to thy wild plaint echoing there.
Draw answering strains from Phoebus' lyre
Till he stirs the dance of the aerial choir   325
And calls from the blessed lips on high
Of a thousand birds, divine reply
To the tones of thy witching melody—

EUELPIDES (*as* PROCNE *now stands erect, ready to call*). Oh, by Zeus, what a sweet little bird. I'm charmed,   330 charmed.

PITHETAERUS.   Sh-h!

EUELPIDES.   What's the matter?

PITHETAERUS.   The King is ready. Procne is ready. They're going to call the birds! (*During the ensuing pas-*   335 *sage* PROCNE *takes the lead, moving in dance rhythm to each promontory on the set and singing a birdlike strain.* EPOPS, *also in dance rhythms, moves to each position after her, keeping on a lower level.*)

PROCNE.   Apopopoi popoi popopopoi popoi!

EPOPS.

> Come hither any bird with plumage like my own,
> Come hither yet that fatten on the acres newly sown,
> On the acres by the farmer newly sown.
> And the myriad tribes that feed on the barley and the
> seed   340
> The tribes that lightly fly, giving out a gentle cry—

PROCNE (*on another promontory*).

> Tio, tio, tio, tio, tiotinx!

EPOPS.

> And ye who in the gardens pleasant harvest glean
> Lurking in the branches of the ivy ever green
> And ye who top the mountains with gay and airy
> flight,   345
> Come hither one and all, come flying to our call—

PROCNE.   Trioto, trioto, totobrinx!

CHORUS (*off faintly*).

> Trioto, trioto, totobrinx!
>
> (*Faintly a whirring of wings begins off, and the
> stage begins to darken as though from a sky filled
> with approaching birds.*)

EPOPS.

> Ye that snap up the gnats, shrilly voiced,
> Mid the deep water-glens of the fens,   350
> And the bird with the gay mottled plumes, come
> away—

PROCNE.   Francolin! Francolin!

EPOPS.   Come away!

CHORUS (*off, louder*).

> Tio, tio, tio, tiotinx.

PITHETAERUS.   See any birds yet?   355

EUELPIDES.   No, but I've got my eyes open.

PITHETAERUS.   That's your mouth, stupid. (EPOPS *and*
PROCNE *now take up a kingly position together on the
rock tower at R and remain still.* EPOPS *speaks climacti-
cally, as the music and the offstage whirring become
louder.*)

EPOPS (*majestically*).

> Ye with the halcyons flitting delightedly
> Over the surge of the infinite sea,
> Come to the great Revolution awaiting us,   360
> Hither, come hither, come hither to me.

(*Now the* CHORUS OF BIRDS *begins to arrive. Some flutter in
from one upstage promontory, others swoop in from another.
They whirr down the formations, crossing one another in
spectacular dance movement.*)

EPOPS.

> All the feathered airy nation—
> Birds of every size and station
> Come in a flurry, with a hurry-scurry—

EUELPIDES.   How they thicken, how they muster!   365

PITHETAERUS.   How they clutter, how they cluster!

EUELPIDES.   How they ramble here and thither,

> How they scramble altogether.
> There's a marsh bird . . .

PITHETAERUS.   . . . a flamingo—   370

EUELPIDES.   Thyme-finch . . .

PITHETAERUS.   . . . ring-dove next, and then

> Rock-dove, stock-dove,
> cuckoo, falcon,
> Fiery crest and willow wren.   375

EUELPIDES.

> Oho for the birds, oho, oho!
> Oho for the blackbirds, ho!

CHORUS (*in final ecstatic movement*).

> Toro, toro, toro, torotinx
> Kikkabau! Kikkabau! Toro, toro, toro, toro lililinx!

(*With the last phrase the* CHORUS OF BIRDS *suddenly becomes still, perching about the stage in a great arc facing
Epops, R.* PITHETAERUS *and* EUELPIDES *are crouching on our
side of a rock L of C. The* CHORUS LEADER *steps forward.*)

LEADER.

> We have answered the call of the King of the
> Birds.   380
> We await his pleasure and attend his words.

EPOPS.

> An envoy, queer and shrewd,
> Begs to address the multitude
> Submitting to their decision
> A surprising proposition—   385

CHORUS (*chattily pleasant, among themselves*).

> News amazing! News auspicious! News delightful,
> we agree.

EPOPS.

> Birds . . . two men of subtlest genius
> Have proposed a plan to me.

CHORUS (*suddenly ruffled, stirring*).

> Who? What? When?

LEADER (*sternly*). Say that again.   390

EPOPS (*indicating* PITHETAERUS *and* EUELPIDES *who now
make bold to arise from behind their rock and present
themselves modestly*).

> Here, I say, have come two humans
> Traveling to the birds from man;
> And they bring with them the kernel
> Of a most stupendous plan.

CHORUS (*aroused now; shocked, angry*). You have   395
made the greatest error, since our life up here began!

EPOPS.   Now, you must'n't be so nervous—

EUELPIDES (*a little worried*). Everybody's *nervous*!

CHORUS (*rising to full height, awesomely*).

> Explain your conduct, if you can!

EPOPS (*patiently, indicating them*).

> I've received two men—   400
> (PITHETAERUS *is about to step forward and
> introduce himself, grandly.*)

CHORUS (*shrill, terrifying, ruffling feathers*).
>Among us? Have you really, truly dared?
EPOPS.   Yes, and I shall introduce them—
EUELPIDES (*trembling*).
>I hate to say it, but I'm getting scared!
CHORUS (*a great blast*). Out! Out upon you!

(PITHETAERUS *and* EUELPIDES, *shaken by the impact, scurry to extreme DR and take shelter behind a ledge, as the* CHORUS OF BIRDS *turns from* EPOPS *and gathers in quick, violent consultation at L.*)

>We are cheated and betrayed, we have suffered
>>shame and wrong!   **405**
>Our comrade and our King, who has fed with us so
>>long,
>Has broken every oath, and his holy plighted troth,
>And the old social customs of our clan!
>He has led us unawares into wiles and into snares—
>He has given us as prey, all helpless and
>>forlorn   **410**
>To those who were our foes from the time that they
>>were born,
>To vile and abominable man!
LEADER (*rising high among the choral group*).
>For the bird our Chief, hereafter he must answer to
>>the state!
>With respect to these intruders, I propose, without
>>debate,
>Bit by bit to tear and rend them—   **415**

(*The* CHORUS OF BIRDS *begins to sharpen their claws and make greedy, slavering sounds.*)

PITHETAERUS.   Here's a horrid mess.
EUELPIDES.   It's all your fault, your fault, you and your cleverness! Why didn't you leave me home?
PITHETAERUS.   I wanted a companion.
EUELPIDES.   Your companion is going to melt into   **420**
tears.
PITHETAERUS.   Don't be silly. How're you going to cry with your eyes pecked out? (EUELPIDES *begins to bawl, loudly.*)
CHORUS (*thunderously, a climax to Euelpides' cry*). Form in rank! Form in rank! (CHORUS OF BIRDS *begins*   **425**
to take military formation at L.)
>Then move forward and outflank them.
>Let us see them overpowered,
>Hacked, demolished, and devoured!
>(*Despairing pantomime by* PITHETAERUS *and*
>EUELPIDES.)
>Both, both of them shall die
>And their bodies shall supply   **430**
>Rare, dainty morsels for our beaks—
>Where's the Captain? What detains him?
>We are ready to proceed!

>On the right there, call the captain!
>Let him form his troop and lead!   **435**

(*The* CAPTAIN, *a very shabby-looking bird, hurries in and proceeds to meet troops at L.*)

PITHETAERUS.   He's a seedy looking Captain.
CAPTAIN (*glancing back, huffily*). I was moulting. (*Gives signal to* BIRDS, *who drop to crouched formation as though ready to spring into air and fly directly at the humans across stage.*)
EUELPIDES (*as* CAPTAIN *pantomimes instructions to the crouched and waiting* CHORUS OF BIRDS). They're coming! They're coming! (*Shakes hands with* PITHETAERUS, *quickly.*) Good-bye. (*Starts directly*   **440**
toward CHORUS OF BIRDS.)
PITHETAERUS (*grabbing him*). Where do you think you're going?
EUELPIDES.   I'm going to give myself up.
PITHETAERUS (*shaking him and roaring*). Stand up and fight! Here! (*Digs into their equipment and hands*   **445**
him a fork.)
EUELPIDES.   Somehow I'm not hungry.
PITHETAERUS.   Use it for a sword!
EUELPIDES.   No. When my eyes are pecked out, I won't be able to see who I'm stabbing. I might stab myself.
PITHETAERUS (*throwing him a stewpot*). Here!   **450**
Shield your eyes!
EUELPIDES (*delighted, trying it on*). Oh, that's nice! Want a test match? (*Begins to feint at* PITHETAERUS, *who slaps him away and digs out a pot and a ladle for his own weapons. At the same time the* CAPTAIN *leaps back from his pantomimed instructions to the* CHORUS OF BIRDS *and shouts.*)
CAPTAIN.   Ready, Birds! Present your beaks! In double time, charge and attack!   **455**
LEADER.   Pounce upon them . . .
CAPTAIN.   . . . smash the potlid—
LEADER.   Clapperclaw them . . .
CAPTAIN.   . . . tear and hack! (*The* CHORUS OF BIRDS *leaps and darts forward and there ensues a slashing duel between the* CHORUS OF BIRDS *and* PITHETAERUS *and* EUELPIDES. *The* CHORUS OF BIRDS *keeps up a great chattering racket throughout. Momentarily* PITHETAERUS *and* EUELPIDES *disappear in a melee of surrounding* BIRDS, *then appear dueling each other. Recognizing their mistake, they separate and take on half the* CHORUS OF BIRDS *each. The* CHORUS OF BIRDS *forces them back to the rock towers,* PITHETAERUS *at R and* EUELPIDES *at L. The two men climb their towers, dueling, the* CHORUS OF BIRDS *pursuing, clawing at them. When both are about to be overcome,* EPOPS *decides to reassert himself, takes C.*)
EPOPS.
>Cease! Most unworthy creatures, scandal of the
>>feathered race;   **460**

Must I see my friends and yours massacred before
my face?

(*The* CHORUS OF BIRDS *pause where they are, but do
not release their hold on the humans.*)

CAPTAIN. Friends? They're *men*. Men invented the
slingshot.

EUELPIDES.   I hope they'll mark my grave.

EPOPS.   But they have abandoned other men, and   465
come to give us advice.

LEADER.   Take advice . . . from an enemy?

EPOPS.   How else do you suppose men learned to build
strong walls, and make new weapons—if not from their
enemies? We always learn from the enemy.   470

LEADER.   Who are these men?

CAPTAIN.   Why have they come to us?

EPOPS.   Because they love you, and wish to share your
life—to dwell and remain with you always.

LEADER.   Are they mad?   475

EPOPS.   The sanest men in the world.

EUELPIDES (*signaling* EPOPS *with his finger*). Don't overdo
it.

LEADER.   Clever men, eh?

EPOPS.   Cleverness itself! Men of the world, cun-   480
ning, ingenious, sly . . . (*Searching for a perfect phrase.*)

PITHETAERUS (*prompting in a loud whisper*). Brave. Brave.

EPOPS.   And brave. They have wonderful plans!

LEADER.   Plans?

EPOPS.   To make us the rulers of the universe! All   485
power, above and below, shall be ours! (*Chattering noises
among the* CHORUS OF BIRDS *to each other;* LEADER *listens and considers.*)

LEADER.   Well. I should like to hear this.

PITHETAERUS (*confident now, adopting an attitude*). Well.
You won't hear it from me.

CHORUS.   What's this? What's this?   490

PITHETAERUS (*moving away toward* R, *stubborn*).
Not a word. I'm a clam.

EUELPIDES (*helpless*). He's changed his mind. He wants to
be a clam.

EPOPS.   You must speak!

PITHETAERUS (*turning, in full command*). Not until   495
we reach an agreement! No more pecking, no more
clawing, no more biting! Is it agreed?

LEADER (*after a glance around at the* CHORUS OF BIRDS,
whose heads bob up and down in encouragement). It is
agreed.

CHORUS.   We swear it. (*Raising one wing each.*)   500

LEADER.   You have my word. And if I break my word . . .
(*Glancing directly out front.*) . . . may the audience
speak unkindly of me in the lobby.

PITHETAERUS.   Very well.

LEADER (*coming directly downstage now and speaking con-
fidentially to the audience*). On the other hand, if   505
I keep my word, mention my performance to your friends.
(*Turns immediately and rejoins* CHORUS OF BIRDS *as*
EPOPS *speaks.*)

EPOPS.   Birds! Gather yourselves and listen! (*In a quick
flurry the* CHORUS OF BIRDS *darts to seated positions at
R extending to C, facing the rock tower at L. As they
speak,* PITHETAERUS *mounts the tower slowly.*)

CHORUS.   Full of wiles, full of guiles, at all times, in all
ways. Are the children of men. Still . . . we'll hear what
he says.   510

EPOPS (*to* PITHETAERUS). Speak!

PITHETAERUS (*surveys the group with slow deliberation,
waiting for absolute silence; finally he speaks softly, for
impressive effect*). I am bursting to speak. (*Pause while
he straightens to full height.*) I have already mixed the
dough of my address and I am ready to knead it. (*Flurry
of wings from the* CHORUS OF BIRDS *as though in
applause.*)

EUELPIDES.   A very pretty image.   515

PITHETAERUS (*takes a deep breath, begins to open his
mouth and raise his arm in gesture; then halts*). Water,
please.

EUELPIDES.   These long pauses are hard on the throat.

(LEADER *scurries to the tower, taps a rock nearby and water
gushes forth.* PITHETAERUS *drinks, wipes his mouth, faces
his assembly again.*)

PITHETAERUS.   I shall say what I have to say in a few, well-
chosen words. (EUELPIDES *yawns loudly;* PITHE-   520
TAERUS *hurls a rock at him;* EUELPIDES *ducks.*)   Birds.
My heart bleeds for you. You . . . who were formerly
Emperors!

A BIRD (*to another near him, chattily*). Did you ever hear
that?   525

LEADER.   Emperors? Over whom?

PITHETAERUS.   Over all that exists! Over me. Over that
man. (*Indicates* EUELPIDES, *who rises and bows.*) Over
Zeus himself! You belong to a race older than Saturn—
older than the Titans—older than the very Earth!   530
(EUELPIDES *applauds, vociferously;* PITHETAERUS *throws
another rock at him.*)

CHORUS.   Than the Earth itself! We never heard that
before.

PITHETAERUS (*warmed up now, the thoroughgoing dema-
gogue*). You never heard that before because you haven't
read your Aesop! Aesop clearly tells us—and I quote—
that the lark—and the lark is a bird—existed   535
before the Earth itself! (*Having reached a climax, he turns
to drink.*)

EUELPIDES (*the unwelcome question*). Where does Aesop
say that?

PITHETAERUS (*stares at him hard, then dismisses it,
speaking with casual rapidity as he takes up a cup and
prepares to get more water*). Oh, in that little story about
how the lark's father died and went unburied for   540
five days, and finally had to be buried in the lark's head.
You know that.

EUELPIDES.   No. I didn't. Now that I do, it doesn't seem to explain anything.

PITHETAERUS (*hurling the cup at him in sudden fury and then plunging directly into his speech*). It ex-   **545** plains this: if the lark had to bury its own father in its own head, that can only have been because there was no earth in which to bury him. Ergo, the lark existed before the Earth. Aesop. (*Pronounces his source with finality; the* CHORUS OF BIRDS *buzzes excitedly among themselves.*) Furthermore. The birds existed before the   **550** gods!

A BIRD (*to another, chattily*). Do you think he's going too far?

PITHETAERUS (*thundering*). The gods stole their power from the birds!   **555**

ANOTHER BIRD (*replying confidentially to the first*). Too far.

PITHETAERUS.   They derive their very authority from the birds! Else why should they carry on their sceptres—the symbol of their authority—a hawk? Why should   **560** Zeus always be seen with an eagle on his head?

LEADER (*interested*). Why, indeed?

EUELPIDES.   And so uncomfortable, too.

PITHETAERUS.   Why should Victory be winged? Why Cupid? And, my friends, I ask you to consider the   **565** rooster.

EUELPIDES (*willing*). All right.

PITHETAERUS.   Just consider the rooster.

EUELPIDES.   All right.

PITHETAERUS (*after a quick, disgusted glance at* EUEL-PIDES). What creature, in all the universe, wears   **570** a crown that will not come off?

EUELPIDES (*after a moment's consideration*). The rooster.

PITHETAERUS (*To* EUELPIDES *annoyed*). That was a rhetorical question.

EUELPIDES.   That was a rhetorical answer.   **575**

PITHETAERUS (*whipping back into his tirade*). All other crowns must be put on and taken off. Only a bird has a natural crown! Consider further. This Great King of old, this rooster, even now is so powerful, so great, so feared by men that the moment he crows at daybreak,   **580** they all jump out of bed. (*Pause for effect.*) What effect does the call of the rooster have?

EUELPIDES.   Scares the hell out of me.

PITHETAERUS.   It makes blacksmiths, potters, tanners, shoemakers, corn-dealers, lyre-makers, and amor-   **585** ers all put on their shoes and go to work even before it is daylight! This is the power of the bird! (*Quick change to pathos.*) And yet . . . how are birds treated today? Stones are thrown at you. Men set snares for you—twigs and nets of all kinds. You are caught. Caught.   **590** Sold in heaps for a banquet. The buyer fingers you over to be sure you are fat enough. (CHORUS OF BIRDS *shudders, emits little cries as* PITHETAERUS *pictures the full*

horror of their existence in juicy tones.) If only . . . if only they would serve you up simply roasted. But no! What do they do? They grate cheese into a mix-   **595** ture of oil and vinegar—they add to this a greasy sauce— and they pour it scalding over your backs for all the world as though you were diseased meat! Oh! (*He cries out, unable to bear it; the* CHORUS OF BIRDS *echos him, takes up his wail.*)

CHORUS.

    Oh! Oh!
    Sad and dismal is the story   **600**
    We have heard this stranger tell
    Of our fathers' ancient glory
    Ere the fated empire fell.
    (*On their knees to* PITHETAERUS.)
    From the depths of degradation
    A benignant happy fate   **605**
    Sends you to restore our nation,
    To redeem and save our state!

PITHETAERUS.   Birds! The hour has come! Your power must be reclaimed—from men, and from the gods above!

EUELPIDES (*frowning*). I just can't see Zeus turning   **610** things over to a woodpecker.

LEADER.   But how shall we do this?

CHORUS.   Tell us how!

PITHETAERUS (*during this he descends slowly and actually mingles with the* CHORUS OF BIRDS, *dramatizing it for them in gestures and whipping up their enthusiasm*). Very well.   **615**

    First I propose that the Air you enclose
    And the space twixt the Earth and the Sky,
    Encircling it all with a brick-builded wall
    Like Babylon's, solid and high.
    As soon as the building is brought to an end   **620**
    A herald or envoy to Zeus we shall send
    To require his immediate and prompt abdication;
    If he refuses, or shows hesitation
    Or evades the demand, we shall further proceed
    With legitimate warfare, avowed and decreed: **625**
    (*In the manner of a proclamation.*)
    "Hereafter no god, neither Zeus nor any of the
    others residing in heaven, may pass through our
    aerial domain for the purpose of impromptu love-
    making down below. Permission must first be
    granted by the Birds, and a small fee paid.   **630**
    Otherwise . . . back to Olympus!"
    (CHORUS OF BIRDS *chatters approval; he resumes his description.*)
    Another ambassador also will go
    To the Earth, and tell those below
    That in future:
    (*Again the style of proclamation.*)
    "Every man wishing to beg favors of the   **635**
    gods, and therefore offering sacrifice to the aforesaid

gods, must first of all make an appropriate sacrifice
to the Birds. For instance, if an ox is to be sacrificed
to Zeus, the Birds must first be appeased by the
sacrifice of one male mosquito!'' **640**
(CHORUS OF BIRDS *licks their chops in anticipation.*)

LEADER.   And what if they will not obey?

EUELPIDES.   What if Zeus lets loose with thunder and
lightning?

LEADER.   What if men ignore us?

PITHETAERUS.   Then you will swoop onto their   **645**
fields and eat up all their seed. (EUELPIDES *pantomimes
this helpfully.*) Nothing will grow. Nor will Zeus be offered any oxen. You will fly to the pastures and peck out
their eyes.

LEADER.   And if they obey us, what do we promise   **650**
in return?

PITHETAERUS.   To defend their fields from insects and
pests, as Zeus never did. Nevermore will they fear the
beetle or roach. You will guide their sailing vessels, flying
back to warn of an oncoming storm, and showing   **655**
them favorable winds.

EUELPIDES (*starting to go*). I'm leaving. I'm going into the
shipping business. (PITHETAERUS *collars him, holds him
steady, as the* CHORUS OF BIRDS *rises and then kneels in
homage, with a burst of triumphant confidence.*)

CHORUS.
All honor to you, oh man!
(PITHETAERUS *takes a self-satisfied stance, and*
EUELPIDES *leaps to the fore to share in the praise.*)
We thought thee at first of our foemen the
worst   **660**
And lo! we have found thee the wisest
And best of our friends. Our nation intends
To do whatsoever this great man advisest.
A spirit so lofty and rare
Thy words have within us excited   **665**
That we lift up our souls and we swear
That if thou wilt with us be united
In bonds that are holy and true
And honest and just and sincere—
If our hearts are attuned to one song,   **670**
We will march on the gods without fear!
Now whatever by muscle and strength can be done,
We birds will assuredly do;
But whatever by prudence and skill must be won,
We leave altogether to you.   **675**

EPOPS (*to* PITHETAERUS). Come. Come with me and we shall
lay our plans.

PITHETAERUS.   Very well. (*To* EUELPIDES, *who has started
off with* EPOPS *too willingly.*) Bring the luggage. (EUEL-
PIDES *wearily goes back for their belongings and drags
them forward. Meanwhile* EPOPS *has leaped to a great
promontory as though to fly off when* PITHETAERUS *intervenes.*) Hi! Wait! Come back here! How are we   **680**
going to keep up with you? We haven't got wings.

EPOPS (*considering*). That's true.

EUELPIDES (*tugging at Pithetaerus' sleeve, confidentially*).
I remember something else from Aesop. When the fox
made an alliance with the eagle, he got the worst of it.
(PITHETAERUS *pushes him away and his load throws him
off balance.*)

EPOPS.   Never fear. You shall eat of a certain root,   **685**
and wings will grow on your shoulders.

LEADER (*to* EPOPS). As you take them to dine, send us
Procne. We wish to sing of our newfound happiness.

EPOPS (*turns on promontory and chants*). Procne! Nightingale! Come forth!   **690**

(PROCNE *darts onto stage from between rocks at UL.*)

LEADER.   Oh, nightingale—who are all melody—help us to
show our joy! (PROCNE *dances to C.*)

EUELPIDES (*as* PITHETAERUS *follows* EPOPS *off L, dragging
after them and looking back at* PROCNE). Oh, that nice
nightingale!

(PITHETAERUS *reappears to collar him.*)

EUELPIDES.   How I should like to kiss her!   **695**

PITHETAERUS.   You fool. She has two sharp points on her
beak.

EUELPIDES (*sighing, lovelorn*). I've got around worse.
(PITHETAERUS *pulls him off with a great jerk, L. Only*
PROCNE *and the* CHORUS OF BIRDS, *with their* LEADER,
*are left. They now dance the following passage as they
speak or sing it:*)

CHORUS (*addressing* PROCNE, *who dances*).
Oh darling, oh tawny-throat!
Love, whom I love the best,   **700**
Dearer than all the rest.
Playmate and partner in all my soft lays,
Thou art come! Thou art come!
Thou art sweet to my gaze
And sweeter thy note . . . nightingale,
nightingale!   **705**

PROCNE.   Oh woodland muse—

CHORUS.   Tio, tio, tio, tiotinx!

PROCNE.
Of varied plume, with whose dear aid
On the mountain top, and the sylvan glade—

CHORUS.   Tio, tio, tio, tiotinx!   **710**

PROCNE.   I, sitting aloft on a leafy ash, full oft—

CHORUS.   Tio, tio, tio, tiotinx!

PROCNE.
Pour forth a warbling note from my little tawny
throat,
Pour festive choral dances to the mountain mother's
praise,
And to Pan the holy music of his own
immortal lays.   **715**

CHORUS.

    Totototototototototinx,
    Tio, tio, tio, tio, tiotinx!

PROCNE (*moving down toward the audience and speaking softly to it*).

    You men who are dimly existing below,
    Who perish and fade as the leaf—
    Pale, woebegone, shadowlike, spiritless—   **720**
    Frail castings in clay who are gone in a day
    Like a dream full of sorrow and sighing,
    Come listen with care to the birds of the air,
    The ageless, the deathless, who flying
    In joy and the freshness of air, are wont   **725**
    To muse on wisdom undying.

CHORUS (*all speaking to the audience*).

    Yes, take us for gods, as is proper and fit,
    And Muses prophetic you'll have at your call,
    Spring, winter, summer, and autumn and all.
    And we won't run away from your worship
        and sit   **730**
    Up above in the clouds, very stately and grand,
    The way that old Zeus does. But, always at hand,
    Health and wealth we'll bestow, as the formula runs,
    On yourselves and your sons and the sons of your
        sons.
    And happiness, plenty, and peace shall belong   **735**
    To you all, and the revel, the dance, and the song
    And laughter, and youth, we'll supply.
    We'll never forsake you.

ONE BIRD (*a trifle giddy with it all*). You'll be quite over-burdened with pleasures and joys!   **740**

CHORUS.   So happy and blest we will make you.

LEADER.

    Is there anyone amongst you, O spectators, who
        would lead
    With the birds a life of pleasure?

CAPTAIN.   Let him come to us with speed!

CHORUS.

    Truly to be clad in feather is the very best of
        things.   **745**
    (*With increasing lightness as they continue to face
        the audience but move to exit positions.*)
    Only fancy, dear spectators, had you each a brace of
        wings,
    Never need you, tired and hungry, at our lengthy
        chorus stay.
    You would lightly, when we bored you, spread your
        wings and fly away!
    Back returning, after luncheon, to enjoy our comic
        play.

(CHORUS OF BIRDS *disappears, slipping away behind various sections of rock. A moment later* PITHETAERUS *and* EUELPIDES *enter from UL, now equipped with great flopping wings which they are unable to manage properly. They test them*

awkwardly, absorbed, finally managing to bang them into one another. With this, PITHETAERUS *pauses and really looks at* EUELPIDES. *He bursts out laughing.*)

EUELPIDES.   What are you laughing at?   **750**

PITHETAERUS.   You. You look like a goose in a paint-bucket.

EUELPIDES.   You look like a blackbird in need of a shave.

PITHETAERUS.   Just think. They're our feathers. All our own.   **755**

EUELPIDES.   D'you suppose we can fly?

PITHETAERUS (*pointing to a high rock*). Go up there and jump off.

EUELPIDES (*sizing it up skeptically*). No, I think I have a loose feather back here. (*Turning around and*   **760** *backing into* PITHETAERUS.) Would you see if I have a loose feather?

PITHETAERUS (*roaring*). Would you get that thing out of my eye? (*In trying to disentangle himself from one of Euel-pides' wings, he becomes enmeshed in the other and as* EUELPIDES *starts to turn around there is a pantomimed melee in which each fights his way through the other's wings. This concludes with* PITHETAERUS *booting* EUEL-PIDES *clear across the stage.*)

EUELPIDES (*looking up from his prone position on the ground*). Did I fly?   **765**

(EPOPS *appears.*)

PITHETAERUS.   Hi, King-o! Look. The wings are very nice. But how do we fly?

EPOPS.   You must go slowly at first, like the newborn bird fresh from the egg. One step at a time. (EPOPS *does one, to show them how.* PITHETAERUS *does his best to imitate it.* EUELPIDES *does a very cautious one, barely taking himself off the ground.*) Now another. (*They try*   **770** *again.*) And another. (*There ensues a dance in which* EPOPS *leads the two men in a series of leaps and bounds, he expertly, they clumsily. At conclusion:*) That will be enough for today.

EUELPIDES.   Same time tomorrow?

PITHETAERUS.   Now. We have work to do.   **775**

EPOPS.   What first?

PITHETAERUS.   Have the birds begun the city?

EPOPS.   They are already hard at work. (*We hear sounds of hammering and building offstage.*) You hear?

(*Several* BIRDS *cross through carrying sticks and straw.*)

EPOPS.   You see?   **780**

(*During remainder of scene occasional* BIRDS *go through in this manner.*)

PITHETAERUS.   Then we must give our city a name.

EUELPIDES.   Yes. We must have an address.

EPOPS.   What shall we call it?

EUELPIDES.   How about The New Athens?

PITHETAERUS.   Not a word about Athens, city of   785
pests!

EUELPIDES.   How about Athens-on-the-Incline?

PITHETAERUS.   Quiet!

EUELPIDES.   How about Sparta?

PITHETAERUS.   You! Into the air with you. Help   790
the workers who are building the wall. Carry up rubble.
Strip yourself to mix the mortar. Take up the hod. Tumble
down the ladder. Post sentinels. (EUELPIDES *has started
in a different direction with each command, and is now
turning every way in a daze.*) Keep the fires burning! Go
round the walls. Ring bells. Dispatch two heralds.   795
One to the gods above. The other to mankind. And don't
stop till you're finished!

(EUELPIDES *finally falls out of sight beyond some rocks. At
intervals during the following dialog he reappears, rushing
messengers in various directions, pushing* BIRDS *carrying
hods, etc.*)

PITHETAERUS (*turning to* EPOPS). Now. Do you have a
priest-bird? To offer sacrifice.

EPOPS.   Surely we're not going to offer sacrifice to   800
the gods! We've just declared war!

PITHETAERUS.   To the bird-gods . . . the new gods!

EPOPS.   Ah! I will call him. (EPOPS *leaps to a high rock
and emits a bird call to summon the* PRIEST-BIRD. *Then
he whirls round to* PITHETAERUS.) But how can we offer
sacrifice when we haven't named the city?   805

PITHETAERUS.   I have named it.

EPOPS.   You have a name?

PITHETAERUS.   Just thought of it.

EPOPS.   What? What is the name?

PITHETAERUS.   Cloud Cuckoo-land!   810

EPOPS (*ravished*). Cloud Cuckoo-land! Brilliant! Brilliant!

(To PRIEST-BIRD, *as he enters.*)

EPOPS.   Here! Do as he tells you! (*To* PITHETAERUS.) I shall
announce to the others our glorious name! (EPOPS *exits,
as* PITHETAERUS *turns to* PRIEST-BIRD.)

PITHETAERUS.   You are a priest-bird?

PRIEST.   As my father before me, and his father   815
before him, and his father before . . . (*This may go on
forever.*)

PITHETAERUS.   All right, all right. Do you know how to
offer sacrifice?

PRIEST (*says nothing but immediately crosses to C, kneels,
throws back his wings*). I begin. (*Throws open his arms,
then stops.*) Where's the sacrifice?   820

PITHETAERUS.   Oh. (*He looks around, goes through the
business of spotting a gnat flying through the air, pursuing and catching it; he then delicately deposits it before
the* PRIEST.)

PRIEST (*peers at gnat dubiously, shrugs, and raises his arms
again*). Oh, birds who preside over the earth, and oh, god
and goddess birds who preside over heaven—

PITHETAERUS (*getting into the act, kneeling down*).
Oh, hawk—oh, god of the storks!

PRIEST (*after a disdainful glance at* PITHETAERUS, *forces
himself to continue, more fulsome*). Oh, swan of   825
Delos, oh, mother of the quails, oh, goldfinch—

PITHETAERUS.   Goldfinch?

PRIEST (*paying no attention*). Oh, ostrich, mother of the gods
and mankind—

PITHETAERUS (*going along with it*). Oh, ostrich—   830

PRIEST.   Grant health and safety to the Cloud Cuckoo-
landers, as well as to all who pay us tribute—

PITHETAERUS.   Yes, put them in.

PRIEST.   Oh, heroes—oh, sons of heroes—oh, sons of the
sons of . . .   835

PITHETAERUS   (*quickly*). Don't get off on that again.

PRIEST.   Oh, porphyrion—

PITHETAERUS (*competing with him now*). Oh, pelican—

PRIEST.   Oh, spoonbill—

PITHETAERUS.   Oh—   840

PRIEST (*before* PITHETAERUS *can get one in*). Oh,
redbreast—

PITHETAERUS.   Oh—

PRIEST (*beating him to it again*). Oh, grouse—(*Hereafter intoning more rapidly so that* PITHETAERUS *cannot do much more than get his mouth open for each
phrase;* PITHETAERUS *becomes increasingly disgusted.*)
Oh, peacock—oh, horned-owl—oh, heron—oh,   845
stormy petrel—oh, woodpecker—oh, titmouse—

PITHETAERUS.   Oh, hell. (*Jumping up.*) That'll be enough
now. Out of here, out of here. You'll drive me crazy. Next
you'll be inviting the vultures. Can't you see there isn't
enough sacrifice for more than one small blue-   850
bird? Out, out, I'll finish it myself.

(*As he is hustling the* PRIEST-BIRD *off the stage,* EUELPIDES
is making the last of his flying trips through, urging a BIRD
before him. PITHETAERUS *grabs him and drags him downstage to position for sacrifice, as the* BIRD *scurries off.*)

PITHETAERUS.   Here. Don't say anything. Just assist me.
(PITHETAERUS *gets down on his knees again,* EUEL-
PIDES *mimics him, puzzled.* PITHETAERUS *spreads his
arms.*) We will address our sacrifice to *all* winged
things—

(*Climbing up from the Earth below, a* POET *appears.*)

POET.   Hello! Anyone here?   855

EUELPIDES (*in an "oh-oh" tone of voice*). Here comes the
first pest.

POET (*in over-ecstatic admiration of the view*). Oh, Muse!
Oh, come, my Muse! Teach me to sing of happy, happy
Cloud Cuckoo-land!   860

PITHETAERUS.   What have we got here? Where'd you come from? Who are you?

POET.   I am, a poet—a warbler—whose language is sweeter than honey. An eager, meagre servant of the Muses. As Homer says.   **865**

PITHETAERUS.   You certainly wear your hair long!

POET.   It flows as my songs do. Ah, I have worn myself out in the service of the Muses. As Homer says.

PITHETAERUS.   Worn your cloak out, too, I see. What ill wind blew you up here?   **870**

POET (*taking out a great sheaf of papers*). I have heard of your city, and I have composed a few small verses in its honor. They are small, but splendid.

PITHETAERUS.   I see. And when did you compose them? How long since?   **875**

POET.   Oh, I've been working at them a long time. Yes, a long, long time.

PITHETAERUS.   That's interesting, considering I've just founded the place. Just named it, like a little baby, two minutes ago.   **880**

POET.   Ah, but you reckon without the Muses, and how quickly they spread the word!
   (*Declamatory.*)
   "Fleet, fleet as twinkling horses' feet
   The airy, fairy rumor of the Muses. Sped to me."
   (*Dropping tone.*)
   I went right to work.   **885**

PITHETAERUS.   And why did you put yourself to such trouble?

POET.   For beauty's sake. Beauty alone. The soul. (*Putting out his hand, with pretended indifference.*) Of course, if you want to give me a little something to keep   **890** body and soul together—

PITHETAERUS.   As Homer says.

POET.   Yes, I find it a little chilly walking the mountains in these old things—(*Indicating his ragged clothes and bravely smiling. Then, by way of suggestion, his teeth begin to chatter.*)

EUELPIDES.   Poor fellow. Give him something.   **895**

PITHETAERUS.   You think we ought to be charitable, do you?

EUELPIDES (*nodding*). The generous man shares his benefits.

PITHETAERUS (*putting his arm around* EUELPIDES). I have misjudged you. You have a kind heart. (*Rips*   **900** *Euelpides' fur jacket off and presents it to the* POET.) Here. Take this fur. Maybe your teeth won't chatter so much.

POET.   My Muse thanks you.

PITHETAERUS.   It was nothing.

EUELPIDES.   It was a fur jacket. (*Euelpides' teeth*   **905** *start to chatter.*)

POET.   Do you remember those lovely lines from Pindar?

PITHETAERUS.   Which ones?

POET.
   "Out among the Scythians yonder
   See poor Straton wander, wander—
   Poor, poor Straton, not possessed   **910**
   Of a warmly woven under-vest.
   What matter his jacket of fur if below
   There's no soft tunic for him to show?"
   (*Quietly.*) Get it? (PITHETAERUS *starts toward* EUELPIDES, *as though to relieve him of something else— he hasn't much else on—but* EUELPIDES *backs away protesting.*)

EUELPIDES.   I don't remember those lines! Don't   **915** remember 'em! (*But* PITHETAERUS *has snatched off another piece of Euelpides' clothing, leaving him in the absolute minimum.*)

PITHETAERUS (*tossing the garment to* POET). Now here and get out. I can't spare another thing.

EUELPIDES.   Not decently.

POET.   I shall go, I shall go. And I shall sing your   **920** praises forever. (*Quoting, as he skips about the stage toward an exit.*)
   "Oh, Muse, on your golden throne
   Prepare me a solemn ditty.
   To the mighty, to the flighty,
   To the cloudy, quivering, shivering,   **925**
   To the snowy, to the blowy lovely city.
   Cloud Cuckoo-land! Cloud Cuckoo-land!
   Tra la la la la la la la la!" (POET *has danced off.*)

PITHETAERUS.   What's he talking about—snowy, blowy? We gave him the clothes off our backs! How   **930** d'you suppose that plague found his way up here already? (EUELPIDES *is about to reply, but his chattering teeth prevent him.*) What are you muttering about? (EUELPIDES *tries helplessly to speak but again breaks down into chattering.*) Come, back to the sacrifice. And don't say a word. (EUELPIDES *motions that he can't, pointing to his chattering teeth; Pithetaerus' arms are spread again.*) Oh, snowbird! (EUELPIDES *worse than ever at this.*)   **935** Oh, penguin—(EUELPIDES *shivering all over.*) Oh, gull of the frosty mountains—! (EUELPIDES *in a state of collapse.*)

(*A* PROPHET *has climbed into view from the Earth below.*)

PROPHET.   Cease! Do not continue the sacrifice!

PITHETAERUS.   Why not?

PROPHET.   All the signs are against it!   **940**

PITHETAERUS.   Who are you?

PROPHET.   I . . . am a prophet, and the author of several prophetic books. (*The* PROPHET *might well speak in a voice resembling that of some contemporary radio or television oracle.*)

PITHETAERUS.   Beat it.

PROPHET.   Fool! Would you fly in the face of destiny? There is a prophecy in my book . . . (*Opens a huge volume he carries.*) . . . which applies exactly to Cloud Cuckoo-land. **945**

PITHETAERUS.   This is a fine time to tell me! Why didn't you mention it while I was on Earth below, before I got everything started? **950**

PROPHET (*wisely*). The time was not propitious. However, since hearing of the foundation of Cloud Cuckoo-land, Apollo has appeared to me in a dream. He has interpreted the prophecy in my book. Which I shall now interpret for you. **955**

PITHETAERUS (*wearily*). All right. Interpret.

PROPHET (*reading portentously*). "When the wolves and the white crows shall dwell together between the spoon and the great bowl . . ." **960**

PITHETAERUS.   Now, see here. What has all this kitchenware got to do with me?

PROPHET.   The great bowl stands for Cloud Cuckoo-land— when you know how to interpret it. It continues: "Before a sacrifice can be offered, those who would offer it must first give to the prophet who reveals these words, a new pair of sandals." (EUELPIDES *just sits down and takes off his shoes.*) **965**

PITHETAERUS.   It says sandals, does it?

PROPHET (*smugly*). Look at the book. (*Reading again.*) "Besides this, he must be given a goblet of wine and a good share of the entrails of the victim sacrificed." (EUELPIDES *peers closely at the gnat, wondering how this is to be done.*) **970**

PITHETAERUS.   It says entrails, does it?

PROPHET.   Look at the book. "If you do as I command, you shall be an eagle among the clouds. If not, you shall be neither turtle-dove, nor eagle, nor woodpecker." **975**

PITHETAERUS.   It says all that, does it?

PROPHET.   Look at the book.

PITHETAERUS.   You know, that's funny. Apollo appeared to me in a dream, too. He told me how to interpret another passage. **980**

PROPHET.   He did?

PITHETAERUS.   Yes. (*Snatching the book.*) Ah, here it is. (*Obviously improvising.*) "If an impostor comes without invitation to annoy you during the sacrifice and to demand a share of the victim, give to this man a sharp blow on the head." **985**

PROPHET.   Ridiculous!

PITHETAERUS.   Look at the book. (*Shoves the book under Prophet's nose.* PROPHET *incredulously peers at it, and* PITHETAERUS *claps it shut on his nose. As* PROPHET *dances away in pain,* PITHETAERUS *batters him with it soundly, driving him to a high rock from which he leaps;* PITHETAERUS *hurls the book down after him, and we hear a faraway howl.*)

EUELPIDES (*holding up his sandals*). All right to put these back on? **990**

PITHETAERUS (*dusting off his hands, coming down*). Yes.

EUELPIDES.   My Muse thanks you.

(EUELPIDES *sneezes while putting them on and thereafter develops a cold, which affects his voice. Meantime, a* REAL ESTATE MAN, *equipped with curious measuring instruments, has climbed from the Earth below.* PITHETAERUS *lets out a mighty roar on seeing him, which frightens* EUELPIDES.)

EUELPIDES.   What? What?

PITHETAERUS.   Another one! **995**

REAL ESTATE MAN (*briskly and efficiently striding C with his instruments.*) Good morning. Good morning. Nice development you have here.

PITHETAERUS.   What are you after? Who are you?

REAL ESTATE MAN.   I am going to survey the plains of the air for you. Then we'll subdivide. **1000**

PITHETAERUS.   What are those things?

REAL ESTATE MAN.   Tools. For measuring the air.

PITHETAERUS.   You can measure the air, can you?

REAL ESTATE MAN.   Oh, yes. With this bent ruler I draw a line from top to bottom. From one of its points I describe a circle with the compass. Then I take the hypotenuse. Follow me? **1005**

PITHETAERUS.   Not at all.

REAL ESTATE MAN (*patronizing throughout*). Well, we can't all understand these things. Next, with a straight ruler I inscribe a square within the circle. Its center will be the marketplace, into which all the straight streets will lead. They will converge to a center like a star, which, although only orbicular, sends forth its rays in a straight line from all sides. Better now? **1010** **1015**

PITHETAERUS.   Come here. I want to talk with you. (*Draws him downstage, confidentially.*)

REAL ESTATE MAN (*beaming*). Yes?

PITHETAERUS.   You don't know this, but I'm a friend of yours.

REAL ESTATE MAN.   Oh, that's nice. **1020**

PITHETAERUS.   Don't let on, but I'm going to slip you a piece of advice.

REAL ESTATE MAN.   Oh, fine. What's that?

PITHETAERUS.   Run. Run like hell.

REAL ESTATE MAN.   Good heavens! Have I an enemy here? **1025**

PITHETAERUS.   Yes.

REAL ESTATE MAN.   Someone in the city?

PITHETAERUS.   Yes. Someone very important. In fact, he's had a law passed. **1030**

REAL ESTATE MAN.   What's that?

PITHETAERUS.   "All quacks, profiteers, and other pests are to be swept from the borders."

REAL ESTATE MAN (*thinking it over a moment*). Oh. Then I'd better be going. (*Starts, hesitates.*) Tell me **1035** one thing. Who is this person I have to fear?

PITHETAERUS (*beckons to him, very confidential, heads together*). Me.

REAL ESTATE MAN. Oh, I see! You're joking! (*Laughs heartily.* PITHETAERUS *joins him in the laugh and, as though slapping him jovially, gives him a smart blow.* REAL ESTATE MAN *sobers at this.*) You *are* joking?

PITHETAERUS (*hitting him harder and laughing*). Yes, yes! **1040**

REAL ESTATE MAN (*reeling from blows, suspiciously*). You're *not* joking!

(*In a roar of laughter,* PITHETAERUS *pummels him severely, driving him across the stage. But before he can get him off, they pass a* TAX INSPECTOR *who has just come up from Earth, equipped with notebook and tax forms.* PITHETAERUS *doubles back in a non-stop movement, grabbing the* TAX INSPECTOR *by the seat of his pants.*)

PITHETAERUS. Here, now! This is the way out!

INSPECTOR (*routine formality*). You will please declare your personal property.

PITHETAERUS. Who sent you? **1045**

INSPECTOR. Government. Tax inspector.

PITHETAERUS. Haven't got any personal property. We've just started to build.

INSPECTOR. Very well. I'll have to leave an estimated bill, based upon what we happen to need at the **1050** moment. (*Having scribbled on form, rips it off and hands it to* PITHETAERUS.)

PITHETAERUS (*tearing it up matter-of-factly*). Very well. And I'm going to make an estimated payment, based upon how I happen to feel at the moment—(*Hits him with a stewpot which* EUELPIDES *has casually handed him, then trips him up.*)

INSPECTOR. You'll go to court . . . you'll go to **1055** court!

(*A* LAWYER *has arrived from Earth during this melee and is already tacking a list of printed regulations to a place on the rocks.* PITHETAERUS *sees him.*)

PITHETAERUS. Here! What are you putting up there?

LAWYER. The new laws for the community. "If a Cloud Cuckoo-lander should commit libel against Athens or any Athenian . . ." **1060**

PITHETAERUS (*tearing down list to look at it*). We don't need any lawyers up here!

LAWYER. Have to have lawyers. Don't want to spend all our time in jail, do we?

PITHETAERUS (*reading*). "The Cloud Cuckoo- **1065** landers shall adopt the same weights and measures as now prevail in . . ."

LAWYER. The standard weights and measures, of course.

PITHETAERUS. No, we have new measures up here. Like this. (*Pushes him backward over* EUELPIDES, *who* **1070** *has prepared himself. At same time* LAWYER *has pulled himself together and from now on, both* PITHETAERUS *and* EUELPIDES *are very busy handling the reappearing pests, no sooner laying hands on one than another pops up, until the stage is a swirl of confused activity.*)

INSPECTOR. You are now liable to penalty of ten thousand . . .

(*As* PITHETAERUS *is getting hold of him,* POET *has reappeared.*)

POET. Tralalalalalalalalala! My Muses are back. They say I should also have a crown. (EUELPIDES *claps the stewpot over his head.*)

LAWYER (*reading from list*). "Should anyone drive **1075** away the magistrates and not receive them, according to the decree duly posted . . ."

EUELPIDES (*calling off to the* BIRDS, *desperate*). Help! Help! We have vermin!

(PROPHET *has also reappeared.*)

PROPHET. I came to tell you that your doom is **1080** sealed. I have just had another chat with Apollo . . . (PITHETAERUS *and* EUELPIDES *cannot keep up with all of them and are losing the battle. The combined nuisances are surrounding them, successfully bending their ears, forcing them into a tight knot DC.*)

REAL ESTATE MAN. What I forgot to mention is that there is a great profit in this for you, personally—

INSPECTOR. Of course, if you would like to offer a small bribe— **1085**

PROPHET. The signs are all very unfavorable—

(PITHETAERUS *and* EUELPIDES *slump exhausted DC, as* POET, PROPHET, REAL ESTATE MAN, TAX INSPECTOR, *and* LAWYER *bend over them, all talking at once, ad libbing in a great yammering babble,* PITHETAERUS *and* EUELPIDES *hold their ears, rocking back and forth. By this time* BIRDS *have begun to appear over the rocks. Some of them, carrying a great net, steal downstage behind the group and, at a signal, throw the net over the yammering nuisances.* PITHETAERUS *and* EUEL- PIDES *immediately duck out from under and the net is drawn tight about the others.*)

PROPHET (*a continuation of his previous line, with net business timed between*). I was so right.

POET. Whither has joy flown? Oh, darkest day!

INSPECTOR (*inside net*). Get me a lawyer!

LAWYER (*right next to him, inside net*). I'm a lawyer. **1090**

PITHETAERUS. There! Now we'll put them all in a man-cage. We'll hang them from the ceiling of Cloud Cuckoo-land, and there they can sing to us all day! Take them away! (PITHETAERUS *and* EUELPIDES *supervise the* BIRDS *as they drag them out of sight beyond rocks and the* CHORUS OF BIRDS *takes over.*)

CHORUS (*a great burst*).

> Hear ye!   **1095**
> Henceforth—our worth,
> Our right, our might,
> Shall be shown,
> Acknowledged, known.
> Mankind shall raise   **1100**
> Prayers, vows, praise
> To the Birds alone! (*Change of tone, lighter.*)
> Oh, the happy clan of birds
> Clad in feather,
> Needing not a woolen vest in   **1105**
> Wintry weather—

(PITHETAERUS *and* EUELPIDES *return, dusting off their hands. The* CHORUS OF BIRDS *are distributing themselves in happy, comfortable, languorous positions, and* PITHETAERUS *and* EUELPIDES *move DC, stretch out, entirely comfortable at last.* BIRDS *bring them fruit and wine, drop grapes into their mouths—in all, the picture of sybaritic luxury.*)

CHORUS.

> Heeding not the warm far-flashing
> Summer ray,
> For within the leafy bosoms
> Of the flowery meads we stay,   **1110**
> When the Chirruper in ecstasy is shrilling forth his
>   tune,
> Maddened with the sunshine and the raptures of the
>   noon.
> And we winter in the caverns' hollow spaces.
> In spring we crop the flowers of the myrtles white
>   and tender,
> Dainties that are fashioned in the gardens of the
>   graces. (*Climax of luxurious passage.*)   **1115**
> Oh, many a herb and many a berry
> Serves to feast and make us merry! (*Pause.*)
> It's a nice life.

(*Real break from choral quality to conversational prose tone.*) And now, just before the intermission, one word to the critics. If the reviews are good tomorrow, we **1120** are prepared to do several nice things for you. We will build nests in your chimneys and sing for you sweetly from time to time. When we die, we will leave you our claws, for use on other occasions. As you sit down to dinner, we may even fly in with some plovers' **1125** eggs, if you happen to like them. (*Slight pause.*) On the other hand, should the reviews be bad tomorrow—and should the critics thereafter just happen to be walking down a public street—well, let them wear hats. (*Portentous, with a slight upward glance.*) Let *them wear hats!*

CURTAIN

END OF ACT ONE

ACT TWO

SCENE: *As before,* PITHETAERUS *discovered asleep on the stage. He wakes up, stretches, yawns, then gets up, pleasantly drowsy. He comes directly downstage and speaks in an easy conversational tone.*

PITHETAERUS (*to audience*). Well, friends. We've got the sacrifice over with and those pests out of the way. So far, so good. Now we'll have to make preparations for a splendid banquet to celebrate the building of the city. Just as soon as it's built. That reminds me. I haven't **5** had any report on how it's coming. There ought to be a messenger, bringing me news. There always is a messenger in these plays. It's not right to have no messenger. Probably produced this thing on a low budget. Still, maybe one will be coming along. We'll have to **10** look. (*Goes to high point, looks off.*) Ah, yes. Swift as lightning, he comes!

(*As* PITHETAERUS *turns to greet him, the* FIRST MESSENGER *speeds in at a terrific rate, passing* PITHETAERUS *altogether and exiting opposite.* PITHETAERUS *looks after him, pokes his way down near where* FIRST MESSENGER *has gone off. At this moment* FIRST MESSENGER *whizzes past him again from opposite direction, and off.* PITHETAERUS *has nearly had his nose clipped off in the process. He now considers a moment, starts toward second exit, but pauses a moment to pick up a rock and weigh it in his hand, then climbs to a point above exit prepared to drop rock on returning First Messenger's head.* FIRST MESSENGER *whizzes in again,* PITHETAERUS *hurls the rock down onto his own foot. His yowl stops the* FIRST MESSENGER, *who turns, but who continues his running motions even as he speaks.*)

FIRST MESSENGER. Where is he? Where, where? Oh, where? Where is he?

PITHETAERUS. Who, dammit?   **15**

FIRST MESSENGER. Our leader, Pithetaerus. Where is he?

PITHETAERUS. Here, you idiot! (*Grabs him to stop his legs from running motions.*)

FIRST MESSENGER (*stepping back, military, breathing hard*). You . . . are . . . Pithetaerus?

PITHETAERUS. Yes, dammit!

FIRST MESSENGER (*a military step forward, with a salute, still breathing hard*). I have a message for you, **20** sir.

PITHETAERUS. That's what I thought. Well, well, what is it? (FIRST MESSENGER *opens mouth to deliver message, then faints dead away on the floor.*) Oh, these bit players! Here! Here! Come to! (*Slapping him vigorously.* **25** FIRST MESSENGER *comes to, dazed, and* PITHETAERUS *lifts him to his feet.* FIRST MESSENGER *immediately begins running again.*) Here, stop! (*Grabs* FIRST MESSENGER.) Now. What's the message?

FIRST MESSENGER. The wall is finished.

PITHETAERUS (*dismissing him, as though finished*). Good.

FIRST MESSENGER (*holding his ground*). And a   **30**
most amazing, magnificent work it is!

PITHETAERUS (*turning back, a gesture of dismissal*). Fine,
fine.

FIRST MESSENGER (*obviously has a set-speech of a part and
is going to deliver it, no matter what*). Big enough for two
chariots to pass on it, driven by steeds as big as   **35**
the Trojan horse. (*Becoming increasingly declamatory,
with gestures.*)

PITHETAERUS.   That's wonderful. Good-bye.

FIRST MESSENGER.   The height—I measured it myself—is
exactly a hundred fathoms.

PITHETAERUS (*being drawn into it now*). Is that so?   **40**
Who could have built such a wall?

FIRST MESSENGER (*making the most of his opportunity,
taking over the stage, walking away from* PITHETAERUS
toward audience).   The Birds! Nobody else, no foreigners, Egyptian bricklayers, workmen or masons. But
they themselves—alone—by their own efforts—

PITHETAERUS (*aware of what he is doing, mockingly
helpful*).   Unaided.   **45**

FIRST MESSENGER (*striding off to another part of stage,
forcing* PITHETAERUS *to follow him*). The birds, I say,
completed everything. I was as surprised as you are. But
I was there. An eyewitness.

PITHETAERUS (*same tone, more mocking*). You saw it.

FIRST MESSENGER (*striding off again*). I saw it.   **50**
There came a body of thirty thousand cranes
With stones from Africa—
I won't be positive. There might have been more.

PITHETAERUS (*irritated, shouting, hoping he'll get on with
it and get off*). All right! There were more.

FIRST MESSENGER.
With stones from Africa in their craws and
gizzards,   **55**
Which the sandpipers and stone-chatterers
Worked into shape and finished.
The mudlarks, too, were busy in their department
Mixing the mortar, while the water birds
As fast as it was wanted, brought water   **60**
To temper and loosen it.

PITHETAERUS (*fascinated by his spiel*). Who were the
masons? Who did you get to carry it?

FIRST MESSENGER.   Carry? Why, the carrion crows, of
course. (*Laughs loudly at the audience, an-*   **65**
nouncing this as a joke. PITHETAERUS *hits him a quieting
slap.*)

PITHETAERUS.   I'll tell the jokes. How did you fill the
hods? How did they manage that?

FIRST MESSENGER.   Oh, capitally, I promise you! (*Demonstrating the following movements ludicrously with his
hands and feet.*)
There were the geese, all barefoot,
Trampling the mortar, and when all was ready   **70**

They handed it into the hods . . . so cleverly—
With their flat feet!
(*He is making a production number out of this.*
PITHETAERUS *says nothing so he repeats the business
without the lines.*)

PITHETAERUS.   All right, you do that very well. Go on.

FIRST MESSENGER.   You should have been there. It was a
sight to see them.   **75**
Trains of ducks, clambering the ladders—
(*Demonstrating again.*)
With their little duck legs, like bricklayer's
prentices,
All dapper and handy, with their little trowels.
(*Shows how they trowel with their beaks.*)

PITHETAERUS (*nailing him down*). Could you finish
this standing still? What of the woodwork? Who   **80**
were the carpenters?

FIRST MESSENGER.   The woodpeckers, of course! And
there they were
Laboring upon the gates, driving and banging
With their hard hatchet beaks, and such a din,   **85**
Such a clatter as they made, hammering and hacking,
In a perpetual peal, pelting away,
Like shipwrights, hard at work in the docks.

PITHETAERUS.   You had a lot to say once you got started,
didn't you?   **90**

FIRST MESSENGER (*exuberantly, for climatic effect*).
And now their work is finished, gates and all,
Staples and bolts, and bars and everything.
The sentries at their posts, patrols appointed,
Watchmen in the towers, the beacons
Prepared for lightning, all their signals set—   **95**
(*Immediate drop to conversational tone.*) And now if
you'll excuse me, I have to wash my hands.

(*Drops off the stage and goes up the aisle of the theatre to
the men's washroom. At same time* EPOPS *and the* CHORUS
OF BIRDS *begin to appear over the rocks.*)

EPOPS.   Well! What do you say to us? Aren't you astonished
at how quick we've been? The city completed and ready?

PITHETAERUS.   By the gods, yes. It's simply not to   **100**
be believed. (*A stir is heard offstage.*) What's that?

LEADER.   A messenger is coming.

PITHETAERUS.   Not another! Well, somebody's got to help
me this time!

(SECOND MESSENGER *darts in, as first one did.* PITHETAERUS
immediately blocks off second exit, causing SECOND MES-
SENGER *to turn and head for another, but the* CHORUS OF
BIRDS *leaps to positions blocking him off one place and another until he is surrounded and crowded in DC, still running
in a static position, facing front. On a signal,* PITHETAERUS
and surrounding CHORUS OF BIRDS *grab him to stop him.*)

SECOND MESSENGER.   Alas, alas, alas, alas, alas!   **105**

PITHETAERUS.   Is that the whole message?

SECOND MESSENGER.   Terrible news!

CHORUS.   What? What news? What's the matter?

PITHETAERUS (*to* CHORUS OF BIRDS). Sh-h-h! Be quiet! (*In shushing them,* PITHETAERUS *has momentarily loosed his hold on* SECOND MESSENGER, *who promptly starts running again.* PITHETAERUS *tackles him in a flying dive.* SECOND MESSENGER *goes down and out.* PITHETAERUS *is bending over him.*) What news? (*No response* **110** *from* SECOND MESSENGER.) Now *he's* out. Here! Here! Answer me!

(*Begins the slapping business. At same time a rope dangles down from the city above and, as* CHORUS OF BIRDS *clears a space,* EUELPIDES *slides down it.*)

EUELPIDES.   Ho, there! Look out below!

PITHETAERUS.   What are you doing?

EPOPS.   He's come from the city.   **115**

EUELPIDES.   I still don't trust these wings.

PITHETAERUS.   Get down out of there!

EUELPIDES.   Did you get the message?

PITHETAERUS.   No, dammit! (*To* EPOPS, *as he glances at knocked-out* SECOND MESSENGER.) Put it on   **120** order right away—stronger messengers!

LEADER.   Tell us! What is this terrible news?

EUELPIDES (*dropping to the stage floor*). A horrible outrage. Horrible!

PITHETAERUS.   Well, get on with it!   **125**

EUELPIDES.   Here's what happened—(*The* SECOND MESSENGER *has been coming to, unnoticed.*) The gods have heard about our intention, and Zeus has already . . .

SECOND MESSENGER (*quickly jumping in, attempting to give the message himself, overlapping* EUELPIDES). The thing is that Zeus has already heard what we plan   **130** to do—(*Both* EUELPIDES *and* SECOND MESSENGER *continue explaining but since they are both talking at once, we cannot understand a word they are saying.*)

PITHETAERUS.   Silence! Shut up! One at a time!

EUELPIDES (*to* SECOND MESSENGER, *quarrelsome*). You lie down.

SECOND MESSENGER.   But I was sent here to . . .   **135**

EUELPIDES.   *I* started to tell this story.

SECOND MESSENGER.   I got here first!

EUELPIDES (*shouting*). You had your chance! You didn't . . .

SECOND MESSENGER.   But they're *my* lines!   **140**

EUELPIDES.   I slid all the way down here, getting several rope burns—(*By now they are shouting at each other at the same time and they begin to rough it up.* PITHETAERUS *pulls them apart.*)

PITHETAERUS.   Here! Here!

SECOND MESSENGER.   I was sent here to relay this information—   **145**

PITHETAERUS.   Look. You've run a long way. Don't you want to wash your hands?

SECOND MESSENGER (*reflective pause*). As a matter of fact, I do.

PITHETAERUS (*pointing down aisle to men's washroom*). Right there.   **150**

SECOND MESSENGER.   Oh. Thank you.

(*Leaps offstage as* FIRST MESSENGER *has done; at same time* FIRST MESSENGER *reappears from men's washroom and they pass each other midway down the aisle, shake hands, and go their ways,* SECOND MESSENGER *to the men's washroom,* FIRST MESSENGER *up onto the stage.*)

PITHETAERUS (*seeing* FIRST MESSENGER *coming*). Now before *he* gets up here with *his* big mouth, will you tell us the news?

EUELPIDES.   A god has penetrated the city.   **155**

CHORUS.   What? A sacrilege, on the day our city was built! Oh, horrible! Let terror strike.

EUELPIDES (*shrugging his shoulders*). Got through somehow.

LEADER.   Who was on guard?   **160**

EUELPIDES.   The jays.

LEADER.   Death to the jays!

EUELPIDES.   But it's one of those minor gods with little wings. That made it tougher.

EPOPS.   Where is this god now?   **165**

EUELPIDES.   We don't know. Flying around somewhere. Liable to turn up any minute.

PITHETAERUS (*to* LEADER). Dispatch thirty thousand hawks of the Legion of Mounted Archers!

LEADER (*hustling some* BIRDS *off and calling offstage to others, bawling orders. A few* BIRDS *remain, gathered about* EPOPS). All hook-clawed birds into the air!   **170** Kestrels, buzzards, vultures, great-horned owls! Cleave the air till it resounds with the flapping of wings. Look everywhere!

CHORUS.   To arms, all, with beak and talon! War, a terrible war, is breaking out between us and the gods!   **175**

LEADER.   Look everywhere! (*A conventional puff of smoke at opposite side of stage.*)

EUELPIDES.   Look right there.

(*ALL huddle at opposite side, staring toward the rock from which the smoke puff has come.* IRIS *appears through the cloud, an unlikely looking goddess with small wings. She stands looking at them, then speaks in a flat, nasal voice.*)

IRIS.   Hello.

PITHETAERUS.   Halt! Don't stir. Not a beat of your wing. Who are you? Where do you come from?   **180**

IRIS.   Me? I come from Olympus, my abode.

PITHETAERUS.   Who are you?

IRIS.   I yam swift Iris.

PITHETAERUS.   Call the buzzards and let them seize her!

IRIS.   Say, I handled plenty of buzzards who tried   **185** to do that.

PITHETAERUS.   Woe to you!

IRIS.   Woe to you, too. What's up?

LEADER.   By which gate did you pass through the wall, wretched goddess?   **190**

IRIS.   I didn't see no gate. I was just out for a short flap.

PITHETAERUS.   Fine, innocent airs she gives herself! (*Mockingly.*) You applied to the pelicans, I suppose? The captain of the cormorants let you in?

IRIS.   Well, I seen a nice captain, but I let it pass.   **195**

PITHETAERUS.   So, you confess! You came without permission! You didn't get a passport. Nobody put a label on you!

IRIS (*instinctively starts to reach with her hand, stops*).   Is that what that was?   **200**

PITHETAERUS.   Without permission from anybody, you ramble and fly through the air—the air that belongs to us!

IRIS.   To you?

CHORUS.   To us!

IRIS.   Where do you think us gods are gonna take   **205** our exercise?

PITHETAERUS.   I don't know and I don't care. But I'll tell you this—let us catch you once more flying through this territory and you're done for. You'll be put to death.

CHORUS.   To death!   **210**

IRIS.   Listen. I'm immortal.

PITHETAERUS.   Don't try to wriggle out of it, now. Mortal or immortal, you'll be put to death. We can't have the whole universe obeying us and you lackadaisical gods floating around where you please.   **215**

IRIS (*snaps her fingers*). Almost forgot. Had an errand to do. (*Starts to promenade across the stage.*)

PITHETAERUS.   Wait a minute, here! What errand?

IRIS.   Zeus sent me. I'm supposed to go down to Earth and tell mankind to sacrifice an ox. Zeus wants a little   **220** heady smoke coming up. Helps his sinus.

PITHETAERUS.   Sacrifice to him?

IRIS.   Who else? Zeus, he's my father. He's a deity.

PITHETAERUS.   Zeus a deity? (*Laughs mockingly.* BIRDS *join him in a great hollow cackling.*)

IRIS.   Best deity going.   **225**

PITHETAERUS (*roaring*).   Silence! Remember—once and for all—that we, the birds, are the only deities, from this time forth!

IRIS.   Huh?

PITHETAERUS.   Man henceforth will sacrifice to us   **230** and not to Zeus, by Zeus!

IRIS (*suddenly going into grand tragic style, beating her breast, clinging dramatically to rocks, writhing on the floor, etc.*).

    Oh, fool, fool, fool! Stir not the mighty wrath
    Of angry gods, lest Justice, with the spade
    Of vengeful Jove, demolish all thy race,
    And fiery vapor, with lightning strokes,   **235**
    Incinerate thy city and thyself!

PITHETAERUS (*matter-of-fact tone*). Now, listen, girl. Never mind the oratory. You can save that speech for some tragedy or other. And if Zeus keeps troubling me, I'll be doing some incinerating myself. (*Slowing down*   **240** *his rate, half-abstracted as he looks at her.*) I'll send eagles carrying fire up into his halls of state, and he'll find out. (*Slower still.*) And as for you, unless you learn to mind your manners—(*Suddenly.*) Say, are you doing anything tonight?   **245**

IRIS (*backing away from him*). I'll tell my father, I'll tell my father—

PITHETAERUS (*giving it up*). Oh, bother. Scuttle away. Convey your person elsewhere. Be brisk. Leave a vacancy. Brush off. (*She has backed away but not*   **250** *gone. He shouts.*) Well?

IRIS (*terrified, as she runs off*). Daddy! Zeus! Daddy!

CHORUS.
    Never again shall the Zeus-born gods
    Never again shall they pass this way!
    Never again through this realm of ours   **255**
    Shall men send up to the heavenly powers
    The smoke of beasts which on earth they slay!
    We, too, shall slay! Slay!

PITHETAERUS.   Now whatever's happened to that herald we sent down to Earth, to tell the people? (*To*   **260** EUELPIDES.) You sent him, didn't you?

EUELPIDES.   I did.

PITHETAERUS.   Why can't we keep these actors around here?

(HERALD *enters on the double, late, obviously having missed his cue, and still fixing his costume.*)

EUELPIDES.   He's in.   **265**

HERALD (*stentorian tones*). Oh, Pithetaerus!

PITHETAERUS.   High time.

HERALD.   Oh, thou wisest, thou best—oh, thou wisest *and* best—thou wisest, deepest, happiest of mankind—happiest, deepest, wisest—   **270**

PITHETAERUS.   Did he play the priest in the first act?

HERALD.   Most glorious Pithetaerus, most . . . (*Snapping his fingers, looking off.*) Prompter! Prompter!

PROMPTER'S VOICE (*off*). Revered of men—

HERALD.   Revered of men, most . . . (*Thinks a*   **275** *moment, then speaks confidentially to* PITHETAERUS.) Let me try it again. (*Takes a step back as though entering anew, begins from the beginning.*) Oh, Pithetaerus!

PITHETAERUS.   No, you don't! Suppose we get on with the message?   **280**

HERALD (*hurt*). All right. But I knew it. (*Stentorian again.*) All men on Earth have been notified, and all are filled with admiration for your wisdom. They acknowledge your leadership, and that of the Birds, and have sent you this golden crown. (*Holds out his hands in motion*   **285** *of giving crown, but they are empty.*)

PITHETAERUS.   Yes?

HERALD (*noticing he has no crown*). Oh, dammit! (*Goes to the wings.*) Where's that crown? Somebody was supposed to hand it to me!

PROMPTER'S VOICE (*off*). You were supposed to   **290**
pick it up!

HERALD (*shouting off, beginning an ad lib quarrel, both talking at once*). When an actor has to make an entrance, he can't be worrying about props! (*There is an almost out-of-sight scuffle between the* HERALD *and some member of the stage crew, whose hands only are seen, over the crown.* PITHETAERUS *wearily breaks in, brings* HERALD *back to position, plants him there, thrusts the crown into his hands, deliberately takes it out again, doing the whole business himself to make sure it gets done, and crams it on his own head in disgust.*)

PITHETAERUS.   Now will you get on with the message?

HERALD (*pulling himself together*). All right. (*In a*   **295**
sudden confidence to PITHETAERUS.) Do you get stage fright? I do.

PITHETAERUS (*roaring*). Get on with it!

HERALD (*opens his mouth to speak, then breaks down completely, a nervous shambles*). I'm sorry. I'll have to turn in my part. I'm a wreck. (*He leaves.*)   **300**

PITHETAERUS.   Does anybody know his lines?

FIRST MESSENGER (*hopping to his feet*). Yes, sir. I do!

PITHETAERUS.   I'd hoped it would be anybody but you. All right.

FIRST MESSENGER (*quickly taking Herald's place*). I, who have just returned from Earth . . . (*Aside*   **305**
to PITHETAERUS.) I haven't, of course. I'm saying *his* lines. (*Back into speech.*) . . . bring you this message. All men accept your reign and themselves wish to become birds. More than ten thousand have followed me here and now await your pleasure. They have gone bird-   **310**
mad.

(HERALD *sticks his head in from the wings.*)

HERALD (*to* FIRST MESSENGER).   I hate you.

(PITHETAERUS *makes a threatening gesture and* HERALD *disappears again. We begin to see the hands and heads of people climbing up from Earth.* PITHETAERUS *is immediately aware of them and he goes to the Earth-entrance and is busy counting heads as the* FIRST MESSENGER *completes his speech.*)

FIRST MESSENGER.   They wish to be supplied with feathers and hooked claws, in honor of their masters. Will you oblige them?   **315**

PITHETAERUS.   Ah, yes. Yes, indeed. Quick! There's no time for idling.

(MEN *enter, arriving from Earth.*)

PITHETAERUS.   Go and fill every hamper, every basket you can find with wings. Bring them to me, and I will welcome our new subjects!   **320**

CHORUS (*as a bustle ensues*).
Shortly shall our noble town
Be populous and gay,
High in honor and renown.

PITHETAERUS (*impatiently*). If I get those wings, it may.

(EUELPIDES *rushes in with a basketful of wings which* PITHETAERUS *snatches and doles out to* MEN *as they pass by him single file. The* MEN *affix their new wings as they file across stage to a promontory and leap off, one by one, rapidly.* EUELPIDES *helps* PITHETAERUS *as* BIRDS *bring several more baskets.*)

CHORUS (*during this business*).
Now rush them forth, in yellow, red, and blue   **325**
Feathers of every form and size and hue.

PITHETAERUS.   Give me a hand, can't you? (EUELPIDES *offers his hand matter-of-factly and gets slapped for it.*)

CHORUS.
Where in all this earthly range
He that wishes for a change
Can he find a seat,   **330**
Joyous and secure as this,
Filled with happiness and bliss,
Such a fair retreat?

PITHETAERUS (*busy distributing wings, to* EUELPIDES). Ask that chorus if it has to be so loud, will you?   **335**
(EUELPIDES *goes to* CHORUS OF BIRDS *to shush them but before he can say anything they double their volume in a great blast which shakes* PITHETAERUS *and nearly blows* EUELPIDES *down.*)

CHORUS.
Here is Wisdom and Wit and each exquisite
Grace
And here the unruffled, benevolent face
Of Quiet, and loving desire.

PITHETAERUS (*shouting*). It is my desire that you *keep* quiet so I won't be so ruffled!   **340**

CHORUS (*wounded*). Don't you *like* choruses?

PITHETAERUS (*to* EUELPIDES, *at the baskets*). Back to business here.

(*As they turn back to the oncoming line of* MEN, *the* POET *bursts from the line.*)

POET.   Wings! Give me wings!

PITHETAERUS.   Ye gods, you're back.   **345**

POET.
On the lightest of wings I shall soar up
on high
And lightly from measure to measure I'll fly.

PITHETAERUS.   You want wings, do you?

POET.

> Let me live and let me sing
> Like a bird upon the wing.   350

PITHETAERUS.   Oh, stop that! Talk prose! What do you want wings for?

POET.   I wish to make a tour among the clouds, collecting images and metaphors and things of that description.

PITHETAERUS.   Oh, you pick all your poems out of   355
the clouds, eh?

POET.   Oh, yes. All modern poetry is very cloudy. Our most brilliant poems now are those that flap their wings in empty space and are clothed in mist. What we want is a dense obscurity. Listen. I'll give you a   360
sample.

PITHETAERUS (*picking up a pair of wings to hit him with*). No, you won't.

POET.   Now this one is *all* air. Listen.

> "Shadowy visions of
> Wing-spreading, air-treading   365
> Taper-necked birds . . ."

(*Changing his tactic,* PITHETAERUS *begins to tickle* POET *with wings.* POET *giggles wildly then turns on* PITHETAERUS *reprovingly.*) You're not listening. (*Dancing now.*)

> "Bounding along on the path to the seas,
> Fain I would float on the streams and the
>   breeze . . ."

(*Behind Poet's back,* PITHETAERUS *signals to several* BIRDS, *who get a blanket and begin to steal up behind* POET.)

> "First do I stray on a southerly way,   370
> Then to the northward my body I bear,"
> "Cutting a harborless furrow of air,
> The air I'll cleave, I'll cleave the sky . . ."

(PITHETAERUS *pushes him over into blanket and they toss him in the air several times.*)

PITHETAERUS (*as they let him down*). How do you like cleaving the air?   375

POET.   If this is how you treat people—

PITHETAERUS.   Off with him! Out! (BIRDS *start dragging him out.*)

POET.   But where are my wings? Wings! I want wings! (BIRDS *get* POET *off, and the remaining* MEN *have now jumped off.*)

PITHETAERUS.   Now! Prepare for the feast! Bring me food to roast, and a spit, and the makings of a fire. Oh,   380
dear, I have to do everything.

(*As* EUELPIDES *and* BIRDS *have scattered in all directions to get supplies, leaving the stage clear,* PROMETHEUS, *a sneaky, shadowy figure, his cloak about his face and carrying an umbrella, has darted on, looked about the stage suspiciously, checking every nook and corner for someone who may be following him.* PITHETAERUS *has spotted him,*

watched him with open-mouthed curiosity, but said nothing. Finally PROMETHEUS *comes directly down to* PITHETAERUS.)

PROMETHEUS.   Is there a god following me?

PITHETAERUS.   Not that I know of. What are you all muffled up about?

PROMETHEUS.   If only Zeus doesn't see me. That   385
Zeus, always looking. Where is Pithetaerus?

PITHETAERUS.   I am Pithetaerus.

PROMETHEUS.   Oh, are you? Good boy. (*Taps him approvingly, darts upstage to look around again.*)

PITHETAERUS.   Who are you?

PROMETHEUS (*coming back to him*). What time is   390
it?

PITHETAERUS.   Time? Oh, about noon. Who are you?

PROMETHEUS.   Only noon? Is that all it is?

PITHETAERUS.   How should I know? Who are you?

PROMETHEUS (*after more darting away*). What's   395
Zeus doing? Is he behind the clouds or is he peeping?

PITHETAERUS (*to audience*). I don't know about you, but I'm getting bored. (*Shouting at* PROMETHEUS.) WHO ARE YOU?

PROMETHEUS (*coming back to him, mysteriously*).
I shall reveal myself.   400

PITHETAERUS.   Well, take your time. Don't rush. (PROMETHEUS *throws the cloak back from his face.* PITHETAERUS *throws open his arms and greets him loudly and delightedly.*) Prometheus! My old friend, Prometheus!

PROMETHEUS (*in a panic*). Shh! Not so loud.

PITHETAERUS.   Why, what's the matter, Prometheus?

PROMETHEUS.   Shh! Don't mention my name. If   405
Zeus hears you, I'm in for it. He mustn't know I'm here.

PITHETAERUS.   Very well.

PROMETHEUS.   Here. If you don't mind. Hold the umbrella over me. Then he can't see us.

PITHETAERUS.   Right. Right. (*They sit down on*   410
edge of stage, umbrella over them, speak quietly.)

PROMETHEUS.   Zeus never liked me, you know.

PITHETAERUS.   No.

PROMETHEUS.   Ever since I stole that fire from him. Gave it to men. My name has been mud. I still get in up there, but he doesn't trust me.   415

PITHETAERUS.   Of course.

PROMETHEUS.   Well. Let me tell you. I've got all the news from Olympus.

PITHETAERUS.   Ah?

PROMETHEUS.   Just listen.   420

PITHETAERUS.   I'm listening.

PROMETHEUS.   Zeus is ruined.

PITHETAERUS (*delighted*). Ah! Since when?

PROMETHEUS.   Since you went to work down here. Built your city. They can't get a message through! Not   425
a thing comes up. No smoke. No incense. Absolutely nothing. They're all on a strict diet up there. The whole bunch. You've done it. (*Shakes Pithetaerus' hand.*)

PITHETAERUS.   Good.

PROMETHEUS.   More than that. Mutiny.   **430**

PITHETAERUS.   Mutiny up there? (PROMETHEUS *nods knowingly*.) Who?

PROMETHEUS.   The new gods. Especially those barbarian gods they took in recently. Hell to pay. Zeus can't meet his commitments. They're furious. Open rebel-   **435** lion. All starving to death. Unless Zeus can get the air lanes open—get traffic started again—he'll be out on his ear. Don't say I told you.

PITHETAERUS.   Not a word. But what's Zeus going to do?

PROMETHEUS.   That's it. That's what I came for.   **440** Zeus is sending a committee. Committee of gods. Ought to be here any minute. I ought to get out of here before they come. One of the barbarian gods is with 'em. Checking up. Anyway. They're going to come to you and sue for peace. Here's the thing. Don't you do it. Don't you   **445** agree to a thing unless Zeus acknowledges the rule of the birds. And . . . are you listening? (PITHETAERUS *nods eagerly*.) Don't stop there. To protect yourself . . . ask for one of the goddesses in marriage. That'll make it stick. Protect your line.   **450**

PITHETAERUS.   Oh.

PROMETHEUS.   Any particular goddess you like?

PITHETAERUS.   Why, yes. Yes! There was a little thing in here today. Iris, her name was.

PROMETHEUS.   Fine. Ask for Iris. (*Getting up.*)   **455** Well, I've got to get out of here. Hell to pay. I only came for a minute. Let you know. But you can count on me. I'm a friend. Steady to the human interest. Always was.

PITHETAERUS.   I never eat a roast without thinking of you.

PROMETHEUS.   I hate these gods, you know.   **460**

PITHETAERUS.   Yes, I know.

PROMETHEUS.   I'm a regular scourge to them, a regular scourge. Well, bye-bye. Give me the umbrella. If anyone asks, you haven't seen me.

PITHETAERUS.   Right.   **465**

PROMETHEUS (*at the exit*). Courage. (*As he goes,* PITHE- TAERUS *begins hopping around excitedly.*)

PITHETAERUS.   Oh, my goodness, I've got to hurry!

(EPOPS *and other* BIRDS *scurry in, carrying an open-fire spit with a pig already on it, together with all the necessary uten- sils—oversize forks, spoons, salt-cellars, etc.*)

PITHETAERUS.   Here! Good! (*The spit is mounted down- stage, a "fire" is built under it, and several* BIRDS *remain nearby to help* PITHETAERUS *as he needs things for the cooking.*)

EPOPS.   We have done your bidding, brave leader. Here is food and a fire and everything you need for a   **470** banquet.

PITHETAERUS.   Fine, fine. Now you must all disappear. I have very important visitors coming. The moment is at hand when our fate will be decided.

EPOPS.   I can bring you armies of birds for support.   **475**

PITHETAERUS.   No, no, no. I must handle this alone. They mustn't think we expect them. Give everything away. I won't even pretend to notice them.

(EUELPIDES *runs on.*)

PITHETAERUS.   Here. Help me here. (*Showing* EUELPIDES *how to turn spit.*) Epops, you stand by in the   **480** rocks and when the meeting is over you can spread the word.

EPOPS.   As you say, oh leader! (EPOPS *disappears.* EUEL- PIDES *is savoring the roasting pig with a loud "Mmmm!" but* PITHETAERUS *slaps him away.*)

PITHETAERUS.   Keep your nose out of that. You'll sniff up all the smell. I'm going to win a war with that smell.   **485**

EUELPIDES.   We got another war? Where's that fork?

(*Snatches up a fork to defend himself with, when there is a sudden smoke puff high up on the rocks.* PITHETAERUS *glances at it, then, with a great show of indifference, resumes his work with the roast.* NEPTUNE, HERCULES, *and a* BAR- BARIAN GOD *come through the smoke, coughing, sneezing, and flailing with their cloaks to drive the smoke puff away.*)

NEPTUNE (*who carries his tined fork and is a pompous, exceedingly dignified god*). This damn smoke. I wish they'd cut that stuff out. (*Pulling himself together.*) On your dignity, gods. This is Cloud Cuckoo-land, whither we come as ambassadors. (*Noticing* BARBARIAN   **490** GOD, *whose cloak is dragging sadly and whose general appearance is sloppy indeed.*) You! Barbarian God! Look at your cloak. What a mess. Throw it over your shoulder. (BARBARIAN GOD *does, striking* NEPTUNE *full in the face with it.* NEPTUNE *seizes him, forcibly straightens his costume.* BARBARIAN GOD *maintains an unrelievedly stupid, open-mouthed, deadpan expres- sion.*) What's the matter with you? You are the most uncouth god I ever saw.   **495**

BARBARIAN GOD (*low, moronic speaking voice*). Leave me alone. Leave me alone.

NEPTUNE (*looking at him*). Oh, democracy! Whither are you leading us?

HERCULES (*bright-faced, simple-minded type*). Come on. Let's be ambassadors.   **500**

NEPTUNE.   You will please wait, my dear nephew, Her- cules, until you have been instructed. Or did you have some plan of your own?

HERCULES (*pointing to* PITHETAERUS, *below*). Certainly. There's the fellow. Let me go strangle him to   **505** death.

NEPTUNE.   My dear nephew, may I remind you that we are ambassadors of peace.

HERCULES.   Sure. When I strangle him, we got peace. What do you want?   **510**

BARBARIAN GOD.   I wanna go back where I came from.

NEPTUNE (*curious*). How is it he hasn't noticed our smoke? I hate to put up with that for nothing. (*Clears his throat loudly.*)

PITHETAERUS (*feigning not to notice gods above, now giving directions to* EUELPIDES *and servant* BIRDS *who assist him, running for equipment, etc.*). Hand me the grater! Get some spice for the sauce. Where's the **515** cheese? (NEPTUNE *clears his throat again.*) And blow up the fire a little bit. More charcoal. (NEPTUNE *now strides downstage, without going too close to* PITHETAERUS. EUELPIDES *is backing in his direction at the moment and turns toward him just as* NEPTUNE *happens to lower his tined fork.* EUELPIDES *whips out his own fork and takes a dueling stance.* HERCULES *lifts* EUELPIDES *bodily out of the way, throws him to one side.*)

NEPTUNE.   Mortal! We three who greet you are gods.

PITHETAERUS (*not looking up from his work, waving them away*). Busy just now. Busy just now. Mixing my sauce. (*To servant* BIRD.)   Where are the pickles? Bring **520** me some pickles.

HERCULES (*sniffing and moving closer*). That sauce smells nice.

PITHETAERUS (*offhand, still not looking up*). Yes. It's my own recipe. **525**

HERCULES.   Uh . . . what you roasting there?

PITHETAERUS.   Pig.

EUELPIDES (*passing, thinking he means him, startled*). Who?

PITHETAERUS.   Later we'll have some nice plump fowl. (*To those around him.*) Salt, please! Get me salt! **530**

HERCULES.   I thought you liked birds. Didn't think you'd roast 'em.

PITHETAERUS (*salting the roast*). Oh, there were some birds who wouldn't join the party. Politically unreliable. (*A servant* BIRD *is passing and* PITHETAERUS *salts its tail, too, just for the hell of it.*) Thyme, please. **535** Wild thyme!

NEPTUNE (*impatient and offended*).   Are you going to cook the whole meal before you acknowledge us?

PITHETAERUS.   What? (*Looking up now, feigning recognition.*) What's that? Neptune! Well, for heaven's **540** sake! Welcome! Didn't see you.

NEPTUNE.   Well. Now that I have your ear . . . we have been sent by the gods to sue for peace.

PITHETAERUS (*wandering back to his roast, absorbed*). Yes, yes. Mustn't let this get too done. There's no more **545** olive oil. More olive oil, please.

HERCULES.   Oh, you gotta have olive oil. Plenty of olive oil.

NEPTUNE (*turning on his heel and stalking away*). I told Zeus I didn't want this job. (*Turning back and rapping the floor with his staff.*) Sir! Sir! **550**

PITHETAERUS.   What? Oh, yes. Excuse me. (*Wiping his hands on his apron, he casually shifts places with*

HERCULES *in such a way that* HERCULES *will be placed directly over the roasting pig, inhaling the aroma.* PITHETAERUS *then crosses to* NEPTUNE.) Wouldn't want to spoil a tasty snack like that. Personally, I'm hungry. (*Watches for effect of this on* NEPTUNE, *who swallows hard, then continues.*)

NEPTUNE.   What we have come to say is this. We do not wish to fight you. We are eager to be your friends, **555** to be of service. I am sure we can negotiate. Now on our part we are willing to supply you constantly with warm weather. Further, to see that you always have rain water in your pools. On these points I am prepared to bargain.

PITHETAERUS.   Well, now, we're just as interested **560** in peace as you are. We have no plans for aggression, and are also ready to bargain. We have just one condition. Zeus must give up. We take the sceptre. Now if you three will simply agree to this, I shall invite you all to dinner.

HERCULES (*nearly fainting with rapture over the aroma from the roast, speaks quickly*). I agree. **565**

NEPTUNE.   You jackass! (*Strides to him quickly and pulls him away from the roast.*) When are you going to stop being a fathead? Just because you're a fool and a glutton, do you want to dethrone your own father?

HERCULES (*wistfully*). He'd be mad, wouldn't he? **570**

PITHETAERUS.   Now, that's not true at all. You're not facing the facts. The gods would be even *more* powerful if they turned things over to the birds.

EUELPIDES (*quietly to* PITHETAERUS, *in passing*). I hope you can sell this one. **575**

PITHETAERUS.   How are things now? You gods are stuck up there, behind all those clouds. You don't see *half* of what's going on down below. Men are doing all kinds of things when your backs are turned, especially on cloudy days. But if you put us in charge, we'll watch out **580** for you. Birds get around. Let's say some man down on Earth has promised to offer a sacrifice if he gets a certain favor. Well, he gets the favor and then he forgets all about the sacrifice. We'll keep track of him and, if he doesn't pay up, peck his eyes out. Or at least we'll pick **585** up double the amount of the sacrifice out of his farm yard for you! (*During his speech he has maneuvered* NEPTUNE *directly over the roast, and* NEPTUNE *is reacting, too.*)

NEPTUNE (*considering*). Of course, there's something in what you say—

HERCULES.   See? I ain't such a fathead. **590**

PITHETAERUS (*going to* BARBARIAN GOD, *who has been standing just where he entered, looking stupidly into space, doing nothing*). How do *you* feel about that?

BARBARIAN GOD.   Oh, if it ain't one damn thing it's another.

PITHETAERUS (*to* NEPTUNE). See? He agrees, too!

NEPTUNE (*looking at* BARBARIAN GOD *dubiously*).
I'm not sure I can accept that as an official vote. **595**
(*Anxious to settle now himself, but worried.*) Oh, Barbarian God, what is your considered opinion?

BARBARIAN GOD. When do we eat?

PITHETAERUS. There you are! Now what do you say?

NEPTUNE. Since I am out-voted, two to one— **600**

EUELPIDES (*looking at* BARBARIAN GOD). Does he get a whole vote?

PITHETAERUS. Shh! Shh!

NEPTUNE. I consent as well. You shall receive the sceptre.
(*With a loud "AHHHH" from* HERCULES, *all three* GODS *start immediately for the spit, drooling. Just as they get there,* PITHETAERUS *speaks.*)

PITHETAERUS. Oh, I almost forgot. (*They turn to* **605**
him warily.) There is one other condition. (GODS *exchange glances.*)

NEPTUNE. And that is?

PITHETAERUS. I must have Iris in marriage. Zeus can have all the others. I only want Iris. (*Pause.*)

NEPTUNE (*pointedly*). Then you *don't* want peace. **610**

PITHETAERUS. Just little Iris.

NEPTUNE (*imposingly*). The gods do not marry beneath them! Come, we must go! (*Signals other two* GODS *and they start away.*)

PITHETAERUS. All right; all right. Doesn't matter to me.
(*He goes back to the spit, indifferently.*) How's **615**
that gravy coming? That's fine, stir it good. (GODS *are slowing down in their exit, looking back yearningly over their shoulders.*) My, it seems to be turning out just right. Did you ever smell anything like that? (*To* EUELPIDES *and servant* BIRDS.) Mmm, mmm, here, taste. (*The* GODS *have tried to force themselves to go, but cannot; they look back to the others relishing a sip of the gravy.*)

HERCULES (*throwing down his club*). I don't want **620**
to go to no war about no woman!

NEPTUNE. It *is* annoying. I never cared much for Iris, anyway. But what can we do?

HERCULES. We can give in.

NEPTUNE. I'm sorry. It's impossible. **625**

HERCULES. You go back. I'm giving in. (*Starting back toward spit.*)

NEPTUNE (*grabbing him*). Listen, you blockhead. Don't you see? It's not simply a matter of Zeus losing everything. You'd lose everything, too. You're his son and heir.

HERCULES. Oh. **630**

PITHETAERUS (*has been listening and intervenes between* NEPTUNE *and* HERCULES). No, you don't. No, you don't. Don't let him take you in with *that* story, friend. Come here. I want a word with you. (*Draws him aside.*) As far as Zeus goes, you may be his son, but you're not his heir.

HERCULES. What do you mean? **635**

PITHETAERUS. I hate to be the one to break it to you. You should have been told. It's been all over Olympus for years.

HERCULES. What has?

PITHETAERUS. I'm sorry, but you're illegitimate. **640**

HERCULES. What!

PITHETAERUS. That's the way it is. You won't get a thing.

NEPTUNE. Here, what are you telling my feeble-minded nephew?

HERCULES. He says I'm a . . . (*Bursts into tears.*) **645**

PITHETAERUS. I was simply mentioning his origins.

HERCULES (*weeping*). Uncle Neptune, is it true?

NEPTUNE (*turns away, bites his lip, braces himself*). Well, Hercules. You're a big boy now. It's time you knew. (HERCULES *bawls louder.*)

EUELPIDES (*to* BARBARIAN GOD). Poor fellow. He **650**
didn't know.

BARBARIAN GOD. What's it to him?

NEPTUNE. Now, now, nephew. Zeus will leave you something in his will.

PITHETAERUS. I'll give you something right now. **655**
Roast pig!

HERCULES (*through tears*). I always knew there was something about me.

PITHETAERUS. Be on my side. I will make you a king and will feed you on bird's milk and honey. **660**

HERCULES. Take me! I wasn't wanted! (EUELPIDES *comforts* HERCULES.)

PITHETAERUS. Neptune! I've got his vote!

NEPTUNE. You haven't got mine.

PITHETAERUS. Then it still depends on old stupid here. (*Turns to* BARBARIAN GOD.) Why do you say? **665**

BARBARIAN GOD. Old Stupid votes yes.

PITHETAERUS. We've done it!

HERCULES (*to* NEPTUNE). And you never told me.

NEPTUNE. All right, all right. I give in. Peace is made.

PITHETAERUS. And just to think—we have the **670**
wedding feast all ready!

HERCULES (*to* NEPTUNE). You go get Iris. I'll keep an eye on the roast.

NEPTUNE No, you're too fat now.

PITHETAERUS. I have it. (*Getting* HERCULES' *arm.*) **675**
You hurry up to Olympus and bring them the news. *That'll* make them respect you! (HERCULES *brightens up.*) Bring me the sceptre . . . and bring me Iris. (*To* EUELPIDES, *as* HERCULES *nods and goes.*) Go get the Birds. Spread the glad tidings. (*To* NEPTUNE.) You. You **680**
turn the roast. And don't burn it!

NEPTUNE (*offended*). I am not the god of the kitchen.

PITHETAERUS. You're taking orders from me now. Remember that! (*Resignedly* NEPTUNE *goes to the spit and tries to turn the roast with his tines, aloofly.* EUELPIDES

has rushed in again with EPOPS.) Oh, Bird-King! 685
The treaty's concluded! The universe is ours!

(*The full* CHORUS OF BIRDS *is in by now.*)

CHORUS.
    Oh, all-successful, more than tongue can tell!
    Oh, this thrice-blessed, winged race of birds
    To have a leader who does so excel
    In wisdom and in courage and in power 690
    No man has ever matched him!
    (PITHETAERUS *has been benevolently patting various*
    of the kneeling BIRDS, *who bow low before him. He*
    goes off. The CHORUS OF BIRDS *changes to a rapid,*
    suspenseful rhythm, as the lights change to a mood
    of revelry.)
    There lies a region out of sight
    Far within the realm of night
    Far from torch and candlelight . . .
    There in feasts of meal and wine, 695
    Men and demigods may join,
    There they banquet, there they dine—

(*The dancing and reveling among the* BIRDS *has begun.*
PROCNE *appears and she and* EPOPS *dance.* EUELPIDES *from*
time to time pursues PROCNE, *but is always intercepted by*
EPOPS.)

CHORUS.
    Whilst the light of day prevails
    Honoring the man—the only man—who never fails!
    (*The revelry reaches a climax, the music stops at a*
    high point, and the BIRDS *make a royal path.*)
    Stand aside and clear the ground, 700
    Spreading in a circle round
    With a worthy welcoming
    To salute our noble King!

(HERALD *enters above.*)

HERALD.   Pithetaerus—the King! (*Coming off his perch, to*
    the others.) And I remembered every word of it. 705

(PITHETAERUS *enters, now clad in dazzling robes which look*
quite pretentious on him.)

CHORUS.
    Mark his entrance,
    Dazzling all eyes, resplendent as a Star.
    Outshining all the golden lights, that beam
    From heaven, even as a summer sun
    Blazing at noon! 710

(IRIS *enters, dressed to kill.*)

CHORUS.
    Now to join him by his side
    Comes his happy, lovely bride.

    Oh, the fair delightful face!
    What a figure! What a grace!
    What a presence! What a carriage! 715
    (IRIS *trips over her own train.*)
    What a noble worthy marriage.
    (BIRDS *have formed a crossed-sword effect as of a*
    military marriage and PITHETAERUS *assists* IRIS
    down the path. Leaving it, they go into a little dance
    of their own.)
    Let the Birds rejoice and sing
    At the wedding of their king,
    Happy to congratulate
    Such a blessing to the state. 720

(*Thunder and lightning. Above,* HERCULES *enters to present*
PITHETAERUS *with the thunderbolt of* ZEUS. NEPTUNE *and the*
BARBARIAN GOD *join him for the ceremony. The thunderbolt*
is presented to PITHETAERUS.)

PITHETAERUS.   I accept this token of heavenly love.
    (*To the* CHORUS OF BIRDS.)
    Your music and verse I applaud and admire
    But rouse your invention and, raising it higher,
    Describe me this terrible engine of Zeus . . .
    . . . Now mine— 725
    The thunder of Earth and the thunder above.
CHORUS.
    Let us sing of the trophies he brings us from heaven,
    The Earth-crashing thunders, deadly and dire,
    And the lightning's angry flashes of fire—
    (PITHETAERUS *is wielding the thunderbolt*
    majestically and lightning and thunder ensues,
    frightening him.)
    Blaze of the lightning, so terribly beautiful, 730
    Golden and grand!
    Fire-flashing javelin, glittering now in
    Our leader's right hand!
    (PITHETAERUS *quickly gets it into his right hand, a*
    little late.)
    Earth-crashing thunder, the hoarsely resounding,
    The bringer of showers! 735
    (PITHETAERUS *gives the thunderbolt another good*
    shake, just to reassert himself; it brings on such a
    blast that he quickly and gingerly tosses the
    thunderbolt away; it is caught accidentally by
    EUELPIDES *who dances uncomfortably about with it*
    and tosses it away himself; it is now caught by the
    HERALD, *who matter-of-factly takes it, as though it*
    were nothing but a prop, and drags it off after him.)
    He is our Master, he that is shaking the
    Earth with his almighty powers!
PITHETAERUS.
    Now follow on, dear feathered tribes,
    To see us wed, to see us wed
    Mount up to Zeus' golden floor 740

But watch your head, yes, watch your head!
(BIRDS *are forming an exit processional as*
PITHETAERUS *turns to* IRIS.)
And oh, my darling, reach thine hand
And take my wing and dance with me,
And I will lightly bear thee up
And carry thee, and carry thee.   **745**
(*He picks her up—it requires a mighty effort—and
begins to ascend the rocks with her.*)

CHORUS.
　　Raise the joyous paean-cry,
　　Raise the song of victory.
　　Io Paean, alalalae
　　Mightiest of powers, to thee!

(*The* BIRDS *dance off, higher and higher, on the rocks as the
lights fade, until only Procne's silhouette is visible, and she,
too, disappears.*)

CURTAIN

FOCUS QUESTIONS

1. Three worlds converge in *The Birds:* human, divine, and bird (animal). What observations, both humorous and serious, does Aristophanes make about each of them?
2. Discuss the contemporary relevance of the play's issues to the society in which you live.
3. How does satire serve Aristophanes' comic intentions?
4. Trace Pithetaerus' rise from lower character type to demigod, showing how he overcomes obstacles through comic inventiveness.
5. Based on your reading of this play, develop a short essay in which you describe and evaluate the characteristics of Aristophanic comedy.
6. Show how the varieties of language (that is, rapid-fire dialogue, monologues, and choral song) enhance both spectacle and meaning in the play.
7. Discuss Aristophanes' use of *parabasis* as an effective theatrical component.

OTHER ACTIVITIES

1. Using reviews, photographs, and other available production documents, assess a twentieth-century production of the play.
2. In contrast with Eldon Elder's design concepts for the 1966 Ypsilanti production, list your own alternatives to visualizing the play.
3. Using a similar theme, develop a prologue that incorporates a fantastic premise or Happy Idea.

BIBLIOGRAPHY

Deardon, C. W. *The Stage of Aristophanes.* London: Athlone Press, 1976.
Dover, K. J. *Aristophanic Comedy.* London: Batsford, 1972.
Ehrenberg, Victor. *The People of Aristophanes.* 2d ed. Oxford: Blackwell, 1943.
Harriott, Rosemary M. *Aristophanes: Poet and Dramatist.* London: Croom Helm, 1986.
Henderson, Jeffrey. *The Maculate Muse.* New Haven, CT: Yale University Press, 1975.
Howarth, W. D., ed. *Comic Drama: The European Heritage.* London: Methuen, 1956.
Lord, Louis E. *Aristophanes: His Plays and His Influence.* London: Harrap, 1925.
McLeish, K. L. *The Theatre of Aristophanes.* London: Thames and Hudson, 1980.
Murray, Gilbert. *Aristophanes.* Oxford: Clarendon Press, 1933.

Norwood, Gilbert. *Greek Comedy*. London: Methuen, 1931.

Sanbach, F. H. *The Comic Theatre of Greece and Rome*. London: Chatto and Windus, 1977.

Sifakis, G. M. *Parabasis and Animal Choruses*. London: Athlone Press, 1971.

Solomos, A. *The Living Aristophanes*. Ann Arbor: University of Michigan Press, 1974.

Walton, J. Michael. *Living Greek Theatre: A Handbook of Classical Performance and Modern Production*. Westport, CT: Greenwood Press, 1987.

Whitman, Cedric Hubbell. *Aristophanes and the Comic Hero*. Cambridge, MA: Harvard University Press, 1964.

RECOMMENDED VIDEOTAPES AND RECORDINGS

Aristophanes' Birds. Two sound cassettes. 141 min. 1983. J. Norton Publishers.

The Birds (Excerpts). VHS. 40 min. 1991. Distributed by Insight Media, New York City.

A Dramatization of Birds *by Aristophanes*. Sound cassette. 59 min. Living Literature.

THE ROPE
Plautus (254–184 B.C.)

We are all indebted to Titus Maccius Plautus, high priest of low comedy, inventor of the genre, builder of the machine on which all theatre humor has run for over two millennia.

—Larry Gelbart

Approaching the New Roman Comedy

When the aftermath of the Peloponnesian War resulted in a victory for Sparta by 404 B.C., Athenian pride was destroyed forever and, as far as comedy was concerned, Aristophanes' trusty targets were no longer suitable for ridicule. Replacing something old with something new, the incumbent order sought to revise its stage comedy as well. But the sound of laughter, recognizable in any corner of the human condition, proved irrepressible. Furthermore, Aristophanes was still active during this time of artistic upheaval, and his last few plays contributed to the renovated comic format, despite the fact that younger practitioners of comedy found little use for the conventions of Old Comedy: the choral songs, the essential *parabasis,* and the formulaic demonstration of a thesis. (See Preface to Aristophanes, p. 35.) They would conveniently replace them with extended dialogue between comic characters, prompting a corrosion of the chorus-as-character. To accommodate these structural adjustments, they also returned to parodying the tragic themes of popular gods and heroes, the same stories and characters that flourished on the stage prior to the audacious, timelier targets introduced by Aristophanes.

Salvaging certain features and discarding others from the transitional **Middle Comedy,** a new breed of comic writers, the most successful of whom were Menander, Diphilus, and Philemon, gradually refashioned a comic spirit that was gentler and more cautious. Their style was further tempered by a realism innovated by Euripides, whose influence these younger playwrights proudly acknowledged. Therefore the masks of Aristophanic and Middle Comedy were carefully transformed into **New Comedy** during the fourth and early third centuries B.C.

Menander (c. 342–291 B.C.), whose comedies *The Arbitration, She Who Was Shorn* and *The Woman of Samos* were excavated in fragments in Egypt in 1905, had a pivotal role in the development of Western drama. When the complete text of his *Dyskolos* (*The Grouch*) was discovered a half-century later and published in its original Greek text by 1959, playgoers had their first glimpse of a complete New Comedy. He made sure that the premise of mistaken or concealed identities—certainly New Comedy's most inspired thematic ingredient—did not sour the comic outcome.

There were several popular scenarios, including the sudden appearance of a child fatefully separated from his or her family at birth. Now grown to adulthood and identified solely by a birth ring or domestic trinket, the child enjoyed the restoration of rank and fortune as soon as certain details of plot were sorted out. Another scenario included the reunion of two lovers, one of whom was abducted into slavery for lascivious purposes; in short, a timely revelation rescued the maiden in distress from her procurer, returned her to protective arms, and transformed a potentially tragic outcome into a happy one. Perhaps we are surprised to discover that these familiar reversals of fortune, replete with familiar imagery that has nurtured our romantic imagination and enriched our popular Western culture, all find their antecedents in New Comedy. A far cry from Aristophanes, both in dramatic form and content, they are the same thematic ingredients that influenced two prominent Roman playwrights: Plautus (c. 254–184 B.C.) and Terence (190–159 B.C.).

In the Roman Empire (founded around 753 B.C.), theatrical performances were presented by the Etruscans in 364 B.C. in an effort to appease the gods. Their contribution was one of three distinct sources of Roman theatre and incorporated a range of styles, including song and dance, juggling, gladiatorial feats, and improvised clowning in which the performers exchanged abusive and obscene insults. The second important influence came from Atella in southern Italy, whose farces were imported to Rome early in the third century B.C. These were short, improvised depictions of domestic life filled with stock characters. The third was the drama of the Greeks, which was imported to Rome by 240 B.C. The Greeks, who, under the leadership of Alexander the Great, had already asserted their powerful influence in such places as the Aegean Isles, Asia Minor, Phoenicia, Palestine, and North Africa, exacted their influence throughout the lower part of Italy. From Naples through Sicily, conquerors built permanent theatre sites along the Mediterranean coast and displaced the native entertainments with their own dramatic repertoire.

The profound impact of these foolproof Greek tragedies and comedies, all of which flourished through translation, imitation, and adaptation, took a new direction when Rome seized power. Determined to dominate the political expansiveness that splintered the Greek states by the middle of the second century B.C., Rome was now strategically fortified to absorb the entrenched Hellenistic culture of which the drama played a vital role. The birth of a new empire marked a turning point for Western drama and the demise of the Greek golden age.

An imitator of Menander, Titus Maccius Plautus won acclaim for his comedies, all composed in Latin between 205 and 184 B.C., twenty of which are the earliest to survive. In addition to the six extant plays attributed to Terence, these constitute the legacy of the Roman drama before the birth of Christ.

As for the performance of Roman tragedy, while it never rivaled its Greek counterpart, the form was nevertheless popular with Roman audiences. Unfortunately its extant fragments have given us little to build on, despite the names of three tragedians—Quintus Ennius, Marcus Pacuvius, and Lucius Accius—who wrote between 200 and 75 B.C. With the birth of Christianity and the appearance of Seneca (3 B.C.–A.D. 65), however, Roman tragedy acquired a craftsman whose turgid verse dramas would influence the English Renaissance stage nearly fifteen hundred years later. While we are unable to determine exactly how Seneca's plays were presented in his own time, if indeed they actually were, we know that the jaded tastes of an already declining Roman empire were easily satisfied by such thrill-seeking entertainments as chariot racing, gladiatorial contests, and *naumachiae* or staged sea battles.

In assessing the historical events that preceded Plautus' timely Umbrian birth, including his career as actor/playwright which paralleled Rome's political ascension, it is no surprise that his theatrical models were from New Comedy. He freely adapted their work through a practice known as **contaminatio,** that is, by combining the different elements of two or more Greek plays into his own literary creation—a technique that would also be imitated by many reputable playwrights after him. But while the atmosphere of his plays, the settings and names of characters—including popular stock characters—remained Greek, the spirit that infused them was always Roman.

Plautus' encounter with New Comedy contributed to his greatest achievement: the transformation of these earlier models into a dramatic literature of the highest order, the style of which skirted the rigid formalities of the Latin language, incorporated the best elements of native Atellanae, and captured the colorful speech patterns of his own characters. This Greek-to-Roman acculturation was further strengthened by the disparate contexts in which classical Western drama was produced. For the early Athenian dramatists, the sole aim was religious, to pay homage to Dionysus; for the later Greek and Roman dramatists, the aim was twofold: to entertain audiences and to make money.

MAJOR WORKS

Plautus' zesty language, sharply drawn characters, clever farce, and attractive themes embellish the best of his work. Listed in uncertain chronological order, they include *Amphitruo* (*Amphitryon*); *Aulularia* (*The Crock of Gold*); *Captivi* (*Prisoners of War*); *Menaechmi* (*The Menaechmus Twins*); *Mostellaria* (*The Haunted House*); *Miles Gloriosus* (*The Braggart Soldier*); *Pseudolus* (*The Trickster*); and *Rudens* (*The Rope*), the last of which has been hailed as his masterpiece. Serving as one of the finest examples of the popular "recognition" play, *The Rope* differs markedly from Plautus' other comedies in its balance of clever themes, sentimental and romantic situations, and characters who are paired off to perfection.

THE ACTION

The constellation Arcturus steps forward to announce how the nefarious deeds of certain characters, not yet introduced, have prompted his conjuring forth a storm to induce a shipwreck. The kidnapped heroine, aptly named Palaestra (the struggler), is washed ashore to the very spot where her father Daemones (the guardian spirit) and mother now dwell in exile. All alone, she laments her fate but is happily reunited with her companion Ampelisca (tender grape). In separate scenes, Palaestra's lover Plesidippus pines for her safe return, while the procurer who kidnapped her, Labrax (the shark), searches for her in the wreckage, still hoping to sell her for the best price he can get.

Meanwhile, Daemones' cunning servant Gripus (the fisherman) retrieves from the sea a satchel that is attached to a rope. Neither father nor daughter can recognize each other without the birth tokens contained in a box within the satchel. Dramatic irony and comic mayhem precipitate a happy ending where both servant and procurer are invited to dine at Daemones' table.

STRUCTURE AND LANGUAGE

Plautus' ironic comedy gently coaxes the Roman audience to put aside all remnant Greek influences and to laugh at its own foibles instead. His colorful characters seem truly ingenuous in speaking their minds to the audience as well as to each other, while inhabiting the stage actions with a genuine down-to-earth gusto and assertiveness. Imitating the style of the New Comedy, Plautus' dialogue fortifies their comic entanglements with metrical cadences, either declaimed or chanted to musical accompaniment, that are further offset by bouncy wordplay, rapid-fire exchanges, poetic alliteration, and suggestive jokes. Except for the brief opening to act 2, the use of the chorus is almost entirely omitted, partly because it was too costly a convention for the impoverished acting troupes to maintain.

Perhaps the most unique aspect of *The Rope* is the symbolic correlation between its physical landscape, "a barren shore near Cyrene," and its emotional one. The indelible yet unseen sea affects the fate of each character and proves regenerative at every turn, becoming an all-pervasive and omniscient force ultimately responsible for reuniting a lost child with her exiled father. The silent intercession of the goddess Venus, whose origins also stem from watery depths and whose shrine—always visible on stage—is an affirmation of rebirth and salvation, foreshadows this joyful outcome and reminds us that "the benevolent influence of the gods is manifested only indirectly through symbolic illuminations of the interaction of nature and man."[1] Thus Plautus' conventional display of comic characters and incidents preserves a serious thematic overtone for some length before revealing its happier purpose in the final act. In fact, his smoothly interwoven themes of nature, familial reconciliation, romantic love, and virtue rewarded—all guided by the catalytic storm—will imbue Shakespeare's *Twelfth Night* (1600), *Pericles* (1608), and *The Tempest* (1611).

Confronting both the comic and tragic implications of having survived "a hurricane right out of a play by Euripides," characters react to the catastrophe from entirely different perspectives: Daemones' servant, Sceparnio, prompts our human interest early by noticing two girls "in a boat, all by themselves. Look at the way the poor things are being tossed about!" Struggling to the unknown shore with a frightened companion behind her, Palaestra courageously assures Ampelisca, "We just have to take things as they come." Meanwhile they little suspect that their unscrupulous procurer Labrax has been washed ashore further down the beach, where he muses wisely, "If anyone wants to become a beggar, just let him trust himself, body and soul, to Father Neptune." Somewhat ironically, the chorus of ragged fishermen has regretfully done so: "What *our* financial status is,/ You see by this here get-up./ These hooks and rods we have are our/ Sole economic set-up." Thus characters are brought sharply into focus before entering the action.

In addition to Plautus' unique mastery of characterization, a fine wisdom underscores much of the comedy. This is demonstrated in act 4, where Gripus' refusal to return the satchel he has retrieved from the sea to its rightful owner fuels his confrontation with Trachalio: "But *I* know how it was found and *I* know who found it and *I* know who owns it now." Both characters match wits—the rope between them—in a tug of war.

When Palaestra and Daemones are reunited much later in that act, however, Daemones admonishes the angry fisherman for almost "getting trapped" by his own greed:

> I hide something brought to me that I know isn't mine? None of that for your old master Daemones, no, sir! The one thing any man of intelligence is always on guard against is consciously taking part in wrongdoing.

Far from unintelligent, the clever Gripus has learned a very different set of values from his impoverished life at sea and is much too cynical to accept his master's world view. As slave to Daemones, he has little choice but to step out of character and comment, albeit ironically, on the incident:

> I've often seen actors in a play deliver themselves of gems of wisdom of this sort— and seen them get a round of applause for having mouthed for the audience all these rules of good behavior. Then, when the audience left and everybody was back in his own home, there wasn't a one who behaved the way he had been told to.

Whether or not Plautus chooses to side with the disillusioned Gripus, his public moralizing through the character of Daemones—that honesty is always the best policy—underscores this important confrontation. Perhaps the playwright's personal reaction may be intuited from the wonderful exit line he gives to Gripus, a line that never quite sabotages the good deed that has resulted in a happy ending: "I hope to god whatever's in that satchel—gold or silver or what not—turns to ashes!"

In spite of the comedy's ominous indicators of a supernatural, watery landscape, Plautus insists that his characters negotiate their destinies on solid ground. This may be why the harmonious settlements are unexpectedly demonstrated by the dinner invitation Daemones extends to the villainous Labrax and the greedy Gripus: to confirm the powerful healing effects of hearth and home. For it is his gesture that matters above everything else, and the audience would also be invited, Daemones tells us, except ''there's nothing decent to eat in the house anyway.'' The joke is on all of us, as Daemones begs our applause (the **plaudite**) and bids us farewell.

About the Translation

Like its Greek counterpart, the Roman drama was written in verse. In the present translation, Lionel Casson mostly elects prose ''to retain the spirit, if not the style, of the original'' to create an aural effect that sounds ''more free than many a translation in verse.''[2] The lively results resound with the rhythms of contemporary speech and all unfamiliar classical references are replaced with their modern equivalent. Best of all, some of Plautus' poetic style is smoothly rendered in Casson's combined use of rhymed and unrhymed verse, highlighting the play's comic and serious overtones respectively.

When Labrax pursues Palaestra and Ampelisca in act 3, the rhythmic but unrhymed lines of Palaestra's song capture the desperation of both women:

> The dread móment's at hánd; now we're útterly hélpless.
> There's just nó one to cóme to our aíd or defénse,
> No release from our danger, no way to find safety.
> And we're both so afraid we can't think where to run.

In contrast, Gripus' typically sour disposition is transformed into a joyful one the moment he retrieves the satchel from the sea. His mood in act 4 is conveyed in highly rhythmic lines ending in rhymed couplets:

> And I'll dó what the míllionaires *dó,*
> Take a róund-the-world crúise, maybe *twó.*
> When I get enough fame and *renown,*
> I'll erect a big fortified *town,*
> A metropolis named Gripopolis,
> A memorial to Gripus, the hero *renowned,*
> The capital of a nation, one that I'll *found!*

Furthermore, Casson has inserted stage directions to facilitate the needs of the text in performance. Act divisions introduced by Plautus' scrupulous editors have been retained despite the fact that the playwright wrote his comedies without breaks.

The Rope-in-Performance

The legacy of Roman comedy remains fairly unchallenged on both quantitative and qualitative grounds. Its innate tendency toward topicality and its unabashed emphasis of form over content have given it remarkable resilience. While it is impossible, if not unfair, to evaluate Roman comedy according to popular audience taste, a short historical overview can enlighten us as to why it has survived.

Like the Greeks whose communities sponsored two dramatic festivals to honor Dionysus, the Romans sponsored spectacles and variety entertainment (**ludi**) on countless holidays that paid tribute to the gods. But while the Greeks constructed permanent civic

Ground plan of a typical
Roman theatre.

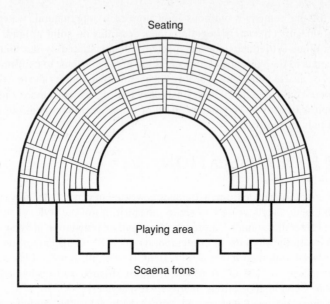

Seating

Playing area

Scaena frons

theatres for their dramas, the Romans built *colisea* only for their *ludi*. Therefore, professional acting troupes performed dramas for a paying audience under makeshift physical conditions for at least three centuries before Pompey built a permanent theatre in Rome in 55 B.C.

Temporary structures, which were erected and dismantled to accommodate the varieties of theatrical performance throughout Italy, demonstrated the flexible uses of the physical stage. These were open-air, curtainless theatres, often supplemented by the already existing Greek theatres that were permanently situated in the hills and would later be remodeled to suit Roman tastes. Hence the original circular performance space, so cherished by the Greeks, would be reduced to a semicircle, which allowed a coterie of Roman citizens to be seated in the *orchestra,* a term still used to designate the frontal seating area in the contemporary theatre. Furthermore, the elimination of the chorus allowed the individual actors to perform on an elevated stage set apart from the spectators.

The single conventional facade or **scaena frons** in the Roman comedy was a painted construction of row houses whose doors opened onto a city street and provided innumerable opportunities to heighten the farce. While it is difficult to imagine how such a facade could serve the barren, storm-swept landscape so essential for *The Rope,* we may safely conclude that convention (in this case, an unrealistic stage set that the Roman audience agreed to tolerate) took precedence over realism. After all, the audience was quite willing to accept men portraying women who, like their Greek predecessors, also wore masks. Costumes probably varied with the type of play, although it is likely that actors performing in *The Rope* adapted some of the same costumes from New Comedy on which Plautus' play was based, in which case everyday Athenian dress was used.

In the dawn of the Renaissance, Plautus was rediscovered and became a literary model. Productions of his plays were given in the palaces of Cardinals, including the Vatican in 1502. Throughout the sixteenth century, Italian playwrights were greatly inspired by Plautine plots of deception and mistaken identity, which they quickly incorporated into their own domestic farces. One of these was Ludovico Dolce, whose adaptation of *The Rope* was called *Il Ruffiano* (1560). The influence soon spread to Spain, Germany, and Holland. In fact, the plays of Plautus and Terence were the only comedies allowed to be performed at the University of Salamanca in 1574.[3] In the seventeenth century, notably in France, the remarkable comic skills of the gifted Molière would remain indebted to the spirit and characters of Plautus and Terence. (See Preface to Molière, p. 352.)

In England, the pre-Shakespearean drama of the sixteenth century took important comic cues from Plautus, while the discovery of Senecan drama influenced the germinating tragic stage. Quick to take advantage of the best that was available to them, Shakespeare and his contemporaries benefited immeasurably from both Roman models. Plautus provided a particularly enduring influence: mischievous twins whose mistaken identities serve as the model for Shakespeare's *Comedy of Errors* (1589); the boastful soldier ("miles gloriosus") whose militaristic pretenses sharpen the portrait of Falstaff in Shakespeare's *Henry IV* (1597); and the parasites who populate Ben Jonson's *Volpone* (1605).

During the early seventeenth century, *The Rope* inspired Jacobean playwright Thomas Heywood to borrow its characters and plot, including several hundred original lines, to fashion his own play which he titled *The Captives* or *The Lost Recovered* (1624). Set in Marseilles, the shipwrecked Palaestea and her companion Scribonia are rescued by an English merchant named Ashburne. When a fisherman's rope hauls a casket from the sea, its contents identify the young woman as Ashburne's long lost daughter. The reunited parties depart for England to live happily ever after, a location Heywood purposely chose to please his London audience.

Plautus' characters and plots have inspired countless character types and storylines for our contemporary stage, screen, and television, even when their repercussions have not always resulted in laughter. Recall the haughty demeanor of a soldier/protagonist in a war drama or the lovesick suitor who is rejected at final curtain. Such familiar types have always shared the stage with grouchy fathers and conniving servants, courtesans, and tricksters, paying homage to the Roman playwright's enduring contribution to the world of drama.

On the lighter side, we need simply turn to one of the most treasured legacies of the twentieth-century theatre, the American musical comedy: Rodgers and Hart's *Boys from Syracuse* (1938); Cole Porter's *Out of This World* (1950); and Sondheim and Gelbart's *A Funny Thing Happened on the Way to the Forum* (1962) have adapted the same proud characters and shifty shenanigans from the original comedies of Plautus, using his technique of *contaminatio* that won the approval of Romans in search of a hearty belly laugh.

REFLECTIONS ON THE ROPE

Larry Gelbart has written for radio, television, film, and the stage. He co-authored with Burt Shevelove the book for the Tony Award-winning musical comedy, A Funny Thing Happened on the Way to the Forum.

The initial idea to do [*Funny Thing*] was the late Burt Shevelove's. Burt had done an embryonic version of a Roman comedy in his university days and had long felt that a professional, full-blown Broadway production would have every chance of success.

Although Burt and I had worked together on many television shows during the 1950s, we had never functioned before as a writing team. Burt produced and directed several comedy/variety shows that I had written in that period; working in separate capacities, we learned that we laughed at the same things and, happily, always at the same time.

Our goal was to construct a musical comedy based on the style and spirit of the twenty-six surviving plays of Titus Maccius Plautus, the third-century Roman playwright, who invented all the devices of theatrical comedy, teaching amphitheater audiences up and down Caesar's Circuit to laugh for the first time at character and situation instead of that old staple they found so amusing, bloodshed.

Continued

Certainly, there was comedy in everyday life before Plautus set quill to parchment, but it was he who created comic conventions and made use of humorous wordplay within the discipline of well-made plays.

With Stephen Sondheim as the third member of the team (it was to be the first Broadway show for which he created words and music; before *Forum*, Steve had *merely* supplied the lyrics for *West Side Story* and *Gypsy*), we began the task of reading and dissecting the writings of and about Plautus, extracting from his works a character here, a relationship there, and then went about creating a considerable amount of new material, both dramatic and musical, as connective tissue to bond our work to his.

What a treat he was to research! How incredibly Plautus' aged, ageless writings based on man's gift for silliness, for pomposity and hypocrisy, have survived; how well it all stood up, the comedy that would serve as fodder not only for the theater, but for future stand-up comedians as well. Digging about as archaeologists might have, what unbelievable treasure we found in his plays, a catacomb filled with nothing but funnybones. It was as though Titus (I feel he would forgive the name-dropping) had written some great and generous last will and testament, a comic estate, and that Burt, Steve, and I had been appointed his heirs.

There they were, in the pages of Plautus, appearing for our pleasure for the first time anywhere: the brash Prologus, working very much in the manner of a modern-day master of ceremonies, addressing his remarks directly to the audience, hitting them with one-liners, warning them to sit up and pay attention and not to go to sleep during the play that was to follow. There were the sly servants, those wily slaves, scheming and plotting and outwitting everyone in sight, constantly getting the upper hand on the upper class, which was largely composed of senile skirt-chasers and henpecked husbands, very often one and the same; domineering matrons, Gorgon-like women, past their prime in every aspect of life but possessiveness; lovesick young men, so much in love they were sickening; and, of course, comely courtesans with hair and hearts of gold that you couldn't bring home without fear of possibly offending your mother—and the certainty of arousing your father; page after page of disguise and mistaken identity, scene after scene of double takes and double meanings.

We were, of course, not Plautus' only benefactors. From the sublime Shakespeare to the somewhat less-so sitcoms, those writers who, through the ages, have presented audiences with surrogate fools acting out of their own foibles (each member of the crowd, secure in the belief that he or she is above ridicule, that it is the person in the *next* seat who is being so portrayed), we are all indebted to Titus Maccius Plautus, high priest of low comedy, inventor of the genre, builder of the machine on which all theater humor has run for over two millennia.

I believe it is safe to say that there is not a joke form, comic character, or farcical situation that exists today that does not find its origin in Plautus' work. *Forum* contains at least one taste of his original flavor. When Miles Gloriosus, the impossibly pompous, braggart warrior, gets a huge laugh (and he always does) by stating "I am a parade!" the audience is responding to a line that is over two thousand years old.

Our goal was not to modernize the master. That is an ongoing process we preferred to leave to others. What we hoped to prove was that Plautus' characters (always one-dimensional) and his style of plotting (which could be as complicated as a Rubik's cube) were timeless. If the three of us occasionally resembled croquet wickets during our labors, it's because we spent so much time bending over backward to avoid using anachronisms (one such line which we rejected, and which we related to the writers of the *Forum* screenplay, found its way into a scene in the movie in which Pseudolus, the leading character, wanting to know the quality of the wine he's being served, asks, "Was 1 a good year?").

We were after more than purity, however. We were not simply out to prove some esoteric point that would have had an appreciative audience of three. We wanted a commercial as well as an artistic success. We were confident we could have both. Cocky would be more accurate. More than simply confidence is needed to get a musical comedy on the boards. Vanity all on its own is not that much help either.

We knew that we were grounding our show in an element that had been long missing from the theater scene. Over the years, Broadway, in its development of the musical comedy had improved the quality of the former at the expense of a good deal of the latter. Musicals had come to be populated by performers who could sell a melody and a set of lyrics but who couldn't deliver a punchline in a handbasket. It was a talent they had no need for, since punchlines had all but disappeared. The Rodgerses and Harts and Hammersteins, the Lerners and Loewes, brilliant men of music and artists of great refinement, had created a vulgarity vacuum, a space we were happy, even anxious to fill.

Our Roman comedy opened in New York on May 8, 1962, complete with leggy showgirls being chased from house to house by cunning slaves who, in drag a few scenes later, found *themselves* being chased by their own lecherous masters, unsuspecting dupes high on love potions prepared by these very same slaves, using recipes that called for such exotic ingredients as mare's sweat.

The show that *Time* magazine called "good clean, dirty fun" has been running somewhere everywhere in the world for the last twenty-seven years . . . Anyone for a comedy tonight?

Larry Gelbart
17 September 1990

From Larry Gelbart's Introduction to A FUNNY THING HAPPENED ON THE WAY TO THE FORUM *by Burt Shevelove, Larry Gelbart and Stephen Sondheim. Copyright © 1991 by Applause Theatre Book Publishers. Reprinted by permission of Applause Theatre Books, 211 West 71st Street, New York, NY 10023.*

Notes

1. *Eleanor Winsor Leach, "Plautus' 'Rudens': Venus Born from a Shell."* TEXAS STUDIES IN LITERATURE AND LANGUAGE *xv.5 (Special Classics Issue, 1974): 916.*
2. *Lionel Casson, ed. and trans.,* PLAUTUS: THE MENAECHMUS TWINS & TWO OTHER PLAYS *(New York: W. W. Norton & Co., 1963), vi.*
3. *Margrete Bieber,* THE HISTORY OF THE GREEK AND ROMAN THEATRE *(Princeton, NJ: Princeton University Press, 1961), 254.*

THE ROPE
Plautus
Translated by Lionel Casson

CHARACTERS

Sceparnio, *Daemones' servant (slave)*

Plesidippus, *a wealthy young Athenian residing in Cyrene*

Daemones, *an elderly Athenian living in straitened circumstances near Cyrene*

Palaestra, *a beautiful young courtesan, the property of Labrax*

Ampelisca, *an attractive young courtesan, also the property of Labrax*

Ptolemocratia, *priestess of the shrine of Venus*

Fishermen

Trachalio, *Plesidippus' valet (slave)*

Labrax, *a slave dealer*

Charmides, *an elderly vagabond who has recently struck up an acquaintance with Labrax*

Roughneck (Turbalio) ⎱ *slaves of*
Cutthroat (Sparax) ⎰ *Daemones*

Gripus, *a fisherman, slave of Daemones*

[Daedalis, *wife of Daemones*]

SCENE

A barren shore near Cyrene. In the background are, stage right, Daemones' simple cottage, and, stage left, a shrine of Venus consisting chiefly of a modest temple with an altar in front. The exit near the temple (stage left) leads to Cyrene. That near the cottage (stage right) leads to the beach; sand and rocks and a patch of reeds are visible near it.

PROLOGUE

(The Prologue, dressed in a spangled costume and wearing a glittering star on his forehead, steps forward. He represents Arcturus, the star that, rising in September and setting in November, marks the period of the equinoctial storms.)

ARCTURUS. I am from the city of the celestials, fellow citizen of him who holds sway over all peoples, all seas, and all lands. My appearance is as you see: a bright star that glitters and gleams, that rises and sets in heaven and on earth, forever and ever, in its season. My name is **5** Arcturus.

At night I shine among the gods in the sky; by day I walk among men on earth. Other stars, too, come down here from heaven: great Jove, lord of gods and men, assigns us stations, one here and another there, **10** all over the world. We find out for him what men are

doing, how they are behaving, particularly which are reverent and honest so that he can show them his favor. If we find people trying to win cases by bearing false witness, or forswearing themselves to deny a **15** debt, we note their names and report them to Jove. From day to day he knows precisely who here on earth is out to do wrong. When rascals go into a trial ready to perjure themselves and trick a judge into awarding them the verdict, *he* reopens the case, reviews it, and passes a **20** sentence so stiff it far outweighs whatever they may have won.

In another set of records he keeps a list of the good. And if the wicked have the idea that they can get on it by winning him over with gifts and offerings, they're **25** wasting their time and money. Why? Because he has no mercy for men who are two-faced. The appeal of the honest man finds favor far more easily than that of the wicked despite all their gifts. And so I advise those of you who are good, who live your lives in reverence and **30** honesty, to go on in this way so that you may reap your reward in time to come.

But now I want to tell you about the play; after all, that's what I'm here for.

(Gesturing toward the scene behind him.) To **35** begin with, this city is Cyrene; that's the way Diphilus[1]

[1]See page 71.

wanted it. This cottage on the seashore and the farm alongside it belong to Daemones. He's an old man who came here as an exile from Athens. He's not a bad man; he didn't leave his homeland because of any wrong **40** he had done. It's simply that, in helping others, he got himself involved and, through his generosity, dissipated a hard-earned fortune. He once had a daughter, and he lost her, too, when she was a little child: she was kidnaped. The kidnaper sold her to a dealer in cour- **45** tesans, one of the worst men alive.

Now the pimp who bought her brought the girl here to Cyrene. A certain young fellow, an Athenian—which makes him the girl's fellow citizen—happened to see her one day as she was coming home from her music **50** lesson. He fell in love with her, went straight to the pimp, and arranged to buy her for seventy-five hundred dollars. He paid a deposit and had a contract drawn up. But the pimp, true to type, didn't care the least bit either about keeping his word or about the contract he had **55** signed. He happened to have staying with him an old fellow from Agrigentum in Sicily, someone just like himself, a scoundrel who'd sell his own mother. This fellow began to rave about how beautiful the girl was, as well as all the others the pimp owned. And he began to **60** talk the pimp into going to Sicily with him: he kept telling him there were lots of fast livers in Sicily, that courtesans made big money there, and that he could become a rich man there. He convinced him. And so the pimp secretly chartered a vessel and, one night, moved every- **65** thing out of his house and put it on board. He told the boy who had bought the girl that he was going to the shrine of Venus to make a sacrifice and pay off an obligation— (*pointing*) this is the shrine right here—and even invited the young fellow to share the remains of the animal **70** and have lunch with him there. Then he went straight to the ship and sailed off with his girls. Word reached the boy of what had happened, that the pimp had left town, but by the time the young fellow made it down to the waterfront the ship was already far out at sea. **75**

When I saw that the pimp was carrying the girl off, I stepped in to help her and hurt him. I raised a storm and stirred up the waves. You all know that I, Arcturus, am the fiercest star of all; things get stormy when I rise and worse when I set. Right now both the pimp and his **80** cohort are castaways, sitting on a rock; their ship's been shattered. The girl and one other from the troupe got frightened and jumped out of the vessel into the ship's boat; at this moment the waves are carrying them to shore near where old Daemones lives in exile. As a **85** matter of fact, the storm ripped off his roof with all its tiles. (*As the door of the cottage opens and a figure comes out.*) That's his servant there, coming out. In a minute you'll see the young fellow who arranged to buy the girl from the pimp. Good-by and good luck! **90**

ACT ONE

(*Daemones' servant,* SCEPARNIO, *"the wood chopper," comes out of the cottage carrying a spade.* SCEPARNIO, *a young fellow in his twenties, is the sort whose face feels more comfortable wearing a scowl than a smile, and his disposition has not been improved by years of work for a penniless master. His expression is even more sour than usual as he looks over the damage done to the cottage during the night.*)

SCEPARNIO (*to the audience*). God in heaven, what a storm we had here last night! The wind took the roof right off the cottage. Wind? That was no wind; that was a hurricane right out of a play by Euripides! Look how it ripped all the tiles off the roof! It's made the cottage a lot **5** brighter—put in some new skylights for us.

(*Unnoticed by* SCEPARNIO, PLESIDIPPUS *enters, stage left, followed by three friends; all are wearing coats and carrying swords.* PLESIDIPPUS *is a good-looking young fellow, well and expensively dressed. His face at the moment shows signs of worry and strain. He and his friends are deep in conversation as they come on stage.*)

PLESIDIPPUS (*apologetically*). And so I rushed you away from your own affairs and all for nothing; I wasn't able to get my hands on that pimp down at the dock. But I didn't want to let up for one minute, I didn't want **10** to give up hope; that's why I've kept you with me all this time. I've come out here to take a look around this shrine of Venus; he told me he was going to make a sacrifice here.

SCEPARNIO (*to himself, eying the spade distastefully*). If I've got any brains, I'd better start getting some **15** of this blasted clay ready.

PLESIDIPPUS (*overhearing, to his friends*). Wait—I hear someone talking.

(*The door of the cottage opens and* DAEMONES *comes out.* DAEMONES *is middle-aged. Though he is dressed in worn work clothes, there is something about his manner and carriage that indicates he was not born a peasant.*)

DAEMONES (*calling*). Hey, Sceparnio!
SCEPARNIO (*as he turns around*). Who wants me? **20**
DAEMONES.   The man who paid good money for you.
SCEPARNIO (*sourly*). Why don't you come right out with it and call me your slave?
DAEMONES.   We're going to need lots of clay, so there's lots of digging for you to do. It looks as if we'll **25** have to reroof the whole cottage. Daylight's coming through everywhere; there are more holes up there than in a sieve.
PLESIDIPPUS (*to* DAEMONES). Good morning, Dad. (*Noticing* SCEPARNIO.) Good morning to you both. **30**
DAEMONES.   Good morning.

SCEPARNIO.   What do you mean by calling him "Dad"? You his—(*Eying his rather dandified dress distastefully.*) What are you anyway, male or female?

PLESIDIPPUS (*astonished*). I? I'm a man.   35

SCEPARNIO.   Well, my man, go find your father farther on.

DAEMONES (*sorrowfully*). I once did have a little daughter, but I lost her. She was the only child I had; I never had a son.

PLESIDIPPUS (*politely*). God will give you one.   40

SCEPARNIO (*snarling*). And he'll give you, whoever you are, what you won't want. Bothering busy people with your blabbering!

PLESIDIPPUS (*pointedly ignoring him, to* DAEMONES; *gesturing toward the cottage*). Do you live here?

SCEPARNIO.   What do you want to know for? What   45
are you doing, casing the place? Looking for someone to rob?

PLESIDIPPUS (*turning on him*). You must be one important and trusted slave to be able to answer for your master when he's present—and insult a gentleman.   50

SCEPARNIO.   And you must be one nervy boor to be able to come up to the house of a total stranger who doesn't owe you the time of day and make a nuisance of yourself.

DAEMONES.   Keep quiet, Sceparnio. (*To* PLESIDIPPUS.) What would you like, my boy?   55

PLESIDIPPUS (*testily*). I'd like to see that slave of yours get what's coming to him for taking it on himself to do the talking when his master's around. (*Politely.*) If you don't mind, there are a few questions I'd like to ask you.

DAEMONES.   Well, I'm busy right now, but I'll be   60
glad to help even so.

SCEPARNIO (*to* DAEMONES, *quickly*). Why don't you go down to the swamp and cut some canes for the roof while the weather's still clear?

DAEMONES (*curtly*). Quiet! (*To* PLESIDIPPUS.) Now,   65
what can I do for you?

PLESIDIPPUS (*eagerly*). Tell me, have you seen a fellow around here with curly gray hair? A sneaking, wheedling, lying—

DAEMONES (*interrupting, grimly*). Lots of them. It's   70
because of men like that that I live the way I do.

PLESIDIPPUS.   I mean right here, at the shrine. Fellow with two girls with him, coming to make a sacrifice? Yesterday or maybe this morning?

DAEMONES (*shaking his head*). No, my boy, I haven't   75
seen anyone come here to make a sacrifice for a good many days now. And when they do, I see them all right—they always drop in to get water or fire or borrow dishes or a knife or a spit or a cooking pot or something. You'd think I kept a kitchen and a well for Venus and not   80
myself. But they've left me alone for quite a while now.

PLESIDIPPUS (*in anguish*). You know what you've just done? Pronounced my death sentence!

DAEMONES.   Believe me, if I had my way, you'd be alive and healthy.   85

SCEPARNIO (*to* PLESIDIPPUS). Listen you, if you're hanging around this shrine to beg some scraps to fill your belly, you'll do a lot better having lunch at home.

DAEMONES (*to* PLESIDIPPUS). What happened? Someone invite you to lunch and not show up?   90

PLESIDIPPUS.   Exactly.

SCEPARNIO.   It's all right; *we* don't mind if you go home from here with your belly empty. Why don't you try Ceres' shrine instead? She handles the commissary; Venus only deals with love.   95

PLESIDIPPUS (*half to himself, bitterly*). The way that man put one over on me is a crying shame!

DAEMONES (*happening to look off, stage right*). Good god! Sceparnio, what are those men doing there in the surf?

SCEPARNIO.   If you ask me, they're going to a   100
fancy breakfast.

DAEMONES.   Why?

SCEPARNIO.   Because they took a bath last night.

DAEMONES (*gazing intently*). They've been wrecked at sea!

SCEPARNIO.   Sure. Take a look at the roof of our   105
cottage—we've been wrecked on land.

DAEMONES.   Poor fellows! Tossed overboard and having to swim for it.

PLESIDIPPUS (*trying to follow the direction of his gaze*). Where do you see these men, anyway?

DAEMONES (*pointing*). There, toward the right.   110
See? Near the beach.

PLESIDIPPUS.   I see them now. (*To his friends.*) Follow me. I only hope one of them is that blasted crook I'm after. (*To* DAEMONES *and* SCEPARNIO.) Well, take care of yourselves. (*They rush off, stage right.*)   115

SCEPARNIO (*calling after him*). We've got it in mind; we don't need any reminders from you. (*Watches them go off, then suddenly gives a start.*) Oh, my god in heaven, what's that I see?

DAEMONES.   What is it?   120

SCEPARNIO (*excitedly*). Two girls in a boat, all by themselves. Look at the way the poor things are being tossed about! (*Gazes intently in silence for a moment.*) Good, good! The waves just carried the boat away from the rocks and toward the shore; there isn't a helmsman   125
alive who could have done better. I don't think I've ever seen the surf this bad in my life! If they can only get clear of those breakers they'll be all right. Now's the moment they have to watch out for—oh, a wave just hit them and one fell overboard—wait, it's shallow there—she   130
can swim out easily. Good work! She's on her feet—she's coming this way—she's safe! (*Turning his head as if looking in a slightly different direction.*) The other's just jumped out of the boat to get on shore—oh, she lost her nerve, she's fallen in the water, she's on her   135
knees—no, she's safe! She's wading out—now she's on the beach—oh, oh, she turned to the right, she's going off in that direction. Damn! That poor girl's going to do a lot of hiking today!

DAEMONES.   What do you care?   **140**

SCEPARNIO (*still gazing intently*).   If she falls off that cliff
she's heading toward, she'll finish her hike in a hurry.

DAEMONES (*with some asperity*). If you were going to eat
at their expense tonight, Sceparnio, I think you should
worry about them. But if you're going to eat at   **145**
mine, you'd better pay attention to me.

SCEPARNIO.   True. You're absolutely right.

DAEMONES.   Follow me.

SCEPARNIO.   I'm right behind.

(*The two enter the cottage. A moment later* PALAESTRA, *"the
struggler," enters, stage right. Her face is haggard, her hair
dripping, her clothing drenched, and she barely has the
energy to drag herself along. Despite all this, we can see
that she is a remarkably fine-looking young girl. She makes
her way downstage and addresses the audience.*)

SONG

PALAESTRA.

The tales they tell of men's mishaps are mild,   **150**
Compared to actual experience.
It seems that Heaven's pleased to leave me thus—
A frightened castaway in lands unknown.
Oh, god, what can I say? That I was born
For this? Have I received this as reward   **155**
For all my honest and devoted prayer?
For me to undergo such hardships would
Be understandable if I had sinned
Against my parents or, perhaps, my god.
But when I've striven so to lead a life   **160**
That's free of all such blame, this treatment is,
O god, unfair, unjust, and undeserved,
What mark hereafter will you place on guilt
If such is the reward for innocence?
If I were conscious that I'd done you wrong,   **165**
Or that my parents had, then I would be
More reconciled to all this misery.

(*Pauses a moment, then resumes with bitterness and
passion.*)

But the crimes of my owner are the cause of my
grief.
It is *his* sins I suffer for—his, and not mine!
All he owned has gone down with his ship in the
sea;   **170**
I am all that is left of his worldly possessions.
And that girl who escaped in the boat at my side,
Even she has been lost; I'm alone, all alone.
If she'd only been saved! Then at least, with her
help,
This sad blow would have been a bit lighter to
bear.   **175**
For what hope have I now or whose help can I seek?

I'm deserted, alone in a desolate spot
Where there's nothing but rocks and the sound of the
sea,
Where there isn't a chance of my meeting a soul.
All I own in this world are the clothes on my
back,   **180**
And I've no idea where to find shelter or food.
Oh, it's hopeless! Why try to go on with my life?
I don't know where I am; it's a place strange to me.
How I wish that some person would come and point
out
Where a road or a path is! I'm so at a loss   **185**
I can't make up my mind to go right or go left;
It's all wild—not a sign of a field can I see.
All the horrors of cold and distraction and fear
Have me now in their grasp. Poor dear parents of
mine,
You can have no idea of your daughter's
despair!   **190**
I was born a free girl, but my birth was in vain—
At this moment how more of a slave could I be
Had I been one from birth? Oh, what good have I
been
All these years to the parents who cherished me so!

(*She staggers back to the rocks on stage right, sinks down
on them, and buries her face in her arms. The next moment
there enters, stage right, the companion she thought had
been lost.* AMPELISCA, *"tender grape," is a pretty girl with
an attractive, gay, vivacious manner. Right now she is as
bedraggled and forlorn as* PALAESTRA. *She makes her way
downstage and addresses the audience.*)

AMPELISCA.

Oh, what act could be better or more suitable
now   **195**
   Than to sever my soul from my body?
For my life is a torment and my breast is beset
   By an army of cares that destroy me!
In the face of all this I've no stomach for life,
   All the hope that once buoyed me is ended: **200**
For I've roamed everywhere, used my voice, eyes,
and ears,
   Crept through thorns, to track down my
companion;
She's been lost without trace, and I have no idea
   Where to turn, in what place to go searching.
And I haven't been able to meet anyone   **205**
   I could speak to and ask for directions.
Why, this region's a desert—in all of the world
   There's just no place so lonely and barren.
Yet as long as I live—granted she's alive too—
   I'll persist in the search till I find her.   **210**

PALAESTRA (*to herself, raising her head in alarm*).
   Whose voice is that I hear?

Was that a sound nearby?
Oh, god, I'm so afraid!
AMPELISCA (*to herself*).
Did I hear someone speak?
PALAESTRA (*in desperation*).
O god of hope! Please help!   215
AMPELISCA (*to herself, hopefully*).
Does this mean my release
From misery and fear?
PALAESTRA (*to herself, listening intently*).
I'm absolutely sure
I heard a woman's voice.
AMPELISCA (*to herself, listening intently*).
A woman's somewhere here—   220
I heard a woman's voice.
PALAESTRA (*dubiously*).
It can't be Ampelisca!
AMPELISCA (*calling uncertainly*).
Palaestra! Is that you?
PALAESTRA (*jumping to her feet, excitedly*).
Oh, I *must* make her hear me—I'll call out her name!
Ampelisca!   225
AMPELISCA (*calling*).
Who's there?
PALAESTRA.
It's Palaestra! It's me!
AMPELISCA (*looking about without seeing her*). I can't see
where you are.
PALAESTRA.
I'm in all sorts of trouble.   230
AMPELISCA.
I've a share in it too—one as big as your own.
But I'm dying to see you.
PALAESTRA.
And I to see you.
AMPELISCA.   Let's both talk and we'll follow the sounds.
Where are you?   235
PALAESTRA.   Over here. Come this way. Now walk up to
me. Come!
AMPELISCA (*walking slowly and hesitantly toward her*). This
is the best I can do.
PALAESTRA (*as she comes near*).
All right, give me your hand.   240
AMPELISCA (*doing so*). Here it is.
PALAESTRA (*grabbing it, pulling her near, and embracing
her*).
Ampelisca! You're safe! You're alive!
AMPELISCA (*tearfully*).
Yes—and now that I'm able to touch you, Palaestra,
You've restored the desire to go on with my life.
But I scarcely believe that you're here in my   245
arms!
Oh, my dear! Hold me tight! How you make me
forget
All my troubles!

PALAESTRA.
You've taken the words from my mouth!
But we ought to get out of this place.
AMPELISCA.
And go where?   250
PALAESTRA.   Shall we follow the beach?
AMPELISCA.
Go wherever you like;
I'll be right at your heels. But we're both sopping
wet—
Are we going to tramp up and down in these clothes?
PALAESTRA.   Yes, we must. We just have to take   255
things as they come.

(*Starts trudging off with* AMPELISCA *close behind and then
suddenly stops and points.*)

What is that, do you think?
AMPELISCA.
What is what?
PALAESTRA.
Don't you see?
There's a shrine over there.   260
AMPELISCA.
Over where?
PALAESTRA.
On the right.
AMPELISCA (*following the direction of her hand*). I can
make out a spot that would serve for a shrine.
PALAESTRA.
It's so pleasant a place that I'm sure we shall
find   265
There are people about. Now let's pray that the god
Dwelling here will have pity on us in our
plight,
And will come to the rescue and bring to a close
All these torments and terrors, these worries and
woes!

(*As the two girls slowly make their way toward the little
temple that marks the shrine, the door opens and* PTOLE-
MOCRATIA, *the priestess, comes out. She is an elderly woman
dressed in flowing white robes that, although spotlessly
clean, have obviously seen better days. Her face is kindly
and serene.*)

PTOLEMOCRATIA (*to herself*).
The sound of prayer just roused me now   270
To step outside. But who has come
To ask my mistress for a favor?
The goddess they implore is quick
To yield, and loath to hide, her grace,
A patroness both kind and good.   275
PALAESTRA (*timidly*). Good morning, Mother.
PTOLEMOCRATIA (*responding perfunctorily*).
Morning, girls.

(Suddenly aware of their appearance.)

> Tell me, where have you come from, my dears?
> You're in rags! And you're both sopping wet!

PALAESTRA.

> Well, right now from a place that's nearby.   **280**
> But our homeland is far, far away.

PTOLEMOCRATIA (*in mock-tragic style*).

> Then you came o'er the blue of the sea
> On a charger of canvas and wood?

PALAESTRA.

> Yes, we did.

PTOLEMOCRATIA (*reproachfully*).

> But you should have come here   **285**
> Dressed in white and prepared to give gifts.
> This is simply unheard of, my dears—
> Coming into this shrine in this way.

PALAESTRA (*taken aback*).

> From two castaways fresh from the sea?
> Tell me, where would you have us find gifts?   **290**

(The two girls drop to the ground and embrace PTOLEMO-CRATIA'S *knees.)*

> Here we are on our knees at your feet.
> We need help! We don't know where we are,
> We don't know what's in store for us next.
> Oh, I beg you, please pity our plight.
> Give us shelter and save us, please do!   **295**
> We are homeless and hopeless, and all
> That we own you can see on our backs!

PTOLEMOCRATIA (*gently*).

> Now I want you to give me your hands
> And get up from your knees, both of you.
> There's no woman alive with a heart   **300**
> That's as tender as mine, I am sure.
> But this shrine's very humble, my girls.
> I can barely keep living myself.
> And the offerings for Venus come from me.

AMPELISCA.

> Then is this one of Venus' shrines?   **305**

PTOLEMOCRATIA.

> Yes, it is, dear. And I am in charge.
> We'll make do. You will both be put up
> Just as well as my means will permit.
> Come with me.

PALAESTRA.

> We're most grateful to you   **310**
> For a welcome so friendly and kind.

PTOLEMOCRATIA.

> It's a duty I've always in mind.

*(*PTOLEMOCRATIA *and the girls enter the temple, and the stage is now empty.)*

ACT TWO

(A group of fishermen, dressed in rags and carrying tackle, enters, stage left.)

FISHERMEN (*to the audience*).

> The poor in every single way
> Find life a sad progression
> Of miseries, especially men
> Without a trade or profession.
> Their living's strictly limited   **5**
> To things in their possession.
> What *our* financial status is,
> You see by this here get-up.
> These hooks and rods we have are our
> Sole economic set-up.   **10**
> Each day we hike from town to beach
> To forage for our rations.
> (It's our substitute for wrestling, gym,
> And other sporting passions.)
> We grub for limpets, oysters, clams,   **15**
> Sea urchins, scallops, mussels.
> And then to try our luck with fish,
> With rod to rock each hustles.
> We fill our bellies from the sea;
> But when the sea's defaulted,   **20**
> We take a swim—if not the fish,
> The fishers get cleaned and salted—
> Then sneak back home and climb in bed
> Without a thing for dinner.
> With seas as rough as they are right now,   **25**
> Our hopes are getting thinner;
> Unless we find a clam or two,
> We've had today's collation.
> To get some help, let's proffer to
> Kind Venus veneration.   **30**

*(*TRACHALIO, *"bull-necked," Plesidippus' servant, enters, stage left. He's a burly young fellow, honest and good-natured at heart, and gay in temperament. He rather fancies himself as a man of importance, and with—or without—provocation often begins orating instead of talking.)*

TRACHALIO (*to himself, worriedly*). And I watched so carefully all the way so's not to miss that master of mine on the road! When he left the house he said he was going to go to the waterfront, and gave me orders to meet him here at the shrine of Venus. (*Catching sight of the fish-*   **35** *ermen.*) Now, that's convenient: there are some fellows over there I can ask. (*Calling.*) Hail, heroes of the hook and half shell, despoilers of the deeps, members of the Honorable Order of the Empty Belly, how're you doing? How're you dying?   **40**

FISHERMAN.   The way fishermen always do—of optimism followed by starvation.

TRACHALIO.   Did you happen to see a young fellow come along while you've been standing here? Husky, red-faced fellow looking as if he meant business? He had   45 three others with him; they were all wearing cloaks and daggers.

FISHERMAN.   Nobody answering to that description's come along, so far as we know.

TRACHALIO.   How about an old guy, pretty big, with   50 a bald forehead like an old satyr, a fat belly, bushy eyebrows, and a dirty look? A low-down, filthy, lying, thieving, swindling crook? Had two good-looking girls with him?

FISHERMAN.   Anyone with those sterling virtues   55 ought to be headed for a town jail, not a temple of Venus.

TRACHALIO.   But did you see him?

FISHERMAN.   No. He hasn't been here. So long. (*They leave, stage right.*)

TRACHALIO (*calling after them*). So long. (*To himself.*) I thought so; I had a suspicion this would happen.   60 They've put one over on that master of mine: that damned pimp skipped town. Took passage on a ship and took the girls away. I'm a prophet, that's what I am. The lousy liar! He even invited Plesidippus for lunch out here. Well, the best thing I can do is wait around here until   65 Plesidippus shows up. And while I'm at it, if I see the priestess, I'll quiz her and find out if she knows anything more about all this. She'll tell me.

(*The door of the temple opens and* AMPELISCA *comes out, carrying a pitcher. Her first words are addressed to the priestess inside.*)

AMPELISCA (*through the doorway*). Yes, I understand. I'm to go to the cottage right next door to the shrine,   70 knock, and ask for water.

TRACHALIO (*pricking up his ears, to himself*). Now whose voice is that the wind has wafted to mine ears?

AMPELISCA (*turning at the sound*). Who's that talking out there, please? (*Seeing him.*) Look who's here!   75

TRACHALIO (*turning, to himself*). Isn't that Ampelisca coming out of the temple?

AMPELISCA (*to herself*). Isn't that Trachalio, Plesidippus' valet, I see?

TRACHALIO (*to himself*). That's who it is, all right.   80

AMPELISCA (*to herself*). That's who it is, all right. (*Calling.*) Trachalio! Hello there!

TRACHALIO (*going up to her*). Hello, Ampelisca. What have you been doing with yourself?

AMPELISCA (*bitterly*). Spending the best years of my   85 life in the worst possible way.

TRACHALIO.   Don't say things like that!

AMPELISCA (*as before*). Sensible people should tell the truth—and listen to it. But where's Plesidippus?

TRACHALIO (*looking at her blankly*). What a ques-   90 tion! He's inside with you people, isn't he?

AMPELISCA (*emphatically*). He is not. He hasn't been here today.

TRACHALIO.   Hasn't been here?

AMPELISCA.   You never said a truer word.   95

TRACHALIO (*grinning*). Rather unusual for me. Well, when will lunch be ready?

AMPELISCA (*taking her turn at looking blank*). What lunch are you talking about?

TRACHALIO.   You people are making a sacrifice   100 here, aren't you?

AMPELISCA.   My dear boy, will you please wake up?

TRACHALIO.   But I know for certain our masters were getting together for lunch here. Labrax invited Plesidippus.

AMPELISCA (*bitterly*). I'm not at all surprised. Ex-   105 actly what you'd expect of a pimp—as ready to cheat a goddess as a man.

TRACHALIO.   You mean you people and Plesidippus *aren't* making a sacrifice here?

AMPELISCA (*scornfully*). You're a prophet.   110

TRACHALIO.   What are you doing around here, then?

AMPELISCA (*breathlessly*). We were in terrible trouble, scared to death, in danger of losing our lives, with not a thing to our name and not a soul to help us. And the priestess here took us in. The two of us—me and   115 Palaestra.

TRACHALIO (*excitedly*). You mean Palaestra's here? His sweetheart's here?

AMPELISCA.   Of course.

TRACHALIO (*as before*). Ampelisca, that's the best   120 possible news you could have brought me. But what was this danger you were in? I'm dying to hear about it.

AMPELISCA.   Trachalio, last night our ship was wrecked!

TRACHALIO.   What ship? What are you talking about?   125

AMPELISCA.   Didn't you hear what happened? The pimp wanted to move all of us to Sicily without anybody knowing about it. So he loaded all his belongings on board a ship. And now he's lost everything!

TRACHALIO (*exulting*). Good work, Father Nep-   130 tune! Congratulations! Nobody can play the game better than you: you hit the jackpot; you gave that liar his lumps. But where is our pimping friend Labrax now?

AMPELISCA.   Probably died of drink. Neptune was serving in the big glasses last night.   135

TRACHALIO (*chuckling*). And he probably insisted on bottoms up, every round. Ampelisca, I love you! You're so sweet! What honeyed words you have for me! (*Suddenly becoming serious.*) But how were you and Palaestra rescued?   140

AMPELISCA.   I'll tell you just how it happened. We saw that the ship was being carried toward the rocks, and we both got so scared we jumped into the ship's boat. Then, while everybody on board was busy having the shakes, I hurried and cast off the rope. The storm carried us away   145 from them, to the right. And then we were tossed about by the wind and waves in the worst way imaginable, all night long. Finally, just this morning, the wind drove us up on the beach. We were half dead!

TRACHALIO.   I know. That's what Neptune always **150** does. (*Grinning.*) Most meticulous purser in the business: any bad merchandise around, and he heaves it right overboard.

AMPELISCA.   Oh, go to the devil!

TRACHALIO.   You almost did, Ampelisca, my girl. **155** (*Becoming serious.*) I knew that pimp would do something like that; I said so all along. You know what I really ought to do? Grow a beard and be a prophet.

AMPELISCA (*tartly*). Considering that you knew all about it, you and that master of yours certainly took good **160** care not to let him get away.

TRACHALIO (*defensively*). What should he have done?

AMPELISCA (*angrily*). If he really loved her, you wouldn't have to ask such a question! He should have kept his eyes open night and day, been on his guard every **165** minute. My god! That Plesidippus of yours certainly took fine care of her! Shows how much she mattered to him!

TRACHALIO (*reproachfully*). Why do you say that?

AMPELISCA (*severely*). It's plain as day, isn't it?

TRACHALIO.   Can't you understand? Why, you **170** take a fellow who goes to a public bath: he watches his clothes like a hawk and still he gets robbed. There are so many people around, he doesn't know which one to keep an eye on. It's easy enough for the crook to spot the man *he* wants to keep his eye on, but it's tough for the **175** fellow who's on guard to spot the crook. (*Quickly changing the subject.*) But how about taking me to Palaestra?

AMPELISCA.   Just go inside the temple here. You'll find her sitting there crying her eyes out. **180**

TRACHALIO.   Crying? That I'm sorry to hear. What's she crying about?

AMPELISCA.   I'll tell you what she's crying about: she's all broken up because the pimp took away a little jewel box she had in which she kept some things that were **185** her only means of identifying her parents. She's afraid it's lost.

TRACHALIO.   Where was this box?

AMPELISCA.   On board with us. He kept it locked up in a satchel. He wanted to make sure she'd never be **190** able to find her parents.

TRACHALIO.   What a criminal thing to do! A girl who ought to be free and he wants to keep her a slave!

AMPELISCA.   It must have gone down to the bottom with the ship. The pimp had all his money in the **195** same satchel.

TRACHALIO (*comfortingly*). Oh, someone's probably dived down and rescued it.

AMPELISCA.   The poor girl is simply miserable at the thought of having lost those things. **200**

TRACHALIO.   All the more reason for me to go in and cheer her up. I don't want her to go on tormenting herself that way. I know for a fact there are lots of people whose affairs turned out much better than they ever expected.

AMPELISCA.   And I know for a fact there are lots **205** who expected their affairs to turn out well and they never did.

TRACHALIO.   When you come down to it, the best medicine for trouble is a level head. Well, if there's nothing more I can do for you, I'll run along inside. (*Enters the* **210** *temple.*)

AMPELISCA.   Go ahead. (*To herself.*) And I'll do that errand for the priestess and ask them next door for some water. She told me they'd give it to me right away if I said it was for her. (*Walking toward the cottage.*) I don't think I've ever met anyone nicer than that old lady. I **215** think she deserves every kindness god or man can do for her. There we were, castaways, frightened to death, drenched to the skin, helpless, half alive, and she took us in and was so sweet and generous and open and unbegrudging—just as if we were her own daughters! **220** She even tucked up her robe and heated the water herself so that we could take a bath. Well, I don't want her to be held up on my account, so I'll go where she told me right now and get some more water. (*Knocking on the door of the cottage.*) Hello there! Anyone inside? Anyone **225** there to open this door? Will someone please come out?

SCEPARNIO (*throwing the door open and looking past her as he does*). Who's the wild animal trying to break this door down?

AMPELISCA.   Here I am.

SCEPARNIO (*breaking into a pleased smile as he sees her, to himself*). Hey, here's a piece of luck. Damn it **230** all, that's one good-looking girl there!

AMPELISCA.   Good morning, mister.

SCEPARNIO.   Good morning to *you*, miss.

AMPELISCA.   I've come here to—

SCEPARNIO (*interrupting with a leer*). It's a little **235** too early in the morning for me to entertain you, my girl. Come back later this evening and I'll really take care of you. (*Putting his arm around her.*) Well, how about it, baby?

AMPELISCA (*deftly fending him off*). Hey, don't you **240** get so familiar with those hands!

SCEPARNIO (*aside*). Lord in heaven, this is Lady Venus herself! Look at those eyes—this girl's the lively type. And those cheeks! Like silt—silk, I mean. And those breasts! And that mouth calls for a kiss. (*Makes another* **245** *pass at her.*)

AMPELISCA (*as before*). Can't you keep your hands off me? I'm for your betters, boy!

SCEPARNIO.   Come on, little one, just one little hug, nice and gentle, like this. (*Tries to get an arm around her again.*)

AMPELISCA.   Later on, when I'm not busy, you and   250
I'll have time to play around, but right now I have a favor
to ask and please just tell me yes or no.

SCEPARNIO.   All right, what do you want?

AMPELISCA (*holding up the pitcher*). If you had any brains,
this would show you what I want.   255

SCEPARNIO (*making an obscene gesture*). And if you had
any, this would show you want *I* want.

AMPELISCA (*remembering her instructions, importantly*).
The priestess of the shrine of Venus sent me to ask you
for some water for her.

SCEPARNIO (*tapping his chest*). *I'm* lord and master   260
around here. Unless you ask me for it, you don't get a
drop. We risked our own necks to dig this well, and we
did it with our own tools. (*Leering.*) And no one gets a
drop without asking me nicely.

AMPELISCA.   What's the matter? You won't give   265
me some water? What any stranger would give to another?

SCEPARNIO.   What's the matter? You won't give me what
any friend would give to another?

AMPELISCA (*enticingly*). I? Of course I will. I'll do anything
you want, honey.   270

SCEPARNIO (*aside*). Congratulations, old boy, you're in; she
just called you "honey." (*To* AMPELISCA.) Sure I'll give
you the water. I don't want you to fall in love with me
and get nothing for it. Give me the pitcher.

AMPELISCA.   Here it is. And please hurry.   275

SCEPARNIO (*taking the pitcher*). You wait here. I'll be right
back—honey. (*Enters the cottage.*)

AMPELISCA (*worriedly*). What should I tell the priestess took
me so long? (*Gazes about abstractedly, and her eye falls
on the sea.*) Ugh! When I look at that water, I get   280
frightened even now. (*Starting.*) Oh, my god, what's that
I see on the beach? It's the pimp and his friend from
Sicily! And I, like a poor fool, thought the two of them
had drowned! That means more trouble in store for us than
we had thought. But what am I waiting for? I've   285
got to hurry into the temple and tell Palaestra so that we
can throw ourselves on the altar before that filthy pimp
comes here and catches us. I'd better run—every minute
counts!

(*She hurries into the temple. A second later* SCEPARNIO
comes out carrying the pitcher.)

SCEPARNIO (*smiling fatuously, to himself*). Lord,   290
oh, lord, I never thought water had so much happiness to
offer. It was a sheer pleasure to draw it—the well never
seemed that shallow before. Practically no work at all to
haul it up. Sceparnio, knock on wood, you're quite a guy.
Got yourself a love affair going today, eh, boy?   295
(*Calling.*) Where's my pretty girl? Here's your water.
(*Putting the bucket on his head and mincing about.*) See?
This is the way I want you to carry it, like a lady. Want
me to like you? Then do it just like this. (*Calling.*)
Sweetie-pie, where are you? Come on and get   300
your water. Where are you? (*Grinning even more fatuously.*) Well, what do you know—the little devil's playing
hide-and-go-seek. Boy, did she fall for me! (*Calling.*)
Where are you? (*After waiting a moment in silence.*) Hey,
are you going to come and get this pitcher? Where   305
are you? Come on, no more games, I'm serious. How
about taking this here pitcher? (*Removes the pitcher from
his head and starts searching in earnest.*) Where the devil
are you? Good god, I don't see her anywhere. Is she
playing a trick on me? (*Slamming the pitcher   310
down, angrily.*) I'll just leave the blasted pitcher right in
the road. (*Starts walking away, then stops abruptly.*) Wait
a second—what if someone walks off with it? That's no
ordinary pitcher; it belongs to the shrine. I'll get into
trouble. (*Excitedly.*) I think that girl framed me—   315
wanted me to get caught with a holy pitcher on me. If
anyone sees me with this thing, the judge'll have every
right to throw the book at me. Look—it's even got its
name on it—it practically shouts to high heaven whose it
is. Holy god, I'm going to call the priestess out   320
here right now to get her pitcher. I'm heading right for
her door! (*Rushes up to the door and starts shouting frantically.*) Hey! Ptolemocratia! Come on out and get your
pitcher! Some blamed girl brought it to me. (*Waits a
moment; then, getting no reply, disgustedly.*) I'll   325
have to carry it in. Fine business if, on top of everything
else, I've got to deliver the water right to the house!

(SCEPARNIO *goes into the temple. A second later* LABRAX,
"*the shark*," *enters, stage right. He is wet, bedraggled, and
shivering.*)

LABRAX (*to himself*). If anyone wants to become a beggar,
just let him trust himself, body and soul, to Father Neptune. Believe me, whenever you do business with   330
him, this (*indicating his appearance*) is the way he sends
you home. I remember a story about a girl who always
refused to set foot on a ship with Hercules—she was a
smart one, all right. But, where's that guest of mine who's
been my ruination? Oh, there he is. Look at him   335
taking his time!

(CHARMIDES *enters, stage right, in the same condition as*
LABRAX.)

CHARMIDES (*sourly*). What the devil's the hurry, Labrax? I
can't keep up when you go that fast.

LABRAX (*bitterly*). I wish to god you had gone to the gallows
in Sicily before I ever set eyes on you. You're to   340
blame for getting me into this!

CHARMIDES.   And I wish to god I had spent the night in
the town jail rather than let you take me home with you
that day. There's only one favor I want from heaven—
that from now on till the end of your days, your   345
guests be the same breed as yourself, every one of them.

LABRAX. The day I took you in I let Bad Luck walk right in the front door. Why did I ever listen to a good-for-nothing like you? Why did I ever leave here? Why did I get aboard that ship? (*Thinking of the money he took from* PLESIDIPPUS.) I've lost even more than I owned! **350**

CHARMIDES. I'm not surprised that ship went down—not when it was carrying a crook like you and all that crooked stuff you had.

LABRAX. You ruined me, you and that slick talk of yours. **355**

CHARMIDES. How about that filthy meal you served me? Believe me, Thyestes and Tereus[2] didn't get worse.

LABRAX (*holding his stomach*). Oh, god, I feel sick. Hold my head, will you? **360**

CHARMIDES. Damn you, I hope you puke up your lungs while you're at it.

LABRAX. Poor Palaestra and Ampelisca. I wonder where they are now.

CHARMIDES. Probably feeding the fish down in the drink. **365**

LABRAX. It's all your doing that I'm a beggar now. I had to listen to that big talk of yours!

CHARMIDES (*grinning maliciously*). You ought to be grateful to me. You never knew how to get along before. I taught you how to get along swimmingly. **370**

LABRAX. Why don't you go straight to hell and leave me alone?

CHARMIDES. That's just what I was going to invite you to do. **375**

LABRAX. God, there isn't a man alive worse off than I am.

CHARMIDES. Oh, yes there is. One lots worse off—me.

LABRAX. How so?

CHARMIDES. Because you deserved what you got. I didn't. **380**

LABRAX. Look at those bulrushes. I envy them. Always nice and dry.

CHARMIDES. I'm practicing to be a Spanish dancer. I'm shivering so much, every time I speak I clack like a castanet. **385**

LABRAX. That Neptune sure runs a cold bathing establishment. I leave the place, have all my clothes on, and I'm still freezing. And he doesn't even have a hot-drink counter. Only drinks he serves are cold and salty.

CHARMIDES. The fellows I envy are the black-smiths. Around a fire all day. Always nice and warm. **390**

LABRAX. What I'd like to be right now is a duck. Come straight out of the water and still be dry.

CHARMIDES. I think I'll get me a job playing a ghost in a theatrical troupe. **395**

LABRAX. Why?

CHARMIDES. Listen to the terrific clatter I can make with my teeth. (*Shaking his head ruefully.*) If you ask me,

being cleaned out of everything I owned was just what was coming to me. **400**

LABRAX. Why?

CHARMIDES. How could I have had the nerve to get aboard a ship with someone like you? I'll bet you made all those waves yourself, just to spite me.

LABRAX. I listened to you, that's what I did. You kept telling me girls made big money where you came from. You promised I'd rake in the cash there. **405**

CHARMIDES. And you expected to swallow up the whole island of Sicily in one gulp, like a damned vulture.

LABRAX. Talk about swallowing, I wonder what whale got my satchel. I had all my money in it. **410**

CHARMIDES. Probably the same one that got my wallet. The inside pocket was full of cash.

LABRAX. Do you know that all I've got left to my name is this shirt and this rag of a coat? I'm done for! **415**

CHARMIDES. You and I could set up a perfect partnership. We'd hold identical shares.

LABRAX. If only my girls were still alive, there'd be some hope. If that young fellow Plesidippus sees me now, the one I took a down payment from for Palaestra, he's going to make real trouble for me—and soon. **420**

CHARMIDES. What are you crying about, stupid? So long as that tongue of yours is alive, you've got what it takes to get you out of any debts you owe.

(*The door of the temple opens, and* SCEPARNIO *comes out, looking puzzled.*)

SCEPARNIO (*to himself*). What's going on here, anyway? Two girls inside the temple, holding on to the altar and crying their eyes out. The poor things are scared to death of someone but I don't know who. They said they'd been shipwrecked last night and tossed up on the beach this morning. **430** **425**

LABRAX (*to* SCEPARNIO, *eagerly*). Say there, mister, where are these girls you're talking about?

SCEPARNIO. Here, in the temple.

LABRAX. How many of them are there?

SCEPARNIO. Two. **435**

LABRAX (*half to himself*). I'll swear they're mine.

SCEPARNIO. And I'll swear I don't know about that.

LABRAX. What do they look like?

SCEPARNIO. Not bad. I could go for either one of them— if I was good and drunk. **440**

LABRAX. They're pretty young, aren't they?

SCEPARNIO. You're pretty much of a nuisance, aren't you? Go on in and take a look if you want.

LABRAX (*to* CHARMIDES, *excitedly*). Charmides! Those girls in there must be mine! **445**

CHARMIDES. Whether they are or they aren't, you can go to hell for all I care.

LABRAX. I'm going into that temple this minute. (*Rushes into the temple.*)

---

[2]Mythological characters who had been served their own sons.

CHARMIDES (*calling after him*). I wish you were going straight to hell this minute. (*To* SCEPARNIO.) Say,   450
how about playing host and giving me a place where I can stretch out and get some sleep?

SCEPARNIO.   Stretch out wherever you want. No one's stopping you. It's a free country.

CHARMIDES.   But look at me—these clothes I'm   455
wearing are wringing wet. How about putting me up in your house and giving me some dry clothes until these get dry? I'll make it up to you sometime.

SCEPARNIO (*pointing to a homely coverall of rushes hanging up alongside the cottage*). See that mat there? That's all I've got. It's dry, and if you want it   460
you're welcome to it. It's my coat, and it doubles as umbrella when there's rain. Here, give me your things and I'll dry them out.

CHARMIDES (*backing away suspiciously*). Oh, no. Isn't the cleaning out I got at sea enough for you? Do you   465
have to put me through it all again on land?

SCEPARNIO.   I don't give a damn whether you get cleaned out or rubbed out. I'm not trusting you with anything of mine without security. Go ahead—freeze to death or sweat to death, get sick or get well. Who cares?   470
I don't want any foreigners around the house, anyway. And that's that. (*Stomps into the cottage.*)

CHARMIDES (*calling after him*). Hey, where are you going? (*To himself.*) Whoever he is, the man must be a slave dealer—doesn't know what it is to feel pity. But   475
what am I standing around here in these wet clothes for? Why don't I go into this temple here and sleep off last night's party? Drank too much; lots more than I wanted. You'd think we were cheap wine, the way Neptune watered us. Maybe he was figuring on giving us   480
a salt-water laxative. When you come right down to it, if he had kept on serving drinks much longer we'd have gone to sleep then and there; this way he let us go home—half alive, but alive. Well, I'll see what my fellow drunk is doing inside here now.   485

(*Enters the temple, and the stage is now empty.*)

ACT THREE

(DAEMONES *comes out of the cottage shaking his head wonderingly.*)

DAEMONES (*to the audience*). It's amazing the way heaven plays tricks on us mortals. The amazing dreams heaven sends you when you're asleep! A person's not left in peace and quiet even in bed. Last night, for example, I had an incredible dream, something unheard of. I   5
dreamed that an ape was trying to climb up to a swallow's nest and get his hands on the swallows, but couldn't quite make it. After a while it came to me to ask for the loan of a ladder. I refused, pointing out that swallows were descended from Philomela[3] and Procne, and I   10
pleaded with it not to do any harm to what were, in effect, my fellow countrymen. That just made it more belligerent than ever, and it threatened to beat me. It hauled me into court. There I lost my temper and, somehow or other, managed to grab the filthy creature around the   15
middle and chain it up. (*Scratching his head perplexedly.*) Now, what does it all mean? I've thought all morning but I just can't figure it out. (*A clamor is heard in the temple.*) What's that? Noise in the shrine next door? That's queer.

(*The door of the temple flies open and* TRACHALIO *bursts out.*)

TRACHALIO (*at the top of his lungs—and at his oratorical best*). Citizens of Cyrene! Farmers! Anyone who   20
lives in the area! In god's name, help for the helpless! Harm for the harmful! Are the merciless to be mightier than the meek who shrink at the very name of crime? Then help right a wrong, give the righteous their reward and the dastards their deserts. Fight the good fight to   25
let us live by law and order and not by fists and force. Everyone here, everyone who hears my voice, in god's name, into this shrine of Venus as fast as you can! Help the poor souls who have entrusted life and limb to the protection of Venus and her priestess in accor-   30
dance with our ancient custom! Wring the neck of wrong before it reaches *you!*

DAEMONES (*impatiently*). What's this all about?

TRACHALIO (*throwing himself on the ground and embracing Daemones' knees*). My dear sir, by these knees, I call upon you, whoever you are—   35

DAEMONES (*interrupting, as before*). Let go of my knees and tell me what this yelling's about. And make it short!

TRACHALIO (*not budging*). I beg you, I implore you! Do you want a good crop on your farm this year? Do you want to see it arrive at an overseas market safe and sound?   40
Do you want to get rid of what ails you? Do you—

DAEMONES (*interrupting*). Are you in your right mind?

TRACHALIO (*unabashed*). Do you want an ample supply of seed for sowing? Then, my dear sir, please don't refuse to do what I'm asking you to.   45

DAEMONES (*testily*). And I call upon *you* by that back of yours and those legs and heels. Do you want a good harvest of birch-rod welts? Do you want a bumper crop of trouble this year? Then you'd better tell me what's going on here and what this shouting's all about.   50

TRACHALIO (*getting up, reproachfully*). You're not fair: I asked only for nice things for you.

DAEMONES (*promptly*). I am so fair: I asked only for what you deserve.

TRACHALIO.   Please! Listen to me!   55

DAEMONES.   What is it?

[3]A mythological princess of Athens.

TRACHALIO.   There are two innocent girls in there. They need your help. The treatment they've had—and are getting this minute—is a blot on the escutcheon of justice and law. Right in the temple of Venus, too! Even **60** the priestess is being manhandled.

DAEMONES (*finally aroused*).   Who would have the gall to lay hands on a priestess? Who are these girls? How are they being mistreated?

TRACHALIO.   If you'll listen to me for a minute, I'll **65** tell you. (*Breathlessly.*) They ran to Venus' altar for safety. Now this fellow has the colossal nerve to want to pull them away. And both of them by rights ought to be free.

DAEMONES.   Who's the man who's so free and easy **70** with priestesses and temples? And no speeches!

TRACHALIO.   A swindler, a crook, a murderer, a liar, a lawbreaker; a foul, filthy, unprincipled—in a word, a pimp. Need I say more?

DAEMONES.   You've said enough. Perfect material **75** for a flogging.

TRACHALIO.   He even tried to strangle the priestess.

DAEMONES.   By god, he's going to pay for that, and pay plenty. (*Shouting to his servants inside.*) Hey! Roughneck and Cutthroat! Come on out here! Where are you, **80** anyway?

TRACHALIO.   Please, I beg you. Go in the temple and rescue them.

(*Two husky slaves rush out of the house and stand at attention before* DAEMONES.)

DAEMONES (*to* TRACHALIO, *reassuringly*).   One word from me will be enough. (*To the slaves.*) Follow me! **85** (*They charge toward the temple.*)

TRACHALIO (*remaining prudently behind and calling to* DAEMONES).   Give it to him! Tell those boys to make believe they're cooks scaling fish and have them scratch his eyes out!

DAEMONES (*to the slaves*).   Drag him out here by the feet, like a stuck pig. **90**

(*The three enter the temple.* TRACHALIO *stands near the door, listening intently.*)

TRACHALIO (*to the audience*).   I hear a racket: the pimp's getting a going-over. I hope they knock every tooth out of the rascal's mouth. (*Stepping back as the door opens.*) Here come the girls. They look scared to death.

(PALAESTRA *and* AMPELISCA *come out and rush past* TRACHALIO *without noticing him.*)

SONG

PALAESTRA (*to the audience*).
> The dread moment's at hand; now we're utterly helpless. **95**

There's just no one to come to our aid or defense,
No release from our danger, no way to find safety.
And we're both so afraid we can't think where to run.
Oh, the vicious and brutal ordeal that that pimp
Put us through just a moment ago in the shrine! **100**
Why, the monster attacked the old priestess, poor thing,
Shoved her this way and that—it was dreadful to see—
And then dragged us by force from the innermost altar.
In the state that we're in, we'd be better off dead.
In the depths of despair what is dearer than death? **105**

TRACHALIO (*to himself*).
> Hey, what's this? What a way for a young girl to talk!
> I must swing into action—they need cheering up. (*Calling.*)
> Hey, Palaestra!

PALAESTRA (*too frightened to turn around*).
> Who's there?

TRACHALIO (*calling*).
> Ampelisca! **110**

AMPELISCA (*clutching* PALAESTRA).
> Who wants me?

PALAESTRA (*as before*).   Who's that calling our names?

TRACHALIO.
> Turn around and you'll see.

PALAESTRA (*turning and seeing him, fervently*).   Oh, some hope for our safety at last! **115**

TRACHALIO (*walking over to them, importantly*).
> Now be calm.
> Take it easy. Trust me.

PALAESTRA.
> Yes—if you'll give your word
> We need fear no more violence and force. Otherwise I'll be brought to a violent act on myself! **120**

TRACHALIO (*as before*).   Now you're just being silly. No more of this talk.

PALAESTRA (*dully*).   Don't try to console me in my misery with mere words. If you don't have some real help to offer, Trachalio, it's all over with us. **125**

AMPELISCA (*wildly*).   I've made up my mind to die rather than suffer at the hands of that pimp any longer. (*Hesitatingly.*) But I'm just a woman, after all; every time I even think of death I get paralyzed with fright. Oh, what a nightmare this day is! **130**

TRACHALIO (*heartily*).   Courage, girls!

PALAESTRA (*dully*).   Courage? Where am I going to find it?

TRACHALIO (*as before*).   Take my word for it, there's no reason to be afraid. (*Pointing to the altar outside the shrine.*) Come, sit down on this altar. **135**

AMPELISCA. Why should this one do us any more good than the one in the shrine? We were clutching it just now when they pulled us away by brute force.

TRACHALIO (*leading them to the altar and seating them on it*). You just sit down. I'll stand guard over here. See? The altar's your fort, here are the walls, and I'm the **140** garrison. With Venus at my side I'm ready to counter the pimp's sneak attacks.

AMPELISCA. All right, we'll do whatever you say. (*Falling on her knees and praying.*) Dear Venus, here we are, both of us, on our knees, in tears, before your altar. **145** We beg of you: guard us, watch over us. Give us our revenge on those criminals who had so little respect for your shrine. Be gracious and let us find safety by this altar. Thanks to Neptune we had a bath last night; please don't be offended or hold it against us if you feel **150** such a washing isn't all that your ritual requires.

TRACHALIO (*looking up toward heaven, importantly*). Venus, if you ask me, that's a perfectly valid request and they deserve to have it granted. You should make allowances for them: the scare they had forced them into this informality. They tell me that you were born from **155** a sea shell; don't leave these poor shells abandoned on the beach! (*As the door of the temple opens.*) Look! Here's your savior and mine—the old man's coming out. He couldn't have picked a better time.

(DAEMONES *comes out followed by the two slaves, who are unceremoniously shoving* LABRAX *ahead of them.*)

DAEMONES (*to* LABRAX). Get out of that shrine, you **160** scum of the earth! (*Turning to address the girls.*) And you two sit down on the altar—where are they?

TRACHALIO. Over here.

DAEMONES. Perfect. Exactly what I wanted. Just let him try to get near them now. (*To* LABRAX.) So you **165** thought you could get away with your lawbreaking inside a temple while we were around, eh? (*To one of the slaves.*) Give him a sock on the jaw.

LABRAX (*blustering*). This is an outrage—and you'll pay for it. **170**

DAEMONES. What's that? You've got the nerve to make threats?

LABRAX (*as before*). You're depriving me of my rights. These are my girls and you took them from me without my consent. **175**

TRACHALIO. You go right down to City Hall here at Cyrene and pick yourself a judge—anyone you want, the most influential you can find. Let *him* decide whether these girls should be yours or should go free—and whether you shouldn't be clapped into jail and **180** stay there until you wear the place out.

LABRAX (*turning on him*). I'm in no mood today for conversation with a blasted slave. (*To* DAEMONES.) It's you I want to talk to.

DAEMONES (*gesturing toward* TRACHALIO). First **185** you'll have it out with this fellow here. He knows you.

LABRAX (*curtly*). My business is with you.

TRACHALIO. But you're going to take it up with me whether you like it or not. So these girls are yours, eh?

LABRAX. That's right. **190**

TRACHALIO. Well, you just try touching either one of them with the tip of your little finger.

LABRAX (*belligerently*). And what'll happen if I do?

TRACHALIO (*very brave with the odds four to one in his favor*). So help me, I'll make a punching bag out of you, that's what'll happen. I'll tie you up and knock **195** the stuffings out of you, you damned liar.

LABRAX (*to* DAEMONES). You mean I can't take my own girls away from that altar?

DAEMONES. That's what I mean. That's the law around here. **200**

LABRAX (*scornfully*). Your laws have nothing to do with me. I'm taking both those girls out of here right now. (*Leering.*) If you're so much in love with them, you old goat, you're going to have to come across with hard cash. And if they're such favorites with Venus, she's **205** welcome to them—if she pays me.

DAEMONES. Pay you! There's something you'd better get straight: if you try the least bit of rough stuff, even as a joke, on these girls, I'll send you away from here in such a state you won't recognize yourself. (*To the* **210** *slaves.*) Listen, you two. The minute I give the signal, knock the eyes out of his head. If you don't, I'll wrap a whip around you like twine on a spool.

LABRAX. So you're going to use force on me, eh?

TRACHALIO (*exploding*). Look who's talking about **215** force! You stinking hypocrite!

LABRAX (*shouting*). No blasted slave can talk to me like that!

TRACHALIO. Sure, I'm a blasted slave and you're a saint—but that doesn't change the fact that these girls should be free. **220**

LABRAX. What do you mean, free?

TRACHALIO. What's more, damn it, you ought to be their slave. They come from the heart of Greece. (*Pointing to* PALAESTRA.) This one was born in Athens. Her parents were respectable Athenians. **225**

DAEMONES (*eagerly*). What's that you say?

TRACHALIO. I said this girl is an Athenian and was no slave when she was born.

DAEMONES. You mean she's from my own city?

TRACHALIO (*surprised*). You weren't born here in **230** Cyrene?

DAEMONES. Oh, no. I'm a native Athenian, born and raised in Athens.

TRACHALIO. Then I implore you to defend your fellow citizens. **235**

DAEMONES (*sighing*). How I'm reminded of my own daughter when I look at this girl! The very thought stirs up old sorrows. Three years old she was, when I lost her, and if she's alive she'd be just that tall, I'm sure of it.

LABRAX.   I paid their owner good money for both   **240**
of them. What do I care whether they come from Athens or Thebes so long as I'm satisfied with the way they slave for me.

TRACHALIO (*confident enough now to assume his orator's manner*).   So, you sneaking cradle snatcher, you think you're going to get away with snatching infants   **245**
from their mother's breast and grinding them to nothingness in your foul trade? I admit I don't know where this other girl comes from. But I know one thing: she's far above scum like you.

LABRAX (*sneering*).   I suppose they belong to you?   **250**

TRACHALIO.   All right. Let's you and I take a back test to see which of us tells the truth. First I'll inspect you. And if that back of yours hasn't more welts from the whip than a ship's hull has nails, *I'm* the world's worst liar. Then you look at me. And if my hide isn't so smooth   **255**
and unblemished that any leatherworker would classify it as absolutely top grade, give me one good reason why I shouldn't tan yours until I get tired of it. (*As* LABRAX *glances toward the altar.*) What are you staring at those girls for? You lay a hand on them and I'll gouge   **260**
your eyes out!

LABRAX (*belligerently*).   You know what? Just because you say I can't do it, I'm going to take them both away with me right now.

DAEMONES (*scornfully*).   And just how do you pro-   **265**
pose to do that?

LABRAX.   You've got Venus on your side? I'll use Vulcan. (*Rushing toward the door of the cottage.*) I'm going for fire.

TRACHALIO (*alarmed*).   Where's he going?   **270**

LABRAX (*as he nears the door*).   Hey! Anybody inside? Hey, there!

DAEMONES (*calling*).   You touch that door and I'll fill that face of yours with fists for you. (*Nods to the two slaves, who run over and haul* LABRAX *back.*)

SLAVE (*to* LABRAX, *grinning*).   We don't use fire. All   **275**
we eat is dried figs.

TRACHALIO.   I'll give you fire all right—I'll light one on your head.

LABRAX.   Damn it, I'll get fire from somewhere else then.

DAEMONES.   And just what are you going to do   **280**
with it when you get it?

LABRAX (*gesturing toward the altar*).   I'll start a bonfire right here.

DAEMONES.   Funeral pyre for yourself, eh?

LABRAX.   No, sir. I'm going to burn the both of   **285**
them alive right here on the altar, that's what I'm going to do.

TRACHALIO.   The minute you try it, I'll heave you in the fire by that beard of yours, haul you out just as you begin to brown, and feed you to the vultures.   **290**

DAEMONES (*to himself*).   Now it comes to me! This is the ape I saw in my dream, the one I wanted to keep from pulling the swallows out of their nest.

TRACHALIO (*to* DAEMONES).   Would you please do me a favor? Would you keep an eye on these girls and   **295**
see that no harm comes to them while I go get my master?

DAEMONES.   Go ahead. Find him and bring him here.

TRACHALIO (*gesturing toward* LABRAX).   But don't let him—

DAEMONES (*interrupting*).   If he lays a hand on them, or even tries to, he'll be sorry.   **300**

TRACHALIO.   Be careful now.

DAEMONES.   I'm being careful. You go along.

TRACHALIO.   But keep an eye on him too, so's he doesn't get away. We agreed to forfeit fifteen thousand dollars to the hangman if we didn't produce him today.   **305**

DAEMONES.   Just run along. I'll take care of everything until you get back.

TRACHALIO.   I'll be back right away. (*Exits, stage right.*)

DAEMONES (*to* LABRAX).   Hey, pimp! I'll give you your choice: you prefer a beating to keep you quiet or   **310**
will you stay still without one?

LABRAX.   I don't give a damn what you say. These girls are mine, and I'm going to drag them off this altar by the hair whether you or Venus or god almighty himself likes it or not.   **315**

DAEMONES.   Just try to touch them.

LABRAX.   Sure I'll touch them.

DAEMONES (*with elaborate cordiality*).   Go right ahead. Step right this way. (*Points toward the altar.*)

LABRAX.   You just tell those boys of yours to step   **320**
back that way. (*Points away from the altar.*)

DAEMONES.   Oh, no. Any stepping they do will be toward you.

LABRAX (*belligerently*).   Oh, yeah? I don't think so.

DAEMONES.   What'll you do if they step closer?   **325**
(*Nods to the slaves, who advance on* LABRAX.)

LABRAX (*taking a hasty step backward*).   I'll move back. Listen, you old goat, if I ever catch you back in town, believe me, I'll have my fun out of you before I let you go, or I'm no pimp.

DAEMONES (*grimly*).   You do that. But, in the mean-   **330**
time, if you lay a hand on these girls I'll let you have it—and hard.

LABRAX.   Yeah? How hard?

DAEMONES.   Hard enough for a pimp.

LABRAX.   I don't give a damn for your threats. I'm   **335**
dragging those girls out of here right now whether you like it or not.

DAEMONES.   Just try to touch them.

LABRAX.   Sure I'll touch them.

DAEMONES.   So you'll touch them, will you? And   **340**
do you know what's going to happen? (*To one of the slaves.*) Roughneck! Hurry into the house and bring out two clubs.

LABRAX (*taken aback*).   Clubs?

DAEMONES (*to the slave*). Be sure they're thick   345
ones. Quick! On the double! (*The slave dashes off. He
turns back to* LABRAX.) I'll see that you get the reception
you deserve.

LABRAX (*to himself*). And I had to lose my helmet in the
wreck! If I still had it, now's the time I could use   350
it. (*To* DAEMONES.) Look, can't I at least talk to them?

DAEMONES.   No, you can't. (*As the slave hurries back carrying two hefty clubs, jovially.*) Look who's here—my
clubman. Couldn't have come at a better time.

LABRAX (*to himself*). Look what's here—an earache.   355
Couldn't have come at a worse time.

DAEMONES (*to the slaves*). Cutthroat, take one of those
clubs. (*Pointing to either side of the altar.*) Now one of
you stand there, and one here. Take your positions. (*Nodding with satisfaction as they do.*) That's the way.   360
Now listen to me. If he lays a finger on them and you
don't lay those clubs on him until he doesn't know which
way is up, so help me, I'll murder you both. If he tries to
talk to either one of them, stay just where you are and
answer instead. And the minute he tries to get   365
away from here, wrap those clubs around his shins as fast
as you can.

LABRAX.   You mean they're not even going to let me leave
here?

DAEMONES (*distastefully*). I've got no more to say   370
to you. (*To the slaves.*) And when that servant who went
for his master gets back here with him, you come right
home. Mind you—do exactly what I told you (*Goes into
the cottage.*)

LABRAX (*to himself*). Amazing how quickly shrines change
around here. A minute ago this one belonged to   375
Venus; now it's Hercules'—that's what it looks like with
these two statues, clubs and all, that the old man just set
up. God almighty, I don't know where I can run to now.
Storms everywhere: first on sea, and now on land.
(*Calling.*) Palaestra!   380

SLAVE.   What do you want?

LABRAX.   Hey, must be some mistake; this Palaestra isn't
the one I know. (*Calling.*) Ampelisca!

SLAVE.   Watch yourself or I'll let you have it.

LABRAX (*to himself*). Not bad advice, even though it   385
comes from a pair of clods like this. (*To the slaves.*) Hey,
you two, I'm talking to you. No harm in my going a little
closer to them, is there?

SLAVE.   Not at all—for us.

LABRAX.   How about for me?   390

SLAVE.   None for you either—if you can keep your eyes
open.

LABRAX.   Keep my eyes open for what?

SLAVE (*brandishing the club*). See this? For a good hard
wallop.   395

LABRAX.   For god's sake, please just let me get out of here!
(*Takes a tentative step away.*)

SLAVE.   Go right ahead, if you want. (*The two take a step
toward him.*)

LABRAX (*backing away in a hurry*). Very kind of you; thanks
very much. No, I think I'll stick around—and you fellows
can stand right where you are. (*To himself.*) God   400
damn it, I'm not doing well at all. (*Settling himself for a
long wait.*) Well, I'll get those girls yet. I'll stay put and
starve them out.

(PLESIDIPPUS *and* TRACHALIO *enter, stage right, deep in
conversation.*)

PLESIDIPPUS (*shocked*). You mean that pimp wanted to drag
my girl away from Venus' altar by brute force?   405

TRACHALIO.   Exactly.

PLESIDIPPUS.   Why didn't you kill him on the spot?

TRACHALIO (*glibly*). I didn't have a sword.

PLESIDIPPUS.   You should have picked up a stick or a rock.

TRACHALIO (*as if appalled at the suggestion*). What?   410
Chase a man with stones like a dog?

PLESIDIPPUS.   That scum? Of course!

LABRAX (*catching sight of them, to himself*). Oh, lord, now
I'm in for it! Here comes Plesidippus. By the time he gets
done, there won't be a speck of me left.   415

PLESIDIPPUS.   Were the girls still sitting on the altar when
you left to get me?

TRACHALIO (*looking toward the altar*). They're there right
now.

PLESIDIPPUS.   Who's minding them?   420

TRACHALIO.   Some old fellow who lives next door to the
shrine. He gave us all the help you could ask for. He and
his servants are standing guard. (*Importantly.*) I ordered
him to.

PLESIDIPPUS.   Take me right to that pimp. Where   425
is he?

LABRAX (*ingratiatingly*). Good morning, Plesidippus.

PLESIDIPPUS.   Don't you good-morning me! You're getting
a rope around your neck: do you prefer to be carried or
dragged? Make up your mind while you still have   430
the chance.

LABRAX (*gulping*). Neither, thanks.

PLESIDIPPUS (*to* TRACHALIO). Trachalio, get down to the
beach on the double. You know those fellows I brought
out here with me to help me hand this creature   435
over to the hangman? Tell them to go back to town and
meet me down at the docks. Then come back here and
stand guard. I'm hauling this godforsaken good-for-
nothing into court. (*As* TRACHALIO *dashes off, stage right,*
PLESIDIPPUS *goes up to* LABRAX *and ties a rope around
his neck.*) Come on, get moving. We're heading   440
for the courthouse.

LABRAX (*with injured innocence*). What did I do?

PLESIDIPPUS (*exploding*). What did you do? I suppose you
didn't take a deposit from me for the girl and then carry
her off?   445

LABRAX.   I did *not* carry her off.

PLESIDIPPUS.   How can you say a thing like that?

LABRAX.   I only carried her on board. It was my damned luck that I wasn't able to carry her off. Look—I told you I'd meet you at the shrine of Venus. Didn't I do 450 just what I said? I'm here, ain't I?

PLESIDIPPUS (*grimly*). Tell it to the judge. There's been enough talk around here. Follow me. (*Starts walking off, jerking* LABRAX *after him at the end of the rope.*)

LABRAX (*shouting*). Charmides! Help! They've tied a rope around my neck and they're hauling me off! 455

CHARMIDES (*appearing in the doorway of the temple*). Who's calling me?

LABRAX (*frantically*). See the way they're hauling me off?

CHARMIDES (*coolly*). I sure do. And I'm delighted to see it.

LABRAX (*unbelievingly*). You mean to say you're not going to help me? 460

CHARMIDES (*disinterestedly*). Who's hauling you off?

LABRAX.   That young fellow Plesidippus.

CHARMIDES (*grinning*). You were out to get him, now keep him. You ought to creep into jail happy as a lark. You've just had happen to you what most people in the 465 world wish for.

LABRAX.   What's that?

CHARMIDES (*as before*). Getting what they've been looking for.

LABRAX (*desperately*). Please, Charmides, stick with 470 me! (*Grabs hold of him.*)

CHARMIDES (*disgustedly*). Just like you to ask a thing like that. You're being hauled off to jail, so you want me to go along too. Come on, let go of me! (*Brushes* LABRAX's *arm away.*)

LABRAX.   I'm sunk! 475

PLESIDIPPUS.   I hope to god you're right. (*Turning to the girls.*) Palaestra, dear, and you, Ampelisca, stay right here until I get back.

SLAVE.   I think they'd be better off in our house until you come back for them. 480

PLESIDIPPUS.   Good idea; thanks very much. (*The two slaves lead the girls into the cottage.*)

LABRAX (*shouting at them*). You're a bunch of robbers!

SLAVE.   What's that? Robbers? (*To* PLESIDIPPUS.) Haul him out of here.

LABRAX (*calling*). Palaestra, please, I beg you— 485

PLESIDIPPUS (*jerking the rope*). Damn you, follow me!

LABRAX (*to* CHARMIDES). My friend—

CHARMIDES (*distastefully*). I'm no friend of yours. You and I are quits.

LABRAX.   So you're throwing me over, eh? 490

CHARMIDES.   That's exactly what I'm doing. One drinking session with you was enough.

LABRAX (*as* PLESIDIPPUS *hauls him off, stage left*). God damn you to hell!

CHARMIDES (*calling after him*). Same to you! (*To* 495 *the audience.*) I'm a believer in the theory that men get turned into different kinds of animals. If you ask me, that pimp is being turned into a bird—a jailbird. He's going to build a nest in the town lockup right now. But I'm going to stand by him in court. Maybe I can help 500 convince the judge to let him go—to jail.

(*Exits, stage left, and the stage is now empty.*)

ACT FOUR

(DAEMONES *comes out of the cottage.*)

DAEMONES (*to the audience*). That was a good turn I did today, helping those girls, and a very pleasant one to do. Now I have a pair of devoted followers—young ones, too, and not bad looking. But that shrew of a wife of mine is watching me like a hawk to make sure I don't start 5 anything with either one of them. (*Looking off, stage right, toward the sea.*) I wonder how my servant Gripus is doing? He took the boat out last night for some fishing. Believe me, he'd have shown more sense if he had stayed in bed. With the weather we had last night, and are 10 having right now, he's wasting his time, his energy, and his nets. Look how rough that water is! I'll be able to fry what he catches on my fingers. (*A call is heard from inside.*) There's my wife calling me for lunch. (*Heaving a sigh.*) I'd better go in; it's time for my earful of 15 her gabble.

(DAEMONES *goes into the cottage. A second later* GRIPUS, *"the fisherman," enters, stage right. He is hauling mightily at his net, dragging along in it a satchel that, to judge by the effort it takes to move it, is no light weight; a rope, tied to the satchel, trails loosely behind.* GRIPUS *is by nature sour and uncommunicative, very much like his fellow slave* SCE- PARNIO; *at the moment, however, his face is wearing an expression that is almost beatific.*)

SONG

GRIPUS (*to the audience*).
I'm sending many thanks down to
My benefactor Neptune, who
Resides where salt and fish abound.
When I left his bailiwick, you see, 20
He sent me off decked royally:
A load of loot and my boat still sound.
Through heavy seas it had carried me
To a rich, new type of fishing ground.
(*Breathlessly.*)
It's a marvel, a freak, to have made such a
    haul! 25
    Best fishing I've ever done yet.
Though I didn't pull in one more ounce of fresh fish
    Than what I've got here in my net.
(*Pauses, then resumes less excitedly.*)

At 1:00 A.M. I jumped from bed—
I felt a chance to get ahead 30
Was better than a good night's sleep.
I had in mind, though the seas were steep,
To see if I could somehow ease
This hard-up family's miseries.
(And help myself as well, I'll add.) 35
I gave the project all I had.
(*Vehemently.*)
Any man who is lazy is not worth a damn;
    The whole bunch of them makes me see red.
If a man wants to finish his work in good time,
    He should know when to get out of bed 40
And not wait for his master to call him to work.
    If a man likes to sleep or to sun, he
Will get plenty of rest, but he'll find there's a quirk:
    It pays off—but in trouble, not money.
(*Rapturously.*)
    I, who've never lazed a day, 45
    Now have found the means for a
    Life of lazing, if I like.
    On the sea this lucky strike
    Came my way. Who knows just what
    This contains—but it weighs a lot! 50
(*Excitedly.*)
Do you know what I think? That there's gold inside
    here!
    Not a soul knows about it but I.
Now's your chance, Gripus boy, to be free as a bird.
    Here's my plan, here's the scheme that I'll try.
I'll go up to the master, and, playing it smart, 55
    Make a very low bid for my head.
I'll keep upping the price till he lets me go free.
    Once I'm free of this life that I've led,
I'll go buy me a farm and a house and some slaves.
    I'll invest next in shipping, that's what. 60
I'll be rolling in money and known far and wide.
    Then I'll build me a luxury yacht,
(*Working himself up.*)
    And I'll do what the millionaires do,
    Take a round-the-world cruise, maybe two.
    When I get enough fame and renown, 65
    I'll erect a big fortified town,
(*Reaching his climax.*)
    A metropolis named Gripopolis,
    A memorial to Gripus, the hero renowned,
    The capital of a nation, one that I'll found!
(*Pauses for a moment transfixed, then comes to.*)
    I'm standing here with big ideas 70
      Of the things I'll do some day,
    When I'd better take this satchel here
      And hide it right away.
    And then, King Gripus, soon you'll munch
    The bread and beans you'll get for lunch! 75

(*As he starts walking toward the cottage,* TRACHALIO *enters, stage left, sees him and his catch—and immediately becomes extremely interested.*)

TRACHALIO (*calling*).
    Hey, wait.
GRIPUS (*suspiciously*).
    What for?
TRACHALIO (*casually reaching down to pick up the trailing rope, cheerily*).
    Your rope is dragging, see?
    I'll coil it up for you.
GRIPUS (*curtly*).
    Just let it be. 80
TRACHALIO (*holding on, brightly*).
    Please let me help. No matter what the
      cost,
    To do good folks good turns is never lost.
GRIPUS (*uneasily*).
    That windstorm yesterday just wouldn't end.
    Don't get ideas—I've got no fish, my friend.
    Why, can't you see I'm dragging back a net 85
    With nothing scaly in it, only wet?
TRACHALIO (*heartily*).
    It's not your fish I want, oh no indeed.
    Your charming conversation's what I need.
GRIPUS (*pulling on the net and trying to walk away*).
    You bore me to tears, whoever you are. Let go!
TRACHALIO (*pulling in the opposite direction and bringing him to a halt*).
    Now, *I'm* not letting you leave this place. So,
      whoa! 90
GRIPUS.
    Hey, what's the big idea of holding me
      back?
    You watch your step or that jaw will get a
      smack.
TRACHALIO.
    Now, listen here—
GRIPUS (*interrupting*).
    I won't.
TRACHALIO (*grimly*).
    You won't right now, 95
    But later on you'll listen, boy, and how!
GRIPUS (*trying, without much success, to sound indifferent*).
    Oh, speak your piece.
TRACHALIO.
    What I want to tell to you,
    You'll find well worth your while to listen to.
GRIPUS (*as before*).
    All right, start talking, you. What's on your
      mind? 100
TRACHALIO (*looking around warily*).
    First look and see if anyone's behind.

GRIPUS (*looks around and turns back; nervously*).
    Is it something to do, say, with me?
TRACHALIO.
    Well, of course! What I'm after, you see,
    Is your view on a matter in doubt.
GRIPUS.
    You just tell me what this is about.   **105**
TRACHALIO.
    Just keep quiet. You'll hear. But I must have fair
        play—
    Do you give me your word you won't give me
        away?
GRIPUS (*anxiously*).
    Whoever you are, here's my word. It's okay.
TRACHALIO (*confidentially*).
    Now then, listen. I happened to see
    A thief rob a man known to me.   **110**
    So I later go up to the crook,
    And I give him this deal, I say, "Look,
    As it happens, I know whom you robbed.
    He'll hear nothing about it at all
    If you'll hand over half of the haul."   **115**
    Now, I've not heard a word from him yet.
    Well, how much of a share should I get?
    I expect you'll say half. Am I right?
GRIPUS (*blurting*).
    God, I'd ask even more! You're all set:
    If he won't come across, don't think twice,   **120**
    Turn him in to his victim on sight!
TRACHALIO (*promptly*).
    Now I'm ready to use your advice.
    (*Pointing a finger at him.*)
    Listen carefully now. It's all true—
    And the crook it applies to is *you!*
GRIPUS (*startled*). What do you mean?   **125**
TRACHALIO.   That satchel there—I've known all along
    whose it is—
GRIPUS (*interrupting, defensively*). What are you talking
    about?
TRACHALIO   —and how it was lost.   **130**
GRIPUS (*heatedly*). But *I* know how it was found and *I* know
    who found it and *I* know who owns it now. What you
    know is none of my business, any more than what I know
    is yours. You know whose it used to be. I know whose it is
    now. (*Grimly.*) There isn't a man alive who can take   **135**
    it away from me, so don't get your hopes up that you can.
TRACHALIO.   You mean you won't give it up if the owner
    comes for it?
GRIPUS.   The owner? Make no mistake about it, my friend,
    there's only one man in this world who owns this   **140**
    thing—me. I caught it when I was fishing.
TRACHALIO.   You did, eh?
GRIPUS (*argumentatively*). You won't deny my right to the
    fish in the sea, will you? If, as, and when I catch any,

they're mine. I keep them; they're my property.   **145**
No one else lays a hand on them or puts in any claims for
any share. They're my goods and I sell them as such in
the fish market. The sea is absolutely public domain;
everybody shares it in common.
TRACHALIO (*promptly*). Agreed. So then, my friend,   **150**
why shouldn't I share this satchel in common? It came
from the sea—public domain, you know.
GRIPUS.   Don't be a wise guy. If the law was the way you
put it, fishermen would be finished. The minute any fish
went up for sale in the market, everyone would   **155**
start claiming a share; no one would buy a thing. Everyone'd say they were caught in the public domain.
TRACHALIO.   Who's the wise guy now? Compare a satchel
to a fish? What a nerve! Are you trying to tell me you
think they're the same?   **160**
GRIPUS (*shrugging*). That's no problem of mine. When I
throw over a net or a line, whatever gets caught there I
pull up. And what my nets or lines catch is mine, absolutely and positively mine.
TRACHALIO.   Oh, no, it isn't. Not if you pulled up   **165**
some pot, say.
GRIPUS (*scornfully*). What are you, a lawyer?
TRACHALIO.   Listen, you stinker, did you ever in your life
see a fisherman catch a satchel-fish or peddle one in the
market? You can't take over just any trade you   **170**
want, not by a long shot. Damn you, you want to be a
fisherman and a satchel-maker all in one. Either you show
me exactly how a satchel is a fish or you don't walk off
with something that doesn't have scales and certainly
wasn't born in salt water.   **175**
GRIPUS (*affecting incredulity*). What? You never heard of a
satchel-fish before?
TRACHALIO.   Cut it out. There's no such thing.
GRIPUS (*assuming the air of an expert*). Oh, yes there is.
I'm a fisherman, I know. But you don't often   **180**
catch them. Isn't a fish around landed less often.
TRACHALIO.   You're wasting your time. You can't kid me,
you crook. All right, what color is it?
GRIPUS (*as before, pointing to the satchel*). Very few are
like this one here. Some of them have a dark red   **185**
skin. Then there are some that are big and black.
TRACHALIO.   Oh, sure. (*Savagely.*) If you want my opin-
ion, you better watch out or you'll turn into a satchel-fish
yourself: that skin of yours is going to get dark red, and
then wind up black—and blue.   **190**
GRIPUS (*half to himself*). The god-damned trouble I had to
run into today!
TRACHALIO (*impatiently*). This argument's getting us nowhere. We're wasting time. Come on, my friend, who do
you want to pick as judge to settle this for us?   **195**
GRIPUS (*eying him balefully*). Judge? The satchel.
TRACHALIO.   Oh, yeah?
GRIPUS.   Yeah.
TRACHALIO (*exasperated*). God, you're stupid!

GRIPUS (*scornfully*). Well, listen to the professor!   **200**

TRACHALIO (*getting a firm grip on the rope*). You're not moving an inch with this thing today—not unless you agree to a third party to hold it or a judge to judge the matter.

GRIPUS.   Look here, are you in your right mind?   **205**

TRACHALIO (*scornfully*). I'm as mad as a hatter.

GRIPUS (*tightening his grip on the net*). Then I'm as crazy as a loon—but I'm not letting go.

TRACHALIO.   You say one more word and I'll sink my fists in your skull. You know what they do to a new   **210** sponge? If you don't let go, that's the way I'll squeeze the juice out of you.

GRIPUS.   You know how I slam the ink out of an octopus? You lay a finger on me and that's what I'll do to you. (*Sticking his chin in Trachalio's face.*) So you   **215** want to fight, eh?

TRACHALIO (*abruptly losing his belligerence*). Why do we have to fight? Why don't you and I just split the swag?

GRIPUS.   Don't get any ideas: the only thing you'll be able to get for yourself out of all this is a sock on the   **220** jaw. (*Starts pulling the net toward the cottage.*) I'm getting out of here.

TRACHALIO (*running ahead and yanking the rope so that the net—and* GRIPUS—*are spun about*). No, you're not getting out of here—I'm putting this ship about. You stay where you are.   **225**

GRIPUS (*between his teeth*). If you're going to play deck hand on this ship, I'll be skipper. (*Roaring.*) Damn you, let go that rope!

TRACHALIO.   Sure I'll let go. You let go that satchel.

GRIPUS.   By god, you're not going to get one   **230** single solitary square inch of this satchel.

TRACHALIO (*standing his ground*). You can't get around me just by saying no. Either you cut me in, or you put up security, or you let a judge decide.

GRIPUS.   What do you mean? Something *I* caught   **235** in the sea—

TRACHALIO (*interrupting*). But *I* saw it from the shore.

GRIPUS (*disregarding him*).—with my own hands, my own net, and my own boat?

TRACHALIO.   I saw you get it from the shore, right?   **240** So, if the owner should come along, then I'm in this thing just as deep as you are, I'm an accomplice, right?

GRIPUS.   Right.

TRACHALIO.   All right, you stinker, you just prove to me how I can be an accomplice and not be entitled   **245** to a cut. Come on, show me how!

GRIPUS (*baffled and confused*).   I don't know. I don't know anything about that legal stuff you city boys do. All I say is that this satchel is mine.

TRACHALIO.   And I say it's mine.   **250**

GRIPUS (*switching suddenly to affability*). Wait a second. I just figured out how you don't have to be an accomplice—or get a cut.

TRACHALIO.   Yeah? How?

GRIPUS.   First you let me leave here. Then you go   **255** your own way—and keep your mouth shut. You don't say a word about me to anybody—and I don't give you anything. You stay mum, and I keep my trap shut. That's the fairest and squarest way to do it.

TRACHALIO.   You mean you're not going to offer   **260** me a deal?

GRIPUS (*promptly*). I already did: that you let go that rope, go away, and stop bothering me.

TRACHALIO.   Wait a second. I've got a counteroffer to make.   **265**

GRIPUS.   Yeah? Well offer to get the hell out of here.

TRACHALIO (*disregarding the last remark, with elaborate casualness*). Do you know anybody hereabouts?

GRIPUS (*evasively*). My own neighbors, naturally.

TRACHALIO (*as before*). Whereabouts do you live?

GRIPUS (*waving vaguely*). Farther on. Lots farther   **270** on. 'Way off at the end of those fields out there.

TRACHALIO (*concealing his satisfaction at the answer, even more casually than before*). How'd you like the fellow who lives in this cottage to be judge?

GRIPUS (*concealing his satisfaction at the suggestion*). Suppose you give me a little slack on that rope so I   **275** can step off to the side and think it over?

TRACHALIO.   Sure. (*Slacks off the rope, letting* GRIPUS *lug the net a few feet off to the side.*)

GRIPUS (*to the audience, jubilantly*). Hooray! I'm in! The swag's mine for keeps. He's inviting me to call in my own master as judge, right here on my own home   **280** grounds. Good old Daemones wouldn't judge anyone in his household out of a penny. This fellow here has no idea what kind of deal he's offering me. Sure I'll take a judge!

TRACHALIO.   Well, what do you say?

GRIPUS (*as if grudgingly*). Even though I know for   **285** sure that by rights this thing is mine, rather than have a fight with you, I'll do it your way.

TRACHALIO (*heartily*). That's what I like to hear.

GRIPUS (*as before*). And even though you're bringing me up before a judge I don't know, if he turns out   **290** honest, I may not know him but I want to; if he doesn't, I may know him but he's the last man in the world I want to. (*The door of the cottage opens and* DAEMONES *and the two girls come out.*)

DAEMONES (*to the girls*). Much as I want to do what you want me to, girls, I'm afraid that wife of mine   **295** will kick me out of the house on account of you. She'll say I'm bringing in a pair of mistresses right under her nose. I'd rather have you two running to that altar for help than me.

PALAESTRA.   Oh, my god! This is the end!   **300**

DAEMONES (*reassuringly*). Don't be afraid. I'll make sure you're safe. (*Noticing that the two slaves with the clubs are tagging along after the girls.*) What are you following them outside for? No one's going to hurt them with me

around. All right, guards, off guard and into the **305**
house, both of you. (*They go back into the cottage.*)

GRIPUS.   Hello, master.

DAEMONES.   Why, Gripus! Hello! How did things go?

TRACHALIO (*startled, to* DAEMONES). Is he your servant?

GRIPUS (*grinning*). His servant, and proud of it.   **310**

TRACHALIO (*glaring at him*). I've got nothing to say to you.

GRIPUS.   Yeah? Then get out of here.

TRACHALIO (*to* DAEMONES). Please, mister, tell me: is he your servant?

DAEMONES.   Yes, he is.   **315**

TRACHALIO (*jubilantly*). Oh, boy! If he's yours, that's the best thing that could have happened! I'll say it for the second time today: I'm mighty glad to meet you.

DAEMONES (*cordially*). Glad to meet you too. Aren't you the one who left here to get your master a little **320** while ago?

TRACHALIO.   I'm the one.

DAEMONES.   Well, what can we do for you?

TRACHALIO.   So he's yours, eh?

DAEMONES.   Yes, he is.   **325**

TRACHALIO (*grinning broadly*). If he's yours, that's the best thing that could have happened.

DAEMONES.   What's this all about?

TRACHALIO (*pointing to* GRIPUS, *vehemently*). That devil there is a damned crook!   **330**

DAEMONES (*patiently*). And just what has the "damned crook" done to you?

TRACHALIO.   I want him drawn and quartered!

DAEMONES.   Now what is this you two are making such a case about?   **335**

TRACHALIO.   I'll tell you.

GRIPUS (*quickly*). Oh, no you don't. I'll tell him.

TRACHALIO (*with elaborate formality*). If I'm not mistaken, I have the right to open this action.

GRIPUS.   If you had any decency, you'd get into **340** action and get out of here.

DAEMONES (*sharply*). Gripus! Shut up and listen.

GRIPUS (*unbelievingly*). You mean he's going to speak first?

DAEMONES (*nodding curtly*). You listen. (*To* TRACHALIO.) And you start talking.   **345**

GRIPUS (*as before*). You're going to let an outsider talk ahead of one of your own household?

TRACHALIO (*eying him balefully*). Isn't there any way to handle this fellow? (*Turning to* DAEMONES.) What I started to tell you was this. Remember that pimp **350** you kicked out of the temple? Well, this fellow has his satchel. (*Pointing.*) See? There it is.

GRIPUS (*trying to edge in front of the net*). I haven't got it.

TRACHALIO.   What do you mean you haven't got it? I'm not blind.   **355**

GRIPUS (*aside*). I only wish you were! (*To* TRACHALIO.) I have it, I don't have it—what are you sticking your nose into my affairs for?

TRACHALIO (*doggedly*). What's more important is how you got it, whether legally or illegally.   **360**

GRIPUS (*to* DAEMONES, *heatedly*). You can string me up by the neck this minute if I didn't find this satchel while I was fishing. (*To* TRACHALIO.) And if I fished it up from the sea with my own net, how do you figure it's yours instead of mine?   **365**

TRACHALIO (*to* DAEMONES). He's trying to pull the wool over your eyes. What I just told you are the facts.

GRIPUS (*menacingly*). What did I hear you say?

TRACHALIO (*to* DAEMONES). He's yours, isn't he? Can't you handle him somehow? Get him to shut up until **370** his betters finish speaking?

GRIPUS (*leering and making an obscene gesture*). So you want me to get what your master gives you, eh? Well, yours may "handle" you, all right, but ours doesn't pull that stuff with us.   **375**

DAEMONES (*to* TRACHALIO, *smiling*). He got the better of you there, my boy. Now, what is it you want? Speak up.

TRACHALIO.   For myself, nothing. I don't want any part of that satchel there, and I never once said it was mine. But there's a little jewel box in it that belongs to this **380** girl here (*gesturing toward* PALAESTRA). She's the one I was telling you earlier was no slave.

DAEMONES (*nodding*). You mean the one you said came from the same city I did?

TRACHALIO.   Exactly. Well, the birth tokens she **385** wore when she was a child are there in that box, and the box is there in that satchel. (*Nodding scornfully in Gripus' direction.*) It's no earthly use to him, but he'll be doing this poor girl a real service if he gives her the only means she has for finding her parents.   **390**

DAEMONES.   Say no more. I'll have him hand it over.

GRIPUS.   So help me, I'm not giving him a thing!

TRACHALIO (*to* DAEMONES). All I'm asking for is the jewel box and birth tokens.

GRIPUS.   Oh, yeah? What if they're gold?   **395**

TRACHALIO.   What difference should that make to you? (*Loftily.*) Any gold or silver will be bought and paid for in cash.

GRIPUS.   All right, my friend, you let me see that cash and I'll let you see the box.   **400**

DAEMONES.   Gripus, shut up or you'll be sorry. (*To* TRACHALIO.) Finish what you started to say.

TRACHALIO (*earnestly*). I have just one favor to ask of you: have pity on this girl—I mean, if the satchel really is that pimp's, as I suspect it is. (*Pointedly.*) You see, at **405** this moment I can't say anything for sure, I can only guess.

GRIPUS (*to* DAEMONES, *excitedly*). Don't you see? That good-for-nothing's trying to lay a trap for us!

TRACHALIO (*to* GRIPUS). Will you let me finish **410** talking? (*To* DAEMONES.) I say the satchel belongs to that filthy pimp. Now, if it does, the girls will be able to recognize it. So will you please make him show it to them?

GRIPUS (*spluttering*). What's that? Show it to them?

DAEMONES (*mildly*). There's nothing wrong with **415** his suggestion, is there, Gripus? Just to show it to them?

GRIPUS (*roaring*). I should say there is! A hell of a lot wrong!

DAEMONES.   How so?

GRIPUS.   Because the minute I show it to them, **420** naturally they'll say they recognize it.

TRACHALIO (*heatedly*). Damn you, you think everybody's as big a liar as you are!

GRIPUS (*gesturing toward* DAEMONES). So long as he's on my side, you can say anything you like; it won't **425** bother me in the least.

TRACHALIO.   He may be standing on your side, but he's going to take his testimony from this side. (*Pointing to the girls.*)

DAEMONES (*sharply*). Gripus, you listen. (*To* TRACHALIO.) And you explain what you want—and make it **430** short.

TRACHALIO (*patiently*). I already did. But if you didn't follow me, I'll do it again. As I've already told you, neither of these girls should be slaves. (*Gesturing toward* PALAESTRA.) This one here was kidnaped from **435** Athens when she was a child.

GRIPUS.   Suppose you explain to me just what their being slaves or not has to do with this satchel?

TRACHALIO (*angrily*). Damn you, you want me to tell the story all over again just to waste the whole day. **440**

DAEMONES (*to* TRACHALIO, *sharply*). Cut out the cursing and do what I asked you.

TRACHALIO.   It's just as I told you before. There should be a little jewel box in that satchel. It contains the birth tokens she can use to identify her parents. She **445** was wearing them when she was snatched from Athens as a child.

GRIPUS (*savagely*). I wish to god someone'd put the snatch on you! What the hell's going on here? (*Gesturing angrily toward the girls.*) What's the matter with them? **450** Are they dumb? Can't they talk for themselves?

TRACHALIO.   Sure. But they're keeping quiet because they know that's what makes a good woman—knowing how to keep quiet and not talk.

GRIPUS.   So help me, by that token you don't make **455** either a good man or a good woman.

TRACHALIO.   Why?

GRIPUS.   Because you're no good whether you talk or keep quiet. (*To* DAEMONES.)   Please! Am I going to get a chance to speak today? **460**

DAEMONES (*turning on him*). One more word out of you today and I'll have your head!

TRACHALIO (*to* DAEMONES). As I was saying, would you please make him give the box back to the girls? If he insists on some sort of reward, he can have one: **465** let him keep whatever else is in the satchel for himself.

GRIPUS.   Finally you said it! And you know why? Because you know very well what my rights in the matter are. A few minutes ago you were out to get half for yourself.

TRACHALIO.   You know what? I still am. **470**

GRIPUS.   I once saw a vulture out to get something, and you know what? He didn't get away with a thing.

DAEMONES (*to* GRIPUS, *angrily*). Do you need a beating to keep you quiet?

GRIPUS (*stubbornly*). If he shuts up, I'll shut up. But **475** if he's going to talk, let me talk too, and give my side of the story.

DAEMONES.   Gripus, hand me that satchel.

GRIPUS.   I'll trust you with it if you promise that, if there's nothing of theirs in it, I get it back. **480**

DAEMONES.   You'll get it back.

GRIPUS (*taking the satchel out of the net and handing it over*). Here it is.

DAEMONES.   Now, Palaestra, and you too, Ampelisca, listen to me. Is this the satchel you say has your box in it? **485**

PALAESTRA (*without hesitation*). Yes, it is.

GRIPUS.   Oh, my god in heaven, I haven't got a chance! She said it was hers before she even got a good look at it!

PALAESTRA (*earnestly*). I know it's confusing, so let **490** me clear things up for you. There should be a little wicker box in that satchel. Now, without your showing me a thing, I'll name every article that's in it. If I make a mistake, then I've wasted my breath and you people keep whatever's in there for yourselves. But if I don't, **495** then please, please let me have my things back.

DAEMONES.   Agreed. In my opinion, what you're asking for is plain and simple justice.

GRIPUS.   And in mine, damn it all, plain and simple injustice. Supposing she's a witch or a fortuneteller **500** and reels off the name of whatever's in there perfectly? Are we going to let some fortuneteller walk off with everything?

DAEMONES (*sharply*). She's not walking off with a thing unless she names every item without a mistake. **505** Fortunetelling won't get her anywhere. Now, unstrap that satchel so that I can find out who's right and who's wrong without wasting another minute.

TRACHALIO (*watching* GRIPUS *unstrap the satchel, aside with satisfaction*). And that settles *his* hash.

GRIPUS (*to* Daemones). The straps are off. **510**

DAEMONES.   Now open it.

PALAESTRA (*excitedly*). I see the box!

DAEMONES (*taking it out and holding it*). Is this it?

PALAESTRA.   That's it! (*Extending her hand and touching it almost caressingly, to herself.*) Dear parents, all **515** I have of you I carry locked up here. Here are stored all my hopes, the only means I have of ever finding you.

GRIPUS (*to himself, growling*). You deserve the wrath of god on your head, whoever you are, for squeezing your parents into something that small.   **520**

DAEMONES (*pointing to a spot at his side*). Gripus, you stand here; this concerns you now. (*To* PALAESTRA.) You stand over there and call off all the things in the box and tell us what each looks like. Mind you, don't leave anything out. And, believe me, if you make the   **525** slightest mistake, don't get any ideas about correcting it later. It'll be a sheer waste of time, my girl. (PALAESTRA *nods and steps a few paces away.*)

GRIPUS (*nodding approvingly*). You're asking only for what's fair.

TRACHALIO.   God knows he wouldn't ask anything   **530** like that of you. You don't know what it is to be fair.

DAEMONES (*to* PALAESTRA). All right, my girl, you can start now. (*As* GRIPUS *opens his mouth.*) Gripus! Shut up and pay attention.

PALAESTRA (*with her back to* DAEMONES *and* GRIPUS). The box has my birth tokens.   **535**

DAEMONES (*holding the box open before him*). I see them.

GRIPUS (*to himself*). Knocked out in the first round! (*Grabbing Daemones' arm to bring the box closer to his chest.*) Wait a second! Don't show them to her!

DAEMONES.   Now tell me what each one of them looks like.   **540**

PALAESTRA.   First there's a miniature gold sword. It's inscribed.

DAEMONES.   What's the inscription say?

PALAESTRA.   My father's name. Next, alongside the sword is a miniature two-headed ax, also of gold and   **545** inscribed; this time it's my mother's name.

DAEMONES.   Wait a second. What is your father's name? I mean the one on the sword?

PALAESTRA.   Daemones.

(DAEMONES *holds the trinket in his hand and stares at the letters in amazement. Slowly he lifts his head to look toward the sky.*)

DAEMONES (*to himself, hoarsely*). God in heaven!   **550** What is happening to all my hopes!

GRIPUS (*aside*). You mean what's happening to all mine!

TRACHALIO (*to* PALAESTRA *and* DAEMONES, *eagerly*). Please! Go on, don't stop!

GRIPUS (*turning on him*). Either you take it easy or   **555** go straight to hell!

DAEMONES (*in a voice so full of emotion it is barely audible*). Tell me, what's the name on the little ax, your mother's name?

PALAESTRA. Daedalis.

DAEMONES (*to himself, choking with emotion*). It   **560** was heaven's will to rescue me!

GRIPUS (*aside*). And throw me overboard!

DAEMONES (*sotto voce to* GRIPUS). Gripus! This girl! She must be my daughter!

GRIPUS (*not exactly overcome by the news, sotto voce*). It's all right with me. (*Looking toward* TRA-   **565** CHALIO, *under his breath.*) God damn you to hell for having gotten a look at me today—and me for being damned fool enough not to have looked around a hundred times to make sure no one was watching before I pulled that net out of the water!   **570**

PALAESTRA (*unaware of the excitement she is causing*). Next a miniature silver sickle, and two clasped hands, and a miniature windlass—

GRIPUS (*aside*). Windlass? I wish to hell you were windless.

PALAESTRA.   —and a gold medallion my father   **575** gave me on my birthday.

DAEMONES (*to himself, ecstatically*). It's she! I must take her in my arms! (*Rushing to her and taking her hands.*) My daughter! I'm your own father! I'm Daemones! Daedalis—your mother—is right inside!   **580**

PALAESTRA (*throwing herself into his arms*). Oh, my father, my father! Who ever imagined this could happen!

DAEMONES (*holding her tightly*). What a joy it is to have you in my arms!

TRACHALIO (*beaming on them*). It's a joy to see   **585** how heaven has rewarded you both for being as good as you are.

DAEMONES.   Trachalio, pick up the satchel if you can and bring it inside. Hurry!

TRACHALIO (*to* GRIPUS, *grinning broadly*). See   **590** where all your dirty tricks got you? My heartiest congratulations on your bad luck.

DAEMONES (*to* PALAESTRA). Come, my daughter, let's go in to your mother. She'll be able to test you further about all this. She used to be with you more, and she's   **595** more familiar with these trinkets of yours.

PALAESTRA.   Let's all go in. Then we can do it all together. (*Turning to* AMPELISCA.) Follow me, Ampelisca.

AMPELISCA (*tearfully*). I'm so happy that god has been so good to you!   **600**

(DAEMONES, TRACHALIO, *and the two girls enter the cottage.*)

GRIPUS (*to himself*). Why the hell did I have to fish that satchel up today? Or, rather, why the hell didn't I stash it away in a safe spot after I fished it up? So help me, it was so rough out there when I found the thing, I knew I'd have a rough time with it. God, I'll bet that satchel's   **605** full of money. The best thing for me to do now is just sneak off and hang myself—at least for a while until the ache goes away! (*Exits, stage right.*)

(*The door of the cottage opens and* DAEMONES *emerges. He is radiant. He walks downstage and addresses the audience.*)

DAEMONES.   I swear I'm the luckiest man in the world! Suddenly, like a bolt from the blue, I found my   **610** daughter. (*Shaking his head wonderingly.*) You know, when heaven wants to do well by a man, somehow he ends up getting his fondest wish—if he's been decent and god-fearing. Take me—today, like a bolt from the blue, I found my daughter, something I had given up 615 hoping for, no longer believed could happen. And I'm going to marry her to a fine young fellow from one of the best families in Athens. What's more, I find that he's a relative of mine. I want him to come out here and see me just as soon as possible, so I've told his servant 620 to step outside; I want to send him to town right away. (*Looking toward the door.*) He hasn't come out yet. I wonder what's keeping him? I think I'd better take a look inside. (*Walks back to the entrance and peers in.*) What's this? My wife hanging on to my daughter's neck? 625 All this hugging and loving is getting to be a silly nuisance. (*Calling through the doorway.*) My dear wife, it's time to stop the kissing and start getting things ready for me. As soon as I come in I want to give a thank offering to our guardian angel for having added to our 630 family the way he has. The lambs and pigs for the sacrifice are all ready. (*Impatiently.*) What are you women keeping Trachalio for? (*Stepping back from the door.*) Good. He's coming out now.

TRACHALIO (*as he hurries out the door, breathlessly*). I don't care where he is, I'll track him down and 635 bring him back here with me. Plesidippus, I mean.

DAEMONES (*nodding approval*). And tell him what happened about my daughter. Ask him to drop everything and come right out here.

TRACHALIO. Right. 640

DAEMONES. Tell him he has my permission to marry her.

TRACHALIO. Right.

DAEMONES. And that I know his father; he's a relative of mine.

TRACHALIO. Right. 645

DAEMONES. And hurry.

TRACHALIO. Right.

DAEMONES. Bring him here right away, so we can start preparing dinner.

TRACHALIO. Right. 650

DAEMONES (*somewhat irritated*). Everything I say is "right," eh?

TRACHALIO. Right. But do you know what I'd like from you? That you remember the promise you made about my getting my freedom today. 655

DAEMONES. Right.

TRACHALIO. You get Plesidippus to agree to set me free.

DAEMONES. Right.

TRACHALIO. And get your daughter to ask him; she'll get it out of him without any trouble. 660

DAEMONES. Right.

TRACHALIO. And arrange to have Ampelisca marry me as soon as I'm free.

DAEMONES. Right.

TRACHALIO. I want to see some tangible appre- 665 ciation for all I've done for you.

DAEMONES. Right.

TRACHALIO. Everything I say is "right," eh?

DAEMONES. Right—I'm just returning the favor. Now, off to the city this minute, on the double, and then 670 come back here.

TRACHALIO. Right. I won't take long. In the meantime you get everything ready that we need.

DAEMONES. Right. (*To himself as* TRACHALIO *dashes off, stage left.*) The devil take him with his "rights"! 675 My ears are ringing: whatever I said, it was nothing but "right," "right," "right."

(*Enter* GRIPUS, *stage right.*)

GRIPUS (*determinedly*). Daemones, when will it be all right to have a word with you?

DAEMONES (*wincing at still another "right"*). What's 680 on your mind, Gripus?

GRIPUS. It's about that satchel. If you've got any sense, you'll have the sense to hold onto something heaven's dropped right in your lap.

DAEMONES (*reproachfully*). Do you think it's right 685 for me to claim somebody else's property as my own?

GRIPUS (*exasperated*). But it's something I found in the sea!

DAEMONES. So much the better for the man who lost it. But that doesn't make it any more your satchel.

GRIPUS (*disgustedly*). That's why you're so poor. 690 It's that sanctified goodness of yours.

DAEMONES (*gently*). Gripus, Gripus, there are so many traps set for men during their lifetime to trick and fool them! What's more, the traps are often baited; if a man's avaricious and goes after the bait greedily, he gets 695 trapped by his own greed. The man who's careful and experienced and astute in watching his step can live a long and honest life on what he's honestly earned. If you ask me, this prize you're so wedded to will fall prize to its owner—and the divorce will cost us money. (*In* 700 *shocked tones.*) I hide something brought to me that I know isn't mine? None of that for your old master Daemones, no, sir! The one thing any man of intelligence is always on guard against is consciously taking part in wrongdoing. I'll have nothing whatsoever to do 705 with making any gains by collusion.

GRIPUS (*eying him pityingly*). I've often seen actors in a play deliver themselves of gems of wisdom of this sort—and seen them get a round of applause for having mouthed for the audience all these rules of good behavior. 710 Then, when the audience left and everybody was back in his own home, there wasn't a one who behaved the way he had been told to.

DAEMONES (*impatiently*). Oh, go inside and stop bothering me. And watch that tongue of yours. Make no 715 mistake about it—I'm not going to give you a thing.

(GRIPUS, *without a word, marches up to the door, opens it, then turns to deliver a parting shot.*)

GRIPUS (*bitterly*). I hope to god whatever's in that satchel—gold or silver or what not—turns into ashes! (*Ducks into the cottage, slamming the door.*)

DAEMONES (*to the audience, shaking his head sadly*). See that attitude? That's the reason we have such bad   **720** servants. Now if that Gripus of mine had gotten together with some other servant, he'd have involved the two of them in grand larceny. He'd have been thinking he had his hands on a prize, and he'd have turned out to be the prize himself. What he caught would have caught   **725** him. Well, I'll go in now and attend to the offering. And then I'll give orders to have dinner ready immediately.

(DAEMONES *goes into the cottage. A moment later* TRA-CHALIO *and* PLESIDIPPUS *enter, stage left. One glance at the latter is enough to reveal that he has gotten the news.*)

PLESIDIPPUS (*ecstatically*). Trachalio, my friend, my freed-man-to-be, no, my patron—more than that, the founder of my household! Tell me that whole story over   **730** again. So Palaestra found her mother and father?

TRACHALIO (*smiling indulgently*). Yes, she did.

PLESIDIPPUS.   And she's an Athenian like me?

TRACHALIO.   I think so.

PLESIDIPPUS.   And she's going to marry me?   **735**

TRACHALIO.   I suspect so.

PLESIDIPPUS.   What do you think, will we become engaged today?

TRACHALIO (*pretending, indulgently, to be under formal interrogation*). Yes, Mr. Chairman.

PLESIDIPPUS.   What do you say, should I congrat-   **740** ulate her father on having found her?

TRACHALIO.   Yes, Mr. Chairman.

PLESIDIPPUS.   How about her mother?

TRACHALIO.   Yes, Mr. Chairman.

PLESIDIPPUS.   Have you anything to tell the chair?   **745**

TRACHALIO.   Yes, Mr. Chairman: yes to whatever the chair asks.

PLESIDIPPUS (*slyly*). All right, can you estimate the chair's net worth?

TRACHALIO (*taken aback*). Me? (*Recovering.*) Yes,   **750** Mr. Chairman—

PLESIDIPPUS (*interrupting*). Look, I'm standing; forget about this "chair" business.

TRACHALIO.   Yes, Mr. Chairman.

PLESIDIPPUS.   Should I rush up to her?   **755**

TRACHALIO.   Yes, Mr. Chairman.

PLESIDIPPUS.   Or should I go up to her quietly, like this? (*Demonstrates.*)

TRACHALIO.   Yes, Mr. Chairman.

PLESIDIPPUS.   Should I shake her hand when I go up to her?

TRACHALIO.   Yes, Mr. Chairman.   **760**

PLESIDIPPUS.   Her father's too?

TRACHALIO.   Yes, Mr. Chairman.

PLESIDIPPUS.   And then her mother's?

TRACHALIO.   Yes, Mr. Chairman.

PLESIDIPPUS.   Should I embrace her father when I   **765** go up to him?

TRACHALIO.   No, Mr. Chairman.

PLESIDIPPUS.   How about her mother?

TRACHALIO.   No, Mr. Chairman.

PLESIDIPPUS (*eagerly*). How about her?   **770**

TRACHALIO.   No, Mr. Chairman. (*Starts walking toward the cottage.*)

PLESIDIPPUS.   Oh, lord! He votes Nay just when I want Aye—and walks out on the meeting.

TRACHALIO (*calling*). You're crazy. Come on!

PLESIDIPPUS.   Lead on, my patron, whither thou will.   **775**

(*The two enter the cottage, and the stage is now empty.*)

ACT FIVE

(*Enter* LABRAX, *stage left.*)

LABRAX (*to the audience*). Is there another man alive right now who's worse off than I am? I've just come from court; Plesidippus got them to condemn me and they made me give Palaestra up. I'm ruined! (*Bitterly.*) If you ask me, pimps were put on this earth just to make people   **5** laugh—that's the way it looks, judging from the general hilarity whenever a poor pimp has to suffer. (*Turning and walking toward the shrine.*) I'm going to see to that other girl of mine in the shrine here. At least I'll take her away with me—the only remnant left of all my property.   **10**

(*The door of the cottage opens and* GRIPUS *comes out. He is holding a spit encrusted with rust—eloquent testimony as to how long it's been since* DAEMONES *last held a party. He turns to speak to those inside.*)

GRIPUS (*through the doorway*). By god, you're not going to lay eyes on me alive after tonight—unless I get that satchel back!

LABRAX (*to himself*). Oh, god! Whenever I hear anyone mention a satchel, it's like the stab of a sword through   **15** my heart.

GRIPUS (*as before*). That damned Trachalio gets his freedom and you refuse to give a single thing to the man who fished the satchel up in his net!

LABRAX (*his attention arrested, to himself*). So help   **20** me, what this fellow is saying sounds very, very interesting.

GRIPUS (*as before*). I'm going right out and post notices everywhere in letters a foot and a half high: "Found. One satchel full of gold and silver. For information see   **25** Gripus." You think you're going to get away with my satchel, don't you? Well, you're not.

LABRAX (*to himself*). By god, I think this fellow knows who has my satchel! I'd better have a talk with him. Lord in heaven, help me now!   **30**

GRIPUS (*as someone calls him to come back inside*). What are you calling me back for? I want to clean this outside here. (*Turns away from the door and starts scraping the spit; to himself.*) My god! You'd think this spit's made of rust instead of iron. The more I scrape it, the redder **35** and skinnier it gets. I think there's a curse on it: the thing's dying of old age right in my hands.

LABRAX (*in his most affable manner*). Hello there.

GRIPUS (*eying him distastefully*). Hello yourself, dirty face.

LABRAX (*as before*). What are you doing with yourself **40** these days?

GRIPUS (*scraping away industriously*). Cleaning a spit.

LABRAX.   Business good around here?

GRIPUS.   What's it to you? You a broker?

LABRAX.   Oh, no. I'm one letter short of that.   **45**

GRIPUS.   Broke, eh?

LABRAX.   You hit the nail on the head.

GRIPUS.   I know. You look it. What happened to you?

LABRAX.   My ship was wrecked last night. Lost everything I had in it.   **50**

GRIPUS.   What did you lose?

LABRAX (*pointedly*). A satchel full of gold and silver.

GRIPUS (*his attention caught*). Do you remember any of the things in this satchel you lost?

LABRAX (*evasively*). What difference does it make?   **55** It's lost, isn't it? Forget it. Let's talk about something else.

GRIPUS.   What if I know who found it? I just want to see if you can prove it's your property.

LABRAX.   Well, there were eight hundred gold pieces **60** in a pouch. Then another hundred gold eagles in a separate leather sack.

GRIPUS (*aside*). God almighty, what a haul! I'm in for a fat reward. There is a providence after all: I'm going to get a load of loot out of this fellow. It's his satchel, no **65** question about it. (*To* LABRAX.) Go on, tell me what else was in it.

LABRAX.   Thirty thousand dollars in silver in a sack, all good coin. And some silverware—a bowl, a bucket, a pitcher, a jug, and a cup.   **70**

GRIPUS.   Wow! That's quite a fortune you had there.

LABRAX.   I "had"; now I don't have a thing. Saddest and worst word in the language, "had."

GRIPUS (*eying him narrowly*). What are you willing to pay the fellow who brings you information about its **75** whereabouts? (*As* LABRAX *hesitates.*) Come on, speak up!

LABRAX.   Fifteen hundred dollars.

GRIPUS (*snorting*). Stop kidding.

LABRAX.   Two thousand.

GRIPUS.   That's a laugh.   **80**

LABRAX.   Two thousand, five hundred.

GRIPUS.   Peanuts.

LABRAX.   Three thousand.

GRIPUS.   Chicken feed.

LABRAX.   I'll give you three thousand, five hundred.   **85**

GRIPUS.   What's the matter? Your mouth hot and you want to air it out?

LABRAX.   I'll give you five thousand dollars.

GRIPUS.   Wake up.

LABRAX.   Not another cent.   **90**

GRIPUS.   All right then, beat it!

LABRAX.   Listen—

GRIPUS (*heading for the door*). Once I leave here, my friend, I'm gone for good.

LABRAX.   Will you take five thousand, five hundred?   **95**

GRIPUS (*walking away*). You're dreaming.

LABRAX (*calling after him*). Name your price.

GRIPUS (*stopping*). Fifteen thousand dollars and you don't have to give me a penny more. But not a penny less! That's it; take it or leave it.   **100**

LABRAX (*shrugging*). What can I say? I've got to take it. All right, I'll give you fifteen thousand.

GRIPUS (*walking over to the altar*). Come on over here; I want Venus to be a party to this deal.

LABRAX (*following him*). Anything you want; just **105** tell me what it is.

GRIPUS.   Put your hand on this altar.

LABRAX.   It's on.

GRIPUS (*grimly*). You've got to swear by Venus here.

LABRAX.   What should I swear?   **110**

GRIPUS.   What I tell you to.

LABRAX.   You say it; I'll swear it. (*Aside, sardonically.*) The old master being told what to swear!

GRIPUS.   Got hold of the altar?

LABRAX.   Right.   **115**

GRIPUS.   Give me your solemn oath you'll pay me the money the day you get your satchel back.

LABRAX.   So be it. (*Raising his eyes to heaven and intoning.*) I solemnly swear in the name of Venus of Cyrene that, if I find the satchel I lost in the shipwreck **120** and regain possession of it with the gold and silver safe inside, I will pay to this man—

GRIPUS (*interrupting*). Say "I will pay to this man Gripus" and touch me at the same time.

LABRAX (*sardonically*). To make it absolutely clear **125** to you, Venus, I will pay to this man Gripus fifteen thousand dollars on the spot.

GRIPUS.   Now say that, if you should welsh, Venus should ruin your body, your soul, and your business. (*Aside.*) And once you've done swearing it, I hope she does it **130** to you anyway.

LABRAX (*intoning*). If I go back on anything I have sworn, may all pimps suffer a life of misery.

GRIPUS.   Don't worry, that'll happen even if you keep your word. (*Walking toward the door.*) You wait there. **135** I'll bring the old man outside right away. As soon as I do, you ask him for your satchel. (*Hurries into the cottage.*)

LABRAX (*looking after him scornfully, to himself*). Even if he gets the satchel back for me, I don't owe him a dime. *I'm the one who decides what I do about what I swear.*   **140** (*The door opens and* GRIPUS *and* DAEMONES *come out lugging the satchel.*) Here he comes with the old man. I'd better shut up.

GRIPUS (*to* DAEMONES). Follow me. This way.

DAEMONES.   Where is that pimp of yours?

GRIPUS (*calling to* LABRAX). Hey, you! (*Pointing*   **145** *to Daemones.*) Here he is. This fellow's got your satchel.

DAEMONES (*to* LABRAX). Yes, I have it and I don't mind telling you that I do. What's more, if it's yours, you're welcome to it. You'll find everything that was in it still there, safe and sound. Here, take it if it's yours.   **150**

LABRAX (*unable to believe his eyes*). Well, what do you know! My satchel! (*Going up to it and fingering it lovingly.*) Greetings, old satchel, greetings!

DAEMONES.   Is it yours?

LABRAX (*getting a firm grip on it*). What a question!   **155** I don't care if it belonged to god almighty himself; it's mine now.

DAEMONES.   Everything in it is safe and sound—with one exception: I took out a little box of trinkets I used in finding my daughter today.   **160**

LABRAX.   Who's that?

DAEMONES.   Palaestra, the girl you used to own. I found out she's my daughter.

LABRAX (*assuming his heartiest manner*). Well, that's just fine! Things have turned out beautifully for you.   **165** Just what you hoped for. I'm delighted.

DAEMONES (*dryly*). I find it a little hard to believe that.

LABRAX (*as before*). It's the god's honest truth. (*Slyly.*) And just to prove my feelings are genuine, you don't have to pay me a cent for her. She's a gift.   **170**

DAEMONES (*as before*). So kind of you.

LABRAX.   Oh, no, nothing at all, really.

GRIPUS (*pointedly*). All right you, you have your satchel now.

LABRAX.   That's right.   **175**

GRIPUS.   Well, let's get on with it.

LABRAX (*producing his blankest look*). Get on with what?

GRIPUS.   Paying me my money.

LABRAX.   I'm not paying you any money. I don't owe you a cent.   **180**

GRIPUS.   Hey, what's going on here! (*Disbelievingly.*) You don't owe me a cent?

LABRAX.   That's right. Not a cent.

GRIPUS.   But you gave me your oath.

LABRAX (*blandly*). I know I did. I'll give you another   **185** right now if I feel like it. This oath business is strictly for holding on to property, not letting it go.

GRIPUS (*shouting*). You hand over that fifteen thousand dollars, you dirty liar!

DAEMONES (*to* GRIPUS). Gripus, what's this fifteen   **190** thousand you're asking him for?

GRIPUS.   He gave me his oath he'd pay it to me.

LABRAX (*to* GRIPUS, *as before*). I get fun out of giving oaths. What are you, the chief justice? Going to try me for perjury?   **195**

DAEMONES (*to* GRIPUS). What did he promise you the money for?

GRIPUS.   He swore he'd give me fifteen thousand dollars if I got his satchel back for him.

LABRAX (*to* GRIPUS, *scornfully*). Pick some free man   **200** to represent you and let's go to court. (*Grinning.*) I'll prove you made me a party to a fraudulent contract, (*the grin widening*) and that I'm still a minor.

GRIPUS (*pointing to* DAEMONES). He'll represent me.

LABRAX (*losing his grin*). No. You'll have to get   **205** someone else.

DAEMONES (*to* LABRAX, *firmly*). I'm not going to let you take a penny away from this boy—unless I find he's done something wrong. Now then, did you promise him the money?   **210**

LABRAX (*unabashed*). Sure I did.

DAEMONES (*promptly*). What you promised a servant of mine is by rights mine. (*As Labrax opens his mouth.*) Don't get the idea you can pull any of your pimp's tricks on me; you won't get away with it.   **215**

GRIPUS (*to* LABRAX, *jubilantly*). So you thought you had gotten your hands on some poor devil you could swindle, eh? You'll pay—and in good money, too. And the minute I get it I'm giving it to this man here (*pointing to Daemones*) to pay for my freedom.   **220**

DAEMONES (*to* LABRAX, reproachfully). When you think of how well I've treated you and that it was all because of me this money was kept safe for you—

GRIPUS (*interrupting angrily*). None of that—all because of me, not you.   **225**

DAEMONES (*turning on him*). If you've got any brains, you'll keep your mouth shut! (*To* LABRAX.)—the least you could do is act decently and reciprocate for all I've done for you.

LABRAX (*softened by Daemones' conciliatory tone*). I   **230** take it you're asking me this because you recognize my rights?

DAEMONES.   I'm not exactly asking you to use them against me, you know.

GRIPUS (*his eyes fixed on Labrax' face, aside*). I'm   **235** in! The pimp's weakening! My freedom's just around the corner!

DAEMONES (*gesturing toward* GRIPUS). First of all, this boy who found that satchel of yours is my servant. Secondly, I kept it safe for you, money and all.   **240**

LABRAX (*nodding his head in agreement*). I'm really very grateful to you. About that fifteen thousand I swore to give that boy of yours—I see no reason why you shouldn't have it.

GRIPUS (*to* LABRAX, *shouting*). Hey, you! You give   **245** it to me, not him! Haven't you got any brains?

DAEMONES (*turning on him*). Will you please shut up!

GRIPUS (*wildly*). You're just pretending to be working for my interests; you're really out for yourself. I may have lost all the rest of the swag in that satchel, but, **250** by god, you're not going to screw me out of this!

DAEMONES (*angrily*). If you say another word, I'll have you whipped!

GRIPUS (*as before*). Go on, kill me! I'll only keep quiet if you gag me with fifteen thousand dollars. There's **255** no other way to shut me up.

LABRAX (*to* GRIPUS, *disgustedly*). Oh, pipe down. He certainly is working for your best interests.

DAEMONES (*beckoning* LABRAX *off to the side*). Step over here, will you? **260**

LABRAX. Sure.

GRIPUS (*calling to them as they move to one side*). Hey, let's keep it in the open! I don't want any of this whispering business.

DAEMONES (*sotto voce*). How much did you pay for **265** that other girl? Ampelisca, I mean.

LABRAX (*sotto voce*). Five thousand dollars.

DAEMONES (*sotto voce*). How'd you like me to make you a good offer for her?

LABRAX (*sotto voce*). I sure would. **270**

DAEMONES (*sotto voce*). I'll split that fifteen thousand with you.

LABRAX (*sotto voce, with pleased surprise*). Thanks!

DAEMONES (*sotto voce*). You take half for letting Ampelisca go free, and give me half. **275**

LABRAX (*sotto voce*). It's a deal.

DAEMONES (*sotto voce*). The half I get will pay for Gripus' freedom. After all, it was because of him that you found your satchel and I my daughter.

LABRAX (*sotto voce*). Thanks very much. I'm much **280** obliged to you.

GRIPUS (*calling*). Hey, how soon am I going to get my money?

DAEMONES. It's all settled, Gripus. I've got it.

GRIPUS. Damn it all, I want me to have it! **285**

DAEMONES. Well, damn it all, you're not getting it, so don't start getting your hopes up. And I want you to let him (*gesturing toward* LABRAX) off his oath.

GRIPUS (*roaring*). Damn it all, that's the end of me. I'm a goner—unless I hang myself. And, damn it all, **290** I'll do it right now—you won't get a second chance to swindle me, no sir!

DAEMONES (*to* LABRAX). How about joining us for dinner?

LABRAX. Thanks. Be glad to.

DAEMONES. Follow me in, both of you. (*Walks* **295** *downstage and addresses the audience.*) Ladies and gentlemen, I'd invite you to dinner too—except that I'm not serving anything, and there's nothing decent to eat in the house anyway; besides, I know you've all got other invitations to eat out tonight. But, if you'd care to **300** give a hearty round of applause to our play, you can all come to a big party at my house—sixteen years from now. (*Turning to* LABRAX *and* GRIPUS.) You two come to dinner.

LABRAX AND GRIPUS. Thank you. **305**

DAEMONES (*to the audience*). Your applause, please.

FOCUS QUESTIONS

1. Discuss the moral lessons that underscore the comedy in *The Rope*.
2. Discuss the significance of the play's title and show why this is a comedy of fate and fortune.
3. A universal theme in *The Rope*—that of a lost child restored to its parents—has found enduring popularity with audiences. Cite a different work of literature (dramatic or non-dramatic) in which this theme is prominently featured and compare its treatment with Plautus'.
4. Briefly analyze the different master/servant relationships in the play, describing how each functions.
5. How does the Gripus/Trachalio confrontation in act 4 advance both plot and character development?

6. Show how certain characters' gender and function are depicted by the playwright, for characters seen or unseen.

7. Listing specific examples from stage, screen, and television, defend Larry Gelbart's comment that "there is not a joke form, comic character, or farcical situation that exists today that does not find its origin in Plautus' work."

OTHER ACTIVITIES

1. Block the prologue as a stylized dumb show (i.e., silent-film style), in which characters and actions are introduced to the audience while Arcturus is speaking.

2. Discuss the influence of Plautus on television "sitcoms" or soap operas.

3. View Richard Lester's 1966 film version of *A Funny Thing Happened on the Way to the Forum* and locate the Plautine sources in the film's numerous characters and subplots.

BIBLIOGRAPHY

Arnott, W. G. *Menander, Plautus, and Terence.* Oxford: Clarendon Press, 1975.

Beare, William. *The Roman Stage: A Short History of Latin Drama in the Time of the Republic.* New York: Barnes & Noble, 1963.

Bieber, Margrete. *The History of the Greek and Roman Theatre.* Princeton, NJ: Princeton University Press, 1961.

Duckworth, George E. *The Nature of Roman Comedy: A Study in Popular Entertainment.* Princeton, NJ: Princeton University Press, 1952.

Handley, E. W. *Menander and Plautus: A Study in Comparison.* London: E. K. Lewis, 1968.

Hunter, R. L. *The New Comedy of Greece and Rome.* New York: Cambridge University Press, 1985.

Kerr, Walter. *Tragedy and Comedy.* New York: Da Capo Press, 1985.

Konstan, David. *Roman Comedy.* Ithaca, NY: Cornell University Press, 1983.

Kurrelmeyer, Carrie Mae. *The Economy of Actors in Plautus.* Graz, Germany: Deutsche vereins-druckerei a.g., 1932.

Norwood, Gilbert. *Plautus and Terence.* New York: Cooper Square Publishers, 1963

Perry, Henry T. Eyck. *Masters of Dramatic Comedy and Their Social Themes.* Cambridge, MA: Harvard University Press, 1939.

Segal, Erich. *Roman Laughter: The Comedy of Plautus.* 2d ed. New York: Oxford University Press, 1987.

Slater, N. W. *Plautus in Performance: The Theatre of the Mind.* Princeton, NJ: Princeton University Press, 1985.

Tatum, James. *Plautus: The Darker Comedies.* Baltimore: Johns Hopkins, 1983.

Zagagi, Netta. *Tradition and Originality in Plautus.* Gottingen: Vandenhoeck and Ruprecht, 1980.

THE SACRIFICE OF ISAAC
ANONYMOUS

With the completed secularization of the drama in the early fourteenth century, play-writing and performance shook off the shackles of the liturgy and, while still closely connected with religion in the choice of subject matter, became an independent, realistic, and thoroughly national art.

—T. M. PARROTT & R. H. BALL

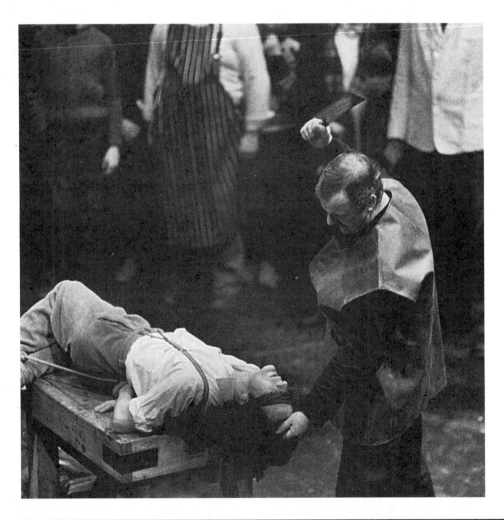

Stephen Pencher (*on the block*) as Isaac and Derek Newark as Abraham in *The Mysteries,* presented by the National Theatre in 1985, under the direction of Bill Bryden. *Photo: Donald Cooper,* © *Photostage.*

APPROACHING ENGLISH MEDIEVAL DRAMA

The conventional forms of classical drama, once recognized by their familiar masks of tragedy and comedy, were not meaningful to a divided Roman Empire. Superseding the dramatic contributions of Plautus and Terence, the licentious and bloody entertainments of the *ludi,* housed in large-scaled amphitheatres such as the Colosseum, drew audiences away from the theatre. These popular gladiatorial spectacles became scandalous and were censored with the acceptance of Christianity by Emperor Constantine. Under this rule, the Church was empowered to condemn theatrical performances altogether. As a result, actors surfaced under the safer guises of traveling minstrels, jugglers, and acrobats.

At the dawn of the tenth century, the same Holy Church was fostering the drama's rebirth. The event was prompted by a set of timely circumstances closely linked to the historical development of drama and performance. Foremost was the demise of the western half of the Roman Empire by the end of the fifth century A.D. Equally important was the establishment of Christianity as the official religion throughout Western Europe. With almost no fanfare whatever, a ritual evolved on medieval church altars that established the direction of Western drama.

It is ironic that this rebirth was harmonious with the daily services of the hours celebrated in the monasteries, which provided the flexibility for the development of antiphonal chanting of dialogue. By the ninth century, these songs led to the development of **tropes,** or extended passages that embellished the text. Early in the tenth century, tropes were incorporated into the Easter service, requiring the responsive singing of two separate choruses: ''Whom seek ye in the tomb?'' asked the chorus of angels, to which the holy women replied, ''Jesus of Nazareth, the crucified.'' ''He is not here; he has risen as he foretold. Go and announce that he has risen from the tomb,'' commanded the angels.

This exchange, known as the ''Quem Quaeritis''—''Whom seek ye?''—trope, held rich theatrical potential for the largely illiterate congregation. There was *representation* (the altar serving as Christ's tomb); *impersonation* (priests and male parishioners acting the roles of holy women and angels); *costumes* (the ornamental liturgical vestments); *dialogue* (the words shared between both choruses); and a hint of *action* (the women approaching and leaving the tomb). In fact, an early account of this ritual/performance appears in the *Concordia Regularis,* dating back to the tenth century. It is documented by Ethelwold, Bishop of Winchester, whose description of the service supports his own unheralded role as playwright and director:

> While the third responsory is being sung, let the remaining three follow, all of them
> vested in capes, and carrying in their hands censers filled with incense; and slowly,
> in the manner of seeking something, let them come before the place of the sepulchre. These things are done in imitation of the angel seated in the monument,
> and of the women coming with spices to anoint the body of Jesus.[1]

Ethelwold's description reveals that members of the chorus took on the roles of the angel and the three Marys as they came forward to perform the actions that depict the discovery of Christ's resurrection. Originally composed in Latin, the chanted exchanges were eventually translated into the vernacular—an important early step toward popularizing the Bible for audiences who neither read nor understood Latin—and were performed on different Holy Days. They were also rewritten to accommodate corresponding celebrations (for example, ''Whom seek ye in the manger, shepherds?'' for the Christmas service) and were gradually embellished by their celebrants until the trope developed into a full ''liturgical'' play. So the medieval drama—religious in nature, didactic in purpose—was born.

What happened next was perfectly in keeping with the central importance of the church to the social life of each community. When the popularity of these dramatic enactments began to attract larger audiences, they were moved from the confined altar setting to the more spacious alcoves of the church. In time, the decision to perform outdoors provided newer alternatives.

Whether the occasion was the simple trope performed by clerics or the cycle plays for the festival of Corpus Christi performed by men in the community about four hundred years later, the plots were based on stories and characters from the Old and New Testaments. *The Fall of Lucifer, The Creation of Eve, Adam and Eve in Eden, The Killing of Abel, The Deluge, The Prophets, The Harrowing of Hell, The Offering of the Magi, The Resurrection of Christ,* and *The Judgment Day* are just a few titles that suggest the range of dramatic content. Furthermore, these liturgical dramas were collaborative efforts whose authorship remained anonymous. The reason was clear enough: they represented the collective contributions of medieval craft guilds much like our trade unions of today.

Guild members—with guidance from the Church—convened to sponsor, organize, and rehearse these plays. Their contribution usually demonstrated some connection between their professional chores and the particular play they represented. The Shipwrights, for example, produced a play about the building of Noah's ark; the Bakers created one for the Last Supper; and the Carpenters performed the Crucifixion. The enormous ingenuity of these craftsmen was reflected in their stage machinery and special effects, which included trap doors for the appearance of the loaves and fishes, flying machines for angels passing between heaven and earth, and the rain for Noah's flood. Chester, York, and Wakefield were just a few of the English towns that gave their names to the multiple episodes or **mysteries**—collectively called ''cycles''—that emerged and grew into elaborate community enterprises.

By the fourteenth and fifteenth centuries, the cycles spread across central Europe, with the twofold purpose of teaching solid lessons from the Bible to young and old alike and entertaining them as well. Throughout Europe, spectators usually assembled around scaffold stages, **mansions,** that were positioned at different locations, or **stations,** designated throughout each town.

The cycles were presented in several distinct ways. The most popular approach was the presentation of individual plays on **pageant wagon** stages that moved in succession from one locale to another within each town. (See the drawing on page 112.) These wagons consisted of a ''wooden platform supported on four wheels, which is likely to have borne a superstructure in the form of a box-frame, also mostly wooden. It appears that three sides of this frame were hung with painted cloth backdrops, leaving the front of the structure open to the audience. It probably resembled a small proscenium stage.''[2] In some towns, however, the wagons were positioned in a circle, allowing spectators to move from one play to another, that is, to follow their connected but episodic enactments one by one. In actual performance, each of the thirty-two plays of the Wakefield Cycle averaged 384 lines. If all of them were performed in order, they would have taken

> over fourteen hours at each station. If however they were performed at one station
> only, and by such an arrangement reducing the time spent in procession and in
> preparation before and after each performance, then the total playing time would
> have stretched from dawn to dusk.[3]

Throughout England, specifically in Cornwall, **rounds** provided circular performance areas in which mansions were erected. Earthen embankments enclosed these spaces. Whatever the approach, the need to create drama was fashionable once again and guilds enjoyed the enthusiastic support of audiences far and wide.

Unquestionably *The Sacrifice of Isaac* play, which dates back to the fourteenth century, is a fascinating example of both the style and content of these short biblical enactments. Named after the Brome Manor in Suffolk, England, where the manuscript is preserved, this version is the most highly representative of five other plays that treat the

Side view of a medieval pageant wagon behind a scaffold stage.

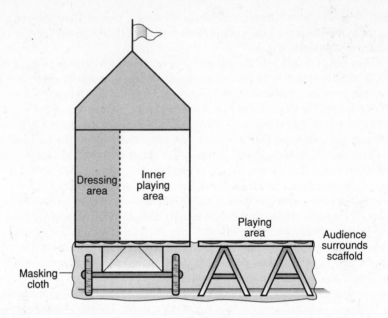

same theme, including the *Abraham* of the Wakefield Cycle and the *Abraham and Isaac* of the Chester Cycle, which it closely resembles. Whether the Brome version actually belonged to a cycle remains uncertain, although there is little doubt that it was performed on the conventional pageant wagon and, like the mysteries, was a form of street theatre.

THE ACTION

God observes Abraham, who kneels in prayer and thanks him for his own healthy son Isaac. To test Abraham's faith and obedience, God commands him to make a blood sacrifice of Isaac. At first reluctant to obey, Abraham fetches Isaac and, with the boy's help, carries wood and fire to the mountaintop for a sacrifice. Laying the wood down, Isaac wonders why his father is clutching a sword, since no sacrificial animal appears in sight. When he realizes that he is to be the sacrificial lamb, Isaac laments that his mother is not there to rescue him. Torn between obedience to God and love for his son, Abraham lifts the terrible blade over Isaac's head until God intervenes.

STRUCTURE AND LANGUAGE

The simple realism of *The Sacrifice of Isaac* is tempered by a rare poignancy and pathos. Its unconventional depiction of the parent/child relationship, always a source of powerful thematic conflict in the drama, resounds on two levels: one spiritual (God vs. Abraham) and the other human (Abraham vs. Isaac), but each is strengthened and unified by important familial bonds. While both pairs of relationships parallel each other and prove mutually enlightening in subtle ways, the anonymous playwright infuses the conflict between Abraham and Isaac with urgent dramatic irony by informing the audience of the victim's fate quite early in the action. Isaac, of course, shares none of this. In contrast, an entirely different but no less effective use of irony stems from the unexpected reprieve exacted by God upon the obedient Abraham at the play's memorable climax.

Furthermore, the playwright loses no time setting these familiar characters on their journey, acknowledging the audience's familiarity with the outcome of this chilling tale of submission and obedience. Nor is he concerned with the creation of vital heroes who over-come obstacles or struggle to assert themselves, one against the other. The reason is ob-vious: life on earth was a testing ground for earning God's forgiveness and enjoying the rewards of heaven. This reality replaces any need for allegorical characters to challenge what is already part of a divine plan. By the same token, the innate theatricality of the Abraham and Isaac story, with its expertly timed reversal of action, cannot help but trans-form urgent moral lessons into gripping drama, while reaffirming the audience's trust in God.

Although character exchanges frequently resonate with recognizable images of obe-dience, terror, love, and death, the language of the play in its close to original form makes unusual demands on the contemporary reader. But the challenge is quietly rewarded by the flowing rhythms and catchy rhymes of the text, all of which become accessible after several readings. For this Brome, like many cycle plays, demonstrates on the simplest of levels the power of poetry in performance, a format that was inspired by the chanted verse of the liturgical tropes. Here Abraham beckons Isaac to the mysterious sacrifice:

> Rysse v́p, my chýld, and fást cum héder,
> My géntyll bárn [child] that árt so wyśse,
> For we to, chyld, must goo to-geder
> And on-to my Lord make sacryffyce.

The smooth integration of iambic meter and rhyme is unmistakenly musical and, lifted from its dramatic context, recalls the warmth of a lullabye. Returned to its proper context, Abra-ham's words grow deceptively powerful in luring Isaac to the journey.

No less remarkable is that the language of all medieval drama, as witnessed in this richly constructed Brome, inspired the indigenous English drama of the early Renaissance. Thus the literary and theatrical blossoming of a much later and more refined golden age has owed no small debt to its primitive medieval ancestry and artistry.

MEDIEVAL DRAMA-IN-PERFORMANCE

It is the theatrical rather than liturgical perspective that enlightens our approach to cycle plays in performance in our own time, since drama and religion are mutually exclusive enterprises in most Western societies. On the other hand, the very impact of the Abraham and Isaac theme remains embedded in our universal consciousness: Christianity embraced its important lesson and the medieval guilds actualized its rich dramatic potential. The result was that, on a designated day, spectators could behold an actor playing God who towers over the characters of Abraham and Isaac in an enactment transpiring before dark.

During the latter half of the twentieth century, England has witnessed a resurgence of mystery cycles in the same towns where they originated. York, Coventry, and Lincoln, among others, have successfully revived them to commemorate the British Commonwealth. Some festivals have refined the original text and staging to accommodate modern conven-tions; others have sought authenticity through the reconstruction of pageant wagons and processions, in the hope of recreating the spirit of medieval performance. In contrast with these commemorative rituals, the mainstream London theatre had largely ignored its me-dieval legacy until 1977 when the National Theatre of Great Britain mounted a production of the cycle plays. These same plays were reworked and adapted by Tony Harrison in 1985 under the title *The Mysteries* for the Cottesloe and Lyceum Theatres, demonstrating their commercial viability.

Outside of England, remnants of this sacrificial motif have been preserved in the renowned *Passion Play* at Oberammergau. Originally performed so that the remaining population could be spared from a plague, the citizens of this village in southern Bavaria,

Germany, have enacted the drama almost every ten years since 1633. In part 3, act 12 of the present Oberammergau text, a prologue, in which the choir sings of Pilate's pronouncement of death for Jesus, is followed by a **tableau** that depicts Isaac bearing the wood to be used for his sacrifice on Mount Moriah. The careful placement of this prologue and tableau as preface to the dramatization of the Way to Golgotha and the Crucifixion supports the popular belief that Abraham's action toward Isaac anticipated God's sacrifice of his only begotten son. While it is difficult to assess the performance ritual at Oberammergau as a modern equivalent to the medieval experience, its communal interaction, episodic design, and liturgical themes pay homage to medieval artistry. Even to this day, the actors at Oberammergau receive a special pardon at the time of performance, so that their enactment of certain evil characters and deeds will not be viewed as sinful.

REFLECTIONS ON THE SACRIFICE OF ISAAC

The following theatre review, written by Ned Chaillet, appeared in
The Wall Street Journal, *January 25, 1985.*

God first came to the National Theatre as a bald Yorkshireman eight years ago. Since then he has from time to time reappeared in the mystery plays with his flat cap and flat Northern vowels to condemn Lucifer to the depths, to build Eden and to command Abraham to kill his son. Audiences have walked with him under a glittering firmament of flickering lights and shiny kitchen implements, with banners of the trade guilds overhead. They have also stood next to a naked Eve as the Serpent tempts her to eat the forbidden fruit, and have been gently nudged aside as Jesus was taken before Pontius Pilate and picked up his cross to go to Calvary.

Not until now, however, have audiences witnessed the Resurrection and seen Jesus (Karl Johnson) and Mary the Mother ascend to Heaven. The continuation of the story, in the play *The Mysteries,* has its risks for the audience, since director Bill Bryden takes the story through to Doomsday and spectators risk being on the wrong side as the Last Judgment is made and souls are consigned to Heaven and to Hell. But even for those caught up with great sinners, there are rewards: an entire day spent watching the medieval mystery plays in Mr. Bryden's production and genuine religious profundity.

Profundity might be the last thing you would expect of a work as secular as this. Mr. Bryden has done everything in his power to try to capture the original feel of a street festival, bringing in an electric folk band, the Home Service, to give a little hoedown spirit to the dances. He has remembered that different guilds traditionally took responsibility for different sections of the play (e.g., nail makers at the Crucifixion), and so he has provided sewer workers for the slimier depths of Hell and laborers to operate the forklift trucks used to elevate God and his angels. But what comes through, however coarse the jokes (rather, however coarse the medieval English), is the fundamental Christian faith.

In the episodes from the Old Testament, the plays might show Mr. and Mrs. Noah as a bickering English couple but their fundamental purpose is to show how God and the Prophets prepared the world for the birth of Christ. The sequence in which Abraham (Derek Newark) trusses Isaac (Stephen Pencher) and puts him on the butcher's block has an almost unbearable tenderness, with Mr. Newark wrenching hearts by the restraint with which he goes about God's will. When the plain-spoken God (Brian Glover) stops the execution, the comprehension of pain transfers to Abraham's promise to sacrifice his own son to save the world, and theology becomes painfully concrete.

There is more than one way to see *The Mysteries*. Those who arrive early can find seats on the two levels above the floor of the Cottesloe Auditorium. Those who choose to wander on to the floor will be given the chance to promenade with the production, moving close to some scenes and standing back from others, perhaps dancing with the company or holding a staff while Christ's persecutors drink wine. Moving between levels gives different views of Mr. Bryden's scenic inventions (as well as the fine designs of William Dudley), and scenes such as Christ's baptism in the river Jordan, where a massive blue cloth becomes the river, are remarkable from an aerial perch.

Served up in three portions—"The Nativity," "The Passion" and "Doomsday"—the plays can be relished separately or, during the Easter period, in marathons with meal breaks. The first two parts have long established their worth in the National's repertory, with a core of talented actors including Jack Shepherd, Edna Dore and Karl Johnson, but "Doomsday" is new to the program and the addition of such actors as Robert Stephens, Don Warrington and Brenda Blethyn adds richness to the acting and renewed power to the earlier parts. There are several moments seen in "Doomsday" that scenically rank with the best London theatre in over 10 years.

Most staggering of the images, with impassioned musical accompaniment, is the sudden appearance of a skeletal globe the width and height of the theater. Inside the prison of meridians, the people of Earth are dangled from the tortuous ferris wheel, carrying them round and round. Hieronymous Bosch could not paint more memorable pictures of earthly torment, and yet it is the suggestive power of the image that is most impressive. Again, the performance presents grounds for religious thought.

Behind all this is a literary sensibility. The poet Tony Harrison has investigated the medieval plays with the company to make a coherent text, and his taut editing and poetic interjections unite the bawdy and the lyrical beauty of the plays. Through the choice of scenes, as well as through the staging, the point is always made that Christianity is about a God who chose to walk in the world among people. A promenade has never been a more apt theatrical metaphor.

From THE WALL STREET JOURNAL, *25 January 1985. Reprinted by permission.*

Notes

1. *Joseph Quincy Adams, ed.,* CHIEF PRE-SHAKESPEAREAN DRAMAS *(Cambridge, MA: Houghton Mifflin, 1924), 9.*
2. *Richard Beadle, ed.,* THE YORK PLAYS *(London: Edward Arnold, 1982), 36.*
3. *Martial Rose, ed.,* THE WAKEFIELD MYSTERY PLAYS *(Garden City, NY: Doubleday & Co., 1962), 28.*

THE SACRIFICE OF ISAAC[1]
ANONYMOUS
EDITED BY JOSEPH QUINCY ADAMS

CHARACTERS

God (Deus) Abraham The Angell
Isaac Doctor

(*On the upper stage* GOD *with his angels; on the lower stage*
ABRAHAM *and his young son* ISAAC. ABRAHAM *kneels in
prayer.*)

ABRAHAM.
> Fader of heuyn omnipotent,
> > With all my hart to the I call.
> Thow hast goffe me both lond and rent;
> And my lyvelod thow hast me sent.
> > I thanke the heyly euer-more of all. 5

> Fyrst off the erth thou madyst Adam,
> > And Eue also to be hys wyffe;
> All other creatures of them too cam.
> And now thow hast grant to me, Abra-
> > ham,
> > Her in thys lond to lede my lyffe. 10

> In my age thou hast grantyd me thys,

> That thys yowng chyld with me shall
> > wone.[2]
> I love no-thyng so myche, i-wysse,
> Except thin owyne selffe, der Fader of
> > blysse,
> > As Yssac her, my owyne swete sone. 15

> I haue dyuerse chyldryn moo,
> > The wych I loue not halffe so wyll;
> Thys fayer swet chyld he schereys[3] me soo
> In euery place wer that I goo,
> > That noo dessece[4] her may I fell. 20

> And therfor, Fadyr of heuyn, I the prey
> > For hys helth and also for hys grace;
> Now, Lord, kepe hym both nyght and
> > day,
> That neuer dessese nor noo fray[5]
> > Cume to my chyld in noo place. 25

(*Rises.*)

> Now cum on, Yssac, my owyne swete
> > chyld;
> > Goo we hom and take owr rest.
ISAAC.
> Abraham, myne owyne fader so
> > myld,
> > To folowe yow I am full prest,[6]
> > > Bothe erly and late.
ABRAHAM.
> Cume on, swete chyld. I love
> > the best 31
> > Of all the chyldryn that ever I be-
> > > gat.

[1]This play, as Miss Lucy Toulmin Smith observes, is superior to the five other extant plays on the same theme. It has often been printed, for it is justly regarded as the best example of pathos in the early religious drama. I have based the text on *The Non-Cycle Mystery Plays,* re-edited from the manuscripts for the Early English Text Society by O. Waterhouse, 1909, but have adopted some emendations made by other editors. The manuscript is preserved at Brome Manor, Suffolk, in a commonplace-book of 1470–80; the original, however, of which this is a transcript must be dated as early as the fourteenth century. Waterhouse suggests that the play was not a part of a cycle, but was designed for representation by itself. We cannot be certain. In form and language it is closely akin to the *Abraham and Isaac* of the Chester Cycle, and it differs in no essential way from the ordinary craft play. And, even if acted separately, "it is to be supposed," says Waterhouse, "that the stage was the usual pageant, and the mode of performance practically identical with that of the regular cycle plays."

[2]Dwell. [3]Cheers. [4]Discomfort, trouble. [5]Harm, terror.
[6]Ready. MS. glad, *corr. by Manly.*

(*They cross to another place.* GOD *speaks above.*)

DEUS.

    Myn angell, fast hey the thy
        wey,
      And on-to medyll-erth anon thou goo;
    Abrams hart now wyll I asay,[7]
      Wether that he be stedfast or noo.   **36**

    Sey I commaw[n]dyd hym for to take
      Yssac, hys yowng sonne, that he love so
        wyll,
    And with hys blood sacryfyce he make,
      Yffe ony off my freynchepe he wyll
        ffell.   **40**

    Schow hym the wey on-to the hylle
      Wer that hys sacryffyce schall be.
    I schall asay, now, hys good wyll,
      Whether he lovyth better hys chyld or
        me.
    All men schall take exampyll be hym
      My commawmentes how they schall
        kepe.   **46**

(*The* ANGEL *descends.* ABRAHAM, *returning, kneels in prayer.*)

ABRAHAM.

    Now, Fader of heuyn, that
        formyd all thyng,
      My preyeres I make to the a-geyn,
    For thys day my tender-offryng[8]
      Here mvst I geve to the, certeyn.
    A! Lord God, allmyty Kyng,   **51**
      Wat maner best woll make the most
        fayn?[9]
    Yff I had ther-of very knoyng,
      Yt schuld be don with all my mayne,
      Full sone anone.
    To don thy plesyng on an hyll,
    Verely yt ys my wyll,
      Dere Fader, God in Trinyte.   **58**

THE ANGELL.

    Abraham! Abraham! wyll
        thou rest!
      Owre Lord comandyth the for to take
    Ysaac, thy yowng sone that thow lovyst
        best,
      And with hys blod sacryfyce that thow
        make.   **62**

    In-to the Lond of V[i]syon thow goo,
      And offer thy chyld on-to thy Lord;

    I schall the lede and schow all-soo.
      Vnto Goddes hest,[10] Abraham, a-cord,   **66**

    And folow me vp-on thys grene.

ABRAHAM.

    Wolle-com to me be my
        Lordes sond,[11]
      And hys hest I wyll not with-stond.
      Yit Ysaac, my yowng sonne in lond,
    A full dere chyld to me haue byn.   **71**

    I had lever,[12] yf God had be plesyd,
      For to a for-bore all the good[13] that I
        haue,
    Than Ysaac my sone schuld a be desessyd,[14]
      So God in heuyn my sowll mot saue!   **75**

    I lovyd neuer thyng soo mych in erde,[15]
      And now I mvst the chyld goo kyll.
    A! Lord God, my conseons ys stronly
        steryd!
    And yit, my dere Lord, I am sore a-ferd
      To groche ony thyng a-gens yowre
        wyll.   **80**

    I love my chyld as my lyffe;
      But yit I love my God myche more.
    For thow my hart woold make ony stryffe,
    Yit wyll I not spare for chyld nor wyffe,
      But don after my Lordes lore.[16]   **85**

    Thow I love my sonne neuer so wyll,
      Yit smythe[17] of hys hed sone I schall.
    A! Fader of heuyn, to the I knell;
    An hard dethe my son schall fell
      For to honor the, Lord, with-all.   **90**

THE ANGELL.

    Abraham! Abraham! thys
        ys wyll seyd!
      And all thys comamentes loke that thou
        kepe.
    But in thy hart be no-thyng dysmayd.

ABRAHAM.

    Nay, nay, for-soth, I hold me
        wyll a-payd[18]
      To plesse my God to the best that I
        haue.[19]   **95**

    For thow my hart be heuely sett
      To see the blood of my owyn dere sone,
    Yit for all thys I wyll not lett,

---

[7]Try, test.   [8]Burnt-offering.   [9]Pleased.

[10]Decree. [11]Messenger. [12]Rather. [13]Goods, possessions.
[14]Injured. [15]MS. erthe, *corr. by Manly.* [16]Precept. [17]Smite.
[18]MS. plesyd: *Manly suggests* a-payd. [19]*Manly suggests* may.

But Ysaac, my son, I wyll goo fett,
  And cum asse fast as euer we can.   100

(ABRAHAM *crosses to the end of the pageant,*
where ISAAC *is kneeling in prayer.*)

  Now, Ysaac, my owyne son dere,
    Wer art thow, chyld? Speke to me.
YSAAC.
  My fader, swet fader, I am here,
    And make my preyrys to the Tren-
      yte.   104
ABRAHAM.
  Rysse vp, my chyld, and fast
    cum heder,
  My gentyll barn[20] that art so wysse,
  For we to, chyld, must goo to-geder
    And on-to my Lord make sacryffyce.   108
YSAAC.
  I am full redy, my fader, loo!
    Yevyn at yowr handes I stand rygth
    here;
  And wat-so-euer ye byd me doo,
    Yt schall be don with glad cher,
      Full wyll and fyne.
ABRAHAM.
  A! Ysaac, my owyn son soo
    dere,
    Godes blyssyng I gyffe the, and
    myn.   115

  Hold thys fagot vpon thi bake,
    And her myselffe fyer schall bryng.
YSAAC.
  Fader, all thys her wyll I packe;
    I am full fayn to do yowr bedyng.
ABRAHAM (*aside*).
  A! Lord of heuyn,
    my handes I wryng,
    Thys chyldes wordes all to-wond my
    harte.   121

  Now, Ysaac [s]on,[21] goo we owr wey
    On-to yon mownte, with all owr mayn.
YSAAC.
  Gowe we, my dere fader, as fast
    I as may;
    To folow yow I am full fayn,
      Allthow I be slendyr.
ABRAHAM (*aside*).
  A! Lord, my hart
    brekyth on tweyn,

Thys chyldes wordes, they be so
  tender.   128

(*They arrive at the Mount.*)

  A! Ysaac, son, anon ley yt down;
    No lenger vpon thi backe yt hold,[22]
  For I mvst make redy bon[23]
    To honowr my Lord God as I schuld.   132
YSAAC.
  Loo, my dere fader, wer yt ys!

(*Lays down the fagot.*)

  To cher yow all-wey I draw me nere.
  But, fader, I mervell sore of thys,
    Wy that ye make thys heuy chere.   136

  And also, fader, euer-more dred I:
    Wer ys yowr qweke[24] best that ye schuld
    kyll?
  Both fyer and wood we haue redy,
    But queke best haue we non on this
    hyll.   140

  A qwyke best, I wot wyll,[25] must be ded[26]
    Yowr sacryfyce for to make.
ABRAHAM.
  Dred the nowgth, my chyld, I
    the red,[27]
  Owr Lord wyll send me on-to thys sted[28]
    Summ maner a best for to take,
    Throw hys swet sond.[29]
YSAAC.
  Ya, fader, but my hart begynnyth
    to quake
    To se that scharpe sword in yowr
    hond.   148

  Wy bere ye yowr sword drawyn soo?
    Off yowre conwnauns[30] I haue mych
    wonder.
ABRAHAM (*aside*).
  A! Fader of heuyn,
    so I am woo!
    Thys chyld her brekys my harte on-
    sonder.[31]   152
YSAAC.
  Tell me, my dere fader, or that ye
    ses,[32]
    Ber ye yowr sword draw[yn][33] for me?

---

[20]Child. [21]MS. on; *I have adopted Manly's emendation.*

[22]MS. bere, *corr. by Kittredge.* [23]Quickly ready. [24]Live.
[25]Well. [26]Killed. [27]Advise. [28]Place. [29]Messenger.
[30]Countenance. [31]MS. on-too, *corr. by Holthausen.* [32]Cease.
[33]*Added by Holthausen.*

ABRAHAM.

    A! Ysaac, swet son, pes! pes!
      For, i-wys, thow breke my harte on
        thre.   **156**

YSAAC.

    Now trewly, sum-what, fader, ye
      thynke,
    That ye morne thus more and more.

ABRAHAM (*aside*).

    A! Lord of heuyn,
      thy grace let synke,
    For my hart was neuer halffe so sore.   **160**

YSAAC.

    I preye yow, fader, that ye wyll
      let me that wyt,[34]
    Wyther schall I haue ony harme or
      noo.

ABRAHAM.

    I-wys, swet son, I may not tell
      the yit,
    My hart ys now soo full of woo.   **164**

YSAAC.

    Dere fader, I prey yow, hyd yt[35]
      not fro me,
    But sum of yowr thowt that ye tell me.

ABRAHAM.

    A! Ysaac, Ysaac, I must kyll
      the!

YSAAC.

    Kyll me, fader? Alasse! wat
      haue I done?   **168**

    Yff I haue trespassyd a-gens yow owt,
      With a yard[36] ye may make me full myld;
    And with yowr scharp sword kyll me nogth,
      For, i-wys, fader, I am but a chyld.   **172**

ABRAHAM.

    I am full sory, son, thy blood
      for to spyll,
    But truly, my chyld, I may not chese.

YSAAC.

    Now I wold to God my moder
      were her on this hyll!
    Sche woold knele for me on both hyr
      kneys
      To save my lyffe.
    And sythyn[37] that my moder ys not here,
    I prey yow, fader, schonge[38] yowr chere,   **179**
      And kyll me not with yowyr knyffe.

ABRAHAM.

    For-sothe, son, but yf[39] I the
      kyll,
    I schuld greve God rygth sore, I drede.
    Yt ys hys commawment, and also hys
      wyll,
    That I schuld do thys same dede.   **184**

    He commawdyd me, son, for serteyn,
      To make my sacryfyce with thy blood.

YSAAC.

    And ys yt Goddes wyll that I
      schuld be slayn?

ABRAHAM.

    Ya, truly, Ysaac, my son soo
      good;
      And ther-for my handes I wryng.   **189**

YSAAC.

    Now, fader, agens my Lordes wyll
    I wyll neuer groche, lowd nor styll.
      He mygth a sent me a better desteny
    Yf yt had a be hys plecer.[40]   **193**

ABRAHAM.

    For-sothe, son, but yf I ded
      this dede,
      Grevosly dysplessyd owr Lord wyll be.

YSAAC.

    Nay, nay, fader, God for-bede
      That euer ye schuld greve hym for
      me.   **197**

    Ye haue other chyldryn, on or too,
      The wyche ye schuld love wyll be kynd.[41]
    I prey yow, fader, make ye no woo;
    For, be I onys ded, and fro yow goo,
      I schall be sone owt of yowre mynd.   **202**

    Ther-for doo owre Lordes byddyng,
      And wan I am ded, than prey for me.
    But, good fader, tell ye my moder no-
      thyng;
    Sey that I am in a-nother cuntre dwellyng.

ABRAHAM.

    A! Ysaac, Ysaac, blyssyd
      mot thow be!   **207**

    My hart be-gynnyth[42] stronly to rysse,
      To see the blood off thy blyssyd body.

YSAAC.

    Fader, syn yt may be noo other
      wysse,
      Let yt passe ouer as wyll as I.   **211**

---

[34]Know. [35]*Manly's reading for* MS. hydygth. [36]Rod.
[37]Since. [38]Change.

[39]Unless. [40]Pleasure. [41]Well by nature. [42]MS. begynnyd, *corr.*
by Manly. Miss Smith and Waterhouse prefer begynnys.

But, fader, or I goo on-to my deth,
   I prey yow blysse me with yowr hand.

(ISAAC *kneels*.)

ABRAHAM.
   Now, Ysaac, with all my breth
     My blyssyng I geve the upon thys lond,
     And Godes also ther-to, i-wys.
     Ysaac, Ysaac, sone, up thow stond,
      Thy fayer swete mowthe that I may
       kys.   218

YSAAC.
   Now for-wyll, my owyne fader so
      fyn;
     And grete wyll my moder in erde.[43]
   But I prey yow, fader, to hyd my eyne,
     That I se not the stroke of yowr scharpe
      swerd,[43]
      That my fleysse schall defyle.   223

ABRAHAM.
   Sone, thy wordes make me to
      weep full sore;
   Now, my dere son Ysaac, speke no more.

YSAAC.
   A! my owyne dere fader, were-
      fore?
     We schall speke to-gedyr her but a
      wylle.   227

And sythyn that I must nedysse be ded,
   Yit, my dere fader, to yow I prey,
Smythe but fewe[44] strokes at my hed,
   And make an end as sone as ye may,
     And tery not to longe.

ABRAHAM.
   Thy meke wordes, child,
      make me afray;
     So, "welawey!" may be my songe,   234

Excepe alonly Godes wyll.
   A! Ysaac, my owyn swete chyld,
Yit kysse me a-gen vp-on thys hyll!
   In all thys war[l]d ys non soo myld.   238

YSAAC.
   Now truly, fader, all thys tery[y]ng
     Yt doth my hart but harme;
   I prey yow, fader, make an enddyng.

ABRAHAM.
   Cume vp, swet son, on-to my
      arme.   242

(*Starts to bind him*.)

   I must bynd thy hand[e]s too,
     All-thow thow be neuer soo myld.

YSAAC.
   A! mercy, fader! wy schuld ye do
      soo?

ABRAHAM.
   That thow schuldyst not let[45]
     [me], my chyld.   246

YSAAC.
   Nay, i-wysse, fader, I wyll not let
     yow.
     Do on, for me, yowre wyll;
   And on the purpos that ye haue set
     yow,
     For Godes love kepe yt for the styll. 250

I am full sory thys day to dey,
   But yit I kepe[46] not my God to greve.
Do on yowre lyst for me hardly;
   My fayer swete fader, I geffe yow
     leve.   254

But, fader, I prey yow euermore,
   Tell ye my moder no dell;[47]
Yffe sche wost[48] yt, sche wold wepe full
     sore,
   For i-wysse, fader, sche lovyt me full
     wyll.
     Goddes blyssyng mot sche haue!   259

   Now for-wyll, my moder so swete!
     We too be leke[49] no mor to mete.

ABRAHAM.
   A! Ysaac, Ysaac! son, thou
      makyst me to gret,
     And with thy wordes thow dystempurst
      me.   263

YSAAC.
   I-wysse, swete fader, I am sory to
      greve yow.
     I cry yow mercy of that I haue donne.
   And of all trespasse that euer I ded meve
     yow;
     Now, dere fader, for-gyffe me that I haue
      donne.
      God of heuyn be with me!   268

ABRAHAM.
   A! dere chyld, lefe of thy
      monys;

---

[43]*Here, and elsewhere, MS. has* erthe *and* sword, *which Manly alters for the sake of the rhyme.*   [44]*MS.* feve, *spelling altered by Manly.*

[45]Hinder.   [46]Desire.   [47]Bit.   [48]Knew.   [49]Like.

In all thy lyffe thow grevyd me neuer onys.
Now blyssyd be thow, body and bonys,
    That euer thow were bred and born!
Thow hast be to me chyld full good.
    But i-wysse, child, thow I morne neuer
        so fast,
    Yit must I nedes here at the last
In thys place sched all thy blood.   276

Ther-for, my dere son, here schall thou lye.

(*Places him on the altar.*)

    On-to my warke I must me stede.[50]
    I-wysse I had as leve my-selffe to dey,
    Yff God wyll [be] plecyd wyth my dede,
        And myn owyn body for to offer.
YSAAC.
    A! mercy, fader, morne ye no
        more!
        Yowr wepyng maketh[51] my hart sore,
            As my owyn deth that I schall suf-
        fer.   284

    Yowr kerche, fader, a-bowt my eyn ye
        wynd.
ABRAHAM.
    So I schall, my swettest chyld
        in erde.
YSAAC.
    Now yit, good fader, haue thys in
        mynd,
        And smyth me not oftyn with yowr
            scharp swerd,
            But hastely that yt be sped.

(*Here* ABRAHAM *leyd a cloth on* YSAACES *face,
thus seyyng:*)

ABRAHAM.
    Now fore-wyll, my chyld, so
        full of grace.
YSAAC.
    A! fader, fader, torne downgward
        my face,
        For of yowre scharpe sword I am euer
            a-dred.   292

ABRAHAM (*aside*).
    To don thys dede I
        am full sory,
        But, Lord, thyn hest[52] I wyll not with-
        stond.
YSAAC.
    A! Fader of heuyn, to the I crye;
        Lord, reseyve me into thy hand.   296

ABRAHAM (*aside*).
    Loo! now ys the
        tyme cum, certeyn,
        That my sword in hys necke schall bite.[53]
    A! Lord, my hart reysyth the[r]-ageyn;
        I may not fynd yt[54] in my harte to
            smygth;
        My hart wyll not now ther-too.   301
    Yit fayn I woold warke my Lordes wyll.
    But thys yowng innosent lygth so styll,
    I may not fynd yt[54] in my hart hym to kyll.
        O! Fader of heuyn, what schall I
            do?   305

YSAAC.
    A! mercy, fader, wy tery ye so,
        And let me ley thus longe on this heth?
    Now I wold to God the stroke were doo!
    Fader, I prey yow hartely, schorte me of
        my woo,
        And let me not loke [thus] after my
            degth.   310

ABRAHAM.
    Now, hart, wy wolddyst not
        thow breke on thre?
        Yit schall thou not make me to my God
            onmyld.
    I wyll no lenger let for the,
    For that my God a-grevyd wold be.
        Now hoold[55] tha stroke, my owyn dere
            chyld.   315

(*Her* ABRAHAM *drew hys stroke and the angel toke
the sword in hys hond soddenly.*)

THE ANGELL.
    I am an angell, thow may-
        ist se blythe,
        That fro heuyn to the ys senth.
    Owr Lord thanke the an C[56] sythe[57]
        For the kepyng of hys commawment.   319

    He knowyt thi wyll, and also thy harte,
        That thow dredyst[58] hym above all
            thyng;
    And sum of thy hevynes for to departe
        A fayr ram yinder I gan brynge;   323

    He standyth teyed, loo! a-mong the
        breres.[59]
        Now, Abraham, amend thy mood,

---

[50]Set myself.   [51]MS. makes, *corr. by Holthausen.*   [52]Command.

[53]MS. synke, *corr. by Holthausen.*   [54]*Manly's reading for* MS.
fyndygth.   [55]Receive.   [56]Hundred.   [57]Times.   [58]Reverest.
[59]Briars.

For Ysaac, thy yowng son that her ys,
   Thys day schall not sched hys blood.   327

Goo, make thy sacryfece with yon rame.
Now forwyll, blyssyd Abraham,
   For onto heuyn I goo now hom;
      The way ys full gayn.[60]
        Take vp thy son soo free. (*Exit.*)   332

ABRAHAM.
   A! Lord, I thanke the of thy
      gret grace,
   Now am I yeyed[61] on dyuers wysse.
   Arysse vp, Ysaac, my dere sunne,
      arysse;
      Arysse vp, swete chyld, and cum to
      me.   336

YSAAC.
   A! mercy, fader, wy smygth ye
      nowt?[62]
   A! smygth on, fader, onys with yowr
      knyffe.
ABRAHAM.
   Pesse, my swet son,[63] and take
      no thowt,
   For owr Lord of heuyn hath grant thi
      lyffe
      Be hys angell now,   341

That thou schalt not dey this day, sunne,
      truly.
YSAAC.
   A! fader, full glad than wer I, —
   I-wys, — fader, — I sey, — i-wys, —
      Yf thys tale wer trew.
ABRAHAM.
   An hundyrd tymys, my son
      fayer of hew,
   For joy thi mowt[h] now wyll I kys.   347

YSAAC.
   A! my dere fader, Abraham,
      Wyll not God be wroth that we do thus!
ABRAHAM.
   Noo, noo! har[de]ly, my swyt
      son,
   For yin same rame he hath vs sent
   Hether down to vs.   352

Yin best schall dey here in thi sted,
   In the worthschup of owr Lord alon.
Goo, fet hym hethyr, my chyld, in-ded.

[60]Direct. [61]Eased. [62]MS. not yit, *corr. by Holthausen.*
[63]MS. sir; *Manly changes to* son.

YSAAC.
   Fader, I wyll goo hent[64] hym be
      the hed,
   And bryng yon best with me anon.   357

(ISAAC, *untying the ram.*)

   A! scheppe, scheppe, blyssyd mot thou be,
      That euer thow were sent down heder!
   Thow schall thys day dey for me
   In the worchup of the Holy Trynyte.   361
      Now cum fast and goo we to-geder
      To my Fader of heuyn.
   Thow thou be neuer so jentyll and good,
   Yit had I leuer thow schedyst thi blood,
      Iwysse, scheppe, than I.   366

(*He leads the ram to his father.*)

   Loo! fader, I haue browt here full smerte
      Thys jentyll scheppe, and hym to yow I
      gyffe.
   But, Lord God, I thanke the with all my
      hart,
      For I am glad that I schall leve,[65]
      And kys onys my dere moder.
ABRAHAM.
   Now be rygth myry, my swete
      chylld,
      For thys qwyke best, that ys so myld,
      Here I schall present before all
      other.   374

YSAAC.
   And I wyll fast begynne to
      blowe;
      Thys fyere schall brene a full good spyd.
   But, fader, wyll I stowppe downe lowe,
   Ye wyll not kyll me with yowr sword, I
      trowe?
ABRAHAM.
   Noo, har[de]ly, swet son; haue
      no dred;
      My mornyng ys past.
YSAAC.
   Ya! but I woold that sword wer
      in a gled,[66]
   For, iwys, fader, yt make me full yll
      agast.   382

(*Here* ABRAHAM *mad hys offryng, knelyng and
seyyng thus:*)

ABRAHAM.
   Now, Lord God of heuen in
      Trynyte,

[64]Seize. [65]Live. [66]Fire.

Allmyty God omnipotent,
My offeryng I make in the worchope of the,
And with thys qweke best I the present.
Lord, reseyve thow myn intent,
 As [thow] art God and grownd of owr
  grace.   **388**

(GOD *speaks above*.)

DEUS.
Abraham, Abraham, wyll mot
  thow sped,
And Ysaac, thi yowng son the by!
Trvly, Abraham, for thys dede
I schall mvltyplye yowres botheres[67] sede
 As thyke as sterres be in the skye, **393**
  Bothe more and lesse;
 And as thyke as gravell in the see,
 So thyke mvltyplyed yowre sede schall
  be.
  Thys grant I yow for yowre good-
   nesse.   **397**

Off yow schall cume frowte gret [won],[68]
 And euer be in blysse withowt yend,
For ye drede me as God a-lon
And kepe my commawmentes eueryschon;
 My blyssyng I geffe, wersoeuer ye
  wend.[69]   **402**

ABRAHAM.
Loo! Ysaac, my son, how
  thynke ye
 Be thys warke that we haue wrogth?
Full glad and blythe we may be,
 Agens the wyll of God that we grocched
  nott,
  Vpon thys fayer hetth.
YSAAC.
A! fader, I thanke owr Lord euery
  dell,[70]
 That my wyt servyd me so wyll
  For to drede God more than my
   detth.   **410**

ABRAHAM.
Why! derewordy son, wer
  thow adred?
 Hardely,[71] chyld, tell me thy lore.[72]
YSAAC.
Ya! be my feyth, fader, now
  haue[73] I red,

I wos neuer soo afrayd before
 As I haue byn at yin hyll.
But, be my feth, fader, I swere
I wyll neuermore cume there
 But yt be a-gens my wyll.   **418**
ABRAHAM.
Ya! cum on with me, my
  owyn swet sonn,
And hom-ward fast now let vs goon.
YSAAC.
Be my feyth, fader, therto I
  grant;
I had neuer so good wyll to gon hom,
 And to speke with my dere moder. **423**
ABRAHAM.
A! Lord of heuyn, I thanke
  the,
 For now may I led hom with me
 Ysaac, my yownge sonn soo fre,
  The gentyllest chyld a-bove all other,
  Thys may I wyll a-voee.   **428**

Now goo we forthe, my blyssyd sonn.
YSAAC.
I grant, fader, and let vs gon;
 For, be my trowthe, wer I at home,
 I wold neuer gon owt vnder that forme.[74]
  I pray God geffe vs grace euermo,
  And all thow[75] that we be holdyng
   to.[76]
(*Exeunt.*)   **434**

(*Enter* DOCTOR.)

DOCTOR.
Lo! sovereyns and sorys,[77] now
  haue we schowyd
 Thys solom story to grete and smale.
It ys good lernyng to lernd and lewyd,[78]
 And the wysest of vs all,
  Wythowtyn ony berryng.[79]
For thys story schoyt[80] yowe [her][81]
How we schuld kepe, to owr po[we]re,[81]
 Goddes commawmentes withowt
  grochyng.   **442**

Trowe ye, sores, and God sent an angell
 And commawndyd yow yowr chyld to
  slayn,[82]
Be yowr trowthe, ys ther ony of yow

---

[67]Both your. [68]Number. *Added by Manly*. [69]Ms. goo, *corr. by Holthausen*. [70]Part. [71]Boldly. [72]Thinking. [73]MS. hath, *corr. by Manly*.

[74]Condition? [75]Those. [76]Beholden to. [77]Sirs. [78]Ignorant. [79]Barring. [80]Showeth. [81]*Added by Manly*. [82]MS. to smygth of your chyldes hed; *emended by Holthausen*.

That eyther wold groche or stryve ther-
    ageyn?
How thyngke ye now, sorys, ther-by?   **447**

    I trow ther be iij or iiij or moo.
And thys women, that wepe so sorowfully
    Whan that hyr chyldryn dey them froo,[83]
        As nater woll and kynd,   **451**
    Yt ys but folly, I may well awooe,[84]
    To groche a-gens God or to greve yow,
    For ye schall neuer se hym myschevyd,
        wyll I knowe,
        Be lond nor watyr, haue thys in
            mynd;   **455**

And groche not a-gens owr Lord God
    In welth or woo, wether that he yow send,

Thow ye be neuer so hard bestad;
    For when he wyll, he may yt a-mend,
Hys commawmentes treuly yf ye kepe with
        goo[d] hart,
    As thys story hath now schowyd you
        be-for[n]e,   **461**
And feytheffully serve hym qwyll ye be
        qvart,[85]
    That ye may plece God bothe euyn and
        morne.
    Now Jesu, that weryt the crown of
        thorne,
        Bryng vs all to heuyn blysse!   **465**

FINIS.

---

[83]From.   [84]Avow.   [85]Safe and sound.

FOCUS QUESTIONS

1. Citing aspects of structure as well as content, show how this Brome conforms with the expectations of medieval drama.
2. Describe the different levels on which the conflict between father and son functions in the play.
3. Discuss the uses of *pathos* in the play.
4. Under what secular circumstances might the Brome be made to have contemporary significance? Justify your response.

OTHER ACTIVITIES

1. Sketch and annotate your own approach to directing this Brome. Discuss why you have chosen to adhere or not adhere to medieval stage practices.

BIBLIOGRAPHY

Bibliographic listings for *The Sacrifice of Isaac* have been placed on pp. 146–147 with those for *Master Pierre Pathelin*.

RECOMMENDED VIDEOTAPES AND RECORDINGS

The Creation and Fall. One sound disc recording. Spoken Word. 1970. Features readings from the Brome, Chester, and Wakefield versions of *Abraham and Isaac* directed by John Barton for BBC.

Medieval Theater: The Play of Abraham and Isaac. VHS. 26 min. 1974. Brome version. Distributed by Insight Media, New York City.

The Mysteries, presented by Britain's National Theatre. VHS, in 3 parts. 5 hrs. 49 min. Distributed by Films for the Humanities and Sciences.

MASTER PIERRE PATHELIN
ANONYMOUS

The farce of *Pathelin* is, without question, the most important work of comedy before Molière.

—EDOUARD FOURNIER

Claude Beauclair (*left*) as Pathelin and David Thornton as the Clothier in *Master Pierre Pathelin*, presented by Compagnie Claude Beauclair, under the direction of Monsieur Beauclair.
Photo: Claude Beauclair.

APPROACHING FRENCH MEDIEVAL DRAMA

The dimensions of the medieval drama expanded throughout Western Europe as play-wrights constructed dramatic plots from folk and popular narrative sources. This was a direct outgrowth of the secularization of biblical stories in the cycle plays. (See Preface to *The Sacrifice of Isaac,* p. 111.) Written by townspeople, these plays had served a dual function: teaching biblical lessons to the largely illiterate public and amusing them with characters who reflected the attitudes, foibles, and preoccupations of contemporary common folk.

In addition to the mysteries, whose themes were fairly interchangeable throughout the Holy Roman Empire, a type known as the **miracle play** gained enormous popularity during the fourteenth century. By drawing on a wider range of subjects, including the lives of saints and the miracles they performed, the plays offset the monotony of familiar biblical stories. Often the Virgin Mary would intervene and, like the classical **deus ex machina,** offer a perfect solution to unraveling the otherwise unsolvable plots created by these anonymous playwrights.

Allegories based on church sermons, called **moralities,** became quite popular much later. The form introduced the ideas of good and evil through a device known as **personification.** In the *Everyman* play, for example, the protagonist prepares for death and the journey to heaven in the company of such characters as Fellowship, Knowledge, and Good Deeds, the last of whom is the only one who completes the journey with him. The actions of these plays taught the spectator the ideals of a good Christian life, and their collective theme of humans in relationship to God and Heaven was gradually replaced by narratives that explored the daily interactions of characters living in the present. The realistic scenes and happy endings in these plays offered lessons in moral behavior. Thus these moralities, which were labeled profane, never lost touch with the religious tradition that inspired them.

Comedy was always a popular form in medieval performance. Its ingredients were incorporated into liturgical drama to heighten realism and provide relief, and its pagan merrymaking paid homage to the cycle of rebirth, just as it had in classical times. Since some of these holy days coincided with pagan festivals, the lighter elements of one ritual were bound to mingle with the other until a comfortable interplay between serious and comic styles was quietly established. By exposing human foibles and concentrating on themes of politics, marriage, and religion, the medieval playwright, particularly in France, became a master of the one-act comedy, which would influence the later comic tradition of French dramatic art. (See Preface to Molière, p. 351.)

Farce developed in France as a dramatic form to serve as comic ''filler'' between the dramatically weightier medieval enactments. In delineating its features under the general heading of comedy, farce was further defined by the mechanical antics of sight gags, coarse wit, and exaggerated incongruities, all of which still characterize the form today. The comedies of the Roman Plautus further inspired the tradition of French farce, but in a rather circuitous way. Not long after the decline of the Roman Empire, Plautus' comedies fell into the hands of an anonymous circle of fourth-century stylists who imitated the Roman playwright's craftsmanship. Fortunately, the narratives they produced carried his characters, dialogue, and storylines into twelfth-century France, when Vital de Blois incorporated selected themes from Plautus into his own writings. By the fifteenth century, the guilds of France were sharpening their own comic skills, and their playwrights fell under the Plautine influence. It was under these circumstances that *Master Pierre Pathelin,* whose authorship remains obscure, was written.

THE ACTION

The lawyer Pathelin's reputation as a cheat has cost him many clients and left him penniless. Still he convinces his wife Guillemette that he can swindle the miserly Clothier out of new cloth. Putting his plan into practice, Pathelin flatters him. Before leaving the shop with merchandise purchased on credit, he invites the Clothier to his house for dinner at which time he promises to pay him nine francs.

When the merchant arrives and demands payment, Guillemette pretends that her husband has been confined to his sickbed these many months and that he never visited the shop. Jabbering wildly from his bed, Pathelin feigns madness. Not wanting to be blamed for aggravating his condition, the Clothier leaves the house. Needing to hold someone responsible for his financial loss, he accuses a local Shepherd of robbing his sheep. When Pathelin is hired to serve as the Shepherd's advocate, the three men must untangle their messy affairs in the presence of the equally confused Judge. In the end, the cheat Pathelin is proven the greatest of gulls.

STRUCTURE AND LANGUAGE

The surprisingly durable *Master Pierre Pathelin* was produced in the early fifteenth century, which is also the time of the action. The very notion of a cheater being tricked at his own game held enormous theatrical appeal that, even today, comes freshly to life in performance. This is largely attributed to the abundant satire, primitive charm, and earthly wisdom introduced by a playwright whose work epitomized the French medieval tradition. Whether the inventive premise or handful of scheming characters prompted the achievement, the work was crowned with an inspired outcome, all of which have made the play foolproof.

The domestic bliss once shared by Pathelin and his wife has been soured by the husband's unethical practices, which have reduced them to poverty. No doubt their dilemma embodied an important moral lesson whose repercussions can still be appreciated. In fact, Guillemette's portrait seems unusually assertive, and she proves to be an equally shifty partner by reminding her husband "to drink on the [next] bargain if you find a gullible creditor." In this case, he turns out to be a Clothier whose own greedy tactics have allowed him to charge Pathelin "24 sous a yard for cloth that's not even worth 20!"

The playwright wastes no time exploring the foibles of these slyly drawn characters who not only become prey to each other but whose unscrupulous schemes swiftly beget others. Thus the angry Clothier proceeds to press charges against the Shepherd "for killing my sheep and for all the losses you've caused me in the last ten years." Confident that he can win the Shepherd's case and be paid handsomely if both of them stand up against the Clothier in court, Pathelin advises his client to "answer only with 'baa,' no matter what they say to you." Indeed the clever strategy works. Mistaking the Shepherd for a "natural-born fool" who has spent too much time in the fields, the Judge grants him pardon. Then he dismisses Pathelin and the Clothier, scolding the latter for trying to bring suit "against fools and simpletons."

Pleased with the outcome, for he will no longer need to pay the Clothier the money he owes him, Pathelin asks the Shepherd for his fee. But his client responds with "Baa!"

Pathelin: Why "baa"? You mustn't say it any more. Just pay me generously.
Shepherd: Baa!
Pathelin: Why do you keep saying "baa"? Speak normally and pay me so I can go.

Shepherd: Baa!

Pathelin: You know what? I'll tell you. I'm asking you, please, without any more bleating around the bush to think about paying me. I've had enough of your baa's. Pay up quickly.

The Shepherd has wisely chosen to stay in character and practice the deceit first taught him by the master trickster Pathelin. It is a wonderful conceit that lets Pathelin's ruination hang on a mere word or, better yet, a bleated syllable echoed by someone smarter than he. Pathelin can see that the Shepherd has tricked him out of the money owed him for Pathelin's legal work, but it is too late to change what the court has already decreed.

Whether we marvel at the cleverness by which themes of deception have traveled full circle or laugh at plot complications resolved so ingeniously, we cannot ignore the playwright's witty exposé of the institutions that these characters represent. Foremost is the law, personified by Pathelin, whose loss of professional ethics has damaged his personal code of behavior. The second is marriage, represented by both Pathelins, not only suggesting that their partnership is capable of darker loyalties but that Guillemette may be its controlling force. Commerce is the third, and is represented by the Clothier who will do anything for a profit. Not coincidentally, his trade held great importance to medieval life. Placing the essential verdict in the hands of an incompetent Judge, the playwright takes a final swing at the corrupt legal system before letting its victims fend for themselves. Never losing sight of its primary aim, which was to delight us, the moral of the farce—that we get what we give—resounds loudly, but nowhere enough to drown out our laughter.

ABOUT THE TRANSLATION

This literal prose rendition by Alan E. Knight preserves all sixteen hundred lines of the *moyen français* or Middle French text, including its outspoken language, energy, and humor. The tone of Pathelin's frustration, which launches the unrelenting action, is established in the opening five lines, cited here in the octosyllabic or eight-syllable pattern with rhyming couplets, that were characteristic of the entire original text.

> Saíncté Máríe, Gúillémétté,
> Póur qúelqúe paíne qúe jé métté
> A cabasser n'a ramasser
> Nous ne pouvons rien amasser.
> Or viz je que j'avocassoye.

Adhering to the same two-sentence length, Knight's prose captures Pathelin's predicament with uncanny precision: "Holy Mary, Guillemette, for all the trouble I take to scrimp and save we just can't get ahead. I've seen the day, though, when I was a real attorney." His translation also retains the first of many important allusions to religious characters, a reminder of *Master Pierre Pathelin*'s roots in the earlier medieval drama.

One of the more rewarding highlights of the present text will be found in scene 5, where Knight uses a variety of authentic dialects or "voices" spouted by Pathelin as gibberish during his bouts of madness. While the intricate passages will convey little sense, if any, to the English-speaking audience unacquainted with Middle French dialects, it suggests the farcical impact that Pathelin's mad episodes had on medieval audiences who understood only the principal dialect in which the play had been written. By restoring these passages in their entirety, Knight pays homage to the powerful linguistic features that knitted these characters to their actions, an achievement of great theatrical and literary importance.

MASTER PIERRE PATHELIN-IN-PERFORMANCE

The *mise-en-scène,* or placement of the farce's many components into an integrated stage picture, complies with the staging of earlier mystery plays. In the open air, the actors performed on an elevated platform or scaffold that was possibly mounted on a wagon. There was no curtain behind which scenes could be changed. In the middle of the scaffold, however, stood four posts around which loose drapes were hung to suggest a room that faced the audience. This scanty space served as the Pathelin bedroom and the Clothier's shop.

A few simple props and pieces of furniture were used to differentiate both settings: a small bed represented the Pathelin household; a trestle signified the Clothier's shop; the Judge, seated on his chair, established the courtroom. The costumes reflected the simple tastes of fifteenth-century life. As mistress of the house, Guillemette wore a long dress with a key chain hanging down her side. Both Pathelin and the Clothier wore knee-length robes. The Shepherd was identified by the crook he held in his hand, and the Judge was attired as a contemporary fifteenth-century *bourgeois* from Paris. The limited production values, simultaneous settings, and basic attire made strong demands on the audience's imagination in creating the world of the play.

While scant performance documentation for *Master Pierre Pathelin* exists prior to the twentieth century, the shrewd Pathelin and his games of deceit have inspired an international coterie of authors no less than the playwright Molière. Thanks to this stage character, the French language inherited the adjective *patelin* and the verb *pateliner*. Even the idiomatic expression, ''Revenons à ces moutons'' (''Let us return to the subject'')—literally ''to these sheep''—became a well-known French proverb not long after the play became popular. This may be attributed to the fact that *Master Pierre Pathelin* was one of the earliest masterpieces of French literature to be officially published.

Between 1486 and 1499, four separate editions became available, one including a series of wood engravings that illustrated the principal scenes from the farce. The popularity of the text continued during the sixteenth century, while newer editions—and amateur performances of the farce—multiplied. In 1614, a Paris edition was published by Pierre Menier, although one hundred years earlier, a Latin adaptation entitled *Veterator* had been performed by students in Paris. In 1706, a popular comedy by Brueys and Palaprat was based on *Master Pierre Pathelin.* The first critical edition of the text was published in France in the nineteenth century, and by the twentieth century, translations and productions of the play could be found all over the world.

The farce appeared in a program of four one-act plays produced by the Washington Square Players at the Bandbox Theatre in New York City in March of 1916. Maurice Relonde was the translator and adaptor. When the company relocated at the Comedy Theatre two months later, the play was performed again. An entirely different production of the comedy opened at the Maxine Elliott Theatre on December 12, 1937, in an adaptation by M. Jagendorf. Produced under the auspices of the WPA Federal Theatre Project, the production reappeared on April 19, 1938, in a series of four matinee performances at the Hippodrome. The famous medieval trickster surfaced on his own native soil in 1941, this time in a performance by Denis d'Inès at the Comédie Française, where the revival scored a triumph. In 1968, the San Francisco Mime Troupe revived the play in the *commedia dell'arte* style. Since the 1970s, Compagnie Claude Beauclair has continued to perform the play throughout the world.

REFLECTIONS ON MASTER PIERRE PATHELIN

Claude Beauclair is co-director with Françoise Mojeret of Compagnie Claude Beauclair.

Since the Compagnie Claude Beauclair was established in 1970, it has traveled every year throughout Europe, the United States, Africa, and Asia. Our wide repertoire has always included the classics, such as Molière, Musset, Corneille, and Racine, and moderns like Sartre, Ionesco, Beckett, and Genet. But one day we thought we would try something unusual and we had the idea to do the medieval farce, *Pierre Pathelin.* When I asked our audiences how they felt about it, many thought it was an interesting idea because it is not very often that anyone has the chance to see this kind of play.

One of our principal concerns with the play was that it was originally written in the old French—and in verse, which is not only difficult for our French-speaking actors, but can be a greater problem for English-speaking audiences as well, many of whom do not understand French. Since we did not want to use the authentic version, we developed a prose adaptation that retained many of the old forms, but updated others for modern ears. We have used this same version no matter where we have performed the play.

Although so many international audiences have responded enthusiastically to both classic and modern works of our repertoire, *Pathelin* has turned out to be one of the most popular. I think this is because audiences really love the story and are impressed with how the more traditional elements of the language and situations can still be meaningful to them today. The play provides a total theatre experience. It happens to be a wonderful comedy, too.

But most of all, actors have a great time with the play because it gives us so many different things to do. All the situations are so well written that we can build our characters just by sticking to the text. Take the role of the Shepherd, for example. His purpose in the play is so clearly defined that even a bad actor can be a triumph in the part and steal the show in the end. Perhaps the most difficult role belongs to the Clothier who must play the same attitude throughout, very much like a straight man to the other characters. As for Guillemette, she is probably the most sympathetic character next to the Shepherd. She loves her husband and tries to help him, right or wrong. After all, she has been taught by a master.

The role of Pathelin is the most theatrical of all. While playing the role, I have discovered so many facets to him. He is *one* type of character with his wife, Guillemette, but through role playing, instantly changes his personality when he confronts the Clothier. When he returns to his house and climbs into his bed, his "madness" gives him more things to do. Depending on our audience, I have improvised different languages in this scene: strange expressions in Italian, German, and even Japanese. On other occasions, I have spoken in French, but with different accents. The audiences always love it! Pathelin is very much the center of the play and all the other characters move around him. But they need him just as much as he needs them.

The original text is so rich that it has allowed us to uncover some very funny gags. In the scene where I'm in bed, Guillemette serves us some wine. She stands at my left and the Clothier at my right. The scene is played entirely in pantomime. First I propose a toast by drinking the wine down to the last drop and tossing my glass behind the bed, at which point a noise of crashing glass is heard. Now the Clothier performs a similar toast: he drinks and tosses his glass behind the bed, but there is no crash this time, only silence. The audience goes wild. I guess Pathelin has demonstrated his magical touch, while the Clothier is reduced to playing the straight man once again.

Ideas such as these turn up in rehearsal or on stage no matter how often we have performed the play. One time during my mad scene I grabbed a broom and started shooting it like a rifle all over the stage. On another occasion, when I was performing the same scene and marching around the room, I got this crazy idea and, all of a sudden, started to whistle that famous marching tune from *The Bridge on the River Kwai.* The audience loved it so much—that unexpected moment of recognition, I suppose—that I kept it in for the rest of the tour. The mad scene is so well constructed that it can afford these improvisational moments without losing its impact. But I never take such liberties in the other scenes. I remain close to where the other characters are and play those scenes as they are written.

We always play the final courtroom scene with humor, but no exaggeration. The judge demonstrates some wonderful facial expressions, but the object of the trial is fairly serious. One of our actors who has played the Shepherd many times is tall and large with a round head. He wears a sheepskin jacket with simple trousers. Whenever the judge asks him a question, he pulls a piece of fur from his jacket, as if to play dumb. The amazing thing about this final scene is that, as soon as the Shepherd says "Baa-baa—!," the audience laughs and no other word spoken by the other characters seems to matter. The situation is so intense that the audience grasps everything even if they don't understand a word of French. The lesson or moral, that Pathelin deserves what is coming back to him, is instantly clear. I'd like to think this scene had the same kind of impact on its medieval audience, with no outside explanations necessary.

A very fine adaptation of *Pierre Pathelin* was written for the Comédie Française by Denis d' Inès, one of the great actors from that company who was also one of my teachers. He was a famous Pathelin in the 1941 production at the Comédie Française. In fact, the first time I went on the stage of the Comédie Française was with d' Inès in *The Miser* by Molière, a comedy that was greatly influenced by *Pathelin.* It is a good feeling to have been a part of that wonderful tradition. *Pierre Pathelin* is always given full-scaled productions at the Comédie Française. That's because the company performs on their own permanent stage and never travels. But we know that the medieval plays moved from one town to another. In much the same way, my own troupe travels to many theatres with a variety of cloths to cover the stage furniture and recreate some of this original performance style. In fact, all of our costumes, props, and accessories are traditional in our performance of this comedy. Nothing is modern-looking.

Our troupe has performed *Pierre Pathelin* on stages both large and small and to audiences of all ages. The play easily adjusts to the size of each stage and always plays well. Our set is divided into three playing areas. Pathelin's house is located on the right side of the stage, with the Clothier's shop on the left. The characters move quickly from one location to the other, and if we are lucky to be playing on a stage where there are steps around the orchestra, the actors will cross down in front of the audience to get to the other side.

Continued

There is always musical accompaniment when we move from one playing area to another. We like to use simple lighting effects to highlight these areas. The important courtroom scene is always played downstage center, where the wise old judge presides.

It is very interesting that when you read the play or see it in performance, you discover so many references to God, the Virgin Mary, St. John, St. Peter, and so many others. Even the devil is mentioned. These references remind us how the play grew out of the tradition of liturgical mysteries that were being performed around the same time. How fascinating that this work remained connected to these sources, even when it chose to make fun of them. And just like other plays that enjoy certain periods of popularity on the stage, *Pathelin* has always been around to exert its influence on later works, including Molière's. For me it's the Monteverdi of the classic French theatre!

The play remains popular because we can find *pathelins* or tricksters everywhere in our society. They exist in all professions. But no matter how hard the character of Pathelin works in performance, the audiences remember the Shepherd best of all. When our audiences return to see us, they always tell us how fantastic the Shepherd was. And all he has to do is "Baaa!!!" But in doing so, he is able to silence Pathelin forever. With one simple word—"Baaa!"—he puts the whole world in his pocket. We don't know who wrote this play, but whoever did had a terrific idea.

MASTER PIERRE PATHELIN
Anonymous
Translated by Alan E. Knight

CHARACTERS

Pathelin (*a lawyer*)
Guillemette (*his wife*)

Guillaume Joceaulme (*a clothier*)
Thibault Aignelet (*a shepherd*)

The Judge

SCENE ONE

PATHELIN.   Holy Mary, Guillemette, for all the trouble I take to scrimp and save we just can't get ahead. I've seen the day, though, when I was a real attorney.

GUILLEMETTE.   By Our Lady of the Law Trade! I was just thinking about that. But now people don't think you're nearly as clever as they used to. I remember when everybody wanted you to take his case. Now they all call you a prattling pettifogger.

PATHELIN.   And I don't mean to brag, of course, but there's not a sharper fellow in the whole circuit, except maybe the mayor.

GUILLEMETTE.   Yes, but he's studied his Latin grammar and he knows how to conjure his verbs.

PATHELIN.   Whose case don't I expedite if I decide to take it on? It's true I don't know much Latin, but when I chant with our priest from the mass-book, it sounds like I've studied for as long as Charlemagne stayed in Spain.

GUILLEMETTE.   But what's it worth to us? Not a thing! We're starving to death, our clothes have as many holes as a sieve, and we have no idea how we can get new ones. So, what's all your knowledge worth to us?

PATHELIN.   Hold your tongue! I swear, if I really put my mind to it, I'll find out where to get some clothes—and some headgear too. God willing, we'll pull out of this and be back on our feet in no time. "God does a deed with all due speed," they say. If I really have to apply myself to further my practice, you won't be able to find my equal.

GUILLEMETTE.   By Saint James, certainly not in swindling. At that you're a past master.

PATHELIN.   By God, you mean a master of proper lawyering.

GUILLEMETTE.   By my faith, you're a master deceiver. I know, because, despite your little learning and less common sense, you're taken for one of the slyest wits in the parish.

PATHELIN.   Nobody knows the finer points of the law the way I do.

GUILLEMETTE.   Or the finer points of cheating, by God. At least that's the reputation you have.

PATHELIN.   And so have those who wear fine clothes of silk and velvet, who claim to be lawyers, but aren't. Enough of this chatter, I'm off to the fair.

GUILLEMETTE.   To the fair?

PATHELIN.   Yes, by Saint John! (*He sings.*) "To the fair, my pretty maid . . ." Would it displease you if I bought some cloth or some other little thing that we need? Our clothes are nothing but rags.

GUILLEMETTE.   But you don't have a penny to bless yourself with. What'll you do there?

PATHELIN.   Don't ask too many questions, my lady. But if I don't bring back enough cloth to outfit us both, then call me a liar to my face. What color would you like? A gray-green, a Brussels black, or what? I need to know.

GUILLEMETTE.   Whatever you can get. Beggars can't be choosers.

PATHELIN (*counting on his fingers*).   Two and a half yards for you and three for me, or maybe four. That makes . . .

GUILLEMETTE.   You count off the yards very generously, but who the Devil will give you that much cloth on credit?

PATHELIN.   What do you care who? Somebody will give it to me and with payment due on Judgment Day, because it won't be paid for any sooner.

GUILLEMETTE.   Very well then. In that case, no matter what happens, we'll be covered.

PATHELIN.   I'll buy some gray or green, Guillemette, and for a waistcoat I'll need three quarters of a yard of fine black cloth . . . or maybe a yard.

GUILLEMETTE.   Indeed! God help me! Go ahead then and don't forget to drink on the bargain if you find a gullible creditor.

PATHELIN.   Take care of things here. (*He leaves.*)

GUILLEMETTE.   Oh God! But what merchant . . . ? Whoever it is, I just pray he's blind as a bat.

SCENE TWO

PATHELIN (*approaching the Clothier's shop*).   Isn't that the one there? No, I don't think so. Yes it is, by Saint Mary. He deals in cloth goods. (*To the Clothier.*) God be with you.

GUILLAUME JOCEAULME, CLOTHIER.   And God give you joy.

PATHELIN.   So help me, you're just the person I wanted to see. How's your health, Guillaume? Are you hale and hearty?

THE CLOTHIER.   Yes, thank God.

PATHELIN.   Here, shake. How are things going?

THE CLOTHIER.   Pretty well. (*They shake.*) At your service. And how are you?

PATHELIN.   By Saint Peter, I'm as well as ever. So, you're enjoying life?

THE CLOTHIER.   Yes, but believe me, merchants can't always do as they please.

PATHELIN.   And how's business? Are you able to keep the wolf from the door?

THE CLOTHIER.   So help me God, Master Pierre, it's hard to say. It's always work, work, work.

PATHELIN.   Ah, what a wise man your father was! God rest his soul. By Our Lady, it seems to me that you're like him in every way. What a good and clever merchant he was. (*He stares at the Clothier.*) Your face resembles his, by God, like a perfect picture. If God ever had mercy on one of his creatures, may he grant true pardon to his soul.

THE CLOTHIER.   Amen! And to us too if it please him.

PATHELIN.   By my faith, he often predicted in great detail the times we live in now; and I often think of what he said, for he was considered one of the best.

THE CLOTHIER.   Please sit down, sir. It's high time I remembered my manners.

PATHELIN.   I'm fine like this. By heaven, your father had . . .

THE CLOTHIER.   Truly, you must sit down.

PATHELIN.   Very well. (*He sits down.*) "Ah," he used to say to me, "you will see great marvels." (*He stares at the Clothier again.*) Look at those eyes, those ears, that nose, that mouth! So help me God, never did a son more closely resemble his father! And look at that dimpled chin; you're really a chip off the old block. If anyone should say to your mother that you're not your father's son, he'd just be itching for a quarrel. Truly I can't imagine how nature in all her works formed two faces so much alike that one is blemished exactly like the other. Why, it's as if somebody had spit you both out in the same way, like two gobs against a wall. You're the very spit and image of your father. By the way, what about the good Laurence, your lovely aunt? Did she pass away?

THE CLOTHIER.   No, certainly not.

PATHELIN.   How beautiful she was when I saw her, tall and straight and graceful. By the precious Mother of God, you resemble her in shape as if someone had made you both of snow. I think there's not a family in the whole region whose members look so much alike. (*He gets up and stares more intently at the Clothier.*) By God, the more I look at you, the more I see your father. You're more alike than two drops of water, without a doubt. What a gentleman he was, what an honest man, who would sell his goods on credit to anyone who asked. May God have mercy on him. He always used to give me a hearty laugh. Would to Christ the worst in the world were like him; then people wouldn't rob and steal from one another the way they do. (*He feels a piece of cloth.*) What a fine piece of cloth this is, so soft and smooth, and so attractive.

THE CLOTHIER.   I had it specially made from the wool of my own sheep.

PATHELIN.   Ah, what a good business man you are! But you wouldn't be your father's son, if you weren't. You just never stop working.

THE CLOTHIER.   So what do you expect? If a man wants to make a living, he's got to toil and sweat.

PATHELIN (*feeling another piece of cloth*).   And this cloth, is it dyed in the wool? It's as strong as leather.

THE CLOTHIER.   It's a very good fabric from Rouen, and well made I assure you.

PATHELIN.   Well, I'm really tempted. By the Lord's passion, I had no intention of buying cloth when I came. I've saved up 80 gold pieces to pay off a debt, but I can see you're going to get 20 or 30 of them. I like that color so much it hurts.

THE CLOTHIER.   Gold pieces? Indeed! Is it possible that the people you're indebted to would take some other coinage instead?

PATHELIN.   Oh yes, if I wanted them to. It doesn't matter to me how it's paid. (*He feels another piece of cloth.*) And what cloth is this? The more I look at it, the crazier I am about it. I'll have to have a coat made of it, and another for my wife.

THE CLOTHIER.   As you know, cloth is very expensive these days. I'll sell you some if you wish, but 10 or 20 francs won't buy very much.

PATHELIN.   That doesn't matter; it's worth the price. Besides, I have a few sous put away that have never seen the light of day.

THE CLOTHIER.   God be praised! By Saint Peter, that doesn't displease me a bit.

PATHELIN.   To be brief, I'm so taken with this cloth that I just have to have some of it.

THE CLOTHIER.   All right. First you must decide how much you need. Take as much as you want. In fact, I could let *you* take the entire bolt even if you didn't have a sou.

PATHELIN.   That's kind of you. Thanks very much.

THE CLOTHIER.   Do you want some of this light blue?

PATHELIN.   First, how much will a yard cost me? Wait, here's a penny. God's share should be paid first; it's only right. "Let no bargain be made before God's share is paid." (*He puts the coin in a collection box.*)

THE CLOTHIER.   By God, that's the talk of an honest man; you've really cheered me up. Do you want my last word on the price?

PATHELIN.   Yes.

THE CLOTHIER.   It will cost *you* only 24 sous per yard.

PATHELIN.   Never! 24 sous? Holy Mother!

THE CLOTHIER.   That's just what it cost me, by my soul! I'll have to charge at least that, if you take it.

PATHELIN.   The Devil take it! It's too much.

THE CLOTHIER.   But you don't realize how much cloth has gone up. All the sheep died last winter in the great freeze.

PATHELIN.   Twenty sous! Twenty sous!

THE CLOTHIER.   I swear to you I have to charge 24. Just wait till market day on Saturday and you'll see what it costs. A fleece that used to cost 20 pence when they were plentiful, cost me 40 pence last July.

PATHELIN.   By God, if that's the way it is, then without more haggling I'll buy. Come on, measure it.

THE CLOTHIER.   How much do you need?

PATHELIN.   That's easy to figure out. What's the width?

THE CLOTHIER.   The standard Brussels width.

PATHELIN.   Three yards for me and two and a half yards for my wife—she's tall. That makes six yards, doesn't it? . . . No it doesn't. How stupid of me!

THE CLOTHIER.   It only lacks half a yard of being six exactly.

PATHELIN.   Then I'll round it off at six. Anyway, I need a hat.

THE CLOTHIER.   Take that end and we'll measure it. I'm sure we've got a good six yards here. One . . . two . . . three . . . four . . . five . . . and six.

PATHELIN.   Saint Peter's gut! It's six on the nose.

THE CLOTHIER.   Shall I measure it again?

PATHELIN.   No, for Pete's sake! There's always a little gain or loss in business deals. How much is that altogether?

THE CLOTHIER.   Let's see. At 24 sous a yard and six yards, it comes to nine francs.

PATHELIN.   That makes six gold pieces, right?

THE CLOTHIER.   That's right, by God.

PATHELIN.   Then, Sir, will you give me that much credit for the short time it takes to come to my house? It's not really credit. You'll have your money, in gold or in francs, as soon as you reach the door.

THE CLOTHIER.   By our Lady! I'd have to go far out of my way to get there.

PATHELIN.   I swear to God, not a word has passed your lips since you failed to speak the gospel truth. You say it's far out of your way. The thing is, you've never wanted to find an occasion to come drink at my house. But this time you will have a drink there.

THE CLOTHIER.   By Saint James, I hardly do anything but drink to seal the bargain with my customers. I'll go, but it's bad luck, you know, to give credit on the first sale of the day.

PATHELIN.   Isn't it worth it if I pay you in gold coins instead of the common currency? By God, we'll even eat the goose that my wife is roasting.

THE CLOTHIER (*aside*).   This man is driving me crazy! (*To Pathelin.*) Go ahead then. I'll come later and bring the cloth.

PATHELIN.   There's no need for that. Will it burden me if I just tuck it under my arm? Not in the least.

THE CLOTHIER.   No, don't bother. It would be more fitting and proper if I carried it.

PATHELIN.   May Mary Magdalene send me misfortune if I put you to that trouble. As I said, under the arm. It'll give me a nice hump. (*He puts the cloth under his arm inside his robe.*) There, that's perfect. You'll have plenty of drink and good cheer before you leave my house.

THE CLOTHIER.   Please give me my money as soon as I arrive.

PATHELIN.   Of course I will. No, I won't, by God, not until you've been well fed. And I'm glad I didn't have any money on me. At least you'll come sample my wine. Your late father, when he passed my house, used to call out: "Hi there, friend," or "What do you say?" or "What's new?" But now you rich people don't care a straw about us poor people.

THE CLOTHIER.   God in heaven, I'm a lot poorer than you are.

PATHELIN.   Well, so long; goodbye. Come to my house as soon as you can and we'll drink well, I promise you.

THE CLOTHIER.   I'll do that. Go on ahead, but see that I get the gold.

PATHELIN.   Gold? I give you my word. And the Devil take me if I ever broke my word. (*He leaves the shop.*) Gold, indeed! Well, hang him! He wouldn't sell to me at my price, only at his. But he'll be paid at mine. He needs gold, does he? Fool's gold he'll get. By God, if he had to run from now till he's paid, he'd get to the end of the world first.

THE CLOTHIER.   Those gold pieces he gives me won't see daylight for a whole year, I swear, unless somebody steals them. Well, there's no buyer so clever that he won't find a seller who can outwit him. That would-be trickster was stupid enough to pay 24 sous a yard for cloth that's not even worth 20!

SCENE THREE

PATHELIN.   Well, did I get it?

GUILLEMETTE.   What?

PATHELIN.   What happened to your old worn-out dress?

GUILLEMETTE.   That's just what it was. What do you want with it?

PATHELIN.   Nothing. Nothing. So did I get it? I told you I would. (*He takes the cloth from beneath his robe.*) How's that for a piece of cloth?

GUILLEMETTE.   Holy Mother! I'll stake my salvation there's been a swindle. Oh, God! What have you gotten us into now? Alas! Alas! Who'll pay for it.

PATHELIN.   Who'll pay for it, you ask. By Saint John, it's paid for. The draper that sold it to me wasn't as crazy as all that, my love. May I be hanged if I didn't bleed him white as a sack of plaster. The thieving ragpicker got what he deserved.

GUILLEMETTE.   How much did it cost?

PATHELIN.   I owe nothing. He's been paid, so don't worry.

GUILLEMETTE.   He's been paid? But you didn't have a penny. What did you use for money?

PATHELIN.   I swear to you, woman, I did have money. I had one Paris penny.

GUILLEMETTE.   You either signed a note or used a magic formula; that's how you got it. And when the note comes due, they'll come and seize all our goods. Everything we have will be taken away.

PATHELIN.   I swear to God, the whole thing cost only a penny.

GUILLEMETTE.   *Benedicite Maria!* Only a penny? That can't be.

PATHELIN.   You can pluck out this eye if he got more than that or ever does get more, no matter what tune he sings.

GUILLEMETTE.   Who's the merchant?

PATHELIN.   It's a certain Guillaume whose last name is Joceaulme, if you must know.

GUILLEMETTE.   But how did you get it for one penny? What was the trick?

PATHELIN.   It was God's penny that sealed the bargain. If I had asked him to drink on it instead, I could have kept the penny. Still, it was a pretty good deal. He and God can divide that penny if they want to, because it's all they'll get from me, no matter how much they rant and rave.

GUILLEMETTE.   How did he decide to let you have the cloth on credit? He's so bullheaded.

PATHELIN.   By Saint Mary, I flattered him and his whole family tree so much that he almost gave it to me. I told him that his late father was such a worthy man. "Oh, my friend," says I, "what good stock you come from! Your lineage," says I, "is the purest in the whole district." But I swear to God that guy comes from the scurviest lot of scoundrels and the vilest riffraff in the country. "Guillaume, my friend," says I, "how much you resemble your good father in looks and in every other way!" God knows I piled on the flattery, and all the while I was throwing in remarks about his cloth. "Holy Mary," says I, "how easily he gave his merchandise on credit, and without pretense! I can see," says I, "that you're his spit and image." But you could pull all the teeth of that sea-hog of a father and that baboon of a son before they'd give you anything on credit or even give you the time of day. Anyway, I talked so fast that he finally gave me six yards on credit.

GUILLEMETTE.   Really? And you never have to return it?

PATHELIN.   That's right. If I return anything to him, it'll be the Devil.

GUILLEMETTE.   That reminds me of the fable of the crow, who was sitting up on a high cross with a piece of cheese in his beak. A fox came by and, seeing the cheese, thought to himself, "How can I get that?" Then he sat directly beneath the crow and said, "Ah, you have such splendid feathers and your song is so melodious." The vain and foolish crow, hearing his song praised like that, opened his beak to sing. His cheese fell to the ground and Master Fox grabbed it in his teeth and ran. That's just the way it was, I'm sure, with this cloth. You got it by flattery and sweet-talk, the same way the fox got the cheese. You really put one over on him.

PATHELIN.   He's supposed to come eat goose with us, so here's what we have to do. I know he'll come whining to have his money immediately and I've planned a good reception for him. I'll go get into bed and pretend to be sick and when he comes you'll say, "Shh! Speak softly," and you'll moan and put on a long face. "Alas," you'll say, "he's been sick for the past six or eight weeks." And if he says to you, "That's a lot of nonsense! He just left my shop a few minutes ago," you'll say, "Alas! This is a poor time to be making jokes." Then I'll make him think he's on a wild goose chase, because that's the only kind of goose or anything else he'll ever get here.

GUILLEMETTE.   I swear I'll play the role to perfection. But if you get caught again and brought to justice, I'm afraid it'll be twice as bad as it was before.

PATHELIN.   Quiet. I know what I'm doing; we have to do exactly what I said.

GUILLEMETTE.   But, for God's sake, think of that Saturday they put you in the pillory. You know how everybody jeered at you for your shady dealings.

PATHELIN.   Enough of such talk. He'll be here any minute now and we've got to keep this cloth. I'm going to get into bed.

GUILLEMETTE.   Go ahead.

PATHELIN.   Now don't laugh.

GUILLEMETTE.   Of course I won't. I'll be crying hot tears.

PATHELIN.   We both have to be serious so he won't suspect anything.

SCENE FOUR

THE CLOTHIER (*in his shop*).   I think it's time for me to have a little drink before I leave. Oh, no I won't. I'll soon be drinking and eating goose at Master Pierre Pathelin's house. By the patron saint of fools, I'll get my money there and the special treat they're preparing, and it won't cost me a sou. I can't sell anything more here, so I'll be going.

SCENE FIVE

THE CLOTHIER (*shouts in front of Pathelin's house*).   Hey There! Master Pierre!

GUILLEMETTE (*opening the door*).   Please sir, for the love of God, if you have something to say, speak softly.

THE CLOTHIER.   God be with you, Madame.

GUILLEMETTE.   Shh! Softer.

THE CLOTHIER.   What's the matter?

GUILLEMETTE.   Bless my soul . . .

THE CLOTHIER.   Where is he?

GUILLEMETTE.   Alas! Where should he be?

THE CLOTHIER.   Who . . . ?

GUILLEMETTE.   Ah, that was ill-spoken, my good sir. "Where is he," indeed! May God in his mercy have pity on him. The poor suffering man is in the same place he's been without budging for eleven weeks now.

THE CLOTHIER.   But who . . . ?

GUILLEMETTE.   Pardon me, but I don't dare speak louder. I think he's resting now; he was a little drowsy. Alas, he's so sick, the poor man.

THE CLOTHIER.   Who?

GUILLEMETTE.   Master Pierre.

THE CLOTHIER.   What? Didn't he come to my shop to get six yards of cloth just now?

GUILLEMETTE.   Who? Him?

THE CLOTHIER.   He just left there, not ten minutes ago. Hurry up! Devil take me, I've stayed too long already. Quick, give me my money and no more foolishness.

GUILLEMETTE.   Hey! No more of *your* foolishness! This is no time to joke around.

THE CLOTHIER.   Are you crazy? My money! Now! You owe me nine francs.

GUILLEMETTE.   Ah, Guillaume, are you making fun of me? This is no asylum for lunatics. Go tell your nonsense to fools like yourself and play your tricks on them.

THE CLOTHIER.   May I renounce God, if I don't get my nine francs!

GUILLEMETTE.   Alas, Sir, not everyone is as eager to laugh and gossip as you are.

THE CLOTHIER.   Please, I beg you, no more joking. Just have Master Pierre come here, for the love of . . .

GUILLEMETTE.   Misfortune strike you down! Will this go on all day?

THE CLOTHIER.   But isn't this the house of Master Pierre Pathelin?

GUILLEMETTE.   Of course! May the patron saint of lunatics (*crosses herself*) addle your brain! Speak low!

THE CLOTHIER.   The Devil take your "speak low"! Shouldn't I ask for what's mine?

GUILLEMETTE.   God help me! Speak low, if you don't want him to wake up.

THE CLOTHIER.   How "low" do you want? In the ear? In the cellar? Or in the bottom of the well?

GUILLEMETTE.   My God, how you drivel on! But that's always been your way.

THE CLOTHIER.   The Devil it has! (*Calming down.*) Now that I think about it, if you want me to speak low, just say so. I'm really not used to arguments like this. The truth is that Master Pierre took six yards of cloth today.

GUILLEMETTE.   What is this? Will this go on all day? The Devil take it! Now, just what do you mean by "took"? Oh, may the one who's lying be hanged! That poor man is in such a pitiful state that he hasn't left his bed in eleven weeks. Then you come along with your wild ideas. Now is that right? By God's passion, you'll leave my house at once. Oh, what misery!

THE CLOTHIER.   You asked *me* to speak so low. Now, by the Holy Virgin, you're screaming.

GUILLEMETTE.   So help me, you're the one who can't speak without quarreling.

THE CLOTHIER.   Look, so I can go, just give me . . .

GUILLEMETTE (*shouting*). Are you going to speak low?

THE CLOTHIER.   But you're going to wake him yourself. Damn it all, you're yelling four times louder than I am. I insist that you pay me.

GUILLEMETTE.   What is this? Are you drunk or just out of your mind? God in heaven!

THE CLOTHIER.   Drunk! Saint Peter curse you! What a question!

GUILLEMETTE.   Please! Speak lower!

THE CLOTHIER.   By Saint George, I demand payment for six yards of cloth!

GUILLEMETTE.   You must have been dreaming. And just who did you give it to?

THE CLOTHIER.   To him.

GUILLEMETTE.   He's in fine shape to be buying cloth. Alas, he can't even move. He has no need for new clothes. He'll never get dressed again, except in graveclothes; and he'll never leave his room again, except feet first.

THE CLOTHIER.   Then this happened since early this morning, because I spoke to him for sure.

GUILLEMETTE (*in a loud voice*). Your voice is so loud. For the love of God, speak lower!

THE CLOTHIER.   You're the one shouting, damn it all, you and nobody else. God help me, this is agony. Will somebody pay me so I can go! By God, every time I've given credit, I've had nothing but trouble.

PATHELIN (*from his bed*). Guillemette, a little rose water. Prop me up. Tuck me in behind. Damn! Who was I talking to? The water jar! Give me a drink! Rub my feet!

THE CLOTHIER.   I hear him in there.

GUILLEMETTE.   Yes.

PATHELIN (*delirious*). Ah, wicked woman! Come here! Did I tell you to open these windows? Come cover me up. Get rid of these people in black! *Marmara carimari carimara!* Take them away from me, away!

GUILLEMETTE.   What's the matter? You're tossing about so. Have you lost your senses?

PATHELIN.   You don't see what I see. There's a monk in black flying around the room. Catch him. Get a stole to exorcise him! The cat! Get the cat! Look how he rises up!

GUILLEMETTE.   What is all this? Aren't you ashamed? This is too much stirring about, for heaven's sake.

PATHELIN.   Those doctors are killing me with all the vile potions they make me drink. And yet we have to believe them; we're like putty in their hands.

GUILLEMETTE (*to the Clothier*). Alas! Come and see him, good sir. He's suffering terribly.

THE CLOTHIER.   Was he taken so ill on returning from the fair?

GUILLEMETTE.   The fair?

THE CLOTHIER.   Yes, by Saint John! I'm sure he was there. Master Pierre! I need the money for the cloth I gave you on credit.

PATHELIN (*pretending to take the Clothier for a doctor*). Ah, Doctor John! I shat two tiny black turds, round as balls and hard as rocks. Should I take another enema?

THE CLOTHIER.   How should I know? What've I got to do with enemas? I want my nine francs or six gold pieces.

PATHELIN.   Those three black sharp things—you call those pills? They nearly busted my jaws. For God's sake don't make me take any more of them, Doctor John. There's nothing in the world more bitter, and they made everything come up again.

THE CLOTHIER.   No they didn't, by God. My nine francs haven't appeared yet.

GUILLEMETTE.   Hang such tiresome people. (*To the Clothier.*) Go away, by all the devils, since it can't be on God's part.

THE CLOTHIER.   I swear to God, I'll get my cloth before I leave, or my nine francs.

PATHELIN (*pretending the Clothier is a doctor*). And my urine specimen, doesn't it show that I'm dying? For God's sake, whatever happens, don't let me die.

GUILLEMETTE (*to the Clothier*). Be off with you! It's terrible to torment him like this.

THE CLOTHIER.   Lord God in heaven! Six yards of cloth! Tell me, do you think it's right that I should lose it?

PATHELIN.   Oh, Doctor John! Do you think you could loosen my bowels? I'm so constipated I don't know how I stand to sit on the throne.

THE CLOTHIER.   I want my nine francs now or by Saint Peter of Rome . . .

GUILLEMETTE.   Alas! You're tormenting this man so. How can you be so cruel? You can see plain as day that he thinks you're his doctor. Alas! The poor soul has had such misfortune. He's been in that bed for eleven straight weeks, the poor man!

THE CLOTHIER.   By God, I don't know how this sickness came about, because today he was in my shop and we did business together—at least it seems we did. Otherwise I don't know what could have happened.

GUILLEMETTE.   By Our Lady, I think your memory is slipping, my friend. If you take my advice, you'll go get some rest. Besides there are a lot of gossips around who'll think you came in here to see me. Go on now; his doctors will be here soon.

THE CLOTHIER.   I don't care if others do think evil of it, because I have no such thoughts. Damn it all, how'd I get into this mess? I swear to God, I thought . . .

GUILLEMETTE.   Again?

THE CLOTHIER.   And don't you have a goose cooking?

GUILLEMETTE.   What a question! Sir, that's not a dish for sick people. Go chase your own goose and don't come here making fun of us. You've got some nerve to do that.

THE CLOTHIER.   Please excuse me, but I really thought . . .

GUILLEMETTE.   Still?

THE CLOTHIER.   By the sacrament! Goodbye! (*He leaves the house.*) Now I've got to figure this out. I know I should have six yards of cloth in one piece. But that woman addles my brain so much I can't think. He really did take the cloth. . . . No, he couldn't have, damn it! It just doesn't fit. I saw Death coming to strike him down—at least he so pretended. . . . Yes he did! He did take the cloth and he put it under his arm, by Saint Mary! . . . No, he didn't. Maybe I'm dreaming. But even in my sleep I'd never give my cloth away to anybody, no matter how much I liked him. I just wouldn't have given credit . . . By God, he did take the cloth! . . . No, damn it all, he didn't. I know he didn't. But where does that leave me! . . . Yes he did, by Our Lady's passion! . . . Misfortune take me, body and soul, if I know who could decide who got the best of this deal, them or me. I just can't figure it out.

PATHELIN.   Is he gone?

GUILLEMETTE.   Quiet, I'm listening. I don't know what he was muttering, but he left grumbling so much that he was almost hysterical.

PATHELIN.   Isn't it time for me to get up? We sure pulled that one off.

GUILLEMETTE.   I don't know if he's coming back or not. (*Pathelin starts to get up.*) No, don't get up yet! Everything would be ruined if he found you out of bed.

PATHELIN.   He's always so suspicious of others, but by God he met his match this time. The joke was on him and it fit like a cross on a steeple.

GUILLEMETTE.   No greedy shark ever took the bait quicker than he did. It serves him right. He never gives a thing in church on Sundays. (*She laughs.*)

PATHELIN.   For God's sake, don't laugh. If he came back and heard you, it would spoil everything. I'm sure he'll be back.

GUILLEMETTE.   Hold in your laughter if you can, but I swear I can't help myself.

THE CLOTHIER (*at his shop*). By the sacred sun that shines, I'm going back to that backwoods barrister, I don't care what anybody says. Oh, God! That phoney financial fraud would fleece his own family. Now, by St. Peter, I know he has my cloth, the sneaky swindler. I gave it to him right on this spot.

GUILLEMETTE.   When I think of the face he made looking at you, I can't help laughing. He was so greedy in asking you for . . .

PATHELIN.   Peace, you cackler! I swear to God, if he came back and heard you, we might as well start running. He's such a sour old bastard.

THE CLOTHIER (*returning to Pathelin's house*).   That addlepated advocate, that bibulous barrister, does he take us all for fools? By damn, the only doctor he needs is a good hangman. I'll renounce God if he doesn't have my cloth. And he played this trick on me, too. (*At the door.*) Hey, in there! Where are you hiding?

GUILLEMETTE.   On my oath, he heard me and he seems to be raving mad.

PATHELIN.   I'll pretend to be delirious. Go to the door.

GUILLEMETTE (*to the Clothier*). My, how you're shouting.

THE CLOTHIER.   By God, you were laughing! My money, now!

GUILLEMETTE.   Holy Mary! What do you think I have to laugh about? There's no sadder person in town. He's fading fast. Never did you hear such an uproar or such raving. He's still delirious. His mind wanders, he sings, he jabbers in so many languages and jumbles them all together. He won't live half an hour longer. I swear, I laugh and cry at the same time.

THE CLOTHIER.   I don't know what you mean about laughing and crying. But to put it bluntly, I must be paid now!

GUILLEMETTE.   For what? Are you insane? Are you going to start that again?

THE CLOTHIER.   I'm not used to being paid with words when I sell my cloth. Would you have me believe the moon is made of green cheese?

PATHELIN (*delirious*). Arise! Make way for the Queen of Guitars. Let her approach without delay. I know she gave birth to four and twenty guitarlings, sired by the Abbot of Iverneaux. I'll have to be the godfather.

GUILLEMETTE.   Alas! Think about God the father, my dear, not about guitars.

THE CLOTHIER.   What a pair of con artists you are! Quick, now, give me my money in gold or silver for the cloth you took.

GUILLEMETTE.   Good God! You were mistaken once, isn't that enough?

THE CLOTHIER.   Do you know what's going on, woman? So help me, I don't know what you mean by "mistaken." But never mind, you'll either pay up or be strung up. How do I wrong you by coming here to ask for what's mine? By Saint Peter of Rome . . .

GUILLEMETTE.   Alas! How you torment this poor man! Truly, I can see in your face that you're losing your wits. If only I had help, sinner that I am, I'd have you tied up. You're a raving lunatic.

THE CLOTHIER.   I'm raving because I don't have my money.

GUILLEMETTE.   Oh, what madness! Cross yourself. *Benedicite!* Make the sign of the cross.

THE CLOTHIER.   May I renounce God if I ever again sell cloth on credit. (*Pathelin stirs.*) What an invalid!

PATHELIN.

Mere de Dieu, la coronade,
Par ma fye, y m'en vuol anar,
Or regni biou, oultre la mar!
Ventre de Diou! z'en dis gigone!
(*He points to the Clothier.*)
Çastuy ça rible et res ne done.
Ne carrilaine! fuy ta none!
Que de l'argent il ne me sone![1]

(*To the Clothier.*) Did you understand, cousin?

GUILLEMETTE.   He had an uncle from Limousin, the brother of his aunt by marriage. I'll bet that's what makes him babble in the Limousin dialect.

THE CLOTHIER.   Damn it, he stole out of my shop with the cloth under his arm.

PATHELIN.

Venez ens, doulce damiselle.
Et que veult ceste crapaudaille?
Alez en arriere, merdaille!
(*He wraps himself in his blanket.*)
Sa! tost! je vueil devenir prestre.
Or sa! que le dyable y puist estre,

---

[1](Limousin dialect.) Mother of God, crowned [queen of Heaven], by my faith, I want to go, or I'll renounce God, to the other side of the sea. God's belly, I say *gigone!* (He points to the Clothier.) That one there steals and gives nothing. Toll not the bell. Take your nap. Let him not speak to me of money!

En chelle vielle prestrerie!
Et faut il que le prestre rie
Quant il dëust chanter sa messe?[2]

GUILLEMETTE.   Alas! Alas! The hour draws near when he'll need the last sacraments.

THE CLOTHIER.   But how does he speak the Picard dialect so well? And why all this silliness?

GUILLEMETTE.   His mother was from Picardy. That's why he speaks it now.

PATHELIN (to the Clothier). Where did you come from, you carnival clown?

Vuacarme, liefe gode man!
Etlbelic beq igluhe golan.
Henrien! Henrien! conselapen.
Ych salgneb nede que maignen.
Grile, grile, scohehonden!
Zilop, zilop, en mon que bouden!
Disticlien unen desen versen.
Mat groet festal ou truit denhersen;
En vuacte vuile! Comme trie!
Cha! a dringuer, I beg of you.
Quoy act semigot yaue.
And put some water in it for me.
Vuste vuille, because of the frost.[3]
Quick, call Father Thomas so I can be shriven.

THE CLOTHIER.   What's going on? Will he never stop jabbering in different languages? If he'd just give me my money, or even a deposit, I'd be on my way.

GUILLEMETTE.   By God's passion, I'm tired of this. You're the weirdest man I ever met. Just what do you want? I don't know how you can be so obstinate.

PATHELIN.

Or cha! Renouart au Tiné!
(He looks into his gown.)
Bé dea, que ma couille est pelouse!
El semble une cate pelouse,
Ou a une mousque a mïel.
Bé! Parlez a moy, Gabriel.
Les play's Dieu! Qu'esse qui s'ataque
A men cul? Esse ou une vaque,
Une mousque, ou ung escarbot?

(He puts his hand into his gown.)
Bé dea! J'é le mau saint Garbot!
Suis je des foureux de Baieux?
Jehan du Quemin sera joyeulz,
Mais qu'i' sache que je le see.
Bee! Par saint Miquiel, je beree
Voulentiers a luy une fes![4]

THE CLOTHIER.   How can he stand to talk so much? He's going stark raving mad.

GUILLEMETTE.   His schoolmaster was from Normandy. Now at the end he's remembering him. He's sinking fast.

THE CLOTHIER.   Holy Mary! This is the craziest mess I've ever gotten myself into. Never would I have doubted that he was at the fair today.

GUILLEMETTE.   You really believed it?

THE CLOTHIER.   I did, by Saint James. But now I see it wasn't so.

PATHELIN.   Is that an ass I hear braying? (To the Clothier.) Alas and alack, good cousin, they all shall bray in great sorrow the day that I see thee no more. And yet I must needs detest thee, for thou hast played false with me. Thy work is naught but deceit.

Ha oul danda oul en ravezeie
Corfha en euf!

GUILLEMETTE (to Pathelin). May God have mercy on you.

PATHELIN.

Huis oz bez ou dronc nos badou
Digaut an tan en hol madou
Empedif dich guicebnuan
Quez queuient ob dre douch aman
Men ez cahet hoz bouzelou
Eny obet grande canou
Maz rehet crux dan hol con
So ol oz merueil grant nacon
Aluzen archet epsy
Har cals amour ha courteisy.[5]

---

[2](Picard dialect.) Come in, sweet damsel. What does that pack of scoundrels want? Get back, you shitten knaves! (He wraps himself in his blanket.) Quick, I want to become a priest. Now, may the Devil be part of that ancient priesthood! And must the priest laugh when he should be chanting his mass?

[3](The meaning of this garbled Flemish is not entirely clear.) Awake, to arms, dear good man! Fortunately I know several books. Henry! Henry! Come to sleep. I shall be well armed. Foolishness, foolishness, crazy inventions! A run, a run, a nun is bound! There are distichs in these verses. But great feasting disturbs the brain. Wait a while! Come quick! Something to drink, I beg of you! Come, look; a gift of God. And put some water in it for me. But wait a while because of the frost.

[4](Norman dialect.) Come here! Renouart au Tiné! (He looks into his gown.) What the Devil! How hairy my balls are! They're furry as a caterpillar or a honeybee. Hey! Speak to me, Gabriel. God's wounds! What's biting my ass? Is it a fly, a dungbeetle, or a cockchafer? (He puts his hand into his gown.) What the Devil! I've got dysentery! Am I one of the loose-boweled of Bayeux? Jean du Quemin would be glad to know that I am. Well, by St. Michael, I'll gladly drink to his health.

[5](The translation of the Breton passage is based on the conjectural reconstruction of J. Loth.) P: May he go to the Devil, body and soul! G: May God have mercy on you. P: May you have dizzy spells all night with much lamenting and with all your relatives praying for you, for fear that you'll vomit your guts out. There will be such weeping and wailing that even the starving dogs will take pity on you. May you receive a coffin as alms out of much love and courtesy.

THE CLOTHIER.   Alas! For God's sake, listen to him. He's going fast. How he rattles on! But what the Devil is he jabbering about? Holy Mary, how he mutters! God's bodkin, he babbles and quacks his words so you can't understand a thing. It's no Christian tongue he's speaking, nor any that makes sense.

GUILLEMETTE.   His father's mother came from Brittany. But he's dying, and all this indicates that it's time for the last sacraments.

PATHELIN.

> Hé, par saint Gigon, tu te mens.
> Voit a Deu! Couille de Lorraine!
> Dieu te mette en bote sepmaine!
> Tu ne vaulx mie une vielz nate.
> Va, sanglante bote savate;
> Va foutre! Va, sanglant paillart!
> Tu me refais trop le gaillart.
> Par la mort bieu! Sa! Vien t'en boire,
> Et baille moy stan grain de poire,
> Car vrayment je le mangera
> Et, par saint George, je bura
> A ty. Que veulx tu que je die?
> Dy, viens tu nient de Picardie?
> Jaques nient se sont ebobis.[6]
> Et bona dies sit vobis,
> Magister amantissime,
> Pater reverendissime.
> Quomodo brulis? Que nova?
> Parisius non sunt ova.
> Quid petit ille mercator?
> Dicat sibi quod trufator,
> Ille qui in lecto jacet,
> Vult ei dare, si placet,
> De oca ad comedendum.
> Si sit bona ad edendum,
> Pete tibi sine mora.[7]

GUILLEMETTE.   I swear, he's going to die making speeches. My, how he Latinizes! Don't you see how highly he esteems the divinity? His humanity is ebbing away. Now I'll remain poor and miserable.

THE CLOTHIER.   It would be better for me to go before he breathes his last. If he has some secret things to confide in you before he dies, I doubt that he would want to say them in front of me. Please forgive me, but I swear to you that I truly believed he had taken my cloth. Farewell, good woman. I beg you in God's name to forgive me.

GUILLEMETTE.   May this day be blessed for you and also for me in my sorrow.

THE CLOTHIER (*leaving the house*). By the gracious Virgin, I'm more confused now than ever. The Devil, in his shape, took my cloth to tempt me. (*Crosses himself.*) *Benedicite.* May he leave me in peace. But since that's the way it is, I give the cloth, in God's name, to whoever took it.

PATHELIN (*getting up*). Now then, didn't I instruct you well? There he goes, the gullible simpleton. Now he's really got some confused ideas under that bonnet of his. I bet he'll have nightmares when he goes to bed tonight.

GUILLEMETTE.   We really put him in his place. Didn't I play my part well?

PATHELIN.   By God, you played it to perfection. Now at least we have enough cloth to make some clothes.

SCENE SIX

THE CLOTHIER (*in his shop*). Damn it all! Everybody feeds me lies; everybody steals from me and takes all he can get. I feel like I'm the king of the wretched. Even the shepherds of the field defraud me. And my own shepherd, to whom I've always been generous, will not get away with cheating me. He'll be begging for mercy, by the Blessed Virgin!

THIBAULT AIGNELET, THE SHEPHERD (*entering the shop*). God grant you a blessed day and a good evening, gentle Master.

THE CLOTHIER.   Aha! There you are, you dung-covered scoundrel! What a good fellow you are! Good for nothing!

THE SHEPHERD.   Begging your pardon, Sir, but some guy, I don't know who, with stripes on his sleeve, and all kind of excited, and carrying a whip handle without a cord, came up and said to me . . . But I don't rightly recollect what it was he said. He talked about you, Master, and some kind of summons, but, Holy Mary, I couldn't make heads or tails out of it. He mixed me up so with his talk about ''sheep'' and ''afternoon session,'' and he made a great fuss about things you had said against me, Sir.

THE CLOTHIER.   If I don't haul you before the judge in two shakes, I pray God to strike me with storm and flood. Never again will you get away with killing my sheep, I swear. And no matter what happens, you'll pay me for those six yards . . . I mean, for killing my sheep and for all the losses you've caused me in the last ten years.

THE SHEPHERD.   You shouldn't believe those poison tongues, good Master, for by my soul . . .

---

[6](Lorraine dialect.) Hey, by St. Gengoux, you're lying! I swear to God! Great balls, may God send you misfortune! You're not worth an old doormat. Get out of here, you bloody old boot; fuck off! Leave, you low-life lecher! You're too malicious, by God! You there! Come have a drink and give me a peppercorn; I'll really eat it and, by St. George, I'll drink to you. What do you expect me to say? Say, are you by chance from Picardy? The peasants there are dumbfounded.

[7](Latin.) Good day to you, beloved master, most reverend father. How are you burning? What's new? There are no eggs in Paris. What does that merchant want? Let him say to himself that the swindler, the one lying in bed, wants to give him, if he will, some goose to eat. If it's good, ask for some without delay.

THE CLOTHIER.   And by Our Lady you'll pay me on Saturday for my six yards of cloth . . . I mean, for what you stole of my sheep.

THE SHEPHERD.   What cloth? Ah, Sir, I believe you're upset about something else. By Saint Lupus, Master, I'm afraid to say anything when I see you like this.

THE CLOTHIER.   Go and leave me in peace. And answer your summons, if you know what's good for you.

THE SHEPHERD.   But Sir, let's settle this now. For God's sake, don't take me to court.

THE CLOTHIER.   Go! The matter is in good hands. Go on, now! I won't make a settlement, by God, and I won't agree to anything but what the judge decides. Damn it all, everybody will cheat me from now on if I don't put a stop to it.

THE SHEPHERD.   Goodbye, Sir. May God give you joy. (*He leaves.*) So now I have to defend myself.

SCENE SEVEN

THE SHEPHERD (*knocking at Pathelin's door*). Is anybody here?

PATHELIN (*to Guillemette*).   I'll be hanged if he hasn't come back.

GUILLEMETTE.   No it can't be! Saint George preserve us. That would be the end.

THE SHEPHERD.   God be with you and keep you.

PATHELIN.   God save you, my good fellow. What is it you want?

THE SHEPHERD.   They're going to fine me for not showing up, if I don't answer my summons, Sir, this afternoon, and if you please, would you, good Master, plead my case for me, 'cause I don't know nothing about it, and I can pay you good, even though I'm dressed so poor.

PATHELIN.   Come here and speak up. Which are you, plaintiff or defendant?

THE SHEPHERD.   Well, Sir, I work for a certain merchant, you know, and for a long time I've taken his sheep out to graze and I guard 'em, and I swear when I think about him paying me next to nothing . . . Do I have to tell everything?

PATHELIN.   Certainly. A client should hide nothing from his counsel.

THE SHEPHERD.   It's true, Sir, it's the truth, I struck 'em down, so that many of 'em were knocked out and fell down dead, even though they were strong and healthy, and then I made him think, so's he wouldn't punish me, that they died of the scab. "Oh," he'd say, "don't leave a diseased one with the others, get rid of it." "I'll be glad to," I'd say; and I'd get rid of it all right, but not the way he thought, for, by Saint John, I ate every one of 'em, 'cause I knew what they really died of. What else can I tell you? I kept doin' this so long and struck down and killed so many that he noticed it, and when he found out he had been deceived, so help me God, he sent somebody to spy on me 'cause you could hear 'em cry out, you know, when you hit 'em. So I was caught red-handed, I can never deny it, and now I come to ask if there ain't some way we can put the old hound off the scent, and don't worry about money, I got enough to pay you good. I know he's got a good case, but you can find some loophole, if you will, to make it worthless.

PATHELIN.   I promise you'll be satisfied with the results. What will you give me if I overturn the claim of your accuser and get you a full pardon?

THE SHEPHERD.   Instead of payin' in sous, I'll pay you in solid gold crowns.

PATHELIN.   Then you'll have an unbeatable case even if it's twice as weak as you say. The stronger the case I argue against, the quicker I can render it null, when I put my mind to it. You'll hear how well I can spiel it off after he's presented his argument. Come over here. By God, you're wily enough to understand the trick. Now tell me, what's your name?

THE SHEPHERD.   By Saint Maurus, it's Thibault Aignelet.

PATHELIN.   Aignelet, did you appropriate many lambs from your master?

THE SHEPHERD.   On my oath, I may have eaten thirty or more in three years.

PATHELIN.   That makes an income of ten a year—the equivalent of a few games at the tavern. (*He thinks for a moment.*) I believe I have a good ruse here. Do you think he can readily find a witness to prove his allegation? That's the most important part of the trial.

THE SHEPHERD.   Prove, Sir? Holy Mary! By all the saints in paradise, instead of one, he'll find ten to testify against me.

PATHELIN.   That's almost enough to ruin your case. Here's what I had in mind. I'll pretend that I'm not on your side and that I've never seen you before.

THE SHEPHERD.   For God's sake, don't do that!

PATHELIN.   No, that's no good. But here's what we have to do. If you speak, they'll trap you one by one on all counts of the indictment, and in such cases confessions are as prejudicial and harmful as the Devil himself. So here's what will make our case: as soon as they call you to appear before the court, you'll answer only with "baa," no matter what they say to you. And if they should curse you, saying, "Hey, you stinking yokel! May God plunge you into misery! Are you making fun of the court?" just answer "baa." "Ha!" I'll say, "he's a poor simpleton who thinks he's talking to his sheep." But even if they knock themselves out yelling at you, make sure no other word comes out of your mouth.

THE SHEPHERD.   Seein' as how this touches me close, I'll make sure I don't say nothin' else and I'll do it right, I promise.

PATHELIN.   Now make sure you stick to your promise. And even to me, no matter what I say or ask, don't answer any other way.

THE SHEPHERD.   Me? Never, by the sacrament! You can cry out that I'm crazy, if I say another word today, to you or anybody else, no matter what they say to me, except "Baa," just like you told me.

PATHELIN.   If you do that, by Saint John, your accuser will be caught in our trap. But also make sure when it's over that I get a payment I'll be proud of.

THE SHEPHERD.   Sir, if I don't pay you at your word, then never believe me again. But please work hard on my case.

PATHELIN.   By Our Lady, I'll bet the judge is already on the bench; he always holds court around six o'clock. Now you come along after me; we won't both go together.

THE SHEPHERD.   That's a good idea, so nobody sees you're my lawyer.

PATHELIN.   And God help you if you don't pay generously.

THE SHEPHERD.   I swear I'll pay at your word; really, Sir, have no fear.

PATHELIN (*alone*). Well now, it may not be raining money, but it's sprinkling. At least I'll get a little something out of this. If everything falls into place, I'll have a gold piece or two for my trouble.

SCENE EIGHT

PATHELIN (*removing his hat to salute the Judge*). Your Honor, God grant you success and whatever your heart desires.

THE JUDGE.   Welcome, Sir. Please don your hat and take your place over there.

PATHELIN (*seeing the Clothier*). Damn! (*To the Judge.*) I'm fine here, Your Honor; I'll have more room to maneuver.

THE JUDGE.   If there is business before the court, let it be done quickly so I can adjourn.

THE CLOTHIER.   My lawyer is coming, Your Honor. He's finishing up some other business. If the court please, we had better wait for him.

THE JUDGE.   Wait? I have cases to hear elsewhere. If the offending party is present, then state the case yourself without delay. Are you not the plaintiff?

THE CLOTHIER.   I am.

THE JUDGE.   Where is the defendant? Is he here in person?

THE CLOTHIER.   Yes, there he is, not saying a word. God only knows what he's thinking.

THE JUDGE.   Since you're both here, state your case.

THE CLOTHIER.   Then here's my complaint against him, Your Honor. The truth is that for the love of God and in charity I fed and clothed him in his childhood; and, to be brief, when I saw that he was strong enough to go to the fields, I made him my shepherd and set him to watching my flock. But as sure as you're sitting there, Your Honor, he wrought such carnage among my wethers and ewes that without a doubt . . .

THE JUDGE.   Just a minute! Wasn't he hired by you?

PATHELIN.   That's a good point! Because if he had finagled to employ him without a contract . . .

THE CLOTHIER (*recognizing Pathelin*). May I disavow God if it isn't you! You, without a doubt!

THE JUDGE.   Why are you holding your hand to your face, Master Pierre? Do you have a toothache?

PATHELIN.   Yes, the pain is so excruciating that never before have I been in such agony. I can't even look up. For God's sake, make him get on with it.

THE JUDGE.   Proceed! Finish your deposition. Come on, be brief about it.

THE CLOTHIER.   It's him and nobody else! By God's cross, it really is! Master Pierre, it was you that I sold six yards of cloth to.

THE JUDGE.   What's he saying about cloth?

PATHELIN.   He's rambling. He thinks he's getting to his opening statement, but he doesn't know how because he isn't used to this.

THE CLOTHIER.   May I be hanged by the bloody neck if anybody else took my cloth.

PATHELIN.   Look how this unworthy man goes to extremes to build his case. He means, and he's very stubborn about it, that his shepherd had sold the wool—that's what I understood—from which the cloth of my robe was made. He seems to be saying that the shepherd's a thief and has been stealing the wool of his sheep.

THE CLOTHIER.   God send me misfortune if you haven't got it!

THE JUDGE.   Silence! The Devil take you for running off at the mouth! Can't you get back to your deposition without delaying the court with such drivel?

PATHELIN (*laughing*). Oh, my tooth aches, but I can't help laughing. He's already so rushed he doesn't know where he left off. We'll have to lead him back to the subject.

THE JUDGE.   Come now, let's get back to those sheep. What happened next?

THE CLOTHIER.   He took six yards of it, worth nine francs.

THE JUDGE.   Do you take us for fools or simpletons? Where do you think you are?

PATHELIN.   I swear to God, he's trying to make an ass of you! And he looks like such a decent man. But I suggest you examine his adversary.

THE JUDGE.   That's a good idea. He sees him often, so he must know him. (*To the Shepherd.*) Step forward! Speak!

THE SHEPHERD.   Baa!

THE JUDGE.   Another vexation! What do you mean, "baa"? Am I a goat! Speak to me!

THE SHEPHERD.   Baa!

THE JUDGE.   The bloody pox take you! Are you trying to make a fool of me!

PATHELIN.   He must be either crazy or pigheaded; or maybe he thinks he's among his sheep.

THE CLOTHIER.   I'll renounce God if you aren't the one that got my cloth—you and nobody else! (*To the Judge.*) Oh, you don't know, Your Honor, by what malice . . .

THE JUDGE.   What! Hold your tongue! Are you dense? Set aside this accessory matter and let's get back to the principal.

THE CLOTHIER.   Very well, Your Honor, but the case concerns me. Nevertheless, I promise I won't say another word about it for the rest of the day. Some other time it may be different; right now I'll just have to swallow it. Now, I was saying in my complaint that I had given six yards . . . I should say, my sheep . . . Please forgive me, Your Honor. . . . This good Master . . . I mean, my shepherd, when he was supposed to be in the fields . . . He told me I would get six gold pieces when I came . . . I mean to say, three years ago my shepherd made an agreement that he would faithfully guard my sheep and would cause me no loss nor do me any wrong, and then . . . Now he brazenly refuses to give me either cloth or money. (To Pathelin.) Ah, Master Pierre, I swear . . . (To the Judge.) This scoundrel here was stealing the wool from my sheep, and he was killing healthy ones by clubbing them on the head. . . . When he put my cloth under his arm, he took off in a great hurry, saying that I should go collect my six gold pieces at his house.

THE JUDGE.   There's neither rime nor reason in any of your railing and ranting. What is this? You mix in one thing and then another. In short, by God, I can't make heads or tails of it. (To Pathelin.) He prattles about cloth, then he jabbers about sheep and jumbles it all up. Nothing he says makes sense.

PATHELIN.   I'll bet anything he's keeping this poor shepherd's wages for himself.

THE CLOTHIER.   You can shut your mouth, by God. It's the gospel truth that my cloth . . . I know better than you or anybody else where my shoe pinches, and by God in heaven, I know you have it!

THE JUDGE.   What does he have?

THE CLOTHIER.   Nothing, Your Honor. But I swear he's the biggest swindler . . . OK, I'll try to control my tongue and I won't say another word about it today, no matter what happens.

THE JUDGE.   Very well, but remember your promise. Now conclude quickly.

PATHELIN.   This shepherd cannot answer the charges against him without counsel, and he's afraid or doesn't know how to ask for it. I would be willing to counsel him, Your Honor, if you so ordered.

THE JUDGE.   Him? I should think that would be wasted effort. He's as poor as a church mouse.

PATHELIN.   I swear I have no thought of gain. Let it be for love of God. Now I'll try to find out from the poor lad what he has to say, and I'll see if he can instruct me as to how to reply to the charges against him. He'd have a hard time getting out of this, if nobody helped him. (To the Shepherd.) Come over here, my friend. Now if we could find . . . Do you understand?

THE SHEPHERD.   Baa!

PATHELIN.   What is this "baa"? By the Holy Blood, are you crazy? Tell me about your case.

THE SHEPHERD.   Baa!

PATHELIN.   What is this "baa"? Do you hear the ewes bleating? Try to understand, this is for your own good.

THE SHEPHERD.   Baa!

PATHELIN.   Come on! Answer yes or no. (Softly.) That's good. Keep it up. (Aloud.) Will you do that?

THE SHEPHERD.   Baa!

PATHELIN.   Speak up, or you'll find yourself in real trouble, I'm afraid.

THE SHEPHERD.   Baa!

PATHELIN.   It takes a real ass to bring such a poor fool to trial. Your Honor, send him back to his sheep. He's just a natural-born fool.

THE CLOTHIER.   You call him a fool? By Saint Savior of Asturias, he's smarter than you are.

PATHELIN (to the Judge).   Send him back to watch his sheep, sine die, never to return. A plague on him who brings charges against such natural-born fools.

THE CLOTHIER.   Will he be sent back before I can be heard?

THE JUDGE.   So help me, since he's a born fool, yes. Why shouldn't he be?

THE CLOTHIER.   But Your Honor, at least allow me to sum up my case first. This isn't something I dreamed up or just idle discourse.

THE JUDGE.   Nothing but vexation comes of bringing suit against fools and simpletons. Now hear this: to stop this senseless babble, the court will be adjourned.

THE CLOTHIER.   Will they go without obligation to return?

THE JUDGE.   And why not?

PATHELIN.   Return! You never saw a greater fool in word or in deed. (Pointing to the Clothier.) And this other one isn't an ounce better. They're both brainless boneheads. By the Blessed Virgin, their brains together wouldn't weigh a carat.

THE CLOTHIER.   You took my cloth by deceit, Master Pierre, without paying. As I'm a poor sinner, that wasn't the deed of an honest man.

PATHELIN.   May I renounce Saint Peter of Rome if he isn't an insidious fool, or well on his way to being one.

THE CLOTHIER.   I recognize you by your speech, by your clothes, and by your face. And I'm not crazy! I'm sane enough to know what's good for me. (To the Judge.) I'll tell you the whole story, Your Honor, upon my conscience. (The Judge grimaces. Laughter in the audience.)

PATHELIN (pointing to the audience).   Please, Your Honor, bring them to order. (To the Clothier.) Aren't you ashamed to haul this poor shepherd into court for three or four grubby old sheep that aren't worth two buttons. (To the Judge.) His litany gets longer and more tedious.

THE CLOTHIER.   What sheep? It's always the same old song! It's you I'm talking to and, by God, you'll give me back my cloth.

THE JUDGE (*to the audience*). You see that? I really get the cases, don't I? He won't stop braying for the rest of the day.

THE CLOTHIER.   I'll bring suit . . .

PATHELIN.   Make him shut up! (*To the Clothier.*) You prattle too much, by God. Let's say he did knock off six or seven sheep, or even a dozen, and ate them—Holy Christmas, you weren't crippled by it. You still earned a lot more than that in the time he's been watching your flock.

THE CLOTHIER.   Look at that, Your Honor, just look! I talk to him about cloth and he answers me in sheep. (*To Pathelin.*) Those six yards of cloth that you stuck under your arm, where are they? Don't you intend to give them back to me?

PATHELIN.   Oh, Sir, would you have him hanged for six or seven sheep? At least think it over. Don't be so harsh on this poor, unfortunate shepherd, who hasn't a thing to his name.

THE CLOTHIER.   You're an expert in changing the subject. The Devil himself made me sell cloth to such a customer. Please, Your Honor, I charge him . . .

THE JUDGE (*thinking the Clothier is charging the Shepherd*). I absolve him of your charges and forbid you to proceed. A fine thing it is to bring suit against a fool. (*To the Shepherd.*) Go back to your sheep.

THE SHEPHERD.   Baa!

THE JUDGE (*to the Clothier*). By our Lady, you've certainly shown what kind of person you are, Sir.

THE CLOTHIER.   But Your Honor, I swear I want him to . . .

PATHELIN.   Can't he shut up?

THE CLOTHIER.   But it's you I have a case against. You tricked me with your eloquent speeches and carried my cloth away like a thief.

PATHELIN.   Your Honor, I solemnly appeal! Are you going to listen to this?

THE CLOTHIER.   So help me God, you're the biggest swindler . . . Your Honor, let me say . . .

THE JUDGE.   It's a three-ring circus with you two—nothing but wrangling and squabbles. So help me, I've got to be going. (*To the Shepherd.*) Go, my son, and don't ever come back, even if an officer serves you with a warrant. The court grants you full pardon.

PATHELIN.   Say "thank you."

THE SHEPHERD.   Baa!

THE JUDGE.   Is that clear? Go now and don't worry about a thing. It's all right.

THE CLOTHIER.   But is it right for him to go like that?

THE JUDGE.   Bah! I have business elsewhere. You're both outrageous mockers and you won't detain me a moment longer. I'm leaving. Will you come to supper with me, Master Pierre?

PATHELIN (*raising his hand to his cheek*). I can't. (*The Judge leaves.*)

SCENE NINE

THE CLOTHIER.   You're an outright thief! Tell me, will I ever be paid?

PATHELIN.   For what? Are you crazy? Who do you think I am anyway? By God, I've been trying to figure out who it is you take me for.

THE CLOTHIER.   Indeed!

PATHELIN.   No just a minute, my good man. I'll tell you right now who it is you take me for. It's the town fool, isn't it? But look! (*He lifts his hat.*) That can't be because he's not bald on top of his head like me.

THE CLOTHIER.   Do you think I'm an imbecile? It was you in person; you, yourself, and nobody but you. Your voice proves it and don't think it doesn't.

PATHELIN.   Me myself, and I? No it wasn't, I swear. Get that out of your head. It was probably John from Noyon; he's about my size.

THE CLOTHIER.   The Devil it was! He doesn't have that besotted, witless face of yours. Didn't I leave you sick a while ago at your house?

PATHELIN.   Now there's a fine bit of evidence! Me, sick? And what was I sick with? Come on, admit your stupidity; it's quite clear now.

THE CLOTHIER.   I'll renounce Saint Peter if it wasn't you—you and nobody else. I know that to be absolutely true.

PATHELIN.   Well don't you believe it, because it positively wasn't me. I never took a yard or even half a yard of cloth from you. I don't have that kind of reputation.

THE CLOTHIER.   Damn it all, I'm going to go back to your house to see if you're there. We won't have to squabble here any more if I find you there.

PATHELIN.   By Our Lady, that's a good idea! That way you'll know for sure. (*The Clothier leaves.*)

SCENE TEN

PATHELIN.   Hey, Aignelet!

THE SHEPHERD.   Baa!

PATHELIN.   Come here. Was your case well disposed of?

THE SHEPHERD.   Baa!

PATHELIN.   Your accuser has gone, so you don't have to say "baa" anymore. I really cooked his goose, didn't I? And didn't I counsel you just right?

THE SHEPHERD.   Baa!

PATHELIN.   Hey, don't worry. Nobody'll hear you. Speak up.

THE SHEPHERD.   Baa!

PATHELIN.   It's time for me to go now, so pay me.

THE SHEPHERD.   Baa!

PATHELIN.   To tell the truth, you played your part very well; you looked good. But what really fooled him was that you kept from laughing.

THE SHEPHERD.   Baa!

PATHELIN.   Why "baa"? You mustn't say it any more. Just pay me generously.

THE SHEPHERD.   Baa!

PATHELIN.   Why do you keep saying "baa"? Speak normally and pay me so I can go.

THE SHEPHERD.   Baa!

PATHELIN.   You know what? I'll tell you. I'm asking you, please, without any more bleating around the bush to think about paying me. I've had enough of your baa's. Pay up quickly.

THE SHEPHERD.   Baa!

PATHELIN.   Is this some kind of joke? Is this all you're going to do? I swear to God, if you don't escape, you're going to pay me, understand? The money! Now!

THE SHEPHERD.   Baa!

PATHELIN.   You've got to be kidding. Is this all I'm going to get from you?

THE SHEPHERD.   Baa!

PATHELIN.   You're running this into the ground. And just who are you trying to fool? Do you know who you're dealing with? Don't babble your baa's to me anymore today; just pay me.

THE SHEPHERD.   Baa!

PATHELIN.   Is this the only pay I'll get? Who do you think you're playing games with? I was taking such pride in your performance; now really make me proud of you.

THE SHEPHERD.   Baa!

PATHELIN.   Are you trying to pull the wool over my eyes? God's curse! Have I lived so long that a shepherd, a sheep in human clothing, a churlish knave can make a fool of me?

THE SHEPHERD.   Baa!

PATHELIN.   Will I get no other word? If you're doing this for a joke, say so and don't make me argue any more. Come and have supper at my house.

THE SHEPHERD.   Baa!

PATHELIN.   By Saint John, you're right: the goslings lead the geese to pasture. (*To himself.*) I thought I was the master in these parts of all the cheaters and swindlers and those who give their word in payment, collectible on Judgment Day; and now a shepherd of the fields outwits me. (*To the Shepherd.*) By Saint James, if I could find an officer, I'd have you arrested.

THE SHEPHERD.   Baa!

PATHELIN.   Baa, yourself! May I be hanged if I don't go find me a good policeman! and misfortune seize him if he doesn't throw you in jail.

THE SHEPHERD (*running away*).   If he finds me, I'll give him a full pardon.

FOCUS QUESTIONS

1. Develop a character sketch of the eponymous protagonist and comment on his central importance to the other characters and action.
2. Defend the play as farce.
3. Discuss the uses and impact of role playing on the action.
4. Discuss Guillemette's role and suggest reasons why she protects her husband.

OTHER ACTIVITIES

1. Develop a short scene in which you carry the action of the play one step further.

BIBLIOGRAPHY

Axton, Richard. *European Drama of the Early Middle Ages*. Pittsburgh: University of Pittsburgh Press, 1975.

Bevington, David, ed. *Medieval Drama*. Boston: Houghton Mifflin, 1975.

Chambers, E. K. *The Mediaeval Stage*. 2 vols. Oxford: Clarendon Press, 1903.

Craig, Barbara. *The Evolution of a Mystery Play: Critical Editions of "The Sacrifice of Abraham."* Orlando, FL: French Literature Publications, Co., 1983.

Emmerson, Richard K., ed. *Medieval English Drama.* New York: Modern Language Association, 1990.

Fifield, Merle. *"The Sacrifice of Isaac:* Tradition and Innovation in Fifteenth Century Dramatizations.'' *Fifteenth Century Studies 8* (1983): 67–88.

Friedman, Saul. *The Oberammergau Passion Play: A Lance Against Civilization.* Carbondale: Southern Illinois University Press, 1984.

Happe, Peter, ed. *Medieval English Drama.* London: Macmillan, 1984.

Kahrl, Stanley J. *Traditions of Medieval English Drama.* Pittsburgh: University of Pittsburgh Press, 1975.

Maddox, Donald. *The Semiotics of Deceit: The Pathelin Era.* Lewisburg, PA: Bucknell University Press, 1984.

Nelson, Alan H. *The Medieval English Stage.* Chicago: University of Chicago Press, 1974.

Prosser, Eleanor. *Drama and Religion in the English Mystery Plays.* Stanford: Stanford University Press, 1961.

Richardson, Christine, and Jackie Johnston. *Medieval Drama.* London: Macmillan Education LTD, 1991.

Southern, Richard. *Medieval Theatre in the Round: A Study of the Staging of "The Castle of Perseverance" and Related Matters.* New York: Theatre Arts Books, 1975.

———. *The Staging of Medieval Plays before Shakespeare.* New York: Theatre Arts Books, 1973.

Taylor, Jerome, and Alan H. Nelson, eds. *Medieval English Drama: Essays Critical and Contextual.* Chicago: University of Chicago Press, 1972.

Wickham, Glynne. *The Medieval Theatre.* New York: Cambridge University Press, 1987.

Woolf, Rosemary. *The English Mystery Plays.* Berkeley: University of California Press, 1980.

KOMACHI AT SEKIDERA
(*SEKIDERA KOMACHI*)
KANZE MOTOKIYO ZEAMI (1363–1443)

Drama is something that happens.
Noh is someone that happens.

—PAUL CLAUDEL

APPROACHING NOH DRAMA

In Japanese culture, the spirits of ancestors are ever present. One way to ensure their benevolence is to recite their deeds on earth and pay homage to them. This is the purpose of the **Noh drama.** The actors become the spirits of the dead who report their glorious or anguished pasts to the living. In this way, the audience is brought to a realization of life's precious yet fleeting qualities, while the sense of tradition and community pride is enhanced. These elements evoke the mood or the emotional state of the legendary event, rather than tell the story. As a result, Noh cannot be viewed according to the standards of Western dramatic action.

Noh's sources include the dances and songs performed by priests; the animal and court dances from China; the popular and folk entertainments (magic, acrobatics, juggling, country harvest dances, and songs) from Japan; and quotations of traditional Japanese literature in a form of dramatic prayer for the longevity of an esteemed person. These forms coalesced in the performances of traveling **sarugaku** troupes during the thirteenth century. Their patronage by the ruling warrior class was instrumental in the creation of Noh as a distinct art form.

When Ashikago Yoshimitsu, the shogun from 1338 to 1394 and a man of impressive poetic as well as martial skill, brought the sarugaku actor Kannami (1333–1384) and his son Zeami to court, he began the great tradition of Noh as the official drama. Under his patronage, Kannami, who is credited with creating the Noh, performed and wrote plays of which eight or ten survive. Of particular importance was his introduction of dialogue between the first actor, or **shite,** and the second actor, or **waki,** and the **kusemai,** a dance performed to irregular drum rhythms.

His son Zeami was the true codifier of the Noh, however. As performer, playwright, and head of the troupe since 1384, he recorded and preserved his father's teachings in a series of treatises. In 1400, he wrote the first treatise, *Kadensho,* which is the fullest account of the training of Noh performers, who are always male. It includes Zeami's concern for the performer's development of **monomane,** the ability to create believable representation through suggestive movement, and **yugen,** the ability to create a fragile and restrained gracefulness. From 1420 to 1423, he completed two other treatises: the *Shikadosho,* dealing with the further development of **hana** or "flower," which is the unique quality of the performer's art; and the *Nosakusho,* dealing with the composition of the Noh's one-act framework. The aesthetics of Noh have been handed down through these writings for over five centuries. In addition to these treatises, Zeami wrote at least 25 of the 240 extant plays in the Noh repertoire.

Zeami gave special attention to those plays requiring the most *yugen,* notably those in which the *shite* performed the role of a woman. An elderly actor who accomplished this task and was able to dazzle the audience despite his age had reached the pinnacle of his creative art. Zeami compared the beauty of his performance to "flowers still blossoming on an aged tree with few remaining leaves."[1] That is why *Komachi at Sekidera,* a play about the poet Ono no Komachi nearing death at one hundred years old, is attributed to him.

THE ACTION

An abbot and his priests take a young disciple to the shrine at Sekidera to observe the celebration of the festival of Tanabata. Hearing that an old woman who resides in a hut at the base of the shrine is an expert in poetry, they go to learn from her. Their questions reveal her identity as Ono no Komachi, a legendary woman of beauty and poetic skill who has been forgotten in her old age.

The young disciple and his teacher invite her to join them in celebrating the festival and offer her a ceremonial cup of wine. Watching the child dance to the festival music, Komachi is moved to dance as well in an effort to recapture her youth. But this memory of a vanished past reduces her to tears. Ashamed of her foolhardy clinging to life, she returns to her hut to wait for death.

STRUCTURE AND LANGUAGE

The aesthetic rule, **jo-ha-kyu,** categorizes the types of plays and determines their order of presentation in the five-play Noh cycle. **Okina,** or god plays, constitute the *jo* (introduction); warrior plays, women plays, and madness plays constitute the *ha* (development); and demon plays constitute the *kyu* (climax or frenzy). The rationale is quite specific: the building of theatrical excitement intensifies with each successive play. By the fifth and most dynamic play, this deliberate and steady mounting of tension works the spectators into a state of emotional exhilaration.

Komachi at Sekidera exemplifies the *ha,* one of the women plays or "wig pieces" valued for the extraordinarily delicate performance demanded of the *shite.* The emphasis is not on representation or *monomane,* but on *yugen,* which Leonard Pronko translates as the presentation of "what lies beneath the surface."[2] As in all Noh plays, the *jo-ha-kyu* also provides the basic structure to the text and must be rigidly adhered to. In the *jo,* or prelude, a flute sounds and the *waki* (second actor) enters with his **wakizure** (companions) and the **kokata** (child actor). He announces himself as a traveling priest and explains the reason for his journey to a famous place, in this case the shrine at Sekidera. His short dance, consisting of a few steps, indicates his arrival. The accompanying poetry, which describes the physical landscape of his journey, portrays a shrine that is decorated with prayer sticks and multicolored streamers.

The *ha* contains two parts. The first discloses the *shite* (the first actor who plays Komachi) seated in the hut and includes the monologue that reveals the character's problem—like all who are old, she is alone, poor, withered, and forgotten. The second is the verbal exchange between the *waki* and the *shite,* in which the *waki*'s catalytic role in unveiling the truth about the old woman's identity is of paramount importance. When the *waki* surmises that she must indeed be Komachi, the old woman acknowledges it with shame.

The *kyu,* or climax, opens with Komachi's sad reminiscences of her past glory as a court poet in the face of her present poverty and loss of physical and creative powers. Aided by the chorus, the *shite* reveals, through the use of quoted lines from Komachi's poems, the theme of the play: the futility of clinging to life as death approaches. The **shimai** or final dance, the culmination of the *kyu,* is signaled when Komachi moves from her hut to take part in the Tanabata celebration. Her feeble recreation of the Harvest Festival dance is as poignant as the last blossoms on a dying tree. Despite its faulty gestures and halting steps, the dance captures the essence of the beauty that mortality has robbed from Komachi. Her former power and grace are now only a vague glimmer.

In addition to their common structures, all Noh plays share a certain intertextuality. They combine narrative and lyrical forms taken from Chinese and Japanese sources found in the traditional literary canon, or *Kokinshu.* These quoted materials become recontextualized in the plays in which they appear. For example, lines adapted from the preface of the *Kokinshu* and the inclusion of the anonymous poem that begins ''I know my lover/ Is coming tonight—'' frame the discussion on the nature of poetry in *Komachi at Sekidera.* As translator Karen Brazell points out in her footnotes, innumerable examples of references and adaptations of lines from earlier Chinese and Japanese works illuminate the essence of old age, which is the play's theme. Such lines as ''Early autumn comes and brings a touch of chill./ We feel it in the wind and in our thinning locks'' not only pay tribute to the well-known poet Po-Chü-i, but also introduce the idea of aging. Equally important for this play, which focuses on a legendary woman poet, are the numerous inclusions of lines from her works. These allusions become both a means for depicting her life and an embodiment of the essential irony of the play: although the poet is mortal, her poetry will never lose its vitality.

It is impossible to describe the complexity of Noh's literary style. Besides juxtaposing sacred scripture and poetic texts with lines of the playwright's own invention, the plays contain symbolic allusions to legendary events and historical sites as well as puns and homonyms that obscure meaning and intensify ambiguity. Brazell points to one such example in her translation in reference to a forest near Kyoto mentioned toward the end of the play. *Hazukashi,* the forest's name, is the same word for *ashamed* in Japanese. Thus the use of the homonym adds another level of meaning to *Komachi at Sekidera.* In this respect, the language is chosen not to enhance the story but to suggest the essence of Komachi and evoke her feelings on the stage.

Noh Drama-in-Performance

Okina, plays originally performed by priests at the Kasuga Shrine as early as the eleventh century, are shamanistic in nature. They reenact the first Noh, which had been transmitted from the world of the gods to a priest through the Yogo Pine under which he danced. The performer dons a mask and stares at his reflection in a mirror until he is possessed by the god's spirit. When he dances on the stage in front of the Yogo Pine painted on the back wall, he has become an incarnation of the god. Every Noh performance since Zeami has begun in this manner.

Yet Noh drama in the form that we encounter today did not become solidified until the seventeenth century when it was performed primarily at court as a ceremony for the upperclasses. Both **Bunraku** and **Kabuki** had supplanted the Noh as popular entertainment forms. No longer needing to create dramatic appeal to satisfy a popular audience, the

Ground plan of a
traditional Noh theatre.

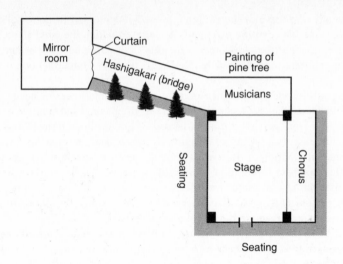

performance style of Noh plays reflected a spiritual subject matter. The performances were deliberate and ritualistic. Dialogue was delivered in a protracted vocal manner and the sung parts became muffled and often unintelligible. Dances that had once been energetic were elongated by slow, subtle movements performed to flute and occasional drum beats. To provide relief from the solemnity of the five-play Noh cycle, humorous **Kyogen,** which satirized the ruling classes, were performed as interludes.

The present Noh stage is inherited from this period, the early seventeenth century until the overthrow of the shogunate in 1868. An eighteen-foot square stage of polished cedar is built to resemble a shrine with four columns supporting a roof. Earthenware jars positioned underneath this stage augment the sound of the foot stamping that is the primary step in the *shite*'s and *waki*'s performances. There are three other parts to the playing area: the rear stage with its pine tree backdrop from which two or three drummers and a flute player accompany the action; the side stage on which the eight to ten chorus members sit facing the performance area throughout the play; and the **hashigakari,** or runway, along which the *shite* enters from the mirror room, where he has prepared to take on the spirit of the mask he wears. As he introduces his character, he walks slowly across this covered bridge passing three pine trees that symbolize heaven, earth, and man. *Komachi at Sekidera* is one of the few plays in which the *shite* makes his entrance from a place on stage other than the mirror room across the runway.

There is no attempt at stage illusion in the Noh. Lights remain up at all times. Props are minimal: a bamboo frame might resemble a boat; a miniature structure might indicate a palace or a mountain; the performers' fans might suggest different objects through the use of mime. In *Komachi at Sekidera,* the line, ''Grinding ink, I dip my brush and write,'' for example, prompts the *shite* to use his fan as if it were a pen. Later, the *kokata* opens his fan and, holding it like a ladle, offers Komachi a drink. Another anti-illusionistic convention is the use of stage assistants dressed in black. While the audience watches, they introduce or remove these few suggestive props without interrupting the play. When the assistants remove the cover from the hut to reveal Komachi, it is as if they are not there at all. Our imagination transforms the scene as they fade into the background.

In the process of Westernization, Japan welcomed the influences of Europe and the United States. As a result, Noh performances became reserved for special occasions, such as the visits of foreign dignitaries from 1868 through 1880. When former President Ulysses S. Grant saw a Noh performance at a nobleman's residence in 1879, his praise prompted the construction of a Noh stage in 1881, making Noh available to the public for the first time since the seventeenth century. Renewed public interest in the art of Noh created a revival in the training of performers that has lasted through the twentieth century.

Perhaps the most decisive factor in the continued interest in Noh as a traditional art form in Japan and as an influence on Western drama and performance was the publication of *Noh: Or Accomplishment* in 1916. Ernest Fenollosa's extensive study of Noh, which included translations of the plays, was arranged and adapted by Ezra Pound. William Butler Yeats used these texts to create his own plays in the Noh style. *At the Hawk's Well* and *Calvary* are two notable examples. Further translations of Noh plays by Arthur Waley and the discovery and translation of Zeami's treatises led to experiments in Noh actor training as early as 1931 by such French theatre practitioners as Jacques Copeau, Charles Dullin, and Jean-Louis Barrault. Witnessing Noh in performance, British composer Benjamin Britten took the text of a Noh play, *Sumidigawa,* and created *Curlew River,* an opera that recreated the performance values of its Japanese original. Equally important, European interest in the Noh and a need to revive the traditional arts since the late 1960s has led Tadashi Suzuki and Yukio Ninagawa, the most innovative teachers and directors in contemporary Japan, to return to Noh for inspiration in their training exercises and production concepts.

REFLECTIONS ON KOMACHI AT SEKIDERA

The challenge for the actor who takes the role of Komachi is to portray the essence of her beauty which, altogether now long past, still lingers like the perfume of a flower. This completely unaffected quality of maturity can only be conveyed by an actor who has perfected so many different roles that he unconsciously projects a sense of accumulated experience. Most actors never perform the role. Those that do, do so only when they are in their seventies or eighties.

Komachi is costumed in a white under-robe with a silver or gold-foiled design, over which is worn a satin robe worn draped at the waist so that embroidered patterns on the sleeves complement patterns around the bottom of the robe. Over this is worn a brocade small-sleeved robe, the bottom of which is folded up at the waist. The colors of the satin and brocade robes are subdued, and usually the color red is not used. Occasionally, however, the lining of the satin robe may be a shade of red. Such a robe would be chosen to refer subtly to the memory of Komachi's past beauty. The waist and wig bands worn are usually white or off-white and embellished with embroidered figures.

Because they visit Komachi on a festival day, the priests wear stiff trouser-skirts over their plain under-robes. Over these they wear thin broad-sleeved silk cloaks belted at the waist with a waistband. They also wear peaked priest's hats. The young boy is dressed in the same style. As he has not yet taken priestly vows, he does not wear a headcovering, but instead wears a wig which is tied to the nape of the neck and turned under, like a low, turned-under ponytail.

Stage attendants bring out a thatch-roofed bamboo hut draped with damask after the musicians and chorus are seated on stage. Komachi is already within this structure when it is brought out on stage. Only after the priests have declared their arrival at the hut is

Continued

the draping removed. The base of the hut is a three-foot square bamboo frame. The four poles forming the structure are covered a third of the way up with white cloth. Crossbars on either side at staggered heights are hung with poem cards. A bamboo staff leans against one of the back poles of the hut.

Little action takes place during the major part of the play. At first, Komachi stays within her hut while she discusses poetry with the priest. At the end of the description of her present life, she turns her fan to use the bamboo end to mime grinding ink and writing as these actions are mentioned. Finally, at the invitation of the priests to join in the festivities, she takes her staff and leaves the hut, going to the starting position upper right where she sits. The child uses his opened fan to represent a pitcher and to pour wine while she is seated there. At the close of the play, Komachi returns to the hut and sits again.

One of the charms of the play is the contrast between the dance by the child and Komachi's dance in response. The short dance of three movements that the boy performs is brisk in tempo. Komachi dances with her staff as well as her fan. She rests periodically during the three movements of her dance. Instead of the usual *jo-ha-kyu* development which brings the dance to a close at a faster tempo than it began, the tempo is reversed. This demonstrates clearly the natural tiring of the old woman as she dances.

From Roy E. Teele, Nicholas J. Teele, and H. Rebecca Teele, trans., ONO NO KOMACHI: POEMS, STORIES, NO PLAYS. *Copyright © 1993, Garland Publishing, New York. Reprinted by permission.*

Notes

1. *Donald Keene,* NO: THE CLASSICAL THEATRE OF JAPAN *(Tokyo: Kodanshu International Ltd., 1973), 33.*
2. *Leonard C. Pronko,* THEATER EAST AND WEST *(Berkeley: University of California Press, 1967), 84.*

KOMACHI AT SEKIDERA
(SEKIDERA KOMACHI)
KANZE MOTOKIYO ZEAMI
TRANSLATED BY KAREN BRAZELL

CHARACTERS

The Abbot of Sekidera (*waki*)   Two Priests (*wakizure*)   A Child (*kokata*)
Ono no Komachi (*shite*)

PLACE: Sekidera in Ōmi Province
TIME: The beginning of autumn: The seventh day of the seventh month

(The stage assistants bring forward a simple construction representing a hut with a thatched roof. It is covered with a cloth. The Old Woman is inside.

As the music begins the Child, the Abbot, and two Priests enter and face each other onstage. The Abbot and the Priests carry rosaries.)

THREE PRIESTS.   So long awaited, autumn has come at last,
So long awaited, the lovers' autumn meeting!
Now let us begin the Festival of Stars.[1]
(The Abbot faces front.)
ABBOT.   I am the chief priest of Sekidera in Ōmi. Today, the seventh day of the seventh month, we come to celebrate the Festival of Stars here in the temple garden. People say that the old woman who has built her hut at the foot of the mountain knows all the secrets of the art of poetry. So, on this festive day dedicated to poetry, I am going to take the young people to hear her stories.
(He turns to the Child.)

THREE PRIESTS.   Early autumn comes and brings a touch of chill.
We feel it in the wind and in our thinning locks.[2]
Soon, soon the Seventh Night will be on us.
(The Abbot faces front.)
ABBOT.   We bring offerings for the festival today,
The music of flutes and strings,
TWO PRIESTS.   And many poems
ABBOT.   Composed in our native tongue.[3]
(He turns to the Child.)
THREE PRIESTS.   Our prayers for skill at poetry are decked
With brightly colored streamers:
Fluttering ribbons, each a token of prayer,
Like silk threads woven into rich brocades
On looms of autumn flowers

---

[1]The Tanabata Festival, of Chinese origin, is still celebrated in Japan on the seventh day of the seventh month. Bamboo branches are decorated with five-colored streamers and with slips on which poems have been written commemorating the lovers' meeting of the two stars.

[2]From some lines by Po Chü-i included in the *Wakan Rōei Shū*, no. 204: "Who could have arranged things so well? The sighing cool wind and my thinning locks at once announce autumn is here." A parallel is drawn between the coming of autumn in the world and the coming of autumn to the person, evidenced by the thinning locks. [3]Many poets wrote in Chinese, especially on formal occasions, but the Japanese preferred their own language for their intimate feelings.

And pampas grass pearly with dew.
The winds in the pines
(*The Abbot faces front, takes a few steps, then returns to his former position, indicating he has made a journey.*)
Blend with the strings of the *koto*
To make music for the offerings tonight,[4]
Our offerings for this festive night.
(*The Abbot and his companions are now at their destination.*)

ABBOT.   Here is the hut now. Let us call on the old woman. (*To the Child.*) But first, please sit down.

(*All kneel. A stage assistant removes the cloth around the hut, revealing the Old Woman seated inside. Paper strips inscribed with poems hang from the crossbars of the hut frame, The Old Woman wears the* uba *mask.*)

OLD WOMAN.   Days go by without a single bowl of food;
Whom can I ask for one?
At night my tattered rags fail to cover me,
But there is no way to patch the rents.
Each passing rain
Ages the crimson of the flowers;
The willows are tricked by the wind
And their green gradually droops.[5]
Man has no second chance at youth;
He grows old. The aged song thrush
Warbles again when spring has come,
But time does not revert to the past.
Oh, how I yearn for the days that are gone!
What would I do to recapture the past!
(*She weeps. The Abbot and the Child rise, and go to kneel before her.*)

ABBOT.   Old woman, we have come to speak with you.

OLD WOMAN.   Who are you?

ABBOT.   I am a priest from Sekidera. These young people are students of poetry. They have heard of your talent, and I have brought them here to question you about poetry and to learn something of your life.

OLD WOMAN.   This is an unexpected visit! The log buried in the earth has been so long forgotten you must not expect it will put forth new sprouts.[6] Just remember this: If you will make your heart the seed and your words the blossoms,[7] if you will steep yourself in the fragrance of the art, you will not fail to accomplish true poetry. But how praiseworthy that mere boys should cherish a love of poetry!

ABBOT.   May I ask you about a poem everyone knows, "The Harbor of Naniwa?"[8] Do you agree that it should be used as a first guide?

OLD WOMAN.   Indeed I do. Poetry goes back to the Age of the Gods, but the meters were then irregular and the meanings difficult to understand. "The Harbor of Naniwa," however, belongs to the Age of Man. It was composed for the joyous occasion of an emperor's enthronement, and has long been beloved for that reason.[9]

ABBOT.   The poem about Mount Asaka, which once soothed the heart of a prince, is also beautifully written.[10]

OLD WOMAN.   Truly, you understand the art,
For those two poems are the parents of all poetry.

ABBOT.   They serve as models for beginners.

OLD WOMAN.   Noblemen and peasantry alike,

ABBOT.   City dwellers and country folk,

OLD WOMAN.   Even commoners like ourselves

ABBOT.   Take pleasure in composing poetry

OLD WOMAN.   Following the promptings of our hearts.

CHORUS.   Though the sands lapped by the waves
Of the lake in Ōmi should run out,
Though the sands of the shore should melt away,
(*The Abbot and the Child return to kneel with the Priests.*)
The words of poetry will never fail.[11]
They are enduring as evergreen boughs of pine,
Continuous as trailing branches of willow;
For poetry, whose source and seed is found
In the human heart, is everlasting.
Though ages pass and all things vanish,
As long as words of poetry remain,
Poems will leave their marks behind,
And the traces of poetry will never disappear.

ABBOT.   Thank you for your words of explanation. It is true that countless poems survive from the past, but they are rarely by women. Few women know as much as you about poetry. Tell me—the poem

---

[4]The above three lines are based on a poem by the Consort Itsukinomiya in the *Shūishū*, no. 451.   [5]Derived from an anonymous poem in Chinese found in a commentary to the historical work *Hyakurenshō*.   [6]Quoted, with slight modifications, from the preface to the *Kokinshū*.   [7]Also from the preface to the *Kokinshū*.

[8]This is the "Naniwazu" poem: "In Naniwa Harbor/ The flowers have come to the trees;/ They slept through the winter,/ But now it is the spring—/ See how the blossoms have opened!" The preface to the *Kokinshū* characterizes this poem and the one on Asakayama, Mount Asaka, as the "father and mother of poetry." Both poems are given considerable attention in *The Reed Cutter*.
[9]The poem was traditionally supposed to have been composed to encourage the future Emperor Nintoku, who reigned in the fourth century A.D., to accept the throne.   [10]The poem runs, literally: "Mount Asaka—/ Its reflection appears In the mountain spring/ That is not shallow, and of you/ My thoughts are not shallow either." The Prince of Kazuraki was sent to the distant province of Mutsu where he was badly received by the governor. He was so angry that he refused to eat, but the governor's daughter cheered him by offering saké and reciting this poem.   [11]Based on lines from the *Kokinshū* preface: "Though you count up my love you could never come to the end, not even if you could count every grain of sand on the shore of the wild sea."

"I know my lover
Is coming tonight—
See how the spider
Spins her web:
That is a sure sign!"[12]
Was that not by a woman?

OLD WOMAN.   Yes, that poem was written long ago by
Princess Sotōri, the consort of Emperor Ingyō. I tried, if
only in form, to master her style.

ABBOT.   Ah! You have studied the style of Princess Sotōri?
I have heard that Ono no Komachi, who's so much talked
of these days, wrote in that style.[13]

"Wretched that I am—
A floating water weed,
Broken from its roots—
If a stream should beckon,
I would follow it, I think."
That poem is by Komachi.

OLD WOMAN.   Yes, once my husband, Ōe no Koreaki,
took up with another woman, and I grieved at the fickle-
ness of the world. Then, Funya no Yasuhide[14] invited me
to accompany him to Mikawa, where he was to be the
governor. I wrote that poem in response to his urging and
to his promises that life in the country would bring solace.

Alas, memories of the past!
So long forgotten, they rise up again
Before me as I talk to you.
Tears well up from my suffering heart.
(She weeps.)

ABBOT.   Strange! This old woman says she wrote the poem
"Wretched that I am." And she says she wrote in the
Sotōri style, just as Komachi did. She must be nearly a
hundred years old, and if Komachi were still alive
today. . . . And is there any reason why she couldn't be?
It must be so! (To the Old Woman.) You are what is left
of Ono no Komachi. Do not deny it.

OLD WOMAN.   Ah, I burn with shame to be called Komachi, I who wrote

"With no outward sign

CHORUS.   It withers—
The flower in the human heart."[15]
How ashamed I am to be seen!
"Wretched that I am—
A floating water weed,
Broken from its roots—
If a stream should beckon,
I would follow it, I think."
How ashamed I am!
(She weeps.)

"Hide them though I may,
The tears keep flowing,
Too many for my sleeves to hold—
A rain of tears dissolving
Everything except the past."[16]
Now that my life has reached its end,
Like a withered flower,
Why should there still be tears?

OLD WOMAN.   "Longing for him,
I fell asleep,
Then he appeared before me . . ."[17]

CHORUS.   The joy I felt when I composed those lines
Is gone forever, but still my life goes on,
Attending the months and years as they come and go.
The dews of spring depart, and autumn frosts appear,
The leaves and grasses turn, and insect voices fade.

OLD WOMAN.   My life is over, and now I see

CHORUS.   It was like a rose of Sharon that knows
Only a single day of glory.[18]
"The living go on dying,
The dead increase in number;
Left in this world, ah—
How long must I go on
Lamenting for the dead?"[19]
And how long must I, who wrote that poem,
Live on, like flowers fallen, like leaves scattered,
With nothing left but life—dewlike, they always said.
Oh, how I long for the past!
My middle years were spent in yearning
For the distant glory of my youth.
Now even those days of wistful recollection
Have become such ancient history
I find myself wishing, if not for youth,
At least for middle age.
Long ago, wherever I spent a single night
My room would be bright with tortoise shell,
Golden flowers hung from the walls,
And in the door were strings of crystal beads.[20]
Brilliant as the Emperor's chair in grand procession
The jewellike gowns I wore, a hundred colors.
I lay on bright brocaded quilts
Within a pillowed bridal chamber.
Look at it now, my mud-daubed hut!
Can this be my resplendent room?

---

[12]An anonymous poem, no. 1110 in the *Kokinshū*. [13]So stated in
the preface to the *Kokinshū*. [14]An early Heian poet, one of the
"Six Immortals of Poetry." The explanation of the "Wretched
that I am" poem was traditional. [15]From poem no. 757 in the
Kokinshū, by Komachi.

[16]A poem by Abe no Kiyoyuki, no. 556 in the *Kokinshū*. [17]The
first part of a poem by Komachi, no. 552 in the *Kokinshū*. The last
two lines run: "If I had known it was a dream/ I should never
have wakened." [18]These lines are based on verses by Po Chü-i,
no. 291 in the *Wakan Rōei Shū*. [19]A poem by Komachi, no. 850
in the *Shinkokinshū*. [20]This description is based on a passage in
the *Tamatsukuri Komachi Sōsuisho*, a work in Chinese, apparently
by a Buddhist priest of the Heian period, describing Komachi's
decline and her eventual salvation.

OLD WOMAN.　The temple bell of Sekidera
CHORUS.　Tolls the vanity of all creation—
　To ancient ears a needless lesson.
　A mountain wind blows down Ōsaka's slope
　To moan the certainty of death;
　Its message still eludes me.
　Yet, when blossoms scatter and leaves fall,
　Still in this hut I find my pleasure:
　Grinding ink, I dip my brush and write.
　My words are all dry, like seaweed on the shore.
　Touching, they once said, but lacking strength[21]—
　My poems lacked strength because they were a woman's.
　Now when I have grown decrepit
　My poems are weaker still. Their life is spent.
　How wretched it is to be old!
　(*She weeps. The Child turns to the Abbot.*)
CHILD.　I'm afraid we'll be late for the Festival of Stars.
　Let's ask the old lady to come with us.
　(*The Abbot kneels before the Old Woman.*)
ABBOT.　Please join us on this Seventh Night, the Festival
　of Stars.
OLD WOMAN.　Alas! An old woman should not intrude on
　such an occasion. I cannot go.
　(*She takes down the paper poem cards.*)
ABBOT.　What harm could come of it? Please come with us.
　(*He goes to the hut and helps the Old Woman to stand.*)
CHORUS.　The Seventh Night—
　How many years since first I offered the gods
　Bamboo tied with colored streamers?
　How long has shriveled old Komachi lived?
　(*Assisted by the Abbot and leaning on a staff, the Old
　　Woman leaves the hut.*)
　Has Ono no Komachi reached a hundred years?
　Or even more?
　I who used to watch the Festival of Stars,
　Familiar of the noblest lords and ladies,
　(*She kneels beside the* shite-*pillar. The Abbot goes back
　　beside the others.*)
　Now stand in shameful hempen rags!
　A sight too painful for eyes to bear!
　(*The Abbot weeps.*)
　Still, tonight we hold the Festival of Stars,
　(*The Child stands and mimes serving wine to the Old
　　Woman.*)
　Tonight we celebrate the Seventh Night
　With multitudes of offerings for the stars.
　Prayer streamers hang from bamboo,
　(*While the following lines are being sung the Child goes
　　to the gazing-pillar, moves clockwise around the
　　stage, then stands at the center preparatory to begin-
　　ning his dance.*)

Music plays and cups of wine go round.
The young dancer—look how gracefully
He twirls his sleeves, like snow
Swirling in the moonlight.
　(*The Old Woman, still seated, watches the Child dance.*)
We celebrate the Festival of Stars,
Streamers flutter from the bamboos. . . .
OLD WOMAN.　May it be celebrated through ages as many
　As the joints of the bamboo!
　(*The Old Woman, hardly aware of what she does, taps
　　the rhythm with her fan.*)
CHORUS.　We pray for eternal prosperity;
　We dance the "Ten Thousand Years."[22]
　(*The Child completes his dance, then sits as before.*)
OLD WOMAN.　How gracefully that boy has danced! I re-
　member how, long ago in the Palace, the Gosechi dancing
　girls swirled their sleeves five times at the Harvest Fes-
　tival. They say that if a madman runs, even the sane will
　run after him. But tonight the proverb is reversed! Enticed
　by the boy's floating sleeves, see how a madwoman
　prances!
　(*She stands with the aid of her staff and begins her
　　dance.*)
One hundred years—
The dance of the butterfly
Who dreamt he had spent
A hundred years enfolded
Within a flower petal.[23]
CHORUS.　How sad it is! It breaks my heart!
　A flowering branch on a withered tree!
OLD WOMAN.　I have forgotten how to move my hands.
CHORUS.　Unsteady feet, uncertain wave of sleeves,
OLD WOMAN.　Billow after billow, floating wave on wave.
CHORUS.　My dancing sleeves rise up,
　But sleeves cannot wave back the past.
　(*She goes before the hut.*)
OLD WOMAN.　I miss those vanished days!
　(*She kneels and weeps.*)
CHORUS.　But as I dance the early autumn night,
　The short night, gives way to dawn.
　The temple bell of Sekidera tolls.
OLD WOMAN.　A chorus of morning birdsong heralds
CHORUS.　The coming dawn, the day's approaching light,
　The dawn's fresh light that reveals my shame!
OLD WOMAN.　Where is the forest of Hazukashi?[24]
　(*She stands, propping herself on her staff.*)

---

[22]The name of a *gagaku* dance, *Manzairaku*.　[23]A reference to a
poem by Ōe no Masafusa in the collection *Horikawa-in Ontoki
Hyakushu Waka*: "This world where I have dwelt a hundred years
lodged in a flower is the dream of a butterfly." The poem in turn
refers to a famous passage in Chuang Tzu. See *The Complete
Works of Chuang Tzu* (New York, 1968), translated by Burton
Watson, p. 49.　[24]Hazukashi, the name of a wood near Kyoto, also
has the meaning "ashamed."

[21]The appraisal of Komachi's poetry given in the preface to the
Kokinshū.

CHORUS.   Where is the forest of Hazukashi?
There is no forest here to hide my shame.
Farewell, I take my leave.
Now, leaning heavily on her stick,
She slowly returns to her straw hut.

(*She enters the hut, sits and weeps.*)
The hundred-year-old woman you have spoken to
Is all that remains of famed Komachi,
Is all that is left of Ono no Komachi.

FOCUS QUESTIONS

1. Discuss how the appearance of the child disciple *(kokata)* and his dance enhance the play's theme on the mutability of life.
2. Show how the introduction of poetic fragments helps evoke the sadness and pain of lost youth that Komachi feels.
3. What elements in the play underscore the bittersweet irony of the mortality of the poet and the immortality of that poet's creation?

OTHER ACTIVITIES

1. Trace the Abbot's role in the play. Describe what purpose the *waki* serves in a Noh drama in terms of both furthering the story and evoking its essential mood.
2. In a short essay, discuss why Noh cannot be viewed according to the standards of Western drama.

BIBLIOGRAPHY

Anderson, G. L. *The Genius of the Oriental Theater*. New York: New American Library, 1966.

Brazell, Karen. *Twelve Plays of the Noh and Kyogen Theaters*. Ithaca, NY: Cornell University East Asia Papers, no. 50, 1988.

Ernst, Earle, ed. *The Japanese Plays from the Traditional Theatre*. New York: Grove Press Inc., 1960.

Inoura, Yoshinobu, and Toshio Kawatake. *The Traditional Theatre of Japan*. New York: Weatherhill Publishers, 1981.

Keene, Donald. *No: The Classical Theatre of Japan*. Tokyo: Kodanshu International Ltd., 1973.

————, ed. *Twenty Plays of the No Theatre*. New York: Columbia University Press, 1970.

Komparu, Kunio. *The Noh Theater: Principles and Perspectives*. New York: John Weatherhill Inc., 1983.

Pronko, Leonard C. *Theater East and West: Perspectives Toward a Total Theater*. Berkeley: University of California Press, 1967.

Teele, Roy E., Nicholas J. Teele, and H. Rebecca Teele, trans. *Ono no Komachi: Poems, Stories, No Plays*. New York: Garland Publishing Inc., 1993.

Tyler, Royall. *Pining Wind: A Cycle of No Plays*. Ithaca, NY: Cornell University East Asia Papers, no. 17, 1978.

Waley, Arthur. *The No Plays of Japan*. New York: Grove Press, 1957.

Yasuda, Kenneth. *Masterworks of the No Theater*. Bloomington: Indiana University Press, 1989.

RECOMMENDED VIDEOTAPES

Noh: The Classical Theater of Japan. VHS. 28 min. 1980. Distributed by Insight Media, New York City.

The Style of the Classical Japanese Noh Theater. VHS. 17 min. Distributed by Insight Media, New York City.

THE PEDANT
ANONYMOUS*

It is astonishing to think that, with such a trifling aid as this, ten or twelve actors are able to keep the public in a gale of laughter for three hours or more and bring to a satisfactory close the argument which has been set for them.

—CARLO GOZZI

The San Francisco Mime Troupe performing in *commedia dell'arte* style in 1968. *Photo: Doug Rives.*

*Recorded by Flaminio Scala.

Approaching the Commedia dell'Arte

A unique form of theatre known as **commedia dell'arte** surfaced in Italy around 1550, drawing on a variety of performance styles: the entertainments provided by traveling acrobats, jugglers, bards, mountebanks, and clowns; the medieval farces in the vernacular; and the revival of classical plays in the Renaissance academies. This form of spectacle was developed and perfected by itinerant troupes of professional actors who specialized in physical action and virtuoso improvisation. Using a mere scenario as a framework, these men and women created full-fledged comedies that incorporated political and social problems as well as current scandals and intrigues with which their audiences were preoccupied.

Since there was no set dialogue to memorize, the players could alter a scenario as a vehicle for biting satire to suit the mood of any crowd. As a result, much of the form's popularity was attributed to its ad-libbed dialogue as well as its agile and often vulgar stage business to elicit laughter across class lines. Its stock cast of characters and their antics appealed equally to simple townsfolk who attended outdoor performances held in their village squares, to wealthy merchants who patronized the performances held in public theatres rented by the companies, and to the nobility who invited the companies to play in their private theatres.

The plotlines for these performances were taken from the plays of Plautus and Terence and the new dramas written in the neoclassical style. There were at least three types of domestic comedies: those in which the old men were cuckolded; those in which the lovers were thwarted by their parents and by a variety of confusions and misunderstandings; and those that focused on the unraveling of intrigue. Such devices as reunions between parents and children or siblings, shipwrecks, the undoing of spells and magic, mistaken identity between twins, disguises, and cross-dressing were not uncommon. Like their classical counterparts, these comedies depended on farce, verbal wit, and most of all, the willingness of audiences to laugh at their own foibles.

Characteristic of *commedia dell'arte* was its adaptability. Few settings, if any, were required. With a platform and either a curtain for a backdrop or a constructed street scene with several houses that had working doors and windows (like the *scaena frons* of the Roman theatre), a scenario could be staged in almost any venue. Each of the ten to twelve members of a company had a set role that he or she developed and would play over many years. As part of their stock-in-trade, the performers collected a variety of material from which to draw dialogue. These included specific phrases, declarations of love, monologues of fatherly advice, set speeches of despair or delirium, and rhyming couplets with which to end an act. They also had a repertoire of gestures and bits of action, **lazzi,** that they worked into the scenario.

Every comedy drew from the same stock characterizations for its **dramatis personae.** Thus casting was only a matter of which roles were needed for that particular performance. Of extreme importance, however, was the sense of ensemble that the spontaneous nature of this theatre demanded: as each performance of a scenario changed to accommodate the audience and the space, the actors had to adapt their improvisations to those of their colleagues with a spontaneity and ingenuity that kept the dialogue moving and the storyline coherent.

Of the numerous individual performers and companies that brought *commedia dell'arte* to the courts and cities of Europe from the mid-sixteenth to the mid-eighteenth century, the earliest to gain recognition was *I Gelosi* (1578–1604), headed by Francesco and Isabella Andreini. Sponsored by the court of Ferrara, this company introduced the plethora of dialects and comic bits and the constellation of recognizable characters of which the *commedia* was comprised. From the ranks of *I Gelosi* came the author/actor Flaminio Scala who published forty-eight **soggetti,** or plot outlines, that he based on scenarios performed by his company. Of these, *The Pedant* is one of the most famous.

THE CAST

Commedia characters never needed introduction for audiences. Their costumes, masks, dialects, and general demeanor easily identified their roles. As soon as the performers appeared on stage, the audience knew their characters and exactly what to expect. Because Scala's *soggetti* contain relatively few character descriptions, some knowledge of their personality and appearance enhances our appreciation of *The Pedant*.

Crucial to each performance are two old men who represent the heads of different households. The first is Pantalone, a wealthy, middle-aged Venetian merchant and prominent citizen dressed in red jacket and tights, black gown, hat, and slippers. Wearing a dark brown leather mask with hooked nose and gray hair, moustache, and pointy beard, he portrays the stingy, avaricious, and credulous father. Still virile, he lusts after younger women. Although he maintains a stronghold over his family, he cannot keep his children in line and they quickly tire of his oppressive fatherly advice. Furthermore, his infidelities are driving his wife to find a lover and to cuckold him.

His foil is Gratiano, a corpulent, middle-aged doctor of medicine or jurisprudence from Bologna who has enjoyed better times financially. His black cloak, doctoral bonnet, white ruff at his neck, black leather mask with large nose, and reddened cheeks identify him as the ineffectual, would-be intellectual. He cannot resist offering opinions on everything, even when he knows nothing, and he is sadly reduced to controlling his children by ''the power of the purse.'' Rather than taking action, he speaks in illogical circumlocutions, resorting to Latin phrases and classical allusions to impress his listeners. His usual role as lascivious charlatan is assumed in *The Pedant* by Cataldo, the **eponymous** character, who ends up the butt of the servants and the young people.

Of equal importance are the three to five masked **zanni,** or clowns. The three who appear in *The Pedant* are Pedrolino, Burattino, and Arlecchino, each of whom speaks in his own dialect but is costumed according to tradition. Pedrolino, the Italian Pierrot from Bergamo, is dressed in baggy tunic and pants and plays the trusted servant of Pantalone. He is outspoken and often tricks others for sport, but always on behalf of his employer. Burattino, dressed in tight-fitting tunic and pants, is a rough and uncouth bawd who is poorly paid by Gratiano. He cheats others out of money or food to make up for what his master cannot provide. Arlecchino from Bergamo, in his irregularly patched clothing with cap and slapstick, is the focal point of the clowning. Although he never initiates an intrigue, he enjoys furthering it along, especially if it is of an amorous nature. His spontaneous and impulsive acrobatics further help him escape punishment. The fact that Pedrolino and Arlecchino both come from Bergamo also gives them the opportunity to perform the *lazzo* of friendship in which they ''recognize each other as fellow countrymen'' and go through the ritual of ridiculous and elaborate handshakes and embraces.

Another important group in the *soggetto* are the lovers, of which there are usually two male and two female roles. These are often played by young, attractive performers who are unmasked, dress fashionably, and speak in a refined Tuscan dialect. Typically, Oratio and Fabritio are handsome innocents who seek their servants' help in overcoming the obstacles to love or to freedom from their fathers. Flaminia is the young daughter of Gratiano who is overly protective. She is pursued by rival suitors, only one of whom is her heart's desire. Isabella, on the other hand, is slightly older in this comedy. Still a beautiful woman in her late thirties, she is the educated and dignified mother of Oratio and wife of Pantalone. Although her honor is important to her, her husband's extramarital exploits tempt her to flirt with others.

The final role is that of Captain Spavento, the Spanish mercenary whose presence in the comedy serves as a catalyst for marital intrigue and as an obstacle to the union of the lovers. He leers and swaggers, flashing his sword to frighten others. Underneath his braggart manner lies the heart of a consummate coward. Vain and conceited in his cape and feathered hat with sword dangling from hip, he prides himself as a lady-killer. But his advances toward the opposite sex go unrewarded and his haughty self-image is ridiculed.

STRUCTURE

The standard opening for the *commedia* performance was a prologue delivered by one of the masked characters in front of the curtain. This often took the form of a madrigal or speech that had no relation to the storyline of the piece to follow. The comedy itself was performed in three acts separated by brief **intermezzi.** During these intervals, the performers had a chance to exhibit their skill at creating character monologues, at dancing, or performing gymnastics. Interspersed throughout the performance were set bits of action, the *lazzi,* which prompted laughter from the audience. These *lazzi* were a repertory of practical jokes or gags handed down from *zanni* to *zanni* and drawn on as needed. They ran the gamut from ''blows, trips, stumbles, starts of causeless fright, pretense of stupidity, misinterpretations of orders with laughable results, puns and satiric repartee, all these ways of rousing mirth.''[1]

In *The Pedant,* the following *lazzi* are some of those chosen to round out the comedy: the one that challenges social class, ''I say,'' as the servants and children question Gratiano's power in act 1; the one of inappropriate behavior, ''friendship,'' referred to earlier; the one that breaks the illusion of performance, ''of the beautiful city,'' in which the Captain and Arlecchino overpraise Venice to the audience. Acrobatic stunts, scatological references, comic violence, and illogic were also displayed. A typical food gag is the macaroni scene in which Arlecchino dutifully serves a dish of pasta to Pedrolino as a gift from his master, Captain Spavento. All three *zanni* partake heartily in the meal, as they weep copiously. When the plate is cleared, Pedrolino and Burattino send their thanks to Captain Spavento and depart weeping. Alone and still tearful, Arlecchino licks the plate clean and exits. The incongruity of the scene and the skill with which it was executed always guaranteed laughter.

To ensure that the comedies were integrated and coherent, despite the detailed directions provided in the *soggetto,* the *corago,* or director of the company, devised a specific interpretation of the scenario that was agreed on in advance. He read the argument that laid out the story and revealed all past events pertinent to his interpretation for the evening's performance. In this way, each actor determined which material to incorporate into his dialogue. The director also suggested specific *lazzi* that he thought would enhance the comedy. With no further rehearsal, each performer went off alone for about an hour to plan the stock phrases and gags to play in performance. The only guideline was a copy of the scenario posted in the wings to remind the players of the order of scenes. Skill at maintaining the ensemble, while creating effective interpretations of their own, is what made these performers so special and their performances so dynamic.

HISTORICAL IMPACT

Commedia troupes toured the countries of Europe for nearly two centuries and left a lasting influence. In Spain, there are traces of the *zanni* in the *graciosos* (clowns) and of the comedies of intrigue in the plays of Lope de Vega. In England, Ben Jonson's *Volpone* and *The Alchemist* and Shakespeare's *Twelfth Night, Merchant of Venice,* and *A Midsummer Night's Dream* are replete with characters and situations found in the two hundred *soggetti* from the Renaissance that still exist. In those countries that were divided into principalities—notably Germany, Poland, and Russia—*commedia* troupes were engaged by the different rulers in the seventeenth and eighteenth centuries. Their presence inspired the development of distinct national theatres that celebrated the folklore and inhabitants of their countries. Of greatest importance was the adoption of *commedia* in France in 1660 when Louis XIV authorized the Comédie Italien to share the Petit Bourbon with Molière's troupe and later to occupy the Hôtel de Bourgogne. Because of this venture, which lasted until 1697, French theatre owes a great debt to the form. From the plays of Molière—whose *Tartuffe* adapts the story of *The Pedant*—to those of Beaumarchais and Marivaux, the crafty servants, thwarted lovers, and doddering old men of *commedia* brightened the stage.

By the end of the eighteenth century, *commedia dell'arte* had faded. The written comedies of Goldoni, which emphasized realism, and those of Gozzi, which emphasized the masks and fantasies, substituted and ultimately suppressed the improvisational style for which Italian comedy was legendary. Although *commedia* troupes continued to train and to perform in Naples through the 1920s, their influence on the mainstream stage was not felt until the twentieth century when *commedia* style was welcomed as an antidote to realism and naturalism.

As early as 1901, Edward Gordon Craig, who had studied the classic scenarios and *zanni,* championed the *commedia dell'arte* tradition in his journal, *The Mask,* and prompted interest in *commedia* throughout Europe. Soviet directors like Meyerhold, Tairov, and Vaktanghov experimented with the stock characters and acrobatic *lazzi* to create a theatre for the populace. In France by the 1930s, teacher and performer Jacques Copeau reintroduced the emphasis on physical and mental agility through the improvisational techniques of Italian comedy into his actor training program. His students Charles Dullin and Jean-Louis Barrault eventually brought *commedia* techniques and images to the French stage. Even modern mime taught by Etienne Decroux and popularized by his students Jacques Lecoq and Marcel Marceau owes a debt to this tradition.

By the 1960s in America, the iconoclastic and satiric qualities that had galvanized *commedia's* popularity led such groups as the San Francisco Mime Troupe and El Teatro Campesino to borrow the form. Adapting the plays of Goldoni and Molière and incorporating current events into the improvised dialogue, the Mime Troupe found *commedia dell'arte* to be a powerful medium through which to protest materialistic values in their productions of *The Dowry* (1962), *Scapin* (1962), and *Tartuffe* (1964) and the escalating of the Vietnamese War in *L'Amant Militaire* (1967). The revival of the *commedia* style for political ends was taken up by another California-based company, Dell-Arte Players, a touring company whose plays touched on social and environmental issues. Their *Performance Anxiety* (1981) used traditional scenarios and the characters of Isabella, Pantalone, and Arlecchino to address issues of birth control responsibility. In 1989, they collaborated with the San Diego Repertory Company to produce Peter Barnes' *Red Noses,* which utilized *lazzi* and *commedia* masks.

Commedia dell'arte continues to be a viable performance style, as demonstrated in the presentation of Leon Katz's version of the scenario *The Three Cuckolds* by The Actors Theatre of Louisville. The production highlighted their 1990 Classics in Context series. Théâtre de la Jeune Lune's presentation of ''*commedia*'' characters in such plays as Goldoni's *Campiello,* performed in 1990, and Gozzi's *The Green Bird,* performed in 1993, has further reinforced the tradition in America. Perhaps the most important descendant of the *commedia* tradition in the last half of the twentieth century, however, is actor/writer/director Dario Fo. His ''throwaway'' radical political plays such as *Accidental Death of an Anarchist* (1970) depend on the improvisation and open-ended form that allowed Scala's *soggetti* to incorporate topical events. In the guise of the anarchic clown Arlecchino in *Mistero Buffo* (1969) or *Helliquin, Arlekin, Arlecchino* (1986), Fo has performed his political satires as the ''blasphemous voice of the people, an alterego of the masses.''[2]

REFLECTIONS ON THE PEDANT

R. G. Davis is founder of The San Francisco Mime Troupe. The following originally appeared in The San Francisco Mime Troupe: The First Ten Years.

We were fortunate in meeting Carlo Mazzone, a mime from the Lecoq School. He had played Brighella under Georgio Strehler at the Piccolo and possessed eight leather *commedia* masks made by Amleto Sartori. Mazzone showed the masks in operation and told us some of their history. The mask-making skill had disappeared with the Renaissance Venetians but Sartori unearthed the process and created these magnificent examples. Each mask, a fine sculpture, fixed the image of a face and needed only a turn of the body to make it come alive. The process of molding the leather to a wooden form was a Sartori family secret but the real genius was the characteristic sculptured expression. Sartori had carved useful props—Pantalone's nose was hooked and his eyes properly almond-shaped; Arlecchino, with eyes like small dots, had a strained forehead with nothing behind it; Brighella's* perpetual wiseguy grin had room for shifty eyes; etc. We had our photographer friend Nata Piaskowski take meticulous pictures of the masks and had people copy them. Our papier-mâché and cheesecloth imitations were often too heavy and the contours not sharp enough. Mazzone left us with a sense of some impossible magic about the masks. In the seven years of playing *commedias,* we found only one artist, Francesca Green, an Art Institute graduate and commercial designer, who could make a few usable masks. In 1968 I realized that there was a simpler method and sent a letter with a check to Sartori.

We went to work on *commedia dell'arte* as we had on the Events—by jumping in and splashing around. We plowed through all the books, Italian, French, and English. We improvised from old scenarios and plays by Molière and Goldoni; wrote our own scenes; tried different characters. We discovered that the stereotypical characters operated both as an escape valve for irritation and as an integrating force. To the liberal, they often appear to show prejudice. However, if you dig the people and the contradictions, the stereotypes are more accurate in describing social conditions than bland generalities. We eventually learned in *commedia,* and later in the Minstrel Show, how to make stereotypes carry the burden of social satire.

In our *commedia* the performer had to be totally involved. There was no open fourth wall; in fact, there were no walls. Therefore, the performer had to keep his thoughts way ahead of the action. This *commedia* was "Brechtian" in that the stage play was a game. We posited that all action on the platform was fake, masked, indicated, enlarged show biz, while everything off stage was real. On stage we were totally committed to the dialogue, *lazzi,* pantomimic or mimetic play and could sustain the fakery of the onstage commitment by admitting the reality of off stage. After exiting behind the drop an actor stepped off the platform, took off his mask and out of character walked around to the side to watch the other actors.

From the first *commedia* our opening format was designed to help the performers warm up in front of an audience and let the audience in on the "secrets" of backstage.

We would set up the stage, get into costume and makeup (or masks), play music, loose and easy, gather into a circle and do warm-up physical exercises while singing songs. At first, the songs were from an Archive record of the Central Middle Ages, often simple rounds, Christmas tunes, and eventually, tunes from Wobblies and political songs from Italy, Mexico, and even some we wrote. When inside we sat behind the drop or "off stage" in the dressing room. In the park, we sang and played to one side of the stage. By

---

*Brighella is a popular *commedia dell'arte* character.

1966–67 the singing and playing (tambourine, recorder, drum, castanets, hand clapping) were interesting and the audience usually joined in. We opened our circle and taught a three-part round, like "Scotland's Burning," but with new words:

> L. A.'s burning, L. A.'s burning, Watts out,
> Watts out. Fire, fire, fire, fire.
> Pour on money [or, Pay your taxes].

Despite political analysis or intellectual message, the job, especially in *commedia,* is always to "get them out." In our "openings" we ad-libbed good and bad jokes, cornball and marvelous, then introduced each individual character with some appropriate wisecrack. The openings took us much time to develop and never were finished until the last moment. We wanted the audience to see and learn about the characters prior to the play (exposition) and we also wanted to get used to each other on stage.

In a highly stylized play, the actor usually has one task—to play the character. In our adaptations we gave our actors three jobs: play yourself, play the character, play an Italian who was a *commedia* performer. The person was to act himself while reading the script, simply to understand the situation, the conditions, the motives of the character and the point of the play. This is then simple Stanislavsky technique where actions and objectives are discovered without trying to perform the text.

The second layer of refinement or the development of the mask requires physical characteristics such as a duck walk for Pantalone; a swinging bravado for the lover; snap, crackle, and suspicious looks for Brighella. And accents—French (for lovers), Italian (Dottore and servants), or Jewish and Mexican with their concurrent gestures. The personal attributes of the actor were changed or extended to create the mask.

The third level—historical imitation of Italian actors—required some study of *commedia dell'arte* and preparation that would produce a rich stage characterization. Each modern actor was to find his/her Italian counterpart. Francesco Andreini played Capitano Spavento (ca. 1600); Guiseppe Biancolelli as Dottore; Isabella Andreini as first lady; Tomasso Fortunati played Brighella; Domenico Biancolelli as Arlecchino.

These levels of reality, one concrete (self) and the other two assumed (mask and Italian actor), allowed for constant shifting of characterization and play. When the actor lost the character's believability or failed to make the audience laugh, he could change to the Italian role and say, "Well, I tried thata one, no?" Or when a dog walked across the stage, the performer could break character as Italian actor and comment from his own vantage point, or if he was skilled enough he might stay inside the mask (role) and deal with the intrusion as the character. The ad lib (improvisational wisecrack) was the oil of transition.

Why go through this elaborate structure? In the twentieth century all three levels made up only an approximation of the sixteenth-century form called *commedia dell'arte.* There was no way of deluding the audience or creating an illusion that we were really *commedia dell'arte* performers just in from the Duke of Mantua's palace.

From Ron Davis, THE SAN FRANCISCO MIME TROUPE: THE FIRST TEN YEARS. *Copyright © 1975, R. G. Davis, Palo Alto, CA. Reprinted by permission.*

Notes

1. *Winifred Smith,* THE COMMEDIA DELL'ARTE *(New York: Avon Press, 1980), 13.*
2. *James Fisher, "Controversy, Cops, Commedia,"* THEATRE SYMPOSIUM *1 (1993): 128.*

THE PEDANT

Recorded by Flaminio Scala

Translated and Edited by Henry F. Salerno

CHARACTERS

Pantalone, *a Venetian*
Isabella, *his wife*
Oratio, *his son*
Pedrolino, *his servant*
Facchino, *the porter*
Doctor Gratiano

Flaminia, *his daughter*
Fabritio, *his son, a beardless youth*
Burattino, *his servant*
Cataldo, *tutor of Oratio*
Captain Spavento, *a stranger*
Arlecchino, *his servant*

Properties

A large copper tub
Three long knives
Three butcher's aprons
A nightshirt for Cataldo
A long cord
A stick

ARGUMENT

There lived in the city of Venice a very rich merchant named Pantalone de Bisognosi who had for a wife a very beautiful young lady named Isabella. By her he had a son named Oratio, who, as was the custom of the time, was tutored by one M. Cataldo, a pedant. Because the said Pantalone was a man who loved wine and women, it happened that more and more he quarreled with his wife, and many times the wife was consoled by the pedant. It happened that one day— after the usual quarrel—the pedant decided to try the wife of Pantalone and awaited the opportunity of more discord and another quarrel between husband and wife to reveal his love for her, pleading with most affectionate words for the return of his love. The lady, who much esteemed her honor, after promising him satisfaction, revealed all to her husband, who worked out a very neat plot and punishment as an example to all other pedants, as will become known in the story.

ACT ONE

VENICE

PANTALONE. ORATIO. Pantalone is scolded by his son Oratio for being a glutton and whoremaster and for leading his mother, Isabella, a terrible life. Pantalone replies he will live according to his own wishes.

CATALDO. At that, Cataldo, the pedant and Oratio's tutor, arrives and comes between them with peaceful words; he leads Pantalone away. Oratio says that his father does not know the wicked nature of the pedant, and they go well together.

ISABELLA. PEDROLINO. FACCHINO. Just then, Isabella enters, beating Pedrolino and the porter, whom she found in the cellar stealing a barrel of wine. The porter flees; Oratio reprimands his mother. Isabella replies that he is a wretch like his father, and she will avenge herself, and she goes into the house. Oratio leaves sorrowfully, and Pedrolino goes off to find Pantalone.

CAPT. SPAVENTO. ARLECCHINO. The Captain enters; having come from Naples on his way to Milan, he says he likes Venice and sings its praises.

ISABELLA. At that, Isabella appears at the window, sees the Captain, and drops her handkerchief. The Captain picks it up. Isabella comes out, and the Captain wants to return her handkerchief, but she refuses to take it. The Captain then gives her a ring which she accepts. The Captain asks if she is married. Isabella, sighing, says yes, as Pedrolino arrives. She sees him and goes in.

PEDROLINO. Pedrolino approaches, but, while still hidden, he heard her sighs and saw the Captain give her the ring; now he jokes with the Captain, telling him that the lady with whom he was talking is his wife. The Captain, offering him much money, asks him to find some beautiful girl to sleep with him. Pedrolino says that he will act as go-between between him and his wife. The Captain, satisfied, leaves with Arlecchino. Pedrolino declares he will tell Pantalone everything to avenge the beating he got from Isabella.

ISABELLA. At that moment, Isabella appears at the window, having heard everything; she mocks Pedrolino by calling him husband. She comes out mimicking him; then, angrily, she calls him villain and tells him she will expose all his knavery to Pantalone. She goes back in, and Pedrolino goes off in despair.

ORATIO. Oratio enters, unhappy because of his father and Flaminia, whom he loves.

FLAMINIA. At that, Flaminia appears at her window and talks with Oratio; they play a love scene. Flaminia then tells him that Fabritio, her brother, wants a favor of him, and she will send him out. She goes into the house, and Oratio waits.

FABRITIO. Then, Fabritio enters and asks Oratio if he would do anything to have his tutor given to him for his education. Oratio agrees, but first Fabritio will have to give him Flaminia, his sister, for wife. Fabritio says, ''When you make me a scholar of your master, then I will give you my sister for wife.'' Immediately his father arrives.

DR. GRATIANO. Gratiano at once says, ''You will not be a scholar of his tutor, nor will that one have my daughter for wife.''

PEDROLINO. Pedrolino enters and declares Fabritio will be a scholar of the pedant, and Oratio will have Gratiano's daughter for wife. Gratiano, laughing, says he will give it to him; Pedrolino replies, ''I shall be the one who gives.'' Gratiano sends Fabritio into the house; then, still laughing at Pedrolino, he leaves. Pedrolino tells Oratio to leave the matter to him, adding that there are many things he wants to say to his mother.

ISABELLA. At that, Isabella appears at her window. She has heard everything; she comes out with a stick and beats Pedrolino hard. Then she turns on Oratio, who, without attempting to defend himself, runs off. Isabella, still threatening Pedrolino, goes into the house. He remains, weeping.

ARLECCHINO. Just then, Arlecchino enters with a dish of macaroni to give to Pedrolino from the Captain. He gives it to Pedrolino, who, weeping, takes it, saying he is weeping because of something that happened to his wife, and thus weeping, he begins to eat. Arlecchino also begins to cry and to eat.

BURATTINO. At that, Burattino enters, sees them eating macaroni and weeping, and he also begins to weep and to eat until all the macaroni is eaten. Pedrolino, still crying, tells Arlecchino to kiss the Captain's hand for him and

goes. Burattino says the same, also crying, and goes. Arlecchino, crying and licking the platter, goes; and thus the first act ends.

ACT TWO

PANTALONE. PEDROLINO. Pantalone enters and learns from Pedrolino that his wife gave a handkerchief to a strange captain, that in return she received a ring as a gift, and that she beat him. Pantalone wonders about it, having never known his wife to be unfaithful.

DR. GRATIANO. At that moment, Gratiano arrives, saying to Pantalone that his servant is trying to marry off the children of others in his own way and urges Pantalone to attend to his own household, reprimanding him for the life he leads, especially as he is an old man.

ARLECCHINO. Then, Arlecchino enters and asks Pedrolino how his wife is, calling him Sir Sensual. Pedrolino tells Pantalone that this fellow is crazy; he drives him off.

CATALDO. Cataldo, the pedant, arrives; he is greeted by all. Pantalone tells him all that occurred between his wife and the Captain, saying that Pedrolino had reported everything.

FABRITIO. At that, Fabritio enters, greets the pedant, to the disgust of his father, who considers the pedant a knave. As the pedant observes that Gratiano knows him for what he is to spite him, he makes much of Fabritio and gives him a book of verse pedantically written by Fidentio, master of all pedants. Pantalone asks Cataldo's advice about what he has told him. The pedant says that Pedrolino is not to repeat what he has said, and Pantalone is to leave his wife to him; he will get the truth from her. Pantalone agrees.

ORATIO. Oratio then arrives and greets his master. The pedant reprimands him for not attending to his studies and to his duties in the house; he reprimands Pantalone for not maintaining discipline; then he consoles them and sends them all off. Alone, he speaks of his life and his vices. Under the pretense of moral sentiments, he says, he hides all his wickedness; he knocks on Isabella's door.

ISABELLA. Isabella comes out; she greets the pedant who, complaining and pretending, reports to her the gossip her husband told him about the ring she received from the Captain. Isabella confesses having done wrong and blames her husband, who chases other women. The pedant tells her that if she wishes to satisfy her desires, she does not have to go to a stranger, but to a person in the household, one known; and with much smooth talk he offers to satisfy her himself, promising to make peace between her and her husband. Isabella, in gay spirits, goes in to placate her husband. The pedant, seeing that Isabella will be content without another, is happy and leaves.

PEDROLINO. Pedrolino, hidden, has heard everything and says the pedant is a rascal and that his mistress is of a mind to go along with him.

FLAMINIA.   At that, Flaminia appears at the window to ask Pedrolino about Oratio.

CAPT. SPAVENTO.   The Captain enters, sees Flaminia, and asks Pedrolino about the young lady. Pedrolino tells him she is the daughter of the husband of the house and that he will speak to her on the Captain's behalf. He plans to entertain the people in the house and thus give the Captain an opportunity to talk to her. Pedrolino goes inside; then appearing behind Flaminia's window and disguising his voice, he tells the Captain to come dressed as a porter within half an hour, that Flaminia will let him into the house without the others suspecting. The Captain goes, and Pedrolino withdraws.

ORATIO.   Oratio, who has heard all, is unhappy.

PEDROLINO.   At that moment, Pedrolino comes out of the house and consoles Oratio by telling him it is a trick. He promises that Flaminia will be his, but they must watch out for the pedant; he takes him off to tell him what to do.

PANTALONE. DR. GRATIANO.   Pantalone enters. He is waiting for the pedant's reply concerning the business between Isabella and the Captain. Gratiano speaks ill of the pedant, whom he considers a knave and an adulterer, but Pantalone defends him. Gratiano knocks at the door of his house.

FABRITIO.   Fabritio comes out. Gratiano asks him if he has seen the pedant. Fabritio says no.

CATALDO.   At that, Cataldo, the pedant, arrives; all greet him. He tells Pantalone that his wife is the most faithful and honorable woman living, and he would like to make permanent peace between them. Pantalone agrees. Cataldo then calls Isabella.

ISABELLA.   Isabella comes out, and at the pleading and persuasion of the pedant, is reconciled to her husband; finally the good pedant declares expansively that peace be with all and kisses everyone, Isabella last; then he leaves. Fabritio does the same and leaves; Gratiano does the same and leaves. Isabella embraces her husband, saying, "Peace be with us," and they go into the house, happy. Here the second act ends.

ACT THREE

ORATIO. PEDROLINO.   Oratio enters, enraged at the pedant and Isabella because of what Pedrolino has told him and swears that he cannot believe such wickedness.

FLAMINIA.   At that, Flaminia comes out, and they play a flirtatious scene. Pedrolino decides that the Captain must be beaten.

CAPT. SPAVENTO.   Just then, the Captain arrives, dressed as a porter. They torment him; then Flaminia plays up to him as if to take him into the house. Then she beats him. The Captain runs off; then Oratio and Flaminia hold hands as a pledge of marriage.

BURATTINO.   At that, Burattino arrives, saying he wishes no one harm; they soothe him, and he goes into the house with Flaminia. Oratio leaves to find his father. Pedrolino remains, still enraged at the pedant.

PANTALONE. ISABELLA.   At that moment, Pantalone enters with Isabella, speaking well of the pedant, who has made peace between them; Isabella, smiling, tells her husband all that has occurred between her and the pedant and that he gave her to understand he would take care of all her wanton desires. Pantalone is thunderstruck, having always taken him for a good man. He asks his wife to prove that he is a rascal. Isabella says she will prove it; she will tell him that the following night her husband will not sleep at home because he must go out of town on important business. Pantalone agrees to her plan; she goes in, and he remains.

DR. GRATIANO.   Then, Gratiano, who has heard all, greets Pantalone and tells him he dreamed that the pedant cuckolded him.

PEDROLINO.   At that, Pedrolino arrives. Pantalone calls him a gossip and a liar. Pedrolino says that what he told him is true, as he will soon find out. Gratiano insists he always took the pedant for a rascal.

CATALDO.   At that moment, Cataldo arrives, speaking fine words and flattering everyone. Pantalone tells him he must go away for three or four days, and that night he will be out of the city. The pedant assures Pantalone that under his watchfulness and loyalty all will be well, that he knows how to care for the family and to keep the peace of his lord; then, with much ceremony, he leaves. Pantalone remarks that he finds it hard to believe that the pedant is a rascal as they say. He leaves Pedrolino on guard, then goes off with Gratiano to the Rialto. Pedrolino hides.

CATALDO.   At that, Cataldo, the pedant, returns. Pedrolino moves farther off; the pedant joyfully says that the opportunity to enjoy Isabella at her convenience has come, and he has recognized in her the desire to find pleasure with him; he knocks on her door.

ISABELLA.   Isabella comes out, sees Cataldo all worked up, and asks him the cause of his sickness. The good pedant tells her that he is dying for love of her, and if she does not return his love, he will die, all the more since her husband has gone out of the city that night. Isabella, to trap him, tells him to go into her room, to undress, and to get up on the bed; that she, meantime, will visit Flaminia to make certain she will not disturb them, as she usually comes to visit when Isabella's husband is out of the city at night. The pedant happily goes in to undress. Pedrolino comes out of hiding; Isabella sends him to tell her husband and her son, and to bring their friends and relations; then she goes to lock the pedant in the room.

ARLECCHINO.   Arlecchino enters and says he cannot find his master. He speaks to Pedrolino, and they recognize each other as fellow countrymen; they recall their many relations and embrace.

ORATIO.   At that, Oratio enters and learns from Pedrolino that Arlecchino is his relative and the pedant is in the house locked in the bedroom.

FLAMINIA.   Flaminia comes out, and Oratio marries her then and there before the two servants.

BURATTINO.   At that moment, Burattino comes out. Pedrolino summons Arlecchino and Burattino, telling them that he needs their help to carry out justice.

PANTALONE. DR. GRATIANO.   Just then, Pantalone and Gratiano enter, hear of the nuptials between Oratio and Flaminia, and are content. Pedrolino tells Pantalone that the pedant is trapped.

ISABELLA.   At that, Isabella comes out, laughing about the pedant, who is locked in the bedroom and waiting; she wonders how they are going to punish him. After many suggestions, they decide to castrate him; the men all go into the room, while the women wait.

FABRITIO.   Fabritio arrives, and Flaminia tells him that he will soon see his master, his new master, nicely altered.

ORATIO. PANTALONE. DR. GRATIANO. PEDROLINO. ARLECCHINO. BURATTINO. CATALDO.   Soon they hear a cry and all the men come out, leading Cataldo, the pedant, in a nightshirt, tied with a strong rope; he screams and pleads with them. Pedrolino, Arlecchino, and Burattino go back into the house. The pedant falls to his knees, begging forgiveness and confessing his knavery, declaring Isabella to be a faithful and honorable young lady.

PEDROLINO. ARLECCHINO. BURATTINO.   At that moment, Pedrolino, Arlecchino, and Burattino enter dressed in butchers' aprons and hog gelders' aprons, holding long knives and a large copper tub.

CAPT. SPAVENTO.   Suddenly, the Captain bursts in on this spectacle. The pedant pleads with him. The Captain says he has no authority, but hearing that they intend to castrate him, he urges them to give him smaller punishment, such as a whipping, or else drive him out of the city. They agree, and with three sticks, they beat him thoroughly; then, shouting and cursing, they drive him away as a disgraceful example to all other pedant rogues and rascals like himself. Then they happily discuss marriage preparations for Flaminia, not forgetting to invite the Captain; and the comedy ends.

FOCUS QUESTIONS

1. Captain Spavento performs different functions to further the actions in the *soggetto*. Describe how each of these elicits our laughter.
2. How does Pedrolino display his loyalty to Pantalone and his family?
3. Develop a character sketch of Isabella.

OTHER ACTIVITIES

1. Select a character and a specific action from *The Pedant* and develop a monologue that illustrates this character. In a subsequent exercise, deliver the monologue while wearing a mask.
2. View Jean Renoir's picturesque film, *La Carrosse D'Or* (*The Golden Coach,* 1953). Evaluate the film's reenactment of the *commedia dell'arte* and discuss some of the film's characters in relation to the *commedia* roles they play.

BIBLIOGRAPHY

Cairns, Christopher, ed. *The Commedia dell'Arte: From the Renaissance to Dario Fo.* Lewiston, NY: The Edwin Mellen Press, 1989.

''Commedia dell'Arte Performance: Contexts and Contents.'' *Theatre Symposium* 1 (1993).

Davis, Ron. *The San Francisco Mime Troupe: The First Ten Years.* Palo Alto, CA: Ramparts Press, 1975.

Duchartre, Pierre L. *The Italian Comedy.* Translated by Randolph T. Weaver. New York: Dover Press, 1966.

Gordon, Mel, ed. *Lazzi: The Comic Routines of the Commedia dell'Arte*. New York: Performing Arts Journal Publications, 1983.

Herrick, Marvin. *Italian Comedy in the Renaissance*. Urbana: University of Illinois Press, 1960.

Lea, Kathleen M. *Italian Popular Comedy: A Study of the Commedia dell'Arte, 1560–1620*. 2 vols. Oxford: Clarendon Press, 1934.

Nicoll, Allardyce. *The World of Harlequin: A Critical Study of the Commedia dell'Arte*. Cambridge: Cambridge University Press, 1963.

Oreglia, Giacomo. *The Commedia dell'Arte*. Translated by Lovett F. Edwards. New York: Hill & Wang, 1968.

Salerno, Henry F., ed. and trans. *Scenarios of the Commedia dell'Arte: Flaminio Scala's ''Il Teatro delle Favole Rappresentative.''* New York: Limelight Editions, 1989.

Smith, Winifred. *The Commedia dell'Arte*. New York: Avon Press, 1980.

RECOMMENDED VIDEOTAPE

Aspects of Commedia dell'Arte. VHS. 14 min. A resource that focuses on the mask characters. Distributed by Insight Media, New York City.

DOCTOR FAUSTUS
CHRISTOPHER MARLOWE (1564–1593)

In Marlowe, for example, there is a voice prematurely silenced, but already having defined its particular timbre.

—GEORGE STEINER

Paula Laurence as Helen of Troy in *Doctor Faustus,* presented by the Federal Theatre in 1937, under the direction of Orson Welles. *Photo: The Billy Rose Theatre Collection, The New York Public Library for the Performing Arts; Astor, Lenox, and Tilden Foundations.*

ENGLISH RENAISSANCE DRAMA

As late as the sixteenth century, English audiences were still enthralled by mystery and morality plays. But the menu for popular entertainment incorporated several kinds of professional performance. On one hand, players fashioned interludes based on classical mythology for the court. On the other, they constructed popular entertainments from a mix of stories drawn from the Bible, history, folklore, and feats of chivalry for the public. These were rivaled by school and university revivals of the classical Greek drama now performed in Latin or English.

The comedies of Plautus and Terence, which had proven quite popular in these performances, inspired some wonderful imitations; two notable ones were Nicholas Udall's *Ralph Roister Doister* (c. 1534–1541) and Master S's *Gammer Gurton's Needle* (c. 1552–1563). In Udall's comedy, the eponymous character was a **miles gloriosus** portrayed in the image of Plautus' braggart and surrounded by the same stock characters from Roman comedy, including the parasite, the lovelorn suitor, and the cunning servant. What was unique about the play, often regarded as the first English comedy of the Renaissance, was its rejection of the didactic mode that marred similar works of this period. So Udall's comedy kept audiences entertained until a burgeoning second wave of theatrical energy introduced the university wits in an era ruled by Elizabeth I (1558–1603), a period popularly known as the Elizabethan Age.

By the middle of the century, the need to commercialize drama in England had become a reality. Professional actors were thriving in playhouses newly erected outside the city, while the direction of English Renaissance drama was in the hands of playwrights like John Lyly (c. 1554–1606), George Peele (c. 1557–1596), Thomas Kyd (1558–1594), and Christopher Marlowe. The appearance of Ben Jonson (1572–1637), who joined this illustrious circle of university wits toward the end of the sixteenth century and became England's poet laureate, suggested that a **playwrights' theatre** was finally at hand.

Credited with some important "firsts," such as creating strong protagonists who emerge as tragic heroes and whose internal struggles are demonstrated through episodic plotlines, Marlowe finally constructed the **chronicle play** when he demonstrated that a coherent story could be fashioned from "diverse historical events by rearranging, telescoping, and altering them to create a sense of causal relationships."[1] Marlowe also fashioned a verse format to support his characterizations and dramatic themes, earning him the reputation as the "first great English poet to make use of the drama as a medium of poetic expression."[2]

While his literary reputation was no doubt heightened by his publicized self-destructive life-style, the four plays he wrote were eloquent harbingers of a brilliant playwriting career that was tragically terminated in a fatal brawl when Marlowe was only twenty-nine. Written for and acted by Edward Alleyn, one of the leading players of the Lord Admiral's Company where Marlowe served as playwright, his plays utilized the technical resources of such theatres as the Rose and the Fortune. Constituting a legacy that would carry Marlowe's name into the twentieth century, these plays whetted the gutsy Elizabethan appetite and liberated the playwriting styles of his contemporaries.

MAJOR WORKS

Marlowe's four plays—*Tamburlaine* (1587–1588), *The Tragical History of Doctor Faustus* (c. 1588), *The Jew of Malta* (c. 1592), and *Edward II* (c. 1592)—demonstrate a certain interchangeability: all are named after their male protagonists and burst with vivid, highly theatricalized stage actions that are similarly patterned around them. Tamburlaine's thirst for power is compelling but, while it wins him many thrones, cannot diminish the violence and bloodshed produced by his barbaric passions. In fact, Marlowe's portrait of the Eastern conqueror proved so popular with audiences that the playwright succumbed to commercial acclaim and wrote a sequel in which his villain-hero was followed to an unrepentant end. Faustus' lust for power, like Tamburlaine's, transcends the limitations set for mortal man. Yet we are excited by these same supernatural forces that animate his actions so that we anticipate, somewhat vicariously, his fiery day of reckoning with a tinge of horror and remorse. In retrospect, Marlowe's instinctive grasp of audience taste and his willingness to exploit his art foreshadow the enterprising tactics of theatrical producers in our own time.

In contrast, the Jew of Malta, whose real name is Barabas, loses all his possessions to the Christians. Yet he holds our sympathy until his revenge suddenly exceeds all bounds and enmeshes him in a web of plots and counterplots. In a theatrical turn that thrills the spectator, Marlowe delivers Barabas into a boiling cauldron that the latter has prepared for his enemy. Marlowe's attempt to write a revenge tragedy was followed by *Edward II,* which proved a touching history play. Based on factual history, specifically Holinshed's *Chronicles,* this dramatization of a king who forfeits both his crown and his life purposely lacked the flamboyant style of the playwright's previous achievements and disappointed his fans who, by now, had different expectations. The blatant political and sexual themes of *Edward II* have garnered favorable critical reception in our own time, although its popularity remains eclipsed by *Doctor Faustus.*

THE ACTION

Bored with the limitations of philosophy, physics, law, and scriptures, Dr. Faustus turns to a study of metaphysics and magic and conjures Mephostophilis with one of his new spells. He draws up a binding contract with the devil and surrenders his soul in exchange for twenty-four years of life, during which time Mephostophilis will serve him and grant him unlimited power.

To ensure that Faustus can never repent, Mephostophilis incites him to ridicule and harass the Pope—an action that wins him papal damnation and excommunication. Years later, as he nears his death, Faustus feels repentant but Mephostophilis forces obedience to Lucifer upon him. Unable to ask for God's mercy, Faustus is dragged to hell, aware of the awful price that has been exacted from him.

STRUCTURE AND LANGUAGE

Doctor Faustus is inspired by the popular Renaissance tale of the historical Johannes Faust, whose story was retold in 1587 and translated from its original German into English in 1592, around the time Marlowe wrote his play. Like all of Marlowe's tragedies, it remains innovative for its unsweetened blank-verse format and its unification of unwieldy dramatic episodes built around a powerful personality whose downfall begins early in the play. Furthermore, its five-act structure, use of chorus, and melodramatic excesses pay homage to Seneca, whose rhetorical tragedies, translated into English in 1581, were already familiar, as Latin exercises to the university-trained Marlowe. Thus Marlowe is often credited for reviving and popularizing important Senecan elements in the drama.

The universality of Marlowe's masterpiece is rooted in its medieval past and its depicted conflict of good and evil, personified by the appearance of Good and Bad Angels who struggle from opposite ends of the stage for Faustus' immortal soul. No playgoer, then or now, can ignore the fateful partnership struck between Faustus (Marlowe's unconventional protagonist) and Mephostophilis: an archetypal rivalry that sharpens as Faustus' magical lease on life runs out. Perhaps Elizabethan audiences recognized a part of Faustus in themselves, but knew that pride must have its fall—a lesson witnessed repeatedly in the medieval cycles, moralities, and interludes, whose powerful repercussions had tempered Marlowe's tragedy. Creating his own emblematic portrait of the Seven Deadly Sins, Marlowe successfully restored poetry to the drama and populated the Elizabethan stage with formidable scenic images, not the least of which introduced Helen of Troy. Her conjured presence epitomized classical antiquity and inspired sensual, immortal longings in Marlowe's protagonist.

His career as playwright was deeply influenced by the secularization of drama that Elizabeth I demanded. God may have been the undeniable center of an earlier medieval universe and may have remained prominently situated in the Elizabethan world picture, but papal authority and Catholic ritual had been renounced by the throne of England. This suited the atheistic Marlowe and gave him ample cause to voice popular anti-clerical sentiment and to dramatize how science and magic inflate human aspiration.

These concerns are demonstrated throughout. In the prologue to act 3, for example, the Chorus tells us that Faustus arrives ''at Rome/ To see the Pope and manner of his court/ And take some part of holy Peter's feast,/ The which this day is highly solemnized.'' When a sumptuous meal is set before his Holiness and Faustus, the food and drink magically disappear. This slapstick encounter concludes with Faustus' striking the Pope, at which point the audience no doubt laughed along with Mephostophilis and the protagonist. Marlowe also made use of the controversy surrounding the scientific progress of the Renaissance, particularly the cosmic discoveries of Galileo and Kepler. Those in England who were exploring these new astronomical findings were considered dangerous practitioners of black magic and inspired Marlowe's adaptation of the Johannes Faust legend.

Marlowe's dramatization of Faustus' rise and fall is dictated by the twenty-four-year pact he signs in blood with the devil. But unlike a medieval allegorical protagonist's journey toward self-discovery and repentance that leads him to God's kingdom, Faustus' quest ends in darkness: eternal life in God's presence is replaced with eternal damnation in Hell. In act 1, Faustus' study is the setting of his initial inquiry, in which he soliloquizes his darkest wish and extolls the power of black magic:

> O, what a world of profit and delight,
> Of power, of honor, and omnipotence
> Is promised to the studious artisan!
> All things that move between the quiet poles
> Shall be at my command: emperors and kings
> Are but obeyed in their several provinces
> But his dominion that exceeds in this
> Stretcheth as far as doth the mind of man:
> A sound magician is a demi-god!

His wish comes true, of course, as depicted ambitiously and imaginatively in the play's five-act circular structure, whose final scenes bring us back to Faustus' study.

In act 5, just moments before the clock strikes eleven, Mephostophilis appears one last time to settle a bargain made long ago. His closing words offer no allowance to his tear-filled victim:

> What, weep'st thou! 'Tis too late, despair, farewell!
> Fools that will laugh on earth, most weep in hell.

But Faustus confronts his last hour on earth, still believing there is time to repent. In a final soliloquy that contains one of the most rapturous poetic images Marlowe ever conceived, Faustus arouses our pity by imagining that salvation is at hand and that the God he rejected will not abandon him:

> O, I'll leap up to my God! Who pulls me down?
> See, see where Christ's blood streams in the firmament!
> One drop of blood will save me.

In our mind's eye, we might imagine a reddish glow suggestive of Christ's blood and highlighted by Faustus' gaze toward heaven. But in that same instant, as he feels the dreaded drift toward death, the reddish hue explodes into fiery flames, the foreshadowing of an eternity spent in Hell. We are not surprised that his cry should go unanswered—after all, a pact is a pact—although his recognition of a fatal decision made two dozen years earlier ennobles his character, renders it pitiable, and even for a few brief moments, betrays a tragic stature. Marlowe's stage directions indicate that the clock strikes twelve and thunder is heard as devils enter, then exit, with Faustus.

The twenty sharply paced scenes in *Doctor Faustus* demonstrate Marlowe's consummate mastery at transforming Renaissance legend into palpable and memorable poetic imagery, and they reflect Elizabethan attitudes toward religion, science, and the cosmos. Except for Mephostophilis, the more than three dozen characters who populate the play—including a Senecan-influenced Chorus most likely portrayed by one actor—are satellites who travel in Faustus' orbit and serve his earthly commands. These characters are mostly one-dimensional portraits, in contrast with the rounder ones of Faustus and Mephostophilis who command the stage throughout.

Depending on which aspect of their relationship we focus our attention, Mephostophilis—in his dual capacity as Faustus' overseer and partner in greatness—enhances the psychological bond of their evolving, now eternal collaboration. Within a modern context, our view of Mephostophilis as Faustus' *alter ego* empowers both characters' on-stage *personae*. That Faustus succumbs to his malignant opponent finally confirms his misplaced and self-destructive value system, as it would befit any human being to choose between good and evil. While Marlowe's audacious individualism and bold theatrical imagination set the stage for Shakespeare's timely entrance, his *Doctor Faustus* has continued to rival the literary masterpieces of every age since.

The Elizabethan Playhouse

Compared with the awesome physical dimensions of both the classical and medieval stages, the innovative structure of the Elizabethan playhouse offered challenging alternatives to artists and audiences alike. These public theatres were round, square, or polygonal in shape, and actors performed on a large elevated rectangular platform that extended from an inside wall of the playhouse and was covered by a roof extension. The wall provided a natural backdrop or setting to the action of the play, against which two or three balcony-like levels offered additional acting areas. More than fifteen hundred spectators sat on wooden benches that lined the three roofed galleries surrounding the three sides of the platform, with sightlines providing an optimum view of the stage and establishing the proper **aesthetic distance**—that is, a comfortable physical and psychological space between actor and audience—which would leave its mark on the modern theatre. For just a few pence, additional spectators or ''groundlings'' could stand in the open yard between the stage and the galleries to view the performance.

The following diary entry enhances our appreciation of the typical playgoer's experience at playhouses such as the Rose, the Swan, and the Globe:

> The places are so built, that they play on a raised platform, and every one can well see it all. There are, however, separate galleries and there one stands more comfortably and moreover can sit, but one pays more for it. Thus anyone who remains on the level standing pays only one English penny: but if he wants to

An Elizabethan public playhouse.

sit, he is let in at a further door, and there he gives another penny. If he desires to sit on a cushion in the most comfortable place of all, where he not only sees everything well, but can also be seen, then he gives yet another English penny at another door. And in the pauses of the comedy food and drink are carried round amongst the people, and one can thus refresh himself at his own cost.[3]

While the diarist makes no direct reference to the activity on stage, it is certain that the stage conventions in practice would have placed enormous demands on his imagination. Much of this stemmed from the more intimate physical staging of the play, which contrasted sharply with the grand scale of its classical and medieval counterparts. A minimal use of stage sets and props, compounded by the fact that all the roles were still played by men—unmasked this time—called for an even greater emphasis on stage-character development. The innovative multiplicity of scenes, the combination of tragic and comic plots, and the use of analogous action in which two separate stories were played against each other expanded the limits of drama and raised audience expectations to even greater heights. Furthermore, all of this happened without pause for a change of scenery or the benefit of a stage curtain; and the blazing light of day could offer no illusion to scenes set at night. But Marlowe and his contemporaries reveled in the exciting possibilities such stage conventions offered them and fashioned a Renaissance drama with total audience support.

DOCTOR FAUSTUS-IN-PERFORMANCE

The first known performance of *Doctor Faustus* was given in 1594 by the Lord Admiral's Company. The play was first published in 1604 and enjoyed great success, especially in Germany, where it was performed in 1608 and remained in repertory throughout the continent during the next two hundred years. When the Puritans closed the English theatres in 1642, Marlowe's stage works were instantly forgotten by his countrymen. With the restoration of the Stuarts in 1660, plays in the French style replaced Elizabethan drama in popularity.

When the Romantic movement rediscovered the Elizabethans during the late eighteenth century, Marlowe's *Doctor Faustus,* long popular in Europe, was suddenly replaced with *Faust* by German poet-playwright Johann Wolfgang von Goethe (1749–1832). He completed his two-part epic, the culmination of his artistic energies, shortly before his death. Devising a happy ending, Goethe embellished the protagonist's legendary escapades quite differently from his Elizabethan predecessor, whose tragedy had initially inspired him. Thus the German *Faust* overshadowed *Doctor Faustus*. During the nineteenth century, the story of Marlowe's disreputable life still preceded his plays, so that Victorian theatre managers were content to ignore him. Besides, the plays of Shakespeare were sufficient to represent the Elizabethan drama.

On the evening of March 18, 1910, Ben Greet produced Marlowe's tragedy at the Garden Theatre in New York City in what appeared to be its first presentation in America. It was played almost in its entirety, except for the scene in which Faustus slapped the Pope—perhaps thought too offensive for New York Catholics who might be sitting in the audience. Greet paid homage to the Elizabethan stage by constructing a canopy under which all the scenes set in Faustus' study were played. But more importantly, Greet had opened a door to performing Marlowe in the twentieth century.

Today *Doctor Faustus* is one of the most frequently performed works of the non-Shakespearean Elizabethan repertoire. The story has also inspired numerous other dramatic masterpieces, ranging from opera to the avant-garde. In 1938, Gertrude Stein wove threads from Marlowe and Goethe to create her own eccentric version in *Doctor Faustus Lights the Lights*.

The achievement of Marlowe's cosmic vision, densely populated with devils and other unearthly apparitions and ruled by the forces of black magic, has challenged some important contemporary theatre practitioners. Adhering to a mostly uncluttered *mise-en-scène,* the play conjures forth disembodied heads that fly through the air; it boasts the Seven Deadly Sins (inspired, in some productions, by the paintings of Hieronymous Bosch); it fills the stage with puffs of smoke and thunder rolls and resorts to an all-purpose trap door at center stage.

These demands were nobly met when Orson Welles (1915–1985) assumed the three-fold responsibility of co-producing (with John Houseman), directing, and heading the cast of Marlowe's play for Project #891 of the WPA's Federal Theatre. The engagement opened on January 8, 1937, at the Maxine Elliott Theatre in New York City. Supported by a favorable critical reception, *Doctor Faustus* played to packed houses for an extended run of 128 performances.

Like Marlowe, whose reputation was firmly established in his twenties, Welles was twenty-one years old at the time. But his intense identification with the play was fortified by his own personal interest in magic, which he practiced as an "aside" to his career as actor/director, and would immerse him totally in the Faustian experience. The production was taking him back more than three centuries "to the heart of *[Doctor Faustus]* and to its vivid recreation on a contemporary American stage."[4]

The precocity that would propel Welles' controversial career some years later was already at work in this production, which he smartly reduced to an intermissionless playing time of less than two hours. The streamlining lost none of Marlowe's intended impact and kept intact his original language and many of his characters. But several inspired ingredients adorned the performance, strengthening its appeal to an audience whose expectations for serious drama were fashioned by the proliferation of Hollywood horror movies of the 1930s.

To begin with, a "tapering apron was built to [Welles'] specifications: it struck prow-like into the auditorium and necessitated the removal of two dozen seats from the center of the orchestra floor."[5] This early example of a "thrust stage," a common phenomenon in contemporary theatre design, improved on the conventional proscenium effect by bringing the actors face-to-face with their audience. The atmosphere was further enhanced by the dissonant musical and sound score created by Paul Bowles and played by an unseen orchestra. Drawing on his radio experiences, Welles knew how carefully monitored sounds could tap the imagination of the spectator and cast the necessary spell.

Perhaps the most imaginative contribution to the production was engineered by Abe Feder, whose lighting designs transformed the cavernous stage of the Maxine Elliott Theatre into magical spaces Marlowe never dreamed of. Feder's use of "eighty-three spot-lights, including over two dozen 1,000-watt spots, plus thirty-one 1,000-watt beam projectors"[6] were operated from three separate switching stations to provide three main areas of light on stage. This heightened the illusion of magical entrances and exits and disguised several trap doors that were strategically coordinated against a complex network of black curtains.

Critics found so much to praise. There were the columnar shafts and cathedral depth of the stage, created by black drapes and patterned light effects. They noted the eloquent performances of Welles in the lead and Jack Carter, who wore a bald red pate as Mephostophilis. Among the smoothly directed efforts of forty-five cast members, critics pointed out the strong comic antics of several supporting actors, as well as the effective voices heard from off-stage. James Cochrane's masks and the parade of the Seven Deadly Sins, portrayed by Bil Baird's puppets and staged in the theatre's upper left box, provided an eerie and spectacular effect. Stark Young wrote:

> Only a variety of emotional pressures on the part of the actor who plays the leading role can register for the audience the stages of Faustus' struggle and his progression toward the climax of his deep damnation. Marlowe's poetry is spoken far above the average by Mr. Orson Welles, who has a beautiful even voice, perfectly placed, and has, too, a remarkable sense of timing. He possesses also both naturally and by study a notable gift for projection, no mean asset for Marlowe's lines.[7]

Brooks Atkinson of *The New York Times* called the production "brilliantly original" and urged his readers "to see how ably Orson Welles and John Houseman have cleared away all the imposing impedimenta that make most classics forbidding and how skillfully they have left 'Dr. Faustus,' grim and terrible, on the stage. By being sensible as well as artists, Mr. Welles and Mr. Houseman have gone a long way toward revolutionizing the staging of Elizabethan plays."[8]

REFLECTIONS ON DOCTOR FAUSTUS

Paula Laurence portrayed Helen of Troy in Orson Welles' production of Doctor Faustus.

In my opinion, *Doctor Faustus* was the most brilliantly executed and realized of all of Orson Welles' theatre productions: in terms of his performance, the style and staging, the sound scheme, the scenic concept, costumes and props, the magic tricks, and a wonderful score by Paul Bowles. At heart, Orson was a magician, and *Faustus* was designed as a magic show. The stage was hung in black velvet and there were black velvet cylinders with spots in them out of which characters noiselessly emerged or disappeared into a limbo. There was a famous scene in Rome—the Pope's banquet—where food flew up into the air and disappeared; flash boxes exploded, and the stage was riddled with trap doors out of which sheets of flame burst, or clouds of mist like those that later heralded my entrance as Helen of Troy. Orson truly believed in the devil and in the forces of evil, so this legend resonated in his soul. Jack Carter, as Mephostophilis—bald-headed, all in black—was the most beautiful of fallen angels. Both actors were very tall, and their scenes together had an absolutely mesmerizing tenderness.

I researched the costumes for the production with Orson's wife. We went to the library with pads of tracing paper and traced cloaks, headdresses, boots, buckles, hairstyles, jewelry, halberds and weapons of all sorts, and anything else we thought might be of interest for the time period of Marlowe's play. The stage crew would leave the Maxine Elliott Theatre around two in the morning, when the official workday was over, after which some of us returned secretly and worked till eight A.M. to rehearse the intricate lighting. There were always a few dedicated groupies—me included—and various wives and loved ones—usually Jack Carter would stay. Orson, John Houseman, and Feder would sit out front to discuss the lighting effects they wanted, while we stood in for all the other actors who had left for the day. There was more work to do than the regular rehearsal schedule allowed. That's how they lit the show.

But John Houseman's contribution must never be underestimated as far as evaluating Orson's work during the years they worked together. He was brilliant on a script, for one thing, but more importantly, he saw to it that Orson's extraordinary demands were met. Orson was left free to create and to pursue his vision. Orson, like so many other gifted people, became pretty paranoid when he got down to the wire. But John had some magical way of diffusing a lot of that, which was very valuable for this production. For example, Orson always suffered a bodily injury the night before an opening. Usually it was his ankle. On the opening night of *King Lear,* which we did at the City Center, he played that part in a wheelchair! Somehow or other, John managed to minimize any opening night disaster with *Faustus.*

John envisioned Helen of Troy, which I played, in very pale makeup. But it had to be a makeup that somehow reflected light. We tried everything that was available, but nothing worked. There was a wonderful puppeteer in the production who assisted Bil Baird. She designed a life-mask of me and taught me how to make the *reverso* of it. John was so delighted with it that I made one for him. My mask had a strange green tinge to it, as I remember, and we painted a gloss on it so it was quite stunning when it was lit.

In actual performance, I arose from the steps of one of the myriad trapdoors, surrounded by buckets of dry ice that contributed to the effect of clouds of smoke. I slowly appeared in the midst of it. I had some pantomimed actions that I performed as I drifted slowly across the stage. Then Orson came upstage to give me his hand, while reciting his famous lines about Helen, until I was no longer visible. Stark Young reviewed me and the mask. It was the first notice I'd ever received that was written in such high-flown literary imagery: "At the back of the stage is Helen, not stupidly classic but looking like Diane de Poitiers on a tapestry in a silver moonlight, the long open bodice, the high breasts, the coif, the stiff folds." I was so thrilled! Audience responses to *Faustus* were absolutely explosive. We even had audience groupies who came several times a week because they couldn't get enough of it.

We were all very close to each other and also to our work during the production. It was an extraordinary experience, given my tender years and lack of much experience at that point to be suddenly in this fantastic, magical world. Of course, we all had an emotional stake in it. It was an important moment—historically and personally. But Orson knew what he wanted, and it was our pleasure to see that he got it.

Notes

1. *Oscar Brockett,* HISTORY OF THE THEATRE, *6th ed. (Boston: Allyn & Bacon, 1991),* *159.*
2. *T. M. Parrott and R. H. Ball,* SHORT VIEW OF ELIZABETHAN DRAMA *(New York:* *Charles Scribner's Sons, 1958), 91.*
3. *A.M. Nagler,* A SOURCE BOOK IN THEATRICAL HISTORY *(New York: Dover* *Publications, 1952), 117–18.*
4. *John Houseman,* RUN THROUGH *(New York: Curtis Books, 1972), 235.*
5. *Ibid., 230.*
6. *Frank Brady,* CITIZEN WELLES *(New York: Charles Scribner's Sons, 1989), 101.*
7. *Houseman,* RUN THROUGH, *240–41.*
8. *Brooks Atkinson,* THE NEW YORK TIMES, *9 Jan. 1937.*

DOCTOR FAUSTUS
CHRISTOPHER MARLOWE

CHARACTERS

Speaking Characters

Chorus

Doctor Faustus

Wagner, *his Student and Servant*

Good Angel

Bad Angel

Valdes ⎫
Cornelius ⎭ Magicians

Three Scholars

Lucifer, *Prince of Devils*

Mephostophilis, *a Devil*

Robin, *a Clown*

Belzebub, *a Devil*

Dick, *a Clown*

Pope Adrian

Raymond, King of Hungary

Pride ⎫
Covetousness |
Envy | the
Wrath | Seven
Gluttony | Deadly
Sloth | Sins
Lechery ⎭

Bruno, *Rival Pope appointed by the Emperor*

Two Cardinals

Archbishop of Rheims

Friars

Vintner

Martino ⎫ Gentlemen at the
Frederick | Emperor's
Benvolio ⎭ Court

The German Emperor, Charles the Fifth

Duke of Saxony

Two Soldiers

Horse-Courser, *a Clown*

Carter, *a Clown*

Hostess of a Tavern

Duke of Vanholt

Duchess of Vanholt

Servant

Old Man

Mute Characters

Darius of Persia, Alexander the Great, Alexander's Paramour, Helen of Troy, Devils, Piper, Cardinals, Monks, Friars, Attendants, Soldiers, Servants, Two Cupids

---

PROLOGUE

Enter CHORUS.[1]

Not marching in the fields of Trasimene[2]
Where Mars did mate[3] the warlike Carthagens,
Nor sporting in the dalliance of love
In courts of kings where state[4] is overturned,
Nor in the pomp of proud audacious deeds   5
Intends our muse[5] to vaunt[6] his heavenly verse.
Only this, gentles—We must now perform
The form of Faustus' fortunes, good or bad:
And now to patient judgments we appeal
And speak for Faustus in his infancy.   10
Now is he born of parents base of stock
In Germany within a town called Rhode;[7]
At riper years to Wittenberg he went
Whereas[8] his kinsmen chiefly brought him up.
So much he profits in divinity   15
That shortly he was graced[9] with doctor's name,

[1]**Chorus** a single actor (here, perhaps, Wagner, Faustus' servant-student) [2]**Trasimene** Lake Trasimene, site of one of Hannibal's victories over the Romans, 217 B.C. (Marlowe is not known to have written on this subject, though lines 3–4 may refer to his *Edward II,* and line 5 to his *Tamburlaine*) [3]**Mars did mate** i.e., the Roman army encountered [4]**state** government

[5]**muse** poet [6]**vaunt** proudly display [7]**Rhode** Roda [8]**Whereas** where [9]**graced** (alluding to the official "grace" permitting the student to take his degree)

Excelling all, and sweetly can dispute
In th' heavenly matters of theology;
Till swoll'n with cunning, of a self-conceit,[10]
His waxen wings[11] did mount above his reach   20
And melting, heavens conspired his overthrow!
For falling to a devilish exercise
And glutted now with learning's golden gifts
He surfeits upon cursèd necromancy:[12]
Nothing so sweet as magic is to him   25
Which he prefers before his chiefest bliss[13]—
And this the man that in his study sits. (*Exit.*)

ACT ONE

SCENE ONE

FAUSTUS *in his study.*[1]

FAUSTUS.

Settle thy studies Faustus, and begin
To sound the depth of that thou wilt profess.[2]
Having commenced,[3] be a divine in show—
Yet level[4] at the end of every art
And live and die in Aristotle's works.   5
Sweet *Analytics*,[5] 'tis thou hast ravished me.
Bene disserere est finis logices.[6]
Is to dispute well logic's chiefest end?
Affords this art no greater miracle?
Then read no more, thou has attained that end.   10
A greater subject fitteth Faustus' wit:[7]
Bid *on kai me on*[8] farewell, and Galen[9] come:
Be a physician Faustus, heap up gold,
And be eternized for some wondrous cure.
Summum bonum medicinae sanitas,[10]   15
The end of physic[11] is our body's health.
Why Faustus hast thou not attained that end?
Are not thy bills[12] hung up as monuments
Whereby whole cities have escaped the plague

And thousand desperate maladies been cured?   20
Yet art thou still but Faustus and a man.
Could'st thou make men to live eternally
Or being dead raise them to life again,
Then this profession were to be esteemed.
Physic farewell! Where is Justinian?[13]   25
*Si una eademque res legatur duobus, alter rem, alter
    valorem rei, et cetera.*[14]
A petty case of paltry legacies.
Exhereditare filium non potest pater, nisi[15]—
Such is the subject of the *Institute*   30
And universal body of the law!
This study fits a mercenary drudge
Who aims at nothing but external trash,
Too servile and illiberal for me.
When all is done, divinity is best.   35
Jerome's Bible,[16] Faustus, view it well.
Stipendium peccati mors est.[17] Ha! *Stipendium et
    cetera.* The reward of sin is death? That's hard:
    *Si peccasse negamus, fallimur, et nulla est in
    nobis veritas.*[18] If we say that we have no sin, we   40
    deceive ourselves, and there is no truth in us.
    Why, then belike, we must sin, and so conse-
    quently die.
Ay, we must die an everlasting death.
What doctrine call you this? *Che serà, serà:*[19]   45
What will be, shall be! Divinity, adieu!
These metaphysics[20] of magicians
And negromantic[21] books are heavenly;
Lines, circles, letters, characters—
Ay, these are those that Faustus most desires.   50
O, what a world of profit and delight,
Of power, of honor, and omnipotence
Is promised to the studious artisan![22]
All things that move between the quiet[23] poles
Shall be at my command: emperors and kings   55

---

[10]**cunning, of a self-conceit** ingenuity, born of arrogance
[11]**waxen wings** (alluding to Icarus, who flew by means of wings
made of feathers waxed to a framework; despite the warning of
his father, Icarus soared too near the sun, the wax melted, and he
plunged to his death) [12]**necromancy** (literally divination by
means of the spirits of the dead, but here probably equivalent to
black magic) [13]**prefers before his chiefest bliss** sets above his
hope of salvation [1]**Faustus in his study** (probably at his last line
the Chorus drew back a curtain at the rear of the stage, disclosing
Faustus) [2]**profess** study and teach [3]**commenced** taken a degree
[4]**level** aim [5]**Analytics** title of two treatises by Aristotle on logic
[6]**Bene . . . logices** the end (i.e., purpose) of logic is to argue well
(Latin) [7]**wit** intelligence [8]**on kai me on** being and not being
(Greek) [9]**Galen** Greek authority on medicine, 2nd century A.D.
[10]**Summum . . . sanitas** health is the greatest good of medicine
(Latin, translated from Aristotle's *Nichomachean Ethics*)
[11]**physic** medicine [12]**bills** prescriptions

[13]**Justinian** Roman emperor and authority on law (483–565) who
ordered the compilation of the *Institutes* (see line 30) [14]**Si . . . et
cetera** if one thing is willed to two persons, one of them shall
have the thing itself, the other the value of the thing, and so forth
(Latin) [15]**Exhereditare . . . nisi** a father cannot disinherit his
son unless (Latin) [16]**Jerome's Bible** the Latin translation made
by St. Jerome (c. 340–420) [17]**Stipendium . . . est** the wages of
sin is death (Romans 6:23; if Faustus had gone on to read the rest
of the verse, he would have found that "the gift of God is eternal
life through Jesus Christ our Lord") [18]**Si . . . veritas** from
I John 1:8, translated in the next two lines; Faustus neglects the
following verse: "If we confess our sins, He is faithful and just to
forgive us our sins, and to cleanse us from all unrighteousness"
[19]**Che serà, serà** (Italian, translated in the first half of the next
line) [20]**metaphysics** subjects lying beyond (or studied after)
physics [21]**negromantic** black magical (though probably here also
associated with "necromantic," i.e., concerned with raising the
spirits of the dead) [22]**artisan** i.e., expert [23]**quiet** motionless

Are but obeyed in their several provinces
But his dominion that exceeds in this[24]
Stretcheth as far as doth the mind of man:
A sound magician is a demi-god!
Here tire my brains to get[25] a deity!   60

Enter WAGNER.

Wagner, commend me to my dearest friends,
The German Valdes and Cornelius.
Request them earnestly to visit me.
WAGNER.   I will, sir. (*Exit.*)
FAUSTUS.
Their conference[26] will be a greater help to me   65
Than all my labors, plod I ne'er so fast.

Enter the (GOOD) ANGEL *and* (*the* EVIL) SPIRIT.[27]

GOOD ANGEL.
O Faustus, lay that damnèd book aside
And gaze not on it lest it tempt thy soul
And heap God's heavy wrath upon thy head!
Read, read the Scriptures—that[28] is blasphemy!   70
BAD ANGEL.
Go forward Faustus, in that famous art
Wherein all nature's treasure is contained.
Be thou on earth as Jove is in the sky,
Lord and commander of these elements! (*Exeunt*
ANGELS.)
FAUSTUS.
How am I glutted with conceit of this![29]   75
Shall I make spirits fetch me what I please?
Resolve me of[30] all ambiguities?
Perform what desperate enterprise I will?
I'll have them fly to India[31] for gold,
Ransack the ocean for orient[32] pearl,   80
And search all corners of the new-found world
For pleasant fruits and princely delicates;
I'll have them read me strange philosophy
And tell the secrets of all foreign kings;
I'll have them wall all Germany with brass   85
And make swift Rhine circle fair Wittenberg;
I'll have them fill the public schools[33] with silk
Wherewith the students shall be bravely[34] clad.
I'll levy soldiers with the coin they bring
And chase the Prince of Parma[35] from our land   90
And reign sole king of all the provinces!

Yea, stranger engines for the brunt[36] of war
Than was the fiery keel[37] at Antwerp bridge
I'll make my servile spirits to invent.

Enter VALDES *and* CORNELIUS.

Come German Valdes and Cornelius   95
And make me blest with your sage conference.
Valdes, sweet Valdes, and Cornelius,
Know that your words have won me at the last
To practice magic and concealèd arts.
Philosophy is odious and obscure,   100
Both law and physic are for petty wits,
Divinity is basest of the three—
Unpleasant, harsh, contemptible, and vile.
'Tis magic, magic, that hath ravished me!
Then, gentle friends, aid me in this attempt   105
And I, that have with subtle syllogisms
Graveled[38] the pastors of the German church
And made the flow'ring pride of Wittenberg
Swarm to my problems[39] as th' infernal spirits
On sweet Musaeus[40] when he came to hell,   110
Will be as cunning as Agrippa[41] was,
Whose shadows made all Europe honor him.
VALDES.
Faustus, these books, thy wit, and our experience
Shall make all nations to canonize us.
As Indian Moors[42] obey their Spanish lords,   115
So shall the spirits of every element
Be always serviceable to us three:
Like lions shall they guard us when we please,
Like Almain rutters[43] with their horsemen's staves
Or Lapland giants trotting by our sides;   120
Sometimes like women or unwedded maids
Shadowing[44] more beauty in their airy brows
Than has the white breasts of the queen of love;
From Venice shall they drag huge argosies
And from America the golden fleece   125
That yearly stuffs old Philip's[45] treasury,
If learnèd Faustus will be resolute.
FAUSTUS.
Valdes, as resolute am I in this
As thou to live; therefore object it not.

---

[24]**this** i.e., magic   [25]**get** beget   [26]**conference** conversation
[27]**Spirit** Bad Angel, devil (the two angels probably enter the stage
from separate doors)   [28]**that** i.e., the book of magic   [29]**conceit of
this** i.e., the conception of being a magician   [30]**Resolve me of**
explain to me   [31]**India** either the West Indies (America) or the
East Indies   [32]**orient** lustrous and precious   [33]**public schools**
universities   [34]**bravely** splendidly   [35]**Prince of Parma** Spanish
governor-general of the Low Countries during 1579–92

[36]**brunt** assault   [37]**fiery keel** burning ship sent by the
Netherlanders in 1585 against a bridge erected by Parma to
blockade Antwerp (Antwerp here is an adjective, not genetive)
[38]**Graveled** confounded   [39]**problems** questions proposed for
disputation   [40]**Musaeus** legendary Greek poet   [41]**Agrippa**
Cornelius Agrippa of Nettesheim (1486–1535), German author of
De occulta philosophia, a survey of Renaissance magic; Agrippa
was believed to have raised spirits (''shadows'') from the dead
[42]**Indian Moors** American Indians   [43]**Almain rutters** German
cavalrymen   [44]**Shadowing** sheltering   [45]**Philip** King Philip II of
Spain (1527–98)

CORNELIUS.

    The miracles that magic will perform   **130**
    Will make thee vow to study nothing else.
    He that is grounded in astrology,
    Enriched with tongues, well seen[46] in minerals,
    Hath all the principles magic doth require.
    Then doubt not Faustus but to be renowned   **135**
    And more frequented for this mystery[47]
    Than heretofore the Delphian oracle.[48]
    The spirits tell me they can dry the sea
    And fetch the treasure of all foreign wracks,
    Yea, all the wealth that our forefathers hid   **140**
    Within the massy[49] entrails of the earth.
    Then tell me Faustus, what shall we three want?[50]

FAUSTUS.

    Nothing, Cornelius. O, this cheers my soul!
    Come, show me some demonstrations magical
    That I may conjure[51] in some bushy grove   **145**
    And have these joys in full possession.

VALDES.

    Then haste thee to some solitary grove,
    And bear wise Bacon's[52] and Albanus'[53] works,
    The Hebrew Psalter, and New Testament;
    And whatsoever else is requisite   **150**
    We will inform thee ere our conference cease.

CORNELIUS.

    Valdes, first let him know the words of art,
    And then, all other ceremonies learned,
    Faustus may try his cunning by himself.

VALDES.

    First I'll instruct thee in the rudiments,   **155**
    And then wilt thou be perfecter than I.

FAUSTUS.

    Then come and dine with me, and after meat
    We'll canvass every quiddity[54] thereof,
    For ere I sleep I'll try what I can do:
    This night I'll conjure though I die therefor!   **160**
    (*Exeunt omnes.*[55])

SCENE TWO

Enter two SCHOLARS.

1 SCHOLAR.   I wonder what's become of Faustus that was
wont to make our schools ring with *sic probo.*[1]

Enter WAGNER.

2 SCHOLAR.   That shall we presently[2] know. Here comes
his boy.[3]

1 SCHOLAR.   How now sirrah,[4] where's thy master?   **5**

WAGNER.   God in heaven knows.

1 SCHOLAR.   Why, dost not thou know then?

WAGNER.   Yes, I know, but that follows not.

1 SCHOLAR.   Go to[5] sirrah, leave your jesting and tell us
where he is.   **10**

WAGNER.   That follows not by force of argument, which
you, being licentiates,[6] should stand upon;[7] therefore acknowledge your error and be attentive.

2 SCHOLAR.   Then you will not tell us?

WAGNER.   You are deceived, for I will tell you. Yet   **15**
if you were not dunces,[8] you would never ask me such a
question. For is he not *corpus naturale?* And is not that
mobile?[9] Then wherefore should you ask me such a question? But that I am by nature phlegmatic,[10] slow to wrath,
and prone to lechery—to love, I would say—it   **20**
were not for you to come within forty foot of the place of
execution[11]—although I do not doubt but to see you both
hanged the next sessions.[12] Thus, having triumphed over
you, I will set my countenance like a precisian[13] and begin
to speak thus: Truly, my dear brethren, my master   **25**
is within at dinner, with Valdes and Cornelius, as this
wine, if it could speak, would inform your worships; and
so, the Lord bless you, preserve you, and keep you, my
dear brethren. (*Exit.*)

1 SCHOLAR.

    O Faustus, then I fear that which I have long
       suspected,   **30**
    That thou art fall'n into that damnèd art
    For which they two are infamous through the world.

2 SCHOLAR.

    Were he a stranger, not allied to me,
    The danger of his soul would make me mourn.
    But come, let us go and inform the rector.[14]   **35**
    It may be his grave counsel may reclaim him.

1 SCHOLAR.   I fear me nothing will reclaim him now.

2 SCHOLAR.   Yet let us see what we can do. (*Exeunt.*)

---

[46]**well seen** skilled   [47]**frequented for this mystery** resorted to for
this art   [48]**Delphian oracle** oracle of Apollo at Delphi   [49]**massy**
massive   [50]**want** lack   [51]**conjure** raise spirits   [52]**Bacon** Roger
Bacon, medieval friar and scientist   [53]**Albanus** perhaps Pietro
d'Abano, medieval writer on medicine and philosophy   [54]**canvass
every quiddity** discuss every essential detail   [55]**omnes** all (Latin)
[1]**sic probo** thus I prove it (Latin)

[2]**presently** at once   [3]**boy** servant (an impoverished student)
[4]**sirrah** (term of address used to an inferior)   [5]**Go to** (exclamation
of impatience)   [6]**licentiates** possessors of a degree preceding
the master's degree   [7]**stand upon** make much of   [8]**dunces**
(1) fools (2) hairsplitters   [9]**corpus naturale . . . mobile** natural
matter . . . movable (Latin, scholastic definition of the subject-
matter of physics)   [10]**phlegmatic** sluggish   [11]**the place of
execution** the place of action, i.e., the dining room (with quibble
on gallows)   [12]**sessions** sittings of a court   [13]**precisian** Puritan
(Wagner goes on to parody the style of the Puritans)   [14]**rector**
head of the university

SCENE THREE

Thunder. Enter LUCIFER *and four* DEVILS.[1] FAUSTUS *to them with this speech.*

FAUSTUS.

Now that the gloomy shadow of the night,
Longing to view Orion's[2] drizzling look,
Leaps from th' antarctic world unto the sky
And dims the welkin[3] with her pitchy breath,
Faustus, begin thine incantations   **5**
And try if devils will obey thy hest,
Seeing thou hast prayed and sacrificed to them.
Within this circle[4] is Jehovah's name
Forward and backward anagrammatized,
Th' abbreviated names of holy saints,   **10**
Figures of every adjunct to[5] the heavens,
And characters of signs and erring stars,[6]
By which the spirits are enforced to rise:
Then fear not, Faustus, to be resolute
And try the utmost magic can perform. *Thunder.* **15**
*Sint mihi dei Acherontis propitii! Valeat numen
triplex Iehovae! Ignei, aerii, aquatici, spiritus, sal-
vete! Orientis princeps, Belzebub inferni ardentis
monarcha, et Demogorgon, propitiamus vos ut ap-
pareat et surgat Mephostophilis! Quid tu
      moraris?*   **20**
*Per Iehovam, Gehennam, et consecratam aquam
quam nunc spargo, signumque crucis quod nunc
facio, et per vota nostra, ipse nunc surgat nobis
dicatus Mephostophilis!*[7]

Enter a DEVIL.[8]

I charge thee to return and change thy shape,   **25**
Thou art too ugly to attend on me.
Go, and return an old Franciscan friar:
That holy shape becomes a devil best. (*Exit* DEVIL.)
I see there's virtue in my heavenly words.
Who would not be proficient in this art?   **30**
How pliant is this Mephostophilis,
Full of obedience and humility,
Such is the force of magic and my spells.

Enter MEPHOSTOPHILIS.

MEPHOSTOPHILIS.   Now Faustus, what wouldst thou have
   me do?   **35**
FAUSTUS.

I charge thee wait upon me whilst I live
To do whatever Faustus shall command,
Be it to make the moon drop from her sphere
Or the ocean to overwhelm the world.
MEPHOSTOPHILIS.

I am a servant to great Lucifer   **40**
And may not follow thee without his leave.
No more than he commands must we perform.
FAUSTUS.   Did not he charge thee to appear to me?
MEPHOSTOPHILIS.   No, I came now hither of mine own
   accord.   **45**
FAUSTUS.   Did not my conjuring raise thee? Speak.
MEPHOSTOPHILIS.

That was the cause, but yet *per accidens:*[9]
For when we hear one rack[10] the name of God,
Abjure the Scriptures and his savior Christ,
We fly in hope to get his glorious[11] soul.   **50**
Nor will we come unless he use such means
Whereby he is in danger to be damned.
Therefore the shortest cut for conjuring
Is stoutly to abjure the Trinity
And pray devoutly to the prince of hell.   **55**
FAUSTUS.

So Faustus hath already done, and holds this
      principle,
There is no chief but only Belzebub:
To whom Faustus doth dedicate himself.
This word "damnation" terrifies not me
For I confound hell in Elysium:[12]   **60**
My ghost[13] be with the old[14] philosophers!
But leaving these vain trifles of men's souls,
Tell me, what is that Lucifer thy lord?
MEPHOSTOPHILIS.   Arch-regent and commander of all
   spirits.[15]   **65**

---

[1]**Enter . . . Devils** (they are invisible to Faustus; perhaps they enter through a trapdoor and climb to the upper playing area, as implied in V.ii.s.d.) [2]**Orion** constellation appearing at the beginning of winter, associated with rain [3]**welkin** sky [4]**circle** circle the conjuror draws around him on the ground, to call the spirits and to protect himself from them [5]**adjunct to** heavenly body fixed to [6]**signs and erring stars** signs of the Zodiac and planets [7]**Sint . . . Mephostophilis** may the gods of the lower region be favorable to me. Away with the trinity of Jehovah. Hail, spirits of fire, air, water. Prince of the east, Belzebub monarch of burning hell, and Demogorgon, we pray to you that Mephostophilis may appear and rise. Why do you delay? By Jehovah, Gehenna, and the holy water which now I sprinkle, and the sign of the cross which now I make, and by our vows, may Mephostophilis himself now rise to serve us (Latin) [8]**Devil** (the word "dragon" oddly appears, after "surgat Mephostophilis," in the preceding conjuration. It makes no sense in the sentence, and it has therefore been omitted from the present text, but perhaps it indicates that a dragon briefly appears at that point, or perhaps the devil referred to in the present stage direction is disguised as a dragon)

[9]**per accidens** the immediate (but not ultimate) cause (Latin)
[10]**rack** torture   [11]**glorious** (1) splendid (2) presumptuous
[12]**confound hell in Elysium** do not distinguish between hell and Elysium   [13]**ghost** spirit   [14]**old** i.e., pre-Christian   [15]**spirits** devils

FAUSTUS.   Was not that Lucifer an angel once?

MEPHOSTOPHILIS.   Yes Faustus, and most dearly loved of
   God.

FAUSTUS.   How comes it then that he is prince of
   devils?   70

MEPHOSTOPHILIS.

   O, by aspiring pride and insolence,
   For which God threw him from the face of heaven.

FAUSTUS.   And what are you that live with Lucifer?

MEPHOSTOPHILIS.

   Unhappy spirits that fell with Lucifer,
   Conspired against our God with Lucifer,   75
   And are forever damned with Lucifer.

FAUSTUS.   Where are you damned?

MEPHOSTOPHILIS.   In hell.

FAUSTUS.   How comes it then that thou art out of hell?

MEPHOSTOPHILIS.

   Why this is hell, nor am I out of it.   80
   Think'st thou that I who saw the face of God
   And tasted the eternal joys of heaven
   Am not tormented with ten thousand hells
   In being deprived of everlasting bliss?
   O Faustus, leave these frivolous demands   85
   Which strikes[16] a terror to my fainting soul!

FAUSTUS.

   What, is great Mephostophilis so passionate[17]
   For being deprivèd of the joys of heaven?
   Learn thou of Faustus manly fortitude
   And scorn those joys thou never shalt possess.   90
   Go bear these tidings to great Lucifer:
   Seeing Faustus hath incurred eternal death
   By desperate thoughts against Jove's deity,
   Say he surrenders up to him his soul
   So he will spare him four and twenty years,   95
   Letting him live in all voluptuousness,
   Having thee ever to attend on me,
   To give me whatsoever I shall ask,
   To tell me whatsoever I demand,
   To slay mine enemies and to aid my friends   100
   And always be obedient to my will.
   Go and return to mighty Lucifer
   And meet me in my study at midnight,
   And then resolve[18] me of thy master's mind.

MEPHOSTOPHILIS.   I will, Faustus.   105

FAUSTUS.

   Had I as many souls as there be stars
   I'd give them all for Mephostophilis.
   By him I'll be great emperor of the world,
   And make a bridge through[19] the moving air

To pass the ocean with a band of men;   110
I'll join the hills that bind the Afric shore
And make that country continent to[20] Spain,
And both contributary to my crown;
The Emperor shall not live but by my leave,
Nor any potentate of Germany.   115
Now that I have obtained what I desired
I'll live in speculation[21] of this art
Till Mephostophilis return again. (*Exit.*)

(*Exeunt* LUCIFER *and* DEVILS.)

SCENE FOUR

Enter WAGNER *and* (ROBIN) THE CLOWN.[1]

WAGNER.   Come hither, sirrah boy.

ROBIN.   Boy! O, disgrace to my person! Zounds,[2] boy in
   your face! You have seen many boys with such pickadevants,[3] I am sure.

WAGNER.   Sirrah, hast thou no comings in?[4]   5

ROBIN.   Yes, and goings out too, you may see sir.

WAGNER.   Alas, poor slave! See how poverty jests in his
   nakedness. I know the villain's out of service, and so
   hungry that I know he would give his soul to the devil for
   a shoulder of mutton, though it were blood-raw.   10

ROBIN.   Not so, neither! I had need to have it well roasted,
   and good sauce to it, if I pay so dear, I can tell you.

WAGNER.   Sirrah, wilt thou be my man and wait on me?
   And I will make thee go like *Qui mihi discipulus.*[5]

ROBIN.   What, in verse?   15

WAGNER.   No, slave, in beaten[6] silk and stavesacre.[7]

ROBIN.   Stavesacre? That's good to kill vermin! Then,
   belike, if I serve you I shall be lousy.

WAGNER.   Why, so thou shalt be, whether thou dost it or
   no; for sirrah, if thou dost not presently bind thy-   20
   self to me for seven years, I'll turn all the lice about thee
   into familiars[8] and make them tear thee in pieces.

ROBIN.   Nay sir, you may save yourself a labor, for they
   are as familiar with me as if they paid for their meat and
   drink, I can tell you.   25

WAGNER.   Well sirrah, leave your jesting and take these
   guilders.[9]

---

[16]**strikes** (it is not unusual to have a plural subject—especially
when it has a collective force—take a verb ending in -s)
[17]**passionate** emotional   [18]**resolve** inform   [19] **through**
(pronounced ''thorough'')

[20]**continent to** continuous with   [21] **speculation** contemplation
[1]**Clown** buffoon   [2]**Zounds** by God's wounds   [3]**pickadevants**
pointed beards   [4]**comings in** income (the Clown then quibbles on
''goings out,'' i.e., expenses and also holes in his clothes through
which his body pokes)   [5]**Qui mihi discipulus** one who is my
disciple, i.e., like the servant of a learned man (the Latin is the
beginning of a poem, familiar to Renaissance schoolboys, on
proper behavior)   [6]**beaten** embroidered (leading to the quibble on
the sense ''hit'')   [7]**stavesacre** preparation from seeds of
delphinium, used to kill vermin   [8]**familiars** attendant demons
[9]**guilders** Dutch coins

ROBIN.   Yes marry[10] sir, and I thank you too.

WAGNER.   So, now thou art to be at an hour's warning whensoever and wheresoever the devil shall fetch thee.   30

ROBIN.   Here, take your guilders, I'll none of 'em!

WAGNER.   Not I, thou art pressed.[11] Prepare thyself, for I will presently raise up two devils to carry thee away. Banio! Belcher!   35

ROBIN.   Belcher! And[12] Belcher come here I'll belch him. I am not afraid of a devil!

Enter two DEVILS.

WAGNER.   How now sir, will you serve me now?

ROBIN.   Ay, good Wagner, take away the devil then.

WAGNER.   Spirits, away! (*Exeunt* DEVILS.) Now sirrah, follow me.   40

ROBIN.   I will sir! But hark you master, will you teach me this conjuring occupation?

WAGNER.   Ay sirrah, I'll teach thee to turn thyself to a dog or a cat or a mouse or a rat or anything.   45

ROBIN.   A dog or a cat or a mouse or a rat? O brave[13] Wagner!

WAGNER.   Villain, call me Master Wagner. And see that you walk attentively, and let your right eye be always diametrally[14] fixed upon my left heel, that thou mayst *quasi vestigiis nostris insistere.*[15]   50

ROBIN.   Well sir, I warrant you. (*Exeunt.*)

ACT TWO

SCENE ONE

Enter FAUSTUS *in his study.*

FAUSTUS.
Now, Faustus, must thou needs be damned;
Canst thou not be saved!
What boots[1] it then to think on God or heaven?
Away with such vain fancies, and despair—
Despair in God and trust in Belzebub!   5
Now go not backward. Faustus, be resolute!
Why waver'st thou? O something soundeth in mine ear,
"Abjure this magic, turn to God again."
Ay, and Faustus will turn to God again.
To God? He loves thee not;   10
The god thou serv'st is thine own appetite
Wherein is fixed the love of Belzebub!
To him I'll build an altar and a church
And offer lukewarm blood of newborn babes!

Enter the two ANGELS.

BAD ANGEL.   Go forward, Faustus, in that famous art.   15

GOOD ANGEL.   Sweet Faustus, leave that execrable art.

FAUSTUS.   Contrition, prayer, repentance, what of these?

GOOD ANGEL.   O, they are means to bring thee unto heaven.

BAD ANGEL.
Rather illusions, fruits of lunacy,   20
That make men foolish that do use them most.

GOOD ANGEL.   Sweet Faustus, think of heaven and heavenly things.

BAD ANGEL.   No Faustus, think of honor and of wealth.
(*Exeunt* ANGELS.)

FAUSTUS.
Wealth!   25
Why, the signory of Emden[2] shall be mine!
When Mephostophilis shall stand by me
What power can hurt me? Faustus, thou art safe.
Cast no more doubts! Mephostophilis, come,
And bring glad tidings from great Lucifer.   30
Is't not midnight? Come Mephostophilis,
Veni, veni, Mephostophile![3]

Enter MEPHOSTOPHILIS.

Now tell me, what saith Lucifer thy lord?

MEPHOSTOPHILIS.
That I shall wait on Faustus whilst he lives,
So he will buy my service with his soul.   35

FAUSTUS.   Already Faustus hath hazarded that for thee.

MEPHOSTOPHILIS.
But now thou must bequeath it solemnly
And write a deed of gift with thine own blood,
For that security craves Lucifer.
If thou deny it I must back to hell.   40

FAUSTUS.
Stay Mephostophilis and tell me
What good will my soul do thy lord?

MEPHOSTOPHILIS.   Enlarge his kingdom.

FAUSTUS.   Is that the reason why he tempts us thus?

MEPHOSTOPHILIS.   *Solamen miseris socios habuisse doloris.*[4]   45

FAUSTUS.   Why, have you any pain that torture other?[5]

MEPHOSTOPHILIS.
As great as have the human souls of men.
But tell me, Faustus, shall I have thy soul—
And I will be thy slave and wait on thee   50
And give thee more than thou hast wit to ask?

FAUSTUS.   Ay, Mephostophilis, I'll give it him.[6]

---

[10]**marry** indeed (a mild oath, from "by the Virgin Mary")
[11]**pressed** enlisted into service   [12]**And if**   [13]**brave** splendid
[14]**diametrally** directly   [15]**quasi vestigiis nostris insistere** as if to step in our footsteps   [1]**boots** avails

[2]**signory of Emden** lordship of the rich German port at the mouth of the Ems   [3]**Veni, veni, Mephostophile** come, come, Mephostophilis (Latin)   [4]**Solamen . . . doloris** misery loves company (Latin)   [5]**other** others   [6]**him** i.e., to Lucifer

MEPHOSTOPHILIS.
>   Then, Faustus, stab thy arm courageously
>   And bind thy soul that at some certain day
>   Great Lucifer may claim it as his own.   **55**
>   And then be thou as great as Lucifer!

FAUSTUS.
>   Lo, Mephostophilis, for love of thee
>   Faustus hath cut his arm and with his proper[7] blood
>   Assures[8] his soul to be great Lucifer's,
>   Chief lord and regent of perpetual night.   **60**
>   View here this blood that trickles from mine arm
>   And let it be propitious for my wish.

MEPHOSTOPHILIS.
>   But Faustus,
>   Write it in manner of a deed of gift.

FAUSTUS.
>   Ay so I do—But Mephostophilis,   **65**
>   My blood congeals and I can write no more.

MEPHOSTOPHILIS.   I'll fetch thee fire to dissolve it
straight. (*Exit.*)

FAUSTUS.
>   What might the staying of my blood portend?
>   Is it unwilling I should write this bill?[9]   **70**
>   Why streams it not that I may write afresh:
>   ''Faustus gives to thee his soul''? O there it stayed.
>   Why shouldst thou not? Is not thy soul thine own?
>   Then write again: "Faustus gives to thee his soul."

Enter MEPHOSTOPHILIS *with the chafer*[10] *of fire.*

MEPHOSTOPHILIS.   See Faustus, here is fire. Set it[11] on. **75**

FAUSTUS.
>   So, now the blood begins to clear again.
>   Now will I make an end immediately.

MEPHOSTOPHILIS (*aside*). What will not I do to obtain his
soul!

FAUSTUS.
>   *Consummatum est!*[12] This bill is ended: **80**
>   And Faustus hath bequeathed his soul to Lucifer.
>   —But what is this inscription on mine arm?
>   *Homo fuge!*[13] Whither should I fly?
>   If unto God, He'll throw me down to hell.
>   My senses are deceived, here's nothing writ.   **85**
>   O yes, I see it plain! Even here is writ
>   *Homo fuge!* Yet shall not Faustus fly!

MEPHOSTOPHILIS (*aside*). I'll fetch him somewhat to
delight his mind. (*Exit.*)

Enter DEVILS *giving crowns and rich apparel to* FAUSTUS.
They dance and then depart.

Enter MEPHOSTOPHILIS.

FAUSTUS.   What means this show? Speak,   **90**
> Mephostophilis.

MEPHOSTOPHILIS.
>   Nothing Faustus, but to delight thy mind
>   And let thee see what magic can perform.

FAUSTUS.   But may I raise such spirits when I please?

MEPHOSTOPHILIS.   Ay Faustus, and do greater things **95**
than these.

FAUSTUS.
>   Then, Mephostophilis, receive this scroll,
>   A deed of gift of body and of soul:
>   But yet conditionally that thou perform
>   All covenants and articles between us both.   **100**

MEPHOSTOPHILIS.
>   Faustus, I swear by hell and Lucifer
>   To effect all promises between us both.

FAUSTUS.
>   Then hear me read it, Mephostophilis:
>   On these conditions following:
>   First, that Faustus may be a spirit[14] in form and
>   substance.   **105**
>   Secondly, that Mephostophilis shall be his servant
>   and be by him commanded.
>   Thirdly, that Mephostophilis shall do for him and
>   bring him whatsoever.
>   Fourthly, that he shall be in his chamber or house
>   invisible.
>   Lastly, that he shall appear to the said John Faustus
>   at all times in what form or shape soever
>   he please: **110**
>   I, John Faustus of Wittenberg, Doctor, by these
>   presents, do give both body and soul to Lucifer,
>   prince of the east, and his minister Mephos-
>   tophilis, and furthermore grant unto them that,
>   four and twenty years being expired, and these **115**
>   articles above written being inviolate,[15] full power
>   to fetch or carry the said John Faustus, body and
>   soul, flesh, blood, or goods, into their habitation
>   wheresoever.
>   By me John Faustus.   **120**

MEPHOSTOPHILIS.   Speak Faustus, do you deliver this as
your deed?

FAUSTUS.   Ay, take it, and the devil give thee good of it!

MEPHOSTOPHILIS.   So now Faustus, ask me what thou
wilt.   **125**

---

[7]**proper** own [8]**Assures** conveys by contract [9]**bill** contract
[10]**chafer** portable grate [11]**it** i.e., the receptacle containing the
congealed blood [12]**Consummatum est** it is finished (Latin; a
blasphemous repetition of Christ's words on the Cross; see John
19:30) [13]**Homo fuge** fly, man (Latin)

[14]**spirit** evil spirit, devil (but to see Faustus as transformed now
into a devil deprived of freedom to repent is to deprive the
remainder of the play of much of its meaning) [15]**inviolate**
unviolated

FAUSTUS.

>First will I question with thee about hell.
>Tell me, where is the place that men call hell?

MEPHOSTOPHILIS.   Under the heavens.

FAUSTUS.   Ay, so are all things else, but whereabouts?

MEPHOSTOPHILIS.

>Within the bowels of these elements   130
>Where we are tortured and remain forever.
>Hell hath no limits nor is circumscribed
>In one self place, but where we are is hell,
>And where hell is there must we ever be.
>And to be short, when all the world dissolves   135
>And every creature shall be purified
>All places shall be hell that is not heaven!

FAUSTUS.   I think hell's a fable.

MEPHOSTOPHILIS.   Ay, think so still—till experience
change thy mind!   140

FAUSTUS.   Why, dost thou think that Faustus shall be
damned?

MEPHOSTOPHILIS.

>Ay, of necessity, for here's the scroll
>In which thou hast given thy soul to Lucifer.

FAUSTUS.

>Ay, and body too; but what of that?   145
>Think'st thou that Faustus is so fond[16] to imagine
>That after this life there is any pain?
>No, these are trifles and mere old wives' tales.

MEPHOSTOPHILIS.

>But I am an instance to prove the contrary,
>For I tell thee I am damned and now in hell!   150

FAUSTUS.

>Nay, and this be hell, I'll willingly be damned—
>What, sleeping, eating, walking, and disputing?
>But leaving this, let me have a wife, the fairest maid
>   in Germany, for I am wanton and lascivious and
>   cannot live without a wife.   155

MEPHOSTOPHILIS.   Well Faustus, thou shalt have a wife.

He fetches in a woman DEVIL *(with fireworks).*

FAUSTUS.   What sight is this?

MEPHOSTOPHILIS.   Now Faustus, wilt thou have a wife?

FAUSTUS.   Here's a hot whore indeed! No, I'll no
wife.   160

MEPHOSTOPHILIS.   Marriage is but a ceremonial toy,[17]
(Exit SHE-DEVIL.*)*

>And if thou lovest me, think no more of it.
>I'll cull thee out[18] the fairest courtesans
>And bring them every morning to thy bed.
>She whom thine eye shall like thy heart shall
>   have,   165
>Were she as chaste as was Penelope,[19]

As wise as Saba,[20] or as beautiful
As was bright Lucifer before his fall.
Here, take this book and peruse it well.
The iterating[21] of these lines brings gold;   170
The framing[22] of this circle on the ground
Brings thunder, whirlwinds, storm, and lightning;
Pronounce this thrice devoutly to thyself,
And men in harness[23] shall appear to thee,
Ready to execute what thou command'st.   175

FAUSTUS.

>Thanks Mephostophilis for this sweet book.
>This will I keep as chary as my life. *(Exeunt.[24])*

SCENE TWO

Enter FAUSTUS *in his study and* MEPHOSTOPHILIS.

FAUSTUS.

>When I behold the heavens, then I repent
>And curse thee, wicked Mephostophilis,
>Because thou has deprived me of those joys.

MEPHOSTOPHILIS.

>'Twas thine own seeking Faustus, thank thyself.
>But think'st thou heaven is such a glorious thing?   5
>I tell thee, Faustus, it is not half so fair
>As thou or any man that breathe on earth.

FAUSTUS.   How prov'st thou that?

MEPHOSTOPHILIS.   'Twas made for man; then he's more
excellent.   10

FAUSTUS.

>If heaven was made for man, 'twas made for me!
>I will renounce this magic and repent.

Enter the two ANGELS.

GOOD ANGEL.   Faustus, repent: yet[1] God will pity thee!

BAD ANGEL.   Thou art a spirit: God cannot pity thee!

FAUSTUS.

>Who buzzeth in mine ears I am a spirit?   15
>Be I a devil, yet God may pity me—
>Yea, God will pity me if I repent.

BAD ANGEL.   Ay, but Faustus never shall repent. *(Exit*
ANGELS.*)*

FAUSTUS.

>My heart is hardened, I cannot repent.
>Scarce can I name salvation, faith, or heaven,   20
>Swords, poison, halters, and envenomed steel

---

[16]**fond** foolish [17]**toy** trifle [18]**cull thee out** select for you
[19]**Penelope** wife of Ulysses, famed for her fidelity

[20]**Saba** the Queen of Sheba [21]**iterating** repetition [22]**framing**
drawing [23]**harness** armor [24]**Exeunt** (a scene following this stage
direction has probably been lost. Earlier Wagner hired the Clown;
later the Clown is an ostler possessed of one of Faustus' conjuring
books. Possibly, then, the lost scene was a comic one, showing
the Clown stealing a book and departing) [1]**yet** still, even now

Are laid before me to dispatch myself.
And long ere this I should have done the deed
Had not sweet pleasure conquered deep despair.
Have not I made blind Homer sing to me   25
Of Alexander's love and Oenon's[2] death?
And hath not he[3] that built the walls of Thebes
With ravishing sound of his melodious harp
Made music with my Mephostophilis?
Why should I die then or basely despair?   30
I am resolved, Faustus shall not repent!
Come Mephostophilis, let us dispute again
And reason of divine astrology.
Speak, are there many spheres above the moon?
Are all celestial bodies but one globe   35
As is the substance of this centric[4] earth?

MEPHOSTOPHILIS.

As are the elements, such[5] are the heavens,
Even from the moon unto the empyreal orb
Mutually folded in each others' spheres,
And jointly move upon one axle-tree,   40
Whose terminè[6] is termed the world's wide pole.
Nor are the names of Saturn, Mars, or Jupiter
Feigned but are erring stars.[7]

FAUSTUS.

But have they all one motion,
Both *situ et tempore?*[8]   45

MEPHOSTOPHILIS.   All move from east to west in four and
   twenty hours upon the poles of the world but differ in
   their motions upon the poles of the zodiac.

FAUSTUS.

These slender questions Wagner can decide.
Hath Mephostophilis no greater skill?   50
Who knows not the double motion of the planets?
That the first is finished in a natural day.[9]
The second thus: Saturn in thirty years;
Jupiter in twelve; Mars in four; the sun, Venus, and
   Mercury in a year; the moon in twenty-eight   55
days. These are freshmen's suppositions.[10] But
tell me, hath every sphere a dominion or *intelli-*
gentia?[11]

MEPHOSTOPHILIS.   Ay.

FAUSTUS.   How many heavens or spheres are there?   60

MEPHOSTOPHILIS.   Nine: the seven planets, the firmament, and the empyreal heaven.

FAUSTUS.   But is there not *coelum igneum et*
   crystallinum?[12]

MEPHOSTOPHILIS.   No Faustus, they be but fables.   65

FAUSTUS.   Resolve me then in this one question. Why are
   not conjunctions, oppositions, aspects, eclipses all at one
   time,[13] but in some years we have more, in some less?

MEPHOSTOPHILIS.   *Per inaqualem motum respectu*
   totius.[14]   70

FAUSTUS.   Well, I am answered. Now tell me, who made
   the world?

MEPHOSTOPHILIS.   I will not.

FAUSTUS.   Sweet Mephostophilis, tell me.

MEPHOSTOPHILIS.   Move[15] me not, Faustus!   75

FAUSTUS.   Villain, have not I bound thee to tell me
   anything?

MEPHOSTOPHILIS.

Ay, that is not against our kingdom.
   This is. Thou art damned. Think thou of hell!

FAUSTUS.   Think, Faustus, upon God, that made the   80
   world.

MEPHOSTOPHILIS.   Remember this! (*Exit.*)

FAUSTUS.

Ay, go accursèd spirit to ugly hell!
   'Tis thou hast damned distressèd Faustus' soul.—
Is't not too late?   85

Enter the two ANGELS.

BAD ANGEL.   Too late.

GOOD ANGEL.   Never too late, if Faustus will repent.

BAD ANGEL.   If thou repent, devils will tear thee in pieces.

GOOD ANGEL.   Repent, and they shall never raze[16] thy
   skin. (*Exeunt* ANGELS.)   90

FAUSTUS.

O Christ, my savior, my savior!
   Help to save distressèd Faustus' soul.

Enter LUCIFER, BELZEBUB, *and* MEPHOSTOPHILIS.

LUCIFER.

Christ cannot save thy soul, for He is just.
   There's none but I have interest in[17] the same.

FAUSTUS.   O, what art thou that look'st so terribly?   95

LUCIFER.

I am Lucifer
   And this is my companion prince in hell.

FAUSTUS.   O Faustus, they are come to fetch thy soul!

BELZEBUB.   We are come to tell thee thou dost injure us.

---

[2]**Alexander . . . Oenone** Paris, also called Alexander, was
Oenone's lover, but he later deserted her for Helen of Troy,
causing the Trojan War, the subject of Homer's *Iliad*   [3]**he**
Amphion, whose music charmed stones to form the walls of
Thebes   [4]**centric** central   [5]**such** i.e., separate but combined; the
idea is that the heavenly bodies are separate but their spheres are
concentric ("folded"), and all—from the nearest (the moon) to
the farthest ("the empyreal orb" or empyrean)—move on one
axletree   [6]**terminè** end, extremity   [7]**erring stars** planets   [8]**situ et**
tempore in place and in time   [9]**natural day** twenty-four hours
[10]**suppositions** premises   [11]**dominion or intelligentia** governing
angel or intelligence (believed to impart motion to the sphere)

[12]**coelum igneum et crystallinum** a heaven of fire and a
crystalline sphere (Latin)   [13]**at one time** i.e., at regular intervals
[14]**Per . . . totius** because of unequal speed within the system
(Latin)   [15]**Move** anger   [16]**raze** scratch   [17]**interest in** legal claim
on

LUCIFER.   Thou call'st on Christ contrary to thy   **100**
   promise.
BELZEBUB.   Thou should'st not think on God.
LUCIFER.   Think on the Devil.
BELZEBUB.   And his dam[18] too.
FAUSTUS.
   Nor will Faustus henceforth. Pardon him for
     this,   **105**
   And Faustus vows never to look to heaven!
   Never to name God or to pray to Him,
   To burn His Scriptures, slay His ministers,
   And make my spirits pull His churches down.
LUCIFER.
   So shalt thou show thyself an obedient servant,   **110**
   And we will highly gratify thee for it.
BELZEBUB.   Faustus, we are come from hell in person to
   show thee some pastime. Sit down and thou shalt behold
   the Seven Deadly Sins[19] appear to thee in their own proper
   shapes and likeness.   **115**
FAUSTUS.   That sight will be as pleasant to me as Paradise
   was to Adam the first day of his creation.
LUCIFER.   Talk not of Paradise or creation but mark the
   show. Go Mephostophilis, fetch them in.

Enter the SEVEN DEADLY SINS (*led by a* PIPER).

BELZEBUB.   Now Faustus, question them of their   **120**
   names and dispositions.
FAUSTUS.   That shall I soon. What art thou, the first?
PRIDE.   I am Pride. I disdain to have any parents. I am like
   to Ovid's flea,[20] I can creep into every corner of a wench:
   sometimes, like a periwig I sit upon her brow;   **125**
   next, like a necklace I hang about her neck; then, like a
   fan of feathers I kiss her; and then, turning myself to a
   wrought smock,[21] do what I list—But fie, what a smell is
   here! I'll not speak a word more for a king's ransom
   unless the ground be perfumed and covered with   **130**
   cloth of arras.[22]
FAUSTUS.   Thou art a proud knave indeed. What art thou,
   the second?
COVETOUSNESS.   I am Covetousness, begotten of an old
   churl in a leather bag;[23] and might I now obtain   **135**
   my wish, this house, you and all, should turn to gold that
   I might lock you safe into my chest. O my sweet gold!
FAUSTUS.   And what art thou, the third?
ENVY.   I am Envy, begotten of a chimney-sweeper and an
   oyster-wife.[24] I cannot read and therefore wish all   **140**

books burned. I am lean with seeing others eat. O, that
there would come a famine over all the world that all
might die and I live alone! Then thou shouldst see how
fat I'd be. But must thou sit and I stand? Come down,
with a vengeance!   **145**
FAUSTUS.   Out, envious wretch! But what art thou, the
   fourth?
WRATH.   I am Wrath. I had neither father nor mother. I
   leapt out of a lion's mouth when I was scarce an hour old
   and ever since have run up and down the world   **150**
   with these case[25] of rapiers, wounding myself when I
   could get none to fight withal. I was born in hell! And
   look to it, for some of you shall be my father.
FAUSTUS.   And what art thou, the fifth?
GLUTTONY.   I am Gluttony. My parents are all   **155**
   dead, and the devil a penny they have left me, but a small
   pension: and that buys me thirty meals a day and ten
   bevers,[26] a small trifle to suffice nature. I come of a royal
   pedigree. My father was a gammon[27] of bacon, and my
   mother was a hogshead of claret wine. My god-   **160**
   fathers were these: Peter Pickled-herring and Martin
   Martlemas-beef.[28] But my godmother, O, she was an ancient gentlewoman: her name was Margery March-beer.[29]
   Now Faustus, thou hast heard all my progeny,[30] wilt thou
   bid me to supper?   **165**
FAUSTUS.   Not I.
GLUTTONY.   Then the devil choke thee!
FAUSTUS.   Choke thyself, glutton! What art thou, the sixth?
SLOTH.   Heigh-ho![31] I am Sloth. I was begotten on a sunny
   bank. Heigh-ho, I'll not speak a word more for a   **170**
   king's ransom.
FAUSTUS.   And what are you, Mistress Minx, the seventh
   and last?
LECHERY.   Who, I, I sir? I am one that loves an inch of raw
   mutton[32] better than an ell of fried stockfish,[33]   **175**
   and the first letter of my name begins with Lechery.
LUCIFER.   Away to hell, away! On, piper! (*Exeunt the*
   SEVEN SINS.)
FAUSTUS.   O, how this sight doth delight my soul!
LUCIFER.   But Faustus, in hell is all manner of delight.
FAUSTUS.   O, might I see hell and return again safe,   **180**
   how happy were I then!
LUCIFER.
     Faustus, thou shalt. At midnight I will send for thee.

---

[18]**dam** mother   [19]**Seven Deadly Sins** (so called because they
cause spiritual death; they are Pride, Covetousness, Envy, Wrath,
Gluttony, Sloth, Lechery)   [20]**Ovid's flea** flea in *Carmen de pulce,*
a lewd poem mistakenly attributed to Ovid   [21]**wrought smock**
decorated petticoat   [22]**cloth of arras** Flemish cloth used for
tapestries   [23]**leather bag** moneybag (?)   [24]**chimney-sweeper . . .
oyster-wife** i.e., dirty and smelly

[25]**these case** this pair   [26]**bevers** snacks (literally drinks)
[27]**gammon** haunch   [28]**Martlemas-beef** cattle slaughtered at
Martinmas (11 November) and salted for winter consumption
[29]**March-beer** strong beer brewed in March   [30]**progeny** ancestry
[31]**Heigh-ho** (a yawn or tired greeting)   [32]**inch of raw mutton** i.e.,
penis (''mutton'' in a bawdy sense commonly alludes to a
prostitute, but since here the speaker is a woman, the allusion
must be to a male)   [33]**an ell of . . . stockfish** forty-five inches of
dried cod

Meanwhile peruse this book and view it thoroughly,
And thou shalt turn thyself into what shape thou
    wilt.

FAUSTUS.
    Thanks mighty Lucifer.   185
    This will I keep as chary[34] as my life.
LUCIFER.   Now Faustus, farewell.
FAUSTUS.   Farewell great Lucifer. Come Mephostophilis.
    (*Exeunt omnes several[35] ways.*)

SCENE THREE

Enter (ROBIN) THE CLOWN.

ROBIN.   What, Dick, look to the horses there till I come
    again! I have gotten one of Doctor Faustus' conjuring
    books, and now we'll have such knavery as't passes.

Enter DICK.

DICK.   What, Robin, you must come away and walk the
    horses.   5
ROBIN.   I walk the horses? I scorn't, 'faith. I have other
    matters in hand. Let the horses walk themselves an[1] they
    will. (*Reading.*) A *per se*[2]—a; t, h, e—the; *o per se*—o;
    deny orgon—gorgon.[3] Keep further from me, O thou il-
    literate and unlearned hostler!   10
DICK.   'Snails,[4] what hast thou got there, a book? Why,
    thou canst not tell ne'er a word on't.
ROBIN.   That thou shalt see presently. Keep out of the
    circle, I say, lest I send you into the hostry[5] with a
    vengeance.   15
DICK.   That's like, 'faith! You had best leave your foolery,
    for an my master come, he'll conjure you, 'faith.
ROBIN.   My master conjure me? I'll tell thee what. An my
    master come here, I'll clap as fair a pair of horns[6] on's
    head as e'er thou sawest in thy life.   20
DICK.   Thou need'st not do that, for my mistress hath done
    it.
ROBIN.   Ay, there be of us here that have waded as deep
    into matters as other men—if they were disposed to talk.
DICK.   A plague take you! I thought you did not   25
    sneak up and down after her for nothing. But I prithee tell
    me in good sadness[7] Robin, is that a conjuring book?
ROBIN.   Do but speak what thou't have me to do, and I'll
    do't. If thou't dance naked, put off thy clothes, and I'll
    conjure thee about presently. Or if thou't go but to   30
    the tavern with me, I'll give thee white wine, red wine,

claret wine, sack,[8] muscadine, malmsey, and whippincrust[9]—hold-belly-hold. And we'll not pay one penny for
it.
DICK.   O brave! Prithee let's to it presently, for I am   35
as dry as a dog.
ROBIN.   Come then, let's away. (*Exeunt.*)

ACT THREE

Enter the CHORUS.

Learnèd Faustus,
To find the secrets of astronomy
Graven in the book of Jove's high firmament,
Did mount him up to scale Olympus' top:
Where, sitting in a chariot burning bright   5
Drawn by the strength of yokèd dragons' necks,
He views the clouds, the planets, and the stars,
The tropics, zones,[1] and quarters of the sky,
From the bright circle[2] of the hornèd moon
Even to the height of *primum mobile:*[3]   10
And whirling round with this circumference
Within the concave compass of the pole,
From east to west his dragons swiftly glide
And in eight days did bring him home again.
Not long he stayed within his quiet house   15
To rest his bones after his weary toil
But new exploits do hale him out again.
And mounted then upon a dragon's back,
That with his wings did part the subtle air,
He now is gone to prove cosmography,[4]   20
That measures coasts and kingdoms of the earth,
And as I guess will first arrive at Rome
To see the Pope and manner of his court
And take some part of holy Peter's feast,
The which this day is highly solemnized. (*Exit.*)   25

SCENE ONE

Enter FAUSTUS *and* MEPHOSTOPHILIS.

FAUSTUS.
    Having now, my good Mephostophilis,
    Passed with delight the stately town of Trier,[1]
    Environed round with airy mountain tops,
    With walls of flint, and deep-entrenchèd lakes,[2]
    Not to be won by any conquering prince: 5
    From Paris next, coasting the realm of France,

---

[34]**chary** carefully   [35]**several** various   [1]**an** if   [2]**per se** by itself
(Latin; the idea is, "A by itself spells A")   [3]**deny orgon—
gorgon** (Robin is trying to read the name "Demogorgon")
[4]**'Snails** by God's nails   [5]**hostry** hostelry, inn   [6]**horns** (as the
next speech indicates, horns were said to adorn the head of a man
whose wife was unfaithful)   [7]**in good sadness** seriously

[8]**sack** sherry   [9]**whippincrust** illiterate pronunciation of
"hippocras," a spiced wine   [1]**zones** segments of the sky   [2]**circle**
orbit   [3]**primum mobile** the outermost sphere, the empyrean
[4]**prove cosmography** test maps, i.e., explore the universe   [1]**Trier**
German city on the Moselle, also known as Trèves   [2]**deep-
entrenchèd lakes** moats

We saw the river Main fall into Rhine,
Whose banks are set with groves of fruitful vines:
Then up to Naples, rich Campania,
Whose buildings fair and gorgeous to the eye,   10
The streets straight forth and paved with finest brick,
Quarters the town in four equivalents.
There saw we learnèd Maro's[3] golden tomb,
The way he cut an English mile in length
Through[4] a rock of stone in one night's space.   15
From thence to Venice, Padua, and the rest,
In one of which a sumptuous temple stands
That threats the stars with her aspiring top,
Whose frame is paved with sundry colored stones
And roofed aloft with curious work in gold.   20
Thus hitherto hath Faustus spent his time.
But tell me now, what resting-place is this?
Hast thou, as erst I did command,
Conducted me within the walls of Rome?

MEPHOSTOPHILIS.
I have, my Faustus, and for proof thereof   25
This is the goodly palace of the Pope,
And 'cause we are no common guests
I choose his privy chamber for our use.

FAUSTUS.
I hope his Holiness will bid us welcome.

MEPHOSTOPHILIS.
All's one, for we'll be bold with his venison.   30
But now my Faustus, that thou may'st perceive
What Rome contains for to delight thine eyes,
Know that this city stands upon seven hills
That underprop the groundwork of the same:
Just through the midst runs flowing Tiber's
    stream   35
With winding banks that cut it in two parts,
Over the which four stately bridges lean[5]
That make safe passage to each part of Rome.
Upon the bridge called Ponte Angelo
Erected is a castle passing strong   40
Where thou shalt see such store of ordinance
As that the double cannons forged of brass
Do match the number of the days contained
Within the compass of one complete year,
Beside the gates and high pyramides[6]   45
That Julius Caesar brought from Africa.

FAUSTUS.
Now, by the kingdoms of infernal rule,
Of Styx, of Acheron, and the fiery lake
Of ever-burning Phlegethon,[7] I swear
That I do long to see the monuments   50

And situation of bright-splendent Rome.
Come therefore, let's away.

MEPHOSTOPHILIS.
Nay stay my Faustus. I know you'd see the Pope
And take some part of holy Peter's feast,
The which this day with high solemnity,   55
This day, is held through Rome and Italy
In honor of the Pope's triumphant victory.

FAUSTUS.
Sweet Mephostophilis, thou pleasest me.
Whilst I am here on earth let me be cloyed
With all things that delight the heart of man.   60
My four and twenty years of liberty
I'll spend in pleasure and in dalliance,
That Faustus' name, whilst this bright frame doth
    stand,
May be admirèd through the furthest land.

MEPHOSTOPHILIS.
'Tis well said, Faustus, come then, stand by me   65
And thou shalt see them come immediately.

FAUSTUS.
Nay stay, my gentle Mephostophilis,
And grant me my request, and then I go.
Thou know'st, within the compass of eight days
We viewed the face of heaven, of earth, and hell.   70
So high our dragons soared into the air
That looking down the earth appeared to me
No bigger than my hand in quantity—
There did we view the kingdoms of the world,
And what might please mine eye I there beheld.   75
Then in this show let me an actor be
That this proud Pope may Faustus' cunning see!

MEPHOSTOPHILIS.
Let it be so, my Faustus, but first stay
And view their triumphs[8] as they pass this way.
And then devise what best contents thy mind   80
By cunning in thine art to cross the Pope
Or dash the pride of this solemnity—
To make his monks and abbots stand like apes
And point like antics[9] at his triple crown,
To beat the beads about the friars' pates,   85
Or clap huge horns upon the cardinals' heads,
Or any villainy thou canst devise—
And I'll perform it, Faustus. Hark, they come!
This day shall make thee be admired[10] in Rome!

Enter the CARDINALS *and* BISHOPS, *some bearing crosiers,
some the pillars;* MONKS *and* FRIARS *singing their procession; then the* POPE *and* RAYMOND KING *of* HUNGARY, *with*
BRUNO[11] *led in chains.*

---

[3]**Maro** Vergil (Publius Vergilius Maro, 70–19 B.C.)   [4]**Through**
(pronounced ''thorough'')   [5]**lean** bend   [6]**pyramides** obelisk
(pronounced py-ràm-i-des)   [7]**Styx, Acheron, Phlegethon** rivers of
the underworld

[8]**triumphs** spectacular displays   [9]**antics** grotesque figures,
buffoons   [10]**admired** wondered at   [11]**Raymond King of
Hungary . . . Bruno** (unhistorical figures; Bruno is the emperor's
nominee for the papal throne)

POPE.   Cast down our footstool.   90
RAYMOND.

                    Saxon Bruno, stoop,
    Whilst on thy back his Holiness ascends
    Saint Peter's chair and state[12] pontifical.
BRUNO.
    Proud Lucifer, that state belongs to me—
    But thus I fall to Peter, not to thee.   95
POPE.
    To me and Peter shalt thou grov'lling lie
    And crouch before the papal dignity!
    Sound trumpets then, for thus Saint Peter's heir
    From Bruno's back ascends Saint Peter's chair!

A flourish[13] while he ascends.

    Thus as the gods creep on with feet of wool   100
    Long ere with iron hands they punish men,
    So shall our sleeping vengeance now arise
    And smite with death thy hated enterprise.
    Lord Cardinals of France and Padua,
    Go forthwith to our holy consistory[14]   105
    And read amongst the statutes decretal[15]
    What by the holy council held at Trent[16]
    The sacred synod[17] hath decreed for him
    That doth assume the papal government
    Without election and a true consent.   110
    Away, and bring us word with speed!
1 CARDINAL.   We go my lord. (*Exeunt* [*two*] CARDINALS.)
POPE.   Lord Raymond—   (*Talks to him apart.*)
FAUSTUS.
    Go haste thee, gentle Mephostophilis,
    Follow the cardinals to the consistory   115
    And as they turn their superstitious books
    Strike them with sloth and drowsy idleness
    And make them sleep so sound that in their shapes
    Thyself and I may parley with this Pope,
    This proud confronter of the Emperor!   120
    —And in despite of all his holiness
    Restore this Bruno to his liberty
    And bear him to the states of Germany!
MEPHOSTOPHILIS.   Faustus, I go.
FAUSTUS.
    Dispatch it soon.   125
    The Pope shall curse that Faustus came to Rome.
      (*Exit* FAUSTUS *and* MEPHOSTOPHILIS.)
BRUNO.
    Pope Adrian, let me have some right of law:
    I was elected by the Emperor.

POPE.
    We will depose the Emperor for that deed
    And curse the people that submit to him.   130
    Both he and thou shalt stand excommunicate
    And interdict from church's privilege
    And all society of holy men.
    He grows too proud in his authority,
    Lifting his lofty head above the clouds,   135
    And like a steeple overpeers the church.
    But we'll pull down his haughty insolence.
    And as Pope Alexander,[18] our progenitor,[19]
    Trod on the neck of German Frederick,
    Adding this golden sentence to our praise: 140
    ''That Peter's heirs should tread on emperors
    And walk upon the dreadful adder's back,
    Treading the lion and the dragon down,
    And fearless spurn the killing basilisk''[20]—
    So will we quell that haughty schismatic   145
    And by authority apostolical
    Depose him from his regal government.
BRUNO.
    Pope Julius swore to princely Sigismond,
    For him and the succeeding Popes of Rome,
    To hold the emperors their lawful lords.   150
POPE.
    Pope Julius did abuse the church's rites
    And therefore none of his decrees can stand.
    Is not all power on earth bestowed on us?
    And therefore though we would, we cannot err.
    Behold this silver belt whereto is fixed   155
    Seven golden keys fast sealed with seven seals
    In token of our sevenfold power from heaven
    To bind or loose, lock fast, condemn, or judge,
    Resign[21] or seal, or whatso pleaseth us.
    Then he and thou and all the world shall stoop—   160
    Or be assurèd of our dreadful curse
    To light as heavy as the pains of hell.

Enter FAUSTUS *and* MEPHOSTOPHILIS *like the cardinals.*

MEPHOSTOPHILIS (*aside*).
    Now tell me Faustus, are we not fitted well?
FAUSTUS (*aside*).
    Yes Mephostophilis, and two such cardinals
    Ne'er served a holy Pope as we shall do.   165
    But whilst they sleep within the consistory
    Let us salute his reverend Fatherhood.
RAYMOND.   Behold my lord, the cardinals are returned.

---

[12]**state** throne   [13]**flourish** trumpet fanfare   [14]**consistory** i.e.,
meeting-place of the papal consistory or senate   [15]**statutes
decretal** i.e., ecclesiastical laws   [16]**council held at Trent**
(intermittently from 1545 to 1563)   [17]**synod** council

[18]**Pope Alexander** Pope Alexander III (d. 1181) compelled the
Emperor Frederick Barbarossa to kneel before him   [19]**progenitor**
predecessor   [20]**basilisk** fabulous monster said to kill with a glance
[21]**Resign** unseal

POPE.

> Welcome grave fathers, answer presently,[22]
> What have our holy council there decreed   **170**
> Concerning Bruno and the Emperor
> In quittance of [23] their late conspiracy
> Against our state and papal dignity?

FAUSTUS.

> Most sacred patron of the church of Rome,
> By full consent of all the synod   **175**
> Of priests and prelates it is thus decreed:
> That Bruno and the German Emperor
> Be held as lollards[24] and bold schismatics
> And proud disturbers of the church's peace.
> And if that Bruno by his own assent,   **180**
> Without enforcement of the German peers,
> Did seek to wear the triple diadem
> And by your death to climb Saint Peter's chair,
> The statutes decretal have thus decreed:
> He shall be straight condemned of heresy   **185**
> And on a pile of fagots burnt to death.

POPE.

> It is enough. Here, take him to your charge
> And bear him straight to Ponte Angelo
> And in the strongest tower enclose him fast.
> Tomorrow, sitting in our consistory   **190**
> With all our college of grave cardinals
> We will determine of his life or death.
> Here, take his triple crown along with you
> And leave it in the church's treasury.
> Make haste again,[25] my good lord cardinals,   **195**
> And take our blessing apostolical.

MEPHOSTOPHILIS (*aside*). So, so! Was never devil thus
blessed before.

FAUSTUS (*aside*).

> Away sweet Mephostophilis, be gone!
> The cardinals will be plagued for this anon.   **200**

Exeunt FAUSTUS *and* MEPHOSTOPHILIS (*with* BRUNO).

POPE.

> Go presently and bring a banquet forth,
> That we may solemnize Saint Peter's feast
> And with Lord Raymond, King of Hungary,
> Drink to our late and happy victory. (*Exeunt*.)

SCENE TWO

A sennet[1] *while the banquet is brought in, and then enter*
FAUSTUS *and* MEPHOSTOPHILIS *in their own shapes*.

MEPHOSTOPHILIS.

> Now Faustus, come prepare thyself for mirth.
> The sleepy cardinals are hard at hand
> To censure Bruno, that is posted hence,
> And on a proud-paced steed as swift as thought
> Flies o'er the Alps to fruitful Germany,   **5**
> There to salute the woeful Emperor.

FAUSTUS.

> The Pope will curse them for their sloth today
> That slept both Bruno and his crown away.
> But now, that Faustus may delight his mind
> And by their folly make some merriment,   **10**
> Sweet Mephostophilis, so charm me here
> That I may walk invisible to all
> And do whate'er I please unseen of any.

MEPHOSTOPHILIS.

> Faustus, thou shalt. Then kneel down presently,

> Whilst on thy head I lay my hand   **15**
> And charm thee with this magic wand.
> First wear this girdle, then appear
> Invisible to all are here:
> The planets seven, the gloomy air,
> Hell, and the Furies' forkèd hair,[2]   **20**
> Pluto's blue fire, and Hecat's[3] tree
> With magic spells so compass thee
> That no eye may thy body see.

> So Faustus, now for all their holiness,
> Do what thou wilt, thou shalt not be discerned.   **25**

FAUSTUS.

> Thanks Mephostophilis. Now friars, take heed
> Lest Faustus make your shaven crowns to bleed.

MEPHOSTOPHILIS.   Faustus, no more. See where the cardinals come.

Enter POPE (*and* FRIARS) *and all the* LORDS (*with* KING RAY-
MOND *and the* ARCHBISHOP OF RHEIMS). *Enter the* (*two*)
CARDINALS *with a book*.

POPE.

> Welcome lord cardinals. Come, sit down.   **30**
> Lord Raymond, take your seat. Friars, attend,
> And see that all things be in readiness
> As best beseems this solemn festival.

1 CARDINAL.

> First may it please your sacred Holiness
> To view the sentence of the reverend synod   **35**
> Concerning Bruno and the Emperor.

---

[22]**presently** immediately   [23]**quittance of** requital for   [24]**lollards**
heretics   [25]**again** i.e., to return   [1]**sennet** set of notes played on a
trumpet signaling an approach or a departure

[2]**Furies' forkèd hair** (the hair of the Furies consisted of snakes,
whose forked tongues may be implied here)   [3]**Hecat** Hecate,
goddess of magic (possibly her ''tree'' is the gallows-tree, but
possibly ''tree'' is a slip for ''three,'' Hecate being the triple
goddess of heaven, earth, and hell)

POPE.

> What needs this question? Did I not tell you
> Tomorrow we would sit i' th' consistory
> And there determine of his punishment?
> You brought us word, even now, it was decreed   40
> That Bruno and the cursèd Emperor
> Were by the holy council both condemned
> For loathèd lollards and base schismatics.
> Then wherefore would you have me view that book?

1 CARDINAL.   Your Grace mistakes. You gave us no   45
such charge.

RAYMOND.

> Deny it not; we all are witnesses
> That Bruno here was late delivered you
> With his rich triple crown to be reserved
> And put into the church's treasury.   50

BOTH CARDINALS.   By holy Paul we saw them not.

POPE.

> By Peter you shall die
> Unless you bring them forth immediately.
> Hale them to prison, lade their limbs with gyves.[4]
> False prelates, for this hateful treachery   55
> Cursed be your souls to hellish misery. (*Exeunt*
>   ATTENDANTS *with two* CARDINALS.)

FAUSTUS.

> So, they are safe. Now Faustus, to the feast.
> The Pope had never such a frolic guest.

POPE.   Lord Archbishop of Rheims, sit down with us.

ARCHBISHOP.   I thank your Holiness.   60

FAUSTUS.   Fall to,[5] the devil choke you an you spare!

POPE.

> Who's that spoke? Friars, look about.
> Lord Raymond, pray fall to. I am beholding
> To the Bishop of Milan for this so rare a present.

FAUSTUS (*aside*). I thank you, sir! (*Snatches the dish.*)   65

POPE.

> How now! Who snatched the meat from me?
> Villains, why speak you not?
> My good Lord Archbishop, here's a most dainty dish
> Was sent me from a cardinal in France.

FAUSTUS (*aside*). I'll have that too! (*Snatches the*   70
dish.)

POPE.

> What lollards do attend our Holiness
> That we receive such great indignity!
> Fetch me some wine.

FAUSTUS (*aside*). Ay, pray do, for Faustus is adry.

POPE.   Lord Raymond, I drink unto your Grace.   75

FAUSTUS (*aside*). I pledge your Grace. (*Snatches the goblet.*)

POPE.

> My wine gone too? Ye lubbers, look about

> And find the man that doth this villainy,
> Or by our sanctitude you all shall die.
> I pray, my lords, have patience at this troublesome
>   banquet.   80

ARCHBISHOP.   Please it your Holiness, I think it be some
ghost crept out of purgatory, and now is come unto your
Holiness for his pardon.

POPE.

> It may be so:
> Go then, command our priests to sing a dirge   85
> To lay the fury of this same troublesome ghost. (*Exit*
>   ATTENDANT.)

(*The* POPE *crosses himself before eating.*)

FAUSTUS.

> How now! Must every bit be spicèd with a cross?
> Nay then, take that! (*Strikes the* POPE.)

POPE.

> O, I am slain! Help me my lords!
> O come and help to bear my body hence.   90
> Damned be this soul forever for this deed. (*Exeunt*
>   *the* POPE *and his train.*)

MEPHOSTOPHILIS.

> Now Faustus, what will you do now?
> For I can tell you, you'll be cursed with bell, book,
> and candle.[6]

FAUSTUS.

> Bell, book, and candle. Candle, book, and bell.   95
> Forward and backward, to curse Faustus to hell!

Enter the FRIARS, *with bell, book, and candle for the dirge.*

1 FRIAR.

> Come brethren, let's about our business with good
>   devotion.
> Cursèd be he that stole his Holiness' meat from the
>   table.
>   *Maledicat Dominus!*[7]
> Cursèd be he that struck his Holiness a blow on the
>   face.   100
>   *Maledicat Dominus!* (FAUSTUS *strikes a* FRIAR.)
> Cursèd be he that took Friar Sandelo a blow on the
>   pate.
>   *Maledicat Dominus!*
> Cursèd be he that disturbeth our holy dirge.
>   *Maledicat Dominus!*   105
> Cursèd be he that took away his Holiness' wine.
>   *Maledicat Dominus!*

(FAUSTUS *and* MEPHOSTOPHILIS) *beat the* FRIARS, *fling fireworks among them and exeunt.*

---

[4]**gyves** fetters   [5]**Fall to** set to work (here, as commonly, ''start eating'')

[6]**bell, book, and candle** implements used in excommunicating (the bell was tolled, the book closed, the candle extinguished)   [7]**Maledicat Dominus** may the Lord curse him (Latin)

SCENE THREE

Enter (ROBIN *the*) CLOWN *and* DICK *with a cup.*

DICK. Sirrah Robin, we were best look that your devil can answer the stealing of this same cup, for the vintner's boy follows us at the hard heels.[1]

ROBIN. 'Tis no matter, let him come! An he follow us I'll so conjure him as he was never conjured in his life, **5** I warrant him. Let me see the cup.

Enter VINTNER.

DICK. Here 'tis. Yonder he comes. Now Robin, now or never show thy cunning.

VINTNER. O, are you here? I am glad I have found you. You are a couple of fine companions![2] Pray, where's **10** the cup you stole from the tavern?

ROBIN. How, how! We steal a cup? Take heed what you say. We look not like cup-stealers, I can tell you.

VINTNER. Never deny't, for I know you have it, and I'll search you. **15**

ROBIN. Search me? Ay, and spare not! (*Aside.*) Hold the cup, Dick.—Come, come. Search me, search me. (VINTNER *searches him.*)

VINTNER. Come on sirrah, let me search you now.

DICK. Ay ay, do do. (*Aside.*) Hold the cup, Robin.— I fear not your searching. We scorn to steal your cups, I **20** can tell you. (VINTNER *searches him.*)

VINTNER. Never outface me for the matter, for sure the cup is between you two.

ROBIN. Nay, there you lie! 'Tis beyond us both.[3]

VINTNER. A plague take you. I thought 'twas your **25** knavery to take it away. Come, give it to me again.

ROBIN. Ay, much! When, can you tell?[4] (*Aside.*) Dick, make me a circle and stand close at my back and stir not for thy life. Vintner, you shall have your cup anon. (*Aside.*) Say nothing, Dick! O *per se,* o; **30** Demogorgon, Belcher, and Mephostophilis!

Enter MEPHOSTOPHILIS. (*Exit* VINTNER.)

MEPHOSTOPHILIS.
　　You princely legions of infernal rule,
　　How am I vexèd by these villains' charms!
　　From Constantinople have they brought me now
　　Only for pleasure of these damnèd slaves. **35**

ROBIN. By lady sir, you have had a shrewd[5] journey of it. Will it please you to take a shoulder of mutton to supper and a tester[6] in your purse and go back again?

DICK. Ay, I pray you heartily, sir. For we called you but in jest, I promise you. **40**

MEPHOSTOPHILIS. To purge the rashness of this cursèd deed,
　　First be thou turnèd to this ugly shape,
　　For apish[7] deeds transformèd to an ape.

ROBIN. O brave! An ape! I pray sir, let me have the **45** carrying of him about to show some tricks.

MEPHOSTOPHILIS. And so thou shalt. Be thou transformed to a dog and carry him upon thy back. Away, be gone!

ROBIN. A dog! That's excellent. Let the maids look **50** well to their porridge-pots, for I'll into the kitchen presently. Come Dick, come. (*Exeunt the two* CLOWNS.)

MEPHOSTOPHILIS.
　　Now with the flames of ever-burning fire
　　I'll wing myself and forthwith fly amain
　　Unto my Faustus, to the Great Turk's court. **55**
(*Exit.*)

ACT FOUR

Enter CHORUS.

　　When Faustus had with pleasure ta'en the view
　　Of rarest things and royal courts of kings,
　　He stayed his course and so returnèd home,
　　Where such as bare his absence but with grief,
　　I mean his friends and nearest companions, **5**
　　Did gratulate[1] his safety with kind words.
　　And in their conference[2] of what befell
　　Touching his journey through the world and air
　　They put forth questions of astrology
　　Which Faustus answered with such learnèd skill **10**
　　As they admired and wondered at his wit.
　　Now is his fame spread forth in every land.
　　Amongst the rest the Emperor is one,
　　Carolus the Fifth,[3] at whose palace now
　　Faustus is feasted 'mongst his noblemen. **15**
　　What there he did in trial of his art
　　I leave untold, your eyes shall see performed. (*Exit.*)

SCENE ONE

Enter MARTINO *and* FREDERICK *at several[1] doors.*

MARTINO.
　　What ho, officers, gentlemen!
　　Hie to the presence[2] to attend the Emperor.
　　Good Frederick, see the rooms be voided straight,[3]

---

[1]**at the hard heels** hard at heel, closely [2]**companions** fellows (contemptuous) [3]**beyond us both** (apparently Robin has managed to place the cup at some distance from where he now stands) [4]**When, can you tell** (a scornful reply) [5]**shrewd** bad [6]**tester** sixpence

[7]**apish** (1) foolish (2) imitative IV Chorus [1]**gratulate** express joy in [2]**conference** discussion [3]**Carolus the Fifth** Charles V (1500–58), Holy Roman Emperor [1]**several** separate [2]**presence** presence-chamber [3]**voided straight** emptied immediately

His Majesty is coming to the hall.
Go back and see the state[4] in readiness.   5
FREDERICK.
But where is Bruno, our elected Pope,
That on a fury's back came post from Rome?
Will not his Grace consort[5] the Emperor?
MARTINO.
O yes, and with him comes the German conjurer,
The learnèd Faustus, fame of Wittenberg,   10
The wonder of the world for magic art:
And he intends to show great Carolus
The race of all his stout progenitors
And bring in presence of his Majesty
The royal shapes and warlike semblances   15
Of Alexander and his beauteous paramour.[6]
FREDERICK.   Where is Benvolio?
MARTINO.
                              Fast asleep, I warrant you.
He took his rouse with stoups[7] of Rhenish wine
So kindly yesternight to Bruno's health   20
That all this day the sluggard keeps his bed.
FREDERICK.   See, see, his window's ope. We'll call to him.
MARTINO.   What ho, Benvolio!

Enter BENVOLIO *above at a window, in his nightcap,*
buttoning.

BENVOLIO.   What a devil ail you two?
MARTINO.
Speak softly sir, lest the devil hear you,   25
For Faustus at the court is late arrived
And at his heels a thousand furies wait
To accomplish whatsoever the doctor please.
BENVOLIO.   What of this?
MARTINO.
Come, leave thy chamber first, and thou shalt see   30
This conjurer perform such rare exploits
Before the Pope[8] and royal Emperor
As never yet was seen in Germany.
BENVOLIO.
Has not the Pope enough of conjuring yet?
He was upon the devil's back late enough!   35
And if he be so far in love with him
I would he would post with him to Rome again.
FREDERICK.   Speak, wilt thou come and see this sport?
BENVOLIO.   Not I.
MARTINO.   Wilt thou stand in thy window and see   40
it then?
BENVOLIO.   Ay, and I fall not asleep i' th' meantime.

MARTINO.
The Emperor is at hand, who comes to see
What wonders by black spells may compassed be.
BENVOLIO.   Well, go you attend the Emperor. I am   45
content for this once to thrust my head out at a window,
for they say if a man be drunk overnight the devil cannot
hurt him in the morning. If that be true, I have a charm
in my head shall control him as well as the conjurer, I
warrant you.   50
    Exit (MARTINO *with* FREDERICK. BENVOLIO *remains*
    at window).[9]

SCENE TWO

A sennet.[1] CHARLES THE GERMAN EMPEROR, BRUNO, (DUKE
OF) SAXONY, FAUSTUS, MEPHOSTOPHILIS, FREDERICK, MAR-
TINO, *and* ATTENDANTS.

EMPEROR.
Wonder of men, renowned magician,
Thrice-learnèd Faustus, welcome to our court.
This deed of thine in setting Bruno free
From his and our professèd enemy,
Shall add more excellence unto thine art   5
Than if by powerful necromantic spells
Thou could'st command the world's obedience.
For ever be beloved of Carolus!
And if this Bruno thou hast late redeemed[2]
In peace possess the triple diadem   10
And sit in Peter's chair despite of chance,
Thou shalt be famous through all Italy
And honored of the German Emperor.
FAUSTUS.
These gracious words, most royal Carolus,
Shall make poor Faustus to his utmost power   15
Both love and serve the German Emperor
And lay his life at holy Bruno's feet.
For proof whereof, if so your Grace be pleased,
The doctor stands prepared by power of art
To cast his magic charms that shall pierce
    through   20
The ebon gates of ever-burning hell,
And hale the stubborn furies from their caves
To compass whatsoe'er your Grace commands.

---

[4]**state** chair of state, throne   [5]**consort** attend   [6]**Alexander and his**
beauteous paramour Alexander the Great and his mistress Thaïs
[7]**took his rouse with stoups** had drinking bouts with full goblets
[8]**the pope** i.e., Bruno

[9]**Benvolio remains at window** (because Benvolio does not leave
the stage, this scene cannot properly be said to be ended. But the
present edition, following its predecessors for convenience of
reference, begins a new scene)   [1]**sennet** trumpet fanfare (the
absence of a verb in the rest of the stage direction perhaps
indicates that the Emperor and his party do not enter but rather are
"discovered," as Faustus may have been discovered at the
beginning of I.i, if the Chorus drew back a curtain)   [2]**redeemed**
freed

BENVOLIO.   Blood! He speaks terribly. But for all that I do
    not greatly believe him. He looks as like a conjurer   25
    as the Pope to a costermonger.[3]
EMPEROR.
    Then Faustus, as thou late didst promise us,
    We would behold that famous conqueror
    Great Alexander and his paramour
    In their true shapes and state majestical,   30
    That we may wonder at their excellence.
FAUSTUS.
    Your Majesty shall see them presently.—
    Mephostophilis away,
    And with a solemn noise of trumpets' sound
    Present before this royal Emperor   35
    Great Alexander and his beauteous paramour.
MEPHOSTOPHILIS.   Faustus, I will. (*Exit.*)
BENVOLIO.   Well master doctor, an your devils come not
    away quickly, you shall have me asleep presently.
    Zounds,[4] I could eat myself for anger to think I   40
    have been such an ass all this while to stand gaping after
    the devils' governor and can see nothing.
FAUSTUS.
    I'll make you feel something anon if my art
    fail me not!
    My lord, I must forewarn your Majesty   45
    That when my spirits present the royal shapes
    Of Alexander and his paramour,
    Your Grace demand no questions of the King
    But in dumb silence let them come and go.
EMPEROR.   Be it as Faustus please; we are content.   50
BENVOLIO.   Ay ay, and I am content too. And thou bring
    Alexander and his paramour before the Emperor, I'll be
    Actaeon[5] and turn myself to a stag.
FAUSTUS (*aside*). And I'll play Diana and send you the horns
    presently.   55

Sennet. Enter at one (*door*) *the* EMPEROR ALEXANDER, *at the
other* DARIUS.[6] *They meet.* DARIUS *is thrown down.* ALEX-
ANDER *kills him, takes off his crown, and offering to go out,
his* PARAMOUR *meets him. He embraceth her and sets*
DARIUS' *crown upon her head, and coming back both salute
the* EMPEROR; *who leaving his state offers to embrace them,
which* FAUSTUS *seeing suddenly stays him. Then trumpets
cease and music sounds.*

    My gracious lord, you do forget yourself.
    These are but shadows, not substantial.
EMPEROR.
    O pardon me, my thoughts are so ravished
    With sight of this renownèd Emperor,

That in mine arms I would have compassed[7] him.   60
But Faustus, since I may not speak to them,
To satisfy my longing thoughts at full,
Let me this tell thee: I have heard it said
That this fair lady whilst she lived on earth,
Had on her neck a little wart or mole.   65
How may I prove that saying to be true?
FAUSTUS.   Your Majesty may boldly go and see.
EMPEROR.
    Faustus, I see it plain!
    And in this sight thou better pleasest me
    Than if I gained another monarchy.   70
FAUSTUS.
    Away, be gone! (*Exit show.*)
    See, see, my gracious lord, what strange beast is
    yon that thrusts his head out at the window!
EMPEROR.
    O wondrous sight! See, Duke of Saxony,
    Two spreading horns most strangely fastened   75
    Upon the head of young Benvolio.
SAXONY.   What, is he asleep or dead?
FAUSTUS.   He sleeps my lord, but dreams not of his horns.
EMPEROR.
    This sport is excellent. We'll call and wake him.
    What ho, Benvolio!   80
BENVOLIO.   A plague upon you! Let me sleep awhile.
EMPEROR.   I blame thee not to sleep much, having such a
    head of thine own.
SAXONY.   Look up Benvolio! 'Tis the Emperor calls.
BENVOLIO.   The Emperor! Where? O zounds, my   85
    head!
EMPEROR.   Nay, and thy horns hold, 'tis no matter for thy
    head, for that's armed sufficiently.
FAUSTUS.   Why, how now Sir Knight? What, hanged by the
    horns?[8] This is most horrible! Fie fie, pull in your   90
    head for shame! Let not all the world wonder at you.
BENVOLIO.   Zounds doctor, is this your villainy?
FAUSTUS.
    Oh, say not so sir: The doctor has no skill,
    No art, no cunning to present these lords
    Or bring before this royal Emperor   95
    The mighty monarch, warlike Alexander.
    If Faustus do it, you are straight resolved
    In bold Actaeon's shape to turn a stag.
    And therefore my lord, so please your Majesty,
    I'll raise a kennel of hounds shall hunt him so   100
    As all his footmanship shall scarce prevail
    To keep his carcass from their bloody fangs.
    Ho, Belimote, Argiron, Asterote!

---

[3]**costermonger** fruit-seller [4]**Zounds** by God's wounds [5]**Actaeon**
legendary hunter who saw the naked goddess Diana bathing. She
transformed him into a stag, and he was torn to pieces by his own
hounds [6]**Darius** King of Persia, defeated by Alexander in
334 B.C.

[7]**compassed** encompassed, embraced [8]**hanged by the horns** (the
spreading horns prevent Benvolio from pulling his head inside of
the window)

BENVOLIO.   Hold, hold! Zounds, he'll raise up a kennel of
    devils I think, anon. Good my lord, entreat for   105
    me. 'Sblood,[9] I am never able to endure these torments.
EMPEROR.
       Then good master doctor,
    Let me entreat you to remove his horns.
    He has done penance now sufficiently.
FAUSTUS.   My gracious lord, not so much for injury   110
    done to me, as to delight your Majesty with some mirth,
    hath Faustus justly requited this injurious[10] knight; which
    being all I desire, I am content to remove his horns.
    Mephostophilis, transform him. And hereafter sir, look
    you speak well of scholars.   115
BENVOLIO (aside). Speak well of ye! 'Sblood, and scholars
    be such cuckold-makers to clap horns of honest men's
    heads o' this order, I'll ne'er trust smooth faces and small
    ruffs[11] more. But an I be not revenged for this, would I
    might be turned to a gaping oyster and drink   120
    nothing but salt water. (Exit.)
EMPEROR.
    Come Faustus, while the Emperor lives,
    In recompense of this thy high desert,
    Thou shalt command the state of Germany
    And live beloved of mighty Carolus.   125
    (Exeunt omnes.)

SCENE THREE

Enter BENVOLIO, MARTINO, FREDERICK, and SOLDIERS.

MARTINO.
    Nay, sweet Benvolio, let us sway thy thoughts
    From this attempt against the conjurer.
BENVOLIO.
    Away! You love me not to urge me thus.
    Shall I let slip[1] so great an injury
    When every servile groom jests at my wrongs   5
    And in their rustic gambols proudly say,
    ''Benvolio's head was graced with horns today''?
    O, may these eyelids never close again
    Till with my sword I have that conjurer slain!
    If you will aid me in this enterprise,   10
    Then draw your weapons and be resolute;
    If not, depart. Here will Benvolio die
    But[2] Faustus' death shall quit[3] my infamy.
FREDERICK.
    Nay, we will stay with thee, betide what may,
    And kill that doctor if he come this way.   15
BENVOLIO.
    Then, gentle Frederick, hie thee to the grove
    And place our servants and our followers

Close in an ambush there behind the trees.
    By this, I know, the conjurer is near.
    I saw him kneel and kiss the Emperor's hand   20
    And take his leave laden with rich rewards.
    Then soldiers, boldly fight. If Faustus die,
    Take you the wealth, leave us the victory.
FREDERICK.
    Come soldiers, follow me unto the grove.
    Who kills him shall have gold and endless love.   25
       (Exit FREDERICK with the SOLDIERS.)
BENVOLIO.
    My head is lighter than it was by th' horns—
    But yet my heart more ponderous than my head,
    And pants until I see that conjurer dead.
MARTINO.   Where shall we place ourselves, Benvolio?
BENVOLIO.
    Here will we stay to bide the first assault.   30
    O, were that damnèd hell-hound but in place
    Thou soon should'st see me quit my foul disgrace.

Enter FREDERICK.

FREDERICK.
    Close, close! The conjurer is at hand
    And all alone comes walking in his gown.
    Be ready then and strike the peasant[4] down!   35
BENVOLIO.
    Mine be that honor then! Now sword, strike home!
    For horns he gave I'll have his head anon.

Enter FAUSTUS with the false head.

MARTINO.   See see, he comes.
BENVOLIO.
               No words. This blow ends
      all! (Strikes FAUSTUS.)
    Hell take his soul, his body thus must fall.   40
FAUSTUS.   O!
FREDERICK.   Groan you, master doctor?
BENVOLIO.
    Break may his heart with groans! Dear Frederick,
      see,
    Thus will I end his griefs immediately.

(Cuts off FAUSTUS' false head.)

MARTINO.   Strike with a willing hand! His head is   45
    off.
BENVOLIO.   The devil's dead, the furies now may laugh.
FREDERICK.
    Was this that stern aspect, that awful frown,
    Made the grim monarch of infernal spirits
    Tremble and quake at his commanding charms?   50

---

[9]**'Sblood** by God's blood   [10]**injurious** insulting   [11]**small ruffs**
(worn by scholars, in contrast to the large ruffs worn by courtiers)
[1]**let slip** ignore   [2]**But** unless   [3]**quit** avenge

[4]**peasant** low fellow

MARTINO.
  Was this that damnèd head whose heart conspired
  Benvolio's shame before the Emperor?
BENVOLIO.
  Ay, that's the head, and here the body lies
  Justly rewarded for his villainies.
FREDERICK.
  Come let's devise how we may add more shame   **55**
  To the black scandal of his hated name.
BENVOLIO.
  First, on his head in quittance of my wrongs
  I'll nail huge forkèd horns and let them hang
  Within the window where he yoked me first
  That all the world may see my just revenge.   **60**
MARTINO.   What use shall we put his beard to?
BENVOLIO.   We'll sell it to a chimney-sweeper. It will
  wear out ten birchen brooms, I warrant you.
FREDERICK.   What shall eyes do?
BENVOLIO.   We'll put out his eyes, and they shall   **65**
  serve for buttons to his lips to keep his tongue from
  catching cold.
MARTINO.   An excellent policy! And now sirs, having di-
  vided him, what shall the body do? (FAUSTUS *rises*.)
BENVOLIO.   Zounds, the devil's alive again!   **70**
FREDERICK.   Give him his head for God's sake!
FAUSTUS.
  Nay keep it. Faustus will have heads and hands,
  Ay, all your hearts, to recompense this deed.
  Knew you not, traitors, I was limited
  For four and twenty years to breathe on earth?   **75**
  And had you cut my body with your swords
  Or hewed this flesh and bones as small as sand,
  Yet in a minute had my spirit returned
  And I had breathed a man made free from harm.
  But wherefore do I dally my revenge?   **80**
  Asteroth, Belimoth, Mephostophilis!

Enter MEPHOSTOPHILIS *and other* DEVILS.

  Go horse these traitors on your fiery backs
  And mount aloft with them as high as heaven,
  Thence pitch them headlong to the lowest hell.
  Yet stay, the world shall see their misery,   **85**
  And hell shall after plague their treachery.
  Go Belimoth, and take this caitiff[5] hence
  And hurl him in some lake of mud and dirt:
  Take thou this other, drag him through the woods
  Amongst the pricking thorns and sharpest briars: **90**
  Whilst with my gentle Mephostophilis
  This traitor flies unto some steepy rock
  That rolling down may break the villain's bones
  As he intended to dismember me.
  Fly hence, dispatch my charge immediately!   **95**

FREDERICK.   Pity us, gentle Faustus, save our lives!
FAUSTUS.   Away!
FREDERICK.   He must needs go that the devil drives.
  (*Exeunt* SPIRITS *with the* KNIGHTS.)

Enter the ambushed SOLDIERS.

1 SOLDIER.
  Come sirs, prepare yourselves in readiness.
  Make haste to help these noble gentlemen.   **100**
  I heard them parley with the conjurer.
2 SOLDIER.   See where he comes, dispatch, and kill the
  slave!
FAUSTUS.
  What's here, an ambush to betray my life?
  Then Faustus, try thy skill. Base peasants, stand! **105**
  For lo, these trees remove[6] at my command
  And stand as bulwarks 'twixt yourselves and me
  To shield me from your hated treachery!
  Yet to encounter this your weak attempt
  Behold an army comes incontinent.[7]   **110**

FAUSTUS *strikes the door, and enter a* DEVIL *playing on a
drum, after him another bearing an ensign, and divers with
weapons:* MEPHOSTOPHILIS *with fireworks: they set upon the*
SOLDIERS *and drive them out.* (*Exeunt all.*)

SCENE FOUR

Enter at several doors BENVOLIO, FREDERICK, *and* MAR-
TINO, *their heads and faces bloody and besmeared with mud
and dirt, all having horns on their heads.*

MARTINO.   What ho, Benvolio!
BENVOLIO.   Here! What, Frederick, ho!
FREDERICK.   O, help me gentle friend. Where is Martino?
MARTINO.
  Dear Frederick, here,
  Half smothered in a lake of mud and dirt,   **5**
  Through which the furies dragged me by the heels.
FREDERICK.   Martino, see, Benvolio's horns again.
MARTINO.   O misery! How now Benvolio?
BENVOLIO.   Defend me, heaven! Shall I be haunted[1] still?
MARTINO.   Nay fear not man, we have no power to   **10**
  kill.
BENVOLIO.
  My friends transformèd thus! O hellish spite,
  Your heads are all set with horns.
FREDERICK.   You hit it right:
  It is your own you mean. Feel on your head.   **15**
BENVOLIO.   Zounds, horns again!

---

[5]**caitiff** wretch

[6]**remove** move   [7]**incontinent** immediately   [1]**haunted** (the
following line suggests that there is a quibble on ''hunted,''
Benvolio now resembling a stag)

MARTINO.   Nay chafe[2] not man, we all are sped.[3]
BENVOLIO.
　What devil attends this damned magician,
　That spite of spite our wrongs are doubled?
FREDERICK.   What may we do that we may hide our   20
shames?
BENVOLIO.
　If we should follow him to work revenge
　He'd join long asses' ears to these huge horns
　And make us laughing-stocks to all the world.
MARTINO.   What shall we then do, dear Benvolio?   25
BENVOLIO.
　I have a castle joining near these woods,
　And thither we'll repair and live obscure
　Till time shall alter this our brutish shapes.
　Sith[4] black disgrace hath thus eclipsed our fame,
　We'll rather die with grief than live with shame.   30
　(*Exeunt omnes.*)

SCENE FIVE

Enter FAUSTUS *and the* HORSE-COURSER.[1]

HORSE-COURSER.   I beseech your worship, accept of these
forty dollars.[2]
FAUSTUS.   Friend, thou canst not buy so good a horse for
so small a price. I have no great need to sell him, but if
thou likest him for ten dollars more, take him, be-   5
cause I see thou hast a good mind to him.
HORSE-COURSER.   I beseech you sir, accept of this. I am
a very poor man and have lost very much of late by horse-
flesh,[3] and this bargain will set me up again.
FAUSTUS.   Well, I will not stand[4] with thee. Give me   10
the money. Now sirrah, I must tell you that you may ride
him o'er hedge and ditch and spare him not. But, do you
hear, in any case ride him not into the water.
HORSE-COURSER.   How sir, not into the water! Why, will
he not drink of all waters?[5]   15
FAUSTUS.   Yes, he will drink of all waters, but ride him not
into the water: o'er hedge and ditch or where thou wilt,
but not into the water. Go bid the hostler deliver him unto
you, and remember what I say.
HORSE-COURSER.   I warrant you sir. O joyful day!   20
Now am I a made man forever. (*Exit.*)
FAUSTUS.
　What art thou, Faustus, but a man condemned
　　to die?
　Thy fatal time[6] draws to a final end;

---

[2]**chafe** fret   [3]**sped** done for, ruined (because of the horns)   [4]**Sith**
since   [1]**Horse-courser** horse trader   [2]**dollars** German coins
[3]**horse-flesh** (the possibility of a quibble on "whores' flesh" is
increased by "set me up" and "stand" in the ensuing dialogue)
[4]**stand** haggle   [5]**drink of all waters** i.e., go anywhere   [6]**fatal
time** life span

Despair doth drive distrust into my thoughts.
Confound these passions with a quiet sleep.   25
Tush, Christ did call the thief upon the cross![7]
Then rest thee Faustus, quiet in conceit.[8]
　(*He sits to sleep.*)

Enter the HORSE-COURSER *wet.*

HORSE-COURSER.   O what a cozening[9] doctor was this! I
riding my horse into the water, thinking some hidden
mystery had been in the horse, I had nothing under   30
me but a little straw and had much ado to escape
drowning. Well, I'll go rouse him and make him give me
my forty dollars again. Ho, sirrah doctor, you cozening
scab! Master doctor, awake and rise, and give me my
money again, for your horse is turned to a bottle[10]   35
of hay. Master doctor! (*He pulls off his leg.*) Alas, I am
undone! What shall I do? I have pulled off his leg.
FAUSTUS.   O help, help! The villain hath murdered me!
HORSE-COURSER.   Murder or not murder, now he has but
one leg I'll outrun him, and cast this leg into some   40
ditch or other. (*Exit.*)
FAUSTUS.   Stop him, stop him, stop him!—Ha, ha, ha!
Faustus hath his leg again, and the horse-courser a bundle
of hay for his forty dollars.

Enter WAGNER.

How now, Wagner? What news with thee?   45
WAGNER.   If it please you, the Duke of Vanholt doth earnestly entreat your company, and hath sent some of his
men to attend you with provision fit for your journey.
FAUSTUS.   The Duke of Vanholt's an honorable gentleman,
and one to whom I must be no niggard of my cun-   50
ning. Come, away! (*Exeunt.*)

SCENE SIX

Enter (ROBIN THE) CLOWN, DICK, HORSE-COURSER, *and a*
CARTER.

CARTER.   Come my masters, I'll bring you to the best beer
in Europe. What ho, hostess! Where be these whores?

Enter HOSTESS.

HOSTESS.   How now? What lack you? What, my old guests,
welcome.
ROBIN (*aside*).   Sirrah Dick, dost thou know why I   5
stand so mute?
DICK (*aside*).   No Robin, why is't?

---

[7]**Christ . . . cross** (in Luke 23:39–43 Christ promised one of the
thieves that he would be with Christ in paradise)   [8]**quiet in
conceit** with a quiet mind   [9]**cozening** deceiving   [10]**bottle** bundle

ROBIN (*aside*). I am eighteen pence on the score.[1] But say nothing. See if she have forgotten me.

HOSTESS.   Who's this that stands so solemnly by **10** himself? What, my old guest!

ROBIN.   O, hostess, how do you? I hope my score stands still.

HOSTESS.   Ay, there's no doubt of that, for methinks you make no haste to wipe it out.   **15**

DICK.   Why hostess, I say, fetch us some beer!

HOSTESS.   You shall, presently.—Look up into th' hall there, ho! (*Exit*.)

DICK.   Come sirs, what shall we do now till mine hostess comes?   **20**

CARTER.   Marry sir, I'll tell you the bravest tale how a conjurer served me. You know Doctor Fauster?

HORSE-COURSER.   Ay, a plague take him! Here's some on's have cause to know him. Did he conjure thee too?

CARTER.   I'll tell you how he served me. As I was **25** going to Wittenberg t'other day with a load of hay, he met me and asked me what he should give me for as much hay as he could eat. Now sir, I thinking that a little would serve his turn, bad him take as much as he would for three farthings. So he presently gave me my money and **30** fell to eating; and as I am a cursen[2] man, he never left eating till he had eat up all my load of hay.

ALL.   O monstrous, eat a whole load of hay!

ROBIN.   Yes yes, that may be, for I have heard of one that has eat a load of logs.[3]   **35**

HORSE-COURSER.   Now sirs, you shall hear how villainously he served me. I went to him yesterday to buy a horse of him, and he would by no means sell him under forty dollars. So sir, because I knew him to be such a horse as would run over hedge and ditch and never tire, I **40** gave him his money. So, when I had my horse, Doctor Fauster bade me ride him night and day and spare him no time. "But," quoth he, "in any case ride him not into the water." Now sir, I thinking the horse had had some quality that he would not have me know of, what **45** did I but rid him into a great river—and when I came just in the midst, my horse vanished away and I sate straddling upon a bottle of hay.

ALL.   O brave doctor!

HORSE-COURSER.   But you shall hear how bravely **50** I served him for it. I went me home to his house, and there I found him asleep. I kept ahallowing and whooping in his ears, but all could not wake him. I seeing that, took him by the leg and never rested pulling till I had pulled me his leg quite off, and now 'tis at home in mine **55** hostry.[4]

DICK.   And has the doctor but one leg then? That's excellent, for one of his devils turned me into the likeness of an ape's face.

CARTER.   Some more drink, hostess!   **60**

ROBIN.   Hark you, we'll into another room and drink awhile, and then we'll go seek out the doctor. (*Exeunt omnes*.)

SCENE SEVEN

Enter the DUKE OF VANHOLT, *his* (SERVANTS,) DUCHESS, FAUSTUS, *and* MEPHOSTOPHILIS.

DUKE.   Thanks master doctor, for these pleasant sights. Nor know I how sufficiently to recompense your great deserts in erecting that enchanted castle in the air, the sight whereof so delighted me,
As nothing in the world could please me more.   **5**

FAUSTUS.   I do think myself, my good lord, highly recompensed in that it pleaseth your Grace to think but well of that which Faustus hath performed.—But gracious lady, it may be that you have taken no pleasure in those sights. Therefore I pray you tell me what is the thing you **10** most desire to have: be it in the world it shall be yours. I have heard that great-bellied[1] women do long for things are rare and dainty.

DUCHESS.   True master doctor, and since I find you so kind, I will make known unto you what my heart **15** desires to have: and were it now summer, as it is January, a dead time of the winter, I would request no better meat[2] than a dish of ripe grapes.

FAUSTUS.   This is but a small matter. Go Mephostophilis, away! (*Exit* MEPHOSTOPHILIS.) Madam, I will do **20** more than this for your content.

Enter MEPHOSTOPHILIS *again with the grapes*.

Here, now taste ye these. They should be good,
For they come from a far country, I can tell you.

DUKE.   This makes me wonder more than all the rest, that at this time of the year when every tree is barren **25** of his fruit, from whence you had these ripe grapes.

FAUSTUS.   Please it your Grace, the year is divided into two circles[3] over the whole world, so that when it is winter with us, in the contrary circle it is likewise summer with them, as in India, Saba, and such countries that lie **30** far east, where they have fruit twice a year. From whence, by means of a swift spirit that I have, I had these grapes brought as you see.

DUCHESS.   And trust me, they are the sweetest grapes that e'er I tasted.   **35**

The CLOWNS (ROBIN, DICK, CARTER, *and* HORSE-COURSER) *bounce*[4] *at the gate within.*

---

[1]**on the score** in debt [2]**cursen** i.e., Christian (dialect form) [3]**eat a load of logs** been drunk [4]**hostry** inn

[1]**great-bellied** i.e., pregnant [2]**meat** food [3]**two circles** i.e., the northern and the southern hemispheres (though later in the speech he talks of east and west rather than of north and south) [4]**bounce** knock

DUKE.

> What rude disturbers have we at the gate?
> Go pacify their fury, set it ope,
> And then demand of them what they would have.

They knock again and call out to talk with FAUSTUS.

A SERVANT.

> Why, how now masters, what a coil⁵ is there!
> What is the reason⁶ you disturb the Duke?   **40**

DICK.   We have no reason for it, therefore a fig for him!

SERVANT.   Why saucy varlets, dare you be so bold!

HORSE-COURSER.   I hope sir, we have wit enough to be more bold than welcome.

SERVANT.

> It appears so. Pray be bold elsewhere   **45**
> And trouble not the Duke.

DUKE.   What would they have?

SERVANT.   They all cry out to speak with Doctor Faustus.

CARTER.   Ay, and we will speak with him.

DUKE.   Will you sir? Commit⁷ the rascals.   **50**

DICK.   Commit with us! He were as good commit with his father as commit with us!

FAUSTUS.

> I do beseech your Grace, let them come in.
> They are good subject for a merriment.

DUKE.   Do as thou wilt, Faustus, I give thee leave.   **55**

FAUSTUS.   I thank your Grace.

Enter (ROBIN) THE CLOWN, DICK, CARTER, *and* HORSE-COURSER.

> Why, how now my good friends?
> 'Faith, you are too outrageous; but come near,
> I have procured your pardons. Welcome all.

ROBIN.   Nay sir, we will be welcome for our money,   **60** and we will pay for what we take. What ho, give's half a dozen of beer here, and be hanged!

FAUSTUS.   Nay, hark you, can you tell me where you are?

CARTER.   Ay, marry can I, we are under heaven.

SERVANT.   Ay, but Sir Sauce-box, know you in what   **65** place?

HORSE-COURSER.   Ay ay, the house is good enough to drink in. Zounds, fill us some beer, or we'll break all the barrels in the house and dash out all your brains with your bottles.   **70**

FAUSTUS.

> Be not so furious. Come, you shall have beer.
> My lord, beseech you give me leave awhile;
> I'll gage⁸ my credit 'twill content your Grace.

DUKE.

> With all my heart, kind doctor, please thyself.
> Our servants and our court's at thy command.   **75**

FAUSTUS.   I humbly thank your Grace.—Then fetch some beer.

HORSE-COURSER.   Ay marry, there spake a doctor indeed! And 'faith, I'll drink a health to thy wooden leg for that word.   **80**

FAUSTUS.   My wooden leg? What dost thou mean by that?

CARTER.   Ha, ha, ha, dost hear him Dick? He has forgot his leg.

HORSE-COURSER.   Ay ay, he does not stand much upon⁹ that.   **85**

FAUSTUS.   No, 'faith, not much upon a wooden leg.

CARTER.   Good lord, that flesh and blood should be so frail with your worship! Do not you remember a horse-courser you sold a horse to?

FAUSTUS.   Yes, I remember I sold one a horse.   **90**

CARTER.   And do you remember you bid he should not ride into the water?

FAUSTUS.   Yes, I do very well remember that.

CARTER.   And do you remember nothing of your leg?

FAUSTUS.   No, in good sooth.   **95**

CARTER.   Then I pray remember your curtsy.¹⁰

FAUSTUS.   I thank you sir.

CARTER.   'Tis not so much worth. I pray you tell me one thing.

FAUSTUS.   What's that?   **100**

CARTER.   Be both your legs bedfellows every night together?

FAUSTUS.   Would'st thou make a colossus¹¹ of me that thou askest me such questions?

CARTER.   No, truly sir, I would make nothing of   **105** you, but I would fain know that.

Enter HOSTESS *with drink*.

FAUSTUS.   Then I assure thee certainly they are.

CARTER.   I thank you, I am fully satisfied.

FAUSTUS.   But wherefore dost thou ask?

CARTER.   For nothing, sir, but methinks you should   **110** have a wooden bedfellow of one of 'em.

HORSE-COURSER.   Why, do you hear sir, did not I pull off one of your legs when you were asleep?

FAUSTUS.   But I have it again now I am awake. Look you here sir.   **115**

ALL.   O horrible! Had the doctor three legs?

CARTER.   Do you remember sir, how you cozened me and eat up my load of— (FAUSTUS *charms him dumb*.)

---

⁵**coil** turmoil   ⁶**reason** (pronounced like "raisin," leading to the quibble on "fig"; a "fig" here is an obscene contemptuous gesture in which the hand is clenched and the thumb is thrust between the first and second fingers, making the thumb resemble the stem of a fig, or a penis)   ⁷**Commit** imprison (Dick proceeds to quibble on the idea of committing adultery)   ⁸**gage** pledge

⁹**stand much upon** (quibble on "attach much importance to")   ¹⁰**curtsy** (also called "a leg," hence there is a quibble on the Carter's previous speech)   ¹¹**colossus** huge statue in the harbor at Rhodes, between whose legs ships were said to have sailed

DICK.   Do you remember how you made me wear an ape's— (FAUSTUS *charms him*.)   **120**

HORSE-COURSER.   You whoreson conjuring scab! Do you remember how you cozened me with a ho— (FAUSTUS *charms him*.)

ROBIN.   Ha' you forgotten me? You think to carry it away with your "hey-pass" and "re-pass"?[12] Do you remember the dog's fa— (FAUSTUS *charms him*.)   **125**
Exeunt CLOWNS.

HOSTESS.   Who pays for the ale? Hear you master doctor, now you have sent away my guests, I pray who shall pay me for my a— (FAUSTUS *charms her*.) *Exit* HOSTESS.

DUCHESS.
    My lord,
    We are much beholding to this learnèd man.   **130**

DUKE.
    So are we madam, which we will recompense
    With all the love and kindness that we may:
    His artful sport drives all sad thoughts away.
        (*Exeunt*.)

ACT FIVE

SCENE ONE

Thunder and lightning. Enter DEVILS *with covered dishes:* MEPHOSTOPHILIS *leads them into* FAUSTUS' *study. Then enter* WAGNER.

WAGNER.   I think my master means to die shortly. He has made his will and given me his wealth: his house, his goods, and store of golden plate—besides two thousand ducats ready coined. I wonder what he means. If death were nigh, he would not frolic thus. He's now at   **5** supper with the scholars, where there's such belly-cheer as Wagner in his life ne'er saw the like! And see where they come. Belike[1] the feast is done.[2] (*Exit*.)

Enter FAUSTUS, MEPHOSTOPHILIS, *and two or three* SCHOLARS.

1 SCHOLAR.   Master Doctor Faustus, since our conference about fair ladies, which was the beautifulest in all   **10** the world, we have determined with ourselves that Helen of Greece was the admirablest lady that ever lived. Therefore master doctor, if you will do us so much favor as to let us see that peerless dame of Greece, whom all the world admires for majesty, we should think our-   **15** selves much beholding unto you.

FAUSTUS.
    Gentlemen,
    For that I know your friendship is unfeigned,

It is not Faustus' custom to deny
The just request of those that wish him well: **20**
You shall behold that peerless dame of Greece
No otherwise for pomp or majesty
Than when Sir Paris crossed the seas with her
And brought the spoils[3] to rich Dardania.[4]
Be silent then, for danger is in words.   **25**

Music sounds. MEPHOSTOPHILIS *brings in* HELEN: *she passeth over the stage.*

2 SCHOLAR.
    Was this fair Helen, whose admired worth
    Made Greece with ten years' wars afflict poor Troy?

3 SCHOLAR.
    Too simple is my wit to tell her worth,
    Whom all the world admires for majesty.

1 SCHOLAR.
    Now we have seen the pride of nature's work,   **30**
    We'll take our leaves, and for this blessèd sight
    Happy and blest be Faustus evermore.

FAUSTUS.   Gentlemen, farewell, the same wish I to you.
    (*Exeunt* SCHOLARS.)

Enter an OLD MAN.

OLD MAN.
    O gentle Faustus, leave this damnèd art,
    This magic that will charm thy soul to hell   **35**
    And quite bereave[5] thee of salvation.
    Though thou hast now offended like a man,
    Do not persever[6] in it like a devil.
    Yet, yet, thou hast an amiable soul[7]
    If sin by custom grow not into nature.   **40**
    Then, Faustus, will repentance come too late!
    Then, thou are banished from the sight of heaven!
    No mortal can express the pains of hell!
    It may be this my exhortation
    Seems harsh and all unpleasant. Let it not.   **45**
    For gentle son, I speak it not in wrath
    Or envy of thee but in tender love
    And pity of thy future misery:
    And so have hope that this my kind rebuke,
    Checking[8] thy body, may amend thy soul.   **50**

FAUSTUS.
    Where art thou, Faustus? Wretch, what hast
    thou done! (MEPHOSTOPHILIS *gives him a dagger*.)
    Hell claims his right and with a roaring voice
    Says "Faustus, come, thine hour is almost come!"
    And Faustus now will come to do thee right!   **55**

OLD MAN.
    O stay, good Faustus, stay thy desperate steps!
    I see an angel hover o'er thy head,

---

[12]**hey-pass, re-pass** conjuring expressions   [1]**Belike** most likely
[2]**I think . . . done** (though printed as prose in the quarto, as here, perhaps this speech should be verse, the lines ending *shortly, wealth, plate, coined, nigh, supper, belly-cheer, like, done*)

[3]**spoils** booty (including Helen)   [4]**Dardania** Troy   [5]**bereave** deprive   [6]**persever** (accent on second syllable)   [7]**an amiable soul** a soul worthy of love   [8]**Checking** rebuking

And with a vial full of precious grace
Offers to pour the same into thy soul:
Then call for mercy and avoid despair.   **60**

FAUSTUS.
O friend,
I feel thy words to comfort my distressèd soul:
Leave me awhile to ponder on my sins.

OLD MAN.
Faustus, I leave thee, but with grief of heart,
Fearing the enemy of thy hapless soul. (*Exit.*)   **65**

FAUSTUS.
Accursèd Faustus! Wretch, what hast thou done!
I do repent, and yet I do despair:
Hell strives with grace for conquest in my breast!
What shall I do to shun the snares of death?

MEPHOSTOPHILIS.
Thou traitor Faustus, I arrest thy soul   **70**
For disobedience to my sovereign lord.
Revolt,[9] or I'll in piecemeal tear thy flesh.

FAUSTUS.
I do repent I e'er offended him.
Sweet Mephostophilis, entreat thy lord
To pardon my unjust presumption,   **75**
And with my blood again I will confirm
The former vow I made to Lucifer.

MEPHOSTOPHILIS.
Do it then, Faustus, with unfeignèd heart
Lest greater dangers do attend thy drift.

FAUSTUS.
Torment, sweet friend, that base and agèd man   **80**
That durst dissuade me from thy Lucifer,
With greatest torment that our hell affords.

MEPHOSTOPHILIS.
His faith is great. I cannot touch his soul.
But what I may afflict his body with
I will attempt, which is but little worth.   **85**

FAUSTUS.
One thing, good servant, let me crave of thee
To glut the longing of my heart's desire:
That I may have unto my paramour
That heavenly Helen which I saw of late,
Whose sweet embraces may extinguish clear   **90**
Those thoughts that do dissuade me from my vow,
And keep mine oath I made to Lucifer.

MEPHOSTOPHILIS.
This or what else my Faustus shall desire
Shall be performed in twinkling of an eye.

Enter HELEN *again, passing over between two* CUPIDS.

FAUSTUS.
Was this the face that launched a thousand ships   **95**
And burnt the topless[10] towers of Ilium?[11]

Sweet Helen, make me immortal with a kiss.
Her lips suck forth my soul. See where it flies!
Come Helen, come, give me my soul again.
Here will I dwell, for heaven is in these lips   **100**
And all is dross that is not Helena.
I will be Paris, and for love of thee
Instead of Troy shall Wittenberg be sacked;
And I will combat with weak Menelaus[12]
And wear thy colors on my plumèd crest.   **105**
Yea, I will wound Achilles[13] in the heel
And then return to Helen for a kiss.
O, thou art fairer than the evening's air
Clad in the beauty of a thousand stars,
Brighter art thou than flaming Jupiter   **110**
When he appeared to hapless Semele,[14]
More lovely than the monarch of the sky
In wanton Arethusa's[15] azure arms,
And none but thou shalt be my paramour. (*Exeunt.*)

SCENE TWO

Thunder. Enter LUCIFER, BELZEBUB, *and* MEPHOSTOPHILIS.[1]

LUCIFER.
Thus from infernal Dis[2] do we ascend
To view the subjects of our monarchy,
Those souls which sin seals the black sons of hell.
'Mong which as chief, Faustus, we come to thee,
Bringing with us lasting damnation   **5**
To wait upon thy soul. The time is come
Which makes it forfeit.

MEPHOSTOPHILIS.
                              And this gloomy night
Here in this room will wretched Faustus be.

BELZEBUB.
And here we'll stay   **10**
To mark him how he doth demean himself.

MEPHOSTOPHILIS.
How should he but in desperate lunacy?
Fond[3] worldling, now his heart blood dries with
     grief,
His conscience kills it, and his laboring brain
Begets a world of idle fantasies   **15**
To overreach the devil; but all in vain:
His store of pleasures must be sauced with pain!

---

[12]**Menelaus** Greek king, deserted by Helen for Paris   [13]**Achilles** greatest of the Greek warriors   [14]**Semele** beloved by Jupiter, who promised to do whatever she wished; she asked to see him in his full splendor, and the sight incinerated her   [15]**Arethusa** a nymph, here apparently loved by Jupiter, "the monarch of the sky"
[1]**Enter Lucifer, Belzebub, and Mephostophilis** (probably they rise out of a trapdoor and ascend to the upper stage, Mephostophilis descending to the main stage at line 93)
[2]**infernal Dis** the underworld (named for its rules)   [3]**Fond** foolish

---

[9]**Revolt** return (to your allegiance)   [10]**topless** i.e., so tall their tops are beyond sight   [11]**Ilium** Troy

He and his servant Wagner are at hand.
Both come from drawing Faustus' latest will.
See where they come.   20

Enter FAUSTUS *and* WAGNER.

FAUSTUS.
Say Wagner, thou hast perused my will;
How dost thou like it?
WAGNER.
                                   Sir, so wondrous well
As in all humble duty I do yield
My life and lasting service for your love.   25

Enter the SCHOLARS.

FAUSTUS.   Gramercies,[4] Wagner.—Welcome gentlemen.
(*Exit* WAGNER.)
1 SCHOLAR.   Now worthy Faustus, methinks your looks are
changed.
FAUSTUS.   O gentlemen!
2 SCHOLAR.   What ails Faustus?   30
FAUSTUS.   Ah my sweet chamber-fellow, had I lived with
thee, then had I lived still!—But now must die eternally.
Look sirs, comes he not, comes he not?
1 SCHOLAR.   O my dear Faustus, what imports this fear?
2 SCHOLAR.   Is all our pleasure turned to melancholy?   35
3 SCHOLAR.   He is not well with being over-solitary.
2 SCHOLAR.   If it be so, we'll have physicians and Faustus
shall be cured.
3 SCHOLAR.   'Tis but a surfeit[5] sir, fear nothing.
FAUSTUS.   A surfeit of deadly sin that hath damned   40
both body and soul!
2 SCHOLAR.   Yet Faustus, look up to heaven and remember
mercy is infinite.
FAUSTUS.   But Faustus' offense can ne'er be pardoned.
The serpent that tempted Eve may be saved, but   45
not Faustus! O gentlemen, hear with patience and
tremble not at my speeches. Though my heart pant and
quiver to remember that I have been a student here these
thirty years, O, would I had never seen Wittenberg,
never read book.—And what wonders I have done   50
all Germany can witness, yea all the world, for which
Faustus hath lost both Germany and the world, yea
heaven itself—heaven, the seat of God, the throne of the
blessèd, the kingdom of joy—and must remain in hell
forever! hell, O hell forever! Sweet friends, what   55
shall become of Faustus being in hell forever?
2 SCHOLAR.   Yet Faustus, call on God.
FAUSTUS.   On God, whom Faustus hath abjured? On God,
whom Faustus hath blasphemed? O my God, I
would weep, but the devil draws in my tears! Gush   60
forth blood instead of tears, yea life and soul! O, he stays

my tongue! I would lift up my hands, but see, they hold
'em, they hold 'em!
ALL.   Who, Faustus?
FAUSTUS.   Why, Lucifer and Mephostophilis. O gen-   65
tlemen, I gave them my soul for my cunning.
ALL.   O, God forbid!
FAUSTUS.   God forbade it indeed, but Faustus hath done it.
For the vain pleasure of four and twenty years hath
Faustus lost eternal joy and felicity. I writ them a   70
bill with mine own blood. The date is expired. This is the
time. And he will fetch me.
1 SCHOLAR.   Why did not Faustus tell us of this before, that
divines might have prayed for thee?
FAUSTUS.   Oft have I thought to have done so, but   75
the devil threatened to tear me in pieces if I named God—
to fetch me body and soul if I once gave ear to divinity;
and now 'tis too late! Gentlemen, away, lest you perish
with me.
2 SCHOLAR.   O, what may we do to save Faustus?   80
FAUSTUS.   Talk not of me but save yourselves and depart.
3 SCHOLAR.   God will strengthen me. I will stay with
Faustus.
1 SCHOLAR.   Tempt not God, sweet friend, but let us into
the next room and pray for him.   85
FAUSTUS.   Ay, pray for me, pray for me. And what noise
soever you hear, come not unto me, for nothing can rescue
me.
2 SCHOLAR.   Pray thou, and we will pray that God may
have mercy upon thee.   90
FAUSTUS.   Gentlemen, farewell! If I live till morning, I'll
visit you. If not, Faustus is gone to hell.
ALL.   Faustus, farewell. (*Exeunt* SCHOLARS.)
MEPHOSTOPHILIS.
Ay, Faustus, now thou hast no hope of heaven.
Therefore, despair! Think only upon hell,   95
For that must be thy mansion, there to dwell.
FAUSTUS.
O thou bewitching fiend, 'twas thy temptation
Hath robbed me of eternal happiness.
MEPHOSTOPHILIS.
I do confess it Faustus, and rejoice.
'Twas I, that when thou wert i' the way to
heaven   100
Dammed up thy passage. When thou took'st the
book
To view the Scriptures, then I turned the leaves
And led thine eye.
What, weep'st thou! 'Tis too late, despair, farewell!
Fools that will laugh on earth, most weep in hell.
(*Exit.*)   105

Enter the GOOD ANGEL *and the* BAD ANGEL *at several doors.*

---

[4]**Gramercies** thank you   [5]**a surfeit** indigestion

GOOD ANGEL.

    O Faustus, if thou hadst given ear to me
    Innumerable joys had followèd thee.
    But thou did'st love the world.

BAD ANGEL.

                       Gave ear to me,
    And now must taste hell's pains perpetually.   **110**

GOOD ANGEL.

    O, what will all thy riches, pleasures, pomps
    Avail thee now?

BAD ANGEL.

               Nothing but vex thee more,
    To want in hell, that had on earth such store.
    Music while the throne[6] descends.

GOOD ANGEL.

    O, thou hast lost celestial happiness,   **115**
    Pleasures unspeakable, bliss without end.
    Had'st thou affected[7] sweet divinity,
    Hell or the devil had had no power on thee.
    Had'st thou kept on that way, Faustus behold
    In what resplendent glory thou had'st sat   **120**
    In yonder throne, like those bright shining saints,
    And triumphed over hell! That hast thou lost.
        (*Throne ascends.*)
    And now, poor soul, must thy good angel leave thee,
    The jaws of hell are open to receive thee. (*Exit.*)
        Hell is discovered.

BAD ANGEL.

    Now Faustus, let thine eyes with horror stare   **125**
    Into that vast perpetual torture-house.
    There are the furies, tossing damnèd souls
    On burning forks. Their bodies boil in lead.
    There are live quarters[8] broiling on the coals,
    That ne'er can die: this ever-burning chair   **130**
    Is for o'er-tortured souls to rest them in.
    These that are fed with sops of flaming fire
    Were gluttons and loved only delicates
    And laughed to see the poor starve at their gates.
    But yet all these are nothing. Thou shalt see   **135**
    Ten thousand tortures that more horrid be.

FAUSTUS.   O, I have seen enough to torture me.

BAD ANGEL.

    Nay, thou must feel them, taste the smart of all:
    He that loves pleasure must for pleasure fall.
    And so I leave thee Faustus, till anon: **140**
    Then wilt thou tumble in confusion.[9] (*Exit.*)
        The clock strikes eleven.

FAUSTUS.

    O Faustus!
    Now hast thou but one bare hour to live
    And then thou must be damned perpetually.

Stand still, you ever-moving spheres of Heaven   **145**
That time may cease and midnight never come:
Fair nature's eye, rise, rise again and make
Perpetual day, or let this hour be but a year,
A month, a week, a natural day—
That Faustus may repent and save his soul.   **150**
O lente lente currite noctis equi![10]
The stars move still, time runs, the clock will strike:
The devil will come, and Faustus must be damned!
O, I'll leap up to my God! Who pulls me down?
See, see where Christ's blood streams in the
    firmament!   **155**
One drop of blood will save me. O my Christ!—
Rend not my heart for naming of my Christ!
Yet will I call on Him! O spare me, Lucifer!—
Where is it now? 'Tis gone: and see where God
Stretcheth out His arm and bends His ireful
    brows!   **160**
Mountains and hills, come, come and fall on me
And hide me from the heavy wrath of God!
No?
Then will I headlong run into the earth.
Gape earth! O no, it will not harbor me.   **165**
You stars that reigned at my nativity,
Whose influence hath allotted death and hell,
Now draw up Faustus like a foggy mist
Into the entrails of yon laboring cloud
That when you vomit forth into the air,   **170**
My limbs may issue from your smoky mouths—
But let my soul mount and ascend to heaven!
    The watch strikes.
O half the hour is passed! 'Twill all be passed anon!
O God,
If thou wilt not have mercy on my soul,   **175**
Yet for Christ's sake, whose blood hath ransomed
    me,
Impose some end to my incessant pain!
Let Faustus live in hell a thousand years,
A hundred thousand, and at last be saved!
No end is limited to[11] damnèd souls!   **180**
Why wert thou not a creature wanting soul?
Or why is this immortal that thou hast?
O, Pythagoras' metempsychosis,[12] were that true
This soul should fly from me and I be changed
Into some brutish beast.   **185**
All beasts are happy, for when they die
Their souls are soon dissolved in elements.

---

[10]**O . . . equi** slowly, slowly run, O horses of the night (Latin, adapted from Ovid's *Amores,* I.xiii.40, where a lover regretfully thinks of the coming of the dawn)   [11]**limited to** set for
[12]**metempsychosis** transmigration of souls (a doctrine held by Pythagoras, philosopher of the sixth century B.C.)

[6]**throne** (symbolic of heaven)   [7]**affected** preferred   [8]**quarters** bodies   [9]**confusion** destruction

But mine must live still[13] to be plagued in hell!
Cursed be the parents that engendered me!
No Faustus, curse thyself, curse Lucifer   **190**
That hath deprived thee of the joys of heaven.
           The clock strikes twelve.
It strikes, it strikes! Now body, turn to air,
Or Lucifer will bear thee quick[14] to hell!
O soul, be changed into small water-drops
And fall into the ocean, ne'er be found.   **195**

Thunder, and enter the DEVILS.

My God, my God! Look not so fierce on me!
Adders and serpents, let me breathe awhile!
Ugly Hell, gape not! Come not Lucifer!
I'll burn my books!—O Mephostophilis!
     Exeunt (DEVILS *with* FAUSTUS.)[15]

SCENE THREE

Enter the SCHOLARS.

1 SCHOLAR.
     Come gentlemen, let us go visit Faustus,
     For such a dreadful night was never seen
     Since first the world's creation did begin!
     Such fearful shrieks and cries were never heard!
     Pray heaven, the doctor have escaped the danger.   **5**
2 SCHOLAR.
     O, help us heaven, see, here are Faustus' limbs
     All torn asunder by the hand of death!

3 SCHOLAR.
     The devils whom Faustus served have torn him thus:
     For 'twixt the hours of twelve and one, methought
     I heard him shriek and call aloud for help,   **10**
     At which self[1] time the house seemed all on fire
     With dreadful horror of these damnèd fiends.
2 SCHOLAR.
     Well gentlemen, though Faustus' end be such
     As every Christian heart laments to think on,
     Yet for he was a scholar once admired   **15**
     For wondrous knowledge in our German schools,
     We'll give his mangled limbs due burial;
     And all the students, clothed in mourning black,
     Shall wait upon[2] his heavy[3] funeral. (*Exeunt.*)

Enter CHORUS.

     Cut is the branch that might have grown full
          straight   **20**
     And burnèd is Apollo's laurel bough[4]
     That sometime grew within this learnèd man.
     Faustus is gone: regard his hellish fall,
     Whose fiendful fortune may exhort the wise
     Only to wonder at[5] unlawful things,   **25**
     Whose deepness doth entice such forward wits
     To practice more than heavenly power permits.
          (*Exit.*)

Terminat hora diem; terminat Author opus.[6]

FINIS

[13]**still** always [14]**quick** alive [15]**Exeunt [Devils with Faustus]**
(possibly the devils drag Faustus into the "hell" that was
"discovered" at V.ii.124, and then toss his limbs onto the stage,
or possibly the limbs are revealed in V.iii.6 by withdrawing a
curtain at the rear of the stage)

[1]**self** same [2]**wait upon** attend [3]**heavy** sad [4]**laurel bough**
symbol of wisdom, here associated with Apollo, god of divination
[5]**Only to wonder at** i.e., merely to observe at a distance, with awe
[6]**Terminat . . . opus** the hour ends the day; the author ends his
work (this Latin tag probably is not Marlowe's but the printer's,
though it is engaging to believe Marlowe wrote it, ending his play
at midnight, the hour of Faustus' death)

FOCUS QUESTIONS

1. Develop a character sketch that illustrates Mephostophilis' ability to control Faustus
   while seeming to serve him.
2. Describe how Marlowe uses clowns and comic action to comment on the play's
   themes.
3. How does Marlowe depict Faustus' continual dilemma? Isolate the devices and
   discuss how they work.
4. Defend Faustus as hero or villain.
5. Comment on the literary and theatrical values of Faustus' closing monologue in act
   5, scene 2.

6. Discuss the circular design of the play and comment on Faustus' pivotal position throughout.
7. Compare Marlowe's version of the Faust story with another stage version (for example, Goethe or Gertrude Stein).

OTHER ACTIVITIES

1. Stage your own interpretation of act 2, scene 2, in which the Seven Deadly Sins appear to Faustus.
2. Using reviews, photographs, and other available production documents, assess one of the following English productions of the play: (a) Royal Shakespeare Theatre (1968), directed by Clifford Williams; (b) Aldwych Theatre (1974), directed by John Barton; or (c) Barbican Pit (1989), directed by Barry Kyle.
3. View the Oxford University film version with Richard Burton and discuss the effectiveness of the play's transference to the screen.

BIBLIOGRAPHY

Bakeless, J. E. *The Tragicall History of Christopher Marlowe.* 2 vols. Westport, CT: Greenwood Press, 1970.

Barroll, J. L., et al. *Revels History of Drama in English.* Vol. 3: 1576–1613. New York: Harper & Row, 1975.

Boas, F. S. *Christopher Marlowe: A Biographical and Critical Study.* Oxford: Clarendon, 1966.

Brockbank, J. P. *Marlowe: Dr. Faustus.* London: E. Arnold, 1962.

Cartelli, Thomas. *Marlowe, Shakespeare, and the Economy of Theatrical Experience.* Philadelphia: University of Pennsylvania Press, 1991.

Cole, Douglas. *Suffering and Evil in the Plays of Christopher Marlowe.* New York: Gordian, 1972.

Farnham, Willard, ed. *Twentieth Century Interpretations of "Doctor Faustus."* Englewood Cliffs, NJ: Prentice-Hall, 1969.

Kernan, Alvin, ed. *Two Renaissance Mythmakers: Christopher Marlowe and Ben Jonson.* Baltimore: Johns Hopkins University Press, 1977.

Levin, Harry. *Christopher Marlowe: The Overreacher.* London: Faber, 1973.

Maclure, Millar, ed. *Marlowe: The Critical Heritage.* London: Routledge & Kegan Paul, 1979.

Orrell, John. *The Human Stage: English Theatre Design, 1567–1640.* New York: Cambridge University Press, 1988.

Rowse, A. L. *Christopher Marlowe: His Life and Work.* New York: Grosset & Dunlap, 1966.

Sewall, Richard. *The Vision of Tragedy.* New York: Paragon House, 1990.

Steane, J. B. *Marlowe: A Critical Study.* London: Cambridge University Press, 1974.

Waith, Eugene M. *The Herculean Hero in Marlowe, Chapman, Shakespeare, and Dryden.* New York: Columbia University Press, 1967.

Weil, Judith. *Christopher Marlowe: Merlin's Prophet.* Cambridge: Cambridge University Press, 1977.

RECOMMENDED VIDEOTAPES AND RECORDINGS

Doctor Faustus. VHS. 93 min. 1967. Starring Richard Burton and Elizabeth Taylor with the Oxford University Dramatic Society, adapted by Nevill Coghill. Distributed by Insight Media, New York City.

Parables of Power: Marlowe's Dr. Faustus. VHS. 26 min. Distributed by Insight Media, New York City.

The Tragical History of Dr. Faustus. One sound cassette. 57 min. 1958. Directed by Howard Sackler. Caedmon Recordings. Featuring Frank Silvera.

MEASURE FOR MEASURE
WILLIAM SHAKESPEARE (1564–1616)

If ever a human being got his work expressed completely, it was Shakespeare.
If ever a mind was incandescent, unimpeded . . . it was Shakespeare's mind.

—VIRGINIA WOOLF

Michael Pennington as the Duke and Paola Dionisotti as Isabella in *Measure for Measure*, presented by the Royal Shakespeare Company in 1978, under the direction of Barry Kyle.
Photo: The Shakespeare Centre Library; Joe Cocks Studio Collection/Copyright Photograph.

APPROACHING SHAKESPEARE

The mention of Shakespeare's name evokes a rich catalogue of responses in the playgoer's imagination: the social, political, and literary forces that fashioned an age named for its ruling monarch, Elizabeth I, in which he served as actor and playwright; the reinvention of a powerful stage language that flexibly accommodated the literary tastes of commoners and aristocrats alike; the profound psychological dimensions of a *dramatis personae* our Western literature has not encountered before or since; and finally, the awesome humanity and universality of his art. These but partly suggest the range and depth of associations conjured by this poet-playwright, born in Stratford-on-Avon, whose actual existence remains so sketchily documented as to stand disputed by scholars of every age since.

Perhaps it was a matter of timing, tempered by an innate genius, that heralded Shakespeare's auspicious debut in London's bustling theatrical scene—"the hub of the universe"—as Virginia Woolf described it. Or perhaps it was the fact that Shakespeare's patron, the Earl of Southampton, bought him a share in the Lord Chamberlain's Men soon after they were refounded in 1594. Writing specifically for a prosperous and stable company of actors, Shakespeare had a chance to draw on the talents and eccentricities of his actors to develop his stage characters. His versatility as a writer was continually utilized until the company emerged as the leading acting troupe in London, performing their repertory across the Thames, at their own public theatre, the Globe. (See Preface to Marlowe, pp. 177–178.) When James I acceded the throne in 1603, the company came under his patronage as the King's Men, occupying the Black Friar's Hall in London as their winter home. This solidified Shakespeare's popularity and his importance to the English stage before his death in 1616.

MAJOR WORKS

Shakespeare's plays, conveniently divided into Tragedies, Comedies, Romances, and Histories, are further categorized into periods before or after 1604, although this date may vary among scholars. Their stylistic differences are the sharpest indicators of the time periods in which each was written. Popular works of his early period include *Richard III, The Taming of the Shrew, Romeo and Juliet, Richard II,* and *A Midsummer Night's Dream.* To point to their superficial characterizations, carefully manipulated plots, and rigid poetic styles in no way lessens their greatness, but pays tribute to the remarkable caliber of Shakespeare's playwriting apprenticeship. The transitional works that follow, including *The Merchant of Venice, Henry IV* parts I and II, *Henry V, As You Like It, Julius Caesar, Twelfth Night, Hamlet, Othello,* and *Measure for Measure,* reflect a considerably matured craftsman whose handling of characterization, stage language, and theatrical devices has grown rich in subtlety. The late period concludes with *King Lear, Macbeth, Antony and Cleopatra, Coriolanus, The Winter's Tale,* and *The Tempest,* all of which demonstrate experimental elements in characterization and language, an abundance of complex poetic imagery, and a balance between dramatic action and meaning still unsurpassed in today's theatre.

Shakespeare borrowed freely from a wide assortment of literary and historical sources. Though his plots were often of his own invention, many of their details were inspired by the works of poets, novelists, and historians. For example, while the multiple-plot structure of *A Midsummer Night's Dream* belongs to the playwright, its characters and actions are suggested by Chaucer, Plutarch, Ovid, and even the folklore of Shakespeare's own time. These are inventively woven into a comic masterpiece whose diverse love themes, magically abetted by the powers of the imagination, incorporate the characters of both real and fairy kingdoms.

On the other hand, a glance at the plays in his popular history cycle (*Richard II, Henry IV* parts I and II, *Henry V*), which is concerned with one central theme—the rise and fall of the House of Lancaster—reveals a different literary inspiration. That the playwright owes some debt to Holinshed, whose *Chronicles* remain well known *because* of Shakespeare's evident use of them, goes without question. But Holinshed's contribution is significantly reduced within the dynamic core of this four-play cycle, and affects little of its poetic context. Furthermore, Shakespeare's invention of Sir John Falstaff, Hal's ''tutor and feeder'' in *Henry IV,* parts I and II, owes nothing to Holinshed. Sir John and his low-comic companions infuse the two central plays with an unforgettable theatrical energy and philosophical wit. Their comic rowdiness and its repercussions further demonstrate how Hal's consorting with the common people will transform him into a worthy king. Shakespeare's poetic imagination, not his sources, once again proves the mightier influence.

Of the entire Shakespeare canon, perhaps no play cuts more sharply or deeply into our contemporary consciousness than *Measure for Measure* (1604). This is accomplished through the outspoken sexuality that permeates the play's political environment and assigns us the role of voyeur, certainly a fascinating psychological space for any playgoer to inhabit. Recalling the stringent moral code of the audience Shakespeare wrote for, including a social hierarchy that elevated its men to the ranks of lord and master, we are quietly provoked by the play's depictions of sexual morality and equality, where women characters, in puppet-like fashion, submit to the lusts of hypocritical men who simultaneously legislate morality and distribute justice. It is equally difficult to ignore the play's bawdy Southwark associations with sex and death or its references to ''plague'' in a modern world where the impact of AIDS has touched our lives.

Hence the moral of this dark comedy, that justice should be tempered with mercy, ironically contradicts the biblical implications of the play's title. But *Measure for Measure* luxuriates in such twists, both in dramatic form and content, which have contributed both to its problematical reputation and enduring fascination. In particular, its rich ambiguities of characterization, language, and dramatic action have provided serious challenges to theatre directors. It is possible, as G. B. Harrison suggests, that Shakespeare confused his original purpose for writing the play by allowing his own humanity to interfere with the playful plot and happy ending he intended, until ''the soul of the play became too great for its body.''[1]

THE ACTION

Under the pretext that he must leave Vienna to visit Poland for some undetermined period of time, Duke Vincentio slyly reenters the city in the guise of a religious friar and negotiates as spiritual confessor to the worldly affairs of his people. Observing Angelo, a man of integrity who has been temporarily empowered ''to enforce or qualify the laws'' during his absence, the Duke uncovers the vast moral chaos incurred by his letting ''evil deeds have their permissive pass.'' In particular, he eavesdrops on the case of one young Claudio, caught in fornication and scheduled to die in accordance with a law recently revived.

On the day before the beheading, Isabella, Claudio's virginal sister who has recently entered a convent, confronts Angelo to beg for mercy and persuade him to free her brother. But her innocence and beauty arouse Angelo's baser instincts and prompt him to consider the very act for which he has condemned Claudio. The scenes that follow are filled with disturbing sexual turns, all guilefully orchestrated by the disguised Duke to produce a dubious comic outcome.

STRUCTURE AND LANGUAGE

In *Measure for Measure,* Shakespeare evades conclusive answers to darker, potentially tragic issues and opts for a sentimental, comic ending that has confounded his critics for centuries. But the play's timelier conflicts between public code and private morality, its problematic view of sex as an easy curative, and its biased portrait of woman—from nun to brothel-keeper—provoke our sense of justice. The play's distorted world, as represented by the Duke's Vienna, where individual codes of morality conveniently bend to accommodate their mutually consenting participants and where sexual repressions prove destructive unless they are quickly addressed, seems uncannily like our own.

In contrast with Shakespeare's usual ease at addressing profound human issues across different historical and cultural planes, the play's solutions, however curiously motivated, further implode: they suggest that the people and behaviors of our real world are never quite what they seem and that a universal system of equality and justice is impossible, despite the Duke's lyrical assertion in act 5 that ''Haste still pays haste, and leisure answers leisure;/ Like doth quit like, and Measure still for Measure.'' A society that empowers a patriarchy like Duke Vincentio's pays lip service to a true utopian harmony and functions as infamously as Shakespeare's imposed happy ending.

So our concerns about the play might include the following: Does the Duke represent a supreme God-head, appropriately reincarnated through religious disguise, now driven to set aright all order gone astray in the world, as symbolized by his own city? Or does he merely function as *deus ex machina,* a theatrical device personified to rescue certain hapless victims from unhappier fates?

Will Isabella's response to Angelo's sexual request that she ''lay down the treasures of [her] body/ . . . or else let [her brother] suffer'' justly confirm her allegiance to a moral order, as symbolized by her religious vocation? Or does her response deservedly renounce any responsibility toward the fornicating Claudio who, to Isabella's horror, further implores her to obey Angelo and ''save a brother's life''?

Granting his good deeds at the play's happy outcome, how morally acceptable or reprehensible is Duke Vincentio's unlawful disguise, which facilitates his manipulating the actions of the play? His real but baser motive is the preservation of Isabella's virginity for his own purpose, which he discloses to her much later: ''Give me your hand and say you will be mine.''

Finally there is the case for Isabella, so shaken by this choice between a brother's life and her maidenhood, that, on one level, she qualifies as true protagonist/antihero in what her words and actions can or cannot achieve in a society governed by men; on another level, she emerges as true heroine, if such an outworn label can be retrieved to name her progressive and humiliating loss of autonomy. Of course her sexual passivity strikes us as pejorative behavior alongside the outspoken assertiveness of Shakespeare's women in other comedies. We must not forget, however, that Isabella's quieter strengths have lacked neither sincerity nor honesty, which cannot be said for the men in the play.

Isabella and the few sketchily painted women who surround her remain subjected to the whims of men, are often indebted to them, and are even reinvented by them to feed their fantasies, much like their counterparts in the real world. Restoring her shattered integrity in the aftermath of a most unsavory ordeal, Isabella has little to smile about, until the Duke, her dubious savior and husband-to-be (for he has shed his religious cloak and she her veil) assures her that all is well. It remains fortuitous that Shakespeare chooses *not* to record Isabella's response to the Duke's sudden gesture, but asks his audience to imagine it instead.

Like all of Shakespeare's plays, *Measure for Measure* is plot-centered in its careful merging of form (how the story will unfold) with content (what the story is about). Whether or not Claudio's life can be saved, and at what expense, becomes the play's most urgent issue and carries significant weight in its ramifications and outcome. In fact, the fate of most of its characters hinges on this outcome and establishes a harmony of character relationships to underscore Shakespeare's darker comic vision. Shakespeare has allowed himself consecutive units of stage time or "scenes," to mirror the multiple places, actions, and time spans Isabella needs to work out her destiny.

He further devises a multiplicity of plot structures: the smaller ones known as **subplots** (for example, the Elbow, Froth, and Pompey business) vs. **analogous actions,** in which certain smaller events are deliberately arranged to mirror each other (for example, the parallel pairings of Claudio/Juliet, Angelo/Mariana, and Lucio with a bawd). Such interwoven actions allow each to comment on the other, until the surprise love match between the Duke and Isabella echoes the previous pairings and provides an ironic touch to the play's comic denouement.

Perhaps the most disturbing element of the play is its use of **dramatic irony** through which Shakespeare permits the ubiquitous Duke, in disguise, to share his incognito with us, while other stage characters must function without such knowledge. The device assumes critical importance as it gives Vincentio control over the effects of comic irony and allows him to atone for his own lax moral leadership of Vienna when he guides Angelo, Claudio, and Lucio through their respective redemptions.

As for the play's language, a close reading of the script reveals Shakespeare's familiar shifts between verse and prose formats, the latter generally assigned to the low-comic roles, although the versatile Duke-as-Friar smoothly adjusts his vocal responses to fit both. The use of **iambic pentameter**—or five-beat metrical cadence—heightens the poetic imagery spoken by these characters without losing its semblance to conversational speech. The occasional irregularity of this metrical cadence further betrays the emotional turmoil they are experiencing, as exemplified by Claudio's reflections on death, when he tries to move Isabella to sin in his behalf:

> Aýe, but to díe, and gó we knów not whére,
> To líe in cóld obstrúction ańd to rót,
> This sénsible wárm mótion tó becóme
> A knéaded clód; and tĥe delíghted spírit
> To báthe in fíery flóods, or tó resíde
> In tĥrilling région of thíck-ríbbed íce.

Claudio alludes to his fragile mortality, his body as a "sensible warm motion" to be dissolved into earth ("a kneaded clod"). Cadence and imagery merge powerfully in his description of instant damnation amid "fiery floods" or, just as bad, in a "region of thick-ribbed ice." In the mouth of this hapless victim, such images acquire an eloquence that might move any listener, but *must* persuade his sister Isabella.

Claudio's fearful images of death provide interesting contrast to the play's more prevalent sexual ones. No sooner does Mistress Overdone tell her cronies of the news of Claudio's impending execution for "getting Madam Julietta with child" than she forthrightly criticizes the closing of her bawdy house: "Thus, what with the war, what with the sweat [plague], what with the gallows, and what with poverty, I am custom-shrunk." Aside from her symbolic nomenclature, which informs us that she is quite "over-the-hill" for her profession, Mistress Overdone has also been "done over" by life's dirty tricks.

Meanwhile Duke Vincentio persuades Friar Thomas (a true religious man) that his need to disguise himself in religious garb has nothing to do with youthful undertakings typically associated with the "dribbling dart of love." While the literal interpretation of this loaded remark discloses the Duke's potential aversion to amorous games, an uncomfortably explicit reference to the symptoms of certain sexually transmitted diseases lurks beneath, despite Shakespeare's light-handed and alliterative reference to a "dribbling dart." The weapon-like image succinctly connotes both the positive and negative effects of love that function in the play.

In the initial confrontation between Isabella and Angelo, Angelo's request that Isabella "lay down the treasures of [her] body" to save Claudio elicits an equally provocative, blatantly masochistic response from her, as if to suggest that her own religious martyrdom is at stake:

> . . . were I under the terms of death,
> Th' impression of keen whips I'd wear as rubies,
> And strip myself to death as to a bed
> That longing have been sick for, ere I'd yield
> My body up to shame.

What powerful imagery from an innocent virgin who has chosen to dedicate her life to Christ! Perhaps her words reveal the darker side of an imagination seeking the control of a cloistered life.

Finally there is Lucio's perceptive observation of Angelo's cold justice, by alluding to "his urine [as] congealed ice;" and the fact that the hypocritical Angelo will execute Claudio only because the former's lust for Isabella, who has refused him, resulted in a "rebellion of [his] codpiece." Whether out of the mouths of bawds, cold-blooded legislators, or displaced saints, the political ramifications of sex abound in *Measure for Measure* and strengthen our appreciation of its wise and wicked ways.

MEASURE FOR MEASURE-IN-PERFORMANCE

Evidence suggests that the King's Men performed *Measure for Measure* for the first time on December 26, 1604, at Whitehall. When the play reappeared in 1662 in William Davenant's adaptation titled *The Law Against Lovers,* the text was considerably altered to suit the taste of its Restoration audience. Charles Gildon's version, which was performed at Lincoln's Inn Fields in 1700 with Thomas Betterton and Anne Bracegirdle as Angelo and Isabella, came closer to presenting Shakespeare's original text.

Adaptations of the play appeared throughout the eighteenth century, largely succeeding as vehicles for the great actors of the period. Mrs. Cibber achieved much notoriety as Isabella from 1737 until her retirement in 1759, after which Mrs. Siddons, in the company of her brothers Charles and John Philip Kemble, incarnated the role until 1812. Her successor at the Covent Garden was Elizabeth O'Neill.

From the late eighteenth to the end of the nineteenth century, Shakespeare's plays were routinely **bowdlerized** by irate censors and egomaniacal actor-managers who selfishly protected their own interests rather than the playwright's. In the case of *Measure for Measure,* suggestive actions and bawdy language were either omitted or replaced. Not until 1893 did the complete original text surface at the Royalty under William Poel's sensitive and responsible direction. Furthermore, the actor-manager's sympathetic impersonation of Angelo was recognized for its innovative departure from the harsh declamatory style of his Victorian predecessors. His subtle psychological nuances shed newer light on Angelo's relationships with the Duke and Isabella, prompting subsequent interpreters to experiment with subtext and style.

The compulsion for directors to make Shakespeare meaningful to audiences everywhere has greatly enhanced his popularity in the twentieth century. While the results have generated controversy, they have also enlightened our appreciation of his texts, even when production choices have failed. No less remarkable is the success of so many unorthodox stagings, thereby confirming the durability of Shakespeare's potent and versatile art.

In several Old Vic productions of the 1930s, the duality of Angelo's sensuality—both unleashed or repressed—vs. Isabella's purity—both real or feigned—reflected director Tyrone Guthrie's personal ambivalence toward these characters. When he confronted the play over a quarter of a century later, however, his direction was shrouded in Christian symbolism and reflected an altogether different sensibility from his earlier approach to the play. The changes were as much a tribute to Guthrie's expanded consciousness as they were to the play's timelessness.

Peter Brook's landmark production at Stratford, England, in 1950 revealed entirely new complexities and dimensions, prophesying the kind of **director's theatre** Brook came to epitomize. His adaptable set of "gray stone pillars and arches [conveyed] an image both of the material prosperity of Vienna and the severity of its penal system" and counterbalanced the play's comic and serious elements, which were strongly emphasized in the production.[2] "If we follow [Shakespeare's] ever-shifting devices," Brook explained, "he will lead us through many different keys. If we follow the movement in *Measure for Measure* . . . we will discover a play about justice, mercy, honesty, forgiveness, virtue, virginity, sex and death: kaleidoscopically one section of the play mirrors the other, it is in accepting the prism as a whole that its meanings emerge."[3]

Since then, notable productions have surfaced in different corners of the world, including China, Austria, France, Australia, and Canada. Their unsettling *mise-en-scènes* have frequently served as barometers for assessing societal turmoils in relation to the play's characters and themes. In a Japanese translation by Tetsuo Anzai, one such production was offered by Tokyo's Gekidan En in 1977. English director Terence Knapp saw Angelo's puritanical rule echoed in Fascist control of Japan from 1939 through 1945. Thus his recreation of the bordello/cabaret atmosphere of the Weimar Republic in the 1930s supplied the landscape for actions taking place in the decadent red light district of Tokyo's Yoshiwara.

Countless interpretations have adorned English-speaking stages during the second half of the twentieth century. Michael Bogdanov, Nicholas Hytner, Mark Lamos, Robin Phillips, Jonathan Miller, John Barton, Charles Marowitz, Robert Egan, David Thacker, and Barry Kyle are but a handful of directors who have investigated the play's moral and psychological complexities, discovering once and for all that the unpleasant world of the play is hardly a stranger to contemporary audiences. Five directors have overseen productions of the play for the New York Shakespeare Festival between 1960 and 1993: Alan Schneider (1960), Michael Kahn (1966), John Pasquin (1976), Joseph Papp (1985), and Michael Rudman (1993), who set the action in the Caribbean just before World War II. Rudman's was the twenty-second production in an ongoing marathon of the complete Shakespeare canon, a project undertaken by the Festival in 1988.

Reflections on MEASURE FOR MEASURE*

Michael Kahn directed Measure for Measure *at the New York Shakespeare Festival in 1966.*

Measure for Measure is a lucky play for me. It started my classical career. Joseph Papp asked me to come up and talk about the play. It was a very right play for me—as a young director—in the late 1960s, because everything that many people think is difficult about the play struck me as being absolutely why I wanted to do it. The complexity of it, the ambiguity of it, the black humor of it were absolutely and totally contemporary.

*Two reflections on MEASURE FOR MEASURE *have been provided. The second, by Barry Kyle, appears on p. 223.*

Continued

First of all, I saw the play as a black comedy, a view that did not meet with the approval of certain people who wanted my approach to be more romantic. So I fought for it. In fact, I went into rehearsals with a different set of leading actors (they had been hired by Joe) from the ones who finally did the play. Now I don't mean "sitcom" comedy; I mean bitter and ironic comedy, and that everybody—with his extremist views—was wrong in the play, and that it was satirical.

The play is called *Measure for Measure,* not so much because it's about an eye for an eye—which is one way of looking at it—but also about the need for balance, the need for personal and political equilibrium. The play is a critique of each character's point of view, which makes it a very modern play. It's not about good people and bad people, that there exists a universe some of these people are defying, and therefore the world goes wrong. It's not about that at all.

Everybody in this play has a strong attitude toward society, and that strong attitude gets them and the society into trouble. First there is the Duke who, seemingly, is trying to discover what is wrong with this society, but he also seems to be a man who ignores his responsibility rather than faces it. I do think he's the hero of the play; otherwise he wouldn't get Isabella at the end. Angelo had for me sort of Tartuffe/Arturo-Ui qualities, and I always thought that there was a way of playing Angelo that suggested the comic. At the time I remember very much wanting Dustin Hoffman to play the part. He came in to read for Elbow. I thought I wanted a funny, not so tall, not leading-man type. I'd play him as a character instead. At that time, Dustin had done some interesting off-Broadway work, and although I tried to talk him into playing Angelo, he wouldn't do it. So Tom Aldredge did it. I wanted a comic character. I wanted an actor who could play a hypocrite and play it with a kind of irony.

And I thought that Isabella was also wrong in her zeal to protect herself from the world, since she was willing to let people die. And that the world was licentious, but it was the real world and needed to be understood and accepted as much as anything. I saw Vienna as a symbol of the world that's gone too far; but on the other hand, I peopled it not only with whores, but with beggars and all other outcasts of society, so it wasn't just a sexually licentious world. After all, this was the 1960s and the sexual revolution was upon us, and I wasn't interested in doing a play which said that sexuality was bad. I think that if I did the play today, I would see that everyone is excessive in the play; and that the play asks for moderation in everything. (P.S. I did the play in 1993 and found some of my attitudes had changed.) The play does not say that sexuality is wrong. It just says that sexuality without relationships is wrong. It also says that oppressive laws breed reaction and that orthodox or fundamentalist ideas of religion and morality are a way of ignoring the real world.

All the characters have fixed ideas about the way they're going to live their lives: whether, like Lucio, they are totally free and have a total cynical freedom, which is a fixed idea; or like Isabella with her fixed morality, which is a sin to go against; or like Angelo who, in denying humanity, has created another fundamentalist state. Shakespeare's critique is of a fixed idea, and I thought that was funny, that it was done through satire.

Quite frankly I welcomed the contradictions of the play's style, and I don't have as big a problem as other people do in terms of how one goes from the serious to the comic and back. But I do remember one of the moments which sort of defined how I saw the play: in the rather strange set of couplets that the Duke speaks with Isabella, supposedly telling Mariana about the bed trick. I'd hired a very clever comic actress—not terribly beautiful but very amusing—to play Mariana. Isabella and she walked upstage as the Duke spoke his couplets. Then at one point Mariana turned to the Duke, who's dressed as a Friar, looking as if to ask "Are you telling me to go to bed with this man?" Then turning to this nun who seemed to suggest the same thing, Mariana fainted. That's where I felt the humor of the play lay. I always looked for the comedy in every situation; I found it a lot. I thought, what would a young woman do if a priest and a nun told her to go to bed with this man. What would she do? She'd be shocked, surprised, and would faint. I think that if you think of a play as a comedy, you'll find the comedy in it. And if you think of it as a black comedy in which tough situations have irony, and a satire on attitudes—which is what I really thought it was—humor comes through.

Furthermore, I don't think there's this realistic tragedy of Isabella, the Duke, and Angelo on one side, and this major comedy of Pompey, Froth, and Lucio on the other. They're all in the same play. Critics seem unwilling to accept the fact that this play can be funny and still do these things at the same time. That's why I never think of *Measure for Measure* as a "problem" play: it's a satire with human elements. And that's why it remains a favorite of mine. I really enjoyed seeing what it would be like for a man, who has never tried to seduce a woman, to try to seduce a nun when he is supposed to be a paragon of virtue. At the time, I thought that was funny—funny because they put themselves in this position. Not funny because the situation was intrinsically funny, but because of who they were, what their public personas had to be, and how that made this funny.

At that time in the sixties, when I was in my twenties and interested in "cool" and satire, this play was perfect. I hired a comic actress, Barbara Baxley, who, as a comedienne, would never have been hired for a role like Isabella. I felt that Shakespeare was making fun of everyone, that everyone had a pretension. The audiences loved the production because of this "take" on the play, which wasn't very humanistic, but was really a "ship of fools."

Measure for Measure is a very urban play. I didn't like the foliage surroundings of Central Park where it was performed, so I asked [our set designer] Ming Cho Lee to build a brick wall and a fire escape, which mirrored an Elizabethan stage. But at the time, I didn't think it was a modern play. I sort of used Brueghel, since his characters seemed right for the play. So there was this tension between Brueghel and this modern construction which I found interesting. But this was the period of Jan Kott and the period of [Arthur Kopit's] *Oh Dad, Poor Dad,* and I saw this play in that ironic, satirical light. I didn't find it stylistically confusing, nor did I find characters good or bad at all. I didn't feel that Shakespeare was a moralist in the way that the Victorians thought he was, and which had been inherited in much of our thinking and teaching of Shakespeare. And that, of course, is because I was living in my times. Anyway, people my age were rebelling against the last vestiges of that kind of thinking.

I didn't find the scholarly work on *Measure for Measure* to be of much value either. There's better work on the play now. But in 1966, much of the scholarship refused to relate Shakespeare to the way we had now come to understand literature: we had come to

Continued

understand not such fixed characterization; we had come to understand that it wasn't an incongruity to integrate different styles in the same performance. In the years since I did the play, it has become a "given" that stylistic differences are not mistakes; that there is an issue of feminism in this particular play; that we are able to see this play as "rougher." In 1966, this was the way the modern theatre was going. So it struck me that Shakespeare was a perfectly modern playwright and I did not have to excuse these things or justify them.

Then there's the notion of the Duke-of-dark-corners. I just thought he was somebody who didn't know how to handle things. He is the leading character and every time you do the play and every time you see the play, you find that out. The story everybody remembers, however, is Angelo and Isabella's. But the thing that ties the play together and finally takes the ending of the play is the Duke and Isabella. If the Duke is not an actor who could command the play, I think the production is skewed. He does seem very cruel to Isabella in letting her believe that Claudio is dead, but I think he does that because he comes into the prison and sees that her religiosity is allowing her to let her brother die. He has to know that. He has to see that. And he has to understand that, in the same way he must help the state, he has to help her because he sees what's wrong and he feels something about her. And through the next set of scenes in which he puts her through torture by telling her Claudio is dead, I think they develop a surprising fondness for each other—one that they both can't talk about because ostensibly she's going to be a nun and he's a priest. So you've got to find where that happens, and it bothers her because this is not in her agenda, and she doesn't think it's possible anyway, because he's celibate. So there's a whole possibility of relationship-building that's not in the text, although there are little places you can play it that I think you have to explore to make the ending work. I think he is perfect for her, because he learns that moderation is necessary. He's put the town in the hands of a zealot and he sees what zealotry can do. And now he's met a young woman who's a zealot in her own way. So he's left to fix everyone up. But the Duke and Isabella are the right people for one another.

As for Claudio, he's not so wrong. In fact, he sort of got it right. He's headstrong and he's young, but he's in love with Juliet, and he doesn't want to die. First he says: alright, let me die, and then he thinks about it; then wants his sister to sleep with somebody to save his life. I thought this a perfectly legitimate and acceptable request to make. The fact that she responds as she does is *her* problem. She makes the excessive demands there. Seeing it as a satire permitted me to accept these things. After all, what does Claudio do that is wrong? He's in love with a young woman and she becomes pregnant. What's wrong with that? It's life. So everything that happened to Claudio was the result of other people's sickness.

On the other hand, the current AIDS phenomenon, in which sex is equated with death, will make future productions of this play more complicated. Directors will simply have to work through how they feel about it, until they realize exactly what they will need to do. While I know what my own politics are, however, I don't want the play to support a growing fundamentalist attitude about sexuality. As a director, I feel very responsible to my audience. Shakespeare already has the answer, and I think that the dilemma of sexuality in a society stricken with AIDS is also his. We will find the way out in Shakespeare.

REFLECTIONS ON MEASURE FOR MEASURE

Barry Kyle directed Measure for Measure *for the Royal Shakespeare Company at Stratford in 1978. The production later opened at the Aldwych Theatre in London.*

I looked at *Measure for Measure* very much in relation to exactly when it was written. I came upon it in that Shakespearean category called "problem plays," a category created by critics who did not know where to put this play. I became very drawn to the crisis of faith the play represented, particularly at a political level. My production was very firmly Jacobean. There were no variations to that. I did the play at a time when the more eclectic treatment of period had not really begun to penetrate Shakespearean production. Things tended to be either modern or they tended to be in the period.

I suppose the biggest event of the day that affected the ideology of the production was the rise of Islamic fundamentalism. I think it was some months before the Iranian Revolution and, while I don't quite remember exactly which came first, I did feel—as I worked on the play—that it was a play about "absolutism." It dealt with that theme in a way that was so schematic. It seemed to me almost like a morality play relocated in a period of faithlessness.

I became very interested in the parallel paths of the Duke and Isabella and very interested in the way in which, in consecutive scenes, they both leave the world. They both seek *initially* almost the same thing, and they both have pressing personal reasons: one political, the other, I think, psychosexual, to leave the world that they are in and to enter a world of perfect spiritual reflection and personal isolation. In both cases, their stories dealt with the testing of absolutist ideologies. I think that contemporary history doesn't so much kick down the door to get into Shakespeare's plays, but rather it can actually be like a rock in the river: it can send the flow into a slightly different direction.

I believed, as I still do, that the destination of the play is to disprove the idea of "measure for measure." The play is like a human experiment set in a crucible in which Shakespeare studies the attraction, the appeal, and the ultimate unreality of absolutist ideals, particularly in the political world. One of the most wonderful lines is the Duke's, in the play's opening scene, when he leaves and says: "Of government the properties to unfold," which has a verse line all to itself, as though there is a pause after it: "Of government!" He is the ruler of a country that has lost its way, because of the longevity of his rule which appears, to me, to be a rule that was characterized by his movement away from fundamentalism. In Shakespearean terms, I felt that this was Shakespeare in 1604, at the time when all the old Elizabethan certainties of political rule, religious faith, the class system, were going through a very great change. It's the play of Shakespeare's political review and what has to be reviewed—is it sixteen years?—of what appeared to me to feel in 1978 like liberalism or like "let's review what was done by the 1960s."

Since I grew up in the sixties and was part of all of that, it felt to me that here was a play where the Duke is looking back at what had happened in that time when the world had changed very remarkably. I'm not saying that the 1590s were the same as the 1960s. They were not. But there was definitely a loosening of fundamentals, a sense that there

Continued

were no fixed points anymore. Anything was possible. I very much felt that the Duke was a man who wanted to give absolutism a chance in the form of Angelo, but knew that he himself, personally, could not do it.

My set was a series of black polished cubicles, very much like a puzzle or a Chinese box, with doors that opened in all kinds of ways. There was a balcony around the top of it, and the first person to go up there and look down was the Duke. The form of this set was essentially a prison: it is, of all the plays, Shakespeare's prison play and the stage designer is most frequently called upon to provide confining spaces. In fact, the front of the stage was almost completely lifted up and actually closed the box on all four sides. And there were doors, and outside it was white. There was a white carpet and you could also stick poles on this box with heads on the top of them. Essentially I wanted to show that the fundamentalist experiments always lead to executions. The history of our century, in terms of the Nazis, the Communists, the Islamic fundamentalists—all of those revolutionary moments which Angelo's political opportunity represents—well, you have to kill people first. So I had the Duke standing amongst these poles with increasing numbers of heads that were being placed on the top of these walls.

The Duke is one of the most wonderful roles in Shakespeare, a role that actors frequently don't want to play. They think Angelo is the star role. That certainly was true in my production. I cast Jonathan Pryce as Angelo and Michael Pennington as the Duke. Jonathan felt that he had very much the play-carrying role, but it became apparent to all of us that it is actually the Duke who runs the show in the fifth act. Literary criticism has told us that Angelo is the better role because he's got the best poetry. But the study of theatrical history has shown us time and again that it is the Duke who runs the play-in-performance because his role is so mysterious.

I did sense a parallel between the journey of the Duke and the journey of Isabella. Through her determination to apply the perfect letter of religious law to her brother's dilemma and the dramatic process through which she comes to realize that you can't shut a door and shut the world out, she and Angelo must discover that whenever they run their revolutionary law courts, Pompey enters to talk about his dishes of prunes and messes things up. So nothing is as clear as Isabella thought it would be.

Then there is the discovery of Mariana, that wonderful relationship, the discovery of the worldly woman—a woman who is loved, is bruised—the discovery of a different kind of beauty in the possibilities of women's lives. That is supremely Shakespearean, as though you can hear the heart of Shakespeare beating underneath the story of these two absolutists, Angelo and Isabella, who try to apply their rigid view of human society and human morality. You can feel the Shakespeare heart beating as he says: life's not like that. These were some of my ideas as I directed.

Of course, you have only a clue about these matters before you start working. You have to set out on a long walk with a map in your hand, but you must be prepared to put the map down and just walk. With good actors—and I had very good actors—in a play like *Measure for Measure,* it has to be kind of a company-wide exploration.

One of the things I'm describing is that the line that the role of Isabella and the role of Angelo take in the play is very pure. Yes, they're very pure acting lines, whereas the line taken by the role of the Duke is extremely complex. And you do come up against really fundamental problems like: why doesn't the Duke tell Isabella that Claudio is alive? One of the most difficult problems in the piece is trying to find whether there is anything other than just pure delight in his own conjury. Michael Pennington felt that this was the hardest part of the role. The solution we worked out, like trying to solve a very complex crossword puzzle, was this: that the destination of the Duke is *not* to step in and undo Angelo's work at any moment. Certainly he could step in to tell Isabella about the head-switching and reveal that Claudio is alive. But the whole point of his leaving society has, at that point, not been fulfilled.

The fulfillment actually comes in the great final challenge he offers Isabella at the end of the play: his perfect argument for an eye for an eye and a tooth for a tooth. He exposes one man's corruption and makes the point about her brother's death. When he quotes: "Haste still pays haste, and leisure answers leisure;/ like doth quit like, and Measure still for Measure," it is a kind of test since the Duke believes the total and absolute *opposite* of what he is saying. But he puts to her the most brilliant and perfect case for capital punishment you could ever put together. Isabella's line, "Let him not die," cracks the code for the play. In other words, the Duke's destination is to release Isabella from absolutism, as though a play got to the point where all of the Iranian clerics in Teheran said, "Okay, we were wrong." Then you can have a happy ending, not before. Because if you have a happy ending earlier, by delivering Claudio back to Isabella, you have not solved the political problem. Somebody must actually see that the way in which human society can finally flourish, the only way, is through the spirit of mercy and compassion. These are not absolutist ideals. When Isabella has arrived at that, however, the Duke proposes marriage. I believe the reason for it is actually to be found more in the world of the morality play and the masque, than it is in the world of just personal motive.

The last image in my production was that Isabella and the Duke never touched. There was no sense that she said yes to his offer. But she threw away her nun's veil and he threw away his monk's garb, and they walked away together. It recalls one of those Stuart drawings in which a perfectly honorable king and a perfectly honorable queen sit side by side on thrones and become the new rulers of the society. Her virtue, the hard-earned human charity that she has found, is now to be placed at the very center of society, in a way that the Czechs did with Vaclav Havel. But I believe their relationship has nothing to do with romance. I believe it has everything to do with the two parallel lines that run through the story and that simply come together at the end.

The happy ending, which is delivered when Shakespeare ends his play, is political, not personal. Perhaps a better way of saying it is that it's an *enlightened* ending. I'm afraid I could never call it a *happy* ending. While I do believe that the Duke-of-dark-corners was not just indulging himself, there was without question a very, very serious political motivation in what he does. I can't think of another play by Shakespeare that is more political than *Measure for Measure.* As far as the balance between tragedy and comedy is concerned, it is really a problem of tone that has been represented more by critics than audiences. The play contains totally modern, mixed sensibilities and multiple responses to reality which, to a modern temperament, can be very very satisfying.

In this respect, the play's treatment of sexuality is a very central issue. In the mid-seventies, one of the problems with Isabella was that audiences were prepared to think, "Who can like a heroine who won't go to bed with someone to save her brother's life?" This was after the swinging sixties, of course. Someone actually suggested that I do the

Continued

play as a fantasy or an allegory. Furthermore, who can believe in a play that deals with a law where people are executed for fornication. What was very interesting was that, within five years, nobody could say this play had to be directed like a fantasy because these things don't happen. In Iran, within the first two weeks of the revolution, they were lining up hundreds of prostitutes against the walls of the prison in Teheran and executing them. That was the moment where many of us in the West started to become aware for the very first time of the nature of strict Islamic observation. So it wasn't a fantasy anymore. In that world, if a brother would ask his sister to sleep with a man to save his life, actually it is the *man* who would be regarded as being unacceptable. A man couldn't possibly ask that of his sister, to dishonor herself in such a way to save his life.

So I directed the play right at the time when the sixties began to swing back and the beginning of the harsh eighties were just around the corner. I remember in my production that when Mistress Overdone was arrested, they brought in a whole load of other whores at the same time and they stripped them all in the prison yard, stripped their clothes off, and their wigs, and they were just a group of women practically naked, shivering. The overtone was like Auschwitz. Pompey, Overdone, and Lucio—all of that Southwark world of brothels that Shakespeare knew so well, I feel he wrote about it with a great deal of compassion and humor. Yet it is interesting that the character who is castigated more than anyone else is Lucio, who is actually exploiting those people. Lucio is unbelievably cruel to Pompey when Pompey is in prison. Again I could hear this heartbeat of Shakespeare I often feel when directing his plays, that Shakespeare likes Pompey, approves of him, even though he's a pimp.

On the other level, the play offers a fascinating exploration of the particular relationship between sexual desire and extreme repression. I can't think of another scene in Shakespeare that explodes with more sexual tension than the second big scene between Angelo and Isabella, where he cannot bring himself to say, "I want you." He has to go through theological phrasing and coded messages. It's like the Hoover Dam breaking. It's magnificent writing.

The play suited the [smaller] Aldwych Theatre more than it suited the Stratford Theatre, because the play is claustrophobic; it's harder to do the play on a more open stage. My stage set wasn't particularly high; it is a prison play, a play of dense argument. Much of the play is carried by two or three actors on stage at the same time. But as I stated earlier about a morality play relocated in the early seventeenth century, I do see the play as a theorem of ideas, although that's not worth five cents unless its fully fleshed out and enacted by human beings. My production was very influenced by the Seven Deadly Sins—pictures of Brueghel, but not the silly shoes, silly hats, and burlap jackets, since ours was quite an elegant Jacobean production. But that world of Brueghel's hell and heaven and earth are very close together, a rather terrifying religious atmosphere. I did try to make the play terrifying. I did try to make the prison, and what was in it, terrifying.

Notes

1. *G. B. Harrison, ed.* SHAKESPEARE: MAJOR PLAYS AND THE SONNETS *(New York: Harcourt Brace & Co., 1948), 746.*

2. "MEASURE FOR MEASURE *on Stage and Screen*" *in* MEASURE FOR MEASURE, *ed. S. Nagarajan (New York: New American Library, 1964), 224–25.*

3. *Peter Brook,* THE EMPTY SPACE *(New York: Avon Books, 1968), 81.*

MEASURE FOR MEASURE
WILLIAM SHAKESPEARE

CHARACTERS

Vincentio, *the Duke*
Angelo, *the Deputy*
Escalus, *an ancient Lord*
Claudio, *a young gentleman*
Lucio, *a fantastic*
Two Other Like Gentlemen
Provost
Thomas }
Peter } two friars

A Justice
Varrius
Elbow, *a simple constable*
Froth, *a foolish gentleman*
Clown (Pompey, *servant to Mistress Overdone*)
Abhorson, *an executioner*
Barnardine, *a dissolute prisoner*

Isabella, *sister to Claudio*
Mariana, *betrothed to Angelo*
Juliet, *beloved of Claudio*
Francisca, *a nun*
Mistress Overdone, *a bawd*
Lords, Officers, Citizens, Boy, and Attendants

SCENE: Vienna

ACT ONE

SCENE ONE (THE DUKE'S PALACE)

Enter DUKE, ESCALUS, LORDS, (*and* ATTENDANTS).

DUKE. Escalus.
ESCALUS.   My lord.
DUKE.
    Of government the properties[1] to unfold,
    Would seem in me t' affect speech and discourse,
    Since I am put to know[2] that your own science[3]   5
    Exceeds, in that, the lists[4] of all advice
    My strength can give you. Then no more remains
    But that, to your sufficiency as your worth is able,[5]
    And let them work. The nature of our people,
    Our city's institutions, and the terms   10
    For common justice, y'are as pregnant in[6]

    As art and practice hath enriched any
    That we remember. There is our commission,
    From which we would not have you warp.[7] Call hither,
    I say, bid come before us Angelo. (*Exit an*   15
    ATTENDANT.)
    What figure[8] of us, think you, he will bear?[9]
    For you must know, we have with special soul[10]
    Elected him our absence to supply;
    Lent him our terror, dressed him with our love,
    And given his deputation all the organs[11]   20
    Of our own pow'r. What think you of it?
ESCALUS.
    If any in Vienna be of worth
    To undergo[12] such ample grace and honor,
    It is Lord Angelo.

Enter ANGELO.

DUKE.   Look where he comes.   25

---

[1]**properties** characteristics [2]**put to know** given to understand [3]**science** knowledge [4]**lists** limits [5]**to your sufficiency . . . able** (perhaps a line is missing after this line) [6]**pregnant in** full of knowledge

[7]**warp** deviate [8]**figure** image [9]**bear** represent [10]**soul** thought [11]**organs** means of action [12]**undergo** enjoy

ANGELO.   Always obedient to your Grace's will,
  I come to know your pleasure.
DUKE.
                  Angelo,
  There is a kind of character[13] in thy life,
  That to th' observer doth thy history   **30**
  Fully unfold. Thyself and thy belongings[14]
  Are not thine own so proper[15] as to waste
  Thyself upon thy virtues, they on thee.
  Heaven doth with us as we with torches do,[16]
  Not light them for themselves; for if our virtues **35**
  Did not go forth of us, 'twere all alike
  As if we had them not. Spirits are not finely
    touched
  But to fine issues,[17] nor Nature never lends
  The smallest scruple[18] of her excellence
  But like a thrifty goddess she determines   **40**
  Herself the glory of a creditor,
  Both thanks and use.[19] But I do bend[20] my
    speech
  To one that can my part in him advertise.[21]
  Hold therefore, Angelo:
  In our remove[22] be thou at full ourself;   **45**
  Mortality and mercy in Vienna
  Live in thy tongue and heart. Old Escalus,
  Though first in question,[23] is thy secondary.[24]
  Take thy commission.
ANGELO.
             Now, good my lord,   **50**
  Let there be some more test made of my mettle[25]
  Before so noble and so great a figure
  Be stamped upon it.
DUKE.
           No more evasion.
  We have with a leavened[26] and preparèd choice **55**
  Proceeded to you; therefore take your honors.
  Our haste from hence is of so quick condition
  That it prefers itself,[27] and leaves unquestioned[28]
  Matters of needful value. We shall write to you,
  As time and our concernings shall importune,   **60**
  How it goes with us, and do look to know
  What doth befall you here. So fare you well.

To th' hopeful execution do I leave you
Of your commissions.
ANGELO.
           Yet give leave, my lord,   **65**
  That we may bring[29] you something on the way.
DUKE.
  My haste may not admit it;
  Nor need you, on mine honor, have to do
  With any scruple; your scope is as mine own,
  So to enforce or qualify the laws   **70**
  As to your soul seems good. Give me your hand.
  I'll privily away; I love the people,
  But do not like to stage me to their eyes.
  Though it do well, I do not relish well
  Their loud applause and aves[30] vehement.   **75**
  Nor do I think the man of safe discretion
  That does affect it. Once more, fare you well.
ANGELO.   The heavens give safety to your purposes.
ESCALUS.   Lead forth and bring you back in happiness.
DUKE.   I thank you; fare you well. (*Exit.*)   **80**
ESCALUS.
  I shall desire you, sir, to give me leave
  To have free speech with you; and it concerns me
  To look into the bottom of my place.[31]
  A pow'r I have, but of what strength and nature,
  I am not yet instructed.   **85**
ANGELO.
  'Tis so with me. Let us withdraw together,
  And we may soon our satisfaction have
  Touching that point.
ESCALUS.   I'll wait upon your honor. (*Exeunt.*)

SCENE TWO (A STREET)

Enter LUCIO *and two other* GENTLEMEN.

LUCIO.   If the Duke, with the other dukes, come not to com-
position[1] with the King of Hungary,[2] why then all the
dukes fall upon the King.
FIRST GENTLEMAN.   Heaven grant us its peace, but not the
King of Hungary's!   **5**
SECOND GENTLEMAN.   Amen.
LUCIO.   Thou conclud'st like the sanctimonious pirate, that
went to sea with the Ten Commandments, but scraped one
out of the table.
SECOND GENTLEMAN.   "Thou shalt not steal"?   **10**
LUCIO.   Ay, that he razed.
FIRST GENTLEMAN.   Why, 'twas a commandment to com-
mand the captain and all the rest from their functions: they

---

[13]**character** secret handwriting [14]**belongings** endowments
[15]**proper** exclusively [16]**Heaven . . . do** (see Luke 11:33: "No
man, when he hath lighted a candle, putteth it in a secret place,
neither under a bushel, but on a candlestick that they which come
in may see the light." Also Matthew 7:16: "Ye shall know them
by their fruits") [17]**Spirits . . . issues** i.e., great qualities are
bestowed only so that they may lead to great achievements
[18]**scruple** 1/24 oz. [19]**use** interest [20]**bend** address [21]**advertise**
display prominently [22]**remove** absence [23]**question** consideration
[24]**secondary** subordinate [25]**mettle** (pun on "metal," i.e.,
material) [26]**leavened** i.e., long-pondered [27]**prefers itself** takes
precedence [28]**unquestioned** unexamined

[29]**bring** escort [30]**aves** salutations [31]**To look . . . place** i.e., to
examine carefully the range of my authority [1]**composition**
agreement [2]**Hungary** (perhaps a pun on "hungry")

put forth to steal. There's not a soldier of us all that, in the thanksgiving before meat, do relish the petition **15** well that prays for peace.

SECOND GENTLEMAN.   I never heard any soldier dislike it.

LUCIO.   I believe thee, for I think thou never wast where grace was said.   **20**

SECOND GENTLEMAN.   No? A dozen times at least.

FIRST GENTLEMAN.   What, in meter?

LUCIO.   In any proportion,[3] or in any language.

FIRST GENTLEMAN.   I think, or in any religion.

LUCIO.   Ay, why not? Grace is grace, despite of all **25** controversy: as, for example, thou thyself art a wicked villain, despite of all grace.

FIRST GENTLEMAN.   Well, there went but a pair of shears between us.[4]

LUCIO.   I grant; as there may between the lists[5] and **30** the velvet. Thou art the list.

FIRST GENTLEMAN.   And thou the velvet. Thou art good velvet; thou'rt a three-piled[6] piece, I warrant thee. I had as lief be a list of an English kersey,[7] as be piled, as thou art piled, for a French velvet.[8] Do I speak feel- **35** ingly[9] now?

LUCIO.   I think thou dost; and, indeed, with most painful feeling[10] of thy speech. I will, out of thine own confession, learn to begin thy health; but, whilst I live, forget to drink after thee.[11]   **40**

FIRST GENTLEMAN.   I think I have done myself wrong, have I not?

SECOND GENTLEMAN.   Yes, that thou hast, whether thou art tainted or free.

Enter BAWD (MISTRESS OVERDONE).

LUCIO.   Behold, behold, where Madam Mitigation **45** comes! I have purchased as many diseases under her roof as come to—

SECOND GENTLEMAN.   To what, I pray?

LUCIO.   Judge.

SECOND GENTLEMAN.   To three thousand dolors[12] **50** a year.

FIRST GENTLEMAN.   Ay, and more.

LUCIO.   A French crown[13] more.

FIRST GENTLEMAN.   Thou art always figuring diseases in me, but thou art full of error. I am sound.   **55**

LUCIO.   Nay, not as one would say, healthy; but so sound as things that are hollow. Thy bones are hollow; impiety[14] has made a feast of thee.

FIRST GENTLEMAN.   How now! Which of your hips has the most profound sciatica?   **60**

MISTRESS OVERDONE.   Well, well; there's one yonder arrested and carried to prison was worth five thousand of you all.

SECOND GENTLEMAN.   Who's that, I pray thee?

MISTRESS OVERDONE.   Marry,[15] sir, that's Claudio, **65** Signior Claudio.

FIRST GENTLEMAN.   Claudio to prison? 'Tis not so.

MISTRESS OVERDONE.   Nay, but I know 'tis so. I saw him arrested; saw him carried away, and which is more, within these three days his head to be chopped off.   **70**

LUCIO.   But, after all this fooling, I would not have it so. Art thou sure of this?

MISTRESS OVERDONE.   I am too sure of it; and it is for getting Madam Julietta with child.

LUCIO.   Believe me, this may be. He promised to **75** meet me two hours since, and he was ever precise in promise-keeping.

SECOND GENTLEMAN.   Besides, you know, it draws something near to the speech we had to such a purpose.

FIRST GENTLEMAN.   But, most of all, agreeing with **80** the proclamation.

LUCIO.   Away! Let's go learn the truth of it.

Exit (LUCIO *with* GENTLEMEN).

MISTRESS OVERDONE.   Thus, what with the war, what with the sweat,[16] what with the gallows, and what with poverty, I am custom-shrunk.   **85**

Enter CLOWN (POMPEY).

How now? What's the news with you?

POMPEY.   Yonder man is carried to prison.

MISTRESS OVERDONE.   Well; what has he done?

POMPEY.   A woman.

MISTRESS OVERDONE.   But what's his offense?   **90**

POMPEY.   Groping for trouts in a peculiar[17] river.

MISTRESS OVERDONE.   What? Is there a maid with child by him?

POMPEY.   No, but there's a woman with maid by him. You have not heard of the proclamation, have you?   **95**

MISTRESS OVERDONE.   What proclamation, man?

POMPEY.   All houses in the suburbs[18] of Vienna must be plucked down.

---

[3]**proportion** length   [4]**there . . . us** i.e., we are cut from the same cloth   [5]**lists** selvage or border of a cloth (usually of a different material from the body)   [6]**three-piled** (1) pile of a treble thickness (2) "piled" (bald) as a result of venereal disease   [7]**kersey** coarse cloth (therefore "plain and honest")   [8]**French velvet** (1) excellent velvet (2) French prostitute (syphilis was also known as "the French disease")   [9]**Do . . . feelingly** i.e., do I touch you there?   [10]**feeling** personal experience   [11]**learn . . . thee** drink to your health but not after you from the same cup (to avoid the infection)   [12]**dolors** (pun on "dollars")   [13]**French crown** (1) écu (2) head that has gone bald from venereal disease

[14]**impiety** immorality   [15]**Marry** (a light oath, from "by the Virgin Mary")   [16]**sweat** sweating sickness, plague   [17]**peculiar** private   [18]**suburbs** (in Shakespeare's London, the area of the brothels)

MISTRESS OVERDONE.   And what shall become of those
in the city?   **100**

POMPEY.   They shall stand for seed: they had gone down
too, but that a wise burgher put in for them.

MISTRESS OVERDONE.   But shall all our houses of resort
in the suburbs be pulled down?

POMPEY.   To the ground, mistress.   **105**

MISTRESS OVERDONE.   Why, here's a change indeed in
the commonwealth! What shall become of me?

POMPEY.   Come, fear not you; good counselors lack no clients. Though you change your place, you need not change
your trade; I'll be your tapster[19] still. Courage,   **110**
there will be pity taken on you; you that have worn your
eyes almost out in the service, you will be considered.

MISTRESS OVERDONE.   What's to do here, Thomas Tapster? Let's withdraw.

POMPEY.   Here comes Signior Claudio, led by the   **115**
provost to prison; and there's Madam Juliet. (*Exeunt.*)

Enter PROVOST, CLAUDIO, JULIET, OFFICERS, LUCIO, *and
two* GENTLEMEN.

CLAUDIO.
   Fellow, why dost thou show me thus to th' world?
   Bear me to prison, where I am committed.

PROVOST.
   I do it not in evil disposition,
   But from Lord Angelo, by special charge.   **120**

CLAUDIO.
   Thus can the demigod Authority
   Make us pay down for our offense by weight.
   The words of heaven: on whom it will, it will;
   On whom it will not, so. Yet still 'tis just.[20]

LUCIO.   Why, how now, Claudio! Whence comes   **125**
this restraint?

CLAUDIO.
   From too much liberty, my Lucio, liberty.
   As surfeit is the father of much fast,
   So every scope by the immoderate use
   Turns to restraint. Our natures do pursue,   **130**
   Like rats that ravin down their proper bane,[21]
   A thirsty evil, and when we drink, we die.

LUCIO.   If I could speak so wisely under an arrest, I would
send for certain of my creditors. And yet, to say the truth,
I had as lief have the foppery[22] of freedom as the   **135**
mortality of imprisonment. What's thy offense, Claudio?

CLAUDIO.   What but to speak of would offend again.

LUCIO.   What, is't murder?

CLAUDIO.   No.

LUCIO.   Lechery?   **140**

CLAUDIO.   Call it so.

PROVOST.   Away, sir, you must go.

CLAUDIO.   One word, good friend. Lucio, a word with you.

LUCIO.   A hundred, if they'll do you any good. Is lechery
so looked after?   **145**

CLAUDIO.
   Thus stands it with me: upon a true contract
   I got possession of Julietta's bed.
   You know the lady, she is fast my wife,
   Save that we do the denunciation[23] lack
   Of outward order. This we came not to,   **150**
   Only for propagation[24] of a dower
   Remaining in the coffer of her friends,[25]
   From whom we thought it meet to hide our love
   Till time had made them for us. But it chances
   The stealth of our most mutual entertainment   **155**
   With character too gross is writ on Juliet.

LUCIO.   With child, perhaps?

CLAUDIO.
                              Unhappily, even so.
   And the new deputy now for the Duke—
   Whether it be the fault and glimpse of
      newness,[26]   **160**
   Or whether that the body public be
   A horse whereon the governor doth ride,
   Who, newly in the seat, that it may know
   He can command, lets it straight feel the spur;
   Whether the tyranny be in his place,   **165**
   Or in his eminence that fills it up,
   I stagger in[27]—but this new governor
   Awakes me all the enrollèd[28] penalties
   Which have, like unscoured armor, hung by th' wall
   So long, that nineteen zodiacs[29] have gone
      round,   **170**
   And none of them been worn; and, for a name,
   Now puts the drowsy and neglected act
   Freshly on me. 'Tis surely for a name.

LUCIO.   I warrant it is, and thy head stands so tickle[30] on
thy shoulders, that a milkmaid, if she be in love,   **175**
may sigh it off. Send after the Duke, and appeal to him.

CLAUDIO.
   I have done so, but he's not to be found.
   I prithee, Lucio, do me this kind service:
   This day my sister should the cloister enter,
   And there receive her approbation.[31]   **180**

---

[19]**tapster** bartender, waiter (here, pimp)   [20]**The words . . . just**
(see Romans 9:15,18: "For he saith to Moses, I will have mercy
on whom I will have mercy, and I will have compassion on
whom I will have compassion. . . . Therefore hath he mercy on
whom he will have mercy, and whom he will he hardeneth")
[21]**ravin . . . bane** greedily devour what is poisonous to them
[22]**foppery** foolishness

[23]**denunciation** formal announcement   [24]**propagation** increase
[25]**friends** relatives   [26]**fault and glimpse of newness** i.e., weakness
arising from the sudden vision of new authority   [27]**stagger in** am
not sure   [28]**enrollèd** inscribed in the rolls of the laws   [29]**zodiacs**
i.e., years   [30]**tickle** insecure   [31]**approbation** novitiate

Acquaint her with the danger of my state;
Implore her, in my voice, that she make friends
To the strict deputy; bid herself assay[32] him.
I have great hope in that; for in her youth
There is a prone[33] and speechless dialect,   **185**
Such as move men; beside, she hath prosperous art
When she will play with reason and discourse,
And well she can persuade.

LUCIO.   I pray she may; as well for the encouragement of
the like, which else would stand under grievous   **190**
imposition, as for the enjoying of thy life, who I would
be sorry should be thus foolishly lost at a game of tick-
tack.[34] I'll to her.

CLAUDIO.   I thank you, good friend Lucio.

LUCIO.   Within two hours.   **195**

CLAUDIO.   Come, officer, away! (*Exeunt.*)

SCENE THREE (A MONASTERY)

Enter DUKE *and* FRIAR THOMAS.

DUKE.
No, holy father; throw away that thought;
Believe not that the dribbling dart[1] of love
Can pierce a complete[2] bosom. Why I desire thee
To give me secret harbor, hath a purpose
More grave and wrinkled[3] than the aims and ends   **5**
Of burning youth.

FRIAR THOMAS.   May your Grace speak of it?

DUKE.
My holy sir, none better knows than you
How I have ever loved the life removed,
And held in idle price to haunt assemblies   **10**
Where youth and cost, witless bravery[4] keeps.
I have delivered to Lord Angelo,
A man of stricture[5] and firm abstinence,
My absolute power and place here in Vienna,
And he supposes me traveled to Poland;   **15**
For so I have strewed it in the common ear,[6]
And so it is received. Now, pious sir,
You will demand of me why I do this.

FRIAR THOMAS.   Gladly, my lord.

DUKE.
We have strict statutes and most biting laws,   **20**
The needful bits and curbs to headstrong weeds,
Which for this fourteen[7] years we have let slip,
Even like an o'ergrown lion in a cave,

That goes not out to prey. Now, as fond fathers,
Having bound up the threat'ning twigs of birch,   **25**
Only to stick it in their children's sight
For terror, not to use; in time the rod
Becomes more mocked than feared; so our decrees,
Dead to infliction,[8] to themselves are dead,
And Liberty[9] plucks Justice by the nose;   **30**
The baby beats the nurse, and quite athwart
Goes all decorum.

FRIAR THOMAS.
                    It rested in your Grace
To unloose this tied-up Justice when you pleased,
And it in you more dreadful would have seemed   **35**
Than in Lord Angelo.

DUKE.
                    I do fear, too dreadful:
Sith[10] 'twas my fault to give the people scope,
'Twould be my tyranny to strike and gall them
For what I bid them do; for we bid this be done   **40**
When evil deeds have their permissive pass,
And not the punishment. Therefore, indeed, my
    father,
I have on Angelo imposed the office,
Who may, in th' ambush[11] of my name, strike home,
And yet my nature never in the fight   **45**
To do it slander. And to behold his sway,
I will, as 'twere a brother of your order,
Visit both prince and people. Therefore, I prithee,
Supply me with the habit[12] and instruct me
How I may formally in person bear   **50**
Like a true friar. Moe[13] reasons for this action
At our more leisure shall I render you;
Only, this one: Lord Angelo is precise,[14]
Stands at a guard with envy;[15] scarce confesses
That his blood flows, or that his appetite   **55**
Is more to bread than stone. Hence shall we see,
If power change purpose, what our seemers be.
                    Exit (*with* FRIAR).

SCENE FOUR (A NUNNERY)

Enter ISABELLA *and* FRANCISCA, *a nun.*

ISABELLA.   And have you nuns no farther privileges?

FRANCISCA.   Are not these large enough?

ISABELLA.
Yes, truly. I speak not as desiring more,
But rather wishing a more strict restraint
Upon the sisterhood, the votarists of Saint Clare.[1]   **5**

LUCIO (*within*).   Ho! Peace be in this place!

---

[32]**assay** test, i.e., attempt to persuade [33]**prone** winning [34]**tick-tack** (literally, a game using a board into which pegs were fitted) [1]**dribbling dart** arrow feebly shot [2]**complete** protected, independent [3]**wrinkled** mature, aged [4]**witless bravery** senseless show [5]**stricture** strictness [6]**common ear** the ear of the people [7]**fourteen** (in I.ii.170 the time has been "nineteen" years. Doubtless the printer's copy in both lines had either xiv or xix and in one line was misread)

[8]**Dead to infliction** utterly unenforced [9]**Liberty** license [10]**Sith** since [11]**in th' ambush** under cover [12]**habit** garment [13]**Moe** more [14]**precise** fastidiously strict [15]**Stands . . . envy** defies all malicious criticism [1]**Saint Clare** (a notably strict order)

ISABELLA.   Who's that which calls?
FRANCISCA.

    It is a man's voice. Gentle Isabella,
    Turn you the key, and know his business of him.
    You may, I may not: you are yet unsworn.   **10**
    When you have vowed, you must not speak with
      men
    But in the presence of the prioress:
    Then, if you speak, you must not show your face,
    Or, if you show your face, you must not speak.
    He calls again; I pray you, answer him. (*Exit*.)   **15**

ISABELLA.   Peace and prosperity! Who is't that calls?

Enter LUCIO.

LUCIO.   Hail, virgin—if you be, as those cheek-roses
    Proclaim you are no less! Can you so stead[2] me
    As bring me to the sight of Isabella,
    A novice of this place and the fair sister   **20**
    To her unhappy brother, Claudio?

ISABELLA.
    Why ''her unhappy brother''? Let me ask,
    The rather for I now must make you know
    I am that Isabella and his sister.

LUCIO.
    Gentle and fair, your brother kindly greets you.   **25**
    Not to be weary with you, he's in prison.

ISABELLA.   Woe me! For what?

LUCIO.
    For that which, if myself might be his judge,
    He should receive his punishment in thanks:
    He hath got his friend with child.   **30**

ISABELLA.   Sir! Make me not your story.[3]

LUCIO.
                    'Tis true.
    I would not, though 'tis my familiar sin
    With maids to seem the lapwing,[4] and to jest,
    Tongue far from heart, play with all virgins so.   **35**
    I hold you as a thing enskied and sainted,
    By your renouncement, an immortal spirit;
    And to be talked with in sincerity,
    As with a saint.

ISABELLA.   You do blaspheme the good in mocking   **40**
  me.

LUCIO.
    Do not believe it. Fewness and truth,[5] 'tis thus:
    Your brother and his lover have embraced;
    As those that feed grow full, as blossoming time
    That from the seedness[6] the bare fallow brings   **45**
    To teeming foison,[7] even so her plenteous womb
    Expresseth his full tilth and husbandry.

ISABELLA.   Someone with child by him? My cousin Juliet?
LUCIO.   Is she your cousin?
ISABELLA.
    Adoptedly, as schoolmaids change their names   **50**
    By vain, though apt, affection.

LUCIO.   She it is.

ISABELLA.   O, let him marry her.

LUCIO.
                This is the point:
    The Duke is very strangely gone from hence;   **55**
    Bore many gentlemen, myself being one,
    In hand and hope of action,[8] but we do learn
    By those that know the very nerves of state,
    His givings-out were of an infinite distance
    From his true-meant design. Upon his place,   **60**
    And with full line of his authority,
    Governs Lord Angelo, a man whose blood
    Is very snow-broth; one who never feels
    The wanton stings and motions of the sense,
    But doth rebate and blunt his natural edge   **65**
    With profits of the mind, study and fast.
    He—to give fear to use and liberty,[9]
    Which have for long run by the hideous law,
    As mice by lions—hath picked out an act,
    Under whose heavy sense[10] your brother's life   **70**
    Falls into forfeit; he arrests him on it,
    And follows close the rigor of the statute,
    To make him an example. All hope is gone,
    Unless you have the grace by your fair prayer
    To soften Angelo. And that's my pith of
      business   **75**
    'Twixt you and your poor brother.

ISABELLA.   Doth he so? Seek his life?

LUCIO.
                  Has censured[11] him
    Already, and, as I hear, the provost hath
    A warrant for's execution.   **80**

ISABELLA.
    Alas, what poor ability's in me
    To do him good?

LUCIO.   Assay the pow'r you have.

ISABELLA.   My power? Alas, I doubt—

LUCIO.
                Our doubts are traitors, **85**
    And makes[12] us lose the good we oft might win,
    By fearing to attempt. Go to Lord Angelo,
    And let him learn to know, when maidens sue,
    Men give like gods; but when they weep and kneel,

---

[2]**stead** help   [3]**story** subject for mirth   [4]**lapwing** pewit (a bird
which runs away from its nest to mislead intruders)   [5]**Fewness
and truth** briefly and truly   [6]**seedness** sowing   [7]**foison** harvest

[8]**Bore . . . action** deluded . . . with the hope of military action
[9]**use and liberty** habitual license   [10]**sense** interpretation
[11]**censured** pronounced judgment on   [12]**makes** (a plural subject
sometimes takes a verb ending in -s)

All their petitions are as freely theirs   90
As they themselves would owe[13] them.
ISABELLA.   I'll see what I can do.
LUCIO.   But speedily.
ISABELLA.
  I will about it straight,
  No longer staying but to give the Mother   95
  Notice of my affair. I humbly thank you;
  Commend me to my brother; soon at night
  I'll send him certain word of my success.[14]
LUCIO.   I take my leave of you.
ISABELLA.   Good sir, adieu. (*Exeunt.*)   100

ACT TWO

SCENE ONE (A ROOM)

Enter ANGELO, ESCALUS, *and* SERVANTS, JUSTICE.

ANGELO.
  We must not make a scarecrow of the law,
  Setting it up to fear the birds of prey,
  And let it keep one shape, till custom make it
  Their perch and not their terror.
ESCALUS.
                              Ay, but yet   5
  Let us be keen, and rather cut[1] a little,
  Than fall,[2] and bruise to death. Alas, this gentleman
  Whom I would save had a most noble father.
  Let but your honor know,
  Whom I believe to be most strait[3] in virtue,   10
  That, in the working of your own affections,[4]
  Had time cohered with place or place with wishing,
  Or that the resolute acting of your blood
  Could have attained th' effect of your own purpose,
  Whether you had not sometime in your life   15
  Erred in this point which now you censure him,
  And pulled the law upon you.
ANGELO.
  'Tis one thing to be tempted, Escalus,
  Another thing to fall. I not deny,
  The jury, passing on the prisoner's life,   20
  May in the sworn twelve have a thief or two
  Guiltier than him they try. What's open made to
      Justice,
  That Justice seizes. What knows the laws
  That thieves do pass on thieves? 'Tis very pregnant,[5]
  The jewel that we find, we stoop and take't   25
  Because we see it; but what we do not see
  We tread upon, and never think of it.
  You may not so extenuate his offense
  For I have had such faults; but rather tell me,

When I, that censure him, do so offend,   30
  Let mine own judgment pattern out my death,
  And nothing come in partial. Sir, he must die.
ESCALUS.   Be it as your wisdom will.
ANGELO.   Where is the provost?

Enter PROVOST.

PROVOST.   Here, if it like your honor.   35
ANGELO.
                          See that Claudio
  Be executed by nine tomorrow morning.
  Bring him his confessor, let him be prepared,
  For that's the utmost of his pilgrimage. (*Exit*
      PROVOST.)
ESCALUS.
  Well, Heaven forgive him, and forgive us all.   40
  Some rise by sin, and some by virtue fall:
  Some run from breaks of ice,[6] and answer none;
  And some condemnèd for a fault[7] alone.

Enter ELBOW, FROTH, CLOWN (POMPEY), OFFICERS.

ELBOW.   Come, bring them away. If these be good people
  in a commonweal that do nothing but use their   45
  abuses in common houses, I know no law. Bring them
  away.
ANGELO.   How now, sir! What's your name? And what's
  the matter?
ELBOW.   If it please your honor, I am the poor   50
  Duke's constable, and my name is Elbow. I do lean upon
  justice, sir, and do bring in here before your good honor
  two notorious benefactors.
ANGELO.   Benefactors? Well, what benefactors are they?
  Are they not malefactors?   55
ELBOW.   If it please your honor, I know not well what they
  are, but precise villains they are, that I am sure of, and
  void of all profanation in the world that good Christians
  ought to have.
ESCALUS.   This comes off well; here's a wise officer.   60
ANGELO.   Go to: what quality[8] are they of? Elbow is your
  name? Why dost thou not speak, Elbow?
POMPEY.   He cannot, sir; he's out at elbow.[9]
ANGELO.   What are you, sir?
ELBOW.   He, sir! A tapster, sir, parcel-bawd,[10] one   65
  that serves a bad woman whose house, sir, was, as they
  say, plucked down in the suburbs, and now she professes
  a hothouse,[11] which, I think, is a very ill house too.
ESCALUS.   How know you that?

---

[13]**owe** own   [14]**success** outcome   [1]**cut** prune   [2]**fall** let the ax fall
[3]**strait** strict   [4]**affections** passions   [5]**pregnant** clear

[6]**Some . . . ice** some escape after gross violations of chastity
(? the passage is much disputed)   [7]**fault** (1) small crack in the ice
(2) act of sex   [8]**quality** profession   [9]**out at elbow** (1) somewhat
seedy (2) speechless (out at the sound of his name)   [10]**parcel-
bawd** partly a bawd   [11]**hothouse** bathhouse

ELBOW.   My wife, sir, whom I detest[12] before   70
Heaven and your honor—

ESCALUS.   How! Thy wife?

ELBOW.   Ay, sir—whom, I thank Heaven, is an honest[13]
woman—

ESCALUS.   Dost thou detest her therefore?   75

ELBOW.   I say, sir, I will detest myself also, as well as she,
that this house, if it be not a bawd's house, it is pity of
her life, for it is a naughty[14] house.

ESCALUS.   How dost thou know that, constable?

ELBOW.   Marry, sir, by my wife, who, if she had   80
been a woman cardinally[15] given, might have been accused in fornication, adultery, and all uncleanliness there.

ESCALUS.   By the woman's means?

ELBOW.   Ay, sir, by Mistress Overdone's means; but as she
spit in his face, so she defied him.   85

POMPEY.   Sir, if it please your honor, this is not so.

ELBOW.   Prove it before these varlets here, thou honorable
man; prove it.

ESCALUS.   Do you hear how he misplaces?

POMPEY.   Sir, she came in great with child; and   90
longing, saving your honor's reverence, for stewed
prunes.[16] Sir, we had but two in the house, which at that
very distant time stood, as it were, in a fruit dish, a dish
of some threepence; your honors have seen such dishes;
they are not china dishes, but very good dishes—   95

ESCALUS.   Go to, go to; no matter for the dish, sir.

POMPEY.   No, indeed, sir, not of a pin; you are therein in
the right; but to the point. As I say, this Mistress Elbow,
being, as I say, with child, and being great-bellied, and
longing, as I said, for prunes; and having but two   100
in the dish, as I said, Master Froth here, this very man,
having eaten the rest, as I said, and, as I say, paying for
them very honestly; for, as you know, Master Froth, I
could not give you threepence again.

FROTH.   No, indeed.   105

POMPEY.   Very well, you being then, if you be rememb'red,
cracking the stones of the foresaid prunes—

FROTH.   Ay, so I did indeed.

POMPEY.   Why, very well; I telling you then, if you be rememb'red, that such a one and such a one were   110
past cure of the thing you wot[17] of, unless they kept very
good diet, as I told you—

FROTH.   All this is true.

POMPEY.   Why, very well, then—

ESCALUS.   Come, you are a tedious fool; to the pur-   115
pose. What was done to Elbow's wife, that he hath cause
to complain of? Come me to what was done to her.

POMPEY.   Sir, your honor cannot come to that yet.[18]

ESCALUS.   No, sir, nor I mean it not.

POMPEY.   Sir, but you shall come to it, by your hon-   120
or's leave. And, I beseech you, look into Master Froth here,
sir, a man of fourscore pound a year, whose father died at
Hallowmas.[19] Was't not at Hallowmas, Master Froth?

FROTH.   All-hallond Eve.[20]

POMPEY.   Why, very well; I hope here be truths.   125
He, sir, sitting, as I say, in a lower chair, sir, 'twas in the
Bunch of Grapes, where, indeed, you have a delight to
sit, have you not?

FROTH.   I have so, because it is an open room, and good
for winter.   130

POMPEY.
Why, very well, then; I hope here be truths.

ANGELO.
This will last out a night in Russia,
When nights are longest there. I'll take my leave,
And leave you to the hearing of the cause,
Hoping you'll find good cause to whip them all.   135

ESCALUS.
I think no less. Good morrow to your lordship. *Exit*
(ANGELO).
Now, sir, come on: what was done to Elbow's wife,
once more?

POMPEY.   Once, sir? There was nothing done to her once.

ELBOW.   I beseech you, sir, ask him what this man did to
my wife.   140

POMPEY.   I beseech your honor, ask me.

ESCALUS.   Well, sir; what did this gentleman to her?

POMPEY.   I beseech you, sir, look in this gentleman's face.
Good Master Froth, look upon his honor; 'tis for a good
purpose. Doth your honor mark his face?   145

ESCALUS.   Ay, sir, very well.

POMPEY.   Nay, I beseech you, mark it well.

ESCALUS.   Well, I do so.

POMPEY.   Doth your honor see any harm in his face?

ESCALUS.   Why, no.   150

POMPEY.   I'll be supposed[21] upon a book, his face is the
worst thing about him. Good, then; if his face be the worst
thing about him, how could Master Froth do the constable's wife any harm? I would know that of your honor.

ESCALUS.   He's in the right. Constable, what say   155
you to it?

ELBOW.   First, and[22] it like you, the house is a respected[23]
house; next, this is a respected fellow; and his mistress is
a respected woman.

POMPEY.   By this hand, sir, his wife is a more re-   160
spected person than any of us all.

---

[12]**detest** i.e., protest [13]**honest** chaste [14]**naughty** immoral
[15]**cardinally** i.e., carnally [16]**stewed prunes** (supposed to be a
favorite dish among prostitutes) [17]**wot** know [18]**Come me . . .
that yet** (the verbs carry a sexual innuendo)

[19]**Hallowmas** All Saints' Day, November 1st [20]**All-hallond Eve**
October 31st [21]**supposed** i.e., deposed [22]**and** if [23]**respected**
i.e., suspected

ELBOW.   Varlet, thou liest; thou liest, wicked varlet! The time is yet to come that she was ever respected with man, woman, or child.

POMPEY.   Sir, she was respected with him before **165** he married with her.

ESCALUS.   Which is the wiser here, Justice or Iniquity?[24] Is this true?

ELBOW.   O thou caitiff! O thou varlet! O thou wicked Hannibal![25] I respected with her before I was married **170** to her! If ever I was respected with her, or she with me, let not your worship think me the poor Duke's officer. Prove this, thou wicked Hannibal, or I'll have mine action of batt'ry on thee.

ESCALUS.   If he took you a box o' th' ear, you **175** might have your action of slander too.

ELBOW.   Marry, I thank your good worship for it. What is't your worship's pleasure I shall do with this wicked caitiff?

ESCALUS.   Truly, officer, because he hath some of- **180** fenses in him that thou wouldst discover if thou couldst, let him continue in his courses till thou know'st what they are.

ELBOW.   Marry, I thank your worship for it. Thou seest, thou wicked varlet, now, what's come upon thee. **185** Thou art to continue now, thou varlet; thou art to continue.

ESCALUS.   Where were you born, friend?

FROTH.   Here in Vienna, sir.

ESCALUS.   Are you of fourscore pounds a year? **190**

FROTH.   Yes, and't please you, sir.

ESCALUS.   So. (*To* POMPEY.) What trade are you of, sir?

POMPEY.   A tapster, a poor widow's tapster.

ESCALUS.   Your mistress' name?

POMPEY.   Mistress Overdone. **195**

ESCALUS.   Hath she had any more than one husband?

POMPEY.   Nine, sir; Overdone by the last.

ESCALUS.   Nine! Come hither to me, Master Froth. Master Froth, I would not have you acquainted with tapsters: they will draw you,[26] Master Froth, and you will hang **200** them. Get you gone, and let me hear no more of you.

FROTH.   I thank your worship. For mine own part, I never come into any room in a taphouse, but I am drawn in.

ESCALUS.   Well, no more of it, Master Froth; farewell. (*Exit* FROTH.) Come you hither to me, Master Tapster. **205** What's your name, Master Tapster?

POMPEY.   Pompey.

ESCALUS.   What else?

POMPEY.   Bum, sir.

ESCALUS.   Troth, and your bum is the greatest thing **210** about you; so that, in the beastliest sense, you are Pompey the Great. Pompey, you are partly a bawd, Pompey, howsoever you color[27] it in being a tapster, are you not? Come, tell me true; it shall be the better for you.

POMPEY.   Truly, sir, I am a poor fellow that would **215** live.

ESCALUS.   How would you live, Pompey? By being a bawd? What do you think of the trade, Pompey? Is it a lawful trade?

POMPEY.   If the law would allow it, sir. **220**

ESCALUS.   But the law will not allow it, Pompey; nor it shall not be allowed in Vienna.

POMPEY.   Does your worship mean to geld and splay all the youth of the city?

ESCALUS.   No, Pompey. **225**

POMPEY.   Truly, sir, in my poor opinion, they will to't, then. If your worship will take order for the drabs and the knaves, you need not to fear the bawds.

ESCALUS.   There is pretty orders beginning, I can tell you; it is but heading[28] and hanging. **230**

POMPEY.   If you head and hang all that offend that way but for ten year together, you'll be glad to give out a commission for more heads; if this law hold in Vienna ten year, I'll rent the fairest house in it after threepence a bay;[29] if you live to see this come to pass, say **235** Pompey told you so.

ESCALUS.   Thank you, good Pompey; and, in requital of your prophecy, hark you: I advise you, let me not find you before me again upon any complaint whatsoever; no, not for dwelling where you do. If I do, Pompey, I **240** shall beat you to your tent, and prove a shrewd Caesar to you; in plain dealing, Pompey, I shall have you whipped. So, for this time, Pompey, fare you well.

POMPEY.

    I thank your worship for your good counsel; (*Aside.*) but I shall follow it as the flesh and fortune shall better determine. **245**

    Whip me? No, no; let carman whip his jade.[30]

    The valiant heart's not whipped out of his trade.

    (*Exit.*)

ESCALUS.   Come hither to me, Master Elbow; come hither, Master constable. How long have you been in this place of constable? **250**

ELBOW.   Seven year and a half, sir.

ESCALUS.   I thought, by the readiness in the office, you had continued in it some time. You say, seven years together?

ELBOW.   And a half, sir.

ESCALUS.   Alas, it hath been great pains to you. **255** They do you wrong to put you so oft upon't.[31] Are there not men in your ward sufficient to serve it?

---

[24]**Justice or Iniquity** (personified characters in morality plays)
[25]**Hannibal** i.e., cannibal, fleshmonger (?)   [26]**draw you** (1) draw drinks for you (2) empty you, disembowel you

[27]**color** camouflage   [28]**heading** beheading   [29]**bay** space under a single gable   [30]**carman whip his jade** (the cartman whipped the whore after carting her through the streets; a "jade" is literally a nag)   [31]**put you so oft upon't** i.e., impose on you the task of being constable

ELBOW.   Faith, sir, few of any wit in such matters. As they are chosen, they are glad to choose me for them; I do it for some piece of money, and go through with **260** all.

ESCALUS.   Look you bring me in the names of some six or seven, the most sufficient of your parish.

ELBOW.   To your worship's house, sir?

ESCALUS.   To my house. Fare you well. (*Exit* **265** ELBOW.) What's o'clock, think you?

JUSTICE.   Eleven, sir.

ESCALUS.   I pray you home to dinner with me.

JUSTICE.   I humbly thank you.

ESCALUS.   It grieves me for the death of Claudio, **270** But there's no remedy.

JUSTICE.   Lord Angelo is severe.

ESCALUS.

It is but needful:
Mercy is not itself, that oft looks so;
Pardon is still[32] the nurse of second woe.   **275**
But yet—poor Claudio! There is no remedy.
Come, sir. (*Exeunt*.)

SCENE TWO (A ROOM)

Enter PROVOST, (*and a*) SERVANT.

SERVANT.   He's hearing of a cause; he will come straight: I'll tell him of you.

PROVOST.

Pray you, do. (*Exit* SERVANT.) I'll know
His pleasure; maybe he will relent. Alas,
He hath but as offended in a dream.   **5**
All sects,[1] all ages smack of this vice; and he
To die for't!

Enter ANGELO.

ANGELO.   Now, what's the matter, provost?

PROVOST.   Is it your will Claudio shall die tomorrow?

ANGELO.   Did not I tell thee yea? Hadst thou not order?   **10**
Why dost thou ask again?

PROVOST.

Lest I might be too rash.
Under your good correction, I have seen,
When, after execution, judgment hath
Repented o'er his doom.   **15**

ANGELO.

Go to; let that be mine.[2]
Do you your office, or give up your place,
And you shall well be spared.

PROVOST.

I crave your honor's pardon.
What shall be done, sir, with the groaning Juliet?   **20**
She's very near her hour.

ANGELO.

Dispose of her
To some more fitter place, and that with speed.

(*Reenter* SERVANT.)

SERVANT.

Here is the sister of the man condemned
Desires access to you.   **25**

ANGELO.   Hath he a sister?

PROVOST.

Ay, my good lord, a very virtuous maid
And to be shortly of a sisterhood,
If not already.

ANGELO.   Well, let her be admitted. (*Exit* SERVANT.) **30**
See you the fornicatress be removed;
Let her have needful, but not lavish, means;
There shall be order for't.

Enter LUCIO *and* ISABELLA.

PROVOST.   'Save your honor.

ANGELO.   Stay a little while. (*To* ISABELLA.) Y'are   **35**
welcome: what's your will?

ISABELLA.

I am a woeful suitor to your honor,
Please but your honor hear me.

ANGELO.   Well; what's your suit?

ISABELLA.

There is a vice that most I do abhor,   **40**
And most desire should meet the blow of justice,
For which I would not plead, but that I must,
For which I must not plead, but that I am
At war 'twixt will and will not.

ANGELO.   Well: the matter?   **45**

ISABELLA.

I have a brother is condemned to die.
I do beseech you, let it be his fault,[3]
And not my brother.

PROVOST (*aside*). Heaven give thee moving graces.

ANGELO.

Condemn the fault, and not the actor of it?   **50**
Why, every fault's condemned ere it be done.
Mine were the very cipher of a function,
To fine the faults whose fine[4] stands in record,
And let go by the actor.

ISABELLA.   O just but severe law!   **55**
I had a brother, then. Heaven keep your honor.

LUCIO (*aside to* ISABELLA).

Give't not o'er so. To him again, entreat him,
Kneel down before him, hang upon his gown;
You are too cold; if you should need a pin,

---

[32]**still** always   [1]**sects** classes   [2]**mine** i.e., my responsibility

[3]**let it be his fault** i.e., condemn his fault, not him   [4]**fine . . . fine** penalize . . . penalty

You could not with more tame a tongue desire it. **60**
  To him, I say!
ISABELLA. Must he needs die?
ANGELO.   Maiden, no remedy.
ISABELLA. Yes; I do think that you might pardon him,
  And neither heaven nor man grieve at the mercy. **65**
ANGELO. I will not do't.
ISABELLA.   But can you, if you would?
ANGELO. Look what[5] I will not, that I cannot do.
ISABELLA.
  But might you do't, and do the world no wrong,
  If so your heart were touched with that remorse[6] **70**
  As mine is to him?
ANGELO.   He's sentenced; 'tis too late.
LUCIO (*aside to* ISABELLA). You are too cold.
ISABELLA.
  Too late? Why, no: I, that do speak a word,
  May call it again. Well, believe this: **75**
  No ceremony[7] that to great ones 'longs,[8]
  Not the king's crown, nor the deputed sword,
  The marshal's truncheon, nor the judge's robe,
  Become them with one half so good a grace
  As mercy does. **80**
  If he had been as you, and you as he,
  You would have slipped like him; but he, like you,
  Would not have been so stern.
ANGELO.   Pray you, be gone.
ISABELLA.
  I would to heaven I had your potency, **85**
  And you were Isabel; should it then be thus?
  No; I would tell what 'twere to be a judge,
  And what a prisoner.
LUCIO (*aside to* ISABELLA). Ay, touch him; there's the vein.
ANGELO.
  Your brother is a forfeit of the law, **90**
  And you but waste your words.
ISABELLA.
                     Alas, alas!
  Why, all the souls that were were forfeit once;
  And He might the vantage best have took
  Found out the remedy. How would you be, **95**
  If He, which is the top of judgment, should
  But judge you as you are? O, think on that,
  And mercy then will breathe within your lips,
  Like man new made.
ANGELO.
                Be you content, fair maid; **100**
  It is the law, not I, condemn your brother.
  Were he my kinsman, brother, or my son,
  It should be thus with him; he must die tomorrow.

ISABELLA.
  Tomorrow! O, that's sudden! Spare him, spare him!
  He's not prepared for death. Even for our
    kitchens **105**
  We kill the fowl of season:[9] shall we serve heaven
  With less respect than we do minister
  To our gross selves? Good, good my lord, bethink
    you:
  Who is it that hath died for this offense?
  There's many have committed it. **110**
LUCIO (*aside to* ISABELLA).   Ay, well said.
ANGELO.
  The law hath not been dead, though it hath slept.
  Those many had not dared to do that evil,
  If the first that did th' edict infringe
  Had answered for his deed. Now 'tis awake, **115**
  Takes note of what is done, and, like a prophet,
  Looks in a glass, that shows what future evils,
  Either new, or by remissness new conceived,[10]
  And so in progress to be hatched and born,
  Are now to have no successive degrees, **120**
  But here they live, to end.
ISABELLA.   Yet show some pity.
ANGELO.
  I show it most of all when I show justice,
  For then I pity those I do not know,
  Which a dismissed[11] offense would after gall; **125**
  And do him right that, answering one foul wrong,
  Lives not to act another. Be satisfied;
  Your brother dies tomorrow; be content.
ISABELLA.
  So you must be the first that gives this sentence,
  And he, that suffers. O, it is excellent **130**
  To have a giant's strength; but it is tyrannous
  To use it like a giant.
LUCIO (*aside to* ISABELLA). That's well said.
ISABELLA.
  Could great men thunder
  As Jove himself does, Jove would ne'er
    be quiet, **135**
  For every pelting,[12] petty officer
  Would use his heaven for thunder.
  Nothing but thunder. Merciful heaven,
  Thou rather with thy sharp and sulfurous bolt
  Splits the unwedgeable and gnarlèd oak **140**
  Than the soft myrtle. But man, proud man,
  Dressed in a little brief authority,
  Most ignorant of what he's most assured,

[5]**Look what** whatever [6]**remorse** compassion [7]**ceremony**
insignia of greatness [8]**'longs** belongs

[9]**of season** in season [10]**future . . . conceived** i.e., evils that will
take place in the future, but that are either now planned or may be
planned later (''remissness'': careless omission of duty)
[11]**dismissed** forgiven [12]**pelting** paltry

His glassy essence,[13] like an angry ape,
Plays such fantastic tricks before high heaven   145
As makes the angels weep; who, with our spleens,[14]
Would all themselves laugh mortal.

LUCIO (*aside to* ISABELLA).
O, to him, to him, wench!
He will relent;
He's coming; I perceive't.   150

PROVOST (*aside*).   Pray heaven she win him.

ISABELLA.
We cannot weigh our brother with ourself:
Great men may jest with saints; 'tis wit in them;
But in the less, foul profanation.

LUCIO.   Thou'rt i' th' right, girl; more o' that.   155

ISABELLA.
That in the captain's but a choleric word,
Which in the soldier is flat blasphemy.

LUCIO (*aside to* ISABELLA). Art avised[15] o that? More on't.

ANGELO.   Why do you put these sayings upon me?

ISABELLA.
Because authority, though it err like others,   160
Hath yet a kind of medicine in itself,
That skins the vice[16] o' th' top; go to your bosom,
Knock there, and ask your heart what it doth know
That's like my brother's fault; if it confess
A natural guiltiness such as is his,   165
Let it not sound a thought upon your tongue
Against my brother's life.

ANGELO (*aside*).
She speaks, and 'tis
Such sense, that my sense breeds with it. (*Aloud.*)
Fare you well.   170

ISABELLA.   Gentle my lord, turn back.

ANGELO.   I will bethink me; come again tomorrow.

ISABELLA.   Hark how I'll bribe you; good my lord, turn
back.

ANGELO.   How? Bribe me?   175

ISABELLA.   Ay, with such gifts that heaven shall share with
you.

LUCIO (*aside to* ISABELLA). You had marred all else.

ISABELLA.
Not with fond sicles[17] of the tested gold,
Or stones whose rate are either rich or poor   180
As fancy values them; but with true prayers
That shall be up at heaven, and enter there
Ere sunrise, prayers from preservèd souls,

From fasting maids whose minds are dedicate
To nothing temporal.   185

ANGELO.   Well; come to me tomorrow.

LUCIO (*aside to* ISABELLA). Go to; 'tis well; away.

ISABELLA.   Heaven keep your honor safe.

ANGELO (*aside*).
Amen:
For I am that way going to temptation,   190
Where prayers cross.[18]

ISABELLA.
At what hour tomorrow
Shall I attend your lordship?

ANGELO.   At any time 'fore noon.

ISABELLA.   'Save your honor.   195

(*Exeunt* ISABELLA, LUCIO, *and* PROVOST.)

ANGELO.
From thee, even from thy virtue!
What's this? What's this? Is this her fault or mine?
The tempter or the tempted, who sins most?
Ha, not she. Nor doth she tempt; but it is **I**
That, lying by the violet in the sun,   200
Do as the carrion does, not as the flow'r,
Corrupt with virtuous season.[19] Can it be
That modesty may more betray our sense
Than woman's lightness? Having waste ground
enough,
Shall we desire to raze the sanctuary,   205
And pitch our evils[20] there? O fie, fie, fie!
What dost thou, or what art thou, Angelo?
Dost thou desire her foully for those things
That make her good? O, let her brother live:
Thieves for their robbery have authority   210
When judges steal themselves. What, do I love her,
That I desire to hear her speak again,
And feast upon her eyes? What is't I dream on?
O cunning enemy, that, to catch a saint,
With saints dost bait thy hook! Most dangerous   215
Is that temptation that doth goad us on
To sin in loving virtue. Never could the strumpet,
With all her double vigor, art and nature,
Once stir my temper; but this virtuous maid
Subdues me quite. Ever till now,   220
When men were fond,[21] I smiled, and wond'red how.
(*Exit.*)

SCENE THREE (THE PRISON)

Enter DUKE (*disguised as a friar*) *and* PROVOST.

DUKE.   Hail to you, provost—so I think you are.

---

[13]**glassy essence** the rational soul which reveals to man, as in a
mirror, what constitutes him a human being (?) fragile nature (?)
[14]**spleens** (the spleen was believed the seat of mirth and anger)
[15]**avised** informed   [16]**skins the vice** i.e., covers the sore of vice
with a skin, but does not heal it (or perhaps ''skims off the visible
layer of vice'')   [17]**fond sicles** foolish shekels

[18]**cross** are at cross purposes   [19]**Corrupt with virtuous season** go
bad in the season that blossoms the flower   [20]**evils** evil structures
(e.g., perhaps whorehouses or privies)   [21]**fond** infatuated

PROVOST.   I am the provost. What's your will, good friar?
DUKE.

    Bound by my charity and my blest order,
    I come to visit the afflicted spirits
    Here in the prison. Do me the common right   **5**
    To let me see them, and to make me know
    The nature of their crimes, that I may minister
    To them accordingly.
PROVOST.   I would do more than that, if more were
    needful.   **10**

Enter JULIET.

    Look, here comes one: a gentlewoman of mine,
    Who, falling in the flaws[1] of her own youth,
    Hath blistered her report:[2] she is with child;
    And he that got it, sentenced; a young man
    More fit to do another such offense   **15**
    Than die for this.
DUKE.   When must he die?
PROVOST.

          As I do think, tomorrow. (*To* JULIET.)
    I have provided for you; stay awhile,
    And you shall be conducted.   **20**
DUKE.   Repent you, fair one, of the sin you carry?
JULIET.   I do, and bear the shame most patiently.
DUKE.

    I'll teach you how you shall arraign[3] your
        conscience,
    And try your penitence, if it be sound
    Or hollowly put on.   **25**
JULIET.   I'll gladly learn.
DUKE.   Love you the man that wronged you?
JULIET.   Yes, as I love the woman that wronged him.
DUKE.

    So, then, it seems your most offenseful act
    Was mutually committed?   **30**
JULIET.   Mutually.
DUKE.   Then was your sin of heavier kind than his.
JULIET.   I do confess it, and repent it, father.
DUKE.   'Tis meet so, daughter. But lest you do repent
    As that the sin hath brought you to this
        shame—   **35**
    Which sorrow is always toward ourselves, not
        heaven,
    Showing we would not spare heaven as we love it,
    But as we stand in fear—
JULIET.

    I do repent me, as it is an evil,
    And take the shame with joy.   **40**
DUKE.

          There rest.
    Your partner, as I hear, must die tomorrow,

And I am going with instruction to him.
    Grace go with you, *Benedicite*![4] (*Exit.*)
JULIET.

    Must die tomorrow! O injurious love,   **45**
    That respites[5] me a life, whose very comfort
    Is still a dying horror.
PROVOST.   'Tis pity of him. (*Exeunt.*)

SCENE FOUR (A ROOM)

Enter ANGELO.

ANGELO.

    When I would pray and think, I think and pray
    To several[1] subjects: heaven hath my empty words,
    Whilst my invention,[2] hearing not my tongue,
    Anchors on Isabel: heaven in my mouth,
    As if I did but only chew his name,   **5**
    And in my heart the strong and swelling evil
    Of my conception.[3] The state,[4] whereon I studied,
    Is like a good thing, being often read,
    Grown seared[5] and tedious; yea, my gravity,
    Wherein, let no man hear me, I take pride,   **10**
    Could I with boot[6] change for an idle plume
    Which the air beats for vain. O place, O form,
    How often dost thou with thy case,[7] thy habit,[8]
    Wrench awe from fools, and tie the wiser souls
    To thy false seeming! Blood, thou art blood.   **15**
    Let's write "good angel" on the devil's horn,[9]
    'Tis not the devil's crest. How now, who's there?

Enter SERVANT.

SERVANT.   One Isabel, a sister, desires access to you.
ANGELO.

    Teach her the way. (*Exit* SERVANT.)
    O heavens,   **20**
    Why does my blood thus muster to my heart,
    Making both it unable for itself,
    And dispossessing all my other parts
    Of necessary fitness?
    So play the foolish throngs with one that
        swounds,[10]   **25**
    Come all to help him, and so stop the air
    By which he should revive; and even so
    The general,[11] subject to a well-wished king,
    Quit their own part, and in obsequious fondness

---

[1]**flaws** sudden gusts of wind [2]**report** reputation [3]**arraign** interrogate

[4]**Benedicite** bless you [5]**respites** saves [1]**several** separate [2]**invention** imagination [3]**conception** thought [4]**state** attitude (?) statecraft (?) [5]**seared** worn out [6]**with boot** with profit [7]**case** (either "chance" or "outside") [8]**habit** (either "behavior" or "garment") [9]**horn** phallus (?) [10]**swounds** swoons [11]**general** multitude

Crowd to his presence, where their untaught
    love   30
Must needs appear offense.

Enter ISABELLA.

                       How now, fair maid?
ISABELLA. I am come to know your pleasure.
ANGELO.
    That you might know it, would much better please
      me
    Than to demand what 'tis. Your brother
      cannot live.   35
ISABELLA. Even so. Heaven keep your honor.
ANGELO.
    Yet may he live awhile, and it may be,
    As long as you or I; yet he must die.
ISABELLA. Under your sentence?
ANGELO. Yea.   40
ISABELLA.
    When? I beseech you that in his reprieve,
    Longer or shorter, he may be so fitted
    That his soul sicken not.
ANGELO.
    Ha! Fie, these filthy vices! It were as good
    To pardon him that hath from nature stol'n   45
    A man already made, as to remit
    Their saucy sweetness[12] that do coin heaven's image
    In stamps that are forbid: 'tis all as easy
    Falsely to take away a life true made,
    As to put metal in restrainèd[13] means   50
    To make a false one.
ISABELLA. 'Tis set down so in heaven, but not in earth.
ANGELO.
    Say you so? Then I shall pose[14] you quickly.
    Which had you rather: that the most just law
    Now took your brother's life; or, to redeem him, 55
    Give up your body to such sweet uncleanness
    As she that he hath stained?
ISABELLA.
                   Sir, believe this:
    I had rather give my body than my soul.
ANGELO.
    I talk not of your soul; our compelled sins   60
    Stand more for number than for accompt.[15]
ISABELLA.   How say you?
ANGELO.
    Nay, I'll warrant that; for I can speak
    Against the thing I say. Answer to this:
    I, now the voice of the recorded law,   65
    Pronounce a sentence on your brother's life;

Might there not be a charity in sin
To save this brother's life?
ISABELLA.
                  Please you to do't,
    I'll take it as a peril to my soul,   70
    It is no sin at all, but charity.
ANGELO.
    Pleased you to do't at peril of your soul,
    Were equal poise[16] of sin and charity.
ISABELLA.
    That I do beg his life, if it be sin,
    Heaven let me bear it. You granting of my suit, 75
    If that be sin, I'll make it my morn prayer
    To have it added to the faults of mine,
    And nothing of your answer.
ANGELO.
                  Nay, but hear me.
    Your sense pursues not mine; either you are
      ignorant,   80
    Or seem so, crafty; and that's not good.
ISABELLA.
    Let me be ignorant, and in nothing good,
    But graciously to know I am no better.
ANGELO.
    Thus wisdom wishes to appear most bright
    When it doth tax[17] itself, as these black masks   85
    Proclaim an enshield[18] beauty ten times louder
    Than beauty could, displayed. But mark me;
    To be receivèd plain, I'll speak more gross:
    Your brother is to die.
ISABELLA. So.   90
ANGELO.
    And his offense is so, as it appears,
    Accountant[19] to the law upon that pain.[20]
ISABELLA. True.
ANGELO.
    Admit no other way to save his life—
    As I subscribe[21] not that, nor any other,   95
    But in the loss of question[22]—that you, his sister,
    Finding yourself desired of such a person
    Whose credit with the judge, or own great place,
    Could fetch your brother from the manacles
    Of the all-binding law; and that there were   100
    No earthly mean to save him, but that either
    You must lay down the treasures of your body
    To this supposed, or else to let him suffer:
    What would you do?
ISABELLA.
    As much for my poor brother as myself: 105
    That is, were I under the terms of death,

---

[12]**to remit . . . sweetness** to pardon their lascivious pleasures
[13]**restrainèd** forbidden [14]**pose** baffle (with a difficult question)
[15]**Stand . . . accompt** are enumerated but not counted against us

[16]**poise** balance [17]**tax** censure [18]**enshield** concealed
[19]**Accountant** accountable [20]**pain** punishment [21]**subscribe**
assent to [22]**But . . . question** except to keep alive the argument

Th' impression of keen whips I'd wear as rubies,
And strip myself to death as to a bed
That longing have been sick for, ere I'd yield
My body up to shame.   **110**

ANGELO.   Then must your brother die.

ISABELLA.
And 'twere the cheaper way.
Better it were a brother died at once
Than that a sister, by redeeming him,
Should die forever.   **115**

ANGELO.
Were not you, then, as cruel as the sentence
That you have slandered so?

ISABELLA.
Ignomy in ransom and free pardon
Are of two houses; lawful mercy
Is nothing kin to foul redemption.   **120**

ANGELO.
You seemed of late to make the law a tyrant,
And rather proved the sliding of your brother
A merriment than a vice.

ISABELLA.
O, pardon me, my lord. It oft falls out,
To have what we would have, we speak not what
we mean.   **125**
I something do excuse the thing I hate
For his advantage that I dearly love.

ANGELO.   We are all frail.

ISABELLA.
                    Else let my brother die,
If not a fedary, but only he   **130**
Owe and succeed thy weakness.[23]

ANGELO.   Nay, women are frail too.

ISABELLA.
Ay, as the glasses where they view themselves,
Which are as easy broke as they make forms.[24]
Women! Help heaven! Men their creation mar   **135**
In profiting by them. Nay, call us ten times frail;
For we are soft as our complexions are,
And credulous[25] to false prints.

ANGELO.
                    I think it well,
And from this testimony of your own sex—   **140**
Since, I suppose, we are made to be no stronger
Than faults may shake our frames—let me be bold:
I do arrest your words.[26] Be that you are,
That is, a woman; if you be more, you're none;
If you be one, as you are well expressed[27]   **145**

By all external warrants, show it now,
By putting on the destined livery.[28]

ISABELLA.
I have no tongue but one; gentle my lord,
Let me entreat you speak the former language.

ANGELO.
Plainly conceive, I love you.   **150**

ISABELLA.
My brother did love Juliet,
And you tell me that he shall die for't.

ANGELO.
He shall not, Isabel, if you give me love.

ISABELLA.
I know your virtue hath a license in't,
Which seems a little fouler than it is,   **155**
To pluck on[29] others.

ANGELO.
                    Believe me, on mine honor,
My words express my purpose.

ISABELLA.
Ha! Little honor to be much believed,
And most pernicious purpose. Seeming,
seeming!   **160**
I will proclaim thee, Angelo; look for't:
Sign me a present pardon for my brother,
Or with an outstretched throat I'll tell the world
aloud
What man thou art.

ANGELO.
                    Who will believe thee, Isabel?   **165**
My unsoiled name, th' austereness of my life,
My vouch[30] against you, and my place i' th' state,
Will so your accusation overweigh,
That you shall stifle in your own report,
And smell of calumny. I have begun,   **170**
And now I give my sensual race the rein.
Fit thy consent to my sharp appetite,
Lay by all nicety and prolixious[31] blushes,
That banish what they sue for; redeem thy brother
By yielding up thy body to my will,[32]   **175**
Or else he must not only die the death,
But thy unkindness shall his death draw out
To ling'ring sufferance.[33] Answer me tomorrow,
Or, by the affection[34] that now guides me most,
I'll prove a tyrant to him. As for you,   **180**
Say what you can, my false o'erweighs your true.
                    (*Exit.*)

ISABELLA.
To whom should I complain? Did I tell this,
Who would believe me? O perilous mouths,

---

[23]**If . . . weakness** (the meaning seems to be: "Let my brother die if he is the only inheritor of human frailty instead of being a mere vassal to it")   [24]**forms** images, appearances   [25]**credulous** receptive   [26]**I do arrest your words** I take you at your word   [27]**expressed** shown to be

[28]**the destined livery** the dress that it is the destiny of a woman to wear   [29]**pluck on** draw on   [30]**vouch** testimony   [31]**prolixious** tediously drawn-out   [32]**will** carnal appetite   [33]**sufferance** torture   [34]**affection** passion

That bear in them one and the selfsame tongue,
Either of condemnation or approof;[35]   185
Bidding the law make curtsy to their will,
Hooking both right and wrong to th' appetite,
To follow as it draws. I'll to my brother.
Though he hath fall'n by prompture of the blood,
Yet hath he in him such a mind of honor,   190
That, had he twenty heads to tender down
On twenty bloody blocks, he'd yield them up,
Before his sister should her body stoop
To such abhorred pollution.
Then, Isabel, live chaste, and, brother, die: 195
More than our brother is our chastity.
I'll tell him yet of Angelo's request,
And fit his mind to death, for his soul's rest. (*Exit*.)

ACT THREE

SCENE ONE (THE PRISON)

Enter DUKE (*as friar*), CLAUDIO, *and* PROVOST.

DUKE.   So then, you hope of pardon from Lord Angelo?
CLAUDIO.
The miserable have no other medicine
But only hope:
I have hope to live, and am prepared to die.
DUKE.
Be absolute[1] for death; either death or life   5
Shall thereby be the sweeter. Reason thus with life:
If I do lose thee, I do lose a thing
That none but fools would keep; a breath thou art,
Servile to all the skyey influences,[2]
That dost this habitation, where thou keep'st,[3]   10
Hourly afflict; merely, thou art death's fool,[4]
For him thou labor'st by thy flight to shun,
And yet run'st toward him still. Thou art not noble,
For all th' accommodations[5] that thou bear'st
Are nursed by baseness. Thou'rt by no means
     valiant,   15
For thou dost fear the soft and tender fork[6]
Of a poor worm. Thy best of rest is sleep,
And that thou oft provok'st;[7] yet grossly fear'st
Thy death, which is no more. Thou art not
     thyself;
For thou exists on many a thousand grains   20
That issue out of dust. Happy thou art not,
For what thou hast not, still thou striv'st to get,
And what thou hast, forget'st. Thou art not certain,[8]

For thy complexion shifts to strange effects,
After the moon.[9] If thou art rich, thou'rt poor.   25
For, like an ass whose back with ingots bows,
Thou bear'st thy heavy riches but a journey,
And death unloads thee. Friend hast thou none,
For thine own bowels,[10] which do call thee sire,
The mere effusion of thy proper loins,[11]   30
Do curse the gout, serpigo,[12] and the rheum,[13]
For ending thee no sooner. Thou hast nor youth nor
     age,
But, as it were, an after-dinner's sleep,
Dreaming on both; for all thy blessèd youth
Becomes as agèd, and doth beg the alms   35
Of palsied eld,[14] and when thou art old and rich,
Thou has neither heat, affection,[15] limb, nor beauty,
To make thy riches pleasant. What's yet in this
That bears[16] the name of life? Yet in this life
Lie hid moe thousand deaths; yet death we fear,   40
That makes these odds all even.
CLAUDIO.
                              I humbly thank you.
To sue to live, I find I seek to die,
And seeking death, find life: let it come on.

Enter ISABELLA.

ISABELLA.   What, ho! Peace here; grace and good   45
     company!
PROVOST.   Who's there? Come in, the wish deserves a
     welcome.
DUKE.   Dear sir, ere long I'll visit you again.
CLAUDIO.   Most holy sir, I thank you.   50
ISABELLA.   My business is a word or two with Claudio.
PROVOST.   And very welcome. Look, signior, here's your
     sister.
DUKE.   Provost, a word with you.
PROVOST.   As many as you please.   55
DUKE.   Bring me to hear them speak, where I may be con-
     cealed. (DUKE *and* PROVOST *withdraw*.)
CLAUDIO.   Now, sister, what's the comfort?
ISABELLA.
Why,
As all comforts are, most good, most good
     indeed.   60
Lord Angelo, having affairs to heaven,
Intends you for his swift ambassador,
Where you shall be an everlasting leiger:[17]
Therefore your best appointment[18] make with speed;
Tomorrow you set on.   65

---

[35]**approof** approval   [1]**absolute** unconditionally prepared   [2]**skyey influences** influence of the stars   [3]**keep'st** dwellest   [4]**fool** (the professional jester in a nobleman's household whose job was to keep his master amused)   [5]**accommodations** necessities   [6]**fork** forked tongue (of a snake)   [7]**provok'st** invokest   [8]**certain** invariable

[9]**For . . . moon** your temperament (desire?) moves to numerous things, changeable as (or "influenced by") the moon   [10]**bowels** offspring   [11]**The mere . . . loins** the very issue of your own loins   [12]**serpigo** a skin disease   [13]**rheum** catarrh   [14]**eld** old age   [15]**affection** feeling   [16]**bears** deserves   [17]**leiger** resident ambassador   [18]**appointment** preparation

CLAUDIO.   Is there no remedy?
ISABELLA.
     None, but such remedy as, to save a head,
     To cleave a heart in twain.
CLAUDIO.   But is there any?
ISABELLA.
     Yes, brother, you may live;   70
     There is a devilish mercy in the judge,
     If you'll implore it, that will free your life,
     But fetter you till death.
CLAUDIO.   Perpetual durance?[19]
ISABELLA.
     Ay, just; perpetual durance, a restraint,   75
     Though all the world's vastidity[20] you had,
     To a determined scope.[21]
CLAUDIO.   But in what nature?
ISABELLA.
     In such a one as, you consenting to't,
     Would bark your honor from that trunk you bear,   80
     And leave you naked.
CLAUDIO.   Let me know the point.
ISABELLA.
     O, I do fear thee, Claudio, and I quake,
     Lest thou a feverous life shouldst entertain,
     And six or seven winters more respect   85
     Than a perpetual honor. Dar'st thou die?
     The sense[22] of death is most in apprehension,[23]
     And the poor beetle that we tread upon
     In corporal sufferance finds a pang as great
     As when a giant dies.   90
CLAUDIO.
                         Why give you me this shame?
     Think you I can a resolution fetch
     From flow'ry tenderness? If I must die,
     I will encounter darkness as a bride,
     And hug it in mine arms.   95
ISABELLA.
     There spake my brother, there my father's grave
     Did utter forth a voice. Yes, thou must die,
     Thou art too noble to conserve a life
     In base appliances.[24] This outward-sainted deputy,
     Whose settled visage and deliberate word   100
     Nips youth i' th' head, and follies doth enmew[25]
     As falcon doth the fowl, is yet a devil;
     His filth within being cast,[26] he would appear
     A pond as deep as hell.
CLAUDIO.   The prenzie[27] Angelo!   105

ISABELLA.
     O, 'tis the cunning livery of hell,
     The damned'st body to invest and cover
     In prenzie guards.[28] Dost thou think, Claudio,
     If I would yield him my virginity,
     Thou mightst be freed?   110
CLAUDIO.   O heavens, it cannot be.
ISABELLA.
     Yes, he would give't thee, from this rank offense,
     So to offend him still. This night's the time
     That I should do what I abhor to name,
     Or else thou diest tomorrow.   115
CLAUDIO.   Thou shalt not do't.
ISABELLA.
     O, were it but my life,
     I'd throw it down for your deliverance
     As frankly as a pin.
CLAUDIO.   Thanks, dear Isabel.   120
ISABELLA.   Be ready, Claudio, for your death tomorrow.
CLAUDIO.
     Yes. Has he affections[29] in him,
     That thus can make him bite the law by th' nose,
     When he would force[30] it? Sure, it is no sin,
     Or of the deadly seven[31] it is the least.   125
ISABELLA.   Which is the least?
CLAUDIO.
     If it were damnable, he being so wise,
     Why would he for the momentary trick
     Be perdurably fined?[32] O Isabel!
ISABELLA.   What says my brother?   130
CLAUDIO.   Death is a fearful thing.
ISABELLA.   And shamèd life a hateful.
CLAUDIO.
     Ay, but to die, and go we know not where,
     To lie in cold obstruction[33] and to rot,
     This sensible[34] warm motion[35] to become   135
     A kneaded clod; and the delighted[36] spirit
     To bathe in fiery floods, or to reside
     In thrilling region of thick-ribbèd ice;
     To be imprisoned in the viewless winds,
     And blown with restless violence round about   140
     The pendent[37] world; or to be worse than worst
     Of those that lawless and incertain thought
     Imagine howling—'tis too horrible!
     The weariest and most loathèd worldly life
     That age, ache, penury, and imprisonment   145

---

[19]**durance** imprisonment   [20]**vastidity** vast spaces   [21]**determined scope** fixed limit (i.e., the reprieve may win him the world, but will cost him his soul)   [22]**sense** feeling   [23]**apprehension** imagination   [24]**appliances** devices   [25]**enmew** drive into the water (as a hawk drives a fowl)   [26]**cast** vomited up   [27]**prenzie** (meaning uncertain; often emended to "princely," or "precise")

[28]**guards** trimmings   [29]**affections** sensual appetites   [30]**force** enforce   [31]**deadly seven** (pride, envy, wrath, sloth, avarice, gluttony, lechery)   [32]**Why . . . fined** i.e., why for the momentary trifle (of sexual intercourse) would he be eternally damned   [33]**obstruction** motionlessness   [34]**sensible** feeling   [35]**motion** organism   [36]**delighted** capable of delight   [37]**pendent** hanging in space

Can lay on nature is a paradise
To what we fear of death.

ISABELLA.   Alas, alas.

CLAUDIO.

Sweet sister, let me live:
What sin you do to save a brother's life,   150
Nature dispenses with[38] the deed so far
That it becomes a virtue.

ISABELLA.

O you beast,
O faithless coward, O dishonest wretch!
Wilt thou be made a man out of my vice?   155
Is't not a kind of incest, to take life
From thine own sister's shame? What should I
think?
Heaven shield my mother played my father fair,
For such a warpèd slip of wilderness[39]
Ne'er issued from his blood. Take my defiance,   160
Die, perish! Might but my bending down
Reprieve thee from thy fate, it should proceed.
I'll pray a thousand prayers for thy death,
No word to save thee.

CLAUDIO.   Nay, hear me, Isabel.   165

ISABELLA.

O, fie, fie, fie!
Thy sin's not accidental, but a trade.
Mercy to thee would prove itself a bawd,
'Tis best that thou diest quickly.

CLAUDIO.   O, hear me, Isabella!   170

(*The* DUKE *comes forward.*)

DUKE.   Vouchsafe a word, young sister, but one word.

ISABELLA.   What is your will?

DUKE.   Might you dispense with your leisure, I would by
and by have some speech with you: the satisfaction I
would require is likewise your own benefit.   175

ISABELLA.   I have no superfluous leisure; my stay must be
stolen out of other affairs, but I will attend you awhile.

DUKE (*aside to* CLAUDIO). Son, I have overheard what hath
passed between you and your sister. Angelo had never the
purpose to corrupt her; only he hath made an   180
assay[40] of her virtue to practice his judgment with the
disposition of natures. She, having the truth of honor in
her, hath made him that gracious denial which he is most
glad to receive. I am confessor to Angelo, and I know this
to be true; therefore prepare yourself to death. Do   185
not satisfy your resolution with hopes that are fallible.
Tomorrow you must die; go to your knees, and make
ready.

CLAUDIO.   Let me ask my sister pardon. I am so out of love
with life, that I will sue to be rid of it.   190

DUKE.   Hold you there; farewell. (*Exit* CLAUDIO.) Provost,
a word with you.

Enter PROVOST.

PROVOST.   What's your will, father?

DUKE.   That now you are come, you will be gone. Leave
me awhile with the maid. My mind promises with   195
my habit[41] no loss shall touch her by my company.

PROVOST.   In good time.[42] (*Exit.*)

DUKE.   The hand that hath made you fair hath made you
good. The goodness that is cheap in beauty makes beauty
brief in goodness; but grace, being the soul of   200
your complexion,[43] shall keep the body of it ever fair. The
assault that Angelo hath made to you, fortune hath conveyed to my understanding, and, but that frailty hath examples for his falling, I should wonder at Angelo. How
will you do to content this substitute, and to save 205
your brother?

ISABELLA.   I am now going to resolve[44] him. I had rather
my brother die by the law than my son should be unlaw-
fully born. But O, how much is the good Duke deceived
in Angelo! If ever he return and I can speak to   210
him, I will open my lips in vain, or discover his
government.[45]

DUKE.   That shall not be much amiss. Yet, as the matter
now stands, he will avoid your accusation: he made trial
of you only. Therefore fasten your ear on my ad-   215
visings; to the love I have in doing good a remedy presents itself. I do make myself believe that you may most
uprighteously do a poor wronged lady a merited benefit;
redeem your brother from the angry law; do no stain to
your own gracious person; and much please the   220
absent Duke, if peradventure he shall ever return to have
hearing of this business.

ISABELLA.   Let me hear you speak farther. I have spirit to
do anything that appears not foul in the truth of my spirit.

DUKE.   Virtue is bold, and goodness never fearful. 225
Have you not heard speak of Mariana, the sister of Frederick, the great soldier who miscarried at sea?

ISABELLA.   I have heard of the lady, and good words went
with her name.

DUKE.   She should this Angelo have married; was   230
affianced to her by oath, and the nuptial appointed: between which time of the contract and limit of the solemnity,[46] her brother Frederick was wracked at sea, having
in that perished vessel the dowry of his sister. But mark
how heavily this befell to the poor gentlewoman: 235
there she lost a noble and renowned brother, in his love

---

[38]**dispenses with** grants a dispensation for   [39]**wilderness** wild
nature without nurture   [40]**assay** test

[41]**habit** religious dress   [42]**In good time** very well   [43]**complexion**
character   [44]**resolve** answer   [45]**discover his government** expose
his rule   [46]**limit of the solemnity** date set for the marriage
ceremony

toward her ever most kind and natural; with him, the portion and sinew of her fortune, her marriage dowry; with both, her combinate[47] husband, this well-seeming Angelo.

ISABELLA.   Can this be so? Did Angelo so leave   **240**
her?

DUKE.   Left her in her tears, and dried not one of them with his comfort; swallowed his vows whole, pretending in her discoveries of dishonor: in few, bestowed her on her own lamentation, which she yet wears for his sake;   **245**
and he, a marble to her tears, is washed with them, but relents not.

ISABELLA.   What a merit were it in death to take this poor maid from the world! What corruption in this life, that it will let this man live! But how out of this can she   **250**
avail?[48]

DUKE.   It is a rupture that you may easily heal, and the cure of it not only saves your brother, but keeps you from dishonor in doing it.

ISABELLA.   Show me how, good father.   **255**

DUKE.   This forenamed maid hath yet in her the continuance of her first affection; his unjust unkindness, that in all reason should have quenched her love, hath, like an impediment in the current, made it more violent and unruly. Go you to Angelo; answer his requiring   **260**
with a plausible obedience; agree with his demands to the point; only refer yourself to this advantage: first, that your stay with him may not be long; that the time may have all shadow and silence in it; and the place answer to convenience. This being granted in course—and now   **265**
follows all—we shall advise this wronged maid to stead up[49] your appointment, go in your place. If the encounter[50] acknowledge itself hereafter, it may compel him to her recompense: and here, by this, is your brother saved, your honor untainted, the poor Mariana   **270**
advantaged, and the corrupt deputy scaled.[51] The maid will I frame[52] and make fit for his attempt. If you think well to carry this, as you may, the doubleness of the benefit defends the deceit from reproof. What think you of it?   **275**

ISABELLA.   The image of it gives me content already, and I trust it will grow to a most prosperous perfection.

DUKE.   It lies much in your holding up. Haste you speedily to Angelo: if for this night he entreat you to his bed, give him promise of satisfaction. I will presently to   **280**
Saint Luke's; there at the moated grange[53] resides this dejected Mariana. At that place call upon me, and dispatch with Angelo, that it may be quickly.

ISABELLA.   I thank you for this comfort. Fare you well, good father. (*Exit*.)   **285**

SCENE TWO (BEFORE THE PRISON)

Enter, (*to the* DUKE,) ELBOW, CLOWN (POMPEY, *and*) OFFICERS.

ELBOW.   Nay, if there be no remedy for it, but that you will needs buy and sell men and women like beasts, we shall have all the world drink brown and white bastard.[1]

DUKE.   O heavens! What stuff is here?

POMPEY.   'Twas never merry world since, of two usu-   **5**
ries,[2] the merriest was put down, and the worser allowed by order of law a furred gown to keep him warm; and furred with fox and lamb skins too, to signify that craft, being richer than innocency, stands for the facing.[3]

ELBOW.   Come your way, sir. 'Bless you, good   **10**
father friar.

DUKE.   And you, good brother father. What offense hath this man made you, sir?

ELBOW.   Marry, sir, he hath offended the law; and, sir, we take him to be a thief too, sir; for we have found   **15**
upon him, sir, a strange picklock, which we have sent to the deputy.

DUKE.
    Fie, sirrah, a bawd, a wicked bawd!
    The evil that thou causest to be done,
    That is thy means to live. Do thou but think   **20**
    What 'tis to cram a maw[4] or clothe a back
    From such a filthy vice; say to thyself,
    From their abominable and beastly touches
    I drink, I eat, array myself, and live.
    Canst thou believe thy living is a life,   **25**
    So stinkingly depending? Go mend, go mend.

POMPEY.   Indeed, it does stink in some sort, sir; but yet, sir, I would prove—

DUKE.
    Nay, if the devil have given thee proofs for sin,
    Thou wilt prove his. Take him to prison, officer.   **30**
    Correction and instruction must both work
    Ere this rude beast will profit.

ELBOW.   He must before the deputy, sir; he has given him warning. The deputy cannot abide a whoremaster; if he be a whoremonger, and comes before him, he were   **35**
as good go a mile on his errand.[5]

DUKE.   That we were all, as some would seem to be,
From our faults, as faults from seeming, free!

Enter LUCIO.

ELBOW.   His neck will come to your waist—a cord,[6] sir.

[1]**bastard** sweet Spanish wine   [2]**two usuries** lending money at interest (a way of breeding barren metal) and fornication   [3]**stands for the facing** represents the trimming   [4]**maw** belly   [5]**he were . . . errand** i.e., he has a hard (or fruitless?) journey ahead   [6]**cord** i.e., the cord around the Friar's waist

[47]**combinate** betrothed   [48]**avail** benefit   [49]**stead up** keep   [50]**encounter** i.e., sexual union   [51]**scaled** weighed   [52]**frame** prepare   [53]**grange** farm

POMPEY.   I spy comfort; I cry bail. Here's a gen-   40
tleman and a friend of mine.

LUCIO.   How now, noble Pompey! What, at the wheels of
Caesar? Art thou led in triumph? What, is there none of
Pygmalion's images,[7] newly made woman, to be had now,
for putting the hand in the pocket and extracting it   45
clutched? What reply, ha? What say'st thou to this tune,
matter and method? Is't not drowned i' th' last rain, ha?
What say'st thou, Trot? Is the world as it was, man?
Which is the way? Is it sad, and few words? Or how? The
trick of it?   50

DUKE.   Still thus, and thus; still worse.

LUCIO.   How doth my dear morsel, thy mistress? Procures
she still, ha?

POMPEY.   Troth, sir, she hath eaten up all her beef,[8] and she
is herself in the tub.[9]   55

LUCIO.   Why, 'tis good. It is the right of it; it must be so:
ever your fresh whore and your powdered bawd, an un-
shunned consequence; it must be so. Art going to prison,
Pompey?

POMPEY.   Yes, faith sir.   60

LUCIO.   Why, 'tis not amiss, Pompey. Farewell; go, say I
sent thee thither. For debt, Pompey? Or how?

ELBOW.   For being a bawd, for being a bawd.

LUCIO.   Well, then, imprison him. If imprisonment be the
due of a bawd, why, 'tis his right. Bawd is he   65
doubtless, and of antiquity too, bawd-born. Farewell,
good Pompey. Commend me to the prison, Pompey, you
will turn good husband[10] now, Pompey, you will keep the
house.

POMPEY.   I hope, sir, your good worship will be my   70
bail.

LUCIO.   No, indeed, will I not, Pompey, it is not the wear.[11]
I will pray, Pompey, to increase your bondage. If you take
it not patiently, why, your mettle[12] is the more. Adieu,
trusty Pompey. 'Bless you, friar.   75

DUKE.   And you.

LUCIO.   Does Bridget paint still, Pompey, ha?

ELBOW.   Come your ways, sir, come.

POMPEY.   You will not bail me then, sir?

LUCIO.   Then, Pompey, nor now. What news abroad,   80
friar, what news?

ELBOW.   Come your ways, sir, come.

LUCIO.   Go to kennel, Pompey, go. (*Exeunt* ELBOW,
POMPEY, *and* OFFICERS.) What news, friar, of the Duke?

DUKE.   I know none. Can you tell me of any?   85

LUCIO.   Some say he is with the Emperor of Russia; other
some, he is in Rome: but where is he, think you?

DUKE.   I know not where; but wheresoever, I wish him
well.

LUCIO.   It was a mad fantastical trick of him to steal   90
from the state, and usurp the beggary he was never born
to. Lord Angelo dukes it well in his absence; he puts
transgression to't.

DUKE.   He does well in't.

LUCIO.   A little more lenity to lechery would do no   95
harm in him; something too crabbed that way, friar.

DUKE.   It is too general a vice, and severity must cure it.

LUCIO.   Yes, in good sooth, the vice is of a great kindred,
it is well allied; but it is impossible to extirp it quite, friar,
till eating and drinking be put down. They say   100
this Angelo was not made by man and woman after this
downright way of creation. Is it true, think you?

DUKE.   How should he be made, then?

LUCIO.   Some report a sea maid[13] spawned him; some, that
he was begot between two stockfishes.[14] But it is   105
certain that when he makes water his urine is congealed
ice; that I know to be true. And he is a motion generative;[15] that's infallible.

DUKE.   You are pleasant, sir, and speak apace.

LUCIO.   Why, what a ruthless thing is this in him,   110
for the rebellion of a codpiece to take away the life of a
man! Would the Duke that is absent have done this? Ere
he would have hanged a man for the getting a hundred
bastards, he would have paid for the nursing a thousand.
He had some feeling of the sport; he knew the   115
service, and that instructed him to mercy.

DUKE.   I never heard the absent Duke much detected for[16]
women; he was not inclined that way.

LUCIO.   O, sir, you are deceived.

DUKE.   'Tis not possible.   120

LUCIO.   Who, not the Duke? Yes, your beggar of fifty, and
his use was to put a ducat in her clack-dish;[17] the Duke
had crotchets[18] in him. He would be drunk too; that let
me inform you.

DUKE.   You do him wrong, surely.   125

LUCIO.   Sir, I was an inward[19] of his. A shy fellow was the
Duke, and I believe I know the cause of his withdrawing.

DUKE.   What, I prithee, might be the cause?

LUCIO.   No, pardon; 'tis a secret must be locked within the
teeth and the lips; but this I can let you under-   130
stand, the greater file[20] of the subject held the Duke to be
wise.

DUKE.   Wise! Why, no question but he was.

---

[7]**Pygmalion's images** i.e., prostitutes (Pompey is compared to
Pygmalion, sculptor of a female statue that came to life)   [8]**beef**
prostitutes (who serve as flesh-food)   [9]**in the tub** taking the cure
for venereal disease (a tub was also used for corning beef, hence
the reference to powdering—pickling—in Lucio's next speech)
[10]**husband** housekeeper, manager   [11]**wear** fashion   [12]**mettle** spirit
(pun on metal of chains)

[13]**sea maid** (to explain his piscatory coldness)   [14]**stockfishes** dried
cod   [15]**motion generative** masculine puppet   [16]**detected for**
accused of   [17]**clack-dish** beggar's bowl (metaphorical here)
[18]**crotchets** whims   [19]**inward** intimate companion   [20]**greater file**
majority

LUCIO.   A very superficial, ignorant, unweighing fellow.

DUKE.   Either this is envy in you, folly, or mis-   **135**
taking. The very stream of his life and the business he
hath helmed must, upon a warranted need,[21] give him a
better proclamation. Let him be but testimonied in his
own bringings-forth,[22] and he shall appear to the envious
a scholar, a statesman, and a soldier. Therefore   **140**
you speak unskillfully; or if your knowledge be more, it
is much dark'ned in your malice.

LUCIO.   Sir, I know him, and I love him.

DUKE.   Love talks with better knowledge, and knowledge
with dearer love.   **145**

LUCIO.   Come, sir, I know what I know.

DUKE.   I can hardly believe that, since you know not what
you speak. But, if ever the Duke return, as our prayers are
he may, let me desire you to make your answer before
him. If it be honest you have spoke, you have   **150**
courage to maintain it. I am bound to call upon you, and
I pray you, your name?

LUCIO.   Sir, my name is Lucio, well known to the Duke.

DUKE.   He shall know you better, sir, if I may live to report
you.   **155**

LUCIO.   I fear you not.

DUKE.   O, you hope the Duke will return no more, or you
imagine me too unhurtful an opposite. But, indeed, I can
do you little harm; you'll forswear this again.

LUCIO.   I'll be hanged first; thou art deceived in   **160**
me, friar. But no more of this. Canst thou tell if Claudio
die tomorrow or no?

DUKE.   Why should he die, sir?

LUCIO.   Why? For filling a bottle with a tundish.[23] I would
the Duke we talk of were returned again; this un-   **165**
genitured[24] agent will unpeople the province with conti-
nency; sparrows must not build in his house-eaves,
because they are lecherous. The Duke yet would have
dark deeds darkly answered; he would never bring them
to light. Would he were returned! Marry, this   **170**
Claudio is condemned for untrussing.[25] Farewell, good
friar; I prithee, pray for me. The Duke, I say to thee again,
would eat mutton on Fridays.[26] He's not past it, yet, and
I say to thee, he would mouth with a beggar, though she
smelled brown bread and garlic. Say that I said   **175**
so. Farewell. (*Exit.*)

DUKE.
    No might nor greatness in mortality
    Can censure 'scape; back-wounding calumny
    The whitest virtue strikes. What king so strong

Can tie the gall up in the slanderous tongue?   **180**
But who comes here?

Enter ESCALUS, PROVOST, *and* (OFFICERS *with*) BAWD (MIS-
TRESS OVERDONE).

ESCALUS.   Go, away with her to prison!

MISTRESS OVERDONE.   Good my lord, be good to me.
Your honor is accounted a merciful man, good my lord.

ESCALUS.   Double and treble admonition, and still   **185**
forfeit in the same kind! This would make mercy swear,
and play the tyrant.

PROVOST.   A bawd of eleven years' continuance, may it
please your honor.

MISTRESS OVERDONE.   My lord, this is one Lu-   **190**
cio's information against me. Mistress Kate Keepdown
was with child by him in the Duke's time; he promised
her marriage; his child is a year and a quarter old, come
Philip and Jacob;[27] I have kept it myself, and see how he
goes about to abuse me.   **195**

ESCALUS.   That fellow is a fellow of much license; let him
be called before us. Away with her to prison. Go to, no
more words. (*Exeunt* OFFICERS *with* MISTRESS OVER-
DONE.) Provost, my brother Angelo will not be altered;
Claudio must die tomorrow. Let him be furnished   **200**
with divines, and have all charitable preparation. If my
brother wrought by my pity, it should not be so with him.

PROVOST.   So please you, this friar hath been with him, and
advised him for th' entertainment of death.

ESCALUS.   Good even, good father.   **205**

DUKE.   Bliss and goodness on you!

ESCALUS.   Of whence are you?

DUKE.
    Not of this country, though my chance is now
    To use it for my time; I am a brother
    Of gracious order, late come from the See   **210**
    In special business from his Holiness.

ESCALUS.   What news abroad i' th' world?

DUKE.   None, but that there is so great a fever on goodness,
that the dissolution of it must cure it,[28] novelty is only in
request,[29] and it is as dangerous to be aged[30] in   **215**
any kind of course as it is virtuous to be constant in any
undertaking. There is scarce truth enough alive to make
societies secure, but security[31] enough to make fellowships[32] accursed. Much upon this riddle runs the wisdom
of the world. This news is old enough, yet it is   **220**
every day's news. I pray you, sir, of what disposition was
the Duke?

---

[21]**upon a warranted need** if proof be demanded   [22]**bringings-
forth** actions   [23]**tundish** funnel   [24]**ungenitured** sexless
[25]**untrussing** undressing   [26]**eat mutton on Fridays** (the Duke
allegedly ate mutton on a Friday, which was a fast day, and also
practiced venery; ''mutton'' also means ''harlot,'' and Friday is
the day of the planet Venus)

[27]**Philip and Jacob** May 1st   [28]**fever . . . cure it** i.e., the
dissolution of the fever alone can now restore goodness to its
pristine health   [29]**novelty is only in request** change is urgently
needed   [30]**aged** old and worn out   [31]**security** heedlessness
[32]**fellowships** human societies

ESCALUS.   One that, above all other strifes, contended especially to know himself.

DUKE.   What pleasure was he given to?   225

ESCALUS.   Rather rejoicing to see another merry, than merry at anything which professed to make him rejoice: a gentleman of all temperance. But leave we him to his events, with a prayer they may prove prosperous, and let me desire to know how you find Claudio pre-   230
pared. I am made to understand that you have lent him visitation.

DUKE.   He professes to have received no sinister measure from his judge, but most willingly humbles himself to the determination of justice; yet had he framed to   235
himself, by the instruction of his frailty, many deceiving promises of life; which I, by my good leisure, have discredited to him, and now is he resolved to die.

ESCALUS.   You have paid the heavens your function, and the prisoner the very debt of your calling. I have   240
labored for the poor gentleman to the extremest shore of my modesty,[33] but my brother justice have I found so severe, that he hath forced me to tell him he is indeed Justice.

DUKE.   If his own life answer the straitness of his   245
proceeding, it shall become him well; wherein if he chance to fail, he hath sentenced himself.

ESCALUS.   I am going to visit the prisoner. Fare you well.

DUKE.   Peace be with you! (*Exeunt* ESCALUS *and* PROVOST.)

> He who the sword of heaven will bear   250
> Should be as holy as severe;
> Pattern in himself to know
> Grace to stand, and virtue go;[34]
> More nor less to others paying
> Than by self-offenses weighing.   255
> Shame to him whose cruel striking
> Kills for faults of his own liking.
> Twice treble shame on Angelo,
> To weed my[35] vice and let his grow.
> O, what may man within him hide,   260
> Though angel on the outward side!
> How may likeness made in crimes,
> Making practice[36] on the times,
> To draw with idle spiders' strings
> Most ponderous and substantial things?   265
> Craft against vice I must apply:
> With Angelo tonight shall lie
> His old betrothèd but despisèd;
> So disguise shall, by th' disguisèd,

Pay with falsehood false exacting,   270
And perform an old contracting. (*Exit.*)

ACT FOUR

SCENE ONE (THE MOATED GRANGE)

Enter MARIANA *and* BOY *singing.*

SONG

> Take, O, take those lips away,
>   That so sweetly were forsworn;
> And those eyes, the break of day,
>   Lights that do mislead the morn;
> But my kisses bring again, bring again;   5
> Seals of love, but sealed in vain, sealed in vain.

Enter DUKE (*disguised as before*).

MARIANA.
> Break off thy song, and haste thee quick away.
> Here comes a man of comfort, whose advice
> Hath often stilled my brawling discontent. (*Exit*
>   BOY.)
> I cry you mercy, sir; and well could wish   10
> You had not found me here so musical.
> Let me excuse me, and believe me so,
> My mirth it much displeased, but pleased my woe.

DUKE.
> 'Tis good; though music oft hath such a charm
> To make bad good, and good provoke to harm.   15
> I pray you, tell me, hath anybody inquired for me
> here today? Much upon this time have I promised
> here to meet.

MARIANA.   You have not been inquired after; I have sat here all day.   20

Enter ISABELLA.

DUKE.   I do constantly believe you. The time is come even now. I shall crave your forbearance a little; may be I will call upon you anon, for some advantage to yourself.

MARIANA.   I am always bound to you. (*Exit.*)

DUKE.
> Very well met, and well come.   25
> What is the news from this good deputy?

ISABELLA.
> He hath a garden circummured[1] with brick,
> Whose western side is with a vineyard backed;
> And to that vineyard is a planchèd[2] gate,
> That makes his opening with this bigger key.   30
> This other doth command a little door
> Which from the vineyard to the garden leads.
> There have I made my promise

---

[33]**extremest shore of my modesty** i.e., as far as is proper
[34]**Pattern . . . go** i.e., he should have a model in himself of grace which will stand if virtue elsewhere ebbs   [35]**my** (used impersonally)   [36]**Making practice** practicing deception

[1]**circummured** walled around   [2]**planchèd** planked

Upon the heavy middle of the night
To call upon him.   **35**
DUKE.   But shall you on your knowledge find this way?
ISABELLA.
I have ta'en a due and wary note upon't.
With whispering and most guilty diligence,
In action all of precept,[3] he did show me
The way twice o'er.   **40**
DUKE.
                              Are there no other tokens
Between you 'greed concerning her observance?[4]
ISABELLA.
No, none, but only a repair i' th' dark,
And that I have possessed[5] him my most stay
Can be but brief; for I have made him know   **45**
I have a servant comes with me along,
That stays upon[6] me, whose persuasion[7] is
I come about my brother.
DUKE.
                              'Tis well borne up.
I have not yet made known to Mariana   **50**
A word of this. What, ho, within! Come forth.

Enter MARIANA.

I pray you, be acquainted with this maid;
She comes to do you good.
ISABELLA.   I do desire the like.
DUKE.   Do you persuade yourself that I respect you?   **55**
MARIANA.   Good friar, I know you do, and have found it.
DUKE.
Take, then, this your companion by the hand,
Who hath a story ready for your ear.
I shall attend your leisure, but make haste;
The vaporous night approaches.   **60**
MARIANA. Will't please you walk aside? *Exit (with*
  ISABELLA*).*
DUKE.
O place and greatness, millions of false eyes
Are stuck upon thee; volumes of report
Run with these false and most contrarious quests[8]
Upon thy doings; thousand escapes[9] of wit   **65**
Make thee the father of their idle dreams,
And rack thee in their fancies.

Enter MARIANA *and* ISABELLA.

                              Welcome, how agreed?
ISABELLA.   She'll take the enterprise upon her, father,
If you advise it.   **70**

DUKE.
                    It is not my consent
But my entreaty too.
ISABELLA.
                              Little have you to say
When you depart from him, but, soft and low,
"Remember now my brother."   **75**
MARIANA.   Fear me not.
DUKE.
Nor, gentle daughter, fear you not at all.
He is your husband on a precontract;[10]
To bring you thus together, 'tis no sin,
Sith that the justice of your title to him   **80**
Doth flourish the deceit. Come, let us go:
Our corn's to reap, for yet our tithe's[11] to sow.
                    (*Exeunt.*)

SCENE TWO (THE PRISON)

Enter PROVOST *and* CLOWN (POMPEY).

PROVOST.   Come hither, sirrah. Can you cut off a man's
head?
POMPEY.   If the man be a bachelor, sir, I can; but if he be
a married man, he's his wife's head,[1] and I can never cut
off a woman's head.   **5**
PROVOST.   Come, sir, leave me your snatches,[2] and yield
me a direct answer. Tomorrow morning are to die Claudio
and Barnardine. Here is in our prison a common executioner, who in his office lacks a helper. If you will take it
on you to assist him, it shall redeem you from   **10**
your gyves;[3] if not, you shall have your full time of imprisonment, and your deliverance with an unpitied whipping, for you have been a notorious bawd.
POMPEY.   Sir, I have been an unlawful bawd time out of
mind, but yet I will be content to be a lawful   **15**
hangman. I would be glad to receive some instruction
from my fellow partner.
PROVOST.   What, ho, Abhorson![4] Where's Abhorson,
there?

Enter ABHORSON.

ABHORSON.   Do you call, sir?   **20**
PROVOST.   Sirrah, here's a fellow will help you tomorrow
in your execution. If you think it meet, compound[5] with
him by the year, and let him abide here with you; if not,
use him for the present, and dismiss him. He cannot plead
his estimation[6] with you; he hath been a bawd.   **25**

---

[3]**In . . . precept** teaching by gestures   [4]**her observance** what she
must do   [5]**possessed** informed   [6]**stays upon** waits for
[7]**persuasion** conviction   [8]**quests** cry of the hound on the scent
[9]**escapes** sallies

[10]**precontract** legally binding betrothal agreement   [11]**tithe** tithe
corn   [1]**he's his wife's head** (see Ephesians 5:23: "For the
husband is the head of the wife")   [2]**snatches** quibbles   [3]**gyves**
shackles   [4]**Abhorson** (pun on "ab, whore, son," son from a
whore)   [5]**compound** settle   [6]**estimation** reputation

ABHORSON.   A bawd, sir? Fie upon him! He will discredit our mystery.[7]

PROVOST.   Go to, sir; you weigh equally; a feather will turn the scale. (*Exit.*)

POMPEY.   Pray, sir, by your good favor—for surely,   30
sir, a good favor[8] you have, but that you have a hanging look—do you call, sir, your occupation a mystery?

ABHORSON.   Ay, sir; a mystery.

POMPEY.   Painting, sir, I have heard say, is a mystery; and
your whores, sir, being members of my occupa-   35
tion, using painting, do prove my occupation a mystery;
but what mystery there should be in hanging, if I should
be hanged, I cannot imagine.

ABHORSON.   Sir, it is a mystery.

POMPEY.   Proof?   40

ABHORSON.   Every true man's apparel fits your thief: if it
be too little for your thief, your true man thinks it big
enough; if it be too big for your thief, your thief thinks it
little enough: so every true man's apparel fits your thief.[9]

Enter PROVOST.

PROVOST.   Are you agreed?   45

POMPEY.   Sir, I will serve him; for I do find your hangman
is a more penitent trade than your bawd; he doth oft'ner
ask forgiveness.[10]

PROVOST.   You, sirrah, provide your block and your ax tomorrow four o'clock.   50

ABHORSON.   Come on, bawd. I will instruct thee in my
trade; follow.

POMPEY.   I do desire to learn, sir; and I hope, if you have
occasion to use me for your own turn,[11] you shall find me
yare;[12] for, truly, sir, for your kindness I owe you   55
a good turn.

PROVOST.   Call hither Barnardine and Claudio.

Exit (POMPEY *with* ABHORSON).

Th' one has my pity; not a jot the other,
Being a murderer, though he were my brother.

Enter CLAUDIO.

Look, here's the warrant, Claudio, for thy death.   60
'Tis now dead midnight, and by eight tomorrow
Thou must be made immortal. Where's Barnardine?

CLAUDIO.
As fast locked up in sleep as guiltless labor
When it lies starkly[13] in the traveler's bones;
He will not wake.   65

PROVOST.
                    Who can do good on him?
Well, go, prepare yourself. (*Knocking within.*) But,
    hark, what noise?—
Heaven give your spirits comfort. (*Exit* CLAUDIO.)
    By and by.   70
I hope it is some pardon or reprieve
For the most gentle Claudio. Welcome, father.

Enter DUKE (*disguised as before*).

DUKE.   The best and wholesom'st spirits of the night
Envelop you, good provost! Who called here of late?

PROVOST.   None since the curfew rung.   75

DUKE.   Not Isabel?

PROVOST.   No.

DUKE.   They will, then, ere't be long.

PROVOST.   What comfort is for Claudio?

DUKE.   There's some in hope.   80

PROVOST.   It is a bitter deputy.

DUKE.
Not so, not so; his life is paralleled
Even with the stroke and line of his great justice.
He doth with holy abstinence subdue
That in himself which he spurs on his pow'r   85
To qualify[14] in others; were he mealed[15] with that
Which he corrects, then were he tyrannous;
But this being so, he's just. (*Knocking within.*)
                    Now are they come. (*Exit* PROVOST.)
This is a gentle provost—seldom when   90
The steelèd jailer is the friend of men. (*Knocking
    within.*)
How now, what noise? That spirit's possessed with
    haste
That wounds th' unsisting[16] postern[17] with these
    strokes.

Enter PROVOST.

PROVOST.
There he must stay until the officer
Arise to let him in; he is called up.   95

DUKE.
Have you no countermand for Claudio yet,
But he must die tomorrow?

PROVOST.   None, sir, none.

DUKE.
As near the dawning, provost, as it is,
You shall hear more ere morning.   100

PROVOST.
                    Happily
You something know; yet I believe there comes

---

[7]**mystery** craft   [8]**favor** countenance   [9]**every . . . thief**
(interpretation uncertain)   [10]**ask forgiveness** (the executioner
always asked the condemned man to forgive him)   [11]**turn**
execution (pun)   [12]**yare** ready   [13]**starkly** stiffly

[14]**qualify** moderate   [15]**mealed** stained   [16]**unsisting** (perhaps
''unassisting,'' perhaps a printer's slip for ''resisting'')
[17]**postern** small door

No countermand; no such example have we.
Besides, upon the very siege[18] of justice
Lord Angelo hath to the public ear   **105**
Professed the contrary.

Enter a MESSENGER.

This is his lord's man.
DUKE.   And here comes Claudio's pardon.
MESSENGER.   My lord hath sent you this note, and by me
this further charge, that you swerve not from the   **110**
smallest article of it, neither in time, matter, or other cir-
cumstance. Good morrow; for, as I take it, it is almost day.
PROVOST.   I shall obey him. (*Exit* MESSENGER.)
DUKE (*aside*).
This is his pardon, purchased by such sin
For which the pardoner himself is in.   **115**
Hence hath offense his quick celerity,
When it is borne in high authority.
When vice makes mercy, mercy's so extended,
That for the fault's love is th' offender friended.
Now, sir, what news?   **120**
PROVOST.   I told you. Lord Angelo, belike[19] thinking me
remiss in mine office, awakens me with this unwonted
putting-on;[20] methinks strangely, for he hath not used it
before.
DUKE.   Pray you, let's hear.   **125**
PROVOST (*reads the letter*).   "Whatsoever you may hear to
the contrary, let Claudio be executed by four of the clock;
and in the afternoon Barnardine. For my better satisfaction, let me have Claudio's head sent me by five. Let this
be duly performed with a thought that more de-   **130**
pends on it than we must yet deliver. Thus fail not to do
your office, as you will answer it at your peril."
What say you to this, sir?
DUKE.   What is that Barnardine who is to be executed in
th' afternoon?   **135**
PROVOST.   A Bohemian born, but here nursed up and bred;
one that is a prisoner nine years old.
DUKE.   How came it that the absent Duke had not either
delivered him to his liberty or executed him? I have heard
it was ever his manner to do so.   **140**
PROVOST.   His friends still wrought reprieves for him; and,
indeed, his fact,[21] till now in the government of Lord
Angelo, came not to an undoubtful proof.
DUKE.   It is now apparent?
PROVOST.   Most manifest, and not denied by   **145**
himself.
DUKE.   Hath he borne himself penitently in prison?
How seems he to be touched?

PROVOST.   A man that apprehends death no more dread-
fully but as a drunken sleep; careless, reckless,   **150**
and fearless of what's past, present, or to come; insensible
of mortality, and desperately mortal.[22]
DUKE.   He wants[23] advice.
PROVOST.   He will hear none. He hath evermore had the
liberty of the prison; give him leave to escape   **155**
hence, he would not: drunk many times a day, if not many
days entirely drunk. We have very oft awaked him, as if
to carry him to execution, and showed him a seeming
warrant for it; it hath not moved him at all.
DUKE.   More of him anon. There is written in your   **160**
brow, provost, honesty and constancy: if I read it not
truly, my ancient skill beguiles me; but, in the boldness
of my cunning,[24] I will lay myself in hazard.[25] Claudio,
whom here you have warrant to execute, is no greater
forfeit to the law than Angelo who hath sentenced   **165**
him. To make you understand this in a manifested
effect,[26] I crave but four days' respite, for the which you
are to do me both a present[27] and a dangerous courtesy.
PROVOST.   Pray, sir, in what?
DUKE.   In the delaying death.   **170**
PROVOST.   Alack, how may I do it, having the hour lim-
ited,[28] and an express command, under penalty, to deliver
his head in the view of Angelo? I may make my case as
Claudio's, to cross this in the smallest.
DUKE.   By the vow of mine Order I warrant you, if   **175**
my instructions may be your guide. Let this Barnardine
be this morning executed, and his head borne to Angelo.
PROVOST.   Angelo hath seen them both, and will discover
the favor.[29]
DUKE.   O, death's a great disguiser; and you may   **180**
add to it. Shave the head, and tie the beard; and say it was
the desire of the penitent to be so bared[30] before his death;
you know the course is common. If anything fall to you
upon this, more than thanks and good fortune, by the saint
whom I profess, I will plead against it with my   **185**
life.
PROVOST.   Pardon me, good father; it is against my oath.
DUKE.   Were you sworn to the Duke, or to the deputy?
PROVOST.   To him, and to his substitutes.
DUKE.   You will think you have made no offense,   **190**
if the Duke avouch the justice of your dealing?
PROVOST.   But what likelihood is in that?
DUKE.   Not a resemblance, but a certainty. Yet since I see
you fearful,[31] that neither my coat, integrity, nor persua-
sion can with ease attempt[32] you, I will go further   **195**
than I meant, to pluck all fears out of you. Look you, sir,

---

[22]**desperately mortal** about to die without hope of the future
[23]**wants** needs   [24]**cunning** knowledge   [25]**lay myself in hazard**
take a risk   [26]**in a manifested effect** by open proof   [27]**present**
immediate   [28]**limited** determined   [29]**discover the favor** recognize
the face   [30]**bared** shaved   [31]**fearful** full of fear   [32]**attempt** move

[18]**siege** seat   [19]**belike** perhaps   [20]**putting-on** urging   [21]**fact** evil
deed

here is the hand and seal of the Duke. You know the character,[33] I doubt not, and the signet is not strange to you.

PROVOST.   I know them both.

DUKE.   The contents of this is the return of the   200
Duke. You shall anon overread it at your pleasure, where
you shall find, within these two days he will be here. This
is a thing that Angelo knows not; for he this very day
receives letters of strange tenor, perchance of the Duke's
death, perchance entering into some monastery,   205
but by chance nothing of what is writ. Look, th' unfolding
star[34] calls up the shepherd. Put not yourself into amazement how these things should be: all difficulties are but
easy when they are known. Call your executioner, and off
with Barnardine's head; I will give him a present   210
shrift,[35] and advise him for a better place. Yet you are
amazed; but this shall absolutely resolve[36] you. Come
away; it is almost clear dawn. *Exit* (with PROVOST).

SCENE THREE (THE PRISON)

Enter CLOWN (POMPEY).

POMPEY.   I am as well acquainted here as I was in our house
of profession: one would think it were Mistress Overdone's own house, for here be many of her old customers.
First, here's young Master Rash; he's in for a commodity[1]
of brown paper and old ginger, ninescore and sev-   5
enteen pounds, of which he made five marks,[2] ready
money; marry, then ginger was not much in request, for
the old women were all dead. Then is there here one
Master Caper, at the suit of Master Three-pile the mercer,
for some four suits of peach-colored satin, which   10
now peaches[3] him a beggar. Then have we here young
Dizzy, and young Master Deep-vow, and Master Copper-
spur,[4] and Master Starve-lackey, the rapier and dagger
man, and young Drop-heir that killed lusty Pudding, and
Master Forthright the tilter,[5] and brave Master   15
Shoe-tie[6] the great traveler, and wild Half-can[7] that
stabbed Pots, and, I think, forty more; all great doers in
our trade, and are now "for the Lord's sake."[8]

Enter ABHORSON.

ABHORSON.   Sirrah, bring Barnardine hither.

POMPEY.   Master Barnardine! You must rise and be   20
hanged, Master Barnardine!

ABHORSON.   What, ho, Barnardine!

BARNARDINE (*within*). A pox o' your throats! Who makes
that noise there? What are you?

POMPEY.   Your friends, sir; the hangman. You must   25
be so good, sir, to rise and be put to death.

BARNARDINE (*within*). Away, you rogue, away! I am sleepy.

ABHORSON.   Tell him he must awake, and that quickly
too.

POMPEY.   Pray, Master Barnardine, awake till you   30
are executed, and sleep afterwards.

ABHORSON.   Go into him, and fetch him out.

POMPEY.   He is coming, sir, he is coming; I hear his straw
rustle.

Enter BARNARDINE.

ABHORSON.   Is the ax upon the block, sirrah?   35

POMPEY.   Very ready, sir.

BARNARDINE.   How now, Abhorson? What's the news
with you?

ABHORSON.   Truly, sir, I would desire you to clap into
your prayers; for, look you, the warrant's come.   40

BARNARDINE.   You rogue, I have been drinking all night;
I am not fitted for't.

POMPEY.   O, the better, sir: for he that drinks all night, and
is hanged betimes[9] in the morning, may sleep the sounder
all the next day.   45

Enter DUKE (*disguised as before*).

ABHORSON.   Look you, sir; here comes your ghostly[10]
father. Do we jest now, think you?

DUKE.   Sir, induced by my charity, and hearing how hastily
you are to depart, I am come to advise you, comfort you,
and pray with you.   50

BARNARDINE.   Friar, not I: I have been drinking hard all
night, and I will have more time to prepare me, or they
shall beat out my brains with billets.[11] I will not consent
to die this day, that's certain.

DUKE.
    O, sir, you must; and therefore I beseech you   55
    Look forward on the journey you shall go.

BARNARDINE.   I swear I will not die today for any man's
persuasion.

DUKE.   But hear you—

BARNARDINE.   Not a word. If you have anything to   60
say to me, come to my ward, for thence will not I today.
(*Exit.*)

Enter PROVOST.

---

[33]**character** handwriting   [34]**unfolding star** morning star
(signaling the shepherd to lead the sheep from the fold)   [35]**shrift**
absolution   [36]**resolve** convince   [1]**commodity** (worthless goods
whose purchase at a heavy price was forced on a debtor in dire
need by a usurious creditor, who thus circumvented the
contemporary laws against usury)   [2]**marks** (a mark was about
two-thirds of a pound)   [3]**peaches** betrays   [4]**Copper-spur** i.e.,
Master Pretentious (copper was a bogus substitute for gold)
[5]**tilter** fighter   [6]**Shoe-tie** rosette (worn by gallants)   [7]**Half-can** (a
larger vessel than a pot)   [8]"**for the Lord's sake**" (the cry of
prisoners begging alms from passers-by)

[9]**betimes** early   [10]**ghostly** spiritual   [11]**billets** cudgels

DUKE.
>Unfit to live or die. O gravel heart!
>After him, fellows; bring him to the block. (*Exeunt*
>>ABHORSON *and* POMPEY.)

PROVOST.   Now, sir, how do you find the prisoner?

DUKE.
>A creature unprepared, unmeet for death;   **65**
>And to transport him in the mind he is
>Were damnable.

PROVOST.
>>>Here in the prison, father,
>There died this morning of a cruel fever
>One Ragozine, a most notorious pirate,   **70**
>A man of Claudio's years, his beard and head
>Just of his color. What if we do omit
>This reprobate till he were well inclined,
>And satisfy the deputy with the visage
>Of Ragozine, more like to Claudio?   **75**

DUKE.
>O, 'tis an accident that heaven provides.
>Dispatch it presently;[12] the hour draws on
>Prefixed[13] by Angelo. See this be done,
>And sent according to command, whiles I
>Persuade this rude wretch willingly to die.   **80**

PROVOST.
>This shall be done, good father, presently;
>But Barnardine must die this afternoon,
>And how shall we continue Claudio,
>To save me from the danger that might come
>If he were known alive?   **85**

DUKE.
>>>Let this be done:
>Put them in secret holds,[14] both Barnardine and
>>Claudio.
>Ere twice the sun hath made his journal[15] greeting
>To yonder generation, you shall find
>Your safety manifested.   **90**

PROVOST.   I am your free dependant.[16]

DUKE.   Quick, dispatch, and send the head to Angelo.
>*Exit* (PROVOST).
>Now will I write letters to Angelo—
>The provost, he shall bear them—whose contents
>Shall witness to him I am near at home,   **95**
>And that by great injunctions I am bound
>To enter publicly. Him I'll desire
>To meet me at the consecrated fount,
>A league below the city; and from thence,
>By cold gradation[17] and well-balanced form,   **100**
>We shall proceed with Angelo.

Enter PROVOST.

PROVOST.   Here is the head; I'll carry it myself.

DUKE.
>Convenient is it. Make a swift return,
>For I would commune with you of such things
>That want[18] no ear but yours.   **105**

PROVOST.   >>>I'll make all speed. (*Exit.*)

ISABELLA (*within*). Peace, ho, be here!

DUKE.
>The tongue of Isabel. She's come to know
>If yet her brother's pardon be come hither.
>But I will keep her ignorant of her good,   **110**
>To make her heavenly comforts of despair
>When it is least expected.

Enter ISABELLA.

ISABELLA.   >>>Ho, by your leave!

DUKE.   Good morning to you, fair and gracious daughter.

ISABELLA.
>The better, given me by so holy a man.   **115**
>Hath yet the deputy sent my brother's pardon?

DUKE.
>He hath released him, Isabel, from the world;
>His head is off, and sent to Angelo.

ISABELLA.   Nay, but it is not so.

DUKE.
>It is no other. Show your wisdom, daughter,   **120**
>In your close[19] patience.

ISABELLA.   O, I will to him and pluck out his eyes!

DUKE.   You shall not be admitted to his sight.

ISABELLA.
>Unhappy Claudio, wretched Isabel,
>Injurious world, most damnèd Angelo!   **125**

DUKE.
>This nor hurts him nor profits you a jot;
>Forbear it therefore, give your cause to heaven.
>Mark what I say, which you shall find
>By every syllable a faithful verity.
>The Duke comes home tomorrow—nay, dry your
>>eyes—   **130**
>One of our covent,[20] and his confessor,
>Gives me this instance:[21] already he hath carried
>Notice to Escalus and Angelo,
>Who do prepare to meet him at the gates,
>There to give up their pow'r. If you can, pace[22]
>>your wisdom   **135**
>In that good path that I would wish it go,
>And you shall have your bosom[23] on this wretch,
>Grace of the Duke, revenges to your heart,
>And general honor.

ISABELLA.   >>>I am directed by you.   **140**

---

[12]**presently** at once   [13]**Prefixed** predetermined   [14]**holds** cells
[15]**journal** daily   [16]**your free dependant** freely at your service
[17]**cold gradation** deliberate steps

[18]**want** need   [19]**close** deep, secret   [20]**covent** convent   [21]**instance**
proof   [22]**pace** conduct   [23]**bosom** desire

DUKE.

> This letter, then, to Friar Peter give;
> 'Tis that he sent me of the Duke's return.
> Say, by this token, I desire his company
> At Mariana's house tonight. Her cause and yours
> I'll perfect him withal, and he shall bring you   145
> Before the Duke; and to the head of Angelo
> Accuse him home and home. For my poor self,
> I am combinèd[24] by a sacred vow,
> And shall be absent. Wend you with this letter;
> Command these fretting waters from your eyes   150
> With a light heart; trust not my holy Order,
> If I pervert your course. Who's here?

Enter LUCIO.

LUCIO.   Good even. Friar, where's the provost?

DUKE.   Not within, sir.

LUCIO.   O pretty Isabella, I am pale at mine heart   155
to see thine eyes so red; thou must be patient. I am fain
to dine and sup with water and bran; I dare not for my
head fill my belly; one fruitful meal would set me to't.
But they say the Duke will be here tomorrow. By my
troth, Isabel, I loved thy brother. If the old fan-   160
tastical Duke of dark corners had been at home, he had
lived. (*Exit* ISABELLA.)

DUKE.   Sir, the Duke is marvelous little beholding to your
reports; but the best is, he lives not in them.

LUCIO.   Friar, thou knowest not the Duke so well   165
as I do; he's a better woodman[25] than thou tak'st him for.

DUKE.   Well, you'll answer this one day. Fare ye well.

LUCIO.   Nay, tarry, I'll go along with thee: I can tell thee
pretty tales of the Duke.

DUKE.   You have told me too many of him already,   170
sir, if they be true; if not true, none were enough.

LUCIO.   I was once before him for getting a wench with
child.

DUKE.   Did you such a thing?

LUCIO.   Yes, marry, did I; but I was fain to for-   175
swear it: they would else have married me to the rotten
medlar.[26]

DUKE.   Sir, your company is fairer than honest. Rest you
well.

LUCIO.   By my troth, I'll go with thee to the lane's   180
end. If bawdy talk offend you, we'll have very little of it.
Nay, friar, I am a kind of burr; I shall stick. (*Exeunt.*)

SCENE FOUR (A ROOM)

Enter ANGELO *and* ESCALUS.

ESCALUS.   Every letter he hath writ hath disvouched other.

ANGELO.   In most uneven and distracted manner. His actions show much like to madness; pray heaven his wisdom
be not tainted. And why meet him at the gates, and re-
deliver our authorities there?   5

ESCALUS.   I guess not.

ANGELO.   And why should we proclaim it in an hour before
his ent'ring, that if any crave redress of injustice, they
should exhibit their petitions in the street?

ESCALUS.   He shows his reason for that: to have a   10
dispatch of complaints, and to deliver us from devices[1]
hereafter which shall then have no power to stand against
us.

ANGELO.   Well, I beseech you, let it be proclaimed. Betimes i' th' morn I'll call you at your house. Give   15
notice to such men of sort and suit[2] as are to meet him.

ESCALUS.   I shall, sir. Fare you well. (*Exit.*)

ANGELO.

> Good night.
> This deed unshapes me quite, makes me unpregnant,[3]
> And dull to all proceedings. A deflow'red maid,   20
> And by an eminent body that enforced
> The law against it! But that her tender shame
> Will not proclaim against her maiden loss,[4]
> How might she tongue me! Yet reason dares her no;
> For my authority bears of a credent bulk,[5]   25
> That no particular scandal once can touch
> But it confounds the breather. He should have lived,
> Save that his riotous youth, with dangerous sense,[6]
> Might in the times to come have ta'en revenge,
> By so receiving a dishonored life   30
> With ransom of such shame. Would yet he had lived!
> Alack, when once our grace we have forgot,
> Nothing goes right; we would, and we would not.
>   (*Exit.*)

SCENE FIVE (OUTSIDE THE TOWN)

Enter DUKE (*in his own habit*) *and* FRIAR PETER.

DUKE.

> These letters at fit time deliver me.[1]
> The provost knows our purpose and our plot.
> The matter being afoot, keep your instruction,
> And hold you ever to our special drift,
> Though sometimes you do blench[2] from this
>   to that,   5
> As cause doth minister. Go call at Flavius' house,
> And tell him where I stay; give the like notice
> To Valencius, Rowland, and to Crassus,

---

[24]**combinèd** bound   [25]**woodman** hunter (here, of women)
[26]**medlar** applelike fruit edible only when partly decayed (here, a
prostitute)

[1]**devices** false complaints   [2]**men of sort and suit** noblemen
[3]**unpregnant** unreceptive   [4]**maiden loss** loss of maidenhood
[5]**bears of a credent bulk** is derived from trusted material   [6]**sense**
feeling   [1]**me** for me   [2]**blench** deviate

And bid them bring the trumpets to the gate;
But send me Flavius first.   10
FRIAR PETER.   It shall be speeded well. (*Exit.*)

Enter VARRIUS.

DUKE.
I thank thee, Varrius; thou hast made good haste.
Come, we will walk. There's other of our friends
Will greet us here anon, my gentle Varrius. (*Exeunt.*)

SCENE SIX (NEAR THE CITY GATE)

Enter ISABELLA *and* MARIANA.

ISABELLA.
To speak so indirectly I am loath:
I would say the truth; but to accuse him so,
That is your part. Yet I am advised to do it,
He says, to veil full purpose.
MARIANA.   Be ruled by him.   5
ISABELLA.
Besides, he tells me that, if peradventure
He speak against me on the adverse side,
I should not think it strange; for 'tis a physic
That's bitter to sweet end.
MARIANA.   I would Friar Peter—   10

Enter FRIAR PETER.

ISABELLA.   O peace! The friar is come.
FRIAR PETER.
Come, I have found you out a stand most fit
Where you may have such vantage[1] on the Duke,
He shall not pass you. Twice have the trumpets
    sounded.
The generous[2] and gravest citizens   15
Have hent[3] the gates, and very near upon
The Duke is ent'ring: therefore, hence, away!
    (*Exeunt.*)

ACT FIVE

SCENE ONE (THE CITY GATE)

Enter DUKE, VARRIUS, LORDS, ANGELO, ESCALUS, LUCIO,
(PROVOST, OFFICERS, *and*) CITIZENS, *at several doors.*

DUKE.
My very worthy cousin,[1] fairly met.
    Our old faithful friend, we are glad to see you.
ANGELO, ESCALUS.   Happy return be to your royal Grace.
DUKE.
Many and hearty thankings to you both.
    We have made inquiry of you, and we hear   5

Such goodness of your justice, that our soul
Cannot but yield you forth to public thanks,
Forerunning more requital.[2]
ANGELO.   You make my bonds still greater.
DUKE.
O, your desert speaks loud, and I should wrong it 10
To lock it in the wards of covert bosom,[3]
When it deserves, with characters of brass,
A forted residence 'gainst the tooth of time
And razure[4] of oblivion. Give me your hand,
And let the subject see, to make them know   15
That outward courtesies would fain proclaim
Favors that keep[5] within. Come, Escalus,
You must walk by us on our other hand—
And good supporters are you.

Enter (FRIAR) PETER *and* ISABELLA.

FRIAR PETER.   Now is your time: speak loud, and   20
kneel before him.
ISABELLA.
Justice, O royal Duke! Vail your regard[6]
Upon a wronged—I would fain have said, a maid.
O worthy prince, dishonor not your eye
By throwing it on any other object   25
Till you have heard me in my true complaint,
And given me justice, justice, justice, justice!
DUKE.
Relate your wrongs. In what? By whom? Be brief.
Here is Lord Angelo shall give you justice;
Reveal yourself to him.   30
ISABELLA.
              O worthy Duke,
You bid me seek redemption of the devil.
Hear me yourself, for that which I must speak
Must either punish me, not being believed,
Or wring redress from you. Hear me, O hear me,
    here!   35
ANGELO.
My lord, her wits, I fear me, are not firm.
She hath been a suitor to me for her brother
Cut off by course of justice—
ISABELLA.   By course of justice!
ANGELO.   And she will speak most bitterly and   40
strange.
ISABELLA.
Most strange, but yet most truly, will I speak.
That Angelo's forsworn, is it not strange?
That Angelo's a murderer, is't not strange?
That Angelo is an adulterous thief,   45

---

[2]**Forerunning more requital** preceding additional reward
[3]**To . . . bosom** i.e., to keep it locked hidden in my heart [4]**razure**
erasure [5]**keep** dwell [6]**Vail your regard** cast your attention

[1]**vantage** advantageous position [2]**generous** highborn [3]**hent**
gathered at   [1]**cousin** (a sovereign's address to a nobleman)

An hypocrite, a virgin-violator;
Is it not strange, and strange?
DUKE.   Nay, it is ten times strange.
ISABELLA.
It is not truer he is Angelo
Than this is all as true as it is strange.   50
Nay, it is ten times true, for truth is truth
To th' end of reck'ning.
DUKE.
                              Away with her! Poor soul,
She speaks this in th' infirmity of sense.
ISABELLA.
O prince, I conjure thee, as thou believ'st   55
There is another comfort than this world,
That thou neglect me not, with that opinion
That I am touched with madness. Make not
    impossible
That which but seems unlike. 'Tis not impossible
But one, the wicked'st caitiff on the ground,   60
May seem as shy, as grave, as just, as absolute[7]
As Angelo; even so may Angelo,
In all his dressings, caracts,[8] titles, forms,
Be an arch-villain. Believe it, royal prince;
If he be less, he's nothing; but he's more,   65
Had I more name for badness.
DUKE.
                              By mine honesty,
If she be mad, as I believe no other,
Her madness hath the oddest frame of sense,
Such a dependency of thing on thing,   70
As e'er I heard in madness.
ISABELLA.
                              O gracious Duke,
Harp not on that; nor do not banish reason
For inequality,[9] but let your reason serve
To make the truth appear where it seems hid,   75
And hide the false seems[10] true.
DUKE.
                              Many that are not mad
Have, sure, more lack of reason. What would you
    say?
ISABELLA.
I am the sister of one Claudio,
Condemned upon the act of fornication   80
To lose his head, condemned by Angelo.
I, in probation[11] of a sisterhood,
Was sent to by my brother, one Lucio
As then the messenger—
LUCIO.
                              That's I, and't like[12] your Grace.   85
I came to her from Claudio, and desired her

To try her gracious fortune with Lord Angelo
For her poor brother's pardon.
ISABELLA.   That's he indeed.
DUKE.   You were not bid to speak.   90
LUCIO.
                              No, my good lord,
Nor wished to hold my peace.
DUKE.
                              I wish you now, then;
Pray you, take note of it, and when you have
A business for yourself, pray heaven you then   95
Be perfect.[13]
LUCIO.   I warrant your honor.
DUKE.   The warrant's[14] for yourself; take heed to't.
ISABELLA.   This gentleman told somewhat of my tale—
LUCIO.   Right.   100
DUKE.
It may be right; but you are i' the wrong
To speak before your time. Proceed.
ISABELLA.
                              I went
To this pernicious caitiff deputy—
DUKE.   That's somewhat madly spoken.   105
ISABELLA.
                              Pardon it;
The phrase is to the matter.[15]
DUKE.   Mended again. The matter: proceed.
ISABELLA.
In brief, to set the needless process by,
How I persuaded, how I prayed, and kneeled,   110
How he refelled[16] me, and how I replied—
For this was of much length—the vild[17] conclusion
I now begin with brief and shame to utter.
He would not, but by gift of my chaste body
To his concupiscible intemperate lust,   115
Release my brother; and after much debatement,
My sisterly remorse[18] confutes mine honor,
And I did yield to him; but the next morn betimes,
His purpose surfeiting,[19] he sends a warrant
For my poor brother's head.   120
DUKE.   This is most likely!
ISABELLA.   O, that it were as like as it is true!
DUKE.
By heaven, fond wretch, thou know'st not what thou
    speak'st,
Or else thou art suborned against his honor
In hateful practice.[20] First, his integrity   125
Stands without blemish. Next, it imports no reason[21]
That with such vehemency he should pursue

---

[7]**absolute** perfect   [8]**caracts** symbols of office   [9]**inequality** injustice   [10]**seems** which seems   [11]**probation** novitiate   [12]**and't like** if it please

[13]**perfect** thoroughly prepared   [14]**warrant** warning   [15]**to the matter** appropriate   [16]**refelled** repelled   [17]**vild** vile   [18]**remorse** pity   [19]**surfeiting** satiating   [20]**practice** plot   [21]**imports no reason** does not attend to reason

Faults proper[22] to himself: if he had so offended,
He would have weighed thy brother by himself,
And not have cut him off. Someone hath set
    you on;   **130**
Confess the truth, and say by whose advice
Thou cam'st here to complain.

ISABELLA.
               And is this all?
Then, O you blessèd ministers above,
Keep me in patience, and with ripened time   **135**
Unfold the evil which is here wrapped up
In countenance. Heaven shield your Grace from woe,
As I, thus wronged, hence unbelievèd go!

DUKE.
I know you'd fain be gone. An officer,
To prison with her! Shall we thus permit   **140**
A blasting and a scandalous breath to fall
On him so near us? This needs must be a practice.
Who knew of your intent and coming hither?

ISABELLA.   One that I would were here, Friar Lodowick.

DUKE.   A ghostly father, belike. Who knows that   **145**
   Lodowick?

LUCIO.
My lord, I know him; 'tis a meddling friar,
I do not like the man. Had he been lay,[23] my lord,
For certain words he spake against your Grace
In your retirement, I had swinged[24] him soundly. **150**

DUKE.
Words against me! This's a good friar, belike!
And to set on this wretched woman here
Against our substitute! Let this friar be found.

LUCIO.
But yesternight, my lord, she and that friar,
I saw them at the prison; a saucy friar,   **155**
A very scurvy[25] fellow.

FRIAR PETER.
Blessed be your royal Grace!
I have stood by, my lord, and I have heard
Your royal ear abused. First, hath this woman
Most wrongfully accused your substitute,   **160**
Who is as free from touch or soil with her
As she from one ungot.

DUKE.
            We did believe no less.
Know you that Friar Lodowick that she speaks of?

FRIAR PETER.
I know him for a man divine and holy;   **165**
Not scurvy, nor a temporary meddler,[26]
As he's reported by this gentleman;
And, on my trust, a man that never yet
Did, as he vouches, misreport your Grace.

LUCIO.   My lord, most villainously; believe it.   **170**

FRIAR PETER.
Well, he in time may come to clear himself,
But at this instant he is sick, my lord,
Of a strange fever. Upon his mere request,
Being come to knowledge that there was complaint
Intended 'gainst Lord Angelo, came I hither,   **175**
To speak, as from this mouth, what he doth know
Is true and false; and what he with his oath
And all probation[27] will make up full clear,
Whensoever he's convented.[28] First, for this woman,
To justify this worthy nobleman,   **180**
So vulgarly and personally accused,
Her shall you hear disprovèd to her eyes,
Till she herself confess it.

DUKE.   Good friar, let's hear it.
   (ISABELLA *is carried off guarded.*)

Enter MARIANA (*veiled*).

Do you not smile at this, Lord Angelo?   **185**
O heaven, the vanity of wretched fools!
Give us some seats. Come, cousin Angelo,
In this I'll be impartial; be you judge
Of your own cause. Is this the witness, friar?
First, let her show her face, and after speak.   **190**

MARIANA.
Pardon, my lord; I will not show my face
Until my husband bid me.

DUKE.   What, are you married?

MARIANA.   No, my lord.

DUKE.   Are you a maid?   **195**

MARIANA.   No, my lord.

DUKE.   A widow, then?

MARIANA.   Neither, my lord.

DUKE.   Why, you are nothing, then: neither maid, widow,
   nor wife?   **200**

LUCIO.   My lord, she may be a punk;[29] for many of them
   are neither maid, widow, nor wife.

DUKE.
Silence that fellow. I would he had some cause
To prattle for himself.

LUCIO.   Well, my lord.   **205**

MARIANA.
My lord, I do confess I ne'er was married,
And I confess, besides, I am no maid.
I have known[30] my husband; yet my husband
Knows not that ever he knew me.

LUCIO.   He was drunk, then, my lord; it can be no   **210**
   better.

DUKE.   For the benefit of silence, would thou wert so too!

LUCIO.   Well, my lord.

---

[22]**proper** belonging [23]**lay** layman [24]**swinged** thrashed [25]**scurvy**
worthless [26]**temporary meddler** meddler in temporal affairs

[27]**probation** proof [28]**convented** sent for [29]**punk** harlot [30]**known**
had intercourse with

DUKE.   This is no witness for Lord Angelo.

MARIANA.

Now I come to't, my lord: 215
She that accuses him of fornication,
In selfsame manner doth accuse my husband,
And charges him, my lord, with such a time
When I'll depose I had him in mine arms
With all th' effect of love.   220

ANGELO.   Charges she moe than me?

MARIANA.   Not that I know.

DUKE.   No? You say your husband?

MARIANA.

Why, just, my lord, and that is Angelo,
Who thinks he knows that he ne'er knew
        my body,   225
But knows he thinks that he knows Isabel's.

ANGELO.   This is a strange abuse. Let's see thy face.

MARIANA.   My husband bids me; now I will unmask.
        (Unveiling.)
This is that face, thou cruel Angelo,
Which once thou swor'st was worth the
        looking on;   230
This is the hand which, with a vowed contract,
Was fast belocked in thine; this is the body
That took away the match[31] from Isabel,
And did supply thee at thy garden house
In her imagined person.   235

DUKE.   Know you this woman?

LUCIO.   Carnally, she says.

DUKE.   Sirrah, no more!

LUCIO.   Enough, my lord.

ANGELO.

My lord, I must confess I know this woman: 240
And five years since there was some speech of
        marriage
Betwixt myself and her, which was broke off,
Partly for that her promisèd proportions[32]
Came short of composition,[33] but in chief,
For that her reputation was disvalued   245
In levity;[34] since which time of five years
I never spake with her, saw her, nor heard from her,
Upon my faith and honor.

MARIANA.

                    Noble prince,
As there comes light from heaven and words from
        breath,   250
As there is sense in truth and truth in virtue,
I am affianced this man's wife as strongly
As words could make up vows; and, my good lord,
But Tuesday night last gone in's garden house
He knew me as a wife. As this is true,   255

Let me in safety raise me from my knees,
Or else forever be confixèd[35] here,
A marble monument.

ANGELO.

                    I did but smile till now;
Now, good my lord, give me the scope of
        justice;   260
My patience here is touched. I do perceive
These poor informal[36] women are no more
But instruments of some more mightier member
That sets them on. Let me have way, my lord,
To find this practice out.   265

DUKE.

                    Ay, with my heart,
And punish them to your height of pleasure.
Thou foolish friar and thou pernicious woman,
Compact[37] with her that's gone, think'st thou thy
        oaths,
Though they would swear down each particular
        saint,   270
Were testimonies against his worth and credit,
That's sealed in approbation?[38] You, Lord Escalus,
Sit with my cousin; lend him your kind pains
To find out this abuse, whence 'tis derived.
There is another friar that set them on;   275
Let him be sent for.

FRIAR PETER.

Would he were here, my lord, for he, indeed,
Hath set the women on to this complaint:
Your provost knows the place where he abides,
And he may fetch him.   280

DUKE.

                    Go, do it instantly. (Exit PROVOST.)
And you, my noble and well-warranted cousin,
Whom it concerns to hear this matter forth,
Do with your injuries as seems you best,
In any chastisement. I for a while   285
Will leave you, but stir not you till you have
Well determined upon these slanderers.

ESCALUS.

My lord, we'll do it thoroughly. Exit (DUKE).
Signior Lucio, did not you say you knew that Friar
Lodowick to be a dishonest person?   290

LUCIO.   Cucullus non facit monachum;[39] honest in nothing
    but in his clothes, and one that hath spoke most villainous
    speeches of the Duke.

ESCALUS.   We shall entreat you to abide here till he come,
    and enforce[40] them against him; we shall find this   295
    friar a notable[41] fellow.

---

[31]**match** meeting [32]**proportions** dowry [33]**composition** previous
agreement [34]**disvalued/In levity** discredited for lightness

[35]**confixèd** fixed firmly [36]**informal** (1) rash (2) informing
[37]**Compact** in collusion [38]**approbation** attested integrity
[39]**Cucullus non facit monachum** the cowl does not make the
monk (Latin) [40]**enforce** urge [41]**notable** notorious

LUCIO.   As any in Vienna, on my word.

ESCALUS.   Call that same Isabel here once again; I would
    speak with her. (*Exit an* ATTENDANT.) Pray you, my lord,
    give me leave to question; you shall see how I'll   **300**
    handle her.

LUCIO.   Not better than he, by her own report.

ESCALUS.   Say you?

LUCIO.   Marry, sir, I think, if you handled her privately,
    she would sooner confess; perchance, publicly,   **305**
    she'll be ashamed.

Enter DUKE (*as friar*), PROVOST, ISABELLA, (*and* OFFICERS).

ESCALUS.   I will go darkly[42] to work with her.

LUCIO.   That's the way; for women are light at midnight.

ESCALUS.   Come on, mistress, here's a gentlewoman denies
    all that you have said.   **310**

LUCIO.   My lord, here comes the rascal I spoke of—here
    with the provost.

ESCALUS.   In very good time. Speak not you to him till we
    call upon you.

LUCIO.   Mum.   **315**

ESCALUS.   Come, sir, did you set these women on to slander
    Lord Angelo? They have confessed you did.

DUKE.   'Tis false.

ESCALUS.   How! Know you where you are?

DUKE.
    Respect to your great place; and let the devil   **320**
    Be sometime honored for his burning throne.
    Where is the Duke? 'Tis he should hear me speak.

ESCALUS.
    The Duke's in us, and we will hear you speak.
    Look you speak justly.

DUKE.
    Boldly, at least. But, O poor souls,   **325**
    Come you to seek the lamb here of the fox?
    Good night to your redress. Is the Duke gone?
    Then is your cause gone too. The Duke's unjust,
    Thus to retort[43] your manifest[44] appeal,
    And put your trial in the villain's mouth   **330**
    Which here you come to accuse.

LUCIO.   This is the rascal; this is he I spoke of.

ESCALUS.
    Why, thou unreverend and unhallowed friar,
    Is't not enough thou hast suborned these women
    To accuse this worthy man, but in foul mouth,   **335**
    And in the witness of his proper[45] ear,
    To call him villain? And then to glance from him
    To th' Duke himself, to tax him with injustice?
    Take him hence; to th' rack with him. We'll touse[46]
        you

Joint by joint, but we will know his purpose.   **340**
What, "unjust"!

DUKE.
                Be not so hot. The Duke
    Dare no more stretch this finger of mine than he
    Dare rack his own: his subject am I not,
    Nor here provincial.[47] My business in this state   **345**
    Made me a looker-on here in Vienna,
    Where I have seen corruption boil and bubble
    Till it o'errun the stew. Laws for all faults,
    But faults so countenanced, that the strong statutes
    Stand like the forfeits[48] in a barber's shop,   **350**
    As much in mock as mark.[49]

ESCALUS.   Slander to th' state! Away with him to prison!

ANGELO.   What can you vouch against him, Signior Lucio?
    Is this the man that you did tell us of?

LUCIO.   'Tis he, my lord. Come hither, goodman   **355**
    bald-pate; do you know me?

DUKE.   I remember you, sir, by the sound of your voice. I
    met you at the prison, in the absence of the Duke.

LUCIO.   O, did you so? And do you remember what you
    said of the Duke?   **360**

DUKE.   Most notedly, sir.

LUCIO.   Do you so, sir? And was the Duke a fleshmonger,
    a fool, and a coward, as you then reported him to be?

DUKE.   You must, sir, change persons with me, ere you
    make that my report. You, indeed, spoke so of   **365**
    him; and much more, much worse.

LUCIO.   O thou damnable fellow! Did not I pluck thee by
    the nose for thy speeches?

DUKE.   I protest I love the Duke as I love myself.

ANGELO.   Hark, how the villain would close[50]   **370**
    now, after his treasonable abuses.

ESCALUS.   Such a fellow is not to be talked withal. Away
    with him to prison! Where is the provost? Away with him
    to prison, lay bolts enough upon him, let him speak no
    more. Away with those giglets[51] too, and with the   **375**
    other confederate companion.

DUKE (*to the* PROVOST).   Stay, sir; stay awhile.

ANGELO.   What, resists he? Help him, Lucio.

LUCIO.   Come, sir; come, sir; come, sir; foh, sir! Why, you
    bald-pated, lying rascal, you must be hooded,   **380**
    must you? Show your knave's visage, with a pox to you.
    Show your sheep-biting[52] face, and be hanged an hour.
    Will't not off? (*Pulls off the friar's hood, and discovers
    the* DUKE.)

DUKE.
    Thou art the first knave that e'er mad'st a Duke.
    First, provost, let me bail these gentle three.   **385**

[42]**darkly** subtly   [43]**retort** refer back   [44]**manifest** clear   [45]**proper**
very   [46]**touse** pull

[47]**provincial** belonging to the province or state   [48]**forfeits**
extracted teeth (barbers acted as dentists)   [49]**As much . . . mark**
to be mocked at as much as to be seen   [50]**close** come to agreement
[51]**giglets** wanton women   [52]**sheep-biting** currish

(*To* LUCIO.) Sneak not away, sir; for the friar and
    you
Must have a word anon. Lay hold on him.
LUCIO.   This may prove worse than hanging.
DUKE (*to* ESCALUS).
    What you have spoke I pardon. Sit you down.
    We'll borrow place of him. (*To* ANGELO.) Sir, by
       your leave.   390
    Hast thou or word, or wit, or impudence,
    That yet can do thee office?[53] If thou hast,
    Rely upon it till my tale be heard,
    And hold no longer out.
ANGELO.
                  O my dread lord,   395
    I should be guiltier than my guiltiness,
    To think I can be undiscernible,
    When I perceive your Grace, like pow'r divine,
    Hath looked upon my passes.[54] Then, good prince,
    No longer session[55] hold upon my shame,   400
    But let my trial be mine own confession.
    Immediate sentence then, and sequent death,
    Is all the grace I beg.
DUKE.
               Come hither, Mariana.
    Say, wast thou e'er contracted to this woman?   405
ANGELO.   I was, my lord.
DUKE.
    Go take her hence, and marry her instantly.
    Do you the office, friar, which consummate,
    Return him here again. Go with him, provost.

Exit (ANGELO *with* MARIANA, FRIAR PETER, *and* PROVOST).

ESCALUS.
    My lord, I am more amazed at his dishonor   410
    Than at the strangeness of it.
DUKE.
              Come hither, Isabel.
    Your friar is now your prince. As I was then
    Advertising and holy[56] to your business,
    Not changing heart with habit, I am still   415
    Attorneyed at your service.
ISABELLA.
               O, give me pardon,
    That I, your vassal, have employed and pained
    Your unknown sovereignty!
DUKE.
            You are pardoned, Isabel: 420
    And now, dear maid, be you as free to us.
    Your brother's death, I know, sits at your heart,
    And you may marvel why I obscured myself,
    Laboring to save his life, and would not rather

Make rash remonstrance of my hidden pow'r   425
Than let him so be lost. O most kind maid,
It was the swift celerity of his death,
Which I did think with slower foot came on,
That brained my purpose. But, peace be with him.
That life is better life, past fearing death,   430
Than that which lives to fear. Make it your comfort,
So happy is your brother.

Enter ANGELO, MARIANA, (FRIAR) PETER, PROVOST.

ISABELLA.   I do, my lord.
DUKE.
    For this new-married man, approaching here,
    Whose salt[57] imagination yet hath wronged   435
    Your well-defended honor, you must pardon
    For Mariana's sake. But as he adjudged your brother,
    Being criminal, in double violation,
    Of sacred chastity, and of promise-breach,
    Thereon dependent, for your brother's life,   440
    The very mercy of the law cries out
    Most audible, even from his proper tongue,
    ''An Angelo for Claudio, death for death!''
    Haste still pays haste, and leisure answers leisure;
    Like doth quit like, and Measure still for
       Measure.[58]   445
    Then, Angelo, thy fault's thus manifested;
    Which, though thou wouldst deny, denies thee
       vantage.
    We do condemn thee to the very block
    Where Claudio stooped to death, and with like haste.
    Away with him.   450
MARIANA.   O my most gracious lord,
    I hope you will not mock me with a husband.
DUKE.
    It is your husband mocked you with a husband.
    Consenting to the safeguard of your honor,
    I thought your marriage fit; else imputation,[59]   455
    For that he knew you, might reproach your life,
    And choke your good to come. For his possessions,
    Although by confiscation they are ours,
    We do instate and widow you withal,
    To buy you a better husband.   460
MARIANA.   O my dear lord,
    I crave no other, nor no better man.
DUKE.   Never crave him; we are definitive.[60]
MARIANA.   Gentle my liege—(*Kneeling*.)

---

[53]**office** service [54]**passes** trespasses [55]**session** trial
[56]**Advertising and holy** attentive and devoted

[57]**salt** lecherous [58]**Measure still for Measure** (see Matthew
7:1–2: ''Judge not, that ye be not judged. For with what judgment
ye judge, ye shall be judged: and with what measure ye mete, it
shall be measured to you again'') [59]**imputation** accusation
[60]**definitive** determined

DUKE.

You do but lose your labor.   **465**
Away with him to death! (*To* LUCIO.) Now, sir, to
    you.

MARIANA.

O my good lord! Sweet Isabel, take my part,
Lend me your knees, and all my life to come
I'll lend you all my life to do you service.

DUKE.

Against all sense you do importune her;   **470**
Should she kneel down in mercy of this fact,[61]
Her brother's ghost his pavèd[62] bed would break,
And take her hence in horror.

MARIANA.

Isabel,
Sweet Isabel, do yet but kneel by me,   **475**
Hold up your hands, say nothing, I'll speak all.
They say, best men are molded out of faults;
And, for the most, become much more the better
For being a little bad; so may my husband.
O Isabel, will you not lend a knee?   **480**

DUKE.   He dies for Claudio's death.

ISABELLA (*kneeling*).

Most bounteous sir,
Look, if it please you, on this man condemned,
As if my brother lived. I partly think
A due sincerity governèd his deeds,   **485**
Till he did look on me. Since it is so,
Let him not die. My brother had but justice,
In that he did the thing for which he died.
For Angelo,
His act did not o'ertake his bad intent,   **490**
And must be buried but as an intent.
That perished by the way. Thoughts are no subjects,[63]
Intents but merely thoughts.

MARIANA.   Merely, my lord.

DUKE.

Your suit's unprofitable; stand up, I say.   **495**
I have bethought me of another fault.
Provost, how came it Claudio was beheaded
At an unusual hour?

PROVOST.   It was commanded so.

DUKE.   Had you a special warrant for the deed?   **500**

PROVOST.   No, my good lord; it was by private message.

DUKE.

For which I do discharge you of your office;
Give up your keys.

PROVOST.

Pardon me, noble lord.
I thought it was a fault, but knew it not;[64]   **505**
Yet did repent me, after more advice;[65]

For testimony whereof, one in the prison,
That should by private order else have died,
I have reserved alive.

DUKE.   What's he?   **510**

PROVOST.   His name is Barnardine.

DUKE.

I would thou hadst done so by Claudio.
Go fetch him hither; let me look upon him. (*Exit*
    PROVOST.)

ESCALUS.

I am sorry, one so learnèd and so wise
As you, Lord Angelo, have still[66] appeared,   **515**
Should slip so grossly, both in the heat of blood,
And lack of tempered judgment afterward.

ANGELO.

I am sorry that such sorrow I procure,
And so deep sticks it in my penitent heart,
That I crave death more willingly than mercy;   **520**
'Tis my deserving, and I do entreat it.

Enter BARNARDINE *and* PROVOST, CLAUDIO (*muffled*),
JULIET.

DUKE.   Which is that Barnardine?

PROVOST.   This, my lord.

DUKE.

There was a friar told me of this man.
Sirrah, thou art said to have a stubborn soul,   **525**
That apprehends no further than this world,
And squar'st[67] thy life according. Thou'rt
    condemned;
But, for those earthly faults, I quit[68] them all,
And pray thee take this mercy to provide
For better times to come. Friar, advise him;   **530**
I leave him to your hand. What muffled fellow's
    that?

PROVOST.

This is another prisoner that I saved,
Who should have died when Claudio lost his head;
As like almost to Claudio as himself. (*Unmuffles*
    CLAUDIO.)

DUKE (*to* ISABELLA).

If he be like your brother, for his sake   **535**
Is he pardoned; and, for your lovely sake,
Give me your hand, and say you will be mine,
He is my brother too; but fitter time for that.
By this Lord Angelo perceives he's safe;
Methinks I see a quick'ning[69] in his eye.   **540**
Well, Angelo, your evil quits you well;
Look that you love your wife; her worth, worth
    yours.
I find an apt remission[70] in myself,

---

[61]**fact** crime   [62]**pavèd** slab-covered   [63]**no subjects** i.e., not subject
to law   [64]**knew it not** was not sure   [65]**advice** thought

[66]**still** ever   [67]**squar'st** regulate   [68]**quit** pardon   [69]**quick'ning**
animation   [70]**remission** wish to forgive

And yet here's one in place I cannot pardon.
(*To* LUCIO.) You, sirrah, that knew me for a fool, a
    coward,   **545**
One all of luxury,[71] an ass, a madman;
Wherein have I so deserved of you,
That you extol me thus?

LUCIO.   'Faith, my lord, I spoke it but according to the
trick.[72] If you will hang me for it, you may; but   **550**
I had rather it would please you I might be whipped.

DUKE.
Whipped first, sir, and hanged after.
Proclaim it, provost, round about the city,
If any woman wronged by this lewd fellow—
As I have heard him swear himself there's one   **555**
Whom he begot with child—let her appear,
And he shall marry her. The nuptial finished,
Let him be whipped and hanged.

LUCIO.   I beseech your highness, do not marry me to a
whore. Your highness said even now, I made you   **560**
a duke: good my lord, do not recompense me in making
me a cuckold.

DUKE.
Upon mine honor, thou shalt marry her.
Thy slanders I forgive; and therewithal
Remit any other forfeits. Take him to prison,   **565**
And see our pleasure herein executed.

[71]**luxury** lust   [72]**trick** fashion

LUCIO.   Marrying a punk, my lord, is pressing to death,
whipping, and hanging.

DUKE.
Slandering a prince deserves it. (*Exeunt* OFFICERS
    with LUCIO.)
She, Claudio, that you wronged, look you
    restore.[73]   **570**
Joy to you, Mariana. Love her, Angelo;
I have confessed her, and I know her virtue.
Thanks, good friend Escalus, for thy much goodness;
There's more behind[74] that is more gratulate.[75]
Thanks, provost, for thy care and secrecy;   **575**
We shall employ thee in a worthier place.
Forgive him, Angelo, that brought you home
The head of Ragozine for Claudio's;
Th' offense pardons itself. Dear Isabel,
I have a motion[76] much imports your good,   **580**
Whereto if you'll a willing ear incline,
What's mine is yours, and what is yours is mine.
So, bring us to our palace, where we'll show
What's yet behind, that's meet[77] you all should
    know. (*Exeunt.*)

FINIS

[73]**restore** i.e., by marriage   [74]**behind** to come   [75]**gratulate**
gratifying   [76]**motion** proposal   [77]**meet** fitting

FOCUS QUESTIONS

1. Why does Shakespeare set his play in Vienna? What ingredients, suggested by scenes from the play, highlight both its historical time period and setting?
2. Love has a variety of contradictory meanings in the play. How do these further the action?
3. Discuss the unexpected shift from tragedy to comedy that divides the play.
4. If Angelo is initially portrayed as an outright sensualist, how does he win the audience's sympathy in the play's comic outcome?
5. How old are these characters, especially Duke Vincentio and Isabella? Why do their respective ages matter?
6. Since Shakespeare gives her no words to speak, discuss how Isabella might respond to the Duke's final offer.

OTHER ACTIVITIES

1. Develop costume sketches for any three characters and briefly annotate your designs.
2. In what specific ways can stage lighting enhance the play's changing moods?
3. Although not presented in the text, how would the reunion between Angelo and Mariana be realized or even *visualized?*
4. In a manner that befits a comedy, restage the play's final scene.

BIBLIOGRAPHY

Barnet, Sylvan. *A Short Guide to Shakespeare.* New York: Harcourt Brace Jovanovich, 1974.

Beckerman, Bernard. *Shakespeare at the Globe, 1599–1609.* New York: Macmillan, 1962.

Bennett, J. W. *"Measure for Measure" as Royal Entertainment.* New York: Columbia University Press, 1966.

Berry, Ralph. *On Directing Shakespeare.* London: Croom Helm, 1977.

Bevington, David. *Shakespeare.* Arlington Heights, IL: A. H. M. Publishing, 1978.

Chute, Marchette. *Shakespeare in London.* New York: Dutton, 1949.

Foakes, R. A. *Shakespeare: The Dark Comedies to the Last Plays.* London: Routledge & Kegan Paul, 1971.

Gay, Penny. *As She Likes It: Shakespeare's Unruly Women.* New York: Routledge, 1994.

Geckle, George L., ed. *Twentieth Century Interpretations of "Measure for Measure."* Englewood Cliffs, NJ: Prentice Hall, 1970.

Gless, Darryl J. *"Measure for Measure," the Law, and the Convent.* Princeton, NJ: Princeton University Press, 1979.

Hawkins, Harriet. *Measure for Measure.* Brighton, England: Harvester Press, 1987.

Miles, Rosalind. *The Problem of "Measure for Measure": A Historical Investigation.* London: Vision Press, 1976.

Muir, Kenneth. *The Sources of Shakespeare's Plays.* New Haven, CT: Yale University Press, 1978.

Shell, Marc. *The End of Kinship: "Measure for Measure," Incest, and the Ideal of Universal Siblinghood.* Stanford, CA: Stanford University Press, 1988.

Stead, C. K., ed. *"Measure for Measure": A Casebook.* London: Macmillan, 1971.

Thomson, Peter. *Shakespeare Theatre.* London: Routledge & Kegan Paul, 1983.

RECOMMENDED VIDEOTAPES AND RECORDINGS

Measure for Measure. Three sound cassettes. 146 min. 1961. Starring John Gielgud, Margaret Leighton, and Sir Ralph Richardson. Directed by Peter Wood. Caedmon Recordings.

Measure for Measure. VHS. 145 min. 1979. Starring Kate Nelligan. Directed by Desmond Davis. BBC Shakespeare Series. Distributed by Insight Media, New York City.

LIFE IS A DREAM
Calderón de la Barca (1600–1681)

As nature and poetry in modern times have never been found more intimately together than in Shakespeare, so the highest culture and poetry have never been found more intimately together than in Calderón.

—Goethe

Cherry Jones as Rosaura and Tom Hewitt as Segismundo in *Life Is a Dream,* presented by the American Repertory Theatre in 1989, under the direction of Anne Bogart. *Photo: Richard Feldman.*

APPROACHING THE GOLDEN AGE OF SPANISH DRAMA

The impact of Columbus' historic voyage of discovery in 1492 quickly elevated Spain's position in the New World and expanded its political horizons through the acquisition of territories both in northern Africa and on the European continent. By the middle of the sixteenth century, it was the most powerful nation in the Western world, until its decline in the mid-seventeenth century. *Siglo de Oro,* or Golden Age, is the name given to the extraordinary one hundred years that followed, between 1580 and 1680, when a burst of creative energy produced an impressive circle of artists and poets, including Spain's greatest playwrights. Ferdinand and Isabella's desire to unify Spain through Christianity in the aftermath of abolishing its Moorish and Jewish occupants gained the support of certain influential literary artists whose attitudes toward politics, women, and honor were esteemed as highly as the Catholic church. As a result, the Spanish drama discovered its purpose and principal themes.

Splitting from its religious roots, the secular drama of Spain had fully emerged by 1500 with works designed for popular and aristocratic audiences. These plays laid the groundwork for a professional theatre. When playwright Lope de Rueda (c. 1510–c. 1565) captured the attention of the court in Valladolid (Spain's capitol at that time), theatrical troupes surfaced in Seville and Madrid. Other cities established their own troupes shortly afterwards. They performed in public theatres that had been constructed as early as 1579. Known as **corrales,** these were based on the found courtyard spaces that these troupes used before permanent theatres were available. Like their Elizabethan counterparts, these theatres included boxes and galleries around a yard or **patio** with a platform stage at one end.

As the demand for new plays grew, playwrights surfaced to accommodate the need. The versatile Juan de la Cueva (1550–1610), for example, drew his themes from classical subjects, Spanish history, and everyday life. Even Miguel de Cervantes (1547–1616) wrote dozens of plays, although only sixteen have survived. But his most popular contribution to Western literature was the novel *Don Quixote.* Cervantes' plays were eventually overshadowed by the work of Lope de Vega, who entered the playwriting circle around 1590.

Lope de Vega (1562–1635) was the most prolific writer of his generation and over four hundred of his plays survive. He often worked with the popular **comedia** structure— the three-act play that was neither strictly comic nor serious and which ignored the neo-classical unities. (See Preface to Racine, p. 317.) His most well-known play in the English-speaking world is *Fuente Ovejuna (The Sheep Well),* which exposed strong revolutionary sentiments. The villagers who serve as protagonists and kill their tyrannical feudal lord are ultimately rescued from torture by their benevolent ruler. Yet this play does not begin to suggest the variety of styles and subject matter of which Lope de Vega was a master.

The prolific Tirso de Molina (c. 1584–1648) was credited with some four hundred plays of which eighty survive. His *Trickster of Seville* deserved all the praise that was bestowed on this earliest dramatization of the Don Juan legend. But his reputation and popularity were seriously challenged by a younger playwright, Calderón de la Barca, whose sublime contributions would solidify the importance of the Golden Age of Spanish drama.

Calderón's reputation as a writer for the court distinguished him from his contemporaries who were primarily associated with the public theatres. Productions at the court of Philip IV were given regularly until the end of the sixteenth century, signaling a shift in attention away from public theatres that contributed to the decline in the Spanish drama. By the time of his death in 1681, Calderón had written some 120 *comedias,* 80 **autos sacramentales** or religious dramas with music, and numerous **entremeses** or interludes during a career that also encompassed his roles as soldier and priest.

MAJOR WORKS

As a university-educated playwright whose artistry was uniquely Spanish and of the highest order, Calderón investigated a range of religious, historical, and philosophical themes in his dramatic writings. The first major phase of his career, between 1622 and 1640, yielded secular works of comedy, intrigue, love, and honor such as *The Phantom Lady* (1629) and *The Physician of His Own Honor* (1635). The second phase reflected the impact of his soldierly responsibilities in the Catalan War between 1640 and 1642, after which he wrote *The Mayor of Zalamea* (c. 1642). Adapting this play of revenge from a similarly titled work by Lope de Vega, he drew inspiration from his own military experiences to depict the spirit of lawlessness that permeated the invasion of Portugal.

The final phase of his career was influenced by his ordination to the priesthood in 1651, when a fierce stoicism characterized the *autos* he wrote until the end of his life, the most well known of which is *The Great World Theatre* (1649). Other major works include *The Constant Prince* (1629), *Devotion to the Cross* (1633), and *The Wonder-Working Magician* (1637). The most famous play of Calderón's secular period, and one that has dominated an international stage repertoire, is *Life Is a Dream* (1636), written during the year Philip IV appointed him court dramatist.

THE ACTION

Since birth, Segismundo, the Prince of Poland, had been imprisoned in a tower by his father, King Basilio, who feared the prophesies that this child would kill him and the queen. The death of Segismundo's mother at childbirth lent credence to the prediction. On his twenty-first birthday, which opens the play, Segismundo is still imprisoned in the tower.

On this special day, however, he is drugged and carried to the palace and, when he awakens, is told that his imprisonment was merely a dream. In response to freedom, he displays an uncontrollable violence that terrifies the court and sends him back to the tower. Drugged once again, he is told upon awakening that he had never been released from his chains and that he only dreamed he was a prince. With no proof whatever to support his claim, Segismundo relinquishes his rage for a more humane disposition.

As the rightful heir, Segismundo leads soldiers in a battle against his father. Instead of slaying the king on the spot, he prostrates himself in token of his new self. Although he has won his freedom, Segismundo is destined to remain a disillusioned, solitary figure who must stand alone in the universe.

STRUCTURE AND LANGUAGE

In concept, *Life Is a Dream* explores the reality of its metaphysical title, which succinctly embodies the play's principal theme. Its pervasive dream motif explores the complex interrelationship of illusion and reality, of art and life. In developing a theme whose roots can be traced to the ancient philosophers and poets, Calderón weaves his mythical tale around a legendary sleeping-prince who is suddenly roused from his uneasy slumber and reconciled with reality: the ultimate journey from darkness to enlightenment, the cycle from death to rebirth.

Basilio's abusive treatment of his son is an attempt to avert the tragic outcome predicted by the stars and to protect his own health and kingship from the accursed prince. The consequences of these actions result in a maze-like construction of poetic language, Christian symbolism, and philosophical discourse. Calderón's rich text, which is remarkably modern in its psychological dimensions, becomes the exemplary precursor to dream works, which underscore an international repertory of twentieth-century plays, films, and works of fiction.

A bold sophistication characterizes *Life Is a Dream* and epitomizes the spirit of its time and place in Spain's history and the literature of world drama. Foremost is Calderón's unique handling of characters. Disguised as a man to conceal her identity from the nobleman Astolfo, who has betrayed her in love, and from a father who long ago abandoned her unwed mother, Rosaura approaches the tower in the company of her manservant Clarín and rouses the enchained Segismundo. Symbolically speaking, she has awakened the enchanted prince—a reversal of the more familiar scenario in which the wandering knight encounters the sleeping princess over whom an evil spell has been cast. Their mutual attraction, more spiritual than sexual, triggers the **analogous actions** that ensue: Segismundo's attempt to overcome the tactics of the selfish king, his father; and Rosaura's revenge on the two men who have forsaken her. Clotaldo, Segismundo's tutor and sole companion for his many years in the tower, immediately recognizes Rosaura as his ''son,'' but, choosing not to acknowledge this discovery, assures her and Clarín safety at the palace. His protection enables Rosaura to resume her woman's garb as an attendant at the court.

While the principal Segismundo/Basilio plot holds precedence over the Rosaura/Clotaldo/Astolfo subplot, the latter continually illuminates the former and relegates Rosaura to an almost sisterly role in her relationship to Segismundo. Thus Segismundo's lustful attraction to her subsides when his more ennobling mission is finally revealed to him. As long as he is in Rosaura's presence, he benefits from her wisdom and courage. Her function in the play is further designated by her name or **symbolic nomenclature,** which closely corresponds with Segismundo's: while he is destined to follow ''the world'' (*seguir/el mundo*) from which he has been so long estranged, she possesses the ''aura'' of the ''rose''—a symbolic attribute of the Blessed Virgin—that will enable him to do so. Holding the key to Segismundo's salvation, Rosaura addresses several important issues of the Golden Age drama: religion, womanhood, and honor.

Sharing the spotlight with these three-dimensional characters is Calderón's formal and richly textured poetic language, at once direct in the strange tale it unfolds but also multilayered in its symbolic associations. Thus the range and variety of metrical constructions and verbal images do more than embellish Calderón's imaginative and complex premise: they also mirror both the stability and disintegration of the Golden Age, which Calderón's life spanned. The confusion of a dream is reflected in the language, dynamically splintered into carefully measured rhymed couplets, irregularly rhymed octosyllabic lines, and soliloquies of inordinate length and complexity, which express Calderón's philosophical arguments. In sharp contrast, carefully measured verbal exchanges establish, identify, and justify the characters.

The theme of the play, that life is a dream, echoes throughout. The motif carries poignant dramatic irony at the conclusion of act 2, in particular, when Segismundo is returned to the tower, this time believing that the royal treatment he received at the palace was only a dream, a mere figment of his imagination. When the King and Clotaldo have exited, Segismundo meditates on the transiency of life: the king who ''dreams he's a king,/ and so he lives with this illusion'' until he is ''transformed to dust and ashes;'' the rich man who ''dreams he's wealthy with all the cares/ it brings him;'' and the poor man who ''dreams/ he's suffering his misery/ and poverty.'' By concluding that ''each man dreams the thing he is,/ though no one sees it so,'' Segismundo achieves immortal status among those protagonists of Western dramatic literature who question the human condition.

ABOUT THE TRANSLATION

Edwin Honig's finely wrought verse translation adheres closely to the verbal and metrical patterns of Calderón's original. Calderón imitated a poetic style initiated by Lope de Vega in which the selection of different metrical patterns reflected the dynamic interchange of characterization and action. Six distinct patterns can be identified in *Life Is a Dream:* the *silva* (comprised of rhymed couplets with alternating lines of seven and eleven syllables, mostly used for dialogue); the *decima* (or ten-line stanza of irregularly rhymed patterns, mostly used for soliloquies by Segismundo); the *romance* (used mainly for narrative purposes); the *quintilla* (or five-line stanza consisting of octosyllabics and used for complimentary dialogues); the *recondilla* (or four-line stanza of octosyllabics used for fast-paced action); and the *octava* (or eight-line stanza of octosyllabics used for portentous moments of dramatic action).[1] The effect of these complex poetic measures is unquestionably musical, especially when we hear the characters of the play shaping Calderón's language, whether in solos, duets, or even small ensembles.

An impression of the original *decima* format from Segismundo's soliloquy in act 2, during which the character comments on the transiency of all humanity, reveals both the simple humility and the philosophical depth of his inquiry into life's meaning:

Yo sueño que estoy aqui,	I dream that I am here
detas prisiones cargado;	manacled in this cell,
y sone que en otro estado	and I dreamed I saw myself
mas lisonjero me vi.	before, much better off.
¿Que es la vida? Un frenesi.	What is life? A frenzy.
¿Que es la vida? Una illusion,	What is life? An illusion,
una sombra, una ficcion,	fiction, passing shadow,
y el mayor bien es pequeño;	and the greatest good the merest dot,
que toda la vida es sueño,	for all of life's a dream, and dreams
y los sueños, sueños son.	themselves are only part of dreaming.

Honig's wish to "reflect the essential poetry of Calderón's language as well as stick to its prose sense" is admirably realized.[2]

LIFE IS A DREAM-IN-PERFORMANCE

Between 1610 and 1640, when the Spanish theatre was at its height, the average acting troupe contained sixteen to twenty players, including both men and women. Little is known of individual acting companies, although by 1615 the number of companies privileged to perform was restricted to twelve by the crown. Nevertheless, records show that many additional troupes existed during this time. While actors were not held in esteem, they were much better off than their French counterparts who were denied religious rites, or their English ones who were always in conflict with civic authorities. Furthermore, the royal council's declaration that no man could perform a woman's role meant that women would perform on stage. However, the council also decreed that no woman could perform unless her husband or father was in the company to protect her. In this way, actors in Spain avoided the amorality associated with them elsewhere. Certainly this was a far cry from the Elizabethan convention, which demanded that all stage roles be performed by men.

The Spanish court theatre reached its zenith during Philip's reign, between 1621 and 1665, with performances of the play staged in a large hall at the Alcazar or in the gardens at Aranjuez, until the 1630s when a new palace was built in Madrid. While there are no specific records of the play's earliest performances at court, we can assume that *Life Is a Dream* was performed in the Italian manner, since Philip IV had rejected the *corrales* for court entertainments. Not wanting to be outdone by the Italian courts, he imported designer Cosmo Lotti from Florence in 1626 to introduce the architectural features and scenic technology of Serlio for court spectacles. By 1640, five years after Philip appointed Calderón as court playwright, Lotti had supervised the building of the Coliseo for the new palace in Madrid. This royal theatre was Spain's first proscenium stage to employ the wing and groove system for changing scenery. (See Preface to Racine, p. 320.)

Life Is a Dream enjoyed a happy fate from its inception at court to its reemergence on the great stages of the world. Fortunately Calderón's brother, Don Joseph, carefully placed it at the head of a collection of twelve plays by the playwright in 1636, making them more available than the work of his rivals and ensuring their popularity. A variety of translations appeared during the seventeenth century alone: several in Italian and Dutch, and one libretto for a German opera. Due to Spain's declining resources, the play might have succumbed to oblivion were it not for the efforts of two German critics—August Wilhelm von Schlegel (1767–1845) and his younger brother Friedrich (1772–1829)—who rediscovered it.

Germany offered the broadest philosophical basis for the strong romantic movement that was establishing itself in Europe, of which Calderón's works, along with Shakespeare's, became a dynamic part. Calderón revealed a deep understanding of human nature, and the passionate behaviors of his characters were essential features of European **romanticism.** August von Schlegel translated Calderón, while Friedrich was convinced that *Life Is a Dream* had solved the riddle of the universe. Another important feature of romanticism was the return to Catholicism. Since Calderón was declared the supreme Catholic poet (he had become a priest when his mistress died in childbirth in 1651), his literary triumph was assured. From the early part of the eighteenth century to 1870, the countless translations and adaptations of this play generated a rather impressive stage history.

In 1812, Goethe produced *Das Leben Ein Traum* at the Weimar Court Theatre. It was the greatest success of a season that included a rich and varied repertory of his own work as well as plays by Schiller, Lessing, Kotzebue, and adaptations of works by Gozzi, Goldoni, Voltaire, and Shakespeare. In fact, Calderón's play was performed three times as often as Shakespeare's *Romeo and Juliet*.

Noted for his innovative stagings of Shakespeare, William Poel directed Edward Fitzgerald's English translation, *Such Stuff as Dreams Are Made Of,* for the Elizabethan Stage Society in 1899 and, in an innovative move, cast the young actress Margaret Halstan, in the role of Segismundo. Hugo von Hofmannsthal's translation, called *The Tower* (1919), was influenced by the events of World War I. Max Kommerell's version, which drew closely from the Spanish, was produced in Berlin in 1943 during the Third Reich. It emphasized the latent political forces of the play.

Calderón's international reputation has rested on *Life Is a Dream*. But it is also the most frequently produced of his plays in America, with performances for both English- and Spanish-speaking audiences. Regardless of the language in which it is played, the production aims are usually twofold: to serve the literal story of the play by emphasizing Calderón's poetic language and to accommodate the vision of the director by exploring the play's symbolic and subtextual overtones.

During the 1964 theatre season, New York City provided its bilingual audiences with two ways of looking at the Calderón classic, in what was believed to be "the first [production] ever given professionally of this work in New York."[3] A Spanish-language production was presented by the Teatro Español de Nueva York at the Astor Place Playhouse two days before an English-language production took place at the same theatre, after which performances continued in rotation. Perhaps the most interesting aspect of this enterprise, whose major financial backing came from the Spanish government, was that each company went its own way: separate directors, casts, sets, costumes, and acting styles all reflected marked contrasts, so that the Spanish production followed a formal approach by actors who ''[knew] the tradition of Spain's classic drama''[4] in contrast with the freer English production that was moderately stylized. The unusual project was a critical success.

Almost a decade later, a darker subtext emerged under Jacques Burdick's direction at the Yale Repertory Theatre, suggesting that Segismundo, as the sleeping prince, ''could in fact be the black man, subjugated by whites, released suddenly and wilfully—with repression always at arm's reach.''[5] While Burdick's direction ''[transmitted] Calderón undistorted and with considerable distinction,'' it challenged audiences to consider the larger philosophical and political ramifications of the play.

Since then, productions have rarely remained impervious to the radical cultural issues and performance demands of the postmodern era. Presented by the Repertorio Español at the Gramercy Arts Theatre in New York City in 1981, stage figures dressed in black and adorned with silver, copper, and brass wire mesh and chains performed against a spider web of steel cables ''[stretched] out from several 'vanishing points' on the stage and into the auditorium.'' These were augmented by three gold spotlights at the back of the stage. On a net of these cables ''the violent and virile prince is discovered, half-naked, writhing in the agony of an unjust confinement.''[6] Director René Buch transformed the small raked stage of his intimate theatre into an eerie labyrinth of illusion and reality, thus heightening both the psychological and physical dimensions of Segismundo's incarceration. The unanimously favorable reactions of both the Spanish- and English-language press attracted audiences to what still remains one of the company's most ambitious endeavors. Not coincidentally, the production paid homage to the three hundredth anniversary of Calderón's death.

Controversial for its surrealistic stage environment and its radical alteration of Calderón's hollowed text was Maria Irene Fornes' modern adaptation, retitled, *Life Is Dream,* and presented in separate Spanish and English versions at the INTAR Hispanic American Theatre of New York in 1981. Also serving as director, Fornes purposely emphasized stark, often haunting visual images, such as the sudden disclosure of the prince in the tower, contorted in a knot of ropes like a caged animal. Her spare free verse cut through Calderón's flowery original, while her inclusion of music in the form of madrigals, chants, and arias substituted for this ornamental language.

Fornes introduced a new character: a winged angel, emblematic of the Renaissance, who floated through the action while singing music composed by George Quincy. The angel's descent from above in a parachute skirt, under which Rosaura found shelter, provided comic relief. It sustained a costume motif that was echoed in Clarín's long skirt and Rosaura's hoop skirt, which dropped over her from above, without her being aware of it, when she assumed the role of a woman at court.

Most of all, Fornes changed the outcome of the play. Convinced that Calderón's conclusion was written to please the Spanish court by invoking the spirit of peace, there seemed to be no reason in the world for Segismundo to marry Estrella. In Fornes' version, Astolfo and Estrella remain together, while Segismundo encourages Rosaura to continue her quest for truth. Praising Rosaura for her integrity, the prince escorts her out with a green flag shared between them.

In 1989, Anne Bogart directed Edwin Honig's translation for the American Repertory Theatre in Cambridge, Massachusetts. The production achieved striking tableaux of foreground and background actions accompanied by unusual lighting and sound effects; prerecorded passages of the text, especially of monologues, mixed with live performance; actors choreographed in slow motion as they addressed each other; and the creation of a chorus whose juxtaposed voices recalled the elements of a dream. ''A formal, ritualistic quality pervades the entire production,'' wrote Edwin Wilson, ''[and leads] the audience into Segismundo's nightmare.''[7]

REFLECTIONS ON LIFE IS A DREAM

Anne Bogart directed Life Is a Dream *at the American Repertory Theatre (ART) in Cambridge, Massachusetts, in 1989.*

Life Is a Dream is a play that fascinates but also frightens me. Its theatricality attracted me. Also its mystery, its poetry, and its philosophy. The problem of translation is a real one. I chose the Edwin Honig translation because it's the clearest, but for me the text is only one part of the whole experience. As a director, it's a mistake to think only of the text. The original intentions of the Spanish text should be translated into the way the movement works, the way light falls, the way timing occurs, and the juxtaposition of all these things.

Theoretically, it fascinates me that Calderón would spend a great deal of effort designing a text which would never speak directly about its real concern. For example, in the first passage, Calderón avoids using the word *horse.* He'll describe a horse in every way he can, using every sort of baroque metaphor. The play is packed with metaphor that forces you to another level of understanding. It begins with a woman dressed as a man in midair, falling off a horse. From then on, layers of metaphors keep revealing themselves, keep opening up to new meanings. The metaphors are in language, and it's my job to translate those into theatrical metaphors.

Like a mirror that splinters and breaks into many pieces, Calderón uses shattered reflections circling around a particular idea. There's always a tension between what is said and what is not said. Now that's very difficult to translate. What it makes me want to do is try to find a way to stage the play true to Calderón's interest in language and the relationship between language and "reality."

Georgio Strehler says that when he stages a play, he's writing an essay on the play and his essay is created in his language, languages of the stage. Rather than writing an essay on the play with words, he's writing it with actors, light, movement, sound. It's my intention to translate my understanding of Calderón into the languages of the stage.

One of the limitations of resident theatre is the shortness of rehearsal time. I find it absolutely necessary—especially with a play that has a production history to it—to have time to meet the play in a non-producing situation, not creating staging but exploring the themes and the movement of the play without being concerned with staging it. The workshop [at ART] allowed me and the Institute actors the luxury of swimming in the themes, the problems, the characters of the play. I got to ask questions like: What does it mean to act a dream? How is that different from acting in a Terrence McNally play? How are events put together in a dream differently than they are put together in waking life? We looked at things like Plato's allegory of the cave in *The Republic,* which is an important part of Calderón's thinking. What does it mean to see life as a reflection of the real thing? The workshop gave us time to meet the play without the pressure of turning that meeting into a result.

There are two things happening in the play. First, a story's being told. Second, a very complex philosophy is being evoked—not told, not explained, but evoked—and evoked in a very theatrical way. What I want to do is play the linear story off the universal philosophy of the play. I want to create an event where the theatre is an echoing chamber. You go through the story but you're always aware of past, future, present. The cave is the theatre, and all the particles of the story are constantly swirling around the story itself.

Every object, every character on stage has its opposite inside it, which is why I find it so modern. Both Rosaura and Segismundo are half woman and half man. I think Rosaura is one of the most wonderful female characters in literature because of her constant confrontation with the world as a woman and how she adapts to it by changing into a man and adapts to it again by being a woman. She's like a chameleon. For a female actress this is an extraordinary challenge. At first glance, Segismundo seems like a cliché Tarzan. But if you look closer you feel there's a strong feminine thread running through him. He's very vulnerable. That's the feminist viewpoint as opposed to the masculine viewpoint. I find Calderón really plays with the contradictions inherent in each gender stereotype, which is something I agree with philosophically, politically, and personally. I find truth in gender contradictions.

To me [Calderón's] theatre world is completely postmodern because of its shattered refraction of reality and its self-referentiality. The contemporary French philosopher, Baudrillard, states that whatever you're looking at is only as real as its image. This approaches Calderón's worldview of reality as a palace of mirrors. In Calderón, human beings are a little off-center in their environment.

I'd like for the audience to feel as though they are in Plato's cave and that they're in the process of turning around to look at the light. I keep thinking of this word *cave* because it means that sounds and images are bouncing off the walls and reverberating against each other. There needs to be a sense of intimacy and distance at the same time. I feel like the audience should feel at first as though they're going through an art gallery from a distant past and little by little it gets closer and closer until it feels as if it's inside you. At first it will feel foreign but it will become more and more understandable.

I'm interested in Calderón's fascination with the artificial as opposed to the natural. I wanted the costumes, sets, lights, and the physicality of the production to embrace the contradiction between an artificial order, represented by the court, and natural chaos. The designs are a meeting of those two worlds with influences from Spanish culture from many different periods, including Calderón's. It should look like little fragments of history that have reinvented themselves into a world in which the play could be physicalized. I wanted to create a feeling, an atmosphere of listening and of being in a world that we know but don't quite know, that is familiar yet we've never seen anything quite like it, that has remnants and artifacts from a number of places in history but also reeks of the play.

When I think of *Life Is a Dream* I keep going back to an episode of "Twilight Zone" with Rod Serling. The guy wakes up from a dream. Something's happening to him, but he realizes he's in a dream. He tries to wake up and he finally does and yet he's in another dream. Then he's living this other life and he's in another dream. It goes on and on to infinity.

Continued

The play speaks directly to every human being struggling with consciousness and waking up. I want to do it in a way which people will not only hear, but see and feel. The production will be a journey for the senses, for the ears. We crave this kind of spectacle today.

Reprinted from A.R.T. NEWS, *April 1989 with permission from the American Repertory Theatre.*

Notes

1. *Edwin Honig, trans.,* LIFE IS A DREAM *(New York: Hill & Wang, 1970), xii.*
2. *Ibid., xv.*
3. NEW YORK HERALD TRIBUNE, *29 Feb. 1964.*
4. *Howard Taubman,* THE NEW YORK TIMES, *18 March 1964.*
5. *Mel Gussow,* THE NEW YORK TIMES, *21 March 1972.*
6. *Glenn Loney,* OTHER STAGES, *4 June 1981.*
7. *Edwin Wilson,* WALL STREET JOURNAL, *June 1989.*

LIFE IS A DREAM
PEDRO CALDERÓN DE LA BARCA
TRANSLATED BY EDWIN HONIG

CHARACTERS

Basilio, *King of Poland*
Segismundo, *Prince*
Astolfo, *Duke of Muscovy*
Clotaldo, *old man*
Clarín, *clownish servant*

Estrella, *Princess*
Rosaura, *lady*
Soldiers
Guards

Musicians
Retinue
Servants
Ladies

The setting of the play is the Polish court, a fortress tower nearby, and an open battlefield.

ACT ONE
SCENE ONE

(On one side, mountain crags; on the other, a tower, with SEGISMUNDO'S *cell at the base. The door, facing the audience, is half open. The action begins at dusk.* ROSAURA *enters, dressed as a man, at the top of a crag and descends to level ground;* CLARÍN *enters behind her.)*

ROSAURA.
    Where have you thrown me, mad horse,
    half griffin? You rage like a storm,
    then flicker like lightning
    outspeeding light, off in a flash
    like a fish without scales,   5
    or a white featherless bird
    in headlong flight. Beast, there's not
    one natural instinct in you—
    tearing your mouth to hurl
    and drag yourself through   10
    this labyrinth of tangled rocks!
    So stick to these heights like
    that fallen sun-driver Phaëthon,
    and be a hero to all
    the wild animals, while I,   15
    desperate and blind, scramble down
    these rugged, twisting, barren crags

    where there is no way but what the laws
    of destiny set down for me,
    here where the wrinkled cliffs   20
    glower at the sun. Poland,
    you greet this stranger harshly,
    writing her entry in blood
    on your sands; she hardly arrives
    before hardship arrives.   25
    Look where I am—doesn't this prove it?
    But when was pity ever showered
    on anyone in misery?
CLARÍN.
    Say any two, including me.
    Misery needs company.   30
    Besides, if it was the two of us
    who left our country searching
    for adventure, surely
    the same two arrived here,
    hard luck, crazy falls down crags   35
    and all; so why shouldn't I complain,
    if in sharing all the pain,
    I don't get half the credit?
ROSAURA.
    I fail to mention you
    in my complaints, Clarín,   40
    because I do not like
    depriving you of the right
    and consolation to voice your own.
    As some philosopher has put it,
    there's so much satisfaction   45

in complaining that troubles
should be cultivated
so we may complain of them.

CLARÍN.
Philosopher? He was
a drunken old graybeard.   50
Someone should have whacked him good and hard
to give him something to complain of.
Well, madame, what are we to do now,
alone and stranded without a horse,
at this late hour on a barren slope,   55
just as the sun is setting?

ROSAURA.
Who'd imagine such strange things
could happen? But if my eyes
do not deceive me and this is not
a fantasy, a trick   60
of failing daylight, I seem to see
a building there.

CLARÍN.
                    My hopes deceive me,
or else I see what you see.

ROSAURA.
Standing there amid huge bare rocks,   65
there's a crude fortress tower, so small
it barely reaches daylight,
and so roughly made among
so many crags and boulders that when
the dying sunlight touches it,   70
it looks like just another rock
fallen down the mountainside.

CLARÍN.
Let's move closer, madame.
We've stared enough; it's better letting
them who live there exercise   75
their hospitality.

ROSAURA.
                    The front door
stands open to . . . what is it,
a mausoleum? And pitch darkness
comes crawling out as though   80
the night itself were born inside.
(The sound of chains is heard.)

CLARÍN.
Good Heavens, what's that I hear?

ROSAURA.
I'm a solid block of ice and fire!

CLARÍN.
It's just a bit of rattling chain.
Destroy me if it's not the ghost   85
of a galley slave. Would **I**
be so scared otherwise?

SEGISMUNDO (within).
Oh misery and wretchedness!

ROSAURA.
Whose unhappy voice was that? Now
I've more suffering to contend with.   90

CLARÍN.
And I, more nightmares.

ROSAURA.
                                Clarín . . .

CLARÍN.
Madame . . .

ROSAURA.
                    This is desolating.
Let's leave this enchanted tower.   95

CLARÍN.
When it comes to that, I haven't
got the strength to run away.

ROSAURA.
Isn't that tiny light
like someone's dying breath
or some faintly flickering star   100
whose pulsing, darting rays
make that dark room even darker
in its wavering glow?
Yes, and even from here
I can make out by its reflection   105
a murky prison cell, a tomb
for some still living carcass.
But even more astonishing,
there's a man lying there
in heavy chains, wearing   110
animal skins, whose only
company is that tiny light.
So, since we cannot run away,
let's listen and find out
what his misfortunes are about.   115

(*The door swings open and* SEGISMUNDO *appears in the tower light in chains, wearing animal skins.*)

SEGISMUNDO.
Heavens above, I cry to you,
in misery and wretchedness,
what crime against you did I commit
by being born, to deserve
this treatment from you?—although   120
I understand my being born
is crime enough, and warrants
your sternest judgment, since
the greatest sin of man
is his being born at all.   125
But to ease my mind I only want
to know what worse offense was mine,
aside from being born, to call
for this, my greater punishment.
Are not all others born as I was?   130
And, if so, what freedom do they have

which I have never known?
A bird is born, fine-feathered
in all its unimagined beauty,
but scarcely does it sprout   135
that small bouquet of plumage
when its wings cut through the halls of air,
scorning safety in the sheltered nest.
Why should I, whose soul is greater
than a bird's, enjoy less liberty?   140
A brute is born, its hide all covered
in brightly painted motley,
which, thanks to nature's brush, is lovely
as the sky in star-strewn panoply,
till learning man's cruel need   145
to lunge and pounce on prey
when it becomes a monster
in a labyrinth. Then why should I,
with instincts higher than a brute's,
enjoy less liberty?   150
A fish is born, and never breathes,
spawned in weed and slime;
then, while still a tiny skiff of scales
it sets itself against the waves,
and twists and darts in all directions,   155
trying out as much immensity
as the frigid sea-womb will permit.
Why should I, with greater freedom
of the will, enjoy less liberty?
A stream is born and freely snakes   160
its way among the flowers;
then, while still a silvery serpent
breaking through, it makes glad music ring,
grateful for its majestic passage,
flowing into the open fields.   165
Why should I, with greater life
in me, enjoy less liberty?
I rise to such a pitch of anger
that I feel like Etna, volcanic;
I want to rip my chest open   170
and tear out pieces of my own heart.
By what law, reason, or judgment
is a man deprived of that sweet gift,
that favor so essential,
which God has granted to a stream,   175
a fish, a brute, a bird?

ROSAURA.
      His words move me. I pity him
      and am afraid.

SEGISMUNDO.
            Who's been listening
      to me? Is that you Clotaldo?   180

CLARÍN (*aside*).
      Say yes.

ROSAURA.
            Only some lost
      unhappy soul among these cold rocks
      who heard you in your misery.

SEGISMUNDO.
      Then I'll kill you at once   185
      so you won't know that I know
      you already know my weaknesses.
      You overheard me—that's enough.
      For that alone, these two strong arms
      of mine must tear you apart.   190

CLARÍN.
      I'm deaf, I couldn't hear a word
      you said.

ROSAURA.
            I throw myself at your feet.
      If you were born human,
      my doing so would free me.   195

SEGISMUNDO.
      Your voice moves and softens me,
      your living presence stops me,
      and your level glance confuses me.
      Who are you? I know so little
      of the world here in this tower,   200
      my cradle and my tomb.
      I was born here (if you call it
      being born), knowing only
      this rugged desert, where I exist
      in misery, a living corpse,   205
      a moving skeleton.
      I've never seen or spoken to
      another human being, except
      the man who hears my lamentations
      and has told me all I know   210
      of earth and heaven; but even
      more amazing (and this will make you
      say I am a human monster,
      living in his fears and fantasies):
      though I'm a beast among men,   215
      a man among beasts, and sunk
      in misery, I've studied
      government, taught by the animals,
      and from the birds I've learned to follow
      the gentle declinations   220
      of the stars—it is you, and you
      alone, who douse the fire of my wrath,
      fill my sight with wonder
      and my hearing with admiration.
      Each time I look at you   225
      the vision overwhelms me
      so that I yearn to look again.
      My eyes must have the dropsy,
      to go on drinking more and more
      of what is fatal to their sight.   230

And yet, seeing that the vision
must be fatal, I'm dying to see more.
So let me look at you and die,
for since I have succumbed and find
that looking at you must be fatal,   235
I do not know what not looking
at you would mean; it would be worse
than fiercest death, madness,
rage, and overwhelming grief.
It would be life—for, as   240
I've had so bitterly to learn,
bringing life to one who's desperate
is the same as taking life away
from one who swims in happiness.

ROSAURA.
　　I look at you astonished,   245
amazed at what I hear, not knowing
what to say to you nor what to ask.
I can only say that Heaven
must have brought me here
to be consoled, if misery   250
finds consolation in seeing
someone still more miserable.
They tell the story of a wise man
who one day was so poor
and miserable he had nothing   255
to sustain him but a few herbs
he picked up. "Can any man,"
he asked himself, "be more wretched
than I am?" Turning his head,
he found the answer where another   260
sage was picking up the leaves
that he had thrown away.
I was living in this world,
complaining of my troubles,
and when I asked myself the question,   265
"Can there be another person
whose luck is worse than mine?"
pitifully you answered me.
Now, coming to my senses,
I find that you have gathered up   270
my troubles and turned them into bliss.
So if by chance any
of my troubles can relieve you,
listen carefully and take your pick
among the leftovers. I am—   275

CLOTALDO (*within*).
　　Cowards, or are you fast asleep!
Is this the way you guard the tower,
letting two people break
into the prison . . .

ROSAURA.
　　　　　　More confusion!   280

SEGISMUNDO.
　　It's Clotaldo, my jailer.
My troubles aren't over yet.

CLOTALDO (*within*).
　　Be quick now, go capture them before
they can defend themselves, or else
kill them.   285

VOICES (*within*).
　　　　　　Treason!

CLARÍN.
　　　　　　Oh prison guards
who let us in here, since there's a choice,
capturing us would be simpler now.
(CLOTALDO *enters with a pistol and the* SOLDIERS,
　　all wearing masks.)

CLOTALDO.
　　Keep your faces covered, everyone.   290
It is most important, while we're here,
to let no one recognize us.

CLARÍN.
　　Here's a little masquerade!

CLOTALDO.
　　You there—you, who out of ignorance,
have trespassed on this forbidden spot   295
against the order of the King,
who has decreed that no one
dare approach the prodigy
secluded here among these rocks—
put down your arms and lives, or else   300
this pistol like a metal snake
will tear the air apart with fire,
and spit out two penetrating
shots of venom.

SEGISMUNDO.
　　　　　　Master tyrant,   305
before you injure them, I'll give up
my life to these blasted chains,
where, by God, with my hands and teeth
I'd sooner tear myself apart
than let you harm them or regret   310
the outrage you may have done them!

CLOTALDO.
　　What's all this bluster, Segismundo?
You know your own misfortunes
are so immense that Heaven
declared you dead before   315
you were even born. You know
these chains are simply a restraint
to curb your mad, proud rages.
Yes, to rein you in and stop you cold.
—Now throw him back in, and shut   320
the door to his narrow cell.

(*He is shut in and speaks from inside.*)

SEGISMUNDO.
> Heavens, you were right to take
> my freedom from me. Otherwise
> I'd be a giant rising up
> against you, piling your jasper   325
> mountains up in stone foundations
> till I reached the top to smash
> the crystal windows of the sun!

CLOTALDO.
> Perhaps your being kept from
> doing it makes you suffer here.   330

ROSAURA.
> Since I see how much pride offends you
> I'd be foolish not to beg you
> humbly, at your feet, to spare my life.
> Let Pity move you, sir;
> it would be bad for me   335
> if you happened to dislike
> Humility as much as Pride.

CLARÍN.
> If neither one can move you (being
> the two stock characters we see
> traipsing on and off stage   340
> in the same old moralities),
> I, who can't say I stand
> for Pride or for Humility
> but for something in between,
> beg only, from where I'm standing,   345
> for your help and your protection.

CLOTALDO.
> You there, soldier!

SOLDIER.
>   Sir?

CLOTALDO.
>   Take away
> their weapons and blindfold them; they're not   350
> to see how or where they're going.

ROSAURA.
> Here is my sword—I can only
> yield it up to you, since you are
> in command here; it may not be
> surrendered to one of lesser rank.   355

CLARÍN (to a SOLDIER).
> Here's mine surrendering itself to
> the least of all of you—take it, man!

ROSAURA.
> And if I must die, I wish you
> to have this as a token
> for your sympathy, a gift worthy   360
> as its master, who once wore it
> at his side. I beg you, guard it well,
> for though I do not know
> precisely what its secret is,
> I know this golden sword   365

> has certain special powers.
> Indeed, trusting to nothing else,
> I came with it to Poland,
> hoping to avenge an insult.

CLOTALDO (aside).
> My God, what's this? Old wounds   370
> reopen, my confusion deepens.
> (Aloud.)
> Who gave this to you?

ROSAURA.
>   A woman.

CLOTALDO.
> Her name?

ROSAURA.
>   I swore not to reveal it.   375

CLOTALDO.
> How do you know, how can you assume
> there's some secret about this sword?

ROSAURA.
> Because she who gave it to me said,
> "Go to Poland, and use your wits,
> your guile, or some ruse to bring   380
> this sword to the attention
> of the noblemen and leaders there.
> For I know that one of them
> will favor you and help you."
> Yet since he may have died,   385
> she did not wish to give his name.

CLOTALDO (aside).
> Heaven help me! What's this I hear?
> I still have no idea
> whether all this has really happened
> or is simply an illusion.   390
> But surely it's the sword
> I left behind with Violante,
> promising that whoever came
> wearing it would find me tender
> and receptive as any father   395
> to his son. But now, my God, what
> can I do in such a quandary?
> He who brings it to me as a gift
> must lose his life for his doing so,
> and by surrendering to me   400
> sentences himself to death.
> What a pass to come to now!
> What a sad and fickle thing is fate!
> Here's my son—as every sign
> would indicate, including   405
> these stirrings in my heart
> which seeing him before me rouses.
> It's as if my heart responded
> like a bird beating its wings
> that can't break out to fly away,   410
> or like someone shut up in a house

who hears some outcry in the street
and can only look out
through a window. Now, hearing
that outcry in the street, and not   415
knowing what's happening, my heart
can only use these eyes of mine,
the windows it looks out of,
and through them dissolve in tears.
Heaven help me, what shall I do?   420
What is there to do? To take him
to the King (oh God!) is to lead him
to his death. But to hide him
is to break my oath of fealty
to the King. That I cannot do.   425
Between my selfish interests,
on the one hand, and my loyalty,
on the other, I'm torn apart.
But come, why do I hesitate?
Does not loyalty to the King   430
come before one's own life and honor?
Let loyalty prevail—let him die!
Just now he said, as I recall,
that he came here in order
to avenge himself, and a man   435
whose honor hasn't been avenged
is in disgrace. No, he's not
my son! He cannot be my son.
He must not have my noble blood.
But if there's really been   440
some accident, from which no man
is ever free—honor being
such a fragile thing, shattered by
the merest touch, tarnished by
the slightest breeze—then what choice   445
had he, what else could he do,
if he's really noble, but risk
everything to come here
to avenge his honor?
Yes, he is my son, he bears my blood.   450
It must be so, since he's so brave.
Now then, between one doubt
and another, the best recourse
would be to go and tell the King,
"Here's my son, and he must die."   455
But if, perhaps, the very scruple
which sustains my honor
moves the King to mercy
and merits having my son spared,
then I'll help him to avenge   460
the insult; but if the King
in strictest justice should execute
my son, than he will die
not knowing I'm his father.
(Aloud.)

Strangers, come with me, and do not fear   465
you are alone in your misfortunes,
for in such dilemmas,
where life or death hangs by
a thread, I cannot tell
whose lot is worse—yours or mine.   470
(They leave.)

SCENE TWO

(*In the capital; a hall in the royal palace.* ASTOLFO *and* SOL-
DIERS *enter on one side; and the* PRINCESS ESTRELLA *and*
LADIES IN WAITING, *on the other. Military music and inter-
mittent salvos are heard offstage.*)

ASTOLFO.
    Drums and trumpets, birds and fountains—
    each responds with its own fanfare
    to your bright rays that once were comets,
    and when joining in the same refrain
    of marveling together   5
    at your celestial beauty,
    some are feathery clarinets,
    others, metallic birds.
    Thus, all alike salute you, madame:
    to cannonade, you are the queen,   10
    to birds, their own Aurora,
    to trumpets, their Minerva,
    and to flowers, Flora.
    Because your coming pales the daylight
    which has banished night away,   15
    yours is the glory of Aurora,
    the peace of sweet Flora,
    Minerva's martial stance,
    who reign as queen of all my heart.
ESTRELLA.
    If what you say is measured   20
    by any human action,
    your gallant courtly phrases
    are belied by all this menacing
    display of arms, which I oppose,
    since your lisping flattery   25
    contradicts the sabre-rattling
    that I've seen. I'll have you know
    such behavior is contemptible
    (deceptive, false, corrupt,
    and, if you will, just beastly),   30
    which uses honeyed words
    to disguise the aim to kill.
ASTOLFO.
    You've been badly misinformed,
    Estrella, if you doubt me
    and think my words are insincere.   35
    I beg you now to hear me out,
    and judge if they make sense or not.

When Eustorgio the Third,
King of Poland, died, his heirs were
Basilio, who succeeded him,   40
and two daughters, of whom we are
the offspring. (I do not wish
to bore you with anything
irrelevant.) But there was Her Grace,
Clorilene, your mother—bless her,   45
gone to a higher kingdom
now veiled among the stars—
and she was the elder sister.
The second daughter was your aunt,
my mother, lovely Recisunda—   50
God rest her soul a thousand years—
and she was married in Muscovy,
where I was born. But to return now
to the other member
of the family. Basilio,   55
both childless and a widower,
suffering the usual decline
of age in time, is given more
to study than to women; so you
and I now both lay claim   60
to the throne. You insist
that being the daughter
of the elder sister gives you
the prior right; and I, that being male,
though born of the younger sister,   65
gives me precedence over you.
We advised the King our uncle
of our claims, and he has called us here
to judge between us—which is
the reason why we came today.   70
Having only this in view,
I left my estates in Muscovy
and came here not to fight with,
but to be subdued by, you.
Now may the all-knowing god of love   75
concur with the subjects of this land
in their prophetic wisdom.
And let such concord lead to your
becoming queen and, as my consort,
reigning over my heart's desire.   80
And, toward your greater honor,
as our uncle yields the crown,
may it reward you for your courage,
and its empire be my love for you!
ESTRELLA.
    The least my heart can hope for   85
in response to so much courtesy
is to wish the crown were mine,
if only that I might rejoice
in giving it to you—
even though my love might still suspect   90

there's reason to mistrust you
in that portrait locket which you wear
dangling over your chest.
ASTOLFO.
    I can explain it all to you
quite easily . . . but those loud drums   95
    (*Sound of drums.*)
cut me off now, announcing
the King and his council.
    (KING BASILIO *enters with retinue.*)
ESTRELLA.
    Wise Thales . . .
ASTOLFO.
                learnèd Euclid . . .
ESTRELLA.
    You who rule . . .   100
ASTOLFO.
            . . . you who are immersed . . .
ESTRELLA.
    Among the signs . . .
ASTOLFO.
           . . . among stars and zodiac . . .
ESTRELLA.
    Plotting their course . . .
ASTOLFO.
         . . . tracing their passage . . .   105
ESTRELLA.
    Charting them . . .
ASTOLFO.
          . . . weighing, judging them.
ESTRELLA.
    Permit me like ivy humbly . . .
ASTOLFO.
    Permit these arms, wide opened . . .
ESTRELLA.
    to cling around your waist.   110
ASTOLFO.
    lovingly to kiss your feet.
BASILIO.
    Come, niece and nephew, embrace me.
Since you so loyally respond
to my affectionate command
and come greeting me so warmly,   115
you may be sure you shall have nothing
to complain of—you will be treated
equally and fairly, both.
So, while I confess I'm tired
of the heavy weight of all my years,   120
I beg only for your silence now.
When everything is told,
my story will no doubt amaze you.
Listen to me, then, beloved niece
and nephew, noble court of Poland,   125
my kinsmen, vassals, friends.

You knew the world in honoring
my years of study has given me
the surname Learnèd. To counteract
oblivion, the paint brush   130
of Timanthes and the marbles
of Lysippus portray me throughout
the world as Basilio the Great.
As you know, the science
I pursue and love the most   135
is subtle mathematics,
through which I steal from time and take
from fame their slow-moving powers
to divulge more and more
of what's new to man each day.   140
For now, perceiving in my tables
all the novelties of centuries
to come, I triumph over time,
forcing it to bring about
the happenings I have foretold.   145
Those snow circles, those glass canopies
which the sun's rays illuminate
and the revolving moon cuts through,
those diamond orbits, crystal globes,
the stars adorn and the zodiac   150
wheels into the open—such have been
my main study all these years.
They are the books of diamond paper
bound in sapphire where Heaven writes
in separate characters   155
on golden lines whatever
is to be in each man's life,
whether adverse or benign.
These I read so swiftly
that only my spirit follows   160
their rapid traces through the sky.
God! before this skill of mine
became a commentary
in their margins, an index
to their pages, I could wish   165
my life itself had been the victim
of their rages, so my tragedy
were totally confined to them.
For those destined to melancholy,
their own merit is a knife-thrust,   170
since he whom knowledge ravages
is most apt to destroy himself!
Though I say this now, my experience
itself tells it more convincingly,
which to give you time to marvel at,   175
I ask again only for your silence.
By my late wife, I had
an ill-starred son, at whose birth
the heavens drained themselves of signs
and portents. Before emerging   180

in the lovely light of day
from the living sepulchre
of the womb (birth and death being
so much alike), time and again
between waking and delirium,   185
she saw a monster in human form
burst savagely out of her womb,
while she, blood-drenched, dying, gave birth
to the human viper of this age.
The prophecies were all fulfilled   190
(rarely if ever are
the cruelest omens proven false).
His horoscope at birth was such
that the sun, all bathed in blood,
clashed in furious combat   195
with the moon, the earth serving
as battleground; the two beacons
of the sky fought light to light,
if not hand to hand, for mastery.
It was the hugest, most horrible   200
eclipse the sun has suffered
since it wept blood at the death of Christ.
The sun sank in living flames, as though
undergoing its last paroxysm.
Skies turned black, buildings shook.   205
Clouds rained with stones, rivers
ran blood. So the sun in frenzy
or delirium saw the birth
of Segismundo, who giving
indication of his nature   210
caused his mother's death, as if
to say ferociously,
"I am a man, since I begin by
repaying good with evil."
Hastening to my studies,   215
I discovered everywhere I looked
that Segismundo would be
the most imprudent of men,
the cruelest prince, the most ungodly
monarch, through whom this kingdom   220
would be split and self-divided,
a school for treason, academy
of all vices, and he,
swept by fury and outrageous crimes,
would trample on me, and while I lay   225
prostrate before him (what an effort
for me to say this!), would see
this white beard on my face
become a carpet for his feet.
Who would disbelieve such danger,   230
especially the danger he witnessed
in his study, where self-love presides?
And so, believing that the fates
correctly prophesied

catastrophe by such dire omens,   235
I decided to imprison
the newborn monster and see
if human wisdom could dominate
the stars. The news went out
the child had died at birth.   240
Thus forewarned, I built a tower
in the crags and rocks of those mountains
where the light almost never enters,
protected by such a dense array
of cliffs and obelisks.   245
Edicts were imposed forbidding anyone
to trespass near the spot,
for reasons I've made clear to you.
There Segismundo lives now, poor
and wretched in captivity,   250
tended, seen, and spoken to,
only by Clotaldo,
his instructor in humane studies
and religious doctrine, who still is
the only witness of his sufferings.   255
Now here are three things to consider:
first, that my respect for you is such
that I would spare you from servitude
and the oppression of a despot.
No ruler that's benevolent   260
would let his subjects and his realm
fall into such jeopardy.
Second, it must be decided
if depriving my own flesh and blood
of rights sanctioned by the laws   265
of man and God would be in keeping
with Christian charity.
There's no law that says that I,
wishing to restrain another
from tyranny and cruelty,   270
should practice them myself;
or that, if my son's a tyrant,
to prevent his committing crimes,
I may commit those crimes myself.
Now here's the third and last point—   275
and that's to see how much in error
I may have been in giving
easy credence to foretold events.
For though temperament impels him
to acts of violence, perhaps   280
they will not wholly master him;
even if the most unbending fate,
the most vicious temperament, the most
destructive planet, sway the will
in one direction, they cannot force   285
the will to do their bidding.
And so, having turned the matter
over so much, and weighing one

alternative after another,
I have come to a conclusion   290
that may shock you. Tomorrow
I will bring him here, who,
without knowing he is my son
and your King, Segismundo
(the name he's always borne),   295
will be seated on my throne,
under this canopy. In a word,
he will take my place here,
to govern and rule over you,
while you bow and take your oaths   300
of fealty to him.
In this way I accomplish
three things, each answering
to the three questions I have put.
First, if he is prudent,   305
wise, benign, and thus wholly
disproves the prophecy about him,
you may all enjoy in him
your native prince as King, who till now
was a courtier in the desert   310
and the neighbor of wild animals.
The second thing is this:
if he's cruel, proud, outrageous, wild,
running the whole gamut
of his vices, I shall then   315
have faithfully discharged
my obligation, for in
disposing of him I shall do so
as a king in just authority,
and his going back to prison   320
will not constitute an act
of cruelty but fair punishment.
And finally, if the Prince
turns out as I say, then I'll give you
(out of the love I bear you all,   325
my subjects) monarchs more worthy
of the crown and scepter—namely these,
my niece and nephew, who,
conjoining their claims and pledging
holy matrimony together,   330
will be tendered what they have deserved.
This is my command to you as King,
this is my desire as father,
this is my advice as sage,
and this, my word to you as elder.   335
And if what Spanish Seneca once said
is true—that a king's a slave
to his own nation—then as slave
I humbly beg this of you.

ASTOLFO.

If it behooves me to reply,   340
who in effect have been

the most interested of parties here,
I would speak for one and all
in saying, Let Segismundo come.
His being your son is enough.   345

ALL.

Give us our Prince, we would
beg him now to be our King.

BASILIO.

My subjects, I thank you all
for your esteem and favor.
And you, my mainstays and supports,   350
retire to your rooms meanwhile
until we meet the Prince tomorrow.

ALL.

Long live King Basilio the Great!
(*All except* BASILIO *leave with* ESTRELLA *and*
        ASTOLFO. *Enter* CLOTALDO, ROSAURA, *and*
        CLARÍN.)

CLOTALDO.

Sire, may I speak with you?

BASILIO.

                    Ah,   355
Clotaldo, you are very welcome.

CLOTALDO.

Sire, I have always felt welcome here
before, but now I fear
some sad, contrary fate annuls
my former privilege   360
under law and the use of custom.

BASILIO.

What's wrong?

CLOTALDO.

                A misfortune,
Sire, overwhelmed me out of what
appeared to be the greatest joy.   365

BASILIO.

Tell me more.

CLOTALDO.

                This handsome youth
recklessly burst into the tower,
Sire, and there saw the Prince,
and he is—   370

BASILIO.

                Don't disturb yourself,
Clotaldo. If this had happened
any other day I confess
I would have been annoyed.
But now that I have let the secret   375
out, it does not matter who knows it.
See me later; there are many things
I must consult with you about,
and many things for you to do.
I warn you now, you must be   380
my instrument in accomplishing

the most amazing thing
the world has ever seen.
And not to have you think I blame you
for any negligence,   385
I pardon your prisoners.
(*He leaves.*)

CLOTALDO.

Great Sire, long life to you!
(*Aside.*)
Heaven's improved our luck;
I'll not tell him he's my son,
since that's no longer necessary.   390
(*Aloud.*)
Strangers, you're free to go.

ROSAURA.

I am in your debt eternally.

CLARÍN.

And I, infernally.
What's a few letters' difference,
more or less, between two friends?   395

ROSAURA.

To you I owe my life, sir;
and since the credit's due to you,
I am your slave forever.

CLOTALDO.

It is not your life you owe me,
for a man of honor can't be said   400
to be alive if his honor's lost.
And if as you have told me
you've come here to avenge an insult,
I have not spared your life,
for you brought none to spare;   405
a life disgraced is no life at all.
(*Aside.*)
Now that should spur him on.

ROSAURA.

Then I admit I have none,
though you have spared it for me.
Yet when I am avenged   410
and my honor's cleansed, with all threats
to it annulled, my life will seem
a gift worth giving you.

CLOTALDO.

Take back this burnished sword
you wore; I know it will suffice,   415
stained with your enemy's blood,
to avenge you, for this which was
my steel . . . I mean that for a while,
the little while, I've held it . . .
has the power to avenge you.   420

ROSAURA.

In your name I put it on again,
and on it swear to get my vengeance,
even though my enemy should be
more powerful.

CLOTALDO.

             Is he—by much?   425

ROSAURA.

    So much so, I may not tell you—
    not that I distrust your confidence
    in such important matters, but that
    your sympathy and favor, which
    move me so, won't be turned against me.   430

CLOTALDO.

    Telling me would only win me
    further; it also would remove
    the possibility of my
    giving aid to your enemy.
    (*Aside.*)
    Oh, if I only knew who he is!   435

ROSAURA.

    Then, not to have you think I value
    your confidence so little,
    know that my adversary is
    no less a personage than
    Astolfo, Duke of Muscovy!   440

CLOTALDO (*aside*).

    This could hardly be more painful.
    The case is worse than I suspected.
    Let us see what lies behind it.
    (*Aloud.*)
    If you were born a Muscovite,
    the man who's ruler of your country   445
    could not possibly dishonor you.
    Go back to your country and give up
    this burning purpose that inflames you.

ROSAURA.

    Though he was my Prince, I know
    he could and did dishonor me.   450

CLOTALDO.

    But he couldn't; even if
    he'd slapped your face, that wouldn't be
    an insult.
    (*Aside.*)
            God, what next?

ROSAURA.

                It was   455
    much worse than that.

CLOTALDO.

             Tell me,
    since you cannot tell me more
    than I already have imagined.

ROSAURA.

    Yes, I'll tell you—though I cannot say   460
    why I regard you with such respect,
    or why I venerate you so,
    or why I hang upon your words
    so that I hardly dare to tell you
    these outer garments are deceptive,   465

and do not belong to me.
Consider this enigma
carefully; if I'm not the person
I appear to be, and he came here
with the view of marrying   470
Estrella, he could dishonor me.
There, I have said enough.
(ROSAURA *and* CLARÍN *leave.*)

CLOTALDO.

    Listen! Wait! Stop! What sort of maze
    is this now, where reason finds no clue?
    It is my honor that's at stake.   475
    The enemy is powerful.
    I'm only a subject, and she—
    she's but a woman. Heavens above,
    show me the way to go.
    There may be none, I know,   480
    since all I see through this abyss
    is one portentous sky
    covering the whole wide world.

ACT TWO

SCENE ONE

(*A room in the palace.*)

CLOTALDO.

    It's all done, just as you directed.

BASILIO.

    Clotaldo, tell me what happened.

CLOTALDO.

    What happened, Sire, was this.
    I brought him the pacifying drink,
    which you ordered to be made,   5
    a mixture of ingredients
    compounding the virtue
    of certain herbs whose great strength
    and secret power so wholly sap
    a man, they steal away   10
    and alienate his reason.
    Emptied of aggression, drained of all
    his faculties and powers,
    he becomes a living corpse.
    We need not question, Sire,   15
    if such a thing is possible.
    Experience shows it often,
    and we know that medicine
    is full of nature's secrets.
    There's no animal, plant, or stone   20
    without its own determined structure,
    and since human malice can
    uncover a thousand fatal drugs,
    is it any wonder that,
    when their virulence is tempered,   25

such drugs, instead of killing,
are merely sleep-inducing?
We can drop the question, then,
since reason and evidence both
prove the matter creditable.   30
And so, taking this drug with me
(actually made up of henbane,
opium, and poppies), I went down
to Segismundo's narrow cell
and talked with him a while about   35
those humane studies taught him
by silent nature under skies
and mountains, that holy school where
he'd learned rhetoric from birds and beasts.
To elevate his spirit further   40
toward the enterprise you had in mind,
I proposed the subject
of the mighty eagle and its speed,
how, in scorning the lower regions
of the wind, it rises   45
to the highest realms of fire
where it becomes plumed lightning
or a shooting star; and thus,
glorifying the eagle's flight,
I said, "Of course, as the king of birds,   50
he should take precedence over them.
That's his right." This was enough
for Segismundo, for on the subject
of royalty his discourse is full
of eager, proud ambition.   55
Thus moved by something in his blood
inciting him to do great things,
he replied, "So even in
the commonwealth of birds someone
requires they swear obedience.   60
The example comforts me
in my misery, since if I'm
anybody's subject here, that's
because I'm forced to be. On my own
I'd never bow to any man."   65
Seeing how the matter, so close
to his own griefs, roused his anger,
I administered the potion.
It scarcely left the glass
and touched his throat when all   70
his vital spirits fell asleep.
A cold sweat made its way through every
vein and member of his body,
so that if I hadn't known
it wasn't death but its counterfeit,   75
I would have doubted he was alive.
Then the people came whom
you'd entrusted to carry out
the experiment; they put him

in a coach and brought him here   80
to your chamber where all
the majesty and grandeur owing
to his person were awaiting him.
He lies there now in your bed where,
when his torpor ends, he'll be treated,   85
Sire, as you directed,
just as if he were yourself.
If I have fulfilled your wishes
well enough to warrant some reward,
I beg you only to tell me (pardon   90
this presumption) what your purpose is
in having Segismundo brought here
to the palace in this way?

BASILIO.
     Clotaldo, your scruple
is justified, and I wish only   95
to satisfy you on it.
You know that the moving star
guiding the destiny of my son
Segismundo threatens
endless tragedy and grief.   100
I would like to know if the stars,
which can't be wrong and have given us
so many further signs
of his bad character,
may still mitigate or even   105
slightly soften their influence,
and be allayed by his valor
and discretion, since man himself
can master his own fate.
This I would like to test   110
by bringing him here, where
he will know he is my son
and where he can show what
his real character is like.
If he's magnanimous he'll rule;   115
if he's tyrannical and cruel,
back to his chains he goes.
But now you'll ask why, in order
to conduct the experiment, have I
brought him sleeping here this way.   120
Since I wish to give you
every satisfaction, I'll answer
every question. If he discovers
that he's my son today,
then wakes up tomorrow   125
to see himself again reduced
to misery in his own cell,
he'll come to know his true condition,
only to despair, for knowing who
he is would be no consolation.   130
So I wish to mitigate
the possibility

by making him believe
that what he saw was something
that he dreamt. In that way   135
two things will be tested:
first, his true character,
for when he wakes he'll act out all
he's dreamt and thought; and secondly,
his consolation, for if he has   140
to see himself obeyed today
and subsequently back in prison,
he'll believe that he was dreaming,
and he'll be right in thinking so,
since everyone alive on earth,   145
Clotaldo, is only dreaming.

CLOTALDO.
There's proof enough, I think,
to make me doubt you will succeed.
But it's too late—there's no other way.
Besides, there are signs he's wakened   150
and is on his way here now.

BASILIO.
Then I'll withdraw, as you, his tutor, stay
and guide him through this new perplexity
by telling him the truth.

CLOTALDO.
You mean you give me leave   155
to tell it to him?

BASILIO.
                Yes, for if
he knows the truth perhaps
he'll grasp the danger facing him
and more easily overcome it.   160

(He leaves; CLARÍN enters.)

CLARÍN.
Four whacks I had to take
to get inside here; they were laid on
by a redheaded halberdier
showing off his livery and beard,
but I had to see what's going on.   165
Now, there's no box seat to be had
that gives a better view of things,
without bothering about tickets,
than the eyes and head a man carries
with him: bright though broke, he can take in   170
any peepshow, cool as you please.

CLOTALDO (aside).
There's Clarín, that girl's servant—
My God! that girl, such a dealer
in misfortunes, bringing my disgrace
all the way from Poland!   175
(Aloud.)
Tell me, Clarín, what's new?

CLARÍN.
What's new, sir, is that Rosaura,
who believes you sympathetic
to her cause of vengeance, has taken
your advice and put on again   180
her proper woman's clothing.

CLOTALDO.
That's good—it's right she dresses
properly.

CLARÍN.
                Also, she's changed her name
and wisely made it known she is your niece,   185
whereby her reputation's risen
till now she's maid of honor here to
the incomparable Estrella.

CLOTALDO.
That's fine—at last I now can stand
responsible for her honor.   190

CLARÍN.
Other news: with some such thing in mind,
she now awaits the time and place
when you can act in her behalf.

CLOTALDO.
Yes, that's the safest course.
Only time itself will see such matters   195
fully settled.

CLARÍN.
                Further news:
she's favored so, being your niece,
she's treated like a queen, while I,
who came with her through thick and thin,   200
I am dying of hunger.
Nobody thinks of me at all.
They forget my name's Clarín—
meaning trumpet—and if I once
sound off, there's a tune will carry all   205
the news there is to Astolfo,
Estrella, and the King,
because Clarín the trumpet
and Clarín the man-servant
are two things which don't keep secrets well.   210
So it may be, if silence
should ever lose its hold, out of me
will pop some refrain like this:

There's nothing sweeter to the ears or eyes
than waking to a trumpet at sunrise.   215

CLOTALDO.
There's something in what you say.
I'll see to it you're better treated.
Meanwhile, you are in my service.

CLARÍN.
Yes, but here comes Segismundo.

(MUSICIANS *enter singing and with* SERVANTS *attending*
SEGISMUNDO, *who appears to be in a state of shock.*)

SEGISMUNDO.

    Heavenly God, what is this?   220
    What's this I see, God help me!
    My wonder makes me fear it less
    than my belief, which doubts it more.
    I, in this sumptuous palace?
    I, in silks and in brocades?   225
    I, surrounded by swarms of servants,
    all so elegant and attentive?
    I, awake from sleep and in a bed
    of such magnificence?
    I, among so many people,   230
    and all eager to dress me?
    To say I'm dreaming would be untrue.
    I know quite well that I'm awake.
    I'm Segismundo, am I not?
    Heavens, tell me if I'm mistaken,   235
    and tell me what happened to my brain
    and my imagination
    while I slept that I should
    find myself in such a place?
    But be that as it may,   240
    why worry over such questions?
    Let them all serve me, come what will.

SERVANT 1 (*aside to* SERVANT 2).

    What a melancholy chap this is!

SERVANT 2.

    Who wouldn't be, considering
    what's happened to him.   245

CLARÍN.

                        I wouldn't.

SERVANT 2.

    You speak to him, go ahead.

SERVANT 1 (*to* SEGISMUNDO).

    Shall they sing again?

SEGISMUNDO.

                 No,
    I don't want them to sing again.   250

SERVANT 1.

    You were so abstracted,
    I had hoped it would divert you.

SEGISMUNDO.

    I don't feel diverted from
    my troubles with your singing voices.
    When the military band   255
    was playing, yes—I liked hearing that.

CLOTALDO.

    Your Majesty and Noble Highness:
    let me kiss your hand and be
    the first to render homage
    and my obedience to you.   260

SEGISMUNDO (*aside*).

    It's Clotaldo—but how can it be
    that he who treated me

    so miserably in prison
    now addresses me respectfully?
    What is happening to me?   265

CLOTALDO.

    In the huge bewilderment
    brought on by your new situation
    you'll find your reason and your
    every utterance beset by doubt.
    I wish, if possible, to free you   270
    from all doubt, because, Sire, you should know
    you are the Crown Prince of Poland.
    If you were kept from others
    and in seclusion till now,
    that was due to fate's bad auguries,   275
    foretelling numberless disasters
    for this kingdom once the proud laurel
    crowned your august brows. But now,
    trusting that your prudence
    may yet overcome the stars,   280
    which a strong man's magnanimity
    can indeed accomplish,
    you were brought here to this palace
    from the tower where you lived,
    your spirit swathed in sleep.   285
    My Lord and King, your father,
    will come to see you, Segismundo,
    and from him you'll learn the rest.

SEGISMUNDO.

    The rest? You infamous, vile traitor!
    Now that I know who I am, what more   290
    do I need to learn in order
    to express my pride and power from
    now on? How do you explain
    your treason to this country,
    you who hid from me, and so denied,   295
    the rank due me by reason and law?

CLOTALDO.

    Alas, unhappy me!

SEGISMUNDO.

    You played treason with the law,
    a wheedling game with the King,
    and a cruel one with me.   300
    And so the law, the King, and I,
    after such monstrous misdeeds,
    condemn you now to die between
    these two bare hands of mine.

SERVANT 2.

    But, my Lord—   305

SEGISMUNDO.

                 Don't interfere now—
    anybody. It's useless. By God,
    if any of you get in front
    of me, I'll throw you out the window!

SERVANT 2.

    Run, Clotaldo.   310

CLOTALDO.
          Alas, for you
cannot know that all this
arrogance you turn on me
is only something that you're dreaming.
    (*He leaves.*)

SERVANT 2.
    But you ought to know—   315

SEGISMUNDO.
               Get out of here!

SERVANT 2.
    —that he was obeying the King.

SEGISMUNDO.
    If his law's unjust, the King
is not to be obeyed.
Besides, I was the Prince.   320

SERVANT 2.
    It's not for him to undertake
to say if any law is good or bad.

SEGISMUNDO.
    I suspect something bad's
about to happen to you,
since you go on arguing with me.   325

CLARÍN.
    The Prince is altogether right,
and you are in the wrong.

SERVANT 2.
    And who asked you to talk?

CLARÍN.
    I just decided to.

SEGISMUNDO.
             And you,   330
who are you, tell me?

CLARÍN.
               A meddling
snoop—I do that job best. In fact,
I'm the biggest busybody
the world has ever known.   335

SEGISMUNDO.
    You're the only one who pleases me
in this brave new world of moribunds.

CLARÍN.
    Sire, I am the greatest pleaser
of whole worlds of Segismundos.
    (ASTOLFO *enters.*)

ASTOLFO.
    Oh Prince and sun of Poland,   340
how fortunate is this day
when you appear and fill it,
from one horizon to the other,
with joyful and blessèd splendor!
For like the sun you rose to come   345
from deep among the mountains.
Come then, and wear the glittering crown

of laurel on your brow, and since
you put it on so late,
may it never wither there.   350

SEGISMUNDO.
    God save you.

ASTOLFO.
           Of course you do not
know me. Only that excuses you
from honoring me properly.
I am Astolfo, born Duke   355
of Muscovy and your cousin.
We are of equal rank.

SEGISMUNDO.
    If my "God save you" doesn't please you
and you complain and make so much
of who you are, next time you see me   360
I'll say "May God *not* save you!"

SERVANT 2 (*aside to* ASTOLFO).
    Your Highness should consider
he is mountain-born and -bred,
and treats everyone this way.
    (*Aside to* SEGISMUNDO.)   365
Sire, Astolfo merits—

SEGISMUNDO.
    I couldn't stand the way he came in
and talked so pompously. Now the first
thing he does is put his hat back on.

SERVANT 1.
    He's a grandee.

SEGISMUNDO.
           And I am grander.   370

SERVANT 2.
    However that may be, it would be
better if more respect were shown
between you than among the rest.

SEGISMUNDO.
    And who asked for your opinion?
    (ESTRELLA *enters.*)

ESTRELLA.
    Your Highness, Noble Sire,   375
you are most welcome to this throne,
which so gratefully receives you
and wishes to secure you,
notwithstanding all false omens,
and henceforth would have you   380
live augustly eminent,
not only for years and years
but for centuries.

SEGISMUNDO (*to* CLARÍN).
           Now you tell me,
who is this proud beauty, this human   385
goddess at whose lovely feet
Heaven strews its radiance?
Who is this splendid woman?

CLARÍN.

    Sire, your star cousin, Estrella.

SEGISMUNDO.

    But more like the sun than a star.   390

    My heart wells up to your well-wishing

    my well-being, though seeing you

    is the only welcome thing

    I can admit today.

    So having found in you a sight   395

    more welcome than I merit,

    your speech of welcome overcomes me.

    Estrella, you can rise

    and in your dawning fill

    the brightest star with happiness.   400

    What's there for the sun to do

    if when you rise the day does too?

    Come, let me kiss that hand of yours

    from whose snowy cup the early breeze

    imbibes its purities.   405

ESTRELLA.

    Your courtliness is more than gallant.

ASTOLFO (aside).

    If he touches her hand,

    I am lost.

SERVANT 2 (aside).

            I know this puts

    Astolfo off. I'll try to stop it.   410

    (Aloud.)

    Consider, Sire, it is not right

    to take such liberties,

    especially with Astolfo here . . .

SEGISMUNDO.

    Haven't I already told you

    I don't care for your opinions?   415

SERVANT 2.

    What I say is no more than right.

SEGISMUNDO.

    That sort of thing infuriates me.

    Nothing's right if it goes against

    the things I want.

SERVANT 2.

            But I heard you say,   420

    Sire, that one must honor and obey

    only what is right and just.

SEGISMUNDO.

    You also heard me say

    I'd throw anyone off

    this balcony who gets me mad.   425

SERVANT 2.

    Such a thing as that just can't be done

    to someone like myself.

SEGISMUNDO.

            No?

    Well, by God, then I'll just try it.

(SEGISMUNDO *lifts him up bodily and goes out; the others follow, then return immediately.*)

ASTOLFO.

    What is this I have just seen?   430

ESTRELLA.

    Quickly, everyone. Go stop him!

    (*She leaves.*)

SEGISMUNDO (*returning*).

    He fell from the balcony

    right into the sea. So, by God,

    it could be done after all!

ASTOLFO.

    Now you should try restraining   435

    your violent temper.

    There's as much difference between

    men and beasts as between living

    in the wilds and in a palace.

SEGISMUNDO.

    Now if you get so righteous   440

    every time you say a word,

    maybe you'll find yourself

    without a head to hang your hat on.

    (ASTOLFO *leaves;* BASILIO *enters.*)

BASILIO.

    What has been going on here?

SEGISMUNDO.

    Nothing's going on. There was   445

    a man who got me mad,

    so I threw him off that balcony.

CLARÍN.

    Be careful, that's the King.

BASILIO.

    So your arrival here

    has cost a man his life,   450

    and on the first day too.

SEGISMUNDO.

    The man said it just couldn't be done,

    so I did it and won the bet.

BASILIO.

    Prince, I am greatly grieved,

    I came to see you, supposing   455

    that, being warned against

    the ascendancy of certain stars,

    you were overcoming adverse fate;

    but I find you in a rage instead,

    and that your first act here   460

    has been a heinous murder.

    How can I welcome you

    with open arms, knowing that yours,

    so cruelly skilled, have dealt out death?

    Who could view the naked knife   465

    still dripping from its fatal thrust

    and not be fearful? Who could approach

    the bloody scene where another man

was killed and not find himself repelled?
From such a deed the bravest man   470
instinctively recoils.
So I withdraw from your embrace,
for there I see your arms
as that death-dealing instrument
still raised above the fatal scene.   475
I who had hoped to meet and clasp you
warmly in fond welcome
can only drop my arms,
afraid of what your own have done.

SEGISMUNDO.
I can do without your fond embrace,   480
as I've done without it till now,
because a father who can treat me
with such uncanny cruelty,
being disposed to cast me off
so scornfully he has me   485
brought up like an animal,
chained up like a freak, and wanting
to see me dead—what does it matter
to me if he embraces me or not,
when he's deprived me of the right   490
to be a human being?

BASILIO.
God in Heaven, if only
I'd never given you a life,
I'd never have to hear your voice
or look at your outrageous face.   495

SEGISMUNDO.
If you'd never given me a life
I'd have no complaint against you,
but since you did and then
deprived me of it, I must complain.
If giving something freely   500
is a rare and noble thing,
to take it back again
is as base as one can be.

BASILIO.
Is this the way you thank me
for making you a prince who were   505
a poor and lowly prisoner?

SEGISMUNDO.
But what's there to thank you for?
What are you really giving me,
tyrant over my free will,
now that you've grown so old and feeble   510
that you're dying? Are you giving me
anything that isn't mine?
You're my father and my King.
And so all this majesty
is what justice and the law   515
of nature already grant me.
While this is my true station,

I am not obliged to you at all,
but could call you to account instead
for all the years you've robbed me   520
of liberty and life and honor.
Indeed, you have me to thank
for making no demands on you,
since it is you who are in my debt.

BASILIO.
Insolent barbarian,   525
you've confirmed the prophecy
of Heaven, to which I now appeal
to look at you, brash and puffed up
with pride. Though now you know
the truth about yourself   530
and are completely undeceived,
and though you see yourself preferred
above all others, I am warning you,
be moderate and humble,
for you may find you're only dreaming   535
though you think yourself awake.
(*He leaves.*)

SEGISMUNDO.
Can it be I'm only dreaming
though I think myself awake?
I am not dreaming, for I know
and feel what I have been   540
and what I am; now you may be
repentant, but that will do no good.
I know who I am, and however
you bemoan it and regret it,
you cannot rob me of the fact   545
that I am the born heir to this throne.
And if you once had me bound in chains,
that was because I had
no notion who I was,
but now I know exactly who I am,   550
and that's knowing I am
partly beast and partly man.
(ROSAURA *enters, dressed as a woman.*)

ROSAURA (*aside*).
Here I come to find Estrella,
but dreading to think that
Astolfo may find me. Clotaldo   555
wishes him not to know who I am
nor to catch sight of me since,
Clotaldo says, it vitally
affects my honor. And I trust
his interest now, grateful   560
for his support of me,
my life and honor both.

CLARÍN (*to* SEGISMUNDO).
What is it here you've liked most among
the things you've seen and wondered at?

SEGISMUNDO.

 Nothing has amazed me here   565
 that I had not foreseen.
 But if there were anything
 in this world that may have struck me,
 it's a woman's beauty.
 Among the books I used to have   570
 I once read that God put
 most of His attention
 into creating man,
 a little world unto himself.
 Instead, I think, it should have been   575
 in His creating woman,
 a little heaven unto herself,
 encompassing in her a beauty
 as superior to a man's
 as Heaven is to earth—   580
 and more, if she's the one
 I'm gazing at this moment.

ROSAURA (*aside*).

 Oh, it's the Prince—I must go back.

SEGISMUNDO.

 Stop, woman—listen to me!
 Coming and going so fast, you push   585
 sunrise and sunset together.
 With the dawn and the dusk colliding
 that way, you cut short my day.
 Can I believe my eyes?

ROSAURA.

 No more than I do mine, believing   590
 and disbelieving them at once.

SEGISMUNDO (*aside*).

 Her beauty—I've seen it somewhere
 before.

ROSAURA (*aside*).

   His magnificence
 and splendor I've seen before—   595
 chained up in a narrow cell.

SEGISMUNDO (*aside*).

 At last I've found my life!
 (*Aloud.*)
 Woman—the most endearing word
 a man can utter—who are you?
 Though I do not know you,   600
 I adore you, claiming you
 on faith alone, and luckily
 I have the feeling that
 I've seen you once before.
 Who are you, lovely woman?   605

ROSAURA (*aside*).

 I must pretend.
 (*Aloud.*)
   Simply
 an unhappy lady
 in Estrella's retinue.

SEGISMUNDO.

 Say no such thing. Say you are the sun   610
 from whose fire that other star,
 Estrella, borrows its flamboyance,
 bathing in the splendor of your light.
 In the realms of fragrance,
 amid whole squadrons of flowers,   615
 I have seen the rose preside
 in its divinity,
 reigning over all the others
 by virtue of its loveliness.
 In that fine academy of mines   620
 among the precious stones,
 I have seen the admired diamond
 ruling over all the rest
 by virtue of its brilliance.
 In the restless commonwealth of stars   625
 I have seen the morning star
 given precedence and chosen
 monarch over all the others.
 Amid Heaven's perfected spheres
 I have seen the sun summoning   630
 to court all its planets and,
 as the clearest oracle of day,
 in command above the rest.
 Now if among the flowers,
 precious stones, the planets, stars,   635
 the whole zodiac itself,
 only the loveliest prevail,
 how is it that you serve
 one of lesser beauty, you
 who all in one are lovelier   640
 than sun and stars, diamond and rose?
 (CLOTALDO *appears at the curtain.*)

CLOTALDO (*aside*).

 I must do something to restrain him;
 I'm responsible, after all,
 I brought him up . . . But what's this now?

ROSAURA.

 I esteem your favor,   645
 but let silence fill the rhetoric
 of my reply. When one finds
 one's reason sluggish, Sire,
 speaking best is speaking least.

SEGISMUNDO.

 Stay here, you do not have to leave!   650
 How can you persist this way
 in evading what it is I mean?

ROSAURA.

 I must ask that permission, Sire.

SEGISMUNDO.

 Your leaving me abruptly
 is not asking it but taking   655
 such permission for granted.

ROSAURA.
> If you don't give it, I must take it.

SEGISMUNDO.
> You'll turn my courtesy
> to impropriety; resistance
> is a poison I can't swallow.   660

ROSAURA.
> But if that poison, full of rage
> and hate and fury, should overcome
> your patience, you still could not,
> you would not dare, dishonor me.

SEGISMUNDO.
> I'll try it, just to see if I can—   665
> once you make me lose the awe
> I feel for your beauty, for when
> a thing's impossible I find
> the challenge to overcome it
> irresistible; only today   670
> I threw a man off that balcony
> who said I couldn't do it.
> So, just to find out if I can—what
> could be simpler?—I'll let your virtue
> go flying out the window.   675

CLOTALDO (aside).
> From bad to worse—he makes
> an issue of it. Lord,
> what am I to do now that mad lust
> threatens my honor a second time?

ROSAURA.
> Then the prophecy was true   680
> foretelling how your tyranny
> would bring to this poor kingdom
> riots of monstrous crimes and deaths,
> treason and furious contention.
> But what's a man like you to do   685
> who is human in name only,
> insolent, insensitive,
> cruel, impulsive, savage,
> and tyrannical, someone
> born and bred among beasts?   690

SEGISMUNDO.
> To keep you from insulting me
> I spoke to you gently,
> hoping that way I might win you.
> But if despite my courtesy
> you still accuse me of such things,   695
> then, by God, I'll give you reason to.
> All of you now, leave us!
> And lock that door behind you.
> Let no one enter.
> (CLARÍN and SERVANTS leave.)

ROSAURA (aside).
> Now I'm lost.   700
> (Aloud.)
> Take care—

SEGISMUNDO.
> I'm a raging brute—
> no use trying to chain me down.

CLOTALDO (aside).
> What a situation to be in!
> I must go out and stop him,   705
> though it may mean my life.
> (Aloud.)
> Sire, look, be lenient—
> (He approaches.)

SEGISMUNDO.
> You've provoked me once again,
> you crazy, weak old man.
> Do my cruelty and fury   710
> mean so little to you?
> How did you get in here?

CLOTALDO.
> This woman's cries brought me here
> to urge you to be more moderate
> if you wish to rule, and not be cruel   715
> because you see yourself
> the master of everything about you,
> for all this may only be a dream.

SEGISMUNDO.
> Spouting that way about illusions
> makes me fighting mad! Now let's see if   720
> killing you is real or just a dream.
> (As SEGISMUNDO tries to draw his dagger,
> CLOTALDO stops him, falling to his knees.)

CLOTALDO.
> Going down upon my knees,
> I hope to save my life.

SEGISMUNDO.
> Take your crazy hand off my dagger!

CLOTALDO.
> I won't let go till someone comes   725
> to check your outrageous fury.

ROSAURA.
> Oh God in Heaven!

SEGISMUNDO.
> Hands off me,
> I tell you—enemy, doddering
> old idiot, or you'll see   730
> (They fight.)
> these arms of mine crushing you to death!

ROSAURA.
> Help, oh, come and help him!
> Clotaldo is being murdered!
> (She leaves. Just as CLOTALDO falls to the ground,
> ASTOLFO appears and stands between them.)

ASTOLFO.
> Well, what's this, magnanimous Prince?
> Is this the way to stain your keen blade,   735
> in an old man's frozen blood?
> Come, sheathe that shining knife of yours.

SEGISMUNDO.
    Not till it runs with your putrid blood.
ASTOLFO.
    Having put his life in
    my protection should do him   740
    some further good.
SEGISMUNDO.
                  Your own death
    will be that further good.
    Now I can avenge myself
    for your piquing me before,   745
    by killing you as well.
ASTOLFO.
    The law justifies my fighting
    royalty in self-defense.
    (ASTOLFO *draws his sword and they duel.*)
CLOTALDO.
    Do not injure him, my lord.
    (BASILIO *appears with* ESTRELLA *and retinue.*)
BASILIO.
    What, drawn swords in my presence?   750
ESTRELLA (*aside*).
    There's Astolfo! I'm full
    of terrible misgivings.
BASILIO.
    Well, what's the reason for this?
ASTOLFO.
    Nothing, Sire, now that you are here.
    (*They sheathe their swords.*)
SEGISMUNDO.
    A great deal—even though you're here, Sire.   755
    I was about to kill that old man.
BASILIO.
    And you had no respect
    for those white hairs?
CLOTALDO.
               You see,
    they are merely mine, Sire; nothing   760
    of importance, you understand.
SEGISMUNDO.
    Such futile nonsense—expecting me
    to honor someone's white hairs!
    (*To the* KING.)
    Perhaps some day you'll see your own
    become a carpet for my feet.   765
    (*He leaves.*)
BASILIO.
    And before you see that day arrive,
    back to your old sleep you'll go,
    where all that's happened to you here
    will come to seem, like all the glories
    of this world, something that you dreamed.   770
    (*The* KING *leaves with* CLOTALDO *and*
        ATTENDANTS.*)

ASTOLFO.
    How rarely fate deceives us
    in foretelling our misfortunes,
    as certain to be right
    in predicting what is evil
    as to be wrong in predicting good.   775
    He'd be a fine astrologer
    whose forecasts were always negative,
    since no doubt they'd always turn out true.
    In such a light, Estrella,
    consider our experiences—   780
    Segismundo's and my own,
    each so different in effect.
    For him the auguries foretold
    violence, catastrophes,
    murder, and despair, and so   785
    his forecast was correct, since all this
    is really happening.
    But consider my case: when, madame,
    I beheld your gaze flashing
    such brilliant rays, it turned the sun   790
    into a shade and the sky
    into a passing cloud;
    so fate seemed to promise great success,
    quick approval, rewards,
    and gains in property.   795
    Fate in this was right, but also wrong:
    right, when promising such favors,
    and wrong, when in effect it deals out
    nothing but disdain and scorn.
ESTRELLA.
    I do not doubt your gallantries   800
    contain a certain weight of truth,
    but they must be intended
    for that other lady
    whose portrait you were wearing
    in a locket on a chain   805
    that hung around your neck
    when you came to see me.
    And so, Astolfo, she alone
    deserves your compliments.
    Go give them to her quickly   810
    so she may reward you,
    for in the court of love,
    as in the court of kings,
    gallantries and vows of fealty
    are not the way to valid titles   815
    when they are addressed to
    other ladies, other kings.
    (ROSAURA *enters, standing aside and listening.*)
ROSAURA (*aside*).
    Thank God I've reached the end
    of my misfortunes, since witnessing
    such sights as this is to fear no more.   820

ASTOLFO.

> I'll see to it that portrait
> is replaced with the image
> of your loveliness against my breast.
> When Estrella lights the way,
> shadows disappear, just as stars do   825
> when the sun itself arrives.
> Let me go and get the locket now.
> (*Aside.*)
> Forgive me, beautiful Rosaura,
> but when it comes to that,
> both men and women are untrue   830
> who are absent from each other.
> (*He leaves.* ROSAURA *comes forward.*)

ROSAURA (*aside*).

> I couldn't hear one word they said,
> I was so afraid they'd see me.

ESTRELLA.

> Astrea!

ROSAURA.

> My lady.   835

ESTRELLA.

> I'm so glad it's you, since you're
> the only one I can confide in.

ROSAURA.

> My lady, you honor me
> in serving you.

ESTRELLA.

> Astrea,   840
> in the short time I have known you,
> you've won my trust completely.
> And so, knowing what you are,
> I dare confide in you what I have
> often kept even from myself.   845

ROSAURA.

> I am all obedience.

ESTRELLA.

> Then, to tell this to you briefly:
> Astolfo, my cousin—
> to call him that should be enough;
> what more he is you can imagine—   850
> he and I are to be married,
> if one stroke of good fortune
> can do away with much that's bad.
> The first day we met I was troubled
> that he wore the portrait   855
> of another woman round his neck.
> I told him so politely.
> Since he's so gallant and in love
> with me, he's gone to get the portrait
> and will bring it to me here.   860
> His giving it to me
> will embarrass me no end.
> Please stay behind and when he comes,
> tell him to give it to you.
> I'll say nothing more than that.   865
> Being lovely and discreet yourself,
> you know what love is all about.
> (*She leaves.*)

ROSAURA.

> Good Lord, if only I didn't!
> Who is there so wise and cool
> he can advise himself   870
> on such a difficult occasion?
> Is there anyone alive
> so heavily weighed down
> by fate's adversities,
> and choked by such bleak sorrows?   875
> What is there for me to do,
> confused, perplexed, when reason
> cannot guide me nor help me find
> a way to any consolation?
> After my first misfortune   880
> nothing new has taken place
> without additional misfortunes,
> as though each one has given birth
> to the next, and so on, endlessly,
> like the phoenix always rising   885
> out of one form into another,
> the living out of the dead,
> and always finding in its grave
> a bed of warm ashes.
> A wise man once said our cares   890
> are cowards—they never come alone.
> I say they're more like heroes—
> always marching on ahead
> and never looking once behind them.
> Anyone who's had to bear them   895
> knows he can do anything;
> knowing they will never leave him,
> he is always fearless.
> I can say this since, whatever else
> has happened to me all my life,   900
> they've never stopped dogging me,
> and they never will grow tired
> till they see me, destroyed by fate,
> fall into the arms of death.
> Good God, what am I to do now?   905
> If I say who I am,
> I offend Clotaldo,
> whom I must loyally support
> since he saved my life; and he tells me
> to wait silently until   910
> my honor has been satisfied.
> But if I do not tell Astolfo
> who I am, and he finds out,
> how can I continue this pretense?
> For though my voice, my tongue, my eyes   915

deny it, my heart will tell him
that I lie. What shall I do?
But what's the use of planning to do
this or that when it's obvious
the more I do to prevent it,   920
the more I plan and mull it over,
when the time comes, my own grief
will blurt the secret out, since no one
can rise above his sorrows.
Since my soul won't dare decide   925
what I must do, let there be an end
to sorrow. Today my grief is over.
Goodbye to doubts and all pretense.
And meanwhile, heaven help me.
(ASTOLFO *enters with the portrait.*)

ASTOLFO.
  Here, madame, is the portrait.   930
  But . . . oh God!
ROSAURA.
                What's so astonishing,
  Your Grace? What stops you?
ASTOLFO.
  Hearing you, Rosaura,
  and seeing you.   935
ROSAURA.
            I, Rosaura?
  Your Grace must be mistaken, thinking
  I'm some other lady. No, I'm
  Astrea; in all humility,
  I do not merit such extreme   940
  regard as your surprise reveals.
ASTOLFO.
  Rosaura, stop pretending,
  one's heart can never lie;
  although I see you as Astrea,
  I love you as Rosaura.   945
ROSAURA.
  Since I cannot understand Your Grace
  I don't know how to answer you.
  I can only tell you
  that Estrella, bright and beautiful
  as Venus, has asked me to wait   950
  for you in her stead; she asked me
  to accept the portrait for her
  which Your Grace would give me
  (a fair enough request), and which I,
  in turn, would bring to her.   955
  This is what Estrella wishes,
  and even in the slightest matters,
  though it result in harm to me,
  this is what Estrella wishes.
ASTOLFO.
  Try as you will, Rosaura,   960
  you are no good at pretending!

Tell your eyes to harmonize
with the music of your voice.
Otherwise they grow discordant
and throw their instrument out of tune,   965
trying to temper their false notes
with the truth of feeling in it.
ROSAURA.
  As I've said, I'm waiting
  only for the portrait.
ASTOLFO.
                All right, then,   970
  since you wish to carry this pretense
  to its conclusion, I'll go along.
  So, Astrea, go tell the Princess,
  in answer to her request,
  that I respect her too much to send   975
  a mere likeness, and instead,
  because I value and esteem her,
  I am sending the original.
  And you are to carry it with you,
  since you already bear it in you,   980
  being yourself the original.
ROSAURA.
  A bold man with a fixed purpose,
  who bravely undertakes a mission,
  then finds a substitute is offered,
  even one of greater value,   985
  would feel balked and foolish
  returning without the prize
  he set out to obtain.
  I was asked to get the portrait;
  if I bring back the original,   990
  though it be more valuable,
  my mission is not accomplished.
  And so, Your Grace, give me the portrait.
  I cannot return without it.
ASTOLFO.
  But if I don't give it to you,   995
  how are you to get it?
ROSAURA.
  This way! Let go of it,
  you scoundrel!
  (*She tries to take it from him.*)
ASTOLFO.
                Impossible!
ROSAURA.
  So help me, I will not see it fall   1000
  into another woman's hands!
ASTOLFO.
  You're a real terror!
ROSAURA.
                And you're a fiend!
ASTOLFO.
  Rosaura, that's enough, my dear.

ROSAURA.

Your what? You lie, you cad!   **1005**
(*They struggle over the portrait.* ESTRELLA *enters.*)

ESTRELLA.

Astolfo, Astrea, what is this?

ASTOLFO (*aside*).

It's Estrella.

ROSAURA (*aside*).

Oh Love, grant me
the wit to get my portrait back!
(*Aloud.*)
My lady, if you like,   **1010**
I'll tell you what it's all about.

ASTOLFO (*aside to* ROSAURA).

What are you up to now?

ROSAURA.

You directed me to wait here
for Astolfo to request
a portrait for you. Being alone,   **1015**
and finding my thoughts drifting
from one thing to another,
and having just heard you speak
of portraits, it occurred to me
that I happened to have my own   **1020**
here in my sleeve. I intended
to look at it, like anyone
alone trying to amuse himself
with little things of that sort.
It fell from my hand to the ground.   **1025**
Coming in just then to give you
the portrait of some other woman,
Astolfo picked mine up, and now
is not only set against
surrendering the one   **1030**
you asked for but also
wants to keep the other one.
I pleaded and protested,
but he would not give it back.
In my anger and annoyance   **1035**
I tried to snatch it from him.
The one he's holding in his hand
is mine; you can tell by looking
if it isn't a likeness of me.

ESTRELLA.

Let me have that portrait, Astolfo.   **1040**
(*She takes it out of his hand.*)

ASTOLFO.

Madame . . .

ESTRELLA.

Yes, indeed, it's close;
the drawing doesn't do you any harm.

ROSAURA.

Would you say it's me?

ESTRELLA.

Who would doubt it?   **1045**

ROSAURA.

Now have him give you the other one.

ESTRELLA.

Take your portrait, and go.

ROSAURA (*aside*).

I've got it back now; let come what will.
(*She leaves.*)

ESTRELLA.

Now give me the portrait I asked for.
Though I'll never look at it   **1050**
or talk to you again, I insist
I won't permit you to keep it,
having been fool enough to beg you
for it.

ASTOLFO (*aside*).

How do I wriggle   **1055**
out of this embarrassment?
(*Aloud.*)
Beautiful Estrella,
though I wish for nothing better
than to serve you obediently,
I cannot possibly give up   **1060**
the portrait you asked for, because—

ESTRELLA.

You're a villain and, as a suitor,
beneath contempt. I don't want it now.
If I had it, it would only
remind me how I had to ask you   **1065**
for it.
(*She leaves.*)

ASTOLFO.

Wait, listen, look, let me say . . .
The good Lord bless you, Rosaura!
How, or why in the world,
did you come to Poland now?   **1070**
Just to ruin me and yourself?
(*He leaves.*)

SCENE TWO

(*The Prince's cell in the tower.* SEGISMUNDO, *in chains and
animal skins, as in the beginning, lies stretched out on the
ground;* CLOTALDO *enters with two* SERVANTS *and* CLARÍN.)

CLOTALDO.

You can leave him here now,
his insolent pride ending
where it began.

A SERVANT.

I'll attach the chain
the way it was before.   **5**

CLARÍN.

Better not wake up, Segismundo,
and see how lost you are, your luck
all gone, and your imaginary

glory passing like life's shadow,
and like death, all in a flash.   10

CLOTALDO.
A man who can turn phrases like that
deserves to have a place apart,
a room where he can go on prattling.
(*To the* SERVANTS.)
Take hold of this man and lock him up
in that cell.   15

CLARÍN.
                        But why me?

CLOTALDO.
Because a tight prison cell
is just the place for trumpeters
who want to blare their secrets out.

CLARÍN.
Did I, by any chance, offer   20
to kill my father? No.
Was I the one who picked up
little Icarus and threw him
off the balcony? Is this a dream
or am I only sleeping?   25
What's the point of locking me up?

CLOTALDO.
Clarín, you're a trumpeter.

CLARÍN.
Well, then, I'll play the cornet,
and a muted one at that; as
an instrument it's miserable!   30
(*They take him away, leaving* CLOTALDO *alone.*
   BASILIO *enters, masked.*)

BASILIO.
Clotaldo.

CLOTALDO.
            Sire! Is it
Your Majesty coming here this way?

BASILIO.
Alas, foolish curiosity
brought me here like this   35
to see what's happening
to Segismundo.

CLOTALDO.
                  See him
lying there in complete abjection.

BASILIO.
Unhappy Prince—oh, the fatal hour   40
you were born! You may wake him now,
his energies and manhood sapped
by the opium he drank.

CLOTALDO.
Sire, he's restless and talking
to himself.   45

BASILIO.
            What can he be dreaming
now? Let's listen to what he says.

SEGISMUNDO (*in his sleep*).
A just prince must punish tyrants.
Clotaldo must be put to death,
and my father kiss my feet.   50

CLOTALDO.
He's threatening to kill me.

BASILIO.
To insult and conquer me.

CLOTALDO.
He plans to take my life.

BASILIO.
And to humiliate me.

SEGISMUNDO (*in his sleep*).
Once my uncontested valor   55
finds its way into the vast
theatre of this world to clinch
its vengeance, they'll all see
how Prince Segismundo subjugates
his father.   60
(*Waking.*)
            But, good Lord,
what's this? Where am I now?

BASILIO (*to* CLOTALDO).
He must not see me. You know
what's to be done. Meanwhile,
I'll step back here and listen.   65
(*He withdraws.*)

SEGISMUNDO.
Is this really me? Can I be he
who now returns to see himself
reduced to such a state, bound up
and clapped in chains? Oh tower,
have you become my sepulcher?   70
Yes, of course. God Almighty,
what things have I been dreaming!

CLOTALDO (*aside*).
That's my cue to play illusionist.

SEGISMUNDO.
Is it time for me to waken now?

CLOTALDO.
Yes, it's time for you to waken.   75
Or would you spend the whole day sleeping?
Have you been awake at all
since I began that disquisition
on the eagle? Were you left behind
while I was following its slow flight?   80

SEGISMUNDO.
Yes, nor have I wakened yet,
Clotaldo, for if I grasp
your meaning, I must be still asleep.

In that I can't be much mistaken,
for if what I felt and saw so clear   85
was something that I dreamt,
then what I'm looking at this moment
would be unreal; so since I now
can see I'm fast asleep, it shouldn't
be surprising that when   90
I am unconscious I dream
that I'm awake.

CLOTALDO.
                Tell me what you dreamt.

SEGISMUNDO.
    If I thought it was a dream
I'd never tell you what I dreamt.   95
But what I saw, Clotaldo—
yes, I'll tell you that. I woke,
I saw myself lying in a bed
—oh, the warmly sinister
deception of it all!—as in   100
some flower bed the spring shoots
through and through with luscious colors.
And gathered there around me
were a thousand noblemen
bowing and calling me their Prince.   105
What they offered me were jewels
and costumes rich and elegant.
Then you yourself appeared,
and changed my quiet numbness into
an ecstasy by telling me   110
(never mind what I look like now)
that I was the Prince of Poland.

CLOTALDO.
    Surely you rewarded me
for bringing you such news.

SEGISMUNDO.
    Just the opposite. In a rage   115
I tried to kill you twice
for being such a traitor.

CLOTALDO.
    Did I deserve the punishment?

SEGISMUNDO.
    I was lord and master there—
of everybody. And I took   120
revenge on all of them,
except for a woman that I loved . . .
I know that that was true, for
it's the only thing that stays with me.
All the rest has disappeared.   125
(*The* KING *leaves.*)

CLOTALDO (*aside*).
    The King was moved by what he heard,
and went away.
    (*Aloud.*)
             So much talk

about eagles put you to sleep
and made you dream of empire. Still   130
it would be better, Segismundo,
if you could dream, instead,
of honoring the one
who took such pains to bring you up;
for even in a dream, remember,   135
it's still worth doing what is right.
(*He leaves.*)

SEGISMUNDO.
    True enough. And so, put down
the beast in us, its avidity
and mad ambition, since we may
just happen to dream again,   140
as we surely will, for the world
we live in is so curious
that to live is but to dream.
And all that's happened to me tells me
that while he lives man dreams   145
what he is until he wakens.
The king dreams he's a king,
and so he lives with this illusion,
making rules, putting things in order,
governing, while all the praise   150
he's showered with is only lent him,
written on the wind, and by death,
his everlasting sorrow,
transformed to dust and ashes.
Who would ever dare to reign,   155
knowing he must wake into
the dream of death? The rich man
dreams he's wealthy with all the cares
it brings him. The poor man dreams
he's suffering his misery   160
and poverty. The fellow
who improves his lot is dreaming,
and the man who toils and only
hopes to, is dreaming too.
And dreaming too, the man   165
who injures and offends.
And so, in this world, finally,
each man dreams the thing he is,
though no one sees it so.
I dream that I am here   170
manacled in this cell,
and I dreamed I saw myself
before, much better off.
What is life? A frenzy.
What is life? An illusion,   175
fiction, passing shadow,
and the greatest good the merest dot,
for all of life's a dream, and dreams
themselves are only part of dreaming.

ACT THREE
SCENE ONE

(*In the tower.*)

CLARÍN.

I'm kept a prisoner
in an enchanted tower
because of what I know.
What will they do to me
because of what I do not know,　　5
since they're so quick to do away
with me for what I do know? To think
a man like me should have to die
of hunger and stay alive!
Of course, I'm sorry for myself.　　10
They'll all say, "You're right to be,"
and they're surely right to say so,
because this silence doesn't jibe
with the name I've got, Clarín.
I just can't keep still, you see.　　15
Who's here to keep me company?
To tell the truth—spiders and rats . . .
Oh, the dear little twitterers!
and my poor head still stuffed
with those nightmares I had last night—　　20
there were a thousand oboes, trumpets,
and what have you, playing to
long processionals of flagellants
and crosses; some staggering up,
others toppling down, still others　　25
fainting at the sight of blood.
As for me, I'm fainting out of
hunger, because I told the truth.
I find I'm in prison where all day
I'm taught the philosophic text　　30
of No-eateries, and all night,
the stuff of No-dineries.
If silence is ever canonized
in a new calendar,
Saint Secrecy should be　　35
my patron saint because
I celebrate his day,
not by feasting but by fasting.
Still, I deserve this punishment
because instead of blabbing, I shut　　40
my mouth, which for a servant
is the greatest sacrilege.

(*The sound of bugles, drums, and voices outside.*)

SOLDIER 1 (*offstage*).

Here's the tower where they put him.
Knock the door down, everyone,
and let's go in.　　45

CLARÍN.

　　　Good Heavens,
it's clear they're looking for me,
since they say I'm in here.
What do they want of me?

SOLDIER 1.

　　　　　Now go in.　　50

(*Several* SOLDIERS *enter.*)

SOLDIER 2.

Here he is.

CLARÍN.

　　　Here he isn't.

ALL SOLDIERS.

　　　　　Sire . . .

CLARÍN (*aside*).

Are they drunk, or what?

SOLDIER 1.

　　　　　You are　　55
our Prince. We want you and won't accept
anyone but a native ruler—
no foreigners! We all kiss your feet.

ALL SOLDIERS.

Long live our mighty Prince!

CLARÍN (*aside*).

Good God, they really mean it! Is it　　60
customary in these parts
to grab someone every day
and make him a prince, then
throw him back into the tower?
Now I see that's just what happens.　　65
Well, so that's the part I'll play.

SOLDIERS.

We're at your feet. Let us have them . . .

CLARÍN.

Impossible. I need my feet.
Besides, what good's a footless prince?

SOLDIERS.

We've told your father, straight out,　　70
we'll recognize only you as Prince,
and not someone from Muscovy.

CLARÍN.

You *told* my father? Oh,
how disrespectful of you!
Then you're nothing but riffraff.　　75

SOLDIER 1.

But it was out of loyalty
we said it—straight from the heart.

CLARÍN.

Loyalty? If so, you're pardoned.

SOLDIER 2.

Come with us and reclaim your kingdom.
Long live Segismundo!　　80

ALL.

　　　Hurray,
Segismundo!

CLARÍN (*aside*).
    So Segismundo's
the one you're after? Oh, well,
then Segismundo must be the name 85
they give all their fictitious princes.
(SEGISMUNDO *enters*.)
SEGISMUNDO.
 Who is it here that's calling
Segismundo?
CLARÍN (*aside*).
    Well, I'll be a—
pseudo-Segismundo. 90
SOLDIER 1.
    Now who is
Segismundo?
SEGISMUNDO.
   I am.
SOLDIER 2 (*to* CLARÍN).
 You pretentious idiot,
how dare you impersonate 95
Segismundo?
CLARÍN.
   Me, Segismundo?
I deny that! Why, you were the ones
who segismundozed me
in the first place. So you're the 100
pretentious idiots, not me.
SOLDIER 1.
 Great Prince Segismundo,
the standards we have brought
are yours, though our faith's sufficient
to acclaim you as our sovereign. 105
The great King Basilio,
your father, fearing Heaven
would fulfill the fate
predicting he'd fall vanquished
at your feet, seeks to deprive you 110
of your lawful right to succeed him
and to give it to Astolfo,
Duke of Muscovy. To achieve this,
he has convened his council,
but the populace, alerted now 115
and knowing there's a native
successor to the crown,
has no wish to see a foreigner
come here to rule over them.
And thus, nobly scorning fate's 120
ominous predictions, they've come
to find you where you've been kept
a prisoner so that, assisted
by their arms, you may leave
this tower and reclaim 125
the kingly crown and scepter
sequestered by a tyrant.

Now come with us, for in this desert
large bands of rebels and plebeians
acclaim you: freedom is yours! 130
It is shouting to you—listen!
VOICES (*offstage*).
 Long live Segismundo!
SEGISMUNDO.
 Heavenly God, do you wish me
once again to dream of grandeur
which time must rip asunder? 135
Do you wish me once again
to glimpse half-lit among the shadows
that pomp and majesty
which vanish with the wind?
Do you wish me once again to taste 140
that disillusionment, the risks
that human power must begin with
and must forever run?
This must not, no, it must not happen!
I cannot bear to see myself 145
bound down again by a private fate.
Knowing as I do that life's a dream,
I say to you, be gone and leave me,
vague shadows, who now pretend
these dead senses have a voice 150
and body, when the truth is they are
voiceless and incorporeal.
Because I'm through with blown-up majesty,
I'm through with pompous fantasies
and with all illusions scattered 155
by the smallest puff of wind,
like the flowering almond tree
surrendering without the slightest
warning to the dawn's first passing breeze,
which dulls and withers the fine 160
rose-lit beauty of its frilly blooms.
I understand you now, yes,
I understand you and I know now
that this game's the game you play
with anyone who falls asleep. 165
For me, no more pretenses, no more
deceptions. My eyes are wide open.
I've learned my lesson well.
I know that life's a dream.
SOLDIER 2.
 If you think we're deceiving you, 170
just cast your eyes up to
those mighty mountains and see
all the people waiting there
for your commands.
SEGISMUNDO.
    Yes, and this 175
is just the thing I saw before,
as clearly and distinctly

as I see it now, and it was all
a dream.
SOLDIER 2.
           Great events, my lord,   180
always are foreseen this way.
That is why, perhaps, you saw them
in your dream first.
SEGISMUNDO.
               You're right.
This was all foreseen; and just in case   185
it turns out to be true,
since life's so short, let's dream,
my soul, let's dream that dream again,
but this time knowing the pleasure's brief
from which we suddenly must waken;   190
knowing that much, the disillusion's
bound to be that much less.
One can make light of injuries
if one's prepared to meet them halfway.
Thus forewarned, and knowing that   195
however much it seems assured
all power is only lent
and must be given back to
its donor, let's dare do anything.
My subjects, I appreciate   200
your loyalty to me.
With my aggressiveness and skill,
I'm the one to lead you
out of servitude to foreigners.
Strike the call to arms; you'll soon have proof   205
of how great-hearted my valor is.
I intend to wage war against
my father, dragging whatever truth
there is out of the stars of Heaven.
I'll see him grovel at my feet . . .   210
(Aside.)
But if I wake before that happens,
perhaps I'd better not mention it,
especially if I don't reach that point.
ALL.
Long live Segismundo!
(CLOTALDO enters.)
CLOTALDO.
Good Lord, what's all this uproar?   215
SEGISMUNDO.
Clotaldo.
          My Lord . . .
CLOTALDO (aside).
              He's sure
to take his fury out on me!
CLARÍN (aside).
I'll bet he throws him off the cliff.   220
CLOTALDO.
I come to lie down at your feet, Sire,
knowing I must die.

SEGISMUNDO.
            Get up,
little father, get up from the ground,
for you're to be my guide,   225
my true North Star. I entrust you
with my first efforts, aware of
how much I owe to your loyalty
for bringing me up. Come, embrace me.
CLOTALDO.
What's that you say?   230
SEGISMUNDO.
            That I'm dreaming,
and "Even in a dream, remember,
it's still worth doing what is right."
CLOTALDO.
Indeed, Sire, if doing right
is to be your motto, then surely   235
it should not offend you if the plea
I make now is in the same cause.
Wage war against your father?
I must tell you that I cannot serve
against my King, thus cannot help you.   240
I am at your feet. Kill me!
SEGISMUNDO (aside).
Traitor! Villain! Ingrate!
God knows, I should control myself,
I don't even know if I'm awake.
(Aloud.)
Clotaldo, your courage   245
is enviable, thank you.
Go now and serve the King;
we'll meet again in combat.
You, there! Strike the call to arms!
CLOTALDO.
You have my deepest gratitude.   250
(He leaves.)
SEGISMUNDO.
Fortune, we go to rule!
Do not wake me, if I sleep,
and if it's real, don't put me
to sleep again; but whether real
or not, to do the right thing   255
is all that matters. If it's true,
then for truth's sake only;
if not, then to win some friends
against the time when we awaken.
(They leave, to the sound of drums.)

SCENE TWO

(A hall in the royal palace. BASILIO and ASTOLFO enter.)

BASILIO.
Astolfo, tell me, what prudence
could restrain a wild horse's fury?

And who could check a coursing river
flowing fast and foaming to the sea?
Can valor keep loose rock   5
from breaking off a mountain top?
Well, any one of these would seem
easier to achieve than putting
down an impudent, rebellious mob.
Once rumor starts up factions   10
you can hear the echoes breaking
far across the mountains: from one side,
Segismundo! and from the other,
Astolfo! while the throne room,
split by duplicity and horror,   15
becomes again the grisly stage where
urgent fate enacts its tragedies.

ASTOLFO.

Then, Sire, we'll defer our happiness
and put aside the tribute
and sweet reward your hand   20
so generously offered me.
For if Poland, which I hope to rule,
now withholds obedience to me,
it's because I have to win it first.
Give me a horse, and let me show   25
my fearlessness, hurling lightning, as
I go, behind my shield of thunder.
(*He leaves.*)

BASILIO.

What must be admits no remedy;
what's foreseen magnifies the peril,
impossible to cope with,   30
while to evade it only brings it on.
This is the circumstance, this the law
grinding on so horribly.
The risk I tried to shun meets me head on;
and I have fallen in the trap   35
I took such pains to sidestep.
Thus I've destroyed my country and myself.
(*ESTRELLA enters.*)

ESTRELLA.

If Your Majesty in person
does not intervene to halt
this riot swelling with each   40
new band fighting in the streets
and squares, you'll see your kingdom
swimming in scarlet waves, and caked
in its own purpling blood.
Sorrow creeps in everywhere,   45
piling tragedy on misfortune
everywhere. The ear grows numb,
the eye falters witnessing
the havoc done your kingdom,
the bloody, heavyhanded blows   50
of sheer calamity.

The sun pulses in amazement,
the wind moves up and back perplexed;
each stone juts out to mark a grave,
each flower garlanding a tomb.   55
Every building has become
a towering sepulcher, every
soldier a living skeleton.
(*CLOTALDO enters.*)

CLOTALDO.

Thank God I've reached you here alive!

BASILIO.

Ah, Clotaldo, what news   60
have you of Segismundo?

CLOTALDO.

A blind and monstrous mob
poured into the tower; out of
its recesses they plucked their Prince,
who, when he saw himself   65
a second time restored to grandeur,
relentlessly displayed his valor
and hoarsely swore he'd drag what truth
there is out of the stars of Heaven.

BASILIO.

Give me my horse. Relentless too,   70
I go in person to put down
an ungrateful son; and, to defend
my crown, will show that where knowledge failed,
my cold steel must succeed.
(*He leaves.*)

ESTRELLA.

And at his royal side, the Sun God,   75
I'll be the invincible Bellona;
hoping to frame my name with his
in glory, I'll stretch my wings
and fly like Pallas Athena,
war goddess and protector.   80
(*She leaves, and the call to arms is sounded;
   ROSAURA enters, detaining CLOTALDO.*)

ROSAURA.

I know that war is everywhere,
but though your valor beckons you
impatiently, listen to me first.
You well remember how I came
to Poland, poor, unhappy,   85
and humiliated, and how,
shielded by your valor,
I took refuge in your sympathy.
Then, alas, you ordered me
to live at court incognito   90
and, while I masked my jealousy,
endeavor to avoid Astolfo.
Finally, he saw me,
but though he recognized me
still persists in trampling   95

on my honor by going nightly
to the garden to meet Estrella.
I've taken the garden key
and can now make it possible
for you to enter there   100
and wipe my cares away.
So, with daring, courage, strength,
you will restore my honor,
determined as you are
to avenge me by killing him.   105

CLOTALDO.
It's true, Rosaura, that from
the moment I met you
I was inclined—as your tears
could testify—to do all
I possibly could for you.   110
My first thought was to have you change
the costume you were wearing, so that
if Astolfo happened to see you,
at least he'd see you as you are,
and not think that your outraged honor   115
had filled you with such mad despair,
it had made you wholly licentious.
Meanwhile I tried to think of some way
to restore your honor, even though
(and this shows how much your honor   120
meant to me) it should involve
murdering Astolfo. But oh,
it must have been the madness
of senility in me!
I do not mean the prospect fazed me.   125
After all, who is he? Surely
not my King. So there I was,
about to kill him when . . . when
Segismundo tried to murder me.
And there was Astolfo, on the spot,   130
to save me—despite the danger.
all heart, all will, and boundless
courage! Now think of me,
touched to the soul with gratitude—
how could I kill the man who saved   135
my life? So here I am,
split between duty and devotion:
what I owe you, since I gave you life,
and what I owe him, who gave me life.
I don't know whom to help   140
nor which one of you to support:
you, to preserve what I have given,
or him, for what I have received.
In the present circumstance, my love
has no recourse at all, since I am   145
both the one to do the deed
and the one to suffer for it too.

ROSAURA.
I'm sure I needn't tell a man
of honor that when it's nobler
to give, it's sheer abjection   150
to receive. Assuming that much, then,
you owe him nothing, for if
he's the one who gave you life,
as you once gave me mine, it's clear
he's forcing you, in good conscience,   155
to do a thing that's mean and base, and
I, a thing that's fine and generous.
By that token, he insults you,
and by it you remain obliged to me
for having given me   160
what you received from him.
Therefore, as giving is worthier
than taking, you must apply yourself
to the mending of my honor,
a cause far worthier than his.   165

CLOTALDO.
While nobility lives on giving,
gratitude depends on taking
what's given. And having learned by now
how to be the giver,
I have the honor to be known   170
as generous; let me now be known
as well for being grateful.
That I can achieve, as I achieved
nobility, by way of being
generous again, and thereby show   175
I love both giving and receiving.

ROSAURA.
When you granted me my life,
you told me then yourself
that to live disgraced
was not to live at all.   180
Therefore, I received nothing from you,
since the life your helping hand held forth
to me was not a life at all.
And if it's generosity
you admire above gratitude   185
(as I've heard you say), then I'm still
waiting for that gift of life
you've neglected giving me.
For the gift grows greater
when before you practice gratitude   190
you indulge your generosity.

CLOTALDO.
You've won; first I'll be generous.
Rosaura, you will have my estate,
but live in a convent.
I've thought the matter through: 195
this way you'll commit yourself
to safety rather than to crime.

Surely at times like these,
with the kingdom so divided,
I could not, as a born nobleman,   200
add to my country's misfortunes.
In following my proposal,
I continue loyal to the crown,
generous to you, and grateful
to Astolfo. Now choose this way   205
which best suits you between extremes.
If I were your father, God knows
I couldn't do more for you.

ROSAURA.
If you were my father,
I'd endure this insult silently.   210
But since you're not, I won't.

CLOTALDO.
Then what do you intend to do?

ROSAURA.
Kill the Duke.

CLOTALDO.
A woman
who has never known her father,   215
and so courageous?

ROSAURA.
Yes.

CLOTALDO.
What inspires you?

ROSAURA.
My good name.

CLOTALDO.
Think of Astolfo as—   220

ROSAURA.
The man who utterly disgraced me.

CLOTALDO.
—your King and Estrella's husband.

ROSAURA.
That, by God, he'll never be!

CLOTALDO.
This is madness!

ROSAURA.
I know it is.   225

CLOTALDO.
Well, control it.

ROSAURA.
I can't.

CLOTALDO.
Then you'll lose—

ROSAURA.
Yes, I know.

CLOTALDO.
—your life and honor.   230

ROSAURA.
Yes, of course.

CLOTALDO.
Why? What do you want?

ROSAURA.
To die.

CLOTALDO.
That's sheer spite.

ROSAURA.
No, it's honor.   235

CLOTALDO.
It's hysteria.

ROSAURA.
It's self-respect.

CLOTALDO.
You're in a frenzy.

ROSAURA.
Angry, outraged!

CLOTALDO.
So there's no way to curb   240
your blind passion?

ROSAURA.
No, there's not.

CLOTALDO.
Who's to help you?

ROSAURA.
Myself.

CLOTALDO.
And no other way?   245

ROSAURA.
No other way.

CLOTALDO.
Consider now, if there's another—

ROSAURA.
Another way to ruin myself, of course.
(*She leaves.*)

CLOTALDO.
Daughter, wait for me—I'll go
with you, and we'll be lost together.   250
(*He leaves.*)

SCENE THREE

(*An open field.* SEGISMUNDO *in animal skins;* SOLDIERS
marching, drum beats; CLARÍN.)

SEGISMUNDO.
If old Rome, in its triumphant
Golden Age, could see me now,
how she'd rejoice at the strange sight
of a wild animal leading
mighty armies, for whom,   5
in his high purposes,
the conquest of the firmament
is but a paltry thing. And yet,
my soul, let us not fly too high,
or the little fame we have   10

will vanish, and when I wake
I'll plague myself for having gained
so much only to lose it all;
so, the less I feel attached to now,
the easier to lose it later.   15
(*A bugle is sounded.*)

CLARÍN.
Mounted on a fire-eating steed
(excuse me if I touch things up
a bit in telling you this story),
on whose hide a map is finely drawn,
for of course his body is the earth,   20
and his heart the fire locked up
in his breast, his froth the sea,
his breath the wind, and in
the sweltering chaos I stand
agape, since heart, froth, body, breath,   25
are monsterized by fire, earth, sea, wind—
mounted on this dappled steed,
which feels the rider's spur
bidding it to gallop (say to fly
instead of gallop), I mean, look here,   30
there's a very lively woman
riding up to meet you.

SEGISMUNDO.
Her light blinds me.

CLARÍN.
                              God, it's Rosaura.
(*He withdraws.*)

SEGISMUNDO.
Heaven has restored her to me.   35
(ROSAURA *enters in the loose blouse and wide skirts*
       of a peasant woman, and wearing a sword and a
       dagger.)

ROSAURA.
Magnanimous Segismundo,
your heroic majesty rises
with the daylight of your deed
out of your shadowy long night.
Like the sun regaining lustre   40
as it rises from Aurora's arms
to shine on plants and roses,
seas and mountains, gazing
golden-crowned abroad and shedding rays
that twinkle in the foam   45
and flash upon the summits,
so too you come now, a bright new sun
of Poland rising in the world.
Oh aid this poor unhappy woman
who lies prostrate at your feet,   50
and help her both because she is
a woman and is unprotected,
two reasons to obligate
any man who prides himself

on being valiant—either one   55
should do or be more than enough.
Three times now I've surprised you and
three times you've failed to recognize me,
because each time you saw me I was
someone else and dressed differently.   60
The first time you took me for a man.
That's when you were heavily confined
in prison, where your life was so
wretched that it made my own sorrows
seem trivial. The next time   65
you admired me as a woman,
when all the pomp of majesty
was to you a dream, a fantasy,
a fleeting shadow. The third time is
today, when I appear before you   70
as a monstrous hybrid:
armed for combat as a man,
but in woman's clothing.
Now to rouse your sympathy,
the better to dispose you   75
to my cause, hear my tragic story.
My mother was a noblewoman
in Muscovy, who, since she was
unfortunate, must have been
most beautiful. Her betrayer   80
saw her there, whose name I cannot tell
because I did not know him, yet know
there was something valiant in him
because the same stuff stirs in me.
Sometimes when I think he fathered me,   85
a perverse idea seizes me:
I'm sorry I wasn't born a pagan
so I could tell myself
he was like one of those gods
who changed himself into a shower   90
of gold, a swan, a bull,
on Danae, Leda, and Europa.
That's odd: I thought I'd just been
rambling on, telling old tales
of treachery, but I find   95
I've told you in a nutshell
how my mother was deceived
by tender love's expression,
being herself more beautiful
than any woman, but like us all,   100
unhappy. His promises
to marry her she took
so guilelessly that to this day
the thought of them starts her weeping.
As Aeneas did on fleeing Troy,   105
this scoundrel fled, leaving her his sword.
It's the same one sheathed here at my side,
which I'll bare before my story ends.

This was the loosely tied knot—
neither binding enough   110
for a marriage nor open
enough to punish as a crime—
out of which I myself was born,
my mother's image, not in beauty
but in bad luck and its aftermath.   115
I needn't stop to tell you how,
having inherited such luck,
my fate has been as grim as hers.
All I can tell you is that the man
who destroyed my honor and good name   120
is . . . Astolfo. Simply naming him
floods and chokes my heart with rage,
as if I'd named my worst enemy.
Astolfo was the faithless wretch
who, forgetting love's delights   125
(for when one's love is past, even
its memory fades away),
came here to Poland, fresh for new
conquest, to marry Estrella,
her torch lit against my setting sun.   130
Who'd have thought after one happy star
had brought two lovers together
that another star (Estrella)
should then rise to pull them apart?
Hurt, insulted, my sadness turned   135
to madness, and I froze up inside—
I mean that all of Hell's confusions
went sweeping through my head
like voices howling out
of my own Tower of Babel   140
I decided to be silent,
and speak my troubles wordlessly,
because there are anxieties
too painful for words and
only feelings may express.   145
Alone with her one day,
my mother Violante
tore wide open in my breast
the prison where these were hidden.
They came swarming out like troops tripping   150
over one another.
I was not ashamed to speak of them.
For, knowing that the person to whom
one confesses one's weaknesses
has herself been prone in the same way   155
makes the telling easier
and the burden lighter.
Sometimes there's purpose in
a bad example. And so,
as she listened to my troubles,   160
she was sympathetic
and tried to console me

by telling me of her own.
How easily can the judge who sinned
excuse that sin in another!   165
Sad experience had taught her
not to entrust the cause of honor
to lapsing time or to occasion.
She applied this lesson
to me in my unhappiness,   170
advising me to follow him
and, with relentless courtesy,
persuade him to restore my honor.
Also, to minimize the risks,
fate designed that I should go   175
disguised as a gentleman.
Mother took down this ancient sword
I wear (and the time approaches,
as I promised, to unsheathe it)
and, trusting in its power, told me,   180
"Go to Poland, and make sure that
those at court see you wearing this blade.
For surely someone among them
will be sympathetic to you
and defend you in your plight."   185
Since it's known and not worth retelling,
I'll only mention the wild horse
that threw me and left me at your cave,
where you saw me and were astonished.
We may also pass over how   190
Clotaldo first became my close
supporter, interceded for me,
and got the King to spare my life;
then, when Clotaldo found out
who I was, convinced me I must   195
change back into my own dress
and join Estrella's retinue,
where I managed rather skillfully
to block Astolfo's courtship
and his plans to marry her.   200
Again we can pass over details:
how you saw me there once more,
dressed as a woman, and how
confused you were by all those changes.
Let's pass on to Clotaldo.   205
Convinced that now the fair Estrella
and Astolfo must marry and rule,
he urged me to drop my prior claim
against the interest of my honor.
And when, oh valiant Segismundo,   210
I now see you, ripe for vengeance,
since Heaven permits you to break out
of your crude prison cell
where your body lay, an animal
to feeling, a rock to suffering,   215
and since you take up arms

against your father and your country,
I have come to help you fight.
You see me wearing both the precious
robes of Diana and the armor   220
of Minerva, for I'm equally
adorned in cloth and steel. And so,
brave captain, let us go together
to prevent the projected marriage,
a matter which concerns us both: 225
me, to keep the man who's vowed
to be my husband from marrying
another, and you, to keep them
from joining forces, whose greater strength
would make our victory doubtful.   230
As a woman I come hoping to win you
over to my honor's cause;
but also as a man would, I come
to swell your heart, battling for your crown.
The woman yearning for your sympathy   235
kneels down here at your feet;
the man who comes offering his service
lends you both his person and his sword.
But should you turn to take
the woman in me as all woman,   240
the man in me would kill you,
in strict defense of my good name;
for, to triumph in the war of love,
I must be both the humbled woman
who appeals to you and the man   245
who's out for honor and for glory.

SEGISMUNDO (*aside*).
If it's true that I'm still dreaming,
oh God, suspend my memory,
for it's impossible to crowd
so many things in one dream.   250
God, let me escape from all this,
or else give up thinking of it!
Who ever found himself confronting
such terrible ambiguities?
If I only dreamed the grandeur   255
in which I saw myself before,
how can this woman bring up details
known patently to me alone?
Then it was all true and not a dream;
but if true—which would only make things   260
more, not less, confusing—
how can my life be called a dream?
Are all glories like dreams—
the true ones taken to be false,
and the false ones, to be true?   265
There's so little difference
between one and the other
that we cannot be sure if what
we're seeing and enjoying

is simple fact or an illusion!   270
Can it be the copy is so like
the original that no one knows
which is which? If this is so,
and one must be prepared to find
all pomp and majesty,   275
all the power and the glory,
vanishing among the shadows, then
let us learn to take advantage
of the little while that's granted us,
because all we can enjoy now   280
is what's to be enjoyed between dreams.
Rosaura's in my power;
my soul adores her beauty . . .
Let's take advantage of the moment.
Let love break all laws of gallantry   285
and the trust that lets her lie there
at my feet. It's all a dream,
and being such, let it be glad;
it'll turn sour soon enough.
My own reasoning convinces me   290
again, but let's see now.
If it's all a dream, all vainglory,
who'd want to substitute vanity
that's human for glory that's divine?
Is not all our former bliss a dream?   295
Does not a man who's known great joy
tell himself, when the thought of it
returns, "Surely it was all a dream"?
If this proves I'm disillusioned,
knowing that pleasure is a lovely flame   300
soon turned to ashes by the wind,
let me aim at what is lasting,
that longer-living glory
where joys are not a dream
nor greatness swallowed in a sleep.   305
Rosaura has lost her honor.
The duty of a prince is not
to take it but to give it back.
By God, then, I shall restore
her reputation before I claim   310
my crown. Meanwhile I turn my back
on her; the temptation
is more than I can bear.
(*To a* SOLDIER.)
Sound the call to arms! This day
must see me fighting before darkness   315
buries its gold rays in dark green waves.

ROSAURA.
But, Sire, is this the way you'd leave me?
Without a single word?
Doesn't my plight affect you?
Doesn't my anguish move you?   320
Sire, how is this possible—

you neither listen nor glance at me.
Won't you even turn and look at me?
SEGISMUNDO.
    Because your honor hangs by a thread,
    Rosaura, I must be cruel now   325
    in order to be kind.
    Words fail me in reply
    so my honor will not fail.
    I do not dare to talk to you,
    because my deeds must do the talking.   330
    I do not even look at you because,
    as someone sworn to look after
    your honor, I have all I can do
    to keep from looking at your beauty.
    (*He leaves with the* SOLDIERS.)
ROSAURA.
    God, why all these riddles now?   335
    After all my troubles,
    to be left with piercing out
    a meaning from such puzzling replies!
    (CLARÍN *enters.*)
CLARÍN.
    Madame, is it all right for me
    to see you?   340
ROSAURA.
              Clarín! Where have you been?
CLARÍN.
    Cooped up in a tower, and reading
    my fortune—life or death—in a deck
    of cards. The first card frowned at me,
    thumbs down: my life is forfeit. Poof!   345
    that's when I came close to bursting.
ROSAURA.
    But why?
CLARÍN.
             Because I know the secret
    of who you are and, in fact,
    Clotaldo . . . But what's all that noise?   350
    (*The sound of drums.*)
ROSAURA.
    What can it be?
CLARÍN.
    An armed squad's left the besieged palace
    to fight and overcome
    Segismundo's wild armies.
ROSAURA.
    Then how can I be such a coward   355
    and not be at his side
    to scandalize the world that basks in
    so much cruelty and anarchy?
    (*She leaves.*)
VOICES.
    Long live our invincible King!

OTHER VOICES.
    Long live our liberty!   360
CLARÍN.
    Long live both—liberty and King!
    Let them live together;
    I don't care what they're called
    as long as I'm not called.
    I'll just take French leave now   365
    from all this ruckus and, like Nero,
    not give a damn who gets it or how,
    unless it's for myself.
    This spot here between the rocks
    looks mighty well protected   370
    and out of the way enough for me
    to watch all the fireworks.
    Death won't find me here—to hell with it!
    (*He hides; drum beats, the call to arms, and*
        BASILIO, CLOTALDO, ASTOLFO *enter, fleeing.*)
BASILIO.
    No king was ever more regretful,
    no father more beset, ill-used.   375
CLOTALDO.
    Your army is beaten,
    and retreating everywhere pell-mell.
ASTOLFO.
    The traitors are victorious.
BASILIO.
    In such wars the victors
    are always considered loyal,   380
    the vanquished, always traitors.
    Clotaldo, let us escape the wrath
    and ruthlessness of a tyrant son.
    (*Shots are fired offstage;* CLARÍN *falls wounded out*
        of his hiding place.)
CLARÍN.
    Heaven help me!
ASTOLFO.
              Who is   385
    this unhappy soldier, fallen
    so bloodily at your feet?
CLARÍN.
    A man whose luck ran out.
    Trying to hide from death,
    I ran straight into it.   390
    I discovered it by fleeing it;
    for death, no place is secret.
    From this you clearly may conclude,
    the man who most avoids its sting
    is stung the quickest. Turn back, therefore—   395
    go back to that bloody battlefield;
    there's more safety in the midst
    of clashing arms and fire
    than in the highest mountain passes.
    And there's no safe highway leading past   400

the force of destiny
or fate's inclemency.
So if by fleeing you now attempt
to free yourselves from death, remember,
you die when it's God's will you die.   405
(*He stumbles out and falls offstage.*)

BASILIO.
"Remember, you die when
it's God's will you die." Good Lord,
how convincingly this corpse
reflects upon our error,
showing our ignorance the way   410
to greater understanding,
and all this spoken from the mouth
of a wound trickling out its gore,
a bloody tongue lengthening
with eloquence, to teach us how vain   415
are men's deliberations when set
against a higher will and cause.
So in endeavoring to free
my country of murder
and sedition, I succeeded   420
only in giving it away
to murderers and traitors.

CLOTALDO.
Although it's true, Sire, that fate
knows all the ways and byways,
and can pick its man out of a crack   425
between two heavy boulders,
still it isn't Christian to believe
there's nothing to pit against fate's wrath.
Because there is—a manly prudence
will conquer fate's adversities.   430
But since you're not yourself exempt
from such contingencies, do something
now, in order to protect yourself.

ASTOLFO.
Clotaldo speaks to you, Sire,
as a man of prudence and ripe years,   435
and I, simply as a valiant youth.
Hidden in some nearby thickets,
there's a horse that runs like lightning.
Take it and escape, and I'll
keep you covered from behind.   440

BASILIO.
If God intends that I should die here,
or death awaits me somewhere nearby,
I should like to meet it face to face.
(*A call to arms;* SEGISMUNDO *and the whole
    company enter.*)

SOLDIER.
Somewhere among these twisting paths
and heavy branches, the King   445
is hiding.

SEGISMUNDO.
            Go after him.
Comb every plant and tree,
trunk by trunk and twig by twig,
until you find him.   450

CLOTALDO.
                Sire, escape now.

BASILIO.
    Why?

CLOTALDO.
        What will you do?

BASILIO.
                Step aside, Astolfo.

CLOTALDO.
What have you in mind?   455

BASILIO.
To do something, Clotaldo,
that has long needed doing.
(*To* SEGISMUNDO.)
If you've come to find me, Prince,
here I am now, at your feet.
(*He kneels.*)
Here's a snowy carpet for you,   460
made out of my white hair.
Here's my neck—stamp on it!
Here's my crown—trample on it!
Smash my honor, disgrace me,
drag down my self-respect.   465
Make sure you take revenge on me.
Chain and use me as your slave!
After all I've done to ward it off,
let fate receive its due, and the word
of Heaven be fulfilled at last.   470

SEGISMUNDO.
Distinguished court of Poland,
witnesses of these astonishing
events, listen to me:
your Prince addresses you.
What's written in the stars,   475
on that blue tablet which
God's hand inscribes with swirling figures
and his ciphers, like so much gold
lettering on blue fields of paper—
such markings never are mistaken,   480
and they never lie. Those who lie
and are mistaken are such men
who'd use them to bad purpose trying
to penetrate the mystery
so as to possess it totally.   485
My father, at my feet here,
using as his excuse
the auguries of my foul nature,
made of me a brute, a half-
human creature, so that   490

even if I'd been born gentle
and sweet-tempered, despite my noble
blood and inbred magnanimity,
such bizarre treatment, such upbringing,
would have been enough to turn me   **495**
into a wild animal.
Strange, because this was what
he wanted to avoid!
If any man were told,
"One day you'll be murdered   **500**
by some inhuman monster,"
would he deliberately go
and rouse the sleeping beast?
If he were told, "That sword
you're wearing at your side   **505**
is the one that will kill you,"
wouldn't it be foolish if,
to keep this from happening,
he unsheathed his sword so as
to turn it toward his chest?   **510**
Suppose that he were told,
"Deep waters, under silvery foam,
will one day be your grave"—
it would be a pity if he
put out to sea when the waves   **515**
were curling whitecaps like
foaming silver mountains.
But this all happened to the man
who, feeling threatened by a brute,
went and woke it up; and to the man   **520**
who, fearing the sword, unsheathed it;
and to the one who, fearing waves,
churned up a storm to jump into.
And, though my rage (listen to me)
were like a sleeping beast,   **525**
my latent fury like a sword still
sheathed, my hidden violence a sea
becalmed—no vengeance nor injustice
would alter the course of fate,
but, if anything, would incite it.   **530**
And so, the man who wishes
to control his fate must use
judgment and be temperate.
He cannot keep an injury
from happening, even though   **535**
he sees it coming; though, of course,
he can mitigate the shock
by resignation, this cannot
be done till after the worst
has happened, since there's no way   **540**
to ward it off. Let this strangest
of spectacles, this most amazing
moment, this awesome, prodigious scene
serve as an example. Because

nothing better shows how,   **545**
after so much had been done
to prevent its happening,
a father and a king lies subject
at his own son's feet. For such was
Heaven's verdict and, do what he might,   **550**
he could not change it. How then can I,
with fewer white hairs, less courage,
and less knowledge, conquer fate
when he could not?
(*To the* KING.)
             Rise, Sire,   **555**
and give me your hand. Now
that Heaven's disabused you
of the illusion that you knew the way
to overcome it, I offer
myself up to you. Take   **560**
your vengeance. I kneel before you.
BASILIO.
    My son—because your noble deed
has re-engendered you in me—
you are a prince indeed!
The laurel and the palm belong to you.   **565**
You've won the day. Your exploits crown you!
ALL.
    Long, long live Segismundo!
SEGISMUNDO.
    If my valor is destined
for great victories, the greatest
must be the one I now achieve   **570**
by conquering myself.
Astolfo, take Rosaura's hand.
You know the debt of honor due her.
I mean to see it paid her now.
ASTOLFO.
    Though it's true I've obligations   **575**
to her, let me point out that she
does not know who she is.
It would be base and infamous
for me to marry a woman who . . .
CLOTALDO.
    Enough, don't say another word now.   **580**
Rosaura is your equal
in nobility, Astolfo,
and I'll defend her with this sword
on the field of honor.
She's my daughter—and that's enough.   **585**
ASTOLFO.
    What's that you say?
CLOTALDO.
             Simply that until
I saw her married, nobly
and honorably, I would not
reveal the fact. It's a long story,   **590**
but it ends with this: she's my daughter.

ASTOLFO.
Well, if that's the case, of course
I'll keep my word.
SEGISMUNDO.
                    And now,
not to leave Estrella downcast,   595
since she has lost this brave
and famous prince, I offer her
my own hand in marriage,
with the virtues and fortune
that go with it, and though   600
they do not exceed, at least
they equal, his. Give me your hand.
ESTRELLA.
I gain by meriting this good fortune.
SEGISMUNDO.
For Clotaldo, who served
my father loyally,   605
my gratitude waits to grant
whatever wish he has.
SOLDIER.
If you're about to honor someone
who treated you dishonorably,
what about me, who incited   610
this kingdom's overthrow,
and took you out of that tower
you were in? What'll you give me?

SEGISMUNDO.
The tower. And—so that you'll never
leave it till you die—a constant guard.   615
Once the cause of treason's past,
there's no need to keep the traitor.
BASILIO.
Your judgment astonishes us all.
ASTOLFO.
What a changed disposition!
ROSAURA.
What prudence, what discretion!   620
SEGISMUNDO.
Why are you surprised? What's there
to wonder at, if my master in this
was a dream, and I still tremble
at the thought that I may waken
and find myself again locked in a cell?   625
Even if this should not happen,
it would be enough to dream it,
since that's the way I've come to know
that all of human happiness
must like a dream come to an end.   630
And now, to take advantage
of the moments that remain, I'd like
to ask your pardon for our mistakes;
for such noble hearts as yours,
it would be fitting to forgive them.   635

FOCUS QUESTIONS

1. Citing specific examples from the text, defend *Life Is a Dream* as a dream work.
2. Trace the Segismundo/Rosaura relationship and explain how each character complements the other.
3. In a short essay, discuss how Segismundo's unique situation enlightens his understanding of the human condition.
4. Describe how *Life Is a Dream* handles one of the following issues: politics, women, honor, and faith.
5. In what ways do the language and imagery of Segismundo's closing soliloquy (II, ii) address one of the play's themes?
6. Describe how one of the supporting characters influences the action of the play.
7. Discuss the play's women, both seen and unseen, and show how they embellish the world of the play.

OTHER ACTIVITIES

1. Using reviews, photographs, and other available production documents, assess a twentieth-century production of the play.
2. Develop a production concept for your own contemporary version, using visual supports wherever possible.
3. Select a soliloquy spoken by Segismundo and establish three different vocal interpretations to presenting it. Defend your stylistic approaches.

BIBLIOGRAPHY

Allen, John J. *The Reconstruction of a Spanish Golden Age Playhouse: El Corral del Principe, 1583–1744.* Gainesville, FL: University Presses of Florida, 1983.

Hesse, Everett W. *Calderón de la Barca.* New York: Twayne Publishers, 1967.

Leavett, Sturgis E. *An Introduction to Golden Age Drama in Spain.* Chapel Hill: University of North Carolina, Dept. of Romance Language, 1971.

McKendrick, Melveena. *Theatre in Spain, 1490–1700.* New York: Cambridge University Press, 1989.

Parker, A. A. *The Allegorical Drama of Calderón.* Oxford and London: Dolphin Book Company, Ltd., 1943.

———. ''The Approach to the Spanish Drama of the Golden Age,'' *The Tulane Drama Review* 4 (1959): 42–59.

Rennert, H. A. *The Spanish Stage in the Time of Lope de Vega.* New York: Dover Publications, 1963.

Sauvage, Micheline. *Calderón: Dramaturge.* Paris: L'Arche, 1959.

Shergold, N. D. *A History of the Spanish Stage from Medieval Times until the End of the 17th Century.* Oxford: Clarendon Press, 1980.

Sloman, Albert E. ''The Structure of Calderón's *La Vida es Sueño*,'' *Modern Language Review* 48 (1953): 293–300.

———. *The Dramatic Craftsmanship of Calderón.* Oxford: Dolphin Book Co., 1969.

Wardropper, Bruce, ed. *Critical Essays on the Theatre of Calderón.* New York: New York University Press, 1965.

Wilson, E. M. ''The Four Elements in the Imagery of Calderón,'' *Modern Language Review* 31 (1936): 34–37.

Wilson, Edward, and Duncan Moir. *A Literary History of Spain: The Golden Age, Drama, 1492–1700.* New York: Barnes & Noble, 1971.

Wilson, Margaret. *Spanish Drama of the Golden Age.* New York: Pergamon Press, 1969.

RECOMMENDED VIDEOTAPE

La Vida es Sueño. VHS. 60 min. 1975. In Spanish. Distributed by Films for the Humanities and Sciences, Princeton, NJ.

PHÈDRE
JEAN RACINE (1639–1699)

And yet it is clear that Racinian tragedy as a whole is a kind of epiphany.

—FRANCIS FERGUSSON

Ludmila Mikaël as Phèdre and Jean-Noël Dalric as Hippolyte in *Phèdre*, presented by the Comédie Française in 1978, under the direction of Jacques Rosner. *Photo:* © *Lipnitzki-Viollet.*

APPROACHING FRENCH NEOCLASSICISM

Fortified with their mastery of religious and profane dramas, all of which had survived the Middle Ages, French playwrights of the mid-sixteenth century found themselves at the crossroads of a strange cultural transformation. Thus, the emergence of a true French theatre to rival Italian opera and the *commedia dell' arte* was a matter of some importance by the end of the seventeenth century. Across the Channel, the playwrights of the Restoration were enjoying immense popularity. On yet another part of the continent, the rich theatrical activity of Spain's Golden Age from 1580 to 1680 generated an international impact equally hard to ignore. But France's triumph, which would dominate the continental stage for the better part of the seventeenth century, had less to do with her Italian and Spanish competition than with her own internal struggle to institutionalize the art of drama.

A major turn had been prompted by a burgeoning interest in the classics. This literary menu, prescribed by a circle of French humanists known as the *Pléiade,* included the Greek and Roman drama. Their mission had inspired countless playwriting imitations, first composed in Latin, then translated into French. Avoiding popular and medieval samples, unless these could be rewritten, the Pleiade had hoped to establish a new vernacular French literature in league with its classical antecedents that would surpass the Italian poetry introduced to France by her foreign queen, Catherine de Medici (1519–1589). Naturally such lofty aims called for an idealism and purity of grammar and prosody that very few poets possessed. While the impact of this early French **neoclassicism** resounded through western Europe, however, its finest examples crystallized in the elitist French theatre of the seventeenth century.

The achievement of this Golden Age of French drama, which became the envy of Europe, did not happen overnight. But its background of literary, political, and religious upheaval sheds important light on both the courtly and commercial aspects of the theatrical scene in Paris, where the greatest activity was centered. By the second half of the sixteenth century, several areas of conflict were set into motion and noisily, if incompletely, resolved: the working relationship between older guilds and newly formed acting troupes; the proliferation of secular plays over religious ones, which triggered the usual censorship problems; and finally, the establishment of Paris as the central theatre district. Issues inevitably revolved around money, with the troupe of players at the Hôtel de Bourgogne asserting inordinate control. By the end of the sixteenth century, Paris became a showcase for traveling companies, while managing her own city-based troupes as well. The repertory was vast, ranging from familiar farces and profane dramas to fashionable **tragicomedies,** even including the less popular imitation tragedies inspired by the Pléiade.

In retrospect, the literary accomplishments of once important playwrights who prompted vital growth in the French theatre have faded considerably, including those of Alexandre Hardy (1576–1632), whose prolific output catered to popular audience taste and sustained his reputation as professional playwright. Yet Cardinal Richelieu's founding of the French Academy in 1635, in an effort to glorify the French language and advance the national literature and drama, was instrumental in establishing the playwriting careers of Pierre Corneille (1606–1684), Molière (1622–1673), and Jean Racine (1639–1699). Their collective achievements adorned the stages of Paris, including the court of Louis XIV, during the seventeenth century. In fact, the glorious decade of the 1660s beheld all three playwrights working simultaneously on the French stage.

Corneille, the oldest of the three, established residency at the Théâtre du Marais, a troupe of men and women whose specialty was the dramatic spectacle. His reputation, which was built on the success of numerous comedies and tragedies, was permanently set by 1637, when his greatest triumph, *Le Cid,* filled the stage of the Marais. Inspired by the play of Guillen de Castro, one of Spain's Golden Age writers, Corneille transformed this story of a famous Spanish hero into a drama that glorified the spirit of the Renaissance.

His poetic language, sharply drawn characters, and single-minded theme of honor also paid homage to Aristotle by putting his ideas into practice. Corneille's general adherence to the unities of time, place, and action was an exemplary step in the right direction, even if the compression of the action of *Le Cid* over many years and places into a twenty-four-hour period overstepped the Academy's rules of **verisimilitude** based on classical models. Indeed the French neoclassical spirit that was instilled by the Pléiade almost a century earlier had found genuine dramatic expression in Corneille's humanizing voice.

As for Jean Baptiste Poquelin, called Molière, his extraordinary comic talent was inspired by an entirely different muse. It is no wonder that the story of his theatrical accomplishments has filled so many volumes. (See Preface to Molière, p. 351.) Molière enhances our appreciation of this Golden Age through his countless comedies, so wonderfully crafted, which exude a magic so different from the austere overtones of Corneille and Racine. Of course such artistry was rooted in an honorable medieval farce tradition and the *commedia dell'arte*. (See Preface to *The Pedant*, p. 162.) His adherence to the spirit of neoclassicism also reflected the influence of ancient masters, so his comic mask effortlessly complemented Racine's tragic one.

Responding to his own upbringing in the Counter Reformation and the Catholic puritanism of Port Royal-Jansenism, Racine often followed his stage characters through the logic of a highly rigid moral universe to their tragic demises. Further adhering to the classical notion that tragedy should deal only with nobility, he resurrected his *dramatis personae* from mythology and the Old Testament and revealed extraordinary psychological insights in his creation of women characters. Conjoined with his playwright contemporaries, their contribution collectively demonstrates the purest range of comedy and tragedy the stage has known since ancient times.

MAJOR WORKS

In spite of Racine's dramatic output of eleven tragedies and one comedy, all of which were numerically outweighed by Corneille's thirty-three and Molière's thirty-four plays, a literary assessment of the quality of these dozen works renders all comparisons superfluous. Racine's profane tragedies include such eponymous titles as *Andromaque* (1667), *Britannicus* (1669), *Bérénice* (1670), *Bajazet* (1672), *Iphigénie* (1674), and *Phèdre* (1677); his two sacred tragedies are *Esther* (1689) and *Athalie* (1691), the former appearing twelve years after *Phèdre,* when Racine had retreated to the confines of Port Royal and married a young wife, Catherine de Romanet, who never read one word of her husband's work. In any event, Racine proclaimed an unhalting allegiance to Aristotelian theory, when, in the preface to his masterpiece *Phèdre,* he wrote that the tragedy possessed "all the qualities that Aristotle expects from his tragic heroes, which are suitable for arousing pity and fear. In fact, Phèdre is neither entirely guilty nor entirely innocent."[1]

THE ACTION

Phèdre's undeclared love for her stepson Hippolyte is slowly destroying her will to live. This perpetual torment is both soothed and provoked by Oenone, her nurse and confidante. Recently married to the philandering Theseus, whom she no longer loves, Phèdre masks her forbidden feelings before Hippolyte, whom she pretends to scorn instead. She is also unaware of Hippolyte's love for Aricie, the daughter of his father's enemy. When rumor reports that Theseus is dead, Oenone encourages Phèdre to reveal her feelings to Hippolyte, but he is horrified and rejects her.

Theseus, still alive, returns home. To protect the queen, Oenone falsely accuses Hippolyte of initiating amorous advances towards Phèdre. The outraged Theseus denounces his son and calls down the gods to punish him. As the wheel comes full circle, Racine's characters embrace despair, suicide, or bloody destruction.

STRUCTURE AND LANGUAGE

While Racine openly acknowledged the *Hippolytus* of Euripides and the *Phaedra* of Seneca as his principal sources, he purposely named the play after Seneca's protagonist to demonstrate her central importance in the action. Then he turned the other characters into bystanders who moved in her orbit. But his inspired transformation of a woman who is ruled and ultimately destroyed by passion was thoroughly original and transcended its formal adherence to Aristotelian theory, even while honoring it. Furthermore, his use of the **confidante** as an expedient way to compress the action by means of exposition was a major innovation.

Racine's characters, all lovers in one way or another, fall prey to the goddess Venus: there is the philandering Theseus whose wanderings welcome the possibility of new love; the young Hippolyte, now the target of Phèdre's love and cruelty, who struggles to overcome the political obstacles that thwart his love for Aricie; and Oenone, whose nurturance, previously rooted in love, has turned into fatal obsession. But the catalytic center of the tragedy, whose unrequited love for her stepson sets the principal characters tumbling to destruction, is Phèdre.

Phèdre's uncontrollable passion is nourished by both the hatred she has fabricated against the man she is forbidden to love and the hatred he shows her in return. Believing that her husband Theseus is dead in act 2, she may now openly pursue this same Hippolyte whom she had previously made an outcast. She succumbs to the timely circumstances surrounding her torment by confessing her love:

> I tried to show myself so odious to you,
> by being hateful and inhuman in your view.
> What good was this great war I waged without success?
> You hated me much more, I did not love you less.

But the appalled Hippolyte can only urge her to "recall your vow:/ Theseus, my father, is your lord and husband now."

Victimized even further by the dramatic irony underlying Oenone's unrelenting protection of Phèdre, Hippolyte boldly proclaims his innocence when the news of "this shameful love" reaches his father's ears in act 4:

> So Phèdre says Hippolyte is guilty of such shame!
> Such excellent excess of horror shakes my frame;
> so many sudden blows must overthrow me now,
> they take away my voice and make me dumb somehow.

Unable to salvage his reputation no matter how eloquently he pleads his case, Hippolyte is banished by an avenging father whose pride and anger disqualify his "criminal" son from mercy:

> Go and invent new friends, whose own dishonesty
> congratulates incest, applauds adultery—
> outlaws without conscience, traitors who know no law,
> able to care for you and share your brazen flaw.

Crystallizing this eternal triangle and casting no judgment on their behavior, Racine has confined its participants to a psychological hell where their repressed feelings are forced to the surface. The outcome, heightened by the compression of time, is a carefully orchestrated clash of wills, a dynamic unveiling of raw emotion, and an unsettling examination of human passion and jealousy.

Luxuriating in rich and resonant imagery, Racine's poetry ultimately ennobles these characters and gives shape to their destinies. In the final moments of the play, when Theseus tells Phèdre that his son's death must be applauded as her victory, Racine gives his protagonist mere seconds to unravel the ever-tightening knot of ironic circumstances that have brought Oenone and Hippolyte to their cruel ends. Disclosing that "Medea's poison now runs all along my veins," she confesses that she was "the one in whom this passion had begun,/ by casting a foul eye on your respectful son." Speaking to "my noble husband whom my being here offends," she hopes that death "which takes away this great disgrace in me,/ gives back the light of day in all its purity." Phèdre's self-incrimination and guilt-ridden suicide as well as Theseus' remorse at the hasty condemnation of his son, establish their tragic grandeur.

Ultimately, Racine believed that deep within the Greek tragic vision was a world of cruelty where human beings were at the mercy of the gods. He imagined that the same crimes and passions enacted by his noble characters were lurking beneath the civilized and elegant facade of the society for which he wrote. Holding this tightly wrought literary masterpiece up to nature, he invited audiences to glimpse at themselves.

Phèdre emerges as a tortured woman for whom there is neither escape nor salvation. Although her uncontrollable desire for Hippolyte is not, strictly speaking, incestuous, it undermines her power of reason and her will. Even her noble bearing cannot diminish the overwhelming pain that her feelings unleash. Whether or not the contemporary spectator is willing to accept the moral premise that guides this lyrical tragedy, *Phèdre* unequivocally remains an awesome theatrical experience.

ABOUT THE TRANSLATION

The classical five-act structure inspired by Seneca is symmetrically unified by Racine's command of **Alexandrine verse:** an ambitious display of six iambic feet to each line, called iambic hexameter. The pattern is further divided by absolute **caesuras,** or clear breaks, after the third foot of each line. An uninterrupted flow of rhymed couplets, in which individual pairs of verse lines terminate with the identical sound, balances the design.

William Packard's poetic achievement responds with English Alexandrines to recreate the style and content of the original. The success of his translation can be measured in this bilingual citation from act 1, scene 3, where Phèdre discloses her condition to Oenone:

N'allons point plus avant.	Demeurons, chère Oenone.
Nŏ móre, Ŏenóne, nŏ móre.	Lĕt me stăy hére aňd wáit.
Je ne me soutiens plus:	ma force m'abandonne.
Mў stréngth iš só mĕagér,	mў wéaknĕss iś sŏ gréat.

Mes yeux sont éblouis du jour que je revoi,
My eyes are dazzled by the bright light of the day,

Et mes genoux tremblants se dérobent sous moi.
my knees are trembling as I feel myself give way.

Hélas!
Alas!

OENONE: Dieux tout-puissant! que nos pleurs vous apaisent.
See how we weep, O gods, and set us free!

The final consonant placement of the rhymed couplet in the first pair of lines (''chère Oenone''/''m'abandonne'') contrasts sharply with the open-vowel placement of the second pair (''revoi''/''sous moi''). Phèdre's interjection, which initiates the fifth line, merges with Oenone's response to complete the rigid Alexandrine design. The effect is sustained for each of more than sixteen hundred verse lines of the tragedy, thereby reflecting Racine's disciplined mastery.

Preserving the iambic hexameter, Packard creates subtle paradoxes by paralleling word choices like ''meager''/''strength'' and ''great''/''weakness'' in the second line. The effect is amplified by the next pair of lines in which Phèdre's life-giving images serve as ironic counterpoint to her physical disintegration. The dramatic ''Alas,'' which temporarily halts her tragic metaphors, seductively beckons Oenone's reply.

Phèdre's sweeping, almost breathless responses might tempt any actor to succumb to the pronounced Alexandrines, an effect that should be avoided in actual stage performance. But the actor's need to uncover the meaning and reality behind Phèdre's character must never be entirely separated from the cadence established by the iambic hexameter: one must nourish the other; the form must serve the content. Careful to create a translation that can facilitate these technicalities, Packard recommends that the actor ''confront the written text itself, to find out exactly what it is [Racine] had in mind, and why he chose this particular way of saying it [and] begin to concern himself with the shape and the form of the words and the rhythms he is supposed to embody.''[2] His mastery of Racine's melodic verse provides a key to characterization and enhances our grasp of Racine's tragic art.

PHÈDRE-IN-PERFORMANCE

The neoclassical stage did not come to France until 1641 when Cardinal Richelieu constructed the Palais Cardinal (Palais-Royal). This stage, which predominated in Europe from the sixteenth to the late nineteenth century, was modeled on the theatre architecture and scenic practices inspired by the classical Vitruvius, whose treatises were rediscovered in 1414. In imitation of the outdoor arenas of Rome, Italian theatres were built in the mid-sixteenth century in accordance with Sebastiano Serlio's *Architettura* (1545), which summed up Vitruvius' descriptions. Rectangular structures seated as few as 250 or as many as 3,500 spectators on elliptical stadium-like benches around a semicircular orchestra. Combining the concept of the *scaena frons* from the classical stage and the developments in painting of linear perspective, Serlio created three stock exterior settings—tragic, comic, and pastoral—which required four sets of flat canvas wings, all painted to give the illusion of three-dimensionality, and placed on a raised stage set at eye level. Thus the king or patron could have an ideal seat in direct line of the vanishing point.

The stage itself consisted of two sections: a **raked stage** floor to increase the sense of depth and a flat **forestage** on which all the action could take place without detracting from the illusion. By the mid-seventeenth century, the static stage picture was no longer sufficient to sustain audience interest; in fact, with the incorporation of Nicola Sabbattini's **wing-and-groove system** and Giacomo Torelli's **pole-and-chariot system,** the Italianate theatre had become a machine for magically transforming the stage picture before the spectators' eyes, an important ingredient in the creation of spectacles reserved for opera and ballet. The last architectural element to be added, as a way of masking the stage machinery, was the permanent proscenium arch, which served as an ornate frame for the spectacle.

In Paris, the two existing public theatres, the Hôtel de Bourgogne and the Théâtre du Marais, which had been converted from a tennis court (**jeu de paume**) in 1634, were remodeled with the Italian stage in mind. Besides incorporating the raked stage, stock perspective scenery, forestage, and proscenium arch, these rectangular auditoriums consisted of a pit for standing audience members; two tiers of boxes along both side walls,

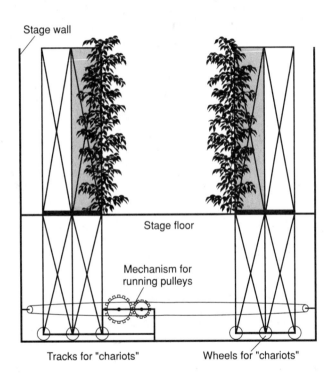

Backstage

Wings and shutters

Proscenium

Ground plan of the Teatro Farnese, an Italianate theatre.

Stage wall

Stage floor

Mechanism for running pulleys

Tracks for "chariots"   Wheels for "chariots"

The pole-and-chariot system.

and one tier across the back; and a third gallery called the *paradis* for standing spectators, which connected to a rising U-shaped amphitheatre at the rear of the hall. The stage was set for Racine's tragic art.

Like a trap that lures its victim, the role of Phèdre has challenged women artists for centuries, establishing theatrical traditions and legends not easily broken or forgotten. Thus certain actors have become curiously identified with Racine's heroine, with success in the part following them to their graves. In fact, the events surrounding the premiere on New Year's Day, 1677, at the Hôtel de Bourgogne, were equally ominous, when its reception was seriously undermined by the simultaneous opening of another "Phèdre" play by a rival of Racine. When the troupe at the Hôtel de Bourgogne eventually merged with the troupe at the Hôtel Guénégaud on August 25, 1680, the Comédie Française—the national theatre of France—was established and Racine's version finally received the acclaim it deserved.

Racine created the role of Phèdre for Marie Champmeslé, who was the principal tragedienne at the Bourgogne as well as the playwright's mistress. Originating the role of Phèdre at the age of thirty-five, she was the first of many who would achieve great notoriety as the tragic queen on the stages of the Comédie Française and other Parisian theatres: Mlles. Lecouvreur, Clairon, Raucourt, Duchenois, Dudlay, S. Weber, Moreno, Silvain, Roch, and Falconetti.

In the nineteenth century, two French artists incarnated Racine's protagonist with memorable results, achieving great international acclaim. The first was Rachel Félix (1821– 1858), who first attempted the role at the age of twenty-three. The other was Sarah Bernhardt (1844–1923), who was thirty when she played Phèdre, although she would keep the role in active repertory until the age of seventy. So cautious were critics to decide which one was the greater Phèdre that they relegated the strengths of each to specific scenes or certain acts and, in retrospect, assessed their individual performances in relation to their respective physical ages at the time each played her.

On the contemporary French stage, Edwige Feuillère and Marie Bell would face similar comparisons in the role, with their own respective strengths and weaknesses bandied by audiences and critics alike, until a professional rivalry was rumored. When in the late 1950s their performances were imported to London, where critics further praised their different approaches to the role, the time seemed ripe for the English stage to tackle the controversial classic on its own terms.

Except for Mary Newcombe's Phaedra in Euripides' *Hippolytus* at the Old Vic in 1935, the lack of an English translation suitable for stage performance had relegated Racine's version to a life on the bookshelf. This was quickly remedied when the actress and French scholar, Margaret Rawlings, appeared in her own translation in 1957. Enjoying a brief London run, including engagements in Cambridge, Scarborough, and Birmingham, Rawlings toured in the production during the next five years and was responsible for generating interest in later London revivals.

The first of these, *Phaedra Britannicus,* was produced at the Old Vic in 1975 under John Dexter's direction in a translation by Tony Harrison. Dexter moved the action from a mythical Grecian landscape to nineteenth-century India. Just as the raging sea encircled Racine's play, his production of classical columns interspersed with tropical blinds was surrounded by the dark jungle. In the title role, Diana Rigg headed a company whose performances demonstrated "uncommon dignity, passion, discipline and weight."[3]

The play returned to the Old Vic in 1984, this time in a translation by Robert Davis MacDonald, under the direction of Philip Prowse. In a production he called "truly outstanding," Michael Coveney described Glenda Jackson's Phèdre "in regal scarlet and a piled-up wig. Her performance is a process of shedding the accoutrements along with her stains of guilt and thwarted passion until, in a stunning final entrance, she achieves a natural untrammelled peace and beauty . . . [It] is a tragic performance on the grand scale."[4]

Phèdre was performed in America for the first time at the Metropolitan Theatre in New York City on September 4, 1855. Rachel Félix, who was thirty-four years old and would be dead less than three years later, starred. But her acknowledged rival, the divine Sarah Bernhardt, made numerous appearances in America assisted by her French company between 1880 and 1910. Visits to New York City inevitably included performances of *Phèdre.* Then, nearly fifty years later, Marie Bell appeared with her company at the Brooks Atkinson Theatre during the 1963 New York theatre season. Her director was André Barsacq.

In 1966, Comédie Française director, Paul Émile Deiber, who had often appeared opposite Marie Bell, first in the role of Hippolyte and later as Theseus, staged a production for the Institute for Advanced Studies in the Theatre Arts (IASTA) at the intimate Greenwich Mews Theatre in New York City. William Packard was commissioned to write the Alexandrine translation. The American cast was headed by Beatrice Straight who made Phèdre "poignant in her wilfulness [and] credible in her passions."[5]

REFLECTIONS ON PHÈDRE

After the collapse of the German Uprising of 1848, Carl Schurz, exiled revolutionist, returned to Berlin under an assumed name. In the fall of 1850, while he was cautiously planning the rescue of a fellow patriot, he risked going to the theatre to see Rachel Felix, who was performing in Berlin. "Impressions of Rachel" documents the occasion.

IMPRESSIONS OF RACHEL

So I saw Rachel. It was one of the most overpowering impressions of my life. The play was Racine's *Phèdre*. I had read most of the tragedies of Corneille, Racine, and Voltaire, and was well enough acquainted with them to follow the dialogue. But I had never liked them much. The stilted artificiality of the diction in the tedious monotony of the rhymed Alexandrine verse had repelled me, and I had always wondered how such plays could be made interesting on the stage. That I was to learn. When Rachel stepped upon the scene, not with the customary stage stride, but with a dignity and majestic grace all her own, there was first a spell of intense astonishment and then a burst of applause. She stood still for a moment, in the folds of her classic robe like an antique statue fresh from the hand of Phidias. The mere sight sent a thrill through the audience: her face a long oval, her forehead, shadowed by black wavy hair, not high, but broad and strong; under her dark arched eyebrows a pair of wondrous eyes that glowed and blazed in their deep sockets like two black suns; a finely chiselled nose with open, quivering nostrils; above an energetic chin a mouth severe in its lines, with slightly lowered corners, such as we may imagine the mouth of the tragic Muse; her stature, sometimes seeming tall, sometimes little, very slender, but the attitude betraying elastic strength; a hand with fine tapering fingers of rare beauty: the whole apparition exciting in the beholder a sensation of astonishment and intense expectancy.

The applause ceasing, she began to speak. In deep tones the first sentences came forth, in tones as deep as if they were rising from the innermost cavities of the chest, aye, from the very earth. Was that the voice of a woman? Of this you felt certain—such a voice you had never heard, never a tone so hollow and yet so full and resonant, so phantomlike and yet so real. But this first surprise soon yielded to new and greater wonders. As her speech went on, that voice, first so deep and cavernous, began, in the changing play of feelings or passions, to rise, and roll, and bound, and fly up and down the scale for an octave or two without the slightest effort or artificiality, like the notes of a musical instrument of apparently unlimited compass and endless variety of tone color. Where was now the stiffness of the Alexandrine verse? Where the tedious monotony of the forced rhymes? That marvelous voice and the effects it created on the listener can hardly be described without a seemingly extravagant resort to metaphor.

Continued

Now her speech would flow on with the placid purl of a pebbly meadow brook; then it poured forth with the dashing vivacity of a mountain stream rushing and tumbling from rock to rock. But, her passion aroused, how that voice heaved and surged like the swelling tide of the sea with the rising tempests behind it, and how then the thunder-storm burst, booming, and pealing, and crashing, as when the lightning strikes close, making you start with terror! All the elementary forces of nature and all the feelings and agitations of the human soul seemed to have found their most powerful and thrilling language in the intonations of that voice and to subjugate the hearer with superlative energy. It uttered an accent of tender emotion, and instantly the tears shot into your eyes; a playful or cajoling turn of expression came, and a happy smile lightened every face in the audience. Its notes of grief or despair would make every heart sink and tremble with agony, and when one of those terrific explosions of wrath and fury broke forth you instinctively clutched the nearest object to save yourself from being swept away by the hurricane. The marvelous modulations of that voice alone sufficed to carry the soul of the listener through all the sensations of joy, sadness, pain, love, hatred, despair, jealousy, contempt, wrath, and rage, even if he did not understand the language, or if he closed his eyes so as not to observe anything of the happenings on the stage.

But who can describe the witcheries of her gestures and the changeful play of her eyes and features? They in their turn seemed to make the spoken work almost superfluous. There was, of course, nothing of that aimless swinging of arms and sawing of the air, and the other perfunctory doings of which Hamlet speaks. Rachel's action was sparing and simple. When that beautiful hand with its slender, almost translucent, fingers, moved, it spoke a language every utterance of which was a revelation to the beholder. When those hands spread out with open palms and remained for a moment in explanatory attitude— an attitude which the richest fancy of the artist could not have imagined anything more beautifully expressive—they made everything intelligible and clear; at once you understood it all and were in accord with her. When those hands stretched themselves out to the friend or the lover, accompanied by one of those smiles which were rare in Rachel's acting, but which, whenever they appeared, would radiate all surroundings like friendly sunbeams breaking through the clouded sky—a tremor of happiness ran all over the house. When she lifted up her noble head with the majestic pride of authority, as if born to rule the world, every one felt like bowing before her. Who would have dared to disobey when, the power of the empire on her front, she raised her hand in a gesture of command? And who could have stood up against the stony glare of contempt in her eye and the haughty toss of her chin, and the disdainful wave of her arm, which seemed to sweep the wretch before her into utter nothingness?

It was in the portrayal of her evil passions and the fiercest emotions that her powers rose to the most tremendous effects. Nothing more terrible can be conceived than her aspect in her great climaxes. Clouds of sinister darkness gathered upon her brow, her eyes, naturally deep-set, began to protrude and to flash and scintillate with a truly hellish fire. Her nostrils fluttered in wild agitation as if breathing flame. Her body shot up to unnatural height. Her face transformed itself into a very Gorgon head, making you feel as if you saw the serpents wriggling in her locks. Her forefinger darted out like a poisoned dagger against the object of her execration; or her fist clenched as though it would shatter the universe at a blow; or her fingers bent like the veriest tiger's claws to lacerate the victim of her fury—a spectacle so terrific that the beholder, shuddering with horror, would feel his blood run cold, and gasp for breath, and moan, "God, help us all."

But I saw her again later in Paris, and still later in America. In fact, I have seen her in all her great characters, in not a few of them several times, and the impression was always identically the same, even during the beginning of her American tour when the beginning of her fatal ailment had already seized upon her, and her powers were said to be on the wane. Endeavoring to account more clearly for those impressions I sometimes asked myself: "But is this really the mirror held up to nature? Did ever a woman in natural life speak in such tones? Have such women as Rachel portrays ever lived?" The answer I uniformly arrived at was that such questions were idle; if Medea, Phèdre, and Roxane ever lived, so they must have been as Rachel showed them; or, rather, Rachel in her acting was happiness, misery, love, jealousy, hatred, revenge, anger, rage—all these things in an ideal grandeur, in their highest poetic potency, in gigantic reality. This may not be a very satisfactory definition, but it is as precise as I can make it. It was to see, to hear, and to be carried away, magically, irresistibly. The waves of delight or of anguish or of horror with which Rachel flooded the souls of her audiences baffled all critical analysis. Criticism floundered about in helpless embarrassment trying to classify her performances, or to measure them by any customary standard. She stood quite alone. To compare her with other actors or actresses seemed futile, for there was between them not a mere difference of degree, but a difference of kind. Various actresses of the time sought to imitate her, but whoever had seen the original simply shrugged his shoulders at the copies. It was the mechanism without the divine breath. I have subsequently seen only three actresses—Ristori, Wolter, and Sarah Bernhardt—who now and then, by some inspired gesture or intonation of voice, reminded me of Rachel; but only at passing moments. On the whole, however, the difference between them was very great. It was the difference between unique genius which irresistibly overpowers and subdues us and to which we involuntarily bow, and extraordinary talent which we simply admire. Rachel has, therefore, remained with me an overshadowing memory; and when in later years in my familiar circle we discussed the merits of contemporaneous stage performances, and someone among us grew enthusiastic about this or that living actor or actress, I could seldom repress the remark—in fact, I fear I made it often enough to become tiresome—"All this is very fine, but, ah!—you should have seen Rachel."

Source: From Carl Schurz, THE REMINISCENCES OF CARL SCHURZ, *Vol. 1, 1829–1852.*

Notes

1. *Editor's translation.*
2. *William Packard, "Spoken Poetry" in* FIRST STAGE, *Spring 1966.*
3. *Robert Cushman,* THE LONDON OBSERVER, *14 Sept. 1975, p. 24.*
4. *Michael Coveney,* FINANCIAL TIMES, *22 Nov. 1984.*
5. *Whitney Bolton,* THE MORNING TELEGRAPH, *12 Feb. 1966.*

PHÈDRE
JEAN RACINE
TRANSLATED BY WILLIAM PACKARD

CHARACTERS

Hippolyte

Théramène

Oenone

Phèdre

Panope

Aricie

Theseus

Ismène

ACT ONE

SCENE ONE: HIPPOLYTE, THÉRAMÈNE

HIPPOLYTE.
    I have made up my mind: I go, dear Théramène,
    and leave the loveliness of staying in Trézène.
    Each day I have new doubts, they drive me to
        distress,
    and I must blush with shame to see my idleness.
    For more than six long months I've missed my
        father's face,   5
    I do not know his fate, I do not know the place
    that could be capable of keeping such a man.

THÉRAMÈNE.
    In what new place, my lord, will you try what new
        plan?
    So far, to satisfy your great uncertainty,
    I've sailed the seas each side of Corinth
        endlessly;   10
    I've asked about Theseus of those who, it is said,
    saw Acheron descend forever to the dead;
    I've visited Elis, and Tenaros, and I
    sailed by where Icarus fell screaming from the sky.
    And now with what new hope, in what new place
        will you   15
    listen for his footsteps or look for what new clue?
    Now who knows truly if the king your father be
    hidden somewhere that must remain a mystery?
    Perhaps we fear for what we both know nothing of,
    perhaps this hero has discovered some new love,   20
    some beautiful young girl he's dying to abuse . . .

HIPPOLYTE.
    Stop now, dear Théramène, you've no right to
        accuse.
    He's given up that vice, he's long ago outgrown
    such bubblings of the blood, he's happier alone;
    for Phèdre has made him shed his old
        inconstancy,   25
    so she no longer fears an unknown rivalry.
    No no, I only go because I know I must,
    and also to escape this place which I distrust.

THÉRAMÈNE.
    Ah, when did you, my lord, begin to hate and fear
    this pleasant peaceful place?—for you grew up
        right here,   30
    and surely you preferred this quiet rest and sport
    to all the pomp and noise of Athens and the court.
    What danger made you change, what dread drives
        you away?

HIPPOLYTE.
    It's not the same, I face a different place today,
    since this Phèdre, the daughter of Minos and
        his wife   35
    Pasiphaë, came here, she has upset my life.

THÉRAMÈNE.
    I guess at your distress, and I know what is true,
    For Phèdre weighs on your mind, and she depresses
        you.
    The first time she met you, she hardly let you smile
    before she ordered your immediate exile.   40
    And yet her raging hate, which had you in its hold,
    has either disappeared, or grown much more
        controlled.

Besides, what can she do, or bring down on your
    head,
this dying woman who desires to be dead?
This Phèdre, who wastes away from what she will
    not say,   **45**
grown weary of herself and of the light of day,
can she do anything against you any more?

HIPPOLYTE.
    I do not fear her hate the way I did before.
    No, Hippolyte must flee another enemy:
    and that is why I fly from this young Aricie,   **50**
    last blood of that bad line which worked against us
        so.

THÉRAMÈNE.
    What?—even you, my lord, you think she is your
        foe?
    She is related to the Pallantides, it's true,
    but should she share the blame of that malicious
        crew?
    And should you hate her face, which lights the
        brightest day?   **55**

HIPPOLYTE.
    If I could hate her face, I would not go away.

THÉRAMÈNE.
    My lord, let me say this before you go too far—
    you are no longer proud of being what you are:
    Hippolyte, the sworn foe of love itself and all
    the slavish laws of love that made your father
        fall.   **60**
    Yet though you may remain cool and aloof in pride,
    Venus may still win out, and take your father's side
    and, placing you among those men who sigh and
        pine,
    she may force you to kneel before her sacred shrine.
    My lord: are you in love?   **65**

HIPPOLYTE.
                     How can you use that word?
    You, who have known my heart since first my spirit
        stirred—
    a heart that only knows such distance and disdain,
    a heart that hardly can return to earth again.
    Son of an Amazon, I drank her milk and drew   **70**
    that strong and stubborn pride which seems to baffle
        you;
    considering myself, the way a young man does,
    I gave myself great praise when I knew who I was.
    You who were close to me, who saw to all my needs,
    you made me learn by heart my famous father's
        deeds.   **75**
    You told me of his life, and once you had begun,
    I was on fire to hear whatever he had done:
    So you described the way this hero had consoled
    mankind for its great loss of Hercules, and told
    me how he slew Sinnis, told how he killed
        Scirron,   **80**

and destroyed Procrustes, and slaughtered Cercyon,
took Epidaurus' bones and spilled them in the mud,
then covered over Crete with Minotaur's life blood,
But when you told of deeds that sounded more like
    crimes,
how Theseus used to break his word a hundred
    times—   **85**
Helen is raped away from Sparta by his lies;
poor Salamis must sit as Periboëa cries—
and there were many more whose names escape me
    now,
who loved him, and believed that he would keep his
    vow:
Ariadne, weeping in silence by the sea,   **90**
Phèdre, too, whom he seduced, although more
    happily;
ah, you remember how I begged you to be brief,
such stories made me grave, they stayed and gave
    me grief;
if it were in my will to wrench them from my brain
so only the brave deeds and glories would
    remain!   **95**
Could I be so enslaved and waste my life away?
Could some god make me cheat, dissemble and
    betray?
Loose and lascivious, I would have twice the shame
of Theseus—I have none of his great claim to fame
no name, and no strange beasts defeated, and no
    right   **100**
to fail as he has failed, or fall from his steep height.
And yet suppose my pride should mellow and grow
    mild,
why should it all be for this Aricie, this child?
Surely I sense, deep in the darkness of my heart,
there is a law that says we two must stay apart?   **105**
My father disapproves, and by a stern decree,
forbids that she enlarge her brother's family:
he fears some bright new life from that guilt-ridden
    line,
therefore each leaf must wilt, and so die on the vine.
This sister must stay chaste forever to the tomb,   **110**
and bury their bad name in her own barren womb.
Should I stand by her side against my father's laws?
Show off my arrogance by taking up her cause?
Should I let love set sail the madness of my
    youth . . .

THÉRAMÈNE.
    My lord, once fate takes place and makes men face
        the truth,   **115**
    not even gods can find what goes on in the mind.
    Theseus has made you see, who tried to keep you
        blind;
    his hate has fanned a love, has nurtured a fine fire,
    has lent this enemy a grace which you admire.

Why are you so afraid of being so in love?   **120**
Perhaps there are strange joys which you know
    nothing of:
or will cruel scruples rule your conscientious days?
Must you scorn Hercules for his few playful ways?
What brave courageous soul has Venus never won?
And you, where would you be if you were not the
    son   **125**
of Antiope, whose breast encouraged a shy fire
for Theseus your father, the thirst of her desire?
What does it matter now, this high pride when you
    speak?
Things have already changed, and over this past
    week
you were not wild, not free, not as you were
    before,   **130**
now racing chariots with loud shouts by the shore,
and now perfecting skills with Neptune as your
    guide,
taking an untamed horse and breaking it to ride.
The woods do not return the echo of your cries;
weary with some great weight, you die before my
    eyes.   **135**
Now there can be no doubt: you are in love, you
    burn,
you hide a fatal pain which no man can discern.
Is it this Aricie has made your spirit bow?

HIPPOLYTE.
    I go, dear Théramène, to find my father now.

THÉRAMÈNE.
    But will you not tell Phèdre why you refuse to stay,
        my lord?   **140**

HIPPOLYTE.
           You can explain, once I have gone away.
    I know I should see her; I shall, before I go.
    But now, why does Oenone seem to be troubled so?

SCENE TWO: HIPPOLYTE, OENONE, THÉRAMÈNE

OENONE.
    Alas my lord alas, whose troubles are like mine?
    The Queen almost begins to end her thin life line.
    Vainly each night and day I stay close by her side:
    she dies of some great pain which she still tries to
        hide.
    Some fatal disarray goes raging through her head,   **5**
    it keeps her wide awake and takes her from her bed.
    This illness makes her long to see the light of day,
    yet she insists that I turn everyone away . . .
    She comes.

HIPPOLYTE.
           Enough, I go: I would not want to wait   **10**
    And let her see a face which she has grown to hate.

SCENE THREE: PHÈDRE, OENONE

PHÈDRE.
    No more, Oenone, no more. Let me stay here and
        wait.
    My strength is so meager, my weakness is so great.
    My eyes are dazzled by the bright light of the day,
    my knees are trembling as I feel myself give way.
    Alas!   **5**

OENONE.
    See how we weep, O gods, and set us free!

PHÈDRE.
    All these vain ornaments, these veils weigh down on
        me!
    What meddling dreadful hands have tried to tie my
        hair
    in such fine tiny knots with such annoying care?
    All things on every side conspire to do me harm.   **10**

OENONE.
    The way you say these things, you cause me great
        alarm!
    When you yourself saw that you were not at your
        best,
    you made me use my hands to get you so well
        dressed;
    and you yourself, because you felt a bit more bright,
    wanted to show yourself and feel the full
        daylight.   **15**
    So here you are, Madam; yet now you try to hide,
    you say you hate the day, so you must go inside.

PHÈDRE.
    Creator of the day, and of my family,
    my mother claimed she came from your fierce
        clarity;
    O now perhaps you burn with shame to see my
        pain: **20**
    Sun, I shall never gaze on your great face again!

OENONE.
    You choose cruel suicide, is that your last desire?
    how often must I hear you curse life's famous fire,
    stand here as you rehearse the farewells to be made?

PHÈDRE.
    Why shouldn't I be there, there in the forest
        shade?   **25**
    Why shouldn't I look out and follow with my eye
    a cloud of dust, and see a chariot race by?

OENONE.
    What, Madam?

PHÈDRE.
        Where am I? and what did I just say?
    have I gone mad, and have my wits begun to
        stray?   **30**
    O I have lost my mind, the great gods are to blame.
    Oenone, see how my face must blush with such great
        shame:

I let you see too much, my sorrow was too plain;
my eyes, in spite of me, are filled with tears again.

OENONE.

Alas, if you must cry, then cry for keeping still,   35
which only aggravates this illness of your will.
So deaf to what we've said, as if you had not heard,
will you be pitiless and die without a word?
What fury must obscure the brilliance of the sun?
What poison has dried up your life before it's
  done?   40
The darkness of three nights has crept across the
  skies
since you have slept, and sleep has rested your sore
  eyes;
the blazing of three days has chased those nights
  along
since you took food, and ate to make your body
  strong.
Have you dreamed up some scheme, some plot to
  stop your breath?   45
What pride gave you the right to bring about your
  death?
O you dismay the gods who gave you your own life,
and you betray the man who took you as his wife;
and finally, you cheat your children by this deed,
they will be left to lead a life of endless need.   50
Suppose on that same day they find their mother
  dead,
their whole inheritance goes somewhere else instead,
to someone else's son, some enemy of yours,
son of that Amazon from far-off distant shores,
this Hippolyte . . .   55

PHÈDRE.

                    O god!

OENONE.

                              That moves you a good deal.

PHÈDRE.

Wretched worthless woman, whose name did you
  reveal?

OENONE.

Now your great hate is not so hard for me to gauge;
it is that fatal name that makes you shake with
  rage.   60
Live, Lady, live, let love and duty rule in you.
Live, do not leave it to your children to undo
this Scythian's one son; you must keep his caprice
from bleeding the best blood that can be found in
  Greece.
Only do not delay, you may die if you wait,   65
quickly, get back your strength before it is too late,
now, while you still have time, the flame of all your
  days
may be brought back again to a substantial blaze.

PHÈDRE.

This has gone on too long, this guile, this guilty
  heart.

OENONE.

What? tell me what remorse is tearing you apart?   70
What crime obsesses you, that no one understands?
Is there some guilty blood remaining on your hands?

PHÈDRE.

Thank god these hands are clean, they've nothing to
  repent.
I only wish my heart were just as innocent.

OENONE.

Then what appalling thing is still to happen here   75
and why does your poor heart still tremble in its
  fear?

PHÈDRE.

No, no I've told enough. The rest is best unsaid.
I die in silence, so my secret shall be dead.

OENONE.

Die then, and try to take your secret to the skies;
just find some other hand to close your sightless
  eyes.   80
Because although your life has almost run its course,
my soul shall be the first to seek its holy source.
So many hopeless roads go headlong to the dead,
and my own sorrow now shall choose the best
  deathbed.
Was I untrue to you about some vow I'd sworn?   85
Remember that these arms held you when you were
  born.
I gave up everything, my home, my family—
Is this the way you pay me for my loyalty?

PHÈDRE.

What can you hope to gain by using so much force?
If I spoke now, you would be frozen with
  remorse.   90

OENONE.

What evil could exceed what I already see?
—that you should try to die right here in front of me.

PHÈDRE.

If you knew my great guilt, what fate makes me
  ashamed,
I would still have to die, but I would die more
  blamed.

OENONE.

Madam, by all these tears that I've already shed,   95
by these knees I embrace, release me from this
  dread,
tell me what deadly doubts have seized you with
  such fear—

PHÈDRE.

It is your wish. Get up.

OENONE.

                    All right. Speak, I can hear.

PHÈDRE.

    God!—what am I to say, or where can I begin?   **100**

OENONE.

    I do not want to hear your fears that are within.

PHÈDRE.

    O Venus! Violence! O fatal rage and hate!
    My mother's love cast her in a distracted state!

OENONE.

    Forget such things, Madam, let all such memories
    keep in the secret peace of the eternities.   **105**

PHÈDRE.

    Ariadne, sister, O I remember you
    were left by those cold stones to die in silence too!

OENONE.

    Madam, why must you choose such hateful things to
        say
    about the blood that moves within your veins today?

PHÈDRE.

    Since it pleases Venus, this blood which is so
        base   **110**
    shall see the last of me and my unhappy race.

OENONE.

    Are you in love?

PHÈDRE.

                I feel that madness in my heart.

OENONE.

    Who is it?

PHÈDRE.

            Who it is, is the most shocking part.   **115**
    I love—(his fatal name makes me become undone)
    I love . . .

OENONE.

         Who?

PHÈDRE.

        —Do you know the Amazon's one son,
    That Prince whom I myself oppressed with hate and
        shame?   **120**

OENONE.

    Hippolyte? O god, god!

PHÈDRE.

         It's you who said his name.

OENONE.

    O god, how all my blood runs cold and turns to ice.
    O guilt! O great disgrace! O race of hidden vice!
    O joyless voyages, through such great storms and
        wars,   **125**
    what fortunes made us land on these tormented
        shores!

PHÈDRE.

    My illness goes far back. For I had hardly wed
    the son of Aegeus, and lain down on his bed,
    and tasted the sweet peace of our long reverie
    when Athens made me see my matchless enemy.   **130**
    I saw him, I was lost—I turned red, I turned pale;

disturbances occurred; I felt my feelings fail;
I could no longer see, I could no longer speak;
my body boiled and froze, then everything grew
    weak.
Great Venus can be seen in these few futile fires   **135**
with which she plagues my race with passionate
    desires.
With reverent strict vows I tried to turn aside:
I built a shrine for her, and tended it with pride;
my knife made sacrifice on beasts of every kind;
I searched through their insides to find my own
    lost mind.   **140**
This was weak treatment for my woeful hopeless
    love!
In vain I burned incense and watched it curl above:
When I prayed to the god, and said her sacred name,
I still loved Hippolyte; I saw him in the flame,
and at the altar where my prayers rose to
    the sky,   **145**
I worshipped someone I dared not identify.
I fled him everywhere—O sickness of despair;
Seeing his father's face, I even found him there!
At last I went to war against this lovely lord;
I persecuted him whom I was so drawn toward.   **150**
I banished this bad foe whom I admired so,
pretending some deep grief, insisting he should go,
I pressed for his exile, and my persistent cries
removed him from his home and from his father's
    eyes.
Then I could breathe, Oenone; once he had gone
    away   **155**
I felt freedom and peace with each new passing day.
Beside my husband now, and hiding my past pain,
I could confine myself to my own home again.
O useless cruel outcome! O destiny of men!
My husband brought me here to settle in
    Trézène—   **160**
once more I face this foe so fatal to my flesh;
my old wound opened wide, and my breast bled
    afresh.
This is no secret heat concealed within my veins;
this is great Venus now, who plagues me with these
    pains.
This guilt has made me ill, I loathe my waste of
    days,   **165**
it makes me hate my life and all its idle ways.
In dying now, at least I leave a noble name,
and I do not expose the full scope of my shame.
I could not bear to see your tears or hear your pleas,
so I told everything, with no apologies.   **170**
Now leave me to myself, because I choose to die,
and do not lecture me about my reasons why;
now all your foolish pleas to make me live must
    cease;
let me seek my release, and find my final peace.

SCENE FOUR: PHÈDRE, OENONE, PANOPE

PANOPE.
> How I would like to hide the sad news which I bring,
> Madam, and yet I know I must say everything.
> Death has been cruel to you, your husband has been killed;
> you are the last to know his greatness has been stilled.

OENONE.
> Panope, what did you say?   5

PANOPE.
>   That the poor Queen must learn
> she cannot pray to god for Theseus to return;
> because the sailing ships that brought this dreadful word
> have just told Hippolyte the news of what occurred.

PHÈDRE.
> God!   10

PANOPE.
> Athens splits itself, in choosing who shall rule,
> Some choose the Prince your son; but others play the fool,
> forgetting all the law and what the state has done,
> they reach beyond their rights and choose a foreign son.
> It's even rumored that a ruthless anarchy   15
> is working to restore the race of Aricie.
> This may be dangerous, I thought you ought to know.
> Already Hippolyte has made his plans to go;
> if he should appear there, there where the storm is loud,
> then he may be able to sway that coward crowd.   20

OENONE.
> Panope, that's quite enough. The Queen, having heard you,
> will not neglect this news, and your own point of view.

SCENE FIVE: PHÈDRE, OENONE

OENONE.
> Madam, I ceased to plead that you should live this through;
> I even could agree that I should die with you;
> I knew you would ignore all tears or talk of force;
> but now this dreadful news dictates a different course.
> Your fortune seems to change and wear a strange new face: 5
> the King is dead, Madam, so you must take his place.
> His death leaves you one son, you owe him everything—

> a slave if you should die; if you should live, a king.
> To what discerning friends could he turn with his fears?
> His ancestors would hear his innocent outcries,   10
> and they would shake with rage across the distant skies.
> O live!—you still possess the honor of your name.
> Your sordid flame becomes an ordinary flame.
> This passion is no crime, now Theseus has died,
> your guilt has gone away, the knots are all untied.   15
> Now Hippolyte is free and you can see him now,
> and you can let him come as close as you allow.
> Perhaps, because he thinks you are still filled with hate,
> he leads a faction now to overthrow the state.
> Make him see his mistake, help him to understand.   20
> He thinks he should be King, Trézène is his homeland.
> But he knows that the law gives your son all the forts,
> all Athens' worldly force, her ramparts and her ports.
> Now you both know you have a common enemy,
> and so you should unite to fight this Aricie.   25

PHÈDRE.
> Your words appeal to me: they please me, I agree.
> Yes, I will live: if life will flow back into me,
> and if my feelings for my son can lift my soul
> and fill me with new hope, I will again be whole.

END OF ACT ONE

ACT TWO
SCENE ONE: ARICIE, ISMÈNE

ARICIE.
> Hippolyte has told you that this is where he'll be?
> Hippolyte will come here to say goodbye to me?
> Ismène, can this be true?—no one is fooling you?

ISMÈNE.
> Now that Theseus has died, you will see much that's new.
> Prepare yourself, Madam, to find on every side   5
> so many friends of yours whom Theseus tried to hide.
> Now Aricie is strong, her freedom is complete,
> and soon all Greece will be kept captive at her feet.

ARICIE.
> Ismène, then these are not mere idle fantasies—
> I cease to be a slave and have no enemies?   10

ISMÈNE.
> From now on, all the fates are tame and will behave;
> and brave Theseus has joined your brothers in the grave.

ARICIE.

Have they said how he died, what led him to the
dead?

ISMÈNE.

Incredible accounts of it are being spread.
Some say that while defiled with infidelity,   15
this fine philanderer was swallowed by the sea.
And others also say, and you will hear them tell,
that with Pirithoüs, descending into hell,
he went to see Cocyte, and through that mood of
doom,
he showed his own live soul to dead men in the
gloom;   20
but he could not come back from that disgraceful
place,
for those were fatal steps which he could not retrace.

ARICIE.

Now how could any man, still filled with his life
breath,
be willing to set forth on the deep sleep of death?
What led him to explore that final finding out?   25

ISMÈNE.

Theseus is dead, Madam, there can be no more
doubt.
Athens is in a storm, Trézène in an uproar,
and all hail Hippolyte as King from shore to shore.
Phèdre is in this palace, and trembling for her son,
seeks counsel from her friends and pleads with
everyone.   30

ARICIE.

Do you think Hippolyte will have more love for me
than his own father had, who gave me slavery?
Will he ease my distress?

ISMÈNE.

                    Madam, I know he will.

ARICIE.

This listless Hippolyte may turn against me still.   35
How can you dare to say he pities and adores
in me, and me alone, a sex which he ignores?
You know that for some time he has avoided me;
he always finds a place where we will never be.

ISMÈNE.

I know the things they say, that Hippolyte
is cold—   40
but coming close to you, he was a bit more bold;
I watched him all the while, I tried to find his pride,
and it occurred to me that everyone had lied.
No, he is not so cold as he has been accused:
when you first looked at him, he seemed to be
confused.   45
He turned his eyes aside to leave your lovely glance,
but they still gazed at you and he was in a trance.
That he should be in love may seem to him absurd;
yet it is in his eyes, if not in his own word.

ARICIE.

I listen, dear Ismène, my heart in all its youth   50
devours what you say, although there's not much
truth!
You who are dear to me, you know my great
distress:
my heart has only known my own soul's loneliness,
I who have been the toy of accident and chance,
how can I know the joy, the folly of romance?   55
The daughter of a King from this great ancient shore,
I only have survived the tragedies of war.
I lost six brothers who were strong and brave and
free,
the hope and flower of a famous family!
The sword tore all of them, the earth was wet with
red,   60
Erectheus was dead when all these sons had bled.
You know that since their death, there was a stern
decree
forbidding any Greek to fall in love with me:
the flame of my desire might kindle in my womb,
and one day light a fire within my brother's tomb.   65
Besides, you ought to know with what a haughty
frown
I viewed this conqueror and what he had set down.
For I had hated love through my disdainful days,
and so I thanked Theseus, and even gave him praise
for making me obey the vows I had begun.   70
But then I had not seen this fearless hero's son.
Not that my eyes alone were held by his fair face,
and made to dwell upon his celebrated grace—
those gifts which nature gives, which anyone would
prize,
he seems to set aside, as something to despise.   75
I love and value him for what makes him unique:
his father's deeds, and not the ways that he was
weak:
I love, and I admire the scope of his high pride,
which never yet was tamed, has never yet been tied.
How Phèdre was taken in by Theseus and his
sighs!   80
I have more self-respect, and my affection flies
from all these easy vows passed out to everyone:
such offers leave me cold, they're something that I
shun.
To teach humility to the inflexible,
to speak of suffering to the insensible,   85
to chain a prisoner with claims that I would make,
which he could strain against, but never really
break—
that is what I desire, that will make me complete;
and yet strong Hercules fought less than Hippolyte;
subdued more often, and seduced more easily,   90
he gave less glory to each lover he would see.

But dear Ismène, alas!—what awful things I dare!
I will come up against more force than I can bear.
Perhaps you may hear me, humble in my despair,
groan under that high pride which now I think so
    fair.   95
Hippolyte fall in love?—how could my hope or fear
affect him in the least . . .

ISMÈNE.
                        Now you yourself shall hear:
for here he comes.

SCENE TWO: HIPPOLYTE, ARICIE, ISMÈNE

HIPPOLYTE.
                        Madam, before I go away,
I have some things to say about your fate today.
My father has just died. My fears which were so
    strong
told me the reason why he had been gone so long.
For death, and death alone, could end his splendid
    deeds   5
and hide from all the world the life a hero leads.
The Fates in their great greed have taken from our
    side
this friend of Hercules who shared the same high
    pride.
I think your hatred may ignore his few defects
and grant his memory these fitting last respects.   10
One hope has opened up and pleased me in my grief:
I can release your soul and give you some relief.
I can revoke the laws that made you suffer so.
Now you can start to live, your heart is yours to
    know.
And here in this Trézène, which I come to control 15
just as old Pittheus, ancestor of my soul;
which calls for a new King, and recognizes me—
I now proclaim you free and give you liberty.

ARICIE.
This is immoderate, your Highness is too kind,
such generosity is madness to my mind;   20
my Lord, it binds me more to all the stern decrees
which you would cast away in an attempt to please.

HIPPOLYTE.
In choosing who shall rule, Athens becomes undone,
speak first of you, then me, and then the Queen's one
    son.

ARICIE.
Of me, my Lord?   25

HIPPOLYTE.
                    I know, no honor to my name,
an ancient famous law seems to reject my claim.
Greece is displeased with me for my strange foreign
    birth.
But if I could compete against my brother's worth,

Madam, I know so well that my rights would win
    out,   30
that I would be made Greek and King without a
    doubt.
But there are strong restraints which make me rest
    my case.
I therefore say to you: this is your proper place,
your sceptre is the one your ancestors received
from that first son of earth so secretly conceived. 35
They say that Aegeus once held it in his hands.
Athens was satisfied in all of its demands
by my own father, who was hailed as its own King,
and your six brothers were deprived of everything.
But Athens calls you now to come within
    her walls.   40
There have been groans enough from all these
    hopeless brawls;
there has been blood enough to soak the open fields
and drown the fertile earth with all the life it yields.
Trézène will obey me. The countryside of Crete
will give the son of Phèdre a sumptuous retreat.   45
You will take Attica. Now I must go at last
and try to reunite the votes which will be cast.

ARICIE.
Astonished and confused by all that I have heard,
I have a secret fear that this is all absurd.
Now am I wide awake, or should I trust this
    dream?   50
What gracious god, my Lord, made you adopt this
    scheme?
How wonderful it is all places know your name!
and how the truth itself exceeds all praise and fame!
Would you betray yourself, like this, all for my
    sake?
Not hating me may be the greatest gift you make,   55
and having kept yourself in everything you do
from this hostility . . .

HIPPOLYTE.
                        Madam, could I hate you?
No matter what they say or how they paint my pride,
do they suppose some beast once carried me
    inside?   60
What mind that is unkind, what heart that may be
    hard,
in viewing you, would not grow soft in its regard?
Could any man resist the charm of what you
    are? . . .

ARICIE.
What? My Lord.

HIPPOLYTE.
                    But I know, now I have gone too far. 65
Reason, I see, gives way to feelings that are real.
I have already said more than I should reveal,
Madam, so I go on: I must inform you of

something which my own heart keeps secret in its
   love.
You see before you here a wretched restless
   Prince,   **70**
epitome of pride too headstrong to convince.
I who fought love and thought my attitude was right;
who laughed at its captives and ridiculed their plight;
who scorned the worst shipwrecks, the first one to
   deplore
the storms of mortals which I witnessed from the
   shore;   **75**
now I have been bowed down to know the common
   lot,
how I have been estranged and changed to what I'm
   not!
One instant has destroyed my childish arrogance:
this soul which was so bold now yields to
   circumstance.
For almost six long months, so hopeless and
   alone,   **80**
and bearing everywhere this torture I have known;
divided in desires, I don't know what to do:
with you, I try to fly; alone, I long for you;
far off in the forest, your image follows me;
the brilliance of the day, the night's obscurity,   **85**
all show me the sly charm which my high pride
   ignores;
all render Hippolyte a prisoner of yours.
Now through this mad pursuit, I've lost my self-
   control,
so I no longer know the scope of my own soul.
I've lost my javelins, my chariot, my bow;   **90**
I've lost Neptune's lessons which I learned long ago;
the woods no longer hear loud shouts as I rejoice,
and my horses ignore the sound of my own voice.
Perhaps the telling of a love so wild and free
might make you blush to see what you have done to
   me.   **95**
What foolish things to say from such a captive heart!
And what a sick victim of all your lovely art!
But you should see in me that which is very dear.
Imagine that I speak another language here;
do not reject my love for its vague awkward
   vow,   **100**
for I have never tried to say this until now.

SCENE THREE: HIPPOLYTE, ARICIE, THÉRAMÈNE, ISMÈNE

THÉRAMÈNE.
   My Lord, the Queen comes here, and I have come
      before.
   She looks for you.
HIPPOLYTE.
            For me?

THÉRAMÈNE.
           My Lord, I know no more.
   But I have just been sent to make sure that you
      stay.   **5**
   Phèdre wants to speak to you before you go away.
HIPPOLYTE.
   Phèdre?—But what can I say?—And what can she
      expect . . .
ARICIE.
   My Lord, you can't refuse, you owe her this respect.
   Although you know too well her old hostility,
   her tears require you to show some sympathy.   **10**
HIPPOLYTE.
   And so you go away. And now I do not know
   if I've offended you whom I admire so!
   I wonder if this heart which I leave in your
      hands . . .
ARICIE.
   Go, Prince, and carry out your generous demands.
   Arrange that Athens be subject to my decree.   **15**
   For I accept these things which you bestow on me.
   But this impressive state, although it is so great,
   is not the gift you give which I praise with most
      weight.

SCENE FOUR: HIPPOLYTE, THÉRAMÈNE

HIPPOLYTE.
   Are we all ready now?—But see, the Queen draws
      near.
   Go now, prepare the way, and gather all our gear.
   Set down the plans, the course, the orders, and then
      come
   to free me from this talk which will be tedium.

SCENE FIVE: PHÈDRE, HIPPOLYTE, OENONE

PHÈDRE.
   There he is. My bad blood refuses to obey.
   Seeing him, I forget what I have come to say.
OENONE.
   Remember that your son depends on you today.
PHÈDRE.
   They say your plans are made, and you are on your
      way.
   To all your miseries I offer you my tears.   **5**
   And I have come to you to speak about my fears.
   My son is fatherless; and I can prophesy
   that he shall see the day when I myself must die.
   A thousand enemies attack this child of mine.
   Now you and you alone can keep them all in line.   **10**
   And yet a new remorse has come before my eyes:
   I fear I may have closed your ears against his cries.
   I tremble when I think he may receive your hate,
   because I am the one you choose to desecrate.

HIPPOLYTE.

> Madam, I am not base, I could not cause such
>   pain.   **15**

PHÈDRE.

> If you detested me, then I would not complain,
> my Lord. I know you know I tried to injure you;
> but what was in my heart, my Lord, you never knew.
> I took enormous care to make your hatred great.
> I could not let you live so close to my estate.   **20**
> Aloud and secretly, I was so proud I swore
> that I would have you sent to some far distant shore.
> I went on to forbid, by an express decree,
> that anyone should speak your name in front of me.
> Yet weigh my crime against the pain that is
>   my fate,   **25**
> and say that my own hate has only caused your hate;
> no woman in this world deserves your pity more,
> no woman whom you have less reason to abhor.

HIPPOLYTE.

> A mother's jealousy may make her rarely fair
> to some adopted son who comes into her care.   **30**
> Madam, I know this well. Curses which disparage
> are the common outcome of a second marriage.
> All mothers would scorn me, and find things to
>   deplore;
> perhaps they would have tried to make me suffer
>   more.

PHÈDRE.

> Ah! My Lord, believe me, that this is not the
>   case!   **35**
> I do not fit that law which rules the human race!
> A very different care consumes me through and
>   through!

HIPPOLYTE.

> Madam, I see no need for this to trouble you.
> Perhaps your husband still bathes in the light of day;
> we weep for his return, and heaven may obey.   **40**
> My father has a god who guards him everywhere;
> Neptune will not ignore my father's fervent prayer.

PHÈDRE.

> One only journeys once to that land of the dead,
> my Lord. Since Theseus has been already led
> to see those dismal shores, no god restores him
>   now—   **45**
> no freedom or release will Acheron allow.
> But still, he is not dead, because he breathes in you.
> Always before my eyes, my husband lives anew.
> I see him, speak to him; and my heart . . . O my
>   Lord,
> I'm mad, my tortured mind shows its perverse
>   discord.   **50**

HIPPOLYTE.

> I see the power now of love that never dies.
> Theseus may be dead, yet he lives in your eyes;
> I seem to see his face irradiating you.

PHÈDRE.

> I long for Theseus, yes, Prince, that much is true.
> I love him, not the way the shades of Hades must,   **55**
> the driven libertine who lives for his own lust,
> who may be making love right now in dead men's
>   beds;
> but rather faithful, proud, the haughtiest of heads,
> so charming and so young, who won all hearts
>   somehow,
> a portrait by a god—or as I see you now.   **60**
> He had your poise, your gaze, your manner and your
>   grace,
> a gentle tender smile that lighted his whole face,
> when he first sailed the sea, without the least conceit,
> receiving the sweet vows of the fair maids of Crete.
> What were you doing then? Where were you,
>   Hippolyte?   **65**
> Why were you not among the famous Greek elite?
> Why were you still too young to join these
>   conquerors
> who came on their swift ships to land on our far
>   shores?
> Seeing the Cretan beast, you could have gained great
>   praise,
> by slaying him within his labyrinthine maze.   **70**
> And so that you would know which way you should
>   be led,
> my sister would have come and made you take the
>   thread.
> No, wait—I would be there, and well ahead of her,
> the love inside of me would be the first to stir.
> Prince, I would be the one to help you learn the
>   ways   **75**
> of staying safe and so escaping from the maze.
> I would have taken pains to hasten your return!
> A thread is not enough to show you my concern.
> I'm sure that it would be a peril I could share,
> and I myself could walk ahead of you through
>   there;   **80**
> so Phèdre would go with you through that great
>   vacant void,
> would have emerged with you, or with you been
>   destroyed.

HIPPOLYTE.

> Gods!—what words have I heard?—Madam, recall
>   your vow:
> Theseus, my father, is your lord and husband now.

PHÈDRE.

> My Lord, what makes you say I've placed this out of
>   mind?   **85**
> or do I need to have my dignity defined?

HIPPOLYTE.

> Madam, please forgive me. See how my face turns
>   red,

for I misunderstood exactly what you said.
My shame cannot stand here and let you look at me;
I go . . .   90
PHÈDRE.
                    You understood too well. O cruelty!
I must have said enough to make it all quite clear.
Well then, prepare to see Phèdre in her fury here.
I am in love. And yet, seeing this sentiment,
do not believe I think that I am innocent,   95
or that the passion which is poisoning my mind
has been encouraged by complacence of some kind.
I am the sick victim of the spite of the skies;
I mightily despise myself in my own eyes.
The gods are my witness, the same great gods who
    lit   100
a fire in my blood and then kept fanning it;
these gods who take delight in their deceit and seek
to seduce and undo a woman who is weak.
Now you yourself know well what happened in the
    past:
I chased you from this place and made you an
    outcast.   105
I tried to show myself so odious to you,
by being hateful and inhuman in your view.
What good was this great war I waged without
    success?
You hated me much more, I did not love you less.
Your sadness gave your face a charm beyond your
    years.   110
I languished, I burned up, in fire and in tears.
Your eyes could witness to the truth of what I say,
if you could lift them up and make them look my
    way.
What am I saying now?—have I become so ill
I could make such a vow, and of my own
    free will?   115
I fear for my one son, I must protect this child,
and so I had begun to ask you to be mild.
The feeble weakness of a heart too full to speak!
Alas, for it is you and you alone I seek.
Revenge yourself, my Lord, on my disgraceful
    shame.   120
Son of a hero who first gave you your own name,
here is your chance to kill another beast of Crete:
the wife of Theseus dares to love Hippolyte!
This terrible monster should not escape you now.
Here is my heart, right here, it's waiting for your
    blow.   125
It is impatient now to pay for its foul lust,
it feels your hand reach out and make the fatal
    thrust.
So strike. Or if you think your hatred should abstain
from granting me at least this last sweet peaceful
    pain,

or if you think my blood would soil your hand, my
    Lord,   130
then do not make a move, yet let me have your
    sword.
Now.
OENONE.
                    What is this, Madam? By all gods far and near!
But someone comes. Quickly, you must not be found
    here;
come, let us leave this place of so much shame and
    dread.   135

SCENE SIX: HIPPOLYTE, THÉRAMÈNE

THÉRAMÈNE.
    Is Phèdre fleeing from us, or is she being led?
    And what are all these signs of suffering, my Lord?
    Why do you stand here with no color, speech or
        sword?
HIPPOLYTE.
    We must fly, Théramène. I feel such wild surprise,
    I find that I despise myself in my own eyes.   5
    Phèdre . . . No, by all the gods!—Let this deep
        secret be
    kept hidden in the dark through all eternity.
THÉRAMÈNE.
    If you are going to go, the ship is in the port.
    My Lord, before you board, listen to this report:
    Athens has made her choice, the voices all avow   10
    your brother is the one. Phèdre has full power now.
HIPPOLYTE.
    Phèdre?
THÉRAMÈNE.
                    An Athenian is coming with a scroll
    to put into her hands, which gives complete control.
    Her son is King, my Lord.   15
HIPPOLYTE.
                    You who look down on us,
    is she so virtuous that you reward her thus?
THÉRAMÈNE.
    However, now they say the King is still alive,
    that he is in Épire, is well and seems to thrive.
    But I have sought him there, my Lord, and I know
        well . . .   20
HIPPOLYTE.
    We must investigate whatever people tell.
    Let us look into this, and trace it to its source:
    if it should prove untrue, I will pursue my course,
    and we will go; and so no matter what it takes,
    we'll choose the ruler who is best for all
        our sakes.   25

END OF ACT TWO

ACT THREE

SCENE ONE: PHÈDRE, OENONE

PHÈDRE.
I wish that they would take this fame and praise
   away!
Now how can you make me see anyone today?
What have you come to say to comfort my despair?
I spoke my secret mind, and I should hide
   somewhere.
My passions all broke out more than I meant to
   show.   5
I have already said what no one else should know.
God, how he listened so!—and how he seemed to be
distracted and obtuse, misunderstanding me!
And how he tried to find some safe way to escape!
His blushing bothered me and made my shame take
   shape!   10
Why did you keep me from my fatal last request?
Alas! when his great sword was resting on my
   breast,
did he grow pale for me?—or snatch it from my
   grasp?
No, no, it was enough for my proud hand to clasp
the handle, and I made that instrument abhorred   15
forever in the eyes of this inhuman Lord.

OENONE.
Your own misfortunes soar and cause you to
   complain,
you feed a fire which you must put out again.
Would it not be discreet and wise as Minos was,
to have much nobler cares than your self-pity
   does?   20
Instead of mourning for this wretch who flies his
   fate,
be Queen, and concentrate on the affairs of State.

PHÈDRE.
Be Queen!—and make the State come under my
   strong rule,
when I myself stand here, a weak and lawless fool!
When I have lost control of the whole world of
   sense!   25
When I can hardly breathe, my shame is so intense!
When I am dying.

OENONE.
         Fly.

PHÈDRE.
            I cannot turn and run.

OENONE.
You dared to banish him, whom now you dare not
   shun.   30

PHÈDRE.
There's no more time for that. He knows my lust at
   last.

All thoughts of modesty and patient tact are past.
I have declared my guilt to this proud hero's eyes;
hope stole into my heart, I could not hold my sighs.
And it was you yourself, ignoring my complaint,   35
reviving my poor life when I was growing faint.
With flattery and guile, who told me your grand
   plan:
you made me seem to see that I could love this man.

OENONE.
Alas!—these pains are not something I could
   contrive,
and what would I not do to make you stay alive?   40
If insults have hurt you, and made you try to hide,
could you forget the scorn of such a haughty pride?
With cruel and stubborn eyes, his obstinate conceit
watched as you almost fell and lay there at his feet!
How his great vanity made me hate him again!   45
If only you had seen, as I could see him then!

PHÈDRE.
Oenone, he could subdue this pride that bothers you.
His ways are just as wild as those woods where he
   grew.
This Hippolyte is rude and savage in his prime,
and now he heard of love perhaps for the first
   time.   50
Perhaps his great surprise gives rise to his silence,
and our complaints perhaps have too much violence.

OENONE.
Remember he was formed and born from a strange
   womb.

PHÈDRE.
That Scythian knew well how true love could
   consume.

OENONE.
He has a fatal hate which sets our sex apart.   55

PHÈDRE.
Then I shall never see a rival in his heart.
But all of your advice is overdue and blind.
Now serve my love, Oenone, and never mind my
   mind.
This man opposes love because his heart is hard:
we must find some new way to gain his kind
   regard.   60
At least the lure of rule appealed to his high pride;
Athens attracted him, that much he could not hide;
already all his ships are turned towards that great
   State,
the sails are in the wind, the men can hardly wait.
Find this ambitious youth whose heart is in
   the skies,   65
Oenone; and make the crown shine brightly in his
   eyes.
The sacred diadem is his possession now;
I only ask that I might place it on his brow.

Give him the power now which is not in my hands.
He will instruct my son in how to give
   commands;   70
perhaps he may consent to play the father's role.
The mother and the son are placed in his control.
Use every trick you know to move him to my view:
your words will do more good than mine could ever
   do.
So plead and weep for me; say Phèdre grows weak
   and dies;   75
and do not be ashamed of begging with your cries.
You can do anything; I send my hopes with you.
So go: I will wait here to learn what I must do.

SCENE TWO: PHÈDRE (ALONE)

PHÈDRE.
O being who can see the shame of my rebuff,
implacable Venus, am I not low enough?
But you should not prolong this useless cruelty.
My downfall is complete; for you have wounded me.
Now if you truly choose your glory should be
   known,   5
attack another heart more stubborn than my own.
This Hippolyte flees you; defying your decrees,
he never sees your shrine nor kneels down on his
   knees.
He has a pride of mind your name cannot assuage.
Goddess, avenge yourself: we share the same
   outrage!   10
Let him love—Here you are, you have come back to
   me,
Oenone?—Then he hates me; he would not hear your
   plea.

SCENE THREE: PHÈDRE, OENONE

OENONE.
Put out of mind this lust, this love that must not be,
Madam. Instead, recall your virtue instantly.
The King they said was dead is very much alive;
they know Theseus is here for they saw him arrive.
So now they rush and run to see his famous face.   5
I searched for Hippolyte in almost every place,
but then a thousand cries went flying to the
   skies . . .
PHÈDRE.
My husband lives, Oenone, give me no more replies.
I have already sworn a love he must abhor.
He lives: that is enough, now I must know
   no more.   10
OENONE.
What?

PHÈDRE.
        I predicted this; but you preferred to doubt.
My own remorse was weak, and your weeping won
   out.
If I had only died this morning, all would mourn;
but I took your advice, so I must die forlorn.   15
OENONE.
You are dying?
PHÈDRE.
        My god! What did I do today?
My husband and his son already on their way!
—this witness who has seen all my deceitful charms
will watch my features greet his father to
   my arms,   20
my heart still filled with sighs which he would not
   accept,
my eyes still wet with tears which he could not
   respect.
To keep the self-respect of Theseus clean and free,
will he now try to hide this love inside of me?
Will he let me betray his father and his King?   25
Can he contain his rage at this dishonoring?
No, he could not be still. Besides, I know my crime,
Oenone, but I have not grown hard in my lifetime,
like some who even seem to take delight in blame,
who wear a smiling face and never blush with
   shame.   30
I know my madness now, I can recall it all.
I feel the ceiling sees, and each great vacant wall
awaits my husband's face, and when Theseus
   appears,
they will speak my disgrace to his astonished ears.
O let me die, let death deliver me instead.   35
I wonder can it be so dreadful to be dead?
Death is not terrible to those in misery.
I only fear the name which I leave after me.
My wretched children shall inherit this chagrin!
The blood of Jupiter should help them to begin;   40
and yet despite their pride in such a great estate,
a mother's wickedness can be a hateful weight.
I fear that they shall hear, alas! the fatal truth,
their mother had such shame when they were in their
   youth.
I fear in later years, when this guilt multiplies,   45
that neither one of them will dare to lift his eyes.
OENONE.
Believe me, I agree, their future makes me grieve;
I feel you are quite right to fear what you perceive.
But why expose them to such terrible insults?
And why accuse yourself of such grotesque
   results?   50
That's that: for they will say that Phèdre, so filled
   with shame,

is racing to escape her husband's rage and blame.
And Hippolyte is glad to see the end of you,
for by your dying you support his point of view.
Now how could I reply to these things he
    accused? 55
Before him I would be too easily confused.
Then I would have to see this Hippolyte rejoice
and tell your tale to all with ears to hear his voice.
I wish I were struck by some fire from the sky!
Now do not lie to me, does he still make
    you sigh? 60
How do you see this Prince, so boastful, so upright?

PHÈDRE.
    I see him as a beast, made frightful to my sight.

OENONE.
    Then why should he achieve an easy victory?
You fear him. Then strike first, and have the bravery
to say he did this crime which he may lay to you. 65
For who will disagree, and claim it is not true?
How fortunate his sword is left here in your hands!
All know your present woe, and each man
    understands
his father heard your words whenever you
    complained,
and it was due to you his exile was obtained. 70

PHÈDRE.
    How can I injure one so innocent of sin?

OENONE.
    My purpose only needs your silence to begin.
I tremble as you do, and I feel some remorse.
To die a thousand times would be a better course.
But I lose you unless you let me have my way, 75
and your life is to me worth more than I can say.
I will speak out. Theseus, when my fierce tale is
    done,
will limit his revenge to banishing his son.
A father, in great rage, still has a father's mind:
and a light punishment is all that he will find. 80
But if in spite of all some guiltless blood must spill,
why should your honor put such things beyond your
    will?
For your integrity should not be thrown away,
and it has certain laws you know you must obey,
Madam; and so to save your threatened honor,
    you 85
must give up everything, perhaps your virtue too.
Who's there?—I see Theseus.

PHÈDRE.
                Ah!—I see Hippolyte;
in his cruel eyes I see my downfall is complete.
Do what you want with me, my heart is torn and
    sore. 90
The way things are right now, I can do nothing
    more.

SCENE FOUR: THESEUS, HIPPOLYTE, PHÈDRE, OENONE, THÉRAMÈNE

THESEUS.
    I am no longer torn by the strong force of fate,
Madam, and to your arms I . . .

PHÈDRE.
                Theseus, you must wait,
do not profane your name by saying anything,
for I do not deserve these greetings that you bring. 5
You are greatly disgraced. Fate labored to debase
your helpless wife while you were absent from this
    place.
Unworthy of your words, and of your fine high
    pride,
from now on I must find the safest way to hide.

SCENE FIVE: THESEUS, HIPPOLYTE, THÉRAMÈNE

THESEUS.
    Why this excitement now at the mere sight of me,
    my son?

HIPPOLYTE.
             Phèdre is the one to solve this mystery.
Yet if my earnest wish can move your brave heart,
    then
let me, my Lord, depart and not see her again.
Your son is so upset that he must disappear 5
from any place your wife decides she may come
    near.

THESEUS.
    My son, you're going to go?

HIPPOLYTE.
               I did not search for her:
you were the one who made her coming here
    occur.
When you had left Trézène, my Lord, by your
    decree, 10
you also chose to leave the Queen and Aricie.
I took good care of them according to my vow.
But what care makes me stay behind in this place
    now?
Far in the forests, I have wasted each new day
by chasing frightened game and slaying my small
    prey. 15
Why can't I fly from this great laziness I'm in,
and find genuine blood to stain my javelin?
When you were in your youth, and not yet my own
    age,
strange beasts were beaten down by your enormous
    rage,
and tyrants felt the crush of your tremendous
    blow; 20
the innocent were safe, the insolent brought low;

you made peace on the sea, protecting all our shores.
Travelers did not fear unnecessary wars;
and Hercules, who heard the ordeals you went
    through,
could lay his labors down and rest because of you. 25
And I, the unknown son who sees my father's fame,
I even envy now my mother's honored name.
Allow my courage now to be put to good use.
If some beast escaped you and is still on the loose,
then let me try to set its corpse before your feet;   **30**
or if I have to die, then let my death be sweet,
so everyone will praise my days so bravely done,
and weigh my famous name, and say I was your son.

THESEUS.
What madness greets my face?—what horror fills
    this place
and makes my family fly off in such disgrace?   **35**
If I come back so feared, so little needed here,
gods, why did you help me and make me persevere?
I only had one friend. Desires plagued his life,
he labored in Épire to take the tyrant's wife;
I helped him to attain this passion of his mind;   **40**
but an outrageous fate dazed us and made us blind.
The tyrant stepped aside and took me by surprise.
I saw Pirithoüs destroyed before my eyes
thrown down and torn apart and eaten by strange
    beasts
who feed on human flesh in their atrocious feasts.   **45**
I was shut far away in dark abysmal caves,
a deep and dismal place, and underneath all graves.
Then after six long months the gods came back to
    me:
and so I could escape by my own subtlety.
The tyrant tried to fight, and when I slaughtered
    him   **50**
his beasts fell on his corpse and tore it limb from
    limb.
So when with joy I thought at last I could come near
the gift of all the gods that is to me most dear;—
what can I say?—when I myself return all right,
and eagerly expect to satisfy my sight,   **55**
my only welcome is a trembling everywhere:
all fly, and all refuse the greetings that I bear.
And I, filled with the fear my coming here has
    brought,
wish I were still kept in the cave where I was
    caught.
Speak to me. Phèdre has said that I have been
    disgraced.   **60**
Who betrayed me?—Why has the traitor not been
    traced?
Would Greece, whom I have saved and served with
    my brave toil,
protect the guilty one on her own sacred soil?

But you do not reply. Then could my own son be
collaborating with his father's enemy?   **65**
My mind is overwhelmed with doubt: I must find out
the criminal and what the crime is all about.
So Phèdre will have to say what has been troubling
    her.

SCENE SIX: HIPPOLYTE, THÉRAMÈNE

HIPPOLYTE.
Why does my blood run dry and make my senses
    blur?
Is Phèdre now giving in to all her inner strife?
Will she accuse herself and lose her right to life?
Gods!—what will the King say?—What fatal hate
    has love
spread over all our heads, that we are dying of?   **5**
And I, fed by a fire which he cannot allow,—
think how he saw me once, and how he sees me
    now!
Forebodings fill the air and terrify me here.
But then, the innocent should have no cause to fear
So let us go, and find some way to state my case   **10**
and make my father say that I am in his grace,
because although he may despise this love today,
no power in the world can make it go away.

END OF ACT THREE

ACT FOUR
SCENE ONE: THESEUS, OENONE

THESEUS.
How can I hear these things? What traitor could
    betray
his father's famous name in this disgraceful way?
The pain of my great fate keeps on pursuing me!
I don't know where I am or where I ought to be.
O all my tenderness so callously paid back!   **5**
The bald audacity of such a bad attack!
In order to achieve his evil intercourse,
this proud insolent Prince resorted to cruel force.
That was his weapon there, I recognized his sword:
he swore brave deeds the day I gave it to this
    Lord.   **10**
Didn't our common blood give him the least
    restraint?
And why did Phèdre delay in voicing her complaint?
Or did her silence try to hide the guilty one?

OENONE.
Her silence tried to hide that you had been undone.
Ashamed that she should be the cause of all
    his sighs   **15**
and of the lawless fire that kindles in his eyes,

Phèdre would have lied, my Lord, and killed herself
    outright,
so closing both her eyes, extinguishing the light.
I saw her raise her arm, and I ran to her side;
I made her save her life for love of your high
    pride.   **20**
Now pitying your shock and her disturbing fears,
I have, despite my vows, interpreted her tears.

THESEUS.

Dishonesty!—I see why he became so pale,
and when we met again, his feelings had to fail.
I was astonished at his lack of happiness;   **25**
his cold embraces stole and froze my tenderness.
But how long has his love so hideously grown?
When he was in Athens was it already known?

OENONE.

My Lord, remember how the Queen complained to
    you.
It was this shameful love, which she already
    knew.   **30**

THESEUS.

This love began again once back here in Trézène?

OENONE.

I've told you everything, my Lord, that happened
    then.
But I have left the Queen alone in her distress;
let me go now and see to her uneasiness.

SCENE TWO: THESEUS, HIPPOLYTE

THESEUS.

Ah, here he is. Good god! Seeing his noble air,
what naive eye would not make the same error there?
Why must the forehead of profane adultery
shine with the sacred grace of virtue's simile?
Are there no secret signs, is there no special art   **5**
to know, with no mistake, a false dishonest heart?

HIPPOLYTE.

Now let me ask of you what hideous disgrace,
my Lord, is on your mind and showing in your face?
Will you not dare to speak this great shame to my
    ear?

THESEUS.

Traitor and slave!—how dare you stand before me
    here?   **10**
Sky's brightest lightning bolt should throw you to
    the void,
almost the last outlaw of those I have destroyed!
After this ugly lust had come into your head
and led you to defame your father's wedding bed,
you still present yourself, and show your hated
    face,   **15**
and so parade your shame throughout this fatal
    place,
and do not go away, under some foreign sun,

where my own name may be unknown to everyone.
Fly, traitor!—do not try to brave my hatred now,
so go, while my great rage is kept inside
    somehow.   **20**
It is enough for me to bear my own despair
for having brought you forth into the living air,
without your death as well dishonoring my name
and spoiling endlessly the splendor of my fame.
Fly; if you do not wish a swift and fatal blow   **25**
to add you to the beasts that I myself brought low,
make sure that that bright sun which shines up in the
    sky
will never see you breathe beneath its flaming eye.
Fly, I say, forever, now never come back here,
do not let your foul face infect our atmosphere.   **30**
And you, Neptune, yes, you: if I was ever brave,
if I have ever raged against the slaves that rave,
remember my reward, your promise to obey
whatever I would ask, whatever I would pray.
In the cruel agonies of a crude prison cell,   **35**
I did not cry for help to free me from that hell.
I held myself in check, I waited in my greed,
until some later day saw some much greater need.
But I implore you now. Revenge a father's heart.
I leave this traitor's life for you to tear apart;   **40**
stifle his filthy vice in his own blood and lust:
I will worship your worth if you do what you must.

HIPPOLYTE.

So Phèdre says Hippolyte is guilty of such shame!
Such excellent excess of horror shakes my frame;
so many sudden blows must overthrow me now,   **45**
they take away my voice and make me dumb
    somehow.

THESEUS.

Traitor, you may have thought that by your keeping
    still
poor Phèdre would try to hide your insults and ill
    will?
You made one great mistake, just now when you
    withdrew,
to take away the sword which now accuses you;   **50**
or rather, you forgot to make your deed complete,
and take away her life to cover your retreat.

HIPPOLYTE.

Now irritated by so foul and black a lie,
I feel I should reveal the truth in my reply,
my Lord, yet I suppress something which touches
    you.   **55**
You should approve my tact, my duty to subdue;
without the slightest wish of stirring up more strife,
remember who I am, and look through my whole life.
Always, some minor sins precede great major
    crimes.
Whoever breaks the law at first for a few times,   **60**

will finally go on to break all sacred rights;
for crime has its degrees, it has its depths and
    heights;
thus one has never seen timidity grow strong
and leap to the extreme of evil and vile wrong.
More than a single day is needed to create   **65**
a monster capable of incest, sin and hate.
Brought up in the chaste gaze of a great heroine,
I never scorned the pride of my own origin.
Old Pittheus, esteemed by all men everywhere,
agreed to teach me when I left my mother's care. **70**
I do not seek to see myself in some great light,
but if I have revealed my worth, however slight,
my Lord, above all things I think I have made clear
my hatred for those crimes I am accused of here.
And Hippolyte is known for this in all of Greece. **75**
My virtue hurts, and yet I work for its increase.
All know I suffer from so strict and harsh an art.
The light of day is not so pure as my own heart.
Yet they say Hippolyte, obsessed with a strange
    flame . . .

THESEUS.
    This is the same high pride that damns you to your
      shame.   **80**
    I see what evil hides behind your cold disguise:
    for only Phèdre alone could charm your brazen eyes;
    and for all other loves your sly and lifeless soul
    would never once catch fire, but kept its self-control.

HIPPOLYTE.
    No, my father, this heart—it's too much to
      conceal—   **85**
    has not refused a love for someone chaste and real.
    Here at your feet I make my great apology:
    I love; I love, it's true, what you forbid to me.
    For I love Aricie: it is already done;
    the daughter of Pallas has overcome your son.   **90**
    I worship her, and I, defying all your laws,
    am lost in my own sighs, of which she is the cause.

THESEUS.
    You love her? God! But no, this trick is to distract:
    act like a criminal to cover up your act.

HIPPOLYTE.
    My Lord, for six long months, I fought this love for
      her.   **95**
    I came here trembling now to tell you this news, sir.
    But how? Can anything erase this great mistake?
    Could any oath I take persuade you for my sake?
    "By this earth, by this sky, by nature all in
      all . . ."

THESEUS.
    Always, false hypocrites perjure their own
      downfall.   **100**
    No, do not bore me now with more of your fine lies,
    if your dishonesty can find no new disguise.

HIPPOLYTE.
    You think all this is false and full of subtlety.
    But Phèdre in her own heart is much more fair to
      me.

THESEUS.
    Ah! how your impudence makes me more angry
      now!   **105**

HIPPOLYTE.
    Where will I be exiled, and how long is your vow?

THESEUS.
    Far beyond the Pillars of Hercules would be
    not far enough, and much too near the heart of me.

HIPPOLYTE.
    Charged with this awful crime, this foul atrocity,
    what friends will pity me, when you abandon
      me?   **110**

THESEUS.
    Go and invent new friends, whose own dishonesty
    congratulates incest, applauds adultery—
    outlaws without conscience, traitors who know no
      law,
    able to care for you and share your brazen flaw.

HIPPOLYTE.
    You keep on speaking of incest, adultery?   **115**
    I do not speak. But Phèdre comes from her family—
    her mother's blood, my Lord, you know it very well,
    is worse than mine, and filled with all the filth of
      hell.

THESEUS.
    What?—have you lost all sense, that you rage to my
      face?
    For the last time, get out, get away from this
      place: **120**
    go, traitor, do not wait for your own father's hand
    to drive you forcefully before you leave this land.

SCENE THREE: THESEUS (ALONE)

THESEUS.
    Wretched, you are running to your own ruin now.
    Neptune, god of that sea which all gods fear
      somehow,
    has given me his word and he will make it good.
    You cannot flee a god, let that be understood.
    I loved you; and I sense, in spite of your great
      crime,   **5**
    the pain you must endure in such a little time.
    But you condemned yourself, and now the deed is
      done.
    Has any father been so outraged by a son?
    O gods, who see the grief which overwhelms me
      here,
    how could I ever cause this monster to appear?   **10**

SCENE FOUR: PHÈDRE, THESEUS

PHÈDRE.

My Lord, I come to you, filled with a ghastly fear.
I heard your strong loud voice as you were speaking
here.
I am afraid your threats have ended in something.
If there is still some time, then spare your own
offspring;
respect your flesh and blood, I dare to beg of you. **5**
I cannot hear the cries of what you plan to do;
do not condemn me to this future misery,
that your own hand has killed one of your family.

THESEUS.

Madam, there is no blood at all on my own hand.
And yet the criminal shall not flee from this land. **10**
For an immortal hand is raised in rage right now.
So you will be revenged, Neptune has made the vow.

PHÈDRE.

Neptune has made the vow! What?—just one angry
word . . .

THESEUS.

What?—now are you afraid that that will not be
heard?
Instead, join with me now in prayers of
righteousness. **15**
Recite his crimes to me in all their foul excess;
arouse my wrath which is too slow and too
restrained.
All of his evil deeds have not yet been explained:
your world is furious with insults in his eyes:
your mouth, he says, is full of foul deceits
and lies; **20**
he swears that Aricie has all his heart and soul,
that he loves her.

PHÈDRE.

                        What's that?

THESEUS.

                            He spoke with self-control.
But I know how to scorn this artificial trick. **25**
May Neptune's justice come, and be most cruel and
quick.
Now I myself will go to worship at his shrine,
and urge him to perform that oath that was divine.

SCENE FIVE: PHÈDRE (ALONE)

PHÈDRE.

He's gone. What news is this which has just struck
my ear?
Now what slow smouldering begins within me here?
O sky, what thunderbolt! what words that shock and
stun!
I came here willingly to save his noble son;

breaking away, I left Oenone's own frightened
arms, **5**
and gave myself to all these torments and alarms.
What if I were found out, and driven to repent?
I might have just confessed, admitting my intent;
if he had not gone on to interrupt my speech,
I might have let the truth go flying out of reach. **10**
For Hippolyte can feel, and does not feel for me!
His heart to Aricie!—his soul to Aricie!
Ah gods!—to my own love this Lord was so unkind,
with his derisive eye, and his high pride of mind,
that I imagined he, with such a hardened heart, **15**
would have to hate my sex and be set far apart.
But now another has attained this famous place;
in his great scornful gaze another has found grace.
Perhaps he has a heart which some can tempt and
lure.
I am the only one that he cannot endure; **20**
so why should I defend what he has been about?

SCENE SIX: PHÈDRE, OENONE

PHÈDRE.

Dear Oenone, do you know what I have just found
out?

OENONE.

No, but I tremble now, I must make you believe
I fear for this mad plan which made you try to leave:
for I distrust the path your fatal passions choose.

PHÈDRE.

I have a rival now: this is my bitter news. **5**

OENONE.

How?

PHÈDRE.

            Hippolyte's in love, consumed by a great flame.
That same cold enemy whom no one else could
tame,
who praised his own chaste days, and hated others'
praise—
this tiger, how I stayed in fear of his wild ways, **10**
and now he has been tamed, he knows a stronger
soul,
for Aricie now keeps his heart in her control.

OENONE.

Aricie?

PHÈDRE.

                Ah, despair which is still unimproved!
Which way is my own heart still waiting to be
moved? **15**
All that I have suffered, my passions and my fears,
the fury of my love, the horror of my tears,
and the cruel injury of having been refused,
were all a warning that I would be more abused.
They are in love! but how? right here before my
face? **20**

how did they meet? and when? and in what secret
    place?
You knew of it. But then, why didn't you tell me?
Why didn't you describe this dear conspiracy?
How often have they talked and walked together
    now?
Far in the forest, did they hope to hide somehow? 25
Alas! once they met there, they were completely
    free.
There the wide open sky smiled on their ecstasy;
they did whatever they themselves desired to do;
and each new day was clear and splendid in their
    view.
While I, the sad outcast of everything in sight, 30
I tried to hide by day and fly from the bright light:
death is the only god I dared to glorify.
I waited for the day I could lie down and die:
filled with this bitterness, alone in my despair,
still in my illness watched by all eyes
    everywhere, 35
I could not find the time to cry as I desired;
that was a fatal joy I privately acquired;
the peaceful features which I wore as my disguise
required that I hide the tears of my own eyes.

OENONE.

What true fruit did they taste from their vain
    endeavor? 40
For they will have to part.

PHÈDRE.

            They will love forever.
And right now, as I speak—ah! what a deadly
    thought!—
they brave the rage of one who raves and is
    distraught.
Despite the long exile which takes them far apart, 45
they swear they will remain within each other's
    heart.
No, no, Oenone, no no, I cannot bear their joy;
take pity on my hate which hastens to destroy.
This Aricie must die. My husband must revive
his wrath against that race he said must not
    survive. 50
And he must not lay down a few light penalties:
this sister has surpassed her brother's blasphemies.
My jealousy will speak and seek ways to cajole.
What am I doing now? have I lost all control?
I, jealous! and Theseus becomes the one I seek! 55
My husband is alive, and love still makes me weak!
For whom? and for whose heart are all my prayers
    addressed?
Each word I say creates new chaos in my breast.
Now all my hopes fly off beyond all scope of crime.
Incest and fraud exist in me at the same time. 60
My own cold reckless hands, restless for violence,

are burning to disturb the breath of innocence.
Wretched! and I still live? I am still in the sight
of that great sacred sun which bore me in its light?
My father is the first of all the gods on high; 65
and my own ancestors still populate the sky.
Where can I hide? far down in the foul dark of hell.
But how? for even there my father casts a spell;
he holds the fatal urn the gods put in his hand:
Minos dooms all who fall to that last ghastly
    land. 70
Ah, just imagine how his spirit will despair
when his own daughter comes into his presence
    there,
confessing all her crimes, with shame in every word,
and sins the underworld perhaps has never heard!
Father, what will you say when I have said it all? 75
I know, your hand will drop, the fatal urn will fall;
then you shall have to choose what torment you
    prefer,
so you yourself can be my executioner.
Forgive me: a cruel god has damned this family;
and he still takes revenge in my anxiety. 80
Alas! and my sad heart has never known the taste
of this forbidden love for which I am disgraced.
Pursued by suffering until my dying breath,
I leave a painful life as I fly towards my death.

OENONE.

Ah, Madam, do reject this insubstantial fear. 85
Do take another look at what has happened here.
You love. And yet we know one cannot conquer fate.
The gods themselves led you into this hateful state.
But then are you so sure your story is unique?
Others, equally strong, have grown equally weak. 90
For flesh is flesh, and frail—unfortunate, but true.
Since you are human, you must do what humans do.
Your woe is a great weight imposed so long ago.
For the Olympians, the greatest gods we know,
who with a dreadful curse condemn all kinds of
    crime, 95
have had their own desires and sinned from time to
    time.

PHÈDRE.

What do I hear? what words of wisdom do you give?
You will still poison me for as long as I live,
you wretch! remember that you ruined me this way;
for it was you that made me face the light
    of day. 100
Your prayers made me forget the duty that I knew;
I fled from Hippolyte; you forced him in my view.
By what right did your words, which were so full of
    shame,
accuse his blameless life and darken his good name?
Perhaps he will be killed, perhaps his father's
    vow 105

to strike him down is done and he is dead right now.
I will not hear your words. Get out, you worthless
    beast!
Leave me my last few days and my own fate at least.
Let heaven pay you back for all that you have done!
And may your punishment petrify everyone—   **110**
all who, like you, may dare to use deceitful speech,
feeding the weakness of each Prince within their
    reach,
luring their hearts to go which way they are inclined,
and daring them to do the crimes in their own mind!
O fatal flatterers, the most destructive things   **115**
which heaven in its rage inflicts on sinful Kings!

OENONE (*alone*).

    Ah gods look down on me, my faith begins to fade.
    So this is what I get. I have been well repaid.

END OF ACT FOUR

ACT FIVE

SCENE ONE: HIPPOLYTE, ARICIE (ISMÈNE)

ARICIE.

    Now you are so unsafe—Speak out, for your own
        sake!
    You leave your father here to make the same
        mistake?
    You are too cruel if you turn from my tears of pain
    and easily agree not to see me again;
    yet if you go away and leave your Aricie,   **5**
    at least you should assure your own security:
    you must defend your name against this shame right
        now,
    and force your father to take back his solemn vow—
    for there is still some time. Why, and by what
        caprice,
    does your accuser keep her freedom in such
        peace?   **10**
    You should tell Theseus all.

HIPPOLYTE.

                Now what have I not said?
    And how could I reveal the shame of his own bed?
    Should I describe the truth in all sincerity
    and watch my father blush at the indignity?   **15**
    For you alone have known the worst of what is true.
    My heart has only told the gods above and you.
    For I loved you that much—from you I could not
        hide
    what I myself despised and tried to keep inside.
    But see the secrecy with which my words are
        sealed: **20**
    forget now, if you can, the things I have revealed,
    Madam, because I pray your lips which are so fair

may never once repeat this tale of foul despair.
The gods are rational and they deserve our trust;
now for their own sake they shall save me and be
    just: **25**
unable to escape her punishment in time,
soon Phèdre will pay at last for her most shameful
    crime.
Your silence is the thing I ask for, at this stage.
And for all else, I give a free rein to my rage:
fly from this hateful state where you have been a
    slave;   **30**
accompany my flight, come with me and be brave;
now tear yourself away and leave this fatal place
where virtue has to breathe the great stench of
    disgrace;
your hope lies in disguise—to hide your swift
    retreat,
use the confusion which is caused by my defeat.   **35**
I can assure you of the safest means of flight:
the guards here are all mine, the only men in sight;
now we will take our cause to powerful allies—
Argos holds out its arms, Sparta will sympathize:
we can count on these friends to hear our just
    appeal;   **40**
for Phèdre must not succeed, keeping what she can
    steal,
for she will seize the throne, and once that prize is
    won,
she will give everything we have to her own son.
This is our perfect chance, and now we must not
    wait . . .
But what fear holds you back? you seem to
    hesitate!   **45**
It's only your own cause that moves me to be bold:
when I am all on fire, why do you seem so cold?
Does my own banishment fill you so full of fear?

ARICIE.

    Such a sweet banishment would be to me most dear!
    What happiness to be tied to your destiny,   **50**
    forgotten by the rest of sad humanity!
    But not united now by any tie so sweet,
    how could I try to leave this place without deceit?
    I know that I can go against all stern commands
    and free myself right now out of your father's
        hands: **55**
    this place is not the home of my own family;
    and flight is right for those who flee from tyranny.
    But you love me, my Lord; and there is my good
        name . . .

HIPPOLYTE.

    No, you are in my care and you shall know no
        shame.
    I have a nobler plan for you and for your life: **60**
    fly from your enemies, and join me as my wife.

We shall be free in grief, and under the same sun,
our loving vows shall not depend on anyone.
A marriage does not need bright torchlight and loud
    sound.
In the ports of Trézène, in the tombs underground, 65
great ancient sepulchres of Princes of my race,
there is a temple there which is a sacred place.
There men would never dare to make their vows in
    vain:
for perjurers receive a penalty of pain;
and fearing to find there their own predestined
    death,   70
liars will never try to take that fatal breath.
There, if you believe me, we can declare our love
and swear it in the sight of the great gods above;
our witness will be He whom they all worship there;
and our father will be all good gods everywhere.   75
To the great sacred ones I will address our plea,
to chaste Diana, and to Juno's majesty,
and all the others there, they see my sweet love now,
and they will guarantee the conscience of my vow.

ARICIE.
    The King comes now: fly, Prince, you must leave
        right away.   80
    No one must know my plans to go, so I shall stay.
    But please leave me someone to show me what to
        do,
    to guide my timid steps and lead my love to you.

SCENE TWO: THESEUS, ARICIE, ISMÈNE

THESEUS.
    O gods, enlighten me and give me by your grace
    the living sight of truth I search for in this place!
ARICIE.
    Remember everything, Ismène; prepare our flight.

SCENE THREE: THESEUS, ARICIE

THESEUS.
    You color now, Madam, and you are seized with
        fright;
    now why did Hippolyte leave her so secretly?
ARICIE.
    My Lord, he came to say his last farewells to me.
THESEUS.
    Your eyes have overcome the high pride of his heart;
    and his first secret sighs are those you made him
        start.   5
ARICIE.
    My Lord, I cannot lie and hide the truth from you:
    nothing could make him take your hateful point of
        view;
    he never treated me like some lost criminal.

THESEUS.
    I know: he swore his love would be perpetual.
    But do not put your trust in his inconstant mind;   10
    for he swore other loves with vows of the same kind.
ARICIE.
    My Lord?
THESEUS.
                    You should have trained this Prince to
        be less vain:
    how could you bear to share his love without great
        pain?
ARICIE.
    How can you bear to say such evil of his ways,   15
    maligning this fair man and darkening his days?
    Have you so little wit to understand his heart?
    Or can you not keep crime and innocence apart?
    Must you see his virtue in some grotesque disguise,
    when it so brightly shines before all other eyes?   20
    You damn him to slander and scandal everywhere.
    Stop it: you should repent of your relentless prayer;
    O you should fear, my Lord, that heaven will fulfill
    its own great hate for you and execute your will.
    Its fatal rage may take away our prey sometimes.   25
    Sometimes its benefits repay us for our crimes.
THESEUS.
    No, now you cannot hide how he has been so lewd:
    your love has made you blind to his ingratitude.
    But I have witnesses who testified right here:
    and I myself have seen fierce tears which are
        sincere.   30
ARICIE.
    Take care, my Lord, take care: for your heroic hands
    have slain the numberless monsters of many lands;
    but all are not destroyed, because you did not seek
    one . . . But your son, my Lord, forbids me now to
        speak.
    Informed of the respect which he still holds
        for you,   35
    I would grieve him too much if I said what I knew.
    So I shall be discreet, and leave your presence now;
    if I stayed I might say more than I should somehow.

SCENE FOUR: THESEUS (ALONE)

THESEUS.
    What went on in her mind? what did her saying
        hide—
    begun, and then cut off, unable to confide?
    Were they to baffle me by their hypocrisy?
    Or do the two of them resort to torture me?
    And meanwhile I myself, despite my self-control,   5
    what is the voice I hear cry out in my own soul?
    A secret pity pleads and weeps in my heart's core.
    I must seek out Oenone and question her once more:

I must find out the truth, my mind must be made
  clear.
Now guards, go find Oenone alone, and bring her
  here.   **10**

SCENE FIVE: THESEUS, PANOPE

PANOPE.

My Lord, I do not know what the Queen means to
  do,
but I fear for the state which she now suffers
  through.
A fatal pale despair is painted on her face,
already, the great dread of death has left its trace.
Already, leaving her and flying shamefully,   **5**
Oenone has thrown herself into the raging sea.
Now no one knows what cruel madness made her
  obey;
we only know the waves have taken her away.

THESEUS.

What do I hear?

PANOPE.

              Her death has not disturbed the Queen;   **10**
the anguish of her soul is so grotesquely seen.
Sometimes, as if to ease the torment of her fears,
she holds her children close and bathes them with
  her tears;
and then, rejecting them, renouncing tenderness,
she pushes them away, far from her best caress;   **15**
she walks as if she lived in some oblivion;
and her distracted gaze does not know anyone;
three times she tried to write; and then, changing her
  mind,
three times she rose and tore the letter up unsigned.
See her, my Lord, see her, and listen to her cry.   **20**

THESEUS.

O gods! Oenone is dead, and Phèdre desires to die!
Recall my son, he must defend himself somehow;
now let him speak to me, I want to hear him now.
The fatal vow must wait, it cannot be begun,
Neptune; I almost wish my prayer could be
  undone.   **25**
Perhaps I have believed people I should not trust,
I may have raged too soon and asked you to be just.
Now into what despair am I led by my vow?

SCENE SIX: THESEUS, THÉRAMÈNE

THESEUS.

Théramène, is it you? And where is my son now?
I trusted him to you in his most tender years.
But now I see you weep: what is behind these tears?
Where is my son?

THÉRAMÈNE.

              Too late, this should have come before!   **5**
Your suit is useless now: Hippolyte is no more.

THESEUS.

O gods!

THÉRAMÈNE.

              I saw him die, this loveliest of men,
and this man had no guilt, my Lord, I say again.

THESEUS.

My son is no more now! I would have been his
  friend,   **10**
but the impatient gods have rushed him to his end!
What blow has taken him? What great stroke of the
  fates?

THÉRAMÈNE.

When he had left Trézène and gone beyond the
  gates,
he drove his chariot; and with a solemn air,
his silent grieving guards were all around him
  there;   **15**
sadly he chose the road to Mycenae, and he
relaxed the reins so that his horses all ran free;
these handsome animals, which once were his own
  choice,
and eager to obey the loud sound of his voice,
now galloped with sad eye and raced with heavy
  head,   **20**
as if responding to his own keen sense of dread.
A frightful cry, which came from far along the shore,
cut through the quiet sky with an ungodly roar;
and from the earth itself there came a great loud
  shout
which terrorized the air and echoed all about.   **25**
Afraid in our stark hearts, our own life blood froze
  cold;
the horses heard and reared and could not be
  controlled.
Just then, erupting from the surface of the sea,
there rose a mound of foam which burst ferociously;
the wave approached, and broke, and vomited to
  sight,   **30**
amidst the waves of foam, a monster of great height.
Its large forehead was armed with long and pointed
  horns;
covered with yellow scales, the beast could be sea-
  born,
a fiery dragon, a wild and raging bull;
the hair along its back was twisted, thick
  and full;   **35**
its shrieking shook the shore and cut across the air.
The sky with horror saw the savage monster there;
the earth quaked, and the sight poisoned the
  atmosphere;

the same great wave of foam it came on, fled with
   fear.
Everyone flew, we knew that now no one was
   brave;   **40**
we sought the safety that a nearby temple gave.
But Hippolyte remained, true to his origin,
halted his horses there, took up his javelin,
threw at the monster's side, and with a perfect aim,
he tore a ghastly wound in its enormous frame.   **45**
The great beast leaped ahead and shrieked with rage
   and pain,
came where the horses were, fell to the earth again,
rolled over, roared, and showed its throat, began to
   choke,
and bathed the horses there with fire, blood and
   smoke.
Fear overwhelmed them then, none of the horses
   heard   **50**
their master shouting out his stern commanding
   word;
he pulled back on the reins, his strength was infinite,
but their mouths overflowed with blood around the
   bit.
Through all this violence they say that one could see
a god with a great whip beating them ruthlessly.   **55**
Spurred on by their own fear, they raced across the
   rocks;
the axle screeched and broke from such outrageous
   shocks:
the chariot flew off its few shattered remains;
but Hippolyte was caught all snarled up in the reins.
Forgive my sorrow now: for knowing what
   I know,   **60**
the sight of this will be a constant source of woe.
For I saw your own son, my Lord, I saw your son
dragged by his horses there wherever they would
   run.
He tried to call a halt, they bolted at the sound,
they ran until he was torn open on the ground.   **65**
The field could feel the pain, and our hearts were
   downcast,
and then the mad horse race began to slow at last:
and finally they stopped near the great ancient tomb
where all his ancestors are kept in the cool gloom.
I ran there breathlessly, and his guards followed
   me: **70**
his blood had formed a trail which everyone could
   see;
the rocks were wet with it; there was red
   everywhere,
even the rough thorns bore his bloody shocks of hair.
I reached him, I cried out; and then, trying to rise,
the dying Hippolyte opened and closed his eyes: **75**
''The sky,'' he said, ''has seized a sinless life from
   me.

When I have died, dear friend, take care of Aricie.
If my own father should someday be told the truth,
and pities the sad fate of an insulted youth,
tell him, to please my blood and give my spirit
   peace,   **80**
that all these injuries to Aricie must cease;
let him give her . . .'' And then, at last, the hero
   died,
leaving his poor torn form to lie there by my side:
a figure which the gods decided to despise,
which his own father now would never
   recognize.   **85**

THESEUS.
   My son! My only hope now taken far away!
   O gods! In your high pride you served me well
      today!
   I know grief is the fate I must forever face!

THÉRAMÈNE.
   Then timid Aricie came up to that sad place:
   she came, my Lord, because you made her try
      to fly;   **90**
   she swore to be his wife by all the gods on high.
   She came up close; she saw the grass was wet and
      bright;
   she saw (and what a thing for a sweet lover's sight!)
   without color or form, how Hippolyte stretched out.
   For a long time she stood, and she had a strong
      doubt;   **95**
   not knowing her own love who lay there at her feet,
   she looked around awhile and called for Hippolyte.
   But satisfied at last this had to be her love,
   she gazed up to the sky and blamed the gods above;
   then cold and so alone, and losing all restraint,   **100**
   she fell there at his feet, insensible and faint.
   Ismène was close to her; and lost in tears, Ismène
   made her come back to life, or back to grief again.
   And I myself came here, hating the light of day,
   to tell you everything he wanted me to say,   **105**
   and finishing, my Lord, this last unpleasant task
   which his fine dying heart had strength enough to
      ask.
   But now I seem to see his deadly enemy.

SCENE SEVEN: THESEUS, PHÈDRE, THÉRAMÈNE, PANOPE (GUARDS)

THESEUS.
   My son has lost his life: this is your victory!
   It is no wonder now I tried to see his side,
   deep in my heart I sensed a doubt I could not hide!
   But Madam, he is dead, so you should claim your
      prey;
   enjoy his having died, guilty or not, today: **5**
   for I agree my eyes must be forever blind.
   He was a criminal, you proved it to my mind.

His death gives me enough to occupy my grief,
without more questions now, to test my disbelief,
since it would do no good nor cause my son to
    live—   **10**
a greater source of pain is all that it would give.
Let me go far from here, and far away from you,
perhaps the sight of death will vanish from my view.
I choke with memory, and to escape this curse,
I would exile myself from the whole universe.   **15**
Everything rises up against me to complain;
the fame of my own name increases my great pain:
if I were less well known, I might hide easily.
I hate all gifts the gods have ever given me;
I shall regret their great murderous favors now,   **20**
and never weary them with any further vow.
What they have given me, cannot at all repay
for that which they have now chosen to take away.

PHÈDRE.

No, Theseus, let me speak, for I cannot keep still;
I must show you your son in his own guiltless
    will: **25**
for he was innocent.

THESEUS.

                              Ah! unfortunate son!
And it was on your word that this damned thing was
    done!
O cruel! and do you think that I could now
    forgive . . .

PHÈDRE.

Moments are dear to me, so hear me while I live: **30**
I am the one in whom this passion had begun,
by casting a foul eye on your respectful son.
The gods lodged him in me until I was obsessed:
detestable Oenone accomplished all the rest.
She feared that Hippolyte, informed of my mad
    lust,   **35**

would tell you of this love which gave him such
    disgust:
and so this meddling wretch, seeing that I was weak,
hurried to greet you here, and she began to speak.
Escaping from my rage, she then began to flee
and sought her judgment in the silence of the sea. **40**
The sword would have served me, and made me face
    my fate,
but I felt the command of virtue was too great:
I wanted to come here, to say what I have said,
so then I could descend more slowly to the dead.
Medea's poison now runs all along my veins,   **45**
and I can feel it work, I understand these pains.
Already, its cruel death is coming on my heart,
I feel an unknown cold in every body part;
already my dim eye no longer comprehends
my noble husband whom my being here offends;   **50**
and death, which takes away this great disgrace in
    me,
gives back the light of day in all its purity.

PANOPE.

She has just died, my Lord.

THESEUS.

                              If this catastrophe
could only wipe away the fatal memory!   **55**
I know my error now, and since it has been done,
I must mingle my tears in the blood of my son!
And I must go embrace his mangled body now,
to expiate the shame of that great hateful vow.
He has deserved his name, his honors will
    increase;   **60**
and so that we are sure his soul will rest in peace,
I shall, despite the guilt of her whole family,
proclaim to all the world my daughter Aricie!

FOCUS QUESTIONS

1. Discuss the dramatic sources of Racine's *Phèdre*.
2. Evaluate the play as a model of French neoclassicism.
3. In a short essay, comment on Racine's remark that Phèdre ''is neither entirely guilty
   nor entirely innocent.''
4. Briefly analyze Racine's treatment of the Phèdre/Oenone relationship.
5. Develop a character sketch of Phèdre.
6. Locate a biographical sketch of Racine and discuss some possible connections
   between his life and the writing of the play.

OTHER ACTIVITIES

1. Compare William Packard's translation of Phèdre's closing confession to Hippolyte in act 2, scene 2 with a different verse or prose version.
2. Discuss your personal approaches to staging *Phèdre,* and develop several sketches to support your interpretation.
3. Using reviews, photographs, and other helpful documents, briefly discuss a contemporary English-language production of the play.
4. The play has inspired two film versions: one featuring Melina Mercouri (1961), the other with Marie Bell (1968). Briefly assess one interpretation.

BIBLIOGRAPHY

Barrera, Madame de. *Memoirs of Rachel*. New York: Harper, 1858.

Barthes, Roland. *On Racine*. Translated by Richard Howard. New York: Performing Arts Journal Press, University of California, 1992.

Bowra, Cecil M. *The Simplicity of Racine*. Oxford: Clarendon Press, 1956.

Brereton, G. *Jean Racine: A Critical Biography*. New York: Barnes & Noble, 1973.

Brownstein, Rachel M. *Tragic Muse: Rachel of the Comédie-Française*. New York: Alfred A. Knopf, 1993.

Clark, A. F. B. *Jean Racine*. Cambridge, MA: Harvard University Press, 1939.

Hawkins, Frederick. *Annals of the French Stage from its Origins to the Death of Racine*. 2 vols. London: Chapman & Hall, 1884.

Lapp, John. *Aspects of Racinian Tragedy*. Toronto: University of Toronto Press, 1978.

Lawrenson, T. E. *The French Stage in the XVIIth Century: A Study in the Advent of Italian Order*. Manchester: Manchester University Press, 1957.

Lockert, Lacy. *Studies in French Classical Tragedy*. Nashville: Vanderbilt University Press, 1967.

Muir, Kenneth. *Racine: Five Plays*. New York: Hill & Wang, 1960.

Sainte-Beuve, C. *Portraits of the Seventeenth Century, Historic and Literary*. Translated by K. P. Wormeley. New York: G. P. Putnam's Sons, 1925.

Schurz, Carl. *The Reminiscences of Carl Schurz*. Vol. 1, *1829–1852*. New York: The McClure Co., 1907.

Tilley, Arthur. *Three French Dramatists: Racine, Marivaux, Musset*. New York: Macmillan, 1933.

Turnell, Martin. *The Classical Moment: Studies in Corneille, Molière and Racine*. Westport, CT: Greenwood Press, 1971.

Vinaver, Eugene. *Racine and Poetic Tragedy*. Translated by P. M. Jones. New York: Hill & Wang, 1959.

Weinberg, Bernard. *The Art of Jean Racine*. Chicago: University of Chicago Press, 1969.

Wheatley, Katherine. *Racine and English Classicism*. Westport, CT: Greenwood Press, 1973.

RECOMMENDED VIDEOTAPES AND RECORDINGS

Aspects of Neo-Classical Theater: Racine's "Phèdre." VHS. 13 min. Scenes in English. Directed by Paul-Émile Deiber. Distributed by Insight Media, New York City.

Phèdre. VHS. 93 min. 1968. Starring Marie Bell. In French with English Subtitles by William Packard. Directed by Pierre Jourdan. Distributed by Insight Media, New York City.

Phèdre. One sound cassette. 1973. Everett/Edwards, World Literature Cassette Curriculum.

THE MISANTHROPE
MOLIÈRE (JEAN-BAPTISTE POQUELIN)
(1622–1673)

Molière's wit is like a running brook, with innumerable fresh lights on it at every turn of the wood through which its business is to find a way . . . Without effort, and with no dazzling flashes of achievement, it is full of healing, the wit of good breeding, the wit of wisdom.

—GEORGE MEREDITH

Georges Descrières as Alceste and Béatrice Agenin as Célimène in *The Misanthrope,* presented by the Comédie Française in 1977, under the direction of Pierre Dux. *Photo: © Lipnitzki-Viollet.*

FRENCH DRAMA IN THE SEVENTEENTH CENTURY

In the tradition of its classical Greek counterpart, French neoclassical drama wore the masks of tragedy and comedy, using Aristotle's *Poetics* and Horace's *Ars Poetica* as models that established standards for each form. Tragedy portrayed the nobility, with its matters of state and downfall of rulers and its heroic figures whose misfortunes were narrated in an elevated poetic style. In contrast, comedy portrayed the middle and lower classes in stories with happy endings drawn from domestic life, sometimes spelled out in prose. Neoclassical rules of the three **unities, decorum,** and **verisimilitude** allowed no compromise, and any dramatist who deviated from them was denounced overnight. At best, his work was considered "illegitimate" and was not paid much critical attention.

While the works of Corneille (1606–1684) and Racine (1639–1699) epitomized neoclassical tragedy in the seventeenth century (see Preface to Racine, p. 316), Molière's did the same for comedy. Born Jean Baptiste Poquelin, he initially studied law and seemed destined for a court position until he joined the acting family, the Bejarts, to found the Théâtre Illustre in 1643. Failing in Paris, the troupe began a tour of the provinces in 1646 and joined forces with another touring company headed by Charles Dufresne. By 1651, Molière had taken charge and began writing plays four years later. Impressing the court through a series of invitational performances, his company, given the title Troupe de Monsieur, was granted use of the court theatre, the Petit Bourbon, for public performances. Eventually they settled in the Palais Royal, a theatre that belonged to the crown, where they performed from 1660 until the time of Molière's death in 1673.

In the triple-threat capacity of actor, director, and playwright, Molière built his reputation around comedies of character and social commentary, although he wrote tragedies as well as comedy-ballets in collaboration with musicians and designers. His plays drew heavily from a variety of sources: the ancient Roman comedy, medieval farce, and the Spanish and Italian comic masters of the Renaissance, the last of which introduced him to the important *commedia dell'arte* tradition. (See Preface to *The Pedant,* p. 162.) He borrowed from the best, but he never copied, which is why his plays have survived the flood of imitations created by colleagues and predecessors. His comedies continue to generate universal appeal and are performed perennially, while the tragic masterpieces of his contemporaries are seldom produced outside of France.

Molière's plays examine the human condition and reflect his preoccupation with the worldly charades practiced by the society he served. He stirred controversy at every turn. He was sanctioned by the Church for holding the hypocrisy of its members up to ridicule, and he angered the nobility whom he targeted. In spite of this, he was championed by Louis XIV who found pleasure in these unflattering caricatures of French society.

His use of satire to reveal monomaniacal traits such as avarice, hypochondria, and conceit and to expose the affectations and posturings of his audience has prompted laughter at characters and situations that other playwrights might have handled seriously. From the stock characters and predicaments inspired by the *commedia dell'arte* in his one-act farces, Molière developed more psychologically complex characters, who are victimized by their own foibles, in his full-length comedies. Their inner conflicts in personal and social relationships continue to have contemporary resonance.

MAJOR WORKS

Molière's plays can be placed into four categories: the farces in the *commedia dell'arte* style, demonstrated by *The Doctor in Spite of Himself* (1666); the comedy-ballets with music by Lully of which *The Would-Be Gentleman* (1670) and *The Imaginary Invalid* (1673) remain the most well known; the tragic farce of *Don Juan* (1665); and the comedies of character and manners for which he is still best known. These include *School for Wives* (1662), *The Miser* (1668), *Tartuffe* (1669), and *The Learned Ladies* (1672). Each of these comedies reveals a grave underside without diminishing the laughter; each imparts great wisdom without sounding preachy or didactic. But it is *The Misanthrope* (1666), whose irrational hero feels compelled to speak the truth, no matter the consequences, that has demonstrated the widest universal appeal.

THE ACTION

Visiting Célimène's salon in Paris, where suitors and friends conveniently gather, Alceste vehemently denounces the deceitful and hypocritical ways of society to his friend Philinte. His candor is quickly put to the test when one of his rivals, Oronte, pays a visit and asks for his opinion of a love sonnet he has recently composed in Célimène's honor. Refusing to compliment his recitation, Alceste tells Oronte that he ''cannot write a line.'' Oronte leaves, feeling scorned and ridiculed, a sworn enemy of his critic.

Célimène, whom Alceste pursues, attracts a roomful of attentive flatterers and rivals, two of whom infuriate Alceste with their gossip. The arrival of Arsinoé complicates matters further; while Arsinoé has been unlucky at seducing Alceste, she is now prepared to offer proof that Célimène has been untrue to him.

A guard appears at the door to summon Alceste to court for insulting Oronte. Alceste not only loses the lawsuit, but is victimized by a dangerous and slanderous rumor. At the same time, Célimène is exposed as a hypocrite and abandoned by her other suitors. Instead of challenging his opponents, Alceste insists that Célimène accompany him in exile. When she refuses, he sulks in his injured idealism and retreats to lonely isolation.

STRUCTURE AND LANGUAGE

Considered Molière's masterpiece and one of the most personal of his works, *The Misanthrope* was produced at the height of the Golden Age of Louis XIV, when the playwright's professional success was upstaged by his own disenchantment with the glittering court-society around him. As a result, his protagonist is like no other character he created. So forthright and critical are Alceste's indictments against the manners of his age that it is difficult *not* to view him, even partially, as a self-portrait of the playwright. These views persist despite the fact that various contemporaries of Molière proudly insisted *they* were the ''genuine'' Alceste—no doubt finding cause for pride in the character's avowed sincerity.

While Alceste commands the stage almost entirely throughout so that other characters are left with no strategic alternative but to confront him, his melancholic obsessions and enigmatic outbursts can offset the play's comic equilibrium. For centuries, therefore, critics have argued over the play as comedy or tragedy, seeming determined to categorize it once and for all. Their efforts have been further frustrated by the play in performance, since the merest shift in the acting style can heighten its comic or tragic overtones.

Ironically Molière offers no easy solution, even when we turn to his characters for helpful clues. Serving as Alceste's confidant and foil, Philinte urges him to ''have an end of rantings and of railings,/ And show some leniency toward human failings.'' As if to counterbalance Philinte's gentle reasoning, Célimène's cousin Éliante—the one magnanimous and wholly sympathetic character in the play—admits that the ''honesty in which [Alceste] takes such pride/ Has—to my mind—its noble, heroic side,'' despite its excesses. As **raisonneurs,** Philinte and Éliante strike a delicate balance in their opposing views of Alceste's malady—a psychological condition that still prompts our laughter, no matter how serious his denunciations are. But if these characters fail to enlighten him or calm his ''spleen,'' a genuine concern for his welfare transforms their mutual admiration into love and adds a rare bright note to an otherwise dark, unsettled finale.

Molière was first and foremost an actor, whose playwriting talent encompassed an innate sense of theatre. But he was a poet as well, whose gift for language illuminated the memorable idiosyncracies of his characters, including their dynamic interactions. Thus Alceste's ''rantings and railings'' needed to be perfectly targeted at a circle of highbrows whose acerbic wordplay is more razor-sharp than his. Since Alceste's problem stems from his candid remarks about Oronte's verse—which is recited for all of us to hear and judge with respect or with laughter—language is the pivotal component of the play.

Regardless of where we choose to eavesdrop, words prove a glamorous weapon in the mouths of these characters. Confiding in her soul mates, Clitandre and Acaste, Célimène exercises her scathing humor in act 2, to undo one of her dreary female friends:

> Whenever she comes to call, I grope about
> To find some topic which will draw her out,
> But, owing to her dry and faint replies,
> The conversation wilts, and droops, and dies.

Not surprisingly, the topic focuses on the art of conversation. Célimène's remarks are filled with words of action that portray her more favorably than her unseen guest. Nor is she above bending the rhyme to accommodate such gossip, when she concludes: ''And though you ask the time, and yawn, and yawn,/ She sits there like a stone and won't be gone.''

Her brand of wit is equally matched by Acaste who, in act 3, flatters himself before the same Clitandre:

> I've wit, of course; and taste in such perfection
> That I can judge without the least reflection,
> And at the theatre, which is my delight,
> Can make or break a play on opening night.

Molière's clever theatrical metaphor serves several purposes: to demonstrate Acaste's naked pomposity in the context of ordinary conversation; to equate this pomposity with the taste of a certain drama critic who no doubt sat in the audience on opening night; and to let the play comment on itself, rather like an ''inside'' joke, which is a familiar and enjoyable device in his plays.

Alceste is fully appreciated only in his relationship with Célimène, who is the celebrated hostess of Parisian society. Empowered from his position on the margins of her world, he flaunts his superiority as one who lets his heart speak by refusing to ''mask [his sentiments] in silly compliments.'' Such behavior, along with the witty backbiting at which Célimène excels, disgusts him. Yet it is curious that she remains the single object of his desire. Thus his love for her reveals his hypocrisy. Although he insists on honesty and would be ''frank with everyone,'' when Célimène points out that ''he's so in love with contradiction,/ He'll turn against his most profound conviction,'' he, like his own victims, lashes out at her. In professing his love for her, he claims that if she ''were wretchedly poor,/ Unloved, uncherished, utterly obscure,'' then he might offer his heart and ''repair the great injustice of [her] plight.'' When his wish is unwittingly granted and she loses the admiration of all, rather than defend her reputation, he expects her to atone. What Alceste has mistaken for love is really rooted in his obsession with himself.

Célimène, who occupies as much of the play's center as Alceste does, also inhabits an equally unbending **persona**. Anxious to remain at the hub of Parisian society, she uses her wit to assassinate the characters of those in her social circle. Her cleverness is the substance on which her world thrives. Yet, when her suitors discover her deceit, she loses all public influence. She is unmasked as someone fearful of showing her true feelings. When, at the close of the play, she asks Alceste—the one she truly loves—to forgive her, he cannot act on his love. Instead he exacts a test, inviting her to renounce the world and go with him to the desert: "To that wild, trackless, solitary place/ In which I shall forget the human race." In response to her unhaltingly self-possessed reply, "What! *I* renounce the world at my young age,/ And die of boredom in some hermitage?" Alceste casts her off. Thus Célimène is left alone and friendless, perhaps to remind us that the soul of the play—whose unified actions have transpired in *her* drawing-room—does not belong entirely to Alceste.

ABOUT THE TRANSLATION

Working within a neoclassical mode, Molière composed most of his plays in sweeping Alexandrine lines, incorporating rhymed couplets for good measure. In this translation of *The Misanthrope,* Richard Wilbur replaces the iambic hexameter with rigid iambic pentameter to recreate the bounce and bite of Molière's original. Achieving the rhythms of ordinary conversation, all realistically placed, his English verse brings Molière's imagery and meaning sharply into focus, especially when it is viewed alongside the original French. In an act 1 exchange between Philinte and Alceste, the content of which ironically foreshadows Alceste's trouble with the law, Philinte advises his friend to rage less at his imaginary opponent. Alceste self-righteously replies:

> Alceste: I assure you I'll do nothing of the sort.
> Je n'en donnerai point, c'est une chose dite.
> Philinte: Then who will plead your case before the court?
> Mai qui voulez-vous donc qui pour vous sollicite?
> Alceste: Reason and right and justice will plead for me.
> Qui je veux? La raison, mon bon droit, l'équité.
> Philinte: Oh, Lord. What judges do you plan to see?
> Aucun juge par vous ne sera visité?
> Alceste: Why, none. The justice of my cause is clear.
> Non. Est-ce que ma cause est injuste ou doutouse?
> Philinte: Of course, man; but there's politics to fear. . . .
> J'en demeure d'accord; mais la brigue est fâcheuse.
> Et . . .
> Alceste: No, I refuse to lift a hand. That's flat.
> Non. J'ai résolu de n'en pas faire en pas.
> I'm either right, or wrong.
> J'ai tort ou j'ai raison.
> Philinte: Don't count on that.
> Ne vous y fiez pas.

A five-beat rhythm, which ends in sets of rhymed couplets, frames this rapidly paced argument. The final line of verse is shared by both speakers, showing how Alceste's haughty confidence is toppled by Philinte's matter-of-fact practicality. Wilbur has admitted that his participation in rehearsals of *The Misanthrope* helped to "sharpen [his] sense of what speakable verse is on the stage." It made him "more sympathetic to [actors'] difficulties, to the trouble one can give them by writing a bad line." Acknowledging the innately different rhythms of both languages, he has succeeded in creating "as much fluidity as possible through the use of run-on lines, ones that don't emphasize the rhyme but keep the rhythm flowing throughout a passage." As for his indelible use of rhymed couplets, Wilbur has insisted that "it by no means gets in the way of individuating one character from another. In fact, it helps underline the distinctions."[1]

THE MISANTHROPE-IN-PERFORMANCE

French theatre was dominated by professionally licensed troupes, which, like those in Spain, included women. Each company had an active repertory of some seventy productions that rotated on a daily change of bill, playing three or four days each week. Members (ten to fifteen in number) played particular character types, while additional salaried actors were hired when necessary. The playwright and the leading actor of the company, who also served as the play's director, made the casting decisions. Once the play opened, actors were expected to perform the play before an audience without further input. In this milieu, Molière spent an apprenticeship that prepared him for the rigorous responsibilities of a lifetime in the theatre.

Still under the influence of the Italian comedic tradition, Molière's Illustre Théâtre "played in tennis courts, inn-yards, or the halls of great houses with little specialized setting and, originally, no proscenium curtain."[2] Spectators stood in a pit or sat in tiers on three sides of the room. Others moved around freely, while theatre-goers wishing to be seen sat on the stage, a practice that, by the late seventeenth century, could number as many as 150 and obviously affect performance styles or any attempt at stage illusion.

In compliance with neoclassical rules, the scenic demands of comedy and tragedy were relatively simple, often requiring one set with no scene change. Thus the scenic decor at Versailles, which was equipped with elaborate stage machinery from the continent, was rarely utilized for Molière's comedies. (See Preface to Racine, p. 320.) In *The Misanthrope,* for example, which takes place in Célimène's salon, several chairs, a table, a desk, and candlesticks might suggest the specific decor as well as her social class. Costuming was not specific to the play, since it was customary for actors to wear the fashionable apparel of the day, a practice that often became the target of Molière's satire.

During its premiere season in 1666, *The Misanthrope* enjoyed twenty-one consecutive performances, although it was not the success that Molière, who incarnated the role of Alceste for its comic value, had expected. After his death in 1673, the role was taken over by the considerably younger Michel Baron, whose handsome and dignified demeanor brought a more humane dimension to the tormented protagonist. Baron reportedly abandoned the traditional declamatory style and interpreted the Alexandrines in a softer conversational tone. After Molière's death, however, the company formed the nucleus of the Comédie Française—the national theatre of France—founded by Louis XIV in 1680.

Making his debut at the Comédie Française in 1685 and eventually heading the troupe, Florent-Carton Dancourt lent his corpulence to the role and played his amorous scenes with Célimène in a chiding manner from 1700 to 1715. During the close of Louis XV's reign, a more humanizing quality once again tempered the fiery Alceste when François-René Molé joined the Comédie Française in 1760, although he restricted himself to a handful of performances each season.

When Abraham-Joseph Fleury joined the company in 1778, his elegant manner and intellectual superiority perfectly suited Alceste. The result was a contemplative protagonist, thoroughly devoid of exaggeration and whimsy. But after his retirement in 1818, the play was scarcely performed during the reigns of Louis XVIII, Charles I, and Louis-Philippe. Edmond Geffroy, who performed with the company between 1830 and 1865, brought melancholic and brooding tones to the role. His style epitomized the Romantic era. Not until the nineteenth century did Alceste find new life at the Comédie Française in the agile but serious acting style of Hippolyte Worms, whose interpretation would dominate the stage during the last three decades of that century.

By the dawn of the twentieth century, Lucien Guitry had firmly established himself as the model actor of his time. A performer of artful restraint and supreme irony, he broke with tradition when he performed the role of Alceste for thirty consecutive performances on a Paris stage *other* than the Comédie Française, just prior to his death in 1925. The important occasion would lead to a rediscovery of the theatrical values of Molière's plays in the twentieth century. Thus the sacred attitudes established by the Comédie Française toward performing Molière were seriously challenged.

In 1906, Richard Mansfield, the British actor-manager, produced the first English version of the play, a production which he brought to America. His interpretation of Alceste was marked by a nervous unrest and a scornful vocal manner, but a certain amount of nobility shone through his pain. By 1922, in celebration of the three-hundredth anniversary of Molière's birth, Jacques Copeau's meditative and cloistered composure at the Vieux Colombier characterized an Alceste who contrasted sharply from the highly comical portrayal he had given in New York City three years earlier.

Jean-Louis Barrault's interpretation of Alceste enjoyed the support of a classically trained ensemble when *The Misanthrope* played at the Winter Garden in 1957. Barrault's blend of charm, seductiveness, and naiveté seemed perfectly suited to the *commedia dell'arte* style that infused the production which he also directed. His emphasis of the play's joyful spirit delighted New York audiences and critics.

No less imaginative or controversial have been the efforts of directors the world over to keep the comedy alive during the second half of the twentieth century. In fact, at the very time Barrault was winning kudos with his *commedia*-inspired production, Ingmar Bergman finally agreed to direct the play—his first Molière—for the Municipal Theater in Malmö, Sweden. It was a project Bergman had dreamed about since his visit to Paris in the summer of 1949, when he saw a production at the Comédie Française. Relying on darker strokes to define a unique directorial style, his production made use of a single chair and a painted backdrop against which the actors, led by Max von Sydow's Alceste, performed in elaborate costumes of the period in which Molière had placed the action.

In 1973, *The Misanthrope* was the popular choice of directors wishing to commemorate the three-hundredth anniversary of the playwright's death. One production, directed by Rudolf Noeltes and featuring Romuald Pekny as Alceste, launched the popular Salzburg Festival. Noeltes' exploration of the play's darker elements uncovered its tragic subtext. The other production proved equally controversial in the hands of John Dexter for the National Theatre at the Old Vic. Working with a new and fairly slangy verse translation by Tony Harrison, Dexter updated the 1666 setting to Charles De Gaulle's France of the mid-1960s and cast two of his country's most charismatic actors, Alec McCowen and Diana Rigg, as the infamous lovers. His inventive direction was filled with unexpected turns and culminated in the final scene when, instead of exiting as Molière's script indicates, Rigg's ''superb and deserted heroine is left sadly contemplating the desolation of her empty house, alone but with all our sympathies.''[3]

Like other time-honored companies faced with the need to satisfy the tastes and expectations of newer audiences, the Comédie Française has responded in ways Molière might never have dreamed but would probably have approved. During the final decades of the twentieth century, certain radical adjustments within a dramatic art bound by three centuries of tradition slowly gained the acceptance of audiences both in France and abroad. Under the direction of Pierre Dux, a Comédie artist who consciously sought to make Molière's comic genius relevant to contemporary audiences, François Beaulieu as Alceste ''[was] a prime example of what must be called new Comédie acting, an admixture of the classical style with Stanislavsky . . . Modern, but not too modern; colloquial, but not scanting the verse; physically loose and agile, but without losing gravity or composure— the new style, as played by Beaulieu, has a lot to recommend it.''[4]

REFLECTIONS ON THE MISANTHROPE

Stephen Porter has directed the plays of Molière in theatres across America.

I did not plan to be a director. I seemed to want to be everything else. Then I took a job teaching. We had a course in English high comedy and I wanted some sort of touchstone to start the class off. I chose *The Misanthrope*—although there was really no good translation available—because I thought it would be the demonstration of high comedy as opposed to romantic comedy, as opposed to farce, as opposed to all kinds of picaresque comedy. It was strictly high comedy on a highly moral issue, and avoided farce and exaggeration and plot complications and things of that sort. I remember telling the class again and again: you're going to have to take my word for it because the play depends on something which, I thought at that time, could not be translated. That is, the relation between the rigidity of the verse form and the wild, chaotic emotions that are expressed through different rhymes and other strict forms of the French theatre.

Eventually I got restless and thought I'd like to go into the professional theatre. But I really didn't know what step to take until the Richard Wilbur translation appeared. I was startled that it was able to do exactly the thing I had thought could not be done. So I optioned it and quit teaching and became a professional director with this play which, in that first off-Broadway production in 1956, I also produced.

After directing it, I thought I'd move on to other things. But in that production was Ellis Rabb who played Alceste and who was to form the A.P.A. Repertory where I was, next to Ellis, the most active director. So in 1968 Ellis asked me to direct *The Misanthrope* again. I was a little reluctant to do it, since I'd done it once before and didn't want to lessen the impact. But it turned out quite nicely with the A.P.A., with Richard Easton playing Alceste and, in the comparatively modest role of Acaste, Brian Bedford, who had joined the company.

Some fifteen years after that, I was directing a lot at the Circle-in-the-Square and they wanted me to direct Brian. The producers then decided to do *The Misanthrope*. I thought, "My God, I've done this twice!" I was a little scared to do it a third time, because I didn't think there was anything more to be said about the play. But as it happens, so much depends on your leading man and woman, who color the production all over again, that you could never repeat yourself even if you tried. So I directed it once again.

I admire the work from a detached point of view, just loving the script. Certainly all the other high comedies I've directed stir the audience more viscerally because they are either more melodramatic or more farcical. Furthermore, other Molière works involve the audience more. It's quite possible for an intelligent person to sit through *The Misanthrope* and not really understand what it's about. Other people connect with it instantly. But what is being made fun of and whose side you're on are very different things to perceive.

The very center of the play is that Alceste has enormous moral superiority where his own emotions are not involved, but when his own emotions *are* involved, he's just a petulant child. This is his tragic or tragicomic flaw. In this respect, nearly all of Molière's plays can be viewed as either comic or tragic, because the central character is almost invariably defeated by an obsession. Alceste's friends say to him, "You will go out of your mind if you don't stop pursuing the track you are pursuing." Crazy or not, Alceste ends up totally alienated which, in terms of the gregarious seventeenth century he lives in, is a kind of madness. He's cut himself off from the society of common sense, of rational human beings.

Although Alceste claims he will abandon the world and live in a desert, I often suspect that he turns up at Célimène's doorstep the next morning and says, "Maybe you didn't understand what I meant!" and goes through the whole thing all over again. But he hasn't changed his position one bit, nor has she changed hers.

One gets such a sense of claustrophobia from the society depicted, which is why the play eludes some people. Alceste is obviously right about everybody else in the play, with the exception of Philinte and Éliante, that one thinks he must be right about everything. But if *he's* not right and *they're* not right, then who's right? You're at a point where you don't quite know where to stand.

People used to say that Philinte and Éliante were right. But recently some French critics have endeavored to rebut this by calling Philinte and Éliante the villains because they compromise. The French love to be revisionists about this sort of thing, but that's an extreme too. On this point, Philinte can get a couple of laughs, more so perhaps in Wilbur than in the original. His idea that other peoples' evil exists to make us grow strong by surmounting it, can be a slightly absurd, slightly extreme position. But Molière often does this to his *raisonneur,* to the person who seems to be in the right. In this case, Molière pushes his *raisonneur* to the extreme.

I don't think one of my three New York productions was better than the others, but that different things came out with the talents of the different actors: whether the chemical balance of a passionate sexual attraction was dominant in one production or a sardonic detachment was dominant in another. The first time I directed it was in a small basement theatre and on a very small physical scale. My actors were dedicated to classic theatre. Besides Ellis Rabb, there was Bill Ball, who later established the American Conservatory Theater and Jacqueline Brookes. They were missionaries for American actors hungry for the chance to master the techniques of speaking verse. Furthermore, there hadn't been a very well-received straight production, realistic and unexaggerated, of any of Molière's plays for a long while. We didn't wink at the audience, we spoke the verse very precisely, and the ladies knew how to handle their fans and so forth. A lot of things that we would now take for granted were very new in 1956, because most people hadn't had the experience that I've been lucky to have, to go to France a great many times during that period in the 1950s and to see French productions and know how simple they were. Not many people had the courage to be very simple on stage.

By the time I directed the play in 1968, that was not a new thing and would no longer be enough to carry us. But I did it for the A.P.A. in a very large proscenium theatre, and there was great vocal resonance with actors like Richard Easton, Christine Pickles, and Brian Bedford. Christine lowered her voice one full octave. She had enough time to accomplish this. Richard was and still is the most stentorian of actors on two continents. He has an enormous voice. So the production was as big as the other one was small. This was partly due to physical circumstances and to the qualities of these particular actors.

Continued

When I directed *The Misanthrope* in 1983 for the Circle-in-the-Square, I found it the most difficult play imaginable for a full arena. Once again, there were the temperamental qualities of the actors around: Brian Bedford, Marybeth Hurt, and Carole Shelley were a different set of people who all came from different directions. They were also at the peak of their careers, technically accomplished but also very nervous precisely because they were "up there" and would be judged so, as opposed to my first production where the actors were new and the material had never been heard before. Now we were dealing with major artists of considerable reputation in a play that, by now, had been done many times all over America.

The Circle-in-the-Square is shaped rather like a lozenge-surfboard, with long entranceways and with spectators sitting around all sides. The actors couldn't suddenly appear on stage. Their entrances were especially tricky because they had to choose an emotion that propelled them forward. For example, Alceste walking on at the beginning of the play, sitting down—so as to seem dejected—before Philinte comes in to ask him what's the matter. All this would have been very different on a smaller stage. Then there's Célimène entering down a rather long and not very pleasant aisle at the opposite end of the stage. Such technical matters can make quite a difference.

Furthermore, an enormous weight is placed on the director when so many spectators are sitting *behind* the actors. But in a play where there is so much psychological and verbal subtlety, it is necessary to get the actors turned around from time to time so the audience can eventually see them, even when the custom of the time is to have them just sit and talk forever. This is particularly vivid in the scene in act 2 where Célimène is gossiping. We defied certain conventions by having her rise and wander among the other actors, and the men *not* rise when she rose, so that the audience would be able to see her over their shoulders. Because if she did rise, and the men rose after her, she would still have been hidden behind their backs.

We devised a convention in which anybody who wanted to "take" the scene would stand up, do his number, then sit down. The action isn't absolutely motivated, except by an external need. I often have to ask the actor to find a motivation to move even when there isn't one, just so that the characters can be seen moving around. The plays I'm asked to direct at the Circle are all very verbal and cerebral, which complicates matters even further. This was a much less demanding matter when I directed *Tartuffe* at the same theatre, since the elements of farce and melodrama, including its many characters and explosive events, made it easier to hold the audience.

It helps in a space like Circle-in-the-Square, where acoustical problems exist, for the play to be in verse. One is constantly reminded, especially by the rhyme, that this is not strict realism. So we don't expect strict realism, which helps with the need to expound. Just as people who wear elaborate clothing take up a lot of space, people who express themselves at great length with rhetorical vehemence are also psychologically inclined to take up a lot of air to speak out. On the subject of how American or English speakers speak Molière's verse and who speaks it better, however, the line has been crossed and any distinction is false. I'm convinced that good actors, whatever their training, bring the same degree of willingness to be real, willingness to fill it out, willingness to say what has to be said. So the ability to handle verse is not geographic.

I've done so much Molière over so many years, that I think I'm more set in my ways than not. When I do a play nowadays, I try very hard *not* to try to get people to do what was done before, even though what was done before might have been better. My choices tend to be, in the literal sense, conservative. That is, one carries with him what one knew before. But I don't want to fall into the trap of getting actors to do what somebody did before: to play it for an audience that no longer exists, with a set of values that no longer exists, or with a sense of discovery that no longer exists.

I've not made my career out of strongly conceptual productions. What I've done best is to try to get inside the play to see what's there, to find some life in the play that has been neglected for some time, rather than to do the arbitrary changes of period, which are very good for some people because they bring out things that weren't in the play before. But I'm always more aware of the passages that won't work when you change the period than the passages that will. Since Molière is hardly an obscure artist, I don't need to show people that this kind of play works. Nor do I have the impulse to deconstruct him.

Tony Harrison's adaptation of *The Misanthrope* succeeded because it was so totally modernized that it seemed transported into another sphere. I talked with him for some time about this when we were both in Paris for a Molière colloquium. It was all very deliberate to try to make the production *not* look like Molière, since the English have always had a notorious resistance to his plays. I recently saw a production of *The Bourgeois Gentleman* at the National Theatre, in a translation by Nick Dear. There was an obscenity in every second line, which made David Mamet by contrast sound like Little Mary Sunshine. I thought, has no one noticed the fact that this bourgeois gentleman is trying to rise in society? Far from being deliberately vulgar, he would—I think—be excessively refined, if anything, since he's trying to pretend to himself that he's an aristocrat. It seems Molière succeeds in England only in the most outrageous adaptations.

The Misanthrope is not typical of Molière, who set out to be anti-dramatic and avoided all the plot devices he normally used, including the comic *lazzi* and other bits. Nor did he use any of those chunks of materials that are repeated throughout his other plays. Instead he set out to do something moral and psychological, without any of the trappings of dramatic conventions of his time or ours. The play was immediately recognized by the court as the best thing he'd ever done, but also rejected by the general public because they didn't know where they were in it. It still remains, even today, challengingly advanced and challengingly simple up against virtually any modern play.

Notes

1. PERFORMING ARTS, *July 1982, p. 15.*
2. *Molière,* THE MISER AND OTHER PLAYS, *trans. John Wood (New York: Penguin Books, 1953), xvii–xviii.*
3. *Harold Hobson,* LONDON SUNDAY TIMES, *25 Feb. 1973.*
4. *Michael Feingold, "Beaulieu Well Placed,"* THE VILLAGE VOICE, *14 May 1979, p. 95.*

THE MISANTHROPE
MOLIÈRE (JEAN-BAPTISTE POQUELIN)
TRANSLATED BY RICHARD WILBUR

CHARACTERS

Alceste, *in love with Célimène*

Philinte, *Alceste's friend*

Oronte, *in love with Célimène*

Célimène, *Alceste's beloved*

Éliante, *Célimène's cousin*

Arsinoé, *a friend of Célimène's*

Acaste ⎱ *marquesses*
Clitandre ⎰

Basque, *Célimène's servant*

A Guard *of the Marshalsea*

Dubois, *Alceste's valet*

The scene throughout is in Célimène's house at Paris.

ACT ONE

SCENE ONE: PHILINTE, ALCESTE

PHILINTE.
    Now, what's got into you?

ALCESTE (*seated*).
                        Kindly leave me alone.

PHILINTE.
    Come, come, what is it? This lugubrious tone . . .

ALCESTE.
    Leave me, I said; you spoil my solitude.

PHILINTE.
    Oh, listen to me, now, and don't be rude.   5

ALCESTE.
    I choose to be rude, Sir, and to be hard of hearing.

PHILINTE.
    These ugly moods of yours are not endearing;
    Friends though we are, I really must insist . . .

ALCESTE (*abruptly rising*).
    Friends? Friends, you say? Well, cross me off your
      list.

    I've been your friend till now, as you well know;   10
    But after what I saw a moment ago
    I tell you flatly that our ways must part.
    I wish no place in a dishonest heart.

PHILINTE.
    Why, what have I done, Alceste? Is this
      quite just?

ALCESTE.
    My God, you ought to die of self-disgust.   15
    I call your conduct inexcusable, Sir,
    And every man of honor will concur.
    I see you almost hug a man to death,
    Exclaim for joy until you're out of breath,
    And supplement these loving demonstrations   20
    With endless offers, vows, and protestations;
    Then when I ask you, ''Who was that?'' I find
    That you can barely bring his name to mind!
    Once the man's back is turned, you cease to love
      him,
    And speak with absolute indifference of him!   25
    By God, I say it's base and scandalous

To falsify the heart's affections thus;
If I caught myself behaving in such a way,
I'd hang myself for shame, without delay.

PHILINTE.
It hardly seems a hanging matter to me;   30
I hope that you will take it graciously
If I extend myself a slight reprieve,
And live a little longer, by your leave.

ALCESTE.
How dare you joke about a crime so grave?

PHILINTE.
What crime? How else are people to behave?   35

ALCESTE.
I'd have them be sincere, and never part
With any word that isn't from the heart.

PHILINTE.
When someone greets us with a show of pleasure,
It's but polite to give him equal measure,
Return his love the best that we know how,   40
And trade him offer for offer, vow for vow.

ALCESTE.
No, no, this formula you'd have me follow,
However fashionable, is false and hollow,
And I despise the frenzied operations
Of all these barterers of protestations,   45
These lavishers of meaningless embraces,
These utterers of obliging commonplaces,
Who court and flatter everyone on earth
And praise the fool no less than the man of
    worth.
Should you rejoice that someone fondles you,   50
Offers his love and service, swears to be true,
And fills your ears with praises of your name,
When to the first damned fop he'll say the same?
No, no: no self-respecting heart would dream
Of prizing so promiscuous an esteem;   55
However high the praise, there's nothing worse
Than sharing honors with the universe.
Esteem is founded on comparison:
To honor all men is to honor none.
Since you embrace this indiscriminate vice,   60
Your friendship comes at far too cheap a price;
I spurn the easy tribute of a heart
Which will not set the worthy man apart:
I choose, Sir, to be chosen; and in fine,
The friend of mankind is no friend of mine.   65

PHILINTE.
But in polite society, custom decrees
That we show certain outward courtesies. . . .

ALCESTE.
Ah, no! we should condemn with all our force
Such false and artificial intercourse.
Let men behave like men; let them display   70
Their inmost hearts in everything they say;

Let the heart speak, and let our sentiments
Not mask themselves in silly compliments.

PHILINTE.
In certain cases it would be uncouth
And most absurd to speak the naked truth;   75
With all respect for your exalted notions,
It's often best to veil one's true emotions.
Wouldn't the social fabric come undone
If we were wholly frank with everyone?
Suppose you met with someone you couldn't
    bear;   80
Would you inform him of it then and there?

ALCESTE.
Yes.

PHILINTE.
Then you'd tell old Emilie it's pathetic
The way she daubs her features with cosmetic
And plays the gay coquette at sixty-four?   85

ALCESTE.
I would.

PHILINTE.
And you'd call Dorilas a bore,
And tell him every ear at court is lame
From hearing him brag about his noble name?

ALCESTE.
Precisely.   90

PHILINTE.
Ah, you're joking.

ALCESTE.
                                    Au contraire:
In this regard there's none I'd choose to spare.
All are corrupt; there's nothing to be seen
In court or town but aggravates my spleen.   95
I fall into deep gloom and melancholy
When I survey the scene of human folly,
Finding on every hand base flattery,
Injustice, fraud, self-interest, treachery. . . .
Ah, it's too much; mankind has grown so base,   100
I mean to break with the whole human race.

PHILINTE.
This philosophic rage is a bit extreme;
You've no idea how comical you seem;
Indeed, we're like those brothers in the play
Called *School for Husbands*, one of whom was
    prey . . .   105

ALCESTE.
Enough, now! None of your stupid similes.

PHILINTE.
Then let's have no more tirades, if you please.
The world won't change, whatever you say or do;
And since plain speaking means so much to you,
I'll tell you plainly that by being frank   110
You've earned the reputation of a crank,
And that you're thought ridiculous when you rage
And rant against the manners of the age.

ALCESTE.

    So much the better; just what I wish to hear.
    No news could be more grateful to my ear.   115
    All men are so detestable in my eyes,
    I should be sorry if they thought me wise.

PHILINTE.

    Your hatred's very sweeping, is it not?

ALCESTE.

    Quite right: I hate the whole degraded lot.

PHILINTE.

    Must all poor human creatures be embraced,   120
    Without distinction, by your vast distaste?
    Even in these bad times, there are surely a few . . .

ALCESTE.

    No, I include all men in one dim view:
    Some men I hate for being rogues; the others
    I hate because they treat the rogues like brothers, 125
    And, lacking a virtuous scorn for what is vile,
    Receive the villain with a complaisant smile.
    Notice how tolerant people choose to be
    Toward that bold rascal who's at law with me.
    His social polish can't conceal his nature;   130
    One sees at once that he's a treacherous creature;
    No one could possibly be taken in
    By those soft speeches and that sugary grin.
    The whole world knows the shady means
        by which
    The low-brow's grown so powerful and rich,   135
    And risen to a rank so bright and high
    That virtue can but blush, and merit sigh.
    Whenever his name comes up in conversation,
    None will defend his wretched reputation;
    Call him knave, liar, scoundrel, and all the rest, 140
    Each head will nod, and no one will protest.
    And yet his smirk is seen in every house,
    He's greeted everywhere with smiles and bows,
    And when there's any honor that can be got
    By pulling strings, he'll get it, like as not.   145
    My God! It chills my heart to see the ways
    Men come to terms with evil nowadays;
    Sometimes, I swear, I'm moved to flee and find
    Some desert land unfouled by humankind.

PHILINTE.

    Come, let's forget the follies of the times   150
    And pardon mankind for its petty crimes;
    Let's have an end of rantings and of railings,
    And show some leniency toward human failings.
    This world requires a pliant rectitude;
    Too stern a virtue makes one stiff and rude;   155
    Good sense views all extremes with detestation,
    And bids us to be noble in moderation.
    The rigid virtues of the ancient days
    Are not for us; they jar with all our ways
    And ask of us too lofty a perfection.   160

    Wise men accept their times without objection,
    And there's no greater folly, if you ask me,
    Than trying to reform society.
    Like you, I see each day a hundred and one
    Unhandsome deeds that might be better done,   165
    But still, for all the faults that meet my view,
    I'm never known to storm and rave like you.
    I take men as they are, or let them be,
    And teach my soul to bear their frailty;
    And whether in court or town, whatever
        the scene,   170
    My phlegm's as philosophic as your spleen.

ALCESTE.

    This phlegm which you so eloquently commend,
    Does nothing ever rile it up, my friend?
    Suppose some man you trust should treacherously
    Conspire to rob you of your property,   175
    And do his best to wreck your reputation?
    Wouldn't you feel a certain indignation?

PHILINTE.

    Why, no. These faults of which you so complain
    Are part of human nature, I maintain,
    And it's no more a matter for disgust   180
    That men are knavish, selfish and unjust,
    Than that the vulture dines upon the dead,
    And wolves are furious, and apes ill-bred.

ALCESTE.

    Shall I see myself betrayed, robbed, torn to bits,
    And not . . . Oh, let's be still and rest our wits. 185
    Enough of reasoning, now. I've had my fill.

PHILINTE.

    Indeed, you would do well, Sir, to be still.
    Rage less at your opponent, and give some thought
    To how you'll win this lawsuit that he's brought.

ALCESTE.

    I assure you I'll do nothing of the sort.   190

PHILINTE.

    Then who will plead your case before the court?

ALCESTE.

    Reason and right and justice will plead for me.

PHILINTE.

    Oh, Lord. What judges do you plan to see?

ALCESTE.

    Why, none. The justice of my cause is clear.

PHILINTE.

    Of course, man; but there's no politics to
        fear. . . .   195

ALCESTE.

    No, I refuse to lift a hand. That's flat.
    I'm either right, or wrong.

PHILINTE.

                        Don't count on that.

ALCESTE.

    No, I'll do nothing.

PHILINTE.

                  Your enemy's influence   **200**
Is great, you know . . .

ALCESTE.

                        That makes no difference.

PHILINTE.

    It will; you'll see.

ALCESTE.

               Must honor bow to guile?
If so, I shall be proud to lose the trial.   **205**

PHILINTE.

    Oh, really . . .

ALCESTE.

             I'll discover by this case
Whether or not men are sufficiently base
And impudent and villainous and perverse
To do me wrong before the universe.   **210**

PHILINTE.

    What a man!

ALCESTE.

          Oh, I could wish, whatever the cost,
Just for the beauty of it, that my trial were lost.

PHILINTE.

    If people heard you talking so, Alceste,
They'd split their sides. Your name would be
      a jest.   **215**

ALCESTE.

    So much the worse for jesters.

PHILINTE.

              May I enquire
Whether this rectitude you so admire,
And these hard virtues you're enamored of
Are qualities of the lady whom you love?   **220**
It much surprises me that you, who seem
To view mankind with furious disesteem,
Have yet found something to enchant your eyes
Amidst a species which you so despise.
And what is more amazing, I'm afraid,   **225**
Is the most curious choice your heart has made.
The honest Éliante is fond of you,
Arsinoé, the prude, admires you too;
And yet your spirit's been perversely led
To choose the flighty Célimène instead,   **230**
Whose brittle malice and coquettish ways
So typify the manners of our days.
How is it that the traits you most abhor
Are bearable in this lady you adore?
Are you so blind with love that you can't
      find them?   **235**
Or do you contrive, in her case, not to mind them?

ALCESTE.

    My love for that young widow's not the kind
That can't perceive defects; no, I'm not blind.
I see her faults, despite my ardent love,
And all I see I fervently reprove.   **240**

And yet I'm weak; for all her falsity,
That woman knows the art of pleasing me,
And though I never cease complaining of her,
I swear I cannot manage not to love her.
Her charm outweighs her faults; I can but aim   **245**
To cleanse her spirit in my love's pure flame.

PHILINTE.

    That's no small task; I wish you all success.
You think then that she loves you?

ALCESTE.

                        Heavens, yes!
I wouldn't love her did she not love me.   **250**

PHILINTE.

    Well, if her taste for you is plain to see,
Why do these rivals cause you such despair?

ALCESTE.

    True love, Sir, is possessive, and cannot bear
To share with all the world. I'm here today
To tell her she must send that mob away.   **255**

PHILINTE.

    If I were you, and had your choice to make,
Éliante, her cousin, would be the one I'd take;
That honest heart, which cares for you alone,
Would harmonize far better with your own.

ALCESTE.

    True, true: each day my reason tells me so;   **260**
But reason doesn't rule in love, you know.

PHILINTE.

    I fear some bitter sorrow is in store;
This love . . .

SCENE TWO: ORONTE, ALCESTE, PHILINTE

ORONTE (*to* ALCESTE).

               The servants told me at the door
That Éliante and Célimène were out,
But when I heard, dear Sir, that you were about,
I came to say, without exaggeration,
That I hold you in the vastest admiration,   **5**
And that it's always been my dearest desire
To be the friend of one I so admire.
I hope to see my love of merit requited,
And you and I in friendship's bond united.
I'm sure you won't refuse—if I may be frank—   **10**
A friend of my devotedness—and rank.

During this speech of ORONTE'S, ALCESTE *is abstracted, and
seems unaware that he is being spoken to. He only breaks
off his reverie when* ORONTE *says:*

    It was for you, if you please, that my words were
      intended.

ALCESTE.

    For me, Sir?

ORONTE.

             Yes, for you. You're not offended?

ALCESTE.
By no means. But this much surprises me. . . .   15
The honor comes most unexpectedly. . . .
ORONTE.
My high regard should not astonish you;
The whole world feels the same. It is your due.
ALCESTE.
Sir . . .
ORONTE.
Why, in all the State there isn't one   20
Can match your merits; they shine, Sir, like the sun.
ALCESTE.
Sir . . .
ORONTE.
You are higher in my estimation
Than all that's most illustrious in the nation.
ALCESTE.
Sir . . .   25
ORONTE.
If I lie, may heaven strike me dead!
To show you that I mean what I have said,
Permit me, Sir, to embrace you most sincerely,
And swear that I will prize our friendship dearly.
Give me you hand. And now, Sir, if you choose,   30
We'll make our vows.
ALCESTE.
Sir . . .
ORONTE.
What! You refuse?
ALCESTE.
Sir, it's a very great honor you extend:
But friendship is a sacred thing, my friend;   35
It would be profanation to bestow
The name of friend on one you hardly know.
All parts are better played when well-rehearsed;
Let's put off friendship, and get acquainted first.
We may discover it would be unwise   40
To try to make our natures harmonize.
ORONTE.
By heaven! You're sagacious to the core;
This speech has made me admire you even more.
Let time, then, bring us closer day by day;
Meanwhile, I shall be yours in every way.   45
If, for example, there should be anything
You wish at court, I'll mention it to the King.
I have his ear, of course; it's quite well known
That I am much in favor with the throne.
In short, I am your servant. And now, dear friend,   50
Since you have such fine judgment, I intend
To please you, if I can, with a small sonnet
I wrote not long ago. Please comment on it,
And tell me whether I ought to publish it.
ALCESTE.
You must excuse me, Sir; I'm hardly fit   55
To judge such matters.

ORONTE.
Why not?
ALCESTE.
I am, I fear,
Inclined to be unfashionably sincere.
ORONTE.
Just what I ask; I'd take no satisfaction   60
In anything but your sincere reaction.
I beg you not to dream of being kind.
ALCESTE.
Since you desire it, Sir, I'll speak my mind.
ORONTE.
Sonnet. It's a sonnet. . . . *Hope* . . . The poem's
addressed
To a lady who wakened hopes within my breast.   65
Hope . . . this is not the pompous sort of thing,
Just modest little verses, with a tender ring.
ALCESTE.
Well, we shall see.
ORONTE.
Hope . . . I'm anxious to hear
Whether the style seems properly smooth and
clear,   70
And whether the choice of words is good or bad.
ALCESTE.
We'll see, we'll see.
ORONTE.
Perhaps I ought to add
That it took me only a quarter-hour to write it.
ALCESTE.
The time's irrelevant, Sir: kindly recite it.   75
ORONTE (*reading*).

Hope comforts us awhile, 'tis true,
Lulling our cares with careless laughter,
And yet such joy is full of rue,
My Phyllis, if nothing follows after.

PHILINTE.
I'm charmed by this already; the style's
delightful.   80
ALCESTE (*sotto voce, to* PHILINTE).
How can you say that? Why, the thing is frightful.
ORONTE.

Your fair face smiled on me awhile,
But was it kindness so to enchant me?
'Twould have been fairer not to smile,
If hope was all you meant to grant me.   85

PHILINTE.
What a clever thought! How handsomely you phrase
it!
ALCESTE (*sotto voce, to* PHILINTE).
You know the thing is trash.
How dare you praise it?

ORONTE.

> *If it's to be my passion's fate*
> *Thus everlastingly to wait,* **90**
> *Then death will come to set me free:*
> *For death is fairer than the fair;*
> *Phyllis, to hope is to despair*
> *When one must hope eternally.*

PHILINTE.

The close is exquisite—full of feeling and grace. **95**

ALCESTE (*sotto voce, aside*).

Oh, blast the close; you'd better close your face
Before you send your lying soul to hell.

PHILINTE.

I can't remember a poem I've liked so well.

ALCESTE (*sotto voce, aside*).

Good Lord!

ORONTE (*to* PHILINTE).

I fear you're flattering me a bit. **100**

PHILINTE.

Oh, no!

ALCESTE (*sotto voce, aside*).

What else d'you call it, you hypocrite?

ORONTE (*to* ALCESTE).

But you, Sir, keep your promise now: don't shrink
From telling me sincerely what you think.

ALCESTE.

Sir, these are delicate matters; we all desire **105**
To be told that we've the true poetic fire.
But once, to one whose name I shall not mention,
I said, regarding some verse of his invention,
That gentlemen should rigorously control
That itch to write which often afflicts the soul; **110**
That one should curb the heady inclination
To publicize one's little avocation;
And that in showing off one's works of art
One often plays a very clownish part.

ORONTE.

Are you suggesting in a devious way **115**
That I ought not . . .

ALCESTE.

Oh, that I do not say.
Further, I told him that no fault is worse
Than that of writing frigid, lifeless verse,
And that the merest whisper of such a shame **120**
Suffices to destroy a man's good name.

ORONTE.

D'you mean to say my sonnet's dull and trite?

ALCESTE.

I don't say that. But I went on to cite
Numerous cases of once-respected men
Who came to grief by taking up the pen. **125**

ORONTE.

And am I like them? Do I write so poorly?

ALCESTE.

I don't say that. But I told this person, "Surely
You're under no necessity to compose;
Why you should wish to publish, heaven knows.
There's no excuse for printing tedious rot **130**
Unless one writes for bread, as you do not.
Resist temptation, then, I beg of you;
Conceal your pastimes from the public view;
And don't give up, on any provocation,
Your present high and courtly reputation, **135**
To purchase at a greedy printer's shop
The name of silly author and scribbling fop."
These were the points I tried to make him see.

ORONTE.

I sense that they are also aimed at me;
But now—about my sonnet—I'd like to be
told . . . **140**

ALCESTE.

Frankly, that sonnet should be pigeonholed.
You've chosen the worst models to imitate.
The style's unnatural. Let me illustrate:

For example, *Your fair face smiled on me awhile*,
Followed by, *'Twould have been fairer not to*
smile! **145**
Or this: *such joy is full of rue;*
Or this: *For death is fairer than the fair;*
Or, *Phyllis, to hope is to despair*
When one must hope eternally!

This artificial style, that's all the fashion, **150**
Has neither taste, nor honesty, nor passion;
It's nothing but a sort of wordy play,
And nature never spoke in such a way.
What, in this shallow age, is not debased?
Our fathers, though less refined, had better taste; **155**
I'd barter all that men admire today
For one old love song I shall try to say:

> *If the King had given me for my own*
> *Paris, his citadel,*
> *And I for that must leave alone* **160**
> *Her whom I love so well,*
> *I'd say then to the Crown,*
> *Take back your glittering town;*
> *My darling is more fair, I swear,*
> *My darling is more fair.* **165**

The rhyme's not rich, the style is rough and old,
But don't you see that it's the purest gold
Beside the tinsel nonsense now preferred,
And that there's passion in its every word?

> *If the King had given me for my own* **170**
> *Paris, his citadel,*

And I for that must leave alone
Her whom I love so well,
I'd say then to the Crown,
Take back your glittering town;   175
My darling is more fair, I swear,
My darling is more fair.

There speaks a loving heart. (*To* PHILINTE.)
You're laughing, eh?
Laugh on, my precious wit. Whatever you say,   180
I hold that song's worth all the bibelots
That people hail today with ah's and oh's.

ORONTE.
And I maintain my sonnet's very good.

ALCESTE.
It's not at all surprising that you should.
You have your reasons; permit me to have mine   185
For thinking that you cannot write a line.

ORONTE.
Others have praised my sonnet to the skies.

ALCESTE.
I lack their art of telling pleasant lies.

ORONTE.
You seem to think you've got no end of wit.

ALCESTE.
To praise your verse, I'd need still more of it.   190

ORONTE.
I'm not in need of your approval, Sir.

ALCESTE.
That's good; you couldn't have it if you were.

ORONTE.
Come now, I'll lend you the subject of my sonnet;
I'd like to see you try to improve upon it.

ALCESTE.
I might, by chance, write something just as
    shoddy;   195
But then I wouldn't show it to everybody.

ORONTE.
You're most opinionated and conceited.

ALCESTE.
Go find your flatterers, and be better treated.

ORONTE.
Look here, my little fellow, pray watch your tone.

ALCESTE.
My great big fellow, you'd better watch your
    own.   200

PHILINTE (*stepping between them*).
Oh, please, please, gentlemen! This will never do.

ORONTE.
The fault is mine, and I leave the field to you.
I am your servant, Sir, in every way.

ALCESTE.
And I, Sir, am your most abject valet.

SCENE THREE: PHILINTE, ALCESTE

PHILINTE.
Well, as you see, sincerity in excess
Can get you into a very pretty mess;
Oronte was hungry for appreciation. . . .

ALCESTE.
Don't speak to me.

PHILINTE.
                                    What?   5

ALCESTE.
                            No more conversation.

PHILINTE.
Really, now . . .

ALCESTE.
                                Leave me alone.

PHILINTE.
                                        If I . . .

ALCESTE.
                    Out of my sight!   10

PHILINTE.
But what . . .

ALCESTE.
                    I won't listen.

PHILINTE.
                                But . . .

ALCESTE.
                                    Silence!

PHILINTE.
                            Now, is it polite . . .   15

ALCESTE.
By heaven, I've had enough. Don't follow me.

PHILINTE.
Ah, you're just joking. I'll keep you company.

ACT TWO

SCENE ONE: ALCESTE, CÉLIMÈNE

ALCESTE.
Shall I speak plainly, Madam? I confess
Your conduct gives me infinite distress,
And my resentment's grown too hot to smother.
Soon, I foresee, we'll break with one another.
If I said otherwise, I should deceive you;   5
Sooner or later, I shall be forced to leave you,
And if I swore that we shall never part,
I should misread the omens of my heart.

CÉLIMÈNE.
You kindly saw me home, it would appear,
So as to pour invectives in my ear.   10

ALCESTE.
I've no desire to quarrel. But I deplore
Your inability to shut the door

On all these suitors who beset you so.
There's what annoys me, if you care to know.
CÉLIMÈNE.

    Is it my fault that all these men pursue me?   **15**
Am I to blame if they're attracted to me?
And when they gently beg an audience,
Ought I to take a stick and drive them hence?
ALCESTE.

    Madam, there's no necessity for a stick;
A less responsive heart would do the trick.   **20**
Of your attractiveness I don't complain;
But those your charms attract, you then detain
By a most melting and receptive manner,
And so enlist their hearts beneath your banner.
It's the agreeable hopes which you excite   **25**
That keep these lovers round you day and night;
Were they less liberally smiled upon,
That sighing troop would very soon be gone.
But tell me, Madam, why it is that lately
This man Clitandre interests you so greatly?   **30**
Because of what high merits do you deem
Him worthy of the honor of your esteem?
Is it that your admiring glances linger
On the splendidly long nail of his little finger?
Or do you share the general deep respect   **35**
For the blond wig he chooses to affect?
Are you in love with his embroidered hose?
Do you adore his ribbons and his bows?
Or is it that this paragon bewitches
Your tasteful eye with his vast German breeches?   **40**
Perhaps his giggle, or his falsetto voice,
Makes him the latest gallant of your choice?
CÉLIMÈNE.

    You're much mistaken to resent him so.
Why I put up with him you surely know:
My lawsuit's very shortly to be tried,   **45**
And I must have his influence on my side.
ALCESTE.

    Then lose your lawsuit, Madam, or let it drop;
Don't torture me by humoring such a fop.
CÉLIMÈNE.

    You're jealous of the whole world, Sir.
ALCESTE.

                          That's true, **50**
Since the whole world is well-received by you.
CÉLIMÈNE.

    That my good nature is so unconfined
Should serve to pacify your jealous mind;
Were I to smile on one, and scorn the rest,
Then you might have some cause to be distressed.   **55**
ALCESTE.

    Well, if I mustn't be jealous, tell me, then,
Just how I'm better treated than other men.
CÉLIMÈNE.

    You know you have my love. Will that not do?

ALCESTE.

    What proof have I that what you say is true?
CÉLIMÈNE.

    I would expect, Sir, that my having said it   **60**
Might give the statement a sufficient credit.
ALCESTE.

    But how can I be sure that you don't tell
The selfsame thing to other men as well?
CÉLIMÈNE.

    What a gallant speech! How flattering to me!
What a sweet creature you make me out to be!   **65**
Well, then, to save you from the pangs of doubt,
All that I've said I hereby cancel out;
Now, none but yourself shall make a monkey of you:
Are you content?
ALCESTE.

                 Why, why am I doomed to love you? **70**
I swear that I shall bless the blissful hour
When this poor heart's no longer in your power!
I make no secret of it: I've done my best
To exorcise this passion from my breast;
But thus far all in vain; it will not go;   **75**
It's for my sins that I must love you so.
CÉLIMÈNE.

    Your love for me is matchless, Sir; that's clear.
ALCESTE.

    Indeed, in all the world it has no peer;
Words can't describe the nature of my passion,
And no man ever loved in such a fashion.   **80**
CÉLIMÈNE.

    Yes, it's a brand-new fashion, I agree:
You show your love by castigating me,
And all your speeches are enraged and rude.
I've never been so furiously wooed.
ALCESTE.

    Yet you could calm that fury, if you chose.   **85**
Come, shall we bring our quarrels to a close?
Let's speak with open hearts, then, and begin . . .

SCENE TWO: CÉLIMÈNE, ALCESTE, BASQUE

CÉLIMÈNE.

    What is it?
BASQUE.

               Acaste is here.
CÉLIMÈNE.

                   Well, send him in.

SCENE THREE: CÉLIMÈNE, ALCESTE

ALCESTE.

    What! Shall we never be alone at all?
You're always ready to receive a call,

And you can't bear, for ten ticks of the clock,
Not to keep open house for all who knock.

CÉLIMÈNE.

    I couldn't refuse him: he'd be most put out.   5

ALCESTE.

    Surely that's not worth worrying about.

CÉLIMÈNE.

    Acaste would never forgive me if he guessed
That I consider him a dreadful pest.

ALCESTE.

    If he's a pest, why bother with him then?

CÉLIMÈNE.

    Heavens! One can't antagonize such men;   10
Why, they're the chartered gossips of the court,
And have a say in things of every sort.
One must receive them, and be full of charm;
They're no great help, but they can do you harm,
And though your influence be ever so great,   15
They're hardly the best people to alienate.

ALCESTE.

    I see, dear lady, that you could make a case
For putting up with the whole human race;
These friendships that you calculate so nicely . . .

SCENE FOUR: ALCESTE, CÉLIMÈNE, BASQUE

BASQUE.

    Madam, Clitandre is here as well.

ALCESTE.

                    Precisely.

CÉLIMÈNE.

    Where are you going?

ALCESTE.

              Elsewhere.

CÉLIMÈNE.

                  Stay.   5

ALCESTE.

                    No, no.

CÉLIMÈNE.

    Stay, Sir.

ALCESTE.

         I can't.

CÉLIMÈNE.

           I wish it.

ALCESTE.

               No, I must go.   10
I beg you, Madam, not to press the matter;
You know I have no taste for idle chatter.

CÉLIMÈNE.

    Stay: I command you.

ALCESTE.

            No, I cannot stay.

CÉLIMÈNE.

    Very well; you have my leave to go away.   15

SCENE FIVE: ÉLIANTE, PHILINTE, ACASTE, CLITANDRE, ALCESTE, CÉLIMÈNE, BASQUE

ÉLIANTE (*to* CÉLIMÈNE).

    The Marquesses have kindly come to call.
Were they announced?

CÉLIMÈNE.

             Yes. Basque, bring chairs for all.

BASQUE *provides the chairs, and exits.*

To ALCESTE. You haven't gone?

ALCESTE.

             No; and I shan't depart   5
Till you decide who's foremost in your heart.

CÉLIMÈNE.

    Oh, hush.

ALCESTE.

        It's time to choose; take them, or me.

CÉLIMÈNE.

    You're mad.

ALCESTE.

        I'm not, as you shall shortly see.   10

CÉLIMÈNE.

    Oh?

ALCESTE.

      You'll decide.

CÉLIMÈNE.

        You're joking now, dear friend.

ALCESTE.

    No, no; you'll choose; my patience is at an end.

CLITANDRE.

    Madam, I come from court, where poor Cléonte   15
Behaved like a perfect fool, as is his wont.
Has he no friend to counsel him, I wonder,
And teach him less unerringly to blunder?

CÉLIMÈNE.

    It's true, the man's a most accomplished dunce;
His gauche behavior charms the eye at once;   20
And every time one sees him, on my word,
His manner's grown a trifle more absurd.

ACASTE.

    Speaking of dunces, I've just now conversed
With old Damon, who's one of the very worst;
I stood a lifetime in the broiling sun   25
Before his dreary monologue was done.

CÉLIMÈNE.

    Oh, he's a wondrous talker, and has the power
To tell you nothing hour after hour:
If, by mistake, he ever came to the point,
The shock would put his jawbone out of joint.   30

ÉLIANTE (*to* PHILINTE).

    The conversation takes its usual turn,
And all our dear friends' ears will shortly burn.

CLITANDRE.

    Timante's a character, Madam.

CÉLIMÈNE.

                          Isn't he, though?
  A man of mystery from top to toe,   **35**
  Who moves about in a romantic mist
  On secret missions which do not exist.
  His talk is full of eyebrows and grimaces;
  How tired one gets of his momentous faces;
  He's always whispering something confidential **40**
  Which turns out to be quite inconsequential;
  Nothing's too slight for him to mystify;
  He even whispers when he says "good-by."

ACASTE.

  Tell us about Géralde.

CÉLIMÈNE.

                    That tiresome ass. **45**
  He mixes only with the titled class,
  And fawns on dukes and princes, and is bored
  With anyone who's not at least a lord.
  The man's obsessed with rank, and his discourses
  Are all of hounds and carriages and horses; **50**
  He uses Christian names with all the great,
  And the word Milord, with him, is out of date.

CLITANDRE.

  He's very taken with Bélise, I hear.

CÉLIMÈNE.

  She is the dreariest company, poor dear.
  Whenever she comes to call, I grope about **55**
  To find some topic which will draw her out,
  But, owing to her dry and faint replies,
  The conversation wilts, and droops, and dies.
  In vain one hopes to animate her face
  By mentioning the ultimate commonplace; **60**
  But sun or shower, even hail or frost
  Are matters she can instantly exhaust.
  Meanwhile her visit, painful though it is,
  Drags on and on through mute eternities,
  And though you ask the time, and yawn,
      and yawn, **65**
  She sits there like a stone and won't be gone.

ACASTE.

  Now for Adraste.

CÉLIMÈNE.

                Oh, that conceited elf
  Has a gigantic passion for himself;
  He rails against the court, and cannot bear it **70**
  That none will recognize his hidden merit;
  All honors given to others give offense
  To his imaginary excellence.

CLITANDRE.

  What about young Cléon? His house, they say,
  Is full of the best society, night and day. **75**

CÉLIMÈNE.

  His cook has made him popular, not he:
  It's Cléon's table that people come to see.

ÉLIANTE.

  He gives a splendid dinner, you must admit.

CÉLIMÈNE.

  But must he serve himself along with it?
  For my taste, he's a most insipid dish **80**
  Whose presence sours the wine and spoils the fish.

PHILINTE.

  Damis, his uncle, is admired no end.
  What's your opinion, Madam?

CÉLIMÈNE.

                    Why, he's my friend.

PHILINTE.

  He seems a decent fellow, and rather clever. **85**

CÉLIMÈNE.

  He works too hard at cleverness, however.
  I hate to see him sweat and struggle so
  To fill his conversation with bons mots.
  Since he's decided to become a wit
  His taste's so pure that nothing pleases it; **90**
  He scolds at all the latest books and plays,
  Thinking that wit must never stoop to praise,
  That finding fault's a sign of intellect,
  That all appreciation is abject,
  And that by damning everything in sight **95**
  One shows oneself in a distinguished light.
  He's scornful even of our conversations:
  Their trivial nature sorely tries his patience;
  He folds his arms, and stands above the battle,
  And listens sadly to our childish prattle. **100**

ACASTE.

  Wonderful, Madam! You've hit him off precisely.

CLITANDRE.

  No one can sketch a character so nicely.

ALCESTE.

  How bravely, Sirs, you cut and thrust at all
  These absent fools, till one by one they fall:
  But let one come in sight, and you'll at once **105**
  Embrace the man you lately called a dunce,
  Telling him in a tone sincere and fervent
  How proud you are to be his humble servant.

CLITANDRE.

  Why pick on us? *Madame's* been speaking, Sir,
  And you should quarrel, if you must, with her. **110**

ALCESTE.

  No, no, by God, the fault is yours, because
  You lead her on with laughter and applause,
  And make her think that she's the more delightful
  The more her talk is scandalous and spiteful.
  Oh, she would stoop to malice far, far less **115**
  If no such claque approved her cleverness.
  It's flatterers like you whose foolish praise
  Nourishes all the vices of these days.

PHILINTE.

  But why protest when someone ridicules

Those you'd condemn, yourself, as knaves
   or fools?   120

CÉLIMÈNE.

Why, Sir? Because he loves to make a fuss.
You don't expect him to agree with us,
When there's an opportunity to express
His heaven-sent spirit of contrariness?
What other people think, he can't abide;   125
Whatever they say, he's on the other side;
He lives in deadly terror of agreeing;
'Twould make him seem an ordinary being.
Indeed, he's so in love with contradiction,
He'll turn against his most profound conviction 130
And with a furious eloquence deplore it,
If only someone else is speaking for it.

ALCESTE.

Go on, dear lady, mock me as you please;
You have your audience in ecstasies.

PHILINTE.

But what she says is true: you have a way   135
Of bridling at whatever people say;
Whether they praise or blame, your angry spirit
Is equally unsatisfied to hear it.

ALCESTE.

Men, Sir, are always wrong, and that's the reason
That righteous anger's never out of season;   140
All that I hear in all their conversation
Is flattering praise or reckless condemnation.

CÉLIMÈNE.

But . . .

ALCESTE.

     No, no, Madam, I am forced to state
That you have pleasures which I deprecate,   145
And that these others, here, are much to blame
For nourishing the faults which are your shame.

CLITANDRE.

I shan't defend myself, Sir; but I vow
I'd thought this lady faultless until now.

ACASTE.

I see her charms and graces, which are many;   150
But as for faults, I've never noticed any.

ALCESTE.

I see them, Sir; and rather than ignore them,
I strenuously criticize her for them.
The more one loves, the more one should object
To every blemish, every least defect.   155
Were I this lady, I would soon get rid
Of lovers who approved of all I did,
And by their slack indulgence and applause
Endorsed my follies and excused my flaws.

CÉLIMÈNE.

If all hearts beat according to your measure,   160
The dawn of love would be the end of pleasure;
And love would find its perfect consummation
In ecstasies of rage and reprobation.

ÉLIANTE.

Love, as a rule, affects men otherwise,
And lovers rarely love to criticize.   165
They see their lady as a charming blur,
And find all things commendable in her.
If she has any blemish, fault, or shame,
They will redeem it by a pleasing name.
The pale-faced lady's lily-white, perforce;   170
The swarthy one's a sweet brunette, of course;
The spindly lady has a slender grace;
The fat one has a most majestic pace;
The plain one, with her dress in disarray,
They classify as *beauté négligée;*   175
The hulking one's a goddess in their eyes,
The dwarf, a concentrate of Paradise;
The haughty lady has a noble mind;
The mean one's witty, and the dull one's kind;
The chatterbox has liveliness and verve,   180
The mute one has a virtuous reserve.
So lovers manage, in their passion's cause,
To love their ladies even for their flaws.

ALCESTE.

But I still say . . .

CÉLIMÈNE.

     I think it would be nice   185
To stroll around the gallery once or twice.
What! You're not going, Sirs?

CLITANDRE AND ACASTE.

       No, Madam, no.

ALCESTE.

You seem to be in terror lest they go.
Do what you will, Sirs; leave, or linger on,   190
But I shan't go till after you are gone.

ACASTE.

I'm free to linger, unless I should perceive
Madame is tired, and wishes me to leave.

CLITANDRE.

And as for me, I needn't go today
Until the hour of the King's *coucher.*   195

CÉLIMÈNE (*to* ALCESTE).

You're joking, surely?

ALCESTE.

     Not in the least; we'll see
Whether you'd rather part with them, or me.

SCENE SIX: ALCESTE, CÉLIMÈNE, ELIANTE, ACASTE, PHILINTE, CLITANDRE, BASQUE

BASQUE (*to* ALCESTE).

Sir, there's a fellow here who bids me state
That he must see you, and that it can't wait.

ALCESTE.

Tell him that I have no such pressing affairs.

BASQUE.
>It's a long tailcoat that this fellow wears,
>With gold all over.   5
CÉLIMÈNE (*to* ALCESTE).
>You'd best go down and see.
>Or—have him enter.

SCENE SEVEN: ALCESTE, CÉLIMÈNE, ELIANTE, ACASTE, PHILINTE, CLITANDRE, GUARD

ALCESTE (*confronting the* GUARD).
>   Well, what do you want with me?
>Come in, Sir.
GUARD.
>   I've a word, Sir, for your ear.
ALCESTE.
>Speak it aloud, Sir; I shall strive to hear.
GUARD.
>The Marshals have instructed me to say   5
>You must report to them without delay.
ALCESTE.
>Who? Me, Sir?
GUARD.
>   Yes, Sir; you.
ALCESTE.
>   But what do they want?
PHILINTE (*to* ALCESTE).
>To scotch your silly quarrel with Oronte.   10
CÉLIMÈNE (*to* PHILINTE).
>What quarrel?
PHILINTE.
>   Oronte and he have fallen out
>Over some verse he spoke his mind about;
>The Marshals wish to arbitrate the matter.
ALCESTE.
>Never shall I equivocate or flatter!   15
PHILINTE.
>You'd best obey their summons; come, let's go.
ALCESTE.
>How can they mend our quarrel, I'd like to know?
>Am I to make a cowardly retraction,
>And praise those jingles to his satisfaction?
>I'll not recant; I've judged that sonnet rightly. 20
>It's bad.
PHILINTE.
>   But you might say so more politely. . . .
ALCESTE.
>I'll not back down; his verses make me sick.
PHILINTE.
>If only you could be more politic!
>But come, let's go.   25
ALCESTE.
>   I'll go, but I won't unsay
>A single word.

PHILINTE.
>   Well, let's be on our way.
ALCESTE.
>Till I am ordered by my lord the King
>To praise that poem, I shall say the thing   30
>Is scandalous, by God, and that the poet
>Ought to be hanged for having the nerve to show it.
>*To* CLITANDRE *and* ACASTE, *who are laughing.*
>By heaven, Sirs, I really didn't know
>That I was being humorous.
CÉLIMÈNE.
>   Go, Sir, go;   35
>Settle your business.
ALCESTE.
>   I shall, and when I'm through,
>I shall return to settle things with you.

ACT THREE

SCENE ONE: CLITANDRE, ACASTE

CLITANDRE.
>Dear Marquess, how contented you appear;
>All things delight you, nothing mars your cheer.
>Can you, in perfect honesty, declare
>That you've a right to be so debonair?
ACASTE.
>By Jove, when I survey myself, I find   5
>No cause whatever for distress of mind.
>I'm young and rich; I can in modesty
>Lay claim to an exalted pedigree;
>And owing to my name and my condition
>I shall not want for honors and position.   10
>Then as to courage, that most precious trait,
>I seem to have it, as was proved of late
>Upon the field of honor, where my bearing,
>They say, was very cool and rather daring.
>I've wit, of course; and taste in such perfection 15
>That I can judge without the least reflection,
>And at the theater, which is my delight,
>Can make or break a play on opening night,
>And lead the crowd in hisses or bravos,
>And generally be known as one who knows.   20
>I'm clever, handsome, gracefully polite;
>My waist is small, my teeth are strong and white;
>As for my dress, the world's astonished eyes
>Assure me that I bear away the prize.
>I find myself in favor everywhere,   25
>Honored by men, and worshiped by the fair;
>And since these things are so, it seems to me
>I'm justified in my complacency.
CLITANDRE.
>Well, if so many ladies hold you dear,
>Why do you press a hopeless courtship here?   30

ACASTE.

    Hopeless, you say? I'm not the sort of fool
    That likes his ladies difficult and cool.
    Men who are awkward, shy, and peasantish
    May pine for heartless beauties, if they wish,
    Grovel before them, bear their cruelties,   35
    Woo them with tears and sighs and bended knees,
    And hope by dogged faithfulness to gain
    What their poor merits never could obtain.
    For men like me, however, it makes no sense
    To love on trust, and foot the whole expense.   40
    Whatever any lady's merits be,
    I think, thank God, that I'm as choice as she;
    That if my heart is kind enough to burn
    For her, she owes me something in return;
    And that in any proper love affair   45
    The partners must invest an equal share.

CLITANDRE.

    You think, then, that our hostess favors you?

ACASTE.

    I've reason to believe that that is true.

CLITANDRE.

    How did you come to such a mad conclusion?
    You're blind, dear fellow. This is sheer delusion.   50

ACASTE.

    All right, then: I'm deluded and I'm blind.

CLITANDRE.

    Whatever put the notion in your mind?

ACASTE.

    Delusion.

CLITANDRE.

            What persuades you that you're right?

ACASTE.

    I'm blind.   55

CLITANDRE.

            But have you any proofs to cite?

ACASTE.

    I tell you I'm deluded.

CLITANDRE.

               Have you, then,
    Received some secret pledge from Célimène?

ACASTE.

    Oh, no: she scorns me.   60

CLITANDRE.

             Tell me the truth, I beg.

ACASTE.

    She just can't bear me.

CLITANDRE.

             Ah, don't pull my leg.
    Tell me what hope she's given you, I pray.

ACASTE.

    I'm hopeless, and it's you who win the day.   65
    She hates me thoroughly, and I'm so vexed
    I mean to hang myself on Tuesday next.

CLITANDRE.

    Dear Marquess, let us have an armistice
    And make a treaty. What do you say to this?
    If ever one of us can plainly prove   70
    That Célimène encourages his love,
    The other must abandon hope, and yield,
    And leave him in possession of the field.

ACASTE.

    Now, there's a bargain that appeals to me;
    With all my heart, dear Marquess, I agree.   75
    But hush.

SCENE TWO: CÉLIMÈNE, ACASTE, CLITANDRE

CÉLIMÈNE.

    Still here?

CLITANDRE.

            'Twas love that stayed our feet.

CÉLIMÈNE.

    I think I heard a carriage in the street.
    Whose is it? D'you know?

SCENE THREE: CÉLIMÈNE, ACASTE, CLITANDRE, BASQUE

BASQUE.

               Arsinoé is here, *Madame*.

CÉLIMÈNE.

    Arsinoé, you say? Oh, dear.

BASQUE.

    Éliante is entertaining her below.

CÉLIMÈNE.

    What brings the creature here, I'd like to know?

ACASTE.

    They say she's dreadfully prudish, but in fact   5
    I think her piety . . .

CÉLIMÈNE.

             It's all an act.
    At heart she's worldly, and her poor success
    In snaring men explains her prudishness.
    It breaks her heart to see the beaux and gallants   10
    Engrossed by other women's charms and talents,
    And so she's always in a jealous rage
    Against the faulty standards of the age.
    She lets the world believe that she's a prude
    To justify her loveless solitude,   15
    And strives to put a brand of moral shame
    On all the graces that she cannot claim.
    But still she'd love a lover; and Alceste
    Appears to be the one she'd love the best.
    His visits here are poison to her pride;   20
    She seems to think I've lured him from her side;
    And everywhere, at court or in the town,

The spiteful, envious woman runs me down.
In short, she's just as stupid as can be,
Vicious and arrogant in the last degree,   25
And . . .

SCENE FOUR: ARSINOÉ, CÉLIMÈNE, CLITANDRE, ACASTE

CÉLIMÈNE.

Ah! What happy chance has brought you here?
I've thought about you ever so much, my dear.
ARSINOÉ.

I've come to tell you something you should know.
CÉLIMÈNE.

How good of you to think of doing so!
CLITANDRE *and* ACASTE *go out, laughing.*

SCENE FIVE: ARSINOÉ, CÉLIMÈNE

ARSINOÉ.

It's just as well those gentlemen didn't tarry.
CÉLIMÈNE.

Shall we sit down?
ARSINOÉ.

That won't be necessary.
Madam, the flame of friendship ought to burn
Brightest in matters of the most concern,   5
And as there's nothing which concerns us more
Than honor, I have hastened to your door
To bring you, as your friend, some information
About the status of your reputation.
I visited, last night, some virtuous folk,   10
And, quite by chance, it was of you they spoke;
There was, I fear, no tendency to praise
Your light behavior and your dashing ways.
The quantity of gentlemen you see
And your by now notorious coquetry   15
Were both so vehemently criticized
By everyone, that I was much surprised.
Of course, I needn't tell you where I stood;
I came to your defense as best I could,
Assured them you were harmless, and declared   20
Your soul was absolutely unimpaired.
But there are some things, you must realize,
One can't excuse, however hard one tries,
And I was forced at last into conceding
That your behavior, Madam, is misleading,   25
That it makes a bad impression, giving rise
To ugly gossip and obscene surmise,
And that if you were more *overtly* good,
You wouldn't be so much misunderstood.
Not that I think you've been unchaste—no! no!   30
The saints preserve me from a thought so low!
But mere good conscience never did suffice:
One must avoid the outward show of vice.

Madam, you're too intelligent, I'm sure,
To think my motives anything but pure   35
In offering you this counsel—which I do
Out of a zealous interest in you.
CÉLIMÈNE.

Madam, I haven't taken you amiss;
I'm very much obliged to you for this;
And I'll at once discharge the obligation   40
By telling you about *your* reputation.
You've been so friendly as to let me know
What certain people say of me, and so
I mean to follow your benign example
By offering you a somewhat similar sample.   45
The other day, I went to an affair
And found some most distinguished people there
Discussing piety, both false and true.
The conversation soon came round to you.
Alas! Your prudery and bustling zeal   50
Appeared to have a very slight appeal.
Your affectation of a grave demeanor,
Your endless talk of virtue and of honor,
The aptitude of your suspicious mind
For finding sin where there is none to find,   55
Your towering self-esteem, that pitying face
With which you contemplate the human race,
Your sermonizings and your sharp aspersions
On people's pure and innocent diversions—
All these were mentioned, Madam, and, in fact,   60
Were roundly and concertedly attacked.
"What good," they said, "are all these outward
    shows,
When everything belies her pious pose?
She prays incessantly; but then, they say,
She beats her maids and cheats them of their pay;   65
She shows her zeal in every holy place,
But still she's vain enough to paint her face;
She holds that naked statues are immoral,
But with a naked *man* she'd have no quarrel."
Of course, I said to everybody there   70
That they were being viciously unfair;
But still they were disposed to criticize you,
And all agreed that someone should advise you
To leave the morals of the world alone,
And worry rather more about your own.   75
They felt that one's self-knowledge should be great
Before one thinks of setting others straight;
That one should learn the art of living well
Before one threatens other men with hell,
And that the Church is best equipped, no doubt,   80
To guide our souls and root our vices out.
Madam, you're too intelligent, I'm sure,
To think my motives anything but pure
In offering you this counsel—which I do
Out of a zealous interest in you.   85

ARSINOÉ.

    I dared not hope for gratitude, but I
    Did not expect so acid a reply;
    I judge, since you've been so extremely tart,
    That my good counsel pierced you to the heart.

CÉLIMÈNE.

    Far from it, Madam. Indeed, it seems to me   **90**
    We ought to trade advice more frequently.
    One's vision of oneself is so defective
    That it would be an excellent corrective.
    If you are willing, Madam, let's arrange
    Shortly to have another frank exchange   **95**
    In which we'll tell each other, *entre nous,*
    What you've heard tell of me, and I of you.

ARSINOÉ.

    Oh, people never censure you, my dear;
    It's me they criticize. Or so I hear.

CÉLIMÈNE.

    Madam, I think we either blame or praise   **100**
    According to our taste and length of days.
    There is a time of life for coquetry,
    And there's a season, too, for prudery.
    When all one's charms are gone, it is, I'm sure,
    Good strategy to be devout and pure: **105**
    It makes one seem a little less forsaken.
    Some day, perhaps, I'll take the road you've taken:
    Time brings all things. But I have time aplenty,
    And see no cause to be a prude at twenty.

ARSINOÉ.

    You give your age in such a gloating tone   **110**
    That one would think I was an ancient crone;
    We're not so far apart, in sober truth,
    That you can mock me with a boast of youth!
    Madam, you baffle me. I wish I knew
    What moves you to provoke me as you do.   **115**

CÉLIMÈNE.

    For my part, Madam, I should like to know
    Why you abuse me everywhere you go.
    Is it my fault, dear lady, that your hand
    Is not, alas, in very great demand?
    If men admire me, if they pay me court   **120**
    And daily make me offers of the sort
    You'd dearly love to have them make to you,
    How can I help it? What would you have me do?
    If what you want is lovers, please feel free
    To take as many as you can from me.   **125**

ARSINOÉ.

    Oh, come. D'you think the world is losing sleep
    Over that flock of lovers which you keep,
    Or that we find it difficult to guess
    What price you pay for their devotedness?
    Surely you don't expect us to suppose   **130**
    Mere merit could attract so many beaux?
    It's not your virtue that they're dazzled by;

    Nor is it virtuous love for which they sigh.
    You're fooling no one, Madam; the world's not
      blind;
    There's many a lady heaven has designed   **135**
    To call men's noblest, tenderest feelings out,
    Who has no lovers dogging her about;
    From which it's plain that lovers nowadays
    Must be acquired in bold and shameless ways,
    And only pay one court for such reward   **140**
    As modesty and virtue can't afford.
    Then don't be quite so puffed up, if you please,
    About your tawdry little victories;
    Try, if you can, to be a shade less vain,
    And treat the world with somewhat less disdain. **145**
    If one were envious of your amours,
    One soon could have a following like yours;
    Lovers are no great trouble to collect
    If one prefers them to one's self respect.

CÉLIMÈNE.

    Collect them then, my dear; I'd love to see   **150**
    You demonstrate that charming theory;
    Who knows, you might . . .

ARSINOÉ.

                        Now, Madam, that will do;
    It's time to end this trying interview.
    My coach is late in coming to your door,   **155**
    Or I'd have taken leave of you before.

CÉLIMÈNE.

    Oh, please don't feel that you must rush away;
    I'd be delighted, Madam, if you'd stay.
    However, lest my conversation bore you,
    Let me provide some better company for you;   **160**
    This gentleman, who comes most apropos,
    Will please you more than I could do, I know.

SCENE SIX: ALCESTE, CÉLIMÈNE, ARSINOÉ

CÉLIMÈNE.

    Alceste, I have a little note to write
    Which simply must go out before tonight;
    Please entertain *Madame;* I'm sure that she
    Will overlook my incivility.

SCENE SEVEN: ALCESTE, ARSINOÉ

ARSINOÉ.

    Well, Sir, our hostess graciously contrives
    For us to chat until my coach arrives;
    And I shall be forever in her debt
    For granting me this little tête-à-tête.
    We women very rightly give our hearts   **5**
    To men of noble character and parts,
    And your especial merits, dear Alceste,
    Have roused the deepest sympathy in my breast.

Oh, how I wish they had sufficient sense
At court, to recognize your excellence!   **10**
They wrong you greatly, Sir. How it must hurt you
Never to be rewarded for your virtue!

ALCESTE.

Why, Madam, what cause have I to feel aggrieved?
What great and brilliant thing have I achieved?
What service have I rendered to the King   **15**
That I should look to him for anything?

ARSINOÉ.

Not everyone who's honored by the State
Has done great services. A man must wait
Till time and fortune offer him the chance.
Your merit, Sir, is obvious at a glance,   **20**
And . . .

ALCESTE.

Ah, forget my merit; I'm not neglected.
The court, I think, can hardly be expected
To mine men's souls for merit, and unearth
Our hidden virtues and our secret worth.   **25**

ARSINOÉ.

Some virtues, though, are far too bright to hide;
Yours are acknowledged, Sir, on every side.
Indeed, I've heard you warmly praised of late
By persons of considerable weight.

ALCESTE.

This fawning age has praise for everyone,   **30**
And all distinctions, Madam, are undone.
All things have equal honor nowadays,
And no one should be gratified by praise.
To be admired, one only need exist,
And every lackey's on the honors list.   **35**

ARSINOÉ.

I only wish, Sir, that you had your eye
On some position at court, however high;
You'd only have to hint at such a notion
For me to set the proper wheels in motion;
I've certain friendships I'd be glad to use   **40**
To get you any office you might choose.

ALCESTE.

Madam, I fear that any such ambition
Is wholly foreign to my disposition.
The soul God gave me isn't of the sort
That prospers in the weather of a court.   **45**
It's all too obvious that I don't possess
The virtues necessary for success.
My one great talent is for speaking plain;
I've never learned to flatter or to feign;
And anyone so stupidly sincere   **50**
Had best not seek a courtier's career.
Outside the court, I know, one must dispense
With honors, privilege, and influence;
But still one gains the right, foregoing these,
Not to be tortured by the wish to please.   **55**

One needn't live in dread of snubs and slights,
Nor praise the verse that every idiot writes,
Nor humor silly Marquesses, nor bestow
Politic sighs on Madam So-and-So.

ARSINOÉ.

Forget the court, then; let the matter rest.   **60**
But I've another cause to be distressed
About your present situation, Sir.
It's to your love affair that I refer.
She whom you love, and who pretends to love you,
Is, I regret to say, unworthy of you.   **65**

ALCESTE.

Why, Madam! Can you seriously intend
To make so grave a charge against your friend?

ARSINOÉ.

Alas, I must. I've stood aside too long
And let that lady do you grievous wrong;
But now my debt to conscience shall be paid: **70**
I tell you that your love has been betrayed.

ALCESTE.

I thank you, Madam; you're extremely kind.
Such words are soothing to a lover's mind.

ARSINOÉ.

Yes, though she *is* my friend, I say again
You're very much too good for Célimène.   **75**
She's wantonly misled you from the start.

ALCESTE.

You may be right; who knows another's heart?
But ask yourself if it's the part of charity
To shake my soul with doubts of her sincerity.

ARSINOÉ.

Well, if you'd rather be a dupe than doubt her,   **80**
That's your affair. I'll say no more about her.

ALCESTE.

Madam, you know that doubt and vague suspicion
Are painful to a man in my position;
It's most unkind to worry me this way
Unless you've some real proof of what you say.   **85**

ARSINOÉ.

Sir, say no more: all doubt shall be removed,
And all that I've been saying shall be proved.
You've only to escort me home, and there
We'll look into the heart of this affair.
I've ocular evidence which will persuade you   **90**
Beyond a doubt, that Célimène's betrayed you.
Then, if you're saddened by that revelation,
Perhaps I can provide some consolation.

ACT FOUR

SCENE ONE: ÉLIANTE, PHILINTE

PHILINTE.

Madam, he acted like a stubborn child;
I thought they never would be reconciled;

In vain we reasoned, threatened, and appealed;
He stood his ground and simply would not yield.
The Marshals, I feel sure, have never heard   5
An argument so splendidly absurd.
"No, gentlemen," said he, "I'll not retract.
His verse is bad: extremely bad, in fact.
Surely it does the man no harm to know it.
Does it disgrace him, not to be a poet?   10
A gentleman may be respected still,
Whether he writes a sonnet well or ill.
That I dislike his verse should not offend him;
In all that touches honor, I commend him;
He's noble, brave, and virtuous—but I fear   15
He can't in truth be called a sonneteer.
I'll gladly praise his wardrobe; I'll endorse
His dancing, or the way he sits a horse;
But, gentlemen, I cannot praise his rhyme.
In fact, it ought to be a capital crime   20
For anyone so sadly unendowed
To write a sonnet, and read the thing aloud."
At length he fell into a gentler mood
And, striking a concessive attitude,
He paid Oronte the following courtesies: 25
"Sir, I regret that I'm so hard to please,
And I'm profoundly sorry that your lyric
Failed to provoke me to a panegyric."
After these curious words, the two embraced,
And then the hearing was adjourned—in haste.   30

ELIANTE.
His conduct has been very singular lately;
Still, I confess that I respect him greatly.
The honesty in which he takes such pride
Has—to my mind—its noble, heroic side.
In this false age, such candor seems outrageous;   35
But I could wish that it were more contagious.

PHILINTE.
What most intrigues me in our friend Alceste
Is the grand passion that rages in his breast.
The sullen humors he's compounded of
Should not, I think, dispose his heart to love;   40
But since they do, it puzzles me still more
That he should choose your cousin to adore.

ELIANTE.
It does, indeed, belie the theory
That love is born of gentle sympathy,
And that the tender passion must be based   45
On sweet accords of temper and of taste.

PHILINTE.
Does she return his love, do you suppose?

ELIANTE.
Ah, that's a difficult question, Sir. Who knows?
How can we judge the truth of her devotion?
Her heart's a stranger to its own emotion.   50
Sometimes it thinks it loves, when no love's there;
At other times it loves quite unaware.

PHILINTE.
I rather think Alceste is in for more
Distress and sorrow than he's bargained for;
Were he of my mind, Madam, his affection   55
Would turn in quite a different direction,
And we would see him more responsive to
The kind regard which he receives from you.

ELIANTE.
Sir, I believe in frankness, and I'm inclined,
In matters of the heart, to speak my mind.   60
I don't oppose his love for her; indeed,
I hope with all my heart that he'll succeed,
And were it in my power, I'd rejoice
In giving him the lady of his choice.
But if, as happens frequently enough   65
In love affairs, he meets with a rebuff—
If Célimène should grant some rival's suit—
I'd gladly play the role of substitute;
Now would his tender speeches please me less
Because they'd once been made without success.   70

PHILINTE.
Well, Madam, as for me, I don't oppose
Your hopes in this affair; and heaven knows
That in my conversations with the man
I plead your cause as often as I can.
But if those two should marry, and so remove   75
All chance that he will offer you his love,
Then I'll declare my own, and hope to see
Your gracious favor pass from him to me.
In short, should you be cheated of Alceste,
I'd be most happy to be second best.   80

ELIANTE.
Philinte, you're teasing.

PHILINTE.
                         Ah, Madam, never fear;
No words of mine were ever so sincere,
And I shall live in fretful expectation
Till I can make a fuller declaration.   85

SCENE TWO: ALCESTE, ELIANTE, PHILINTE

ALCESTE.
Avenge me, Madam! I must have satisfaction,
Or this great wrong will drive me to distraction!

ELIANTE.
Why, what's the matter? What's upset you so?

ALCESTE.
Madam, I've had a mortal, mortal blow.
If Chaos repossessed the universe,   5
I swear I'd not be shaken any worse.
I'm ruined. . . . I can say no more. . . . My
    soul . . .

ELIANTE.
Do try, Sir, to regain your self-control.

ALCESTE.

    Just heaven! Why were so much beauty and grace
    Bestowed on one so vicious and so base?   **10**

ÉLIANTE.

    Once more, Sir, tell us. . . .

ALCESTE.

                My world has gone to wrack;
    I'm—I'm betrayed; she's stabbed me in the back:
    Yes, Célimène (who would have thought it of her?)
    Is false to me, and has another lover.   **15**

ÉLIANTE.

    Are you quite certain? Can you prove these things?

PHILINTE.

    Lovers are prey to wild imaginings
    And jealous fancies. No doubt there's some
        mistake. . . .

ALCESTE.

    Mind your own business, Sir, for heaven's sake.

To ÉLIANTE.

    Madam, I have the proof that you demand   **20**
    Here in my pocket, penned by her own hand.
    Yes, all the shameful evidence one could want
    Lies in this letter written to Oronte—
    Oronte! whom I felt sure she couldn't love,
    And hardly bothered to be jealous of.   **25**

PHILINTE.

    Still, in a letter, appearances may deceive;
    This may not be so bad as you believe.

ALCESTE.

    Once more I beg you, Sir, to let me be;
    Tend to your own affairs; leave mine to me.

ÉLIANTE.

    Compose yourself; this anguish that you
        feel . . .   **30**

ALCESTE.

    Is something, Madam, you alone can heal.
    My outraged heart, beside itself with grief,
    Appeals to you for comfort and relief.
    Avenge me on your cousin, whose unjust
    And faithless nature has deceived my trust;   **35**
    Avenge a crime your pure soul must detest.

ÉLIANTE.

    But how, Sir?

ALCESTE.

              Madam, this heart within my breast
    Is yours; pray take it; redeem my heart from her,
    And so avenge me on my torturer.   **40**
    Let her be punished by the fond emotion,
    The ardent love, the bottomless devotion,
    The faithful worship which this heart of mine
    Will offer up to yours as to a shrine.

ÉLIANTE.

    You have my sympathy, Sir, in all you suffer;   **45**
    Nor do I scorn the noble heart you offer;

    But I suspect you'll soon be mollified,
    And this desire for vengeance will subside.
    When some belovèd hand has done us wrong
    We thirst for retribution—but not for long;   **50**
    However dark the deed that she's committed,
    A lovely culprit's very soon acquitted.
    Nothing's so stormy as an injured lover,
    And yet no storm so quickly passes over.

ALCESTE.

    No, Madam, no—this is no lovers' spat;   **55**
    I'll not forgive her; it's gone too far for that;
    My mind's made up; I'll kill myself before
    I waste my hopes upon her any more.
    Ah, here she is. My wrath intensifies.
    I shall confront her with her tricks and lies,   **60**
    And crush her utterly, and bring you then
    A heart no longer slave to Célimène.

SCENE THREE: CÉLIMÈNE, ALCESTE

ALCESTE (*aside*).

    Sweet heaven, help me to control my passion.

CÉLIMÈNE (*aside*).

    Oh, Lord.

    To ALCESTE.

          Why stand there staring in that fashion?
    And what d'you mean by those dramatic sighs,
    And that malignant glitter in your eyes?   **5**

ALCESTE.

    I mean that sins which cause the blood to freeze
    Look innocent beside your treacheries;
    That nothing Hell's or Heaven's wrath could do
    Ever produced so bad a thing as you.

CÉLIMÈNE.

    Your compliments were always sweet and pretty.   **10**

ALCESTE.

    Madam, it's not the moment to be witty.
    No, blush and hang your head; you've ample reason,
    Since I've the fullest evidence of your treason.
    Ah, this is what my sad heart prophesied;
    Now all my anxious fears are verified;   **15**
    My dark suspicion and my gloomy doubt
    Divined the truth, and now the truth is out.
    For all your trickery, I was not deceived;
    It was my bitter stars that I believed.
    But don't imagine that you'll go scot-free;   **20**
    You shan't misuse me with impunity.
    I know that love's irrational and blind;
    I know the heart's not subject to the mind,
    And can't be reasoned into beating faster;
    I know each soul is free to choose its master;   **25**
    Therefore had you but spoken from the heart,
    Rejecting my attentions from the start,
    I'd have no grievance, or at any rate
    I could complain of nothing but my fate.

Ah, but so falsely to encourage me—   30
That was a treason and a treachery
For which you cannot suffer too severely,
And you shall pay for that behavior dearly.
Yes, now I have no pity, not a shred;
My temper's out of hand; I've lost my head;   35
Shocked by the knowledge of your double-dealings,
My reason can't restrain my savage feelings;
A righteous wrath deprives me of my senses,
And I won't answer for the consequences.

CÉLIMÈNE.
    What does this outburst mean? Will you please
        explain?   40
    Have you, by any chance, gone quite insane?

ALCESTE.
    Yes, yes, I went insane the day I fell
    A victim to your black and fatal spell,
    Thinking to meet with some sincerity
    Among the treacherous charms that beckoned me.   45

CÉLIMÈNE.
    Pooh. Of what treachery can you complain?

ALCESTE.
    How sly you are, how cleverly you feign!
    But you'll not victimize me any more.
    Look: here's a document you've seen before.
    This evidence, which I acquired today,   50
    Leaves you, I think, without a thing to say.

CÉLIMÈNE.
    Is this what sent you into such a fit?

ALCESTE.
    You should be blushing at the sight of it.

CÉLIMÈNE.
    Ought I to blush? I truly don't see why.

ALCESTE.
    Ah, now you're being bold as well as sly;   55
    Since there's no signature, perhaps you'll claim . . .

CÉLIMÈNE.
    I wrote it, whether or not it bears my name.

ALCESTE.
    And you can view with equanimity
    This proof of your disloyalty to me!

CÉLIMÈNE.
    Oh, don't be so outrageous and extreme.   60

ALCESTE.
    You take this matter lightly, it would seem.
    Was it no wrong to me, no shame to you,
    That you should send Oronte this billet-doux?

CÉLIMÈNE.
    Oronte! Who said it was for him?

ALCESTE.
                            Why, those   65
    Who brought me this example of your prose.
    But what's the difference? If you wrote the letter
    To someone else, it pleases me no better.
    My grievance and your guilt remain the same.

CÉLIMÈNE.
    But need you rage, and need I blush for shame,   70
    If this was written to a *woman* friend?

ALCESTE.
    Ah! Most ingenious. I'm impressed no end;
    And after that incredible evasion
    Your guilt is clear. I need no more persuasion.
    How dare you try so clumsy a deception?   75
    D'you think I'm wholly wanting in perception?
    Come, come, let's see how brazenly you'll try
    To bolster up so palpable a lie:
    Kindly construe this ardent closing section
    As nothing more than sisterly affection!   80
    Here, let me read it. Tell me, if you dare to,
    That this is for a woman . . .

CÉLIMÈNE.
                            I don't care to.
    What right have you to badger and berate me,
    And so highhandedly interrogate me?   85

ALCESTE.
    Now, don't be angry; all I ask of you
    Is that you justify a phrase or two . . .

CÉLIMÈNE.
    No, I shall not. I utterly refuse,
    And you may take those phrases as you choose.

ALCESTE.
    Just show me how this letter could be meant   90
    For a woman's eyes, and I shall be content.

CÉLIMÈNE.
    No, no, it's for Oronte; you're perfectly right.
    I welcome his attentions with delight,
    I prize his character and his intellect,
    And everything is just as you suspect.   95
    Come, do your worst now; give your rage free rein;
    But kindly cease to bicker and complain.

ALCESTE (*aside*).
    Good God! Could anything be more inhuman?
    Was ever a heart so mangled by a woman?
    When I complain of how she has betrayed me,   100
    She bridles, and commences to upbraid me!
    She tries my tortured patience to the limit;
    She won't deny her guilt; she glories in it!
    And yet my heart's too faint and cowardly
    To break these chains of passion, and be free,   105
    To scorn her as it should, and rise above
    This unrewarded, mad, and bitter love.
To CÉLIMÈNE.
    Ah, traitress, in how confident a fashion
    You take advantage of my helpless passion,
    And use my weakness for your faithless charms   110
    To make me once again throw down my arms!
    But do at least deny this black transgression;
    Take back that mocking and perverse confession;
    Defend this letter and your innocence,

And I, poor fool, will aid in your defense.   115
Pretend, pretend, that you are just and true,
And I shall make myself believe in you.
CÉLIMÈNE.
Oh, stop it. Don't be such a jealous dunce,
Or I shall leave off loving you at once.
Just why should I *pretend?* What could
impel me   120
To stoop so low as that? And kindly tell me
Why, if I loved another, I shouldn't merely
Inform you of it, simply and sincerely!
I've told you where you stand, and that admission
Should altogether clear me of suspicion;   125
After so generous a guarantee,
What right have you to harbor doubts of me?
Since women are (from natural reticence)
Reluctant to declare their sentiments,
And since the honor of our sex requires   130
That we conceal our amorous desires,
Ought any man for whom such laws are broken
To question what the oracle has spoken?
Should he not rather feel an obligation
To trust that most obliging declaration?   135
Enough, now. Your suspicions quite disgust me;
Why should I love a man who doesn't trust me?
I cannot understand why I continue,
Fool that I am, to take an interest in you.
I ought to choose a man less prone to doubt,   140
And give you something to be vexed about.
ALCESTE.
Ah, what a poor enchanted fool I am;
These gentle words, no doubt, were all a sham;
But destiny requires me to entrust
My happiness to you, and so I must.   145
I'll love you to the bitter end, and see
How false and treacherous you dare to be.
CÉLIMÈNE.
No, you don't really love me as you ought.
ALCESTE.
I love you more than can be said or thought;
Indeed, I wish you were in such distress   150
That I might show my deep devotedness.
Yes, I could wish that you were wretchedly poor,
Unloved, uncherished, utterly obscure;
That fate had set you down upon the earth
Without possessions, rank, or gentle birth;   155
Then, by the offer of my heart, I might
Repair the great injustice of your plight;
I'd raise you from the dust, and proudly prove
The purity and vastness of my love.
CÉLIMÈNE.
This is a strange benevolence indeed!   160
God grant that I may never be in need. . . .
Ah, here's Monsieur Dubois, in quaint disguise.

SCENE FOUR: CÉLIMÈNE, ALCESTE,
DUBOIS

ALCESTE.
Well, why this costume? Why those frightened eyes?
What ails you?
DUBOIS.
                    Well, Sir, things are most mysterious.
ALCESTE.
What do you mean?
DUBOIS.
                         I fear they're very serious.   5
ALCESTE.
What?
DUBOIS.
                    Shall I speak more loudly?
ALCESTE.
                                                  Yes; speak out.
DUBOIS.
Isn't there someone here, Sir?
ALCESTE.
                                     Speak, you lout!   10
Stop wasting time.
DUBOIS.
                    Sir, we must slip away.
ALCESTE.
How's that?
DUBOIS.
                    We must decamp without delay.
ALCESTE.
Explain yourself.   15
DUBOIS.
                    I tell you we must fly.
ALCESTE.
What for?
DUBOIS.
                    We mustn't pause to say good-by.
ALCESTE.
Now what d'you mean by all of this, you clown?
DUBOIS.
I mean, Sir, that we've got to leave this town.   20
ALCESTE.
I'll tear you limb from limb and joint from joint
If you don't come more quickly to the point.
DUBOIS.
Well, Sir, today a man in a black suit,
Who wore a black and ugly scowl to boot,
Left us a document scrawled in such a hand   25
As even Satan couldn't understand.
It bears upon your lawsuit, I don't doubt;
But all hell's devils couldn't make it out.
ALCESTE.
Well, well, go on. What then? I fail to see
How this event obliges us to flee.   30

DUBOIS.

 Well, Sir: an hour later, hardly more,
 A gentleman who's often called before
 Came looking for you in an anxious way.
 Not finding you, he asked me to convey
 (Knowing I could be trusted with the same) 35
 The following message. . . . Now, what *was* his
  name?

ALCESTE.

 Forget his name, you idiot. What did he say?

DUBOIS.

 Well, it was one of your friends, Sir, anyway.
 He warned you to begone, and he suggested
 That if you stay, you may well be arrested. 40

ALCESTE.

 What? Nothing more specific? Think, man, think!

DUBOIS.

 No, Sir. He had me bring him pen and ink,
 And dashed you off a letter which, I'm sure,
 Will render things distinctly less obscure.

ALCESTE.

 Well—let me have it! 45

CÉLIMÈNE.

     What *is* this all about?

ALCESTE.

 God knows; but I have hopes of finding out.
 How long am I to wait, you blitherer?

DUBOIS (*after a protracted search for the letter*).

 I must have left it on your table, Sir.

ALCESTE.

 I ought to . . . 50

CÉLIMÈNE.

    No, no, keep your self-control;
 Go find out what's behind this rigmarole.

ALCESTE.

 It seems that fate, no matter what I do,
 Has sworn that I may not converse with you;
 But Madam, pray permit your faithful lover 55
 To try once more before the day is over.

ACT FIVE

SCENE ONE: ALCESTE, PHILINTE

ALCESTE.

 No, it's too much. My mind's made up, I tell you.

PHILINTE.

 Why should this blow, however hard, compel
  you . . .

ALCESTE.

 No, no, don't waste your breath in argument;
 Nothing you say will alter my intent;
 This age is vile, and I've made up my mind 5
 To have no further commerce with mankind.
 Did not truth, honor, decency, and the laws
 Oppose my enemy and approve my cause?

 My claims were justified in all men's sight;
 I put my trust in equity and right; 10
 Yet, to my horror and the world's disgrace,
 Justice is mocked, and I have lost my case!
 A scoundrel whose dishonesty is notorious
 Emerges from another lie victorious!
 Honor and right condone his brazen fraud, 15
 While rectitude and decency applaud!
 Before his smirking face, the truth stands charmed,
 And virtue conquered, and the law disarmed!
 His crime is sanctioned by a court decree!
 And not content with what he's done to me, 20
 The dog now seeks to ruin me by stating
 That I composed a book now circulating,
 A book so wholly criminal and vicious
 That even to speak its title is seditious!
 Meanwhile Oronte, my rival, lends his credit 25
 To the same libelous tale, and helps to spread it!
 Oronte! a man of honor and of rank,
 With whom I've been entirely fair and frank;
 Who sought me out and forced me, willy-nilly,
 To judge some verse I found extremely silly; 30
 And who, because I properly refused
 To flatter him, or see the truth abused,
 Abets my enemy in a rotten slander!
 There's the reward of honesty and candor!
 The man will hate me to the end of time 35
 For failing to commend his wretched rhyme!
 And not this man alone, but all humanity
 Do what they do from interest and vanity;
 They prate of honor, truth, and righteousness,
 But lie, betray, and swindle nonetheless. 40
 Come then: man's villainy is too much to bear;
 Let's leave this jungle and this jackal's lair.
 Yes! treacherous and savage race of men,
 You shall not look upon my face again.

PHILINTE.

 Oh, don't rush into exile prematurely; 45
 Things aren't as dreadful as you make them, surely.
 It's rather obvious, since you're still at large,
 That people don't believe your enemy's charge.
 Indeed, his tale's so patently untrue
 That it may do more harm to him than you. 50

ALCESTE.

 Nothing could do that scoundrel any harm:
 His frank corruption is his greatest charm,
 And, far from hurting him, a further shame
 Would only serve to magnify his name.

PHILINTE.

 In any case, his bald prevarication 55
 Has done no injury to your reputation,
 And you may feel secure in that regard.
 As for your lawsuit, it should not be hard
 To have the case reopened, and contest
 This judgment . . . 60

ALCESTE.

                No, no, let the verdict rest.
Whatever cruel penalty it may bring,
I wouldn't have it changed for anything.
It shows the times' injustice with such clarity
That I shall pass it down to our posterity   **65**
As a great proof and signal demonstration
Of the black wickedness of this generation.
It may cost twenty thousand francs; but I
Shall pay their twenty thousand, and gain thereby
The right to storm and rage at human evil,   **70**
And send the race of mankind to the devil.

PHILINTE.

    Listen to me. . . .

ALCESTE.

                Why? What can you possibly say?
Don't argue, Sir; your labor's thrown away.
Do you propose to offer lame excuses   **75**
For men's behavior and the times' abuses?

PHILINTE.

    No, all you say I'll readily concede:
This is a low, conniving age indeed;
Nothing but trickery prospers nowadays,
And people ought to mend their shabby ways.   **80**
Yes, man's a beastly creature; but must we then
Abandon the society of men?
Here in the world, each human frailty
Provides occasion for philosophy,
And that is virtue's noblest exercise;   **85**
If honesty shone forth from all men's eyes,
If every heart were frank and kind and just,
What could our virtues do but gather dust
(Since their employment is to help us bear
The villainies of men without despair)?   **90**
A heart well-armed with virtue can endure. . . .

ALCESTE.

    Sir, you're a matchless reasoner, to be sure;
Your words are fine and full of cogency;
But don't waste time and eloquence on me.
My reason bids me go, for my own good.   **95**
My tongue won't lie and flatter as it should;
God knows what frankness it might next commit,
And what I'd suffer on account of it.
Pray let me wait for Célimène's return
In peace and quiet. I shall shortly learn,   **100**
By her response to what I have in view,
Whether her love for me is feigned or true.

PHILINTE.

    Till then, let's visit Éliante upstairs.

ALCESTE.

    No, I am too weighed down with somber cares.
Go to her, do; and leave me with my gloom   **105**
Here in the darkened corner of this room.

PHILINTE.

    Why, that's no sort of company, my friend;
I'll see if Éliante will not descend.

SCENE TWO: CÉLIMÈNE, ORONTE, ALCESTE

ORONTE.

    Yes, Madam, if you wish me to remain
Your true and ardent lover, you must deign
To give me some more positive assurance.
All this suspense is quite beyond endurance.
If your heart shares the sweet desires of mine,   **5**
Show me as much by some convincing sign;
And here's the sign I urgently suggest:
That you no longer tolerate Alceste,
But sacrifice him to my love, and sever
All your relations with the man forever.   **10**

CÉLIMÈNE.

    Why do you suddenly dislike him so?
You praised him to the skies not long ago.

ORONTE.

    Madam, that's not the point. I'm here to find
Which way your tender feelings are inclined.
Choose, if you please, between Alceste and me,   **15**
And I shall stay or go accordingly.

ALCESTE (*emerging from the corner*).

    Yes, Madam, choose; this gentleman's demand
Is wholly just, and I support his stand.
I too am true and ardent; I too am here
To ask you that you make your feelings clear.   **20**
No more delays, now; no equivocation;
The time has come to make your declaration.

ORONTE.

    Sir, I've no wish in any way to be
An obstacle to your felicity.

ALCESTE.

    Sir, I've no wish to share her heart with you;   **25**
That may sound jealous, but at least it's true.

ORONTE.

    If, weighing us, she leans in your direction . . .

ALCESTE.

    If she regards you with the least affection . . .

ORONTE.

    I swear, I'll yield her to you there and then.

ALCESTE.

    I swear I'll never see her face again.   **30**

ORONTE.

    Now, Madam, tell us what we've come to hear.

ALCESTE.

    Madam, speak openly and have no fear.

ORONTE.

    Just say which one is to remain your lover.

ALCESTE.

    Just name one name, and it will all be over.

ORONTE.

    What! Is it possible that you're undecided?   35

ALCESTE.

    What! Can your feelings possibly be divided?

CÉLIMÈNE.

    Enough: this inquisition's gone too far:
    How utterly unreasonable you are!
    Not that I couldn't make the choice with ease;
    My heart has no conflicting sympathies;   40
    I know full well which one of you I favor,
    And you'd not see me hesitate or waver.
    But how can you expect me to reveal
    So cruelly and bluntly what I feel?
    I think it altogether too unpleasant   45
    To choose between two men when both are present;
    One's heart has means more subtle and more kind
    Of letting its affections be divined,
    Nor need one be uncharitably plain
    To let a lover know he loves in vain.   50

ORONTE.

    No, no, speak plainly; I for one can stand it.
    I beg you to be frank.

ALCESTE.

                  And I demand it.
    The simple truth is what I wish to know,
    And there's no need for softening the blow.   55
    You've made an art of pleasing everyone,
    But now your days of coquetry are done:
    You have no choice now, Madam, but to choose,
    For I'll know what to think if you refuse;
    I'll take your silence for a clear admission   60
    That I'm entitled to my worst suspicion.

ORONTE.

    I thank you for this ultimatum, Sir,
    And I may say I heartily concur.

CÉLIMÈNE.

    Really, this foolishness is very wearing:
    Must you be so unjust and overbearing?   65
    Haven't I told you why I must demur?
    Ah, here's Éliante; I'll put the case to her.

SCENE THREE: ÉLIANTE, PHILINTE, CÉLIMÈNE, ORONTE, ALCESTE

CÉLIMÈNE.

    Cousin, I'm being persecuted here
    By these two persons, who, it would appear,
    Will not be satisfied till I confess
    Which one I love the more, and which the less,
    And tell the latter to his face that he   5
    Is henceforth banished from my company.
    Tell me, has ever such a thing been done?

ÉLIANTE.

    You'd best not turn to me; I'm not the one
    To back you in a matter of this kind:
    I'm all for those who frankly speak their mind.   10

ORONTE.

    Madam, you'll search in vain for a defender.

ALCESTE.

    You're beaten, Madam, and may as well surrender.

ORONTE.

    Speak, speak, you must; and end this awful strain.

ALCESTE.

    Or don't, and your position will be plain.

ORONTE.

    A single word will close this painful scene.   15

ALCESTE.

    But if you're silent, I'll know what you mean.

SCENE FOUR: ARSINOÉ, CÉLIMÈNE, ÉLIANTE, ALCESTE, PHILINTE, ACASTE, CLITANDRE, ORONTE

ACASTE (*to* CÉLIMÈNE).

    Madam, with all due deference, we two
    Have come to pick a little bone with you.

CLITANDRE (*to* ORONTE *and* ALCESTE).

    I'm glad you're present,
    Sirs; as you'll soon learn,
    Our business here is also your concern.   5

ARSINOÉ (*to* CÉLIMÈNE).

    Madam, I visit you so soon again
    Only because of these two gentlemen,
    Who came to me indignant and aggrieved
    About a crime too base to be believed.
    Knowing your virtue, having such confidence
        in it,   10
    I couldn't think you guilty for a minute,
    In spite of all their telling evidence;
    And, rising above our little difference,
    I've hastened here in friendship's name to see
    You clear yourself of this great calumny.   15

ACASTE.

    Yes, Madam, let us see with what composure
    You'll manage to respond to this disclosure.
    You lately sent Clitandre this tender note.

CLITANDRE.

    And this one, for Acaste, you also wrote.

ACASTE (*to* ORONTE *and* ALCESTE).

    You'll recognize this writing,   20
    Sirs, I think;
    The lady is so free with pen and ink
    That you must know it all too well, I fear.
    But listen: this is something you should hear.

''How absurd you are to condemn my lighthearted- **25**
edness in society, and to accuse me of being happiest in
the company of others. Nothing could be more unjust; and
if you do not come to me instantly and beg pardon for
saying such a thing, I shall never forgive you as long as
I live. Our big bumbling friend the Viscount . . .'' **30**

What a shame that he's not here.

''Our big bumbling friend the Viscount, whose name
stands first in your complaint, is hardly a man to my taste;
and ever since the day I watched him spend three-quarters
of an hour spitting into a well, so as to make circles **35**
in the water, I have been unable to think highly of him.
As for the little Marquess . . .''

In all modesty, gentlemen, that is I.

''As for the little Marquess, who sat squeezing my hand
for such a long while yesterday, I find him in all **40**
respects the most trifling creature alive; and the only
things of value about him are his cape and his sword. As
for the man with the green ribbons . . .''

To ALCESTE.

It's your turn now, Sir.

''As for the man with the green ribbons, he **45**
amuses me now and then with his bluntness and his
bearish ill-humor; but there are many times indeed when
I think him the greatest bore in the world. And as for the
sonneteer . . .''

To ORONTE.

Here's your helping. **50**

''And as for the sonneteer, who has taken it into his
head to be witty, and insists on being an author in the
teeth of opinion, I simply cannot be bothered to listen to
him, and his prose wearies me quite as much as his poetry.
Be assured that I am not always so well-entertained **55**
as you suppose; that I long for your company, more than
I dare to say, at all these entertainments to which people
drag me; and that the presence of those one loves is the
true and perfect seasoning to all one's pleasures.''

CLITANDRE.

And now for me. **60**

''Clitandre, whom you mention, and who so pesters me
with his saccharine speeches, is the last man on earth for
whom I could feel any affection. He is quite mad to suppose that I love him, and so are you, to doubt that you are
loved. Do come to your senses; exchange your sup- **65**
positions for his; and visit me as often as possible, to help
me bear the annoyance of his unwelcome attentions.''

It's a sweet character that these letters show,
And what to call it, Madam, you well know.
Enough. We're off to make the world acquainted **70**
With this sublime self-portrait that you've painted.

ACASTE.

Madam, I'll make you no farewell oration;
No, you're not worthy of my indignation.

Far choicer hearts than yours, as you'll discover,
Would like this little Marquess for a lover. **75**

SCENE FIVE: CÉLIMÈNE, ÉLIANTE, ARSINOÉ, ALCESTE, ORONTE, PHILINTE

ORONTE.

So! After all those loving letters you wrote,
You turn on me like this, and cut my throat!
And your dissembling, faithless heart, I find,
Has pledged itself by turns to all mankind!
How blind I've been! But now I clearly see; **5**
I thank you, Madam, for enlightening me.
My heart is mine once more, and I'm content;
The loss of it shall be your punishment.
To ALCESTE.
Sir, she is yours; I'll seek no more to stand
Between your wishes and this lady's hand. **10**

SCENE SIX: CÉLIMÈNE, ÉLIANTE, ARSINOÉ, ALCESTE, PHILINTE

ARSINOÉ (*to* CÉLIMÈNE).

Madam, I'm forced to speak. I'm far too stirred
To keep my counsel, after what I've heard.
I'm shocked and staggered by your want of morals.
It's not my way to mix in others' quarrels;
But really, when this fine and noble spirit, **5**
This man of honor and surpassing merit,
Laid down the offering of his heart before you,
How *could* you . . .

ALCESTE.

Madam, permit me, I implore you,
To represent myself in this debate. **10**
Don't bother, please, to be my advocate.
My heart, in any case, could not afford
To give your services their due reward;
And if I chose, for consolation's sake,
Some other lady, 'twould not be you I'd take. **15**

ARSINOÉ.

What makes you think you could, Sir? And how dare
you
Imply that I've been trying to ensnare you?
If you can for a moment entertain
Such flattering fancies, you're extremely vain.
I'm not so interested as you suppose **20**
In Célimène's discarded gigolos.
Get rid of that absurd illusion, do.
Women like me are not for such as you.
Stay with this creature, to whom you're so attached;
I've never seen two people better matched. **25**

SCENE SEVEN: CÉLIMÈNE, ÉLIANTE, ALCESTE, PHILINTE

ALCESTE (*to* CÉLIMÈNE).

Well, I've been still throughout this exposé,
Till everyone but me has said his say.
Come, have I shown sufficient self-restraint?
And may I now . . .

CÉLIMÈNE.

      Yes, make your just complaint. 5
Reproach me freely, call me what you will;
You've every right to say I've used you ill.
I've wronged you, I confess it; and in my shame
I'll make no effort to escape the blame.
The anger of those others I could despise; 10
My guilt toward you I sadly recognize.
Your wrath is wholly justified, I fear;
I know how culpable I must appear,
I know all things bespeak my treachery,
And that, in short, you've grounds for hating me. 15
Do so; I give you leave.

ALCESTE.

      Ah, traitress—how,
How should I cease to love you, even now?
Though mind and will were passionately bent
On hating you, my heart would not consent. 20
To ÉLIANTE *and* PHILINTE.
Be witness to my madness, both of you;
See what infatuation drives one to;
But wait; my folly's only just begun,
And I shall prove to you before I'm done
How strange the human heart is, and how far 25
From rational we sorry creatures are.
To CÉLIMÈNE.
Woman, I'm willing to forget your shame,
And clothe your treacheries in a sweeter name;
I'll call them youthful errors, instead of crimes,
And lay the blame on these corrupting times. 30
My one condition is that you agree
To share my chosen fate, and fly with me
To that wild, trackless, solitary place
In which I shall forget the human race.
Only by such a course can you atone 35
For those atrocious letters; by that alone
Can you remove my present horror of you,
And make it possible for me to love you.

CÉLIMÈNE.

What! *I* renounce the world at my young age,
And die of boredom in some hermitage? 40

ALCESTE.

Ah, if you really loved me as you ought,
You wouldn't give the world a moment's thought;
Must you have me, and all the world beside?

CÉLIMÈNE.

Alas, at twenty one is terrified
Of solitude. I fear I lack the force 45
And depth of soul to take so stern a course.
But if my hand in marriage will content you,
Why, there's a plan which I might well consent to,
And . . .

ALCESTE.

    No, I detest you now. I could excuse 50
Everything else, but since you thus refuse
To love me wholly, as a wife should do,
And see the world in me, as I in you,
Go! I reject your hand, and disenthrall
My heart from your enchantments, once for all. 55

SCENE EIGHT: ÉLIANTE, ALCESTE, PHILINTE

ALCESTE (*to* ÉLIANTE).

Madam, your virtuous beauty has no peer;
Of all this world, you only are sincere;
I've long esteemed you highly, as you know;
Permit me ever to esteem you so,
And if I do not now request your hand, 5
Forgive me, Madam, and try to understand.
I feel unworthy of it; I sense that fate
Does not intend me for the married state,
That I should do you wrong by offering you
My shattered heart's unhappy residue, 10
And that in short . . .

ÉLIANTE.

      Your argument's well taken:
Nor need you fear that I shall feel forsaken.
Were I to offer him this hand of mine,
Your friend Philinte, I think, would not decline. 15

PHILINTE.

Ah, Madam, that's my heart's most cherished goal,
For which I'd gladly give my life and soul.

ALCESTE (*to* ÉLIANTE *and* PHILINTE).

May you be true to all you now profess,
And so deserve unending happiness.
Meanwhile, betrayed and wronged in everything, 20
I'll flee this bitter world where vice is king,
And seek some spot unpeopled and apart
Where I'll be free to have an honest heart.

PHILINTE.

Come, Madam, let's do everything we can
To change the mind of this unhappy man. 25

FOCUS QUESTIONS

1. Show how Alceste's need to speak the truth at all costs affects the action of the play.
2. Recalling Éliante's reference to his ''noble, heroic side,'' defend Alceste as a tragic hero.
3. Defend Alceste as a comic hero, citing examples of character interaction, dialogue, or incidents from the play.
4. In a short essay, defend *The Misanthrope* as a dark comedy.
5. What does *The Misanthrope* tell us about the manners, taste, and fashion of the period?
6. In what ways is Célimène victimized by social pretensions and by Alceste's excessive nature?
7. Discuss the dramatic functions of any two supporting characters in the play.

OTHER ACTIVITIES

1. Using reviews, photographs, and other available production documents, evaluate the performance of a contemporary stage actor who has portrayed Alceste.
2. Mindful that the entire action takes place in Célimène's salon, design a stage set that will accommodate these characters and actions.
3. Block scenes 7 and 8 of act 5 in ways that will illuminate their subtexts.

BIBLIOGRAPHY

Arnott, Peter. *Ballet of Comedians*. New York: Macmillan, 1971.

Ashton, H. *Molière*. New York: E. P. Dutton, 1930.

Bermel, Albert. *Molière's Theatrical Bounty: A New View of the Plays*. Carbondale: Southern Illinois University Press, 1990.

Fernandez, Ramón. *Molière: The Man Seen Through the Plays*. New York: Hill & Wang, 1958.

Gossman, Lionel. *Men and Masks: A Study of Molière*. Baltimore: Johns Hopkins University Press, 1963.

Gross, Nathan. *From Gesture to Idea: Esthetics and Ethics in Molière's Comedy*. New York: Columbia University Press, 1982.

Guicharnaud, Jacques, ed. *Molière: A Collection of Critical Essays*. Englewood Cliffs, NJ: Prentice-Hall, 1964.

Herzel, Roger W. *The Original Casting of Molière's Plays*. Ann Arbor, MI: UMI Research Press, 1981.

Hope, Quentin M. ''Society in *Le Misanthrope*.'' *French Review* 32 (1959): 329–36.

Howarth, W. D. *Molière: A Playwright and His Audience*. London and Cambridge: Cambridge University Press, 1982.

Howarth, W. D. and M. Thomas, eds. *Molière: Stage and Study*. Oxford and London: Oxford University Press, 1973.

Hubert, Judd. *Molière and the Comedy of Intellect*. Berkeley: University of California Press, 1973.

Lawrence, Francis L. *Molière: The Comedy of Unreason*. New Orleans: Loyola University Press, 1968.

Mander, Gertrude. *Molière*. New York: Ungar, 1973.

Moore, W. G. *Molière: A New Criticism*. Oxford: Clarendon Press, 1949.

Yarrow, Philip. ''A Reconsideration of Alceste.'' *French Studies* 13 (1959): 314–31.

RECOMMENDED VIDEOTAPES AND RECORDINGS

The Comedy of Manners, Molière: The Misanthrope. VHS. 52 min. Starring Edward
    Petherbridge. In English, translation by Richard Wilbur. Distributed by Films for the
    Humanities and Sciences, Princeton, NJ.

The Misanthrope. Two sound cassettes. 90 min. 1969. APA-Phoenix production. Directed by
    Stephen Porter. Richard Wilbur translation. Caedmon Recordings.

Molière and the Comédie Française. VHS. 17 min. Excerpts from *The Misanthrope* and
    Tartuffe. Directed by Jacques Charon. Distributed by Insight Media, New York City.

THE ROVER
Aphra Behn (1640–1689)

All women together ought to let flowers fall upon the tomb of Aphra Behn
. . . for it was she who earned them the right to speak their minds.

—Virginia Woolf

Myra Taylor (*far left*) as Moretta, Robin Strasser as Angelica Bianca, Christopher Reeve as Willmore, and Faye Grant as Hellena in *The Rover,* presented by the Williamstown Theatre Festival in 1987, under the direction of John Rubinstein. *Photo: Nina Krieger.*

APPROACHING RESTORATION DRAMA

When Oliver Cromwell led the Puritan Revolution that closed the public theatres of England in 1642, the Elizabethan drama had already been displaced some forty years earlier by the Jacobean Age. Although Ben Jonson and William Shakespeare were still writing after James I assumed the throne in 1603, the new monarchy nurtured its own impressive enclave of playwrights that included Beaumont and Fletcher, Thomas Dekker, Thomas Heywood, Cyril Tourneur, John Webster, and John Ford, among others. When James I died in 1625, the last of the Jacobean playwrights saw their works produced until the Puritan takeover. It was not too long after Cromwell's death in 1658 that theatre-goers, having sustained the termination of England's potent dramatic art, were suddenly privy to its reemergence in 1660, when Charles II was restored to the throne. But the backlash to the Puritan repression was about to unfurl some rather startling surprises, in the theatre of all places, where a parade of worldly stage characters would lace their illicit behaviors with an acid-tongued wit. Thus the **Restoration drama** was born.

In contrast with the Elizabethan and Jacobean periods, when all classes of London society flocked to the public playhouses, the Restoration drama catered exclusively to the society surrounding Charles II until his death. Charles' fashion, wit, and sexual abandon set the tone. In terms of the stage, he brought his theatre-going experiences from Paris, a luxury reserved for the aristocrats and wealthy merchant families, as a model for the new theatres of London. Foremost was the appearance for the first time in England of women performers. Therefore the Restoration drama, like its French neighbor, held a mirror up to nature to reflect the precious language and wit of its upper-class subjects. Contributing to the critical development of the Western drama, the Restoration playwrights promoted the classical dramatic principles with which Jonson experimented but which had hardly influenced Shakespeare and his contemporaries. They substantially altered the differently shaped Elizabethan and Jacobean dramas of their playwright-predecessors to accommodate the newly constructed playhouses—now complete with movable painted flats—which were built when the king granted monopolies on theatrical productions in London to Thomas Killigrew (head of the King's Company) and William Davenant (head of the Duke's Company) in 1660.

While the Restoration drama flourished for nearly three decades, its rich examples of tragedy and comedy reflected the soul of the society it served. The latter, which became known as the **Comedy of Manners,** would finally prove the more popular and lasting. But the most significant outcome of this emancipation from Puritanism was the impact of women on the English stage. This innovation—now the rule, rather than the exception—prompted a new dimension of realism in the portrayal of stage life by forcing the playwrights to create roles for specific actors and actresses of the licensed acting companies. The true-to-life interactions between men and women resulted in dramatic confrontations that English playwrights were exploring in a new way. This equality between genders *as represented in live performance* was a matter not to be taken lightly. Comic writers in particular were not about to abandon the opportunities for sexual innuendo and for putting women on display.

By contrast, the Restoration's powerful authorial patriarchy boasted the glittering dramatic achievements of John Dryden, George Etherege, William Wycherley, John Vanbrugh, William Congreve, Thomas Shadwell, and George Farquhar, as each brought his own variation of sexual flirtation and seduction to front and center stage. While heroic tragedies depicted a world of absolutes in elegantly patterned blank verse, prose writers mastered a highly conversational comic tone to steer their wayward characters through boudoirs and bedchambers and down garden paths. Whether comic or tragic, the language was decidedly focused on the human personality. Their literary debt, of course, belonged not only to Molière, whose comedies of manners were centered on sexual conflicts and performed by men and women alike, but also to that master of English comedy, Ben Jonson, and the rich continuity of stage characters who followed after. That the craft of playwriting still belonged exclusively to men—a discrimination that would remain indelible for several more centuries—seemed all the more ironic, therefore, when the entrance of the Restoration actress was shared by the appearance of England's first successful woman playwright, Aphra Behn.

The achievement of Behn cannot be separated from certain biographical data that precipitated her debut as professional playwright: her marriage in c. 1664 to a Dutch merchant named Behn, whose apparent death during the plague of 1666 led to abandonment and poverty; her well-publicized espionage work in the Dutch Wars, where services, albeit unpaid, drove her back to London and, for a time, to debtor's prison; and her friendship with Thomas Killigrew who persuaded her to pursue the theatrical profession as a way of settling her pressing financial needs. Such circumstances apparently worked to her advantage when her play, *The Forc'd Marriage,* was produced in 1670, not by Killigrew, but by the Duke's Company. The romantic tragicomedy, also written in verse—for Behn had already achieved some renown as a poet—displayed her natural playwriting skills at once. With reference to the fact that this first play was written by a woman, her prologue playfully admonished the men in the audience: ''Discourage but this first attempt, and then/ They'll hardly dare to sally out again.''

In retrospect, the forces that previously conspired against Behn's reputation as Restoration author and further suppressed the performances of her more acclaimed works have since lost their impact. Her prolific output of some sixteen plays far outnumbered those of her colleagues Wycherley, who wrote four, and Congreve, who wrote six. In fact, she was one of the most frequently performed playwrights of her time. Her reappearance during the late twentieth century, fostered by caring scholars who have demystified the gender biases that stifled her celebrity, has allowed her documented achievements as playwright, novelist, poet, and translator to overshadow her controversial life and acknowledged commercialism. Granting that her assertive claims for women's rights to their own sexuality and for total sexual equality were only covertly demonstrated in her plays, she had no choice but to appease her audiences with the same debauchery, sexual intrigue, and bawdy humor as her male counterparts in order to see her work produced.

Perhaps it was fortuitous that the crystallization of the Restoration drama, to which Behn made noteworthy contributions, proved a unique but all too brief phenomenon. But its select audience and narrow concentration on upper-class manners were not the reasons for its demise. Religion was. A year after the ''bloodless revolution'' and abdication of James II in 1688, his Protestant daughter Mary and her husband William of Orange assumed the throne. England now became a constitutional monarchy with rulers who were sympathetic to the working middle class. The new conservatism that took control renewed its hostility toward the theatre. Its most persuasive argument was delivered by Jeremy Collier, whose *Short View of the Immorality and Profaneness of the English Stage* (1698) railed against the obscenities of English stage comedy. A blow had been delivered to salacious wit, once again forcing the drama to rethink its agenda.

MAJOR WORKS

The Amorous Prince (1671), Behn's second tragicomedy, scrutinizes the most promiscuous of rakes who is reformed just in the nick of time. The play enjoyed as equally an excellent run as *The Forc'd Marriage*. While critics were less kind to her third offering, a comedy of intrigue called *The Dutch Lover* (1673), its notoriety was sufficient enough to win her money, friends, and a respectable reputation. Other notable successes included *Abdelazer* (1676), her only pure tragedy; *The Town Fop* (1676), a comedy with brothel scenes; *Sir*

Patient Fancy (1678), adapted from Molière's *Imaginary Invalid; The Feigned Courtesans* (1679), a comedy; *The Roundheads* (1681), a historical comedy; *The City Heiress* (1682), an anti-Whig political lampoon; *The Lucky Chance* (1686), a comedy; and *The Emperor of the Moon* (1687), a strikingly original *commedia*-style farce. But her greatest stage success was *The Rover,* subtitled *The Banished Cavaliers* (1677), which prompted a sequel, *The Rover,* Part II (1681). Often regarded as her finest comedy, the play launched her comeback in the late twentieth century.

The Action

Arriving in Naples to carouse with the local inhabitants, a band of cavaliers encounters several young women who disguise themselves in masks to celebrate the carnival. Although Florinda has previously exchanged vows of love with the cavalier named Belvile, both her brother Don Pedro and her father plan to marry her to their rich friend Antonio. Meanwhile, Florinda's sister Hellena amorously pursues Belvile's friend—a cavalier named Willmore (the Rover). But Willmore also seeks the services of Angelica Bianca, a courtesan who happens to fall in love with him.

Sexual intrigue and rivalry mount steadily and prompt Florinda's escape from her father's house to the quarters of Ned Blunt, another fellow-cavalier. His lustful advances toward Florinda are interrupted by the arrival of Belvile, Willmore, and Don Pedro. Willing to accept his sister's love for Belvile, Don Pedro summons a priest to unite them at once. Angelica Bianca suddenly appears with a pistol aimed at Willmore but is disarmed by Antonio. She leaves angrily, relinquishing her Rover to Hellena.

Structure and Language

Behn's debt to an outside literary source—in this case, Thomas Killigrew's unproduced earlier play, *Thomaso* (1654)—was openly acknowledged in her postscript to *The Rover.* For that matter, Killigrew's play had been directly influenced by Ben Jonson and his literary circle. Nevertheless, the charge of plagiarism persisted, despite the fact that adapting the works of other authors was not an unfashionable practice. That such conduct was especially unbecoming to a woman, even of Behn's background and reputation, further aggravated the situation. But Behn's artistry surpassed Killigrew's at every turn, thus enabling her, according to Montague Summers, to clothe "dry bones with flesh, and to have given her creation a witty and supple tongue."[1]

Behn's newly transformed libertines still played their amorous games in true Restoration style, with moonlit gardens and perfumed boudoirs always conveniently visible on stage. Furthermore, her exotic locale, far from the city of London, evoked a certain nostalgia for the interregnum—the duration Charles II spent in exile—when followers like Willmore and his companions wandered across the continent in search of adventure while anticipating their ruler's return.

Setting the action in the pre-Lenten season when appetites for feasting and carousing need to be satisfied before the fasting begins, Behn lets her woman characters instigate the sexual innuendoes. Both sisters mock the ridiculous suitors chosen for Florinda by a father and a brother, then rail against the convent life for which Hellena is obviously unsuited. When Callis admits to a "youthful itch" in her eagerness to chaperone them to the carnival, all serious concerns for familial duty and religious discipline are tossed to the wind in response to baser yearnings. Of far greater importance to these ladies is their colorful gypsy attire, which should attract many onlookers yet keep them discreetly disguised.

The tone of the second scene mirrors the first, as Behn introduces her banished cavaliers whose own unadulterated lusts have driven them to this convenient carnival port.

When Willmore notices how the celebrants seem to enjoy "a kind of legal authorized fornication, where the men are not chided for it, nor the women despised, as among our dull English," he justifies his own promiscuity by attacking the same Puritan ethic at which Behn's comedy has been carefully aimed.

Willmore is instantly drawn to Hellena who flirts with him unashamedly then asks if he would climb a nunnery-wall to win her. His clever reply, "There's no sinner like a young saint," is hardly a subtle plea to know her better. While the oppression of marriage provides no attractive alternative for either of them, Hellena instinctively knows that submitting to Willmore's advances may rob her of honor and fortune in exchange for a "cradle full of noise and mischief." Certainly a far safer recourse is to tease him to the altar, which establishes her comic mission in the play. In the meantime, Florinda and Belvile renew their vow of love, agreeing to meet in secrecy later that night, and Florinda's kinswoman Valeria captures the attention of Frederick. The smooth coupling and verbal dueling, all of which infuse the contrivances of act 1, exude a seductive playfulness and wit that not only pay homage to the Restoration style, but also owe a debt to Plautus and Shakespeare with the unfolding mistaken identities, disguises, cross-dressings, and chases that follow.

But Willmore's attraction to Hellena is suddenly interrupted by the mention of the name "Angelica Bianca," an infamous courtesan familiar to all the young men in Naples, whose availability for a price "quenches all manner of fire" in him and temporarily displaces his feelings for Hellena. The unsavory actions that draw Angelica into Willmore's orbit and victimize her reveal the play's darker agenda.

Once in Angelica's arms, the penniless Willmore ascends to the heights of verse as he begs for her favors:

> There's not a joy thou hast in store
> I shall not then command:
> For which I'll pay thee back my soul, my life.
> Come, let's begin th'account this happy minute.

Furious with the oppressive male double standard that has determined her profession and driven her to cold financial bargainings, Angelica is weakened by Willmore's seductive powers, which have strangely rekindled the glimmer of love she has always kept hidden in her heart. When she asks, "And will you pay me then the price I ask?" he quite understandably misinterprets her ambiguous tone. So she clarifies the request, which now becomes a confession of her love: "The pay I mean is but thy love for mine./ —Can you give that?" Capable of feeling only lust for her, since this is how society has taught him to treat whores, Willmore answers with a lie: "Intirely—come, let's withdraw: where I'll renew my vows,—and breathe 'em with such ardour, thou shalt not doubt my zeal." Deceived by his powerful charm, Angelica submits to the most abhorred fate of her trade which, echoed by her servant Moretta, is to love "a pirate beggar, whose business is to rifle, and be gone."

The playful tug-of-war between Hellena and Willmore contrasts sharply with the more insidious one Angelica wages against Willmore, as she now pursues him with the soul of vengeance, especially when she discovers his heart belongs to another. "Who made the laws by which you judge me?" she asks him and then answers, "Men! Men who would rove and ramble, but require that women must be nice." It is conceivable that Angelica Bianca's points of view, considering her initials, might have belonged to the playwright. Out of this fallen woman's pain emerges Behn's political cry for sexual equality, a cry that was deliberately muffled by the play's wit and rambunctious comedy. But the message had been heard by an outspoken society whose liberal catechism harbored a double-standard code of honor, the repercussions of which would survive long after the Restoration.

Ground plan of the Restoration stage.

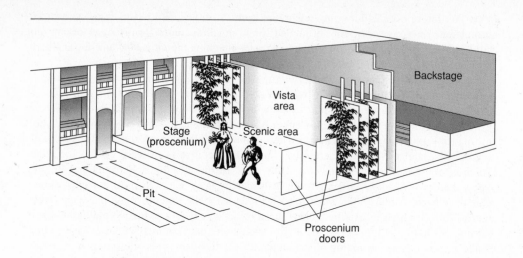

THE ROVER-IN-PERFORMANCE

Behn's comedy not only enjoyed the benefit of real stage actresses but also the more intimate surroundings of the Dorset Garden Theatre which, like other private Restoration playhouses, had a seating capacity between five and eight hundred. Aside from being smaller than the Elizabethan public theatres, the shape of the playhouse was also markedly different, drawing its architectural inspiration from the theatre practices of France. The actors performed on an extensive **apron** stage in front of a proscenium whose arch framed the painted perspective scenes of boudoir, bedroom, garden, or street, which were now operated by the **wing-and-groove** system. Stage characters stood apart from the flat scenic surfaces behind them, as if *in relief,* so that their mannered gestures welcomed a more presentational and less realistic style of acting.

The first documented performance of *The Rover* took place on March 24, 1677. William Smith assumed the role of Willmore and Thomas Betterton, who also served as joint manager of the Duke of York's company, played Belvile. Betterton's wife Mary appeared as Florinda, Anne Quin was Angelica, and Elizabeth Barry played Hellena. The popular low comedian, Cave Underhill, took the part of Ned Blunt. The comedy was so well received, in fact, that it immediately joined the company's repertory and was performed regularly through the end of the century. Actor William Mountford, in particular, achieved great success as the eponymous rake, prompting Queen Mary to remark that "it was dangerous to see him act, he made vice so alluring."[2]

From the start, the eighteenth century was renowned for its great actors, many of whom assumed the challenges of Behn's comedy, which was performed many times through the middle of the century at such theatres as the Drury Lane, Haymarket, and Lincoln's Inn Fields. Notable actors who played Willmore included Wilks, Verbruggen, Ryan, and Smith; Hellena attracted such artists as Mrs. Bracegirdle, Mrs. Oldfield, and in the 1757 revival at Covent Garden, Peg Wolfington. Despite the great success of this mid-century production, which was extended over the next four seasons, the comedy suddenly dropped out of sight until March 8, 1790, when J. P. Kemble presented his own adaptation at Drury Lane, calling it *Love in Many Masks.* Kemble's unfortunate rewrite resulted in the comedy's lengthy demise.

The resurgence of interest in neglected women authors, initially fueled by the landmark women's movement during the second half of the twentieth century, led to the reinstatement of Behn's reputation and the reconstruction of several of her plays. In the summer of 1984, two Behn revivals surfaced almost simultaneously in the same London district where her fame had originated two hundred years earlier: *The Rover* was presented by the Upstream Theatre, while the Women's Playhouse Trust produced *The Lucky Chance* at the Royal Court. Scheduled for limited runs, both productions drew sufficient critical praise to reclaim Behn's position among her esteemed Restoration colleagues. When the Royal Shakespeare Company mounted a lavish production of *The Rover* at the Swan Theatre in Stratford-upon-Avon on July 3, 1986, the unanimous kudos ushered it to London's Mermaid Theatre where it reopened on November 6, 1987. The rest, as they say, was history.

The occasion owed much of its success to the inspired, often tactful direction of John Barton, who confronted Behn's text with the right touch of daring. First of all, he removed some 550 lines, replacing them with 350 lines from the earlier Killigrew source, thus ironing out some of the wrinkles in the action. Valeria was introduced earlier in the play and Angelica's contribution was expanded considerably. Barton also reset the play in an unidentified Spanish colony, which facilitated his assigning one of the romantic leads (Belvile) to a black actor who plays a soldier of fortune rather than a cavalier. But most of all, he cast the usually cool and sophisticated Jeremy Irons as his swashbuckling hero, a coup that paid off handsomely on all sides. Michael Billington praised Barton's ''vigorous revival that justifies *The Rover*'s return'' and was especially impressed with Irons' Willmore ''as a Restoration hippy in red bandana and flowing locks'' and Stephanie Beacham's turn as Angelica Bianca ''with a light Spanish accent, sausage-curls and a good deal of sexual wit.''[3]

The Rover reached America for one of its earliest professional visits on July 21, 1987, under John Rubinstein's direction at the Williamstown Theatre Festival in Massachusetts. The cast featured Christopher Reeve (the Rover), Stephen Collins (Belvile), Harry Groener (Frederick), Edward Herrmann (Blunt), Kate Burton (Florinda), Faye Grant (Hellena), Ann Reinking (Moretta), and Robin Strasser (Angelica Bianca). Frank Rich found the direction ''sympathetic to the polemical undertow delicately illuminated by Ms. Grant and Ms. Strasser'' and credited the women for delivering ''the punch in Williamstown's hunk-heavy rendition of Behn's pioneering play.''[4] A less conventional staging of the work was offered by the Guthrie Theatre in 1994, under the direction of JoAnne Akalaitis.

REFLECTIONS ON THE ROVER

John Rubinstein directed The Rover
at the Williamstown Theatre in 1987.

I was celebrating the Fourth of July when the phone rang. It was my friend, Nikos Psacharopoulos, who ran the Williamstown Theatre. He wanted me to act in this play called *The Rover*. When he told me it was a Restoration comedy, I immediately felt my heart sink. We'd done a few Restoration plays at UCLA. I had never been in them, but I always found them sort of lame and heavy-handed. The language was so stilted that the jokes didn't play, and so the actors went out of their way to do shtick, to be funny in spite of

Continued

the story. This was my rather jaundiced view, of course. So I said, "Oh, dear! Well, who else is in it?" Then he read me the list. Quite a cast! I said, "Oh, well gee, it sounds like you've given all the best parts away. What do you want me to play?" He named the role of Don Pedro. So I picked up a copy of the script, and I read it through, and I must say it struck me like Restoration comedy. You know, the language was a little thick, the scenes were a little long, and the jokes weren't all that funny. The character of Don Pedro blustered around, but I didn't really get it.

I called Nikos back and told him I didn't want to play the part. Then I asked him who was directing, because I hadn't asked that the first time and sort of thought it was him. He said he didn't know, but that rehearsals were supposed to have started two days ago. And without thinking about it, I said, "Okay, I'll play the part, and why don't you let me direct it too?" I've never said those words to anybody. He asked if I'd ever directed before. I told him I'd done two productions at NYU that I was proud of, a *Three Sisters* and a *Macbeth,* both of which I didn't even feel humble about. I felt they were almost the best versions I'd ever seen in my life. So he put me on hold for about forty-five seconds, and then he punched back and said okay, and that I had to be up there the next day.

Paul Steinberg, the set designer, met me at dawn the following morning and we rented a car and drove from New York to Williamstown. Now, mind you, I'd flipped through this play only once and hadn't (a) liked it very much, or (b) understood it. With that thick language you really have to spend your time and do your work, which I hadn't time to do. So in our drive to Williamstown, Paul and I spoke about what the set should be. I didn't really know the play well enough, but he had some wonderful ideas. So I said, "Hey, that sounds great! Put it on paper!"

We finally got up there, parked the car, and walked into this rehearsal room where the cast was assembled. There was Ann Reinking who had been in *Pippin* with me. She was to play Lucetta, the whore, Angelica Bianca's colleague. And there were apprentices and younger actors I didn't know. Steven Collins was a friend of mine because I'd done a television movie with him and I knew Kate Burton. So there was a little bit of a sense of— I don't want to say family, but having had some connections with the group in some indirect or direct way—I can't even use the word *comfortable.* I was actually scared to death, because I take directing very seriously. I take acting very seriously. I take the theatre very seriously. They are my life! And here I was, standing with a bunch of really experienced and knowledgeable and gifted actors, not students, looking at me like hungry puppies looking at the person opening the Alpo. They had no director and they had been sitting around for two or three days and wondering what to do about it. Any one of them was experienced enough to take control, but they wanted a director. And of course, Williamstown works with a very tight schedule. Ours had already been cut. So I had nine days, in fact ten days, including that day.

Well, they were all as sweet as pie. Nobody looked at me as if to say what the hell are you doing as our director? So I sat everybody in a circle and we read the play. I even cast the minor parts which hadn't been cast yet with some of the apprentices sitting there. I mostly listened to the play, desperately hoping that by the time it was over I would know it well enough to begin directing with some kind of intelligence. Having rushed through it a day or so earlier, I didn't remember what the story was. But this time I fell in love with the play. It was funny and it got to me. So it was just a matter of getting it on its feet.

It happened very easily. We just read it once and then that afternoon we started blocking it in a rehearsal studio next to the theatre. Meanwhile Paul was madly putting together the set. He made me some drawings so that I had some idea of the floor plan. The set was being built twenty-four hours a day while we were rehearsing, so I'd go and visit it often. It grew and grew into a giant-like wall with balconies and staircases and windows. It was a massive, beautiful set which we used for interiors and exteriors alike. When we lit the interior, it seemed like the windows looked out; and when we lit the exterior, it was like you were outside, looking in. There was a big archway that we used as a grand entrance to the living room, but that also served as the city gates through which our four heroes entered at the very beginning. Meanwhile I saw drawings of the costumes, then approved them or made alterations. Suddenly there were costumes the next day.

But several days later I realized that I was not going to play Don Pedro. I didn't have the time to learn the lines. There was too much directing to do, and music to write. I mean, it was like I was going out of my mind. So I finally cast David Purdham who recently played Hamlet with me, Off-Broadway, in a production of *Rosencrantz and Guildenstern Are Dead*. He almost made me die laughing, because he was so funny as Don Pedro. And this was the part that I had read and said I didn't know what to do with.

I don't even remember having to do any "business" to make a single moment of *The Rover* work. One of my objections to playing Restoration or to some of the Shakespeare comedies you see done is the paranoid acting that you get from comic actors who, for instance, get to one of the bawdy references and invariably indicate it with two hands doing exaggerated masturbatory gestures so that we "get" the joke. Sometimes the language makes the humor a bit obscure to our modern ears. Now Shakespeare uses dirty language in a very subtle, roundabout kind of way. So these poor actors standing up there saying oh, geez, I'm making a joke about my crotch and nobody's gonna get it. I won't get a laugh. So what I'll do, oh, here's an original idea, I'll indicate a giant phallus and it works and it gets a laugh. Well that always makes me squirm in my seat, because it's not the gesture of the man in the situation saying what he's saying; it's the gesture of a laugh-crazed actor trying to nail his laugh.

We didn't have to invent any kind of stupid behavior to make the stuff funny. It was all there, and the actors just had to play it honestly. I've heard hundreds of actors say that it's got to be real, because it's the reality that makes you laugh. Certain comic actors throughout history and till today can get a laugh by doing their own personal brand of stage business, be it rubber-walking—you know, people have funny legs—or they can just look funny, amazing face-making and mugging, gestures and indications like I've just been talking about. All of these can get laughs and illuminate. Although I admire actors who do that, and I join with the rest of the audience laughing at something that's really funny, I finally find myself getting annoyed because the laughter is from the actor on the stage and for his or her brilliance. But as legitimate as that may be, my enjoyment as an audience member, and therefore my ambition as an actor or director, is for the reality of the situation and the words of the author to be funny.

There's always a lot of talk about "style" among actors, directors, and producers. Restoration "style." But I think it's a bunko word. It's misused. Naturally, there's a style to anything. When you're doing something in ancient costumes, you need to undo what is

Continued

purely of your own time and substitute it for anything you choose that illuminates the text. It's going to be relevant if it's relevant. It's not going to be relevant if it's not relevant. Often you'll get an actor playing Shakespeare in some sort of classical "style," and usually affecting a British accent and doing all kinds of old-fashioned gestures, especially if he's schooled in them. Very good, mind you. But he might as well be in a British company, you know. In the same production will be some woman or some man playing another part in their own native Brooklyn accent, sitting in the giant hoop skirt, as though it were a mini-skirt, not doing anything at all to alter who and what they are, and getting laughs. And making anachronistic, ironic points by saying Shakespeare's words in such a modern reading that the laughs are from that fact. We laugh at how funny the words sound coming through that person's mouth who is obviously from Delaney Street.

So I insisted we all use American accents. Nobody was allowed to do British, which immediately took away that phony sense of style. But the moment somebody was getting a laugh illegitimately, by doing a phallus gesture or talking in a New York accent or a California valley girl accent, I would say, "No, don't do that. That's not the way it goes." I personally helped people with their enunciation. We even had a vocal coach. We did the play as honestly as we could. That was my intention and that took care of any further discussion about style, about Restoration Comedy, about the history of such plays. So, for instance, David Purdham played the moral outrage against his sister *in extremis* and that's what made it funny. But it was never shticky, never phony. He just heightened it, played it big, because if it were soap opera, you would play it relatively small. Although we played it the way we wanted to play it, it was definitely set in the period Aphra Behn was writing about.

What Behn was doing is comparable to what we have to do today if we work on television. You've got to please the sponsor, selling Colgate toothpaste, for example, and he wants to offend no one. But you also want to say something. You don't want to just put a bland cartoon up there. You have to say it, but you still have to provide television "entertainment" that will get the largest amount of people watching. Behn certainly knew how to do that. She had a lot of bawdy stuff, girls undressing on stage and very masculine sexy guys and swordplay. But the theme of the play becomes terribly clear. I mean the liberation of women. Now the bad guy is Don Pedro who allows himself all kinds of sexual freedom, as do our other heroes. But the women are not supposed to have anything to do with this. They're not supposed to join the celebration; they're not supposed to be free and open about their emotions and their sexual desires. Not by reading any relevancy or con-temporaneity into it, but by just reading the play, they win out.

The scenes between Chris Reeve and Robin Strasser were the most difficult in the play. I tried to get their characters to tell the truth and to make sense or, to the degree that they were lying and pretending, to lie and pretend fully. And it really made a lot of sense. I think that if Aphra Behn wrote that the whore should fall in love in order to please the men in her audience, that might have been her candy-coating to the pill she was giving them about women being free. Women should be in charge of their own destiny, and their stupid fathers and brothers shouldn't be the masters of their daily lives, much less their destiny.

I don't believe too many people in our audience had even heard of the playwright, unless they were teachers or students. I would bet that, unless they'd been to London and seen John Barton's production, if I'd gotten up in front of them and asked if anyone heard of the two words—Aphra Behn—they would have said it was some kind of German car. But she wrote a wonderfully colorful and entertaining play. In fact, this was the first professional production I'd ever directed. Everybody pitched in to make it a total delight. That's the whole point of Williamstown. Egos are left behind, from big movie stars to directors. They give somebody a shot, like me, to direct their big money mainstage productions. Nikos just trusted me.

I remember one of our matinee performances. There was a tremendous rain and wind storm. So right in the big scene with Ed Hermann and Annie Reinking, the electricity went off in Williamstown and, of course, in the theatre as well. Some sort of weird emergency lights came on, and we barely finished the first act. We cancelled the rest of the performance until we could restore the power. We walked around with flashlights and wondered if we would be able to do the evening performance. When night fell, it was completely dark. Nobody could see anything. There were still no lights. The cast returned with candles and flashlights. There was word that they were fixing the power lines in town and that the electricity might be restored. The audience all came and the parking attendants guided them toward the theatre with flashlights.

We couldn't let the audience into the theatre, however, because it was dangerous. The storm was now over, so they gathered on the big lawn under the huge trees. The wind was still blowing, and the actors were in the dressing rooms putting on their makeup and costumes by candlelight. Talk about going back to the period! Meanwhile, I was running around madly lobbying for a performance on the lawn, but they fought me and finally said no, just in case somebody slipped on the wet grass and broke an ankle. I was frustrated because the audience wanted a play. It seems to me that around 9:15 on the evening of an 8:00 curtain, with actors in costume and ready to go—Bingo!—the lights went on. Just as the house manager was about to make the announcement that we were going to cancel the performance, she announced instead that the play would begin. Nobody had left, of course. By then it had turned into a kind of party atmosphere. The audience had mingled with the actors, drinking punch and coffee on the grass and chatting under the trees in candlelight. That performance was the best one we ever gave.

Notes

1. *Montague Summers, ed.,* THE WORKS OF APHRA BEHN, *vol. I (New York: Phaeton Press, 1967), 5.*
2. *Ibid., 5.*
3. *Michael Billington,* MANCHESTER GUARDIAN, *9 Nov. 1987.*
4. *Frank Rich,* THE NEW YORK TIMES, *27 July 1987.*

THE ROVER

OR, THE BANISH'D CAVALIERS
APHRA BEHN

CHARACTERS

Men

Don Antonio, *the Vice-Roy's Son*

Don Pedro, *a Noble Spaniard, his Friend*

Belvile, *an English Colonel in love with Florinda*

Willmore, *the ROVER*

Frederick, *an English Gentleman, and Friend to Belvile and Blunt*

Blunt, *an English Country Gentleman*

Stephano, *Servant to Don Pedro*

Philippo, *Lucetta's Gallant*

Sancho, *Pimp to Lucetta*

Bisky *and* Sebastian, *two Bravoes to Angelica*

Diego, *Page to Don Antonio*

Page *to Hellena*

Boy, *Page to Belvile*

Blunt's Man

Officers and Soldiers

Women

Florinda, *Sister to Don Pedro*

Hellena, *a gay young Woman design'd for a Nun, and Sister to Florinda*

Valeria, *a Kinswoman to Florinda*

Angelica Bianca, *a famous Curtezan*

Moretta, *her Woman*

Callis, *Governess to Florinda and Hellena*

Lucetta, *a jilting Wench*

Servants, other Masqueraders, Men and Women

SCENE: Naples, in Carnival-time

PART ONE
PROLOGUE

WRITTEN BY A PERSON OF QUALITY

WITS, like Physicians, never can agree,
When of a different Society;
And Rabel's Drops were never more cry'd down
By all the Learned Doctors of the Town,
Than a new Play, whose Author is unknown:　　5
Nor can those Doctors with more Malice sue
(And powerful Purses) the dissenting Few,
Than those with an insulting Pride do rail
At all who are not of their own Cabal.
　　If a Young Poet hit your Humour right,　　10

You judge him then out of Revenge and Spite;
So amongst Men there are ridiculous Elves,
Who Monkeys hate for being too like themselves:
So that the Reason of the Grand Debate,
Why Wit so oft is damn'd, when good Plays take,　　15
Is, that you censure as you love or hate.
Thus, like a learned Conclave, Poets sit
Catholick Judges both of Sense and Wit,
And damn or save, as they themselves think fit.
Yet those who to others Faults are so severe,　　20
Are not so perfect, but themselves may err.
Some write correct indeed, but then the whole
(Bating their own dull Stuff i' th' Play) is stole:
As Bees do suck from Flowers their Honey-dew,

So they rob others, striving to please you.   25
  Some write their Characters genteel and fine,
But then they do so toil for every Line,
That what to you does easy seem, and plain,
Is the hard issue of their labouring Brain.
And some th' Effects of all their Pains we see,   30
Is but to mimick good Extempore.
Others by long Converse about the Town,
Have Wit enough to write a leud Lampoon,
But their chief Skill lies in a Baudy Song.
In short, the only Wit that's now in Fashion   35
Is but the Gleanings of good Conversation.
As for the Author of this coming Play,
I ask'd him what he thought fit I should say,
In thanks for your good Company to day:
He call'd me Fool, and said it was well known,   40
You came not here for our sakes, but your own.
New Plays are stuff'd with Wits, and with
  Debauches,
That crowd and sweat like Cits in May-day Coaches.

ACT ONE

SCENE ONE. A CHAMBER.

Enter FLORINDA *and* HELLENA.

FLORINDA.   What an impertinent thing is a young Girl bred in a Nunnery! How full of Questions! Prithee no more, *Hellena;* I have told thee more than thou understand'st already.

HELLENA.   The more's my Grief; I wou'd fain know   5
as much as you, which makes me so inquisitive; nor is't enough to know you're a Lover, unless you tell me too, who 'tis you sigh for.

FLORINDA.   When you are a Lover, I'll think you fit for a Secret of that nature.   10

HELLENA.   'Tis true, I was never a Lover yet—but I begin to have a shreud Guess, what 'tis to be so, and fancy it very pretty to sigh, and sing, and blush and wish, and dream and wish, and long and wish to see the Man; and when I do, look pale and tremble; just as you did   15
when my Brother brought home the fine *English* Colonel to see you—what do you call him? Don *Belvile.*

FLORINDA.   Fie, *Hellena.*

HELLENA.   That Blush betrays you—I am sure 'tis so—or is it Don *Antonio* the Vice-Roy's Son?—or per-   20
haps the rich old Don *Vincentio,* whom my father designs for your Husband?—Why do you blush again?

FLORINDA.   With Indignation, and how near soever my Father thinks I am to marrying that hated Object, I shall let him see I understand better what's due to my   25
Beauty, Birth and Fortune, and more to my Soul, than to obey those unjust Commands.

HELLENA.   Now hang me, if I don't love thee for that dear Disobedience. I love Mischief strangely, as most of our Sex

do, who are come to love nothing else—But tell me,   30
dear *Florinda,* don't you love that fine *Anglese?*—for I vow next to loving him my self, 'twill please me most that you do so, for he is so gay and so handsom. .

FLORINDA.   *Hellena,* a Maid design'd for a Nun ought not to be so curious in a Discourse of Love.   35

HELLENA.   And dost thou think that ever I'll be a Nun? Or at least till I'm so old, I'm fit for nothing else. Faith no, Sister; and that which makes me long to know whether you love *Belvile,* is because I hope he has some mad Companion or other, that will spoil my Devotion; nay   40
I'm resolv'd to provide my self this Carnival, if there be e'er a handsom Fellow of my Humour above Ground, tho I ask first.

FLORINDA.   Prithee be not so wild.

HELLENA.   Now you have provided your self with a   45
Man, you take no Care for poor me—Prithee tell me, what dost thou see about me that is unfit for Love—have not I a world of Youth? a Humour gay? a Beauty passable? a Vigour desirable? well shap'd? clean limb'd? sweet breath'd? and Sense enough to know how all these   50
ought to be employ'd to the best Advantage: yes, I do and will. Therefore lay aside your Hopes of my Fortune, by my being a Devotee, and tell me how you came acquainted with this *Belvile;* for I perceive you knew him before he came to *Naples.*   55

FLORINDA.   Yes, I knew him at the Siege of *Pampelona,* he was then a Colonel of *French* Horse, who when the Town was ransack'd, nobly treated my Brother and my self, preserving us from all Insolencies; and I must own, (besides great Obligations) I have I know not what,   60
that pleads kindly for him about my Heart, and will suffer no other to enter—But see my Brother.

Enter DON PEDRO, STEPHANO, *with a Masquing Habit, and* CALLIS.

PEDRO.   Good morrow, Sister. Pray, when saw you your Lover Don *Vincentio?*

FLORINDA.   I know not, Sir—*Callis,* when was he   65
here? for I consider it so little, I know not when it was.

PEDRO.   I have a Command from my Father here to tell you, you ought not to despise him, a Man of so vast a Fortune, and such a Passion for you—*Stephano,* my things—(*Puts on his Masquing Habit.*)   70

FLORINDA.   A Passion for me! 'tis more than e'er I saw, or had a desire should be known—I hate *Vincentio,* and I would not have a Man so dear to me as my Brother follow the ill Customs of our Country, and make a Slave of his Sister—And Sir, my Father's Will, I'm sure, you   75
may divert.

PEDRO.   I know not how dear I am to you, but I wish only to be rank'd in your Esteem, equal with the *English* Colonel *Belvile*—Why do you frown and blush? Is there any Guilt belongs to the Name of that Cavalier?   80

FLORINDA.   I'll not deny I value *Belvile:* when I was ex-
pos'd to such Dangers as the licens'd Lust of common
Soldiers threatned, when Rage and Conquest flew thro the
City—then *Belvile,* this Criminal for my sake, threw himself into all Dangers to save my Honour, and will   85
you not allow him my Esteem?

PEDRO.   Yes, pay him what you will in Honour—but you
must consider Don *Vincentio's* Fortune, and the Jointure
he'll make you.

FLORINDA.   Let him consider my Youth, Beauty   90
and Fortune; which ought not to be thrown away on his
Age and Jointure.

PEDRO.   'Tis true, he's not so young and fine a Gentleman
as that *Belvile*—but what Jewels will that Cavalier present
you with? those of his Eyes and Heart?   95

HELLENA.   And are not those better than any Don *Vincentio*
has brought from the *Indies?*

PEDRO.   Why how now! Has your Nunnery-breeding
taught you to understand the Value of Hearts and Eyes?

HELLENA.   Better than to believe *Vincentio* de-   100
serves Value from any woman—He may perhaps encrease
her Bags, but not her Family.

PEDRO.   This is fine—Go up to your Devotion, you are not
design'd for the Conversation of Lovers.

HELLENA.   Nor Saints yet a while I hope. (*Aside.*)   105
Is't not enough you make a Nun of me, but you must cast
my Sister away too, exposing her to a worse confinement
than a religious Life?

PEDRO.   The Girl's mad—Is it a Confinement to be carry'd
into the Country, to an antient Villa belonging to   110
the Family of the *Vincentio's* these five hundred Years,
and have no other Prospect than that pleasing one of
seeing all her own that meets her Eyes—a fine Air, large
Fields and Gardens, where she may walk and gather
Flowers?   115

HELLENA.   When? By Moon-Light? For I'm sure she dares
not encounter with the heat of the Sun; that were a Task
only for Don *Vincentio* and his *Indian* Breeding, who
loves it in the Dog-days—And if these be her daily Divertisements, what are those of the Night? to lie in   120
a wide Moth-eaten Bed-Chamber with Furniture in
Fashion in the Reign of King *Sancho* the First; the Bed
that which his Forefathers liv'd and dy'd in.

PEDRO.   Very well.

HELLENA.   This Apartment (new furbisht and fitted   125
out for the young Wife) he (out of Freedom) makes his
Dressing-room; and being a frugal and a jealous Coxcomb, instead of a Valet to uncase his feeble Carcase, he
desires you to do that Office—Signs of Favour, I'll assure
you, and such as you must not hope for, unless   130
your Woman be out of the way.

PEDRO.   Have you done yet?

HELLENA.   That Honour being past, the Giant stretches it
self, yawns and sighs a Belch or two as loud as a Musket,
throws himself into Bed, and expects you in his   135
foul Sheets, and e'er you can get your self undrest, calls
you with a Snore or two—And are not these fine Blessings
to a young Lady?

PEDRO.   Have you done yet?

HELLENA.   And this man you must kiss, nay, you   140
must kiss none but him too—and nuzle thro his Beard to
find his Lips—and this you must submit to for threescore
Years, and all for a Jointure.

PEDRO.   For all your Character of Don *Vincentio,* she is as
like to marry him as she was before.   145

HELLENA.   Marry Don *Vincentio!* hang me, such a Wedlock
would be worse than Adultery with another Man: I had
rather see her in the *Hostel de Dieu,* to waste her Youth
there in Vows, and be a Handmaid to Lazers and Cripples,
than to lose it in such a Marriage.   150

PEDRO.   You have consider'd, Sister, that *Belvile* has no
Fortune to bring you to, is banisht his Country, despis'd
at home, and pity'd abroad.

HELLENA.   What then? the Vice-Roy's Son is better than
that Old Sir Fisty. Don *Vincentio!* Don *Indian!* he   155
thinks he's trading to *Gambo* still, and wou'd barter himself (that Bell and Bawble) for your Youth and Fortune.

PEDRO.   *Callis,* take her hence, and lock her up all this
Carnival, and at Lent she shall begin her everlasting Penance in a Monastery.   160

HELLENA.   I care not, I had rather be a Nun, than be oblig'd
to marry as you wou'd have me, if I were design'd for't.

PEDRO.   Do not fear the Blessing of that Choice—you shall
be a Nun.

HELLENA.   Shall I so? you may chance to be mis-   165
taken in my way of Devotion—A Nun! yes I am like to
make a fine Nun! I have an excellent Humour for a Grate:
No, I'll have a Saint of my own to pray to shortly, if I
like any that dares venture on me. (*Aside.*)

PEDRO.   *Callis,* make it your Business to watch   170
this wild Cat. As for you, *Florinda,* I've only try'd you
all this while, and urg'd my Father's Will; but mine is,
that you would love *Antonio,* he is brave and young, and
all that can compleat the Happiness of a gallant Maid—
This Absence of my Father will give us oppor-   175
tunity to free you from *Vincentio,* by marrying here,
which you must do to morrow.

FLORINDA.   To morrow!

PEDRO.   To morrow, or 'twill be too late—'tis not my
Friendship to *Antonio,* which makes me urge this,   180
but Love to thee, and Hatred to *Vincentio*—therefore resolve upon't to morrow.

FLORINDA.   Sir, I shall strive to do, as shall become your
Sister.

PEDRO.   I'll both believe and trust you—Adieu.   185
(*Exit* PEDRO *and* STEPHANO.)

HELLENA.   As become his Sister!—That is, to be as resolved your way, as he is his—(HELLENA *goes to* CALLIS.)

FLORINDA.
> I ne'er till now perceiv'd my Ruin near,
> I've no Defence against *Antonio's* Love,
> For he has all the Advantages of Nature,   **190**
> The moving Arguments of Youth and Fortune.

HELLENA.   But hark you, *Callis,* you will not be so cruel to lock me up indeed: will you?

CALLIS.   I must obey the Commands I hate—besides, do you consider what a Life you are going to lead?   **195**

HELLENA.   Yes, *Callis,* that of a Nun: and till then I'll be indebted a World of Prayers to you, if you let me now see, what I never did, the Divertisements of a Carnival.

CALLIS.   What, go in Masquerade? 'twill be a fine farewell to the World I take it—pray what wou'd you do   **200**
there?

HELLENA.   That which all the World does, as I am told, be as mad as the rest, and take all innocent Freedom—Sister, you'll go too, will you not? come prithee be not sad— We'll out-wit twenty Brothers, if you'll be ruled   **205**
by me—Come put off this dull Humour with your Clothes, and assume one as gay, and as fantastick as the Dress my Cousin *Valeria* and I have provided, and let's ramble.

FLORINDA.   *Callis,* will you give us leave to go?   **210**

CALLIS.   I have a youthful Itch of going my self. (*Aside.*) —Madam, if I thought your Brother might not know it, and I might wait on you, for by my troth I'll not trust young Girls alone.

FLORINDA.   Thou see'st my Brother's gone al-   **215**
ready, and thou shalt attend and watch us.

Enter STEPHANO.

STEPHANO.   Madam, the Habits are come, and your Cousin Valeria is drest, and stays for you.

FLORINDA.   'Tis well—I'll write a Note, and if I chance to see *Belvile,* and want an opportunity to speak   **220**
to him, that shall let him know what I've resolv'd in favour of him.

HELLENA.   Come, let's in and dress us. (*Exeunt.*)

SCENE TWO. A LONG STREET.

Enter BELVILE, *melancholy,* BLUNT *and* FREDERICK.

FREDERICK.   Why, what the Devil ails the Colonel, in a time when all the World is gay, to look like mere Lent thus? Hadst thou been long enough in *Naples* to have been in love, I should have sworn some such Judgment had befall'n thee.   **5**

BELVILE.   No, I have made no new Amours since I came to Naples.

FREDERICK.   You have left none behind you in Paris.

BELVILE.   Neither.

FREDERICK.   I can't divine the Cause then; unless   **10**
the old Cause, the want of Mony.

BLUNT.   And another old Cause, the want of a Wench— Wou'd not that revive you?

BELVILE.   You're mistaken, *Ned.*

BLUNT.   Nay, 'Sheartlikins, then thou art past Cure.   **15**

FREDERICK.   I have found it out; thou hast renew'd thy Acquaintance with the Lady that cost thee so many Sighs at the Siege of *Pampelona*—pox on't, what d'ye call her— her Brother's a noble *Spaniard*—Nephew to the dead General—*Florinda*—ay,   *Florinda*—And   will   **20**
nothing serve thy turn but that damn'd virtuous Woman, whom on my Conscience thou lov'st in spite too, because thou seest little or no possibility of gaining her?

BELVILE.   Thou art mistaken, I have Interest enough in that lovely Virgin's Heart, to make me proud and vain,   **25**
were it not abated by the Severity of a Brother, who perceiving my Happiness—

FREDERICK.   Has civilly forbid thee the House?

BELVILE.   'Tis so, to make way for a powerful Rival, the Vice-Roy's Son, who has the advantage of me, in   **30**
being a Man of Fortune, a *Spaniard,* and her Brother's Friend; which gives him liberty to make his Court, whilst I have recourse only to Letters, and distant Looks from her Window, which are as soft and kind as those which Heav'n sends down on Penitents.   **35**

BLUNT.   Hey day! 'Sheartlikins, Simile! by this Light the Man is quite spoil'd—*Frederick,* what the Devil are we made of, that we cannot be thus concern'd for a Wench?— 'Sheartlikins, our *Cupids* are like the Cooks of the Camp, they can roast or boil a Woman, but they have none   **40**
of the fine Tricks to set 'em off, no Hogoes to make the Sauce pleasant, and the Stomach sharp.

FREDERICK.   I dare swear I have had a hundred as young, kind and handsom as this *Florinda;* and Dogs eat me, if they were not as troublesom to me i'th' Morning   **45**
as they were welcome o'er night.

BLUNT.   And yet, I warrant, he wou'd not touch another Woman, if he might have her for nothing.

BELVILE.   That's thy Joy, a cheap Whore.

BLUNT.   Why, 'dsheartlikins, I love a frank Soul—   **50**
When did you ever hear of an honest Woman that took a Man's Mony? I warrant 'em good ones—But, Gentlemen, you may be free, you have been kept so poor with Parliaments and Protectors, that the little Stock you have is not worth preserving—but I thank my Stars, I have   **55**
more Grace than to forfeit my Estate by Cavaliering.

BELVILE.   Methinks only following the Court should be sufficient to entitle 'em to that.

BLUNT.   'Sheartlikins, they know I follow it to do it no good, unless they pick a hole in my Coat for   **60**
lending you Mony now and then; which is a greater Crime to my Conscience, Gentlemen, than to the Commonwealth.

Enter WILLMORE.

WILLMORE.   Ha! dear *Belvile!* noble Colonel!

BELVILE.   *Willmore!* welcome ashore, my dear   **65**
Rover!—what happy Wind blew us this good Fortune?

WILLMORE.   Let me salute you my dear *Frederick,* and
then command me—How is't honest Lad?

FREDERICK.   Faith, Sir, the old Complement, infinitely the
better to see my dear mad *Willmore* again—Prithee   **70**
why camest thou ashore? and where's the Prince?

WILLMORE.   He's well, and reigns still Lord of the watery
Element—I must aboard again within a Day or two, and
my Business ashore was only to enjoy my self a little this
Carnival.   **75**

BELVILE.   Pray know our new Friend, Sir, he's but bashful,
a raw Traveller, but honest, stout, and one of us. (*Embraces* BLUNT.)

WILLMORE.   That you esteem him, gives him an Interest
here.

BLUNT.   Your Servant, Sir.   **80**

WILLMORE.   But well—Faith I'm glad to meet you again
in a warm Climate, where the kind Sun has its god-like
Power still over the Wine and Woman.—Love and Mirth
are my Business in *Naples;* and if I mistake not the Place,
here's an excellent Market for Chapmen of my   **85**
Humour.

BELVILE.   See here be those kind Merchants of Love you
look for.

*Enter several Men in masquing Habits, some playing on
Musick, others dancing after; Women drest like Curtezans,
with Papers pinn'd to their Breasts, and Baskets of Flowers
in their Hands.*

BLUNT.   'Sheartlikins, what have we here!

FREDERICK.   Now the Game begins.   **90**

WILLMORE.   Fine pretty Creatures! may a stranger have
leave to look and love?—What's here—*Roses for every
Month!* (*Reads the Paper.*)

BLUNT.   Roses for every Month! what means that?

BELVILE.   They are, or wou'd have you think they're   **95**
Curtezans, who here in *Naples* are to be hir'd by the
Month.

WILLMORE.   Kind and obliging to inform us—Pray where
do these Roses grow? I would fain plant some of 'em in
a Bed of mine.   **100**

WOMAN.   Beware such Roses, Sir.

WILLMORE.   A Pox of fear: I'll be bak'd with thee between
a pair of Sheets, and that's thy proper Still, so I might but
strow such Roses over me and under me—Fair one, wou'd
you wou'd give me leave to gather at your Bush   **105**
this idle Month, I wou'd go near to make some Body smell
of it all the Year after.

BELVILE.   And thou hast need of such a Remedy, for thou
stinkest of Tar and Rope-ends, like a Dock or Pesthouse.

(*The Woman puts her self into the Hands of a Man, and Exit.*)

WILLMORE.   Nay, nay, you shall not leave me so.   **110**

BELVILE.   By all means use no Violence here.

WILLMORE.   Death! just as I was going to be damnably in
love, to have her led off! I could pluck that Rose out of
his Hand, and even kiss the Bed, the Bush it grew in.

FREDERICK.   No Friend to Love like a long Voyage   **115**
at Sea.

BLUNT.   Except a Nunnery, *Frederick.*

WILLMORE.   Death! but will they not be kind, quickly be
kind? Thou know'st I'm no tame Sigher, but a rampant
Lion of the Forest.   **120**

*Two Men drest all over with Horns of several sorts, making
Grimaces at one another, with Papers pinn'd on their Backs,
advance from the farther end of the Scene.*

BELVILE.   Oh the fantastical Rogues, how they are dress'd!
'tis a Satir against the whole Sex.

WILLMORE.   Is this a Fruit that grows in this warm
Country?

BELVILE.   Yes: 'Tis pretty to see these *Italian* start,   **125**
swell, and stab at the Word *Cuckold,* and yet stumble at
Horns on every Threshold.

WILLMORE.   See what's on their Back—*Flowers for every
Night.* (*Reads.*) —Ah Rogue! And more sweet than Roses
of ev'ry Month! This is a Gardiner of *Adam's*   **130**
own breeding. (*They dance.*)

BELVILE.   What think you of those grave People?—is a
Wake in *Essex* half so mad or extravagant?

WILLMORE.   I like their sober grave way, 'tis a kind of
legal authoriz'd Fornication, where the Men are   **135**
not chid for't, nor the Women despis'd, as amongst our
dull *English;* even the Monsieurs want that part of good
Manners.

BELVILE.   But here in *Italy* a Monsieur is the humblest best-
bred Gentleman—Duels are so baffled by Bravo's   **140**
that an age shews not one, but between a *Frenchman* and
a Hang-man, who is as much too hard for him on the
Piazza, as they are for a *Dutchman* on the new Bridge—
But see another Crew.

Enter FLORINDA, HELLENA, *and* VALERIA, *drest like Gipsies;*
CALLIS *and* STEPHANO, LUCETTA, PHILIPPO *and* SANCHO *in
Masquerade.*

HELLENA.   Sister, there's your *Englishman,* and   **145**
with him a handsom proper Fellow—I'll to him, and instead of telling him his Fortune, try my own.

WILLMORE.   Gipsies, on my Life—Sure these will prattle
if a Man cross their Hands. (*Goes to* HELLENA.) Dear
pretty (and I hope) young Devil, will you tell an   **150**
amorous Stranger what Luck he's like to have?

HELLENA.   Have a care how you venture with me, Sir, lest
I pick your Pocket, which will more vex your *English*
Humour, than an *Italian* Fortune will please you.

WILLMORE.   How the Devil cam'st thou to know   **155**
my Country and Humour?

HELLENA.   The first I guess by a certain forward Impudence, which does not displease me at this time; and the Loss of your Money will vex you, because I hope you have but very little to lose.   **160**

WILLMORE.   Egad Child, thou'rt i'th' right; it is so little, I dare not offer it thee for a Kindness—But cannot you divine what other things of more value I have about me, that I would more willingly part with?

HELLENA.   Indeed no, that's the Business of a   **165** Witch, and I am but a Gipsy yet—Yet, without looking in your Hand, I have a parlous Guess, 'tis some foolish Heart you mean, an inconstant *English* Heart, as little worth stealing as your Purse.

WILLMORE.   Nay, then thou dost deal with the   **170** Devil, that's certain—Thou hast guess'd as right as if thou hadst been one of that Number it has languisht for—I find you'll be better acquainted with it; nor can you take it in a better time, for I am come from Sea, Child; and *Venus* not being propitious to me in her own Element, I   **175** have a world of Love in store—Wou'd you would be good-natur'd, and take some on't off my Hands.

HELLENA.   Why—I could be inclin'd that way—but for a foolish Vow I am going to make—to die a Maid.

WILLMORE.   Then thou art damn'd without Re-   **180** demption; and as I am a good Christian, I ought in charity to divert so wicked a Design—therefore prithee, dear Creature, let me know quickly when and where I shall begin to set a helping hand to so good a Work.

HELLENA.   If you should prevail with my tender   **185** Heart (as I begin to fear you will, for you have horrible loving Eyes) there will be difficulty in't that you'll hardly undergo for my sake.

WILLMORE.   Faith, Child, I have been bred in Dangers, and wear a Sword that has been employ'd in a worse   **190** Cause, than for a handsom kind Woman—Name the Danger—let it be any thing but a long Siege, and I'll undertake it.

HELLENA.   Can you storm?

WILLMORE.   Oh, most furiously.   **195**

HELLENA.   What think you of a Nunnery-wall? for he that wins me, must gain that first.

WILLMORE.   A Nun! Oh how I love thee for't! there's no Sinner like a young Saint—Nay, now there's no denying me: the old Law had no Curse (to a Woman) like   **200** dying a Maid; witness *Jephtha's* Daughter.

HELLENA.   A very good Text this, if well handled; and I perceive, Father Captain, you would impose no severe Penance on her who was inclin'd to console her self before she took Orders.   **205**

WILLMORE.   If she be young and handsom.

HELLENA.   Ay, there's it—but if she be not—

WILLMORE.   By this Hand, Child, I have an implicit Faith, and dare venture on thee with all Faults—besides, 'tis more meritorious to leave the World when thou hast   **210** tasted and prov'd the Pleasure on't; then 'twill be a Virtue in thee, which now will be pure Ignorance.

HELLENA.   I perceive, good Father Captain, you design only to make me fit for Heaven—but if on the contrary you should quite divert me from it, and bring me   **215** back to the World again, I should have a new Man to seek I find; and what a grief that will be—for when I begin, I fancy I shall love like any thing: I never try'd yet.

WILLMORE.   Egad, and that's kind—Prithee, dear Creature, give me Credit for a Heart, for faith, I'm a   **220** very honest Fellow—Oh, I long to come first to the Banquet of Love; and such a swimming Appetite I bring—Oh, I'm impatient. Thy Lodging, Sweetheart, thy Lodging, or I'm a dead man.

HELLENA.   Why must we be either guilty of For-   **225** nication or Murder, if we converse with you Men?—And is there no difference between leave to love me, and leave to lie with me?

WILLMORE.   Faith, Child, they were made to go together.

LUCETTA.   Are you sure this is the Man? (*Pointing*   **230** *to* BLUNT.)

SANCHO.   When did I mistake your Game?

LUCETTA.   This is a stranger, I know by his gazing; if he be brisk he'll venture to follow me; and then, if I understand my Trade, he's mine: he's *English* too, and they say that's a sort of good natur'd loving People, and   **235** have generally so kind an opinion of themselves, that a Woman with any Wit may flatter 'em into any sort of Fool she pleases.

BLUNT.   'Tis so—she is taken—I have Beauties which my false Glass at home did not discover.   **240**

(*She often passes by* BLUNT *and gazes on him; he struts, and cocks, and walks, and gazes on her.*)

FLORINDA.   This Woman watches me so, I shall get no Opportunity to discover my self to him, and so miss the intent of my coming—But as I was saying, Sir—by this Line you should be a Lover. (*Looking in his Hand.*)

BELVILE.   I thought how right you guess'd, all Men   **245** are in love, or pretend to be so—Come, let me go, I'm weary of this fooling. (*Walks away.*)

FLORINDA.   I will not, till you have confess'd whether the Passion that you have vow'd *Florinda* be true or false. (*She holds him, he strives to get from her.*)

BELVILE.   *Florinda!* (*Turns quick towards her.*)   **250**

FLORINDA.   Softly.

BELVILE.   Thou hast nam'd one will fix me here for ever.

FLORINDA.   She'll be disappointed then, who expects you this Night at the Garden-gate, and if you'll fail not—as let me see the other Hand—you will go near to   **255** do—she vows to die or make you happy. (*Looks on* CALLIS, *who observes 'em.*)

BELVILE.   What canst thou mean?

FLORINDA.   That which I say—Farewel. (*Offers to go.*)

BELVILE.   Oh charming Sybil, stay, complete that Joy, which, as it is, will turn into Distraction!—Where must I be? at the Garden-gate? I know it—at night you say—I'll sooner forfeit Heaven than disobey.   260

Enter DON PEDRO *and other Masquers, and pass over the Stage.*

CALLIS.   Madam, your Brother's here.

FLORINDA.   Take this to instruct you farther. (*Gives him a Letter, and goes off.*)

FREDERICK.   Have a care, Sir, what you promise; this may be a Trap laid by her Brother to ruin you.   265

BELVILE.   Do not disturb my Happiness with Doubts. (*Opens the Letter.*)

WILLMORE.   My dear pretty Creature, a Thousand Blessings on thee; still in this Habit, you say, and after Dinner at this Place.   270

HELLENA.   Yes, if you will swear to keep your Heart, and not bestow it between this time and that.

WILLMORE.   By all the little Gods of Love I swear, I'll leave it with you; and if you run away with it, those Deities of Justice will revenge me. (*Exit all the Women except* LUCETTA.)   275

FREDERICK.   Do you know the Hand?

BELVILE.   'Tis *Florinda's*. All Blessings fall upon the virtuous Maid.

FREDERICK.   Nay, no Idolatry, a sober Sacrifice I'll allow you.   280

BELVILE.   Oh Friends! the welcom'st News, the softest Letter!—nay, you shall see it; and could you now be serious, I might be made the happiest Man the Sun shines on.

WILLMORE.   The Reason of this mighty Joy.   285

BELVILE.   See how kindly she invites me to deliver her from the threaten'd Violence of her Brother—will you not assist me?

WILLMORE.   I know not what thou mean'st, but I'll make one at any Mischief where a Woman's concern'd—but she'll be grateful to us for the Favour, will she not?   290

BELVILE.   How mean you?

WILLMORE.   How should I mean? Thou know'st there's but one way for a Woman to oblige me.   295

BELVILE.   Don't prophane—the Maid is nicely virtuous.

WILLMORE.   Who pox, then she's fit for nothing but a Husband; let her e'en go, Colonel.

FREDERICK.   Peace, she's the Colonel's Mistress, Sir.

WILLMORE.   Let her be the Devil; if she be thy Mistress, I'll serve her—name the way.   300

BELVILE.   Read here this postcript. (*Gives him a Letter.*)

WILLMORE. (*Reads.*) *At Ten at night—at the Garden-Gate—of which, if I cannot get the Key, I will contrive a way over the Wall—come attended with a Friend or two.*—Kind heart, if we three cannot weave a String to   305

let her down a Garden-Wall, 'twere pity but the Hangman wove one for us all.

FREDERICK.   Let her alone for that: your Woman's Wit, your fair kind Woman, will out-trick a Brother or a Jew, and contrive like a Jesuit in Chains—but see, *Ned Blunt* is stoln out after the Lure of a Damsel. (*Exit* BLUNT *and* LUCETTA.)   310

BELVILE.   So he'll scarce find his way home again, unless we get him cry'd by the Bell-man in the Market-place, and 'twou'd sound prettily—a lost *English* Boy of Thirty.   315

FREDERICK.   I hope 'tis some common crafty Sinner, one that will fit him; it may be she'll sell him for *Peru*, the Rogue's sturdy and would work well in a Mine; at least I hope she'll dress him for our Mirth; cheat him of all, then have him well-favour'dly bang'd, and turn'd out naked at Midnight.   320

WILLMORE.   Prithee what Humour is he of, that you wish him so well?

BELVILE.   Why, of an *English* Elder Brother's Humour, educated in a Nursery, with a Maid to tend him till Fifteen, and lies with his Grand-mother till he's of Age; one that knows no Pleasure beyond riding to the next Fair, or going up to *London* with his right Worshipful Father in Parliament-time; wearing gay Clothes, or making honourable Love to his Lady Mother's Landry-Maid; gets drunk at a Hunting-Match, and ten to one then gives some Proofs of his Prowess—A pox upon him, he's our Banker, and has all our Cash about him, and if he fail we are all broke.   325   330   335

FREDERICK.   Oh let him alone for that matter, he's of a damn'd stingy Quality, that will secure our Stock. I know not in what Danger it were indeed, if the Jilt should pretend she's in love with him, for 'tis a kind believing Coxcomb; otherwise if he part with more than a Piece of Eight—geld him: for which offer he may chance to be beaten, if she be a Whore of the first Rank.   340

BELVILE.   Nay the Rogue will not be easily beaten, he's stout enough; perhaps if they talk beyond his Capacity, he may chance to exercise his Courage upon some of them; else I'm sure they'll find it as difficult to beat as to please him.   345

WILLMORE.   'Tis a lucky Devil to light upon so kind a Wench!

FREDERICK.   Thou hadst a great deal of talk with thy little Gipsy, coud'st thou do no good upon her? for mine was hard-hearted.   350

WILLMORE.   Hang her, she was some damn'd honest Person of Quality, I'm sure, she was so very free and witty. If her Face be but answerable to her Wit and Humour, I would be bound to Constancy this Month to gain her. In the mean time, have you made no kind Acquaintance since you came to Town?—You do not use to be honest so long, Gentlemen.   355

FREDERICK.   Faith Love has kept us honest, we   **360**
have been all fir'd with a Beauty newly come to Town,
the famous *Paduana Angelica Bianca.*

WILLMORE.   What, the Mistress of the dead *Spanish*
General?

BELVILE.   Yes, she's now the only ador'd Beauty of   **365**
all the Youth in *Naples,* who put on all their Charms to
appear lovely in her sight, their Coaches, Liveries, and
themselves, all gay, as on a Monarch's Birth-Day, to attract the Eyes of this fair Charmer, while she has the
Pleasure to behold all languish for her that see her.   **370**

FREDERICK.   'Tis pretty to see with how much Love the
Men regard her, and how much Envy the Women.

WILLMORE.   What Gallant has she?

BELVILE.   None, she's exposed to Sale, and four Days in the
Week she's yours—for so much a Month.   **375**

WILLMORE.   The very Thought of it quenches all manner
of Fire in me—yet prithee let's see her.

BELVILE.   Let's first to Dinner, and after that we'll pass the
Day as you please—but at Night ye must all be at my
Devotion.   **380**

WILLMORE.   I will not fail you. (*Exeunt.*)

ACT TWO

SCENE ONE. THE LONG STREET.

Enter BELVILE *and* FREDERICK *in Masquing-Habits, and*
WILLMORE *in his own Clothes, with a Vizard in his Hand.*

WILLMORE.   But why thus disguis'd and muzzl'd?

BELVILE.   Because whatever Extravagances we commit in
these Faces, our own may not be oblig'd to answer 'em.

WILLMORE.   I should have chang'd my Eternal Buff too:
but no matter, my little Gipsy wou'd not have found   **5**
me out then: for if she should change hers, it is impossible
I should know her, unless I should hear her prattle—A
Pox on't, I cannot get her out of my Head: Pray Heaven,
if ever I do see her again, she prove damnable ugly, that
I may fortify my self against her Tongue.   **10**

BELVILE.   Have a care of Love, for o' my conscience she
was not of a Quality to give thee any hopes.

WILLMORE.   Pox on 'em, why do they draw a Man in then?
She has play'd with my Heart so, that 'twill never lie still
till I have met with some kind Wench, that will   **15**
play the Game out with me—Oh for my Arms full of soft,
white, kind—Woman! such as I fancy *Angelica.*

BELVILE.   This is her House, if you were but in stock to get
admittance; they have not din'd yet; I perceive the Picture
is not out.   **20**

Enter BLUNT.

WILLMORE.   I long to see the Shadow of the fair Substance,
a Man may gaze on that for nothing.

BLUNT.   Colonel, thy Hand—and thine, *Frederick.* I have
been an Ass, a deluded Fool, a very Coxcomb from my
Birth till this Hour, and heartily repent my little   **25**
Faith.

BELVILE.   What the Devil's the matter with thee *Ned?*

BLUNT.   Oh such a Mistress, *Frederick,* such a Girl!

WILLMORE.   Ha! where? *Frederick,* Ay where!

BLUNT.   So fond, so amorous, so toying and fine!   **30**
and all for sheer Love, ye Rogue! Oh how she lookt and
kiss'd! and sooth'd my Heart from my Bosom. I cannot
think I was awake, and yet methinks I see and feel her
Charms still—*Frederick.*—Try if she have not left the
Taste of her balmy Kisses upon my Lips—(*Kisses*   **35**
him.)

BELVILE.   Ha, ha, ha! *Willmore,* Death Man, where is
she?

BLUNT.   What a Dog was I to stay in dull *England* so
long—How have I laught at the Colonel when he sigh'd
for Love! but now the little Archer has reveng'd   **40**
him, and by his own Dart, I can guess at all his Joys,
which then I took for Fancies, mere Dreams and Fables—
Well, I'm resolved to sell all in *Essex,* and plant here for
ever.

BELVILE.   What a Blessing 'tis, thou hast a Mistress   **45**
thou dar'st boast of; for I know thy Humour is rather to
have a proclaim'd Clap, than a secret Amour.

WILLMORE.   Dost know her Name?

BLUNT.   Her Name? No, 'sheartlikins: what care I for
Names?—She's fair, young, brisk and kind, even   **50**
to ravishment: and what a Pox care I for knowing her by
another Title?

WILLMORE.   Didst give her anything?

BLUNT.   Give her!—Ha, ha, ha! why, she's a Person of
Quality—That's a good one, give her! 'sheartlikins   **55**
dost think such Creatures are to be bought? Or are we
provided for such a Purchase? Give her, quoth ye? Why
she presented me with this Bracelet, for the Toy of a Diamond I us'd to wear: No, Gentlemen, *Ned Blunt* is not
every Body—She expects me again to night.   **60**

WILLMORE.   Egad that's well; we'll all go.

BLUNT.   Not a Soul: No, Gentlemen, you are Wits; I am a
dull Country Rogue, I.

FREDERICK.   Well, Sir, for all your Person of Quality, I
shall be very glad to understand your Purse be   **65**
secure; 'tis our whole Estate at present, which we are loth
to hazard in one Bottom: come, Sir, unload.

BLUNT.   Take the necessary Trifle, useless now to me, that
am belov'd by such a Gentlewoman—'sheartlikins
Money! Here take mine too.   **70**

FREDERICK.   No, keep that to be cozen'd, that we may
laugh.

WILLMORE.   Cozen'd!—Death! wou'd I cou'd meet with
one, that wou'd cozen me of all the Love I cou'd spare to
night.   **75**

FREDERICK.   Pox 'tis some common Whore upon my Life.

BLUNT.   A Whore! yes with such Clothes! such Jewels!
such a House! such Furniture, and so attended! a Whore!

BELVILE.   Why yes, Sir, they are Whores, tho they'll neither
entertain you with Drinking, Swearing, or Baudy;   **80**

are Whores in all those gay Clothes, and right Jewels; are Whores with great Houses richly furnisht with Velvet Beds, Store of Plate, handsome Attendance, and fine Coaches, are Whores and errant ones.

WILLMORE.   Pox on't, where do these fine Whores   85
live?

BELVILE.   Where no Rogue in Office yclep'd Constables dare give 'em laws, nor the Wine-inspired Bullies of the Town break their Windows; yet they are Whores, tho this *Essex* Calf believe them Persons of Quality.   90

BLUNT.   'Sheartlikins, y'are all Fools, there are things about this *Essex* Calf, that shall take with the Ladies, beyond all your Wits and Parts—This Shape and Size, Gentlemen, are not to be despis'd; my Waste tolerably long, with other inviting Signs, that shall be   95 nameless.

WILLMORE.   Egad I believe he may have met with some Person of Quality that may be kind to him.

BELVILE.   Dost thou perceive any such tempting things about him, should make a fine Woman, and of   100 Quality, pick him out from all Mankind, to throw away her Youth and Beauty upon, nay, and her dear Heart too?—no, no, *Angelica* has rais'd the Price too high.

WILLMORE.   May she languish for Mankind till she die, and be damn'd for that one Sin alone.   105

Enter two Bravoes, and hang up a great Picture of ANGEL-ICA'S, *against the Balcony, and two little ones at each side of the Door.*

BELVILE.   See there the fair Sign to the Inn, where a Man may lodge that's Fool enough to give her Price. (WILL-MORE *gazes on the Picture.*)

BLUNT.   'Sheartlikins, Gentlemen, what's this?

BELVILE.   A famous Curtezan that's to be sold.

BLUNT.   How! to be sold! nay then I have nothing   110 to say to her—sold! what Impudence is practis'd in this Country?—With Order and Decency Whoring's estab-lished here by virtue of the Inquisition—Come let's be gone, I'm sure we're no Chapmen for this Commodity.

FREDERICK.   Thou art none, I'm sure, unless thou   115 could'st have her in thy Bed at the Price of a Coach in the Street.

WILLMORE.   How wondrous fair she is—a Thousand Crowns a Month—by Heaven as many Kingdoms were too little. A plague of this Poverty—of which I   120 ne'er complain, but when it hinders my Approach to Beauty, which Virtue ne'er could purchase. (*Turns from the Picture.*)

BLUNT.   What's this?—(*Reads.*) *A Thousand Crowns a Month!*

—'Sheartlikins, here's a Sum! sure 'tis a mistake.   125

—Hark you, Friend, does she take or give so much by the Month!

FREDERICK.   A Thousand Crowns! Why, 'tis a Portion for the *Infanta.*

BLUNT.   Hark ye, Friends, won't she trust?   130

BRAVO.   This is a Trade, Sir, that cannot live by Credit.

Enter DON PEDRO *in Masquerade, follow'd by* STEPHANO.

BELVILE.   See, here's more Company, let's walk off a while. (PEDRO *Reads.*) (*Exeunt* ENGLISH.)

Enter ANGELICA *and* MORETTA *in the Balcony, and draw a Silk Curtain.*

PEDRO.   Fetch me a Thousand Crowns, I never wish to buy this Beauty at an easier Rate. (*Passes off.*)

ANGELICA.   Prithee what said those Fellows to thee?   135

BRAVO.   Madam, the first were Admirers of Beauty only, but no purchasers; they were merry with your Price and Picture, laught at the Sum, and so past off.

ANGELICA.   No matter, I'm not displeas'd with their ral-lying; their Wonder feeds my Vanity, and he that   140 wishes to buy, gives me more Pride, than he that gives my Price can make me Pleasure.

BRAVO.   Madam, the last I knew thro all his disguises to be Don *Pedro,* Nephew to the General, and who was with him in *Pampelona.*   145

ANGELICA.   Don *Pedro!* my old Gallant's Nephew! When his Uncle dy'd, he left him a vast Sum of Money; it is he who was so in love with me at *Padua,* and who us'd to make the General so jealous.

MORETTA.   Is this he that us'd to prance before our   150 Window and take such care to shew himself an amorous Ass? if I am not mistaken, he is the likeliest Man to give your Price.

ANGELICA.   The Man is brave and generous, but of an Humour so uneasy and inconstant, that the vic-   155 tory over his Heart is as soon lost as won; a Slave that can add little to the Triumph of the Conqueror: but in-constancy's the Sin of all Mankind, therefore I'm resolv'd that nothing but Gold shall charm my Heart.

MORETTA.   I'm glad on't; 'tis only interest that   160 Women of our Profession ought to consider: tho I wonder what has kept you from that general Disease of our Sex so long, I mean that of being in love.

ANGELICA.   A kind, but sullen Star, under which I had the Happiness to be born; yet I have had no time for   165 Love; the bravest and noblest of Mankind have purchas'd my Favours at so dear a Rate, as if no Coin but Gold were current with our Trade—But here's Don *Pedro* again, fetch me my Lute—for 'tis for him or Don *Antonio* the Vice-Roy's Son, that I have spread my Nets.   170

Enter at one Door Don PEDRO, *and* STEPHANO; *Don* AN-TONIO *and* DIEGO (*his page*), *at the other Door, with People following him in Masquerade, antickly attir'd, some with Musick: they both go up to the Picture.*

ANTONIO.   A thousand Crowns! had not the Painter flatter'd her, I should not think it dear.

PEDRO.   Flatter'd her! by Heaven he cannot. I have seen
the Original, nor is there one Charm here more than
adorns her Face and Eyes; all this soft and sweet,   **175**
with a certain languishing Air, that no Artist can
represent.

ANTONIO.   What I heard of her Beauty before had fir'd my
Soul, but this confirmation of it has blown it into a flame.

PEDRO.   Ha!   **180**

DIEGO.   Sir, I have known you throw away a Thousand
Crowns on a worse Face, and tho y' are near your Marriage, you may venture a little Love here; *Florinda*—will
not miss it.

PEDRO.   Ha! *Florinda!* Sure 'tis *Antonio.* (*Aside.*)   **185**

ANTONIO.   *Florinda!* name not those distant Joys, there's
not one thought of her will check my Passion here.

PEDRO.   *Florinda* scorn'd! and all my Hopes defeated of
the Possession of *Angelica!* (*A noise of a Lute above.* AN-
TONIO *gazes up.*) Her Injuries by Heaven he shall   **190**
not boast of. (*Song to a Lute above.*)

SONG

When Damon *first began to love,*
He languisht in a soft Desire,
And knew not how the Gods to move,
To lessen or increase his Fire,   **195**
For Cælia *in her charming Eyes*
Wore all Love's Sweet, and all his Cruelties.

II

But as beneath a Shade he lay,
Weaving of Flow'rs for Cælia's *Hair,*
She chanc'd to lead her Flock that way,   **200**
And saw the am'rous Shepherd there.
She gaz'd around upon the Place,
And saw the Grove (resembling Night)
To all the Joys of Love invite,
Whilst guilty Smiles and Blushes drest her
*   Face.*   **205**
At this the bashful Youth all Transport grew,
And with kind Force he taught the Virgin how
To yield what all his Sighs cou'd never do.

ANTONIO.   By Heav'n she's charming fair!

(ANGELICA *throws open the Curtains, and bows to* ANTONIO,
who pulls off his Vizard, and bows and blows up Kisses.
PEDRO *unseen looks in his Face.*)

PEDRO.   'Tis he, the false *Antonio!*   **210**

ANTONIO.   Friend, where must I pay my offering of Love?
(*To the* BRAVO.) My Thousand Crowns I mean.

PEDRO.
That Offering I have design'd to make,
And yours will come too late.

ANTONIO.
Prithee be gone, I shall grow angry else,   **215**
And then thou art not safe.

PEDRO.
My Anger may be fatal, Sir, as yours;
And he that enters here may prove this Truth.

ANTONIO.   I know not who thou art, but I am sure thou'rt
worth my killing, and aiming at *Angelica.* (*They*   **220**
draw and fight.)

Enter WILLMORE *and* BLUNT, *who draw and part 'em.*

BLUNT.   'Sheartlikins, here's fine doings.

WILLMORE.   Tilting for the Wench I'm sure—nay gad, if
that wou'd win her, I have as good a Sword as the best of
ye—Put up—put up, and take another time and place, for
this is design'd for Lovers only. (*They all put up.*)   **225**

PEDRO.   We are prevented; dare you meet me to morrow
on the *Molo?*
For I've a Title to a better quarrel,
That of *Florinda,* in whose credulous Heart
Thou'st made an Int'rest, and destroy'd my Hopes.   **230**

ANTONIO.   Dare?
I'll meet thee there as early as the Day.

PEDRO.   We will come thus disguis'd, that whosoever
chance to get the better, he may escape unknown.

ANTONIO.   It shall be so. (*Exit* PEDRO *and* STE-   **235**
PHANO.) Who shou'd this Rival be? unless the *English*
Colonel, of whom I've often heard Don *Pedro* speak; it
must be he, and time he were removed, who lays a Claim
to all my Happiness.

(WILLMORE *having gaz'd all this while on the Picture, pulls*
down a little one.)

WILLMORE.
This posture's loose and negligent,   **240**
The sight on't wou'd beget a warm desire
In Souls, whom Impotence and Age had chill'd.
—This must along with me.

BRAVO.   What means this rudeness, Sir?—restore the
Picture.   **245**

ANTONIO.   Ha! Rudeness committed to the fair *An-*
gelica!—Restore the Picture, Sir.

WILLMORE.   Indeed I will not, Sir.

ANTONIO.   By Heav'n but you shall.

WILLMORE.   Nay, do not shew your Sword; if you   **250**
do, by this dear Beauty—I will shew mine too.

ANTONIO.   What right can you pretend to't?

WILLMORE.   That of Possession which I will maintain—
you perhaps have 1000 Crowns to give for the Original.

ANTONIO.   No matter, Sir, you shall restore the   **255**
Picture.

ANGELICA.   Oh, *Moretta!* what's the matter? (ANGELICA
and MORETTA *above.*)

ANTONIO.   Or leave your Life behind.

WILLMORE. Death! you lye—I will do neither.

ANGELICA. Hold, I command you, if for me you 260
fight.

(*They fight, the Spaniards join with* ANTONIO, BLUNT *laying on like mad. They leave off and bow.*)

WILLMORE. How heavenly fair she is!—ah Plague of her Price.

ANGELICA. You Sir in Buff, you that appear a Soldier, that first began this Insolence. 265

WILLMORE. 'Tis true, I did so, if you call it Insolence for a Man to preserve himself; I saw your charming Picture, and was wounded: quite thro my Soul each pointed Beauty ran; and wanting a Thousand Crowns to procure my Remedy, I laid this little Picture to my 270 Bosom—which if you cannot allow me, I'll resign.

ANGELICA. No, you may keep the Trifle.

ANTONIO. You shall first ask my leave, and this. (*Fight again as before.*)

Enter BELVILE *and* FREDERICK *who join with the* ENGLISH.

ANGELICA. Hold; will you ruin me?—*Biskey, Sebastian,* part them. (*The* SPANIARDS *are beaten off.*) 275

MORETTA. Oh Madam, we're undone, a pox upon that rude Fellow, he's set on to ruin us: we shall never see good days, till all these fighting poor Rogues are sent to the Gallies.

Enter BELVILE, BLUNT, *and* WILLMORE, *with his shirt bloody.*

BLUNT. 'Sheartlikins, beat me at this Sport, and 280 I'll ne'er wear Sword more.

BELVILE. The Devil's in thee for a mad Fellow, thou art always one at an unlucky Adventure.—Come, let's be gone whilst we're safe, and remember these are *Spaniards,* a sort of People that know how to revenge 285 an Affront.

FREDERICK. You bleed; I hope you are not wounded. (*To* WILLMORE.)

WILLMORE. Not much:—a plague upon your Dons, if they fight no better they'll ne'er recover *Flanders.*—What the Devil was't to them that I took down the Picture? 290

BLUNT. Took it! 'Sheartlikins, we'll have the great one too; 'tis ours by Conquest.—Prithee, help me up, and I'll put it down.—

ANGELICA. Stay, Sir, and e'er you affront me further, let me know how you durst commit this Outrage— 295
To you I speak, Sir, for you appear like a Gentleman.

WILLMORE. To me, Madam?—Gentlemen, your Servant.
(BELVILE *stays him.*)

BELVILE. Is the Devil in thee? Do'st know the danger of entring the house of an incens'd Curtezan?

WILLMORE. I thank you for your care—but there 300 are other matters in hand, there are, tho we have no great Temptation.—Death! let me go.

FREDERICK. Yes, to your Lodging, if you will, but not in here.—Damn these gay Harlots—by this Hand I'll have as sound and handsome a Whore for a 305 Patacoone.—Death, Man, she'll murder thee.

WILLMORE. Oh! fear me not, shall I not venture where a Beauty calls? a lovely charming Beauty? for fear of danger! when by Heaven there's none so great as to long for her, whilst I want Money to purchase her. 310

FREDERICK. Therefore 'tis loss of time, unless you had the thousand Crowns to pay.

WILLMORE. It may be she may give a Favour, at least I shall have the pleasure of saluting her when I enter, and when I depart. 315

BELVILE. Pox, she'll as soon lie with thee, as kiss thee, and sooner stab than do either—you shall not go.

ANGELICA. Fear not, Sir, all I have to wound with, is my Eyes.

BLUNT. Let him go, 'Sheartlikins, I believe the 320 Gentlewoman means well.

BELVILE. Well, take thy Fortune, we'll expect you in the next Street.—Farewell Fool,—farewell—

WILLMORE. B'ye Colonel—(*Goes in.*)

FREDERICK. The Rogue's stark mad for a Wench. 325
(*Exeunt.*)

SCENE TWO. A FINE CHAMBER.

Enter WILLMORE, ANGELICA, *and* MORETTA.

ANGELICA. Insolent Sir, how durst you pull down my Picture?

WILLMORE. Rather, how durst you set it up, to tempt poor amorous Mortals with so much Excellence? which I find you have but too well consulted by the unmerciful 5 price you set upon't.—Is all this Heaven of Beauty shewn to move Despair in those that cannot buy? and can you think the effects of that Despair shou'd be less extravagant than I have shewn?

ANGELICA. I sent for you to ask my Pardon, Sir, not 10 to aggravate your Crime.—I thought I shou'd have seen you at my Feet imploring it.

WILLMORE. You are deceived, I came to rail at you, and talk such Truths, too, as shall let you see the Vanity of that Pride, which taught you how to set such a Price 15 on Sin. For such it is, whilst that which is Love's due is meanly barter'd for.

ANGELICA. Ha, ha, ha, alas, good Captain, what pity 'tis your edifying Doctrine will do no good upon me—*Moretta,* fetch the Gentleman a Glass, and let him 20 survey himself, to see what Charms he has,—and guess my Business. (*Aside in a soft tone.*)

MORETTA. He knows himself of old, I believe those Breeches and he have been acquainted ever since he was beaten at *Worcester*.   **25**

ANGELICA.   Nay, do not abuse the poor Creature.—

MORETTA. Good Weather-beaten Corporal, will you march off? we have no need of your Doctrine, tho you have of our Charity; but at present we have no Scraps, we can afford no kindness for God's sake; in fine,   **30** Sirrah, the Price is too high i'th' Mouth for you, therefore troop, I say.

WILLMORE.   Here, good Fore-Woman of the Shop, serve me, and I'll be gone.

MORETTA.   Keep it to pay your Landress, your Linen   **35** stinks of the Gun-Room; for here's no selling by Retail.

WILLMORE.   Thou hast sold plenty of thy stale Ware at a cheap Rate.

MORETTA.   Ay, the more silly kind Heart I, but this is an Age wherein Beauty is at higher Rates.—In fine,   **40** you know the price of this.

WILLMORE.   I grant you 'tis here set down a thousand Crowns a Month—Baud, take your black Lead and sum it up, that I may have a Pistole-worth of these vain gay things, and I'll trouble you no more.   **45**

MORETTA.   Pox on him, he'll fret me to Death:—abominable Fellow, I tell thee, we only sell by the whole Piece.

WILLMORE.   'Tis very hard, the whole Cargo or nothing—Faith, Madam, my Stock will not reach it, I cannot be your Chapman.—Yet I have Countrymen in Town,   **50** Merchants of Love, like me; I'll see if they'l put for a share, we cannot lose much by it, and what we have no use for, we'll sell upon the *Friday's* Mart, at—*Who gives more?* I am studying, Madam, how to purchase you, tho at present I am unprovided of Money.   **55**

ANGELICA.   Sure, this from any other Man would anger me—nor shall he know the Conquest he has made—Poor angry Man, how I despise this railing.

WILLMORE.

    Yes, I am poor—but I'm a Gentleman,
    And one that scorns this Baseness which you
       practise.   **60**
    Poor as I am, I would not sell my self,
    No, not to gain your charming high-priz'd Person.
    Tho I admire you strangely for your Beauty,
    Yet I contemn your Mind.
    —And yet I wou'd at any rate enjoy you;   **65**
    At your own rate—but cannot—See here
    The only Sum I can command on Earth;
    I know not where to eat when this is gone:
    Yet such a Slave I am to Love and Beauty,
    This last reserve I'll sacrifice to enjoy you.   **70**
    —Nay, do not frown, I know you are to be bought,
    And wou'd be bought by me, by me,
    For a mean trifling Sum, if I could pay it down.
    Which happy knowledge I will still repeat,

    And lay it to my Heart, it has a Virtue in't,   **75**
    And soon will cure those Wounds your Eyes have
      made.
    —And yet—there's something so divinely powerful
      there—
    Nay, I will gaze—to let you see my Strength.
    (*Holds her, looks on her, and pauses and sighs.*)
    By Heaven, bright Creature—I would not for the
      World
    Thy Fame were half so fair as is thy Face.   **80**
    (*Turns her away from him.*)

ANGELICA.   His words go thro me to the very Soul. (*Aside.*) —If you have nothing else to say to me.

WILLMORE.

    Yes, you shall hear how infamous you are—
    For which I do not hate thee:
    But that secures my Heart, and all the Flames it
      feels   **85**
    Are but so many Lusts,
    I know it by their sudden bold intrusion.
    The Fire's impatient and betrays, 'tis false—
    For had it been the purer Flame of Love,
    I should have pin'd and languish'd at your Feet,   **90**
    E'er found the Impudence to have discover'd it.
    I now dare stand your Scorn, and your Denial.

MORETTA.   Sure she's bewitcht, that she can stand thus tamely, and hear his saucy railing.—Sirrah, will you be gone?   **95**

ANGELICA.   How dare you take this liberty?—Withdraw. (*To* MORETTA.)—Pray, tell me, Sir, are not you guilty of the same mercenary Crime? When a Lady is proposed to you for a Wife, you never ask, how fair, discreet, or virtuous she is; but what's her Fortune—which if   **100** but small, you cry—She will not do my business—and basely leave her, tho she languish for you.—Say, is not this as poor?

WILLMORE.   It is a barbarous Custom, which I will scorn to defend in our Sex, and do despise in yours.   **105**

ANGELICA.

    Thou art a brave Fellow! put up thy Gold, and know,
    That were thy Fortune large, as is thy Soul,
    Thou shouldst not buy my Love,
    Couldst thou forget those mean Effects of Vanity,
    Which set me out to sale; and as a Lover, prize   **110**
    My yielding Joys.
    Canst thou believe they'l be entirely thine,
    Without considering they were mercenary?

WILLMORE.   I cannot tell, I must bethink me first—ha, Death, I'm going to believe her. (*Aside.*)   **115**

ANGELICA.   Prithee, confirm that Faith—or if thou canst not—flatter me a little, 'twill please me from thy Mouth.

WILLMORE.

    Curse on thy charming Tongue! dost thou return
    My feign'd Contempt with so much subtilty?
    (*Aside.*)

Thou'st found the easiest way into my Heart, 120
Tho I yet know that all thou say'st is false.
(*Turning from her in a Rage.*)

ANGELICA.
By all that's good 'tis real,
I never lov'd before, tho oft a Mistress.
—Shall my first Vows be slighted?

WILLMORE. What can she mean? (*Aside.*) 125

ANGELICA. I find you cannot credit me. (*In an angry tone.*)

WILLMORE.
I know you take me for an errant Ass,
An Ass that may be sooth'd into Belief,
And then be us'd at pleasure.
—But, Madam I have been so often cheated 130
By perjur'd, soft, deluding Hypocrites,
That I've no Faith left for the cozening Sex,
Especially for Women of your Trade.

ANGELICA.
The low esteem you have of me, perhaps
May bring my Heart again: 135
For I have Pride that yet surmounts my Love.
(*She turns with Pride, he holds her.*)

WILLMORE.
Throw off this Pride, this Enemy to Bliss,
And shew the Power of Love: 'tis with those Arms
I can be only vanquisht, made a Slave.

ANGELICA.
Is all my mighty Expectation vanisht? 140
—No, I will not hear thee talk,—thou hast a Charm
In every word, that draws my Heart away.
And all the thousand Trophies I design'd,
Thou hast undone—Why art thou soft?
Thy Looks are bravely rough, and meant
    for War. 145
Could thou not storm on still?
I then perhaps had been as free as thou.

WILLMORE.
Death! how she throws her Fire about my Soul!
(*Aside.*)
—Take heed, fair Creature, how you raise my Hopes,
Which once assum'd pretend to all Dominion. 150
There's not a Joy thou hast in store
I shall not then command:
For which I'll pay thee back my Soul, my Life.
Come, let's begin th' account this happy minute.

ANGELICA.
And will you pay me then the Price I ask? 155

WILLMORE.
Oh, why dost thou draw me from an awful Worship,
By shewing thou art no Divinity?
Conceal the Fiend, and shew me all the Angel;
Keep me but ignorant, and I'll be devout,
And pay my Vows for ever at this Shrine. 160
— (*Kneels, and kisses her Hand.*)

ANGELICA. The Pay I mean is but thy Love for mine.
—Can you give that?

WILLMORE. Intirely—come, let's withdraw: where I'll
renew my Vows—and breathe 'em with such Ardour,
thou shalt not doubt my Zeal. 165

ANGELICA. Thou hast a Power too strong to be resisted.
(*Exit* WILLMORE *and* ANGELICA.)

MORETTA. Now my Curse go with you—Is all our Project
fallen to this? to love the only Enemy to our Trade? Nay,
to love such a Shameroon, a very Beggar; nay, a Pirate-
Beggar, whose Business is to rifle and be gone, a 170
No-Purchase, No-Pay Tatterdemalion, an *English* Piccaroon; a Rogue that fights for daily Drink, and takes a Pride
in being loyally lousy—Oh, I could curse now, if I durst—
This is the Fate of most Whores.

Trophies, which from believing Fops we win, 175
Are Spoils to those who cozen us again.

ACT THREE

SCENE ONE. A STREET.

Enter FLORINDA, VALERIA, HELLENA, *in Antick different
Dresses from what they were in before,* CALLIS *attending.*

FLORINDA. I wonder what should make my Brother in so
ill a Humour: I hope he has not found out our Ramble this
Morning.

HELLENA. No, if he had, we should have heard on't at both
Ears, and have been mew'd up this Afternoon; 5
which I would not for the World should have happen'd—
Hey ho! I'm sad as a Lover's Lute.

VALERIA. Well, methinks we have learnt this Trade of Gipsies as readily as if we had been bred upon the Road to
Loretto: and yet I did so fumble, when I told the 10
Stranger his Fortune, that I was afraid I should have told
my own and yours by mistake—But methinks *Hellena* has
been very serious ever since.

FLORINDA. I would give my Garters she were in love, to
be reveng'd upon her, for abusing me—How is't, 15
Hellena?

HELLENA. Ah!—would I had never seen my mad Monsieur—and yet for all your laughing I am not in love—
and yet this small Acquaintance, o' my Conscience, will
never out of my Head. 20

VALERIA. Ha, ha, ha—I laugh to think how thou art fitted
with a Lover, a Fellow that, I warrant, loves every new
Face he sees.

HELLENA. Hum—he has not kept his Word with me here—
and may be taken up—that thought is not very 25
pleasant to me—what the Duce should this be now that I
feel?

VALERIA. What is't like?

HELLENA. Nay, the Lord knows—but if I should be
hanged, I cannot chuse but be angry and afraid, 30

when I think that mad Fellow should be in love with any Body but me—What to think of my self I know not—Would I could meet with some true damn'd Gipsy, that I might know my Fortune.

VALERIA.   Know it! why there's nothing so easy;   **35**
thou wilt love this wandring Inconstant till thou find'st thy self hanged about his Neck, and then be as mad to get free again.

FLORINDA.   Yes, *Valeria;* we shall see her bestride his Baggage-horse, and follow him to the Campaign.   **40**

HELLENA.   So, so; now you are provided for, there's no care taken of poor me—But since you have set my Heart a wishing, I am resolv'd to know for what. I will not die of the Pip, so I will not.

FLORINDA.   Art thou mad to talk so? Who will like   **45**
thee well enough to have thee, that hears what a mad Wench thou art?

HELLENA.   Like me! I don't intend every he that likes me shall have me, but he that I like: I shou'd have staid in the Nunnery still, if I had lik'd my Lady Abbess   **50**
as well as she lik'd me. No, I came thence, not (as my wise Brother imagines) to take an eternal Farewel of the World, but to love and to be belov'd; and I will be belov'd, or I'll get one of your Men, so I will.

VALERIA.   Am I put into the Number of Lovers?   **55**

HELLENA.   You! my Couz, I know thou art too good natur'd to leave us in any Design: Thou wou't venture a Cast, tho thou comest off a Loser, especially with such a Gamester—I observ'd your Man, and your willing Ears incline that way; and if you are not a Lover, 'tis an Art   **60**
soon learnt—that I find. (*Sighs.*)

FLORINDA.   I wonder how you learnt to love so easily, I had a thousand Charms to meet my Eyes and Ears, e'er I cou'd yield; and 'twas the knowledge of *Belvile's* Merit, not the surprising Person, took my Soul—Thou art   **65**
too rash to give a Heart at first sight.

HELLENA.   Hang your considering Lover; I ne'er thought beyond the Fancy, that 'twas a very pretty, idle, silly kind of Pleasure to pass ones time with, to write little, soft, nonsensical Billets, and with great difficulty and   **70**
danger receive Answers; in which I shall have my Beauty prais'd, my Wit admir'd (tho little or none) and have the Vanity and Power to know I am desirable; then I have the more Inclination that way, because I am to be a Nun, and so shall not be suspected to have any such earthly   **75**
Thoughts about me—But when I walk thus—and sigh thus—they'll think my Mind's upon my Monastery, and cry, how happy 'tis she's so resolv'd—But not a Word of Man.

FLORINDA.   What a mad Creature's this!   **80**

HELLENA.   I'll warrant, if my Brother hears either of you sigh, he cries (gravely)—I fear you have the Indiscretion to be in love, but take heed of the Honour of our House, and your own unspotted Fame; and so he conjures on till he has laid the soft-wing'd God in your Hearts, or   **85**

broke the Birds-nest—But see here comes your Lover: but where's my inconstant? let's step aside, and we may learn something. (*Go aside.*)

Enter BELVILE, FREDERICK, *and* BLUNT.

BELVILE.   What means this? the Picture's taken in.

BLUNT.   It may be the Wench is good-natur'd, and   **90**
will be kind *gratis.* Your Friend's a proper handsom Fellow.

BELVILE.   I rather think she has cut his Throat and is fled: I am mad he should throw himself into Dangers—Pox on't, I shall want him to night—let's knock and ask for   **95**
him.

HELLENA.   My heart goes a-pit a-pat, for fear 'tis my Man they talk of. (*Knock,* MORETTA *above.*)

MORETTA.   What would you have?

BELVILE.   Tell the Stranger that enter'd here about   **100**
two Hours ago, that his Friends stay here for him.

MORETTA.   A Curse upon him for *Moretta,* would he were at the Devil—but he's coming to you. (*Enter* WILLMORE.)

HELLENA.   I, I, 'tis he. Oh how this vexes me.

BELVILE.   And how, and how, dear Lad, has For-   **105**
tune smil'd? Are we to break her Windows, or raise up Altars to her! hah!

WILLMORE.   Does not my Fortune sit triumphant on my Brow? dost not see the little wanton God there all gay and smiling? have I not an Air about my Face and   **110**
Eyes, that distinguish me from the Croud of common Lovers? By Heav'n, *Cupid's* Quiver has not half so many Darts as her Eyes—Oh such a *Bona Roba,* to sleep in her Arms is lying in Fresco, all perfum'd Air about me.

HELLENA.   Here's fine encouragement for me to   **115**
fool on. (*Aside.*)

WILLMORE.   Hark ye, where didst thou purchase that rich Canary we drank to-day? Tell me, that I may adore the Spigot, and sacrifice to the Butt: the Juice was divine, into which I must dip my Rosary, and then bless all   **120**
things that I would have bold or fortunate.

BELVILE.   Well, Sir, let's go take a Bottle, and hear the Story of your Success.

FREDERICK.   Would not *French* Wine do better?

WILLMORE.   Damn the hungry Balderdash; cheer-   **125**
ful Sack has a generous Virtue in't, inspiring a successful Confidence, gives Eloquence to the Tongue, and Vigour to the Soul; and has in a few Hours compleated all my Hopes and Wishes. There's nothing left to raise a new Desire in me—Come let's be gay and   **130**
wanton—and, Gentlemen, study, study what you want, for here are Friends,—that will supply, Gentlemen,—hark! what a charming sound they make—'tis he and she Gold whilst here, shall beget new Pleasures every moment.   **135**

BLUNT.   But hark ye, Sir, you are not married, are you?

WILLMORE.   All the Honey of Matrimony, but none of the Sting, Friend.

BLUNT.   'Sheartlikins, thou'rt a fortunate Rogue.

WILLMORE.   I am so, Sir, let these inform you.—   140
Ha, how sweetly they chime! Pox of Poverty, it makes a
Man a Slave, makes Wit and Honour sneak, my Soul grew
lean and rusty for want of Credit.

BLUNT.   'Sheartlikins, this I like well, it looks like my
lucky Bargain! Oh how I long for the Approach   145
of my Squire, that is to conduct me to her House again.
Why! here's two provided for.

FREDERICK.   By this light y're happy Men.

BLUNT.   Fortune is pleased to smile on us, Gentlemen,—to
smile on us.   150

Enter SANCHO, *and pulls* BLUNT *by the Sleeve. They go
aside.*

SANCHO.   Sir, my Lady expects you—she has remov'd all
that might oppose your Will and Pleasure—and is impatient till you come.

BLUNT.   Sir, I'll attend you—Oh the happiest Rogue! I'll
take no leave, lest they either dog me, or stay me.   155
(*Exeunt with* SANCHO.)

BELVILE.   But then the little Gipsy is forgot?

WILLMORE.   A Mischief on thee for putting her into my
thoughts; I had quite forgot her else, and this Night's
Debauch had drunk her quite down.

HELLENA.   Had it so, good Captain? (*Claps him on*   160
the Back.)

WILLMORE.   Ha! I hope she did not hear.

HELLENA.   What, afraid of such a Champion!

WILLMORE.   Oh! you're a fine Lady of your word, are you
not? to make a Man languish a whole day—

HELLENA.   In tedious search of me.   165

WILLMORE.   Egad, Child, thou'rt in the right, hadst thou
seen what a melancholy Dog I have been ever since I was
a Lover, how I have walkt the Streets like a *Capuchin*,
with my Hands in my Sleeves—Faith, Sweetheart, thou
wouldst pity me.   170

HELLENA.   Now, if I should be hang'd, I can't be angry with
him, he dissembles so heartily—Alas, good Captain, what
pains you have taken—Now were I ungrateful not to
reward so true a Servant.

WILLMORE.   Poor Soul! that's kindly said, I see   175
thou bearest a Conscience—come then for a beginning
shew me thy dear Face.

HELLENA.   I'm afraid, my small Acquaintance, you have
been staying that swinging stomach you boasted of this
morning; I remember then my little Collation   180
would have gone down with you, without the Sauce of a
handsom Face—Is your Stomach so quesy now?

WILLMORE.   Faith long fasting, Child, spoils a Man's Appetite—yet if you durst treat, I could so lay about me still.

HELLENA.   And would you fall to, before a Priest   185
says Grace?

WILLMORE.   Oh fie, fie, what an old out-of-fashion'd thing
hast thou nam'd? Thou could'st not dash me more out of
Countenance, shouldst thou shew me an ugly Face.

Whilst he is seemingly courting HELLENA, *enter* ANGELICA,
MORETTA, BISKEY, *and* SEBASTIAN, *all in Masquerade:* AN-
GELICA *sees* WILLMORE *and starts.*

ANGELICA.   Heavens, is't he? and passionately   190
fond to see another Woman?

MORETTA.   What cou'd you expect less from such a
Swaggerer?

ANGELICA.
Expect! as much as I paid him, a Heart intire,
Which I had pride enough to think when e'er
I gave   195
It would have rais'd the Man above the Vulgar,
Made him all Soul, and that all soft and constant.

HELLENA.   You see, Captain, how willing I am to be
Friends with you, till Time and Ill-luck make us Lovers;
and ask you the Question first, rather than put   200
your Modesty to the blush, by asking me: for alas, I know
you Captains are such strict Men, severe Observers of
your Vows to Chastity, that 'twill be hard to prevail with
your tender Conscience to marry a young willing Maid.

WILLMORE.   Do not abuse me, for fear I should   205
take thee at thy word, and marry thee indeed, which I'm
sure will be Revenge sufficient.

HELLENA.   O' my Conscience, that will be our Destiny, because we are both of one humour; I am as inconstant as
you, for I have considered, Captain, that a   210
handsom Woman has a great deal to do whilst her Face
is good, for then is our Harvest-time to gather Friends;
and should I in these days of my Youth, catch a fit of
foolish Constancy, I were undone; 'tis loitering by daylight in our great Journey: therefore declare, I'll   215
allow but one year for Love, one year for Indifference,
and one year for Hate—and then—go hang your self—for
I profess myself the gay, the kind, and the inconstant—
the Devil's in't if this won't please you.

WILLMORE.   Oh most damnably!—I have a Heart   220
with a hole quite thro it too, no Prison like mine to keep
a Mistress in.

ANGELICA.   Perjur'd Man! how I believe thee now! (*Aside.*)

HELLENA.   Well, I see our Business as well as Humours are
alike, yours to cozen as many Maids as will trust   225
you, and I as many Men as have Faith—See if I have not
as desperate a lying look, as you can have for the heart of
you. (*Pulls off her Vizard; he starts.*)—How do you like
it, Captain?

WILLMORE.   Like it! by Heav'n, I never saw so   230
much Beauty. Oh the Charms of those sprightly black
Eyes, that strangely fair Face, full of Smiles and Dimples!
those soft round melting cherry Lips! and small even
white Teeth! not to be exprest, but silently adored!—Oh

one Look more, and strike me dumb, or I shall   **235**
repent nothing else till I am mad. (*He seems to court her
to pull off her Vizard: she refuses.*)

ANGELICA.   I can endure no more—nor is it fit to interrupt
him; for if I do, my Jealousy has so destroy'd my
Reason,—I shall undo him—Therefore I'll retire. And
you *Sebastian* (*To one of her Bravoes*) follow that   **240**
Woman, and learn who 'tis; while you tell the Fugitive, I
would speak to him instantly. (*To the other Bravo.*) (*Exit.*)

(*This while* FLORINDA *is talking to* BELVILE, *who stands sullenly.* FREDERICK *courting* VALERIA.)

VALERIA.   Prithee, dear Stranger, be not so sullen; for tho
you have lost your Love, you see my Friend frankly offers
you hers, to play with in the mean time.   **245**

BELVILE.   Faith, Madam, I am sorry I can't play at her
Game.

FREDERICK.   Pray leave your Intercession, and mind your
own Affair, they'll better agree apart; he's a model Sigher
in Company, but alone no Woman escapes him.   **250**

FLORINDA.   Sure he does but rally—yet if it should be
true—I'll tempt him farther—Believe me, noble Stranger,
I'm no common Mistress—and for a little proof on't—
wear this Jewel—nay, take it, Sir, 'tis right, and Bills of
Exchange may sometimes miscarry.   **255**

BELVILE.   Madam, why am I chose out of all Mankind to be
the Object of your Bounty?

VALERIA.   There's another civil Question askt.

FREDERICK.   Pox of's Modesty, it spoils his own Markets,
and hinders mine.   **260**

FLORINDA.   Sir, from my Window I have often seen you;
and Women of Quality have so few opportunities for
Love, that we ought to lose none.

FREDERICK.   Ay, this is something! here's a Woman!—
When shall I be blest with so much kindness from   **265**
your fair Mouth?—Take the Jewel, Fool. (*Aside to*
BELVILE.)

BELVILE.   You tempt me strangely, Madam, every way.

FLORINDA.   So, if I find him false, my whole Repose is
gone. (*Aside.*)

BELVILE.   And but for a Vow I've made to a very   **270**
fine Lady, this Goodness had subdu'd me.

FREDERICK.   Pox on't be kind, in pity to me be kind, for I
am to thrive here but as you treat her Friend.

HELLENA.   Tell me what did you in yonder House, and I'll
unmasque.   **275**

WILLMORE.   Yonder House—oh—I went to—a—to—
why, there's a Friend of mine lives there.

HELLENA.   What a she, or a he Friend?

WILLMORE.   A Man upon my Honour! a Man—A She
Friend! no, no, Madam, you have done my Busi-   **280**
ness, I thank you.

HELLENA.   And was't your Man Friend, that had more
Darts in's Eyes than *Cupid* carries in a whole Budget of
Arrows?

WILLMORE.   So—   **285**

HELLENA.   Ah such a *Bona Roba:* to be in her Arms is lying
in *Fresco,* all perfumed Air about me—Was this your
Man Friend too?

WILLMORE.   So—

HELLENA.   That gave you the He, and the She—   **290**
Gold, that begets young Pleasures.

WILLMORE.   Well, well, Madam, then you see there are
Ladies in the World, that will not be cruel—there are,
Madam, there are—

HELLENA.   And there be Men too as fine, wild, in-   **295**
constant Fellows as your self, there be, Captain, there be,
if you go to that now—therefore I'm resolv'd—

WILLMORE.   Oh!

HELLENA.   To see your Face no more—

WILLMORE.   Oh!   **300**

HELLENA.   Till to morrow.

WILLMORE.   Egad you frighted me.

HELLENA.   Nor then neither, unless you'l swear never to
see that Lady more.

WILLMORE.   See her!—why! never to think of   **305**
Womankind again?

HELLENA.   Kneel, and swear. (*Kneels, she gives him her
hand.*)

HELLENA.   I do, never to think—to see—to love—nor lie
with any but thy self.

WILLMORE.   Kiss the Book.   **310**

WILLMORE.   Oh, most religiously. (*Kisses her Hand.*)

HELLENA.   Now what a wicked Creature am I, to damn a
proper Fellow.

CALLIS.   Madam, I'll stay no longer, 'tis e'en dark. (*To*
FLORINDA.)

FLORINDA.   However, Sir, I'll leave this with   **315**
you—that when I'm gone, you may repent the opportunity
you have lost by your modesty. (*Gives him the Jewel,
which is her Picture, and Exit he gazes after her.*)

WILLMORE.   'Twill be an Age till to morrow,—and till then
I will most impatiently expect you—Adieu, my dear
pretty Angel. (*Exit all the Women.*)   **320**

BELVILE.   Ha! *Florinda's* Picture! 'twas she her self—what
a dull Dog was I? I would have given the World for one
minute's discourse with her.—

FREDERICK.   This comes of your Modesty,—ah pox on
your Vow, 'twas ten to one but we had lost the   **325**
Jewel by't.

BELVILE.   *Willmore!* the blessed'st Opportunity lost!—
Florinda, Friends, *Florinda!*

WILLMORE.   Ah Rogue! such black Eyes, such a Face, such
a Mouth, such Teeth,—and so much Wit!   **330**

BELVILE.   All, all, and a thousand Charms besides.

WILLMORE.   Why, dost thou know her?

BELVILE.   Know her! ay, ay, and a Pox take me with all my
Heart for being modest.

WILLMORE.   But hark ye, Friend of mine, are you   **335**
my Rival? and have I been only beating the Bush all this
while?

BELVILE.   I understand thee not—I'm mad—see here—
(*Shews the Picture.*)

WILLMORE.   Ha! whose Picture is this?—'tis a fine Wench.

FREDERICK.   The Colonel's Mistress, Sir.   **340**

WILLMORE.   Oh, oh, here—I thought it had been another
Prize—come, come, a Bottle will set thee right again.
(*Gives the Picture back.*)

BELVILE.   I am content to try, and by that time 'twill be late
enough for our Design.

WILLMORE.   Agreed.   **345**

> *Love does all day the Soul's great Empire keep,*
> *But Wine at night lulls the soft God asleep. (Exeunt.)*

SCENE TWO. LUCETTA'S HOUSE.

Enter BLUNT *and* LUCETTA *with a Light.*

LUCETTA.   Now we are safe and free, no fears of the coming
home of my old jealous Husband, which made me a little
thoughtful when you came in first—but now Love is all
the business of my Soul.

BLUNT.   I am transported—Pox on't, that I had but   **5**
some fine things to say to her, such as Lovers use—I was
a Fool not to learn of *Frederick* a little by Heart before I
came—something I must say.—(*Aside.*)
'Sheartlikins, sweet Soul, I am not us'd to complement, but
I'm an honest Gentleman, and thy humble Servant.   **10**

LUCETTA.   I have nothing to pay for so great a Favour, but
such a Love as cannot but be great, since at first sight of
that sweet Face and Shape it made me your absolute
Captive.

BLUNT.   Kind heart, how prettily she talks! Egad I'll   **15**
show her Husband a *Spanish* Trick; send him out of the
World, and marry her: she's damnably in love with me,
and will ne'er mind Settlements, and so there's that sav'd.
(*Aside.*)

LUCETTA.   Well, Sir, I'll go and undress me, and be with
you instantly.   **20**

BLUNT.   Make haste then, for 'dsheartlikins, dear Soul,
thou canst not guess at the pain of a longing Lover, when
his Joys are drawn within the compass of a few minutes.

LUCETTA.   You speak my Sense, and I'll make haste to provide it. (*Exit.*)   **25**

BLUNT.   'Tis a rare Girl, and this one night's enjoyment
with her will be worth all the days I ever past in Essex.—
Would she'd go with me into *England,* tho to say truth,
there's plenty of Whores there already.—But a pox on
'em they are such mercenary prodigal Whores, that   **30**
they want such a one as this, that's free and generous, to
give 'em good Examples:—Why, what a House she has!
how rich and fine!

Enter SANCHO.

SANCHO.   Sir, my Lady has sent me to conduct you to her
Chamber.   **35**

BLUNT.   Sir, I shall be proud to follow—Here's one of her
Servants, too: 'dsheartlikins, by his Garb and Gravity he
might be a Justice of Peace in *Essex,* and is but a Pimp
here. (*Exeunt.*)

*The Scene changes to a Chamber with an Alcove-Bed in it,
a Table, &c.* LUCETTA *in Bed. Enter* SANCHO *and* BLUNT,
who takes the Candle of SANCHO *at the Door.*

SANCHO.   Sir, my Commission reaches no farther.   **40**

BLUNT.   Sir, I'll excuse your Complement:—what, in Bed,
my sweet Mistress?

LUCETTA.   You see, I still out-do you in kindness.

BLUNT.   And thou shalt see what haste I'll make to quit
scores—oh the luckiest Rogue! (*Undresses him-*   **45**
self.)

LUCETTA.   Shou'd you be false or cruel now!

BLUNT.   False, 'Sheartlikins, what dost thou take me for a
Jew? an insensible Heathen,—A Pox of thy old jealous
Husband: and he were dead, egad, sweet Soul, it shou'd
be none of my fault, if I did not marry thee.   **50**

LUCETTA.   It never shou'd be mine.

BLUNT.   Good Soul, I'm the fortunatest Dog!

LUCETTA.   Are you not undrest yet?

BLUNT.   As much as my Impatience will permit. (*Goes towards the Bed in his Shirt and Drawers.*)

LUCETTA.   Hold, Sir, put out the Light, it may betray   **55**
us else.

BLUNT.   Any thing, I need no other Light but that of thine
Eyes!—'sheartlikins, there I think I had it. (*Aside.*) (*Puts
out the Candle, the Bed descends, he gropes about to find
it.*)—Why—why—where am I got? what, not yet?—
where are you sweetest?—ah, the Rogue's silent   **60**
now—a pretty Love-trick this—how she'll laugh at me
anon!—you need not, my dear Rogue! you need not! I'm
all on a fire already—come, come, now call me in for
pity—Sure I'm enchanted! I have been round the
Chamber, and can find neither Woman, nor Bed—   **65**
I lockt the Door, I'm sure she cannot go that way; or if
she cou'd, the Bed cou'd not—Enough, enough, my pretty
Wanton, do not carry the Jest too far—Ha, betray'd!
Dogs! Rogues! Pimps! help! help! (*Lights on a Trap, and
is let down.*)

Enter LUCETTA, PHILIPPO, *and* SANCHO *with a Light.*

PHILIPPO.   Ha, ha, ha, he's dispatcht finely.   **70**

LUCETTA.   Now, Sir, had I been coy, we had mist of this
Booty.

PHILIPPO.   Nay when I saw 'twas a substantial Fool, I was
mollified; but when you doat upon a Serenading
Coxcomb, upon a Face, fine Clothes, and a Lute,   **75**
it makes me rage.

LUCETTA.   You know I never was guilty of that Folly, my
dear *Philippo,* but with your self—But come let's see
what we have got by this.

PHILIPPO.   A rich Coat!—Sword and Hat!—these   **80**
Breeches too—are well lin'd!—see here a Gold Watch!—
a Purse—ha! Gold!—at least two hundred Pistoles! a
bunch of Diamond Rings; and one with the Family
Arms!—a Gold Box!—with a Medal of his King! and his
Lady Mother's Picture!—these were sacred Re-   **85**
liques, believe me!—see, the Wasteband of his Breeches
have a Mine of Gold!—Old Queen *Bess's.* We have a
Quarrel to her ever since *Eighty Eight,* and may therefore
justify the Theft, the Inquisition might have committed it.

LUCETTA.   See, a Bracelet of bow'd Gold, these his   **90**
Sister ty'd about his Arm at parting—but well—for all
this, I fear his being a Stranger may make a noise, and
hinder our Trade with them hereafter.

PHILIPPO.   That's our security; he is not only a Stranger to
us, but to the Country too—the Common-Shore   **95**
into which he is descended, thou know'st, conducts him
into another Street, which this Light will hinder him from
ever finding again—he knows neither your Name, nor the
Street where your House is, nay, nor the way to his own
Lodgings.   **100**

LUCETTA.   And art not thou an unmerciful Rogue, not to
afford him one Night for all this?—I should not have been
such a *Jew.*

PHILIPPO.   Blame me not, *Lucetta,* to keep as much
of thee as I can to my self—come, that thought   **105**
makes me wanton,—let's to Bed,—*Sancho,* lock up
these.

>   *This is the Fleece which Fools do bear,*
>   *Design'd for witty Men to sheer. (Exeunt.)*

The Scene changes, and discovers BLUNT, *creeping out of a
Common Shore, his Face, &c., all dirty.*

BLUNT.   Oh Lord! (*Climbing up.*) I am got out at last,   **110**
and (which is a Miracle) without a Clue—and now to
Damning and Cursing,—but if that would ease me, where
shall I begin? with my Fortune, my self, or the Quean that
cozen'd me—What a dog was I to believe in Women! Oh
Coxcomb—ignorant conceited Coxcomb! to fancy   **115**
she cou'd be enamour'd with my Person, at the first sight
enamour'd—Oh, I'm a cursed Puppy, 'tis plain, Fool was
writ upon my Forehead, she perceiv'd it,—saw the *Essex*
Calf there—for what Allurements could there be in this
Countenance? which I can indure, because I'm   **120**
acquainted with it—Oh, dull silly Dog! to be thus sooth'd
into a Cozening! Had I been drunk, I might fondly have
credited the young Quean! but as I was in my right Wits,
to be thus cheated, confirms I am a dull believing *English*
Country Fop.—But my Comrades! Death and the   **125**
Devil, there's the worst of all—then a Ballad will be sung

to Morrow on the *Prado,* to a lousy Tune of the enchanted
Squire, and the annihilated Damsel—But *Frederick* that
Rogue, and the Colonel, will abuse me beyond all Christian patience—had she left me my Clothes, I have   **130**
a Bill of Exchange at home wou'd have sav'd my Credit—
but now all hope is taken from me—Well, I'll home (if I
can find the way) with this Consolation, that I am not the
first kind believing Coxcomb; but there are, Gallants,
many such good Natures amongst ye.   **135**

>   *And tho you've better Arts to hide your Follies,*
>   *Adsheartlikins y'are all as errant Cullies.*

SCENE THREE. THE GARDEN,
IN THE NIGHT.

Enter FLORINDA *undress'd, with a Key, and a little Box.*

FLORINDA.   Well, thus far I'm in my way to Happiness; I
have got my self free from *Callis;* my Brother too, I find
by yonder light, is gone into his Cabinet, and thinks not
of me: I have by good Fortune got the Key of the Garden
Back-door,—I'll open it, to prevent *Belvile's*   **5**
knocking,—a little noise will now alarm my Brother.
Now am I as fearful as a young Thief. (*Unlocks the Door.*)
Hark,—what noise is that?—Oh, 'twas the Wind that
plaid amongst the Boughs.—*Belvile* stays long, methinks—it's time—stay—for fear of a surprize, I'll   **10**
hide these Jewels in yonder Jessamin. (*She goes to lay
down the Box.*)

Enter WILLMORE *drunk.*

WILLMORE.   What the Devil is become of these Fellows,
Belvile and *Frederick?* They promis'd to stay at the next
corner for me, but who the Devil knows the corner of a
full Moon?—Now—whereabouts am I?—hah—   **15**
what have we here? a Garden!—a very convenient place
to sleep in—hah—what has God sent us here?—a
Female—by this light, a Woman; I'm a Dog if it be not a
very Wench.—

FLORINDA.   He's come!—hah—who's there?   **20**

WILLMORE.   Sweet Soul, let me salute thy Shoe-string.

FLORINDA.   'Tis not my *Belvile*—good Heavens, I know
him not.—Who are you, and from whence come you?

WILLMORE.   Prithee—prithee, Child—not so many hard
Questions—let it suffice I am here, Child—Come,   **25**
come kiss me.

FLORINDA.   Good Gods! what luck is mine?

WILLMORE.   Only good luck, Child, parlous good luck.—
Come hither,—'tis a delicate shining Wench,—by this
Hand she's perfum'd, and smells like any   **30**
Nosegay.—Prithee, dear Soul, let's not play the Fool, and
lose time,—precious time—for as Gad shall save me, I'm
as honest a Fellow as breathes, tho I am a little disguis'd
at present.—Come, I say,—why, thou may'st be free with

me, I'll be very secret. I'll not boast who 'twas   35
oblig'd me, not I—for hang me if I know thy Name.

FLORINDA.   Heavens! what a filthy beast is this!

WILLMORE.   I am so, and thou oughtst the sooner to lie
with me for that reason,—for look you, Child, there will
be no Sin in't, because 'twas neither design'd nor   40
premeditated; 'tis pure Accident on both sides—that's a
certain thing now—Indeed should I make love to you, and
you vow Fidelity—and swear and lye till you believ'd and
yielded—Thou art therefore (as thou art a good Christian)
oblig'd in Conscience to deny me nothing. Now—   45
come, be kind, without any more idle prating.

FLORINDA.   Oh, I am ruin'd—wicked Man, unhand me.

WILLMORE.   Wicked! Egad, Child, a Judge, were he young
and vigorous, and saw those Eyes of thine, would know
'twas they gave the first blow—the first provoca-   50
tion.—Come, prithee let's lose no time, I say—this is a
fine convenient place.

FLORINDA.   Sir, let me go, I conjure you, or I'll call out.

WILLMORE.   Ay, ay, you were best to call Witness to see
how finely you treat me—do.—   55

FLORINDA.   I'll cry Murder, Rape, or any thing, if you do
not instantly let me go.

WILLMORE.   A Rape! Come, come, you lye, you Baggage,
you lye: What, I'll warrant you would fain have the World
believe now that you are not so forward as I. No,   60
not you,—why at this time of Night was your Cobweb-
door set open, dear Spider—but to catch Flies?—Hah
come—or I shall be damnably angry.—Why what a Coil
is here.—

FLORINDA.   Sir, can you think—   65

WILLMORE.   That you'd do it for nothing? oh, oh, I find
what you'd be at—look here, here's a Pistole for you—
here's a work indeed—here—take it, I say.—

FLORINDA.   For Heaven's sake, Sir, as you're a Gentleman—   70

WILLMORE.   So—now—she would be wheedling me for
more—what, you will not take it then—you're resolv'd
you will not.—Come, come, take it, or I'll put it up again;
for, look ye, I never give more.—Why, how now, Mistress, are you so high i'th' Mouth, a Pistole won't   75
down with you?—hah—why, what a work's here—in
good time—come, no struggling, be gone—But an y'are
good at a dumb Wrestle, I'm for ye,—look ye,—I'm for
ye.— (*She struggles with him.*)

Enter BELVILE *and* FREDERICK.

BELVILE.   The Door is open, a Pox of this mad   80
Fellow, I'm angry that we've lost him, I durst have sworn
he had follow'd us.

FREDERICK.   But you were so hasty, Colonel, to be gone.

FLORINDA.   Help, help,—Murder!—help—oh, I'm ruin'd.

BELVILE.   Ha, sure that's *Florinda's* Voice. (*Comes   85
up to them.*)—A Man! Villain, let go that Lady. (*A noise.*)
(WILLMORE *turns and draws,* FREDERICK *interposes.*)

FLORINDA.   *Belvile!* Heavens! my Brother too is coming,
and 'twill be impossible to escape.—*Belvile,* I conjure
you to walk under my Chamber-window, from whence
I'll give you some instructions what to do—This   90
rude Man has undone us. (*Exit.*)

WILLMORE.   *Belvile!*

Enter PEDRO, STEPHANO, *and other Servants with Lights.*

PEDRO.   I'm betray'd; run, *Stephano,* and see if *Florinda* be
safe. (*Exit* STEPHANO.) So whoe'er they be, all is not well,
I'll to *Florinda's* Chamber. (*They fight, and* PED-   95
RO's *Party beats 'em out; going out, meets* STEPHANO.)

STEPHANO.   You need not, Sir, the poor Lady's fast asleep,
and thinks no harm: I wou'd not wake her, Sir, for fear
of frightning her with your danger.

PEDRO.   I'm glad she's there—Rascals, how came the
Garden-Door open?   100

STEPHANO.   That Question comes too late, Sir: some of my
Fellow-Servants Masquerading I'll warrant.

PEDRO.   Masquerading! a leud Custom to debauch our
Youth—there's something more in this than I imagine.
(*Exeunt.*)

SCENE FOUR. CHANGES TO THE STREET.

Enter BELVILE *in Rage,* FREDERICK *holding him, and* WILL-
MORE *melancholy.*

WILLMORE.   Why, how the Devil shou'd I know *Florinda?*

BELVILE.   Ah plague of your ignorance! if it had not been
Florinda, must you be a Beast?—a Brute, a senseless
Swine?

WILLMORE.   Well, Sir, you see I am endu'd with   5
Patience—I can bear—tho egad y're very free with me
methinks,—I was in good hopes the Quarrel wou'd have
been on my side, for so uncivilly interrupting me.

BELVILE.   Peace, Brute, whilst thou'rt safe—oh, I'm
distracted.   10

WILLMORE.   Nay, nay, I'm an unlucky Dog, that's certain.

BELVILE.   Ah curse upon the Star that rul'd my Birth! or
whatsoever other Influence that makes me still so
wretched.

WILLMORE.   Thou break'st my Heart with these   15
Complaints; there is no Star in fault, no Influence but
Sack, the cursed Sack I drank.

FREDERICK.   Why, how the Devil came you so drunk?

WILLMORE.   Why, how the Devil came you so sober?

BELVILE.   A curse upon his thin Skull, he was always   20
before-hand that way.

FREDERICK.   Prithee, dear Colonel, forgive him, he's sorry
for his fault.

BELVILE.   He's always so after he has done a mischief—a
plague on all such Brutes.   25

WILLMORE.   By this Light I took her for an errant Harlot.

BELVILE.   Damn your debaucht Opinion: tell me, Sot, hadst thou so much sense and light about thee to distinguish her to be a Woman, and could'st not see something about her Face and Person, to strike an awful Reverence into thy Soul?   **30**

WILLMORE.   Faith no, I consider'd her as mere a Woman as I could wish.

BELVILE.   'Sdeath I have no patience—draw, or I'll kill you.

WILLMORE.   Let that alone till to morrow, and if I set not all right again, use your Pleasure.   **35**

BELVILE.
To morrow, damn it.
The spiteful Light will lead me to no happiness.
To morrow is *Antonio's,* and perhaps
Guides him to my undoing;—oh that I could meet   **40**
This Rival, this powerful Fortunate.

WILLMORE.   What then?

BELVILE.   Let thy own Reason, or my Rage instruct thee.

WILLMORE.   I shall be finely inform'd then, no doubt; hear me, Colonel—hear me—shew me the Man and I'll do his Business.   **45**

BELVILE.   I know him no more than thou, or if I did, I should not need thy aid.

WILLMORE.   This you say is *Angelica's* House, I promis'd the kind Baggage to lie with her to Night. (*Offers to go in.*)   **50**

Enter ANTONIO *and his Page.* ANTONIO *knocks on the Hilt of his Sword.*

ANTONIO.   You paid the thousand Crowns I directed?

PAGE.   To the Lady's old Woman, Sir, I did.

WILLMORE.   Who the Devil have we here?

BELVILE.   I'll now plant my self under *Florinda's* Window, and if I find no comfort there, I'll die. (*Exit* BEL-   **55**
VILE *and* FREDERICK.)

Enter MORETTA.

MORETTA.   Page!

PAGE.   Here's my Lord.

WILLMORE.   How is this, a Piccaroon going to board my Frigate! here's one Chase-Gun for you.

(*Drawing his Sword, justles* ANTONIO *who turns and draws. They fight,* ANTONIO *falls.*)

MORETTA.   Oh, bless us, we are all undone! (*Runs*   **60**
in, and shuts the Door.)

PAGE.   Help, Murder! (BELVILE *returns at the noise of fighting.*)

BELVILE.   Ha, the mad Rogue's engag'd in some unlucky Adventure again.

Enter two or three Masqueraders.

MASQUERADERS.   Ha, a Man kill'd!

WILLMORE.   How! a Man kill'd! then I'll go home   **65**
to sleep. (*Puts up, and reels out. Exit Masqueraders an-other way.*)

BELVILE.   Who shou'd it be! pray Heaven the Rogue is safe, for all my Quarrel to him. (*As* BELVILE *is groping about, enter an Officer and six Soldiers.*)

SOLDIERS.   Who's there?

OFFICER.   So, here's one dispatcht—secure the   **70**
Murderer.

BELVILE.   Do not mistake my Charity for Murder: I came to his Assistance. (*Soldiers seize on* BELVILE.)

OFFICER.   That shall be tried, Sir.—St. *Jago,* Swords drawn in the Carnival time! (*Goes to* ANTONIO.)   **75**

ANTONIO.   Thy Hand prithee.

OFFICER.   Ha, Don *Antonio!* look well to the Villain there.—How is't, Sir?

ANTONIO.   I'm hurt.

BELVILE.   Has my Humanity made me a Criminal?   **80**

OFFICER.   Away with him.

BELVILE.   What a curst Chance is this! (*Exit Soldiers with* BELVILE.)

ANTONIO.   This is the Man that has set upon me twice— carry him to my Apartment till you have further Orders from me. (*To the Officer. Exit.* ANTONIO led.)   **85**

ACT FOUR

SCENE ONE. A FINE ROOM.

Discovers BELVILE, *as by Dark alone.*

BELVILE.   When shall I be weary of railing on Fortune, who is resolv'd never to turn with Smiles upon me?—Two such Defeats in one Night—none but the Devil and that mad Rogue could have contriv'd to have plagued me with—I am here a Prisoner—but where?—Heaven   **5**
knows—and if there be Murder done, I can soon decide the Fate of a Stranger in a Nation without Mercy—Yet this is nothing to the Torture my Soul bows with, when I think of losing my fair, my dear *Florinda.*—Hark—my Door opens—a Light—a Man—and seems of Quality—   **10**
arm'd too.—Now shall I die like a Dog without defence.

Enter ANTONIO *in a Night-Gown, with a Light; his Arm in a Scarf, and a Sword under his Arm: He sets the Candle on the Table.*

ANTONIO.   Sir, I come to know what Injuries I have done you, that could provoke you to so mean an Action, as to attack me basely, without allowing time for my Defence.   **15**

BELVILE.   Sir, for a Man in my Circumstances to plead In-nocence, would look like Fear—but view me well, and you will find no marks of a Coward on me, nor any thing that betrays that Brutality you accuse me of.

ANTONIO.
In vain, Sir, you impose upon my Sense,   **20**

You are not only he who drew on me last Night,
But yesterday before the same house, that of
    Angelica.
Yet there is something in your Face and Mein—

BELVILE.
I own I fought to day in the defence of a Friend
of mine, with whom you (if you're the same) and
    your   25
Party were first engag'd.
Perhaps you think this Crime enough to kill me,
But if you do, I cannot fear you'll do it basely.

ANTONIO.   No, Sir, I'll make you fit for a Defence with
this. (*Gives him the Sword.*)   30

BELVILE.   This Gallantry surprizes me—nor know I how to
use this Present, Sir, against a Man so brave.

ANTONIO.
You shall not need;
For know, I come to snatch you from a Danger
That is decreed against you;   35
Perhaps your Life, or long Imprisonment:
And 'twas with so much Courage you offended,
I cannot see you punisht.

BELVILE.   How shall I pay this Generosity?

ANTONIO.
It had been safer to have kill'd another,   40
Than have attempted me:
To shew your Danger, Sir, I'll let you know my
    Quality;
And 'tis the Vice-Roy's Son whom you have
    wounded.

BELVILE.
The Vice-Roy's Son!
Death and Confusion! was this Plague reserved   45
To compleat all the rest?—oblig'd by him!
The Man of all the World I would destroy.
(*Aside.*)

ANTONIO.   You seem disorder'd, Sir.

BELVILE.
Yes, trust me, Sir, I am, and 'tis with pain
That Man receives such Bounties,   50
Who wants the pow'r to pay 'em back again.

ANTONIO.
To gallant Spirits 'tis indeed uneasy;
—But you may quickly over-pay me, Sir.

BELVILE.
Then I am well—kind Heaven! but set us even,
That I may fight with him, and keep my Honour
    safe.   55
(*Aside.*)
—Oh, I'm impatient, Sir, to be discounting
The mighty Debt I owe you; command me quickly—

ANTONIO.
I have a Quarrel with a Rival, Sir,
About the Maid we love.

BELVILE.
Death, 'tis *Florinda* he means—   60
That Thought destroys my Reason, and I shall kill
    him—
(*Aside.*)

ANTONIO.
My Rival, Sir.
Is one has all the Virtues Man can boast of.

BELVILE.   Death! who shou'd this be? (*Aside.*)

ANTONIO.
He challeng'd me to meet him on the *Molo,*   65
As soon as Day appear'd; but last Night's quarrel
Has made my Arm unfit to guide a Sword.

BELVILE.
I apprehend you, Sir, you'd have me kill the Man
That lays a claim to the Maid you speak of.
—I'll do't—I'll fly to do it.   70

ANTONIO.   Sir, do you know her?

BELVILE.   No, Sir, but 'tis enough she is admired by you.

ANTONIO.
Sir, I shall rob you of the Glory on't,
For you must fight under my Name and Dress.

BELVILE.
That Opinion must be strangely obliging that
    makes   75
You think I can personate the brave *Antonio,*
Whom I can but strive to imitate.

ANTONIO.
You say too much to my Advantage.
Come, Sir, the Day appears that calls you forth.
Within, Sir, is the Habit.   80
(*Exit* ANTONIO.)

BELVILE.
Fantastick Fortune, thou deceitful Light,
That cheats the wearied Traveller by Night,
Tho on a Precipice each step you tread,
I am resolv'd to follow where you lead.
(*Exit.*)

SCENE TWO. THE MOLO.

Enter FLORINDA *and* CALLIS *in Masques, with* STEPHANO.

FLORINDA.
I'm dying with my fears; *Belvile's* not coming,
As I expected, underneath my Window,
Makes me believe that all those Fears are true.
(*Aside.*)
—Canst thou not tell with whom my Brother fights?

STEPHANO.   No, Madam, they were both in Mas-   5
querade, I was by when they challeng'd one another, and
they had decided the Quarrel then, but were prevented by
some Cavaliers; which made 'em put it off till now—but
I am sure 'tis about you they fight.

FLORINDA.   Nay then 'tis with *Belvile,* for what   10
other Lover have I that dares fight for me, except *Antonio?*

and he is too much in favour with my Brother—If it be he, for whom shall I direct my Prayers to Heaven? (*Aside*.)

STEPHANO.   Madam, I must leave you; for if my Master see me, I shall be hang'd for being your Con-   15
ductor.—I escap'd narrowly for the Excuse I made for you last night i'th' Garden.

FLORINDA.   And I'll reward thee for't—prithee no more.
(*Exit* STEPHANO.)

Enter Don PEDRO *in his Masquing Habit.*

PEDRO.   *Antonio's* late to day, the place will fill, and we may be prevented. (*Walks about*.)   20

FLORINDA.   *Antonio!* sure I heard amiss. (*Aside*.)

PEDRO.
But who would not excuse a happy Lover.
When soft fair Arms comfine the yielding Neck;
And the kind Whisper languishingly breathes,
Must you be gone so soon?   25
Sure I had dwelt for ever on her Bosom.
—But stay, he's here.

Enter BELVILE *drest in* ANTONIO's *Clothes.*

FLORINDA.   'Tis not *Belvile*, half my Fears are vanisht.

PEDRO.   *Antonio!*—

BELVILE.
This must be he. (*Aside*.)   30
You're early, Sir,—I do not use to be out-done this way.

PEDRO.
The wretched, Sir, are watchful, and 'tis enough
You have the advantage of me in *Angelica*.

BELVILE.
Angelica!
Or I've mistook my Man! Or else *Antonio*,   35
Can he forget his Interest in *Florinda*,
And fight for common Prize? (*Aside*.)

PEDRO.   Come, Sir, you know our terms—

BELVILE.
By Heaven, not I. (*Aside*.)
—No talking, I am ready, Sir.   40
(*Offers to fight.* FLORINDA *runs in.*)

FLORINDA.
Oh, hold! whoe'er you be, I do conjure you hold.
If you strike here—I die—(*To* BELVILE.)

PEDRO.   *Florinda!*

BELVILE.   *Florinda* imploring for my Rival!

PEDRO.   Away, this Kindness is unseasonable.   45

(*Puts her by, they fight; she runs in just as* BELVILE *disarms* PEDRO.)

FLORINDA.   Who are you, Sir, that dare deny my Prayers?

BELVILE.
Thy Prayers destroy him; if thou wouldst preserve him.
Do that thou'rt unacquainted with, and curse him.
(*She holds him.*)

FLORINDA.
By all you hold most dear, by her you love,
I do conjure you, touch him not.   50

BELVILE.
By her I love!
See—I obey—and at your Feet resign
The useless Trophy of my Victory.
(*Lays his sword at her Feet.*)

PEDRO.   *Antonio*, you've done enough to prove you love *Florinda*.   55

BELVILE.
Love *Florinda!*
Does Heaven love Adoration, Pray'r, or Penitence?
Love her! here Sir,—your Sword again.
(*Snatches up the Sword, and gives it him.*)
Upon this Truth I'll fight my Life away.

PEDRO.   No, you've redeem'd my Sister, and my   60
Friendship.

BELVILE.   Don *Pedro!* (*He gives him* FLORINDA *and pulls off his Vizard to shew his Face, and puts it on again.*)

PEDRO.
Can you resign your Claims to other Women,
And give your Heart intirely to *Florinda?*

BELVILE.
Intire, as dying Saints Confessions are.   65
I can delay my happiness no longer.
This minute let me make *Florinda* mine:

PEDRO.
This minute let it be—no time so proper,
This Night my Father will arrive from *Rome*,
And possibly may hinder what we propose.   70

FLORINDA.   Oh Heavens! this Minute! (*Enter Masqueraders, and pass over.*)

BELVILE.   Oh, do not ruin me!

PEDRO.   The place begins to fill; and that we may not be observ'd, do you walk off to St. *Peter's* Church, where I will meet you, and conclude your Happiness.   75

BELVILE.   I'll meet you there—if there be no more Saints Churches in *Naples*. (*Aside*.)

FLORINDA.
Oh stay, Sir, and recall your hasty Doom:
Alas I have not yet prepar'd my Heart
To entertain so strange a Guest.   80

PEDRO.   Away, this silly Modesty is assum'd too late.

BELVILE.   Heaven, Madam! what do you do?

FLORINDA.
Do! despise the Man that lays a Tyrant's Claim
To what he ought to conquer by Submission.

BELVILE.   You do not know me—move a little this   85
way. (*Draws her aside.*)

FLORINDA.

    Yes, you may even force me to the Altar,
    But not the holy Man that offers there
    Shall force me to be thine.
    (PEDRO *talks to* CALLIS *this while.*)

BELVILE.

    Oh do not lose so blest an opportunity!   **90**
    See—'tis your *Belvile*—not *Antonio,*
    Whom your mistaken Scorn and Anger ruins.
    (*Pulls off his Vizard.*)

FLORINDA.

    Belvile!
    Where was my Soul it cou'd not meet thy Voice,
    And take this knowledge in?   **95**

(*As they are talking, enter* WILLMORE *finely drest, and* FREDERICK.)

WILLMORE. No Intelligence! no News of *Belvile* yet—
well I am the most unlucky Rascal in Nature—ha!—am I
deceiv'd—or is it he—look, *Frederick*—'tis he—my dear
Belvile. (*Runs and embraces him.* BELVILE'S *Vizard falls
out on's Hand.*)

BELVILE. Hell and Confusion seize thee!   **100**

PEDRO. Ha! *Belvile!* I beg your Pardon, Sir. (*Takes* FLOR-
INDA *from him.*)

BELVILE. Nay, touch her not, she's mine by Conquest, Sir.
I won her by my Sword.

WILLMORE. Did'st thou so—and egad, Child, we'll keep
her by the Sword. (*Draws on* PEDRO, BELVILE   **105**
goes between.)

BELVILE.

    Stand off.
    Thou'rt so profanely leud, so curst by Heaven,
    All Quarrels thou espousest must be fatal.

WILLMORE.

    Nay, an you be so hot, my Valour's coy,
    And shall be courted when you want it next.   **110**
    (*Puts up his Sword.*)

BELVILE.

    You know I ought to claim a Victor's Right,
    (*To* PEDRO.)
    But you're the Brother to divine *Florinda,*
    To whom I'm such a Slave—to purchase her,
    I durst not hurt the Man she holds so dear.

PEDRO.

    'Twas by *Antonio's,* not by *Belvile's* Sword,   **115**
    This Question should have been decided, Sir:
    I must confess much to your Bravery's due,
    Both now, and when I met you last in Arms.
    But I am nicely punctual in my word,
    As Men of Honour ought, and beg your
        Pardon.   **120**
    —For this Mistake another Time shall clear.
    —This was some Plot between you and *Belvile:*
    But I'll prevent you. (*Aside to* FLORINDA *as they are
    going out.*)

(BELVILE *looks after her, and begins to walk up and down
in a Rage.*)

WILLMORE. Do not be modest now, and lose the Woman:
but if we shall fetch her back, so—   **125**

BELVILE. Do not speak to me.

WILLMORE. Not speak to you!—Egad, I'll speak to you,
and will be answered too.

BELVILE. Will you, Sir?

WILLMORE. I know I've done some mischief, but   **130**
I'm so dull a Puppy, that I am the Son of a Whore,
if I know how, or where—prithee inform my
Understanding.—

BELVILE. Leave me I say, and leave me instantly.

WILLMORE. I will not leave you in this humour,   **135**
nor till I know my Crime.

BELVILE. Death, I'll tell you, Sir—(*Draws and runs at*
WILLMORE *he runs out;* BELVILE *after him,* FREDERICK
interposes.)

Enter ANGELICA, MORETTA, *and* SEBASTIAN.

ANGELICA. Ha—*Sebastian*—Is not that *Willmore?* haste,
haste, and bring him back.

FREDERICK. The Colonel's mad—I never saw him   **140**
thus before; I'll after 'em, lest he do some mischief, for I
am sure *Willmore* will not draw on him. (*Exit.*)

ANGELICA.

    I am all Rage! my first desires defeated
    For one, for ought he knows, that has no
    Other Merit than her Quality,—   **145**
    Her being Don *Pedro's* Sister—He loves her:
    I know 'tis so—dull, dull, insensible—
    He will not see me now tho oft invited;
    And broke his Word last night—false perjur'd Man!
    —He that but yesterday fought for my Favours,   **150**
    And would have made his Life a Sacrifice
    To've gain'd one Night with me,
    Must now be hired and courted to my Arms.

MORETTA. I told you what wou'd come on't, but *Moretta's*
an old doating Fool—Why did you give him five   **155**
hundred Crowns, but to set himself out for other Lovers?
You shou'd have kept him poor, if you had meant to have
had any good from him.

ANGELICA.

    Oh, name not such mean Trifles.—Had I given him
        all
    My Youth has earn'd from Sin,   **160**
    I had not lost a Thought nor Sigh upon't.
    But I have given him my eternal Rest,
    My whole Repose, my future Joys, my Heart;
    My Virgin Heart. *Moretta!* oh 'tis gone!

MORETTA.

    Curse on him, here he comes;   **165**
    How fine she has made him too!

Enter WILLMORE *and* SEBASTIAN. ANGELICA *turns and walks away.*

WILLMORE.
> How now, turn'd Shadow?
> Fly when I pursue, and follow when I fly!
> (*Sings.*)

> > *Stay gentle Shadow of my Dove,*
> > *And tell me e'er I go,*   **170**
> > *Whether the Substance may not prove*
> > *A fleeting Thing like you.*
> There's a soft kind Look remaining yet.
> (*As she turns she looks on him.*)

ANGELICA.   Well, Sir, you may be gay; all Happiness, all Joys pursue you still, Fortune's your Slave, and   **175** gives you every hour choice of new Hearts and Beauties, till you are cloy'd with the repeated Bliss, which others vainly languish for—But know, false Man, that I shall be reveng'd. (*Turns away in a Rage.*)

WILLMORE.   So, 'gad, there are of those faint-   **180** hearted Lovers, whom such a sharp Lesson next their Hearts would make as impotent as Fourscore—pox o' this whining—my Bus'ness is to laugh and love—a pox on't; I hate your sullen Lover, a Man shall lose as much time to put you in Humour now, as would serve to gain   **185** a new Woman.

ANGELICA.   I scorn to cool that Fire I cannot raise,
Or do the Drudgery of your virtuous Mistress.

WILLMORE.   A virtuous Mistress! Death, what a thing thou hast found out for me! why what the Devil should   **190** I do with a virtuous Woman?—a fort of ill-natur'd Creatures, that take a Pride to torment a Lover. Virtue is but an Infirmity in Women, a Disease that renders even the handsom ungrateful; whilst the ill-favour'd, for want of Sollicitations and Address, only fancy them-   **195** selves so.—I have lain with a Woman of Quality, who has all the while been railing at Whores.

ANGELICA.
> I will not answer for your Mistress's Virtue,
> Tho she be young enough to know no Guilt:
> And I could wish you would persuade my Heart,   **200**
> 'Twas the two hundred thousand Crowns you
> > courted.

WILLMORE.   Two hundred thousand Crowns! what Story's this?—what Trick?—what Woman?—ha.

ANGELICA.   How strange you make it! have you forgot the Creature you entertain'd on the Piazza last night?   **205**

WILLMORE.   Ha, my Gipsy worth two hundred thousand Crowns!—oh how I long to be with her—pox, I knew she was of Quality. (*Aside.*)

ANGELICA.
> False Man, I see my Ruin in thy Face.
> How many vows you breath'd upon my Bosom,   **210**
> Never to be unjust—have you forgot so soon?

WILLMORE.   Faith no, I was just coming to repeat 'em— but here's a Humour indeed—would make a Man a Saint—Wou'd she'd be angry enough to leave me, and command me not to wait on her. (*Aside.*)   **215**

Enter HELLENA, *drest in Man's Clothes.*

HELLENA.   This must be *Angelica,* I know it by her mumping Matron here—Ay, ay, 'tis she: my mad Captain's with her too, for all his swearing—how this unconstant Humour makes me love him:—pray, good grave Gentlewoman, is not this *Angelica?*   **220**

MORETTA.   My too young Sir, it is—I hope 'tis one from Don *Antonio.* (*Goes to* ANGELICA.)

HELLENA.   Well, something I'll do to vex him for this. (*Aside.*)

ANGELICA.   I will not speak with him; am I in humour to receive a Lover?   **225**

WILLMORE.   Not speak with him! why I'll be gone—and wait your idler minutes—Can I shew less Obedience to the thing I love so fondly? (*Offers to go.*)

ANGELICA.   A fine Excuse this—stay—

WILLMORE.   And hinder your Advantage: should I   **230** repay your Bounties so ungratefully?

ANGELICA.
> Come hither, Boy,—that I may let you see
> How much above the Advantages you name
> I prize one Minute's Joy with you.

WILLMORE.   Oh, you destroy me with this Endear-   **235** ment. (*Impatient to be gone.*)—Death, how shall I get away?—Madam, 'twill not be fit I should be seen with you—besides, it will not be convenient—and I've a Friend—that's dangerously sick.

ANGELICA.   I see you're impatient—yet you shall   **240** stay.

WILLMORE.   And miss my Assignation with my Gipsy. (*Aside, and walks about impatiently.*)

HELLENA.
> Madam, (MORETTA *brings* HELLENA, *who addresses*
> > *her self to* ANGELICA.)
> You'l hardly pardon my Intrusion,
> When you shall know my Business;   **245**
> And I'm too young to tell my Tale with Art:
> But there must be a wondrous store of Goodness
> Where so much Beauty dwells.

ANGELICA.   A pretty Advocate, whoever sent thee,— Prithee proceed—Nay, Sir, you shall not go. (*To*   **250** WILLMORE *who is stealing off.*)

WILLMORE.   Then shall I lose my dear Gipsy for ever.— Pox on't, she stays me out of spite. (*Aside.*)

HELLENA.
> I am related to a Lady, Madam,
> Young, rich, and nobly born, but has the fate
> To be in love with a young *English* Gentleman.   **255**
> Strangely she loves him, at first sight she
> > lov'd him,

But did adore him when she heard him speak;
For he, she said, had Charms in every word,
That fail'd not to surprize, to wound, and conquer—

WILLMORE.   Ha, Egad I hope this concerns me.   260
(*Aside.*)

ANGELICA.
'Tis my false Man, he means—wou'd he were gone.
This Praise will raise his Pride and ruin me—Well,
Since you are so impatient to be gone,
I will release you, Sir.
(*To* WILLMORE.)

WILLMORE.
Nay, then I'm sure 'twas me he spoke of, this   265
cannot be the Effects of Kindness in her.
(*Aside.*)
—No, Madam, I've consider'd better on't,
And will not give you cause of Jealousy.

ANGELICA.   But, Sir, I've—business, that—

WILLMORE.   This shall not do, I know 'tis but to   270
try me.

ANGELICA.   Well, to your Story, Boy,—tho 'twill undo me.
(*Aside.*)

HELLENA.
With this Addition to his other Beauties,
He won her unresisting tender Heart,
He vow'd and sigh'd, and swore he lov'd her
dearly;   275
And she believ'd the cunning Flatterer,
And thought her self the happiest Maid alive:
To day was the appointed time by both,
To consummate their Bliss;
The Virgin, Altar, and the Priest were drest,   280
And whilst she languisht for the expected
Bridegroom,
She heard, he paid his broken Vows to you.

WILLMORE.   So, this is some dear Rogue that's in love with
me, and this way lets me know it; or if it be not me, she
means some one whose place I may supply. (*Aside.*) 285

ANGELICA.
Now I perceive
The cause of thy Impatience to be gone,
And all the business of this glorious Dress.

WILLMORE.   Damn the young Prater, I know not what he
means.   290

HELLENA.
Madam,
In your fair Eyes I read too much concern
To tell my farther Business.

ANGELICA.
Prithee, sweet Youth, talk on, thou may'st perhaps
Raise here a Storm that may undo my Passion,   295
And then I'll grant thee any thing.

HELLENA.
Madam, 'tis to intreat you, (oh unreasonable!)
You wou'd not see this Stranger;
For if you do, she vows you are undone,

Tho Nature never made a Man so excellent;   300
And sure he'ad been a God, but for Inconstancy.

WILLMORE.   Ah, Rogue, how finely he's instructed!
(*Aside.*)—'Tis plain some Woman that has seen me *en
passant.*

ANGELICA.   Oh, I shall burst with Jealousy! do you   305
know the Man you speak of?—

HELLENA.   Yes, Madam, he us'd to be in Buff and Scarlet.

ANGELICA.   Thou, false as Hell, what canst thou say to
this? (*To* WILLMORE.)

WILLMORE.   By Heaven—   310

ANGELICA.   Hold, do not damn thy self—

HELLENA.   Nor hope to be believ'd. (*He walks about, they
follow.*)

ANGELICA.
Oh, perjur'd Man!
Is't thus you pay my generous Passion back?

HELLENA.   Why wou'd you, Sir, abuse my Lady's   315
Faith?

ANGELICA.   And use me so inhumanly?

HELLENA.   A Maid so young, so innocent—

WILLMORE.   Ah, young Devil!

ANGELICA.   Dost thou not know thy Life is in my   320
Power?

HELLENA.   Or think my Lady cannot be reveng'd?

WILLMORE.   So, so, the Storm comes finely on. (*Aside.*)

ANGELICA.   Now thou art silent, Guilt has struck thee
dumb. Oh, hadst thou still been so, I'd liv'd in   325
safety. (*She turns away and weeps.*)

WILLMORE.   Sweetheart, the Lady's Name and House—
quickly: I'm impatient to be with her.—

(*Aside to* HELLENA, *looks towards* ANGELICA *to watch her
turning; and as she comes towards them, he meets her.*)

HELLENA.   So now is he for another Woman. (*Aside.*)

WILLMORE.
The impudent'st young thing in Nature!   330
I cannot persuade him out of his Error, Madam.

ANGELICA.
I know he's in the right,—yet thou'st a Tongue
That wou'd persuade him to deny his Faith.
(*In Rage walks away.*)

WILLMORE.   Her Name, her Name, dear Boy—
(*Said softly to* HELLENA.)

HELLENA.   Have you forgot it, Sir?   335

WILLMORE.   Oh, I perceive he's not to know I am a
Stranger to his Lady. (*Aside.*)—Yes, yes, I do know—
but—I have forgot the—(ANGELICA *turns.*)—By Heaven,
such early confidence I never saw.

ANGELICA.
Did I not charge you with this Mistress, Sir?   340
Which you denied, tho I beheld your Perjury.

This little Generosity of thine has render'd back my
Heart. (*Walks away.*)

WILLMORE.
So, you have made sweet work here, my little
mischief;
Look your Lady be kind and good-natur'd now, or
I shall have but a cursed Bargain on't.   345
(ANGELICA *turns towards them.*)
—The Rogue's bred up to Mischief,
Art thou so great a Fool to credit him?

ANGELICA.   Yes, I do; and you in vain impose upon me.—
Come hither, Boy—Is not this he you speak of?

HELLENA.   I think—it is; I cannot swear, but I vow   350
he has just such another lying Lover's look. (HELLENA
looks in his Face, he gazes on her.)

WILLMORE.
Hah! do not I know that Face?—
By Heaven, my little Gipsy! what a dull Dog was I?
Had I but lookt that way, I'd known her.
Are all my hopes of a new Woman banisht?   355
(*Aside.*)
—Egad, if I don't fit thee for this, hang me.
—Madam, I have found out the Plot.

HELLENA.   Oh Lord, what does he say? am I discover'd
now?

WILLMORE.   Do you see this young Spark here?   360

HELLENA.   He'll tell her who I am.

WILLMORE.   Who do you think this is?

HELLENA.   Ay, ay, he does know me.—Nay, dear Captain,
I'm undone if you discover me.

WILLMORE.   Nay, nay, no cogging; she shall know   365
what a precious Mistress I have.

HELLENA.   Will you be such a Devil?

WILLMORE.   Nay, nay, I'll teach you to spoil sport you will
not make.—This small Ambassador comes not from a
Person of Quality, as you imagine, and he says;   370
but from a very errant Gipsy, the talkingst, pratingst, can-
tingst little Animal thou ever saw'st.

ANGELICA.   What news you tell me! that's the thing I mean.

HELLENA.   Wou'd I were well off the place.—If ever I go
a Captain-hunting again.—(*Aside.*)   375

WILLMORE.   Mean that thing? that Gipsy thing? thou
may'st as well be jealous of thy Monkey, or Parrot as her:
a *German* Motion were worth a dozen of her, and a Dream
were a better Enjoyment, a Creature of Constitution fitter
for Heaven than Man.   380

HELLENA.   Tho I'm sure he lyes, yet this vexes me. (*Aside.*)

ANGELICA.   You are mistaken, she's a *Spanish* Woman
Made up of no such dull Materials.

WILLMORE.   Materials! Egad, and she be made of any that
will either dispense, or admit of Love, I'll be   385
bound to continence.

HELLENA.   Unreasonable Man, do you think so? (*Aside to
him.*)

WILLMORE.   You may Return, my little Brazen Head, and
tell your Lady, that till she be handsom enough to be belov'd, or I dull enough to be religious, there will   390
be small hopes of me.

ANGELICA.   Did you not promise then to marry her?

WILLMORE.   Not I, by Heaven.

ANGELICA.   You cannot undeceive my fears and torments,
till you have vow'd you will not marry her.   395

HELLENA.   If he swears that, he'll be reveng'd on me indeed
for all my Rogueries.

ANGELICA.   I know what Arguments you'll bring against
me, Fortune and Honour.

WILLMORE.   Honour! I tell you, I hate it in your   400
Sex; and those that fancy themselves possest of that Foppery, are the most impertinently troublesom of all
Woman-kind, and will transgress nine Commandments to
keep one: and to satisfy your Jealousy I swear—

HELLENA.   Oh, no swearing, dear Captain—(*Aside*   405
to him.)

WILLMORE.   If it were possible I should ever be inclin'd to
marry, it should be some kind young Sinner, one that has
Generosity enough to give a favour handsomely to one
that can ask it discreetly, one that has Wit enough to
manage an Intrigue of Love—oh, how civil such   410
a Wench is, to a Man than does her the Honour to marry
her.

ANGELICA.   By Heaven, there's no Faith in any thing he
says.

Enter SEBASTIAN.

SEBASTIAN.   Madam, *Don Antonio*—   415

ANGELICA.   Come hither.

HELLENA.   Ha, *Antonio!* he may be coming hither, and he'll
certainly discover me, I'll therefore retire without a Ceremony. (*Exit* HELLENA.)

ANGELICA.   I'll see him, get my Coach ready.   420

SEBASTIAN.   It waits you, Madam.

WILLMORE.   This is lucky: what, Madam, now I may be
gone and leave you to the enjoyment of my Rival?

ANGELICA.
Dull Man, that canst not see how ill, how poor
That false dissimulation looks—Be gone,   425
And never let me see thy cozening Face again,
Lest I relapse and kill thee.

WILLMORE.
Yes, you can spare me now,—farewell till you
are in a better Humour—I'm glad of this release—
Now for my Gipsy: 430
For tho to worse we change, yet still we find
New Joys, New Charms, in a new Miss that's kind.
(*Exit* WILLMORE.)

ANGELICA.
He's gone, and in this Ague of My Soul
The shivering Fit returns;

Oh with what willing haste he took his leave,   435
As if the long'd for Minute were arriv'd,
Of some blest Assignation.
In vain I have consulted all my Charms,
In vain this Beauty priz'd, in vain believ'd
My eyes cou'd kindle any lasting Fires.   440
I had forgot my Name, my Infamy,
And the Reproach that Honour lays on those
That dare pretend a sober passion here.
Nice Reputation, tho it leave behind
More Virtues than inhabit where that dwells,   445
Yet that once gone, those virtues shine no more.
—Then since I am not fit to belov'd,
I am resolv'd to think on a Revenge
On him that sooth'd me thus to my undoing.
(*Exeunt.*)

SCENE THREE. A STREET.

Enter FLORINDA *and* VALERIA *in Habits different from what they have been seen in.*

FLORINDA.   We're happily escap'd, yet I tremble still.
VALERIA.   A Lover and fear! why, I am but half a one, and yet I have Courage for any Attempt. Would *Hellena* were here. I wou'd fain have had her as deep in this Mischief as we, she'll fare but ill else I doubt.   5
FLORINDA.   She pretended a Visit to the *Augustine* Nuns, but I believe some other design carried her out, pray Heavens we light on her.
—Prithee what didst do with *Callis?*
VALERIA.   When I saw no Reason wou'd do good on   10
her, I follow'd her into the Wardrobe, and as she was looking for something in a great Chest, I tumbled her in by the Heels, snatcht the Key of the Apartment where you were confin'd, lockt her in, and left her bauling for help.
FLORINDA.   'Tis well you resolve to follow my For-   15
tunes, for thou darest never appear at home again after such an Action.
VALERIA.   That's according as the young Stranger and I shall agree—But to our business—I deliver'd your Letter, your Note to *Belvile,* when I got out under pretence   20
of going to Mass, I found him at his Lodging, and believe me it came seasonably; for never was Man in so desperate a Condition. I told him of your Resolution of making your escape to day, if your Brother would be absent long enough to permit you; if not, die rather than be   25
Antonio's.
FLORINDA.   Thou shou'dst have told him I was confin'd to my Chamber upon my Brother's suspicion, that the Business on the *Molo* was a Plot laid between him and I.
VALERIA.   I said all this, and told him your Brother   30
was now gone to his Devotion, and he resolves to visit every Church till he find him; and not only undeceive him in that, but caress him so as shall delay his return home.

FLORINDA.   Oh Heavens! he's here, and *Belvile* with him too. (*They put on their Vizards.*)   35

Enter Don PEDRO, BELVILE, WILLMORE; BELVILE *and Don* PEDRO *seeming in serious Discourse.*

VALERIA.   Walk boldly by them, I'll come at a distance, lest he suspect us. (*She walks by them, and looks back on them.*)
WILLMORE.   Ha! A Woman! and of an excellent Mien!
PEDRO.   She throws a kind look back on you.
WILLMORE.   Death, tis a likely Wench, and that   40
kind look shall not be cast away—I'll follow her.
BELVILE.   Prithee do not.
WILLMORE.   Do not! By Heavens to the Antipodes, with such an Invitation. (*She goes out, and* WILLMORE *follows her.*)
BELVILE.   'Tis a mad Fellow for a Wench.   45

Enter FREDERICK.

FREDERICK.   Oh Colonel, such News.
BELVILE.   Prithee what?
FREDERICK.   News that will make you laugh in spite of Fortune.
BELVILE.   What, *Blunt* has had some damn'd Trick   50
put upon him, cheated, bang'd, or clapt?
FREDERICK.   Cheated, Sir, rarely cheated of all but his Shirt and Drawers; the unconscionable Whore too turn'd him out before Consummation, so that traversing the Streets at Midnight, the Watch found him in this *Fresco,*   55
and conducted him home: By Heaven 'tis such a slight, and yet I durst as well have been hang'd as laugh at him, or pity him; he beats all that do but ask him a Question, and is in such an Humour—
PEDRO.   Who is't has met with this ill usage, Sir?   60
BELVILE.   A Friend of ours, whom you must see for Mirth's sake. I'll imploy him to give *Florinda* time for an escape. (*Aside.*)
PEDRO.   Who is he?
BELVILE.   A young Countryman of ours, one that has been educated at so plentiful a rate, he yet ne'er knew   65
the want of Money, and 'twill be a great Jest to see how simply he'll look without it. For my part I'll lend him none, and the Rogue knows not how to put on a borrowing Face, and ask first. I'll let him see how good 'tis to play our parts whilst I play his—Prithee, *Frederick* do   70
go home and keep him in that posture till we come. (*Exeunt.*)

Enter FLORINDA *from the farther end of the Scene, looking behind her.*

FLORINDA.   I am follow'd still—hah—my Brother too advancing this way, good Heavens defend me from being seen by him. (*She goes off.*)

Enter WILLMORE, *and after him* VALERIA, *at a little distance.*

WILLMORE.   Ah! There she sails, she looks back as   **75**
she were willing to be boarded, I'll warrant her Prize. (*He
goes out,* VALERIA *following.*)

Enter HELLENA, *just as he goes out, with a Page.*

HELLENA.   Hah, is not that my Captain that has a Woman
in chase?—'tis not *Angelica*. Boy, follow those People at
a distance, and bring me an Account where they go in.—
I'll find his Haunts, and plague him every where.—   **80**
ha—my Brother! (*Exit Page.*) (BELVILE, WILLMORE,
PEDRO *cross the Stage:* HELLENA *runs off.*)

Scene changes to another Street. Enter FLORINDA.

FLORINDA.   What shall I do, my Brother now pursues me.
Will no kind Power protect me from his Tyranny?—Hah,
here's a Door open, I'll venture in, since nothing can be
worse than to fall into his Hands, my Life and   **85**
Honour are at stake, and my Necessity has no choice. (*She
goes in.*)

Enter VALERIA, *and* HELLENA'S *Page peeping after*
FLORINDA.

PAGE.   Here she went in, I shall remember this House. (*Exit
Boy.*)

VALERIA.   This is *Belvile's* Lodgings; she's gone in
as readily as if she knew it—hah—here's that mad Fellow again, I dare not venture in—I'll watch my   **90**
Opportunity. (*Goes aside.*)

Enter WILLMORE, *gazing about him.*

WILLMORE.   I have lost her hereabouts—Pox on't she must
not scape me so. (*Goes out.*)

Scene changes to BLUNT'S *Chamber, discovers him sitting
on a Couch in his Shirt and Drawers, reading.*

BLUNT.   So, now my Mind's a little at Peace, since I have
resolv'd Revenge—A Pox on this Taylor tho, for   **95**
not bringing home the Clothes I bespoke; and a Pox of all
poor Cavaliers, a Man can never keep a spare Suit for
'em; and I shall have these Rogues come in and find me
naked; and then I'm undone; but I'm resolv'd to arm my
self—the Rascals shall not insult over me too   **100**
much. (*Puts on an old rusty Sword and Buff-Belt.*)—Now,
how like a Morrice-Dancer I am equipt—a fine Lady-like
Whore to cheat me thus, without affording me a Kindness
for my Money, a Pox light on her, I shall never be reconciled to the Sex more, she has made me as   **105**
faithless as a Physician, as uncharitable as a Churchman,
and as ill-natur'd as a Poet. O how I'll use all Women-
kind hereafter! what wou'd I give to have one of 'em
within my reach now! any Mortal thing in Petticoats, kind

Fortune, send me; and I'll forgive thy last Night's   **110**
Malice—Here's a cursed Book too, (a Warning to all
young Travellers) that can instruct me how to prevent
such Mischiefs now 'tis too late. Well 'tis a rare convenient thing to read a little now and then, as well as hawk
and hunt. (*Sits down again and reads.*)   **115**

Enter to him FLORINDA.

FLORINDA.   This House is haunted sure, 'tis well furnisht
and no living thing inhabits it—hah—a Man! Heavens
how he's attir'd! sure 'tis some Rope-dancer, or Fencing-
Master; I tremble now for fear, and yet I must venture
now to speak to him—Sir, if I may not interrupt   **120**
your Meditations—(*He starts up and gazes.*)

BLUNT.   Hah—what's here? Are my wishes granted? and is
not that a she Creature? Adsheartlikins 'tis! what
wretched thing art thou—hah!

FLORINDA.   Charitable Sir, you've told your self   **125**
already what I am; a very wretched Maid, forc'd by a
strange unlucky Accident, to seek a safety here, and must
be ruin'd, if you do not grant it.

BLUNT.   Ruin'd! Is there any Ruin so inevitable as that
which now threatens thee? Dost thou know, mis-   **130**
erable Woman, into what Den of Mischiefs thou art
fall'n? what a Bliss of Confusion?—hah—dost not see
something in my looks that frights thy guilty Soul, and
makes thee wish to change that Shape of Woman for any
humble Animal, or Devil? for those were safer   **135**
for thee, and less mischievous.

FLORINDA.   Alas, what mean you, Sir? I must confess your
Looks have something in 'em makes me fear; but I be-
seech you, as you seem a Gentleman, pity a harmless
Virgin, that takes your House for Sanctuary.   **140**

BLUNT.   Talk on, talk on, and weep too, till my faith return.
Do, flatter me out of my Senses again—a harmless Virgin
with a Pox, as much one as t'other, adsheartlikins. Why,
what the Devil can I not be safe in my House for you? not
in my Chamber? nay, even being naked too   **145**
cannot secure me. This is an Impudence greater than has
invaded me yet.—Come, no Resistance. (*Pulls her
rudely.*)

FLORINDA.   Dare you be so cruel?

BLUNT.   Cruel, adsheartlikins as a Gally-slave, or a *Spanish*
Whore: Cruel, yes, I will kiss and beat thee all   **150**
over; kiss, and see thee all over; thou shalt lie with me
too, not that I care for the Injoyment, but to let you see I
have ta'en deliberated Malice to thee, and will be revenged on one Whore for the Sins of another; I will smile
and deceive thee, flatter thee, and beat thee, kiss   **155**
and swear, and lye to thee, imbrace thee and rob thee, as
she did me, fawn on thee, and strip thee stark naked, then
hang thee out at my Window by the Heels, with a Paper
of scurvey Verses fasten'd to thy Breast, in praise of damnable Women—Come, come along.   **160**

FLORINDA.   Alas, Sir, must I be sacrific'd for the Crimes of the most infamous of my Sex? I never understood the Sins you name.

BLUNT.   Do, persuade the Fool you love him, or that one of you can be just or honest; tell me I was not an 165 easy Coxcomb, or any strange impossible Tale: it will be believ'd sooner than thy false Showers or Protestations. A Generation of damn'd Hypocrites, to flatter my very Clothes from my back! dissembling Witches! are these the Returns you make an honest Gentleman that 170 trusts, believes, and loves you?—But if I be not even with you—Come along, or I shall— (*Pulls her again.*)

Enter FREDERICK.

FREDERICK.   Hah, what's here to do?

BLUNT.   Adsheartlikins, *Frederick.* I am glad thou art come, to be a Witness of my dire Revenge. 175

FREDERICK.   What's this, a Person of Quality too, who is upon the Ramble to supply the Defects of some grave impotent Husband?

BLUNT.   No, this has another Pretence, some very unfortunate Accident brought her hither, to save a Life 180 pursued by I know not who, or why, and forc'd to take Sanctuary here at Fools Haven. Adsheartlikins to me of all Mankind for Protection? Is the Ass to be cajol'd again, think ye? No, young one, no Prayers or Tears shall mitigate my Rage; therefore prepare for both my 185 Pleasure of Enjoyment and Revenge, for I am resolved to make up my Loss here on thy Body, I'll take it out in kindness and in beating.

FREDERICK.   Now, Mistress of mine, what do you think of this? 190

FLORINDA.   I think he will not—dares not be so barbarous.

FREDERICK.   Have a care, *Blunt,* she fetch'd a deep Sigh, she is inamour'd with thy Shirt and Drawers, she'll strip thee even of that. There are of her Calling such unconscionable Baggages, and such dexterous Thieves, 195 they'll flea a Man, and he shall ne'er miss his Skin, till he feels the Cold. There was a Country-man of ours robb'd of a Row of Teeth whilst he was sleeping, which the Jilt made him buy again when he wak'd—You see, Lady, how little Reason we have to trust you. 200

BLUNT.   'Dsheartlikins, why, this is most abominable.

FLORINDA.   Some such Devils there may be, but by all that's holy I am none such, I entered here to save a Life in danger.

BLUNT.   For no goodness I'll warrant her. 205

FREDERICK.   Faith, Damsel, you had e'en confess the plain Truth, for we are Fellows not to be caught twice in the same Trap: Look on that Wreck, a tight Vessel when he set out of Haven, well trim'd and laden, and see how a Female Piccaroon of this Island of Rogues has 210 shatter'd him, and canst thou hope for any Mercy?

BLUNT.   No, no, Gentlewoman, come along, adsheartlikins we must be better acquainted—we'll both lie with her, and then let me alone to bang her.

FREDERICK.   I am ready to serve you in matters of 215 Revenge, that has a double Pleasure in't.

BLUNT.   Well said. You hear, little one, how you are condemn'd by publick Vote to the Bed within, there's no resisting your Destiny, Sweetheart. (*Pulls her.*)

FLORINDA.   Stay, Sir, I have seen you with *Belvile,* 220 an English Cavalier, for his sake use me kindly; you know how, Sir.

BLUNT.   *Belvile!* why, yes, Sweeting, we do know *Belvile,* and wish he were with us now, he's a Cormorant at Whore and Bacon, he'd have a Limb or two of thee, my 225 Virgin Pullet: but 'tis no matter, we'll leave him the Bones to pick.

FLORINDA.   Sir, if you have any Esteem for that *Belvile,* I conjure you to treat me with more Gentleness; he'll thank you for the Justice. 230

FREDERICK.   Hark ye, *Blunt,* I doubt we are mistaken in this matter.

FLORINDA.   Sir, If you find me not worth *Belvile's* Care, use me as you please; and that you may think I merit better treatment than you threaten—pray take this 235 Present— (*Gives him a Ring: He looks on it.*)

BLUNT.   Hum—A Diamond! why, 'tis a wonderful Virtue now that lies in this Ring, a mollifying Virtue; adsheartlikins there's more persuasive Rhetorick in't, than all her Sex can utter. 240

FREDERICK.   I begin to suspect something; and 'twou'd anger us vilely to be truss'd up for a Rape upon a Maid of Quality, when we only believe we ruffle a Harlot.

BLUNT.   Thou art a credulous Fellow, but adsheartlikins I have no Faith yet; why, my Saint prattled as par- 245 lously as this does, she gave me a Bracelet too, a Devil on her: but I sent my Man to sell it to day for Necessaries, and it prov'd as counterfeit as her Vows of Love.

FREDERICK.   However let it reprieve her till we see *Belvile.*

BLUNT.   That's hard, yet I will grant it. 250

Enter a Servant.

SERVANT.   Oh, Sir, the Colonel is just come with his new Friend and a *Spaniard* of Quality, and talks of having you to Dinner with 'em.

BLUNT.   'Dsheartlikins, I'm undone—I would not see 'em for the World: Harkye, *Frederick* lock up the 255 Wench in your Chamber.

FREDERICK.   Fear nothing, Madam, whate'er he threatens, you're safe whilst in my Hands. (*Exit* FREDERICK *and* FLORINDA.)

BLUNT.   And, Sirrah—upon your Life, say—I am not at home—or that I am asleep—or—or any thing— 260 away—I'll prevent them coming this way. (*Locks the Door and Exeunt.*)

ACT FIVE

SCENE ONE. BLUNT'S CHAMBER.

After a great knocking as at his Chamber-door, enter BLUNT *softly, crossing the Stage in his Shirt and Drawers, as before.*

Ned, Ned Blunt, Ned Blunt. (*Call within.*)

BLUNT.   The Rogues are up in Arms, 'dsheartlikins, this villainous *Frederick* has betray'd me, they have heard of my blessed Fortune.

Ned Blunt, Ned, Ned— (*And knocking within.*)

BELVILE.   Why, he's dead, Sir, without dispute dead, he has not been seen to day; let's break open the Door—   5
here—Boy—

BLUNT.   Ha, break open the Door! 'dsheartlikins that mad Fellow will be as good as his word.

BELVILE.   Boy, bring something to force the Door. (*A great noise within at the Door again.*)

BLUNT.   So, now must I speak in my own Defence,   10
I'll try what Rhetorick will do—hold—hold, what do you mean, Gentleman, what do you mean?

BELVILE.   Oh Rogue, art alive? prithee open the Door, and convince us.

BLUNT.   Yes, I am alive, Gentlemen—but at present   15
a little busy.

BELVILE.   How! *Blunt* grown a man of Business! come, come, open, and let's see this Miracle. (*Within.*)

BLUNT.   No, no, no, no, Gentlemen, 'tis no great Busi-ness—but—I am—at—my Devotion,—'dsheartli-   20
kins, will you not allow a man time to pray?

BELVILE.   Turn'd religious! a greater Wonder than the first, therefore open quickly, or we shall unhinge, we shall. (*Within.*)

BLUNT.   This won't do—Why, hark ye, Colonel; to tell you the plain Truth, I am about a necessary Affair of   25
Life.—I have a Wench with me—you apprehend me? the Devil's in't if they be so uncivil as to disturb me now.

WILLMORE.   How, a Wench! Nay, then we must enter and partake; no Resistance,—unless it be your Lady of Quality, and then we'll keep our distance.   30

BLUNT.   So, the Business is out.

WILLMORE.   Come, come, lend more hands to the Door,—now heave altogether—so, well done, my Boys—(*Breaks open the Door.*)

Enter BELVILE, WILLMORE, FREDERICK, PEDRO *and* BELVILE's *Page:* BLUNT *looks simply, they all laugh at him, he lays his hand on his Sword, and comes up to* WILLMORE.

BLUNT.   Hark ye, Sir, laugh out your laugh quickly, d'ye hear, and be gone, I shall spoil your sport else;   35
'dsheartlikins, Sir, I shall—the Jest has been carried on too long,—a Plague upon my Taylor—(*Aside.*)

WILLMORE.   'Sdeath, how the Whore has drest him! Faith, Sir, I'm sorry.

BLUNT.   Are you so, Sir? keep't to your self then,   40
Sir, I advise you, d'ye hear? for I can as little endure your Pity as his Mirth. (*Lays his Hand on's Sword.*)

BELVILE.   Indeed, *Willmore*, thou wert a little too rough with *Ned Blunt's* Mistress; call a Person of Quality Whore, and one so young, so handsome, and so   45
eloquent!—ha, ha, ha.

BLUNT.   Hark ye, Sir, you know me, and know I can be angry; have a care—for 'dsheartlikins I can fight too—I can, Sir,—do you mark me—no more.

BELVILE.   Why so peevish, good *Ned*? some Disap-   50
pointments, I'll warrant—What! did the jealous Count her Husband return just in the nick?

BLUNT.   Or the Devil, Sir,—d'ye laugh? (*They laugh.*) Look ye, settle me a good sober Countenance, and that quickly too, or you shall know *Ned Blunt* is not—   55

BELVILE.   Not every Body, we know that.

BLUNT.   Not an Ass, to be laught at, Sir.

WILLMORE.   Unconscionable Sinner, to bring a Lover so near his Happiness, a vigorous passionate Lover, and then not only cheat him of his Moveables, but his De-   60
sires too.

BELVILE.   Ah, Sir, a Mistress is a Trifle with *Blunt*, he'll have a dozen the next time he looks abroad; his Eyes have Charms not to be resisted: There needs no more than to expose that taking Person to the view of the Fair,   65
and he leads 'em all in Triumph.

PEDRO.   Sir, tho I'm a stranger to you, I'm ashamed at the rudeness of my Nation; and could you learn who did it, would assist you to make an Example of 'em.

BLUNT.   Why, ay, there's one speaks sense now, and   70
handsomly; and let me tell you Gentlemen, I should not have shew'd my self like a Jack-Pudding, thus to have made you Mirth, but that I have revenge within my power; for know, I have got into my possession a Female, who had better have fallen under any Curse, than the   75
Ruin I design her: 'dsheartlikins, she assaulted me here in my own Lodgings, and had doubtless committed a Rape upon me, had not this Sword defended me.

FREDERICK.   I knew not that, but o' my Conscience thou hadst ravisht her, had she not redeem'd her self   80
with a Ring—let's see't, *Blunt*. (BLUNT *shews the Ring.*)

BELVILE.   Hah!—the Ring I gave *Florinda* when we ex-chang'd our Vows!—hark ye, *Blunt*—(*Goes to whisper to him.*)

WILLMORE.   No whispering, good Colonel, there's a Woman in the case, no whispering.   85

BELVILE.   Hark ye, Fool, be advis'd, and conceal both the Ring and the Story, for your Reputation's sake; don't let People know what despis'd Cullies we *English* are: to be cheated and abus'd by one Whore, and another rather bribe thee than be kind to thee, is an Infamy to our   90
Nation.

WILLMORE.   Come, come, where's the Wench? we'll see her, let her be what she will, we'll see her.

PEDRO.   Ay, ay, let us see her, I can soon discover whether she be of Quality, or for your Diversion.   **95**

BLUNT.   She's in *Frederick's* Custody.

WILLMORE.   Come, come, the Key. (*To* FREDERICK *who gives him the Key, they are going.*)

BELVILE.   Death! what shall I do?—stay, Gentlemen—yet if I hinder 'em, I shall discover all—hold, let's go one at once—give me the Key.   **100**

WILLMORE.   Nay, hold there, Colonel, I'll go first.

FREDERICK.   Nay, no Dispute, *Ned* and I have the property of her.

WILLMORE.   Damn Property—then we'll draw Cuts. (BELVILE *goes to whisper* WILLMORE.) Nay, no Corruption, good Colonel: come, the longest Sword carries her.—(*They all draw, forgetting Don* PEDRO, *being a Spaniard, had the longest.*)   **105**

BLUNT.   I yield up my Interest to you Gentlemen, and that will be Revenge sufficient.

WILLMORE.   The Wench is yours—(*To* PEDRO.) Pox of his *Toledo*, I had forgot that.   **110**

FREDERICK.   Come, Sir, I'll conduct you to the Lady. (*Exit* FREDERICK *and* PEDRO.)

BELVILE.   To hinder him will certainly discover—(*Aside.*) Dost know, dull Beast, what Mischief thou has done? (WILLMORE *walking up and down out of Humour.*)

WILLMORE.   Ay, ay, to trust our Fortune to Lots, a Devil on't, 'twas madness, that's the Truth on't.   **115**

BELVILE.   Oh intolerable Sot!

Enter FLORINDA, *running masqu'd,* PEDRO *after her,* WILLMORE *gazing round her.*

FLORINDA.   Good Heaven, defend me from discovery. (*Aside.*)

PEDRO.   'Tis but in vain to fly me, you are fallen to my Lot.

BELVILE.   Sure she is undiscover'd yet, but now I fear there is no way to bring her off.   **120**

WILLMORE.   Why, what a Pox is not this my Woman, the same I follow'd but now? (PEDRO *talking to* FLORINDA, *who walks up and down.*)

PEDRO.   As if I did not know ye, and your Business here.

FLORINDA.   Good Heaven! I fear he does indeed—   **125** (*Aside.*)

PEDRO.   Come, pray be kind, I know you meant to be so when you enter'd here, for these are proper Gentlemen.

WILLMORE.   But, Sir—perhaps the Lady will not be impos'd upon, she'll chuse her Man.

PEDRO.   I am better bred, than not to leave her Choice free.   **130**

Enter VALERIA, *and is surpriz'd at the Sight of Don* PEDRO.

VALERIA.   Don *Pedro* here! there's no avoiding him. (*Aside.*)

FLORINDA.   *Valeria!* then I'm undone—(*Aside.*)

VALERIA.   Oh! have I found you, Sir—(*To* PEDRO, *running to him.*)—The strangest Accident—if I had breath—to tell it.   **135**

PEDRO.   Speak—is *Florinda* safe? *Hellena* well?

VALERIA.   Ay, ay, Sir—*Florinda*—is safe—from any fears of you.

PEDRO.   Why, where's *Florinda?*—speak.   **140**

VALERIA.   Ay, where indeed, Sir? I wish I could inform you,—But to hold you no longer in doubt—

FLORINDA.   Oh, what will she say! (*Aside.*)

VALERIA.   She's fled away in the Habit of one of her Pages, Sir—but *Callis* thinks you may retrieve her yet,   **145** if you make haste away; she'll tell you, Sir, the rest—if you can find her out. (*Aside.*)

PEDRO.   Dishonourable Girl, she has undone my Aim— Sir—you see my necessity of leaving you, and I hope you'll pardon it: my Sister, I know, will make her   **150** flight to you; and if she do, I shall expect she should be render'd back.

BELVILE.   I shall consult my Love and Honour, Sir. (*Exit* PEDRO.)

FLORINDA.   My dear Preserver, let me imbrace thee. (*To* VALERIA.)

WILLMORE.   What the Devil's all this?   **155**

BLUNT.   Mystery by this Light.

VALERIA.   Come, come, make haste and get your selves married quickly, for your Brother will return again.

BELVILE.   I am so surpriz'd with Fears and Joys, so amaz'd to find you here in safety, I can scarce persuade   **160** my Heart into a Faith of what I see—

WILLMORE.   Harkye, Colonel, is this that Mistress who has cost you so many Sighs, and me so many Quarrels with you?

BELVILE.   It is—Pray give him the Honour of your   **165** Hand. (*To* FLORINDA.)

WILLMORE.   Thus it must be receiv'd then. (*Kneels and kisses her Hand.*) And with it give your Pardon too.

FLORINDA.   The Friend to *Belvile* may command me anything.   **170**

WILLMORE.   Death, wou'd I might, 'tis a surprizing Beauty. (*Aside.*)

BELVILE.   Boy, run and fetch a Father instantly. (*Exit Boy.*)

FREDERICK.   So, now do I stand like a Dog, and have not a Syllable to plead my own Cause with: by this   **175** Hand, Madam, I was never thorowly confounded before, nor shall I ever more dare look up with Confidence, till you are pleased to pardon me.

FLORINDA.   Sir, I'll be reconcil'd to you on one Condition, that you'll follow the Example of your Friend, in   **180** marrying a Maid that does not hate you, and whose Fortune (I believe) will not be unwelcome to you.

FREDERICK.   Madam, had I no Inclinations that way, I shou'd obey your kind Commands.

BELVILE.   Who, *Frederick* marry; he has so few In-   **185** clinations for Womankind, that had he been possest of

Paradise, he might have continu'd there to this Day, if no
Crime but Love cou'd have disinherited him.

FREDERICK.   Oh, I do not use to boast of my Intrigues.

BELVILE.   Boast! why thou do'st nothing but boast;   **190**
and I dare swear, wer't thou as innocent from the Sin of
the Grape, as thou art from the Apple, thou might'st yet
claim that right in *Eden* which our first Parents lost by
too much loving.

FREDERICK.   I wish this Lady would think me so   **195**
modest a Man.

VALERIA.   She shou'd be sorry then, and not like you half
so well, and I shou'd be loth to break my Word with you;
which was, That if your Friend and mine are agreed, it
shou'd be a Match between you and I. (*She gives*   **200**
him her Hand.)

FREDERICK.   Bear witness, Colonel, 'tis a Bargain. (*Kisses
her Hand.*)

BLUNT.   I have a Pardon to beg too; but adsheartlikins I am
so out of Countenance, that I am a Dog if I can say any
thing to purpose. (*To* FLORINDA.)

FLORINDA.   Sir, I heartily forgive you all.   **205**

BLUNT.   That's nobly said, sweet Lady—*Belvile,* prithee
present her her Ring again, for I find I have not Courage
to approach her my self. (*Gives him the Ring, he gives it
to* FLORINDA.)

Enter BOY.

BOY.   Sir, I have brought the Father that you sent for.

BELVILE.   'Tis well, and now my dear *Florinda,*   **210**
let's fly to compleat that mighty Joy we have so long
wish'd and sigh'd for.—Come, *Frederick* you'll follow?

FREDERICK.   Your Example, Sir, 'twas ever my Ambition
in War, and must be so in Love.

WILLMORE.   And must not I see this juggling Knot   **215**
ty'd?

BELVILE.   No, thou shalt do us better Service, and be our
Guard, lest Don *Pedro's* sudden Return interrupt the
Ceremony.

WILLMORE.   Content; I'll secure this Pass. (*Exit*   **220**
BELVILE, FLORINDA, FREDERICK, *and* VALERIA.)

BOY.   Sir, there's a Lady without wou'd speak to you. (*To*
WILLMORE.)

WILLMORE.   Conduct her in, I dare not quit my Post.

BOY.   And, Sir, your Taylor waits you in your Chamber.

BLUNT.   Some comfort yet, I shall not dance naked at the
Wedding. (*Exit* BLUNT *and* BOY.)   **225**

Enter again the BOY, *conducting in* ANGELICA *in a masquing
Habit and a Vizard,* WILLMORE *runs to her.*)

WILLMORE.   This can be none but my pretty Gipsy—Oh, I
see you can follow as well as fly—Come, confess thy self
the most malicious Devil in Nature, you think you have
done my Bus'ness with *Angelica*—

ANGELICA.   Stand off, base Villain—(*She draws a*   **230**
Pistol and holds to his Breast.)

WILLMORE.   Hah, 'tis not she: who art thou? and what's
thy Business?

ANGELICA.   One thou hast injur'd, and who comes to kill
thee for't.

WILLMORE.   What the Devil canst thou mean?   **235**

ANGELICA.   By all my Hopes to kill thee—(*Holds still the
Pistol to his Breast, he going back, she following still.*)

WILLMORE.   Prithee on what Acquaintance? for I know
thee not.

ANGELICA.
Behold this Face!—so lost to thy Remembrance!
And then call all thy Sins about thy Soul,   **240**
(*Pulls off her Vizard.*)
And let them die with thee.

WILLMORE.   *Angelica!*

ANGELICA.   Yes, Traitor.
Does not thy guilty Blood run shivering thro thy
Veins?
Hast thou no Horrour at this Sight, that
tells thee,   **245**
Thou hast not long to boast thy shameful Conquest?

WILLMORE.   Faith, no Child, my Blood keeps its old Ebbs
and Flows still, and that usual Heat too, that cou'd oblige
thee with a Kindness, had I but opportunity.

ANGELICA.   Devil! dost wanton with my Pain—   **250**
have at thy Heart.

WILLMORE.
Hold, dear Virago! hold thy Hand a little,
I am not now at leisure to be kill'd—hold and hear
me—
Death, I think she's in earnest. (*Aside.*)

ANGELICA.
Oh if I take not heed,   **255**
My coward Heart will leave me to his Mercy.
(*Aside, turning from him.*)
—What have you, Sir, to say?—but should I hear
thee,
Thoud'st talk away all that is brave about me:
(*Follows him with the Pistol to his Breast.*)
And I have vow'd thy Death, by all that's sacred.

WILLMORE.   Why, then there's an end of a proper   **260**
handsom Fellow, that might have liv'd to have done good
Service yet:—That's all I can say to't.

ANGELICA.   Yet—I wou'd give thee—time for Penitence.
(*Pausingly.*)

WILLMORE.   Faith, Child, I thank God, I have ever took
care to lead a good, sober, hopeful Life, and am   **265**
of a Religion that teaches me to believe, I shall depart in
Peace.

ANGELICA.
So will the Devil: tell me

How many poor believing Fools thou has undone;
How many Hearts thou hast betray'd to ruin!   270
—Yet these are little Mischiefs to the Ills
Thou'st taught mine to commit: thou'st taught it
    Love.

WILLMORE.   Egad, 'twas shrewdly hurt the while.

ANGELICA.
—Love, that has robb'd it of its Unconcern,
Of all that Pride that taught me how to value it,   275
And in its room a mean submissive Passion was
    convey'd,
That made me humbly bow, which I ne'er did
To any thing but Heaven.
—Thou, perjur'd Man, didst this, and with thy
    Oaths,
Which on thy Knees thou didst devoutly make,   280
Soften'd my yielding Heart—And then, I was a
    Slave—
Yet still had been content to've worn my Chains,
Worn 'em with Vanity and Joy for ever,
Hadst thou not broke those Vows that put them on.
—'Twas then I was undone.   285
(All this while follows him with a Pistol to his
    Breast.)

WILLMORE.
Broke my Vows! why, where has thou lived?
Amongst the Gods! For I never heard of mortal Man,
That has not broke a thousand Vows.

ANGELICA.   Oh, Impudence!

WILLMORE.
Angelica! that Beauty has been too long
    tempting,   290
Not to have made a thousand Lovers languish,
Who in the amorous Favour, no doubt have sworn
Like me; did they all die in that Faith? still adoring?
I do not think they did.

ANGELICA.   No, faithless Man: had I repaid their   295
Vows, as I did thine, I wou'd have kill'd the ungrateful
that had abandon'd me.

WILLMORE.   This old General has quite spoil'd thee,
nothing makes a woman so vain, as being flatter'd; your
old Lover ever supplies the Defects of Age, with   300
intolerable Dotage, vast Charge, and that which you call
Constancy; and attributing all this to your own Merits,
you domineer, and throw your Favours in's Teeth, up-
braiding him still with the Defects of Age, and cuckold
him as often as he deceives your Expectations.   305
But the gay, young, brisk Lover, that brings his equal
Fires, and can give you Dart for Dart, he'll be as nice as
you sometimes.

ANGELICA.
All this thou'st made me know, for which I hate
    thee.
Had I remain'd in innocent Security,   310
I shou'd have thought all Men were born my Slaves;

And worn my Pow'r like Lightning in my Eyes,
To have destroy'd at Pleasure when offended.
—But when Love held the Mirror, the undeceiving
    Glass
Reflected all the Weakness of my Soul, and made me
    know,   315
My richest Treasure being lost, my Honour,
All the remaining Spoil cou'd not be worth
The Conqueror's Care or Value.
—Oh how I fell like a long worship'd Idol,
Discovering all the Cheat!   320
Wou'd not the Incense and rich Sacrifice,
Which blind Devotion offer'd at my Altars,
Have fall'n to thee?
Why woud'st thou then destroy my fancy'd Power?

WILLMORE.
By Heaven thou art brave, and I admire thee
    strangely.   325
I wish I were that dull, that constant thing,
Which thou woud'st have, and Nature never meant
    me:
I must, like chearful Birds, sing in all Groves,
And perch on every Bough,
Billing the next kind She that flies to meet me;   330
Yet after all cou'd build my Nest with thee,
Thither repairing when I'd lov'd my round,
And still reserve a tributary Flame.
—To gain your Credit, I'll pay you back your
    Charity,
And be oblig'd for nothing but for Love.   335
(Offers her a Purse of Gold.)

ANGELICA.
Oh that thou wert in earnest!
So mean a Thought of me,
Wou'd turn my Rage to Scorn, and I shou'd pity
    thee,
And give thee leave to live;
Which for the publick Safety of our Sex,   340
And my own private Injuries, I dare not do.
Prepare—(Follows still, as before.)
—I will no more be tempted with Replies.

WILLMORE.   Sure—

ANGELICA.   Another Word will damn thee! I've   345
heard thee talk too long. (She follows him with a Pistol
ready to shoot: he retires still amaz'd.)

Enter Don ANTONIO, his Arm in a Scarf, and lays hold on
the Pistol.

ANTONIO.   Hah! Angelica!

ANGELICA.   Antonio! What Devil brought thee hither?

ANTONIO.   Love and Curiosity, seeing your Coach at
Door. Let me disarm you of this unbecoming In-   350
strument of Death.—(Takes away the Pistol.)
Amongst the Number of your Slaves, was there not
    one

worthy the Honour to have fought your Quarrel?
—Who are you, Sir, that are so very wretched
To merit Death from her?   355

WILLMORE.   One, Sir, that cou'd have made a better End
of an amorous Quarrel without you, than with you.

ANTONIO.   Sure 'tis some Rival—hah—the very Man took
down her Picture yesterday—the very same that set on me
last night—Blest opportunity—(*Offers to shoot*   360
him.)

ANGELICA.   Hold, you're mistaken, Sir.

ANTONIO.   By Heaven the very same!—Sir, what pretensions have you to this Lady?

WILLMORE.   Sir, I don't use to be examin'd, and am ill at
all Disputes but this—(*Draws,* ANTONIO *offers to*   365
shoot.)

ANGELICA.
     Oh, hold! you see he's arm'd with certain Death:
     (*To* WILLMORE.)
     —And you, *Antonio,* I command you hold,
     By all the Passion you've so lately vow'd me.

Enter Don PEDRO, *sees* ANTONIO, *and stays.*

PEDRO.   Hah, *Antonio!* and *Angelica!* (*Aside.*)

ANTONIO.
     When I refuse Obedience to your Will,   370
     May you destroy me with your mortal Hate.
     By all that's Holy I adore you so,
     That even my Rival, who has Charms enough
     To make him fall a Victim to my Jealousy,
     Shall live, nay, and have leave to love on still.   375

PEDRO.   What's this I hear? (*Aside.*)

ANGELICA.
     Ah thus, 'twas thus he talk'd, and I believ'd.
     (*Pointing to* WILLMORE.)
     —*Antonio,* yesterday,
     I'd not have sold my Interest in his Heart,
     For all the Sword has won and lost in Battle.   380
     —But now to show my utmost of Contempt,
     I give thee Life—which if thou would'st preserve,
     Live where my Eyes may never see thee more,
     Live to undo some one, whose Soul may prove
     So bravely constant to revenge my Love.   385
     (*Goes out,* ANTONIO *follows, but* PEDRO *pulls him*
     back.)

PEDRO.   *Antonio*—stay.

ANTONIO.   Don *Pedro*—

PEDRO.   What Coward Fear was that prevented thee
From meeting me this Morning on the *Molo?*

ANTONIO.   Meet thee?   390

PEDRO.   Yes me; I was the Man that dar'd thee to't.

ANTONIO.
     Hast thou so often seen me fight in War,
     To find no better Cause to excuse my Absence?
     —I sent my Sword and one to do thee Right,
     Finding my self uncapable to use a Sword.   395

PEDRO.
     But 'twas *Florinda's* Quarrel that we fought,
     And you to shew how little you esteem'd her,
     Sent me your Rival, giving him your Interest.
     —But I have found the Cause of this Affront,
     But when I meet you fit for the Dispute,   400
     —I'll tell you my Resentment.

ANTONIO.   I shall be ready, Sir, e'er long to do you
Reason. (*Exit* ANTONIO.)

PEDRO.   If I cou'd find *Florinda,* now whilst my Anger's
high, I think I shou'd be kind, and give her to   405
Belvile in Revenge.

WILLMORE.   Faith, Sir, I know not what you wou'd do, but
I believe the Priest within has been so kind.

PEDRO.   How! my Sister married?

WILLMORE.   I hope by this time she is, and bedded   410
too, or he has not my longings about him.

PEDRO.   Dares he do thus? Does he not fear my Pow'r?

WILLMORE.   Faith not at all. If you will go in, and thank
him for the Favour he has done your Sister, so; if not, Sir,
my Power's greater in this House than yours; I   415
have a damn'd surly Crew here, that will keep you till the
next Tide, and then clap you an board my Prize; my Ship
lies but a League off the *Molo,* and we shall show your
Donship a damn'd *Tramontana* Rover's Trick.

Enter BELVILE.

BELVILE.   This Rogue's in some new Mischief—   420
hah, *Pedro* return'd!

PEDRO.   Colonel *Belvile,* I hear you have married my
Sister.

BELVILE.   You have heard truth then, Sir.

PEDRO.   Have I so? then, Sir, I wish you Joy.   425

BELVILE.   How!

PEDRO.   By this Embrace I do, and I glad on't.

BELVILE.   Are you in earnest?

PEDRO.   By our long Friendship and my Obligations to
thee, I am. The sudden Change I'll give you Rea-   430
sons for anon. Come lead me into my Sister, that she may
know I now approve her Choice. (*Exit* BELVILE *with*
PEDRO.)

(WILLMORE *goes to follow them. Enter* HELLENA *as before*
in Boy's Clothes, and pulls him back.)

WILLMORE.   Ha! my Gipsy—Now a thousand Blessings on
thee for this Kindness. Egad, Child, I was e'en in despair
of ever seeing thee again; my Friends are all pro-   435
vided for within, each Man his kind Woman.

HELLENA.   Hah! I thought they had serv'd me some such
Trick.

WILLMORE.   And I was e'en resolv'd to go aboard, condemn my self to my lone Cabin, and the Thoughts   440
of thee.

HELLENA. And cou'd you have left me behind? wou'd you have been so ill-natur'd?

WILLMORE. Why, 'twou'd have broke my Heart, Child— but since we are met again, I defy foul Weather **445** to part us.

HELLENA. And wou'd you be a faithful Friend now, if a Maid shou'd trust you?

WILLMORE. For a Friend I cannot promise, thou art of a Form so excellent, a Face and Humour too good **450** for cold dull Friendship; I am parlously afraid of being in love, Child, and you have not forgot how severely you have us'd me.

HELLENA. That's all one, such Usage you must still look for, to find out all your Haunts, to rail at you to **455** all that love you, till I have made you love only me in your own Defence, because no body else will love.

WILLMORE. But hast thou no better Quality to recommend thy self by?

HELLENA. Faith none, Captain—Why, 'twill be **460** the greater Charity to take me for thy Mistress, I am a lone Child, a kind of Orphan Lover; and why I shou'd die a Maid, and in a Captain's Hands too, I do not understand.

WILLMORE. Egad, I was never claw'd away with Broad-Sides from any Female before, thou hast one **465** Virtue I adore, good-Nature; I hate a coy demure Mistress, she's as troublesom as a Colt, I'll break none; no, give me a mad Mistress when mew'd, and in flying on[e] I dare trust upon the Wing, that whilst she's kind will come to the Lure. **470**

HELLENA. Nay, as kind as you will, good Captain, whilst it lasts, but let's lose no time.

WILLMORE. My time's as precious to me, as thine can be; therefore, dear Creature, since we are so well agreed, let's retire to my Chamber, and if ever thou were **475** treated with such savory Love—Come—My Bed's prepar'd for such a Guest, all clean and sweet as thy fair self; I love to steal a Dish and a Bottle with a Friend, and hate long Graces—Come, let's retire and fall to.

HELLENA. 'Tis but getting my Consent, and the **480** Business is soon done; let but old Gaffer *Hymen* and his Priest say Amen to't, and I dare lay my Mother's Daughter by as proper a Fellow as your Father's Son, without fear or blushing.

WILLMORE. Hold, hold, no Bugg Words, Child, **485** Priest and *Hymen:* prithee add Hangman to 'em to make up the consort—No, no, we'll have no Vows but Love, Child, nor Witness but the Lover; the kind Diety injoins naught but love and enjoy. *Hymen* and Priest wait still upon Portion, and Joynture; Love and Beauty **490** have their own Ceremonies. Marriage is as certain a Bane to Love, as lending Money is to Friendship: I'll neither ask nor give a Vow, tho I could be content to turn Gipsy,

and become a Left-hand Bridegroom, to have the Pleasure of working that great Miracle of making a Maid **495** a Mother, if you durst venture; 'tis upse Gipsy that, and if I miss, I'll lose my Labour.

HELLENA. And if you do not lose, what shall I get? A Cradle full of Noise and Mischief, with a Pack of Repentance at my Back? Can you teach me to weave **500** Incle to pass my time with? 'Tis upse Gipsy that too.

WILLMORE. I can teach thee to weave a true Love's Knot better.

HELLENA. So can my Dog.

WILLMORE. Well, I see we are both upon our Guard, and I see there's no way to conquer good Nature, but **505** by yielding—here—give me thy Hand—one Kiss and I am thine—

HELLENA. One Kiss! How like my Page he speaks; I am resolv'd you shall have none, for asking such a sneaking Sum—He that will be satisfied with one Kiss, will **510** never die of that Longing; good Friend single-Kiss, is all your talking come to this? A Kiss, a Caudle! farewel, Captain single-Kiss. (*Going out he stays her.*)

WILLMORE. Nay, if we part so, let me die like a Bird upon a Bough, at the Sheriff's Charge. By Heaven, **515** both the *Indies* shall not buy thee from me. I adore thy Humour and will marry thee, and we are so of one Humour, it must be a Bargain—give me thy Hand— (*Kisses her hand.*) And now let the blind ones (Love and Fortune) do their worst. **520**

HELLENA. Why, God-a-mercy, Captain!

WILLMORE. But harkye—The Bargain is now made; but is it not fit we should know each other's Names? That when we have Reason to curse one another hereafter, and People ask me who 'tis I give to the Devil, I may **525** at least be able to tell what Family you came of.

HELLENA. Good reason, Captain; and where I have cause, (as I doubt not but I shall have plentiful) that I may know at whom to throw my—Blessings—I beseech ye your Name. **530**

WILLMORE. I am call'd *Robert the Constant.*

HELLENA. A very fine Name! pray was it your Faulkner or Butler that christen'd you? Do they not use to whistle when they call you?

WILLMORE. I hope you have a better, that a Man **535** may name without crossing himself, you are so merry with mine.

HELLENA. I am call'd *Hellena the Inconstant.*

Enter PEDRO, BELVILE, FLORINDA, FREDERICK, VALERIA.

PEDRO. Hah! *Hellena!*

FLORINDA. *Hellena!* **540**

HELLENA. The very same—hah my Brother! now, Captain, shew your Love and Courage; stand to your Arms, and defend me bravely, or I am lost for ever.

PEDRO.   What's this I hear? false Girl, how came you
hither, and what's your Business? Speak. (*Goes*   545
roughly to her.)

WILLMORE.   Hold off, sir, you have leave to parly only.
(*Puts himself between*.)

HELLENA.   I had e'en as good tell it, as you guess it. Faith,
Brother, my Business is the same with all living Creatures
of my Age, to love, and be loved, and here's the Man.

PEDRO.   Perfidious Maid, hast thou deceiv'd me   550
too, deceiv'd thy self and Heaven?

HELLENA.   'Tis time enough to make my Peace with that:
Be you but kind, let me alone with Heaven.

PEDRO.   *Belvile,* I did not expect this false Play from you;
was't not enough you'd gain *Florinda* (which I   555
pardon'd) but your leud Friends too must be inrich'd with
the Spoils of a noble Family?

BELVILE.   Faith, Sir, I am as much surpriz'd at this as you
can be: Yet, Sir, my Friends are Gentlemen, and ought to
be esteem'd for their Misfortunes, since they   560
have the Glory to suffer with the best of Men and Kings;
'tis true, he's a Rover of Fortune, yet a Prince aboard his
little wooden World.

PEDRO.   What's this to the maintenance of a Woman or her
Birth and Quality?   565

WILLMORE.   Faith, Sir, I can boast of nothing but a Sword
which does me Right where-e'er I come, and has defended
a worse Cause than a Woman's: and since I lov'd her
before I either knew her Birth or Name, I must pursue my
Resolution, and marry her.   570

PEDRO.   And is all your holy Intent of becoming a Nun
debauch'd into a Desire of Man?

HELLENA.   Why—I have consider'd the matter, Brother,
and find the Three hundred thousand Crowns my Uncle
left me (and you cannot keep from me) will be   575
better laid out in Love than in Religion, and turn to as
good an Account—let most Voices carry it, for Heaven
or the Captain?

ALL CRY.   A Captain, a Captain.

HELLENA.   Look ye, Sir, 'tis a clear Case.   580

PEDRO.   Oh I am mad—if I refuse, my Life's in Danger—
(*Aside*.)—Come—There's one motive induces me—take
her—I shall now be free from the fear of her Honour;
guard it you now, if you can, I have been a Slave to't long
enough. (*Gives her to him*.)   585

WILLMORE.   Faith, Sir, I am of a Nation, that are of opinion
a Woman's Honour is not worth guarding when she has
a mind to part with it.

HELLENA.   Well said, Captain.

PEDRO.   This was your Plot, Mistress, but I hope   590
you have married one that will revenge my Quarrel to
you—(*To* VALERIA.)

VALERIA.   There's no altering Destiny, Sir.

PEDRO.   Sooner than a Woman's Will, therefore I forgive
you all—and wish you may get my Father's   595
Pardon as easily; which I fear.

Enter BLUNT *drest in a* Spanish *Habit, looking very ridiculously; his Man adjusting his Band.*

MAN.   'Tis very well, Sir.

BLUNT.   Well, Sir, 'dsheartlikins I tell you 'tis damnable
ill, Sir—a Spanish Habit, good Lord! cou'd the Devil and
my Taylor devise no other Punishment for me,   600
but the Mode of a Nation I abominate?

BELVILE.   What's the matter, *Ned?*

BLUNT.   Pray view me round, and judge—(*Turns round*.)

BELVILE.   I must confess thou art a kind of an odd Figure.

BLUNT.   In a Spanish Habit with a Vengeance! I   605
had rather be in the Inquisition for Judaism, than in this
Doublet and Breeches; a Pillory were an easy Collar to
this, three Handfuls high; and these Shoes too are worse
than the Stocks, with the Sole an Inch shorter than my
Foot: In fine, Gentlemen, methinks I look alto-   610
gether like a Bag of Bays stuff'd full of Fools Flesh.

BELVILE.   Methinks 'tis well, and makes thee look *en Cavalier:* Come, Sir, settle your Face, and salute our Friends,
Lady—

BLUNT.   Hah! Say'st thou so, my little Rover? (*To*   615
HELLENA.) Lady—(if you be one) give me leave to kiss
your Hand, and tell you, adsheartlikins, for all I look so,
I am your humble Servant—A Pox of my *Spanish* Habit.

WILLMORE.   Hark—what's this? (*Musick is heard to Play*.)

Enter BOY.

BOY.   Sir, as the Custom is, the gay People in Mas-   620
querade, who make every Man's House their own, are
coming up.

*Enter several Men and Women in masquing Habits, with
Musick, they put themselves in order and dance.*

BLUNT.   Adsheartlikins, wou'd 'twere lawful to pull off
their false Faces, that I might see if my Doxy were not
amongst 'em.   625

BELVILE.   Ladies and Gentlemen, since you are come so *a
propos,* you must take a small Collation with us. (*To the
Masqueraders*.)

WILLMORE.   Whilst we'll to the Good Man within, who
stays to give us a Cast of his Office. (*To* HELLENA.)—
Have you no trembling at the near approach?   630

HELLENA.   No more than you have in an Engagement or a
Tempest.

WILLMORE.

    Egad, thou'rt a brave Girl, and I admire thy Love
      and Courage.
    Lead on, no other Dangers they can dread,
    Who venture in the Storms o'th' Marriage-Bed.   635
(*Exeunt*.)

EPILOGUE

THE *banisht Cavaliers! a Roving Blade!*
A popish Carnival! a Masquerade!
The Devil's in't if this will please the Nation,
In these our blessed Times of Reformation,
When Conventicling is so much in Fashion.   5
And yet—
That mutinous Tribe less Factions do beget,
Than your continual differing in Wit;
Your Judgment's (as your Passions) a Disease:
Nor Muse nor Miss your Appetite can please;   10
You're grown as nice as queasy Consciences,
Whose each Convulsion, when the Spirit moves,
Damns every thing that Maggot disapproves.
    With canting Rule you wou'd the Stage refine,
And to dull Method all our Sense confine.   15
With th' Insolence of Common-wealths you rule,
Where each gay Fop, and politick brave Fool
On Monarch Wit impose without controul.
As for the last who seldom sees a Play,
Unless it be the old Black-Fryers way,   20
Shaking his empty Noddle o'er Bamboo,
He crys—Good Faith, these Plays will never do.
—Ah, Sir, in my young days, what lofty Wit,
What high-strain'd Scenes of Fighting there were
        writ:
These are slight airy Toys. But tell me, pray,   25
What has the House of Commons done to day?
Then shews his Politicks, to let you see
Of State Affairs he'll judge as notably,
As he can do of Wit and Poetry.
    The younger Sparks, who hither do resort,   30
Cry—
Pox o' your gentle things, give us more Sport;
—Damn me, I'm sure 'twill never please the Court.
    Such Fops are never pleas'd, unless the Play
Be stuff'd with Fools, as brisk and dull as they: 35
Such might the Half-Crown spare, and in a Glass
At home behold a more accomplisht Ass,
Where they may set their Cravats, Wigs and Faces,
And practice all their Buffoonry Grimaces;

See how this—Huff becomes—this Dammy—flare— **40**
Which they at home may act, because they dare,
But—must with prudent Caution do elsewhere.
Oh that our Nokes, or Tony Lee could show
A Fop but half so much to th' Life as you.

POST-SCRIPT

THIS *Play had been sooner in Print, but for a*
Report about the Town (made by some either very
Malitious or very Ignorant) that 'twas Thomaso
alter'd; which made the Book-sellers fear some
trouble from the Proprietor of that Admirable Play,
which indeed has Wit enough to stock a Poet, and is
not to be piec't or mended by any but the Excellent
Author himself; That I have stol'n some hints from it
may be a proof, that I valu'd it more than to pretend
to alter it: had I had the Dexterity of some Poets
who are not more expert in stealing than in the Art
of Concealing, and who even that way out-do the
Spartan-*Boyes I might have appropriated all to*
myself, but I, vainly proud of my Judgment hang out
the Sign of ANGELICA *(the only Stol'n Object) to*
give Notice where a great part of the Wit dwelt;
though if the Play of the Novella *were as well worth*
remembering as Thomaso, *they might (bating the*
Name) have as well said, I took it from thence: I will
only say the Plot and Bus'ness (not to boast on't) is
my own: as for the Words and Characters, I leave
the Reader to judge and compare 'em with Thomaso,
to whom I recommend the great Entertainment of
reading it, tho' had this succeeded ill, I shou'd have
had no need of imploring that Justice from the
Critics, who are naturally so kind to any that
pretend to usurp their Dominion, they wou'd
doubtless have given me the whole Honour on't.
Therefore I will only say in English *what the famous*
Virgil *does in Latin: I make Verses and others have*
the Fame.

FOCUS QUESTIONS

1. Defend Willmore as *miles gloriosus*.
2. Show how the behaviors and actions of these characters fulfill the expectations of Restoration comedy.
3. With specific reference to the dialogue, evaluate Behn's mixture of prose and verse formats.
4. Develop a character sketch of Angelica Bianca and discuss her function as a mouthpiece for the playwright.
5. Develop a character sketch of Hellena and pay special attention to the impact of her disguises.
6. Analyze Behn's treatment of the ''battle between the sexes.''
7. Defend or refute Behn's reputation as a feminist playwright, basing your discussion on *The Rover*.
8. In what ways do Behn's women characters—in the words of Virginia Woolf—''speak their minds''?

OTHER ACTIVITIES

1. Show how Behn's use of a foreign locale might affect specific production ingredients of the play in performance.
2. Using reviews, photographs, and other available production documentation, assess a contemporary production of the play.

BIBLIOGRAPHY

Avery, Emmet L., and Arthur H. Scouten. *The London Stage, 1660–1700: A Critical Introduction.* Carbondale: Southern Illinois University Press, 1968.

Brown, John Russell, and Bernard Harris, eds. *Restoration Theatres,* Stratford-upon-Avon Studies 6. London: Edward Arnold Publishers, 1965.

Cotton, Nancy. *Women Playwrights in England, c. 1363–1750.* Lewisburg: Bucknell University Press, 1980.

Duffy, Maureen. *The Passionate Shepherdess.* London: Methuen, 1989.

Goreau, Angeline. *Reconstructing Aphra.* New York: Oxford University Press, 1980.

Howe, Elizabeth. *The First English Actresses: Women and Drama 1660–1700.* New York: Cambridge University, 1992.

Link, Frederick M. *Behn.* New York: Twayne, 1968.

Powell, Jocelyn. *Restoration Theatre Production.* London: Routledge & Kegan Paul, 1981.

Price, Cecil. *Theatre in the Age of Garrick.* Oxford: Blackwell, 1973.

Summers, Montague. *The Restoration Theatre.* New York: Humanities Press, 1934.

Wilcox, J. *The Relation of Molière to Restoration Comedy.* New York: Benjamin Blom, 1938.

Wilson, J. H. *All the King's Ladies.* Chicago: University of Chicago Press, 1974.

———. *The Court Wits of the Restoration.* New York: Octagon Books, 1967.

SHE STOOPS TO CONQUER
OLIVER GOLDSMITH (1730–1774)

Whether, indeed, we take him as a poet,—as a comick writer,—or as a historian, he stands in the first rank.

—DR. SAMUEL JOHNSON

Susannah Harker as Kate and Iain Glen as Marlow in *She Stoops to Conquer,* presented by the Chichester Festival Theatre in 1992, under the direction of Peter Wood. *Photo: John Haynes*

APPROACHING EIGHTEENTH-CENTURY ENGLISH DRAMA

In the early eighteenth century, the excitement of Restoration tragedy and the vitality of Comedy of Manners, which had mirrored its upper-class audience through the use of polish and wit, subtle ridicule, and sexual innuendo, were greatly tamed. (See Preface to Behn, p. 390.) In a move toward didacticism and moralizing, playwrights depicted stage characters who displayed sentimental emotions and bourgeois values of home, family, and friendship. Colley Cibber's *Love's Last Shift* (1696), in which a rake's natural goodness elicits his change of heart, exemplified the move toward sentimentalism that now appealed to the heart rather than the intellect and focused on individuality and social class hierarchy rather than observing the world through the narrow lens of upper-class manners.

The drama of this period also signaled the popularity of women playwrights whose many new works were produced between 1695 and 1715. Mary Pix (1666–1706), Delarivière Manley (c. 1672–1724), Catharine Trotter (1679–1749), and Susanna Centlivre (c. 1670–1723) were no doubt inspired by their predecessor Aphra Behn (1640–1689). Furthermore, by the first quarter-century, the drama witnessed a radical change in *dramatis personae* drawn from the merchant class and the London poor whose innate goodness won them an end to their trials and tribulations. The sentimentalism and tragic overtones of Nicholas Rowe's *The Tragedy of Jane Shore* (1714) and George Lillo's *The London Merchant* (1731) proved very successful with audiences who felt uplifted by their own sympathies for virtuous protagonists in distress. The domestic comedy of Richard Steele's *The Conscious Lovers* (1722) beheld its penniless heroine restored to her fortune.

The drama also witnessed a sharp increase in productivity and audience attendance. The wide range of performance styles brought a renewed excitement to the London stage and played to packed houses. Such styles included pantomimes, particularly those created by John Rich; ballad operas, notably John Gay's *The Beggar's Opera* (1728); and satiric **burlesques,** the finest of which were written by Henry Fielding. In addition, many of Shakespeare's plays were adapted and performed between 1700 to 1741, restoring his popularity. This remarkable period of expansion was abruptly halted by the Lord Chamberlain's Licensing Act of 1737, which limited operating permission to only two theatres: the Drury Lane and Covent Garden.

Sentimental comedy found its fullest expression in Hugh Kelly's *False Delicacy* (1768) and Richard Cumberland's *The West Indian* (1771), and thanks to David Garrick, manager at the Drury Lane, these plays were quickly adopted in response to popular audience taste. In contrast, George Colman produced two plays by Oliver Goldsmith at Covent Garden, in which the playwright's unabashed demonstration of ''laughing comedy'' proved an assault on sentimentality. The themes in these two works were typical, but their style differed markedly. Goldsmith simply rejected the genteel strains, the delicacy in dialogue and action, and the heavy-handed moralizing that characterized the sentimental drama. He criticized these traits in his famous *Essay on the Theatre; or, A Comparison Between Sentimental and Laughing Comedy* (1773), where he insisted that ''comedy should excite our laughter, by ridiculously exhibiting the follies of the lower part of mankind.''[1]

MAJOR WORKS

Born in Ireland, Goldsmith studied at Trinity College, Dublin, and trained as a doctor in Edinburgh. In 1755, he traveled through Europe and settled in England to work as a physician until he began earning his living as a writer in 1757. His literary works included *The Vicar of Wakefield* (1766), a novel; *The Deserted Village* (1770), a pastoral poem; *The*

History of the Earth and Animated Nature (1774), in eight volumes; and two plays: *The Good-Natured Man* (1768), which met with difficulties when it was produced, and *She Stoops to Conquer* (1773), whose unexpected success influenced the development of English stage comedy.

Although Goldsmith died the year after his Covent Garden triumph with *She Stoops to Conquer,* his opposition to sentimentalism was carried out by the twenty-three-year old Richard Brinsley Sheridan, whose play *The Rivals* opened on January 17, 1775. Sheridan exposed the foibles of fashionable society through laughter but, unlike his predecessor, rekindled the scintillating wit that had filled the London theatres a century earlier.

The Action

Thanks to the pranks of Tony Lumpkin, Marlow and Hastings are directed to a country inn which, unbeknownst to them, is actually the Hardcastle residence. This was the very destination where Marlow hoped to meet his yet unseen fiancée Kate. Mistaking Hardcastle for the innkeeper, Hastings and Marlow treat him rudely. Yet, when Marlow meets the fashionable Kate, he is reduced to a bashful stammer that makes her question his suitability. Hardcastle is left to wonder if this man is the same brazen guest he confronted earlier.

Disguised as a maid, Kate becomes a woman with whom Marlow can feel comfortable. Revealing his more gallant side, he tries to kiss her. Discovering that the maid is really Kate in disguise, he is too smitten with love to care. In spite of Mrs. Hardcastle's pursuit of a match between her niece Constance and her son Tony, Constance has fallen in love with Hastings and Tony asserts his independence. Thus the mistakes of a night are ''crowned with a merry morning.''

Structure and Language

Goldsmith's ironic premise prompts a merry-go-round of comic confusion, mistaken identity, pairs of lovers opposed to their parents or guardians, and endless clever dialogue. The pervasive question as to which is preferable—life in the country or life in town—further underscores the comedy and inspires numerous character confrontations that often turn farcical. The tone is initially established by Mr. Hardcastle, an honest and agreeable country gentleman who is proud of his old-fashioned ideals: ''I love everything that's old: old friends, old times, old manners, old books, old wine; and I believe, Dorothy (taking her hand), you'll own I have been pretty fond of an old wife.'' Unlike her husband, Mrs. Hardcastle yearns to ''take a trip to town now and then, to rub off the rust a little,'' although the snobbery of London is gently mocked through the crafty ''awkward booby'' embodied in the ubiquitous and aptly named Tony Lumpkin, her son by an earlier marriage.

In contrast with the singularly opinionated attitudes of her parents, Kate Hardcastle knows the pleasures of both life-styles, but willingly accedes to her father's preference for country values. ''You know our agreement, Sir,'' she reminds him. ''You allow me the morning to receive and pay visits, and to dress in my own manner; and in the evening, I put on my housewife's dress to please you.'' Thus her smooth switch from town to country attire foreshadows an important disguise that is central to the play's comic action.

Goldsmith's satiric swing at sentimental comedy is chiefly demonstrated by young Marlow: the perennially immature protagonist, overbearing on some occasions and unsure of himself on others, whose insecurity with women of his own class exposes his somewhat dual personality. When the stylish Kate is suddenly confronted by his timid and stammering demeanor, she laughingly reflects on the hypocrisy of what she has witnessed: ''Was there ever such a sober, sentimental interview?'' But when ''she stoops to conquer'' Marlow somewhat later in the play in the disguise of a lowly maid, he eloquently rises to the occasion and wins her hand, an event that sparks the unraveling of plot entanglements and pays tribute to Goldsmith's comic inventiveness.

The heart of the comedy lies in the pivotal portrait of Tony Lumpkin, whose pranks ensnare every character in sight, including a doting mother who regards him as the "very pink of perfection." Initiating the confusion from his first encounter with Marlow at the inn, Tony controls the comedy's delirious conclusion in which he finally breaks free of his mother's apron-strings to become "his own man again" and pursue his never-seen-but-always-talked-about Betty Bouncer. Taking his best cues from *commedia's* clowns, Molière's comic servants, and Shakespeare's Puck in *A Midsummer Night's Dream,* he laughs heartily at the follies of his victims while maneuvering their mishaps.

Under Tony's inspired instigation, Goldsmith's extended prank follows a smooth line of comic development that is dramatically unified by real time, as suggested by the play's alternate title, *The Mistakes of a Night*. His wide assortment of sparkling characters, so carefully paired and juxtaposed, supports the nonstop mayhem throughout. But if credibility was not Goldsmith's aim, then laughter was, which is demonstrated by a range of dialogue—from the formal to the colloquial—whose freshness strikes a contemporary note. In their act 3 reunion, the newly poised but suddenly thirsty Marlow catches the eye of a woman he presumes to be the maid. His manner is forthright and his language welcomes the **double-entendre:**

> Marlow: Suppose I should call for a taste, just by way of trial, of the nectar
> of your lips; perhaps I might be disappointed in that, too!
> Miss Hardcastle: Nectar! nectar! that's a liquor there's no call for in these parts.
> French, I suppose. We keep no French wines here, sir.

Delivered in a regional accent that preserves her disguise, Kate's clever response thwarts Marlow's advance by undermining its sexual overtone, noting instead that his wine of choice is unavailable.

The character of Marlow belongs to the tradition of innocent young heroes from the Roman comedy, attractive but immature, and usually quite helpless as lovers. Kate Hardcastle is a refreshing contrast to the bloodless heroines of sentimental comedy. In her scheming wordplay to fool young Marlow, she is a close descendant of the quick-witted, self-possessed heroines of Restoration comedy, although her roots can be found in such Shakespeare heroines as Rosalind in *As You Like It,* Viola in *Twelfth Night,* and Kate in *Taming of the Shrew*. Sporting a keen sense of fun and a warmly assertive manner, she takes delight in her mission to cure Marlow of his shyness and nimbly proves that love conquers everything. No matter how consciously Goldsmith intended Kate's portrait, her "intelligence, resourcefulness, and charm make her easily the most attractive heroine in eighteenth-century British drama; and the way in which she combines filial duty with a sprightly independence of judgement attests to the integrity of her character."[2]

On the other hand, Tony's language reflects his low-comic character, but is also capable of suggesting a music or poetry of its own. Preserving his real identity from Marlow and Hastings when he meets them early in the play, he refers to Hardcastle's daughter as "a tall, trapesing, trolloping, talkative maypole," and to the old man's son—really himself, of course—as "a pretty, well-bred, agreeable youth, that everybody is fond of!" He is no less eloquent when he pokes fun at Constance Neville, Kate's confidante, whose romance with Hastings parallels the Kate/Marlow relationship and provides the play with an important comic subplot. Calling Constance "a cantankerous toad," capable of "as many tricks as a hare in a thicket" and "as loud as a hog in a gate," Tony's brazen animal imagery matches his rustic manner. Instead of crediting her down-to-earth demeanor, his vocabulary consciously serves the comic muse.

She Stoops to Conquer successfully exemplified Goldsmith's theory of comedy, although his attempt to rekindle a laughing tradition was relatively short-lived. Fortunately the abundant merits of his work still remain unsurpassed. Important themes of conflict—between the country and the city, between old values and new, between the generations and the sexes—are eloquently demonstrated by a cast of exceedingly likable characters whose improbable behaviors comically undermine and satirize the foibles of every age. But the good taste and genuine skill with which Goldsmith handled the proceedings have only enhanced the popularity of his dramatic achievement.

SHE STOOPS TO CONQUER-IN-PERFORMANCE

The eighteenth century has been hailed as the century of great acting. During this time, the best actors—male and female—began to take control of their own destinies by becoming theatre managers and extending professional status to other performers whom they placed under formal contract. The styles of acting varied from formal to realistic, so it was not unusual to see both displayed in the same production. In spite of the common practice of letting actors punctuate their dialogue with vocal vigor and declamatory gesture to win the applause of the audience, David Garrick (1717–1779) advanced a more naturalistic style of acting.

Stage architecture in such theatres as the Drury Lane, Lincoln's Inn Fields, the King's, the Haymarket, and the Covent Garden was inspired by those of the *jeu de paume* theatres of Paris, imported to London during the Restoration. (See Preface to Racine, p. 320.) No longer sufficient to accommodate the rising number of bourgeois spectators, these intimate theatres of the seventeenth century were remodeled. To allow for more rows in the pit, the stage apron was reduced to a small forestage just beyond the proscenium arch. The need for additional seating was so great that audience members sat on stage benches.

Scenic practices were also imported from Europe. Elaborate systems of wings and grooves, borders, shutters, and **drops** created spectacular scene changes when they were moved into place by stagehands at the sound of a whistle. Each theatre had a large space in which stock scenery representing standard locales could be constructed and stored. Rather than creating new settings for each production, this stock scenery was used during the theatrical season. Thus *She Stoops to Conquer* utilized the rural landscape, street or roadway, garden, and chamber sets with accompanying properties brought out from the large backstage or basement storage area of the Covent Garden, the house in which Goldsmith's two plays were staged. Because technology for illusionistic stage lighting was not yet perfected, the auditorium remained lit during performance. Since the actors had been forced upstage into the scenery, footlights and lights masked by the wings illuminated them as well.

The theatrical season ran from mid-September and continued through the end of May or early June. The playbill opened with a short musical interlude, followed by a prologue, the full-length play with between-act entertainment, and an afterpiece. The performance usually closed with a song and dance. The largely middle-class audience at Covent Garden, which numbered around 2,500 when *She Stoops to Conquer* was performed, was the nucleus of a prosperous theatre season. At that time, the company contained 66 principal actors, 26 principal dancers, 9 singers, and 5 musicians. A competent cast was assembled, despite the fact that several of the leading players still objected to the playwright's emphasis on ''low'' character types.

Several well-known actors contributed to the success of the play's opening night on March 15, 1773, including Edward Shuter as Hardcastle, Mary Bulkley as Kate, and John Quick as Tony Lumpkin. The critics were full of praise. *The London Magazine* applauded its blow against "that monster Sentimental Comedy." Although *The Westminster Magazine* hesitated to recommend it as "a pattern for imitation," *The Gentleman's Magazine* called the play "truly comic" and its humor "irresistible." *The Evening Post* reported that "the audience is kept in a continual roar." Dr. Johnson's remarks in *Life* summed up the occasion quite well: "I know of no comedy for many years that has so much exhilarated an audience, that has answered so much the great end of comedy—making an audience merry."

The play was performed twenty-five times during its first season; and, during the summer of 1773, Samuel Foote brought the production to the Haymarket Theatre where he also played the part of Tony Lumpkin. Three months later, productions appeared throughout England, in Dublin, and in New York City. In America, *She Stoops to Conquer* was the last important new play given in New York before the Revolutionary War led to the closing of theatres in 1774. A New York company kept the play in repertory as it traveled to Charleston and then to Kingston, Jamaica, until the war ended. When the company eventually returned, the play was featured as a "Lecture on the Disadvantages of Improper Education Exemplified in the History of Tony Lumpkin" in deference to the Quakers.

The nineteenth-century London stage saw Goldsmith's play revived often. Charles Kemble played Marlow early in the century, and during the 1860s, Miss Herbert, manager of the Saint James Street Theatre, was acclaimed for her Kate and Walter Lacy for his Tony. During the 1870s and 1880s, Forbes-Robertson alternated in the roles of Marlow and Hastings, and Lilly Langtry made her professional stage debut as Kate at the Haymarket in 1881, before touring America in the role in 1883.

The comedy has attracted many important theatre artists during the twentieth century. In England, Laurence Olivier triumphed as Tony Lumpkin with the Birmingham Repertory in 1927, and actors like Peggy Ashcroft, Roger Livesey, Anthony Quayle, John Mills, Diana Churchill, and Michael Redgrave brought their own special talents to a variety of West End productions by mid-century. Back in New York, a Players' Club revival premiered at the Empire Theatre on June 9, 1924, with a stellar cast romping through the comic action in leading and cameo performances, not the least of whom was Helen Hayes as Constance Neville.

Exactly a quarter century later, a major New York revival took place at City Center and featured Celeste Holm as Kate and Brian Aherne as Marlow, with the inspired casting of the American actor/folksinger Burl Ives as Mr. Hardcastle. Brooks Atkinson commended the actor as "direct and forceful, and portly as well, giving a fine specific gravity to the whole affair." The critic also found Goldsmith's comedy, which was presented under the artistic direction of Maurice Evans, "affectionately restored."[3]

She Stoops to Conquer has enjoyed countless revivals in regional theatres throughout North America. It has inspired two operas and numerous musicals, including an adaptation by Worth Gardner and Barbara Carlisle presented at Cincinnati's Playhouse-in-the-Park in 1987, which recalled the "free-wheeling excitement of the early rock musicals such as *Hair, Two Gentlemen of Verona,* and *Grease.*" The all-black ensemble "rapped, rocked, strutted, and jived" through its evocation of the Reagan era and its search for universal themes, using "everything from exercise bicycles to the modern equivalent of the *post chaise:* a souped-up, car-phoned, cardboard sports car that circled the Playhouse's revolving stage during the 'mistakes of the night.' "[4] Kate's stooping to barmaid was transformed into a 1980s streetwise woman's dressing down to attract her man, while Tony Lumpkin emerged as an Eddie Murphy-type prankster. The Hardcastles tried to stay young through trendy exercise routines and clothes too youthful for them. For better or worse, such controversial directorial choices have tested the timelessness and durability of Goldsmith's comedy.

In England, the comedy has remained a durable commodity with contemporary audiences, no matter how often it is revived. To celebrate its thirtieth-anniversary season, the

Chichester Festival presented the Goldsmith classic for the first time in the summer of 1992, under the direction of Peter Wood. One year later, Peter Hall directed the play for the Thorndike Theatre in Leatherhead in a production that was moved to the Queen's Theatre in the heart of London's West End on October 25, 1993. The all-star cast featured Donald Sinden and Miriam Margolyes as Mr. and Mrs. Hardcastle, with David Essex as Tony Lumpkin.

REFLECTIONS ON SHE STOOPS TO CONQUER

The following theatre review, written by Charles Spencer, appeared in the Daily Telegraph, *August 14, 1992.*

The temporary madness which afflicted the Chichester Festival Theatre when it decided to stage Melvyn Bragg's preposterous *King Lear in New York* has lifted. With Peter Wood's affectionate production of Oliver Goldsmith's *She Stoops to Conquer* (1773), sanity is restored and the theatre has a real hit with which to end the season.

This is one of the most purely enjoyable of all English plays, combining a superbly inventive plot with a wonderful generosity of spirit. It is an extraordinarily efficient laughter machine, which sets the audience in "a continual roar," as a critic at the first night noted, but it is also a genuinely touching work, glowing with a benevolence that is worlds removed from the vicious licentiousness of the Restoration comedies of 100 years earlier.

Peter Wood is a specialist in this period and, as always, treats the text with respect. There is no attempt at updating, no "fresh" or "revealing" directorial slant. My one reservation is that there are moments when you feel the play has been prettified.

There is more than a touch of Walt Disney in David Walker's design, with its back-drop of Mr. Hardcastle's house framed by giant 18th-century books; something a little sanitised about the happily laughing servants and the cute little boy who comes on and plays a music box between scenes with a live mouse sitting on his shoulder.

For all its good nature, there are darker shadows in *She Stoops to Conquer*. Goldsmith was rebelling against the "sentimental comedy" of his day and there is an element of cruelty in the plot, in which the hero Marlow is persuaded that Mr. Hardcastle's house is an inn, his prospective father-in-law the innkeeper. The dramatist has some sharp things to say, too, about class and sexual double standards, but these tend to be muted in the production's search for laughs.

The star of the evening is Iain Glen, and significantly he shows us the unattractive side of Marlow as well as his more amiable qualities. There is something faintly repulsive about a man who sets about seducing the lower orders with gusto but becomes entirely tongue-tied with women of his own class, and Glen's prissily fastidious performance lets us see the arrogance that is often the reverse side of shyness.

But the point isn't laboured, and the character is redeemed by comic suffering. In Kate Hardcastle's presence he becomes so overwhelmed that just sitting on a chair becomes a nightmare of stiff, unwieldy limbs while his protracted stammering, the single word *Madam* holding him up for as long as 20 seconds before he finally spits it out, is as agonising as it is hilarious. This is comic acting of a very high order.

Continued

The captivating Susannah Harker brings both sense and sensuality to the role of Kate, and the tender relationship with her father, played with a cherishable mixture of kindness and indignation by Denis Quilley, is beautifully observed. Jonathon Morris is too blandly amiable as Tony Lumpkin, a booby whose character contains a streak of real malevolence, and Mrs. Hardcastle isn't quite the uncomplicated figure of fun that Jean Boht makes her.

But as the play's "mistakes of a night" reach their climax, and harmony is finally restored, such niggling reservations are forgotten in an aura of infectious happiness.

From Charles Spencer, DAILY TELEGRAPH. *Copyright © The Telegraph plc, London, 1992.*

Notes

1. Oliver Goldsmith, "Essay," in CRITICISM: THE MAJOR TEXTS, *ed. Walter Jackson Bate* (New York: Harcourt, Brace & World, 1952), 251.
2. Oliver W. Ferguson, "Kate's Strategem and the Naming of SHE STOOPS TO CONQUER," RESTORATION RESEARCH *(Winter 1991): 27.*
3. M. K. Danziger, OLIVER GOLDSMITH AND RICHARD BRINSLEY SHERIDAN *(New York: Ungar Publications, 1978), 63.*
4. Steve Reynolds, *review of* SHE STOOPS TO CONQUER, THEATRE JOURNAL *(May 1988): 271.*

SHE STOOPS TO CONQUER

OR, THE MISTAKES OF A NIGHT
OLIVER GOLDSMITH

CHARACTERS

Men

Sir Charles Marlow
Young Marlow (*his Son*)
Hardcastle
Hastings

Tony Lumpkin
Diggory

Women

Mrs. Hardcastle

Miss Hardcastle
Miss Neville
Maid
Landlords, Servants,
  &c., &c.

PROLOGUE
BY DAVID GARRICK, ESQ.

Enter MR. WOODWARD, *dressed in black, and holding a Handkerchief to his Eyes.*

EXCUSE me, sirs, I pray—I can't yet speak—
I'm crying now—and have been all the week!
'Tis not alone this mourning suit, good masters;
I've that within—for which there are no plasters!
Pray would you know the reason why I'm crying?
The Comic muse, long sick, is now a-dying!
And if she goes, my tears will never stop:
For as a player, I can't squeeze out one drop:
I am undone, that's all—shall lose my bread—
I'd rather, but that's nothing—lose my head.
When the sweet maid is laid upon the bier,
Shuter and I shall be chief mourners here.
To *her* a mawkish drab of spurious breed,
Who deals in *sentimentals* will succeed!
Poor *Ned* and I are dead to all intents,
We can as soon speak *Greek as sentiments!*
Both nervous grown, to keep our spirits up,
We now and then take down a hearty cup.
What shall we do?—If Comedy forsake us!
They'll turn us out, and no one else will take us,
But why can't I be moral?—Let me try—
My heart thus pressing—fix'd my face and eye—
With a sententious look, that nothing means
(Faces are blocks, in sentimental scenes),
Thus I begin—*All is not gold that glitters,*
Pleasure seems sweet, but proves a glass of bitters.
When ignorance enters, folly is at hand;
Learning is better far than house and land.
Let not your virtue trip, who trips may stumble,
And virtue is not virtue, if she tumble.
  I give it up—morals won't do for me;
To make you laugh I must play tragedy.
One hope remains—hearing the maid was ill,
A *doctor* comes this night to show his skill.
To cheer her heart, and give your muscles motion,
He in *five draughts* prepar'd, presents a potion:
A kind of magic charm—for be assur'd,
If you will *swallow* it, the maid is cur'd.
But desperate the Doctor, and her case is,
If you reject the dose, and make wry faces!
This truth he boasts, will boast it while he lives.
No *poisonous drugs* are mix'd in what he gives;
Should he succeed, you'll give him his degree;
If not, within he will receive no fee!
The college *you,* must his pretentions back,
Pronounce him *regular,* or dub him *quack.*

ACT ONE

SCENE—A CHAMBER IN AN OLD-FASHIONED HOUSE

Enter MRS. HARDCASTLE *and* MR. HARDCASTLE.

MRS. HARDCASTLE.   I vow, Mr. Hardcastle, you're very particular. Is there a creature in the whole country, but ourselves, that does not take a trip to town now and then, to rub off the rust a little? There's the two Miss Hoggs, and our neighbour, Mrs. Grigsby, go to take a month's polishing every winter.

HARDCASTLE.   Ay, and bring back vanity and affectation to last them the whole year. I wonder why London cannot keep its own fools at home. In my time, the follies of the town crept slowly among us, but now they travel faster than a stage-coach. Its fopperies come down, not only as inside passengers, but in the very basket.

MRS. HARDCASTLE.   Ay, *your* times were fine times, indeed; you have been telling us of *them* for many a long year. Here we live in an old rumbling mansion, that looks for all the world like an inn, but that we never see company. Our best visitors are old Mrs. Oddfish, the curate's wife, and little Cripplegate, the lame dancing-master: And all our entertainment your old stories of Prince Eugene and the Duke of Marlborough. I hate such old-fashioned trumpery.

HARDCASTLE.   And I love it. I love everything that's old: old friends, old times, old manners, old books, old wine; and, I believe, Dorothy (*taking her hand*), you'll own I have been pretty fond of an old wife.

MRS. HARDCASTLE.   Lord, Mr. Hardcastle, you're for ever at your Dorothys and your old wifes. You may be a Darby, but I'll be no Joan, I promise you. I'm not so old as you'd make me, by more than one good year. Add twenty to twenty, and make money of that.

HARDCASTLE.   Let me see; twenty added to twenty, makes just fifty and seven!

MRS. HARDCASTLE.   It's false, Mr. Hardcastle: I was but twenty when I was brought to bed of Tony, that I had by Mr. Lumpkin, my first husband; and he's not come to years of discretion yet.

HARDCASTLE.   Nor ever will, I dare answer for him. Ay, you have taught *him* finely!

MRS. HARDCASTLE.   No matter, Tony Lumpkin has a good fortune. My son is not to live by his learning. I don't think a boy wants much learning to spend fifteen hundred a year.

HARDCASTLE.   Learning, quotha! A mere composition of tricks and mischief!

MRS. HARDCASTLE.   Humour, my dear: nothing but humour. Come, Mr. Hardcastle, you must allow the boy a little humour.

HARDCASTLE.   I'd sooner allow him a horse-pond! If burning the footmen's shoes, frightening the maids, and worrying the kittens, be humour, he has it. It was but yesterday he fastened my wig to the back of my chair, and when I went to make a bow, I popped my bald head in Mrs. Frizzle's face!

MRS. HARDCASTLE.   And am I to blame? The poor boy was always too sickly to do any good. A school would be his death. When he comes to be a little stronger, who knows what a year or two's Latin may do for him?

HARDCASTLE.   Latin for him! A cat and fiddle! No, no, the alehouse and the stable are the only schools he'll ever go to!

MRS. HARDCASTLE.   Well, we must not snub the poor boy now, for I believe we shan't have him long among us. Anybody that looks in his face may see he's consumptive.

HARDCASTLE.   Ay, if growing too fat be one of the symptoms.

MRS. HARDCASTLE.   He coughs sometimes.

HARDCASTLE.   Yes, when his liquor goes the wrong way.

MRS. HARDCASTLE.   I'm actually afraid of his lungs.

HARDCASTLE.   And truly, so am I; for he sometimes whoops like a speaking-trumpet—(TONY *hallooing behind the scenes.*)—O, there he goes.—A very consumptive figure, truly!

Enter TONY, *crossing the stage.*

MRS. HARDCASTLE.   Tony, where are you going, my charmer? Won't you give papa and I a little of your company, lovey?

TONY.   I'm in haste, mother, I cannot stay.

MRS. HARDCASTLE.   You shan't venture out this raw evening, my dear: You look most shockingly.

TONY.   I can't stay, I tell you. The Three Pigeons expects me down every moment. There's some fun going forward.

HARDCASTLE.   Ay; the alehouse, the old place: I thought so.

MRS. HARDCASTLE.   A low, paltry set of fellows.

TONY.   Not so low, neither. There's Dick Muggins the exciseman, Jack Slang the horse doctor, Little Aminadab that grinds the music-box, and Tom Twist that spins the pewter platter.

MRS. HARDCASTLE.   Pray, my dear, disappoint them for one night, at least.

TONY.   As for disappointing *them,* I should not much mind; but I can't abide to disappoint *myself!*

MRS. HARDCASTLE (*detaining him*).   You shan't go.

TONY.   I will, I tell you.

MRS. HARDCASTLE.   I say you shan't.

TONY.   We'll see which is strongest, you or I. (*Exit hauling her out.*)

HARDCASTLE *solus.*

HARDCASTLE.   Ay, there goes a pair that only spoil each other. But is not the whole age in a combination to drive sense and discretion out of doors? There's my pretty darling Kate; the fashions of the times have almost infected her too. By living a year or two in town, she is as fond of gauze, and French frippery, as the best of them.

Enter MISS HARDCASTLE.

HARDCASTLE.   Blessings on my pretty innocence! Dressed out as usual, my Kate! Goodness! What a quantity of superfluous silk hast thou got about thee, girl! I could never teach the fools of this age that the indigent world could be clothed out of the trimmings of the vain.

MISS HARDCASTLE.   You know our agreement, sir. You allow me the morning to receive and pay visits, and to dress in my own manner; and in the evening, I put on my housewife's dress, to please you.

HARDCASTLE.   Well, remember, I insist on the terms of our agreement; and, by-the-bye, I believe I shall have occasion to try your obedience this very evening.

MISS HARDCASTLE.   I protest, sir, I don't comprehend your meaning.

HARDCASTLE.   Then to be plain with you, Kate, I expect the young gentleman I have chosen to be your husband from town this very day. I have his father's letter, in which he informs me his son is set out, and that he intends to follow himself shortly after.

MISS HARDCASTLE.   Indeed! I wish I had known something of this before. Bless me, how shall I behave? It's a thousand to one I shan't like him; our meeting will be so formal, and so like a thing of business, that I shall find no room for friendship or esteem.

HARDCASTLE.   Depend upon it, child, I'll never control your choice; but Mr. Marlow, whom I have pitched upon, is the son of my old friend, Sir Charles Marlow, of whom you have heard me talk so often. The young gentleman has been bred a scholar, and is designed for an employment in the service of his country. I am told he's a man of an excellent understanding.

MISS HARDCASTLE.   Is he?

HARDCASTLE.   Very generous.

MISS HARDCASTLE.   I believe I shall like him.

HARDCASTLE.   Young and brave.

MISS HARDCASTLE.   I'm sure I shall like him.

HARDCASTLE.   And very handsome.

MISS HARDCASTLE.   My dear papa, say no more (*kissing his hand*), he's mine, I'll have him!

HARDCASTLE.   And, to crown all, Kate, he's one of the most bashful and reserved young fellows in all the world.

MISS HARDCASTLE.   Eh! You have frozen me to death again. That word *reserved* has undone all the rest of his accomplishments. A reserved lover, it is said, always makes a suspicious husband.

HARDCASTLE.   On the contrary, modesty seldom resides in a breast that is not enriched with nobler virtues. It was the very feature in his character that first struck me.

MISS HARDCASTLE.   He must have more striking features to catch me, I promise you. However, if he be so young, so handsome, and so everything, as you mention, I believe he'll do still. I think I'll have him.

HARDCASTLE.   Ay, Kate, but there is still an obstacle. It is more than an even wager, he may not have *you*.

MISS HARDCASTLE.   My dear papa, why will you mortify one so?—Well, if he refuses, instead of breaking my heart at his indifference, I'll only break my glass for its flattery, set my cap to some newer fashion, and look out for some less difficult admirer.

HARDCASTLE.   Bravely resolved! In the meantime I'll go prepare the servants for his reception; as we seldom see company, they want as much training as a company of recruits the first day's muster. (*Exit.*)

MISS HARDCASTLE *sola*.

MISS HARDCASTLE.   Lud, this news of papa's puts me all in a flutter. Young, handsome; these he put last; but I put them foremost. Sensible, good-natur'd; I like all that. But then reserved, and sheepish, that's much against him. Yet can't he be cured of his timidity, by being taught to be proud of his wife? Yes, and can't I—But I vow I'm disposing of the husband before I have secured the lover!

Enter MISS NEVILLE.

MISS HARDCASTLE.   I'm glad you're come, Neville, my dear. Tell me, Constance, how do I look this evening? Is there anything whimsical about me? Is it one of my well-looking days, child? Am I in face to-day?

MISS NEVILLE.   Perfectly, my dear. Yet, now I look again—bless me!—sure no accident has happened among the canary birds or the goldfishes? Has your brother or the cat been meddling? Or has the last novel been too moving?

MISS HARDCASTLE.   No; nothing of all this. I have been threatened—I can scarce get it out—I have been threatened with a lover!

MISS NEVILLE.   And his name—

MISS HARDCASTLE.   Is Marlow.

MISS NEVILLE.   Indeed!

MISS HARDCASTLE.   The son of Sir Charles Marlow.

MISS NEVILLE.   As I live, the most intimate friend of Mr. Hastings, *my* admirer. They are never asunder. I believe you must have seen him when we lived in town.

MISS HARDCASTLE.   Never.

MISS NEVILLE.   He's a very singular character, I assure you. Among women of reputation and virtue, he is the modestest man alive: but his acquaintance give him a very different character among creatures of another stamp: you understand me?

MISS HARDCASTLE.   An odd character, indeed! I shall never be able to manage him. What shall I do? Pshaw, think no more of him, but trust to occurrences for success. But how goes on your own affair, my dear? Has my mother been courting you for my brother Tony, as usual?

MISS NEVILLE.   I have just come from one of our agreeable *tête-à-têtes*. She has been saying a hundred tender things, and setting off her pretty monster as the very pink of perfection.

MISS HARDCASTLE.   And her partiality is such, that she actually thinks him so. A fortune like yours is no small temptation. Besides, as she has the sole management of it, I'm not surprised to see her unwilling to let it go out of the family.

MISS NEVILLE.   A fortune like mine, which chiefly consists in jewels, is no such mighty temptation. But, at any rate, if my dear Hastings be but constant, I make no doubt to be too hard for her at last. However, I let her suppose that I am in love with her son, and she never once dreams that my affections are fixed upon another.

MISS HARDCASTLE.   My good brother holds out stoutly. I could almost love him for hating you so.

MISS NEVILLE.   It is a good-natur'd creature at bottom, and I'm sure would wish to see me married to anybody but himself. But my aunt's bell rings for our afternoon's walk through the improvements. *Allons.* Courage is necessary, as our affairs are critical.

MISS HARDCASTLE.   Would it were bed-time and all were well. (*Exeunt.*)

SCENE—*An Alehouse Room. Several shabby fellows, with punch and tobacco.* TONY *at the head of the table, a little higher than the rest, a mallet in his hand.*

OMNES.   Hurrea, hurrea, hurrea, bravo!

FIRST FELLOW.   Now, gentlemen, silence for a song. The 'Squire is going to knock himself down for a song.

OMNES.   Ay, a song, a song.

TONY.   Then I'll sing you, gentlemen, a song I made upon this alehouse, the Three Pigeons.

SONG

Let school-masters puzzle their brain,
  With grammar, and nonsense, and learning;
Good liquor, I stoutly maintain,
  Gives genus *a better discerning,*
Let them brag of their Heathenish Gods,
  Their Lethes, their Styxes, and Stygians;
Their Quis, and their Quæs, and their Quods,
  They're all but a parcel of Pigeons.
      Toroddle, toroddle, toroll!
When Methodist preachers come down,
  A-preaching that drinking is sinful,
I'll wager the rascals a crown,
  They always preach best with a skinful.
But when you come down with your pence,
  For a slice of their scurvy religion,
I'll leave it to all men of sense,
  But you, my good friend, are the pigeon.
      Toroddle, toroddle, toroll!
Then come, put the jorum about,
  And let us be merry and clever,

Our hearts and our liquors are stout,
  Here's the Three Jolly Pigeons for ever.
Let some cry up woodcock or hare,
  Your bustards, your ducks, and your widgeons:
But of all the birds in the air,
  Here's a health to the Three Jolly Pigeons.
      Toroddle, toroddle, toroll!

OMNES.   Bravo, bravo!

FIRST FELLOW.   The 'Squire has got spunk in him.

SECOND FELLOW.   I loves to hear him sing, bekeays he never gives us nothing that's *low.*

THIRD FELLOW.   O damn anything that's *low,* I cannot bear it!

FOURTH FELLOW.   The genteel thing is the genteel thing at any time. If so be that a gentleman bees in a concatenation accordingly.

THIRD FELLOW.   I like the maxum of it, Master Muggins. What, though I am obligated to dance a bear, a man may be a gentleman for all that. May this be my poison if my bear ever dances but to the very genteelest of tunes: Water Parted, or the minuet in Ariadne.

SECOND FELLOW.   What a pity it is the 'Squire is not come to his own. It would be well for all the publicans within ten miles round of him.

TONY.   Ecod, and so it would, Master Slang. I'd then show what it was to keep choice of company.

SECOND FELLOW.   O, he takes after his own father for that. To be sure, old 'Squire Lumpkin was the finest gentleman I ever set my eyes on. For winding the straight horn, or beating a thicket for a hare, or a wench, he never had his fellow. It was a saying in the place, that he kept the best horses, dogs, and girls in the whole county.

TONY.   Ecod, and when I'm of age I'll be no bastard, I promise you. I have been thinking of Bet Bouncer and the miller's grey mare to begin with. But come, my boys, drink about and be merry, for you pay no reckoning. Well, Stingo, what's the matter?

Enter LANDLORD.

LANDLORD.   There be two gentlemen in a post-chaise at the door. They have lost their way upo' the forest; and they are talking something about Mr. Hardcastle.

TONY.   As sure as can be, one of them must be the gentleman that's coming down to court my sister. Do they seem to be Londoners?

LANDLORD.   I believe they may. They look woundily like Frenchmen.

TONY.   Then desire them to step this way, and I'll set them right in a twinkling. (*Exit* LANDLORD.) Gentlemen, as they mayn't be good enough company for you, step down for a moment, and I'll be with you in the squeezing of a lemon. (*Exeunt* MOB.)

TONY *solus*.

TONY.   Father-in-law has been calling me whelp, and hound, this half year. Now, if I pleased, I could be so revenged upon the old grumbletonian. But then I'm afraid—afraid of what? I shall soon be worth fifteen hundred a year, and let him frighten me out of *that* if he can!

Enter LANDLORD, *conducting* MARLOW *and* HASTINGS.

MARLOW.   What a tedious uncomfortable day have we had of it! We were told it was but forty miles across the country, and we have come above threescore!

HASTINGS.   And all, Marlow, from that unaccountable reserve of yours, that would not let us enquire more frequently on the way.

MARLOW.   I own, Hastings, I am unwilling to lay myself under an obligation to every one I meet; and often stand the chance of an unmannerly answer.

HASTINGS.   At present, however, we are not likely to receive any answer.

TONY.   No offence, gentlemen. But I'm told you have been enquiring for one Mr. Hardcastle, in these parts. Do you know what part of the country you are in?

HASTINGS.   Not in the least, sir, but should thank you for information.

TONY.   Nor the way you came?

HASTINGS.   No, sir, but if you can inform us—

TONY.   Why, gentlemen, if you know neither the road you are going, nor where you are, nor the road you came, the first thing I have to inform is, that—you have lost your way.

MARLOW.   We wanted no ghost to tell us that.

TONY.   Pray, gentlemen, may I be so bold as to ask the place from whence you came?

MARLOW.   That's not necessary towards directing us where we are to go.

TONY.   No offence; but question for question is all fair, you know. Pray, gentlemen, is not this same Hardcastle a cross-grained, old-fashioned, whimsical fellow with an ugly face, a daughter, and a pretty son?

HASTINGS.   We have not seen the gentleman, but he has the family you mention.

TONY.   The daughter, a tall, trapesing, trolloping, talkative maypole——The son, a pretty, well-bred, agreeable youth, that everybody is fond of!

MARLOW.   Our information differs in this. The daughter is said to be well-bred and beautiful; the son, an awkward booby, reared up and spoiled at his mother's apron-string.

TONY.   He-he-hem—then, gentlemen, all I have to tell you is, that you won't reach Mr. Hardcastle's house this night, I believe.

HASTINGS.   Unfortunate!

TONY.   It's a damned long, dark, boggy, dirty, dangerous way. Stingo, tell the gentlemen the way to Mr.

Hardcastle's. (*Winking upon the* LANDLORD.) Mr. Hardcastle's of Quagmire Marsh, you understand me.

LANDLORD.   Master Hardcastle's! Lack-a-daisy, my masters, you're come a deadly deal wrong! When you came to the bottom of the hill, you should have crossed down Squash Lane.

MARLOW.   Cross down Squash Lane!

LANDLORD.   Then you were to keep straight forward, until you came to four roads.

MARLOW.   Come to where four roads meet!

TONY.   Ay, but you must be sure to take only one of them.

MARLOW.   O, sir, you're facetious!

TONY.   Then, keeping to the right, you are to go sideways till you come upon Crack-skull Common: there you must look sharp for the track of the wheel, and go forward, till you come to Farmer Murrain's barn. Coming to the farmer's barn, you are to turn to the right, and then to the left and then to the right about again, till you find out the old mill——

MARLOW.   Zounds, man! we could as soon find out the longitude!

HASTINGS.   What's to be done, Marlow?

MARLOW.   This house promises but a poor reception, though, perhaps, the landlord can accommodate us.

LANDLORD.   Alack, master, we have but one spare bed in the whole house.

TONY.   And to my knowledge, that's taken up by three lodgers already. (*After a pause, in which the rest seem disconcerted.*) I have hit it. Don't you think, Stingo, our landlady could accommodate the gentlemen by the fireside, with——three chairs and a bolster?

HASTINGS.   I hate sleeping by the fireside.

MARLOW.   And I detest your three chairs and a bolster.

TONY.   You do, do you?—then let me see—what—if you go on a mile further, to the Buck's Head; the old Buck's Head on the hill, one of the best inns in the whole country?

HASTINGS.   Oh, oh! so we have escaped an adventure for this night, however.

LANDLORD (*apart to* TONY). Sure, you ben't sending them to your father's as an inn, be you?

TONY.   Mum, you fool, you. Let *them* find that out. (*To them.*) You have only to keep on straight forward, till you come to a large old house by the roadside. You'll see a pair of large horns over the door. That's the sign. Drive up the yard, and call stoutly about you.

HASTINGS.   Sir, we are obliged to you. The servants can't miss the way?

TONY.   No, no: but I tell you though, the landlord is rich, and going to leave off business; so he wants to be thought a gentleman, saving your presence, he! he! he! He'll be for giving you his company, and, ecod, if you mind him, he'll persuade you that his mother was an alderman, and his aunt a justice of the peace!

LANDLORD. A troublesome old blade, to be sure; but 'a keeps as good wines and beds as any in the whole country.

MARLOW. Well, if he supplies us with these, we shall want no further connection. We are to turn to the right, did you say?

TONY. No, no; straight forward. I'll just step myself, and show you a piece of the way. (*To the* LANDLORD.) Mum.

LANDLORD. Ah, bless your heart, for a sweet, pleasant— damned mischievous son of a whore. (*Exeunt.*)

ACT TWO

SCENE—AN OLD-FASHIONED HOUSE.

Enter HARDCASTLE, *followed by three or four awkward* SERVANTS.

HARDCASTLE. Well, I hope you're perfect in the table exercise I have been teaching you these three days. You all know your posts and your places, and can show that you have been used to good company, without ever stirring from home.

OMNES. Ay, ay.

HARDCASTLE. When company comes, you are not to pop out and stare, and then run in again, like frightened rabbits in a warren.

OMNES. No, no.

HARDCASTLE. You, Diggory, whom I have taken from the barn, are to make a show at the side-table; and you, Roger, whom I have advanced from the plough, are to place yourself behind *my* chair. But you're not to stand so, with your hands in your pockets. Take your hands from your pockets, Roger; and from your head, you blockhead, you. See how Diggory carries his hands. They're a little too stiff, indeed, but that's no great matter.

DIGGORY. Ay, mind how I hold them. I learned to hold my hands this way, when I was upon drill for the militia. And so being upon drill——

HARDCASTLE. You must not be so talkative, Diggory. You must be all attention to the guests. You must hear us talk, and not think of talking; you must see us drink and not think of drinking; you must see us eat and not think of eating.

DIGGORY. By the laws, your worship, that's parfectly unpossible. Whenever Diggory sees yeating going forward, ecod, he's always wishing for a mouthful himself.

HARDCASTLE. Blockhead! Is not a bellyful in the kitchen as good as a bellyful in the parlour? Stay your stomach with that reflection.

DIGGORY. Ecod, I thank your worship, I'll make a shift to stay my stomach with a slice of cold beef in the pantry.

HARDCASTLE. Diggory, you are too talkative. Then, if I happen to say a good thing, or tell a good story at table, you must not all burst out a-laughing, as if you made part of the company.

DIGGORY. Then, ecod, your worship must not tell the story of Ould Grouse in the gun-room: I can't help laughing at that—he! he! he!—for the soul of me! We have laughed at that these twenty years—ha! ha! ha!

HARDCASTLE. Ha! ha! ha! The story is a good one. Well, honest Diggory, you may laugh at that—but still remember to be attentive. Suppose one of the company should call for a glass of wine, how will you behave? A glass of wine, sir, if you please (*to* DIGGORY)—Eh, why don't you move?

DIGGORY. Ecod, your worship, I never have courage till I see the eatables and drinkables brought upo' the table, and then I'm as bauld as a lion.

HARDCASTLE. What, will nobody move?

FIRST SERVANT. I'm not to leave this pleace.

SECOND SERVANT. I'm sure it's no pleace of mine.

THIRD SERVANT. Nor mine for sartain.

DIGGORY. Wauns, and I'm sure it canna be mine.

HARDCASTLE. You numskulls! and so while, like your betters, you are quarrelling for places, the guests must be starved. O, you dunces! I find I must begin all over again.—But don't I hear a coach drive into the yard? To your posts, you blockheads! I'll go in the meantime and give my old friend's son a hearty reception at the gate. (*Exit* HARDCASTLE.)

DIGGORY. By the elevens, my pleace is gone quite out of my head!

ROGER. I know that my pleace is to be everywhere!

FIRST SERVANT. Where the devil is mine?

SECOND SERVANT. My pleace is to be nowhere at all; and so I'ze go about my business. (*Exeunt* SERVANTS, *running about as if frighted, different ways.*)

Enter SERVANTS *with Candles, showing in* MARLOW *and* HASTINGS.

SERVANT. Welcome, gentlemen, very welcome. This way.

HASTINGS. After the disappointments of the day, welcome once more, Charles, to the comforts of a clean room and a good fire. Upon my word, a very well-looking house; antique but creditable.

MARLOW. The usual fate of a large mansion. Having first ruined the master by good housekeeping, it at last comes to levy contributions as an inn.

HASTINGS. As you say, we passengers are to be taxed to pay for all these fineries. I have often seen a good sideboard, or a marble chimney-piece, though not actually put in the bill, inflame a reckoning confoundedly.

MARLOW. Travellers, George, must pay in all places. The only difference is, that in good inns, you pay dearly for luxuries; in bad inns, you are fleeced and starved.

HASTINGS. You have lived pretty much among them. In truth, I have been often surprised, that you who have seen so much of the world, with your natural good sense, and your many opportunities, could never yet acquire a requisite share of assurance.

MARLOW.   The Englishman's malady. But tell me, George, where could I have learned that assurance you talk of? My life has been chiefly spent in a college, or an inn, in seclusion from that lovely part of the creation that chiefly teaches men confidence. I don't know that I was ever familiarly acquainted with a single modest woman—except my mother—but among females of another class, you know—

HASTINGS.   Ay, among them you are impudent enough of all conscience!

MARLOW.   They are of *us,* you know.

HASTINGS.   But in the company of women of reputation I never saw such an idiot, such a trembler; you look for all the world as if you wanted an opportunity of stealing out of the room.

MARLOW.   Why, man, that's because I *do* want to steal out of the room. Faith, I have often formed a resolution to break the ice, and rattle away at any rate. But I don't know how, a single glance from a pair of fine eyes has totally overset my resolution. An impudent fellow may counterfeit modesty, but I'll be hanged if a modest man can ever counterfeit impudence.

HASTINGS.   If you could but say half the fine things to them that I have heard you lavish upon the barmaid of an inn, or even a college bedmaker——

MARLOW.   Why, George, I can't say fine things to them. They freeze, they petrify me. They may talk of a comet, or a burning mountain, or some such bagatelle. But to me, a modest woman, dressed out in all her finery, is the most tremendous object of the whole creation.

HASTINGS.   Ha! ha! ha! At this rate, man, how can you ever expect to marry!

MARLOW.   Never, unless, as among kings and princes, my bride were to be courted by proxy. If, indeed, like an Eastern bridegroom, one were to be introduced to a wife he never saw before, it might be endured. But to go through all the terrors of a formal courtship, together with the episode of aunts, grandmothers, and cousins, and at last to blurt out the broad staring question of, *Madam, will you marry me?* No, no, that's a strain much above me, I assure you!

HASTINGS.   I pity you. But how do you intend behaving to the lady you are come down to visit at the request of your father?

MARLOW.   As I behave to all other ladies. Bow very low. Answer yes, or no, to all her demands—But for the rest, I don't think I shall venture to look in her face, till I see my father's again.

HASTINGS.   I'm surprised that one who is so warm a friend can be so cool a lover.

MARLOW.   To be explicit, my dear Hastings, my chief inducement down was to be instrumental in forwarding your happiness, not my own. Miss Neville loves you, the family don't know you, as my friend you are sure of a reception, and let honour do the rest.

HASTINGS.   My dear Marlow! But I'll suppress the emotion. Were I a wretch, meanly seeking to carry off a fortune, you should be the last man in the world I would apply to for assistance. But Miss Neville's person is all I ask, and that is mine, both from her deceased father's consent and her own inclination.

MARLOW.   Happy man! You have talents and art to captivate any woman. I'm doomed to adore the sex, and yet to converse with the only part of it I despise. This stammer in my address, and this awkward prepossessing visage of mine, can never permit me to soar above the reach of a milliner's apprentice, or one of the duchesses of Drury Lane. Pshaw! this fellow here to interrupt us.

Enter HARDCASTLE.

HARDCASTLE.   Gentlemen, once more you are heartily welcome. Which is Mr. Marlow? Sir, you're heartily welcome. It's not my way, you see, to receive my friends with my back to the fire. I like to give them a hearty reception in the old style at my gate. I like to see their horses and trunks taken care of.

MARLOW (*aside*).   He has got our names from the servants already. (*To him.*) We approve your caution and hospitality, sir. (*To* HASTINGS.) I have been thinking, George, of changing our travelling dresses in the morning. I am grown confoundedly ashamed of mine.

HARDCASTLE.   I beg, Mr. Marlow, you'll use no ceremony in this house.

MARLOW.   I fancy, George, you're right: the first blow is half the battle. I intend opening the campaign with the white and gold.

HARDCASTLE.   Mr. Marlow—Mr. Hastings—gentlemen—pray be under no constraint in this house. This is Liberty Hall, gentlemen. You may do just as you please here.

MARLOW.   Yet, George, if we open the campaign too fiercely at first, we may want ammunition before it is over. I think to reserve the embroidery to secure a retreat.

HARDCASTLE.   Your talking of a retreat, Mr. Marlow, puts me in mind of the Duke of Marlborough, when we went to besiege Denain. He first summoned the garrison——

MARLOW.   Don't you think the *ventre d'or* waistcoat will do with the plain brown?

HARDCASTLE.   He first summoned the garrison, which might consist of about five thousand men——

HASTINGS.   I think not: brown and yellow mix but very poorly.

HARDCASTLE.   I say, gentlemen, as I was telling you, he summoned the garrison, which might consist of about five thousand men——

MARLOW.   The girls like finery.

HARDCASTLE.   Which might consist of about five thousand men, well appointed with stores, ammunition, and other implements of war. "Now," says the Duke of Marlborough to George Brooks, that stood next to him—you must have heard of George Brooks; "I'll pawn my Dukedom," says he, "but I take that garrison without spilling a drop of blood!" So——

MARLOW.   What, my good friend, if you gave us a glass of punch in the meantime, it would help us to carry on the siege with vigour.

HARDCASTLE.   Punch, sir!——(*Aside.*) This is the most unaccountable kind of modesty I ever met with!

MARLOW.   Yes, sir, punch! A glass of warm punch, after our journey, will be comfortable. This is Liberty Hall, you know.

HARDCASTLE.   Here's a cup, sir.

MARLOW (*aside*).   So this fellow, in his Liberty Hall, will only let us have just what he pleases.

HARDCASTLE (*taking the cup*).   I hope you'll find it to your mind. I have prepared it with my own hands, and I believe you'll own the ingredients are tolerable. Will you be so good as to pledge me, sir? Here, Mr. Marlow, here is our better acquaintance! (*Drinks.*)

MARLOWE (*aside*).   A very impudent fellow this! but he's a character, and I'll humour him a little. Sir, my service to you. (*Drinks.*)

HASTINGS (*aside*).   I see this fellow wants to give us his company, and forgets that he's an innkeeper, before he has learned to be a gentleman.

MARLOW.   From the excellence of your cup, my old friend, I suppose you have a good deal of business in this part of the country. Warm work, now and then, at elections, I suppose?

HARDCASTLE.   No, sir, I have long given that work over. Since our betters have hit upon the expedient of electing each other, there's no business *for us that sell ale.*

HASTINGS.   So, then you have no turn for politics, I find.

HARDCASTLE.   Not in the least. There was a time, indeed, I fretted myself about the mistakes of government, like other people; but finding myself every day grow more angry, and the government growing no better, I left it to mend itself. Since that, I no more trouble my head about *Heyder Ally* or *Ally Cawn,* than about *Ally Croker.* Sir, my service to you.

HASTINGS.   So that, with eating above stairs, and drinking below, with receiving your friends within, and amusing them without, you lead a good pleasant bustling life of it.

HARDCASTLE.   I do stir about a great deal, that's certain. Half the differences of the parish are adjusted in this very parlour.

MARLOW (*after drinking*).   And you have an argument in your cup, old gentleman, better than any in Westminster Hall.

HARDCASTLE.   Ay, young gentleman, that, and a little philosophy.

MARLOW (*aside*).   Well, this is the first time I ever heard of an innkeeper's philosophy.

HASTINGS.   So then, like an experienced general, you attack them on every quarter. If you find their reason manageable, you attack it with your philosophy; if you find they have no reason, you attack them with this. Here's your health, my philosopher. (*Drinks.*)

HARDCASTLE.   Good, very good, thank you; ha! ha! Your generalship puts me in mind of Prince Eugene, when he fought the Turks at the battle of Belgrade. You shall hear.

MARLOW.   Instead of the battle of Belgrade, I believe it's almost time to talk about supper. What has your philosophy got in the house for supper?

HARDCASTLE.   For supper, sir!——(*Aside.*) Was ever such a request to a man in his own house!

MARLOW.   Yes, sir, supper, sir; I begin to feel an appetite. I shall make devilish work to-night in the larder, I promise you.

HARDCASTLE (*aside*).   Such a brazen dog sure never my eyes beheld. (*To him.*) Why, really, sir, as for supper I can't well tell. My Dorothy, and the cook maid, settle these things between them. I leave these kind of things entirely to them.

MARLOW.   You do, do you?

HARDCASTLE.   Entirely. By-the-bye, I believe they are in actual consultation upon what's for supper this moment in the kitchen.

MARLOW.   Then I beg they'll admit *me* as one of their privy council. It's a way I have got. When I travel, I always choose to regulate my own supper. Let the cook be called. No offence, I hope, sir.

HARDCASTLE.   O, no, sir, none in the least; yet, I don't know how: our Bridget, the cook maid, is not very communicative upon these occasions. Should we send for her, she might scold us all out of the house.

HASTINGS.   Let's see your list of the larder, then. I ask it as a favour. I always match my appetite to my bill of fare.

MARLOW (*to* HARDCASTLE, *who looks at them with surprise*).   Sir, he's very right, and it's my way, too.

HARDCASTLE.   Sir, you have a right to command here. Here, Roger, bring us the bill of fare for to-night's supper. I believe it's drawn out. Your manner, Mr. Hastings, puts me in mind of my uncle, Colonel Wallop. It was a saying of his, that no man was sure of his supper till he had eaten it.

HASTINGS (*aside*).   All upon the high ropes! His uncle a colonel! We shall soon hear of his mother being a justice of the peace. But let's hear the bill of fare.

MARLOW (*perusing*). What's here? For the first course; for the second course; for the dessert. The devil, sir, do you think we have brought down the whole Joiners' Company, or the Corporation of Bedford, to eat up such a supper? Two or three little things, clean and comfortable, will do.

HASTINGS.   But let's hear it.

MARLOW (*reading*). For the first course at the top, a pig, and prune sauce.

HASTINGS.   Damn your pig, I say!

MARLOW.   And damn your prune sauce, say I!

HARDCASTLE.   And yet, gentlemen, to men that are hungry, pig, with prune sauce, is very good eating.

MARLOW.   At the bottom, a calf's tongue and brains.

HASTINGS.   Let your brains be knocked out, my good sir; I don't like them.

MARLOW.   Or you may clap them on a plate by themselves, I do.

HARDCASTLE (*aside*). Their impudence confounds me. (*To them.*) Gentlemen, you are my guests, make what alterations you please. Is there anything else you wish to retrench or alter, gentlemen?

MARLOW.   Item. A pork pie, a boiled rabbit and sausages, a florentine, a shaking pudding, and a dish of tiff—taff—taffety cream!

HASTINGS.   Confound your made dishes, I shall be as much at a loss in this house as at a green and yellow dinner at the French ambassador's table. I'm for plain eating.

HARDCASTLE.   I'm sorry, gentlemen, that I have nothing you like, but if there be anything you have a particular fancy to——

MARLOW.   Why, really, sir, your bill of fare is so exquisite, that any one part of it is full as good as another. Send us what you please. So much for supper. And now to see that our beds are aired, and properly taken care of.

HARDCASTLE.   I entreat you'll leave all that to me. You shall not stir a step.

MARLOW.   Leave that to you! I protest, sir, you must excuse me, I always look to these things myself.

HARDCASTLE.   I must insist, sir, you'll make yourself easy on that head.

MARLOW.   You see I'm resolved on it.—(*Aside.*) A very troublesome fellow this, as ever I met with.

HARDCASTLE.   Well, sir, I'm resolved at least to attend you.—(*Aside.*) This may be modern modesty, but I never saw anything look so like old-fashioned impudence. (*Exeunt* MARLOW *and* HARDCASTLE.)

HASTINGS *solus.*

HASTINGS.   So I find this fellow's civilities begin to grow troublesome. But who can be angry at those assiduities which are meant to please him! Miss Neville, by all that's happy!

Enter MISS NEVILLE.

MISS NEVILLE.   My dear Hastings! To what unexpected good fortune? to what accident am I to ascribe this happy meeting?

HASTINGS.   Rather let me ask the same question, as I could never have hoped to meet my dearest Constance at an inn.

MISS NEVILLE.   An inn! sure you mistake! my aunt, my guardian, lives here. What could induce you to think this house an inn?

HASTINGS.   My friend, Mr. Marlow, with whom I came down, and I, have been sent here as to an inn, I assure you. A young fellow whom we accidentally met at a house hard by directed us hither.

MISS NEVILLE.   Certainly it must be one of my hopeful cousin's tricks, of whom you have heard me talk so often, ha! ha! ha! ha!

HASTINGS.   He whom your aunt intends for you? He of whom I have such just apprehensions?

MISS NEVILLE.   You have nothing to fear from him, I assure you. You'd adore him if you knew how heartily he despises me. My aunt knows it too, and has undertaken to court me for him, and actually begins to think she has made a conquest.

HASTINGS.   Thou dear dissembler! You must know, my Constance, I have just seized this happy opportunity of my friend's visit here to get admittance into the family. The horses that carried us down are now fatigued with their journey, but they'll soon be refreshed; and then if my dearest girl will trust in her faithful Hastings, we shall soon be landed in France, where even among slaves the laws of marriage are respected.

MISS NEVILLE.   I have often told you, that though ready to obey you, I yet should leave my little fortune behind with reluctance. The greatest part of it was left me by my uncle, the India Director, and chiefly consists in jewels. I have been for some time persuading my aunt to let me wear them. I fancy I'm very near succeeding. The instant they are put into my possession you shall find me ready to make them and myself yours.

HASTINGS.   Perish the baubles! Your person is all I desire. In the meantime, my friend Marlow must not be let into his mistake. I know the strange reserve of his temper is such, that if abruptly informed of it, he would instantly quit the house before our plan was ripe for execution.

MISS NEVILLE.   But how shall we keep him in the deception? Miss Hardcastle is just returned from walking; what if we still continue to deceive him?—This; this way—— (*They confer.*)

Enter MARLOW.

MARLOW.   The assiduities of these good people tease me beyond bearing. My host seems to think it ill manners to leave me alone, and so he claps not only himself, but his old-fashioned wife on my back. They talk of coming to sup with us, too; and then, I suppose, we are to run the gauntlet through all the rest of the family.—What have we got here?—

HASTINGS.   My dear Charles! Let me congratulate you!—The most fortunate accident!—Who do you think is just alighted?

MARLOW.   Cannot guess.

HASTINGS.   Our mistresses, boy, Miss Hardcastle and Miss Neville. Give me leave to introduce Miss Constance Neville to your acquaintance. Happening to dine in the neighbourhood, they called, on their return to take fresh horses, here. Miss Hardcastle has just stept into the next room, and will be back in an instant. Wasn't it lucky? eh!

MARLOW (aside).   I have just been mortified enough of all-conscience, and here comes something to complete my embarrassment.

HASTINGS.   Well! but wasn't it the most fortunate thing in the world?

MARLOW.   Oh! yes. Very fortunate—a most joyful encounter——But our dresses, George, you know, are in disorder——What if we should postpone the happiness till to-morrow?——To-morrow at her own house——It will be every bit as convenient——And rather more respectful——To-morrow let it be. (Offering to go.)

MISS NEVILLE.   By no means, sir. Your ceremony will displease her. The disorder of your dress will shew the ardour of your impatience. Besides, she knows you are in the house, and will permit you to see her.

MARLOW.   O! the devil! how shall I support it? Hem! hem! Hastings, you must not go. You are to assist me, you know. I shall be confoundedly ridiculous. Yet, hang it! I'll take courage. Hem!

HASTINGS.   Pshaw, man! it's but the first plunge, and all's over. She's but a woman, you know.

MARLOW.   And of all women, she that I dread most to encounter!

Enter MISS HARDCASTLE, as returned from walking, a Bonnet, &c.

HASTINGS (introducing them).   Miss Hardcastle, Mr. Marlow, I'm proud of bringing two persons of such merit together, that only want to know, to esteem each other.

MISS HARDCASTLE (aside).   Now, for meeting my modest gentleman with a demure face, and quite in his own manner. (After a pause, in which he appears very uneasy and disconcerted.) I'm glad of your safe arrival, sir—— I'm told you had some accidents by the way.

MARLOW.   Only a few, madam. Yes, we had some. Yes, madam, a good many accidents, but should be sorry—madam—or rather glad of any accidents—that are so agreeably concluded. Hem!

HASTINGS (to him).   You never spoke better in your whole life. Keep it up, and I'll insure you the victory.

MISS HARDCASTLE.   I'm afraid you flatter, sir. You that have seen so much of the finest company can find little entertainment in an obscure corner of the country.

MARLOW (gathering courage).   I have lived, indeed, in the world, madam; but I have kept very little company. I have been but an observer upon life, madam, while others were enjoying it.

MISS NEVILLE.   But that, I am told, is the way to enjoy it at last.

HASTINGS (to him).   Cicero never spoke better. Once more, and you are confirmed in assurance for ever.

MARLOW (to him).   Hem! Stand by me, then, and when I'm down, throw in a word or two to set me up again.

MISS HARDCASTLE.   An observer, like you, upon life, were, I fear, disagreeably employed, since you must have had much more to censure than to approve.

MARLOW.   Pardon me, madam. I was always willing to be amused. The folly of most people is rather an object of mirth than uneasiness.

HASTINGS (to him).   Bravo, bravo. Never spoke so well in your whole life. Well, Miss Hardcastle, I see that you and Mr. Marlow are going to be very good company. I believe our being here will but embarrass the interview.

MARLOW.   Not in the least, Mr. Hastings. We like your company of all things. (To him.) Zounds! George, sure you won't go? How can you leave us?

HASTINGS.   Our presence will but spoil conversation, so we'll retire to the next room. (To him.) You don't consider, man, that we are to manage a little tête-à-tête of our own. (Exeunt.)

MISS HARDCASTLE (after a pause).   But you have not been wholly an observer, I presume, sir. The ladies, I should hope, have employed some part of your addresses.

MARLOW (relapsing into timidity).   Pardon me, madam, I—I—I—as yet have studied—only—to—deserve them.

MISS HARDCASTLE.   And that some say is the very worst way to obtain them.

MARLOW.   Perhaps so, madam. But I love to converse only with the more grave and sensible part of the sex.——But I'm afraid I grow tiresome.

MISS HARDCASTLE.   Not at all, sir; there is nothing I like so much as grave conversation myself: I could hear it for ever. Indeed, I have often been surprised how a man of sentiment could ever admire those light airy pleasures, where nothing reaches the heart.

MARLOW.   It's—a disease—of the mind, madam. In the variety of tastes there must be some who, wanting a relish for—um-a-um.

MISS HARDCASTLE.   I understand you, sir. There must be some, who, wanting a relish for refined pleasures, pretend to despise what they are incapable of tasting.

MARLOW.   My meaning, madam, but infinitely better expressed. And I can't help observing—a——

MISS HARDCASTLE (*aside*).   Who could ever suppose this fellow impudent upon some occasions? (*To him.*) You were going to observe, sir——

MARLOW.   I was observing, madam——I protest, madam, I forget what I was going to observe.

MISS HARDCASTLE (*aside*).   I vow and so do I. (*To him.*) You were observing, sir, that in this age of hypocrisy—something about hypocrisy, sir.

MARLOW.   Yes, madam. In this age of hypocrisy, there are few who upon strict enquiry do not—a—a—a——

MISS HARDCASTLE.   I understand you perfectly, sir.

MARLOW (*aside*).   Egad! and that's more than I do myself!

MISS HARDCASTLE.   You mean that in this hypocritical age there are few that do not condemn in public what they practise in private, and think they pay every debt to virtue when they praise it.

MARLOW.   True, madam; those who have most virtue in their mouths, have least of it in their bosoms. But I'm sure I tire you, madam.

MISS HARDCASTLE.   Not in the least, sir; there's something so agreeable and spirited in your manner, such life and force——pray, sir, go on.

MARLOW.   Yes, madam. I was saying——that there are some occasions——when a total want of courage, madam, destroys all the——and puts us——upon a——a a——

MISS HARDCASTLE.   I agree with you entirely, a want of courage upon some occasions assumes the appearance of ignorance, and betrays us when we most want to excel. I beg you'll proceed.

MARLOW.   Yes, Madam. Morally speaking, madam——but I see Miss Neville expecting us in the next room. I would not intrude for the world.

MISS HARDCASTLE.   I protest, sir, I never was more agreeably entertained in all my life. Pray go on.

MARLOW.   Yes, Madam. I was——But she beckons us to join her. Madam, shall I do myself the honour to attend you?

MISS HARDCASTLE.   Well then, I'll follow.

MARLOW (*aside*).   This pretty smooth dialogue has done for me. (*Exit.*)

MISS HARDCASTLE *sola.*

MISS HARDCASTLE.   Ha! ha! ha! Was there ever such a sober sentimental interview? I'm certain he scarce looked in my face the whole time. Yet the fellow, but for his unaccountable bashfulness, is pretty well, too. He has good sense, but then so buried in his fears, that it fatigues one more than ignorance. If I could teach him a little confidence, it would be doing somebody that I know of a piece of service. But who is that somebody?—that, faith, is a question I can scarce answer. (*Exit.*)

Enter TONY *and* MISS NEVILLE, *followed by* MRS. HARDCASTLE *and* HASTINGS.

TONY.   What do you follow me for, cousin Con? I wonder you're not ashamed to be so very engaging.

MISS NEVILLE.   I hope, cousin, one may speak to one's own relations, and not be to blame.

TONY.   Ay, but I know what sort of a relation you want to make me, though; but it won't do. I tell you, cousin Con, it won't do, so I beg you'll keep your distance, I want no nearer relationship. (*She follows coquetting him to the back scene.*)

MRS. HARDCASTLE.   Well! I vow, Mr. Hastings, you are very entertaining. There's nothing in the world I love to talk of so much as London, and the fashions, though I was never there myself.

HASTINGS.   Never there! You amaze me! From your air and manner, I concluded you had been bred all your life either at Ranelagh, St. James's, or Tower Wharf.

MRS. HARDCASTLE.   O! sir, you're only pleased to say so. We country persons can have no manner at all. I'm in love with the town, and that serves to raise me above some of our neighbouring rustics; but who can have a manner, that has never seen the Pantheon, the Grotto Gardens, the Borough, and such places where the nobility chiefly resort? All I can do is to enjoy London at second-hand. I take care to know every *tête-à-tête* from the Scandalous Magazine, and have all the fashions as they come out, in a letter from the two Miss Rickets of Crooked Lane. Pray how do you like this head, Mr. Hastings?

HASTINGS.   Extremely elegant and *degagée,* upon my word, madam. Your friseur is a Frenchman, I suppose?

MRS. HARDCASTLE.   I protest, I dressed it myself from a print in the Ladies' Memorandum-book for the last year.

HASTINGS.   Indeed. Such a head in a side-box, at the Playhouse, would draw as many gazers as my Lady Mayoress at a City Ball.

MRS. HARDCASTLE.   I vow, since inoculation began, there is no such thing to be seen as a plain woman; so one must dress a little particular or one may escape in the crowd.

HASTINGS.   But that can never be your case, madam, in any dress! (*Bowing.*)

MRS. HARDCASTLE.   Yet, what signifies *my* dressing when I have such a piece of antiquity by my side as Mr. Hardcastle? All I can say will never argue down a single button from his clothes. I have often wanted him to throw off his great flaxen wig, and where he was bald, to plaster it over like my Lord Pately, with powder.

HASTINGS.   You are right, madam; for, as among the ladies there are none ugly, so among the men there are none old.

MRS. HARDCASTLE.   But what do you think his answer was? Why, with his usual Gothic vivacity, he said I only wanted him to throw off his wig to convert it into a *tête* for my own wearing!

HASTINGS.   Intolerable! At your age you may wear what you please, and it must become you.

MRS. HARDCASTLE.   Pray, Mr. Hastings, what do you take to be the most fashionable age about town?

HASTINGS.   Some time ago forty was all the mode; but I'm told the ladies intend to bring up fifty for the ensuing winter.

MRS. HARDCASTLE.   Seriously. Then I shall be too young for the fashion!

HASTINGS.   No lady begins now to put on jewels till she's past forty. For instance, Miss there, in a polite circle, would be considered as a child, as a mere maker of samplers.

MRS. HARDCASTLE.   And yet Mrs. Niece thinks herself as much a woman, and is as fond of jewels as the oldest of us all.

HASTINGS.   Your niece, is she? And that young gentleman, a brother of yours, I should presume?

MRS. HARDCASTLE.   My son, sir. They are contracted to each other. Observe their little sports. They fall in and out ten times a day, as if they were man and wife already. (*To them.*) Well, Tony, child, what soft things are you saying to your cousin Constance, this evening?

TONY.   I have been saying no soft things; but that it's very hard to be followed about so. Ecod! I've not a place in the house now that's left to myself but the stable.

MRS. HARDCASTLE.   Never mind him, Con, my dear. He's in another story behind your back.

MISS NEVILLE.   There's something generous in my cousin's manner. He falls out before faces to be forgiven in private.

TONY.   That's a damned confounded——crack.

MRS. HARDCASTLE.   Ah! he's a sly one. Don't you think they're like each other about the mouth, Mr. Hastings? The Blenkinsop mouth to a T. They're of a size, too. Back to back, my pretties, that Mr. Hastings may see you. Come, Tony.

TONY.   You had as good not make me, I tell you. (*Measuring.*)

MISS NEVILLE.   O lud! he has almost cracked my head.

MRS. HARDCASTLE.   O, the monster! For shame, Tony. You a man, and behave so!

TONY.   If I'm a man, let me have my fortin. Ecod! I'll not be made a fool of no longer.

MRS. HARDCASTLE.   Is this, ungrateful boy, all that I'm to get for the pains I have taken in your education? I that have rocked you in your cradle, and fed that pretty mouth with a spoon! Did not I work that waistcoat to make you genteel? Did not I prescribe for you every day, and weep while the receipt was operating?

TONY.   Ecod! you had reason to weep, for you have been dosing me ever since I was born. I have gone through every receipt in the complete housewife ten times over; and you have thoughts of coursing me through *Quincy*

next spring. But, ecod! I tell you, I'll not be made a fool of no longer.

MRS. HARDCASTLE.   Wasn't it all for your good, viper? Wasn't it all for your good?

TONY.   I wish you'd let me and my good alone, then. Snubbing this way when I'm in spirits. If I'm to have any good, let it come of itself; not to keep dinging it, dinging it into one so.

MRS. HARDCASTLE.   That's false; I never see you when you're in spirits. No, Tony, you then go to the alehouse or kennel. I'm never to be delighted with your agreeable, wild notes, unfeeling monster!

TONY.   Ecod! Mamma, your own notes are the wildest of the two.

MRS. HARDCASTLE.   Was ever the like? But I see he wants to break my heart, I see he does.

HASTINGS.   Dear Madam, permit me to lecture the young gentleman a little. I'm certain I can persuade him to his duty.

MRS. HARDCASTLE.   Well! I must retire. Come, Constance, my love. You see, Mr. Hastings, the wretchedness of my situation. Was ever poor woman so plagued with a dear, sweet, pretty, provoking, undutiful boy? (*Exeunt* MRS. HARDCASTLE *and* MISS NEVILLE.)

HASTINGS, TONY.

TONY (*singing*). *There was a young man riding by, and fain would have his will. Rang do didlo dee.* Don't mind her. Let her cry. It's the comfort of her heart. I have seen her and sister cry over a book for an hour together, and they said, they liked the book the better the more it made them cry.

HASTINGS.   Then you're no friend to the ladies, I find, my pretty young gentleman?

TONY.   That's as I find 'um.

HASTINGS.   Not to her of your mother's choosing, I dare answer! And yet she appears to me a pretty, well-tempered girl.

TONY.   That's because you don't know her as well as I. Ecod! I know every inch about her; and there's not a more bitter cantankerous toad in all Christendom!

HASTINGS (*aside*). Pretty encouragement, this, for a lover.

TONY.   I have seen her since the height of that. She has as many tricks as a hare in a thicket, or a colt the first day's breaking.

HASTINGS.   To me she appears sensible and silent!

TONY.   Ay, before company. But when she's with her playmates she's as loud as a hog in a gate.

HASTINGS.   But there is a meek modesty about her that charms me.

TONY.   Yes, but curb her never so little, she kicks up, and you're flung in a ditch.

HASTINGS.   Well, but you must allow her a little beauty.—Yes, you must allow her some beauty.

TONY. Bandbox! She's all a made up thing, mun. Ah! could you but see Bet Bouncer of these parts, you might then talk of beauty. Ecod, she has two eyes as black as sloes, and cheeks as broad and red as a pulpit cushion. She'd make two of she.

HASTINGS. Well, what say you to a friend that would take this bitter bargain off your hands?

TONY. Anon.

HASTINGS. Would you thank him that would take Miss Neville, and leave you to happiness and your dear Betsy?

TONY. Ay; but where is there such a friend, for who would take *her?*

HASTINGS. I am he. If you but assist me, I'll engage to whip her off to France, and you shall never hear more of her.

TONY. Assist you! Ecod, I will, to the last drop of my blood. I'll clap a pair of horses to your chaise that shall trundle you off in a twinkling, and may be get you a part of her fortin besides, in jewels, that you little dream of.

HASTINGS. My dear 'Squire, this looks like a lad of spirit.

TONY. Come along then, and you shall see more of my spirit before you have done with me. (*Singing.*)

> We are the boys
> That fears no noise
> Where the thundering cannons roar. (*Exeunt.*)

ACT THREE

Enter HARDCASTLE *solus.*

HARDCASTLE. What could my old friend Sir Charles mean by recommending his son as the modestest young man in town? To me he appears the most impudent piece of brass that ever spoke with a tongue. He has taken possession of the easy chair by the fireside already. He took off his boots in the parlour, and desired me to see them taken care of. I'm desirous to know how his impudence affects my daughter.—She will certainly be shocked at it.

Enter MISS HARDCASTLE *plainly dressed.*

HARDCASTLE. Well, my Kate, I see you have changed your dress as I bid you; and yet, I believe, there was no great occasion.

MISS HARDCASTLE. I find such a pleasure, sir, in obeying your commands, that I take care to observe them without ever debating their propriety.

HARDCASTLE. And yet, Kate, I sometimes give you some cause, particularly when I recommended my *modest* gentleman to you as a lover to-day.

MISS HARDCASTLE. You taught me to expect something extraordinary, and I find the original exceeds the description!

HARDCASTLE. I was never so surprised in my life! He has quite confounded all my faculties!

MISS HARDCASTLE. I never saw anything like it: and a man of the world, too!

HARDCASTLE. Ay, he learned it all abroad,—what a fool was I, to think a young man could learn modesty by travelling. He might as soon learn wit at a masquerade.

MISS HARDCASTLE. It seems all natural to him.

HARDCASTLE. A good deal assisted by bad company and a French dancing-master.

MISS HARDCASTLE. Sure, you mistake, papa! a French dancing-master could never have taught him that timid look,—that awkward address,—that bashful manner——

HARDCASTLE. Whose look? whose manner? child!

MISS HARDCASTLE. Mr. Marlow's: his *mauvaise honte,* his timidity struck me at the first sight.

HARDCASTLE. Then your first sight deceived you; for I think him one of the most brazen first sights that ever astonished my senses!

MISS HARDCASTLE. Sure, sir, you rally! I never saw anyone so modest.

HARDCASTLE. And can you be serious! I never saw such a bouncing swaggering puppy since I was born. Bully Dawson was but a fool to him.

MISS HARDCASTLE. Surprising! He met me with a respectful bow, a stammering voice, and a look fixed on the ground.

HARDCASTLE. He met me with a loud voice, a lordly air, and a familiarity that made my blood freeze again.

MISS HARDCASTLE. He treated me with diffidence and respect; censured the manners of the age; admired the prudence of girls that never laughed; tired me with apologies for being tiresome; then left the room with a bow, and, *Madam, I would not for the world detain you.*

HARDCASTLE. He spoke to me as if he knew me all his life before. Asked twenty questions, and never waited for an answer. Interrupted my best remarks with some silly pun, and when I was in my best story of the Duke of Marlborough and Prince Eugene, he asked if I had not a good hand at making punch. Yes, Kate, he asked your father if he was a maker of punch!

MISS HARDCASTLE. One of us must certainly be mistaken.

HARDCASTLE. If he be what he has shown himself, I'm determined he shall never have my consent.

MISS HARDCASTLE. And if he be the sullen thing I take him, he shall never have mine.

HARDCASTLE. In one thing then we are agreed—to reject him.

MISS HARDCASTLE. Yes. But upon conditions. For if you should find him less impudent, and I more presuming; if you find him more respectful, and I more importunate— I don't know—the fellow is well enough for a man—Certainly we don't meet many such at a horse race in the country.

HARDCASTLE.   If we should find him so——But that's impossible. The first appearance has done my business. I'm seldom deceived in that.

MISS HARDCASTLE.   And yet there may be many good qualities under that first appearance.

HARDCASTLE.   Ay, when a girl finds a fellow's outside to her taste, she then sets about guessing the rest of his furniture. With her, a smooth face stands for good sense, and a genteel figure for every virtue.

MISS HARDCASTLE.   I hope, sir, a conversation begun with a compliment to my good sense won't end with a sneer at my understanding?

HARDCASTLE.   Pardon me, Kate. But if young Mr. Brazen can find the art of reconciling contradictions, he may please us both, perhaps.

MISS HARDCASTLE.   And as one of us must be mistaken, what if we go to make further discoveries?

HARDCASTLE.   Agreed. But depend on't I'm in the right.

MISS HARDCASTLE.   And depend on't I'm not much in the wrong. (*Exeunt.*)

Enter TONY *running in with a casket.*

TONY.   Ecod! I have got them. Here they are. My cousin Con's necklaces, bobs and all. My mother shan't cheat the poor souls out of their fortin neither. O! my genus, is that you?

Enter HASTINGS.

HASTINGS.   My dear friend, how have you managed with your mother? I hope you have amused her with pretending love for your cousin, and that you are willing to be reconciled at last? Our horses will be refreshed in a short time, and we shall soon be ready to set off.

TONY.   And here's something to bear your charges by the way. (*Giving the casket.*) Your sweetheart's jewels. Keep them, and hang those, I say, that would rob you of one of them!

HASTINGS.   But how have you procured them from your mother?

TONY.   Ask me no questions, and I'll tell you no fibs. I procured them by the rule of thumb. If I had not a key to every drawer in mother's bureau, how could I go to the alehouse so often as I do? An honest man may rob himself of his own at any time.

HASTINGS.   Thousands do it every day. But to be plain with you; Miss Neville is endeavouring to procure them from her aunt this very instant. If she succeeds, it will be the most delicate way at least of obtaining them.

TONY.   Well, keep them, till you know how it will be. But I know how it will be well enough, she'd as soon part with the only sound tooth in her head!

HASTINGS.   But I dread the effects of her resentment, when she finds she has lost them.

TONY.   Never you mind her resentment, leave *me* to manage that. I don't value her resentment the bounce of a cracker. Zounds! here they are! Morrice! Prance! (*Exit* HASTINGS.)

TONY, MRS. HARDCASTLE, MISS NEVILLE.

MRS. HARDCASTLE.   Indeed, Constance, you amaze me. Such a girl as you want jewels? It will be time enough for jewels, my dear, twenty years hence, when your beauty begins to want repairs.

MISS NEVILLE.   But what will repair beauty at forty, will certainly improve it at twenty, madam.

MRS. HARDCASTLE.   Yours, my dear, can admit of none. That natural blush is beyond a thousand ornaments. Besides, child, jewels are quite out at present. Don't you see half the ladies of our acquaintance, my Lady Kill-daylight, and Mrs. Crump, and the rest of them, carry their jewels to town, and bring nothing but paste and marcasites back?

MISS NEVILLE.   But who knows, madam, but somebody that shall be nameless would like me best with all my little finery about me?

MRS. HARDCASTLE.   Consult your glass, my dear, and then see, if with such a pair of eyes, you want any better sparklers. What do you think, Tony, my dear, does your cousin Con want any jewels, in your eyes, to set off her beauty?

TONY.   That's as thereafter may be.

MISS NEVILLE.   My dear aunt, if you knew how it would oblige me.

MRS. HARDCASTLE.   A parcel of old-fashioned rose and table-cut things. They would make you look like the court of King Solomon at a puppet-show. Besides, I believe I can't readily come at them. They may be missing, for aught I know to the contrary.

TONY (*apart to* MRS. HARDCASTLE). Then why don't you tell her so at once, as she's so longing for them? Tell her they're lost. It's the only way to quiet her. Say they're lost, and call me to bear witness.

MRS. HARDCASTLE (*apart to* TONY). You know, my dear, I'm only keeping them for you. So if I say they're gone, you'll bear me witness, will you? He! he! he!

TONY.   Never fear me. Ecod! I'll say I saw them taken out with my own eyes.

MISS NEVILLE.   I desire them but for a day, madam. Just to be permitted to show them as relics, and then they may be locked up again.

MRS. HARDCASTLE.   To be plain with you, my dear Constance, if I could find them, you should have them. They're missing, I assure you. Lost, for aught I know; but we must have patience wherever they are.

MISS NEVILLE.   I'll not believe it; this is but a shallow pretence to deny me. I know they're too valuable to be so slightly kept, and as you are to answer for the loss.

MRS. HARDCASTLE.   Don't be alarmed, Constance. If they be lost, I must restore an equivalent. But my son knows they are missing, and not to be found.

TONY.   That I can bear witness to. They are missing, and not to be found, I'll take my oath on't!

MRS. HARDCASTLE.   You must learn resignation, my dear; for though we lose our fortune, yet we should not lose our patience. See me, how calm I am!

MISS NEVILLE.   Ay, people are generally calm at the misfortunes of others.

MRS. HARDCASTLE.   Now, I wonder a girl of your good sense should waste a thought upon such trumpery. We shall soon find them; and, in the meantime, you shall make use of my garnets till your jewels be found.

MISS NEVILLE.   I detest garnets!

MRS. HARDCASTLE.   The most becoming things in the world to set off a clear complexion. You have often seen how well they look upon me. You *shall* have them. (*Exit.*)

MISS NEVILLE.   I dislike them of all things. You shan't stir.—Was ever anything so provoking to mislay my own jewels, and force me to wear her trumpery.

TONY.   Don't be a fool. If she gives you the garnets, take what you can get. The jewels are your own already. I have stolen them out of her bureau, and she does not know it. Fly to your spark, he'll tell you more of the matter. Leave me to manage *her.*

MISS NEVILLE.   My dear cousin!

TONY.   Vanish. She's here, and has missed them already. Zounds! how she fidgets and spits about like a Catherine wheel!

Enter MRS. HARDCASTLE.

MRS. HARDCASTLE.   Confusion! thieves! robbers! We are cheated, plundered, broke open, undone!

TONY.   What's the matter, what's the matter, mamma? I hope nothing has happened to any of the good family!

MRS. HARDCASTLE.   We are robbed. My bureau has been broke open, the jewels taken out, and I'm undone!

TONY.   Oh! is that all? Ha! ha! ha! By the laws, I never saw it better acted in my life. Ecod, I thought you was ruined in earnest, ha, ha, ha!

MRS. HARDCASTLE.   Why, boy, I *am* ruined in earnest. My bureau has been broke open, and all taken away.

TONY.   Stick to that; ha, ha, ha! stick to that. I'll bear witness, you know, call me to bear witness.

MRS. HARDCASTLE.   I tell you, Tony, by all that's precious, the jewels are gone, and I shall be ruined for ever.

TONY.   Sure I know they're gone, and I am to say so.

MRS. HARDCASTLE.   My dearest Tony, but hear me. They're gone, I say.

TONY.   By the laws, mamma, you make me for to laugh, ha! ha! I know who took them well enough, ha! ha! ha!

MRS. HARDCASTLE.   Was there ever such a blockhead, that can't tell the difference between jest and earnest! I tell you I'm not in jest, booby!

TONY.   That's right, that's right! You must be in a bitter passion, and then nobody will suspect either of us. I'll bear witness that they are gone.

MRS. HARDCASTLE.   Was there ever such a cross-grained brute, that won't hear me! Can you bear witness that you're no better than a fool? Was ever poor woman so beset with fools on one hand, and thieves on the other?

TONY.   I can bear witness to that.

MRS. HARDCASTLE.   Bear witness again, you blockhead, you, and I'll turn you out of the room directly. My poor niece, what will become of *her?* Do you laugh, you unfeeling brute, as if you enjoyed my distress?

TONY.   I can bear witness to that.

MRS. HARDCASTLE.   Do you insult me, monster? I'll teach you to vex your mother, I will!

TONY.   I can bear witness to that. (*He runs off, she follows him.*)

Enter MISS HARDCASTLE *and* MAID.

MISS HARDCASTLE.   What an unaccountable creature is that brother of mine, to send them to the house as an inn, ha! ha! I don't wonder at his impudence.

MAID.   But what is more, madam, the young gentleman as you passed by in your present dress, asked me if you were the barmaid? He mistook you for the barmaid, madam!

MISS HARDCASTLE.   Did he? Then as I live I'm resolved to keep up the delusion. Tell me, Pimple, how do you like my present dress? Don't you think I look something like Cherry in the Beaux' Stratagem?

MAID.   It's the dress, madam, that every lady wears in the country, but when she visits or receives company.

MISS HARDCASTLE.   And are you sure he does not remember my face or person?

MAID.   Certain of it!

MISS HARDCASTLE.   I vow, I thought so; for though we spoke for some time together, yet his fears were such, that he never once looked up during the interview. Indeed, if he had, my bonnet would have kept him from seeing me.

MAID.   But what do you hope from keeping him in his mistake?

MISS HARDCASTLE.   In the first place, I shall be *seen,* and that is no small advantage to a girl who brings her face to market. Then I shall perhaps make an acquaintance, and that's no small victory gained over one who never addresses any but the wildest of her sex. But my chief aim is to take my gentleman off his guard, and like an invisible champion of romance examine the giant's force before I offer to combat.

MAID.   But you are sure you can act your part, and disguise your voice, so that he may mistake that, as he has already mistaken your person?

MISS HARDCASTLE.   Never fear me. I think I have got the true bar cant.—Did your honour call?——Attend the Lion there.——Pipes and tobacco for the Angel.—The Lamb has been outrageous this half hour!

MAID.   It will do, madam. But he's here. (*Exit* MAID.)

Enter MARLOW.

MARLOW.   What a bawling in every part of the house; I have scarce a moment's repose. If I go to the best room, there I find my host and his story. If I fly to the gallery, there we have my hostess with her curtsey down to the ground. I have at last got a moment to myself, and now for recollection. (*Walks and muses.*)

MISS HARDCASTLE.   Did you call, sir? did your honour call?

MARLOW (*musing*).   As for Miss Hardcastle, she's too grave and sentimental for me.

MISS HARDCASTLE.   Did your honour call? (*She still places herself before him, he turning away.*)

MARLOW.   No, child! (*Musing.*) Besides, from the glimpse I had of her, I think she squints.

MISS HARDCASTLE.   I'm sure, sir, I heard the bell ring.

MARLOW.   No! no! (*Musing.*) I have pleased my father, however, by coming down, and I'll to-morrow please myself by returning. (*Taking out his tablets, and perusing.*)

MISS HARDCASTLE.   Perhaps the other gentleman called, sir?

MARLOW.   I tell you, no.

MISS HARDCASTLE.   I should be glad to know, sir. We have such a parcel of servants.

MARLOW.   No, no, I tell you. (*Looks full in her face.*) Yes, child, I think I did call. I wanted——I wanted——I vow, child, you are vastly handsome!

MISS HARDCASTLE.   O la, sir, you'll make one ashamed.

MARLOW.   Never saw a more sprightly malicious eye. Yes, yes, my dear, I did call. Have you got any of your—a— what d'ye call it in the house?

MISS HARDCASTLE.   No, sir, we have been out of that these ten days.

MARLOW.   One may call in this house, I find, to very little purpose. Suppose I should call for a taste, just by way of trial, of the nectar of your lips; perhaps I might be disappointed in that, too!

MISS HARDCASTLE.   Nectar! nectar! that's a liquor there's no call for in these parts. French, I suppose. We keep no French wines here, sir.

MARLOW.   Of true English growth, I assure you.

MISS HARDCASTLE.   Then it's odd I should not know it. We brew all sorts of wines in this house, and I have lived here these eighteen years.

MARLOW.   Eighteen years! Why one would think, child, you kept the bar before you were born. How old are you?

MISS HARDCASTLE.   O! sir, I must not tell my age. They say women and music should never be dated.

MARLOW.   To guess at this distance, you can't be much above forty. (*Approaching.*) Yet nearer I don't think so much. (*Approaching.*) By coming close to some women they look younger still; but when we come very close indeed—(*Attempting to kiss her.*)

MISS HARDCASTLE.   Pray, sir, keep your distance. One would think you wanted to know one's age as they do horses, by mark of mouth.

MARLOW.   I protest, child, you use me extremely ill. If you keep me at this distance, how is it possible you and I can be ever acquainted?

MISS HARDCASTLE.   And who wants to be acquainted with you? I want no such acquaintance, not I. I'm sure you did not treat Miss Hardcastle that was here awhile ago in this obstropalous manner. I'll warrant me, before her you looked dashed, and kept bowing to the ground, and talked, for all the world, as if you was before a justice of the peace.

MARLOW (*aside*).   Egad! she has hit it, sure enough. (*To her.*) In awe of her, child? Ha! ha! ha! A mere awkward, squinting thing, no, no! I find you don't know me. I laughed, and rallied her a little; but I was unwilling to be too severe. No, I could not be too severe, curse me!

MISS HARDCASTLE.   O! then, sir, you are a favourite, I find, among the ladies?

MARLOW.   Yes, my dear, a great favourite. And yet, hang me, I don't see what they find in me to follow. At the Ladies' Club in town I'm called their agreeable Rattle. Rattle, child, is not my real name, but one I'm known by. My name is Solomons. Mr. Solomons, my dear, at your service. (*Offering to salute her.*)

MISS HARDCASTLE.   Hold, sir; you were introducing me to your club, not to yourself. And you're so great a favourite there, you say?

MARLOW.   Yes, my dear. There's Mrs. Mantrap, Lady Betty Blackleg, the Countess of Sligo, Mrs. Longhorns, old Miss Biddy Buckskin, and your humble servant, keep up the spirit of the place.

MISS HARDCASTLE.   Then it's a very merry place, I suppose.

MARLOW.   Yes, as merry as cards, suppers, wine, and old women can make us.

MISS HARDCASTLE.   And their agreeable Rattle, ha! ha! ha!

MARLOW (*aside*).   Egad! I don't quite like this chit. She looks knowing, methinks. You laugh, child!

MISS HARDCASTLE.   I can't but laugh to think what time they all have for minding their work or their family.

MARLOW (*aside*).   All's well, she don't laugh at me. (*To her.*) Do *you* ever work, child?

MISS HARDCASTLE.   Ay, sure. There's not a screen or a quilt in the whole house but what can bear witness to that.

MARLOW.   Odso! Then you must show me your embroidery. I embroider and draw patterns myself a little. If you want a judge of your work you must apply to me. (*Seizing her hand.*)

MISS HARDCASTLE.   Ay, but the colours don't look well by candlelight. You shall see all in the morning. (*Struggling.*)

MARLOW.   And why not now, my angel? Such beauty fires beyond the power of resistance.——Pshaw! the father here! My old luck: I never nicked seven that I did not throw ames-ace three times following. (*Exit* MARLOW.)

Enter HARDCASTLE, *who stands in surprise.*

HARDCASTLE.   So, madam! So I find *this* is your *modest* lover. This is your humble admirer that kept his eyes fixed on the ground, and only adored at a humble distance. Kate, Kate, art thou not ashamed to deceive your father so?

MISS HARDCASTLE.   Never trust me, dear papa, but he's still the modest man I first took him for, you'll be convinced of it as well as I.

HARDCASTLE.   By the hand of my body, I believe his impudence is infectious! Didn't I see him seize your hand? Didn't I see him haul you about like a milkmaid? and now you talk of his respect and his modesty, forsooth!

MISS HARDCASTLE.   But if I shortly convince you of his modesty, that he has only the faults that will pass off with time, and the virtues that will improve with age, I hope you'll forgive him.

HARDCASTLE.   The girl would actually make one run mad! I tell you I'll not be convinced. I am convinced. He has scarcely been three hours in the house, and he has already encroached on all my prerogatives. You may like his impudence, and call it modesty. But my son-in-law, madam, must have very different qualifications.

MISS HARDCASTLE.   Sir, I ask but this night to convince you.

HARDCASTLE.   You shall not have half the time, for I have thoughts of turning him out this very hour.

MISS HARDCASTLE.   Give me that hour then, and I hope to satisfy you.

HARDCASTLE.   Well, an hour let it be then. But I'll have no trifling with your father. All fair and open, do you mind me?

MISS HARDCASTLE.   I hope, sir, you have ever found that I considered your commands as my pride; for your kindness is such, that my duty as yet has been inclination. (*Exeunt.*)

ACT FOUR

Enter HASTINGS *and* MISS NEVILLE.

HASTINGS.   You surprise me! Sir Charles Marlow expected here this night? Where have you had your information?

MISS NEVILLE.   You may depend upon it. I just saw his letter to Mr. Hardcastle, in which he tells him he intends setting out a few hours after his son.

HASTINGS.   Then, my Constance, all must be completed before he arrives. He knows me; and should he find me here, would discover my name, and perhaps my designs, to the rest of the family.

MISS NEVILLE.   The jewels, I hope, are safe.

HASTINGS.   Yes, yes. I have sent them to Marlow, who keeps the keys of our baggage. In the meantime, I'll go to prepare matters for our elopement. I have had the 'Squire's promise of a fresh pair of horses; and, if I should not see him again, will write him further directions. (*Exit.*)

MISS NEVILLE.   Well! success attend you. In the meantime, I'll go amuse my aunt with the old pretence of a violent passion for my cousin. (*Exit.*)

Enter MARLOW, *followed by a* SERVANT.

MARLOW.   I wonder what Hastings could mean by sending me so valuable a thing as a casket to keep for him, when he knows the only place I have is the seat of a post-coach at an inn door. Have you deposited the casket with the landlady, as I ordered you? Have you put it into her own hands?

SERVANT.   Yes, your honour.

MARLOW.   She said she'd keep it safe, did she?

SERVANT.   Yes, she said she'd keep it safe enough; she asked me how I came by it? and she said she had a great mind to make me give an account of myself. (*Exit* SERVANT.)

MARLOW.   Ha! ha! ha! They're safe, however. What an unaccountable set of beings have we got amongst! This little barmaid though runs in my head most strangely, and drives out the absurdities of all the rest of the family. She's mine, she must be mine, or I'm greatly mistaken!

Enter HASTINGS.

HASTINGS.   Bless me! I quite forgot to tell her that I intended to prepare at the bottom of the garden. Marlow here, and in spirits too!

MARLOW.   Give me joy, George! Crown me, shadow me with laurels! Well, George, after all, we modest fellows don't want for success among the women.

HASTINGS.   Some women, you mean. But what success has your honour's modesty been crowned with now, that it grows so insolent upon us?

MARLOW.   Didn't you see the tempting, brisk, lovely little thing that runs about the house with a bunch of keys to its girdle?

HASTINGS.   Well! and what then?

MARLOW.   She's mine, you rogue, you. Such fire, such motion, such eyes, such lips——but egad! she would not let me kiss them though.

HASTINGS.   But are you sure, so very sure of her?

MARLOW.   Why, man, she talked of showing me her work above-stairs, and I am to improve the pattern.

HASTINGS.   But how can *you*, Charles, go about to rob a woman of her honour?

MARLOW.   Pshaw! pshaw! we all know the honour of the barmaid of an inn. I don't intend to *rob* her, take my word for it, there's nothing in this house, I shan't honestly *pay* for!

HASTINGS.   I believe the girl has virtue.

MARLOW.   And if she has, I should be the last man in the world that would attempt to corrupt it.

HASTINGS.   You have taken care, I hope, of the casket I sent you to lock up? It's in safety?

MARLOW.   Yes, yes. It's safe enough. I have taken care of it. But how could you think the seat of a post-coach at an inn door a place of safety? Ah! numskull! I have taken better precautions for you than you did for yourself.—— I have——

HASTINGS.   What!

MARLOW.   I have sent it to the landlady to keep for you.

HASTINGS.   To the landlady!

MARLOW.   The landlady.

HASTINGS.   You did!

MARLOW.   I did. She's to be answerable for its forthcoming, you know.

HASTINGS.   Yes, she'll bring it forth with a witness.

MARLOW.   Wasn't I right? I believe you'll allow that I acted prudently upon this occasion?

HASTINGS (*aside*). He must not see my uneasiness.

MARLOW.   You seem a little disconcerted, though, methinks. Sure nothing has happened?

HASTINGS.   No, nothing. Never was I in better spirits in all my life. And so you left it with the landlady, who, no doubt, very readily undertook the charge?

MARLOW.   Rather too readily. For she not only kept the casket, but, through her great precaution, was going to keep the messenger too. Ha! ha! ha!

HASTINGS.   He! he! he! They're safe, however.

MARLOW.   As a guinea in a miser's purse.

HASTINGS (*aside*). So now all hopes of fortune are at an end, and we must set off without it. (*To him.*) Well, Charles, I'll leave you to your meditations on the pretty barmaid, and, he! he! he! may you be as successful for yourself as you have been for me. (*Exit.*)

MARLOW.   Thank ye, George! I ask no more. Ha! ha! ha!

Enter HARDCASTLE.

HARDCASTLE.   I no longer know my own house. It's turned all topsy-turvy. His servants have got drunk already. I'll bear it no longer, and yet, from my respect for his father, I'll be calm. (*To him.*) Mr. Marlow, your servant. I'm your very humble servant. (*Bowing low.*)

MARLOW.   Sir, your humble servant. (*Aside.*) What's to be the wonder now?

HARDCASTLE.   I believe, sir, you must be sensible, sir, that no man alive ought to be more welcome than your father's son, sir. I hope you think so?

MARLOW.   I do, from my soul, sir. I don't want much entreaty. I generally make my father's son welcome wherever he goes.

HARDCASTLE.   I believe you do, from my soul, sir. But though I say nothing to your own conduct, that of your servants is insufferable. Their manner of drinking is setting a very bad example in this house, I assure you.

MARLOW.   I protest, my very good sir, that's no fault of mine. If they don't drink as they ought *they* are to blame. I ordered them not to spare the cellar, I did, I assure you. (*To the side scene.*) Here, let one of my servants come up. (*To him.*) My positive directions were, that as I did not drink myself, they should make up for my deficiencies below.

HARDCASTLE.   Then they had your orders for what they do! I'm satisfied!

MARLOW.   They had, I assure you. You shall hear from one of themselves.

Enter SERVANT, *drunk*.

MARLOW.   You, Jeremy! Come forward, sirrah! What were my orders? Were you not told to drink freely, and call for what you thought fit, for the good of the house?

HARDCASTLE (*aside*). I begin to lose my patience.

JEREMY.   Please your honour, liberty and Fleet Street for ever! Though I'm but a servant, I'm as good as another man. I'll drink for no man before supper, sir, dammy! Good liquor will sit upon a good supper, but a good supper will not sit upon——hiccup——upon my conscience, sir.

MARLOW.   You see, my old friend, the fellow is as drunk as he can possibly be. I don't know what you'd have more, unless you'd have the poor devil soused in a beer-barrel.

HARDCASTLE.   Zounds! He'll drive me distracted if I contain myself any longer. Mr. Marlow, sir; I have submitted to your insolence for more than four hours, and I see no likelihood of its coming to an end. I'm now resolved to be master here, sir, and I desire that you and your drunken pack may leave my house directly.

MARLOW.   Leave your house!—Sure, you jest, my good friend! What, when I'm doing what I can to please you!

HARDCASTLE.   I tell you, sir, you don't please me; so I desire you'll leave my house.

MARLOW.   Sure, you cannot be serious! At this time of night, and such a night! You only mean to banter me!

HARDCASTLE.   I tell you, sir, I'm serious; and, now that my passions are roused, I say this house is mine, sir; this house is mine, and I command you to leave it directly.

MARLOW.   Ha! ha! ha! A puddle in a storm. I shan't stir a step, I assure you. (*In a serious tone.*) This your house, fellow! It's my house. This is my house. Mine, while I choose to stay. What right have you to bid me leave this house, sir? I never met with such impudence, curse me, never in my whole life before!

HARDCASTLE.   Nor I, confound me if ever I did! To come to my house, to call for what he likes, to turn me out of my own chair, to insult the family, to order his servants to get drunk, and then to tell me *This house is mine, sir.* By all that's impudent, it makes me laugh. Ha! ha! ha! Pray, sir, (*bantering*) as you take the house, what think you of taking the rest of the furniture? There's a pair of silver candlesticks, and there's a fire-screen, and here's a pair of brazen-nosed bellows, perhaps you may take a fancy to them?

MARLOW.   Bring me your bill, sir, bring me your bill, and let's make no more words about it.

HARDCASTLE.   There are a set of prints, too. What think you of the Rake's Progress for your own apartment?

MARLOW.   Bring me your bill, I say; and I'll leave you and your infernal house directly.

HARDCASTLE.   Then there's a mahogany table, that you may see your own face in.

MARLOW.   My bill, I say.

HARDCASTLE.   I had forgot the great chair, for your own particular slumbers, after a hearty meal.

MARLOW.   Zounds! bring me my bill, I say, and let's hear no more on't.

HARDCASTLE.   Young man, young man, from your father's letter to me, I was taught to expect a well-bred modest man, as a visitor here, but now I find him no better than a coxcomb and a bully; but he will be down here presently, and shall hear more of it. (*Exit.*)

MARLOW.   How's this! Sure, I have not mistaken the house? Everything looks like an inn. The servants cry "coming." The attendance is awkward; the barmaid, too, to attend us. But she's here, and will further inform me. Whither so fast, child? A word with you.

Enter MISS HARDCASTLE.

MISS HARDCASTLE.   Let it be short, then. I'm in a hurry.— (*Aside.*) I believe he begins to find out his mistake, but it's too soon quite to undeceive him.

MARLOW.   Pray, child, answer me one question. What are you, and what may your business in this house be?

MISS HARDCASTLE.   A relation of the family, sir.

MARLOW.   What? A poor relation?

MISS HARDCASTLE.   Yes, sir. A poor relation appointed to keep the keys, and to see that the guests want nothing in my power to give them.

MARLOW.   That is, you act as the barmaid of this inn.

MISS HARDCASTLE.   Inn! O law!—What brought that in your head? One of the best families in the county keep an inn! Ha, ha, ha, old Mr. Hardcastle's house an inn!

MARLOW.   Mr. Hardcastle's house! Is this house Mr. Hardcastle's house, child?

MISS HARDCASTLE.   Ay, sure. Whose else should it be?

MARLOW.   So then all's out, and I have been damnably imposed on. O, confound my stupid head, I shall be laughed at over the whole town. I shall be stuck up in caricature in all the print-shops. The Dullissimo Macaroni. To mistake this house of all others for an inn, and my father's old friend for an innkeeper! What a swaggering puppy must he take me for. What a silly puppy do I find myself. There again, may I be hanged, my dear, but I mistook you for the barmaid!

MISS HARDCASTLE.   Dear me! dear me! I'm sure there's nothing in my *behaviour* to put me upon a level with one of that stamp.

MARLOW.   Nothing, my dear, nothing. But I was in for a list of blunders, and could not help making you a subscriber. My stupidity saw everything the wrong way. I mistook your assiduity for assurance, and your simplicity for allurement. But it's over—this house I no more show *my* face in!

MISS HARDCASTLE.   I hope, sir, I have done nothing to disoblige you. I'm sure I should be sorry to affront any gentleman who has been so polite, and said so many civil things to me. I'm sure I should be sorry (*pretending to cry*) if he left the family upon my account. I'm sure I should be sorry people said anything amiss, since I have no fortune but my character.

MARLOW (*aside*). By heaven, she weeps. This is the first mark of tenderness I ever had from a modest woman, and it touches me. (*To her.*) Excuse me, my lovely girl, you are the only part of the family I leave with reluctance. But to be plain with you, the difference of our birth, fortune and education makes an honourable connexion impossible; and I can never harbour a thought of seducing simplicity that trusted in my honour, or bringing ruin upon one whose only fault was being too lovely.

MISS HARDCASTLE (*aside*). Generous man! I now begin to admire him. (*To him.*) But I'm sure my family is as good as Miss Hardcastle's, and though I'm poor, that's no great misfortune to a contented mind, and, until this moment, I never thought that it was bad to want fortune.

MARLOW.   And why now, my pretty simplicity?

MISS HARDCASTLE.   Because it puts me at a distance from one, that if I had a thousand pound I would give it all to.

MARLOW (*aside*). This simplicity bewitches me, so that if I stay I'm undone. I must make one bold effort, and leave her. (*To her.*) Your partiality in my favour, my dear, touches me most sensibly, and were I to live for myself alone, I could easily fix my choice. But I owe too much to the opinion of the world, too much to the authority of a father, so that—I can scarcely speak it—it affects me! Farewell! (*Exit.*)

MISS HARDCASTLE.   I never knew half his merit till now. He shall not go, if I have power or art to detain him. I'll still preserve the character in which I stooped to conquer, but will undeceive my papa, who, perhaps, may laugh him out of his resolution. (*Exit.*)

Enter TONY, MISS NEVILLE.

TONY.   Ay, you may steal for yourselves the next time. I have done my duty. She has got the jewels again, that's a sure thing; but she believes it was all a mistake of the servants.

MISS NEVILLE.   But, my dear cousin, sure, you won't forsake us in this distress. If she in the least suspects that I am going off, I shall certainly be locked up, or sent to my aunt Pedigree's, which is ten times worse.

TONY.   To be sure, aunts of all kinds are damned bad things. But what can I do? I have got you a pair of horses that will fly like Whistlejacket, and I'm sure you can't say but I have courted you nicely before her face. Here she comes, we must court a bit or two more, for fear she should suspect us. (*They retire, and seem to fondle.*)

Enter MRS. HARDCASTLE.

MRS. HARDCASTLE.   Well, I was greatly fluttered, to be sure. But my son tells me it was all a mistake of the servants. I shan't be easy, however, till they are fairly married, and then let her keep her own fortune. But what do I see! Fondling together, as I'm alive! I never saw Tony so sprightly before. Ah! have I caught you, my pretty doves! What, billing, exchanging stolen glances, and broken murmurs! Ah!

TONY.   As for murmurs, mother, we grumble a little now and then, to be sure. But there's no love lost between us.

MRS. HARDCASTLE.   A mere sprinkling, Tony, upon the flame, only to make it burn brighter.

MISS NEVILLE.   Cousin Tony promises to give us more of his company at home. Indeed, he shan't leave us any more. It won't leave us, cousin Tony, will it?

TONY.   O! it's a pretty creature. No, I'd sooner leave my horse in a pound, than leave you when you smile upon one so. Your laugh makes you so becoming.

MISS NEVILLE.   Agreeable cousin! Who can help admiring that natural humour, that pleasant, broad, red, thoughtless (*patting his cheek*), ah! it's a bold face.

MRS. HARDCASTLE.   Pretty innocence!

TONY.   I'm sure I always loved Cousin Con's hazel eyes, and her pretty long fingers, that she twists this way and that, over the haspicholls, like a parcel of bobbins.

MRS. HARDCASTLE.   Ah, he would charm the bird from the tree. I was never so happy before. My boy takes after his father, poor Mr. Lumpkin, exactly. The jewels, my dear Con, shall be yours incontinently. You shall have them. Isn't he a sweet boy, my dear? You shall be married to-morrow, and we'll put off the rest of his education, like Dr. Drowsy's sermons, to a fitter opportunity.

Enter DIGGORY.

DIGGORY.   Where's the 'Squire? I have got a letter for your worship.

TONY.   Give it to my mamma. She reads all my letters first.

DIGGORY.   I had orders to deliver it into your own hands.

TONY.   Who does it come from?

DIGGORY.   Your worship mun ask that of the letter itself.

TONY.   I could wish to know, though. (*Turning the letter, and gazing on it.*)

MISS NEVILLE (*aside*). Undone, undone! A letter to him from Hastings. I know the hand. If my aunt sees it we are ruined for ever. I'll keep her employed a little if I can. (*To* MRS. HARDCASTLE.) But I have not told you, madam, of my cousin's smart answer just now to Mr. Marlow. We so laughed—you must know, madam—this way a little, for he must not hear us. (*They confer.*)

TONY   (*still gazing*). A damned cramp piece of penmanship, as ever I saw in my life. I can read your print-hand very well. But here there are such handles, and shanks, and dashes, that one can scarce tell the head from the tail. *To Anthony Lumpkin, Esquire*. It's very odd, I can read the outside of my letters, where my own name is, well enough. But when I come to open it, it's all—buzz. That's hard, very hard; for the inside of the letter is always the cream of the correspondence.

MRS. HARDCASTLE.   Ha! ha! ha! Very well, very well. And so my son was too hard for the philosopher!

MISS NEVILLE.   Yes, madam; but you must hear the rest, madam. A little more this way, or he may hear us. You'll hear how he puzzled him again.

MRS. HARDCASTLE.   He seems strangely puzzled now himself, me-thinks.

TONY (*still gazing*). A damned up-and-down hand, as if it was disguised in liquor. (*Reading.*) *Dear Sir*. Ay, that's that. Then there's an *M*, and a *T*, and an *S*, but whether the next be an *izzard* or an *R*, confound me, I cannot tell!

MRS. HARDCASTLE.   What's that, my dear? Can I give you any assistance?

MISS NEVILLE.   Pray, aunt, let me read it. Nobody reads a cramp hand better than I. (*Twitching the letter from her.*) Do you know who it is from?

TONY.   Can't tell, except from Dick Ginger the feeder.

MISS NEVILLE.   Ay, so it is. (*Pretending to read.*) Dear 'Squire, Hoping that you're in health, as I am at this present. The gentlemen of the Shakebag club has cut the gentlemen of Goose-green quite out of the feather. The odds—um—odd battle—um—long fighting—um, here, here, it's all about cocks, and fighting; it's of no consequence, here, put it up, put it up. (*Thrusting the crumpled letter upon him.*)

TONY.   But I tell you, miss, it's of all the consequence in the world! I would not lose the rest of it for a guinea! Here, mother, do you make it out? Of no consequence! (*Giving* MRS. HARDCASTLE *the letter.*)

MRS. HARDCASTLE.   How's this! (*Reads.*) Dear 'Squire, I'm now waiting for Miss Neville, with a post-chaise and pair, at the bottom of the garden, but I find my horses yet unable to perform the journey. I expect you'll assist us with a pair of fresh horses, as you promised. Dispatch is necessary, as the *hag* (ay, the hag) your mother, will otherwise suspect us. Yours, Hastings. Grant me patience. I shall run distracted! My rage chokes me.

MISS NEVILLE.   I hope, madam, you'll suspend your resentment for a few moments, and not impute to me any impertinence, or sinister design that belongs to another.

MRS. HARDCASTLE (*curtseying very low*).   Fine spoken, madam, you are most miraculously polite and engaging, and quite the very pink of courtesy and circumspection, madam. (*Changing her tone.*) And you, you great ill-fashioned oaf, with scarce sense enough to keep your mouth shut. Were you too joined against me? But I'll defeat all your plots in a moment. As for you, madam, since you have got a pair of fresh horses ready, it would be cruel to disappoint them. So, if you please, instead of running away with your spark, prepare, this very moment, to run off with *me.* Your old aunt Pedigree will keep you secure. I'll warrant me. You too, sir, may mount your horse, and guard us upon the way. Here, Thomas, Roger, Diggory, I'll show you that I wish you better than you do yourselves. (*Exit.*)

MISS NEVILLE.   So now I'm completely ruined.

TONY.   Ay, that's a sure thing.

MISS NEVILLE.   What better could be expected from being connected with such a stupid fool, and after all the nods and signs I made him?

TONY.   By the laws, miss, it was your own cleverness, and not my stupidity, that did your business. You were so nice and so busy with your Shakebags and Goose-greens, that I thought you could never be making believe.

Enter HASTINGS.

HASTINGS.   So, sir, I find by my servant, that you have shown my letter, and betrayed us. Was this well done, young gentleman?

TONY.   Here's another. Ask miss there who betrayed you. Ecod, it was her doing, not mine.

Enter MARLOW.

MARLOW.   So I have been finely used here among you. Rendered contemptible, driven into ill manners, despised, insulted, laughed at.

TONY.   Here's another. We shall have old Bedlam broke loose presently.

MISS NEVILLE.   And there, sir, is the gentleman to whom we all owe every obligation.

MARLOW.   What can I say to him, a mere boy, an idiot, whose ignorance and age are a protection?

HASTINGS.   A poor contemptible booby that would but disgrace correction.

MISS NEVILLE.   Yet with cunning and malice enough to make himself merry with all our embarrassments.

HASTINGS.   An insensible cub.

MARLOW.   Replete with tricks and mischief.

TONY.   Baw! damme, but I'll fight you both one after the other,——with baskets.

MARLOW.   As for him, he's below resentment. But your conduct, Mr. Hastings, requires an explanation. You knew of my mistakes, yet would not undeceive me.

HASTINGS.   Tortured as I am with my own disappointments, is this a time for explanations? It is not friendly, Mr. Marlow.

MARLOW.   But, sir—

MISS NEVILLE.   Mr. Marlow, we never kept on your mistake, till it was too late to undeceive you. Be pacified.

Enter SERVANT.

SERVANT.   My mistress desires you'll get ready immediately, madam. The horses are putting to. Your hat and things are in the next room. We are to go thirty miles before morning. (*Exit* SERVANT.)

MISS NEVILLE.   Well, well; I'll come presently.

MARLOW (*to* HASTINGS).   Was it well done, sir, to assist in rendering me ridiculous? To hang me out for the scorn of all my acquaintance? Depend upon it, sir, I shall expect an explanation.

HASTINGS.   Was it well done, sir, if you're upon that subject, to deliver what I entrusted to yourself, to the care of another, sir?

MISS NEVILLE.   Mr. Hastings. Mr. Marlow. Why will you increase my distress by this groundless dispute? I implore, I entreat you——

Enter SERVANT.

SERVANT.   Your cloak, madam. My mistress is impatient.

MISS NEVILLE.   I come. Pray be pacified. If I leave you thus, I shall die with apprehension!

Enter SERVANT.

SERVANT. Your fan, muff, and gloves, madam. The horses are waiting.

MISS NEVILLE. O, Mr. Marlow! if you knew what a scene of constraint and ill-nature lies before me, I'm sure it would convert your resentment into pity.

MARLOW. I'm so distracted with a variety of passions, that I don't know what I do. Forgive me, madam. George, forgive me. You know my hasty temper, and should not exasperate it.

HASTINGS. The torture of my situation is my only excuse.

MISS NEVILLE. Well, my dear Hastings, if you have that esteem for me that I think, that I am sure you have, your constancy for three years will but increase the happiness of our future connection. If—

MRS. HARDCASTLE (*within*). Miss Neville. Constance, why, Constance, I say.

MISS NEVILLE. I'm coming. Well, constancy. Remember, constancy is the word. (*Exit.*)

HASTINGS. My heart! How can I support this! To be so near happiness, and such happiness!

MARLOW (*to* TONY). You see now, young gentleman, the effects of your folly. What might be amusement to you, is here disappointment, and even distress.

TONY (*from a reverie*). Ecod, I have hit it. It's here. Your hands. Yours and yours, my poor Sulky. My boots there, ho! Meet me two hours hence at the bottom of the garden; and if you don't find Tony Lumpkin a more good-natur'd fellow than you thought for, I'll give you leave to take my best horse, and Bet Bouncer into the bargain! Come along. My boots, ho! (*Exeunt.*)

ACT FIVE

SCENE—CONTINUES.

Enter HASTINGS *and* SERVANT.

HASTINGS. You saw the old lady and Miss Neville drive off, you say?

SERVANT. Yes, your honour. They went off in a post-coach, and the young 'Squire went on horseback. They're thirty miles off by this time.

HASTINGS. Then all my hopes are over.

SERVANT. Yes, sir. Old Sir Charles is arrived. He and the old gentleman of the house have been laughing at Mr. Marlow's mistake this half hour. They are coming this way.

HASTINGS. Then I must not be seen. So now to my fruitless appointment at the bottom of the garden. This is about the time. (*Exit.*)

Enter SIR CHARLES *and* HARDCASTLE.

HARDCASTLE. Ha! ha! ha! The peremptory tone in which he sent forth his sublime commands.

SIR CHARLES. And the reserve with which I suppose he treated all your advances.

HARDCASTLE. And yet he might have seen something in me above a common innkeeper, too.

SIR CHARLES. Yes, Dick, but he mistook you for an uncommon innkeeper, ha! ha! ha!

HARDCASTLE. Well, I'm in too good spirits to think of anything but joy. Yes, my dear friend, this union of our families will make our personal friendships hereditary: and though my daughter's fortune is but small——

SIR CHARLES. Why, Dick, will you talk of fortune to *me?* My son is possessed of more than a competence already, and can want nothing but a good and virtuous girl to share his happiness and increase it. If they like each other, as you say they do——

HARDCASTLE. *If,* man! I tell you they *do* like each other. My daughter as good as told me so.

SIR CHARLES. But girls are apt to flatter themselves, you know.

HARDCASTLE. I saw him grasp her hand in the warmest manner myself; and here he comes to put you out of your *ifs,* I warrant him.

Enter MARLOW.

MARLOW. I come, sir, once more, to ask pardon for my strange conduct. I can scarce reflect on my insolence without confusion.

HARDCASTLE. Tut, boy, a trifle. You take it too gravely. An hour or two's laughing with my daughter will set all to rights again. She'll never like you the worse for it.

MARLOW. Sir, I shall be always proud of her approbation.

HARDCASTLE. Approbation is but a cold word, Mr. Marlow; if I am not deceived, you have something more than approbation thereabouts. You take me?

MARLOW. Really, sir, I have not that happiness.

HARDCASTLE. Come, boy, I'm an old fellow, and know what's what, as well as you that are younger. I know what has passed between you; but mum.

MARLOW. Sure, sir, nothing has passed between us but the most profound respect on my side, and the most distant reserve on hers. You don't think, sir, that my impudence has been passed upon all the rest of the family?

HARDCASTLE. Impudence! No, I don't say that—Not quite impudence—Though girls like to be played with, and rumpled a little too, sometimes. But she has told no tales, I assure you.

MARLOW. I never gave her the slightest cause.

HARDCASTLE. Well, well, I like modesty in its place well enough. But this is over-acting, young gentleman. You *may* be open. Your father and I will like you the better for it.

MARLOW. May I die, sir, if I ever——

HARDCASTLE. I tell you, she don't dislike you; and as I'm sure you like her——

MARLOW.   Dear sir—I protest, sir——

HARDCASTLE.   I see no reason why you should not be joined as fast as the parson can tie you.

MARLOW.   But hear me, sir——

HARDCASTLE.   Your father approves the match, I admire it, every moment's delay will be doing mischief, so——

MARLOW.   But why won't you hear me? By all that's just and true, I never gave Miss Hardcastle the slightest mark of my attachment, or even the most distant hint to suspect me of affection. We had but one interview, and that was formal, modest, and uninteresting.

HARDCASTLE (*aside*). This fellow's formal modest impudence is beyond bearing.

SIR CHARLES.   And you never grasped her hand, or made any protestations!

MARLOW.   As heaven is my witness, I came down in obedience to your commands. I saw the lady without emotion, and parted without reluctance. I hope you'll exact no further proofs of my duty, nor prevent me from leaving a house in which I suffer so many mortifications. (*Exit.*)

SIR CHARLES.   I'm astonished at the air of sincerity with which he parted.

HARDCASTLE.   And I'm astonished at the deliberate intrepidity of his assurance.

SIR CHARLES.   I dare pledge my life and honour upon his truth.

HARDCASTLE.   Here comes my daughter, and I would stake my happiness upon her veracity.

Enter MISS HARDCASTLE.

HARDCASTLE.   Kate, come hither, child. Answer us sincerely, and without reserve; has Mr. Marlow made you any professions of love and affection?

MISS HARDCASTLE.   The question is very abrupt, sir! But since you require unreserved sincerity, I think he has.

HARDCASTLE (*to* SIR CHARLES). You see.

SIR CHARLES.   And pray, madam, have you and my son had more than one interview?

MISS HARDCASTLE.   Yes, sir, several.

HARDCASTLE (*to* SIR CHARLES). You see.

SIR CHARLES.   But did he profess any attachment?

MISS HARDCASTLE.   A lasting one.

SIR CHARLES.   Did he talk of love?

MISS HARDCASTLE.   Much, sir.

SIR CHARLES.   Amazing! And all this formally?

MISS HARDCASTLE.   Formally.

HARDCASTLE.   Now, my friend, I hope you are satisfied.

SIR CHARLES.   And how did he behave, madam?

MISS HARDCASTLE.   As most professed admirers do. Said some civil things of my face, talked much of his want of merit, and the greatness of mine; mentioned his heart, gave a short tragedy speech, and ended with pretended rapture.

SIR CHARLES.   Now I'm perfectly convinced, indeed. I know his conversation among women to be modest and submissive. This forward, canting, ranting manner by no means describes him, and I am confident he never sat for the picture.

MISS HARDCASTLE.   Then what, sir, if I should convince you to your face of my sincerity? If you and my papa, in about half-an-hour, will place yourselves behind that screen, you shall hear him declare his passion to me in person.

SIR CHARLES.   Agreed. And if I find him what you describe, all my happiness in him must have an end. (*Exit.*)

MISS HARDCASTLE.   And if you don't find him what I describe—I fear my happiness must never have a beginning. (*Exeunt.*)

SCENE—CHANGES TO THE BACK OF THE GARDEN.

Enter HASTINGS.

HASTINGS.   What an idiot am I, to wait here for a fellow, who probably takes a delight in mortifying me. He never intended to be punctual, and I'll wait no longer. What do I see? It is he, and perhaps with news of my Constance.

Enter TONY, *booted and spattered.*

HASTINGS.   My honest 'Squire! I now find you a man of your word. This looks like friendship.

TONY.   Ay, I'm your friend, and the best friend you have in the world, if you knew but all. This riding by night, by-the-bye, is cursedly tiresome. It has shook me worse than the basket of a stage-coach.

HASTINGS.   But how? Where did you leave your fellow-travellers? Are they in safety? Are they housed?

TONY.   Five and twenty miles in two hours and a half is no such bad driving. The poor beasts have smoked for it: rabbit me, but I'd rather ride forty miles after a fox, then ten with such *varmint.*

HASTINGS.   Well, but where have you left the ladies? I die with impatience.

TONY.   Left them? Why, where should I leave them, but where I found them?

HASTINGS.   This is a riddle.

TONY.   Riddle me this, then. What's that goes round the house, and round the house, and never touches the house?

HASTINGS.   I'm still astray.

TONY.   Why, that's it, mon. I have led them astray. By jingo, there's not a pond or slough within five miles of the place but they can tell the taste of.

HASTINGS.   Ha, ha, ha, I understand; you took them in a round, while they supposed themselves going forward. And so you have at last brought them home again.

TONY.   You shall hear. I first took them down Feather-bed Lane, where we stuck fast in the mud. I then rattled them crack over the stones of Up-and-down Hill—I then introduced them to the gibbet on Heavy-tree Heath, and from that, with a circumbendibus, I fairly lodged them in the horse-pond at the bottom of the garden.

HASTINGS.   But no accident, I hope.

TONY.   No, no. Only mother is confoundedly frightened. She thinks herself forty miles off. She's sick of the journey, and the cattle can scarce crawl. So, if your own horses be ready, you may whip off with cousin, and I'll be bound that no soul here can budge a foot to follow you.

HASTINGS.   My dear friend, how can I be grateful?

TONY.   Ay, now it's dear friend, noble 'Squire. Just now, it was all idiot, cub, and run me through the guts. Damn *your* way of fighting, I say. After we take a knock in this part of the country, we kiss and be friends. But if you had run me through the guts, then I should be dead, and you might go kiss the hangman.

HASTINGS.   The rebuke is just. But I must hasten to relieve Miss Neville; if you keep the old lady employed, I promise to take care of the young one. (*Exit* HASTINGS.)

TONY.   Never fear me. Here she comes. Vanish. She's got from the pond, and draggled up to the waist like a mermaid.

Enter MRS. HARDCASTLE.

MRS. HARDCASTLE.   Oh, Tony, I'm killed. Shook. Battered to death. I shall never survive it. That last jolt that laid us against the quickset hedge has done my business.

TONY.   Alack, mamma, it was all your own fault. You would be for running away by night, without knowing one inch of the way.

MRS. HARDCASTLE.   I wish we were at home again. I never met so many accidents in so short a journey. Drenched in the mud, overturned in a ditch, stuck fast in a slough, jolted to a jelly, and at last to lose our way! Whereabouts do you think we are, Tony?

TONY.   By my guess we should be upon Crack-skull Common, about forty miles from home.

MRS. HARDCASTLE.   O lud! O lud! the most notorious spot in all the country. We only want a robbery to make a complete night on't.

TONY.   Don't be afraid, mamma, don't be afraid. Two of the five that kept here are hanged, and the other three may not find us. Don't be afraid. Is that a man that's galloping behind us? No; it's only a tree. Don't be afraid.

MRS. HARDCASTLE.   The fright will certainly kill me.

TONY.   Do you see anything like a black hat moving behind the thicket?

MRS. HARDCASTLE.   O death!

TONY.   No, it's only a cow. Don't be afraid, mamma, don't be afraid.

MRS. HARDCASTLE.   As I'm alive, Tony, I see a man coming towards us. Ah! I'm sure on't. If he perceives us, we are undone.

TONY (*aside*).   Father-in-law, by all that's unlucky, come to take one of his night walks. (*To her.*) Ah, it's a highwayman, with pistols as long as my arm. A damned ill-looking fellow.

MRS. HARDCASTLE.   Good heaven defend us! He approaches.

TONY.   Do you hide yourself in that thicket, and leave me to manage him. If there be any danger I'll cough and cry hem. When I cough be sure to keep close. (MRS. HARDCASTLE *hides behind a tree in the back scene.*)

Enter HARDCASTLE.

HARDCASTLE.   I'm mistaken, or I heard voices of people in want of help. Oh, Tony, is that you? I did not expect you so soon back. Are your mother and her charge in safety?

TONY.   Very safe, sir, at my aunt Pedigree's. Hem.

MRS. HARDCASTLE (*from behind*).   Ah! I find there's danger.

HARDCASTLE.   Forty miles in three hours; sure, that's too much, my youngster.

TONY.   Stout horses and willing minds make short journeys, as they say. Hem.

MRS. HARDCASTLE (*from behind*).   Sure he'll do the dear boy no harm.

HARDCASTLE.   But I heard a voice here; I should be glad to know from whence it came.

TONY.   It was I, sir, talking to myself, sir. I was saying that forty miles in four hours was very good going. Hem. As to be sure it was. Hem. I have got a sort of cold by being out in the air. We'll go in if you please. Hem.

HARDCASTLE.   But if you talked to yourself, you did not answer yourself. I am certain I heard two voices, and am resolved (*raising his voice*) to find the other out.

MRS. HARDCASTLE (*from behind*).   Oh! he's coming to find me out. Oh!

TONY.   What need you go, sir, if I tell you? Hem. I'll lay down my life for the truth—hem—I'll tell you all, sir. (*Detaining him.*)

HARDCASTLE.   I tell you I will not be detained. I insist on seeing. It's in vain to expect I'll believe you.

MRS. HARDCASTLE (*running forward from behind*).   O lud, he'll murder my poor boy, my darling. Here, good gentleman, whet your rage upon me. Take my money, my life, but spare that young gentleman, spare my child, if you have any mercy.

HARDCASTLE.   My wife! as I'm a Christian. From whence can she come, or what does she mean?

MRS. HARDCASTLE (*kneeling*).   Take compassion on us, good Mr. Highwayman. Take our money, our watches, all we have, but spare our lives. We will never bring you to justice, indeed we won't, good Mr. Highwayman.

HARDCASTLE.   I believe the woman's out of her senses. What, Dorothy, don't you know *me?*

MRS. HARDCASTLE.   Mr. Hardcastle, as I'm alive! My fears blinded me. But who, my dear, could have expected to meet you here, in this frightful place, so far from home? What has brought you to follow us?

HARDCASTLE.   Sure, Dorothy, you have not lost your wits! So far from home, when you are within forty yards of your own door! (*To him.*) This is one of your old tricks, you graceless rogue, you! (*To her.*) Don't you know the gate, and the mulberry-tree; and don't you remember the horse-pond, my dear?

MRS. HARDCASTLE.   Yes, I shall remember the horse-pond as long as I live; I have caught my death in it. (*To* TONY.) And is it to you, you graceless varlet, I owe all this? I'll teach you to abuse your mother, I will.

TONY.   Ecod, mother, all the parish says you have spoiled me, and so you may take the fruits on't.

MRS. HARDCASTLE.   I'll spoil you, I will. (*Follows him off the stage. Exit.*)

HARDCASTLE.   There's morality, however, in his reply. (*Exit.*)

Enter HASTINGS *and* MISS NEVILLE.

HASTINGS.   My dear Constance, why will you deliberate thus? If we delay a moment, all is lost for ever. Pluck up a little resolution, and we shall soon be out of the reach of her malignity.

MISS NEVILLE.   I find it impossible. My spirits are so sunk with the agitations I have suffered, that I am unable to face any new danger. Two or three years' patience will at last crown us with happiness.

HASTINGS.   Such a tedious delay is worse than inconstancy. Let us fly, my charmer. Let us date our happiness from this very moment. Perish fortune. Love and content will increase what we possess beyond a monarch's revenue. Let me prevail.

MISS NEVILLE.   No, Mr. Hastings, no. Prudence once more comes to my relief, and I will obey its dictates. In the moment of passion, fortune may be despised, but it ever produces a lasting repentance. I'm resolved to apply to Mr. Hardcastle's compassion and justice for redress.

HASTINGS.   But though he had the will, he has not the power to relieve you.

MISS NEVILLE.   But he has influence, and upon that I am resolved to rely.

HASTINGS.   I have no hopes. But since you persist, I must reluctantly obey you. (*Exeunt.*)

SCENE—CHANGES.

Enter SIR CHARLES *and* MISS HARDCASTLE.

SIR CHARLES.   What a situation am I in! If what you say appears, I shall then find a guilty son. If what he says be true, I shall then lose one that, of all others, I most wished for a daughter.

MISS HARDCASTLE.   I am proud of your approbation; and, to show I merit it, if you place yourselves as I directed, you shall hear his explicit declaration. But he comes.

SIR CHARLES.   I'll to your father, and keep him to the appointment. (*Exit* SIR CHARLES.)

Enter MARLOW.

MARLOW.   Though prepared for setting out, I come once more to take leave, nor did I, till this moment, know the pain I feel in the separation.

MISS HARDCASTLE (*in her own natural manner*). I believe these sufferings cannot be very great, sir, which you can so easily remove. A day or two longer, perhaps, might lessen your uneasiness, by showing the little value of what you think proper to regret.

MARLOW (*aside*). This girl every moment improves upon me. (*To her.*) It must not be, madam. I have already trifled too long with my heart. My very pride begins to submit to my passion. The disparity of education and fortune, the anger of a parent, and the contempt of my equals begin to lose their weight; and nothing can restore me to myself but this painful effort of resolution.

MISS HARDCASTLE.   Then go, sir. I'll urge nothing more to detain you. Though my family be as good as hers you came down to visit, and my education, I hope, not inferior, what are these advantages without equal affluence? I must remain contented with the slight approbation of imputed merit; I must have only the mockery of your addresses, while all your serious aims are fixed on fortune.

Enter HARDCASTLE *and* SIR CHARLES *from behind.*

SIR CHARLES.   Here, behind this screen.

HARDCASTLE.   Ay, ay, make no noise. I'll engage my Kate covers him with confusion at last.

MARLOW.   By heavens, madam, fortune was ever my smallest consideration. Your beauty at first caught my eye; for who could see that without emotion? But every moment that I converse with you, steals in some new grace, heightens the picture, and gives it stronger expression. What at first seemed rustic plainness, now appears refined simplicity. What seemed forward assurance, now strikes me as the result of courageous innocence, and conscious virtue.

SIR CHARLES.   What can it mean? He amazes me!

HARDCASTLE.   I told you how it would be. Hush!

MARLOW.   I am now determined to stay, madam, and I have too good an opinion of my father's discernment, when he sees you, to doubt his approbation.

MISS HARDCASTLE.   No, Mr. Marlow, I will not, cannot detain you. Do you think I could suffer a connection, in which there is the smallest room for repentance? Do you think I would take the mean advantage of a transient passion, to load you with confusion? Do you think I could ever relish that happiness, which was acquired by lessening yours?

MARLOW.   By all that's good, I can have no happiness but what's in your power to grant me. Nor shall I ever feel repentance, but in not having seen your merits before. I will stay, even contrary to your wishes; and though you should persist to shun me, I will make my respectful assiduities atone for the levity of my past conduct.

MISS HARDCASTLE.   Sir, I must entreat you'll desist. As our acquaintance began, so let it end, in indifference. I might have given an hour or two to levity; but, seriously, Mr. Marlow, do you think I could ever submit to a connection, where *I* must appear mercenary, and *you* imprudent? Do you think I could ever catch at the confident addresses of a secure admirer?

MARLOW (*kneeling*). Does this look like security? Does this look like confidence? No, madam, every moment that shows me your merit, only serves to increase my diffidence and confusion. Here let me continue——

SIR CHARLES.   I can hold it no longer. Charles, Charles, how hast thou deceived me! Is this your indifference, your uninteresting conversation!

HARDCASTLE.   Your cold contempt! your formal interview! What have you to say now?

MARLOW.   That I'm all amazement! What can it mean?

HARDCASTLE.   It means that you can say and unsay things at pleasure. That you can address a lady in private, and deny it in public; that you have one story for us, and another for my daughter!

MARLOW.   Daughter!—this lady your daughter!

HARDCASTLE.   Yes, sir, my only daughter. My Kate, whose else should she be?

MARLOW.   Oh, the devil.

MISS HARDCASTLE.   Yes, sir, that very identical tall, squinting lady you were pleased to take me for. (*Curtseying.*) She that you addressed as the mild, modest, sentimental man of gravity, and the bold, forward, agreeable Rattle of the Ladies' Club: ha, ha, ha!

MARLOW.   Zounds, there's no bearing this; it's worse than death!

MISS HARDCASTLE.   In which of your characters, sir, will you give us leave to address you? As the faltering gentleman, with looks on the ground, that speaks just to be heard, and hates hypocrisy: or the loud, confident creature, that keeps it up with Mrs. Mantrap, and old Miss Biddy Buckskin, till three in the morning: ha, ha, ha!

MARLOW.   Oh, curse on my noisy head. I never attempted to be impudent yet, that I was not taken down. I must be gone.

HARDCASTLE.   By the hand of my body, but you shall not. I see it was all a mistake, and I am rejoiced to find it. You shall not, sir, I tell you. I know she'll forgive you. Won't

you forgive him, Kate? We'll all forgive you. Take courage, man. (*They retire, she tormenting him, to the back scene.*)

Enter MRS. HARDCASTLE, TONY.

MRS. HARDCASTLE.   So, so, they're gone off. Let them go, I care not.

HARDCASTLE.   Who gone?

MRS. HARDCASTLE.   My dutiful niece and her gentleman, Mr. Hastings, from town. He who came down with our modest visitor, here.

SIR CHARLES.   Who, my honest George Hastings? As worthy a fellow as lives, and the girl could not have made a more prudent choice.

HARDCASTLE.   Then, by the hand of my body, I'm proud of the connection.

MRS. HARDCASTLE.   Well, if he has taken away the lady, he has not taken her fortune, that remains in this family to console us for her loss.

HARDCASTLE.   Sure, Dorothy, you would not be so mercenary?

MRS. HARDCASTLE.   Ay, that's my affair, not yours. But you know, if your son when of age, refuses to marry his cousin, her whole fortune is then at her own disposal.

HARDCASTLE.   Ay, but he's not of age, and she has not thought proper to wait for his refusal.

Enter HASTINGS *and* MISS NEVILLE.

MRS. HARDCASTLE (*aside*). What! returned so soon? I begin not to like it.

HASTINGS (*to* HARDCASTLE). For my late attempt to fly off with your niece, let my present confusion be my punishment. We are now come back, to appeal from your justice to your humanity. By her father's consent, I first paid her my addresses, and our passions were first founded in duty.

MISS NEVILLE.   Since his death, I have been obliged to stoop to dissimulation to avoid oppression. In an hour of levity, I was ready even to give up my fortune to secure my choice. But I'm now recovered from the delusion, and hope from your tenderness what is denied me from a nearer connection.

MRS. HARDCASTLE.   Pshaw, pshaw! this is all but the whining end of a modern novel.

HARDCASTLE.   Be it what it will, I'm glad they're come back to reclaim their due. Come hither, Tony, boy. Do you refuse this lady's hand whom I now offer you?

TONY.   What signifies my refusing? You know I can't refuse her till I'm of age, father.

HARDCASTLE.   While I thought concealing your age, boy, was likely to conduce to your improvement, I concurred with your mother's desire to keep it secret. But since I find she turns it to a wrong use, I must now declare, you have been of age these three months.

TONY.   Of age! Am I of age, father?

HARDCASTLE.   Above three months.

TONY.   Then you'll see the first use I'll make of my liberty. (*Taking* MISS NEVILLE'S *hand.*) Witness all men by these presents, that I, Anthony Lumpkin, Esquire, of BLANK place, refuse you, Constantia Neville, spinster, of no place at all, for my true and lawful wife. So Constance Neville may marry whom she pleases, and Tony Lumpkin is his own man again!

SIR CHARLES.   O brave 'Squire!

HASTINGS.   My worthy friend!

MRS. HARDCASTLE.   My undutiful offspring!

MARLOW.   Joy, my dear George, I give you joy sincerely. And could I prevail upon my little tyrant here to be less arbitrary, I should be the happiest man alive, if you would return me the favour.

HASTINGS (*to* MISS HARDCASTLE). Come, madam, you are now driven to the very last scene of all your contrivances. I know you like him, I'm sure he loves you, and you must and shall have him.

HARDCASTLE (*joining their hands*). And I say so, too. And Mr. Marlow, if she makes as good a wife as she has a daughter, I don't believe you'll ever repent your bargain. So now to supper, to-morrow we shall gather all the poor of the parish about us, and the Mistakes of the Night shall be crowned with a merry morning; so, boy, take her; as you have been mistaken in the mistress, my wish is, that you may never be mistaken in the wife.

EPILOGUE
BY DR. GOLDSMITH

WELL, having stooped to conquer with success,
And gained a husband without aid from dress,
Still as a Barmaid, I could wish it too,
As I have conquered him to conquer you:
And let me say, for all your resolution,
That pretty Barmaids have done execution.
Our life is all a play, composed to please,
"We have our exits and our entrances."
The first act shows the simple country maid,
Harmless and young, of everything afraid;
Blushes when hired, and with unmeaning action,
I hopes as how to give you satisfaction.
Her second act displays a livelier scene,—
Th' unblushing Barmaid of a country inn.
Who whisks about the house, at market caters,
Talks loud, coquets the guests, and scolds the waiters.
Next the scene shifts to town, and there she soars,
The chop-house toast of ogling connoisseurs.
On 'Squires and Cits she there displays her arts,
And on the gridiron broils her lovers' hearts—
And as she smiles, her triumphs to complete,
Even Common Councilmen forget to eat.
The fourth act shows her wedded to the 'Squire,
And madam now begins to hold it higher;
Pretends to taste, at Operas cries *caro,*
And quits her *Nancy Dawson,* for *Che Faro.*
Dotes upon dancing, and in all her pride,
Swims round the room, the *Heinel* of Cheapside:
Ogles and leers with artificial skill,
Till having lost in age the power to kill,
She sits all night at cards, and ogles at spadille.
Such, through our lives, the eventful history—
The fifth and last act still remains for me.
The Barmaid now for your protection prays,
Turns female Barrister, and pleads for Bayes.

EPILOGUE
BY J. CRADOCK, ESQ.

TO BE SPOKEN IN THE CHARACTER OF TONY LUMPKIN

WELL—now all's ended—and my comrades gone,
Pray what becomes of *mother's nonly son?*
A hopeful blade!—in town I'll fix my station,
And try to make a bluster in the nation.
As for my cousin Neville, I renounce her,
Off—in a crack—I'll carry big Bet Bouncer.
    Why should not I in the great world appear?
I soon shall have a thousand pounds a year;
No matter what a man may here inherit,
In London—'gad, they've some regard for spirit.
I see the horses prancing up the streets,
And big Bet Bouncer bobs to all she meets;
Then hoicks to jigs and pastimes ev'ry night—
Not to the plays—they say it a'n't polite,
To Sadler's-Wells perhaps, or Operas go,
And once by chance, to the roratorio.
Thus here and there, for ever up and down,
We'll set the fashions too, to half the town;
And then at auctions—money ne'er regard,
Buy pictures like the great, ten pounds a yard:
Zounds, we shall make these London gentry say,
We know what's damned genteel, as well as they.

FOCUS QUESTIONS

1. How does Goldsmith's comedy depict the society of eighteenth-century England? In particular, how are the differences between town and country manners portrayed?
2. Show how games, disguise, and sentiment influence the characters and dramatic action.
3. Develop a character study of Tony Lumpkin in which you describe his influence on characters and actions.
4. Discuss the correlation between the women in the play and those of eighteenth-century society. Briefly note the uses of comedy and satire in your discussion.
5. Defend Kate Hardcastle as "the most attractive heroine in eighteenth-century British drama."
6. With reference to the play's subtitle, "*The Mistakes of a Night*," show how the play's unity of time serves both "place" and "action."
7. Briefly analyze Goldsmith's comical handling of male/female relationships in the play. Can you draw any conclusions?
8. Discuss Goldsmith's use of comic irony.

OTHER ACTIVITIES

1. Based on costume sketches from the period, suggest a wardrobe to accommodate Kate Hardcastle's life-style in both the country and the city.
2. Develop sketches for a production that focuses on contemporary American bourgeois values as seen in 1950–1970 suburbia.

BIBLIOGRAPHY

Bevis, Richard. *The Laughing Tradition: Stage Comedy in Garrick's Day*. Athens: University of Georgia Press, 1980.

Bloom, Harold, ed. *Oliver Goldsmith*. New York: Chelsea House, 1987.

Danziger, M. K. *Oliver Goldsmith and Richard Brinsley Sheridan*. New York: Ungar Publishing Co., 1978.

Dixon, Peter. *Oliver Goldsmith Revisited*. Boston: Twayne Publishers, 1991.

Ginger, John. *The Notable Man: The Life and Times of Oliver Goldsmith*. London: Hamish Hamilton, 1977.

Hopkins, Robert H. *The True Genius of Oliver Goldsmith*. Baltimore: Johns Hopkins University Press, 1969.

Hume, Robert D. *The Rakish Stage: Studies in English Drama, 1660–1800*. Carbondale: Southern Illinois University Press, 1983.

Quintana, Ricardo. *Oliver Goldsmith, A Georgian Study*. New York: Macmillan, 1967.

Rousseau, G. S., ed. *Goldsmith: the Critical Heritage*. London: Routledge & Kegan Paul, 1974.

Smith, John T. "Tony Lumpkin and the Country Booby Type in Antecedent English Comedy." *PMLA* 58 #4: 1038–1049, Dec. 1944.

Swarbrick, Andrew, ed. *The Art of Oliver Goldsmith*. London: Vision Press, 1984.

Wardle, Ralph. *Oliver Goldsmith*. Lawrence: University of Kansas Press, 1957.

Woods, Samuel H. *Oliver Goldsmith: A Reference Guide*. Boston: G. K. Hall, 1982.

Worth, Katharine. *Sheridan and Goldsmith*. New York: St. Martin's Press, 1992.

RECOMMENDED VIDEOTAPE

She Stoops to Conquer. VHS. 119 min. 1976. Starring Tom Courtney, Sir Ralph Richardson, and Juliet Mills, directed by Cedric Messina for BBC Television. Distributed by Time-Life Multimedia.

HERNANI
VICTOR HUGO (1802–1885)

The old Classical edifice had itself been crumbling for years, and Hugo was the demolition man. He was the one who arrived at the eleventh hour, when all that was needed was to give a push.

—ÉMILE ZOLA

Geneviève Casile as Doña Sol and François Beaulieu (*right*) as Hernani in *Hernani,* presented by the Comédie Française in 1974, under the direction of Robert Hossein. *Photo:© Lipnitski-Viollet.*

APPROACHING FRENCH ROMANTICISM

Romanticism had its beginnings in the writings of French philosopher and man of letters, Jean Jacques Rousseau (1712–1778), who expressed a vision of humanity that countered the one proposed by the Enlightenment. He argued that people should be guided by feelings, emotions, and instinct rather than reason; that the Noble Savage, with his simpler life close to nature, should be envied and imitated. His blueprint for humanity pressed for a government that could diminish the superiority and authority of the aristocracy and monarchy and, at the same time, equalize the populace as well as promote the individual. His writings sparked the movements that led to the American Revolution in 1776 and the French Revolution in 1789.

His compatriot and fellow philosopher, Voltaire (1694–1778), was also instrumental in instigating political and cultural changes. Of particular importance to the history of the theatre was his introduction of Shakespeare's works to France after 1730. Finding the French neoclassical ideals too restrictive, he championed Shakespeare's episodic structures, complex plots, use of comic relief in tragedy, and inclusion of the supernatural. In his own plays, Voltaire introduced ghosts, sudden recognition scenes, and displays of violence. He also exploited the public's growing interest in national history and local color by demanding accuracy in both the settings and costumes designed for his dramas. His enthusiasm for Shakespeare was echoed throughout Europe where translations and adaptations began appearing as early as 1770.

It is ironic that the seeds for the growth of Romanticism and the subsequent demise of neoclassicism arose in France, the last European nation to accept its aesthetic premises. The Revolution had inspired artists, musicians, and poets to question the traditions and authority of the country's institutions, which had become the arbiters of European culture. Not only were the French unwilling to give up this place of cultural superiority, they also saw the acceptance of the new movement, which already had a stronghold in Germany and England through the works of August Wilhelm Schlegel, as an act of surrender to their political foes.

Further retarding the growth of Romanticism was Napoleonic rule. As the seat of the new empire, Paris was envisioned as a new Rome. Neoclassical style in dress and in drama, now sanctioned by the emperor, were fully embraced by the bourgeoisie and the aristocracy. When Mme. de Stael (1766–1817) published her description of the Romantic movement, *Of Germany,* in 1810, the book was suppressed not only because its author was Napoleon's bitter enemy, but because it challenged the classical traditions he favored. Although the book had been circulated privately during Napoleon's reign, it did not reappear until 1814, after his downfall. At this time, its message of the new art form was taken up by poets and artists alike.

Undaunted by the emperor's preferences, the vaudevilles and melodramas that emerged during the eighteenth century continued to gain in popularity. They also laid a foundation for France's burgeoning Romantic movement. The offerings in the boulevard theatres exploited the public demands for sentimentality, spectacle, and local color. Gothic and medieval settings, folkloric legends, emotional thrills, plot entanglements, heroes who were thieves or bandits, tragedy interspersed with farce, and realistic dialogue were traits found in the entertainments catering to the tastes of the common people.

By the 1820s an *avant-garde* movement determined to overthrow the entrenched neoclassicism established by the French Academy was gaining momentum. Stendhal (1783–1842) took up the dispute in his work, *Racine and Shakespeare,* written between 1823 and 1825, in which he proclaimed Shakespeare the superior playwright. Despite his importance and the growing reputations of Alfred de Vigny and Alexandre Dumas *père,* it was Victor Hugo, not Stendhal, who became the spokesman for Romanticism. In the preface to his never-completed play, *Cromwell,* written in 1827, he issued an artistic manifesto, calling for the abandonment of the unities of time, place, and action. He advocated the mixing of tragic and comic forms, an emphasis on historical milieu in individual scenes, and the use of narrative to determine the passage of time from one scene to the next. Hugo wanted to create dramas of epic proportion to demonstrate his panoramic view of life, rather than focusing on single catastrophic moments. The drama should assault audience sensibility, he thought, and move them from "paroxysms of mirth to heart rending emotions, from the grave to the sweet, from the pleasant to the severe."[1]

To achieve more realistic stage characters, Hugo rejected the ideals of decorum and nobility in favor of displaying both the sublime or spiritual and the grotesque or animal in human nature. He believed that characters—no matter what their social class—should represent a dynamic mix of angelic and demonic forces, of beautiful and monstrous impulses. His preface challenged his fellow poets to "take the hammer to poetic systems [and] throw down the old plastering that conceals the facade of art. There are neither rules nor models; or rather, there are no other rules than the general laws of Nature."[2]

The success of Charles Kemble's troupe of English actors who performed Shakespeare in 1827 and William Charles Macready's company who imported new English plays in 1828 proved that Paris audiences were ready to accept Romanticism. French lyric poets who heeded Hugo's manifesto now wanted to see their own plays and adaptations of Shakespeare produced on the official French stage, the Comédie Française. Fortunately, Baron Taylor, recently appointed as theatre director in 1825, was sympathetic to the new aesthetic and eager to produce plays whose visual effects, realistic details, and sharply paced actions would attract enthusiastic audiences. Not until 1829 did French romantic verse drama finally reach the stage of the Comédie Française, with de Vigny's *The Moor of Venice,* adapted from Shakespeare's *Othello;* Dumas *père*'s *Henri III and His Court;* and Hugo's *Marion de Lorme,* banned after several performances. The conservative aristocrats who sat in boxes laughed at the display of tender emotion and at the realistic poses of actors. But their reactions only hinted at the steps they would take to halt the spread of Romanticism on stage. It was not until February 25, 1830, when Taylor slated Hugo's *Hernani* for its premiere, that Paris beheld the final showdown.

MAJOR WORKS

Hugo's literary reputation rests primarily with his poetry and his novels, particularly *The Hunchback of Notre-Dame* (1831) and *Les Miserables* (1862), which eventually were dramatized, both on film and the latter on the musical stage. Although he began his playwrighting career in 1816 with a neoclassical tragedy called *Irtamene,* his most famous were those written in verse after the battle over *Hernani* subsided. These centered on historic, high-born figures who were the products of Hugo's imagination. In creating these stage characters, he continued to explore such themes as the selfishness and immorality of the aristocracy (despite his political stance as a royalist); the capacity that resides in all human beings for love and devotion on one hand and for moral depravity on the other; and the unlimited range of emotion and passion that motivates human action. These verse dramas include *Le Roi S'Amuse* (1832), which inspired the libretto for Verdi's opera *Rigoletto; Lucrèce Borgia* (1833) and *Marie Tudor* (1833)—both written in prose; *Angelo, Tyran de Padoue* (1835); *Ruy Blas* (1838); and *Les Burgraves* (1843). From 1851 until 1870, Hugo's works were banned while the writer lived in exile in England after conspiring against the forces of Louis Bonaparte. Yet he continued to write novels and poetry during this twenty-year absence. Shortly after his triumphant return to Paris, he became a member of the French Academy and an elected statesman, but continued to write plays until his death.

THE ACTION

Doña Sol has three suitors: Don Carlos, the king who would abduct her; Hernani, the bandit to whom she has sworn her love; and Don Ruy Gomez de Silva, her guardian who wishes her for himself. Their intense rivalry in pursuing her hand forces Hernani into hiding. In Hernani's absence, Doña Sol agrees to marry Ruy Gomez.

In disguise, Hernani returns on their wedding day. Although Ruy Gomez feels betrayed when Hernani's identity is revealed, he refuses to surrender his rival to Don Carlos. As a result, Doña Sol becomes the king's hostage. Promising to surrender his life at the duke's command, Hernani joins Ruy Gomez in a plot to avenge her honor.

On the day Don Carlos is elected Holy Roman Emperor, the conspirators, Hernani and Ruy Gomez, are captured and sentenced to death. In order to die a nobleman, Hernani reveals his true identity as Duke of Segorbe and Cardona. As Emperor, Don Carlos rescinds all charges against his rival and sanctions his union with Doña Sol. But Ruy Gomez remains jealous. His cruel demand that Hernani fulfill his promise before consummating his marriage to Doña Sol propels the play to its tragic conclusion.

STRUCTURE AND LANGUAGE

Exemplifying a new aesthetic freed from the stringent neoclassical format, each of *Hernani*'s five acts crosses the boundaries of time and space. While the first two acts unfold at the palace of the Silva family in Sargossa in northern Spain around 1519, twenty-four hours elapse between them. In the third act, sufficient time has passed for Doña Sol and Ruy Gomez to reach the Silva ancestral home, a castle in the mountains of Aragon—the same mountain range as the Pyrenees—for their wedding. Act 4 is set in the Papal palace at Aix-la-Chapelle in southern France, where the further passage of time gives Hernani and Ruy Gomez an opportunity to join a conspiracy against Don Carlos. The final act returns to the Silva palace in Sargossa, across a mountain range and miles from the seat of the Holy Roman Empire at Aix-la-Chapelle.

Hugo celebrates the new aesthetic through elaborate stage directions that demand the sumptuous spectacle of historically and regionally accurate costumes, props, and settings, the last of which re-create the Gothic and Moorish designs of Spain and the Romanesque designs of Lombardy. The sweep of the action across landscapes is achieved by altering the painted backdrops. Full sets of armor from different eras, an ornate ducal throne, and Doña Sol's numerous Castilian gowns and nuptial jewelry are described by Hugo in meticulous detail. Furthermore, the character of Doña Sol is allotted approximately eighty-seven acting directions, most of which describe her emotional responses to the surrounding actions.

Of equal importance is Hugo's rejection of decorum, in which protagonists of noble birth speak in an elevated style to reflect their class. In contrast, the aristocratic characters of *Hernani* possess ignoble qualities and often speak as commoners. They are motivated by contradictory emotional forces such as duty, hatred, jealousy, ambition, lust, fear of death, and love. In keeping with the play's grandiose design, these feelings are richly demonstrated in the first three acts, each of which focuses on one of Doña Sol's three suitors and is so named: The King, The Bandit, and The Old Man. Each speaks of her in language that quickly reveals the nature of his love.

In the opening moments of act 1, Don Carlos disobeys the rules of propriety by entering Doña Sol's room in disguise, threatening to kill her duenna if she utters a word, and hiding in a closet like a common criminal. ''Is this the stable where you keep your broomstick between rides?'' he asks the duenna as she reluctantly leads him to the cramped hiding space. Given the unusual circumstances and characters at play, the effect is surprisingly comical. Later, in act 2, as Don Carlos anxiously awaits the dark of night so that Doña Sol can ''shine like a star in all this blackness,'' his poetic expressiveness is abruptly punctuated by the question, ''What time is it?'' rendered so matter-of-factly, that it quickly reduces his eloquence to everyday speech. Such elements of stage dialogue, according to Theophile Gautier, violated the accepted dramatic form and prompted a critical fracas that resounded through the corridors of the Comédie Française long after opening night.[3]

Hugo's unflattering portrait of Don Carlos, with his unsatisfied lust for Doña Sol and his unrelenting, blustering self-importance, serves a special dramatic purpose, which becomes evident in act 4 when he undergoes a radical transformation. In his ambitious bid for the title of Holy Roman Emperor, he has beheld the pettiness of kings, much like himself, whose votes he could easily buy. In an important monologue that closes this act, he invokes the spirit of the first emperor, Charlemagne, and humbly seeks permission to follow in his path:

> May I join my helmet to the Roman miter? Have I the right to bend the fortunes
> of the world? Have I a firm and steady foot, one that may walk upon this path, all
> strewn with vandal's ruins, that you have beaten out for us with your broad sandals?
> Have I caught your flame to kindle my own torch? And understood the voice that
> sounds within your tomb?

Questioning his capacity to shoulder the enormous responsibility of ruling over Europe, he emerges from Charlemagne's tomb newly enlightened and strengthened for his sacred office. Having learned that clemency, not the exercise of power, is the best way to rule, he also relinquishes all claims to Doña Sol. The once selfish and profligate king has become a magnanimous and wise ruler.

The hero of the play, who is the focus of act 2, is not a nobleman but a poor mountaineer who leads a band of outlaws. Hernani, the exiled son of an executed duke, is—despite his reputation—a ''nobler'' match than his rival for the aristocratic Doña Sol, who would rather live in exile with him than become wife to Don Carlos. Selflessly concerned for her welfare, he pleads that she fly from him and save herself: ''It would be a crime to wrench out the flower as I fall into the abyss! No, I have breathed its perfume, and that is enough. Go link the life I've troubled to another man's.'' But her unfaltering love has already transformed him from the bandit he has become to the nobleman he was meant to be. Hernani is further ennobled by the intensity of his conflicting passions: his strong sense of honor, which drives his hatred and need for revenge, versus his self-sacrificing love for Doña Sol, which places her above himself. Thus their first embrace at the close of act 2 seems destined to be their last.

Don Ruy Gomez de Silva, the descendant of an ancient line of noblemen, reveals the nature of his love for Doña Sol in act 3. By marrying Doña Sol, he hopes to cling to life as he nears the grave. In spite of the fact that she does not love him, but has agreed to marry him, he is still jealous of his youthful rivals. When Hernani appears on the eve of their wedding, Ruy Gomez must choose between dishonoring his family name by surrendering Hernani to Don Carlos or saving Doña Sol from being carried off as Don Carlos' hostage. Obedience to the ancestral code of honor prevails. Yet it is his jealousy and not his honor that propels his cruel insistence to end Hernani's life for daring to love Doña Sol. Masked as Death, Ruy Gomez reclaims his bond: ''The bells you rang this morning tolled your death . . . Shall I go alone to death? Young man, you must come with me!'' Ruy Gomez has become the very force he has feared most.

ABOUT THE TRANSLATION

Hugo's unique poetic gifts are profusely evident in *Hernani*. His characters are nourished by a vivid verse structure that sustains intense emotions at every turn of the dramatic action. But confronting the play without the music of its metrical cadences and powerful rhyming couplets is to experience only one side of its mysterious romantic fascination. Fortunately the present translation into English prose by Linda Asher accommodates our contemporary consciousness, while remaining sensitive to the performance expectations of Hugo's dramatic achievement: the deliberate shifts between bold and delicate verbal imagery; the repeated passionate outbursts that must never grow tiresome; the carefully measured solos, duets, trios, and chorus structures that stress the hidden music of the play; and the inevitable tragic denouement.

The tone is set early in act 1 with Doña Sol's first declaration of love: "J'ai besoin de vous voir et de vous voir encore/ Et de vous voir toujours." The urgency of her desire is captured as follows: "I need to see you, and must have you near, and have you all the time." But Hugo's poetic imagery swells as Doña Sol rhapsodizes further:

> Quand le bruit de vos pas
> S'efface, alors je crois que mon coeur ne bat pas,
> Vous me manquez, je suis absente de moi-même;
> Mais dès qu'enfin ce pas que j'attends et que j'aime
> Vient frapper mon oreille, alors il me souvient
> Que je vis, et je sens mon âme qui revient!

These images are richly served by the following:

> When the sound of your step fades, then I think that my heart has stopped its beat; you are gone, and I am gone from myself. But no sooner does that beloved footfall sound in my ear again, than I remember life and feel my soul come back to me!

Asher's adherence to the original French reproduces the lyrical content, if not the form, of Hugo's masterpiece.

HERNANI-IN-PERFORMANCE

The premiere of *Hernani* on February 25, 1830, proved to be one of the most notorious evenings in stage history. Followers of Hugo had been gathering forces since the previous October when the play had been announced and were especially determined to enjoy a smooth reception. Since the paid **claque** of the Comédie Française had refused to applaud the works of the Romantic playwrights during the 1829 season, Hugo was taking no chances. He sent fellow writers and artists, including Theophile Gautier, Hector Berlioz, Gerard de Nerval, Honoré de Balzac, and Stendhal, to seek out further supporters among the young Bohemians living in the Latin Quarter, distributing tickets to them to serve as his personal *claque* during the performance. In addition, red paper squares on which were written the Spanish word "hierro" (iron)—symbolic of the courage and faith required to do battle—were handed out to nearly ninety Hugo partisans who were scattered throughout the theatre. On the morning of the opening, Hugo himself visited Philante Chasles, the critic for *Le Temps,* urging him to join the fight by carrying a yellow paper with the inscription, "Hierro Yerro"—"I am of iron."

Instead of an ordinary opening night, the occasion was shaping into a battleground. By mid-afternoon, Hugo's supporters were sequestered inside the theatre to lie in wait for the arrival of the patrons. One strategy was to create a barrier in the orchestra pit between the audience and the stage; another was to detract hecklers from disrupting the performance. Hanging around long hours before the doors were officially opened, they ate, drank, sang, and recited Hugo's poetry. Like troops in the trenches, they acted out their revolutionary fervor by littering the hallowed auditorium and urinating at the entrances to the boxes and galleries.

Thus the fashionable and conservative aristocracy entered this desecrated temple of neoclassicism. Under Hugo's direction, the actors of the Comédie Française, particularly Mme. Mars as Doña Sol, Michelot as Don Carlos, Joanny as Ruy Gomez, and Firman as Hernani, abandoned their accustomed **declamatory style.** This unexpected move toward realistic acting, played against the spectacular sets by Pierre-Luc-Charles Ciceri and Louis Boulanger, created a sensation. But despite some cries of consternation at the drama unfolding on stage, *Hernani* proved a success. The excessive emotions, implausible characters, and unexpected shifts from farce to high drama prompted the very response Hugo had hoped for so that by the evening's end, he was offered a contract to publish his play. When *Hernani* ended its first season in June, its forty-five-performance engagement asserted the triumph of Romanticism.

James Kenney adapted the play for its English premiere at the Drury Lane in 1831. Seven years later, with Romanticism securely in place on stage, the Comédie Française revived *Hernani* with Marie-Thomas Dorval as Doña Sol, thus making it a permanent fixture in its repertoire. On March 9, 1844, at the Teatro la Fenice, Venice, the public was treated to the first performance of *Ernani,* the opera by Giuseppe Verdi with a libretto by Francesco Maria Piave, based on Hugo's play. It is in this form that *Hernani* remains best known and widely performed today.

From 1867, when the fall of Louis Bonaparte lifted the ban against Hugo's works, until 1952, the number of performances of *Hernani* at the Comédie Française exceeded 2,600. The most important of these was the 1877 revival with Sarah Bernhardt as Doña Sol. Her real-life love affair with Mounet-Sully, who played Hernani, was common knowledge, so audiences were openly grief-stricken when the dying lovers collapsed in each other's arms. Hugo was so elated at seeing Bernhardt play the role exactly as he conceived it that he sent her a diamond in the shape of a tear drop on a gold bracelet to express his admiration. *Hernani* proved the great hit of the season, playing 116 performances between November 19, 1877, and December 31, 1878.

Bernhardt brought her triumphant Doña Sol to New York City's Booth's Theatre on November 19, 1880. Following her successful appearance, English actor Lawrence Barrett revised James Kenney's adaptation at both the Chestnut Theatre in Philadelphia and the Star Theatre in New York in 1886. His appearance in the title role and his streamlining the script received critical praise. When Bernhardt appeared at the Star Theatre in 1887 in the final performance of her American tour, the cheers that greeted her would never ring as loudly again. By the time Mounet-Sully played *Hernani* in New York on March 27, 1894, the American public had lost interest in the play. A reporter for *The New York Times* thought Hernani's oath and self-sacrifice seemed more ridiculous than stirring to an audience whose tastes, at the turn of the century, seemed noticeably influenced by matters of commerce.

During the second half of the twentieth century, the play's revolutionary spirit demonstrated a resurgence of interest after the student uprisings in Paris in 1968. Decrying the limitations of history and the suffocating ideologies and traditions of the old guard, students and thinkers like Barthes, Derrida, and Foucault were analogous to those Hugo partisans who championed the overthrow of neoclassicism. To quote Anne Ubersfeld,

It is impossible to see the last act of *Hernani* as anything other than an allegory of the old society, the old forces and old laws still sufficiently powerful to remove all future vision for the young. At the same time, Hernani's despair no longer appears as that of a neurotic individual, an absurd fool, but as the symbol of the powerlessness to which an ossified society condemns the young man and his desire to live and to act.[4]

So when *Hernani* was revived at the Comédie Française in 1974, its excesses were no longer viewed with a jaundiced eye or with derision. To the contrary, Hugo's political and artistic aims were greeted with renewed enthusiasm.

REFLECTIONS ON HERNANI

The following excerpt is taken from a New York Times *review of* Hernani. *The Comédie Française production, which starred Sarah Bernhardt as Doña Sol, opened at Booth's Theatre in New York City in November 1880. [No reviewer was listed.]*

As to Mlle. Bernhardt's impersonation of Doña Sol, that has been viewed by French critics and by M. Hugo himself as a positive and brilliant embodiment of the character, it has done more, perhaps, than any other of her undertakings to establish her place among the great artists of the stage. The power and the art displayed in Mlle. Bernhardt's Doña Sol are, of course, the power and the art already more or less displayed in each of her three previous performances; but Doña Sol, unlike her other characters, is a creature of poetry and romance, and some new aspects of the actress's versatility were, in consequence, brought to light here for the first time last night. Her exquisite treatment of verse, her sense of the picturesque, and her strong sympathies with the actions of the romantic drama, were made apparent throughout the representation, and it is these traits of her performance that chiefly call for notice.

Mlle. Bernhardt comprehends perfectly the difference between realism and romanticism, and this is clearly shown in her manner of combining the two; her performance was truthful and natural, and yet it had all the force of a delineation which needs to be colored deeply and treated poetically. Her declamation, for instance, was in no instance stilted or artificial, and was, on the other hand, as full of art and harmony as Hugo's verse. Her gestures were remarkably picturesque, her movements vivid with life and contrast, and her transitions striking. If we were to select the chief beauty of this performance for special comment, Mlle. Bernhardt's declamation would certainly be chosen; for, though we have heard the French verse recited by all the leading actors of the Comédie Française, we have never heard it read with such variety of effect, distinctiveness of enunciation, clearness of meaning, and musical sweetness as by this actress last night. Her tones, it has been already stated here, are of a fine, bell-like quality, and are clearly heard in all their modulations, and her manner of delivery is singularly fine. Join to her natural vocal resources and to the accomplishments that are the result of training, a thorough sense of rhythm, and a true poetic feeling, and some idea of her diction may be formed. Her reading, like her acting, was a charming blend of the natural and the poetic.

Doña Sol cannot be called in any sense a "heavy part" until the fifth act is reached, for, throughout the previous portion of the play is precisely as M. Hugo has described it— simple, grave, ardent, concentrated. The mingling in her nature of pride and purity, of course, steadfast honor, and tenderness, and of a certain passionateness that never becomes exuberant passion—all this is indicated with delicate art by Mlle. Bernhardt, and there is nothing here that taxes her strength unduly or lies beyond her talent. Her appearance is romantic to the point of pre-Raphaelism; and the picturesqueness of her gestures, the dignity of her bearing, and the expressive face and manners, help to make her embodiment an idea that satisfies both the eye and the imagination.

In general, Mlle. Bernhardt treated all her scenes with great care and skill, and made no effort to be theatrical at the expense of truth and poetry; her performance was even singularly quiet at times, and seemed to disdain applause; but it was admirably dramatic in the third act, and simply exquisite throughout the last act. Nothing more melodious than her delivery of the love passages at the close of the play has been heard upon our stage, and her accompanying actions were full of restrained passion. The death of Doña Sol was portrayed with a touching fidelity.

Notes

1. *Charles Affron,* A STAGE FOR POETS: STUDIES IN THE THEATRE OF HUGO AND MUSSET *(Princeton, NJ: Princeton University Press, 1971), 23.*
2. THE NEW YORK TIMES, *review (undated) in* THE MODERN THEATRE IN REVOLT *by John Mason Brown (New York: W. W. Norton & Co., 1929).*
3. *Marvin Carlson,* "HERNANI*'s Revolt from the Tradition of French Stage Composition,"* THEATRE SURVEY *(May 1972): 4–5.*
4. COMÉDIE FRANÇAISE *program, no. 31 (September 1974), translated by editors.*

HERNANI
VICTOR HUGO
TRANSLATED BY LINDA ASHER

CHARACTERS

Hernani	Don Sancho	First Conspirator
Don Carlos	Don Matias	A Mountaineer
Don Ruy Gomez de Silva	Don Ricardo	Iaquez
Doña Sol de Silva	Don Garci Suarez	Doña Josefa Duarte
Duke of Bavaria	Don Francisco	A Lady
Duke of Gotha	Don Juan de Haro	Other Conspirators, Mountaineers,
Duke of Lutzelburg	Don Gil Tellez Giron	Lord, Soldiers, Pages, etc.

The action of the play takes place in Spain, in 1519.

ACT ONE
THE KING

(*Saragossa: a bedchamber. It is night. A lamp on the table.*)

SCENE ONE

(DOÑA JOSEFA DUARTE, *an old woman in black, with the bodice of her gown ornamented in jet, in the style of Isabella the Catholic; she draws the crimson window drapes and arranges a few chairs. There is a knock at a small hidden door on the right. She listens; there is a second knock.*)

DOÑA JOSEFA. Has he arrived already? (*Another knock.*) It *is* from the secret stairway, no doubt of that. (*A fourth knock.*) Quick, then—I must open it. (*She opens the covered door.* DON CARLOS *enters, his cloak across his lower face, and his hat low over his eyes.*) Good evening to you, sir. (*She leads him in. He opens his cloak and reveals a rich outfit of velvet and silk, in the fashion of Castile in 1519. She looks at him more closely, and draws back, astonished.*) What? Señor Hernani—but it is not you! Help! Guards!

DON CARLOS (*gripping her arm*). Two more words out of you, old woman, and you die! (*He stares hard at her; she subsides into terrified silence.*) Is this the apartment that belongs to Doña Sol? They tell me she is promised to her uncle, the old duke—a gracious lord, proud, venerable, and decrepit. They say this beauty spurns all other men, but that she loves a smooth-faced youth, and every night she meets this young lover—without whiskers or mustache—beneath the very nose of the old man. Is this all true? (*She is silent; he shakes her arm.*) Well? Will you answer me?

DOÑA JOSEFA. You forbade me to speak even two words, my lord.

DON CARLOS. I asked for only one—a yes or no. Doña Sol de Silva *is* your mistress? Speak.

DOÑA JOSEFA. Yes. Why?

DON CARLOS. No matter. And her old fiancé, the duke—he is out at present?

DOÑA JOSEFA. Yes.

DON CARLOS. She must be awaiting her young man, then?

DOÑA JOSEFA. Yes.

DON CARLOS. Oh, I could die!

DOÑA JOSEFA.   Yes.

DON CARLOS.   Duenna—is this where they meet?

DOÑA JOSEFA.   Yes.

DON CARLOS.   Hide me here somehow!

DOÑA JOSEFA.   Hide you!

DON CARLOS.   Yes.

DOÑA JOSEFA.   But why?

DON CARLOS.   No matter why.

DOÑA JOSEFA.   You're asking me to hide you?

DON CARLOS.   Yes—somewhere here.

DOÑA JOSEFA.   Never!

DON CARLOS (*drawing a knife and a purse at once from his sash*). Madame, do me the honor of choosing—this purse or else this blade.

DOÑA JOSEFA (*taking the purse*). You must be the devil.

DON CARLOS.   Yes, I am.

DOÑA JOSEFA (*opening a narrow closet in the wall*). Come in here.

DON CARLOS (*looking in*). This box?

DOÑA JOSEFA (*closing it*). If it does not suit you, leave.

DON CARLOS (*opening it again and examining it*). It will do perfectly. (*With another glance inside.*) Is this the stable where you keep your broomstick between rides? (*He cramps himself into it with difficulty.*) Ouff!

DOÑA JOSEFA (*clasping her hands in horror*). A man—here in this room!

DON CARLOS (*from the still-open closet*). Oh, then your lady was expecting a woman?

DOÑA JOSEFA.   Good heavens—I hear her coming now— please, my lord, close the door, quickly! (*She pushes the door shut.*)

DON CARLOS (*from inside*). Remember, duenna—say one word, and you shall die.

DOÑA JOSEFA (*alone*). Who is this man, Good Jesus! Shall I call for help? But whom can I call? Except my lady and myself, all the palace is asleep. Well, the other one will be arriving soon, and this is his affair—he has a good sword. May the Lord save us from perdition! (*Weighs the purse in her hand.*) After all, it's not as though he were a common thief.

(DOÑA SOL *enters, in white;* DOÑA JOSEFA *hides the purse.*)

SCENE TWO

DOÑA SOL.   Josefa!

DOÑA JOSEFA.   My lady?

DOÑA SOL.   I am afraid—Hernani should be here by now. (*Sound of steps at the small door.*) Listen—I hear him now on the stair. Open before he knocks—and be quick— hurry!

(JOSEFA *opens the tiny door.* HERNANI *enters, in a great cloak and broad hat. Underneath he is dressed as an Aragonese mountaineer, in gray, with a leather jerkin; a sword, a dagger, and a horn are at his waist.*)

DOÑA SOL (*running to him*). Hernani!

HERNANI.   Doña Sol! At last you stand before me, and the voice I hear is yours! Ah, why must fate set my path so far from yours? I need you to help me forget the rest of this unhappy life.

DOÑA SOL.   Your cloak is drenched! Is it raining so hard?

HERNANI.   I do not know.

DOÑA SOL.   You must be chilled.

HERNANI.   It is nothing.

DOÑA SOL.   Take off that cloak.

HERNANI.   Doña Sol, my beloved, tell me this—when you fall to rest at night, all calm, and innocent and pure— when a happy sleep half opens your fresh lips, and when its finger closes your dark eyes—does some angel come and tell you how dear a thing you are to me, a man deserted and rebuffed by all the world?

DOÑA SOL.   You are so late, my lord! But tell me, are you cold?

HERNANI.   Beside you I only burn! When a fierce love rages in my head, when my heart swells with its own swirling tempests—then how can I feel nature's cloud outside, with all its flash and storming?

DOÑA SOL (*unfastening his cloak*). Come—give me your cape. And your sword too.

HERNANI.   No—this is another friend, as innocent and loyal as you. Doña Sol, the old duke, your uncle, your promised husband—is he away?

DOÑA SOL.   Yes, this hour belongs to us.

HERNANI.   This hour, and nothing more! No more than just an hour for our love! And afterwards, I must forget, or die. My angel, one hour with you when I would ask for all of life and all eternity!

DOÑA SOL.   My Hernani!

HERNANI (*bitterly*). How fortunate I am, that the duke has left the palace! Like a miserable thief I force the door— I creep within and see you, and steal an hour of your sweet song and gaze from the old man. And I am lucky, and others envy me for stealing an hour from him, while he steals my whole life.

DOÑA SOL.   Please, Hernani. (*Handing the cloak to the old woman.*) Josefa, dry his cloak. (JOSEFA *goes out.* DOÑA SOL *sits down, and gestures to* HERNANI *to come closer.*) Come here by me.

HERNANI (*not hearing her*). So the duke is away from the castle. . . .

DOÑA SOL (*smilingly*). How tall you are!

HERNANI.   He is gone awhile—

DOÑA SOL.   Dear Hernani, let us not think about the duke.

HERNANI.   But we must think about him! That old man loves you, and will marry you. . . . He took a kiss from you the other day—not think about him!

DOÑA SOL (*laughing*). Is that what's thrown you into such despair? An uncle's kiss—and on the brow, besides! Almost a fatherly caress. . . .

HERNANI.   No; a lover's kiss, a husband's—the kiss of a jealous man. Oh, my lady, you will soon belong to him! Do you realize that? The foolish, stooped old man, he needs a wife to end his journey and complete his day— and so the chilly specter takes himself a young girl! The mad old man! Does he not see that while he marries you with one hand, death weds him by the other? He comes so heedlessly to thrust himself into our love—when he should instead be measuring himself for the gravedigger! Doña Sol, who made this match? You were forced to it, I hope?

DOÑA SOL.   The king desires it, they say.

HERNANI.   The king! the king! My father died upon the gallows, condemned by his! And though we have grown older since that day, my hatred is still fresh toward the old king's ghost, his widow, and his son—toward all his flesh. He is dead, he counts no more; but when I was a child I made a vow to avenge my father on his son. Carlos, king of the Castiles—I have sought you everywhere, for the loathing between our houses does not die! Our fathers struggled without pity or remorse for thirty years; now, with our fathers dead, nothing has changed. They died in vain, for their enmity lives on; peace has not yet come to them, for their sons still stand, and still pursue the duel. So it is you, Carlos, who made this shameful match! So much the better. I sought for you, and here you are astride my path.

DOÑA SOL.   You frighten me.

HERNANI.   I have sworn to carry out a curse, and I must frighten even myself. Listen. The man they have betrothed you to, Don Ruy de Silva, is duke of Pastraña; he is a nobleman of Aragon, a count and grandee of Castile. He cannot give you youth, my sweet young girl; but in its place he offers you such gold, such jewels and gems that your brow will shine among the glittering crowns of royalty. His duchess will hold such power and pride, splendor and wealth, that many a queen could envy her. Such is the duke. While I—I am poor; as a child I had nothing but the forests where I roamed barefoot. I too may own some glowing coat of arms, hid now by clotted blood; I too may have rights that now are cloaked in the folds and shadows of a black gallows-cloth; unless my waiting be in vain, perhaps one day those rights will flash out from this sheath again as I draw my sword. Meanwhile, a jealous heaven has granted me nothing but air, and light, and water—no more than the dowry it offers every man. Let me free you now from one of us, the duke or me. You must choose between us: marry him, or come with me.

DOÑA SOL.   I shall go with you.

HERNANI.   To live among my rough companions? They are outlaws, whose names the hangman already knows, men whose blades never grow blunt, nor their hearts tender—each of them with some blood vengeance that whips him on. Would you come and be the queen of such a band? For I never told you this—I am an outlaw! When I was hunted through the land of Spain, only old Catalonia welcomed me like a mother into her forests, her harsh mountains, her rough rocks where only the soaring eagle peers. Among her highlanders, her solemn, poor, free men, I grew to manhood; and tomorrow if I sound this horn, three thousand of them will come. . . . You shiver—think again. Would you follow me into the trees, over the hills, along the river's edge? To the land of men who look like the devils in your dreams? And live in doubt, suspecting everything—eyes, voices, footfalls, rustlings—and sleep on the bare grass, and drink from the stream; and as you nurse some waking child at night, to hear musket balls go hissing by your ear?

Would you be an outlawed wanderer with me, and if need be, follow me to where I shall follow my father— onto the scaffold?

DOÑA SOL.   I will follow you.

HERNANI.   The duke is prosperous and powerful—his life is good. There is no stain on his old family name. The duke can do what he will. He offers you not just his hand, but treasure, titles, and contentment.

DOÑA SOL.   We will leave tomorrow. Hernani, do not condemn me for my new boldness. Are you my demon or my angel? I cannot tell—but I am your slave. Wherever you go I will go. Stay, or depart—I belong to you. Why? I cannot say. I need to see you, and must have you near, and have you all the time. When the sound of your step fades, then I think that my heart has stopped its beat; you are gone, and I am gone from myself. But no sooner does that beloved footfall sound in my ear again, than I remember life and feel my soul come back to me!

HERNANI (*taking her in his arms*).   My love!

DOÑA SOL.   At midnight, then, tomorrow. Bring your men to my window, and clap your hands three times. You will see—I will be strong and brave.

HERNANI.   Do you realize now what I am?

DOÑA SOL.   My lord, what does it matter? I am going with you.

HERNANI.   No—since you want to follow me, impulsive woman, you must learn what name, what rank, what soul, what destiny is hidden in this rough Hernani. You would take a brigand; but would you have a banished man?

DON CARLOS (*clattering the cupboard door open*).   Will you never finish telling her your tale? Do you suppose it's pleasant, cramped into this closet?

(HERNANI *starts back, astonished.* DOÑA SOL *cries out and flies into his arms, staring fearfully at* DON CARLOS.)

HERNANI (*his hand on his sword hilt*).   Who is this man?

DOÑA SOL.   Great heavens! Help! Help, guards!

HERNANI.   Quiet, Doña Sol! You'll waken angry eyes! When I am with you, please, whatever comes, never call for any hand but mine to aid you. (*To* DON CARLOS.) What were you doing there?

DON CARLOS.   I can hardly claim I was out for a gallop through the woods.

HERNANI.   When a man banters after he offends, only his heir is likely to enjoy the joke.

DON CARLOS.   One good line deserves another. Sir, let us speak frankly. You love this lady; you come to watch your eyes in hers each night: very good. I love her too, and want to know who it is I have seen so often entering by the window while I stay at the door.

HERNANI.   I swear you shall leave the way I enter, sir.

DON CARLOS.   We shall see. So then, I offer my lady my love too. Let us share her, shall we? I've seen such goodness in her soul, so much tender feeling, that I should think she had enough for two lovers. And so, tonight, I thought to bring my plans to fruit. I was mistaken for you, and slipped in by surprise; I hid, I listened—you see how frank I am—but in this slot I hardly heard a word, and nearly suffocated. Besides, my French vest was crumpling badly. I am coming out.

HERNANI.   My dagger is uneasy in its hiding place too, and eager to come out.

DON CARLOS (*acknowledging the challenge*). As you like, sir.

HERNANI (*drawing his sword*). En garde!

(DON CARLOS *draws his own.*)

DOÑA SOL (*throwing herself between them*). Hernani! No!
DON CARLOS.   Peace, señora.
HERNANI.   Tell me your name.
DON CARLOS.   Tell me your own!
HERNANI.   I am keeping it a deadly secret for another man—one day he will lie beneath my conquering knee and feel my name in his ear, and my knife at his heart.
DON CARLOS.   Then what is that man's name?
HERNANI.   What can it mean to you? On guard! Defend yourself!

(*They cross swords.* DOÑA SOL *falls trembling onto a chair. Knocking at the main door.*)

DOÑA SOL (*rising in alarm*). Someone is at the door! (*The duel stops.* JOSEFA *enters through the small door, highly agitated.*)
HERNANI (*to* JOSEFA). Who is knocking there?
DOÑA JOSEFA (*to* DOÑA SOL). My lady, a terrible thing! The duke has just returned!
DOÑA SOL (*wringing her hands*). The duke! Then there is no hope. . . .
DOÑA JOSEFA (*glancing about her*). Gracious Lord—the stranger, and these swords—they're battling! This is a fine affair!

(*The two adversaries slip their swords back into the sheaths.* DON CARLOS *wraps himself in his cloak and pulls his hat down over his eyes. The knock is heard again.*)

HERNANI.   What shall we do?

(*Another knock.*)

A VOICE OUTSIDE.   Doña Sol, open the door. It is I.

(DOÑA JOSEFA *takes a step toward the door, but* HERNANI *stops her.*)

HERNANI.   No.
DOÑA JOSEFA (*fingering her rosary*). Good Saint James, help us through this trial!

(*More knocking.*)

HERNANI.   We must hide. (*He points to the closet.*)
DON CARLOS.   In that closet again?
HERNANI (*opening its door*). Go on in, yes; it will hold the two of us.
DON CARLOS.   Lord no, it's far too small.
HERNANI.   Let us leave then, through the secret door.
DON CARLOS.   Good night. I shall stay here.
HERNANI.   You will pay for this! (*To* DOÑA SOL.) Can I barricade the door?
DON CARLOS (*to* JOSEFA). Open it.
HERNANI.   What is he saying?
DON CARLOS.   Open it, I say! (*She is standing bewildered. The knocking is repeated.* DOÑA JOSEFA *goes trembling to answer it.*)
DOÑA SOL.   Lord in heaven, help me!

SCENE THREE

DON RUY GOMEZ DE SILVA (*white-haired, white-bearded, dressed in black*). Men at this hour in my niece's room! Guards, come closer—this calls for brighter light! (*To* DOÑA SOL.) By Saint John of Avila, there are three of us here—two more than should be, madam! (*To the young men.*) You young cavaliers, what business have you here? When the Cid lived, and in Bernardo's day, those two giants of Spain and of the world moved through the Castiles doing honor to the aged and granting women the safeguard of their shields. Those were powerful men—their iron and their steel rode lighter on their shoulders than your velvet does on you. Those men respected a gray beard; they brought their love to consecration in the church and betrayed no man, and their reason was that they must keep the honor of their line. When they desired a woman, they wed her unsullied and in full daylight before the eyes of all, and with their sword, or halberd, or lance firmly in hand. But these criminals who skulk by dark, trusting only the night with their shameful deeds—who steal a woman's honor behind her husband's back—I tell you that the Cid, the ancestor of us all, would have named them vile and forced them to their knees. He would degrade their rank, for they are mere usurpers of nobility; he would deface their coat of arms with a slap of his sword.

Ah, what regret I feel as I think of it—how those men of other times would deal with men today!

Why are you here? To tell me I am an old man, at whom the young shall sneer? Will they laugh at me, who fought at Zamora? When I pass by, white-headed, will they laugh? Not you—no, you at least will not be there to laugh!

HERNANI. Duke—

DON RUY. Silence! . . . You have your swords, your daggers, your lances; you have hunting, and banquets, festivals, and falcons; songs to sing at evening under a balcony, plumes in your hats, and cloaks of silk, and balls and tournaments, and youth, and joy—and yet you children weary of all that! You must have a new plaything; you cast about and pick an old man for it—and now, you have smashed the toy! But God willing, the pieces will spring up whole again and burst in your very teeth! Come out with me!

HERNANI. My lord duke—

DON RUY. Come out with me! Draw your swords! Gentlemen, was this only a whim? Was it? There is a treasure in my house—a young girl's honor, the honor of a woman and of a whole family. I love this girl; she is my niece, and soon she will exchange her ring for the one I wear. I believe her to be chaste and pure, and sacred to all men. It happens that I leave the house an hour, and a thief slips in through the door to steal my honor. Wash off your hands, you soulless men—by no more than a touch you taint our women. Or better—have I still something more for you? (*He pulls off his gold collar of knighthood.*) Here, take and trample this, my Golden Fleece! (*Throws off his hat.*) Wrench out my hair, make it a lowly thing, and tomorrow go and boast throughout the town that never in their shameless games have scoundrels defiled a nobler head, nor whiter hairs.

DOÑA SOL. My lord—

DON RUY (*to his servants*). Guards—my hatchet, and my knife, and my Toledo blade. And you two, come out with me now!

DON CARLOS (*stepping forward*). Duke, there is more pressing business first. I came to tell you of Maximilian, emperor of Germany: he is dead. (*He throws off his cloak, and uncovers his face.*)

DON RUY. Are you joking? . . . God, it is the king!

DOÑA SOL. The king!

HERNANI (*his eyes flaring*). The king of Spain!

DON CARLOS. Yes, Carlos of Spain. My lord duke, then, do you understand? My grandsire the emperor has died; I heard this only now, and hastened here in person to tell you of the news, as a loyal and beloved subject. I came

by dark, and incognito, to ask your guidance—all quite simple, and yet see what confusion you arouse!

(DON RUY *sends his servants away with a sign. He draws closer to* DON CARLOS, *whom* DOÑA SOL *watches in fear and surprise.* HERNANI *gazes attentively on, from his corner.*)

DON RUY GOMEZ. But why that long delay before the door was opened?

DON CARLOS. With good reason—you come with a whole escort. When a state secret brings me to your house, am I expected to confide in all your men?

DON RUY. Highness, forgive me! Appearances—

DON CARLOS. Good father, I named you governor of the Figueras castle. Now who will govern you?

DON RUY. Forgive me—

DON CARLOS. Enough. We'll talk no more of it, my lord. Well. The emperor is dead.

DON RUY. Your highness' grandfather—he is dead?

DON CARLOS. I stand before you now heavy with grief.

DON RUY. Who will succeed him?

DON CARLOS. A Saxon duke, perhaps; or Francis the First of France, who is one of the contenders.

DON RUY. Where will the electors meet?

DON CARLOS. At Aix-la-Chapelle, I think, or Spires or Frankfurt.

DON RUY. And our own Spanish king, whose days God guard, has he never considered the throne of empire for himself?

DON CARLOS. Incessantly.

DON RUY. It goes to you by right.

DON CARLOS. I know it.

DON RUY. Your father was archduke of Austria; and I hope the electors will recall that the man who has just fallen from the imperial purple to the shroud was your ancestor.

DON CARLOS. Besides, I am a citizen of Ghent.

DON RUY. I saw your grandfather once when I was young—alas, I am the last survivor of a whole century; everyone else has died now. He was a superb, a mighty emperor.

DON CARLOS. Rome is on my side.

DON RUY. Valiant, firm—and yet no tyrant—that head well suited the old Germanic body! (*He bends to kiss the king's hands.*) I pity you—so young and made to know so terrible a grief.

DON CARLOS. Sicily belongs to me; the pope wants it back again. An emperor cannot own Sicily; thus he makes me emperor; and I, the docile son, give Naples over. Let us first win the eagle and then we'll see whether I let his wings be clipped!

DON RUY. What joy that old ruler would feel to see your already broad brow assume his crown. My lord, we weep with you for that very great and good and Christian emperor!

DON CARLOS. The holy father is nimble. What is Sicily, after all: an island dangling from my realm; a ragged tag, a remnant that hangs off Spain and trails along beside her. He will say this: "What use have you, my son, for that misshapen shred of land that clings by a mere thread to the imperial world? Your empire is badly shaped. Quick now, the shears, and let us cut it off."

    Most holy Father, thanks! For if fortune is good to me, I shall expect to stitch a couple of those pieces back again onto the holy empire; and if some few strips are missing here and there, I'll patch my estates together again with duchies and with islands!

DON RUY. May you find consolation. There is an empire of just men where the dead are found again, still holier and grander than they were in life.

DON CARLOS. This King Francis the First is an ambitious man. No sooner does the emperor die than he ogles the throne! He already has his France—a fine piece of Christian land, and well worth holding to. My grandfather the emperor used to say to King Louis, "If I were God the Father, and I had two sons, I should make the elder God, and the other king of France." (*To the duke*.) Do you suppose that Francis has a chance?

DON RUY. He has a habit of success.

DON CARLOS. Everything would have to be amended. The Golden Bull forbids a foreigner to reign.

DON RUY. But in that respect, Your Highness, you are king of Spain.

DON CARLOS. But I am a citizen of Ghent.

DON RUY. His latest campaign has made King Francis very strong.

DON CARLOS. The eagle who may hatch upon my crest can spread his wings wide too.

DON RUY. Does Your Highness know Latin?

DON CARLOS. Only poorly.

DON RUY. That is a pity. The German nobles like to be addressed in Latin.

DON CARLOS. They will be satisfied with a noble Spanish. For mark my words, it makes small difference what tongue a voice may speak, if it speaks strongly enough.

    I am setting out for Flanders. Your king, dear Silva, must return to you as emperor. The king of France will do all that he can to win his way; I must overtake him. I shall go shortly.

DON RUY. Will you leave us, sire, with Aragon still unpurged of these new bandits who raise their brazen heads throughout our mountainland?

DON CARLOS. I shall leave orders with the Duke of Arcos to wipe them out.

DON RUY. And will you also command their leader to let himself be taken?

DON CARLOS. Who is their leader—his name?

DON RUY. I do not know it. But he is said to be a formidable man.

DON CARLOS. Nonsense. I know that just now he is hidden in Galicia, and can be taken with a few militia troops.

DON RUY. Then the rumors are false that say he is nearby?

DON CARLOS. Completely false. . . . You will give me a bed for the night.

DON RUY (*bowing to the floor*). Thank you, sire. (*Calling his servants.*) All of you, do honor to the king, my guest.

(*The servants bring torches, and the duke orders them into two rows to the door in rear. Meanwhile* DOÑA SOL *draws imperceptibly closer to* HERNANI; *the king watches the pair of them.*)

DOÑA SOL (*low to* HERNANI). Tomorrow at midnight, beneath my window—do not fail. And clap three times.

HERNANI (*softly*). Tomorrow night . . .

DON CARLOS (*to himself*). Tomorrow! (*And aloud to* DOÑA SOL, *toward whom he moves with courtly gesture.*) Allow me to escort you. (*He leads her to the door; she exits.*)

HERNANI (*his hand inside his breast, on the pommel of his dagger*). My faithful blade! . . .

DON CARLOS (*returning, aside*). Our friend has the expression of a man who is trapped. (*He draws Hernani aside.*) I did you the honor, sir, of touching your sword. I could mistrust you for a hundred different reasons—but King Carlos has no taste for betrayals. Go. I am willing to protect you in your flight.

DON RUY (*coming closer and indicating* HERNANI). Who is this gentleman?

DON CARLOS. One of my followers. He is leaving now.

(*They go out with the servants and the torches, the duke ahead of the king, with a candle in his hand.*)

SCENE FOUR

HERNANI (*alone*). One of your followers—yes, King! Your follower, true! Night and day, and step by step, I follow you. A knife in my fist I go, my eye fixed on your trail— my race in me pursues your race in you. And now besides, you are become my rival. For a moment I hung hesitant between love and hatred; my heart was not large enough to hold both you and her. In loving her I forgot the hatred for you that weighs on me; but since you wish it, since you yourself come to remind me, good! I remember! My love bends the uncertain scales, and falls now wholly to the side of hatred. Yes, I am one of your followers. No courtier dancing in your accursed halls, no noble lord kissing your shadow, no steward denying his own man's heart for your heart's whim, no palace dog trained to slink at the king's heel, will dog your step more diligently than I! All that those Castilian grandees want of you is some pointless title, some shiny trinket, some golden sheep to hang about their throats; I'm not so foolish as to yearn so small! What I want from you is no vain favor—it is your body's soul, your vein's blood; I want what a fuming, conquering knife can dredge out from a heart's dark root. Lead on before me! I shall follow you. My vengeance is alert, it moves with me and speaks into my ear. Lead! I am here, I watch and I listen; my step seeks yours soundlessly, pursues it, and draws close. By day, my king, you'll never turn your head but you shall find me motionless and dark amid your celebration. By night you shall not turn your eyes, my king, but you shall see my burning eyes glow hot behind you! (*He goes out the small door.*)

ACT TWO
THE BANDIT

(*Saragossa. A patio in the Silva palace. At left, the palace's high walls, with a balconied window. Beneath the window is a small door. At right and rear are houses and streets. It is night. Here and there in the buildings a few windows are still showing light.*)

SCENE ONE

(DON CARLOS, DON SANCHO SANCHEZ DE ZUÑIGA, DON MATIAS CENTURION, DON RICARDO DE ROXAS, *all four arrive onstage, with* DON CARLOS *at their head. Their hats are pulled low and they are enveloped in long cloaks whose lower edges are lifted by their spears.*)

DON CARLOS (*surveying the balcony*). There is the balcony, and the door, just as she said. . . . My blood is boiling hot. (*Pointing to the unlit window.*) No light there yet! (*His eyes rove over the other lighted casements.*) Lights everywhere that are no use to me, and none where I would see one!

DON SANCHO.   That traitor; my lord—you simply let him leave?

DON CARLOS.   Yes.

DON MATIAS.   And he may have been the bandit general!

DON CARLOS.   He might have been their general or their drummer boy, but no sceptered king ever bore himself more nobly.

DON SANCHO.   What was his name, my lord?

DON CARLOS (*his eyes on the casement window*). Muñoz— . . . Fernan— . . . (*He suddenly remembers something.*) A name that ends in *i*.

DON SANCHO.   Hernani, possibly?

DON CARLOS.   Yes.

DON MATIAS.   Hernani? Then it *was* the chief!

DON SANCHO (*to the king*). Do you remember anything of what he said?

DON CARLOS (*who has not taken his eyes from the window*). I could not hear a thing in their damned closet.

DON SANCHO.   But why let him go when he was in your hands?

DON CARLOS (*turning slowly and staring at him*). Count of Monterey, do you question me? (*The two lords draw back and are silent.*) Besides, that is not what concerns me now. I want his mistress, not his head. I want her black eyes, friends! The loveliest in the world! Two mirrors! Two black beams of light, two dark torches! I heard nothing of their babble but these few words: "Tomorrow, come at midnight"—but they are the important ones. A perfect arrangement, gentlemen, I think you will agree: while this winsome bandit dallies at some murder or other, or digging someone's grave, I come at my ease and make off with his dove.

DON RICARDO.   Your Highness, it were more decisive to take the dove by killing off the vulture.

DON CARLOS (*to* DON RICARDO). A valuable suggestion, Count! Your hand is quick!

DON RICARDO (*bowing deeply*). By what title does the king please to name me count?

DON SANCHO (*angrily*). That was an error!

DON RICARDO (*to* DON SANCHO). The king called me count.

DON CARLOS.   That's enough. (*To* DON RICARDO.) I dropped that title. Pick it up.

DON RICARDO (*bowing again*). Thank you, Highness.

DON SANCHO (*to* DON MATIAS). A fine count—a count by accident!

(*The king walks about stage rear, looking at the lighted windows impatiently. The two noblemen converse in the foreground.*)

DON MATIAS (*to* DON SANCHO). But what will the king do, once he has the woman?

DON SANCHO (*watching* RICARDO *out of the corner of his eye*). Make her a countess, and then a lady in waiting; then, if he has a son by her, it will be king.

DON MATIAS.   Oh, come now. A bastard? Count, even a king can never draw a king out of a countess.

DON SANCHO.   He'll make her a marquise then, my dear marquis.

DON MATIAS.   Bastards are brought up to be the viceroys of conquered countries—that is how they are used.

(DON CARLOS *comes back.*)

DON CARLOS (*looking about at all the lighted windows*). They are watching us like dozens of jealous eyes. . . . Well, finally—two have just gone out. Now for the rest of them! Gentlemen, how long these waiting minutes! Who can make the time move faster?

DON SANCHO.   We often wonder in Your Highness' court.

DON CARLOS.   And meanwhile my people are saying it of you. (*The last bright window dims.*) The last of them is out! (*He turns toward the balcony of* DOÑA SOL'S *room; it is still dark.*) You damned glass, when will you turn light? This night is very dark. Doña Sol, come shine like a star in all this blackness! (*To* DON RICARDO.) What time is it?

DON RICARDO. Nearly midnight.

DON CARLOS. This business must be done with soon—the other one may come at any moment!

(DOÑA SOL'S *window brightens. Her shadow is visible on the lighted panes.*) Friends—a torch—her shadow at the window! No dawn was ever more beautiful to me than this one. I must be quick: give the signal she is waiting for, and clap my hands three times. In an instant, friends, you'll see her! . . . But our number will frighten her, perhaps—go, the three of you, into the shadow there, and watch for him. We'll share the loving pair among us—I take the lady, and you three the brigand.

DON RICARDO. A thousand thanks.

DON CARLOS. If he comes, get to him quickly and stun him with your swords. Then, while he is still unconscious, I'll go off with the girl; we shall meet later. But be sure not to kill him. He is a valiant man, and a man's death is a serious thing.

(*The two noblemen bow and leave.* DON CARLOS *waits till they disappear, then claps twice. At the second, the window opens, and* DOÑA SOL *appears on the balcony.*)

SCENE TWO

DOÑA SOL (*from the balcony*). Is it you, Hernani?

DON CARLOS (*to himself*). I must not speak! (*He claps his hands once more.*)

DOÑA SOL. I shall come down.

(*She closes the window, and the light goes out. A moment later, the small door opens and she emerges, a lantern in her hand and a cloak over her shoulders.*)

DOÑA SOL. Hernani! (DON CARLOS *pulls his hat low over his face, and hurries to her.*) That is not his step! (*She turns to go back.* DON CARLOS *runs to her and holds her by the arm.*)

DON CARLOS. Doña Sol!

DOÑA SOL. And not his voice!

DON CARLOS. What more adoring voice could you desire? It is still a lover's voice, and a royal lover's besides.

DOÑA SOL. The king!

DON CARLOS. Wish or command—a kingdom is yours to have! For the man whose gentle grasp you would break is the king your lord, and Carlos is your slave!

DOÑA SOL (*struggling to free herself*). Hernani, help me!

DON CARLOS. You fear the wrong man—this is not your bandit holding you; it is the king!

DOÑA SOL. No. *You* are the bandit! Do you feel no shame? I blush with it for you. Are these the exploits for a king to boast? To come by night and take a woman by force? My bandit is worth a thousand of you! If a man's birth

matched his nobility—if God gave rank according to men's hearts, then he would be the king, and you the criminal!

DON CARLOS (*trying to draw her with him*). Madame—

DOÑA SOL. Have you forgotten that my father was a count?

DON CARLOS. I shall make you a duchess.

DOÑA SOL (*pushing him away*). Shame! (*She draws back a few steps.*) There can be nothing of the sort between us, Don Carlos. My aged father poured out his blood for you. I am a noblewoman, I come from that proud blood—too haughty for a concubine, and too lowly for a bride.

DON CARLOS. Princess!

DOÑA SOL. Go offer your love games to common girls, King Carlos; else, if you dare to treat me in such disgraceful manner, I can show you quite clearly that I am a lady and a woman both.

DON CARLOS. Well then, come share my throne and my name too. Come—you shall be queen, and empress besides—

DOÑA SOL. No. That is a ruse. Besides, Your Highness, I must speak honestly—no matter if you were another man, I would rather wander with Hernani, my own king; rather live outside the world, and the law, in hunger, and thirst, forever hunted and in flight, rather share his sorry destiny from day to day, share his solitude, his battles and his exile, his grief, his poverty, his fear—I would rather all that than be empress to any emperor.

DON CARLOS. How fortunate he is!

DOÑA SOL. He is a pitiful exile!

DON CARLOS. But fortunate even so, for he is loved. I am alone, and an angel walks with him. Do you loathe me?

DOÑA SOL. I do not love you.

DON CARLOS (*seizing her violently*). Whether you love me or not can make no difference—you will come! My hand is stronger than yours—you will come. I want you! We shall soon see if I am king of Spain and of the Indies for nothing.

DOÑA SOL (*struggling*). Have pity on me, my lord! You are king! You are royal! You have but to select a duchess, a marquise, or a countess. The loyal ladies of the court can always find a love that's ready made to answer yours. But my exiled beloved, what did the miserly heavens ever grant to him? You have Castile, Aragon, and Navarre; and Murcia and León; ten other realms, and Flanders; you have India with all its golden mines! You own an empire vast beyond any other king's, a domain so wide it never sees a setting sun! And with all of this, could you, the king, take a poor girl from him who has nothing else? (*She throws herself to her knees. He tries to draw her away.*)

DON CARLOS. Come! I do not hear your words. Come, and if you will, I give you any four of my Spains. Which will you have? Come, choose them! (*She struggles in his arms.*)

DOÑA SOL.   For my honor's sake, I want nothing of you but this dagger, sir! (*She wrenches the knife from his belt. He releases her and falls back.*) Come forward now! Take a single step!

DON CARLOS.   So that is how she plays! I do not wonder now that she should love a rebel! (*He moves to take a step; she raises the dagger.*)

DOÑA SOL.   One step and I kill you and myself. (*He draws back again. She turns away and cries loudly.*) Hernani! Hernani!

DON CARLOS.   Quiet!

DOÑA SOL (*the knife ready*). One step, and all is over!

DON CARLOS.   Madam! Now you have gone too far; I can be gentle no longer. I have three men here to force you . . .

HERNANI (*springing from behind him*). There is one you did not count!

(*The king turns and sees* HERNANI *poised behind him in the shadows, his arms crossed under his long cloak, and the broad border of his hat raised.* DOÑA SOL *cries out, runs to* HERNANI, *and throws her arms around him.*)

SCENE THREE

HERNANI (*motionless, his arms still crossed and his glittering eyes set on the king*). As God is my witness, I did not want to confront you now, nor here.

DOÑA SOL.   Hernani, save me from him!

HERNANI.   Be calm, my love.

DON CARLOS.   What are my men doing in the town to have let this gypsy chieftain pass? Monterey! (*He calls.*)

HERNANI.   Your men are in the hands of mine—no use to cry out for their powerless swords. For any three that came to your call, sixty would run to mine. Sixty, and every one of them worth four of yours. So . . . we shall settle our quarrel between the two of us. You raised your hand against this girl! It was an unwise move, my lord king of Castile; a coward's act.

DON CARLOS (*smiling disdainfully*). My lord bandit, let there be no reproach from you to me.

HERNANI.   He laughs! I am no king; but when a king insults me, and then scoffs, my rage springs up and lifts me to his height. Beware, for when I am offended, men fear my angry brow more than any kingly crest! You are mad if you have some illusion of hope. (*He seizes the king.*) Do you know whose hand grips you now? Listen. Your father sentenced mine to death. For that I hate you. You took my title and my estate. For that I hate you. We love the same woman, both of us. For that I hate you, I hate you for everything—I hate you from my soul!

DON CARLOS.   Very well.

HERNANI.   And yet this evening my hatred seemed far away. I felt only one desire, one heat, one need—Doña Sol! I hastened here, full of love—and I find you in this vile attempt on her! I had forgotten you, but you are set across my path! You are mad, Don Carlos! You are caught in your own snare without help, or hope of escape. I have you in my hand! You are alone, surrounded by furious enemies. What will you do?

DON CARLOS (*proudly*). You dare to question me!

HERNANI.   I will not have you struck down by some strange hand—my vengeance must not elude me now. No one but I shall touch you; defend yourself. (*He draws his sword.*)

DON CARLOS.   I am the king, your master. Strike; but I will not duel with you.

HERNANI.   If you recall, only yesterday you crossed your blade with mine.

DON CARLOS.   Yesterday it still could be. I did not know your name, nor you my rank. Today you know who I am and I know you.

HERNANI.   Perhaps.

DON CARLOS.   No duel, then. Assassinate me.

HERNANI.   Do you suppose that kings are sacred to me? Draw your sword!

DON CARLOS.   You must murder me. (HERNANI *draws back.* DON CARLOS *sets his eagle eyes on him.*) Do you believe your bandit gangs can roam through our towns at will? Striped with gore and stained with murder as you are, do you believe that you can still strut and pose as noble men, and expect that we should dignify your knives by striking ours against them? Are we such gullible victims? No, crime holds you in its grip; it trails you where you go. And we—are we to duel with you? Never. Murder me.

HERNANI (*brooding and thoughtful, stands for a few seconds gripping and releasing the hilt of his sword; then he turns abruptly back to the king, and snaps the swordblade against the flagstones*). Then leave here. (*The king half turns back toward him, and stares haughtily at him.*) Go.

DON CARLOS.   Very well, sir. In a few hours I shall return. My first concern will be to call for the prosecutor. Is there a price already set upon your head?

HERNANI.   Yes.

DON CARLOS.   From this day forward you shall be considered a traitor and a rebel. I warn you of this; I shall pursue you everywhere. I hereby place you under the ban of the kingdom.

HERNANI.   I am already banished.

DON CARLOS.   Good.

HERNANI.   But France is close by Spain; it will be a haven.

DON CARLOS.   I shall be emperor. I set you under the ban of all the empire.

HERNANI.   As you will. I have the rest of the world to defy you from. There are many other lands where your power cannot reach me.

DON CARLOS.   And when I have the world?

HERNANI.   Then I shall have my grave.

DON CARLOS.   I will put an end to your insolent activities.

HERNANI.   Revenge is lame; it comes with halting steps— but it does come.

DON CARLOS (*half laughing, disdainful*). That I should touch the woman this outlaw loves!

HERNANI (*his eyes blazing again*). Have you forgotten you are still within my grasp? You would-be Roman Caesar, do not remind me that you lie frail and small in my hand's cup; that if I were to clench this too-honorable fist, I should crush the imperial eagle in the egg!

DON CARLOS.   Then do so.

HERNANI.   Go! Leave this place! (*He takes off his mantle and throws it over the king's shoulders.*) Take my cloak, and go; without it you could not pass alive among my men. (*The king wraps himself in the cloak.*) You may leave in safety now. My thirsting rage will let no hand but mine cut off your life.

DON CARLOS.   Remember how you spoke to me tonight, and ask no mercy of me when we meet again. (*He goes out.*)

SCENE FOUR

DOÑA SOL (*seizing HERNANI'S hand*). Let us go now quickly!

HERNANI (*holding her away, with gentle gravity*). My love, you have determined to join more firmly in my misery each day; to hold to it always, and to share my days without reserve until they end. Your scheme is a noble one, and one that is worthy of so steadfast a heart. But Lord God, you can see it is too late now to accept so much of her, and heedlessly to carry off to my lair this beauteous gem a king wants for his own; to have my Doña Sol follow me and to own her, to take her life and wed it to my own, to lead her off with no shame or remorse—there is no time! The scaffold looms too near!

DOÑA SOL.   What are you saying?

HERNANI.   I defied the king to his face, and he will punish me for having dared to free him. He is gone; perhaps already in his palace, gathering his men, his soldiers, and his noblemen; calling his executioners . . .

DOÑA SOL.   Hernani! I am frightened! Then hurry—we must leave now together!

HERNANI.   Together . . . no. No. The time for that is past. Doña Sol, when first you revealed yourself to me, so good, and kind enough to love me with a willing love, I dared to offer you everything I have: my mountain, my woods, my stream. Your sympathy emboldened me; I offered you my outlaw's bread, and half the green and tufted bed the forest gives me. But to offer you half my gallows—oh no, my Doña Sol—the gallows is mine alone.

DOÑA SOL.   Yet you promised to share everything.

HERNANI (*falling to his knees*). My saint! At this moment when death perhaps is near, when my dark destiny draws to a dark close, I must tell you this: banished, and burdened by a solemn mission born in a bloody cradle; and as black as is the grief that shades my life—I am a happy man, and call upon all men to envy me! For you have loved me, for you have told me so, for you have leaned and blessed my cursed brow!

DOÑA SOL (*bending over him*). Hernani!

HERNANI.   How kind is the fate that set this flower at the chasm's edge for me! (*He rises.*) And I speak not for your sake; I speak for the listening heavens, and for God.

DOÑA SOL.   Let me go with you.

HERNANI.   It would be a crime to wrench out the flower as I fall into the abyss! No, I have breathed its perfume, and that is enough. Go link the life I've troubled to another man's. Marry the old duke. I myself unbind you. I return into my night. And you—be happy, and forget!

DOÑA SOL.   No, I shall come with you. I want my share of your shroud! I shall go where you go!

HERNANI (*grasping her in his arms*). Ah, let me go alone! (*He turns from her with a convulsive movement.*)

DOÑA SOL (*mournfully, and clasping her hands*). Hernani, you would go from me! So, foolish woman, you give your life and see it turned away; and after so much love, and so much pain, you do not earn even the joy of dying by his side.

HERNANI.   I am a banished man! I am outlawed! I bring misfortune!

DOÑA SOL.   You are a thankless man.

HERNANI (*turning back to her*). Then no! no, I shall stay. You desire it—then I am here. Come . . . oh come into my arms! I shall stay, and for as long as you shall want me. Let us forget the others. We shall stay here. (*He seats her on a bench.*) Sit here on this stone. (*He settles at her feet.*) Flames from your eyes wash over my lids; sing me some song as you used to sing at evening, with tears in your dark eyes. Let us be happy! And drink, for the cup is filled, for this hour is ours, and all the rest is madness. Speak to me, sing, and say: Is it not sweet to love and to know you are adored? To be true? To be alone? And is it not sweet to speak our love at night, when all's at rest? . . . Oh let me sleep and dream upon your breast. Doña Sol! My love, my beauty!

(*Sound of alarm bells in the distance.*)

DOÑA SOL (*rising, frightened*). The alarm! Do you hear it? The alarm!

HERNANI (*still on his knees*). No . . . they are tolling our marriage. (*The sound of bells grows louder. There are cries, torches, and lights at all the windows, on all the roofs, in every street.*)

DOÑA SOL.   Hernani, flee! Almighty God! All Saragossa is alight!

HERNANI (*half rising*). Our wedding shall be lit by torches!

DOÑA SOL.   A deathly wedding! A marriage of the tomb!

(*Sounds of swords and cries.*)

HERNANI (*reclining again on the stone bench*). Come lie here in my arms!

(*A* MOUNTAINEER *runs in, his sword in hand.*)

MOUNTAINEER. Sir, long columns of militia and police are entering the square! Be quick, my lord! (HERNANI *rises.*)

DOÑA SOL (*pale*). You were right; he did prepare this.

MOUNTAINEER. Men—to the rescue!

HERNANI (*to the* MOUNTAINEER). I am ready. All is well. (*Cries offstage:* ''Death to the bandit!'') Your sword. (*To* DOÑA SOL.) Then farewell!

DOÑA SOL. You are lost through my doing! Where will you go? (*Pointing to the small door.*) Come this way! We can leave by that open door.

HERNANI. Abandon my comrades? What are you saying?

DOÑA SOL. This clamor stabs my heart. (*She holds* HERNANI.) Remember that if you die, I die!

HERNANI (*holding her close*). One kiss!

DOÑA SOL. My husband! My Hernani! Oh, my master!

HERNANI (*kissing her brow*). Alas!—it is our first.

DOÑA SOL. It is perhaps our last.

(*He leaves. She falls to the bench.*)

ACT THREE

THE OLD MAN

(*The Silva Castle, in the mountains of Aragon. The portrait gallery of the Silva family: a large hall in which the portraits form the decor, in rich frames with ducal coronets and golden blazons. In rear, a tall gothic door. Between every two portraits stands a full panoply of armor, a suit representing each of the different centuries.*)

SCENE ONE

(DOÑA SOL, *pale, standing by a table;* DON RUY GOMEZ DE SILVA, *seated in his great ducal chair of oak.*)

DON RUY GOMEZ. At last! Today, within an hour, you shall be my duchess, and I no longer an uncle. And you will embrace me—but have you forgiven me? I was wrong, I know; I caused you shame, and made your cheek turn pale. My doubts surged up too soon; I should not have condemned you thus before I heard you. How false appearances can be—how unjust we are! Two fine young men were there indeed with you; still, I should not have believed my eyes. But what can you expect, my poor child, from an old man like me?

DOÑA SOL (*motionless and grave*). You still return to that. Who has blamed you for it?

DON RUY GOMEZ. I myself! I was wrong. I should have known a Doña Sol would allow no lovers courting—not such a woman as you, nor one whose heart is flushed with good Spanish blood.

DOÑA SOL. It is good and pure blood indeed, my lord; perhaps it will soon be seen.

DON RUY GOMEZ (*rising and going toward her*). Understand, a man is not master over himself, when he loves as I love you, and when he is old. Why might a man be jealous, and even cruel? Because he is old. Because grace and fairness, youth in another man all make for fear, all threaten him. Because he is envious of others, and ashamed of himself. What a mockery is this limping love—it brings a drunken fire back to the heart, it makes the soul young again, but it forgets the body! Often when some young shepherd goes by—ah yes, it's come to that—as we pass, he singing and I musing, he to his green pasture, I to my dark halls, often I murmur low beneath my breath ''How gladly I would give my battlements, my ancient ducal keep; and I would give my fields and forestlands, and the vast herds that browse upon my hills, my ancient name, my title, and all my ruins, and all my old forbears who soon will welcome me among them—I would give it all for his new-thatched cottage and for his youthful brow!'' His hair is black, his eye gleams like your own; you might see him and say ''A young man!'' And then think of me who am old. I know this. I bear the Silva name, but it is no longer enough. And my mind is ever running on this theme. You see how great a love I bear you. I would give all I have to be young and fair as you. But what am I dreaming of, I young and fair? I who must go so long before you to the grave!

DOÑA SOL. Who can tell?

DON RUY GOMEZ. But believe me, Doña Sol; such gay gallants as those can give no love more lasting than fine phrases. Let a girl love and give her faith to such a man, she may die of it and he will laugh. All those young cockerels, with their bright wings and with their languid song—their love molts like their plumage. The aged ones, whose tone and tints are muted by the years, have a more trusty wing and they are better, though less fair to see. We love well. Our steps may be heavy, our eyes dull, perhaps, and our brows deep-lined—but the heart does not show the crease of age. Alas! When an old man loves, one must go gently; the heart is always young, and it still can bleed. My love is no crystal toy that gleams and trembles; it is a stern and solid love—deep, sure, paternal, friendly, carved of the same oak as my ducal throne. See then how I love you—and I love you too a hundred other ways, as one loves the dawn, as one loves flowers, and as one loves the skies. To know that I shall see you every day—you with your graceful step and your pure brow, the rich fire in your proud eye—I laugh, and in my soul I feel an endless joy.

DOÑA SOL. Alas!

DON RUY GOMEZ. And then, you know, when a man is waning limb by limb, when he stumbles against the marble of the tomb—the world thinks well of the woman watching over him; an innocent dove, an angel sheltering him and suffering a useless antique good only for death. It is a sacred work, and they are right to praise it, when a devoted heart performs this crowning good—to console a dying man until he ends his day—and even perhaps without love, has all the look of love.

Ah, you shall be my woman-hearted angel, who still sweetens the soul of a pitiful old man, and helps to bear the weight of his last years—a daughter in respect, a sister in compassion.

DOÑA SOL. Far from preceding me, you may well follow, my lord. Youth is not reason enough for living. Often the old ones linger, the younger go before; suddenly their eyelids drop like an open tomb whose stone falls back to place.

DON RUY GOMEZ. What mournful talk! I must scold you, my child—a day like this is holy and joyful. But the hour is late; how is it you are not ready for the chapel? Hurry then, and dress yourself. I shall count every second. Put on your wedding gown!

DOÑA SOL. There still is time.

DON RUY GOMEZ. Not much of it. (A PAGE enters.) What does Iaquez want of us?

PAGE. My lord, a man—a pilgrim or a beggar—is at the door and asks you for asylum.

DON RUY GOMEZ. Whatever he may be, good fortune enters with the stranger. Let him come. Has there been a report from the outside? What do they say of the treacherous bandit who fills our forests with his rebel acts?

PAGE. Hernani is done for; the mountain lion is finished.

DOÑA SOL (aside). Oh God!

DON RUY GOMEZ. What?

PAGE. The band has been destroyed. They say the king himself set after them. Hernani's head is worth a thousand crowns; but I have heard he is dead.

DOÑA SOL (aside). Without me, Hernani!

DON RUY GOMEZ. Thanks be to heaven! the rebel's dead! Now, my dear, we can truly rejoice. Go and prepare yourself, my love, my pride! Today's a double holiday!

DOÑA SOL (aside). . . . A wedding dress for widow's weeds! . . . (She goes out.)

DON RUY GOMEZ (to the page). Send her the jewel case I prepared for her. (He sits down again in his armchair.) I want to see her adorned like a madonna; I want her gentle eyes and all my jewels to make her so beautiful a pilgrim would fall upon his knees at sight of her. Oh—and the one who has begged shelter of us, tell him to enter, and ask his pardon. Quickly. (The PAGE salutes and goes out.) Leaving a guest to linger at the door! A shameful thing.

(The rear door opens. HERNANI appears, disguised as a pilgrim. The duke rises and goes toward him.)

SCENE TWO

HERNANI (stopping on the threshold). My lord, peace and happiness!

DON RUY GOMEZ (saluting him with a gesture of his hand). Peace and happiness to you, my guest! (HERNANI enters. The duke sits again.) You are a pilgrim?

HERNANI. Yes. (He bows.)

DON RUY GOMEZ. You come from Armillas?

HERNANI. No. I took another road. There was fighting there.

DON RUY GOMEZ. The outlaw's men?

HERNANI. I do not know.

DON RUY GOMEZ. And Hernani, their leader—what of him? Do you know?

HERNANI. Who is this man, my lord?

DON RUY GOMEZ. You do not know him? A pity, then you shall not win the bounty for him. Hernani is a rebel who has gone too long unpunished. If you go to Madrid, you still may see him hang.

HERNANI. I am not going there.

DON RUY GOMEZ. The reward goes to whatever man can take him.

HERNANI (aside). Let them come!

DON RUY GOMEZ. Where are you bound for, good pilgrim?

HERNANI. My lord, I go to Saragossa.

DON RUY GOMEZ. For a vow made to some saint? to Our Lady?

HERNANI. Yes, Duke—to Our Lady.

DON RUY GOMEZ. Of Pilar?

HERNANI. Of Pilar.

DON RUY GOMEZ. It would be an empty soul that did not fulfill the vows made to the saints. But when you have accomplished yours, have you no further plans? To see the Lady of the Pillar is all you want?

HERNANI. Yes, I want to see the torches and the candles burn; to see Our Lady glowing in her brilliant shrine, with all her golden vestments, and then turn home again.

DON RUY GOMEZ. Very good. Your name, my brother? I am Ruy de Silva.

HERNANI (hesitating). My name . . . ?

DON RUY GOMEZ. You need not pronounce it, if you so choose. None has the right to demand it here. Have you not come to ask asylum?

HERNANI. Yes, Duke.

DON RUY GOMEZ. Thank you. Be welcome; stay here, my friend, and want for nothing. As for your name, you are called my guest. Whoever you be, it is well. I'd welcome Satan himself with peace of mind, if God sent him to me.

(The double door at rear opens. DOÑA SOL enters, dressed in Castilian wedding costume of the period. Behind her are pages and attendants; two women carry upon a velvet cushion a chiseled silver box which they place upon a table.

It holds a rich array of jewels, a duchess' coronet, bracelets, collars, necklaces, pearls, and diamonds in a tumbled heap. HERNANI, *breathless and startled, his eyes burning, stares at* DOÑA SOL *without listening to the duke.)*

SCENE THREE

DON RUY GOMEZ (*continuing*). Here is my own holy lady. A prayer to her will bring you good fortune. (*He goes to offer his hand to* DOÑA SOL, *who is still pale and grave.*) My lovely bride, come forward. What? You wear no ring, and still no coronet?

HERNANI (*in a thunderous voice*). Who here would earn a thousand crowns? (*All turn toward him, astonished. He rips off his pilgrim's robe, throws it to the door, and appears in his mountaineer's outfit.*) I am Hernani.

DOÑA SOL (*aside, joyfully*). He is alive!

HERNANI (*to the valets*). I am the man they seek. (*To the duke.*) You asked if I were called—what, Perez, or Diego? No, I am named Hernani. It is a name much greater, an exile's name, an outlaw's name! You see this head? It is worth enough to pay for your whole feast! (*To the attendants.*) I offer it to all of you. You will be well rewarded! Take it! Tie my hands, and bind my feet—bind them! No, that is needless; there is a chain that holds me and that I shall never break!

    (*Horror on* DOÑA SOL'S *part.*)

DON RUY GOMEZ. Madness—my guest is a madman!

HERNANI. Your guest is a bandit.

DOÑA SOL. Do not listen to him!

HERNANI. I have said what I have said.

DON RUY GOMEZ. A thousand golden crowns! Sir, the sum is a high one, and I cannot be sure of all my men.

HERNANI. What does it matter? So much the better if there is one among them who will do it. (*To the attendants.*) Give me up! Sell me!

DON RUY GOMEZ (*trying to quiet him*). Be still! Someone may take you at your word.

HERNANI. My friends, it is a matchless opportunity! I tell you I am the criminal, the rebel—I am Hernani!

DON RUY GOMEZ. Quiet!

HERNANI. Hernani!

DOÑA SOL (*her voice faint, in his ear*). Oh be still, my love!

HERNANI (*half turning toward her*). There is a wedding here! and I shall share in it! My bride awaits me too. (*To the duke.*) She is less lovely than your own, my lord, but no less faithful. Her name is Death. (*To the servants.*) Not one of you steps forward?

DOÑA SOL (*low*). Have pity on me!

HERNANI (*to the servants*). Hernani! A thousand crowns in gold!

DON RUY GOMEZ. It is the devil himself!

HERNANI (*to the young servant*). Come, you there; you can win the bounty; you shall be rich, and from a servant

become a man again. (*To the other unmoving men.*) And you, you tremble too! Oh, have I not misery enough!

DON RUY GOMEZ. Brother, in touching your head they risk their own. Were you Hernani, were you a thousand times worse; if the reward for your head were more than gold, were it a whole empire, I still must protect you in this house against he king himself, for as my guest you are here by will of God. May I die if a single hair falls from your brow. (*To* DOÑA SOL.) My niece, within the hour you shall be my wife. Go to your rooms. I must order the castle armed, and bar the door. (*He goes out, and the servants follow him.*)

HERNANI (*glancing despairingly at his weaponless sash*). Not even a knife!

(*When the duke has gone,* DOÑA SOL *starts to follow her ladies off, then stops. When they have disappeared, she comes anxiously back to* HERNANI.)

SCENE FOUR

(HERNANI *gazes coldly at the nuptial jewel casket on the table, and seems almost unaware of her. Then he raises his head abruptly, and his eyes flare.*)

HERNANI. I compliment you! You cannot imagine how thoroughly charming I find your ornaments . . . Enchanting; really, quite admirable. (*He moves to the casket.*) The ring is most tasteful; I like the coronet; the necklace is lovely work, the bracelet quite rare—but a hundred, a hundred times less so than the woman who can hide such perfidy behind so pure a brow! (*He examines the box again.*) And what have you paid for all of this? A little of your love? Why, excellent! That is nothing at all. Good God! To so betray, to feel no shame, and still live on! (*Looking through the jewel box.*) But perhaps though, after all, these are no more than painted pearls, and copper that seems gold, and glass and lead; unreal diamonds, false sapphires, false gems and glittering stones! If that is so, then your heart is false as well, Duchess—false as these ornaments, and you are only gilt! (*He goes back to the case.*) But no. No. It is all real, all good, and every piece is fine. He would not dare to cheat, so near the grave. There is nothing lacking. (*He takes one piece after another from the case.*) Necklets, brilliants, ear pendants . . . a ducal coronet, a ring of gold—marvelous! A fitting thanks to steadfast, true, and deepest love—the precious jewel case!

DOÑA SOL (*going to the casket; she reaches beneath the jewels, and draws out a dagger*). You have not reached deep enough. Here is the knife I took from King Carlos with my holy Lady's help, when he was offering me a throne; and I refused, for you who vilify me.

HERNANI (*dropping to her feet*). Oh—I beg from my knees—let me wipe those bitter beloved tears out from your sorrowing eyes. Take my blood for your tears!

DOÑA SOL (*softened*). Hernani! I love you and forgive you. I feel only love for you.

HERNANI. She has forgiven me, and loves me! But how can I forgive and love myself again, after what I have said? My heavenly angel, show me where you have walked, and let me kiss the pavement where it was.

DOÑA SOL. My love!

HERNANI. No, I cannot be but hateful to my eyes! Listen, say to me: ''I love you!'' Assure a doubtful heart, and tell me. Often a woman's lips have healed many pains with those few words.

DOÑA SOL (*absorbed, unhearing*). How could he think my love so short of memory? That lusterless men could shrink a heart wherein his name has entered down to the size of other loves, however noble the world might think them!

HERNANI. I have blasphemed! Doña Sol, if I were in your stead, I should have had enough; I should be weary of this wild fool, of this brooding, senseless man who knows not how to kiss till he has wounded. I should tell him ''Go.'' Turn me away, you must! And I shall only bless you, for you were good, and kind; for you have borne me far too long already, for I am evil—I would darken your days with my black nights.

It is too much—your spirit is high and good and pure; if I am bad, why should you suffer for it? Wed the old duke, he is a good man, and noble; he owns Olmedo from his mother, Alcala from his father. Once more I bid you, be rich with him; be happy! Do you know what splendid gifts my own generous hand can offer you? A dowry of sorrow. A choice between blood and tears. Exile, chains, death, the constant fear around me—there is your golden necklace, and your handsome crown, and never has proud husband offered his bride a richer treasure chest of pain and mourning! Marry the old man, I tell you. He deserves you. Who would ever match my doomed head with your clear brow? Who ever, seeing the two of us—you calm and fair, me violent and perilous, you tranquil and blossoming like a shaded flower, me storm-tossed against a thousand different reefs—who would think to say our fates are joined by a single law? No. God, who determines good things, did not make you for me. I have no heaven-sent right to you. I am resigned. I have your heart, but I have it by theft. I hand it to another, worthier man. Heaven has never consented to our love. When I told you it was your destiny, I lied. And in any case, farewell to all revenge and love! My day is done. I'll go then, futile, with my double dream, unable either to win love or to punish. I should have been built to hate, but I can only love! Forgive me, and flee! These prayers are all I ask; do not refuse them, for they are my last. You live, and I am dead. You must not wall yourself into my tomb with me.

DOÑA SOL. Ungrateful love!

HERNANI. Mountains of Aragon! Galicia, Estremadura! I bring misfortune to all who join with me. I have taken your best sons to serve my claims; relentless, I have sent them into battle, and they are dead of it. They were the most valiant in all of valiant Spain. And they are dead. They have fallen in the mountains, all of them upon their backs as brave men do, before God; if they were to open their eyes again, they would see the blue heavens. And this is what I do to all who join me. Is this a destiny that you should want to share? Doña Sol, take the duke—take hell itself, take the king! Anyone is better! There is not one friend left who thinks of me; everything else has gone, and now your turn has come to leave me too, for I must live alone. Flee my contamination; do not make a religion of love. Oh, have mercy on yourself, and flee! . . . Perhaps you think me a man like all the rest, a rational thing who first perceives his goal and then will move straight toward it. Do not be fooled—I am not such a man. I am a resistless energy—the blind and deafened agent of doleful mysteries, a soul of sorrows bound together with darkness. Where am I bound? I cannot say. But yet I feel myself hurled on by some impulsive gale, some wild determination. I fall, and fall, and never do I rest. . . . If once, gasping for breath, I dare to turn my head, a voice commands ''Go on!''; and the chasm is a deep one, and the depth of it is red with blood or flame! And meanwhile, along my headlong course, all things are crushed, or die. Woe to him who comes close to me! Oh, flee! Turn from my fated path. Against my will I'll do you injury!

DOÑA SOL. Oh God!

HERNANI. My devil is a fearsome one—the single miracle he cannot work is my happiness. And you are happiness! So you are not meant for me; seek out another man. Heaven has rejected me; if ever it should smile upon my fate, do not believe in it! It would only be in irony. Marry the duke.

DOÑA SOL. It still was not enough—you tore my heart and now you crush it. You do not love me now.

HERNANI. You are my heart, my soul! The glowing hearth that warms me by its flames is you! Do not hate me that I flee, my love.

DOÑA SOL. I do not hate you. But I shall die of it.

HERNANI. Die? For whom? For me? Could you die for so little?

DOÑA SOL (*letting her tears come*). It is all!

HERNANI (*sitting beside her*). You weep, and once more through my doing. And who will punish me? For you, I know, will pardon me again. Can you ever know what pain I feel when even a single tear drowns the radiance in your eyes? For their brightness is my joy. Oh, my friends are dead! I am a fool. Forgive me. I want to love, but I do not know the way—and yet I love so deeply! Weep no more—let's rather die. If I owned a world I would give it to you. What misery this is!

DOÑA SOL (*throwing herself at his neck*). Oh my proud, my noble lion! I love you.

HERNANI.   How supreme a blessing love would be, if one could die of loving too well!

DOÑA SOL.   I love you, my lord! I love you and I am wholly yours!

HERNANI (*dropping his head onto her shoulder*). How sweet a dagger blow would be from you. . . .

DOÑA SOL (*imploring*). Have you no fear that God will punish you for words like those?

HERNANI (*still leaning on her breast*). Let him unite us then! . . . You wish it—let it be! I have fought against it!

(*They gaze ecstatically at one another in an embrace, hearing nothing, seeing nothing else, and totally absorbed in their own gaze.* DON RUY GOMEZ *enters by the door at rear. He sees them and stops frozen on the doorsill.*)

SCENE FIVE

DON RUY GOMEZ (*motionless, his arms crossed, on the threshold*). Then this is hospitality's reward!

DOÑA SOL.   It is the duke! (*The two turn as if shocked awake.*)

DON RUY GOMEZ (*still unmoving*). Are these my wages, guest? Run, my lord host, and see if the wall is high enough, if the gate is strongly barred and the archer in his tower; go look once, and once again, about your castle for our sake. Look through your arsenal for armor that will fit—try on your battle trappings again at sixty years! And here's our kind of loyalty in payment for your good faith. You do that for us; we shall do this for you. Saints in heaven! I have lived more than sixty years, and seen a hundred bandits, with lawless and untrammeled soul; often, as I drew my dagger from its sheath, I have flushed the hangman's game where I walked. I have seen murderers, forgers, traitors; and faithless grooms serve poison to their masters. I have seen men die without the cross, and without prayer. I saw Sforza, and Borgia; I see Luther now—but never have I seen evil so great as to betray one's host in the face of heaven's thunder! I come from other times. So black a treason petrifies an old man on the threshold of his home; the aging master, as he waits to fall, takes on the aura of a statue carved for his own tomb. Moors and Castilians! Tell me, what is this man? (*He raises his eyes and runs them over the portraits that circle the hall.*) Oh all ye Silvas who hear me now, forgive me if I say this to you—forgive me if my wrath pronounces hospitality a poor adviser!

HERNANI (*rising*). Duke—

DON RUY.   Silence! (*He takes three or four slow steps into the hall, and again looks about him at the Silva portraits on the walls.*) Sacred departed ones! My ancestors! Men of iron! You who see all that comes from heaven and hell—tell me, my lords, tell me—what is this man? He is not Hernani, no; his name is Judas! Oh strain to speak, and tell me who he is! (*Crossing his arms.*) Have you ever in your times seen such a thing? No!

HERNANI.   My lord duke—

DON RUY GOMEZ (*still to the portraits*). Do you see this? This villain wants to speak! But you can read better in his soul than I. Oh do not hear him, he is a knave! He will tell you he sees that my own hand longs to drench my house with blood; that perhaps my heart is brewing some revenge amid its storm, some vengeance like the feast of the Seven Heads.[1] He will declare he is an exile, and that the name of Silva will ring with all the horror of the Lara name. He will say he is my guest, and yours as well. . . . My fathers, oh my sires, say, am I to blame? Judge now between us!

HERNANI.   Ruy Gomez de Silva, if ever a noble brow was raised to heaven, if ever there was fine heart, or lofty soul, they are yours, my lord! I who speak to you am guilty; I have nothing more to say than that I am most surely damned. Yes, I desired to take your bride from you; I did wish to soil your marriage bed, and that is infamous. I have life and blood in me—you have the right to spill it, then wipe your sword, and think no more of it.

DOÑA SOL.   My lord, the fault is mine, not his! Strike me instead!

HERNANI.   Be silent, Doña Sol. This moment is supreme; this time belongs to me, and it is all I own. Then let me talk to the duke. Sir, believe these last words from my lips: I swear that I am guilty, but be at peace, for she is innocent. That is the whole tale—I guilty and she pure. Your good faith must go to her, and the thrust of a sword or knife to me. Then toss the body away and wash the floor if you wish; it matters not.

DOÑA SOL.   No! I alone have done it all! Because I love him. (DON RUY *starts at this word, and turns a terrible gaze on* DOÑA SOL. *She throws herself to her knees.*) Yes, forgive me. I love him, my lord.

DON RUY GOMEZ.   You love him! (*To* HERNANI.) Then tremble! (*A blare of trumpets outside. The* PAGE *enters. To the* PAGE:) What is that sound?

PAGE.   It is the king himself, my lord, with a troop of archers, and his herald.

DOÑA SOL.   The king! A final stab of fate!

PAGE (*to the duke*). He demands to know the reason why the gate is closed, and wants it opened.

DON RUY GOMEZ.   Open to the king. (*The* PAGE *bows and leaves.*)

DOÑA SOL.   He is lost!

(DON RUY *goes to one of the paintings, which is his own portrait, the last on the left; he touches a spring, the portrait turns out like a door, and shows a hiding place in the wall. He turns to* HERNANI.)

---

[1] The heads of his seven children were served up to their father at table by their uncle, Ruy Velasquez de Lara.

DON RUY GOMEZ.   Step in here, sir.

HERNANI.   My life belongs to you. Surrender it, my lord; I hold it ready. I am your prisoner.

(*He steps into the hiding place.* DON RUY *touches the spring again, and the painting moves back into place.*)

PAGE (*returning*). His Highness the King. (DOÑA SOL *quickly lowers her veil. The double door opens.* DON CARLOS *enters outfitted for war, followed by a crowd of gentlemen armed as he is, and halberdiers, arquebusiers, and crossbowmen.*)

SCENE SIX

(DON CARLOS *advances slowly, his left hand on the hilt of his sword, his right inside his bosom, and stares at the duke in anger. The duke steps before the king and bows deeply. Silence. Suspense and fear in the atmosphere. Finally the king, reaching the duke, lifts his own head abruptly.*)

DON CARLOS.   How is it that today, my cousin, your gate is so firmly locked? By the very saints, I had thought your blade more rusty by now! I should not have imagined it would be so quick to flash in your fist again when we should come to see you. (DON RUY GOMEZ *attempts to speak, but the king continues, with an imperious gesture.*) It is a little late to play the young man! Do we wear a turban? Are we named Boabdil, or Mohammed, and not Carlos—answer!—that you should lower the portcullis or raise the bridge before us?

DON RUY GOMEZ (*bowing*). Highness—

DON CARLOS (*to his men*). Take the keys and seize the gates. (*Two officers go out. Several others arrange the soldiers into triple file in the hall, from the king to the main door.* DON CARLOS *turns again toward the duke.*) So, you yearn to awaken dead mutinies: God in heaven— if you dukes assume such airs with me, the king will act the king! I shall go about among the lofty mountain peaks and crush their lordships in their battlemented nests with my own warring hands!

DON RUY GOMEZ (*straightening*). Highness, the Silvas are loyal—

DON CARLOS (*interrupting him*). Answer me without guile, Duke, or I shall have your eleven towers razed to earth. A spark still glows from the extinguished blaze; from all the slaughtered bandits, their chief survives. Who is concealing him? It is you! This Hernani, this vicious rebel— you are hiding him here within your castle now!

DON RUY GOMEZ.   My lord, it is true.

DON CARLOS.   Very well. I want his head—or else your own, you understand, my cousin?

DON RUY GOMEZ (*bowing*). You shall be satisfied.

(DOÑA SOL *hides her face in her hands and falls into a chair.*)

DON CARLOS (*softening*). Ah, you improve. Now give me my prisoner.

(*The duke crosses his arms, lowers his head, and remains thoughtful for a few moments. The king and* DOÑA SOL *watch him in silence, and with contrary emotions. Finally the duke raises his head, goes to the king, takes his hand, and leads him slowly up to the oldest of the portraits, the one starting the row at the spectator's right.*)

DON RUY GOMEZ (*showing the portrait to the king*). This is the oldest of the Silvas, the forefather, the ancestor, the great man! Don Silvius, who three times was Roman consul. (*Moving to the next portrait.*) Here is Don Galceran de Silva, the other Cid. At Toro, near Valladolid, there is a golden case that holds his remains, and a thousand candles burn around the shrine. He liberated León from the tribute of the hundred virgins.[2] (*He passes to another.*) Don Blas, who by his own decision and his conscience placed himself in exile, for having given the king poor counsel. (*At another.*) Christoval. At the battle of Escalona, the king Don Sancho was forced to flee on foot, and the furious blows fell harshest around his royal white plume. He cried out "Christoval!" Christoval took on the plume and gave his horse. (*At the next.*) Don Jorge, who paid the ransom for Ramirez, king of Aragon.

DON CARLOS (*crossing his arms and looking at* DON RUY *from head to toe*). Don Ruy, by God, I wonder at you! I want my prisoner now!

DON RUY (*moving to another portrait*). This is Ruy Gomez de Silva; he was named Grand Master of Saint James and of Calatrava.[3] His giant armor would far surpass our size. He took three hundred flags, won thirty battles; he conquered Motril for the king, and Antequera, Suez, and Nijar, and died a pauper. Highness, salute them. (*He himself bows and uncovers his head, then goes on to another. The king listens to him with growing impatience and anger.*) Beside him, Gil his son, beloved by noble hearts. His hand upon an oath was worth a king's. (*At another.*) Don Gaspard, the glory of Mendoza and of Silva! Every noble house has some alliance with the Silvas, Highness. The house of Sandoval dreads and weds us in alternation; Manrico's line is envious, the Laras jealous, and Alencastro hates us. Our feet touch all the dukes at once, and our foreheads all the kings.

DON CARLOS (*annoyed*). Do you make sport of us?

DON RUY (*going to other portraits*). Here is Don Vasquez, called the Wise; and Don Jaime, called the Strong. One day as he went by he stopped Zamet and a hundred Moors alone. I shall pass over others, some better still! (*As the king makes an angry gesture, he moves past a great many of the paintings, and stops at the last three portraits at the spectator's left.*) My noble grandfather. He lived for sixty years, keeping his promised word even to Jews. (*At*

---

[2]A yearly levy extorted by the victorious Moors there.
[3]Orders of chivalry.

the next-to-last.) This old man, this holy face—this is my father. He was a great man, although he came the last. The Moors at Granada had taken prisoner Count Alvar Giron, his friend. But my father gathered six hundred soldiers to find and free him. He had a Count Alvar Giron carved out in stone, and carried the statue with him, swearing by his patron saint that never would he turn back until the stony count itself should turn about and seek retreat. He battled, reached the count, and saved him.

DON CARLOS. My prisoner, Duke!

DON RUY GOMEZ. He was a Gomez de Silva. When in this house one sees the portraits of these heroes, this is what one says—

DON CARLOS. My prisoner, and instantly!

(DON RUY GOMEZ *bows deeply before the king, takes his hand and leads him to the last portrait, the one behind which he has hidden* HERNANI. DOÑA SOL *watches him anxiously, and the others are silent and attentive.*)

DON RUY GOMEZ. This portrait is my own. And I thank you, King Carlos; for what you ask is that on seeing it, all men should say ''This last one, the son of such heroic race—he was a traitor that sold his guest away.''

(*Joy on* DOÑA SOL'S *face; a murmur of astonishment among the others present. The king, disconcerted, moves off in fury, and keeps silence for several moments, his lips trembling and eyes blazing.*)

DON CARLOS. Duke, your castle is in my way, and I shall throw it down!

DON RUY GOMEZ. For you would indeed pay me for his head, Your Highness, would you not?

DON CARLOS. For such defiance as this, I shall level all its towers, and order nettles sown where once it stood.

DON RUY GOMEZ. Better that nettles grow where my towers rose, than that a stain should mark the Silva name. (*To the portraits.*) Is that not so, my fathers?

DON CARLOS. Duke, his head is ours, and you had promised me—

DON RUY GOMEZ. I promised one or the other. (*To the portraits.*) Is that not so, my sires? (*Touching his own head; to the king.*) I give you this one. Take it.

DON CARLOS. I thank you, Duke—but I lose by this arrangement. The head I need is young; once severed, it must be lifted by the hair before the people. But yours! What use have I for it? The headsman would seek in vain to grasp its hair. You have not even enough to fill the hand!

DON RUY GOMEZ. Highness, do not insult me! My head is still a good one, and easily worth a rebel's thatch, I think. You disdain a Silva head?

DON CARLOS. Give us Hernani!

DON RUY GOMEZ. My lord, I have spoken.

DON CARLOS (*to his men*). Search everywhere! In every wing, in every cellar and tower—

DON RUY GOMEZ. My dungeon is as faithful as myself. Alone it knows the secret that I know, and both of us will guard it well.

DON CARLOS. I am the king.

DON RUY GOMEZ. Unless they build my tomb up, stone by stone, from my demolished castle, they will find nothing.

DON CARLOS. Pleas and threats are all in vain! Give me the bandit, Duke, or I will demolish head and castle both!

DON RUY GOMEZ. I have spoken.

DON CARLOS. Well then, instead of one, I shall take two heads. (*To the* DUKE OF ALCALA.) Jorge, arrest the duke.

DOÑA SOL (*tearing off her veil and throwing herself between the duke and the guards*). Carlos, you are an evil king!

DON CARLOS. Good Lord, what is this? Doña Sol!

DOÑA SOL. Highness, you have not a Spaniard's heart!

DON CARLOS (*disturbed and hesitant*). Madam, you are too harsh toward the king. (*He approaches* DOÑA SOL, *and speaks low to her.*) You yourself have put this fury in my heart. A man turns saint or monster by your touch. How quickly one grows evil when one is loathed! I was already great; if you had wished it, perhaps I might have been the lion of Castile! You have made me its tiger with your rage. And now that tiger roars. Be silent, then. (DOÑA SOL *looks at him. He bows.*) However, I'll obey. (*He turns back to the duke.*) My cousin, I respect you. Your scruples after all have something worthy in them. Be loyal to your guest, and disloyal to your king. Very well, I pardon you and am the better man. I shall only take your niece with me as hostage.

DON RUY GOMEZ. Only!

DOÑA SOL (*shocked and frightened*). Take me, my lord?

DON CARLOS. Yes, you!

DON RUY GOMEZ. So you exact no more than that of me? Oh, what splendid clemency! Oh, generous victor, to spare the head and torture the heart instead! Fine mercy, this!

DON CARLOS. Make your choice—Doña Sol or the traitor. I must have one of them.

DON RUY GOMEZ. Ah, you are the master!

(DON CARLOS *approaches* DOÑA SOL *to take her away. She retreats toward* DON RUY GOMEZ.)

DOÑA SOL. Save me, my lord! (*She stops; then, to herself.*) But I must! My uncle's head or his—no, sooner myself. (*To the king.*) I go with you.

DON CARLOS (*aside*). By all the saints! What an excellent idea this was! You shall have to soften finally, my girl! (DOÑA SOL *moves with deliberate step toward the box that holds the jewels; she opens it and takes the dagger out, hiding it in her bosom.* DON CARLOS *comes up beside her and offers her his hand.*) What have you there?

DOÑA SOL.   Nothing.

DON CARLOS.   Some precious jewel?

DOÑA SOL.   Yes.

DON CARLOS (*smiling*). Let us see it.

DOÑA SOL.   Later you shall. (*She gives him her hand and prepares to go with him.* DON RUY GOMEZ, *who has remained motionless and deeply absorbed in thought, turns and takes a few steps, shouting.*)

DON RUY GOMEZ.   Doña Sol! Heaven and earth, my Doña Sol! . . . Since this man has no heart in him—castle, come to my aid! Crumble, you weapons and fortress walls, fall in upon us all! (*He runs to the king.*) Leave me my child! I have nothing but her, my king!

DON CARLOS (*dropping* DOÑA SOL'S *hand*). My prisoner, then!

(*The duke drops his head, and seems caught by a tortured hesitation; then he raises his eyes and gazes at the portraits, clasping and stretching his hands toward them imploringly.*)

DON RUY GOMEZ.   Have pity on me, my fathers! (*He takes a step toward the hiding place;* DOÑA SOL'S *eyes follow him in anguish. He turns back toward the portraits; to them:*) Oh, hide your eyes—your gaze will hold me back! (*He advances falteringly as far as his portrait, then turns back to the king again.*) It is your will?

DON CARLOS.   Yes.

(*The duke raises his trembling hand toward the spring.*)

DOÑA SOL.   God in heaven!

DON RUY GOMEZ.   No! (*He throws himself at the king's feet.*) Have pity, take my head!

DON CARLOS.   Your niece!

DON RUY GOMEZ (*rising*). Then take her! And leave me my honor.

DON CARLOS (*gripping* DOÑA SOL'S *trembling hand*). Farewell, Duke.

DON RUY GOMEZ.   Until we meet again. (*His eyes follow the king, who moves slowly off with* DOÑA SOL; *then he puts his hand to his dagger.*) God protect you, Highness! (*He comes forward again, and stands motionless, hearing and seeing nothing; his gaze is fixed, his arms crossed on his chest, which rises and falls in a convulsive rhythm. Meanwhile, the king goes out with* DOÑA SOL, *and all the courtiers go gravely after him, two by two, each in order of his rank. They speak low among themselves.*)

DON RUY (*to himself*). King, as you leave my home rejoicing, my ancient loyalty leaves my weeping heart. (*He raises his eyes, looks about him, and sees that he is alone. He dashes to the wall, takes down two swords from a display there, compares and examines them, and sets them on a table. This done, he goes to the portrait, pushes the spring, and opens the secret door.*)

SCENE SEVEN

DON RUY.   Come out. (HERNANI *appears at the doorway of the hiding place.* DON RUY *points to the two swords on the table.*) Choose one of them. Don Carlos has left my house; now you must settle with me. Choose, and do it swiftly. . . . Come now! Your hand is trembling!

HERNANI.   A duel! Old man, we cannot fight one another.

DON RUY GOMEZ.   And why not? Are you afraid? Or is it that you are not noble? Damnation! Noble or not, any man who injures me is gentleman enough to cross his sword with mine!

HERNANI.   Old man—

DON RUY GOMEZ.   Kill me, or die yourself.

HERNANI.   Die—yes. You have saved me despite my will, and so my life is yours to take.

DON RUY GOMEZ.   That is your wish? (*To the portraits.*) You see that he asks it. (*To* HERNANI.) Very well; then say your prayer.

HERNANI.   I make my last to you, my lord.

DON RUY GOMEZ.   Address the other Lord.

HERNANI.   No—no, to you! Old man, strike me, with anything, knife, dagger, sword! But grant me this last joy, in pity's name—Duke, before I die, let me see her!

DON RUY GOMEZ.   See her!

HERNANI.   Or at least let me hear her voice once more—only one last time!

DON RUY GOMEZ.   Hear her voice!

HERNANI.   My lord, I understand your jealousy; but death already clutches at my young life—forgive me. Tell me that I may hear her voice again, even if it must be without the sight of her. And I shall die tonight. Only to hear her! Fill my last longing—how contented I should breathe out my life, if you would let my soul look into hers again, into her eyes, before I fly to heaven! I shall not speak to her—you will be there, my father. And take me afterwards!

DON RUY GOMEZ (*looking amazed at the open door of the cupboard*). Can that closet be so deep, so tightly sealed, that he heard nothing?

HERNANI.   I heard nothing at all.

DON RUY GOMEZ.   I was forced to yield him Doña Sol, or you.

HERNANI.   Yield her to whom?

DON RUY GOMEZ.   The king.

HERNANI.   You fool! He loves her!

DON RUY GOMEZ.   Loves her!

HERNANI.   He has stolen her from us! He is our rival!

DON RUY GOMEZ.   My God! . . . Men! To your horses, your horses! We must go after the abductor!

HERNANI.   Listen. Vengeance that is well planned makes far less noise as it comes. I belong to you; you have the right to kill me. But do you wish to use me first, to avenge your niece and her honor? Let me share in your revenge! Ah, grant me that share—if I must fall and kiss your feet,

I do it, but let us both pursue the king! Come, I shall be your striking arm—I shall avenge you, Duke. And afterwards you can slay me.

DON RUY GOMEZ.   And then, just as today, you will give yourself up to death?

HERNANI.   Yes, Duke.

DON RUY GOMEZ.   How do you swear it?

HERNANI.   Upon my father's head.

DON RUY GOMEZ.   And will you swear to recall the vow yourself?

HERNANI (*handing him the horn he takes from his belt*). Take this horn. Whatever may happen, when you wish it, lord, and in whatever place, when you feel that it is time for me to die, then sound this trumpet, nothing more. It shall be done.

DON RUY GOMEZ (*offering him his hand*). Your hand. (*They clasp hands. Then, to the portraits:*) And you, my fathers—you all are witness to it!

ACT FOUR

THE TOMB

(*Aix-la-Chapelle: the underground crypt that holds the tomb of Charlemagne. The great vaults of Lombard architecture, arches, massive low pillars, their capitals carved with birds and flowers. To the right, Charlemagne's tomb with a small bronze door, low and arched. A single lamp hung from the height of an arch picks out its inscription: Carolus Magnus. It is dark. The far end of the cavern cannot be seen; it is lost among the arcades, the stairs and pillars that merge and disappear into the dimness.*)

SCENE ONE

(DON CARLOS *and* DON RICARDO DE ROXAS, *with a lantern in his hand. Full cloaks, hatbrims pulled low.*)

DON RICARDO (*his hat in his hand*). This is the place.

DON CARLOS.   It is here that the conspiracy will meet— and I shall have them all in the hollow of my hand! My Lord Elector of Treves, this is the place and you have lent it to them. . . . It is an admirable choice—a black plot flourishes in the air of catacombs, and tombstones are good for sharpening stilettos. And yet the game is crucial—a life is at stake, my lords assassins. We shall see. Well, they are wise indeed to choose a sepulcher for such a conference; they will have less distance to go. (*To* DON RICARDO.) Do these caverns stretch far beneath the ground?

DON RICARDO.   Down to the castle-fort.

DON CARLOS.   More space than I shall need.

DON RICARDO.   Others on this side go as far as the monastery of Altenheim. . . .

DON CARLOS.   Where Rudolph killed Lothair. Good— now once again, Count, recite me all the names and grievances: where, why, and how.

DON RICARDO.   Gotha—

DON CARLOS.   I know why that good duke would plot with them: he wants a German emperor for Germany.

DON RICARDO.   Hohenburg—

DON CARLOS.   Hohenburg, I think, would rather choose hell with Francis at its head, then heaven itself with me.

DON RICARDO.   Don Gil Tellez Giron—

DON CARLOS.   Saint Mary and Castile! So he is in revolt against his king, the traitor!

DON RICARDO.   They say he found you with Lady Giron, the evening of the day you made him baron. He would avenge the honor of his sweet wife.

DON CARLOS.   And thus turns rebel against Spain? . . . Who else is there?

DON RICARDO.   The Reverend Vasquez, the bishop of Avila, is said to be among them.

DON CARLOS.   Is that to avenge his wife's dishonor too?

DON RICARDO.   Then Guzman de Lara is discontent; he wants the collar of your knighthood.

DON CARLOS.   Ah! Guzman de Lara—if he wants only a collar, he will have it.

DON RICARDO.   The duke of Lutzelburg. As for his intentions—

DON CARLOS.   The duke of Lutzelburg stands just a head too tall.

DON RICARDO.   And Juan de Haro, who wants Astorga.

DON CARLOS.   Those Haros have always earned the headsman twice his wages.

DON RICARDO.   That is the list.

DON CARLOS.   You have named only seven, Count, and I had been warned of more.

DON RICARDO.   There are some bandits besides, engaged by Treves, or France. . . .

DON CARLOS.   Men without a true allegiance, whose ever-ready knives turn toward the fattest purse like compass needles toward the pole.

DON RICARDO.   I did make out two more conspirators, both of them newly arrived. One young, one old.

DON CARLOS.   Their names? (DON RICARDO *shrugs his shoulders; he does not know.*) Their ages then?

DON RICARDO.   The younger one seems twenty.

DON CARLOS.   What a pity!

DON RICARDO.   The elder, sixty at least.

DON CARLOS.   The one is too young, the other too old. Too bad; I shall take care of them. The headsman can count upon my help when it is needed. My sword will not be kind to treachery, and I shall lend it when his ax grows dull; and if the scaffold cloth should prove too small, I shall stitch my imperial purple onto it. But shall I indeed be emperor?

DON RICARDO.   The college of electors is gathered now to vote.

DON CARLOS.   I cannot tell—they will name Francis the First, or else their Saxon, their Frederick the Wise—ah,

Luther is right, Europe is in bad times! Fine men to choose a sacred majesty, reasons of gold alone can sway their mood. A Saxon heretic! An imbecilic count palatine, and a primate of Treves who is a libertine! The Bohemian king will vote for me. But Hessian princes even smaller than their fiefs—young idiots and debauched old men. Oh, crowns—there are many crowns, but heads? only try to find one! Dwarfs all of them, that laughable council, whom I could carry off like Hercules draped in my lion-skin. Without their purple mantles, they would none of them have a skull as large as Triboulet's[4] . . .

I lack three voices, Ricardo! And lacking them, I shall lack everything! Oh, I would give Toledo, Ghent, and Salamanca or any three cities they could wish, for three more votes! For those three voices—mark thee, Count, I would give up three cities in Castile or in Flanders! For I could take them back another time. (DON RICARDO *bows deeply to the king, and puts his hat on his head.*) You cover your head before me?

DON RICARDO.   My lord, you called me "thou"; (*He bows again.*) thus I am made a grandee.

DON CARLOS (*aside*). Ah, you pitiful things, so ambitious for a pittance! A self-seeking breed of animals, who follow their single strand of purpose through our own concerns! This is a shabby barnyard where they beg shamelessly of the king, and he dispenses scraps of greatness to all these famished beasts. (*Reflectively.*) Only God and the emperor are great—and the holy father. The rest, the kings and dukes—what are they?

DON RICARDO.   Indeed, I hope they will select Your Highness for the throne.

DON CARLOS (*aside*). Highness! Am I still only highness? Must misfortune follow me? If I should remain only king . . .

DON RICARDO (*aside*). Enough—emperor or not, I am now a grandee of Spain.

DON CARLOS.   How will they announce his name when they elect the German emperor?

DON RICARDO.   If it is the duke of Saxony, a single cannon shot. Two for the king of France, and three if it is Your Highness.

DON CARLOS.   And then Doña Sol! Everything has joined to irritate and wound me! Count, if fortune falls my way and makes me emperor, quickly bring her here. Perhaps she will find a Caesar more to her taste.

DON RICARDO (*smiling*). Your Highness is most generous.

DON CARLOS (*interrupting him haughtily*). Silence, upon that subject! I have not yet said what I wish opinion to be. When will we know the council's choice?

DON RICARDO.   Within the hour at latest, I think.

[4]Fool at the courts of Louis XII and Francis I; main character in *Le roi s'amuse* (1832), which play Verdi later adopted for *Rigoletto*.

DON CARLOS.   Three voices more! Only three. . . . But first we must crush this plotting rabble here, and afterwards see who will have the empire. (*He counts on his fingers and stamps his foot.*) Still three votes too few! The others have it! Yet that Cornelius Agrippa predicted them—he saw thirteen stars in the celestial sea come sailing swiftly toward my northern one. I'll have the empire then! . . . But on the other hand, they say that Abbé Jean Trithème prophesied for Francis. I should have helped the auguries along by military means, for then fate would be clear! Predictions by the best of sorcerers come best to birth when a good army serves as midwife; an army with its cannon and its pikes, with soldiers, horsemen and with marching tunes will lead a wavering fate in the right direction. Which of the two is better, Cornelius Agrippa or Jean Trithème? The one with regiments behind his words; the one who makes his points with iron lance, who underlines them with troops and mercenaries; their swords can set imperfect fortune straight, and mold the event according to the prophet.

They are poor fools who aim to have the empire of the world, who with proud eye and brow declare "It is my right!" They have a thousand cannon stretched in rows, whose hot breath could melt cities; they've vassals, soldiers, horses, and one assumes that they will march to their goal over the conquered peoples. . . . But no! When they have reached the great crossroads of human destiny, where many paths lead to the pit and one leads to the throne, they hardly take three steps but stop in indecision; wondering, they try in vain to read the book of fate; they hesitate, uncertain of themselves; and, caught by doubt, go running to the neighboring necromancer, to ask their way!

(*To* DON RICARDO.) Leave me now; the traitors' league will soon be here. Oh—and the key to the tomb?

DON RICARDO (*handing it to him*). My lord, you will remember the Count of Limburg, the guardian here? He gave me the key, and he does all that's in his power for your sake.

DON CARLOS (*dismissing him*). Do everything as I have ordered you. Everything!

DON RICARDO (*bowing*). I go at once, Your Highness.

DON CARLOS.   I need three cannon shots, you said?

(DON RICARDO *bows and leaves.* DON CARLOS, *left alone, falls into a deep reverie. His arms cross, his head falls to his chest; then he lifts it and turns toward the tomb.*)

SCENE TWO

DON CARLOS.   Charlemagne, forgive me! These silent vaults should not reverberate with any but solemn words. You must be indignant at hearing our ambition hum about your monument. . . . Charlemagne is here! You somber sepulcher, how can you hold so great a spirit and yet not burst? Are you truly there, giant creator of a world? And can you stretch your length within those walls? . . . It is a spectacle to astound the mind, as it was before he came, and as he later made it! A vast structure with two men at its top, elected lords to whom each king is subject. Each state and duchy, military fief, kingdom, and march—almost all are hereditary reigns; yet the people sometimes have their pope or Caesar. The mechanism works, and one chance corrects another; so equilibrium comes, and order triumphs. Electors in cloth of gold, and scarlet cardinals—the sacred double senate that stirs the earth—are but display, and God will have His will. An idea may rise one day born of the times; it grows, and burns, and spreads, and mingles with all things; takes human form, grips hearts, and carves a furrow; many a king will trample it underfoot, or gag its voice. But if one day it penetrates the diet, or the papal conclave, then suddenly the kings will see the once-enslaved idea loom up, with globe in hand or the tiara on its brow, and bow their royal heads beneath its feet.

The pope and emperor are everything. Nothing is on earth but for or by them. A sublime mystery dwells in them, and heaven, from which they hold their privilege, endows them with a feast of peoples and of kings; heaven keeps them underneath its thunderous canopy of cloud, seated alone at table where God serves them up the world. Side by side, they sit to rule and sentence, arranging the universe as a reaper does his field. All that is occurs between those two. The kings stand at the door, breathing the savory steam of dishes carried past, staring through the window, watchful, agitated, and rising on their toes to see. Beneath them the world falls into ranks and groups. They do and they undo. One absolves, the other cuts. The one is truth, the other might. Their purpose is contained within them; they are because they are. When they emerge from the sanctuary, both equal, the one in purple, the other in his white soutane, the dazzled universe in terror regards these two halves of God, the pope and the emperor.

Emperor! To be emperor—oh fury, not to be, and to feel one's heart filled with courage! How fortunate was he who sleeps within this tomb; how great was he! And it was still finer in his time. The pope and the emperor: they were more than two men. Peter and Caesar—in themselves the two Romes were joined, each fertilized the other by mystic marriage, giving new form and soul to human kind; melding peoples and kingdoms as they wished to form a new Europe, and both of them by their hands refashioning the bronze that still remained of the old Roman world. A lofty fate—and yet, this tomb is his. Is all so trivial then, that this is where it ends? To have been prince, and king, and emperor—to have been the sword and been the law . . . a giant, with Germany for his pedestal, with Caesar for his title, and Charlemagne

for name! To have been greater than Hannibal, or than Attila, as great as all the world—and this is where it ends!

Then scheme for empire, and see the dust an emperor leaves! Cover the earth entire with fanfare and with tumult; raise and build your endless empire; slash and carve out an enormous edifice—do you know what will remain one day? Ah, lunacy—this stone! And of the title and the triumphal name? A few letters, that serve to teach a child his spelling! However high the goal your pride envisions, here is the last limit! Oh empire! I do not care—I touch at it, and find it to my liking. Something tells me: ''You shall have it.'' It shall be mine . . . if it only were! Oh heaven, to be what is beginning! Alone, upright, atop the enormous spiral; to be the keystone in the arch of all the states arranged one on the other, to see beneath one all the many kings, and wipe one's sandals on them.

To see beneath the kings the feudal houses, margraves and cardinals, doges, and dukes with floral seals; then bishops, abbots, heads of clans, great barons! Then priests and soldiers next; then in the shadow, far below the peak whereon we stand—deep within the chasm—are men!

Men—a mass, a sea, great rumbling, tears and cries, sometimes a bitter laugh—a whole lament that wakes the startled earth, and through a hundred thousand echoes reaches us as a skirl of trumpets! Men! . . . Cities, towers, a vast swarm of high church belfries to ring their gongs! (*Musingly.*) A base of human nations, bearing on their shoulders the enormous pyramid that leans on the two poles; living waves that grasp it always in their hollows, and float it pitching on their vast swells; waves that shift everything about, and at its upper reaches topple thrones like footstools, so that all kings cease their vain disputes and raise their eyes to heaven.

Kings! Look down beneath you! Ah, the people—that ocean—that never-resting wave, where nought can be cast in but stirs the whole! A swell that may crush a throne or rock a tomb! Mirror wherein a king will rarely find a handsome image of himself. If he should sometimes gaze into that dark swell, he'd see at bottom numberless empires, great shipwrecked vessels swaying in its ebb and flow—empires that had disturbed the ocean's stream and now exist no more!

To think of ruling over all of that! To mount up to that pinnacle if the electors call—to climb there, conscious that one is but a man! To see the chasm below! If only I do not at that same moment grow dazed with vertigo— oh, shifting pyramid of kings and countries, your summit is so narrow! Woe to the fearful foot! By whom should I hold steady? Suppose I stumble at feeling the world shudder beneath my feet! At feeling the earth live, and surge, and pulse! Or when I have that globe between my hands, what then? Shall I be capable of carrying it? What is there in me? Emperor, my God! to fill the role of king was hard for me! Surely the man is rare whose soul can stretch with fortune. But I—who shall make me great? Who will be my guide and give me counsel?

(*He falls to his knees before the tomb.*) Charlemagne— you shall! Since God, before whom all obstacles fall back, has taken our two majesties and set them face to face, then from the depths of this your grave imbue my heart with something sublime! Ah, show me all things from their every aspect, show me that the world is small, for I dare not lay my hand on it. Show me that within this tower of Babel, rising from shepherd to Caesar to the skies, each man at his own rank delights himself, admires what he is, observes the man beneath him and cannot help but mock. Teach me your secrets of conquest and of rule, and tell me that it is better to punish than forgive—is this not so? If it is true that sometimes the world's clatter wakes a great shadow in his lonely resting place; if it is true his wide bright tomb can open suddenly, and throw the world a flare in its dark night—if these things are true, emperor of Germany, then tell me, what can a man do when he comes after Charlemagne?

Speak! Though it mean your sovereign breath in speaking must crack this bronze door across my brow! Or rather let me enter alone within your sanctuary, and see your face in death—do not repulse me by an icy breath, but raise yourself upon your bed of stone, and let us talk. Yes, even though you should tell me, in your fateful voice, of matters that darken the eye and pale the brow! Speak, and do not blind your fearful son, for your tomb must be so full with light! Or else, if you will say nothing, let me study that deeply peaceful head, as if it were a world; let me measure you carefully, oh giant, for nothing here below is great as is thy dust! Let the ashes guide me if the spirit would not.

(*He puts the key to the lock.*) We shall go in. (*He draws back.*) But what if he should speak to me indeed? if he is there, awake and upright, walking with slow steps! And I should reappear with my hair white! Still—I shall enter. (*Sound of footsteps.*) Someone is approaching. Who but I could dare to come here at this hour, and rouse the home of such a corpse? Who is it? (*The noise is closer.*) Ah, I had forgotten—it is my murderers. Let us go in then.

(*He opens the door to the tomb and closes it behind him. Several men come on, with muffled steps, hidden in their cloaks and hats.*)

SCENE THREE

(*The conspirators; they move about among themselves, clasping hands and exchanging a few words in low voices.*)

FIRST CONSPIRATOR (*who alone carries a lighted torch*). *Ad augusta.*
SECOND CONSPIRATOR.   *Per angusta.*
FIRST.   May the saints protect us.
THIRD.   May the dead serve us.

FIRST.   God keep us.

(*Sounds of steps in the darkness.*)

SECOND.   Who goes there?
VOICE.   *Ad augusta.*
SECOND.   *Per angusta.*

(*Other conspirators appear. Sound of footsteps again.*)

FIRST CONSPIRATOR (*to the* THIRD). Look there, another's coming.
THIRD.   Who goes there?
VOICE IN SHADOWS.   *Ad augusta.*
THIRD.   *Per angusta.*

(*Still others appear, with signs of greeting.*)

FIRST.   Good, we are all here. Gotha, give us your report. My friends, the dark awaits the light.

(*All the conspirators seat themselves on tombs in a half circle. The first conspirator passes among them, and from his torch each lights a candle and holds it in his hand. Then the first conspirator takes a seat silently upon a tomb at the center of the circle and higher than the others.*)

DUKE OF GOTHA (*rising*). Friends, this Charles of Spain, a foreigner through his mother, lays claim to the Holy Empire.
FIRST CONSPIRATOR.   He shall have the grave instead.
GOTHA (*throwing his torch to the ground and grinding it out with his foot*). May his skull be as this flame!
ALL.   May it be!
FIRST.   Death to him!
GOTHA.   May he die!
ALL.   May he be slain!
DON JUAN DE HARO.   His father was a German.
DUKE OF LUTZELBURG.   His mother was Spanish.
GOTHA.   He is Spanish no longer, and not a German. Death!
ONE OF THE CONSPIRATORS.   What if the electors were to name him emperor at this moment?
FIRST.   They name him? Never!
DON GIL TELLEZ GIRON.   What does that matter, friends! If we strike the head, the crown will die with it.
FIRST.   Whatever he may be, if he wins the Holy Empire, he becomes mighty and august, and only God can touch him.
GOTHA.   The surest way is to act before he gains that state.
FIRST.   He shall not be elected.
ALL.   He shall not have the Empire!
FIRST.   How many hands are needed to wind him in his shroud?
ALL.   Only one.
FIRST.   How many strokes to the heart?
ALL.   Only one!

FIRST.   Who will do it?

ALL.   All of us!

FIRST.   Our victim is a traitor. They are choosing an emperor; let us make a high priest. We shall draw lots.

(*All the conspirators write their names on their tablets, tear off the sheet, roll it up, and go one after the other to drop it into the urn on one of the tombs.*)

FIRST CONSPIRATOR.   Let us pray. (*They all kneel. The* FIRST *rises.*) May the chosen one put his faith in God, strike like a Roman, and die like a Hebrew! He must brave the wheel and pincers, sing at the rack, and laugh at the fiery brand; he must do all to kill and die in resignation! (*He draws one of the parchment sheets from the urn.*)

ALL.   What name is it?

FIRST (*loudly*). Hernani.

HERNANI (*emerging from the group*). I've won! Ah revenge, I have you now, you whom I have pursued so long!

DON RUY GOMEZ (*moving through the crowd and taking* HERNANI *aside*). Let me take your place!

HERNANI.   No, upon my life! My lord, do not grudge me my fortune! It is the first time that luck has come to me!

DON RUY.   You have nothing. Then listen—I give you my fiefs, my castles, and my vassalages—a hundred thousand peasants in my three hundred villages—I give them all to you, my friend, for the right to strike that blow!

HERNANI.   No!

GOTHA.   Your weaker arm would strike with less effect, old man.

DON RUY GOMEZ.   Silence! If not the arm, I have the spirit for it! Do not judge the blade by the rust that coats its scabbard. (*To* HERNANI.) You belong to me.

HERNANI.   My life is yours, yes. But his belongs to me!

DON RUY GOMEZ (*drawing the horn from his waist*). Listen, my friend: I give you back this horn.

HERNANI (*shaken*). What? My life? Ah, what does it mean to me? My vengeance is at hand! God is with me in this. I have my father to avenge, and more perhaps! Would you give her to me?

DON RUY GOMEZ.   Never! But I yield up this horn!

HERNANI.   No.

DON RUY GOMEZ.   Reflect upon it, boy!

HERNANI.   Duke, leave me my prey.

DON RUY.   Then be accursed for denying me that joy. (*He replaces the horn in his belt.*)

FIRST CONSPIRATOR (*to* HERNANI). Brother, before they can elect him, it would be well to watch for Carlos on this very night—

HERNANI.   Fear not! I know how to put a man into his grave.

FIRST.   May any treason fall back upon the traitor, and God be with us! And if he should fall without having slain, then, counts and barons, we shall continue it! Let us swear to strike, each of us in turn, without evasion—for Carlos must die.

ALL.   We swear it!

GOTHA (*to the* FIRST CONSPIRATOR). Upon what, my brother?

DON RUY GOMEZ (*upending his sword, taking it by the tip and raising it over his head*). Let us swear upon this cross!

ALL (*raising their swords*). May he die unrepentant.

(*A far-off cannon is heard. They all stop, silent. The door to the tomb opens slightly;* DON CARLOS *appears on the threshold. Pale, he listens. A second shot. A third. He opens the door wide, but without stepping forward; he stands motionless on the doorsill.*)

SCENE FOUR

DON CARLOS.   Go on, my lords! The emperor is listening. (*All the torches go out at once. Deep silence. He moves a step in the shadows, so dark that the mute and motionless conspirators are scarcely visible.*) Silence and darkness! the swarm emerges from the black, and now returns there. Do you believe somehow that all of this will seem a dream, and that because you have put out your flares, I shall take you all for stone figures seated on their tombs? But a moment since, my statues, your voices were still loud! Come now! raise up your lowered heads, for Charles the Fifth is here! Strike me now—take even a step. Let us see it, do you dare? No, you dare not. Your torches flamed like blood beneath these vaults; and my breath alone sufficed to put them out. But look, turn your quavering eyes—I did extinguish many, but I light many more. (*He strikes the iron key on the bronze door of the tomb; at the sound, the depths of the cavern fill with soldiers bearing torches and halberds. At their head are the* DUKE OF ALCALA *and the* MARQUIS OF ALMUÑAN.) Come here, my falcons! I have the nest, and I have the prey! (*To the* CONSPIRATORS.) Now I bring light in my turn. Look, the sepulcher's aflame. (*To the soldiers.*) Come forward, all of you; this is a flagrant crime.

HERNANI (*looking at the soldiers*). That is better now. Alone, he seemed too large. At first I thought that it was Charlemagne; it is only Charles the Fifth.

DON CARLOS (*to the* DUKE OF ALCALA). Constable of Spain! (*To the* MARQUIS OF ALMUÑAN.) Admiral of Castile, come forward! Disarm them all. (*The plotters are surrounded and disarmed.*)

DON RICARDO (*running up and bowing to the ground*). Majesty!

DON CARLOS.   I name thee alcalde of the palace.

DON RICARDO (*bowing again*). Two electors are come to congratulate Your Sacred Majesty, in the name of the Golden Chamber.

DON CARLOS.   Let them come in. (*Low, to* RICARDO.) Doña Sol.

(RICARDO *salutes and leaves. The* KING OF BOHEMIA *and the* DUKE OF BAVARIA *enter with torches and trumpet flourishes; both are clothed in their gold-embroidered mantles, with* crowns on their heads. A large cortege follows them, made up of German lords carrying the imperial banner—the two-headed eagle with the Spanish shield at its center. The soldiers form an aisle to the emperor for the two electors. They salute him deeply and he returns it by raising his hat.)

DUKE OF BAVARIA.   Charles, King of the Romans, Most Sacred Majesty, Emperor! The world is now within your hands, for the Empire is yours. Yours, the throne that every monarch covets. Frederick, Duke of Saxony, was first elected; but he judged you more worthy of it, and declined. Come then, receive this crown and take the globe. The Holy Empire, King, invests you with its purple robe; it arms you with its sword, and you are great.

DON CARLOS.   I shall thank the council on my return. Go now, my lords. Thank you, my brother Bohemia, and my cousin Bavaria. Go now—and I myself must leave.

KING OF BOHEMIA.   Charles, our ancestors were friends; my father loved your father, and their sires too loved each other. Charles, you are so young a man to face disturbing fortunes—tell me, would you wish that I should be your brother among brothers? I knew you as a child, and I cannot forget—

DON CARLOS (interrupting him). King of Bohemia, you are most familiar! (He presents his hand for the KING to kiss, and to the DUKE OF BAVARIA, then dismisses the two electors, who bow deeply.) Go now. (They leave with their suites.)

CROWD.   Long live the emperor!

DON CARLOS (aside). I am emperor! And everything has made way for me. Emperor! through the refusal, though, of Frederick the Wise!

(DOÑA SOL enters, led by RICARDO.)

DOÑA SOL.   Soldiers! and the emperor—oh God, I did not expect this! Hernani!

HERNANI.   Doña Sol!

DON RUY (beside HERNANI, to himself). She does not even see me!

(DOÑA SOL runs to HERNANI; his defiant stare stops her.)

HERNANI.   My lady!

DOÑA SOL (drawing the knife from her bodice). I have his dagger still.

HERNANI.   My beloved!

DON CARLOS.   Silence, all of you. (To the plotters.) Have you recovered your determination? It is fitting that I show the world a lesson here. Lara the Castilian, and Saxon Gotha—all of you—what did you come here to do? Speak!

HERNANI (stepping forward). Sire, it is a simple thing, and we can tell you of it: we were writing the sentence upon Balthazar's wall. (He draws his knife and brandishes it.) We render unto Caesar what is Caesar's.

DON CARLOS.   I see. (To DON RUY GOMEZ.) And you, Silva—a traitor!

DON RUY GOMEZ.   Which of us two is traitor, sire?

HERNANI (turning to the other CONSPIRATORS). He has what he desires—our heads and empire both! (To the EMPEROR.) A king's blue robe could hinder your steps. This purple suits you better; it does not show blood.

DON CARLOS (to DON RUY GOMEZ). My cousin Silva—this is crime enough to strike your barony from your coat of arms. It is high treason, Don Ruy; consider that well.

DON RUY GOMEZ.   Count Julians are made by King Rodrigos.[5]

DON CARLOS (to the DUKE OF ALCALA). Take only the dukes or counts. The rest—

(DON RUY GOMEZ, the DUKE OF LUTZELBURG, the DUKE OF GOTHA, DON JUAN DE HARO, DON GUZMAN DE LARA, DON GIL TELLEZ GIRON, and the BARON OF HOHENBURG step out of the group; HERNANI remains with it. The DUKE OF ALCALA surrounds the lords with guards.)

DOÑA SOL (aside). He is safe!

HERNANI (stepping forward). I claim my place among these others! (To DON CARLOS.) Since this is a matter of the ax; since Hernani the humble peasant would slip beneath your feet unpunished; since his brow is no longer worthy of your sword; since one must be a nobleman to die, I rise. God who awards the scepter and who gave it you, God made me Duke of Segorbia and Cardona, the Marquis of Monroy, Count Albatera and Viscount of Gor—and lord of lands whose number or whose names I cannot count. I am Juan of Aragon, grand master of Avis, born in exile—the banished son of a father slaughtered by your father's word, King Carlos of Castile! Murder is a family affair between us. You have the scaffold; we have the knife. Thus, heaven made me a duke, and exile a mountaineer. I have whetted my sword against the hills and tempered it in rushing streams; but since all my preparation must come to nothing—(He puts on his hat, and says to the other conspirators:)—cover your heads, all you grandees of Spain! (All the nobles do so. To DON CARLOS.) Yes, King—our heads have the right to fall before you covered! (To the prisoners.) Silva, Haro, Lara—men of title and of race—open your ranks to Juan of Aragon! Dukes and counts, give me my place! (To the courtiers and guards.) I am Juan of Aragon, king, headsmen and grooms. And if your scaffolds are too small, change them for others! (He joins the group of captured lords.)

DOÑA SOL.   Why did he speak?

DON CARLOS.   True, I had forgotten that whole story.

---

[5]This Visigoth king defiled the count's daughter, and was killed by him.

HERNANI. The man whose flesh has bled remembers better. And the wrong forgotten by the offender lives on still active in the injured heart.

DON CARLOS.   Then I am the son of men who felled your fathers' heads—that is title enough for me.

DOÑA SOL (*throwing herself to her knees before the emperor*). Sire, pardon! Pity, sire—be merciful! Or else then kill us both by the same stroke, for he is my beloved, my husband! I live in him alone. Oh, I tremble, sire; find the compassion to kill the two of us together! Majesty, I lie at your sainted feet! I love him! He is mine, as the empire is yours! Oh mercy! (DON CARLOS *watches her, impassive.*) What dark idea absorbs you now?

DON CARLOS.   Rise, Duchess of Segorbia, Countess Albatera, Marchioness of Monroy. . . . (*To* HERNANI.) What are your other names, Don Juan?

HERNANI.   Who is it says these things? The king?

DON CARLOS.   No, the emperor.

DOÑA SOL (*rising*). Great heavens!

DON CARLOS (*indicating her to* HERNANI). Duke, here is your wife.

HERNANI (*his eyes raised to heaven, and* DOÑA SOL *in his arms*). God of justice!

DON CARLOS (*to* DON RUY GOMEZ). Cousin, you are jealous and proud in your nobility, I know. But an Aragon may wed a Silva.

DON RUY GOMEZ (*darkly*). It is not for my nobility.

HERNANI (*gazing lovingly at* DOÑA SOL, *and holding her close*). Ah, I feel my hatred vanishing. . . . (*He throws down his dagger.*)

DON RUY GOMEZ (*watching the pair*). Shall my rage burst from me? Ah no—senseless love, and senseless grief. . . . They would pity your old Spanish head. Burn flameless, old man—love and suffer secretly. Let your heart be consumed, but not a cry, for they would laugh.

DOÑA SOL (*still in* HERNANI'*s arms*). My duke!

HERNANI.   I have nothing left in my heart but love.

DOÑA SOL.   What happiness . . .

DON CARLOS (*aside, his hand upon his breast*). Quiet, my heart that still is young and full of love! Let intellect rule now, for too long you have had your way. Henceforward all your loves, and alas, your only mistresses are Germany and Flanders and old Spain. (*He eyes his banner.*) The emperor is like the eagle, his companion: in the heart's stead there hangs only an escutcheon.

HERNANI.   You are Caesar indeed!

DON CARLOS (*to* HERNANI). Your heart is worthy of your noble line, Don Juan. (*Indicating* DOÑA SOL.) And worthy too of her. On your knees, Duke! (HERNANI *kneels.* DON CARLOS *takes off the collar of the Golden Fleece, and sets it around* HERNANI'*s neck.*) Receive this collar. (DON CARLOS *draws his sword and taps him three times upon the shoulder.*) Be faithful. In the name of Saint Stephen, Duke, I name thee knight. (*He raises and embraces him.*)

But you have the best and sweetest collar yet, one I have not, and one that even the highest rank can lack: the arms of a beloved woman loving you. Ah, you shall be happy; and I, I am emperor. . . . (*To the conspirators.*) I know your names no more, sirs. Hatred and anger—I would forget them all. Go then; I pardon you. This is the lesson I must give the world. It shall not be in vain that the emperor Charles the Fifth succeeds to Charles the First, the king; nor that, before a mourning, orphaned Europe, a law should change a Catholic highness into a sacred majesty.

(*The plotters fall to their knees.*)

CONSPIRATORS.   Glory to Carlos! Hail!

DON RUY GOMEZ (*to* DON CARLOS). And so I alone remain condemned to suffering.

DON CARLOS.   And I.

DON RUY (*aside*). But unlike him, I have not forgiven!

HERNANI.   Who is it has changed us all?

ALL (SOLDIERS, CONSPIRATORS, NOBLES).   Long live Germany and Charles the Fifth!

DON CARLOS (*turning toward the tomb*). Honor to Charlemagne! Leave the two of us together now. (ALL *exeunt.*)

SCENE FIVE

DON CARLOS (*alone; he bows before the tomb*). Are you content with me? Have I stripped away the pettiness of kings, Charlemagne, and am I indeed become another man? May I join my helmet to the Roman miter? Have I the right to bend the fortunes of the world? Have I a firm and steady foot, one that may walk upon this path, all strewn with vandal's ruins, that you have beaten out for us with your broad sandals? Have I caught your flame to kindle my own torch? And understood the voice that sounds within your tomb? Ah, I was alone and lost before an empire, a whole howling world that plots and threatens me—there is the Dane to punish, the Holy Father to pay; Venice and Suleiman; Luther, Francis the First—a thousand jealous blades already gleaming in the dark, snares and hidden reefs, and enemies unnumbered; twenty peoples, and each of them enough to frighten twenty kings— all hurrying and urgent, all to do at once. And I cried out to you: "How shall I start?" And you replied: "My son, by clemency!"

ACT FIVE
THE WEDDING

(*Saragossa. A terrace of the palace of Aragon. At stage rear, a flight of stairs down into the garden. At right and left, two doors opening onto the terrace, which is enclosed by a balustrade topped by two rows of Moorish arcades; above and through them are visible the palace gardens, fountains in the* shade, clumps of trees with lights moving among them, and beyond it all the Gothic and Arab lines of the brightly lit palace. It is night. We hear faraway trumpet flourishes. Persons in masks and dominoes, single or in groups, cross over the terrace here and there. In the foreground, a group of young lords, their masks in hand, are laughing and chattering noisily.)

SCENE ONE

(DON SANCHO SANCHEZ DE ZUÑIGA, DON MATIAS CENTURION, DON RICARDO DE ROXAS, DON FRANCISCO DE SOTOMAYER, DON GARCI SUAREZ DE CARBAJAL.)

DON GARCI. Well, here's to joy, and long live the lovely bride!

DON MATIAS (*watching the balcony*). All Saragossa is hanging out of its windows tonight.

DON GARCI. And so it should! There has never been a wedding with gayer lights, nor a gentler night, nor for a handsomer pair!

DON MATIAS. The emperor is good!

DON SANCHO. Marquis, I remember a dusky night when we went out with him to try our chance. Who could have told that it would end this way?

DON RICARDO (*interrupting him*). I was there too. (*To the others.*) Listen to this tale. Three lovers—one a bandit destined for the block, and a duke, and then a king—all three lay siege to a single woman's heart. When the battle clears, who holds it? It is the bandit.

DON FRANCISCO. But nothing is astonishing in that. In Spain as everywhere, love and luck turn on a play of loaded dice. The thief will always win!

DON RICARDO. And I, I've made my fortune by watching the course of love. First count, then grandee, then alcalde of the court; I have spent my time quite well, and none observed me.

DON SANCHO. Your secret is to hang about the king's path . . .

DON RICARDO. And turn my rights and actions to advantage.

DON GARCI. You profited by his preoccupation.

DON MATIAS. What is the old duke doing now? Having his coffin built?

DON SANCHO. Marquis, do not scoff. He is a valiant man. And he loved Doña Sol. Sixty years had turned his hair to gray, and one day made it white.

DON GARCI. He has not appeared again in Saragossa, they say.

DON SANCHO. Would you have this festival send him sooner to the grave?

DON FRANCISCO. And the emperor? how is he?

DON SANCHO. The emperor is sad today; Luther distresses him.

DON RICARDO. That Luther is fine cause for worry and alarm! With three or four armed men I'd take him easily.

DON MATIAS. He is disturbed by Suleiman as well.

DON GARCI. Oh, Luther, Suleiman, Neptune, the devil, Jupiter—what are they all to me? The women are pretty, the masquerade's a good one, and I've laughed all evening long!

DON SANCHO. Those are the things that count.

DON RICARDO. Garci is right—on holidays I am no longer myself; when I pull on a mask I fully believe I have a different head entirely!

DON SANCHO (*low to* MATIAS). If only each day were a holiday!

DON FRANCISCO (*pointing to the door at right*). My lords, is that not the bridal apartment?

DON GARCI (*nodding*). They will appear in just a moment.

DON FRANCISCO. Do you think so?

DON GARCI. I am sure of it!

DON FRANCISCO. Good! The bride is so very beautiful.

DON RICARDO. How generous the emperor is—to think this rebel Hernani should have the Golden Fleece—and be wed—and pardoned too! If he had taken my advice, the emperor would have given the outlaw a bed of stone, and the lady one of down.

DON SANCHO (*low to* DON MATIAS). Ah, how my blade would love to slit his throat—that false, tinsel lord, all patched together with string! A count's doublet stuffed with a steward's soul!

DON RICARDO (*drawing near*). What are you saying?

DON MATIAS (*low to* DON SANCHO). Count, let's have no quarrels here! (*Aloud to* DON RICARDO.) He was singing me one of Petrarch's sonnets to his love.

DON GARCI. Gentlemen, among the flowers and the women, and all these brightly colored costumes, have you noticed that specter leaning at the parapet and dimming the feast with his black domino?

DON RICARDO. I have indeed!

DON GARCI. Who is it?

DON RICARDO. Well, from his height, his manner, it must be Don Prancasio, the admiral.

DON FRANCISCO. No.

DON GARCI. He has not taken off his mask.

DON FRANCISCO. He has been cautious not to. It is the duke of Soma, who wants to draw attention—nothing more.

DON RICARDO. No, the duke spoke to me.

DON GARCI. Who is he then? Look now, there he goes.

(*A black domino slowly crosses the terrace at the rear. All turn to watch him, without his seeming to notice.*)

DON SANCHO. If the dead walk, that is their step.

DON GARCI (*approaching the dark figure*). Good sir! . . . (*The figure turns and stops;* GARCI *draws back.*) Gentlemen, I swear, a flame gleams in his eyes!

DON SANCHO. If he is the devil, he has found the man to talk to. (*He goes to the black domino, who stands motionless.*) Evil one! Have you come to us from hell?

MASKED FIGURE.   I do not come; I go there. (*He continues his progress and disappears by the flight of stairs. All watch him go with a kind of horror.*)

DON MATIAS.   His voice comes from the grave!

DON GARCI.   Enough now! what's frightening otherwise is only amusing at a ball!

DON SANCHO.   It is some sorry joke!

DON GARCI.   Or if it's Lucifer who's stopped to watch us dance while on his way to hell, then let us dance!

DON SANCHO.   It is certainly some game.

DON MATIAS.   We shall find out tomorrow.

DON SANCHO (*to* DON MATIAS). Look below, I beg you. Where is he now?

DON MATIAS (*leaning over the balustrade*). He has gone down the staircase. I see no more of him.

DON SANCHO.   A droll trick . . . (*musingly*) it is strange. . . .

DON GARCI (*to a lady passing by*). Marquise, shall we dance this one together? (*He bows and presents his hand.*)

LADY.   My dear sir, you know my husband counts the ones we dance together.

DON GARCI.   Only the more reason. If he finds pleasure in that, he shall count, and we shall dance, you and I. (*The lady gives him her hand, and they go out.*)

DON SANCHO (*thoughtfully*). It is curious, indeed.

DON MATIAS.   Here is the bridal pair! Silence!

(*Enter* HERNANI *and* DOÑA SOL *hand in hand.* DOÑA SOL *wears a magnificent bridal costume;* HERNANI *is all in black velvet, the Golden Fleece about his neck. Behind them, a crowd of masked figures, ladies and lords forming a retinue. Two halberdiers in rich livery follow them, and four pages precede them. All present separate and bow as they pass. Fanfare.*)

SCENE TWO

HERNANI (*saluting*). My dear friends!

DON RICARDO (*going up to him and bowing*). Your happiness is ours, Excellency!

DON FRANCISCO (*gazing at* DOÑA SOL). Holy Saint James! . . .

DON SANCHO (*to* DON MATIAS). It is late. Shall we go now?

(*All of them move forward to greet the pair and then leave, some through the door, others by the stairway in rear.*)

HERNANI (*moving with them*). God keep you all!

DON SANCHO (*the last to go, grips his hand*). I wish you joy. (*He leaves.*)

(HERNANI *and* DOÑA SOL *remain alone. The sound of footsteps and voices fades and disappears completely. Throughout the beginning of the following scene, the faraway trumpets and the lights diminish gradually, and darkness and silence return.*)

SCENE THREE

DOÑA SOL.   They all have gone, at last.

HERNANI (*attempting to draw her into his arms*). My dearest love!

DOÑA SOL (*blushing and drawing back*). It—it is late, I think.

HERNANI.   My angel, it is always late for us to come together!

DOÑA SOL.   All the activity was tiring me. Do you not find, my dear lord, that so much gaiety turns happiness numb?

HERNANI.   It is true. Happiness is a thing of gravity. It seeks for hearts of bronze, and carves itself there slowly; pleasure startles it away by tossing flowers to it. Joy's smile is much more close to tears than it is to laughter.

DOÑA SOL.   In your eyes, that smile is daybreak. (HERNANI *tries to lead her toward the door. She flushes.*) Soon.

HERNANI.   I am your slave—yes, linger, linger! Do what you will, I ask you nothing. You know what you would have; you can do only good. I shall laugh if you desire it, or sing. My soul burns. Ah, tell the volcano to smother its flame—the volcano shall close its gaping chasms, and rim its sides with flowers and green grass. For the giant is held captive, Vesuvius is enslaved; its lava-boiling heart must not affect you. It is flowers you would have? Very well! Then the spitting volcano must do its best to burst with blossom!

DOÑA SOL.   How kind you are to a poor woman, Hernani my heart!

HERNANI.   What name is that, my lady? Ah, never call me by that name again, I beg of you! You remind me then of all I have forgotten. I know that once upon a time, in some dream, there lived a Hernani, whose eye glinted like a sword—a man of night and of the mountains, an outlaw who wore the word "revenge" scrawled everywhere upon him, a miserable man who trailed a curse behind him! But I do not know this Hernani. I am a man who loves the meadows, and flowers, and woods, and the nightingale's soft song; I am Juan of Aragon, and wed to Doña Sol! I am a happy man!

DOÑA SOL.   I too am happy!

HERNANI.   What do I care for the rags I left behind me at the door? Here I am returned to my saddened palace; an angel of the Lord awaits me on the stair. I enter, and set upright the shattered columns; I light the fire, I open wide the casements, and tear the growth from between the flagstones in the court—I am nothing now but joy, enchantment, love.

Let them return my towers, my cellars and bastilles, my crest and seat within the council of the Castiles; give me my Doña Sol, all flushed, and her brow bent low—let the two of us be left alone, and the rest is past, forgotten. I have seen nothing, said and done nothing. I begin anew, wipe everything away, forget! Be it wisdom or madness, I have you, I love you, and you are all my joy!

DOÑA SOL (*examining his collar*). How handsome this collar is against the velvet black!

HERNANI.   You saw the king dressed thus before myself.

DOÑA SOL.   I did not notice it. What is another man to me? And then besides, is it the velvet, or the satin? No, my duke, it is your throat that suits the gold so well. You are noble and proud, my lord. (*He urges her off again.*) Soon! A moment yet! Look at me, do you see? This is joy, and I am weeping with it! Come look upon the lovely night! (*She goes to the balustrade.*) Only a moment, my duke! Only for long enough to breathe and gaze. All is dimmed now, the flares and festive tunes. Only the night and us. Perfect delight. . . . Say then, do you not feel that dreaming nature still half watches over us with love? There is not a cloud. All is at rest, as we are. Come, breathe the rose-perfumed air with me. No torches, not a sound. All is still. A while ago the moon climbed up from the horizon, and as you spoke your voice and its trembling light both pierced my heart together. I felt myself joyful and calm, oh my beloved; I should have liked to die then.

HERNANI.   Who'd not forget all things at that celestial voice? Your tones are a song that has nothing human left in it. And like a traveler carried on a stream, who slips upon the waters through a summer night, and sees a thousand flowery fields slide past him, my bewitched spirit goes wandering in your reveries. . . .

DOÑA SOL.   This silence is too dark, this peace is too profound. Would you not set a star there in the sky? Or hear a night voice sing out suddenly, all tender and sweet? . . .

HERNANI (*smiling*). Capricious girl—only a moment since, you yearned for the light and singing to be done!

DOÑA SOL.   The celebration, yes! But a bird who would sing above the meadow, a single nightingale amid the moss and shadow, or else a distant flute. . . . Such music is sweet; it brings its harmony into the soul, and sets a thousand voices singing in the heart like heavenly choirs! Oh, how lovely it would be! (*The distant sound of a horn is heard.*) God! My prayer is answered!

HERNANI (*starting; aside*). Ah no, it cannot be!

DOÑA SOL.   An angel heard my thought—your guardian angel!

HERNANI (*bitterly*). Yes, my guardian angel! (*The horn is heard again. Aside.*) Again!

DOÑA SOL (*smilingly*). Don Juan, I recognize the sound of your own horn!

HERNANI.   Yes.

DOÑA SOL.   Have you then some part in this serenade?

HERNANI.   Some part—yes.

DOÑA SOL.   Unpleasant wedding feast—how much more I love the horn deep in the wood. And then besides, it is your horn, and so like your own voice.

(*Sound of the horn again.*)

HERNANI (*aside*). The tiger is there, and howling for his prey!

DOÑA SOL.   Its music fills my heart with delight, Don Juan.

HERNANI (*rising, in terrible fury*). Call me Hernani! Hernani! For I have not yet done with that terrible name!

DOÑA SOL (*trembling*). What is wrong?

HERNANI.   The old man!

DOÑA SOL.   My God! What horror in your eyes! What is it?

HERNANI.   The old man, laughing in the dark! Can you not see him?

DOÑA SOL.   What wildness is this? What old man?

HERNANI.   The old man!

DOÑA SOL (*falling to her knees*). I beg you from my knees, tell me, what secret tears at you? What is it?

HERNANI.   I gave my oath!

DOÑA SOL.   Your oath? (*She watches all his movements anxiously. He stops suddenly and wipes his hand over his brow.*)

HERNANI (*aside*). What did I nearly tell? I must spare her. (*Aloud.*) Nothing, nothing. What did I say to you?

DOÑA SOL.   You said—

HERNANI.   No—no. I was distressed. I am a little ill, it is nothing. . . . I did not mean to frighten you.

DOÑA SOL.   Is there something you need? Tell me, I am your servant!

(*The horn begins again.*)

HERNANI (*aside*). He demands it, and he has my pledge! (*He feels at his waist, but finds no sword, no dagger.*) Nothing there! It should be done by now!

DOÑA SOL.   Do you suffer such pain?

HERNANI.   An old wound, one I thought had healed. It has reopened. (*Aside.*) She must be sent away. (*Aloud.*) Doña Sol, beloved, listen. The box I carried with me always in less happy days—

DOÑA SOL.   I know the one you mean—what do you want of it?

HERNANI.   There is a vial inside; it holds a remedy to end the pain I feel. Go!

DOÑA SOL.   I go, my lord. (*She leaves by the door of the marriage chamber.*)

SCENE FOUR

HERNANI (*alone*). So this is what he would make of my good fortune! This is the fateful finger that gleams upon the wall! Oh, how sardonically fate laughs at me! (*He falls into a deep, convulsive reverie; then turns abruptly.*) Well? . . . But all is still. . . . I hear nothing approach. . . . Could I have been mistaken?

(*The masked figure in its black domino appears at the head of the stairs. HERNANI stops, frozen.*)

SCENE FIVE

MASK.   ''Whatever may happen, when you wish it, and in whatever place—when you feel that it is time for me to die, then sound this trumpet, nothing more. It shall be done.'' The dead were witness to that pact. Well now, and is it done?

HERNANI (*his voice low*).   It is he!

MASK.   I come now to your home, and tell you it is time. Now is the hour I choose. I find you late.

HERNANI.   Very well. What is your will? What would you do with me? Speak.

MASK.   You may choose—the knife or poison. I have brought both with me. We shall go together.

HERNANI.   So be it.

MASK.   Shall we pray?

HERNANI.   What does it matter?

MASK.   Which will you take?

HERNANI.   The poison.

MASK.   Very well. Give me your hand. (*He gives a small flask to* HERNANI, *who takes it, paling.*) Now drink—and let me finish it.

HERNANI.   Oh, Duke, have pity! Tomorrow! Ah, if you have still a heart, or even a soul—if you are more than a specter from the flames, one of the damned dead, a phantom or a demon till eternity—if God has not yet set the hideous mark of ''Never'' on your brow—if you have known this highest joy, to love at twenty years of age, and to marry your beloved—if ever a cherished woman has trembled in your arms, then wait until tomorrow! Tomorrow come for me!

MASK.   What a fool you are to say this! Tomorrow! Tomorrow! You must be mocking me! The bells you rang this morning tolled your end! What would become of me, this night! I should die of it, and who would come and take you afterwards? Shall I go alone to death? Young man, you must come with me!

HERNANI.   No! No, you devil, I free myself from you—I shall not obey!

MASK.   I suspected you would not. Very well. For after all, how did you swear this vow? On nothing so important, after all—only your father's head. That can be overlooked. Youth's vows are frivolous.

HERNANI.   My father! Father! Oh, I shall go mad!

MASK.   No, it is only perjury and treason.

HERNANI.   Duke!

MASK.   Since the sons of Spanish houses play so lightly now with pledges and denials, farewell! (*He makes as if to go.*)

HERNANI.   Stay!

MASK.   Well then—

HERNANI.   Cruel old man! (*He raises the vial.*) I turn about and trace my steps back to the door of heaven!

(DOÑA SOL *returns, but does not see the masked figure, who stands at the rear.*)

SCENE SIX

DOÑA SOL.   I could not find your box—

HERNANI (*aside*).   She has returned! And at so terrible a moment!

DOÑA SOL.   I startle him, he shudders at my voice! . . . What have you in your hand? No—what have you in your hand? Answer me! (*The domino approaches and unmasks. She cries out as she recognizes* DON RUY.) It is poison!

HERNANI.   Great heaven!

DOÑA SOL (*to* HERNANI). What have I done to you? What hellish mystery! You meant to betray me, Don Juan!

HERNANI.   I should have hid it from you. When the duke saved me I promised him that I would die at his command. Aragon must pay its debt to Silva.

DOÑA SOL.   You belong to me, and not to him. What do I care for any other of your vows? (*To* DON RUY GOMEZ.) Duke, love makes me strong. I shall defend him, against you and all the world.

DON RUY GOMEZ (*immobile*). Defend him if you can against a sworn pledge.

DOÑA SOL.   What pledge?

HERNANI.   I did swear it.

DOÑA SOL.   No, no—nothing shall bind you! It cannot be! It is a crime! Murder! Madness!

DON RUY GOMEZ.   Duke, let us proceed.

(HERNANI *makes as if to obey.* DOÑA SOL *tries to draw him away.*)

HERNANI.   No, Doña Sol; I must. The Duke has my word, and my father is watching from above.

DOÑA SOL (*to* DON RUY GOMEZ). You would do better to tear their young from the tigers than the one I love from me! Do you know this Doña Sol? For a long while, compassion for your age and for your sixty years made me the docile daughter, all innocent and mild. But now you see my eyes are wet with tears of rage. (*She draws a dagger from her bodice.*) And do you see this dagger? Ah, you mad old man, do you not fear the knife, when the eye has already sent its threat? Take care, Don Ruy, my uncle; I am of your line! Listen to me. Were I your very daughter, woe to you if you should lift your hand against my husband! (*She throws down the knife, and falls to her knees before the duke.*) Mercy! Alas, my lord, I am only a woman! I am weak, my strength stops short within my soul. I break too easily. I fall to your feet! Ah, I implore you, have pity on us!

DON RUY GOMEZ.   Doña Sol!

DOÑA SOL.   Forgive! We Spaniards speak our pain in hasty words, you know that. You were not cruel before! Have pity! Uncle, you kill me in wounding him! Pity—I love him so!

DON RUY GOMEZ (*darkly*). You love him too well!

HERNANI (*to* DOÑA SOL). Do you weep?

DOÑA SOL.   No, no, my love—you must not die! No, I will not let you! (*To* DON RUY.) Be merciful today! I shall be fond of you as well!

DON RUY GOMEZ.   After him! Do you think to appease the thirst that harrows me with such remnants of love—of friendship—no, even less than that! (*Pointing to* HERNANI.) He is the only one. He is everything. But I, what need have I for pity? What can I do with your affection? Oh, fury! He, he would have your heart, your love, the throne, and he would offer me the alms of a kind glance from you! And if a word were needed to calm my wild desires, he would tell you "Say this, and nothing more," cursing below his breath the avid beggar who gets the leavings in the empty cup. Shame! and mockery! No. It must be ended. Drink!

HERNANI.   He has my word, and I must keep it.

DON RUY GOMEZ.   Drink!

(HERNANI *brings the vial to his lips.* DOÑA SOL *throws herself upon his arm.*)

DOÑA SOL.   Not yet! Both of you, ah hear me!

DON RUY GOMEZ.   The grave is open, and I cannot wait.

DOÑA SOL.   A moment! My lord, and my Don Juan! Ah, both of you, you are so harsh! What do I ask of them? An instant only, I ask no more! A moment to let this sorry woman speak what is in her heart! Oh let me speak!

DON RUY GOMEZ (*to* HERNANI). I cannot wait.

DOÑA SOL.   My lords, you make me tremble! What have I done to you?

HERNANI.   Her cry undoes me!

DOÑA SOL (*still clutching his arm*). You see I have a thousand things to say!

DON RUY GOMEZ (*to* HERNANI). Death is waiting.

DOÑA SOL (*still hanging from* HERNANI'S *arm*). Don Juan, when I have spoken, you shall do what you will. (*She snatches the vial from him.*) I have it now! (*She raises the vial to the gaze of* HERNANI *and the astonished old man.*)

DON RUY GOMEZ.   Since I must deal here with two women, Don Juan, I shall go elsewhere to seek souls. You make fine vows upon the blood you spring from; I shall go now among the dead and speak of it to your father. Farewell. (*He takes a few steps away.* HERNANI *holds him back.*)

HERNANI.   Duke, stop! (*To* DOÑA SOL.) Alas, I implore you, would you see me a man of false word, a felon, a perjurer? Would you have me go about the world with treason written on my brow? For pity's sake, give me back that poison! by our love, by our immortal souls . . . !

DOÑA SOL (*somberly*). You wish it? (*She drinks.*) Here, take it now.

DON RUY GOMEZ (*aside*). Then it was meant for her!

DOÑA SOL (*handing* HERNANI *the half-empty vial*). Take it, I tell you!

HERNANI (*to* DON RUY). You see this, vile old man!

DOÑA SOL.   Do not be angry with me; I saved your share for you.

HERNANI (*taking the vial*). Lord God!

DOÑA SOL.   You would not have left mine for me. You! You have not the heart a Christian wife has. You cannot love as a Silva loves. But I have drunk first and am at peace. Go on! Drink if you wish!

HERNANI.   Alas, what have you done, my wretched love!

DOÑA SOL.   It is you who forced me to it.

HERNANI.   It is a hideous death!

DOÑA SOL.   No, why should it be?

HERNANI.   This potion takes us to the grave!

DOÑA SOL.   Were we not to sleep together through this night? What difference in what bed?

HERNANI.   My father, you have your revenge on me, for I forgot you! (*He puts the vial to his lips.*)

DOÑA SOL (*throwing herself upon him*). Ah heaven! What unearthly agony! Ah, throw that flask far from you! My reason's wandering. Stop! Alas, my Don Juan, this poison is a living thing! It opens out a hundred-toothed hydra in the heart that gnaws and then devours! Ah, I did not know one could feel such hideous pain! What is that thing? Pure fire! Do not drink it! You would suffer too horribly!

HERNANI (*to* DON RUY). Ah, your soul is wicked! Could you not choose a different way for her? (*He drinks, and throws down the vial.*)

DOÑA SOL.   What are you doing?

HERNANI.   What have you done?

DOÑA SOL.   Come, oh my young love, come to my arms. (*They sit by one another.*) Is it not a terrible pain?

HERNANI.   No.

DOÑA SOL.   So now begins our wedding night! Am I not strangely pale for a young bride?

HERNANI.   Ah!

DON RUY GOMEZ.   Now destiny is done.

HERNANI.   What torment! That Doña Sol should suffer, and I watch!

DOÑA SOL.   Be calm. It is better now. Soon we shall open our wings together, and move toward some new brightness. Let us fly side by side toward a better world. . . . A kiss, though; only a kiss! (*They embrace.*)

DON RUY GOMEZ.   Oh, what pain to see them. . . .

HERNANI (*his voice weakening*). Oh, blessed be heaven; it gave me a life hemmed in by chasms and haunted by shades; but when I wearied of so hard a road, it let me drop to sleep, with my lips pressed to your hand!

DON RUY GOMEZ.   They are happy!

HERNANI (*his voice weaker and weaker*). Come, come . . . Doña Sol . . . it is dark. Are you in pain?

DOÑA SOL (*her voice as faint*). Nothing, nothing now. . . .

HERNANI.   Do you see flames within the shade?

DOÑA SOL.   Not yet.

HERNANI (*with a sigh*). Here . . . (*He falls.*)

DON RUY GOMEZ (*raising his head, then dropping it*). Dead!

DOÑA SOL (*disheveled, half rising from her bench*). Dead! No, not dead! we are asleep. He sleeps. You see, he is my husband. We love one another. This is where we shall lie. It is our bridal night (*Her voice failing.*) Do not awaken him. He is weary. (*She turns* HERNANI'S *head to her.*) Turn your face to me, my love. Nearer . . . nearer still. . . . (*She falls back.*)

DON RUY GOMEZ. Dead! Oh, I am damned! (*He kills himself.*)

FOCUS QUESTIONS

1. Cite and describe three elements of French Romanticism that are prominently featured in *Hernani*.
2. Comment on the use and effectiveness of Hugo's stage directions.
3. Write a character sketch of one of the leading male characters and discuss the nature and consequences of his relationship to Doña Sol.
4. Discuss the themes that propel the action of the play.
3. Analyze Doña Sol's pivotal function in the play.
6. Show how character dualities and physical disguises contribute to the dramatic outcome.
7. Show how styles of language reflect stage characters in *Hernani*.

OTHER ACTIVITIES

1. Research visual documentation for the historical period in which Hugo sets his play and suggest how these might be realized in stage performance.
2. Discuss the similarities and differences between Verdi's opera libretto to *Ernani* and Hugo's play.
3. Using reviews, sketches, and other available production documents, assess a Comédie Française production of *Hernani*.

BIBLIOGRAPHY

Affron, Charles. *A Stage of Poets: Studies in the Theatre of Hugo and Musset*. Princeton, NJ: Princeton University Press, 1971.

Carlson, Marvin. *The French Stage in the Nineteenth Century*. Metuchen, NJ: Scarecrow Press, 1972.

———. "*Hernani's* Revolt from the Tradition of French Stage Composition," in *Theatre Survey*, May 1972.

Clement, N. H. *Romanticism in France*. New York: Modern Language Association of America, 1939.

Houston, John Porter. *Victor Hugo*. Rev. ed. Boston: G. K. Hall & Co., 1988.

Pendell, William D. *Victor Hugo's Acted Drama and the Contemporary Press*. Baltimore: Johns Hopkins Press, 1947.

Richardson, Joanna. *Victor Hugo*. New York: St. Martin's Press, 1976.

RECOMMENDED RECORDING

Hernani. Selections in French. One sound disk. 33⅓ rpm. Spoken Arts.

UNDER THE GASLIGHT
AUGUSTIN DALY (1838–1899)

He made the Theatre important, and he kept it worthy of the sympathy and
support of the most refined taste and the best intellect of his time.

—WILLIAM WINTER

From the 1972 Carnegie-Mellon University production of *Under the Gaslight*, directed by Richard
Shank. *Photo: Carnegie-Mellon University, Department of Drama.*

APPROACHING AMERICAN MELODRAMA

It is no surprise that **melodrama** was the first type of theatre to originate in America, since its citizens were neophytes to the theatre, much like the French bourgeois audience for whom René Charles Guilbert de Pixérécourt (1773–1844) created the dramatic form *melodrame*. When these audiences frequented the theatre, they wanted to see ordinary, uncomplicated people like themselves in domestic situations. Expecting to be dazzled by the lavish costumes and spectacular realistic sets changing magically before their eyes, they clamored for throbbing emotions, thrilling acts of violence and narrow escapes, and happy endings. They also called for moral lessons that confirmed their values of hard work, marriage, family, capitalism, and the triumph of goodness. In the absence of native playwrights, the plays of Pixérécourt and his German counterpart August Friedrich Ferdinand von Kotzebue (1761–1819) were translated into English and imported to the metropolitan centers of the United States where they became popular.

Here was entertainment that suited a rough-hewn country without traditions. Its depiction of the rewards of the work ethic and Christian ideals suited the puritanical pragmatism of the industrialized northeast. Its reliance on action and sensation merely reflected the adventures awaiting those who went westward into the frontier. Its fictional world in which any individual could achieve wealth and happiness, where the underdog had the best chance to catch the brass ring, and even the criminal could reform and start life anew appealed to American optimism, naiveté, and sense of justice. Americans saw the facts of their existence held up before them: life in the new country was a great gamble where good or bad luck determined one's economic success or financial ruin.

A distinct literary sensibility had been quietly responding to these same native experiences, finding its most eloquent expression during the nineteenth-century American Renaissance, chiefly in the prose writings of Emerson, Thoreau, Melville, Hawthorne, and Whitman. While their works were tempered by the indelible strains of New England puritanism, their voices were genuine and original. Equally important, they contributed to a literary genre which, in its private demands on the reader, fulfilled their artistic intentions even under the scrutiny of outside forces. For better or worse, this was not the case at the inception of American drama, where the playwright's dynamic collaboration with actor and audience was communal and public, open to censorship, and in need of patronage to achieve its artistic purpose or else fail. Those Americans wealthy enough to attend the theatre were unwilling to acknowledge these playwrights whose works were perceived as unworthy commodities. They snobbishly preferred the plays of London and Paris.

This distrust of American dramatic expression resulted directly from the fact that its beginnings were guided by England. The first acting company to tour America had arrived from London in 1752 to perform Shakespeare in Williamsburg. Other English classics followed, but were often advertised as moral lectures in order to meet approval. Thanks to home-grown touring companies that were spawned by these English models, theatrical entertainments had spread quickly across America in covered wagons and boats. But the dramas written by American playwrights were not yet produced.

In fact, American playwrights faced numerous obstacles in the development of their craft. English actors who toured America brought their tastes along with them. They demanded that playwrights imitate the romantic dramas from abroad. This forced practice reaped artificial results that proved foreign to any established national style. Only when loyalties to English custom had started to fade did plays with a true local flavor appear on stage. The earliest examples included the satire of Royall Tyler's *The Contrast* (1787) and the comedy of Anna Cora Mowatt's *Fashion* (1845). Once international acclaim followed the European tour of George Aiken's adaptation of Harriet Beecher Stowe's novel, *Uncle Tom's Cabin* (1852), an American tradition of playwriting had been launched. Theatre patrons were finally persuaded that American themes and regional settings were equally promising theatrical fare. When Augustin Daly—playwright, drama critic, theatre manager, and director—promoted melodrama to an art form, he ensured its place on the legitimate stage.

Ten years' experience reviewing performances for five New York newspapers, most notably *The New York Times,* gave Augustin Daly important insights into the theatrical scene, particularly the tastes of the patrons. As he covered the innumerable offerings of romantic, melodramatic plays freely adapted from contemporary European models, he developed theories about what kind of theatre American playwrights should be writing. He advocated dramas that presented a moral view of life, but were entertaining as well; they should contain both the sadness and the folly of human beings and should promote a code of ethics. He further advocated production principles that would later define the director's role in the modern theatre: the manager must exert complete control over the acting and the visual elements. For him, pleasing the audience came first. Thus the theatre he championed depicted both sensational and realistic scenes from life in which the stage pictures and the ensemble of characters were part of a unified concept.

These years as critic proved invaluable to his playwriting as well. His theatre-going sharpened his tastes while schooling him in the formulas requisite to writing melodrama. His first success in this genre was a dramatization of S. H. van Mosenthal's *Deborah,* entitled *Leah, the Forsaken* (1862), first produced in Boston and then revived at Niblo's Garden in New York in 1863, before touring London. Once accepted by London theatregoers, Daly became the preferred writer of scripts to meet the needs of the leading American actors of his time. They requested plays from him, providing him with the plotlines and situations; so all he needed to do was construct the play according to the proven formula. Following the practice of his European contemporaries, he dramatized novels or translated and adapted successful scripts from the French, English, and German stages that were not yet protected by international copyright laws.

What made it possible for him to continue writing reviews for newspapers and churning out scripts was the close collaboration he established with his brother. Unacknowledged, Joseph Daly substituted for Augustin as a reviewer and later helped create the dialogue for the plays. This arrangement continued throughout Augustin's lifetime and facilitated his capacity to provide scripts on demand.

In 1867, he wrote and produced his first original melodrama, *Under the Gaslight.* After the play's successful runs in New York and London, Daly embarked on the second phase of his career: managing and directing his own theatre company. In 1869, he resigned from all of his newspaper responsibilities and rented the Fifth Avenue Theatre in order to produce plays. His mission was to present "whatever is novel, original, entertaining and unobjectionable and the revival of whatever is rare and worthy in legitimate dramas."[1]

Over the course of the next thirty years, until his death, Daly produced adaptations of contemporary English and European works, his own melodramas, as well as classics by Sheridan and Shakespeare. As theatre manager, he oversaw all aspects of production: the design and construction of sets and costumes; the ordering of curtains, furniture and decorative props to complete the realistic stage sets; and the casting and acting style of his performers. When audiences came to a Daly show, they expected a perfect work of entertainment. As the reviewer from the *New York Herald* wrote on September 6, 1871: "The prevailing feature is a naturalness in dialogue and action and a finish which invests even the most commonplace scenes with interest . . . Whether the scene be in a drawing room, a garden, the country, the illusion is perfect . . . to transport the audience from the theatre to the scene of the action." It was his expectations of the actors that had the most consequence, however. The range of produced plays required that actors switch from comic to serious roles and portray heroic as well as villainous characters. With autocratic discipline and absolute rejection of the star system, Daly created an ensemble of actors who became America's foremost company.

During his career as America's first *regisseur,* or "autocrat of the stage," he raised the standards of American theatre to refined entertainment. His demands for excellence had created the possibility for artful production, the growth of talented artists, the introduction of realistic and elaborate staging, a new order of drama, and an ensemble approach to acting. Although he was never a playwright of exceptional literary stature, his theatrical effects and perfectionism profoundly influenced the development of a viable American drama that held a prominent position in world literature of the twentieth century.

MAJOR WORKS

From 1856 until his death in 1899, Augustin Daly wrote over ninety plays in the romantic style and in the **well-made-play** tradition of French writers Scribe and Sardou, who had constructed and popularized a playwriting formula that relied on the cause-and-effect arrangement of events, the building of dramatic incidents to a climax, and the uses of suspense and sudden reversals. The bulk of Daly's literary output were adaptations of French and German farces, melodramas, operettas, and **vaudevilles.** With his considerable knowledge of the types of entertainment popular with contemporary audiences, he also wrote stage adaptations of novels by such authors as Harriet Beecher Stowe, Charles Dickens, Anthony Trollope, and Émile Zola.

His most important literary contributions to American theatre were his ten original stage plays. Perhaps the most memorable of these were the sensational melodramas that relied on a single climactic moment heightened by a theatrical trick. These included *Under the Gaslight* (1867), *A Flash of Lightning* (1869), *The Red Scarf* (1869), and *The Undercurrent* (1883). Influenced by his romantic counterparts who incorporated a notable amount of regional or local color into their writings, he also wrote a frontier play, *Horizon* (1871). Finally, taking a cue from his great success with urban settings, he emphasized the seamier, more threatening aspects of metropolitan life in New York City in *Round the Clock: Or New York by Dark* (1871), *Roughing It!* (1873), and *The Dark City and Its Bright Side* (1877). Of all his stage works, however, *Under the Gaslight* proved one of his most popular and enduring contributions to the art of American melodrama.

THE ACTION

News of socialite Laura Courtland's humble origins spreads throughout upper-class society, forcing her fiancé Ray Trafford to break off their engagement. Humiliated and betrayed, she sets herself up in a basement flat as a photographer's assistant, her only friend a young girl from the streets named Peachblossom.

Both Ray and Byke, the villain who claims to be her father, discover her whereabouts. Byke abducts her as part of a plan to blackmail her upper-class family. Yet he is stopped at the pier by Ray and Snorkey, a one-armed Civil War veteran, which allows Laura to escape. Byke tracks her down at the Courtland home in Long Branch, New Jersey, and she is forced to leave. Foiled in her effort to return to New York by train, she engineers the hair-raising rescue of Snorkey, whom Byke has tied to the railroad tracks.

In the last act, when Laura is discovered to be a true Courtland after all, loose plot ends are tied; villains are served their just reward; the lovers, Laura and Ray, are reunited; and a new romance is kindled between Peachblossom and Snorkey.

STRUCTURE AND LANGUAGE

In his effort to tap the heartbeat and pulse of America's giant metropolis and to expose both the high and low life that shared its vital rhythms, Augustin Daly's melodramatic portrait of urban life in New York City left little to the dramatic imagination of his nineteenth-century audiences. Curious to see exactly how the other half lived, upper-class theatre-goers attended *Under the Gaslight* and took their lesson from the actions on stage. Furthermore, it was from the perspective of one of their own kind—in this case, the "belle of society" Laura Courtland—that they not only glimpsed at their tendency to judge each other on the basis of wealth and family pedigree, but also gained entrance to that forbidding nether world of poverty and criminality. Like carefully etched postcards, scene after scene depicted the heartrending circumstances that followed Laura's fall from grace.

From the top of the action, set in the most elegant Fifth Avenue parlor interior late one evening with snow falling outside the lamp-lit deep window, not a moment is wasted before "a strange man has forced himself in at the door and asks to see [her], but will give no name." Thus we confront the villain of the play, Byke, whose appearance elicits the truth of Laura's disreputable past. The disclosure becomes gossip for the fashionable society that waltzes leisurely at Delmonico's towards the end of act 1. Bereft of reputation and fortune, Laura is forced to exit from this once idyllic landscape and find her place in another. But the journey charted by the playwright is a dark and downward one.

The unprotected, squalid basement interior of the humbly furnished second act—"street and railings seen through window at back"—is made slightly more palatable by the presence of Peachblossom, a companion to Laura (now called Miss Nina) who has taken refuge there with her. Polishing the stove, Peachblossom sings wistfully about a mythical damsel-in-distress who is rescued just in time to find happiness-ever-after. Of course, the song is really about her and Miss Nina, and its happy ending briefly foreshadows fairer weather for both young women. But reality soon knocks at the door with the sudden appearance of Old Judas—"the right hand of Byke"—who mirrors his impact from act 1, suggesting that Laura's safety is still at risk. "I'd know her anywheres!" whispers Judas when she surmises who Miss Nina really is, then exits to plot more mischief.

The highly structured format of suspense and reversals is firmly established in these first two acts. But more impressively, Daly creates a realistic dimension through the variety of localized scenes whose actions never transpire in the light of day, but unfold in shadowy, half-lit spaces like the coatroom and Blue Room at Delmonico's or the subterranean basement quarters where Laura hides from her past. Furthermore, while Byke's unseen presence is initially described to us—he stands by a "street lamp lighted" before he enters Laura's home and destroys her happiness—the description triggers the play's sinister title and the nefarious deeds that ensue.

Nor can we ignore the name of the opening setting for act 3, the Tombs Police Court, which conjures forth the suffocating and hopeless atmosphere of its cavernous stage reality. For it is in this doom-filled setting that Byke successfully wins the sympathy of Justice Bowling, who promptly delivers Laura into his custody and orders her "to love him as a daughter should." Not only has our villain duped the court system, but the ineffectuality of the law to administer justice is blatantly scrutinized through the playwright's clever use of dramatic irony.

By the final scene of act 3, in which the stage set re-creates the foot of Pier 30 at the North River and is shadowed once again "by starlight," the sound of real water splashing against the dark stage enables Byke and Old Judas to propel a small boat with oars to carry out Laura's abduction. But the need to interrupt the suspenseful actions by addressing the lighter side of his rich melodramatic formula proves irresistible to Daly. He provides un-expected comic relief when Snorkey arrives at the scene to rescue Laura. Accompanied by Bermudas, who resides with Peanuts and a band of ragamuffins in a hole along the side of the very dock where Byke and Old Judas are conspiring, Snorkey is entertained by Ber-mudas' lively banjo playing as the boys jubilantly dance ''according to capacity and talent.'' The noise attracts a police sergeant ''entering in [a] patrol boat'' and the harmless entertainment is halted. Dramatic timing still sides with the forces of evil, however, and the sergeant exits just prior to the water-drenched final showdown between Snorkey and the villains. Since the law has failed at its responsibility once again, Laura must swim to shore where further perils await her.

Several of the major stock characters who populate *Under the Gaslight* are infused with feeling and originality, producing a stage realism that whets audience interest, but never stretches the melodrama's capacity for theatrical effects. The achievement can be credited to Daly's earlier journalistic writing on the lives of single working girls and crim-inals, the experience of which enhanced his treatment of characters and dialogue. Foremost is Snorkey, the Civil War veteran now reduced to messenger work because of the loss of an arm. His willingness to assist Ray Trafford in rescuing Laura stems from his chivalric code of honor: ''I was on Columbia's side for four years and I'll fight for her daughters for the rest of my life, if you say so. If there's any fightin' count me in, Cap'n.'' But in an ironic twist of fate during the hair-raising final seconds of the fourth act, it is Laura who courageously frees Snorkey from the tracks as ''the train of cars rushes past with roar and whistle from left to right.'' ''And these are the women who ain't to have a vote!'' Snorkey exclaims, still defending the rights of all free citizens as the curtain descends.

As for the protagonist, Laura Courtland, whose perilous journey has not dimmed her innate optimism, a fifth-act reconciliation with family and friends and a determination to leave the past behind rekindle all hopes for the kind of happiness prophesied by Peach-blossom in her second-act song. While Ray's melancholic final words, ''It is night always for me,'' sustain the haunting gaslight motif that has enshrouded the actions of the play, they are quickly counteracted by Laura's expectation that tomorrow ''will bring the long sought sunlight of our lives.'' Echoing the sentiment of the playwright, Laura symbolizes those cherished American ideals such as liberty and justice for all.

UNDER THE GASLIGHT-IN-PERFORMANCE

The premiere of *Under the Gaslight: Life and Love in These Times* took place on August 12, 1867, at the New York Theatre where it ran until October 1. The lively cast was headed by Rose Eytinge as Laura Courtland and J. K. Mortimer as Snorkey. New York locales, topical references, and the timely inclusion of railroad technology won the admiration of enthusiastic audiences.

For unexpected reasons, opening night fell somewhat short of the professional stan-dards that characterized Daly's later productions. Foremost was the inebriated entrance by the actor playing Justice Bowling, an incident that prompted Daly to institute stiff fines for such misconduct once he managed his own company. Next was the celebrated train-rescue scene at the end of act 4. As suspense built with the noise of the steam whistle and the rumble of the approaching engine only seconds after Laura freed Snorkey from the tracks, the train broke in two the instant it appeared on stage, ruining the climactic effect. The reviews of the period indicate that the technical difficulty was corrected in subsequent performances.

Pleased with their first major success, the Worrell sisters, who managed the theatre, revived the play later that year and assumed the leading women's roles: Irene played Laura,

Sophie played Pearl, and Jennie played Peachblossom. When the show closed on January 29, 1868, it had chalked up more than one hundred performances.

Adding a further subtitle, "A Drama of American Life," Daly took *Under the Gaslight* to England, where it opened at the Tyne Theatre in Newcastle on April 20, 1868, before opening at the Pavilion Theatre in London on July 20. The success of American melodrama was evidenced by Miss Hazlewood's adaptation entitled, *London by Gaslight,* produced at Sadler's Wells Theatre two months later. Thus the play was "pirated" for the English stage in the same way that Daly had adapted English, French, and German plays to the American stage.

Not all of these borrowings would bode well for Daly. When rival playwright-producer Dion Boucicault lifted the train-rescue effect for his own production of *After Dark* in 1868, the incident sparked legal consequences as soon as Daly discovered that his claim to the device was not protected by copyright laws. Convinced that the scene was patentable, Daly filed a lawsuit when *After Dark* was sold to Jarrett and Palmer for production at Niblo's Garden in November 1868. The court granted him the judgment and Palmer was forced to pay Daly royalties for its use. For the next twenty-five years, Daly continued to seek injunctions against other producers of *After Dark*. Although his 1889 case against William Brady was lost on a technicality, his 1893 case against the same producer was overturned by the Circuit Court of Appeals and he was granted a judgment of $61,000. In the end, such lawsuits helped to establish stringent copyright regulations.

Until the mid-1880s, *Under the Gaslight* was revived regularly in New York. One of the most famous engagements was presented by Daly's company at the Grand Old Opera House in April 1873, where performances played to near-capacity houses. The play was produced at the Boston Theatre around this time, while touring companies reached Denver, Salt Lake City, and San Francisco, where David Belasco is believed to have acted in a production.

In 1900, the play was so popular that reviewers attending a revival at the Castle Square Theatre in Boston commented on its durable status as a crowd-pleaser. It became such a familiar icon to the melodramatic stage that in his novel *Sister Carrie,* Theodore Dreiser wrote about an amateur production of the play which his heroine attends.

From the 1920s through the 1970s, the play was produced many times by university and community theatre groups, professional showcases, and stock companies. The majority of these revivals exaggerated the play's sentimentality and even burlesqued it. They emphasized the recreation of nineteenth-century theatre-going practices with their various entr'acte entertainments over the presentation of the play itself. Especially innovative was the setting in Denise Hamilton's adaptation for the New York Theatre Ensemble in 1979: the elite African-American society that resided in Brooklyn around 1890. Thus the play became a vehicle for exposing the nature of life for one of the city's oldest minority populations a generation after the end of the Civil War.

Perhaps the most original twentieth-century revival was produced by Larry Fay and Alex Yokel at Fay's People's Bowery Theatre on April 2, 1929. Complete with a lobby bar where beer and peanuts were served before the first curtain and between the acts, the production not only restored Daly's play, but also the conditions in which it had been viewed by audiences more than fifty years earlier. The actors played their parts in earnest, avoiding the spoofing of characters. James Meighan as Ray played with nobility, Helene Dumas portrayed Laura's broken-hearted agonies with authenticity, and Earl Mitchell embodied the unshaven and wicked Byke. Hissing the villain and applauding the heroes, audiences greeted the play with the same exuberance they exhibited at the silent-film showings that were currently popular. This was not surprising. After all, these films were the descendants of melodrama and relied on the sensationalism and formulaic plots that Daly's play had made famous.

REFLECTIONS ON UNDER THE GASLIGHT

The following review by J. Brooks Atkinson appeared in
THE NEW YORK TIMES *on April 3, 1929.*

When the whisky-voiced villain was foiled at about 11:15 last evening in Fay's Bowery The-atre, during a revival of Augustin Daly's *Under the Gaslight,* the audience succeeded in making its pleasure both rowdy and genuine. All during that act the foul villainies had come thick and fast. While one-armed Snorkey, veteran of the Civil War, struggled with the rope that bound him to the track, the pitiless white glare of the locomotive headlight blinked the symbol of his peril. It seemed already too late when Laura Courtland, belle of society, smashed her way out of the freight house with an axe, loosened the victim's thongs and pulled him off the track just as the cardboard locomotive shot out of the wings and ground its ruthless course across the stage. Having waited all evening for such a frenetic scene, the audience let go and roared.

Yet this attempt to transport Hoboken to the Bowery was not always so successful. Perhaps the actors played too well. Perhaps the scenery lacked sentimental imagination. Per-haps Augustin Daly's old thriller was either better or worse than its successor, *After Dark,* or the pace was too slow. Or perhaps twice-told tales should not be related a third time. At any rate, the wish was not father to the thought without some show of effort, and the hisses, the boos, the throwing of missiles and the salvos of applause did not come altogether sponta-neously. In short, you suspected the excitement of being synthetic. Even in Hoboken la-borious pleasure can temper enjoyment.

The attempt to imitate Hoboken was not particularly subtle. In its admonitions to the audience the management had taken the trouble to reproduce, substantially word for word, the cautionary notice that is being distributed these Spring evenings to the effervescent theatre-goers across the river. But perhaps the old jealousy of *Under the Gaslight* for *After Dark* still persists. Way back in the '60s when the melodramas are supposed to have been genuinely exciting, *After Dark*'s tardy interpolation of the hair-raising railroad scene was the subject of legal proceedings. Daly's stupendous originality in having thought of it first was recognized and solemnly applauded by the law; apparently no hero could be in peril on a railroad track without first doffing his torn cap to the preeminence of *Under the Gaslight.*

The similarities between the two plays extend also to the priceless mystery of birth, the wharf-front hostelry, and the superciliousness of high society—which is still the delight and the amiable weakness of modish playmakers. They have a good villain down on the Bowery, a broken-hearted hero, and a one-armed war veteran so loyal to his country that the patriots in the audience thundered their approval last evening and cheered his homely sentiments to the echo. Although *After Dark* may have imitated *Under the Gaslight* in the '60s, the current revivals wear the shoe on the other foot. The audience's voluble and shrill delight is interesting if true. If it is not true, it is a little empty. But then, you can say that of Hoboken.

Note

1. *William Winter,* VAGRANT MEMORIES *(New York: George Doran, 1915), 273.*

UNDER THE GASLIGHT
AUGUSTIN DALY

CHARACTERS

Ray Trafford, *one of the New York "Bloods"*

Snorkey, *a returned veteran, established as a soldier messenger, but open to anything else*

Byke, *one of the men whom the law is always reaching for and never touches*

Ed. Demilt, *one of the rising Wall Street generation*

Windel, *his friend, "sound on the street"*

Justice Bowling, *of the Tombs Police Court*

Counsellor Splinter, *an attorney of the Tombs Court*

Bermudas, *one of the under crust, a sidewalk merchant prince, with a "banjo swarry"*

Peanuts, *a rival operator in papers and matches*

Sam, *a colored citizen, ready for suffrage when it is ready for him*

Rafferdi, *nee Rafferty, an Italian organist from Cork*

The Sergeant of the River Patrol

Policeman 9–9–9

Martin

Peter Rich, *the boy who was committed*

The Signalman at Shrewsbury Bend

Members of the Tuesday Sociable, Court Officers, Dock Boys, etc.

Laura Courtland, *the belle of society*

Pearl Courtland, *pretty, but no heart*

Peachblossom, *a girl who was never "brought up," with the doleful ditty of "the Knight, the Dame, and the Murderous Rival"*

Old Judas, *the right hand of Byke*

Mrs. Van Dam, *one of the voices of society*

Sue Earlie, *one of the echoes of the voice*

Lizzie Liston, *another echo*

ACT ONE
SCENE ONE

Parlor at the Courtlands; deep window at back showing snowy exterior; street lamp lighted; time, night; the place elegantly furnished; chandelier. RAY TRAFFORD *is discovered lounging on a tete-a-tete.* PEARL *is at door taking leave of* DEMILT, WINDEL, MRS. VAN DAM, *and* SUE EARLIE, *who are all dressed and muffled to go out.*

MRS. VAN DAM. Good night! Of course we'll see you on Tuesday.

PEARL. To be sure you will.

DEMILT. Never spent a jollier hour. Good night, Ray.

RAY (*on sofa*). Good night.

MRS. VAN DAM. You won't forget the Sociable on Tuesday, Ray?

RAY. O, I won't forget.

ALL (*at door*). Good night—good night! (*Exit.*)

PEARL. Good night. (*Coming forward.*) O, dear! now they're gone, and the holiday's gone with them. (*Goes to the window.*) There they go. (*Laughter without.*) Ray, do come and look at the Van Dam's new sleigh. How they have come out.

RAY. Yes, it's the gayest thing in the Park!

PEARL (*still at window*). I wonder where they got the money, I thought you said Van Dam had failed!

RAY. Well, yes. He failed to pay, but he continues to spend.

PEARL (*as if to those outside*). Good night! (*Response from without as sleigh bells jingle—"Good night."*) I wish I was in there with you. It's delightful for a sleigh ride, if it wasn't New Year's. O! there's Demilt over! (*Laughter outside—cracking of whips—Ray saunters up to window. Sleigh bells jingle, sleigh music heard to die away. Ray and Pearl wave their handkerchiefs. Ray comes down and sits.*)

PEARL (*closing lace curtains*). Isn't it a frightful thing to be shut up here on such a beautiful night, and New Year's of all others. Pshaw, we've had nothing but mopes all day. O, dear! I hate mourning, though it does become me, and I hate everything but fun, larks and dancing. (*Comes down.*)

PEARL.   Where in the world is Laura?

RAY.   O! do forget her for a second, can't you? She'll be here presently. You're not in the house a minute but it's, "Where's Laura?" "Why don't Laura come?"

RAY (*taking her hand*).   Well, if anybody in the world could make me forget her, it would be you. But if you had a lover, wouldn't you like him to be as constant as that?

PEARL.   That's quite another thing.

RAY.   But this doesn't answer my question—Where is she?

PEARL.   I sent for her as soon as I saw you coming. She has hardly been down here a moment all this evening. O, dear! Now don't you think I'm a victim, to be cooped up in this way instead of receiving calls as we used to?

RAY.   You forget that your mother died only last summer. (*Rising.*)

PEARL.   No, I don't forget. Pshaw! You're just like Laura. She's only my cousin, and yet she keeps always saying— "Poor aunt Mary! let us not forget how she would have sorrowed for us."

RAY (*going towards back*).   Well, don't you know she would, too.

PEARL.   I don't know anything about it. I was always at boarding school, and she only saw me once a year. Laura was always at home, and it's very different. But don't let's talk about it. To die—ugh! I don't want to die till I don't want to live—and that'll not be for a million of years. Come, tell me—where have you been to-day? How many calls did you make? (*Sitting in tete-a-tete.*)

RAY.   About sixty.

PEARL.   That's all? You're lazy. Demilt and Windel made a hundred and thirty, and they say that's nothing. Won't you have a cup of coffee?

RAY.   No.

PEARL.   Ain't you hungry?

RAY.   No—you torment.

PEARL.   O, dear! I suppose it's because you're going to be married shortly to Laura. If there's one time that a man's stupid to his friends, it's when he's going to be married shortly. Tell me whom you saw. (*Ray has sauntered off and is looking over cards on table.*) Where are you? Oh, you needn't be so impatient to see her. Do be agreeable; sit here and tell me something funny, or I shall drop down and fall asleep.

RAY (*over her shoulder*).   You witch! Why didn't I fall in love with you?

PEARL (*laughing*).   I don't know; why didn't you?

RAY.   You never keep me waiting. (*Listening.*) Ah, that's her step! No.

PEARL.   Do sit down.

RAY (*sitting*).   This calling's a great bore; but as you and Laura insisted I should go through it, I did. First I— (*Jumping up.*) I knew it was she. (*Goes to door, meets Laura, who enters.*) How you did keep me waiting. (*Kisses both her hands.*)

LAURA.   And you, sir, we have been looking for you since eight o'clock.

RAY.   O, I was fulfilling your orders. I've been engaged in the business of calling, from ten o'clock in the morning, till now—(*Looks at watch—*) ten at night.

LAURA.   Well, you can make this your last one, for you have leave to spend a nice long hour chatting here before you go. Won't you have some supper. (*Goes to bell.*)

RAY.   I don't care if I do. I'm rather famished.

PEARL.   Well, I declare! Did Laura bring your appetite with her? (*Laura rings.*)

RAY.   I don't know how it is, but she brings me a relish for everything in life, I believe. Laura, I think if I were to lose you I'd mope to death and starve to death.

LAURA.   Well, that's as much as to say I'm a sort of Life Pill. (*Martin enters door.*) Supper. (*Martin exits.*)

RAY.   You may joke about it,—but it's so. You take the lounge. (*Laura and Pearl sit on tete-a-tete.*)

PEARL.   You don't want me to go away, do you? (*Putting her head on Laura's shoulder.*)

LAURA.   Certainly not. What an idea!

PEARL.   I'm sure you'll have time enough to be alone when you are married. And I do so want to talk and be talked to.

LAURA.   Well, Ray shall talk to you.

PEARL.   He was just going to tell me about his calls to-day.

LAURA.   That's exactly what we want to hear about. Did you call on every one we told you to?

RAY.   Every one. There was Miss—

PEARL.   Did you go to Henrietta Liston's first?

RAY.   Yes, and wasn't she dressed! Speaking of dress, are you going to have your new pink for the Sociable, Tuesday?

LAURA.   Yes, Pearl, and I will do credit to the occasion, as it is our first for a year.

RAY (*taking Laura's hand*).   And *our* last.

PEARL.   Our last!

RAY.   Laura's and mine. For when we are married, you know we shall be tabooed—where maids and bachelors only are permitted.

PEARL.   O bless me! (*Rising.*) How do you do Mrs. Trafford.

LAURA (*rising sadly*).   I wish you hadn't said that Pearl. You know the old proverb: "Call a maid by a married name."

RAY.   Nonsense! (*Putting his arm about Laura's waist.*) It's only a few days to wait, and we'll live long enough, you know. For nothing but death shall separate us. (*Martin appears at door.*)

PEARL.   O, here's supper.

MARTIN.   Beg pardon, Miss.

LAURA.   What's the matter?

MARTIN.   There's a person below, Miss, who says he's been sent with a bouquet for you, Miss, and must deliver it in person.

LAURA.   For me? Whose servant is it?

MARTIN.   I don't know, Miss, he looks like one of those soldier Messengers—red cap and all that.

LAURA.   Show him up here. (*Exit Martin.*)

PEARL.   How romantic. So late at night. It's a rival in disguise, Ray.

(*Martin re-enters showing in Snorkey, with an air of disdain. Snorkey has a large bouquet in his hand, and his hat is under the stump of his right arm, which is cut off.*)

LAURA.   You wished to see me?

SNORKEY.   Are you Miss Laura Courtland?

LAURA.   Yes.

SNORKEY.   Then I was told to give you this.

LAURA.   By whom?

SNORKEY.   Now, that's what I don't know myself! You see I was down by the steps of the Fifth Avenue Hotel, taking a light supper off a small toothpick, when a big chap dressed in black came by, and says he: "Hallo, come with me if you want to earn a quarter." That (*confidentially to all*) being my very frame of mind, I went up one street and down another, till we came here. "Just you take this up there," says he, "and ask for Miss Laura Courtland, and give it to her and no one else."

LAURA.   It is some folly of our late visitors.

SNORKEY.   I'm one of the Soldier Messengers, Miss. We take to it very well, considering we had so little running in Uncle Sam's service.

RAY.   Stop a moment, my man. Were you not one of the Twenty-second's recruits?

SNORKEY.   Yes, Captain; I remember you joined us in New York, and left us at Washington. Real fighting wasn't funny, you thought, and I began to think so too at Fredericksburg.

RAY.   Poor devil.

SNORKEY.   There was a South Carolina gentleman took such a fancy to me at Fredericksburg! Wouldn't have no denial, cut off my arm to remember me by; he was very fond of me. I wasn't any use to Uncle Sam then, so I came home, put a red band round my blue cap, and with my empty sleeve, as a character from my last place, set up for light porter and general messenger. All orders executed with neatness and dispatch.

PEARL.   And Uncle Sam has forgotten you.

SNORKEY.   Ah! Miss, don't blame Uncle Sam for that, he's got such a big family to look after, I can't find fault if he don't happen to remember all us poor stumps of fellows.

RAY.   So it seems.

LAURA (*Pearl takes bouquet*). Poor fellow! (*To servant.*) Martin, be sure and give him a glass of wine before he goes.

SNORKEY.   I'm much obliged, Miss—but I don't think it would be good for me on an empty stomach—after fasting all day.

LAURA.   Well, Martin shall find you some supper, too.

SNORKEY.   Is this Martin? What a nice young man. Mayn't he have a drop of something, too? He must have caught cold letting me in, he has got such a dreadful stiffness in the back of his neck. (*Martin exits.*)

RAY (*giving penciled address*). Call on me at this place tomorrow and you shan't regret it.

SNORKEY.   All right, Cap'n! I haven't forgot the Army Regulations about punctuality and promotion. Ladies, if ever either of you should want a Light Porter, think of Joe Snorkey—wages no objection. (*Exit.*)

PEARL (*who has been examining the bouquet*). O! Laura, only look—here's a billet-doux!

RAY.   Nonsense! Crazy head! Who would dare (*takes bouquet*)—a letter! (*Takes a paper from bouquet.*)

LAURA.   A letter?

PEARL.   I am crazy—am I?

RAY (*reads superscription*). "For Miss Laura Courtland. Confidential."

LAURA (*laughs*). Ha! Ha! from some goose who has made one call too many today. Read it, Ray—(*Offering letter.*)

RAY.   "Dear Laura . . . " (*Refusing the letter, and going to Pearl.*)

LAURA (*looks at it a moment, when the whole expression of face changes. Then reads slowly and deliberately*). "I respectfully beg you to grant me the favor of an interview to-night. I have waited until your company retired. I am waiting across the street, now."

PEARL (*runs to window*). A tall man in black is just walking away.

LAURA.   "If you will have the door opened as soon as you get this I will step over; if you don't, I will ring; under all circumstances I will get in. There is no need to sign my name; you will remember me as the strange man whom you once saw talking with your mother in the parlor, and who frightened you so much." What can be the meaning of this?—Pearl—no—(*Goes to bell on table and rings.*)

RAY.   Laura, you—

LAURA.   Ask me nothing. I will tell you by and by. (*Enter Martin.*)

MARTIN.   Miss—

LAURA.   Admit no one till you bring me the name.

MARTIN.   I was about to tell you, Miss, that a strange man has forced himself in at the door and asks to see you, but will give no name.

RAY.   Kick the rascal out!

PEARL.   Oh! don't let him come here.

MARTIN.   He's a very strange-looking person, Miss.

RAY.   I'll find out what this means! (*Is going to door when Byke appears at it smiling and bowing.*)

BYKE. I'll spare you the trouble, if you'll hear me a minute.

RAY (*violently*). Who are you, fellow?

BYKE. Don't, I beg you. Don't speak so crossly; I might answer back—then you'd kick me out—and you'd never forgive yourself for it as long as I lived.

RAY. Your business? Come! Speak quickly and begone.

BYKE. Business! On this happy day! I came for pleasure— to see Miss Courtland, my little pupil—grown so—only think, sir! I knew her when she was only a little child. I taught her music—she was so musical—and so beautiful— I adored her, and her mother told me I needn't come again—But I did—and her mother was glad to see me. Wasn't she, little pupil?—(*To Laura, who is pale with terror, leaning on Pearl.*)—and begged me to stay—but I said no—I'd call occasionally—to see my dear little pupil, and to receive any trifling contribution her mother might give me. Won't you shake hands, little pupil? (*Advances suddenly, when Ray grasps him by the collar— Byke glares at him a moment. Then, quickly as before.*) Don't please, don't! The stuff is old, and I've no other.

RAY. The fellow's drunk! Leave the house.

BYKE. What! after sending that touching bouquet?

LAURA. It was you, then? I knew it.

BYKE. You see she knows me. Ah! memory how it blooms again where the plough of time has passed.

LAURA. Leave this house at once.

BYKE. Not until I have spoken to you.

RAY (*seizing him*). You miserable rascal.

BYKE. Don't, pray don't! I weigh a hundred and ninety-eight pounds, and if you attempt to throw me about you'll strain yourself.

LAURA (*crossing*). Go. To-morrow in the morning I will see you.

BYKE. Thanks! I thank you, Miss, for your forebearance. (*To Ray.*) I am also obliged to you, sir, for not throwing me out at the window. I am indeed. I wish you good night, and many happy returns of the day. (*Bows and turns to go. Then familiarly to servant.*) Many calls to-day, John? (*Exit.*)

RAY (*runs to Laura, who is pale*).

LAURA (*pointing after Byke*). See that he goes. (*Exit Ray.*)

LAURA (*taking both of Pearl's hands in her own*). Pearl, he must know everything.

PEARL. O, dear! this is dreadful! I do hate scenes.

LAURA. He must know everything, I tell you; and you must relate all. He will question—he will ponder—leave him nothing to ask.

PEARL. If you wish it, but—

LAURA. I desire it; speak of me as you will—but tell him the truth. (*Ray enters hastily.*) Stay with her. Don't follow me. (*Exit.*)

RAY. Pearl, what does this mean.

PEARL. O, it's only a little cloud that I want to clear up for you.

RAY. Cloud—how? where?

PEARL. Don't I tell you I am going to tell you. Sit down here by me. (*She sinks into tete-a-tete.*)

RAY (*promenading*). He said he knew her. And she gave him an interview for to-morrow. That drunken wretch—

PEARL. Do sit down. I can never speak while you are walking about so. (*Gets up, brings him to a chair and makes him sit.*) Sit by me, won't you? For I've got something strange to tell you.

RAY. *You* serious! I'd as soon expect to see the lightning tamed. Well, I listen.

PEARL. I have something to say to you, Ray, which you must settle with your own heart. You love Laura, do you not?

RAY. Pearl, I do more, I adore her. I adore the very air that she breathes. I will never be happy without her. I can swear *that*.

PEARL. Laura is twenty now. How do you think she looked when I first saw her?

RAY. Were you at home when she first came into this earthly sphere?

PEARL. Yes.

RAY. Well then, I suppose she looked very small and very pink.

PEARL. She was covered with rags, barefooted, unkempt, crying and six years old.

RAY (*shocked*). Explain.

PEARL. One night father and mother were going to the Opera. When they were crossing Broadway, the usual crowd of children accosted them for alms. As mother felt in her pocket for some change, her fingers touched a cold and trembling hand which had clutched her purse.

RAY. A pickpocket! Well.

PEARL. This hand my mother grasped in her own, and so tightly that a small, feeble voice uttered an exclamation of pain. Mother looked down, and there beside her was a little ragged girl.

RAY. The thief.

PEARL. Yes, but a thief hardly six years old, with a face like an angel's. "Stop!" said my mother. "What are you doing?" "Trying to steal," said the child. "Don't you know that it's wicked to do so?" asked my father. "No," said the girl, "but it's dreadful to be hungry." "Who told you to steal?" asked my mother. "She—there!" said the child, pointing to a squalid woman in a doorway opposite, who fled suddenly down the street. "That is Old Judas," said the girl.

RAY. Old Judas. What a name! But how does this story interest us?

PEARL. That child was Laura. My father was about to let her go unharmed—but my mother said, "No, it is not enough. We have a duty to perform, even to her," and acting on a sudden impulse, took her to our home. On

being questioned there, the child seemed to have no recollection, save of misery and blows. My mother persuaded father, and the girl was sent to a country
clergyman's for instruction, and there she remained for
several years.

RAY.   Pearl, you are joking with me.

PEARL.   In beauty, and accomplishments, and dignity,
Laura (as mother named her) exceeded every girl of her
age. In gratitude she was all that father could have wished.
She was introduced as you know, into society as my
cousin, and no one dreams of her origin.

RAY (*starting up*). Laura, an outcast—a thief!

PEARL (*rising*). No, that is what she might have been.

RAY.   And this man—to-night?

PEARL.   All I know about him is, that four years ago this
man came with a cruel looking woman, to see mother.
There was a fearful scene between them, for Laura and I
sat trembling on the stairs, and overheard some awful
words. At last they went away, the man putting money
into his pocket as he left.

RAY.   But who were they?

PEARL.   Laura never told me, and mother would not. But,
of course, they must have been Laura's father and mother.
(*Ray sinks on chair as if overcome.*)

PEARL.   Mother made me promise never to tell anybody
this, and you would have known nothing had not Laura
made me speak. You see, she would not conceal anything
from you. (*Going to him.*) Ray, why don't you speak—
shall I go after Laura? Shall I tell her to come to you?
Why don't you answer? (*Going.*) I'll go and tell her you
want to see her. (*Pausing as she goes.*) I'm going to send
her to you, Ray. (*Goes off still looking back at him.*)

RAY (*starting up*). What a frightful story. Laura Courtland a
thief! A drunken wretch who knows her history, and a
squalid beggar woman who can claim her at any moment
as their child. And I was about to marry her. Yes, and I
love her. But what would my mother think? My friends?
Society? No—no—no—I cannot think of it. I will write
her—I will tell her—pshaw! she knows of course that I
cannot wed her now. (*Goes to table.*) Here is paper. (*Sits.*)
What am I about to do? What will be said of me? But I
owe a duty to myself—to society—I must perform it.
(*Writes.*) "Laura, I have heard all from your sister." What
have I said—(*Crosses out last word*)—"from Pearl. You
know that I love you, but my mother will demand of me
a wife who will not blush to own her kindred, and who is
not the daughter of obscurity and crime." It is just; it is
I who have been deceived. (*Folds letter and addresses it.*)
I will leave it for her. (*Puts on light overcoat, which hangs
on chair at back.*) I must go before she returns. Her step—
too late! (*Crams the letter into pocket of overcoat. Laura
enters.*)

LAURA (*gently*). Ray.

RAY.   Miss—Miss Courtland. (*Laura looks at him a
moment, smiles and then crosses without further noticing

him, and sits down on tete-a-tete.*) What have I said? What
ought I to have said? (*He takes a step towards her—she
rises, without looking at him goes to window—looks out,
then looks over books on table.*)

RAY.   Laura—I—

LAURA.   Pshaw, where is my book?

RAY.   What book do you want, Laura?

LAURA.   Sir.

RAY (*repulsed*). Oh!—(*Pause*)—I've been a fool. How
lovely she looks. (*He follows her mechanically to table.*)
Can I find it for you? (*Laura picks up a book and reseats
herself.*)

LAURA.   Don't trouble yourself I beg.

RAY (*coming forward and leaning over her seat*). Laura.

LAURA (*without lifting her head*). Well.

RAY (*toying with her hair*). Look at me.

LAURA (*turns round and looks full at him*).

RAY.   No, no, not that way; as you used to. You act as if I
were a stranger.

LAURA.   They are only strangers who call me Miss Courtland. (*Resumes reading.*)

RAY.   Forgive me, I beg you to forgive me. (*Coming round
and sitting beside her.*) I was mad—it was so sudden—
this miserable story—but I don't care what they say. O!
do listen to me. I thought you hated reading.

LAURA.   I often wish that I were ugly, wretched and repulsive, like the heroine in this story. (*Seats herself.*)

RAY (*behind her*). Why?

LAURA.   Because, then I could tell who really loved me.

RAY.   And don't you know?

LAURA.   No; I do not.

RAY.   Well, I know.

LAURA.   Do tell me then, please.

RAY.   He has told you so himself a hundred times.

LAURA.   You.

RAY.   I.

LAURA (*laughing heartily at him, then seriously*). How
happy must those women be, who are poor, and friendless, and plain, when some true heart comes and says: I
wish to marry you.

RAY.   Laura, you act very strangely to-night.

LAURA.   Will you put this book away?

RAY (*throws it on table*). There Laura. (*Seats himself beside
her.*)

LAURA (*rising*). There's Pearl calling me.

RAY (*rising and taking her hand*). Laura, why don't you let
me speak to you.

LAURA.   About what?

RAY.   About my love.

LAURA.   For whom? Not me. This is only marriage and
giving in marriage. I hate the very word.

RAY.   You did not think so once.

LAURA.   I wish I had. I am frightened now; I begin to understand myself better.

RAY.   And I am frightened because I understand you less.

LAURA.   Do not try to; good night. (*Stops by door as she is going out.*) Good night Mr. Trafford. (*Exit laughing.*)

RAY.   I've been an ass. No, I wrong that noble animal. The ass recognized the angel, and I, like Balaam, was blind. But I see now. After all what have I to fear? (*Takes letter from pocket.*) No one knows of this, (*puts it in his pocket again*). Let things go on, we'll be married, go straight to Europe, and live there ten years. That's the way we'll fix it. (*Exit. Scene closes in.*)

SCENE TWO

1st Grooves—The Gentlemen's coat-room at Delmonico's— opening for hat and coat. Chairs. Pier-glass on flat.

(*Enter Windel and Demilt muffled, and with umbrellas. They proceed to disrobe.*)

DEMILT.   Phew! wet as the deuce, and cold, too. There'll be nobody here.

WINDEL.   It's an awful night. The rooms are almost empty.

DEMILT.   Sam! Where the dickens is that darkey? (*Enter Sam fetching in a chair, and boot-black, box and brush.*)

SAM.   Here, sah.

DEMILT (*sitting in a chair*). Hurry up with my boots. Who's here?

SAM.   Berry few gemman, sah; only lebben overcoats and ten overshoes. Bless de Lord—dem overshoes is spilin the polishin business.

DEMILT.   Look out and don't give me any knocks.

WINDEL (*handing in his coat at window and getting check for it*). I wonder if the Courtland girls have come yet.

DEMILT.   What did Laura Courtland ever see in Trafford to fall in love with? The Van Dam party is my fancy.

WINDEL (*brushing his hair at glass*). She's ten years older than you, and has a husband.

DEMILT.   Yes, a fine old banker, on whom she can draw for everything but attention and affection. She has to get that by her own business tact.

(*Other parties enter, exchange good-nights, and deposit their coats; some go out at once, some arrange themselves at glass.*)

DEMILT.   That'll do, Sam, take my coat. (*Enter Ray.*)

WINDEL.   Hallo! Trafford, this is a night, ain't it? Have the Courtlands come?

RAY.   Not with me. Here, Sam, take my coat. (*His coat is pulled off by Sam, and four letters drop out.*) Stupid!

DEMILT.   Save the pieces. Mind the love letters.

RAY (*picking them up*). Look out well next time. There's that cursed letter I was going to send to Laura. Confound it, I must destroy it when I go home. (*Puts letters back in overcoat pocket. Ray gets his boots touched up.*)

DEMILT.   I say, Trafford, what'll you take, and let a fellow read those? Windel, I guess if the girls could get into the cloak room, it would be better than the dead-letter office. What a time they'd have! Are you ready?

WINDEL.   What's the use of hurrying? There's no life in the party till Laura Courtland comes. By Jove, Trafford! you're in luck. She's the prettiest girl in New York.

RAY.   And the best. (*March music is heard.*)

DEMILT.   There's the march music; let's go. (*Gets a final brush as they all go off.*)

RAY.   Come along. (*Exeunt.*)

SAM (*picking up a letter dropped from Ray's pocket*). Dere's anoder of dem billy dooses; wonder if it am Mist' Trafford's. Eh golly! musn't mix dem gentlemen's letters,— musn't mix 'em nohow,—or an oberruling providence wouldn't be able to stop fighting in dis city for de nex month. (*Exit, carrying a chair.*)

(*Scene draws off to dance music. Wait till change of music before change of Scene.*)

SCENE THREE

The Blue Room at Delmonico's. Waltz-music as the Scene opens. Waltzers in motion. Pearl is dancing with Mrs. Van Dam.

(*Enter Trafford, Demilt, and Windel.*)

PEARL.   There's Ray. I've had enough; I want to speak with him. (*Bursts away from Mrs. Van Dam, runs up to Trafford. Demilt goes up to Mrs. Van Dam.*)

PEARL (*to Ray*). You lazy fellow, where have you been?

DEMILT.   You're not tired, are you?

MRS. VAN DAM.   I feel as fresh as a daisy.

DEMILT.   Have a waltz with me. (*Waltz music, piano, as they dance. Windel goes to Sue Earlie.*)

RAY (*coming down with Pearl*). Where's Laura?

PEARL.   She wasn't ready, and I was dying to come. Been fixed since eight o'clock; so I came with Sue Earlie. So you made it up with Laura.

RAY.   Yes. Don't say anything more about the horrid subject. We've made it all up. But what on earth keeps her to-night? It's eleven already. (*Looking at watch.*) Confound it, I tremble every moment she's out of my sight. I fear that terrible man and his secret.

MRS. VAN DAM (*coming up with Demilt*). Trafford, you look very uneasy. What's the matter?

RAY.   O, nothing. I think I ought to go for Laura. I will, too. (*Servant passes at back.*) Here! go upstairs for my overcoat. (*Gives the man a card, and he goes out.*)

MRS. VAN DAM.   Nonsense! She'll be here in good time. You shan't leave us. Hold him, Pearl. We want a nine-pin quadrille, we haven't half enough gentlemen. Come, be jolly about it. You lovers are always afraid some one will carry your girls away.

RAY (*uneasy*). I? I'm not afraid.

PEARL.   Come, come! I never saw such a restless fellow.

(*Servant enters with coat.*)

SERVANT.   Here's your coat, sir.

MRS. VAN DAM.   Give it to me. I'm determined you shan't go. (*Takes coat carelessly.*) I'll make you a promise—if Laura isn't here in fifteen minutes you shall have your coat, and may go for her.

RAY.   Well, I suppose I'll have to wait.

MRS. VAN DAM.   There; take him off, Pearl. (*Ray goes up with Pearl. To Servant.*) Here take this back. (*Flings coat to Servant. As she does so, letters drop from it.*) Well, there's a mess. (*Sue Earlie and another lady run forward and pick up the letters.*) Love letters, of course!— (*Smelling them.*) Perfumed to suffocation.

SUE EARLIE.   Here's one for Laura. It's unsealed and not delivered.

MRS. VAN DAM (*tremolo waltz music*). A fair prize! Let's see it. (*Music. Takes and opens it. Puts on eye-glasses and reads.*) ''Laura''—Well, come! That's cool for a lover. ''I have heard all from''—something scratched out—ah!—''Your sister, Pearl—Your obscure origin—terrible family connexions—the secret of the tie which binds you to a drunken wretch—My mother, Society—will demand of me a wife who will not blush to own her kindred,—or start at the name of outcast and thief! Signed, Ray Trafford.''

(*All stand speechless and look at each other. All this time the rest have been dancing.*)

SUE EARLIE.   What can it mean?

MRS. VAN DAM.   It means that the rumors of ten years ago are proven. It was then suspected that the girl whom Mrs. Courtland brought every year from some unnamed place in the country, and introduced to everybody as her niece, was an imposter, which that foolish woman, in a freak of generosity, was thrusting upon society. The rumors died out for want of proof—and before Laura's beauty and dignity—but now they are confirmed. She is some beggar's child.

SUE EARLIE.   What do you think we ought to do? (*Trafford surrenders Pearl to Demilt and comes down.*)

MRS. VAN DAM.   Tell it—tell it everywhere, of course. The best blood of New York is insulted by the girl's presence. (*Trafford coming down.*)

RAY.   What have you three girls got your heads together for? Some conspiracy, I know.

MRS. VAN DAM (*to ladies*). Go girls—tell it everywhere.

RAY (*as the ladies distribute themselves about the groups*). What is it all about? Your face is a portrait of mystery.

MRS. VAN DAM (*showing letter*). Look at this, and tell me what it means.

RAY (*quickly*). Where did you get this?

MRS. VAN DAM.   It is you who must answer—and Society that will question. So Laura is not a Courtland?

RAY (*overcome*). You know, then,—

MRS. VAN DAM.   Everything; and will you marry this creature! You cannot. Society will not permit your sacrifice.

RAY.   This is not your business. Give me that letter.

MRS. VAN DAM.   Certainly; take it. But let me say one word—its contents are known. In an hour every tongue will question you about this secret,—every eye will inquire.

RAY.   I implore you! Do not breathe a word for her sake. (*She turns scornfully away.*)

MRS. VAN DAM.   The secret's not mine.

RAY.   Who knows it?

MRS. VAN DAM.   Look! (*Points to others who are grouped about whispering and motioning towards Ray. Pearl enters here and speaks to lady and gents.*)

RAY (*wildly*). What will they do?

MRS. VAN DAM.   Expose her! Expel her from society in which she is an intruder!

RAY.   You dare not. (*Pearl comes forward.*)

PEARL.   O, Ray! What is the meaning of this?

RAY (*bitterly*). It means that society is a terrible avenger of insult. Have you ever heard of the Siberian wolves? When one of the pack falls through weakness, the others devour him. It is not an elegant comparison—but there is something wolfish in society. Laura has mocked it with a pretense, and society, which is made up of pretenses, will bitterly resent the mockery.

MRS. VAN DAM.   Very good! This handsome thief has stolen your breeding as well as your brains, I see.

RAY.   If you speak a word against her, I will say that what you utter is a lie!

MRS. VAN DAM.   As you please, we will be silent. But you will find that the world speaks most forcibly when it utters no sound.

PEARL.   O, go and prevent her coming here.

RAY.   That I can do. (*Going up hastily sees Laura entering.*) Too late. (*He retreats.*)

MRS. VAN DAM.   Come girls! Let us look after our things. They are no longer safe when such an accomplished thief enters.

(*Music low as Laura enters, continues while all except Pearl and Ray pass out, eyeing her superciliously.*)

PEARL.   Ray, Ray, why do you not come to her?

MRS. VAN DAM (*surrounded by others*). Are you not coming with us Trafford?

PEARL (*to Laura*). Let us go home.

LAURA.   No; stay with him. (*Pointing to Ray, who has held off.*) He shall not suffer the disgrace long! (*About to faint, Ray runs forward—she proudly waves him away.*) It is Heaven's own blow!

Picture—Quick Curtain

END OF ACT ONE

ACT TWO

SCENE ONE

Interior of a basement. Street and railings seen through window at back. Stove with long pipe in fire-place. Table between two windows at back, with flowers, etc. Humble furniture. Table and three chairs. Closet (2nd Grooves). PEACH-BLOSSOM *is discovered polishing stove, a slip-shod girl a la Fanchon.*

SONG—PEACHBLOSSOM

> A lordly knight and a lovely dame, were walking in
>   the meadow,
> But a jealous rival creeping came a-watching in the
>   shadow;
> They heeded not, but he whet his knife and dogg'd
>   them in the shadow.
> The knight was brave, and the dame was true, the
>   rival fared but badly;
> For the knight he drew and ran him through, and left
>   him groaning sadly,
> The knight and dame soon wedded were, with bells
>   a-chiming gladly.

PEACHBLOSSOM (*talking while working*). The stove won't shine. It's the fault of the polish I know. That boy that comes here, just fills the bottles with mud, and calls it stove polish. Only let me catch him. Ah! Ah! (*threatening gesture with brush*) I declare I'd give it up if I didn't want to make everything look smart, before Miss Nina comes in. Miss Nina is the only friend I ever had, since I ran away from Mother Judas. I wonder where old Judas is now? I know she's drunk; she always was; perhaps that's why she never tried to find out what became of me. If she did she could not take me away. Miss Nina begged me off a policeman. I belong to her. I wonder why she ain't got any other friends? She's awful mysterious. Tells me never to let any strangers see her. She's afraid of some-body, I know. It looks just as if she was hiding. I thought only bad girls, such as I, had to hide. If I was good and pretty like her, I wouldn't hide from the President. (*Still polishing. Judas appears at window with basket of ornaments.*)

JUDAS.   Hum! Is your ma in my dear?

PEACHBLOSSOM (*starting*). Oh! (*Aside.*) Old Judas! She's found me out at last. No she h'aint, or she'd have got me by the hair before she spoke. That's *her* way.

JUDAS (*coming in at door. Peachblossom keeps her back towards her*). Any old clothes to change for chany, my dear? Where's your ma's old skirts and shawls, my pet. Get 'em quick before mother comes in, and I'll give you a beautiful chany mug or a tea-pot for them. Come here, my ducky—see the pretty—(*recognizes Peachblossom.*) Eh! why you jail-bird what are you doing here? Are you

sneakin' it? Answer me, or I'll knock your head agin the wall. (*Catches her by the hair.*)

PEACHBLOSSOM.   You just leave me be. I'm honest I am! I'm good.

JUDAS.   You're good? Where's my shoe? I'll take the good-ness out of you.

PEACHBLOSSOM.   Oh, oh! please don't beat me. I ain't good. I'm only trying to be.

JUDAS.   You're only trying to be, eh? Trying to be good, and here's me as was a-weeping every night, thinking as you was sent up for six months. Who're you living with—you ain't a-keeping house, are you?

PEACHBLOSSOM.   I'm living with Miss Nina.

JUDAS.   Nina, what's she, concert-saloon girl?

PEACHBLOSSOM.   No, she's a lady.

JUDAS.   A lady—and have such baggage as you about. Where's my shoe, I'll make you speak the truth.

PEACHBLOSSOM.   I don't know what she is. She met me when the police was taking me up for loafin' down Hudson Street, and she begged me off.

JUDAS.   Has she any money?

PEACHBLOSSOM.   No, she's poor.

JUDAS.   Any nice clothes?

PEACHBLOSSOM.   O, she's got good clothes.

JUDAS.   Where are they?

PEACHBLOSSOM.   Locked up, and she's got the key.

JUDAS.   You're lying, I see it in your eye. You're always shamefaced when you are telling the truth, and now you're as bold as brass. Where's my shoe? (*Making a dash at her.*)

PEACHBLOSSOM (*shouting*). There's Miss Nina (*As if curt-seying to some one behind Judas.*) Good morning, miss.

JUDAS (*changing her tone*). Ah! my pretty dear! What a good lady to take you in and give you a home. (*Turns and dis-covers the deception—in a rage.*) You hussy, (*Peach-blossom retreats.*) wait till I get you in my clutches again, my lady; and it won't be long. Miss Nina takes care of you, does she. Who will take care of her? Let her look to it. (*Laura enters plainly dressed, at back.*) Beg pardon, Miss, I just called to see if you had any old clothes you'd like to exchange.

LAURA.   No, I don't want anything, my good woman.

JUDAS (*eyeing her sharply and going to door*). That's her—I'd know her anywheres! (*Malicious glance, and exit.*)

LAURA.   You've been very good this morning, Blossom. The room is as nice as I could wish.

PEACHBLOSSOM.   Please 'm, I tried because you are so good to me (*Laura taking off her shawl and things.*) Shall I sweep out the airy? (*Laura does not answer.*) I guess I'd better—then she'll be alone, as she loves to be. (*Takes broom and exit.*)

LAURA (*solus. Opening a package and taking out photo-graphs*). No pay yet for coloring, 'till I have practiced a week longer. Then I shall have all the work I can do. They say at the photographer's I color well, and the best pictures will be given me. The best! Already I have had beneath my brush so many faces that I know, friends of the old days. The silent eyes seem to wonder at me for bringing them to this strange and lowly home. (*Picking up letters from table.*) Letters; ah! answers to my advertisement for employment. No, only a circular ''To the lady of this house.'' What's that! (*starting*) only Blossom sweeping. Every time there is a noise I dread the entrance of some one that knows me. But they could never find me in New York, I left them all too secretly and suddenly. None of them can expect I would have descended to this. But it is natural, everything will find its level. I sprang from poverty, and I return to it. Poor Pearl. How she must have wondered the next morning—Laura gone? But three months have passed, and they have forgotten me. Ray will cheer her. (*Wrangling outside, Peachblossom bursts in dragging Bermudas, with his professional tape, pins, blacking and baskets.*)

PEACHBLOSSOM.   Here he is m'm.

BERMUDAS.   Leave go, I tell yer, or I'll make yer.

LAURA.   What is the matter?

PEACHBLOSSOM.   He's the boy that sold me that stove polish what isn't stove polish.

BERMUDAS.   What is it then—s-a-a-y?

PEACHBLOSSOM.   It's mud! it's mud at ten pence a bottle.

BERMUDAS.   Ah! Where could I get mud? Ain't the streets clean? Mud's dearer than stove polish now.

PEACHBLOSSOM.   And your matches is wet, and your pins won't stick, and your shoe-strings is rotten, there now!

BERMUDAS.   Well, how am I to live; it ain't my fault, it's the taxes. Ain't I got to pay my income tax, and how am I to pay it if I gives you your money's worth? Do you think I'm Stewart—Sa-a-y?

LAURA.   Do let the boy alone, Blossom. Send him away. (*Enter Peanuts at door flat.*)

PEANUTS.   Extra! Hollo, Bermudas! how's your sister? Papers, Miss. Extra! Revolution in Mexico!

LAURA.   Dear, dear, this is the way I'm worried from morning till night.

BERMUDAS.   Here, just you get out! This is my beat.

PEANUTS.   Vell, I ain't blacking or hairpins now, I'm papers—How'm I hurting you?

BERMUDAS.   Vell, I'm papers at four o'clock, and this is my beat. Take care of me, I'm in training for a fight. I'm a bruiser, I am.

PEANUTS.   Hold yer jaw. (*They fight.*)

PEACHBLOSSOM (*beats them with broom*). Get out with you. Both of you (*Grand escapade and exit of boys.*)

LAURA.   Don't let's be troubled in this way again. Have you got the things for dinner?

PEACHBLOSSOM.   Lor, no, miss! It's twelve o'clock and I forgot! (*Peachblossom gets shawl, bit bonnet from hooks on the wall, basket from closet, while Laura opens her pocket-book for money.*)

LAURA.   What did we have for dinner yesterday, Blossom?

PEACHBLOSSOM.   Beefsteak, 'm. Let's have some leg o'mutton to-day. We've never had that.

LAURA.   But I don't know how to cook it. Do you?

PEACHBLOSSOM.   No, but I'd just slap it on, and it's sure to come out right.

LAURA.   Slap it on what?

PEACHBLOSSOM.   The gridiron.

LAURA (*giving money*). No, we'd better not try a leg of mutton to-day. Get some lamb chops, we know how to manage them.

PEACHBLOSSOM (*as she is going*). Taters, as usual, 'mum?

LAURA.   Yes; and stop Blossom—while you're buying the chops, just ask the butcher—off hand—you know—how he would cook a leg of mutton, if he were going to eat it himself—as if you wanted to know for yourself.

PEACHBLOSSOM.   Yes'm—but I'm sure it's just as good broiled as fried. (*Exit.*)

LAURA.   Now to be cook. (*Laughing.*) ''The Tuesday Sociable'' ought to see me now. Artist in the morning, cook at noon, artist in the afternoon. (*Snorkey raps at the door and enters.*)

SNORKEY (*with letter*). Beg pardon, is there anybody here as answers to the name of A. B. C.?

LAURA (*aside*). My advertisement for work.—Yes, give it to me.

SNORKEY (*seeing her face*). If I'd been taking something this morning, I'd say that I'd seen that face in a different sort of place from this.

LAURA.   Is there anything to pay? Why do you wait?

SNORKEY.   Nothing, Miss. It's all right. (*Going—and aside.*) But it ain't all right, Snorkey, old boy! (*Goes out after looking at her, stops at window, and gazes in.*)

LAURA (*without noticing him, opening letter*). Yes, an answer to my advertisement. (*Reads.*) To A. B. C.: ''Your advertisement promises that you are a good linguist, and can teach children of any age. I have two daughters for whom I wish to engage your services while on a tour of Europe. Call at seven o'clock, this evening, at No. 207 W. 34th Street. Annersley.'' Hope at last—a home, and in another land soon. I was sure the clouds would not always be black above me! (*Kisses letter. Snorkey re-entering.*)

SNORKEY.   Miss, I say, Miss. (*Laura starts.*)—Sh—

LAURA.   What do you want?

SNORKEY.   Only one word—and perhaps it may be of service to you. I'd do anything to serve you.

LAURA.   And why me?

SNORKEY.   I'm a blunt fellow, Miss, but I hope my way don't offend. Ain't you the lady that I brought a bouquet to on New Year's night—not here, but in a big house, all bright and rich—and who was so kind to a poor soldier?

LAURA (*faint and leaning against chair*). Whoever you may be, promise to tell no one you saw me here.

SNORKEY.   No fear, Miss! I promise.

LAURA.   Sacredly!

SNORKEY.   No need to do more than promise, Miss—I keeps my word. I promised Uncle Sam I'd stick to the flag—though they tore my arm off, and by darnation I stuck. I don't want to tell on you Miss. I want to tell on some one else.

LAURA.   What do you mean?

SNORKEY.   They're looking for you.

LAURA.   Who?

SNORKEY.   Byke. (*Laura utters a loud cry and sinks on chair.*) He's on it day and night. I've got his money in my pocket now, and you've got his letter in your hand this minute. (*Laura drops the letter in dismay.*)

LAURA.   This?

SNORKEY.   Yes, it's his writin'—looks like a woman's, don't it? Lord! the snuff that man's up to, would make Barnum sneeze his head off. He's kept me in hand, 'cause he thinks I know you, having seen you that once. Every day he reads the advertisements, and picks out a dozen or so and says to me: "Snorkey, that's like my little pet" and then he sits down and answers them and gets the advertisers to make appointments with him, which he keeps regularly, and regularly comes back cussing at his ill luck. See here Miss, I've a bundle of answers to deliver, as usual, to advertisers. I calls 'em Byke's Target Practice, and this time, you see, he's accidentally hit the mark.

LAURA.   For Heaven's sake do not betray me to him! I've got very little money, I earn it hardly; but take it, take it—and save me. (*Offers money.*)

SNORKEY.   No, Miss; not a cent of it. Though Byke is a devil and would kick me hard if he thought I would betray him.

LAURA.   I don't want you to suffer for my sake, take the money.

SNORKEY.   No, I stood up to be shot at for thirteen dollars a month, and I can take my chances of a kickin' for nothing. But Byke ain't the only one Miss, there's another's looking for you.

LAURA (*her look of joy changing to fear*). Another! Who?

SNORKEY (*approaching smilingly and confidential*). Mr. Trafford. (*Laura turns aside despairingly.*) He's been at me every day for more than six weeks. "Snorkey" says he, "do you remember that beautiful young lady you brought the bouquet to on New Year's night?" "Well," says I, "Capt'n, the young lady I slightly disremember, but the cakes and wine I got there that night I shall never forget." "Search for that young lady," says he, "and when you find her"—

LAURA.   No, no, no; not even he must know. Do you hear—not he—not anyone. You have served them well; serve me and be silent.

SNORKEY.   Just as you please, Miss, but I hate to serve you by putting your friends off the track—it don't seem natural—Byke I don't mind; but the Capt'n wouldn't do you

any harm. Just let me give him a bit of a hint. (*Laura makes an entreating gesture.*) Well I'm mum, but as I've got only one hand, it's hard work to hold my tongue. (*Going.*) Not the least bit of a hint? (*Laura appealingly and then turns away.*) They say when a woman says no, she means yes! I wonder if I dare tell her that he's not far off. Perhaps I'd better not. But I can tell him. (*Exit.*)

LAURA.   How shall I ever escape that dreadful man? And Ray searching for me too! Our friends then remember us as well as our enemies. (*Peachblossom enters quickly shutting the door behind her, with basket which she places on table.*)

PEACHBLOSSOM.   Miss Nina, whatever is into the people? There's a strange man coming down the entry. I heard him asking that red cap fellow about you.

LAURA.   Byke! Fasten the door quick. (*Peachblossom runs to door, it is slightly opened, she pushes it against some one on the other side.*)

PEACHBLOSSOM.   O dear! He is powerful strong, I can't keep it shut. Go away, you willin! (*The door is forced and Ray enters.*)

RAY (*advancing*). Laura—It is I.

LAURA.   Ray! (*Shrinks from him.*)

RAY.   Dear Laura! (*He stops as he becomes conscious that Blossom with her basket on her arm and her bonnet hanging on her back is staring at him.*) I say, my girl, havn't you some particular business somewhere else to attend to?

PEACHBLOSSOM (*seriously*). No, sir; I've swept the sidewalk and gone a marketing, and now I'm indoors and I mean to stay.

RAY.   And wouldn't you oblige me by going for a sheet of paper and an envelope? Here's a dollar—try and see how slow you can be.

PEACHBLOSSOM (*firmly*). You can't sheet of paper me, mister, I'm protecting Miss Nina, and I'm not going to be enveloped.

LAURA.   Go as the gentleman asks you, Blossom.

PEACHBLOSSOM.   Oh! (*Takes money, fixes her bonnet.*) First it's "Keep the man out," now it's "Let him stay in alone with me." But I suppose she's like all of us—it makes a great difference which man it is. (*Exit.*)

RAY (*after watching Peachblossom out*). Laura, when I approached you, you shrank from me. Why did you so?

LAURA.   Look around you and find your answer.

RAY (*shuddering*). Pardon me, I did not come here to insult your misery. When I saw you I forgot everything else.

LAURA.   And now it's time for us to remember everything. I told you to look around that you might understand that in such a place I am no longer Laura Courtland, nor anything I used to be. But I did not ask your pity. There is no misery here.

RAY.   Alone, without means, exposed to every rudeness, unprotected, is this not misery for you?

LAURA (*laughing*). Oh, it's not so bad as that.

RAY. Laura, don't trifle with me. You cannot have exchanged everything that made you happy, for this squalid poverty, and not feel it deeply.

LAURA. I have not time to feel anything deeply. (*Takes basket up, goes to table, busies herself about preparing dinner.*) I work from sunrise till night, and I sleep so soundly that I have not even dreams to recall the past. Just as you came in I was about to cook our dinner. Only think—lamp chops!

RAY. Lamb chops! It makes me shudder to hear you speak.

LAURA. Does it? Then wait till I get the gridiron on the fire, and you'll shiver. And if you want to be transfixed with horror, stop and take dinner.

RAY. I will not hear you mock yourself thus, Laura. I tell you in this self-banishment you have acted thoughtlessly—you have done wrong.

LAURA. Why?

RAY. Because, let the miserable creatures who slandered you say what they might, you had still a home and friends.

LAURA. A home! Where the very servants would whisper and point. Friends who would be ashamed to acknowledge me. You are mistaken. That is neither home nor friendship.

RAY. And you are resolved to surrender the past forever.

LAURA. The past has forgotten me in spite of myself.

RAY. Look at me.

LAURA (*coming down*). Well then, there's one who has not forgotten me, but I desire that he may. You speak to me of bitterness. Your presence, your words, cause me the first pang I have felt since the night I fled unnoticed from my chamber, and began my life anew. Therefore I entreat you to leave me, to forget me.

RAY. Laura, by the tie that once bound us—

LAURA (*going up*). Yes, *once*. It *is* a long time ago.

RAY. What have I said?—the tie which still—

LAURA (*sharply turning*). Mr. Trafford must I remind you of that night, when all arrayed themselves so pitilessly against me? When a gesture from you might have saved me! And you saw me sink without stretching a finger to the woman who had felt the beating of your heart. No, you made your choice then—the world without me. I make my choice now—the wide, wide world without you.

RAY. I have been bitterly punished, for we are never so humiliated as when we despise ourselves. But, by the Heaven above us both I love you Laura, I have never ceased to love you.

LAURA. I thank you. I know how to construe the love which you deny in the face of society, to offer me behind its back.

RAY. Will you drive me mad! I tell you Laura, your misery, your solicitude is as nothing to the anguish I have suffered. The maniac who in his mental darkness, stabs to the heart the friend he loved, never felt in returning reason the remorse my error has earned me. Every day it says to me: ''You have been false to the heart that loved you, and you shall account for it to your conscience all your life. You shall find that the bitterest drops in the cup of sorrow, are the tears of the woman you have forsaken.'' And it is true. O, forgive me—have pity on me.

LAURA (*moved*). I forgive you. Yes, and I pity you—and, so good-bye, forever.

RAY. Of course, I am nothing to you now. That is some comfort to me. I have only to be sorry on my account. But, I come to you on behalf of others.

LAURA. Whom?

RAY. My mother and Pearl. They ask for you. For them I have sought you, to urge you to return to them.

LAURA. Dear little Pearl.

RAY. Yes, she has been quite ill.

LAURA. She has been ill?

RAY. Think of those two hearts which you have caused to suffer and do not drive me from you. It is not only wealth, luxury and refinement which you have surrendered—you have also cast away those greater riches: loving and devoted friends. But they shall persuade you themselves. Yes, I'll go and bring them to you, you cannot resist their entreaties.

LAURA. No, no, they must not come here. They must never know where I hide my shame, and you must never reveal it.

RAY. I promise it, if you will go to them with me. Think, they will insist on coming unless you do.

LAURA. Poor Pearl! If I go with you, you promise not to detain me—to permit me to come back, and to trouble me and my poor life no more?

RAY. I promise; but I know you will release me from it when you see them. I will get a carriage. So that no one will meet you. Wait for me, I shall not be long. Is it agreed?

LAURA (*smiling*). Yes, it is agreed.

(*Enter Peachblossom, with a sheet of paper, foolscap, and some enormous envelopes.*)

PEACHBLOSSOM. Here they are.

RAY. That's a good girl, keep them till I come back. In half an hour. Laura be ready. (*Exit.*)

PEACHBLOSSOM (*with an air*). What's he going to do in half an hour?

LAURA. He's going to take me away with him for a little while Blossom, and while I'm gone, I wish you to be a good girl, and watch the house, and take care of it till I return.

PEACHBLOSSOM. I don't believe it. You won't return. (*Crying.*) That's what our Sal said when she went off with her young man, and she never came back at all. You shan't go; I hate him. He shan't take you away.

LAURA.   Blossom! (*Who is getting ready, putting her hat on, etc.*)

PEACHBLOSSOM.   I don't care. If you go away, I'll go away; I'd bit and scratch him if he comes back. (*Fiercely tearing up the paper and envelopes.*) Let him come back. Let him dare come back.

LAURA.   Blossom, you're very wicked. Go into the corner this minute and put your apron over your head.

PEACHBLOSSOM (*crying at Laura's feet*). O, please, Miss Nina, let me go with you. Let me ask him to let me go with you. (*Figure passes the window.*) Here he is, I see him coming.

LAURA.   Run! run! open the door. (*Peachblossom runs to door; throws it open, disclosing Byke. Exclamation of horror from Laura.*)

BYKE (*advancing*). Ah, my dear little runaway! Found you at last,—and just going out. How lucky! I wanted you to take a walk with me.

LAURA.   Instantly leave this place!

BYKE.   How singular! you are always ordering me out and I am always coming in. We want a change. I will go out and I request you to come with me.

LAURA.   Blossom, go find an officer. Tell him this wretch is insulting me.

BYKE.   Blossom? ah,—exactly! Here you, Judas! (*Judas appears at door. Peachblossom crosses to Laura.*)

PEACHBLOSSOM.   O, Miss, save me!

BYKE (*throws Peachblossom over to Judas*). Take care of that brat. And as for you, daughter—come with me.

LAURA.   Daughter!

BYKE.   Yes; it is time to declare myself. Paternal feeling has been long smothered in my breast. Come to my arms, my child, my long-estranged child! (*Takes out dirty handkerchief and presses his eyes with pretended feeling.*)

LAURA.   God! is there no help coming? (*She attempts to escape. Byke seizes her.*)

BYKE.   What, unfilial girl! You take advantage of a father's weakness, and try to bolt! (*Clutching her by the arm.*) Come, go with me; and cheer my old age. Ain't I good, to take you back after all these years?

Picture—Quick Curtain

END OF ACT TWO

ACT THREE

SCENE ONE

The Tombs Police Court. Long high desk with three seats, across back from right to left on platform. Railing in front. Railing around with open center. In front of railing, a bench. Gate in center of railing. Judge Bowling and another Justice seated behind high desk with clerk. Justice is reading paper, with his feet upon desk. Policeman 9–9–9 at right and left.

Policeman at gate. Hard-looking set of men and women on benches. Lawyer Splinter is talking to Rafferdi, an organ-man, who is in crowd. As the curtain rises noisy buzz is heard.

BOWLING.   Smithers, keep those people quiet. (*9–9–9 handling people roughly.*) Here—easy, officer; treat those poor people decently. Well, whom have you got there?

9–9–9 (*going to one and dragging urchin within railing*). Pickpocket, your Honor. Caught in the act.

BOWLING.   What's he got to say for himself? Nothing, eh? What's his name?

9–9–9 (*stooping down to boy as if asking him*). Says his name is Peter Rich.

BOWLING.   You stand a poor chance, Rich! Take him away. (*Bowling consults with other Justice, as the boy is taken off.*)

SPLINTER (*to Rafferdi, who has his monkey and organ*). So you want to get out, eh? How much money have you got?

RAFFERDI.   Be jabers! half a dollar in cents is all the money I'm worth in the world.

SPLINTER.   Give it to me. I thought you organ fellows were Italians.

RAFFERDI.   Devil doubt it! Ain't I got a monkey?

9–9–9.   Here, you; come up here. (*Takes Rafferdi inside the railing.*)

BOWLING.   Now, then; what's this officer?

9–9–9 (*Rafferdi takes stand*). Complaint of disturbing the neighborhood.

BOWLING.   What have you got to say for yourself?

SPLINTER.   If your Honor please, I appear for this man.

BOWLING.   Well what have you got to say for him?

SPLINTER.   Here is an unfortunate man, your Honor—a native of Sunny Italy. He came to our free and happy country, and being a votary of music, he bought an organ and a monkey, and tried to earn his bread. But the myrmidons of the law were upon him, and the Eagle of Liberty drooped his pinions as Rafferdi was hurried to his dungeon.

BOWLING.   Rafferdi!—You're an Irishman, ain't you? What do you mean by deceiving us?

RAFFERDI.   Sure I didn't. It's the lawyer chap there. I paid him fifty pints and he's lying out the worth of it.

BOWLING.   You fellows are regular nuisances! I've a great mind to commit you.

SPLINTER.   Commit him! If the Court please—reflect—commit him—to prison—what will become of his monkey?

BOWLING.   Well, I'll commit him too.

SPLINTER.   You cannot. I defy the Court to find anything in the statutes authorizing the commital of the monkey.

BOWLING.   Well, we'll leave out the monkey.

SPLINTER.   And if the Court please, what is the monkey to do in the wide world, with his natural protector in prison?

I appeal to those kindlier feelings in your honor's breast—which must ever temper justice with mercy. This monkey is perhaps an orphan!

BOWLING (*laughing*). Take them both away, and don't let me catch you here again Mr. Rafferdi or you'll go to jail. (*Exit Rafferdi. Splinter goes down, Rafferdi exits.*)

9–9–9 (*pulling Sam who is drunk out of a crowd*). Get up here.

SAM (*noisily*). Look yah—don't pull me around.

BOWLING. Silence there! what's all this noise about?

SAM. Whar's de Court? I want to see de Judge.

SPLINTER (*approaching him*). My colored friend, can I assist you?

SAM. Am you a Counsellor-at-Law?

SPLINTER. Yes, retain me! How much money have you got?

SAM. I ain't got no money—but I've got a policy ticket. It bound to draw a prize.

SPLINTER. Got any pawn tickets?

SAM. Of course. (*Giving him a handful.*)

BOWLING. Well, what's the charge?

9–9–9. Drunk and disorderly.

BOWLING. Well, my man, what have you to say?

SAM. Dis here gemman represents me.

SPLINTER. We admit, if the Court please, that we were slightly intoxicated, but we claim the privilege, as the equal of the white man.

BOWLING (*to Clerk*). Very good! Commit him for ten days.

SPLINTER. But this is an outrage, your honor.

BOWLING (*to Officer*). Take him off! (*Motioning to Sam, who is very wroth.*)

SAM. What?

BOWLING. Take him away.

SAM. Look here, judge, hab you read the Civil Right Bill? You can't send dis nigger to prison while dat bill am de law of de land.

BOWLING. That'll do—remove him.

SAM. I ain't no gipsy, I'm one of de Eureau niggers, I am. Where am de law? Don't touch me, white man! Dis am corruption—dis am 'ficial delinquency.

9–9–9 (*collars him and carries him off*).

SAM. Mr. Stevens! Thaddeus! (*Exit.*)

BOWLING. Any more prisoners? (*Noise.*) What noise is that? (*Officer goes out. Byke enters, followed by the officer who escorts Laura.*)

BYKE. Where is the judge? O, where is the good, kind judge?

BOWLING. Well, my dear sir, what is the matter?

BYKE. O, sir, forgive my tears. I'm a broken-hearted man!

BOWLING. Be calm, my dear sir. Officer, bring this gentleman a chair. (*Officer hands chair.*)

BYKE. Ah, sir, you are very good to a poor distressed father whose existence has been made a desert on account of his child.

BOWLING. Repress your emotion, and tell me what you want.

BYKE. I want my child.

BOWLING. Where is she?

BYKE. She is here, sir—here—my darling, my beautiful child, and so unfilial—so unnatural.

BOWLING. How is this, young lady?

LAURA (*standing inside railing*). It is all a lie. He is not my father.

BYKE. Not your father? Oh, dear, oh, dear, you will break my heart.

BOWLING. This needs some explanation. If not his child, who are you?

LAURA. I am—I dare not say it. I know not who I am, but I feel that he cannot be my father.

BYKE. O, dear—O—

BOWLING (*sharply*). Silence! (*To Laura, sternly.*) You say you don't know who you are. Do you know this man?

LAURA. Yes.

BOWLING. Where, and with whom do you live?

LAURA. I have lived alone for four months.

BOWLING. And with whom did you live before that?

LAURA. O, forgive me, if I seem disobedient—but I cannot tell.

BOWLING. Then I must look to this gentleman for information.

BYKE. And I will gladly give it. Yes, sir, I will gladly tell. She was taken from me years ago, when she was but a little child, by rich people who wanted to adopt her. I refused—they paid me—I was poor—I was starving—I forebore to claim her—she was happy, but they turned her forth four months ago into the street. I could not see her suffer—my child—the prop of my declining days. I begged her to come—she refused. Me enemies had poisoned my daughter's mind against *me*, her father. I am still poor. I taught school, but I have saved a little money, only for her.

BOWLING. How old is she?

BYKE. Nineteen.

BOWLING (*to Laura*). Your father is your legal guardian during your minority, and is entitled to your custody. Why are you so undutiful? Try to correct this.

BYKE. Oh, bless you, dear, good judge for those words.

LAURA. O, have I no friends, must I go with him?

BOWLING. Certainly.

LAURA. Anything, then. Exposure! Disgrace, rather than that. (*Judges consult. Enter Snorkey—goes opposite to Laura and signals her.*)

BYKE (*aside*). Snorkey! The devil!

SNORKEY (*crossing to Laura*). Can I help you miss? Only tell me what to do, and if it takes my other arm off, I'll save you.

LAURA. Yes, yes, you can help me! (*To Judge.*) Will you let me send a message?

BOWLING.   You may do that.

LAURA.   Run to that house—not my house—but the one in which you saw me first. Do you remember it?

SNORKEY.   Don't I, and the wine and cakes.

LAURA.   Ask for Miss Pearl. Tell her where I am. Tell her to come instantly. (*Snorkey going.*) Stay—tell her to bring the ebony box in mother's cabinet. Can you recollect?

SNORKEY.   Can I what? Gaze at this giant intellect and don't ask me! The ebony box—all right—I'm off. (*Exit.*)

BOWLING.   It would have been as well, young lady, to have answered frankly at first.

BYKE.   O, sir! Don't be harsh with her! Don't be harsh with my poor child!

BOWLING.   Your father has a most Christian disposition.

LAURA.   Sir, I have told you and I now solemnly repeat it, that this man is no relation of mine. I desire to remain unknown, for I am most unfortunate; but the injustice you are about to commit forces me to reveal myself, though in doing so I shall increase a sorrow already hard to bear. (*Splinter talks with Laura aside.*)

BOWLING.   We sit here to do right, according to the facts before us. And let me tell you, young lady, that your obstinate silence has more than convinced us that your father's statement is correct. Further, unless the witnesses you have sent for can directly contradict him, we shall not alter our decision.

LAURA.   Let it be so. He says he gave me into the care of certain wealthy people when I was a little child.

BYKE.   I am willing to swear to it.

LAURA (*Splinter watching effect of question*). Then he will be able to describe the clothes in which I was dressed at the time. They were safely kept. I have sent for them.

BYKE.   Let them be produced—and I will recognize every little precious garment. (*Aside.*) This is getting ferociously hot for me! Ha! (*Re-enter Snorkey with Ray hastily.*)

SNORKEY (*excitedly*). Here's a witness! Here's evidence! (*9–9–9 admonishes him.*)

LAURA (*Ray takes her hand through the rail*). Ray?

BOWLING.   Who is this?

RAY.   I am a friend, sir, of this lady.

BYKE.   He is a dreadful character—a villain who wants to lead my child astray! Don't—please don't let him contaminate her!

BOWLING.   Silence! (*To Ray.*) Can you disprove that this young lady is his daughter?

RAY.   His daughter? (*Looks at Laura.*)

LAURA.   He knows nothing.

BOWLING.   Let him answer. Come—have you any knowledge of this matter?

RAY.   I had been told, sir, that—(*Laura looks at him.*) No—I know nothing.

LAURA.   Have you brought the ebony box? It contained the clothes which I wore when—

RAY.   I understand; but in my haste, and not knowing your peril I brought nothing. But can you not remember them yourself?

LAURA.   Perfectly.

RAY.   Write, then! (*Handing her a memorandum book. To Bowling.*) Sir, this lady will hand you a description of those articles which she wore when she was found, thirteen years ago. Then let this scoundrel be questioned—and if he fail to answer, I will accuse him of an attempted abduction.

BOWLING.   That's the way.

BYKE (*aside*). It will not be a great effort for me to remember.

BOWLING (*taking the book from Ray*). Now sir, I will listen to you. (*Ray and Laura are eager and expectant.*)

BYKE (*deliberately*). A soiled gingham frock, patched and torn. (*Laura gives a shudder and turns aside.*)

BOWLING.   What kind of shoes and stockings?

BYKE.   Her feet were bare.

BOWLING.   And the color of her hood?

BYKE.   Her dear little head was uncovered.

BOWLING (*handing book back*). He has answered correctly.

LAURA.   It is useless to struggle more! Heaven alone can help me!

RAY.   You can see, sir, that this lady cannot be his daughter. Look at her and at him!

BOWLING.   I only see that he has pretty well proven his case. She must go with him, and let her learn to love him as a daughter should.

RAY.   She shall not! I will follow him wherever he goes.

BYKE (*taking Laura's hand*). I appeal to the Court.

BOWLING.   Officer, take charge of that person, until this gentleman is gone.

BYKE (*coming forward with Laura who is dumb and despairing*). My child, try and remember the words of the good judge. ''You must learn to love me as a daughter should.'' (*Leading her out.*)

SNORKEY (*to Ray*). Stay here, sir, I'll track him. No one suspects me!

(*Music. Tableau. Scene closes in.*)

SCENE TWO

Exterior of the Tombs, with ballads on strings upon the railings. Enter Judas followed by Peachblossom.

PEACHBLOSSOM.   Only tell me where he has taken her, and I'll go with you—indeed I will.

JUDAS.   We don't want you, we wouldn't be bothered with you; she's our game.

PEACHBLOSSOM.   What are you going to do with her?

JUDAS.   Do? why we'll coin her. Turn her into dollars. We've had it on foot for a long time.

PEACHBLOSSOM.   What! Is she the rich young lady I heard you and Byke speak of so often before I got away from you?

JUDAS (*savagely*). Heard me speak of! What did you hear?

PEACHBLOSSOM (*dancing off*). O, I know! I know more than you suppose. When you used to lock me up in the back cellar for running away, you forgot that doors had key-holes.

JUDAS (*aside*). This girl must be silenced.

PEACHBLOSSOM.   What are you muttering about—don't you know how Byke used to throw you down and trample on you for muttering?

JUDAS.   I'll have you yet, my beauty.

PEACHBLOSSOM.   I think you are a great fool, Judas.

JUDAS.   Likely, likely.

PEACHBLOSSOM.   Why don't you give up Miss Nina to that handsome young gentleman? He'd pay you well for the secret. He'd give his whole fortune for her, I know, I saw it in his face. And he'd treat you better than Byke does.

JUDAS.   Not yet my chicken; besides, what does he care for her now? Isn't he going to marry the other girl—she's the one will pay when the time comes—but we intend to hold the goods 'till the price is high.

PEACHBLOSSOM.   Then, if you won't, I'll tell all as I knows. I'll tell him all I used to overhear about babies and cradles, and he'll understand it perhaps, if I don't.

JUDAS (*aside*). Hang her—she'll make mischief. (*Aloud.*) Well, come along with me, my beauty, and I'll talk it over with you.

PEACHBLOSSOM.   Don't touch me, I won't trust you with your hands on me. (*Judas makes a dart at her.*) I knew that was your game. But I'll be even with you yet. (*Dancing off tantalizingly before Judas. Both exit.*)

(*Enter Snorkey.*)

SNORKEY (*despondent*). I'm no more use than a gun without a trigger. I tried to follow Byke, but he smoked me in a minute. Then I tried to make up with him, but he swore that I went against him in Court, and so he wouldn't have me at no price. Then after I ran after the carriage that he got into with the lady, till a damned old woman caught me for upsetting her applestand and bursting up her business. What am I to do now? I'm afraid to go back to the Cap'n, *he* won't have me at any price either, I suppose. (*Gazing at ballads, hands in his pockets—going from one to the other. Enter Bermudas with ballads in his hands and preparing to take others off the line as if to shut up shop.*)

BERMUDAS (*after gazing at Snorkey*). What are you a-doing of—S-a-ay? (*Snorkey takes no notice.*) This here's one of the fellows as steals bread of the poor man. Reading all the songs for nothin, and got bags of gold at home. Sa-ay!

SNORKEY.   Well, youngster, what are you groaning about? Have you got the cholera?

BERMUDAS.   Ah! What are you doing? Taking the bloom off my songs? You've read them 'ere ballads till they're in rags.

SNORKEY.   I was looking for the "Prairie Bird."

BERMUDAS.   Perary Bird! eh? There aint no perary bird. There's a "Perary Flower."

SNORKEY.   Now don't go into convulsions. I'll find it. (*Turns to the songs.*)

BERMUDAS.   S-a-ay—you needn't look no further for that bird! I've found him, and no mistake. He's a big Shanghae with a red comb and no feathers.

SNORKEY.   He's dropped on me.

BERMUDAS.   Ain't you a mean cuss, sa-a-y? Why don't you come down with your two cents, and support trade?

SNORKEY.   But I ain't got two cents. What's a fellow to do if he hasn't got a red?

BERMUDAS (*toning down*). Haint you? Where's your messages?

SNORKEY.   Havn't had one go to-day.

BERMUDAS.   Where do you hang out?

SNORKEY.   Nowheres.

BERMUDAS.   My eye—no roost?

SNORKEY.   No.

BERMUDAS.   I tell you what, come along with us—we've got a bully place—no rent—no taxes—no nothin.

SNORKEY.   Where is it?

BERMUDAS.   Down under the pier!—I discovered it. I was in swimmin and seed a hole and I went in. Lots of room, just the place for a quiet roost. We has jolly times every night I tell you on the dock; and when it is time to turn in we goes below, and has it as snug as a hotel; come down with us.

SNORKEY.   I will! These young rascals will help me track that scoundrel yet.

BERMUDAS.   Now, help me to take in my show windows; it's time to shut up shop.

(*Enter Ray Trafford.*)

RAY.   If what that crazy girl has told me can be true, Laura may yet be restored to her friends if not to me, for I have dispelled that dream for ever. But that villain must be traced immediately, or he will convey his victim far beyond our reach or rescue.

(*Snorkey helping to take down songs sees Trafford, who has crossed.*)

SNORKEY.   Hollo! Cap'n!

RAY.   The man of all I wanted. You tracked him?

SNORKEY.   They was too much for me, sir—two horses was—but I saw them turn into Greenwich Street, near Jay.

RAY.   This may give us a clue. I have learned from a girl who knows this fellow, that he has some hiding place over the river, and owns a boat which is always fastened near the pier where the Boston Steamers are.

SNORKEY.   Well, Cap'n, if anything's to be done, you'll find me at Pier—what's the number of our pier, Shorty?

BERMUDAS.   Pier 30!—Down stairs!

SNORKEY.   Pier 30. That's my new home, and if you want me, say the word.

RAY.   You will help me?

SNORKEY.   You bet, Cap'n. I was on Columbia's side for four years and I'll fight for her daughters for the rest of my life, if you say so. If there's any fightin' count me in, Cap'n.

RAY.   Thank you, brave fellow. Here take this—no nonsense—take it. Pier 30 is it?

SNORKEY.   Pier 30. (*Exit Trafford.*)

BERMUDAS (*eyeing money*). How much, Perary?

SNORKEY.   One—two—three—four—four dollars.

BERMUDAS.   Four dollars! Sa-a-y—Don't you want to buy a share in a paying business? I'm looking out for a partner with a cash capital, for the ballad business. Or I tell you what to do. Lay your money on me in a mill. I'm going to be a prize fighter, and get reported in the respectable dailies. "Rattling Mill, 99th round, Bermudas the victor, having knocked his antagonist into nowheres."

SNORKEY.   Come along, you young imp. I could floor you with my own arm, and then the report would be: "25th round—Snorkey came up first, while his antagonist showed great signs of distress."

BERMUDAS.   Say, Perary, what are you going to do with all that money?

SNORKEY.   I won't bet it on you, sure.

BERMUDAS.   I'll tell you what to do, let's go and board at the Metropolitan Hotel for an hour.

SNORKEY.   What will we do for toothpicks?

BERMUDAS.   Oh, go along. You can't get anything to eat for four dollars. (*Exit Snorkey, Bermudas squaring off.*)

SCENE THREE

Foot of Pier 30, North River. Sea cloth down and working— A pier projecting into the river. A large cavity in front. Bow of a vessel at back, and other steamers, vessels and piers in perspective on either side. The flat gives view of Jersey City and the river shipping by starlight. Music of distant serenade heard.

(*Byke enters sculling a boat, and fastens his boat to the pier. Old Judas is on the pier, smoking pipe, looking down.*)

JUDAS.   Have you fixed everything across the river?

BYKE.   Yes, I have a horse and wagon waiting near the shore to carry her to the farm. Has any one been around here?

JUDAS.   Not a soul. I've been waiting here for an hour. What made you so long?

BYKE.   I pulled down the river for a spell to throw any spies off the track. It was necessary after what you told me of that girl's threat to blab about the Boston pier.

JUDAS.   Pshaw! she'd never dare.

BYKE.   Never mind, it's best to be certain. Is the prize safe?

JUDAS.   Yes, she was worn out, and slept when I came away. How her blood tells—she wouldn't shed a tear.

BYKE.   Bah! if she'd been more of a woman and set up a screaming, we shouldn't have been able to get her at all. Success to all girls of spirit, say I.

JUDAS.   Don't you think it might be worth while to treat this young spark, Trafford, and hear what he has to offer?

BYKE.   Satan take him! no. That'll spoil your game about the other girl, Pearl. He was making up to her all right, and if he gets this one back he'll upset the whole game by marrying her. I tell you he's got the old feeling for her, spite of her running away. Now you can judge for yourself, and do as you please.

JUDAS.   Then I do as you do—get her out of the city. When Pearl is married to him we can treat for Laura's ransom, by threatening them with the real secret.

BYKE.   Then that's settled. (*Taking out flask.*) Here's the precious infant's health. Do you think she'll go easy, or shall we drug her?

JUDAS.   Just tell her it's to meet her beau and get her ransom, or give her a reason and she'll be as mild as a lamb.

BYKE.   Ha! let me get hold of her, and I'll answer she goes across, reason or no reason. (*Bermudas calls outside.*) There's a noise.

JUDAS.   It's only the market boys coming down for a swim.

BYKE.   Softly then, come along. (*Music, exeunt.*)

(*Enter Bermudas, Peanuts, and a couple other boys.*)

BERMUDAS.   Say, Peanuts, go down and see if any of the fellows is come yet. (*Peanuts scrambles down to hole in front on side of dock; comes out again.*)

PEANUTS.   There's nobody there.

SNORKEY (*without*). Hollo!

BERMUDAS.   Hollo! That's our new chum. Hollo! follow your front teeth, and you'll get here afore you knows it. (*Enter Snorkey with more boys.*)

SNORKEY.   What a very airy location.

BERMUDAS.   It's a very convenient hotel. Hot and cold salt-water baths at the very door of your bedrooms, and sometimes when the tide rises we has the bath brought to us in bed—doesn't we, Peanuts?

PEANUTS.   That's so.

SNORKEY.   Come, what do you do before you go to bed?

BERMUDAS.   We has a swarry. Say, one of you fellows, go down and bring up the piany forty. (*Peanuts goes into hole and gets banjo.*) What'll I give you?

SNORKEY.   Something lively. (*Music, and dance by boys, ensue,—given according to capacity and talent. At the end of it, a general shout of jubilee; when—*)

SERGEANT OF PATROL (*outside*). Here, boys! less noise.

BERMUDAS.   It's Acton and the police. Let's go to bed. (*Bermudas and boys get down into hole.*)

SERGEANT (*entering in patrol boat*). If you boys don't make less noise, I'll have to clear you out.

BERMUDAS (*on the pier*). It's an extra occasion, Mr. Acton;—we're having a distinguished military guest, and we're entertaining him. (*Boat passes out.*) Come along, Perary, let's go to bed. (*Snorkey is about to descend.*)

(*Enter Ray Trafford, on pier.*)

RAY.   Is that you, Snorkey?

SNORKEY (*quickly whispering*).   Here, sir. Anything turned up?

RAY.   Byke was overheard to say he intended crossing the river to-night; he will doubtless use that boat which he keeps by the Boston Pier. The river patrol are on the watch for him. But I will meet him before he can embark.

SNORKEY.   Which Boston Pier is it, Cap'n? there are three on this river.

RAY.   Three!

SNORKEY.   Yes; one of them is two slips below. I tell you what, Cap'n: You get the officers, go by the shore way, search all the slips; I'll find a boat about here, and will drop down the river, and keep an eye around generally.

VOICES (*without*).   This way, sir.

RAY.   That's the patrol calling me. Your idea is a good one. Keep a sharp eye down the stream. (*Exit.*)

SNORKEY (*alone*).   Now for my lay.

BERMUDAS (*popping his head up*).   Say, can't I do nothin? I'm the Fifth-Ward Chicken, and if there's any muss, let me have a shy.

SNORKEY.   No; get in and keep quiet. (*Bermudas disappears.*) I wonder where I can find a boat. There ought to be plenty tied up about here. My eye! (*Discovering Byke's.*) Here's one for the wishin'; sculls too. I'm in luck. Say, Bermuda, whose boat is this?

BERMUDAS.   Yours, if you like. Tie it loose. (*Jumps down, enters boat, pushes off.*)

BERMUDAS (*inside*).   Keep your toe out of my ear! (*Pause.*)

(*Byke, Laura, and Judas enter on pier.*)

LAURA.   Is this the place? There's no one here; you have deceived me.

BYKE.   Well, we have but we won't do so any longer.

LAURA.   What do you mean?

BYKE (*drawing pistol*).   Do you see this? It is my dog Trusty. It has a very loud voice and a sharp bite; and if you scream out, I'll try if it can't outscream you. Judas, unfasten the boat.

LAURA.   What are you going to do? You will not murder me?

BYKE.   No; we only mean to take you to the other shore, where your friends won't think of finding you. Quick, Judas.

JUDAS.   The boat's gone.

BYKE.   Damn you, what do you mean? Where is it? Here, hold her. (*Judas clutches Laura.*) Where the devil is that boat?

SNORKEY (*re-appearing in boat*).   Here!

BYKE.   Snorkey! We're betrayed. Come. (*Drags Laura towards exit.*)

SNORKEY.   The police are there! Turn, you coward! Don't run from a one-armed man!

BYKE.   Judas, take her! (*Snorkey strikes at him with oar. Byke takes oar from him and strikes him; he falls in boat. The boys hear the noise, and scramble up at back. The patrol boat appears with lights.*)

SNORKEY.   Help! Bermudas!

BERMUDAS.   Hi! Ninety-ninth round! first blood for Bermudas! (*Jumps at Byke.*)

BYKE (*flinging Bermudas off*).   Judas, toss her over!

(*Judas throws Laura over back of pier. Ray enters. Boys all get on pier and surround Byke, fighting him. Officers enter at left. Ray leaps into water after Laura.*)

Curtain. Moonlight on during scene.

END OF ACT THREE

ACT FOUR
SCENE ONE

Long Branch. Ground floor of an elegant residence—open windows from floor to ceiling at back—opening upon a balcony or promenade. Perspective of the shore and sea in distance. Door right and left. Sunset.

(*As the curtain rises to lively music, enter Pearl, Mrs. Van Dam, Sue Earlie, and other ladies in summer costume, Demilt and Windel with them.*)

PEARL.   And so the distinguished foreigner is in love with me? I thought he looked excessively solemn at the hop last night. Do you know, I can't imagine a more serious spectacle than a French man or an Italian in love. One always imagines them to be sick. (*To Mrs. Van Dam.*) Do fasten my glove—there's a dear.

MRS. VAN DAM.   Where's Ray?

PEARL.   O, he's somewhere. I never saw such another. Isn't he cheerful? He never smiles, and seldom talks.

MRS. VAN DAM.   But the foreigner does. What an ecstasy he was in over your singing; sing us a verse, won't you, while we're waiting for Ray?

ALL.   It will be delightful—do.

PEARL.   Well! (*Song introduced.*)

(*Air; "When the War is Over, Mary."*)

I.

Now the summer days are fading,
Autumn send its dreary blast
Moaning through the silent forest
Where the leaves are falling fast.

Soon dread winter will enfold us—
Chilling in its arms of snow,
Flowers that the summer cherished,
Birds that sing, and streams that flow.
Say, shall all things droop and wither,
That are born this Summer day?
Shall the happy love it brought us—
Like the flowers fade away?
No; be still thou flutt'ring bosom—
Seasons change and years glide by,
They may not harm what is immortal—
Darling—love shall never die!

PEARL.   Now, I've sung that to Ray a dozen times, and he never even said it was nice. He hasn't any soul for music; O, dear, what a creature!

MRS. VAN DAM.   Yes, and what a victim you will be with a husband who has $60,000 per annum income.

PEARL.   That's some comfort, isn't it?

RAY (enters bowing to others). Going out, Pearl?

PEARL.   Yes, we're off the Shrewsbury. Quite a party's going—four carriages—and we mean to stay and ride home by moonlight.

RAY.   Couldn't you return a little earlier?

MRS. VAN DAM.   Earlier! Pshaw! What's in you, Trafford? (The ladies and gents go up.)

RAY (to Pearl). You know that Laura will be quite alone and she is still suffering.

PEARL.   Well, she'll read and read, as she always did, and never miss me.

RAY.   But, at least, she ought to have some little attention.

PEARL.   Dear, dear, what an unreasonable fellow you are. Isn't she happy now—didn't you save her from drowning, and havn't I been as good to her as I can be—what more do you want?

RAY.   I don't like to hear you talk so, Pearl, and remember what she and you were once. And you know that she was something else once—something that you are now to me. And yet how cheerful, how gentle she is. She has lost everything and does not complain.

PEARL.   Well, what a sermon! There, I know you're hurt and I'm a fool. But I can't help it. People say she's good-looking but she's got no heart! I'd give anything for one, but they ain't to be bought.

RAY.   Well, don't moan about it, I didn't mean to reprove you.

PEARL.   But you do reprove me. I'm sure I havn't been the cause of Laura's troubles. I didn't tell the big, ugly man to come and take her away, although I was once glad he did.

RAY.   Pearl!

PEARL.   Because I thought I had gained you by it. (Ray turns away.) But now I've got you, I don't seem to make you happy. But I might as well complain that you don't make me happy—but I don't complain, I am satisfied, and I want you to be satisfied. There, are you satisfied?

MRS. VAN DAM (who with others has been promenading up and down the balcony). Here are the carriages.

PEARL.   I'm coming. Can't you get me my shawl, Ray. (Ray gets it from chair.)

MRS. VAN DAM.   And here's you foreign admirer on horseback.

(Sue Earlie, Demilt and Windel exit.)

PEARL.   Bye, bye, Ray. (Exit.)

MRS. VAN DAM.   Are you not coming, Trafford?

RAY.   I? No!

MRS. VAN DAM.   Do come on horseback, here's a horse ready for you.

PEARL (without). Ray! Ray!

MRS. VAN DAM.   Pearl's calling you. Be quick or Count Carom will be before you, and hand her in the carriage.

RAY (taking his hat slowly). O, by all means, let the Count have some amusement.

MRS. VAN DAM (taking Ray's arm). You're a perfect icicle. (They exit.)

(Noise of whips and laughter. Plaintive music as Laura enters and gazes out at them.)

LAURA.   Poor Pearl. It is a sad thing to want for happiness but it is a terrible thing to see another groping about blindly for it when it is almost within the grasp. And yet she can be very happy with him. Her sunny temper, and her joyous face will brighten any home. (Sits at table, on which are books.) How happy I feel to be alone with these friends, who are ever ready to talk to me—with no long-ings for what I may not have—my existence hidden from all, save two in the wide world, and making my joy out of the joy of that innocent child who will soon be his wife.

(Peachblossom appears at back looking in cautiously, grotesquely attired.)

PEACHBLOSSOM.   If you please.

LAURA (aloud). Who is there?

PEACHBLOSSOM (running in window). O, it's Miss Nina! O, I'm so glad; I've had such a hunt for you. Don't ask me nothing yet. I'm so happy. I've been looking for you for so long, and I've had such hard luck. Lord what a tramp—miles on miles.

LAURA.   Did any one see you come here? How did you find me?

PEACHBLOSSOM.   I asked 'em at the hotel where Mr. Trafford was, and they said at Courtlands, and I asked 'em where Courtlands was, and they said down the shore, and I walked down lookin' at every place till I came here.

LAURA.   Speak low, Blossom. My existence is a secret, and no one must hear you.

PEACHBLOSSOM.   Well, Miss, I says to Snorkey—says I—

LAURA.   Is he with you?

PEACHBLOSSOM.   No, Miss, but we are great friends. He wants me to keep house for him some day. I said to him—''I want to find out where Miss Nina's gone,'' and so he went to Mr. Trafford's and found he was come to Long Branch, but never a word could we hear of you.

LAURA.   And the others—those dreadful people?

PEACHBLOSSOM.   Byke and old Judas? Clean gone! They hasn't been seen since they was took up for throwing you into the water, and let off because no one came to Court agin 'em. Bermudas says he's seen 'em in Barnum's wax-work show, but Bermudas is *such* a liar. He brought me up here.

LAURA.   Brought you up here.

PEACHBLOSSOM.   Yes, he sells papers at Stetson's; he's got the exclusive trade here, and he has a little wagon and a horse, and goes down to the junction every night to catch the extras from the Express train what don't come here. He says he'll give me lots of nice rides if I'll stay here.

LAURA.   But you must not stay here. You must go back to New York this evening.

PEACHBLOSSOM.   Back! No, I won't.

LAURA.   Blossom!

PEACHBLOSSOM.   I won't, I won't, I won't! I'll never let you away again. I did it once and you was took away and dragged about and chucked overboard and almost drowned. I won't be any trouble, indeed I won't. I'll hire out at the hotel, and run over when my work is done at night, when nobody can see me, to look up at your window. Don't send me away. You're the only one as ever was good to me.

LAURA (*aside*).   It's too dangerous. She certainly would reveal me sooner or later. I must send her back.

PEACHBLOSSOM.   Besides, I've got something to tell you. Dreadful! dreadful! about old Judas and Byke—a secret.

LAURA.   A secret! what in the world are you saying?

PEACHBLOSSOM.   Is it wicked to listen at doors when people talk?

LAURA.   It is very wicked.

PEACHBLOSSOM.   Well, I suppose that's why I did it. I used to listen to Byke and Judas when they used to talk about a rich lady whom they called Mrs. Courtland.

LAURA.   Ah!

PEACHBLOSSOM.   Judas used to be a nurse at Mrs. Courtland's, and was turned off for stealing. And wasn't she and Byke going to make money off her! and Byke was to pretend to be some beautiful lady's father. Then, when they took you, Judas says to me: ''Did you ever hear of children being changed in their cradles?''—and that you wasn't her child, but she was going to make money off the real one at the proper time.

LAURA.   What do you tell me?

PEACHBLOSSOM.   Oh! I'm not crazy. I know a heap, don't I? And I want you to think I'm somebody, and not send me away.

LAURA (*to herself*).   She must speak the truth. And yet if I were to repeat her strange words here, I should be suspected of forging some tale to abuse the ear of society. No! better let it rest as it is. She must go—and I must go too.

PEACHBLOSSOM.   You ain't mad with me?

LAURA.   No, no; but you must go away from here. Go back to the hotel to your friend—anywhere, and wait for me; I will come to you.

PEACHBLOSSOM.   Is it a promise?

LAURA (*nervously*).   Yes, go.

PEACHBLOSSOM.   Then I'll go; for I know you always keep your word—you ain't angry, cause I came after you? I did it because I loved you—because I wanted to see you put in the right place. Honor bright, you ain't sending me away now? Well, I'll go; good bye! (*Exit.*)

LAURA (*animated*).   I must return to the city, no matter what dangers may lurk there. It is dangerous enough to be concealed here, with a hundred Argus-eyed women about me every day, but with this girl, detection would be certain. I must go—secretly if I can—openly if I must.

RAY (*outside*).   No, I shall not ride again. Put him up. (*Entering.*) Laura, I knew I should find you here.

LAURA (*sitting and pretending composure*).   I thought you had gone with Pearl?

RAY.   I did go part of the way, but I left the party a mile down the road.

LAURA.   You and Pearl had no disagreement?

RAY.   No—yes; that is, we always have. Our social barometers always stand at ''cloudy'' and ''overcast.''

LAURA (*rising*).   And whose fault is that?

RAY (*pettishly*).   Not mine. I know I do all I can—I say all I can—but she—(*crossing*).

LAURA.   But she is to be your wife. Ray—my friend—courtship is the text from which the whole solemn sermon of married life takes its theme. Do not let yours be discontented and unhappy.

RAY.   To be my wife; yes. In a moment of foolishness, dazzled by her airs and teased by her coquettishness, I asked her to be my wife.

LAURA.   And you repent already?

RAY (*taking her hand*).   I lost you, and I was at the mercy of any flirt that chose to give me an inviting look. It was your fault—you know it was! Why did you leave me?

LAURA (*after conflict with her feelings*).   Ray, the greatest happiness I have ever felt, has been the thought that all your affections were forever bestowed upon a virtuous lady, your equal in family fortune and accomplishments. What a revelation do you make to me now! What is it makes you continually war with your happiness?

RAY.   I don't know what it is. I was wrong to accuse you. Forgive me! I have only my own cowardice to blame for my misery. But Pearl—

LAURA.   You must not accuse her.

RAY. When you were gone, she seemed to have no thought—no wish—but for my happiness. She constantly invited me to her house, and when I tried to avoid her, met me at every turn. Was she altogether blameless?

LAURA. Yes, it was her happiness she sought, and she had a right to seek it.

RAY. Oh! men are the veriest fools on earth; a little attention, a little sympathy, and they are caught—caught by a thing without soul or brains, while some noble woman is forsaken and forgotten.

LAURA (*Ray throws himself into a seat*). Ray, will you hear me?

RAY (*looking at her hopefully*). Yes, speak to me as you used to speak. Be to me as you used to be.

LAURA (*smiling sadly*). I cannot be that to you; but I can speak as the spirit of the Laura who is dead to you forever.

RAY. Be it as you will.

LAURA (*standing beside him*). Let the woman you look upon be wise or vain, beautiful or homely, rich or poor, she has but one thing she can really give or refuse—her heart! Her beauty, her wit, her accomplishments, she may sell to you—but her love is the treasure without money and without price.

RAY. How well I have learned that.

LAURA. She only asks in return, that when you look upon her your eyes shall speak a mute devotion; that when you address her your voice shall be gentle, loving and kind. That you shall not despise her because she cannot understand, all at once, your vigorous thoughts and ambitious designs: for when misfortune and evil have defeated your greatest purposes—her love remains to console you. You look to the trees for strength and grandeur—do not despise the flowers, because their fragrance is all they have to give. Remember—love is all a woman has to give; but it is the only earthly thing which God permits us to carry beyond the grave.

RAY (*rising*). You are right. You are always right. I asked Pearl to be my wife, knowing what she was, and I will be just to her. I will do my duty though it break my heart.

LAURA. Spoken like a hero.

RAY. But it is to you I owe the new light that guides me; and I will tell her—

LAURA. Tell her nothing—never speak of me. And when you see her say to her it is she, and she alone, whom you consult and to whom you listen.

RAY. And you—

LAURA. You will see me no more.

RAY. You will leave me?

LAURA. Something of me will always be with you—my parting words—my prayers for your happiness. (*Distant music heard.*)

RAY (*falling on his knees*). O, Laura, you leave me to despair.

LAURA. No; to the happiness which follows duty well performed. Such happiness as I feel in doing mine.

(*Picture. Scene closes in. During last of this scene the sun has set, and night come on. Stage dark.*)

SCENE TWO

Woods near Shrewsbury Station.

(*Enter Byke shabbily dressed.*)

BYKE. It's getting darker and darker, and I'm like to lose my way. Where the devil is Judas? It must be nine o'clock, and she was to be at the bend with the wagon half an hour ago. (*Rumble of wheels heard.*) Humph—at last.

JUDAS (*entering*). Is that you Byke?

BYKE. Who did you suppose it was? I've been tramping about the wet grass for an hour.

JUDAS. It was a hard job to get the horse and wagon.

BYKE. Give me a match. (*Lights pipe and leans against a tree.*) Did you get the bearing of the crib?

JUDAS. Yes, it is on the shore, well away from the other cottages and hotels.

BYKE. That's good. Nothing like peace and quietness. Who's in the house?

JUDAS. Only the two girls and the servants.

BYKE. How many of them?

JUDAS. Four.

BYKE. It'll be mere child's play to go through that house. Have you spied about the swag?

JUDAS. They have all their diamonds and jewels there; Pearl wears them constantly; they're the talk of the whole place.

BYKE. We'll live in luxury off that girl all our lives. She'll settle a handsome thing on us, won't she? when she knows what we know, and pays us to keep dark;—if t'other one don't spoil the game.

JUDAS. Curse her! I could cut her throat.

BYKE. O, I'll take care of that!

JUDAS. You always do things for the best, dear old Byke!

BYKE. Of course I do. What time is it?

JUDAS. Not ten yet.

BYKE. An hour to wait.

JUDAS. But, Byke, you won't peach on me before my little pet is married, will you?

BYKE. What's the fool about now?

JUDAS. I can't help trembling; nothing is safe while Laura is there.

BYKE. I've provided for that. I've had the same idea as you—while she's in the way, and Trafford unmarried, our plans are all smoke, and we might as well be sitting on the hob with a keg of powder in the coals.

JUDAS. That we might. But what have you thought to do?

BYKE. Why, I've thought what an unfortunate creature Laura is—robbed of her mother, her home, and her lover; nothing to live for; it would be a mercy to put her out of the way.

JUDAS.   That's it; but how—how—how—

BYKE.   It's plain she wasn't born to be drowned, or the materials are very handy down here. What made you talk about cutting her throat? It was very wrong! When 'a thing gets into my head, it sticks there.

JUDAS.   You oughtn't to mind me.

BYKE.   Make your mind easy on that score.

JUDAS (*alarmed*). Byke, I heard some one in the bushes just there. (*Points.*)

BYKE (*nervously and quickly*). Who? Where?

JUDAS.   Where the hedge is broken. I could swear I saw the shadow of a man.

BYKE.   Stop here. I'll see. (*Exits.*)

JUDAS (*solus*). I begin to shiver. But it must be done or we starve. Why should I tremble? it's the safest job we ever planned. If they discover us, our secret will save us:—we know too much to be sent to jail.

(*Re-enter Byke, slowly.*)

BYKE.   There are traces, but I can see no one. (*Looking off.*)

JUDAS.   Suppose we should have been overheard!

BYKE (*glaring at her*). Overheard? Bah! no one could understand.

JUDAS.   Come, let us go to the wagon and be off.

BYKE (*always looking off*). Go you, I will follow. Bring it round by the station, and wait for me in the shadows of the trees and I will follow. (*Judas goes off. Byke, after a moment,—still looking,—buttons up his coat and hides behind wood.*) Heigho! I must be off.

(*Enter Snorkey, slowly.*)

SNORKEY.   Tracked 'em again! We're the latest fashionable arrivals at Long Branch. "Mr. Byke and Lady, and Brigadier-General Snorkey, of New York;"—there's an item for the papers! With a horse and wagon, they'll be at the seaside in two hours; but in the train I think I'll beat 'em. Then to find Cap'n Trafford, and give him the wink, and be ready to receive the distinguished visitors with all the honors. Robbery; Burglary; Murder;—that's Byke's catechism:—"What's to be done when you're hard up? Steal! What's to be done if you're caught at it? Kill!'' It's short and easy, and he lives up to it like a good many Christians don't live up to their laws. (*Looking off.*) They're out of sight. Phew! it's midsummer, but I'm chilled to the bone; something like a piece of ice has been stuck between my shoulders all day, and something like a black mist is always before me. (*Byke is behind tree.*) Just like old Nettly told me he felt, the night before Fredericksburg;—and next day he was past all feeling,—hit with a shell, and knocked into so many pieces, I didn't know which to call my old friend. Well, (*slapping his chest*) we've all got to go; and if I can save *them*, I'll have some little capital to start the next world on. The next world perhaps I shan't be the maimed beggar *there*

that I am in this. (*Takes out pistol, examines cap; goes off, Byke gliding after him.*)

SCENE THREE

Railroad Station at Shrewsbury Bend. The station shed, platform around it, and door at side, window in front. Clump of shrubs and tree. The Railroad Track runs from left to right. View of Shrewsbury River in perspective. Night. Moonlight. The switch, with a red lantern and Signalman's coat hanging on it. The signal lamp and post beside it.

(*As the scene opens, several packages are lying about the stage, among them a bundle of axes. The Signalman is wheeling in a small barrel, whistling at his work. Enter Laura in walking dress, feebly.*)

LAURA.   It is impossible for me to go further. A second time I've fled from home and friends, but now they will never find me. The trains must all have passed, and there are no conveyances till to-morrow. (*She sits at clump.*)

SIGNALMAN.   Beg pardon, ma'am, looking for anybody?

LAURA.   Thank you, no. Are you the man in charge of this station?

SIGNALMAN.   Yes, ma'am.

LAURA.   When is there another train for New York?

SIGNALMAN.   New York? Not till morning. We've only one more train to-night; that's the down one; it'll be here in about twenty minutes—"Express Train."

LAURA.   What place is that?

SIGNALMAN.   That? That's the signal station shed. It serves for store-room, depot, baggage-room, and everything.

LAURA.   Can I stay there to-night?

SIGNALMAN.   There? Well it's an odd place, and I should think you would hardly like it. Why don't you go to the hotel?

LAURA.   I have my reasons—urgent ones. It is not because I want money. You shall have this (*producing portmonnaie*) if you let me remain here.

SIGNALMAN.   Well, I've locked up a good many things in there over night, but I never had a young lady for freight before. Besides, ma'am, I don't know anything about you. You know it's odd that you won't go to a decent hotel, and plenty of money in your pocket.

LAURA.   You refuse me—well—I shall only have to sit here all night.

SIGNALMAN.   Here, in the open air? Why, it would kill you.

LAURA.   So much the better.

SIGNALMAN.   Excuse me for questions, Miss, but you're a running away from some one, ain't you?

LAURA.   Yes.

SIGNALMAN.   Well, I'd like to help you. I'm a plain man you know and I'd like to help you, but there's one thing would go agin' me to assist in. (*Laura is interested.*) I'm on to fifty years of age, and I've many children, some on 'em daughters grown. There's a many temptations for young gals, and sometimes the old man has to put on the brakes a bit, for some young men who are wicked enough to persuade the gals to steal out of their father's house in the dead of night, and go to shame and misery. So tell me this—it ain't the old man, and the old man's home you've left, young lady?

LAURA.   No; you good, honest fellow—no—I have no father.

SIGNALMAN.   Then, by Jerusalem! I'll do for you what I can. Anything but run away from them that have not their interest but yours at heart. Come, you may stay there, but I'll have to lock you in.

LAURA.   I desire that you should.

SIGNALMAN.   It's for your safety as much as mine. I've got a patent lock on that door that would give a skeleton key the rheumatism to fool with it. You don't mind the baggage. I'll have to put it in with you, hoes, shovels, mowing machines, and what is this—axes. Yes, a bundle of axes. If the Superintendent finds me out, I'll ask him if he was afraid you'd run off with these. (*Laughs.*) So, if you please, I'll first tumble 'em in. (*Puts goods in house, Laura sitting on platform looking at him. When all in, he comes towards her, taking up cheese-box to put it in Station.*) I say, Miss, I ain't curious—but, of course, it's a *young man* you're a going to?

LAURA.   So far from that, it's a young man I'm running away from.

SIGNALMAN (*dropping box*). Running away from a young man! Let me shake hands with you. (*Shakes her hand.*) Lord, it does my heart good! At your age, too! (*Seriously.*) I wish you'd come and live down in my neighborhood a while, among my gals. (*Shaking his head.*) You'd do a power of good. (*Putting box in station.*)

LAURA.   I've met an excellent friend. And here at least I can be concealed until to-morrow—then for New York. My heart feels lighter already—it's a good omen.

SIGNALMAN.   Now, Miss, bless your heart, here's your hotel ready. (*Goes to switch and takes coat off, putting it on.*)

LAURA.   Thanks, my good friend; but not a word to any one—till to-morrow; not even—not even to your girls.

SIGNALMAN.   Not a word, I promise you. If I told my girls, it would be over the whole village before morning. (*She goes in. He locks the door. Laura appears at window facing audience.*)

LAURA.   Lock me in safely.

SIGNALMAN.   Ah! be sure I will. There! (*Tries door.*) Safe as a jail. (*Pulls out watch, and then looking at track with lantern.*) Ten minutes and down she comes. It's all safe this way, my noisy beauty, and you may come as soon as you like. Good night, Miss!

LAURA (*at window*). Good night.

SIGNALMAN.   Running away from young man. Ha! ha! ha! (*He goes to track, then looks down—lights his pipe and is trudging off when enter Snorkey.*)

SNORKEY.   Ten minutes before the train comes. I'll wait here for it. (*To Signalman, who re-enters.*) Hollo, I say, the train won't stop here too long, will it?

SIGNALMAN.   Too long? It won't stop here at all.

SNORKEY.   I must reach the shore to-night. There'll be murder done, unless I can prevent it!

SIGNALMAN.   Murder, or no murder, the train can't be stopped.

SNORKEY.   It's a lie. By waving the red signal for danger, the engineer must stop, I tell you!

SIGNALMAN.   Do you think I'm a fool! What! disobey orders and lose my place; then what's to become of my family? (*Exit.*)

SNORKEY.   I won't be foiled. I will confiscate some farmer's horse about here, and get there before them somehow. (*Byke enters at back with loose coil of rope in his hand.*) Then when Byke arrives in his donkey cart he'll be ready to sit for a picture of surprise. (*Byke enters suddenly throwing coil over Snorkey.*)

BYKE.   Will he?

SNORKEY.   Byke!

BYKE.   Yes, Byke. Where's that pistol of yours? (*Tightening rope around his arm.*)

SNORKEY.   In my breast pocket.

BYKE (*taking it*). Just what I wanted.

SNORKEY.   You ain't a going to shoot me?

BYKE.   No!

SNORKEY.   Well, I'm obliged to you for that.

BYKE (*leading him to platform*). Just sit down a minute, will you.

SNORKEY.   What for? (*Laura appears horror struck at window.*)

BYKE.   You'll see.

SNORKEY.   Well, I don't mind if I do take a seat. (*Sits down. Byke coils the rope round his legs.*) Hollo! what's this?

BYKE.   You'll see. (*Picks the helpless Snorkey up.*)

SNORKEY.   Byke, what are you going to do!

BYKE.   Put you to bed. (*Lays him across the railroad track.*)

SNORKEY.   Byke, you don't mean to—My God, you are a villain!

BYKE (*fastening him to rails*). I'm going to put you to bed. You won't toss much. In less than ten minutes you'll be sound asleep. There, how do you like it? You'll get down to the Branch before me, will you? You dog me and play the eavesdropper, eh! Now do it if you can. When you hear the thunder under your head and see the lights dancing in your eyes, and feel the iron wheels a foot from your neck, remember Byke! (*Exit.*)

LAURA.   O, Heavens! he will be murdered before my eyes! How can I aid him?

SNORKEY.   Who's that?

LAURA.   It is I. Do you not know my voice?

SNORKEY.   That I do; but I almost thought I was dead, and it was an angel's. Where are you?

LAURA.   In the station.

SNORKEY.   I can't see you, but I can hear you. Listen to me, Miss, for I've got only a few minutes to live.

LAURA (*shaking door*). God help me! and I cannot aid you.

SNORKEY.   Never mind me, Miss. I might as well die now, and here, as at any other time. I'm not afraid. I've seen death in almost every shape, and none of them scare me; but, for the sake of those you love, I would live. Do you hear me?

LAURA.   Yes! yes!

SNORKEY.   They are on the way to your cottage—Byke and Judas—to rob and murder.

LAURA (*in agony*). O, I must get out! (*Shakes window bars.*) What shall I do?

SNORKEY.   Can't you burst the door?

LAURA.   It is locked fast.

SNORKEY.   Is there nothing in there?—no hammer?—no crowbar?

LAURA.   Nothing! (*Faint steam whistle heard in the distance.*) O, heavens! The train! (*Paralysed for an instant.*) The axe!!!

SNORKEY.   Cut the woodwork! Don't mind the lock—cut round it! How my neck tingles! (*A blow at door is heard.*) Courage! (*Another.*) Courage! (*The steam whistle heard again—nearer, and rumble of train on track. Another blow.*) That's a true woman! Courage! (*Noise of locomotive heard—with whistle. A last blow; the door swings open, mutilated—the lock hanging—and Laura appears, axe in hand.*)

SNORKEY.   Here—quick! (*She runs and unfastens him. The locomotive lights glare on the scene.*) Victory! Saved! Hooray! (*Laura leans exhausted against switch.*) And these are the women who ain't to have a vote!

(*As Laura takes his head from the track, the train of cars rushes past with roar and whistle from left to right.*)

END OF ACT FOUR

ACT FIVE

An elegant boudoir at Courtland's cottage, Long Branch; open window and balcony at back; moonlight exterior; tree overhanging balcony. Bed and toilette table; arm chair; door; lighted lamp of toilette table; dresses on chair by bed and by window. Music.

(*Pearl is discovered en negligee brushing her hair out at table before mirror.*)

PEARL.   I don't feel a bit sleepy. What a splendid drive we had! I like that foreigner. What an elegant fellow he is! Ray is nothing to him. I wonder if I'm in love with him. Pshaw! What an idea! I don't believe I could love anybody much. How sweetly he writes!—(*Picks up letter and sits on chair.*) "You were more lovely than ever to-night; with one more thing, you'd be an angel!" Now, that's perfectly splendid: "with one more thing, you'd be an angel—that one thing is love. They tell me Mr. Trafford is your professed admirer. I'm sure he could never be called your lover—for he seems incapable of any passion but

Melancholy." It's quite true. Ray does not comprehend me. (*Takes up another letter.*) "Pearl, forgive me if I have been cross and cold. For the future, I will do my duty, as your affianced husband, better." Now, did ever anyone hear such talk as that from a lover? Lover!—O, dear! I begin to feel that he can love, but not me. Well, I'd just as soon break—if he'd be the first to speak. How nice and fresh the air is!—(*She turns down lamp.*) It's much nicer here, than going to bed. (*Settles her self in tete-a-tete for a nap. Pause.*)

(*Moonbeams fall on Byke, who appears above the balcony. He gets over the rail and enters.*)

BYKE.   Safely down! I've made no mistake—no, this is her room. What a figure I am for a lady's chamber. (*Goes to table, picks up delicate lace handkerchief, and wipes his face.*) Phew! Hot! (*Puts handkerchief in his pocket.*) Now for my bearings. (*Taking huge clasp-knife from his pocket.*) There's the bed where she's sleeping like a precious infant, and here—(*Sees Pearl in chair and steals round at back, looking down at her.*) It's so dark—I can't recognize the face. It's a wonder she don't feel me in the air and dream of me. If she does she'll wake sure—but it's easy to settle that. (*Takes phial of chloroform from his pocket, saturates the handkerchief he picked up, and applies it.*) So!—now my charmer—we'll have the earrings. (*Takes them out.*) What's here? (*Going to table.*) Bracelets—diamonds! (*Going to dresses, and feeling in the pockets.*) Money! That's handy. (*He puts all in a bag, and hands them over balcony.*) Now for the drawers, there's where the treasure must be. Locked? (*Tries them with bunch of keys.*) Patent lock, of course! It amuses me to see people buying patent locks, when there's one key will fit 'em all. (*Produces small crowbar, and just as he is about to force the drawer, a shout is heard, and noise of wagon.*) What's that? (*Jumps, catching at bureau, which falls over.*) Damnation!

PEARL (*starting up*). Who's there? What's that?

BYKE.   Silence, or I'll kill you!

PEARL.   Help! Help!

BYKE (*running to bureau for knife*). You will have it my pretty one. (*Pearl runs to door.*)

PEARL.   Save me! Save me! (*Byke pursues her, the door bursts open and Ray and Laura enter. Byke turns and runs to balcony, and confronts Snorkey and Bermudas, who have clambered over.*)

LAURA.   Just in time.

RAY (*seizing Byke*). Scoundrel!

SNORKEY.   Hold him, Governor! Hold him! (*Assists Ray to bind Byke in chair.*)

BERMUDAS.   Sixty-sixth and last round. The big 'un floored, and Bermudas as fresh as a daisy.

PEARL.   Dear, dear Laura, you have saved me.

RAY.   Yes, Pearl; from more than you can tell.

LAURA.   No, no, her saviors are there. (*Pointing to Bermudas and Snorkey.*) Had it not been for the one, I should never have learned your danger, and but for the other, we could never have reached you in time.

SNORKEY.   Bermudas and his fourth editions did it. Business enterprise and Bermudas' pony express worked the oracle this time.

BERMUDAS.   The way we galloped! Sa-a-y, my pony must have thought the extras was full of lively intelligence.

PEARL.   Darling Laura, you shall never leave us again.

RAY.   No! never.

SNORKEY.   Beg pardon, Cap'n, what are we to do with this here game we've brought down?

RAY.   The Magistrates will settle with him.

SNORKEY.   Come, old fellow!

BYKE.   One word, I beg. My conduct, I know, has been highly reprehensible. I have acted injudiciously, and have been the occasion of more or less inconvenience to every one here. But I wish to make amends, and therefore I tender you all in this public manner my sincere apologies. I trust this will be entirely satisfactory.

RAY.   Villain!

BYKE.   I have a word to say to you, sir.

SNORKEY.   Come, that's enough.

BYKE.   My good fellow, don't interrupt gentlemen who are conversing together. (*To Ray.*) I address you, sir—you design to commit me to the care of the officers of the law?

RAY.   Most certainly.

BYKE.   And you will do your best towards having me incarcerated in the correctional establishments of this country? (*Ray bows.*)

SNORKEY.   How very genteel!

BYKE.   Then I have to say if you will, I shall make a public exposure of certain matters connected with a certain young lady.

LAURA.   Do not think that will deter us from your punishment. I can bear even more than I have—for the sake of justice.

BYKE.   Excuse me, but I did not even remotely refer to you.

LAURA.   To whom, then?

BYKE (*pointing to Pearl*). To her.

RAY.   Miss Courtland?

BYKE.   O, dear! no, sir. The daughter of old Judas—the spurious child placed in *your* cradle, Miss Laura Courtland, when you were abducted from it by your nurse.

PEARL.   What does he say?

BYKE.   That you're a beggar's child—we have the proofs! Deliver me to prison, and I produce them.

RAY.   Wretch!

PEARL.   Then it's you, dear Laura, have been wronged—while I—

LAURA.   You are my sister still—whatever befalls!

PEARL.   Oh, I'm so glad it's so! Ray won't want to marry me, now—at least, I hope so; for I know he loves you—he always loved you—and you will be happy together.

RAY.   Pearl, what are you saying?

PEARL.   Don't interrupt me! I mean every word of it. Laura, I've been very foolish, I know. I ought to have tried to reunite you—but there is time.

RAY.   Dear Laura! Is there, indeed, still time? (*She gives her hand.*)

BYKE.   Allow me to suggest that a certain proposition I had the honor to submit has not yet been answered.

RAY.   Release him. (*Snorkey undoes his cords.*)

BYKE.   Thank you—not so rough! Thank you.

RAY.   Now, go—but remember, if you ever return to these parts you shall be tried, not only for this burglary, but for the attempt to kill that poor fellow.

BYKE.   Thank you. Good-bye. (*To Snorkey.*) Good-bye, my dear friend; overlook our little dispute, and write to me. (*Aside.*) They haven't caught Judas, and she shall make them pay handsomely for her silence, yet.

(*Enter Peachblossom.*)

PEACHBLOSSOM.   O Miss! O, such an accident—old Judas!

LAURA & BYKE.   Well?

PEACHBLOSSOM.   She was driving along the road away from here—just now, when her horse dashed close to the cliff and tumbled her down all of a heap. They've picked her up, and they tell me she is stone dead.

BYKE (*aside*). Dead! And carried her secret with her! All's up. I'll have to emigrate. (*Aloud.*) My friends, pardon my emotion—this melancholy event has made me a widower. I solicit your sympathies in my bereavement. (*Exit.*)

BERMUDAS.   Go to Hoboken and climb a tree! I guess I'll follow him and see he don't pick up anything on his way out. (*Exit Bermudas.*)

SNORKEY.   Well there goes a pretty moment of grief. Ain't he a cool 'un? If I ever sets up an ice cream saloon, I'll have him for a head freezer.

PEACHBLOSSOM.   O, Miss Laura, mayn't I live with you now, and never leave no more.

LAURA.   Yes, you shall live with me as long as you please.

SNORKEY.   That won't be long if I can help it. (*Peachblossom blushes.*) Beg pardon. I suppose we'd better be going. The ladies must be tired, Cap'n, at this time of night.

RAY.   Yes, it is night! It is night always for me. (*Moving towards door.*)

LAURA (*placing one hand on his shoulder, taking his hand*). But there is a to-morrow. You see it cannot be dark forever.

PEARL.   Hope for to-morrow, Ray.

LAURA.   We shall have cause to bless it, for it will bring the long sought sunlight of our lives.

Curtain.

END

FOCUS QUESTIONS

1. Show how Daly uses *Under the Gaslight* to critique upper-class society.
2. Develop character sketches of Snorkey and Peachblossom in which you contrast their lower societal values.
3. How does Daly depict the criminal world through characters like Byke and Old Judas?
4. Develop your own definition of melodrama using *Under the Gaslight* as an example.
5. List ways in which the use of music/songs and other production details evoke the mood and atmosphere of post-Civil War New York.
6. Discuss how physical settings create a panoramic view of New York in this period.
7. How does the play promote the ideals of democracy?

OTHER ACTIVITIES

1. Research and collect into a scrapbook the visual documentation that illustrates the contemporary period of which Daly wrote.
2. Discuss the influence of Daly's sensational train-rescue scene on American silent film.
3. Stage the Tombs court scene (III, i), re-creating the acting style of melodrama.

BIBLIOGRAPHY

Daly, Augustin. ''The American Dramatist.'' *The North American Review* 142 (May 1886).

Daly, Joseph F. *The Life of Augustin Daly*. New York: Macmillan, 1917.

Felheim, Marvin. *The Theater of Augustin Daly*. New York: Greenwood Press, 1969.

Gerould, Daniel, ed. *American Melodrama*. New York: PAJ Publications, 1983.

McConachie, Bruce A. *Melodramatic Formations: American Theatre and Society, 1820–1870*. Iowa City: University of Iowa Press, 1992.

Quinn, Arthur Hobson. *A History of the American Drama, from the Civil War to the Present Day*. New York: Appleton-Century-Crofts, 1936.

Shaal, David. ''The Rehearsal Situation at Daly's Theatre.'' *Educational Theatre Journal* 14 (March 1962).

Skinner, Otis. *Footlights and Spotlights*. Indianapolis: Bobbs-Merrill, 1924.

Towse, J. Ranken. ''An American School of Dramatic Art: A Critical Review of Daly's Theatre.'' *Century Magazine* 56 (1898).

Wilmeth, Don, and Rosemary Cullen, eds. *Plays*. New York: Cambridge University Press: 1984.

Winter, William. *Vagrant Memories*. New York: George Doran, 1915.

RECOMMENDED VIDEOTAPE

Under the Gaslight. VHS. 118 min. 1969. Indiana University at South Bend.

GHOSTS
HENRIK IBSEN (1828–1906)

Ibsen supplies the want left by Shakespeare.

—BERNARD SHAW

APPROACHING REALISM

Reconciling as equal but separate and diverse cultural traditions of the ancient Norse lands, now Sweden, Norway, Denmark, and Iceland—the Scandinavian drama has survived political challenges and maintained strong artistic ties with the European continent. Yet it has been misunderstood by those unacquainted with the Scandinavian languages, especially when the quality and availability of important works in translation have remained scarce. It has been further undermined by the "geographical-climatological fallacy"[1] that has exaggerated the influence of a cold climate and barren terrain on the Scandinavian artistic temperament. Fortunately such cultural misconceptions have had little negative impact on the reputation of Norway's foremost poet and playwright, Henrik Ibsen, whose dramatic achievements immortalized Scandinavia's theatrical tradition during the second half of the nineteenth century, just as they continue to resonate powerfully on contemporary stages all over the world.

Ibsen belongs to a distinctive circle of playwrights whose works have been tempered by the events of human history. His prolific dramatic art proved an eloquent harbinger of major literary reform, prompted by political and social upheaval that swept through Europe in 1848, when bloody skirmishes signaled the demise of the Second Empire and artists and writers turned to folklore and the common people for inspiration and strength. Although Ibsen, at twenty years of age, was only a helpless bystander, the impact of this spirit of nationalism triggered his imagination and spawned the bold themes and powerful characters of his prose plays almost thirty years later.

Ibsen also witnessed the call for **realism** sweeping the continent on its stages, in its novels, and on its canvases. Historically accurate and realistic stage pictures dominated productions of melodrama and the plays of Shakespeare, Schiller, and Hugo. (See Preface to Hugo, p. 476.) Mid-nineteenth-century novelists like Balzac, Flaubert, and Stendhal were establishing a new genre that focused on the impact of the social milieu on the bourgeoisie. In the art world, painters like Turner and Courbet, who claimed that "beauty afforded by nature [stood] above all artistic conventions . . . I give you real nature, crudities, violences and all," attempted to capture realistic landscapes.[2]

While these movements toward realism were brewing on the continent, Ibsen distracted himself with his duties as artistic director of the Christiania Norsk Theater from 1857 to its collapse in 1862. (He had previously served as playwright-in-residence at Bergen's Norsk Theater.) But the theatre scene in Norway at the second half of the nineteenth century seemed as colorless as the first half: superficial and bourgeois entertainments sponsored by the Royal Theatre of Copenhagen; many inexperienced acting companies; tired revivals of familiar works; and, worst of all, a conspicuous absence of new Norwegian plays. Discouraged that his menial tasks provided no workable solutions to these artistic shortcomings, he decided to withdraw from theatre management altogether and apply himself solely to the ideals of literature and to the creation of a new drama. So he exiled himself to Italy during the summer of 1864 and remained an infrequent visitor to his homeland during the next twenty-seven years.

What happened in Italy reflected the creative turmoil of one who must first liberate *himself* before he can liberate his art. It was clear that, at the age of thirty-six, his instincts as a poet, renewed by this joy of freedom, had been nourished by other influential sources. One was the Danish philosopher and theologian, Søren Kierkegaard (1813–1855), whose free-thinking ideas permeated the fashionable literary circles Ibsen carefully avoided back in Norway. Kierkegaard's cry for self-liberation and a revolution of the spirit of humankind echoed Ibsen's, although the playwright claimed to have "read little of Kierkegaard and understood less."[3] Still the need to find oneself and *become* that person at all costs had already seized his creative powers and would not let go. Another source hard to ignore was the German philosopher, Friedrich Hegel (1770–1831), whose popular theory of the all-embracing unity of the spirit was harmonious with Ibsen's own crusade for freedom and spiritual growth. Whether intentional or not, the playwright's journey toward selfhood attracted inspiring company.

This personal quest for liberation soon became the single most eloquent theme of Ibsen's new playwriting phase, despite the controversial, often negative repercussions it would generate on the stage. *Brand* (1866) and *Peer Gynt* (1867) epitomized his brooding romantic spirit during these early years of exile. Originally conceived as epic poems for dramatic readings, they heralded his role as national playwright and thinker and proved notable for their eccentric protagonists and ambitious themes. (The eponymous Brand was believed to be partly modeled on Kierkegaard.) Produced nine years after it was written and enhanced by Edvard Grieg's musical score, *Peer Gynt* would find renewed popularity in twentieth-century performances.

Ibsen was reluctant at first to abandon the well-established verse format that had previously enhanced the historical characters and events of plays he wrote between 1849 and 1862. As he witnessed European theatre practices steadily responding to the modern sensibilities of the audience, he was left with little choice but to explore the wider artistic options of realistic prose, a style noted as his awesome contribution to the literature of the modern stage.

MAJOR WORKS

Ibsen's prose plays include *The Pillars of Society* (1877); *A Doll House* (1879); *Ghosts* (1881); *An Enemy of the People* (1882); *The Wild Duck* (1884); *Rosmersholm* (1886); *The Lady from the Sea* (1888); *Hedda Gabler* (1890); *The Master Builder* (1892); *Little Eyolf* (1894); *John Gabriel Borkman* (1896); and *When We Dead Awaken* (1899). Their powerful themes include the inequality of the sexes; the endangerment of political systems; the conflict of reality and illusion; the destructive price of material success; and the tyranny of ideals. While each of his works is memorable for its own special reasons, *Ghosts* has endured as one of the most controversial.

THE ACTION

Helene Alving has built an orphanage to commemorate her late husband, the respected Captain Alving. Their son Osvald has returned from Paris for the occasion. During the preparation for the dedication ceremony, painful memories and truths are brought to light: that Captain Alving led a dissolute life that destroyed his wife's happiness; that the man she really loved had forced her to return to Alving; that Osvald is deteriorating from venereal disease inherited from his father; and that the household servant is really Captain Alving's illegitimate daughter.

At the end of the day, the orphanage as well as the myths surrounding the Captain's memory have been destroyed. When Osvald is alone with his mother, he reveals the gruesome details of his disease to her and exposes a lethal dose of morphine, which he urges her to administer before he is reduced to idiocy. As he speaks, his mind collapses and the panic-stricken Mrs. Alving must decide what to do.

STRUCTURE AND LANGUAGE

Ghosts was written immediately after *A Doll House,* whose protagonist Nora follows the convictions of her newly raised consciousness by leaving her husband and children to find equality and respect elsewhere. The play was followed by *An Enemy of the People,* where pollution—literally and metaphorically—informs the dramatic action. Hence the shattered ideals of marriage and the consequences of living with lies, important themes that identify both of these anchor plays, converge in *Ghosts* and enlighten the emerging patterns of Ibsen's prose cycle. Yet each play would remain independent of the other, either as a reading experience or in performance.

Environment has always shaped human destiny in the Alving household, whether we observe its inhabitants in action or listen to them sermonize on their pasts. Even the unrelenting "devil's rain," as Regina Engstrand sarcastically calls it, drenches the bleak landscape against which this domestic drama unfolds. Rain is an ironic contrast to the sun and warmth of Sorrento and Rome, where Ibsen wrote the play, and its presence would suggest that he was not impervious to the influence of nature on his characters' behaviors after all. Osvald's artistic vision has been filled "with light and sun," while his morbid preoccupation with "the sun—the sun" gives the play its shattering final image. But unlike his European contemporaries whose prosaic styles often blurred their investigation of newer theatrical forms, Ibsen's visionary poetic principles and powerful use of subtext guide the play's characters, theme, and design from an expository first act to its unsettling conclusion.

When Osvald first appears in act 1, dressed in his father's overcoat and smoking his father's pipe, Pastor Manders instantly recognizes "a look around the corners of the mouth, something about the lips, that's the very picture of Alving." Although Helene Alving is quick to deny any resemblance, she knows at once that the ghost of her dead husband is alive in her son, despite her wish that Osvald not "inherit the least little thing from his father." Protecting her responsibility for Osvald's emotional and financial needs, she assures Manders that "everything my son inherits will come from me, and no one else." Her words are ironically prophetic, for she has not only unknowingly transmitted the physical infection that ravages Osvald's brain, but has innocently confirmed Osvald's conviction that "the sins of the fathers are visited upon the children," a motif sounded earlier by Euripides, echoed in the Bible, and suggested by the findings of Darwin.

The Alving household is observed through several different psychological perspectives, all of which surround the unseen Captain. The crippled Engstrand and the self-righteous Manders, both bearing physical and spiritual stigmas, represent aspects of evil and repression. They are the human remains of old attitudes and dead ideologies that still contaminate the present. In contrast, Osvald and Regina, the play's youthful inheritors, might have anticipated happy futures were it not for the shocking disclosure early in act 3 that thwarts their relationship and hastens their respective physical and spiritual demises. Finally, as guardian of her dead husband's sexual profligacy—an ironic legacy that pervades the oppressive *mise-en-scène*—Helene Alving must not only attend to what happens when truth is suppressed in behalf of the ideal, but must also suffer the consequences.

Ghosts is Ibsen's most compact play, whose issues—in spite of their apparent directness—remain hidden. Its dark vision and spare design recall the classical Greek drama, whose protagonists suffer tragic consequences when they attempt to impose their own sense of order. But Ibsen inverts the classical design by introducing a woman whose crisis is the result of accepting the established order. Furthermore, his concern with contemporary issues and his wish that audiences could feel "they are listening to something that is happening in real life"[4] are enhanced by the same well-made-play features that Eugene Scribe had popularized. (See Preface to Augustin Daly, p. 518.) Characters serve specific ends; events, both on stage and off, remain logically connected and sharply paced; and whispered disclosures hinge upon each other, culminating in a climactic third-act confrontation. Yet Ibsen was convinced that *Ghosts* was "a picture of life."[5]

On one hand, *Ghosts* is markedly naturalistic because of its thematic, almost clinical preoccupation with heredity—just one aspect of its title. On the other hand, its symbolism exposes the more insidious theme of hypocrisy, that is, the corrupt value system which Helene Alving has dutifully upheld in the name of respectability but which Ibsen chooses

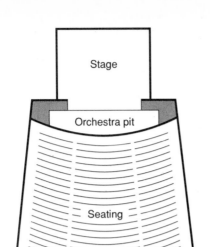

Ground plan of a modern proscenium arch theatre.

to attack. What emerges is hardly a conflict of old and new playwriting conventions. Rather it is a revision of the well-made design that accommodates *Ghosts'* unresolved moral dilemma, which Ibsen has cleverly placed into the audience's hands.

GHOSTS-IN-PERFORMANCE

The realization of Ibsen's mature prose plays in performance was facilitated by the steady development of Scandinavian stage techniques during the 1880s. His scripts suited the modern tastes of European directors who were experimenting with the **fourth wall** conventions of the **box set,** whose carefully constructed interiors reflected their characters' personalities and the environment in which they lived. At the same time, the advent of electric stage lighting further enriched the illusion of stage reality so vital to the intimate settings of Ibsen's plays.

Published in Copenhagen on December 13, 1881, but quickly removed from bookshelves when its content was deemed shocking and offensive, *Ghosts* experienced an equally controversial reception when it reached the stage. Ironically, its world premiere took place in America, at the Aurora Turner Hall in Chicago on May 20, 1882. Having been rejected by all the Scandinavian theatres, the play was sponsored by the Norwegian-Danish Society and performed by local immigrants in a mixture of Norwegian and Danish. Helge Bluhme, who had performed briefly at the Mollergaten Theatre in Christiania, originated the role of Mrs. Alving. Unfortunately, the performance—believed to be the first on record of any Ibsen play in America—was not covered by the local press, which is why so little is known about it.

From late August to mid-October of 1883, productions appeared successively in Sweden, Denmark, and Norway. The German premiere took place on April 14, 1886 under the direction of Georg II, Duke of Saxe-Meiningen. Four years later, on May 30, 1890, the play was produced by the Théâtre Libre under the artistic direction of André Antoine, who also portrayed Osvald. By March 13, 1891, England's Independent Theatre introduced *Ghosts* to London audiences at the Royalty Theatre. Reflecting on the scathing critical reception the play received there, Bernard Shaw came to Ibsen's defense: ''[Their] horror at *Ghosts* is a striking proof of the worthlessness of mere Bohemianism, which has all the idle sentimentality and idolatry of conventionality without any of its backbone of contract and law.''[6]

In America, where Ibsen's popularity has been demonstrated in countless productions of his plays, *Ghosts* has challenged many stage artists, especially in the role of Helene Alving. Almost to prove that Ibsen could succeed in America, a Bostonian named Mary Shaw (1860–1929) garnered important critical acclaim in a single performance of *Ghosts* at New York's Carnegie Lyceum Theatre in 1899. Playing Mrs. Alving with ''appalling realism,'' wrote critic Charles Henry Meltzer, the actress ''outdid herself in the interpretation of the sorrowful mother . . . Her repose in the long opening scenes was admirable. Her anguish when the climax came was heartrending.'' In his final confrontation with his mother, John Blair's Osvald was quietly pathetic and ''did not cry out for the sun. He babbled. His tongue thickened. He became a hopeless idiot.'' Meltzer thought the effect was ''infinitely greater than could be produced by more melodramatic readings.''[7]

As an outspoken feminist and Ibsenite, both on stage and off, Mary Shaw's association with *Ghosts* continued for many years. In 1903, she repeated the role, then traveled to Chicago, where she followed the engagement with a thirty-seven-week tour across America in an endless string of one-night stands, totaling 225 performances. On May 7, 1917, the Washington Square Players revived the play and invited her to head the cast. Her fans cheered loudly, and Ibsen's play was again praised by critics and audiences alike.

In 1923, the legendary Eleonora Duse (1859–1924) brought a repertory of international plays to New York, where they were performed in Italian at both the Metropolitan Opera and Century Theatre. *Ghosts* was among them. The sympathetic and fragile portrait of Helene Alving was ''full of memorable details,'' thanks to Duse's distinctive use of hands, face, and voice. Revealing a passive demeanor on occasion, and daring to upstage herself by showing her back to the audience, Duse dominated every scene ''by the mood of her tragic suffering.''[8] Critic John Corbin was especially impressed by Memo Benassi, who played Osvald ''with fine reticence, sparing us the clinical details so often stressed.''[9] But the world tour ended tragically with Duse's death in Pittsburgh, less than six months later.

A different side to the character surfaced in the performance of Minnie Maddern Fiske (1865–1932) at the Mansfield Theatre in New York on January 10, 1927, in a production that gave twenty-seven performances. Audiences already familiar with the play were surprised to discover that Mrs. Fiske, as she was popularly called, had uncovered ''the inner laughter'' of Ibsen's protagonist ''in her amusement towards the blundering Manders and the hypocritical Engstrand.''[10] Furthermore, she managed to turn Mrs. Alving into a ''quick-witted, shrewd-tongued woman, aware of polite scorns, practiced with ready ironies.''[11] Fiske made a lasting impression on audiences who were eager by now for less conventional interpretations of Ibsen's work.

When the Russian-born Alla Nazimova (1879–1945) stepped on the stage of New York's Empire Theatre on December 12, 1935, in an elaborate staging that she also directed, Ibsen's slightly dusty reputation was greatly invigorated. The Alving drawing-room contained high clear walls with panels set back and framed by tall windows. An immense upstage window opened on two mountains in the distance, beyond which the fjord and clean sky could be seen. Amid such splendid decor, the imperious Nazimova ''[brought] the play forward, out of argument into the eternal realities of human feeling and experience.''[12]

In her final scene with Harry Ellerbe, who brought ''unusual distinction and harmony to the whole production''[13] she ''took the morphine from Osvald's outstretched hand, wavered for an agonizing moment between 'Yes' and 'No,' exclaimed with tremendous finality and decisiveness, 'Yes!' and crossed resolutely to the stricken Osvald as the curtain fell.''[14] Nazimova's production gave eighty-one performances.

By mid-century, audience taste was radically altered in the aftermath of World War II, and while Ibsen's plays were still regarded as masterpieces, they fell under sharper critical scrutiny. Thus it was no simple task for theatre artists to ''present Ibsen'' as if nothing had happened at home or abroad. This might account for the mixed critical reception that greeted the first professional New York revival of *Ghosts* since Nazimova's triumph, when Eva Le Gallienne (1899–1991) appeared as Helene Alving at the Cort Theatre in New York during the 1947–48 theatre season.

Born in London, but establishing herself quite early as one of America's most versatile stage artists, Le Gallienne founded her own Civic Repertory Theatre which, over many years, introduced a wide range of international plays to American audiences. Her earlier appearances in other Ibsen plays had won the respect of critics, and now, under Margaret Webster's direction, she was appearing in her own translation of *Ghosts*. (She would eventually translate all of Ibsen's twelve prose plays for publication between 1950 and 1960.)

But *Ghosts* had gained acceptance since its controversial reception in 1881, and Webster's production, according to Brooks Atkinson, ''needed more than respectability to make it come to life.''[15] Le Gallienne's performance became the focus of attention. Howard Barnes admired her ''tremendous authority, whether she [was] disclosing infamous secrets to a minister and her unwanted step-daughter, or preparing to relieve her rotting son from a terrible affliction. There is one point in which she cries unashamedly on the stage. There can be no question that the tears are real.''[16] Alfred Ryder did ''a particularly good job with Osvald, describing the whole progress of the character from filial affability through mounting terror to madness.''[17]

Ghosts continues to attract and repel. Its confrontation with the unspeakable, in terms of sex, marriage, and religious propriety, has challenged international stage directors and prompted some highly unconventional interpretations. Addressing a world plagued with disease, the repercussions of which are never defined, *Ghosts* forces the audience to grapple with its dilemmas.

REFLECTIONS ON GHOSTS

Rolf Fjelde's translations have served many English-language productions of Ibsen's plays.

Some years ago I taught my first introductory drama course with an anthology which contained the obligatory Ibsen play. In this case, it was *Hedda Gabler*. I was appalled by the quality of the translation. It was [William] Archer, and I had to apologize to my students, since this was *not* what Ibsen was. Here one had George Tesman bleating out repeatedly, "FAHN-cy that!" It was British to the core!

I had initially thought about translating *Peer Gynt,* having much admired that masterpiece of poetic drama. I had gone to Scandinavia on a fellowship and was in Copenhagen just before Christmas. It was one of those crisp, blue transitions into dusk when the wonderful clear northern air has the power of revelation. The first snowflakes were falling from an impending storm, and I walked into a bookstore and strolled down an aisle of books, saw *Peer Gynt* on the shelf, and pulled it out. There it was in verse, with illustrations, and I thought: I've been a poet and a publisher of poets. I've had contact and acquaintance with

Continued

Ezra Pound, T. S. Eliot, William Carlos Williams, e. e. cummings, and Marianne Moore. And here is Ibsen who began as a poet, as I had, and moved—for economic reasons, but also a need for utterance in a larger dimension—toward the field of drama. That, too, I had earlier experienced at the Yale Drama School, where I had first written plays. So I thought: here is a vital congruence of interests and talents that I share with Ibsen. And my indignation gave them force and form: that my students had to endure such abysmal translations. In fact, whenever Ibsen's name came up at literary cocktail parties in those days, people would say "He's a great writer, obviously. A pillar of the theatre! But those translations!" So I felt this was something I could usefully do.

At that time I was publishing a poetry magazine, and because we had done one of Ezra Pound's *Cantos,* I visited him at St. Elizabeth's Hospital many times, where we talked mainly about contemporary poetry. He was very adamant on finding something one could do to add to the general store of literature. I guess in a kind of subtle suasion he pointed me toward productively exploring my Scandinavian heritage. And of course, he was very strong on translation. He had done those beautiful, stunningly lucid translations from the Chinese. And Ibsen does share a quality of the pure immediacy of Chinese poetry. *Peer Gynt* was written in verse. *Ghosts* is a prose play. But when you get into that prose, it has a biblical, spare simplicity that reflects the mind and sensibility of a poet.

So I said to myself, this is what has been missing. This is what Archer and so many of the other translators lacked. Eva Le Gallienne had a splendid background in theatre; but she was not a poet, she was not a writer. So I thought I could make Ibsen's prose plays luminous and resonant with image and metaphor and all the things Ibsen had put into them. I had to understand what was in the Norwegian. But what I crucially had was a love for the English language and for American speech, and the capacity to bring across—in a way that was natural—the innate poetry which was in the originals.

Years ago one of my professors remarked that the triumph of style is to be unaware of its existence. In Ibsen's style, you can feel the impulse of passions under the surface, of depths of language which demand a unique kind of mastery; and yet the language in its aptness and its concision is so completely in touch with the underlying reality that you feel the style is invisible. We're dealing with actual human beings; one senses that this is the way—*naturally*—they would talk. Their dialogue has a tremendous authenticity and artfulness in its Norwegian expression to challenge the American translator. What *Ghosts,* for example, has that is so often missed by an insensitive translator is the same immensity of implication that belongs to great poetry. Poetry is allusive. Poetry takes us deep into the psyche, into the cosmos, into the body politic, as Shakespeare's plays do. Ibsen has that same kind of enormous implication, which means that *Ghosts*—although it seems to be and has been produced wrongly as a naturalistic case study—is ultimately about the loving history of Western civilization at a time of profound crisis.

We meet Mrs. Alving, whose name is Helene, almost identical with the Greek "Helena." Pastor Manders is the Christian overlay, which has darkened and repressed her natural Greek pride in and love of life. As Osvald says: "Not a glimmer of sunlight the whole day long!" So Ibsen tries to rescue these two characters who were meant to be together, but were separated by their basic beliefs. Helene recalls how she went to him in the middle of the night, crying "Take me in!" She loved him, as he loved her. But he couldn't open to her because of his doctrinaire religious convictions, which are merely external and have died into a static formality—the Second Empire, as Ibsen calls it. Manders' only concern is how the community will regard him. So he tells her to go back to her abusive husband, pick up her cross and bear it. In this symbolic attraction between Helene and Manders is that natural Greek spontaneity, that love of color and light and sound that enchanted Ibsen when he went to Italy and learned about the classic world firsthand. Being separated from what is the most natural sort of union is the man of God, whom Ibsen mocks here, not because he mocks God (Ibsen was a deeply religious human being) but because he does not believe in a rote-learned, alienated Christianity. Osvald should have been the child of both of them, but instead is the product of Captain Alving, who himself was maimed.

Perhaps the greatest spiritual unfolding of the play lies in Helene Alving's admission that she is at fault. In the first act, she refers only to what Alving did to her, but by the third act, she recognizes her error in judging her husband from Manders' narrow point of view: namely, that the reason we are in this vale of tears is to suffer and to find salvation in an afterlife. But Ibsen says no! Salvation is *here* in *this* life, through recovering the seeds of glory that this life consists in, but at the same time, transcends in a dimension of meaning which can only be thought of as religious. In fact, all of Ibsen's characters tell us lessons about where the place of the evolving spirit is in our world picture. If they fail, if they miss it, their shortcomings are also part of the growing truth.

With Ibsen the question is always: how can we be whole? How can we be what we are meant to be? Which is what Peer Gynt's quest is all about. Ibsen proclaimed in one of his letters that the age of Shakespeare was over, that he could no longer strive to write in magnificent verse, but must write in truthful prose and specifically about the actual lives we live. That's why his prose plays all interrelate in atmosphere, themes, and characters. I don't believe he deliberately sat down to write these plays as one cycle. But as he began writing, he gradually realized that they were moving into a cycle format. The nineteenth century was the age of cycle works anyway—Balzac, Wagner, Zola—so Ibsen felt comfortable shaping this total panorama as such. *Ghosts* has a meaning in itself, but it also has a greater meaning—as it has an integral place—within this larger structure.

When I translate, I "play" all the parts. Recalling Stanislavski's teaching about the illusion of the first time, I make it a point *not* to read the material I'm going to translate for some months beforehand. Then I approach each speech as the advancing edge of consciousness: nobody knows anything more about the play than has happened up to that moment of dialogue. I suspect that Ibsen was every character in each play, which is one reason why there are no one-hundred percent bad characters or good characters. Every Ibsen character who seems bad has a germ of goodness. Every person who is good has a germ of evil. It's much like the *yin-yang* symbol, because in one part of this sigmoid shape is the dot which is the opposite that's present in it. Justifiably there are productions which say, this is going to be an Osvald-focused production; or this is going to be a Mrs. Alving-focused production. Or I'm going to do it in a Brechtian style of exposé and show Pastor Manders as the dead hand of religion casting an opiate pall on everything.

As translator, I am trying to convey the complete multifaceted reality that Ibsen created, in the same sense that he once said: my plays are not plays, they are real life. We know he spent two years on each prose play, thinking and rethinking it, usually doing a

Continued

first draft, a second draft, then a final one, in which we can trace the stages in the growing complexity of each work, to the point of our seeing Ibsen walking around and circumspecting each of his characters. Out of my own background as a poet, a playwright, a Norwegian descendant, with even a nineteenth-century family connection with Ibsen himself, all of these points of congruency have given me an immense satisfaction, helping me, as translator, to play all of these characters—some one-hundred and eight parts in the prose cycle.

I translate both for the actor as well as the reader, and view this as a mutually reinforcing process. But I was unusually fortunate in that Ibsen himself saw it this way, too. We know that with every one of his plays, he prepared a text for the Christmas book market. That was the time when Scandinavians bought books and exchanged them as gifts. So he first saw his work "premiered" to the public in a readable version which, as soon as possible, was then transferred to the stage. While his plays easily addressed both audiences, earlier translations failed to achieve this duality: they were either too theatrical without a sense of literary resonance, or they were too literary without a sense of the theatrical. In the European theatre today, where the tradition is stronger than in America, men and women of the theatre are, as well, *literarily* trained. In America, however, theatre people get unduly nervous when they are around "literary people" because they think the play will not be theatrical. In the ideal, however, in the highest achievements of the greatest periods of the drama, it has always been the summit of both: from the ancient Greeks, to Shakespeare, to Racine and Molière. Ibsen represents another one of those summits.

Translation has to be distinguished from adaptation. Adaptation has its place in the theatre, but is only justified when the culture is too far removed either in time or space, that you really have to change elements of the actuality of the situation to make them intelligible for the audience here. Now Ibsen is so very close to us that one does not have to adapt in that sense. But occasionally I have had to do what I call a "mini-adaptation" regarding a phrase I did not find intelligible. It struck me, for example, as superb that Engstrand says to Regina, "Come along, wench, you'll live soft as a yoke in an egg." Every listener recognizes this, and I didn't have to adapt it. But later, I have Regina say, "I'll be barefoot at Christmas," adapted from the Norwegian, which says that she'll find herself out in the bare hills. This is a traditional folk expression, an idiomatic phrase, that lacks immediacy to an English-speaking listener.

Where does Osvald get his desire for the sun in the chilling final scene? Recent studies have told us that one of the things that happens frequently in this kind of schizophrenic breakdown is an obsession with the sun. Somehow Ibsen knew this psychopathology. But he also knew it poetically, since the sun is centrally implied by its very absence, as everything about the play's initial environment is hidden from the light. But Osvald additionally talks about it in regard to what painting was becoming in Paris at the time. So the sun as well appears in a verbalized description of a painting. Was Ibsen alluding to the great painting movement which, at that time, was Impressionism? The sun as an image appears on the stage in relation to something Osvald wants to get back to and artistically realize: he wants to return to his impressionistic painting. So there are these fascinating webs of correspondence.

Nothing ever terminates in an Ibsen play. This is a very important point to understand and is another of Ibsen's major breaks with the past. Instead, Ibsen throws the play at his audience as if to say: my works are only meaningful as they complete themselves in *your* experience. This was a part of his "New Age" vision, so to speak, in an attempt to affect and change our lives. He's given us the very healing apparatus we need to deal with: a revelatory experience that has a beginning, a middle, and an end. But the end is not really an end, because he's saying it ends in us. As readers, we are exactly in the position he wanted his audience to be in: seekers for wholeness along with him.

Ghosts is a play about euthanasia. It is also about venereal disease as a descending curse that comes down in a way that metaphorically expresses how the past imprisons us, just as it is about the yearning for self-liberation. For ours is a time of epochal transition in history. We are capable today of so much more, and yet—as he says in one of his famous poems—"we are sailing with a corpse in the cargo." We are surrounded by "ghosts." Not just our past, but all of these dead ideas that hold us back. We are enmeshed in ghosts and are so miserably afraid of the light. We are living with polluted lives. It's fascinating that the next play Ibsen writes—*An Enemy of the People*—is targeted at pollution in a public water supply. And once again, he's asking how we can clear the pollution out of our lives. It's not just cities that are polluted, it's not just rivers that are polluted, it's human lives that have been polluted by unhealthy, destructive thinking.

I think it would be wrong to rewrite the play, as I once saw it done, as if this were Ibsen writing about the AIDS crisis. I've always found that Ibsen is most effective when he is played in period with the references he sets up, so that, at some point, people look at each other or think within their privacy, "My God, this is the same as . . . " Ibsen is always on the brink of the future, writing like a prophet who sees the future implicit in the present. Ibsen's concern must involve an infectious disease, a "social" disease, which was a shocking thing to discuss at the time he wrote the play. Incidentally, this is another great part of the sanity and indispensability of Ibsen's mind: he believes *we must discuss these things.* The raising and amplification of consciousness is part of Ibsen's whole moral quest. It represents the prophetic resonance, the contemporary analogy that refuses to be spelled out so completely. That's why audiences discover that this heartrending play is not happening in 1882, but is happening now. That's why Ibsen never died. Helene Alving's symbolic nomenclature represents the continual coming of the light.

Regarding a German translation, Ibsen once said that all of his characters in all of his plays have their individual modes of speaking. Ibsen was angry that the translator failed to capture this. Ibsen is not a univocal playwright, one who is filled with *me*. Life is greater than art, which is the message of Ibsen's last play, *When We Dead Awaken*. We will all discover that we should have given ourselves first to life, rather than art. Of course, Ibsen is always bigger than his characters, and every one of his plays gives itself to life. How beauteous is mankind that contains such various creatures, although Ibsen simply embodies, but doesn't make that exclamation.

I interfere as little as possible with the production of one of my Ibsen translations, because it's always the new production that teaches me something new about the play. Sometimes I can clear up some technical points; but I want every production not to violate a concept I have established, but to show me another dimension within which the play can be appreciated. An acquaintance of mine was responsible for the first Jordanian production of *Ghosts,* in my translation. It created such tension that it was almost grounds for closing

Continued

the theatre. If we still think this is pretty steamy stuff to be talking about in public, in Islamic Jordan it was unthinkable. It was only the presence in the audience of one of the country's leaders that permitted *Ghosts* to go on. These plays are still detonating life-enhancing and life-affirming responses all over the world, saying: think for yourself; act out of truth; examine and bear witness to your own reality. All over the world, actors continue to find indelible and imperishable meaning in Ibsen's work.

Copyright © Rolf Fjelde.

Notes

1. *F. J. Marker and L. L. Marker,* THE SCANDINAVIAN THEATRE: A SHORT HISTORY *(Oxford: Basil Blackwell, 1975), ix.*
2. *Childe Reese, "Experts Disagree,"* MAGAZINE OF ART *(April 1945): 148.*
3. *Meyer,* IBSEN, *176.*
4. *Ibid, 518.*
5. *Toby Cole, ed.,* PLAYWIGHTS ON PLAYWRITING *(New York: Hill & Wang, 1961), 154.*
6. THE QUINTESSENCE OF IBSENISM *(New York: Hill & Wang, 1957), 94.*
7. CRITERION, *3 June 1899.*
8. *Percy Hammond,* NEW YORK TRIBUNE, *9 Nov. 1923.*
9. THE NEW YORK TIMES, *9 Nov. 1923.*
10. *Alexander Woollcott,* NEW YORK WORLD, *11 Jan. 1927.*
11. BOSTON TRANSCRIPT, *22 March 1927.*
12. *Stark Young,* NEW REPUBLIC, *1 Jan. 1936, p. 230.*
13. *Ibid.*
14. *Schanke,* IBSEN IN AMERICA, *110.*
15. THE NEW YORK TIMES, *17 Feb. 1948.*
16. NEW YORK HERALD TRIBUNE, *17 Feb. 1948.*
17. *Atkinson, 17 Feb. 1948.*

GHOSTS
Henrik Ibsen
Translated by Rolf Fjelde

CHARACTERS

Mrs. Helene Alving, *widow of Captain Alving, late Court Chamberlain*

Osvald Alving, *her son, a painter*
Pastor Manders
Engstrand, *a carpenter*

Regina Engstrand, *in service with Mrs. Alving*

The action takes place on Mrs. Alving's country estate by a large fjord in West Norway.

ACT ONE

A large garden room, with a door in the left-hand wall, and two doors in the wall to the right. In the middle of the room a round table with chairs grouped about it; on the table lie books, magazines, and newspapers. In the left foreground, a window, and next to it a small sofa with a sewing table in front of it. In the background, the room is extended into a somewhat smaller greenhouse, whose walls are great panes of glass. From the right side of the greenhouse, a door leads into the garden. Through the glass walls a somber fjord landscape can be glimpsed, half hidden by the steady rain.

ENGSTRAND is standing by the garden door. His left leg is partly deformed; under his bootsole he has a wooden block. REGINA, with an empty garden syringe in her hand, is trying to keep him from entering.

REGINA (*in a low voice*). What do you want? Just stay where you are. Why, you're dripping wet.
ENGSTRAND. It's God's own rain, my girl.
REGINA. The devil's rain, it is!
ENGSTRAND. Jeez, how you talk, Regina. (*Hobbles a few steps into the room.*) But now, what I wanted to say—
REGINA. Stop stomping about with that foot, will you! The young master's sleeping upstairs.
ENGSTRAND. Still sleeping? In broad daylight?

REGINA. That's none of your business.
ENGSTRAND. I was out on a binge last night—
REGINA. I can imagine.
ENGSTRAND. Yes, because we mortals are weak, my girl—
REGINA. Yes, so we are.
ENGSTRAND. And temptations are manifold in this world, you see— But for all of that, I was on the job, so help me God, five thirty this morning early.
REGINA. All right now, get out of here. I'm not going to stand around, having a rendezvous with you.
ENGSTRAND. You're not going to have any what?
REGINA. I'm not going to have anyone meeting you here. So—on your way.
ENGSTRAND (*a few steps closer*). Damned if I'll go before I've had my say with you. This afternoon I'll be done with my work down at the schoolhouse, and then I'll rip right back to town by the night boat.
REGINA (*mutters*). Pleasant trip!
ENGSTRAND. Thank you, my girl. Tomorrow they'll be dedicating the orphanage, and there'll probably be all kinds of carrying-on here, and hard liquor, you know. And nobody's going to say about Jacob Engstrand that he can't put temptation behind him.
REGINA. Ha!

ENGSTRAND. Yes, because you know a lot of the best people'll be here tomorrow. Pastor Manders is expected from town.

REGINA. He's coming today.

ENGSTRAND. There, you see. And I'll be damned if he's going to get anything on me.

REGINA. Ah, so *that's* it!

ENGSTRAND. What do you mean, *that?*

REGINA (*looks knowingly at him*). Just what are you out to trick him into this time?

ENGSTRAND. Shh, are you crazy? Would *I* trick the pastor into anything? Oh no, Pastor Manders, he's been much too good to me for that. But it's what I wanted to talk to you about, see—that I'll be leaving for home then, tonight.

REGINA. The sooner the better.

ENGSTRAND. Yes, but I want you along with me, Regina.

REGINA (*open-mouthed*). You want me along—? What did you say?

ENGSTRAND. I'm saying I want you back home with me.

REGINA (*scornfully*). Back home with you? Never. Not a chance!

ENGSTRAND. Oh, we'll see about that.

REGINA. Yes, you can bet we will, all right. *I,* who've been brought up by Mrs. Alving—? Been taken in like one of the family—? *I* should move back with *you?* To a house like that? Pah!

ENGSTRAND. What the devil is this? You trying to cross your own father, you slut?

REGINA (*mutters, without looking at him*). You've always said I had no part of you.

ENGSTRAND. Ahh, never mind about that—

REGINA. How many times haven't you cursed me and called me a—*fi donc!*

ENGSTRAND. So help me God if I've ever used such a dirty word.

REGINA. Oh, I haven't forgotten the word you used.

ENGSTRAND. Yes, but that was only when I had some drink in me—hm. Temptations are manifold in this world, Regina.

REGINA. Ugh!

ENGSTRAND. And when your mother got nasty, see—then I had to find something to needle her with. Always made herself so refined. (*Mimics.*) ''Let go of me, Engstrand! Leave me be! I've been three years in service to Chamberlain Alving at Rosenvold!'' (*Laughs.*) Jeez, that was something she never could forget—that the captain was made a chamberlain while she was in service there.

REGINA. Poor mother—you bullied the life out of her soon enough.

ENGSTRAND (*with a shrug*). Yes, that's right; I get the blame for everything.

REGINA (*in an undertone, as she turns away*). Ugh—! And that leg.

ENGSTRAND. What did you say, my girl?

REGINA. *Pied de mouton.*

ENGSTRAND. What's that—German?*

REGINA. Yes.

ENGSTRAND. Oh yes, you got some learning out here, and that's going to come in handy now, Regina.

REGINA (*after a short silence*). And what was it you wanted with me in town?

ENGSTRAND. How can you ask what a father wants with his only child? Aren't I a lonely, forsaken widower?

REGINA. Oh, don't give me that garbage. Why do you want me in town?

ENGSTRAND. All right, I'll tell you—I've been thinking of striking into something new.

REGINA (*with a snort*). You've done that so often, and it always goes wrong.

ENGSTRAND. Ah, but this time, Regina, you wait and see! Hell's bells—!

REGINA (*stamps her foot*). Stop swearing!

ENGSTRAND. Sh, sh! Perfectly right you are, my girl! I only wanted to say—I've put by a nice piece of change out of the work on this new orphanage.

REGINA. Have you? Well, that's good for you.

ENGSTRAND. Because what can you spend your money on here, out in the country?

REGINA. Well, so?

ENGSTRAND. Yes, so you see, I thought I might put the money into something that'd turn a profit. It was going to be a sort of hotel for seamen—

REGINA. Ugh-ah!

ENGSTRAND. A regular, first-class inn, you understand—not just any old pigsty for sailors. No, damn it all—it's going to be for ship captains and mates and—and real fine people, you understand.

REGINA. And how do I—?

ENGSTRAND. You? You get to help, see. Just for the look of things, if you follow me. There wouldn't be so damn much to do. You can have it just like you want it.

REGINA. I'll bet!

ENGSTRAND. But there've got be women on the premises, that's clear as day. Because we want a little life in the evenings—singing and dancing and that sort of thing. You have to remember, these are wayfaring seamen on the ocean of life. (*Comes nearer.*) Now don't be stupid and hold yourself back, Regina. What can you come to out here? What good can it do you, all this learning Mrs. Alving's paid out for? You're supposed to take care of the children, I hear, in the new orphanage. Is *that* anything for you, uh? Have you such a hunger to run yourself ragged for the sake of those filthy brats?

---

*''English,'' in the original, which loses meaning in an English translation.

REGINA.   No, if things go the way *I* want, then— And it could happen, all right. Yes, it could!

ENGSTRAND.   What could?

REGINA.   None of your business. Is it—quite a bit of money you made out here?

ENGSTRAND.   Between this and that, I'd say up to seven, eight hundred crowns.

REGINA.   That's not so bad.

ENGSTRAND.   It's enough for a start, my girl.

REGINA.   Don't you think you might give me some of that money?

ENGSTRAND.   No, I don't think I might!

REGINA.   Don't you think you could send me at least some cloth for a dress?

ENGSTRAND.   Just come with me into town, and you'll have dresses to burn.

REGINA.   Pah! I can do as well on my own, if I care to.

ENGSTRAND.   No, but it goes better, Regina, with a father's guiding hand. There's a nice house I can get now in Little Harbor Street. They don't want too much money down; and it could make some kind of seamen's home, all right.

REGINA.   But I don't want to stay with you! I've got no business with you. Get out!

ENGSTRAND.   You wouldn't stay so damn long with me, girl. No such luck—if you know how to show off yourself. A wench as good-looking as you've turned out these last two years—

REGINA.   Yes—?

ENGSTRAND.   It wouldn't be long before some ship's officer—maybe even a captain—

REGINA.   I'm not marrying any of those. Sailors don't have any *savoir-vivre.*

ENGSTRAND.   They don't have any what?

REGINA.   Let me tell you, I know about sailors. They aren't any sort to marry.

ENGSTRAND.   Then forget about getting married. That can pay just as well. (*More confidentially.*) Him—the Englishman—the one with the yacht—he gave three hundred dollars, he did—and she was no better looking than you.

REGINA (*advancing on him*). Get out of here!

ENGSTRAND (*steps back*). Easy now, you don't want to hit me.

REGINA.   Don't I! Talk about Mother, and you'll find out. Get out of here, I said! (*She forces him back toward the garden door.*) And no slamming doors; young Mr. Alving—

ENGSTRAND.   Yes, he's asleep. It's something all right, how you worry about young Mr. Alving— (*Dropping his voice.*) Ho-ho! It just wouldn't be that *he*—?

REGINA.   Out of here, quick! You're all mixed up! No not that way. There's Pastor Manders coming. Down the kitchen stairs.

ENGSTRAND (*moving to the right*). All right, I'm going. But you talk with *him* that's coming in. He's the one who'll

tell you what a child owes her father. Because, after all, I *am* your father, you know. I can prove it in the parish register.

(*He goes out by the farther door, which* REGINA *has opened, closing it after him. She hurriedly glances at herself in the mirror, fans herself with her handkerchief and straightens her collar, then busies herself with the flowers.* PASTOR MANDERS, *in an overcoat, carrying an umbrella along with a small traveling bag on a strap over his shoulder, comes through the garden door into the greenhouse.*)

MANDERS.   Good morning, Miss Engstrand.

REGINA (*turning with a pleasantly surprised look*). Why, Pastor Manders, good morning! The boat's already come?

MANDERS.   It just arrived. (*Entering the room.*) It's certainly tedious weather we've been having these days.

REGINA (*following him*). It's a godsend for the farmers, Pastor.

MANDERS.   Yes, you're quite right. That's something we townspeople hardly think of. (*He starts taking his overcoat off.*)

REGINA.   Oh, let me help you—that's it. My, how wet it is! I'll just hang it up in the hall. And the umbrella, too— I'll leave it open to dry.

(*She goes off with the things through the farther door on the right.* MANDERS *removes his traveling bag and sets it and his hat down on a chair, as* REGINA *returns.*)

MANDERS.   Ah, but it's good to be indoors. So—everything's going well out here?

REGINA.   Yes, thank you.

MANDERS.   But terribly busy, I suppose, getting ready for tomorrow?

REGINA.   Oh yes, there's plenty to do.

MANDERS.   And, hopefully, Mrs. Alving's at home?

REGINA.   Why, of course. She just went upstairs to bring the young master some hot chocolate.

MANDERS.   Yes, tell me—I heard down at the pier that Osvald was supposed to have come.

REGINA.   He got in the day before yesterday. We hadn't expected him before today.

MANDERS.   In the best of health, I hope?

REGINA.   Yes, just fine, thank you. But awfully tired after his trip. He came straight from Paris without a break—I mean, he went the whole route without changing trains. I think he's sleeping a little now, so we should talk just a tiny bit softer.

MANDERS.   Shh! We'll be so quiet.

REGINA (*as she moves an armchair up to the table*). Please now, do sit down, Pastor, and make yourself comfortable. (*He sits; she slips a footstool under his feet.*) That's it! Is that all right, Pastor?

MANDERS.   Just perfect, thank you. (*Regarding her.*) You know, Miss Engstrand, I definitely think you've grown since I saw you last.

REGINA.   Do you think so, Pastor? Mrs. Alving says that I've filled out, too.

MANDERS.   Filled out—? Well, yes, maybe a little—but acceptably. (*A short pause.*)

REGINA.   Shall I tell Mrs. Alving you're here?

MANDERS.   Oh, thank you, there's no hurry, my dear child—well, uh—but tell me now, Regina, how's it been going for your father out here?

REGINA.   Fairly well, Pastor, thank you.

MANDERS.   He was in to see me when he was last in town.

REGINA.   Really? He's always so happy when he can talk with you.

MANDERS.   And you make it your rule, of course, to look in on him daily.

REGINA.   I? Oh, yes, of course—whenever I have some time—

MANDERS.   Your father is not very strong in character, Miss Engstrand. He's woefully in need of a guiding hand.

REGINA.   Yes, I'm sure of that.

MANDERS.   He needs to have someone around him that he can love, and whose judgment carries some weight. He confessed as much quite frankly when he was last up to see me.

REGINA.   Yes, he said something like that to me. But I don't know if Mrs. Alving could spare me—especially now, when we've got the new orphanage to manage. And then I'd be so awfully unhappy to leave Mrs. Alving—she's always been so kind to me.

MANDERS.   But, my dear girl, a daughter's duty— Naturally, we'd first have to obtain Mrs. Alving's consent.

REGINA.   But I don't know if it would do for me, at my age, to keep house for a single man.

MANDERS.   What! But, my dear Miss Engstrand, this is your own father we're speaking of!

REGINA.   Yes, maybe so, but all the same—you see, if it were a *good* house, with a real gentleman—

MANDERS.   But, my dear Regina—

REGINA.   One I could care for and look up to, almost like a daughter—

MANDERS.   Yes, but my dear child—

REGINA.   Because I'd like so much to live in town. Out here it's terribly lonely—and you know yourself, Pastor, what it is to stand alone in the world. And I think I can say that I'm both capable and willing. Mr. Manders, don't you know of a place like that for me?

MANDERS.   I? No, I don't, for the life of me.

REGINA.   But dear, dear Mr. Manders—you will think of me, in any case, if ever—

MANDERS (*getting up*).   Yes, I'll remember, Miss Engstrand.

REGINA.   Yes, because if I—

MANDERS.   Perhaps you'll be good enough to tell Mrs. Alving I've come.

REGINA.   I'll go call her right away, Pastor.

(*She goes out left.* MANDERS *paces back and forth in the room a couple of times, then stands for a moment at the far end of the room, hands behind his back, looking out into the garden. He then returns to the table, picks up a book and looks at the title page, starts, and inspects several others.*)

MANDERS.   Hm—aha! Well!

(MRS. ALVING *comes in by the door, left. She is followed by* REGINA, *who immediately goes out by the nearer door to the right.*)

MRS. ALVING (*extending her hand*).   So good to see you, Mr. Manders.

MANDERS.   Good morning, Mrs. Alving. Here I am, just as I promised.

MRS. ALVING.   Always on the dot.

MANDERS.   But you can imagine, it was touch and go for me, getting away. All those blessed boards and committees—

MRS. ALVING.   All the more kind of you to come so promptly. Now we can get our business done before lunch. But where do you have your bags?

MANDERS (*hurriedly*).   My things are down at the general store—I took a room there for tonight.

MRS. ALVING (*repressing a smile*).   You can't be persuaded even yet to spend the night here in my house?

MANDERS.   No, no, really; thank you so much, but I'll stay down there as usual. It's so convenient to the boat.

MRS. ALVING.   Well, you do as you wish. But I really thought instead that two old people like us—

MANDERS.   Gracious me, the way you joke! Yes, of course you're in rare spirits today. First the celebration tomorrow, and then you've got Osvald home.

MRS. ALVING.   Yes, can you imagine how happy I am! It's more than two years since he was home last. And then he's promised to stay with me this whole winter.

MANDERS.   No, has he really? That's certainly a nice gesture for a son to make—because there must be other, quite different attractions to life in Rome and Paris, I'm sure.

MRS. ALVING.   Yes, but he has his mother here at home, you see. Oh, that dear, blessed boy—he still has room in his heart for me!

MANDERS.   It would really be tragic if distance and devotion to anything like art should dull his natural feelings.

MRS. ALVING.   You're perfectly right. But there's no chance at all of that with him. Oh, I'm going to be so curious to see if you still recognize him. He'll be down shortly; he's just stretched out to rest a little on the sofa upstairs. But now, my dear Mr. Manders—do sit down.

MANDERS.   Thank you. It *is* convenient, then—?

MRS. ALVING.   Why, of course. (*She sits at the table.*)

MANDERS.   Good. Then let's have a look— (*Goes over to the chair where his bag lies, takes out a sheaf of papers, sits at the opposite side of the table, and searches for a space to lay the papers out.*) Now here, first, we have— (*Breaks off.*) Tell me, Mrs. Alving, where did these books come from?

MRS. ALVING.   These books? I'm reading them.

MANDERS.   You read this sort of thing?

MRS. ALVING.   Yes, of course I do.

MANDERS.   Do you think you've grown any better or happier for this kind of reading?

MRS. ALVING.   I think it makes me feel more secure.

MANDERS.   That's astonishing. What do you mean?

MRS. ALVING.   Well, I find it clarifies and reinforces so many ideas I've been thinking out all to myself. Yes, that's the strange part, Mr. Manders—there's actually nothing really new in these books, nothing beyond what most people think and believe. It's simply that most people don't like to face these things, or what they imply.

MANDERS.   Oh, my dear God! You don't seriously consider that most people—?

MRS. ALVING.   Yes, I certainly do.

MANDERS.   Well, but not here in our society? Not among us?

MRS. ALVING.   Yes, definitely—among us, too.

MANDERS.   Well, I must say, really—!

MRS. ALVING.   But what exactly do you object to in these books?

MANDERS.   Object to? You surely don't think I waste my time exploring that kind of publication?

MRS. ALVING.   In other words, you know nothing of what you're condemning?

MANDERS.   I've read quite enough about these writings to disapprove of them.

MRS. ALVING.   Yes, but your own opinion—

MANDERS.   My dear Mrs. Alving, there are many circumstances in life where one has to entrust oneself to others. That's the condition of this world, and it's all for the best. How else could society function?

MRS. ALVING.   That's true; maybe you're right.

MANDERS.   Besides, I wouldn't deny that there's a certain fascination about such writings. And I can't blame you either for wanting to become acquainted with the intellectual currents that, I hear, are quite prevalent in the larger world—where you've let your son wander so long. But—

MRS. ALVING.   But—?

MANDERS (*dropping his voice*). But one needn't talk about it, Mrs. Alving. One doesn't have to recount to all and sundry everything one reads and thinks within one's own four walls.

MRS. ALVING.   No, of course not. I agree.

MANDERS.   Remember your obligations to the orphanage, which you decided to found at a time when your attitude toward things of the mind and spirit was so very different from now—at least as *I* see it.

MRS. ALVING.   Yes, I admit it, completely. But it was about the orphanage—

MANDERS.   It was about the orphanage we wanted to speak, yes. All the same—prudence, my dear Mrs. Alving! And now, let's turn to business. (*Opens a folder and takes out some papers.*) You see these?

MRS. ALVING.   The deeds?

MANDERS.   The whole set—in perfect order. You can imagine it hasn't been easy to get them in time. I actually had to apply some pressure. The authorities are almost painfully scrupulous when it comes to decisions. But here they are, in any case. (*Leafing through the papers.*) See, here's the duly recorded conveyance of title of the Solvik farm, said property being part of the Rosenvold estate, together with all buildings newly erected thereon, including the schoolhouse, the staff residence, and the chapel. And here's the official charter for the institution—and the by-laws governing its operation. You see—(*Reads.*) "By-laws governing the Captain Alving Memorial Orphan's Home."

MRS. ALVING (*looking at the papers for a long moment*). So—there it is.

MANDERS.   I chose "Captain" for the title, rather than "Court Chamberlain." "Captain" seems less ostentatious.

MRS. ALVING.   Yes, whatever you think.

MANDERS.   And here you've got the bankbook showing interest on capital reserved to cover the running expenses of the orphanage.

MRS. ALVING.   Thank you—but please, won't you hold onto it, for convenience' sake?

MANDERS.   Yes, gladly. I think we can leave the money in the bank for a time. It's true, the interest rate isn't very attractive: four percent, with a six-month withdrawal notice. If we could come across a good mortgage later on—naturally, it would have to be a first mortgage, of unquestionable security—then we could reconsider the situation.

MRS. ALVING.   Yes, dear Mr. Manders, you know best about all that.

MANDERS.   Anyway, I'll keep an eye out. But now there's one more thing I've meant several times to ask you.

MRS. ALVING.   And what's that?

MANDERS.   Should the orphanage be insured or not?

MRS. ALVING.   Why, of course, it has to be insured.

MANDERS.   Ah, not too fast, Mrs. Alving. Let's study this question a bit.

MRS. ALVING.   Everything I own is insured—buildings, furniture, crops, livestock.

MANDERS.   Obviously, when it's your own property. I do the same, naturally. But here, you see, it's a very different matter. This orphanage is going to be, so to say, consecrated to a higher calling.

MRS. ALVING.   Yes, but if—

MANDERS.   From my personal standpoint, I wouldn't find the slightest objection to insuring us against all eventualities—

MRS. ALVING.   No, I wouldn't either.

MANDERS.   But how would that sit with the public opinion hereabouts? You know better than I.

MRS. ALVING.   Public opinion, hm—

MANDERS.   Is there any considerable segment of opinion—I mean, really important opinion—that might take offense?

MRS. ALVING.   Well, what do you mean, exactly, by important opinion?

MANDERS.   I was thinking mainly of people of such independent and influential position that one could hardly avoid giving their opinions a certain weight.

MRS. ALVING.   There are a few like that here who might possibly take offense if—

MANDERS.   There, you see! In town we have any number of them. The congregations of other churches, for example. It would be the easiest thing in the world for them to construe this as neither you nor I having adequate faith in Divine Providence.

MRS. ALVING.   But, my dear Mr. Manders, as long as you know to your own satisfaction—

MANDERS.   Yes, I know, I know—I have my own inner conviction, quite so. But the fact remains that we wouldn't be able to counter a false and damaging impression—and that, in turn, could easily hamper the work of the orphanage.

MRS. ALVING.   Well, if that's the case, then—

MANDERS.   Also, I can hardly ignore the difficult—I might just as well say, painful—position I'd probably be in myself. Among the best circles in town there's a good deal of interest in the orphanage. After all, it's partly being established to benefit the town as well, and hopefully it's going to have a sizable effect in lowering our local public welfare taxes. But since I've been your adviser in this and made all the business arrangements, I'm afraid those bigots would concentrate all their fire on me—

MRS. ALVING.   No, you shouldn't be exposed to that.

MANDERS.   Not to mention the charges that would doubtless be leveled against me in certain papers and magazines that—

MRS. ALVING.   Enough, Mr. Manders; that settles it.

MANDERS.   Then you won't want the insurance?

MRS. ALVING.   No, we'll let that be.

MANDERS (leaning back in his chair). But now, if there should be an accident—one never knows, after all—would you be able to make good the losses?

MRS. ALVING.   I can tell you right now, I absolutely wouldn't.

MANDERS.   Ah, but you know, Mrs. Alving—then it's a grave responsibility we're taking on.

MRS. ALVING.   But what else do you see that we can do?

MANDERS.   No, that's just the thing: we can't do anything else. We shouldn't expose ourselves to unfavorable opinion; and we certainly have no right to stir dissension in the community.

MRS. ALVING.   Especially you, as a clergyman.

MANDERS.   And also I really do believe that we can depend on a project like this carrying some luck along with it—standing, so to say, under a special protection.

MRS. ALVING.   Let's hope so, Mr. Manders.

MANDERS.   Then we'll leave things as they are?

MRS. ALVING.   Yes, of course.

MANDERS.   Right. As you wish. (Jotting a note.) No insurance.

MRS. ALVING.   It's strange you happened to speak about this just today—

MANDERS.   I've often thought to ask you about it—

MRS. ALVING.   Because yesterday we nearly had a fire down there.

MANDERS.   What!

MRS. ALVING.   Well, there wasn't anything to it, really. Some shavings caught fire in the carpenter shop.

MANDERS.   Where Engstrand works?

MRS. ALVING.   Yes. They say he's often so careless with matches.

MANDERS.   He has so much on his mind, that man—so many tribulations. Praise be to God, he's now making a real effort to lead a blameless life, I hear.

MRS. ALVING.   Oh? Who's been saying that?

MANDERS.   He', assured me of it himself. And he's a capable workman, too.

MRS. ALVING.   Why, yes, as long as he's sober—

MANDERS.   Ah, that distressing weakness! But he tells me he frequently has to resort to it for the sake of his ailing leg. Last time he was in town, I really was quite moved by him. He stopped in and thanked me so sincerely for getting him this work out here, so he could be together with Regina.

MRS. ALVING.   But he hardly ever sees her.

MANDERS.   No, he speaks with her every day—he told me that himself.

MRS. ALVING.   Yes—well, it's possible.

MANDERS.   He feels so positively that he needs someone there who can restrain him when temptation looms. That's what's so engaging about Jacob Engstrand, the way he comes to one so utterly helpless and accuses himself and admits his faults. Just this last time that he talked to me—Mrs. Alving, if it became a vital necessity for him to have Regina home with him again—

MRS. ALVING (rising impulsively). Regina!

MANDERS.   Then you mustn't set yourself against it.

MRS. ALVING.   Yes, I'm decidedly set against it. And besides—Regina will have a position at the orphanage.

MANDERS.   But remember, he is her father—

MRS. ALVING.   I know all too well what kind of father he's been to her. No, she'll never have my blessings to go to him.

MANDERS (rising). But my dear Mrs. Alving, don't take it so violently. It's such a pity, the way you misjudge Engstrand. Really, it's as if you were somehow afraid—

MRS. ALVING (*more calmly*). Never mind about that. I've taken Regina in here, and she'll stay here with me. (*Listens.*) Shh, now! Dear Mr. Manders, let's not talk of this anymore. (*Her face radiating joy.*) Hear that! Osvald's coming downstairs. Now we'll think only of him.

(OSVALD ALVING, *wearing a light overcoat, hat in hand, and smoking a large meerschaum pipe, comes in through the door to the left.*)

OSVALD (*pausing in the doorway*). Oh, I'm sorry—I thought you were in the study. (*Comes in.*) Good morning, Pastor Manders.

MANDERS (*stares at him*). Ah—! That's amazing—!

MRS. ALVING. Yes, what do you think of him, Mr. Manders?

MANDERS. Well, I must say—no, but—is it really—?

OSVALD. Yes, really—the prodigal son, Pastor.

MANDERS. But my dear boy—

OSVALD. Well, the homecoming son, anyway.

MRS. ALVING. Osvald's thinking of the time when you were so against his becoming a painter.

MANDERS. From our human viewpoint, you know, many a step looks doubtful that later turns out— (*Shaking his hand.*) Ah, welcome, welcome back! Imagine, my dear Osvald—may I still call you by your first name?

OSVALD. What else could you think of calling me?

MANDERS. Good. What I meant to say, my dear Osvald— was that you mustn't suppose that I categorically condemn the artist's life. I assume there are quite a few who keep their inner selves uncorrupted even in those circumstances.

OSVALD. Let's hope so.

MRS. ALVING (*beaming with pleasure*). I know one who's kept both his inner and outer selves incorruptible. You only have to look at him, Mr. Manders.

OSVALD (*pacing about the room*). Yes, all right, Mother dear—that's enough.

MANDERS. Completely so—that's undeniable. And you've already begun to make your name. You're often mentioned in the papers—and most favorably, too. Though lately, I should say, there seems to be less.

OSVALD (*near the greenhouse*). I haven't been painting so much lately.

MRS. ALVING. Even artists need a rest now and then.

MANDERS. That I can understand. A time to prepare oneself and gather strength for the great work to come.

OSVALD. Yes. Mother, are we eating soon?

MRS. ALVING. In just half an hour. He certainly has an appetite, thank goodness.

MANDERS. And likes his tobacco, too.

OSVALD. I found Father's pipe upstairs in the bedroom—

MANDERS. Ah, that explains it!

MRS. ALVING. What?

MANDERS. When Osvald came through the door there with that pipe in his mouth, it was as if I saw his father in the flesh.

OSVALD. Really?

MRS. ALVING. Oh, how can you say that? Osvald takes after me.

MANDERS. Yes, but there's a look around the corners of the mouth, something about the lips, that's the very picture of Alving—especially now that he's smoking.

MRS. ALVING. No, it's nothing like him, not at all. To me, Osvald has more of a minister's look about the mouth.

MANDERS. Yes, Yes, a number of my colleagues have a similar expression.

MRS. ALVING. But put the pipe down, dear. I don't want smoking in this room.

OSVALD (*sets the pipe down*). All right. I only thought I'd try it because I'd once smoked it as a child.

MRS. ALVING. You?

OSVALD. Yes, I was very small then. And I remember going up to Father's room one evening when he was in such a marvelous humor.

MRS. ALVING. Oh, you don't remember anything from those years.

OSVALD. Oh yes, I distinctly remember him taking me on his knee and letting me smoke his pipe. "Smoke, boy," he said, "smoke it for real!" And I smoked for all I was worth, till I felt myself go pale, and the great drops of sweat stood out on my forehead. Then he shook all over with laughter—

MANDERS. That's most peculiar.

MRS. ALVING. I'm sure it's just something that Osvald dreamed.

OSVALD. No, Mother, it was definitely no dream. Because—don't you remember—then you came in and carried me off to the nursery. I was sick then, and I could see you were crying. Did Father often play such tricks?

MANDERS. When he was young he was always full of life—

OSVALD. And still he got so much accomplished—so much that was good and useful, for all that he died so early.

MANDERS. Yes, Osvald Alving—it's a strong and worthy name you've inherited. Well, let's hope it'll inspire you—

OSVALD. It certainly ought to.

MANDERS. And it was good of you to come home for the ceremonies in his honor.

OSVALD. It's the least I could do for Father.

MRS. ALVING. And that he'll remain with me here so long—that's the best of his goodness.

MANDERS. Yes, I hear you're staying all winter.

OSVALD. I'll be staying on indefinitely, Pastor. Oh, it's wonderful to be home again.

MRS. ALVING (*radiant*). Yes, how true!

MANDERS (*looks sympathetically at him*). You were out in the world quite early, Osvald, weren't you?

OSVALD.   Yes, I wonder sometimes if it wasn't too early.

MRS. ALVING.   Nonsense! There's nothing better for a healthy boy, especially when he's an only child. He shouldn't be kept home and coddled by his mother and father.

MANDERS.   That's a highly debatable proposition, Mrs. Alving. A child's rightful place is and always will be his parental home.

OSVALD.   I have to agree with Mr. Manders there.

MANDERS.   Now take your own son, for instance. Yes, we can discuss this in front of him. What effect has this had on him? He's grown to age twenty-six or -seven without any chance to experience a normal home life.

OSVALD.   Excuse me, Mr. Manders—but you're quite wrong about that.

MANDERS.   Really? I thought you'd been moving almost entirely in artistic circles.

OSVALD.   I have.

MANDERS.   And mainly among the younger artists.

OSVALD.   Yes.

MANDERS.   But I thought most of those people hadn't the means to start a family and make a home.

OSVALD.   It's true that a number of them haven't the means to get married—

MANDERS.   Well, that's what I'm saying.

OSVALD.   But they can still have a home life. And several of them do—one that's quite normal and pleasant.

(MRS. ALVING, *following attentively, nods but says nothing.*)

MANDERS.   But it's not a bachelor life I'm talking about. By home life I mean a family home, where a man lives with his wife and his children.

OSVALD.   Yes, or with his children and his children's mother.

MANDERS (*jolted, clasping his hands together*). Merciful God—!

OSVALD.   What—?

MANDERS.   Lives together with—his children's mother!

OSVALD.   Well, would you rather have him abandon her?

MANDERS.   But you're talking about illicit relations! About plain, irresponsible free love!

OSVALD.   I've never noticed anything particularly irresponsible about the way these people live.

MANDERS.   But how is it possible that—that even moderately decent young men or women could accept living in that manner—before the eyes of the world!

OSVALD.   But what else can they do? A poor young artist—a poor young girl—and marriage so expensive. What can they do?

MANDERS.   What can they do? Well, Mr. Alving, I'll tell you what they can do. They ought to keep each other at a distance right from the start—that's what they ought to do!

OSVALD.   You won't get very far with that advice among warm-blooded young people in love.

MRS. ALVING.   No, you certainly won't!

MANDERS (*persisting*). And to think the authorities tolerate such things! That it's allowed to go on openly. (*To* MRS. ALVING.) You see what good reason I've had to be concerned about your son. In circles where immorality is flaunted, and even seems to be prized—

OSVALD.   Let me tell you something, Pastor. I've been a frequent Sunday guest in a couple of these so-called unconventional homes—

MANDERS.   Sunday, no less!

OSVALD.   Yes, the day of rest and relaxation—and yet I've never once heard an offensive word, nor have I ever witnessed anything that could be called immoral. But do you know when and where I *have* met immorality among artists?

MANDERS.   No, thank God, I don't

OSVALD.   Well, then let me tell you. I've met it when one or another of our exemplary husbands and fathers—on a trip away from home and out to see a little life—did the artists the honor of dropping in on them in their poor cafés. Then we had our ears opened wide. Those gentlemen could tell us about things and places we never dreamed existed.

MANDERS.   What? Are you suggesting that respectable men from here at home would—?

OSVALD.   Have you never—when these same respectable men came home from their trips—have you never heard them carrying on about the monstrous immorality abroad?

MANDERS.   Why, of course—

MRS. ALVING.   I have, too.

OSVALD.   Well, you can trust their word for it—they're experts, many of them. (*Clasps his head.*) Oh, that the beautiful freedom of that life—could be made so foul!

MRS. ALVING.   You mustn't provoke yourself, Osvald. It's not good for you.

OSVALD.   No, you're right, Mother. It's bad for my health. It's this damnable fatigue, you know. Well, I'll go for a little walk now before lunch. I'm sorry, Pastor. You can't share my feelings about this—but it's the way I see it. (*He goes out through the farther door to the right.*)

MRS. ALVING.   My poor boy—!

MANDERS.   Yes, you can well say that. How far he's strayed! (MRS. ALVING *looks at him, saying nothing.* MANDERS *paces up and down.*) He called himself the prodigal son. Yes, it's sad—sad! (MRS. ALVING *continues to look at him.*) And what do you say to all this?

MRS. ALVING.   I say Osvald was right in every word that he said.

MANDERS (*stops short*). Right? Right! With such principles?

MRS. ALVING.   Here in my solitude I've come to the same conclusions, Mr. Manders—though I've never dared breathe a word of it. All well and good—my boy can speak for me now.

MANDERS. You're a woman much to be pitied, Mrs. Alving. Now I must talk seriously with you. It's no longer as your business adviser, nor as your and your husband's childhood friend, that I'm standing before you now—but as your priest, exactly as I once did at the most bewildered hour of your life.

MRS. ALVING. And what does my priest have to tell me?

MANDERS. First, let me call up some memories. It's a suitable moment. Tomorrow is the tenth anniversary of your husband's death; tomorrow the memorial will be unveiled in his honor; tomorrow I'll be speaking to all those assembled—but today I want to speak to you alone.

MRS. ALVING. All right, Mr. Manders—speak!

MANDERS. Do you recall how, after barely a year of marriage, you stood on the very edge of the abyss? That you left house and home—deserted your husband—yes, Mrs. Alving, deserted, deserted, and refused to go back to him, for all that he begged and implored you to?

MRS. ALVING. Have you forgotten how unutterably miserable I was that first year?

MANDERS. But this is the very essence of the rebellious spirit, to crave happiness here in this life. What right have we human beings to happiness? No, we must do our duty, Mrs. Alving! And your duty was to stand by that man you once had chosen, and to whom you were joined by a sacred bond.

MRS. ALVING. You know well enough what kind of life Alving led in those days—and the appetites he indulged.

MANDERS. I know quite well the rumors that circulated about him; and to the extent that those rumors were true, I'd be the last to condone such conduct as his then. But a wife isn't required to be her husband's judge. It was your proper role to bear with a humble heart that cross that a higher will saw fit to lay upon you. But instead, you rebelliously cast away the cross, left the groping soul you should have aided, went off and risked your good name and reputation and—nearly ruined other reputations in the bargain.

MRS. ALVING. Other reputations? Just one, I think you mean.

MANDERS. It was exceedingly thoughtless of you to seek refuge with me.

MRS. ALVING. With our pastor? With an old, close friend?

MANDERS. Yes, for that very reason. You should thank Almighty God that I had the necessary inner strength—that I got you to drop your hysterical plans, and that it was given me to lead you back to the path of duty, and home to your lawful husband.

MRS. ALVING. Yes, Pastor Manders, that certainly was your doing.

MANDERS. I was only a humble instrument directed by a higher power. And that I bent your will to duty and obedience—hasn't that grown as a great blessing, from that time on, in all the days of your life? Didn't it go the way I foretold? Didn't Alving turn away from his depravities, as a man must, and take up a loving and blameless life with you right to the end? Didn't he become a benefactor of the community, and uplift you as well into his own sphere of activities to share them all? And how effectively you shared them, too—that I know, Mrs. Alving; I'll give you *that* credit. But now I come to the next great mistake in your life.

MRS. ALVING. What do you mean?

MANDERS. Just as you once evaded the duties of a wife, you've since evaded those of a mother.

MRS. ALVING. Ah—!

MANDERS. All your life you've been governed by an incorrigible spirit of willfullness. Instinctively you've been drawn to all that's undisciplined and lawless. You never can bear the least constraint. Everything that inconveniences your life you've carelessly and irresponsibly thrown aside—as if it were baggage you could leave behind if you chose. It didn't agree with you to be a wife any longer, so you left your husband. You found it troublesome to be a mother, so you put your child out with strangers.

MRS. ALVING. Yes, it's true—that's what I did.

MANDERS. And for that same reason you've become a stranger to him.

MRS. ALVING. No, no, I'm *not!*

MANDERS. You are. You had to be! And what sort of son have you gotten back? Think well, Mrs. Alving. You were terribly unfair to your husband—you admit as much by raising this monument to him. Now admit as well how unfair you've been to your son; there may still be time to lead him back from the paths of error. Change your ways—and save what's still left to be saved in him. For truly, Mrs. Alving—(*With an admonishing forefinger.*)—you're profoundly guilty as a mother! I've considered it my duty to tell you this.

(*Silence.*)

MRS. ALVING (*deliberately, controlling herself*). You've said your piece, Pastor; and tomorrow you'll be speaking publicly in my husband's memory. Tomorrow I'll make no speeches; but now I want to say something to you, exactly as you've just spoken to me.

MANDERS. Naturally, you want to make excuses for your conduct—

MRS. ALVING. No. Only to tell a few facts.

MANDERS. Well—?

MRS. ALVING. All that you've been saying here about me and my husband and our life together—after, as you put it, you led me back to the path of duty—all this is something you don't know the least thing about at firsthand. From that moment on, you, our dearest friend, never set foot in our house again.

MANDERS.   But you and your husband moved out of town right after that.

MRS. ALVING.   Yes, and you never came out here to see us while my husband was living. It was business that impelled you to visit me, since you were involved with the orphanage, too.

MANDERS (*in a low, hesitant voice*). Helene—if that's meant as a reproach, then I ask you to consider—

MRS. ALVING.   The respect you owed to your calling, yes. And I, after all, was a runaway wife. One can never be careful enough with such reckless women.

MANDERS. Dear—Mrs. Alving, that is a flagrant exaggeration—

MRS. ALVING.   Yes, yes, all right, then forget that. I simply wanted to say that when you make judgments on my married life, you're basing them on no more than common gossip.

MANDERS.   Granted. Well, what of it?

MRS. ALVING.   But now, Mr. Manders, now I'll tell you the truth! I swore to myself that one day you were going to hear it—you alone.

MANDERS.   And what, then, is the truth?

MRS. ALVING.   The truth is—that my husband died just as dissolute as he'd lived every day of his life.

MANDERS (*groping for a chair*). What did you say?

MRS. ALVING.   After nineteen years of marriage, just as dissolute—in his desires, in any case—as he was before you married us.

MANDERS.   But these mistakes of his youth, these confusions—dissipations, if you want—you call them a dissolute life?

MRS. ALVING.   It's the phrase our doctor used.

MANDERS.   I don't understand you.

MRS. ALVING.   You don't have to.

MANDERS.   It makes my head spin. You mean the whole of your marriage—all those many years together with your husband—were nothing more than a hollow mockery?

MRS. ALVING.   Exactly. Now you know.

MANDERS.   This—I find this so hard to believe. I can't understand it! It doesn't make sense! But how was it possible to—? How could it be kept a secret?

MRS. ALVING.   That was the constant battle I had, day after day. When Osvald was born, I thought things might go better with Alving—but it didn't last long. So then I had to redouble my efforts, fight with a vengeance so no one would know what kind of man my child's father was. And you know, of course, how charming Alving could be. No one thought anything but good of him. He was one of those people whose lives never detract from their reputations. But then, Mr. Manders—and this you also have to hear—then came the most sickening part of the whole business.

MANDERS.   More sickening than what you've told me!

MRS. ALVING.   I'd borne with him, even though I knew very well what was going on in secret away from this house. But when the infection came right within our own four walls—

MANDERS.   You mean—here!

MRS. ALVING.   Yes, here in our own house. In there— (*Pointing to the nearer door on the right.*)—in the dining room, that was where I first discovered it. I had something to get inside, and the door was ajar. I heard the maid come up from the garden with water for the plants—

MANDERS.   And—?

MRS. ALVING.   A moment later I heard Alving come in after her. I could hear him saying something to her. And then I heard— (*With an abrupt laugh.*) —oh, I can hear it still, as something both so shattering and so ludicrous— my own maid whispering: "Let go of me, Captain Alving! Leave me be!"

MANDERS.   How terribly gross and thoughtless of him! Oh, but Mrs. Alving, it was no more than a moment's thoughtlessness, believe me.

MRS. ALVING.   I soon learned what to believe. The captain had his way with the girl—and that affair had its after-effects, Pastor Manders.

MANDERS (*as if stunned into stone*). And all that in this house! In this house!

MRS. ALVING.   I've endured a lot in this house to keep him home in the evenings—and nights. I had to become his drinking companion as he got sodden over his bottle, holed up in his room. There I had to sit alone with him, forcing myself through his jokes and toasts and all his maundering, abusive talk, and then fight him bare-handed to drag him into bed—

MANDERS (*shaken*). That you were able to bear all that!

MRS. ALVING.   I had my little boy, and I bore it for him— at least until that final humiliation, when my own maid—! Then I swore to myself: that was the end! So I took charge of the house—complete charge—over him and everything else. Because now, you see, I had a weapon against him; he couldn't let out a word of protest. It was then I sent Osvald away. He was going on seven and starting to notice things and ask questions, the way children do. All that was too much for me, Manders. I thought the child would be poisoned just breathing this polluted air. That's why I sent him away. And now you can understand, too, why he never set foot in this house as long as his father lived. No one will know what that cost me.

MANDERS.   What a trial your life has been!

MRS. ALVING.   I could never have gotten through it if it hadn't been for my work. And I *have* worked, I can tell you. All the additions to the property, all the improvements and technical innovations that Alving got fame and credit for—do you think those were *his* doing? *He,* sprawled all day on the sofa, reading old government journals! No, I can tell you as well; it was *I* who got him moving whenever he had his lucid moments; and it was I who had to pull the whole load when he fell back in his old wild ways or collapsed in groveling misery.

MANDERS.   And for this man, you're raising a monument!

MRS. ALVING.   There's the power of a bad conscience.

MANDERS.   A bad—? What do you mean?

MRS. ALVING.   It always seemed inevitable to me that the truth would have to come out someday and be believed. So the orphanage was meant to spike all the rumors and dispel the doubts.

MANDERS.   Well, you've certainly accomplished that, Mrs. Alving.

MRS. ALVING.   And I had still another reason. I didn't want Osvald, my own son, to inherit the least little thing from his father.

MANDERS.   Then it's with Alving's money that—?

MRS. ALVING.   Yes. The sums I've contributed year after year to the orphanage add up to just the amount—I've figured it out exactly—just the amount that made Lieutenant Alving such a good catch at the time.

MANDERS.   Then, if I understand you—

MRS. ALVING.   It was my selling price. I don't want that money passing into Osvald's hands. Everything my son inherits will come from me, and no one else.

(OSVALD *enters by the farther door to the right. He has left his hat and overcoat outside.*)

MRS. ALVING (*moving toward him*). You back again, dear?

OSVALD.   Yes. What can anyone do outside in this interminable rain? But I hear lunch is ready. That's good news!

(REGINA *enters from the dining room with a package.*)

REGINA.   A parcel just came for you, ma'am. (*Handing it to her.*)

MRS. ALVING (*with a quick look at* MANDERS). The choir music for tomorrow, most likely.

MANDERS.   Hm—

REGINA.   And lunch is served.

MRS. ALVING.   Good. We'll be along in a moment; I just want to— (*Starts opening the package.*)

REGINA (*to* OSVALD). Will Mr. Alving have red wine, or white?

OSVALD.   Both, Miss Engstrand.

REGINA.   *Bien.* Very good, Mr. Alving. (*She goes into the dining room.*)

OSVALD.   I better help her uncork the bottles— (*He follows her into the dining room, the door swinging half shut behind him.*)

MRS. ALVING (*who has unwrapped the package*). Yes, quite so—it's the choir music, Mr. Manders.

MANDERS (*with folded hands*). How I'll ever be able to give my speech tomorrow with any conviction—!

MRS. ALVING.   Oh, you'll manage all right.

MANDERS (*softly, so as not to be heard in the dining room*). Yes, we mustn't stir up any scandal.

MRS. ALVING (*in a quiet, firm voice*). No. And then this long, horrible farce will be over. After tomorrow, it will really seem as if the dead had never lived in this house. There'll be no one else here but my son and me.

(*From the dining room comes the sound of a chair knocked over, along with* REGINA's *voice in a sharp whisper.*)

REGINA.   Osvald! Are you crazy? Let me go!

MRS. ALVING (*starting in terror*). Ah—!

(*She stares distractedly at the half-open door.* OSVALD *is heard to cough within and start humming. A bottle is uncorked.*)

MANDERS (*shaken*). But what happened, Mrs. Alving? What was that?

MRS. ALVING (*hoarsely*). Ghosts. Those two from the greenhouse—have come back.

MANDERS.   You mean—! Regina—? Is *she*—?

MRS. ALVING.   Yes. Come. Not a word—!

(*She grips* PASTOR MANDER's *arm and moves falteringly toward the dining room.*)

ACT TWO

The same room. A thick mist still veils the landscape. MANDERS *and* MRS. ALVING *enter from the dining room.*

MRS. ALVING.   Why, you're very welcome, Mr. Manders. (*Speaking into the dining room.*) Aren't you joining us, Osvald?

OSVALD (*from within*). No, thanks; I think I'll go out for a while.

MRS. ALVING.   Yes, do that. It's clearing a little now. (*She shuts the dining room door, goes over to the hall door and calls.*) Regina!

REGINA (*from without*). Yes, ma'am.

MRS. ALVING.   Go down to the laundry room and help out with the decorations.

REGINA.   Very good, ma'am.

(MRS. ALVING *makes certain* REGINA *has gone, then shuts the door.*)

MANDERS.   You're sure he can't hear us in there?

MRS. ALVING.   Not with the door closed. Anyway, he's going out soon.

MANDERS.   I'm still in a daze. I can't understand how I ever managed to devour one morsel of that heavenly meal.

MRS. ALVING (*pacing up and down, suppressing her anxiety*). Nor I, either. But what's to be done?

MANDERS.   Yes, what's to be done? Believe me, I just don't know; I'm so utterly inexperienced in such matters.

MRS. ALVING.   I'm convinced nothing serious has happened so far.

MANDERS.   God forbid! But it's still an unsavory business.

MRS. ALVING.   It's just a foolish fancy of Osvald's, you can be sure of that.

MANDERS.   Well, as I said, I'm not really up on these things; but it definitely seems to me—

MRS. ALVING.   She'll have to get out of this house. Immediately. That's clear as day—

MANDERS.   Yes, that's obvious.

MRS. ALVING.   But where? We can't simply—

MANDERS.   Where? Home to her father, of course.

MRS. ALVING.   To whom, did you say?

MANDERS.   To her—ah, but of course, Engstrand isn't—! Good Lord, Mrs. Alving, how is this possible? You must be mistaken, really.

MRS. ALVING.   Unfortunately, I'm not the least bit mistaken. Joanna had to confess everything to me—and Alving couldn't deny it. There was nothing else to do, then, but have the whole thing hushed up.

MANDERS.   Yes, that was essential.

MRS. ALVING.   The girl was turned out at once and given a fairly sizable amount to keep quiet. She managed the rest for herself when she got back to town. She revived an old friendship with Engstrand—probably dropped a few hints, I would guess, about all the money she had— and spun him some tale of a foreigner on a yacht berthed here for the summer. So she and Engstrand were married straight off—well, you married them yourself.

MANDERS.   But I don't see how—? I distinctly remember when Engstrand came to arrange the wedding. He was so woefully penitent, accusing himself so bitterly of the casual ways he and his fiancée had allowed themselves.

MRS. ALVING.   Well, naturally he had to take the blame himself.

MANDERS.   But the hypocrisy of the man? And with *me!* I absolutely never would have believed that of Jacob Engstrand. Well, I'll have to be very severe with him; he better be ready for that. And the immorality of such a marriage—all for money! How much did the girl get?

MRS. ALVING.   Three hundred dollars.

MANDERS.   Yes, can you imagine—to go and get married to a fallen woman for a paltry three hundred dollars!

MRS. ALVING.   Then what's your opinion of me, who let herself be married to a fallen man?

MANDERS.   God of mercy, what are you saying? A fallen man!

MRS. ALVING.   Do you think my husband was any better when I went with him to the altar than Joanna when Engstrand married her?

MANDERS.   But—there's a world of difference between you and her—

MRS. ALVING.   Much less than a world, I think. There was a considerable difference in price—a paltry three hundred dollars as against a whole fortune.

MANDERS.   But there's just no comparison here. After all, you'd listened to the counsels of your own heart, and those of your family.

MRS. ALVING (*not looking at him*). I thought you understood where I'd lost what you call my heart at the time.

MANDERS (*withdrawn*). If I'd understood any such thing, I would never have become a regular visitor in your husband's house.

MRS. ALVING.   Anyway, one thing is clear: I never really listened to myself.

MANDERS.   Well, to your nearest kin then, as it's ordained you should: your mother and your two aunts.

MRS. ALVING.   Yes, how true. The three of them wrote up my bill of sale. Oh, it's amazing how neatly they figured it out, that it would be stark madness to turn down an offer like that. If Mother could come back and see me now, where all those splendors got me.

MANDERS.   No one's responsible for the outcome. At least there's this to be said: your marriage was carried through with every respect for law and order.

MRS. ALVING (*at the window*). Yes, always law and order! I often think they're the root of all our miseries on earth.

MANDERS.   Mrs. Alving, that's a sinful thought.

MRS. ALVING.   Yes, perhaps it is. But I can't stand it any longer, with all these webs of obligation. I can't stand it! I've got to work my way out to freedom.

MANDERS.   What do you mean by that?

MRS. ALVING (*drumming on the windowpane*). I never should have covered up Alving's life. It was all I dared do then—not for Osvald, but to spare myself. What a coward I was!

MANDERS.   Coward?

MRS. ALVING.   If people had known anything of what went on, they would have said: "Poor man, it's no wonder he strays at times; his wife ran away, you know."

MANDERS.   And they could say that with some right, too.

MRS. ALVING (*looking straight at him*). If I were all I should have been, I would have taken Osvald aside and said: "Listen, my boy, your father was a degenerate human being—"

MANDERS.   Good Lord—!

MRS. ALVING.   Then I ought to have told him everything— word for word as I've told it to you.

MANDERS.   I find you almost frightening, Mrs. Alving.

MRS. ALVING.   I'm aware of that. Yes, I'm quite aware! I frighten myself by the thought. (*Coming away from the window.*) That's the coward I am.

MANDERS.   And you call it cowardice to do your bounden duty? Have you forgotten that a child should love and honor his father and mother?

MRS. ALVING.   Oh, don't let's talk abstractions! Why don't we ask, should Osvald love and honor Captain Alving?

MANDERS.   Isn't there something that tells you, as a mother, not to destroy your son's ideals?

MRS. ALVING.   Yes, but what of the truth—?

MANDERS.   Yes, but what of his ideals—?

MRS. ALVING.   Oh—ideals, ideals! If I only weren't the coward I am!

MANDERS.   Don't demolish ideals, Mrs. Alving—that can have cruel repercussions. And especially now, with Osvald. He hasn't too many ideals, sad to say—but as far as I can make out, his father is some sort of ideal to him.

MRS. ALVING.   Yes, you're right about that.

MANDERS.   And the impressions he has you've instilled and nourished yourself, through your letters.

MRS. ALVING.   Yes, I felt it was my duty and obligation— so year after year, I've gone on lying to my own child. Oh, what a coward—what a coward I've been!

MANDERS.   You've built up a beautiful image in your son's imagination—and that's something you mustn't take lightly.

MRS. ALVING.   Hm—who knows how good that's been, after all. But, in any case, I'm not going to have any trifling with Regina. He's not going to get that poor girl in trouble.

MANDERS.   Good God, that would be dreadful!

MRS. ALVING.   If I knew he was serious about it, and that it would make him happy—

MANDERS.   Yes? Then what?

MRS. ALVING.   But it wouldn't work out. Regina just isn't the type.

MANDERS.   How so? What do you mean?

MRS. ALVING.   If I weren't such a wretched coward, then I'd say to him: "Marry her, or live any way you like— but just be honest together."

MANDERS.   Heavens above—! A legal marriage, no less! That would be barbarous—! It's unheard of—!

MRS. ALVING.   Unheard of, you say? Word of honor, Pastor Manders—haven't you heard that, out here in the country, there are numbers of married couples who are just as closely related?

MANDERS.   I really don't understand you.

MRS. ALVING.   Oh yes you do, very well.

MANDERS.   Well, you mean cases where possibly they—? Yes, unfortunately family life isn't always as pure as it ought to be, that's true. But what you're referring to is hardly ever known—at least, not conclusively. But here, instead—you, the mother, are willing to let your own—!

MRS. ALVING.   But I'm not willing. I don't want to encourage it for anything in the world—that's just what I was saying.

MANDERS.   No, because you're a coward, as you put it. But if you weren't a coward—! Almighty God—what a monstrous union!

MRS. ALVING.   Well, as far as that goes, it's been rumored that we're all descended from a similar union. And who was it who thought up that arrangement, Pastor?

MANDERS.   I will not discuss such questions with you, Mrs. Alving—because you're not in the proper state of mind. But, that you can dare call it cowardice on your part—!

MRS. ALVING.   You have to understand what I mean by that. I'm anxious and fearful because of the ghosts that haunt me, that I can't get rid of.

MANDERS.   Because of—what did you say?

MRS. ALVING.   Ghosts. When I heard Regina and Osvald in there, it was as if I was seeing ghosts. But I almost believe we *are* ghosts, all of us, Pastor. It's not only what we inherit from our fathers and mothers that keeps on returning in us. It's all kinds of old dead doctrines and opinions and beliefs, that sort of thing. They aren't alive in us; but they hang on all the same, and we can't get rid of them. I just have to pick up a newspaper, and it's as if I could see the ghosts slipping between the lines. They must be haunting our whole country, ghosts everywhere—so many and thick, they're like grains of sand. And there we are, the lot of us, so miserably afraid of the light.

MANDERS.   Ah! So this is the outgrowth of all your reading. Fine fruit, I must say! Oh, these disgusting, insidious freethinking books!

MRS. ALVING.   My dear Mr. Manders, you're wrong. It was you yourself who set me to thinking—and for that I'll always be grateful.

MANDERS.   *I?*

MRS. ALVING.   Yes, when you made me give in to what you called duty and obligation; when you praised as right and proper what I rebelled against heart and soul as something loathsome—that's when I started going over your teachings, seam by seam. I just wanted to pull out a single thread; but after I'd worked it loose, the whole design fell apart. And then I realized it was only basted.

MANDERS (*quietly, with feeling*). Is that all that was won by the hardest battle of my life?

MRS. ALVING.   You mean your most shameful defeat.

MANDERS.   It was the greatest victory I've known, Helene—victory over myself.

MRS. ALVING.   It was a crime against us both.

MANDERS.   That I entreated you by saying, "Woman, go home to your lawful husband," when you came to me distracted, crying, "Here I am, take me!" Was that a crime?

MRS. ALVING.   Yes, I think so.

MANDERS.   We two don't understand each other.

MRS. ALVING.   Not anymore, at least.

MANDERS.   Never—never, in even my most secret thoughts, have I seen you as anything but another man's wife.

MRS. ALVING.   You believe that?

MANDERS.   Helene—!

MRS. ALVING.   One forgets so easily.

MANDERS.   I don't. I'm the same as I always was.

MRS. ALVING (*shifting her tone abruptly*). Yes, yes, well—let's stop talking about the old days. Now you're up to your ears in boards and committees; and I go around here struggling with ghosts, inside me and outside both.

MANDERS.   At least I can help you manage the outer ones. After all the disturbing things I've heard from you today, my conscience won't suffer a defenseless young girl to remain in this house.

MRS. ALVING.   It would be best, don't you think, if we could see her established? I mean, decently married.

MANDERS.   Undoubtedly. I'd say it's desirable for her in every respect. Regina's already at an age when—of course, I'm really no judge of these things, but—

MRS. ALVING.   Regina matured quite early.

MANDERS.   Yes, didn't she, though? It's my impression she was unusually well developed physically when I was preparing her for confirmation. But temporarily, in all events, she ought to go home, under her father's supervision—ah, but of course, Engstrand isn't—to think that he—that *he* could conceal the truth from me like that!

(*There is a knock at the hall door.*)

MRS. ALVING.   Who can that be? Come in!

(ENGSTRAND, *in his Sunday clothes, appears in the doorway.*)

ENGSTRAND.   I beg your pardon most humbly, but—

MANDERS.   Aha! Hm—

MRS. ALVING.   Oh, it's you, Engstrand.

ENGSTRAND.   There were none of the maids about, so I made myself so bold as to give a knock.

MRS. ALVING.   Well, all right, come in. You want to talk to me about something?

ENGSTRAND (*coming in*). No, thanks all the same. It was the pastor, actually, I wanted to have a little word with.

MANDERS (*walking up and down*). Oh, yes? You want to talk to me? Is that it?

ENGSTRAND.   Yes, I'd be grateful no end—

MANDERS (*stopping in front of him*). Well, may I ask what this is about?

ENGSTRAND.   See, it's like this, Pastor; we've gotten paid off down there now—with all thanks to you, ma'am—and now we've finished everything up. And so I was thinking how nice and fitting it'd be if all us honest craftsmen who've been working together all this time—I was thinking, we ought to round things off with a little prayer meeting this evening.

MANDERS.   A prayer meeting? Down at the orphanage?

ENGSTRAND.   Yes. But of course if the pastor's not agreeable, then—

MANDERS.   Oh, it's a splendid thought, but—hm—

ENGSTRAND.   I've been holding a few evening prayers down there myself now and then—

MRS. ALVING.   You have?

ENGSTRAND.   Yes, now and then. Just a little meditation, so to speak. But then I'm a common, ordinary man, with no special gifts, God help me—and so I was thinking, since the pastor was out here—

MANDERS.   Now look, Engstrand, first I have to ask you a question. Are you in a proper frame of mind for this kind of meeting? Do you feel your conscience is free and clear?

ENGSTRAND.   Oh, Lord help us, Pastor, there's no point going on talking about my conscience.

MANDERS.   Ah, but it's exactly what we *are* going to talk about. Well, what's your answer?

ENGSTRAND.   My conscience? Yes, that can be pretty nasty at times, it can.

MANDERS.   Well, at least you're owning up to it. Now will you tell me, without any subterfuge—just what is your relationship to Regina?

MRS. ALVING (*quickly*). Mr. Manders!

MANDERS (*calming her*). If you'll leave it to me—

ENGSTRAND.   To Regina! Jeez, you gave me a turn there! (*Looking at* MRS. ALVING.) There's nothing wrong with Regina, is there?

MANDERS.   We hope not. What I mean is, just exactly how are you related to her? You pass for her father, don't you? Well?

ENGSTRAND (*vaguely*). Why—hm—you know, Pastor, this business with me and poor Joanna.

MANDERS.   Stop bending the truth. Your late wife told Mrs. Alving everything before she left her service.

ENGSTRAND.   But it's supposed to—! She did that, really?

MANDERS.   So your secret's out, Engstrand.

ENGSTRAND.   And after she swore on a stack of Bibles—!

MANDERS.   She swore—!

ENGSTRAND.   I mean, she gave me her word. But with such sincerity.

MANDERS.   And all these years you've hidden the truth from me. From *me,* who put my absolute trust in you.

ENGSTRAND.   Yes, I'm afraid that's just what I've done.

MANDERS.   Have I deserved this from you, Engstrand? Haven't I always been ready to help you out in every way, so far as I possibly could? Answer! Haven't I?

ENGSTRAND.   There's plenty of times things would've looked pretty bad for me, if it wasn't for Pastor Manders.

MANDERS.   And this is the way you pay me back. Get me to make false entries in the parish register, and for years after withhold information you owed as a matter of respect both to me and the plain truth. Your conduct has been unpardonable, Engstrand: and from now on we're through with each other.

ENGSTRAND (*with a sigh*). Well, that's it, I guess.

MANDERS.   Yes. Because how can you ever justify yourself?

ENGSTRAND.   But how could she go around shaming herself the more by talking about it? If you could just imagine, Pastor, yourself in the same trouble as poor Joanna—

MANDERS.   I!

ENGSTRAND.   Jeez now, I don't mean the very same. But I mean, supposing you had something to be ashamed of in the eyes of the world, as they say. We menfolk oughtn't to judge a poor woman too hard, Pastor.

MANDERS.   But that's not what I'm doing. It's you that I blame.

ENGSTRAND.   If I might ask your Reverence one tiny little question—?

MANDERS.   Yes, go ahead.

ENGSTRAND.   Isn't it right and proper of a man that he raises up the fallen?

MANDERS.   Why, of course.

ENGSTRAND.   And isn't a man obliged to keep his word of honor?

MANDERS.   Certainly he is, but—

ENGSTRAND.   At the same time Joanna had her downfall at the hands of that Englishman—or maybe it was an American, or a Russian, or whatever—well, it was then she came back to town. Poor thing, she'd turned me down once or twice already; she only had eyes for the handsome ones, see—and I had this crook in my leg. Yes, you remember, Pastor, how I once took it on myself to go into a dance hall where common seamen were rioting in drink and dissipation, like they say. And when I tried to arouse them to seek out a better life—

MRS. ALVING (*over by the window*). Hm—

MANDERS.   Yes, I know, Engstrand; those ruffians threw you downstairs. You've told me that before. Your disability does you great credit.

ENGSTRAND.   I'm not priding myself on it, Pastor. But what I wanted to say was that then she came and confessed the whole thing to me, streaming down tears and gnashing her teeth. And I have to say, Pastor, it just about ripped the heart out of me to listen.

MANDERS.   All of *that,* Engstrand. Well! Then what?

ENGSTRAND.   Yes, so I said to her: that American, he's beating over the seas of the world, he is. And you, Joanna, I said—you've had your downfall, and you're a sinful, fallen creature. But Jacob Engstrand, I said, he stands on two stout legs—yes, I meant it like a manner of speaking, Pastor.

MANDERS.   Yes, I quite understand. Go on.

ENGSTRAND.   Well, so that's how I raised her up and gave her an honorable marriage, so no one'd ever find out about her wild carrying-on with foreigners.

MANDERS.   That was all quite commendable of you. What I cannot approve is that you could bring yourself to accept money—

ENGSTRAND.   Money? I? Not a penny.

MANDERS (*with an inquiring glance at* MRS. ALVING). But—?

ENGSTRAND.   Oh, yes—just a minute; now I remember. Joanna did have a little odd change, all right—but I wanted nothing of *that.* Faugh! I said: Mammon, that's the wages of sin, it is. We'll take that greasy gold—or banknotes, whatever it was—and heave it back into the American's face, I said. But he was off and gone over the rolling sea, Pastor.

MANDERS.   Was that it, my dear Engstrand?

ENGSTRAND.   That's right. So I and Joanna agreed that the money ought to be put toward the child's bringing up, and that's where it went; and I can give a true reckoning of every penny.

MANDERS.   But that changes things substantially.

ENGSTRAND.   That's the way it worked out, Pastor. And I'll be bold enough to say I've been a real father to Regina, as far as it lay in my power—for I have to admit, I'm only a poor, frail mortal.

MANDERS.   There, there, Engstrand—

ENGSTRAND.   But I will say that I brought up the child and looked after my poor, dear Joanna and made them a home, like the gospel says. But it never would have occurred to me to go up to Pastor Manders, priding myself and making much out of a good deed done in this world. No, when that sort of thing happens to Jacob Engstrand, he keeps it to himself, he does. Though it happens none too often, sorry to say. No, when I come to see Pastor Manders, then it's all I can do just to talk out my sins and errors. Because to say what I said before—my conscience does turn pretty nasty at times.

MANDERS.   Give me your hand, Jacob Engstrand.

ENGSTRAND.   Oh, Jeez, Pastor—

MANDERS.   No fuss now. (*Grasping his hand.*) There!

ENGSTRAND.   And if I can dare to beg your pardon, Pastor, most humbly—

MANDERS.   You? Quite the contrary, I'm the one who should beg your pardon—

ENGSTRAND.   Oh, no, no!

MANDERS.   Yes, definitely. And I do, with all my heart. Forgive me that I could so misjudge you. If only I could give you some sign of my sincere regret, and the goodwill I have toward you—

ENGSTRAND.   You'd like that, Pastor?

MANDERS.   It would please me no end.

ENGSTRAND.   Because there's a real good opportunity for that right now. With the bit of honest coin I've put aside from my work out here, I was thinking of founding a kind of seaman's home back in town.

MRS. ALVING.   *You?*

ENGSTRAND.   Yes, it'd be sort of a refuge for the orphans of the sea, so to speak. Temptations are so manifold for a sailor when he comes wandering ashore. But in this house of mine he could live like under a father's protection, that was my thought.

MANDERS.   What do you say to that, Mrs. Alving?

ENGSTRAND.   It's not much I have to begin with, Lord knows; but if I could just take hold of a helping hand—

MANDERS. Yes, yes, we have to consider this further. Your project interests me enormously. But now, go on down and get things ready—and light some candles, to give it a ceremonial touch. And then we'll have our devotional hour together, my dear Engstrand, for now I'm sure you're in the right frame of mind.

ENGSTRAND. I really do think so, yes. So good-bye, Mrs. Alving, and thanks for everything. And take good care of Regina for me. (*Brushes a tear from his eye.*) Poor Joanna's child—um, isn't it amazing—but it's just as if that girl had grown a part of my very heart. Yes, sir, and that's a fact. (*He bows and goes out.*)

MANDERS. Well, what do you think of the man now, Mrs. Alving? That's quite a different picture of things we got from him.

MRS. ALVING. Yes, quite so, indeed.

MANDERS. There you see how scrupulously careful one has to be about judging one's fellowman. But it's also a wonderful joy to discover one's made a mistake. Well, what do you say?

MRS. ALVING. I say you are and you always will be a big baby, Manders.

MANDERS. I?

MRS. ALVING (*placing both hands on his shoulders*). And I say I could easily wrap you up in a great, big hug.

MANDERS (*pulling back quickly*). Oh, bless you, no! What an impulse!

MRS. ALVING (*with a smile*). Oh, don't be afraid of me.

MANDERS (*by the table*). You sometimes have the most outrageous way of expressing yourself. Now I first want to collect these documents together and put them in my bag. (*Doing so.*) There now. And so good-bye for the moment. Keep your eye on Osvald when he comes back. I'll be looking in on you later.

(*He takes his hat and goes out by the hall door. MRS. ALVING sighs, gazes a moment out of the window, straightens the room up a bit and starts into the dining room, then stops with a stifled cry in the doorway.*)

MRS. ALVING. Osvald! Are you still at the table?

OSVALD (*from the dining room*). I'm just finishing my cigar.

MRS. ALVING. I thought you'd gone for a walk.

OSVALD. In such weather?

(*The chink of a glass and decanter. MRS. ALVING leaves the door open and settles down with her knitting on the sofa by the window.*)

OSVALD. Wasn't that Pastor Manders who left just now?

MRS. ALVING. Yes, he went down to the orphanage.

OSVALD. Hm.

(*Again, the chink of glass and decanter.*)

MRS. ALVING (*with an anxious glance*). Osvald, dear, you ought to go easy with the liqueur. It's strong.

OSVALD. It keeps the dampness out.

MRS. ALVING. Wouldn't you rather come in here with me?

OSVALD. But I can't smoke in there.

MRS. ALVING. Now you know a cigar is all right.

OSVALD. Oh, well, then I'll come in. Just a tiny drop more—ah, there. (*He enters, smoking his cigar, and shuts the door after him. Short silence.*) Where'd the pastor go?

MRS. ALVING. I told you, he went down to the orphanage.

OSVALD. Oh yes, that's right.

MRS. ALVING. You shouldn't go on sitting at the table so long, Osvald.

OSVALD (*holding his cigar behind his back*). But I think it's so cozy, Mother. (*Patting and fondling her.*) Imagine—what it is for me, coming home, to sit at my mother's own table, in my mother's room, and enjoy her delectable meals.

MRS. ALVING. My dear, dear boy!

OSVALD (*somewhat impatiently, walking about and smoking*). And what else am I going to do here? I can't accomplish anything—

MRS. ALVING. Can't you?

OSVALD. In all this murk? Not a glimmer of sunlight the whole day long? (*Pacing about.*) Oh, this—! This not being able to work—!

MRS. ALVING. Perhaps it wasn't such a good idea for you to come home.

OSVALD. No, Mother, that was essential.

MRS. ALVING. Because I'd ten times rather give up the joy of having you home with me, if it meant that you—

OSVALD (*stops by the table*). Now tell me, Mother—is it really such a great joy for you to have me home?

MRS. ALVING. What a question to ask!

OSVALD (*crumpling a newspaper*). I should have thought it hardly mattered to you whether I was here or not.

MRS. ALVING. You have the heart to say that to your mother, Osvald?

OSVALD. But you lived without me very well before.

MRS. ALVING. Yes, I've lived without you—that's true.

(*Silence. The twilight gradually deepens. OSVALD paces the floor, back and forth. He has set his cigar down.*)

OSVALD (*stops by MRS. ALVING*). Do you mind if I sit beside you on the sofa?

MRS. ALVING (*making room for him*). Please sit down, dear.

OSVALD (*sitting*). There's something I have to tell you, Mother.

MRS. ALVING (*nervously*). What?

OSVALD (*staring ahead into space*). Because I can't go on bearing it any longer.

MRS. ALVING. Bearing what? What is it?

OSVALD (*as before*). I couldn't bring myself to write you about it; and ever since I came home—

MRS. ALVING (*gripping his arm*). But, Osvald, what *is* it?

OSVALD.   All yesterday and today I've been trying to drive these thoughts away—and free myself. But it doesn't work.

MRS. ALVING (*rising*). You've got to speak out, Osvald!

OSVALD (*drawing her down on the sofa again*). Sit still, and I'll try to tell you—I've been complaining so about my tiredness after the trip here—

MRS. ALVING.   Yes? Well?

OSVALD.   But that isn't what's wrong with me, not any ordinary tiredness—

MRS. ALVING (*starts to rise*). Osvald, you're not ill!

OSVALD (*draws her down again*). Sit still, Mother. Just be calm about it. I'm not exactly ill—at least not ill in the ordinary sense. (*Puts his hands to his head.*) Mother, it's my mind that's broken down—out of control—I'll never be able to work again! (*Hands over his face, he throws himself down in her lap and bursts into deep sobs.*)

MRS. ALVING (*pale and trembling*). Osvald! Look at me! No, no, it isn't true.

OSVALD (*looks up despairingly*). Never able to work again! Never—never! It's like a living death! Mother, can you imagine anything as horrible?

MRS. ALVING.   My poor boy! How did this awful thing happen to you?

OSVALD (*sitting up again*). That's just what I don't understand. I can't figure it out. I've never lived a wild life—not in any respect. You have to believe me, Mother—that's something I've never done!

MRS. ALVING.   I believe you, Osvald.

OSVALD.   And yet it's come on me—this horrible thing!

MRS. ALVING.   Oh, but dearest, it's going to be all right. It's no more than nervous exhaustion, believe me.

OSVALD (*heavily*). That's what I thought at first—but it's not so.

MRS. ALVING.   Tell me everything, right from the start.

OSVALD.   Yes, I want to.

MRS. ALVING.   When did you first notice anything?

OSVALD.   It was just after my last visit home, and I'd returned to Paris. I began having such tremendous pains in my head—mostly toward the back, it seemed. It felt like a tight iron band squeezing me from my neck up—

MRS. ALVING.   Go on.

OSVALD.   At first I thought they were nothing more than the old, familiar headaches I've been bothered by ever since I was little.

MRS. ALVING.   Yes, yes—

OSVALD.   But I soon found out: that wasn't it. I couldn't work any longer. I wanted to start a new large painting, but it was as if all my talents had flown, and all my strength was paralyzed; I couldn't focus any of my thoughts; everything swam—around and around. Oh, it was a terrifying state to be in! Finally I sent for a doctor—and through him I discovered the truth.

MRS. ALVING.   What do you mean?

OSVALD.   He was one of the foremost doctors down there. He had me describe exactly what I was feeling; and then he began asking me a whole lot of questions that didn't seem to bear at all. I couldn't grasp what he was after—

MRS. ALVING.   So—?

OSVALD.   At last he said: Right from your birth, your whole system has been more or less worm-eaten. The actual expression he used was *vermoulu*.

MRS. ALVING (*anxiously*). What did he mean by that?

OSVALD.   I didn't understand either, so I asked him to be more specific. And then that old cynic said— (*Clenching his fist.*) Oh—!

MRS. ALVING.   What—?

OSVALD.   He said: The sins of the fathers are visited upon the children.

MRS. ALVING (*slowly stands up*). The sins of the fathers—!

OSVALD.   I almost hit him in the face.

MRS. ALVING (*moving across the room*). The sins of the fathers—

OSVALD (*smiles sadly*). Yes, can you imagine? Of course I assured him that was absolutely out of the question. But do you think he gave way? No, he had his mind made up; and it was only when I brought out your letters and translated all the parts to him that dealt with Father—

MRS. ALVING.   What then—?

OSVALD.   Well, then naturally he had to admit he'd been on the wrong track; and that's when I learned the truth—the incredible truth: that this beautiful, soul-stirring life with my young artist friends was something I should never have entered. It was too much for my strength. So—everything's my own fault.

MRS. ALVING.   Osvald, no! You mustn't believe that!

OSVALD.   There was no other way to explain it, he said. *That's* the worst of it. The whole of my life ruined beyond repair—all because of my own carelessnesss. So much that I wanted to do in this world—I don't dare think of it anymore—I'm not *able* to think of it. Oh, if I only could live my life over—and wipe out what I've done!

(*He throws himself face down on the sofa. *MRS. ALVING* wrings her hands and walks silently back and forth, locked in inner struggle. After a moment, *OSVALD* looks up, propping himself on his elbows.*)

OSVALD.   If it had only *been* something inherited—something that wasn't my fault. But this! In a shameful, mindless, trivial way, to have thrown away health, happiness, a world of possibility—my future, my life—!

MRS. ALVING.   No, no, my own dearest—it can't be! (*Bending over him.*) Things aren't as desperate as you think.

OSVALD.   Oh, you don't know— (*Leaps to his feet.*) And then all the pain that I'm causing you, Mother! How often I could almost hope and wish you wouldn't care for me so much.

MRS. ALVING.   Oh, Osvald, my only boy! You're all I have in this world, and all I care to have.

OSVALD (*grasps both her hands and kisses them*). Yes, yes, now I see. When I'm home I see it so well. And it's part of what weighs on me— Anyway, now you know the whole story. And let's not talk about it anymore today. I can't bear thinking about it very long. (*Walking about the room.*) Give me something to drink, Mother!

MRS. ALVING.   To drink? What do you want to drink now?

OSVALD.   Oh, anything. You must have some cold punch in the house.

MRS. ALVING.   Oh, but Osvald, dear—!

OSVALD.   Don't refuse me that, Mother. Be good now! I've got to have something to drown all these gnawing thoughts. (*Goes into the greenhouse.*) And how—how dark it is here!

(MRS. ALVING *goes over to the bell-pull, right, and rings.*)

And this interminable rain. Week after week it can go on; whole months at a time. In all my visits home, I never once remember seeing the sun shine.

MRS. ALVING.   Osvald—you're thinking of leaving me!

OSVALD.   Hm— (*Sighs deeply.*) I'm not thinking of anything. I can't think of anything! (*In a low tone.*) I've given that up.

REGINA (*entering from the dining room*). You rang, ma'am?

MRS. ALVING.   Yes, bring the lamp in.

REGINA.   Right away, ma'am. It's already lit. (*Goes out.*)

MRS. ALVING (*going over to* OSVALD). Osvald, don't keep anything from me.

OSVALD.   I won't, Mother. (*Moves to the table.*) I've told you a lot, I think.

(REGINA *comes in with the lamp and sets it on the table.*)

MRS. ALVING.   Yes, and Regina, you might bring us a half bottle of champagne.

REGINA.   Yes, ma'am. (*Goes out again.*)

OSVALD (*clasping* MRS. ALVING *about the neck*). That's the way it should be. I knew you wouldn't let your boy go thirsty.

MRS. ALVING.   Ah, my poor dear Osvald—how could I refuse you anything now?

OSVALD (*bouyantly*). Is that true, Mother? You mean it?

MRS. ALVING.   Mean what—?

OSVALD.   That you won't refuse me *anything*?

MRS. ALVING.   But Osvald dear—

OSVALD.   Shh!

(REGINA *returns with a half bottle of champagne and two glasses on a tray, which she sets down on the table.*)

REGINA.   Should I open it—?

OSVALD.   No, thanks, I'll do it.

(REGINA *goes out again.*)

MRS. ALVING (*seating herself at the table*). What did you mean—that I shouldn't refuse you?

OSVALD (*busy opening the bottle*). First a glass—maybe two.

(*The cork pops; he fills one glass and is about to pour the second.*)

MRS. ALVING (*holds her hand over it*). Thanks—not for me.

OSVALD.   Well, for me then. (*He drains the glass, refills it, drains it again, then sits down at the table.*)

MRS. ALVING (*expectantly*). Well?

OSVALD (*not looking at her*). Say, tell me—I thought you and Mr. Manders looked so strange—hm, so quiet during lunch.

MRS. ALVING.   You noticed that?

OSVALD.   Yes. Hm—(*A short silence.*) Tell me, what do you think of Regina?

MRS. ALVING.   What do I think?

OSVALD.   Yes, isn't she splendid?

MRS. ALVING.   Osvald, dear, you don't know her as well as I do—

OSVALD.   So—?

MRS. ALVING.   It's too bad Regina lived at home for so long. I should have taken her in earlier.

OSVALD.   Yes, but she's magnificent to look at, isn't she, Mother?

MRS. ALVING.   Regina has a good many serious flaws—

OSVALD.   Oh, but what does that matter? (*He drinks again.*)

MRS. ALVING.   Even so, I'm fond of her; and I'm responsible for her. I wouldn't for the world want anything to hurt her.

OSVALD (*springing to his feet*). Mother, Regina's my only hope!

MRS. ALVING (*rising*). What do you mean by that?

OSVALD.   I can't bear this anguish all by myself.

MRS. ALVING.   But you have your mother to help you bear it, don't you?

OSVALD.   Yes, I thought so—and that's why I came home to you. But it won't work that way. I can see; it won't work. I can't make a life out here.

MRS. ALVING.   Osvald!

OSVALD.   I have to live differently, Mother. So I will have to leave you. I don't want you to see all this.

MRS. ALVING.   Oh, my miserable child! But, Osvald, when you're sick as you are—

OSVALD.   If it were only the illness, I'd stay with you, Mother—I would. For you're my best friend in this world.

MRS. ALVING.   Yes, it's true; I am, aren't I?

OSVALD (*striding restlessly about*). But it's all the torment, agony, remorse—and the great deathly fear. Oh—this hideous fear!

MRS. ALVING (*following him*). Fear? What fear? What do you mean?

OSVALD.   Oh, don't ask me anymore about it. I don't know. I can't describe it to you.

(Mrs. Alving *crosses to the bell-pull, right, and rings.*)

OSVALD.   What do you want?

MRS. ALVING.   I want my boy to be happy, that's what. He mustn't go around brooding. (*To* REGINA, *who has appeared at the door.*) More champagne. A whole bottle.

(REGINA *goes.*)

OSVALD.   Mother!

MRS. ALVING.   Don't you think, in the country too, we know how to live?

OSVALD.   Isn't she magnificent-looking? The figure she has! And the glow of her health!

MRS. ALVING.   Sit down, Osvald, and let's have a quiet talk.

OSVALD (*sits*). You wouldn't know this, Mother, but I have a wrong to make right with Regina.

MRS. ALVING.   You!

OSVALD.   Or a little indiscretion—you might call it. Quite innocent, actually. When I was home last—

MRS. ALVING.   Yes?

OSVALD.   She asked me so many times about Paris, and I told her bits and pieces about the life down there. And I remember that one day I chanced to say, "Wouldn't you like to go there yourself?"

MRS. ALVING.   Well?

OSVALD.   I could see her blushing all shades of red, and then she said, "Yes, I'd very much like to." "All right," I said, "I expect that can be arranged"—or something like that.

MRS. ALVING.   Oh?

OSVALD.   Of course I forgot the whole thing completely; but then the day before yesterday I happened to ask her if she was glad I'd be staying so long at home this time—

MRS. ALVING.   Yes?

OSVALD.   And she gave me such a peculiar look and said, "But what about my trip to Paris?"

MRS. ALVING.   Her trip!

OSVALD.   And then I got it out of her that she'd taken the whole thing seriously, that she'd been thinking of me all this while, and that she'd even started to learn some French—

MRS. ALVING.   So that's why—

OSVALD.   Mother—when I saw her there in front of me, that splendid girl, so alive with health and beauty—it was as if I'd never noticed her before—but now she was standing there as if her arms were simply waiting to take me in—

MRS. ALVING.   Osvald!

OSVALD.   Then it struck me that in her was my salvation, because I saw how the joy of life was in her.

MRS. ALVING (*with a start*). The joy of life—? Is there salvation in that?

REGINA (*entering from the dining room with a bottle of champagne*). I'm sorry for taking so long, but I had to go down in the cellar— (*Sets the bottle down on the table.*)

OSVALD.   And get one more glass.

REGINA (*looks at him in surprise*). But Mrs. Alving has her glass.

OSVALD.   Yes, but bring one for yourself, Regina.

(REGINA *looks startled and flashes a quick, shy glance at* MRS. ALVING.)

OSVALD.   Well?

REGINA (*her voice low and hesitant*). Is that your wish, Mrs. Alving—?

MRS. ALVING.   Get the glass, Regina.

(REGINA *goes out into the dining room.*)

OSVALD (*his eyes following her*). Can you see the way she walks? So firm and fearless.

MRS. ALVING.   Osvald, this can't happen—!

OSVALD.   The thing is settled. You must see that. There's no use denying it.

(REGINA *returns with an empty glass in her hands.*)

OSVALD.   Sit down, Regina.

(REGINA *looks uncertainly at* MRS. ALVING.)

MRS. ALVING.   Sit down.

(REGINA *sits on a chair by the dining-room door, still holding the empty glass in her hand.*)

MRS. ALVING.   What were you saying, Osvald, about the joy of life?

OSVALD.   Yes, the joy of life, Mother—you don't know much about that here at home. I never feel it here.

MRS. ALVING.   Not even with me?

OSVALD.   Not when I'm home. But how could you understand that?

MRS. ALVING.   Oh, yes, yes. I think I'm beginning to understand—now.

OSVALD.   That—and the joy of work. Yes, they're really the same thing, basically. But no one understands that here, either.

MRS. ALVING.   Maybe you're right. Go on, I want to hear more of this.

OSVALD.   I mean, here everyone's brought up to believe that work is a curse and a punishment, and that life is a miserable thing that we're best off to be out of as soon as possible.

MRS. ALVING.   A vale of tears, yes. And we ingeniously manage to make it that.

OSVALD.   But they won't hear of such things down there. Nobody abroad believes in that sort of outlook anymore. Down there, simply to be alive in the world is held for a kind of miraculous bliss. Mother, have you noticed how everything I've painted is involved with this joy of life? Always and invariably, the joy of life. With light and sun and holiday scenes—and faces radiant with human content. That's why I'm afraid to stay on at home with you.

MRS. ALVING. Afraid? What are you afraid of here with me?

OSVALD. I'm afraid that everything that's most alive in me will degenerate into ugliness here.

MRS. ALVING (looking fixedly at him). Would that happen, do you think?

OSVALD. I'm sure it would. Live here the same as down there—and it still wouldn't be the same life.

MRS. ALVING (who has been listening intently, rises, her eyes large and thoughtful). Now I see how it all fits together.

OSVALD. What do you see?

MRS. ALVING. I see it now, for the first time. And now I can speak.

OSVALD (getting up). I don't understand you, Mother.

REGINA (who has also gotten up). Shouldn't I go?

MRS. ALVING. No, stay here. Now I can speak. Now, my son, you have to know everything—and then you can choose. Osvald! Regina!

OSVALD. Quiet! The pastor—

MANDERS (entering by the hall door). Well, we've really had a heart-warming session together.

OSVALD. We also.

MANDERS. Engstrand needs help with his seaman's home. Regina will have to move back and accommodate him—

REGINA. No, thank you, Pastor.

MANDERS (just noticing her). What—? Here—with a glass in your hand!

REGINA (hurriedly putting the glass down). Pardon—!

OSVALD. Regina's leaving with me, Pastor.

MANDERS. Leaving—with you!

OSVALD. Yes, as my wife—if she wants that.

MANDERS. Merciful heavens—!

REGINA. It wasn't my doing, Mr. Manders.

OSVALD. Or she'll stay here if I stay.

REGINA (involuntarily). Here!

MANDERS. You petrify me, Mrs. Alving.

MRS. ALVING. Neither one nor the other will happen—because now I can speak out freely.

MANDERS. But you can't do that! No, no, no!

MRS. ALVING. I both can and will. And without demolishing any ideals.

OSVALD. Mother, what is it you're hiding from me?

REGINA (listening). Mrs. Alving! Listen! People are shouting out there. (She goes into the greenhouse and looks out.)

OSVALD (moving toward the window, left). What's going on? What's that light in the sky?

REGINA (cries out). The orphanage—it's burning!

MRS. ALVING (hurrying to the window). Burning!

MANDERS. Burning? Impossible. I was just down there.

OSVALD. Where's my hat? Oh, never mind—! Father's orphanage—! (He runs out through the garden door.)

MRS. ALVING. My shawl, Regina! It's all ablaze!

MANDERS. How awful! Mrs. Alving, this is God's fiery judgment on a wayward house!

MRS. ALVING. Yes, no doubt. Come along, Regina.

(She and REGINA hurry out the hall door.)

MANDERS (clasping his hands together). And then—no insurance! (He follows them out.)

ACT THREE

The room as before. All the doors stand open. The lamp is still burning on the table. It is dark outside, with only a faint red glow in the background to the left. MRS. ALVING, with a large shawl over her head, is standing in the greenhouse, gazing out. REGINA, also with a shawl about her, stands slightly behind her.

MRS. ALVING. Completely burned out—right to the ground.

REGINA. It's burning still in the basement.

MRS. ALVING. Why doesn't Osvald come up—? There's nothing to save.

REGINA. Should I go down to him with his hat?

MRS. ALVING. He hasn't even got his hat?

REGINA (pointing into the hall). No, it's hanging in there.

MRS. ALVING. Oh, leave it be. He has to come up soon. I'll look for him myself. (She goes into the garden.)

MANDERS (entering from the hall). Isn't Mrs. Alving here?

REGINA. She just went into the garden.

MANDERS. This is the most frightful night I've ever experienced.

REGINA. Yes, it's a terrible catastrophe, isn't it, Pastor?

MANDERS. Oh, don't speak of it! I can hardly think of it even.

REGINA. But how could it have happened—?

MANDERS. Don't ask me, Miss Engstrand. How should I know? You're not also going to—? Isn't it enough that your father—?

REGINA. What about him?

MANDERS. He's got me completely confused.

ENGSTRAND (entering from the hall). Pastor—!

MANDERS (turning away, appalled). Are you after me even here!

ENGSTRAND. Yes, God strike me dead, but I have to—! Good grief, what a mess this is, Pastor!

MANDERS (pacing back and forth). Dreadful, dreadful!

REGINA. What's going on?

ENGSTRAND. Oh, it was on account of this here meeting, see? (In an undertone.) Now we've got the old bird snared, my girl. (*Aloud.*) And to think it's all my fault that it's Pastor Manders' fault for something like this!

MANDERS.   But I assure you, Engstrand—

ENGSTRAND.   But there was nobody besides the pastor who messed around with the candles down there.

MANDERS (*stopping*). Yes, that's what you say. But I absolutely cannot remember ever having a candle in my hand.

ENGSTRAND.   And I saw so plainly how the pastor took that candle and pinched it out with his fingers and flicked the tip of the wick down into those shavings.

MANDERS.   You saw me do that?

ENGSTRAND.   Plain as day, I saw it.

MANDERS.   I just don't understand it. It's never been a habit of mine to snuff a candle in my fingers.

ENGSTRAND.   Yes, it did look pretty sloppy to me, all right. But could it really do that much damage, Pastor?

MANDERS (*walking restlessly back and forth*). Oh, don't ask me.

ENGSTRAND (*walking along with him*). And then your Reverence hadn't insured it either, had you?

MANDERS (*keeps walking*). No, no, no—you heard me.

ENGSTRAND (*keeps following him*). Not insured. And then to go straight over and set the whole works afire. Lord love us—what awful luck!

MANDERS (*wiping the sweat from his brow*). Yes, you can say that again, Engstrand.

ENGSTRAND.   And to think it would happen to a charitable institution that was meant to serve the whole community, so to speak. The papers'll handle you none too gently, Pastor, I can bet.

MANDERS.   No, that's just what I've been thinking about. That's almost the worst part of the whole business—all these vicious attacks and innuendoes—! Oh, it's too upsetting to think about!

MRS. ALVING (*coming from the garden*). I can't pull him away from the embers.

MANDERS.   Ah, you're back, Mrs. Alving.

MRS. ALVING.   So you got out of making your speech, Mr. Manders.

MANDERS.   Oh, I would have been only too glad—

MRS. ALVING (*her voice subdued*). It's best that it went like this. This orphanage was never made for anyone's benefit.

MANDERS.   You think it wasn't?

MRS. ALVING.   You think it was?

MANDERS.   It was a frightful misfortune, in any case.

MRS. ALVING.   Let's discuss it purely as a business arrangement—Are you waiting for the pastor, Engstrand?

ENGSTRAND (*by the hall door*). Well, actually I was.

MRS. ALVING.   Then sit down and rest a moment.

ENGSTRAND.   Thanks, I can stand all right.

MRS. ALVING (*to* MANDERS). I suppose you'll be leaving by the steamer?

MANDERS.   Yes. It goes an hour from now.

MRS. ALVING.   Would you be so good as to take all the papers back with you. I don't want to hear another word about this thing. I've got other matters to think about—

MANDERS.   Mrs. Alving—

MRS. ALVING.   I'll shortly be sending you power of attorney to settle everything however you choose.

MANDERS.   I'll be only too glad to take care of it. Of course the original terms of the bequest will have to be changed completely now, I'm afraid.

MRS. ALVING.   That's understood.

MANDERS.   Just offhand, it strikes me that I might arrange it so the Solvik property is made over to the parish. The land itself can hardly be written off as worthless; it can always be put to some use or other. And the interest on the balance of capital in the bank—I could probably apply that best to support some project or other that might be considered of benefit to the town.

MRS. ALVING.   Whatever you wish. The whole thing's utterly indifferent to me now.

ENGSTRAND.   Think of my seaman's home, Pastor!

MANDERS.   Yes, definitely, that's a possibility. Well, it will bear some investigation.

ENGSTRAND.   The hell with investigating—oh, Jeez!

MANDERS (*with a sigh*). And then too, unfortunately I have no idea how long I'll be able to handle these affairs—or if public opinion won't force me to drop them. That depends entirely on the results of the inquest into the fire.

MRS. ALVING.   What are you saying?

MANDERS.   And those results aren't predictable in advance.

ENGSTRAND (*approaching him*). Oh yes, they are! Because here's old Jacob Engstrand, right beside you.

MANDERS.   Yes, but—?

ENGSTRAND (*lowering his voice*). And Jacob Engstrand's not the man to go back on a worthy benefactor in his hour of need, as the expression goes.

MANDERS.   Yes, but my dear fellow—how can you—?

ENGSTRAND.   Jacob Engstrand's sort of like your guardian angel, Pastor, see?

MANDERS.   No, no, that I absolutely cannot accept.

ENGSTRAND.   Oh, it's how it's going to be, anyway. It's not like somebody here hasn't taken the blame for somebody else before, you know.

MANDERS.   Jacob! (*Grasps his hand.*) You're a rare individual. Well, you're going to have every bit of help you need for your seaman's home, you can count on that.

(ENGSTRAND *tries to thank him, but is overcome by emotion.*)

MANDERS (*slipping the strap of his traveling bag over his shoulder*). Well, time to be off. We can travel together.

ENGSTRAND (*by the dining-room door*). Come along with me, wench! You'll live soft as a yoke in an egg.

REGINA (*tossing her head*). *Merci!* (*She goes out in the hall and fetches* MANDERS' *overcoat and umbrella.*)

MANDERS.   Good-bye, Mrs. Alving. And may the spirit of law and order soon dwell again in this house.

MRS. ALVING.   Good-bye, Manders. (*She goes into the greenhouse as she notices* OSVALD *coming in through the garden door.*)

ENGSTRAND (*as he and* REGINA *help* MANDERS *on with his coat*). Good-bye, my girl. And if you're ever in any trouble, well, you know where to find Jacob Engstrand. (*Quietly.*) Little Harbor Street, hm—! (*To* MRS. ALVING *and* OSVALD.) And my house for wayfaring seamen— that's going to be known as "Captain Alving's Home," yes. And if I get to run that house after my own devices, I think I can promise you it'll be truly worthy of that great man's memory, bless him.

MANDERS (*in the doorway*). Hm—hm! Come along, my dear Engstrand. Good-bye, good-bye!

(*He and* ENGSTRAND *go out the hall door.*)

OSVALD (*going toward the table*). What is this house he was speaking of?

MRS. ALVING.   It's some sort of home that he and the pastor want to establish.

OSVALD.   It'll burn up like all this here.

MRS. ALVING.   Why do you say that?

OSVALD.   Everything will burn. There'll be nothing left in memory of Father. And here I'm burning up, too.

(REGINA *stares perplexed at him.*)

MRS. ALVING.   Osvald! Poor boy—you shouldn't have stayed down there so long.

OSVALD (*sitting at the table*). I guess you're right.

MRS. ALVING.   Let me dry your face, dear; you're dripping wet.

OSVALD (*gazing indifferently into space*). Thank you, Mother.

MRS. ALVING.   Aren't you tired, Osvald? Perhaps you could sleep?

OSVALD (*anxiously*). No, no—not sleep! I never sleep; I only pretend to. (*Dully.*) That comes soon enough.

MRS. ALVING (*looking worriedly at him*). You know, dearest, you really are ill.

REGINA (*tensely*). Is Mr. Alving ill?

OSVALD (*impulsively*). And shut all the doors! This racking fear—!

MRS. ALVING.   Shut them, Regina.

(REGINA *shuts the doors and remains standing by the hall door.* MRS. ALVING *removes her shawl;* REGINA *does the same.*)

MRS. ALVING (*draws a chair over beside* OSVALD *and sits by him*). There, now I'll sit with you—

OSVALD.   Yes, do that. And Regina must stay here, too. I always want her close to me. You'll give me your help, Regina—won't you?

REGINA.   I don't understand—

MRS. ALVING.   Help?

OSVALD.   Yes—when it's needed.

MRS. ALVING.   Osvald, don't you have your mother to give you help?

OSVALD.   You? (*Smiles.*) No, Mother, that kind of help you'd never give me. (*With a mournful laugh.*) You! Ha, ha! (*Looks soberly at her.*) Although you're the obvious choice. (*Vehemently.*) Regina, why are you so reserved toward me? Why can't you call me Osvald?

REGINA (*softly*). I don't think Mrs. Alving would like it.

MRS. ALVING.   You'll have every right to soon—so won't you sit down with us here?

(*After a moment,* REGINA *sits down with shy dignity at the other side of the table.*)

And now, my poor, troubled boy, I'm going to take all this weight off your mind—

OSVALD.   You, Mother?

MRS. ALVING.   Everything you call the agony of remorse and self-reproach.

OSVALD.   Do you think you can?

MRS. ALVING.   Yes, Osvald, now I can. You were speaking earlier about the joy of life: and as you said those words, it was as if a new light had been shed over the whole of my life.

OSVALD (*shaking his head*). I don't understand this.

MRS. ALVING.   You should have known your father when he was just a young lieutenant. *He* had the joy of life, he did!

OSVALD.   Yes, I know.

MRS. ALVING.   It was like a holiday just to look at him. And all the energy, the unquenchable power that was in him!

OSVALD.   Well—?

MRS. ALVING.   And then, so full of that very joy, this child—because he *was* like a child then, really—had to make a life here in a mediocre town that had no joys to offer—only distractions. He had to get along here with no real goal in life—only a routine job to hold down. He never found any activity he could throw himself in heart and soul—only business affairs. He never had one single friend with the slightest sense of what the joy of life can mean—no one but drifters and drunkards—

OSVALD.   Mother—!

MRS. ALVING.   And finally the inevitable happened.

OSVALD.   The inevitable?

MRS. ALVING.   You said yourself, earlier this evening, what would happen to you if you stayed at home.

OSVALD.   Your'e saying that Father—?

MRS. ALVING.   Your poor father never found any outlet for the overpowering joy of life that he had. And I'm afraid I couldn't make his home very festive, either.

OSVALD.   You, too?

MRS. ALVING.   They'd drilled me so much in duty and things of that kind that I went on here all too long putting my faith in them. Everything resolved into duties—*my* duties, and *his* duties, and—I'm afraid I made this home unbearable for your poor father.

OSVALD.   Why didn't you ever write me any of this?

MRS. ALVING.   I've never seen it before as anything I could mention to you—his son.

OSVALD.   And how, then, did you see it?

MRS. ALVING (*slowly*).   I only saw the one thing: that your father was a ravaged man before you were born.

OSVALD (*with a strangled cry*). Ah—! (*He stands up and goes to the window.*)

MRS. ALVING.   And then day after day I had only one thought on my mind: that Regina in reality belonged here in this house—just as much as my own son.

OSVALD (*wheeling about*). Regina—!

REGINA (*brought shaken to her feet, in a choked voice*). I—!

MRS. ALVING.   Yes, now you both know.

OSVALD.   Regina!

REGINA (*to herself*). So that's what she was.

MRS. ALVING.   Your mother was decent in many ways, Regina.

REGINA.   Yes, but she was that kind, all the same. Well, I sometimes thought so, but—then, Mrs. Alving, if you don't mind, may I leave right away, at once?

MRS. ALVING.   Do you really want to, Regina?

REGINA.   Yes, of course I want to.

MRS. ALVING.   Naturally you can do as you wish, but—

OSVALD (*going over to* REGINA). Leave now? But you belong here.

REGINA.   *Merci*, Mr. Alving—yes, I guess I can call you Osvald now. But it's certainly not the way I wanted to.

MRS. ALVING.   Regina, I haven't been straightforward with you—

REGINA.   That's putting it mild! If I'd known that Osvald was sick, why— And now that there isn't a chance of anything serious between us— No, I really can't stay out in the country and run myself ragged for invalids.

OSVALD.   Not even for someone this close to you?

REGINA.   Not on your life, I can't! A poor girl's only got her youth; she'd better use it—or else she'll find herself barefoot at Christmas before she knows it. And I've got this joy of life too, Mrs. Alving—in *me!*

MRS. ALVING.   Yes, I'm afraid so. Only don't throw yourself away, Regina.

REGINA.   Oh, things go as they go. If Osvald takes after his father, then I take after my mother, I guess. May I ask, Mrs. Alving, if Pastor Manders knows all this about me?

MRS. ALVING.   Pastor Manders knows everything.

REGINA (*busy putting on her shawl*). Then I really better see if I can catch the boat out of here as quick as I can. The pastor's so nice to deal with, and I definitely think I've got just as much right to some of that money as he does— that rotten carpenter.

MRS. ALVING.   You're quite welcome to it, Regina.

REGINA (*looking sharply at her*). You know, Mrs. Alving, you could have raised me as a gentleman's daughter— and I would've been a lot better off. (*Tossing her head.*) But, hell—what's the difference! (*With a bitter glance at the unopened bottle.*) I'll get my champagne in society yet, just see if I don't.

MRS. ALVING.   If you ever need a home, Regina, you can come to me.

REGINA.   No, thank you, ma'am. Pastor Manders'll look out for me, all right. And if things really go wrong, I still know a house where I'll do just fine.

MRS. ALVING.   Where?

REGINA.   In "Captain Alving's Home."

MRS. ALVING.   Regina—I can see now—you'll go to your ruin!

REGINA.   Ahh, ffft! *Adieu.* (*She curtsies and goes out the hall door.*)

OSVALD (*standing at the window, looking out*). Has she gone?

MRS. ALVING.   Yes.

OSVALD (*murmuring to himself*). I think it's insane, all this.

MRS. ALVING (*goes over behind him, placing her hands on his shoulders*). Osvald, dear—has this disturbed you terribly?

OSVALD (*turning his face toward her*). All that about Father, you mean?

MRS. ALVING.   Yes, about your poor father. I'm afraid it's been too much of a shock for you.

OSVALD.   Why do you think so? It came as quite a surprise, of course; but basically it can hardly make any difference to me.

MRS. ALVING (*withdrawing her hands*). No difference! That your father was so enormously unhappy!

OSVALD.   Naturally I can feel sympathy for him as for any human being, but—

MRS. ALVING.   Nothing more—for your own father—!

OSVALD (*impatiently*). Yes, Father—Father! I never knew a father. My only memory of him is that he once got me to vomit.

MRS. ALVING.   That's a dreadful thought! Surely a child ought to feel some love for his father, no matter what.

OSVALD.   When that child has nothing to thank him for? Hasn't even known him? Do you really hang on to that old superstition—you, so enlightened in everything else?

MRS. ALVING.   And is that just a superstition—!

OSVALD.   Yes, you must realize that, Mother. It's one of these ideas that materialize in the world for a while, and then—

MRS. ALVING (*with a shudder*). Ghosts!

OSVALD (*pacing the floor*). Yes, you could very well call them ghosts.

MRS. ALVING (*in an outcry*). Osvald—you don't love me either!

OSVALD. I know you, at least—

MRS. ALVING. Yes, I know—but is that all?

OSVALD. And I know how much you care for me, and I have to be grateful to you for that. And you can be especially useful to me, now that I'm ill.

MRS. ALVING. Yes, I can, Osvald, can't I? Oh, I could almost bless this illness that forced you home to me, because it's made me see you're really not mine; you still have to be won.

OSVALD (*impatiently*). Yes, yes, yes, that's all just a manner of speaking. You have to remember I'm a sick man, Mother. I can't be concerned very much with others; I have enough just thinking about myself.

MRS. ALVING (*softly*). I'll be patient and forebearing.

OSVALD. And cheerful, Mother!

MRS. ALVING. Yes, dearest, you're right. (*Going over to him.*) Now have I taken away all your remorse and self-reproach?

OSVALD. Yes, you have. But who'll take away the fear?

MRS. ALVING. The fear?

OSVALD (*pacing about the room*). Regina would have done it for the asking.

MRS. ALVING. I don't understand. What is all this about fear—and Regina?

OSVALD. Is it very late, Mother?

MRS. ALVING. It's nearly morning. (*Looking out through the greenhouse.*) There's the first light of dawn already on the mountains. It's going to be clear, Osvald! In a little while you'll see the sun.

OSVALD. I look forward to that. Oh, there can be so much still to look forward to, and live for—!

MRS. ALVING. I'm sure there will be!

OSVALD. And even though I can't work, I'll—

MRS. ALVING. Oh, my dearest, you'll find yourself working again so soon. Because now you won't have these worrisome, depressing thoughts to brood on any longer.

OSVALD. Yes, it was good that you could rid me of all those fantasies of mine. And now, if I can only face this one thing more— (*She sits down on the sofa.*) Mother, we have to talk together—

MRS. ALVING. Yes, let's. (*She pushes an armchair over by the sofa and sits beside him.*)

OSVALD. And meanwhile the sun will rise. And by then, you'll know—and I won't have this fear any longer.

MRS. ALVING. Tell me, what will I know?

OSVALD (*not listening*). Mother, didn't you say earlier this evening that there wasn't anything in the world you wouldn't do for me if I asked you?

MRS. ALVING. Why, yes, of course!

OSVALD. And you meant it, Mother?

MRS. ALVING. That you can depend on. You're my one and only boy; I have nothing else to live for but you.

OSVALD. All right, then listen. You have a strong, resilient mind, I know that. I want you to sit very quiet as I tell this.

MRS. ALVING. But what is it that's so terrible—?

OSVALD. You mustn't scream. Do you hear? Promise me that? We're going to sit and speak of it quietly. Mother, promise me?

MRS. ALVING. Yes, yes, I promise—just tell me!

OSVALD. Well, then you've got to realize that all this about tiredness—and my incapacity for thinking in terms of my work—isn't the real illness—

MRS. ALVING. What is the real illness?

OSVALD. The one that I inherited, the illness—(*Points to his forehead and speaks very softly.*)—that's seated here.

MRS. ALVING (*nearly speechless*). Osvald! No—no!

OSVALD. Don't scream; I can't bear it. Yes, it sits in here and waits. And any day, at any time, it can strike.

MRS. ALVING. Oh, how horrible—!

OSVALD. Just stay calm. So, that's how things are with me.

MRS. ALVING (*springing to her feet*). It's not true, Osvald! It's impossible! It can't be!

OSVALD. I had one attack down there. It soon passed off—but when I found out how things stood with me, then this anxiety took hold, racking me like a cold fever; and with that, I started home here to you as fast as I could.

MRS. ALVING. So that's the fear—!

OSVALD. Yes, I can't tell you how excruciating it is. Oh, if it only had been some ordinary disease that would kill me—I'm not so afraid of dying, though I want to live as long as I can.

MRS. ALVING. Yes, yes, Osvald, you must!

OSVALD. But the thought of it *is* excruciating. To revert back to a helpless child again. To have to be fed, to have to be—oh, it's unspeakable.

MRS. ALVING. My child has his mother to nurse him.

OSVALD (*leaps up*). No, never! That's just what I won't have! I can't abide the thought of lying here like that for years—turning old and gray. And in the meantime you might die before me. (*Sits in* MRS. ALVING'*s chair.*) Because the doctor said it needn't be fatal at once. He called it a kind of "softening of the brain"—some phrase like that. (*Smiles sadly.*) I think that expression sounds so nice. It always makes me think of cherry-red velvet draperies—something soft to stroke.

MRS. ALVING (*screams*). Osvald!

OSVALD (*leaps up again and paces the floor*). And now you've taken Regina away from me! If I'd only had her. She would have helped me out, I'm sure.

MRS. ALVING (*going over to him*). My dear boy, what do you mean? Is there any help in this world that I wouldn't willingly give you?

OSVALD.   After I'd recovered from the attack down there, the doctor told me that, when it struck again—and it *would* strike—there'd be no more hope.

MRS. ALVING.   That he could be so heartless—

OSVALD.   I demanded it of him. I told him I had certain arrangements to make. (*With a shy smile.*) And so I had. (*Brings out a small box from his inner breast pocket.*) Mother, you see this?

MRS. ALVING.   What's that?

OSVALD.   Morphine pills.

MRS. ALVING (*looks at him in horror*). Osvald—my child!

OSVALD.   I've saved up twelve of them—

MRS. ALVING (*snatching at it*). Give me the box, Osvald!

OSVALD.   Not yet, Mother. (*He returns the box to his pocket.*)

MRS. ALVING.   I can't live through this!

OSVALD.   You'll have to. If I'd had Regina here now, I'd have told her what state I was in—and asked for her help with this one last thing. She'd have helped me, I'm positive of that.

MRS. ALVING.   Never!

OSVALD.   If this horrible thing struck me down, and she saw me lying there like an infant child, helpless, and beyond help, lost, hopeless—incurable—

MRS. ALVING.   Regina never would have done that!

OSVALD.   Yes, she would have. Regina was so wonderfully lighthearted. She soon would have gotten tired of tending an invalid like me.

MRS. ALVING.   Then thank God Regina's not here!

OSVALD.   So now, Mother, you've got to give me that help.

MRS. ALVING (*in a loud outcry*). I!

OSVALD.   What more obvious choice than you?

MRS. ALVING.   I! Your mother!

OSVALD.   Exactly the reason.

MRS. ALVING.   I, who gave you life!

OSVALD.   I never asked you for life. And what is this life you gave me? I don't want it! You can take it back!

MRS. ALVING.   Help! Help! (*She runs out into the hall.*)

OSVALD (*right behind her*). Don't leave me! Where are you going?

MRS. ALVING (*in the hall*). To get the doctor, Osvald! Let me out!

OSVALD (*also in the hall*). You don't leave. And no one comes in.

(*The sound of a key turning in a lock.*)

MRS. ALVING (*coming in again*). Osvald—Osvald—my child!

OSVALD (*following her*). Have you no mother-love for me at all—to see me suffer this unbearable fear!

MRS. ALVING (*after a moment's silence, controlling her voice*). Here's my hand on it.

OSVALD.   Then you will—?

MRS. ALVING.   If it becomes necessary. But it won't be necessary. No, no, that's simply impossible!

OSVALD.   Well, that we can hope. And now let's live together as long as we can. Thank you, Mother.

(*He settles down in the armchair that* MRS. ALVING *had moved over to the sofa. The day is breaking; the lamp still burns on the table.*)

MRS. ALVING.   Now do you feel all right?

OSVALD.   Yes.

MRS. ALVING (*bending over him*). What a fearful nightmare this has been for you, Osvald—but it was all a dream. Too much excitement—it hasn't been good for you. But now you can have your rest, at home with your mother near, my own, my dearest boy. Anything you want you can have, just like when you were a little child. There now, the pain is over. You see how quickly it went. Oh, I knew it would— And look, Osvald, what a lovely day we'll have. Bright sunlight. Now you really can see your home.

(*She goes to the table and puts out the lamp. Sunrise. The glaciers and peaks in the background shine in the brilliant light of morning. With his back toward the distant view,* OSVALD *sits motionless in the armchair.*)

OSVALD (*abruptly*). Mother, give me the sun.

MRS. ALVING (*by the table, looks at him, startled*). What did you say?

OSVALD (*repeats in a dull monotone*). The sun. The sun.

MRS. ALVING (*moves over to him*). Osvald, what's the matter?

(OSVALD *appears to crumple inwardly in the chair; all his muscles loosen; the expression leaves his face; and his eyes stare blankly.*)

MRS. ALVING (*shaking with fear*). What is it? (*In a shriek.*) Osvald! What's wrong! (*Drops to her knees beside him and shakes him.*) Osvald! Osvald! Look at me! Don't you know me?

OSVALD (*in the same monotone*). The sun—the sun.

MRS. ALVING (*springs to her feet in anguish, tears at her hair with both hands and screams*). I can't bear this! (*Whispers as if paralyzed by fright.*) I can't bear it! Never! (*Suddenly.*) Where did he put them? (*Her hand skims across his chest.*) Here! (*She shrinks back several steps and shrieks.*) No, no, no!—Yes!—No, no! (*She stands a few steps away from him, her fingers thrust into her hair, staring at him in speechless horror.*)

OSVALD (*sitting motionless, as before*). The sun—the sun.

FOCUS QUESTIONS

1. Discuss the controversy surrounding *Ghosts* and explain why its issues still remain relevant in today's society.
2. In a short essay, evaluate the exposition of the play and its importance to Ibsen's dramatic intentions.
3. Exactly what is Ibsen promulgating when he attacks Pastor Manders? Or Jakob Engstrand?
4. Discuss how Ibsen's handling of mood and atmosphere contributes to the design and effect of the play.
5. What specific functions do characters serve in *Ghosts?*
6. How does Ibsen's play depict the society of nineteenth-century Norway? Does the playwright imply any need for change?
7. How does the reality of Osvald's physical condition serve as metaphor? Evaluate any implications.

OTHER ACTIVITIES

1. Using reviews, photographs, and other available documents, assess an English-language production of the play.
2. Construct a short dialogue between Mrs. Alving and the late Captain Alving. Assume that she has recently learned about Osvald's illness.
3. View Gabriel Axel's *Babette's Feast* (1987), in which the issues of ''sacrifice'' and ''life choices'' are crucial to both theme and dramatic action. Discuss the similarities between this film and *Ghosts*.

BIBLIOGRAPHY

Bradbrook, M. C. *Ibsen the Norwegian: A Revaluation.* London: Chatto & Windus, 1966.
Durbach, Errol, ed. *Ibsen and the Theatre.* London: Macmillan, 1980.
Fjelde, Rolf, ed. *Ibsen: A Collection of Critical Essays.* Englewood Cliffs, NJ: Prentice Hall, 1965.
Johnston, Brian. *Text and Supertext in Ibsen's Drama.* University Park, PA: Pennsylvania State University Press, 1989.
Lyons, Charles. *Henrik Ibsen: The Divided Consciousness.* Carbondale: Southern Illinois University Press, 1972.
Marker, F. J., and L. L. Marker. *Ibsen's Lively Art: A Performance Study of the Major Plays.* New York: Cambridge University Press, 1989.
Meyer, Michael. *Ibsen.* New York: Doubleday & Co., 1971.
Northam, John. *Ibsen: A Critical Study.* New York: Cambridge University Press, 1973.
Schanke, Robert. *Ibsen in America: A Century of Change.* Metuchen, NJ: Scarecrow Press, 1988.
Shaw, Bernard. *The Quintessence of Ibsenism.* New York: Hill & Wang, 1957.
Tennant, P. F. D. *Ibsen's Dramatic Technique.* Cambridge: Bower & Bower, 1948.
Valency, Maurice. *The Flower and the Castle.* London: Macmillan, 1963.
Weigand, H. J. *The Modern Ibsen: A Reconsideration.* New York: Books for Libraries Press, 1970.

RECOMMENDED VIDEOTAPES AND RECORDINGS

Ghosts. VHS. 90 min. Distributed by Films for the Humanities and Sciences, Princeton, NJ. Starring Dorothy Tutin, Richard Pasco, and Ronald Fraser.
Ghosts. One sound cassette. 1974. A classic Theatre Guild Production. Adapted by Elayne Carroll and Robert M. Culp. Listening Library.

THE SEA GULL
ANTON CHEKHOV (1860–1904)

There is only one road for the playwrights of the future, and that is the road of Chekhov.

—NEMIROVICH-DANCHENKO

From the 1987 Tokyo Engeki Ensemble production of *The Sea Gull*, under the direction of Tsunetoshi Hirowatari. *Photo: Tokyo Engeki Ensemble.*

APPROACHING REALISM IN RUSSIA

The artistic temperament that flourished in Czarist Russia during the second half of the nineteenth century has had an enduring impact on Western performance. The prolific, highly individualized literary achievements of Fyodor Dostoyevski (1821–1881) and Leo Tolstoy (1828–1910), the lush musical lyricism of Peter Ilich Tchaikovsky (1840–1893), and the heartrending dramas of Anton Chekhov certainly rank among the most popular and evocative symbols of Russia's cultural past. They have survived the demise of several political orders, each of which had its own aesthetic agenda.

Russia's theatrical tradition, which gained world status more than a century before the revolution of 1917, was prompted by the invasion of Napoleon Bonaparte, whose stunning defeat by Russian armies captured the attention of western Europe. Occurring under the leadership of Alexander I, who ruled between 1801 and 1825, the military triumph infused artists with a patriotic fervor and a renewed hope for liberating the serfs. When Nicholas I assumed the throne in 1825, his thirty-year reign created an upsurge in artistic activity shared by the older St. Petersburg and the new cultural capital, Moscow. Adhering to the strictly enforced code of censorship that permeated Russian society, the lively arts of opera, ballet, and drama filled the numerous imperial theatres that flourished under his reign.

Alexander Griboyedov (1795–1829), Alexander Pushkin (1799–1837), and Mikhail Lermontov (1814–1841) were the renowned masters of dramatic art and poetry during the first half of the nineteenth century. Reflecting a dwindling loyalty to the European neoclassical model approved by the censorial Russian court, their literary styles gradually embraced the romantic spirit best exemplified by French melodrama, thereby generating countless imitations on the Russian stage. But hints of a more powerful theatrical art were present from the start. The neoclassical style of Griboyedov's *Woe from Wit,* for example, was no barrier to its satiric treatment of Czarist corruption. Often regarded as his masterpiece, the play anticipated the thrust toward realism so fully evident in the eccentric characters and themes of Nikolai Gogol (1809–1852). In fact, Gogol's stage achievements would inspire Ivan Turgenev (1818–1883) and Alexander Ostrovsky (1823–1886), whose emphasis on domestic detail and symbolism quietly set the stage for Chekhov. When Tolstoy finally turned from novels to playwriting, his reliance on **naturalism** paid homage to a Russian spirit that was fully prepared for Chekhov's timely entrance.

In the theatre, initial steps in what proved to be a highly productive direction were taken by two established practitioners, Vladimir Nemirovich-Danchenko (1858–1943) and Konstantin Stanislavsky (1863–1938), who co-founded an independent company in 1898 which they called the Moscow Art Theatre. Opposing the outworn conventions that permeated the domestic repertoire currently available in Moscow, both artists nurtured a gifted acting ensemble and drew up manifestos for a renovated agenda in all aspects of stage production. Their goals called for change.

In spite of the ever-watchful eye of the state censor, their hope of introducing a new kind of stage realism was facilitated by the company's timely association with Chekhov, whose play *The Sea Gull* had been unsuccessfully performed at the Alexandrinsky Theatre in St. Petersburg in 1896. Nemirovich-Danchenko wanted to stage it at the Moscow Art Theatre, which he did with the playwright's reluctant approval and under Stanislavsky's direction on December 17, 1898. The success of the production not only brought new life and critical acclaim to the play, but ensured the company's aim at producing "works of art of the highest possible excellence quite free of official restriction or the pressures of popular taste."[1] Thus a new era in Russian drama was born.

In fact, Chekhov's overnight success in the theatre had taken some years to achieve. Having used his writing skills to support both his education and a large family of parents, brothers, and a sister, he was a paid author by the time of his graduation from the medical college of Moscow University at the age of twenty-four. His close to three hundred short literary pieces, written under a pseudonym, had already gained a respectable readership. Although the theatre was his great love, he chose to write stories instead, because he could have them published easily and would be paid just enough to cover his expenses.

While juggling both careers, Chekhov became an outspoken critic of Russian literature and stage performance, much of which invariably bored him. Bemoaning the fact that the provinces were besieged with amateur acting companies and that mediocre works from the past were continually revived, he commented extensively in his informal letters to colleagues about the criteria he deemed essential for the art of playwriting. Among these, he sought originality in stage characters and advocated that they not reflect the playwright entirely, but be allowed to speak for themselves. He insisted on a certain compactness in the play's design and verbal expressiveness. Finally he wanted his plays to impart humanity and a high moral purpose, recalling Dr. Dorn's advice to the young playwright in *The Sea Gull,* that "a work of art decidedly should express a great idea. Only what is serious can be beautiful."

What evolved was a powerful mastery of characterization, dramatic mood, and subtlety of incident, all of which contributed to his esteemed literary reputation. His narrative skills had prepared him for his immersion into playwriting. Above all, his professional association with Nemirovich-Danchenko and Stanislavsky, which was characterized by well-documented clashes, resulted in a dramatic style filled with psychological innovations and finely etched stage characters more evocative of the approaching revolutionary spirit than of Russia's conventional literary past. As for Chekhov's uneventful medical practice, which he maintained out of his own humanitarian interests, it had produced an acute scientific eye that, in turn, enhanced his imagination and sharpened his powers of observation.

Major Works

Chekhov wrote countless short stories and nearly a dozen one-act plays between 1877 and 1894, followed by six full-length plays on which his fame as a dramatist became permanently established. Two earlier works, *Platonov* (1881) and *Ivanov* (1887), evoked a special brand of stage realism which, the playwright later described, was not only designed to show "life as it is" but "life as it should be."[2] Both plays foreshadowed his unique handling of tragedy and comedy, the elements of which were seamlessly fused in four major works that epitomized his dramatic art: *The Sea Gull* (1896), *Uncle Vanya* (1897), *Three Sisters* (1901), and *The Cherry Orchard* (1904). Social, political, and emotional inertia, helplessness at effecting change, and the inability to escape the past are motifs that echo throughout, converging in a complex network of character interactions and dramatic subtexts. Yet one major theme is voiced repeatedly: the need to endure despite life's frustrations. Correlating life with art, specifically the art of the theatre, *The Sea Gull* remains unique in its depiction of the playwright's struggle to reinvent his craft.

The Action

The performance of Konstantin Gavrilovich's newest play, presented to his family and friends and featuring his girlfriend Nini Zarechnaya as its solo performer, is interrupted by the laughter of his mother, the well-known actress Arkadina. Days later, Konstantin shoots a sea gull which he places at Nina's feet, telling her he will kill himself in the same manner one day. Arkadina's lover Trigorin notices the sea gull and makes a note of it in his book, thinking it a unique idea for a story about a man who meets a young girl and, having nothing better to do, ''destroys her, just like this sea gull here.'' A week later, Konstantin has attempted suicide and recovered. Nina has decided to join Trigorin in Moscow and become an actress.

Two years have passed. Nina has had an affair with Trigorin and given birth to a child who died. While Konstantin contemplates his own failure as a writer, the abandoned and exhausted Nina appears and talks confusedly about her stage career. When she leaves, Konstantin destroys his manuscripts, exits from the drawing room, then shoots himself.

STRUCTURE AND LANGUAGE

Chekhov's innovative literary style departs from the traditional design of Western drama rooted in conflict and built on rising actions, climax, and denouement. Understating the dramatic action but never eliminating it entirely, Chekhov has created a character-centered work that thrives on indirect actions. While certain crucial events occur offstage, their repercussions force the characters to play their interior lives against each other, but always before our eyes.

Konstantin's play-within-a-play is an indelible opening metaphor around which the subsequent actions continually resound. Its interruption swiftly launches these hapless characters into the larger design of Chekhov's play: in this case, the unique and often undefinable relationship between human life and creative art. Chekhov uses the older generation to critique the spiritual malaise permeating Russian society. ''I do have some money,'' Arkadina exclaims, ''but I am an actress, and my costumes alone are enough to ruin me.'' Her artistic values are rooted in material success, and she is coldly indifferent to the nobler aims of her profession. Her lover Trigorin revels in his own brand of cynicism as well: ''I've never had a will of my own . . . Flabby, soft, always submissive—how can that appeal to a woman?'' Their complaints reflect a jaded outlook that sharply contrasts with the youthful idealism and energy of the upcoming generation. When Konstantin and Nina threaten their facade of well-being, Arkadina and Trigorin impede their futures and hasten their destruction.

No matter how hard the worldly Arkadina and Trigorin try to distance themselves from the simpler country folk who cater to their demands, they are, like the characters who surround them, encumbered by their own frustrated lives. Equally important, their cynical indifference shifts our attention back to Konstantin and Nina, whose destinies ultimately consume the play's center and whose reunion and final separation in act 4 eloquently merge Chekhov's thematic concerns for life and art—but only after a fatal price has been paid.

Chekhov the artist captures the poetry of his characters at every turn, ordinary people ultimately ennobled by life's ordinary events. But on another level, they achieve more profound dimensions through the playwright's allusion to *Hamlet*—Shakespeare's universal tragedy. The domestic entanglement of son, mother, lover—the Konstantin-Arkadina-Trigorin triangle—proves as problematical as the significantly darker relationship of Hamlet-Gertrude-Claudius and prompts our contemplation of life's unanswerable mysteries, a matter of great philosophical importance to Chekhov as well as Shakespeare.

In his most heated confrontation with Arkadina, Konstantin perceives the truth about her and Trigorin: ''You, with your hackneyed conventions, have usurped the foremost places in art, and consider nothing genuine and legitimate except what you yourselves do—everything else you stifle and suppress! I do not accept you! I accept neither you nor him!'' But Konstantin, like Hamlet, is helpless to act on this knowledge, thereby elevating a simple family quarrel to almost tragic proportions.

Further animated by delicately nuanced rhythms, Chekhov's dialogue achieves a poetic lyricism enhanced by internalized responses, **asides,** and **soliloquies** that illuminate the emotional impact. One of the earliest notes is sounded by Nina in her solo performance as the world soul of Konstantin's experimental play: "I am all alone. Once in a hundred years I open my mouth to speak, my voice echoes dolefully in this void, and no one hears it . . . Like a prisoner cast into a deep and empty well, I know not where I am or what awaits me." No matter how empty this dialogue sounds, something transcendent occurs when its images are echoed by Konstantin in his final confrontation with her. Several years have passed and their lives have been tinged by unhappiness and failure. Suddenly he exclaims, "I am alone, I have no one's affection to warm me, I am as cold as if I were living in a dungeon, and no matter what I write, it's dry, hard, dark." This time the effect is chilling and recalls Dorn's first-act advice to the aspiring young playwright after his play had been laughed at: "You must know what you are writing for, otherwise, if you just move along some esthetic road without a definite aim, you'll be lost and your talent will destroy you." Somewhat prophetically, Konstantin's fate has been tragically conjoined to his art. But Nina—his sea gull—will survive, as she reminds him that the future is "not so painful now, and when I think of my vocation, I'm not afraid of life."

Mindful of the pathetic destinies of his two young protagonists, Chekhov seems to redefine the conventional view of comedy to accommodate the fundamental absurdities of the human condition. Not surprisingly, the characters' thwarted dreams and the barriers to communication that underlie *The Sea Gull* prompt its themes of loneliness and alienation which pay homage to these absurdities. The new stage realism achieved by the playwright thrives on our viewing the dramatic action from some safe distance, while recognizing the flashes of truth in his characters' emotions. When that rare Chekhovian balance between the comic and the tragic is achieved in live performance, we may smile at their tears or cry at their laughter.

About the Translation

The art of rendering Chekhov's world faithfully and clearly to the contemporary English-speaking reader has been masterfully achieved in this fairly literal translation by Ann Dunnigan. Leaving the structure of Chekhov's text for *The Sea Gull* intact, including his indelible punctuation, Dunnigan uncovers a comparable musicality inherent in the original Russian and captures much of that essential spirit that has made his spoken dialogue so natural for the stage. In the memorable final confrontation between Konstantin and Nina, for example, Nina's halting speech rhythms are reflective of her mental confusion but adhere completely to Chekhov's style, including his careful use of ellipsis. Furthermore, the closely aligned negatives in Nina's "No, no . . . Don't go with me, I'll go alone . . . My horses are not far," duplicate the Russian, creating an urgency that smoothly counterpoints Konstantin's despondent disposition. Occasionally Dunnigan opts for the underlying sense of the character's remark instead. When Konstantin confesses to Nina, "I have no faith," his brief remark provides an eloquent variation of Chekhov's "I do not believe." It is understandable why Dunnigan's renditions of Chekhov's plays have served many American stage productions.

The Sea Gull-in-Performance

If Chekhov's last four plays had been produced posthumously, their production histories might never have proven so rich or controversial. Chekhov's outspoken, even negative reactions to the initial performances of *The Sea Gull,* both at the Alexandrinsky (1896) and the Moscow Art Theatre (1898), prompted a set of standards and expectations that subsequent theatre artists in and outside of Russia have found impossible to ignore and difficult to achieve. The onstage results have often been the measure of success or failure for international theatre companies, the lack of **ensemble** acting usually generating the sharpest criticism.

Stanislavsky's strenuous and lengthy rehearsal for *The Sea Gull,* with a cast that featured Olga Knipper as Arkadina, Vsevolod Meyerhold as Konstantin, M. P. Roksanova as Nina, and the director himself as Trigorin won a glowing critical reception that enhanced the reputations of all involved. Yet the playwright was unhappy with the performances of Stanislavsky and Roksanova, who were later replaced by Vassily Kachalov and Maria Lilina. When a revival of the play proved unsuccessful in 1905, the blame was placed on Stanislavsky's gimmicky direction and *The Sea Gull* was dropped from the repertory.

During the forty years that followed the October Revolution, 262 new productions of Chekhov's plays appeared throughout Russia, of which 28 were of *The Sea Gull.* But only in the second half of the twentieth century has any real effort been made to break away from the Chekhovian style established by Stanislavsky's productions. In 1946, a radical attempt had been made by Alexander Tairov, director of the Kamerny Theatre, who interpreted the play to accommodate his own artistic vision and to incorporate some of the experimental forms that Chekhov's protagonist, Konstantin, hoped to explore in his own interrupted playlet from act 1. Greeted with public disapproval, Tairov's use of **symbolism** proved too sharp a contrast from the more traditional renditions of the play which, under the influence of Soviet censorship, were still preferred by Russian stage artists and audiences.

In Europe, George and Ludmilla Pitoëff staged *The Sea Gull* in Paris in 1921 and again in 1939. Adhering to the abstract and imaginative style that they popularized on the Paris stage prior to World War II, their productions of Chekhov played against black canvas flats pleased audiences and enhanced the playwright's reputation in France. Elsewhere on the continent, Giorgio Strehler's 1948 production at the Piccolo Teatro in Milan echoed Stanislavsky's *mise-en-scène.* Strehler's success not only confirmed his directorial skill at age twenty-seven, but drew international acclaim to other Chekhov works performed in Italy.

The Sea Gull received its first British production on November 2, 1909, at the Royalty Theatre in Glasgow in a translation by George Calderon, who also served as director. The first London production took place on March 31, 1912, at the Little Theatre under the direction of Maurice Elvey. A revival directed by Esme Filmer at the Little Theatre on October 19, 1925, featured the young John Gielgud in the role of Konstantin. Eleven years later, Gielgud would play Trigorin opposite Edith Evans as Arkadina and Peggy Ashcroft as Nina at the New Theatre. This production became notable because its director/designer was Fyodr Komissarzhevsky, brother of the actress Vera Komissarzhevskaya, who originated the role of Nina at the Alexandrinsky.

The United States premiere of the play was performed in Russian in New York on December 22, 1905, by the St. Petersburg Dramatic Company. The first production of the play in English was offered by the Washington Square Players at the Bandbox Theatre in New York City on May 22, 1916. Directed by Edward Goodman and designed by Lee Simonson, the effort was not successful and lasted only a week. The company gradually evolved into the renowned Theatre Guild, under whose auspices *The Sea Gull* was produced at the Shubert Theatre in New York on March 28, 1938. Lynn Fontanne (Arkadina), Alfred Lunt (Trigorin), and Uta Hagen (Nina) led the cast under Robert Milton's direction, with sets and costumes by Robert Edmond Jones.

The play continues to be showcased around the world, often attracting artists of the highest calibre. During the 1980–1981 season, English-language productions were given at the Stratford Festival in Ontario and at the New York Shakespeare Festival. The Canadian production featured Maggie Smith and Brian Bedford under Robin Phillips' direction, while Rosemary Harris and Christopher Walken headed the New York company under the direction of Andrei Serban. Jon Jory directed *The Sea Gull* in 1989 for the Actors Theater of

Louisville as part of its Classics in Context celebration of the arts in Russia. During the 1992–1993 Broadway season, Tyne Daly and Jon Voight were directed by Marshall Mason for the National Actors Theatre. Dublin's Gate Theatre produced the play during its 1993–1994 season, transposing the action to the West of Ireland in the late nineteenth century. Fascination for the play has been shown by the film industry as well. In 1968, Sidney Lumet directed an international cast that featured Simone Signoret and Vanessa Redgrave. A Russian film version appeared in 1971.

Indicative of the universality of Chekhov's characters and themes is their appeal to Japanese artists. The Tokyo Engeki Ensemble, for example, has built its reputation around an international repertory of plays from the works of its own modern Japanese playwrights to the Western drama of Shakespeare and Chekhov. *The Sea Gull,* in a translation by Jun Makihara, has won great acclaim for the company since it was first directed by Tsunetoshi Hirowatari in 1973 and later televised throughout Japan. Set designs of Shigeo Okajima transformed the raised circular performance space of their warehouse theatre into an earth-toned environment quietly perched at the edge of a shadowy universe. The uncluttered space, which slowly increased its stage props as the four acts progressed, was enhanced by Sumio Yoshii's vertical beams of light from a circular ring above the stage, projected in sharp painterly fashion to envelop the actors below. The abstract mood was enriched by a soft babbling brook of real running water that flowed along the downstage half of the stage, and whose rippling sounds quietly suggested the watery landscape of Sorin's estate. To enter the acting space, cast members crossed the brook by means of a narrow bridge positioned downstage-center.

In act 1, an abstract, drape-like configuration hung in full view from the upstage edge of the acting circle. Somewhat emblematically, it reflected the experimental nature of Konstantin's play which unfolded before it. The somersaulting Konstantin was dressed in silky-white garments. His youthful athleticism and idealism seemed the right match for Nina's innocence, suggested by her flowing, soft-white tunic. The worldlier dispositions of the other characters were mirrored in the comparatively darker monochromatic hues of their Westernized clothing.

Konstantin's first-act playlet was embellished with vibrant choreography. The stage was bathed in blue light as Nina delivered her monologue. She was surrounded by four ghost-like figures, while mechanical fireflies swirled above the stage. Lights shifted to red, then back to blue. To view Konstantin's play, the other stage characters crossed back over the bridge and positioned themselves alongside the real spectators who sat in semicircular rows facing the stage. Arkadina's laughter pierced the atmosphere. When Konstantin halted his play, she reentered the performance space, haughtily smoking a cigarette.

The abstract configuration was removed in act 2. Arkadina, Dorn, and Masha were stretched out on the stage, as though resting after a long hot afternoon. They seemed frozen and stared into space as they spoke their lines. When they were joined by the other actors, the physical movement of the scene accelerated. Some actors played into the center; others played out to the audience. Occasionally one strolled the circumference of the stage as he spoke. The act was highlighted by the confrontation between Konstantin and Nina. When he tossed the dead sea gull at her feet, he was bathed momentarily in white light, as a chilling musical chord rose and faded. They confronted each other eye to eye, but the lifeless sea gull created a wall between them.

Adhering closely to the design of the play, Hirowatari quickened the pace of the final two acts by his use of sharper stage movements and heightened vocalization. Konstantin raged at his mother, while she rapidly paced the diameter of the stage, dragging his loose bandages behind her, as though they were part of her attire. She consoled him only after their explosive confrontation subsided. Yet Hirowatari steadily intensified the smaller moments: the sound of the running brook seemed louder; an offstage piano played western music as an intoxicated Masha waltzed tearfully around the stage; helpless characters huddled around the dying Sorin, now confined to a wheelchair. Then, in one striking tableau illuminated by shadowy stage lighting, the director recaptured the lakeside reverie of Konstantin's interrupted play from act 1 as fireflies swirled around the stage and leaves fell to the ground. The tableau faded out of sight.

Konstantin approached his neatly organized writing desk downstage center as though it were a sacred altar. He knelt before it as Nina entered in a dress that was considerably darker than what she had worn in the previous act. Her shortened hair suggested a toughened and weary demeanor. When she threw her body across Konstantin's writing space, the bold laughter of Arkadina and Trigorin resounded suddenly offstage. In an ironic foreshadowing of Konstantin's tragic fate, she drank from the running stream and deliberately held her head under the water until Konstantin came to her rescue.

The play's final moments belonged to Konstantin who, in a slow, ritualized gesture, tore the pages of his manuscript one-by-one. Sealing his writing pen with a sense of completion, he exited as the lights faded to black. The shadowy effect of the rippling water shimmered upon the stage for a few moments, just before the other characters returned as the lights came up and a gunshot was heard.

REFLECTIONS ON THE SEA GULL

Tsunetoshi Hirowatari has directed THE SEA GULL *for the Tokyo Engeki Ensemble.*

I had no reason to be attracted to *The Sea Gull.* Yet I was fascinated by its strange mood when I discovered it in my late teens at the end of the world war, in a translation by Masao Yonegawa. It was no coincidence, however, that I read it over and over again, eventually directed it three times, and would be planning a fourth production.

I recall my earliest experience with Chekhov's play. I worked as an assistant editor for the Workers' Theatre Union—an organization established for recruiting theatre audiences. I also participated in student theatre activities at Tokyo University and at Waseda University, started a theatre group at a university in Kyushu, and finally entered the professional theatre company, Haiyuza, as a member of its directing staff. Then war broke out in Korea. Although I temporarily returned to my hometown in Kyushu, I could not give up my career in the theatre. I chose *The Sea Gull* as the subject of a paper I submitted when I joined Haiyuza.

As members of the Chekhov Study Group at Haiyuza, we searched for ways to perform the play, using the Stanislavsky system and creating certain exercises to relate physical action to theme. It was a hopeless task. We really needed to discover our own kind of realism. So we established a small theatre which later became the Tokyo Engeki Ensemble. But it was not until 1973 that we finally achieved our dream of producing the play.

My notes for our first production, which opened at the Haiyuza Theatre in 1973, mention the following:

> I long dreamed of directing *The Sea Gull* but hesitated every time. It is a Russian play that recalls my own youth. The life described in the play seems to me very much like the life in this country at the present time, not life in the 1880s.

> You may read it as a story of Konstantin. It will become the story of Meyerhold who also aimed at a revolution of the theatre.

This modern age is too grotesque for Masha who loves Konstantin. She is tired of expecting something which can never be realized. Here is the story of Masha who is betrayed by everything and is trying to live a life by lying to herself.

How about reading the play as Nina's story? She chooses Trigorin, leaving Konstantin behind. Longing for fame and glory, she realizes after her downfall that endurance is everything. Meyerhold is shot. Konstantin shoots himself in the head. Is it merely the theme for a short story? No, it is not.

Dorn looks at the various lives of the people around him and asks Konstantin to tell him about Nina's downfall. All these characters dreamed of a better life. They want to *be* someone but cannot. Dorn does not give medicine to Sorin who is dying. A card game is started. It is a trifle, but helps them forget. It is like our life. Trigorin wins the game.

You can tell the story of *The Sea Gull* any way you like. No matter how you tell it, however, you can never explain it fully. The world of the play is outside the story. Chekhov silently challenges his critics.

Here are my notes from our 1980 production:

I cannot explain why I chose to direct this play again, but I still like it very much. Perhaps it's because it deals with an artist revolting against the established theatre—the Shingeki in this country.

It might be that my interpretation changes from time to time. We might be Konstantin, or Nina, or Masha, and our lives depend on how we interpret the play, or vice-versa.

Arkadina and Trigorin are very handsome people. Arkadina is a star and Trigorin is a popular artist. But Konstantin does not accept the establishment. The love between him and Nina should have grown when they violated the establishment and created a new art form. But Konstantin's art has toppled before the establishment, and Nina has left him for Trigorin.

Konstantin will imitate Trigorin, just as Nina will follow Arkadina's path. Konstantin cannot bear to see his former lover become like Arkadina. So he kills himself.

The lives described here might be ours. Frustrated and crushed people who convert themselves into the establishment. *The Sea Gull* is about all of us.

Reflecting on my feelings when I wrote this, I now realize that there is no single interpretation of this play, that Chekhov must have smiled cynically at me.

At the end of World War II, Bertolt Brecht asked, "Is it possible for the theatre to express our world today?" He probably knew it could not, which is why he established "epic" theatre. But Chekhov had asked the same question a half-century earlier. He found the answer when he returned from his long and difficult journey to Sakhalin and expressed it in *The Sea Gull*. He revolted against the ruling principles of his contemporary theatre. He put necessity aside and wrote a work of pure accident. Its bold and epoch-making dramaturgy even surpassed Stanislavsky's comprehension.

Continued

My notes for *The Sea Gull* produced at the Aoyama Round Theatre in 1987 include the following:

> I am filled with the feeling that I have finally reached a small port after drifting for a long time. Is this port merely an illusion? The characters in this play are polarized from positive to negative, negative to positive. A man who seemed confident suddenly feels uneasy. He who was high-spirited becomes resigned. He who wanted to be somebody finds himself nobody. He who wanted to live a better life cannot change his life at all. He waits in futility. Such a man is ludicrously lonely. Such people only think of themselves and cannot hear the words of others. They are egoists lost unto themselves. A manor with a beautiful lake turns into a shuddering space. The rich Russian landscape becomes a grotesque, rocky desert against which Chekhov's aimless characters are seen, not unlike the modern Tokyo in which we live.
>
> Chekhov destroyed the need for pat solutions which Realism called for. He welcomed an endless darkness for those who have no way but "to bump their heads into walls." His all-pervasive theme—the alienation of daily existence—has been reflected in the condition of urbanization in the twentieth century. By bumping our heads into walls, we also experience the depth of Chekhov's darkness.

We can hardly imagine how serious this isolation has become in our highly industrialized society. It is impossible to keep our identity. We are estranged and manipulated. Must we become egotistical and selfish to survive? Urbanization has brought about a spiritual illness so serious that neither Baudelaire nor Benjamin Franklin, who described the gloomy city of Paris in the nineteenth century, could have imagined contemporary Tokyo.

A harsh, shuddering sensation spreads across the theatre. Loose, slovenly people appear on the empty stage. They are all isolated egoists. Water flows along the side of the circular space. Nina, Konstantin, Masha, and the others jump over the flowing water to reach the stage. The boxed set has been replaced by a polyphonic stage. The play is a collection of particles controlled by an accident. Chekhov's dialogue never conveys messages, but is merely spoken. It finds its existence in performance. The stage characters cannot communicate with one another. No one listens to what is said. Perhaps our performance of *The Sea Gull* merely adds one more misinterpretation to the long production history of this play. But it is obvious that the Tokyo Engeki Ensemble has reached the end of another pilgrimage toward discovering Chekhov.

Courtesy of Tsunetoshi Hirowatari. Excerpted from A PILGRIMAGE TO "THE SEA GULL."

Notes

1. Maurice Valency, THE BREAKING STRING: THE PLAYS OF ANTON CHEKHOV (*New York: Oxford University Press, 1966*), *162.*
2. David Magarshack, CHEKHOV THE DRAMATIST (*New York: Hill & Wang, 1960*), *41.*

THE SEA GULL

A COMEDY IN FOUR ACTS

ANTON CHEKHOV

TRANSLATED BY ANN DUNNIGAN

CHARACTERS

Arkadina, Irina Nikolayevna,
(Madame Trepleva), *an actress*
Treplev, Konstantin Gavrilovich, *her
son, a young man*
Sorin, Pyotr Nikolayevich, *her
brother*
Zarechnaya, Nina Mikhailovna, *a
young girl, the daughter of a
wealthy landowner*

Shamrayev, Ilya Afanasyevich, *a
retired lieutenant, Sorin's
steward*
Polina Andreyevna, *his wife*
Masha, *his daughter*
Trigorin, Boris Alekseyevich, *a
writer*

Dorn, Yevgeny Sergeyevich,
a doctor
Medvedenko, Semyon
Semyonovich, *a schoolmaster*
Yakov, *a workman*
A Cook (male)
A Housemaid

The action takes place on Sorin's estate.
Between the third and fourth acts there is an interval of two years.

ACT ONE

(*A section of the park on* SORIN's *estate. A wide avenue,
leading away from the spectators into the depths of the park
toward a lake, is obstructed by a stage hurriedly put together
for amateur theatricals, so that the lake is not visible. There
are bushes left and right of the stage. A few chairs, a small
table. The sun has just set.*

YAKOV *and other workmen are on the stage behind the
curtain; sounds of coughing and hammering are heard.*
MASHA *and* MEDVEDENKO *enter from the left, returning from
a walk.*)

MEDVEDENKO.   Why do you always wear black?
MASHA.   I am in mourning for my life. I am unhappy.
MEDVEDENKO.   Why? (*Pondering.*) I don't understand.
. . . You are in good health, and your father, though not
rich, is well off. My life is much harder than yours.

I get only twenty-three rubles a month, and out of that
they take something for the pension fund, but I don't wear
mourning.

(*They sit down.*)

MASHA.   It isn't a question of money. Even a beggar can
be happy.
MEDVEDENKO.   Yes, in theory, but in practice it's like
this: there's me, my mother, my two sisters, and a little
brother—on a salary of only twenty-three rubles. People
have to eat and drink, don't they? And they need tea and
sugar? And tobacco? It's not easy to make ends meet.
MASHA (*glancing toward the stage*). The performance will
begin soon.
MEDVEDENKO.   Yes. Nina Zarechnaya is going to act, and
the play was written by Konstantin Gavrilovich. They are

in love with each other, and today their souls will be merged in the desire to create a single artistic image. But your soul and mine have no common point of contact. I love you, I'm so miserable I can't stay at home, every day I walk six versts here and six versts back, but I get nothing but indifference from you. It's quite understandable. I am without means, I have a large family. . . . Who wants to marry a man who hasn't even got enough to eat?

MASHA.   Nonsense. (*Takes a pinch of snuff.*) Your love touches me, but I can't return it, that's all. (*Holding out the snuff box to him.*) Have some.

MEDVEDENKO.   I don't feel like it. (*Pause.*)

MASHA.   It's sultry; there'll probably be a thunderstorm tonight. You are always philosophizing or talking about money. You think there's no greater misfortune than poverty, but in my opinion, it's a thousand times easier to be a beggar and wear rags than . . . however, that's something you wouldn't understand. . . .

(SORIN *and* TREPLEV *enter from the right.*)

SORIN (*leaning on a cane*).   For some reason, my boy, I'm not quite myself in the country, and, it stands to reason, I'll never get accustomed to it. I went to bed at ten o'clock last night and woke up at nine this morning feeling as though my brain were stuck to my skull from sleeping so long, and all that sort of thing. (*Laughs.*) And after dinner I accidentally fell asleep again, and now I'm a complete wreck. I feel as if I were in a nightmare, and . . . so forth and so on. . . .

TREPLEV.   You're right, Uncle, you really ought to live in town. (*Catching sight of* MASHA *and* MEDVEDENKO.) Look, my friends, when the play begins, we'll call you, but you can't stay here now. I'll have to ask you to go.

SORIN (*to* MASHA).   Maria Ilyinichna, be so good as to ask your papa to have the dog let off its chain, otherwise it howls. My sister was kept awake again the whole night.

MASHA.   You'll have to speak to my father yourself. I won't do it, so please don't ask me. (*To* MEDVEDENKO.) Let's go!

MEDVEDENKO (*to* TREPLEV).   Then you will let us know before it begins.

(MASHA *and* MEDVEDENKO *go out.*)

SORIN.   That means the dog will howl all night again. The trouble is, I've never lived as I wanted to in the country. I used to take a month's leave and come here to rest and all, but as soon as I got here they began to pester me so with all sorts of nonsense that by the next day I was ready to leave. (*Laughs.*) It was always a pleasure to go. . . . Well, now I'm retired, and I have no place to go, and all that. Like it or not, you've got to live. . . .

YAKOV (*to* TREPLEV).   We're going for a swim, Konstantin Gavrilovich.

TREPLEV.   Very well, only be in your places in ten minutes. (*Looks at his watch.*) We're going to begin soon.

YAKOV.   Yes, sir. (*Goes out.*)

TREPLEV (*looking over the stage*).   There's a theater for you. A curtain, two wings, and beyond that—open space. No scenery at all. There's a clear view to the lake and the horizon. We'll raise the curtain at half past eight, as the moon is rising.

SORIN.   Magnificent.

TREPLEV.   If Nina is late, then, of course, the whole effect will be spoiled. It's time she was here. Her father and stepmother keep such a close watch over her that it's as hard for her to get out of the house as a prison. (*Straightens his uncle's necktie.*) Your hair and beard are untidy. Maybe you ought to have them trimmed. . . .

SORIN (*combing his beard*).   The tragedy of my life. Even when I was young I used to look as if I had been drinking for days, and all that. The ladies never loved me. (*Sitting down.*) Why is my sister in such a bad mood?

TREPLEV.   Why? She's bored. (*Sits down beside him.*) And jealous. She's set against me, against the performance, and against my play, because Nina—and not she—is acting in it. She hasn't even read the play, but she already hates it.

SORIN (*laughing*).   You just imagine that, really. . . .

TREPLEV.   It actually annoys her that here, on this tiny stage, it will be Nina, and not she, who's a success. (*Looking at his watch.*) A psychological curiosity—my mother. Unquestionably talented, intelligent, she can sob over a book, reel off the whole of Nekrasov by heart, nurse the sick like an angel; but just try praising Duse in her presence! Oh, ho! You must praise no one but her; you must write about her, rave about her, go into ecstasies over her acting in *La Dame aux Camélias* or *The Fumes of Life;* but here in the country, where she can't get these opiates, she's bored, bad-tempered, and we are all her enemies, we're all to blame. And she's superstitious—she's afraid of three candles and the number thirteen. And stingy. She has seventy thousand rubles in the bank in Odessa—I know this for a fact—but ask her for a loan and she'll burst into tears.

SORIN.   You've got it into your head that your mother doesn't like your play, and now you're upset and all that. Don't worry, your mother adores you.

TREPLEV (*pulling the petals off a flower*).   She loves me—she loves me not; she loves me—she loves me not; she loves me—she loves me not. (*Laughs.*) You see, my mother doesn't love me. Of course not! She wants to live, to love, to wear bright dresses, and here I am, twenty-five years old, a constant reminder that she is no longer young. When I'm not there, she's only thirty-two, but when I am, she's forty-three—and for that she hates me. Besides, she knows I don't accept the theater. She loves the theater, she thinks she is serving humanity and the sacred cause of art, while in my opinion, the theater of today is hidebound and conventional. When the curtain goes up, and, in a room with three walls and artificial light, those great geniuses, those priests of holy art, show me how people eat, drink, love, walk about, and wear their jackets; when from those banal scenes and phrases they try to fish out a moral—some little moral that is easily grasped and suitable for domestic use; when, in a thousand variations, I am served the same thing over and over and over again—then I flee, as Maupassant fled from the Eiffel Tower, which made his brain reel with its vulgarity.

SORIN.   We can't do without the theater.

TREPLEV.   We need new forms. New forms are needed, and if we can't have them, then we had better have nothing at all. (*Looks at his watch.*) I love my mother, love her very much; but she leads a senseless life, always fussing over that writer of hers, her name constantly bandied about in the papers—I find all that very tiresome. Sometimes the simple egoism of an ordinary mortal makes me regret that I have a mother who's a famous actress, and it seems to me that if she had been an ordinary woman I should have been happier. Uncle, what could be more hopeless and absurd than my position: she's always been surrounded by celebrities—actors, authors—and among them all, I alone was nothing; they tolerated me only because I was her son. Who am I? What am I? I left the university in my third year, because of circumstances, as they say, over which the editors have no control; I have no special talent, no money of my own, and, according to my passport, I am—just a Kiev petty bourgeois. My father, you see, was a petty bourgeois from Kiev, though he was also a well-known actor. So whenever those actors and writers who frequented her drawing room would bestow their gracious attentions on me, I felt their eyes were measuring my insignificance—I could guess their thoughts and I suffered from humiliation.

SORIN.   By the way, what sort of man is this writer? I can't make him out. He never opens his mouth.

TREPLEV.   He's an intelligent man, simple, and rather melancholy, it seems. Very decent. He's well under forty, and already famous and extremely well off. . . . As for his writing . . . well . . . what shall I say? Charming, shows talent, but . . . after Tolstoy or Zola, you don't feel much like reading Trigorin.

SORIN.   But I love writers, my boy. There was a time when I passionately wanted two things: I wanted to get married, and I wanted to become a writer; but I didn't succeed in doing either. Yes . . . even to be a minor writer must be pleasant, and all that sort of thing.

TREPLEV (*listens*). I hear footsteps. (*Embraces his uncle.*) I can't live without her. . . . Even the sound of her footsteps is beautiful. . . . I am insanely happy! (*Quickly goes to meet* NINA ZARECHNAYA *as she enters.*) My enchantress—my dream!

NINA.   I'm not late . . . surely I'm not late . . .

TREPLEV (*kissing her hands*). No, no, no. . . .

NINA   I've been worried all day, and so frightened! I was afraid father wouldn't let me come . . . but he just went out with my stepmother. The sky turned red, the moon was beginning to rise, and I kept urging and urging the horse on. . . . (*Laughs.*) But now I'm happy. (*Warmly shakes* SORIN's *hand.*)

SORIN (*laughs*). Those little eyes look as if they had been shedding tears. . . . Ah-ah! That's not right!

NINA.   It's nothing. . . . You see how out of breath I am. I'll have to go in half an hour, we must hurry. I can't stay, I really can't, so don't, for Heaven's sake, detain me. My father doesn't know I'm here.

TREPLEV.   It's time to begin, anyhow. I'll go and call the others.

SORIN.   I'll go, and all that. I'll go at once. (*Starts off right singing "The Two Grenadiers" then stops.*) Once I began singing like that and the Assistant Prosecutor said to me: "You have a strong voice, Your Excellency." Then he thought a moment and added: "Strong, but revolting."

NINA.   My father and his wife won't let me come here. They say it's Bohemian . . . they're afraid I might go on the stage. . . . But I am drawn here to this lake, like a sea gull. . . . My heart is full of you. (*Glances back.*)

TREPLEV.   We are alone.

NINA.   I think someone is there . . .

TREPLEV.   There's no one. . . . (*Kisses her.*)

NINA.   What kind of tree is that?

TREPLEV.   An elm.

NINA.   Why is it so dark?

TREPLEV.   Because it's evening, and everything looks darker. Don't go early, please don't.

NINA.   I must.

TREPLEV.   And if I come to you, Nina? I'll stand all night in the garden, gazing at your window.

NINA.   No, you mustn't, the watchman would see you. And Trésor isn't used to you, he would bark.

TREPLEV.   I love you.

NINA.   Sh-sh!

TREPLEV (*hearing footsteps*). Who's there? Is that you, Yakov?

YAKOV (*behind the stage*). Yes, sir.

TREPLEV.   Take your places. It's time to begin. The moon is rising, isn't it?

YAKOV.   Yes, sir.

TREPLEV.   Have you got the methylated spirit? Is the sulfur there? When the red eyes appear, there's got to be a smell of sulfur. (*To* NINA.) You'd better go now, everything's ready. Are you nervous?

NINA.   Yes, very. It's not so much your mother . . . I'm not afraid of her, but there's Trigorin. . . . I feel ashamed and terrified to act before him. . . . A famous author . . . Is he young?

TREPLEV.   Yes.

NINA.   What wonderful stories he writes!

TREPLEV (*coldly*). I don't know, I don't read them.

NINA.   It's difficult to act in your play. There are no living characters in it.

TREPLEV.   Living characters! One must portray life not as it is, and not as it ought to be, but as it appears in our dreams.

NINA.   There's not very much action in the play, only reciting. And I do think a play ought to have love in it. . . .

(*They go behind the stage. Enter* POLINA ANDREYEVNA *and* DORN.)

POLINA ANDREYEVNA.   It's getting damp. Go back and put on your galoshes.

DORN.   I'm hot.

POLINA ANDREYEVNA.   You don't take care of yourself. It's just stubbornness. You're a doctor, and you know perfectly well the damp air is bad for you, but you love making me miserable; you sat out on the veranda all last evening on purpose. . . .

DORN (*softly singing*). "Never say that youth is wasted . . ."

POLINA ANDREYEVNA.   You were so fascinated by your conversation with Irina Nikolayevna . . . you didn't even notice the cold. You may as well confess, you find her attractive. . . .

DORN.   I'm fifty-five years old.

POLINA ANDREYEVNA.   Fiddlesticks! For a man that's not old. You're very well preserved, and you're still attractive to women!

DORN.   Well, what do you want me to do about it?

POLINA ANDREYEVNA.   You are all ready to fall on your knees before an actress. Every one of you!

DORN (*singing*). "Again I stand before you . . ." If society loves artists and treats them differently from . . . merchants, let us say, that is in the nature of things. That's— idealism.

POLINA ANDREYEVNA.   Women have always fallen in love with you and hung on your neck. Was that also idealism?

DORN (*shrugging his shoulders*). Well . . . there was always a great deal that was fine in their relations to me. What they chiefly loved in me was an excellent physician. Ten or fifteen years ago, you remember, I was the only decent obstetrician in the whole province. And then, I've always been honest.

POLINA ANDREYEVNA (*clasping his hand*). My darling!

DORN.   Hush—they're coming.

(*Enter* ARKADINA *on* SORIN'S *arm*, TRIGORIN, SHAMRAYEV, MEDVEDENKO, *and* MASHA.)

SHAMRAYEV.   In 1873, at the Poltava Fair, she played astoundingly! Sheer delight! Marvelous acting! Would you happen to know where Chadin—the comedian Pavel Semyonovich Chadin—is at present? His Rasplyuev was inimitable, better than Sadovsky's, I assure you, most esteemed lady. Where is he now?

ARKADINA.   You keep asking me about antediluvians. How should I know? (*Sits down.*)

SHAMRAYEV (*sighing*). Pashka Chadin! Nobody like that now. The theater has declined, Irina Nikolayevna! In the old days there were mighty oaks, but now we see nothing but stumps.

DORN.   There are fewer brilliant talents today, that's true, but the general level is much higher.

SHAMRAYEV.   I can't agree with you. However, it's a matter of taste. *De gustibus aut bene, aut nihil.*

(TREPLEV *comes out from behind the stage*.)

ARKADINA.   My dear son, when is it going to begin?

TREPLEV.   In a moment. Please have patience.

ARKADINA.   My son! (*reciting from* Hamlet.)
"Thou turn'st mine eyes into my very soul;
And there I see such black and grainèd spots
As will not leave their tint."

TREPLEV (*paraphrasing* Hamlet).
Nay, but to live
In wickedness, to seek love
In the depths of sin . . .

(*A horn is sounded behind the stage.*)

TREPLEV.   Ladies and gentlemen, we are about to begin! Attention, please! (*Pause.*) I shall begin. (*Taps with a stick and recites in a loud voice.*) Oh, you ancient, venerable shades, that float above this lake by night, darken our eyes with sleep, and bring us dreams of what will be two hundred thousand years from now!

SORIN.   There'll be nothing two hundred thousand years from now.

TREPLEV.   Then let them portray that nothing to us.

ARKADINA.   Let them. We are asleep.

(*The curtain rises, revealing a view of the lake; the moon, above the horizon, is reflected in the water;* NINA, *all in white, is seated on a large rock.*)

NINA.   Men, lions, eagles, and partridges, horned deer, geese, spiders, silent fish that dwell in the deep, starfish, and creatures invisible to the eye—these and all living things, all, all living things, having completed their sad cycle, are no more. . . . For thousands of years the earth has borne no living creature. And now in vain this poor moon lights her lamp. Cranes no longer wake and cry in meadows, May beetles are heard no more in linden groves. Cold, cold, cold. Empty, empty, empty. Awful, awful, awful. (*Pause.*) The bodies of all living creatures having turned to dust, eternal matter has transformed them into stones, water, clouds, and all their souls have merged into one. That great world soul—is I . . . I . . . . In me are the souls of Alexander, of Caesar, Shakespeare, and Napoleon, and of the lowest worm. In me the consciousness of man is merged with the instincts of animals, and I remember all, all, all, and in me each several life is lived anew.

(*Will-o'-the-wisps appear.*)

ARKADINA (*in a low voice*). There's something decadent about this.

TREPLEV (*reproachfully imploring her*). Mother!

NINA.   I am all alone. Once in a hundred years I open my mouth to speak, my voice echoes dolefully in this void, and no one hears it. . . . And you, pale lights, you do not hear me. . . . The stagnant marsh begets you before dawn, you drift till daybreak without thought, without will, without the throb of life. Fearing lest life should spring up in you, the devil, father of eternal matter, at every instant produces in you a continual interchange of atoms, as in stones and in water, and you are ceaselessly being changed. Within the universe, spirit alone remains constant and unaltered. (*Pause.*) Like a prisoner cast into a deep and empty well, I know not where I am or what awaits me. One thing only is not hidden from me: in the cruel, persistent struggle with the devil, the principle of the forces of matter, I am destined to be victorious, then matter and spirit shall merge in glorious harmony, and the kingdom of universal will shall be at hand. But this will come only little by little, after a long, long succession of millennia, when the moon, bright Sirius, and the earth have turned to dust. . . . Until then . . . horror, horror . . . (*Pause; in the background two red spots appear over the lake.*) Behold, my powerful enemy, the devil, approaches. I see his awful, blood-red eyes. . . .

ARKADINA.   There's a smell of sulfur. Is that necessary?

TREPLEV.   Yes.

ARKADINA (*laughs*). Oh, it's a stage effect!

TREPLEV.   Mother!

NINA.   He yearns for man . . .

POLINA ANDREYEVNA (*to* DORN). You've taken off your hat. Put it on or you'll catch cold.

ARKADINA.   The doctor has taken off his hat to the devil, the father of eternal matter.

TREPLEV (*flaring up, loudly*). The play is over! That's enough! Curtain!

ARKADINA.   Why are you angry?

TREPLEV.   Enough! Curtain! Bring down the curtain! (*Stamping his foot.*) Curtain! (*The curtain falls.*) You must forgive me. I overlooked the fact that only the chosen few can write plays and act in them. I have infringed on a monopoly! To me . . . I . . . (*Tries to continue, then, with a gesture of resignation, goes out left.*)

ARKADINA.   What's the matter with him?

SORIN.   Irina, my dear, you shouldn't wound a young man's pride like that.

ARKADINA.   But what have I said to him?

SORIN.   You've hurt his feelings.

ARKADINA.   He told us himself it was going to be a joke, so I treated it as a joke.

SORIN.   All the same . . .

ARKADINA.   Now it appears he has written a great work! Oh, really! Evidently he got up this performance and fumigated us with sulfur, not as a joke but as a demonstration. . . . He wanted to teach us how one ought to write, and what one ought to act in. After all, this is getting tiresome! These continual sallies at my expense, these gibes, if you please, would try anyone's patience! He's a conceited, capricious boy!

SORIN.   He meant to give you pleasure.

ARKADINA.   Yes? Then why didn't he choose the usual sort of play instead of forcing us to listen to these decadent ravings? I don't mind listening even to raving if it's a joke, but here we have pretensions to new forms, a new era in art. To my way of thinking this has nothing at all to do with new forms, it's simply bad temper.

TRIGORIN.   Everyone writes as he likes and as he can.

ARKADINA.   Let him write as he likes and as he can, so long as he leaves me in peace.

DORN.   Jupiter, you grow angry—

ARKADINA.   I'm not Jupiter, I'm a woman. (*Lights a cigarette.*) And I'm not angry, I'm merely annoyed that a young man should spend his time in such a tiresome way. I didn't mean to hurt his feelings.

MEDVEDENKO.   Nobody has any grounds for separating spirit from matter, for it may be that this very spirit is an aggregation of material atoms. (*Eagerly, to* TRIGORIN.) You know, someone ought to write a play describing how we teachers live, and put that on. It's a hard, hard life!

ARKADINA.   You may be quite right, but let's not talk about plays or atoms. It's such a lovely evening! Do you hear them singing? (*Listens.*) How pleasant!

POLINA ANDREYEVNA.   It's on the other side of the lake.

ARKADINA (*to* TRIGORIN). Sit here beside me. Ten or fifteen years ago you could hear music and singing on this lake almost every night. There are six country houses here on the lake. I remember the laughter, the noise, the shooting . . . and the love affairs, always love affairs. . . . The *jeune premier* and idol of all six houses was our friend here—(*Nods toward* DORN.) I give you Dr. Yevgeny Sergeyevich. He's fascinating now, but he was irresistible then. . . . Oh, my conscience is beginning to torment me. Why did I hurt my poor boy's feelings? I'm so troubled. (*Loudly.*) Kostya! Son! Kostya!

MASHA.   I'll go and look for him.

ARKADINA.   Please do, my dear.

MASHA (*going to the left*). Aa-oo! Konstantin Gavrilovich! Aa-oo! (*Goes out.*)

(*Enter* NINA *from behind the stage.*)

NINA.   Apparently we're not going on, so I may as well come out. Good evening! (*Kisses* ARKADINA *and* POLINA ANDREYEVNA.)

SORIN.   Bravo! Bravo!

ARKADINA.   Bravo! Bravo! We were enchanted! With your looks and that marvelous voice, you really cannot remain in the country—it's a sin! I wouldn't be surprised if you have talent. Do you hear? You simply must go on the stage!

NINA.   Oh, that is my dream! (*Sighing*.) But it will never come true.

ARKADINA.   Who knows? But let me present Boris Alekseyevich Trigorin.

NINA.   Oh, I'm so glad to . . . (*overcome with embarrassment*.) I'm always reading your . . .

ARKADINA (*making her sit down beside them*).   Don't be embarrassed, dear. He's a celebrity, but he has a simple heart. You see, he's embarrassed himself.

DORN.   I suppose we may raise the curtain now—it looks rather sinister as it is.

SHAMRAYEV.   Yakov, my boy, pull up the curtain.

(*The curtain goes up.*)

NINA (*to* TRIGORIN).   It's a strange play, isn't it?

TRIGORIN.   I didn't understand a word, but I enjoyed watching it. You acted with great sincerity. And the scenery was lovely. (*Pause.*) I expect there are a lot of fish in that lake.

NINA.   Yes.

TRIGORIN.   I love to fish. For me there is no greater pleasure than to sit on the bank of a river toward evening watching a float.

NINA.   But I should have thought that for anyone who had experienced the joy of creation, no other pleasure could exist.

ARKADINA (*laughing*).   You mustn't talk like that. When people make him pretty speeches, it simply floors him.

SHAMRAYEV.   I recall one evening at the opera house in Moscow when the famous Silva took a low C. It so happened that the bass from our church choir was sitting in the gallery, and suddenly—you can imagine our utter amazement—we heard: "Bravo, Silva" from the gallery—but a whole octave lower! Like this: (*in a deep bass*.) Bravo, Silva. . . . The audience was thunderstruck. (*Pause.*)

DORN.   The angel of silence has flown over us.

NINA.   It's time for me to go. Good-bye.

ARKADINA.   Where are you off to? Why so early? We won't let you go.

NINA.   Papa is expecting me. . . .

ARKADINA.   What a man, really . . . (*Kisses her*.) Well, it can't be helped. I'm so sorry, so sorry to let you go.

NINA.   If you only knew how hard it is for me to go!

ARKADINA.   Someone ought to see you home, little one.

NINA (*frightened*).   Oh, no, no!

SORIN (*entreating her*).   Do stay!

NINA.   I can't, Pyotr Nikolayevich.

SORIN.   Just stay for an hour, and all . . . Come, now, do. . . .

NINA (*after a moment's thought, through tears*).   I can't! (*Shakes hands and quickly goes.*)

ARKADINA.   A most unfortunate girl, really. They say her mother left her father her entire, enormous fortune, everything, to the last kopeck, and now this girl has nothing; and the father has already made a will leaving it all to his second wife. It's shocking!

DORN.   Yes, her papa is a pretty thorough swine, to give him his due.

SORIN (*rubbing his hands to warm them*).   Let us go, too, my friends, it's getting damp. My legs ache.

ARKADINA.   It's just like having wooden legs, you can hardly walk. Well, come along, you poor old man. (*Takes his arm.*)

SHAMRAYEV (*offering his arm to his wife*).   Madam?

SORIN.   I hear that dog howling again. (*To* SHAMRAYEV.) Ilya Afanasyevich, be so good as to have them let it off the chain.

SHAMRAYEV.   Can't be done, Pyotr Nikolayevich, I'm afraid of thieves breaking into the barn. I've got millet in there. (*To* MEDVEDENKO, *walking beside him.*) Yes, a whole octave lower: "Bravo, Silva!" And not even a singer, mind you, just an ordinary church chorister.

MEDVEDENKO.   What salary does a church chorister get?

(*All go out except* DORN.)

DORN (*alone*).   I don't know, perhaps I don't understand these things, or maybe I've gone off my head, but I like the play. There's something in it. When that girl talked of solitude, and afterward when the red eyes of the devil appeared, my hands trembled with excitement. It's fresh, ingenuous. . . . Here he comes, I believe. I'd like to say everything nice I possibly can to him. . . .

(*Enter* TREPLEV.)

TREPLEV.   They've all gone.

DORN.   I'm here.

TREPLEV.   Masha's been hunting all over the park for me. Insufferable creature!

DORN.   Konstantin Gavrilovich, I liked your play enormously. It's somewhat strange, and, of course, I haven't heard the end, but even so, it made a strong impression on me. You're a talented man, and you must go on.

(TREPLEV *warmly presses his hand, then impulsively embraces him.*)

DORN.   Whew, what a nervous fellow! Tears in your eyes . . . Now, what did I want to say? You took a subject from the realm of abstract ideas. That's as it should be, because a work of art decidedly should express a great idea. Only what is serious can be beautiful. . . . How pale you are!

TREPLEV.   So you're telling me—to keep at it?

DORN.   Yes. . . . But write only of what is important and eternal. You know, I've lived a varied and discriminating life, I'm satisfied, but if it had ever been my lot to experience the exaltation that comes to artists in their moments of creation, I believe I should have despised this material shell of mine and all that pertains to it, and I'd have soared to the heights, leaving earthly things behind me.

TREPLEV.   Excuse me, where is Nina?

DORN.   And here's another thing. In a work of art there should be a clear, definite idea. You must know what you are writing for, otherwise, if you just move along some esthetic road without a definite aim, you'll be lost and your talent will destroy you.

TREPLEV (*impatiently*).   Where is Nina?

DORN.   She went home.

TREPLEV (*in despair*).   What shall I do? I want to see her. . . . I must see her. . . . I'm going . . .

(*Enter* MASHA.)

DORN (*to* TREPLEV).   Calm yourself, my friend.

TREPLEV.   But all the same I am going. I must go.

MASHA.   Come into the house, Konstantin Gavrilovich. Your mother wants you. She's worried.

TREPLEV.   Tell her I've gone away. And please, all of you, leave me in peace! Leave me alone! Don't keep following me!

DORN.   Come, come, come, my boy . . . you mustn't . . . That's not right.

TREPLEV (*through tears*).   Good-bye, Doctor. Thank you. . . . (*Goes out.*)

DORN (*sighing*).   Youth, youth!

MASHA.   When there's nothing else to say, people always say: youth, youth . . . (*Takes a pinch of snuff.*)

DORN (*takes the snuff box from her and flings it into the bushes*).   That's disgusting! (*Pause.*) They seem to be playing there in the house. We'd better go in.

MASHA.   Wait.

DORN.   What is it?

MASHA.   I want to tell you once more . . . I feel like talking . . . (*Agitated.*) I don't love my father . . . but I am fond of you. For some reason I feel with all my heart that you are close to me. . . . Help me. Help me, or I'll do something stupid—I'll make a mockery of my life, ruin it. . . . I can't go on. . . .

DORN.   What is it? Help you how?

MASHA.   I am suffering. No one, no one knows what I am suffering! (*Lays her head on his breast, softly.*) I love Konstantin.

DORN.   How nervous you all are! How nervous! And so much love! Oh, that betwitching lake! (*Tenderly.*) But what can I do, my child? What? What?

ACT TWO

(*A croquet lawn, flowerbeds. In the background on the right is the house with a large veranda; on the left, the lake, glimmering in the sunlight. It is midday and hot. At the side of the croquet lawn* ARKADINA, DORN, *and* MASHA *are sitting on a bench in the shade of an old linden tree.* DORN *has an open book on his lap.*)

ARKADINA (*to* MASHA).   Come, let's stand up. (*Both get up.*) Side by side. You are twenty-two and I am nearly twice that. Yevgeny Sergeyevich, which of us looks the younger?

DORN.   You, of course.

ARKADINA.   There you are! And why? Because I work, I feel, I am always on the go, while you stay in the same place all the time, you don't live. . . . And I make it a rule not to look into the future. I never think about old age or death. What is to be, will be.

MASHA.   And I feel as if I had been born a long, long time ago; I drag my life behind me like an endless train. . . . Sometimes I haven't the slightest desire to go on living. (*Sits down.*) Of course, that's all nonsense. I ought to shake myself and throw it off.

DORN (*sings softly*).   "Tell her, pretty flowers . . . "

ARKADINA.   Besides, I'm as correct as an Englishman. Yes, my dear, I keep myself in hand, as they say. I'm always dressed, and my hair is always *comme il faut*. Do you think I'd permit myself to go out of the house, even here into the garden, in a dressing gown or without my hair being done? Never. That's why I've kept young, because I was never dowdy, never let myself go as some women do. . . . (*Walks up and down the lawn, arms akimbo.*) You see—light as a bird. I could play a girl of fifteen.

DORN.   Well, I may as well continue. (*Takes up his book.*) We left off at the corn merchants and the rats.

ARKADINA.   Yes, the rats. Go on. (*Sits down.*) No, give it to me, I'll read. It's my turn, anyhow. (*She takes the book and looks for the place.*) And the rats . . . Here it is. . . . (*Reads.*) "And it goes without saying that for society people to pamper novelists and entice them into their own circle is as dangerous as for corn merchants to breed rats in their barns. And yet they are loved. Thus, when a woman has chosen a writer whom she wishes to capture, she lays siege to him by means of compliments, courtesies, and favors. . . . " Well, that may be true of the French, but with us there's nothing like that, we have no set rules. Here, if you please, a woman is generally head over heels in love herself before she sets out to capture a writer. To go no further, take Trigorin and me . . .

(*Enter* SORIN, *leaning on a cane, with* NINA *at his side.* MEDVEDENKO *pushing an empty wheelchair after them.*)

SORIN (*in the caressing tone one uses to a child*). Yes? We're delighted, aren't we? And we're cheerful today, and all that sort of thing? (*To his sister.*) We're delighted! Father and stepmother have gone off to Tver, and now we're free for three whole days.

NINA (*sits down beside* ARKADINA *and embraces her*). I'm so happy! Now I belong to you.

SORIN (*sits in his wheelchair*). She's looking very pretty today.

ARKADINA. And very smartly dressed, interesting. . . . There's a clever girl. (*Kisses her.*) But we mustn't praise her too much—it's bad luck. Where is Boris Alekseyevich?

NINA. He's down by the bathhouse, fishing.

ARKADINA. You'd think he'd get sick of it! (*About to go on reading.*)

NINA. What is that?

ARKADINA. Maupassant's "On the Water," my dear. (*Reads a few lines to herself.*) Well, the rest is uninteresting and untrue. (*Closes book.*) I'm worried. Tell me, what is the matter with my son? Why is he so sad and so austere? He spends whole days by the lake, and I hardly ever see him.

MASHA. His heart is troubled. (*To* NINA, *timidly.*) Please read something from his play.

NINA (*shrugs her shoulders*). Do you really want me to? It's so uninteresting!

MASHA (*restraining her enthusiasm*). When he reads anything himself, his eyes glow and his face turns pale. He has a beautiful, sad voice and the manner of a poet.

(SORIN *can be heard snoring.*)

DORN. Good night!

ARKADINA. Petrusha!

SORIN. Eh?

ARKADINA. Are you asleep?

SORIN. Not at all.

(*A pause.*)

ARKADINA. You're not having any medical treatment, and that's not right, my dear.

SORIN. I'd be glad to, but the doctor here doesn't want me to.

DORN. Take medicine at sixty!

SORIN. Even at sixty one wants to live.

DORN (*with vexation*). Ach! Well, then, take valerian drops.

ARKADINA. I think it would do him good to take a cure at some mineral spring.

DORN. Well . . . it might. Or it might not.

ARKADINA. And how is one supposed to understand that?

DORN. There's nothing to understand. It's quite clear.

(*A pause.*)

MEDVEDENKO. Pyotr Nikolayevich ought to give up smoking.

SORIN. Nonsense.

DORN. No, it's not nonsense. Wine and tobacco rob us of our personalities. After a cigar or a glass of vodka, you are no longer Pyotr Nikolayevich, but Pyotr Nikolayevich plus somebody else; your ego becomes diffused, and you begin to see yourself as a third person—as he.

SORIN (*laughs*). It's all very well for you to talk, you have lived your life, but what about me? I served in the Department of Justice for twenty-eight years, but I've never lived, never experienced anything, and so forth and so on, and it's natural that I should feel very much like living. You've had your fill and you don't care any more, so you're inclined to be philosophical, but I want to live, and that's why I drink sherry at dinner and smoke cigars, and all that sort of thing. And there you have it.

DORN. One must take life seriously, but to go in for cures at sixty and to regret that one has not sufficiently enjoyed one's youth is, if you will forgive me, frivolous.

MASHA (*getting up*). It must be time for lunch. (*Walking with an indolent, lagging gait.*) My foot has gone to sleep. . . . (*Goes out.*)

DORN. Now she'll go and have a couple of glasses before lunch.

SORIN. She's not happy in her personal life, poor thing.

DORN. Ridiculous, Your Excellency!

SORIN. You argue like a man who's had his fill.

ARKADINA. Oh, what could be more boring than this sweet country boredom! It's hot, quiet, nobody does anything, everyone philosophizes. . . . It's good to be with you, my friends, pleasant to listen to you, but . . . to be sitting in a hotel room learning a part—how much better!

NINA (*ecstatically*). Oh, yes! I understand you!

SORIN. Of course, it's better in town. You sit in your study, the footman lets no one in unannounced, there's a telephone . . . cabs in the streets, and all that sort of thing. . . .

DORN (*sings*). "Tell her, pretty flowers . . ."

(*Enter* SHAMRAYEV, *followed by* POLIN ANDREYEVNA.)

SHAMRAYEV. Here they are! Good morning! (*Kisses* ARKADINA*'s hand, then* NINA*'s.*) Delighted to see you looking so well. (*To* ARKADINA.) My wife tells me that you are planning on driving into town with her today. Is that right?

ARKADINA. Yes, we are planning on it.

SHAMRAYEV. Hm! That's splendid, but how do you intend to travel, most esteemed lady? We're carting the rye today, and all the men are busy. And what horses would you take, may I ask?

ARKADINA. What horses? How should I know what horses!

SORIN. We have carriage horses.

SHAMRAYEV (*growing excited*). Carriage horses? And where am I to get the collars? Where am I to get the collars? It's amazing! Inconceivable! Most esteemed lady! Excuse me, I have the greatest reverence for your talent, I would give ten years of my life for you, but I cannot let you have the horses!

ARKADINA.   And if I have to go? This is a strange state of affairs!

SHAMRAYEV.   My dear lady, you don't realize what farming means!

ARKADINA (*flaring up*). The same old story! In that case I'll leave for Moscow today. Order horses for me from the village, or I'll walk to the station!

SHAMRAYEV (*flaring up*). In that case, I resign! Find yourself another steward! (*Goes out.*)

ARKADINA.   Every summer it's like this, every summer they insult me here! I'll never set foot in this place again!

(*She goes off left in the direction of the bathhouse; a moment later she is seen going into the house, followed by* TRIGORIN *carrying fishing rods and a pail.*)

SORIN (*flaring up*). This is insolence! It's beyond everything! I'm sick and tired of it . . . and so forth. Have all the horses brought around at once!

NINA (*to* POLINA ANDREYEVNA). To refuse Irina Nikolayevna, the famous actress! Surely any wish of hers, even the least whim, is more important than your farming? It's simply unbelievable!

POLINA ANDREYEVNA (*in despair*). What can I do? Put yourself in my position: what can I do?

SORIN (*to* NINA). Let us go to my sister. . . . We'll all plead with her not to go. Shall we? (*Looking in the direction of* SHAMRAYEV'*s departure.*) Insufferable man! Despot!

NINA (*preventing him from getting up*). Sit still, sit still. . . . We'll wheel you in. . . . (*She and* MEDVEDENKO *push the wheelchair.*) Oh, how dreadful this is!

SORIN.   Yes, yes, it is dreadful. . . . But he won't leave. I'll talk to him presently.

(*They go out.* DORIN *and* POLINA ANDREYEVNA *are left alone.*)

DORN.   People are tiresome. As a matter of fact, what they ought to do is simply to kick your husband out, but instead it will end in that old woman Pyotr Nikolayevich and his sister both begging the man's pardon. You'll see!

POLINA ANDREYEVNA.   He's even put the carriage horses into the field. Every day there are these misunderstandings. If you only knew how it upsets me! It's making me ill; you see how I am trembling. I can't endure his coarseness. (*Entreating.*) Yevgeny, my dearest, my beloved, let me come to you. Our time is passing, we're not young any more, if only—for the end of our lives, at least—we could stop hiding and lying . . .

DORN.   I'm fifty-five; it's too late for me to change my life.

POLINA ANDREYEVNA.   I know why you refuse me—because there are other women besides me who are close to you. You can't take them all to live with you. I understand. Forgive me, you are tired of me.

(NINA *appears near the house, she is picking flowers.*)

DORN.   No, it's all right.

POLINA ANDREYEVNA.   I am tormented by jealousy. Of course, you are a doctor, you can't escape women. I understand. . . .

DORN (*to* NINA, *who has joined them*). How are things going in there?

NINA.   Irina Nikolayevna is crying, and Pyotr Nikolayevich is having an attack of asthma.

DORN (*gets up*). I'll go and give them both some valerian drops.

NINA (*handing him the flowers*). For you!

DORN.   *Merci bien.* (*Goes toward the house.*)

POLINA ANDREYEVNA (*going with him*). What pretty flowers! (*Nearing the house, in a choked voice.*) Give me those flowers! Give me those flowers!

(*He gives them to her, and she tears them to pieces and flings them away. They go into the house.*)

NINA.   How strange to see a famous actress cry, and for such a trivial reason! And isn't it strange that a celebrated author, adored by the public, written about in all the papers, his photograph for sale, his works translated into foreign languages, should spend the whole day fishing, and be delighted that he has caught two chub? I thought that famous people were proud, unapproachable, that they despised the crowd, and that with the luster of their names, and all their glory, they somehow revenged themselves on the world for placing rank and wealth above everything. But here they are crying, fishing, playing cards, laughing, and losing their tempers just like everybody else. . . .

(*Enter* TREPLEV, *without a hat, carrying a gun and a dead sea gull.*)

TREPLEV.   Are you alone here?

NINA.   Alone. (TREPLEV *lays the sea gull at her feet.*) What does that mean?

TREPLEV.   I was so low as to kill this sea gull today. I lay it at your feet.

NINA.   What's the matter with you? (*Picks up the sea gull and looks at it.*)

TREPLEV (*after a pause*). Soon, in the same way, I shall kill myself.

NINA.   I hardly know you.

TREPLEV.   Yes, ever since I began to feel that I no longer know you. You have changed toward me, your eyes are cold, I'm in your way.

NINA.   You've become so irritable lately, and whenever you say anything I can't understand you, it's as if you were talking in symbols. This sea gull, I suppose, is another symbol, but, forgive me, I don't understand. . . . (*Lays the sea gull on the bench*.) I am too simple to understand you.

TREPLEV.   This began the evening that my play failed so stupidly. Women never forgive failure. I've burnt it all, everything, to the last scrap. If you only knew how unhappy I am! Your coldness is awful, unbelievable. . . . It's as if I had woken up and found that this lake had suddenly dried up or sunk into the earth. You said just now that you are too simple to understand me. Oh, what is there to understand? My play was not liked, you despise my inspiration, you already consider me mediocre, insignificant, like so many others. . . . (*Stamps his foot.*) How well I understand it, how well! I feel as if I had a spike in my brain, may it be damned along with my pride, which is sucking my blood, sucking it like a viper. . . . (*Seeing* TRIGORIN, *who enters reading a book.*) Here comes the real genius, walking like Hamlet—and with a book. (*Mimicking.*) "Words, words, words . . . " This sun has hardly reached you, but already you are smiling, your glance is melting in its rays. I won't stand in your way. (*Quickly goes.*)

TRIGORIN (*making a note in his notebook*). Takes snuff and drinks vodka . . . always in black. The schoolmaster in love with her . . .

NINA.   Good morning, Boris Alekseyevich!

TRIGORIN.   Good morning. Things have taken an unexpected turn, and it appears we are leaving today. It's not very likely that we shall meet again. I am sorry. I don't often meet young girls . . . youthful and interesting. I've forgotten how it feels to be eighteen or nineteen, I can't picture it very clearly, that's why the young girls in my novels and stories are generally false. I'd like to be in your shoes, if only for an hour, to find out how you think, and, in general, what a pretty young girl is like.

NINA.   And I should like to be in your shoes.

TRIGORIN.   Why?

NINA.   To find out how it feels to be a famous, gifted writer. What does it feel like to be famous? How does it affect you?

TRIGORIN.   How? Not at all, I expect. I've never thought about it. (*After a moment's thought.*) One of two things: either you exaggerate my fame, or it's . . . just not something that one feels.

NINA.   But if you read about yourself in the papers?

TRIGORIN.   When they praise me, I'm pleased; when they abuse me, I'm in a bad mood for a couple of days.

NINA.   A wonderful world! How I envy you, if you only knew! People's destinies are so different. Some can barely drag out their dull, obscure existences, all very much alike, and all miserable, while others, like you, for example—but you are one in a million—are given a life that is brilliant, interesting, full of meaning. . . . You are fortunate. . . .

TRIGORIN.   I? (*Shrugging his shoulders.*) Hm . . . You talk of fame, of happiness, of some sort of brilliant, interesting life, but to me all these fine words, if you will forgive me, are like sugar plums—which I never eat. You are very young and very kind.

NINA.   Your life is beautiful!

TRIGORIN.   What's so good about it? (*Looks at his watch.*) I must get to my writing directly. Excuse me, I haven't time to . . . (*Laughs.*) You've stepped on my pet corn, as they say, and here I am getting excited and rather cross. Well, then, let's talk. We'll talk about my beautiful, brilliant life. . . . Where shall we begin? (*After a moment's thought.*) There are such things as fixed ideas, when a man keeps thinking day and night, about the moon, for instance. I have just such a moon. Day and night I am haunted by one thought: I must write, I must write, I must. . . . I have scarcely finished one novel when, for some reason, I have to write another, then a third, and after that a fourth. . . . I write incessantly, at a furious rate, I can't work any other way. What is brilliant and beautiful about that, I ask you? Oh, what a preposterous life! Here I am talking to you, I'm excited, yet not for a moment do I forget that my unfinished novel is waiting for me. I see that cloud, it looks like a grand piano. I think: must remember to put into a story somewhere that a cloud floats by looking like a grand piano. There's a scent of heliotrope. I quickly make a mental note: cloying smell, widow's color, use when describing a summer evening. I catch up every word and phrase we utter, and lock them in my literary storeroom—they may be useful. When I finish work, I hurry off to the theater or go fishing, and there's where I ought to rest and forget, but—no, a great, heavy cannon ball begins rolling around in my head—a new subject for a story; and once more I am pulled back to my desk and have to rush to start writing and writing again. And it's always like that, always; I have no rest from myself, and I feel that I am consuming my own life, that for the sake of the honey I give to someone in a void, I despoil my finest flowers of their pollen, tear them up, trample on their roots. Do you think I am mad? Do you think my relatives and friends treat me as if I were sane? "What are you scribbling now? What are you going to present us with next?" It's always the same, and I begin to think that these attentions on the part of my friends, all this praise and admiration—is nothing but a sham, that they're deceiving me as one does an invalid; and I sometimes fear that at any moment they may steal up from behind, seize me, and carry me off, like Poprishchin, to a madhouse. As for the years of my youth, my best years, when I was just beginning, my writing was one continuous torture. A minor writer, especially when he has no luck, feels clumsy, awkward, and superfluous; he is nervous, overwrought, he can't resist hanging around people connected with literature and the arts; he is unrecognized, unnoticed, afraid to look anyone straight in the eye—exactly like a man who has a passion for gambling but no money. I'd never seen my readers, but for some reason, I pictured them as unfriendly and suspicious. I was afraid of the public, it terrified me, and whenever a new play of mine was produced, it seemed to me that all the dark-haired people in the audience were hostile and all the fair-haired ones cold and indifferent. Oh, how awful it was! What agony!

NINA.   But surely inspiration and the very process of creation have given you moments of exalted happiness?

TRIGORIN.   Yes, while I'm writing I enjoy it. And I like reading the proofs, but . . . as soon as it appears in print, I can't bear it, I see that it's all wrong, a mistake, that it ought never to have been written, and I feel vexed and miserable. . . . (*Laughs.*) Then the public reads it: "Yes, charming, clever. . . . Charming but a far cry from Tolstoy"; or, "A fine thing, but Turgenev's *Fathers and Sons* is better." And so it will be to my dying day: charming and clever, charming and clever—nothing more; and when I die my friends will walk by my grave and say: "Here lies Trigorin: a good writer, but Turgenev was better."

NINA.   Forgive me, but I give up trying to understand you. You are simply spoiled by success.

TRIGORIN.   What success? I have never pleased myself. I don't like myself as a writer. The worst of it is that I'm in some sort of haze and often don't understand what I am writing. . . . I love this water here, the trees, the sky, I have a feeling for nature, it arouses in me a passionate, irresistible desire to write. But, you see, I'm not just a landscape painter, I'm a citizen besides, I love my country and its people, I feel that if I am a writer it is my duty to write about them, about their sufferings, their future, and to write about science, the rights of man, and so on, and so I write about everything, I am hurried, driven from all sides, people get angry at me, I dash back and forth like a fox brought to bay by the hounds; I see that life and science keep moving farther and farther ahead, while I fall farther and farther behind, like a peasant who has missed the train, and, in the end, I feel that I only know how to paint landscapes and in all the rest I am false—false to the marrow of my bones.

NINA.   You have worked too hard and you have neither the time nor the inclination to realize your own importance. You may be dissatisfied with yourself, but to others you are a great and wonderful person! If I were such a writer as you, I'd give my whole life to the people, but I should know that the only happiness for them would be in rising to my level, and they would harness themselves to my chariot.

TRIGORIN.   My chariot! What am I—Agamemnon? (*They both smile.*)

NINA.   For the happiness of being a writer or an actress, I would endure poverty, disillusionment, the hatred of my family; I would live in a garret and eat black bread, suffer dissatisfaction with myself, and the recognition of my own imperfections, but in return I should demand fame . . . real, resounding fame. . . . (*Covers her face with her hands.*) My head is swimming . . . Ough!

(*The voice of* ARKADINA *from the house: "Boris Alekseyevich!"*)

TRIGORIN.   I am being called . . . to pack, I suppose. But I don't feel like leaving. (*Glances back at the lake.*) Just look—what a paradise! . . . Lovely!

NINA.   Do you see the house with the garden on the other side of the lake?

TRIGORIN.   Yes.

NINA.   It belonged to my mother when she was alive. I was born there. I've spent my whole life by this lake, I know every little island on it.

TRIGORIN.   It's lovely here! (*Seeing the sea gull.*) And what is this?

NINA.   A sea gull. Konstantin Gavrilovich shot it.

TRIGORIN.   A beautiful bird. I really don't want to go. Try to persuade Irina Nikolayevna to stay. (*Makes a note in his book.*)

NINA.   What are you writing?

TRIGORIN.   Just making a note. . . . An idea occurred to me. (*Putting away notebook.*) Subject for a short story: a young girl like you lives all her life beside a lake; she loves the lake like a sea gull, and, like a sea gull, is happy and free. A man comes along by chance, sees her, and having nothing better to do, destroys her, just like this sea gull here.

(*A pause;* ARKADINA *appears at the window.*)

ARKADINA.   Boris Alekseyevich, where are you?

TRIGORIN.   Coming! (*Goes, then looks back at* NINA; *to* ARKADINA *at the window.*) What is it?

ARKADINA.   We're staying.

(TRIGORIN *goes into the house.*)

NINA (*comes down to the footlights; after a moment's reflection*). A dream!

ACT THREE

(*The dining room in* SORIN's *house. Doors on the right and left. A sideboard, a medicine cupboard, and, in the middle of the room, a table. A trunk and hat boxes; signs of preparations for departure.* TRIGORIN *is having lunch;* MASHA *is standing by the table.*)

MASHA.   I'm telling you all this because you're a writer. You may be able to use it. I tell you honestly: if he had seriously wounded himself, I would not have gone on living another minute. But I have courage, all the same. I've made up my mind to tear this love out of my heart—tear it out by the roots.

TRIGORIN.   How are you going to do that?

MASHA.   I'm going to get married. To Medvedenko.

TRIGORIN.   That's the schoolmaster?

MASHA.   Yes.

TRIGORIN.   I don't understand the necessity for that.

MASHA.   To love without hope . . . to spend whole years waiting for something . . . But when I marry, there'll be no more of that, new cares will stifle the old. Anyhow, it will be a change. Shall we have another?

TRIGORIN.   Haven't you had enough?

MASHA.   Oh, come! (*Fills their glasses.*) Don't look at me like that. Women drink more often than you imagine. Only a few drink openly as I do, the majority drink in secret. Yes. . . . And it's always vodka or cognac. (*Clinks glasses with him.*) Good luck! You're a very unassuming person, I'm sorry to be parting from you. (*They drink.*)

TRIGORIN.   I don't feel like going myself.

MASHA.   You should ask her to stay.

TRIGORIN.   No, she won't stay now. Her son is behaving most tactlessly. First he shoots himself, and now they say he's going to challenge me to a duel. And what for? He sulks, sneers, preaches new forms. . . . But there's room for all, the old and the new—why elbow?

MASHA.   Well, there's jealousy, too. However, that's not my affair.

(*Pause.* YAKOV *crosses from right to left carrying a suitcase;* NINA *comes in and stops near the window.*)

MASHA.   My schoolmaster is none too clever, but he's kind, and a poor soul, and he loves me very much. I'm sorry for him. And I'm sorry for his old mother. Well, I wish you all the best. Don't think badly of me. (*Warmly shakes his hand.*) I'm very grateful to you for your friendly interest. Do send me your books, and be sure to autograph them. Only don't write: "To my esteemed friend"; but simply: "To Maria, who doesn't know where she comes from or why she is living in this world." Good-bye! (*Goes out.*)

NINA (*holding out her hand with the fist closed to* TRIGORIN). Odd or even?

TRIGORIN.   Even.

NINA (*sighing*). No. I had only one pea in my hand. I was trying to tell my fortune—whether to go on the stage or not. If only someone would advise me!

TRIGORIN.   It's impossible to advise anyone about that. (*A pause.*)

NINA.   We are parting and . . . perhaps we shall never meet again. Will you take this little medallion as a remembrance? I had it engraved with your initials . . . and on the other side the title of your book, *Days and Nights.*

TRIGORIN.   How charming! (*Kisses the medallion.*) An enchanting gift!

NINA.   Think of me sometimes.

TRIGORIN.   I shall think of you. I shall think of you as you were on that sunny day—do you remember—a week ago, when you were wearing a light dress . . . we were talking . . . and a white sea gull lay there on the bench beside us.

NINA (*pensively*). Yes, the sea gull. . . . (*Pause.*) We can't talk any more, someone's coming. . . . Let me have two minutes with you before you go, I beg you . . . (*Goes out left.*)

(*At the same moment* ARKADINA *enters right with* SORIN, *who wears a dress coat with a decoration, then* YAKOV, *busy with the luggage.*)

ARKADINA.   Stay at home, old man. Are you really up to gadding about visiting people with your rheumatism? (*To* TRIGORIN.) Who was it that just went out? Nina?

TRIGORIN.   Yes.

ARKADINA.   *Pardon,* we interrupted you. . . . (*Sits down.*) I believe I've packed everything. I'm exhausted.

TRIGORIN (*reading the inscription on the medallion*). *Days and Nights,* page one twenty-one, lines eleven and twelve.

YAKOV (*clearing the table*). Am I to pack your fishing rods, too?

TRIGORIN.   Yes, I shall be wanting them again. But the books you can give away.

YAKOV.   Yes, sir.

TRIGORIN (*to himself*). Page one twenty-one, lines eleven and twelve. What are those lines? (*To* ARKADINA.) Are there copies of my books in the house?

ARKADINA.   Yes, in my brother's study, in the corner bookcase.

TRIGORIN.   Page one twenty-one . . . (*Goes out.*)

ARKADINA.   Really Petrusha, you'd better stay at home. . . .

SORIN.   You're going away. . . . It will be miserable for me here without you.

ARKADINA.   But what is there in town?

SORIN.   Nothing special, but all the same . . . (*Laughs.*) There'll be the laying of the cornerstone for the town hall, and all that sort of thing. . . . I'd like to shake myself free of this gudgeon existence, if only for an hour or two. I've been lying around like an old cigarette holder for too long. I've ordered the horses for one o'clock, so we'll be setting off at the same time.

ARKADINA (*after a pause*). Come, stay at home, don't be bored . . . and don't catch cold. Look after my son. Take care of him. Guide him. (*Pause.*) Here I am going away, and I shall never know why Konstantin tried to shoot himself. I believe that jealousy was the chief reason, and the sooner I take Trigorin away from here the better.

SORIN.   How shall I say it? There were other reasons. It's not hard to understand; an intelligent young man living in this remote place in the country, without money, without position, without future. No occupation whatsoever. Ashamed, and afraid of his idleness. I am extremely fond of him, and he's attached to me, but all the same, when it comes to it, he feels superfluous in this house, like a parasite, a hanger-on. It's only natural, his pride. . . .

ARKADINA.   He's such a worry to me! (*Pondering.*) He might go into the service, perhaps. . . .

SORIN (*begins to whistle, then, irresolutely*). It seems to me the best thing would be if you were to . . . give him a little money. In the first place, he ought to be able to dress like a human being, and all that. Just look at him, he's been going around in the same miserable jacket for the last three years, he has no overcoat. . . . (*Laughs.*) Yes, it wouldn't do him any harm to have a little fun . . . to go abroad, maybe. . . . It doesn't cost much.

ARKADINA.   Well . . . I might manage the suit, but as for going abroad . . . No, at the moment I can't even manage the suit. (*Peremptorily.*) No, I haven't any money!

(SORIN *laughs.*)

ARKADINA.   I haven't!

SORIN (*begins to whistle*). Quite so. Forgive me, my dear, don't be angry. I believe you. . . . You are a generous, noble-hearted woman.

ARKADINA (*through tears*). I have no money!

SORIN.   If I had any money, naturally, I'd give it to him myself, but I have nothing, not a kopeck. (*Laughs.*) My steward takes my entire pension and spends it on agriculture, cattle raising, beekeeping. . . . And my money all goes for nothing. The bees die, the cattle die, and he never lets me have the horses. . . .

ARKADINA.   I do have some money, but I'm an actress, and my costumes alone are enough to ruin me.

SORIN.   You are very kind, my dear. . . . I respect you. . . . Yes . . . But something's wrong with me again. . . . (*Staggers.*) I'm dizzy. (*Holds onto the table.*) I feel ill, and all that. . . .

ARKADINA (*alarmed*). Petrusha! (*Trying to support him.*) Petrusha, my dear! (*Calls.*) Help me! Help!

(*Enter* TREPLEV, *his head bandaged, and* MEDVEDENKO.)

ARKADINA.   He's ill!

SORIN.   It's nothing, it's nothing. . . . (*Smiles and drinks some water.*) It's passed off already, and so forth. . . .

TREPLEV (*to his mother*). Don't be frightened, Mother, it's not serious. This often happens to Uncle now. (*To his uncle.*) You must lie down for a while, Uncle.

SORIN.   For a little while, yes. . . . But I'm going to town all the same. . . . I'll lie down for a bit, and then I'm going. . . . It stands to reason . . . (*Goes out, leaning on his stick.*)

MEDVEDENKO (*gives him his arm*). There's a riddle: what goes on four legs in the morning, on two legs at noon, and on three in the evening? . . .

SORIN (*laughs*). Precisely. And on the back at night. Thank you, I can manage alone.

MEDVEDENKO.   Come, now, such formality! (*They go out.*)

ARKADINA.   How he frightened me!

TREPLEV.   It's not good for him to live in the country. He gets depressed. If you'd just have a sudden burst of generosity, Mother, and lend him fifteen hundred or two thousand rubles, he could live a whole year in town.

ARKADINA.   I haven't any money. I'm an actress, not a banker. (*A pause.*)

TREPLEV.   Mother, change my bandage. You do it so well.

ARKADINA (*takes iodoform and a box of bandage material out of the medicine cupboard*). The doctor is late.

TREPLEV.   He promised to be here at ten, but it's already noon.

ARKADINA.   Sit down. (*Takes the bandage off his head.*) You look as if you were wearing a turban. Yesterday some passer-by asked them in the kitchen what nationality you were. . . . But it's almost entirely healed. What's left is the merest trifle. (*Kisses him on the head.*) And no more click-click while I'm away?

TREPLEV.   No, Mother, that was a moment of insane despair, when I couldn't control myself. It won't happen again. (*Kisses her hand.*) You have magic fingers. I remember, a long time ago, when you were still playing in the state theater—I was little then—there was a fight in our courtyard, and one of the tenants, a washerwoman, was badly beaten. Do you remember? She was picked up unconscious. . . . You looked after her, took medicines to her, washed her children in the trough. Don't you remember?

ARKADINA.   No. (*Puts on a fresh bandage.*)

TREPLEV.   Two ballet dancers were living in the same house with us then. . . . They used to come and have coffee with you. . . .

ARKADINA.   That I do remember.

TREPLEV.   They were so devout. (*Pause.*) Lately, these last few days, I have loved you as tenderly and as completely as when I was a child. I have no one left but you now. Only why, why have you succumbed to the influence of that man?

ARKADINA.   You don't understand him, Konstantin. He is a very noble character.

TREPLEV.   And yet, when he was told I was going to challenge him to a duel, his nobility of character did not prevent him from playing the coward. He is leaving. An ignominious retreat.

ARKADINA.   What nonsense! It is I who am asking him to go.

TREPLEV.   A very noble character! Here you and I are nearly quarreling over him, and at this very moment he is somewhere in the garden or the drawing room laughing at us . . . developing Nina, trying to convince her once and for all that he's a genius.

ARKADINA.   You take delight in saying disagreeable things to me. I respect that man, and I ask you not to speak ill of him in my presence.

TREPLEV.   And I don't respect him. You want me to consider him a genius, too, but forgive me, I can't lie, his books make me sick.

ARKADINA.   That's envy. There's nothing left for people who lay claim to a talent they haven't got but to disparage real talent. A fine consolation, I must say!

TREPLEV (*ironically*). Real talent! (*Wrathfully.*) I have more talent than all of you put together, if it comes to that! (*Tears the bandage off his head.*) You, with your hackneyed conventions, have usurped the foremost places in art, and consider nothing genuine and legitimate except what you yourselves do—everything else you stifle and suppress! I do not accept you! I accept neither you nor him!

ARKADINA.   You decadent!

TREPLEV.   Go back to your charming theater and play in your miserable, worthless plays!

ARKADINA.   I have never acted in such plays! Leave me! You're incapable of writing so much as a paltry little vaudeville sketch. You're nothing but a Kiev petty bourgeois! You sponger!

TREPLEV.   Miser!

ARKADINA.   Beggar!

(TREPLEV *sits down and quietly weeps.*)

ARKADINA.   Nonentity! (*Walking up and down in agitation.*) Don't cry. You mustn't cry. . . . (*Weeps.*) Don't. . . . (*Kisses him on the forehead, the cheeks, the head.*) My darling child, forgive me. . . . Forgive your sinful mother. Forgive miserable me!

TREPLEV (*embraces her*). If you only knew! I have lost everything. She does not love me, I can no longer write. . . . All my hopes are gone. . . .

ARKADINA.   Don't despair. . . . It will all pass. He's going away now. She will love you again. (*Dries his tears.*) That's enough. Now we have made peace.

TREPLEV (*kisses her hands*). Yes, Mother.

ARKADINA (*tenderly*). Make it up with him, too. You don't want a duel. . . . Do you?

TREPLEV.   Very well. . . . Only, Mother, don't make me see him. It's too painful . . . it's more than I can bear. . . . (TRIGORIN *comes in.*) There he is. . . . I'm going . . . (*Hurriedly puts dressings in the cupboard.*) The doctor can put on the bandage. . . .

TRIGORIN (*looking through a book*). Page one twenty-one . . . lines eleven and twelve. . . . Here it is. . . . (*Reads.*) "If ever my life can be of use to you, come and take it."

(TREPLEV *picks up the bandage from the floor and goes out.*)

ARKADINA (*looking at her watch*). The horses will be here soon.

TRIGORIN (*to himself*). "If ever my life can be of use to you, come and take it."

ARKADINA.   Your things are all packed, I hope?

TRIGORIN (*impatiently*). Yes, yes. . . . (*Musing.*) Why is it that in this appeal from a pure soul I have a presentiment of sorrow, and it wrings my heart? . . . "If ever my life can be of use to you, come and take it." (*To* ARKADINA.) Let us stay one more day!

(ARKADINA *shakes her head.*)

TRIGORIN.   Do let us stay!

ARKADINA.   Darling, I know what's keeping you here, but have some self-control. You're a little intoxicated, try to be sober.

TRIGORIN.   And you be sober, too, be wise and reasonable, I beg you; look at this like a true friend. . . . (*Presses her hand.*) You are capable of sacrifice. . . . Be a friend to me, let me go. . . .

ARKADINA (*violently agitated*). Are you so infatuated with her?

TRIGORIN.   I am attracted to her! Perhaps this is just what I need.

ARKADINA.   The love of a provincial girl! Oh, how little you know yourself!

TRIGORIN.   Sometimes people are walking about but asleep; that's how it is with me now. . . . I am talking to you, but it's as if I were asleep and dreaming of her. I am possessed by sweet, wonderful dreams. . . . Let me go. . . .

ARKADINA (*trembling*). No, no. . . . I am just an ordinary woman, you can't talk to me like this. Don't torture me, Boris . . . it frightens me. . . .

TRIGORIN.   You could be an extraordinary woman if you wanted to be. A youthful love, alluring, poetic, carrying one off into a world of dreams—the only thing on earth that can give happiness! I have never known a love like that. . . . In my youth there wasn't time, I was always haunting the editors' offices, fighting off poverty. . . . And now that love has come at last, and is beckoning me. . . . What sense is there in running away from it?

ARKADINA (*furiously*). You've gone out of your mind!

TRIGORIN.   And why not?

ARKADINA.   You are all in a conspiracy to torment me today! (*Weeps.*)

TRIGORIN (*clutching his head*). She doesn't understand! She doesn't want to understand!

ARKADINA.   Am I really so old and ugly that you feel no constraint in talking to me about other women? (*Puts her arms around him and kisses him.*) Oh, you madman! My beautiful, wonderful . . . You are the last chapter of my life! (*Falls on her knees.*) My joy, my pride, my bliss. . . . (*Embraces his knees.*) If you leave me, even for one hour, I won't survive it, I'll lose my mind, my wonderful, magnificent one, my master. . . .

TRIGORIN.   Someone may come in. (*Helps her to her feet.*)

ARKADINA.   Let them, I'm not ashamed of my love for you. (*Kisses his hands.*) My precious, my reckless boy, you want to be mad, but I won't have it, I won't let you. . . . (*Laughs.*) You are mine . . . mine. . . . This brow is mine, these eyes, this lovely, silky hair is mine. . . . You are all mine. You are so talented, so clever, the best of all modern writers, the hope of Russia. . . . You have such sincerity, such simplicity, freshness, such robust humor. . . . In one stroke you can convey the essence of a person or a landscape, your characters are like living people. Oh, it's impossible to read you without delight! You think this is just adulation—that I'm flattering you? Come, look into my eyes . . . look at me. . . . Do I look like a liar? I am the only one who knows how to appreciate you, the only one who tells you the truth, my darling, wonderful one. . . . Will you come with me? Yes? You won't leave me?

TRIGORIN.   I have no will of my own . . . I've never had a will of my own. . . . Flabby, soft, always submissive— how can that appeal to a woman? Take me, carry me off, only don't let me go one step away from you. . . .

ARKADINA (*to herself*). Now he is mine. (*Casually, as if nothing had happened.*) But, of course, if you want to, you can stay. I'll go by myself, and you can come later, in a week. After all, why should you hurry?

TRIGORIN.   No, we may as well go together.

ARKADINA.   As you wish. We'll go together then. . . .

(*A pause;* TRIGORIN *writes in a notebook.*)

ARKADINA.   What are you writing?

TRIGORIN.   I heard a good expression this morning: "Vestal forest. . . ." It might do for a story. (*Stretches.*) So, we're off? Again the railway carriages, the stations, refreshment bars, the stews, and conversations. . . .

(*Enter* SHAMRAYEV.)

SHAMRAYEV.   I have the honor to inform you, with regret, that the horses are here. It is time, most esteemed lady, to leave for the station; the train comes in at five minutes past two. You will do me the favor, Irina Nikolayevna, and not forget to inquire about the actor Suzdaltsev—if he is alive and in good health? There was a time when we used to drink together. . . . He was inimitable in *The Mail Robbery*. And at Elisavetgrad, I remember, the tragedian Izmailov—also a remarkable character—played in

the same company with him. Don't be in a hurry, most esteemed lady, you still have five minutes. Once, in some melodrama, they were playing conspirators, and when they suddenly were discovered and Izmailov was supposed to say: "We're caught in a trap," he said: "We're traught in a cap." (*Laughs.*) A cap!

(*While he is speaking,* YAKOV *is busy with the luggage; a* MAID *brings* ARKADINA's *hat, cloak, parasol, and gloves; the* COOK *glances in at the door left and a moment later hesitantly comes in. Enter* POLINA ANDREYEVNA, *then* SORIN *and* MEDVEDENKO.)

POLINA ANDREYEVNA (*with a small basket*). Here are some plums for the journey. . . . They're very sweet. You may feel like having a little something. . . .

ARKADINA.   You are very kind, Polina Andreyevna.

POLINA ANDREYEVNA.   Good-bye, my dear! If there has been anything . . . not quite as it should be, forgive it. (*Weeps.*)

ARKADINA (*embraces her*). Everything has been lovely, everything. Only you mustn't cry.

POLINA ANDREYEVNA.   Our time is passing.

ARKADINA.   What can we do?

(*Enter* SORIN *in an overcoat with a cape, his hat on, and carrying a cane; he comes in from door on the left and crosses the stage.*)

SORIN.   Sister, it's time to start, if you don't want to be late and all that. . . . I'll go and get into the carriage. (*Goes out.*)

MEDVEDENKO.   I'm going to walk to the station to see you off. I'll be there in no time. . . . (*Goes out.*)

ARKADINA.   Good-bye, my dears. . . . If we are alive and well, we'll meet again next summer. . . . (*The* MAID, YAKOV, *and the* COOK *kiss her hand.*) Don't forget me. (*Gives the* COOK *a ruble.*) Here's a ruble for the three of you.

COOK.   We humbly thank you, madam. A happy journey to you! We are most grateful.

YAKOV.   Godspeed to you!

SHAMRAYEV.   You might make us happy with a letter. Good-bye, Boris Alekseyevich!

ARKADINA.   Where's Konstantin? Tell him that I'm leaving. I must say good-bye to him. Well, think kindly of me. (*To* YAKOV.) I gave a ruble to the cook. It's for the three of you.

(*All go out on the right. The stage is empty. Offstage there are the customary sounds of people being seen off. The* MAID *comes back for the basket of plums on the table and goes out.*)

TRIGORIN (*returning*). I forgot my stick. It must be out there on the veranda. (*Goes toward the door on the left and meets* NINA *coming in.*) It's you! We are leaving.

NINA. I felt that we should see each other once more. (*Excitedly.*) Boris Alekseyevich, I have come to an irrevocable decision, the die is cast, I am going on the stage. Tomorrow I shall no longer be here, I am leaving my father, giving up everything, and beginning a new life. . . . I am going to Moscow . . . like you. . . . We shall see each other there.

TRIGORIN (*glancing back*). Stay at the Slavyansky Bazaar. . . . Send me word at once . . . Molchanovka, Grokholsky House. . . . I must hurry. . . .

(*A pause.*)

NINA. One minute more . . .

TRIGORIN (*in an undertone*). You are so lovely. . . . Oh, what happiness to think that we shall meet soon! (*She leans on his breast.*) I shall see these wonderful eyes, this inexpressibly beautiful, tender smile . . . this sweet face with its expression of angelic purity. . . . My darling . . . (*A prolonged kiss.*)

(*Two years pass between the third and fourth acts.*)

ACT FOUR

(*One of the drawing rooms in* SORIN's *house, which has been turned into a study by* KONSTANTIN TREPLEV. *Doors right and left leading to other parts of the house, and French windows center leading to the veranda. Besides the usual drawing-room furniture, there is a desk in the right corner, a sofa and a bookcase near the door left, and books lying on window sills and chairs. Evening. A single lamp with a shade is lighted. The room is in semidarkness. Sounds of trees rustling and wind howling in the chimneys. The watchman is tapping. Enter* MEDVEDENKO *and* MASHA.)

MASHA (*calling*). Konstantin Gavrilovich! Konstantin Gavrilovich! (*Looking around.*) Nobody here. The old man keeps asking: where's Kostya, where's Kostya? . . . He can't live without him. . . .

MEDVEDENKO. He's afraid of being alone. (*Listening.*) What terrible weather! Two whole days of it!

MASHA (*turns up the lamp*). There are waves on the lake . . . tremendous ones.

MEDVEDENKO. It's dark in the garden. We ought to have told them to pull down that stage. It stands there bare and ugly, like a skeleton, and the curtain flaps in the wind. Last night as I walked by I thought I heard somebody crying inside.

MASHA. What next? . . . (*Pause.*)

MEDVEDENKO. Let's go home, Masha.

MASHA (*shakes her head*). I'm going to stay here tonight.

MEDVEDENKO (*imploring*). Masha, do let us go! The baby may be hungry.

MASHA. Nonsense. Matryona will feed him. (*Pause.*)

MEDVEDENKO. It's a shame. . . . Three nights now without his mother.

MASHA. You're becoming tiresome. In the old days you'd at least philosophize a little, but now it's always home and baby, home and baby—that's all I ever hear from you.

MEDVEDENKO. Do come, Masha.

MASHA. Go yourself.

MEDVEDENKO. Your father won't let me have a horse.

MASHA. He will if you ask him.

MEDVEDENKO. Very well. I'll try. Then you'll come tomorrow?

MASHA (*taking snuff*). Yes, tomorrow. Don't bother me. . . .

(*Enter* TREPLEV *and* POLINA ANDREYEVNA; TREPLEV *with pillows and a blanket,* POLINA ANDREYEVNA *with sheets and pillow cases; they lay them on the sofa, then* TREPLEV *goes to his desk and sits down.*)

MASHA. What's this for, Mama?

POLINA ANDREYEVNA. Pyotr Nikolayevich asked us to make up a bed for him in Kostya's room.

MASHA. Let me. . . . (*Makes the bed.*)

POLINA ANDREYEVNA (*sighing*). Old people are like children. . . . (*Goes to the desk, leans on her elbow and looks at a manuscript. A pause.*)

MEDVEDENKO. Well, I'm going. Good-bye, Masha. (*Kisses his wife's hand.*) Good-bye, Mother. (*Tries to kiss his mother-in-law's hand.*)

POLINA ANDREYEVNA (*with annoyance*). Well, go if you're going!

MEDVEDENKO. Good-bye, Konstantin Gavrilovich.

(*TREPLEV gives him his hand without speaking;* MEDVEDENKO *goes out.*)

POLINA ANDREYEVNA (*glancing at the manuscript*). Nobody ever thought or dreamed that you'd turn out to be a real author, Kostya. And here you are, God be praised, getting money from the magazines. (*Passing her hand over his hair.*) And you've grown handsome. . . . Dear, good Kostya, be a little kinder to my Mashenka!

MASHA (*making the bed*). Leave him alone, Mama.

POLINA ANDREYEVNA (*to* TREPLEV). She's a good girl. . . . (*Pause.*) A woman doesn't ask for much, Kostya, so long as you give her a kind look. I know from myself.

(*TREPLEV gets up from the desk and goes out without speaking.*)

MASHA. Now you've made him angry. Why did you have to pester him?

POLINA ANDREYEVNA. I'm sorry for you, Mashenka.

MASHA. A lot of good that does!

POLINA ANDREYEVNA. My heart aches for you. I see it all, you know, I understand.

MASHA.   It's simply nonsense. Hopeless love—there's no such thing except in novels. It's of no consequence. The only thing is you mustn't let yourself go, and always be expecting something, waiting for the tide to turn. . . . When love plants itself in your heart, you have to clear it out. They've promised to transfer my husband to another district. Once we're there, I shall forget it all—I'll tear it out of my heart by the roots.

(*Two rooms away a melancholy waltz is being played.*)

POLINA ANDREYEVNA.   Kostya is playing. That means he's depressed.

MASHA (*takes a few waltz steps in silence*). The most important thing, Mama, is not to have him constantly before my eyes. If only they give my Semyon his transfer, believe me, within a month I'll have forgotten. It's all nonsense.

(*The door on the left opens and* DORN *and* MEDVEDENKO *wheel in* SORIN.)

MEDVEDENKO.   I've got six in my house now. And flour at two kopecks a pound.

DORN.   It's a tight squeeze.

MEDVEDENKO.   It's all very well for you to laugh. You've got more money than you know what to do with.

DORN.   Money? After thirty years of practice, an onerous practice, my friend, when day and night I couldn't call my soul my own, I managed to save only two thousand rubles, and that I've just spent on a holiday abroad. I have nothing.

MASHA (*to her husband*). Haven't you gone?

MEDVEDENKO (*guiltily*). Well . . . how can I go when they won't let me have a horse?

MASHA (*with bitter vexation, in an undertone*). I wish I had never set eyes on you!

(SORIN, *in the wheel chair, remains on the left side of the room;* POLINA ANDREYEVNA, MASHA, *and* DORN *sit down near him;* MEDVEDENKO, *chagrined, moves to one side.*)

DORN.   What a lot of changes you have made here . . . this drawing room turned into a study. . . .

MASHA.   It's more convenient for Konstantin Gavrilovich to work there. He can go out into the garden and think whenever he feels like it.

(*The watchman is heard tapping.*)

SORIN.   Where is my sister?

DORN.   She has gone to the station to meet Trigorin. She'll be back soon.

SORIN.   If you found it necessary to send for my sister, I must be seriously ill. (*After a brief silence.*) It's very odd, I'm seriously ill, yet they don't give me any medicine.

DORN.   What do you want? Valerian drops? Soda? Quinine?

SORIN.   Now the philosophy begins. Oh, what an infliction! (*Nods his head in the direction of the sofa.*) Has that been made up for me?

POLINA ANDREYEVNA.   For you, Pyotr Nikolayevich.

SORIN.   Thank you.

DORN (*sings softly*). "The moon floats in the evening sky . . ."

SORIN.   You know, I'd like to give Kostya a subject for a story. It should be called: "The Man Who Wished"— "L'Homme qui a voulu." There was a time in my youth when I wished to become a writer—but I didn't. I wanted to speak well, too—and I speak abominably: (*Mimicking himself.*) "and all that sort of thing, and so forth and so on . . ." When I used to try to sum anything up I'd drag on and on till I broke out in a perspiration. I wanted to marry—and I never married. I always wanted to live in town—and here I am ending my life in the country, and so forth and so on.

DORN.   You wanted to become a Councilor of State—and you became one.

SORIN (*laughs*). I didn't seek that, it came of itself.

DORN.   To express dissatisfaction with life at sixty-two is, you must admit, not very magnanimous.

SORIN.   What an obstinate fellow you are! Can't you understand, one wants to live!

DORN.   That's frivolous. It's a law of nature that every life must have its end.

SORIN.   You argue like a man who's had his fill. You're satisfied, and so nothing means anything to you. You're indifferent to life. But when it comes to dying, you'll be afraid, too.

DORN.   The fear of death is an animal fear. . . . One must overcome it. It's reasonable only for those who believe in eternal life and are in terror because of their sins. But, in the first place, you are not religious, and in the second place, what sins have you committed? You served in the department of justice for twenty-five years—that's all.

SORIN (*laughs*). Twenty-eight. . . .

(TREPLEV *enters and sits on a stool at* SORIN'*s feet.* MASHA *never takes her eyes off him.*)

DORN.   We're keeping Konstantin Gavrilovich from his work.

TREPLEV.   No, it doesn't matter.

(*A pause.*)

MEDVEDENKO.   If I may ask, Doctor, which city appealed to you most in your travels?

DORN.   Genoa.

TREPLEV.   Why Genoa?

DORN.   Because of the wonderful street crowds there. You go out of your hotel in the evening, and the street is filled with people. You wander aimlessly up and down, in and out, mingling with the crowd, psychologically entering into its life, and you begin to believe there might actually be a world soul, like the one Nina Zarechnaya acted in your play. By the way, where is she now? How is she getting on?

TREPLEV.   All right, I suppose.

DORN.   I was told she'd been leading a rather peculiar life. What does that mean?

TREPLEV.   It's a long story, Doctor.

DORN.   Well, you can make it short.

(*A pause.*)

TREPLEV.   She ran away from home and had an affair with Trigorin. You knew that, didn't you?

DORN.   Yes, I knew that.

TREPLEV.   She had a child. The child died. Trigorin got tired of her and resumed his former attachments, as might have been expected. In fact, he had never given them up, but, in his spineless way, had somehow contrived to be everywhere at once. As far as I can make out from what I have heard, Nina's personal life is a complete failure.

DORN.   And the stage?

TREPLEV.   Even worse, I believe. She made her debut in a summer theater near Moscow, then went to the provinces. At that time I never lost sight of her; wherever she went, I followed. She always attempted big parts, but she acted crudely, tastelessly, with stiff gestures and strident intonations. There were moments when she showed talent—when she uttered a cry or had a dying scene—but those were only moments.

DORN.   She does have talent, then?

TREPLEV.   It was hard to tell. I suppose she has. I went to see her, but she didn't want to see me, and the maid would never let me in at her hotel. I understood how she felt and didn't insist on a meeting. (*Pause.*) What more can I tell you? Afterward, when I had come back home, I received letters from her—clever, warm, interesting letters; she didn't complain, but I felt that she was profoundly unhappy; there was not a line that didn't betray her sick, strained nerves. And her imagination was somewhat distracted. She always signed herself "The Sea Gull." The miller in *The Mermaid* says that he's a raven, and in the same way she kept repeating that she was a sea gull. She's here now.

DORN.   What do you mean—here?

TREPLEV.   In town, staying at the inn. She's been here for five days. I was on the point of going to see her, but Masha went, and she won't see anyone. Semyon Semyonovich is convinced that he saw her last night after dinner in the fields a couple of versts from here.

MEDVEDENKO.   Yes, I did see her. She was walking in the opposite direction, toward town. I bowed to her and asked her why she didn't come to see us. She said she would come.

TREPLEV.   She won't. (*Pause.*) Her father and stepmother will have nothing to do with her. They've put watchmen everywhere so that she can't even go near the house. (*Goes toward his desk with the doctor.*) How easy it is, Doctor, to be a philosopher on paper, and how difficult in life.

SORIN.   She was a charming girl.

DORN.   What's that?

SORIN.   She was a charming girl, I say. State Councilor Sorin was positively in love with her for a while.

DORN.   You old Lovelace!

(SHAMRAYEV's *laugh is heard*.)

POLINA ANDREYEVNA.   I think they've come back from the station. . . .

TREPLEV.   Yes, I hear Mother.

(*Enter* ARKADINA *and* TRIGORIN *followed by* SHAMRAYEV.)

SHAMRAYEV.   We all grow old and weather-beaten under the influence of the elements, but you, most esteemed lady, are still young. . . . Light blouse, sprightly . . . graceful . . .

ARKADINA.   That's enough to bring me bad luck, you tiresome man!

TRIGORIN (*to* SORIN). How do you do, Pyotr Nikolayevich! Still ailing? That's bad! (*Seeing* MASHA, *delighted.*) Maria Ilyinichna!

MASHA.   You remember me? (*Shakes hands.*)

TRIGORIN.   Married?

MASHA.   Long ago.

TRIGORIN.   Happy? (*Bows to* DORN *and* MEDVEDENKO, *then hesitantly approaches* TREPLEV.) Irina Nikolayevna tells me that you have forgotten the past and are no longer angry.

(TREPLEV *holds out his hand.*)

ARKADINA (*to her son*). Look, Boris Alekseyevich has brought the magazine with your new story in it.

TREPLEV (*taking the magazine, to* TRIGORIN). Thank you. You're very kind.

TRIGORIN.   Your admirers send their greetings. . . . In Petersburg and Moscow there's a great deal of interest in your work, and I'm always being asked about you. They want to know what you are like, how old you are, whether you are dark or fair. For some reason they all think you are no longer young. And nobody knows your real name, of course, since your work is always published under a pseudonym. You're as mysterious as the Iron Mask.

TREPLEV.   Will you be with us long?

TRIGORIN.   No, tomorrow I think I'll go to Moscow. I must. I'm in a hurry to finish my novel, and besides, I've promised to give them something for an anthology. In short—the same old story.

(*While they are talking,* ARKADINA *and* POLINA ANDREY-EVNA *set up a card table in the middle of the room.* SHAM-RAYEV *lights the candles and arranges the chairs. A game of lotto is brought out of the cupboard.*)

TRIGORIN.   The weather has not given me a very friendly welcome. There's a cruel wind. If it dies down tomorrow morning I'm going to the lake to fish. And I want to have a look at the garden and the place—do you remember?—where your play was performed. I've got an idea for a story all worked out, I only want to refresh my memory of the place where it is laid.

MASHA (*to her father*). Papa, please let my husband have a horse! He must go home.

SHAMRAYEV (*mimicking*). A horse . . . must go home. . . . (*Sternly.*) You can see for yourself they've just been to the station. They'll not go out again.

MASHA.   But there are other horses. . . . (*Seeing that her father does not answer, makes a gesture of resignation.*) There's no use trying to do anything with you. . . .

MEDVEDENKO.   I can walk, Masha. Really . . .

POLINA ANDREYEVNA (*sighing*). Walk, in such weather. . . . (*Sits down at the card table.*) Come and sit down, friends.

MEDVEDENKO.   It's only six versts, after all. . . . Good-bye . . . (*Kisses his wife's hand.*) Good-bye, Mama. (*His mother-in-law reluctantly holds out her hand.*) I shouldn't have troubled anyone, but the baby. . . . (*Bows to them.*) Good-bye. . . . (*Goes out apologetically.*)

SHAMRAYEV.   He can walk all right! He's not a general.

POLINA ANDREYEVNA (*taps on the table*). Please, friends. Let's not lose time, they'll be calling us to supper soon.

(SHAMRAYEV, MASHA, *and* DORN *sit down at the table.*)

ARKADINA (*to* TRIGORIN). When the long autumn evenings commence they always play lotto here. Look, it's the same old lotto set we had when Mother used to play with us as children. Don't you want to have a game with us till supper? (*She and* TRIGORIN *sit down at the table.*) It's a dull game, but it's not bad when you get used to it. (*Deals three cards to each.*)

TREPLEV (*turning the pages of the magazine*). He's read his own story, but he hasn't even cut the pages of mine. (*Puts the magazine down on his desk, then goes toward the door left; as he passes his mother, kisses her on the head.*)

ARKADINA.   What about you, Kostya?

TREPLEV.   Sorry, I don't feel like it somehow. . . . I'm going for a walk. (*Goes out.*)

ARKADINA.   The stake is ten kopecks. Put it down for me, will you, Doctor?

DORN.   Right.

MASHA.   Have you all put down your stakes? I begin—twenty-two!

ARKADINA.   I have it.

MASHA.   Three!

DORN.   Right.

MASHA.   Did you put down three? Eight! Eighty-one! Ten!

SHAMRAYEV.   Not so fast.

ARKADINA.   What a reception they gave me in Kharkov! Goodness, my head is still spinning!

MASHA.   Thirty-four!

(*A melancholy waltz is played offstage.*)

ARKADINA.   The students gave me an ovation . . . three baskets of flowers . . . two garlands, and look. . . . (*Unfastens a brooch and tosses it onto the table.*)

SHAMRAYEV.   Now, that is something. . . .

MASHA.   Fifty!

DORN.   Exactly fifty?

ARKADINA.   I had a marvelous costume. . . . You may say what you like, but I do know how to dress.

POLINA ANDREYEVNA.   Kostya is playing. He's depressed, poor boy.

SHAMRAYEV.   They've been abusing him in the newspapers.

MASHA.   Seventy-seven!

ARKADINA.   He needn't take any notice of that!

TRIGORIN.   He has no luck. He never manages to find a genuine style of his own. There's always something strange, vague, at times almost resembling a delirium. And not one living character.

MASHA.   Eleven!

ARKADINA (*looking at* SORIN). Petrusha, are you bored? (*Pause.*) He's asleep.

DORN.   The State Councilor sleeps.

MASHA.   Seven! Ninety!

TRIGORIN.   If I lived in a place like this, by a lake, do you think I'd write? I should overcome this passion of mine and do nothing but fish.

MASHA.   Twenty-eight!

TRIGORIN.   To catch a perch or a bass—what bliss!

DORN.   I believe in Konstantin Gavrilovich. He's got something! He's got something! He thinks in images, his stories are vivid, striking, and I am deeply moved by them. It's only a pity that he has no definite purpose. He creates impressions, nothing more, and, of course, you don't get very far on impressions alone. Irina Nikolayevna, are you glad to have a son who's a writer?

ARKADINA.   Imagine, I haven't read anything of his yet. There's never time.

MASHA.   Twenty-six!

(TREPLEV *quietly enters and goes to his desk.*)

SHAMRAYEV (*to* TRIGORIN). We've still got that thing of yours here, Boris Alekseyevich.

TRIGORIN.   What thing?

SHAMRAYEV.   Konstantin Gavrilovich shot a sea gull once, and you told me to have it stuffed for you.

TRIGORIN.   I don't remember. (*Musing.*) I don't remember.

MASHA.   Sixty-six! One!

TREPLEV (*throws open the window and stands listening*). How dark it is! I don't know why I feel so uneasy.

ARKADINA.   Kostya, shut the window, there's a draft.

(TREPLEV *shuts the window.*)

MASHA.   Eighty-eight!

TRIGORIN.   Ladies and gentlemen, the game is mine.

ARKADINA.   Bravo! Bravo!

SHAMRAYEV.   Bravo!

ARKADINA.   This man is lucky in everything! (*Gets up.*) And now, let's go and have a bite to eat. Our great man has not dined today. After supper we'll go on. (*To her son.*) Kostya, leave your manuscript and come have something to eat.

TREPLEV.   I don't want to, Mother, I'm not hungry.

ARKADINA.   Just as you like. (*Wakes* SORIN.) Petrusha, supper! (*Takes* SHAMRAYEV'S *arm.*) Let me tell you about my reception in Kharkov. . . .

(POLINA ANDREYEVNA *blows out the candles on the table, then she and* DORN *wheel out* SORIN'S *chair. All go out by the door on the left;* TREPLEV *is left alone at his desk.*)

TREPLEV (*preparing to write, reads through what he has already written*). I've talked so much about new forms, and now I feel that little by little I myself am falling into a convention. (*Reads.*) "The placards on the fence proclaimed . . . " "A pale face framed by dark hair . . . " Proclaimed . . . framed by dark hair . . . That's banal. (*Scratches out what he has written.*) I'll begin where the hero is awakened by the sound of rain, and throw out all the rest. The description of the moonlight night is long and artificial. Trigorin has worked out a method, it's easy for him. . . . With him a broken bottleneck glitters on the dam and the mill wheel casts a black shadow—and there you have a moonlight night; but with me there's the shimmering light, the silent twinkling of the stars, the distant sounds of a piano dying away on the still, fragrant air. . . . It's agonizing. (*A pause.*) Yes, I'm becoming more and more convinced that it's not a question of old and new forms, but that one writes, without even thinking about forms, writes because it pours freely from the soul. (*Someone taps on the window nearest the desk.*) What's that? (*Looks out the window.*) I don't see anything. (*Opens the French windows and peers into the garden.*) Someone ran down the steps. (*Calls.*) Who's there? (*Goes out; he can be heard walking rapidly along the veranda; a moment later returns with* NINA ZARECHNAYA.) Nina! Nina!

(NINA *lays her head on his breast and quietly sobs.*)

TREPLEV (*moved*). Nina! Nina! It's you . . . you. . . . It's as though I had a presentiment, all day long my soul has been in terrible torment. (*Takes off her hat and cloak.*) Oh, my precious darling, she has come at last! Don't let us cry, don't!

NINA.   There's someone here.

TREPLEV.   No one.

NINA.   Lock the doors, someone might come in.

TREPLEV.   No one will come in.

NINA.   I know Irina Nikolayevna is here. Lock the doors.

TREPLEV (*locks the right door, goes to the door left*). There's no lock on this one. I'll put a chair against it. (*Puts an armchair against the door.*) Don't be afraid, no one will come in.

NINA (*looking intently into his face*). Let me look at you. (*Looking around.*) It's warm, cozy. . . . This used to be the drawing room. Am I very much changed?

TREPLEV.   Yes. . . . You are thinner, and your eyes have grown bigger. Nina, it seems so strange to be seeing you. Why wouldn't you let me come to see you? Why didn't you come sooner? I know you've been here almost a week. . . . I went there several times every day and stood under your window like a beggar.

NINA.   I was afraid you might hate me. Every night I dream that you are looking at me and don't recognize me. If you only knew! Ever since I arrived I've been walking here . . . by the lake. I came near the house many times, but I couldn't bring myself to come in. Let's sit down. (*They sit down.*) Let's sit and talk, and talk. . . . It's nice here, warm and cozy. . . . Listen—the wind! There's a passage in Turgenev: "Happy the man who on such a night has a roof over his head, who has a warm corner of his own." I am a sea gull. . . . No, that's not it. (*Rubs her forehead.*) What was I saying? Yes . . . Turgenev . . . "And may the Lord help all homeless wanderers." . . . It doesn't matter. (*Sobs.*)

TREPLEV.   Nina, you're crying again—Nina!

NINA.   Never mind, it does me good. . . . I haven't cried for two years. Yesterday, in the late evening, I came into the garden to see if our theater was still there. It's still standing. I began to cry, for the first time in two years, and I felt relieved, my soul felt clear. See, I'm not crying now. (*Takes his hand.*) And so you have become a writer. . . . You are a writer—and I am an actress. . . . We, too, have been drawn into the whirlpool. . . . I used to live happily, like a child—I'd wake up in the morning singing; I loved you and I dreamed of fame . . . and now? Tomorrow, early in the morning, I must go to Yelets, third class . . . traveling with peasants, and at Yelets the educated merchants will pester me with their attentions. It's a coarse life.

TREPLEV.   Why to Yelets?

NINA.   I've accepted an engagement for the whole winter. It's time I was going.

TREPLEV.   Nina, I cursed you, I hated you, I tore up all your letters and photographs, but every minute I was conscious that my soul was bound to yours forever. I can never stop loving you. Ever since I lost you, and my work began to be published, my life has been unbearable—I am miserable. . . . All of a sudden my youth was snatched from me, and now I feel as if I had been living in this world for ninety years. I call to you, I kiss the ground you walked on; wherever I look I see your face, that tender smile that used to shine on me in the best years of my life. . . .

NINA (*confused*). Why does he talk like that, why does he talk like that?

TREPLEV.   I am alone, I have no one's affection to warm me, I am as cold as if I were living in a dungeon, and no matter what I write, it's dry, hard, dark. Stay here, Nina, I implore you, or let me go with you!

(NINA *quickly puts on her hat and cloak.*)

TREPLEV.   Nina, why? For God's sake, Nina. . . . (*Looks at her putting on her things.*)

(*A pause.*)

NINA.   My horses are waiting at the gate. Don't see me off. I'll go by myself. . . . (*Through tears.*) Give me some water. . . .

TREPLEV (*gives her a glass of water*). Where are you going now?

NINA.   To town. (*Pause.*) Is Irina Nikolayevna here?

TREPLEV.   Yes. . . . On Thursday, Uncle was ill and we telegraphed her to come.

NINA.   Why do you say you kissed the ground I walked on? I ought to have been killed. (*Leans on the table.*) I'm so tired! If I could rest . . . rest! (*Raising her head.*) I am a sea gull. . . . No, that's not it. . . . I'm an actress. Ah, well! (*Hears* ARKADINA *and* TRIGORIN *laughing, listens, then runs to the door on the left and looks through the keyhole.*) So, he's here, too. . . . (*Goes to* TREPLEV.) Well, it doesn't matter. . . . He didn't believe in the theater, he always laughed at my dreams, and gradually I too ceased believing and lost heart. And then there was the anxiety of love, the jealousy, the constant fears for my baby. . . . I grew petty, trivial, my acting was insipid. . . . I didn't know what to do with my hands, I didn't know how to stand on the stage, I couldn't control my voice. You can't imagine what it's like to feel that you are acting abominably. I am a sea gull. No, that's not it. . . . Do you remember, you shot a sea gull? A man came along by chance, saw it, and having nothing better to do, destroyed it. . . . A subject for a short story. . . . No, that's not it. . . . (*Rubs her forehead.*) What was I saying? . . . I was talking about the stage. . . . I'm not like that now. . . . Now I'm a real actress, I act with delight, with rapture, I'm intoxicated when I'm on the stage, and I feel that I act beautifully. And since I have been here, I've been walking, continually walking and

thinking . . . and I think and feel that my soul is growing stronger with each day. . . . I know now, I understand, that in our work, Kostya—whether it's acting or writing—what's important is not fame, not glory, not the things I used to dream of, but the ability to endure. To be able to bear one's cross and have faith. I have faith, and it's not so painful now, and when I think of my vocation, I'm not afraid of life.

TREPLEV (*sadly*). You have found your way, you know where you are going, but I'm still drifting in a chaos of images and dreams, without knowing why it is necessary, or for whom. . . . I have no faith, and I don't know what my vocation is.

NINA (*listening*). Sh-sh! . . . I'm going. Good-bye. When I become a great actress, come and see me. Promise? And now. . . . (*Presses his hand.*) It's late. I can hardly stand on my feet. . . . I'm exhausted and hungry. . . .

TREPLEV.   Stay, I'll give you supper. . . .

NINA.   No, no. . . . Don't go with me, I'll go alone. . . . My horses are not far. . . . So, she brought him with her? Well, it doesn't matter. When you see Trigorin, don't say anything to him. . . . I love him. I love him even more than before. . . . A subject for a short story . . . I love him, love him passionately, desperately. . . . How good life used to be, Kostya! Do you remember? How clear, how pure, warm, and joyous, and our feelings—our feelings were like tender, delicate flowers. . . . Do you remember? (*Recites.*) "Men, lions, eagles, and partridges, horned deer, geese, spiders, silent fish that dwell in the deep, starfish, and creatures invisible to the eye—these and all living things, all, all living things, having completed their sad cycle, are no more. . . . For thousands of years the earth has borne no living creature. And now in vain this poor moon lights her lamp. Cranes no longer wake and cry in meadows, May beetles are heard no more in linden groves." . . . (*Impulsively embraces* TREPLEV *and runs out through the French windows.*)

TREPLEV   (*after a pause*). It would be too bad if someone were to meet her in the garden and tell Mother. That might upset Mother. . . .

(TREPLEV *spends the next few minutes in silence, tearing up all his manuscripts and throwing them under the desk, then he unlocks the door on the right and goes out.*)

DORN (*trying to open the door on the left*). That's strange. This door seems to be locked. . . . (*Comes in and puts the armchair in its place.*) An obstacle race.

(*Enter* ARKADINA, POLINA ADREYEVNA, *followed by* YAKOV *carrying bottles, then* MASHA, SHAMRAYEV, *and* TRIGORIN.)

ARKADINA.   Put the red wine, and the beer for Boris Alekseyevich, here on the table. We'll have our drinks as we play. Let's sit down, friends.

POLINA ANDREYEVNA (*to* YAKOV). Bring the tea now, too. (*Lights the candles and sits down at the card table.*)
SHAMRAYEV (*leading* TRIGORIN *to the cupboard*). Here's that thing I was telling you about. . . . (*Takes a stuffed sea gull from the cupboard.*) Just as you ordered.
TRIGORIN (*looking at the sea gull*). I don't remember. . . . (*Musing.*) I don't remember. . . .

(*There is the sound of a shot offstage right. Everyone jumps.*)

ARKADINA (*alarmed*). What was that?
DORN.   Nothing. Probably something in my medical case exploded. Don't be alarmed. (*Goes out at the door on the right and returns a moment later.*) That's what it was. A bottle of ether blew up. (*Sings.*) "Again I stand before you, enchanted" . . .

ARKADINA (*sitting down at the table*). Ough, how that frightened me! It reminded me of the time. . . . (*Covers her face with her hands.*) Everything went black for a minute. . . .
DORN (*turning the pages of a magazine, to* TRIGORIN). There was an article in here a couple of months ago . . . a letter from America, and I wanted to ask you about it . . . (*putting his arm around* TRIGORIN, *leads him down to the footlights.*) since I'm very much interested in this question. . . . (*Lowers his voice.*) Get Irina Nikolayevna away from here somehow. The fact is, Konstantin Gavrilovich has shot himself. . . .

FOCUS QUESTIONS

1. Trace and discuss the interrelationship between crucial actions (occurring offstage) and character reactions (depicted onstage).
2. Develop a character sketch of Arkadina.
3. After analyzing the dialogue of certain characters, describe Chekhov's views on creative art.
4. Discuss the significance and repercussions of the play's title.
5. List the ways in which the dramatic action reflects Chekhov's themes of survival, loneliness, and alienation.
6. In a short essay, discuss Chekhov's fusion of tragic and comic elements.
7. Analyze the Arkadina-Konstantin relationship and comment on its familial and artistic repercussions.

OTHER ACTIVITIES

1. Study Nina's fourth-act soliloquy and enact two different but appropriate dramatic interpretations. List and discuss these differences.
2. Placing *The Sea Gull* in a contemporary setting, assemble some production sketches to reflect your ideas.
3. View the 1971 Russian version of *The Sea Gull* and discuss the effectiveness of the play's transference to the screen.

BIBLIOGRAPHY

Balukhaty, S. D., ed. *"The Seagull" Produced by Stanislavsky*. New York: Theatre Arts Books, 1952.
Emiljanow, Victor, ed. *Chekhov: The Critical Heritage*. London: Routledge, 1981.
Hingley, Ronald. *Chekhov, A Biographical and Critical Study*. London: Unwin Books, 1966.
———. *A New Life of Chekhov*. London: Oxford University Press, 1976.

Jackson, R. L., ed. *Chekhov: A Collection of Critical Essays*. Englewood Cliffs, NJ: Prentice-
    Hall, 1967.
Magarshack, David. *Chekhov the Dramatist*. New York: Hill & Wang, 1960.
———. *The Real Chekhov: An Introduction to Chekhov's Last Plays*. New York: Harper &
    Row, 1973.
Nemirovich-Danchanko, V. I. *My Life in the Russian Theatre*. New York: Theatre Arts
    Books, 1968.
Slonin, Marc. *Russian Theatre from the Empire to the Soviets*. New York: Macmillan, 1962.
Stanislavsky, Konstantin. *My Life in Art*. London: Methuen, 1985.
Styan, J. L. *Chekhov in Performance: A Commentary on the Major Plays*. New York:
    Cambridge University Press, 1971.
Valency, Maurice. *The Breaking String: The Plays of Anton Chekhov*. New York: Oxford
    University Press, 1966.
Williams, Raymond. *Drama in Performance*. London: Watts, 1968.

RECOMMENDED VIDEOTAPES AND RECORDINGS

The Seagull. Two sound discs. 89 min. 1964 BBS Transcription Service.
The Seagull. VHS. 99 min. 1971. Starring Alla Demidova, Lyudmila Savelyeva, and Yuri
    Yakolev. Directed by Yuri Karasik. In Russian with English subtitles. Distributed by
    Insight Media, New York City.

ARMS AND THE MAN
BERNARD SHAW (1856–1950)

Whether people admire or dislike him, whether they find his plays didactically boring or morally stimulating, they fail to take account of the fact that it is the enchantment of a highly accomplished art which has brought them to and kept them in the playhouse.

—EDMUND WILSON

Andrew Gillies as Sergius and Elizabeth Brown as Raina in *Arms and the Man,* presented by the Shaw Festival in 1994, under the direction of Jim Mezon. *Photo: David Cooper.*

Approaching Modern British Drama

The playwriting genius of Dublin-born Bernard Shaw, who settled in London when he was twenty years old, restored the tradition of English drama to the level of artistic excellence it had achieved before the nineteenth century. At the time of Shaw's arrival in 1876 and for the duration of Queen Victoria's long and steadfast reign (1837–1901), London's theatrical scene was unremarkable at best and could claim but a few lasting contributions to world drama. Although numerous melodramatic offerings with their superficial plots and character entanglements brought countless pleasures to West End audiences, the entrenched formulaic patterns of playwriting had set emotional and intellectual limitations on original plays being produced, thus reducing the theatre to a fairly conventional status.

As a young man who had seen almost nothing of the world before his journey from Ireland to England but had felt the intensity of certain artistic and intellectual forces around him, Shaw was ready to listen and respond to everything. In his capacity as a London music/theatre critic and political activist during the final quarter of the nineteenth century, he was not afraid to assert his convictions publicly. He was acquainted with cultural matters and prepared to write about both dramatic and musical performances, for his mother taught music and sang. Shaw was also in touch with the theatrical circuit and suspected that the creative energy burgeoning across the channel in response to the serious study of human behavior was nowhere to be found on the London stage.

Indeed, his suspicions were soon confirmed. Amid the commercially successful melodrama of Tom Taylor (1817–1880), Henry James Byron (1834–1884) and Dion Boucicault (1822–1890) stood T. W. Robertson (1829–1871), whose mid-Victorian playwriting voice became one of the first to grapple with realistic issues, albeit faintly. In time, Robertson's need to reconcile with the moral climate around him only softened any further attempts. Somewhat louder echoes belonged to Henry Arthur Jones (1851–1929) and Arthur Wing Pinero (1855–1934), each of whom constructed plays that spoke out against conventional values. But even their most interesting efforts settled into solemn moralizing by final curtain.

Shaw was particularly critical of the undue praise heaped upon Pinero, who used his artistry for commercial ends by substituting "dead machinery and lay figures for vital action and real characters."[1] Although the plays of Jones and Pinero spawned many popular but forgettable imitations, their authors are remembered today for the occasional farce or comedy of manners that surprises the playgoer's expectations in contemporary performance. As for W. S. Gilbert and Arthur Sullivan, the former of whom was a successful dramatist in his own right, their collaborative light-operatic concoctions probably had as much to say to Victorian audiences of the 1870s and 1880s as any of their dramatic colleagues.

The literary example set by Oscar Wilde (1856–1900), who was absolutely determined that his dramatic art must never debase itself by imitating life, was another matter altogether. His lifelong attack on Victorian smugness immediately caught the attention and silent admiration of his fellow-Irishman. The scintillating verbal style of Wilde's colorful stage characters, despite their brittle veneers, inspired Shaw to create characters who were no less articulate but far more assertive in expressing his philosophical convictions.

In an unheralded move away from journalism and fiction, Shaw began to write plays that were an extension of nineteenth-century theatre, though in opposition to its ethos. Affinities to the dramas of Henrik Ibsen, the music of Richard Wagner, and the philosophical teachings of such notable renegades as Schopenhauer, Nietzsche, and Bergson helped bring his aesthetics into focus. His first play, *Widowers' Houses,* premiered in 1892. Its attack on slums owned by absentee landlords pleased the socialists in the audience (Shaw himself was a lifelong member of the Fabian Society), but rankled just about everyone else who was present. Nevertheless, Shaw must have had Zola's naturalistic aims foremost in mind when he brought his playwriting skills to the British stage. (See Preface to Ibsen, p. 550.)

The producer of the play, J. T. Grien, had introduced Ibsen's *Ghosts* to London audiences one year earlier, and the aims of his Independent Theatre were aligned with Shaw's. Although their partnership did not result in a commercial success, because the play's content was unpleasant and did not conform to conventional expectations, it signaled the arrival of a modern theatre in England. Shaw knew other plays would be forthcoming and that, sooner or later, audiences and critics would return to hear him. He was absolutely right. By the end of the nineteenth century, his astonishing Augustan prose style and provocative themes had jolted London audiences, creating a modern dimension in theatrical performance that was distinctly world class. Awarded the Nobel Prize for Literature in 1925, and completing his last play the year before his death at the age of ninety-four, Shaw is universally recognized as the most important British dramatist of the twentieth century.

MAJOR WORKS

For nearly sixty years, Shaw's major plays, often accompanied by extravagantly detailed prefaces, echoed lifetime concerns: the elimination of poverty; the pretensions of morality and patriotism; the ineffectuality of professionals such as churchmen, lawyers, and doctors; the hollowness of war and military heroism; and in response to controversial Darwinian theory, the exaltation of the talented or superior person as demonstrated through a Life Force. The following representation of selected works, listed here in order of their initial productions, reflects these issues on one level or another: *Arms and the Man* (1894); *Candida* (1897); *The Devil's Disciple* (1897); *Mrs. Warren's Profession* (1902); *Man and Superman* (1905); *Major Barbara* (1905); *The Doctor's Dilemma* (1906); *Caesar and Cleopatra* (1906); *Pygmalion* (1913); *Heartbreak House* (1920); *Back to Methuselah* (1922); *Saint Joan* (1923); *The Apple Cart* (1929); and *Buoyant Billions* (1949)—the last completed just a year before his death. While it is impossible to single out a Shavian masterpiece from more than fifty short and full-length works, critics have unanimously cited *Arms and the Man* among his finest.

THE ACTION

Set in Bulgaria in 1885, where the Bulgarians have been fighting the Servians, Raina Petkoff receives news that her fiancé, Major Sergius Saranoff, has led a Bulgarian cavalry charge with extraordinary success. Moments later, she shelters a man who is dressed in the tattered blue coat of the enemy.

Three months later, Major Petkoff, Raina's father, and Sergius have returned from battle. Finding himself bored with his fiancée Raina, Sergius tries to seduce her servant Louka. A ''Captain Bluntschli'' arrives unexpectedly to return an overcoat given to him by a young lady to ensure his disguise as he escaped from her home three months earlier. Raina instantly recognizes Bluntschli but, to her surprise, her father and Sergius greet him affectionately as the professional Swiss mercenary who fought with the Servians.

Louka reveals to Sergius the compromising circumstances under which Raina and Bluntschli met. When Sergius breaks his engagement in order to marry Louka, Bluntschli eagerly takes his place. Major Petkoff approves of the marriage proposal upon learning of the young man's wealthy inheritance.

STRUCTURE AND LANGUAGE

Like the best of his work, the literary style of *Arms and the Man* is reinforced by several important factors. The first, the indelible Anglo-Irish upbringing, introduced Shaw to the unspoiled English of his fellow-Dubliners, that was reminiscent of the purity of eighteenth-century style. After settling in London, he heard a polyphony of dialects that expanded his appreciation for the richness of the English language. He would later fashion such variety into realistic dialogue.

The second factor is the undeniable impact of music. Certain rhythmical patterns find their natural counterpart in both the language and design of the play, enhancing its smaller motifs and grander themes. These are expressed through solo passages in which outspoken characters like Sergius and Bluntschli present conflicting points of view to listeners on stage and in the audience; the flirtatious duets of lovers quite adept at verbal sparring; and trios in which argumentative dialogues are suddenly counterpointed by the intrusive but calming wisdom of a third party.

Although structure and content must be reconciled in any literary work of art, in Shaw's case we find ourselves drawn less to *what* his characters tell us in their customary didactic fashion, than *how* they communicate. There is a distinct advantage to this Shavian trademark, for it allows audiences to enjoy this combination of rich characterization, brilliant dialogue, clever plots, and potent themes, even if they disagree with his arguments. Their dynamic contrasts have both enlivened and enlightened his art and reputation.

That most critical dimension for which his playwriting would garner universal acclaim—his modernism—comes boldly to life in *Arms and the Man,* despite its broadly drawn characters and clearly well-made plot, both of which owed no small debt to the popular romantic melodrama that Shaw had attacked as a critic. In fact, Shaw was deliberately satirizing such familiar theatrical devices as disguise, the daring entrance of a nameless enemy soldier into the boudoir of an unprotected maiden; misplaced documents, the words Raina inscribes on the back of her own photograph slipped into the pocket of the overcoat she gives the stranger; fashionable stage entrances, notably Raina's two well-timed ones in the second act; and a *deus ex machina* that wins her a financially independent dream soldier.

No less familiar are the historically inspired prototypes emulated by these characters: the *miles gloriosus* or braggart soldier of which Bluntschli, Sergius, and Major Petkoff offer refreshing variations; a pair of crafty servants, Louka and Nicola, whose battle of the sexes concerning class distinctions serves a no-less-likable subplot; and two shamelessly doting parents whose genuine concern for their daughter's happiness can be allayed for a price.

Apparently Shaw's need to create protagonists who were mouthpieces for his own arguments was unswervingly in place by the time he wrote *Arms and the Man*. Taking his title from Dryden's version of Virgil's *Aeneid*—"I sing of arms and the man"—he built his thematic concerns around love and war, specifically the romanticism of the former and the follies of the latter, both of which are spelled out quite early in the action. Playing the mysterious intruder aptly named for his blunt and ingenuous charm, the antiheroic Bluntschli displays an unkempt and bloody appearance that cannot disguise his "trim soldierlike carriage and energetic manner." He proves an attractive partner to Raina, who, just moments before their moonlit confrontation, had been "intensely conscious of the romantic beauty of the night, and of the fact that her own youth and beauty is a part of it."

Unable to subdue his attraction to her, Bluntschli confesses that he would just as easily have "joined the Bulgarian army instead of the Servian," had he known of her existence. His pacifist attitude toward war, shared by the playwright, is no less disarming: in place of ammunition, he carries chocolate—"and I finished the last cake of that yesterday." Such honesty triggers surprising consequences when Raina runs to her chest of drawers and ''returns with the box of confectionery in her hand'' to satisfy his hunger. ''Creams! Delicious!'' he exclaims and ravenously devours the contents. Following in the footsteps of Raina's favorite operatic hero Ernani, this intruder has also found refuge ''in the castle of his bitterest enemy''—an occasion that not only fuels Raina's romantic yearnings but once again heightens the kind of intrigue popularly displayed in melodrama. Yet Shaw refuses to take an easy way out, by creating in Bluntschli a realistic hero who almost fails to recognize the true bond between himself and Raina.

Instead, he opens the second act from an entirely different comic perspective. Peace has been declared and Bluntschli comes to the Petkoff home to return the coat, which happens to belong to Raina's father. Carefully reestablishing the comraderie of the three soldiers prior to Raina's appearance—''Welcome, our friend the enemy!'' exclaims Sergius—Shaw demonstrates his supreme use of comic irony when Raina enters only to discover that her father and Sergius have befriended the nameless intruder. The playwright turns first-act implications into second-act complications, as his heroine valiantly struggles to recover from her embarrassment and romantic delusions.

Reminiscent of the drawing-room settings which beheld the *denouements* of many nineteenth-century melodramas, Major Petkoff's library is transformed into ''a most comfortable sitting-room'' in act 3 where the comically ironic repercussions of Raina's earlier indiscretion are sorted out and resolved. Gathering all his characters together, Shaw orchestrates an eloquent round of recriminations and reconciliations to reinforce his ingenious farcical structure, after which the dazed participants emerge newly enlightened.

Spurred by Louka's intention to rise above her station, the cynical Nicola reminds her that ''the way to get on as a lady is the same as the way to get on as a servant: you've got to know your place.'' Certain that Raina will marry Bluntschli, Louka provokes Sergius by insisting that he ''has beaten you in love. He may beat you in war.'' Accepting her remarks as a challenge to his Byronic ideals and manhood, he succumbs to her amorous advances and proposes marriage. By loving a woman who believes in him as a man, not an ideal, Sergius becomes a genuine hero.

The battle between Raina and Bluntschli is waged on less cynical ground as the latter confesses to lapsing into a romantic disposition: ''I came sneaking back here to have another look at the young lady when any other man of my age would have sent the coat back.'' Yet he claims his ripe age of thirty-four is a barrier to loving a girl not much more than seventeen who scribbled an affectionate farewell to her chocolate cream soldier. In reply, Raina gently scolds him for not knowing ''the difference between a schoolgirl of seventeen and a woman of twenty-three.'' She has stepped down from her pedestal, abandoning her artificial infatuation with Sergius to enjoy a more honest and practical relationship with Bluntschli.

As a light-hearted model of Shavian comedy, *Arms and the Man* avoids the heavyhanded wit of his later works. Although its anti-militaristic and anti-romantic love themes offended those eminent Victorians who held their country's military prowess and chivalric codes of honor as sacred, and although it punctured every idea and notion by which romantic melodrama survived, the play has endured precisely because of its grace, good humor, and honesty. Unlike Sergius, who proudly admits that his hand ''is more accustomed to the sword than to the pen,'' Shaw was more accustomed to the power of words for expressing his anti-romantic sentiments on love and war and for enriching our stage literature.

ARMS AND THE MAN-IN-PERFORMANCE

Originally titled *Alps and Balkans,* in reference to the Servo-Bulgarian war of 1885 that provides background to the dramatic action, *Arms and the Man* premiered on April 21, 1894, at the Avenue Theatre (later to become The Playhouse) in London, where it gave fifty performances before touring the provinces. In spite of an opening-night success heralded by cheering playgoers who brought him to the stage for a curtain call, Shaw was convinced that this theatrical laugh machine had unintentionally diverted them from his more serious purposes. As a result, he would forever regard the play as a failure, no matter that it earned him the reputation of professional playwright.

Heading the original cast were Alma Murray (Raina), Yorke Stephens (Bluntschli), and Bernard Gould (Sergius), each of whom performed astonishingly well despite scant rehearsals. The results drew praise and condemnation from the critics, among whom was William Butler Yeats, who called this anti-romantic comedy "the first contest between the old commercial school of theatrical folk and the new artistic school."[2] While the critics were less enthusiastic than the audience and suggested that Shaw's somewhat bloodless characters were composed with "more head than heart," they could not ignore his directorial accomplishment at helping the actors "achieve comedy without sacrificing realism." Yorke Stephens was complimented for adopting "a solemnity of demeanor and earnestness of tone when speaking comic lines which were very effective." Alma Murray "conveyed realistically the assumed operatic aspect of [Raina's] character and the natural, unpretentious side."[3]

This was Shaw's fourth play, but marked his first appearance in the commercial theatre in the role of director as well, a responsibility he would assume for numerous London productions of his major plays. He approached the task with gusto, scrutinizing stage lighting, properties, and actors' makeup, as well as sketching floor plans and costumes and devising movements for his actors to ensure that the overall interpretation of the play was consistent, even for the different productions that followed. Specific stage directions varied for later works, which were published before their initial stage productions. Thus *Arms and the Man,* which was published four years after its first production, gained immeasurably from the playwright's firsthand experience with his script in performance.

West End revivals that the playwright either directed or supervised took place at the Savoy (1907), the Criterion (1911), and the Duke of York's (1919). Other revivals quickly followed at the Everyman in 1922 and 1926 and at the Court (1929). In the Savoy production, a rehearsal note to Lillah McCarthy advised that "what Raina wants is the extremity of style—style *Comédie Française,* Queen of Spain style." He urged an actor in a touring production to play Sergius "as if he were acting Hamlet . . . Let him read Byron—Sarah—the Corsair, etc. etc.—and play and feel like that, leaving the irony to come from the words."[4] By no means was Shaw asking his actors to exaggerate their portrayals. Rather his concern for realistic detail and comic effect demanded a certain broadness that must never slip into cliché.

The two most notable London productions in the first half of the twentieth century were offered by the Old Vic. The first opened on February 16, 1931, and featured Marie Ney (Raina), Ralph Richardson (Bluntschli), and John Gielgud (Sergius). While Shaw was no longer directing, clues to his former technique were still evident. Gielgud recalls how the playwright's reading of the play to the company just prior to rehearsals "was far more amusing and complete than ours could possibly hope to be. He seemed to enjoy himself thoroughly, as he illustrated bits of business, and emphasized the correct inflexions for his lines."[5] The second production opened on September 5, 1944, under John Burrell's direction. Seeming to own the role of Bluntschli by now, Richardson was joined this time by Laurence Olivier and Margaret Leighton. The actors traveled through Europe with the play, further enhancing Shaw's international reputation and uncovering, two world wars later, its prophetic message.

Other prominent West End revivals have taken place at the Mermaid (1962) with Jane Merrow (Raina), Joss Ackland (Bluntschli), and David Knight (Sergius) under the direction of Colin Ellis; and at The Lyric Theatre (1981), where Jonathan Lynn directed Alice Krige, Richard Briers, and Peter Egan. Sheridan Morley praised the latter production's remarkable pairing of Briers and Egan who "look as though they have been at it all their professional lives, complementing and counterbalancing each other like a Ruritanian Laurel and Hardy."[6] Casper Wrede revived the play at the Royal Exchange in Manchester (1988) with Catherine Russell, Paul Herzberg, and Adrian Lukis.

Arms and the Man was the first Shaw play to be performed in America, Germany, Norway, Sweden, and Russia (St. Petersburg, 1904). It generated controversy as well, notably in Vienna where a production was censored because of its treatment of the Balkan question. Not coincidentally, Bulgarians have demonstrated against the play, objecting to its comments on their habits and manners. The plot has been used without Shaw's permission for the highly successful operetta, *The Chocolate Soldier,* with music by Oscar Strauss. An English film version of the play appeared in 1932, and a German one, titled *Helden,* was produced in 1958.

The American premiere on September 17, 1894, at the Herald Square Theatre in New York City prompted a storm of critical praise for the play itself and the performance of Richard Mansfield as Bluntschli. The prominent actor revived it during his 1896 and 1899 repertory seasons. Arnold Daly staged the play at New York's Lyric Theatre on April 16, 1906, for a run of forty-eight performances, then returned with it to the Garrick Theatre in New York on May 3, 1915.

Ten years later, the Theatre Guild's revival with Alfred Lunt and Lynn Fontanne added to its impressive list of Shavian productions. Opening at the Guild Theatre on September 14, 1925, to a subscription audience, the production proved so successful that it continued its run at the Garrick Theatre for a total of 180 performances. In his opening-night review, Alexander Woollcott observed that Lunt as Bluntschli "did more than his share in the collaboration. He was handsome and, if I may be permitted another cliché, Shavian, not to say human and readily understandable."[7] Percy Hammond called Fontanne's portrayal of Raina "lovely and shrewd," adding that she brought to the role "all of her dependable fascinations."[8] Arthur Hornblow complimented Lee Simonson's sets as "admirably adroit in their picturesque coloring."[9]

Arms and the Man has sparked a merry-go-round of successful commercial revivals in New York and has become a staple of community, university, and regional theatres across America. It has inspired some exciting acting ensembles that have had little difficulty making Shaw's realistic intentions comically palatable: director Robert Allan Ackerman worked with Blythe Danner (Raina), Edward Herrmann (Bluntschli), and Richard Chamberlain (Sergius) at the Williamstown Theater Festival in 1981; Nikos Psacharopoulos led Lisa Eichorn, Richard Thomas, and John Rubinstein at the Pasadena Playhouse in 1986; and Frank Hauser directed Roma Downey, Daniel Gerroll, and Christopher Noth at New York's Roundabout Theatre in 1989. The Circle-in-the-Square attracted some of the greatest notoriety of its long history in 1985 when Glenne Headly (Raina), Kevin Kline (Bluntschli), and Raul Julia (Sergius) incarnated Shaw's trio of protagonists under John Malkovich's direction. Bowing to the farcical occasion, Walter Kerr conceded that "everything has mysteriously, perhaps miraculously, fallen into place so that the laughs come equally and explosively from all four sides of the house. It's weird, but you can't resist it."[10]

The first Canadian production of *Arms and the Man* took place at the Princess Theatre, Toronto, on May 8, 1923. The Shaw Festival in Niagra-on-the-Lake, which is the only theatre in the world to specialize exclusively in plays by Shaw and his contemporaries, presented a centennial production of the play during its 1994 season.

REFLECTIONS ON ARMS AND THE MAN

"Exit the Hero, Enter the Superman" by Ronald Bryden,
Literary Advisor to the Shaw Festival.

There's a famous story about the first night of *Arms and The Man*. On April 21, 1894, George Bernard Shaw stepped before the curtain of the Avenue Theatre in response to cries of "Author!" and was met by wild applause and a single loud "Boo!" from the gallery. Raising his eyes toward his invisible critic, Shaw said drily, "My dear fellow, I quite agree with you. But what are we two against so many?"

The rest of the story is not so famous. Shaw meant what he said. The evening had been both triumph and torture for him. He knew it had made his reputation as the most brilliant and ruthless new wit on the London stage. He knew also that this was the wrong reputation for him to make. "I had the curious experience," he wrote to his fellow dramatist Henry Arthur Jones, "of witnessing an apparently insane success, with the actors and actresses almost losing their heads with the intoxication of laugh after laugh, and of going before the curtain to thunderous applause, the only person in the theatre who knew that the whole affair was a ghastly failure."

It was a failure, to Shaw's mind, because the audience in its headlong laughter had failed to recognize the serious argument and emotions on which he had built his comedy. He found it ghastly that this riotous success could saddle him for life with the public image of a heartless joker, a satirist with the smile of a cut-throat razor, in the manner of W. S. Gilbert. To make it ghastlier, that comparison was made by his friend, the critic William Archer, in a review that accused Shaw of draining all the red corpuscles from his characters' veins.

"Gilbert is simply a paradoxically humorous cynic," Shaw wrote furiously to Archer. "He accepts the conventional ideals implicitly, but observes that people do not really live up to them. This he regards as a failure on their part which he mocks bitterly. This position is precisely that of Sergius in the play . . . I do not accept the conventional ideals . . . My whole secret is that I have got clean through the old categories of good and evil, and no longer use them even for dramatic effect. Sergius is ridiculous through the breakdown of his ideals, not odious from his falling short of them." Elsewhere he described Sergius as "a movingly human figure whose tragicomedy is the true theme of the play."

Shaw was partly to blame for misreadings of his play. Before it opened, he published an imaginary interview with himself in which he pretended to have written it initially as a timeless, placeless comic theorem, then taken the advice of his Fabian friend Sidney Webb to set it during the Serbo-Bulgarian War of 1885–86. The story will not hold water. Shaw's allegedly placeless first draft bore the title *Alps and Balkans*. The whole strategy of the first act depends on the audience discovering that a scene of apparent Dumas romance is happening during Europe's most recent war. In any case, it's impossible to believe that Shaw's start on the play, recorded in his diary on November 26, 1893, owed nothing to the lengthy newspaper reports a week earlier of the death of Alexander of Battenberg, first prince of Bulgaria. The Prince died on November 18, the eighth anniversary of the battle of Slivnitza in which he had led his nation to victory over the Serbs; Sergius' tragicomedy is, to a great extent, a domestic distillation of that of poor Sandro Battenberg.

The Battenbergs now are better known by the name their English branch adopted during World War I: Mountbatten. They descend from a spirited Grand Duchess of Hesse who, bored with her husband, set up a separate domicile managed for her by her Swiss master-of-horse. There she gave birth to two children, Marie and Alexander, whose good looks bore little resemblance to their Hessian siblings but a marked one to the handsome Switzer.

Marie's Cinderella beauty caught the eye of the Tsarevitch Alexander of Russia, touring the courts of Europe in search of a bride. Her brother accompanied her to Moscow for her wedding, but had to be sent home in disgrace for beguiling an imperial princess and then seducing an imperial lady-in-waiting. As a consolation prize for marrying her, he was granted the title Prince of Battenberg, and it was their string of handsome, penniless sons who made the name known and feared in every European palace housing marriageable daughters.

Louis, the eldest, married Queen Victoria's granddaughter and became Britain's First Lord of the Admiralty. Henry, the idlest, outdid him by snaring Victoria's youngest daughter, and never worked again. But Sandro, the handsomest, found himself a throne. His uncle the Tsar Alexander II nominated him as first ruling prince of Bulgaria, wrested by Russia from the Turks in 1878. The Tsar's plan was to establish a Balkan puppet who would help Russia to corner Balkan railway construction and Danube trade. But Sandro, a newly minted Bulgarian, had discovered the pleasures of patriotism. When he turned on his patron to befriend British and German interests, the enraged Tsar recalled the Russian officers who commanded Bulgaria's tiny untrained army. Seizing his chance, the king of neighboring Serbia ordered three divisions to cross the Bulgarian border.

The Serbo-Bulgarian War was Sandro's finest hour. He led his army, commanded now by inexperienced young Bulgarians, on a forced march from the Turkish border over the Balkan mountains to defend Sofia, the capital. Sandro himself rode at their head to meet the oncoming Serbs before the village of Slivnitza. For two days the battle swayed back and forth. On the third, the Bulgarian cavalry led by Captain Benderev broke the Serbian line, triggering the panic retreat over the Dragoman Pass which opens Shaw's play. With his advance guard, Sandro crossed the Serbian frontier and prepared to march on Belgrade. Before he could do so, Austria's ambassador to Serbia arrived at Sandro's command post. Any further Bulgarian advance, he warned, would be met by Austrian troops and artillery.

Piece by piece Sandro saw his victory taken from him. The Powers were not prepared to see him upset their balance of influence in the Balkans. Bismarck and the new Tsar Alexander III, who had never liked his matinee-idol cousin, agreed that Sandro must go. In August 1886 a group of Russian-paid officers, Benderev among them, kidnapped the prince from his palace, bundled him down the Danube in the royal yacht, and handed him over to the Tsar's police at the nearest Russian port. Given the choice of yielding up his throne or seeing Bulgaria disappear, Sandro abdicated. He returned to life as a cavalry officer in the Austrian army, happily married to an attractive commoner. His death in 1893 was caused by a burst appendix. In his deathbed delirium, he believed he was back on the field of Slivnitza, and died crying "Victory! Victory!"

Continued

Shaw in *Arms and the Man* pointed the moral of Sandro's war: patriotism and gallantry count for nothing in modern warfare beside armaments, power politics, and political calculation. Does this mean he found Sandro, or his theatrical representative Sergius, ridiculous as well as pitiful? Not, surely, when Sergius recognizes the tragedy into which his inhumanly romantic ideals have led him. But it took forty years for Shaw criticism to reach the insight of Edmund Wilson's essay in *The Triple Thinkers,* which argues that what made the playwright great was his ability to hold two contradictory truths in his mind at the same time. *Arms and the Man* is the first of the great plays in which Shaw does this. It is at once a comedy of a perfect rationalist—Shaw's first Superman—who points where the world must go, and the tragedy of a heroic romantic who embodies what the world will lose by going there.

For the rest of his life, Shaw harangued actors and managers about the casting of his play; urging Richard Mansfield to play Sergius rather than Bluntschli, begging Firmin Gémier to find for the first Paris production a Sergius as superb, magnetic and handsome as the leading tragedian of the Comédie Française, Mounet-Sully. It's not clear whether Florence Farr believed Shaw, when he persuaded her to play Louka, that she was abandoning the feminine lead to play the strongest part in the script. But one need only compare the precision of Shaw's details with the fairy tale that Anthony Hope wove around Sandro's kidnapping in *The Prisoner of Zenda* (published some weeks after the play opened) to see that Shaw was interested in human realities, not Balkan romance. Perhaps with a real Balkan war to shed its light on *Arms and The Man* on its hundredth birthday, we may have a better chance to see the play as Shaw intended.

Ronald Bryden's "Exit the Hero, Enter the Superman" was originally printed for the Shaw Festival's centennial production of ARMS AND THE MAN (1994). *Used by permission.*

Notes

1. *Michael Holroyd,* BERNARD SHAW: THE SEARCH FOR LOVE, 1856–1898 *(New York: Random House, 1988), 338.*
2. *Ibid., 303.*
3. *Bernard F. Dukore,* BERNARD SHAW'S "ARMS AND THE MAN": A COMPOSITE PRODUCTION BOOK *(Carbondale: Southern Illinois University Press, 1982) xxx–xxxi.*
4. *Christopher Innes,* MODERN BRITISH DRAMA: 1890–1990 *(New York: Cambridge University Press, 1992), 28.*
5. *John Gielgud,* EARLY STAGES *(London: Macmillan, 1939), 184.*
6. PUNCH, *October 1981.*
7. NEW YORK WORLD, *15 Sept. 1925.*
8. THE TRIBUNE, *15 Sept. 1925.*
9. THEATRE MAGAZINE, *(Nov. 1925): 18.*
10. THE NEW YORK TIMES, *23 June 1985.*

ARMS AND THE MAN
BERNARD SHAW

ACT ONE*

Night: A lady's bedchamber in Bulgaria, in a small town near the Dragoman Pass, late in November in the year 1885. Through an open window with a little balcony a peak of the Balkans, wonderfully white and beautiful in the starlit snow, seems quite close at hand, though it is really miles away. The interior of the room is not like anything to be seen in the west of Europe. It is half rich Bulgarian, half cheap Viennese. Above the head of the bed, which stands against a little wall cutting off the left hand corner of the room, is a painted wooden shrine, blue and gold, with an ivory image of Christ, and a light hanging before it in a pierced metal ball suspended by three chains. The principal seat, placed towards the other side of the room and opposite the window, is a Turkish ottoman. The counterpane and hangings of the bed, the window curtains, the little carpet, and all the ornamental textile fabrics in the room are oriental and gorgeous; the paper on the walls is occidental and paltry. The washstand, against the wall on the side nearest the ottoman and window, consists of an enamelled iron basin with a pail beneath it in a painted metal frame, and a single towel on the rail at the side. The dressing table, between the bed and the window, is a common pine table, covered with a cloth of many colors, with an expensive toilet mirror on it. The door is on the side nearest the bed; and there is a chest of drawers between. This chest of drawers is also covered by a variegated native cloth; and on it there is a pile of paper backed novels, a box of chocolate creams, and a miniature easel with a large photograph of an extremely handsome officer, whose lofty bearing and magnetic glance can be felt even from the portrait. The room is lighted by a candle on the chest of drawers, and another on the dressing table with a box of matches beside it.

The window is hinged doorwise and stands wide open. Outside, a pair of wooden shutters, opening outwards, also stand open. On the balcony a young lady, intensely conscious of the romantic beauty of the night, and of the fact that her own youth and beauty are part of it, is gazing at the snowy Balkans. She is in her nightgown, well covered by a long mantle of furs, worth, on a moderate estimate, about three times the furniture of her room.

Her reverie is interrupted by her mother, Catherine Petkoff, a woman over forty, imperiously energetic, with magnificent black hair and eyes, who might be a very splendid specimen of the wife of a mountain farmer, but is determined to be a Viennese lady, and to that end wears a fashionable tea gown on all occasions.

CATHERINE (*entering hastily, full of good news*). Raina! (*She pronounces it Rah-eena, with the stress on the ee.*) Raina! (*She goes to the bed, expecting to find Raina there.*) Why, where—? (*Raina looks into the room.*) Heavens, child! are you out in the night air instead of in your bed? Youll catch your death. Louka told me you were asleep.

RAINA (*dreamily*). I sent her away. I wanted to be alone. The stars are so beautiful! What is the matter?

CATHERINE. Such news! There has been a battle.

RAINA (*her eyes dilating*). Ah! (*She comes eagerly to Catherine.*)

CATHERINE. A great battle at Slivnitza! A victory! And it was won by Sergius.

RAINA (*with a cry of delight*). Ah! (*They embrace rapturously.*) Oh, mother! (*Then, with sudden anxiety*) Is father safe?

CATHERINE. Of course: he sends me the news. Sergius is the hero of the hour, the idol of the regiment.

RAINA. Tell me, tell me. How was it? (*Ecstatically.*) Oh, mother! mother! mother! (*She pulls her mother down on the ottoman; and they kiss one another frantically.*)

CATHERINE (*with surging enthusiasm*). You cant guess how splendid it is. A cavalry charge! think of that! He defied our Russian commanders—acted without orders—led a charge on his own responsibility—headed it himself— was the first man to sweep through their guns. Cant you see it, Raina: our gallant splendid Bulgarians with their swords and eyes flashing, thundering down like an avalanche and scattering the wretched Serbs and their dandified Austrian officers like chaff. And you! you kept Sergius waiting a year before you would be betrothed to him. Oh, if you have a drop of Bulgarian blood in your veins, you will worship him when he comes back.

*Editor's note: Shaw does not list a cast of characters for this play.

RAINA. What will he care for my poor little worship after the acclamations of a whole army of heroes? But no matter: I am so happy! so proud! (*She rises and walks about excitedly.*) It proves that all our ideas were real after all.

CATHERINE (*indignantly*). Our ideas real! What do you mean?

RAINA. Our ideas of what Sergius would do. Our patriotism. Our heroic ideals. I sometimes used to doubt whether they were anything but dreams. Oh, what faithless little creatures girls are! When I buckled on Sergius's sword he looked so noble: it was treason to think of disillusion or humiliation or failure. And yet—and yet—(*She sits down again suddenly.*) Promise me youll never tell him.

CATHERINE. Dont ask me for promises until I know what I'm promising.

RAINA. Well, it came into my head just as he was holding me in his arms and looking into my eyes, that perhaps we only had our heroic ideas because we are so fond of reading Byron and Pushkin, and because we were so delighted with the opera that season at Bucharest. Real life is so seldom like that! indeed never, as far as I knew it then. (*Remorsefully.*) Only think, mother: I doubted him: I wondered whether all his heroic qualities and his soldiership might not prove mere imagination when he went into a real battle. I had an uneasy fear that he might cut a poor figure there beside all those clever officers from the Tsar's court.

CATHERINE. A poor figure! Shame on you! The Serbs have Austrian officers who are just as clever as the Russians; but we have beaten them in every battle for all that.

RAINA (*laughing and snuggling against her mother*). Yes: I was only a prosaic little coward. Oh, to think that it was all true! that Sergius is just as splendid and noble as he looks! that the world is really a glorious world for women who can see its glory and men who can act its romance! What happiness! what unspeakable fulfilment!

They are interrupted by the entry of Louka, a handsome proud girl in a pretty Bulgarian peasant's dress with double apron, so defiant that her servility to Raina is almost insolent. She is afraid of Catherine, but even with her goes as far as she dares.

LOUKA. If you please, madam, all the windows are to be closed and the shutters made fast. They say there may be shooting in the streets. (*Raina and Catherine rise together, alarmed.*) The Serbs are being chased right back through the pass; and they say they may run into the town. Our cavalry will be after them; and our people will be ready for them, you may be sure, now theyre running away. (*She goes out on the balcony, and pulls the outside shutters to; then steps back into the room.*)

CATHERINE (*businesslike, housekeeping instincts aroused*). I must see that everything is made safe downstairs.

RAINA. I wish our people were not so cruel. What glory is there in killing wretched fugitives?

CATHERINE. Cruel! Do you suppose they would hesitate to kill you—or worse?

RAINA (*to Louka*). Leave the shutters so that I can just close them if I hear any noise.

CATHERINE (*authoritatively, turning on her way to the door*). Oh no, dear: you must keep them fastened. You would be sure to drop off to sleep and leave them open. Make them fast, Louka.

LOUKA. Yes, madam. (*She fastens them.*)

RAINA. Dont be anxious about me. The moment I hear a shot, I shall blow out the candles and roll myself up in bed with my ears well covered.

CATHERINE. Quite the wisest thing you can do, my love. Goodnight.

RAINA. Goodnight. (*Her emotion comes back for a moment.*) Wish me joy. (*They kiss.*) This is the happiest night of my life—if only there are no fugitives.

CATHERINE. Go to bed, dear; and dont think of them. (*She goes out.*)

LOUKA (*secretly to Raina*). If you would like the shutters open, just give them a push like this (*She pushes them: they open: she pulls them to again.*) One of them ought to be bolted at the bottom; but the bolt's gone.

RAINA (*with dignity, reproving her*). Thanks, Louka; but we must do what we are told. (*Louka makes a grimace.*) Goodnight.

LOUKA (*carelessly*). Goodnight. (*She goes out, swaggering.*)

Raina, left alone, takes off her fur cloak and throws it on the ottoman. Then she goes to the chest of drawers, and adores the portrait there with feelings that are beyond all expression. She does not kiss it or press it to her breast, or shew it any mark of bodily affection; but she takes it in her hands and elevates it, like a priestess.

RAINA (*looking up at the picture*). Oh, I shall never be unworthy of you any more, my soul's hero: never, never, never. (*She replaces it reverently. Then she selects a novel from the little pile of books. She turns over the leaves dreamily; finds her page; turns the book inside out at it; and, with a happy sigh, gets into bed and prepares to read herself to sleep. But before abandoning herself to fiction, she raises her eyes once more, thinking of the blessed reality, and murmurs*) My hero! my hero!

A distant shot breaks the quiet of the night. She starts, listening; and two more shots, much nearer, follow, startling her so that she scrambles out of bed, and hastily blows out the candle on the chest of drawers. Then, putting her fingers in her ears, she runs to the dressing table, blows out the light there, and hurries back to bed in the dark, nothing being visible but the glimmer of the light in the pierced ball before the image, and the starlight seen through the slits at the top of the shutters. The firing breaks out again: there is a startling fusillade quite close at hand. Whilst it is still echoing, the shutters disappear, pulled open from without; and for an instant the rectangle of snowy starlight flashes out with the figure of a man silhouetted in black upon it. The shutters close immediately; and the room is dark again. But the silence is now broken by the sound of panting. Then there is a scratch; and the flame of a match is seen in the middle of the room.

RAINA (*crouching on the bed*). Who's there? (*The match is out instantly.*) Who's there? Who is that?

A MAN'S VOICE (*in the darkness, subduedly, but threateningly*). Sh—sh! Dont call out; or youll be shot. Be good; and no harm will happen to you. (*She is heard leaving her bed, and making for the door.*) Take care: it's no use trying to run away.

RAINA. But who—?

THE VOICE (*warning*). Remember: if you raise your voice my revolver will go off. (*Commandingly.*) Strike a light and let me see you. Do you hear. (*Another moment of silence and darkness as she retreats to the chest of drawers. Then she lights a candle; and the mystery is at an end. He is a man of about 35, in a deplorable plight, bespattered with mud and blood and snow, his belt and the strap of his revolver-case keeping together the torn ruins of the blue tunic of a Serbian artillery officer. All that the candlelight and his unwashed unkempt condition make it possible to discern is that he is of middling stature and undistinguished appearance, with strong neck and shoulders, roundish obstinate looking head covered with short crisp bronze curls, clear quick eyes and good brows and mouth, hopelessly prosaic nose like that of a strong minded baby, trim soldierlike carriage and energetic manner, and with all his wits about him in spite of his desperate predicament: even with a sense of the humor of it, without, however, the least intention of trifling with it or throwing away a chance. Reckoning up what he can guess about Raina: her age, her social position, her character, and the extent to which she is frightened, he continues, more politely but still most determinedly.*) Excuse my disturbing you; but you recognize my uniform? Serb! If I'm caught I shall be killed. (*Menacingly.*) Do you understand that?

RAINA.   Yes.

THE MAN.   Well, I don't intend to get killed if I can help it. (*Still more formidably.*) Do you understand that? (*He locks the door quickly but quietly.*)

RAINA (*disdainfully*). I suppose not. (*She draws herself up superbly, and looks him straight in the face, adding, with cutting emphasis.*) Some soldiers, I know, are afraid to die.

THE MAN (*with grim goodhumor*). All of them, dear lady, all of them, believe me. It is our duty to live as long as we can. Now, if you raise an alarm—

RAINA (*cutting him short*). You will shoot me. How do you know that *I* am afraid to die?

THE MAN (*cunningly*). Ah; but suppose I dont shoot you, what will happen then? A lot of your cavalry will burst into this pretty room of yours and slaughter me here like a pig; for I'll fight like a demon: they shant get me into the street to amuse themselves with: I know what they are. Are you prepared to receive that sort of company in your present undress? (*Raina, suddenly conscious of her nightgown, instinctively shrinks and gathers it more closely about her neck. He watches her and adds pitilessly.*) Hardly presentable, eh? (*She turns to the ottoman. He raises his pistol instantly, and cries*) Stop! (*She stops.*) Where are you going?

RAINA (*with dignified patience*). Only to get my cloak.

THE MAN (*passing swiftly to the ottoman and snatching the cloak*). A good idea! I'll keep the cloak; and youll take care that nobody comes in and sees you without it. This is a better weapon than the revolver: eh? (*He throws the pistol down on the ottoman.*)

RAINA (*revolted*). It is not the weapon of a gentleman!

THE MAN.   It's good enough for a man with only you to stand between him and death. (*As they look at one another for a moment, Raina hardly able to believe that even a Serbian officer can be so cynically and selfishly unchivalrous, they are startled by a sharp fusillade in the street. The chill of imminent death hushes the man's voice as he adds*) Do you hear? If you are going to bring those blackguards in on me you shall receive them as you are. *Clamor and disturbance. The pursuers in the street batter at the house door, shouting* Open the door! Open the door! Wake up, will you! *A man servant's voice calls to them angrily from within* This is Major Petkoff's house: you cant come in here; *but a renewal of the clamor, and a torrent of blows on the door, end with his letting a chain down with a clank, followed by a rush of heavy footsteps and a din of triumphant yells, dominated at last by the voice of Catherine, indignantly addressing an officer with* What does this mean, sir? Do you know where you are? *The noise subsides suddenly.*

LOUKA (*outside, knocking at the bedroom door*). My lady! my lady! get up quick and open the door. If you dont they will break it down.

The fugitive throws up his head with the gesture of a man who sees that it is all over with him, and drops the manner he has been assuming to intimidate Raina.

THE MAN (*sincerely and kindly*). No use, dear: I'm done for. (*Flinging the cloak to her.*) Quick! wrap yourself up: they're coming.

RAINA.   Oh, thank you. (*She wraps herself up with intense relief.*)

THE MAN (*between his teeth*). Dont mention it.

RAINA (*anxiously*). What will you do?

THE MAN (*grimly*). The first man in will find out. Keep out of the way; and dont look. It wont last long; but it will not be nice. (*He draws his sabre and faces the door, waiting.*)

RAINA (*impulsively*). I'll help you. I'll save you.

THE MAN.   You cant.

RAINA.   I can. I'll hide you. (*She drags him towards the window.*) Here! behind the curtains.

THE MAN (*yielding to her*). Theres just half a chance, if you keep your head.

RAINA (*drawing the curtain before him*). S-sh! (*She makes for the ottoman.*)

THE MAN (*putting out his head*). Remember—

RAINA (*running back to him*). Yes?

THE MAN.   —nine soldiers out of ten are born fools.

RAINA.   Oh! (*She draws the curtain angrily before him.*)

THE MAN (*looking out at the other side*). If they find me, I promise you a fight: a devil of a fight.

She stamps at him. He disappears hastily. She takes off her cloak, and throws it across the foot of the bed. Then, with a sleepy, disturbed air, she opens the door. Louka enters excitedly.

LOUKA.   One of those beasts of Serbs has been seen climbing up the waterpipe to your balcony. Our men want to search for him; and they are so wild and drunk and furious. (*She makes for the other side of the room to get as far from the door as possible.*) My lady says you are to dress at once and to—(*She sees the revolver lying on the ottoman, and stops, petrified.*)

RAINA (*as if annoyed at being disturbed*). They shall not search here. Why have they been let in?

CATHERINE (*coming in hastily*). Raina, darling, are you safe? Have you seen anyone or heard anything?

RAINA.   I heard shooting. Surely the soldiers will not dare come in here?

CATHERINE.   I have found a Russian officer, thank Heaven: he knows Sergius. (*Speaking through the door to someone outside*) Sir: will you come in now. My daughter will receive you.

A young Russian officer, in Bulgarian uniform, enters, sword in hand.

OFFICER (*with soft feline politeness and stiff military carriage*). Good evening, gracious lady. I am sorry to intrude; but there is a Serb hiding on the balcony. Will you and the gracious lady your mother please to withdraw whilst we search?

RAINA (*petulantly*). Nonsense, sir: you can see that there is no one on the balcony. (*She throws the shutters wide open and stands with her back to the curtain where the man is hidden, pointing to the moonlit balcony. A couple of shots are fired right under the window; and a bullet shatters the glass opposite Raina, who winks and gasps, but stands*

her ground; whilst Catherine screams, and the officer, with a cry of Take care! *rushes to the balcony.*)

THE OFFICER (*on the balcony, shouting savagely down to the street*). Cease firing there, you fools: do you hear? Cease firing, damn you! (*He glares down for a moment; then turns to Raina, trying to resume his polite manner.*) Could anyone have got in without your knowledge? Were you asleep?

RAINA.   No: I have not been to bed.

THE OFFICER (*impatiently, coming back into the room*). Your neighbors have their heads so full of runaway Serbs that they see them everywhere. (*Politely.*) Gracious lady: a thousand pardons. Goodnight. (*Military bow, which Raina returns coldly. Another to Catherine, who follows him out.*)

Raina closes the shutters. She turns and sees Louka, who has been watching the scene curiously.

RAINA.   Dont leave my mother, Louka, until the soldiers go away.

Louka glances at Raina, at the ottoman, at the curtain; then purses her lips secretively, laughs insolently, and goes out. Raina, highly offended by this demonstration, follows her to the door, and shuts it behind her with a slam, locking it violently. The man immediately steps out from behind the curtain, sheathing his sabre. Then, dismissing the danger from his mind in a businesslike way, he comes affably to Raina.

THE MAN.   A narrow shave; but a miss is as good as a mile. Dear young lady: your servant to the death. I wish for your sake I had joined the Bulgarian army instead of the other one. I am not a native Serb.

RAINA (*haughtily*). No: you are one of the Austrians who set the Serbs on to rob us of our national liberty, and who officer their army for them. We hate them!

THE MAN.   Austrian! not I. Dont hate me, dear young lady. I am a Swiss, fighting merely as a professional soldier. I joined the Serbs because they came first on the road from Switzerland. Be generous: youve beaten us hollow.

RAINA.   Have I not been generous?

THE MAN.   Noble! Heroic! But I'm not saved yet. This particular rush will soon pass through; but the pursuit will go on all night by fits and starts. I must take my chance to get off in a quiet interval. (*Pleasantly.*) You dont mind my waiting just a minute or two, do you?

RAINA (*putting on her most genteel society manner*). Oh, not at all. Wont you sit down?

THE MAN.   Thanks. (*He sits on the foot of the bed.*)

Raina walks with studied elegance to the ottoman and sits down. Unfortunately she sits on the pistol, and jumps up with a shriek. The man, all nerves, shies like a frightened horse to the other side of the room.

THE MAN (*irritably*). Dont frighten me like that. What is it?

RAINA. Your revolver! It was staring that officer in the face all the time. What an escape!

THE MAN (*vexed at being unnecessarily terrified*). Oh, is that all?

RAINA (*staring at him rather superciliously as she conceives a poorer and poorer opinion of him, and feels proportionately more and more at her ease*). I am sorry I frightened you. (*She takes up the pistol and hands it to him.*) Pray take it to protect yourself against me.

THE MAN (*grinning wearily at the sarcasm as he takes the pistol*). No use, dear young lady: theres nothing in it. It's not loaded. (*He makes a grimace at it, and drops it disparingly into his revolver case.*)

RAINA. Load it by all means.

THE MAN. I've no ammunition. What use are cartridges in battle? I always carry chocolate instead; and I finished the last cake of that hours ago.

RAINA (*outraged in her most cherished ideals of manhood*). Chocolate! Do you stuff your pockets with sweets—like a schoolboy—even in the field?

THE MAN (*grinning*). Yes: isnt it contemptible? (*Hungrily.*) I wish I had some now.

RAINA. Allow me. (*She sails away scornfully to the chest of drawers, and returns with the box of confectionery in her hand.*) I am sorry I have eaten them all except these. (*She offers him the box.*)

THE MAN (*ravenously*). Youre an angel! (*He gobbles the contents.*) Creams! Delicious! (*He looks anxiously to see whether there are any more. There are none: he can only scrape the box with his fingers and suck them. When that nourishment is exhausted he accepts the inevitable with pathetic goodhumor, and says, with grateful emotion*) Bless you, dear lady! You can always tell an old soldier by the inside of his holsters and cartridge boxes. The young ones carry pistols and cartridges: the old ones, grub. Thank you. (*He hands back the box. She snatches it contemptuously from him and throws it away. He shies again, as if she had meant to strike him.*) Ugh! Dont do things so suddenly, gracious lady. It's mean to revenge yourself because I frightened you just now.

RAINA (*loftily*). Frighten me! Do you know, sir, that though I am only a woman, I think I am at heart as brave as you.

THE MAN. I should think so. You havnt been under fire for three days as I have. I can stand two days without shewing it much; but no man can stand three days: I'm nervous as a mouse. (*He sits down on the ottoman, and takes his head in his hands.*) Would you like to see me cry?

RAINA (*alarmed*). No.

THE MAN. If you would, all you have to do is to scold me just as if I were a little boy and you my nurse. If I were in camp now, theyd play all sorts of tricks on me.

RAINA (*a little moved*). I'm sorry. I wont scold you. (*Touched by the sympathy in her tone, he raises his head and looks gratefully at her: she immediately draws back and says stiffly*) You must excuse me: our soldiers are not like that. (*She moves away from the ottoman.*)

THE MAN. Oh yes they are. There are only two sorts of soldiers: old ones and young ones. I've served fourteen years: half of your fellows never smelt powder before. Why, how is it that youve just beaten us? Sheer ignorance of the art of war, nothing else. (*Indignantly.*) I never saw anything so unprofessional.

RAINA (*ironically*). Oh! was it unprofessional to beat you?

THE MAN. Well, come! is it professional to throw a regiment of cavalry on a battery of machine guns, with the dead certainty that if the guns go off not a horse or man will ever get within fifty yards of the fire? I couldn't believe my eyes when I saw it.

RAINA (*eagerly turning to him, as all her enthusiasm and her dreams of glory rush back on her*). Did you see the great cavalry charge? Oh, tell me about it. Describe it to me.

THE MAN. You never saw a cavalry charge, did you?

RAINA. How could I?

THE MAN. Ah, perhaps not. No: of course not! Well, it's a funny sight. It's like slinging a handful of peas against a window pane: first one comes; then two or three close behind him; and then all the rest in a lump.

RAINA (*her eyes dilating as she raises her clasped hands ecstatically*). Yes, first One! the bravest of the brave!

THE MAN (*prosaically*). Hm! you should see the poor devil pulling at his horse.

RAINA. Why should he pull at his horse?

THE MAN (*impatient of so stupid a question*). It's running away with him, of course: do you suppose the fellow wants to get there before the others and be killed? Then they all come. You can tell the young ones by their wildness and their slashing. The old ones come bunched up under the number one guard: they know that theyre mere projectiles, and that it's no use trying to fight. The wounds are mostly broken knees, from the horses cannoning together.

RAINA. Ugh! But I dont believe the first man is a coward. I know he is a hero!

THE MAN (*goodhumoredly*). Thats what youd have said if youd seen the first man in the charge today.

RAINA (*breathless, forgiving him everything*). Ah, I knew it! Tell me. Tell me about him.

THE MAN. He did it like an operatic tenor. A regular handsome fellow, with flashing eyes and lovely moustache, shouting his war-cry and charging like Don Quixote at the windmills. We did laugh.

RAINA. You dared to laugh!

THE MAN. Yes; but when the sergeant ran up as white as a sheet, and told us theyd sent us the wrong ammunition, and that we couldnt fire a round for the next ten minutes, we laughed at the other side of our mouths. I never felt so sick in my life; though Ive been in one or two very tight places. And I hadnt even a revolver cartridge: only chocolate. We'd no bayonets: nothing. Of course, they just cut us to bits. And there was Don Quixote flourishing like a drum major, thinking he'd done the cleverest thing ever known, whereas he ought to be courtmartialled for it. Of all the fools ever let loose on a field of battle, that man must be the very maddest. He and his regiment simply committed suicide; only the pistol missed fire: thats all.

RAINA (*deeply wounded, but steadfastly loyal to her ideals*). Indeed! Would you know him again if you saw him?

THE MAN. Shall I ever forget him!

She again goes to the chest of drawers. He watches her with a vague hope that she may have something more for him to eat. She takes the portrait from its stand and brings it to him.

RAINA. That is a photograph of the gentleman—the patriot and hero—to whom I am betrothed.

THE MAN (*recognizing it with a shock*). I'm really very sorry. (*Looking at her.*) Was it fair to lead me on? (*He looks at the portrait again.*) Yes: thats Don Quixote: not a doubt of it. (*He stifles a laugh.*)

RAINA (*quickly*). Why do you laugh?

THE MAN (*apologetic, but still greatly tickled*). I didnt laugh, I assure you. At least I didnt mean to. But when I think of him charging the windmills and imagining he was doing the finest thing—(*He chokes with suppressed laughter.*)

RAINA (*sternly*). Give me back the portrait, sir.

THE MAN (*with sincere remorse*). Of course. Certainly. I'm really very sorry. (*He hands her the picture. She deliberately kisses it and looks him straight in the face before returning to the chest of drawers to replace it. He follows her, apologizing.*) Perhaps I'm quite wrong, you know: no doubt I am. Most likely he had got wind of the cartridge business somehow, and knew it was a safe job.

RAINA. That is to say, he was a pretender and a coward! You did not dare say that before.

THE MAN (*with a comic gesture of despair*). It's no use, dear lady: I cant make you see it from the professional point of view. (*As he turns away to get back to the ottoman, a couple of distant shots threaten renewed trouble.*)

RAINA (*sternly, as she sees him listening to the shots*). So much the better for you!

THE MAN (*turning*). How?

RAINA. You are my enemy; and you are at my mercy. What would I do if I were a professional soldier?

THE MAN. Ah, true, dear young lady: youre always right. I know how good youve been to me: to my last hour I shall remember those three chocolate creams. It was unsoldierly; but it was angelic.

RAINA (*coldly*). Thank you. And now I will do a soldierly thing. You cannot stay here after what you have just said

about my future husband; but I will go out on the balcony and see whether it is safe for you to climb down into the street. (*She turns to the window.*)

THE MAN (*changing countenance*). Down that waterpipe! Stop! Wait! I cant! I darent! The very thought of it makes me giddy. I came up it fast enough with death behind me. But to face it now in cold blood—!(*He sinks on the ottoman.*) It's no use: I give up: I'm beaten. Give the alarm. (*He drops his head on his hands in the deepest dejection.*)

RAINA (*disarmed by pity*). Come: dont be disheartened. (*She stoops over him almost maternally: he shakes his head.*) Oh, you are a very poor soldier: a chocolate cream soldier! Come, cheer up! it takes less courage to climb down than to face capture: remember that.

THE MAN (*dreamily, lulled by her voice*). No: capture only means death; and death is sleep: oh, sleep, sleep, sleep, undisturbed sleep! Climbing down the pipe means doing something—exerting myself—thinking! Death ten times over first.

RAINA (*softly and wonderingly, catching the rhythm of his weariness*). Are you as sleepy as that?

THE MAN. Ive not had two hours undisturbed sleep since I joined. I havnt closed my eyes for forty-eight hours.

RAINA (*at her wit's end*). But what am I to do with you?

THE MAN (*staggering up, roused by her desperation*). Of course. I must do something. (*He shakes himself; pulls himself together; and speaks with rallied vigor and courage.*) You see, sleep or no sleep, hunger or no hunger, tired or not tired, you can always do a thing when you know it must be done. Well, that pipe must be got down: (*he hits himself on the chest.*) do you hear that, you chocolate cream soldier? (*He turns to the window.*)

RAINA (*anxiously*). But if you fall?

THE MAN. I shall sleep as if the stones were a feather bed. Goodbye. (*He makes boldly for the window; and his hand is on the shutter when there is a terrible burst of firing in the street beneath.*)

RAINA (*rushing to him*). Stop! (*She seizes him recklessly, and pulls him quite round.*) Theyll kill you.

THE MAN (*coolly, but attentively*). Never mind: this sort of thing is all in my day's work. I'm bound to take my chance. (*Decisively.*) Now do what I tell you. Put out the candle; so that they shant see the light when I open the shutters. And keep away from the window, whatever you do. If they see me theyre sure to have a shot at me.

RAINA (*clinging to him*). Theyre sure to see you: it's bright moonlight. I'll save you. Oh, how can you be so indifferent! You want me to save you, dont you?

THE MAN. I really dont want to be troublesome. (*She shakes him in her impatience.*) I am not indifferent, dear young lady, I assure you. But how is it to be done?

RAINA. Come away from the window. (*She takes him firmly back to the middle of the room. The moment she releases him he turns mechanically towards the window again. She seizes him and turns him back, exclaiming)* Please! *(He becomes motionless, like a hypnotized rabbit, his fatigue gaining fast on him. She releases him, and addresses him patronizingly.)* Now listen. You must trust to our hospitality. You do not yet know in whose house you are. I am a Petkoff.

THE MAN.   A pet what?

RAINA *(rather indignantly)*. I mean that I belong to the family of the Petkoffs, the richest and best known in our country.

THE MAN.   Oh yes, of course. I beg your pardon. The Petkoffs, to be sure. How stupid of me!

RAINA.   You know you never heard of them until this moment. How can you stoop to pretend!

THE MAN.   Forgive me: I'm too tired to think; and the change of subject was too much for me. Dont scold me.

RAINA.   I forgot. It might make you cry. *(He nods, quite seriously. She pouts and then resumes her patronizing tone.)* I must tell you that my father holds the highest command of any Bulgarian in our army. He is *(proudly.)* a Major.

THE MAN *(pretending to be deeply impressed)*. A Major! Bless me! Think of that!

RAINA.   You shewed great ignorance in thinking that it was necessary to climb up to the balcony because ours is the only private house that has two rows of windows. There is a flight of stairs inside to get up and down by.

THE MAN.   Stairs! How grand! You live in great luxury indeed, dear young lady.

RAINA.   Do you know what a library is?

THE MAN.   A library? A roomful of books?

RAINA.   Yes. We have one, the only one in Bulgaria.

THE MAN.   Actually a real library! I should like to see that.

RAINA *(affectedly)*. I tell you these things to shew you that you are not in the house of ignorant country folk who would kill you the moment they saw your Serbian uniform, but among civilized people. We go to Bucharest every year for the opera season; and I have spent a whole month in Vienna.

THE MAN.   I saw that, dear young lady. I saw at once that you knew the world.

RAINA.   Have you ever seen the opera of Ernani?

THE MAN.   Is that the one with the devil in it in red velvet, and a soldiers' chorus?

RAINA *(contemptuously)*. No!

THE MAN *(stifling a heavy sigh of weariness)*. Then I dont know it.

RAINA.   I thought you might have remembered the great scene where Ernani, flying from his foes just as you are tonight, takes refuge in the castle of his bitterest enemy, an old Castilian noble. The noble refuses to give him up. His guest is sacred to him.

THE MAN *(quickly, waking up a little)*. Have your people got that notion?

RAINA *(with dignity)*. My mother and I can understand that notion as you call it. And if instead of threatening me with your pistol as you did you had simply thrown yourself as a fugitive on our hospitality, you would have been as safe as in your father's house.

THE MAN.   Quite sure?

RAINA *(turning her back on him in disgust)*. Oh, it is useless to try to make you understand.

THE MAN.   Dont be angry: you see how awkward it would be for me if there was any mistake. My father is a very hospitable man: he keeps six hotels; but I couldnt trust him as far as that. What about your father?

RAINA.   He is away at Slivnitza fighting for his country. I answer for your safety. There is my hand in pledge of it. Will that reassure you? *(She offers him her hand.)*

THE MAN *(looking dubiously at his own hand)*. Better not touch my hand, dear young lady. I must have a wash first.

RAINA *(touched)*. That is very nice of you. I see that you are a gentleman.

THE MAN *(puzzled)*. Eh?

RAINA.   You must not think I am surprised. Bulgarians of really good standing—people in our position—wash their hands nearly every day. So you see I can appreciate your delicacy. You may take my hand. *(She offers it again.)*

THE MAN *(kissing it with his hands behind his back)*. Thanks, gracious young lady: I feel safe at last. And now would you mind breaking the news to your mother? I had better not stay here secretly longer than is necessary.

RAINA.   If you will be so good as to keep perfectly still whilst I am away.

THE MAN.   Certainly. *(He sits down on the ottoman.)*

Raina goes to the bed and wraps herself in the fur cloak. His eyes close. She goes to the door. Turning for a last look at him, she sees that he is dropping off to sleep.

RAINA *(at the door)*. You are not going asleep, are you? *(He murmurs inarticulately: she runs to him and shakes him.)* Do you hear? Wake up: you are falling asleep.

THE MAN.   Eh? Falling aslee—? Oh no: not the least in the world: I was only thinking. It's all right: I'm wide awake.

RAINA *(severely)*. Will you please stand up while I am away. *(He rises reluctantly.)* All the time, mind.

THE MAN *(standing unsteadily)*. Certainly. Certainly: you may depend on me.

Raina looks doubtfully at him. He smiles weakly. She goes reluctantly, turning again at the door, and almost catching him in the act of yawning. She goes out.

THE MAN *(drowsily)*. Sleep, sleep, sleep, sleep, slee—*(The words trail off into a murmur. He wakes again with a shock on the point of falling.)* Where am I? Thats what I want to know: where am I? Must keep awake. Nothing keeps me awake except danger: remember that: *(intently.)* danger, danger, danger, dan—*(trailing off again: another* shock.) Wheres danger? Mus' find it. (*He starts off vaguely round the room in search of it.*) What am I looking for? Sleep—danger—dont know. (*He stumbles against the bed.*) Ah yes: now I know. All right now. I'm to go to bed, but not to sleep. Be sure not to sleep, because of danger. Not to lie down either, only sit down. (*He sits on the bed. A blissful expression comes into his face.*) Ah! (*With a happy sigh he sinks back at full length; lifts his boots into the bed with a final effort; and falls fast asleep instantly.*)

Catherine comes in, followed by Raina.

RAINA (*looking at the ottoman*). He's gone! I left him here.

CATHERINE.   Here! Then he must have climbed down from the—

RAINA (*seeing him*). Oh! (*She points.*)

CATHERINE (*scandalized*). Well! (*She strides to the bed, Raina following until she is opposite her on the other side.*) He's fast asleep. The brute!

RAINA (*anxiously*). Sh!

CATHERINE (*shaking him*). Sir! (*Shaking him again, harder.*) Sir!! (*Vehemently, shaking very hard.*) Sir!!!

RAINA (*catching her arm*). Dont, mamma; the poor darling is worn out. Let him sleep.

CATHERINE (*letting him go, and turning amazed to Raina*). The poor darling! Raina!!! (*She looks sternly at her daughter.*)

The man sleeps profoundly.

ACT TWO

The sixth of March, 1886. In the garden of Major Petkoff's house. It is a fine spring morning: the garden looks fresh and pretty. Beyond the paling the tops of a couple of minarets can be seen, shewing that there is a valley there, with the little town in it. A few miles further the Balkan mountains rise and shut in the landscape. Looking towards them from within the garden, the side of the house is seen on the left, with a garden door reached by a little flight of steps. On the right the stable yard, with its gateway, encroaches on the garden. There are fruit bushes along the paling and house, covered with washing spread out to dry. A path runs by the house, and rises by two steps at the corner, where it turns out of sight. In the middle, a small table, with two bent wood chairs at it, is laid for breakfast with Turkish coffee pot, cups, rolls, etc.; but the cups have been used and the bread broken. There is a wooden garden seat against the wall on the right.

Louka, smoking a cigaret, is standing between the table and the house, turning her back with angry disdain on a man servant who is lecturing her. He is a middle-aged man of cool temperament and low but clear and keen intelligence, with the complacency of the servant who values himself on his rank in servitude, and the imperturbability of the accurate calculator who has no illusions. He wears a white Bulgarian costume: jacket with embroidered border, sash, wide knickerbockers, and decorated gaiters. His head is shaved up to the crown, giving him a high Japanese forehead. His name is Nicola.

NICOLA.   Be warned in time, Louka: mend your manners. I know the mistress. She is so grand that she never dreams that any servant could dare be disrespectful to her; but if she once suspects that you are defying her, out you go.

LOUKA.   I do defy her. I will defy her. What do I care for her?

NICOLA.   If you quarrel with the family, I never can marry you. It's the same as if you quarrelled with me!

LOUKA.   You take her part against me, do you?

NICOLA (*sedately*). I shall always be dependent on the good will of the family. When I leave their service and start a shop in Sofia, their custom will be half my capital: their bad word would ruin me.

LOUKA.   You have no spirit. I should like to catch them saying a word against me!

NICOLA (*pityingly*). I should have expected more sense from you, Louka. But youre young: youre young!

LOUKA.   Yes; and you like me the better for it, dont you? But I know some family secrets they wouldnt care to have told, young as I am. Let them quarrel with me if they dare!

NICOLA (*with compassionate superiority*). Do you know what they would do if they heard you talk like that?

LOUKA.   What could they do?

NICOLA.   Discharge you for untruthfulness. Who would believe any stories you told after that? Who would give you another situation? Who in this house would dare be seen speaking to you ever again? How long would your father be left on his little farm? (*She impatiently throws away the end of her cigaret, and stamps on it.*) Child: you dont know the power such high people have over the like of you and me when we try to rise out of our poverty against them. (*He goes close to her and lowers his voice.*) Look at me, ten years in their service. Do you think I know no secrets? I know things about the mistress that she wouldnt have the master know for a thousand levas. I know things about him that she wouldnt let him hear the last of for six months if I blabbed them to her. I know things about Raina that would break off her match with Sergius if—

LOUKA (*turning on him quickly*). How do you know? I never told you!

NICOLA (*opening his eyes cunningly*). So thats your little secret, is it? I thought it might be something like that. Well, you take my advice and be respectful; and make the mistress feel that no matter what you know or dont know, she can depend on you to hold your tongue and serve the family faithfully. Thats what they like; and thats how youll make most out of them.

LOUKA (*with searching scorn*). You have the soul of a servant, Nicola.

NICOLA (*complacently*). Yes: thats the secret of success in service.

A loud knocking with a whip handle on a wooden door is heard from the stable yard.

MALE VOICE OUTSIDE.   Hollo! Hollo there! Nicola!

LOUKA.   Master! back from the war!

NICOLA (*quickly*). My word for it, Louka, the war's over. Off with you and get some fresh coffee. (*He runs out into the stable yard.*)

LOUKA (*as she collects the coffee pot and cups on the tray, and carries it into the house*). Youll never put the soul of a servant into me.

Major Petkoff comes from the stable yard, followed by Nicola. He is a cheerful, excitable, insignificant, unpolished man of about 50, naturally unambitious except as to his income and his importance in local society, but just now greatly pleased with the military rank which the war has thrust on him as a man of consequence in his town. The fever of plucky patriotism which the Serbian attack roused in all the Bulgarians has pulled him through the war; but he is obviously glad to be home again.

PETKOFF (*pointing to the table with his whip*). Breakfast out here, eh?

NICOLA.   Yes, sir. The mistress and Miss Raina have just gone in.

PETKOFF (*sitting down and taking a roll*). Go in and say Ive come; and get me some fresh coffee.

NICOLA.   It's coming, sir. (*He goes to the house door. Louka, with fresh coffee, a clean cup, and a brandy bottle on her tray, meets him.*) Have you told the mistress?

LOUKA.   Yes: she's coming.

Nicola goes into the house. Louka brings the coffee to the table.

PETKOFF.   Well: the Serbs havnt run away with you, have they?

LOUKA.   No, sir.

PETKOFF.   Thats right. Have you brought me some cognac?

LOUKA (*putting the bottle on the table*). Here, sir.

PETKOFF.   That's right. (*He pours some into his coffee.*)

Catherine, who, having at this early hour made only a very perfunctory toilet, wears a Bulgarian apron over a once brilliant but now half worn-out dressing gown, and a colored handkerchief tied over her thick black hair, comes from the house with Turkish slippers on her bare feet, looking astonishingly handsome and stately under all the circumstances. Louka goes into the house.

CATHERINE.   My dear Paul: what a surprise for us! (*She stoops over the back of his chair to kiss him.*) Have they brought you fresh coffee?

PETKOFF.   Yes: Louka's been looking after me. The war's over. The treaty was signed three days ago at Bucharest; and the decree for our army to demobilize was issued yesterday.

CATHERINE (*springing erect, with flashing eyes*). Paul: have you let the Austrians force you to make peace?

PETKOFF (*submissively*). My dear: they didnt consult me. What could *I* do? (*She sits down and turns away from him.*) But of course we saw to it that the treaty was an honorable one. It declares peace—

CATHERINE (*outraged*). Peace!

PETKOFF (*appeasing her*).—but not friendly relations: remember that. They wanted to put that in; but I insisted on its being struck out. What more could I do?

CATHERINE.   You could have annexed Serbia and made Prince Alexander Emperor of the Balkans. Thats what I would have done.

PETKOFF.   I dont doubt it in the least, my dear. But I should have had to subdue the whole Austrian Empire first; and that would have kept me too long away from you. I missed you greatly.

CATHERINE (*relenting*). Ah! (*She stretches her hand affectionately across the table to squeeze his.*)

PETKOFF.   And how have you been, my dear?

CATHERINE.   Oh, my usual sore throats: thats all.

PETKOFF (*with conviction*). That comes from washing your neck every day. Ive often told you so.

CATHERINE.   Nonsense, Paul!

PETKOFF (*over his coffee and cigaret*). I dont believe in going too far with these modern customs. All this washing cant be good for the health: it's not natural. There was an Englishman at Philippopolis who used to wet himself all over with cold water every morning when he got up. Disgusting! It all comes from the English: their climate makes them so dirty that they have to be perpetually washing themselves. Look at father! he never had a bath in his life; and he lived to be ninety-eight, the healthiest man in Bulgaria. I dont mind a good wash once a week to keep up my position; but once a day is carrying the thing to a ridiculous extreme.

CATHERINE.   You are a barbarian at heart still, Paul. I hope you behaved yourself before all those Russian officers.

PETKOFF.   I did my best. I took care to let them know that we have a library.

CATHERINE.   Ah; but you didnt tell them that we have an electric bell in it? I have had one put up.

PETKOFF.   What's an electric bell?

CATHERINE.   You touch a button; something tinkles in the kitchen; and then Nicola comes up.

PETKOFF.   Why not shout for him?

CATHERINE.   Civilized people never shout for their servants. Ive learnt that while you were away.

PETKOFF.   Well, I'll tell you something Ive learnt too. Civ- ilized people dont hang out their washing to dry where visitors can see it; so youd better have all that (*indicating the clothes on the bushes*) put somewhere else.

CATHERINE.   Oh, thats absurd, Paul: I dont believe really refined people notice such things.

SERGIUS (*knocking at the stable gates*). Gate, Nicola!

PETKOFF.   Theres Sergius. (*Shouting.*) Hollo, Nicola!

CATHERINE.   Oh, dont shout, Paul: it really isnt nice.

PETKOFF.   Bosh! (*He shouts louder than before.*) Nicola!

NICOLA (*appearing at the house door*). Yes, sir.

PETKOFF.   Are you deaf? Dont you hear Major Saranoff knocking? Bring him round this way. (*He pronounces the name with the stress on the second syllable: Sarahnoff.*)

NICOLA.   Yes, Major. (*He goes into the stable yard.*)

PETKOFF.   You must talk to him, my dear, until Raina takes him off our hands. He bores my life out about our not promoting him. Over my head, if you please.

CATHERINE.   He certainly ought to be promoted when he marries Raina. Besides, the country should insist on having at least one native general.

PETKOFF.   Yes; so that he could throw away whole brigades instead of regiments. It's no use, my dear: he hasnt the slightest chance of promotion until we're quite sure that the peace will be a lasting one.

NICOLA (*at the gate, announcing*). Major Sergius Saranoff! (*He goes into the house and returns presently with a third chair, which he places at the table. He then withdraws.*)

Major Sergius Saranoff, the original of the portrait in Rai- na's room, is a tall romantically handsome man, with the physical hardihood, the high spirit, and the susceptible imagination of an untamed mountaineer chieftain. But his remarkable personal distinction is of a characteristically civilized type. The ridges of his eyebrows, curving with an interrogative twist round the projections at the outer cor- ners; his jealously observant eye; his nose, thin, keen, and apprehensive in spite of the pugnacious high bridge and large nostril; his assertive chin would not be out of place in a Parisian salon, shewing that the clever imaginative bar- barian has an acute critical faculty which has been thrown into intense activity by the arrival of western civilization in the Balkans. The result is precisely what the advent of nine- teenth century thought first produced in England: to wit, By- ronism. By his brooding on the perpetual failure, not only of others, but of himself, to live up to his ideals; by his conse- quent cynical scorn for humanity; buy his jejune credulity as to the absolute validity of his concepts and the unworthi- ness of the world in disregarding them; by his wincings and mockeries under the sting of the petty disillusions which every hour spent among men brings to his sensitive obser- vation, he has acquired the half tragic, half ironic air, the mysterious moodiness, the suggestion of a strange and ter- rible history that has left nothing but undying remorse, by

which Childe Harold fascinated the grandmothers of his En- glish contemporaries. It is clear that here or nowhere is Rai- na's ideal hero. Catherine is hardly less enthusiastic about him than her daughter, and much less reserved in shewing her enthusiasm. As he enters from the stable gate, she rises effusively to greet him. Petkoff is distinctly less disposed to make a fuss about him.

PETKOFF.   Here already, Sergius! Glad to see you.

CATHERINE.   My dear Sergius! (*She holds out both her hands.*)

SERGIUS (*kissing them with scrupulous gallantry*). My dear mother, if I may call you so.

PETKOFF (*drily*). Mother-in-law, Sergius: mother-in-law! Sit down; and have some coffee.

SERGIUS.   Thank you: none for me. (*He gets away from the table with a certain distaste for Petkoff's enjoyment of it, and posts himself with conscious dignity against the rail of the steps leading to the house.*)

CATHERINE.   You look superb. The campaign has im- proved you, Sergius. Everybody here is mad about you. We were all wild with enthusiasm about that magnificent cavalry charge.

SERGIUS (*with grave irony*). Madam: it was the cradle and the grave of my military reputation.

CATHERINE.   How so?

SERGIUS.   I won the battle the wrong way when our worthy Russian generals were losing it the right way. In short, I upset their plans, and wounded their self-esteem. Two Cossack colonels had their regiments routed on the most correct principles of scientific warfare. Two major- generals got killed strictly according to military etiquette. The two colonels are now major-generals; and I am still a simple major.

CATHERINE.   You shall not remain so, Sergius. The women are on your side; and they will see that justice is done you.

SERGIUS.   It is too late. I have only waited for the peace to send in my resignation.

PETKOFF (*dropping his cup in amazement*). Your resignation!

CATHERINE.   Oh, you must withdraw it!

SERGIUS (*with resolute measured emphasis, folding his arms*). I never withdraw.

PETKOFF (*vexed*). Now who could have supposed you were going to do such a thing?

SERGIUS (*with fire*). Everyone that knew me. But enough of myself and my affairs. How is Raina; and where is Raina?

RAINA (*suddenly coming round the corner of the house and standing at the top of the steps in the path*). Raina is here.

She makes a charming picture as they turn to look at her. She wears an underdress of pale green silk, draped with an overdress of thin ecru canvas embroidered with gold. She is crowned with a dainty eastern cap of gold tinsel. Sergius goes impulsively to meet her. Posing regally, she presents her hand: he drops chivalrously on one knee and kisses it.

PETKOFF (*aside to Catherine, beaming with parental pride*). Pretty, isnt it? She always appears at the right moment.

CATHERINE (*impatiently*). Yes; she listens for it. It is an abominable habit.

Sergius leads Raina forward with splendid gallantry. When they arrive at the table, she turns to him with a bend of the head: he bows; and thus they separate, he coming to his place, and she going behind her father's chair.

RAINA (*stooping and kissing her father*). Dear father! Welcome home!

PETKOFF (*patting her cheek*). My little pet girl. (*He kisses her. She goes to the chair left by Nicola for Sergius, and sits down.*)

CATHERINE.   And so youre no longer a soldier, Sergius.

SERGIUS.   I am no longer a soldier. Soldiering, my dear madam, is the coward's art of attacking mercilessly when you are strong, and keeping out of harm's way when you are weak. That is the whole secret of successful fighting. Get your enemy at a disadvantage; and never, on any account, fight him on equal terms.

PETKOFF.   They wouldnt let us make a fair stand-up fight of it. However, I suppose soldiering has to be a trade like any other trade.

SERGIUS.   Precisely. But I have no ambition to shine as a tradesman; so I have taken the advice of that bagman of a captain that settled the exchange of prisoners with us at Pirot, and given it up.

PETKOFF.   What! that Swiss fellow? Sergius: Ive often thought of that exchange since. He over-reached us about those horses.

SERGIUS.   Of course he over-reached us. His father was a hotel and livery stable keeper; and he owed his first step to his knowledge of horse-dealing. (*With mock enthusiasm.*) Ah, he was a soldier: every inch a soldier! If only I had bought the horses for my regiment instead of foolishly leading it into danger, I should have been a field-marshall now!

CATHERINE.   A Swiss? What was he doing in the Serbian army?

PETKOFF.   A volunteer, of course: keen on picking up his profession. (*Chuckling.*) We shouldnt have been able to begin fighting if these foreigners hadnt shewn us how to do it: we knew nothing about it; and neither did the Serbs. Egad, there'd have been no war without them!

RAINA.   Are there many Swiss officers in the Serbian Army?

PETKOFF.   No. All Austrians, just as our officers were all Russians. This was the only Swiss I came across. I'll never trust a Swiss again. He humbugged us into giving him fifty ablebodied men for two hundred worn out chargers. They werent even eatable!

SERGIUS.   We were two children in the hands of that consummate soldier, Major: simply two innocent little children.

RAINA.   What was he like?

CATHERINE.   Oh, Raina, what a silly question!

SERGIUS.   He was like a commercial traveller in uniform. Bourgeois to his boots!

PETKOFF (*grinning*). Sergius: tell Catherine that queer story his friend told us about how he escaped after Slivnitza. You remember. About his being hid by two women.

SERGIUS (*with bitter irony*). Oh yes: quite a romance! He was serving in the very battery I so unprofessionally charged. Being a thorough soldier, he ran away like the rest of them, with our cavalry at his heels. To escape their sabres he climbed a waterpipe and made his way into the bedroom of a young Bulgarian lady. The young lady was enchanted by his persuasive commercial traveller's manners. She very modestly entertained him for an hour or so, and then called in her mother lest her conduct should appear unmaidenly. The old lady was equally fascinated; and the fugitive was sent on his way in the morning, disguised in an old coat belonging to the master of the house, who was away at the war.

RAINA (*rising with marked stateliness*). Your life in the camp has made you coarse, Sergius. I did not think you would have repeated such a story before me. (*She turns away coldly.*)

CATHERINE (*also rising*). She is right, Sergius. If such women exist, we should be spared the knowledge of them.

PETKOFF.   Pooh! nonsense! what does it matter?

SERGIUS (*ashamed*). No, Petkoff: I was wrong. (*To Raina, with earnest humility*) I beg your pardon. I have behaved abominably. Forgive me, Raina. (*She bows reservedly.*) And you too, madam. (*Catherine bows graciously and sits down. He proceeds solemnly, again addressing Raina.*) The glimpses I have had of the seamy side of life during the last few months have made me cynical; but I should not have brought my cynicism here: least of all into your presence, Raina, I—(*Here, turning to the others, he is evidently going to begin a long speech when the Major interrupts him.*)

PETKOFF.   Stuff and nonsense, Sergius! Thats quite enough fuss about nothing: a soldier's daughter should be able to stand up without flinching to a little strong conversation. (*He rises.*) Come: it's time for us to get to business. We have to make up our minds how those three regiments are to get back to Philippopolis: theres no forage for them on the Sofia route. (*He goes towards the house.*) Come along. (*Sergius is about to follow him when Catherine rises and intervenes.*)

CATHERINE.   Oh, Paul, cant you spare Sergius for a few moments? Raina has hardly seen him yet. Perhaps I can help you settle about the regiments.

SERGIUS (*protesting*). My dear madam, impossible: you—

CATHERINE (*stopping him playfully*). You stay here, my dear Sergius: theres no hurry. I have a word or two to say to Paul. (*Sergius instantly bows and steps back.*) Now, dear (*taking Petkoff's arm*): come and see the electric bell.

PETKOFF.   Oh, very well, very well.

They go into the house together affectionately. Sergius, left alone with Raina, looks anxiously at her, fearing that she is still offended. She smiles, and stretches out her arms to him.

SERGIUS (*hastening to her*). Am I forgiven?

RAINA (*placing her hands on his shoulders as she looks up at him with admiration and worship*). My hero! My king!

SERGIUS.   My queen! (*He kisses her on the forehead.*)

RAINA.   How I have envied you, Sergius! You have been out in the world, on the field of battle, able to prove yourself there worthy of any woman in the world; whilst I have had to sit at home inactive—dreaming—useless—doing nothing that could give me the right to call myself worthy of any man.

SERGIUS.   Dearest: all my deeds have been yours. You inspired me. I have gone through the war like a knight in a tournament with his lady looking down at him!

RAINA.   And you have never been absent from my thoughts for a moment. (*Very solemnly.*) Sergius: I think we two have found the higher love. When I think of you, I feel that I could never do a base deed, or think an ignoble thought.

SERGIUS.   My lady and my saint! (*He clasps her reverently.*)

RAINA (*returning his embrace*). My lord and my—

SERGIUS.   Sh—sh! Let me be the worshipper, dear. You little know how unworthy even the best man is of a girl's pure passion!

RAINA.   I trust you. I love you. You will never disappoint me, Sergius. (*Louka is heard singing within the house. They quickly release each other.*) I cant pretend to talk indifferently before her: my heart is too full. (*Louka comes from the house with her tray. She goes to the table, and begins to clear it, with her back turned to them.*) I will get my hat; and then we can go out until lunch time. Wouldnt you like that?

SERGIUS.   Be quick. If you are away five minutes, it will seem five hours. (*Raina runs to the top of the steps, and turns there to exchange looks with him and wave him a kiss with both hands. He looks after her with emotion for a moment; then turns slowly away, his face radiant with the loftiest exaltation. The movement shifts his field of vision, into the corner of which there now comes the tail of Louka's double apron. His attention is arrested at once. He takes a stealthy look at her, and begins to twirl his moustache mischievously, with his left hand akimbo on his hip. Finally striking the ground with his heels in*

something of a cavalry swagger, he strolls over to the other side of the table, opposite her, and says) Louka: do you know what the higher love is?

LOUKA (*astonished*). No, sir.

SERGIUS.   Very fatiguing thing to keep up for any length of time, Louka. One feels the need of some relief after it.

LOUKA (*innocently*). Perhaps you would like some coffee, sir? (*She stretches her hand across the table for the coffee pot.*)

SERGIUS (*taking her hand*). Thank you, Louka.

LOUKA (*pretending to pull*). Oh, sir, you know I didnt mean that. I'm surprised at you!

SERGIUS (*coming clear of the table and drawing her with him*). I am surprised at myself, Louka. What would Sergius, the hero of Slivnitza, say if he saw me now? What would Sergius, the apostle of the higher love, say if he saw me now? What would the half dozen Sergiuses who keep popping in and out of this handsome figure of mine say if they caught us here? (*Letting go her hand and slipping his arm dexterously round her waist.*) Do you consider my figure handsome, Louka?

LOUKA.   Let me go, sir. I shall be disgraced. (*She struggles: he holds her inexorably.*) Oh, will you let go?

SERGIUS (*looking straight into her eyes*). No.

LOUKA.   Then stand back where we cant be seen. Have you no common sense?

SERGIUS.   Ah! thats reasonable. (*He takes her into the stable yard gateway, where they are hidden from the house.*)

LOUKA (*plaintively*). I may have been seen from the windows: Miss Raina is sure to be spying about after you.

SERGIUS (*stung: letting her go*). Take care, Louka. I may be worthless enough to betray the higher love; but do not you insult it.

LOUKA (*demurely*). Not for the world, sir, I'm sure. May I go on with my work, please, now?

SERGIUS (*again putting his arm round her*). You are a provoking little witch, Louka. If you were in love with me, would you spy out of windows on me?

LOUKA.   Well, you see, sir, since you say you are half a dozen different gentlemen all at once, I should have a great deal to look after.

SERGIUS (*charmed*). Witty as well as pretty. (*He tries to kiss her.*)

LOUKA (*avoiding him*). No: I dont want your kisses. Gentlefolk are all alike: you making love to me behind Miss Raina's back; and she doing the same behind yours.

SERGIUS (*recoiling a step*). Louka!

LOUKA.   It shews how little you really care.

SERGIUS (*dropping his familiarity, and speaking with freezing politeness*). If our conversation is to continue, Louka, you will please remember that a gentleman does not discuss the conduct of the lady he is engaged to with her maid.

LOUKA.   It's so hard to know what a gentleman considers right. I thought from your trying to kiss me that you had given up being so particular.

SERGIUS (*turning from her and striking his forehead as he comes back into the garden from the gateway*). Devil! devil!

LOUKA.   Ha! ha! I expect one of the six of you is very like me, sir; though I am only Miss Raina's maid. (*She goes back to her work at the table, taking no further notice of him.*)

SERGIUS (*speaking to himself*). Which of the six is the real man? thats the question that torments me. One of them is a hero, another a buffoon, another a humbug, another perhaps a bit of a blackguard. (*He pauses, and looks furtively at Louka as he adds, with deep bitterness*) And one, at least, is a coward: jealous, like all cowards. (*He goes to the table.*) Louka.

LOUKA.   Yes?

SERGIUS.   Who is my rival?

LOUKA.   You shall never get that out of me, for love or money.

SERGIUS.   Why?

LOUKA.   Never mind why. Besides, you would tell that I told you; and I should lose my place.

SERGIUS (*holding out his right hand in affirmation*). No! on the honor of a—(*He checks himself; and his hand drops, nerveless, as he concludes sardonically*)—of a man capable of behaving as I have been behaving for the last five minutes. Who is he?

LOUKA.   I dont know. I never saw him. I only heard his voice through the door of her room.

SERGIUS.   Damnation! How dare you?

LOUKA (*retreating*). Oh, I mean no harm: youve no right to take up my words like that. The mistress knows all about it. And I tell you that if that gentleman ever comes here again, Miss Raina will marry him, whether he likes it or not. I know the difference between the sort of manner you and she put on before one another and the real manner.

Sergius shivers as if she had stabbed him. Then, setting his face like iron, he strides grimly to her, and grips her above the elbows with both hands.

SERGIUS.   Now listen you to me.

LOUKA (*wincing*). Not so tight: youre hurting me.

SERGIUS.   That doesnt matter. You stained my honor by making me a party to your eavesdropping. And you have betrayed your mistress.

LOUKA (*writhing*). Please—

SERGIUS.   That shews that you are an abominable little clod of common clay, with the soul of a servant. (*He lets her go as if she were an unclean thing, and turns away, dusting his hands of her, to the bench by the wall, where he sits down with averted head, meditating gloomily.*)

LOUKA (*whimpering angrily with her hands up her sleeves, feeling her bruised arms*). You know how to hurt with your tongue as well as with your hands. But I dont care, now Ive found out that whatever clay I'm made of, youre made of the same. As for her, she's a liar; and her fine airs are a cheat; and I'm worth six of her. (*She shakes the pain off hardily; tosses her head; and sets to work to put the things on the tray.*)

He looks doubtfully at her. She finishes packing the tray, and laps the cloth over the edges, so as to carry all out together. As she stoops to lift it, he rises.

SERGIUS.   Louka! (*She stops and looks defiantly at him.*) A gentleman has no right to hurt a woman under any circumstances. (*With profound humility, uncovering his head.*) I beg your pardon.

LOUKA.   That sort of apology may satisfy a lady. Of what use is it to a servant?

SERGIUS (*rudely crossed in his chivalry, throws it off with a bitter laugh, and says slightingly*). Oh! you wish to be paid for the hurt? (*He puts on his shako, and takes some money from his pocket.*)

LOUKA (*her eyes filling with tears in spite of herself*). No: I want my hurt made well.

SERGIUS (*sobered by her tone*). How?

She rolls up her left sleeve; clasps her arm with the thumb and fingers of her right hand; and looks down at the bruise. Then she raises her head and looks straight at him. Finally, with a superb gesture, she presents her arm to be kissed. Amazed, he looks at her; at the arm; at her again; hesitates; and then, with shuddering intensity, exclaims Never! *and gets away as far as possible from her.*

Her arm drops. Without a word, and with unaffected dignity, she takes her tray, and is approaching the house when Raina returns, wearing a hat and jacket in the height of the Vienna fashion of the previous year, 1885. Louka makes way proudly for her, and then goes into the house.

RAINA.   I'm ready. Whats the matter? (*Gaily.*) Have you been flirting with Louka?

SERGIUS (*hastily*). No, no. How can you think such a thing?

RAINA (*ashamed of herself*). Forgive me, dear: it was only a jest. I am so happy today.

He goes quickly to her, and kisses her hand remorsefully. Catherine comes out and calls to them from the top of the steps.

CATHERINE (*coming down to them*). I am sorry to disturb you, children; but Paul is distracted over those three regiments. He doesnt know how to send them to Philippopolis; and he objects to every suggestion of mine. You must go and help him, Sergius. He is in the library.

RAINA (*disappointed*). But we are just going out for a walk.

SERGIUS.   I shall not be long. Wait for me just five minutes. (*He runs up the steps to the door.*)

RAINA (*following him to the foot of the steps and looking up at him with timid coquetry*). I shall go round and wait in full view of the library windows. Be sure you draw father's attention to me. If you are a moment longer than five minutes, I shall go in and fetch you, regiments or no regiments.

SERGIUS (*laughing*). Very well. (*He goes in.*)

Raina watches him until he is out of her sight. Then, with a perceptible relaxation of manner, she begins to pace up and down the garden in a brown study.

CATHERINE.   Imagine their meeting that Swiss and hearing the whole story! The very first thing your father asked for was the old coat we sent him off in. A nice mess you have got us into!

RAINA (*gazing thoughtfully at the gravel as she walks*). The little beast!

CATHERINE.   Little beast! What little beast?

RAINA.   To go and tell! Oh, if I had him here, I'd cram him with chocolate creams til he couldnt ever speak again!

CATHERINE.   Dont talk such stuff. Tell me the truth, Raina. How long was he in your room before you came to me?

RAINA (*whisking round and recommencing her march in the opposite direction*). Oh, I forget.

CATHERINE.   You cannot forget! Did he really climb up after the soldiers were gone; or was he there when that officer searched the room?

RAINA.   No. Yes: I think he must have been there then.

CATHERINE.   You think! Oh, Raina! Raina! Will anything ever make you straightforward? If Sergius finds out, it will be all over between you.

RAINA (*with cool impertinence*). Oh, I know Sergius is your pet. I sometimes wish you could marry him instead of me. You would just suit him. You would pet him, and spoil him, and mother him to perfection.

CATHERINE (*opening her eyes widely indeed*). Well, upon my word!

RAINA (*capriciously: half to herself*). I always feel a longing to do or say something dreadful to him—to shock his propriety—to scandalize the five senses out of him. (*To Catherine, perversely.*) I dont care whether he finds out about the chocolate cream soldier or not. I half hope he may. (*She again turns and strolls flippantly away up the path to the corner of the house.*)

CATHERINE.   And what should I be able to say to your father, pray?

RAINA (*over her shoulder, from the top of the two steps*). Oh, poor father! As if he could help himself! (*She turns the corner and passes out of sight.*)

CATHERINE (*looking after her, her fingers itching*). Oh, if you were only ten years younger! (*Louka comes from the house with a salver, which she carries hanging down by her side.*) Well?

LOUKA.   Theres a gentleman just called, madam. A Serbian officer.

CATHERINE (*flaming*). A Serb! And how dare he—(*checking herself bitterly.*) Oh, I forgot. We are at peace now. I suppose we shall have them calling every day to pay their compliments. Well: if he is an officer why dont you tell your master? He is in the library with Major Saranoff. Why do you come to me?

LOUKA.   But he asks for you, madam. And I dont think he knows who you are: he said the lady of the house. He gave me this little ticket for you. (*She takes a card out of her bosom; puts it on the salver; and offers it to Catherine.*)

CATHERINE (*reading*). "Captain Bluntschli"? Thats a German name.

LOUKA.   Swiss, madam, I think.

CATHERINE (*with a bound that makes Louka jump back*). Swiss! What is he like?

LOUKA (*timidly*). He has a big carpet bag, madam.

CATHERINE.   Oh Heavens! he's come to return the coat. Send him away: say we're not at home: ask him to leave his address and I'll write to him. Oh stop: that will never do. Wait! (*She throws herself into a chair to think it out. Louka waits.*) The master and Major Saranoff are busy in the library, arnt they?

LOUKA.   Yes, madam.

CATHERINE (*decisively*). Bring the gentleman out here at once. (*Peremptorily.*) And be very polite to him. Dont delay. Here (*impatiently snatching the salver from her*): leave that here; and go straight back to him.

LOUKA.   Yes, madam (*Going.*)

CATHERINE.   Louka!

LOUKA (*stopping*). Yes, madam.

CATHERINE.   Is the library door shut?

LOUKA.   I think so, madam.

CATHERINE.   If not, shut it as you pass through.

LOUKA.   Yes, madam (*Going.*)

CATHERINE.   Stop. (*Louka stops.*) He will have to go that way (*indicating the gate of the stable yard*). Tell Nicola to bring his bag here after him. Dont forget.

LOUKA (*surprised*). His bag?

CATHERINE.   Yes: here: as soon as possible. (*Vehemently.*) Be quick! (*Louka runs into the house. Catherine snatches her apron off and throws it behind a bush. She then takes up the salver and uses it as a mirror, with the result that the handkerchief tied round her head follows the apron. A touch to her hair and a shake to her dressing gown make her presentable.*) Oh, how? how? how can a man be such a fool! Such a moment to select! (*Louka appears at the door of the house, announcing* Captain Bluntschli. *She stands aside at the top of the steps to let him pass before she goes in again. He is the man of the midnight adventure in Raina's room, clean, well brushed, smartly uniformed, and out of trouble, but still unmistakably the same man. The moment Louka's back is turned, Catherine swoops on him with impetuous, urgent, coaxing appeal.*)

Captain Bluntschli: I am very glad to see you; but you must leave this house at once. (*He raises his eyebrows.*) My husband has just returned with my future son-in-law; and they know nothing. If they did, the consequences would be terrible. You are a foreigner: you do not feel our national animosities as we do. We still hate the Serbs: the effect of the peace on my husband has been to make him feel like a lion baulked of his prey. If he discovers our secret, he will never forgive me; and my daughter's life will hardly be safe. Will you, like the chivalrous gentleman and soldier you are, leave at once before he finds you here?

BLUNTSCHLI (*disappointed, but philosophical*). At once, gracious lady. I only came to thank you and return the coat you lent me. If you will allow me to take it out of my bag and leave it with your servant as I pass out, I need detain you no further. (*He turns to go into the house.*)

CATHERINE (*catching him by the sleeve*). Oh, you must not think of going back that way. (*Coaxing him across to the stable gates.*) This is the shortest way out. Many thanks. So glad to have been of service to you. Good-bye.

BLUNTSCHLI.   But my bag?

CATHERINE.   It shall be sent on. You will leave me your address.

BLUNTSCHLI.   True. Allow me. (*He takes out his card-case, and stops to write his address, keeping Catherine in an agony of impatience. As he hands her the card, Petkoff, hatless, rushes from the house in a fluster of hospitality, followed by Sergius.*)

PETKOFF (*as he hurries down the steps*). My dear Captain Bluntschli—

CATHERINE.   Oh Heavens! (*She sinks on the seat against the wall.*)

PETKOFF (*too preoccupied to notice her as he shakes Bluntschli's hand heartily*). Those stupid people of mine thought I was out here, instead of in the—haw!—library. (*He cannot mention the library without betraying how proud he is of it.*) I saw you through the window. I was wondering why you didnt come in. Saranoff is with me: you remember him, dont you?

SERGIUS (*saluting humorously, and then offering his hand with great charm of manner*). Welcome, our friend the enemy!

PETKOFF.   No longer the enemy, happily. (*Rather anxiously.*) I hope youve called as a friend, and not about horses or prisoners.

CATHERINE.   Oh, quite as a friend, Paul. I was just asking Captain Bluntschli to stay to lunch; but he declares he must go at once.

SERGIUS (*sardonically*). Impossible, Bluntschli. We want you here badly. We have to send on three cavalry regiments to Philippopolis; and we dont in the least know how to do it.

BLUNTSCHLI (*suddenly attentive and businesslike*). Philippopolis? The forage is the trouble, I suppose.

PETKOFF (*eagerly*). Yes: thats it. (*To Sergius.*) He sees the whole thing at once.

BLUNTSCHLI.   I think I can shew you how to manage that.

SERGIUS.   Invaluable man! Come along! (*Towering over Bluntschli, he puts his hand on his shoulder and takes him to the steps, Petkoff following.*)

Raina comes from the house as Bluntschli puts his foot on the first step.

RAINA.   Oh! The chocolate cream soldier!

Bluntschli stands rigid. Sergius, amazed, looks at Raina, then at Petkoff, who looks back at him and then at his wife.

CATHERINE (*with commanding presence of mine*). My dear Raina, dont you see that we have a guest here? Captain Bluntschli: one of our new Serbian friends.

Raina bows. Bluntschli bows.

RAINA.   How silly of me! (*She comes down into the centre of the group, between Bluntschli and Petkoff.*) I made a beautiful ornament this morning for the ice pudding; and that stupid Nicola has just put down a pile of plates on it and spoilt it. (*To Bluntschli, winningly.*) I hope you didnt think that you were the chocolate cream soldier, Captain Bluntschli.

BLUNTSCHLI (*laughing*). I assure you I did. (*Stealing a whimsical glance at her.*) Your explanation was a relief.

PETKOFF (*suspiciously, to Raina*). And since when, pray, have you taken to cooking?

CATHERINE.   Oh, whilst you were away. It is her latest fancy.

PETKOFF (*testily*). And has Nicola taken to drinking? He used to be careful enough. First he shews Captain Bluntschli out here when he knew quite well I was in the library; and then he goes downstairs and breaks Raina's chocolate soldier. He must—(*Nicola appears at the top of the steps with the bag. He descends; places it respectfully before Bluntschli; and waits for further orders. General amazement. Nicola, unconscious of the effect he is producing, looks perfectly satisfied with himself. When Petkoff recovers his power of speech, he breaks out at him with*) Are you mad, Nicola?

NICOLA (*taken aback*). Sir?

PETKOFF.   What have you brought that for?

NICOLA.   My lady's orders, major. Louka told me that—

CATHERINE (*interrupting him*). My orders! Why should I order you to bring Captain Bluntschli's luggage out here? What are you thinking of, Nicola?

NICOLA (*after a moment's bewilderment, picking up the bag as he addresses Bluntschli with the very perfection of servile discretion*). I beg your pardon, captain, I am sure. (*To Catherine.*) My fault, madam: I hope youll overlook it. (*He bows, and is going to the steps with the bag, when Petkoff addresses him angrily.*)

PETKOFF.   Youd better go and slam that bag, too, down on Miss Raina's ice pudding! (*This is too much for Nicola. The bag drops from his hand almost on his master's toes, eliciting a roar of*) Begone, you butter-fingered donkey.

NICOLA (*snatching up the bag, and escaping into the house*). Yes, major.

CATHERINE.   Oh, never mind. Paul: dont be angry.

PETKOFF (*blustering*). Scoundrel! He's got out of hand while I was away. I'll teach him. Infernal blackguard! The sack next Saturday! I'll clear out the whole establishment— (*He is stifled by the caresses of his wife and daughter, who hang round his neck, petting him.*)

CATHERINE ⎱ (*together*). ⎰ Now, now, now, it mustnt be
RAINA ⎰   ⎱ Wow, wow, wow: not on your

⎰ angry. He meant no harm. Be good to
⎱ first day at home. I'll make another ice
⎱ please me, dear, Sh-sh-sh-sh!
⎰ pudding. Tch-ch-ch!

PETKOFF (*yielding*). Oh well, never mind. Come, Bluntschli: lets have no more nonsense about going away. You know very well youre not going back to Switzerland yet. Until you do go back youll stay with us.

RAINA.   Oh, do, Captain Bluntschli.

PETKOFF (*to Catherine*). Now, Catherine: it's of you he's afraid. Press him; and he'll stay.

CATHERINE.   Of course I shall be only too delighted if (*appealingly*) Captain Bluntschli really wishes to stay. He knows my wishes.

BLUNTSCHLI (*in his driest military manner*). I am at madam's orders.

SERGIUS (*cordially*). That settles it!

PETKOFF (*heartily*). Of course!

RAINA.   You see you must stay.

BLUNTSCHLI (*smiling*). Well, if I must, I must.

Gesture of despair from Catherine.

ACT THREE

In the library after lunch. It is not much of a library. Its literary equipment consists of a single fixed shelf stocked with old paper covered novels, broken backed, coffee stained, torn and thumbed; and a couple of little hanging shelves with a few gift books on them: the rest of the wall space being occupied by trophies of war and the chase. But it is a most comfortable sitting room. A row of three large windows shews a mountain panorama, just now seen in one of its friendliest aspects in the mellowing afternoon light. In the corner next the right hand window a square earthenware stove, a perfect tower of glistening pottery, rises nearly to the ceiling and guarantees plenty of warmth. The ottoman is like that in Raina's room, and similarly placed; and the window seats are luxurious with decorated cushions. There is one object, however, hopelessly out of keeping with its surroundings. This is a small kitchen table, much the worse

for wear, fitted as a writing table with an old canister full of pens, an eggcup filled with ink, and a deplorable scrap of heavily used pink blotting paper.

At the side of this table, which stands to the left of anyone facing the window, Bluntschli is hard at work with a couple of maps before him, writing orders. At the head of it sits Sergius, who is supposed to be also at work, but is actually gnawing the feather of a pen, and contemplating Bluntschli's quick, sure, businesslike progress with a mixture of envious irritation at his own incapacity and awestruck wonder at an ability which seems to him almost miraculous, though its prosaic character forbids him to esteem it. The Major is comfortably established on the ottoman, with a newspaper in his hand and the tube of his hookah within easy reach. Catherine sits at the stove, with her back to them, embroidering. Raina, reclining on the divan, is gazing in a daydream out at the Balkan landscape, with a neglected novel in her lap.

The door is on the same side as the stove, farther from the window. The button of the electric bell is at the opposite side, behind Bluntschli.

PETKOFF (*looking up from his paper to watch how they are getting on at the table*). Are you sure I cant help you in any way, Bluntschli?

BLUNTSCHLI (*without interrupting his writing or looking up*). Quite sure, thank you. Saranoff and I will manage it.

SERGIUS (*grimly*). Yes: we'll manage it. He finds out what to do; draws up the orders; and I sign em. Division of labor! (*Bluntschli passes him a paper.*) Another one? Thank you. (*He plants the paper squarely before him; sets his chair carefully parallel to it; and signs with his cheek on his elbow and his protruded tongue following the movements of his pen.*) This hand is more accustomed to the sword than to the pen.

PETKOFF.   It's very good of you, Bluntschli: it is indeed, to let yourself be put upon in this way. Now you are quite sure I can do nothing?

CATHERINE (*in a low warning tone*). You can stop interrupting, Paul.

PETKOFF (*starting and looking round at her*). Eh? Oh! Quite right, my love: quite right. (*He takes his newspaper up again, but presently lets it drop.*) Ah, you havnt been campaigning, Catherine: you dont know how pleasant it is for us to sit here, after a good lunch, with nothing to do but enjoy ourselves. Theres only one thing I want to make me thoroughly comfortable.

CATHERINE.   What is that?

PETKOFF.   My old coat. I'm not at home in this one: I feel as if I were on parade.

CATHERINE.   My dear Paul, how absurd you are about that old coat! It must be hanging in the blue closet where you left it.

PETKOFF.   But my dear Catherine, I tell you I've looked there. Am I to believe my own eyes or not? (*Catherine rises and crosses the room to press the button of the electric bell.)* What are you shewing off that bell for? *(She looks at him majestically, and silently resumes her chair and her needlework.)* My dear: if you think the obstinacy of your sex can make a coat out of two old dressing gowns of Raina's, your waterproof, and my mackintosh, youre mistaken. Thats exactly what the blue closet contains at present.

Nicola presents himself.

CATHERINE.   Nicola: go to the blue closet and bring your master's old coat here: the braided one he wears in the house.

NICOLA.   Yes, madam. *(He goes out.)*

PETKOFF.   Catherine.

CATHERINE.   Yes, Paul.

PETKOFF.   I bet you any piece of jewellery you like to order from Sofia against a week's housekeeping money that the coat isnt there.

CATHERINE.   Done, Paul!

PETKOFF *(excited by the prospect of a gamble)*. Come: heres an opportunity for some sport. Wholl bet on it? Bluntschli: I'll give you six to one.

BLUNTSCHLI *(imperturbably)*. It would be robbing you, major. Madam is sure to be right. *(Without looking up, he passes another batch of papers to Sergius.)*

SERGIUS *(also excited)*. Bravo, Switzerland! Major: I bet my best charger against an Arab mare for Raina that Nicola finds the coat in the blue closet.

PETKOFF *(eagerly)*. Your best char—

CATHERINE *(hastily interrupting him)*. Dont be foolish, Paul. An Arabian mare will cost you 50,000 levas.

RAINA *(suddenly coming out of her picturesque revery)*. Really, mother, if you are going to take the jewellery, I dont see why you should grudge me my Arab.

Nicola comes back with the coat, and brings it to Petkoff, who can hardly believe his eyes.

CATHERINE.   Where was it, Nicola?

NICOLA.   Hanging in the blue closet, madam.

PETKOFF.   Well, I am d—

CATHERINE *(stopping him)*. Paul!

PETKOFF.   I could have sworn it wasnt there. Age is beginning to tell on me. I'm getting hallucinations. *(To Nicola.)* Here: help me to change. Excuse me, Bluntschli. *(He begins changing coats, Nicola acting as valet.)* Remember: I didnt take that bet of yours, Sergius. Youd better give Raina that Arab steed yourself, since youve roused her expectations. Eh, Raina? *(He looks round at her; but she is again rapt in the landscape. With a little gush of parental affection and pride, he points her out to them, and says)* She's dreaming, as usual.

SERGIUS.   Assuredly she shall not be the loser.

PETKOFF.   So much the better for her. *I* shant come off so cheaply, I expect. *(The change is now complete. Nicola goes out with the discarded coat.)* Ah, now I feel at home at last. *(He sits down and takes his newspaper with a grunt of relief.)*

BLUNTSCHLI *(to Sergius, handing a paper)*. Thats the last order.

PETKOFF *(jumping up)*. What! Finished?

BLUNTSCHLI.   Finished.

PETKOFF *(with childlike envy)*. Havent you anything for me to sign?

BLUNTSCHLI.   Not necessary. His signature will do.

PETKOFF *(inflating his chest and thumping it)*. Ah well, I think weve done a thundering good day's work. Can I do anything more?

BLUNTSCHLI.   You had better both see the fellows that are to take these. *(Sergius rises.)* Pack them off at once; and shew them that Ive marked on the orders the time they should hand them in by. Tell them that if they stop to drink or tell stories—if theyre five minutes late, theyll have the skin taken off their backs.

SERGIUS *(suffering indignantly)*. I'll say so. *(He strides to the door.)* And if one of them is man enough to spit in my face for insulting him, I'll buy his discharge and give him a pension. *(He goes out.)*

BLUNTSCHLI *(confidentially)*. Just see that he talks to them properly, major, will you?

PETKOFF *(officiously)*. Quite right, Bluntschli, quite right. I'll see to it. *(He goes to the door importantly, but hesitates on the threshold.)* By the bye, Catherine, you may as well come too. Theyll be far more frightened of you than of me.

CATHERINE *(putting down her embroidery)*. I daresay I had better. You would only splutter at them. *(She goes out, Petkoff holding the door for her and following her.)*

BLUNTSCHLI.   What an army! They make cannons out of cherry trees; and the officers send for their wives to keep discipline! *(He begins to fold and docket the papers.)*

Raina, who has risen from the divan, marches slowly down the room with her hands clasped behind her, and looks mischievously at him.

RAINA.   You look ever so much nicer than when we last met. *(He looks up, surprised.)* What have you done to yourself?

BLUNTSCHLI.   Washed; brushed; good night's sleep and breakfast. Thats all.

RAINA.   Did you get back safely that morning?

BLUNTSCHLI.   Quite, thanks.

RAINA.   Were they angry with you for running away from Sergius's charge?

BLUNTSCHLI *(grinning)*. No: they were glad; because theyd all just run away themselves.

RAINA (*going to the table, and leaning over it towards him*). It must have made a lovely story for them: all that about me and my room.

BLUNTSCHLI.   Capital story. But I only told it to one of them: a particular friend.

RAINA.   On whose discretion you could absolutely rely?

BLUNTSCHLI.   Absolutely.

RAINA.   Hm! He told it all to my father and Sergius the day you exchanged the prisoners. (*She turns away and strolls carelessly across to the other side of the room.*)

BLUNTSCHLI (*deeply concerned, and half incredulous*). No! You dont mean that, do you?

RAINA (*turning, with sudden earnestness*). I do indeed. But they dont know that it was in this house you took refuge. If Sergius knew, he would challenge you and kill you in a duel.

BLUNTSCHLI.   Bless me! then dont tell him.

RAINA.   Please be serious, Captain Bluntschli. Can you not realize what it is to me to deceive him? I want to be quite perfect with Sergius: no meanness, no smallness, no deceit. My relation to him is the one really beautiful and noble part of my life. I hope you can understand that.

BLUNTSCHLI (*sceptically*). You mean that you wouldnt like him to find out that the story about the ice pudding was a—a—a—You know.

RAINA (*wincing*). Ah, dont talk of it in that flippant way. I lied: I know it. But I did it to save your life. He would have killed you. That was the second time I ever uttered a falsehood. (*Bluntschli rises quickly and looks doubtfully and somewhat severely at her.*) Do you remember the first time?

BLUNTSCHLI.   I! No. Was I present?

RAINA.   Yes; and I told the officer who was searching for you that you were not present.

BLUNTSCHLI.   True. I should have remembered it.

RAINA (*greatly encouraged*). Ah, it is natural that you should forget it first. It cost you nothing: it cost me a lie! A lie!

She sits down on the ottoman, looking straight before her with her hands clasped around her knee. Bluntschli, quite touched, goes to the ottoman with a particularly reassuring and considerate air, and sits down beside her.

BLUNTSCHLI.   My dear young lady, dont let this worry you. Remember: I'm a soldier. Now what are the two things that happen to a soldier so often that he comes to think nothing of them? One is hearing people tell lies (*Raina recoils*): the other is getting his life saved in all sorts of ways by all sorts of people.

RAINA (*rising in indignant protest*). And so he becomes a creature incapable of faith and of gratitude.

BLUNTSCHLI (*making a wry face*). Do you like gratitude? I dont. If pity is akin to love, gratitude is akin to the other thing.

RAINA.   Gratitude! (*Turning on him.*) If you are incapable of gratitude you are incapable of any noble sentiment. Even animals are grateful. Oh, I see now exactly what you think of me! You were not surprised to hear me lie. To you it was something I probably did every day! every hour!! That is how men think of women. (*She paces the room tragically.*)

BLUNTSCHLI (*dubiously*). Theres reason in everything. You said youd told only two lies in your whole life. Dear young lady: isnt that rather a short allowance? I'm quite a straightforward man myself; but it wouldnt last me a whole morning.

RAINA (*staring haughtily at him*). Do you know, sir, that you are insulting me?

BLUNTSCHLI.   I cant help it. When you strike that noble attitude and speak in that thrilling voice, I admire you; but I find it impossible to believe a single word you say.

RAINA (*superbly*). Captain Bluntschli!

BLUNTSCHLI (*unmoved*). Yes?

RAINA (*standing over him, as if she could not believe her senses*). Do you mean what you said just now? Do you know what you said just now?

BLUNTSCHLI.   I do.

RAINA (*gasping*). I! I! I!!! (*She points to herself incredulously, meaning "I, Raina Petkoff tell lies!" He meets her gaze unflinchingly. She suddenly sits down beside him, and adds, with a complete change of manner from the heroic to a babyish familiarity.*) How did you find me out?

BLUNTSCHLI (*promptly*). Instinct, dear young lady. Instinct, and experience of the world.

RAINA (*wonderingly*). Do you know, you are the first man I ever met who did not take me seriously?

BLUNTSCHLI.   You mean, dont you, that I am the first man that has ever taken you quite seriously?

RAINA.   Yes: I suppose I do mean that. (*Cosily, quite at her ease with him.*) How strange it is to be talked to in such a way! You know, Ive always gone on like that.

BLUNTSCHLI.   You mean the—?

RAINA.   I mean the noble attitude and the thrilling voice. (*They laugh together.*) I did it when I was a tiny child to my nurse. She believed in it. I do it before my parents. They believe in it. I do it before Sergius. He believes in it.

BLUNTSCHLI.   Yes: he's a little in that line himself, isnt he?

RAINA (*startled*). Oh! Do you think so?

BLUNTSCHLI.   You know him better than I do.

RAINA.   I wonder—I wonder is he? If I thought that—! (*Discouraged.*) Ah, well: what does it matter? I suppose, now youve found me out, you despise me.

BLUNTSCHLI (*warmly, rising*). No, my dear young lady, no, no, no a thousand times. It's part of your youth: part of your charm. I'm like all the rest of them: the nurse, your parents, Sergius: I'm your infatuated admirer.

RAINA (*pleased*). Really?

BLUNTSCHLI (*slapping his breast smartly with his hand, German fashion*). Hand aufs Herz! Really and truly.

RAINA (*very happy*). But what did you think of me for giving you my portrait?

BLUNTSCHLI (*astonished*). Your portrait! You never gave me your portrait.

RAINA (*quickly*). Do you mean to say you never got it?

BLUNTSCHLI.   No. (*He sits down beside her, with renewed interest, and says, with some complacency.*) When did you send it to me?

RAINA (*indignantly*). I did not send it to you. (*She turns her head away, and adds, reluctantly*) It was in the pocket of that coat.

BLUNTSCHLI (*pursing his lips and rounding his eyes*). Oh-o-oh! I never found it. It must be there still.

RAINA (*springing up*). There still! for my father to find the first time he puts his hand in his pocket! Oh, how could you be so stupid?

BLUNTSCHLI (*rising also*). It doesnt matter: I suppose it's only a photograph: how can he tell who it was intended for? Tell him he put it there himself.

RAINA (*bitterly*). Yes: that is so clever! isnt it? (*Distractedly.*) Oh! what shall I do?

BLUNTSCHLI.   Ah, I see. You wrote something on it. That was rash.

RAINA (*vexed almost to tears*). Oh, to have done such a thing for you, who care no more—except to laugh at me—oh! Are you sure nobody has touched it?

BLUNTSCHLI.   Well, I cant be quite sure. You see, I couldnt carry it about with me all the time: one cant take much luggage on active service.

RAINA.   What did you do with it?

BLUNTSCHLI.   When I got through to Pirot I had to put it in safe keeping somehow. I thought of the railway cloak room; but thats the surest place to get looted in modern warfare. So I pawned it.

RAINA.   Pawned it!!!

BLUNTSCHLI.   I know it doesnt sound nice; but it was much the safest plan. I redeemed it the day before yesterday. Heaven only knows whether the pawnbroker cleared out the pockets or not.

RAINA (*furious: throwing the words right into his face*). You have a low shopkeeping mind. You think of things that would never come into a gentleman's head.

BLUNTSCHLI (*phlegmatically*). Thats the Swiss national character, dear lady. (*He returns to the table.*)

RAINA.   Oh, I wish I had never met you. (*She flounces away, and sits at the window fuming.*)

Louka comes in with a heap of letters and telegrams on her salver, and crosses, with her bold free gait, to the table. Her left sleeve is looped up to the shoulder with a brooch, shewing her naked arm, with a broad gilt bracelet covering the bruise.

LOUKA (*to Bluntschli*). For you. (*She empties the salver with a fling on to the table.*) The messenger is waiting. (*She is determined not to be civil to an enemy, even if she must bring him his letters.*)

BLUNTSCHLI (*to Raina*). Will you excuse me: the last postal delivery that reached me was three weeks ago. These are the subsequent accumulations. Four telegrams: a week old. (*He opens one.*) Oho! Bad news!

RAINA (*rising and advancing a little remorsefully*). Bad news?

BLUNTSCHLI.   My father's dead. (*He looks at the telegram with his lips pursed, musing on the unexpected change in his arrangements. Louka crosses herself hastily.*)

RAINA.   Oh, how very sad!

BLUNTSCHLI.   Yes: I shall have to start for home in an hour. He has left a lot of big hotels behind him to be looked after. (*He takes up a fat letter in a long blue envelope.*) Here's a whacking letter from the family solicitor. (*He pulls out the enclosures and glances over them.*) Great Heavens! Seventy! Two hundred! (*In a crescendo of dismay.*) Four hundred! Four thousand!! Nine thousand six hundred!!! What on earth am I do with them all?

RAINA (*timidly*). Nine thousand hotels?

BLUNTSCHLI.   Hotels! nonsense. If you only knew! Oh, it's too ridiculous! Excuse me: I must give my fellow orders about starting. (*He leaves the room hastily, with the documents in his hand.*)

LOUKA (*knowing instinctively that she can annoy Raina by disparaging Bluntschli*). He has not much heart, that Swiss. He has not a word of grief for his poor father.

RAINA (*bitterly*). Grief! A man who has been doing nothing but killing people for years! What does he care? What does any soldier care? (*She goes to the door, restraining her tears with difficulty.*)

LOUKA.   Major Saranoff has been fighting too; and he has plenty of heart left. (*Raina, at the door, draws herself up haughtily and goes out.*) Aha! I thought you wouldn't get much feeling out of your soldier. (*She is following Raina when Nicola enters with an armful of logs for the stove.*)

NICOLA (*grinning amorously at her*). Ive been trying all the afternoon to get a minute alone with you, my girl. (*His countenance changes as he notices her arm.*) Why, what fashion is that of wearing your sleeve, child?

LOUKA (*proudly*). My own fashion.

NICOLA.   Indeed! If the mistress catches you, she'll talk to you. (*He puts the logs down, and seats himself comfortably on the ottoman.*)

LOUKA.   Is that any reason why you should take it on yourself to talk to me?

NICOLA.   Come! dont be co contrary with me. Ive some good news for you. (*She sits down beside him. He takes out some paper money. Louka, with an eager gleam in her eyes, tries to snatch it; but he shifts it quickly to his left hand, out of her reach.*) See! a twenty leva bill! Sergius gave me that, out of pure swagger. A fool and his money are soon parted. Theres ten levas more. The Swiss gave me that for backing up the mistress's and Raina's lies about him. He's no fool, he isnt. You should have heard old Catherine downstairs as polite as you please to me, telling me not to mind the Major being a little impatient; for they knew what a good servant I was—after making a fool and a liar of me before them all! The twenty will go to our savings; and you shall have the ten to spend if youll only talk to me so as to remind me I'm a human being. I get tired of being a servant occasionally.

LOUKA.   Yes: sell your manhood for 30 levas, and buy me for 10! (*Rising scornfully.*) Keep your money. You were born to be a servant. I was not. When you set up your shop you will only be everybody's servant instead of somebody's servant. (*She goes moodily to the table and seats herself regally in Sergius's chair.*)

NICOLA (*picking up his logs, and going to the stove*). Ah, wait til you see. We shall have our evenings to ourselves; and I shall be master in my own house, I promise you. (*He throws the logs down and kneels at the stove.*)

LOUKA.   You shall never be master in mine.

NICOLA (*turning, still on his knees, and squatting down rather forlornly on his calves, daunted by her implacable disdain*). You have a great ambition in you, Louka. Remember: if any luck comes to you, it was I that made a woman of you.

LOUKA.   You!

NICOLA (*scrambling up and going at her*). Yes, me. Who was it made you give up wearing a couple of pounds of false black hair on your head and reddening your lips and cheeks like any other Bulgarian girl! I did. Who taught you to trim your nails, and keep your hands clean, and be dainty about yourself, like a fine Russian lady? Me: do you hear that? me! (*She tosses her head defiantly; and he turns away, adding, more coolly.*) Ive often thought that if Raina were out of the way, and you just a little less of a fool and Sergius just a little more of one, you might come to be one of my grandest customers, instead of only being my wife and costing me money.

LOUKA.   I believe you would rather be my servant than my husband. You would make more out of me. Oh, I know that soul of yours.

NICOLA (*going closer to her for emphasis*). Never you mind my soul; but just listen to my advice. If you want to be a lady, your present behavior to me wont do at all, unless when we're alone. It's too sharp and impudent; and impudence is a sort of familiarity: it shews affection for me. And dont you try being high and mighty with me, either. Youre like all country girls: you think it's genteel to treat a servant the way I treat a stableboy. Thats only your ignorance; and dont you forget it. And dont be so ready to defy everybody. Act as if you expected to have your own way, not as if you expected to be ordered about. The way to get on as a lady is the same as the way to get on as a servant: youve got to know your place: thats the secret of it. And you may depend on me to know my place if you get promoted. Think over it, my girl. I'll stand by you: one servant should always stand by another.

LOUKA (*rising impatiently*). Oh, I must behave in my own way. You take all the courage out of me with your cold-blooded wisdom. Go and put those logs on the fire: thats the sort of thing you understand.

Before Nicola can retort, Sergius comes in. He checks himself a moment on seeing Louka; then goes to the stove.

SERGIUS (*to Nicola*). I am not in the way of your work, I hope.

NICOLA (*in a smooth, elderly manner*). Oh no, sir: thank you kindly. I was only speaking to this foolish girl about her habit of running up here to the library whenever she gets a chance, to look at the books. Thats the worst of her education, sir: it gives her habits above her station. (*To Louka.*) Make that table tidy, Louka, for the Major. (*He goes out sedately.*)

Louka, without looking at Sergius, pretends to arrange the papers on the table. He crosses slowly to her, and studies the arrangement of her sleeve reflectively.

SERGIUS.   Let me see: is there a mark there? (*He turns up the bracelet and sees the bruise made by his grasp. She stands motionless, not looking at him: fascinated, but on her guard.*) Ffff! Does it hurt?

LOUKA.   Yes.

SERGIUS.   Shall I cure it?

LOUKA (*instantly withdrawing herself proudly, but still not looking at him*). No. You cannot cure it now.

SERGIUS (*masterfully*). Quite sure? (*He makes a movement as if to take her in his arms.*)

LOUKA.   Dont trifle with me, please. An officer should not trifle with a servant.

SERGIUS (*indicating the bruise with a merciless stroke of his forefinger*). That was no trifle, Louka.

LOUKA (*flinching; then looking at him for the first time*). Are you sorry?

SERGIUS (*with measured emphasis, folding his arms*). I am never sorry.

LOUKA (*wistfully*). I wish I could believe a man could be as unlike a woman as that. I wonder are you really a brave man?

SERGIUS (*unaffectedly, relaxing his attitude*). Yes: I am a brave man. My heart jumped like a woman's at the first shot; but in the charge I found that I was brave. Yes: that at least is real about me.

LOUKA.   Did you find in the charge that the men whose fathers are poor like mine were any less brave than the men who are rich like you?

SERGIUS (*with bitter levity*). Not a bit. They all slashed and cursed and yelled like heroes. Psha! the courage to rage and kill is cheap. I have an English bull terrier who has as much of that sort of courage as the whole Bulgarian nation, and the whole Russian nation at its back. But he lets my groom thrash him, all the same. Thats your soldier all over! No, Louka: your poor men can cut throats; but they are afraid of their officers; they put up with insults and blows; they stand by and see one another punished like children: aye, and help to do it when they are ordered. And the officers!!! Well (*With a short hard laugh.*) I am an officer. Oh, (*fervently*) give me the man who will defy to the death any power on earth or in heaven that sets itself up against his own will and conscience: he alone is the brave man.

LOUKA.   How easy it is to talk! Men never seem to me to grow up: they all have schoolboy's ideas. You dont know what true courage is.

SERGIUS (*ironically*). Indeed! I am willing to be instructed. (*He sits on the ottoman, sprawling magnificently.*)

LOUKA.   Look at me! How much am I allowed to have my own will? I have to get your room ready for you: to sweep and dust, to fetch and carry. How could that degrade me if it did not degrade you to have it done for you? But (*with subdued passion*) if I were Empress of Russia, above everyone in the world, then!! Ah then, though according to you I could shew no courage at all, you should see, you should see.

SERGIUS.   What would you do, most noble Empress?

LOUKA.   I would marry the man I loved, which no other queen in Europe has the courage to do. If I loved you, though you would be as far beneath me as I am beneath you, I would dare to be the equal of my inferior. Would you dare as much if you loved me? No: if you felt the beginnings of love for me you would not let it grow. You would not dare: you would marry a rich man's daughter because you would be afraid of what other people would say of you.

SERGIUS (*bounding up*). You lie: it is not so, by all the stars! If I loved you, and I were the Czar himself, I would set you on the throne by my side. You know that I love another woman, a woman as high above you as heaven is above earth. And you are jealous of her.

LOUKA.   I have no reason to be. She will never marry you now. The man I told you of has come back. She will marry the Swiss.

SERGIUS (*recoiling*). The Swiss!

LOUKA.   A man worth ten of you. Then you can come to me; and I will refuse you. You are not good enough for me. (*She turns to the door.*)

SERGIUS (*springing after her and catching her fiercely in his arms*). I will kill the Swiss; and afterwards I will do as I please with you.

LOUKA (*in his arms, passive and steadfast*). The Swiss will kill you, perhaps. He has beaten you in love. He may beat you in war.

SERGIUS (*tormentedly*). Do you think I believe that she— she! whose worst thoughts are higher than your best ones, is capable of trifling with another man behind my back?

LOUKA.   Do you think she would believe the Swiss if he told her now that I am in your arms?

SERGIUS (*releasing her in despair*). Damnation! Oh, damnation! Mockery! mockery everywhere! everything I think is mocked by everything I do. (*He strikes himself frantically on the breast.*) Coward! liar! fool! Shall I kill myself like a man, or live and pretend to laugh at myself? (*She again turns to go.*) Louka! (*She stops near the door.*) Remember: you belong to me.

LOUKA (*turning*). What does that mean? An insult?

SERGIUS (*commandingly*). It means that you love me, and that I have had you here in my arms, and will perhaps have you there again. Whether that is an insult I neither know nor care: take it as you please. But (*vehemently*) I will not be a coward and a trifler. If I choose to love you, I dare marry you, in spite of all Bulgaria. If these hands ever touch you again, they shall touch my affianced bride.

LOUKA.   We shall see whether you dare keep your word. And take care. I will not wait long.

SERGIUS (*again folding his arms and standing motionless in the middle of the room*). Yes: we shall see. And you shall wait my pleasure.

Bluntschli, much preoccupied, with his papers still in his hand, enters, leaving the door open for Louka to go out. He goes across to the table, glancing at her as he passes. Sergius, without altering his resolute attitude, watches him steadily. Louka goes out, leaving the door open.

BLUNTSCHLI (*absently, sitting at the table as before, and putting down his papers*). Thats a remarkable looking young woman.

SERGIUS (*gravely, without moving*). Captain Bluntschli.

BLUNTSCHLI.   Eh?

SERGIUS.   You have deceived me. You are my rival. I brook no rivals. At six o'clock I shall be in the drilling-ground on the Klissoura road, alone, on horseback, with my sabre. Do you understand?

BLUNTSCHLI (*staring, but sitting quite at his ease*). Oh, thank you: thats a cavalry man's proposal. I'm in the artillery; and I have the choice of weapons. If I go, I shall take a machine gun. And there shall be no mistake about the cartridges this time.

SERGIUS (*flushing, but with deadly coldness*). Take care, sir. It is not our custom in Bulgaria to allow invitations of that kind to be trifled with.

BLUNTSCHLI (*warmly*). Pooh! dont talk to me about Bulgaria. You dont know what fighting is. But have it your own way. Bring your sabre along. I'll meet you.

SERGIUS (*fiercely delighted to find his opponent a man of spirit*). Well said, Switzer. Shall I lend you my best horse?

BLUNTSCHLI.   No: damn your horse! thank you all the same, my dear fellow. (*Raina comes in, and hears the next sentence.*) I shall fight you on foot. Horseback's too dangerous: I dont want to kill you if I can help it.

RAINA (*hurrying forward anxiously*). I have heard what Captain Bluntschli said, Sergius. You are going to fight. Why? (*Sergius turns away in silence, and goes to the stove, where he stands watching her as she continues, to Bluntschli.*) What about?

BLUNTSCHLI.   I dont know: he hasnt told me. Better not interfere, dear young lady. No harm will be done: Ive often acted as sword instructor. He wont be able to touch me; and I'll not hurt him. It will save explanations. In the morning I shall be off home; and youll never see me or hear of me again. You and he will then make it up and live happily ever after.

RAINA (*turning away deeply hurt, almost with a sob in her voice*). I never said I wanted to see you again.

SERGIUS (*striding forward*). Ha! That is a confession.

RAINA (*haughtily*). What do you mean?

SERGIUS.   You love that man!

RAINA (*scandalized*). Sergius!

SERGIUS.   You allow him to make love to you behind my back, just as you treat me as your affianced husband behind his. Bluntschli: you knew our relations; and you deceived me. It is for that that I call you to account, not for having received favors *I* never enjoyed.

BLUNTSCHLI (*jumping up indignantly*). Stuff! Rubbish! I have received no favors. Why, the young lady doesnt even know whether I'm married or not.

RAINA (*forgetting herself*). Oh! (*Collapsing on the ottoman.*) Are you?

SERGIUS.   You see the young lady's concern, Captain Bluntschli. Denial is useless. You have enjoyed the privilege of being received in her own room, late at night—

BLUNTSCHLI (*interrupting him pepperily*). Yes, you blockhead! she received me with a pistol at her head. Your cavalry were at my heels. I'd have blown out her brains if she'd uttered a cry.

SERGIUS (*taken aback*). Bluntschli! Raina: is this true?

RAINA (*rising in wrathful majesty*). Oh, how dare you, how dare you?

BLUNTSCHLI.   Apologize, man: apologize. (*He resumes his seat at the table.*)

SERGIUS (*with the old measured emphasis, folding his arms*). I never apologize!

RAINA (*passionately*). This is the doing of that friend of yours, Captain Bluntschli. It is he who is spreading this horrible story about me. (*She walks about excitedly.*)

BLUNTSCHLI.   No: he's dead. Burnt alive.

RAINA (*stopping, shocked*). Burnt alive!

BLUNTSCHLI.   Shot in the hip in a woodyard. Couldnt drag himself out. Your fellows' shells set the timber on fire and burnt him, with half a dozen other poor devils in the same predicament.

RAINA.   How horrible!

SERGIUS.   How ridiculous! Oh, war! war! the dream of patriots and heroes! A fraud, Bluntschli. A hollow sham, like love.

RAINA (*outraged*). Like love! You say that before me!

BLUNTSCHLI.   Come, Saranoff: that matter is explained.

SERGIUS.   A hollow sham, I say. Would you have come back here if nothing had passed between you except at the muzzle of your pistol? Raina is mistaken about your friend who was burnt. He was not my informant.

RAINA.   Who then? (*Suddenly guessing the truth.*) Ah, Louka! my maid! my servant! You were with her this morning all that time after—after—Oh, what sort of god is this I have been worshipping! (*He meets her gaze with sardonic enjoyment of her disenchantment. Angered all the more, she goes closer to him, and says, in a lower, intenser tone*) Do you know that I looked out of the window as I went upstairs, to have another sight of my hero; and I saw something I did not understand then. I know now that you were making love to her.

SERGIUS (*with grim humor*). You saw that?

RAINA.   Only too well. (*She turns away, and throws herself on the divan under the centre window, quite overcome.*)

SERGIUS (*cynically*). Raina: our romance is shattered. Life's a farce.

BLUNTSCHLI (*to Raina, whimsically*). You see: he's found himself out now.

SERGIUS (*going to him*). Bluntschli: I have allowed you to call me a blockhead. You may now call me a coward as well. I refuse to fight you. Do you know why?

BLUNTSCHLI.   No; but it doesnt matter. I didnt ask the reason when you cried on; and I dont ask the reason now that you cry off. I'm a professional soldier! I fight when I have to, and am very glad to get out of it when I havnt to. Youre only an amateur: you think fighting's an amusement.

SERGIUS (*sitting down at the table, nose to nose with him*). You shall hear the reason all the same, my professional. The reason is that it takes two men—real men—men of heart, blood and honor—to make a genuine combat. I could no more fight with you than I could make love to an ugly woman. Youve no magnetism: youre not a man: youre a machine.

BLUNTSCHLI (*apologetically*). Quite true, quite true. I always was that sort of chap. I'm very sorry.

SERGIUS.   Psha!

BLUNTSCHLI.   But now that youve found that life isnt a farce, but something quite sensible and serious, what further obstacle is there to your happiness?

RAINA (*rising*). You are very solicitous about my happiness and his. Do you forget his new love—Louka? It is not you that he must fight now, but his rival, Nicola.

SERGIUS.   Rival!! (*Bounding half across the room.*)

RAINA.   Dont you know that theyre engaged?

SERGIUS.   Nicola! Are fresh abysses opening? Nicola!!

RAINA (*sarcastically*). A shocking sacrifice, isnt it? Such beauty! such intellect! such modesty! wasted on a middle-aged servant man. Really, Sergius, you cannot stand by and allow such a thing. It would be unworthy of your chivalry.

SERGIUS (*losing all self-control*). Viper! Viper! (*He rushes to and fro, raging.*)

BLUNTSCHLI.   Look here, Saranoff: youre getting the worst of this.

RAINA (*getting angrier*). Do you realize what he has done, Captain Bluntschli? He has set this girl as a spy on us; and her reward is that he makes love to her.

SERGIUS.   False! Monstrous!

RAINA.   Monstrous! (*Confronting him.*) Do you deny that she told you about Captain Bluntschli being in my room?

SERGIUS.   No; but—

RAINA (*interrupting*). Do you deny that you were making love to her when she told you?

SERGIUS.   No; but I tell you—

RAINA (*cutting him short contemptuously*). It is unnecessary to tell us anything more. That is quite enough for us. (*She turns away from him and sweeps majestically back to the window.*)

BLUNTSCHLI (*quietly, as Sergius, in an agony of mortification, sinks on the ottoman, clutching his averted head between his fists*). I told you you were getting the worst of it, Saranoff.

SERGIUS.   Tiger cat!

RAINA (*running excitedly to Bluntschli*). You hear this man calling me names, Captain Bluntschli?

BLUNTSCHLI.   What else can he do, dear lady? He must defend himself somehow. Come (*very persuasively*): dont quarrel. What good does it do?

Raina, with a gasp, sits down on the ottoman, and after a vain effort to look vexedly at Bluntschli, falls victim to her sense of humor, and actually leans back babyishly against the writhing shoulder of Sergius.

SERGIUS.   Engaged to Nicola! Ha! ha! Ah well, Bluntschli, you are right to take this huge imposture of a world coolly.

RAINA (*quaintly to Bluntschli, with an intuitive guess at his state of mind*). I daresay you think us a couple of grown-up babies, dont you?

SERGIUS (*grinning savagely*). He does: he does. Swiss civilization nursetending Bulgarian barbarism, eh?

BLUNTSCHLI (*blushing*). Not at all, I assure you. I'm only very glad to get you two quieted. There! there! let's be pleasant and talk it over in a friendly way. Where is this other young lady?

RAINA.   Listening at the door, probably.

SERGIUS (*shivering as if a bullet had struck him, and speaking with quiet but deep indignation*). I will prove that that, at least, is a calumny. (*He goes with dignity to the door and opens it. A yell of fury bursts from him as he looks out. He darts into the passage, and returns dragging in Louka, whom he flings violently against the table, exclaiming*) Judge her, Bluntschli. You, the cool impartial man: judge the eavesdropper.

Louka stands her ground, proud and silent.

BLUNTSCHLI (*shaking his head*). I mustnt judge her. I once listened myself outside a tent when there was a mutiny brewing. It's all a question of the degree of provocation. My life was at stake.

LOUKA.   My love was at stake. I am not ashamed.

RAINA (*contemptuously*). Your love! Your curiosity, you mean.

LOUKA (*facing her and retorting her contempt with interest*). My love, stronger than anything you can feel, even for your chocolate cream soldier.

SERGIUS (*with quick suspicion, to Louka*). What does that mean?

LOUKA (*fiercely*). It means—

SERGIUS (*interrupting her slightingly*). Oh, I remember: the ice pudding. A paltry taunt, girl!

Major Petkoff enters, in his shirtsleeves.

PETKOFF.   Excuse my shirtsleeves, gentlemen. Raina: somebody has been wearing that coat of mine: I'll swear it. Somebody with a differently shaped back. It's all burst open at the sleeve. Your mother is mending it. I wish she'd make haste: I shall catch cold. (*He looks more attentively at them.*) Is anything the matter?

RAINA.   No. (*She sits down at the stove, with a tranquil air.*)

SERGIUS.   Oh no. (*He sits down at the end of the table, as at first.*)

BLUNTSCHLI (*who is already seated*). Nothing. Nothing.

PETKOFF (*sitting down on the ottoman in his old place*). Thats all right. (*He notices Louka.*) Anything the matter, Louka?

LOUKA.   No, sir.

PETKOFF (*genially*). Thats all right. (*He sneezes.*) Go and ask your mistress for my coat, like a good girl, will you?

Nicola enters with the coat. Louka makes a pretence of having business in the room by taking the little table with the hookah away to the wall near the windows.

RAINA (*rising quickly as she sees the coat on Nicola's arm*). Here it is papa. Give it to me Nicola; and do you put some more wood on the fire. (*She takes the coat, and brings it to the Major, who stands up to put it on. Nicola attends to the fire.*)

PETKOFF (*to Raina, teasing her affectionately*). Aha! Going to be very good to poor old papa just for one day after his return from the wars, eh?

RAINA (*with solemn reproach*). Ah, how can you say that to me, father?

PETKOFF.   Well, well, only a joke, little one. Come: give me a kiss. (*She kisses him.*) Now give me the coat.

RAINA.   No: I am going to put it on for you. Turn your back. (*He turns his back and feels behind him with his arms for the sleeves. She dexterously takes the photograph from the pocket and throws it on the table before Bluntschli, who covers it with a sheet of paper under the very nose of Sergius, who looks on amazed, with his suspicions roused in the highest degree. She then helps Petkoff on with his coat.*) There, dear! Now are you comfortable?

PETKOFF.   Quite, little love. Thanks. (*He sits down; and Raina returns to her seat near the stove.*) Oh, by the bye, Ive found something funny. Whats the meaning of this? (*He puts his hand into the picked pocket.*) Eh? Hallo! (*He tries the other pocket.*) Well, I could have sworn—! (*Much puzzled, he tries the breast pocket.*) I wonder— (*Trying the original pocket.*) Where can it—? (*He rises exclaiming*) Your mother's taken it!

RAINA (*very red*). Taken what?

PETKOFF.   Your photograph, with the inscription: ''Raina, to her Chocolate Cream Soldier: a Souvenir.'' Now you know theres something more in this than meets the eye; and I'm going to find it out. (*Shouting.*) Nicola!

NICOLA (*coming to him*). Sir!

PETKOFF.   Did you spoil any pastry of Miss Raina's this morning?

NICOLA.   You heard Miss Raina say that I did, sir.

PETKOFF.   I know that, you idiot. Was it true?

NICOLA.   I am sure Miss Raina is incapable of saying anything that is not true, sir.

PETKOFF.   Are you? Then I'm not. (*Turning to the others.*) Come: do you think I dont see it all? (*He goes to Sergius, and slaps him on the shoulder.*) Sergius: youre the chocolate cream soldier, arnt you?

SERGIUS (*starting up*). I! A chocolate cream soldier! Certainly not.

PETKOFF.   Not! (*He looks at them. They are all very serious and very conscious.*) Do you mean to tell me that Raina sends things like that to other men?

SERGIUS (*enigmatically*). The world is not such an innocent place as we used to think, Petkoff.

BLUNTSCHLI (*rising*). It's all right, Major. I'm the chocolate cream soldier. (*Petkoff and Sergius are equally astonished.*) The gracious young lady saved my life by giving me chocolate creams when I was starving: shall I ever forget their flavour! My late friend Stolz told you the story of Pirot. I was the fugitive.

PETKOFF.   You! (*He gasps.*) Sergius: do you remember how those two women went on this morning when we mentioned it? (*Sergius smiles cynically. Petkoff confronts Raina severely.*) Youre a nice young woman, arnt you?

RAINA (*bitterly*). Major Saranoff has changed his mind. And when I wrote that on the photograph, I did not know that Captain Bluntschli was married.

BLUNTSCHLI (*startled into vehement protest*). I'm not married.

RAINA (*with deep reproach*). You said you were.

BLUNTSCHLI.   I did not. I positively did not. I never was married in my life.

PETKOFF (*exasperated*). Raina: will you kindly inform me, if I am not asking too much, which of these gentlemen you are engaged to.?

RAINA.   To neither of them. This young lady (*introducing Louka, who faces them all proudly*) is the object of Major Saranoff's affections at present.

PETKOFF.   Louka! Are you mad, Sergius? Why, this girl's engaged to Nicola.

NICOLA.   I beg your pardon, sir. There is a mistake. Louka is not engaged to me.

PETKOFF.   Not engaged to you, you scoundrel! Why, you had twenty-five levas from me on the day of your betrothal; and she had that gilt bracelet from Miss Raina.

NICOLA (*with cool unction*). We gave it out so, sir. But it was only to give Louka protection. She had a soul above her station; and I have been no more than her confidential servant. I intend, as you know, sir, to set up a shop later on in Sofia; and I look forward to her custom and recommendation should she marry into the nobility. (*He goes out with impressive discretion, leaving them all staring after him.*)

PETKOFF (*breaking the silence*). Well, I am—hm!

SERGIUS.   This is either the finest heroism or the most crawling baseness. Which is it, Bluntschli?

BLUNTSCHLI.   Never mind whether it's heroism or baseness. Nicola's the ablest man Ive met in Bulgaria. I'll make him manager of a hotel if he can speak French and German.

LOUKA (*suddenly breaking out at Sergius*). I have been insulted by everyone here. You set them the example. You owe me an apology.

Sergius, like a repeating clock of which the spring has been touched, immediately begins to fold his arms.

BLUNTSCHLI (*before he can speak*). It's no use. He never apologizes.

LOUKA.   Not to you, his equal and his enemy. To me, his poor servant, he will not refuse to apologize.

SERGIUS (*approvingly*). You are right. (*He bends his knee in his grandest manner.*) Forgive me.

LOUKA.   I forgive you. (*She timidly gives him her hand, which he kisses.*) That touch makes me your affianced wife.

SERGIUS (*springing up*). Ah! I forgot that.

LOUKA (*coldly*). You can withdraw if you like.

SERGIUS.   Withdraw! Never! You belong to me. (*He puts his arm about her.*)

Catherine comes in and finds Louka in Sergius's arms, with all the rest gazing at them in bewildered astonishment.

CATHERINE.   What does this mean?

Sergius releases Louka.

PETKOFF.   Well, my dear, it appears that Sergius is going to marry Louka instead of Raina. (*She is about to break out indignantly at him: he stops her by exclaiming testily*) Dont blame me: Ive nothing to do with it. (*He retreats to the stove.*)

CATHERINE.   Marry Louka! Sergius: you are bound by your word to us!

SERGIUS (*folding his arms*). Nothing binds me.

BLUNTSCHLI (*much pleased by this piece of common sense*). Saranoff: your hand. My congratulations. These heroics of yours have their practical side after all. (*To Louka.*) Gracious young lady: the best wishes of a good Republican! (*He kisses her hand, to Raina's great disgust, and returns to his seat.*)

CATHERINE.   Louka: you have been telling stories.

LOUKA.   I have done Raina no harm.

CATHERINE (*haughtily*). Raina!

Raina, equally indignant, almost snorts at the liberty.

LOUKA.   I have a right to call her Raina: she calls me Louka. I told Major Saranoff she would never marry him if the Swiss gentleman came back.

BLUNTSCHLI (*rising, much surprised*). Hallo!

LOUKA (*turning to Raina*). I thought you were fonder of him than of Sergius. You know best whether I was right.

BLUNTSCHLI.   What nonsense! I assure you, my dear Major, my dear Madam, the gracious young lady simply saved my life, nothing else. She never cared two straws for me. Why, bless my heart and soul, look at the young lady and look at me. She, rich, young, beautiful, with her imagination full of fairy princes and noble natures and cavalry charges and goodness knows what! And I, a commonplace Swiss soldier who hardly knows what a decent life is after fifteen years of barracks and battles: a vagabond, a man who has spoiled all his chances in life through an incurably romantic disposition, a man—

SERGIUS (*starting as if a needle had pricked him and interrupting Bluntschli in incredulous amazement*). Excuse me, Bluntschli: what did you say had spoiled your chances in life?

BLUNTSCHLI (*promptly*). An incurably romantic disposition. I ran away from home twice when I was a boy. I went into the army instead of into my father's business. I climbed the balcony of this house when a man of sense would have dived into the nearest cellar. I came sneaking back here to have another look at the young lady when any other man of my age would have sent the coat back—

PETKOFF.   My coat!

BLUNTSCHLI.   —yes: thats the coat I mean—would have sent it back and gone quietly home. Do you suppose I am the sort of fellow a young girl falls in love with? Why, look at our ages! I'm thirty-four: I dont suppose the young lady is much over seventeen. (*This estimate produces a marked sensation, all the rest turning and staring at one another. He proceeds innocently.*) All that adventure which was life or death to me, was only a schoolgirl's game to her—chocolate creams and hide and seek. Heres the proof! (*He takes the photograph from the table.*) Now, I ask you, would a woman who took the affair seriously have sent me this and written on it ''Raina, to her Chocolate Cream Soldier: a Souvenir''? (*He exhibits the photograph triumphantly, as if it settled the matter beyond all possibility of refutation.*)

PETKOFF.   Thats what I was looking for. How the deuce did it get there? (*He comes from the stove to look at it, and sits down on the ottoman.*)

BLUNTSCHLI (*to Raina, complacently*). I have put everything right, I hope, gracious young lady.

RAINA (*going to the table to face him*). I quite agree with your account of yourself. You are a romantic idiot. (*Bluntschli is unspeakably taken aback.*) Next time, I hope you will know the difference between a schoolgirl of seventeen and a woman of twenty-three.

BLUNTSCHLI (*stupefied*). Twenty-three!

Raina snaps the photograph contemptuously from his hand; tears it up; throws the pieces in his face; and sweeps back to her former place.

SERGIUS (*with grim enjoyment of his rival's discomfiture*). Bluntschli: my one last belief is gone. Your sagacity is a fraud, like everything else. You have less sense than even I!

BLUNTSCHLI (*overwhelmed*). Twenty-three! Twenty-three!! (*He considers.*) Hm! (*Swiftly making up his mind and coming to his host.*) In that case, Major Petkoff, I beg to propose formally to become a suitor for your daughter's hand, in place of Major Saranoff retired.

RAINA.   You dare!

BLUNTSCHLI. If you were twenty-three when you said those things to me this afternoon, I shall take them seriously.

CATHERINE (*loftily polite*). I doubt, sir, whether you quite realize either my daughter's position or that of Major Sergius Saranoff, whose place you propose to take. The Petkoffs and the Saranoffs are known as the richest and most important families in the country. Our position is almost historical: we can go back for twenty years.

PETKOFF. Oh, never mind that, Catherine. (*To Bluntschli.*) We should be most happy, Bluntschli, if it were only a question of your position; but hang it, you know, Raina is accustomed to a very comfortable establishment. Sergius keeps twenty horses.

BLUNTSCHLI. But who wants twenty horses? We're not going to keep a circus.

CATHERINE (*severely*). My daughter, sir, is accustomed to a first-rate stable.

RAINA. Hush, mother: youre making me ridiculous.

BLUNTSCHLI. Oh well, if it comes to a question of an establishment, here goes! (*He darts impetuously to the table; seizes the papers in the blue envelope; and turns to Sergius.*) How many horses did you say?

SERGIUS. Twenty, noble Switzer.

BLUNTSCHLI. I have two hundred horses. (*They are amazed.*) How many carriages?

SERGIUS. Three.

BLUNTSCHLI. I have seventy. Twenty-four of them will hold twelve inside, besides two on the box, without counting the driver and conductor. How many tablecloths have you?

SERGIUS. How the deuce do I know?

BLUNTSCHLI. Have you four thousand?

SERGIUS. No.

BLUNTSCHLI. I have. I have nine thousand six hundred pairs of sheets and blankets, with two thousand four hundred eider-down quilts. I have ten thousand knives and forks, and the same quantity of dessert spoons. I have three hundred servants. I have six palatial establishments, besides two livery stables, a tea garden, and a private house. I have four medals for distinguished services; I have the rank of an officer and the standing of a gentleman; and I have three native languages. Shew me any man in Bulgaria that can offer as much!

PETKOFF (*with childish awe*). Are you Emperor of Switzerland?

BLUNTSCHLI. My rank is the highest known in Switzerland: I am a free citizen.

CATHERINE. Then, Captain Bluntschli, since you are my daughter's choice—

RAINA (*mutinously*). He's not.

CATHERINE (*ignoring her*). —I shall not stand in the way of her happiness. (*Petkoff is about to speak.*) This is Major Petkoff's feeling also.

PETKOFF. Oh, I shall be only too glad. Two hundred horses! Whew!

SERGIUS. What says the lady?

RAINA (*pretending to sulk*). The lady says that he can keep his tablecloths and his omnibuses. I am not here to be sold to the highest bidder. (*She turns her back on him.*)

BLUNTSCHLI. I wont take that answer. I appealed to you as a fugitive, a beggar, and a starving man. You accepted me. You gave me your hand to kiss, your bed to sleep in, and your roof to shelter me.

RAINA. I did not give them to the Emperor of Switzerland.

BLUNTSCHLI. Thats just what I say. (*He catches her by the shoulders and turns her face-to-face with him.*) Now tell us whom you did give them to.

RAINA (*succumbing with a shy smile*). To my chocolate cream soldier.

BLUNTSCHLI (*with a boyish laugh of delight*). Thatll do. Thank you. (*He looks at his watch and suddenly becomes businesslike.*) Time's up, Major. Youve managed those regiments so well that youre sure to be asked to get rid of some of the infantry of the Timok division. Send them home by way of Lom Palanka. Saranoff: dont get married until I come back: I shall be here punctually at five in the evening on Tuesday fortnight. Gracious ladies (*his heels click*) good evening. (*He makes them a military bow, and goes.*)

SERGIUS. What a man! Is he a man!

FOCUS QUESTIONS

1. In a short essay, show how *Arms and the Man* grew out of the Victorian tradition, yet helped pave the way for a modern British theatre.
2. List specific ways in which the play pokes fun at conventional melodrama.
3. Why did Shaw regard his play as an "anti-romantic comedy"?
4. Compare/contrast any two characters and show how their stereotypes originated from earlier drama.
5. What serious message(s) did Shaw hope to communicate to his audience?
6. How does the popular romantic triangle affect the play's larger design?
7. Cite specific examples of dialogue and describe how they demonstrate the playwright's unique mastery of language.

OTHER ACTIVITIES

1. Develop scenic designs for your own production of *Arms and the Man* and show how they respond to Shaw's call for realism.
2. Direct two actors to read Raina's and the stranger's initial (act 1) confrontation in a broad or farcical manner; then repeat the scene, playing it more dramatically this time. Discuss the differences with your actors and audience.
3. Using reviews, photographs, and other available documents, assess an American production of the play.

BIBLIOGRAPHY

Colbourne, Maurice. *The Real Bernard Shaw*. Boston: B. Humphries, 1931.

Dukore, Bernard F. *Bernard Shaw Director*. Seattle: University of Washington Press, 1971.

———. *Bernard Shaw's "Arms and the Man": A Composite Production Book*. Carbondale: Southern Illinois University Press, 1982.

Elliott, R. C. "Shaw's Captain Bluntschli: A Latter-Day Falstaff." *Modern Language Notes* 67 (7): 461–65 (November 1952).

Holroyd, Michael. *Bernard Shaw: The Search for Love, 1856–1898*. New York: Random House, 1988.

Innes, Christopher. *Modern British Drama, 1890–1990*. New York: Cambridge University Press, 1992.

Styan, J. L. *The Elements of Drama*. New York: Cambridge University Press, 1960.

West, E. J. " 'Arma Virumque' Shaw did not Sing." *Colorado Quarterly* 1 (3): 267–80 (Winter 1953).

———. "Hollywood and Mr. Shaw: Some Reflections of Shavian Drama-Into-Cinema." *Educational Theatre Journal* 5 (October 1953): 223–32.

———, ed. *Shaw on the Theatre*. New York: Hill & Wang, 1958.

RECOMMENDED VIDEOTAPES AND RECORDINGS

Arms and the Man. One sound cassette. 1982. Starring Sir Ralph Richardson, Vanessa Redgrave, and Sir John Gielgud. The Talking Tape Co. Ltd., Great Britain.

Omnibus. Two video cassettes. 90 min. 1953. A CBS Television Network production of *Arms and the Man* starring Nanette Fabray and Walter Slezak. Directed by John Burrell. Ford Foundation.

Arms and the Man. Two audiocassettes of the 1994 Shaw Festival Production; CBC Radio Works.

A DREAM PLAY
AUGUST STRINDBERG (1849–1912)

For me, [Strindberg] remains . . . the master, still to this day more modern
than any of us, still our leader.

—EUGENE O'NEILL

From the 1986 Royal Dramatic Theatre production of *The Dream Play,* under the direction of
Ingmar Bergman. *Photo: © Bengt Wanselius.*

APPROACHING EXPRESSIONISM

The Scandinavian drama achieved international recognition through the efforts of two dissimilar playwrights, Henrik Ibsen and August Strindberg, whose respective celebrations of their own artistic freedom contributed to the emergence of the modern theatre. Prompted by the professional rivalry that underscored their controversial reputations in theatres across Scandinavia and western Europe, the accomplishments of each remained oddly irreconcilable, despite overlapping cultural backgrounds and literary influences. Like a coin whose unmatched halves reflect whole but separate images, both playwrights illuminated vastly different landscapes of the dramatic art they served.

In contrast with the Norwegian Ibsen (see Preface to Ibsen, p. 550), whose dramatic imagination was stirred by an austere but balanced temperament, the Swedish Strindberg projected his feelings with fiery abandon, producing an introspective body of work that often blurred the distinction between autobiography and fiction. In turn, critical assessments have either explored his life and art as totally unrelated entities or, at the opposite extreme, reveled in their mutually dynamic dependency. A truly valid assessment of Strindberg's plays must rest somewhere in the middle, since their fascinating themes and rich subtexts are indeed illuminated by relevant biographical associations. Even without them, however, his innate theatrical craftsmanship has stood on solid ground. Furthermore, his innovative use of the sustained confessional narrative, often realized as the externalization of the dream state, has inspired a reputable circle of twentieth-century playwrights ranging from Eugene O'Neill and Edward Albee to Luigi Pirandello, Samuel Beckett, and Harold Pinter. His final works have innovated trends as far reaching as the **Theatre of the Absurd.**

Playwriting dominated Strindberg's prolific and versatile accomplishments as novelist, essayist, short-story writer, poet, painter and scientist, roles that also disclosed his pessimistic view of humanity. Yet his artistic vision drew inspiration from a variety of powerful sources, even when he denied their influence: Schopenhauer, Nietzsche, Swedenborg, Buddhism, the Bible, and world mythology. One of his more enduring convictions was spawned by his misogyny and enhanced by his preoccupation with the impossibility of marriage, thereby becoming a provocative and recurring theme in his work. Still his obsession with women was an undeniable part of his creativity, as his three marriages demonstrated. In fact, two of his wives, Siri von Essen and Harriet Bosse, were prominently featured actresses in his plays. Another was his belief that earth was Hell itself and that answers to life's riddles, to human pain and suffering, and to the ambivalences of love and hate were denied us in this lifetime. No doubt this second conviction sprang from the first, since he viewed women as the source of all material life and imperfection in the world.

When his published assaults on the Swedish establishment were vehemently criticized, he sought voluntary exile in Europe in 1883. While visiting Paris, he learned of his first theatrical success back in Sweden, *Lucky Per's Journey* (1883). But two groundbreaking plays, *The Father* (1887) and *Miss Julie* (1888), brought him notoriety for very different reasons. The first opened to warm applause and good reviews in Denmark, but failed in Sweden. Its lethal battle of the sexes involved a woman's power over her husband through the unexpected disclosure that he might not be the father of their child. This dubious paternity leads to his insanity and death. The second work was attacked for immorality upon publication. It presented a different battle of the sexes, waged under more violent circumstances, in which an aristocratic young woman provokes her father's lackey to the point of sexual aggression and then suffers humiliation and destruction at his hands.

Both plays charted a bold new direction for Strindberg and the modern drama, by introducing characters who were motivated by irrational forces rather than by the tired contrivances previously portrayed on stage. Suspecting that the controversial *Miss Julie* demanded special treatment in actual performance, Strindberg composed a lengthy preface in which he introduced his theories for a ''new drama,'' including approaches to staging, lighting, makeup, and acting. Premieres of *Miss Julie* took place in Denmark, Germany, England, France, Russia, and America before its official Swedish premiere in 1906, exactly eighteen years after its publication. In spite of its subject matter, *Miss Julie*'s intimate and realistic depiction of sexuality advanced the causes of naturalistic tragedy and the treatment of sex on stage.

Returning to Sweden in 1889, he wrote several more plays—his last for the next six years—then left for Berlin in 1892, where his scientific experimentation and dabblings in the occult instigated a five-year odyssey across the continent. Teetering between sanity and madness, he survived this period of crisis, the experience of which he described in his novel, *Inferno* (1897). Emerging with renewed creative energy and a sense of integration with the universe, he now entered the most productive period of his life, only to discover that the repercussions of his *inferno* had radically altered his artistic vision.

This post-*Inferno* phase lifted his stage work from the earthy domain of **naturalism,** with its unrelenting turmoil and violence, to the sublime realm of **symbolism**. Championing the theories and dramaturgical insights of the Belgian playwright, Maurice Maeterlinck (1862–1949), whose intimate chamber plays provided striking alternatives to naturalism through their static form and symbolic content, Strindberg founded the Intimate Theatre in Stockholm in 1907, for which he wrote his own chamber pieces. But this quest to expand the symbolic overtones of his work found its surest solutions in **expressionism,** whose psychological dimensions accommodated his unconventional artistic needs.

Borrowed from the post-impressionist phase of painting with which he was already acquainted, expressionism gave him license to objectify on stage his subjective responses to characterization, action, and theme and to uncover the truth beneath surface reality through bold visual images and provocative stage language. In collaboration with other stage artists, the result in the theatre was a distortion of reality, an abstraction of objects or moods through which Strindberg's internal feelings, including his intellectual and moral impressions, were prominently delineated. This unique theatrical style was not only congruent with the present art movement, but was timely in its corroboration with the psychoanalytical theory promulgated by Sigmund Freud (1856–1939) in this early dawn of the twentieth century.

While it is impossible to reduce the psychological and philosophical complexities of these post-*Inferno* plays to a common denominator, their expansive range of characters and events is more clearly understood as the unified perceptions of a conscious dreamer—often personified in the dramatic action as ''the Stranger'' or ''the Student''—who orchestrates them in a timeless and spaceless void. To what extent this dreamer represents the author can never be fully determined. But if Strindberg's **persona** is evident, its purpose is not to confront society in outworn and conventional ways, but rather to glance inward. Thus his quest for self-enlightenment or need to construct the meaning of existence out of nothing has infused his most influential stage achievements with a totally modern sensibility.

MAJOR WORKS

In addition to novels, short fiction, essays, and poetry, the exceedingly prolific Strindberg wrote sixty plays. Less than a third of these have been performed outside of Sweden, while others, including notable historical dramas, remain untranslated because of their concerns with Swedish history. Impressing audiences toward the end of the 1880s with naturalistic plays like *Comrades, The Father, Miss Julie,* and *Creditors,* Strindberg strove to achieve what consumed him totally—the reality of his own emotions. This led him to incorporate symbolism and expressionism into the writing periods that followed.

Between 1898 to 1903, he wrote twenty-six plays. These include such historical dramas as *Queen Christina, The Saga of the Folkungs, Gustav Vasa,* and *Erik the Fourteenth,* as well as the expressionist *To Damascus,* Parts I, II, and III (1898–1901); the realistic *The Dance of Death,* Parts I and II (1900); and *A Dream Play* (1901). His four chamber pieces, all written in 1907, are *Storm, A Burned House, The Ghost Sonata,* and *The Pelican.* The merging of symbolist and expressionist styles that characterize these plays, however, is memorably illustrated in his earlier work, *A Dream Play,* which, in the playwright's own words, "has attempted to imitate the disconnected but seemingly logical form of a dream."

THE ACTION

Indra's daughter descends to earth and is reincarnated as Agnes. She meets an Officer who is imprisoned in a castle and helps him to escape. Later the Officer waits for someone named Victoria in the alley outside an opera house. His hair turns white with age as time passes, but he continuously waits for her.

Agnes offers her love to a Lawyer. They spend their lives in torment, yet agree to compromise for the sake of their child. The Officer returns and persuades Agnes to go with him to Fairhaven, where the sun always shines. Instead they end up at Foulport, a port plagued with cholera. In spite of the disease, a Poet appears and announces that "love conquers all."

When the Lawyer arrives to take Agnes home or, if she refuses, to court, the Officer disappears. Unwilling to return to humiliation and filth, Agnes chooses to relinquish her human shape. To do so, she must open the door to reveal life's secret. She leads the Poet to Fingal's Grotto, where she interprets the sighing of the wind and reads the Poet's thoughts. But the "right-thinking" people angrily demand the answer to life's riddle. In response, Agnes leads the Poet to the castle and enters, disclosing the secret. The castle turns into flames as "the flower bud on the roof bursts into a giant chrysanthemum."

STRUCTURE AND LANGUAGE

The external, more accessible design of *A Dream Play* is the circular journey in which Indra's Daughter descends to earth to endure a term of human existence until her safe return to Nirvana. But its internal design imitates a dream in which "anything can happen, everything is possible and plausible" [Author's Note]. This potent theatrical metaphor allows Strindberg to conceptualize the raw material of his *inferno,* including his own upward journey from despair to enlightenment, and to abandon the conventional boundaries of stage realism in the hope of discovering what "is concealed behind the door." Equally important, the format accommodates his fullest exploration of expressionism, in which haunting, staccato-like character interactions contrast sharply with more internalized monologues. Furthermore, his success at fashioning a dream state out of this radical theatrical style incorporates the less jarring elements of symbolism to humanize his pessimistic message.

Critics have also viewed the play's rich assortment of allusions as biographical, prompted by the fact that Strindberg's former wife, Harriet Bosse, created the role of Indra's Daughter, the conscious, self-possessed dreamer who remains impervious to the play's assaulting actions and is the driving force behind each male/female encounter. Were they meant to show aspects of Bosse's own personal and artistic relationship with the playwright, as seen through *his* eyes? Sensing some need to qualify the unique design of the play but not exploit its subjective overtones, other critics have interpreted these allusions as reflections of Strindberg's views on art and the unconscious self in relation to his creative process. If either view is valid, then never was the meaning of a play so obscured by its plot, which may have been Strindberg's intention.

A haunting and poetic Eastern mythology frames the play once the Daughter of Indra, the principal god of the Vedas, has descended to a world shattered long ago by ''an act of disobedience followed by crimes, which had to be suppressed.'' Strindberg juxtaposes two worldviews in the prologue: one inspired by his discovery of Buddhism, the spiritual source that rescued him from his *inferno;* the second inspired by a Christian world that lives in the shadow of Adam's sin, wherein his wife Eve was the erring seductress. Wondering if the earth's inhabitants have ever known happiness, Indra's Daughter discovers that ''complaining is their mother tongue!'' Once she takes it upon herself to find out why, her episodic journey—the principal action of the play—finds shape and meaning in the seemingly formless sequence of characters and events that envelop her. Like a second Christ who has come to redeem humankind, she is incarnated as Agnes, the vulnerable but always courageous reflector of characters who know only pain and ''are to be pitied.'' In short, she embodies the human and the divine.

Her first earthly sight is a castle growing out of manure but crowned with a flower bud. The image evokes strong symbolic resonance with its upward striving toward beauty and the ideal, as well as sexual fulfillment, and it embodies the eternal struggle between flesh and spirit, the triumph of life over death. The castle also imprisons an Officer—one of several important male characters who serve symbolic functions but remain nameless throughout—whose freedom becomes Agnes' urgent responsibility. When she liberates him and acquires a shawl into which she hopes to gather all of the world's pain, her journey toward selfhood begins. Equally important, the castle grounds continue to generate growth, and the bud atop its tower matures throughout the dramatic action.

Agnes' human experiences, the kaleidoscopic nature of which contributes to the play's expressionist design, have no boundaries. They include the conventional but transient realities of love, marriage, and motherhood; the gradual onset of spiritual disillusionment and despair; the confrontation with physical disease and suffering; the juxtaposition of images from Heaven and Hell; even the sublime appearance of Christ—once crucified by all the right-thinking people—walking again upon the water. Their cumulative impact recalls the medieval morality play. Even the higher human faculties, personified by philosophy, theology, medicine, and law, fall under Strindberg's scrutiny of their failure to provide us with answers.

The appearance of the selfless Poet, who is the one best able to articulate the artist's pain despite his ingenuous conviction that ''love conquers all,'' prompts a major turning point in the action. Accompanying Agnes/Indra's Daughter to Fingal's Grotto where the Lord of Heaven ''listens to the lamentations of mortals,'' the Poet learns that human beings must ''live as best they can,/ one day at a time.'' The message is delivered in poetry, the language spoken by the gods and first heard in the prologue, which Strindberg now incorporates into the remaining prose text. In response, the Daughter interprets one of the Poet's questions: ''If we are made in God's own image,/ why must we endure this form?'' and then chides him for finding fault with his Creator since ''the riddle of life has yet to be solved.'' When the Grotto ''has changed back to the stage door alley'' where all the right-thinking people threaten to stone Agnes unless she will answer them, the door finally opens. ''What was concealed behind the door?'' asks the Chancellor. ''Nothing! That's the solution to the riddle of the world,'' answers the angry Dean of Theology.

The concluding action is set near the castle of the earlier scene, except that the ''chrysanthemum bud [is] ready to burst into bloom.'' Closing her mortal journey before returning to Indra, the Daughter explains to the Poet that the sinful seduction of Brahman (the divine) by Maya (the worldly) produced human beings who are ''only an illusion, a phantom, a dream image.'' Hence the struggle for redemption can be found only through ''self-denial and suffering,'' despite the woeful clinging of humans to earthly materialism, now represented by ''a wall of human faces, questioning, grieving, despairing'' against the illuminated backdrop to the burning castle. Strindberg's hard message that reality is illusory, perhaps even meaningless, is the stuff of which dreams are made.

ABOUT THE TRANSLATION

In keeping with its innovative expressionist style, any effective presentation of *A Dream Play* must reflect the triumphant merging of heightened production ingredients and strongly imagistic language. While stage directors have necessarily altered specific aspects of Strindberg's script to suit the strengths of their respective acting companies and performance spaces, they have had no choice but to respect the playwright's daring and imaginative dream concept, without which the play's center would quickly topple.

Sensitive to these sweeping and flexible demands, translator Harry G. Carlson has rendered Strindberg's images into an American English "with something approximating the impact they have (or had) in Swedish, even if it means totally recasting certain metaphors to make them more meaningful to an audience with very different expectations than the one Strindberg wrote for."[1] Enlightened by what he saw and heard in live rehearsals, he has preserved the playability and literary accuracy of the original text. The results keep Strindberg's intentions intact.

A DREAM PLAY-IN-PERFORMANCE

The first performance of *A Dream Play* took place at the Swedish Theatre (formerly the Nya Teatern) in Stockholm on April 17, 1907. Under Victor Castegren's heavy-handed direction, the production fell considerably short of Strindberg's expectations, achieving neither the expressionistic, stylized murals nor the dreamlike overtones demanded by the problematical stage directions. Background projections provided by a **stereopticon** failed to enhance the production whose effects were too materialized for a dream. Nevertheless, audiences and critics were sufficiently challenged by the playwright's imaginative script to deem the occasion a success. Although Strindberg wanted to produce the play at his Intimate Theatre, which opened later that year, he was discouraged from doing so as a result of its small stage and limited physical resources.

As *Ein Traumspiel,* the play opened in Berlin on March 17, 1916, in its first production outside Sweden. With strong technical assistance from the Danish scenic designer, Svend Gade, director Rudolph Bernauer successfully met the playwright's expressionistic demands. Later that year, Mauritz Stiller directed a production in Göteborg, Sweden. By the time Max Reinhardt was invited to direct *A Dream Play* at the Royal Dramatic Theatre in Stockholm in 1921, however, the work was officially recognized as one that offered its greatest challenges to the director. Several months later, Reinhardt restaged it at the Deutsches Theatre in Berlin to even greater acclaim. Julius Weissmann's opera version premiered in Duisburg in 1925, confirming the high esteem in which German audiences held this work.

Elsewhere, productions of *A Dream Play* were sporadic, drawing attention to those more adventurous circles for whom theatrical experimentation was the rule, such as the Provincetown Playhouse in New York City where the American premiere took place on January 20, 1926, in a translation by Edwin Bjorkman. The sets were designed by Cleon Throckmorton, and James Light directed. Lasting twenty-seven performances, the production proved memorable for a young American playwright named Eugene O'Neill, whose career had been launched at the Provincetown a few years earlier and would become inspired by Strindberg's influence. The results of O'Neill's experimentation firmly established a generation of American expressionists at work on the New York stage and in league with their continental counterparts. (See Preface to O'Neill, p. 708.)

A Dream Play eventually triggered a more controversial response in Paris in June 1928, when Antonin Artaud's version, *Le Songe, Ou Jeu des Rêves*—the French translation by Strindberg himself—was presented for two matinee performances by the Théâtre Alfred Jarry. Artaud also portrayed the Dean of Theology. The highly unorthodox production sparked both damnation and praise from all sides, but Artaud's irrepressible need to break dramaturgical conventions had found kindred support in Strindberg's work.

A Dream Play found its most inspired realization back at the Royal Dramatic Theatre (Dramaten) in Stockholm under Olof Molander's imaginative direction on October 25, 1935. Molander eventually directed six more productions, not including two radio versions over the next thirty years, preparing yet another at the time of his death in 1966. Each of these—in Copenhagen (1940), Malmö (1947), Göteborg (1947), back in Stockholm (1955), Norrköping (1963), and finally Oslo, Norway (1965), at the New Theatre, which he personally considered his finest to date—responded instinctively to Strindberg's profound theatrical vision. But these productions also reflected Molander's personal beliefs and professional growth of awareness: his long conversion to Catholicism and the catastrophic events of World War II, the effects of which were demonstrated in the smallest details of his vastly divergent interpretations. Equally important was that Molander's commitment to this and other Strindberg plays would establish the playwright's reputation permanently both at home and abroad during the 1940s and 1950s.

During the second half of the twentieth century, a darker and more austere level to *A Dream Play* was uncovered by film director Ingmar Bergman. Prompted by his successful version for the Swedish Radio Theater on May 2, 1963, Bergman's first stage production opened at the Dramaten's intimate 350-seat studio theatre (Lilla Scenen) on March 14, 1970. Adapted as a chamber work and re-titled *The Dream Play,* the *mise-en-scène* consisted of two circular staircases, a few wooden chairs, several folding screens, and a table around which important stage actions were blocked—a radical departure from the elaborate sets and visual effects established by Molander. Emphasizing stark stage imagery, a nondescript red design was hung at the rear stage wall in contrast with the gray and black stage void. Bergman rehearsed his twenty-four actors in their forty-three identified stage characters during a strenuous three-month period, concentrating on the actors' movements, including pantomime and frozen *tableaux,* and spoken language to create the illusion of the play. A more intimate actor-audience relationship was created by the elimination of the proscenium and the extension of the stage floor over the first rows of seats. There was no proscenium curtain. Finally, Bergman condensed the script into fifteen compact scenes that played for an intermissionless hour and forty-five minutes.

By stripping the performance space down to its barest essentials and eliminating the more obvious approaches to expressionism, including the Eastern mysticism, Bergman focused attention on his actors whose task was to expose the nerve of Strindberg's dream, the pain of human existence. His ironic directorial coup, which lost none of the play's expressionistic resonance, remained true to the spare landscapes that characterized much of his work for stage and screen. Having gathered all human suffering into her gray shawl, which she carefully wrapped around herself, Agnes sat anxiously alone on the empty stage in the play's final *tableau.*

REFLECTIONS ON A DREAM PLAY

Ingmar Bergman staged his fourth production of A Dream Play *in Stockholm in 1986. The following reminiscence of that experience originally appeared in his autobiography,* The Magic Lantern.

In 1986, I was to direct Strindberg's *A Dream Play* for the fourth time, a decision that seemed good. *Miss Julie* and *A Dream Play* within the same production year. My room at the Royal Dramatic Theatre, always known as Dramaten, had been repaired. I moved in and felt at home.

Continued

I had been dissatisfied with my previous three productions of this seminal play. The Swedish TV version had come to grief owing to technical disasters (video tapes couldn't even be edited in those days); the performance on the Small Stage [Lilla Scenen] turned out poor despite excellent actors; and the German adventure had been ruined by over-whelming sets.

This time I wanted to play the text with no changes or deletions, just as the writer had written it. My intention was also to translate the very complicated stage directions into technically possible and beautiful solutions. I wanted the audience to experience the stench of the backyard of the Advocate's office, the cold beauty of Fagervik's summer countryside in snow, the sulphurous mist and glint of hell in Skamsund and the magnificent flowers round the Rising Castle, the old theatre behind the theatre corridor.

The small stage at Dramaten was impractical, cramped and shabby, in reality a con-verted cinema which had not had any major repairs since it was opened in the early 1940s. To achieve space and intimacy, we decided to remove four rows of seats and extend the stage by five metres.

In that way, we obtained an outer room and an inner room. The outer room, nearest to the audience, was to be the Writer's domain with his desk by a multi-coloured art-nouveau window, the palm with its coloured lights, the bookcase with its secret door. To the right of the stage was a heap of rubbish dominated by a large but damaged crucifix and the mysterious pantry door. In the corner, as if buried in the dusty junk, "Ugly Edith" sat at her piano. The actress was a skilled pianist, accompanying the events with both action and music.

The front room, achieved by extending the stage, opened on to a magical back room. Ten strong projectors were acquired to play on to five specially constructed screens. We didn't know what images they were to show, but we considered we had plenty of time to think about that. The stage floor was covered with a soft greyish blue carpet, and a ceiling of the same colour was fixed above the outer room. Thus the unusually unpredictable acous-tics on the Small Stage became stable and extremely sensitive. The actors could speak quickly and lightly; the chamber music principle was established.

Then things became more difficult for the producer of *A Dream Play*. Skamsund was followed by Favervik, the inspiration stumbled and tripped rather as if, in the insoluble fugue in Beethoven's Hammerklavier sonata, the precision were to be replaced by too many notes. If you eliminated too much, the scenes died; if you acted it all, the audience tired.

It meant keeping a cool head and introducing a rhythm that had been lost. That was possible and paid dividends, as the text was still strong, harsh, amusing, and poetically tenable. The unexpected intrusion of the school scene, for instance, is splendid. On the other hand, the unhappy coal-heavers are a taxing affair. *A Dream Play* is no longer a dream play, but a topical review with one number of doubtful quality.

However, the most complex problems remained. First Fingal's Cave . . . Indra's Daughter takes the Writer by the hand and, unfortunately for him, leads him to the Fingal's Cave farthest out to sea, where they declaim beautiful and worthless verses about each other, the vilest and the most lovely side by side.

A producer who doesn't give up but lets Strindberg stew in his own juice is faced with almost insuperable problems. How to create Fingal's Cave so that it doesn't sabotage itself? How shall I maneuver the Writer's great lament directed at Indra? It consists largely of complaints. How shall I create that storm, the shipwreck and, most difficult of all, Christ walking on the water?

I tried to make a small theatre performance within the performance. The Writer arranges an acting space with a screen, a chair and a horn gramophone. He wraps Indra's Daughter in an oriental shawl. He crowns himself in front of the mirror with a crown of thorns from the crucifix. He gives some manuscript pages to his fellow player. They slide from playing games into seriousness, from parody into irony, seriousness again, the joy of the amateur, great theatre and pure simple harmony. The sublime stays sublime and what is governed by time is given a touch of tender-hearted irony.

We are pleased with our solution; at last we have found a practical way.

The following scene in the theatre corridor is dull and says nothing, but cannot be excluded. The game with the Righteous, the Secret behind the door and the Advocate's murder of the Daughter's soul runs perfectly smoothly, hastily sketched and never deeply gone into. The only way to overcome this is lightness, swiftness and menace. The Righteous must unconditionally become dangerous when they are seized with anxiety when faced with the emptiness behind the open door.

Despite everything, the final scene at the altar is superb and the Daughter's departure simply gripping. It is preceded by a strange excrescence: Indra's Daughter betrays the Solution of the Mystery of Life. According to his diary, Strindberg was reading about Indian mythology and philosophy at the time of the final production of the drama. He threw the fruits of his reading into the pot and stirred it. They refused to sink to the bottom or give the dish any taste, remaining a piece of Indian saga with no place in the rest of the text.

In the final scene, and in the brisk opening scene, there is an insoluble but well-concealed problem. At the beginning a child is apparently speaking to his father: "The Castle is still growing out of the earth. Do you see how much it has grown since last year?" At the very end, an aging writer is speaking: "Oh, now I feel the whole pain of existence. So this is what it is to be a human being." At first a child and at the end an old man, a human life in between. I shared Indra's Daughter between three actresses. That paid dividends. The beginning glowed, the end was adequate, and even the Mystery of Life became a moving saga in the life experience and sincerity of a great actress. The adult Daughter was to be strong, inquisitive, vital, cheerful, capricious and tragic as she walked through life.

I had never before found the solution to a production with so much labour or so aggravatingly slowly. It had meant wiping out memories of earlier results.

On Friday 14 March we had the first run-through, letting it all go through without interruptions or re-runs. In my diary I wrote: "Frustrating run-through. Sitting there glaring. Totally outside. Totally unmoved. Well, time enough." (The premiere had been planned for 17 April, seventy-nine years to the day after the world premiere.)

On Wednesday 9 April we completed our last day in the rehearsal room. I wrote: "Apprehensions verified and reinforced. Must drive on harder. Sad, but by no means crushed."

Then we moved down to the crush and discomforts of the Small Stage. Distance and the bright working light mercilessly showed up the unevenness in the play. We corrected and changed things, lighting, costumes, masks. My laboriously constructed house of cards collapsed, everything chafing, creaking, refractory.

Continued

The morning after the assassination of Olof Palme, we assembled in the waiting room of the rehearsal hall. It was impossible to start the day's work. We spoke uncertainly and fumblingly, trying to get through to each other. Someone was crying. Our profession becomes so peculiar when reality smashes its way in and massacres our illusory games.

But now Olof Palme had been murdered. How should we behave in our confusion? Should we cancel the rehearsal? Should we cancel the evening performance? Let's abandon *A Dream Play* forever. One can't put on a play about someone going around preaching that "it isn't easy to be a human being." An unendurably out-of-date artistic product, beautiful but distant, perhaps dead.

"Maybe I'm wrong," said one of the young actresses, "but I think we should rehearse, I think we should go on. Whoever killed Palme wanted chaos. If we abandon it, we just add to the chaos. We let our emotions take over. This is something more than incidental private feelings. Chaos mustn't decide."

Slowly and hesitantly, *A Dream Play* became a performance. We rehearsed to an audience. Sometimes they were attentive and enthusiastic, sometimes silent and withdrawn. A cautious optimism began to colour our cheeks. Colleagues were complimentary, we received letters and encouragement.

On Thursday 24 April at seven in the evening (the fact that no one was allowed in after the start of the performance had been announced in all the papers), at last the dress rehearsal started. The actors sensed a slight whiff of success and were cheerfully light-hearted. I took pains to share their happy expectations. Somewhere deep down in my consciousness I had already registered our failure, not that I was dissatisfied with our performance, on the contrary. After all our afflictions, a first-class, well-thought-through and, under the circumstances, well-acted performance was at last on stage. There was no reason for self-reproach.

Nevertheless, I already knew our venture would not make it.

After the dress rehearsal, we assembled in one of the new rehearsal rooms above the Small Stage for sandwiches and champagne. The atmosphere was happy, but also melancholy. It is always hard to part company after a long and close association. I felt a helpless love for these people. The umbilical cord had been cut, but my whole body hurt.

The candles on the table burnt down and flickered, candlegrease dribbling. It was time to part. We embraced and kissed each other as if we were never to meet again. We would meet the next morning, for Christ's sake, we said and laughed. The premiere was the next day.

From THE MAGIC LANTERN *by Ingmar Bergman. Translation copyright © 1988 by Joan Tate. Original copyright © 1987 by Ingmar Bergman. Used by permission of Viking Penguin, a division of Penguin Books USA Inc.*

Note

1. *August Strindberg* FIVE PLAYS *Harry G. Carlson, trans., (Berkeley: University of California Press, 1981), 14.*

A DREAM PLAY
AUGUST STRINDBERG
TRANSLATED BY HARRY G. CARLSON

AUTHOR'S NOTE

In this dream play, as in his earlier dream play, *To Damascus,* the author has attempted to imitate the disconnected but seemingly logical form of a dream. Anything can happen, everything is possible and plausible. Time and space do not exist. Upon an insignificant background of real life events, the imagination spins and weaves new patterns: a blend of memories, experiences, pure inventions, absurdities, and improvisations. (Those who follow the author during the brief hours of his sleepwalker route will perhaps find a certain similarity between the apparent jumble of a dream and life's motley, unmanageable canvas, woven by the "World Weaveress," who sets up the "warp" of human destinies and then constructs the "woof" from our intersecting interests and variable passions.)*

The characters split, double, redouble, evaporate, condense, fragment, cohere. But one consciousness is superior to them all: that of the dreamer. For him there are no secrets, no inconsistencies, no scruples, no laws. He neither condemns nor acquits, only relates. And since dreams are more often painful than happy, a tone of melancholy, and of compassion for all living things, runs through the swaying narrative. Sleep, supposedly a liberator, is often a torturer, but when the torment is at its worst, an awakening reconciles the sufferer with reality. No matter how agonizing reality can be, at this moment, compared with a tormenting dream, it is a pleasure.

CHARACTERS*

The Voice of Indra	The Billposter	The One-Eyed Clerk
Indra's Daughter, *Agnes*	The Voice of Victoria	Three Doctoral Candidates
The Glazier	A Ballet Dancer	Kristine
The Officer, *Alfred*	A Singer	The Quarantine Master
His Father	The Prompter	The Dandy, *Don Juan*
His Mother, *Kristina*	The Policeman	His Attendant
Lina	The Lawyer, *Axel*	The Coquette
The Stage Doorkeeper	The One-Armed Clerk	Her "Friend"

*There is no list of characters in the original (translator).

CHARACTERS

The Poet	The Schoolmaster	The Chancellor of the University
He	A Boy, *Nils*	The Dean of Theology
She, *Victoria*	A Newlywed Husband	The Dean of Philosophy
The Retired Man	A Newlywed Wife	The Dean of Medicine
Three Maids	The Blind Man	The Dean of Law
Ugly Edith	The First Coal Heaver	Dancers and Chorus Members of
Edith's Mother	The Second Coal Heaver	the Opera Company, Children,
The Naval Officer	The Gentleman	Schoolboys, and Sailors
Alice	His Wife	

PROLOGUE

(*The backdrop represents banks of clouds that resemble crumbling slate mountains with ruins of castles and fortresses. The constellations of Leo, Virgo, and Libra can be seen. Between them is the planet Jupiter, shining brightly.* INDRA'S DAUGHTER *is standing on the highest cloud.*)

INDRA'S VOICE (*from above*). Where are you daughter, where?

INDRA'S DAUGHTER.   Here, Father, here!

INDRA'S VOICE.
> You have strayed, child,
> Beware, you're falling . . .
> How did you get here?

INDRA'S DAUGHTER.
> Racing on a cloud, I followed a lightning beam
> from the highest ether . . .
> But the cloud fell, and is still falling . . .
> Oh, great Father Indra, god of gods, what regions
>   have I come to?
> Why is it so close,
> so hard to breathe?

INDRA'S VOICE.
> You have left the second world and entered a third.
> Far from Śukra, the Morning Star,
> you have come to a circle of vapors called Earth.
> Mark there the seventh house of the sun,
> Libra, where the star of day lights the balance scale
>   of autumn
> and day and night weigh the same . . .

INDRA'S DAUGHTER.   You speak of the Earth, is that this dark and heavy world lit by the moon?

INDRA'S VOICE.   It is the densest and heaviest of the spheres that wander space.

INDRA'S DAUGHTER.   Does the sun never shine there?

INDRA'S VOICE.   Of course the sun shines there, but not all the time . . .

INDRA'S DAUGHTER.   My cloud is opening and I can see what's there . . .

INDRA'S VOICE.   What do you see, child?

INDRA'S DAUGHTER.   I see . . . that it is fair . . . with green forests, blue waters, white mountains, and golden fields . . .

INDRA'S VOICE.
> Yes it is fair, as is all Brahmā created . . .
> but it was fairer still
> once, in the dawn of time.
> Then something happened,
> a disturbance in the orbit, perhaps something else,
> an act of disobedience followed by crimes, which
>   had to be suppressed . . .

INDRA'S DAUGHTER.   Now I hear sounds from down below . . . What kind of creatures dwell there?

INDRA'S VOICE.
> Descend and see . . . I'll not slander the Creator's
>   children.
> What you hear is their speech.

INDRA'S DAUGHTER.   It sounds like . . . There's no happiness in it.

INDRA'S VOICE.
> Yes, I know. Complaining
> is their mother tongue!
> They're an ungrateful race,
> impossible to please . . .

INDRA'S DAUGHTER.
> Don't say that, now I hear shouts of joy,
> and shots and boomings, see lightning flashes,
> now bells are ringing, fires are lit,
> and a thousand times a thousand voices
> sing praise and thanks to heaven . . .

(*Pause.*)

You judge them too hard, oh Father . . .

INDRA'S VOICE.

Descend and see, listen and return.

Tell me then if they have cause and reason

for complaints and lamentations . . .

INDRA'S DAUGHTER.   So be it. I'll descend, but come with me, Father!

INDRA'S VOICE.   No, I cannot breathe there . . .

INDRA'S DAUGHTER.

My cloud is descending. The air is close; I'm

suffocating . . .

What I breathe is not air, but smoke and water . . .

So heavy, it draws me down, down,

and now I can feel it turning and rolling.

This third world is surely not the best . . .

INDRA'S VOICE.

Not the best, but not the worst.

This globe of dust spins around like all the others,

and so its creatures sometimes suffer a dizziness

bordering between foolishness and madness ———

Have courage, my child, this is but a trial.

INDRA'S DAUGHTER (*on her knees as the cloud descends*).

I'm falling!

(*The backdrop now represents a forest of giant hollyhocks in bloom: white, pink, sulphur-yellow, violet. Above them rises the gilded roof of a castle topped by a crown-shaped flower bud. Spread out below the foundation walls of the castle are piles of straw, covering manure from the castle stables. On the wings, which remain in place for the entire play, are stylized paintings representing a mixture of interiors, exteriors, and landscapes. The* GLAZIER *and the* DAUGHTER *enter.*)

DAUGHTER.   The castle keeps growing up out of the earth . . . Father, do you see how much it's grown since last year?

GLAZIER (*to himself*). I have never seen this castle before . . . have never heard of a castle growing . . . but ——— (*To the* DAUGHTER *with strong conviction.*) Yes, it's grown seven and a half feet, but that's because it's been fertilized . . . and if you look closely, you'll see that a wing has sprouted on the sunny side.

DAUGHTER.   It should bloom soon since we're past midsummer.

GLAZIER.   Don't you see the flower up there?

DAUGHTER.   Oh, yes, I see it! (*Clapping her hands.*) Tell me, why do flowers grow up out of filth?

GLAZIER (*gently*). They don't like the filth, and so they hurry out of it as fast as they can, up toward the light, to bloom and die.

DAUGHTER.   Do you know who lives in the castle?

GLAZIER.   I used to know, but I forgot.

DAUGHTER.   I think there's a prisoner inside . . . and I'm sure he's waiting for me to set him free.

GLAZIER.   But at what price?

DAUGHTER.   You don't bargain about what you have to do. Let's go in the castle! . . .

GLAZIER.   Yes, let's go!

(*They cross toward the backdrop, which slowly divides to reveal a simple, bare room with a table and a few chairs. On one of the chairs sits an* OFFICER, *wearing a very unusual contemporary military uniform. He is rocking in the chair and striking the table with a saber. The* DAUGHTER *crosses to him and slowly takes the saber out of his hand.*)

DAUGHTER.   No, no, you mustn't do that!

OFFICER.   Oh, please, Agnes, let me keep my saber!

DAUGHTER.   No, you're chopping the table to pieces. (*To the* GLAZIER.) Father, you go down to the harness room and replace the windowpane. We'll see each other later. (*He leaves.*) You're a prisoner in your own room. I've come to set you free.

OFFICER.   I guess I've been expecting this, but I wasn't sure you'd want to.

DAUGHTER.   The castle is strong, with seven walls, but it can be done . . . Do you want to or not?

OFFICER.   To be honest, I don't know. Either way I'll suffer. You have to pay for every joy in life with twice the sorrow. It's hard sitting here, but if I have to buy my freedom, I'll suffer threefold. ——— Agnes, I'd just as soon put up with it, as long as I can see you.

DAUGHTER.   What do you see in me?

OFFICER.   The beauty that gives harmony to the universe. ——— I see in you lines I find only in the orbits of the solar system, in a lovely chord of music, in the vibrations of light. ——— You are a child of heaven . . .

DAUGHTER.   So are you.

OFFICER.   Then why do I have to look after horses? Clean stables and shovel manure?

DAUGHTER.   So that you'll long to get out of here.

OFFICER.   I do, but it's so hard to tear myself away.

DAUGHTER.   But everyone has an obligation to seek freedom in the light.

OFFICER.   Obligation? What about life's obligations to me?

DAUGHTER.   You feel life has wronged you?

OFFICER.   Yes. It's been unjust . . .

(*Voices are heard from behind a screen, which divides the stage. The screen is drawn aside. The* OFFICER *and the* DAUGHTER *look in that direction, then freeze in place. The* MOTHER, *sickly, sits at a table. In front of her burns a tallow candle, and she trims the wick from time to time with a pair of snuffers. On the table are piles of newly sewn shirts, which she is marking with marking ink and a quill pen. A brown wardrobe stands to the left. The* FATHER *brings her a silk shawl.*)

FATHER (*gently*). Don't you want it?

MOTHER.   A silk shawl for me? What use is that, dear? I'll soon be dead.

FATHER.   Then you believe what the doctor said?

MOTHER.   Yes, that too, but mostly I believe the voice I hear inside me.

FATHER (*sorrowfully*).   Then it really is serious . . . And you're thinking of your children, first and last.

MOTHER.   They've been my whole life, my reason for being . . . my joy, and my sorrow . . .

FATHER.   Kristina, forgive me . . . for everything.

MOTHER.   For what? Forgive me, dear. We've tormented each other . . . and why? Neither of us knows. We couldn't do otherwise . . . Anyway, here are the children's new shirts . . . See that they change twice a week, Wednesdays and Sundays, and that Louisa washes them . . . all over . . . Are you going out?

FATHER.   I have to be up at school at eleven.

MOTHER.   Ask Alfred to come in before you go.

FATHER (*pointing to the* OFFICER).   But sweetheart, he's standing right here.

MOTHER.   My eyesight is going too . . . It's getting so dark . . . (*Trims the candle.*) Alfred, come here! (*The* FATHER, *nodding good-bye, walks out through the wall. The* OFFICER *crosses to the* MOTHER.)

MOTHER.   Who is that girl?

OFFICER (*whispering*).   That's Agnes.

MOTHER.   Oh, so that's Agnes. Do you know what they're saying? . . . That she's the daughter of the god Indra, and that she asked to come down to Earth to feel what it's like to be a human being . . . But don't say anything . . .

OFFICER.   She's a divine creature, that's for certain.

MOTHER (*aloud*).   Alfred, my dear, I'm soon going to leave you and your brothers and sisters . . . There's something I want you to remember for the rest of your life.

OFFICER (*sadly*).   Of course, Mother.

MOTHER.   Just one thing: never quarrel with God!

OFFICER.   What do you mean, Mother?

MOTHER.   You mustn't go around feeling that life has wronged you.

OFFICER.   But I've been treated unjustly.

MOTHER.   You're still brooding about the time you were punished for stealing a coin which was later found.

OFFICER.   Yes. That injustice warped my whole life . . .

MOTHER.   I see! Now go over to the wardrobe . . .

OFFICER (*ashamed*).   So, you know. It's . . .

MOTHER.   The copy of *The Swiss Family Robinson* . . . that . . .

OFFICER.   Don't say any more! . . .

MOTHER.   That your brother got punished for . . . when it was *you* who tore it up and hid the pieces.

OFFICER.   Imagine! That wardrobe is still standing there after more than twenty years . . . And we moved so many times, and my mother died ten years ago!

MOTHER.   What difference does that make? Why must you always question everything and spoil the best that life has to offer? . . . Look, there's Lina!

LINA (*enters*).   Ma'am, I'm very grateful, but I can't go to the christening . . .

MOTHER.   Why not, child?

LINA.   I have nothing to wear.

MOTHER.   You can borrow my shawl.

LINA.   That's very kind, but I couldn't do that.

MOTHER.   I don't understand you. I'll never be able to use it again myself.

OFFICER.   What will Father say? It's a present from him . . .

MOTHER.   What small minds you all have . . .

FATHER (*sticking his head in*).   Are you lending my present to one of the maids?

MOTHER.   Don't talk like that . . . Remember, I was a servant once myself . . . Why must you hurt an innocent person?

FATHER.   Why must you hurt me, your husband? . . .

MOTHER.   Oh, what a world! You try to do the right thing and there's always someone who thinks it's wrong . . . If you help one person, you hurt another. What a world! (*She trims the candle so that it goes out. The stage is darkened, and the screen is drawn again.*)

DAUGHTER.   Human beings are to be pitied.

OFFICER.   You think so?

DAUGHTER.   Yes, life is hard, but love conquers all! Come and see! (*They cross upstage.*)

(*The backdrop is raised to reveal a new backdrop which represents an old, dirty, free-standing fire wall. In the middle of the wall a gate opens on an alley, which leads to a brightly lit green area where a giant blue monkshood [aconitum] can be seen. To the left of the gate, in front of a booth, sits the* STAGE DOORKEEPER, *a woman with a shawl over her head and shoulders. She is crocheting a star-patterned comforter. To the right a gas lamp hangs over a billboard which the* BILLPOSTER *is cleaning. Beside him stands a fishing net with a green handle. Farther to the right is a door with an air hole in the shape of a four-leaf clover. To the left of the gate stands a small linden tree with a pitch-black trunk and several pale green leaves. Next to it is a cellar air vent.*)

DAUGHTER (*crossing to the* DOORKEEPER).   Isn't the star comforter finished yet?

DOORKEEPER.   No, dear child. Twenty-six years is no time at all for a piece of work like this.

DAUGHTER.   And your young man never came back?

DOORKEEPER.   No, but it wasn't his fault. He just *had* to leave . . . poor man. That was thirty years ago.

DAUGHTER (*to the* BILLPOSTER).   She was a ballet dancer, wasn't she? Up there, in the opera?

BILLPOSTER.   She was the prima ballerina there . . . but when *he* left, it was as if he took her dancing with him . . . She never got any more parts . . .

DAUGHTER.   Everyone complains, with their eyes if not with their voices . . .

BILLPOSTER.   Oh, I don't complain much any more . . . not since I got a scoop net and green fish box.

DAUGHTER.   And that makes you happy?

BILLPOSTER.   Yes, very happy, very . . . It was my childhood dream and now it's come true. Of course, I just turned fifty . . .

DAUGHTER.   Fifty years for a net and a fish box . . .

BILLPOSTER.   A *green* fish box . . . a *green* one . . .

DAUGHTER (*to the* DOORKEEPER). Give me the shawl now, so I can sit and watch the children of man. But you must stand behind me and tell me about them. (*Puts on the shawl and sits down by the gate.*)

DOORKEEPER.   It's the last performance of the season today and the opera is closing . . . Now they find out if they're rehired . . .

DAUGHTER.   What happens to those who aren't?

DOORKEEPER.   Lord Jesus, you'll see . . . I always pull the shawl over my head . . .

DAUGHTER.   Poor people!

DOORKEEPER.   Look, here comes one! . . . She's not among the chosen ones . . . Do you see how she's crying? . . . (*The* SINGER *rushes out through the gate, her handkerchief covering her eyes. She stops for a moment outside the gate and leans her head against the wall. Then she runs off.*)

DAUGHTER.   Human beings are to be pitied! . . .

DOORKEEPER.   But look: here's the way a happy person looks!

(*The* OFFICER *comes down the alley wearing a frock coat and top hat. He is carrying a bouquet of roses and looks radiantly happy.*)

DOORKEEPER.   He's going to marry Miss Victoria! . . .

OFFICER (*downstage, looks up and sings*). Victoria!

DOORKEEPER.   She'll be right down.

OFFICER.   Fine! I've got the carriage waiting, the table set, and the champagne on ice . . . May I embrace you, ladies? (*Embraces the* DOORKEEPER *and the* DAUGHTER; *sings.*) Victoria!

WOMAN'S VOICE (*singing from above*). I'm here!

OFFICER (*begins to stroll around*). Well, I'm waiting!

DAUGHTER.   Don't you know me?

OFFICER.   No, I know only one woman . . . Victoria! For seven years I've been walking here and waiting for her . . . at noon, when the sun reaches the chimney tops, and in the evening, when darkness begins to fall . . . Look at the pavement here, worn down by a faithful lover. Hurrah! She's mine! (*Sings.*) Victoria! (*There is no answer.*) Oh well, she's probably getting dressed. (*To the* BILLPOSTER.) I see you have a fishing net. Everybody at the Opera is crazy about fishing nets . . . or rather, fish! That's because fish can't sing! . . . What does a thing like that cost?

BILLPOSTER.   It's pretty expensive.

OFFICER (*sings*). Victoria! . . . (*Shakes the linden tree.*) Look, it's getting new leaves again! For the eighth time! . . . (*Sings.*) Victoria! . . . Now she's fixing her hair! . . . (*To the* DAUGHTER.) Ma'am, can I go up and fetch my bride? . . .

DOORKEEPER.   No one is allowed on stage!

OFFICER.   Seven years I've been walking up and down here. Seven times three hundred and sixty-five makes two thousand five hundred and fifty-five! (*Stops and pokes at the door with the clover-shaped hole.*) . . . And I've looked at this door two thousand five hundred and fifty-five times without finding out where it leads to. And this cloverleaf opening to let in light . . . light for whom? Is there someone inside? Does anyone live there?

DOORKEEPER.   I don't know. I've never seen it opened . . .

OFFICER.   It looks like a pantry door I saw when I was four years old and one Sunday afternoon went off with the maid. Off to other houses, other maids. But I never got beyond the kitchen, and I sat between the water barrel and the salt tub. I've seen so many kitchens in my day, and the pantry was always in the entry hall, with round bored holes and a cloverleaf in the door . . . But how can the Opera have a pantry when it has no kitchen? (*Sings.*) Victoria! . . . Listen, she can't leave by any other way, can she, ma'am?

DOORKEEPER.   No, there's no other way out.

OFFICER.   Good, then I can't miss her. (*Theatre people come rushing out, scrutinized by the* OFFICER.) She's got to come out soon! . . . Ma'am, that blue monkshood out there. I saw one like that when I was a child . . . Could it be the same flower? . . . I remember it in a minister's garden when I was seven. There were usually two doves, blue doves, under the hood. . . . But that time a bee came and went into the hood, and I thought: "Now I've got you," and I squeezed the flower. But the bee stung me, right through it, and I cried. And the minister's wife came and put some wet dirt on it. . . . Then we got wild strawberries and milk for supper! . . . I think it's dark already ——— (*To the* BILLPOSTER.) Where are you going?

BILLPOSTER.   Home for supper.

OFFICER (*rubbing his eyes*). Supper? At this time of day? ——— Say . . . can I go in for a moment and phone the Growing Castle?

DAUGHTER.   What for?

OFFICER.   I want to tell the Glazier to put in double windows. It's winter soon and I'm really freezing. (*Goes past the* DOORKEEPER *into her booth.*)

DAUGHTER.   Who is Miss Victoria?

DOORKEEPER.   She's his beloved.

DAUGHTER.   Of course, I see! What she is to other people doesn't interest him. All she is is what she means to him . . . (*It suddenly grows dark.*)

DOORKEEPER (*lights the gas lamp*). It's getting dark quickly today.

DAUGHTER.   For the gods a year is like a minute.

DOORKEEPER.   And for human beings a minute can be as long as a year. (*The* OFFICER *enters again. He looks dusty; his roses have wilted.*)

OFFICER.   She hasn't come yet?

DOORKEEPER.   No.

OFFICER.   She'll come, all right! . . . She'll come! (*Strolls around.*) But maybe it would be wise to phone and cancel lunch, anyway . . . since it's already evening . . . Yes, I'll do that. (*Goes in to telephone.*)

DOORKEEPER (*to the* DAUGHTER). Can I have my shawl back now?

DAUGHTER.   No, my friend, you rest a while longer. I'll do your work . . . I want to know about people and life, to find out if it's as hard as they say.

DOORKEEPER.   But they don't let you sleep on this job, never sleep, day or night . . .

DAUGHTER.   Not sleep at night?

DOORKEEPER.   Well, if you can, with a bell cord tied to your arm. You see, there are night watchmen on the stage, and they're relieved every three hours . . .

DAUGHTER.   But that must be torture . . .

DOORKEEPER.   Maybe you think so, but we're happy to get jobs like this. If you knew how envied I am . . .

DAUGHTER.   Envied? People envy someone who's tortured?

DOORKEEPER.   Yes . . . But do you know what's worse than night work and drudgery and drafts and cold and dampness? Having to listen, as I do, to all the stories of unhappiness up there . . . They all come to me. Why? Maybe they see the lines of suffering in my face and read sympathy there . . . Hidden in this shawl, my dear, are thirty years of anguish, mine and others'! . . .

DAUGHTER.   It's heavy too, and it stings like nettles . . .

DOORKEEPER.   Wear it as long as you like . . . When it gets too heavy, call me, and I'll come and relieve you.

DAUGHTER.   Good-bye. If you could stand it, surely I can.

DOORKEEPER.   We'll see . . . But be kind to my little friends and be patient with their complaining. (*She disappears down the alley.*)

(*Blackout. When the lights come up, the setting is changed: the linden tree has lost its leaves, the blue monkshood is almost withered, and the green area at the end of the alley is autumn brown. The* OFFICER *enters. He now has gray hair and a gray beard. His clothes are dilapidated, his collar black and limp. Only a few petals are left in the bouquet of roses. He strolls around.*)

OFFICER.   All the signs are that summer is over and autumn is near. —— I see that from the linden tree and the monkshood . . . (*Strolling.*) But autumn is my *spring*

because that's when the theatre reopens. And then she must come. Ma'am, would you please let me sit in that chair for awhile.

DAUGHTER.   You sit, my friend, I'll stand.

OFFICER (*sits*). If only I could sleep a little, I'd feel better . . . (*He dozes off for a moment, then jumps up and continues strolling, stopping before the door with the clover-leaf opening and poking at it.*) This door won't give me any peace . . . What's behind it? There must be something! (*Soft music sounds from above in dance rhythm.*) Oh! Rehearsals have begun! (*The lights flash on and off as if the stage were illuminated by a lighthouse beacon.*) What's this? (*In time with the flashes.*) Light and dark; light and dark?

DAUGHTER (*imitating him*). Day and night, day and night! . . . A merciful Providence wants to shorten your waiting. And so the days fly by, chasing the nights! (*The lights remain on again. The* BILLPOSTER *enters, carrying his net and posting equipment.*)

OFFICER.   There's the Billposter, with his net . . . Has the fishing been good?

BILLPOSTER.   Oh, yes! The summer was hot and a bit long . . . The net was pretty good, but not *quite* as I imagined . . .

OFFICER (*stressing the words*). Not quite as I imagined! . . . That's very well put. Nothing is ever as I imagined it! . . . It's always greater in my imagination, better than it turns out to be . . . (*Strolls around striking the walls with the bouquet so that the last petals fall.*)

BILLPOSTER.   Hasn't she come yet?

OFFICER.   No, not yet, but she'll come soon! . . . Do you know what's behind that door?

BILLPOSTER.   No, I've never seen that door open.

OFFICER.   I'm going to phone for a locksmith to come and open it. (*He goes in to phone. The* BILLPOSTER *pastes up a poster and starts exiting right.*)

DAUGHTER.   What's wrong with the net?

BILLPOSTER.   Wrong? Well, there's nothing really wrong . . . It's just not as I imagined it, and so I didn't enjoy it quite as much as . . .

DAUGHTER.   How did you imagine the net?

BILLPOSTER.   How? . . . I can't say exactly . . .

DAUGHTER.   Maybe I can . . . It was different in your imagination. It was green, but not *that* green!

BILLPOSTER.   Yes, you understand, you do! You know everything—and that's why everyone comes to you with their troubles . . . maybe you'd listen to me too, sometime . . .

DAUGHTER.   Of course I will . . . Come over here and tell me what's bothering you . . . (*She goes in her booth. The* BILLPOSTER *stands outside and speaks to her through the window.*)

(*Blackout. When the lights come up, the linden tree has leaves again, the monkshood is in flower, and the open area at the end of the alley shines green in the sun. The* OFFICER *enters. He is now old and white-haired. His clothes are tattered and his shoes worn out. The bouquet is a handful of twigs. He still strolls around, but slowly, like an old man. He reads a poster. A* BALLET DANCER *enters right.*)

OFFICER.   Has Miss Victoria gone?

BALLET DANCER.   No, she hasn't.

OFFICER.   Then I'll wait. She's coming soon, isn't she?

BALLET DANCER (*earnestly*). I'm sure she will.

OFFICER.   Don't go, you'll be able to see what's behind this door. I've sent for the locksmith.

BALLET DANCER.   It'll really be interesting to see that door opened. The door and the Growing Castle. Do you know the Growing Castle?

OFFICER.   Do I? ——— I was a prisoner there.

BALLET DANCER.   No, was that you? Say, why did they have so many horses there?

OFFICER.   It was a horse castle, of course . . .

BALLET DANCER (*painfully*). How stupid of me. I should have known. (*A* SINGER *enters right.*).

OFFICER.   Has Miss Victoria gone?

SINGER (*earnestly*). No, she hasn't gone. She never goes.

OFFICER.   That's because she loves me! . . . Don't leave before the locksmith gets here. He's going to open the door.

SINGER.   Oh, is the door going to be opened? What fun! . . . I just want to ask the Doorkeeper something. (*The* PROMPTER *enters right.*)

OFFICER.   Prompter, has Miss Victoria gone?

PROMPTER.   No, not that I know.

OFFICER.   You see! Didn't I say she was waiting for me? ——— Don't go. The door's going to be opened.

PROMPTER.   What door?

OFFICER.   Is there more than one door?

PROMPTER.   Oh, I know: the one with the cloverleaf . . . I'll have to stay for that! Just want to have a little word with the Doorkeeper. (*The* BALLET DANCER, *the* SINGER, *and the* PROMPTER *gather around the* BILLPOSTER *outside the* DOORKEEPER'*s window, where they take turns speaking to the* DAUGHTER. *The* GLAZIER *enters through the gate.*)

OFFICER.   Are you the locksmith?

GLAZIER.   No, the locksmith had company. A glazier will do just as well.

OFFICER.   Certainly . . . of course. You brought your diamond, didn't you?

GLAZIER.   Naturally! Did you ever hear of a glazier without his diamond?

OFFICER.   Never! ——— Let's get to work! (*He claps his hands. Everyone gathers in a circle around the door. Singers in costumes for* Die Meistersinger *and female dancers from* Aïda *enter right and join them.*) Locksmith—uh, rather, Glazier—do your duty! (*The* GLAZIER *advances with his diamond.*) There aren't many moments

like this in a person's life. And so, dear friends, I beg you . . . consider carefully . . .

POLICEMAN (*entering*). In the name of the law I forbid the opening of this door!

OFFICER.   Oh, God, what a fuss there is when you try to do something new and important! . . . We'll take it to court! . . . Let's go to the Lawyer! We'll see what the law has to say! ——— To the Lawyer!

(*The scene changes, in full view of the audience, to the* LAWYER'*s office: the gate remains and now functions as the gate in an office railing, which extends across the entire stage. The* DOORKEEPER'*s booth turns to open toward the audience and becomes the niche for the* LAWYER'*s desk. The linden tree, leafless, is a clothes tree. The billboard is hung with royal proclamations and court decisions. The door with the four-leaf clover opening is now part of a filing cabinet.*

The LAWYER, *in white tie and tails, is seated on the left inside the railing at a high desk covered with papers. His face bears witness to extraordinary suffering; it is chalk-white, lined, and with purple shadows. He is ugly and his face reflects all the crime and vice his profession has compelled him to come in contact with. He has two* CLERKS, *one of whom has only one arm, the other one eye.*

The people who assembled to observe "the opening of the door" remain but are now clients waiting for the LAWYER *and seem to have been standing there forever. The* DAUGHTER *[in her shawl] and the* OFFICER *are standing downstage.*)

LAWYER (*crossing to the* DAUGHTER). Sister, may I take your shawl? . . . I'll hang it in here until I get a fire going in the stove. Then I'll burn it with all its sorrows and miseries . . .

DAUGHTER.   Not yet, my brother, I want it to be quite full first, and more than anything I want to be able to gather in all your pain, all the confidences you've had to share about crime and vice and unjust imprisonment, about slander and libel . . .

LAWYER.   Your shawl wouldn't be big enough, my child. Look at these walls! Doesn't it seem as if the wallpaper is stained with every kind of sin? Look at these papers: the records I keep of injustice. Look at me . . . I never see any smiles on the people who come here, nothing but angry looks, bared teeth, clenched fists . . . And they spit out all their anger, envy, and suspicions on me . . . You see how black my hands are? I can never get them clean. You see how they're cracked and bleeding . . . I can never wear the same clothes for more than a day or two; they stink of other people's crimes . . . Sometimes I try fumigating the place with smoking sulphur, but it doesn't help. I sleep in the next room and dream of nothing but crimes . . . I have a murder case right now, but as terrible as that is, do you know what's worse? . . . Separating husbands and wives! ——— It's as if heaven and earth cried out against the betrayal—betrayal of Nature, virtue, love . . . And do you know, after all the mutual accusations have filled reams of paper, and someone sympathetic finally grabs one of the parties by the ear, pulls him or her aside, and in a friendly way asks the simple question: ''What have you actually got against your husband or wife?''—they just stand there speechless. They don't know. Oh yes, in one case the trouble started with an argument over a salad. Another time it was a single word, or something equally trivial. But the pain, the suffering! These I have to bear! . . . Look at me! And tell me if you believe that I could win a woman's love with this criminal's face! Or that anyone would even want to be friends with the person responsible for collecting all the unpaid debts in town! . . . You try to act like a human being and you get nothing but misery in return!

DAUGHTER.   Human beings are to be pitied.

LAWYER.   That they are! And what they live on is a mystery to me. They get married on an income of two thousand crowns when they need four thousand . . . Which means they borrow, of course, everybody borrows! They live from hand to mouth till the day they die. And they always leave debts behind them. Who will pay the final reckoning? Tell me that.

DAUGHTER.   He who feeds the birds.

LAWYER.   Yes. But if He who feeds the birds would come down to the earth He made and see what wretches human beings are, maybe He would have some compassion . . .

DAUGHTER.   They are to be pitied.

LAWYER.   They are indeed. (*To the* OFFICER.) What can I do for you?

OFFICER.   I just wanted to ask if Miss Victoria has gone.

LAWYER.   No, she hasn't. You can rest assured of that. Why are you poking at my filing cabinet?

OFFICER.   I was thinking that this door resembles . . .

LAWYER.   No, it doesn't! Absolutely not! (*Church bells can be heard.*)

OFFICER.   Is there a funeral in town?

LAWYER.   No, it's a commencement exercise. Doctoral degrees will be awarded. I was just going over to receive my doctorate in law. Would you like to get a degree and a laurel wreath?

OFFICER.   Sure, why not? I could use a little diversion . . .

LAWYER.   It's an impressive ceremony, and we should probably leave for it right away. ———— Just go and change your clothes.

(*The* OFFICER *exits. Blackout. The setting is changed to a church chancel. The office railing remains but now serves as the balustrade in front of the high altar. The billboard becomes the announcement board for psalms. The linden/clothes tree becomes a candelabra. The* LAWYER'*s desk becomes the* CHANCELLOR'*s lectern. The door with the cloverleaf opening now leads to the vestry . . . The* CHORUS *from* **Die Meistersinger** *become* HERALDS *with staffs, and the*

DANCERS *carry laurel wreaths. The rest of the people are spectators. The backdrop rises, and the new backdrop represents a giant organ; above the keyboard is a mirror. Music sounds. At the sides stand representatives of the four faculties:* PHILOSOPHY, THEOLOGY, MEDICINE, *and* LAW. *The stage is empty for a moment. The* HERALDS *enter right, followed by the* DANCERS, *holding their laurel wreaths out before them. The three* CANDIDATES *enter left, one after the other, are crowned by the* DANCERS, *and exit right. The* LAWYER *advances to receive his wreath. The* DANCERS *turn away, refusing to crown him, and leave. The* LAWYER, *shaken, leans against a pillar. Everyone else exits, leaving him alone. The* DAUGHTER *enters with a white veil over her head and shoulders.*)

DAUGHTER.   Look, I've washed the shawl . . . But why are you standing here? Didn't you get your wreath?

LAWYER.   No, I wasn't worthy.

DAUGHTER.   Why not? Because you defended poor people, spoke up for prisoners' rights, lightened the burdens of the guilty, won reprieves for the condemned . . . Oh these human beings . . . They're no angels; they are pitiful creatures.

LAWYER.   Don't speak badly of them. I can plead their case.

DAUGHTER (*leaning against the organ*). But why must they hurt their own friends so?

LAWYER.   They don't know any better.

DAUGHTER.   Then we'll enlighten them, you and I, together. Shall we?

LAWYER.   They won't accept enlightenment . . . If only our complaints could reach the gods in heaven . . .

DAUGHTER.   They shall reach the throne . . . (*At the organ.*) Do you know what I see in this mirror? . . . The world as it really is! . . . Before it got turned around.

LAWYER.   How did it get turned around?

DAUGHTER.   When the copy was made . . .

LAWYER.   Of course, that's it! The copy . . . I've always felt that this was a false copy . . . and when I began to sense what the original must have been like, I became dissatisfied with everything . . . People called me malcontent and troublemaker and worse . . .

DAUGHTER.   It is a crazy world! Take those representatives of the four university faculties, for example! . . . The government is afraid of change, so it supports all four: theology, the study of God's truth, is always being attacked and ridiculed by philosophy, which claims to be wisdom itself! And medicine, which always challenges philosophy and calls theology not an academic discipline but a superstition . . . And they all sit together on a council which is supposed to teach young people respect—for the university. It's nothing but a madhouse! And heaven help the first persons to see the truth!

LAWYER.   That'll be the theologians. They begin their studies with philosophy, which teaches them that theology is nonsense. Later, in theology, they learn that philosophy is nonsense. Madmen, right?

DAUGHTER. And then there's law, the servant of all, except those who serve it.

LAWYER. All for the sake of justice, in whose name terrible wrongs are committed! . . . By the just, who are so often unjust!

DAUGHTER. That's the way you've arranged things, you children of man! Yes, *children!* ——— Come, I'll give you a wreath . . . one that'll suit you better. (*Puts a crown of thorns on his head.*) Now I'll play for you. (*She sits at the organ and plays a "kyrie," but instead of organ tones, human voices are heard.*)

CHILDREN'S VOICES. Eternal One! Eternal One! (*The last note is held.*)

WOMEN'S VOICES. Have mercy upon us! (*The last note is held.*)

MEN'S VOICES (*tenors*). Save us, for Thy sake!

MEN'S VOICES (*basses*). Spare Thy children, Lord, and be not wrathful against us!

ALL. Have mercy upon us! Hear us! Pity us mortals! ——— Eternal One, why art Thou so far from us? . . . Out of the depths we call: mercy, Eternal One! Make not the burden too heavy for Thy children! Hear us! Hear us!

(*The lights fade. The* DAUGHTER *rises and approaches the* LAWYER. *The lights transform the organ into Fingal's Grotto. The sea swells in between basalt pillars, producing a sound ensemble, a harmony of wind and waves.*)

LAWYER. Where are we, sister?

DAUGHTER. What do you hear?

LAWYER. I hear drops falling . . .

DAUGHTER. Those are tears, human tears . . . What else do you hear?

LAWYER. Sighing . . . moaning . . . wailing . . .

DAUGHTER. The complaints of mortals have reached this far . . . but no further. Why this eternal complaining? Has life no joy to offer?

LAWYER. Yes, the sweetest which is also the bitterest, love! Wife and home; the best things and the worst.

DAUGHTER. Let me try it!

LAWYER. You mean with me?

DAUGHTER. With you! You know the pitfalls, the stumbling blocks. We can avoid them.

LAWYER. But I'm poor.

DAUGHTER. What does that matter, as long as we love each other? And a little beauty doesn't cost anything.

LAWYER. Maybe the things I like you'll dislike.

DAUGHTER. Then we'll compromise.

LAWYER. And if we tire of each other?

DAUGHTER. Then a child will come and bring us delights that are always new!

LAWYER. And you'll have me, an outcast: poor and ugly and despised?

DAUGHTER. Yes! Let us join our destinies!

LAWYER. So be it, then.

(*A very simple room adjoining the* LAWYER'S *office. To the right a large curtained double bed near a window. To the left an iron stove with cooking utensils.* KRISTINE *is pasting over all the cracks between the window and its sash. A door upstage leads to the office, where poor people can be seen waiting to see the* LAWYER. *The* DAUGHTER, *pale and worn, sits by the stove.*)

KRISTINE. I'm pasting, I'm pasting!

DAUGHTER. You're cutting off all the air. I'm suffocating . . .

KRISTINE. There's only one little crack left.

DAUGHTER. Let in some air! I can't breathe.

KRISTINE. I'm pasting, I'm pasting!

LAWYER. That's right, Kristine. Heat costs money.

DAUGHTER. Oh, it's as if you're pasting my mouth shut!

LAWYER (*in the doorway with a paper in his hand*). Is the baby asleep?

DAUGHTER. Yes, finally.

LAWYER (*gently*). Its crying is scaring away my clients.

DAUGHTER (*sympathetically*). What can we do about it?

LAWYER. Nothing.

DAUGHTER. We'll have to get a larger apartment.

LAWYER. We can't afford it.

DAUGHTER. Can't I open the window? This bad air is suffocating me.

LAWYER. Then the heat will escape and we'll freeze.

DAUGHTER. This is dreadful . . . Can we scrub the office then?

LAWYER. You don't have the strength to scrub, neither do I, and Kristine has to paste. She has to paste every crack in the place, ceilings, floors, and walls.

DAUGHTER. I was prepared to be poor, not filthy.

LAWYER. Poverty and filth go together.

DAUGHTER. This is much worse than I dreamed.

LAWYER. It could be a lot worse. We still have food in the house.

DAUGHTER. But what food! . . .

LAWYER. Cabbage is cheap, nourishing and good.

DAUGHTER. For people who like cabbage. To me it's disgusting.

LAWYER. Why haven't you said that before?

DAUGHTER. Because I loved you. I was willing to make a sacrifice.

LAWYER. Then I'll have to give up cabbage. Sacrifices must be mutual.

DAUGHTER. What'll we eat then? Fish? You hate fish.

LAWYER. And it's expensive.

DAUGHTER. This is much harder than I expected.

LAWYER (*sympathetically*). You see how hard it is? . . . And the child, who should have been a blessing, a bond that brought us together . . . is only driving us apart.

DAUGHTER. Dearest! I'm dying in this air, in this room, with its window that looks out on nothing but a backyard, with its endless nights where I lie awake listening to a child crying, and with those people out there, always moaning and quarreling and accusing . . . I'm dying in here.

LAWYER.   My poor little flower, with no light, no air . . .

DAUGHTER.   And you say there are those who have it harder.

LAWYER.   I'm among the most envied people in the neighborhood.

DAUGHTER.   I could manage if only I had a little beauty in my home.

LAWYER.   You mean a flower, don't you, maybe a heliotrope? But it costs one and a half crowns. That's six liters of milk or a half bushel of potatoes.

DAUGHTER.   If I could have my flower, I'd gladly do without food.

LAWYER.   There's one kind of beauty that doesn't cost anything, and when that's absent in a home, it's pure torture for someone with any sense of beauty.

DAUGHTER.   What is that?

LAWYER.   If I tell you, you'll get angry.

DAUGHTER.   We agreed not to get angry.

LAWYER.   We did agree . . . All right, Agnes, providing we can avoid getting snide or sarcastic . . . You know what I mean, don't you?

DAUGHTER.   We won't use harsh tones.

LAWYER.   Not if it's up to me.

DAUGHTER.   Now tell me!

LAWYER.   Well, when I come into a home, the first thing I look for is how the curtains are draped . . . (*Crosses to the window curtains and straightens them.*) . . . If they hang like a string or a rag . . . I leave right away . . . Then I glance at the chairs . . . If they're placed properly, I stay . . . (*Straightens a chair against the wall.*) After that I look at the candles . . . If they're leaning over instead of standing straight, the house is crooked . . . (*Straightens a candle on the bureau.*) That, my dear, is the beauty that doesn't cost anything!

DAUGHTER (*bowing her head*). Not that harsh tone, Axel!

LAWYER.   It wasn't harsh!

DAUGHTER.   Yes, it was!

LAWYER.   Goddamn it! . . .

DAUGHTER.   What sort of language is that?

LAWYER.   Forgive me, Agnes. But I've suffered as much from your untidiness as you have from the dirt. And I didn't dare straighten up things myself, because you'd take it as criticism and get angry . . . Ugh! Shall we stop now?

DAUGHTER.   It's terribly hard to be married . . . harder than anything else. I think you have to be an angel.

LAWYER.   Yes, I think so too.

DAUGHTER.   I'm starting to hate you after all this.

LAWYER.   God help us! Let's try to prevent hatred. I promise never again to comment on your housekeeping . . . even though it's torture for me.

DAUGHTER.   And I'll eat cabbage, even though it's a torment for me.

LAWYER.   And so living together is a torment. One person's pleasure is another's pain.

DAUGHTER.   Human beings are to be pitied!

LAWYER.   You realize that?

DAUGHTER.   Yes. But in God's name, now that we know the pitfalls so well, let's try to avoid them!

LAWYER.   Let's do that! After all, we're enlightened and considerate people. We can forgive and forget.

DAUGHTER.   And we can smile at trifles.

LAWYER.   Yes, we can, of course we can . . . Do you know, I read in the newspaper today . . . By the way—where is the paper?

DAUGHTER (*embarrassed*). Which paper?

LAWYER (*harshly*). Do I get more than one paper?

DAUGHTER.   Try to smile and don't speak harshly . . . I started the fire with your paper . . .

LAWYER (*violently*). Goddamn it!

DAUGHTER.   Remember, smile! . . . I burned it because it ridiculed the things I believe in . . .

LAWYER.   And that I don't believe in. Well! . . . (*Smashes his fist in his hand furiously.*) Oh, I'll smile. I'll smile so hard every tooth will show . . . I'll be considerate and keep my opinions to myself, and be evasive and hypocritical. So, you've burned up my newspaper! Well! (*Adjusts the hanging on the bedpost.*) You see! Here I am tidying up again, and making you angry! . . . Agnes, this is simply impossible!

DAUGHTER.   Of course it is!

LAWYER.   And yet we must put up with it, not because of our vows, but for the sake of the child.

DAUGHTER.   That's true. For the child. Oh! ——— Oh! . . . We must put up with it!

LAWYER.   I have to go out to my clients. Listen to them: buzzing impatiently! They can't wait to tear at each other, to have each other fined and imprisoned . . . lost souls.

DAUGHTER.   Poor, poor human beings! And this pasting! (*She bows her head in silent despair.*)

KRISTINE.   I'm pasting. I'm pasting. (*The* LAWYER *stands at the door, twisting the doorknob nervously.*)

DAUGHTER.   Oh, how the doorknob screeches. It's as if you were twisting a knife in my heart . . .

LAWYER.   I'm twisting, I'm twisting . . .

DAUGHTER.   Please, don't!

LAWYER.   I'm twisting . . .

DAUGHTER.   No!

LAWYER.   I'm . . .

OFFICER (*inside the office, grasps the doorknob*). May I?

LAWYER (*releasing the doorknob*). Of course! After all, you've got your doctorate.

OFFICER.   The whole world is mine! All roads are open to me. I've climbed Parnassus. The laurel wreath is won. Immortality, honor, it's all mine!

LAWYER.   But what will you live on?

OFFICER.   Live on?

LAWYER.   Aren't you going to have a home, clothes, food?

OFFICER.   That's no problem, as long as you have someone who loves you.

LAWYER.   Oh, naturally, of course . . . Of course! Paste, Kristine! Paste! Until no one can breathe! (*He backs out, nodding.*)

KRISTINE.   I'm pasting, I'm pasting! Until no one can breathe!

OFFICER.   Are you coming along now?

DAUGHTER.   Right away! But where?

OFFICER.   To Fairhaven! A summer resort where the sun is shining and there are young people, children, and flowers! With singing and dancing, parties, and feasting!

DAUGHTER.   That's where I want to go!

OFFICER.   Come on!

LAWYER (*entering again*). And I'll return to my first hell . . . this was the second . . . and the worst! The sweetest of all but the worst hell . . . Look, she's dropped hairpins on the floor again . . . (*Picks one up.*)

OFFICER.   Oh, that's nothing!

LAWYER.   Isn't it? . . . Look at it! Two prongs, but one pin. It's two, but it's one. If I straighten it out, it's a single piece. If I bend it, it's two, without ceasing to be one. "And the two shall become as one." But if I break it— like this—then the two are two. (*Breaks the hairpin and throws away the pieces.*)

OFFICER.   What a wonderful image! . . . But in order for you to break it, the prongs have to diverge. If they converge, they hold together!

LAWYER.   But if they're parallel, they never meet, never come together . . . It's like ice on water that neither bears nor breaks.

OFFICER.   The hairpin must be the most perfect thing ever created: both a straight line and two parallel lines at the same time!

LAWYER.   A lock that fastens when it is open!

OFFICER.   Fastening open a braid of hair which remains open when it is fastened . . .

LAWYER.   Like this door. When I close it, I open the way out, for you, Agnes! (*Withdraws and closes the door.*)

DAUGHTER.   And now?

(*Scene change: the bed and canopy are transformed into a tent; the iron stove remains; the backdrop rises. In the foreground to the right charred hills are visible, covered with red heather and tree stumps left black and white after a forest fire; red pigsties and outhouses. Below this is an open-air gymnasium for hospital patients who exercise on machines resembling instruments of torture. In the foreground to the left a section of the quarantine station complex: open sheds with furnaces, boilers, and pipes. Beyond the foreground is a strait of water. The backdrop depicts another island: a beautiful wooded shoreline with flag-bedecked piers where white boats are moored, some with sails hoisted, some not. Between the trees on the shore small country estates with gazebos, kiosks, and marble statues can be seen.*

On the shore of the island in the foreground the QUARANTINE MASTER, *dressed as a Moor, is walking. The* OFFICER *crosses to him and shakes his hand.*)

OFFICER.   If it isn't old Bombast! So you ended up here.

MASTER.   Yes, I did. I'm the Quarantine Master here.

OFFICER.   This is Fairhaven, isn't it?

MASTER.   No, that's over there. This is Foulport.

OFFICER.   Then we came to the wrong place!

MASTER.   We? ——— Aren't you going to introduce me?

OFFICER.   Oh, I couldn't do that. (*Whispering.*) She's Indra's own daughter!

MASTER.   Indra's? And I thought it was the god Varuna himself! . . . Aren't you surprised that I'm wearing a black mask?

OFFICER.   My son, I'm over fifty, so nothing surprises me any more . . . I just assumed you were going to a masquerade this afternoon.

MASTER.   You're absolutely right. And I hope you'll come along.

OFFICER.   Certainly, for there's nothing very . . . appealing about this place. What sort of people do you have staying here?

MASTER.   Sick people. Healthy people are over on the other island.

OFFICER.   Nothing but poor people here, eh?

MASTER.   On the contrary, they're all rich. You see that one being stretched on the rack? He's eaten so much goose liver with truffles and drunk so much burgundy that his feet are curling up on themselves.

OFFICER.   Curling up?

MASTER.   Yes, he's got curly feet . . . And that one over there—lying on the guillotine—he's drunk so much cognac we have to pull him through rollers to straighten his back out.

OFFICER.   And that's no fun, I bet.

MASTER.   Everyone staying on this island has something terrible to hide. Take that one coming now, for example. (*An* Attendant *rolls an elderly* DANDY *in a wheelchair, accompanied by a gaunt, ugly, sixty-year-old* COQUETTE, *dressed in the latest fashion. She is attended by a forty-year-old male* "FRIEND.")

OFFICER.   Why that's the Major! He was in school with us.

MASTER.   Don Juan! And he's still in love with that scarecrow who's with him. He doesn't see that she's grown old, that she's ugly, unfaithful, cruel.

OFFICER.   That's true love! I never would've believed someone that fickle could be capable of loving so deeply and seriously.

MASTER.   What a beautiful way to look at it.

OFFICER.   I've been in love myself with Victoria . . . Yes, I still wait for her in the alley outside the Opera.

MASTER. So, you're the one who waits in the alley?

OFFICER. That's me!

MASTER. And have you gotten the door open yet?

OFFICER. No, the case is still pending . . . The Billposter is out fishing with his new net, you see, so he hasn't testified yet . . . Meanwhile, the Glazier has put in window panes in the castle, which has grown half a story . . . It's been an unusually good year . . . warm and humid.

MASTER. Not as warm as it is here with me!

OFFICER. How hot does it get in those ovens?

MASTER. When we disinfect people suspected of carrying cholera, the temperature is 140 degrees.

OFFICER. Is cholera going around again?

MASTER. Didn't you know? . . .

OFFICER. Yes, of course I did, but I so often forget what I know.

MASTER. I often wish I could forget what I know, especially about myself. That's why I'm always on the lookout for masquerades, fancy dress balls, and spectacular parties.

OFFICER. What've you been up to?

MASTER. If I talk about it, people say I'm boasting. If I keep my mouth shut, they call me a hypocrite.

OFFICER. So that's why you've blackened your face?

MASTER. Yes. A little blacker than I really am.

OFFICER. Who's that coming?

MASTER. Oh, he's a poet, come for his mud bath. (*The* POET *enters, staring up at the sky and carrying a bucket of mud.*)

OFFICER. What? Shouldn't someone like that be bathing in light and air?

MASTER. No, he spends so much time on higher planes that he gets homesick for the mud . . . Wallowing in mire makes his skin as tough as a pig's. Then he can't feel the stings of the critics.

OFFICER. What a strange world of contradictions.

POET (*ecstatically*). Out of clay the creator god Ptah made man on a potter's wheel, a lathe, ——— (*Skeptically.*) ——— or some other damned thing! . . . (*Ecstatically.*) Out of clay the sculptor creates his more or less immortal masterpieces ——— (*Skeptically.*) ——— which are mostly junk! (*Ecstatically.*) Out of clay are manufactured those vessels so necessary in the kitchen and pantry, and which we call jars and plates, ——— (*Skeptically.*) ——— though I don't give a damn what they're called! (*Ecstatically.*) This is clay! In its liquid state it's called mud ——— *C'est mon affaire!* (*Shouting.*) Lina! (LINA *enters carrying a bucket.*) Lina, let Miss Agnes see you . . . She met you ten years ago, when you were a young, happy, and, let's say, pretty girl . . . Look at her now! Five children and a house full of drudgery, screaming, beatings, and starvation. Do you see how her beauty has faded, her joy disappeared? All drained away by duties and responsibilities that should have made her feel fulfilled.

MASTER (*putting his hand over the* POET'S *mouth*). That's enough, shut up!

POET. That's what they all say! And if you do keep quiet, they tell you to speak out! These impossible human beings!

DAUGHTER (*crossing to* LINA). Tell me your troubles.

LINA. No, I don't dare to! Things would only get worse!

DAUGHTER. Who could be that cruel?

LINA. I don't dare talk about it! They'd beat me!

POET. She's right. But I'll talk about it, even if the Moor tries to knock my teeth out! . . . I'll tell how unjust things can be sometimes . . . Agnes, daughter of the gods! Do you hear that music and dancing up there on the hill? . . . Well, that's for Lina's sister, who's come home from town, where she . . . went astray, if you know what I mean . . . Now they're slaughtering the fatted calf for her, while Lina, who stayed at home, has to carry buckets to feed the pigs! . . .

DAUGHTER. But there's rejoicing there, not just because a child came home, but because someone who went astray found the right path again! Don't you see?

POET. Then make it festive every night for this poor woman who never went astray! Do that! . . . But no one will. When Lina has any time off, she goes to prayer meeting where she's scolded for not being perfect! Is that justice?

DAUGHTER. Your questions are so hard to answer . . . Problems I never expected . . .

POET. That's what he said, too—Harun the Just, Caliph of Baghdad! . . . He just sat calmly, up there on his throne, too remote from the troubles of the common people. Finally, their complaints reached his exalted ear. One fine day he stepped down, disguised himself, and walked unnoticed among his subjects to see how justice was being kept.

DAUGHTER. You don't think I'm like Harun the Just, do you?

OFFICER. Let's talk about something else! . . . Here come visitors! (*From the left a white ship shaped like a dragon glides in, with a light blue silk sail flying from a golden yard and a rose-colored pennant flapping on a golden mast.* HE *and* SHE *sit at the helm with their arms around each other.*) Look at them! There's perfect happiness for you, bliss without limits, the triumph of young love! (*The stage becomes brighter.*)

HE (*rises in the boat and sings*).

Hail to thee, fair bay,
where the springtimes of my youth were spent,
where I dreamed those early, rosy dreams!
You have me back again,
but no longer alone!
Greet her,
groves and bays,
sea and sky!

My love, my bride!
My sun, my life!

(*The flags on Fairhaven's piers dip in greeting; white hand-kerchiefs wave from the estates and the beaches, and a chord played on harps and violins sounds over the strait.*)

POET.   See how radiant they are! Listen to that sound across the water! . . . Eros!

OFFICER.   It's Victoria!

MASTER.   Well, what are you going to do about it?

OFFICER.   He has his Victoria and I have mine! And mine no one may see! . . . Hoist the quarantine flag, and I'll haul in the net! (*The* QUARANTINE MASTER *waves a yellow flag. The* OFFICER *pulls on a line, and the boat turns toward Foulport.*) Heave to there! (HE *and* SHE *now notice the dreadful landscape and are horrified.*)

MASTER.   Oh yes! You have to pay the price! Anyone and everyone coming from a contaminated area has to stop here!

POET.   How can you treat them like that, even talk like that to people in love? Leave them alone! Interfering with love is high treason! . . . Alas! Everything beautiful is dragged down, down in the mud. (HE *and* SHE *come ashore, sad and ashamed.*)

HE.   Have pity on us! What have we done?

MASTER.   You don't need to have done anything to be contaminated by life's little troubles.

SHE.   Must joy and happiness be so brief?

HE.   How long must we stay here?

MASTER.   Forty days and forty nights.

SHE.   We'd rather throw ourselves in the sea!

HE.   Live here, among charred hills and pigsties?

POET.   Love conquers all, even sulphur fumes and carbolic acid!

(*The* QUARANTINE MASTER *lights the oven. Blue sulphur fumes rise.*)

MASTER.   I've lit the sulphur! You're welcome to step in!

SHE.   Oh! My blue dress will lose its color.

MASTER.   And turn white! Your red roses will also turn white.

HE.   And your cheeks too. In forty days.

SHE (*to the* OFFICER). This must please you.

OFFICER.   No, it doesn't! . . . It's true that your happiness caused me suffering, but . . . it doesn't matter—I have my doctorate now and a job on that other island . . . Oh yes, I do. This autumn I'll be working in a school there . . . teaching boys the same lessons I had to learn all the time I was growing up, all the time, over and over. And now it'll be the same lessons again, for the rest of my life, the same lessons. How much is two times two? How many times does two go evenly into four? . . . Until I retire, on a pension, with—nothing to do but wait around for meals and newspapers—until finally they carry me out to the crematorium to be burned up . . . Have you got any retired people here? The worst thing I know next to two times two is four is having to begin school again when you already have your doctorate. Asking the same questions over and over until you die . . . (*An elderly man walks past, his hands behind his back.*) Look, there goes a retired person, waiting away his life. He's probably a captain who never made major, or a law clerk who never became a judge—many are called, but few are chosen . . . Nothing to do but wait for his lunch . . .

RETIRED MAN.   No, for the paper! The morning paper!

OFFICER.   And he's only fifty-four years old. He can go on for another twenty-five years waiting for meals and newspapers . . . Isn't that awful?

RETIRED MAN.   Tell me what isn't awful! Go ahead, tell me!

OFFICER.   Yes, whoever can! . . . Now I'll have to teach boys that two and two are four! How many times does two go evenly into four? (*He scratches his head in despair.*) And Victoria, whom I loved and therefore wished the greatest happiness on earth . . . Now she has that happiness, more than she's ever known, and I'm suffering . . . suffering, suffering!

SHE.   Do you think I can be happy when I see you suffering? How can you believe that? Maybe it'll easy your pain that I'll be a prisoner here for forty days and nights. It will, won't it?

OFFICER.   Yes and no! How can I enjoy your suffering? Oh!

HE.   And do you think I can build my happiness on your anguish?

OFFICER.   We're all to be pitied—all of us! (ALL *stretch their hands toward heaven and utter a cry of pain that sounds like a dissonant chord:* "Oh!")

DAUGHTER.   Eternal One, hear them! Life is evil! Human beings are to be pitied! (ALL *cry out again:* "Oh!")

(*The stage grows completely dark for a moment, during which everyone either leaves or changes places. When the lights come up again, Fairhaven's beach is visible in the foreground, but lies in shadow. Beyond the foreground is the strait of water and beyond that Foulport; both are brightly lit. To the right a corner of the resort's clubhouse; through its open windows couples can be seen dancing. Standing on an empty box outside are three* MAIDS, *their arms about each other's waists, watching the dancing. On the terrace of the building is a bench where* UGLY EDITH *is sitting, bareheaded and sad, her massive head of hair tousled. In front of her is a piano, its keyboard open. To the left a yellow frame house. Outside, two children in summer clothes are throwing a ball.*

At the rear of the foreground is a pier with white boats and flags flying from flagpoles. Out in the strait is a white, square-rigged warship with gunports.

But the landscape itself is winter-clad, with snow on the bare trees and ground. The DAUGHTER *and the* OFFICER *enter.*)

DAUGHTER.   It's vacation time, with everyone relaxed and happy! All work has stopped and there's a party every day. Everyone's dressed in holiday finery and there's music and dancing, even in the mornings. (*To the* MAIDS.) Why don't you girls go in and dance?

FIRST MAID.   Us?

OFFICER.   But they're servants!

DAUGHTER.   That's true! . . . But why is Edith sitting there instead of dancing? (EDITH *hides her face in her hands.*)

OFFICER.   Leave her alone! She's been sitting there for three hours and no one has asked her . . . (*He enters the yellow house to the left.*)

DAUGHTER.   What a cruel game! (EDITH's MOTHER, *in a décolleté dress, comes out of the clubhouse and crosses to her daughter.*)

MOTHER.   Why haven't you gone in as I told you to?

EDITH.   Because . . . I can't just invite myself. No one wants to dance with me because I'm ugly, I know that. I don't have to be reminded of it! (*She begins to play J. S. Bach's "Toccata and Fugue" No. 10 on the piano.*)

(*The waltz being played inside the clubhouse can be heard only faintly at first. Then it grows louder, as if to challenge the Bach Toccata. But* EDITH's *playing subdues the waltz music. Clubhouse guests appear in the doorway to hear her play. Everyone on stage listens raptly.*

Then a NAVAL OFFICER *grabs* ALICE, *one of the clubhouse guests, around the waist, and leads her down to the pier.*)

NAVAL OFFICER.   Come quickly! (EDITH *breaks off playing, rises and watches them, her heart broken. She remains standing, as if turned to stone.*)

(*The wall on the yellow house now rises to reveal the interior.* SCHOOLBOYS *sit on three benches. In among them is the* OFFICER, *who looks ill at ease and troubled. The* SCHOOLMASTER, *wearing glasses, and with chalk and a cane in his hands, stands before them.*)

SCHOOLMASTER (*to the* OFFICER). Well, my boy, can you tell me how much two times two is? (*The* OFFICER *remains seated, struggling painfully but unsuccessfully to remember the answer.*) Stand up when you're asked a question!

OFFICER (*rises, tormented*). Two . . . times two . . . Let me see! . . . It's two twos.

SCHOOLMASTER.   I see! You haven't done your homework!

OFFICER (*ashamed*). Yes, I have, but . . . I know what it is, but I can't say it . . .

SCHOOLMASTER.   Don't try that with me, boy! You know it, but can't *say* it! Maybe I can help you! (*He pulls the* OFFICER's *hair.*)

OFFICER.   Ow, this is awful, awful!

SCHOOLMASTER.   Yes, it is awful that a big boy like you has no ambition . . .

OFFICER (*in agony*). A *big* boy! Yes, I *am* big, much bigger than the others here. I'm grown up. I've finished school . . . (*As if awakening.*) . . . Why, I have my doctorate . . . Then what am I doing here? Didn't I get my doctorate?

SCHOOLMASTER.   Yes, of course, but you'll sit here until you're mature, do you understand? You've got to mature . . . That's only right, isn't it?

OFFICER (*clutching his forehead*). Yes, yes, it's only right. You have to mature . . . Two times two . . . is two! And I can prove it by an analogy, the highest form of proof! Listen! One times one is one, therefore two times two is two! What applies to one, applies to the other!

SCHOOLMASTER.   Your proof follows the laws of logic precisely, but the answer is wrong!

OFFICER.   Something that follows the laws of logic can't be wrong. Here's another proof: one goes into one once, therefore two goes into two twice!

SCHOOLMASTER.   Absolutely correct, according to the proof of analogy. But then how much is one times three?

OFFICER.   Three!

SCHOOLMASTER.   Then consequently two times three is also three!

OFFICER (*contemplatingly*). No, that can't be right . . . it can't be . . . otherwise . . . (*Sits down in despair.*) No, I'm not mature yet!

SCHOOLMASTER.   No, you're not, far from it . . .

OFFICER.   But then how long will I have to sit here?

SCHOOLMASTER.   How long? Do you think time and space exist? . . . If time does exist, you should be able to tell me what it is. What is time?

OFFICER.   Time . . . (*Thinking.*) I can't say, but I know what it is: ergo, I *can* know how much two times two is and still not be able to say it! Can you tell me what time is, sir?

SCHOOLMASTER.   Certainly I can!

ALL THE BOYS.   Tell us then!

SCHOOLMASTER.   Time? . . . Let me see! (*Standing motionless, his finger alongside his nose.*) While we speak, time flies. Therefore, time is something that flies while I speak.

A BOY (*rising*). The teacher is speaking, and while he speaks, I fly. Therefore, I am time! (*Flees.*)

SCHOOLMASTER.   That's absolutely correct, according to the laws of logic.

OFFICER.   But then the laws of logic must be crazy! Nils can't be time just because he's flying off!

SCHOOLMASTER.   That's also absolutely correct according to the laws of logic. Although you're right, it is crazy.

OFFICER.   Then logic is crazy!

SCHOOLMASTER.   It really looks that way. But if logic is crazy, then the whole world is crazy . . . And I'll be damned if I stand here teaching you such nonsense! . . . If someone will buy us all a drink, we'll go for a swim!

OFFICER.   But that's a *posterus prius* or turned-around world. You're supposed to swim first and then have a drink! You old fogey!

SCHOOLMASTER.   Don't get arrogant, *Doctor!*

OFFICER.   Officer, if you please! I'm an officer, and I can't understand why I have to sit here among schoolboys and be scolded . . .

SCHOOLMASTER (*raising his finger*).   Because we've got to mature! (*The* QUARANTINE MASTER *enters.*)

MASTER.   The quarantine is beginning!

OFFICER.   Oh, it's you! Can you imagine, this man has me sitting on a school bench, even though I have my doctorate!

MASTER.   Well, why don't you get up and leave?

OFFICER.   Listen to that! . . . Leave? It's not so easy.

SCHOOLMASTER.   No, I bet it isn't. Try!

OFFICER (*to the* QUARANTINE MASTER).   Save me! Save me from his eyes!

MASTER.   Come on! . . . Come on and help us dance . . . We have to dance before the plague breaks out! We have to!

OFFICER.   Then the naval ship is leaving?

MASTER.   Yes, it's the first to leave . . . That'll mean a lot of weeping, of course.

OFFICER.   Always weeping: when it arrives and when it leaves . . . Let's go! (*They exit. The* SCHOOLMASTER *continues his lesson. The* MAIDS, *who were standing at the clubhouse window, now move sadly down toward the pier.* EDITH, *who had been standing by the piano as if turned to stone, follows them slowly.*)

DAUGHTER (*to the* OFFICER).   Isn't there a single happy human being in this paradise?

OFFICER.   Yes, those newlyweds! Listen to them! (*The newlyweds enter.*)

HUSBAND (*to his* WIFE).   My happiness is so great at this moment I wish I could die . . .

WIFE.   Why die?

HUSBAND.   Because in the midst of happiness grows a seed of unhappiness. Happiness consumes itself like a flame. It can't burn forever; sooner or later it must die. And that knowledge destroys the joy for me, right at its peak.

WIFE.   Let us die together then, right now!

HUSBAND.   Die? Very well. I'm afraid of happiness. It's deceitful! (*They cross toward the sea.*)

DAUGHTER (*to the* OFFICER).   Life is cruel. Human beings are to be pitied!

OFFICER.   Do you see that man coming now? He is the most envied person on the island. (*The* BLIND MAN *is led in.*) He owns all the hundred country estates here. All these bays, inlets, beaches, and woods are his, all the fish in the water, the birds in the air, the game in the woods. These thousand people are *his* tenants, and the sun rises on *his* sea and sets on *his* lands . . .

DAUGHTER.   And does he complain too?

OFFICER.   Yes, and with good reason. He can't see.

MASTER.   He's blind . . .

DAUGHTER.   The most envied person of all.

OFFICER.   He's come to see the ship sail. His son is on board.

BLIND MAN.   I can't see, but I can hear! I hear the claw of the anchor tearing at the clay at the bottom of the sea. It's like when you pull the hook out of a fish's throat and the heart follows with it . . . My son, my only child, will travel to foreign lands on the great wide sea. I can only follow him with my thoughts . . . Now I hear the anchor chain screeching . . . and . . . something snapping and flapping like wash hanging on a line . . . wet handkerchiefs perhaps . . . And I hear sobbing and sniffling, like people crying . . . Is it the waves lapping at the ship's planking or the girls on the shore? . . . the abandoned ones . . . inconsolable . . . I once asked a child why the ocean was salty. And the child, whose father was away on a long voyage, answered without hesitation: "The ocean is salty because sailors cry so much." "And why do sailors cry so much?" I asked. "Well," he answered, "because they always have to go away . . . And that's why they always dry their handkerchiefs up in the masts!" . . . "Why do people cry when they're sad?" I continued . . . "Well," he said, "because sometimes you have to wash the windows of your eyes to see more clearly!" . . . (*The ship has set sail and glides away. The girls on the shore alternate waving good-bye with their handkerchiefs and drying their tears. On the foremast the signal "yes" is hoisted, a red ball on a white field.* ALICE *waves joyfully in response.*)

DAUGHTER (*to the* OFFICER).   What does the flag mean?

OFFICER.   It means "yes." The Lieutenant is affirming his love in red, as red as the blood in his heart, etched against the blue of the sky.

DAUGHTER.   And what does "no" look like?

OFFICER.   Blue, as blue as the unclean blood in his veins . . . Look how jubilant Alice is!

DAUGHTER.   While Edith weeps! . . .

BLIND MAN.   Meeting each other and leaving each other. Leaving and meeting. That's what life is! I met his mother. And then she left. But I still had my son, and now he's gone!

DAUGHTER.   He'll come back, you'll see!

BLIND MAN. Who's that speaking to me? I've heard that voice before; in my dreams, in my youth when summer holidays began, then when I got married, and when my child was born. Every time life smiled I heard that voice, like the murmur of the south wind, like a chord of music from above when the angels greet Christmas . . . (*The* LAWYER *enters, crosses to the* BLIND MAN, *and whispers something to him.*)

BLIND MAN. Is that right?

LAWYER. Yes, it is. (*Crossing to the* DAUGHTER.) You've seen just about everything, but you haven't experienced the worst thing of all.

DAUGHTER. What could that be?

LAWYER. The endless repetitions . . . Doing the same things over and over . . . Learning the same lessons again and again . . . Come!

DAUGHTER. Where?

LAWYER. Back to your duties.

DAUGHTER. What are they?

LAWYER. Everything you dread doing. Whatever you don't want to do but must! It means giving up things, denying yourself, going without, leaving behind . . . It's everything unpleasant, disgusting, painful . . .

DAUGHTER. Are there no pleasant duties?

LAWYER. Only those that are already done . . .

DAUGHTER. And no longer exist . . . So duty is everything unpleasant. What's pleasant then?

LAWYER. What's pleasant is what's sinful.

DAUGHTER. Sinful?

LAWYER. And so must be punished. Yes. If I have a really pleasant day and evening, a guilty conscience makes me suffer the pangs of hell the next day.

DAUGHTER. How strange!

LAWYER. Yes, I wake up in the morning with a headache and have to relive the whole experience, only this time totally differently. What was beautiful, witty, and enjoyable the night before, seems ugly, stupid, and disgusting the morning after. It's as if the pleasure turned sour, and the joy dissolved. What people call success is only preparation for the next failure. All the successes in my life have contributed to my ruin. It's human instinct to dread someone else becoming prosperous. People think it's unjust of fate to favor one person over another. So they try to restore the balance by putting obstacles in the paths of others. To have talent can cost you your life, for you can easily starve to death! . . . Anyway, it's either return to your duties or I take you to court, and, if necessary, appeal the case to the highest level!

DAUGHTER. Return? To the iron stove and the cabbage pot, the baby's clothes . . .

LAWYER. That's right. In fact, there's a big load of laundry today. All the handkerchiefs have to be washed . . .

DAUGHTER. Oh, and I have to do all that again?

LAWYER. That's all life is: doing the same things over and over again . . . take the new schoolteacher here . . . He got his doctorate yesterday, with a laurel wreath and the firing of cannon. He ascended Parnassus and was embraced by the king . . . Today he starts back in the schoolhouse again, asking how much two and two are, and will continue until he dies . . . Anyway, come back, to your home!

DAUGHTER. I'd rather die than that!

LAWYER. Die? It's not allowed! First of all, suicide is against the law; second, it means the loss of God's grace—it's a mortal sin!

DAUGHTER. It's never easy being a human being!

ALL. True!

DAUGHTER. I won't return with you to humiliation and filth! . . . I want to go back where I came from, but . . . first, the door must be opened so that I'll know the secret . . . I want the door to be opened!

LAWYER. Then you'll have to retrace your steps, take the same road back, put up with all the horrors of a courtroom trial: reliving and repeating everything, over and over . . .

DAUGHTER. So be it, but first I must seek seclusion in the wilderness to find myself once more. We'll meet again. (*To the* POET.) Come with me! (*Cries of woe sound from Foulport in the distance.*) What was that?

LAWYER. Those are the lost souls in Foulport.

DAUGHTER. But why are they complaining more than usual today?

LAWYER. Because the sun is shining over here, because there's music, dancing, and young people. It makes their suffering so much worse.

DAUGHTER. We must set them free!

LAWYER. Go ahead and try. There was once someone else who wanted to set mankind free, but they hung Him on a cross.

DAUGHTER. Who did?

LAWYER. All the right-thinking people.

DAUGHTER. Who are they?

LAWYER. You mean you don't know who the right-thinking people are? We'll have to introduce you.

DAUGHTER. Were they the ones who denied you your degree?

LAWYER. Yes.

DAUGHTER. Then I know who they are.

(*The Riviera. To the left in the foreground is a white wall above which the tops of fruit-laden orange trees can be seen. Upstage are estates and a casino with a terrace. To the right a large pile of coal with two wheelbarrows. To the right upstage a blue strip of the sea.*

Two COAL HEAVERS, *naked to the waist, their faces, hands, and other exposed parts of their bodies blackened, sit on their wheelbarrows in despair. The* DAUGHTER *and the* LAWYER *appear upstage.*)

DAUGHTER. This is paradise!

1ST COAL HEAVER.   This is hell!

2ND COAL HEAVER.   It's a hundred and fifteen in the shade!

1ST COAL HEAVER.   Shall we cool off in the water?

2ND COAL HEAVER.   The police'll come. You're not allowed to swim here.

1ST COAL HEAVER.   What about picking one of those oranges?

2ND COAL HEAVER.   No, the police would come then too.

1ST COAL HEAVER.   But I can't work in this heat. I'm walking out.

2ND COAL HEAVER.   Then you'll get arrested . . . (*Pause.*) . . . and they'll put you on bread and water . . .

1ST COAL HEAVER.   Bread and water! We work the hardest and get the least to eat! . . . And the rich people, who don't do anything, get the most! . . . If the truth be known, I call that unjust . . . What does the daughter of the gods think?

DAUGHTER.   I don't know what to say . . . What have you done that you should have to work so hard and get so dirty?

1ST COAL HEAVER.   What have we done? We were born poor, and our parents weren't very respectable . . . And maybe we got arrested a couple of times.

DAUGHTER.   Arrested?

1ST COAL HEAVER.   That's right . . . The ones who didn't get arrested are sitting up there in the casino, eating eight-course dinners with wine.

DAUGHTER (*to the* LAWYER). Can that be true?

LAWYER.   For the most part, yes! . . .

DAUGHTER.   Do you mean that everyone has at least once in his life done something to be arrested for?

LAWYER.   Yes.

DAUGHTER.   You too?

LAWYER.   Yes.

DAUGHTER.   Is it true that these poor people can't swim in the sea here?

LAWYER.   Yes, not even with their clothes on. Only people caught trying to drown themselves get away without paying a fine. But I hear the police beat them up later in the station house.

DAUGHTER.   Why don't they go where the beaches aren't private?

LAWYER.   All the beaches are private.

DAUGHTER.   But I mean outside of town, in the country, where the land doesn't belong to anyone.

LAWYER.   It all belongs to someone.

DAUGHTER.   Even the sea? The great, open . . .

LAWYER.   Everything! If you're out on the sea in a boat, you can't even come ashore without getting permission and paying a fee. Beautiful, isn't it?

DAUGHTER.   This is no paradise!

LAWYER.   No, it isn't, I promise you.

DAUGHTER.   Why don't people do something to reform things? . . .

LAWYER.   Oh, they do. But all reformers end up in prison or the madhouse . . .

DAUGHTER.   Who puts them in prison?

LAWYER.   All the right-thinking people, all those honorable . . .

DAUGHTER.   Who puts them in the madhouse?

LAWYER.   Their own despair, when they realize how hopeless their efforts are.

DAUGHTER.   Hasn't anyone ever thought that there might be a hidden reason why things are as they are?

LAWYER.   That's exactly what the people who have it good believe.

DAUGHTER.   That things are good as they are? . . .

1ST COAL HEAVER.   And yet we're the foundations of society. Without the coal we deliver, everything would die out or ground to a halt: the stove in the kitchen, the furnace in the basement, the machine in the factory, the lights on the streets, in the stores, in the homes. Cold and darkness would descend over everything . . . And so we sweat like hell to bring you that black coal . . . What do you give us in return?

LAWYER (*to the* DAUGHTER). Help them . . . (*Pause.*) I can understand that there can't be absolute equality for everyone, but does there have to be this much inequality? (*A* GENTLEMAN *and his* WIFE *cross the stage.*)

WIFE.   Are you going to come and play cards?

GENTLEMAN.   No, I have to take a walk to work up an appetite.

1ST COAL HEAVER.   Work up an appetite?

2ND COAL HEAVER.   Work up an . . . ? (*Children enter and scream in terror when they see the* HEAVERS.)

1ST COAL HEAVER.   They scream when they see us! They scream . . .

2ND COAL HEAVER.   Damn it to hell! . . . It's time to bring out the guillotines and chop away the corruption . . .

1ST COAL HEAVER.   You said it! Goddamn it! (*Spits in disgust.*)

LAWYER (*to the* DAUGHTER). It's all so crazy! But it's not people who are bad . . . it's . . .

DAUGHTER.   What? . . .

LAWYER.   The way they're forced to live . . .

DAUGHTER (*covering her face as she leaves*). This is no paradise!

COAL HEAVERS.   No, it's hell, that's what it is!

(*Fingal's Grotto. Long green waves roll slowly into the cave. In the foreground a red bell buoy bobs on the waves; during the scene it sounds only in the places indicated. The music of the winds. The music of the waves. The* DAUGHTER *and the* POET *enter.*)

POET.   Where have you led me?

DAUGHTER.   Far from the murmur and moaning of the children of man, to the ends of the ocean, to this grotto we call the Ear of Indra since they say that the Lord of Heaven listens here to the lamentations of mortals.

POET. Here? How?

DAUGHTER. Don't you see how the grotto is shaped like a seashell? Yes, of course you do. Don't you realize that your ear is shaped like a seashell? You do, but you haven't thought about it. (*She picks up a shell from the beach.*) Didn't you ever as a child hold a seashell to your ear and listen . . . listen to the buzzing of your heart's blood, the murmur of thoughts in your brain, the bursting of thousands of tiny threads in the fabric of your body . . . These things you could hear in a little shell, imagine what you'll hear in one this big!

POET (*listening*). I hear nothing but the sighing of the wind . . .

DAUGHTER. Then I'll interpret it for you! Listen! The lamentation of the winds. (*Reciting to soft music.*)

Born under heaven's clouds
we were chased by Indra's thunderbolts
down to this dusty earth . . .
The mud of the fields soiled our feet.
We suffered
the smoke of the highways,
the soot of the cities,
the pungent smells of food and wine
and human breath . . .
So we raced out across the open sea
to clean our lungs,
shake our wings,
wash our feet.
Indra, Lord of Heaven,
hear us!
Hear us when we sigh!
The earth is not clean,
life is not good,
human beings are not evil,
nor are they good.
They live as best they can,
one day at a time.
Sons of dust in dust they wander,
of dust they were born
to dust they return.
Instead of wings,
they have only feet to plod with.
If they become dusty,
is the fault theirs
or thine?

POET. This is familiar . . .

DAUGHTER. Hush! The winds sing on! (*Reciting to soft music.*)

We winds, children of the air,
sing the lamentations of men.
Have you heard our song
on autumn nights

in oven doors,
in window cracks,
in the weeping of the rain on the roof tiles,
or on a winter night
in a snowy wood?
Have you heard on a wind-blown sea
the weeping and wailing
in the tackle and sails? . . .
It is we, the winds,
children of the air.
Men breathed us in
and taught us
these songs of pain . . .
In the sickroom, on the battlefield,
but mostly in the nursery,
where the newborn cry
and wail and scream
from the pain of being.
It is we, we, the winds,
who whine and wail
woe! woe! woe!

POET. I'm sure I've heard this . . .

DAUGHTER. Hush! The waves are singing now. (*Reciting to soft music.*)

It is we, the waves,
who rock the winds
to sleep!
Green cradles, we waves.
Wet we are, and salt;
flaming up like fire,
wet flames are we.
Quenching, burning,
bathing, cleansing,
begetting, bearing.
We, we, the waves,
that rock the winds
to sleep!

False waves and faithless. Everything on earth that isn't burned is drowned—in waves. ——— Look here. (*Pointing to a heap of flotsam.*) See what the sea has plundered and smashed . . . All that's left of these sunken ships are their figureheads . . . and their names: Justice, Friendship, Golden Peace, Hope—this is all that's left of hope . . . deceitful hope! . . . Spars, oarlocks, bailers! And look: the lifebuoy . . . it saved itself and let those in distress perish!

POET (*searching in the flotsam*). Here's the nameboard for the Justice. That was the ship that left Fairhaven with the Blind Man's son. Now it's sunk. And Alice's fiancé was on board: Edith's hopeless love.

DAUGHTER. The Blind Man? Fairhaven? I must have dreamed these things. And Alice's fiancé, ugly Edith, Foulport and the quarantine station, the sulphur and carbolic acid, the commencement in the church, the lawyer's office, the stage door alley and Victoria, the Growing Castle and the Officer . . . All these things were in my dreams . . .

POET.   All these things were in my poems . . .

DAUGHTER.   Then you know what poetry is . . .

POET.   Then I know what dreams are . . . What is poetry?

DAUGHTER.   Not reality, but more than reality . . . not dreams, but waking dreams, reveries . . .

POET.   And the children of man think we only play . . . only make-believe!

DAUGHTER.   It's just as well, my friend. Otherwise nothing would ever get done in this world. If people took you seriously, they would only lie on their backs and look up at the sky. No one would touch a plow or a shovel, a pick or a hoe.

POET.   What do you know of these things, Daughter of Indra? You're from another world.

DAUGHTER.   You're right to reproach me. I've stayed too long down here, bathing in mud, like you . . . My thoughts no longer soar: they have clay on their wings, earth on their feet . . . and I ——— (*Lifting her arms.*) ——— feel myself sinking, sinking . . . Help me, Father, Lord of Heaven! (*Silence.*) I can't hear his answers any more! The ether no longer carries the sound from his lips to the shell of my ear . . . the silver thread has snapped . . . Alas! I am earthbound!

POET.   Then you intend to return . . . soon?

DAUGHTER.   As soon as I have burned away this mortal clay . . . for the waters of the ocean cannot make me clean. Why do you ask?

POET.   Because I . . . I have a prayer . . . a petition . . .

DAUGHTER.   What kind of petition? . . .

POET.   A petition from mankind to the ruler of the world, drawn up by a dreamer . . .

DAUGHTER.   To be presented by . . . ?

POET.   By Indra's Daughter . . .

DAUGHTER.   Can you speak the words?

POET.   I can.

DAUGHTER.   Then speak them.

POET.   Better that you should.

DAUGHTER.   Where can I read them?

POET.   In my thoughts, or here! (*Hands her a scroll.*)

DAUGHTER (*takes the scroll but reads aloud without looking at it*). Very well, then I'll speak them.
> "Child of man, why must you be born in pain?
> Why must you hurt your mother so
> to bring her the joy of motherhood,
> joy of joys?
> Why do you awaken to life
> and greet the light
> with a scream of outrage and pain?
> Why don't you smile at life,
> child of man, since the gift of life
> is happiness itself?

> Why are we born like animals,
> we descendents of gods and men?
> The spirit craves other garb
> than this of blood and filth!
> If we are made in God's own image,
> why must we endure this form? . . .''
> . . . Hush! Inquisitive one . . .
> a creation shouldn't find fault with its Creator!
> The riddle of life has yet to be solved! . . .
> ''And thus the pilgrimage begins
> over thorns, stones and thistles.
> The beaten path, you'll find,
> is closed to you.
> If you pick a flower, you learn
> it belongs to someone else.
> If your road is blocked by a field,
> and you must go on,
> you'll trample others' crops
> as others will trample yours
> to even the score.
> Every happiness you enjoy
> brings sorrow to others,
> but your sorrow makes no one happy,
> because sorrow begets only sorrow.
> And when the journey ends in one man's death,
> its purpose seems to give another man breath.''

Son of mortal clay, is this the way you intend to approach the All Highest . . . ?

POET.
> How can a son of mortal clay find
> words luminous, pure and airy enough
> to rise from the earth?
> Child of the gods, will you translate
> our lament into language
> the Immortal One understands?

DAUGHTER.   I will.

POET (*indicating the buoy*). What's that floating there? . . . A buoy?

DAUGHTER.   Yes.

POET.   It looks like a lung with a windpipe.

DAUGHTER.   It's the watchman of the sea. When danger threatens, it sings.

POET.   The sea seems to be rising, and the waves are beginning to . . .

DAUGHTER.   Yes, you're right!

POET.   Oh! What's that? It's a ship . . . beyond the reef.

DAUGHTER.   What ship is it?

POET.   I think it's the ghost ship.

DAUGHTER.   What's that?

POET.   The Flying Dutchman.

DAUGHTER.   Him? Why is he punished so severely, and why does he never come ashore?

POET.   Because he had seven unfaithful wives.

DAUGHTER.   Must he be punished for that?

POET. Yes! All the right-thinking people condemned him . . .

DAUGHTER. Strange world! . . . How can he be set free from the curse?

POET. Free? You have to be careful about setting people free . . .

DAUGHTER. Why?

POET. Because . . . No, it's not the Dutchman! It's just an ordinary ship in distress! . . . Why doesn't the buoy cry out? . . . Look, the sea is rising, the waves getting higher. We'll soon be trapped in this grotto! . . . The ship's bell is ringing! —— We'll soon have another figurehead . . . Cry out, buoy! Do your duty, watchman! . . . (*The buoy sounds a four-part chord in fifths and sixths, resembling a foghorn's signal.*) . . . The crew is waving to us . . . but we ourselves are perishing!

DAUGHTER. Don't you want to be set free?

POET. Yes, of course, of course I do, but not now . . . and not by water!

THE CREW (*singing in four-part*). Christ Kyrie!

Christ Ky- ri- e!

POET. They're calling and the sea is calling. But no one hears.

THE CREW (*as before*). Christ Kyrie!

DAUGHTER. Who's that coming there?

POET. Walking on the water? There's only One who walks upon the water. —— It couldn't be Peter, the rock, for he sank like a stone . . . (*A shimmering white light appears out on the water.*)

THE CREW. Christ Kyrie!

DAUGHTER. Is it He?

POET. It is He, the one they crucified . . .

DAUGHTER. Why—tell me, why was He crucified?

POET. Because He tried to set men free . . .

DAUGHTER. I've forgotten—who crucified Him?

POET. All the right-thinking people.

DAUGHTER. What a strange world!

POET. The sea is rising! It's getting dark . . . The storm's getting worse . . . (THE CREW *screams.*) The crew is screaming in horror now that they see their Savior . . . And . . . they're jumping overboard, in terror of the Redeemer . . . (THE CREW *screams again.*) Now they're screaming because they're going to die! They scream when they're born, and they scream when they die! (*The rising waves in the grotto threaten to drown them.*)

DAUGHTER. If I were sure it was a ship . . .

POET. Actually . . . I don't think it is a ship . . . It's a two-story house with trees outside it . . . and . . . a telephone tower . . . a tower reaching into the clouds . . . It's a modern Tower of Babel, sending wires upward—to communicate with those above . . .

DAUGHTER. Child, human thought needs no wires to travel on . . . The prayers of the faithful penetrate all worlds . . . It's definitely not the Tower of Babel. If you want to storm heaven, do it with your prayers!

POET. No, it's not a house . . . not a telephone tower either . . . Do you see?

DAUGHTER. What do you see?

POET. I see a snow-covered heath, a drill field . . . The winter sun is shining behind a church on a hill, and the church tower casts a long shadow on the snow . . . A troop of soldiers is marching across the heath. They're marching across the tower's shadow, toward the top of the spire. Now they're on the cross, and I sense that the first one to step on the weathercock will die . . . They're getting closer . . . The corporal is in the lead . . . Aha! A cloud is moving over the heath, blotting out the sun, of course . . . Now everything is gone . . . the water of the cloud has quenched the fire of the sun! —— The sun's rays created the dark shadow of the tower, but the dark shadow of the cloud smothered the tower . . . (*During the* POET'S *speech, the setting has changed back to the stage door alley.*)

DAUGHTER (*to the* DOORKEEPER). Has the Chancellor of the university come yet?

DOORKEEPER. No.

DAUGHTER. What about the Deans?

DOORKEEPER. No.

DAUGHTER. Then call them at once because the door is going to be opened . . .

DOORKEEPER. Is it that urgent?

DAUGHTER. Yes, it is. People think that the solution to the riddle of the world is hidden there . . . So, call the Chancellor and the Deans of the four faculties! (*The* DOORKEEPER *blows a whistle.*) And don't forget the Glazier and his diamond. Without him we can't do anything. (*Theatre people enter from left as in the beginning of the play. The* OFFICER *enters from upstage wearing a frock coat and a top hat. He is carrying a bouquet of roses and looks radiantly happy.*)

OFFICER. Victoria!

DOORKEEPER. She's coming soon!

OFFICER. Fine! I've got the carriage waiting, the table set, and the champagne on ice . . . May I embrace you, ma'am? (*Embraces the* DOORKEEPER.) Victoria!

WOMAN'S VOICE (*singing from above*). I'm here!

OFFICER (*begins to stroll around*). Well, I'm waiting!

POET. I think I've been through this before . . .

DAUGHTER. Me too.

POET.   Maybe it was a dream.

DAUGHTER.   Or a poem.

POET.   Or a poem.

DAUGHTER.   Then you know what poetry is.

POET.   Then I know what dreams are.

DAUGHTER.   It seems to me we said these words before, somewhere else.

POET.   Then you'll soon know what reality is.

DAUGHTER.   Or dreams.

POET.   Or poetry. (*The* CHANCELLOR *enters with the* DEANS *of* THEOLOGY, PHILOSOPHY, MEDICINE, *and* LAW.)

CHANCELLOR.   It's this business about the door, of course! ———What do you think about it, as Dean of Theology?

DEAN OF THEOLOGY.   Speaking theologically, I don't think, I believe . . . *credo* . . .

DEAN OF PHILOSOPHY.   Speaking philosophically, I consider . . .

DEAN OF MEDICINE.   Speaking medically, I know . . .

DEAN OF LAW.   Speaking legally, I withhold judgment until I've seen the evidence and heard the witnesses.

CHANCELLOR.   They're starting to fight again . . . Let me hear first from theology.

DEAN OF THEOLOGY.   I believe this door must not be opened since it conceals dangerous truths.

DEAN OF PHILOSOPHY.   The truth is never dangerous.

DEAN OF MEDICINE.   What is truth?

DEAN OF LAW.   Whatever can be proven by the testimony of two witnesses.

DEAN OF THEOLOGY.   With two false witnesses anything can be proven—by a crooked lawyer.

DEAN OF PHILOSOPHY.   Truth is wisdom, and wisdom and knowledge are the core of philosophy . . . Philosophy is the science of sciences, the sum of all learning, and all other sciences are its servants.

DEAN OF MEDICINE.   The only science is natural science. Philosophy is not a science. It's only empty speculations.

DEAN OF THEOLOGY.   Bravo!

DEAN OF PHILOSOPHY (*to the* DEAN OF THEOLOGY). So, you say bravo! And what are you? You're the archenemy of all learning, the very opposite of science. You are ignorance and darkness . . .

DEAN OF MEDICINE.   Bravo!

DEAN OF THEOLOGY (*to the* DEAN OF MEDICINE). Look who's shouting bravo now! Someone who can't see beyond the end of his nose except through a magnifying glass! Someone who believes only what his deceptive senses tell him: your eye, for example, which could be far-sighted, near-sighted, bleary-eyed, cross-eyed, one-eyed, color-blind, red-blind, green-blind, just plain blind . . .

DEAN OF MEDICINE.   Idiot!

DEAN OF THEOLOGY.   Jackass! (*They begin to fight.*)

CHANCELLOR.   Stop that! I won't have my deans squabbling among themselves.

DEAN OF PHILOSOPHY.   If I had to choose between the two—theology or medicine—it would be neither!

DEAN OF LAW.   And if I were the judge in a case involving the three of you, I'd find against you all! . . . You can't agree on a single thing and never could . . . Back to the business at hand! Chancellor, what is your opinion about this door and whether it should be opened?

CHANCELLOR.   Opinion? I don't have any opinions. I was appointed by the government only to see to it that you educate students instead of breaking each other's arms and legs in committee meetings. Opinions? No, I'm very careful about holding opinions. I once had some opinions, which I debated, but my opponent immediately refuted them . . . Perhaps now we can open the door, even at the risk that it conceals dangerous truths.

DEAN OF LAW.   What is truth? Where is it?

DEAN OF THEOLOGY.   I am the truth and the life . . .

DEAN OF PHILOSOPHY.   I am the science of all sciences . . .

DEAN OF MEDICINE.   I am exact science . . .

DEAN OF LAW.   And I object! (*They begin to fight.*)

DAUGHTER.   Shame on you! Shame! Teachers of the young!

DEAN OF LAW.   Chancellor, as representative of the government and head of the faculty, it's up to you to bring charges against this woman! To say "shame on you" to us is libel, and that sneering way she calls us "teachers of the young" amounts to defamation of character.

DAUGHTER.   Poor students.

DEAN OF LAW.   By pitying the students, she's accusing us! Chancellor, bring charges!

DAUGHTER.   Yes, I accuse you, all of you, of sowing doubt and dissension in the minds of the young.

DEAN OF LAW.   Listen to her! She's raising doubts herself in the young about our authority and then accuses us of raising doubts. I ask you—all right-thinking people—is this not a criminal action?

ALL THE RIGHT-THINKING PEOPLE.   Yes, it's criminal.

DEAN OF LAW.   All the right-thinking people have condemned you! ——— Go in peace with your gains. Otherwise . . .

DAUGHTER.   My gains? ——— Otherwise? Otherwise what?

DEAN OF LAW.   Otherwise you'll be stoned.

POET.   Or crucified.

DAUGHTER.   I'm going. Come with me and learn the answer to the riddle.

POET.   What riddle?

DAUGHTER.   What did he mean by my "gains"? . . .

POET.   Probably nothing. That's what we call chatter. He was chattering.

DAUGHTER.   But that hurt me more than anything!

POET.   That's why he said it, I guess . . . Human beings are like that.

ALL THE RIGHT-THINKING PEOPLE.   Hurray! The door is opened!

CHANCELLOR.   What was concealed behind it?

GLAZIER.   I can't see anything.

CHANCELLOR.   You can't? Well, that's not surprising . . . Deans! What was concealed behind the door?

DEAN OF THEOLOGY.   Nothing! That's the solution to the riddle of the world . . . In the beginning God created Heaven and Earth out of nothing.

DEAN OF PHILOSOPHY.   Out of nothing comes nothing.

DEAN OF MEDICINE.   Nonsense! That's what nothing is.

DEAN OF LAW.   I'm suspicious. This looks like fraud to me. I appeal to all the right-thinking people.

DAUGHTER (to the POET).   Who are the right-thinking people?

POET.   Good question. It depends on which way the wind is blowing. Today the right-thinking people are me and mine, tomorrow they're you and yours. ——— It's something you're nominated for, or rather, you nominate yourself for.

ALL THE RIGHT-THINKING PEOPLE.   We've been cheated!

CHANCELLOR.   Who cheated you?

ALL THE RIGHT-THINKING PEOPLE.   Indra's Daughter!

CHANCELLOR (to the DAUGHTER).   Will you kindly tell us what you intended by having the door opened?

DAUGHTER.   No, my friends! If I told you, you wouldn't believe it.

DEAN OF MEDICINE.   But there's nothing.

DAUGHTER.   That's it exactly. ——— But you haven't understood it.

DEAN OF MEDICINE.   She's talking nonsense.

ALL THE RIGHT-THINKING PEOPLE.   Nonsense!

DAUGHTER (to the POET).   I pity them.

POET.   Are you serious?

DAUGHTER.   Always serious.

POET.   You pity the right-thinking people too?

DAUGHTER.   Maybe them most of all.

POET.   And the four deans of the faculty?

DAUGHTER.   Even them, and not the least. Four heads, four minds, on one body. Who made this monster?

ALL THE RIGHT-THINKING PEOPLE.   She won't answer about the door!

CHANCELLOR.   Then stone her!

DAUGHTER.   I did answer you.

CHANCELLOR.   Listen, she's answering.

ALL THE RIGHT-THINKING PEOPLE.   Stone her! She's answering!

DAUGHTER.   It's "stone her" if I answer and "stone her" if I don't! . . . Come, poet and seer, I'll tell you the answer to the riddle, but far from here, out in the wilderness, where no one can hear us, or see us! Because . . .

LAWYER (coming forward to take the DAUGHTER by the arm).   Have you forgotten your duties?

DAUGHTER.   Oh, God, no! But I have higher duties.

LAWYER.   And your child?

DAUGHTER.   My child! What about it?

LAWYER.   Your child is calling for you.

DAUGHTER.   My child! Alas! I am earthbound! . . . And this pain in my breast, this anguish . . . what is it?

LAWYER.   Don't you know?

DAUGHTER.   No!

LAWYER.   The pangs of conscience.

DAUGHTER.   The pangs of conscience?

LAWYER.   Yes. You feel them after every neglected duty, after every pleasure, even the most innocent, if there is such a thing as an innocent pleasure, which is doubtful. And you feel them after every suffering you've caused to those closest to you.

DAUGHTER.   And there's no cure?

LAWYER.   Yes, but only one: to do your duty without hesitation . . .

DAUGHTER.   You look like a demon when you say that word "duty" ——— But what if a person has two duties, as I have?

LAWYER.   First do one and then the other!

DAUGHTER.   Then the highest one first . . . Will you look after my child, so I can fulfill my duty? . . .

LAWYER.   Your child misses you terribly . . . Can you let another human being suffer because of you?

DAUGHTER.   Suddenly my soul can find no peace . . . It's torn in two directions!

LAWYER.   Life's little problems will do that.

DAUGHTER.   But they're tearing me apart!

POET.   If you had any idea how much disappointment and grief I caused by fulfilling my highest duty—my calling—you wouldn't want to take my hand!

DAUGHTER.   How could that be?

POET.   My father placed all his hopes in me, his only son. I was to take over his business . . . But I ran away from business school, and he . . . worried himself to death. My mother wanted me to be religious . . . but I couldn't . . . She disowned me . . . I had a friend who helped me through hard times . . . but he exploited the very people whose cause I was pleading in my poems. To save my soul I was forced to strike down my friend and benefactor. Since then I've had no peace. People call me traitor and scum of the earth. It doesn't help when my conscience tells me I was right because the next moment it tells me I was wrong. Such is life.

DAUGHTER.   Come with me into the wilderness!

LAWYER.   But your child!

DAUGHTER (indicating everyone around her).   Here are my children. Individually they are good and kind, but when they get together, they fight and turn into demons . . . Farewell!

(Outside the castle. The setting is the same as the earlier scene, but the ground at the foot of the castle is now covered *with flowers [blue monkshood, aconite]. Atop a small tower on the roof of the castle is a chrysanthemum bud ready to burst into bloom. The castle windows are illuminated by candles. The* POET *and the* DAUGHTER *appear.*)

DAUGHTER.   The moment is near when I shall rise again into the ether with the help of fire . . . This is what mortals call death and which you approach with fear.

POET.   Fear of the unknown.

DAUGHTER.   Which you know.

POET.   Who knows it?

DAUGHTER.   Everyone! Why won't you believe your prophets?

POET.

> Prophets have never been believed. I wonder why? ———
>
> And "if God has spoken, why will the people then not believe?"
>
> His power to persuade should be irresistible.

DAUGHTER.   Have you always doubted?

POET.   No! I've had certainty often, but after a time it would vanish, like a dream when you wake up.

DAUGHTER.   It's not easy to be a human being.

POET.   You really know that now, don't you? . . .

DAUGHTER.   Yes.

POET.   Tell me, wasn't it Indra who once sent his Son to earth to hear the complaints of mankind?

DAUGHTER.   Yes, it was. How was He received?

POET.   To answer with a question: did He accomplish His mission?

DAUGHTER.   To answer with another: weren't conditions improved for mankind after His visit to earth? Answer truthfully!

POET.   Improved? . . . Yes, a little. Very little! . . . But instead of all these questions: will you tell me the answer to the riddle?

DAUGHTER.   Yes, but what good will it do? You won't believe me.

POET.   I want to believe you, for I know who you are.

DAUGHTER.   Very well, I'll tell you.

> In the dawn of time, before the sun shone, Brahman, the divine primal force, allowed itself to be seduced by Māyā, the world mother, into propagating. This contact between divine and earthly substances was heaven's original sin. And so the world, life and human beings are only an illusion, a phantom, a dream image . . .

POET.   My dream!

DAUGHTER.   A dream become reality! . . . But to be set free from this earthly substance, Brahman's descendents seek self-denial and suffering. . . . There you have suffering as liberator . . . But this yearning for suffering comes in conflict with the desire for pleasure, or love . . . Do you understand then why love is sublime joy and the greatest pain, the sweetest and the bitterest? Do you understand then what woman is? Woman, through whom sin and death entered life?

POET.   I understand! . . . And the outcome? . . .

DAUGHTER.   What you already know . . . A struggle between the torment of pleasure and the suffering that brings release . . . the pangs of remorse and the joys of sensuality . . .

POET.   Nothing but struggle?

DAUGHTER.   Struggle between opposites generates power, as when fire and water make steam . . .

POET.   But what of peace? Rest?

DAUGHTER.   Hush, you mustn't ask any more and I mustn't answer! . . . The altar is already decked for the sacrifice . . . The flowers stand watch, the candles are lit . . . Death is near . . .

POET.   You say this so calmly, as if suffering didn't exist for you.

DAUGHTER.   Not exist? . . . I've suffered all your suffering, but a hundredfold, because my senses were sharper . . .

POET.   Tell me your sorrows!

DAUGHTER.   Poet, could you tell me yours so completely that every word counted? Have you ever found words equal to the moment?

POET.   No, you're right. I've always thought of myself as a deaf mute. Whenever my songs were admired, they seemed only noise to me . . . That's why I always blushed when people praised me.

DAUGHTER.   And yet you want *me* to . . . ? Look into my eyes.

POET.   I can't bear to . . .

DAUGHTER.   How then could you bear my words, if I were to speak in my own language?

POET.   Tell me anyway, before you go: what did you suffer most from here?

DAUGHTER.   From just—being alive: from sensing my vision dimmed by my eyes, my hearing muffled by my ears, and my thoughts, my bright, airy thoughts trapped in that labyrinth of fatty coils in my brain. You've seen a brain . . . those devious turns, those secret paths . . .

POET.   So that's why all the right-thinking people think so deviously.

DAUGHTER.   That was cruel, always cruel, but so are you all! . . .

POET.   How can we be otherwise?

DAUGHTER.   First I must shake the dust from my feet . . . the earth, the clay . . . (*She takes off her shoes and puts them in the fire.*)

DOORKEEPER (*enters and puts her shawl in the fire*). Perhaps I may burn my shawl too? (*Exits.*)

OFFICER (*enters*). And I my roses . . . only the thorns are left. (*Exits.*)

BILLPOSTER (*enters*). The posters can go, but never my scoop net! (*Exits.*)

GLAZIER (*enters*). The diamond that opened the door. Goodbye. (*Exits.*)

LAWYER (*enters*). The trial proceedings from great cases involving the Pope's beard or the depleted water supply at the sources of the river Ganges. (*Exits.*)

QUARANTINE MASTER (*enters*). A small contribution: the black mask that made me a blackamoor against my own will. (*Exits.*)

VICTORIA (*enters*). My beauty, my sorrow. (*Exits.*)

EDITH (*enters*). My ugliness, my sorrow. (*Exits.*)

THE BLIND MAN (*enters and sticks his hand in the fire*). A hand for an eye! (*Exits.*)

DON JUAN (*enters in his wheelchair with the* COQUETTE *and her* "FRIEND"). Hurry up, hurry up, life is short! (*They exit.*)

POET. I've read that when life is ending, everything and everyone passes in review . . . Is this the end?

DAUGHTER. For me, yes. Farewell!

POET. Won't you say a parting word?

DAUGHTER. No, I can't. Do you still believe that words can express your thoughts?

DEAN OF THEOLOGY (*enters, raging*). I've been abandoned by God, persecuted by men, rejected by the government, and scorned by my colleagues! How can I have faith when no one else has faith . . . How can I defend a God who won't defend His own people? It's all nonsense! (*Throws a book in the fire and exits.*)

POET (*snatching the book from the fire*). Do you know what this is? . . . A Book of Martyrs, a calendar with a martyr for each day in the year.

DAUGHTER. A martyr?

POET. Yes, someone tortured and killed for his faith. Tell me why! Do you think everyone who's tortured suffers and that everyone who's killed feels pain? Isn't suffering redemption and death deliverance?

KRISTINE (*enters with strips of paper*). I paste, I paste till there's nothing more to paste . . .

POET. And if the dome of heaven itself cracked, you'd try to paste that together too . . . Go!

KRISTINE. Are there no double windows in the castle?

POET. No, Kristine, not in there.

KRISTINE (*exiting*). Then I'll go.

DAUGHTER.

Our parting time has come and the end approaches.
Farewell, you child of man, you dreamer,
you poet, who understands best how to live.
Hovering on your wings above the world,
you plunge to earth from time to time,
but just to brush against it, not be trapped by it!

——————————————————

Now as I go . . . in the moment of parting,
leaving behind a friend, a place,
how great I feel the loss of all I loved
how great the regret for all I offended . . .
Oh, now I know all the pain of being,
this is what it's like to be human . . .
You miss even things you didn't value,
regret even wrongs you didn't commit . . .
You want to go, and you want to stay . . .
And so the heart is divided,
as if wild horses were pulling it apart,
torn by contradiction, indecision, uncertainty . . .

———

Farewell! Tell my brothers and sisters I shall
    remember them
where I now go, and their lament
I shall bear in your name to the throne.
Farewell!

(*She goes into the castle. Music can be heard! The backdrop is illuminated by the burning castle and reveals a wall of human faces, questioning, grieving, despairing . . . As the castle burns, the flower bud on the roof bursts open into a giant chrysanthemum.*)

FOCUS QUESTIONS

1. Select and discuss three expressionistic features of *A Dream Play*.
2. Discuss the significance of the play's title.
3. Describe how Strindberg's use of Eastern and Western mythologies enhances his motifs and themes.
4. Trace and discuss the consequences of the journey of Indra's Daughter.
5. Develop a character sketch of the Lawyer and describe how his relationship with Agnes contributes to the theme of sexual conflict.
6. Which special attributes characterize the Poet and his function in the play?
7. Identify the play's poetic images and describe how they reveal the dramatic themes.
8. What do these characters tell us about the playwright's view of the human condition?

OTHER ACTIVITIES

1. Describe your approaches to staging the opening and closing scenes.
2. Using reviews, photographs, and other available production documents, assess an English-language production of the play.

BIBLIOGRAPHY

Adam. (London). Strindberg Centenary Issue, 1949.

Carlson, Harry G. *Strindberg and the Poetry of Myth.* Berkeley: University of California, 1982.

Cima, Gay Gibson. *Performing Women: Female Characters, Male Playwrights and the Modern Stage.* Ithaca, NY: Cornell University Press, 1993.

Dahlstrom, Carl. *Strindberg's Dramatic Expressionism.* Ann Arbor: University of Michigan Press, 1930.

Hillestrom, Gustaf. *Swedish Theatre during Five Decades.* Stockholm: Swedish Institute, 1962.

Johnson, Walter. ''*A Dream Play:* Plans and Fulfillment.'' in *Scandinavica* (1971).

———. *Structures of Influence.* Chapel Hill: University of North Carolina Press, 1981.

Lucas, F. L. *The Dreams of Ibsen and Strindberg.* New York: Macmillan Co., 1963.

Marker, F. J. and L. L. Marker. *The Scandinavian Theatre: A Short History.* Totowa, NJ: Rowman & Littlefield, 1975.

———. *Ingmar Bergman: Four Decades in the Theatre.* New York: Cambridge University Press, 1982.

Meyer, Michael. *Strindberg.* New York: Random House, 1985.

Morgan, Margery M. ''Strindberg and the English Theatre.'' in *Modern Drama VII* (September, 1964), 161–73.

Reinert, Otto, ed. *Strindberg: A Collection of Critical Essays.* Englewood Cliffs, NJ: Prentice-Hall, 1971.

Smedmark, C. R., ed. *Essays on Strindberg.* Stockholm: Strindberg Society, 1966.

Sprinchorn, Evert. *Strindberg as Dramatist.* New Haven, CT: Yale University Press, 1982.

Swerling, Anthony. *Strindberg's Impact in France, 1920–1960.* Cambridge, (II Covent Garden): Trinity Lane Press, 1971.

RECOMMENDED RECORDING

A Dream Play. One sound cassette. University of Minnesota Radio Guild for the Fifth Annual Summer Drama Festival. University of Colorado, National Center for Audio Tapes.

RIDERS TO THE SEA
John Millington Synge (1871–1909)

John Millington Synge came close to creating an age in Ireland: he more than any other changed the shape of Irish dramatic writing; he more than any other showed Ireland to the world, and it was an Ireland neither of fact nor of fiction but of a creative revelation.

—Micheál MacLiammóir

Honor Lavelle, Sara Allgood, and Emma Vernon in an early production of *Riders to the Sea*. *Photo: The Abbey Theatre.*

APPROACHING THE IRISH LITERARY REVIVAL

The swift ascendancy of Ireland's literary stature at the end of the nineteenth century was heralded by two remarkable events. Foremost was the liberating spirit of European nationalism, finally asserting itself upon an ancient soil whose rich Gaelic language and colorful sagas had been suppressed under British domination. The second was the timely appearance of John Millington Synge, whose unique poetic voice effortlessly transformed the native Irish experience into a world class drama.

Backed by a movement to gain Home Rule and independence from England as early as the 1870s, many scholarly and artistic efforts were spawned to reclaim Ireland's cultural heritage. The publication in 1878 of O'Grady's *History of Ireland: Heroic Period*—translations of Celtic folktales into Anglo-Irish—made the heroes, manners, and ancient way of life accessible for the first time to the generations of Irish people who had lost their linguistic birthright. As a result, cultural and political societies proudly conducted classes in Irish language, folklore, and history.

In 1892, the National Literary Society was founded for the express purpose of cultivating a renaissance of poetry, fiction, and drama in the Anglo-Irish tradition. The unique crystallization would be known as the Irish Literary Revival. The first step in transforming Dublin's theatrical center from English to native drama, however, was the founding of the Irish Literary Theatre (1889–1902). Under the leadership of writers Edward Martyn, George Moore, Lady Augusta Gregory, and William Butler Yeats, this theatre took shape in response to the Théâtre Libre in France, the Freie Bühne in Germany, and the National Theatre of Norway, the last of which had been profoundly influenced by the folk themes and domestic realism of Henrik Ibsen's plays (See Preface to Ibsen, p. 550). Goals to promote new theatrical practices and to produce Celtic and Irish dramatic literature were gradually set into place. In 1902, Frank and William Fay, who had established the Ormand Dramatic Society ten years earlier, joined forces with Yeats and Lady Gregory to produce the first program ever of Irish plays performed by Irish actors: George Russell's *Deirdre* and Yeats' peasant drama *Kathleen Ni Houlihan.* So successful was their venture that the company was restructured as the Irish National Theatre Society with Yeats at the helm.

Yeats met Synge in Paris in 1896. Discovering that the young Anglo-Irishman had studied Gaelic at Trinity College in Dublin and was deeply interested in Irish folklore and history, Yeats encouraged him to investigate the peasant life on the Aran Islands off the west coast of Ireland. He suspected that their rich but unexplored traditions might fire Synge's literary imagination, which they did indeed. Between 1889 and 1902, Synge made four trips to this remote and rugged landscape and recorded his impressions, which were eventually published in his book *The Aran Islands* (1907). But he also discovered that playwriting best accommodated his literary talent. Under the auspices of the National Theatre Society, Lady Gregory and Yeats produced Synge's *The Shadow of the Glen,* his one-act play about an Irish tramp who runs off with a Wicklow woman when she is rejected by a jealous husband and a ne'er-do-well lover. Its unromanticized depiction of Irish peasantry prompted controversial responses from its audiences, not the first he would experience. The play opened in October 1903. Four months later the company produced *Riders to the Sea,* a one-act play set on the Aran Islands.

Synge officially joined the National Theatre Society in 1904 and, until his early death in 1909, wrote exclusively for the company, which became the Abbey Theatre in 1905. His insistence that ''originality is not enough unless it has the characteristic of a particular time and locality, and the life that was in it'' became the manifesto for his use of Anglo-Irish dialect and peasant lore, as well as the hallmark for all Irish national drama to follow.[1]

MAJOR WORKS

In the tradition of *The Shadow of the Glen* (1902) and *Riders to the Sea* (1902), Synge's sparse but qualitatively rich dramatic output was inspired by his concerns with life of the Irish countryside in places like Kerry, Wicklow, and Galway: the conflict between freedom and religious domination in *The Well of the Saints* (1905); the hypocrisy of hero-worship in *Playboy of the Western World* (1907); and the farcical treatment of marriage and the clergy in *The Tinker's Wedding* (1909). While Synge's rich portraits of Irish characters and customs have elicited sharp criticism, they have always satirized the failings of the Irish without bitterness or rancor. In his final play, *Deidre of the Sorrows* (1909), Synge departed from the realistic mode and the events of the present to retell the tragic love story of the legendary Irish beauty Deidre and her beloved Naisi. The play was produced post-humously by the Abbey Players in 1910 in a version edited by Lady Gregory from Synge's unfinished work.

THE ACTION

Resigned to the fact that she has lost another son, Michael, to the sea, Maurya tries to dissuade Bartley from going off to sell the family horses at the Galway fair. Despite her warnings about the dangerous voyage and her plea that her youngest and only living son is needed at home, Bartley rides off to catch the boat. His sisters send Maurya out of the house to reconcile with him. In her absence, they examine the evidence that identifies Michael's body as the one washed up on the coast. In spite of their efforts to keep this news from her, Maurya is assured of Michael's fate when she sees his ghost riding on the horse harnessed directly behind Bartley. Distraught, she returns to her cottage only to discover that the sea has claimed Bartley as well.

STRUCTURE AND LANGUAGE

Riders to the Sea pays tribute to human perseverance in the face of adversity and death. It is a deeply moving account of women who must endure the loss of husbands and sons to the merciless sea. A tragic **motif,** that children who die before their mothers often die without reason, is eloquently sounded by Maurya: "In the big world the old people do be leaving things after them for their sons and children, but in this place it is the young men do be leaving things behind for them that do be old." If there is heroism in these women, it rests in their ability to accept the inextricable connection between life and death, but also to mourn from a depth of pain that is commensurate with the raging sea. In Synge's ironic universe, "this place" becomes a microcosm of "the big world," where survival is never certain but death always is.

As keepers of the hearth, these women are preoccupied with matters of the practical world: the spinning of wool, the maintenance of a turf fire, and the baking of bread. But they have also confronted life's realities, in sharp contrast with the difficult reasoning of their menfolk whose needs are so imperative as to override the risks of being lost at sea. Because their possessions are meager and often of their own making, each item bears significance, including the number of stitches in the stocking from a drowned man's body to identify him as Michael. But answers only trigger more questions: "What is the price of a thousand horses against a son where there is one son only?" implores Maurya. Her faith has also convinced a local priest that God will surely listen to her prayers and spare her Bartley, the last of these sons. But Maurya's maternal instincts know better. Supported by the kind of experience only a mother can acquire if she is unfortunate to live so long, she knows that Bartley will never return.

By retelling a story from the Aran Islands about a mother's vision of her dead son riding a horse to market, Synge pits the minute, naturalistic details of peasant life against the power of superstition and the simple wisdom of country folk. Maurya's failure to bless Bartley or give him the bread to sustain him on the journey as well as her vision of Michael's ghost dressed in city finery on a gray horse bear the mark of authenticity throughout. But the tragic circumstances are illuminated by Synge's language. Unable to fulfill the superstitious ritual of blessing a sailor before his journey, an omission that might have contributed to Bartley's death, Maurya expresses her sorrow in the powerful cadences of the Anglo-Irish dialect.

As the villagers prepare the table and lay upon it Bartley's drenched body wrapped in a sail, the present quietly echoes the past as Maurya asks, "Is it Patch, or Michael, or what is it at all?" The answer hardly matters, since this drowned man symbolizes all men who have gone before him. While the traditional Irish *caoine* (lamentation for the dead) rises from the chorus of women who stand beside her, the threnody is broken by Maurya as she blesses her son with the resignation that no man or woman is immortal. Synthesizing the emotional sweep and verbal clarity of characters who accept their fate through tears, Synge achieves a work of poetic art which, according to Christopher Fitz-Simon, is "probably the greatest, shortest tragedy of the modern Western theatre."[2]

RIDERS TO THE SEA-IN-PERFORMANCE

In his effort to establish an Irish literary drama, Yeats published Synge's one-act tragedy in the journal *Samhain* in October 1903, prior to its premiere at Molesworth Hall in Dublin on February 25, 1904. He called Synge's play "the finest piece of tragic work done in Ireland of late years. One finds in it, from first to last, the presence of the sea, and a sorrow that has majesty as in the work of some ancient poet."[3] The small opening-night audience was highly enthusiastic, but the Dublin press found the work too depressing.

Most remarkable was the naturalistic detail of the staging. Set in an auditorium that seated fewer than three hundred people, the interior of an Aran Island cottage was constructed on the small stage. An authentic spinning wheel borrowed from a nunnery in Gort was one hundred years old. Pampooties, or cowskin shoes, were delivered to the actors by a young Aran man who also served as consultant in the reproduction of native island costumes. Even the turf baskets and panniers were gathered from the Irish countryside to complete the kitchen set. The playwright himself insisted that the actresses be coached on the traditional keening from the women of Galway.

For Irish and English audiences who attended more than eighty-eight performances given between 1904 and 1908, these naturalistic elements of the production gave the play an exotic dimension. Equally important, the realistic details counteracted the stage image of the Irish man or woman that had been perpetuated in British dramas. When *Riders to the Sea* traveled to Galway, however, audiences were repelled by subject matter that hit so close to home. One Galway playgoer told William Fay that *Riders to the Sea* "was not a play at all, at all."[4] When the play reached England four years later, the critic for the *Manchester Guardian* praised Sara Allgood's portrayal of Maurya as "the finest of tragic acting that any English speaking actress has done in our time."[5]

The publication of the play expanded its international popularity and inspired some interesting translations, including one into Bohemian by Karel Musak, and one into Italian by James Joyce. Joyce later directed an English production at the Pfauen Theatre in Zurich in 1918, in which his wife Nora played one of the daughters. The first American production was mounted at Emerson College in Boston in 1906. In 1924, the play was the source for Henri Rabaud's opera *L'Appel de la Mer,* written for the Opera Comique in Paris. Further homage was paid when Ralph Vaughan Williams used Synge's script for his opera libretto produced at the Royal College of Music in 1937.

The Abbey Theatre production of *Riders to the Sea* was filmed on location in Connemara in 1935 with Sara Allgood recreating the role of Maurya. As late as the 1960s, two television versions emerged: one in 1960 for the BBC with Sybil Thorndike as Maurya and Sean Connery as Bartley, and the other in 1962 for WNET with Maureen Stapleton.

Unquestionably the most important productions of Synge's play took place from the early century to the mid 1930s. These were presented by the Abbey Theatre's Irish Players on tours through Europe and America. Their first American performance was at the Maxine Elliott Theatre in New York City on December 5, 1911, with Sara Allgood, J. M. Kerrigan, Maire ni Shibhlaugh, and Eileen O'Doherty. The impact was so tremendous that the company returned to New York on April 21, 1915.

In repertory with other peasant dramas, *Riders to the Sea* demonstrated a sharp influence on American playwrights. The attention to realistic detail and the celebration of folklore in a distinctly Irish idiom inspired writers to experiment with folk plays for America's "little theatres." Those written by Paul Green, Ridgely Torrence, and DuBose and Dorothy Heywood for the Carolina Playmakers and those written by Susan Glaspell and Eugene O'Neill for the Provincetown Playhouse contributed to the development of an indigenous American drama. In 1923, O'Neill wrote: "It was seeing the Irish Players . . . that gave me a glimpse of my opportunity. I went to see everything they did. I thought then and I still think that they demonstrated the possibilities of naturalistic acting better than any other company."[6]

The Irish Players performed *Riders to the Sea* at the Martin Beck Theatre in New York City in November of 1932, with Eileen Crowe, Denis O'Dea, Rea Mooney, and May Craig. But it was no longer the play's exotic flavor or rhythms of dialect that touched the audience. Rather it was what critic Richard Watts called its "haunting, mournful Beauty," its realization of traditional Gaelic keening, and its evocation of the "grim, storm-swept shores of those western islands of Aran."[7] Its universal themes also aroused great empathy from playgoers who were witnessing the breadlines and cardboard shanty towns of New York City in the Great Depression.

REFLECTIONS ON RIDERS TO THE SEA

From OUR IRISH THEATRE: A CHAPTER OF AUTOBIOGRAPHY,
by Lady Augusta Gregory.

Our Theatre, when it set out, had in its repertory Mr. Yeats's beautiful verse-plays, and some prose ones in the Ibsen tradition, written by Mr. E. Martyn. But it was caught into the current, and it is that current, as I believe, that has brought it on its triumphant way. It is chiefly known now as a folk theatre; it has not only the great mass of primitive material, of primitive culture to draw on, but it has been made a living thing by the excitement of that discovery. Mr. Yeats himself was swept into the current. Compare his *Land of Heart's Desire,* written a little from the outside, with his *Kathleen Ni Houlihan.* You may like one better than the other, but you see what the influence has been. Mr. Synge was caught in, and with him it was all for good. In his return to Ireland just at that time of imaginative awakening, he found fable, emotion, style. He tells what he owes to that collaboration with the people; and in spite of all attacks, he has given back to them what they will one day thank him for. He has put into perfect and lasting form in his *Riders to the Sea* the sorrow,

Continued

the struggle against a force too strong for them, of those islanders among whom he made his dwelling for a while. Their Gaelic songs are full of the pity of the unequal fight; he has shaped it so that there are now many who cannot hear Aran spoken of without a pulling at the heartstrings. The return to the people, the reunion after separation, the taking and giving again, is it not the perfect circle, the way of nature, the eternal wedding ring?

From THE DRAMATIC IMAGINATION *by Robert Edmond Jones.*

I am thinking of the company of Irish Players from the Abbey Theatre in Dublin who first gave us the dramas of Synge and Yeats in 1910. As one watched these players, one saw what they knew. I kept saying to myself on that first evening: Who are these rare beings? Where did they come from? How have they spent their lives? Who are their friends? What music they must have heard, what books they must have read, what emotions they must have felt! They literally enchanted me. They put me under a spell. And when the curtain came down at the end of the play, they had become necessary to me. I have often asked myself since that time how it was that actors could make me feel such strange emotions of trouble and wonder; and I find the answer now, curiously enough, in an address spoken by a modern Irish poet to the youth of Ireland—*Keep in your souls some images of magnificence.* These Irish players had kept in their souls some images of magnificence.

Exceptional people, distinguished people, superior people, people who can say, as the old Negro said, "I got a-plenty music in me." These are the actors the theatre needs.

Notes

1. *Denis Johnston,* JOHN MILLINGTON SYNGE *(New York: Columbia University Press, 1965),* 6.
2. *Christopher Fitz-Simon,* THE IRISH THEATRE *(New York: Thames & Hudson, 1983),* 153.
3. EXPLORATIONS *(London: Macmillan Press, 1962),* 106.
4. *Brenna Katz Clarke,* THE EMERGENCE OF THE IRISH PEASANT PLAY AT THE ABBEY THEATRE *(Ann Arbor: UMI Research Press, 1982),* 62.
5. MANCHESTER GUARDIAN, *13 April 1908.*
6. *Arthur and Barbara Gelb,* O'NEILL *(New York: Harper & Row, 1962),* 172.
7. HERALD TRIBUNE, *5 Nov. 1932.*

RIDERS TO THE SEA
John Millington Synge

CHARACTERS

Maurya, *an old woman*

Bartley, *her son*

Cathleen, *her daughter*

Nora, *a younger daughter*

Men and Women

SCENE: An Island off the West of Ireland

Cottage kitchen, with nets, oilskins, spinning-wheel, some new boards standing by the wall, etc. Cathleen, a girl of about twenty, finishes kneading cake, and puts it down in the pot-oven by the fire; then wipes her hands, and begins to spin at the wheel. Nora, a young girl, puts her head in at the door.

NORA (*in a low voice*). Where is she?

CATHLEEN. She's lying down, God help her, and maybe sleeping, if she's able.

(Nora comes in softly, and takes a bundle from under her shawl.)

CATHLEEN (*spinning the wheel rapidly*). What is it you have?

NORA. The young priest is after bringing them. It's a shirt and a plain stocking were got off a drowned man in Donegal.

(Cathleen stops her wheel with a sudden movement, and leans out to listen.)

NORA. We're to find out if it's Michael's they are, some time herself will be down looking by the sea.

CATHLEEN. How would they be Michael's, Nora? How would he go the length of that way to the far north?

NORA. The young priest says he's known the like of it. 'If it's Michael's they are,' says he, 'you can tell herself he's got a clean burial, by the grace of God; and if they're not his, let no one say a word about them, for she'll be getting her death,' says he, 'with crying and lamenting.'

(The door which Nora half closed is blown open by a gust of wind.)

CATHLEEN (*looking out anxiously*). Did you ask him would he stop Bartley going this day with the horses to the Galway fair?

NORA. 'I won't stop him,' says he; 'but let you not be afraid. Herself does be saying prayers half through the night, and the Almighty God won't leave her destitute,' says he, 'with no son living.'

CATHLEEN. Is the sea bad by the white rocks, Nora?

NORA. Middling bad, God help us. There's a great roaring in the west, and it's worse it'll be getting when the tide's turned to the wind. (*She goes over to the table with the bundle.*) Shall I open it now?

CATHLEEN. Maybe she'd wake up on us, and come in before we'd done. (*Coming to the table.*) It's a long time we'll be, and the two of us crying.

NORA (*goes to the inner door and listens*). She's moving about on the bed. She'll be coming in a minute.

CATHLEEN. Give me the ladder, and I'll put them up in the turf loft, the way she won't know of them at all, and maybe when the tide turns she'll be going down to see would he be floating from the east.

(They put the ladder against the gable of the chimney; Cathleen goes up a few steps and hides the bundle in the turf loft. Maurya comes from the inner room.)

MAURYA (*looking up at Cathleen and speaking querulously*). Isn't it turf enough you have for this day and evening?

CATHLEEN.   There's a cake baking at the fire for a short space (*throwing down the turf*), and Bartley will want it when the tide turns if he goes to Connemara.

(*Nora picks up the turf and puts it round the pot-oven.*)

MAURYA (*sitting down on a stool at the fire*). He won't go this day with the wind rising from the south and west. He won't go this day, for the young priest will stop him surely.

NORA.   He'll not stop him, mother; and I heard Eamon Simon and Stephen Pheety and Colum Shawn saying he would go.

MAURYA.   Where is he itself?

NORA.   He went down to see would there be another boat sailing in the week, and I'm thinking it won't be long till he's here now, for the tide's turning at the green head, and the hooker's tacking from the east.

CATHLEEN.   I hear someone passing the big stones.

NORA (*looking out*). He's coming now, and he in a hurry.

BARTLEY (*comes in and looks round the room. Speaking sadly and quietly*). Where is the bit of new rope, Cathleen, was bought in Connemara?

CATHLEEN (*coming down*). Give it to him, Nora; it's on a nail by the white boards. I hung it up this morning, for the pig with the black feet was eating it.

NORA (*giving him a rope*). Is that it, Bartley?

MAURYA.   You'd do right to leave that rope, Bartley, hanging by the boards. (*Bartley takes the rope.*) It will be wanting in this place, I'm telling you, if Michael is washed up to-morrow morning, or the next morning, or any morning in the week; for it's a deep grave we'll make him, by the grace of God.

BARTLEY (*beginning to work with the rope*). I've no halter the way I can ride down on the mare, and I must go now quickly. This is the one boat going for two weeks or beyond it, and the fair will be a good fair for horses, I heard them saying below.

MAURYA.   It's a hard thing they'll be saying below if the body is washed up and there's no man in it to make the coffin, and I after giving a big price for the finest white boards you'd find in Connemara. (*She looks round at the boards.*)

BARTLEY.   How would it be washed up, and we after looking each day for nine days, and a strong wind blowing a while back from the west and south?

MAURYA.   If it isn't found itself, that wind is raising the sea, and there was a star up against the moon, and it rising in the night. If it was a hundred horses, or a thousand horses you had itself, what is the price of a thousand horses against a son where there is one son only?

BARTLEY (*working at the halter, to Cathleen*). Let you go down each day, and see the sheep aren't jumping in on the rye, and if the jobber comes you can sell the pig with the black feet if there is a good price going.

MAURYA.   How would the like of her get a good price for a pig?

BARTLEY (*to Cathleen*). If the west winds holds with the last bit of the moon let you and Nora get up weed enough for another cock for the kelp. It's hard set we'll be from this day with no one in it but one man to work.

MAURYA.   It's hard set we'll be surely the day you're drowned with the rest. What way will I live and the girls with me, and I an old woman looking for the grave?

(*Bartley lays down the halter, takes off his old coat, and puts on a newer one of the same flannel.*)

BARTLEY (*to Nora*). Is she coming to the pier?

NORA (*looking out*). She's passing the green head and letting fall her sails.

BARTLEY (*getting his purse and tobacco*). I'll have half an hour to go down, and you'll see me coming again in two days, or in three days, or maybe in four days if the wind is bad.

MAURYA (*turning round to the fire, and putting her shawl over her head*). Isn't it a hard and cruel man won't hear a word from an old woman, and she holding him from the sea?

CATHLEEN.   It's the life of a young man to be going on the sea, and who would listen to an old woman with one thing and she saying it over?

BARTLEY (*taking the halter*). I must go now quickly. I'll ride down on the red mare, and the grey pony 'ill run behind me. . . . The blessing of God on you. (*He goes out.*)

MAURYA (*crying out as he is in the door*). He's gone now, God spare us, and we'll not see him again. He's gone now, and when the black night is falling I'll have no son left me in the world.

CATHLEEN.   Why wouldn't you give him your blessing and he looking round in the door? Isn't it sorrow enough is on every one in this house without your sending him out with an unlucky word behind him, and a hard word in his ear?

(*Maurya takes up the tongs and begins raking the fire aimlessly without looking round.*)

NORA (*turning towards her*). You're taking away the turf from the cake.

CATHLEEN (*crying out*). The Son of God forgive us, Nora, we're after forgetting his bit of bread. (*She comes over to the fire.*)

NORA.   And it's destroyed he'll be going till dark night, and he after eating nothing since the sun went up.

CATHLEEN (*turning the cake out of the oven*). It's destroyed he'll be surely. There's no sense left on any person in a house where an old woman will be talking for ever. (*Maurya sways herself on her stool.*)

CATHLEEN (*cutting off some of the bread and rolling it in a cloth; to Maurya*). Let you go down now to the spring well and give him this and he passing. You'll see him then and the dark word will be broken, and you can say 'God speed you,' the way he'll be easy in his mind.

MAURYA (*taking the bread*). Will I be in it as soon as himself?

CATHLEEN. If you go now quickly.

MAURYA (*standing up unsteadily*). It's hard set I am to walk.

CATHLEEN (*looking at her anxiously*). Give her the stick, Nora, or maybe she'll slip on the big stones.

NORA. What stick?

CATHLEEN. The stick Michael brought from Connemara.

MAURYA (*taking a stick Nora gives her*). In the big world the old people do be leaving things after them for their sons and children, but in this place it is the young men do be leaving things behind for them that do be old. (*She goes out slowly. Nora goes over to the ladder.*)

CATHLEEN. Wait, Nora, maybe she'd turn back quickly. She's that sorry, God help her, you wouldn't know the thing she'd do.

NORA. Is she gone round by the bush?

CATHLEEN (*looking out*). She's gone now. Throw it down quickly, for the Lord knows when she'll be out of it again.

NORA (*getting the bundle from the loft*). The young priest said he'd be passing to-morrow, and we might go down and speak to him below if it's Michael's they are surely.

CATHLEEN (*taking the bundle*). Did he say what way they were found?

NORA (*coming down*). 'There were two men,' said he, 'and they rowing round with poteen before the cocks crowed, and the oar of one of them caught the body, and they passing the black cliffs of the north.'

CATHLEEN (*trying to open the bundle*). Give me a knife, Nora; the string's perished with the salt water, and there's a black knot on it you wouldn't loosen in a week.

NORA (*giving her a knife*). I've heard tell it was a long way to Donegal.

CATHLEEN (*cutting the string*). It is surely. There was a man in here a while ago—the man sold us that knife—and he said if you set off walking from the rocks beyond, it would be in seven days you'd be in Donegal.

NORA. And what time would a man take, and he floating?

(*Cathleen opens the bundle and takes out a bit of a shirt and a stocking. They look at them eagerly.*)

CATHLEEN (*in a low voice*). The Lord spare us, Nora! isn't it a queer hard thing to say if it's his they are surely?

NORA. I'll get his shirt off the hook the way we can put the one flannel on the other. (*She looks through some clothes hanging in the corner.*) It's not with them, Cathleen, and where will it be?

CATHLEEN. I'm thinking Bartley put it on him in the morning, for his own shirt was heavy with the salt in it. (*Pointing to the corner.*) There's a bit of a sleeve was of the same stuff. Give me that and it will do.

(*Nora brings it to her and they compare the flannel.*)

CATHLEEN. It's the same stuff, Nora; but if it is itself, aren't there great rolls of it in the shops of Galway, and isn't it many another man may have a shirt of it as well as Michael himself?

NORA (*who has taken up the stocking and counted the stitches, crying out*). It's Michael, Cathleen, it's Michael; God spare his soul, and what will herself say when she hears this story, and Bartley on the sea?

CATHLEEN (*taking the stocking*). It's a plain stocking.

NORA. It's the second one of the third pair I knitted, and I put up three-score stitches, and I dropped four of them.

CATHLEEN (*counts the stitches*). It's that number is in it. (*Crying out.*) Ah, Nora, isn't it a bitter thing to think of him floating that way to the far north, and no one to keen him but the black hags that do be flying on the sea?

NORA (*swinging herself half round, and throwing out her arms on the clothes*). And isn't it a pitiful thing when there is nothing left of a man who was a great rower and fisher but a bit of an old shirt and a plain stocking?

CATHLEEN (*after an instant*). Tell me is herself coming, Nora? I hear a little sound on the path.

NORA (*looking out*). She is, Cathleen. She's coming up to the door.

CATHLEEN. Put these things away before she'll come in. Maybe it's easier she'll be after giving her blessing to Bartley, and we won't let on we've heard anything the time he's on the sea.

NORA (*helping Cathleen to close the bundle*). We'll put them here in the corner.

(*They put them into a hole in the chimney corner. Cathleen goes back to the spinning-wheel.*)

NORA. Will she see it was crying I was?

CATHLEEN. Keep your back to the door the way the light'll not be on you.

(*Nora sits down at the chimney corner, with her back to the door. Maurya comes in very slowly, without looking at the girls, and goes over to her stool at the other side of the fire. The cloth with the bread is still in her hand. The girls look at each other, and Nora points to the bundle of bread.*)

CATHLEEN (*after spinning for a moment*). You didn't give him his bit of bread?

(*Maurya begins to keen softly, without turning round.*)

CATHLEEN. Did you see him riding down? (*Maurya goes on keening.*)

CATHLEEN (*a little impatiently*). God forgive you; isn't it a better thing to raise your voice and tell what you seen, than to be making lamentation for a thing that's done? Did you see Bartley, I'm saying to you?

MAURYA (*with a weak voice*). My heart's broken from this day.

CATHLEEN (*as before*). Did you see Bartley?

MAURYA.   I seen the fearfullest thing.

CATHLEEN (*leaves her wheel and looks out*). God forgive you; he's riding the mare now over the green head, and the grey pony behind him.

MAURYA (*starts so that her shawl falls back from her head and shows her white tossed hair. With a frightened voice*). The grey pony behind him. . . .

CATHLEEN (*coming to the fire*). What is it ails you at all?

MAURYA (*speaking very slowly*). I've seen the fearfullest thing any person has seen since the day Bride Dara seen the dead man with the child in his arms.

CATHLEEN AND NORA.   Uah.

(*They crouch down in front of the old woman at the fire.*)

NORA.   Tell us what it is you seen.

MAURYA.   I went down to the spring well, and I stood there saying a prayer to myself. Then Bartley came along, and he riding on the red mare with the grey pony behind him. (*She puts up her hands, as if to hide something from her eyes.*) The Son of God spare us, Nora!

CATHLEEN.   What is it you seen?

MAURYA.   I seen Michael himself.

CATHLEEN (*speaking softly*). You did not, mother. It wasn't Michael you seen, for his body is after being found in the far north, and he's got a clean burial, by the grace of God.

MAURYA (*a little defiantly*). I'm after seeing him this day, and he riding and galloping. Bartley came first on the red mare, and I tried to say 'God speed you,' but something choked the words in my throat. He went by quickly; and 'The blessing of God on you,' says he, and I could say nothing. I looked up then, and I crying, at the grey pony, and there was Michael upon it—with fine clothes on him, and new shoes on his feet.

CATHLEEN (*begins to keen*). It's destroyed we are from this day. It's destroyed, surely.

NORA.   Didn't the young priest say the Almighty God won't leave her destitute with no son living?

MAURYA (*in a low voice, but clearly*). It's little the like of him knows of the sea. . . . Bartley will be lost now, and let you call in Eamon and make me a good coffin out of the white boards, for I won't live after them. I've had a husband, and a husband's father, and six sons in this house—six fine men, though it was a hard birth I had with every one of them and they coming into the world—and some of them were found and some of them were not found, but they're gone now the lot of them. . . . There were Stephen and Shawn were lost in the great wind, and found after in the Bay of Gregory of the Golden Mouth, and carried up the two of them on one plank, and in by that door.

(*She pauses for a moment, the girls start as if they heard something through the door that is half open behind them.*)

NORA (*in a whisper*). Did you hear that, Cathleen? Did you hear a noise in the north-east?

CATHLEEN (*in a whisper*). There 's someone after crying out by the seashore.

MAURYA (*continues without hearing anything*). There was Sheamus and his father, and his own father again, were lost in a dark night, and not a stick or sign was seen of them when the sun went up. There was Patch after was drowned out of a curragh that turned over. I was sitting here with Bartley, and he a baby lying on my two knees, and I seen two women, and three women, and four women coming in, and they crossing themselves and not saying a word. I looked out then, and there were men coming after them, and they holding a thing in the half of a red sail, and water dripping out of it—it was a dry day, Nora— and leaving a track to the door.

(*She pauses again with her hand stretched out towards the door. It opens softly and old women begin to come in, crossing themselves on the threshold, and kneeling down in front of the stage with red petticoats over their heads.*)

MAURYA (*half in a dream, to Cathleen*). Is it Patch, or Michael, or what is it at all?

CATHLEEN.   Michael is after being found in the far north, and when he is found there how could he be here in this place?

MAURYA.   There does be a power of young men floating round in the sea, and what way would they know if it was Michael they had, or another man like him, for when a man is nine days in the sea, and the wind blowing, it's hard set his own mother would be to say what man was in it.

CATHLEEN.   It's Michael, God spare him, for they're after sending us a bit of his clothes from the far north.

(*She reaches out and hands Maurya the clothes that belonged to Michael. Maurya stands up slowly, and takes them in her hands. Nora looks out.*)

NORA.   They're carrying a thing among them, and there's water dripping out of it and leaving a track by the big stones.

CATHLEEN (*in a whisper to the women who have come in*). Is it Bartley it is?

ONE OF THE WOMEN.   It is, surely, God rest his soul.

(*Two younger women come in and pull out the table. Then men carry in the body of Bartley, laid on a plank, with a bit of a sail over it, and lay it on the table.*)

CATHLEEN (*to the women as they are doing so*). What way was he drowned?

ONE OF THE WOMEN.   The grey pony knocked him over into the sea, and he was washed out where there is a great surf on the white rocks.

(*Maurya has gone over and knelt down at the head of the table. The women are keening softly and swaying themselves with a slow movement. Cathleen and Nora kneel at the other end of the table. The men kneel near the door.*)

MAURYA (*raising her head and speaking as if she did not see the people around her*). They're all gone now, and there isn't anything more the sea can do to me. . . . I'll have no call now to be up crying and praying when the wind breaks from the south, and you can hear the surf is in the east, and the surf is in the west, making a great stir with the two noises, and they hitting one on the other. I'll have no call now to be going down and getting Holy Water in the dark nights after Samhain, and I won't care what way the sea is when the other women will be keening. (*To Nora.*) Give me the Holy Water, Nora; there's a small sup still on the dresser. (*Nora gives it to her.*)

MAURYA (*drops Michael's clothes across Bartley's feet, and sprinkles the Holy Water over him*). It isn't that I haven't prayed for you, Bartley, to the Almighty God. It isn't that I haven't said prayers in the dark night till you wouldn't know what I'd be saying; but it's a great rest I'll have now, and it's time, surely. It's a great rest I'll have now, and great sleeping in the long nights after Samhain, if it's only a bit of wet flour we do have to eat, and maybe a fish that would be stinking.

(*She kneels down again, crossing herself, and saying prayers under her breath.*)

CATHLEEN (*to an old man*). Maybe yourself and Eamon would make a coffin when the sun rises. We have fine white boards herself bought, God help her, thinking Michael would be found, and I have a new cake you can eat while you'll be working.

THE OLD MAN (*looking at the boards*). Are there nails with them?

CATHLEEN.   There are not, Colum; we didn't think of the nails.

ANOTHER MAN.   It's a great wonder she wouldn't think of the nails, and all the coffins she's seen made already.

CATHLEEN.   It's getting old she is, and broken.

(*Maurya stands up again very slowly and spreads out the pieces of Michael's clothes beside the body, sprinkling them with the last of the Holy Water.*)

NORA (*in a whisper to Cathleen*). She's quiet now and easy; but the day Michael was drowned you could hear her crying out from this to the spring well. It's fonder she was of Michael, and would any one have thought that?

CATHLEEN (*slowly and clearly*). An old woman will be soon tired with anything she will do, and isn't it nine days herself is after crying and keening, and making great sorrow in the house?

MAURYA (*puts the empty cup mouth downwards on the table, and lays her hands together on Bartley's feet*). They're all together this time, and the end is come. May the Almighty God have mercy on Bartley's soul, and on Michael's soul, and on the souls of Sheamus and Patch, and Stephen and Shawn (*bending her head*); and may He have mercy on my soul, Nora, and on the soul of every one is left living in the world.

(*She pauses, and the keen rises a little more loudly from the women, then sinks away.*)

MAURYA (*continuing*). Michael has a clean burial in the far north, by the grace of the Almighty God. Bartley will have a fine coffin out of the white boards, and a deep grave surely. What more can we want than that? No man at all can be living for ever, and we must be satisfied.

(*She kneels down again and the curtain falls slowly.*)

FOCUS QUESTIONS

1. Discuss how the play resembles or contrasts with classical Greek tragedy.
2. Analyze the relationship between Maurya and Bartley to illustrate how the power of the sea—their only source of livelihood—affects the lives of the islanders.
3. Describe how pagan superstition and Christian symbolism and beliefs are juxtaposed in the play.

OTHER ACTIVITIES

1. Make a chart of the various uses for each prop: as part of exposition, as part of establishing the economic and social world of the characters, as symbolic of the play's themes.
2. Using reviews, photographs, and other available production documents, assess an Abbey Theatre production of the play.

BIBLIOGRAPHY

Benson, Eugene. *J. M. Synge*. New York: Grove Press, 1982.

Clarke, Brenna Katz. *The Emergence of the Irish Peasant Play at the Abbey Theatre*. Ann Arbor: UMI Research Press, 1982.

Gerstenberger, Donna. *John Millington Synge*. Boston: Twayne Publishers, 1990.

Greene, David, and Edward Stephens. *J. M. Synge, 1871–1909*. New York: New York University Press, 1989.

Grene, Nicholas. *Synge: A Critical Study of the Plays*. London: Macmillan, 1975.

Hogan, Robert, and James Kilroy. *The Abbey Theatre: The Years of Synge, 1905–1909*. The Modern Irish Drama: Documentary History 3. Highlands, NJ: Humanities Press, 1978.

Johnston, Denis. *John Millington Synge*. Columbia Essays on Modern Writers, 12. New York: Columbia University Press, 1965.

Kiberd, Declan. *Synge and the Irish Language*. Totowa, NJ: Rowan and Littlefield, 1979.

King, Mary. *The Drama of J. M. Synge*. Syracuse, NY: Syracuse University Press, 1985.

Kopper, Edward A. *A J. M. Synge Literary Companion*. New York: Greenwood Press, 1988.

Mikhail, E. H., ed. *J. M. Synge: Interview and Recollections*. New York: Barnes & Noble, 1977.

Thornton, Weldon. *J. M. Synge and the Western Mind*. Gerrard's Cross, Buckinghamshire, England: Colin Smythe, 1979.

Van Laan, Thomas. "Form as Agent in Synge's *Riders to the Sea*." *Drama Survey* 3 (February 1964): 352–66.

RECOMMENDED VIDEOTAPES AND RECORDINGS

Riders to the Sea. VHS. 40 min. 1987. Starring Geraldine Page, Amanda Plummer, Sachi Parker, and Barry McGovern. Directed by Roman O'Leary. Diamond Entertainment.

Riders to the Sea and *In the Shadow of the Glen*. Two sound cassettes. 145 min. 1983. A radio Eireann Players production. Spoken Arts.

Riders to the Sea. One sound cassette. 43 min. 1976. World Literature Sound Recording. Everett/Edwards.

THE HAIRY APE
EUGENE O'NEILL (1888–1953)

One of the marks of O'Neill's genius is that he was able to convert what happened to him into the drama of what has happened to us. His own story has become American history.

—TENNESSEE WILLIAMS

Roland Schäfer (*upstage center*) as Yank in *The Hairy Ape,* presented by the Schaubühne in 1986, under the direction of Peter Stein. *Photo: © Ruth Walz.*

APPROACHING MODERN AMERICAN DRAMA

Early in the twentieth century, when Europe continued to nurture important literary experimentation, a relatively young American drama still lagged noticeably behind. Although a substantial body of stage work held a mirror up to American society to demonstrate a sensibility that was both original and unique, its well-made conventions continued to pay homage to the aging muse of **melodrama.** (See Preface to Daly, p. 516.) In several curious ways, such conventionality echoed the climate of London's West End prior to the arrival of Bernard Shaw. (See Preface to Shaw, p. 622.) America had moved headlong into the twentieth century, but its theatrical standards were still tied to the past.

Such was the theatrical environment inhabited by the American actor, James O'Neill (1847–1920), whose son Eugene would become a natural heir to the nineteenth-century melodrama of which his father was a chief icon. Equally important, James was Irish-born, the repercussions of which would haunt his son's identity and later prompt the creation of powerful stage characters whose personalities would be forged from the immigrant experience. Angry with his father for squandering a brilliant acting career in the title role of Charles Fechter's dramatization of *The Count of Monte Cristo* (1883) by Alexandre Dumas—the play had amassed the actor easy fortunes over many years of performing in it—Eugene O'Neill at last revolted against the artifice and convention symbolized by his father's world.

It was no coincidence that playwriting became the outlet for his revolt. He had already incorporated some of his personal experiences into several one-act plays dealing with the sea, that mystical ally with which his youthful wanderings had brought him in close contact. Nevertheless, his debut as playwright happened under fortuitous circumstances during the summer of 1915 at an artists' colony in Provincetown, Massachusetts. A friend urged him to retrieve some one-acts locked away in a suitcase to help the Provincetown Players complete a program of short plays. The performance was a resounding success and O'Neill's career was launched. But neither the playwright nor his artistic circle could have imagined that, during the next few years, the results of that evening in Provincetown would transform the American drama into a modern art.

The Provincetown Players had discovered a powerful new spokesperson to represent their experimental vision. Joining them at their permanent headquarters on Macdougal Street in Greenwich Village, O'Neill fit comfortably into the unconventional enclave and wallowed in the creative energies around him. Here, Robert Edmond Jones and Kenneth Macgowan—two visionaries who had spent much time observing theatrical performances in Europe and recording their impressions—steered O'Neill's artistic inclinations toward the continental stagecraft, until he was convinced that any solution to the stagnation of the American drama would probably be found in the experimental climate from abroad.

Artificial realism, which had turned the theatre into a lifeless photograph but still reigned unchallenged in the American theatre, was a dead issue to O'Neill when he began to write for the Provincetown Players. Inspiration came from every direction, most especially from the expressionist writings of August Strindberg whom O'Neill called "the most modern of moderns, the greatest interpreter in the theatre of the uncharacteristic spiritual conflicts which constitute the drama—the blood—of our lives today."[1] Expressionism, as demonstrated through European art and literature and manifested so memorably in the works of the controversial Swedish playwright, emphasized the artist's subjective approach to objectifying certain psychological states on the stage. Its most visible feature in the drama was the distortion of physical perspectives to reflect the protagonist's emotional makeup. (See Preface to Strindberg, p. 661.)

Expressionism, as it turned out, found support in the New York theatre, leaving its impact on a wide circle of artists. Shortly after O'Neill left the Provincetown Players to work more independently as a playwright, theatrical experimentation that took place there continued to surface in the works of Alfred Kreymborg, Susan Glaspell, Edmund Wilson, e. e. cummings, and Paul Green. The legacy continued under the auspices of the Theatre Guild, whose productions of the European avant-garde drama seemed quite at home with American expressionists like Elmer Rice and John Howard Lawson. O'Neill eventually saw six of his own plays produced by the Guild, three of which bore the jagged imprint of this style. Countless artists as different from each other as Sophie Treadwell and William Carlos Williams made notable contributions to the expressionist drama in America, while others borrowed from its palette only when they needed.

O'Neill's prolific output ultimately reflected his extraordinarily diverse range of interest in writers like Nietzsche, Schopenhauer, Ibsen, Kaiser, Toller, Melville, Aeschylus, and Freud; and in religious and philosophical movements ranging from Oriental mysticism and pantheism to the more local varieties of puritanism, political anarchism, and his own Irish-Catholicism. So universal in scope, yet so personal in feeling was the impact of his dramatic art by the 1930s, that he was awarded the Nobel Prize for literature in 1936. Ironically, some of his best work still lay ahead.

MAJOR WORKS

Approaching O'Neill's canon from a stylistic standpoint enhances our appreciation of the different phases of his career. His more than two dozen early one-acts, mostly characterized by an unadorned realism, include the popular plays of the sea, all written between 1916 and 1918: *In the Zone, The Long Voyage Home, The Moon of the Caribbees, Bound East for Cardiff, Where the Cross is Made, 'Ile,* and *The Rope.* Full-length works that reveal impressive variations on this realistic mode include *Beyond the Horizon* (1920), *Anna Christie* (1921), *Desire Under the Elms* (1924), and *Marco Millions* (1928). His experiments with masks in *The Great God Brown* (1926) and *Lazarus Laughed* (1928) were intended to meet the psychological needs of modern audiences, while his equally controversial use of the **stream of consciousness** technique in *Strange Interlude* (1928) attracted great notoriety. His creation of a modern trilogy in *Mourning Becomes Electra* (1931) was built along the lines of its classical Greek counterpart, drawing resounding applause from critics and audiences alike. Still he demonstrated a unique mastery of comedy in *Ah, Wilderness!* (1933).

His final achievements, most of which were produced posthumously, were the result of great personal turmoil. *The Iceman Cometh* (1946), *Long Day's Journey into Night* (1956), *A Moon for the Misbegotten* (1957), *A Touch of the Poet* (1958), and *More Stately Mansions* (1967)—listed here in order of their New York productions—would not only demonstrate some of his finest writing and strongest characters under the banner of realism, but would also generate much controversy among his biographers for what they revealed about the playwright himself.

While these late plays have remained among the most popular and frequently produced of his work, they have also served as contrast to his earlier and equally remarkable productivity at the Provincetown Playhouse, where theatrical experimentation established his professional reputation. When his purest expressionist play, *The Emperor Jones,* premiered on the evening of November 1, 1920, O'Neill was convinced that its jarring style held a key to the unconscious and to that restorative Dionysiac spirit so vital to the drama. The two experimental works that followed, *The Hairy Ape* (1922) and *All God's Chillun Got Wings* (1924), explored the uses of expressionism on the American stage even further. But *The Hairy Ape* rightly epitomized the playwright's daring and imagination.

THE ACTION

The first four scenes take place on a ship where a stoker named Yank asserts that brute strength is his badge of superiority. When the socialite Mildred Douglas is invited to visit the stokehole, she faints at the sight of Yank's naked and raw animality. The last four scenes take place on shore, where the confused and insulted Yank searches for Mildred. He approaches Fifth Avenue on a Sunday morning but is hauled to jail for disturbing the peace. Hearing about the Industrial Workers of the World and hoping to find acceptance there, he breaks through the bars of his cell. The local IWW is not amused by Yank's intention to "knock all de steel in de woild up to de moon," so they throw him out. Determined to find a place where he can belong, Yank wanders into the monkey house at the zoo where he meets his fate.

STRUCTURE AND LANGUAGE

Ironically subtitled "A Comedy of Ancient and Modern Life," *The Hairy Ape* displays its fierce and eloquent temper through eight episodic but sharply etched scenes: from the "steel framework of [the stokehole] cage" to the steel bars of a gorilla house; from the protagonist's invincible strength in the bowels of a ship to his fatal homecoming at the hands of a brute he calls "brother." Its landscape of powerful images, both aural and visual, is accentuated by bristling dialogue and accelerated tempos, almost seeming to anatomize a protagonist who stands in relief against O'Neill's larger expressionist canvas.

Viewing Yank through a purely subjective lens, the playwright adheres firmly to the aesthetics of expressionism to create a work of audacious originality. While steel is the unifying and all-encompassing metaphor that empowers Yank's brutish *persona,* it is also the stuff of which cages are made. The resulting images of entrapment, which dissonantly permeate the *mise-en-scène,* enlighten our grasp of Yank's predicament and add poignant, almost tragic resonance to his final self-disclosure: "I ain't on oith and I ain't in heaven, get me? I'm in the middle tryin' to separate 'em, takin' all de woist punches from bot' of 'em. Maybe dat's what dey call hell, huh?"

The bold opening image that launches the action—"the steel framework of a cage"— pays homage to the melting-pot motif, an echo of America's nineteenth-century heritage. It is brought to life by a cacophony of voices belonging to the anonymous stokers and led by the symbolically nicknamed "Yank," an American whose thick speech defines him as a New York waterfront tough. Their raw vocal music generates powerful expressionist rhythms:

> Gif me a trink dere, you!
> 'Ave a wet!
> Salute!
> Gesundheit!
> Skoal!
> Drunk as a lord, God stiffen you!
> Here's how!
> Luck! . . .

Suddenly Yank merges his voice, first to identify with them, but also to establish himself as steel: "And I'm steel—steel—steel! I'm de muscles in steel, de punch behind it." Shifting from the collective chorus to the solitary figure, from the masses to the individual, O'Neill preserves the character of the mob to underscore Yank's alienation, his feeling "caged" in a dehumanized and hostile world. The critical theme is articulated swiftly and sharply.

By eliminating the realistic mode almost entirely, O'Neill's painterly style emerges from richly detailed stage directions: the emphasis on geometric perspectives and scenic distortions; the tightly juxtaposed areas of light and dark, white and black, heaven (the promenade deck where Mildred rests) and hell (the fiery stokehole where she later appears "all in white"); and Yank's hunched pose "in the attitude of Rodin's 'The Thinker,' " a silent image that humorously assigns to him an identity for which he is hopelessly miscast.

The expressionist canvas established in scene 1 becomes more fully actualized as Yank's thematic quest "to belong" intensifies back on shore in his futile search for Mildred. While her superficiality and lifelessness have already been established as the antithesis of Yank's animal strength, she emerges as his antagonist. Her appearance in the dramatic action is curiously confined to scenes 2 and 3. Nevertheless, she is symbolically represented in scene 5 by the mechanical procession of church-goers who resemble "gaudy marionettes." When Yank deliberately bumps into them to taunt them into reacting, the stage direction indicates that "it is he who recoils after each collision." Yank's painful invisibility is once again established, a further reminder of his powerlessness on land, away from the stokehole.

When the altercation lands him in jail, the dominant steel-cage motif in scene 6 achieves newer eloquence by isolating Yank, quite literally, from the world. It also foreshadows his visit to the zoo. Except for the voices of unseen cellmates and a guard who appears briefly, Yank alone occupies the stage. But O'Neill's canvas has acquired yet more ominous shadings designated by the "one electric bulb from the low ceiling of the narrow corridor [that] sheds its light through the heavy steel bars of the cell" to expose Yank. The stark simplicity of this stage picture demonstrates once and for all how effectively stage lighting can serve as character to advance dramatic theme.

Scene 8 at the monkey house contributes less to the tone of the play than the previous scenes have, but proves memorable for its humanistic dimension. Yank shares the stage with his nemesis, who initially "makes no sound or move" but then growls at certain intervals in response to Yank's remarks. In spite of the suggestive exchange between both parties, Yank's riveting monologue essentially functions as **soliloquy,** since his identification with the beast often dissolves into self-reflection, as if he were talking to himself: "So yuh're what she seen when she looked at me, de white-faced tart! I was you to her, get me? On'y outa de cage—broke out—free to moider her, see?" While the beast is incapable of understanding him, Yank's intended revenge on Mildred has been revealed. Ironically, his own destruction will be enacted before the scene has ended.

Another kind of closure is also established in this final *tableau,* since the off-stage "chorus of angry chattering and screeching [gorillas]" echoes scene 1, where Yank triumphed over the cacophony of his fellow-stokers. But this triumph was short-lived and marked the start of his journey downward. Although the link O'Neill draws between humankind and beasts has been forcefully demonstrated throughout, this kinship is suddenly juxtaposed to yield its tragic irony. While Yank's strength has kept him alienated until the end, his single victory, found "in a murderous hug" from the gorilla, has given him the chance to belong.

THE HAIRY APE-IN-PERFORMANCE

When *The Hairy Ape* opened at the Playwrights' Theatre on March 9, 1922, O'Neill was hardly a stranger to New York audiences. Scoring a major triumph with *The Emperor Jones,* he was awarded Pulitzer Prizes for *Beyond the Horizon* and *Anna Christie,* which were produced at centrally located Broadway theatres. Thus his commercial viability was assured. But the premiere of *The Hairy Ape,* with its political extremism and its stylistic daring, exceeded all expectations and catapulted the playwright to the highest rank of the literary vanguard.

The production was directed by James Light with the assistance of Arthur Hopkins. Designer Cleon Throckmorton approached the problematical sets with the help of Robert Edmond Jones. Inspired by O'Neill's explicit descriptions, the combined artistry of Throckmorton and Jones transformed the notoriously small stage of the theatre into the "cramped space in the bowels of a ship," bringing to life the nightmarish landscape of Yank's journey. Impressed with the assaultive effect of the stokehole scene when the boiler doors were suddenly opened, critic Walter Prichard Eaton eloquently described how "six red, searing searchlight-glares strike into the eyeballs of the audience like flashes from the Inferno."[2] Futhermore, the plaster dome and cyclorama at the Provincetown, which had created such wondrous effects in *The Emperor Jones,* performed similar magic in *The Hairy Ape,* when the illusion of endless angular perspectives for scene 1 was replaced by the "sunshine on the [promenade] deck" for scene 2. The jarring contrast was exactly what the play demanded.

The role of Yank was assigned to a forty-year-old ex-college football star-turned-actor named Louis Wolheim, who proved to be an outstanding choice and whose admiration for Yank inspired the ensemble around him. Complementing the visual eloquence established in the stokehole was the jail in which Yank sat alone in darkness, the door of his cell lit by a single beam of pallid light. Suddenly from the dark "comes the husky voice of the prisoner . . . and then rises a score of other voices, howling, jeering, cursing, groaning—the terrific strophe of the caged."[3]

The potential for experimentation at rehearsals was particularly evident in the Fifth Avenue scene. Although never specified in the stage directions, the idea of masks was suggested to O'Neill by Blanche Hays, who then proceeded to design full featherlike ones on which the church-goers' identically haughty and vacant features were painted. The effect was successful at creating what the playwright had described in his stage description, "the relentless horror of Frankenstein monsters in their detached, mechanical awareness," and encouraged O'Neill to experiment with masks in later plays.

Completing its limited engagement at the Playwrights' Theatre, *The Hairy Ape* moved uptown to the Plymouth Theatre on April 17, 1922, ringing up a total of 127 performances. By the end of the decade, it would be produced all over the world by theatre companies craving such adventurous works. Opening in Russia as early as 1923, it reappeared at the Kamerny Theatre under Alexander Tairov's controversial direction in 1926, in a production that later toured Europe and South America. Tairov's friendship with Japanese actor Yoshi Hijikata eventually led to productions of O'Neill's work, including *The Hairy Ape*, at the Tsukiji Little Theatre between 1924 and 1929.

Inspired by a London premiere, Hilton Edwards and Micheál MacLiammóir helped to establish the experimental wing of Dublin's Gate Theatre with their production of *The Hairy Ape,* which opened on October 28, 1928. Edwards himself played Yank. An opening-night critic found the production "very meritorious. The small stage cramps a play which demands space, but the producer, Mr. Hilton Edwards, made the best of everything at his disposal. The settings designed by Micheál MacLiammóir expressed fully the dramatist's desires."[4] One year later, *The Hairy Ape* opened at the Théâtre des Arts in Paris, under George Pitoëff's direction. Productions had been previously staged in Czechoslovakia (1927) and Hungary (1928), thereby establishing O'Neill's status as a world dramatist.

Germany's response to O'Neill during the twentieth century has warranted particular attention, since unconventional plays such as *The Emperor Jones* and *The Hairy Ape* were directly inspired by the German expressionist movement. By 1922, the German theatre was looking abroad for materials to satisfy its fluctuating tastes in drama. When *The Hairy Ape* opened at the Tribune on October 31, 1924, under the direction of Eugen Robert, the largely favorable if not enthusiastic critical reception seemed hardly surprising. For the expressionist movement, which once enjoyed great popularity in the German theatre, had changed directions after World War I, so that O'Neill's play was reviving an earlier style. Thus *The Hairy Ape* became conspicuously absent for decades, a situation not helped by the fact that O'Neill's plays were censured by the Third Reich. But O'Neill's name had already drifted into German consciousness so that the plays he would write during the final stage of his career would renew his popularity with German audiences during the second half of the twentieth century.

In 1986, more than sixty years after its German premiere, director Peter Stein unveiled *The Hairy Ape (Der Haarige Affe)* at the Schaubühne in West Berlin in a production that very much belonged to the German tradition and, in the words of English critic Michael Billington, "widen[ed] our experience of world drama."[5] Acknowledging Stein's imaginative direction and an extraordinary acting ensemble headed by Roland Schäfer's hypnotic Yank, the production emphasized Lucio Fanti's sets, which exhumed the power of German expressionism to reinvent O'Neill's nightmarish world.

The audience confronted a gigantic wall of three riveted steel plates, the full height of the curtainless stage—horizontally but unevenly leveled—which were lifted to expose the different layers of the ship's world. The central plate revealed the cramped quarters of the forecastle, barely six feet high, compelling Yank and his comrades to assume their bent, animalistic poses, as they drank, sang, fought, and slept, accompanied by sirens, throbbing engines, and accordion music. Stein's "sculptural frieze of pale, coal-choked bodies comes to life in a wide slit so low some can barely stand up in it," wrote critic Michael Ratcliffe.[6]

From the promenade deck of the upper-third tier, Mildred started her slow and cautious descent, the entire height of the stage, down the long flight of stairs to the stokehole below. The bottom plate was lifted to reveal a row of men, naked to the waist, who groaned and cursed as they shoveled coal into the fifteen fiery boilers of the ship's furnace. Dressed to resemble a white plastic doll with blood-red lips, Mildred lifted her arms in a puppet-like gesture briefly suggestive of a benediction, swooned at Yank's animal ugliness, and was quickly carried off by the second engineer. Yank hurled his shovel after them and swore to avenge her contempt.

In the last four scenes, in contrast to the first four on the ship, Stein evoked an equally provocative *mise-en-scène,* suggesting a world askew. The results were angular, theatrical, and dizzyingly expressionistic. Against a sharply raked stage, skyscraper cutouts and blinking neon-dollar signs sailed in from side to center stage, at one point revealing Yank—in King-Kong fashion—beating his chest atop one of the skyscrapers, surrounded by Fifth Avenue city-dwellers in red masks. At the close of the scene, Yank was surrounded by Keystone Kops who brutally assaulted him as the sounds of jazz muffled their attack.

The jail scene offered a two-tiered perspective of cages "with white hands fluttering through the bars like doves"[7] and beating spoons deafeningly against the prison bars. The black and white effect contrasted with the IWW set, which was bathed in a pool of warm light, like an Edward Hopper painting—both realistic and dreamlike—with its remembered ideal of labor at its most purposeful and law-abiding.

In the final scene, Yank confronted a gorilla in an eerie zoo set "where primates shaggily dangle[d] from perches"[8] of gigantic circular cages,[8] like a chattering chorus reacting to his bitter soliloquy. With cages tilted to the right, but set against skyscraper cutouts angled toward the left, Yank was choreographed among sixteen vocally orchestrated gorillas—an effect that utilized the entire Schaubühne company in gorilla suits. The final image conveyed the artistic merging of director Stein and set designer Fanti in actualizing the irony O'Neill sought: that a common laborer, despised as a hairy ape, should end up dead in the same cage of the very beast whom, in a gesture of brotherhood, he had set free.

REFLECTIONS ON THE HAIRY APE

The following theatre review, written by Alexander Woollcott, appeared in The
New York Times *on March 10, 1922.*

The little theatre of Provincetownsmen in Macdougal Street was packed to the doors with astonishment last evening as scene after scene unfolded in the new play by Eugene O'Neill. This was *The Hairy Ape,* a bitter, brutal, wildly fantastic play of nightmare hue and nightmare distortion. It is a monstrously uneven piece, now flamingly eloquent, now choked and thwarted and inarticulate. Like most of his writing for the theatre, it is the worse here and there for the lack of a fierce, unintimidated blue pencil, but it has a little greatness in it, and it seems rather absurd to fret overmuch about the undisciplined imagination of the young playwright towering so conspicuously above the milling, mumbling crowd of playwrights who have no imagination at all.

The Hairy Ape has been superbly produced. There is a rumor abroad that Arthur Hopkins, with a proprietary interest in the piece, has been lurking around its rehearsals and the program confesses that Robert Edmond Jones went down to Macdougal Street and took a hand with Cleon Throckmorton in designing the eight pictures which the play calls for. That preposterous little theatre has one of the most cramped stages New York has ever known, and yet on it the artists have created the illusion of vast spaces and endless perspectives. They drive one to the conclusion that when a stage seems pinched and little, it is the mind of the producer that is pinched and little. This time O'Neill, unbridled, set them a merry pace in the eccentric gait of his imaginings. They kept up with him.

O'Neill begins his fable by posing before you the greatest visible contrast in social and physical circumstance. He leads you up the gangplank of a luxurious liner bound for Europe. He plunges you first into the stokers' pit, thrusting you down among the men as they stumble in from the furnaces, hot, sweaty, choked with coal dust, brutish. Squirm as you may, he holds you while you listen to the rumble of their discontent, and while you listen, also, to speech more squalid than an American audience heard before in an American theatre, it is true talk, all of it, and only those who have been so softly bred that they have never really heard the vulgate spoken in all its richness would venture to suggest that he has exaggerated it by so much as a syllable in order to agitate the refined. On the contrary.

Then, in a twinkling, he drags you (as the ghosts drag Scrooge) up out of all this murk and thudding avengeance and brawling of speech to a cool, sweet, sunlit stretch of the hurricane deck, where, at lazy ease, lies the daughter of the President of the line's board of directors, a nonchalant dilettante who has found settlement work frightfully interesting and is simply crazy to go down among the stokers and see how the other half lives aboard ship.

Then follows the confrontation—the fool fop of a girl and the huge animal of a stoker who had taken sort of a dizzy romantic pride in himself and his work as something that was real in an unreal world, as something that actually counted, as something that was and had force. Her horrified recoil from him as from some loathsome, hairy ape is the first notice served on him by the world that he doesn't belong. The remaining five scenes are the successive blows by which this is driven in on him, each scene, as written, as acted and as intensified by the artists, taking on more and more of the nightmare quality with which O'Neill seemed possessed to endow his fable.

The scene on Fifth Avenue when the hairy ape comes face to face with a little parade of wooden-faced church-goers who walk like automata and prattle of giving a "Hundred Percent American Bazaar" as a contribution to the solution of discontent among the lower classes: the scene on Blackwell's Island with the endless row of cells and the argot of the prisoners floating out of the darkness: the care with which each scene ends in a retributive and terrifying closing in upon the bewildered fellow—all these preparations induce you at last, to accept as natural and inevitable and right that the hairy ape should, by the final curtain, be found dead inside the cage of the gorilla in the Bronx Zoo.

Except for the role of the girl, which is pretty badly played by Mary Blair, the cast captured for *The Hairy Ape* is an exceptionally good one. Louis Wolheim, though now and then rather painfully off the beat in his cooperation with the others, gives a capital impersonation of the stoker, and lesser parts are well managed by Harry O'Neill as an Irish fireman dreaming of the old days of sailing vessels, and Harold West as a cockney agitator who is fearfully annoyed because of the hairy ape's concentrating his anger against this one little plutocrat instead of maintaining an abstract animosity against plutocrats in general.

In Macdougal Street now and doubtlessly headed for Broadway, we have a turbulent and tremendous play, so full of blemishes that the merest fledgling among the critics could point out a dozen, yet so vital and interesting and teeming with life that those playgoers who let it escape them will be missing one of the real events of the year.

Notes

1. *Helen Deutsch and Stella Hanau,* THE PROVINCETOWN: A STORY OF THE THEATRE *(New York: Russell & Russell, 1931), 191.*
2. *Jordan Miller,* PLAYWRIGHT'S PROGRESS *(Chicago: Scott Foresman, 1965), 34.*
3. *Ibid.*
4. IRISH TIMES, *29 Oct. 1928.*
5. *Michael Billington,* MANCHESTER GUARDIAN, *13 May 1987.*
6. OBSERVER, *7 Dec. 1986.*
7. *Billington.*
8. *Peter Kemp,* INDEPENDENT, *13 May 1987.*

THE HAIRY APE

A COMEDY OF ANCIENT AND MODERN LIFE IN EIGHT SCENES
EUGENE O'NEILL

CHARACTERS

Robert Smith, "Yank" Mildred Douglas A Guard
Paddy Her Aunt A Secretary of an Organization
Long Second Engineer Stokers, Ladies, Gentlemen, etc.

SCENES

SCENE 1: The firemen's forecastle of an ocean liner an hour after sailing from New York.
SCENE 2: Section of promenade deck, two days out—morning.
SCENE 3: The stokehole. A few minutes later.
SCENE 4: Same as Scene One. Half an hour later.
SCENE 5: Fifth Avenue, New York. Three weeks later.
SCENE 6: An island near the city. The next night.
SCENE 7: In the city. About a month later.
SCENE 8: In the city. Twilight of the next day.

SCENE ONE

The firemen's forecastle of a transatlantic liner an hour after sailing from New York for the voyage across. Tiers of narrow, steel bunks, three deep, on all sides. An entrance in rear. Benches on the floor before the bunks. The room is crowded with men, shouting, cursing, laughing, singing—a confused, inchoate uproar swelling into a sort of unity, a meaning—the bewildered, furious, baffled defiance of a beast in a cage. Nearly all the men are drunk. Many bottles are passed from hand to hand. All are dressed in dungaree pants, heavy ugly shoes. Some wear singlets, but the majority are stripped to the waist.

The treatment of this scene, or of any other scene in the play, should by no means be naturalistic. The effect sought after is a cramped space in the bowels of a ship, imprisoned by white steel. The lines of bunks, the uprights supporting them, cross each other like the steel framework of a cage. The ceiling crushes down upon the men's heads. They cannot stand upright. This accentuates the natural stooping posture which shoveling coal and the resultant overdevelopment of back and shoulder muscles have given them. The men themselves should resemble those pictures in which the appearance of Neanderthal Man is guessed at. All are hairy-chested, with long arms of tremendous power, and low, receding brows above their small, fierce, resentful eyes. All the civilized white races are represented, but except for the slight differentiation in color of hair, skin, eyes, all these men are alike.

The curtain rises on a tumult of sound. YANK *is seated in the foreground. He seems broader, fiercer, more truculent, more powerful, more sure of himself than the rest. They respect his superior strength—the grudging respect of fear. Then, too, he represents to them a self-expression, the very last word in what they are, their most highly developed individual.*

VOICES.
>Gif me trink dere, you!
>'Ave a wet!
>Salute!
>Gesundheit!
>Skoal!
>Drunk as a lord, God stiffen you!
>Here's how!
>Luck!
>Pass back that bottle, damn you!
>Pourin' it down his neck!
>Ho, Froggy! Where the devil have you been?
>*La Touraine.*
>I hit him smash in yaw, py Gott!
>Jenkins—the First—he's a rotten swine——
>And the coppers nabbed him—and I run——
>I like peer better. It don't pig head gif you.
>A slut, I'm sayin'. She robbed me aslape—
>To hell with 'em all!
>You're a bloody liar!
>Say dot again! (*Commotion. Two men about to fight are pulled apart.*)
>No scrappin' now!
>Tonight——
>See who's the best man!
>Bloody Dutchman!
>Tonight on the for'ard square.
>I'll bet on Dutchy.
>He packa da wallop, I tell you!
>Shut up, Wop!
>No fightin', maties. We're all chums, ain't we?
>(*A voice starts bawling a song.*)
>"Beer, beer, glorious beer!
>Fill yourselves right up to here."

YANK (*for the first time seeming to take notice of the uproar about him, turns around threateningly—in a tone of contemptuous authority*). Choke off dat noise! Where d'yuh get dat beer stuff? Beer, hell! Beer's for goils—and Dutchmen. Me for somep'n wit a kick to it! Gimme a drink, one of youse guys. (*Several bottles are eagerly offered. He takes a tremendous gulp at one of them; then, keeping the bottle in his hand, glares belligerently at the owner, who hastens to acquiesce in this robbery by saying*) All righto, Yank. Keep it and have another. (YANK *contemptuously turns his back on the crowd again. For a second there is an embarrassed silence. Then——*)

VOICES.
>We must be passing the Hook.
>She's beginning to roll to it.
>Six days in hell—and then Southampton.
>Py Yesus, I vish somepody take my first vatch for me!
>Gittin' seasick, Square-head?
>Drink up and forget it!
>What's in your bottle?
>Gin.
>Dot's a nigger trink.
>Absinthe? It's doped. You'll go off your chump, Froggy!
>Cochon!
>Whisky, that's the ticket!
>Where's Paddy?
>Going asleep.
>Sing us that whisky song, Paddy.

(*They all turn to an old, wizened Irishman who is dozing, very drunk, on the benches forward. His face is extremely monkey-like with all the sad, patient pathos of that animal in his small eyes.*)

>Singa da song, Caruso Pat!
>He's gettin' old. The drink is too much for him.
>He's too drunk.

PADDY (*blinking about him, starts to his feet resentfully, swaying, holding on to the edge of a bunk*). I'm never too drunk to sing. 'Tis only when I'm dead to the world I'd be wishful to sing at all. (*With a sort of sad contempt.*) "Whisky Johnny," ye want? A chanty, ye want? Now that's a queer wish from the ugly like of you. God help you. But no mather, (*He starts to sing in a thin, nasal, doleful tone.*)

>"Oh, whisky is the life of man!
>   Whisky! O Johnny! (*They all join in on this.*)
>Oh, whisky is the life of man!
>   Whisky for my Johnny! (*Again chorus.*)
>Oh, whisky drove my old man mad!
>   Whisky! O Johnny!
>Oh, whisky drove my old man mad!
>   Whisky for my Johnny!"

YANK (*again turning around scornfully*). Aw hell! Nix on dat old sailing ship stuff! All dat bull's dead, see? And you're dead, too, yuh damned old Harp, on'y yuh don't know it. Take it easy, see. Give us a rest. Nix on de loud noise. (*With a cynical grin.*) Can't youse see I'm tryin' to t'ink?

ALL (*repeating the word after him as one with the same cynical amused mockery*). Think! (*The chorused word has a brazen metallic quality as if their throats were phonograph horns. It is followed by a general uproar of hard, barking laughter.*)

VOICES.

> Don't be cracking your head wit ut, Yank.
> You gat headache, py yingo!
> One thing about it—it rhymes with drink!
> Ha, ha, ha!
> Drink, don't think!
> Drink, don't think!
> Drink, don't think! (*A whole chorus of voices has taken up this refrain, stamping on the floor, pounding on the benches with fists.*)

YANK (*taking a gulp from his bottle—good-naturedly*). Aw right. Can de noise. I got yuh de foist time. (*The uproar subsides. A very drunken sentimental tenor begins to sing.*)

> "Far away in Canada
>   Far across the sea,
> There's a lass who fondly waits
>   Making a home for me——"

YANK (*fiercely contemptuous*). Shut up, yuh lousy boob! Where d'yuh get dat tripe? Home? Home, hell! I'll make a home for yuh! I'll knock yuh dead. Home! T'hell wit home! Where d'yuh get dat tripe? Dis is home, see? What d'yuh want wit home? (*Proudly.*) I runned away from mine when I was a kid. On'y too glad to beat it, dat was me. Home was lickings for me, dat's all. But yuh can bet your shoit no one ain't never licked me since! Wanter try it, any of youse? Huh! I guess not. (*In a more placated but still contemptuous tone.*) Goils waitin' for yuh, huh? Aw, hell! Dat's all tripe. Dey don't wait for no one. Dey'd double-cross yuh for a nickel. Dey're all tarts, get me? Treat 'em rough, dat's me. To hell wit 'em. Tarts, dat's what, de whole bunch of 'em.

LONG (*very drunk, jumps on a bench excitedly, gesticulating with a bottle in his hand*). Listen 'ere, Comrades. Yank 'ere is right. 'E says this 'ere stinkin' ship is our 'ome. And 'e says as 'ome is 'ell. And 'e's right! This is 'ell. We lives in 'ell, Comrades—and right enough we'll die in it. (*Raging.*) And who's ter blame, I arsks yer? We ain't. We wasn't born this rotten way. All men is born free and ekal. That's in the bleedin' Bible, maties. But what d'they care for the Bible—them lazy, bloated swine what travels first cabin? Them's the ones. They dragged us down 'til we're on'y wage slaves in the bowels of a bloody ship, sweatin', burnin' up, eatin' coal dust! Hit's them's ter blame—the damned Capitalist clarss! (*There had been a gradual murmur of contemptuous resentment rising among the men until now he is interrupted by a storm of catcalls, hisses, boos, hard laughter.*)

VOICES.

> Turn it off!
> Shut up!
> Sit down!
> Closa da face!
> Tamn fool! (*Etc.*)

YANK (*standing up and glaring at* LONG). Sit down before I knock yuh down! (LONG *makes haste to efface himself.* YANK *goes on contemptuously.*) De Bible, huh? De Cap'tlist class, huh? Aw nix on dat Salvation Army-Socialist bull. Git a soapbox! Hire a hall! Come and be saved, huh? Jerk us to Jesus, huh? Aw g'wan! I've listened to lots of guys like you, see. Yuh're all wrong. Wanter know what I t'ink? Yuh ain't no good for no one. Yuh're de bunk. Yuh ain't got no noive, get me? Yuh're yellow, dat's what. Yellow, dat's you. Say! What's dem slobs in de foist cabin got to do wit us? We're better men dan dey are, ain't we? Sure! One of us guys could clean up de whole mob wit one mit. Put one of 'em down here for one watch in de stokehole, what'd happen? Dey'd carry him off on a stretcher. Dem boids don't amount to nothin'. Dey're just baggage. Who makes dis old tub run? Ain't it us guys? Well den, we belong, don't we? We belong and dey don't. Dat's all. (*A loud chorus of approval.* YANK *goes on.*) As for dis bein' hell—aw, nuts! Yuh lost your noive, dat's what. Dis is a man's job, get me? It belongs. It runs dis tub. No stiffs need apply. But yuh're a stiff, see? Yuh're yellow, dat's you.

VOICES (*with a great hard pride in them*).

> Righto!
> A man's job!
> Talk is cheap, Long.
> He never could hold up his end.
> Divil take him!
> Yank's right. We make it go.
> Py Gott, Yank say right ting!
> We don't need no one cryin' over us.
> Makin' speeches.
> Throw him out!
> Yellow!
> Chuck him overboard!
> I'll break his jaw for him!
> (*They crowd around* LONG *threateningly.*)

YANK (*half good-natured again—contemptuously*). Aw, take it easy. Leave him alone. He ain't woith a punch. Drink up. Here's how, whoever owns dis. (*He takes a long swallow from his bottle. All drink with him. In a flash all is hilarious amiability again, back-slapping, loud talk, etc.*)

PADDY (*who has been sitting in a blinking, melancholy daze—suddenly cries out in a voice full of old sorrow*). We belong to this, you're saying? We make the ship to go, you're saying? Yerra then, that Almighty God have pity on us! (*His voice runs into the wail of a keen, he rocks back and forth on his bench. The men stare at him, startled and impressed in spite of themselves.*) Oh, to be back in the fine days of my youth, ochone! Oh, there was fine beautiful ships them days—clippers wid tall masts touching the sky—fine strong men in them—men that was sons of the sea as if 'twas the mother that bore them. Oh, the clean skins of them, and the clear eyes, the straight backs and full chests of them! Brave men they was, and bold men surely! We'd be sailing out, bound down round the Horn maybe. We'd be making sail in the dawn, with a fair breeze, singing a chanty song wid no care to it. And astern the land would be sinking low and dying out, but we'd give it no heed but a laugh, and never a look behind. For the day that was, was enough, for we was free men— and I'm thinking 'tis only slaves do be giving heed to the day that's gone or the day to come—until they're old like me. (*With a sort of religious exaltation.*) Oh, to be scudding south again wid the power of the Trade Wind driving her on steady through the nights and the days! Full sail on her! Nights and days! Nights when the foam of the wake would be flaming wid fire, when the sky'd be blazing and winking wid stars. Or the full of the moon maybe. Then you'd see her driving through the gray night, her sails stretching aloft all silver and white, not a sound on the deck, the lot of us dreaming dreams, till you'd believe 'twas no real ship at all you was on but a ghost ship like the *Flying Dutchman* they say does be roaming the seas forevermore widout touching a port. And there was the days, too. A warm sun on the clean decks. Sun warming the blood of you, and wind over the miles of shiny green ocean like strong drink to your lungs. Work— aye, hard work—but who'd mind that at all? Sure, you worked under the sky and 'twas work wid skill and daring to it. And wid the day done, in the dog watch, smoking me pipe at ease, the lookout would be raising land maybe, and we'd see the mountains of South Americy wid the red fire of the setting sun painting their white tops and the clouds floating by them! (*His tone of exaltation ceases. He goes on mournfully.*) Yerra, what's the use of talking? 'Tis a dead man's whisper. (*To* YANK *resentfully.*) 'Twas them days men belonged to ships, not now. 'Twas them days a ship was part of the sea, and a man was part of a ship, and the sea joined all together and made it one. (*Scornfully.*) Is it one wid this you'd be, Yank—black smoke from the funnels smudging the sea, smudging the decks—the bloody engines pounding and throbbing and shaking—wid divil a sight of sun or a breath of clean air— choking our lungs wid coal dust—breaking our backs and hearts in the hell of the stokehole—feeding the bloody furnace—feeding our lives along wid the coal, I'm thinking—caged in by steel from a sight of the sky like bloody apes in the Zoo! (*With a harsh laugh.*) Ho-ho, divil mend you! Is it to belong to that you're wishing? Is it a flesh and blood wheel of the engines you'd be?

YANK (*who has been listening with a contemptuous sneer, barks out the answer*). Sure ting! Dat's me. What about it?

PADDY (*as if to himself—with great sorrow*). Me time is past due. That a great wave wid sun in the heart of it may sweep me over the side sometime I'd be dreaming of the days that's gone!

YANK.   Aw, yuh crazy Mick! (*He springs to his feet and advances on Paddy threateningly—then stops, fighting some queer struggle within himself—lets his hands fall to his side—contemptuously.*) Aw, take it easy. Yuh're aw right, at dat. Yuh're bugs, dat's all—nutty as a cuckoo. All dat tripe yuh been pullin'—Aw, dat's all right. On'y it's dead, get me? Yuh don't belong no more, see. Yuh don't get de stuff. Yuh're too old. (*Disgustedly.*) But aw say, come up for air onct in a while, can't yuh? See what's happened since yuh croaked. (*He suddenly bursts forth vehemently, growing more and more excited.*) Say! Sure! Sure I meant it! What de hell—Say, lemme talk! Hey! Hey, you old Harp! Hey, youse guys! Say, listen to me— wait a moment—I gotta talk, see. I belong and he don't. He's dead but I'm livin'. Listen to me! Sure I'm part of de engines! Why de hell not? Dey move, don't dey? Dey're speed, ain't dey? Dey smash trou, don't dey? Twenty-five knots a hour! Dat's goin' some! Dat's new stuff! Dat belongs! But him, he's too old. He gets dizzy. Say, listen. All dat crazy tripe about nights and days; all dat crazy tripe about stars and moons; all dat crazy tripe about suns and winds, fresh air and de rest of it—Aw hell, dat's all a dope dream! Hittin' de pipe of de past, dat's what he's doin'. He's old and don't belong no more. But me, I'm young! I'm in de pink! I move wit it! It, get me! I mean de ting dat's de guts of all dis. It ploughs trou all de tripe he's been sayin'. It blows dat up! It knocks dat dead! It slams dat offen de face of de oith! It, get me! De engines and de coal and de smoke and all de rest of it! He can't breathe and swallow coal dust, but I kin, see? Dat's fresh air for me! Dat's food for me! I'm new, get me? Hell in de stokehole? Sure! It takes a man to work in hell. Hell, sure, dat's my fav'rite climate. I eat it up! I git fat on it! It's me makes it hot! It's me makes it roar! It's me makes it move! Sure, on'y for me everyting stops. It all goes dead, get me? De noise and smoke and all de engines movin' de woild, dey stop. Dere ain't nothin' no more! Dat's what I'm sayin'. Everyting else dat makes de woild move, somep'n makes it move. It can't move witout somep'n else, see? Den yuh get down to me. I'm at de bottom, get me! Dere ain't nothin' foither. I'm de end! I'm de start! I start somep'n and de woild moves! It— dat's me!—de new dat's moiderin' de old! I'm de ting in coal dat makes it boin; I'm steam and oil for de engines; I'm de ting in noise dat makes yuh hear it; I'm smoke and express trains and steamers and factory whistles; I'm de ting in gold dat makes money! And I'm what makes iron into steel! Steel, dat stands for de whole ting! And I'm steel—steel—steel! I'm de muscles in steel, de punch behind it. (*As he says this he pounds with his fist against the steel bunks. All the men, roused to a pitch of frenzied self-glorification by his speech, do likewise. There is a deafening metallic roar, through which* YANK'S *voice can be heard bellowing.*) Slaves, hell! We run de whole woiks. All de rich guys dat tink dey're somep'n, dey ain't nothin'! Dey don't belong. But us guys, we're in de move, we're at de bottom, de whole ting is us! (PADDY *from the start of* YANK'S *speech has been taking one gulp after another from his bottle, at first frightenedly, as if he were afraid to listen, then desperately, as if to drown his senses, but finally has achieved complete indifferent, even amused, drunkenness.* YANK *sees his lips moving. He quells the uproar with a shout.*) Hey, youse guys, take it easy! Wait a moment! De nutty Harp is sayin' somep'n.

PADDY (*is heard now—throws his head back with a mocking burst of laughter*). Ho-ho-ho-ho-ho——

YANK (*drawing back his fist, with a snarl*). Aw! Look out who yuh're givin' the bark!

PADDY (*begins to sing "The Miller of Dee" with enormous good nature*).

　　"I care for nobody, no, not I,
　　And nobody cares for me."

YANK (*good-natured himself in a flash, interrupts* PADDY *with a slap on the bare back like a report*). Dat's de stuff! Now yuh're gettin' wise to somep'n. Care for nobody, dat's de dope! To hell wit 'em all! And nix on nobody else carin'. I kin care for myself, get me! (*Eight bells sound, muffled, vibrating through the steel walls as if some enormous brazen gong were imbedded in the heart of the ship. All the men jump up mechanically, file through the door silently close upon each other's heels in what is very like a prisoners' lockstep.* YANK *slaps* PADDY *on the back.*) Our watch, yuh old Harp! (*Mockingly.*) Come on down in hell. Eat up de coal dust. Drink in de heat. It's it, see! Act like yuh like it, yuh better—or croak yuhself.

PADDY (*with jovial defiance*). To the divil wid it! I'll not report this watch. Let him log me and be damned. I'm no slave the like of you. I'll be sittin' here at me ease, and drinking, and thinking, and dreaming dreams.

YANK (*contemptuously*). Tinkin' and dreamin', what'll that get yuh? What's tinkin' got to do wit it? We move, don't we? Speed, ain't it? Fog, dat's all you stand for. But we drive trou dat, don't we? We split dat up and smash trou—twenty-five knots a hour! (*Turns his back on* PADDY *scornfully.*) Aw, yuh make me sick! Yuh don't belong! (*He strides out the door in rear. Paddy hums to himself, blinking drowsily.*)

(*The curtain falls.*)

SCENE TWO

Two days out. A section of the promenade deck. MILDRED DOUGLAS *and her aunt are discovered reclining in deck chairs. The former is a girl of twenty, slender, delicate, with a pale, pretty face marred by a self-conscious expression of disdainful superiority. She looks fretful, nervous and discontented, bored by her own anemia. Her aunt is a pompous and proud—and fat—old lady. She is a type even to the point of* a double chin and lorgnettes. *She is dressed pretentiously, as if afraid her face alone would never indicate her position in life.* MILDRED *is dressed all in white.*

The impression to be conveyed by this scene is one of the beautiful, vivid life of the sea all about—sunshine on the deck in a great flood, the fresh sea wind blowing across it. In the midst of this, these two incongruous, artificial figures, inert and disharmonious, the elder like a gray lump of dough touched up with rouge, the younger looking as if the vitality of her stock had been sapped before she was conceived, so that she is the expression not of its life energy but merely of the artificialities that energy had won for itself in the spending.

MILDRED (*looking up with affected dreaminess*). How the black smoke swirls back against the sky! Is it not beautiful?

AUNT (*without looking up*). I dislike smoke of any kind.

MILDRED.　My great-grandmother smoked a pipe—a clay pipe.

AUNT (*ruffling*). Vulgar!

MILDRED.　She was too distant a relative to be vulgar. Time mellows pipes.

AUNT (*pretending boredom but irritated*). Did the sociology you took up at college teach you that—to play the ghoul on every possible occasion, excavating old bones? Why not let your great-grandmother rest in her grave?

MILDRED (*dreamily*). With her pipe beside her—puffing in Paradise.

AUNT (*with spite*). Yes, you are a natural born ghoul. You are even getting to look like one, my dear.

MILDRED (*in a passionless tone*). I detest you, Aunt. (*Looking at her critically.*) Do you know what you remind me of? Of a cold pork pudding against a background of linoleum tablecloth in the kitchen of a—but the possibilities are wearisome. (*She closes her eyes.*)

AUNT (*with a bitter laugh*). Merci for your candor. But since I am and must be your chaperon—in appearance—at least—let us patch up some sort of armed truce. For my part you are quite free to indulge any pose of eccentricity that beguiles you—as long as you observe the amenities—

MILDRED (*drawling*). The inanities?

AUNT (*going on as if she hadn't heard*). After exhausting the morbid thrills of social service work on New York's East Side—how they must have hated you, by the way, the poor that you made so much poorer in their own eyes!—you are now bent on making your slumming international. Well, I hope Whitechapel will provide the needed nerve tonic. Do not ask me to chaperon you there, however. I told your father I would not. I loathe deformity. We will hire an army of detectives and you may investigate everything—they allow you to see.

MILDRED (*protesting with a trace of genuine earnestness*). Please do not mock at my attempts to discover how the other half lives. Give me credit for some sort of groping sincerity in that at least. I would like to help them. I would like to be of some use in the world. Is it my fault I don't know how? I would like to be sincere, to touch life somewhere. (*With weary bitterness.*) But I'm afraid I have neither the vitality nor integrity. All that was burnt out in our stock before I was born. Grandfather's blast furnaces, flaming to the sky, melting steel, making millions—then father keeping those home fires burning, making more millions—and little me at the tail-end of it all. I'm a waste product in the Bessemer process—like the millions. Or rather, I inherit the acquired trait of the by-product, wealth, but none of the energy, none of the strength of the steel that made it. I am sired by gold and damned by it, as they say at the race track—damned in more ways than one. (*She laughs mirthlessly.*)

AUNT (*unimpressed—superciliously*). You seem to be going in for sincerity today. It isn't becoming to you, really—except as an obvious pose. Be as artificial as you are, I advise. There's a sort of sincerity in that, you know. And, after all, you must confess you like that better.

MILDRED (*again affected and bored*). Yes, I suppose I do. Pardon me for my outburst. When a leopard complains of its spots, it must sound rather grotesque. (*In a mocking tone.*) Purr, little leopard. Purr, scratch, tear, kill, gorge yourself and be happy—only stay in the jungle, where your spots are camouflage. In a cage they make you conspicuous.

AUNT.   I don't know what you are talking about.

MILDRED.   It would be rude to talk about anything to you. Let's just talk. (*She looks at her wrist watch.*) Well, thank goodness, it's about time for them to come for me. That ought to give me a new thrill, Aunt.

AUNT (*affectedly troubled*). You don't mean to say you're going? The dirt—the heat must be frightful——

MILDRED.   Grandfather started as a puddler. I should have inherited an immunity to heat that would make a salamander shiver. It will be fun to put it to the test.

AUNT.   But don't you have to have the captain's—or someone's—permission to visit the stokehole?

MILDRED (*with a triumphant smile*). I have it—both his and the chief engineer's. Oh, they didn't want to at first, in spite of my social service credentials. They didn't seem a bit anxious that I should investigate how the other half lives and works on a ship. So I had to tell them that my father, the president of Nazareth Steel, chairman of the board of directors of this line, had told me it would be all right.

AUNT.   He didn't.

MILDRED.   How naïve age makes one! But I said he did, Aunt. I even said he had given me a letter to them—which I had lost. And they were afraid to take the chance that I might be lying. (*Excitedly.*) So it's ho! for the stokehole. The second engineer is to escort me. (*Looking at her watch again.*) It's time. And here he comes, I think. (*The

SECOND ENGINEER *enters. He is a husky, fine-looking man of thirty-five or so. He stops before the two and tips his cap, visibly embarrassed and ill-at-ease.*)

SECOND ENGINEER.   Miss Douglas?

MILDRED.   Yes. (*Throwing off her rugs and getting to her feet.*) Are we all ready to start?

SECOND ENGINEER.   In just a second, ma'am. I'm waiting for the Fourth. He's coming along.

MILDRED (*with a scornful smile*). You don't care to shoulder this responsibility alone, is that it?

SECOND ENGINEER (*forcing a smile*). Two are better than one. (*Disturbed by her eyes, glances out to sea—blurts out.*) A fine day we're having.

MILDRED.   Is it?

SECOND ENGINEER.   A nice warm breeze——

MILDRED.   It feels cold to me.

SECOND ENGINEER.   But it's hot enough in the sun——

MILDRED.   Not hot enough for me. I don't like Nature. I was never athletic.

SECOND ENGINEER (*forcing a smile*). Well, you'll find it hot enough where you're going.

MILDRED.   Do you mean hell?

SECOND ENGINEER (*flabbergasted, decides to laugh*). Ho-ho! No, I mean the stokehole.

MILDRED.   My grandfather was a puddler. He played with boiling steel.

SECOND ENGINEER (*all at sea—uneasily*). Is that so? Hum, you'll excuse me, ma'am, but are you intending to wear that dress?

MILDRED.   Why not?

SECOND ENGINEER.   You'll likely rub against oil and dirt. It can't be helped.

MILDRED.   It doesn't matter. I have lots of white dresses.

SECOND ENGINEER.   I have an old coat you might throw over——

MILDRED.   I have fifty dresses like this. I will throw this one into the sea when I come back. That ought to wash it clean, don't you think?

SECOND ENGINEER (*doggedly*). There's ladders to climb down that are none too clean—and dark alleyways——

MILDRED.   I will wear this very dress and none other.

SECOND ENGINEER.   No offense meant. It's none of my business. I was only warning you——

MILDRED.   Warning? That sounds thrilling.

SECOND ENGINEER (*looking down the deck—with a sigh of relief*). There's the Fourth now. He's waiting for us. If you'll come——

MILDRED.   Go on. I'll follow you. (*He goes. MILDRED turns a mocking smile on her aunt.*) An oaf—but a handsome, virile oaf.

AUNT (*scornfully*). Poser!

MILDRED.   Take care. He said there were dark alleyways——

AUNT (*in the same tone*). Poser!

MILDRED (*biting her lips angrily*). You are right. But would that my millions were not so anemically chaste!

AUNT.   Yes, for a fresh pose I have no doubt you would drag the name of Douglas in the gutter!

MILDRED.   From which it sprang. Good-by, Aunt. Don't pray too hard that I may fall into the fiery furnace.

AUNT.   Poser!

MILDRED (*viciously*). Old hag! (*She slaps her aunt insultingly across the face and walks off, laughing gaily.*)

AUNT (*screams after her*). I said poser!

(*The curtain falls.*)

SCENE THREE

The stokehole. In the rear, the dimly-outlined bulks of the furnaces and boilers. High overhead one hanging electric bulb sheds just enough light through the murky air laden with coal dust to pile up masses of shadows everywhere. A line of men, stripped to the waist, is before the furnace doors. They bend over, looking neither to right nor left, handling their shovels as if they were part of their bodies, with a strange, awkward, swinging rhythm. They use the shovels to throw open the furnace doors. Then from these fiery round holes in the black a flood of terrific light and heat pours full upon the men who are outlined in silhouette in the crouching, inhuman attitudes of chained gorillas. The men shovel with a rhythmic motion, swinging as on a pivot from the coal which lies in heaps on the floor behind to hurl it into the flaming mouths before them. There is a tumult of noise—the brazen clang of the furnace doors as they are flung open or slammed shut, the grating, teeth-gritting grind of steel against steel, of crunching coal. This clash of sounds stuns one's ears with its rending dissonance. But there is order in it, rhythm, a mechanical regulated recurrence, a tempo. And rising above all, making the air hum with the quiver of liberated energy, the roar of leaping flames in the furnace, the monotonous throbbing beat of the engines.

As the curtain rises, the furnace doors are shut. The men are taking a breathing spell. One or two are arranging the coal behind them, pulling it into more accessible heaps. The others can be dimly made out leaning on their shovels in relaxed attitudes of exhaustion.

PADDY (*from somewhere in the line—plaintively*). Yerra, will this divil's own watch nivir end? Me back is broke. I'm destroyed entirely.

YANK (*from the center of the line—with exuberant scorn*). Aw, yuh make me sick! Lie down and croak, why don't yuh? Always beefin', dat's you! Say, dis is a cinch! Dis was made for me! It's my meat, get me! (*A whistle is blown—a thin, shrill note from somewhere overhead in the darkness.* YANK *curses without resentment.*) Dere's de damn engineer crackin' de whip. He tinks we're loafin'.

PADDY (*vindictively*). God stiffen him!

YANK (*in an exultant tone of command*). Come on, youse guys! Git into de game! She's gettin' hungry! Pile some grub in her. Trow it into her belly! Come on now, all of youse! Open her up! (*At this last all the men, who have followed his movements of getting into position, throw open their furnace doors with a deafening clang. The fiery light floods over their shoulders as they bend round for the coal. Rivulets of sooty sweat have traced maps on their backs. The enlarged muscles form bunches of high light and shadow.*)

YANK (*chanting a count as he shovels without seeming effort*). One—two—tree—(*His voice rising exultantly in the joy of battle.*) Dat's de stuff! Let her have it! All togedder now! Sling it into her! Let her ride! Shoot de piece now! Call de toin on her! Drive her into it! Feel her move. Watch her smoke! Speed, dat's her middle name! Give her coal, youse guys! Coal, dat's her booze! Drink it up, baby! Let's see yuh sprint! Dig in and gain a lap! Dere she go-o-es. (*This last in the chanting formula of the galley gods at the six-day bike race. He slams his furnace door shut. The others do likewise with as much unison as their wearied bodies will permit. The effect is of one fiery eye after another being blotted out with a series of accompanying bangs.*)

PADDY (*groaning*). Me back is broke. I'm bate out—bate—(*There is a pause. Then the inexorable whistle sounds again from the dim regions above the electric light. There is a growl of cursing rage from all sides.*)

YANK (*shaking his fist upward—contemptuously*). Take it easy dere, you! Who d'yuh tinks runnin' dis game, me or you? When I git ready, we move. Not before! When I git ready, get me!

VOICES (*approvingly*).
> That's the stuff!
> Yank tal him, py golly!
> Yank ain't afeerd.
> Goot poy, Yank!
> Give him hell!
> Tell 'im 'e's a bloody swine!
> Bloody slave-driver!

YANK (*contemptuously*). He ain't got no noive. He's yellow, get me? All de engineers is yellow. Dey got streaks a mile wide. Aw, to hell with him! Let's move, youse guys. We had a rest. Come on, she needs it! Give her pep! It ain't for him. Him and his whistle, dey don't belong. But we belong, see! We gotter feed de baby! Come on! (*He turns and flings his furnace door open. They all follow his lead. At this instant the* SECOND *and* FOURTH ENGINEERS *enter from the darkness on the left with* MILDRED *between them. She starts, turns paler, her pose is crumbling, she shivers with fright in spite of the blazing heat, but forces herself to leave the* ENGINEERS *and take a few steps near the men. She is right behind* YANK. *All this happens quickly while the men have their backs turned.*)

YANK.   Come on, youse guys! (*He is turning to get coal when the whistle sounds again in a peremptory, irritating note. This drives* YANK *into a sudden fury. While the other men have turned full around and stopped dumbfounded by the spectacle of* MILDRED *standing there in her white dress,* YANK *does not turn far enough to see her. Besides, his head is thrown back, he blinks upward through the murk trying to find the owner of the whistle, he brandishes his shovel murderously over his head in one hand, pounding on his chest, gorilla-like, with the other, shouting.*) Toin off dat whistle! Come down outa dere, yuh yellow, brass-buttoned, Belfast bum, yuh! Come down and I'll knock yer brains out! Yuh lousy, stinkin, yellow mut of a Catholic-moiderin' bastard! Come down and I'll moider yuh! Pullin' dat whistle on me, huh? I'll show yuh! I'll crash yer skull in! I'll drive yer teet' down yer troat! I'll slam yer nose trou de back of yer head! I'll cut yer guts out for a nickel, yuh lousy boob, yuh dirty, crummy, muck-eatin' son of a—— (*Suddenly he becomes conscious of all the other men staring at something directly behind his back. He whirls defensively with a snarling, murderous growl, crouching to spring, his lips drawn back over his teeth, his small eyes gleaming ferociously. He sees* MILDRED, *like a white apparition in the full light from the open furnace doors. He glares into her eyes, turned to stone. As for her, during his speech she has listened, paralyzed with horror, terror, her whole personality crushed, beaten in, collapsed, by the terrific impact of this unknown, abysmal brutality, naked and shameless. As she looks at his gorilla face, as his eyes bore into hers, she utters a low, choking cry and shrinks away from him, putting both hands up before her eyes to shut out the sight of his face, to protect her own. This startles* YANK *to a reaction. His mouth falls open, his eyes grow bewildered.*)

MILDRED (*about to faint—to the* ENGINEERS, *who now have her one by each arm—whimperingly*). Take me away! Oh, the filthy beast! (*She faints. They carry her quickly back, disappearing in the darkness at the left, rear. An iron door clangs shut. Rage and bewildered fury rush back on* YANK. *He feels himself insulted in some unknown fashion in the very heart of his pride. He roars.*) God damn yuh! (*And hurls his shovel after them at the door which has just closed. It hits the steel bulkhead with a clang and falls clattering on the steel floor. From overhead the whistle sounds again in a long, angry, insistent command.*)

(*The curtain falls.*)

SCENE FOUR

The firemen's forecastle. YANK'S *watch has just come off duty and had dinner. Their faces and bodies shine from a soap and water scrubbing but around their eyes, where a hasty dousing does not touch, the coal dust sticks like black make-up, giving them a queer, sinister expression.* YANK *has not washed either face or body. He stands out in contrast to them, a blackened, brooding figure. He is seated forward on a bench in the exact attitude of Rodin's "The Thinker." The others, most of them smoking pipes, are staring at* YANK *half-apprehensively, as if fearing an outburst; half-amusedly, as if they saw a joke somewhere that tickled them.*

VOICES.
    He ain't ate nothin'.
    Py golly, a fallar gat to gat grub in him.
    Divil a lie.
    Yank feeda da fire, no feeda da face.
    Ha-ha.
    He ain't even washed hisself.
    He's forgot.
    Hey, Yank, you forgot to wash.
YANK (*sullenly*). Forgot nothin'! To hell wit washin'.
VOICES.
    It'll stick to you.
    It'll get under your skin.
    Give yer the bleedin' itch, that's wot.
    It makes spots on you—like a leopard.
    Like a piebald nigger, you mean.
    Better wash up, Yank.
    You sleep better.
    Wash up, Yank.
    Wash up! Wash up!
YANK (*resentfully*). Aw say, youse guys. Lemme alone. Can't youse see I'm tryin' to tink?
ALL (*repeating the word after him as one with cynical mockery*). Think! (*The word has a brazen, metallic quality as if their throats were phonograph horns. It is followed by a chorus of hard, barking laughter.*)
YANK (*springing to his feet and glaring at them belligerently*). Yes, tink! Tink, dat's what I said! What about it? (*They are silent, puzzled by his sudden resentment at what used to be one of his jokes.* YANK *sits down again in the same attitude of "The Thinker."*)
VOICES.
    Leave him alone.
    He's got a grouch on.
    Why wouldn't he?
PADDY (*with a wink at the others*). Sure I know what's the matther. 'Tis aisy to see. He's fallen in love, I'm telling you.
ALL (*repeating the word after him as one with cynical mockery*). Love! (*The word has a brazen, metallic quality as if their throats were phonograph horns. It is followed by a chorus of hard, barking laughter.*)
YANK (*with a contemptuous snort*). Love, hell! Hate, dat's what. I've fallen in hate, get me?
PADDY (*philosophically*). 'Twould take a wise man to tell one from the other. (*With a bitter, ironical scorn, increasing as he goes on.*) But I'm telling you it's love

that's in it. Sure what else but love for us poor bastes in the stokehole would be bringing a fine lady, dressed like a white quane, down a mile of ladders and steps to be havin' a look at us? (*A growl of anger goes up from all sides.*)

LONG (*jumping on a bench—hecticly*). Hinsultin' us! Hinsultin' us, the bloody cow! And them bloody engineers! What right 'as they got to be exhibitin' us 's if we was bleedin' monkeys in a menagerie? Did we sign for hinsults to our dignity as 'onest workers? Is that in the ship's articles? You kin bloody well bet it ain't! But I knows why they done it. I arsked a deck steward 'o she was and 'e told me. 'Er old man's a bleedin' millionaire, a bloody Capitalist! 'E's got enuf bloody gold to sink this bleedin' ship! 'E makes arf the bloody steel in the world! 'E owns this bloody boat! And you and me, Comrades, we're 'is slaves! And the skipper and mates and engineers, they're 'is slaves! And she's 'is bloody daughter and we're all 'er slaves, too! And she gives 'er orders as 'ow she wants to see the bloody animals below decks and down they take 'er! (*There is a roar of rage from all sides.*)

YANK (*blinking at him bewilderedly*). Say! Wait a moment! Is all dat straight goods?

LONG.   Straight as string! The bleedin' steward as waits on 'em, 'e told me about 'er. And what're we goin' ter do, I arsks yer? 'Ave we got ter swaller 'er hinsults like dogs? It ain't in the ship's articles. I tell yer we got a case. We kin go to law——

YANK (*with abysmal contempt*). Hell! Law!

ALL (*repeating the word after him as one with cynical mockery*). Law! (*The word has a brazen metallic quality as if their throats were phonograph horns. It is followed by a chorus of hard, barking laughter.*)

LONG (*feeling the ground slipping from under his feet—desperately*). As voters and citizens we kin force the bloody governments—

YANK (*with abysmal contempt*). Hell! Governments!

ALL (*repeating the word after him as one with cynical mockery*). Governments! (*The word has a brazen metallic quality as if their throats were phonograph horns. It is followed by a chorus of hard, barking laughter.*)

LONG (*hysterically*). We're free and equal in the sight of God——

YANK (*with abysmal contempt*). Hell! God!

ALL (*repeating the word after him as one with cynical mockery*). God! (*The word has a brazen metallic quality as if their throats were phonograph horns. It is followed by a chorus of hard, barking, laughter.*)

YANK (*witheringly*). Aw, join de Salvation Army!

ALL.   Sit down! Shut up! Damn fool! Sea-lawyer! (LONG *slinks back out of sight.*)

PADDY (*continuing the trend of his thoughts as if he had never been interrupted—bitterly*). And there she was standing behind us, and the Second pointing at us like a man you'd hear in a circus would be saying: In this cage is a queerer kind of baboon than ever you'd find in darkest Africy. We roast them in their own sweat—and be damned if you won't hear some of thim saying they like it! (*He glances scornfully at* YANK.)

YANK (*with a bewildered uncertain growl*). Aw!

PADDY.   And there was Yank roarin' curses and turning round wid his shovel to brain her—and she looked at him, and him at her——

YANK (*slowly*). She was all white. I thought she was a ghost. Sure.

PADDY (*with heavy, biting sarcasm*). 'Twas love at first sight, divil a doubt of it! If you'd seen the endearin' look on her pale mug when she shriveled away with her hands over her eyes to shut out the sight of him! Sure, 'twas as if she'd seen a great hairy ape escaped from the Zoo!

YANK (*stung—with a growl of rage*). Aw!

PADDY.   And the loving way Yank heaved his shovel at the skull of her, only she was out the door! (*A grin breaking over his face.*) 'Twas touching, I'm telling you! It put the touch of home, swate home in the stokehole. (*There is a roar of laughter from all.*)

YANK (*glaring at* PADDY *menacingly*). Aw, choke dat off, see!

PADDY (*not heeding him—to the others*). And her grabbin' at the Second's arm for protection. (*With a grotesque imitation of a woman's voice.*) Kiss me, Engineer dear, for it's dark down here and me old man's in Wall Street making money! Hug me tight, darlin', for I'm afeerd in the dark and me mother's on deck makin' eyes at the skipper! (*Another roar of laughter.*)

YANK (*threateningly*). Say! What yuh tryin' to do, kid me, yuh old Harp?

PADDY.   Divil a bit! Ain't I wishin' myself you'd brained her?

YANK (*fiercely*). I'll brain her! I'll brain her yet, wait 'n' see! (*Coming over to* PADDY *slowly.*) Say, is dat what she called me—a hairy ape?

PADDY.   She looked it at you if she didn't say the word itself.

YANK (*grinning horribly*). Hairy ape, huh? Sure! Dat's de way she looked at me, aw right. Hairy ape! So dat's me, huh? (*Bursting into rage—as if she were still in front of him.*) Yuh skinny tart! Yuh white-faced bum, yuh! I'll show yuh who's a ape! (*Turning to the others, bewilderment seizing him again.*) Say, youse guys. I was bawlin' him out for pullin' de whistle on us. You heard me. And den I seen youse lookin' at somep'n and I tought he'd sneaked down to come up in back of me, and I hopped round to knock him dead wit de shovel. And dere she was wit de light on her! Christ, yuh coulda pushed me over with a finger! I was scared, get me? Sure! I tought she was a ghost, see? She was all in white like dey wrap around stiffs. You seen her. Kin yuh blame me? She didn't belong, dat's what. And den when I come to and seen it was a real skoit and seen de way she was lookin' at me—like Paddy said—Christ, I was sore, get me? I don't stand for dat stuff from nobody. And I flung de shovel—on'y she'd beat it. (*Furiously.*) I wished it'd banged her! I wished it'd knocked her block off!

LONG.   And be 'anged for murder or 'lectrocuted? She ain't bleedin' well worth it.

YANK.   I don't give a damn what! I'd be square wit her, wouldn't I? Tink I wanter let her put somep'n over on me? Tink I'm goin' to let her git away wit dat stuff? Yuh don't know me! No one ain't never put nothin' over on me and got away wit it, see!—not dat kind of stuff—no guy and no skoit neither! I'll fix her! Maybe she'll come down again——

VOICE.   No chance, Yank. You scared her out of a year's growth.

YANK.   I scared her? Why de hell should I scare her? Who de hell is she? Ain't she de same as me? Hairy ape, huh? (*With his old confident bravado.*) I'll show her I'm bet-ter'n her, if she on'y knew it. I belong and she don't, see! I move and she's dead! Twenty-five knots a hour, dat's me! Dat carries her but I make dat. She's on'y baggage. Sure! (*Again bewilderedly.*) But, Christ, she was funny lookin'! Did yuh pipe her hands? White and skinny. Yuh could see de bones through 'em. And her mush, dat was dead white, too. And her eyes, dey was like dey'd seen a ghost. Me, dat was! Sure! Hairy ape! Ghost, huh? Look at dat arm! (*He extends his right arm, swelling out the great muscles.*) I coulda took her wit dat, wit' just my little finger even, and broke her in two. (*Again bewil-deredly.*) Say, who is dat skoit, huh? What is she? What's she come from? Who made her? Who give her de noive to look at me like dat? Dis ting's got my goat right. I don't get her. She's new to me. What does a skoit like her mean, huh? She don't belong, get me! I can't see her. (*With growing anger.*) But one ting I'm wise to, aw right, aw right! Youse all kin bet your shoits I'll git even wit her. I'll show her if she tinks she—She grinds de organ and I'm on de string, huh? I'll fix her! Let her come down again and I'll fling her in de furnace! She'll move den! She won't shiver at nothin' den! Speed, dat'll be her! She'll belong den! (*He grins horribly.*)

PADDY.   She'll never come. She's had her bellyfull, I'm telling you. She'll be in bed now, I'm thinking, wid ten doctors and nurses feedin' her salts to clean the fear out of her.

YANK (*enraged*). Yuh tink I made her sick, too, do yuh? Just lookin' at me, huh? Hairy ape, huh? (*In a frenzy of rage.*) I'll fix her! I'll tell her where to git off! She'll git down on her knees and take it back or I'll bust de face offen her! (*Shaking one fist upward and beating on his chest with the other.*) I'll find yuh! I'm comin', d'yuh hear! I'll fix yuh, God damn yuh! (*He makes a rush for the door.*)

VOICES.
    Stop him!
    He'll get shot!
    He'll murder her!
    Trip him up!
    Hold him!
    He's gone crazy!
    Gott, he's strong!
    Hold him down!
    Look out for a kick!
    Pin his arms!

(*They have all piled on him and, after a fierce struggle, by sheer weight of numbers have borne him to the floor just inside the door.*)

PADDY (*who has remained detached*). Kape him down till he's cooled off. (*Scornfully.*) Yerra, Yank, you're a great fool. Is it payin' attention at all you are to the like of that skinny sow widout one drop of rale blood in her?

YANK (*frenziedly, from the bottom of the heap*). She's done me doit! She done me doit, didn't she? I'll git square wit her! I'll get her some way! Git offen me, youse guys! Lemme up! I'll show her who's a ape!

(*The curtain falls.*)

SCENE FIVE

Three weeks later. A corner of Fifth Avenue in the Fifties on a fine Sunday morning. A general atmosphere of clean, well-tidied, wide street; a flood of mellow, tempered sunshine; gentle, genteel breezes. In the rear, the show windows of two shops, a jewelry establishment on the corner, a furrier's next to it. Here the adornments of extreme wealth are tantaliz-ingly displayed. The jeweler's window is gaudy with glit-tering diamonds, emeralds, rubies, pearls, etc., fashioned in ornate tiaras, crowns, necklaces, collars, etc. From each piece hangs an enormous tag from which a dollar sign and numerals in intermittent electric lights wink out the incred-ible prices. The same in the furrier's. Rich furs of all vari-eties hang there bathed in a downpour of artificial light. The general effect is of a background of magnificence cheapened and made grotesque by commercialism, a background in tawdry disharmony with the clear light and sunshine on the street itself.

Up the side street YANK *and* LONG *come swaggering. LONG is dressed in shore clothes, wears a black Windsor tie, cloth cap. YANK is in his dirty dungarees. A fireman's cap with black peak is cocked defiantly on the side of his head. He has not shaved for days and around his fierce, resentful eyes—as around those of LONG to a lesser degree—the black smudge of coal dust still sticks like make-up. They hesitate and stand together at the corner, swaggering, looking about them with a forced, defiant contempt.*

LONG (*indicating it all with an oratorical gesture*). Well, 'ere we are. Fif' Avenoo. This 'ere's their bleedin' private lane, as yer might say. (*Bitterly.*) We're trespassers 'ere. Proletarians keep orf the grass!

YANK (*dully*). I don't see no grass, yuh boob. (*Staring at the sidewalk.*) Clean, ain't it? Yuh could eat a fried egg offen it. The white wings got some job sweepin' dis up. (*Looking up and down the avenue—surlily.*) Where's all de white-collar stiffs yuh said was here—and de skoits—her kind?

LONG.   In church, blarst 'em! Arskin' Jesus to give 'em more money.

YANK.   Choich, huh? I useter go to choich onct—sure—when I was a kid. Me old man and woman, dey made me. Dey never went demselves, dough. Always got too big a head on Sunday mornin', dat was dem. (*With a grin.*) Dey was scrappers for fair, bot' of dem. On Satiday nights when dey bot' got a skinful dey could put up a bout oughter been staged at de Garden. When dey got trough dere wasn't a chair or table with a leg under it. Or else dey bot' jumped on me for somep'n. Dat was where I loined to take punishment. (*With a grin and a swagger.*) I'm a chip offen de old block, get me?

LONG.   Did yer old man follow the sea?

YANK.   Naw. Worked along shore. I runned away when me old lady croaked with de tremens. I helped at truckin' and in de market. Den I shipped in de stokehole. Sure. Dat belongs. De rest was nothin'. (*Looking around him.*) I ain't never seen dis before. De Brooklyn waterfront, dat was where I was dragged up. (*Taking a deep breath.*) Dis ain't so bad at dat, huh?

LONG.   Not bad? Well, we pays for it wiv our bloody sweat, if yer wants to know!

YANK (*with sudden angry disgust*). Aw, hell! I don't see no one, see—like her. All dis gives me a pain. It don't belong. Say, ain't dere a back room around dis dump? Let's go shoot a ball. All dis is too clean and quiet and dolled-up, get me? It gives me a pain.

LONG.   Wait and yer'll bloody well see——

YANK.   I don't wait for no one. I keep on de move. Say, what yuh drag me up here for, anyway? Tryin' to kid me, yuh simp, yuh?

LONG.   Yer wants to get back at 'er, don't yer? That's what yer been sayin' every bloomin' hour since she hinsulted yer.

YANK (*vehemently*). Sure ting I do! Didn't I try to get even wit her in Southampton? Didn't I sneak on de dock and wait for her by de gangplank? I was goin' to spit in her pale mug, see! Sure, right in her pop-eyes! Dat woulda made me even, see? But no chanct. Dere was a whole army of plainclothes bulls around. Dey spotted me and gimme de bum's rush. I never seen her. But I'll git square wit her yet, you watch! (*Furiously.*) De lousy tart! She tink she kin get away with moider—but not wit me! I'll fix her! I'll tink of a way!

LONG (*as disgusted as he dares to be*). Ain't that why I brought yer up 'ere—to show yer? Yer been lookin' at this 'ere 'ole affair wrong. Yer been actin' an' talkin' 's if it was all a bleedin' personal matter between yer and that bloody cow. I wants to convince yer she was on'y a representative of 'er clarss. I wants to awaken yer bloody clarss consciousness. Then yer'll see it's 'er clarss yer've got to fight, not 'er alone. There's a 'ole mob of 'em like 'er, Gawd blind 'em!

YANK (*spitting on his hands—belligerently*). De more de merrier when I gits started. Bring on de gang!

LONG.   Yer'll see 'em in arf a mo', when that church lets out. (*He turns and sees the window display in the two stores for the first time.*) Blimey! Look at that, will yer? (*They both walk back and stand looking in the jeweler's.* LONG *flies into a fury.*) Just look at this 'ere bloomin' mess! Just look at it! Look at the bleedin' prices on 'em—more'n our 'ole bloody stokehole makes in ten voyages sweatin' in 'ell! And they—'er and 'er bloody clarss—buys 'em for toys to dangle on 'em! One of these 'ere, would buy scoff for a starvin' family for a year!

YANK.   Aw, cut de sob stuff! T' hell wit de starvin' family! Yuh'll be passin' de hat to me next. (*With naïve admiration.*) Say, dem tings is pretty, huh? Bet yuh dey'd hock for a piece of change aw right. (*Then turning away, bored.*) But aw hell, what good are dey? Let 'er have 'em. Dey don't belong no more'n she does. (*With a gesture of sweeping the jewelers into oblivion.*) All dat don't count, get me?

LONG (*who has moved to the furrier's—indignantly*). And I s'pose this 'ere don't count neither—skins of poor, 'armless animals slaughtered so as 'er and 'ers can keep their bleedin' noses warm!

YANK (*who has been staring at something inside—with queer excitement*). Take a slant at dat! Give it de once-over! Monkey fur—two t'ousand bucks! (*Bewilderedly.*) Is dat straight goods—monkey fur? What de hell——?

LONG (*bitterly*). It's straight enuf. (*With grim humor.*) They wouldn't bloody well pay that for 'airy ape's skin—no, nor for the 'ole livin' ape with all 'is 'ead, and body, and soul thrown in!

YANK (*clenching his fists, his face growing pale with rage as if the skin in the window were a personal insult*). Trowin' it up in my face! Christ! I'll fix her!

LONG (*excitedly*). Church is out. 'Ere they come, the bleedin' swine. (*After a glance at* YANK'S *lowering face—uneasily.*) Easy goes, Comrade. Keep yer bloomin' temper. Remember force defeats itself. It ain't our weapon. We must impress our demands through peaceful means—the votes of the on-marching proletarians of the bloody world!

YANK (*with abysmal contempt*). Votes, hell! Votes is a joke, see. Votes for women! Let dem do it!

LONG (*still more uneasily*). Calm, now. Treat 'em wiv the proper contempt. Observe the bleedin' parasites but 'old yer 'orses.

YANK (*angrily*). Git away from me! Yuh're yellow, dat's what. Force, dat's me! De punch, dat's me every time, see! (*The crowd from church enter from the right, sauntering slowly and affectedly, their heads held stiffly up, looking neither to right nor left, talking in toneless, simpering voices. The women are rouged, calcimined, dyed, overdressed to the nth degree. The men are in Prince Alberts, high hats, spats, canes, etc. A procession of gaudy marionettes, yet with something of the relentless horror of Frankenstein monsters in their detached, mechanical unawareness.*)

VOICES.
> Dear Doctor Caiaphas! He is so sincere!
> What was the sermon? I dozed off.
> About the radicals, my dear—and the
> false doctrines that are being preached.
> We must organize a hundred per cent American
> bazaar.
> And let everyone contribute one one-hundredth per
> cent of their income tax.
> What an original idea!
> We can devote the proceeds to rehabilitating the veil
> of the temple.
> But that has been done so many times.

YANK (*glaring from one to the other of them—with an insulting snort of scorn*). Huh! Huh! (*Without seeming to see him, they make wide detours to avoid the spot where he stands in the middle of the sidewalk.*)

LONG (*frightenedly*). Keep yer bloomin' mouth shut, I tells yer.

YANK (*viciously*). G'wan! Tell it to Sweeney! (*He swaggers away and deliberately lurches into a top-hatted gentleman, then glares at him pugnaciously.*) Say, who d'yuh tink yuh're bumpin? Tink yuh own de oith?

GENTLEMAN (*coldly and affectedly*). I beg your pardon. (*He has not looked at* YANK *and passes on without a glance, leaving him bewildered.*)

LONG (*rushing up and grabbing* YANK'S *arm*). 'Ere! Come away! This wasn't what I meant. Yer'll 'ave the bloody coppers down on us.

YANK (*savagely—giving him a push that sends him sprawling*). G'wan!

LONG (*picks himself up—hysterically*). I'll pop orf then. This ain't what I meant. And whatever 'appens yer can't blame me. (*He slinks off left.*)

YANK. T' hell wit youse! (*He approaches a lady—with a vicious grin and a smirking wink.*) Hello, Kiddo. How's every little ting? Got anyting on for tonight? I know an old boiler down to de docks we kin crawl into. (*The lady stalks by without a look, without a change of pace.* YANK *turns to others—insultingly.*) Holy smokes, what a mug! Go hide yuhself before de horses shy at yuh. Gee, pipe de heine on dat one! Say, youse, yuh look like de stoin of a ferryboat. Paint and powder! All dolled up to kill! Yuh look like stiffs laid out for de boneyard! Aw, g'wan, de lot of youse! Yuh give me de eyeache. Yuh don't belong, get me! Look at me, why don't youse dare? I belong, dat's me! (*Pointing to skyscraper across the street which is in process of construction—with bravado.*) See dat building goin' up dere? See de steel work? Steel, dat's me! Youse guys live on it and tink yuh're somep'n. But I'm *in* it, see! I'm de-hoistin' engine dat makes it go up! I'm it—de inside and bottom of it! Sure! I'm steel and steam and smoke and de rest of it! It moves—speed—twenty-five stories up—and me at de top and bottom—movin'! Youse simps don't move. Yuh're on'y dolls I winds up to see 'm spin. Yuh're de garbage, get me—de leavins—der ashes we dump over de side! Now, what's 'a' yuh gotta say? (*But as they seem neither to see nor hear him, he flies into a fury.*) Bums! Pigs! Tarts! Bitches! (*He turns in rage on the men, bumping viciously into them but not jarring them the least bit. Rather it is he who recoils after each collision. He keeps growling.*) Git off de oith! G'wan, yuh bum! Look where yuh're goin', can't yuh? Git outa here! Fight, why don't yuh? Put up yer mits! Don't be a dog! Fight or I'll knock yuh dead! (*But, without seeming to see him, they all answer with mechanical affected politeness.*) I beg your pardon. (*Then at a cry from one of the women they all scurry to the furrier's window.*)

THE WOMAN (*ecstatically, with a gasp of delight*). Monkey fur! (*The whole crowd of men and women chorus after her in the same tone of affected delight.*) Monkey fur!

YANK (*with a jerk of his head back on his shoulders, as if he had received a punch full in the face—raging*). I see yuh, all in white! I see yuh, yuh white-faced tart, yuh! Hairy ape, huh? I'll hairy ape yuh! (*He bends down and grips at the street curbing as if to pluck it out and hurl it. Foiled in this, snarling with passion, he leaps to the lamp-post on the corner and tries to pull it up for a club. Just at that moment a bus is heard rumbling up. A fat, high-hatted, spatted gentleman runs out from the side street. He calls out plaintively.*) Bus! Bus! Stop there! (*And runs full tilt into the bending straining* YANK, *who is bowled off his balance.*)

YANK (*seeing a fight—with a roar of joy as he springs to his feet*). At last! Bus, huh! I'll bust yuh! (*He lets drive a terrific swing, his fist landing full on the fat gentleman's face. But the gentleman stands unmoved as if nothing had happened.*)

GENTLEMAN. I beg your pardon. (*Then irritably.*) You have made me lose my bus. (*He claps his hands and begins to scream.*) Officer! Officer! (*Many police whistles shrill out on the instant and a whole platoon of policemen rush in on* YANK *from all sides. He tries to fight but is clubbed to the pavement and fallen upon. The crowd at the window have not moved or noticed this disturbance. The clanging gong of the patrol wagon approaches with a clamoring din.*)

(*The curtain falls.*)

SCENE SIX

Night of the following day. A row of cells in the prison on Blackwell's Island. The cells extend back diagonally from right front to left rear. They do not stop, but disappear in the dark background as if they ran on, numberless, into infinity. One electric bulb from the low ceiling of the narrow corridor sheds its light through the heavy steel bars of the cell at the extreme front and reveals part of the interior. YANK *can be seen within, crouched on the edge of his cot in the attitude of Rodin's "The Thinker." His face is spotted with black and blue bruises. A blood-stained bandage is wrapped around his head.*

YANK (*suddenly starting as if awakening from a dream, reaches out and shakes the bars—aloud to himself, wonderingly*). Steel. Dis is de Zoo, huh? (*A burst of hard barking laughter comes from the unseen occupants of the cells, runs back down the tier, and abruptly ceases.*)

VOICES (*mockingly*).
    The Zoo? That's a new name for this coop—a damn good name!
    Steel, eh? You said a mouthful. This is the old iron house.
    Who is that boob talkin'?
    He's the bloke they brung in out of his head. The bulls had beat him up fierce.

YANK (*dully*). I musta been dreamin'. I tought I was in a cage at de Zoo—but de apes don't talk, do dey?

VOICES (*with mocking laughter*).
    You're in a cage aw right.
    A coop!
    A pen!
    A sty!
    A kennel! (*Hard laughter—a pause.*)
    Say, guy! Who are you? No, never mind lying. What are you?
    Yes, tell us your sad story. What's your game?
    What did they jug yuh for?

YANK (*dully*). I was a fireman—stokin' on de liners. (*Then with sudden rage, rattling his cell bars.*) I'm a hairy ape, get me? And I'll bust youse all in de jaw if yuh don't lay off kiddin' me.

VOICES.
    Huh! You're a hard-boiled duck, ain't you!
    When you spit, it bounces! (*Laughter.*)
    Aw, can it. He's a regular guy. Ain't you?
    What did he say he was—a ape?

YANK (*defiantly*). Sure ting! Ain't dat what youse all are—apes? (*A silence. Then a furious rattling of bars from down the corridor.*)

A VOICE (*thick with rage*). I'll show yuh who's a ape, yuh bum!

VOICES.
    Ssshh! Nix!
    Can de noise!
    Piano!
    You'll have the guard down on us!

YANK (*scornfully*). De guard? Yuh mean de keeper, don't yuh? (*Angry exclamations from all the cells.*)

VOICE (*placatingly*). Aw, don't pay no attention to him. He's off his nut from the beatin'-up he got. Say, you guy! We're waitin' to hear what they landed you for—or ain't yuh tellin'?

YANK. Sure, I'll tell youse. Sure! Why de hell not? On'y—youse won't get me. Nobody gets me but me, see? I started to tell de Judge and all he says was: "Toity days to tink it over." Tink it over! Christ, dat's all I been doin' for weeks! (*After a pause.*) I was tryin' to git even with someone, see?—someone dat done me doit.

VOICES (*cynically*).
    De old stuff, I bet. Your goil, huh?
    Give yuh the double-cross, huh?
    That's them every time!
    Did yuh beat up de odder guy?

YANK (*disgustedly*). Aw, yuh're all wrong! Sure dere was a skoit in it—but not what youse mean, not dat old tripe. Dis was a new kind of skoit. She was dolled up all in white—in de stokehole. I tought she was a ghost. Sure. (*A pause.*)

VOICES (*whispering*).
    Gee, he's still nutty.
    Let him rave. It's fun listenin'.

YANK (*unheeding—groping in his thoughts*). Her hands—dey was skinny and white like dey wasn't real but painted on somep'n. Dere was a million miles from me to her—twenty-five knots an hour. She was like some dead ting de cat brung in. Sure, dat's what. She didn't belong. She belonged in de window of a toy store, or on de top of a garbage can, see! Sure! (*He breaks out angrily.*) But would yuh believe it, she had de noive to do me doit. She lamped me like she was seein' somep'n broke loose from de menagerie. Christ, yuh'd oughter seen her eyes! (*He rattles the bars of his cell furiously.*) But I'll get back at her yet, you watch! And if I can't find her I'll take it out on de gang she runs wit. I'm wise to where dey hangs out now. I'll show her who belongs! I'll show her who's in de move and who ain't. You watch my smoke!

VOICES (*serious and joking*).
    Dat's de talkin'!
    Take her for all she's got!
    What was this dame, anyway? Who was she, eh?

YANK. I dunno. First cabin stiff. Her old man's a millionaire, dey says—name of Douglas.

VOICES.
    Douglas? That's the president of the Steel Trust, I bet.
    Sure. I seen his mug in de papers.
    He's filthy with dough.

VOICE. Hey, feller, take a tip from me. If you want to get back at that dame, you better join the Wobblies. You'll get some action, then.

YANK. Wobblies? What de hell's dat?

VOICE. Ain't you ever heard of the I. W. W.?

YANK. Naw. What is it?

VOICE. A gang of blokes—a tough gang. I been readin' about 'em today in the paper. The guard give me the *Sunday Times*. There's a long spiel about 'em. It's from a speech made in the Senate by a guy named Senator Queen. (*He is in the cell next to* YANK'S. *There is a rustling of paper.*) Wait'll I see if I got light enough and I'll read you. Listen. (*He reads.*) ''There is a menace existing in this country today which threatens the vitals of our fair Republic—as foul a menace against the very life-blood of the American Eagle as was the foul conspiracy of Cataline against the eagles of ancient Rome!''

VOICE (*disgustedly*). Aw, hell! Tell him to salt de tail of dat eagle!

VOICE (*reading*). ''I refer to that devil's brew of rascals, jailbirds, murderers and cutthroats who libel all honest working men by calling themselves the Industrial Workers of the World; but in the light of their nefarious plots, I call them the Industrious Wreckers of the World!''

YANK (*with vengeful satisfaction*). Wreckers, dat's de right dope! Dat belongs! Me for dem!

VOICE. Ssshh! (*Reading.*) ''This fiendish organization is a foul ulcer on the fair body of our Democracy——''

VOICE. Democracy, hell! Give him the boid, fellers—the raspberry! (*They do.*)

VOICE. Ssshh! (*Reading.*) ''Like Cato I say to this Senate, the I. W. W. must be destroyed! For they represent an ever-present dagger pointed at the heart of the greatest nation the world has ever known, where all men are born free and equal, with equal opportunities to all, where the Founding Fathers have guaranteed to each one happiness, where Truth, Honor, Liberty, Justice, and the Brotherhood of Man are a religion absorbed with one's mother's milk, taught at our father's knee, sealed, signed, and stamped upon in the glorious Constitution of these United States!'' (*A perfect storm of hisses, catcalls, boos, and hard laughter.*)

VOICES (*scornfully*).
Hurrah for de Fort' of July!
Pass de hat!
Liberty!
Justice!
Honor!
Opportunity!
Brotherhood!

ALL (*with abysmal scorn*). Aw, hell!

VOICE. Give that Queen Senator guy the bark! All togedder now—one—two—tree——(*A terrific chorus of barking and yapping.*)

GUARD (*from a distance*). Quiet, there, youse—or I'll get the hose. (*The noise subsides.*)

YANK (*with growling rage*). I'd like to catch dat senator guy alone for a second. I'd loin him some trute!

VOICE. Ssshh! Here's where he gits down to cases on the Wobblies. (*Reads.*) ''They plot with fire in one hand and dynamite in the other. They stop not before murder to gain their ends, nor at the outraging of defenseless womanhood. They would tear down society, put the lowest scum in the seats of the mighty, turn Almighty God's revealed plan for the world topsy-turvy, and make of our sweet and lovely civilization a shambles, a desolation where man, God's masterpiece, would soon degenerate back to the ape!''

VOICE (*to* YANK). Hey, you guy. There's your ape stuff again.

YANK (*with a growl of fury*). I got him. So dey blow up tings, do dey? Dey turn tings round, do dey? Hey, lend me dat paper, will yuh?

VOICE. Sure. Give it to him. On'y keep it to yourself, see. We don't wanter listen to no more of that slop.

VOICE. Here you are. Hide it under your mattress.

YANK (*reaching out*). Tanks. I can't read much but I kin manage. (*He sits, the paper in the hand at his side, in the attitude of Rodin's ''The Thinker.'' A pause. Several snores from down the corridor. Suddenly* YANK *jumps to his feet with a furious groan as if some appalling thought had crashed on him—bewilderedly.*) Sure—her old man—president of de Steel Trust—makes half de steel in de world—steel—where I tought I belonged—drivin' trou—movin'—in dat—to make* her*—and cage me in for her to spit on! Christ (*He shakes the bars of his cell door till the whole tier trembles. Irritated, protesting exclamations from those awakened or trying to get to sleep.*) He made dis—dis cage! Steel!* It *don't belong, dat's what! Cages, cells, locks, bolts, bars—dat's what it means—holdin' me down wit him at de top! But I'll manage trou! Fire, dat melts it! I'll be fire—under de heap—fire dat never goes out—hot as hell—breakin' out in de night—(*While he has been saying this last he has shaken his cell door to a clanging accompaniment. As he comes to the ''breakin' out'' he seizes one bar with both hands and, putting his two feet up against the others so that his position is parallel to the floor like a monkey's, he gives a great wrench backwards. The bar bends like a licorice stick under his tremendous strength. Just at this moment the* PRISON GUARD *rushes in, dragging a hose behind him.*)

GUARD (*angrily*). I'll loin youse bums to wake me up! (*Sees* YANK.) Hello, it's you, huh? Got the D.T.s, hey? Well, I'll cure 'em. I'll drown your snakes for yuh! (*Noticing the bar.*) Hell, look at dat bar bended! On'y a bug is strong enough for dat!

YANK (*glaring at him*). Or a hairy ape, yuh big yellow bum! Look out! Here I come! (*He grabs another bar.*)

GUARD (*scared now—yelling off left*). Toin de hose on, Ben!—full pressure! And call de others—and a strait-jacket! (*The curtain is falling. As it hides* YANK *from view, there is a splattering smash as the stream of water hits the steel of* YANK'S *cell.*)

(*The curtain falls.*)

SCENE SEVEN

Nearly a month later. An I. W. W. local near the waterfront, showing the interior of a front room on the ground floor, and the street outside. Moonlight on the narrow street, buildings massed in black shadow. The interior of the room, which is general assembly room, office, and reading room, resembles some dingy settlement boys' club. A desk and high stool are in one corner. A table with papers, stacks of pamphlets, chairs about it, is at center. The whole is decidedly cheap, banal, commonplace and unmysterious as a room could well be. The Secretary is perched on the stool making entries in a large ledger. An eye shade casts his face into shadows. Eight or ten men, longshoremen, iron workers, and the like are grouped about the table. Two are playing checkers. One is writing a letter. Most of them are smoking pipes. A big signboard is on the wall at the rear, "Industrial Workers of the World—Local No. 57."

YANK (*comes down the street outside. He is dressed as in Scene Five. He moves cautiously, mysteriously. He comes to a point opposite the door; tiptoes softly up to it, listens, is impressed by the silence within, knocks carefully, as if he were guessing at the password to some secret rite. Listens. No answer. Knocks again a bit louder. No answer. Knocks impatiently, much louder*).

SECRETARY (*turning around on his stool*). What the hell is that—someone knocking? (*Shouts.*) Come in, why don't you? (*All the men in the room look up.* YANK *opens the door slowly, gingerly, as if afraid of an ambush. He looks around for secret doors, mystery, is taken aback by the commonplaceness of the room and the men in it, thinks he may have gotten in the wrong place, then sees the signboard on the wall and is reassured.*)

YANK (*blurts out*). Hello.

MEN (*reservedly*). Hello.

YANK (*more easily*). I tought I'd bumped into de wrong dump.

SECRETARY (*scrutinizing him carefully*). Maybe you have. Are you a member?

YANK. Naw, not yet. Dat's what I come for—to join.

SECRETARY. That's easy. What's your job—longshore?

YANK. Naw. Fireman—stoker on de liners.

SECRETARY (*with satisfaction*). Welcome to our city. Glad to know you people are waking up at last. We haven't got many members in your line.

YANK. Naw. Dey're all dead to de woild.

SECRETARY. Well, you can help to wake 'em. What's your name? I'll make out your card.

YANK (*confused*). Name? Lemme tink.

SECRETARY (*sharply*). Don't you know your own name?

YANK. Sure; but I been just Yank for so long—Bob, dat's it—Bob Smith.

SECRETARY (*writing*). Robert Smith. (*Fills out the rest of the card.*) Here you are. Cost you half a dollar.

YANK. Is dat all—four bits? Dat's easy. (*Gives the SECRETARY the money.*)

SECRETARY (*throwing it in drawer*). Thanks. Well, make yourself at home. No introductions needed. There's literature on the table. Take some of those pamphlets with you to distribute aboard ship. They may bring results. Sow the seed, only go about it right. Don't get caught and fired. We got plenty out of work. What we need is men who can hold their jobs—and work for us at the same time.

YANK. Sure. (*But he still stands, embarrassed and uneasy.*)

SECRETARY (*looking at him—curiously*). What did you knock for? Think we had a coon in uniform to open doors?

YANK. Naw. I tought it was locked—and dat yuh'd wanter give me the once-over trou a peephole or somep'n to see if I was right.

SECRETARY (*alert and suspicious but with an easy laugh*). Think we were running a crap game? That door is never locked. What put that in your nut?

YANK (*with a knowing grin, convinced that this is all camouflage, a part of the secrecy*). Dis burg is full of bulls, ain't it?

SECRETARY (*sharply*). What have the cops got to do with us? We're breaking no laws.

YANK (*with a knowing wink*). Sure. Youse wouldn't for woilds. Sure. I'm wise to dat.

SECRETARY. You seem to be wise to a lot of stuff none of us knows about.

YANK (*with another wink*). Aw, dat's aw right, see. (*Then made a bit resentful by the suspicious glances from all sides.*) Aw, can it! Youse needn't put me trou de toid degree. Can't youse see I belong? Sure! I'm reg'lar. I'll stick, get me? I'll shoot de woiks for youse. Dat's why I wanted to join in.

SECRETARY (*breezily, feeling him out*). That's the right spirit. Only are you sure you understand what you've joined? It's all plain and aboveboard; still, some guys get a wrong slant on us. (*Sharply.*) What's your notion of the purpose of the I. W. W.?

YANK. Aw, I know all about it.

SECRETARY (*sarcastically*). Well, give us some of your valuable information.

YANK (*cunningly*). I know enough not to speak outa my toin. (*Then resentfully again.*) Aw, say! I'm reg'lar. I'm wise to de game. I know yuh got to watch your step wit a stranger. For all youse know, I might be a plain-clothes dick, or somep'n, dat's what yuh're tinkin', huh? Aw, forget it! I belong, see? Ask any guy down to de docks if I don't.

SECRETARY.   Who said you didn't?

YANK.   After I'm 'nitiated, I'll show yuh.

SECRETARY (*astounded*). Initiated? There's no initiation.

YANK (*disappointed*). Ain't there no password—no grip nor nothin'?

SECRETARY.   What'd you think this is—the Elks—or the Black Hand?

YANK.   De Elks, hell! De Black Hand, dey're a lot of yellow backstickin' Ginees. Naw. Dis is a man's gang, ain't it?

SECRETARY.   You said it! That's why we stand on our two feet in the open. We got no secrets.

YANK (*surprised but admiringly*). Yuh mean to say yuh always run wide open—like dis?

SECRETARY.   Exactly.

YANK.   Den yuh sure got your noive wit youse!

SECRETARY (*sharply*). Just what was it made you want to join us? Come out with that straight.

YANK.   Yuh call me? Well, I got noive, too! Here's my hand. Yuh wanter blow tings up, don't yuh? Well, dat's me! I belong!

SECRETARY (*with pretended carelessness*). You mean change the unequal conditions of society by legitimate direct action—or with dynamite?

YANK.   Dynamite! Blow it offen de oith—steel—all de cages—all de factories, steamers, buildings, jails—de Steel Trust and all dat makes it go.

SECRETARY.   So—that's your idea, eh? And did you have any special job in that line you wanted to propose to us? (*He makes a sign to the men, who get up cautiously one by one and group behind* YANK.)

YANK (*boldly*). Sure, I'll come out wit it. I'll show youse I'm one of de gang. Dere's dat millionaire guy, Douglas——

SECRETARY.   President of the Steel Trust, you mean? Do you want to assassinate him?

YANK.   Naw, dat don't get yuh nothin'. I mean blow up de factory, de woiks, where he makes de steel. Dat's what I'm after—to blow up de steel, knock all de steel in de woild up to de moon. Dat'll fix tings! (*Exactly, with a touch of bravado.*) I'll do it by me lonesome! I'll show yuh! Tell me where his woiks is, how to git there, all de dope. Gimme de stuff, de old butter—and watch me do de rest! Watch de smoke and see it move! I don't give a damn if dey nab me—long as it's done! I'll soive life for it—and give 'em de laugh! (*Half to himself.*) And I'll write her a letter and tell her de hairy ape done it. Dat'll square tings.

SECRETARY (*stepping away from* YANK). Very interesting. (*He gives a signal. The men, huskies all, throw themselves on* YANK *and before he knows it they have his legs and arms pinioned. But he is too flabbergasted to make a struggle, anyway. They feel him over for weapons.*)

MAN.   No gat, no knife. Shall we give him what's what and put the boots to him?

SECRETARY.   No. He isn't worth the trouble we'd get into. He's too stupid. (*He comes closer and laughs mockingly in* YANK'S *face.*) Ho-ho! By God, this is the biggest joke they've put up on us yet. Hey, you Joke! Who sent you—Burns or Pinkerton? No, by God, you're such a bonehead. I'll bet you're in the Secret Service! Well, you dirty spy, you rotton agent provocator, you can go back and tell whatever skunk is paying you blood-money for betraying your brothers that he's wasting his coin. You couldn't catch a cold. And tell him that all he'll ever get on us, or ever has got, is just his own sneaking plots that he's framed up to put us in jail. We are what our manifesto says we are, neither more nor less—and we'll give him a copy of that any time he calls. And as for you—— (*He glares scornfully at* YANK, *who is sunk in an oblivious stupor.*) Oh, hell, what's the use of talking? You're a brainless ape.

YANK (*aroused by the word to fierce but futile struggles*). What's dat, yuh Sheeny bum, yuh!

SECRETARY.   Throw him out, boys. (*In spite of his struggles, this is done with gusto and éclat. Propelled by several parting kicks,* YANK *lands sprawling in the middle of the narrow cobbled street. With a growl he starts to get up and storm the closed door, but stops bewildered by the confusion in his brain, pathetically impotent. He sits there, brooding, in as near to the attitude of Rodin's "Thinker" as he can get in his position.*)

YANK (*bitterly*). So dem boids don't tink I belong, neider. Aw, to hell wit 'em! Dey're in de wrong pew—de same old bull—soapboxes and Salvation Army—no guts! Cut out an hour offen de job a day and make me happy! Gimme a dollar more a day and make me happy! Tree square a day, and cauliflowers in de front yard—ekal rights—a woman and kids—a lousy vote—and I'm all fixed for Jesus, huh? Aw, hell! What does dat get yuh? Dis ting's in your inside, but it ain't your belly. Feedin' your face—sinkers and coffee—dat don't touch it. It's way down—at de bottom. Yuh can't grab it, and yuh can't stop it. It moves, and everything moves. It stops and de whole woild stops. Dat's me now—I don't tick, see?—I'm a busted Ingersoll, dat's what. Steel was me, and I owned de woild. Now I ain't steel, and de woild owns me. Aw, hell! I can't see—it's all dark, get me? It's all wrong! (*He turns a bitter mocking face up like an ape gibbering at the moon.*) Say, youse up dere, Man in de Moon, yuh look so wise, gimme de answer, huh? Slip me de inside dope, de information right from de stable—where do I get off at, huh?

A POLICEMAN (*who has come up the street in time to hear this last—with grim humor*). You'll get off at the station, you boob, if you don't get up out of that and keep movin'.

YANK (*looking up at him—with a hard, bitter laugh*). Sure! Lock me up! Put me in a cage! Dat's de on'y answer yuh know. G'wan, lock me up!

POLICEMAN.   What you been doin'?

YANK.   Enuf to gimme life for! I was born, see? Sure, dat's de charge. Write it in de blotter. I was born, get me!

POLICEMAN (*jocosely*). God pity your old woman! (*Then matter-of-fact.*) But I've no time for kidding. You're soused. I'd run you in but it's too long a walk to the station. Come on now, get up, or I'll fan your ears with this club. Beat it now! (*He hauls* YANK *to his feet.*)

YANK (*in a vague mocking tone*). Say, where do I go from here?

POLICEMAN (*giving him a push—with a grin, indifferently*). Go to hell.

(*The curtain falls.*)

SCENE EIGHT

Twilight of the next day. The monkey house at the Zoo. One spot of clear gray light falls on the front of one cage so that the interior can be seen. The other cages are vague, shrouded in shadow from which chatterings pitched in a conversational tone can be heard. On the one cage a sign from which the word "gorilla" stands out. The gigantic animal himself is seen squatting on his haunches on a bench in much the same attitude as Rodin's "Thinker." YANK enters from the left. Immediately a chorus of angry chattering and screeching breaks out. The gorilla turns his eyes but makes no sound or move.

YANK (*with a hard, bitter laugh*). Welcome to your city, huh? Hail, hail, de gang's all here! (*At the sound of his voice the chattering dies away into an attentive silence. YANK walks up to the gorilla's cage and, leaning over the railing, stares in at its occupant, who stares back at him, silent and motionless. There is a pause of dead stillness. Then YANK begins to talk in a friendly confidential tone, half-mockingly, but with a deep undercurrent of sympathy.*) Say, yuh're some hard-lookin' guy, ain't yuh? I seen lots of tough nuts dat de gang called gorillas, but yuh're de foist real one I ever seen. Some chest yuh got, and shoulders, and dem arms and mits! I bet yuh got a punch in eider fist dat'd knock 'em all silly. (*This with genuine admiration. The gorilla, as if he understood, stands upright, swelling out his chest and pounding on it with his fist. YANK grins sympathetically.*) Sure, I get yuh. Yuh challenge de whole woild, huh? Yuh got what I was sayin' even if yuh muffed de woids. (*Then bitterness creeping in.*) And why wouldn't yuh get me? Ain't we both members of de same club—de Hairy Apes? (*They stare at each other—a pause—then YANK goes on slowly and bitterly.*) So yuh're what she seen when she looked at me, de white-faced tart! I was you to her, get me? On'y outa de cage—broke out—free to moider her, see? Sure! Dat's what she tought. She wasn't wise dat I was in a cage, too—worser'n yours—sure—a damn sight—'cause you got some chanct to bust loose—but me——(*He grows confused.*) Aw, hell! It's all wrong, ain't it? (*A pause.*) I s'pose yuh wanter know what I'm doin' here, huh? I been warmin' a bench down to de Battery—ever since last night. Sure. I seen de sun come up. Dat was pretty, too—all red and pink and green. I was lookin' at de skyscrapers—steel—and all de ships comin' in, sailin' out, all over de oith—and dey was steel, too. De sun was warm, dey wasn't no clouds, and dere was a breeze blowin'. Sure, it was great stuff. I got it aw right—what Paddy said about dat bein' de right dope—on'y I couldn't get *in* it, see? I couldn't belong in dat. It was over my head. And I kept tinkin'—and den I beat it up here to see what youse was like. And I waited till dey was all gone to git yuh alone. Say, how d'yuh feel sittin' in dat pen all de time, havin' to stand for 'em comin' and starin' at yuh—de white-faced, skinny tarts and de boobs what marry 'em—makin' fun of yuh, laughin' at yuh, gittin' scared of yuh—damn 'em! (*He pounds on the rail with his fist. The gorilla rattles the bars of his cage and snarls. All the other monkeys set up an angry chattering in the darkness. YANK goes on excitedly.*) Sure! Dat's de way it hits me, too. On'y yuh're lucky, see? Yuh don't belong wit 'em and you know it. But me, I belong wit 'em—but I don't, see? Dey don't belong wit me, dat's what. Get me? Tinkin' is hard——(*He passes one hand across his forehead with a painful gesture. The gorilla growls impatiently. YANK goes on gropingly.*) It's dis way, what I'm drivin' at. Youse can sit and dope dream in de past, green woods, de jungle and de rest of it. Den yuh belong and dey don't. Den yuh kin laugh at 'em, see? Yuh're de champ of de woild. But me—I ain't got no past to tink in, nor nothin' dat's comin', on'y what's now—and dat don't belong. Sure, you're de best off! Yuh can't tink, can yuh? Yuh can't talk neider. But I kin make a bluff at talkin' and tinkin'—a'most git away wit it—a'most—and dat's where de joker comes in. (*He laughs.*) I ain't on oith and I ain't in heaven, get me? I'm in de middle tryin' to separate 'em, takin' all de woist punches from bot' of 'em. Maybe dat's what dey call hell, huh? But you, yuh're at de bottom. You belong! Sure! Yuh're de on'y one in de woild dat does, yuh lucky stiff! (*The gorilla growls proudly.*) And dat's why dey gotter put yuh in a cage, see? (*The gorilla roars angrily.*) Sure! Yuh get me. It beats it when you try to tink it or talk it—it's way down—deep—behind—you 'n' me we feel it. Sure! Bot' members of dis club! (*He laughs—then in a savage tone.*) What de hell! T' hell wit it! A little action, dat's our meat! Dat belongs! Knock 'em down and keep bustin' 'em till dey croaks yuh wit a gat—wit steel! Sure! Are yuh game? Dey've looked at youse, ain't dey—in a cage? Wanter get even? Wanter wind up like a sport 'stead of croakin' slow in dere? (*The gorilla roars an emphatic affirmative.* YANK *goes on with a sort of furious exaltation.*) Sure! Yuh're reg'lar! Yuh'll stick to de finish! Me 'n' you, huh?—bot' members of this club! We'll put up one last star bout dat'll knock 'em offen deir seats! Dey'll have to make de cages stronger after we're trou! (*The gorilla is straining at his bars, growling, hopping from one foot to the other,* YANK *takes a jimmy from under his coat and forces the lock on the cage door. He throws this open.*) Pardon from de governor! Step out and shake hands! I'll take yuh for a walk down Fif' Avenoo. We'll knock 'em offen de oith and croak with de band playin'. Come on, Brother. (*The gorilla scrambles gingerly out of his cage. Goes to* YANK *and stands looking at him.* YANK *keeps his mocking tone—holds out his hand.*) Shake—de secret grip of our order. (*Something, the tone of mockery, perhaps, suddenly enrages the animal. With a spring he wraps his huge arms around* YANK *in a murderous hug. There is a crackling snap of crushed ribs—a gasping cry, still mocking, from* YANK.) Hey, I didn't say kiss me! (*The gorilla lets the crushed body slip to the floor; stands over it uncertainly, considering; then picks it up, throws it in the cage, shuts the door, and shuffles off menacingly into the darkness at left. A great uproar of frightened chattering and whimpering comes from the other cages. Then* YANK *moves, groaning, opening his eyes, and there is silence. He mutters painfully.*) Say—dey oughter match him—wit Zybszko. He got me, aw right. I'm trou. Even him didn't tink I belonged. (*Then, with sudden passionate despair.*) Christ, where do I get off at? Where do I fit in? (*Checking himself as suddenly.*) Aw, what de hell! No squawkin', see! No quittin', get me! Croak wit your boots on! (*He grabs hold of the bars of the cage and hauls himself painfully to his feet—looks around him bewilderedly—forces a mocking laugh.*) In de cage, huh? (*In the strident tones of a circus barker.*) Ladies and gents, step forward and take a slant at de one and only—(*His voice weakened.*)—one and original—Hairy Ape from de wilds of—— (*He slips in a heap on the floor and dies. The monkeys set up a chattering, whimpering wail. And, perhaps, the Hairy Ape at last belongs.*)

(*The curtain falls.*)

FOCUS QUESTIONS

1. Select and discuss three expressionistic features of *The Hairy Ape*.
2. Trace and discuss the cage motif used through the play.
3. Develop a character sketch of Robert ''Yank'' Smith, emphasizing his function as pivotal character.
4. How do the dramatic actions reflect themes of alienation and ''belonging?''
5. Discuss the allegorical implications of the play: for example, the upper-deck as Heaven; the stokehole as Hell; Yank's circular journey; the characters as symbols.
6. Describe the style and content of Paddy's monologue in scene 1 and assess its overall effectiveness.
7. Discuss the social implications of the play, paying close attention to its subtitle.
8. Comment on Yank's progress by the end of the play.

OTHER ACTIVITIES

1. Choose three different settings from the play and coordinate their color schemes for staging them.
2. Discuss the blocking for scene 8, finding ways to emphasize Yank's alienation.

BIBLIOGRAPHY

Baum, Bernard. "*Tempest* and *The Hairy Ape*—The Literary Incarnation of Mythos." *Modern Language Quarterly* 14 (3) (Sept. 1953): 258–73.

Bogard, Travis. *Contour in Time: The Plays of Eugene O'Neill.* New York: Oxford University Press, 1972.

Chothia, Jean. *Forging a Language: A Study of the Plays of Eugene O'Neill.* New York: Cambridge University Press, 1979.

———. "Theatre Language: Word and Image in *The Hairy Ape*." In *Eugene O'Neill and the Emergence of American Drama,* edited by Marc Maufort. Amsterdam: Rodopi, 1989.

Clark, Marden J. "Tragic Effect in *The Hairy Ape*." *Modern Drama* 10 (Feb. 1968): 372–82.

Egri, Peter. "'Belonging' Lost: Alienation and Dramatic Form in Eugene O'Neill's *The Hairy Ape*." In *Critical Essays on Eugene O'Neill,* edited by James J. Martine. Boston: G. K. Hall & Co., 1984.

Gump, Margaret. "From Ape to Man and from Man to Ape." *Kentucky Foreign Language Quarterly* 4 (1957): 268–82.

Kalson, Albert E. "Up-Staged and Off-Staged by the Director and Designer: *The Hairy Ape* and *Desire Under the Elms* in London." In *The Eugene O'Neill Newsletter* (Summer–Fall 1987): 36–40.

MacGowan, Kenneth. "Experiment on Broadway." *Theatre Arts* 7 (July 1923): 175–85.

Roy, Emil. "Eugene O'Neill's *The Emperor Jones* and *The Hairy Ape* as Mirror Plays." *Comparative Drama* 2 (Spring 1968): 21–31.

Tiusanen, Timo. *O'Neill's Scenic Images.* Princeton, NJ: Princeton University Press, 1968.

Tornqvist, Egil. *A Drama of Souls: Studies in O'Neill's Super-Naturalistic Technique.* New Haven, CT: Yale University Press, 1969.

Valgemae, Mardi. *Accelerated Grimace: Expressionism in the American Drama of the 1920s.* Carbondale, IL: Southern Illinois University Press, 1972.

Wainscott, Ronald H. *Staging O'Neill: The Experimental Years, 1920–1934.* New Haven, CT: Yale University Press, 1988.

RECOMMENDED VIDEOTAPES AND RECORDINGS

The Hairy Ape. VHS. 90 min. 1944. Starring William Bendix and Susan Hayward, directed by Alfred Santell. Distributed by Facets Video, Chicago.

The Hairy Ape. One sound cassette. 32 min. With author Jordan Y. Miller. Everett/Edwards.

THE THREEPENNY OPERA
BERTOLT BRECHT (1898–1956)

Life in a Brecht production is laid out before you as comprehensively as in a Breughel painting with many of the same colors—browns, grays and off whites. It does not seize you by the lapel and yell secrets into your ear. Humanity itself, not the romantic individualist, is what it is seeking to explore.

—KENNETH TYNAN

From the 1981 Berliner Ensemble production of *The Threepenny Opera*. Photo: © *Vera Tenshert.*

APPROACHING THE EPIC THEATRE

The effects of rapid advances in technology and new findings in the field of psychology toward the end of the nineteenth century prompted the rise of the **avant-garde,** particularly symbolism and expressionism. (See Preface to Strindberg, p. 661.) Following the devastation of Europe in World War I, these artistic movements reflected a new cynicism and despair. Disillusioned by the loss of the war, Germany faced the disintegration of its national identity, symbolized by the Kaiser's abdication in 1918. As the country floundered to reestablish itself as a republic, artists embraced **Dada** and created a new expressionism out of their nihilistic view of society.

The playwrights among them—Walter Hasenclever (1890–1940), Georg Kaiser (1878–1945), and Ernst Toller (1893–1939)—used theatre to challenge the repressive moral codes, excessive materialism, and the dehumanization of a mechanized world. Ironically their plays also provided vicarious emotions and thrills, which bourgeois audiences eagerly sought, while ignoring the blatant social critiques. This decadence of the audience was further fueled by titillating themes of sexuality and madness in revivals of plays by Georg Büchner (1813–1837) and Frank Wedekind (1864–1918), which had influenced the expressionists.

Once the economic and political stability of the new Weimar Republic was shaken by rising inflation around 1923, expressionism was no longer viable. The time had come for a Marxist theatre concerned with the issues affecting the masses, a Volksbühne or people's theatre, promoted by Erwin Piscator (1893–1966). Instead of focusing on individual psychology or personal and private fate, the new plays centered around historical narratives or current issues and emphasized the effect of social and political forces on human behavior. They included adaptations of classics to reflect current trends in Germany, new social critiques such as *Hurrah, We Live!* by Toller, and history plays like Bernard Shaw's *Saint Joan,* which Max Reinhardt directed in 1924. Audiences were expected to judge the dramatic action rather than merely empathize with the characters.

Bertolt Brecht began his apprenticeship as a theatre practitioner and playwright during this whirlwind of change in the German theatre. From a synthesis of theatrical styles surrounding him and his own traumatic experiences as a medical orderly on the front lines, he created his own drama. In his earliest works he, like the expressionists, was greatly influenced by the themes and episodic format of dramas by Büchner and Wedekind. His first play, *Baal* (1918), was a series of twenty-two scenes centering around a bawdy poet whose insatiable drinking and womanizing drive women to suicide and lead him to commit murder. These anarchistic themes were taken up in Brecht's second play, *Drums in the Night* (1919), which promoted procreation rather than revolution. Produced in Munich in 1922, the play garnered the Kleist Prize.

After 1924 when he moved to Berlin, Brecht was introduced to three new theatrical trends: the analytical and self-critical stance of the actors who addressed the audience directly in Luigi Pirandello's *Six Characters in Search of an Author;* the writings of Karl Marx, which proposed a dialectical approach to history and economic inequality; and the documentary, **epic style** of Piscator, which utilized theatre machinery, projections and film to tell a historical narrative. In response to these stimuli, Brecht wrote *A Man's a Man* (1926), a scathing parable about the remaking of an ordinary man into a fighting machine in the service of British imperialism in India.

Hearing the 1927 broadcast of this play, composer Kurt Weill (1900–1950) approached Brecht with the idea of collaborating on an opera based on the scatological and explicitly sexual poems from the playwright's *Domestic Breviary* collection. Instead they created a songspiel, *The Little Mahagonny* (1928), the precursor to their later opera, *The Rise and Fall of the City of Mahagonny* (1930). This project was interrupted when theatre director, Ernst Josef Aufricht, approved of the unfinished translation of John Gay's *The*

Beggar's Opera to open the Theatre am Schiffbauerdam. Over the course of two months, Brecht and Weill reworked the text, keeping the original's satirical plotline. The resulting script—a montage of dialogue, songs, and asides to the audience—became *The Threepenny Opera* (1928), their most successful commercial venture and the only playtext that Brecht never revised.

The Threepenny Opera* was a pivotal work in Brecht's career. While it was the culmination of his use of expressionistic techniques and hedonistic themes, it also marked the beginning of his conception of an **epic theatre**. This new form differed from Piscator's definition. Instead of creating a technological spectacle of history, Brecht opted for ''a clear unreeling of a sequence of episodes so as to tell a complicated story, complete with its social implications, by means of a linear montage in which all the joins should be visible.''[1] It showed how the visuals, the text, and the music could serve as independent elements that undercut and commented on each other while creating a narrative. Beginning with his ''Notes to *Threepenny Opera*'' written in 1930, Brecht continued to rework and refine the theories of production and acting that supported this anti-illusionary, didactic theatre. These theories would have lasting impact on the creation of political theatre, including the anarchistic works of Julian Beck and Judith Malina as early as the 1950s in the United States, to the plays written by English playwright Edward Bond in the late 1960s and early 1970s, and to the street theatre performances of Brazilian director Augusto Boal.

MAJOR WORKS

Brecht's playwriting career can be divided into three distinct periods. The first was his preoccupation with anarchic and nihilistic themes best illustrated in *Baal* (1918), *Drums in the Night* (1919), *In the Jungle of Cities* (1923), *Edward II* (1924), *A Man's a Man* (1924), and *The Threepenny Opera* (1928). Once steeped in the teachings of Marx, Brecht wrote a series of austere, didactic plays—*lehrstücke*, teaching plays, and *schuloper*, school operas—that were clearly forms of **agitprop**. The full-length political plays of this period include his only epic opera, *The Rise and Fall of the City of Mahagonny* (1929); *St. Joan of the Stockyards* (1930); and *The Mother* (1930). The final period in which Brecht wrote his most important dramas encompasses those years spent in exile, from 1933 to 1948, in France, Scandinavia, and the United States, before his return to Europe after the House Un-American Activities Committee investigated his political affiliations. With the exception of the overwhelming popularity of *The Threepenny Opera,* it is the literary output from these years—*Señora Carrar's Rifles* (1937), *Mother Courage and Her Children* (1939), *Galileo* (1939), *The Good Woman of Setzuan* (1940), *Herr Puntila and His Man Matti* (1940), and *The Caucasian Chalk Circle* (1945)—as well as his theoretical essays that have had a lasting impact on international theatre.

THE ACTION

Polly Peachum, the daughter of London's beggar King, elopes with MacHeath (Mackie the Knife), a notorious arsonist, burglar, forger, and bigamist. Outraged at losing his daughter, Peachum orders MacHeath's arrest. Sheriff Brown, Mackie's old army buddy and father-in-law, has been on the take and thus has protected his friend from the law till now. Peachum threatens to order his band of beggars to disrupt the Queen's coronation unless MacHeath is brought into custody. Obliged to comply, Brown arrests MacHeath, who then escapes from jail with the help of his first wife Lucy, Brown's daughter. But he is betrayed to the police by his favorite prostitute, Ginny Jenny. As he is about to be executed, he is saved from the gallows by order of the Queen.

STRUCTURE AND LANGUAGE

The Threepenny Opera, which Brecht loosely adapted from John Gay's *The Beggar's Opera* (1728), uses the plot and ballad structure of the original work to satirize bourgeois society and expose the "pursuit of happiness" as fallacious. The play juxtaposes the underworld of the Soho district in mid-nineteenth-century London with the jazz clubs and speakeasies of 1920s Chicago. Using the conceit that gangsters like MacHeath and Peachum and prostitutes like Jenny share the mores and values found in the urban middle class, Brecht underscores the latent decadence in the self-serving and indulgent aspirations of the bourgeoisie.

The biting satire of the play is enhanced by the infectious zest of Weill's impudent music that comments on Brecht's lyrics. This is evident from the moment J. J. Peachum opens his school for beggars: "Wake up, you old image of Gawd!/ Get on with your sinful existence/ Just prove you're a rascal and fraud/ And the Lord will reward your persistence." Like a minister intoning an anthem, he informs the audience that the difficulty beggars have earning a living is the direct result of the ease with which human beings become inured to pitiful stories of the destitute. Beggars come to him to rent outfits of misery, especially prepared to move others to charitable feelings, and he issues licenses that allow them to panhandle in particular districts of London. There is an obvious parallel between the bureaucratic red tape that the beggars have to go through in order to work the streets and that required by most local governments in order to open small businesses.

An even bolder demonstration of parody is the wedding celebration. Apologizing for the uncouth behavior of his men, MacHeath acts out an exaggerated version of gentility as he and Polly sit on overly ornate furniture and eat food stolen for the occasion in a stable that they do not own: "You'll have a lot to do, Polly, before you can teach these oafs to behave like proper men." When she imitates a barmaid in the "Pirate Jenny Song" to entertain them all, Polly is castigated by Mackie for behaving improperly. The entire scene juxtaposes the pretensions of bourgeois etiquette with the sordid world of beggars, murderers, and whores, concluding with a duet mocking traditional love songs with its insistence that "love endures or does not endure in many and many a town."

Similarly, Polly's plea for her parents' approval of her "marriage" to MacHeath is no different from that of any young girl's. With the exception of her husband's occupation, her present situation and plans for the future seem fairly respectable:

> Please consider him. Is he handsome? No. But he makes a living. He offers me an existence. He is a first class burglar—and also a far-sighted and experienced thief. I know exactly the amount of his savings. I could even tell you the figure. A few more successful enterprises and we shall be able to retire to a little house in the country, just like Mr. Shakespeare whom Father admires so much.

In fact, MacHeath's business is run like that of any middle-class entrepreneur. He keeps accounts of each of his workers and sends the profits to a banking house in Manchester for legitimate reinvestment. As he places Polly in charge of the business in his absence, he reveals that he wants her to change over to banking exclusively in a few weeks because it is safer and more profitable. Once the band of thieves is turned over to the police, she and MacHeath will be free and clear to live as respectable citizens.

Brecht's premise is quite simple: that human moral conduct depends on one's ability to secure life's essentials—food, clothing, shelter, and sexual pleasure—in order to survive. Since the complexities of an industrial, democratic society often make this difficult or impossible, the middle class is forced into a life of petty crime and hedonistic pleasure. To achieve dreams of happiness, one must lie, cheat in love and in business, engage in illegal activities, and not get caught.

The theme is echoed in the finales to each act. In the first, "The Uncertainty of Human Circumstances," Peachum sings with Bible in hand, "There is one right to which man is entitled—/ That he may call some happiness his own/ Enjoying all the pleasures life can offer/ Being given bread to eat and not a stone/ . . . But sad to say there's been no case recorded/ Of any man who got his share—oh no!" The entire family joins in the lament in which the force of circumstances—that "the world is poor and man is base"—is the cause of this dilemma. At the end of act 2, MacHeath and Jenny sing "The Survival of Mankind," about the lengths to which the poor must go in order to exist. They ask, "For how can man survive?" and then answer, "By simply getting/ Others under, cheating and exploiting all he can./ He only can survive by sheer forgetting—/ Forgetting that he ever was a man."

In the finale to act 3, "The Arrival of the Mounted Messenger," the audience hears about injustice in a world where people grow hungry and do not have their share of the basic necessities of life. Mrs. Peachum remarks "how calm and peaceful would our life be always, if a messenger came from the king whenever he wanted." But the moment is rare when those who have been forced to steal and lie are saved from punishment, that is, if they are caught. Brecht suggests that they may not be any guiltier than the complacent members of the middle class who selfishly hoard their wealth and goods while pretending to be upstanding citizens.

ABOUT THE TRANSLATION

Most English-speaking audiences have been introduced to Brecht's plays through Eric Bentley's fine translations. This English version of *The Threepenny Opera,* which Bentley co-translated with Desmond Vesey, is no exception. It not only reproduces important features of Brecht's original, most notably in the explosive merging of musical format and dramatic content, but also captures every bit of the vitality and spirit that infused Brecht's work.

The sound and sense of Brecht's bumpy prose rhythms guide our descent into the play's mythical underworld. The colorful dialogue welcomes the bold intrusion of songs that effortlessly assert themselves in an outspoken cabaret style. In act 2, scene 2, MacHeath reminisces about the one girl, Ginny Jenny, "whom I loved best of all the girls" ["die mir die liebste war unter den Mädchen"], and pays ironic homage to her in "The Ballad of the Fancy-Man" ["Die Zuhalterballade"], recalling those happy days spent together in the bordello:

> Und wenn ein Freier kam, kroch ich aus unserm Bett
> And when a stranger came, I left our little bed
>
> Und druckte mich zu 'n Kirsch und war sehr nett
> And had a drink or two and showed myself well-bred
>
> Und wenn er blechte, sprach ich su ihm: Herr
> And when he paid, I said: Auf Wiederseh'n
>
> Wenn sie mal wieder wollen—bitte sehr.
> If any time you'd care to—come again.

Brecht's loose adherence to an iambic-pentameter verse format successfully incorporates a variety of different actions and literary effects into a single musical statement. The "Und/ And" repetitions reveal MacHeath as a streetwise person who experiences life as a series of happenings, devoid of causality and interrelations. The characterization sustains its credibility both in stage dialogue and song, while the parallel construction enhances the poetry of Brecht's libretto. Two sets of rhyming couplets—"Bett/nett" and "Herr/sehr"—provide an unexpected sense of balance to an otherwise seductive lyric about a world out of kilter, while the second couplet exposes a saucy *double-entendre*.

When MacHeath's recollection ends, Jenny appears to sing her version in words that paint a harsh picture of her former lover, yet duplicate the rhyme and rhythm of the verse he just sang. Both conclude with the refrain, ''That was a time of days now long ago'' [''Zu jener Zeit, die nun vergangen ist''], then go into their dance until Constable Smith interrupts the action and apprehends MacHeath. Thus the musical interlude has served as a pretext for MacHeath's betrayal and arrest. But the powerful stage English of the Bentley/Vesey translation has retained the flavor of the German throughout, which is why this version has proven so indispensable to subsequent English translations and adaptations.

THE THREEPENNY OPERA-IN-PERFORMANCE

More revolutionary than the politics of The Threepenny Opera was Brecht's approach to this 1928 production: theatre with the critical distance of a boxing match or cabaret performance, which allowed the audience to remain cognizant that they were in a theatre. After consultations with co-director Erich Engel and designer Caspar Neher, Brecht exposed the lighting apparatus and placed the musicians in full view of the audience to avoid the mystery of theatrical illusion. Another device to ensure that the audience would not get caught up in the suspense of the plot were signs projected on screens to announce the essential storyline, or fable, for each scene. By dimming the oil lamps hanging from above for each of Kurt Weill's songs, the signs became ironic commentaries on the characters' words and actions and prevented the audience from experiencing empathy.

Last-minute alterations in the script, casting changes due to illness, the actors' dissatisfaction with their parts, and squabbles between Engel and Brecht threatened to make a travesty of the production. The play managed to open on August 31, 1928, with Harold Paulsen as MacHeath, Roma Bahn as Polly, Lotte Lenya as Jenny, Erich Ponto as Peachum, and Kurt Gerron as Tiger Brown. The audience sat through the first two scenes without reaction. Then, as the ''Cannon Song'' ended, ''the breakthrough came. The audience did not slowly thaw but boiled over. Clapping, yelling, stomping, they demanded an encore . . . From this moment on every sentence and every note was a success.''[2] The audience left the theatre singing the lyrics and humming Weill's music. Critics urged everyone to see the play and, within days, Berlin was struck with ''Threepenny Opera'' fever, totally oblivious to the underlying seriousness of its message. The exceptions were the Hitlerites, who attempted to stop the performance when they saw the play as an attack on the Nazi party. In fact, until 1933 when Hitler relegated the music of Kurt Weill to his Museum of Degenerate Art, The Threepenny Opera continued to be staged throughout Germany and Austria as well as to generate translations and productions in Hungary, Czechoslovakia, Russia, Denmark, Poland, and Holland.

Unhappy with the play's anarchic rather than Marxist themes, Brecht attempted to create a movie version with a stronger political message. His scenario was entitled The Bruise. When Nero Films rejected it in 1930, he started court proceedings against them. In the meantime, G. W. Pabst was hired as the director. In spite of Brecht's protests and lawsuit, the film that Pabst created was strongly based on the author's scenario. In it MacHeath becomes a financier at the National Deposit Bank. By marrying Polly, he enters into a capital venture with his father-in-law, the head of a Begging trust. The 1931 movie, which featured Carola Neher, Lotte Lenya, Rudolf Forster, and Ernst Busch, was well received.

Since the end of World War II, there have been many international productions of The Threepenny Opera. As early as 1945, E. F. Burian staged an adaptation at Theatre D46 in Prague, in which the audience observed the theatre electricians hanging large spotlights between the actions. Burian emphasized the difficulties of survival in the post-war era by ending the play before MacHeath's rescue.

Ten years later, Georgio Strehler corresponded with Brecht in preparation for his production at the Piccolo Teatro in Milan, which opened in 1957. With the playwright's approval, Strehler updated the play to New York's Little Italy circa 1917, introducing the policemen as Keystone Kops and bringing a Model T on stage. In 1964, Liviu Ciulei's contemporized version at the Lucia Sturdza Bulandra Theatre in Bucharest used a play of lights on a permanent setting. He created the atmosphere of a gangster film in which the suburb, the jail, the bordello, and the beggar's school were interconnected. Ciulei saw Brecht's characters as both victims and victimizers. The prostitutes were mere merchandise, however, having lost their sense of good and evil. Mackie was obsessed with physical power but wielded just enough economic power to buy his freedom from society's sanctions.

There was even an Indian adaptation by Teen Paishar Pala in Bengal in 1969. Set in Calcutta around the mid 1870s with slide projections and posters and signs indicating the locale, MacHeath became a romantic rebel against the British imperial police force. Traditional Indian music replaced Weill's and traditional theatrical forms were used to visualize the play. Of particular note was the Queen's messenger who was depicted as a man dressed as Shiva in a tiger skin.

In the United States, New York audiences were reintroduced in March 1954 to the Brecht/Weill opera, which had failed when Gifford Cochran and Jerrold Krimsky produced it in 1933. The verve and charm of Marc Blitzstein's **bowdlerized** version seemed perfectly at home in the intimate quarters of the Theatre de Lys situated in the heart of Greenwich Village, where the production won instant approval from post-war audiences. Featuring Beatrice Arthur, Scott Merrill, Jo Sullivan, Charlotte Rae, and Leon Lishner in the original cast, the play drew capacity crowds both in New York and on tour over the next five years. Among its casts for more than two thousand performances were Lotte Lenya, Estelle Parsons, Tony LoBianco, John Astin, Jerry Orbach, Jerry Stiller, Edward Asner, and Gypsy Rose Lee.

It was not until the 1970s that English language versions of the play exposed the dark and vulgar language of the German original. When Tony Richardson opened his post-Theatre of Cruelty production at the Prince of Wales in London in 1972, he chose Michael Feingold's translation. The cast included Vanessa Redgrave as Polly. When Richard Foreman was asked to stage the opera for the New York Shakespeare Festival, he worked with the Ralph Manheim/John Willett translation. His 1976 production opened on May Day with Raul Julia as MacHeath and Ellen Greene as Jenny. Harsh lighting created a cold, sleek production in browns, blacks, and grays and underscored the bold language, anarchic themes, and cynical social commentary of the original. As usual, Foreman relied on his own visual style, whose static poses and odd movement patterns made the characters puppet-like, their potential for violence always lurking beneath the surface.

A resurgence of interest in *The Threepenny Opera* occurred in different corners of the world during the 1980s. When the ban on Brecht was lifted in Spain, a Castilian production was staged in Barcelona. By 1984, a Catalan and Castilian version opened at the National Theatre of Madrid. Not only was the play a success at the box office, it was honored as the best foreign play of that year. Two years later, in Poland, Jerzy Grzegorzewski directed a totally theatricalized production at the Teatr Studio of Warsaw in which the **prompter's box** was turned into the prison visitors' room and the messenger from the Queen was a puppet on a horse. The two major English language productions for that decade, however, were Peter Wood's 1986 direction of Tim Curry as MacHeath and Sally Dexter as Polly for London's National Theatre and John Dexter's 1989 direction of rock star Sting as MacHeath and Maureen McGovern as Polly in a new Michael Feingold translation. The latter was staged at the Lunt-Fontanne Theatre in New York. When Patrick Mason directed Frank McGuinness' adaptation for the Gate Theatre in Dublin in 1991, the production emphasized the oppressiveness of class distinctions characteristic of London in the 1950s.

REFLECTIONS ON THE THREEPENNY OPERA

Douglas Watt's review of the New York Shakespeare Festival production
of The Threepenny Opera *was originally published on May 3, 1976,*
in the New York Daily News.

A BRILLIANT 'THREEPENNY OPERA'

A fantastic and sensationally theatrical production of "The Threepenny Opera" opened Saturday night at the Beaumont under the auspices of the New York Shakespeare Festival. It is a rebirth, rather than a revival, of a blazing 20th-century masterpiece grafted onto an 18th-century one, a collaboration that, though almost 50 years old, seems as immediate as tomorrow's headlines. Be warned, it will mesmerize, thrill, blind, and perhaps blister you. And underlying its bitter cynicism lies a pity that makes it, finally, a work of feverish beauty.

Richard Foreman, whose unusual and visually arresting creations have heretofore been confined to Off Off Broadway, has conceived "Threepenny Opera" (the article has been dropped) as a sort of gigantic robot show whose dehumanized characters perform with mechanical predictability the inhuman acts of man. There are strong echoes, both in staging and design, of Foreman's "Hotel for Criminals" a season ago.

A new translation by Ralph Manheim and John Willett is blunter and allegedly more faithful to the Brecht original than is the Marc Blitzstein one, though at the same time it is often more difficult to sing. The Blitzstein adaptation was, of course, of tremendous importance in establishing "The Threepenny Opera" in this country during its six-year run Off Broadway during the '50s. But the new treatment is more compelling. With Kurt Weill's brilliantly poisonous score, which can lift you right out of your seat in number after number, the total effect is devastating.

Though most of the action takes place directly before us on a raised stage, the full depth of the Beaumont is used as the beggars, whores, cutthroats and other specimens of Victorian London approach us in a straight line from the murky distance at the beginning, and return to it at the finish. In Douglas W. Schmidt's richly atmospheric setting, suggestive of earlier Foreman productions, mortised sections along the forestage create pits in which the human refuse can huddle.

Raul Julia is a tall, mustached, monocled and elegant Mack the Knife given to walking with head tilted slightly forward and feet carefully lifted and set down like the hooves of a horse in dressage steps. We first glimpse him in transit along the back wall as The Ballad Singer, Roy Brocksmith, sings the famous "Moritat" with vacant eyes while cranking a hurdy-gurdy.

Julia sheds his mannequin image at times most notably in the "Cannon Song" duet with police chief Tiger Brown, a civilized rogue as played by David Sabin, and in the gallows scene when he delivers the "Call From the Grave" and "Ballad in Which Macheath Begs All Men for Forgiveness" with passion.

But the most electrifying performance comes from Ellen Greene as the whore Jenny who turns her lover Macheath in for a few shillings. Her account of the bitter aria "Pirate Jenny" is enthralling, and the tango "Ballad of Immoral Earnings" will dissolve you as presented by Miss Greene, Julia and the small band (off to one side) under the excellent direction of Stanley Silverman, Foreman's longtime composing associate.

C. K. Alexander is fascinating as a short, corpulent, insatiably greedy and sternly methodical Peachum, ruler of London's beggar business. Caroline Kava brings a cultivated speaking and singing voice to bear on the role of a dumbly smiling Polly Peachum, Macheath's bride, and Elizabeth Wilson is an efficient Mrs. Peachum. Blair Brown makes an exceptionally pretty Lucy, the police chief's pregnant daughter who springs her lover Macheath from Old Bailey. Tony Azito, who plays Peachum's assistant as a haunting, slow-motion figure, and Ed Zang, as a slyly humble beggar's apprentice, are also effective. Adding handsomely to the garish scene are Theoni V. Aldredge's costumes and Pat Collins' lighting, sometimes glaring and at other times dim.

Though this is purportedly Victorian London superimposed on 18th-century London, we are unmistakably in the decadent environment of pre-Hitler Berlin. When Macheath, at rope's end, asks, "What's breaking into a bank compared with founding a bank? What's murdering a man compared with hiring a man?," he is giving voice to the misery in postwar Germany as well as elsewhere. And as, in the second-act finale—the catechistic "What Keeps Mankind Alive?"—the chorus announces, "Mankind is kept alive by bestial acts," there emerges from behind this putrid society a vision of man's potential, all the clearer for the boldness and honesty of the scene before us.

Notes

1. *Willett,* ARTS AND POLITICS IN THE WEIMAR PERIOD *(New York: Pantheon Books, 1978), 154.*
2. *Aufricht quoted in Fuegi,* BERTOLT BRECHT *(Cambridge: Cambridge University Press, 1987), 62.*

THE THREEPENNY OPERA
BERTOLT BRECHT
TRANSLATED BY DESMOND VESEY AND ERIC BENTLEY

CHARACTERS

A Ballad Singer
Mr. J. J. Peachum
Mrs. Peachum
Polly Peachum
MacHeath, *called Mackie the Knife*
Reverend Kimball
John Brown, *called Tiger Brown*

Ginny Jenny
Filch
Money Matthew
Hookfinger Jacob
Robert, *called Robert the Saw*
Ede
Jimmy the Second
Walter, *called Wally the Weeper*
} The Gang

Vixen
Dolly
Betty
Molly
} Whores
Smith
Lucy Brown
Beggars, Whores, Policemen, etc.

PROLOGUE

BALLAD OF MACKIE THE KNIFE

(*Market Day in Soho. Beggars are begging, thieves thieving, whores whoring. A ballad singer sings a ballad.*)

And the shark, he has his teeth and
In his face they glisten white.
And MacHeath, he has his jack-knife
But he keeps it out of sight.

When the shark bites through his victim
There is scarlet on shagreen.
But MacHeath has fancy gloves on
So the blood is never seen.

By the river's cold green waters
People suddenly drop down.
But it's neither plague nor chol'ra
And 'tis said MacHeath's in town.

On the pavement, one fine Sunday,
Lies a body robbed of life.
And a man slips round the corner
Whom they call MacHeath the Knife.

Solly Meyer now has vanished—
Just another rich young man.
And MacHeath has all his money.
Try to prove it, if you can!

(PEACHUM *with his wife and daughter walk slowly across the stage from left to right.*)

Jenny Towler was discovered
With a jack-knife in her breast,
And MacHeath strolls down the quayside,
Knows no more than all the rest.

Where is Alphonse Glite, the coachman,
Missing seven days ago?
Maybe someone has the answer,
But MacHeath would never know.

Seven children and their granddad
Burnt to death in old Soho
In the crowd MacHeath stands watching—
Isn't asked and doesn't know.

And the seventeen-year-old widow,
She whose name has spread abroad,
Woke one night and was assaulted.
Mackie, what was your reward?

(There is a burst of laughter from the whores, and a man steps out from among them and walks quickly across the stage and exits.)

GINNY JENNY.   Look! That was Mackie the Knife!

ACT ONE
SCENE ONE

IN ORDER TO COMBAT THE INCREASING HARD-HEARTEDNESS OF MANKIND, MR. J. J. PEACHUM, MERCHANT, HAS OPENED A SHOP IN WHICH THE POOREST OF THE POOR MAY ACQUIRE AN APPEARANCE CALCULATED TO MOVE EVEN THE STONIEST OF HEARTS.

(The wardrobe room of Jonathan Jeremiah Peachum's establishment for beggars. MR. PEACHUM *sings his* MORNING ANTHEM.*)*

> Wake up, you old Image of Gawd!
> Get on with your sinful existence
> Just prove you're a rascal and fraud
> And the Lord will reward your persistence.
>
> Double-cross your own brother, you sot!
> And sell your wife's honor, you knave!
> Is *your* life dependent on God?
> You'll know when you rise from the grave!

PEACHUM *(to the audience).* I see I shall have to try something new. This business is far too difficult: trying to arouse human pity! You know there *are* a few things that will move people to pity, a very few; but after they've been used once or twice, they no longer work. Man has the horrid capacity of being able to make himself heartless at will. So it happens, for example, that a man who sees a man standing at the street corner with only a stump of an arm will probably be so horrified the first time that he will give him sixpence. But the second time he will only give threepence; and if he sees him a third time, he'll brutally hand him over to the police. It's just the same with these old spiritual aids.

(A large board is let down from above, and on it is written: "To give is more blessed than to receive.")

What is the use of the finest and most appealing slogans painted on the most enticing posters, when they so quickly lose their effect? In the Bible there are some four or five sayings that really touch the heart; but as soon as they're used up, one's starving again. Take an example—this one hanging here—"Give and it shall be given unto you"—that lasted exactly three weeks. One must always be offering some new attraction. So one has to turn to the Bible again. But how often can *that* be done?

(There is a knock, PEACHUM *opens the door, and a young man named* FILCH *enters.)*

FILCH.   Peachum & Co.?

PEACHUM.   Peachum.

FILCH.   Then you're the owners of the firm called "The Beggars' Friend"? I was told to come to you. Oh! Those are fine slogans. They're a goldmine. I suppose you've got a whole library full of such things? That's something quite new. Fellows like us—we'd never get an idea like that, never; and then, not being properly educated, how could we make a good business out of it?

PEACHUM.   Your name?

FILCH.   Well, you see, Mr. Peachum, I've had bad luck ever since I was a boy. My mother was a drunkard and my father gambled, and so from an early age I had to fend for myself; and without the loving hand of a mother to guide me I sank deeper and deeper into the morass of the great city. I never knew a father's care or the blessings of a happy home. And so now you see me . . .

PEACHUM.   And so now I see you . . .

FILCH *(confused).* . . . see me . . . completely destitute, a prey to my own miserable desires.

PEACHUM.   Like a wreck on the high seas, and so on. Now tell me, you worm-eaten wreck, in which district do you recite this nursery rhyme?

FILCH.   What do you mean, Mr. Peachum?

PEACHUM.   I presume you deliver this speech in public?

FILCH.   Well, you see, Mr. Peachum, there was an unfortunate little incident yesterday in Highland Street. I was standing quietly and miserably yesterday at the corner, hat in hand, not intending any harm . . .

PEACHUM *(turning over the pages of a notebook).* Highland Street. Yes. That's the one. You're the crawling blackleg whom Honey and Sam found yesterday. You had the impertinence to solicit passers-by in District 10. We let it go at a good beating, since we took it you didn't know where God lives. But if you let yourself be seen there again, we shall have to use the saw. Understand?

FILCH.   But please, Mr. Peachum, please. What can I *do* then, Mr. Peachum? The gentlemen really beat me black and blue, and then they gave me your business card. If I were to take off my coat, you'd think you were looking at a haddock.

PEACHUM.   My young friend, if you don't look like a flounder my people were a sight too easy with you. Pah! This young sprout comes along and imagines that if he sticks out his paws, he'll be all set for a fine living. What would you say if somebody came and took the best fish out of *your* pond?

FILCH.   But you see, Mr. Peachum—I haven't got a pond.

PEACHUM.   Well, licenses are only supplied to professionals. *(Points in business-like way to a large map of London.)* London is divided into fourteen districts. Every man-jack who wishes to practice the trade of begging in any of them has to have a license from Jonathan Jeremiah Peachum and Company. Ha! Anyone could come along—a prey to his own miserable desires!

FILCH.   Mr. Peachum. Only a few shillings stand between me and complete ruin. Something must turn up, with only two shillings . . .

PEACHUM.   One pound.

FILCH.   Mr. Peachum!

(*He points beseechingly at a poster which reads: "Shut not your ears to misery." PEACHUM points to a curtain in front of a show-case, on which is written: "Give and it shall be given unto you."*)

Ten shillings.

PEACHUM.   And fifty per cent of the weekly takings. Including outfit, seventy per cent.

FILCH.   And what does the outfit consist of?

PEACHUM.   The Firm decides that.

FILCH.   Well, what district can I start on?

PEACHUM.   2-104 Baker Street. That will be a little cheaper. It is only fifty per cent there, including outfit.

FILCH.   Thank you.

PEACHUM.   Your name?

FILCH.   Charles Filch.

PEACHUM.   Correct. (*Writes.*)—Mrs. Peachum! (MRS. PEACHUM *enters.*) This is Filch. Number three hundred and fourteen. Baker Street District. I'll enter it myself.— Of course, you would want to start now, just before the Coronation; the one opportunity in a lifetime when it's possible to earn a little money.—Outfit C. for you. (*He draws back the linen curtain in front of a show-case in which are standing five wax models.*)

FILCH.   What's that?

PEACHUM.   These are the five best types of misery for touching the human heart. The sight of them rouses a man to that unnatural condition in which he is actually willing to give money away. Outfit A: Victim of Modern Traffic Development. The cheerful cripple, always good-tempered, always carefree. (*He demonstrates it.*) Effect heightened by a mutilated arm.
Outfit B: Victim of the Art of War. The troublesome twitcher, annoys the pedestrians, works by arousing disgust. (*He demonstrates it.*) Modified by medals.
Outfit C: Victim of the Industrial Boom. The Pitiable Blind, or the High School of the Art of Begging.

(PEACHUM *displays him, advancing unsteadily towards* FILCH. *At the moment when he bumps into* FILCH, *the latter screams with horror.* PEACHUM *immediately stops, gazes at him in astonishment, and suddenly shouts.*)

He feels *pity! Pity! You'll* never make a beggar—not in a hundred years. A creature like you is only fit to be begged *from!* Then it's outfit D!—Celia, you've been drinking again, and now you're cockeyed! Number 136 has been complaining about his neck-rag. How often must I tell you that a gentleman will *not* have filthy clothing next to his skin. Number 136 has paid for a new costume. Stains— the only thing about it that could arouse pity—stains have

to be produced—by ironing in candle wax. You never trouble to think! I always have to do everything myself! (*To* FILCH.) Undress and put this on. But mind you keep it in good condition.

FILCH.   And what happens to *my* things?

PEACHUM.   Property of the Firm—Outfit E: Young man who's seen better days, preferably one who "never thought he would come down to this."

FILCH.   Oh, so you use that as well? Why can't *I* have the better days outfit?

PEACHUM.   Because nobody believes in another's real misery, my lad. If you've got the stomach-ache and say so, it only sounds disgusting.—And besides, it's not for you to ask questions, just put these things on.

FILCH.   Aren't they rather dirty? (PEACHUM *gives him a piercing glance.*) I'm sorry, Mr. Peachum, I didn't mean that.

MRS. PEACHUM.   Come on, hurry up, young man. I'm not going to hold your trousers till Christmas.

FILCH (*suddenly, with great determination*). But I'm not going to take off my shoes! Not for anyone. I'd rather chuck the whole thing. They were the only present I had from my poor mother, and never never, however low I may have fallen . . .

MRS. PEACHUM.   Don't talk rubbish. I know you've got dirty feet.

FILCH.   And where do you expect me to wash my feet? In the middle of winter!

(MRS. PEACHUM *leads him behind a folding screen, then sits down left and begins ironing candle-grease into a suit.*)

PEACHUM.   Where is your daughter?

MRS. PEACHUM.   Polly? Upstairs.

PEACHUM.   Was that man here again yesterday? The one who always comes when I'm out.

MRS. PEACHUM.   Don't be so suspicious, Jonathan! There isn't a finer gentleman alive, and the Captain seems to take quite an interest in our Polly.

PEACHUM.   Um.

MRS. PEACHUM.   And if I can see an inch before my nose, Polly is fond of him too.

PEACHUM.   There you go, Celia! Throwing my daughter about as if I were a millionaire! So she's going to marry! And do you think our miserable business would last another week if these filthy customers had only *our* legs to look at?—A husband! *He'd* soon have us in his clutches. I know he would! D' you think your daughter would be any better than you at keeping her mouth shut in bed?

MRS. PEACHUM.   You've got a nice opinion of your daughter!

PEACHUM.   The worst! The very worst! She's nothing but a lump of sensuality!

MRS. PEACHUM.   Well, she certainly doesn't get that from you!

PEACHUM.   Marry!—My daughter should be to me what bread is to the starving. (*He thumbs through a book.*) That's even in the Bible somewhere. Marriage is a nasty business, anyhow. I'll soon beat the marriage out of her.

MRS. PEACHUM.   Jonathan, you're just ignorant.

PEACHUM.   Ignorant! Then what's his name, this gentleman?

MRS. PEACHUM.   People just call him "the Captain."

PEACHUM.   So you haven't even asked him his name! Veery nice!

MRS. PEACHUM.   Well, we wouldn't be so ill-bred as to ask him for his birth certificate; especially him being such a gentleman, inviting us to the Octopus for a dance.

PEACHUM.   *Where!?*

MRS. PEACHUM.   To the Octopus. For a little dance.

PEACHUM.   Captain? Octopus Hotel? I see—

MRS. PEACHUM.   The gentleman never touched me and my daughter except with kid gloves on his hands.

PEACHUM.   Kid gloves!

MRS. PEACHUM.   Now I come to think, he always had kid gloves on—white kid gloves.

PEACHUM.   Ah. He had white kid gloves and a stick with an ivory handle and spats on his shoes and patent leather shoes and a nice polite manner and a scar . . .

MRS. PEACHUM.   On his neck. How do you know all this about him? (FILCH *comes out from behind the screen.*)

FILCH.   Mr. Peachum, could you give me a few tips on what to do? I always prefer to have a system and not go at things haphazard.

MRS. PEACHUM.   So he wants a system now!

PEACHUM.   He can go and be an idiot; it'll come natural.— Come back this evening at six and you'll be given the necessaries.—Now, get out!

FILCH.   Thank you so much, Mr. Peachum, thank you very much. (*Exit* FILCH.)

PEACHUM.   Fifty per cent—And now I'll tell you who this gentleman with the kid gloves is—Mackie the Knife! (*He runs up the stairs into* POLLY'S *bedroom.*)

MRS. PEACHUM.   Lord save us! Mackie the Knife! Heaven help us!—Polly! Where's Polly? (PEACHUM *comes slowly downstairs.*)

PEACHUM.   Polly? Polly hasn't been home. Her bed's not touched.

MRS. PEACHUM.   Then she's been having supper with that wool-merchant. I'm certain of it, Jonathan.

PEACHUM.   For our sake, I hope it was the wool-merchant.

(MR. *and* MRS. PEACHUM *step in front of the curtain and sing. Song illumination: a golden light. The organ is lit up. Three lights come down on a bar from above, and on a board is written:* THE DESPITE-THE-FACT SONG.)

PEACHUM.
> Despite the fact
> That they should be at home now, sleeping in their beds,

They want to act
Just as though some special treat had sent them almost off their heads.

MRS. PEACHUM.
> But that is the moon over Soho
> That is the seductive "Can-you-feel-my-heart-beating" sigh
> That is the "Wherever you go, I shall go with you, Johnny"
> When their love grows warmer and the moon is high.

PEACHUM.
> Despite the fact
> That they should do the useful things which we intend,
> They go and act
> As they think best and then come to a dirty end.

BOTH.
> And where is then their moon over Soho?
> What's left of their seductive "Can-you-feel-my-heart-beating" sigh?
> Where is then their "Wherever you go, I shall go with you, Johnny"?
> When love has faded and in filth they die?

ACT ONE
SCENE TWO

DEEP IN THE HEART OF SOHO, MACKIE THE KNIFE CELEBRATES HIS WEDDING WITH POLLY PEACHUM, DAUGHTER OF THE KING OF THE BEGGARS.

(*An empty stable.*)

MATTHEW (*carrying a lantern and pointing a revolver round the stable*). Hands up! Anyone there?

(MACHEATH *enters and walks across the front of the stage.*)

MACHEATH.   Well, is anyone here?

MATTHEW.   Not a soul. We can have the marriage here safe enough.

POLLY (*enters in a wedding dress*). But this is a stable!

MACHEATH.   Sit down on the crib for a little while, Polly. (*To the audience.*) Today, in this stable, will be celebrated my marriage to Miss Polly Peachum, who for love has followed me and promised to spend the rest of her life with me.

MATTHEW.   A lot of people will be saying this is the riskiest thing you've ever done, enticing Mr. Peachum's daughter out of his own house.

MACHEATH.   Who *is* Mr. Peachum?

MATTHEW.   If you were to ask him, he'd say he was the poorest man in London.

POLLY.   But surely you're not thinking of having our marriage here? This is a nasty, common stable. You can't invite the clergyman here—and besides, it isn't even ours.

We really ought not to begin our new life with a burglary, Mac. And this is the happiest day in our lives.

MACHEATH.   My dearest, everything shall be just as you wish. Not so much as a stone shall be left to touch your little feet. The furnishings are being brought along at this very moment.

MATTHEW.   Here comes the furniture.

(*There is a sound outside of heavy wagons arriving. Half a dozen men come in, carrying carpets, furniture, crockery, etc., and soon the stable is transformed into an over-ornate living-room.*)

MACHEATH.   Junk!

(*The GENTLEMEN place their presents down on the left, congratulate the bride, and report to the bridegroom.*)

JACOB.   Here's luck! At 14 Ginger Street there were some people on the second floor and we had to smoke 'em out first.

ROBERT THE SAW.   Good luck! A copper in the Strand got in our way. We had to beat him up, I'm afraid.

MACHEATH.   Amateurs!

EDE.   We did what we could, but three people down West are goners. Good luck!

MACHEATH.   Amateurs and bunglers.

JIMMY.   An old gentleman got something he wasn't expecting, but I don't think it's serious. Luck!

MACHEATH.   My orders were: bloodshed to be avoided. It makes me feel quite sick when I think of it. *You'll* never make business-men. Cannibals—but never business-men!

WALTER.   Good luck! Half an hour ago, madam, that piano still belonged to the Duchess of Devizes.

POLLY.   Whatever furniture is this?

MACHEATH.   How do you like it, Polly?

POLLY (*crying*). All those poor people robbed, just for a few bits of furniture.

MACHEATH.   And what furniture! Junk! You're quite right to be angry. A rosewood piano—and a Renaissance sofa. That's unforgivable. And where is a table?

WALTER.   A table? (*They lay planks across the feeding troughs.*)

POLLY.   Oh, Mac, I'm so unhappy. I do hope the clergyman won't come here.

MATTHEW.   Of course he will. *We* told him the way all right.

WALTER (*pushes forward the improvised table*). A table!

MACHEATH (*seeing POLLY crying*). My wife is upset. And where are the other chairs? A piano and no chairs! Never trouble to think! How often does that happen when I have a wedding? Shut your trap, Weeper! How often does it happen, I'm asking, that I leave anything to you? It makes my wife unhappy from the start.

EDE.   Dear Polly . . .

MACHEATH (*knocking his hat from his head*). ''Dear Polly''! I'll knock your head into your chest with your ''Dear Polly,'' you sewer rat! Whoever heard such a thing—''Dear Polly.'' Perhaps you've slept with her, too?

POLLY.   But Mac!

EDE.   I swear that . . .

WALTER.   If there's anything more you'd like, we'll go out again . . .

MACHEATH.   A rosewood piano and no chairs! (*Laughs.*) What do *you* say to that, as the bride?

POLLY.   Oh, well, it might be worse.

MACHEATH.   Two chairs and a sofa, and the bridal pair sit on the ground!

POLLY.   Yes, that would be a fine thing.

MACHEATH (*sharply*). Saw the legs off the piano! Come on! Get on with it! (*Four men saw the legs off the piano and sing.*)

FOUR MEN.
>   Bill Lawton took Mary Sawyer
>   To be his true and lawful wedded wife.
>   But when they stood before the Registrar,
>   *He* didn't know she lived at Temple Bar
>   And *she* learnt his name for the first time in her life.
>   Ho!

WALTER.   And so, miss, all's well and we have another bench.

MACHEATH.   Might I now request you gentlemen to take off your rags and dress yourselves respectably. After all, this isn't the wedding of a mere Nobody. And Polly, may I ask *you* to get busy with the food hampers?

POLLY.   Is that the wedding-breakfast? Is it all stolen, Mac?

MACHEATH.   Of course, of course.

POLLY.   I'd like to know what you'd do if the Police Commissioner were to knock on the door and come in now.

MACHEATH.   I'd show you what your husband *can* do.

MATTHEW.   Not a chance of it today. All the police are guarding the streets. The queen's arriving for the coronation on Friday.

POLLY.   Two knives and fourteen forks! A knife for each chair!

MACHEATH.   What a fine job of work! You're more like a lot of apprentices than trained men! Haven't you any idea what style means? You should be able to tell the difference by now between Chippendale and Louis Quatorze.

(*The rest of the gang now return, wearing smart evening dress, but their behavior during the rest of the scene is not in keeping with their attire.*)

WALTER.   We wanted to bring the most valuable things. Look at that wood! The material is all of the very best.

MATTHEW.   Ssst! Ssst! Permit me, Captain . . .

MACHEATH.   Come here, Polly. (*The two of them pose for congratulation.*)

MATTHEW.   Permit me, Captain, on behalf of all, on the finest day of your life, the springtide of your career—its turning-point, one might say—to offer you our heartiest and most—er—importunate congratulations and so on and so forth. I hate this long-winded stuff. Well, what I mean is: (*Shakes* MACHEATH's *hand.*) heads up, old pal!

MACHEATH.   Thank you. That was kind of you, Matthew.

MATTHEW (*shaking* POLLY's *hand, after having patted* MACHEATH *affectionately on the back*). I mean it. Well, never let your head get down, you old rascal. That is, never let down what you can keep up.

(*Roars of laughter from the guests.* MACHEATH *suddenly catches hold of* MATTHEW *and jerks him to the floor.*)

MACHEATH.   Hold your gab. And keep your dirty jokes for your beautiful Kitty: she's the right slut to hear them.

POLLY.   Mac, don't be so common.

MATTHEW.   I object to your calling Kitty a slut . . .

MACHEATH.   So you object, do you?

MATTHEW.   And what's more, I never tell a dirty joke when I'm with her. I respect Kitty far too much for that. Which you perhaps can't understand, being like you are. And *you* ought to know about sluts! Do you think Kitty hasn't told me what *you've* said to her? And what's more, I'm a kid-glove gent compared to that. (MACHEATH *gives him a fierce glance.*)

JACOB.   Stop it. After all, this is a wedding. (*They pull him back.*)

MACHEATH.   A fine wedding, eh, Polly? Having to see these gutter-rats all round you on the day of your marriage. You didn't think your huband would be let down by his friends like this! But you live and learn.

POLLY.   I think it's quite nice.

ROBERT.   There's no one letting you down. A little difference of opinion can happen any time. (*To* MATTHEW.) Your Kitty is as good as any other. But now come on with your wedding present, cocky.

ALL.   Come on, get on with it!

MATTHEW (*offended*). There.

POLLY.   Oh! A wedding present! But that's sweet of you, Mr. Cocky-Matthew. Look, Mac, what a lovely nightdress.

MATTHEW.   Perhaps a dirty joke too, eh, Captain?

MACHEATH.   All right. No offence meant on this great day.

WALTER.   Well, and this? Chippendale! (*He uncovers an immense grandfather clock.*)

MACHEATH.   Quatorze.

POLLY.   That's wonderful. I'm so happy. I can't think of words to thank you. Your attentions are so marvelous. It's a pity we haven't got a house for it, isn't it, Mac?

MACHEATH.   Well, think of it as a beginning. It's always difficult to begin. Thanks too, Walter. Now clear the stuff away. The food!

JACOB (*while the others are laying the table*). Of course, *I've* forgotten to bring anything. (*Emphatically to* POLLY.) Believe me, young woman, I feel very embarrassed.

POLLY.   Don't mention it, Mr. Hook-Finger Jacob.

JACOB.   All the boys throw their presents around and I stand here with nothing. Put yourself in my place.—But that always happens to me. I could tell you of some fixes I've been in! You wouldn't believe me! The other day I met Ginny Jenny, and I said to her: "Well, my little bitch . . ."

(*Suddenly sees* MACHEATH *standing behind him and walks away without a word.*)

MACHEATH.   Come on. (*Leads* POLLY *to her seat.*) This is the finest food you'll get anywhere today, Polly. Shall we start? (*They all sit down to the wedding breakfast.*)

EDE (*pointing to the service*). Lovely plates. Savoy Hotel.

JACOB.   The mayonnaise eggs are from Selfridge's. We had a jar of gooseliver, too. But on the way here Jimmy ate it out of spite, because he said he had an empty belly.

WALTER.   One doesn't say "belly" among respectable people.

JIMMY.   Don't gobble your eggs so, Ede, specially today!

MACHEATH.   Can't someone sing something? Something edifying?

MATTHEW (*choking with laughter*). Something edifying! That's a proper word! (*Under* MACHEATH's *annihilating glance, he sits down, embarrassed.*)

MACHEATH (*knocking a dish out of someone's hand*). As a matter of fact, I didn't wish to start eating yet. Instead of this "on-with-the-food-and-into-the-trough" exhibition from you men, I'd rather hoped you would have given us something festive to start with. Other people always have some such thing on an occasion like this.

JACOB.   What sort of thing?

MACHEATH.   Must I think of everything myself? I'm not asking for an opera here. But you might have arranged something more than just eating and telling dirty jokes. Well, a day like this just shows how much one can count on one's friends.

POLLY.   The salmon's wonderful, Mac.

EDE.   Yes, I'll bet you've never ate one like that. But Mac has them every day. You're in the honeypot all right. I always have said: Mac will make a fine match for a girl who has higher feelings. I said that to Lucy yesterday.

POLLY.   Lucy? Who is Lucy, Mac?

JACOB (*embarrassed*). Lucy? Well, you know, you mustn't take it too seriously.

(MATTHEW *has stood up and is making furious gestures behind* POLLY *to silence* JACOB.)

POLLY (*sees him*). Are you wanting something? The salt perhaps? What were you going to say, Mr. Jacob?

JACOB.   Oh, nothing. Nothing at all. I really wanted to say nothing. I'll be getting into trouble here.

MACHEATH.   What have you got in your hand, Jacob?

JACOB.   A knife, Captain.

MACHEATH.   And what have you got on your plate?

JACOB.   A trout, Captain.

MACHEATH.   I see, and with the knife, I believe, you are eating the trout. Jacob, that is disgusting. Have you ever seen such a thing, Polly? Eating fish with a knife! A person who does that is a pig, do you understand me, Jacob? You'll live and learn. You'll have a lot to do, Polly, before you can teach these oafs to behave like proper men. Do you even know what that means: a proper man?

WALTER.   I know the difference from a woman!

POLLY.   But Mr. Walter!

MACHEATH.   So you don't want to sing a song. Nothing to brighten up the day a bit. This is to be just another sad, ordinary damned day like always.—And is anyone standing outside the door? I've got to see to that myself, I suppose. Perhaps you'd like me to stand at the door today of all days, so you can stuff yourselves here at my expense?

WALTER (*sullenly*).   What d'you mean: at your expense?

JIMMY.   Shut up, Wally. I'll go out. Who'd come here anyway? (*Exit* JIMMY.)

JACOB.   It would be funny if all the wedding guests were copped today!

JIMMY (*bursts in*).   'St! Captain, cops!

WALTER.   Tiger Brown!

MATTHEW.   Gerr, it's the Reverend Kimball. (KIMBALL *enters.*)

ALL (*shout*).   Good evening, Mr. Kimball!

KIMBALL.   Ah, well, I've found you at last. A small place, indeed, but your own.

MACHEATH.   The Duke of Hampstead's.

POLLY.   Good day, sir. Oh, I'm so happy that you've come on the most wonderful day of my life . . .

MACHEATH.   And now I request an anthem for the Reverend Kimball.

MATTHEW.   How would "Bill Lawton and Mary Sawyer" do?

JACOB.   That's right, Bill Lawton.

KIMBALL.   It would be most pleasant to hear your voices raised in song, my men.

MATTHEW.   Then let's begin.

(*Three men stand up and sing, hesitating, flat and uncertain,* THE WEDDING SONG FOR POORER PEOPLE.)

> Bill Lawton took Mary Saywer
> To be his true and lawful wedded wife.
> Long may they live, ho, ho, ho!
> But when they stood before the Registrar
> *He* didn't know she lived at Temple Bar
> And *she* learnt his name for the first time in her life.
>
> HO!
>
> D'you know what your wife is doing? No!
> D'you let her do what she used to do? No!

> Long may they live, ho, ho, ho!
> Billy Lawton said to me: It's fine
> So long as just one part of her is mine.
> The swine!
>
> HO!

MACHEATH.   Is that all? Contemptible!

MATTHEW (*choking again*).   Contemptible! That's a good word, boys—contemptible!

MACHEATH.   Hold your trap!

MATTHEW.   No, that's what I meant—no life, no swing, nothing.

POLLY.   If nobody will do anything, then I myself will sing a little song as best I can, and in it I am going to imitate a girl I once saw in a tiny bar in Soho. She was the barmaid, and you must understand that everyone always laughed at her, and then one day she spoke to the customers and told them the things that I am going to sing to you now. So this is the little bar—you must imagine it being very dirty—which she stood behind every morning and every evening. There is the washing-up bowl and that's the cloth which she used for drying the glasses. Where you are sitting, sat the men who laughed at her. You can laugh, too, so that everything is just as it was; but if you can't, then you needn't. (*She begins, pretending to wash glasses and muttering to herself.*) Now one of you must say—you for instance: (*Pointing at* WALTER.) And when is your ship coming home, Jenny?

WALTER.   And when is your ship coming home, Jenny?

POLLY.   And another says—you, perhaps: Do you still wash up glasses, oh! Jenny the Pirate's Bride?

MATTHEW.   Do you still wash up glasses, oh! Jenny the Pirate's Bride?

POLLY.   Good, and now I begin.

(*Song illumination: golden light. The organ is lit up. Three lights on a bar come down from above, and on a board is written:* JENNY THE PIRATE'S BRIDE.)

> Gentlemen, today you see me washing up the glasses
> And making beds for each who stays here.
> And you throw me a penny and I thank you for it as well,
> And you see my shabby costume and this dirty old hotel
> And you think that I shall end my days here.
> But one fine evening there'll be a shout down by the harbor,
> And you'll ask: what's the reason for that shout?
> And you'll see me smiling as I wash my glasses,
> And you'll ask: what has she to smile about?
>
> For a ship with eight sails
> And with fifty great cannon
> Sailed in with the tide.

But you'll say: go wash your glasses, my girl.
And you'll throw your pennies to me,
And I'll take all your pennies
And tuck the beds up tight
But no one is going to sleep in them tonight,
For you still have no idea who I may be.
But one evening there'll be a roar down by the
   harbor
And you'll ask: what's the reason for that roar?
And you'll see me standing staring through the
   window
And you'll ask: now what's she grinning for?

> And the ship with eight sails
> And with fifty great cannon
> Will start shooting the town.

Then, gentlemen, you'll soon take that laugh off
   your faces,
For your houses will fly in the air
And when the whole town is razed to the ground
Just a dirty old hotel will be standing safe and sound
And you'll ask: what famous person lives in there?
And all through night there'll be a shouting round
   the hotel
And you'll ask: why has that hotel survived?
And you'll see me step out of the front door in the
   morning
And you'll ask: is that where *she* once lived?

> And the ship with eight sails
> And with fifty great cannon
> Will run flags up the mast.

And at midday you will see a hundred men come
   ashore
Who will search the shadows so still now.
And they'll capture every single living person they
   can see
And put them in chains and bring them to me
And ask: which of these shall we kill now?
And when the sun stands at noon there'll be a hush
   down by the harbor
As they ask me which of these are doomed to die
And then you'll hear me saying to them: All o'
   them!
And when their heads fall, I shall shout: Hoppla!

> And the ship with eight sails
> And with fifty great cannon
> Will sail homewards with me.

MATTHEW.   Very nice, that's good, eh? And how she does
  it all, the young lady!

MACHEATH.   What do you mean, nice? That's not nice,
  you fool! That's art. You did it wonderfully, Polly. But
  in front of such scum—pardon me, your reverence—it's
  wasted. (*In an undertone to* POLLY.) And what's more I
  don't like you doing this play-acting, so oblige me by
  stopping it in future. (*Loud laughter at the table. The
  gang are making fun of the parson.*) And what have you
  got in your hand, your reverence?

JACOB.   Two knives, Capt'n.

MACHEATH.   What have you got on your plate, your
  reverence?

KIMBALL.   Smoked salmon, I think.

MACHEATH.   I see. And with the knife you're eating
  salmon, is that it?

JACOB.   Have you ever seen the like, eating his fish with a
  knife; a person who does that is nothing more than a . . .

MACHEATH.   Pig. Understand me, Jacob? You'll learn in
  time.

JIMMY (*bursting in*). Hi, Captain! Police! The Commissioner
  himself.

WALTER.   Brown! Tiger Brown!

MACHEATH.   Tiger Brown. The same Tiger Brown who is
  Commissioner of Police, the pillar of the Old Bailey; and
  who will shortly enter Captain MacHeath's miserable
  dwelling. Now you'll live and learn! (*The gang creep
  away.*)

JACOB.   Then it's the gallows for us. (BROWN *enters.*)

BROWN.   Hallo, Mac! I haven't much time and I've got to
  leave almost at once. Why *must* you pick on somebody
  else's stable? That's another burglary!

MACHEATH.   But Jacky, it's so convenient. I'm glad
  you've come to partake of old Mac's wedding feast. May
  I introduce my wife, Polly, née Peachum. Polly, this is
  Tiger Brown. What do you think of her, old man? (*Slaps
  him on the back.*) And these are my friends, Jacky; you've
  probably seen them all before.

BROWN (*in embarrassment*). But I'm here privately, Mac.

MACHEATH.   So are they. (*He calls them. They come, one
  by one, hands up.*) Hi, Jacob!

BROWN.   That's Hook-Finger Jacob, the biggest scoundrel
  living.

MACHEATH.   Here! Jimmy! Robert! Walter!

BROWN.   Well, we'll forget everything for today.

MACHEATH.   Hi, Ede! Matthew!

BROWN.   Sit down, gentlemen, sit down.

ALL.   Thank you, sir.

BROWN.   Happy to meet the charming wife of my old
  friend Mac.

POLLY.   Don't mention it, sir.

MACHEATH.   Sit yourself down, you old rascal, and start
  in on the whiskey!—Polly! Gentlemen! Today you see in
  your midst a man whom the king's inscrutable wisdom
  has chosen to set high over his fellow men, and who yet
  has remained through fair weather and foul—*my friend.*

You all know who I mean, and you do too, Jacky. Ah, Jacky, do you remember when you were a soldier and I was a soldier and we served together in India? Well, Jacky, old man, shall we sing the Army Song?

(*They sit side by side on the table. Song illumination: a golden light. The organ is lit up. Three lights come down from above on a bar, and on a board is written:* THE ARMY SONG.)

Johnny and Jimmy were both on the scene
And George had his promotion order
For the Army doesn't ask what a man has been:
They were all marching north to the border.

The Army's story
Is guns and glory
From the Cape to Cutch Behar
When they are at a loss
And chance to come across
New and unruly races
With brown or yellow faces
They chop them into little bits of beefsteak
tartare!

Warm whiskey went to Johnny's head
And Jimmy was cold every night,
But George took them both by the arm and said:
The Army lasts forever, and might is right.

The Army's story
Is guns and glory
From the Cape to Cutch Behar.
When they are at a loss
And chance to come across
New and unruly races
With brown or yellow faces
They chop them into little bits of beefsteak
tartare!

Now Jim is missing and George is dead
And whiskey has sent Johnny barmy
But blood is blood and still runs red—
They're recruiting again for the army!!

(*As they all sit there, they march in time with their feet.*)

The Army's story
Is guns and glory
From the Cape to Cutch Behar
When they are at a loss
And chance to come across
New and unruly races
With brown or yellow faces
They chop them into little bits of beefsteak
tartare!

MACHEATH.   We were boyhood friends together, and yet, though life in its great flood has torn us far apart, although our professional interests are so different—some people might even say, diametrically opposed—our friendship has survived it all. Take a lesson from that! Castor and Pollux. Hector and Andromache. Seldom have I, the simple workman—well, you know what I mean—seldom have I undertaken even the smallest job of work without giving my friend Brown a share of the proceeds (a considerable share, my good Brown) as a present and a proof of my unswerving loyalty to him; and seldom has the all-powerful Commissioner—take that knife out of your mouth, Jacob—organized a raid without previously giving a little tip to me, the friend of his youth. Well, and so it goes on; everything depends on reciprocity. Learn from that. (*He takes* BROWN *by the arm.*) And now, Jacky, I'm glad you've come. That's real friendship. (*A pause while* BROWN *sorrowfully regards a carpet.*) Genuine Persian Shirah.

BROWN.   From the Oriental Carpet Company.

MACHEATH.   Yes, we get all our carpets there. Do you know, I had to have you here today, Jacky. I hope you don't feel too uncomfortable, being in the position you are.

BROWN.   You know, Mac, I can't refuse you anything. But I must go, I have so much to do; if anything should happen at the coronation . . .

MACHEATH.   Jacky, my father-in-law is an unpleasant old swine. If he were to raise some kind of a stink, are there any records in Scotland Yard that could be used against me?

BROWN.   In Scotland Yard there is absolutely nothing against you, Mac.

MACHEATH.   Of course.

BROWN.   I saw to all that. And now, good-night.

MACHEATH.   Aren't you going to stand up?

BROWN (*to* POLLY). The best of luck. (*Exit* BROWN, *accompanied by* MACHEATH.)

JACOB (*who meanwhile with* MATTHEW *and* WALTER *has been talking to* POLLY). I must admit I could not help getting the needle, when I heard Tiger Brown was coming.

MATTHEW.   You know, ma'am, we have our connections with the highest official circles.

WALTER.   Yes. Mac always has an extra iron in the fire which we never suspect. But we have our little irons in the fire too. Gentlemen, it is half past nine.

MATTHEW.   And now comes the high spot.

(*All retire to the back left, behind a hanging carpet which conceals something.* MACHEATH *enters.*)

MACHEATH.   Well, what's up?

MATTHEW.   A little surprise, Captain.

(Behind the carpet they sing THE WEDDING SONG FOR POORER PEOPLE, *but this time quite softly and full of feeling. However, when they get to the end of the first verse,* MATTHEW *tears down the carpet and they sing on, bawling at the tops of their voices and beating time on a bed which stands behind.)*

Bill Lawton took Mary Sawyer
To be his true and lawful wedded wife.
Long may they live, ho, ho, ho!
But when they stood before the Registrar
He didn't know she lived at Temple Bar
And *she* learnt his name for the first time in her life.

HO!

D'you know what your wife is doing? No!
D'you let her do what she used to do? No!
Long may they live, ho, ho, ho!
Billy Lawton said to me: It's fine
So long as just one part of her is mine.
The swine!

HO!

MACHEATH.   I thank you, friends, I thank you.

WALTER.   And now the unobstrusive departure. *(The gang exeunt.)*

MACHEATH.   And now sentiment must come into its own, lest a man become a mere slave to his work. Sit down, Polly. Do you see the moon over Soho? *(Music.)*

POLLY.   I see it, dearest. Can you feel my heart beating, beloved?

MACHEATH.   I can feel it, beloved.

POLLY.   Wherever you go, I shall go with you.

MACHEATH.   And where you stay, there too shall I stay.

TOGETHER *(singing).*

And though there's no license to show your name
Also no flowers for the happy pair
And though you don't know whence your wedding
    dress came
And no myrtles are twined in your hair—
The platter from which you are eating your bread,
Don't you keep it long, throw it down;
For love endures or does not endure
In many and many a town.

ACT ONE

SCENE THREE

FOR PEACHUM, WHO KNOWS THE HARDNESS OF THE WORLD, THE LOSS OF HIS DAUGHTER MEANS NOTHING SHORT OF COMPLETE RUIN.

*(*PEACHUM'S *establishment for beggars. Right,* PEACHUM *and* MRS. PEACHUM. *In the doorway stands* POLLY, *in hat and coat, a small suitcase in her hand.)*

MRS. PEACHUM.   Married? First we hang her back and front with dresses and hats and gloves and finery, and then when she's cost as much as a sailing ship to rig out, she throws herself away in the gutter like a rotten tomato. So you've gone and got married?

(Song illumination; golden light. The organ is lit up. Three lights come down on a bar, and on a board is written: IN THE BARBARA SONG POLLY TELLS HER PARENTS OF HER MARRIAGE WITH MACHEATH.)*

1.

Once I believed when I was pure and young—
And that I was once, just as much as you—
Perhaps one day a man will come to me
And then I'll have to know what to do.
And if he's a rich man
And if he's a nice man
And keeps his collar clean as collars go
And if he knows how to behave when with a lady
Then I shall say to him: "No"
And so one holds one's head up higher
And is still on public show.
I know the moon shines bright the whole night long
I know the boat will gently drift along
But further things can't go.
Oh! one cannot just lie down peacefully
Oh no, one must be cold as winter snow
Oh! there's so much can happen suddenly
The only thing to say is: NO

2.

The first who came was a man from Kent
He was all that a man should be.
The second had three ships of his own
And the third was mad about me.
And since they were rich men
And since they were nice men
And they kept their collars clean as collars go
And since they knew how to behave when with a
    lady
I said to each one: "No"
And so I held my head up higher
And remained on public show.
I knew the moon shone bright the whole night long
I knew the boat would gently drift along
But further things couldn't go.
Oh! one cannot just lie down peacefully
I had to be as cold as winter snow
For so much might have happened suddenly
The only thing to say is: NO

3.

But one summer's day, and the day was blue,
Came a man who didn't ask when
And he hung his hat up on the nail inside my
    bedroom
And I didn't know what I did then.
And since he wasn't rich

And since he wasn't nice
And his collar was not clean as collars go
And he didn't know how to behave when with a lady
To him I never said: ''No''
So I didn't hold my head up high
Being no longer for public show.
Ah, the moon shone bright the whole night long
And the boat this time was tied up fast and strong
And it all had to be just so
Oh! one must simply lie down peacefully,
Oh! one couldn't be cold as winter snow
For so much had to happen suddenly
And there wasn't such a word as NO

PEACHUM.   So that's the sort of a crook's hussy she's become. Very nice. That's lovely.

MRS. PEACHUM.   If you're already so immoral as to have to marry at all, why must it be a horse-thief and a murderer? That'll cost you dear some day! I should have seen it coming. Even as a child she had a head as swollen as if she'd been queen of England.

PEACHUM.   So she has really got married.

MRS. PEACHUM.   Yes. Yesterday afternoon at five o'clock.

PEACHUM.   To a notorious criminal! Come to think it over, it shows great courage on the part of this man. But if I have to give away my daughter, the last support of my old age, my house will fall in on me and my last dog will desert me. Why, I couldn't even give away the dirt under my fingernails without risking death from starvation. If all three of us can live through the winter on one log of wood, we may perhaps see the next year. Perhaps.

MRS. PEACHUM.   What are you thinking of? This is the reward for all we've done, Jonathan. I shall go mad. Everything is going round in my head. I can't control myself any longer. Oh! (*She faints.*) A glass of brandy!

PEACHUM.   There! Now you see what you have done to your mother. Quick! Just a crook's hussy, that's fine. Strange how the poor old woman has taken it to heart. (POLLY *returns with a bottle of brandy.*) That's the last consolation left to your poor mother.

POLLY.   Go on, give her two glasses. Mother can carry twice as much when she's not quite herself. That'll put her on her legs again. (*During the whole of this scene she has had a radiantly happy expression on her face.*)

MRS. PEACHUM (*revived*).   Oh, now she's showing her wicked false sympathy and kindness again. (*Five men enter.*)

A BEGGAR.   I won't have it. This thing isn't a proper stump, and I'm not going to waste my money on it.

PEACHUM.   What do you want? That's as good a stump as all the others, only you don't keep it clean.

BEGGAR.   Is that so? Then why don't I earn as much as all the others? No, you can't put that over me. (*Hurls the stump away.*) I might as well cut off my own leg, if I wanted junk like that.

PEACHUM.   Well, what *do* you want? What can I do about it if people have hearts as hard as granite. I can't give you five stumps! In five minutes I can make such a miserable wreck out of a man that a dog would weep if he saw him. What can I do, if *people* won't weep? There's another stump, if one's not enough for you. But take care of your things!

BEGGAR.   That'll do.

PEACHUM (*tries a mutilated arm on another beggar*).   Leather is bad, Celia. Rubber is more horrible. (*To the third.*) The boil is going down, and it's your last. Now we can start from the beginning again. (*Examining the fourth.*) Of course natural scars are never the same as artificial ones. (*To the fifth.*) What's the matter with you? You have been eating again. I shall have to make an example of you.

BEGGAR.   Mr. Peachum, I really haven't eaten much, my fat's just unnatural, I can't help it.

PEACHUM.   Neither can I. You're dismissed. (*Turning to the second beggar.*) Between ''arousing pity'' and ''getting on people's nerves'' there naturally exists a considerable difference, my friend. Yes, I need artists. Only an artist can arouse pity in people's hearts. If you'd work properly, your public would be forced to appreciate and applaud you. But you never think of anything. So, of course, I cannot extend your engagement. (THE BEGGARS *exeunt.*)

POLLY.   Please consider him. Is he handsome? No. But he makes a living. He offers me an existence. He is a first class burglar—and also a far-sighted and experienced thief. I know exactly the amount of his savings. I could even tell you the figure. A few more successful enterprises and we shall be able to retire to a little house in the country, just like Mr. Shakespeare whom Father admires so much.

PEACHUM.   Well, it's all quite simple—You're married. What does one do when one's married? Don't bother to think. One gets a divorce, eh? It's not so difficult, is it?

POLLY.   I don't know what you mean.

MRS. PEACHUM.   Divorce.

POLLY.   But I love him, so how can I think of divorce?

MRS. PEACHUM.   Polly, aren't you ashamed of yourself?

POLLY.   Mother, if you've ever been in love . . .

MRS. PEACHUM.   In love! Those damned books you've been reading have turned your head. Polly, everyone does it.

POLLY.   Then I shall be an exception.

MRS. PEACHUM.   Then I'll tan your bottom, you exception!

POLLY.   Yes, all mothers do that, but it doesn't do any good. Love is greater than a tanned bottom.

MRS. PEACHUM.   Polly, don't try my patience too far.

POLLY.   I won't be robbed of my love.

MRS. PEACHUM.   Another word and you'll get a box on the ears.

POLLY.   But love is the greatest thing in the world.

MRS. PEACHUM.   That creature has several women. When he's hanged, there'll be a half dozen females presenting themselves as widows, and each one will have a brat in her arms. Oh, Jonathan!

PEACHUM.   Hanged! How did you come to think of hanging? It's an idea! Go outside, Polly. (*Exit* POLLY *who remains listening outside the door.*) You're right. That'll be worth forty pounds.

MRS. PEACHUM.   I think I know what you mean. Tell the police.

PEACHUM.   Naturally. And besides, like that we can get him hanged free . . . It'll be two birds with one stone. Only we've got to find out where he's hiding.

MRS. PEACHUM.   I can tell you that, my dear. He's hiding with his whores.

PEACHUM.   But they won't give him up.

MRS. PEACHUM.   Just leave it to me. Money rules the world. I'll go straight to Wapping and talk to the girls there. If this fine gentleman meets one of them two hours from now, he's done for.

POLLY (*enters*). My dear Mama, you can save yourself the trouble of going all that way. Before Mac would meet such women, he'd give himself up to the police. And if he did go to the police, the Commissioner would offer him a drink and a cigar, and then they'd discuss a certain business in this street where things aren't quite as they should be either. For, dear Papa, this Commissioner was very jolly at my wedding.

PEACHUM.   What is the name of the Commissioner?

POLLY.   He's called Brown. But you'd only know him as Tiger Brown. All who are afraid of him call him Tiger Brown. But my husband, you might like to know, calls him Jacky. To him he's just his dear Jacky. They were boyhood friends.

PEACHUM.   I see, they're friends. The Commissioner and the notorious criminal. Then they're probably the only friends in this fine city.

POLLY (*poetically*). Whenever they had a drink together, they would stroke one another's cheeks and say: "If you'll have another, I'll have another." And whenever one went out, the other one's eyes grew moist and he would say: "Wherever you go, I shall go with you." There's nothing against Mac in Scotland Yard.

PEACHUM. Well, well. From Tuesday evening till Thursday morning Mr. MacHeath—a gentleman who has certainly been married several times—enticed my daughter Polly Peachum from her parental home under the pretence of marriage. Before the week is over this will prove a sufficient excuse for bringing him to the gallows, which he so richly deserves. "Mr. MacHeath, you once had white kid gloves and a stick with an ivory handle and a scar on your neck, and you frequented the Octopus Hotel. All that now remains is your scar, which is probably the least valuable of your distinguishing marks, and now you only frequent gaols, and very soon you won't frequent anywhere . . . "

MRS. PEACHUM.   Oh, Jonathan, you'll never succeed; you know you're dealing with Mackie the Knife, the most dangerous criminal in London. He takes what he wants.

PEACHUM.   Who is Mackie the Knife? Get ready, we're going to the Sheriff of London. And you're going to Wapping.

MRS. PEACHUM.   To his whores.

PEACHUM.   For the wickedness of the world is so great that one has to run one's legs off, to avoid having them stolen.

POLLY.   And I, Papa, will be very glad to shake Mr. Brown by the hand again.

(*All three walk to the front of the stage, and, to song illumination, sing the first finale. On a board is written:* FIRST FINALE—THE UNCERTAINTY OF HUMAN CIRCUMSTANCES.)

POLLY.

> What I ask for, is it much?
> Just a man who's strong and tender
> One to whom I can surrender.
> Is that then so very much?

PEACHUM (*holding a Bible in his hand*).

> There is one right to which man is entitled—
> That he may call some happiness his own
> Enjoying all the pleasures life can offer
> Being given bread to eat and not a stone.
> That is one right to which he is entitled.
> But sad to say there's been no case recorded
> Of any man who got his share—oh no!
> Who wouldn't claim this right, if chance afforded,
> But force or circumstance won't have it so!

MRS. PEACHUM.

> Gladly would I give to you
> All the things you ever wanted,
> Let your dearest wish be granted.
> Such things give us pleasure too.

PEACHUM.

> Be good and kind! Could anything be dearer?
> Each giving to the poor in brotherly love.
> If all were good, *His* Kingdom would be nearer
> And we could bask in radiance from above.
> Be good and kind! Could anything be dearer?
> But sad to say this happy state comes never
> For means are scarce and man is far too low.
> Who wouldn't choose to live in peace forever?
> But force of circumstance won't have it so!

POLLY & MRS. PEACHUM.

> And sad to say, he states the case.
> The world is poor and man is base.

PEACHUM.

> Of course I state the very case
> The world is poor and man is base.

Who wouldn't like a Paradise below?
But would our circumstances have it so?
No, that could never be the case.
Your brother may be fond of you
But when the food's too short for two
He'll go and slap you in the face.
Oh Loyalty!—we need that grace.
But when your wife, who's fond of you,
Decides your love for her won't do
She'll go and slap you in the face.
Oh Gratitude!—we need that grace.
And then your child who's fond of you,
If your pension's not enough for two
He'll go and slap you in the face.
Oh Kindness!—we all need that grace.

POLLY & MRS. PEACHUM.

Yes, that's the truth about it,
The silly truth about it.
The world is poor and man is base,
And sad to say he states the case.

PEACHUM.

Of course I state the very case
The world is poor and man is base.
We should be good—instead of low,
But force of circumstance won't have it so.

ALL THREE.

So there is nothing we can do
The world is rotten through and through!

PEACHUM.

The world is poor and man is base,
And sad to say I state the case.

ALL THREE.

Yes, that's the truth about it,
The silly truth about it.
And so there's nothing we can do
For the world is rotten through and through!

ACT TWO

SCENE ONE

THURSDAY AFTERNOON. MACHEATH TAKES LEAVE OF HIS
WIFE, BEFORE FLEEING TO HIGHGATE TO ESCAPE HIS FATHER-
IN-LAW.

(*The stable.*)

POLLY (*enters*). Mac! Mac! Don't be afraid, it's me.
MACHEATH (*lying on a bed*). What's the matter? What are
you looking like that for, Polly?
POLLY. I've just been to see Brown, and my father was
there, too, and they've arranged that they're going to
catch you; my father threatened something terrible and
Brown stuck up for you, but then he gave in and he thinks
you ought to go as quickly as possible and disappear for
a time. Mac, you must pack!

MACHEATH. What! Pack? Nonsense! Come here, Polly.
We're going to do something quite different from
packing.
POLLY. No, we can't do it now. I'm so frightened. They
talked about hanging all the time.
MACHEATH. I don't like it, Polly, when you're moody.
There's nothing against *me* in Scotland Yard.
POLLY. Maybe not yesterday, but today there's something
awful against you all of a sudden. Listen, I can tell you—
I've brought the list of charges with me, I don't know
whether I shall get through it, it's so long it never seems
to end—listen, you've killed two shop-keepers, and committed more than thirty burglaries, twenty-three street-
robberies, arson, attempted murder, forgeries, perjury—
and all in six months. You're a terrible person, Mac. And
in Winchester you seduced two young sisters under the
age of consent.
MACHEATH. They told me they were over twenty-one.
And what did Brown say?

(*He stands up slowly and walks to the right, along the footlights, whistling.*)

POLLY. He caught me up in the corridor and said he
couldn't do anything more for you. Oh, Mac! (*She throws
her arms around his neck.*)
MACHEATH. Well then, if I *must* go you'll have to take
over the running of the business.
POLLY. Don't talk of business now. I can't bear to hear of
it! Mac, kiss your poor Polly again and swear you'll
never, never . . .

(MACHEATH *interrupts her and leads her to the table where
he pushes her down into a chair.*)

MACHEATH. These are the account books. Listen care-
fully. This is a list of the staff. (*Reads.*) Hook-Finger
Jacob, a year and a half in the business; let's see what
he's brought in. One, two, three, four, five gold watches.
It's not much, but it's skilled work. Don't sit on my lap,
I'm not feeling like it any more. And here's Wally the
Weeper, an unreliable swine. Fences stuff of his own
accord. Three weeks' grace for him, then up. You will
simply report him to Brown.
POLLY (*sobbing*). I will simply report him to Brown.
MACHEATH. Jimmy the Second, an impudent customer;
profitable but impudent. Pinches the sheets from under
the finest ladies in the land. Give him a rise.
POLLY. I'll give him a rise.
MACHEATH. Robert the Saw, a petty thief, without a trace
of genius. He won't end on the gallows, but he'll never
come to anything.
POLLY. Never come to anything.
MACHEATH. Otherwise you'll carry on the same as
before: get up at seven, wash, take one bath a day, and so
on.

POLLY. You're quite right, Mac, I shall just have to set my teeth and keep an eye on the business. What's yours is now mine, too, isn't it, Mackie? And Mac, what about your rooms? Shall I give them up? It would be such waste to pay the rent!

MACHEATH. No, I need them still.

POLLY. But why? They only cost us money.

MACHEATH. You seem to think I'm never going to come back.

POLLY. What do you mean? You can take them again! Mac . . . Mac, I can't stand it any longer. I keep looking at your mouth and yet I don't hear what you're saying. Will you be faithful to me, Mac?

MACHEATH. Of course I shall be faithful to you. I shall repay like for like. Do you think I don't love you? It's just that I look further ahead than you.

POLLY. I'm so glad, Mac. Think only of me when the others are after you like bloodhounds . . .

(*At the word "bloodhounds" he stiffens, stands up, crosses to the right, takes off his coat and starts washing his hands.*)

MACHEATH (*hurriedly*). Send all the profits to Jack Poole's banking house in Manchester. Between ourselves, it's only a question of weeks before I change over to banking exclusively. It's safer as well as more profitable. In six weeks at the most the money must all be out of this business, and then you'll go to Brown and hand the list over to the police. In eight weeks at the most all this scum of humanity will be sitting in the Old Bailey.

POLLY. But, Mac! How can you look them in the eyes when you're going to doublecross them like this and they're as good as hanged? Can you still shake them by the hand?

MACHEATH. Who? Robert the Saw, Money Matthew, Hook-Finger Jacob? Those gaol-birds? (*Enter the gang.*) Gentlemen, I'm glad to see you.

POLLY. Good-day, gentlemen.

MATTHEW. Capt'n, I've got the plans for the Coronation here. It looks as though there's days of good hard work ahead of us. The Archbishop of Canterbury arrives in half an hour.

MACHEATH. When?

MATTHEW. Five-thirty. We must start at once, Captain.

MACHEATH. Yes, you must go at once.

ROBERT. What do you mean: *you?*

MACHEATH. As far as I'm concerned I'm afraid I've got to take a short trip to the country.

ROBERT. What! Are they going to nab you?

MATTHEW. And just before the Coronation, too! The Coronation without you will be like tea without sugar.

MACHEATH. Shut up! Because of this, I'm handing over the management of the business to my wife for a short time. Polly!

(*He pushes her to the front and then retires to the back, where he watches her.*)

POLLY. Men, I think our Captain can go away without having to worry. We shall manage all right and get along fine, eh?

MATTHEW. I've got nothing to say. But I don't know if a woman at a time like this . . . I'm not saying anything against *you,* ma'am.

MACHEATH (*from the back*). What do you say to that, Polly?

POLLY. You lousy swine, that's a good beginning. (*Screaming*). Of course you're not saying anything against me: or these men here would have had your trousers off and tanned your bottom long ago. Isn't that so, gentlemen? (*A short pause, then they all clap like mad.*)

JACOB. She's all right, and she means what she says.

WALTER. Bravo, our new captain knows all the answers. Hurrah for Polly!

ALL. Hurrah for Polly!

MACHEATH. A pity, I can't be in London for the Coronation. It'll be a hundred per cent business. During the day every house empty, and at night all the best people drunk. That reminds me, Matthew—you drink too much. Last week you made it obvious that it was *you* who set fire to the children's hospital at Greenwich. If that sort of thing happens again, you're sacked. Who set fire to the children's hospital?

MATTHEW. I did.

MACHEATH (*to the others*). Who set it on fire?

THE OTHERS. You did, Captain.

MACHEATH. Well, who did?

MATTHEW (*sullenly*). You. Going on this way, ones like us will never come up in the world.

MACHEATH (*with a gesture of hanging*). You'll come up all right if you think you can compete with me. Have you ever heard of an Oxford professor letting his scientific mistakes be made by some assistant or other? Of course not, he makes them himself.

ROBERT. Ma'am, you're in command of us while your husband is away. Accounts settled every Thursday, ma'am.

POLLY. Every Thursday, men. (*Exit gang.*)

MACHEATH. And now, good-bye, my love. Keep fresh and don't forget to make up every day, just as if I were there. That's very important, Polly.

POLLY. And you, Mac, promise me you'll never look at another woman and that you'll go away immediately. Believe me, your little Polly doesn't say this out of jealousy, but because it's very important, Mac.

MACHEATH. But, Polly, why should *I* bother with any second-hand goods? I only love you. When it's dark enough I shall start out, and before you can see the moon from your window, I shall be far beyond Highgate.

POLLY. Oh, Mac, don't tear my heart from my body. Stay with me and let us be happy together.

MACHEATH. But I have to tear my own heart from my body: I have to go and no one knows when I shall return.

POLLY.   It lasted such a little while, Mac.

MACHEATH.   Is it over already?

POLLY.   Mac, last night I had a dream. I was looking out of the window and I heard laughter in the street, and when I looked up, I saw our moon, and the moon was quite thin, like a penny that is all worn away. Don't forget me, Mac, in strange places.

MACHEATH.   Of course I shall never forget you, Polly. Kiss me, Polly.

POLLY.   Good-bye, Mac.

MACHEATH.   Good-bye, Polly. (*Music.*)

POLLY.

> And he will never come back again. (*The bells begin to ring.*)
>
> The Queen is now in London on her way.
>
> Where shall we be on Coronation Day? (*Sings.*)
>
> Sweet while it lasted, and now it is over,
> Tear out your heart, say ''Good-bye, my lover.''
> What use is my weeping (O Virgin restore me!)
> When 'tis plain my mother knew all this before me?

MACHEATH (*sings*).

> For love endures or does not endure
> In many and many a town.

INTERLUDE

(MRS. PEACHUM *and* GINNY JENNY *step out in front of the curtain.*)

MRS. PEACHUM.   So if you see Mackie the Knife, run to the nearest policeman and report him; and you'll get ten shillings for it.

GINNY JENNY.   But do you think we'll see him if the police are after him? When the hunt starts, he won't be wasting any time with us.

MRS. PEACHUM.   I can tell you this much, Jenny: even if the whole of London were after him, MacHeath is not the man to give up his old habits. (*She sings* THE BALLAD OF SEXUAL SLAVERY.)

> Now here's a man who fights the devil's battle.
> The butcher, he! And all the others, cattle!
> A dirty crook! No man has taken him in!
> Who gets him down, that gets 'em all down?
>   Women!
> Whether he will or not,—he must comply.
> Such is the law of sexual slavery.
>
>> He pays no heed to the Bible. He laughs at the
>>   S. P. G.
>> He will persist that he's an egoist
>> Knows that with a woman no one can resist.
>> So keeps them all from his vicinity.
>> But in the day he need not feel elated
>> For when the night falls, he's again prostrated.

> And many a man saw many a man's confusion:
> The noble soul descends to prostitution!
> And they who saw it swore no one took them in—
> Yet when they were corpses, who interred 'em?
>   Women!
> Whether they will or not,—they must comply.
> Such is the law of sexual slavery.
>
>> He fastens on to the Bible. He enlists in the S. P. G.
>> He's Methodist! Becomes an Anarchist!
>> Has celery deleted from his midday dinner list
>> The afternoon is spent in thinking patiently.
>> By evening he says: I feel elevated
>> And when the night falls, he's again prostrated.

ACT TWO

SCENE TWO

THE CORONATION BELLS HAVE NOT YET RUNG OUT AND MACKIE THE KNIFE IS ALREADY SITTING AMONG HIS WHORES AT WAPPING. THE GIRLS BETRAY HIM. IT IS THURSDAY EVENING.

(*A brothel in Wapping. An ordinary early evening. The girls, mostly in their underclothes, are ironing, playing draughts, washing themselves; a peaceful bourgeois idyll. HOOK-FINGER JACOB is reading the newspaper, paying not the slightest attention to anyone around him. In fact, he is rather in the way.*)

JACOB.   He won't come today.

WHORE.   Do you think so?

JACOB.   I don't think he'll *ever* come again.

WHORE.   That would be a pity.

JACOB.   Would it? If I know him, he's already well away by now. This time it's—clear out!

(*Enter* MACHEATH, *hangs his hat on a nail, sits on the sofa behind the table.*)

MACHEATH.   My coffee!

VIXEN (*astounded*). ''My coffee''! (*Repeats this in amazement several times.*)

JACOB (*horrified*). Why aren't you in Highgate?

MACHEATH.   Today is my Thursday. I cannot let such trifles disturb my habits. (*Throws his charge-sheet on the floor.*) Besides, it's raining.

GINNY JENNY (*reads the charge-sheet*). In the name of the Queen, Captain MacHeath is herewith charged with triple . . .

JACOB (*snatching it from her*). Am I there too?

MACHEATH.   Of course, the whole staff.

GINNY JENNY (*to the other whore*). Look, those are the charges. (*Pause.*) Mac, give me your hand. (*He holds out his hand.*)

DOLLY.   Yes, Jenny, read his hand; you know how to do it better than anyone. (*Holds forward a paraffin lamp.*)

MACHEATH.   A rich legacy!

GINNY JENNY.   No, not a rich legacy.

BETTY.   Why are you looking like that, Jenny? It's enough to give anyone the shivers.

MACHEATH.   A long journey in the near future?

GINNY JENNY.   No, not a long journey.

VIXEN.   What do you see then?

MACHEATH.   Only good news, please—no bad!

GINNY JENNY.   Oh well! I see a narrow darkness there and a little light. And then I see a large T, which means the treachery of a woman. Then I see . . .

MACHEATH.   Stop. I'd like to know a few details about the narrow darkness and the treachery; for example, the name of the treacherous woman.

GINNY JENNY.   I can only see that it begins with J.

MACHEATH.   Then it's wrong. It begins with P.

GINNY JENNY.   Mac, when the Coronation bells ring out in Westminster, you will have a difficult time.

MACHEATH.   Go on. (JACOB *laughs raucously.*) What's the matter? (*He goes across to* JACOB, *and reads too.*) Quite wrong, there were only three.

JACOB (*laughs*). I know.

MACHEATH.   Nice underclothes you have here.

WHORE.   From the cradle to the coffin, underclothes always come first.

OLD WHORE.   I never use silk. The gentlemen always think you're ill if you do. (GINNY JENNY *edges quietly out of the door.*)

2ND WHORE (*to* GINNY JENNY). Where are you going, Jenny?

GINNY JENNY.   You'll see. (*Exit.*)

MOLLY.   But homespun linen puts them off.

OLD WHORE.   I have had great success with linen.

VIXEN.   That's because the gentlemen feel quite at home.

MACHEATH (*to* BETTY). Have you still got the black braid?

BETTY.   Yes, still got the black braid.

MACHEATH.   And what sort of underclothes do *you* wear?

2ND WHORE.   Oh dear, I'm quite ashamed. I can never bring anyone into my room, my aunt is so mad about men; and in doorways, you know, I can't wear any underclothes at all. (JACOB *laughs.*)

MACHEATH.   Have you finished?

JACOB.   No, I'm just at the rapes.

MACHEATH (*again sitting on the sofa*). But where's Jenny now? Ladies, long before my star rose over this town . . .

VIXEN.   Long before my star rose over this town . . .

MACHEATH.   . . . I lived in the direst poverty with one of you ladies. And even though I am Mackie the Knife now, in present happiness I shall never forget the companions of darker days: above all Jenny, whom I loved best of all the girls. Listen to me!

(*As* MACHEATH *sings* THE BALLAD OF THE FANCY-MAN, GINNY JENNY *stands outside the window right and beckons to a* POLICEMAN. *Then* MRS. PEACHUM *joins her. The three stand under the street lamp and look towards the left.*)

MACHEATH.

There was a time, in days now long ago,
When we two lived together, I and she
And my brains told her body what to do,
I guarded her and she took care of me.
One can do different, but that way does too.
And when a stranger came, I left our little bed
And had a drink or two and showed myself well-bred
And when he paid, I said: Auf Wiederseh'n
If any time you'd care to—come again.
So six months long we lived a happy life
In that bordel where we were man and wife.

(*Enter* GINNY JENNY *through the door: behind her the* POLICEMAN.)

GINNY JENNY.

But in that time of days so long ago
Between us there was many an angry rift
And when the cash was short he'd curse and shout
And he would say: now I must pawn your shift.
A shift will do, but one can do without
But sometimes I grew angry—all come to it—
And I would ask him outright, how he dared to do it
And then he'd start to knock my face about
And then I'd sometimes really feel put out!

BOTH.

Those six long months we lived a happy life
In that bordel where we were man and wife.

BOTH (*together and alternating*). That was a time of days now long ago.

HE.

Before our simple happiness was broken

SHE.

When every day we shared a bed for two

HE.

For nightly, as I said, she was bespoken
(The night is usual, but the day will do)

SHE.

And one fine day I felt a young MacHeath

HE.

And so we worked it out: that I lay underneath

SHE.

Because he knew an unborn child so often crushes

HE.

Though the child was always destined for the rushes.
Too soon we ended our six months of life
In that bordel where we were man and wife.

(*Dance.* MACHEATH *picks up his swordstick; she hands him his hat; and he is still dancing when* CONSTABLE SMITH *lays a hand on his shoulder.*)

SMITH.   Well, now we can get going.

MACHEATH.   Has this rat-hole *still* only got one exit?

(SMITH *attempts to handcuff* MACHEATH. MACHEATH *thrusts against his chest, so that he stumbles over backwards. Then* MACHEATH *jumps out of the window. But outside are standing* MRS. PEACHUM *and the* POLICE.)

MACHEATH (*calmly and very politely*). Good evening, madam.

MRS. PEACHUM.   My dear Mr. MacHeath. My husband always says: the greatest heroes of history always tripped up over such small obstacles.

MACHEATH.   May I enquire how your husband is?

MRS. PEACHUM.   Better again. Unfortunately you must now take leave of these charming ladies here. Constable! Take this gentleman to his new lodgings. (*He is led off.* MRS. PEACHUM *speaks through the window*.) Ladies, if any of you should wish to visit him, you will always find him at home. The gentleman lives from now on in the Old Bailey.—I knew he'd be here with his whores. I myself will pay what is owing. Farewell, ladies. (*Exit* MRS. PEACHUM.)

GINNY JENNY.   Hey, Jacob! Something's happened.

JACOB (*who, on account of his intensive reading, has noticed nothing*). Where is Mac?

GINNY JENNY.   The police were here!

JACOB.   God save us! And here I was, reading and reading and reading . . . Boys, boys, boys! (*Exit.*)

ACT TWO

SCENE THREE

BETRAYED BY HIS WHORES, MACHEATH IS FREED FROM PRISON BY THE LOVE OF ANOTHER WOMAN.

(*Prison in the Old Bailey. A barred cage. The death cell. Enter* BROWN.)

BROWN.   If only my men don't catch him! Oh God, I hope he's far beyond Highgate by now and thinking of his old friend Jacky. But he's so light-hearted, like all great men. If they should bring him in now, and he were to look at me with his faithful friendly eyes, I couldn't stand it. Thank God, there's at least a moon shining, and when he gets into the country he won't get lost. (*Noise outside.*) What's that? Oh God, they've got him.

MACHEATH (*tied with heavy ropes and guarded by six policemen, he enters proudly*). Well, my faithful minions, here we are again, thank God, once more in our old home. (*He sees* BROWN *who has retreated to the farthest corner of the cell.*)

BROWN (*after a long pause, under the fearful gaze of his former friend*). Mac, I didn't do it . . . I did everything I could . . . don't look at me like that, Mac . . . I can't bear it . . . Your silence is too terrible. (*Shouts at a policeman.*) Don't pull him with that rope, you swine! Say something, Mac. Say something to your old friend . . .

Give him a word in his dark . . . (*Rests his head against the wall and weeps.*) He doesn't think me worth even a word. (*Exit.*)

MACHEATH.   That miserable Brown. That evil conscience incarnate. And such a creature is made commissioner of police. Lucky I didn't bawl him out. At first I thought of doing something of the sort. But then I thought a good, piercing, punishing stare would send the shivers down his back. The idea found its mark. I looked at him and he wept bitterly. That's a trick I got from the Bible. (*Enter* SMITH *with handcuffs.*) Well, Mr. Overseer, I suppose those are the heaviest you could find. With your permission, I should like to ask for a more comfortable pair. (*He draws out his check book.*)

SMITH.   Certainly, Captain, we have them here at all prices. It depends what you want to pay. From one to ten guineas.

MACHEATH.   How much do none at all cost?

SMITH.   Fifty.

MACHEATH (*writes out a check*). The devil of it is, that all that business with Lucy will now come out. And when Brown hears what I've done to his daughter behind his friendly back, he'll turn into a real tiger for the first time in his life.

SMITH.   Yes, you've made your bed: now lie on it.

MACHEATH.   I'll bet that slut is waiting outside. I shall have a fine time from now till the execution.

So, gentlemen, is this what you'd call living?
I find no pleasure in such ribaldry
When still a child I heard with great misgiving:
Only the well-to-do live pleasantly.

(*Song illumination: golden light. The organ is illuminated. Three lights come down on a bar from above—and on a board is written:* THE BALLAD OF THE PLEASANT LIFE.)

Some say that we should live like famous sages
On empty stomachs and ascetic reading
Within a hovel where the rats are breeding.
Preserve me from such lunatics in cages!
Let those who like it live the simple way
I've had (between ourselves) too much by far.
No animal from here to Zanzibar
Would live that simple life a single day.
What help is freedom? What good to me?
Only the well-to-do live pleasantly!

Those brave adventurers of light and leading
Who risk their skins in search of new sensations
In order that their truthful publications
May give the bourgeoisie exciting reading—
Just look at them in their domestic station
See how they go with frigid wives to bed,
Their gloomy thoughts five thousand years ahead
And one ear cocked for further acclamation.
Can we call that living? Don't you agree:
Only the well-to-do live pleasantly?

And I myself have felt the inclination
To lead a great and solitary existence
But when I saw such men at shorter distance
I told myself—that's not your occupation.
Poverty makes you sad as well as wise
And bravery brings with fame a bitter grave:
So you are poor and lonely, wise and brave,
And now not even greatness satisfies.
Then let this adage your motto be:
Only the well-to-do live pleasantly! (*Enter* LUCY.)

LUCY. You miserable wretch, you—how can you look me in the face after all that has happened between us?

MACHEATH. Lucy, haven't you a heart? When you see your own husband before you in this condition!

LUCY. My husband! You brute! So you think I know nothing of what's been happening with Miss Peachum. I could scratch your eyes out!

MACHEATH. Lucy, seriously, you're not so stupid as to be jealous of Polly?

LUCY. So you're not married to her, you beast?

MACHEATH. Married! That's a good one! I go to a certain house. I talk to her. Now and then I give her a sort of kiss, and now the silly bitch runs around boasting all over the place that she's married to me. My darling Lucy, I'm ready to do anything to reassure you, if you really believe that she and I are married. What more can a gentleman say? He cannot say more.

LUCY. Oh, Mac, I only want to become an honest woman.

MACHEATH. If you think you'll become an honest woman by marrying me—good. What more can a gentleman say? He cannot say more. (*Enter* POLLY.)

POLLY. Where's my husband? Oh, Mac, there you are. Don't look away, you needn't be ashamed in front of me. After all, I am your wife.

LUCY. Oh, you miserable wretch.

POLLY. Mackie in prison! Why didn't you escape? You told me you wouldn't go to those women any more. I knew what they'd do to you; but I didn't say anything because I believed you. Mac, I shall stay with you to the death.—Not a word, Mac, not a look! Oh, Mac, think what your Polly's suffering when she sees you like this before her!

LUCY. The slut!

POLLY. What's that? Mac, who is that woman? Tell her at least who I am. Tell her, please, that I'm your wife. Am I not your wife? Look at me—am I not your wife?

LUCY. You treacherous brute, have you got two wives, you monster?

POLLY. Say something, Mac. Am I not your wife? Haven't I done everything for you? When I married, I was pure and innocent, you know that. And you handed everything over to me as we arranged, and I was to tell Jacob to . . .

MACHEATH. If you two would shut your mouths for five minutes I could explain everything. This is more than any man can stand.

POLLY. Yes, my love, it's clear that the wife . . .

LUCY. The wife!!

POLLY. . . . The wife has a sort of natural priority. At least outwardly, my love. It's too bad. It's enough to drive anyone mad, this aggravation.

LUCY. Aggravation, that's a good one. And what have you picked up for yourself? This dirty slut! That's your great conquest! That's your beauty of Soho!

(*Song illumination: golden light. The organ is illuminated. Three lights come down on a bar from above and on a board is written:* THE JEALOUSY DUET.)

LUCY.
Come right out, you beauty of Soho!
Show your lovely legs for my inspection!
I too would like to see a thing of beauty
For there's no one can rival your perfection!
You seem to have thought it was you my husband
was after!

POLLY.
Did I then, did I then?

LUCY.
Yes, that really makes me roar with laughter!

POLLY.
Does it then, does it then?

LUCY.
Ha, how everyone would laugh!

POLLY.
You think everyone would laugh?

LUCY.
If Mac should fall for such a calf!

POLLY.
If Mac should fall for such a calf?

LUCY.
Ha, ha, ha, ha, ha! A man for her!
No one cares a damn for her!

POLLY.
Well, we'll soon find out the truth

LUCY.
Yes, we'll soon find out the truth!

TOGETHER.
Mackie and me, we're two birds of a feather
He loves me, we'll always stick together.
And so I must contend it
Our love cannot be ended
When such a creature crops up!
Ridiculous!

POLLY.
Yes, I'm called the beauty of Soho
My lovely legs are worthy of inspection.

LUCY.
D'you think so?

POLLY.
For people like to see a thing of beauty
And they say no one can rival my perfection.

LUCY.
    You hussy!
POLLY.
    Hussy yourself!
    I knew it was always me that my husband was after.
LUCY.
    Was it so? Was it so?
POLLY.
    So I can afford to roar with laughter.
LUCY.
    Can you then? Can you then?
POLLY.
    And how everyone would laugh!
LUCY.
    You think everyone would laugh?
POLLY.
    If no one loved my pretty calf!
LUCY.
    If no one loved your pretty calf?
POLLY (*to the audience*).
    D'*you* think there's no man for me?
    No one cares a damn for me?
LUCY.
    Well, we'll soon find out the truth.
POLLY.
    Yes, we'll soon find out the truth.
TOGETHER.
    Mackie and me, we're two birds of a feather
    He loves just me, we'll always stick together.
    And so I must contend it
    Our love cannot be ended
    When such a creature crops up!
    Ridiculous!
MACHEATH.   And now, dear Lucy, be calm. This is simply a trick of Polly's. She wants to make trouble between you and me. They are going to hang me, and she wants to be able to call herself my widow. Really, Polly, this is not the right time for such things.
POLLY.   You have the heart to deny me?
MACHEATH.   And you have the heart to go on chattering about my being married to you? Why must you add to my misery, Polly? (*Shakes his head reproachfully.*) Polly, Polly!
LUCY.   Really, Miss Peachum, you're only making a show of yourself. Quite apart from the fact that it is monstrous of you to excite a poor gentleman in this condition!
POLLY.   The simplest rules of behavior, my dear madam, would teach you, I believe, that a person should behave with somewhat more modesty towards a man in the presence of his wife.
MACHEATH.   Seriously, Polly, that's carrying a joke too far.
LUCY.   And if you, madam, want to start a row in the prison here, I shall find myself compelled to summon a warder and tell him to show you the door. I should be sorry to have to do it, Miss Peachum.

POLLY.   Mrs! Mrs! Mrs! Permit me to tell you this—Miss!—these airs that you're giving yourself don't suit you in the least. My duty compels me to remain by my husband.
LUCY.   What do you say to that! What do you say to that! So she won't go! She stands there and waits to be thrown out and won't go! Shall I speak more plainly?
POLLY.   Hold your filthy mouth, you slattern, or else I'll give you a smack on the jaw, dear madam!
LUCY.   You're going to be thrown out, you impertinent creature! It's no use mincing words with you. You don't understand delicacy.
POLLY.   Your delicacy! Oh, I'm only compromising my own dignity! And I'm too good for that . . . I am. (*She cries.*)
LUCY.   Well, look at me, you slut! (*She has a fat stomach.*) Does *that* come out of thin air? (*Pause.*) Now are your eyes beginning to open?
POLLY.   Oh! So that's how you are! I suppose you're hoping to make something out of it? You shouldn't have let him in, you fine lady!
MACHEATH.   Polly!
POLLY (*sobbing*). That's really too much. Mac, this shouldn't have happened. I don't know what I shall do now. (*Enter* MRS. PEACHUM.)
MRS. PEACHUM.   I knew it. She's with that man. You hussy, come here immediately. When your husband is hanged, you can hang yourself with him. A fine way to behave to your poor mother: she has to come and fetch you out of prison. And he has two at the same time—that Nero!
POLLY.   Leave me alone, mama; you don't know . . .
MRS. PEACHUM.   Come home—*immediately!*
LUCY.   Listen to that, your mother has to tell you how to behave.
MRS. PEACHUM.   Quick.
POLLY.   All right. Only I must . . . I must tell him something else . . . Really . . . It's very important.
MRS. PEACHUM (*giving her a box on the ear*). And that's important too. Get on!
POLLY.   Oh, Mac! (*She is dragged off.*)
MACHEATH.   Lucy, you behaved wonderfully. Of course I was sorry for her. That's why I couldn't treat the girl as she deserved. You thought at first there was some truth in what she said? Am I right?
LUCY.   Yes, I did think so, dearest.
MACHEATH.   If it had been true, her mother would never have got me into this mess. Have you heard what she did to me? A mother only behaves like that to a seducer, never to a son-in-law.
LUCY.   It makes me so happy, when you speak from the bottom of your heart like that. I love you so much, I'd almost rather see you hanged than in the arms of another girl.

MACHEATH.   Lucy, I would like to owe my life to you.

LUCY.   It's wonderful the way you say that; say it again.

MACHEATH.   Lucy, I would like to owe my life to you.

LUCY.   Shall I escape with you, dearest?

MACHEATH.   But you know it will be hard to hide if we escape together; as soon as the search is over, I'll have you fetched and by express post!

LUCY.   How can I help you?

MACHEATH.   Bring me my hat and stick.

(LUCY *exits and returns with his hat and stick and throws them into his cell.*)

Lucy, the fruit of our love which you carry beneath your heart will forever bind us together.

(*Exit* LUCY. SMITH *enters, goes into the cage and says to* MACHEATH.)

SMITH.   Give me that stick. (*After a short chase in which* SMITH, *armed with a chair and crow-bar, drives* MAC-HEATH *before him,* MACHEATH *climbs over the bars. The Police start to pursue him.*)

BROWN (*off*). Hello, Mac. Mac, please answer! It's Jacky here. Mac, please be kind and answer, I can't bear it any longer. (*Enters.*) Mackie! What's up? He's gone, thank God! (*He sits down on the bench.*) (*Enter* PEACHUM.)

PEACHUM (*to* SMITH). My name is Peachum. I have come to claim the forty pounds which is offered for the capture of the robber, MacHeath. (*Appears in front of the cage.*) Hey! Is Mr. MacHeath there? (BROWN *remains silent.*) Ah! So the other gentleman has gone out for a little walk? I come here to visit a criminal and whom do I find but Mr. Brown! Tiger Brown in prison and his friend MacHeath out.

BROWN (*groaning*). Mr. Peachum, it's not my fault.

PEACHUM.   Of course not. You would never be . . . to get yourself into this situation . . . impossible, Brown.

BROWN.   Mr. Peachum, I am beside myself.

PEACHUM.   I believe you. You must feel horrible.

BROWN.   Yes, it's this feeling of helplessness that paralyses one. The men do just what they like. It's terrible, terrible.

PEACHUM.   Wouldn't you like to lie down a little? Just shut your eyes and behave as though nothing had happened. Imagine you're lying on a beautiful green field with little white clouds overhead. The main thing is to get this nasty affair off your mind. Everything that's happened, and above all what's still to come.

BROWN (*uneasily*). What do you mean by that?

PEACHUM.   It's wonderful the way you're taking it. If I were in your position, I'd simply collapse and go to bed and drink hot tea. And what's more I'd arrange to have a nice cool hand stroking my forehead.

BROWN.   Damn you! I can't help it if the man escapes. The police can't do anything about it.

PEACHUM.   So the police can't do anything about it? You don't think we shall see Mr. MacHeath here again? (BROWN *shrugs his shoulders.*) Then it will be a nasty injustice, what happens to you. Of course people will say the police shouldn't have let him escape. And so I can't see that brilliant coronation procession quite yet.

BROWN.   What do you mean?

PEACHUM.   I might remind you of an historic example which, although it aroused considerable excitement in its time, fourteen hundred years before Christ, is unknown to the larger public today. After the Egyptian king, Ramses the Second, died, the chief of police of Nineveh, and also of Cairo, was guilty of some petty injustice towards the lower classes of the people. The results at that time were terrible. The coronation procession of the new queen, Semiramis, was, as the history books state, ''a succession of catastrophes caused by the all too lively participation of the lower classes.'' The historians are far too squeamish to describe what Semiramis had done to her chief of police. I only remember vaguely; but there was some talk of snakes which she nourished at his bosom.

BROWN.   Really?

PEACHUM.   The Lord be with you, Brown. (*Exit.*)

BROWN.   Now only an iron hand can do any good. Sergeant, a conference. Send out a general alarm.

(*Curtain.* MACHEATH *and* GINNY JENNY *step in front of the curtain and sing. On a board is written:* SECOND FINALE—THE SURVIVAL OF MANKIND.)

MACHEATH.

    All you who try in righteous paths to lead us,
    Who tell us to avoid all carnal sin
    Your elementary duty is to feed us
    Then start your preaching: that's how to begin.
    You who love your stomachs and praise our honesty
    Read, mark, and learn before it is too late:
    However you may use your ingenuity,
    Till we've had dinner, morality can wait.
    First even poorer people must be able
    To satisfy their appetites at table.

VOICE OFF.   For how can man survive?

MACHEATH.

    For how can man survive? By simply getting
    Others under, cheating and exploiting all he can.
    He only can survive by sheer forgetting—
    Forgetting that he ever was a man.

CHORUS OFF.

    So gentlemen, to this fact be alive:
    That only by misdeeds can man survive.

GINNY JENNY.

    You think that moral laws should be decreed us
    On when to lift our skirts and when to grin
    But first of all your duty is to feed us
    Then start your preaching: that's how to begin.

You need our shame to feed your promiscuity
But here is something you should take to heart:
However you may use your ingenuity
First comes the cart horse—afterwards the cart.
First even poorer people must be able
To satisfy their appetites at table.

VOICE OFF. For how can man survive?

GINNY JENNY.

For how can man survive? By simply getting
Others under, cheating and exploiting all he can.
He only can survive by sheer forgetting—
Forgetting that he ever was a man.

CHORUS OFF.

So gentlemen, to this fact be alive:
That only by misdeeds can man survive!

ACT THREE

SCENE ONE

THE SAME NIGHT PEACHUM PREPARES FOR ACTION. BY MEANS OF A DEMONSTRATION OF MISERY HE HOPES TO DISORGANIZE THE CORONATION PROCESSION.

(*The wardrobe-room of Peachum's establishment. The Beggars are painting boards with such inscriptions as "I gave my eye for my King," etc.*)

PEACHUM. Gentlemen, at this very hour, in our eleven branches between here and Wapping, there are one thousand four hundred and thirty-two men working on such boards as these in order to attend the Coronation of our Queen.

MRS. PEACHUM. Come on, come on! If you won't work, you can't beg. You hope to be a blind man, and you can't even write a proper K. That's supposed to be a child's handwriting, not an old man's. (*Roll of drums.*)

BEGGAR. There's the guard of honor lining up, and they'd never dream that today, the grandest day of their military life, they've got to deal with us. (FILCH *enters and announces.*)

FILCH. A dozen benighted birds are coming along this way, Mrs. Peachum. They say they're to be given money here. (*Enter the Whores.*)

GINNY JENNY. Madam . . .

MRS. PEACHUM. Well, well, well, you look as though you've all fallen off your perches. I suppose you've come for the money for your Mr. MacHeath. Well, you'll get nothing, do you understand me, absolutely nothing.

GINNY JENNY. And how may we understand that, madam?

MRS. PEACHUM. Bursting into my room in the middle of the night! Coming to a respectable house at three in the morning! You'd do better to sleep off the effects of business. You all look like skimmed milk.

GINNY JENNY. So we're not going to get our reward for having Mr. MacHeath arrested, madam?

MRS. PEACHUM. Quite correct. In fact, you'll get something you don't like, instead of your blood-money.

GINNY JENNY. And why, madam?

MRS. PEACHUM. Because this wonderful Mr. MacHeath has again vanished into thin air. That's why. And now get out of my house, ladies.

GINNY JENNY. Don't you try that on with us. I give you fair warning. Not with us.

MRS. PEACHUM. Filch, the ladies wish to be shown the door. (FILCH *approaches the girls.* GINNY JENNY *pushes him away.*)

GINNY JENNY. I'd advise you to keep your dirty mouth shut, or it might happen that . . . (*Enter* PEACHUM.)

PEACHUM. What's happening here? I hope you haven't given them any money. Well, what's the matter, ladies? Is Mr. MacHeath in prison or is he not?

GINNY JENNY. Let me in peace with your Mr. MacHeath. You're not a patch on him. I had to send a gentleman away tonight because I wanted to cry in the pillow every time I thought how I had sold Mackie to you. Yes, and what do you think happened this morning? Not an hour ago I had just cried myself to sleep when I heard a whistle, and there in the street below stood the gentleman for whom I'd been weeping for, and he asked me to throw the key down to him. He wished to forget the wrong I had done him in my arms. He's the last gentleman left in London, ladies. And if our colleague, Sukey Tawdry, isn't with us now, it's because he went from me to her, to comfort her as well.

PEACHUM (*himself*). Sukey Tawdry . . .

GINNY JENNY. So now you know you're dirt compared to him. You low-down, dirty, sneaking spies.

PEACHUM. Filch, run quickly to the nearest police station and say that Mr. MacHeath is staying with Sukey Tawdry. (*Exit* FILCH.) But, ladies, why are we quarreling? The money will be paid you, of course. My dear Celia, it would be better if you went and made coffee for the ladies instead of insulting them.

MRS. PEACHUM.

Sukey Tawdry! (*Sings.*)
Now here's a man is facing execution
The burning lime awaits his dissolution.
It won't be long before the noose does him in
But what absorbs his whole attention? Women!
Though near the gallows—still he must comply.
Such is the law of sexual slavery.

And now he has been sold. There's nothing
    left to save.
A female Judas has the money in her hand.
And now he just begins to understand:
The charms of women lead but to the grave.
And, though his fury rages unabated,
Before the night falls he's again prostrated.
(*Exit* MRS. PEACHUM.)

PEACHUM.   Come on, come on! You'd all be rotting in the sewers of Wapping if I hadn't spent sleepless nights discovering how to earn a few pence from your poverty. And I did discover something:—that the rich of the earth indeed *create* misery, but cannot bear to *see* misery. For they are weaklings and fools, just like you. So long as they have enough to eat to the end of their days and can grease their floors with butter, so that even the crumbs that fall from their tables grow fat, they cannot look with indifference on a man collapsing from hunger—although, of course, it must be in front of *their* house that he collapses. (*Enter* MRS. PEACHUM *with a tray full of coffee cups.*)

MRS. PEACHUM.   You can come to the shop tomorrow and fetch your money; but *after* the Coronation.

GINNY JENNY.   Mrs. Peachum, you leave me speechless.

PEACHUM.   Fall in! We assemble in an hour outside Buckingham Palace. Quick! (*The Beggars fall in.*)

FILCH (*bursts in*).   The police! I never got as far as the station. The police are already here!!

PEACHUM.   Hide yourselves! (*To* MRS. PEACHUM.) Get the orchestra ready, quickly. And when you hear me say ''harmless,'' understand me, ''harmless'' . . .

MRS. PEACHUM.   Harmless? I understand nothing.

PEACHUM.   Of course you understand nothing. But when I say ''harmless'' . . . (*There is a knocking on the door.*) That's the cue, *harmless*, then play some sort of music or other. Now get out!

(*Exit* MRS. PEACHUM. *The Beggars, excepting a girl with the board ''A victim of Military Despotism,'' hide with their things behind the clothes racks right. Enter* BROWN *and several policemen.*)

BROWN.   And now, Mr. Beggars' Friend, we take action. Handcuff him, Smith. Ah, so those are a few of your charming notices. (*To the girl.*) ''A Victim of Military Despotism''—is that you?

PEACHUM.   Good morning, Mr. Brown, good morning. Slept well?

BROWN.   Eh?

PEACHUM.   Morning, Brown.

BROWN.   Is he speaking to me? Does he know any of you? I don't think I have the pleasure of your acquaintance.

PEACHUM.   Haven't you? Morning, Brown.

BROWN.   Knock his hat off his head. (SMITH *does so.*)

PEACHUM.   Listen, Brown, since your way leads you *by* my house—I said *by*, Brown—I can now ask you to put a certain MacHeath finally under lock and key.

BROWN.   The man is mad. Don't laugh, Smith. Tell me, Smith, how is it possible that this notorious criminal is allowed to be at large in London?

PEACHUM.   Because he's your friend, Brown.

BROWN.   Who?

PEACHUM.   Mackie the Knife. Not me. I'm not a criminal. I'm only a poor man, Brown. You can't treat me badly.

And listen to me, Brown. You're on the verge of the worst hour of your life. Would you like a cup of coffee? (*To the whores.*) Children, give the Commissioner of Police a drink, that's not the way to behave. After all, we're all friends here. We all obey the law! And the law is simply and solely made for the exploitation of those who do not understand it. Or of those who, for naked need, cannot obey it. And whoever would pick up the crumbs of this exploitation must keep strictly to the law.

BROWN.   So you think our judges are bribable!

PEACHUM.   On the contrary, sir, on the contrary. Our judges are totally unbribable; there's no amount of money can bribe them to dispense justice! (*A second roll of drums.*) Departure of the troops to line the route. The departure of the poorest of the poor takes place half an hour later.

BROWN.   Quite right, Mr. Peachum. The departure of the poorest of the poor takes place in half an hour. They're departing for their winter-quarters in prison. (*To the policemen.*) Well, boys, gather in everything that you can find. All the patriots that are here. (*To the beggars.*) Have you ever heard of Tiger Brown? Tonight, Mr. Peachum, I have found the solution, and, I may also add, I have saved a friend from death. I shall smoke out your whole nest. And then I shall lock you all up for—yes, what for? For street-begging. You seem to have warned me that you were going to bother me and the Queen with your beggars. These beggars I shall now arrest. That will teach you.

PEACHUM.   Very nice, only—what beggars?

BROWN.   Well, these cripples here. Smith, we'll take the gentlemen with us right away.

PEACHUM.   Brown, I can save you from overstepping your duty. Thank God, you came to me. Of course you can arrest these few people, they are harmless, *harmless* . . .

(*Music starts and plays a few introductory bars of the* SONG OF THE INADEQUACY OF HUMAN ENDEAVOR.)

BROWN.   What's that?

PEACHUM.   Music. They're playing as well as they can. ''The Song of Inadequacy.'' Don't you know it? It will teach you something.

(*Song illumination: golden light. The organ is lit up. Three lights come down from above on a bar, and on a board is written:* THE SONG OF THE INADEQUACY OF HUMAN ENDEAVOR.)

> A man lives by his head
> But it does not suffice.
> Just try it, and you'll find your head
> Won't raise a pair of lice.
>
>> In this world forever
>> Man cannot be sharp enough
>> Ever to discover
>> All the tricks and bluff.

Well, make yourself a plan
Just be a leading light!
And then work out a second plan
And neither will come right.

In this world forever
Man is never bad enough.
Yet his high endeavor
Shows that he's good stuff.

Well, run in search of luck
But take care not to fall
For all men run in search of luck
And luck runs last of all.

In this world forever
Man is never meek and mild enough
So all his endeavor
Is a great self-bluff.

Your plan was ingenious, Brown, but impracticable. All that you can arrest here are a few young people who have arranged a small fancy-dress dance in celebration of the Coronation of their Queen. But when the really poor ones come—there's not a single one here now—they'll come in thousands. That's it: you have forgotten the monstrous number of the poor. If they were to stand there in front of the Abbey, it would not be a very cheerful sight. They don't look very nice. Do you know what erysipelas is, Brown? Well, think of a hundred people with erysipelas on their faces. And then these mutilated creatures. At the door of the Abbey. We would rather avoid that, Brown. You say the police will make short work of us poor people. But you do not believe that yourself. And what will it look like if six hundred poor cripples have to be struck down with your truncheons because of the Coronation? It will look very bad. It will be disgusting. Enough to make one sick. I feel ill, Brown, when I think of it. A small chair, please.

BROWN (*to* SMITH). It's a threat. It's blackmail. One can't do anything to this man; in the interests of public safety it's impossible to do anything to him. Such a thing has never happened before.

PEACHUM. But it has happened now. I'll tell you something: you can do what you like to the Queen of England, but you can't even tread on the toes of the poorest man in London—or you're done for, Mr. Brown.

BROWN. So I'm to arrest Mackie the Knife? Arrest him? But it's all very well for you to talk. You've got to catch your man before you can arrest him.

PEACHUM. When you say that, I cannot contradict you. So I shall produce the man for you; we'll soon see if there's any morality left. Jenny, where is Mr. MacHeath at the present moment?

GINNY JENNY. With Sukey Tawdry, at 21 Oxford Street.

BROWN. Smith, go immediately to 21 Oxford Street, Sukey Tawdry's flat, arrest MacHeath, and bring him to the Old Bailey. In the meantime I must change into my full-dress uniform. At times like these I have to wear full-dress.

PEACHUM. Brown, if he's not hanged by six . . .

BROWN. Oh, Mac, it was no good. (*Exit* BROWN *with the Policemen.*)

PEACHUM (*calling after him*). Now you've learnt something, Brown! (*A third roll of drums.*) Drums for the third time. A fresh plan of campaign. New destination: the Old Bailey. Quick march! (*Exeunt the Beggars singing.*)

Since man is far from good
Just hit him on the head
And if you do it properly
He's either good or dead.

In this world forever
Man is never good enough
So to make him clever
You must treat him rough!

INTERLUDE

(*In front of the curtain appears* GINNY JENNY *with a hurdy-gurdy. She sings* THE SONG OF SOLOMON.)

You've heard of wise old Solomon
You know his history.
He understood all things on earth
And saw that all was vanity
And cursed the moment of his birth.
How great and wise was Solomon!
And then, behold, ere it was night
The world saw all that followed on:
His wisdom brought him to that dreadful plight—
Oh, who would envy such a one!

You've heard of lovely Cleopatra
You know her history!
All men were victim to her lust
And yet she died in agony
And passed away and fell to dust.
How fine and great was Babylon!
And then, behold, ere it was night
The world saw all that followed on:
Her beauty brought her to that dreadful plight—
Oh, who would envy such a one!

You've heard of Caesar bold and brave
You know his history!
He sat like god enthroned in light
And yet he was murdered openly
When his career had reached its height.
And loud he cried "You too, my son!"
And then, behold, ere it was night

The world saw all that followed on:
His boldness brought him to that dreadful plight—
Oh, who would envy such a one!

You know the studious-minded Brecht
You've sung him now and then.
Too often he inquired the source
Of all the wealth of wealthy men
They hunted him out of his home, of course.
How studious was my poor old mother's son!
And then, behold, ere it was night
The world saw all that followed on:
His studiousness had brought him to this plight—
Oh, who would envy such a one!

And now you see our friend MacHeath
His head hangs by a hair!
So long as he had commonsense
And robbed his victims everywhere
His fame and fortune were immense.
But then his heart got on the run!
And now, behold, ere it is night
The world sees all that follows on:
His passions brought him to this dreadful plight—
Oh, who would envy such a one!

ACT THREE

Scene Two

The Battle for Possession
(*A room in the Old Bailey.*)

SMITH.   Miss. Mrs. Polly MacHeath would like to speak to you.

LUCY.   Mrs. MacHeath? Show her in.

POLLY.   Good morning, madam. Madam, good morning!

LUCY.   What can I do for you?

POLLY.   You recognize me?

LUCY.   Of course I recognize you.

POLLY.   I've come here to-day to beg your pardon for my behavior yesterday.

LUCY.   Well?

POLLY.   I have really no excuse for my behavior yesterday except—my unhappiness.

LUCY.   Yes, yes.

POLLY.   Miss Brown, you must forgive me. I was very upset yesterday by Mr. MacHeath's behavior. He really shouldn't have placed us in this position, don't you agree? And you can tell him so, too, when you see him.

LUCY.   I—I—don't see him.

POLLY.   You've already seen him.

LUCY.   I have not seen him.

POLLY.   I'm sorry.

LUCY.   After all, he's very fond of you.

POLLY.   Oh no, he only loves you, I know that well enough.

LUCY.   Very kind of you.

POLLY.   But, Miss Brown, a man is always afraid of a woman who loves him too much. Naturally, the result is that he neglects that woman and avoids her. I saw at first glance that he was bound to you in a way which I naturally couldn't all at once guess.

LUCY.   Do you mean that honestly?

POLLY.   Certainly, of course, very honestly. Believe me.

LUCY.   Dear Miss Peachum, we have both loved him too much.

POLLY.   Perhaps that was it. (*Pause.*) And now, Miss Brown, I'll explain to you how it all came about. Ten days ago I saw Mr. MacHeath for the first time in the Octopus Hotel. My mother was there too. About a week later, that is, the day before yesterday, we were married. Yesterday I discovered that the police wanted him for a great many crimes. And today I don't know what will happen. Twelve days ago I wouldn't have dreamt I could ever have fallen for a man. (*Pause.*)

LUCY.   I quite understand now, Miss Peachum.

POLLY.   Mrs. MacHeath.

LUCY.   Mrs. MacHeath.

POLLY.   And indeed, during the last few hours I have been thinking a lot about this man. It's not so simple. For you see, Miss Brown, I have every reason to envy you for his behavior towards you the other day. When I had to leave you, compelled, I must admit, by my mother, he showed not the slightest sign of regret. But perhaps he hasn't got a heart at all, just a stone in his breast instead. What do you think, Lucy?

LUCY.   Yes, dear Miss Peachum. But I am not quite sure if the fault lies entirely with Mr. MacHeath. You should have kept to your own sort, Miss Peachum.

POLLY.   Mrs. MacHeath.

LUCY.   Mrs. MacHeath.

POLLY.   You're quite right—or at least I ought to have conducted everything, as my father says, "on a business basis."

LUCY.   Of course.

POLLY. (*weeps*). He was my only possession.

LUCY.   My dear, that's a misfortune that can happen even to the cleverest woman. But you are legally his wife, you can comfort yourself with that. But, child, I can't bear to go on seeing you so depressed. Can I offer you a little something?

POLLY.   What?

LUCY.   Something to eat!

POLLY.   Oh, yes, please, a little something to eat. (*Exit* LUCY.) (*To herself.*) The great fool! (LUCY *returns with coffee and cakes.*)

LUCY.   Now, that should be enough.

POLLY.   You're really giving yourself too much trouble. (*Pause. She eats.*) That's a lovely picture you have of him. When did he bring it?

LUCY.   What do you mean—bring?

POLLY (*innocently*). I meant, when did he bring it up to you?

LUCY.   He didn't bring it.

POLLY.   Did he give it to you right in this room?

LUCY.   He never was in this room.

POLLY.   I see. But it wouldn't have mattered, would it? The paths of fate are terribly complicated.

LUCY.   Don't go on talking such nonsense. You came here to spy around.

POLLY.   It's true, isn't it, that you know where he is?

LUCY.   I? Don't *you* know?

POLLY.   Tell me where he is immediately.

LUCY.   I haven't the slightest idea.

POLLY.   Then you don't know where he is? Word of honor?

LUCY.   No, I do not know. And don't you know either?

POLLY.   No, this is terrible. (POLLY *laughs and* LUCY *weeps.*) He's got two responsibilities, and he's gone.

LUCY.   I can't bear it any longer. Oh, Polly, it's so awful.

POLLY (*happily*). But I'm so glad that at the end of this tragedy I've found a friend like you. In spite of everything. Will you have something more to eat? Another cake?

LUCY.   Something more. Oh, Polly, don't be so kind to me. Really, I don't deserve it. Oh, Polly, men aren't worth it.

POLLY.   Of course men aren't worth it, but what can one do?

LUCY.   Nothing! I'll tell you the truth. Polly, will you be very angry with me?

POLLY.   What is it?

LUCY.   It's not real.

POLLY.   What isn't real?

LUCY.   *That!* (*She points to her fat stomach.*) And all on that cheap crook's account.

POLLY (*laughs*). Oh, that's wonderful. So it was all a trick? Oh, you're a card. Listen—do you want Mackie? I'll give him to you. Take him as you find him! (*There is a sound of voices and steps outside.*) What's that?

LUCY (*at the window*). Mackie! They've caught him again.

POLLY (*collapses*). Then everything is over. (*Enter* MRS. PEACHUM.)

MRS. PEACHUM.   Ah, Polly, so here you are. Change your dress quickly; your husband is about to be hanged. I've brought the mourning clothes with me. (POLLY *undresses and puts on her widow's weeds.*) You'll look lovely as a widow. But try and look a little cheerful, too.

ACT THREE

SCENE THREE

FRIDAY MORNING, FIVE O'CLOCK, MACKIE THE KNIFE, WHO ONCE MORE WENT BACK TO HIS WHORES, HAS AGAIN BEEN BETRAYED BY THEM. HE IS NOW ABOUT TO BE HANGED.

(*Barred cage. The Death Cell. The bells of the City are ringing. Police bring* MACHEATH, *handcuffed, into the cell.*)

SMITH.   In here with him. The bells have already rung for the first time. Try and behave like a man. I don't know how you manage to make yourself look such a broken-down wreck. I believe you're ashamed. (*To the policemen.*) When the bells ring for the third time, and that will be at six o'clock, he's to be hanged. Get everything ready.

A CONSTABLE.   Every street outside has been jammed with people for the last quarter of an hour. It's impossible to get through now.

SMITH.   Extraordinary! How do they know already?

CONSTABLE.   If it goes on like this, the whole of London will know in half an hour. Then the people who were going to the Coronation will all come here instead. And the Queen will have to drive through empty streets.

SMITH.   So we shall have to be quick about it. If we're finished by six the people will be able to be back at their places on the Coronation route by seven. Now get on with it.

MACHEATH.   Hi, Smith, what's the time?

SMITH.   Haven't you got eyes? Four minutes past five.

MACHEATH.   Four minutes past five.

(*As* SMITH *shuts the door of the cell from the outside,* BROWN *enters.*)

BROWN (*questioning* SMITH, *with his back to the cell*). Is he in there?

SMITH.   Do you want to see him?

BROWN.   No, no, no, for God's sake, manage it all yourself. (*Exit* BROWN.)

MACHEATH (*suddenly bursting into a soft and rapid torrent of speech*). But, Smith, I won't say anything, nothing about bribery, don't be afraid of that. I know everything. If you let yourself be bribed, you must at least flee from the country. Yes, you must. Also you must have enough money to live on. A thousand pounds, will that do? Don't say anything. In twenty minutes I'll let you know whether you can have that thousand pounds by mid-day. I'm not talking about anyone's feelings. Go outside and think it over carefully. Life is short and so is money. And I'm not even sure whether I can raise any. But let anyone in here who wants to see me.

SMITH (*slowly*). You're talking nonsense, Mr. MacHeath. (*Exit* SMITH.)

MACHEATH (*sings softly and very quickly* THE EPISTLE TO HIS FRIENDS).

Now hear the voice which calls on you to save.
MacHeath lies not on leaves of gentle brown,
Nor under hawthorn trees—but in a grave
Where Fate in bitter wrath has struck him down!
God grant that you may hear his final plea!
For now thick walls surround and hold him fast!
My friends, do you not ask where he may be?
If he is dead, then drink to all the past.

But while he lives, stand by and set him free!
Or shall his torment last eternity?

(MATTHEW *and* JACOB *appear in the passage. Both approach*
MACHEATH.)

Five twenty-five. You've taken your time.
JACOB.   Well, after all, we had to . . .
MACHEATH.   After all, after all, I'm going to be hanged,
man! But I've got no time left to quarrel with you. Five
twenty-eight. Well, how much can you draw out of your
private deposits immediately?
MATTHEW.   From our banks, at five o'clock in the
morning?
JACOB.   Is it really as bad as all that?
MACHEATH.   Four hundred pounds, can you manage that?
JACOB.   Yes, and what about us? That's all we've got.
MACHEATH.   Are you going to be hanged, or am I?
MATTHEW (*excitedly*). Did *we* go and sleep with Sukey
Tawdry instead of making ourselves scarce? Do *we* have
Sukey Tawdry or do you?
MACHEATH.   Shut up! I'll soon be sleeping somewhere
else, and not with that slut. Five-thirty.
JACOB.   Then I suppose we shall have to do it, Matthew.
SMITH (*enters*). Mr. Brown told me to ask you what you
would like to have—for breakfast.
MACHEATH.   Leave me alone. (*To* MATTHEW.) Now will
you or will you not? (*To* SMITH.) Asparagus.
MATTHEW.   I'm certainly not going to be shouted at.
MACHEATH.   I'm not shouting at you. That's only because
. . . Now, Matthew, are you going to let me be hanged?
MATTHEW.   Of course I won't let you be hanged. Whoever
suggested I would? But that's all. Four hundred pounds
is all that's there. One's still allowed to say that, I
suppose.
MACHEATH.   Five thirty-eight.
JACOB.   Then hurry, Matthew, or it will be no use at all.
MATTHEW.   If only we can get through; the streets are
blocked. This rabble!
MACHEATH.   If you're not here by five minutes to six,
you'll never see me again. (*Shouts.*). You'll never see me
again . . .
SMITH.   They're off. Well, how goes it? (*Makes a gesture
of paying out money.*)
MACHEATH.   Four hundred.

(SMITH *goes away, shrugging his shoulders.* MACHEATH,
calling after him.)

I must speak to Brown.
SMITH (*returns with policeman*). You've got the soap?
POLICEMAN.   But not the right sort.
SMITH.   You will be able to set up the thing in ten minutes.
POLICEMAN.   But the trap is not working yet.
SMITH.   It *must* work, the bells have already rung for the
second time.

POLICEMAN.   A fine piece of apparatus! (*Exit policeman.*)
MACHEATH (*sings* THE EPISTLE TO HIS FRIENDS).
O come and see his wretched destiny
Now he is really done for, as you say.
And you who think the last authority
Is vested in the dirty cash you pay
Beware lest you go down as well as he!
Now hurry all of you to see the queen
And speak to her of him and plead his cause
Run headlong like the swine of Gadarene
For still his teeth are long as eagles' claws.
Or shall his torment last eternity?
SMITH.   I can't let you in. Your number is sixteen and it's
not your turn yet.
POLLY.   What do you mean: my number is sixteen? You're
not a bureaucrat. I am his wife, I must speak to him.
SMITH.   Then five minutes at the most.
POLLY.   What do you mean, five minutes! It's ridiculous.
Five minutes! You can't say it. It's not as simple as all
that. This is farewell forever. There's a terrible lot to be
said between man and wife . . . Where is he then?
SMITH.   Can't you see him?
POLLY.   Of course. Thank you
MACHEATH.   Polly!
POLLY.   Yes, Mackie, here I am.
MACHEATH.   Of course.
POLLY.   How are you? Are you very done up? It's terribly
difficult!
MACHEATH.   And what will *you* do? What will become of
you?
POLLY.   Oh, our business is doing very well. That's the least
of our troubles. Mackie, are you very nervous? . . . Who
actually was your father? There's so much you haven't
told me. I don't understand it at all. You were really quite
healthy always.
MACHEATH.   Polly, can't you help me out?
POLLY.   Yes, of course.
MACHEATH.   With money, I mean. I talked to the warder
here . . .
POLLY (*slowly*). The money has gone to Manchester.
MACHEATH.   And you have none?
POLLY.   No, I've got nothing. But do you know, Mac, I
could perhaps speak to someone . . . I might even be able
to ask the Queen personally. (*She breaks down.*) Oh,
Mackie!
SMITH (*pulling* POLLY *away*). Now have you got your thou-
sand pounds?
POLLY.   Good luck, Mac, take care of yourself and never
forget me.

(*Exit* POLLY. A CONSTABLE *brings on a table with a plate of
asparagus on it.*)

SMITH.   Is the asparagus tender?
CONSTABLE.   It is. (*Exit* CONSTABLE. BROWN *enters and
walks over to* SMITH.)

BROWN.   Smith, what does he want with me? I'm glad you waited for me with the table. We'll take it with us when we go in to him, so he'll see how thoughtful we are. (*They both carry the table into the cell. Exit* SMITH. *Pause.*) Hallo, Mac. Here's your asparagus. Won't you have a little?

MACHEATH.   Don't trouble yourself, Mr. Brown, there are other people who will do me the last honors.

BROWN.   But Mackie!

MACHEATH.   I should like the account! Forgive me if I eat in the meanwhile. After all, this is my last meal. (*Eats.*)

BROWN.   Good appetite! Oh, Mac, you wound me with red-hot irons.

MACHEATH.   The account, sir, please, the account. No sentimentality.

BROWN (*sighing, draws a little notebook out of a pocket*). I've brought it with me, Mac. Here is the account for the last six months.

MACHEATH (*cuttingly*). I see. So you have only come to get your money out of me.

BROWN.   But you know that's not true . . .

MACHEATH.   All right, I don't want you to be the loser. What do I owe you? I'm sorry, but I shall need a detailed statement. Life has made me mistrustful . . . And you're the one who will understand that best.

BROWN.   Mac, when you speak like that, I can't even think. (*There is a sound of loud banging behind.*)

SMITH (*voice*). All right, that will hold.

MACHEATH.   The account, Brown.

BROWN.   Very well, if you really want it—first of all there are the rewards for the arrests of the murderers which you or your people made possible. You received from the Government in all . . .

MACHEATH.   Three cases at forty pounds each makes a hundred and twenty pounds. So a quarter of that for you is thirty pounds, which we therefore owe you.

BROWN.   Yes—yes—but I really don't know, Mac, at the last minute like this if we can . . .

MACHEATH.   Please leave that stuff out. Thirty pounds, and for the one in Dover eight pounds.

BROWN.   Why only eight pounds, that was . . .

MACHEATH.   Do you or do you not believe me? As a result of the last half year you receive thirty-eight pounds.

BROWN (*sobbing loudly*). A whole lifetime . . . I've known your every thought . . .

BOTH.   By just looking in your eyes.

MACHEATH.   Well, well, three years in India—Johnny and Jimmy were both on the scene—five years in London, and that's all the thanks I get. (*In the meanwhile he shows what he will look like when hanged.*)

> Here hangs MacHeath who never did you wrong,
> Sold by a faithless friend of former days.
> And dangling from a rope a fathom long
> He knows at last how much his bottom weighs.

BROWN.   Mac, if you're going to behave to me like that . . . who attacks my honor attacks me. (*Runs angrily out of the cage.*)

MACHEATH.   Your honor . . .

BROWN.   Yes, my honor. Smith, begin! Let the people in! (*To* MACHEATH.) Excuse me, please.

SMITH (*quickly to* MACHEATH). I can still get you away, but in a minute it will be too late. Have you got the money?

MACHEATH.   Yes, as soon as the boys get back.

SMITH.   They're not in sight. Well—that's off.

(*People are let in:* PEACHUM, MRS. PEACHUM, POLLY, LUCY, THE WHORES, THE CLERGYMAN, MATTHEW *and* JACOB.)

GINNY JENNY.   They didn't want to let us in, but I said to them: if you don't take your something heads out of my way, you'll know Ginny Jenny better than you like.

PEACHUM.   I am his father-in-law. Pardon me, but which of these present is Mr. MacHeath?

MACHEATH (*presents himself*). I am MacHeath.

PEACHUM (*walks past the cage and stands right, as do all the others subsequently*). Fate, Mr. MacHeath, decreed that you should become my son-in-law without my knowing you. The circumstances in which I meet you for the first time are very tragic. Mr. MacHeath, you once had white kid gloves, a stick with an ivory handle and a scar on your neck, and you frequented the Octopus Hotel. There remains the scar on your neck, which is probably the least valuable of your distinguishing marks, and now you only frequent gaols, and very soon you won't frequent anywhere . . . (POLLY *walks sobbing past the cage and stands right.*)

MACHEATH.   What a pretty dress you're wearing. (MATTHEW *and* JACOB *come past the cage and stand right.*)

MATTHEW.   We couldn't get through on account of the crowd. But we ran so fast I thought Jacob was going to have a stroke. If you don't believe us . . .

MACHEATH.   What do the men say? Have they got good places?

MATTHEW.   There, Captain, we knew you'd understand us. But look, we don't get a Coronation every day. The men have to earn when they can. They asked to be remembered to you.

JACOB.   Kindly.

MRS. PEACHUM (*walks past the cage and stands right*). Mr. MacHeath, who would have thought of this when a week ago we had a little dance together in the Octopus Hotel.

MACHEATH.   Yes, a little dance.

MRS. PEACHUM.   But Fate is cruel.

BROWN (*to the clergyman at the back*). And with this man I stood at Aserbaijan, shoulder to shoulder, under withering fire.

GINNY JENNY (*comes past the cage*). Us girls are all in an awful fix. Not a soul has gone to the Coronation. They all want to see you. (*Stands right.*)

MACHEATH.   To see me.

SMITH.   Now, come on. Six o'clock.

MACHEATH.   We will not keep the people waiting. Ladies and gentlemen, you see here the vanishing representative of a vanishing class. We artisans of the lower middle class, who work with honest jemmies on the cash-boxes of small shop-keepers, are being ruined by large concerns backed by the banks. What is a picklock to a bank-share? What is the burglary of a bank to the founding of a bank? What is the murder of a man to the employment of a man? Fellow citizens, I herewith take my leave of you. I thank you all for coming. Some of you have been very close to me. That Jenny should have given me up astonishes me greatly. It is a clear proof that the world will always be the same. The concurrence of several unfortunate circumstances has brought about my fall. Good—I fall.

(*Song illumination: golden light. The organ is lit up. Three lights come down from above on a bar and on a board is written:* BALLADE IN WHICH MACHEATH BEGS THE FORGIVENESS OF ALL.)

> You people who survive us when we die
> Let not your hearts be hard against our action
> And laugh not when we hang against the sky
> A stupid laugh of bitter satisfaction.
> Nor curse against us, though we be defeated,
> Be not, as was the Law to us, unkind.
> Not all of us possess a lawful mind.
> My friends, be not light-hearted nor conceited.
> My friends, let this our fate a warning be
> And pray to God that He will pardon me.
>
> The rains now wash us down and wash us clean
> And wash the flesh we overfed before.
> And those which saw too much and asked for
>   more—
> Our eyes—are pecked by ravens perched between.
> We tried indeed to climb above our station
> And now we hang on high as though in pride
> Attacked by hungry birds on every side
> Like refuse waiting for disintegration.
> Oh brothers, let our fate a warning be
> And pray to God that He will pardon me.
>
> And girls who flaunt their buxom beauty
> To catch the eyes of men with yearnings
> And thieves who watch them when on duty
> To confiscate their sinful earnings
> And murderers and brothel-keepers
> And pickpockets and such as we
> Abortionists and crossing-sweepers
> I pray that they will pardon me.
> Not so the police, scum of the nation,
> Who every evening, every morning
> Caused me endless tribulation

> And usually without a warning.
> Oh, I could curse them to damnation
> But for today I'll let that be
> To save all further explanation
> I pray they too will pardon me.
>
> *With iron hammers smash their faces*
> *And smash them till they cease to be*
> *But now I would forget their faces*
> *And pray that they will pardon me.*

SMITH.   If you please, Mr. MacHeath.

MRS. PEACHUM.   Polly and Lucy, stand by your husband in his last hour.

MACHEATH.   Ladies, whatever there may have been between us . . .

SMITH (*leads him off*). Come on!

(*Passage to the Gallows. All exeunt then re-enter from the other side of the stage, carrying hurricane-lamps. When* MACHEATH *is standing on the gallows,* PEACHUM *speaks.*)

PEACHUM.

> Most honored public, thus far we have come
> MacHeath should now be hanged and justice done
> For in the whole of Christendom
> There's nothing granted free to anyone.
>
> But just in case you should have been misled
> And think that *we* approve this execution
> MacHeath will *not* be hanged till he be dead,
> For we've thought out a different solution.
>
> In order that, in opera anyway,
> Mercy may prevail over justice once a year
> And also since we wish you well today
> The royal messenger will now appear.

(*On a board is written:* THIRD FINALE—THE ARRIVAL OF THE MOUNTED MESSENGER.)

CHORUS.

> Hark, who comes! Hark, who comes!
> The royal messenger riding comes!

BROWN (*enters on horseback and sings recitative*). On account of her Coronation, our gracious Queen commands that a certain MacHeath shall at once be released. (*All cheer.*) At the same time he is raised to the permanent ranks of the nobility. (*Cheers.*) The castle Marmorell and an income of ten thousand pounds are his as long as he shall live. And to the happy couples here the Queen presents her royal and cordial felicitations.

MACHEATH.   A rescue! A rescue! I was sure of it! Where the need is greatest, there God's help will be nearest.

POLLY.   A rescue! A rescue! My dearest MacHeath has been rescued. I am so happy.

MRS. PEACHUM.   So the whole thing has a happy ending. How calm and peaceful would our life be always, if a messenger came from the king whenever we wanted.

PEACHUM.   Therefore all remain standing where you are now and sing the chorale of the poorest of the poor, of whose difficult life you have shown us something today. But in real life their end is always bad. Mounted messengers from the queen come far too seldom, and if you kick a man he kicks you back again. Therefore never be too ready to condemn injustice.

ALL (*singing to the accompaniment of the organ, they advance to the front of the stage. The words they sing appear on a board or screen*).
> Condemn injustice not with overboldness
> Since it is cold, its death is sure but slow.
> Consider all the darkness and the coldness
> Which fill this vale of misery and woe.

FOCUS QUESTIONS

1. Choose one of the following songs and discuss how it reflects on the character in the scene and on the play's theme: ''The Pirate Jenny Song,'' ''The Army Song,'' or ''The Barbara Song.''
2. Why is Peachum distressed at Polly's marriage to MacHeath? Explain his reasons for wishing to condemn her new husband to death.
3. By examining all of the beggars in Peachum's employment, discuss Brecht's attitude toward the middle classes.
4. Discuss how MacHeath's criminal gang reflects the dynamics of employer/employee relationships in legitimate businesses.
5. In a brief essay, discuss the unlikely relationship that develops between Lucy and Polly.
6. Discuss the women characters as perpetrators of capitalist values.
7. Using the Moritat and other dramatic actions of the play, develop a character sketch of MacHeath.
8. Examine the finales to each act and develop a thesis that reveals the themes of the entire opera.

OTHER ACTIVITIES

1. Create a scrapbook of contemporary photographic images of political or newsworthy figures who might be used to illustrate the play's main characters or the subject matter of the songs.
2. View the 1931 Pabst film version of *The Threepenny Opera* and evaluate its effectiveness in relation to Brecht's play.

BIBLIOGRAPHY

Bentley, Eric. *The Brecht Commentaries: 1943–1980.* New York: Grove Press, 1981.

Brooker, Peter. *Bertolt Brecht: Dialectics, Poetry, Politics.* London: Croom Helm, 1988.

Demetz, Peter. *Brecht: A Collection of Critical Essays.* Englewood Cliffs, NJ: Prentice-Hall, 1962.

Esslin, Martin. *Brecht: The Man and His Work.* New York: Doubleday & Co., 1961.

Ewen, Frederic. *Bertolt Brecht: His Life, His Art, and His Times.* New York: Citadel Press, 1967.

Fuegi, John. *Bertolt Brecht: Chaos According to Plan.* Cambridge: Cambridge University Press, 1987.

———. *The Essential Brecht.* Los Angeles: Hennessey & Ingalls, Inc., 1972.

Gray, Ronald. *Brecht the Dramatist.* Cambridge: Cambridge University Press, 1976.

Hill, Claude. *Bertolt Brecht.* Boston: Twayne Publishers, 1975.

Kiebuzinska, Christine Olga. *Revolutionaries in the Theatre.* Ann Arbor: UMI Research Press, 1988.

Lyons, Charles. *Bertolt Brecht: The Despair and the Polemic.* Carbondale: Southern Illinois University Press, 1968.

Mews, Siegfried. *Critical Essays on Bertolt Brecht.* Boston: G. K. Hall & Co., 1989.

Speirs, Ronald. *Bertolt Brecht.* New York: St. Martin's Press, 1992.

Weber, Betty Nance, and Hubert Heiner. *Bertolt Brecht: Political Theory and Literary Practice.* Athens: University of Georgia Press, 1980.

Willett, John. *Art and Politics in the Weimar Period: The New Sobriety 1917–1933.* New York: Pantheon Books, 1978.

———. *Brecht in Context: Comparative Approaches.* London: Methuen, 1984.

———. *Brecht on Theatre.* New York: Hill & Wang, 1964.

———. *The Theatre of Bertolt Brecht.* New York: New Directions Books, 1968.

RECOMMENDED VIDEOTAPES AND RECORDINGS

Threepenny Opera. VHS. 114 min. 1931. Starring Lotte Lenya. Directed by G. W. Pabst in German with English subtitles. Distributed by Facets Video, Chicago. Also available on Laserdisc.

Threepenny Opera. One sound disc. 54 min. 1954. Theatre de Lys Production starring Lotte Lenya, Scott Merrill, Charlotte Rae, and Beatrice Arthur. Polydor.

Threepenny Opera. VHS. 97 min. 1962. Starring Curt Jurgens and Sammy Davis, Jr., with Marc Blitzstein lyrics. Kurt Ulrich Films.

Threepenny Opera. One sound disc. 57 min. 1976. New York Shakespeare Festival Production. Directed by Richard Foreman. CBS Records.

CAT ON A HOT TIN ROOF
TENNESSEE WILLIAMS (1914–1983)

Mr. Williams is the man of our time who comes closest to hurling the actual blood and bone of life onto the stage; he is also the man whose prose comes closest to being an incisive natural poetry.

—WALTER KERR

Pat Hingle (*left*) as Big Daddy and James Morrison as Brick in *Cat on a Hot Tin Roof*, presented by the Mark Taper Forum in 1983, under the direction of José Quintero. *Photo: Jay Thompson.*

APPROACHING POETIC REALISM IN CONTEMPORARY AMERICAN DRAMA

The seeds for a modern American drama were sown shortly after the Abbey Theatre completed its tour of the United States in 1912. Modeling themselves on this newly established company of Irish players, little theatres across the country envisioned a **folk drama** of their own that might pay tribute to the urban and rural poor who struggled to survive. Playwrights and practitioners who eventually founded these theatres were also inspired by the plays and production techniques from the continental theatre that they had studied in recently established programs at Carnegie Institute of Technology or under the guidance of mentors like George Pierce Baker at Harvard and Frederick Koch who later established the Carolina Players. These folk playwrights assimilated certain European influences with their own realistic portrayals of the diverse religious, ethnic, and racial heritages that represented America.

Thus a serious literary theatre was launched by the end of World War I. Its playwrights were regionalists insofar as each reflected the lore and customs of a different American experience. DuBose and Dorothy Heywood wrote about rural southern blacks, while Susan Glaspell captured the spirit of midwestern life. Clifford Odets vividly portrayed the lives of Jewish and Italian immigrant families in New York City. Although a young Eugene O'Neill was caught between the lure of the New York dockside and the puritanism of tragic New Englanders, his playwriting interests smartly encompassed the expansive range of a rapidly maturing American theatre during the 1920s and 1930s. (See Preface to O'Neill, p. 708.) A far cry from the tradition of melodrama that defined popular entertainment during the second half of the nineteenth century, the drama was as much a weapon as it was a palliative for the society it addressed. Its themes concerned human rights and class struggles, the fear of annihilation in the aftermath of the Great War, the loss of human dignity in a bureaucratic society, women's rights, and the elusiveness of the American Dream.

When American troops returned from Asia and Europe at the end of World War II, a different psychological climate began to assert itself in the American consciousness. By 1945, a new generation of artists brought fresh perspectives to a literary era now viewed as contemporary. Their sociopolitical concerns, radically altered in the aftermath of this second war, were underscored by the fact that life in America might not be representative of the democratic principles and tolerance for human differences for which soldiers had fought and died.

The South, where a tradition of social class distinctions remained intact despite the repercussions of recent world turmoil, was a continuing source for investigating the illusory promises of American democracy. Literary artists were especially sensitive to how southerners from every facet of society responded to the struggle between the status quo and the need for change. Foremost was William Faulkner (1897–1962), whose novels and short stories explored a complex psychological network of characters and themes both tragic and universal in dimension. Regional writers like Thomas Wolfe, Carson McCullers, Flannery O'Connor, Katherine Anne Porter, Truman Capote, and Eudora Welty responded in eloquent voices that were often tinged with nostalgia for a South that no longer existed. Their writings triggered the curiosity of outsiders whose imaginations were now given access to a world very different from their own. On a somewhat smaller scale, the drama was represented by an enclave of playwrights that included Paul Green, Lillian Hellman, and a young Mississippian named Thomas Lanier Williams, who preferred the nickname Tennessee.

Earning some recognition through the publication of several short plays, including a few regional stagings and one brief but unsuccessful association with the Theatre Guild, Tennessee Williams achieved wide critical acclaim when *The Glass Menagerie* opened in

New York City on March 31, 1945. During the next ten years, he would establish himself as the most important American playwright to appear since O'Neill. But the strengths of his dramatic art, sharply demonstrated in *The Glass Menagerie* and more fully delineated in his production notes for that play, borrowed little from the commercial theatre around him. In fact, he vehemently rejected the photographic realism that dominated the commercial theatre in New York, preferring a softer application of certain experimental techniques from the continent, whose one valid aim was "a closer approach to truth."[1] He arrived at a compromise by merging the elements he had absorbed from American stage realism and expressionism as well as European symbolism. His art, best described as **poetic realism,** met his dramatic aims and found support from Broadway audiences and critics alike.

Foremost was Williams' unusual gift for stage dialogue. It was naturally poetic without sounding like "poetry" and achieved an unflinching vitality in the mouths of realistic characters. A clue to this achievement may be heard in the difference between **poetry *in* the theatre,** by which the characters speak in metrical verse (for example, Euripides, Shakespeare, and Molière), and **poetry *of* the theatre,** by which the patterns of verbal images and symbols are conveyed through prose. Accomplishing the latter, Williams' unique dialogue did more than merely state: it *illuminated* the embattled world of his characters. As a result, the same Broadway establishment that acclaimed the playwrights of O'Neill's generation, including Elmer Rice, Maxwell Anderson, Sidney Howard, Philip Barry, William Saroyan, and Thornton Wilder, instinctively recognized the artistry of this southern writer who stood tall in the company of newer playwright/contemporaries like Arthur Miller, William Inge, Robert Anderson, and Edward Albee.

Possessing a thoroughly uninhibited and original style, Williams showed an oblique fascination for the disintegrating American Dream—that nineteenth-century spirit of idealism that had weakened under the pressure of materialist expectations and had come to haunt so many artists of his contemporary post-war generation. Equally important was his preoccupation with the seamy side of human behavior, specifically in eccentric southern characters whose ironclad wills at first seemed impervious to decadence of any kind. While these aberrations did not please all tastes, they had a strong commercial appeal through characters and themes that were surprisingly palatable, even when Williams meant to shock conventional standards. Fortunately, by mid-century, psychological theories were already incorporated into American life-styles and the practice of psychiatry had been democratized. So the idiosyncrasies and borderline psychoses of Williams' *dramatic personae* were not unfamiliar to New York playgoers. In fact, his stage characters quickly found acceptance abroad.

At closer glance, his writing paid homage to a sturdy literary stock: August Strindberg, whose focus on the deadly war of the sexes established a male/female dynamic that served Williams' creative needs time and again; D. H. Lawrence, whose primitive psychological studies—populated with childlike adults—infused Williams' characters with an Edenic innocence; William Faulkner, whose themes of survival validated his fellow-Mississippian's preoccupation with the emotional chaos of the human condition; and Eugene O'Neill, whose transformation of personal trauma into powerful theatre inspired Williams to investigate his own pain. "We're under a life-long sentence to solitary confinement inside our own lonely skins for as long as we live on this earth," exclaims Lady Torrance in *Orpheus Descending,* exposing the emotional and psychological wounds through which the playwright spoke.

MAJOR WORKS

In addition to extensive non-theatrical works, including three novels, two volumes of poetry, and numerous short stories, some of whose characters and situations were reworked into his full-length plays, Williams' most representative one-acts are collected in

27 Wagons Full of Cotton and Other Plays (1945), *American Blues* (1948), and *Dragon Country* (1970). But the stage work that followed the success of *The Glass Menagerie* sustained his prolific career, winning him numerous Drama Critics Circle Awards, Antoinette Perry Awards, Pulitzer Prizes, and great international acclaim as well.

Williams was most at home with the **well-made play** format, which accommodated his unusual blend of realism and poetic language, yet invited unexpected turns in the inevitable flow of dramatic action. His philosophical premises always remained consistent: that humankind was pitiable and that the weak must be protected from the strong; that economic survival determined happiness; that positive sexual adjustment—whether heterosexual or homosexual—was equated with a certain kind of happiness but, when it failed, led to frustration, degradation, and even madness. Such premises were eloquently demonstrated in *A Streetcar Named Desire* (1947), *Summer and Smoke* (1948), *The Rose Tattoo* (1951), *Orpheus Descending* (1957), *Sweet Bird of Youth* (1959), *Period of Adjustment* (1960), *Night of the Iguana* (1961), and *Vieux Carré* (1977). He occasionally risked experimentation with dramatic structures in works like *Camino Real* (1953) and *Slapstick Tragedy* (1966).

When *Cat on a Hot Tin Roof* opened on Broadway in 1955, its unsentimental exploration of the human condition, including its battle of the sexes, represented a new peak in Williams' career as playwright. Years later, it would be acclaimed by many critics as his finest play and one that Williams himself called "a work of art and a work of craft."[2]

THE ACTION

The relationship between Brick Pollitt, Big Daddy's favorite son, and Brick's wife Maggie is strained by insinuations of homosexuality that torment Brick and have driven him to drink. Act 1 centers on the family's celebration of Big Daddy's birthday. Refusing to join the party, Brick remains in his bedroom to nurse a broken leg. Maggie reminds him that his brother Gooper and sister-in-law Mae, whose greedy eyes are set on the largest share of the ailing man's fortune, may inherit everything.

In act 2, Big Daddy forces Brick to face the truth behind his excessive drinking, and Brick counters with the knowledge that his father is dying of cancer. In act 3, the family breaks the news to Big Mama, who refuses to believe them. In response to Gooper's insistence that they discuss the inheritance, Maggie announces that she is pregnant, a disclosure intended to anchor Brick's claim to his father's inheritance. Now both are left alone to face each other.

STRUCTURE AND LANGUAGE

Of the many memorable family plays that have given shape to an international repertory of contemporary stage literature, *Cat on a Hot Tin Roof* towers over the best, both for its unconventional design and unorthodox subject matter. Its larger-than-life characters and frank discussion of intensely personal themes, such as cancer, homosexuality, and alcoholism, fascinate us for all the wrong reasons. Hints of voyeurism and illicit relationships, including the outspokenness of Big Daddy's perverse hatred of Big Mama, seem to point in this direction until we confront the play's profound moral subtext: the cry for truth, compassion, and total communication between human beings at all costs.

Enlightening all aspects of the *mise-en-scène,* Williams embellishes the play with exhaustive production notes and stage directions so that the controversial subject matter will not be marred by misinterpretation or conventionality. An inordinate concern for physical details, characteristic of most of his plays, also serves the cause of poetic realism in actual stage performance. Thus an essential feature in *Cat on a Hot Tin Roof* is that the action occupies "precisely the time of its performance" and is unified by the unchanging physical space in which it unfolds, whose "walls below the ceiling should dissolve mysteriously into air; the set should be roofed by the sky; stars and moon suggested by traces of milky pallor, as if they were observed through a telescope lens out of focus." This ethereal, somewhat painterly description guides the play imperceptibly toward a more subjective or psychological realm where its emotional subtext finds unlimited resonance in the playgoer's imagination. Equally important, the blurred image of the telescope softens our critical assessment of human lives painfully askew, but striving to remain connected and visible.

Two important production details frame the play. The first, which asks the scenic designer "to give the actors room to move about freely (to show their restlessness, their passion for breaking out) as if it were a set for a ballet," elevates the play to a cosmic dance by introducing the dimension of eternity to its basically realistic design and content. The second, and certainly more jarring, is the presence of "a big double bed which staging should make a functional part of the set as often as suitable, the surface of which should be slightly raked to make figures on it seen more easily." No stage property or production symbol unifies the vital issues of this play as urgently as this item, an essential key to the resurrection or annihilation of Maggie and Brick's relationship. Like a silent character, the bed serves as the crucible or hard trial that both characters must endure alone but together.

Like much of his work, *Cat on a Hot Tin Roof* is character-centered. Setting specific issues before us and watching them explode through sharp verbal confrontation, these stage characters hold the clues to their inner anxieties in clenched fists. All the Pollitts participate in the conflict, of course, but the leading contenders are Maggie, Big Daddy, and Brick, whose often unsympathetic but powerful portraits are never diminished by whatever truths or denials cross their lips. Whether we like them or not, we are compelled to listen and let ourselves be drawn into their pain.

Conveying a healthy and vibrant sexuality that is established early in the action, Maggie introduces the issues of the play with bold remarks and feisty humor. They affect her directly and place her strategically at the center where she carefully observes the machinations of characters around her. She is further identified with the loneliness and desire of the eponymous cat in heat who would rather stay on her hot tin roof as long as she has to than jump off and "land on [her] four feet uninjured." In this respect, Maggie's sexual *persona* is marked by an ambiguity of tone and purpose that initially distract us from the moral underpinnings of the play, but ultimately lure us to its core.

Maggie shares a special wavelength with Big Daddy, a dying man who cherishes life in much the same way she does. Trying to get Brick's attention, she teases him with the news that his father "harbors a little unconscious 'lech' "for her. The freewheeling design of her one-sided conversation with Brick infuses act 1 with colorful speech rhythms and biting sarcasm, all of which set the stage for Big Daddy's entrance. But Williams never underplays Maggie's emotional connection to subsequent actions and never lets her or her concerns fall from our sight. When Brick wonders how she expects "to have a child by a man that can't stand you," her response—"That's a problem that I will have to work out"—functions like a survival mechanism, revealing her determination to hold on tightly and to secure a comfortable future for herself.

Big Daddy and Brick occupy front and center stage during act 2, where the powerful lesson passed from father to son—that Brick's "disgust with mendacity" is disgust with himself—nurtures the play's two regenerative themes: the need to live a life unblemished by lies and the redemptive power of love. The first is eloquently and ironically represented by the dying man who, immensely relieved by a false medical diagnosis, boasts to Brick that he has "just now returned from the other side of the moon, death's country, son, and I'm not easy to shock by anything here." Shifting effortlessly between his role as confessor to a helpless son and role as *raisonneur* to the issues at large, Big Daddy achieves, in Williams' own words, a crude eloquence like "no other character of my creation."[3]

The second equally urgent theme prompts several important disclosures during the action, not the least of which is the playwright's plea for tolerating the different faces of human love. "One thing you can grow on a big place more important than cotton!—is *tolerance!*—I grown it," exclaims Big Daddy to Brick. He has told him the story of two homosexual lovers, Jack Straw and Peter Ochello, whose mutual devotion and hard work helped build the plantation that eventually became Big Daddy's and who occupied—until their deaths—the same room belonging to Brick and Maggie. In a less than subtle way, this story feeds into Brick's present torment, although it is meant to enlighten his course of moral action. But when Big Daddy accuses Brick of digging the grave of his friend Skipper and kicking him in it "before you'd face truth with him," the words are more than Brick can bear.

Brick is one of the playwright's most enigmatic creations. Walking with a crutch that is symbolic of deeper spiritual and psychological wounds, he is one of those "weak, beautiful people!—who give up," which is how Maggie describes him in the closing lines of the play when she offers to take hold of him "gently, with love!" But as she "turns out the rose-silk lamp [and] the curtain begins to fall slowly," there is some implication—for those who want to see it happen—that she and Brick are "going to make the lie [of her pregnancy] true," that some glimmer of love has redeemed their marriage.

No matter what is spelled out or implied in the action, Williams has expressed that "the moral paralysis of Brick was a root thing in his tragedy" and that the confrontation with Big Daddy could not affect "so immediate a change in the heart or even conduct of a person in Brick's state of spiritual disrepair."[4] There is strong insistence that the original third act, published here, is true to the playwright's intentions whether or not the characters are transformed. Perhaps this very absence of resolution gives the play its indelible power.

CAT ON A HOT TIN ROOF-IN-PERFORMANCE

A curious aspect of Tennessee Williams' dramatic art is that so much of it has been dynamically rewritten over the course of a long and productive career. Williams not only incorporated elements of his non-dramatic works into his plays, including characters, incidents, and themes, but often revised the original version after a professional production of the play failed to live up to his own critical expectations. Since his work attracted artists and producers who were quite willing to support these altered enterprises, although this was not always so in later years, Williams continued to experiment, even when the need to revise was prompted by personal or professional insecurity rather than by the need to perfect his craft.

Cat on a Hot Tin Roof has reflected its share of literary transformations. When the play opened at the Morosco Theatre in New York on March 24, 1955, with Barbara Bel Geddes (Maggie), Ben Gazzara (Brick), Burl Ives (Big Daddy), Mildred Dunnock (Big Mama), Pat Hingle (Gooper), and Madeleine Sherwood (Sister Woman), audiences never suspected that its entire third act was a revision of the one Williams originally wrote. Having serious reservations with textual choices initially made by the playwright, director Elia Kazan insisted that Big Daddy "was too vivid and important a character to disappear from the play" after the second act; that Brick "should undergo some apparent mutation" after his second-act confrontation with Big Daddy; and that Maggie needed to be "more clearly sympathetic" to the audience.[5]

Not wanting to lose Kazan's directorial support, for their productive collaboration had become one of the American theatre's most cherished assets, Williams wrote a new third act "that resulted from [Kazan's] creative influence on the play."[6] The positive critical reception chalked up a total of 694 performances in its original New York run. While commercial success more than justified Williams' decision to listen to his director, it never prevented him from wondering if "*Cat* number one would have done just as well."[7] The playwright revised the ending yet again when the play was produced by the American Shakespeare Festival in Stratford, Connecticut, in 1974 with Elizabeth Ashley in the role of Maggie under Michael Kahn's direction.

Not surprisingly, subsequent productions of the play in America and throughout the world have shown a distinct preference for the original third act. Peter Hall insisted on using it when he directed the play in its London premiere on January 30, 1958, at the Comedy Theatre. American actress Kim Stanley played Maggie, with Paul Massie as Brick and Leo McKern as Big Daddy. The performance was conducted under private club conditions when the play failed to meet censorship standards.

A major revival of the work took place thirty years later in London, but this time under very different conditions. Lindsay Duncan (Maggie), Ian Charleson (Brick), and Eric Porter (Big Daddy) stepped upon the Lyttleton stage of the National Theatre on February 3, 1988, under Howard Davies' direction, in what proved to be one of London's most critically successful productions of a Tennessee Williams play. Like Peter Hall, Davies opted for the original text. The acclaim prompted American producers to invite Davies to New York, where he would direct an American cast. His success was repeated when the play opened in March 1990 with Kathleen Turner as Maggie, Daniel Hugh Kelly as Brick, and Charles Durning as Big Daddy.

Unlike other Williams plays that have not had difficulty reaching worldwide audiences once their New York premieres took place, *Cat on a Hot Tin Roof* has experienced a somewhat bumpy journey to international stages. This has been attributed to its controversial ingredients. While the 1961 production of *Orpheus Descending* was the first play by Williams to be staged in Russia, *Cat on a Hot Tin Roof* did not play there until 1982, when Goncharov directed it at the Mayakovsky Theatre in Moscow. Artist Mark Ketaev designed a round pavilion-like stage surrounded by transparent walls, responding to the play's poetic dimensions. In spite of the play's late arrival to Russia, Williams has remained one of the most frequently staged Western playwrights. His themes have been interpreted as a denunciation of the capitalist system, and his characters, often doomed to psychological isolation, recall Chekhov and Dostoevsky.

That the play has reared its head in some of the most unexpected corners of the world further points to its enduring popularity and universality. One of the first non-English-speaking productions to be staged outside of the United States took place at the Kanssal-isteatterin in Helsinki in 1956. Then in 1967, in a Hungary less restricted after the Revolution, the play was staged at the National Theatre of Budapest. When it was revived there in 1985 under Miklos Szurdi's direction, the production drew negative reactions from the press who criticized Williams for being too lenient on American capitalism and not judgmental enough of the society around him. An outspoken ''Big Daddy'' and a vulgar ''Big Mama'' retained their nomenclatures, suggesting that there were no adequate substitutions for these difficult American stereotypes. Attila Csikos' naturalistic stage set brought the right touch of credibility to the recurring patterns of hysteria and tranquility shared by the four principals. The translation, which belonged to Geyza Banya and had been used in the 1967 production as well, followed the third-act version inspired by Kazan.

The work was staged as *Cat on a Hot [Iron] Roof* by the Shanghai University Drama Institute in 1987, which appears to have been the first professional production of this play in Communist China. It was performed in Pretoria, South Africa, in 1988 under the Afrikaans title *Katvoet Oor Die Kole* and has recently surfaced in Spain as *La Gata Sobre el Tejado de Zinc Caliente*.

The play has generated several American television versions, both highly edited, in 1976 and 1985 respectively. The Hollywood treatment premiered at Radio Music Hall on September 19, 1958, and proved to be one of the most successful screen adaptations of a Williams play. Heavily revised for popular audience consumption, it offered Elizabeth Taylor and Paul Newman two memorable film roles. But more important, it preserved the essence of Burl Ives' stage performance.

REFLECTIONS ON CAT ON A HOT TIN ROOF

Madeleine Sherwood originated the role of Mae, Sister Woman, in Cat on a Hot Tin Roof.

The first time I connected with Tennessee Williams' play was through the usual channels. I don't know how they do it today, but in those days it was auditioning. I lived in New York and I hadn't done terribly much. I played Abigail in *The Crucible* and once again was struggling to find another acting job. I went to see Elia Kazan who was directing "Cat" and I auditioned for him. He said he liked me, but that Tennessee had to approve of everybody. So he gave me an appointment for a second audition. This time, Kazan was inside his office with Tennessee and I stood outside shivering and shaking. He came up to me and said, "Oh, hello! It's Madeleine, isn't it?" And I said yes. Then he said, "If you can make Tennessee laugh, you're in." This was a great way to set up the audition, because I was simply terrified.

I walked in and noticed this little leprechaun with his cigarette holder. He seemed very shy. I was introduced to him and he slunk down in his chair and waved a little bit and that was all. Then I thought, how am I going to make this man laugh? But I did make him laugh and I got the job. The really funny part is that some time afterwards, Tennessee was sitting in the Green Room when we were actually doing the play. He was laughing so hard. I said something to him about his laughter and Kazan said, "Oh, Tennessee laughs at everything. He's the easiest person in the world to make laugh." It seemed kind of funny after what Kazan had said to me at the audition.

It was a wonderful experience to play Mae, Sister Woman. I have always loved that role. Most people who have seen the play or the movie, which I also did, will say to me, "Oh, I just *hated* you in that role." And that's supposed to be a compliment. So I say, "Thank you very much." What else can I say? However, I have always felt that if you examine the play very carefully, you see that Mae and Gooper indeed are doing everything they're supposed to do. They're having babies. He's running the business. He's the lawyer. The other two, you know, are layabouts. Brick's a drunk and concerned about his sexuality and, in those days, of course, nobody was able to be honest about it. We weren't allowed to mention anything about his problem. We weren't even allowed to say the word *cancer*. It was almost like a dirty word.

The golden couple, Maggie and Brick, were thought to be the hero and heroine, of course. But all actors, I guess, have the feeling that we must turn our character—the role we're playing—into the hero. Even if the audience doesn't perceive us as such, we still try to make the play about *us,* about ourselves. And that's what I proceeded to do. I think it's one of the reasons why my performance was as strong as it was, because I believed whole-heartedly in the goodness of Mae. And I still do. I think that she was doing what she was supposed to do.

I'll admit she was a climber. But you can't say that Maggie wasn't a climber. Very definitely a climber, you know? I believe that Tennessee had all of these people of that era very definitely tagged. He writes about these people so beautifully. I had never been South at that time, and yet I felt as though I knew them intimately as I worked on the play. I know that Kazan must have felt the same way, that he knew southerners, white southerners upside down. I don't know whether he's changed his mind or not, because I don't think any of us know a place or people unless we are living there, indigenous to it or living there, at least for a time.

Tennessee and Kazan used to confer very softly as they sat in the orchestra seats during rehearsals. Kazan also talked to the actors very individually. His arm would go around your shoulder, and he'd walk you away and have this nice little conversation where he would be saying something about the weather or your mother or your boyfriend. Then all of a sudden he would interject something to the effect, "I don't think Sister Woman's really ready to give in yet." From that you would infer that you were coming on too strong or not strong enough or whatever. Occasionally Kazan pulled Pat Hingle and me aside together and talked to us, because we were husband and wife. But every once in a while, I would see him taking Pat away and I'd think to myself, Mmmm, he's going to give him something that I'm going to feel. Of course, the whole thrust of acting is the surprise element, you know, the mystery of what my partner is going to do next and how I'm going to react.

Above all, Kazan had the ability to make you trust him completely. He gave you the feeling that you were the only person that mattered. He was in charge, but he never took advantage of that or showed it. He was like a guardian angel. He was going to take care of you, no matter what happened. He was going to take care of you against all those expectant people in the audience who might not laugh or cry. But he was going to make you feel good when you needed to feel good, and if he needed to scold, he would scold you gently. I mean, he was the opposite of someone like Jed Harris, who was the meanest man in the whole world when he directed *The Crucible,* my first Broadway play. Mr. Harris was an extremely talented man and *sadistic.*

Unlike a lot of playwrights, however, Tennessee never for a moment spoke to the actors. He spoke to us at parties as we drank together. But even then, he never said a word about his play. Not one word. He never talked to us about our interpretation. Of course, this was an ironclad rule in the theatre. I know it isn't now, because I've been in enough plays to know that it doesn't always turn out that way. But most certainly it was then. As for laughter, he sat in that audience every single rehearsal, morning, noon, and night, in and out of town, and laughed at things that nobody else laughed at. You always knew where he was sitting because you'd hear him laughing. He just loved his plays, but he would also say afterwards, "I don't understand why they don't laugh on that line. I think it's funny." He was a very, very convivial human being. He loved to be around people. Genuinely loved to be around us during rehearsals.

Tennessee was always honing his "Cat." He was always rewriting. I know that he and Kazan had tremendous battles because Kazan was unhappy about the ending. The controversy of the third act surfaced a little bit as we were rehearsing, but not a whole lot. Because that was their privacy which they kept between them. Along with that was Tennessee's reluctance to open up any controversy in front of actors. I remember that we had a lot of changes, and my original script is in an absolutely horrendous state. The pages are dog-eared and I've lost the covers. But there was no replacement of one act with another. The third act just went through its changes. I realized afterwards that "Cat" had fewer

Continued

problems than a lot of other plays I've been involved with since then. I think this was partly due to superb writing on Tennessee's part to start with and partly due to superb directing. Tennessee and Kazan were very well mated. They really understood each other. They were so different in personality and life-styles and everything else. But they matched each other when it came to the profession and when it actually came to working together.

You could see the results on stage, especially in the casting of Burl Ives as Big Daddy. Burl was a country music person who had never done much straight acting. Kazan was responsible for the excitement of the second act in that long confrontation between Brick and Big Daddy. You see, there was no way you could get Burl to look directly *at* you. He looked over there, or up there, or down there, but he never looked *at* you. That drove Ben Gazzara nuts, of course, because Ben was trained at the Actors Studio. If you go back to certain production photos, you notice that Kazan worked with a thrust stage. He had a couple of front rows removed from the Morosco Theatre so that Jo Mielziner could construct this triangular point. Kazan finally placed Brick on one side and Big Daddy on the other, blocking them as far down as they could go, with the point always left empty. Their scene was played like a tennis match with an invisible net stretched across the stage.

Both actors delivered their lines dead front, like a vaudeville routine and, every once in a while, Kazan would have them turn, you know, on a confrontational note. But then they would turn right back out again, so that you really had no time to notice that they weren't looking at each other. So Gazzara had no time to get upset. It made for a very dramatic piece of staging and ended up creating more of a sense of confrontation than anything else could have, including a flat proscenium stage. That's how their great scene came to be directed.

The script for *Cat on a Hot Tin Roof* changed radically in the movie version, however. It's amazing how well it stands up as a film. It was directed by Richard Brooks, of course, because of Kazan's trouble with the House of Un-American Activities at that time. George Cukor was supposed to direct it. I sent him a telegram telling him I had played it on the stage and, if he had seen me, then he should know I was perfect to play Mae in the film. I was very daring at that time. He telephoned me from Hollywood and asked me why I thought I was so right for the role. I told him that I played it for two years on Broadway and that I'd never heard anybody say anything except that I was wonderful. He said he agreed with that and that he had seen me on Broadway. Then he told me he'd think about it, and so that was that. The next thing I know, he's not directing it. So I called up Richard Brooks, told him my name, and he said, "Oh, yeah! George told me about you." And I got the role! Sometimes you have to do the most amazing things to get cast. Sometimes it works and sometimes it doesn't.

I was very excited again, because it was such a good movie role. And the people in it were wonderful. Burl Ives and I were the only two from the original. Richard Brooks knew how to handle Burl very well. Kazan started it with Big Daddy and I'm sure Richard took his cue from that. The movie was cut very differently. There was much more movement in it, and the characters went down into the basement and so on and so forth. But I still feel as though Richard was aware of Paul Newman's need to make eye contact with Burl, much like Ben Gazzara's need on the stage. For myself, Brooks let me give the interpretation that I'd given on Broadway. The only thing he told me was that I didn't need as much volume as all that. I suppose I was so geared up, having played it for two years and then filming it almost immediately afterwards.

The powerful themes Tennessee dealt with continue to be written for the stage today, except that they happen differently. I think we respond to any author who writes about communication, no matter how he or she approaches it. I think Tennessee was well aware of how difficult it is to bring people together, to communicate on any level. Brick communicates with liquor for much of this play. Maggie longs to communicate with Brick. Even Big Mama has had her good times with Big Daddy. She says she loves him, he says he can't stand her, but I think that's another way in which people communicate. He certainly knows damn well that she takes good care of him. I think one of the most wrenching scenes in the play involved Big Mama and myself and Gooper and Maggie and Brick, when we try to get Big Mama to sign everything away. It became really hard to play that scene night after night, mostly because of this communication barrier and what couldn't be put into words.

Gooper and Mae communicate with each other, but whether you like them or you don't like them, they're a team. They're a couple. In some ways, they communicate better than the other characters in the play. I personally believe that communication is the absolute essential for all of us, and that each of us finds a different way to communicate. But the hardest thing is to communicate rawly, one on one. One against, well, not against, but one next to the other, only to communicate. That's the hardest.

Instead we camouflage in all sorts of ways. Tennessee dealt with this magnificently. He was a poet. We have his poems, his short stories, his autobiography. We have all these other works besides his plays that give us awareness of how truly human he was. He loved men. He loved women. He loved children. He adored dogs. Above all, unlike many playwrights, he loved *actors!* And possibly Mae and Gooper are people he would have respected or loved. He certainly understood them—their crassness, their loyalty—whatever. And there is wonderful comedy in their characters, too, which is why I was supposed to make Tennessee laugh at my audition. And I did make him laugh, you know?

Notes

1. *Tennessee Williams,* MEMOIRS *(New York: Doubleday, 1975), 135.*
2. *Ibid., 168.*
3. *Ibid.*
4. *Tennessee Williams,* CAT ON A HOT TIN ROOF *(New York: New American Library, 1985), 125.*
5. *Ibid., 124–125.*
6. *Ibid., 125.*
7. *Ibid.*

CAT ON A HOT TIN ROOF
Tennessee Williams

CHARACTERS

Margaret

Brick

Mae, *sometimes called* Sister Woman

Big Mama

Dixie, *a little girl*

Big Daddy

Reverend Tooker

Gooper, *sometimes called* Brother Man

Doctor Baugh, *pronounced "Baw"*

Lacey, *a Negro servant*

Sookey, *another*

Another little girl and two small boys

(The playing script of Act III also includes Trixie, another little girl, also Daisy, Brightie, and Small, servants.)

NOTES FOR THE DESIGNER

The set is the bed-sitting-room of a plantation home in the Mississippi Delta. It is along an upstairs gallery which probably runs around the entire house; it has two pairs of very wide doors opening onto the gallery; showing white balustrades against a fair summer sky that fades into dusk and night during the course of the play, which occupies precisely the time of its performance, excepting, of course, the fifteen minutes of intermission.

Perhaps the style of the room is not what you would expect in the home of the Delta's biggest cotton-planter. It is Victorian with a touch of the Far East. It hasn't changed much since it was occupied by the original owners of the place, Jack Straw and Peter Ochello, a pair of old bachelors who shared this room all their lives together. In other words, the room must evoke some ghosts; it is gently and poetically haunted by a relationship that must have involved a tenderness which was uncommon. This may be irrelevant or unnecessary, but I once saw a reproduction of a faded photograph of the verandah of Robert Louis Stevenson's home on that Samoan Island where he spent his last years, and there was a quality of tender light on weathered wood, such as porch furniture made of bamboo and wicker, exposed to tropical suns and tropical rains, which came to mind when I thought about the set for this play, bringing also to mind the grace and comfort of light, the reassurance it gives, on a late and fair afternoon in summer, the way that no matter what, even dread of death, is gently touched and soothed by it. For the set is the background for a play that deals with human extremities of emotion, and it needs that softness behind it.

The bathroom door, showing only pale-blue tile and silver towel racks, is in one side wall; the hall door in the opposite wall. Two articles of furniture need mention: a big double bed which staging should make a functional part of the set as often as suitable, the surface of which should be slightly raked to make figures on it seen more easily; and against the wall space between the two huge double doors upstage: a monumental monstrosity peculiar to our times, a *huge* console combination of radio-phonograph (Hi-Fi with three speakers) TV set *and* liquor cabinet, bearing and containing many glasses and bottles, all in one piece, which is a composition of muted silver tones, and the opalescent tones of reflecting glass, a chromatic link, this thing, between the sepia (tawny gold) tones of the interior and the cool (white and blue) tones of the gallery and sky. This piece of furniture (?!), this monument, is a very complete and compact little shrine to virtually all the comforts and illusions behind which we hide from such things as the characters of the play are faced with. . . . The set should be far less realistic than I have so far implied in this description of it. I think the walls below the ceiling should dissolve mysteriously into air; the set should be roofed by the sky; stars and moon suggested by traces of milky pallor, as if they were observed through a telescope lens out of focus.

Anything else I can think of? Oh, yes, fanlights (transoms shaped like an open glass fan) above all the doors in the set, with panes of blue and amber, and above all, the designer should take as many pains to give the actors room to move about freely (to show their restlessness, their passion for breaking out) as if it were a set for a ballet.

An evening in summer. The action is continuous, with two intermissions.

ACT ONE

At the rise of the curtain someone is taking a shower in the bathroom, the door of which is half open. A pretty young woman, with anxious lines in her face, enters the bedroom and crosses to the bathroom door.

MARGARET (*shouting above roar of water*). One of those no-neck monsters hit me with a hot buttered biscuit so I have t' change! (*Margaret's voice is both rapid and drawling. In her long speeches she has the vocal tricks of a priest delivering a liturgical chant, the lines are almost sung, always continuing a little beyond her breath so she has to gasp for another. Sometimes she intersperses the lines with a little wordless singing, such as ''Da-da-daaaa!''*)

(*Water turns off and Brick calls out to her, but is still unseen. A tone of politely feigned interest, masking indifference, or worse, is characteristic of his speech with Margaret.*)

BRICK.   Wha'd you say, Maggie? Water was on s' loud I couldn't hearya. . . .
MARGARET.   Well, I!—just remarked that!—one of th' no-neck monsters messed up m' lovely lace dress so I got t'—cha-a-ange. . . . (*She opens and kicks shut drawers of the dresser.*)
BRICK.   Why d'ya call Gooper's kiddies no-neck monsters?
MARGARET.   Because they've got no necks! Isn't that a good enough reason?
BRICK.   Don't they have any necks?

MARGARET.   None visible. Their fat little heads are set on their fat little bodies without a bit of connection.
BRICK.   That's too bad.
MARGARET.   Yes, it's too bad because you can't wring their necks if they've got no necks to wring! Isn't that right, honey? (*She steps out of her dress, stands in a slip of ivory satin and lace.*) Yep, they're no-neck monsters, all no-neck people are monsters . . . (*Children shriek downstairs.*) Hear them? Hear them screaming? I don't know where their voice-boxes are located since they don't have necks. I tell you I got so nervous at that table tonight I thought I would throw back my head and utter a scream you could hear across the Arkansas border an' parts of Louisiana an' Tennessee. I said to your charming sister-in-law, Mae, honey, couldn't you feed those precious little things at a separate table with an oilcloth cover? They make such a mess an' the lace cloth looks *so* pretty! She made enormous eyes at me and said, ''Ohhh, noooooo! On Big Daddy's birthday? Why, he would never forgive me!'' Well, I want you to know, Big Daddy hadn't been at the table two minutes with those five no-neck monsters slobbering and drooling over their food before he threw down his fork an' shouted, ''Fo' God's sake, Gooper, why don't you put them pigs at a trough in th' kitchen?''—Well, I swear, I simply could have di-ieed!
Think of it, Brick, they've got five of them and number six is coming. They've brought the whole bunch down here like animals to display at a county fair. Why, they have those children doin' tricks all the time! ''Junior,

show Big Daddy how you do this, show Big Daddy how you do that, say your little piece fo' Big Daddy, Sister. Show your dimples, Sugar. Brother, show Big Daddy how you stand on your head!''—It goes on all the time, along with constant little remarks and innuendos about the fact that you and I have not produced any children, are totally childless and therefore totally useless!—Of course it's comical but it's also disgusting since it's so obvious what they're up to!

BRICK (*without interest*). What are they up to, Maggie?

MARGARET.   Why, you know what they're up to!

BRICK (*appearing*). No, I don't know what they're up to.

(*He stands there in the bathroom doorway drying his hair with a towel and hanging onto the towel rack because one ankle is broken, plastered and bound. He is still slim and firm as a boy. His liquor hasn't started tearing him down outside. He has the additional charm of that cool air of detachment that people have who have given up the struggle. But now and then, when disturbed, something flashes behind it, like lightning in a fair sky, which shows that at some deeper level he is far from peaceful. Perhaps in a stronger light he would show some signs of deliquescence, but the fading, still warm, light from the gallery treats him gently.*)

MARGARET.   I'll tell you what they're up to, boy of mine!—They're up to cutting you out of your father's estate, and— (*She freezes momentarily before her next remark. Her voice drops as if it were somehow a personally embarrassing admission.*) —Now we know that Big Daddy's dyin' of —cancer. . . . (*There are voices on the lawn below: long-drawn calls across distance. Margaret raises her lovely bare arms and powders her armpits with a light sigh.*) (*She adjusts the angle of a magnifying mirror to straighten an eyelash, then rises fretfully saying:*) There's so much light in the room it—

BRICK (*softly but sharply*). Do we?

MARGARET.   Do we what?

BRICK.   Know Big Daddy's dyin' of cancer?

MARGARET.   Got the report today.

BRICK.   Oh . . .

MARGARET (*letting down bamboo blinds which cast long, gold-fretted shadows over the room*). Yep, got th' report just now . . . it didn't surprise me, Baby. . . . (*Her voice has range, and music; sometimes it drops low as a boy's and you have a sudden image of her playing boys' games as a child.*) I recognized the symptoms soon's we got here last spring and I'm willin' to bet you that Brother Man and his wife were pretty sure of it, too. That more than likely explains why their usual summer migration to the coolness of the Great Smokies was passed up this summer in favor of—hustlin' down here ev'ry whipstitch with their whole screamin' tribe! And why so many allusions have been made to Rainbow Hill lately. You know what Rainbow Hill is? Place that's famous for treatin' alcoholics an' dope fiends in the movies!

BRICK.   I'm not in the movies.

MARGARET.   No, and you don't take dope. Otherwise you're a perfect candidate for Rainbow Hill, Baby, and that's where they aim to ship you—over my dead body! Yep, over my dead body they'll ship you there, but nothing would please them better. Then Brother Man could get a-hold of the purse strings and dole out remittances to us, maybe get power-of-attorney and sign checks for us and cut off our credit wherever, whenever he wanted! Son-of-a-bitch!—How'd you like that, Baby?— Well, you've been doin' just about ev'rything in your power to bring it about, you've just been doin' ev'rything you can think of to aid and abet them in this scheme of theirs! Quittin' work, devoting yourself to the occupation of drinkin'!—Breakin' your ankle last night on the high school athletic field: doin' what? Jumpin' hurdles? At two or three in the morning? Just fantastic! Got in the paper. *Clarksdale Register* carried a nice little item about it, human interest story about a well-known former athlete stagin' a one-man track meet on the Glorious Hill High School athletic field last night, but was slightly out of condition and didn't clear the first hurdle! Brother Man Gooper claims he exercised his influence t' keep it from goin' out over AP or UP or every goddam ''P.'' But, Brick? You still have one big advantage!

(*During the above swift flood of words, Brick has reclined with contrapuntal leisure on the snowy surface of the bed and has rolled over carefully on his side or belly.*)

BRICK (*wryly*). Did you *say* something, Maggie?

MARGARET.   Big Daddy dotes on you, honey. And he can't stand Brother Man and Brother Man's wife, that monster of fertility, Mae; she's downright odious to him! Know how I know? By little expressions that flicker over his face when that woman is holding fo'th on one of her choice topics such as—how she refused twilight sleep!— when the twins were delivered! Because she feels motherhood's an experience that a woman ought to experience fully!—in order to fully appreciate the wonder and beauty of it! HAH! (*This loud ''HAH'' is accompanied by a violent action such as slamming a drawer shut.*) —and how she made Brother Man come in an' stand beside her in the delivery room so he would not miss out on the ''wonder and beauty'' of it either!—producin' those no-neck monsters. . . . (*A speech of this kind would be antipathetic from almost anybody but Margaret; she makes it oddly funny, because her eyes constantly twinkle and her voice shakes with laughter which is basically indulgent.*) —Big Daddy shares my attitude toward those two! As for me, well—I give him a laugh now and then and he tolerates me. In fact!—I sometimes suspect that Big Daddy harbors a little unconscious ''lech'' fo' me. . . .

BRICK.   What makes you think that Big Daddy has a lech for you, Maggie?

MARGARET.   Way he always drops his eyes down my body when I'm talkin' to him, drops his eyes to my boobs an' licks his old chops! Ha ha!

BRICK.   That kind of talk is disgusting.

MARGARET.   Did anyone ever tell you that you're an ass-aching Puritan, Brick?

I think it's mighty fine that that ole fellow, on the doorstep of death, still takes in my shape with what I think is deserved appreciation!

And you wanta know something else? Big Daddy didn't know how many little Maes and Goopers had been produced! "How many kids have you got?" he asked at the table, just like Brother Man and his wife were new acquaintances to him! Big Mama said he was jokin', but that ole boy wasn't jokin', Lord, no!

And when they infawmed him that they had five already and were turning out number six!—the news seemed to come as a sort of unpleasant surprise . . . (*Children yell below.*) Scream, monsters! (*Turns to Brick with a sudden, gay, charming smile which fades as she notices that he is not looking at her but into fading gold space with a troubled expression.*) (*It is constant rejection that makes her humor "bitchy."*) Yes, you should of been at that supper-table, Baby. (*Whenever she calls him "baby" the word is a soft caress.*) Y'know, Big Daddy, bless his ole sweet soul, he's the dearest ole thing in the world, but he does hunch over his food as if he preferred not to notice anything else. Well, Mae an' Gooper were side by side at the table, direckly across from Big Daddy, watchin' his face like hawks while they jawed an' jabbered about the cuteness an' brilliance of th' no-neck monsters! (*She giggles with a hand fluttering at her throat and her breast and her long throat arched.*)

(*She comes downstage and recreates the scene with voice and gesture.*)

And the no-neck monsters were ranged around the table, some in high chairs and some on th' *Books of Knowledge,* all in fancy little paper caps in honor of Big Daddy's birthday, and all through dinner, well, I want you to know that Brother Man an' his partner never once, for one moment, stopped exchanging pokes an' pinches an' kicks an' signs an' signals!—Why, they were like a couple of cardsharps fleecing a sucker.—Even Big Mama, bless her ole sweet soul, she isn't th' quickest an' brightest thing in the world, she finally noticed, at last, an' said to Gooper, "Gooper, what are you an' Mae makin' all these signs at each other about?"—I swear t' goodness, I nearly choked on my chicken!

(*Margaret, back at the dressing-table, still doesn't see Brick. He is watching her with a look that is not quite definable.— Amused? shocked? contemptuous?—part of those and part of something else.*)

Y'know—your brother Gooper still cherishes the illusion he took a giant step up on the social ladder when he married Miss Mae Flynn of the Memphis Flynns. (*Margaret moves about the room as she talks, stops before the mirror, moves on.*) But I have a piece of Spanish news for Gooper. The Flynns never had a thing in this world but money and they lost that, they were nothing at all but fairly successful climbers. Of course, Mae Flynn came out in Memphis eight years before I made my debut in Nashville, but I had friends at Ward-Belmont who came from Memphis and they used to come to see me and I used to go to see them for Christmas and spring vacations, and so I know who rates an' who doesn't rate in Memphis society. Why, y'know ole Papa Flynn, he barely escaped doing time in the Federal pen for shady manipulations on th' stock market when his chain stores crashed, and as for Mae having been a cotton carnival queen, as they remind us so often, lest we forget, well, that's one honor that I don't envy her for!—Sit on a brass throne on a tacky float an' ride down Main Street, smilin', bowin', and blowin' kisses to all the trash on the street— (*She picks out a pair of jeweled sandals and rushes to the dressing-table.*) Why, year before last, when Susan McPheeters was singled out fo' that honor, y'know what happened to her? Y'know what happened to poor little Susie McPheeters?

BRICK (*absently*). No. What happened to little Susie McPheeters?

MARGARET.   Somebody spit tobacco juice in her face.

BRICK (*dreamily*). Somebody spit tobacco juice in her face?

MARGARET.   That's right, some old drunk leaned out of a window in the Hotel Gayoso and yelled, "Hey, Queen, hey, hey, there, Queenie!" Poor Susie looked up and flashed him a radiant smile and he shot out a squirt of tobacco juice right in poor Susie's face.

BRICK.   Well, what d'you know about that.

MARGARET (*gaily*). What do I know about it? I was there, I saw it!

BRICK (*absently*). Must have been kind of funny.

MARGARET.   Susie didn't think so. Had hysterics. Screamed like a banshee. They had to stop th' parade an' remove her from her throne an' go on with— (*She catches sight of him in the mirror, gasps slightly, wheels about to face him. Count ten.*) —Why are you looking at me like that?

BRICK (*whistling softly, now*). Like what, Maggie?

MARGARET (*intensely, fearfully*). The way y' were lookin' at me just now, befo' I caught your eye in the mirror and you started t' whistle! I don't know how t' describe it but it froze my blood!—I've caught you lookin' at me like that so often lately. What are you thinkin' of when you look at me like that?

BRICK.   I wasn't conscious of lookin' at you, Maggie.

MARGARET.   Well, I was conscious of it! What were you thinkin'?

BRICK.   I don't remember thinking of anything, Maggie.

MARGARET.   Don't you think I know that—? Don't you—?—Think I know that—?

BRICK (*coolly*). Know *what*, Maggie?

MARGARET (*struggling for expression*). That I've gone through this—*hideous!*—transformation, become—*hard! Frantic!* (*Then she adds, almost tenderly.*) —*cruel!!*

That's what you've been observing in me lately. How could y' help but observe it? That's all right. I'm not—thin-skinned any more, can't afford t' be thin-skinned any more. (*She is now recovering her power.*) —But Brick? Brick?

BRICK.   Did you say something?

MARGARET.   I was *goin'* t' say something: that I get—lonely. Very!

BRICK.   Ev'rybody gets that . . .

MARGARET.   Living with someone you love can be lonelier—than living entirely *alone!*—if the one that y' love doesn't love you. . . .

(*There is a pause. Brick hobbles downstage and asks, without looking at her:*)

BRICK.   Would you like to live alone, Maggie? (*Another pause: then—after she has caught a quick, hurt breath:*)

MARGARET.   *No!—God!—I wouldn't!* (*Another gasping breath. She forcibly controls what must have been an impulse to cry out. We see her deliberately, very forcibly, going all the way back to the world in which you can talk about ordinary matters.*) Did you have a nice shower?

BRICK.   Uh-huh.

MARGARET.   Was the water cool?

BRICK.   No.

MARGARET.   But it made y' feel fresh, huh?

BRICK.   Fresher. . . .

MARGARET.   I know something would make y' feel *much* fresher!

BRICK.   What?

MARGARET.   An alcohol rub. Or cologne, a rub with cologne!

BRICK.   That's good after a workout but I haven't been workin' out, Maggie.

MARGARET.   You've kept in good shape, though.

BRICK (*indifferently*). You think so, Maggie?

MARGARET.   I always thought drinkin' men lost their looks, but I was plainly mistaken.

BRICK (*wryly*). Why, thanks, Maggie.

MARGARET.   You're the only drinkin' man I know that it never seems t' put fat on.

BRICK.   I'm gettin' softer, Maggie.

MARGARET.   Well, sooner or later it's bound to soften you up. It was just beginning to soften up Skipper when—(*She stops short.*) I'm sorry. I never could keep my fingers off a sore—I wish you *would* lose your looks. If you did it would make the martyrdom of Saint Maggie a little more bearable. But no such goddam luck. I actually believe you've gotten better looking since you've gone on the bottle. Yeah, a person who didn't know you would think you'd never had a tense nerve in your body or a strained muscle. (*There are sounds of croquet on the lawn below: the click of mallets, light voices, near and distant.*) Of course, you always had that detached quality as if you were playing a game without much concern over whether you won or lost, and now that you've lost the game, not lost but just quit playing, you have that rare sort of charm that usually only happens in very old or hopelessly sick people, the charm of the defeated.—You look so cool, so cool, so enviably cool. (*Music is heard.*) They're playing croquet. The moon has appeared and it's white, just beginning to turn a little bit yellow. . . .

You were a wonderful lover. . . .

Such a wonderful person to go to bed with, and I think mostly because you were really indifferent to it. Isn't that right? Never had any anxiety about it, did it naturally, easily, slowly, with absolute confidence and perfect calm, more like opening a door for a lady or seating her at a table than giving expression to any longing for her. Your indifference made you wonderful at lovemaking—*strange?*—but true. . . .

You know, if I thought you would never, never, *never* make love to me again—I would go downstairs to the kitchen and pick out the longest and sharpest knife I could find and stick it straight into my heart, I swear that I would!

But one thing I don't have is the charm of the defeated, my hat is still in the ring, and I am determined to win! (*There is the sound of croquet mallets hitting croquet balls.*)

—What is the victory of a cat on a hot tin roof?—I wish I knew. . . .

Just staying on it, I guess, as long as she can. . . . (*More croquet sounds.*) Later tonight I'm going to tell you I love you an' maybe by that time you'll be drunk enough to believe me. Yes, they're playing croquet. . . .

Big Daddy is dying of cancer. . . .

What were you thinking of when I caught you looking at me like that? Were you thinking of Skipper?

(*Brick takes up his crutch, rises.*)

Oh, excuse me, forgive me, but laws of silence don't work! No, laws of silence don't work. . . .

(*Brick crosses to the bar, takes a quick drink, and rubs his head with a towel.*)

Laws of silence don't work. . . .

When something is festering in your memory or your imagination, laws of silence don't work, it's just like shutting a door and locking it on a house on fire in hope of forgetting that the house is burning. But not facing a fire doesn't put it out. Silence about a thing just magnifies it. It grows and festers in silence, becomes malignant. . . .

Get dressed, Brick.

(*He drops his crutch.*)

BRICK.   I've dropped my crutch.

(*He has stopped rubbing his hair dry but still stands hanging onto the towel rack in a white towel-cloth robe.*)

MARGARET.   Lean on me.
BRICK.   No, just give me my crutch.
MARGARET.   Lean on my shoulder.
BRICK.   *I don't want to lean on your shoulder, I want my crutch!* (*This is spoken like sudden lightning.*) Are you going to give me my crutch or do I have to get down on my knees on the floor and—
MARGARET.   *Here, here, take it, take it!* (*She has thrust the crutch at him.*)
BRICK (*hobbling out*). Thanks . . .
MARGARET.   We mustn't scream at each other, the walls in this house have ears. . . .

(*He hobbles directly to liquor cabinet to get a new drink.*)

—but that's the first time I've heard you raise your voice in a long time, Brick. A crack in the wall?—Of composure?

—I think that's a good sign. . . .

A sign of nerves in a player on the defensive!

(*Brick turns and smiles at her coolly over his fresh drink.*)

BRICK.   It just hasn't happened yet, Maggie.
MARGARET.   What?
BRICK.   The click I get in my head when I've had enough of this stuff to make me peaceful. . . .

Will you do me a favor?
MARGARET.   Maybe I will. What favor?
BRICK.   Just keep your voice down!
MARGARET (*in a hoarse whisper*). I'll do you that favor, I'll speak in a whisper, if not shut up completely, if *you* will do *me* a favor and make that drink your last one till after the party.
BRICK.   What party?
MARGARET.   Big Daddy's birthday party.
BRICK.   Is this Big Daddy's birthday?
MARGARET.   You know this is Big Daddy's birthday!
BRICK.   No, I don't, I forgot it.
MARGARET.   Well, I remembered it for you. . . .

(*They are both speaking as breathlessly as a pair of kids after a fight, drawing deep exhausted breaths and looking at each other with faraway eyes, shaking and panting together as if they had broken apart from a violent struggle.*)

BRICK.   Good for you, Maggie.
MARGARET.   You just have to scribble a few lines on this card.
BRICK.   You scribble something, Maggie.
MARGARET.   It's got to be your handwriting; it's your present, I've given him my present; it's got to be your handwriting!

(*The tension between them is building again, the voices becoming shrill once more.*)

BRICK.   I didn't get him a present.
MARGARET.   I got one for you.
BRICK.   All right. You write the card, then.
MARGARET.   And have him know you didn't remember his birthday?
BRICK.   I didn't remember his birthday.
MARGARET.   You don't have to prove you didn't!
BRICK.   I don't want to fool him about it.
MARGARET.   Just write "Love, Brick!" for God's—
BRICK.   No.
MARGARET.   You've *got* to!
BRICK.   I don't have to do anything I don't want to do. You keep forgetting the conditions on which I agreed to stay on living with you.
MARGARET (*out before she knows it*). I'm not living with you. We occupy the same cage.
BRICK.   You've got to remember the conditions agreed on.
MARGARET.   They're impossible conditions!
BRICK.   Then why don't you—?
MARGARET.   HUSH! Who is out there? Is somebody at the door?

(*There are footsteps in the hall.*)

MAE (*outside*). May I enter a moment?
MARGARET.   Oh, *you!* Sure. Come in, Mae.

(*Mae enters bearing aloft the bow of a young lady's archery set.*)

MAE.   Brick, is this thing yours?
MARGARET.   Why, Sister Woman—that's my Diana Trophy. Won it at the intercollegiate archery contest on the Ole Miss campus.
MAE.   It's a mighty dangerous thing to leave exposed round a house full of nawmal rid-blooded children attracted t'weapons.
MARGARET.   "Nawmal rid-blooded children attracted t'weapons" ought t'be taught to keep their hands off things that don't belong to them.
MAE.   Maggie, honey, if you had children of your own you'd know how funny that is. Will you please lock this up and put the key out of reach?
MARGARET.   Sister Woman, nobody is plotting the destruction of your kiddies. —Brick and I still have our special archers' license. We're goin' deer-huntin' on Moon Lake

as soon as the season starts. I love to run with dogs through chilly woods, run, run, leap over obstructions— (*She goes into the closet carrying the bow.*)

MAE.   How's the injured ankle, Brick?

BRICK.   Doesn't hurt. Just itches.

MAE.   Oh, my! Brick—Brick, you should've been downstairs after supper! Kiddies put on a show. Polly played the piano, Buster an' Sonny drums, an' then they turned out the lights an' Dixie an' Trixie puhfawmed a toe dance in fairy costume with *spahkluhs!* Big Daddy just beamed! He just beamed!

MARGARET (*from the closet with a sharp laugh*). Oh, I bet. It breaks my heart that we missed it! (*She reenters.*) But Mae? Why did y'give dawgs' names to all your kiddies?

MAE.   *Dogs'* names?

(*Margaret has made this observation as she goes to raise the bamboo blinds, since the sunset glare has diminished. In crossing she winks at Brick.*)

MARGARET (*sweetly*). Dixie, Trixie, Buster, Sonny, Polly!— Sounds like four dogs and a parrot . . . animal act in a circus!

MAE.   Maggie? (*Margaret turns with a smile.*) Why are you so catty?

MARGARET.   Cause I'm a cat! But why can't *you* take a joke, Sister Woman?

MAE.   Nothin' pleases me more than a joke that's funny. You know the real names of our kiddies. Buster's real name is Robert. Sonny's real name is Saunders. Trixie's real name is Marlene and Dixie's—(*Someone downstairs calls for her. "Hey, Mae!"—She rushes to door, saying:*) Intermission is over!

MARGARET (*as Mae closes door*). I wonder what Dixie's real name is?

BRICK.   Maggie, being catty doesn't help things any . . .

MARGARET.   I know! WHY!—Am I so catty?—Cause I'm consumed with envy an' eaten up with longing?—Brick, I've laid out your beautiful Shantung silk suit from Rome and one of your monogrammed silk shirts. I'll put your cuff-links in it, those lovely star sapphires I get you to wear so rarely. . . .

BRICK.   I can't get trousers on over this plaster cast.

MARGARET.   Yes, you can, I'll help you.

BRICK.   I'm not going to get dressed, Maggie.

MARGARET.   Will you just put on a pair of white silk pajamas?

BRICK.   Yes, I'll do that, Maggie.

MARGARET.   *Thank* you, thank you so *much!*

BRICK.   Don't mention it.

MARGARET.   *Oh, Brick!* How long does it have t' go on? This punishment? Haven't I done time enough, haven't I served my term, can't I apply for a—pardon?

BRICK.   Maggie, you're spoiling my liquor. Lately your voice always sounds like you'd been running upstairs to warn somebody that the house was on fire!

MARGARET.   Well, no wonder, no wonder. Y'know what I feel like, Brick?

(*Children's and grownups' voices are blended, below, in a loud but uncertain rendition of "My Wild Irish Rose."*)

I feel all the time like a cat on a hot tin roof!

BRICK.   Then jump off the roof, jump off it, cats can jump off roofs and land on their four feet uninjured!

MARGARET.   Oh, yes!

BRICK.   Do it—fo' God's sake, do it . . .

MARGARET.   Do what?

BRICK.   Take a lover!

MARGARET.   I can't see a man but you! Even with my eyes closed, I just see you! Why don't you get ugly, Brick, why don't you please get fat or ugly or something so I could stand it? (*She rushes over to hall door, opens it, listens.*) The concert is still going on! Bravo, no-necks, bravo! (*She slams and locks door fiercely.*)

BRICK.   What did you lock the door for?

MARGARET.   To give us a little privacy for a while.

BRICK.   You know better, Maggie.

MARGARET.   No, I don't know better. . . . (*She rushes to gallery doors, draws the rose-silk drapes across them.*)

BRICK.   Don't make a fool of yourself.

MARGARET.   I don't mind makin' a fool of myself over you!

BRICK.   I mind, Maggie. I feel embarrassed for you.

MARGARET.   Feel embarrassed! But don't continue my torture. I can't live on and on under these circumstances.

BRICK.   You agreed to—

MARGARET.   I know but—

BRICK.   —Accept that condition!

MARGARET.   *I CAN'T! CAN'T! CAN'T!* (*She seizes his shoulder.*)

BRICK.   Let go! (*He breaks away from her and seizes the small boudoir chair and raises it like a lion-tamer facing a big circus cat.*)

(*Count five. She stares at him with her fist pressed to her mouth, then bursts into shrill, almost hysterical laughter. He remains grave for a moment, then grins and puts the chair down.*)

(*Big Mama calls through closed door.*)

BIG MAMA.   Son? Son? Son?

BRICK.   What is it, Big Mama?

BIG MAMA (*outside*). Oh, son! We got the most wonderful news about Big Daddy. I just had t' run up an' tell you right this— (*She rattles the knob.*) —What's this door doin', locked, faw? You all think there's robbers in the house?

MARGARET.   Big Mama, Brick is dressin', he's not dressed yet.

BIG MAMA.   That's all right, it won't be the first time I've seen Brick not dressed. Come on, open this door!

(Margaret, with a grimace, goes to unlock and open the hall door, as Brick hobbles rapidly to the bathroom and kicks the door shut. Big Mama has disappeared from the hall.)

MARGARET.   Big Mama?

(Big Mama appears through the opposite gallery doors behind Margaret, huffing and puffing like an old bulldog. She is a short, stout woman; her sixty years and 170 pounds have left her somewhat breathless most of the time; she's always tensed like a boxer, or rather, a Japanese wrestler. Her "family" was maybe a little superior to Big Daddy's, but not much. She wears a black or silver lace dress and at least half a million in flashy gems. She is very sincere.)

BIG MAMA *(loudly, startling Margaret)*. Here—I come through Gooper's and Mae's gall'ry door. Where's Brick? Brick—Hurry on out of there, son, I just have a second and want to give you the news about Big Daddy.—I hate locked doors in a house. . . .

MARGARET *(with affected lightness)*. I've noticed you do, Big Mama, but people have got to have *some* moments of privacy, don't they?

BIG MAMA.   No, ma'am, not in *my* house. *(Without pause)* Whacha took off you' dress faw? I thought that little lace dress was so sweet on yuh, honey.

MARGARET.   I thought it looked sweet on me, too, but one of m' cute little table-partners used it for a napkin so—!

BIG MAMA *(picking up stockings on floor)*. What?

MARGARET.   You know, Big Mama, Mae and Gooper's so touchy about those children—thanks, Big Mama . . . *(Big Mama has thrust the picked-up stockings in Margaret's hand with a grunt.)* —that you just don't dare to suggest there's any room for improvement in their—

BIG MAMA.   Brick, hurry out!—Shoot, Maggie, you just don't like children.

MARGARET.   I do SO like children! Adore them!—well brought up!

BIG MAMA *(gentle—loving)*. Well, why don't you have some and bring them up well, then, instead of all the time pickin' on Gooper's an' Mae's?

GOOPER *(shouting up the stairs)*. Hey, hey, Big Mama, Betsy n' Hugh got to go, waitin' t' tell yuh g'by!

BIG MAMA.   Tell 'em to hold their hawses, I'll be right down in a jiffy! *(She turns to the bathroom door and calls out.)* Son? Can you hear me in there? *(There is a muffled answer.)* We just got the full report from the laboratory at the Ochsner Clinic, completely negative, son, ev'rything negative, right on down the line! Nothin' a-tall's wrong with him but some little functional thing called a spastic colon. Can you hear me, son?

MARGARET.   He can hear you, Big Mama.

BIG MAMA.   Then why don't he say something? God Almighty, a piece of news like that should make him shout. It made *me* shout, I can tell you. I shouted and sobbed and fell right down on my knees—Look! *(She pulls up her skirt.)* See the bruises where I hit my kneecaps? Took both doctors to haul me back on my feet! *(She laughs— she always laughs like hell at herself.)* Bid Daddy was furious with me! But ain't that wonderful news? *(Facing bathroom again, she continues.)* After all the anxiety we been through to git a report like that on Big Daddy's birthday? Big Daddy tried to hide how much of a load that news took off his mind, but didn't fool *me*. He was mighty close to crying about it *himself*! *(Goodbyes are shouted downstairs, and she rushes to door.)* Hold those people down there, don't let them go!—Now, git dressed, we're all comin' up to this room fo' Big Daddy's birthday party because of your ankle.—How's his ankle, Maggie?

MARGARET.   Well, he broke it, Big Mama.

BIG MAMA.   I know he broke it. *(A phone is ringing in hall. A Negro voice answers: "Mistuh Polly's res'dence.")* I mean does it hurt him much still.

MARGARET.   I'm afraid I can't give you that information, Big Mama. You'll have to ask Brick if it hurts much still or not.

SOOKEY *(in the hall)*. It's Memphis, Mizz Polly, it's Miss Sally in Memphis.

BIG MAMA.   Awright, Sookey. *(Big Mama rushes into the hall and is heard shouting on the phone:)* Hello, Miss Sally. How are you, Miss Sally?—Yes, well, I was just gonna call you about it. Shoot!— *(She raises her voice to a bellow.) Miss Sally? Don't ever call me from the Gayoso Lobby, too much talk goes on in that hotel lobby, no wonder you can't hear me!* Now listen, Miss Sally. They's nothin' serious wrong with Big Daddy. We got the report just now, they's nothin' wrong but a thing called a— spastic! SPASTIC!—colon . . . *(She appears at the hall door and calls to Margaret.)* —Maggie, come out here and talk to that fool on the phone. I'm shouted breathless!

MARGARET *(goes out and is heard sweetly at phone)*. Miss Sally? This is Brick's wife, Maggie. So nice to hear your voice. Can you hear *mine?* Well, good!—Big Mama just wanted you to know that they've got the report from the Ochsner Clinic and what Big Daddy has is a spastic colon. Yes. Spastic colon, Miss Sally. That's right, spastic colon. *G'bye, Miss Sally, hope I'll see you real soon! (Hangs up a little before Miss Sally was probably ready to terminate the talk. She returns through the hall door.)* She heard me perfectly. I've discovered with deaf people the thing to do is not shout at them but just enunciate clearly. My rich old Aunt Cornelia was deaf as the dead but I could make her hear me just by sayin' each word slowly, distinctly, close to her ear. I read her the *Commercial Appeal* ev'ry night, read her the classified ads in it, even, she never missed a word of it. But was she a mean ole thing! Know what I got when she died? Her unexpired subscriptions to five magazines and the Book-of-the-Month Club and a LIBRARY full of ev'ry dull book ever written! All else went to her hellcat of a sister . . . meaner than she was, even!

(*Big Mama has been straightening things up in the room during this speech.*)

BIG MAMA (*closing closet door on discarded clothes*). Miss Sally sure is a case! Big Daddy says she's always got her hand out fo' something. He's not mistaken. That poor ole thing always has her hand out fo' somethin'. I don't think Big Daddy gives her as much as he should. (*Somebody shouts for her downstairs and she shouts:*) I'm comin'!

(*She starts out. At the hall door, turns and jerks a forefinger, first toward the bathroom door, then toward the liquor cabinet, meaning: "Has Brick been drinking?" Margaret pretends not to understand, cocks her head and raises her brows as if the pantomimic performance was completely mystifying to her.*)
(*Big Mama rushes back to Margaret:*) Shoot! Stop playin' so dumb!—I mean has he been drinkin' that stuff much yet?

MARGARET (*with a little laugh*). Oh! I think he had a high-ball after supper.
BIG MAMA.   Don't laugh about it!—Some single men stop drinkin' when they git married and others start! Brick never touched liquor before he—!
MARGARET (*crying out*). *THAT'S NOT FAIR!*
BIG MAMA.   Fair or not fair I want to ask you a question, one question: D'you make Brick happy in bed?
MARGARET.   Why don't you ask if he makes *me* happy in bed?
BIG MAMA.   Because I know that—
MARGARET.   *It works both ways!*
BIG MAMA.   Something's not right! You're childless and my son drinks! (*Someone has called her downstairs and she has rushed to the door on the line above. She turns at the door and points at the bed.*) —When a marriage goes on the rocks, the rocks are *there*, right *there*!
MARGARET.   That's— (*Big Mama has swept out of the room and slammed the door.*) —not—*fair* . . .

(*Margaret is alone, completely alone, and she feels it. She draws in, hunches her shoulders, raises her arms with fists clenched, shuts her eyes tight as a child about to be stabbed with a vaccination needle. When she opens her eyes again, what she sees is the long oval mirror and she rushes straight to it, stares into it with a grimace and says: "Who are you?"—Then she crouches a little and answers herself in a different voice which is high, thin, mocking: "I am Maggie the Cat!"—Straightens quickly as bathroom door opens a little and Brick calls out to her.*)

BRICK.   Has Big Mama gone?
MARGARET.   She's gone.

(*He opens the bathroom door and hobbles out, with his liquor glass now empty, straight to the liquor cabinet. He is whistling softly. Margaret's head pivots on her long, slender throat to watch him.*)

(*She raises a hand uncertainly to the base of her throat, as if it was difficult for her to swallow, before she speaks:*) You know, our sex life didn't just peter out in the usual way, it was cut off short, long before the natural time for it to, and it's going to revive again, just as sudden as that. I'm confident of it. That's what I'm keeping myself attractive for. For the time when you'll see me again like other men see me. Yes, like other men see me. They still see me, Brick, and they like what they see. Uh-huh. Some of them would give their—Look, Brick! (*She stands before the long oval mirror, touches her breast and then her hips with her two hands.*) How high my body stays on me!—Nothing has fallen on me—not a fraction. . . . (*Her voice is soft and trembling: a pleading child's. At this moment as he turns to glance at her—a look which is like a player passing a ball to another player, third down and goal to go—she has to capture the audience in a grip so tight that she can hold it till the first intermission without any lapse of attention.*) Other men still want me. My face looks strained, sometimes, but I've kept my figure as well as you've kept yours, and men admire it. I still turn heads on the street. Why, last week in Memphis everywhere that I went men's eyes burned holes in my clothes, at the country club and in restaurants and department stores, there wasn't a man I met or walked by that didn't just eat me up with his eyes and turn around when I passed him and look back at me. Why, at Alice's party for her New York cousins, the best lookin' man in the crowd—followed me upstairs and tried to force his way in the powder room with me, followed me to the door and tried to force his way in!
BRICK.   Why didn't you let him, Maggie?
MARGARET.   Because I'm not that common, for one thing. Not that I wasn't almost tempted to. You like to know who it was? It was Sonny Boy Maxwell, that's who!
BRICK.   Oh, yeah, Sonny Boy Maxwell, he was a good end-runner but had a little injury to his back and had to quit.
MARGARET.   He has no injury now and has no wife and still has a lech for me!
BRICK.   I see no reason to lock him out of a powder room in that case.
MARGARET.   And have someone catch me at it? I'm not that stupid. Oh, I might sometime cheat on you with someone, since you're so insultingly eager to have me do it!—But if I do, you can be damned sure it will be in a place and a time where no one but me and the man could possibly know. Because I'm not going to give you any excuse to divorce me for being unfaithful or anything else. . . .
BRICK.   Maggie, I wouldn't divorce you for being unfaithful or anything else. Don't you know that? Hell. I'd be relieved to know that you'd found yourself a lover.
MARGARET.   Well, I'm taking no chances. No, I'd rather stay on this hot tin roof.
BRICK.   A hot tin roof's 'n uncomfo'table place t' stay on. . . . (*He starts to whistle softly.*)

MARGARET (*through his whistle*). Yeah, but I can stay on it just as long as I have to.

BRICK.   You could leave me, Maggie. (*He resumes whistle. She wheels about to glare at him.*)

MARGARET.   *Don't want to and will not!* Besides if I did, you don't have a cent to pay for it but what you get from Big Daddy and he's dying of cancer! (*For the first time a realization of Big Daddy's doom seems to penetrate to Brick's consciousness, visibly, and he looks at Margaret.*)

BRICK.   Big Mama just said he *wasn't*, that the report was okay.

MARGARET.   That's what she thinks because she got the same story that they gave Big Daddy. And was just as taken in by it as he was, poor ole things. . . .
But tonight they're going to tell her the truth about it. When Big Daddy goes to bed, they're going to tell her that he is dying of cancer. (*She slams the dresser drawer.*) —It's malignant and it's terminal.

BRICK.   Does Big Daddy know it?

MARGARET.   Hell, do they *ever* know it? Nobody says, ''You're dying.'' You have to fool them. They have to fool *themselves*.

BRICK.   Why?

MARGARET.   *Why?* Because human beings dream of life everlasting, that's the reason! But most of them want it on earth and not in heaven. (*He gives a short, hard laugh at her touch of humor.*) Well. . . . (*She touches up her mascara.*) That's how it is, anyhow. . . . (*She looks about.*) Where did I put down my cigarette? Don't want to burn up the home-place, at least not with Mae and Gooper and their five monsters in it! (*She has found it and sucks at it greedily. Blows out smoke and continues:*) So this is Big Daddy's last birthday. And Mae and Gooper, they know it, oh, *they* know it, all right. They got the first information from the Ochsner Clinic. That's why they rushed down here with their no-neck monsters. Because. Do you know something? Big Daddy's made no will? Big Daddy's never made out any will in his life, and so this campaign's afoot to impress him, forcibly as possible, with the fact that you drink and I've borne no children!

(*He continues to stare at her a moment, then mutters something sharp but not audible and hobbles rather rapidly out onto the long gallery in the fading, much faded, gold light.*)

MARGARET (*continuing her liturgical chant*). Y'know, I'm *fond* of Big Daddy, I am genuinely fond of that old man, I really *am*, you know. . . .

BRICK (*faintly, vaguely*). Yes, I know you are. . . .

MARGARET.   I've always sort of admired him in spite of his coarseness, his four-letter words and so forth. Because Big Daddy *is* what he *is*, and he makes no bones about it. He hasn't turned gentleman farmer, he's still a Mississippi red neck, as much of a red neck as he must have been when he was just overseer here on the old Jack Straw and Peter Ochello place. But he got hold of it an' built it into th' biggest an' finest plantation in the Delta—I've always *liked* Big Daddy. . . . (*She crosses to the proscenium.*) Well, this is Big Daddy's last birthday. I'm sorry about it. But I'm facing the facts. It takes money to take care of a drinker and that's the office that I've been elected to lately.

BRICK.   You don't have to take care of me.

MARGARET.   Yes, I do. Two people in the same boat have got to take care of each other. At least you want money to buy more Echo Spring when this supply is exhausted, or will you be satisfied with a ten-cent beer?
Mae an' Gooper are plannin' to freeze us out of Big Daddy's estate because you drink and I'm childless. But we can defeat that plan. We're *going* to defeat that plan!
Brick, y'know, I've been so God damn disgustingly poor all my life!—That's the *truth*, Brick!

BRICK.   I'm not sayin' it isn't.

MARGARET.   Always had to suck up to people I couldn't stand because they had money and I was poor as Job's turkey. You don't know what that's like. Well, I'll tell you, it's like you would feel a thousand miles away from Echo Spring!—And had to get back to it on that broken ankle . . . without a crutch!
That's how it feels to be as poor as Job's turkey and have to suck up to relatives that you hated because they had money and all you had was a bunch of hand-me-down clothes and a few old moldy three per cent government bonds. My daddy loved his liquor, he fell in love with his liquor the way you've fallen in love with Echo Spring!— And my poor Mama, having to maintain some semblance of social position, to keep appearances up, on an income of one hundred and fifty dollars a month on those old government bonds!
When I came out, the year that I made my debut, I had just two evening dresses! One Mother made me from a pattern in *Vogue*, the other a hand-me-down from a snotty rich cousin I hated!
—The dress that I married you in was my grandmother's weddin' gown. . . .
So that's why I'm like a cat on a hot tin roof!

(*Brick is still on the gallery. Someone below calls up to him in a warm Negro voice, ''Hiya, Mistuh Brick, how yuh feelin'?'' Brick raises his liquor glass as if that answered the question.*)

MARGARET.   You can be young without money but you can't be old without it. You've got to be old *with* money because to be old without it is just too awful, you've got to be one or the other, either *young* or *with money*, you can't be old and *without* it.—That's the truth, Brick. . . . (*Brick whistles softly, vaguely.*) Well, now I'm dressed, I'm all dressed, there's nothing else for me to do. (*Forlornly, almost fearfully.*) I'm dressed, all dressed, nothing else for me to do. . . . (*She moves about restlessly, aimlessly, and speaks, as if to herself.*) I know when I made my mistake.—What am I—? Oh!—my bracelets. . . . (*She starts working a collection of bracelets over her hands onto her wrists, about six on each, as she talks.*) I've thought a whole lot about it and now I know when I made my mistake. Yes, I made my mistake when I told you the truth about that thing with Skipper. Never should have confessed it, a fatal error, tellin' you about that thing with Skipper.

BRICK.   Maggie, shut up about Skipper. I mean it, Maggie; you got to shut up about Skipper.

MARGARET.   You ought to understand that Skipper and I—

BRICK.   You don't think I'm serious, Maggie? You're fooled by the fact that I am saying this quiet? Look, Maggie. What you're doing is a dangerous thing to do. You're—you're—you're—foolin' with something that—nobody ought to fool with.

MARGARET.   This time I'm going to finish what I have to say to you. Skipper and I made love, if love you could call it, because it made both of us feel a little bit closer to you. You see, you son of a bitch, you asked too much of people, of me, of him, of all the unlucky poor damned sons of bitches that happen to love you, and there was a whole pack of them, yes, there was a pack of them besides me and Skipper, you asked too goddam much of people that loved you, you—superior creature!—you godlike being!—And so we made love to each other to dream it was you, both of us! Yes, yes, yes! Truth, truth! What's so awful about it? I like it, I think the truth is—yeah! I shouldn't have told you. . . .

BRICK (*holding his head unnaturally still and uptilted a bit*). It was Skipper that told me about it. Not you, Maggie.

MARGARET.   I told you!

BRICK.   After he told me!

MARGARET.   What does it matter who—? (*Brick turns suddenly out upon the gallery and calls.*)

BRICK.   Little girl! Hey, little girl!

LITTLE GIRL (*at a distance*). What, Uncle Brick?

BRICK.   Tell the folks to come up!—Bring everybody upstairs!

MARGARET.   I can't stop myself! I'd go on telling you this in front of them all, if I had to!

BRICK.   Little girl! Go on, go on, will you? Do what I told you, call them!

MARGARET.   Because it's got to be told and you, you!—you never let me! (*She sobs, then controls herself, and continues almost calmly.*) It was one of those beautiful, ideal things they tell about in the Greek legends, it couldn't be anything else, you being you, and that's what made it so sad, that's what made it so awful, because it was love that never could be carried through to anything satisfying or even talked about plainly. Brick, I tell you, you got to believe me, Brick, I *do* understand all about it! I—I think it was—*noble*! Can't you tell I'm sincere when

I say I respect it? My only point, the only point that I'm making, is life has got to be allowed to continue even after the *dream* of life is—all—over. . . . (*Brick is without his crutch. Leaning on furniture, he crosses to pick it up as she continues as if possessed by a will outside herself:*) Why I remember when we double-dated at college, Gladys Fitzgerald and I and you and Skipper, it was more like a date between you and Skipper. Gladys and I were just sort of tagging along as if it was necessary to chaperone you!—to make a good public impression—

BRICK (*turns to face her, half lifting his crutch*). Maggie, you want me to hit you with this crutch? Don't you know I could kill you with this crutch?

MARGARET.   Good Lord, man, d' you think I'd care if you did?

BRICK.   One man has one great good true thing in his life. One great good thing which is true!—I had friendship with Skipper.—You are naming it dirty!

MARGARET.   I'm not naming it dirty! I am naming it clean.

BRICK.   Not love with you, Maggie, but friendship with Skipper was that one great true thing, and you are naming it dirty!

MARGARET.   Then you haven't been listenin', not understood what I'm saying! I'm naming it so damn clean that it killed poor Skipper!—You two had something that had to be kept on ice, yes, incorruptible, yes!—and death was the only icebox where you could keep it. . . .

BRICK.   I married you, Maggie. Why would I marry you, Maggie, if I was—?

MARGARET.   Brick, don't brain me yet, let me finish!—I know, believe me I know, that it was only Skipper that harbored even any *unconscious* desire for anything not perfectly pure between you two!—Now let me skip a little. You married me early that summer we graduated out of Ole Miss, and we were happy, weren't we, we were blissful, yes, hit heaven together ev'ry time that we loved! But that fall you an' Skipper turned down wonderful offers of jobs in order to keep on bein' football heroes—pro-football heroes. You organized the Dixie Stars that fall, so you could keep on bein' team-mates forever! But somethin' was not right with it!—*Me included!*—between you. Skipper began hittin' the bottle . . . you got a spinal injury—couldn't play the Thanksgivin' game in Chicago, watched it on TV from a traction bed in Toledo. I joined Skipper. The Dixie Stars lost because poor Skipper was drunk. We drank together that night all night in the bar of the Blackstone and when cold day was comin' up over the Lake an' we were comin' out drunk to take a dizzy look at it, I said, "SKIPPER, STOP LOVIN' MY HUSBAND OR TELL HIM HE'S GOT TO LET YOU ADMIT IT TO HIM!"—one way or another!

HE SLAPPED ME HARD ON THE MOUTH!—then turned and ran without stopping once, I am sure, all the way back into his room at the Blackstone. . . .

—When I came to his room that night, with a little scratch like a shy little mouse at his door, he made that pitiful, ineffectual little attempt to prove that what I had said wasn't true. . . .

(*Brick strikes at her with crutch, a blow that shatters the gemlike lamp on the table.*) —In this way, I destroyed him, by telling him truth that he and his world which he was born and raised in, yours and his world, had told him could not be told?

—From then on Skipper was nothing at all but a receptacle for liquor and drugs. . . .

—*Who shot cock-robin? I with my*— (*She throws back her head with tight shut eyes.*) —*merciful arrow!* (*Brick strikes at her; misses.*) Missed me!—Sorry,—I'm not tryin' to whitewash my behavior, Christ, no! Brick, I'm not good. I don't know why people have to pretend to be good, nobody's good. The rich or the well-to-do can afford to respect moral patterns, conventional moral patterns, but I could never afford to, yeah, but—I'm honest! Give me credit for just that, will you *please?*—Born poor, raised poor, expect to die poor unless I manage to get us something out of what Big Daddy leaves when he dies of cancer! But Brick?!—*Skipper is dead! I'm alive!* Maggie the cat is— (*Brick hops awkwardly forward and strikes at her again with his crutch.*) —*alive! I am alive, alive! I am* . . . (*He hurls the crutch at her, across the bed she took refuge behind, and pitches forward on the floor as she completes her speech.*) —*alive!*

(*A little girl, Dixie, bursts into the room, wearing an Indian war bonnet and firing a cap pistol at Margaret and shouting: "Bang, bang, bang!"*)

(*Laughter downstairs floats through the open hall door. Margaret had crouched gasping to bed at child's entrance. She now rises and says with cool fury:*) Little girl, your mother or someone should teach you—(*Gasping.*)—to knock at a door before you come into a room. Otherwise people might think that you—lack—good breeding. . . .

DIXIE.   Yanh, yanh, yanh, what is Uncle Brick doin' on th' floor?

BRICK.   I tried to kill your Aunt Maggie, but I failed—and I fell. Little girl, give me my crutch so I can get up off th' floor.

MARGARET.   Yes, give your uncle his crutch, he's a cripple, honey, he broke his ankle last night jumping hurdles on the high school athletic field!

DIXIE.   What were you jumping hurdles for, Uncle Brick?

BRICK.   Because I used to jump them, and people like to do what they used to do, even after they've stopped being able to do it. . . .

MARGARET.   That's right, that's your answer, now go away, little girl. (*Dixie fires cap pistol at Margaret three times.*) Stop, you stop that, monster! You little no-neck monster!

(*She seizes the cap pistol and hurls it through gallery doors.*)

DIXIE (*with a precocious instinct for the cruelest thing*). You're *jealous!*—You're just jealous because you can't have babies! (*She sticks out her tongue at Margaret as she sashays past her with her stomach stuck out, to the gallery. Margaret slams the gallery doors and leans panting against them. There is a pause. Brick has replaced his spilt drink and sits, faraway, on the great four-poster bed.*)

MARGARET.   You see?—they gloat over us being childless, even in front of their five little no-neck monsters! (*Pause. Voices approach on the stairs.*) Brick?—I've been to a doctor in Memphis, a—a gynecologist. . . .

I've been completely examined, and there is no reason why we can't have a child whenever we want one. And this is my time by the calendar to conceive. Are you listening to me? Are you? Are you LISTENING TO ME!

BRICK.   Yes. I hear you, Maggie. (*His attention returns to her inflamed face.*)—But how in hell on earth do you imagine—that you're going to have a child by a man that can't stand you?

MARGARET.   That's a problem that I will have to work out. (*She wheels about to face the hall door.*) Here they come!

(*The lights dim.*)

CURTAIN

ACT TWO

There is no lapse of time. Margaret and Brick are in the same positions they held at the end of Act I.

MARGARET (*at door*). Here they come!

(*Big Daddy appears first, a tall man with a fierce, anxious look, moving carefully not to betray his weakness even, or especially, to himself.*)

BIG DADDY.   Well, Brick.
BRICK.   Hello, Big Daddy.—Congratulations!
BIG DADDY.   —Crap. . . .

(*Some of the people are approaching through the hall, others along the gallery: voices from both directions. Gooper and Reverend Tooker become visible outside gallery doors, and their voices come in clearly.*)
(*They pause outside as Gooper lights a cigar.*)

REVEREND TOOKER (*vivaciously*). Oh, but St. Paul's in Grenada has three memorial windows, and the latest one is a Tiffany stained-glass window that cost twenty-five hundred dollars, a picture of Christ the Good Shepherd with a Lamb in His arms.

GOOPER.   Who give that window, Preach?

REVEREND TOOKER.   Clyde Fletcher's widow. Also presented St. Paul's with a baptismal font.

GOOPER.   Y'know what somebody ought t' give your church is a *coolin'* system, Preach.

REVEREND TOOKER.   Yes, siree, Bob! And y'know what Gus Hamma's family gave in his memory to the church at Two Rivers? A complete new stone parish-house with a basketball court in the basement and a—

BIG DADDY (*uttering a loud barking laugh which is far from truly mirthful*). Hey, Preach! What's all this talk about memorials, Preach? Y' think somebody's about t' kick off around here? 'S that it?

(*Startled by this interjection, Reverend Tooker decides to laugh at the question almost as loud as he can.*)

(*How he would answer the question we'll never know, as he's spared that embarrassment by the voice of Gooper's wife, Mae, rising high and clear as she appears with "Doc" Baugh, the family doctor, through the hall door.*)

MAE (*almost religiously*). —Let's see now, they've had their *tyyy*-phoid shots, and their tetanus shots, their diphtheria shots and their hepatitis shots and their polio shots, they got *those* shots every month from May through September, and—Gooper? Hey! Gooper!—What all have the kiddies been shot faw?

MARGARET (*overlapping a bit*). Turn on the Hi-Fi, Brick! Let's have some music t' start off th' party with!

(*The talk becomes so general that the room sounds like a great aviary of chattering birds. Only Brick remains unengaged, leaning upon the liquor cabinet with his faraway smile, an ice cube in a paper napkin with which he now and then rubs his forehead. He doesn't respond to Margaret's command. She bounds forward and stoops over the instrument panel of the console.*)

GOOPER.   We gave 'em that thing for a third anniversary present, got three speakers in it.

(*The room is suddenly blasted by the climax of a Wagnerian opera or a Beethoven symphony.*)

BIG DADDY.   Turn that dam thing off!

(*Almost instant silence, almost instantly broken by the shouting charge of Big Mama, entering through hall door like a charging rhino.*)

BIG MAMA.   Wha's my Brick, wha's mah precious baby!!
BIG DADDY.   Sorry! Turn it back on!

(*Everyone laughs very loud. Big Daddy is famous for his jokes at Big Mama's expense, and nobody laughs louder at these jokes than Big Mama herself, though sometimes they're pretty cruel and Big Mama has to pick up or fuss with something to cover the hurt that the loud laugh doesn't quite cover.*)

(*On this occasion, a happy occasion because the dread in her heart has also been lifted by the false report on Big Daddy's condition, she giggles, grotesquely, coyly, in Big Daddy's direction and bears down upon Brick, all very quick and alive.*)

BIG MAMA.   Here he is, here's my precious baby! What's that you've got in your hand? You put that liquor down, son, your hand was made fo' holdin' somethin' better than that!

GOOPER.   Look at Brick put it down! (*Brick has obeyed Big Mama by draining the glass and handing it to her. Again everyone laughs, some high, some low.*)

BIG MAMA.   Oh, you bad boy, you, you're my bad little boy. Give Big Mama a kiss, you bad boy, you!—Look at him shy away, will you? Brick never liked bein' kissed or made a fuss over, I guess because he's always had too much of it!

Son, you turn that thing off! (*Brick has switched on the TV set.*) I can't stand TV, radio was bad enough but TV has gone it one better, I mean—(*Plops wheezing in chair.*)—one worse, ha ha! Now what'm I sittin' down here faw? I want t' sit next to my sweetheart on the sofa, hold hands with him and love him up a little!

(*Big Mama has on a black and white figured chiffon. The large irregular patterns, like the markings of some massive animal, the luster of her great diamonds and many pearls, the brilliants set in the silver frames of her glasses, her riotous voice, booming laugh, have dominated the room since she entered. Big Daddy has been regarding her with a steady grimace of chronic annoyance.*)

BIG MAMA (*still louder*). Preacher, Preacher, hey, Preach! Give me you' hand an' help me up from this chair!
REVEREND TOOKER.   None of your tricks, Big Mama!
BIG MAMA.   What tricks? You give me you' hand so I can get up an'— (*Reverend Tooker extends her his hand. She grabs it and pulls him into her lap with a shrill laugh that spans an octave in two notes.*) Ever seen a preacher in a fat lady's lap? Hey, hey, folks! Ever seen a preacher in a fat lady's lap?

(*Big Mama is notorious throughout the Delta for this sort of inelegant horseplay. Margaret looks on with indulgent humor, sipping Dubonnet "on the rocks" and watching Brick, but Mae and Gooper exchange signs of humorless anxiety over these antics, the sort of behavior which Mae thinks may account for their failure to quite get in with the smartest young married set in Memphis, despite all. One of the Negroes, Lacy or Sookey, peeks in, cackling. They are waiting for a sign to bring in the cake and champagne. But Big Daddy's not amused. He doesn't understand why, in spite of the infinite mental relief he's received from the doctor's report, he still has these same old fox teeth in his guts.*)

"This spastic thing sure is something," he says to himself, but aloud he roars at Big Mama:)

BIG DADDY.   *BIG MAMA, WILL YOU QUIT HORSIN'?—* You're too old an' too fat fo' that sort of crazy kid stuff an' besides a woman with your blood-pressure—she had two hundred last spring!—is riskin' a stroke when you mess around like that. . . .

BIG MAMA.   *Here comes Big Daddy's birthday!*

(*Negroes in white jackets enter with an enormous birthday cake ablaze with candles and carrying buckets of champagne with satin ribbons about the bottle necks.*)
(*Mae and Gooper strike up song, and everybody, including the Negroes and Children, joins in. Only Brick remains aloof.*)

EVERYONE.
>   Happy birthday to you.
>   Happy birthday to you.
>   Happy birthday, Big Daddy—
>   (*Some sing: "Dear, Big Daddy!"*)
>   Happy birthday to you.
>   (*Some sing: "How old are you?"*)

(*Mae has come down center and is organizing her children like a chorus. She gives them a barely audible: "One, two, three!" and they are off in the new tune.*)

CHILDREN.
>   Skinamarinka—dinka—dink
>   Skinamarinka—do
>   We love you.
>   Skinamarinka—dinka—dink
>   Skinamarinka—do
>   (*All together, they turn to Big Daddy.*)
>   Big Daddy, you!
>   (*They turn back front, like a musical comedy
>   chorus.*)
>   We love you in the morning;
>   We love you in the night.
>   We love you when we're with you,
>   And we love you out of sight.
>   Skinamarinka—dinka–dink
>   Skinamarinka—do.
>   (*Mae turns to Big Mama.*)
>   Big Mama, too!
>   (*Big Mama bursts into tears. The Negroes leave.*)

BIG DADDY.   Now Ida, what the hell is the matter with you?

MAE.   She's just so happy.

BIG MAMA.   I'm just so happy, Big Daddy, I have to cry or something. (*Sudden and loud in the hush:*) Brick, do you know the wonderful news that Doc Baugh got from the clinic about Big Daddy? Big Daddy's one hundred per cent!

MARGARET.   Isn't that wonderful?

BIG MAMA.   He's just one hundred per cent. Passed the examination with flying colors. Now that we know there's nothing wrong with Big Daddy but a spastic colon, I can tell you something. I was worried sick, half out of my mind, for fear that Big Daddy might have a thing like— (*Margaret cuts through this speech, jumping up and exclaiming shrilly:*)

MARGARET.   Brick, honey, aren't you going to give Big Daddy his birthday present? (*Passing by him, she snatches his liquor glass from him.*) (*She picks up a fancily wrapped package.*) Here it is, Big Daddy, this is from Brick!

BIG MAMA.   This is the biggest birthday Big Daddy's ever had, a hundred presents and bushels of telegrams from—

MAE (*at the same time*). What is it, Brick?

GOOPER.   I bet 500 to 50 that Brick don't *know* what it is.

BIG MAMA.   The fun of presents is not knowing what they are till you open the package. Open your present, Big Daddy.

BIG DADDY.   Open it you'self. I want to ask Brick somethin! Come here, Brick.

MARGARET.   Big Daddy's callin' you, Brick. (*She is opening the package.*)

BRICK.   Tell Big Daddy I'm crippled.

BIG DADDY.   I see you're crippled. I want to know how you got crippled.

MARGARET (*making diversionary tactics*). Oh, look, oh, look, why, it's a cashmere robe! (*She holds the robe up for all to see.*)

MAE.   You sound surprised, Maggie.

MARGARET.   I never saw one before.

MAE.   That's funny.—*Hah!*

MARGARET (*turning on her fiercely, with a brilliant smile*). Why is it funny? All my family ever had was family— and luxuries such as cashmere robes still surprise me!

BIG DADDY (*ominously*). Quiet!

MAE (*heedless in her fury*). I don't see how you could be so surprised when you bought it yourself at Loewenstein's in Memphis last Saturday. You know how I know?

BIG DADDY.   I said, Quiet!

MAE.   —I know because the salesgirl that sold it to you waited on me and said, Oh, Mrs. Pollitt, your sister-in-law just bought a cashmere robe for your husband's father!

MARGARET.   Sister Woman! Your talents are wasted as a housewife and mother, you really ought to be with the FBI or—

BIG DADDY.   QUIET! (*Reverend Tooker's reflexes are slower than the others'. He finishes a sentence after the bellow.*)

REVEREND TOOKER (*to Doc Baugh*). —the Stork and the Reaper are running neck and neck! (*He starts to laugh gaily when he notices the silence and Big Daddy's glare. His laugh dies falsely.*)

BIG DADDY.   Preacher, I hope I'm not butting in on more talk about memorial stained-glass windows, am I, Preacher? (*Reverend Tooker laughs feebly, then coughs dryly in the embarrassed silence.*) Preacher?

BIG MAMA.   Now, Big Daddy, don't you pick on Preacher!

BIG DADDY (*raising his voice*). You ever hear that expression all hawk and no spit? You bring that expression to mind with that little dry cough of yours, all hawk an' no spit. . . .

(*The pause is broken only by a short startled laugh from Margaret, the only one there who is conscious of and amused by the grotesque.*)

MAE (*raising her arms and jangling her bracelets*). I wonder if the mosquitoes are active tonight?

BIG DADDY.   What's that, Little Mama? Did you make some remark?

MAE.   Yes, I said I wondered if the mosquitoes would eat us alive if we went out on the gallery for a while.

BIG DADDY.   Well, if they do, I'll have your bones pulverized for fertilizer!

BIG MAMA (*quickly*). Last week we had an airplane spraying the place and I think it done some good, at least I haven't had a—

BIG DADDY (*cutting her speech*). Brick, they tell me, if what they tell me is true, that you done some jumping last night on the high school athletic field?

BIG MAMA.   Brick, Big Daddy is talking to you, son.

BRICK (*smiling vaguely over his drink*). What was that, Big Daddy?

BIG DADDY.   They said you done some jumping on the high school track field last night.

BRICK.   That's what they told me, too.

BIG DADDY.   Was it jumping or humping that you were doing out there? What were you doing out there at three A.M., layin' a woman on that cinder track?

BIG MAMA.   Big Daddy, you are off the sick-list, now, and I'm not going to excuse you for talkin' so—

BIG DADDY.   Quiet!

BIG MAMA.   —*nasty* in front of Preacher and—

BIG DADDY.   *QUIET!*—I ast you, Brick, if you was cuttin' you'self a piece o' poon-tang last night on that cinder track? I thought maybe you were chasin' poon-tang on that track an' tripped over something in the heat of the chase—'sthat it?

(*Gooper laughs, loud and false, others nervously following suit. Big Mama stamps her foot, and purses her lips, crossing to Mae and whispering something to her as Brick meets his father's hard, intent, grinning stare with a slow, vague smile that he offers all situations from behind the screen of his liquor.*)

BRICK.   No, sir, I don't think so. . . .

MAE (*at the same time, sweetly*). Reverend Tooker, let's you and I take a stroll on the widow's walk. (*She and the preacher go out on the gallery as Big Daddy says:*)

BIG DADDY.   Then what the hell were you doing out there at three o'clock in the morning?

BRICK.   Jumping the hurdles, Big Daddy, runnin' and jumpin' the hurdles, but those high hurdles have gotten too high for me, now.

BIG DADDY.   Cause you was drunk?

BRICK (*his vague smile fading a little*). Sober I wouldn't have tried to jump the *low* ones. . . .

BIG MAMA (*quickly*). Big Daddy, blow out the candles on your birthday cake!

MARGARET (*at the same time*). I want to propose a toast to Big Daddy Pollitt on his sixty-fifth birthday, the biggest cotton-planter in—

BIG DADDY (*bellowing with fury and disgust*). *I told you to stop it, now stop it, quit this—!*

BIG MAMA (*coming in front of Big Daddy with the cake*). Big Daddy, I will not allow you to talk that way, not even on your birthday, I—

BIG DADDY.   I'll talk like I want to on my birthday, Ida, or any other goddam day of the year and anybody here that don't like it knows what they can do!

BIG MAMA.   You don't mean that!

BIG DADDY.   What makes you think I don't mean it?

(*Meanwhile various discreet signals have been exchanged and Gooper has also gone out on the gallery.*)

BIG MAMA.   I just know you don't mean it.

BIG DADDY.   You don't know a goddam thing and you never did!

BIG MAMA.   Big Daddy, you don't mean that.

BIG DADDY.   Oh, yes, I do, oh, yes, I do, I mean it! I put up with a whole lot of crap around here because I thought I was dying. And you thought I was dying and you started taking over, well, you can stop taking over now, Ida, because I'm not gonna die, you can just stop now this business of taking over because you're not taking over because I'm not dying, I went through the laboratory and the goddam exploratory operation and there's nothing wrong with me but a spastic colon. And I'm not dying of cancer which you thought I was dying of. Ain't that so? Didn't you think that I was dying of cancer, Ida?

(*Almost everybody is out on the gallery but the two old people glaring at each other across the blazing cake.*) (*Big Mama's chest heaves and she presses a fat fist to her mouth.*)

(*Big Daddy continues, hoarsely:*) Ain't that so, Ida? Didn't you have an idea I was dying of cancer and now you could take control of this place and everything on it? I got that impression, I seemed to get that impression. Your loud voice everywhere, your fat old body butting in here and there!

BIG MAMA.   Hush! The Preacher!

BIG DADDY.   Rut the goddam preacher!

(*Big Mama gasps loudly and sits down on the sofa which is almost too small for her.*)

Did you hear what I said? I said rut the goddam preacher!

(*Somebody closes the gallery doors from outside just as there is a burst of fireworks and excited cries from the children.*)

BIG MAMA.   I never seen you act like this before and I can't think what's got in you!

BIG DADDY.   I went through all that laboratory and operation and all just so I would know if you or me was boss here! Well, now it turns out that I am and you ain't—and that's my birthday present—and my cake and champagne!—because for three years now you been gradually taking over. Bossing. Talking. Sashaying your fat old body around the place I made! I made this place! I was overseer on it! I was the overseer on the old Straw and Ochello plantation. I quit school at ten! I quit school at ten years old and went to work like a nigger in the fields. And I rose to be overseer of the Straw and Ochello plantation. And old Straw died and I was Ochello's partner and the place got bigger and bigger and bigger and bigger and bigger! I did all that myself with no goddam help from you, and now you think you're just about to take over. Well, I am just about to tell you that you are not just about to take over, you are not just about to take over a God damn thing. Is that clear to you, Ida? Is that very plain to you, now? Is that understood completely? I been through the laboratory from A to Z. I've had the goddam exploratory operation, and nothing is wrong with me but a spastic colon—made spastic, I guess, by *disgust!* By all the goddam lies and liars that I have had to put up with, and all the goddam hypocrisy that I lived with all these forty years that we been livin' together! Hey! Ida!! Blow out the candles on the birthday cake! Purse up your lips and draw a deep breath and blow out the goddam candles on the cake!

BIG MAMA.   Oh, Big Daddy, oh, oh, oh, Big Daddy!

BIG DADDY.   What's the matter with you?

BIG MAMA.   *In all these years you never believed that I loved you??*

BIG DADDY.   Huh?

BIG MAMA.   *And I did, I did so much, I did love you!*—I even loved your hate and your hardness, Big Daddy! (*She sobs and rushes awkwardly out onto the gallery.*)

BIG DADDY (*to himself*). *Wouldn't it be funny if that was true. . . .*

(*A pause is followed by a burst of light in the sky from the fireworks.*)

BRICK! HEY, BRICK! (*He stands over his blazing birthday cake.*)

(*After some moments, Brick hobbles in on his crutch, holding his glass.*)

(*Margaret follows him with a bright, anxious smile.*)

I didn't call you, Maggie. I called Brick.

MARGARET.   I'm just delivering him to you. (*She kisses Brick on the mouth which he immediately wipes with the back of his hand. She flies girlishly back out. Brick and his father are alone.*)

BIG DADDY.   Why did you do that?

BRICK.   Do what, Big Daddy?

BIG DADDY.   Wipe her kiss off your mouth like she'd spit on you.

BRICK.   I don't know. I wasn't conscious of it.

BIG DADDY.   That woman of yours has a better shape on her than Gooper's but somehow or other they got the same look about them.

BRICK.   What sort of look is that, Big Daddy?

BIG DADDY.   I don't know how to describe it but it's the same look.

BRICK.   They don't look peaceful, do they?

BIG DADDY.   No, they sure in hell don't.

BRICK.   They look nervous as cats?

BIG DADDY.   That's right, they look nervous as cats.

BRICK.   Nervous as a couple of cats on a hot tin roof?

BIG DADDY.   That's right, boy, they look like a couple of cats on a hot tin roof. It's funny that you and Gooper being so different would pick out the same type of woman.

BRICK.   Both of us married into society, Big Daddy.

BIG DADDY.   Crap . . . I wonder what gives them both that look?

BRICK.   Well. They're sittin' in the middle of a big piece of land, Big Daddy, twenty-eight thousand acres is a pretty big piece of land and so they're squaring off on it, each determined to knock off a bigger piece of it than the other whenever you let it go.

BIG DADDY.   I got a surprise for those women. I'm not gonna let it go for a long time yet if that's what they're waiting for.

BRICK.   That's right, Big Daddy. You just sit tight and let them scratch each other's eyes out. . . .

BIG DADDY.   You bet your life I'm going to sit tight on it and let those sons of bitches scratch their eyes out, ha ha ha. . . .

But Gooper's wife's a good breeder, you got to admit she's fertile. Hell, at supper tonight she had them all at the table and they had to put a couple of extra leafs in the table to make room for them, she's got five head of them, now, and another one's comin'.

BRICK.   Yep, number six is comin'. . . .

BIG DADDY.   Brick, you know, I swear to God, I don't know the way it happens?

BRICK.   The way what happens, Big Daddy?

BIG DADDY.   You git a piece of land, by hook or crook, an' things start growin' on it, things accumulate on it, and the first thing you know it's completely out of hand, completely out of hand!

BRICK.   Well, they say nature hates a vacuum, Big Daddy.

BIG DADDY.   That's what they say, but sometimes I think that a vacuum is a hell of a lot better than some of the stuff that nature replaces it with.

Is someone out there by that door?

BRICK.   Yep.

BIG DADDY.   Who? (*He has lowered his voice.*)

BRICK.   Someone int'rested in what we say to each other.

BIG DADDY.   Gooper?—*GOOPER!*

(*After a discreet pause, Mae appears in the gallery door.*)

MAE.   Did you call Gooper, Big Daddy?

BIG DADDY.   Aw, it was you.

MAE.   Do you want Gooper, Big Daddy?

BIG DADDY.   No, and I don't want you. I want some privacy here, while I'm having a confidential talk with my son Brick. Now it's too hot in here to close them doors, but if I have to close those rutten doors in order to have a private talk with my son Brick, just let me know and I'll close 'em. Because I hate eavesdroppers, I don't like any kind of sneakin' an' spyin'.

MAE.   Why, Big Daddy—

BIG DADDY.   You stood on the wrong side of the moon, it threw your shadow!

MAE.   I was just—

BIG DADDY.   You was just nothing but *spyin'* and you *know* it!

MAE (*begins to sniff and sob*). Oh, Big Daddy, you're so unkind for some reason to those that really love you!

BIG DADDY.   Shut up, shut up, shut up! I'm going to move you and Gooper out of that room next to this! It's none of your goddam business what goes on in here at night between Brick an' Maggie. You listen at night like a couple of rutten peek-hole spies and go and give a report on what you hear to Big Mama an' she comes to me and says they say such and such and so and so about what they heard goin' on between Brick an' Maggie, and Jesus, it makes me sick. I'm goin' to move you an' Gooper out of that room, I can't stand sneakin' and spyin', it makes me sick. . . .

(*Mae throws back her head and rolls her eyes heavenward and extends her arms as if invoking God's pity for this unjust martyrdom; then she presses a handkerchief to her nose and flies from the room with a loud swish of skirts.*)

BRICK (*now at the liquor cabinet*). They listen, do they?

BIG DADDY.   Yeah. They listen and give reports to Big Mama on what goes on in here between you and Maggie. They say that— (*He stops as if embarrassed.*) —You won't sleep with her, that you sleep on the sofa. Is that true or not true? If you don't like Maggie, get rid of Maggie!—What are you doin' there now?

BRICK.   Fresh'nin up my drink.

BIG DADDY.   Son, you know you got a real liquor problem?

BRICK.   Yes, sir, yes, I know.

BIG DADDY.   Is that why you quit sports-announcing, because of this liquor problem?

BRICK.   Yes, sir, yes, sir, I guess so. (*He smiles vaguely and amiably at his father across his replenished drink.*)

BIG DADDY.   Son, don't guess about it, it's too important.

BRICK (*vaguely*). Yes, sir.

BIG DADDY.   And listen to me, don't look at the damn chandelier. . . . (*Pause. Big Daddy's voice is husky.*) —Somethin' else we picked up at th' big fire sale in Europe. (*Another pause.*) Life is important. There's nothing else to hold onto. A man that drinks is throwing his life away. Don't do it, hold onto your life. There's nothing else to hold onto. . . .

Sit down over here so we don't have to raise our voices, the walls have ears in this place.

BRICK (*hobbling over to sit on the sofa beside him*). All right, Big Daddy.

BIG DADDY.   Quit!—how'd that come about? Some disappointment?

BRICK.   I don't know. Do you?

BIG DADDY.   I'm askin' you, God damn it! How in hell would I know if you don't?

BRICK.   I just got out there and found that I had a mouth full of cotton. I was always two or three beats behind what was goin' on on the field and so I—

BIG DADDY.   Quit!

BRICK (*amiably*). Yes, quit.

BIG DADDY.   Son?

BRICK.   Huh?

BIG DADDY (*inhales loudly and deeply from his cigar; then bends suddenly a little forward, exhaling loudly and raising a hand to his forehead*). —Whew!—ha ha!—I took in too much smoke, it made me a little light-headed. . . . (*The mantel clock chimes.*) Why is it so damn hard for people to talk?

BRICK.   Yeah. . . . (*The clock goes on sweetly chiming till it has completed the stroke of ten.*) —Nice peaceful-soundin' clock, I like to hear it all night. . . . (*He slides low and comfortable on the sofa; Big Daddy sits up straight and rigid with some unspoken anxiety. All his gestures are tense and jerky as he talks. He wheezes and pants and sniffs through his nervous speech, glancing quickly, shyly, from time to time, at his son.*)

BIG DADDY.   We got that clock the summer we wint to Europe, me an' Big Mama on that damn Cook's Tour, never had such an awful time in my life, I'm tellin' you, son, those gooks over there, they gouge your eyeballs out in their grand hotels. And Big Mama bought more stuff than you could haul in a couple of boxcars, that's no crap. Everywhere she wint on this whirlwind tour, she bought,

bought, bought. Why, half that stuff she bought is still crated up in the cellar, under water last spring! (*He laughs.*) That Europe is nothin' on earth but a great big auction, that's all it is, that bunch of old worn-out places, it's just a big fire-sale, the whole rutten thing, an' Big Mama wint wild in it, why, you couldn't hold that woman with a mule's harness! Bought, bought, bought!—lucky I'm a rich man, yes siree, Bob, an' half that stuff is mildewin' in th' basement. It's lucky I'm a rich man, it sure is lucky, well, I'm a rich man, Brick, yep, I'm a mighty rich man. (*His eyes light up for a moment.*) Y'know how much I'm worth? Guess, Brick! Guess how much I'm worth! (*Brick smiles vaguely over his drink.*) Close on ten million in cash an' blue chip stocks, outside, mind you, of twenty-eight thousand acres of the richest land this side of the valley Nile! (*A puff and crackle and the night sky blooms with an eerie greenish glow. Children shriek on the gallery.*) But a man can't buy his life with it, he can't buy back his life with it when his life has been spent, that's one thing not offered in the Europe fire-sale or in the American markets or any markets on earth, a man can't buy his life with it, he can't buy back his life when his life is finished. . . .

That's a sobering thought, a very sobering thought, and that's a thought that I was turning over in my head, over and over and over—until today. . . .

I'm wiser and sadder, Brick, for this experience which I just gone through. They's one thing else that I remember in Europe.

BRICK.   What is that, Big Daddy?

BIG DADDY.   The hills around Barcelona in the country of Spain and the children running over those bare hills in their bare skins beggin' like starvin' dogs with howls and screeches, and how fat the priests are on the streets of Barcelona, so many of them and so fat and so pleasant, ha ha!—Y'know I could feed that country? I got money enough to feed that goddam country, but the human animal is a selfish beast and I don't reckon the money I passed out there to those howling children in the hills around Barcelona would more than upholster one of the chairs in this room, I mean pay to put a new cover on this chair!

Hell, I threw them money like you'd scatter feed corn for chickens, I threw money at them just to get rid of them long enough to climb back into th' car and—drive away. . . .

And then in Morocco, them Arabs, why, prostitution begins at four or five, that's no exaggeration, why, I remember one day in Marrakech, that old walled Arab city, I set on a broken-down wall to have a cigar, it was fearful hot there and this Arab woman stood in the road and looked at me till I was embarrassed, she stood stock still in the duty hot road and looked at me till I was embarrassed. But listen to this. She had a naked child with her, a little naked girl with her, barely able to toddle, and after a while she set this child on the ground and give her a push and whispered something to her. This child come toward me, barely able t' walk, come toddling up to me and—

Jesus, it makes you sick t' remember a thing like this! It stuck out its hand and tried to unbutton my trousers! That child was not yet five! Can you believe me? Or do you think that I am making this up? I wint back to the hotel and said to Big Mama, Git packed! We're clearing out of this country. . . .

BRICK.   Big Daddy, you're on a talkin' jag tonight.

BIG DADDY (*ignoring this remark*). Yes, sir, that's how it is, the human animal is a beast that dies but the fact that he's dying don't give him pity for others, no, sir, it——Did you say something?

BRICK.   Yes.

BIG DADDY.   What?

BRICK.   Hand me over that crutch so I can get up.

BIG DADDY.   Where you goin'?

BRICK.   I'm takin' a little short trip to Echo Spring.

BIG DADDY.   To where?

BRICK.   Liquor cabinet. . . .

BIG DADDY.   Yes, sir, boy— (*He hands Brick the crutch.*) —the human animal is a beast that dies and if he's got money he buys and buys and buys and I think the reason he buys everything he can buy is that in the back of his mind he has the crazy hope that one of his purchases will be life everlasting—Which it never can be. . . . The human animal is a beast that—

BRICK (*at the liquor cabinet*). Big Daddy, you sure are shootin' th' breeze here tonight. (*There is a pause and voices are heard outside.*)

BIG DADDY.   I been quiet here lately, spoke not a word, just sat and stared into space. I had something heavy weighing on my mind but tonight that load was took off me. That's why I'm talking.—The sky looks diff'rent to me. . . .

BRICK.   You know what I like to hear most?

BIG DADDY.   What?

BRICK.   Solid quiet. Perfect unbroken quiet.

BIG DADDY.   Why?

BRICK.   Because it's more peaceful.

BIG DADDY.   Man, you'll hear a lot of that in the grave. (*He chuckles agreeably.*)

BRICK.   Are you through talkin' to me?

BIG DADDY.   Why are you so anxious to shut me up?

BRICK.   Well, sir, ever so often you say to me, Brick, I want to have a talk with you, but when we talk, it never materializes. Nothing is said. You sit in a chair and gas about this and that and I look like I listen. I try to look like I listen, but I don't listen, not much. Communication is— awful hard between people an'—somehow between you and me, it just don't—

BIG DADDY. Have you ever been scared? I mean have you ever felt downright terror of something? (*He gets up.*) Just one moment. I'm going to close these doors. . . . (*He closes doors on gallery as if he were going to tell an important secret.*)

BRICK. What?

BIG DADDY. Brick?

BRICK. Huh?

BIG DADDY. Son, I thought I had it!

BRICK. Had what? Had what, Big Daddy?

BIG DADDY. Cancer!

BRICK. Oh . . .

BIG DADDY. I thought the old man made out of bones had laid his cold and heavy hand on my shoulder!

BRICK. Well, Big Daddy, you kept a tight mouth about it.

BIG DADDY. A pig squeals. A man keeps a tight mouth about it, in spite of a man not having a pig's advantage.

BRICK. What advantage is that?

BIG DADDY. Ignorance—of mortality—is a comfort. A man don't have that comfort, he's the only living thing that conceives of death, that knows what it is. The others go without knowing which is the way that anything living should go, go without knowing, without any knowledge of it, and yet a pig squeals, but a man sometimes, he can keep a tight mouth about it. Sometimes he— (*There is a deep, smoldering ferocity in the old man.*) —can keep a tight mouth about it. I wonder if—

BRICK. What, Big Daddy?

BIG DADDY. A whiskey highball would injure this spastic condition?

BRICK. No, sir, it might do it good.

BIG DADDY (*grins suddenly, wolfishly*). Jesus, I can't tell you! The sky is open! Christ, it's open again! It's open, boy, it's open! (*Brick looks down at his drink.*)

BRICK. You feel better, Big Daddy?

BIG DADDY. Better? Hell! I can breathe!—All of my life I been like a doubled up fist. . . . (*He pours a drink.*) —Poundin', smashin', drivin'!—now I'm going to loosen these doubled up hands and touch things *easy* with them. . . . (*He spreads his hands as if caressing the air.*) You know what I'm contemplating?

BRICK (*vaguely*). No, sir. What are you contemplating?

BIG DADDY. Ha ha!—*Pleasure!*—pleasure with *women!* (*Brick's smile fades a little but lingers.*) Brick, this stuff burns me!—

—Yes, boy. I'll tell you something that you might not guess. I still have desire for women and this is my sixty-fifth birthday.

BRICK. I think that's mighty remarkable, Big Daddy.

BIG DADDY. Remarkable?

BRICK. *Admirable,* Big Daddy.

BIG DADDY. You're damn right it is, remarkable and admirable both. I realize now that I never had me enough. I let many chances slip by because of scruples about it, scruples, convention—crap. . . . All that stuff is bull, bull, bull!—It took the shadow of death to make me see it. Now that shadow's lifted, I'm going to cut loose and have, what is it they call it, have me a—ball!

BRICK. A ball, huh?

BIG DADDY. That's right, a ball, a ball! Hell!—I slept with Big Mama till, let's see, five years ago, till I was sixty and she was fifty-eight, and never even liked her, never did!

(*The phone has been ringing down the hall. Big Mama enters, exclaiming:*)

BIG MAMA. Don't you men hear that phone ring? I heard it way out on the gall'ry.

BIG DADDY. There's five rooms off this front gall'ry that you could go through. Why do you go through this one?

(*Big Mama makes a playful face as she bustles out the hall door.*)

Hunh!—Why, when Big Mama goes out of a room, I can't remember what that woman looks like, but when Big Mama comes back into the room, boy, then I see what she looks like, and I wish I didn't! (*Bends over laughing at this joke till it hurts his guts and he straightens with a grimace. The laugh subsides to a chuckle as he puts the liquor glass a little distrustfully down on the table.*)

(*Brick has risen and hobbled to the gallery doors.*)

Hey! Where you goin'?

BRICK. Out for a breather.

BIG DADDY. Not yet you ain't. Stay here till this talk is finished, young fellow.

BRICK. I thought it was finished, Big Daddy.

BIG DADDY. It ain't even begun.

BRICK. My mistake. Excuse me. I just wanted to feel that river breeze.

BIG DADDY. Turn on the ceiling fan and set back down in that chair.

(*Big Mama's voice rises, carrying down the hall.*)

BIG MAMA. Miss Sally, you're a case! You're a caution, Miss Sally. Why didn't you give me a chance to explain it to you?

BIG DADDY. Jesus, she's talking to my old maid sister again.

BIG MAMA. Well, goodbye, now, Miss Sally. You come down real soon, Big Daddy's dying to see you! Yaisss, goodbye, Miss Sally. . . .

(*She hangs up and bellows with mirth. Big Daddy groans and covers his ears as she approaches.*)

(*Bursting in:*) Big Daddy, that was Miss Sally callin' from Memphis again! You know what she done, Big Daddy?

She called her doctor in Memphis to git him to tell her what that spastic thing is! Ha-*HAAAA!*—and called back to tell me how relieved she was that—Hey! Let me in! (*Big Daddy has been holding the door half closed against her.*)

BIG DADDY.   Naw I ain't. I told you not to come and go through this door. You just back out and go through those five other rooms.

BIG MAMA.   Big Daddy? Big Daddy? Oh, Big Daddy!—You didn't mean those things you said to me, did you? (*He shuts door firmly against her but she still calls.*) Sweetheart? Sweetheart? Big Daddy? You didn't mean those awful things you said to me?—I know you didn't. I know you didn't mean those things in your heart. . . .

(*The childlike voice fades with a sob and her heavy footsteps retreat down the hall. Brick has risen once more on his crutches and starts for the gallery again.*)

BIG DADDY.   All I ask of that woman is that she leave me alone. But she can't admit to herself that she makes me sick. That comes of having slept with her too many years. Should of quit much sooner but that old woman she never got enough of it—and I was good in bed . . . I never should of wasted so much of it on her. . . . They say you got just so many and each one is numbered. Well, I got a few left in me, a few, and I'm going to pick me a good one to spend 'em on! I'm going to pick me a choice one, I don't care how much she costs, I'll smother her in—minks! Ha ha! I'll strip her naked and smother her in minks and choke her with diamonds! Ha ha! I'll strip her naked and choke her with diamonds and smother her with minks and hump her from hell to breakfast. *Ha aha ha ha ha!*

MAE (*gaily at door*).   Who's that laughin' in there?

GOOPER.   Is Big Daddy laughin' in there?

BIG DADDY.   Crap!—them two—*drips*. . . . (*He goes over and touches Brick's shoulder.*) Yes, son. Brick, boy.—I'm—*happy!* I'm happy, son, I'm happy! (*He chokes a little and bites his under lip, pressing his head quickly, shyly against his son's head and then, coughing with embarrassment, goes uncertainly back to the table where he set down the glass. He drinks and makes a grimace as it burns his guts. Brick sighs and rises with effort.*) What makes you so restless? Have you got ants in your britches?

BRICK.   Yes, sir . . .

BIG DADDY.   Why?

BRICK.   —Something—hasn't—happened. . . .

BIG DADDY.   Yeah? What is that!

BRICK (*sadly*).   —the click. . . .

BIG DADDY.   Did you say click?

BRICK.   Yes, click.

BIG DADDY.   What click?

BRICK.   A click that I get in my head that makes me peaceful.

BIG DADDY.   I sure in hell don't know what you're talking about, but it disturbs me.

BRICK.   It's just a mechanical thing.

BIG DADDY.   What is a mechanical thing?

BRICK.   This click that I get in my head that makes me peaceful. I got to drink till I get it. It's just a mechanical thing, something like a—like a—like a—

BIG DADDY.   Like a—

BRICK.   Switch clicking off in my head, turning the hot light off and the cool night on and—(*He looks up, smiling sadly.*) —all of a sudden there's—peace!

BIG DADDY (*whistles long and soft with astonishment; he goes back to Brick and clasps his son's two shoulders*).   Jesus! I didn't know it had gotten that bad with you. Why, boy, you're—*alcoholic!*

BRICK.   That's the truth, Big Daddy. I'm alcoholic.

BIG DADDY.   This shows how I—let things go!

BRICK.   I have to hear that little click in my head that makes me peaceful. Usually I hear it sooner than this, sometimes as early as—noon, but—

—Today it's—dilatory. . . .

—I just haven't got the right level of alcohol in my blood-stream yet! (*This last statement is made with energy as he freshens his drink.*)

BIG DADDY.   Uh—huh. Expecting death made me blind. I didn't have no idea that a son of mine was turning into a drunkard under my nose.

BRICK (*gently*).   Well, now you do, Big Daddy, the news has penetrated.

BIG DADDY.   UH-huh, yes, now I do, the news has—penetrated. . . .

BRICK.   And so if you'll excuse me—

BIG DADDY.   No, I won't excuse you.

BRICK.   —I'd better sit by myself till I hear that click in my head, it's just a mechanical thing but it don't happen except when I'm alone or talking to no one. . . .

BIG DADDY.   You got a long, long time to sit still, boy, and talk to no one, but now you're talkin' to me. At least I'm talking to you. And you set there and listen until I tell you the conversation is over!

BRICK.   But this talk is like all the others we've ever had together in our lives. It's nowhere, nowhere!—it's—it's *painful*, Big Daddy. . . .

BIG DADDY.   All right, then let it be painful, but don't you move from that chair!—I'm going to remove that crutch. . . . (*He seizes the crutch and tosses it across the room.*)

BRICK.   I can hop on one foot, and if I fall, I can crawl!

BIG DADDY.   If you ain't careful you're gonna crawl off this plantation and then, by Jesus, you'll have to hustle your drinks along Skid Row!

BRICK.   That'll come, Big Daddy.

BIG DADDY.   Naw, it won't. You're my son and I'm going to straighten you out; now that *I'm* straightened out, I'm going to straighten out you!

BRICK.   Yeah?

BIG DADDY.   Today the report come in from Ochsner Clinic. Y'know what they told me? (*His face glows with triumph.*) The only thing that they could detect with all the instruments of science in that great hospital is a little spastic condition of the colon! And nerves torn to pieces by all that worry about it.

(*A little girl bursts into room with a sparkler clutched in each fist, hops and shrieks like a monkey gone mad and rushes back out again as Big Daddy strikes at her.*)
(*Silence. The two men stare at each other. A woman laughs gaily outside.*)

I want you to know I breathed a sigh of relief almost as powerful as the Vicksburg tornado!

BRICK.   You weren't ready to go?

BIG DADDY.   GO WHERE?—crap. . . .
—When you are gone from here, boy, you are long gone and no where! The human machine is not no different from the animal machine or the fish machine or the bird machine or the reptile machine or the insect machine! It's just a whole God damn lot more complicated and consequently more trouble to keep together. Yep. I thought I had it. The earth shook under my foot, the sky come down like the black lid of a kettle and I couldn't breathe!—Today!!—that lid was lifted, I drew my first free breath in—how many years?—*God!*—*three.* . . .

(*There is laughter outside, running footsteps, the soft, plushy sound and light of exploding rockets.*)
(*Brick stares at him soberly for a long moment; then makes a sort of startled sound in his nostrils and springs up on one foot and hops across the room to grab his crutch, swinging on the furniture for support. He gets the crutch and flees as if in horror for the gallery. His father seizes him by the sleeve of his white silk pajamas.*)

Stay here, you son of a bitch!—till I say go!

BRICK.   I can't.

BIG DADDY.   You sure in hell will, God damn it.

BRICK.   No, I can't. We talk, you talk, in—circles! We get nowhere, nowhere! It's always the same, you say you want to talk to me and don't have a ruttin' thing to say to me!

BIG DADDY.   Nothin' to say when I'm tellin' you I'm going to live when I thought I was dying?!

BRICK.   Oh—*that!*—Is that what you have to say to me?

BIG DADDY.   Why, you son of a bitch! Ain't that, ain't that—*important?!*

BRICK.   Well, you said that, that's said, and now I—

BIG DADDY.   Now you set back down.

BRICK.   You're all balled up, you—

BIG DADDY.   I ain't balled up!

BRICK.   You are, you're all balled up!

BIG DADDY.   Don't tell me what I am, you drunken whelp! I'm going to tear this coat sleeve off if you don't set down!

BRICK.   Big Daddy—

BIG DADDY.   Do what I tell you! I'm the boss here, now! I want you to know I'm back in the driver's seat now! (*Big Mama rushes in, clutching her great heaving bosom.*) What in hell do you want in here, Big Mama?

BIG MAMA.   Oh, Big Daddy! Why are you shouting like that? I just cain't *stainnnnnnnd*—it. . . .

BIG DADDY (*raising the back of his hand above his head*). GIT!—outa here. (*She rushes back out, sobbing.*)

BRICK (*softly, sadly*). Christ. . . .

BIG DADDY (*fiercely*). Yeah! Christ!—is right . . . (*Brick breaks loose and hobbles toward the gallery.*)

(*Big Daddy jerks his crutch from under Brick so he steps with the injured ankle. He utters a hissing cry of anguish, clutches a chair and pulls it over on top of him on the floor.*)

Son of a—tub of—hog fat. . . .

BRICK.   Big Daddy! Give me my crutch. (*Big Daddy throws the crutch out of reach.*) Give me that crutch, Big Daddy.

BIG DADDY.   Why do you drink?

BRICK.   Don't know, give me my crutch!

BIG DADDY.   You better think why you drink or give up drinking!

BRICK.   Will you please give me my crutch so I can get up off this floor?

BIG DADDY.   First you answer my question. Why do you drink? Why are you throwing your life away, boy, like somethin' disgusting you picked up on the street?

BRICK (*getting onto his knees*). Big Daddy, I'm in pain, I stepped on that foot.

BIG DADDY.   Good! I'm glad you're not too numb with the liquor in you to feel some pain!

BRICK.   You—spilled my—drink . . .

BIG DADDY.   I'll make a bargain with you. You tell me why you drink and I'll hand you one. I'll pour you the liquor myself and hand it to you.

BRICK.   Why do I drink?

BIG DADDY.   Yeah! Why?

BRICK.   Give me a drink and I'll tell you.

BIG DADDY.   Tell me first!

BRICK.   I'll tell you in one word.

BIG DADDY.   What word?

BRICK.   DISGUST! (*The clock chimes softly, sweetly. Big Daddy gives it a short, outraged glance.*) Now how about that drink?

BIG DADDY.   What are you disgusted with? You got to tell me that, first. Otherwise being disgusted don't make no sense!

BRICK.   Give me my crutch.

BIG DADDY.   You heard me, you got to tell me what I asked you first.

BRICK. I told you, I said to kill my disgust!

BIG DADDY. DISGUST WITH WHAT!

BRICK. You strike a hard bargain.

BIG DADDY. What are you disgusted with?—an' I'll pass you the liquor.

BRICK. I can hop on one foot, and if I fall, I can crawl.

BIG DADDY. You want liquor that bad?

BRICK (*dragging himself up, clinging to bedstead*). Yeah, I want it that bad.

BIG DADDY. If I give you a drink, will you tell me what it is you're disgusted with, Brick?

BRICK. Yes, sir, I will try to. (*The old man pours him a drink and solemnly passes it to him.*)

(*There is silence as Brick drinks.*)

Have you ever heard the word "mendacity"?

BIG DADDY. Sure. Mendacity is one of them five dollar words that cheap politicians throw back and forth at each other.

BRICK. You know what it means?

BIG DADDY. Don't it mean lying and liars?

BRICK. Yes, sir, lying and liars.

BIG DADDY. Has someone been lying to you?

CHILDREN (*chanting in chorus offstage*).
    We want Big Dad-dee!
    We want Big Dad-dee!
    (*Gooper appears in the gallery door.*)

GOOPER. Big Daddy, the kiddies are shouting for you out there.

BIG DADDY (*fiercely*). Keep out, Gooper!

GOOPER. 'Scuse *me*! (*Big Daddy slams the doors after Gooper.*)

BIG DADDY. Who's been lying to you, has Margaret been lying to you, has your wife been lying to you about something, Brick?

BRICK. Not her. That wouldn't matter.

BIG DADDY. Then who's been lying to you, and what about?

BRICK. No one single person and no one lie. . . .

BIG DADDY. Then what, what then, for Christ's sake?

BRICK. —The whole, the whole—thing. . . .

BIG DADDY. Why are you rubbing your head? You got a headache?

BRICK. No, I'm tryin' to—

BIG DADDY. —Concentrate, but you can't because your brain's all soaked with liquor, is that the trouble? Wet brain! (*He snatches the glass from Brick's hand.*) What do you know about this mendacity thing? Hell! I could write a book on it! Don't you know that? I could write a book on it and still not cover the subject? Well, I could, I could write a goddam book on it and still not cover the subject anywhere near enough!!—Think of all the lies I got to put up with!—Pretenses! Ain't that mendacity?

Having to pretend stuff you don't think or feel or have any idea of? Having for instance to act like I care for Big Mama!—I haven't been able to stand the sight, sound, or smell of that woman for forty years now!—even when I *laid* her!—regular as a piston. . . . Pretend to love that son of a bitch of a Gooper and his wife Mae and those five same screechers out there like parrots in a jungle? Jesus! Can't stand to look at 'em!

Church!—it bores the Bejesus out of me but I go!—I go an' sit there and listen to the fool preacher!

Clubs!—Elks! Masons! Rotary!—*crap!* (*A spasm of pain makes him clutch his belly. He sinks into a chair and his voice is softer and hoarser.*) You I *do* like for some reason, did always have some kind of real feeling for—affection—respect—yes, always. . . .

You and being a success as a planter is all I ever had any devotion to in my whole life!—and that's the truth. . . . I don't know why, but it is!

I've lived with mendacity!—Why can't *you* live with it? Hell, you *got* to live with it, there's nothing *else* to *live* with except mendacity, is there?

BRICK. Yes, sir. Yes, sir there is something else that you can live with!

BIG DADDY. What?

BRICK (*lifting his glass*). This!—Liquor. . . .

BIG DADDY. That's not living, that's dodging away from life.

BRICK. I want to dodge away from it.

BIG DADDY. Then why don't you kill yourself, man?

BRICK. I like to drink. . . .

BIG DADDY. Oh, God, I can't talk to you. . . .

BRICK. I'm sorry, Big Daddy.

BIG DADDY. Not as sorry as I am. I'll tell you something. A little while back when I thought my number was up— (*This speech should have torrential pace and fury.*) —before I found out it was just this—spastic—colon, I thought about you. Should I or should I not, if the jig was up, give you this place when I go—since I hate Gooper an' Mae an' know that they hate me, and since all five same monkeys are little Maes an' Goopers.—And I thought, No!—Then I thought, Yes!—I couldn't make up my mind. I hate Gooper and his five same monkeys and that bitch Mae! Why should I turn over twenty-eight thousand acres of the richest land this side of the valley Nile to not my kind?—But why in hell, on the other hand, Brick—should I subsidize a goddam fool on the bottle?— Liked or not liked, well, maybe even—*loved!*—Why should I do that?—Subsidize worthless behavior? Rot? Corruption?

BRICK (*smiling*). I understand.

BIG DADDY. Well, if you do, you're smarter than I am, God damn it, because I don't understand. And this I will tell you frankly. I didn't make up my mind at all on that

question and still to this day I ain't made out no will!—
Well, now I don't *have* to. The pressure is gone. I can just
wait and see if you pull yourself together or if you don't.

BRICK.   That's right, Big Daddy.

BIG DADDY.   You sound like you thought I was kidding.

BRICK (*rising*). No, sir, I know you're not kidding.

BIG DADDY.   But you don't care—?

BRICK (*hobbling toward the gallery door*). No, sir, I don't
care. . . .

Now how about taking a look at your birthday fireworks
and getting some of that cool breeze off the river?

(*He stands in the gallery doorway as the night sky turns pink
and green and gold with successive flashes of light.*)

BIG DADDY.   *WAIT!*—Brick. . . . (*His voice drops. Suddenly there is something shy, almost tender, in his restraining gesture.*) Don't let's—leave it like this, like
them other talks we've had, we've always—talked around
things, we've—just talked around things for some rutten
reason. I don't know what, it's always like something was
left not spoken, something avoided because neither of us
was honest enough with the—other. . . .

BRICK.   I never lied to you, Big Daddy.

BIG DADDY.   Did I ever to *you?*

BRICK.   No, sir. . . .

BIG DADDY.   Then there is at least two people that never
lied to each other.

BRICK.   But we've never *talked* to each other.

BIG DADDY.   We can *now.*

BRICK.   Big Daddy, there don't seem to be anything much
to say.

BIG DADDY.   You say that you drink to kill your disgust
with lying.

BRICK.   You said to give you a reason.

BIG DADDY.   Is liquor the only thing that'll kill this
disgust?

BRICK.   Now. Yes.

BIG DADDY.   But not once, huh?

BRICK.   Not when I was still young an' believing. A
drinking man's someone who wants to forget he isn't still
young an' believing.

BIG DADDY.   Believing what?

BRICK.   Believing. . . ,

BIG DADDY.   Believing *what?*

BRICK (*stubbornly evasive*). Believing. . . .

BIG DADDY.   I don't know what the hell you mean by believing and I don't think you know what you mean by
believing, but if you still got sports in your blood, go back
to sports announcing and—

BRICK.   Sit in a glass box watching games I can't play?
Describing what I can't do while players do it? Sweating
out their disgust and confusion in contests I'm not fit for?
Drinkin' a coke, half bourbon, so I can stand it? That's
no goddam good any more, no help—time just outran me,
Big Daddy—got there first . . .

BIG DADDY.   I think you're passing the buck.

BRICK.   You know many drinkin' men?

BIG DADDY (*with a slight, charming smile*). I have known
a fair number of that species.

BRICK.   Could any of them tell you why he drank?

BIG DADDY.   Yep, you're passin' the buck to things like
time and disgust with ''mendacity'' and—crap!—if you
got to use that kind of language about a thing, it's ninety-
proof bull, and I'm not buying any.

BRICK.   I had to give you a reason to get a drink!

BIG DADDY.   You started drinkin' when your friend
Skipper died.

(*Silence for five beats. Then Brick makes a startled movement, reaching for his crutch.*)

BRICK.   What are you suggesting?

BIG DADDY.   I'm suggesting nothing. (*The shuffle and clop
of Brick's rapid hobble away from his father's steady,
grave attention.*) —But Gooper an' Mae suggested that
there was something not right exactly in your—

BRICK (*stopping short downstage as if backed to a wall*).
''Not right''?

BIG DADDY.   Not, well, exactly *normal* in your friendship
with—

BRICK.   They suggested that, too? I thought that was Maggie's suggestion.

(*Brick's detachment is at last broken through. His heart is
accelerated; his forehead sweat-beaded; his breath becomes
more rapid and his voice hoarse. The thing they're discussing, timidly and painfully on the side of Big Daddy,
fiercely, violently on Brick's side, is the inadmissible thing
that Skipper died to disavow between them. The fact that if
it existed it had to be disavowed to ''keep face'' in the world
they lived in, may be at the heart of the ''mendacity'' that
Brick drinks to kill his disgust with. It may be the root of his
collapse. Or maybe it is only a single manifestation of it, not
even the most important. The bird that I hope to catch in the
net of this play is not the solution of one man's psychological
problem. I'm trying to catch the true quality of experience
in a group of people, that cloudy, flickering, evanescent—
fiercely charged!—interplay of live human beings in the
thundercloud of a common crisis. Some mystery should be
left in the revelation of character in a play, just as a great
deal of mystery is always left in the revelation of character
in life, even in one's own character to himself. This does not
absolve the playwright of his duty to observe and probe as
clearly and deeply as he legitimately can: but it should steer
him away from ''pat'' conclusions, facile definitions which
make a play just a play, not a snare for the truth of human
experience.*)

(*The following scene should be played with great concentration, with most of the power leashed but palpable in what is
left unspoken.*)

Who else's suggestion is it, is it *yours?* How many others thought that Skipper and I were—

BIG DADDY (*gently*). Now, hold on, hold on a minute, son.—I knocked around in my time.

BRICK. What's that got to do with—

BIG DADDY. I said 'Hold on!'—I bummed, I bummed this country till I was—

BRICK. Whose suggestion, who else's suggestion is it?

BIG DADDY. Slept in hobo jungles and railroad Y's and flophouses in all cities before I—

BRICK. Oh, *you* think so, too, you call me your son and a queer. Oh! Maybe that's why you put Maggie and me in this room that was Jack Straw's and Peter Ochello's, in which that pair of old sisters slept in a double bed where both of 'em died!

BIG DADDY. *Now just don't go throwing rocks at—*

(*Suddenly Reverend Tooker appears in the gallery doors, his head slightly, playfully, fatuously cocked, with a practiced clergyman's smile, sincere as a bird-call blown on a hunter's whistle, the living embodiment of the pious, conventional lie.*)
(*Big Daddy gasps a little at this perfectly timed, but incongruous, apparition.*) —What're you lookin' for, Preacher?

REVEREND TOOKER. The gentlemen's lavatory, ha ha!—heh, heh . . .

BIG DADDY (*with strained courtesy*). —Go back out and walk down to the other end of the gallery, Reverend Tooker, and use the bathroom connected with my bedroom, and if you can't find it, ask them where it is!

REVEREND TOOKER. Ah, thanks. (*He goes out with a deprecatory chuckle.*)

BIG DADDY. It's hard to talk in this place . . .

BRICK. Son of a—!

BIG DADDY (*leaving a lot unspoken*). —I seen all things and understood a lot of them, till 1910. Christ, the year that—I had worn my shoes through, hocked my—I hopped off a yellow dog freight car half a mile down the road, slept in a wagon of cotton outside the gin—Jack Straw an' Peter Ochello took me in. Hired me to manage this place which grew into this one.—When Jack Straw died—why, old Peter Ochello quit eatin' like a dog does when its master's dead, and died, too!

BRICK. Christ!

BIG DADDY. I'm just saying I understand such—

BRICK (*violently*). Skipper is dead. I have not quit eating!

BIG DADDY. No, but you started drinking. (*Brick wheels on his crutch and hurls his glass across the room shouting.*)

BRICK. YOU THINK SO, TOO?

BIG DADDY. *Shhh!*

(*Footsteps run on the gallery. There are women's calls.*)

(*Big Daddy goes toward the door.*) Go way!—Just broke a glass. . . . (*Brick is transformed, as if a quiet mountain blew suddenly up in volcanic flame.*)

BRICK. You think so, too? You think so, too? You think me an' Skipper did, did, did!—*sodomy!*—together?

BIG DADDY. Hold—!

BRICK. That what you—

BIG DADDY. —*ON*—a minute!

BRICK. You think we did dirty things between us, Skipper an'—

BIG DADDY. Why are you shouting like that? Why are you—

BRICK. —Me, is that what you think Skipper, is that—

BIG DADDY. —so excited? I don't think nothing. I don't know nothing. I'm simply telling you what—

BRICK. You think that Skipper and me were a pair of dirty old men?

BIG DADDY. Now that's—

BRICK. Straw? Ochello? A couple of—

BIG DADDY. Now just—

BRICK. —ducking sissies? Queers? Is that what you—

BIG DADDY. Shhh.

BRICK. —think? (*He loses his balance and pitches to his knees without noticing the pain. He grabs the bed and drags himself up.*)

BIG DADDY. Jesus!—Whew. . . . Grab my hand!

BRICK. Naw, I don't want your hand. . . .

BIG DADDY. Well, I want yours. Git up! (*He draws him up, keeps an arm about him with concern and affection.*) You broken out in a sweat! You're panting like you'd run a race with—

BRICK (*freeing himself from his father's hold*). Big Daddy, you shock me, Big Daddy, you, you—*shock* me! Talkin' so— (*He turns away from his father.*) —casually!—about a—thing like that . . .

—Don't you know how people *feel* about things like that? How, how *disgusted* they are by things like that? Why, at Ole Miss when it was discovered a pledge to our fraternity, Skipper's and mine, did a, *attempted* to do a, unnatural thing with—

We not only dropped him like a hot rock!—We told him to git off the campus, and he did, he got!—All the way to— (*He halts, breathless.*)

BIG DADDY. —Where?

BRICK. —North Africa, last I heard!

BIG DADDY. Well, I have come back from further away than that. I have just now returned from the other side of the moon, death's country, son, and I'm not easy to shock by anything here. (*He comes downstage and faces out.*) Always, anyhow, lived with too much space around me to be infected by ideas of other people. One thing you can grow on a big place more important than cotton!—is *tolerance!*—I grown it. (*He returns toward Brick.*)

BRICK.   Why can't exceptional friendship, *real, real, deep, deep friendship!* between two men be respected as something clean and decent without being thought of as—

BIG DADDY.   It can, it is, for God's sake.

BRICK.   —Fairies. . . . (*In his utterance of this word, we gauge the wide and profound reach of the conventional mores he got from the world that crowned him with early laurel.*)

BIG DADDY.   I told Mae an' Gooper—

BRICK.   Frig Mae and Gooper, frig all dirty lies and liars!—Skipper and me had a clean, true thing between us!—had a clean friendship, practically all our lives, till Maggie got the idea you're talking about. Normal? No!—It was too rare to be normal, any true thing between two people is too rare to be normal. Oh, once in a while he put his hand on my shoulder or I'd put mine on his, oh, maybe even, when we were touring the country in pro-football an' shared hotel-rooms we'd reach across the space between the two beds and shake hands to say goodnight, yeah, one or two times we—

BIG DADDY.   Brick, nobody thinks that that's not normal!

BRICK.   Well, they're mistaken, it was! It was a pure an' true thing an' that's not normal. (*They both stare straight at each other for a long moment. The tension breaks and both turn away as if tired.*)

BIG DADDY.   Yeah, it's—hard t'—talk. . . .

BRICK.   All right, then, let's—let it go. . . .

BIG DADDY.   Why did Skipper crack up? Why have you?

(*Brick looks back at his father again. He has already decided, without knowing that he has made this decision, that he is going to tell his father that he is dying of cancer. Only this could even the score between them: one inadmissible thing in return for another.*)

BRICK (*ominously*).   All right. You're asking for it, Big Daddy. We're finally going to have that real true talk you wanted. It's too late to stop it, now, we got to carry it through and cover every subject. (*He hobbles back to the liquor cabinet.*) Uh-huh. (*He opens the ice bucket and picks up the silver tongs with slow admiration of their frosty brightness.*) Maggie declares that Skipper and I went into pro-football after we left "Ole Miss" because we were scared to grow up . . . (*He moves downstage with the shuffle and clop of a cripple on a crutch. As Margaret did when her speech became "recitative," he looks out into the house, commanding its attention by his direct, concentrated gaze—a broken, "tragically elegant" figure telling simply as much as he knows of "the Truth":*) —Wanted to—keep on tossing—those long, long!—high, high!—passes that—couldn't be intercepted except by time, the aerial attack that made us famous! And so we did, we did, we kept it up for one season, that aerial attack, we held it high!—Yeah, but—

—that summer, Maggie, she laid the law down to me, said, Now or never, and so I married Maggie. . . .

BIG DADDY.   How was Maggie in bed?

BRICK (*wryly*).   Great! the greatest! (*Big Daddy nods as if he thought so.*) She went on the road that fall with the Dixie Stars. Oh, she made a great show of being the world's best sport. She wore a—wore a—tall bearskin cap! A shako, they call it, a dyed moleskin coat, a moleskin coat dyed red!—Cut up crazy! Rented hotel ballrooms for victory celebrations, wouldn't cancel them when it—turned out—defeat. . . .

MAGGIE THE CAT! Ha ha! (*Big Daddy nods.*) —But Skipper, he had some fever which came back on him which doctors couldn't explain and I got that injury—turned out to be just a shadow on the X-ray plate—and a touch of bursitis. . . .

I lay in a hospital bed, watched our games on TV, saw Maggie on the bench next to Skipper when he was hauled out of the game for stumbles, fumbles!—Burned me up the way she hung on his arm!—Y'know, I think that Maggie had always felt sort of left out because she and me never got any closer together than two people just get in bed, which is not much closer than two cats on a—fence humping. . . .

So! She took this time to work on poor dumb Skipper. He was a less than average student at Ole Miss, you know that, don't you?!—Poured in his mind the dirty, false idea that what we were, him and me, was a frustrated case of that ole pair of sisters that lived in this room, Jack Straw and Peter Ochello!—He, poor Skipper, went to bed with Maggie to prove it wasn't true, and when it didn't work out, he thought it *was* true!—Skipper broke in two like a rotten stick—nobody ever turned so fast to a lush—or died of it so quick. . . .

—Now are you satisfied? (*Big Daddy has listened to this story, dividing the grain from the chaff. Now he looks at his son.*)

BIG DADDY.   Are *you* satisfied?

BRICK.   With what?

BIG DADDY.   That half-ass story!

BRICK.   What's half-ass about it?

BIG DADDY.   Something's left out of that story. What did you leave out?

(*The phone has started ringing in the hall. As if it reminded him of something, Brick glances suddenly toward the sound and says:*)

BRICK.   Yes!—I left out a long-distance call which I had from Skipper, in which he made a drunken confession to me and on which I hung up!—last time we spoke to each other in our lives. . . .

(*Muted ring stops as someone answers phone in a soft, indistinct voice in hall.*)

BIG DADDY.   You hung up?

BRICK.   Hung up. Jesus! Well—

BIG DADDY. Anyhow now!—we have tracked down the lie with which you're disgusted and which you are drinking to kill your disgust with, Brick. You been passing the buck. This disgust with mendacity is disgust with yourself.

You!—dug the grave of your friend and kicked him in it!—before you'd face truth with him!

BRICK. *His* truth, not *mine!*

BIG DADDY. His truth, okay! But you wouldn't face it with him!

BRICK. Who *can* face truth? Can *you?*

BIG DADDY. Now don't start passin' the rotten buck again, boy!

BRICK. *How about these birthday congratulations, these many, many happy returns of the day, when ev'rybody but you knows there won't be any!*

(*Whoever has answered the hall phone lets out a high, shrill laugh; the voice becomes audible saying: "no, no, you got it all wrong! Upside down! Are you crazy?"*)

(*Brick suddenly catches his breath as he realized that he has made a shocking disclosure. He hobbles a few paces, then freezes, and without looking at his father's shocked face, says:*)

Let's, let's—go out, now, and—(*Big Daddy moves suddenly forward and grabs hold of the boy's crutch like it was a weapon for which they were fighting for possession.*)

BIG DADDY. Oh, no, no! No one's going out. What did you start to say?

BRICK. I don't remember.

BIG DADDY. "Many happy returns when they know there won't be any"?

BRICK. Aw, hell, Big Daddy, forget it. Come on out on the gallery and look at the fireworks they're shooting off for your birthday. . . .

BIG DADDY. First you finish that remark you were makin' before you cut off. "Many happy returns when they know there won't be any"?—Ain't that what you just said?

BRICK. Look, now. I can get around without that crutch if I have to but it would be a lot easier on the furniture an' glassware if I didn't have to go swinging along like Tarzan of th'—

BIG DADDY. FINISH! WHAT YOU WAS SAYIN'!

(*An eerie green glow shows in sky behind him.*)

BRICK (*sucking the ice in his glass, speech becoming thick*). Leave th' place to Gooper and Mae an' their five little same little monkeys. All I want is—

BIG DADDY. "LEAVE TH' PLACE," did you say?

BRICK (*vaguely*). All twenty-eight thousand acres of the richest land this side of the valley Nile.

BIG DADDY. Who said I was "leaving the place" to Gooper or anybody? This is my sixty-fifth birthday! I got fifteen years or twenty years left in me! I'll outlive *you!* I'll bury you an' have to pay for your coffin!

BRICK. Sure. Many happy returns. Now let's go watch the fireworks, come on, let's—

BIG DADDY. Lying, have they been lying? About the report from th'—clinic? Did they, did they—find something?—*Cancer.* Maybe?

BRICK. Mendacity is a system that we live in. Liquor is one way out an' death's the other. . . . (*He takes the crutch from Big Daddy's loose grip and swings out on the gallery leaving the doors open.*)

(*A song, "Pick a Bale of Cotton," is heard.*)

MAE (*appearing in door*). Oh, Big Daddy, the field-hands are singin' fo' you!

BIG DADDY (*shouting hoarsely*). BRICK! BRICK!

MAE. He's outside drinkin', Big Daddy.

BIG DADDY. *BRICK!*

(*Mae retreats, awed by the passion of his voice. Children call Brick in tones mocking Big Daddy. His face crumbles like broken yellow plaster about to fall into dust.*)

(*There is a glow in the sky. Brick swings back through the doors, slowly, gravely, quite soberly.*)

BRICK. I'm sorry, Big Daddy. My head don't work any more and it's hard for me to understand how anybody could care if he lived or died or was dying or cared about anything but whether or not there was liquor left in the bottle and so I said what I said without thinking. In some ways I'm no better than the others, in some ways worse because I'm less alive. Maybe it's being alive that makes them lie, and being almost *not* alive makes me sort of accidentally truthful—I don't know but—anyway—we've been friends . . .

—And being friends is telling each other the truth. . . . (*There is a pause.*) You told *me!* I told *you!*

(*A child rushes into the room and grabs a fistful of firecrackers and runs out again.*)

CHILD (*screaming*). Bang, bang, bang, bang bang, bang, bang, bang, bang!

BIG DADDY (*slowly and passionately*). CHRIST—DAMN—ALL—LYING SONS OF—LYING BITCHES! (*He straightens at last and crosses to the inside door. At the door he turns and looks back as if he had some desperate question he couldn't put into words. Then he nods reflectively and says in a hoarse voice:*) Yes, all liars, all liars, all lying dying liars! (*This is said slowly, slowly, with fierce revulsion. He goes on out.*) —Lying! Dying! Liars! (*His voice dies out. There is the sound of a child being slapped. It rushes, hideously bawling, through room and out the hall door.*)

(*Brick remains motionless as the lights dim out and the curtain falls.*)

CURTAIN

ACT THREE

There is no lapse of time.
Mae enters with Reverend Tooker.

MAE.   Where is Big Daddy! Big Daddy?

BIG MAMA (*entering*). Too much smell of burnt fireworks makes me feel a little bit sick at my stomach.—Where is Big Daddy?

MAE.   That's what I want to know, where has Big Daddy gone?

BIG MAMA.   He must have turned in, I reckon he went to baid. . . . (*Gooper enters.*)

GOOPER.   Where is Big Daddy?

MAE.   We don't know where he is!

BIG MAMA.   I reckon he's gone to baid.

GOOPER.   Well, then, now we can talk.

BIG MAMA.   What *is* this talk? *what* talk? (*Margaret appears on gallery, talking to Dr. Baugh.*)

MARGARET (*musically*). My family freed their slaves ten years before abolition, my great-great-grandfather gave his slaves their freedom five years before the war between the States started!

MAE.   Oh, for God's sake! Maggie's climbed back up in her family tree!

MARGARET (*sweetly*). What, Mae?—Oh, where's Big Daddy?! (*The pace must be very quick. Great Southern animation.*)

BIG MAMA (*addressing them all*). I think Big Daddy was just worn out. He loves his family, he loves to have them around him, but it's a strain on his nerves. He wasn't himself tonight, Big Daddy wasn't himself, I could tell he was all worked up.

REVEREND TOOKER.   I think he's remarkable.

BIG MAMA.   Yaisss! Just remarkable. Did you all notice the food he ate at that table? Did you all notice the supper he put away? Why, he ate like a hawss!

GOOPER.   I hope he doesn't regret it.

BIG MAMA.   Why, that man—ate a huge piece of cawn-bread with molasses on it! Helped himself twice to hoppin' john.

MARGARET.   Big Daddy loves hoppin' john.—We had a real country dinner.

BIG MAMA (*overlapping Margaret*). Yais, he simply adores it! An' candied yams? That man put away enough food at that table to stuff a nigger *field*-hand!

GOOPER (*with grim relish*). I hope he don't have to pay for it later on. . . .

BIG MAMA (*fiercely*). What's *that*, Gooper?

MAE.   Gooper says he hopes Big Daddy doesn't suffer tonight.

BIG MAMA.   Oh, shoot, Gooper says, Gooper says! Why should Big Daddy suffer for satisfying a normal appetite? There's nothin' wrong with that man but nerves, he's sound as a dollar! And now he knows he is an' that's why

he ate such a supper. He had a big load off his mind, knowin' he wasn't doomed t'—what he thought he was doomed to. . . .

MARGARET (*sadly and sweetly*). Bless his old sweet soul. . . .

BIG MAMA (*vaguely*). Yais, bless his heart, wher's Brick?

MAE.   Outside.

GOOPER.   —Drinkin' . . .

BIG MAMA.   I know he's drinkin'. You all don't have to keep tellin' *me* Brick is drinkin'. Cain't I see he's drinkin' without you continually tellin' me that boy's drinkin'?

MARGARET.   Good for you, Big Mama! (*She applauds.*)

BIG MAMA.   Other people *drink* and *have* drunk an' will *drink*, as long as they make that stuff an' put it in bottles.

MARGARET.   That's the truth. I never trusted a man that didn't drink.

MAE.   Gooper never drinks. Don't you trust Gooper?

MARGARET.   Why, Gooper don't you drink? If I'd known you didn't drink, I wouldn't of made that remark—

BIG MAMA.   *Brick?*

MARGARET.   —at least not in your presence. (*She laughs sweetly.*)

BIG MAMA.   *Brick!*

MARGARET.   He's still on the gall'ry. I'll go bring him in so we can talk.

BIG MAMA (*worriedly*). I don't know what this mysterious family conference is about. (*Awkward silence. Big Mama looks from face to face, then belches slightly and mutters, "Excuse me. . . ." She opens an ornamental fan suspended about her throat, a black lace fan to go with her black lace gown, and fans her wilting corsage, sniffing nervously and looking from face to face in the uncomfortable silence as Margaret calls "Brick?" and Brick sings to the moon on the gallery.*) I don't know what's wrong here, you all have such long faces! Open that door on the hall and let some air circulate through here, will you please, Gooper?

MAE.   I think we'd better leave that door closed, Big Mama, till after the talk.

BIG MAMA.   Reveren' Tooker, will *you* please open that door?!

REVEREND TOOKER.   I sure will, Big Mama.

MAE.   I just didn't think we ought t' take any chance of Big Daddy hearin' a word of this discussion.

BIG MAMA.   *I swan!* Nothing's going to be said in Big Daddy's house that he cain't hear if he wants to!

GOOPER.   Well, Big Mama, it's—

(*Mae gives him a quick, hard poke to shut him up. He glares at her fiercely as she circles before him like a burlesque ballerina, raising her skinny bare arms over her head, jangling her bracelets, exclaiming:*)

MAE.   *A breeze! A breeze!*

REVEREND TOOKER.   I think this house is the coolest house in the Delta.—Did you all know that Halsey Banks' widow put air-conditioning units in the church and rectory at Friar's Point in memory of Halsey?

(*General conversation has resumed; everybody is chatting so that the stage sounds like a big bird-cage.*)

GOOPER.   Too bad nobody cools your church off for you. I bet you sweat in that pulpit these hot Sundays, Reverend Tooker.

REVEREND TOOKER.   Yes, my vestments are drenched.

MAE (*at the same time to Dr. Baugh*).   You reckon those vitamin B$_{12}$ injections are what they're cracked up t' be, Doc Baugh?

DOCTOR BAUGH.   Well, if you want to be stuck with something I guess they're as good to be stuck with as anything else.

BIG MAMA (*at gallery door*).   Maggie, Maggie, aren't you comin' with Brick?

MAE (*suddenly and loudly, creating a silence*).   *I have a strange feeling, I have a peculiar feeling!*

BIG MAMA (*turning from gallery*).   What feeling?

MAE.   That Brick said somethin' he shouldn't of said t' Big Daddy.

BIG MAMA.   Now what on earth could Brick of said t' Big Daddy that he shouldn't say?

GOOPER.   Big Mama, there's somethin'—

MAE.   NOW, WAIT! (*She rushes up to Big Mama and gives her a quick hug and kiss. Big Mama pushes her impatiently off as the Reverend Tooker's voice rises serenely in a little pocket of silence:*)

REVEREND TOOKER.   Yes, last Sunday the gold in my chasuble faded into th' purple. . . .

GOOPER.   Reveren', you must of been preachin' hell's fire last Sunday! (*He guffaws at this witticism but the Reverend is not sincerely amused. At the same time Big Mama has crossed over to Dr. Baugh and is saying to him:*)

BIG MAMA (*her breathless voice rising high-pitched above the others*).   In my day they had what they call the Keeley cure for heavy drinkers. But now I understand they just take some kind of tablets, they call them ''Annie Bust'' tablets. But *Brick* don't need to take *nothin'*.

(*Brick appears in gallery doors with Margaret behind him.*)

BIG MAMA (*unaware of his presence behind her*).   That boy is just broken up over Skipper's death. You know how poor Skipper died. They gave him a big, big dose of that sodium amytal stuff at his home and then they called the ambulance and give him another big, big dose of it at the hospital and that and all of the alcohol in his system fo' months an' months just proved too much for his heart. . . . I'm scared of needles! I'm more scared of a needle than the knife. . . . I think more people have been needled out of this world than— (*She stops short and wheels about.*) OH!—here's Brick! My precious baby— (*She turns upon Brick with short, fat arms extended, at the same time uttering a loud, short sob, which is both comic and touching.*)

(*Brick smiles and bows slightly, making a burlesque gesture of gallantry for Maggie to pass before him into the room. Then he hobbles on his crutch directly to the liquor cabinet and there is absolute silence, with everybody looking at Brick as everybody has always looked at Brick when he spoke or moved or appeared. One by one he drops ice cubes in his glass, then suddenly, but not quickly, looks back over his shoulder with a wry, charming smile, and says:*)

BRICK.   I'm sorry! Anyone else?

BIG MAMA (*sadly*).   No, son. I *wish* you wouldn't!

BRICK.   I wish I didn't have to, Big Mama, but I'm still waiting for that click in my head which makes it all smooth out!

BIG MAMA.   Aw, Brick, you—BREAK MY HEART!

MARGARET (*at the same time*).   Brick, go sit with Big Mama!

BIG MAMA.   I just cain't *staiiiiiiiii-nnnnnd*—it. . . . (*She sobs.*)

MAE.   Now that we're all assembled—

GOOPER.   We kin talk. . . .

BIG MAMA.   Breaks my heart. . . .

MARGARET.   Sit with Big Mama, Brick, and hold her hand. (*Big Mama sniffs very loudly three times, almost like three drum beats in the pocket of silence.*)

BRICK.   You do that, Maggie. I'm a restless cripple. I got to stay on my crutch. (*Brick hobbles to the gallery door; leans there as if waiting.*)

(*Mae sits beside Big Mama, while Gooper moves in front and sits on the end of the couch, facing her. Reverend Tooker moves nervously into the space between them; on the other side, Dr. Baugh stands looking at nothing in particular and lights a cigar. Margaret turns away.*)

BIG MAMA.   Why are you all *surroundin'* me—like this? Why're you all starin' at me like this an' makin' signs at each other? (*Reverend Tooker steps back startled.*)

MAE.   Calm yourself, Big Mama.

BIG MAMA.   Calm you'self, *you'self*, Sister Woman. How could I calm myself with everyone starin' at me as if big drops of blood had broken out on m'face? What's this all about, Annh! What? (*Gooper coughs and takes a center position.*)

GOOPER.   Now, Doc Baugh.

MAE.   Doc Baugh?

BRICK (*suddenly*).   SHHH! (*Then he grins and chuckles and shakes his head regretfully.*) —Naw!—that wasn't th' click.

GOOPER.   Brick, shut up or stay out there on the gallery with your liquor! We got to talk about a serious matter. Big Mama wants to know the complete truth about the report we got today from the Ochsner Clinic.

MAE (*eagerly*). —on Big Daddy's condition!

GOOPER.   Yais, on Big Daddy's condition, we got to face it.

DOCTOR BAUGH.   Well. . . .

BIG MAMA (*terrified, rising*). Is there? Something? Something that I? Don't—Know?

(*In these few words, this startled, very soft, question, Big Mama reviews the history of her forty-five years with Big Daddy, her great, almost embarrassingly true-hearted and simple-minded devotion to Big Daddy, who must have had something Brick has, who made himself loved so much by the "simple expedient" of not loving enough to disturb his charming detachment, also once coupled, like Brick's, with virile beauty.*)

(*Big Mama has a dignity at this moment: she almost stops being fat.*)

DOCTOR BAUGH (*after a pause, uncomfortably*). Yes?—Well—

BIG MAMA.   I!!!—want to—knowwwwwww. . . . (*Immediately she thrusts her fist to her mouth as if to deny that statement.*) (*Then, for some curious reason, she snatches the withered corsage from her breast and hurls it on the floor and steps on it with her short, fat feet.*) —Somebody must be lyin'!—I want to know!

MAE.   Sit down, Big Mama, sit down on this sofa.

MARGARET (*quickly*). Brick, go sit with Big Mama.

BIG MAMA.   *What is it, what is it?*

DOCTOR BAUGH.   I never have seen a more thorough examination than Big Daddy Pollitt was given in all my experience with the Ochsner Clinic.

GOOPER.   It's one of the best in the country.

MAE.   It's *THE* best in the country—bar none! (*For some reason she gives Gooper a violent poke as she goes past him. He slaps at her hand without removing his eyes from his mother's face.*)

DOCTOR BAUGH.   Of course they were ninety-nine and nine-tenths percent sure before they even started.

BIG MAMA.   Sure of what, sure of what, sure of—what?—what! (*She catches her breath in a startled sob. Mae kisses her quickly. She thrusts Mae fiercely away from her, staring at the doctor.*)

MAE.   Mommy, be a brave girl!

BRICK (*in the doorway, softly*).
    "By the light, by the light,
    Of the sil-ve-ry mo-ooo-n . . ."

GOOPER.   Shut up!—Brick.

BRICK.   —Sorry. . . . (*He wanders out on the gallery.*)

DOCTOR BAUGH.   But now, you see, Big Mama, they cut a piece off this growth, a specimen of the tissue and—

BIG MAMA.   Growth? You told Big Daddy—

DOCTOR BAUGH.   Now wait.

BIG MAMA (*fiercely*). You told me and Big Daddy there wasn't a thing wrong with him but—

MAE.   Big Mama, they always—

GOOPER.   Let Doc Baugh talk, will yuh?

BIG MAMA.   —little spastic condition of— (*Her breath gives out in a sob.*)

DOCTOR BAUGH.   Yes, that's what we told Big Daddy. But we had this bit of tissue run through the laboratory and I'm sorry to say the test was positive on it. It's—well—malignant. . . . (*Pause.*)

BIG MAMA.   —Cancer?! Cancer?! (*Dr. Baugh nods gravely.*) (*Big Mama gives a long gasping cry.*)

MAE and GOOPER.   Now, now, now, Big Mama, you had to know. . . .

BIG MAMA.   *WHY DIDN'T THEY CUT IT OUT OF HIM? HANH? HANH?*

DOCTOR BAUGH.   Involved too much, Big Mama, too many organs affected.

MAE.   Big Mama, the liver's affected and so's the kidneys, both! It's gone way past what they call a—

GOOPER.   A surgical risk.

MAE.   —Uh-huh. . . . (*Big Mama draws a breath like a dying gasp.*)

REVEREND TOOKER.   Tch, tch, tch, tch, tch!

DOCTOR BAUGH.   Yes, it's gone past the knife.

MAE.   *That's why he's turned yellow, Mommy!*

BIG MAMA.   *Git away from me, git away from me, Mae!* (*She rises abruptly.*) *I want Brick! Where's Brick? Where is my only son?*

MAE.   Mama! Did she say "*only* son"?

GOOPER.   What does that make *me?*

MAE.   A sober responsible man with five precious children!—*Six!*

BIG MAMA.   I want Brick to tell me! Brick! Brick!

MARGARET (*rising from her reflections in a corner*). Brick was so upset he went back out.

BIG MAMA.   *Brick!*

MARGARET.   Mama, let *me* tell you!

BIG MAMA.   No, no, leave me alone, you're not my blood!

GOOPER.   *Mama, I'm your son!* Listen to *me!*

MAE.   Gooper's your son, he's your first-born!

BIG MAMA.   Gooper never liked Daddy.

MAE (*as if terribly shocked*). That's not TRUE! (*There is a pause. The minister coughs and rises.*)

REVEREND TOOKER (*to Mae*). I think I'd better slip away at this point.

MAE (*sweetly and sadly*). Yes, Doctor Tooker, you go.

REVEREND TOOKER (*discreetly*). Goodnight, goodnight, everybody, and God bless you all . . . on this place. . . . (*He slips out.*)

DOCTOR BAUGH.   That man is a good man but lacking in tact. Talking about people giving memorial windows—if he mentioned one memorial window, he must have spoke of a dozen, and saying how awful it was when somebody died intestate, the legal wrangles, and so forth. (*Mae coughs, and points at Big Mama.*)

DOCTOR BAUGH.   Well, Big Mama. . . . (*He sighs.*)

BIG MAMA.   It's all a mistake, I know it's just a bad dream.

DOCTOR BAUGH.   We're gonna keep Big Daddy as comfortable as we can.

BIG MAMA.   Yes, it's just a bad dream, that's all it is, it's just an awful dream.

GOOPER.   In my opinion Big Daddy is having some pain but won't admit that he has it.

BIG MAMA.   Just a dream, a bad dream.

DOCTOR BAUGH.   That's what lots of them do, they think if they don't admit they're having the pain they can sort of escape the fact of it.

GOOPER (*with relish*).   Yes, they get sly about it, they get real sly about it.

MAE.   Gooper and I think—

GOOPER.   Shut up, Mae!—Big Daddy ought to be started on morphine.

BIG MAMA.   Nobody's going to give Big Daddy morphine.

DOCTOR BAUGH.   Now, Big Mama, when that pain strikes it's going to strike mighty hard and Big Daddy's going to need the needle to bear it.

BIG MAMA.   I tell you, nobody's going to give him morphine.

MAE.   Big Mama, you don't want to see Big Daddy suffer, you know you— (*Gooper standing beside her gives her a savage poke.*)

DOCTOR BAUGH (*placing a package on the table*).   I'm leaving this stuff here, so if there's a sudden attack you all won't have to send out for it.

MAE.   I know how to give a hypo.

GOOPER.   Mae took a course in nursing during the war.

MARGARET.   Somehow I don't think Big Daddy would want Mae to give him a hypo.

MAE.   You think he'd want *you* to do it? (*Dr. Baugh rises.*)

GOOPER.   Doctor Baugh is goin'.

DOCTOR BAUGH.   Yes, I got to be goin'. Well, keep your chin up, Big Mama.

GOOPER (*with jocularity*).   She's gonna keep *both* chins up, aren't you Big Mama? (*Big Mama sobs.*) Now stop that, Big Mama.

MAE.   Sit down with me, Big Mama.

GOOPER (*at door with Dr. Baugh*).   Well, Doc, we sure do appreciate all you done. I'm telling you, we're surely obligated to you for— (*Dr. Baugh has gone out without a glance at him.*)

GOOPER.   —I guess that doctor has got a lot on his mind but it wouldn't hurt him to act a little more human. . . . (*Big Mama sobs.*) Now be a brave girl, Mommy.

BIG MAMA.   It's not true, I know that it's just not true!

GOOPER.   Mama, those tests are infallible!

BIG MAMA.   Why are you so determined to see your father daid?

MAE.   Big Mama!

MARGARET (*gently*).   I know what Big Mama means.

MAE (*fiercely*).   Oh, do you?

MARGARET (*quietly and very sadly*).   Yes, I think I do.

MAE.   For a newcomer in the family you sure do show a lot of understanding.

MARGARET.   Understanding is needed on this place.

MAE.   I guess you must have needed a lot of it in your family, Maggie, with your father's liquor problem and now you've got Brick with his!

MARGARET.   Brick does not have a liquor problem at all. Brick is devoted to Big Daddy. This thing is a terrible strain on him.

BIG MAMA.   Brick is Big Daddy's boy, but he drinks too much and it worries me and Big Daddy, and, Margaret, you've got to cooperate with us, you've got to cooperate with Big Daddy and me in getting Brick straightened out. Because it will break Big Daddy's heart if Brick don't pull himself together and take hold of things.

MAE.   Take hold of *what* things, Big Mama?

BIG MAMA.   The place. (*There is a quick violent look between Mae and Gooper.*)

GOOPER.   Big Mama, you've had a shock.

MAE.   Yais, we've all had a shock, but. . . .

GOOPER.   Let's be realistic—

MAE.   —Big Daddy would never, would *never,* be foolish enough to—

GOOPER.   —put this place in irresponsible hands!

BIG MAMA.   Big Daddy ain't going to leave the place in anybody's hands; Big Daddy is *not* going to die. I want you to get that in your heads, all of you!

MAE.   Mommy, Mommy, Big Mama, we're just as hopeful an' optimistic as you are about Big Daddy's prospects, we have faith in *prayer*—but nevertheless there are certain matters that have to be discussed an' dealt with, because otherwise—

GOOPER.   Eventualities have to be considered and now's the time. . . . Mae, will you please get my briefcase out of our room?

MAE.   Yes, honey. (*She rises and goes through the hall door.*)

GOOPER (*standing over Big Mama*).   Now Big Mom. What you said just now was not at all true and you know it. I've always loved Big Daddy in my own quiet way. I never made a show of it, and I know that Big Daddy has always been fond of me in a quiet way, too, and he never made a show of it neither. (*Mae returns with Gooper's briefcase.*)

MAE.   Here's your briefcase, Gooper, honey.

GOOPER (*handing the briefcase back to her*).   Thank you. . . . Of cou'se, my relationship with Big Daddy is different from Brick's.

MAE.   You're eight years older'n Brick an' always had t'carry a bigger load of th' responsibilities than Brick ever had t'carry. He never carried a thing in his life but a football or a highball.

GOOPER.   Mae, will y' let me talk, please?

MAE.   Yes, honey.

GOOPER.   Now, a twenty-eight thousand acre plantation's a mighty big thing t'run.

MAE.   Almost singlehanded.

(*Margaret has gone out onto the gallery, and can be heard calling softly to Brick.*)

BIG MAMA.   You never had to run this place! What are you talking about? As if Big Daddy was dead and in his grave, you had to run it? Why, you just helped him out with a few business details and had your law practice at the same time in Memphis!

MAE.   Oh, Mommy, Mommy, Big Mommy! Let's be fair! Why, Gooper has given himself body and soul to keeping this place up for the past five years since Big Daddy's health started failing. Gooper won't say it, Gooper never thought of it as a duty, he just did it. And what did Brick do? Brick kept living in his past glory at college! Still a football player at twenty-seven!

MARGARET (*returning alone*).   Who are you talking about, now? Brick? A football player? He isn't a football player and you know it. Brick is a sports announcer on TV and one of the best-known ones in the country!

MAE.   I'm talking about what he was.

MARGARET.   Well, I wish you would just stop talking about my husband.

GOOPER.   I've got a right to discuss my brother with other members of MY OWN family which don't include *you*. Why don't you go out there and drink with Brick?

MARGARET.   I've never seen such malice toward a brother.

GOOPER.   How about his for me? Why, he can't stand to be in the same room with me!

MARGARET.   This is a deliberate campaign of vilification for the most disgusting and sordid reason on earth, and I know what it is! It's *avarice, avarice, greed, greed!*

BIG MAMA.   *Oh, I'll scream! I will scream in a moment unless this stops!*

(*Gooper has stalked up to Margaret with clenched fists at his sides as if he would strike her. Mae distorts her face again into a hideous grimace behind Margaret's back.*)

MARGARET.   We only remain on the place because of Big Mama and Big Daddy. If it is true what they say about Big Daddy we are going to leave here just as soon as it's over. Not a moment later.

BIG MAMA (*sobs*).   Margaret. Child. Come here. Sit next to Big Mama.

MARGARET.   Precious Mommy. I'm sorry. I'm sorry, I—! (*She bends her long graceful neck to press her forehead to Big Mama's bulging shoulder under its black chiffon.*)

GOOPER.   How beautiful, how touching, this display of devotion!

MAE.   Do you know why she's childless? She's childless because that big beautiful athlete husband of hers won't go to bed with her!

GOOPER.   You jest won't let me do this in a nice way, will yah? Aw right—Mae and I have five kids with another one coming! I don't give a goddam if Big Daddy likes me or don't like me or did or never did or will or will never! I'm just appealing to a sense of common decency and fair play. I'll tell you the truth. I've resented Big Daddy's partiality to Brick ever since Brick was born, and the way I've been treated like I was just barely good enough to spit on and sometimes not even good enough for that. Big Daddy is dying of cancer, and it's spread all through him and it's attacked all his vital organs including the kidneys and right now he is sinking into uremia, and you all know what uremia is, it's poisoning of the whole system due to the failure of the body to eliminate its poisons.

MARGARET (*to herself downstage, hissingly*).   *Poisons, poisons! Venomous thoughts and words! In hearts and minds!—That's poisons!*

GOOPER (*overlapping her*).   I am asking for a square deal, and I expect to get one. But if I don't get one, if there's any peculiar shenanigans going on around here behind my back, or before me, well, I'm not a corporation lawyer for nothing, I know how to protect my own interests.—*OH! A late arrival!*

(*Brick enters from the gallery with a tranquil, blurred smile, carrying an empty glass with him.*)

MAE.   Behold the conquering hero comes!

GOOPER.   The fabulous Brick Pollitt! Remember him?— Who could forget him!

MAE.   He looks like he's been injured in a game!

GOOPER.   Yep, I'm afraid you'll have to warm the bench at the Sugar Bowl this year, Brick! (*Mae laughs shrilly.*) Or was it the Rose Bowl that he made that famous run in?

MAE.   The punch bowl, honey. It was in the punch bowl, the cut-glass punch bowl!

GOOPER.   Oh, that's right, I'm getting the bowls mixed up!

MARGARET.   Why don't you stop venting your malice and envy on a sick boy?

BIG MAMA.   *Now you two hush, I mean it, hush, all of you, hush!*

GOOPER.   All right, Big Mama. A family crisis brings out the best and the worst in every member of it.

MAE.   *That's the truth.*

MARGARET.   Amen!

BIG MAMA.   *I said, hush! I won't tolerate any more catty talk in my house.*

(*Mae gives Gooper a sign indicating briefcase.*) (*Brick's smile has grown both brighter and vaguer. As he prepares a drink, he sings softly.*)

BRICK.
Show me the way to go home,
I'm tired and I wanta go to bed,
I had a little drink about an hour ago—

GOOPER (*at the same time*). Big Mama, you know it's necessary for me t'go back to Memphis in th' mornin' t'represent the Parker estate in a lawsuit.

(*Mae sits on the bed and arranges papers she has taken from the briefcase.*)

BRICK (*continuing the song*).
> Wherever I may roam,
> On land or sea or foam.

BIG MAMA.   Is it, Gooper?

MAE.   Yaiss.

GOOPER.   That's why I'm forced to—bring up a problem that—

MAE.   Somethin' that's too important t' be put off!

GOOPER.   If Brick was sober, he ought to be in on this.

MARGARET.   Brick is present; we're here.

GOOPER.   Well, good. I will now give you this outline my partner, Tom Bullitt, an' me have drawn up—a sort of dummy—trusteeship.

MARGARET.   Oh, that's it! You'll be in charge an' dole out remittances, will you?

GOOPER.   This we did as soon as we got the report on Big Daddy from th' Ochsner Laboratories. We did this thing, I mean we drew up this dummy outline with the advice and assistance of the Chairman of the Boa'd of Directors of th' Southern Plantahs Bank and Trust Company in Memphis, C. C. Bellowes, a man who handles estates for all th' prominent fam'lies in West Tennessee and th' Delta.

BIG MAMA.   Gooper?

GOOPER (*crouching in front of Big Mama*). Now this is not—not final, or anything like it. This is just a preliminary outline. But it does provide a basis—a design—a—possible, feasible—*plan!*

MARGARET.   Yes, I'll bet.

MAE.   It's a plan to protect the biggest estate in the Delta from irresponsibility an'—

BIG MAMA.   Now, you listen to me, all of you, you listen here! They's not goin' to be any more catty talk in my house! And Gooper, you put that away before I grab it out of your hand and tear it right up! I don't know what the hell's in it, and I don't want to know what the hell's in it. I'm talkin' in Big Daddy's language now; I'm his *wife,* not his *widow,* I'm still his *wife!* And I'm talkin' to you in his language an'—

GOOPER.   Big Mama, what I have here is—

MAE.   Gooper explained that it's just a plan. . . .

BIG MAMA.   I don't care what you got there. Just put it back where it came from, an' don't let me see it again, not even the outside of the envelope of it! Is that understood? Basis! Plan! Preliminary! Design! I say—what is it Big Daddy always says when he's disgusted?

BRICK (*from the bar*). Big Daddy says "crap" when he's disgusted.

BIG MAMA (*rising*). That's right—*CRAP!* I say *CRAP* too, like Big Daddy!

MAE.   Coarse language doesn't seem called for in this—

GOOPER.   Somethin' in me is *deeply outraged* by hearin' you talk like this.

BIG MAMA.   *Nobody's goin' to take nothin'!*—till Big Daddy lets go of it, and maybe, just possibly, not—not even then! No, not even then!

BRICK.
> You can always hear me singin' this song,
> Show me the way to go home.

BIG MAMA.   Tonight Brick looks like he used to look when he was a little boy, just like he did when he played wild games and used to come home all sweaty and pink-cheeked and sleepy, with his—red curls shining. . . .

(*She comes over to him and runs her fat shaky hand through his hair. He draws aside as he does from all physical contact and continues the song in a whisper, opening the ice bucket and dropping in the ice cubes one by one as if he were mixing some important chemical formula.*)

BIG MAMA (*continuing*). Time goes by so fast. Nothin' can outrun it. Death commences too early—almost before you're half-acquainted with life—you meet with the other. . . .

Oh, you know we just got to love each other an' stay together, all of us, just as close as we can, especially now that such a *black* thing has come and moved into this place without invitation. (*Awkwardly embracing Brick, she presses her head to his shoulder.*)

(*Gooper has been returning papers to Mae who has restored them to briefcase with an air of severely tried patience.*)

GOOPER.   Big Mama? Big Mama? (*He stands behind her, tense with sibling envy.*)

BIG MAMA (*oblivious of Gooper*). Brick, you hear me, don't you?

MARGARET.   Brick hears you, Big Mama, he understands what you're saying.

BIG MAMA.   Oh, Brick, son of Big Daddy! Big Daddy does so love you! Y'know what would be his fondest dream come true? If before he passed on, if Big Daddy has to pass on, you gave him a child of yours, a grandson as much like his son as his son is like Big Daddy!

MAE (*zipping briefcase shut: an incongruous sound*). Such a pity that Maggie an' Brick can't oblige!

MARGARET (*suddenly and quietly but forcefully*). Everybody listen. (*She crosses to the center of the room, holding her hands rigidly together.*)

MAE.   Listen to what, Maggie?

MARGARET.   I have an announcement to make.

GOOPER.   A sports announcement, Maggie?

MARGARET.   Brick and I are going to—*have a child!* (*Big Mama catches her breath in a loud gasp.*) (*Pause. Big Mama rises.*)

BIG MAMA.   Maggie! Brick! This is too good to believe!

MAE.   That's right, too good to believe.

BIG MAMA.   Oh, my, my! This is Big Daddy's dream, his dream come true! I'm going to tell him right now before he—

MARGARET.   We'll tell him in the morning. Don't disturb him now.

BIG MAMA.   I want to tell him before he goes to sleep, I'm going to tell him his dream's come true this minute! And Brick! A child will make you pull yourself together and quit this drinking! (*She seizes the glass from his hand.*) The responsibilities of a father will— (*Her face contorts and she makes an excited gesture; bursting into sobs, she rushes out, crying.*) I'm going to tell Big Daddy right this minute! (*Her voice fades out down the hall.*)

(*Brick shrugs slightly and drops an ice cube into another glass. Margaret crosses quickly to his side, saying something under her breath, and she pours the liquor for him, staring up almost fiercely into his face.*)

BRICK (*coolly*). Thank you, Maggie, that's a nice big shot.

(*Mae has joined Gooper and she gives him a fierce poke, making a low hissing sound and a grimace of fury.*)

GOOPER (*pushing her aside*). Brick, could you possibly spare me one small shot of that liquor?

BRICK.   Why, help yourself, Gooper boy.

GOOPER.   I will.

MAE (*shrilly*). Of course we know that this is—

GOOPER.   *Be still, Mae!*

MAE.   I won't be still! I know she's made this up!

GOOPER.   God damn it, I said to shut up!

MARGARET.   Gracious! I didn't know that my little announcement was going to provoke such a storm!

MAE.   *That* woman isn't *pregnant!*

GOOPER.   Who said she was?

MAE.   *She* did.

GOOPER.   The doctor didn't. Doc Baugh didn't.

MARGARET.   I haven't gone to Doc Baugh.

GOOPER.   Then who'd you go to, Maggie?

MARGARET.   One of the best gynecologists in the South.

GOOPER.   Uh huh, uh huh!—I see. . . . (*He takes out pencil and notebook.*) —May we have his name, please?

MARGARET.   No, you may not, Mister Prosecuting Attorney!

MAE.   He doesn't have any name, he doesn't exist!

MARGARET.   Oh, he exists all right, and so does my child, Brick's baby!

MAE.   You can't conceive a child by a man that won't sleep with you unless you think you're—

(*Brick has turned on the phonograph. A scat song cuts Mae's speech.*)

GOOPER.   *Turn that off!*

MAE.   We know it's a lie because we hear you in here; he won't sleep with you, we hear you! So don't imagine you're going to put a trick over on us, to fool a dying man with a— (*A long drawn cry of agony and rage fills the house. Margaret turns phonograph down to a whisper.*) (*The cry is repeated.*)

MAE (*awed*). Did you hear that, Gooper, did you hear that?

GOOPER.   Sounds like the pain has struck.

MAE.   Go see, Gooper!

GOOPER.   Come along and leave these love birds together in their nest! (*He goes out first. Mae follows but turns at the door, contorting her face and hissing at Margaret.*)

MAE.   Liar! (*She slams the door.*) (*Margaret exhales with relief and moves a little unsteadily to catch hold of Brick's arm.*)

MARGARET.   Thank you for—keeping still . . .

BRICK.   OK, Maggie.

MARGARET.   It was gallant of you to save my face!

BRICK.   —It hasn't happened yet.

MARGARET.   What?

BRICK.   The click. . . .

MARGARET.   —the click in your head that makes you peaceful, honey?

BRICK.   Uh-huh. It hasn't happened. . . . I've got to make it happen before I can sleep. . . .

MARGARET.   —I—know what you—mean. . . .

BRICK.   Give me that pillow in the big chair, Maggie.

MARGARET.   I'll put it on the bed for you.

BRICK.   No, put it on the sofa, where I sleep.

MARGARET.   Not tonight, Brick.

BRICK.   I want it on the sofa. That's where I sleep. (*He has hobbled to the liquor cabinet. He now pours down three shots in quick succession and stands waiting, silent. All at once he turns with a smile and says:*) There!

MARGARET.   What?

BRICK.   The *click.* . . .

(*His gratitude seems almost infinite as he hobbles out on the gallery with a drink. We hear his crutch as he swings out of sight. Then, at some distance, he begins singing to himself a peaceful song.*)

(*Margaret holds the big pillow forlornly as if it were her only companion, for a few moments, then throws it on the bed. She rushes to the liquor cabinet, gathers all the bottles in her arms, turns about undecidedly, then runs out of the room with them, leaving the door ajar on the dim yellow hall. Brick is heard hobbling back along the gallery, singing his peaceful song. He comes back in, sees the pillow on the bed, laughs lightly, sadly, picks it up. He has it under his arm as Margaret returns to the room. Margaret softly shuts the door and leans against it, smiling softly at Brick.*)

MARGARET.   Brick, I used to think that you were stronger than me and I didn't want to be overpowered by you. But now, since you've taken to liquor—you know what?—I guess it's bad, but now I'm stronger than you and I can love you more truly!

Don't move that pillow. I'll move it right back if you do!—Brick? (*She turns out all the lamps but a single rose-silk-shaded one by the bed.*) I really have been to a doctor and I know what to do and—Brick?—this is my time by the calendar to conceive!

BRICK.   Yes, I understand, Maggie. But how are you going to conceive a child by a man in love with his liquor?

MARGARET.   By locking his liquor up and making him satisfy my desire before I unlock it!

BRICK.   Is that what you've done, Maggie?

MARGARET.   Look and see. That cabinet's mighty empty compared to before!

BRICK.   Well, I'll be a son of a— (*He reaches for his crutch but she beats him to it and rushes out on the gallery, hurls the crutch over the rail and comes back in, panting.*)

(*There are running footsteps. Big Mama bursts into the room, her face all awry, gasping, stammering.*)

BIG MAMA.   Oh, my God, oh, my God, oh, my God, where is it?

MARGARET.   Is this what you want, Big Mama? (*Margaret hands her the package left by the doctor.*)

BIG MAMA.   I can't bear it, oh, God! Oh, Brick! Brick, baby! (*She rushes at him. He averts his face from her sobbing kisses. Margaret watches with a tight smile.*) My son, Big Daddy's boy! Little Father! (*The groaning cry is heard again. She runs out, sobbing.*)

MARGARET.   And so tonight we're going to make the lie true, and when that's done, I'll bring the liquor back here and we'll get drunk together, here, tonight, in this place that death has come into. . . .

—What do you say?

BRICK.   I don't say anything. I guess there's nothing to say.

MARGARET.   Oh, you weak people, you weak, beautiful people!—who give up.—What you want is someone to— (*She turns out the rose-silk lamp.*)—take hold of you.— Gently, gently, with love! And— (*The curtain begins to fall slowly.*) I *do* love you, Brick, I do!

BRICK (*smiling with charming sadness*). Wouldn't it be funny if that was true?

THE CURTAIN COMES DOWN
THE END

FOCUS QUESTIONS

1. Briefly discuss the kinds of marital relationships depicted in the play and show how each contributes to the play's principal themes.
2. Develop a character sketch of Big Daddy and comment on his tactics with Brick.
3. In a short essay, discuss Williams' portrait of the South as represented by the characters and actions of the play.
4. Cite Williams' use of symbolism and assess its effect on the poetic-realistic design of the play.
5. Evaluate the work as a family drama.
6. Choose one of the play's controversial issues and discuss its impact on the society in which you live.
7. Analyze the playwright's treatment of the male characters in the play; compare this with his treatment of the female characters.

OTHER ACTIVITIES

1. Read the third-act version inspired by Elia Kazan and compare it to Williams' original.
2. Using references to available documentation on various productions of the play, develop a critical analysis of Brick as he has been portrayed by a variety of actors.
3. View the 1958 Taylor/Newman film version of *Cat on a Hot Tin Roof* and discuss the effectiveness of the play's transference to the screen.

BIBLIOGRAPHY

Bloom, Harold, ed. *Tennessee Williams*. New York: Chelsea House, 1987.

Day, Christine, and Bob Woods, eds. *Where I Live: Selected Essays*. New York: New Directions, 1978.

Falk, Signi. *Tennessee Williams*. Boston: Twayne, 1978.

Heilman, Robert. *The Iceman, the Arsonist, and the Troubled Agent*. Seattle: University of Washington Press, 1973.

Hirsch, Foster. *A Portrait of the Artist: The Plays of Tennessee Williams*. Port Washington, NY: Kennikat, 1979.

Isaac, Dan. "Big Daddy's Dramatic Word Strings." *American Speech* 40 (1965): 272–78.

Jackson, Esther. *The Broken World of Tennessee Williams*. Madison: University of Wisconsin Press, 1966.

Leavitt, Richard, ed. *The World of Tennessee Williams*. New York: Putnam, 1978.

Lolli, Giorgio. "Alcoholism and Homosexuality in Tennessee Williams's *Cat on a Hot Tin Roof*." *Quarterly Journal of Studies in Alcohol* 17 (1956): 543–53.

Londré, Felicia Hardison. *Tennessee Williams*. New York: Ungar, 1979.

Murphy, Brenda. *Tennessee Williams and Elia Kazan: A Collaboration in the Theatre*. Cambridge: Cambridge University Press, 1992.

Peterson, William. "Williams, Kazan, and the Two *Cats*." *New Theatre Magazine* 7 (1967): 14–20.

Reck, Tom. "The First *Cat on a Hot Tin Roof*." *University Review* 34 (1968): 187–92.

Sacksteder, William. "The Three *Cats*: A Study in Dramatic Structure." *Drama Survey* 5 (Winter 1966–67): 252–66.

Stanton, Stephen, ed. *Tennessee Williams: A Collection of Critical Essays*. Englewood Cliffs, NJ: Prentice-Hall, 1977.

Tharpe, Jac, ed. *Tennessee Williams: A Tribute*. Jackson: University Press of Mississippi, 1977.

Williams, Tennessee. *Memoirs*. New York: Doubleday, 1975.

RECOMMENDED VIDEOTAPES AND RECORDINGS

Cat on a Hot Tin Roof. VHS. 108 min. 1958. Distributed by CBS Video. Richard Brooks, director. Starring Paul Newman, Elizabeth Taylor, Burl Ives, Judith Anderson, Jack Carson, and Madeleine Sherwood.

Cat on a Hot Tin Roof. Two videodiscs. 122 min. 1986. Distributed by Vestron Video, Stamford, CT. Jack Hofsis, director. Starring Jessica Lange, Tommy Lee Jones, Rip Torn, Kim Stanley, Penny Fuller, and David Dukes.

THE BIRTHDAY PARTY
HAROLD PINTER (1930–   )

Pinter, obsessed with the boundaries Man makes to control his world, sets out to use the realistic conventions in order to go beyond them. No emotional security is certain—language, personality, even stage formula have a way of dissolving in the irrational movement of a man's history.

—JOHN LAHR

Jean Stapleton (*foreground*) as Meg, with Richard Riehle (*left*) and David Strathairn in *The Birthday Party,* presented by the Classic Stage Company in 1988, under the direction of Carey Perloff. *Photo: Tom Chargin.*

APPROACHING THE COMEDY OF MENACE

English theatre prior to World War II was dominated by revivals of the classics and the aristocratic, sophisticated, and witty plays of Noel Coward (1899–1973) and Somerset Maugham (1874–1965). Besides the continued success of the plays of Bernard Shaw (1856–1950), there were few alternatives to these drawing room comedies: the religious verse dramas of T. S. Eliot (1888–1965), and Christopher Fry (1907–   ), the simpler realistic plays of Terence Rattigan (1911–1977) and Graham Greene (1904–1991), and the mysteries of Agatha Christie (1890–1976) and J. B. Priestley (1894–1984).

After the war, unlike its European counterpart which rallied with productions of new plays, English theatre suffered from a lack of new playwrights. It was not until the plays of existentialists Jean Paul Sartre and Albert Camus, and those of absurdists Samuel Beckett, Eugene Ionesco, and Jean Genet were translated and brought to London for production in the early 1950s that the stagnation plaguing the English stage came to a halt. Inspired by the increasing willingness of commercial producers to experiment, a new breed of playwrights surfaced. Although they rejected the primary metaphysical premise that life is absurd, they were as equally disillusioned with the status quo as their European counterparts. Their focus was on what traditional English drama had neglected: the struggles of the working class and the rising disappointment with the politics of the welfare state felt by university-educated young people. When John Osborne's *Look Back in Anger* was produced by the English Stage Company in 1956, the protagonist Jimmy Porter became the spokesperson for a new rebellious generation. Osborne's anger against the social hierarchy and corrupt government practices was reflected in the socially conscious plays of John Arden and Arnold Wesker.

Harold Pinter, one of the most important playwrights to develop out of the disillusionment with post–World War II England, entered this playwriting arena in the mid-1950s. A successful actor who had already published poetry and fiction, he was not interested in writing about contemporary social problems. Although he experienced the same anger as his English peers, he was more fascinated with the structure of language in everyday speech and the nature of silence as a medium of communication. According to Pinter, ''We communicate only too well, in our silence, in what is unsaid, and that what takes place is continual evasion, desperate rearguard attempts to keep ourselves to ourselves. Communication is too alarming. To enter into someone else's life is too frightening. To disclose to others the poverty within us is too fearsome a possibility.''[1] Thus the words that people do choose are often just another form of silence, a torrent of excuses and dodges that serve as weapons or as masks behind which they hide. Like Chekhov, Pinter became a writer for whom **subtext** rather than the signification of words was of paramount importance. (See Preface to Chekhov, p. 588.)

Besides investigating how human beings interact through speech and gestures, Pinter was also interested in depicting how they experience the pain of existence in a society to which they are forced to conform. The son of a Jewish tailor in London's East End, he had experienced the violent anti-Semitism perpetrated by the rise of fascist sentiment during his childhood and the war years. As a result, he was drawn to the Outsider as a character type, who finds it difficult to assimilate because of religious or racial differences or chooses to drop out of the social order by living in rented rooms where pasts and identities remain unknown.

Affected profoundly by Franz Kafka's novel *The Trial* and the stories of Jews in hiding who were rooted out by the SS, Pinter wanted to explore what happens when the tenuously secure world of the Other is invaded. By focusing on the bizarre and arbitrary violence used against them, he wanted to highlight the fear and anxiety of these victims and their strategies for dodging the inevitable. Instead of using the plays to illustrate themes or social truths, Pinter presented the audience with unexplained actions and feelings, leaving them the task to provide meanings and rationales from their own life experiences.

These preoccupations and his practical experience with what works on the stage coalesced into a distinct and unique theatrical voice. What Pinter captured in his dialogue and silences was a realistic portrayal of the way people interact. Yet the choice of words, the rhythms of language, and the use of pauses were all carefully scored. Using the conventions of dialogue found in popular entertainments—interrogation scenes from gangster movies, music hall patter and repartee, and domestic comedy repetitions and *non sequiturs,* as well as the mundane subjects of everyday speech, Pinter developed verbal exchanges between his characters that, on one hand, had the feel of realistic discourse because of their familiarity and, on the other hand, were controlled and formulaic. This interplay of dialogue structures gave the plays their incongruous mix of humor and terror.

Like Osborne, Arden, and Wesker, all of whom were labeled ''kitchen sink'' realists, Pinter was indebted to conventions of that style. The settings in his plays were real environments inhabited by real people, in which something always happened. The plays were often structured according to Scribe's well-made model, even though the world Pinter created on stage was not realistic. Although the audience witnessed events that seemed familiar, there was never any given exposition of the past, any specific insight into characters, nor explanation of why the actions had taken place. This lack of omniscience had a disconcerting effect: the audience, like the characters, had to read the signs as they were presented to them with no further clues. In addition to building up expectations for answers that were rarely provided, the plays were impelled by an unrelieved dramatic suspense. Kept off balance, the audience experienced the same menacing uncertainty as the characters in the play.

This new, jarring mixture of realistic conventions and absurdist preoccupation with contradiction, bizarre situations, and incomprehensibility of life both baffled and intrigued Pinter's audiences. In spite of the intense theatricality of the plays, the absence of clearly defined themes infuriated the critics whose negative reviews prompted the first London production of *The Birthday Party* to close after five days. As Pinter's work continued to be produced and create powerful effects on playgoers, however, the predictions of the play's one champion, Harold Hobson of the *London Times,* came to fruition: ''. . . on the evidence of his work, [Pinter] possesses the most original, disturbing and arresting talent in theatrical London . . . and will be heard of again.''[2]

Major Works

One of England's foremost playwrights, screenwriters, and adaptors for film and television since the 1960s, Pinter wrote his first play, *The Room* (1957), at the request of a friend who needed a play to direct for a student project at Bristol University. Its characteristic room as insecure haven into which strangers intrude and precipitate an act of unexplained violence prompted a series of dramas that were labeled ''comedies of menace.'' These included *The Dumbwaiter* (1959), *The Caretaker* (1960), *The Dwarfs* (1960), and two radio plays— *A Slight Ache* (1959) and *A Night Out* (1960).

Pinter then moved his exploration of language as a tool of evasion and power from the arena of interractions between strangers to the exploitative relationships between spouses and family members. Works with this focus included such teleplays as *The Collection* (1961), *The Lover* (1963), *The Tea Party* (1964), and his full-length stage play, *The Homecoming* (1965). His interest in the nature of personal secrets and selective memory as a way to protect oneself was the subject of *Landscape* and *Silence* (1969), *Old Times* (1970), and *No Man's Land* (1975).

In his later plays, Pinter has presented more concrete examinations of how people communicate. The most important of these are *Betrayal* (1978), which deals with marital infidelity, and *Moonlight* (1993); as well as *One for the Road* (1984) and *Mountain Language* (1988), the last two of which investigate how governments limit individual rights through repressive interrogation and the outlawing of native dialects. What has remained constant throughout Pinter's work since his menacing play, *The Birthday Party* (1958), is that silence, words, and gestures are part of the power game in interpersonal communication and have the capacity to obscure as well as elucidate, to victimize as well as comfort.

THE ACTION

Stanley Webber has been the only guest at the seaside boardinghouse run by Meg and Petey Boles. Inertia prevents him from leaving the house, despite Meg's overprotection and neediness. One morning, this secure yet stifling cocoon is invaded by two strangers. It becomes evident that their mission is to take Stanley away with them. That evening, at a birthday party they have organized in his honor, they break his spirit and render him inarticulate under brutal verbal assault. By morning they have taken him away without Meg's knowledge and despite Petey's feeble attempt to stop them.

STRUCTURE AND LANGUAGE

When Pinter wrote *The Birthday Party,* he was adamant about not using the theatre as a platform for dogmatism or universal truths. His reasoning was that if the playwright provided the meanings of the play to the audience, then the audience remained outside the theatrical event and the play became meaningless. He envisioned the theatre as an experience that involves the audience through the building up of expectations and suspense that are never satisfactorily resolved. This forces the audience to seek their own interpretation from the structure of the events, words, and gestures they witness on the stage.

In *The Birthday Party* Pinter engages the audience by relying on the popular well-made-play structure: the narrative typically unfolds through exposition and a rising action in which the climax is reached through a pattern of discoveries. When the fortunes of the protagonist are reversed, the denouement resolves the action and what has happened is explained. The twist on the formula employed by Pinter is that the information revealed in the play is never certain. Contradictions and gaps in the narrative make it impossible to piece together exactly why things happen. Yet despite this, Pinter's dialogue still serves as a means for constructing the nature of the relationships between the characters and for revealing their feelings about those relationships and the situations in which they find themselves.

The first act introduces the odd domestic triangle of the Boles household. Preparing her husband's breakfast, Meg greets Petey in a ritualized banter that is banal and mildly antagonistic:

> Meg: Is that you, Petey? (Pause)
>   Petey, is that you? (Pause)
>   Petey?
> Petey: What?
> Meg: Is that you?
> Petey: Yes, it's me.
> Meg: What? (Her face appears at the hatch.) Are you back?
> Petey: Yes.

Husband and wife vie for power through words. Her questions become a kind of challenge to his identity: she even questions his very presence in the room when she asks if he is back after looking through the hatch to see for herself. Holding up the newspaper and replying with short, clipped answers are his only line of defense. Meg seems to have won the round.

That Petey has a rival for Meg's attention and affection is established early:

Meg: Is Stanley up yet?
Petey: I don't know. Is he?
Meg: I don't know. I haven't seen him down yet.
Petey: Well, then, he can't be up.

The use of clever wordplay and repetition appears throughout their conversation about ''nice cornflakes'' and ''nice bits'' from the newspaper, creating a humor reminiscent of domestic sitcoms that exploit a mundane game of one-upmanship.

Until Stanley appears, he is referred to as a boy who sleeps too much and ''goes through his socks.'' But the assumptions that he is Meg's young son are overthrown when an unshaven man in his mid-thirties, dressed in a pajama top, enters for breakfast. Although he may replace the son Meg never had, there are intimations that he may once have been her lover.

Quite suddenly a piece of news surfaces: two men seeking a room are expected that morning. Stanley's reaction signals that this is an unwelcome invasion, while Meg's proprietary hold on him is challenged by the arrival of McCann and Goldberg. Although he is a stranger and newly arrived boarder, Goldberg initiates control over Stanley's birthday as an occasion to host a party.

What is unusual about Pinter's exposition thus far is that the audience knows nothing with certainty, such as the nature of Meg and Stanley's relationship or the identity of McCann and Goldberg. Why have the latter two come? Perhaps it has something to do with Stanley, whose panic increases with news of the strangers' impending arrival. While mystery and suspense mount, audience expectations for answers are frustrated. A further ingredient is the story Stanley tells Meg, as if to threaten her: that men with a van will be looking for someone today and will take that person away in a wheelbarrow. When a knock is heard at the door, Meg calmly goes to answer despite her alarm at Stanley's story. When Stanley hides behind the door to listen, it is evident that he has reason to fear his prophetic and menacing story more than she.

In the second act, Stanley tries to protect himself. But his attempt to gain control is met with little success when he confronts Goldberg and is reduced to the bravado and feeble outcries of a vulnerable child:

Stanley: Let me—just make this clear. You don't bother me. To me you're nothing
          but a dirty joke. But I have a responsibility towards people in this house.
          They've been down here too long. They've lost their sense of smell. I haven't.
          And nobody's going to take advantage of them while I'm here. *(A little less
          forceful)* Anyway, this house isn't your cup of tea. There's nothing here for
          you, from any angle. So why don't you just go, without any more fuss?

Wasting no words, his opponent simply replies: ''Mr. Webber, sit down.''

Stanley is subjected to a merciless barrage of clichéd and contradictory *non sequiturs* designed to make him crack: ''What were you doing yesterday?'' ''What have you done with your wife?'' ''Why did you never get married?'' ''Why did the chicken cross the road?'' ''Which came first? Chicken? Egg?'' McCann and Goldberg end with the accusation, ''You're dead . . . You're nothing but an odour!'' provoking Stanley to strike back. But why they have victimized him and what they intend to do with him still remain a mystery.

As if to reassert the well-made design of his play, Pinter constructs a third act whose denouement offers a reprise of the play's opening. It is breakfast time and once again Petey enters to read the paper as Meg calls out from behind the kitchen hatch. But this time the morning rituals have altered:

Meg: Is that you, Stan? *(Pause)* Stanny?
Petey: Yes?
Meg: Is that you?
Petey: It's me.
Meg: *(appearing at the hatch)* Oh, it's you. I've run out of cornflakes.
Petey: Well, what else have you got?
Meg: Nothing.

Perhaps out of some vague sense of guilt, Meg asks for Stan rather than Petey. There is nothing for breakfast; the intruders have eaten everything. Even Meg's questions about her husband's newspaper, in a feeble effort to recapture the usual banter, have changed. She asks if it is "good," not "nice," and Petey acknowledges her questions with "Not bad," rather than sparring with a repetitious "very good." Pinter has turned this ritual power game into a conspiracy of denial.

The play's last image is of Stanley transformed: he is washed, shaven, in a suit and bowler hat. He can no longer speak or make excuses for himself. In fact, he has no response to McCann and Goldberg's litany of bourgeois rewards for towing the line and following the rules—a "season ticket," "tuppence off [his] morning tea," use of the club bar, as well as the promise of wealth, success, and power. Why they do this is never fully explained. Perhaps neither man knows the reasons. Perhaps they are just following orders, reciting words that they have committed to memory for the express purpose of fulfilling their task. All that we can surmise is that Stanley has been accused of being different. By becoming an unemployed recluse, he has dropped out from society and the "organization" has come to reclaim him and recreate him in their image.

THE BIRTHDAY PARTY-IN-PERFORMANCE

When *The Birthday Party* was first produced in April of 1958 under Peter Wood's direction, audiences were not prepared for Pinter's radical dramatic style. As a result, the critical reception was mixed. Richard Pearson, who played Stanley, recalled that Cambridge audiences "admitted they didn't 'get' the play, but they knew that they had shared a strong emotional experience."[3] Attending the play, Bamber Gascoigne cited Beatrix Lehmann's "angular and macabre performance" and the "zany dialogue" between John Slater's Goldberg and John Stratton's McCann as the "music-hall Jew and Irishman."[4]

At its next stop in Woverhampton, before opening at the Lyric Theatre, Hammersmith, the production was despised by audiences who "resented being put through something hair-raising without knowing why."[5] London critics voiced their unanimous disapproval, causing the play to close on May 24, 1958, only four days after it had opened. The very next day, Harold Hobson chastised his colleagues for failing to acknowledge the play's unique qualities:

> Peter Wood has directed the play with an absolute response to its most delicate nuances. It has six players, every one of them is superb. Beatrix Lehmann is strangely funny and macabrely touching as the landlady. John Slater builds impeccably the facade of eloquence that hides Goldberg's secret quaking. John Stratton finely points McCann's nameless fears (his paper-tearing, with its horrible pause at the end, is unforgettable). Richard Pearson's Stanley, excellent throughout, is very moving in its hurt wonder when he is given the child's drum as a birthday present. Wendy Hutchinson's Lulu is an acceptable saucy young chit: this is a rarer achievement than one might think; and Willoughby Gray's husband is solid and believable.[6]

Hobson, like those Cambridge audiences weeks earlier, acclaimed Pinter's artistry and rallied to his side. The result was that *The Birthday Party* was given another chance, this time in a television version produced by the BBC in 1960. Aided by recent exposure to his two successful London revues, *Pieces of Eight* and *One to Another,* and to a successful production of *The Caretaker* which was playing at the Arts Theatre in London, audiences accepted Pinter as their most promising new playwright. Before long, professional and amateur productions of *The Birthday Party* surfaced all over Britain, while televised versions in Australia, Germany, Denmark, and Canada quickly established Pinter's international reputation. Since then there have been stage productions in Berlin, Vienna, Cape Town, Johannesburg, Amsterdam, Copenhagen, Dublin, Sydney, Wellington, Ankara, and Tel-Aviv.

Perhaps the most important revival of the play was under Pinter's own direction for the Royal Shakespeare Company (RSC) in June 1964. Having successfully co-directed *The Collection* with Peter Hall in 1962, Pinter was determined to address his dissatisfaction with Peter Wood's original direction of the play. He stressed the familiarity of the setting and the ordinariness of the characters, underplaying the intensity of the subtext and heightening the elusiveness of the play's meanings. This time around, the play enjoyed a successful run at the Aldwych Theatre until it was supplanted by the company's presentation of another Pinter work, *The Homecoming.*

The American premiere of *The Birthday Party* took place at the Actors Workshop in San Francisco in July 1960 under the direction of English scholar Glynne Wyckham. The reception was as uneven as its English opening in 1958. But while audiences were mystified and bothered by the play, the critics were enthralled. The production ran for two consecutive seasons.

By the time the play reached Broadway in 1967, Harold Pinter was already canonized as a major contemporary playwright. Under Alan Schneider's direction, *The Birthday Party* opened at the Booth Theatre on October 3 with Henderson Forsythe (Petey), Ruth White (Meg), James Patterson (Stanley), Alexandra Berlin (Lulu), Ed Flanders (Goldberg), and Edward Winters (McCann). Audiences were stunned, but laughter filled the house, proving once and for all that Pinter's style, popularly coined ''Pinteresque,'' had become fashionable. Supported by a pervasive discontent, Schneider used the play to comment on life in America, whose optimistic surface belied a social and political apparatus in need of repair.

What was particularly effective was Schneider's direction of Stanley's birthday party, about which John Lahr wrote the following:

> At the celebration of a birthdate Stanley denies, the party is playing blind man's bluff when the lights go out, plunging them from shadowy sight to obsidian darkness. . . . When a flashlight scans the stage, the solidity of the room has changed. Forms lurk like massive waves ready to overwhelm the company. The light shines on objects assuring us that they exist, but they seem less than real. The walls which have protected Stanley, now incarcerate him as Goldberg and McCann force a flashlight grotesquely into his face.[7]

The compelling nature of the protagonist's performance garnered a Tony Award for James Patterson.

One year later, Pinter adapted his play for the screen. Under William Friedkin's direction, Robert Shaw, Sidney Tafler, Dandy Nichols, and Patrick Magee, who was creating his role of McCann from the RSC production, won the kudos of both the British and American press. Since then, the play has enjoyed countless regional theatre revivals, including the 1971 production by Jules Irving, which captured a certain music hall quality at Lincoln Center's intimate Forum Stage; the idiosyncratic 1986 production by Stephen Kanee at the Guthrie Theatre, which emphasized the play's stylized and symbolic imagery over its realistic aspects; and the 1986 production by Ben Levit for Boston's Huntington Theatre Company, which benefited from a certain **hyperrealism**.

Carey Perloff's 1988 production at the Classic Stage Company in New York City proved to be an auspicious American revival. Her attention to Pinter's language, with its rhythms, humor, and suspense, won her critical accolades and the playwright's respect as well. She eventually revived *The Birthday Party* in a double-bill with Pinter's one-act, *Mountain Language*. In the dual role of Meg in *The Birthday Party* and an elderly woman in *Mountain Language,* Jean Stapleton reflected on how far actors and audiences have come to understanding Pinter's work: ''I don't know how much hope he has for all of us, but if he just uncovers the darkness of our human condition, we may understand it and learn how to cope with it.''[8]

REFLECTIONS ON THE BIRTHDAY PARTY

Carey Perloff directed The Birthday Party *at CSC in 1988.*

Harold Pinter has always been my greatest inspiration. The reason that I'm in the theatre could be attributed as much to him as to anything else. I'm an enormous admirer of his work, and I felt that *The Birthday Party* was truly a classic that deserved another look. It had been I think twenty-five years since the play had a major production in New York and I had a real affinity for it. I'm married to an Englishman, and it's a kind of comedy that attracts me enormously. I felt that it was a play that New Yorkers could be particularly drawn to. In a way, it's Pinter's most Jewish play.

I knew we could cast it well and, although it was a long battle to get the rights and make it happen, it was worth it. I didn't know Pinter at all, and when we applied for the rights, his agent—whom I've since become very friendly with—turned us down. I think we must have called every day for three months. When I finally did get them, I asked his agent, "Why did you put us through that?" She said, "Well, I just wanted to make sure you were really interested." So I think there were a lot of issues there. I think that Pinter had been unhappy with other American productions of his work. He's not someone who's very interested in over-psychologizing his plays or in applying sort of method-acting concepts to his work, and that's something that happens upon occasion here. So I don't think he was desperately anxious to have it done again, especially since he didn't know me.

What finally convinced him is that he's quite close to a British poet called Tony Harrison whom I had worked with on his version of *Phaedra* at CSC. Tony came to see the play as well as my production of Pound's *Electra,* which he loved. So I called Tony Harrison and asked, "Do you know Pinter?" He did, and I said, "Would you call and tell him I'll do well by his play." Since Tony felt strongly that language was important to me and that that's what was most important to Pinter, he felt confident going to Pinter and saying this is someone you should trust and who could really do your work. I quickly got a return phone call from his agent saying that Pinter had agreed to give us the rights.

That brought on the first production, which was extremely successful. Then we developed a relationship with Pinter, and he came to see it. He also met the cast. I had spoken to him very briefly about his then new play, *Mountain Language* and, six months after that,

I got a phone call from his agent in the middle of a rehearsal one day asking if I would like to do the American premiere of *Mountain Language* with *The Birthday Party,* because we had wanted to revive *The Birthday Party.*

It was very different the second time around, and that was partly because Pinter was present at the rehearsals. We spent a great deal of time working on *The Birthday Party.* *Mountain Language* is a very dark, very intense play, and there's only so many hours a day that you can work on something like that without losing your mind. So we tended to split the rehearsal day and work on *Mountain Language* for half the day and *The Birthday Party* for the other half. I didn't think Pinter would be terribly interested in working on *The Birthday Party* again since he's not only directed it but been in it a few times. But he was absolutely riveted and sat in the back row, laughed continuously the entire time, and offered totally invaluable advice to us, when asked. He's a wonderful playwright to work with in rehearsal, because he only offers advice if you ask him something very specific. So *The Birthday Party* production was quite different the second time around.

In general he seemed much more interested in keeping it as subtle as possible. Although the text says that McCann and Goldberg should be wearing bowler hats, he said that he wasn't interested in doing that any more, that he felt that was too obvious. He kept saying to Peter Riegert who was playing Goldberg, "Just imagine you're coming to sell shoes. Don't play the menace. Don't play the heavy. When it gets dark, it will get dark." He really liberated us from any notions we might have had about the symbolism of the piece. To Pinter, it's not at all an abstract play; it's extremely real. He talked about those characters as if they were people he knew. It amused him, you know, and irritates him I think at times, that people label his work Theatre of the Absurd, because in his mind he was writing what he knew.

He stayed with us for about ten days. By then the actors were up on their feet, and most of them were off book. It's a terribly difficult play to do rhythmically. It not only takes a level of training, but you have to be in very, very good shape to do something like Pinter. I remember the first time we did it, the first couple of run-throughs, by the end, Peter Riegert was just lying on the ground. It's intellectually and emotionally exhausting because there is no let up. There's nothing casual in Pinter. There's no blocking that's unnecessary. There's no gesture that's unnecessary. The language is very economical, very precise, and requires intense concentration. You can't paraphrase a line. So it took us about three weeks into the run of the first production to really be in top possible shape to do this. I think the second time they knew much better how to anticipate the rigor and the demands that the play placed on them as actors. The cast of the second production was exactly the same except for Jean Stapleton who played Meg.

The Birthday Party is so incredibly economical and beautifully chosen. I think the trick to doing Pinter is that every element that exists on stage has to be real, but all of reality does not have to be represented. In other words, I think it's a big mistake with Pinter's work to do a literal living-room set with all of the chotchkas and detail filled in, because the play isn't written that way. It's a bit disingenuous when Pinter will say, "Well, all I did is listen to how people really talked and record that." He has the most perfect theatrical ear of almost any playwright I know. So he can take what he hears and sculpt it rhythmically in order to create a poetic language that we now call Pinteresque.

Continued

You have to be extremely attentive to all the rhythmical markings in the play. And he was. When we did a run-through, he wouldn't take any notes. He'd watch carefully and then say, "I think they missed a pause in the second line." I mean, he remembered exactly. Because it's written like music. So it isn't realistic in that sense, that actors can just sort of walk on stage and casually deliver lines. We were absolutely religious about pacing the piece the way it was written. On the other hand, you can't play it as a symbol either. It is menacing, because life is menacing, because into an empty room two men appear who don't belong there, and begin to interrogate the third man, and that action is frightening. But if you have actors who are complex enough so that these multiple layers can be happening at the same time, the menace is very palpable without playing the characters as symbols of anything.

I think our group of actors did extraordinarily well, but it was because they were very, very carefully chosen. I deliberately chose actors whom I knew had a very strong sense of language and a very strong sense of comedy, and had done work—either Mamet or classical work—that I thought would give them the kind of ear that this took. Even so, there were times that it was very difficult. One of the funniest scenes in the play is when Lulu descends the staircase after she's been—what we gather—raped by Goldberg. She comes downstairs the next morning with her dress half hanging off and has this encounter with him. It's a hilarious scene. It's also unbelievably disturbing. He is totally callous to her. The actress playing Lulu came down playing the situation, which is "I have been raped by this man. I am destroyed and I want to get out of here." Well, if that's the intention, then the scene's over before it begins, or it becomes sort of classic American melodrama. And clearly that's not the way the play's written, and we spent endless hours trying to make that scene work.

Most of what it takes to play Pinter well is to understand the subtext and then figure out how perfectly you can mask it. Because if you tip your hand, you will be devoured. Pinter sets up a world that is completely predatory in which everyone is out to destroy everyone else all the time. He has a pretty deeply cynical view—quite realistically, I think—of human nature. So the way his characters operate is to mask feeling, so that they render themselves as invulnerable as possible to the predators around them. So if Lulu comes down the stairs and she dissolves in tears in front of Goldberg, she's only asking to be raped again. She's only making herself more vulnerable. And what we realized is it had to be an exercise if she wants to have a scene with him. She wants to make him apologize. She's ready to have words with him, but she can't afford to fall apart. The subtext is still there, it is critical, because otherwise the scene becomes completely superficial and flat. But playing the scene is a matter of deciding when your character is going to expose him or herself.

American actors are trained the way American people are in general, which is to confess. American culture is very confessional. We're sort of trained to believe that, if you confess everything, you will be absolved. You know, that telling people what you feel is important. Well, the British don't believe that. The British are a completely unconfessional culture—they are extremely protected and completely guarded about revealing emotional life to anyone. It's partly just a cultural makeup. Americans are very quick to show what they feel, and while that may be a nice cultural characteristic, it's not nearly as interesting a dramatic characteristic, because drama is about what is unsaid. What makes drama interesting is the tension between what is being revealed and what is being hidden. So you have to encourage American actors to believe that even if they don't show it, we will understand what they're feeling through the language, which is hard to convince them of at times.

Take Jean Stapleton, for example. She's a dream actress to work with, because she's completely directable. I mean, Jean is the most open actor I've ever worked with. She's completely receptive to a work process that may be different from her own. But she's also the kind of actor who just understands this material. I think Jean's greatest talent is that she never judges the character she's playing. So she never played Meg as being a stupid woman. She completely understood her behavior and her love for Petey, and she played the situation. She's an incredibly specific actress. So it was never a big issue. I didn't have to talk her out of bad habits or anything like that. She's also unbelievably funny. I mean, she had Pinter on the floor. He thought she was the dream Meg, that she was the actress for whom he'd written that role.

I found the stage at CSC a very liberating space to direct this play. One of our challenges was to take plays that had been written for a proscenium and try to do them in a thrust. The great advantage of CSC is that it was always extraordinarily intimate, and it had very good acoustics. So you could do difficult language plays. I think the fun challenge for me in doing Pinter's work in a thrust is that it really is written to be done in a proscenium. Even Pinter laughed and said, "You know, I'm really very conventional, and all of my plays are written for very conventional theatres." When he initially heard that CSC was a thrust, he was nervous about how that would work, and he said he hadn't ever seen *The Birthday Party* done that way. I actually loved it, because it stripped away any temptation we might have had to make this a literal sitting room and kitchen or anything like that.

It was truly a platform suspended in space. When the actors stepped onto the platform, they entered that world, and for the acting process it avoided a lot of very unuseful questions that actors tend to ask: "If I'm coming from the beach, why don't I have sand on my shoes?" These kinds of questions are not very useful to Pinter. His characters don't exist except when they're on stage. Because otherwise you wind up in an endless situation in which you're trying to figure out if Stanley and Goldberg really knew each other in the past. Well, of course, it doesn't matter! If Goldberg makes Stanley believe that he knew him in the past, then he did. That's the truth! So you have to encourage actors to ask the interesting questions and not to get bogged down in the kind of biographical quote/unquote "truth" that you're never going to resolve in Pinter, because the whole point of Pinter is that there is no way of verifying the past.

That's why to do it on a set that was itself highly theatrical and stripped away and just had the iconographic elements that we needed, was actually very useful to the actors. The rule of thumb was always: did the icons that Pinter put in the play really pop. If there was too much detail on the set they didn't. I mean, clearly the icon in the first part of the play is the box of cornflakes. Eating cornflakes is the ritual that ties Meg and Petey together. It's also the comedy of the whole first part of the play. So that box of cornflakes has to become an element in and of itself of great ritual. You have to be very, very careful that you don't put in so much other stuff, that you can't really highlight the individual elements that you want to. And it allowed the audience a way into the play that was very particular. It made it very immediate.

Continued

Pinter enjoyed the experience very much. I think he felt very nostalgic coming to rehearse at CSC because he'd been in recent years doing his work in a much more elegant theatre such as the National, but here he was at a theatre that he said reminded him of his earlier days in the theatre. You know, a sort of downtown, Off-Off Broadway set up. He seemed to enjoy that a lot and was very responsive and helpful in very particular, interesting ways to the actors.

What is amazing about Pinter is that his work hasn't dated. That's because it isn't about formal tricks, to the degree that Albee or Ionesco or Pirandello are. Often with those writers, once you are onto the formal games that are being played and can anticipate them, it isn't enormously interesting anymore. Whereas with Pinter, the resonances and the characters are so complex, and there are all kinds of things buried in his plays that people haven't even begun to look at. The politics of the plays, for example, and the whole masking of the Jewish question. There's a lot of veiled homosexuality, too. They're just enormously resonant plays that live within an extremely beautiful and precise form. But it isn't just about the form. That's why I think to call Pinter's work Theatre of the Absurd is as reductive as to say that about Beckett. The writers that will really survive are Pinter and Beckett, to my mind. I think that's what I learned more than anything else about *The Birthday Party*. I think it's an absolutely timeless play that will continue to have resonance as long as individuals remain in conflict with society.

Notes

1. *Pinter quoted in Harold Bloom, ed.,* MODERN CRITICAL VIEWS *(New York: Chelsea House, 1986), 26.*
2. *Harold Hobson,* LONDON TIMES, *25 May 1958.*
3. *Ronald Knowles,* THE BIRTHDAY PARTY AND THE CARETAKER *(New York: Macmillan Education Co., 1988), 50.*
4. THE LONDON OBSERVER WEEKEND REVIEW, *21 June 1964.*
5. *Pearson quoted in Knowles,* THE BIRTHDAY PARTY AND THE CARETAKER, *50.*
6. *Harold Hobson,* SUNDAY LONDON TIMES, *25 May 1958.*
7. *John Lahr,* WESTSIDE NEWS, *12 Oct. 1967.*
8. *Louis Botto, "Pinter on the Double,"* PLAYBILL *89 (December 1989): 59.*

THE BIRTHDAY PARTY
HAROLD PINTER

CHARACTERS

Petey   Stanley   Goldberg
Meg   Lulu   McCann

ACT ONE

The living-room of a house in a seaside town. A door leading to the hall down left. Back door and small window up left. Kitchen hatch, centre back. Kitchen door up right. Table and chairs, centre.

    PETEY *enters from the door on the left with a paper and sits at the table. He begins to read.* MEG'S *voice comes through the kitchen hatch.*

MEG.   Is that you, Petey?

Pause.

    Petey, is that you?

Pause.

    Petey?
PETEY.   What?
MEG.   Is that you?
PETEY.   Yes, it's me.
MEG.   What? (*Her face appears at the hatch.*) Are you back?
PETEY.   Yes.
MEG.   I've got your cornflakes ready. (*She disappears and reappears.*) Here's your cornflakes.

He rises and takes the plate from her, sits at the table, props up the paper and begins to eat. MEG *enters by the kitchen door.*

    Are they nice?
PETEY.   Very nice.
MEG.   I thought they'd be nice. (*She sits at the table.*) You got your paper?
PETEY.   Yes.

MEG.   Is it good?
PETEY.   Not bad.
MEG.   What does it say?
PETEY.   Nothing much.
MEG.   You read me out some nice bits yesterday.
PETEY.   Yes, well, I haven't finished this one yet.
MEG.   Will you tell me when you come to something good?
PETEY.   Yes.

Pause.

MEG.   Have you been working hard this morning?
PETEY.   No. Just stacked a few of the old chairs. Cleaned up a bit.
MEG.   Is it nice out?
PETEY.   Very nice.

Pause.

MEG.   Is Stanley up yet?
PETEY.   I don't know. Is he?
MEG.   I don't know. I haven't seen him down yet.
PETEY.   Well then, he can't be up.
MEG.   Haven't you seen him down?
PETEY.   I've only just come in.
MEG.   He must be still asleep.

She looks round the room, stands, goes to the sideboard and takes a pair of socks from a drawer, collects wool and a needle and goes back to the table.

    What time did you go out this morning, Petey?
PETEY.   Same time as usual.
MEG.   Was it dark?
PETEY.   No, it was light.
MEG (*beginning to darn*). But sometimes you go out in the morning and it's dark.

PETEY.   That's in the winter.

MEG.   Oh, in winter.

PETEY.   Yes, it gets light later in winter.

MEG.   Oh.

Pause.

What are you reading?

PETEY.   Someone's just had a baby.

MEG.   Oh, they haven't! Who?

PETEY.   Some girl.

MEG.   Who, Petey, who?

PETEY.   I don't think you'd know her.

MEG.   What's her name?

PETEY.   Lady Mary Splatt.

MEG.   I don't know her.

PETEY.   No.

MEG.   What is it?

PETEY (*studying the paper*).   Er—a girl.

MEG.   Not a boy?

PETEY.   No.

MEG.   Oh, what a shame. I'd be sorry. I'd much rather have a little boy.

PETEY.   A little girl's all right.

MEG.   I'd much rather have a little boy.

Pause . . . Vaguely.

PETEY.   I've finished my cornflakes.

MEG.   Were they nice?

PETEY.   Very nice.

MEG.   I've got something else for you.

PETEY.   Good.

She rises, takes his plate and exits into the kitchen. She then appears at the hatch with two pieces of fried bread on a plate.

MEG.   Here you are, Petey.

He rises, collects the plate, looks at it, sits at the table. MEG *re-enters.*

Is it nice?

PETEY.   I haven't tasted it yet.

MEG.   I bet you don't know what it is.

PETEY.   Yes, I do.

MEG.   What is it, then?

PETEY.   Fried bread.

MEG.   That's right.

He begins to eat.
She watches him eat.

PETEY.   Very nice.

MEG.   I knew it was.

PETEY (*turning to her*).   Oh, Meg, two men came up to me on the beach last night.

MEG.   Two men?

PETEY.   Yes. They wanted to know if we could put them up for a couple of nights.

MEG.   Put them up? Here?

PETEY.   Yes.

MEG.   How many men?

PETEY.   Two.

MEG.   What did you say?

PETEY.   Well, I said I didn't know. So they said they'd come round to find out.

MEG.   Are they coming?

PETEY.   Well, they said they would.

MEG.   Had they heard about us, Petey?

PETEY.   They must have done.

MEG.   Yes, they must have done. They must have heard this was a very good boarding house. It is. This house is on the list.

PETEY.   It is.

MEG.   I know it is.

PETEY.   They might turn up today. Can you do it?

MEG.   Oh, I've got that lovely room they can have.

PETEY.   You've got a room ready?

MEG.   I've got the room with the armchair all ready for visitors.

PETEY.   You're sure?

MEG.   Yes, that'll be all right then, if they come today.

PETEY.   Good.

She takes the socks etc. back to the sideboard drawer.

MEG.   I'm going to wake that boy.

PETEY.   There's a new show coming to the Palace.

MEG.   On the pier?

PETEY.   No. The Palace, in the town.

MEG.   Stanley could have been in it, if it was on the pier.

PETEY.   This is a straight show.

MEG.   What do you mean?

PETEY.   No dancing or singing.

MEG.   What do they do then?

PETEY.   They just talk.

Pause.

MEG.   Oh.

PETEY.   You like a song, eh, Meg?

MEG.   I like listening to the piano. I used to like watching Stanley play the piano. Of course, he didn't sing. (*Looking at the door.*) I'm going to call that boy.

PETEY.   Didn't you take him up his cup of tea?

MEG.   I always take him up his cup of tea. But that was a long time ago.

PETEY.   Did he drink it?

MEG.   I made him. I stood there till he did. I'm going to call him. (*She goes to the door.*) Stan! Stanny! (*She listens.*) Stan! I'm coming up to fetch you if you don't come down! I'm coming up! I'm going to count three! One!

Two! Three! I'm coming to get you! (*She exits and goes upstairs. In a moment, shouts from* STANLEY, *wild laughter from* MEG. PETEY *takes his place to the hatch. Shouts. Laughter.* PETEY *sits at the table. Silence. She returns.*) He's coming down. (*She is panting and arranges her hair.*) I told him if he didn't hurry up he'd get no breakfast.

PETEY.   That did it, eh?

MEG.   I'll get his cornflakes.

MEG *exists to the kitchen.* PETEY *reads the paper.* STANLEY *enters. He is unshaven, in his pyjama jacket and wears glasses. He sits at the table.*

PETEY.   Morning, Stanley.

STANLEY.   Morning.

Silence. MEG *enters with the bowl of cornflakes, which she sets on the table.*

MEG.   So he's come down at last, has he? He's come down at last for his breakfast. But he doesn't deserve any, does he, Petey? (STANLEY *stares at the cornflakes.*) Did you sleep well?

STANLEY.   I didn't sleep at all.

MEG.   You didn't sleep at all? Did you hear that, Petey? Too tired to eat your breakfast, I suppose? Now you eat up those cornflakes like a good boy. Go on.

He begins to eat.

STANLEY.   What's it like out today?

PETEY.   Very nice.

STANLEY.   Warm?

PETEY.   Well, there's a good breeze blowing.

STANLEY.   Cold?

PETEY.   No, no, I wouldn't say it was cold.

MEG.   What are the cornflakes like, Stan?

STANLEY.   Horrible.

MEG.   Those flakes? Those lovely flakes? You're a liar, a little liar. They're refreshing. It says so. For people when they get up late.

STANLEY.   The milk's off.

MEG.   It's not. Petey ate his, didn't you, Petey?

PETEY.   That's right.

MEG.   There you are then.

STANLEY.   All right, I'll go on to the second course.

MEG.   He hasn't finished the first course and he wants to go on to the second course!

STANLEY.   I feel like something cooked.

MEG.   Well, I'm not going to give it to you.

PETEY.   Give it to him.

MEG (*sitting at the table, right*). I'm not going to.

Pause.

STANLEY.   No breakfast.

Pause.

All night long I've been dreaming about this breakfast.

MEG.   I thought you said you didn't sleep.

STANLEY.   Day-dreaming. All night long. And now she won't give me any. Not even a crust of bread on the table.

Pause.

Well, I can see I'll have to go down to one of those smart hotels on the front.

MEG (*rising quickly*). You won't get a better breakfast there than here.

She exits to the kitchen. STANLEY *yawns broadly.* MEG *appears at the hatch with a plate.*

Here you are. You'll like this.

PETEY *rises, collects the plate, brings it to the table, puts it in front of* STANLEY, *and sits.*

STANLEY.   What's this?

PETEY.   Fried bread.

MEG (*entering*). Well, I bet you don't know what it is.

STANLEY.   Oh yes I do.

MEG.   What?

STANLEY.   Fried bread.

MEG.   He knew.

STANLEY.   What a wonderful surprise.

MEG.   You didn't expect that, did you?

STANLEY.   I bloody well didn't.

PETEY (*rising*). Well, I'm off.

MEG.   You going back to work?

PETEY.   Yes.

MEG.   Your tea! You haven't had your tea!

PETEY.   That's all right. No time now.

MEG.   I've got it made inside.

PETEY.   No, never mind. See you later. Ta-ta, Stan.

STANLEY.   Ta-ta.

PETEY *exists, left.*

Tch, tch, tch, tch.

MEG (*defensively*). What do you mean?

STANLEY.   You're a bad wife.

MEG.   I'm not. Who said I am?

STANLEY.   Not to make your husband a cup of tea. Terrible.

MEG.   He knows I'm not a bad wife.

STANLEY.   Giving him sour milk instead.

MEG.   It wasn't sour.

STANLEY.   Disgraceful.

MEG.   You mind your own business, anyway. (STANLEY *eats.*) You won't find many better wives than me, I can tell you. I keep a very nice house and I keep it clean.

STANLEY.   Whoo!

MEG.   Yes! And this house is very well known, for a very good boarding house for visitors.

STANLEY. Visitors? Do you know how many visitors you've had since I've been here?

MEG. How many?

STANLEY. One.

MEG. Who?

STANLEY. Me! I'm your visitor.

MEG. You're a liar. This house is on the list.

STANLEY. I bet it is.

MEG. I know it is.

He pushes his plate away and picks up the paper.

Was it nice?

STANLEY. What?

MEG. The fried bread.

STANLEY. Succulent.

MEG. You shouldn't say that word.

STANLEY. What word?

MEG. That word you said.

STANLEY. What, succulent—?

MEG. Don't say it!

STANLEY. What's the matter with it?

MEG. You shouldn't say that word to a married woman.

STANLEY. Is that a fact?

MEG. Yes.

STANLEY. Well, I never knew that.

MEG. Well, it's true.

STANLEY. Who told you that?

MEG. Never you mind.

STANLEY. Well, if I can't say it to a married woman who can I say it to?

MEG. You're bad.

STANLEY. What about some tea?

MEG. Do you want some tea? (STANLEY *reads the paper.*) Say please.

STANLEY. Please.

MEG. Say sorry first.

STANLEY. Sorry first.

MEG. No. Just sorry.

STANLEY. Just sorry!

MEG. You deserve the strap.

STANLEY. Don't do that!

She takes his plate and ruffles his hair as she passes. STANLEY *exclaims and throws her arm away. She goes into the kitchen. He rubs his eyes under his glasses and picks up the paper. She enters.*

MEG. I brought the pot in.

STANLEY (*absently*). I don't know what I'd do without you.

MEG. You don't deserve it though.

STANLEY. Why not?

MEG (*pouring the tea, coyly*). Go on. Calling me that.

STANLEY. How long has that tea been in the pot?

MEG. It's good tea. Good strong tea.

STANLEY. This isn't tea. It's gravy!

MEG. It's not.

STANLEY. Get out of it. You succulent old washing bag.

MEG. I am not! And it isn't your place to tell me if I am!

STANLEY. And it isn't your place to come into a man's bedroom and—wake him up.

MEG. Stanny! Don't you like your cup of tea of a morning—the one I bring you?

STANLEY. I can't drink this muck. Didn't anyone ever tell you to warm the pot, at least?

MEG. That's good strong tea, that's all.

STANLEY (*putting his head in his hands*). Oh God, I'm tired.

Silence. MEG *goes to the sideboard, collects a duster, and vaguely dusts the room, watching him. She comes to the table and dusts it.*

Not the bloody table!

Pause.

MEG. Stan?

STANLEY. What?

MEG (*shyly*). Am I really succulent?

STANLEY. Oh, you are. I'd rather have you than a cold in the nose any day.

MEG. You're just saying that.

STANLEY (*violently*). Look, why don't you get this place cleared up! It's a pigsty. And another thing, what about my room? It needs sweeping. It needs papering. I need a new room!

MEG (*sensual, stroking his arm*). Oh, Stan, that's a lovely room. I've had some lovely afternoons in that room.

He recoils from her hand in disgust, stands and exits quickly by the door on the left. She collects his cup and the teapot and takes them to the hatch shelf. The street door slams. STANLEY *returns.*

MEG. Is the sun shining? (*He crosses to the window, takes a cigarette and matches from his pyjama jacket, and lights his cigarette.*) What are you smoking?

STANLEY. A cigarette.

MEG. Are you going to give me one?

STANLEY. No.

MEG. I like cigarettes. (*He stands at the window, smoking. She crosses behind him and tickles the back of his neck.*) Tickle, tickle.

STANLEY (*pushing her*). Get away from me.

MEG. Are you going out?

STANLEY. Not with you.

MEG. But I'm going shopping in a minute.

STANLEY. Go.

MEG. You'll be lonely, all by yourself.

STANLEY. Will I?

MEG. Without your old Meg. I've got to get things in for the two gentlemen.

A pause. STANLEY *slowly raises his head. He speaks without turning.*

STANLEY.   What two gentlemen?
MEG.   I'm expecting visitors.

He turns.

STANLEY.   What?
MEG.   You didn't know that, did you?
STANLEY.   What are you talking about?
MEG.   Two gentlemen asked Petey if they could come and stay for a couple of nights. I'm expecting them. (*She picks up the duster and begins to wipe the cloth on the table.*)
STANLEY.   I don't believe it.
MEG.   It's true.
STANLEY (*moving to her*).   You're saying it on purpose.
MEG.   Petey told me this morning.
STANLEY (*grinding his cigarette*).   When was this? When did he see them?
MEG.   Last night.
STANLEY.   Who are they?
MEG.   I don't know.
STANLEY.   Didn't he tell you their names?
MEG.   No.
STANLEY (*pacing the room*).   Here? They wanted to come here?
MEG.   Yes, they did. (*She takes the curlers out of her hair.*)
STANLEY.   Why?
MEG.   This house is on the list.
STANLEY.   But who are they?
MEG.   You'll see when they come.
STANLEY (*decisively*).   They won't come.
MEG.   Why not?
STANLEY (*quickly*).   I tell you they won't come. Why didn't they come last night, if they were coming?
MEG.   Perhaps they couldn't find the place in the dark. It's not easy to find in the dark.
STANLEY.   They won't come. Someone's taking the Michael. Forget all about it. It's a false alarm. A false alarm. (*He sits at the table.*) Where's my tea?
MEG.   I took it away. You didn't want it.
STANLEY.   What do you mean, you took it away?
MEG.   I took it away.
STANLEY.   What did you take it away for?
MEG.   You didn't want it!
STANLEY.   Who said I didn't want it?
MEG.   You did!
STANLEY.   Who gave you the right to take away my tea?
MEG.   You wouldn't drink it.

STANLEY *stares at her.*

STANLEY (*quietly*).   Who do you think you're talking to?
MEG (*uncertainly*).   What?
STANLEY.   Come here.

MEG.   What do you mean?
STANLEY.   Come over here.
MEG.   No.
STANLEY.   I want to ask you something. (MEG *fidgets nervously. She does not go to him.*) Come on. (*Pause.*) All right. I can ask it from here just as well. (*Deliberately.*) Tell me, Mrs. Boles, when you address yourself to me, do you ever ask yourself who exactly you are talking to? Eh?

Silence. He groans, his trunk falls forward, his head falls into his hands.

MEG (*in a small voice*).   Didn't you enjoy your breakfast, Stan? (*She approaches the table.*) Stan? When are you going to play the piano again? (STANLEY *grunts.*) Like you used to? (STANLEY *grunts.*) I used to like watching you play the piano. When are you going to play it again?
STANLEY.   I can't, can I?
MEG.   Why not?
STANLEY.   I haven't got a piano, have I?
MEG.   No, I meant like when you were working. That piano.
STANLEY.   Go and do your shopping.
MEG.   But you wouldn't have to go away if you got a job, would you? You could play the piano on the pier.

He looks at her, then speaks airily.

STANLEY.   I've . . . er . . . I've been offered a job, as a matter of fact.
MEG.   What?
STANLEY.   Yes. I'm considering a job at the moment.
MEG.   You're not.
STANLEY.   A good one, too. A night club. In Berlin.
MEG.   Berlin?
STANLEY.   Berlin. A night club. Playing the piano. A fabulous salary. And all found.
MEG.   How long for?
STANLEY.   We don't stay in Berlin. Then we go to Athens.
MEG.   How long for?
STANLEY.   Yes. Then we pay a flying visit to . . . er . . . whatsisname. . . .
MEG.   Where?
STANLEY.   Constantinople. Zagreb. Vladivostock. It's a round the world tour.
MEG (*sitting at the table*).   Have you played the piano in those places before?
STANLEY.   Played the piano? I've played the piano all over the world. All over the country. (*Pause.*) I once gave a concert.
MEG.   A concert?
STANLEY (*reflectively*).   Yes. It was a good one, too. They were all there that night. Every single one of them. It was a great success. Yes. A concert. At Lower Edmonton.
MEG.   What did you wear?

STANLEY (*to himself.*) I had a unique touch. Absolutely unique. They came up to me. They came up to me and said they were grateful. Champagne we had that night, the lot. (*Pause.*) My father nearly came down to hear me. Well, I dropped him a card anyway. But I don't think he could make it. No, I—I lost the address, that was it. (*Pause.*) Yes. Lower Edmonton. Then after that, you know what they did? They carved me up. Carved me up. It was all arranged, it was all worked out. My next concert. Somewhere else it was. In winter. I went down there to play. Then, when I got there, the hall was closed, the place was shuttered up, not even a caretaker. They'd locked it up. (*Takes off his glasses and wipes them on his pyjama jacket.*) A fast one. They pulled a fast one. I'd like to know who was responsible for that. (*Bitterly.*) All right, Jack, I can take a tip. They want me to crawl down on my bended knees. Well I can take a tip . . . any day of the week. (*He replaces his glasses, then looks at* MEG.) Look at her. You're just an old piece of rock cake, aren't you? (*He rises and leans across the table at her.*) That's what you are, aren't you?

MEG.   Don't you go away again, Stan. You stay here. You'll be better off. You stay with your old Meg. (*He groans and lies across the table.*) Aren't you feeling well this morning, Stan. Did you pay a visit this morning?

He stiffens, then lifts himself slowly, turns to face her and speaks lightly, casually.

STANLEY.   Meg. Do you know what?
MEG.   What?
STANLEY.   Have you heard the latest?
MEG.   No.
STANLEY.   I'll bet you have.
MEG.   I haven't.
STANLEY.   Shall I tell you?
MEG.   What latest?
STANLEY.   You haven't heard it?
MEG.   No.
STANLEY (*advancing*). They're coming today.
MEG.   Who?
STANLEY.   They're coming in a van.
MEG.   Who?
STANLEY.   And do you know what they've got in that van?
MEG.   What?
STANLEY.   They've got a wheelbarrow in that van.
MEG (*breathlessly*). They haven't.
STANLEY.   Oh yes they have.
MEG.   You're a liar.
STANLEY (*advancing upon her*). A big wheelbarrow. And when the van stops they wheel it out, and they wheel it up the garden path, and then they knock at the front door.
MEG.   They don't.
STANLEY.   They're looking for someone.
MEG.   They're not.

STANLEY.   They're looking for someone. A certain person.
MEG (*hoarsely*). No, they're not!
STANLEY.   Shall I tell you who they're looking for?
MEG.   No!
STANLEY.   You don't want me to tell you?
MEG.   You're a liar!

A sudden knock on the front door. LULU'S *voice: Ooh-ooh!* MEG *edges past* STANLEY *and collects her shopping bag.* MEG *goes out.* STANLEY *sidles to the door and listens.*

VOICE (*through letter box*). Hullo, Mrs. Boles . . .
MEG.   Oh, has it come?
VOICE.   Yes, it's just come.
MEG.   What, is that it?
VOICE.   Yes. I thought I'd bring it round.
MEG.   Is it nice?
VOICE.   Very nice. What shall I do with it?
MEG.   Well, I don't . . . (*Whispers.*)
VOICE.   No, of course not . . . (*Whispers.*)
MEG.   All right, but . . . (*Whispers.*)
VOICE.   I won't . . . (*Whispers.*) Ta-ta, Mrs. Boles.

STANLEY *quickly sits at the table. Enter* LULU.

LULU.   Oh, hullo.
STANLEY.   Ay-ay.
LULU.   I just want to leave this in here.
STANLEY.   Do. (LULU *crosses to the sideboard and puts a solid, round parcel upon it.*) That's a bulky object.
LULU.   You're not to touch it.
STANLEY.   Why would I want to touch it?
LULU.   Well, you're not to, anyway.

LULU *walks upstage.*

LULU.   Why don't you open the door? It's all stuffy in here.

She opens the back door.

STANLEY (*rising*). Stuffy? I disinfected the place this morning.
LULU (*at the door*). Oh, that's better.
STANLEY.   I think it's going to rain to-day. What do you think?
LULU.   I hope so. You could do with it.
STANLEY.   Me! I was in the sea at half past six.
LULU.   Were you?
STANLEY.   I went right out to the headland and back before breakfast. Don't you believe me!

She sits, takes out a compact and powders her nose.

LULU (*offering him the compact*). Do you want to have a look at your face? (STANLEY *withdraws from the table.*) You could do with a shave, do you know that? (STANLEY *sits, right, at the table.*) Don't you ever go out? (*He does not answer.*) I mean, what do you do, just sit around the house like this all day long? (*Pause.*) Hasn't Mrs. Boles got enough to do without having you under her feet all day long?

STANLEY.   I always stand on the table when she sweeps the floor.

LULU.   Why don't you have a wash? You look terrible.

STANLEY.   A wash wouldn't make any difference.

LULU (*rising*). Come out and get a bit of air. You depress me, looking like that.

STANLEY.   Air? Oh, I don't know about that.

LULU.   It's lovely out. And I've got a few sandwiches.

STANLEY.   What sort of sandwiches?

LULU.   Cheese.

STANLEY.   I'm a big eater, you know.

LULU.   That's all right. I'm not hungry.

STANLEY (*abruptly*). How would you like to go away with me?

LULU.   Where.

STANLEY.   Nowhere. Still, we could go.

LULU.   But where could we go?

STANLEY.   Nowhere. There's nowhere to go. So we could just go. It wouldn't matter.

LULU.   We might as well stay here.

STANLEY.   No. It's no good here.

LULU.   Well, where else is there?

STANLEY.   Nowhere.

LULU.   Well, that's a charming proposal. (*He gets up.*) Do you have to wear those glasses?

STANLEY.   Yes.

LULU.   So you're not coming out for a walk?

STANLEY.   I can't at the moment.

LULU.   You're a bit of a washout, aren't you?

She exits, left. STANLEY *stands. He then goes to the mirror and looks in it. He goes into the kitchen, takes off his glasses and begins to wash his face. A pause. Enter, by the back door,* GOLDBERG *and* MCCANN. MCCANN *carries two suitcases,* GOLDBERG *a briefcase. They halt inside the door, then walk downstage.* STANLEY, *wiping his face, glimpses their backs through the hatch.* GOLDBERG *and* MCCANN *look round the room.* STANLEY *slips on his glasses, sidles through the kitchen door and out of the back door.*

MCCANN.   Is this it?

GOLDBERG.   This is it.

MCCANN.   Are you sure?

GOLDBERG.   Sure I'm sure.

Pause.

MCCANN.   What now?

GOLDBERG.   Don't worry yourself, McCann. Take a seat.

MCCANN.   What about you?

GOLDBERG.   What about me?

MCCANN.   Are you going to take a seat?

GOLDBERG.   We'll both take a seat. (MCCANN *puts down the suitcases and sits at the table, left.*) Sit back, McCann. Relax. What's the matter with you? I bring you down for a few days to the seaside. Take a holiday. Do yourself a favour. Learn to relax, McCann, or you'll never get anywhere.

MCCANN.   Ah sure, I do try, Nat.

GOLDBERG (*sitting at the table, right*). The secret is breathing. Take my tip. It's a well-known fact. Breathe in, breathe out, take a chance, let yourself go, what can you lose? Look at me. When I was an apprentice yet, McCann, every second Friday of the month my Uncle Barney used to take me to the seaside, regular as clockwork. Brighton, Canvey Island, Rottingdean—Uncle Barney wasn't particular. After lunch on Shabbuss we'd go and sit in a couple of deck chairs—you know, the ones with canopies—we'd have a little paddle, we'd watch the tide coming in, going out, the sun coming down—golden days, believe me, McCann. (*Reminiscent.*) Uncle Barney. Of course, he was an impeccable dresser. One of the old school. He had a house just outside Basingstoke at the time. Respected by the whole community. Culture? Don't talk to me about culture. He was an all-round man, what do you mean? He was a cosmopolitan.

MCCANN.   Hey, Nat. . . .

GOLDBERG (*reflectively*). Yes. One of the old school.

MCCANN.   Nat. How do we know this is the right house?

GOLDBERG.   What?

MCCANN.   How do we know this is the right house?

GOLDBERG.   What makes you think it's the wrong house?

MCCANN.   I didn't see a number on the gate.

GOLDBERG.   I wasn't looking for a number.

MCCANN.   No?

GOLDBERG (*settling in the armchair*). You know one thing Uncle Barney taught me? Uncle Barney taught me that the word of a gentleman is enough. That's why, when I had to go away on business I never carried any money. One of my sons used to come with me. He used to carry a few coppers. For a paper, perhaps, to see how the M.C.C. was getting on overseas. Otherwise my name was good. Besides, I was a very busy man.

MCCANN.   What about this, Nat? Isn't it about time someone came in?

GOLDBERG.   McCann, what are you so nervous about? Pull yourself together. Everywhere you go these days it's like a funeral.

MCCANN.   That's true.

GOLDBERG.   True? Of course it's true. It's more than true. It's a fact.

MCCANN.   You may be right.

GOLDBERG.   What is it, McCann? You don't trust me like you did in the old days?

MCCANN.   Sure I trust you, Nat.

GOLDBERG.   But why is it that before you do a job you're all over the place, and when you're doing the job you're as cool as a whistle?

McCANN.   I don't know, Nat. I'm just all right once I know what I'm doing. When I know what I'm doing, I'm all right.

GOLDBERG.   Well, you do it very well.

McCANN.   Thank you, Nat.

GOLDBERG.   You know what I said when this job came up. I mean naturally they approached me to take care of it. And you know who I asked for?

McCANN.   Who?

GOLDBERG.   You.

McCANN.   That was very good of you, Nat.

GOLDBERG.   No, it was nothing. You're a capable man, McCann.

McCANN.   That's a great compliment, Nat, coming from a man in your position.

GOLDBERG.   Well, I've got a position, I won't deny it.

McCANN.   You certainly have.

GOLDBERG.   I would never deny that I had a position.

McCANN.   And what a position!

GOLDBERG.   It's not a thing I would deny.

McCANN.   Yes, it's true, you've done a lot for me. I appreciate it.

GOLDBERG.   Say no more.

McCANN.   You've always been a true Christian.

GOLDBERG.   In a way.

McCANN.   No, I just thought I'd tell you that I appreciate it.

GOLDBERG.   It's unnecessary to recapitulate.

McCANN.   You're right there.

GOLDBERG.   Quite unnecessary.

Pause. McCANN *leans forward.*

McCANN.   Hey Nat, just one thing. . . .

GOLDBERG.   What now?

McCANN.   This job—no, listen—this job, is it going to be like anything we've ever done before?

GOLDBERG.   Tch, tch, tch.

McCANN.   No, just tell me that. Just that, and I won't ask any more.

GOLDBERG *sighs, stands, goes behind the table, ponders, looks at* McCANN, *and then speaks in a quiet, fluent, official tone.*

GOLDBERG.   The main issue is a singular issue and quite distinct from your previous work. Certain elements, however, might well approximate in points of procedure to some of your other activities. All is dependent on the attitude of our subject. At all events, McCann, I can assure you that the assignment will be carried out and the mission accomplished with no excessive aggravation to you or myself. Satisfied?

McCANN.   Sure. Thank you, Nat.

MEG *enters, left.*

GOLDBERG.   Ah, Mrs. Boles?

MEG.   Yes?

GOLDBERG.   We spoke to your husband last night. Perhaps he mentioned us? We heard that you kindly let rooms for gentlemen. So I brought my friend along with me. We were after a nice place, you understand. So we came to you. I'm Mr. Goldberg and this is Mr. McCann.

MEG.   Very pleased to meet you.

They shake hands.

GOLDBERG.   We're pleased to meet you, too.

MEG.   That's very nice.

GOLDBERG.   You're right. How often do you meet someone it's a pleasure to meet?

McCANN.   Never.

GOLDBERG.   But today it's different. How are you keeping, Mrs. Boles?

MEG.   Oh, very well, thank you.

GOLDBERG.   Yes? Really?

MEG.   Oh yes, really.

GOLDBERG.   I'm glad.

GOLDBERG *sits at the table, right.*

GOLDBERG.   Well, so what do you say? You can manage to put us up, eh, Mrs. Boles?

MEG.   Well, it would have been easier last week.

GOLDBERG.   It would, eh?

MEG.   Yes.

GOLDBERG.   Why? How many have you got here at the moment?

MEG.   Just one at the moment.

GOLDBERG.   Just one?

MEG.   Yes. Just one. Until you came.

GOLDBERG.   And your husband, of course?

MEG.   Yes, but he sleeps with me.

GOLDBERG.   What does he do, your husband?

MEG.   He's a deck-chair attendant.

GOLDBERG.   Oh, very nice.

MEG.   Yes, he's out in all weathers.

She begins to take her purchases from her bag.

GOLDBERG.   Of course. And your guest? Is he a man?

MEG.   A man?

GOLDBERG.   Or a woman?

MEG.   No. A man.

GOLDBERG.   Been here long?

MEG.   He's been here about a year now.

GOLDBERG.   Oh yes. A resident. What's his name?

MEG.   Stanley Webber.

GOLDBERG.   Oh yes? Does he work here?

MEG.   He used to work. He used to be a pianist. In a concert party on the pier.

GOLDBERG.   Oh yes? On the pier, eh? Does he play a nice piano?

MEG.   Oh, lovely. (*She sits at the table.*) He once gave a concert.

GOLDBERG.   Oh? Where?

MEG (*falteringly*). In . . . a big hall. His father gave him champagne. But then they locked the place up and he couldn't get out. The caretaker had gone home. So he had to wait until the morning before he could get out. (*With confidence.*) They were very grateful. (*Pause.*) And then they all wanted to give him a tip. And so he took the tip. And then he got a fast train and he came down here.

GOLDBERG.   Really?

MEG.   Oh yes. Straight down.

Pause.

MEG.   I wish he could have played tonight.

GOLDBERG.   Why tonight?

MEG.   It's his birthday today.

GOLDBERG.   His birthday?

MEG.   Yes. Today. But I'm not going to tell him until tonight.

GOLDBERG.   Doesn't he know it's his birthday?

MEG.   He hasn't mentioned it.

GOLDBERG (*thoughtfully*). Ah! Tell me. Are you going to have a party?

MEG.   A party?

GOLDBERG.   Weren't you going to have one?

MEG (*her eyes wide*). No.

GOLDBERG.   Well, of course, you must have one. (*He stands.*) We'll have a party, eh? What do you say?

MEG.   Oh yes!

GOLDBERG.   Sure. We'll give him a party. Leave it to me.

MEG.   Oh, that's wonderful, Mr. Gold—

GOLDBERG.   Berg.

MEG.   Berg.

GOLDBERG.   You like the idea?

MEG.   Oh, I'm so glad you came today.

GOLDBERG.   If we hadn't come today we'd have come tomorrow. Still, I'm glad we came today. Just in time for his birthday.

MEG.   I wanted to have a party. But you must have people for a party.

GOLDBERG.   And now you've got McCann and me. McCann's the life and soul of any party.

McCANN.   What?

GOLDBERG.   What do you think of that, McCann? There's a gentleman living here. He's got a birthday today, and he's forgotten all about it. So we're going to remind him. We're going to give him a party.

McCANN.   Oh, is that a fact?

MEG.   Tonight.

GOLDBERG.   Tonight.

MEG.   I'll put on my party dress.

GOLDBERG.   And I'll get some bottles.

MEG.   And I'll invite Lulu this afternoon. Oh, this is going to cheer Stanley up. It will. He's been down in the dumps lately.

GOLDBERG.   We'll bring him out of himself.

MEG.   I hope I look nice in my dress.

GOLDBERG.   Madam, you'll look like a tulip.

MEG.   What colour?

GOLDBERG.   Er—well, I'll have to see the dress first.

McCANN.   Could I go up to my room?

MEG.   Oh, I've put you both together. Do you mind being both together?

GOLDBERG.   I don't mind. Do you mind, McCann?

McCANN.   No.

MEG.   What time shall we have the party?

GOLDBERG.   Nine o'clock.

McCANN (*at the door*). Is this the way?

MEG (*rising*). I'll show you. If you don't mind coming upstairs.

GOLDBERG.   With a tulip? It's a pleasure.

MEG *and* GOLDBERG *exit laughing, followed by* McCANN. STANLEY *appears at the window. He enters by the back door. He goes to the door on the left, opens it and listens. Silence. He walks to the table. He stands. He sits, as* MEG *enters. She crosses and hangs her shopping bag on a hook. He lights a match and watches it burn.*

STANLEY.   Who is it?

MEG.   The two gentlemen.

STANLEY.   What two gentlemen?

MEG.   The ones that were coming. I just took them to their room. They were thrilled with their room.

STANLEY.   They've come?

MEG.   They're very nice, Stan.

STANLEY.   Why didn't they come last night?

MEG.   They said the beds were wonderful.

STANLEY.   Who are they?

MEG (*sitting*). They're very nice, Stanley.

STANLEY.   I said, who are they?

MEG.   I've told you, the two gentlemen.

STANLEY.   I didn't think they'd come.

He rises and walks to the window.

MEG.   They have. They were here when I came in.

STANLEY.   What do they want here?

MEG.   They want to stay.

STANLEY.   How long for?

MEG.   They didn't say.

STANLEY (*turning*). But why here? Why not somewhere else?

MEG.   This house is on the list.

STANLEY (*coming down*). What are they called? What are their names?

MEG.   Oh, Stanley, I can't remember.

STANLEY.   They told you, didn't they? Or didn't they tell you?

MEG.   Yes, they. . . .

STANLEY.   Then what are they? Come on. Try to remember.

MEG.   Why, Stan? Do you know them?

STANLEY.   How do I know if I know them until I know their names?

MEG.   Well . . . he told me, I remember.

STANLEY.   Well?

She thinks.

MEG.   Gold—something.

STANLEY.   Goldsomething?

MEG.   Yes. Gold. . . .

STANLEY.   Yes?

MEG.   Goldberg.

STANLEY.   Goldberg?

MEG.   That's right. That was one of them.

STANLEY *slowly sits at the table, left.*

Do you know them?

STANLEY *does not answer.*

Stan, they won't wake you up, I promise. I'll tell them they must be quiet.

STANLEY *sits still.*

They won't be here long, Stan. I'll still bring you up your early morning tea.

STANLEY *sits still.*

You mustn't be sad today. It's your birthday.

A pause.

STANLEY (*dumbly*). Uh?

MEG.   It's your birthday, Stan. I was going to keep it a secret until tonight.

STANLEY.   No.

MEG.   It is. I've brought you a present. (*She goes to the sideboard, picks up the parcel, and places it on the table in front of him.*) Here. Go on. Open it.

STANLEY.   What's this?

MEG.   It's your present.

STANLEY.   This isn't my birthday, Meg.

MEG.   Of course it is. Open your present.

He stares at the parcel, slowly stands, and opens it. He takes out a boy's drum.

STANLEY (*flatly*). It's a drum. A boy's drum.

MEG (*tenderly*). It's because you haven't got a piano. (*He stares at her, then turns and walks towards the door, left.*) Aren't you going to give me a kiss? (*He turns sharply,*

and stops. He walks back towards her slowly. He stops at her chair, looking down upon her. Pause. His shoulders sag, he bends and kisses her on the cheek.*) There are some sticks in there. (STANLEY *looks into the parcel. He takes out two drumsticks. He taps them together. He looks at her.*)

STANLEY.   Shall I put it round my neck?

She watches him, uncertainly. He hangs the drum around his neck, taps it gently with the sticks, then marches round the table, beating it regularly. MEG, *pleased, watches him. Still beating it regularly, he begins to go round the table a second time. Halfway round the beat becomes erratic, uncontrolled.* MEG *expresses dismay. He arrives at her chair, banging the drum, his face and the drumbeat now savage and possessed.*

CURTAIN

ACT TWO

MCCANN *is sitting at the table tearing a sheet of newspaper into five equal strips. It is evening. After a few moments* STANLEY *enters from the left. He stops upon seeing* MCCANN, *and watches him. He then walks towards the kitchen, stops, and speaks.*

STANLEY.   Evening.

MCCANN.   Evening.

Chuckles are heard from outside the back door, which is open.

STANLEY.   Very warm tonight. (*He turns towards the back door, and back.*) Someone out there?

MCCANN *tears another length of paper.* STANLEY *goes into the kitchen and pours a glass of water. He drinks it looking through the hatch. He puts the glass down, comes out of the kitchen and walks quickly towards the door, left.* MCCANN *rises and intercepts him.*

MCCANN.   I don't think we've met.

STANLEY.   No, we haven't.

MCCANN.   My name's McCann.

STANLEY.   Staying here long?

MCCANN.   Not long. What's your name?

STANLEY.   Webber.

MCCANN.   I'm glad to meet you, sir. (*He offers his hand.* STANLEY *takes it, and* MCCANN *holds the grip.*) Many happy returns of the day. (STANLEY *withdraws his hand. They face each other.*). Were you going out?

STANLEY.   Yes.

MCCANN.   On your birthday?

STANLEY.   Yes. Why not?

MCCANN.   But they're holding a party here for you tonight.

STANLEY.   Oh really? That's unfortunate.

MCCANN.   Ah no. It's very nice.

Voices from outside the back door.

STANLEY.   I'm sorry. I'm not in the mood for a party tonight.
MCCANN.   Oh, is that so? I'm sorry.
STANLEY.   Yes, I'm going out to celebrate quietly, on my own.
MCCANN.   That's a shame.

They stand.

STANLEY.   Well, if you'd move out of my way—
MCCANN.   But everything's laid on. The guests are expected.
STANLEY.   Guests? What guests?
MCCANN.   Myself for one. I had the honour of an invitation.

MCCANN *begins to whistle "The Mountains of Morne."*

STANLEY (*moving away*). I wouldn't call it an honour, would you? It'll just be another booze-up.

STANLEY *joins* MCCANN *in whistling "The Mountains of Morne." During the next five lines the whistling is continuous, one whistling while the other speaks, and both whistling together.*

MCCANN.   But it is an honour.
STANLEY.   I'd say you were exaggerating.
MCCANN.   Oh no. I'd say it was an honour.
STANLEY.   I'd say that was plain stupid.
MCCANN.   Ah no.

They stare at each other.

STANLEY.   Who are the other guests?
MCCANN.   A young lady.
STANLEY.   Oh yes? And. . . . ?
MCCANN.   My friend.
STANLEY.   Your friend?
MCCANN.   That's right. It's all laid on.

STANLEY *walks round the table towards the door.* MCCANN *meets him.*

STANLEY.   Excuse me.
MCCANN.   Where are you going?
STANLEY.   I want to go out.
MCCANN.   Why don't you stay here?

STANLEY *moves away, to the right of the table.*

STANLEY.   So you're down here on holiday?
MCCANN.   A short one. (STANLEY *picks up a strip of paper.* MCCANN *moves in.*) Mind that.
STANLEY.   What is it?
MCCANN.   Mind it. Leave it.

STANLEY.   I've got a feeling we've met before.
MCCANN.   No we haven't.
STANLEY.   Ever been anywhere near Maidenhead?
MCCANN.   No.
STANLEY.   There's a Fuller's teashop. I used to have my tea there.
MCCANN.   I don't know it.
STANLEY.   And a Boots Library. I seem to connect you with the High Street.
MCCANN.   Yes?
STANLEY.   A charming town, don't you think?
MCCANN.   I don't know it.
STANLEY.   Oh no. A quiet, thriving community. I was born and brought up there. I lived well away from the main road.
MCCANN.   Yes?

Pause.

STANLEY.   You're here on a short stay?
MCCANN.   That's right.
STANLEY.   You'll find it very bracing.
MCCANN.   Do you find it bracing?
STANLEY.   Me? No. But you will. (*He sits at the table.*) I like it here, but I'll be moving soon. Back home. I'll stay there too, this time. No place like home. (*He laughs.*) I wouldn't have left, but business calls. Business called, and I had to leave for a bit. You know how it is.
MCCANN (*sitting at the table, left*). You in business?
STANLEY.   No. I think I'll give it up. I've got a small private income, you see. I think I'll give it up. Don't like being away from home. I used to live very quietly—played records, that's about all. Everything delivered to the door. Then I started a little private business, in a small way, and it compelled me to come down here—kept me longer than I expected. You never get used to living in someone else's house. Don't you agree? I lived so quietly. You can only appreciate what you've had when things change. That's what they say, isn't it? Cigarette?
MCCANN.   I don't smoke.

STANLEY *lights a cigarette. Voices from the back.*

STANLEY.   Who's out there?
MCCANN.   My friend and the man of the house.
STANLEY.   You know what? To look at me, I bet you wouldn't think I'd led such a quiet life. The lines on my face, eh? It's the drink. Been drinking a bit down here. But what I mean is . . . you know how it is . . . away from your own . . . all wrong, of course . . . I'll be all right when I get back . . . but what I mean is, the way some people look at me you'd think I was a different person. I suppose I have changed, but I'm still the same man that I always was. I mean, you wouldn't think, to look at me, really . . . I mean, not really, that I was the sort of bloke to—to cause any trouble, would you? (MCCANN *looks at him.*) Do you know what I mean?

McCANN.   No. (*As* STANLEY *picks up a strip of paper.*) Mind that.

STANLEY (*quickly*).   Why are you down here?

McCANN.   A short holiday.

STANLEY.   This is a ridiculous house to pick on. (*He rises.*)

McCANN.   Why?

STANLEY.   Because it's not a boarding house. It never was.

McCANN.   Sure it is.

STANLEY.   Why did you choose this house?

McCANN.   You know, sir, you're a bit depressed for a man on his birthday.

STANLEY (*sharply*).   Why do you call me sir?

McCANN.   You don't like it?

STANLEY (*to the table*).   Listen. Don't call me sir.

McCANN.   I won't, if you don't like it.

STANLEY (*moving away*).   No. Anyway, this isn't my birthday.

McCANN.   No?

STANLEY.   No. It's not till next month.

McCANN.   Not according to the lady.

STANLEY.   Her? She's crazy. Round the bend.

McCANN.   That's a terrible thing to say.

STANLEY (*to the table*).   Haven't you found that out yet? There's a lot you don't know. I think someone's leading you up the garden path.

McCANN.   Who would do that?

STANLEY (*leaning across the table*).   That woman is mad!

McCANN.   That's slander.

STANLEY.   And you don't know what you're doing.

McCANN.   Your cigarette is near that paper.

Voices from the back.

STANLEY.   Where the hell are they? (*Stubbing his cigarette.*) Why don't they come in? What are they doing out there?

McCANN.   You want to steady yourself.

STANLEY *crosses to him and grips his arm.*

STANLEY (*urgently*).   Look—

McCANN.   Don't touch me.

STANLEY.   Look. Listen a minute.

McCANN.   Let go my arm.

STANLEY.   Look. Sit down a minute.

McCANN (*savagely, hitting his arm*).   Don't do that!

STANLEY *backs across the stage, holding his arm.*

STANLEY.   Listen. You knew what I was talking about before, didn't you?

McCANN.   I don't know what you're at at all.

STANLEY.   It's a mistake! Do you understand?

McCANN.   You're in a bad state, man.

STANLEY (*whispering, advancing*).   Has he told you anything? Do you know what you're here for? Tell me. You needn't be frightened of me. Or hasn't he told you?

McCANN.   Told me what?

STANLEY (*hissing*).   I've explained to you, damn you, that all those years I lived in Basingstoke I never stepped outside the door.

McCANN.   You know, I'm flabbergasted with you.

STANLEY (*reasonably*).   Look. You look an honest man. You're being made a fool of, that's all. You understand? Where do you come from?

McCANN.   Where do you think?

STANLEY.   I know Ireland very well. I've many friends there. I love that country and I admire and trust its people. I trust them. They respect the truth and they have a sense of humour. I think their policemen are wonderful. I've been there. I've never seen such sunsets. What about coming out to have a drink with me? There's a pub down the road serves draught Guinness. Very difficult to get in these parts—(*He breaks off. The voices draw nearer.* GOLDBERG *and* PETEY *enter from the back door.*)

GOLDBERG (*as he enters*).   A mother in a million. (*He sees* STANLEY.) Ah.

PETEY.   Oh hullo, Stan. You haven't met Stanley, have you, Mr. Goldberg?

GOLDBERG.   I haven't had the pleasure.

PETEY.   Oh well, this is Mr. Goldberg, this is Mr. Webber.

GOLDBERG.   Pleased to meet you.

PETEY.   We were just getting a bit of air in the garden.

GOLDBERG.   I was telling Mr. Boles about my old mum. What days. (*He sits at the table, right.*) Yes. When I was a youngster, of a Friday, I used to go for a walk down the canal with a girl who lived down my road. A beautiful girl. What a voice that bird had! A nightingale, my word of honour. Good? Pure? She wasn't a Sunday school teacher for nothing. Anyway, I'd leave her with a little kiss on the cheek—I never took liberties—we weren't like the young men these days in those days. We knew the meaning of respect. So I'd give her a peck and I'd bowl back home. Humming away I'd be, past the children's playground. I'd tip my hat to the toddlers, I'd give a helping hand to a couple of stray dogs, everything came natural. I can see it like yesterday. The sun falling behind the dog stadium. Ah! (*He leans back contentedly.*)

McCANN.   Like behind the town hall.

GOLDBERG.   What town hall?

McCANN.   In Carrikmacross.

GOLDBERG.   There's no comparison. Up the street, into my gate, inside the door, home. "Simey!" my old mum used to shout, "quick before it gets cold." And there on the table what would I see? The nicest piece of gefilte fish you could wish to find on a plate.

McCANN.   I thought your name was Nat.

GOLDBERG.   She called me Simey.

PETEY.   Yes, we all remember our childhood.

GOLDBERG.   Too true. Eh, Mr. Webber, what do you say? Childhood. Hot water bottles. Hot milk. Pancakes. Soap suds. What a life.

Pause.

PETEY (*rising from the table*). Well, I'll have to be off.
GOLDBERG.   Off?
PETEY.   It's my chess night.
GOLDBERG.   You're not staying for the party?
PETEY.   No, I'm sorry, Stan. I didn't know about it till just now. And we've got a game on. I'll try and get back early.
GOLDBERG.   We'll save some drink for you, all right? Oh, that reminds me. You'd better go and collect the bottles.
MCCANN.   Now?
GOLDBERG.   Of course, now. Time's getting on. Round the corner, remember? Mention my name.
PETEY.   I'm coming your way.
GOLDBERG.   Beat him quick and come back, Mr. Boles.
PETEY.   Do my best. See you later, Stan.

Petey and McCann go out, left. Stanley moves to the centre.

GOLDBERG.   A warm night.
STANLEY (*turning*). Don't mess me about!
GOLDBERG.   I beg your pardon?
STANLEY (*moving downstage*). I'm afraid there's been a mistake. We're booked out. Your room is taken. Mrs. Boles forgot to tell you. You'll have to find somewhere else.
GOLDBERG.   Are you the manager here?
STANLEY.   That's right.
GOLDBERG.   Is it a good game?
STANLEY.   I run the house. I'm afraid you and your friend will have to find other accommodation.
GOLDBERG (*rising*). Oh, I forgot, I must congratulate you on your birthday. (*Offering his hand.*) Congratulations.
STANLEY (*ignoring hand*). Perhaps you're deaf.
GOLDBERG.   No, what makes you think that? As a matter of fact, every single one of my senses is at its peak. Not bad going, eh? For a man past fifty. But a birthday, I always feel, is a great occasion, taken too much for granted these days. What a thing to celebrate—birth! Like getting up in the morning. Marvellous! Some people don't like the idea of getting up in the morning. I've heard them. Getting up in the morning, they say, what is it? Your skin's crabby, you need a shave, your eyes are full of muck, your mouth is like a boghouse, the palms of your hands are full of sweat, your nose is clogged up, your feet stink, what are you but a corpse waiting to be washed? Whenever I hear that point of view I feel cheerful. Because I know what it is to wake up with the sun shining, to the sound of the lawnmower, all the little birds, the smell of the grass, church bells, tomato juice—
STANLEY.   Get out.

Enter McCann, with bottles.

Get that drink out. These are unlicensed premises.

GOLDBERG.   You're in a terrible humour today, Mr. Webber. And on your birthday too, with the good lady getting her strength up to give you a party.

McCann puts the bottles on the sideboard.

STANLEY.   I told you to get those bottles out.
GOLDBERG.   Mr. Webber, sit down a minute.
STANLEY.   Let me—just make this clear. You don't bother me. To me, you're nothing but a dirty joke. But I have a responsibility towards the people in this house. They've been down here too long. They've lost their sense of smell. I haven't. And nobody's going to take advantage of them while I'm here. (*A little less forceful.*) Anyway, this house isn't your cup of tea. There's nothing here for you, from any angle, any angle. So why don't you just go, without any more fuss?
GOLDBERG.   Mr. Webber, sit down.
STANLEY.   It's no good starting any kind of trouble.
GOLDBERG.   Sit down.
STANLEY.   Why should I?
GOLDBERG.   If you want to know the truth, Webber, you're beginning to get on my breasts.
STANLEY.   Really? Well, that's—
GOLDBERG.   Sit down.
STANLEY.   No.

Goldberg sighs, and sits at the table right.

GOLDBERG.   McCann.
MCCANN.   Nat?
GOLDBERG.   Ask him to sit down.
MCCANN.   Yes, Nat. (*McCann moves to Stanley.*) Do you mind sitting down?
STANLEY.   Yes, I do mind.
MCCANN.   Yes now, but—it'd be better if you did.
STANLEY.   Why don't you sit down?
MCCANN.   No, not me—you.
STANLEY.   No thanks.

Pause.

MCCANN.   Nat.
GOLDBERG.   What?
MCCANN.   He won't sit down.
GOLDBERG.   Well, ask him.
MCCANN.   I've asked him.
GOLDBERG.   Ask him again.
MCCANN (*to Stanley*). Sit down.
STANLEY.   Why?
MCCANN.   You'd be more comfortable.
STANLEY.   So would you.

Pause.

MCCANN.   All right. If you will I will.
STANLEY.   You first.

McCANN *slowly sits at the table, left.*

McCANN.   Well?

STANLEY.   Right. Now you've both had a rest you can get out!

McCANN (*rising*). That's a dirty trick! I'll kick the shite out of him!

GOLDBERG (*rising*). No! I have stood up.

McCANN.   Sit down again!

GOLDBERG.   Once I'm up I'm up.

STANLEY.   Same here.

McCANN (*moving to* STANLEY). You've made Mr. Goldberg stand up.

STANLEY (*his voice rising*). It'll do him good!

McCANN.   Get in that seat.

GOLDBERG.   McCann.

McCANN.   Get down in that seat!

GOLDBERG (*crossing to him*). Webber. (*Quietly.*) SIT DOWN. (*Silence.* STANLEY *begins to whistle "The Mountains of Morne." He strolls casually to the chair at the table. They watch him. He stops whistling. Silence. He sits.*)

STANLEY.   You'd better be careful.

GOLDBERG.   Webber, what were you doing yesterday?

STANLEY.   Yesterday?

GOLDBERG.   And the day before. What did you do the day before that?

STANLEY.   What do you mean?

GOLDBERG.   Why are you wasting everybody's time, Webber? Why are you getting in everybody's way?

STANLEY.   Me? What are you—

GOLDBERG.   I'm telling you, Webber. You're a washout. Why are you getting on everybody's wick? Why are you driving that old lady off her conk?

McCANN.   He likes to do it!

GOLDBERG.   Why do you behave so badly, Webber? Why do you force that old man out to play chess?

STANLEY.   Me?

GOLDBERG.   Why do you treat that young lady like a leper? She's not the leper, Webber!

STANLEY.   What the—

GOLDBERG.   What did you wear last week, Webber? Where do you keep your suits?

McCANN.   Why did you leave the organization?

GOLDBERG.   What would your old mum say, Webber?

McCANN.   Why did you betray us?

GOLDBERG.   You hurt me, Webber. You're playing a dirty game.

McCANN.   That's a Black and Tan fact.

GOLDBERG.   Who does he think he is?

McCANN.   Who do you think you are?

STANLEY.   You're on the wrong horse.

GOLDBERG.   When did you come to this place?

STANLEY.   Last year.

GOLDBERG.   Where did you come from?

STANLEY.   Somewhere else.

GOLDBERG.   Why did you come here?

STANLEY.   My feet hurt!

GOLDBERG.   Why did you stay?

STANLEY.   I had a headache!

GOLDBERG.   Did you take anything for it?

STANLEY.   Yes.

GOLDBERG.   What?

STANLEY.   Fruit salts!

GOLDBERG.   Enos or Andrews?

STANLEY.   En—An—

GOLDBERG.   Did you stir properly? Did they fizz?

STANLEY.   Now, now, wait, you—

GOLDBERG.   Did they fizz? Did they fizz or didn't they fizz?

McCANN.   He doesn't know!

GOLDBERG.   You don't know. When did you last have a bath?

STANLEY.   I have one every—

GOLDBERG.   Don't lie.

McCANN.   You betrayed the organization. I know him!

STANLEY.   You don't!

GOLDBERG.   What can you see without your glasses?

STANLEY.   Anything.

GOLDBERG.   Take off his glasses.

McCANN *snatches his glasses and as* STANLEY *rises, reaching for them, takes his chair downstage centre, below the table,* STANLEY *stumbling as he follows.* STANLEY *clutches the chair and stays bent over it.*

Webber, you're a fake. (*They stand on each side of the chair.*) When did you last wash up a cup?

STANLEY.   The Christmas before last.

GOLDBERG.   Where?

STANLEY.   Lyons Corner House.

GOLDBERG.   Which one?

STANLEY.   Marble Arch.

GOLDBERG.   Where was your wife?

STANLEY.   In—

GOLDBERG.   Answer.

STANLEY (*turning, crouched*). What wife?

GOLDBERG.   What have you done with your wife?

McCANN.   He's killed his wife!

GOLDBERG.   Why did you kill your wife?

STANLEY (*sitting, his back to the audience*). What wife?

McCANN.   How did he kill her?

GOLDBERG.   How did you kill her?

McCANN.   You throttled her.

GOLDBERG.   With arsenic.

McCANN.   There's your man!

GOLDBERG.   Where's your old mum?

STANLEY.   In the sanatorium.

McCANN.   Yes!

GOLDBERG.   Why did you never get married?

McCANN.   She was waiting at the porch.

GOLDBERG. You skedaddled from the wedding.

MCCANN. He left her in the lurch.

GOLDBERG. You left her in the pudding club.

MCCANN. She was waiting at the church.

GOLDBERG. Webber! Why did you change your name?

STANLEY. I forgot the other one.

GOLDBERG. What's your name now?

STANLEY. Joe Soap.

GOLDBERG. You stink of sin.

MCCANN. I can smell it.

GOLDBERG. Do you recognise an external force?

STANLEY. What?

GOLDBERG. Do you recognise an external force?

MCCANN. That's the question!

GOLDBERG. Do you recognise an external force, responsible for you, suffering for you?

STANLEY. It's late.

GOLDBERG. Late! Late enough! When did you last pray?

MCCANN. He's sweating!

GOLDBERG. When did you last pray?

MCCANN. He's sweating!

GOLDBERG. Is the number 846 possible or necessary?

STANLEY. Neither.

GOLDBERG. Wrong! Is the number 846 possible or necessary?

STANLEY. Both.

GOLDBERG. Wrong! It's necessary but not possible.

STANLEY. Both.

GOLDBERG. Wrong! Why do you think the number 846 is necessarily possible?

STANLEY. Must be.

GOLDBERG. Wrong! It's only necessarily necessary! We admit possibility only after we grant necessity. It is possible because necessary but by no means necessary through possibility. The possibility can only be assumed after the proof of necessity.

MCCANN. Right!

GOLDBERG. Right? Of course right! We're right and you're wrong, Webber, all along the line.

MCCANN. All along the line!

GOLDBERG. Where is your lechery leading you?

MCCANN. You'll pay for this.

GOLDBERG. You stuff yourself with dry toast.

MCCANN. You contaminate womankind.

GOLDBERG. Why don't you pay the rent?

MCCANN. Mother defiler!

GOLDBERG. Why do you pick your nose?

MCCANN. I demand justice!

GOLDBERG. What's your trade?

MCCANN. What about Ireland?

GOLDBERG. What's your trade?

STANLEY. I play the piano.

GOLDBERG. How many fingers do you use?

STANLEY. No hands!

GOLDBERG. No society would touch you. Not even a building society.

MCCANN. You're a traitor to the cloth.

GOLDBERG. What do you use for pyjamas?

STANLEY. Nothing.

GOLDBERG. You verminate the sheet of your birth.

MCCANN. What about the Albigensenist heresy?

GOLDBERG. Who watered the wicket in Melbourne?

MCCANN. What about the blessed Oliver Plunkett?

GOLDBERG. Speak up Webber. Why did the chicken cross the road?

STANLEY. He wanted to—he wanted to—he wanted to. . . .

MCCANN. He doesn't know!

GOLDBERG. Why did the chicken cross the road?

STANLEY. He wanted to—he wanted to. . . .

GOLDBERG. Why did the chicken cross the road?

STANLEY. He wanted. . . .

MCCANN. He doesn't know. He doesn't know which came first!

GOLDBERG. Which came first?

MCCANN. Chicken? Egg? Which came first?

GOLDBERG and MCCANN. Which came first? Which came first? Which came first?

STANLEY *screams*.

GOLDBERG. He doesn't know. Do you know your own face?

MCCANN. Wake him up. Stick a needle in his eye.

GOLDBERG. You're a plague, Webber. You're an overthrow.

MCCANN. You're what's left!

GOLDBERG. But we've got the answer to you. We can sterilise you.

MCCANN. What about Drogheda?

GOLDBERG. Your bite is dead. Only your pong is left.

MCCANN. You betrayed our land.

GOLDBERG. You betray our breed.

MCCANN. Who are you, Webber?

GOLDBERG. What makes you think you exist?

MCCANN. You're dead.

GOLDBERG. You're dead. You can't live, you can't think, you can't love. You're dead. You're a plague gone bad. There's no juice in you. You're nothing but an odour!

Silence. They stand over him. He is crouched in the chair. He looks up slowly and kicks GOLDBERG *in the stomach.* GOLDBERG *falls.* STANLEY *stands.* MCCANN *seizes a chair and lifts it above his head.* STANLEY *seizes a chair and covers his head with it.* MCCANN *and* STANLEY *circle.*

GOLDBERG. Steady, McCann.

STANLEY (*circling*). Uuuuuhhhhh!

MCCANN. Right, Judas.

GOLDBERG (*rising*). Steady, McCann.

MCCANN.   Come on!

STANLEY.   Uuuuuuuhhhhh!

MCCANN.   He's sweating.

STANLEY.   Uuuuuhhhhh!

GOLDBERG.   Easy, McCann.

MCCANN.   The bastard sweatpig is sweating.

A loud drumbeat off left, descending the stairs. GOLDBERG *takes the chair from* STANLEY. *They put the chairs down. They stop still. Enter* MEG, *in evening dress, holding sticks and drum.*

MEG.   I brought the drum down. I'm dressed for the party.

GOLDBERG.   Wonderful.

MEG.   You like my dress?

GOLDBERG.   Wonderful. Out of this world.

MEG.   I know. My father gave it to me. (*Placing drum on table.*) Doesn't it make a beautiful noise?

GOLDBERG.   It's a fine piece of work. Maybe Stan'll play us a little tune afterwards.

MEG.   Oh yes. Will you, Stan?

STANLEY.   Could I have my glasses?

GOLDBERG.   Ah yes. (*He holds his hand out to* MCCANN. MCCANN *passes him his glasses.*) Here they are. (*He holds them out for* STANLEY, *who reaches for them.*) Here they are. (STANLEY *takes them.*) Now. What have we got here? Enough to scuttle a liner. We've got four bottles of Scotch and one bottle of Irish.

MEG.   Oh, Mr. Goldberg, what should I drink?

GOLDBERG.   Glasses, glasses first. Open the Scotch, McCann.

MEG (*at the sideboard*). Here's my very best glasses in here.

MCCANN.   I don't drink Scotch.

GOLDBERG.   You've got the Irish.

MEG (*bringing the glasses*). Here they are.

GOLDBERG.   Good. Mrs. Boles, I think Stanley should pour the toast, don't you?

MEG.   Oh yes. Come on, Stanley. (STANLEY *walks slowly to the table*). Do you like my dress, Mr. Goldberg?

GOLDBERG.   It's out on its own. Turn yourself round a minute. I used to be in the business. Go on, walk up there.

MEG.   Oh no.

GOLDBERG.   Don't be shy. (*He slaps her bottom.*)

MEG.   Oooh!

GOLDBERG.   Walk up the boulevard. Let's have a look at you. What a carriage. What's your opinion, McCann? Like a Countess, nothing less. Madam, now turn about and promenade to the kitchen. What a deportment!

MCCANN (*to* STANLEY). You can pour my Irish too.

GOLDBERG.   You look like a Gladiola.

MEG.   Stan, what about my dress?

GOLDBERG.   One for the lady, one for the lady. Now madam—your glass.

MEG.   Thank you.

GOLDBERG.   Lift your glasses, ladies and gentlemen. We'll drink a toast.

MEG.   Lulu isn't here.

GOLDBERG.   It's past the hour. Now—who's going to propose the toast? Mrs. Boles, it can only be you.

MEG.   Me?

GOLDBERG.   Who else?

MEG.   But what do I say?

GOLDBERG.   Say what you feel. What you honestly feel. (MEG *looks uncertain.*) It's Stanley's birthday. Your Stanley. Look at him. Look at him and it'll come. Wait a minute, the light's too strong. Let's have proper lighting. McCann, have you got your torch?

MCCANN (*bringing a small torch from his pocket*). Here.

GOLDBERG.   Switch out the light and put on your torch. (MCCANN *goes to the door, switches off the light, comes back, shines the torch on* MEG. *Outside the window there is still a faint light.*) Not on the lady, on the gentleman! You must shine it on the birthday boy. (MCCANN *shines the torch in* STANLEY'S *face.*) Now, Mrs. Boles, it's all yours.

Pause.

MEG.   I don't know what to say.

GOLDBERG.   Look at him. Just look at him.

MEG.   Isn't the light in his eyes?

GOLDBERG.   No, no. Go on.

MEG.   Well—it's very, very nice to be here tonight, in my house, and I want to propose a toast to Stanley, because it's his birthday, and he's lived here for a long while now, and he's my Stanley now. And I think he's a good boy, although sometimes he's bad. (*An appreciative laugh from* GOLDBERG.) And he's the only Stanley I know, and I know him better than all the world, although he doesn't think so. (*"Hear—hear" from* GOLDBERG.) Well, I could cry because I'm so happy, having him here and not gone away, on his birthday, and there isn't anything I wouldn't do for him, and all you good people here tonight. . . . (*She sobs.*)

GOLDBERG.   Beautiful! A beautiful speech. Put the light on, McCann. (MCCANN *goes to the door.* STANLEY *remains still.*) That was a lovely toast. (*The light goes on.* LULU *enters from the door, left.* GOLDBERG *comforts* MEG.) Buck up now. Come on, smile at the birdy. That's better. Ah, look who's here.

MEG.   Lulu.

GOLDBERG.   How do you do, Lulu? I'm Nat Goldberg.

LULU.   Hallo.

GOLDBERG.   Stanley, a drink for your guest. You just missed the toast, my dear, and what a toast.

LULU.   Did I?

GOLDBERG.   Stanley, a drink for your guest. Stanley. (STANLEY *hands a glass to* LULU.) Right. Now raise your glasses. Everyone standing up? No, not you, Stanley. You must sit down.

MCCANN.   Yes, that's right. He must sit down.

GOLDBERG. You don't mind sitting down a minute? We're going to drink to you.

MEG. Come on!

LULU. Come on!

STANLEY *sits in a chair at the table.*

GOLDBERG. Right. Now Stanley's sat down. (*Taking the stage.*) Well, I want to say first that I've never been so touched to the heart as by the toast we've just heard. How often, in this day and age, do you come across real, true warmth? Once in a lifetime. Until a few minutes ago, ladies and gentlemen, I, like all of you, was asking the same question. What's happened to the love, the bonhomie, the unashamed expression of affection of the day before yesterday, that our mums taught us in the nursery?

McCANN. Gone with the wind.

GOLDBERG. That's what I thought, until today. I believe in a good laugh, a day's fishing, a bit of gardening. I was very proud of my old greenhouse, made out of my own spit and faith. That's the sort of man I am. Not size but quality. A little Austin, tea in Fullers, a library book from Boots, and I'm satisfied. But just now, I say just now, the lady of the house said her piece and I for one am knocked over by the sentiments she expressed. Lucky is the man who's at the receiving end, that's what I say. (*Pause.*) How can I put it to you? We all wander on our tod through this world. It's a lonely pillow to kip on. Right!

LULU (*admiringly*). Right!

GOLDBERG. Agreed. But tonight, Lulu, McCann, we've known a great fortune. We've heard a lady extend the sum total of her devotion, in all its pride, plume and peacock, to a member of her own living race. Stanley, my heartfelt congratulations. I wish you, on behalf of us all, a happy birthday. I'm sure you've never been a prouder man than you are today. Mazoltov! And may we only meet at Simchahs! (LULU *and* MEG *applaud.*) Turn out the light, McCann, while we drink the toast.

LULU. That was a wonderful speech.

McCANN *switches out the light, comes back, and shines the torch in* STANLEY'S *face. The light outside the window is fainter.*

GOLDBERG. Lift your glasses. Stanley—happy birthday.

McCANN. Happy birthday.

LULU. Happy birthday.

MEG. Many happy returns of the day, Stan.

GOLDBERG. And well over the fast.

They all drink.

MEG (*kissing him*). Oh, Stanny. . . .

GOLDBERG. Lights!

McCANN. Right! (*He switches on the lights.*)

MEG. Clink my glass, Stan.

LULU. Mr. Goldberg—

GOLDBERG. Call me Nat.

MEG (*to* McCANN). You clink my glass.

LULU (*to* GOLDBERG). You're empty. Let me fill you up.

GOLDBERG. It's a pleasure.

LULU. You're a marvellous speaker, Nat, you know that? Where did you learn to speak like that?

GOLDBERG. You liked it, eh?

LULU. Oh yes!

GOLDBERG. Well, my first chance to stand up and give a lecture was at the Ethical Hall, Bayswater. A wonderful opportunity. I'll never forget it. They were all there that night. Charlotte Street was empty. Of course, that's a good while ago.

LULU. What did you speak about?

GOLDBERG. The Necessary and the Possible. It went like a bomb. Since then I always speak at weddings.

STANLEY *is still.* GOLDBERG *sits left of the table.* MEG *joins* McCANN *downstage, right,* LULU *is downstage, left.* McCANN *pours more Irish from the bottle, which he carries, into his glass.*

MEG. Let's have some of yours.

McCANN. In that?

MEG. Yes.

McCANN. Are you used to mixing them?

MEG. No.

McCANN. Give me your glass.

MEG *sits on a shoe-box, downstage, right.* LULU, *at the table, pours more drink for* GOLDBERG *and herself, and gives* GOLDBERG *his glass.*

GOLDBERG. Thank you.

MEG (*to* McCANN). Do you think I should?

GOLDBERG. Lulu, you're a big bouncy girl. Come and sit on my lap.

McCANN. Why not?

LULU. Do you think I should?

GOLDBERG. Try it.

MEG (*sipping*). Very nice.

LULU. I'll bounce up to the ceiling.

McCANN. I don't know how you can mix that stuff.

GOLDBERG. Take a chance.

MEG (*to* McCANN). Sit down on this stool.

LULU *sits on* GOLDBERG'S *lap.*

McCANN. This?

GOLDBERG. Comfortable?

LULU. Yes, thanks.

McCANN (*sitting*). It's comfortable.

GOLDBERG. You know, there's a lot in your eyes.

LULU. And in yours, too.

GOLDBERG. Do you think so?

LULU (*giggling*). Go on!

McCANN (*to* MEG). Where'd you get it?

MEG.   My father gave it to me.

LULU.   I didn't know I was going to meet you here tonight.

McCANN (*to* MEG). Ever been to Carrikmacross?

MEG (*drinking*). I've been to King's Cross.

LULU.   You came right out of the blue, you know that?

GOLDBERG (*as she moves*). Mind how you go. You're cracking a rib.

MEG (*standing*). I want to dance! (LULU *and* GOLDBERG *look into each other's eyes.* McCANN *drinks.* MEG *crosses to* STANLEY.) Stanley. Dance. (STANLEY *sits still.* MEG *dances round the room alone, then comes back to* McCANN, *who fills her glass. She sits.*)

LULU (*to* GOLDBERG). Shall I tell you something?

GOLDBERG.   What?

LULU.   I trust you.

GOLDBERG (*lifting his glass*). Gesundheit.

LULU.   Have you got a wife?

GOLDBERG.   I had a wife. What a wife. Listen to this. Friday, of an afternoon, I'd take myself for a little constitutional, down over the park. Eh, do me a favour, just sit on the table a minute, will you? (LULU *sits on the table. He stretches and continues.*) A little constitutional. I'd say hullo to the little boys, the little girls—I never made distinctions—and then back I'd go, back to my bungalow with the flat roof. "Simey," my wife used to shout, "quick, before it gets cold!" And there on the table what would I see? The nicest piece of rollmop and pickled cucumber you could wish to find on a plate.

LULU.   I thought your name was Nat.

GOLDBERG.   She called me Simey.

LULU.   I bet you were a good husband.

GOLDBERG.   You should have seen her funeral.

LULU.   Why?

GOLDBERG (*draws in his breath and wags head*). What a funeral.

MEG (*to* McCANN). My father was going to take me to Ireland once. But then he went away by himself.

LULU (*to* GOLDBERG). Do you think you knew me when I was a little girl?

GOLDBERG.   Were you a nice little girl?

LULU.   I was.

MEG.   I don't know if he went to Ireland.

GOLDBERG.   Maybe I played piggy-back with you.

LULU.   Maybe you did.

MEG.   He didn't take me.

GOLDBERG.   Or pop goes the weasel.

LULU.   Is that a game?

GOLDBERG.   Sure it's a game!

McCANN.   Why didn't he take you to Ireland?

LULU.   You're tickling me!

GOLDBERG.   You should worry.

LULU.   I've always liked older men. They can soothe you.

They embrace.

McCANN.   I know a place. Roscrea. Mother Nolan's.

MEG.   There was a night-light in my room, when I was a little girl.

McCANN.   One time I stayed there all night with the boys. Singing and drinking all night.

MEG.   And my Nanny used to sit up with me, and sing songs to me.

McCANN.   And a plate of fry in the morning. Now where am I?

MEG.   My little room was pink. I had a pink carpet and pink curtains, and I had musical boxes all over the room. And they played me to sleep. And my father was a very big doctor. That's why I never had any complaints. I was cared for, and I had little sisters and brothers in other rooms, all different colours.

McCANN.   Tullamore, where are you?

MEG (*to* McCANN). Give us a drop more.

McCANN (*filling her glass and singing*). Glorio, Glorio, to the bold Fenian men!

MEG.   Oh, what a lovely voice.

GOLDBERG.   Give us a song, McCann.

LULU.   A love song!

McCANN (*reciting*). The night that poor Paddy was stretched, the boys they all paid him a visit.

GOLDBERG.   A love song!

McCANN (*in a full voice, sings*).

    Oh, the Garden of Eden has vanished, they say,
    But I know the lie of it still.
    Just turn to the left at the foot of Ben Clay
    And stop when halfway to Coote Hill.
    It's there you will find it, I know sure enough,
    And it's whispering over to me:
    Come back, Paddy Reilly, to Bally-James-Duff,
    Come home, Paddy Reilly, to me!

LULU (*to* GOLDBERG). You're the dead image of the first man I ever loved.

GOLDBERG.   It goes without saying.

MEG (*rising*). I want to play a game!

GOLDBERG.   A game?

LULU.   What game?

MEG.   Any game.

LULU (*jumping up*). Yes, let's play a game.

GOLDBERG.   What game?

McCANN.   Hide and seek.

LULU.   Blind man's buff.

MEG.   Yes!

GOLDBERG.   You want to play blind man's buff?

LULU and MEG.   Yes!

GOLDBERG.   All right. Blind man's buff. Come on! Everyone up! (*Rising.*) McCann. Stanley—Stanley!

MEG.   Stanley. Up.

GOLDBERG.   What's the matter with him?

MEG (*bending over him*). Stanley, we're going to play a game. Oh, come on, don't be sulky, Stan.

LULU. Come on.

STANLEY *rises.* MCCANN *rises.*

GOLDBERG. Right! Now—who's going to be blind first?
LULU. Mrs. Boles.
MEG. Not me.
GOLDBERG. Of course you.
MEG. Who, me?
LULU (*taking her scarf from her neck*). Here you are.
MCCANN. How do you play this game?
LULU (*tying her scarf round* MEG'S *eyes*). Haven't you ever played blind man's buff? Keep still, Mrs. Boles. You mustn't be touched. But you can't move after she's blind. You must stay where you are after she's blind. And if she touches you then you become blind. Turn around. How many fingers am I holding up?
MEG. I can't see.
LULU. Right.
GOLDBERG. Right! Everyone move about. McCann. Stanley. Now stop. Now still. Off you go!

STANLEY *is downstage, right,* MEG *moves about the room.* GOLDBERG *fondles* LULU *at arm's length.* MEG *touches* MCCANN.

MEG. Caught you!
LULU. Take off your scarf.
MEG. What lovely hair!
LULU (*untying the scarf*). There.
MEG. It's you!
GOLDBERG. Put it on, McCann.
LULU (*tying it on* MCCANN). There. Turn round. How many fingers am I holding up?
MCCANN. I don't know.
GOLDBERG. Right! Everyone move about. Right. Stop! Still!

MCCANN *begins to move.*

MEG. Oh, this is lovely!
GOLDBERG. Quiet! Tch, tch, tch. Now—all move again. Stop! Still!

MCCANN *moves about.* GOLDBERG *fondles* LULU *at arm's length.* MCCANN *draws near* STANLEY. *He stretches his arm and touches* STANLEY'S *glasses.*

MEG. It's Stanley!
GOLDBERG (*to* LULU). Enjoying the game?
MEG. It's your turn, Stan.

MCCANN *takes off the scarf.*

MCCANN (*to* STANLEY). I'll take your glasses.

MCCANN *takes* STANLEY'S *glasses.*

MEG. Give me the scarf.

GOLDBERG (*holding* LULU). Tie his scarf, Mrs. Boles.
MEG. That's what I'm doing. (*To* STANLEY.). Can you see my nose?
GOLDBERG. He can't. Ready? Right! Everyone move. Stop! And still!

STANLEY *stands blindfolded.* MCCANN *backs slowly across the stage to the left. He breaks* STANLEY'S *glasses, snapping the frames.* MEG *is downstage, left,* LULU *and* GOLDBERG *upstage centre, close together.* STANLEY *begins to move, very slowly, across the stage to the left.* MCCANN *picks up the drum and places it sideways in* STANLEY'S *path.* STANLEY *walks into the drum and falls over with his foot caught in it.*

MEG. Ooh!
GOLDBERG. Sssh!

STANLEY *rises. He begins to move towards* MEG, *dragging the drum on his foot. He reaches her and stops. His hands move towards her and they reach her throat. He begins to strangle her.* MCCANN *and* GOLDBERG *rush forward and throw him off.*

BLACKOUT

There is now no light at all through the window. The stage is in darkness.

LULU. The lights!
GOLDBERG. What's happened?
LULU. The lights!
MCCANN. Wait a minute.
GOLDBERG. Where is he?
MCCANN. Let go of me!
GOLDBERG. Who's this?
LULU. Someone's touching me!
MCCANN. Where is he?
MEG. Why has the light gone out?
GOLDBERG. Where's your torch? (MCCANN *shines the torch in* GOLDBERG'S *face.*) Not on me! (MCCANN *shifts the torch. It is knocked from his hand and falls. It goes out.*)
MCCANN. My torch!
LULU. Oh God!
GOLDBERG. Where's your torch? Pick up your torch!
MCCANN. I can't find it.
LULU. Hold me. Hold me.
GOLDBERG. Get down on your knees. Help him find the torch.
LULU. I can't.
MCCANN. It's gone.
MEG. Why has the light gone out?
GOLDBERG. Everyone quiet! Help him find the torch.

Silence. Grunts from MCCANN *and* GOLDBERG *on their knees. Suddenly there is a sharp, sustained rat-a-tat with a stick on the side of the drum from the back of the room. Silence. Whimpers from* LULU.

GOLDBERG.   Over here. McCann!
McCANN.   Here.
GOLDBERG.   Come to me, come to me. Easy. Over there.

GOLDBERG *and* McCANN *move up left of the table.* STANLEY *moves down right of the table.* LULU *suddenly perceives him moving towards her, screams and faints.* GOLDBERG *and* McCANN *turn and stumble against each other.*

GOLDBERG.   What is it?
McCANN.   Who's that?
GOLDBERG.   What is it?

In the darkness STANLEY *picks up* LULU *and places her on the table.*

MEG.   It's Lulu!

GOLDBERG *and* McCANN *move downstage, right.*

GOLDBERG.   Where is she?
McCANN.   She fell.
GOLDBERG.   Where?
McCANN.   About here.
GOLDBERG.   Help me pick her up.
McCANN (*moving downstage, left*). I can't find her.
GOLDBERG.   She must be somewhere.
McCANN.   She's not here.
GOLDBERG (*moving downstage, left*). She must be.
McCANN.   She's gone.

McCANN *finds the torch on the floor, shines it on the table and* STANLEY. LULU *is lying spread-eagled on the table,* STANLEY *bent over her.* STANLEY, *as soon as the torchlight hits him, begins to giggle.* GOLDBERG *and* McCANN *move towards him. He backs, giggling, the torch on his face. They follow him upstage, left. He backs against the hatch, giggling. The torch draws closer. His giggle rises and grows as he flattens himself against the wall. Their figures converge upon him.*

CURTAIN

ACT THREE

The next morning. PETEY *enters, left, with a newspaper and sits at the table. He begins to read.* MEG'S *voice comes through the kitchen hatch.*

MEG.   Is that you, Stan? (*Pause.*) Stanny?
PETEY.   Yes?
MEG.   Is that you?
PETEY.   It's me.
MEG (*appearing at the hatch*). Oh, it's you. I've run out of cornflakes.
PETEY.   Well, what else have you got?
MEG.   Nothing.

PETEY.   Nothing?
MEG.   Just a minute. (*She leaves the hatch and enters by the kitchen door.*) You got your paper?
PETEY.   Yes.
MEG.   Is it good?
PETEY.   Not bad.
MEG.   The two gentlemen had the last of the fry this morning.
PETEY.   Oh, did they?
MEG.   There's some tea in the pot though. (*She pours tea for him.*) I'm going out shopping in a minute. Get you something nice.
MEG.   I've got a splitting headache.
PETEY (*reading*). You slept like a log last night.
MEG.   Did I?
PETEY.   Dead out.
MEG.   I must have been tired. (*She looks about the room and sees the broken drum in the fireplace.*) Oh, look. (*She rises and picks it up.*) The drum's broken. (PETEY *looks up.*) Why is it broken?
PETEY.   I don't know.

She hits it with her hand.

MEG.   It still makes a noise.
PETEY.   You can always get another one.
MEG (*sadly*). It was probably broken in the party. I don't remember it being broken though, in the party. (*She puts it down.*) What a shame.
PETEY.   You can always get another one, Meg.
MEG.   Well, at least he did have it on his birthday, didn't he? Like I wanted him to.
PETEY (*reading*). Yes.
MEG.   Have you seen him down yet? (PETEY *does not answer.*) Petey.
PETEY.   What?
MEG.   Have you seen him down?
PETEY.   Who?
MEG.   Stanley.
PETEY.   No.
MEG.   Nor have I. That boy should be up. He's late for his breakfast.
PETEY.   There isn't any breakfast.
MEG.   Yes, but he doesn't know that. I'm going to call him.
PETEY (*quickly*). No, don't do that, Meg. Let him sleep.
MEG.   But you say he stays in bed too much.
PETEY.   Let him sleep . . . this morning. Leave him.
MEG.   I've been up once, with his cup of tea. But Mr. McCann opened the door. He said they were talking. He said he'd made him one. He must have been up early. I don't know what they were talking about. I was surprised. Because Stanley's usually fast asleep when I wake him. But he wasn't this morning. I heard him talking. (*Pause.*) Do you think they know each other? I think they're old friends. Stanley had a lot of friends. I know he did.

(*Pause.*) I didn't give him his tea. He'd already had one. I came down again and went on with my work. Then, after a bit, they came down to breakfast. Stanley must have gone to sleep again.

Pause.

PETEY.   When are you going to do your shopping, Meg?

MEG.   Yes, I must. (*Collecting the bag.*) I've got a rotten headache. (*She goes to the back door, stops suddenly and turns.*) Did you see what's outside this morning?

PETEY.   What?

MEG.   That big car.

PETEY.   Yes.

MEG.   It wasn't there yesterday. Did you . . . did you have a look inside it?

PETEY.   I had a peep.

MEG (*coming down tensely, and whispering*). Is there anything in it?

PETEY.   In it?

MEG.   Yes.

PETEY.   What do you mean, in it?

MEG.   Inside it.

PETEY.   What sort of thing?

MEG.   Well . . . I mean . . . is there . . . is there a wheelbarrow in it?

PETEY.   A wheelbarrow?

MEG.   Yes.

PETEY.   I didn't see one.

MEG.   You didn't? Are you sure?

PETEY.   What would Mr. Goldberg want with a wheelbarrow?

MEG.   Mr. Goldberg?

PETEY.   It's his car.

MEG (*relieved*). His car? Oh, I didn't know it was his car.

PETEY.   Of course it's his car.

MEG.   Oh, I feel better.

PETEY.   What are you on about?

MEG.   Oh, I do feel better.

PETEY.   You go and get a bit of air.

MEG.   Yes, I will. I will. I'll go and get the shopping. (*She goes towards the back door. A door slams upstairs. She turns.*) It's Stanley! He's coming down—what am I going to do about his breakfast? (*She rushes into the kitchen.*) Petey, what shall I give him? (*She looks through the hatch.*) There's no cornflakes. (*They both gaze at the door. Enter* GOLDBERG. *He halts at the door, as he meets their gaze, then smiles.*)

GOLDBERG.   A reception committee!

MEG.   Oh, I thought it was Stanley.

GOLDBERG.   You find a resemblance?

MEG.   Oh no. You look quite different.

GOLDBERG (*coming into the room*). Different build, of course.

MEG (*entering from the kitchen*). I thought he was coming down for his breakfast. He hasn't had his breakfast yet.

GOLDBERG.   Your wife makes a very nice cup of tea, Mr. Boles, you know that?

PETEY.   Yes, she does sometimes. Sometimes she forgets.

MEG.   Is he coming down?

GOLDBERG.   Down? Of course he's coming down. On a lovely sunny day like this he shouldn't come down? He'll be up and about in next to no time. (*He sits at the table.*) And what a breakfast he's going to get.

MEG.   Mr. Goldberg.

GOLDBERG.   Yes?

MEG.   I didn't know that was your car outside.

GOLDBERG.   You like it?

MEG.   Are you going to go for a ride?

GOLDBERG (*to* PETEY). A smart car, eh?

PETEY.   Nice shine on it all right.

GOLDBERG.   What is old is good, take my tip. There's room there. Room in the front, and room in the back. (*He strokes the teapot.*) The pot's hot. More tea, Mr. Boles?

PETEY.   No thanks.

GOLDBERG (*pouring tea*). That car? That car's never let me down.

MEG.   Are you going to go for a ride?

GOLDBERG (*ruminatively*). And the boot. A beautiful boot. There's just room . . . for the right amount.

MEG.   Well, I'd better be off now. (*She moves to the back door, and turns.*) Petey, when Stanley comes down. . . .

PETEY.   Yes?

MEG.   Tell him I won't be long.

PETEY.   I'll tell him.

MEG (*vaguely*). I won't be long. (*She exits.*)

GOLDBERG (*sipping his tea*). A good woman. A charming woman. My mother was the same. My wife was identical.

PETEY.   How is he this morning?

GOLDBERG.   Who?

PETEY.   Stanley. Is he any better?

GOLDBERG (*a little uncertainly*). Oh . . . a little better, I think, a little better. Of course, I'm not really qualified to say, Mr. Boles, I mean, I haven't got the . . . the qualifications. The best thing would be if someone with the proper . . . mnn . . . qualifications . . . was to have a look at him. Someone with a few letters after his name. It makes all the difference.

PETEY.   Yes.

GOLDBERG.   Anyway, Dermot's with him at the moment. He's . . . keeping him company.

PETEY.   Dermot?

GOLDBERG.   Yes.

PETEY.   It's a terrible thing.

GOLDBERG (*sighs*). Yes. The birthday celebration was too much for him.

PETEY.   What came over him?

GOLDBERG (*sharply*). What came over him? Breakdown, Mr. Boles. Pure and simple. Nervous breakdown.

PETEY.   But what brought it on so suddenly?

GOLDBERG (*rising, and moving upstage*). Well, Mr. Boles, it can happen in all sorts of ways. A friend of mine was telling me about it only the other day. We'd both been concerned with another case—not entirely similar, of course, but . . . quite alike, quite alike. (*He pauses.*) Anyway, he was telling me, you see, this friend of mine, that sometimes it happens gradual—day by day it grows and grows and grows . . . day by day. And then other times it happens all at once. Poof! Like that! The nerves break. There's no guarantee how it's going to happen, but with certain people . . . it's a foregone conclusion.

PETEY.   Really?

GOLDBERG.   Yes. This friend of mine—he was telling me about it—only the other day. (*He stands uneasily for a moment, then brings out a cigarette case and takes a cigarette.*) Have an Abdullah.

PETEY.   No, no, I don't take them.

GOLDBERG.   Once in a while I treat myself to a cigarette. An Abdullah, perhaps, or a . . . (*He snaps his fingers.*)

PETEY.   What a night. (GOLDBERG *lights his cigarette with a lighter.*) Came in the front door and all the lights were out. Put a shilling in the slot, came in here and the party was over.

GOLDBERG (*coming downstage*). You put a shilling in the slot?

PETEY.   Yes.

GOLDBERG.   And the lights came on.

PETEY.   Yes, then I came in here.

GOLDBERG (*with a short laugh*). I could have sworn it was a fuse.

PETEY (*continuing*). There was dead silence. Couldn't hear a thing. So I went upstairs and your friend—Dermot—met me on the landing. And he told me.

GOLDBERG (*sharply*). Who?

PETEY.   Your friend—Dermot.

GOLDBERG (*heavily*). Dermot. Yes. (*He sits.*)

PETEY.   They get over it sometimes though, don't they? I mean, they can recover from it, can't they?

GOLDBERG.   Recover? Yes, sometimes they recover, in one way or another.

PETEY.   I mean, he might have recovered by now, mightn't he?

GOLDBERG.   It's conceivable. Conceivable.

PETEY *rises and picks up the teapot and cup.*

PETEY.   Well, if he's no better by lunchtime I'll go and get hold of a doctor.

GOLDBERG (*briskly*). It's all taken care of, Mr. Boles. Don't worry yourself.

PETEY (*dubiously*). What do you mean? (*Enter* MCCANN *with two suitcases.*) All packed up?

PETEY *takes the teapot and cups into the kitchen.* MCCANN *crosses left and puts down the suitcases. He goes up to the window and looks out.*

GOLDBERG.   Well? (MCCANN *does not answer.*) McCann. I asked you well.

MCCANN (*without turning*). Well what?

GOLDBERG.   What's what? (MCCANN *does not answer.*)

MCCANN (*turning to look at* GOLDBERG, *grimly*). I'm not going up there again.

GOLDBERG.   Why not?

MCCANN.   I'm not going up there again.

GOLDBERG.   What's going on now?

MCCANN (*moving down*). He's quiet now. He stopped all that . . . talking a while ago.

PETEY *appears at the kitchen hatch, unnoticed.*

GOLDBERG.   When will he be ready?

MCCANN (*sullenly*). You can go up yourself next time.

GOLDBERG.   What's the matter with you?

MCCANN (*quietly*). I gave him. . . .

GOLDBERG.   What?

MCCANN.   I gave him his glasses.

GOLDBERG.   Wasn't he glad to get them back?

MCCANN.   The frames are bust.

GOLDBERG.   How did that happen?

MCCANN.   He tried to fit the eyeholes into his eyes. I left him doing it.

PETEY (*at the kitchen door*). There's some Sellotape somewhere. We can stick them together.

GOLDBERG *and* MCCANN *turn to see him. Pause.*

GOLDBERG.   Sellotape? No, no, that's all right, Mr. Boles. It'll keep him quiet for the time being, keep his mind off other things.

PETEY (*moving downstage*). What about a doctor?

GOLDBERG.   It's all taken care of.

MCCANN *moves over right to the shoe-box, and takes out a brush and brushes his shoes.*

PETEY (*moves to the table*). I think he needs one.

GOLDBERG.   I agree with you. It's all taken care of. We'll give him a bit of time to settle down, and then I'll take him to Monty.

PETEY.   You're going to take him to a doctor?

GOLDBERG (*staring at him*). Sure. Monty.

Pause. MCCANN *brushes his shoes.*

So Mrs. Boles has gone out to get us something nice for lunch?

PETEY.   That's right.

GOLDBERG.   Unfortunately we may be gone by then.

PETEY.   Will you?

GOLDBERG.   By then we may be gone.

Pause.

PETEY.   Well, I think I'll see how my peas are getting on, in the meantime.

GOLDBERG.   The meantime?

PETEY.   While we're waiting.

GOLDBERG.   Waiting for what? (PETEY *walks towards the back door*.) Aren't you going back to the beach?

PETEY.   No, not yet. Give me a call when he comes down, will you, Mr. Goldberg?

GOLDBERG (*earnestly*). You'll have a crowded beach today . . . on a day like this. They'll be lying on their backs, swimming out to sea. My life. What about the deck-chairs? Are the deck-chairs ready?

PETEY.   I put them all out this morning.

GOLDBERG.   But what about the tickets? Who's going to take the tickets?

PETEY.   That's all right. That'll be all right, Mr. Goldberg. Don't you worry about that. I'll be back.

He exits. GOLDBERG *rises, goes to the window and looks after him.* MCCANN *crosses to the table, left, sits, picks up the paper and begins to tear it into strips.*

GOLDBERG.   Is everything ready?

MCCANN.   Sure.

GOLDBERG *walks heavily, brooding, to the table. He sits right of it noticing what* MCCANN *is doing.*

GOLDBERG.   Stop doing that!

MCCANN.   What?

GOLDBERG.   Why do you do that all the time? It's childish, it's pointless. It's without a solitary point.

MCCANN.   What's the matter with you today?

GOLDBERG.   Questions, questions. Stop asking me so many questions. What do you think I am?

MCCANN *studies him. He then folds the paper, leaving the strips inside.*

MCCANN.   Well?

Pause. GOLDBERG *leans back in the chair, his eyes closed.*

MCCANN.   Well?

GOLDBERG (*with fatigue*). Well what?

MCCANN.   Do we wait or do we go and get him?

GOLDBERG (*slowly*). You want to go and get him?

MCCANN.   I want to get it over.

GOLDBERG.   That's understandable.

MCCANN.   So do we wait or do we go and get him?

GOLDBERG (*interrupting*). I don't know why, but I feel knocked out. I feel a bit . . . It's uncommon for me.

MCCANN.   Is that so?

GOLDBERG.   It's unusual.

MCCANN (*rising swiftly and going behind* GOLDBERG'S *chair. Hissing*). Let's finish and go. Let's get it over and go. Get the thing done. Let's finish the bloody thing. Let's get the thing done and go!

Pause.

Will I go up?

Pause.

Nat!

GOLDBERG *sits humped.* MCCANN *slips to his side.*

Simey!

GOLDBERG (*opening his eyes, regarding* MCCANN). What—did—you—call—me?

MCCANN.   Who?

GOLDBERG (*murderously*). Don't call me that! (*He seizes* MCCANN *by the throat.*) NEVER CALL ME THAT!

MCCANN (*writhing*). Nat, Nat, Nat, NAT! I called you NAT. I was asking you, Nat. Honest to God. Just a question, that's all, just a question, do you see, do you follow me?

GOLDBERG (*jerking him away*). What question?

MCCANN.   Will I go up?

GOLDBERG (*violently*). Up? I thought you weren't going to go up there again?

MCCANN.   What do you mean? Why not?

GOLDBERG.   You said so!

MCCANN.   I never said that!

GOLDBERG.   No?

MCCANN (*from the floor, to the room at large*). Who said that? I never said that! I'll go up now!

He jumps up and rushes to the door, left.

GOLDBERG.   Wait!

He stretches his arms to the arms of the chair.

Come here.

MCCANN *approaches him very slowly.*

I want your opinion. Have a look in my mouth.

He opens his mouth wide.

Take a good look.

MCCANN *looks.*

You know what I mean?

MCCANN *peers.*

You know what? I've never lost a tooth. Not since the day I was born. Nothing's changed. (*He gets up.*) That's why I've reached my position, McCann. Because I've always been as fit as a fiddle. All my life I've said the same. Play up, play up, and play the game. Honour thy father and thy mother. All along the line. Follow the line, the line, McCann, and you can't go wrong. What do you think, I'm a self-made man? No! I sat where I was told to sit. I kept my eye on the ball. School? Don't talk to me about school. Top in all subjects. And for why? Because I'm telling you, I'm telling you, follow my line? Follow my mental? Learn by heart. Never write down a thing. And don't go too near the water. And you'll find—that what I say is true.

Because I believe that the world . . . (*Vacant.*). . . .
Because I believe that the world . . . (*Desperate.*). . . .
BECAUSE I BELIEVE THAT THE WORLD . . . (*Lost.*). . . .

He sits in chair.

Sit down, McCann, sit here where I can look at you.

MCCANN *kneels in front of the table.*

(*Intensely, with growing certainty.*) My father said to me, Benny, Benny, he said, come here. He was dying. I knelt down. By him day and night. Who else was there? Forgive, Benny, he said, and let live. Yes, Dad. Go home to your wife. I will, Dad. Keep an eye open for low-lives, for schnorrers and for layabouts. He didn't mention names. I lost my life in the service of others, he said, I'm not ashamed. Do your duty and keep your observations. Always bid good morning to the neighbours. Never, never forget your family, for they are the rock, the constitution and the core! If you're ever in any difficulties Uncle Barney will see you in the clear. I knelt down. (*He kneels, facing* MCCANN:) I swore on the good book. And I knew the word I had to remember—Respect! Because McCann— (*Gently.*) Seamus—who came before your father? His father. And who came before him? Before him? . . . (*Vacant—triumphant.*) Who came before your father's father but your father's father's mother! Your great-gran-granny.

Silence. He slowly rises.

And that's why I've reached my position, McCann. Because I've always been as fit as a fiddle. My motto. Work hard and play hard. Not a day's illness.

GOLDBERG *sits.*

GOLDBERG.   All the same, give me a blow. (*Pause.*) Blow in my mouth.

MCCANN *stands, puts his hands on his knees, bends, and blows in* GOLDBERG'S *mouth.*

One for the road.

MCCANN *blows again in his mouth.* GOLDBERG *breathes deeply, smiles.*

GOLDBERG.   Right!

Enter LULU. MCCANN *looks at them, and goes to the door.*

MCCANN (*at the door*). I'll give you five minutes. (*He exits with the expander.*)

GOLDBERG.   Come over here.
LULU.   What's going to happen?
GOLDBERG.   Come over here.
LULU.   No, thank you.
GOLDBERG.   What's the matter? You got the needle to Uncle Natey?
LULU.   I'm going.
GOLDBERG.   Have a game of pontoon first, for old time's sake.
LULU.   I've had enough games.
GOLDBERG.   A girl like you, at your age, at your time of health, and you don't take to games?
LULU.   You're very smart.
GOLDBERG.   Anyway, who says you don't take to them?
LULU.   Do you think I'm like all the other girls?
GOLDBERG.   Are all the other girls like that, too?
LULU.   I don't know about any other girls.
GOLDBERG.   Nor me. I've never touched another woman.
LULU (*distressed*). What would my father say, if he knew? And what would Eddie say?
GOLDBERG.   Eddie?
LULU.   He was my first love, Eddie was. And whatever happened, it was pure. With him! He didn't come into my room at night with a briefcase!
GOLDBERG.   Who opened the briefcase, me or you? Lulu, schmulu, let bygones be bygones, do me a turn. Kiss and make up.
LULU.   I wouldn't touch you.
GOLDBERG.   And today I'm leaving.
LULU.   You're leaving?
GOLDBERG.   Today.
LULU (*with growing anger*). You used me for a night. A passing fancy.
GOLDBERG.   Who used who?
LULU.   You made use of me by cunning when my defences were down.
GOLDBERG.   Who took them down?
LULU.   That's what you did. You quenched your ugly thirst. You taught me things a girl shouldn't know before she's been married at least three times!
GOLDBERG.   Now you're a jump ahead! What are you complaining about?

Enter MCCANN *quickly.*

LULU.   You didn't appreciate me for myself. You took all those liberties only to satisfy your appetite. Oh Nat, why did you do it?
GOLDBERG.   You wanted me to do it, Lulula, so I did it.
MCCANN.   That's fair enough. (*Advancing.*) You had a long sleep, Miss.
LULU (*backing upstage left*). Me?
MCCANN.   Your sort, you spend too much time in bed.
LULU.   What do you mean?
MCCANN.   Have you got anything to confess?

LULU.   What?

MCCANN (*savagely*). Confess!

LULU.   Confess what?

MCCANN.   Down on your knees and confess!

LULU.   What does he mean?

GOLDBERG.   Confess. What can you lose?

LULU.   What, to him?

GOLDBERG.   He's only been unfrocked six months.

MCCANN.   Kneel down, woman, and tell me the latest!

LULU (*retreating to the back door*). I've seen everything that's happened. I know what's going on. I've got a pretty shrewd idea.

MCCANN (*advancing*). I've seen you hanging about the Rock of Cashel, profaning the soil with your goings-on. Out of my sight!

LULU.   I'm going.

She exits. MCCANN *goes to the door, left, and goes out. He ushers in* STANLEY, *who is dressed in a dark well cut suit and white collar. He holds his broken glasses in his hand. He is clean-shaven.* MCCANN *follows and closes the door.* GOLDBERG *meets* STANLEY, *seats him in a chair.*

GOLDBERG.   How are you, Stan?

Pause.

Are you feeling any better?

Pause.

What's the matter with your glasses?

GOLDBERG *bends to look.*

They're broken. A pity.

STANLEY *stares blankly at the floor.*

MCCANN (*at the table*). He looks better, doesn't he?

GOLDBERG.   Much better.

MCCANN.   A new man.

GOLDBERG.   You know what we'll do?

MCCANN.   What?

GOLDBERG.   We'll buy him another pair.

They begin to woo him, gently and with relish. During the following sequence STANLEY *shows no reaction. He remains, with no movement, where he sits.*

MCCANN.   Out of our own pockets.

GOLDBERG.   It goes without saying. Between you and me, Stan, it's about time you had a new pair of glasses.

MCCANN.   You can't see straight.

GOLDBERG.   It's true. You've been cockeyed for years.

MCCANN.   Now you're even more cockeyed.

GOLDBERG.   He's right. You've gone from bad to worse.

MCCANN.   Worse than worse.

GOLDBERG.   You need a long convalescence.

MCCANN.   A change of air.

GOLDBERG.   Somewhere over the rainbow.

MCCANN.   Where angels fear to tread.

GOLDBERG.   Exactly.

MCCANN.   You're in a rut.

GOLDBERG.   You look anaemic.

MCCANN.   Rheumatic.

GOLDBERG.   Myopic.

MCCANN.   Epileptic.

GOLDBERG.   You're on the verge.

MCCANN.   You're a dead duck.

GOLDBERG.   But we can save you.

MCCANN.   From a worse fate.

GOLDBERG.   True.

MCCANN.   Undeniable.

GOLDBERG.   From now on, we'll be the hub of your wheel.

MCCANN.   We'll renew your season ticket.

GOLDBERG.   We'll take tuppence off your morning tea.

MCCANN.   We'll give you a discount on all inflammable goods.

GOLDBERG.   We'll watch over you.

MCCANN.   Advise you.

GOLDBERG.   Give you proper care and treatment.

MCCANN.   Let you use the club bar.

GOLDBERG.   Keep a table reserved.

MCCANN.   Help you acknowledge the fast days.

GOLDBERG.   Bake you cakes.

MCCANN.   Help you kneel on kneeling days.

GOLDBERG.   Give you a free pass.

MCCANN.   Take you for constitutionals.

GOLDBERG.   Give you hot tips.

MCCANN.   We'll provide the skipping rope.

GOLDBERG.   The vest and pants.

MCCANN.   The ointment.

GOLDBERG.   The hot poultice.

MCCANN.   The fingerstall.

GOLDBERG.   The abdomen belt.

MCCANN.   The ear plugs.

GOLDBERG.   The baby powder.

MCCANN.   The back scratcher.

GOLDBERG.   The spare tyre.

MCCANN.   The stomach pump.

GOLDBERG.   The oxygen tent.

MCCANN.   The prayer wheel.

GOLDBERG.   The plaster of Paris.

MCCANN.   The crash helmet.

GOLDBERG.   The crutches.

MCCANN.   A day and night service.

GOLDBERG.   All on the house.

MCCANN.   That's it.

GOLDBERG.   We'll make a man of you.

MCCANN.   And a woman.

GOLDBERG.   You'll be re-orientated.

MCCANN.   You'll be rich.

GOLDBERG.   You'll be adjusted.

MCCANN.   You'll be our pride and joy.

GOLDBERG.   You'll be a mensch.

MCCANN.   You'll be a success.

GOLDBERG.   You'll be integrated.

MCCANN.   You'll give orders.

GOLDBERG.   You'll make decisions.

MCCANN.   You'll be a magnate.

GOLDBERG.   A statesman.

MCCANN.   You'll own yachts.

GOLDBERG.   Animals.

MCCANN.   Animals.

GOLDBERG *looks at* MCCANN.

GOLDBERG.   I said animals. (*He turns back to* STANLEY.) You'll be able to make or break, Stan. By my life. (*Silence.* STANLEY *is still.*) Well? What do you say?

STANLEY'S *head lifts very slowly and turns in* GOLDBERG'S *direction.*

GOLDBERG.   What do you think? Eh, boy?

STANLEY *begins to clench and unclench his eyes.*

MCCANN.   What's your opinion, sir? Of this prospect, sir?

GOLDBERG.   Prospect. Sure. Sure it's a prospect.

STANLEY'S *hands clutching his glasses begin to tremble.*

What's your opinion of such a prospect? Eh, Stanley?

STANLEY *concentrates, his mouth opens, he attempts to speak, fails and emits sounds from his throat.*

STANLEY.   Uh-gug . . . uh-gug . . . eeehhh-gag . . . (*On the breath.*) Caahh. . . . caahh. . . .

They watch him. He draws a long breath which shudders down his body. He concentrates.

GOLDBERG.   Well, Stanny boy, what do you say, eh?

They watch. He concentrates. His head lowers, his chin draws into his chest, he crouches.

STANLEY.   Uh-gughh . . . uh-gughhh. . . .

MCCANN.   What's your opinion, sir?

STANLEY.   Caaahhh . . . caaahhh. . . .

MCCANN.   Mr. Webber! What's your opinion?

GOLDBERG.   What do you say, Stan? What do you think of the prospect?

MCCANN.   What's your opinion of the prospect?

STANLEY'S *body shudders, relaxes, his head drops, he becomes still again, stooped.* PETEY *enters from door, downstage, left.*

GOLDBERG.   Still the same old Stan. Come with us. Come on, boy.

MCCANN.   Come along with us.

PETEY.   Where are you taking him?

They turn. Silence.

GOLDBERG.   We're taking him to Monty.

PETEY.   He can stay here.

GOLDBERG.   Don't be silly.

PETEY.   We can look after him here.

GOLDBERG.   Why do you want to look after him?

PETEY.   He's my guest.

GOLDBERG.   He needs special treatment.

PETEY.   We'll find someone.

GOLDBERG.   No. Monty's the best there is. Bring him, McCann.

They help STANLEY *out of the chair.* GOLDBERG *puts the bowler hat on* STANLEY'S *head. They all three move towards the door, left.*

PETEY.   Leave him alone!

They stop. GOLDBERG *studies him.*

GOLDBERG (*insidiously*). Why don't you come with us, Mr. Boles?

MCCANN.   Yes, why don't you come with us?

GOLDBERG.   Come with us to Monty. There's plenty of room in the car.

PETEY *makes no move. They pass him and reach the door.* MCCANN *opens the door and picks up the suitcases.*

PETEY (*broken*). Stan, don't let them tell you what to do!

They exit.

Silence. PETEY *stands. The front door slams. Sound of a car starting. Sound of a car going away. Silence.* PETEY *slowly goes to the table. He sits on a chair, left. He picks up the paper and opens it. The strips fall to the floor. He looks down at them.* MEG *comes past the window and enters by the back door.* PETEY *studies the front page of the paper.*

MEG (*coming downstage*). The car's gone.

PETEY.   Yes.

MEG.   Have they gone?

PETEY.   Yes.

MEG.   Won't they be in for lunch?

PETEY.   No.

MEG.   Oh, what a shame. (*She puts her bag on the table.*) It's hot out. (*She hangs her coat on a hook.*) What are you doing?

PETEY.   Reading.

MEG.   Is it good?

PETEY.   All right.

She sits by the table.

MEG.   Where's Stan?

Pause.

   Is Stan down yet, Petey?
PETEY.   No . . . he's. . . .
MEG.   Is he still in bed?
PETEY.   Yes, he's . . . still asleep.
MEG.   Still? He'll be late for his breakfast.
PETEY.   Let him . . . sleep.

Pause.

MEG.   Wasn't it a lovely party last night?
PETEY.   I wasn't there.
MEG.   Weren't you?
PETEY.   I came in afterwards.
MEG.   Oh.

Pause.

It was a lovely party. I haven't laughed so much for years. We had dancing and singing. And games. You should have been there.
PETEY.   It was good, eh?

Pause.

MEG.   I was the belle of the ball.
PETEY.   Were you?
MEG.   Oh yes. They all said I was.
PETEY.   I bet you were, too.
MEG.   Oh, it's true. I was.

Pause.

   I know I was.

CURTAIN

FOCUS QUESTIONS

1. Discuss how Pinter's use of the well-made play structure enhances the play's suspense.
2. Explain the significance of the play's title in terms of dramatic action.
3. In a short essay, evaluate why outsiders to English society—Goldberg, a Jew, and McCann, an Irishman—are the appropriate agents of Stanley's torture. Note how their change from acts 1 to 3 presents a case for your argument.
4. Isolate a dialogue between any two characters and discuss how language is used either combatively or seductively.
5. Describe how Petey's relationship to Meg changes over the course of the play and suggest why this change has occurred.
6. In a short essay evaluate how specific props (for example, the drum, the flashlight, and the glasses) are used to convey meaning.
7. Describe Lulu's function in relation to Stanley and Goldberg.
8. Isolate the identifying characteristics for each character in the play and discuss their purpose and meaning.

OTHER ACTIVITIES

1. Out of the experience of performing the first act up to Lulu's entrance, provide a written subtext for each of the three characters.
2. Using reviews, photographs, and other available documents, assess the original New York production of *The Birthday Party*.

BIBLIOGRAPHY

Baker, William, and Stephen Tabachnik. *Harold Pinter*. Edinburgh: Oliver & Boyd, 1973.

Bloom, Harold, ed. *Modern Critical Views*. New York: Chelsea House, 1986.

Bold, Alan, ed. *Harold Pinter: You Never Heard Such Silence*. New York: Vision and Barnes & Noble, 1984.

Burkman, Katherine H. *The Dramatic World of Harold Pinter: Its Basis in Ritual*. Athens, OH: Ohio University Press, 1971.

———and John L. Kundert-Gibbs, eds. *Pinter at Sixty*. Bloomington: Indiana University Press, 1993.

Diamond, Elin. *Pinter's Comic Play*. Lewisburg, PA: Bucknell University Press, 1985.

Dukore, Bernard. *Harold Pinter*. New York: Grove Press, 1982.

Esslin, Martin. *Pinter: The Playwright*. London: Methuen, 1984.

Gale, Stephen, ed. *Harold Pinter: Critical Approaches*. Rutherford, NJ: Fairleigh Dickinson University Press, 1986.

Gussow, Mel. *Conversations with Pinter*. London: Nick Hern Books, 1994.

Hinchcliffe, Arnold. *Harold Pinter*. Boston: Twayne Publishers, 1981.

Homan, Sidney. *The Audience as Actor and Character*. Lewisburg, PA: Bucknell University Press, 1989.

Knowles, Ronald. *"The Birthday Party" and "The Caretaker": Text and Performance*. New York: Macmillan Education Co., 1988.

Merritt, Susan Hollis. *Pinter in Play*. Durham, NC: Duke University Press, 1990.

Quigley, Austin. *The Pinter Problem*. Princeton, NJ: Princeton University Press, 1975.

Scott, Michael, ed. *Harold Pinter: "The Birthday Party," "The Caretaker," "The Homecoming": A Casebook*. London: Macmillan, 1986.

RECOMMENDED RECORDING

The Birthday Party. One sound cassette. 35 min. 1971. Author Lois Gordon. Everett/Edwards.

PLAY
Samuel Beckett (1906–1989)

Beckett might be said to write paintings, images of reality best glimpsed
behind closed eyelids.

—Alan Schneider

From *left* to *right*:
JoAnne Akalaitis, David
Warrilow, and Ruth
Maleczech in *Play*,
presented by Mabou
Mines in 1975, under the
direction of Lee Breuer.
Photo: Tony Kent.

APPROACHING THE THEATRE OF THE ABSURD

Twice in the twentieth century have the foundations of society—namely its governments and religious institutions—been shaken by world conflagration, thereby generating powerful critical repercussions. In 1918, by the end of World War I, the senseless destruction of countless human lives prompted such artistic movements as **dadaism,** which assumed an indifferent or nihilistic attitude as an antidote to war; and **expressionism** and **surrealism,** both of which presented the human condition through the distorted lenses of the dream world and the subconscious. By the end of World War II, however, a more paralyzing despair and disillusionment had taken hold. Neither the rhetoric of politicians nor sermons from the pulpit could undo the alienation and *Weltschmerz,* or pessimistic outlook on the world, that resulted from rampant demagoguery, genocide, and cold-war threats of nuclear annihilation.

Nurtured by an intellectual climate centered in Paris, Jean Paul Sartre (1905–1980) and Albert Camus (1913–1960) embraced the belief that human life was inexplicable, perhaps even meaningless. In spite of this chaos, human beings were compelled to construct a rationale for their existence. Articulating a philosophy popularly known as **existentialism,** they attracted a circle of international writers, including the Rumanian Eugene Ionesco (1912–1994), the Armenian Arthur Adamov (1903–1970), the French Jean Genet (1910–1986), and the Irish Samuel Beckett, all of whom shared similar feelings of anomie. Each developed his own artistic response to the dilemma, while their collective literary accomplishments shared identical themes: the boredom of existence, the futility of action, and the impossibility of human relationships and even of meaningful human communication. Out of their achievement emerged a powerful core of non-realistic dramatic works which Martin Esslin aptly termed the **theatre of the absurd.**

Although he objected to this characterization of his drama, Beckett stood at the forefront. An Anglo-Irish Dubliner who had studied languages at Trinity College, he was inspired by a fellow-Irishman, James Joyce, whom he met in Paris in 1929. Leaving the academic world to travel and write novels, Beckett settled permanently in Paris in 1937. His literary career began with such novels as *More Pricks than Kicks* (1935), *Murphy* (1938), and *Watt* (1945), which he wrote in English. Subsequently he wrote in French for the linguistic discipline and economy it forced on him and later translated his own works into English.

After working for the French Resistance during the Nazi occupation, Beckett completed a trilogy of novels in French: *Molloy* (1951), *Malone Meurt* (1951), and *L'Innommable* (1953). Then he turned to playwriting, suspecting that its stringent demands would pare his prose style down to the bone. In turn, he could use the presentational quality of images of human existence to convey meaning. The astonishing, highly innovative results were further dictated by his own conversational manner. JoAnne Akalaitis remembers her meeting with him: ''Talk was not unmeditated; conversation was not casual. Beckett's words came from a place deep inside. They possessed a kind of inevitability that is not part of ordinary social disclosure. In that moment speech was measured, definite, authentic in both its form and expression.''[1]

Beckett's first stage success, *Waiting for Godot,* was published in French in 1952. In this two-act play, time passes but nothing happens, at least in the conventional sense, as two tramps anticipate someone or something that will give their lives meaning. The play's chief novelty was that it neither narrated a story nor resolved any conflicts. But its powerful allegorical implications mirrored the absurdity of the human condition between waking and sleeping, between birth and death. Equally important, the play eloquently asserted Beckett's inimitable stage voice.

Changes were soon apparent in Beckett's subsequent works, especially when he began to minimize their dramatic structures and heighten their ambiguity. In time, his dramatic art had succeeded in chiseling all human interaction down to its most isolated sounds and starkest images, a goal he had set out to achieve earlier. The effect transformed his bleak landscapes into microcosms—both comical and tragic—whose unique iconography was characterized by a cohesive sound structure (the dialogue), spare visual imagery (the action), and silence. Gathering momentum and gaining coherence on stage, the dramatic impact bore no small resemblance to music with its repetitions, variations, and juxtapositions. Roland Barthes has identified Beckett's formula by claiming that he wrote plays at the "zero degree," so that the transparency of language allowed the ideas and events on stage to resonate meaning without commentary or explanation. For his contribution, Beckett was awarded the Nobel Prize for Literature in 1969.

MAJOR WORKS

Following the controversial success of *Waiting for Godot,* Beckett wrote three plays that explored the existential dilemma in highly theatrical and absurdist terms: *Endgame* (1957), a four-character homage to the vestiges of human life, perhaps in the wake of nuclear annihilation; *Krapp's Last Tape* (1958), a monologue in which an old man re-encounters lost moments from his past; and *Happy Days* (1961), whose optimistic protagonist is slowly swallowed by the earth beneath her feet. Other experimental pieces were inspired by his writing for radio: *All That Fall* (1957), *Embers* (1959), *Words and Music* (1962), and *Cascando* (1963). Of his more than forty short pieces for radio and stage, the most interesting include *Come and Go* (1966), a 121-line stylized work for three women; *Breath* (1969), a thirty-second look at a garbage heap accompanied by a breath and a cry; *Not I* (1972), an accelerated monologue in which an actor's mouth—spouting *non sequiturs*—is the only thing visible on stage; and *Rockabye* (1981), a final solo work in which an old woman, reminiscing from her rocking chair, merges with eternity. Of Beckett's entire experimental *oeuvre,* it was *Play* (1963) that marked a turning point in its complex but minimalist stage achievement. Its haunting imagery and compelling theme, that death is a metaphor for life, have won approval from audiences who were baffled at its inception.

THE ACTION

Entrapped in urns up to their necks, but unaware that they are in each other's company, a First Woman (w1), Man (M), and Second Woman (w2) speak of their love triangle. The event has happened earlier in time, when all three were alive. Throughout the action, a spotlight strikes their faces, prompting each to disclose his or her version of the sordid details and reflect on his or her current condition. Beckett's cue—"Repeat play"—signals a return to the beginning.

STRUCTURE AND LANGUAGE

Using as its starting point that banal but strident tone of a soap opera—"Give him up, she screamed, he's mine"—*Play* quickly discloses its darker subtext: the tormenting effects of obsessive memory. But instead of fully characterized stage enactments, three stationary heads provide the disembodied voices of existences now condemned to remembering the past. Provoked by "a spotlight projected on faces alone," their speculations, self-doubts, and recriminations brutally expose the futility of the lives they once led. Literally helpless in the glare of an unrelenting light, a sort of Grand Inquisitor who forces them to dredge up the past, they are unable to find release from the torture of consciousness. Choosing the musical-like *da capo* format which necessitates a repeated play, Beckett suggests that these voices will continue through eternity. Perhaps there is some tinge of recognition regarding this predicament when the Man quietly exclaims, "I know now, all this was just . . . play. And all this? When will all this—." But he dare not supply the missing word, for there can be no "end" to his journey.

The dynamics of *Play* resemble a sonata that seamlessly combines three distinct movements: the Chorus, the Narration, and the Meditation, each of which is embellished by its own coloration of sound and light. The chorus provides an introduction as the spot illuminates three faces whose muted, staccato-like, but unintelligible voices merge:

W1	Yes strange	darkness best	and the darker	the worse
W2	Yes perhaps	a shade gone	I suppose	some might say
M	Yes peace	one assumed	all out	all the pain

Harold Clurman has described the choral effect as a "a semi-murmur—like the rustling of leaves or the whisperings of the dead."[2]

In the narrative section, the spotlight is bright and the voices speak in a normal conversational manner. They intone their recollections as distinct phrases involuntarily triggered by the light. We can piece together their story from these fragments and decipher their deceptions, jealousies, and flaws.

With no explanation of when or how these characters have arrived at this place in time, *Play* approaches its third movement, the meditation, in which each character now reflects on his or her own fantasies and death. But a radical alteration in style and tone alerts our attention. This time the spotlight moves with a difference, as though it has acquired a personality of its own. For it not only prompts them to speak, its primary function until now, but it exerts a force in controlling what they have to say.

The trio effect of the first two movements evolves into a discordant quartet by the presence of this fourth character whose contribution to the ensemble seems actively assertive. The First Woman asks if the end will come when she tells the truth, suggesting that the shifting light demands something more from her. The Second Woman thinks that the light is ignoring her, that it follows her without will. The Man only wants an end to his suffering and fantasizes that it is he who empowers the light, yet doubts that he is seen at all. While efforts to create meaning out of their disembodied state ultimately prove futile, the spotlight emerges as the triumphant force of this third movement, capable of tormenting these characters and, as Beckett's title implies, playing with them as well.

On second hearing, the audience is able to catch more of the dialogue. But this time Beckett calls for a new set of dynamics: "a clear progression by which each subsection is both faster and softer than the preceding one."[3] What is implied is that the intensity and speed of the voices are inextricably linked to the intensity of the light shining. Thus form mirrors content: W1, W2, and M will continue to repeat their unenlightened litanies of selfhood, picked out in an order ruled by the spotlight's caprice, until the light—a probing, yet fading intelligence—goes to black. For the purposes of the performance, however, Beckett provides an ending in the form of a coda. When M repeats, "We were not long together—" and the lights go out, it provides closure for the audience but not those on stage.

PLAY-IN-PERFORMANCE

Beckett's plays demand an absolute fidelity to his stage directions. *Play* is no exception, allowing directors little opportunity to exercise their own interpretive powers. The pacing of the spoken vignettes, the varying intensities of the spotlight, and the timing of voices as cued by the light require a remarkable collaboration of artistry.

The world premiere of *Play* took place in Ulm, Germany, in June 1963. Actors Gerhard Winter, Nancy Illig, and Sigrid Pfeiffer were led through the linguistic maze by Deryk Mendel's precise direction. While many spectators were put off by the play's eccentric content, critics were impressed with Beckett's evocation of death and with his transformation of a sordid love triangle into what critic Barbara Bray called "an astonishing, hilarious and moving experience."[4]

In the following year, there were three international productions. The first was the American premiere directed by Alan Schneider, one of the definitive directors of Beckett, which opened at the Cherry Lane Theatre in New York City on January 6, 1964. Michael Lipton, Frances Sternhagen, and Marian Reardon intoned the play as a haunting ritual. But critical attention was mainly focused on the synchronicity between the beam of light and the voices engineered by Robert Currie, who manipulated the spot. The play itself was exposed as a theatrical stunt and praised as a brilliantly orchestrated fugue in merging what Louis Chapin of the *Christian Science Monitor* called its "heard words and seen music."[5] Despite a mixed critical reception, the production was awarded the 1964 Obie for Best Foreign Play.

Overseeing Jean-Marie Serreau directing the French premiere that opened in March 1964, Beckett allowed a variation in the production. During the *da capo,* the order of each character's speeches was left to the whim of the person controlling the spotlight. This approach was used in the production that George Devine co-directed with Beckett at the Old Vic in London on April 12, 1964, featuring Billie Whitelaw, Rosemary Harris, and Robert Stephens. The performance was especially important to Whitelaw's development as the consummate actress of Beckett's later works. She recalled, "When I read *Play,* I knew exactly what I had to get, roughly what direction I was heading."[6]

Other international productions have included a 1978 German one entitled *Spiel,* which Beckett directed in a slightly revised text. In 1985, the Polish scholar and translator Antoni Libere staged *Comedie* at the Teatr Studio in Warsaw. Creating an authentic production that honored the author's intentions, the director measured each light change to six seconds so that there would be no emotional variation.

Among its numerous American productions, the most unique version was staged by Mabou Mines at the Theater for the New City in October 1975. In his presentation of three Beckett pieces—*Play, Come and Go,* and *The Lost Ones,* Lee Breuer created an environmental space that required spectators to move from one area to another in order to witness each play. Incarnating Beckett's ritual, JoAnne Akalaitis, David Warrilow, and Ruth Maleczech were encased in urns with their faces encrusted.

In addition to its American premiere, Alan Schneider created two more productions of *Play:* at Washington DC's Arena Stage in 1976 and at the American Place Theatre in New York City in 1983. Schneider's reminiscences succinctly sum up the play's challenges:

> So what did I do, after all, with that urn play of Beckett's. I picked the actors, . . . I decided on the curve and shape and size and texture and location of the urns in question. I worked out the aesthetics and mechanics (fascinating and difficult) of that omnipresent light beam, which in essence became not only the categorical imperative but the seeing eye of the author. Over our three rehearsal weeks, our ten inadequate days of technical rehearsals, as well as a week of invaluable previews, I was able to arrange and rearrange and select and sample and change and change again the symphony of tones and volumes and rhythms and sounds and silences which together determined the particular texture and shape of this particular production of Beckett's *Play.*[7]

===

REFLECTIONS ON PLAY

David Warrilow has appeared in numerous world premieres of Samuel Beckett's work.

It was in the 60s in Paris that I first read anything at all by Samuel Beckett. Someone gave me a copy of *Waiting for Godot* and asked me if I would play one of the roles in an English-language production in Paris—playing just one night a week. Well, it never actually came to pass. But what did come to pass is that I read the play, and I didn't know what this was, but I found it absolutely irresistible! Sometime later I actually met Beckett very briefly when he okayed me to understudy a role in a production of *Endgame* that was going to take place in Paris. But I couldn't do that either because the rehearsals moved to London. But it was just like signals and signposts along the way, for soon after that I met Lee Breuer, Ruth Maleczech, and JoAnne Akalaitis.

Lee asked me if I would be willing to work on a project, just the four of us and not with a view to performing. Well, that was fine with me, because I had a job for one thing, and I was so intrigued by the idea of working on something for the theatre without planning to perform it. I thought that was really astounding. I was fascinated by these strange people and I said yes! So we did four months of sort of open-ended work on *Play*. Lee's idea was that even though he felt sure that Beckett's strictures and technical requirements for doing the play were correct, he wanted to break the whole thing apart and take it right down to its improvisational base.

So what we did was to meet and improvise, using these character specifics and the situations we felt were being described. We just went at it, hammer and tongs, and very gradually Lee brought us to sitting position, for example, and then—with a flashlight—very gradually got us to the point where we were doing it at breakneck speed. We eventually did two performances in Paris.

I suppose the major discovery was that it didn't matter what all of this meant. What was important was the music, that the singing of the music was absolutely vital to the experience. It was only later when I got to know Beckett that I discovered what a musician he was. You know, he used to love to play the piano, and Shubert was his favorite composer. There were veiled references, but the biggest reference of all was his own musicality. It ran through a tremendous amount of his work. And obviously *Play* is written a bit like a trio.

Lee was smart enough to get us to come up with very distinct vocal lines and tones so that when the voices came one after another there'd be this almost comical change of pitch. It was thrilling to do a piece of work that one knew was absolutely extraordinarily wonderful and not care what anybody thought about it. That was a big issue for me, because until then, it always bothered me a lot if people were not going to like or accept or love something difficult that I might be involved with. But that all changed with *Play*. It's an exquisite piece of wordplay and hangs with all the rest of his work. I mean, it looks very different on the page and the scheme of it is very special, but in a way it's like all the other plays, with its human voices.

Performing Beckett liberated me from psychology. I needed that because I wasn't even an actor when I was doing this work. But I was inside and I picked up a tremendous amount of information, aurally and visually, so obviously I was using that to try to work myself into this job called acting. Then suddenly I realized that the psychology just wasn't important. I mean, for every author that I've come to do—and I've done some great ones, especially Shakespeare—exactly the same things apply. If you come to understand that he does the work, then what you do is sing his music. You must absolutely respect the punctuation, because a great writer knows exactly how to punctuate for the voice, and the indications of breath are very often the overall musical, emotional structure of a piece of writing. If you're loyal to that, then you're way ahead. Certainly Lee Breuer was, which is why he did such great work directing this play.

When we finally came to New York to form a company and work together formally as Mabou Mines in 1970, we decided to do *Play* again. This time it became the kernel of an evening of three Beckett plays we presented at Theater for the New City. *Play* was really a seminal experience. I can remember the terror of it even now. It was so frightening, and a real physical feat as well. I could never really be comfortable because it was always so tricky to get the visual image correct.

In the first place, a lot of juggling had to be done with the levels just below the stage, and the urns had to be constructed and dealt with in such a way that actors of different heights would come out the same height. There was also something very anguishing about knowing that you could not move for nineteen minutes, which doesn't seem like a long time. We entered the urns from an opening in the back. The jars were constructed out of chicken wire and papier-mâché, then painted. So you wore the urn like a suit of armor. They were shorter than our own body height, so that our feet were below the level of the bottom of the urn. There was a hole in the stage platform, which was made for the urns to stand in. Then we had to have our heights adjusted in order to come out at the same level.

The terrifying thing was forgetting a line, which I did at one performance. The light came on me and I didn't know the line. So I opened my mouth and shut it again, and Lee just switched the light to the next actor who picked up the cue and went on, thank god. But it was a terrifying moment, because it's like prison. In a case like that, you really can't start improvising because it would just be all over the place. Lee operated the light, of course. The person who does must breathe the play as well as the actors, because you can't consult the script. It goes too fast.

As always with Beckett, you look at his stage instructions, and they look childishly simple. Then you try to realize them and discover they're not simple at all. In fact, they're enormously complicated. We decided we wanted these urns to look as if they had been buried for centuries, and a light is now suddenly coming upon them, but they are to look as much like the earth and as much like urns as possible. To achieve this, since the urns themselves had this very gnarled, clay-like, dusty aspect, we took Quaker Oats, mixed them with water, and scraped bits of makeup—gray, black, and a little white—into them, until it made this porridge. Then we plastered this on our hair and faces while it dried into a mask that itched and burned us. It took so much preparation to do this play. Yet we repeated this entire process for each performance.

Continued

There was nothing easy about performing *Play,* but it was tremendously effective. I still think the success of our production had to do with the attention to the music and the really wonderful speed that we were able to achieve. The moment we started the second time through, there was this sort of feeling—you could sense it in the audience—of people thinking, "Oh, we're going to hear it again! Maybe we can understand it this time!" It also meant they listened harder because they knew it was going to be a difficult experience. Then the laughter started. They laughed a lot. But they didn't dare laugh too much for fear of missing something. They laughed because of the lines and because it was going so fast. But this time they were getting a clearer idea of what was being said. It was deliberately difficult to understand the first time through, and it created this psychology—this real need to listen and pay attention. So all in all it was a difficult experience on both sides, but tremendously rewarding.

Play is hugely comical. I don't necessarily agree with the way Samuel Beckett saw the world or our lives, but I really appreciate his sense of the comic—what Lily Tomlin once said—that we're all in this alone. He had a very wry look at human beings, and a tremendous compassion for them at the same time, and I think he thought the whole thing was just so peculiar. He had this great love for people, and I think that's clear in his plays.

Beckett will never go away. I mean, what is nice is that with time he becomes less oppressive for young writers. What's been a difficulty for quite some time, I think, is that he was this Olympus and young writers knew they had to deal with him, but they didn't know how to get beyond there. I think that's over now, which is great. In any given time in our history of civilization, creators go through similar experiences as they bring out a new mode, a new way of expressing themselves. Now Beckett opened some doors, right? So there was no real way to be a pioneer without somehow taking notice of those doors.

Once I asked him if he really accepted being called an absurdist writer, and he said, "Good god, no!" Just as I asked him one day, "Do you understand what you write?" He answered, "Of course not!" I said okay, thank you. As an actor, I was pretty sure about that myself, because I'm constantly being asked and refuse to talk about the meaning of what I do, because that's not my job. You know, I'm quite sure that Mozart didn't understand what he did—he was just driven to it! I guess one of the reasons we're drawn to Beckett is because he's not definable.

Notes

1. *"Meeting Beckett,"* THE DRAMA REVIEW *34(3) (Fall 1990): 12.*
2. THE NATION, *January 1964, 106–7.*
3. *Cohn,* JUST PLAY: BECKETT'S THEATRE *(Princeton, NJ: Princeton University Press, 1980), 125.*
4. THE OBSERVER WEEKEND, *18 June 1963.*
5. *Christian Science Monitor, 7 Jan. 1964.*
6. *Linda Ben-Zvi, ed.,* WOMEN IN BECKETT *(Urbana: University of Illinois Press, 1990), 6.*
7. *Cohn, 196–97.*

PLAY

A STAGE PLAY
SAMUEL BECKETT

CHARACTERS

w1   First Woman   w2   Second Woman   M   Man

Front centre, touching one another, three identical grey urns (see page 875) about one yard high. From each a head protrudes, the neck held fast in the urn's mouth. The heads are those, from left to right as seen from auditorium, of w2, M, and w1. They face undeviatingly front throughout the play. Faces so lost to age and aspect as to seem almost part of urns. But no masks.

Their speech is provoked by a spotlight projected on faces alone. See page 875.

The transfer of light from one face to another is immediate. No blackout, i.e., return to almost complete darkness of opening, except where indicated.

The response to light is not quite immediate. At every solicitation a pause of about one second before utterance is achieved, except where a longer delay is indicated.

Faces impassive throughout. Voices toneless except where an expression is indicated.

Rapid tempo throughout.

The curtain rises on a stage in almost complete darkness. Urns just discernible. Five seconds.

Faint spots simultaneously on three faces. Three seconds. Voices faint, largely unintelligible.

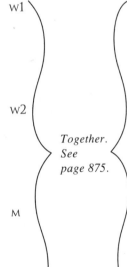

w1
w2
Together.
See
page 875.
M

Yes, strange, darkness best, and the darker the worse, till all dark, then all well, for the time, but it will come, the time will come, the thing is here, you'll see it, get off me, keep off me, all dark, all still, all over, wiped out——

Yes, perhaps, a shade gone, I suppose, some might say, poor thing, a shade gone, just a shade, in the head—(*faint wild laugh*)—just a shade, but I doubt it, *I* doubt it, not really, I'm all right, still all right, do my best, all I can——

Yes, peace, one assumed, all out, all the pain, all as if . . . never been, it will come—(*hiccup*)—pardon, no sense in this, oh I know . . . none the less, one assumed, peace . . . I mean . . . not merely all over, but as if . . . never been——

Spots off. Blackout. Five seconds. Strong spots simultaneously on three faces. Three seconds. Voices normal strength.

W1 ⎫
W2 ⎬ *Together.* ⎰ I said to him, Give her up——
M   ⎭   ⎱ One morning as I was sitting——
                 ⎱ We were not long together——

Spots off. Blackout. Five seconds. Spot on W1.

W1.   I said to him, Give her up. I swore by all I held most sacred——

Spot from W1 *to* W2.

W2.   One morning as I was sitting stitching by the open window she burst in and flew at me. Give him up, she screamed, he's mine. Her photographs were kind to her. Seeing her now for the first time full length and in the flesh I understood why he preferred me.

Spot from W2 *to* M.

M.   We were not long together when she smelled the rat. Give up that whore, she said, or I'll cut my throat—(*hiccup*) pardon—so help me God. I knew she could have no proof. So I told her I did not know what she was talking about.

Spot from M *to* W2.

W2.   What are you talking about? I said, stitching away. Someone yours? Give up whom? I smell you off him, she screamed, he stinks of bitch.

Spot from W2 *to* W1.

W1.   Though I had him dogged for months by a first-rate man, no shadow of proof was forthcoming. And there was no denying that he continued as . . . assiduous as ever. This, and his horror of the merely Platonic thing, made me sometimes wonder if I were not accusing him unjustly. Yes.

Spot from W1 *to* M.

M.   What have you to complain of? I said. Have I been neglecting you? How could we be together in the way we are if there were someone else? Loving her as I did, with all my heart, I could not but feel sorry for her.

Spot from M *to* W2.

W2.   Fearing she was about to offer me violence I rang for Erskine and had her shown out. Her parting words, as he could testify, if he is still alive, and has not forgotten, coming and going on the earth, letting people in, showing people out, were to the effect that she would settle my hash. I confess this did alarm me a little, at the time.

Spot from W2 *to* M.

M.   She was not convinced. I might have known. I smell her off you, she kept saying. There was no answer to this. So

I took her in my arms and swore I could not live without her. I meant it, what is more. Yes, I am sure I did. She did not repulse me.

Spot from M *to* W1.

W1.   Judge then of my astoundment when one fine morning, as I was sitting stricken in the morning room, he slunk in, fell on his knees before me, buried his face in my lap and . . . confessed.

Spot from W1 *to* M.

M.   She put a bloodhound on me, but I had a little talk with him. He was glad of the extra money.

Spot from M *to* W2.

W2.   Why don't you get out, I said, when he started moaning about his home life, there is obviously nothing between you any more. Or is there?

Spot from W2 *to* W1.

W1.   I confess my first feeling was one of wonderment. What a male!

Spot from W1 *to* M. *He opens his mouth to speak. Spot from* M *to* W2.

W2.   Anything between us, he said, what do you take me for, a something machine? And of course with him no danger of the . . . spiritual thing. Then why don't you get out? I said. I sometimes wondered if he was not living with her for her money.

Spot from W2 *to* M.

M.   The next thing was the scene between them. I can't have her crashing in here, she said, threatening to take my life. I must have looked incredulous. Ask Erskine, she said, if you don't believe me. But she threatens to take her own, I said. Not yours? she said. No, I said, hers. We had fun trying to work this out.

Spot from M *to* W1.

W1.   Then I forgave him. To what will love not stoop! I suggested a little jaunt to celebrate, to the Riviera or our darling Grand Canary. He was looking pale. Peaked. But this was not possible just then. Professional commitments.

Spot from W1 *to* W2.

W2.   She came again. Just strolled in. All honey. Licking her lips. Poor thing. I was doing my nails, by the open window. He has told me all about it, she said. Who he, I said filing away, and what it? I know what torture you must be going through, she said, and I have dropped in to say I bear you no ill-feeling. I rang for Erskine.

Spot from W2 *to* M.

M.   Then I got frightened and made a clean breast of it. She was looking more and more desperate. She had a razor in her vanity-bag. Adulterers, take warning, never admit.

Spot from M *to* W1.

W1.   When I was satisfied it was all over I went to have a gloat. Just a common tart. What he could have found in her when he had me——

Spot from W1 *to* W2.

W2.   When he came again we had it out. I felt like death. He went on and on about why he had to tell her. Too risky and so on. That meant he had gone back to her. Back to that!

Spot from W2 *to* W1.

W1.   Pudding face, puffy, spots, blubber mouth, jowls, no neck, dugs you could——

Spot from W1 *to* W2.

W2.   He went on and on. I could hear a mower. An old hand mower. I stopped him and said that whatever I might feel I had no silly threats to offer—but not much stomach for her leavings either. He thought that over for a bit.

Spot from W2 *to* W1.

W1.   Calves like a flunkey—

Spot from W1 *to* M.

M.   When I saw her again she knew. She was looking— (*hiccup*)—wretched. Pardon. Some fool was cutting grass. A little rush, then another. The problem was how to convince her that no . . . revival of intimacy was involved. I couldn't. I might have known. So I took her in my arms and said I could not go on living without her. I don't believe I could have.

Spot from M *to* W2.

W2.   The only solution was to go away together. He swore we should as soon as he had put his affairs in order. In the meantime we were to carry on as before. By that he meant as best we could.

Spot from W2 *to* W1.

W1.   So he was mine again. All mine. I was happy again. I went about singing. The world——

Spot from W1 *to* M.

M.   At home all heart to heart, new leaf and bygones bygones. I ran into your ex-doxy, she said one night, on the

pillow, you're well out of that. Rather uncalled for, I thought. I am indeed, sweetheart, I said, I am indeed. God what vermin women. Thanks to you, angel, I said.

Spot from M *to* W1.

W1.   Then I began to smell her off him again. Yes.

Spot from W1 *to* W2.

W2.   When he stopped coming I was prepared. More or less.

Spot from W2 *to* M.

M.   Finally it was all too much. I simply could no longer——

Spot from M *to* W1.

W1.   Before I could do anything he disappeared. That meant she had won. That slut! I couldn't credit it. I lay stricken for weeks. Then I drove over to her place. It was all bolted and barred. All grey with frozen dew. On the way back by Ash and Snodland——

Spot from W1 *to* M.

M.   I simply could no longer——

Spot from M *to* W2.

W2.   I made a bundle of his things and burnt them. It was November and the bonfire was going. All night I smelt them smouldering.

Spot off W2. *Blackout. Five seconds. Spots half previous strength simultaneously on three faces. Three seconds. Voices proportionately lower.*

W1		
W2	*Together.*	Mercy, mercy——
M		To say I am——
		When first this change——

Spots off. Blackout. Five seconds. Spot on M.

M.   When first this change I actually thanked God. I thought, It is done, it is said, now all is going out——

Spot from M *to* W1.

W1.   Mercy, mercy, tongue still hanging out for mercy. It will come. You haven't seen me. But you will. Then it will come.

Spot from W1 *to* W2.

W2.   To say I am not disappointed, no, I am. I had anticipated something better. More restful.

Spot from W2 *to* W1.

W1.   Or you will weary of me. Get off me.

Spot from w1 *to* M.

M.   Down, all going down, into the dark, peace is coming, I thought, after all, at last, I was right, after all, thank God, when first this change.

Spot from M *to* w2.

w2.   Less confused. Less confusing. At the same time I prefer this to . . . the other thing. Definitely. There are endurable moments.

Spot from w2 *to* M.

M.   I thought.

Spot from M *to* w2.

w2.   When you go out—and I go out. Some day you will tire of me and go out . . . for good.

Spot from w2 *to* w1.

w1.   Hellish half-light.

Spot from w1 *to* M.

M.   Peace, yes, I suppose, a kind of peace, and all that pain as if . . . never been.

Spot from M *to* w2.

w2.   Give me up, as a bad job. Go away and start poking and pecking at someone else. On the other hand——

Spot from w2 *to* w1.

w1.   Get off me! (*Vehement.*) Get off me!

Spot from w1 *to* M.

M.   It will come. Must come. There is no future in this.

Spot from M *to* w2.

w2.   On the other hand things may disimprove, there is that danger.

Spot from w2 *to* M.

M.   Oh of course I know now——

Spot from M *to* w1.

w1.   Is it that I do not tell the truth, is that it, that some day somehow I may tell the truth at last and then no more light at last, for the truth?

Spot from w1 *to* w2.

w2.   You might get angry and blaze me clean out of my wits. Mightn't you?

Spot from w2 *to* M.

M.   I know now, all that was just . . . play. And all this? When will all this——

Spot from M *to* w1.

w1.   Is that it?

Spot from w1 *to* w2.

w2.   Mightn't you?

Spot from w2 *to* M.

M.   All this, when will all this have been . . . just play?

Spot from M *to* w1.

w1.   I can do nothing . . . for anybody . . . any more . . . thank God. So it must be something I have to say. How the mind works still!

Spot from w1 *to* w2.

w2.   But I doubt it. It would not be like you somehow. And you must know I am doing my best. Or don't you?

Spot from w2 *to* M.

M.   Perhaps they have become friends. Perhaps sorrow——

Spot from M *to* w1.

w1.   But I have said all I can. All you let me. All I——

Spot from w1 *to* M.

M.   Perhaps sorrow has brought them together.

Spot from M *to* w2.

w2.   No doubt I make the same mistake as when it was the sun that shone, of looking for sense where possibly there is none.

Spot from w2 *to* M.

M.   Perhaps they meet, and sit, over a cup of that green tea they both so loved, without milk or sugar, not even a squeeze of lemon——

Spot from M *to* w2.

w2.   Are you listening to me? Is anyone listening to me? Is anyone looking at me? Is anyone bothering about me at all?

Spot from w2 *to* M.

M.   Not even a squeeze of——

Spot from M *to* w1.

w1.   Is it something I should do with my face, other than utter? Weep?

Spot from W1 *to* W2.

W2.   Am I taboo, I wonder. Not necessarily, now that all danger is averted. That poor creature—I can hear her—that poor creature——

Spot from W2 *to* W1.

W1.   Bite off my tongue and swallow it? Spit it out? Would that placate you? How the mind works still to be sure!

Spot from W1 *to* M.

M.   Meet, and sit, now in the one dear old place, now in the other, and sorrow together, and compare—(*hiccup*) pardon—happy memories.

Spot from M *to* W1.

W1.   If only I could think, There is no sense in this . . . either, none whatsoever. I can't.

Spot from W1 *to* W2.

W2.   That poor creature who tried to seduce you, what ever became of her, do you suppose?—I can hear her. Poor thing.

Spot from W2 *to* M.

M.   Personally I always preferred Lipton's.

Spot from M *to* W1.

W1.   And that all is falling, all fallen, from the beginning, on empty air. Nothing being asked at all. No one asking me for anything at all.

Spot from W1 *to* W2.

W2.   They might even feel sorry for me, if they could see me. But never so sorry as I for them.

Spot from W2 *to* W1.

W1.   I can't.

Spot from W1 *to* W2.

W2.   Kissing their sour kisses.

Spot from W2 *to* M.

M.   I pity them in any case, yes, compare my lot with theirs, however blessed, and——

Spot from M *to* W1.

W1.   I can't. The mind won't have it. It would have to go. Yes.

Spot from W1 *to* M.

M.   Pity them.

Spot from M *to* W2.

W2.   What do you do when you go out? Sift?

Spot from W2 *to* M.

M.   Am I hiding something? Have I lost——

Spot from M *to* W1.

W1.   She had means, I fancy, though she lived like a pig.

Spot from W1 *to* W2.

W2.   Like dragging a great roller, on a scorching day. The strain . . . to get it moving, momentum coming——

Spot off W2. *Blackout. Three seconds. Spot on* W2.

W2.   Kill it and strain again.

Spot from W2 *to* M.

M.   Have I lost . . . the thing you want? Why go out? Why go——

Spot from M *to* W2.

W2.   And you perhaps pitying me, thinking, Poor thing, she needs a rest.

Spot from W2 *to* W1.

W1.   Perhaps she has taken him away to live . . . somewhere in the sun.

Spot from W1 *to* M.

M.   Why go down? Why not—

Spot from M *to* W2.

W2.   I don't know.

Spot from W2 *to* W1.

W1.   Perhaps she is sitting somewhere, by the open window, her hands folded in her lap, gazing down out over the olives——

Spot from W1 *to* M.

M.   Why not keep on glaring at me without ceasing? I might start to rave and—(*hiccup*)—bring it up for you. Par——

Spot from M *to* W2.

W2.   No.

Spot from W2 *to* M.

M.   —don.

Spot from M *to* W1.

w1.   Gazing down out over the olives, then the sea, wondering what can be keeping him, growing cold. Shadow stealing over everything. Creeping. Yes.

Spot from w1 *to* M.

M.   To think we were never together.

Spot from M *to* w2.

w2.   Am I not perhaps a little unhinged already?

Spot from w2 *to* w1.

w1.   Poor creature. Poor creatures.

Spot from w1 *to* M.

M.   Never woke together, on a May morning, the first to wake to wake the other two. Then in a little dinghy——

Spot from M *to* w1.

w1.   Penitence, yes, at a pinch, atonement, one was resigned, but no, that does not seem to be the point either.

Spot from w1 *to* w2.

w2.   I say, Am I not perhaps a little unhinged already? (*Hopefully.*) Just a little? (*Pause.*) I doubt it.

Spot from w2 *to* M.

M.   A little dinghy——

Spot from M *to* w1.

w1.   Silence and darkness were all I craved. Well, I get a certain amount of both. They being one. Perhaps it is more wickedness to pray for more.

Spot from w1 *to* M.

M.   A little dinghy, on the river, I resting on my oars, they lolling on air-cushions in the stern . . . sheets. Drifting. Such fantasies.

Spot from M *to* w1.

w1.   Hellish half-light.

Spot from w1 *to* w2.

w2.   A shade gone. In the head. Just a shade. I doubt it.

Spot from w2 *to* M.

M.   We were not civilized.

Spot from M *to* w1.

w1.   Dying for dark—and the darker the worse. Strange.

Spot from w1 *to* M.

M.   Such fantasies. Then. And now——

Spot from M *to* w2.

w2.   I doubt it.

Pause. Peal of wild laughter from w2 *cut short as spot from her to* w1.

w1.   Yes, and the whole thing there, all there, staring you in the face. You'll see it. Get off me. Or weary.

Spot from w1 *to* M.

M.   And now, that you are . . . mere eye. Just looking. At my face. On and off.

Spot from M *to* w1.

w1.   Weary of playing with me. Get off me. Yes.

Spot from w1 *to* M.

M.   Looking for something. In my face. Some truth. In my eyes. Not even.

Spot from M *to* w2. *Laugh as before from* w2 *cut short as spot from her to* M.

M.   Mere eye. No mind. Opening and shutting on me. Am I as much——

Spot off M. *Blackout. Three seconds. Spot on* M.

M.   Am I as much as . . . being seen?

Spot off M. *Blackout. Five seconds. Faint spots simultaneously on three faces. Three seconds. Voices faint, largely unintelligible.*

w1		
w2	*Together.*	Yes, strange, etc.
M		Yes, perhaps, etc.
		Yes, peace, etc.

Repeat play.

M (*closing repeat*). Am I as much as . . . being seen?

Spot off M. *Blackout. Five seconds. Strong spots simultaneously on three faces. Three seconds. Voices normal strength.*

w1		
w2	*Together.*	I said to him, Give her up——
M		One morning as I was sitting——
		We were not long together——

Spots off. Blackout. Five seconds. Spot on M.

M.   We were not long together——

Spot off M. *Blackout. Five seconds.*

LIGHT

The source of light is single and must not be situated outside the ideal space (stage) occupied by its victims.

The optimum position for the spot is at the centre of the footlights, the faces being thus lit at close quarters and from below.

When exceptionally three spots are required to light the three faces simultaneously, they should be as a single spot branching into three.

Apart from these moments a single mobile spot should be used, swivelling at maximum speed from one face to another as required.

The method consisting in assigning to each face a separate fixed spot is unsatisfactory in that it is less expressive of a unique inquisitor than the single mobile spot.

CHORUS

w1	Yes strange	darkness best	and the darker	the worse
w2	Yes perhaps	a shade gone	I suppose	some might say
M	Yes peace	one assumed	all out	all the pain
w1	till all dark	then all well	for the time	but it will come
w2	poor thing	a shade gone	just a shade	in the head

M	all as if	never been	it will come	(hiccup) pardon
w1	the time will come	the thing is there		you'll see it
w2	(laugh– – – – –)	just a shade		but I doubt it
M	no sense in this	oh I know		none the less
w1	get off me	keep off me	all dark	all still
w2	I doubt it	not really	I'm all right	still all right
M	one assumed	peace I mean	not merely	all over
w1	all over	wiped out——		
w2	do my best	all I can——		
M	but as if	never been——		

URNS

In order for the urns to be only one yard high, it is necessary either that traps be used, enabling the actors to stand below stage level, or that they kneel throughout play, the urns being open at the back.

The sitting posture results in urns of unacceptable bulk and is not to be considered.

FOCUS QUESTIONS

1. Discuss how each of the three sections of the play—Chorus, Narration, and Meditation—deals with a different aspect of the human condition.
2. *Play* deals with the human need to explain oneself when confronted by another. Focusing on the spotlight as a character in the drama, discuss its relationship to the three disembodied voices in the urns and its effect on each.
3. By piecing together the fragments of the story as told by these voices, describe the nature of the different relationships once shared by these characters.

OTHER ACTIVITIES

1. Create a monologue in which the spotlight becomes a character responding to the words of those he or she is questioning.
2. Assemble from Beckett's fragments a set of monologues for one of the three characters. Show how the monologue reveals the character's struggle to be released from the torture of obsessive memory.

BIBLIOGRAPHY

Ben-Zvi, Linda, ed. *Women in Beckett: Performance and Critical Perspectives*. Urbana: University of Illinois Press, 1990.

Brater, Enoch. *Beyond Minimalism: Beckett's Late Style in the Theatre*. New York: Oxford University Press, 1987.

————. *Why Beckett*. London: Thames & Hudson, 1989.

Burkman, Katherine, ed. *Myth and Ritual in the Plays of Samuel Beckett*. Rutherford, NJ: Fairleigh Dickinson University Press, 1987.

Cohn, Ruby. *Just Play: Beckett's Theater*. Princeton, NJ: Princeton University Press, 1980.

Esslin, Martin. *The Theatre of the Absurd*. New York: Anchor Books, 1961.

Fletcher, Beryl S., and John Fletcher. *A Student's Guide to the Plays of Samuel Beckett*. London: Faber, 1985.

Fletcher, John, and John Spurling. *Beckett: A Study of His Plays*. New York: Hill & Wang, 1972.

Gontarski, S. E. *The Intent of Undoing in Samuel Beckett's Dramatic Texts*. Bloomington: Indiana University Press, 1985.

————. *On Beckett: Essays and Criticism*. New York: Grove Press, 1983.

Homan, Sidney. *Beckett's Theaters: Interpretations for Performance*. Lewisburg, PA: Bucknell University Press, 1984.

Kalb, Jonathan. *Beckett in Performance*. Cambridge: Cambridge University Press, 1989.

Kennedy, Arthur. *Samuel Beckett*. New York: Cambridge University Press, 1989.

Kenner, Hugh. *A Reader's Guide to Samuel Beckett*. New York: Farrar, Straus & Giroux, 1973.

Knowlson, James, and John Pilling. *Frescoes of the Skull: The Later Prose and Drama of Samuel Beckett*. New York: Grove Press, 1980.

McMillan, Douglas, and Martha Fehsenfeld. *Beckett in the Theatre: the Author as Practical Playwright and Director*. London: John Calder Books, 1988.

Vanden Heuvel, Michael. *Performing Drama/Dramatizing Performance*. Ann Arbor: University of Michigan Press, 1991.

RECOMMENDED VIDEOTAPE

Samuel Beckett: Silence to Silence. VHS. 80 min. Readings by Billie Whitelaw, Jack McGowran, and Patrick Magee. Narrated by David Warrilow. Distributed by Films for the Humanities and Sciences, Princeton, NJ.

DUTCHMAN
Amiri Baraka (LeRoi Jones) (1934–   )

Part of Baraka's brilliance as a dramatist is to transform familiar situations into twisted, inflamed projections of the future, prophecies of what is to come in America's racial struggle.

—Darryl Pinckney

Megan Butler as Lula and Jihmi Kennedy as Clay in *Dutchman,* presented by the Mark Taper Forum in 1990, under the direction of Ethan Silverman. *Photo: Jay Thompson.*

APPROACHING REVOLUTIONARY BLACK THEATRE

In the first decades of the twentieth century during the Harlem Renaissance, W. E. B. Dubois and Dr. Alain Locke called for the development of a distinct dramatic idiom written by black artists for a black audience. Writers and teachers responded to what Dubois called "the embargo which white wealth lays on full Negro expression."[1] They wrote social protest dramas and historical plays that celebrated the life of blacks in America. Yet most of their plays never saw commercial production. Only a handful of them by William Richardson, Garland Anderson, Frank Wilson, Wallace Thurman, William Jordan Rapp, and Langston Hughes reached Broadway between 1923 and 1935, and their efforts to counteract the stereotyped roles created for black performers by white authors—overburdened mammies, faithful Uncle Toms, superstitious peasants, and violent brutes—went virtually unnoticed by the playgoing public.

During the Depression, the Federal Theatre Project's Writer's Laboratory and the various political theatre groups that sought plays about the inequities of capitalism and exploitation of workers proved viable training grounds for new black playwrights. By the end of World War II, the need to deal honestly with the problems of racial hatred, ghetto life, and the elusiveness of the American Dream for this country's black population was even more keenly felt. Black soldiers were faced with the fact that the freedoms they had risked their lives to protect in Europe were denied them at home. Their stories needed to be told.

Using realism and surrealism as well as satire, playwrights William Branch, Loften Mitchell, Alice Childress, and Adrienne Kennedy protested this continuing victimization of blacks in white America in their dramas which proliferated on the experimental stages of New York's Greenwich Village and the growing neighborhood theatres of Harlem. With Lorraine Hansberry's landmark Broadway production of *A Raisin in the Sun* (1959), the African-American playwright was finally recognized as an artist to be reckoned with. Yet, for playwriting to become a unique vehicle for voicing the concerns of the African-American community, it would take the influence of poet, novelist, essayist, and playwright Amiri Baraka who, according to Sherley Anne Williams, "came closest to articulating a necessary fusion of politics and aesthetics, making that fusion a potent political force."[2]

Born LeRoi Jones, son of a social worker and a postal employee, Baraka had inherited the integrationist, middle-class values of the Newark public schools and Howard University from which he graduated with a degree in English in 1954. Seeking alternatives to the sterility of bourgeois life, he settled in Greenwich Village and aligned himself with Bohemian poets Allen Ginsberg, Gary Snyder, Gregory Corso, and Jack Kerouac as well as jazz musicians Thelonius Monk and John Coltrane.

As a jazz critic, poet, and founding editor of an alternative literary magazine, *Yugen* (1958–1962), as well as Totem and Corinth Presses, Jones was at the forefront of the beat generation's critical stance on American politics and social conformity. After visiting Cuba in 1960, he abandoned the Zen-based aesthetics of his poet friends and became politically active as a mediator between the white and black communities. One of his earliest plays, *The Eighth Ditch* (1961), used surrealism to explore the double-sided nature of what it means to be black and American, an issue with which he was becoming involved.

Over the next three years, he wrote plays that highlighted the viciousness of a dehumanizing American society. In *The Toilet* (1964), about a black gang-beating of a white homosexual who dared to write their leader a love letter, Jones ended the action with the gang leader cradling his admirer's head in his arms. In *Baptism* (1964), he used obscenity and profanity to burlesque the hypocrisy of "so-called" Christians who have no tolerance or compassion for people who are different. In *Dutchman* (1963) and *The Slave* (1964), Jones abandoned universal themes about the victimization of those who are different to explore the effects of racism on the black artist in particular. In spite of the primarily white audiences' discomfort with these plays, *Dutchman* won the Obie for Best Drama of the 1963–64 season and Jones was hailed by New York theatre critics as an important new voice.

Shortly afterwards, under the growing influence of Malcolm X and black nationalists, Jones left his white wife, his circle of Bohemian friends, and his newly won celebrity. He founded the Black Arts Repertory Theatre in Harlem and then Spirit House in Newark while writing plays and essays that sent out the charge for a revolution in theatre. As a follower of the Nation of Islam from 1964 until 1970, he became Imamu Amiri Baraka, the dominant force in the Black Arts Movement. Rejecting Western theatrical conventions, he encouraged other black playwrights to use African mythology, ritual, African-American history, and music as the means to discover new performance modes that would move their audiences to action and transform their lives rather than to wallow in self-pity. As a result of his influence, a generation of playwrights began to meet the challenges set forth by Dubois and Locke more than half a century earlier.

MAJOR WORKS

Baraka's playwriting career after the success of *Dutchman* is divided into two periods. From 1964 to 1970, he wrote pageants, **agitprop** plays, parodies, and rituals that celebrated black nationalism and self-determination for community audiences in Harlem and Newark. Among these are *Experimental Death Unit #1* (1964), *J-E-L-L-O* (1964), *A Black Mass* (1966), *Slave Ship* (1967), *Madheart* (1967), *Great Goodness of Life* (*A Coon Show*) (1967), and *Home on the Range* (1968). Abandoning Islam and adopting a Marxist-Leninist ideology in 1974, Baraka dropped the title signifying his self-appointed role as a Black Muslim community leader, Imamu, from his name and wrote polemical plays about working class issues including *Sidnee Poet Heroical* (1975), *S-1* (1976), *The Motion of History* (1977), *Boy & Tarzan Appear in a Clearing* (1981), and *Money* (1982). Baraka's essays and poetry have also had a profound impact on African-American aesthetics, but *Dutchman* remains his best-known and most frequently anthologized work.

THE ACTION

On his way to a friend's party, a young middle-class black man, Clay, is accosted on the subway by an attractive, white, Bohemian woman, Lula, who begins an audacious flirtation with him. Intrigued, he agrees to take her to the party. As passengers enter the car, Lula's advances become an overt sexual challenge. When he fails to join her wild dance, she verbally assaults his race and bourgeois aspirations. No longer able to contain his rage, Clay launches into a tirade through which he reveals his contempt and deep-seated hatred for whites. Lula responds, first by silencing him with words, then with her knife. The passive onlookers dispose of the body and exit at the next stop, leaving Lula alone. As the train is about to pull out of the station, another young, unsuspecting black man enters the car and sits down.

STRUCTURE AND LANGUAGE

Dutchman represents a stylistic duel, simultaneously sexual, racial, and metaphorical, which is enacted both physically and verbally. Lula is a liberated, white, Bohemian seductress who offers apples, like Eve, and unbridled sex to her unsuspecting victims. Like the mythical Flying Dutchman, who is cursed and condemned to wander the universe in his phantom ship until he can find the woman who will redeem him, Lula travels "in the flying underbelly of the city" to find the man who will release her. Clay, the middle-class, university-educated black man, is one among many she will confront on her unending journey.

Clay hides behind the safety of a suit and tie, and a mask of passive rationality. Caught outside his bourgeois moorings, he is slow to pick up on the lines Lula feeds him and is awkward at fielding her sexual advances. He also does not understand the unconventional script she is writing for him. When she grabs his thigh and asks, "What are you thinking about?" all he can reply is, "Watch it now, you're gonna excite me for real." When she claims that he should not wear a three-button suit because his grandfather was a slave, his incredulous response is without rancor: "My grandfather was a night watchman." As the first scene ends, Lula continues to push him to reveal murderous feelings that he hides even from himself: "You're a murderer, Clay, and you know it . . . You know goddam well what I mean," to which Clay questions: "I do?"

The blackout before the second scene shifts the direction and momentum of the duel. Lula becomes the spirit of America, which teases and invites and ultimately kills those who are tempted by her crassness. As she presents their fantasy date, which allows them to be "free of their histories," Clay takes on the voices not only of African-American men but all those whose principles and cultural heritage are shaken by the false promises of the American dream. Alone on the train, their date has plausibility. But as more passengers enter the car, the real world encroaches and their racial differences and perspectives on the American experience can no longer be ignored.

Lula miscalculates her knowledge of middle-class black men: they are not necessarily willing to accept Bohemian iconoclasm as a way to fight American bourgeois conformity. In fact, Clay will not take up her challenge to "do the nasty" or the "gritty grind" and lose his dignity in front of the audience of passengers. She demands that he "scream meaningless shit in these hopeless faces" as a way to break out and heal himself. When he refuses to accept her Dada explosion, she mocks him by calling him "Uncle Tom," provoking those on the train to laugh at him.

Clay cannot be shamed into compliance. Instead he erupts with rage and challenges Lula's prescription for his sanity as ignorant. He claims that all she knows about the African-American experience is "what is there for you to see. An Act. Lies. Device. Not the pure heart, the pumping black heart." Although the blues and jazz and, in Clay's case, poetry have helped him to sublimate the anguish of being black and American, he knows that murder, revenge for all the injustices that his people have had to suffer, is the only real avenue for the black man to break out of the chains of oppression. Yet Clay would rather retreat behind his accepting mask and remain a rational, albeit neurotic, individual than chance the violence.

Once the anger underneath this mask has been revealed, his safe position is untenable. For Lula to ensure that she remain alive, that the American Dream can prevail, Clay must lie and say he loves her. But he has been forced to expose his hatred of her and all she represents and can no longer pretend to want her dream. Therefore Lula must kill him in order to win the physical and ideological battle. That is her curse.

DUTCHMAN-IN-PERFORMANCE

In the aftermath of the March on Washington for Jobs and Freedom in August 1963 and the assassination of John F. Kennedy later that November, Theatre 1964—a producing enterprise to promote American plays in the style of Theatre of the Absurd—presented *Dutchman* at the Cherry Lane Theatre in March on a triple bill with Arrabal's *The Two Executioners* and Beckett's *Play*. By April, Edward Albee's *The American Dream* replaced the Arrabal and Beckett offerings, and Baraka's play, directed by Edward Parone with Robert Hooks as Clay and Jennifer West as Lula, was launched in a run of the two one-acts that lasted over 350 performances.

Critics took issue with the play's uncompromising candor and violent message. They were shocked by its scathing hatred, its obscenities, and its driving and explosive power. As Howard Taubman reflected, *Dutchman*'s importance as a document of centuries of racial conflict could not be ignored: "If this is the way the Negroes really feel about the white world around them, there's more rancor buried in the breasts of colored conformists than anyone can imagine. If this is the way even one Negro feels, there is ample cause for guilt as well as alarm, and for a hastening of change."[3] The play was published in August of that year.

Controversy followed the April 1965 production directed by Burgess Meredith and performed by Al Freeman, Jr. and Shirley Knight at the Warner Playhouse in Los Angeles. Police attempted to prevent theatres from producing the play, and newspapers declined to place advertisements for the double bill of *Dutchman* and *The Toilet*. Despite the near-boycott of the production, its anger and bristling dialogue were not lost on the critics. With the riots in the Watts district of Los Angeles as well as the increasingly fervent call for Black Power and subsequent murder of Black nationalist Malcolm X only months away, Baraka's play became a prophetic and frightening image of the rage just below the surface of the civil rights movement.

When the Metropolitan Transit Authority refused to allow the play to be filmed in the New York subway, the Los Angeles cast went to London. Using a replica of a New York City subway car, Anthony Harvey directed a fifty-five-minute film version of the play, which later won a Cannes Film Festival Critics Award and garnered the Venice Film Festival Best Actress Award for Shirley Knight.

Besides Baraka's 1965 revival of the play uptown at his Black Arts Repertory Theatre in Harlem, the play was produced in English and in translation on stages across Europe. These included the touring company version at the Festival of Two Worlds in Spoleto, Italy (1965) and at the Théâtre de Poche in Paris (1965) as well as new productions in Stockholm (1966), London (1967), and the Theatr Kameralny in Warsaw (1967). Performed by all-white casts in Sweden and Poland, the play held new meaning for its audiences. Theatre historian Andrzej Ceynowa speculates that the Polish audience, in particular, saw *Dutchman* as a political play not about racism but "about honesty towards oneself and the wages of betraying one's people in the hour of confrontation with a suppressive, alien power."[4] The play's wide popularity in Europe was further witnessed when Tega Piegela directed an all-German cast in a performance on a streetcar in downtown Munich (1986). As the streetcar moved through the city, passengers served as an audience for the play that was transpiring in front of them.

Although there have been many revivals of the play in college and community theatres throughout the United States, *Dutchman* is rarely seen on commercial stages. One attempt, Gene Frankel's 1988 production in the East Village of New York, was criticized as a powerless artifact from a bygone era. When the Mark Taper Forum revived the play in 50/60 Vision—an eight-week retrospective of one-acts from the 1950s and 1960s— *Dutchman* was seen as part of American experimentation within the European absurdist tradition. Conceived and produced by Edward Parone, the director of the world premiere of *Dutchman,* the 1990 retrospective restored the original context in which the play's vitriolic language and message had been truly shocking. Parone's program note assesses the experience quite succinctly: "These plays were written by writers in love with language— the ordering of words that turns chaos into poetry, art: work that not only *means* something but *is* something, something that never existed before, work that not only characterizes an age but is among the most eloquent expressions of it."

REFLECTIONS ON DUTCHMAN

Edward Parone directed the world premiere of Dutchman.

The success of *Dutchman* began with Edward Albee. When I worked as an agent at William Morris, a play called *The Zoo Story* came across my desk. Also *The Death of Bessie Smith*. I read them and I thought, "This is what I became an agent for!" I knew [producer] Richard Barr and I sold *The Zoo Story* to him. That part is history.

I quit the agency and went to California to work on a movie. While I was out there, I produced and directed Edward's short plays, all four of them, over a two-year period. Till then I had never directed. When I came back to New York in 1963, Edward, Richard Barr and Clinton Wilder had just opened *Who's Afraid of Virginia Woolf* and were making a lot of money. So they formed the Playwrights' Unit which was to be down at the Cherry Lane Theatre. They made me its first managing director.

I didn't pick the playwrights, but there was everybody—from Lanford [Wilson] and Terrence McNally and John Guare to Megan Terry and Jean-Claude [van Itallie], the whole schmeer of new writers. I was in Washington, DC working on another movie at the time, getting ready to come to New York in September. It was in Washington that I began reading these plays and came across *Dutchman*. I'd heard of LeRoi Jones and knew his poetry during my years as a publisher. I was galvanized by his play and wanted to direct it for the Playwrights' Unit. I picked a date sometime in January of 1964 to do it. In the meantime, we started working at a theatre down on Vandamm Street when the Cherry Lane got booked with other plays.

I chose *Dutchman* not because it was revolutionary, which it was (I was a friend of Jimmy Baldwin for more than ten years, so I was aware of what was going on in the black movement and had been acquainted with lots of black actors. So it was a kind of gravitational pull); I chose it because I liked him as a writer. I never choose plays for propaganda purposes. I choose them for aesthetic reasons. I just found it was a wonderful play—very funny and very well-written and, of course, very revolutionary. It was going to be the first time anybody black had gotten on a stage and said, "This is how I really feel!"

I hired an actress I had known in California—but nobody in New York had ever heard of—named Jennifer West, because I knew she was exactly right for Lula. She'd come from the Midwest somewhere. I also knew a black actor out there named Al Freeman, Jr. who to me was one of the best actors around of *any* color. We rehearsed for two weeks. Roi wasn't around very much. He'd stop by now and then, but there was no interference.

Anyway, our workshop production was a last-minute scramble to put on. We took care of everything ourselves, including Lula's now-famous black- and white-striped dress. What a helluva time Jennifer and I had trying to find a summer dress for her in January in New York City. The one we found was made of wool, and even though it looked like summer to the audience, she died in it when she wore it on stage.

Now there was another play on the bill with an actor named Roscoe Lee Browne. There were a lot of extras in *Dutchman,* and not until the last day of rehearsals did I think what I was going to do about them. Then I grabbed people from the other play and made them the passengers in the subway. They had little rehearsal at all, rather off-the-cuff. But my two actors were terrific.

We did two opening performances: one at two o'clock and one at five in the afternoon. About forty-five minutes before the two-o'clock performance, Al said to me, "I can't do this play!" We got into this argument in the basement of the theatre. "I can't get up on that stage and say these things!" he kept insisting. He meant Clay's lengthy monologue. "What are you talking about?" I said. "It's the heart of the play!" One thing led to another, but he reluctantly got up and did it.

Roscoe had invited a lot of people to come to see *his* play. Among them were Leontyne Price and several other black artists. I had invited just a few friends. The other play, which was presented first, was a disaster. But when *Dutchman* came on, I didn't know how explosive it was going to be. It was like a trigger had been pulled. The audience started talking back to the stage. After the performance, several people said to me, "That's the first time I've ever been scared to death in the theatre." I guess they really thought somehow it was going to explode. At five o'clock, when we did the second performance, Mr. Barr, Mr. Wilder, and Mr. Albee were in the audience. The theatre blew up all over again. I can't describe it. It's something that happens to you once in a lifetime, when you do something you *think* is going to work and *does* work. It did, as it could happen only in New York. It was the talk of the town immediately. It was the first successful play in this series we did that whole year, by all these writers.

When they decided to produce the play Off-Broadway, Al opted out. Around the same time, Jimmy Baldwin had written *Blues for Mister Charlie*. So Al decided he wanted to be in Jimmy's play. He did it against my advice. The girl was all set, of course, but there was a scramble about who would replace Al. Then I began to audition and an actor named Bobby Lee Hooks appeared. We changed his name to Robert Hooks. He played Clay at our official Off-Broadway opening. And very well too!

Dutchman really galvanized the black theatre and the black community. Lorraine Hansberry's *A Raisin in the Sun* was a Broadway play and it was different. But this was really like revolution. John Kennedy had just been killed and everything was in turmoil. Hansberry's play was mainstream in a funny way and Jimmy's play [*Blues for Mister Charlie*] turned out to be a failure. But Roi had an instinct for the theatre, for the theatrical, because he was a poet. It won the Obie Award and established him immediately, put him on the map, I would say. In fact, it put a lot of us on the map. Then black theatre started to happen. Douglas Turner Ward opened his Negro Ensemble Company. I really credit all of this to Roi's play, not to me, but to *him*.

The play was entirely his. The one change that occurred was at the end. The stage direction indicates that a black conductor comes back at the end and says to a second young black man, "Hey, brother!" as though they have a connection. But I had no conductor. Roi wanted a black man to come back and say that the girl didn't win. But I told him it was already clear, that he was adding a political coda that really didn't work. The point is she goes on and on and on doing this. Nobody cares. Everybody knows she's really not going to win. But you know the cycle will be repeated. After all, Lula's the Flying Dutchman who goes on forever.

I was conscious of the literary parallels in the play but never paid much attention to them. There were hundreds of girls in New York in those days going with black guys. It was a common occurrence. So I played it like that—absolutely real all the way. The only thing that mattered was the writing. The play was so beautifully written that we didn't need to change a word.

Continued

I cast it very well, both times. But there's an interesting story about the play that concerns its language. After I cast it the first time and we were in rehearsals, Roi brought in an actress from the Actors Studio and asked me to let her read for the play. So I handed her a script. When she got on stage, she turned to me and asked, "You don't care if I don't use the words, do you?" I mean, a play by a *poet* that is *all* words. I said, "Yes, I mind very much!" Of course, Roi knew at once that the actress would not work out.

Once the play opened, everybody came to see it. A representative from a Berlin theatre festival happened to be in the audience one night and invited us to perform it there. Roi came with us. It turned out to be an international avant-garde festival where we shared one of the programs with a Czech production of *Ubu Roi*. The following summer, we were invited to the Spoleto Festival.

Almost thirty years later, when I produced 50/60 Vision at the Mark Taper and included *Dutchman* among the works presented, it was no longer 1964. The political times had changed. The whole reason for the festival was to see the seminal works of a period. These were the important plays that launched the theatre of the 1960s. But they weren't all American. I did Genet, Pinter, Ionesco, and of course, Beckett. The Americans were Albee and LeRoi Jones. Many years had passed and I wanted to see what they meant to audiences.

Every actor with even a minor name turned these plays down. They didn't want to be working in the theatre. They wanted to be working in movies and television. Lots of famous black actors turned down the role of Clay. When I eventually found the actors, they didn't know these plays, or how to act them, how to approach this kind of language. They wanted to improvise, to distort the plays or to make them something else. That's the fashion nowadays. The director is the important person, not the writer. So it was really uphill all the way. I understand that the situation is not much different in New York either. But our *audiences* at the Mark Taper were very interested and thought the plays were terrific.

Dutchman is still powerful, and certain elements in it can jolt the audience in performance. For example, Lula says something about a "wire," and Clay answers, "You must be Jewish. All you can think about is wire." Now there's a large Jewish audience in Los Angeles who go to the theatre and there was a kind of gasp because they thought it was anti-Semitic. In the 1960s, audiences weren't so sensitive. In the first place, it means concentration camp. At least that's the image you get immediately. It isn't an anti-Semitic remark in the context. But now everybody is so politically sensitive about the slightest *anything*. So there were a couple of moments like that where the dialogue was taken differently, where the political "correctness" was not the same. There was no political correctness in 1964. *Dutchman* happened in its moment, and is a document of its own time, mostly because it puts blacks into the New York theatre in a big way, I think. A lot came out of it. A lot.

Notes

1. THE CRISIS 37 (May 1930): 162.
2. "Anonymous in America," BOUNDARY 2 (Winter 1978): 434–35.
3. THE NEW YORK TIMES, 25 March 1964.
4. "The Dramatic Structure of DUTCHMAN," BLACK AMERICAN LITERATURE FORUM 17:1 (Spring 1983): 18.

DUTCHMAN
Amiri Baraka (LeRoi Jones)

CHARACTERS

Clay, *twenty-year-old Negro*
Lula, *thirty-year-old white woman*

Riders of Coach, *white and black*
Young Negro

Conductor

In the flying underbelly of the city. Steaming hot, and summer on top, outside. Underground. The subway heaped in modern myth.

Opening scene is a man sitting in a subway seat, holding a magazine but looking vacantly just above its wilting pages. Occasionally he looks blankly toward the window on his right. Dim lights and darkness whistling by against the glass. (Or paste the lights, as admitted props, right on the subway windows. Have them move, even dim and flicker. But give the sense of speed. Also stations, whether the train is stopped or the glitter and activity of these stations merely flashes by the windows.)

The man is sitting alone. That is, only his seat is visible, though the rest of the car is outfitted as a complete subway car. But only his seat is shown. There might be, for a time, as the play begins, a loud scream of the actual train. And it can recur throughout the play, or continue on a lower key once the dialogue starts.

The train slows after a time, pulling to a brief stop at one of the stations. The man looks idly up, until he sees a woman's face staring at him through the window; when it realizes that the man has noticed the face, it begins very premeditatedly to smile. The man smiles too, for a moment, without a trace of self-consciousness. Almost an instinctive though undesirable response. Then a kind of awkwardness or embarrassment sets in, and the man makes to look away, is further embarrassed, so he brings back his eyes to where the face was, but by now the train is moving again, and the face would seem to be left behind by the way the man turns his head to look back through the other windows at the slowly fading platform. He smiles then; more comfortably confident, hoping perhaps that his memory of this brief encounter will be pleasant. And then he is idle again.

SCENE ONE

Train roars. Lights flash outside the windows.

LULA *enters from the rear of the car in bright, skimpy summer clothes and sandals. She carries a net bag full of paper books, fruit, and other anonymous articles. She is wearing sunglasses, which she pushes up on her forehead from time to time.* LULA *is a tall, slender, beautiful woman with long red hair hanging straight down her back, wearing only loud lipstick in somebody's good taste. She is eating an apple, very daintily. Coming down the car toward* CLAY.

She stops beside CLAY's *seat and hangs languidly from the strap, still managing to eat the apple. It is apparent that she is going to sit in the seat next to* CLAY, *and that she is only waiting for him to notice her before she sits.*

CLAY *sits as before, looking just beyond his magazine, now and again pulling the magazine slowly back and forth in front of his face in a hopeless effort to fan himself. Then he sees the woman hanging there beside him and he looks up into her face, smiling quizzically.*

LULA. Hello.
CLAY. Uh, hi're you?
LULA. I'm going to sit down. . . . O.K.?
CLAY. Sure.
LULA (*swings down onto the seat, pushing her legs straight out as if she is very weary*). Oooof! Too much weight.
CLAY. Ha, doesn't look like much to me. (*Leaning back against the window, a little surprised and maybe stiff.*)
LULA. It's so anyway.

(*And she moves her toes in the sandals, then pulls her right leg up on the left knee, better to inspect the bottoms of the sandals and the back of her heel. She appears for a second not to notice that* CLAY *is sitting next to her or that she has spoken to him just a second before.* CLAY *looks at the magazine, then out the black window. As he does this, she turns very quickly toward him.*)

Weren't you staring at me through the window?

CLAY (*wheeling around and very much stiffened*). What?

LULA.   Weren't you staring at me through the window? At the last stop?

CLAY.   Staring at you? What do you mean?

LULA.   Don't you know what staring means?

CLAY.   I saw you through the window . . . if that's what it means. I don't know if I was staring. Seems to me you were staring through the window at me.

LULA.   I was. But only after I'd turned around and saw you staring through that window down in the vicinity of my ass and legs.

CLAY.   Really?

LULA.   Really. I guess you were just taking those idle potshots. Nothing else to do. Run your mind over people's flesh.

CLAY.   Oh boy. Wow, now I admit I was looking in your direction. But the rest of that weight is yours.

LULA.   I suppose.

CLAY.   Staring through train windows is weird business. Much weirder than staring very sedately at abstract asses.

LULA.   That's why I came looking through the window . . . so you'd have more than that to go on. I even smiled at you.

CLAY.   That's right.

LULA.   I even got into this train, going some other way than mine. Walked down the aisle . . . searching you out.

CLAY.   Really? That's pretty funny.

LULA.   That's pretty funny. . . . God, you're dull.

CLAY.   Well, I'm sorry, lady, but I really wasn't prepared for party talk.

LULA.   No, you're not. What are you prepared for? (*Wrapping the apple core in a Kleenex and dropping it on the floor.*)

CLAY (*takes her conversation as pure sex talk. He turns to confront her squarely with this idea*). I'm prepared for anything. How about you?

LULA (*laughing loudly and cutting it off abruptly*). What do you think you're doing?

CLAY.   What?

LULA.   You think I want to pick you up, get you to take me somewhere and screw me, huh?

CLAY.   Is that the way I look?

LULA.   You look like you been trying to grow a beard. That's exactly what you look like. You look like you live in New Jersey with your parents and are trying to grow a beard. That's what. You look like you've been reading Chinese poetry and drinking lukewarm sugarless tea. (*Laughs, uncrossing and recrossing her legs.*) You look like death eating a soda cracker.

CLAY (*cocking his head from one side to the other, embarrassed and trying to make some comeback, but also intrigued by what the woman is saying . . . even the sharp city coarseness of her voice, which is still a kind of gentle sidewalk throb*). Really? I look like all that?

LULA.   Not all of it. (*She feints a seriousness to cover an actual somber tone.*) I lie a lot. (*Smiling.*) It helps me control the world.

CLAY (*relieved and laughing louder than the humor*). Yeah, I bet.

LULA.   But it's true, most of it, right? Jersey? Your bumpy neck?

CLAY.   How'd you know all that? Huh? Really, I mean about Jersey . . . and even the beard. I met you before? You know Warren Enright?

LULA.   You tried to make it with your sister when you were ten. (CLAY *leans back hard against the back of the seat, his eyes opening now, still trying to look amused.*) But I succeeded a few weeks ago. (*She starts to laugh again.*)

CLAY.   What're you talking about? Warren tell you that? You're a friend of Georgia's?

LULA.   I told you I lie. I don't know your sister. I don't know Warren Enright.

CLAY.   You mean you're just picking these things out of the air?

LULA.   Is Warren Enright a tall skinny black black boy with a phony English accent?

CLAY.   I figured you knew him.

LULA.   But I don't. I just figured you would know somebody like that. (*Laughs.*)

CLAY.   Yeah, yeah.

LULA.   You're probably on your way to his house now.

CLAY.   That's right.

LULA (*putting her hand on Clay's closest knee, drawing it from the knee up to the thigh's hinge, then removing it, watching his face very closely, and continuing to laugh, perhaps more gently than before*). Dull, dull, dull. I bet you think I'm exciting.

CLAY.   You're O.K.

LULA.   Am I exciting you now?

CLAY.   Right. That's not what's supposed to happen?

LULA.   How do I know? (*She returns her hand, without moving it, then takes it away and plunges it in her bag to draw out an apple.*) You want this?

CLAY.   Sure.

LULA (*she gets one out of the bag for herself*). Eating apples together is always the first step. Or walking up uninhabited Seventh Avenue in the twenties on weekends. (*Bites and giggles, glancing at Clay and speaking in loose sing-song.*) Can get you involved . . . boy! Get us involved. Um-huh. (*Mock seriousness.*) Would you like to get involved with me, Mister Man?

CLAY (*trying to be as flippant as Lula, whacking happily at the apple*). Sure. Why not? A beautiful woman like you. Huh, I'd be a fool not to.

LULA. And I bet you're sure you know what you're talking about. (*Taking him a little roughly by the wrist, so he cannot eat the apple, then shaking the wrist.*) I bet you're sure of almost everything anybody ever asked you about . . . right? (*Shakes his wrist harder*). Right?

CLAY. Yeah, right. . . . Wow, you're pretty strong, you know? Whatta you, a lady wrestler or something?

LULA. What's wrong with lady wrestlers? And don't answer because you never knew any. Huh. (*Cynically.*) That's for sure. They don't have any lady wrestlers in that part of Jersey. That's for sure.

CLAY. Hey, you still haven't told me how you know so much about me.

LULA. I told you I didn't know anything about *you* . . . you're a well-known type.

CLAY. Really?

LULA. Or at least I know the type very well. And your skinny English friend too.

CLAY. Anonymously?

LULA (*settles back in seat, single-mindedly finishing her apple and humming snatches of rhythm and blues song*). What?

CLAY. Without knowing us specifically?

LULA. Oh boy. (*Looking quickly at Clay.*) What a face. You know, you could be a handsome man.

CLAY. I can't argue with you.

LULA (*vague, off-center response*). What?

CLAY (*raising his voice, thinking the train noise has drowned part of his sentence*). I can't argue with you.

LULA. My hair is turning gray. A gray hair for each year and type I've come through.

CLAY. Why do you want to sound so old?

LULA. But it's always gentle when it starts. (*Attention drifting.*) Hugged against tenements, day or night.

CLAY. What?

LULA (*refocusing*). Hey, why don't you take me to that party you're going to?

CLAY. You must be a friend of Warren's to know about the party.

LULA. Wouldn't you like to take me to the party? (*Imitates clinging vine.*) Oh, come on, ask me to your party.

CLAY. Of course I'll ask you to come with me to the party. And I'll bet you're a friend of Warren's.

LULA. Why not be a friend of Warren's? Why not? (*Taking his arm.*) Have you asked me yet?

CLAY. How can I ask you when I don't know your name?

LULA. Are you talking to my name?

CLAY. What is it, a secret?

LULA. I'm Lena the Hyena.

CLAY. The famous woman poet?

LULA. Poetess! The same!

CLAY. Well, you know so much about me . . . what's my name?

LULA. Morris the Hyena.

CLAY. The famous woman poet?

LULA. The same. (*Laughing and going into her bag.*) You want another apple?

CLAY. Can't make it, lady. I only have to keep one doctor away a day.

LULA. I bet your name is . . . something like . . . uh, Gerald or Walter. Huh?

CLAY. God, no.

LULA. Lloyd, Norman? One of those hopeless colored names creeping out of New Jersey? Leonard? Gag. . . .

CLAY. Like Warren?

LULA. Definitely. Just exactly like Warren. Or Everett.

CLAY. Gag. . . .

LULA. Well, for sure, it's not Willie.

CLAY. It's Clay.

LULA. Clay? Really? Clay what?

CLAY. Take your pick. Jackson, Johnson, or Williams.

LULA. Oh, really? Good for you. But it's got to be Williams. You're too pretentious to be a Jackson or Johnson.

CLAY. Thass right.

LULA. But Clay's O.K.

CLAY. So's Lena.

LULA. It's Lula.

CLAY. Oh?

LULA. Lula the Hyena.

CLAY. Very good.

LULA (*starts laughing again*). Now you say to me, "Lula, Lula, why don't you go to this party with me tonight?" It's your turn, and let those be your lines.

CLAY. Lula, why don't you go to this party with me tonight, Huh?

LULA. Say my name twice before you ask, and no huh's.

CLAY. Lula, Lula, why don't you go to this party with me tonight?

LULA. I'd like to go, Clay, but how can you ask me to go when you barely know me?

CLAY. That is strange, isn't it?

LULA. What kind of reaction is that? You're supposed to say, "Aw, come on, we'll get to know each other better at the party."

CLAY. That's pretty corny.

LULA. What are you into anyway? (*Looking at him half sullenly but still amused.*) What thing are you playing at, Mister? Mister Clay Williams? (*Grabs his thigh, up near the crotch.*) What are *you* thinking about?

CLAY. Watch it now, you're gonna excite me for real.

LULA (*taking her hand away and throwing her apple core through the window*). I bet. (*She slumps in the seat and is heavily silent.*)

CLAY. I thought you knew everything about me? What happened?

(LULA *looks at him, then looks slowly away, then over where the other aisle would be. Noise of the train. She reaches in her bag and pulls out one of the paper books. She puts it on her leg and thumbs the pages listlessly.* Clay *cocks his head to see the title of the book. Noise of the train.* Lula *flips pages and her eyes drift. Both remain silent.*)

Are you going to the party with me, Lula?

Lula (*bored and not even looking*). I don't even know you.

Clay.   You said you know my type.

Lula (*strangely irritated*). Don't get smart with me, Buster. I know you like the palm of my hand.

Clay.   The one you eat the apples with?

Lula.   Yeh. And the one I open doors late Saturday evening with. That's my door. Up at the top of the stairs. Five flights. Above a lot of Italians and lying Americans. And scrape carrots with. Also . . . (*Looks at him.*) the same hand I unbutton my dress with, or let my skirt fall down. Same hand. Lover.

Clay.   Are you angry about anything? Did I say something wrong?

Lula.   Everything you say is wrong. (*Mock smile.*) That's what makes you so attractive. Ha. In that funnybook jacket with all the buttons. (*More animate, taking hold of his jacket.*) What've you got that jacket and tie on in all this heat for? And why're you wearing a jacket and tie like that? Did your people ever burn witches or start revolutions over the price of tea? Boy, those narrow-shoulder clothes come from a tradition you ought to feel oppressed by. A three-button suit. What right do you have to be wearing a three-button suit and striped tie? Your grandfather was a slave, he didn't go to Harvard.

Clay.   My grandfather was a night watchman.

Lula.   And you went to a colored college where everybody thought they were Averell Harriman.

Clay.   All except me.

Lula.   And who did you think you were? Who do you think you are now?

Clay (*laughs as if to make light of the whole trend of the conversation*). Well, in college I thought I was Baudelaire. But I've slowed down since.

Lula.   I bet you never once thought you were a black nigger.

(*Mock serious, then she howls with laughter.* Clay *is stunned but after initial reaction, he quickly tries to appreciate the humor.* Lula *almost shrieks.*)

A black Baudelaire.

Clay.   That's right.

Lula.   Boy, are you corny. I take back what I said before. Everything you say is not wrong. It's perfect. You should be on television.

Clay.   You act like you're on television already.

Lula.   That's because I'm an actress.

Clay.   I thought so.

Lula.   Well, you're wrong. I'm no actress. I told you I always lie. I'm nothing, honey, and don't you ever forget it. (*Lighter.*) Although my mother was a Communist. The only person in my family ever to amount to anything.

Clay.   My mother was a Republican.

Lula.   And your father voted for the man rather than the party.

Clay.   Right!

Lula.   Yea for him. Yea, yea for him.

Clay.   Yea!

Lula.   And yea for America where he is free to vote for the mediocrity of his choice! Yea!

Clay.   Yea!

Lula.   And yea for both your parents who even though they differ about so crucial a matter as the body politic still forged a union of love and sacrifice that was destined to flower at the birth of the noble Clay . . . what's your middle name?

Clay.   Clay.

Lula.   A union of love and sacrifice that was destined to flower at the birth of the noble Clay Clay Williams. Yea! And most of all yea yea for you, Clay Clay. The Black Baudelaire! Yes! (*And with knifelike cynicism.*) My Christ. My Christ.

Clay.   Thank you, ma'am.

Lula.   May the people accept you as a ghost of the future. And love you, that you might not kill them when you can.

Clay.   What?

Lula.   You're a murderer, Clay, and you know it. (*Her voice darkening with significance.*) You know goddam well what I mean.

Clay.   I do?

Lula.   So we'll pretend the air is light and full of perfume.

Clay (*sniffing at her blouse*). It is.

Lula.   And we'll pretend the people cannot see you. That is, the citizens. And that you are free of your own history. And I am free of my history. We'll pretend that we are both anonymous beauties smashing along through the city's entrails. (*She yells as loud as she can.*) GROOVE!

Black

Scene Two

Scene is the same as before, though now there are other seats visible in the car. And throughout the scene other people get on the subway. There are maybe one or two seated in the car as the scene opens, though neither Clay *nor* Lula *notices them.* Clay's *tie is open.* Lula *is hugging his arm.*

Clay.   The party!

Lula.   I know it'll be something good. You can come in with me, looking casual and significant. I'll be strange, haughty, and silent, and walk with long slow strides.

Clay.   Right.

Lula.   When you get drunk, pat me once, very lovingly on the flanks, and I'll look at you cryptically, licking my lips.

CLAY.   It sounds like something we can do.

LULA.   You'll go around talking to young men about your mind, and to old men about your plans. If you meet a very close friend who is also with someone like me, we can stand together, sipping our drinks and exchanging codes of lust. The atmosphere will be slithering in love and half-love and very open moral decision.

CLAY.   Great. Great.

LULA.   And everyone will pretend they don't know your name, and then . . . (*She pauses heavily.*) later, when they have to, they'll claim a friendship that denies your sterling character.

CLAY (*kissing her neck and fingers*). And then what?

LULA.   Then? Well, then we'll go down the street, late night, eating apples and winding very deliberately toward my house.

CLAY.   Deliberately?

LULA.   I mean, we'll look in all the shopwindows, and make fun of the queers. Maybe we'll meet a Jewish Buddhist and flatten his conceits over some very pretentious coffee.

CLAY.   In honor of whose God?

LULA.   Mine.

CLAY.   Who is . . . ?

LULA.   Me . . . and you?

CLAY.   A corporate Godhead.

LULA.   Exactly. Exactly. (*Notices one of the other people entering.*)

CLAY.   Go on with the chronicle. Then what happens to us?

LULA (*a mild depression, but she still makes her description triumphant and increasingly direct*). To my house, of course.

CLAY.   Of course.

LULA.   And up the narrow steps of the tenement.

CLAY.   You live in a tenement?

LULA.   Wouldn't live anywhere else. Reminds me specifically of my novel form of insanity.

CLAY.   Up the tenement stairs.

LULA.   And with my apple-eating hand I push open the door and lead you, my tender big-eyed prey, into my . . . God, what can I call it . . . into my hovel.

CLAY.   Then what happens?

LULA.   After the dancing and games, after the long drinks and long walks, the real fun begins.

CLAY.   Ah, the real fun. (*Embarrassed, in spite of himself.*) Which is . . . ?

LULA (*laughs at him*). Real fun in the dark house. Hah! Real fun in the dark house, high up above the street and the ignorant cowboys. I lead you in, holding your wet hand gently in my hand . . .

CLAY.   Which is not wet?

LULA.   Which is dry as ashes.

CLAY.   And cold?

LULA.   Don't think you'll get out of your responsibility that way. It's not cold at all. You Fascist! Into my dark living room. Where we'll sit and talk endlessly, endlessly.

CLAY.   About what?

LULA.   About what? About your manhood, what do you think? What do you think we've been talking about all this time?

CLAY.   Well, I didn't know it was that. That's for sure. Every other thing in the world but that. (*Notices another person entering, looks quickly, almost involuntarily up and down the car, seeing the other people in the car.*) Hey, I didn't even notice when those people got on.

LULA.   Yeah, I know.

CLAY.   Man, this subway is slow.

LULA.   Yeah, I know.

CLAY.   Well, go on. We were talking about my manhood.

LULA.   We still are. All the time.

CLAY.   We were in your living room.

LULA.   My dark living room. Talking endlessly.

CLAY.   About my manhood.

LULA.   I'll make you a map of it. Just as soon as we get to my house.

CLAY.   Well, that's great.

LULA.   One of the things we do while we talk. And screw.

CLAY (*trying to make his smile broader and less shaky*). We finally got there.

LULA.   And you'll call my rooms black as a grave. You'll say, "This place is like Juliet's tomb."

CLAY (*laughs*). I might.

LULA.   I know. You've probably said it before.

CLAY.   And is that all? The whole grand tour?

LULA.   Not all. You'll say to me very close to my face, many, many times, you'll say, even whisper, that you love me.

CLAY.   Maybe I will.

LULA.   And you'll be lying.

CLAY.   I wouldn't lie about something like that.

LULA.   Hah. It's the only kind of thing you will lie about. Especially if you think it'll keep me alive.

CLAY.   Keep you alive? I don't understand.

LULA (*bursting out laughing, but too shrilly*). Don't understand? Well, don't look at me. It's the path I take, that's all. Where both feet take me when I set them down. One in front of the other.

CLAY.   Morbid. Morbid. You sure you're not an actress? All that self-aggrandizement.

LULA.   Well, I told you I wasn't an actress . . . but I also told you I lie all the time. Draw your own conclusions.

CLAY.   Morbid. Morbid. You sure you're not an actress? All scribed? There's no more?

LULA.   I've told you all I know. Or almost all.

CLAY.   There's no funny parts?

LULA.   I thought it was all funny.

CLAY.   But you mean peculiar, not ha-ha.

LULA.   You don't know what I mean.

CLAY.   Well, tell me the almost part then. You said almost all. What else? I want the whole story.

LULA (*searching aimlessly through her bag. She begins to talk breathlessly, with a light and silly tone*). All stories are whole stories. All of 'em. Our whole story . . . nothing but change. How could things go on like that forever? Huh? (*Slaps him on the shoulder, begins finding things in her bag, taking them out and throwing them over her shoulder into the aisle.*) Except I do go on as I do. Apples and long walks with deathless intelligent lovers. But you mix it up. Look out the window, all the time. Turning pages. Change change change. Till, shit, I don't know you. Wouldn't, for that matter. You're too serious. I bet you're even too serious to be psychoanalyzed. Like all those Jewish poets from Yonkers, who leave their mothers looking for other mothers, or others' mothers, on whose baggy tits they lay their fumbling heads. Their poems are always funny, and all about sex.

CLAY.   They sound great. Like movies.

LULA.   But you change. (*Blankly.*) And things work on you till you hate them.

(*More people come into the train. They come closer to the couple, some of them not sitting, but swinging drearily on the straps, staring at the two with uncertain interest.*)

CLAY.   Wow. All these people, so suddenly. They must all come from the same place.

LULA.   Right. That they do.

CLAY.   Oh? You know about them too?

LULA.   Oh yeah. About them more than I know about you. Do they frighten you?

CLAY.   Frighten me? Why should they frighten me?

LULA.   'Cause you're an escaped nigger.

CLAY.   Yeah?

LULA.   'Cause you crawled through the wire and made tracks to my side.

CLAY.   Wire?

LULA.   Don't they have wire around plantations?

CLAY.   You must be Jewish. All you can think about is wire. Plantations didn't have any wire. Plantations were big open whitewashed places like heaven, and everybody on 'em was grooved to be there. Just strummin' and hummin' all day.

LULA.   Yes, yes.

CLAY.   And that's how the blues was born.

LULA.   Yes, yes. And that's how the blues was born.

(*Begins to make up a song that becomes quickly hysterical. As she sings she rises from her seat, still throwing things out of her bag into the aisle, beginning a rhythmical shudder and twistlike wiggle, which she continues up and down the aisle, bumping into many of the standing people and tripping over the feet of those sitting. Each time she runs into a person she lets out a very vicious piece of profanity, wiggling and stepping all the time.*)

And that's how the blues was born. Yes. Yes. Son of a bitch, get out of the way. Yes. Quack. Yes. Yes. And that's how the blues was born. Ten little niggers sitting on a limb, but none of them ever looked like him. (*Points to* CLAY, *returns toward the seat, with her hands extended for him to rise and dance with her.*) And that's how blues was born. Yes. Come on, Clay. Let's do the nasty. Rub bellies. Rub bellies.

CLAY (*waves his hands to refuse. He is embarrassed, but determined to get a kick out of the proceedings*). Hey, what was in those apples? Mirror, mirror on the wall, who's the fairest one of all? Snow White, baby, and don't you forget it.

LULA (*grabbing for his hands, which he draws away*). Come on, Clay. Let's rub bellies on the train. The nasty. The nasty. Do the gritty grind, like your ol' rag-head mammy. Grind till you lose your mind. Shake it, shake it, shake it, shake it! OOOOweeee! Come on, Clay. Let's do the choo-choo train shuffle, the navel scratcher.

CLAY.   Hey, you coming on like the lady who smoked up her grass skirt.

LULA (*becoming annoyed that he will not dance, and becoming more animated as if to embarrass him still further*). Come on, Clay . . . let's do the thing. Uhh! Uhh! Clay! Clay! You middle-class black bastard. Forget your social-working mother for a few seconds and let's knock stomachs. Clay, you liver-lipped white man. You would-be Christian. You ain't no nigger, you're just a dirty white man. Get up, Clay. Dance with me, Clay.

CLAY.   Lula! Sit down, now. Be cool.

LULA (*mocking him, in wild dance*). Be cool. Be cool. That's all you know . . . shaking that wildroot cream-oil on your knotty head, jackets buttoning up to your chin, so full of white man's words. Christ. God. Get up and scream at these people. Like scream meaningless shit in these hopeless faces. (*She screams at people in train, still dancing.*) Red trains cough Jewish underwear for keeps! Expanding smells of silence. Gravy snot whistling like sea birds. Clay. Clay, you got to break out. Don't sit there dying the way they want you to die. Get up.

CLAY.   Oh, sit the fuck down. (*He moves to restrain her.*) Sit down, goddamn it.

LULA (*twisting out of his reach*). Screw yourself, Uncle Tom. Thomas Woolly-head. (*Begins to dance a kind of jig, mocking Clay with loud forced humor.*) There is Uncle Tom . . . I mean, Uncle Thomas Woolly-Head. With old white matted mane. He hobbles on his wooden cane. Old Tom. Old Tom. Let the white man hump his ol' mama, and he jes' shuffle off in the woods and hide his gentle gray head. Ol' Thomas Woolly-Head.

(*Some of the other riders are laughing now. A drunk gets up and joins* LULA *in her dance, singing, as best he can, her "song."* CLAY *gets up out of his seat and visibly scans the faces of the other riders.*)

CLAY.   Lula! Lula! (*She is dancing and turning, still shouting as loud as she can. The drunk too is shouting, and waving his hands wildly.*) Lula . . . you dumb bitch. Why don't you stop it? (*He rushes half stumbling from his seat, and grabs one of her flailing arms.*)

LULA.   Let me go! You black son of a bitch. (*She struggles against him.*) Let me go! Help!

(CLAY *is dragging her towards her seat, and the drunk seeks to interfere. He grabs* CLAY *around the shoulders and begins wrestling with him.* CLAY *clubs the drunk to the floor without releasing* LULA, *who is still screaming.* CLAY *finally gets her to the seat and throws her into it.*)

CLAY.   Now you shut the hell up. (*Grabbing her shoulders.*) Just shut up. You don't know what you're talking about. You don't know anything. So just keep your stupid mouth closed.

LULA.   You're afraid of white people. And your father was. Uncle Tom Big Lip!

CLAY (*slaps her as hard as he can, across the mouth.* LULA's *head bangs against the back of the seat. When she raises it again,* CLAY *slaps her again*). Now shut up and let me talk.

(*He turns toward the other riders, some of whom are sitting on the edge of their seats. The drunk is on one knee, rubbing his head, and singing softly the same song. He shuts up too when he sees* CLAY *watching him. The others go back to newspapers or stare out the windows.*)

Shit, you don't have any sense, Lula, nor feelings either. I could murder you now. Such a tiny ugly throat. I could squeeze it flat, and watch you turn blue, on a humble. For dull kicks. And all these weak-faced ofays squatting around here, staring over their papers at me. Murder them too. Even if they expected it. That man there . . . (*Points to well-dressed man.*) I could rip that *Times* right out of his hand, as skinny and middle-classed as I am, I could rip that paper out of his hand and just as easily rip out his throat. It takes no great effort. For what? To kill you soft idiots? You don't understand anything but luxury.

LULA.   You fool!

CLAY (*pushing her against the seat*). I'm not telling you again, Tallulah Bankhead! Luxury. In your face and your fingers. You telling me what I ought to do. (*Sudden scream frightening the whole coach.*) Well, don't! Don't you tell me anything! If I'm a middle-class fake white man . . . let me be. And let me be in the way I want. (*Through his teeth.*) I'll rip your lousy breasts off! Let me be who I feel like being. Uncle Tom. Thomas. Whoever. It's none of your business. You don't know anything except what's there for you to see. An act. Lies. Device. Not the pure heart, the pumping black heart. You don't ever know that. And I sit here, in this buttoned-up suit, to keep myself from cutting all your throats. I mean wantonly. You great liberated whore! You fuck some black man, and right away you're an expert on black people.

What a lotta shit that is. The only thing you know is that you come if he bangs you hard enough. And that's all. The belly rub? You wanted to do the belly rub? Shit, you don't even know how. You don't know how. That ol' dipty-dip shit you do, rolling your ass like an elephant. That's not my kind of belly rub. Belly rub is not Queens. Belly rub is dark places, with big hats and overcoats held up with one arm. Belly rub hates you. Old bald-headed four-eyed offays popping their fingers . . . and don't know yet what they're doing. They say, "I love Bessie Smith." And don't even understand that Bessie Smith is saying, "Kiss my ass, kiss my black unruly ass." Before love, suffering, desire, anything you can explain, she's saying, and very plainly, "Kiss my black ass." And if you don't know that, it's you that's doing the kissing.

Charlie Parker? Charlie Parker. All the hip white boys scream for Bird. And Bird saying, "Up your ass, feeble-minded ofay! Up your ass." And they sit there talking about the tortured genius of Charlie Parker. Bird would've played not a note of music if he just walked up to East Sixty-seventh Street and killed the first ten white people he saw. Not a note! And I'm the great would-be poet. Yes. That's right! Poet. Some kind of bastard literature . . . all it needs is a simple knife thrust. Just let me bleed you, you loud whore, and one poem vanished. A whole people of neurotics, struggling to keep from being sane. And the only thing that would cure the neurosis would be your murder. Simple as that. I mean if I murdered you, then other white people would begin to understand me. You understand? No. I guess not. If Bessie Smith had killed some white people she wouldn't have needed that music. She could have talked very straight and plain about the world. No metaphors. No grunts. No wiggles in the dark of her soul. Just straight two and two are four. Money. Power. Luxury. Like that. All of them. Crazy niggers turning their backs on sanity. When all it needs is that simple act. Murder. Just murder! Would make us all sane. (*Suddenly weary.*) Ahhh. Shit. But who needs it? I'd rather be a fool. Insane. Safe with my words, and no deaths, and clean, hard thoughts, urging me to new conquests. My people's madness. Hah! That's a laugh. My people. They don't need me to claim them. They got legs and arms of their own. Personal insanities. Mirrors. They don't need all those words. They don't need any defense. But listen, though, one more thing. And you tell this to your father, who's probably the kind of man who needs to know at once. So he can plan ahead. Tell him not to preach so much rationalism and cold logic to these niggers. Let them alone. Let them sing curses at you in code and see your filth as simple lack of style. Don't make the mistake, through some irresponsible surge of Christian charity, of talking too much about the advantages of Western rationalism, or the great intellectual legacy of the white man, or maybe they'll begin to listen.

And then, maybe one day, you'll find they actually do understand exactly what you are talking about, all these fantasy people. All these blues people.. And on that day, as sure as shit, when you really believe you can ''accept'' them into your fold, as half-white trusties late of the subject peoples. With no more blues, except the very old ones, and not a watermelon in sight, the great missionary heart will have triumphed, and all of those ex-coons will be stand-up Western men, with eyes for clean hard useful lives, sober, pious and sane, and they'll murder you. They'll murder you, and have very rational explanations. Very much like your own. They'll cut your throats, and drag you out to the edge of your cities so the flesh can fall away from your bones, in sanitary isolation.

LULA (*her voice takes on a different, more businesslike quality*). I've heard enough.

CLAY (*reaching for his books*). I bet you have. I guess I better collect my stuff and get off this train. Looks like we won't be acting out that little pageant you outlined before.

LULA.   No. We won't. You're right about that, at least. (*She turns to look quickly around the rest of the car.*) All right! (*The others respond.*)

CLAY (*bending across the girl to retrieve his belongings*). Sorry, baby, I don't think we could make it.

(*As he is bending over her, the girl brings up a small knife and plunges it into CLAY's chest. Twice. He slumps across her knees, his mouth working stupidly.*)

LULA.   Sorry is right. (*Turning to the others in the car who have already gotten up from their seats.*) Sorry is the rightest thing you've said. Get this man off me! Hurry, now! (*The others come and drag CLAY's body down the aisle.*) Open the door and throw his body out. (*They throw him off.*) And all of you get off at the next stop.

(*LULA busies herself straightening her things. Getting everything in order. She takes out a notebook and makes a quick scribbling note. Drops it in her bag. The train apparently stops and all the others get off, leaving her alone in the coach.*

Very soon a young Negro of about twenty comes into the coach, with a couple of books under his arm. He sits a few seats in back of LULA. When he is seated she turns and gives him a long slow look. He looks up from his book and drops the book on his lap. Then an old Negro conductor comes into the car, doing a sort of restrained soft shoe, and half mumbling the words of some song. He looks at the young man, briefly, with a quick greeting.)

CONDUCTOR.   Hey, brother!
YOUNG MAN.   Hey.

(*The conductor continues down the aisle with his little dance and the mumbled song. LULA turns to stare at him and follows his movements down the aisle. The conductor tips his hat when he reaches her seat, and continues out the car.*)

CURTAIN

FOCUS QUESTIONS

1. Assuming the play title is an allusion to the Flying Dutchman myth, analyze Lula's behaviors and reactions that show she is searching for the ideal mate.
2. Lula's view of Clay's middle-class aspirations is often cited as an astute evaluation of the dilemma inherent for educated African Americans. Outline the major points of her critique and discuss what they reveal about her negative attitudes about America, and how those attitudes make her shortsighted with respect to Clay.
3. In an essay that analyzes Clay's important monologue, discuss why he has made the choice to be a Eurocentric poet rather than an Afrocentric rebel.
4. Using the subway as a metaphor, discuss Baraka's themes about growing up male and black in America today.

OTHER ACTIVITIES

1. Construct a narrative that describes Lula's life before she meets Clay on the train.
2. Take the perspective of one of the passengers in the subway car and write a monologue that expresses his or her thoughts witnessing the interchange between Lula and Clay.

BIBLIOGRAPHY

Benston, Kimberly W. *Baraka: The Renegade and the Mask.* New Haven: Yale University Press, 1976.

———, ed. *Imamu Amiri Baraka (LeRoi Jones): A Collection of Critical Essays.* Englewood Cliffs, NJ: Prentice-Hall, 1978.

Bigsby, C. W. E., ed. *The Black American Writer.* 2 vols. Baltimore: Penguin Books, 1969.

———. *Confrontation and Commitment: A Study of Contemporary American Drama, 1959–1966.* Columbia: University of Missouri Press, 1968.

———. *The Second Black Renaissance: Essays in Black Literature.* Westport, CT: Greenwood Press, 1980.

Brown, Lloyd W. *Amiri Baraka.* New York: Twayne Publishers, 1980.

Gayle, Addison., ed. *Black Expression: Essays by and About Black Americans in the Creative Arts.* New York: Weybright and Talley, 1969.

Gibson, Donald, ed. *Five Black Writers: Essays on Wright, Ellison, Baldwin, Hughes and LeRoi Jones.* New York: New York University Press, 1970.

Hudson, Theodore. *From LeRoi Jones to Amiri Baraka: The Literary Works.* Durham, NC: Duke University Press, 1973.

Jones, LeRoi. *Home.* New York: Morrow Publishing Co., 1966.

Lacey, Henry C. *To Raise, Destroy and Create: The Poetry, Drama and Fiction of Imamu Amiri Baraka (LeRoi Jones).* Troy, NY: Whitson Publishing Company, 1981.

Little, John David. *Black on White: A Critical Survey of Writing by American Negroes.* New York: Viking Press, 1966.

Sollors, Werner. *Amiri Baraka/LeRoi Jones: The Quest for a "Populist Modernism."* New York: Columbia University Press, 1978.

Weales, Gerald. *The Jumping Off Place: American Drama in the 1960s.* New York: Macmillan, 1969.

RECOMMENDED VIDEOTAPE

Dutchman. VHS. 55 min. (1967). Starring Al Freeman and Shirley Knight. Distributed by Insight Media, New York City.

WINE IN THE WILDERNESS
ALICE CHILDRESS (1920–1994)

One gets the feeling that Childress loves the people she writes about. Love of life and people, accent on struggle, humor as a cultural weapon . . . These are the hallmarks of her craft, of her artistry; these, like a trademark or a fingerprint.

—JOHN O. KILLENS

APPROACHING BLACK FEMINIST THEATRE

As early as the founding of the NAACP and the appearance of its newsmagazine *Crisis* in 1910, African-American playwrights entered writing contests and saw their works published. These scripts were eventually produced in community theatres, churches, meeting halls, schools, and libraries throughout the urban ghettoes of New York, Washington, DC, Cleveland, and Chicago. In contrast with highly successful musicals like *Shuffle Along* by Aubrey Lyles, Flournoy Miller, Eubie Blake, and Noble Sissle, which were brought from Harlem to Broadway for the enjoyment of white audiences, these were serious plays of social protest, celebrations of folk culture, and depictions of black historical or mythological figures.

By 1917, there was a movement in American drama to create a folk idiom around the southern and urban black experience. White playwrights Ridgely Torrence, Paul Green, DuBose and Dorothy Heywood, and Eugene O'Neill created an audience for the exotic and primitive black characters whose struggles with poverty and nature they depicted on the stage. In 1926, impelled by the success of these plays by white authors, the Krigwa Players of Harlem called for black writers to seize ownership of this genre and produce their own truthful images of black life. Wallace Thurman, Hall Johnson, and Langston Hughes responded with plays that were produced on Broadway at the height of the Harlem Renaissance when the novels, stories, and musical and dance works created in Harlem were enjoying great popular acclaim.

Choosing **realism** as a way to represent the black experience on stage, these playwrights eschewed the black stereotypes that white authors had invented for the melodramas and folk plays of the nineteenth and early twentieth centuries. Their ''slices of life'' promoted an authentic folk culture with characters drawn from firsthand observations of local neighborhoods. Besides transforming the image of blacks on stage, they also wrote problem plays in the tradition of predecessors like Ibsen and Shaw, which focused on social injustices in America.

Contributing to this movement were nine women playwrights: Angelina Weld Grimke, Alice Dunbar-Nelson, Georgia Douglas Johnson, May Miller, Mary Burrill, Myrtle

Smith Livingston, Ruth Gaines-Shelton, Eulalie Spence, and Marita Bonner. Many were graduates of Howard University and had submitted one-act plays to *Crisis* and *Opportunity* magazines. Like their male counterparts, they wrote historical plays to educate young people as well as protest plays to give credence to the struggle facing blacks in America. They saw the importance of creating works that dealt with specific rather than universal themes. But while these artists were human beings above everything else, they were also black and female. Thus their dramas focused on issues of particular relevance to black women: miscegenation with its taint of white men's exploitation of their bodies; lynching, which threatened their husbands and sons; the endless cycle of poverty exacerbated by the lack of birth control information; and the injustice of black men fighting and often dying in foreign wars for the same freedoms denied them at home.

Although many of these plays were deemed too controversial or propagandistic for commercial production, some of them extended human rights issues to include the middle-class snobbery within the black community and the unfair treatment of black women by their lovers and husbands. Exposing the black community's foibles and injustices to public scrutiny, these dramas were tantamount to heresy. As a result, these women were over-shadowed by their male colleagues and almost forgotten by the end of the Depression, despite the fact that they taught the craft of playwriting to others and provided havens for young, aspiring black intellectuals of New York and Washington, DC.

Their mission to portray the black woman's experience as truthfully as possible was taken up again in the 1950s by Alice Childress. A young aspiring actor with the American Negro Theatre, a company dedicated to promoting the acting profession among black artists, Childress decried the fact that the only stage roles being written for black actresses were hard-working matriarchs, maids, and prostitutes. Setting out to write and direct her own plays and to expand the availability of realistic stage characters, she wrote *Florence* (1949), whose theme—the aspirations of young black women—emerges from the dramatic confrontation between a rich, white, self-styled liberal and a black woman whose daughter struggles to make a living in the theatre. Childress would later explore the impact of racism on a black actress in her Obie Award-winning play, *Trouble in Mind* (1955).

Like the black women playwrights who preceded her, Childress also found poetry in the lives of ordinary black people who were twice denied by race and class differences yet often "[came] through such experiences with [their] head[s] up, ready for the next round."[1] Unlike her predecessors, she had been forced to drop out of high school when she was orphaned, but supported herself with odd jobs and met all types of working-class people who left their indelible mark on her. When she began to write about the poor and disenfranchised, she was guided by a wealth of shared experiences. Thus her purpose in writing was "to explain pain to those who inflict it" and to "concentrate on portraying have-nots in a *have* society, those seldom singled out by mass media, except as source material for derogatory humor and/or condescending clinical, social analysis."[2]

Childress' characters and plots emerged from years of impressions she gathered by observing people and weaving stories around their lives. Inspired by the strength of her mother and grandmother, she witnessed the heroic stamina and remarkable resilience of women who often stood alone in the face of poverty and earned pennies doing domestic or factory work, yet would get up at weekly church meetings to share their troubles with the congregation. Church-goers rallied around them to offer comfort and support in response to stories of imprisoned sons, family illness, poverty, and suicide. The dignity of these women in their everyday struggles as well as the church community's healing ritual became the foundation of Childress' art.

In the 1960s as the Black Power movement gathered momentum, the oppression of black women took a new turn. The image held up for emulation, according to Omofolabo Ajayi-Soyinka, was that of "a silent, submissive African queen who is poised, regal, beautiful, but with no authority . . . who exists mainly as fodder to the man's ego, is his source of sexual gratification, acts as his baby factory, and occasionally the punching sack of his frustrations."[3] For Childress, the further repression of black women in the guise of promoting liberation for all African Americans was "too easy and too misleading a conclusion."[4] Not only was this message an unconscionable denial of freedom to them, but it also threatened the viability of their community by denying the history of struggle in the face of poverty, Jim Crow laws in the south, and the lack of opportunity in racist America which the strong, independent black woman represented. *Wine in the Wilderness* (1969) was written as a critique of this movement.

In the more than four decades in which her plays have been published and produced, Childress maintained her commitment to using theatre as a weapon against racial, economic, and gender-biased inequality and as a tool for creating community solidarity. She inspired a whole generation of black women playwrights—most notably Lorraine Hansberry who wrote *A Raisin in the Sun* after reviewing Childress' plays in Harlem and watching *Trouble in Mind* at the Greenwich Mews Theatre. Although the depiction of intermarriage in her play *Wedding Band* and her use of realism rather than an Afrocentric aesthetic were criticized at the height of the Black Power movement in the 1960s, her truthful vision of the complex range of African-American experiences continues to win her accolades that echo the words of Paul Robeson:

> Seldom is it given to one person to penetrate into the very hearts and minds of a whole people, to be sensitive in the highest degree to their joys, their hopes, their humor and their sorrows, to catch their quiet laughter and their overwhelming outbursts of merriment, their happy smiles and bitter ones, their righteous anger and deep nobility. In the stories of Alice Childress, you will find this all-inclusive richness and breadth.[5]

MAJOR WORKS

In a writing career committed to heightening the social and political consciousness of her audience, Alice Childress wrote novels for adolescent readers—*A Hero Ain't Nothin' but a Sandwich* (1973) and *Rainbow Jordan* (1981)—that won awards for their honest treatment of black history and urban problems. But her seventeen plays, all of which explore sociopolitical, romantic, biographical, historical, and feminist themes, represent a truly unique and powerful contribution to black theatre.

After her playwriting and directing debut with *Florence* (1949), in which she also starred, Childress continued to write for the American Negro Theatre: *Just a Little Simple* (1950), a musical review based on the stories of Langston Hughes; and *Gold Through the Trees* (1952), a variety entertainment that celebrated African and modern dance, the Blues, and historical moments from Harriet Tubman to the desegregation movement in the South. When these works were presented at the Club Baron in Harlem, the Harlem Stagehands' Union received contracts for the first time, thanks to the intercession of the playwright. Her efforts further ensured the viability of the Negro branch of Actor's Equity Association and resulted in her becoming the first black woman to receive professional productions of her plays.

Childress returned to realism to explore an actress' confrontation with racism in *Trouble in Mind* (1955), then wrote about miscegenation and racism in the South after World War II in *Wedding Band* (1966). With *String* (1969) Childress adapted a story by Guy de Maupassant to illustrate how appearances can lead to faulty accusations. In *Mojo: A Black Love Story* (1970), she used the shared experiences of racism to show how a divorced couple bond when the ex-wife must face surgery. Two later works, *Gullah* (1984), a play with music that celebrates the Sea Island culture off the coast of South Carolina and Georgia, and *Moms, A Praise Play for a Black Comedienne* (1986), based on the life of

Jackie "Moms" Mabley, employed variety formats. But it is *Wine in the Wilderness* (1969), about the fragmentation of the black community along class and gender lines, that has prompted a re-examination of her work from a feminist perspective.

THE ACTION

While a race riot rages outside his Harlem studio apartment, painter Bill Jameson waits for his friends Sonny-Man and Cynthia, a black professional couple. They are introducing him to a homeless woman, Tommy-Marie, who they believe will be the perfect grassroots, sexless model for the final panel of his triptych. Meanwhile, Bill explains the two completed panels to Oldtimer, a sixty-year-old man from the neighborhood.

Uneducated factory worker Tommy-Marie arrives, thinking that her new friends have brought her to meet Bill socially. Embarrassed by her shabby appearance, she is reluctant to allow Bill to paint her, but agrees when he bribes her with food. Believing that Bill's telephone description of his beautiful "Mother Africa" panel is about her, Tommy drapes herself in an African throw and discards her wig. Bill is mesmerized by her transformation. Acknowledging a mutual attraction, Tommy spends the night.

The next morning Tommy discovers that she had been invited to Bill's studio to model for the "messed-up chick." Enraged by this betrayal, she lashes out at Bill and his friends as snobs who are deluded into believing that they are superior to her. Touched by the truth of her words and the dignity of her pride and independence, Bill removes the fantasy portrait from his easel and begins to sketch a new triptych that will depict Sonny-Man and Cynthia as the hope of the future, Oldtimer as the man broken by racism, and Tommy as the "Wine in the Wilderness" from which they all gain sustenance.

STRUCTURE AND LANGUAGE

In *Wine in the Wilderness,* Childress addresses the charge by the Black Power movement that black women are culprits in the subjugation of black men. She counters these allegations by exploring the effects of institutionalized racism that have forced black women to become brash and self-reliant, then urges the African-American community to band together in their struggle for freedom. Hence the riot that rages outside Bill's apartment symbolizes the consequences of racism on the community, where residents lash out at each other in anger instead of fighting for better housing and equal opportunity. Their shooting threatens the lives of innocent bystanders and the looting and arson hurt local merchants and those who dwell above the stores. Tomorrow-Marie, the play's aptly named protagonist, is one such victim.

Tommy has inherited a legacy of oppression since slavery, a matter that assigns social and political weight to her central position in the play. Once the concubines of their masters, freed women slaves were subjugated further when laws passed during Emancipation declared that their children were only legitimate offspring of their mothers. This allowed white as well as black men freedom from paternal responsibility. More often than not, these women and their daughters and granddaughters had to feed, raise, and educate their children without help. If they were lucky enough to find a man with whom to share their lives, they would either have to protect him from the mobs waiting to lynch him—particularly if he were successful as a farmer or entrepreneur—or suffer his frustrations and humiliation when no one would hire him. To survive, these women worked and took charge.

Abandoned by her husband, Tommy's mother was head of a household where she "didn't have nothin' to rule over, not a pot nor a window." In fact, she could only claim her man after he was dead. Rather than follow her mother's example, Tommy quit school and got a job, knowing that if she did not "do" for herself, she would not survive. Her dream is not to find a man to be her "meal ticket" but someone "who'll treat [her] just half-way decent . . . Somebody in [her] corner." The play articulates her determination to prevail despite the poverty she has known in her childhood and the elusiveness of her present dream.

Childress uses Bill's apartment, the single setting in which all the action takes place, to criticize young, college-educated blacks who have returned to gentrify Harlem. The apartment is "in a beautiful, rather artistic state of disorder . . . and reflects an interest in other darker peoples of the world," but its "broken out walls" suggest a deeper turmoil and disrepair, no doubt the result of Bill's complacent reliance on fantasies and dreams rather than practical solutions. In similar fashion, he imagines a better life for blacks in America but remains outside any actions for social change. He merely answers the economic and social problems facing his people with either criticism or rationalizations: "The brothers and sisters are tired, weary of the endless get-no-where struggle." His black consciousness consists of verbally assaulting the American system of government and education and hanging up photographs of figures from the African-American past to remind him of his black heritage. He does not perceive that the historical struggle for freedom and those privileges he takes for granted were won by simple, church-going people like those from Tommy's world.

As imagined through Bill's eyes, Tommy is an "ignorant, unfeminine, coarse, rude . . . vulgar . . . poor, dumb chick that's had her behind kicked until it's numb," a woman who certainly fits the description of his subject for the unpainted panel. When Tommy reveals certain truths about her life, however, she is transformed into a courageous, self-sufficient fighter with integrity: forthright and honest about her feelings, embarrassed by her appearance, and angry with those who have set fire to the grocery store above which she used to make her home.

In contrast, Cynthia is guarded and hypocritical. Although she is a social worker, she has studied poverty rather than lived it. Devoid of any understanding of the need for self-reliance that faces black women who are poor, she spouts the rhetoric of Black Power: the need for black women to "let the black man have his manhood again" by being softer, sexier, and more dependent. On the other hand, she is a career woman who balks when her husband suggests that she "can run down to our house and fix [Tommy] some eggs." She does not need to be submissive to have a positive relationship with him. Rather than insult her or react negatively to her sarcastic "that's such a lovely idea," Sonny-Man responds good-naturedly, "Thank you, darlin', I'm in there, . . . on the beam." When Cynthia discovers what kind of person Tommy is, she still denies their sisterhood and withholds the fact that she and Sonny-Man had picked her out as a model for Bill's "mural thing" to exploit her "in her moment of tragedy." Tommy is as much victimized by Cynthia's silent complicity as she is by the riot and by the men's insensitivity.

Tommy is the only character with enough practical experience to know that in racist America "a black man see a hard way to go," and that black men and women have to "pull together" in order to achieve. She knows her roots and, out of this sense of shared oppression, loves all black people. It is she, after all, who discovers Oldtimer's real name— Edmond Lorenzo Matthews—and shows him the respect denied him by the other characters. While the bond shared between Tommy and Oldtimer is rooted in poverty, homelessness, and lack of education, it symbolizes the "we-ness and us-ness" Tommy offers the other characters as their first survival lesson. Acknowledging that "this riot blew [her] life," Tommy is fully prepared to start over, to continue the struggle. Aware that her friends have played her cheap, she refuses to submit to their educated tactics and enlightens them with strong racist reality: that the word *nigger* means "educated you and uneducated me."

Over the play's twelve-hour time period, Childress has introduced five characters whose speech styles not only reflect her own impassioned concerns as playwright but also her practiced skill at capturing the details of these personalities through language differences and idiomatic rhythms. There is the quick-tongued Bill Jameson whose vocabulary is cluttered with the names of black heroes who have sharpened his artistic sensibilities but not his political ones. The similarly educated Cynthia and Sonny-Man have adopted a convincing genteel manner to compliment their upper-middle-class yearnings. In contrast, Oldtimer puts himself down as ignorant. Weary and defeated by life, he philosophizes that ''when hard luck fall it just keep fallin'.''

The message of the play, which lies hidden in the triptych, is ultimately deciphered by Childress' intuitive female protagonist whose language is an unadulterated celebration of her gender and class: ''I'm 'Wine In The Wilderness' . . . alive and kickin', me . . . Tomorrow-Marie, cussin' and fightin' and lookin' out for my damn self.'' Mother Africa, who ''has come through everything that has been put on her'' without losing a semblance that is ''regal . . . grand . . . magnificent, fantastic,'' need not be a figment of Bill's artistic imagination but can be incarnated by women like Tommy. Through her, Childress demonstrates how the ''revolution for liberation'' will be won only when divisions along gender and class lines are eradicated and when African Americans join hands in acknowledging each other—the educated men and women, the men denied opportunities for work and education, and, most of all, the women who have overcome the triple threat of racism, classism, and sexism. Until then, there will be no real ''Tomorrow'' but only ''a promise that can never happen.''

WINE IN THE WILDERNESS-IN-PERFORMANCE

Wine in the Wilderness has not had a rich production history, despite the importance of the play in understanding Childress' contribution to drama. The play was first presented for National Educational Television on October 7, 1969, as the first in a series entitled *On Being Black*. Bruce Mannix directed Abbey Lincoln (Tommy-Marie), Israel Hicks (Bill), Marilyn Berry (Cynthia), Cashmere Ellis (Sonny-Man), and John Marriott (Oldtimer) in this one-hour drama which was a tour de force for its leading lady. Deviating from conventional protest dramas familiar to white television audiences, the play explored ''problems that blacks encounter among themselves, without using the whites as verbal whipping posts'' and exposed a neglected aspect of racism: the mistreatment of black women by black men who take out their frustrations with living in white America on their ''sisters.''[6]

In November 1970, the first major stage production of the play opened for a three-week engagement and shared the bill with *Mojo: A Black Love Story* at the New Heritage Repertory Theatre, a community theatre located in Harlem. The importance of the event was marked by the opening-night presence of such luminaries as Alice Childress, Ossie Davis, Ed Bullins, Roseanne Carter, Clarice Taylor, and Al Fann. Millie Hassle and Georgia Gowan alternated in the role of Tommy, and the cast, which also included John Byrd as Bill, Charles Griffiths as Oldtimer, Christine Anderson as Cynthia, and Roger Parris and Carl Mussa alternating as Sonny-Man, was commended for its realistic performances under Roger Furman's strong direction.

The play enjoyed numerous productions soon afterwards, including ones with the Kuumba Workshop in Chicago in 1971 and with the Howard University Players, Washington, DC, in 1972. Perhaps its most important revival was given in June of 1978 by the National Black Theatre in Harlem. On a double-bill with Lonnie Elder's *Seven Comes Up, Seven Comes Down*, the play was recognized for its timely political and feminist dimensions. But its appeal, according to Townsend Brewster who reviewed the performance for the Harlem Cultural Council, was not the vindication of African-American women but the ''castigation of self-styled militants who actually scorn those whom they boast of trying to uplift.''[7] This production was an important step for the experimental theatre movement in Harlem because it encouraged more traditional African-American plays in an effort to celebrate the creativity of community artists.

REFLECTIONS ON WINE IN THE WILDERNESS

Abbey Lincoln originated the role of Tommy-Marie in Wine in the Wilderness.

Alice Childress was a mentor of mine. I thought of her as a master of the theatre, of the written word. She was also an actress who knew how to build characters. I was involved in another play she wrote called *Wedding Band.* But after I made the film, *For Love of Ivy,* in 1968, Alice asked me to do *Wine in the Wilderness.* I didn't even read the script, but just took her word that the role suited me. It was because of our friendship and my great respect for her that I agreed to do it.

We filmed it in Boston. I mostly remember how, in one of my scenes, Alice had written a dissertation on the word *nigger.* Had it not been her play, I would have been afraid to use this word over and over again to a man that I cared for. You know, the word is a curse against our ancestors and has reference to a mentality that was developed during slavery—of self-deprecation and self-contempt.

But Tommy-Marie—the character I was asked to play—was what they called "grass roots." She was a real person who had high self-esteem. People didn't have to tell her she was wonderful—she knew it, because she was human and very bright. I was grateful for the chance to develop such a beautiful character. I also knew Alice to be a person with taste and honor and insight. So when I looked further at this difficult scene, I began to understand exactly what she had in mind, that Tommy-Marie was talking about Bill's lack of respect for himself, which is why she called him *nigger* over and over again. It wasn't carelessly done.

Bill inherited a way of life that was very sad. It didn't help any of the people in the world and in America to practice slavery, because it gave us all false values. People today don't know how holy work is. They think you're supposed to have something and not do anything to earn it. You're supposed to get it for nothing. That's one of the things we've inherited.

Things have changed a lot since then. The middle classes got bigger and the poor got poorer. People no longer care about what happens to neighborhoods like the one in the play. They've been abandoned by the middle class and the so-called rich. Furthermore, the people who are outside the community have refused to lend their support or respect to it.

Unfortunately, Tomorrow-Marie is still a long way off. It's still tomorrow. I don't know if Alice suspected this at the time she wrote the play, but I wouldn't be surprised because she had spiritual insight. I myself hadn't yet lived in Harlem when I did the play. So I went there to see what it was like, because if you can't live around your relatives, you might as well kill yourself. I stayed up there for six years. But it wasn't spiritually uplifting, and I eventually moved further downtown where I could relax. But I still hear the curses and screams and madness down here.

I grew up on a farm in Michigan. I wasn't raised as a ghettoized person. Tommy-Marie and I share the same background; otherwise she wouldn't have known how to have respect for herself. I've never played a character who didn't have respect for herself. It's funny that my name also happens to be Marie—Anna Marie. So Tomorrow-"Marie"— I thought, oh, yeah, that's me! But Alice had already written the script, and I doubt that she had me in mind when she wrote it.

Continued

I remember I had just started wearing my hair in braids after I made *For Love of Ivy.* I saw a woman coming down the street with two little girls, and she had braided their hair wonderfully and carefully and very beautifully. I had never seen this before except in pictures of African children. I thought that's really what I wanted to do with my hair. My sister said, "Oh, I know how to do that." She braided my hair just around the time I was rehearsing *Wine in the Wilderness,* which was how I wore my hair in the play.

Alice wrote a bitter play, and life has remained bitter for the African-American woman. She lives in a time when her image has been smeared. She's a raped, dirty, conniving, masochistic bitch. This is where she lives, although she refuses to hear about it. I think it's a sad time for African-American women to be living and, if you have values, it's probably much more difficult now than it was then. Still I'm glad that I've known Tomorrow-Marie and Ivy and Josie in *Nothing But a Man.* These are the women I have played, who worshipped the true and living God that is within them and never took themselves lightly and always paid whatever dues they had to pay to be who they are.

When Dr. King was still here, we thought that we would discover we were really somebody. Instead we discovered that we were really not anybody at all. We still don't know who we are. That's why Tommy-Marie remains an oddity in America. Furthermore I don't see any difference between the whites and the blacks. We all worship the same gods; we all need money, and we all know how to be abusive to one another. We all have the same values. But some of us don't know our ancestors and we don't know what our names used to be.

We won the world and then we lost it. But the enemy is always within. We never talked about who the enemy was. We talked about "whitey," but we forgot to talk about "blacky." We still don't talk about it. We just make excuses because we're black, but it's not good for the spirit. We finally became a despotic people who can't see their own flaws and are always pointing to other people. We are divided by cultures and tradition. But there's only one human being. If a man and a woman lie down in a bed and produce a baby, that newborn is a human being, no matter what nation his parents represent. We all had hopes for tomorrow, but we got destructive instead. Although the woman of tomorrow is suggested by her name, Tomorrow-Marie is no fantasy. She really does exist. I'm glad I had the chance to play her.

Notes

1. Alice Childress, *"Those Were the Days, My Friend,"* NEW YORK DAILY NEWS, *3 Dec. 1972.*
2. Alice Childress, *"A Candle in the Wind,"* in BLACK WOMEN WRITERS (1950–1980): A CRITICAL EVALUATION, *ed. Mari Evans (New York: Doubleday Anchor Books, 1984), 112–13.*
3. *"Black Feminist Criticism and Drama: Thoughts on Double Patriarchy,"* JOURNAL OF DRAMATIC THEORY AND CRITICISM *7:2 (Spring 1993): 163.*
4. *"The Negro Woman in Literature,"* FREEDOMWAYS 6 *(First Quarter, 1966): 14.*
5. *A response to* LIKE ONE OF THE FAMILY: CONVERSATIONS FROM A DOMESTIC'S LIFE *(New York Public Library: Schomberg Collection, 1956).*
6. Kay Gardella, *"What's On?"* NEW YORK DAILY NEWS, *8 Oct. 1969.*
7. Townsend Brewster, HARLEM CULTURAL REVIEW, *October 1978, 4.*

WINE IN THE WILDERNESS
ALICE CHILDRESS

CHARACTERS

Bill Jameson, *an artist aged thirty-three*

Oldtimer, *an old roustabout character in his sixties*

Sonny-man, *a writer aged twenty-seven*

Cynthia, *a social worker aged twenty-five. She is Sonny-man's wife*

Tommy, *a woman factory worker aged thirty*

TIME: The summer of 1964. Night of a riot.
PLACE: Harlem, New York City, New York, U.S.A.

SCENE: *A one room apartment in a Harlem Tenement. It used to be a three-room apartment but the tenant has broken out walls and is half finished with a redecorating job. The place is now only partly reminiscent of its past tawdry days, plaster broken away and lathing exposed right next to a new brick-faced portion of wall. The kitchen is now a part of the room. There is a three-quarter bed covered with an African throw, a screen is placed at the foot of the bed to insure privacy when needed. The room is obviously black dominated, pieces of sculpture, wall hangings, paintings. An artist's easel is standing with a drapery thrown across it so the empty canvas beneath it is hidden. Two other canvases the same size are next to it, they too are covered and conceal paintings. The place is in a beautiful, rather artistic state of disorder. The room also reflects an interest in other darker peoples of the world . . . A Chinese incense-burner Buddha, an American Indian feathered war helmet, a Mexican serape, a Japanese fan, a West Indian travel poster. There is a kitchen table, chairs, floor cushions, a couple of box crates, books, bookcases, plenty of artist's materials. There is a small raised platform for model posing. On the platform is a backless chair.*

The tail end of a riot is going on out in the street. Noise and screaming can be heard in the distance, . . . running feet, voices shouting over loudspeakers.

OFFSTAGE VOICES. Offa the street! Into your homes! Clear the street! (*The whine of a bullet is heard.*) Cover that roof! It's from the roof!

(BILL *is seated on the floor with his back to the wall, drawing on a large sketch pad with charcoal pencil. He is very absorbed in his task but flinches as he hears the bullet sound, ducks and shields his head with upraised hand, . . . then resumes sketching. The telephone rings, he reaches for phone with caution, pulls it toward him by the cord in order to avoid going near window or standing up.*)

BILL. Hello? Yeah, my phone is on. How the hell I'm gonna be talkin' to you if it's not on? (*Sound of glass breaking in the distance.*) I could lose my damn life answerin' the phone. Sonny-man, what the hell you callin' me up for! I thought you and Cynthia might be downstairs dead. I banged on the floor and hollered down the air-shaft, no answer. No stuff! Thought yall was dead. I'm sittin' here drawin' a picture in your memory. In a bar! Yall sittin' in a bar? See there, you done blew the picture that's in your memory . . . No kiddin', they wouldn't let you in the block? Man, they can't keep you outta your own house. Found? You found who? Model? What model? Yeah, yeah, thanks, . . . but I like to find my own models. No! Don't bring nobody up here in the middle of a riot . . . Hey, Sonny-man! Hey! (*Sound of yelling and rushing footsteps in the hall.*)

WOMAN'S VOICE (*offstage*). Dammit, Bernice! The riot is over! What you hidin' in the hall for? I'm in the house, your father's in the house, . . . and you out here hidin' in the hall!

GIRL'S VOICE (*offstage*). The house might burn down!

BILL.   Sonny-man, I can't hear you!

WOMAN'S VOICE (*offstage*). If it do burn down, what the hell you gon' do, run off and leave us to burn up by ourself? The riot is over. The police say it's over! Get back in the house! (*Sound of running feet and a knock on the door.*)

BILL.   They say it's over. Man, they oughta let you on your own block, in your own house . . . Yeah, we still standin', this seventy year old house got guts. Thank you, yeah, thanks but I like to pick my own models. You drunk? Can't you hear when I say not to . . . Okay, all right, bring her . . . (*Frantic knocking at the door.*) I gotta go. Yeah, yeah, bring her. I gotto go . . . (*Hangs up phone and opens the door for* OLDTIMER. *The old man is carrying a haul of loot . . . two or three bottles of liquor, a ham, a salami and a suit with price tags attached.*) What's this! Oh, no, no no, Oldtimer, not here . . . (*Faint sound of a police whistle.*) The police after you? What you bring that stuff in here for?

OLDTIMER (*runs past* BILL *to center as he looks for a place to hide the loot*). No, no, they not really after me but . . . I was in the basement so I could stash this stuff, . . . but a fella told me they pokin' round down there . . . in the back yard pokin' round . . . the police doin' a lotta pokin' round.

BILL.   If the cops are searchin' why you wanna dump your troubles on me?

OLDTIMER.   I don't wanta go to jail. I'm too old to go to jail. What we gonna do?

BILL.   We can throw it the hell outta the window. Didn't you think of just throwin' it away and not worry 'bout jail?

OLDTIMER.   I can't do it. It's like . . . I'm Oldtimer but my hands and arms is somebody else that I don' know-a-tall. (BILL *pulls stuff out of* OLDTIMER's *arms and places loot on the kitchen table.* OLDTIMER's *arms fall to his sides.*) Thank you, son.

BILL.   Stealin' ain't worth a bullet through your brain, is it? You wanna get shot down and down and drown in your own blood, . . . for what? A suit, a bottle of whiskey? Gonna throw your life away for a damn ham?

OLDTIMER.   But I ain't really stole nothin', Bill, cause I ain' no thief. Them others, . . . they smash the windows, they run in the stores and grab and all. Me, I pick up what they left scatter in the street. Things they drop . . . things they trample underfoot. What's in the street ain' like stealin'. This is leavin's. What I'm gon' do if the police come?

BILL (*starts to gather the things in the tablecloth that is on the table*). I'll throw it out the airshaft window.

OLDTIMER (*places himself squarely in front of the air-shaft window*). I be damn. Uh-uh, can't let you do it, Billy-Boy. (*Grabs the liquor and holds on.*)

BILL (*wraps the suit, the ham and the salami in the tablecloth and ties the ends together in a knot*). Just for now, then you can go down and get it later.

OLDTIMER (*getting belligerent*). I say I ain' gon' let you do it.

BILL.   Sonny-man calls this "The people's revolution." A revolution should not be looting and stealing. Revolutions are for liberation. (OLDTIMER *won't budge from before the window.*) Okay, man, you win, it's all yours. (*Walks away from* OLDTIMER *and prepares his easel for sketching.*)

OLDTIMER.   Don't be mad with me, Billy-Boy, I couldn't help myself.

BILL (*at peace with the old man*). No hard feelin's.

OLDTIMER (*as he uncorks bottle*). I don't blame you for bein' fed up with us, . . . fella like you oughta be fed up with your people sometime. Hey, Billy, let's you and me have a little taste together.

BILL.   Yeah, why not.

OLDTIMER (*at table pouring drinks*). You mustn't be too hard on me. You see, you talented, you got somethin' on the ball, you gonna make it on past these white folk, . . . but not me, Billy-boy, it's too late in the day for that. Time, time, time, . . . time done put me down. Father Time is a bad white cat. Whatcha been paintin' and drawin' lately? You can paint me again if you wanta, . . . no charge. Paint me 'cause that might be the only way I get to stay in the world after I'm dead and gone. Somebody'll look up at your paintin' and say, . . . "Who's that?" And you say, . . . "That's Oldtimer." (BILL *joins* OLDTIMER *at table and takes one of the drinks.*) Well, here's lookin' at you and goin' down me. (*Gulps drink down.*)

BILL (*raising his glass*). Your health, Oldtimer.

OLDTIMER.   My day we didn't have all this grants and scholarship like now. Whatcha been doin'?

BILL.   I'm working on the third part of a triptych.

OLDTIMER.   A what tick?

BILL.   A triptych.

OLDTIMER.   Hot-damn, that call for another drink. Here's to the trip-tick. Down the hatch. What is one-a-those?

BILL.   It's three paintings that make one work . . . three paintings that make one subject.

OLDTIMER.   Goes together like a new outfit . . . hat, shoes and suit.

BILL.   Right. The title of my triptych is . . . "Wine In The Wilderness" . . . Three canvases on black womanhood. . . .

OLDTIMER (*eyes light up*). Are they naked pitchers?

BILL (*crosses to paintings*). No, all fully clothed.

OLDTIMER (wishing it was a naked picture). Man, ain' nothin' dirty 'bout naked pitchers. That's art. What you call artistic.

BILL. Right, right, right, but these are with clothes. That can be artistic too. (Uncovers one of the canvases and reveals painting of a charming little girl in Sunday dress and hair ribbon.) I call her. . . ''Black girlhood.''

OLDTIMER. Awwwww, that's innocence! Don't know what it's all about. Ain' that the little child that live right down the street? Yeah. That call for another drink.

BILL. Slow down, Oldtimer, wait till you see this. (Covers the painting of the little girl, then uncovers another canvas and reveals a beautiful woman, deep mahogany complexion, she is cold but utter perfection, draped in startling colors of African material, very ''Vogue'' looking. She wears a golden head-dress sparkling with brilliants and sequins applied over the paint.) There she is . . . ''Wine In The Wilderness'' . . . Mother Africa, regal, black womanhood in her noblest form.

OLDTIMER. Hot damn, I'd die for her, no stuff, . . . oh, man, ''Wine In The Wilderness.''

BILL. Once, a long time ago, a poet named Omar told us what a paradise life could be if a man had a loaf of bread, a jug of wine and . . . a woman singing to him in the wilderness. She is the woman, she is the bread, she is the wine, she is the singing. This Abyssinian maiden is paradise, . . . perfect black womanhood.

OLDTIMER (pours for Bill and himself). To our Abyssinian maiden.

BILL. She's the Sudan, the Congo River, the Egyptian Pyramids . . . Her thighs are African Mahogany . . . she speaks and her words pour forth sparkling clear as the waters . . . Victoria Falls.

OLDTIMER. Ow! Victoria Falls! She got a pretty name.

BILL (covers her up again). Victoria Falls is a waterfall not her name. Now, here's the one that calls for a drink. (Snatches cover from the empty canvas.)

OLDTIMER (stunned by the empty canvas). Your . . . your pitcher is gone.

BILL. Not gone, . . . she's not painted yet. This will be the third part of the triptych. This is the unfinished third of ''Wine In The Wilderness.'' She's gonna be the kinda chick that is grass roots, . . . no, not grass roots. . . I mean she's underneath the grass roots. The lost woman, . . . what the society has made out of our women. She's as far from my African queen as a woman can get and still be female, she's as close to the bottom as you can get without crackin' up . . . she's ignorant, unfeminine, coarse, rude. . . vulgar . . . a poor, dumb chick that's had her behind kicked until it's numb . . . and the sad part is . . . she ain't together, you know, . . . there's no hope for her.

OLDTIMER. Oh, man, you talkin' 'bout my first wife.

BILL. A chick that ain' fit for nothin' but to . . . to . . . just pass her by.

OLDTIMER. Yeah, later for her. When you see her, cross over to the other side of the street.

BILL. If you had to sum her up in one word it would be nothin'!

OLDTIMER (roars with laughter). That call for a double!

BILL (beginning to slightly feel the drinks. He covers the canvas again). Yeah, that's a double! The kinda woman that grates on your damn nerves. And Sonny-man just called to say he found her runnin' round in the middle-a this riot, Sonny-man say she's the real thing from underneath them grass roots. A back-country chick right outta the wilds of Mississippi. . . but she ain' never been near there. Born in Harlem, raised right here in Harlem, . . but back country. Got the picture

OLDTIMER (full of laughter). When . . . when . . . when she get here let's us stomp her to death.

BILL. Not till after I paint her. Gonna put her right here on this canvas. (Pats the canvas, walks in a strut around the table.) When she gets put down on canvas, . . . then trip-tych will be finished.

OLDTIMER (joins him in the strut). Trip-tick will be finish trip-tick will be finish . . .

BILL. Then ''Wine In The Wilderness'' will go up against the wall to improve the view of some post office . . . or some library . . . or maybe a bank . . . and I'll win a prize . . . and the queen, my black queen will look down from the wall so the messed up chicks in the neighborhood can see what a woman oughta be . . . and the innocent child on one side of her and the messed up chick on the other side of her.

OLDTIMER (turning the strut into a dance). Wine in the wilderness . . . up against the wall . . . wine in the wilderness . . . up against the wall-ness

WOMAN FROM UPSTAIRS APT (offstage). What's the matter! The house on fire?

BILL (calls upstairs through the air-shaft window). No, baby! We down here paintin' pictures! (Sound of police siren in distance.)

WOMAN FROM UPSTAIRS APT (offstage). So much-a damn noise! Cut out the noise! (To her husband, hysterically.) Percy! Percy! You hear a police siren! Percy! That a fire engine?!

BILL. Another messed up chick. (Gets a rope and ties it to Oldtimer's bundle.) Got an idea. We'll tie the rope to the bundle, . . . then . . . (Lowers bundle out of window.) lower the bundle outta the window . . . and tie it to this nail here behind the curtain. Now! Nobody can find it except you and me. . . Cops come, there's no loot. (Ties rope to nail under curtain.)

OLDTIMER. Yeah, yeah, loot long gone 'til I want it. (Makes sure window knot is secure.) It'll be swingin' in the breeze free and easy. (There is knocking on the door.)

SONNY-MAN. Open up! Open up! Sonny-man and company.

BILL (*putting finishing touches on securing knot to nail*). Wait, wait, hold on. . . .

SONNY-MAN. And-a here we come! (*Pushes the door open. Enters room with his wife* CYNTHIA *and* TOMMY. SONNY-MAN *is in high spirits. He is in his late twenties, his wife* CYNTHIA *is a bit younger. She wears her hair in a natural style, her clothing is tweedy and in good, quiet taste.* SONNY-MAN *is wearing slacks and a dashiki over a shirt.* TOMMY *is dressed in a mis-matched skirt and sweater, wearing a wig that is not comical, but is wiggy looking. She has the habit of smoothing it every once in a while, patting to make sure it's in place. She wears sneakers and bobby sox, carries a brown paper sack.*)

CYNTHIA. You didn't think it was locked, did you?

BILL. Door not locked? (*Looking over* TOMMY.)

TOMMY. You oughta run him outta town, pushin' open people's door.

BILL. Come right on in.

SONNY-MAN (*standing behind* TOMMY *and pointing down at her to draw* BILL's *attention*). Yes, sireeeeee.

CYNTHIA. Bill, meet a friend-a ours . . . This is Miss Tommy Fields. Tommy, meet a friend-a ours . . . this is Bill, Jameson . . . Bill, Tommy.

BILL. Tommy, if I may call you that . . .

TOMMY (*likes him very much*). Help yourself, Bill. It's a pleasure. Bill Jameson, well, all right.

BILL. The pleasure is all mine. Another friend-a ours, Oldtimer.

TOMMY (*with respect and warmth*). How are you, Mr. Timer?

BILL (*laughs along with others,* OLDTIMER *included*). What you call him, baby?

TOMMY. Mr. Timer, . . . ain't that what you say? (*They all laugh expansively.*)

BILL. No, sugar pie, that's not his name, . . . we just say . . . "Oldtimer," that's what everybody call him . . .

OLDTIMER. Yeah, they all call me that . . . everybody say that . . . OLDTIMER.

TOMMY. That's cute, . . . but what's your name?

BILL. His name is . . . er . . . er . . . What *is* your name?

SONNY-MAN. Dog-bite, what's your name, man? (*There is a significant moment of self-consciousness as* CYNTHIA, SONNY *and* BILL *realize they don't know* OLDTIMER's *name.*).

OLDTIMER. Well, it's . . . Edmond L. Matthews.

TOMMY. Edmond L. Matthews. What's the L for?

OLDTIMER. Lorenzo, . . . Edmond Lorenzo Matthews.

BILL AND SONNY-MAN. Edmond Lorenzo Matthews.

TOMMY. Pleased to meetcha, Mr. Matthews.

OLDTIMER. Nobody call me that in a long, long time.

TOMMY. I'll call you Oldtimer like the rest but I like to know who I'm meetin'. (OLDTIMER *gives her a chair.*) There you go. He's a gentleman too. Bet you can tell my feet hurt. I got one corn . . . and that one is enough. Oh,

it'll ask you for somethin'. (*General laughter.* BILL *indicates to* SONNY-MAN *that* TOMMY *seems right.* CYNTHIA *and* OLDTIMER *take seats near* TOMMY.)

BILL. You rest yourself, baby, er . . . er . . . Tommy. You did say Tommy.

TOMMY. I cut it to Tommy . . . Tommy-Marie, I use both of 'em sometime.

BILL. How 'bout some refreshment?

SONNY-MAN. Yeah, how 'bout that. (*Pouring drinks.*)

TOMMY. Don't yall carry me too fast, now.

BILL (*indicating liquor bottles*). I got what you see and also some wine . . . couple-a cans-a beer.

TOMMY. I'll take the wine.

BILL. Yeah, I knew it.

TOMMY. Don't wanta start nothin' I can't keep up. (OLD-TIMER *slaps his thigh with pleasure.*)

BILL. That's all right, baby, you just a wine-o.

TOMMY. You the one that's got the wine, not me.

BILL. I use this for cookin'.

TOMMY. You like to get loaded while you cook? (OLD-TIMER *is having a ball.*)

BILL (*as he pours wine for* TOMMY). Oh, baby, you too much.

OLDTIMER (*admiring* TOMMY). Oh, Lord, I wish, I wish, I wish I was young again.

TOMMY (*flirtatiously*). Lively as you are, . . . I don't know what we'd do with you if you got any younger.

OLDTIMER. Oh, hush now!

SONNY-MAN (*whispering to* BILL *and pouring drinks*). Didn't I tell you! Know what I'm talkin' about. You dig? All the elements, man.

TOMMY (*worried about what the whispering means*). Let's get somethin' straight I didn't come bustin' in on the party, . . . I was asked. If you married and any wives or girl-friends round here . . . I'm innocent. Don't wanta get shot at, or jumped on. Cause I wasn't doin' a thing but mindin' my business! . . . (*Saying the last in loud tones to be heard in other rooms.*)

OLDTIMER. Jus' us here, that's all.

BILL. I'm single, baby. Nobody wants a poor artist.

CYNTHIA. Oh, honey, we wouldn't walk you into a jealous wife or girl friend.

TOMMY. You paint all-a these pitchers? (BILL *and* SONNY-MAN *hand out drinks.*)

BILL. Just about. Your health, baby, to you.

TOMMY (*lifts her wine glass*). All right, and I got one for you . . . Like my grampaw used-ta say, . . . Here's to the men's collars and the women's skirts, . . . may they never meet. (*General laughter.*)

OLDTIMER. But they ain't got far to go before they do.

TOMMY (*suddenly remembers her troubles*). Niggers, niggers . . . niggers, . . . I'm sick-a niggers, ain't you? A nigger will mess up everytime . . . Lemmie tell you what the niggers done . . .

BILL. Tommy, baby, we don't use that word around here. We can talk about each other a little better than that.

CYNTHIA.   Oh, she doesn't mean it.

TOMMY.   What must I say?

BILL.   Try Afro-Americans.

TOMMY.   Well, . . . the Afro-Americans burnt down my house.

OLDTIMER.   Oh, no they didn't!

TOMMY.   Oh, yes they did . . . it's almost burn down. Then the firemen nailed up my door . . . the door to my room, nailed up shut tight with all I got in the world.

OLDTIMER.   Shame, what a shame.

TOMMY.   A *damn* shame. My clothes . . . Everything gone. This riot blew my life. All I got is gone like it never was.

OLDTIMER.   I know it.

TOMMY.   My transistor radio . . . that's gone.

CYNTHIA.   Ah, gee.

TOMMY.   The transistor . . . and a brand new pair-a shoes I never had on one time . . . (*Raises her right hand.*) If I never move, that's the truth . . . new shoes gone.

OLDTIMER.   Child, when hard luck fall it just keep fallin'.

TOMMY.   And in my top dresser drawer I got a my-on-ase jar with forty-one dollars in it. The fireman would not let me in to get it . . . And it was a Afro-American fireman, don'tcha know.

OLDTIMER.   And you ain't got no place to stay. (BILL *is studying her for portrait possibilities.*)

TOMMY (*rises and walks around room*). That's a lie. I always got some place to go. I don't wanta boast but I ain't never been no place that I can't go back the second time. Woman I use to work for say . . . ''Tommy, any time, any time you want a sleep-in place you come right here to me.'' . . . And that's Park Avenue, my own private bath and T.V. set . . . But I don't want that . . . so I make it on out here to the dress factory. I got friends . . . not a lot of 'em . . . but a few *good* ones. I call my friend—girl and her mother . . . they say . . . ''Tommy, you come here, bring yourself over here.'' So Tommy got a roof with no sweat. (*Looks at torn wall.*) Looks like the Afro-Americans got to you too. Breakin' up, breakin' down, . . . that's all they know.

BILL.   No, Tommy, . . . I'm re-decorating the place . . .

TOMMY.   You mean you did this to yourself?

CYNTHIA.   It's gonna be wild . . . brick-face walls . . . wall to wall carpet.

SONNY-MAN.   She was breakin' up everybody in the bar . . . had us all laughin' . . . crackin' us up. In the middle of a riot . . . she's gassin' everybody!

TOMMY.   No need to cry, it's sad enough. They hollerin' whitey, whitey . . . but who they burn out? Me.

BILL.   The brothers and sisters are tired, weary of the endless get-no-where struggle.

TOMMY.   I'm standin' there in the bar . . . tellin' it like it is . . . next thing I know they talkin' 'bout bringin' me to meet you. But you know what I say? Can't nobody pick

nobody for nobody else. It don't work. And I'm standin' there in a mis-match skirt and top and these sneaker-shoes. I just went to put my dresses in the cleaner . . . Oh, Lord, wonder if they burn down the cleaner. Well, no matter, when I got back it was all over . . . They went in the grocery store, rip out the shelves, pull out all the groceries . . . the hams . . . the . . . the . . . the can goods . . . everything . . . and then set fire . . . Now who you think live over the grocery? Me, that's who. I don't even go to the store lookin' this way . . . but this would be the time, when . . . folks got a fella they want me to meet.

BILL (*suddenly self-conscious*). Tommy, they thought . . . they thought I'd like to paint you . . . that's why they asked you over.

TOMMY (*pleased by the thought but she can't understand it*). Paint me? For what? If he was gonna paint somebody seems to me it'd be one of the pretty girls they show in the beer ads. They even got colored on television now, . . . brushin' their teeth and smokin' cigarettes, . . . some of the prettiest girls in the world. He could get them, . . . couldn't you?

BILL.   Sonny-man and Cynthia were right. I want to paint you.

TOMMY (*suspiciously*). Naked, with no clothes on?

BILL.   No, baby, dressed just as you are now.

OLDTIMER.   Wearin' clothes is also art.

TOMMY.   In the cleaner I got a white dress with a orlon sweater to match it, maybe I can get it out tomorrow and pose in that. (CYNTHIA, OLDTIMER and SONNY-MAN *are eager for her to agree.*)

BILL.   No, I will paint you today, Tommy, just as you are, holding your brown paper bag.

TOMMY.   Mmmmmm, me holdin' the damn bag, I don't know 'bout that.

BILL.   Look at it this way, tonight has been a tragedy.

TOMMY.   Sure in hell has.

BILL.   And so I must paint you tonight, . . . Tommy in her moment of tragedy.

TOMMY.   I'm tired.

BILL.   Damn, baby, all you have to do is sit there and rest.

TOMMY.   I'm hungry.

SONNY-MAN.   While you're posin' Cynthia can run down to our house and fix you some eggs.

CYNTHIA (*gives her husband a weary look*). Oh, Sonny, that's such a lovely idea.

SONNY-MAN.   Thank you, darlin', I'm in there, . . . on the beam.

TOMMY (*ill at ease about posing*). I don't want no eggs. I'm goin' to find me some Chinee food.

BILL.   I'll go. If you promise to stay here and let me paint you, . . . I'll get you anything you want.

TOMMY (*brightening up*). Anything I want. Now, how he sound? All right, you comin' on mighty strong there. ''Anything you want.'' When last you heard somebody say that? . . . I'm warnin' you, now, . . . I'm free, single and disengage, . . . so you better watch yourself.

BILL (*keeping her away from ideas of romance*). Now this is the way the program will go down. First I'll feed you, then I'll paint you.

TOMMY.   Okay, I'm game, I'm a good sport. First off, I want me some Chinee food.

CYNTHIA.   Order up, Tommy, the treat's on him.

TOMMY.   How come it is you never been married? All these girls runnin' round Harlem lookin' for husbands. (*To* CYNTHIA.) I don't blame 'em, 'cause I'm lookin' for somebody myself.

BILL.   I've been married, married and divorced, she divorced me, Tommy, so maybe I'm not much of a catch.

TOMMY.   Look at it this-a-way. Some folks got bad taste. That woman had bad taste. (*All laugh except* BILL *who pours another drink.*) Watch it, Bill, you gonna rust the linin' of your stomach. Ain't this a shame? The riot done wipe me out and I'm sittin' here havin' me a ball. Sittin' here ballin'! (*As* BILL *refills her glass.*) Hold it, that's enough. Likker ain' my problem.

OLDTIMER.   I'm havin' me a good time.

TOMMY.   Know what I say 'bout divorce. (*Slaps her hands together in a final gesture.*) Anybody don' wantcha, . . . later, let 'em go. That's bad taste for you.

BILL.   Tommy, I don't wanta ever get married again. It's me and my work. I'm not gettin' serious about anybody . . .

TOMMY.   He's spellin' at me, now. Nigger, . . . I mean Afro-American . . . I ain' ask you nothin'. You hinkty, I'm hinkty too. I'm independent as a hog on ice, . . . and a hog on ice is dead, cold, well-preserved . . . and don't need a mother-grabbin' thing. (*All laugh heartily except* BILL *and* CYNTHIA.) I know models get paid. I ain' no square but this is a special night and so this one'll be on the house. Show you my heart's in the right place.

BILL.   I'll be glad to pay you, baby.

TOMMY.   You don't really like me, do you? That's all right, sometime it happen that way. You can't pick for *nobody*. Friends get to matchin' up friends and they mess up everytime. Cynthia and Sonny-man done messed up.

BILL.   I like you just fine and I'm glad and grateful that you came.

TOMMY.   Good enough. (*Extends her hand. They slap hands together.*) You 'n me friends?

BILL.   Friends, baby, friends. (*Putting rock record on.*)

TOMMY (*trying out the model stand*). Okay, Dad! Let's see 'bout this *anything I want* jive. Want me a bucket-a Egg Foo Yong, and you get you a shrimp-fry rice, we split that and each have some-a both. Make him give you the soy sauce, the hot mustard and the duck sauce too.

BILL.   Anything else, baby?

TOMMY.   Since you ask, yes. If your money hold out, get me a double order egg roll. And a half order of the sweet and sour spare ribs.

BILL (*to* OLDTIMER *and* SONNY-MAN). Come on, come on. I need some strong men to help me bring back your order, baby.

TOMMY (*going into her dance . . . simply standing and going through some boo-ga-loo motions*). Better go get it 'fore I think up some more to go 'long with it. (*The men laugh and vanish out of the door. Steps heard descending stairs.*) Turn that off. (CYNTHIA *turns off record player.*) How could I forget your name, good as you been to me this day. Thank you, Cynthia, thank you. I *like* him. Oh, I *like* him. But I don't wanta push him too fast. Oh, I got to play these cards right.

CYNTHIA (*a bit uncomfortable*). Oh, Honey, . . . Tommy, you don't want a poor artist.

TOMMY.   Tommy's not lookin' for a meal ticket. I been doin' for myself all my life. It takes two to make it in this high-price world. A black man see a hard way to go. The both of you gotta pull together. That way you accomplish.

CYNTHIA.   I'm a social worker . . . and I see so many broken homes. Some of these men! Tommy, don't be in a rush about the marriage thing.

TOMMY.   Keep it to yourself, . . . but I was thirty my last birthday and haven't ever been married. I coulda been. Oh, yes, indeed, coulda been. But I don't want any and everybody. What I want with a no-good piece-a nothin'? I'll never forget what the Reverend Martin Luther King said . . . "I have a dream." I liked him sayin' it 'cause truer words have never been spoke. (*Straightening the room.*) I have a dream, too. Mine is to find a man who'll treat me just half-way decent . . . just to meet me half-way is all I ask, to smile, be kind to me. Somebody in my corner. Not to wake up by myself in the mornin' and face this world all alone.

CYNTHIA.   About Bill, it's best not to ever count on anything, anything at all, Tommy.

TOMMY (*this remark bothers her for a split second but she shakes it off*). Of course, Cynthia, that's one of the foremost rules of life. Don't count on *nothin'!*

CYNTHIA.   Right, don't be too quick to put your trust in these men.

TOMMY.   You put your trust in one and got yourself a husband.

CYNTHIA.   Well, yes, but what I mean is . . . Oh, you know. A man is a man and Bill is also an artist and his work comes before all else and there are other factors . . .

TOMMY (*sits facing* CYNTHIA). What's wrong with me?

CYNTHIA.   I don't know what you mean.

TOMMY.   Yes you do. You tryin' to tell me I'm aimin' too high by lookin' at Bill.

CYNTHIA.   Oh, no, my dear.

TOMMY.   Out there in the street, in the bar, you and your husband were so sure that he'd *like* me and want to paint my picture.

CYNTHIA.   But he does want to paint you, he's very eager to . . .

TOMMY.   But why? Somethin' don't fit right.

CYNTHIA (*feeling sorry for* TOMMY). If you don't want to do it, just leave and that'll be that.

TOMMY.   Walk out while he's buyin' me what I ask for, spendin' his money on me? That'd be too dirty. (*Looks at books. Takes one from shelf.*) Books, books, books everywhere. "Afro-American History." I like that. What's wrong with me, Cynthia? Tell me, I won't get mad with you, I swear. If there's somethin' wrong that I can change, I'm ready to do it. Eighth grade, that's all I had of school. You a social worker, I know that mean college. I come from poor people. (*Examining the book in her hands.*) Talkin' 'bout poverty this and poverty that and studyin' it. When you *in* it you don' be studyin' 'bout it. Cynthia, I remember my mother tyin' up her stockin's with strips-a rag 'cause she didn't have no garters. When I get home from school she'd say, . . . "Nothin' much here to eat." Nothin' much might be grits, or bread and coffee. I got sick-a all that, got me a job. Later for school.

CYNTHIA.   The Matriarchal Society.

TOMMY.   What's that?

CYNTHIA.   A Matriarchal Society is one in which the women rule . . . the women have the power . . . the women head the house.

TOMMY.   We didn't have nothin' to rule over, not a pot nor a window. And my papa picked hisself up and run off with some finger-poppin' woman and we never hear another word 'til ten, twelve years later when a undertaker call up and ask if Mama wanta come claim his body. And don'cha know, mama went on over and claim it. A woman need a man to claim, even if it's a dead one. What's wrong with me? Be honest.

CYNTHIA.   You're a fine person . . .

TOMMY.   Go on, I can take it.

CYNTHIA.   You're too brash. You're too used to looking out for yourself. It makes us lose our femininity . . . It makes us hard . . . it makes us seem very hard. We do for ourselves too much.

TOMMY.   If I don't, who's gonna do for me?

CYNTHIA.   You have to let the black man have his manhood again. You have to give it back, Tommy.

TOMMY.   I didn't take it from him, how I'm gonna give it back? What else is the matter with me? You had school, I didn't. I respect that.

CYNTHIA.   Yes, I've had it, the degree and the whole bit. For a time I thought I was about to move into another world, the so-called "integrated" world, a place where knowledge and know-how could set you free and open all the doors, but that's a lie. I turned away from that idea. The first thing I did was give up dating white fellas.

TOMMY.   I never had none to give up. I'm not soundin' on you. White folks, nothin' happens when I look at 'em. I

don't hate 'em, don't love 'em, . . . just nothin' shakes a-tall. The dullest people in the world. The way they talk . . . "Oh, hooty, hooty, hoo" . . . Break it down for me to A, B, C's. That Bill . . . I like him, with his black, uppity, high-handed ways. What do you do to get a man you want? A social worker oughta tell you things like that.

CYNTHIA.   Don't chase him . . . at least don't let it look that way. Let him pursue you.

TOMMY.   What if he won't? Men don't chase me much, not the kind I like.

CYNTHIA (*rattles off instructions glibly*). Let him do the talking. Learn to listen. Stay in the background a little. Ask his opinion . . . "What do *you* think, Bill?"

TOMMY.   Mmmmm, "Oh, hooty, hooty, hoo."

CYNTHIA.   But why count on him? There are lots of other nice guys.

TOMMY.   You don't think he'd go for me, do you?

CYNTHIA (*trying to be diplomatic*). Perhaps you're not really his type.

TOMMY.   Maybe not, but he's mine. I'm so lonesome . . . I'm *lonesome* . . . I want somebody to love. Somebody to say . . . "That's all-right," when the World treats me mean.

CYNTHIA.   Tommy, I think you're too good for Bill.

TOMMY.   I don't wanta hear that. The last man that told me I was too good for him . . . was trying' to get away. He's good enough for me. (*Straightening room.*)

CYNTHIA.   Leave the room alone. What we need is a little more sex appeal and a little less washing, cooking and ironing. (TOMMY *puts down the room straightening.*) One more thing, . . . do you have to wear that wig?

TOMMY (*a little sensitive*). I like how *your* hair looks. But some of the naturals I don't like. Can see all the lint caught up in the hair like it hasn't been combed since know not when. You a Muslim?

CYNTHIA.   No.

TOMMY.   I'm just sick-a hair, hair, hair. Do it this way, don't do it, leave it natural, straighten it, process, no process. I get sick-a hair and talkin' 'bout it and foolin' with it. That's why I wear the wig.

CYNTHIA.   I'm sure your own must be just as nice or nicer than that.

TOMMY.   It oughta be. I only paid nineteen ninety five for this.

CYNTHIA.   You ought to go back to usin' your own.

TOMMY (*tensely*). I'll be givin' that some thought.

CYNTHIA.   You're pretty nice people just as you are. Soften up, Tommy. You might surprise yourself.

TOMMY.   I'm listenin'.

CYNTHIA.   Expect more. Learn to let men open doors for you . . .

TOMMY.   What if I'm standin' there and they don't open it?

CYNTHIA (*trying to level with her*). You're a fine person. He wants to paint you, that's all. He's doing a kind of mural thing and we thought he would enjoy painting you. I'd hate to see you expecting more out of the situation than what's there.

TOMMY.   Forget it, sweetie-pie, don' nothin' that's not suppose to. (*Sound of laughter in the hall.* BILL, OLD-TIMER *and* SONNY-MAN *enter.*)

BILL.   No Chinese restaurant left, baby! It's wiped out. Gone with the revolution.

SONNY-MAN (*to* CYNTHIA). Baby, let's move, split the scene, get on with it, time for home.

BILL.   The revolution is here. Whatta you do with her? You paint her!

SONNY-MAN.   You write her . . . you write the revolution into a novel nine hundred pages long.

BILL.   Dance it! Sing it! "Down in the cornfield Hear dat mournful sound . . . (SONNY-MAN *and* OLDTIMER *harmonize.*) Dear old Massa am-a sleepin' A-sleepin' in the cold, cold ground." Now for "Wine In The Wilderness!" Triptych will be finished.

CYNTHIA (*in* BILL's *face*). "Wine In The Wilderness," huh? Exploitation!

SONNY-MAN.   Upstairs, all out, come on, Oldtimer. Folks can't create in a crowd. Cynthia, move it, baby.

OLDTIMER (*starting toward the window*). My things! I got a package.

SONNY-MAN (*heads him off*). Up and out. You don't have to go home, but you have to get outta here. Happy paintin', yall. (*One backward look and they are all gone.*)

BILL.   Whatta night, whatta night, whatta night, baby. It will be painted, written, sung and discussed for generations.

TOMMY (*notices nothing that looks like Chinese food. He is carrying a small bag and a container*). Where's the Foo-Yong?

BILL.   They blew the restaurant, baby. All I could get was a couple-a franks and a orange drink from the stand.

TOMMY (*tersely*). You brought me a frankfooter? That's what you think-a me, a frankfooter?

BILL.   Nothin' to do with what I think. Place is closed.

TOMMY (*quietly surly*). This is the damn City-a New York, any hour on the clock they sellin' the chicken in the basket, barbecue ribs, pizza pie, hot pastrami samitches; and you brought me a frank-footer?

BILL.   Baby, don't break bad over somethin' to eat. The smart set, the jet set, the beautiful people, kings and queens eat frankfurters.

TOMMY.   If a queen sent you out to buy her a bucket-a Foo-yung, you wouldn't come back with no lonely-ass frank-footer.

BILL.   Kill me 'bout it, baby! Go 'head and shoot me six times. That's the trouble with our women, yall always got your mind on food.

TOMMY.   Is that our trouble? (*Laughs.*) Maybe you right. Only two things to do. Either eat the frankfooter or walk on outta here. You got any mustard?

BILL (*gets mustard from the refrigerator*). Let's face it, our folks are not together. The brothers and sisters have busted up Harlem, . . . no plan, no nothin'. There's your black revolution, heads whipped, hospital full and we still in the same old bag.

TOMMY (*seated at the kitchen table*). Maybe what everybody need is somebody like you, who know how things oughta go, to get on out there and start some action.

BILL.   You still mad about the frankfurter?

TOMMY.   No. I keep seein' pitchers of what was in my room and how it all must be spoiled now. (*Sips the orange drink.*) A orange never been near this. Well, it's cold. (*Looking at an incense burner.*) What's that?

BILL.   An incense burner, was given to me by the Chinese guy, Richard Lee. I'm sorry they blew his restaurant.

TOMMY.   Does it help you to catch the number?

BILL.   No, baby, I just burn incense sometime.

TOMMY.   For what?

BILL.   Just 'cause I feel like it. Baby, ain't you used to nothin'?

TOMMY.   Ain't used to burnin' incent for nothin'.

BILL (*laughs*). Burnin' what?

TOMMY.   That stuff.

BILL.   What did you call it?

TOMMY.   Incent.

BILL.   It's not incent, baby. It's incense.

TOMMY.   Like the sense you got in your head. In-sense. Thank you. You're a very correctable person, ain't you?

BILL.   Let's put you on canvas.

TOMMY (*stubbornly*). I have to eat first.

BILL.   That's another thing 'bout black women, they wanta eat 'fore they do anything else. Tommy, . . . Tommy, . . . I bet your name is Thomasina. You look like a Thomasina.

TOMMY.   You could sit there and guess til your eyes pop out and you never would guess my first name. You might could guess the middle name but not the first one.

BILL.   Tell it to me.

TOMMY.   My name is Tomorrow.

BILL.   How's that?

TOMMY.   Tomorrow, . . . like yesterday and *tomorrow,* and the middle name is just plain Marie. That's what my father name me, Tomorrow Marie. My mother say he thought it had a pretty sound.

BILL.   Crazy! I never met a girl named Tomorrow.

TOMMY.   They got to callin' me Tommy for short, so I stick with that. Tomorrow Marie, . . . Sound like a promise that can never happen.

BILL (*straightens chair on stand. He is very eager to start painting*). That's what Shakespeare said, . . . "Tomorrow and tomorrow and tomorrow." Tomorrow, you will be on this canvas.

TOMMY (*still uneasy about being painted*). What's the hurry? Rome wasn't built in a day, . . . that's another saying.

BILL.   If I finish in time, I'll enter you in an exhibition.

TOMMY (*loses interest in the food. Examines the room. Looks at portrait on the wall*). He looks like somebody I know or maybe saw before.

BILL.   That's Frederick Douglass. A man who used to be a slave. He escaped and spent his life trying to make us all free. He was a great man.

TOMMY.   Thank you, Mr. Douglass. Who's the light colored man? (*Indicates a frame next to the Douglass.*)

BILL.   He's white. That's John Brown. They killed him for tryin' to shoot the country outta the slavery bag. He dug us, you know. Old John said, "Hell no, slavery must go."

TOMMY.   I heard all about him. Some folks say he was crazy.

BILL.   If he had been shootin' at *us* they wouldn't have called him a nut.

TOMMY.   School wasn't a great part-a my life.

BILL.   If it was you wouldn't-a found out too much 'bout black history cause the books full-a nothin' but whitey, . . . all except the white ones who dug us, . . . they not there either. Tell me, . . . who was Elijah Lovejoy?

TOMMY.   Elijah Lovejoy, . . . Mmmmmmm. I don't know. Have to do with the Bible?

BILL.   No, that's another white fella, . . . Elijah had a printin' press and the main thing he printed was "Slavery got to go." Well the man moved in on him, smashed his press time after time . . . but he kept puttin' it back together and doin' his thing. So, one final day, they came in a mob and burned him to death.

TOMMY (*blows her nose with sympathy as she fights tears*). That's dirty.

BILL (*as TOMMY glances at titles in book case*). Who was Monroe Trotter?

TOMMY.   Was he white?

BILL.   No, soul brother. Spent his years tryin' to make it all right. Who was Harriet Tubman?

TOMMY.   I heard-a her. But don't put me through no test, Billy. (*Moving around studying pictures and books.*) This *room* is full-a things I don't know nothin' about. How'll I get to know?

BILL.   Read, go to the library, book stores, ask somebody.

TOMMY.   Okay, I'm askin'. Teach me things.

BILL.   Aw, baby, why torment yourself? Trouble with our women, . . . they all wanta be great brains. Leave something' for a man to do.

TOMMY (*eager to impress him*). What you think-a Martin Luther King?

BILL.   A great guy. But it's too late in the day for the singin' and prayin' now.

TOMMY.   What about Malcolm X.?

BILL.   Great cat . . . but there again . . . Where's the program?

TOMMY.   What about Adam Powell? I voted for him. That's one thing 'bout me. I vote. Maybe if everybody vote for the right people . . .

BILL.   The ballot box. It would take me all my life to straighten you on that hype.

TOMMY.   I got the time.

BILL.   You gonna wind up with a king size headache. The Matriarchy gotta go. Yall throw them suppers together, keep your husband happy, raise the kids.

TOMMY.   I don't have a husband. Course, that could be fixed. (*Leaving the unspoken proposal hanging in the air.*)

BILL.   You know the greatest thing you could do for your people? Sit up there and let me put you down on canvas.

TOMMY.   Bein' married and havin' a family might be good for your people as a race, but I was thinkin' bout myself a little.

BILL.   Forget yourself sometime, sugar. On that canvas you'll be givin' and givin' and givin' . . . That's where you can do your thing best. What you stallin' for?

TOMMY (*returns to table and sits in chair*). I . . . I don't want to pose in this outfit.

BILL (*patience is wearing thin*). Why, baby, why?

TOMMY.   I don't feel proud-a myself in this.

BILL.   Art, baby, we talkin' art. Whatcha want . . . Ribbons? Lace? False eyelashes?

TOMMY.   No, just my white dress with the orlon sweater, . . . or anything but this what I'm wearin'. You oughta see me in that dress with my pink linen shoes. Oh, hell, the shoes are gone. I forgot 'bout the fire . . .

BILL.   Oh, stop fightin' me! Another thing . . . our women don't know a damn thing bout bein' feminine. *Give in* sometime. It won't kill you. You tellin' me how to paint? Maybe you oughta hang out your shingle and give art lessons! You too damn opinionated. You gonna pose or you not gonna pose? Say somethin'!

TOMMY.   You makin' me nervous! Hollerin' at me. My mama never holler at me. Hollerin'.

BILL.   I'll soon be too tired to pick up the brush, baby.

TOMMY (*eye catches picture of white woman on the wall*). That's a white woman! Bet you never hollered at her and I bet she's your girlfriend . . . too, and when she posed for her pitcher I bet yall was laughin' . . . and you didn't buy her no frankfooter!

BILL (*feels a bit smug about his male prowess*). Awww, come on, cut that out, baby. That's a little blonde, blue-eyed chick who used to pose for me. That ain't where it's at. This is a new day, the deal is goin' down different. This is the black moment, doll. Black, black, black is bee-yoo-tee-full. Got it? *Black is beautiful.*

TOMMY.   Then how come it is that I don't *feel* beautiful when you *talk* to me?!!

BILL.   That's your hang-up, not mine. You supposed to stretch forth your wings like Ethiopia, shake off them chains that been holdin' you down. Langston Hughes said let 'em see how beautiful you are. But you determined not to ever be beautiful. Okay, that's what makes you Tommy.

TOMMY.   Do you *have* a girl friend? And who is she?

BILL (*now enjoying himself to the utmost*). Naw, naw, naw, doll. I *know* people, but none-a this "tie-you-up-and-I-own-you" jive. I ain't mistreatin' nobody and there's enough-a me to go around. That's another thing with our women, . . . they wanta *latch* on. Learn to play it by ear, roll with the punches, cut down on some-a this "got-you-to-the-grave" kinda relationship. Was today all right? Good, be glad, . . . take what's at hand because tomorrow never comes, it's always today. (*She begins to cry.*) Awwww, I didn't mean it that way . . . I forgot your name. (*He brushes her tears away.*) You act like I belong to you. You're jealous of a picture?

TOMMY.   That's how women are, always studyin' each other and wonderin' how they look up 'gainst the next person.

BILL (*a bit smug*). That's human nature. Whatcha call healthy competition.

TOMMY.   You think she's pretty?

BILL.   She was, perhaps still is. Long, silky hair. She could sit on her hair.

TOMMY (*with bitter arrogance*). Doesn't *everybody*?

BILL.   You got a head like a rock and gonna have the last word if it kills you. Baby, I bet you could knock out Mohamud Ali in the first round, then rare back and scream like Tarzan . . . "Now, I am the greatest!" (*He is very close to her and is amazed to feel a great sense of physical attraction.*) What we arguin' bout? (*Looks her over as she looks away. He suddenly wants to put the conversation on a more intimate level. His eye is on the bed.*) Maybe tomorrow would be a better time for paintin'. Wanna freshen up, take a bath, baby? Water's nice n' hot.

TOMMY (*knows the sound and turns to check on the look. Notices him watching the bed. Starts weeping*). No, I don't! Nigger!

BILL.   Was that nice? What the hell, let's paint the picture. Or are you gonna hold that back too?

TOMMY.   I'm posin'. Shall I take off the wig?

BILL.   No, it's a part of your image, ain't it? You must have reason for wearin' it. (*TOMMY snatches up her orange drink and sits in the model's chair.*)

TOMMY (*with defiance*). Yes, I wear it cause you and those like you go for long, silky hair, and this is the only way I can have some without burnin' my mother-grabbin' brains out. Got it? (*She accidentally knocks over container of orange drink into her lap.*) Hell, I can't wear this. I'm soaked through. I'm not gonna catch no double pneumonia sittin' up here wringin' wet while you paint and holler at me.

BILL.   Bitch!

TOMMY.   You must be talkin' bout your mama!

BILL.   Shut up! Aw, shut-up! (*Phone rings. He finds an African throw-cloth and hands it to her.*) Put this on. Relax, don't go way mad, and all the rest-a that jazz. Change,

will you? I apologize. I'm sorry. (*He picks up phone.*) Hello, survivor of a riot speaking. Who's calling? (*TOMMY retires behind the screen with the throw. During the conversation she undresses and wraps the throw around her. We see* TOMMY *and* BILL, *but they can't see each other.*) Sure, told you not to worry. I'll be ready for the exhibit. If you don't dig it, don't show it. Not time for you to see it yet. Yeah, yeah, next week. You just make sure your exhibition room is big enough to hold the crowds that's gonna congregate to see this fine chick I got here. (*This perks* TOMMY's *ears up.*) You oughta see her. The finest black woman in the world . . . No, . . . the finest *any* woman in the world . . . This gorgeous satin chick is . . . is . . . black velvet moonlight . . . an ebony queen of the universe . . . (*TOMMY can hardly believe her ears.*) One look at her and you go back to Spice Islands . . . She's Mother Africa. . . . You flip, double flip. She has come through everything that has been put on her . . . (*He unveils the gorgeous woman he has painted* . . . "*Wine In The Wilderness*." TOMMY *believes he is talking about her.*) Regal . . . grand . . . magnificent, fantastic. . . . You would vote her the woman you'd most like to meet on a desert island, or around the corner from anywhere. She's here with me now . . . and I don't know if I want to show her to you or anybody else . . . I'm beginnin' to have this deep attachment . . . She sparkles, man, Harriet Tubman, Queen of the Nile . . . sweetheart, wife, mother, sister, friend. . . . The night . . . a black diamond . . . A dark, beautiful dream . . . A cloud with a silvery lining . . . Her wrath is a storm over the Bahamas. "Wine In The Wilderness" . . . The memory of Africa . . . The *now* of things . . . but best of all and most important . . . She's tomorrow . . . she's my tomorrow . . . (*TOMMY is dressed in the African wrap. She is suddenly awakened to the feeling of being loved and admired. She removes the wig and fluffs her hair. Her hair under the wig must not be an accurate, well-cut Afro* . . . *but should be rather attractive natural hair. She studies herself in a mirror. We see her taller, more relaxed and sure of herself. Perhaps braided hair will go well with Afro robe.*) Aw, man, later. You don't believe in nothin'! (*He covers* "Wine In The Wilderness." *Is now in a glowing mood.*) Baby, whenever you ready. (*She emerges from behind the screen. Dressed in the wrap, sans wig. He is astounded.*) Baby, what . . . ? Where . . . where's the wig?

TOMMY.   I don't think I want to wear it, Bill.

BILL.   That is very becoming . . . the drape thing.

TOMMY.   Thank you.

BILL.   I don't know what to say.

TOMMY.   It's time to paint. (*Steps up on the model stand and sits in the chair. She is now a queen, relaxed and smiling her appreciation for his last speech to the art dealer. Her feet are bare.*)

BILL (*mystified by the change in her. Tries to do a charcoal sketch*). It is quite late.

TOMMY.   Makes me no difference if it's all right with you.

BILL (*wants to create the other image*). Could you put the wig back on?

TOMMY.   You don't really like wigs, do you?

BILL.   Well, no.

TOMMY.   Then let's have things the way you like.

BILL (*has no answer for this. He makes a haphazard line or two as he tries to remember the other image*). Tell me something about yourself, . . . anything.

TOMMY (*now on sure ground*). I was born in Baltimore, Maryland and raised here in Harlem. My favorite flower is "Four O'clocks," that's a bush flower. My wearin' flower, corsage flower, is pink roses. My mama raised me, mostly by herself, God rest the dead. Mama belonged to "The Eastern Star." Her father was a "Mason." If a man in the family is a "Mason" any woman related to him can be an "Eastern Star." My grandfather was a member of "The Prince Hall Lodge." I had a uncle who was an "Elk," . . . a member of "The Improved Benevolent Protective Order of Elks of the World": "The Henry Lincoln Johnson Lodge." You know, the white "Elks" are called "The Benevolent Protective Order of Elks" but the black "Elks" are called "The *Improved* Benevolent Protective Order of Elks of *the World*." That's because the black "Elks" got the copyright first but the white "Elks" took us to court about it to keep us from usin' the name. Over fifteen hundred black folk went to jail for wearin' the "Elk" emblem on their coat lapel. Years ago, . . . that's what you call history.

BILL.   I didn't know about that.

TOMMY.   Oh, it's understandable. Only way I heard bout John Brown was because the black "Elks" bought his farmhouse where he trained his men to attack the government.

BILL.   The black "Elks" bought the John Brown Farm? What did they do with it?

TOMMY.   They built a outdoor theater and put a perpetual light in his memory, . . . and they buildin' cottages there, one named for each state in the union and . . .

BILL.   How do you know about it?

TOMMY.   Well, our "Elks" helped my cousin go through school with a scholarship. She won a speaking contest and wrote a composition titled "Onward and Upward, O, My Race." That's how she won the scholarship. Coreen knows all that Elk history.

BILL (*seeing her with new eyes*). Tell me some more about you, Tomorrow Marie. I bet you go to church.

TOMMY.   Not much as I used to. Early in life I pledged myself in the A.M.E. Zion Church.

BILL (*studying her face, seeing her for the first time*). A.M.E.

TOMMY.   A.M.E. That's African Methodist Episcopal. We split off from the white Methodist Episcopal and started

our own in the year Seventeen hundred and ninety six. We built our first buildin' in the year 1800. How 'bout that?

BILL.   That right?

TOMMY.   Oh, I'm just showin' off. I taught Sunday School for two years and you had to know the history of A.M.E. Zion . . . or else you couldn't teach. My great, great grandparents was slaves.

BILL.   Guess everybody's was.

TOMMY.   Mine was slaves in a place called Sweetwater Springs, Virginia. We tried to look it up one time but somebody at Church told us that Sweetwater Springs had become a part of Norfolk . . . so we didn't carry it any further . . . As it would be a expense to have a lawyer trace your people.

BILL (*throws charcoal pencil across room*). No good! It won't work! I can't work anymore.

TOMMY.   Take a rest. Tell me about you.

BILL (*sits on bed*). Everybody in my family worked for the Post Office. They bought a home in Jamaica, Long Island. Everybody on that block bought an aluminum screen door with a duck on it, . . . or was it a swan? I guess that makes my favorite flower crab grass and hedges. I have a lot of bad dreams. (TOMMY *massages his temples and the back of his neck.*) A dream like suffocating, dying of suffocation. The worst kinda dream. People are standing in a weird looking art gallery, they're looking and laughing at everything I've ever done. My work begins to fade off the canvas, right before my eyes. Everything I've ever done is laughed away.

TOMMY.   Don't be so hard on yourself. If I was smart as you I'd wake up singin' every mornin'. (*There is the sound of thunder. He kisses her.*) When it thunders that's the angels in heaven playin', with their hoops, rollin' their hoops and bicycle wheels in the rain. My Mama told me that.

BILL.   I'm glad you're here. Black *is* beautiful, you're beautiful, A.M.E. Zion, Elks, pink roses, bush flower, . . . blooming out of the slavery of Sweetwater Springs, Virginia.

TOMMY.   I'm gonna take a bath and let the riot and the hell of living go down the drain with the bath water.

BILL.   Tommy, Tommy, Tomorrow Marie, let's save each other, let's be kind and good to each other while it rains and the angels roll those hoops and bicycle wheels.

(*They embrace. The sound of rain. Music in as lights come down. As lights fade down to darkness, music comes in louder. There is a flash of lightning. We see* TOMMY *and* BILL *in each other's arms. It is very dark. Music up louder, then softer and down to very soft. Music is mixed with the sound of rain beating against the window. Music slowly fades as gray light of dawn shows at window. Lights go up gradually. The bed is rumpled and empty.* BILL *is in the bathroom.* TOMMY *is at the stove turning off the coffee pot. She sets table with cups and saucers, spoons.* TOMMY's *hair is natural, she wears another throw [African design] draped around her. She sings and hums a snatch of a joyous spiritual.*)

TOMMY.   ''Great day, Great day, the world's on fire, Great day . . .'' (*Calling out to* BILL *who is in the bath.*) Honey, I found the coffee, and it's ready. Nothin' here to go with it but a cucumber and a Uneeda biscuit.

BILL (*offstage. Joyous yell from offstage*). Tomorrow and tomorrow and tomorrow! Good mornin', Tomorrow!

TOMMY (*more to herself than to* BILL). ''Tomorrow and tomorrow.'' That's Shakespeare. (*Calls to* BILL.) You say that was Shakespeare?

BILL (*offstage*). Right, baby, right!

TOMMY.   I bet Shakespeare was black! You know how we love poetry. That's what give him away. I bet he was passin'. (*Laughs.*)

BILL (*offstage*). Just you wait, one hundred years from now all the honkeys gonna claim our poets just like they stole our blues. They gonna try to steal Paul Laurence Dunbar and LeRoi and Margaret Walker.

TOMMY (*to herself*). God moves in a mysterious way, even in the middle of a riot. (*A knock on the door.*) Great day, great day the world's on fire . . . (*Opens the door.* OLDTIMER *enters. He is soaking wet. He does not recognize her right away.*)

OLDTIMER.   'Scuse me, I must be in the wrong place.

TOMMY (*patting her hair*). This is me. Come on in, Edmond Lorenzo Matthews. I took off my hair-piece. This is me.

OLDTIMER (*very distracted and worried*). Well, howdy-do and good mornin'. (*He has had a hard night of drinking and sleeplessness.*) Where Billy-boy? It pourin' down some rain out there. (*Makes his way to the window.*)

TOMMY.   What's the matter?

OLDTIMER (*raises the window and starts pulling in the cord, the cord is weightless and he realizes there is nothing on the end of it*). No, no, it can't be. Where is it? It's gone! (*Looks out the window.*)

TOMMY.   You gonna catch your death. You wringin' wet.

OLDTIMER.   Yall take my things in? It was a bag-a loot. A suit and some odds and ends. It was my loot. Yall took it in?

TOMMY.   No. (*Realizes his desperation. She calls to* BILL *through the closed bathroom door.*) Did you take in any loot that was outside the window?

BILL (*offstage*). No.

TOMMY.   He said ''no.''

OLDTIMER (*yells out window*). Thieves, . . . dirty thieves . . . lotta good it'll do you . . .

TOMMY (*leads him to a chair, dries his head with a towel*). Get outta the wet things. You smell just like a whiskey still. Why don't you take care of yourself. (*Dries off his hands.*)

OLDTIMER.   Drinkin' with the boys. Likker was everywhere all night long.

TOMMY.   You got to be better than this.

OLDTIMER.   Everything I ever put my hand and mind to do, it turn out wrong, . . . Nothin' but mistakes . . . When you don' know, you don' know. I don' know nothin'. I'm ignorant.

TOMMY.   Hush that talk . . . You know lotsa things, everybody does. (*Helps him remove wet coat.*)

OLDTIMER.   Thanks. How's the trip-tick?

TOMMY.   The what?

OLDTIMER.   *Trip-tick.* That's a paintin'.

TOMMY.   See there, you know more about art than I do. What's a trip-tick? Have some coffee and explain me a trip-tick.

OLDTIMER (*proud of his knowledge*). Well, I tell you, . . . a trip-tick is a paintin' that's in three parts . . . but they all belong together to be looked at all at once. Now . . . this is the first one . . . a little innocent girl . . . (*Unveils picture.*)

TOMMY.   She's sweet.

OLDTIMER.   And this is ''Wine In The Wilderness'' . . . The Queen of the Universe . . . the finest chick in the world.

TOMMY (TOMMY *is thoughtful as he unveils the second picture*). That's not me.

OLDTIMER.   No, you gonna be this here last one. The worst gal in town. A messed-up chick that—that— (*He unveils the third canvas and is face to face with the almost blank canvas, then realizes what he has said. He turns to see the stricken look on* TOMMY's *face.*)

TOMMY.   The messed-up chick, *that's* why they brought me here, ain't it? That's why he wanted to paint me! Say it!

OLDTIMER.   No, I'm lyin', I didn't mean it. It's the society that messed her up. Awwwwww, Tommy, don't look that-a-way. It's art, . . . it's only art . . . He couldn't mean you . . . it's art . . . (*The door opens.* CYNTHIA *and* SONNY-MAN *enter.*)

SONNY-MAN.   Anybody want a ride down . . . down . . . down . . . downtown? What's wrong? Excuse me . . . (*Starts back out.*)

TOMMY (*blocking the exit to* CYNTHIA *and* SONNY-MAN). No, come on in. Stay with it . . . ''Brother'' . . . ''Sister.'' Tell 'em what a trip-tick is, Oldtimer.

CYNTHIA (*very ashamed*). Oh, no.

TOMMY.   You don't have to tell 'em. They already know. The messed-up chick! How come you didn't pose for that, my sister? The messed-up chick lost her home last night, . . . burnt out with no place to go. You and Sonny-man gave me comfort, you cheered me up and took me in, . . . *took me in!*

CYNTHIA.   Tommy, we didn't know you, we didn't mean . . .

TOMMY.   It's all right! I was lost but now I'm found! Yeah, the blind can see! (*She dashes behind the screen and puts on her clothing, sweater, skirt, etc.*)

OLDTIMER (*goes to bathroom door*). Billy, come out!

SONNY-MAN. Billy, step out here, please! (BILL *enters shirtless, wearing dungarees.*) Oldtimer let it out 'bout the triptych.

BILL. The rest of you move on.

TOMMY (*looking out from behind screen*). No, don't go a step. You brought me here, see me out!

BILL. Tommy, let me explain it to you.

TOMMY (*coming out from behind screen*). I gotta check out my apartment, and my clothes and money. Cynthia, . . . I can't wait for anybody to open the door or look out for me and all that kinda crap you talk. A bunch-a liars!

BILL. Oldtimer, why you . . .

TOMMY. Leave him the hell alone. He ain't said nothin' that ain' so!

SONNY-MAN. Explain to the sister that some mistakes have been made.

BILL. Mistakes have been made, baby. The mistakes were yesterday, this is today . . .

TOMMY. Yeah, and I'm Tomorrow, remember? Trouble is I was Tommin' to you, to all of you, . . . "Oh, maybe they gon' like me." . . . I was your fool, thinkin' writers and painters know moren' me, that maybe a little bit of you would rub off on me.

CYNTHIA. We are wrong. I knew it yesterday. Tommy, I told you not to expect anything out of this . . . this arrangement.

BILL. This is a relationship, not an arrangement.

SONNY-MAN. Cynthia, I tell you all the time, keep outta other people's business. What the hell you got to do with who's gonna get what outta what? You and Oldtimer, yakkin' and hakkin'. (*to* OLDTIMER.) Man, your mouth gonna kill you.

BILL. It's me and Tommy. Clear the room.

TOMMY. Better not. I'll kill him! The "black people" this and the "Afro-American" . . . that . . . You ain't got no use for none-a us. Oldtimer, you their fool too. 'Til I got here they didn't even know your damn name. There's something inside-a me that says I ain' suppose to let *nobody* play me cheap. Don't care how much they know! (*She sweeps some of the* books *to the floor.*)

BILL. Don't you have any forgiveness in you? Would I be beggin' you if I didn't care? Can't you be generous enough . . .

TOMMY. Nigger, I been too damn generous with you, already. All-a these people know I wasn't down here all night posin' for no pitcher, nigger!

BILL. Cut that out, Tommy, and you not going anywhere!

TOMMY. You wanna bet? Nigger!

BILL. Okay, you called it, baby, I did act like a low, degraded person . . .

TOMMY (*combing out her wig with her fingers while holding it*). Didn't call you no low, degraded person. Nigger! (*To* CYNTHIA *who is handing her a comb.*) "Do you have to wear a wig?" Yes! To soften the blow when yall go up side-a my head with a baseball bat. (*Going back to taunting* BILL *and ignoring* CYNTHIA'*s comb.*) Nigger!

BILL. That's enough-a that. You right and you're wrong too.

TOMMY. Ain't a-one-a us you like that's alive and walkin' by you on the street . . . you don't like flesh and blood niggers.

BILL. Call me that, baby, but don't call yourself. That what you think of yourself?

TOMMY. If a black somebody is in a history book, or printed on a pitcher, or drawed on a paintin', . . . or if they're a statue, . . . dead, and outta the way, and can't talk back, then you dig 'em and full-a so much-a damn admiration and talk 'bout "*our*" history. But when you run into us livin' and breathin' ones, with the life's blood still pumpin' through us, . . . then you comin' on 'bout how we ain' never together. You hate us, that's what! *You hate black me!*

BILL (*stung to the heart, confused and saddened by the half truth which applies to himself*). I never hated you, I never will, no matter what you or any of the rest of you do to *make* me hate you. I won't! Hell, woman, why do you say that! Why would I hate you?

TOMMY. Maybe I look too much like the mother that give birth to you. Like the Ma and Pa that worked in the post office to buy you a house and a screen door with a damn duck on it. And you so ungrateful you didn't even like it.

BILL. No, I didn't, baby. I don't like screen doors with ducks on 'em.

TOMMY. You didn't like who was livin' behind them screen doors. Phoney Nigger!

BILL. That's all! Damnit! don't go there no more!

TOMMY. Hit me, so I can tear this place down and scream bloody murder.

BILL (*somewhere between laughter and tears*). Looka here, baby, I'm willin' to say I'm wrong, even in fronta the room fulla people . . .

TOMMY (*through clenched teeth*). Nigger.

SONNY-MAN. The sister is upset.

TOMMY. And you stop callin' me "the" sister, . . . if you feelin' so brotherly why don't you say "*my*" sister? Ain't no we-ness in your talk. "The" Afro-American, "the" black man, there's no we-ness in you. Who you think *you* are?

SONNY-MAN. I was talkin' in general er . . . *my* sister, 'bout the masses.

TOMMY. There he go again. "The" masses. Tryin' to make out like we pitiful and you got it made. You the masses your damn self and don't even know it. (*Another angry look at* BILL.) Nigger.

BILL (*pulls dictionary from shelf*). Let's get this ignorant "nigger" talk squared away. You can stand some education.

TOMMY.   You *treat* me like a nigger, that's what. I'd rather be called one than treated that way.

BILL (*questions* TOMMY). What is a nigger? (*Talks as he is trying to find word.*) A nigger is a low, degraded person, *any* low degraded person. I learned that from my teacher in the fifth grade.

TOMMY.   Fifth grade is a liar! Don't pull that dictionary crap on me.

BILL (*pointing to the book*). Webster's New World Dictionary of The American Language, College Edition.

TOMMY.   I don't need to find out what no college white folks say nigger is.

BILL.   I'm tellin' you it's a low, degraded person. Listen. (*Reads from the book.*) Nigger, N-i-g-g-e-r, . . . A Negro . . . A member of any dark-skinned people . . . Damn. (*Amazed by dictionary description.*)

SONNY-MAN.   Brother Malcolm *said* that's what they meant, . . . nigger is a Negro, Negro is a nigger.

BILL (*slowly finishing his reading*). A vulgar, offensive term of hostility and contempt. Well, so much for the fifth grade teacher.

SONNY-MAN.   No, they do not call low, degraded white folks niggers. Come to think of it, did you ever hear whitey call Hitler a nigger? Now if some whitey digs us, . . . the others might call him a nigger-*lover,* but they don't call him no nigger.

OLDTIMER.   No, they don't.

TOMMY (*near tears*). When they say "nigger," just dry-long-so, they mean educated you and uneducated me. They hate you and call you "nigger," I called you "nigger" but I love you. (*There is dead silence in the room for a split second.*)

SONNY-MAN (*trying to establish peace*). There you go. There you go.

CYNTHIA (*cautioning* SONNY-MAN). Now is not the time to talk, darlin'.

BILL.   You love me? Tommy, that's the greatest compliment you could . . .

TOMMY (*sorry she said it*). You must be runnin' a fever, nigger, I ain't said nothin' 'bout lovin' you.

BILL (*in a great mood*). You did, yes, you did.

TOMMY.   Well, you didn't say it to *me.*

BILL.   Oh, Tommy, . . .

TOMMY (*cuts him off abruptly*). And don't you dare say it now. I'm tellin' you, . . . it ain't to be said now. (*Checks through her paper bag to see if she has everything. Starts to put on the wig, changes her mind, holds it to end of scene. Turns to the others in the room.*) Oldtimer, . . . my brothers and my sister.

OLDTIMER.   I wish I was a thousand miles away, I'm so sorry. (*He sits at the foot of the model stand.*)

TOMMY.   I don't stay mad, it's here today and gone tomorrow. I'm sorry your feelin's got hurt, . . . but when I'm hurt I turn and hurt back. Somewhere, in the middle of last night, I thought the old me was gone, . . . lost forever, and gladly. But today was flippin' time, so back I flipped. Now it's "turn the other cheek" time. If I can go through life other-cheekin' the white folk, . . . guess yall can be other-cheeked too. But I'm goin' back to the nitty-gritty crowd, where the talk is we-ness and us-ness. I hate to do it but I have to thank you 'cause I'm walkin' out with much more than I brought in. (*Goes over and looks at the queen in the "Wine In The Wilderness" painting.*) Tomorrow-Marie had such a lovely yesterday. (BILL *takes her hand, she gently removes it from his grasp.*) Bill, I don't have to wait for anybody's by-your-leave to be a "Wine In The Wilderness" woman. I can be it if I wanta, . . . and I *am.* I am. I am. I'm not the one you made up and painted, the very pretty lady who can't talk back, . . . but I'm "Wine In The Wilderness" . . . alive and kickin', me . . . Tomorrow-Marie, cussin' and fightin' and lookin' out for my damn self 'cause ain' nobody else 'round to do it, dontcha know. And, Cynthia, if my hair is straight, or if it's natural, or if I wear a wig, or take it off, . . . that's all right; because wigs . . . shoes . . . hats . . . bags . . . and even this . . . (*She picks up the African throw she wore a few moments before . . . fingers it.*) They're just what what you call . . . access . . . (*Fishing for the word.*) . . . like what you wear with your Easter outfit . . .

CYNTHIA.   Accessories.

TOMMY.   Thank you, my sister. Accessories. Somethin' you add on or take off. The real thing is takin' place on the inside . . . that's where the action is. That's "Wine In The Wilderness," . . . a woman that's a real one and a good one. And yall just better believe I'm it. (*She proceeds to the door.*)

BILL.   Tommy. (*She turns. He takes the beautiful queen, "Wine In The Wilderness" from the easel.*) She's not it at all, Tommy. This chick on the canvas, . . . nothin' but accessories, a dream I drummed up outta the junk room of my mind. (*Places the "queen" to one side.*) *You* are and . . . (*Points to* OLDTIMER.) . . . Edmund Lorenzo Matthews . . . the real beautiful people, . . . Cynthia . . .

CYNTHIA (*bewildered and unbelieving*). Who? Me?

BILL.   Yeah, honey, you and Sonny-man, don't know how beautiful you are. (*Indicates the other side of model stand.*) Sit there.

SONNY-MAN (*places cushions on the floor at the foot of the model stand*). Just sit here and be my beautiful self. (*To* CYNTHIA.) Turn on, baby, we gonna get our picture took. (CYNTHIA *smiles.*)

BILL.   Now there's Oldtimer, the guy who was here before there were scholarships and grants and stuff like that, the guy they kept outta the schools, the man the factories wouldn't hire, the union wouldn't let him join . . .

SONNY-MAN.   Yeah, yeah, rap to me. Where you goin' with it, man? Rap on.

BILL.   I'm makin' a triptych.

SONNY-MAN.   Make it, man.

BILL (*indicating* CYNTHIA *and* SONNY-MAN). On the other side, Young Man and Woman, workin' together to do our thing.

TOMMY (*quietly*). I'm goin' now.

BILL.   But you belong up there in the center, "Wine In The Wilderness" . . . that's who you are. (*Moves the canvas of "the little girl" and places a sketch pad on the easel.*) The nightmare, about all that I've done disappearing before my eyes. It was a good nightmare. I was painting in the dark, all head and no heart. I couldn't see until you came, baby. (*To* CYNTHIA, SONNY-MAN *and* OLDTIMER.) Look at Tomorrow. She came through the biggest riot of all, . . . somethin' called "Slavery," and she's even comin' through the "now" scene, . . . folks laughin' at her, even her own folks laughin' at her. And look *how* . . . with her head high like she's poppin' her fingers at the world. (*Takes up charcoal pencil and tears old page off sketch pad so he can make a fresh drawing.*) Aw, let me put it down, Tommy. "Wine In The Wilderness," you gotta let me put it down so all the little boys and girls can look up and see you on the wall. And you know what they're gonna say? "Hey, don't she look like somebody we know?" (TOMMY *slowly returns and takes her seat on the stand.* TOMMY *is holding the wig in her lap. Her hands are very graceful looking against the texture of the wig.*) And they'll be right, you're somebody they know . . . (*He is sketching hastily. There is a sound of thunder and the patter of rain.*) Yeah, roll them hoops and bicycle wheels. (*Music in low. Music up higher as* BILL *continues to sketch. Curtain.*)

FOCUS QUESTIONS

1. In a brief essay, discuss the differences between Bill's and Tommy's upbringings and how these differences have shaped their selfhood as African Americans.

2. Both Tommy and Oldtimer use defenses to preserve their pride. Analyze the similarities between these characters and show how gender affects the differences in their attitudes about themselves.

3. The men in the play are united through their humor at the expense of women. Discuss examples of how these put-downs bond them together.

4. If Childress' dialogue is a clue to each character's social class and educational background, show how idiomatic expressions and dialect reveal these differences.

5. Bill, Cynthia, and Sonny-Man are somewhat removed from their community. Analyze the ways in which they have set themselves apart, mindful of their insistence that they are promoting African-American culture. Observe their dialogue and nonverbal behaviors for clues.

6. Each character experiences an epiphany, that is, some moment in which he or she recognizes a self-deception. Select three characters, isolate this moment for each of them, and discuss how each is changed by the experience.

7. Based on the information provided by Childress, why is Bill ashamed of the house in which he grew up, despite the privileges he has enjoyed?

OTHER ACTIVITES

1. Make a scrapbook of images that illustrate the African-American community of Childress' play. Include contemporary as well as historical material.

2. Choose either Sonny-Man, Cynthia, or Oldtimer and create a personal history that would help an actor create a realistic characterization.

3. Stage one of the exchanges between characters of different social classes to demonstrate the dynamics between them. Choose one of the following: a scene between Cynthia and Tommy, Bill and Oldtimer, or Bill and Tommy.

BIBLIOGRAPHY

Abramson, Doris E. *Negro Playwrights in the American Theatre*. New York: Columbia University Press, 1967.

Austin, Gayle, ed. *Feminist Theories for Dramatic Criticism*. Ann Arbor: University of Michigan Press, 1990.

Betsko, Kathleen, and Rachel Koenig. *Interviews with Contemporary Women Playwrights*. New York: Beechtree/Morrow Press, 1987.

Brown, Janet. *Feminist Drama*. Metuchen, NJ: Scarecrow Press, 1979.

Brown-Guillory, Elizabeth. *Their Place on the Stage*. Westport, CT: Greenwood Press, 1988.

Bryer, Jackson R. ed. *The Playwright's Act: Conversations with Contemporary American Dramatists*. New Brunswick: NJ: Rutger's University Press, 1995.

Evans, Mari, ed. *Black Women Writers (1950–1980): A Critical Evaluation*. New York: Doubleday Anchor Books, 1984.

Miller, R. Baxter, ed. *Black American Literature and Humanism*. Lexington: University Press of Kentucky, 1981.

Mitchell, Loften. *Black Drama: The Story of the American Negro in the Theatre*. New York: Hawthorne Books, 1966.

Mitchell, Loften, ed. *Voices of the Black Theatre*. Clifton, NJ: James T. White, 1975.

BERNABÉ
Luis Valdez (1940–   )

This was ritual theatre, political theatre, and mythical theatre performed along Highway 99, like a modern recreation of the Crusades. From one community to another, sometimes performing in parking lots and sometimes indoors, the Teatro Campesino established itself as the outward symbol of a workers' struggle.

—Jorge A. Huerta

Clifton Gonzalez-Gonzalez as the title character in *Bernabé* at Theatre Geo in 1993, under the direction of Barbara Martinez-Jittner. *Photo: Barbara Martinez-Jittner.*

APPROACHING CHICANO THEATRE

During the social and political turmoil of the mid-1960s, when issues of civil rights stirred the hearts and minds of human rights activists across America, the National Farm Workers Association under Cesar Chavez joined the Agricultural Workers Organizing Committee in a strike against a powerful lobby of wealthy grape growers. The incident occurred in Delano, California, and brought worldwide attention to Mexican Americans who first settled in the American Southwest in the early nineteenth century. They were called *Chicanos,* a word whose political connotation spoke of their isolation from America's socioeconomic mainstream and of their efforts to remain a united race (La Raza), preserving their American Indian and Spanish ancestry against assimilation by "Anglos." The *huelga* (strike) prompted an ongoing spirit of resistance among its supporters. In the aftermath, there occurred a rebirth of rich artistic productivity—*el renacimiento*—in which Chicano artists of every kind expressed their newly heightened political consciousness.

But the fortuitous circumstances surrounding the inception of El Teatro Campesino (The Farmworkers Theatre), under the inspired guidance of Luis Valdez, further celebrated the transformative power of theatre. It was not the first time that drama had become a weapon, in this case against the bullets and insecticides that were sprayed at thousands of migrant Chicano and Filipino *campesinos* (farmworkers) who were striking against intolerable work conditions. When twenty-five-year-old Valdez joined the strike in 1965 and saw the need to pull unyielding colleagues into the fight, he "hung signs saying *Huelgista* (striker) on two of the men and *Esquirol* (scab) on a third who was instructed to act like a scab. The *Huelgistas* started shouting at the scab and everyone began laughing."[1] From its inception, the striking farmworkers were cast as the heroes, while the grape growers, the strikebreakers, and the labor contractors were portrayed as villains.

What emerged was a short bilingual skit constructed from the joint contributions of several outspoken participants. Satiric in the effortless merging of propaganda with humor and, equally important, portable in its unadorned outdoor staging, the message could travel from town to town on a flat-bed truck. Valdez's resourceful use of strikers as performers had been largely influenced by the improvisatory techniques he mastered that previous summer while working with the San Francisco Mime Troupe whose performers were trained in *commedia dell'arte*. (See Preface to *The Pedant,* p. 162.) His imagination was probably stirred as well by the company's political activism. Its **agitprop** or pure guerrilla tactics proved useful to the needs of oppressed Chicano *huelgistas*. On the other hand, Valdez was an educated man who had studied drama and written plays while in college— he wrote and directed his first full-length play, *The Shrunken Head of Pancho Villa* in 1964—and was the natural heir to a rich cultural heritage. He was acquainted with the works of his Spanish and Mexican literary predecessors, although this refined taste would become subordinate to the more urgent needs of the ongoing strikers.

Armed with a troupe of farmworkers who picketed by day and performed skits— called **actos**—by night, Valdez's mission to raise money and attract sympathizers for the cause fully engaged his enterprising efforts during the next few years. Eventually the troupe faced an inevitable showdown: to continue working under the auspices of the union, whose full-time tasks required the undivided attention of the *teatro* actors, or to become an independent company. Choosing the latter, a decision that provided a natural turning point to the development of Chicano theatre, enabled the troupe to fulfill its already growing reputation as "the only true example of a labor theatre of sustaining value in our era."[2]

As part of the company's independence, headquarters were established in 1967 in Del Rey, just north of Delano, while a second move in 1969 to the more densely populated Fresno brought a change of perspective to their creative goals as well. For when it appeared that the labor demands of the farmworkers were finally being met, the troupe chose to pay

less attention to the *huelga* and to focus instead on timelier issues such as the barrio, racial discrimination, and Vietnam, all of which were having a powerful impact on daily life.

On the political homefront, circumstances reached a shattering climax in Los Angeles in 1970 during a protest of the exploitation of Chicanos in the military. A riot erupted and ended with the mysterious death of Ruben Salazar, the esteemed intellectual leader of the Chicano community. Suspecting that his Teatro's street-theatre tactics might have generated a propensity toward violence, Valdez was all the more determined to close this chapter of his theatre work. As the *huelga* slowly disappeared from view, so did the *acto* that had drawn life from it. But this period of adjustment, which Valdez viewed as one phase of the troupe's evolutionary process, prompted a shift in performance style, stretching and challenging the Teatro's collective resources.

Actos, after all, had been produced, directed, designed, and acted by the *campesinos* themselves. They were intended to inspire the audience "to social action. Illuminate specific points about social problems. Satirize the opposition. Show or hint at a solution. Express what people are feeling."[3] Without abandoning these important objectives or alarming his company of hard-working performers, all of whom were passionately committed to their unique theatrical enterprise, Valdez was nevertheless determined to push the troupe forward, but in a different direction.

When El Teatro Campesino moved to its permanent home in San Juan Bautista in 1971, it settled as well on a new, more mystical dramatic form called the **mito** (myth), which explored the dynamic interaction between cosmic forces and everyday human existence. The process of discovery was based on the troupe's celebration of ancient Mayan practices, which became fully integrated into their new communal life-style. Embracing the need for harmony between people and the universe, Valdez asserted that the "rejection of white western European (*gabacho*) proscenium theatre makes the birth of new Chicano forms necessary, thus, *los actos y los mitos;* one through the eyes of man, the other through the eyes of God."[4]

But public acceptance of the new *mito* format did not come easily. In the first place, the audience Valdez served was still poor and Catholic but was now expected to adjust to a primitive iconography quite unlike the one they were worshipping daily. Secondly, numerous Chicano theatre companies had already molded themselves around El Teatro Campesino and were confronting important political issues on one hand as well as social aspirations toward middle-class values on the other. Valdez's departure from the *acto* was bound to have negative repercussions when he supplanted its highly successful format with a more sublime one rooted in Mayan myths. Ultimately Valdez was forced to explore further performance concepts that would suit the simpler tastes of his audience.

By 1972, El Teatro Campesino introduced one such concept by returning to the traditional *corridos* or narrative folk ballads that wove musical elements around themes of love, death, and heroism and had been popular at the turn of the century. This reinvented version blended the more effective elements from the *acto* (the use of masks, stock characters, exaggerated gestures, audience participation, and simple dialogue used confrontationally and satirically) as well as the *mito* (the appearance of El Diablo, the Devil; La Muerte, Death depicted as a skeleton; and an assortment of Aztec-Mayan deities). Valdez retained the familiar label to encourage the attendance of an audience whose political enlightenment had begun seven years earlier on the picket lines. The evolutionary process from *actos* to *mitos* to *corridos* as well as the mingling of elements from each style expanded a performance agenda that was no longer overtly political. Furthermore the new *corridos* enabled El Teatro Campesino to recapture their vital cultural past and reinforce community solidarity as well.

A brief assessment of El Teatro Campesino's important contribution to Chicano culture and identity must not overlook factors underlying a largely unscripted theatre enlightened by fierce subjectivity. After working in the pure *acto* style, the troupe's collective approach to creating performances loosened considerably to accommodate Valdez's more defined role as director and playwright. While simple scripts originally grew out of improvisation, longer ones became difficult to create collaboratively. As a result, the workshop approach to scripting performances came to an end by 1975 and Valdez returned to writing his own plays.

A particularly controversial aspect of El Teatro Campesino has concerned its patriarchal structure, a phenomenon partly attributed to a male-dominated culture. Thus the *teatro*'s ''female characters typically engage in activities that are accessory to those of males . . . [and] do not enjoy the space necessary for the unfolding of a character.''[5] In spite of these stereotypical women's roles that result when traditional culture is promoted, the vital legacy of El Teatro Campesino remains indisputable. Whether homage is paid to Valdez, to the entire *teatro,* or to both, there is little doubt that the achievement has charted a new Chicano reality filled with hope and commitment.

MAJOR WORKS

Las Dos Caras del Patroncito (The Two Faces of the Boss, 1965) and *La Quinta Temporada* (The Fifth Season, 1966) were the earliest *actos* of El Teatro Campesino to address the landmark strike. *Los Vendidos* (1967) dealt with Chicano stereotyping and, as the title suggests, the problems of assimilating or ''selling out'' to an Anglo society. Other *actos* have included *La Conquista de Mexico* (a puppet play, 1968); *No Saco Nada de la Escuela* (1969); *The Militants* (1969); *Vietnam Campesino* (1970), and *Soldado Razo* (1970), both of which denounced the Vietnam War; and *Huelgistas* (1970). The *mitos* have included *Bernabé* (1970), *El Virgen del Tepeyac* (1971), *Dark Root of a Scream* (1971), and *Los Olivos Pits* (1972).

Since the work of El Teatro Campesino reflects a dynamic evolution of styles, both the *acto* and the *mito* have contributed to the development of the *corrido,* with no one style overriding the others. *La Gran Carpa de los Rasquachis* (The Tent of the Underdogs, 1972) introduced audiences to Valdez's exploration of the *corrido* and, in its several revisions, moved the Chicano reality from farm to city. *El Baille de los Gigantes* (The Dance of the Giants, 1974) demonstrated the troupe's total immersion in Mayan ritual and was performed against the pyramids of Mexico, with spectators perched on the Pyramid of the Moon. *El Fin del Mundo* (The End of the World, 1975), also reworked under the title *Mundo,* took its name and inspiration from the protagonist, Reimundo, or ''king of the world,'' whose kaleidoscopic adventures lead him through the fantasy and real worlds of Chicano life.

The troupe's most famous *corrido, Zoot Suit* (1978), was written and directed by Valdez for the Mark Taper Forum in Los Angeles, where it enjoyed a long and successful run. Telling the story of the Zoot Suit riots of the 1940s, it introduced Valdez to mainstream audiences and became the first Chicano play to open on Broadway. *I Don't Have to Show You No Stinking Badges* was produced in Los Angeles in 1986, shortly before Valdez directed his first film, *La Bamba* (1987). *Bandido!,* a play about the notorious California bandit, Tiburcio Vasquez, premiered at the Mark Taper in 1994, with book and lyrics by Valdez and music by Lalo Schifrin. Luis Valdez received an Obie Award in 1969 and the Los Angeles Critics' Circle Award in 1969 and 1972 for his work with El Teatro Campesino.

Bernabé is one of the first fully realized, full-length works conceived by Valdez and represents El Teatro Campesino's formal exploration of the *mito* style. While the eponymous protagonist of this poignant work is both victim and survivor of a symbolic and mystical union with the Earth, the political overtones of his earthly mission resound through the play.

THE ACTION

Nagged by a selfish and overprotective mother, Bernabé hides from her by escaping to "a hole in the ground covered with planks." Feeling sorry for Bernabé and convinced that he needs the companionship of a woman, a cousin takes him to a local prostitute named Consuelo. Frightened, Bernabé is dragged into her room and imagines he is making love to his mother. He cries out for La Tierra and escapes into the hallway where Consuelo's pimp, Torres, complains about the commotion. Bernabé comes to Consuelo's rescue by attacking Torres and, thinking he has killed him, retreats to his hiding place in the moonlit field.

As he is about to remove the planks, La Luna (the Moon) appears and playfully reprimands Bernabé for spending "almost every night" with his sister, La Tierra. When she emerges from the hole, she tells Bernabé that, if he truly loves her, he will need to win the approval of El Sol. Bernabé is sacrificed and, after his body is laid out, rises to La Tierra's embrace. The following morning, the body of a dead son found "buried in the earth" is brought home to a sorrowful mother.

STRUCTURE AND LANGUAGE

Bernabé is a theatricalized response to the Chicano dream of partaking of the earth's gifts, not as abused farmworkers who must spend their lives toiling for the benefit of others, but as free American citizens enjoying the rights of cultivating their own land. To demonstrate the powerful implication that grew out of the historical strike issues handled in the earlier *actos,* Valdez has assembled nine recognizable stage characters—both popular stereotypes and historical archetypes from real and mythical worlds—who play out the consequences of being denied their dream. Mindful of the critical socio-political context from which the concerns of *La Raza* have arisen, he has imposed a mythical, neo-Aztec dimension on the literal enactment of this right to ownership, hoping that its ritualized climax will inspire a practical solution. It is the *mito* style, above all, that facilitates the exploration of these communal needs.

The time of the play (the early 1960s) purposely coincides with the political unrest that permeates its economically depressed California setting ("a small squat town"), the latter of which "is necessarily abstract—a design that blends myth with reality" to accommodate the elemental perceptions of a thirty-seven-year-old protagonist who lives "in direct relationship to earth, moon, sun, and stars." Bernabé's interior life belongs to this primitive world, although his outward journey will bear mythic repercussions as he hastens from one action to another and tangles with characters who challenge his strange wish to buy "all the tierra on earth." But Bernabé is well aware of what people say of him: "Tierra, they think I'm crazy. But you know I love you. (Looks around.) See you tonight, eh? . . . like always. (He kisses the ground and exits.)"

The *mito* opens on the timely note of Bernabé's attempt to escape once more from a mother who has frightened him into believing that, if he does not behave, "the moon is going to come down and swallow [him] alive." While this comic note of cosmic foreshadowing lightens her oppressive demeanor, it triggers a self-fulfilling prophesy in the life of her innocent son, this small-town Everyman who like every Chicano wants to possess the earth. Bernabé embodies the belief that "ultimate freedom for the farmworkers means ownership of the land he works" and the play illustrates El Teatro Campesino's understanding that "[their] art grows out of [their] way of life."[6] In its symbolic depiction of this struggle, the play rises to the level of **allegory**.

Equally important, *Bernabé* represents that rare Chicano family play whose appeal is strengthened by a mother-son relationship that harbors tragic overtones. In spite of the fact that Bernabé's mother is made less endearing by constantly badgering her son, she is a true Mexican whose sufferings have much in common with women of the *barrio*. She courageously protects Bernabé because he is all she has in the world. As *La Madre,* her title in the *dramatis personae,* she is an earthly symbol of a Mexican mother who "represents a force opposite that of the father, El Sol, the Supreme Giver of Life" and to whom she will eventually lose Bernabé.[7] Like all Mexicans portrayed in the Chicano drama, she invites compassion and respect and, in the final scene of the play, wins our sympathy.

But her son breathes the air of an altogether different reality from the earthbound characters who move in his orbit. In failing to recognize his connection with the cosmos, they reinforce his role as village idiot. The **dramatic irony** of this situation intensifies the outcome. Bernabé's convictions are so strong, that his unexpected encounter with La Luna, La Tierra, and El Sol seems nowhere as extraordinary to him as it does to the audience. Furthermore, Valdez has cushioned Bernabé's confrontation with these archetypal forces by indicating in the cast list that they be impersonated, both in our mind's eye and in actual stage performance, by the same actors who portray Torres, Consuelo, and El Tio (Bernabé's uncle) respectively.

This purely artistic choice produces revealing consequences once the play has transcended its realistic boundaries. As a businessman and landowner who prostitutes the earth as well as its women, for example, Torres pretends to play Bernabé's game: "I'll rent her to you. (Laughs.) Give me a few bucks, and I'll let you have her—for the night!" By assigning the role of La Luna to the actor who plays Torres, these roles intersect. The actor exudes the same gruff manner as the familiar *pachuco* (old man) in a Zoot suit who shares his marijuana joint with Bernabé and uses street talk laced with sexual innuendo. Not coincidentally, both characters set up Bernabé with a woman, although La Luna joins him to La Tierra in a union blessed by El Sol.

Introduced as the local prostitute, Consuelo later returns as La Tierra in the costume of Mexico's much honored historical archetype, *la soldadera* (soldier woman). This time her night with Bernabé will last for eternity. At first, this emblemized dichotomy of whore and virgin is disturbing as a representation of womanhood and is compounded by Bernabé's feelings of guilt which make him confuse Consuelo with his mother's image. But this final transformation from physical to spiritual planes becomes the pivotal metaphor of the play, uniting these images of womanhood in La Tierra as she pays tribute to her beloved Bernabé: "He has always come to my arms seeking my warmth. He loves me with an intensity most men cannot even imagine . . . for in his eyes I am woman . . . I am Madre."

Valdez's decision to make the mystical portraits of La Luna and La Tierra recognizable to his audience has served the accessibility and popularity of the *mito* style. Only El Sol is attired in Aztec regalia as the Sun God Tonatiuh, since his ceremonial ritual authenticates Bernabé's transfiguration and union with his daughter without offending the taste of a mostly Chicano and Catholic audience. In the haunting climax of the play, when he hears Bernabé speak about the love he has for La Tierra, El Sol acknowledges him as the "last of a great noble lineage of men I once knew in ancient times, and the first of a new raza cosmica that shall inherit the earth." Through the sacrifice of Bernabé, a good and innocent person who is mourned on earth but immortalized with the gods, Luis Valdez pays homage to his ancestral roots.

BERNABÉ-IN-PERFORMANCE

Written in 1970, *Bernabé* premiered at the first Chicano Theatre Festival in Fresno that year. Exploring themes about the environment and individual responsibility, and introducing a memorable protagonist who is crippled both emotionally and physically because he has not been properly cared for, its social and political concerns rallied audience responses to produce one of the company's most durable theatre pieces. The play was originally designed to be played indoors on a conventional proscenium stage, but was also played outdoors, that is, on *commedia* stages where spectators gathered around the actors who worked before a black-curtain backdrop. It was even performed in Mexico at the Casa del Lago Amphitheatre in Chapultepec Park before an audience of five thousand. No doubt these productions altered the play's form and content considerably.

Three triangular, movable flats painted by the artist Ernesto Palomino were constructed for the Fresno production. One represented the hills of California, another the Cantina, while a third served as backdrop against which was projected a silent film of Bernabé "riding his bicycle through barrio streets, working in the fields, waiting in contractors's buses and trucks. In each shot, he is seen eyeing some girl's short skirt, her knees, or legs. The short film [stresses] double themes of longing and exploitation."[8] Neither the triangles nor the film footage were retained when the play took to the road. Even the playwright's Spanish text evolved into an English one.

The actors wore traditional *campesino* clothing, with La Madre always dressed in the black garment that was typical of that era. Their simple attire contrasted sharply with the bold costumes of La Luna, La Tierra, and the extravagant plumage of El Sol who infused the final ritual of the play. No elevation was created on stage to depict Bernabé's underground refuge. Instead, his descent was achieved through the illusion of slits in the stage curtain.

Bernabé was produced at its new permanent home in San Juan Bautista in 1972. But the Teatro's first major revival of the play took place at the Campesino Playhouse on July 6, 1985, to commemorate the company's twentieth anniversary. It was a workshop production performed mostly in English, with a good deal of the humor spoken in Spanish. Tony Curiel directed a cast that featured Herbert Siguenza (Bernabé), Rosemary Ramos (La Madre), and Dolores De Angelo (Consuelo). Critic Steve Hauk praised Curiel's "sense of dramatic rhythm and visual power," noting that "no medium other than the theater can convey so hauntingly" the opening image—performed in shadow with musical accompaniment—as Bernabé "marches in place to his destiny trailed by his hounding Madre." [*The Herald,* 1985]

Under Barbara Martinez-Jittner's direction, *Bernabé* opened at Theatre Geo in Los Angeles in June of 1993, in a production that was part of the United Farm Workers' tribute to Cesar Chavez.

Reflections on BERNABÉ

Barbara Martinez-Jittner has worked with El Teatro Campesino and directed Bernabé.

I directed *Bernabé* as part of the first United Farm Workers' Union-sponsored tribute to Cesar Chavez in a festival of Chicano art done in Los Angeles. I had attended Cesar Chavez's funeral on April 23, 1993, and witnessed forty thousand farmworkers from all over the country come and flood the streets of Delano in solemn procession in honor of his life. I realized that the time had come for me to honor Cesar, but as an artist. Having been a member of El Teatro Campesino for eight years and worked very closely with Luis Valdez, I saw that the same conditions and the same reality in Delano and the San Joaquin Valley still existed, and that for all the work that Cesar had done, there was all this work yet to do. I wanted to do this tribute to Cesar to remind people that, although he's gone, our

Continued

work still continues, and that it's very important that all of us artists and people within the Chicano community now empower ourselves and say, "Hey! The ball is passed into our court. Together we can shine as brightly as Cesar did."

Our movement is La Causa and started with Cesar, with the United Farm Workers' Union, and with people fighting for their own dignity and power. So I chose one of Luis Valdez's earliest plays, written at a time when El Teatro Campesino had left Delano and was evolving from being the United Farmworkers' propaganda arm into a full-fledged Theatre Company. What was beautiful and special about *Bernabé* is that it marked the birth of the Chicano movement. This is the first play that explored the myth and ritual of pre-Colombian Mexico and connected it to the Chicano. It is also probably the first full-length play to have a "campesino," a Mexican farmworker, as its hero. The language in the play, in English or in Spanish, is the language of the "campesino." This slang—"calo," this new language of the Mexican-American was first heard on stage with Bernabé.

The play is about the rites of passage. Bernabé is mentally retarded and his character is based on a person Luis actually knew. He's a virgin who's taken to a whorehouse. He embraces La Tierra. Then he goes through this ritual with the Sun and becomes a new man. That's what Luis is talking about in terms of the Chicano movement, that we have this in order to become new again. I think that El Sol's very lengthy and important speech to Bernabé is the crux and essence of the play, when he talks about cosmic memory and how he remembers Bernabé a thousand years ago, that this is who you are, so don't let anyone call you crazy. This is your power. At that point, I think Luis really did—in terms of the Teatro—embrace that power and become what he is today—part of a huge cultural movement along with the UFW. This play is very special because it is Luis saying to himself and to a community, "Embrace yourself, become a new man, shed your old skin, die, and be born again!" In fact, that's what El Sol says: "Levántate! Rise! Be born again!"

I worked on a production of the play in 1985 at El Teatro Campesino Playhouse, under Tony Curiel's direction. It was a very literal one. I had also worked with Jerzy Grotowski for three years and with Peter Brook and Peter Sellars, and I had a background of avant-garde theatre which attracted me to the Teatro. So I took the play from Bernabé's point of view, that we're seeing the world through this special farmworker who is very in touch with the cosmic reality and the Indio reality, the truths that are passed down through his heritage. That's why he's a campesino who works with the earth and has a relationship with it.

My production went back to the world of the 1960s and what was special about that campesino world: a mixture of the connection of the Aztec-Mayan-Indio belief systems and realities that are still present with the modern-day Chicano. The first part took place in a typical farmworking town which could be seen anywhere in California with its archetypical characteristics: the cantina, the shack, the whorehouse, and, of course, the fields; and with all the archetypical characters: the farmworker, the drunk, the whore, and the labor contractor. In the second part of the play we see the mestizo, the Chicano, as the child of the Americas; that he draws his truth and belief systems from the ancient civilizations of America—from the Aztecs, Olmecs, and Mayans, and not necessarily from Europe. In my 1993 Los Angeles production, however, I did not make a distinction between the first and second half.

I was constantly trying to find strains back into that Aztec or Mayan reality through music and dance, even when it wasn't called for in the *mito* section. It became a through-line with Bernabé weaving this tapestry, so when he finally confronted the moon and the sun and all these deities, it turned out that they were always part of his daily life.

I choreographed the whole piece with a tremendous amount of music and dance because we are in his dream, we are in his reality. My production wasn't realistic. The characters outside of Bernabé were extended and came from the *commedia dell'arte*. But he himself was very pure and very naturalistic and very centered. So we saw it was really the world *around* him that was crazy, but was calling him *el loco*.

I choreographed La Madre with a cross because she was crucified and represented the Church, prayed the rosary, and was dressed in black. The drunk, who's El Tio, was very, very drunk. Usually the drunk becomes El Sol. But I changed that by adding a character called *el campesino,* who's a very poor old man. He was played by a seventy-three-year-old man who really was a campesino. Later this campesino becomes El Sol, the ultimate power because he knows a truth that nobody else knows. That was my tribute to Cesar, the campesino who becomes the ultimate power.

Consuelo is the classic whore, Mary Magdalene, who then becomes, of course, the Virgin Mary—La Virgen de Guadalupe actually. Her encounter with Bernabé was largely suggested through dance. She and Bernabé go upstairs to her bedroom in darkness. In the first part of the scene, when the voices are clearly Bernabé's and Consuelo's, the stage is black except for a little candle. She has an altar to Our Lady of Guadalupe whom she later becomes. So except for the little candle, you mostly hear their sounds. Then when the light comes up, instead of seeing Consuelo, Bernabé sees La Madre in her black robe praying the rosary. I used a lot of the images of the Virgin to make Consuelo as La Tierra because La Virgen de Guadalupe is based on the Aztec Goddess of the Earth. After Consuelo becomes La Tierra, she wears a *calavera,* or death mask, and performs the dance of this Aztec creature. So Bernabé becomes one with his Aztec mythology.

The play is a prayer of sorts, which is why I refused to have an intermission. It ran about an hour and fifteen minutes and was played as an unbroken, ritualistic celebration. The production was completely stylized. After all, Luis borrowed from the San Francisco Mime Troupe who borrowed from *commedia dell'arte*. Movement and gesture were really the text, more than the words. I went with that idea because of my own background with Grotowski. Even Bernabé had an Aztec-influenced dance with La Tierra. The music I used were real songs from *missas* (Masses), songs from the Azteca tradition that were brought into Catholicism, and a lot of popular Latino music.

We performed in a state-of-the-art theatre, the Theatre Geo in West Hollywood. There was no curtain, no real proscenium. It was obviously a theatre piece performed on a stage. I didn't try to make it a happening. The set was a kind of arid mountainous ground. On the left side of the stage was this hole which was both phallic and womb-like, because it was a huge mound that rose up but was also hollowed out. Bernabé crawled into it, but there was this top layer that people saw. But what I did was to slice the hole in half as if we were looking into an embryo. The other characters walked above Bernabé and didn't know that he was below. In fact, they were looking out at a different horizon.

Continued

On the right side of the stage was a cantina which I designed like a prison. Consuelo's bedroom was on a platform right above it and looked like a prison cell. Around the set was a fence. The stars shone through the **scrim** so that when Bernabé got into the elements we arrived from something oppressive into something that was really beautiful and magical. Constructed from a burlap fabric, the earth seemed to move and have a life of her own. She was lit from within and she glowed.

The play focuses on man's relationship with the earth. The issues facing farmworkers right now are pesticides and what we are doing to the earth without any real awareness, and that it's poisoning us. When we talk about La Tierra as our Mother Earth in the play, and how her embrace kills Bernabé in the end, it's much like Consuelo being poisoned, that prostitutes on drugs are being poisoned so that the johns can get more out of them. The same idea is that the growers are putting pesticides into the earth—the same as the drugs—to get more out of her. I've emphasized this in the play with Luis' permission, of course, to be more specific about the pesticide issue that affects the farmworkers. So our festival was not only a celebration to honor Cesar, but it was also a step that this is what we need to look at as a community and as artists within that community.

I believe Luis is saying that there has to be a new relationship between man and the earth. That's why Bernabé says that a man should never own a woman just like a man should never own the earth. It's not really about owning, it's about having a relationship. The whole thing about dignity is that we *are* from America, despite the unbelievable atrocities that have happened to our Mexicano and Chicano populations. So this powerful but rarely performed play helps us celebrate where we have come from and where we are going in the twenty-first century.

Notes

1. *Theodore Shank*, AMERICAN ALTERNATIVE THEATER *(New York: Grove Press, 1982), 74–75.*

2. *Jorge A. Huerta, "Labor Theatre, Street Theatre, and Community Theatre in the Barrios, 1965–1983," in* HISPANIC THEATRE IN THE UNITED STATES, *ed. Nicholas Kanellos (Houston: Arte Publico Press, 1984), 63.*

3. *"The Actos," in* EARLY WORKS, *Luis Valdez (Houston: Arte Publico Press, 1990), 12.*

4. *Ibid., 11.*

5. *Yolanda Broyles-Gonzalez, "Toward a Re-Vision of Chicano Theatre History: The Women of El Teatro Campesino," in* MAKING A SPECTACLE: FEMINIST ESSAYS ON CONTEMPORARY WOMEN'S THEATRE, *ed. Lynda Hart (Ann Arbor: University of Michigan Press, 1989), 214.*

6. *Donald H. Frischmann, "El Teatro Campesino y su mito* Bernabé: *un regresso a la madre tierra,"* AZTLAN *12 (Autumn 1981): 264.*

7. *"From Stereotypes to Archetypes: Chicano Theater's Reflection of the Mexicano in the United States," in* MISSIONS IN CONFLICT: ESSAYS ON U.S.-MEXICAN RELATIONS AND CHICANO CULTURE, *ed. Renata von Bardeleber, Dietrich Briesemeister, and Juan Bruce-Novoq (Tübingen: Gunter Narr Verlag, 1986), 77.*

8. *Early draft, courtesy El Teatro Campesino Archive, University of California at Santa Barbara.*

BERNABÉ
Luis Valdez

CHARACTERS

Bernabé
Madre

El Primo
El Tío/El Sol

Torres/La Luna
Consuelo/La Tierra

The protagonist, Bernabé, better known as *el tonto* in this play, is the prototype of the proverbial village idiot so popular in world literature. Traditionally, this literary figure has been employed to symbolize such human virtues as purity, truth, innocence, and love. Bernabé is no exception. His role is to symbolize man's lost love for Earth. He feels that man, especially the white man, has abused and exploited Earth's natural resources, and that it will take human sacrifice or an act of love to keep man from further destroying Earth. In order to conceive this act of love, Bernabé becomes the sacrificial lamb.

The action takes place in a rural town in the San Joaquin Valley of California. The time is the early 1960s. It is summer—not a cloud in the sky, not a breeze in the air. The crops lie majestically over the landscape, over the immensity of the fecund earth. The valley is sweltering under the heat. The sun is lord and master.

Rising abruptly on the flatness of the land is Burlap, California—a small squat town not picturesque enough to be called a village, too large to be a labor camp—population 2,100, one of hundreds of similar tank towns that dot the long flat immensity of the valley, covered with dust and crankcase oil. The town has a Main Street, the commercial center of town, consisting of a gas station, general store, bank, hardware, cafe, Mexican show, and Torres Bar & Hotel. Amid these business establishments are empty lots littered with debris.

This is the world of Bernabé, a mentally-retarded farmworker in his early thirties touched with cosmic madness. The world of man he inhabits judges him insane but harmless—a source of amusement and easy stoop labor. In his own world, however—a world of profoundly elemental perceptions—he is a human being living in direct relationship to earth, moon, sun, and stars.

The set, then, is necessarily abstract—a design that blends myth and reality—the paradoxical vision of a cosmic idiot simply known as Bernabé. For he is a man who draws his full human worth not from the tragicomic daily reality of men, but from the collective, mythical universality of Mankind.

ONE

Midday: a scorcher in the San Joaquin Valley. Under an infinite pale blue sky, the dusty streets of Burlap, California are empty. No signs of life. Near Torres Bar & Hotel, BER-NABE comes walking down the hot sidewalk at a steady clip. He is followed at some distance by his MADRE. Holding a transistor radio to his ear, BERNABE is listening to Tex-Mex music, oblivious to the heat.

MADRE (*stopping*). Bernabé . . . (BERNABE *keeps going*.) Berna-BEH! (BERNABE *stops with a sly grin*.)
BERNABE. What?
MADRE. Wait . . . ¡Ay, Dios—this heat! (MADRE *waddles forward, sweating and gasping for air—a wizened vision of old age in black, with a shawl wrapped tightly around her head.*)

BERNABE (*rudely*). What do you want?

MADRE.   Don't go so fast, hijo. You leave me behind.

BERNABE.   Well, step on it, you old bag.

MADRE (*angered*). Don't be ill-bred, hombre! I don't know why you have to get so far ahead of me. What if I fall down, eh? Is that what you want—to see me dead in the streets?

BERNABE (*grumbling*). . . . always dying of something.

MADRE (*sharply*). ¿Qué?

BERNABE.   Nothing.

MADRE (*fiercely*). Be careful how you speak to me, eh? I'm your madre! Do you want the ground to open up and swallow you? That's what happens to sons who don't respect their mothers. The earth opens up and swallows them alive, screaming to the heavens!

BERNABE (*looking down*). La tierra? . . . Chale, not me. (*We hear a distant drone high above. Distracted,* BERNABE *looks up at the sky. Smiling.*) Look . . . an airplane. It's a crop duster.

MADRE (*hitting him*). Aren't you listening to me, hombre? I'm getting too old to be out chasing you in the streets— and in this hot sun! Dios mío, you should feel this headache I'm suffering. ¿Sabes qué? You better go on to the store without me. Here. (*She pulls out a small money purse and turns away, digging out coins.* BERNABE *peeks over her shoulder.*) Get back. (BERNABE *backs off.* MADRE *unfolds a ten dollar bill and hands it to him preciously.*) Take this. Buy some eggs, a pound of coffee, and a dozen tortillas. Do you think you can remember that?

BERNABE (*nodding*). Eggs . . . coffee . . . tortillas. (*Pause.*) No pan dulce?

MADRE.   No! And be careful with the change, eh? Don't let them cheat you. God knows what we're going to do till you find work. (CONSUELO *comes down the sidewalk, heading for the bar.* BERNABE *ogles her the moment she appears.* MADRE *scandalized.*) ¡Válgame Dios! Bernabé, turn around!

BERNABE (*grinning*). ¿Por qué?

MADRE.   ¡Qué importa! (*She turns him around.* CONSUELO *pauses for a second, smiling cynically, then exits into Torres Bar.*) Shameless viejas! ¡Descaradas! Don't ever let me catch you going into the cantinas, Bernabé—the shame would kill me! Andale, pues, get to the store. Go on . . . (MADRE *starts to exit.* BERNABE *pauses and picks up an empty beer can on the street.*)

BERNABE.   Oiga, can I buy me . . . (*Looks at the beer can and hides it.*) . . . an ice cream?

MADRE (*turning*). No, no, no! Qué ice cream ni qué mugre! There's no money for sweets. And if you see Señor Torres, the labor contractor, ask him for work. Tell him your leg is fine now. Get going! (BERNABE *starts to go, and* MADRE *exits in the opposite direction.* BERNABE *stops, once she is out of sight, and comes back to the bar.*

He crouches in the doorway looking in, as EL PRIMO *and* TORRES *come down the sidewalk from the other side.*)

TORRES.   So how was Tijuana?

PRIMO.   A toda ème, boss.

TORRES.   No problems, eh?

PRIMO (*cool and secretive*). Chale. They had the carga waiting, I slipped them la lana, and I came back de volada. I got the stuff with me . . . fine shit, boss. The girls'll dig it.

TORRES.   Let's go inside.

PRIMO.   Orale.

TORRES (*spotting* BERNABE). Well, well—look who's here. Your cousin! (*He kicks* BERNABE *playfully.*)

BERNABE (*jumping*). ¡Ay! Baboso, hijo de la . . .

TORRES (*laughing*). Don't get mad, loco.

PRIMO (*feeling bad*). He's only playing with you, primo.

TORRES.   ¿Qué pues? Aren't you going to say hello?

BERNABE (*uneasy*). Hello, Torres.

TORRES (*in a joking mood*). Say, Eddie, did you know Bernabé has himself an old lady?

PRIMO (*humoring him*). No, really, cousin?

BERNABE (*surprised*). How do you know?

TORRES.   The whole town knows. You've been sleeping with her.

PRIMO.   No, really? (BERNABE *smiles mysteriously.*) Who is it, cousin? La Betty?

BERNABE.   No.

PRIMO.   La fat Mary?

BERNABE (*laughing*). Chale.

PRIMO.   Who, pues?

TORRES.   Who else? The old lady who still gives him chichi. His mamá! (TORRES *laughs boisterously.*)

PRIMO (*offended*). Orale, boss, you're laughing at my tía, man.

TORRES.   Just kidding, hombre. ¿Qué traes? (*Getting back to business.*) Bueno, Bernabé, we got work to do. Let's go, Eddie.

PRIMO.   Ahi te watcho, cousin. (TORRES *and* PRIMO *start to go into the bar.*)

TORRES.   Está más loco . . .

BERNABE (*boldly*). Hey, Torres!

TORRES (*stopping*). What? (*Long pause.* BERNABE *searches for words.*)

PRIMO.   What is it, primo?

BERNABE (*smiling slyly*). I wanna be with my ruca.

PRIMO.   Your ruca? What ruca?

BERNABE.   The one that's right here.

TORRES.   Here in my cantina?

BERNABE.   No, here outside.

PRIMO.   The sidewalk's empty, ese.

BERNABE (*insanely vague*). The sidewalk's cement. She's over here . . . where the ground is . . . and out in the fields . . . and in the hills. (*Looking up.*) She loves the rain.

TORRES (*laughing*). ¿Sabes qué? Something tells me this idiot wants to go upstairs.

PRIMO (*smiling*). You mean—to visit Connie?

TORRES.   He's got the itch. Isn't that it, Bernabé? You want one of my chamacas?

BERNABE.   No!

TORRES.   ¿Cómo que no? Your tongue's hanging out, loco. Look, if you tell me what you want, I'll get it for you. Compliments of the house.

BERNABE.   With my ruca?

TORRES.   The one you like.

BERNABE (*pause*). I want a job.

TORRES (*puzzled*). Job?

BERNABE.   In the fields.

PRIMO (*laughs*). He's got you now, Torres! You're gonna have to give him a chamba. The cousin's not as crazy as you think!

BERNABE (*laughs*). Simón, I ain't crazy.

TORRES (*scoffing*). You can't work with that crooked leg of yours.

BERNABE.   It's okay now.

TORRES.   And what about your head, loco? I can't have you throwing another fit and falling off the truck. Five men couldn't handle you.

PRIMO.   Aliviánate, boss—it was only a heat stroke. Besides, Bernabé's the best swamper you ever had. How many potato sacks did you load last year, cousin? Two hundred, five hundred, mil?

BERNABE.   Vale madre, mil!

PRIMO.   A thousand sacos a day, man!

BERNABE.   How about it, Torres?

TORRES (*shaking his head*). Ni modo, Quasimodo. Tell your mother to try the Welfare.

BERNABE.   I need money to buy la tierra.

TORRES.   What tierra?

BERNABE.   This one. Here and there and all over.

PRIMO (*humoring him*). You wanna buy a ranchito?

BERNABE (*emphatically*). No, a big rancho—with lots of tierra! All the tierra on earth. She's all mine.

TORRES.   Yours?

BERNABE.   My woman. We're gonna get married.

TORRES (*bursting out laughing*). Pinche loco! Vámonos, Eddie. His woman! What this idiot needs is a vieja. (*He exits laughing.*)

PRIMO.   Llévatela suave, primo. (PRIMO *exits. Long pause.* BERNABE *kneels on the earth.*)

BERNABE (*slyly*). Tierra, they think I'm crazy. But you know I love you. (*Looks around.*) See you tonight, eh? . . . like always. (*He kisses the ground and exits.*)

TWO

The scene is above and below the earth. Above, BERNABE's *house, a small unpainted shack, sits back from the street on a narrow lot. Below,* BERNABE *sits in a hole in the ground covered with planks, lighting candles to a sexy Aztec goddess pictured on a calendar from Wong's Market.* MADRE *emerges from the house. It is sundown.*

MADRE (*calling*). Bernabé? Bernabé, come and eat! Válgame Dios, where is this hombre? BER–NA–BE! (BERNABE *ignores her.* EL PRIMO *enters on the street.*)

PRIMO.   Buenas tardes, tía. What's wrong? Lose Bernabé again?

MADRE.   No, qué lose! He hides just to make me suffer. Have you seen him, hijo?

PRIMO.   This morning, outside the cantina.

MADRE (*alarmed*). La cantina?

PRIMO.   I mean, the store, tía. The Chinaman's supermarket.

MADRE (*relieved*). Pues, sí. I sent him to buy a few things for me. I have a week now with a headache that won't go away. If you only knew, hijo—how much I suffer and worry. Our rent is almost up, and Bernabé without work. (*Pause.*) You do have a job, no m'ijo?

PRIMO (*nods*). I'm working with Torres.

MADRE.   Ay, pos sí, ¿no? They say that Señor Torres is rich. He always has money.

PRIMO.   Almost all the men in town are unemployed, tía. There won't be anything till the picking starts. Look, let me lend you ten bucks.

MADRE (*self-righteous*). No, Eduardo. What would your mother say? May God forbid it. I know my sister only too well. When it's about money, she's an owl. No, no, no!

PRIMO (*holding out a ten spot*). Here, tía.

MADRE.   No, hijo, gracias.

PRIMO.   Andele. Take it. (*He tries to put the money in her hand.*)

MADRE (*folding her arms*). No, no—y no!

PRIMO (*shrugging*). Well . . .

MADRE (*quickly*). Well, okay, pues! (MADRE *snatches the ten dollars with lightning reflexes and stuffs it in her bosom hypocritically.*) And how is your madrecita?

PRIMO.   Fine, like always.

MADRE.   Gracias a Dios. Bueno, if you see m'ijo, send him straight home, eh? I don't know what will become of him. One of these days they'll put him in the crazy house, then what will I do?

PRIMO.   Try not to worry, tía. Adiós. (MADRE *exits into her house.* PRIMO *starts to move on.* EL TIO *enters down the street.*)

TIO.   ¡Oye. sobrino! Eddie!

PRIMO.   Orale, tío—how you been?

TIO.   Pos, ¿cómo? Hung-over. Oye, you wouldn't happen to have two bits? Un tostón—for the cure, you know? With 35 cents I can buy me a mickey y ya 'stuvo. (PRIMO *gives him the money.*) N'ombre! That's a real nephew. Say, I couldn't help notice you slipped some money to my little sister, eh?

PRIMO.   A few bolas. So what?

TIO (*scratching his head*). No, nothing, but I bet you she didn't even say gracias, right? Sure, don't deny it! Don't be a sucker. Guaro—haven't I told you? That old dried prune don't appreciate nothing. Look at me. How many years did I bust my ass in the fields to support her, her idiot son, and your own sweet mother who I love more than anybody? You know, when I go over to your house, your 'amá never fails to offer me a cup of coffee, a plate of beans—vaya, whatever, no? But this other miserable sister I got won't even give me a glass of water. Instead she tells me to get the hell on my way, because she has to feed Bernabé, and she don't like nobody to watch him eat! (PRIMO *laughs*.) Isn't that so? That's how she is.

PRIMO.   Orale, pues, tío. And speaking of the primo, you seen him?

TIO (*suspiciously*). ¿Por qué? Is that old coyota looking for him? ¡Qué caray! (*Pause.*) Look, you know where the poor loco is?—but don't tell his madre, eh? . . . he's right there, in the field by his house.

PRIMO.   The empty lot?

TIO.   Sí, hombre, the little llano where the kids play. He's got a hole there he dug into the ground, see? That's where he crawls in and hides. At first he used to get into rock fights with the snot-noses, but lately he's been waiting till dark to go down there, so nobody bothers him.

PRIMO (*puzzled*). How do you know all this, tío?

TIO.   I've seen him. He disappears like a gopher and don't come out for two or three hours.

PRIMO.   What does he do?

TIO.   ¡Sabrá Judas! I even went and got into the hole myself once—when he was downtown with his madre, but I didn't see nothing . . . except for the dirt, soft and warm—like he crawls in and squirms around it.

PRIMO.   In the dirt?

TIO.   What else is there?

PRIMO (*pause*). Chale. It can't be.

TIO.   ¿Qué?

PRIMO.   Forget it. He's not that crazy.

TIO.   Sure he's crazy. Completely nuts.

PRIMO.   Can he be that far gone?

TIO.   Cracked and eaten by burros! What's on your mind?

PRIMO.   Just something he told me and Torres this morning.

TIO (*pause*). What?

PRIMO.   Nothing much. It's impossible.

TIO (*exasperated*). Well, what is it, hombre? You got me standing on my toenails!

PRIMO (*pause*). He said he has a girlfriend.

TIO.   Girlfriend?

PRIMO.   La Tierra.

TIO.   You mean the dirt?

PRIMO (*nods*). And that they're gonna get married.

TIO (*pause*). And you think he . . . ? No, hombre! He can't be that crazy!

PRIMO.   Didn't I tell you?

TIO (*pause*). A hole in the ground? (*Angered.*) Pos, mira qué loco tan cochino, hombre! How can he be doing such a dirty thing? Fucking idiot!

PRIMO.   Easy, tío.

TIO.   It's disgusting, Guaro, He's not your nephew.

PRIMO.   He's a cousin.

TIO.   Pos, ¡ahi 'ta! He's disgracing the whole family. We got the same blood, hombre. Chihuahua! What's his madre going to say if she finds him out? I bet you she suspects something already.

PRIMO.   Chale.

TIO.   Si, señor. You think I don't know my own sister?

MADRE (*offstage*). Berna-beh!

TIO.   Listen! Here she comes again. (PRIMO *and* TIO *hide in the shadows, as* MADRE *re-enters. She spots* BERNA-BE's *hole in the ground and approaches it suspiciously. Lifting a plank, she suddenly spots him.*)

MADRE (*gasping*). Bernabé? Por Dios, come out of there!

PRIMO.   She's got him.

TIO.   ¡Pobre loco! He's going to get it now. (MADRE *starts tearing off the planks, as* BERNABE *cowers in his hole.*)

MADRE.   ¡Ave María Purísima! ¡Virgencita pura, ayúdame! (PRIMO *and* TIO *rush to the hole.*)

TIO.   Quihubo pues, sister? What's the matter?

MADRE.   Don't bother me now, Teodoro! I've got too many troubles.

TIO.   Huy, pos—what's new?

MADRE.   Don't even talk to me, hombre! You can be a disgraceful wino if you want, but I have to look out for m'ijo!

PRIMO.   Did you find Bernabé, tía?

MADRE.   Sí, hijo! Look where he is—in a filthy hole! Come out of there, Bernabé!

BERNABE (*refusing to come out*). CHALE!

MADRE.   ¡Sal de ahi te digo!

BERNABE (*cursing*). ¡Vieja cabrona, píntese!

MADRE (*shocked*). What? ¡Bendito sea Dios? Did you hear what he called me?

TIO (*smiling*). What's he doing?

MADRE (*pushing him back*). None of your business! You up here—staggering in the streets, and my son down there risking death, verdad?

TIO.   What death? Stop exaggerating.

MADRE (*fuming*). Exaggerating? Exaggerating! And if the ground falls on top of him, what can happen, eh? Dios mío, he'll suffocate! Do you hear me, Bernabé? Come out of that dark, ugly hole!

PRIMO.   The tía's right, primo. Come on out.

MADRE.   Talk to him, Eduardo. Please! Before I die of the . . .

TIO.   Exaggeration.

MADRE (*lashing at him*). ¡Cállate el hocico! Just get out of here, sabes? Leave!

TIO.   You leave! Pos, mira qué chirrión.

MADRE.   Come out, Bernabé! ¡Ahorita mismo!

PRIMO (*reaching in*). Come on, primo.

BERNABE (*shaking his head*). What are you going to do to me?

MADRE.   Nothing. Just come out.

PRIMO.   Grab my hand, ese. (BERNABE *grabs* PRIMO's *hand and slowly emerges from the pit.*)

BERNABE (*fearful*). Are you going to hit me, oiga?

MADRE.   Come on, Bernabé!

BERNABE (*coming out*). If you lay a finger on me, I'll kick your ass.

MADRE (*gasps*). ¡Válgame Dios, Bernabé! (*She grabs him.*) Now I am going to hit you, for your filthy mouth! ¡Malcriado! (*She beats him.*)

BERNABE (*cowering*). ¡Ay! ¡No! ¡No, mamá!

TIO.   That's enough, let him alone!

PRIMO.   Don't hit him, tía.

MADRE (*incensed*). Stay out of this—both of you! Bernabé's my son and I have the right to punish him. (*She hits him again.*)

TIO.   But he's a man. Not a kid! (*Stopping her.*)

MADRE.   I don't care! I'm his madre. And so long as God gives me life, I'll go on punishing him when he does wrong! Let go of me!

BERNABE (*weeping like a child*). I didn't do nothing!

MADRE.   Sí, nothing! You think I'm blind, eh? What were you doing in that hole? You think I don't know what dirty things you do in there? I can just imagine! But one of these nights the moon is going to come down and swallow you alive—¡por cochino!

BERNABE (*with fear*). No, 'amá, la luna no.

MADRE.   Yes, you'll see! ¡Vamos, ándale! Into the house! ¡Ave María Santísima! (MADRE *exits with* BERNABE, *pulling him by the hair.* PRIMO *and* TIO *look at each other sorrowfully.*)

TIO.   Pobre loco.

PRIMO.   She treats him like a kid.

TIO.   That's what he is. You saw him—he really believes the moon can come down and swallow him. But I know what you mean. In a few weeks, he'll be in the fields, working and sweating like an animal. And do you think my sister appreciates it? No, hombre, she rents him like a burro!

PRIMO.   Say, tío—how old is Bernabé?

TIO.   Pos, lemme see . . . thirty four? No, wait . . . thirty seven!

PRIMO.   And how many girlfriends has he had?

TIO.   Are you serious?

PRIMO.   Simón. (*Pause.*) None, am I right?

TIO.   Ninguna.

PRIMO.   ¡Orale! Then it's not craziness.

TIO.   What?

PRIMO.   All the funny stuff about la tierra and the hole and everything, tío. Figure it out. (*Pause.*) Look, will you help me do the cousin a favor?

TIO.   Like what?

PRIMO.   Pos, ya sabe. You know Consuelo, the hot mamma that works over in Torres Club?

TIO.   ¿La p . . . ?

PRIMO.   ¡Simón, la chavalona!

TIO.   No, Guaro, I don't get into those things no more.

PRIMO.   So what? Look, go to the club and tell her to wait for me in one hour. Tell her Eddie wants to talk to her. Understand?

TIO.   And why don't you go?

PRIMO.   Because I'm bringing the primo.

TIO (*scoffing*). Oh, sure. His madre's gonna let him go straight to the cantina! Forget it, sobrino. You're a bigger fool than I thought.

PRIMO (*smiling*). You just leave the tía to me. She and I get along fine. If I tell her I'm taking Bernabé to see Torres about a job, no hay pedo. I'll have him there. ¿Juega?

TIO.   Pos, qué caray, okay pues. ¡Juega!

PRIMO (*taking out money*). Then here—have a few cold beers while you wait for us.

TIO (*taking the money eagerly*). ¡Ay, chirrión! You mean I have to wait?

PRIMO.   Don't you want to see your nephew happy?

TIO.   What nephew? That pitiful idiot?

PRIMO.   He's not such an idiot, tío. You'll see. Bueno, trucha pues. Torres Club, eh? Around nine. (PRIMO *and* TIO *start to go in opposite directions.*)

TIO (*stopping*). ¡Epa! And what's the name of the . . . ?

PRIMO.   Consuelo. She's got the big chamorrotes (thighs).

TIO.   Pos, you ought to know. I don't.

PRIMO (*laughing*). Orale, pues, ahi nos watchamos later. I'm going to eat with the tía. (*Starts to go again.*)

TIO (*stopping again*). ¡Oye! And if Bernabé doesn't want to . . . tú sabes . . .

PRIMO.   Then the favor's for you, tío. (*Exits.*)

TIO (*starts to exit*). Ha! For me . . . (*Stops. Reconsiders, tilts head, smiles.*) Consuelo, eh? (*He exits.*)

THREE

Torres Club. Outside in the back alley. BERNABE *comes out of the cantina with a beer can. The moon is bright.*

BERNABE (*looking down*). Tierra? It's me . . . out here in this alley. See, that's Torres' cantina . . . Look—a cerveza. You know what? My primo went and covered the hole where we get together. Mi 'amá sent him. But who cares, huh? It's just some boards. Tomorrow I'll take 'em off! Anyway, you're here, and over there, and way over there. And right, right here. We're always together! (*Laughs and kisses the earth.* TORRES *enters. Sees* BERNABE, *laughs to himself, shaking his head.* BERNABE *scoops up a handful of dirt.*)

TORRES.   Oye, oye, stop feeling her up!

BERNABE (*startled*). Uh?

TORRES (*laughs*). Don't get scared, loco. It's me. How's the girlfriend, okay?

BERNABE.   Simón, okay. (*He rises.*)

TORRES.   Nice and cool, eh? Pos, qué suave. Chihuahua, it's hot, hombre! The sun went down and the night stayed hot. What are you doing here so late?

BERNABE.   Nothing. (*Hiding his handful of dirt.*)

TORRES.   And that beer?

BERNABE.   My primo bought it for me. We came to look for work.

TORRES.   So where's Eddie? Inside?

BERNABE (*nodding*). Talking to Torres.

TORRES.   Oh sí, eh? And who am I? La Luna?

BERNABE (*startled*). Chale.

TORRES (*laughs*). No, ¿verdad? There's the moon up there. Look how big she is! I wonder if she's jealous? The moon's a woman too, eh? Or maybe not. Maybe he's the brother of your ruca. Watch it, Bernabé, he's gonna take her away!

BERNABE.   ¡Pura madre! Nobody can take her away!

TORRES.   Well, don't get pissed.

BERNABE.   She's mine. (*Looks at his handful.*)

TORRES (*tongue in cheek*). Then tell that to the gabachos. See if they give her back.

BERNABE.   What gabachos?

TORRES.   The landowners, manito. Banks, corporations.

BERNABE.   They ain't nobody.

TORRES (*pause*). Hey—and if I wanted the land too, Bernabé? What do I do?

BERNABE (*laughs*). Aguántate. You just wait!

TORRES.   But she's my mamá.

BERNABE.   ¿La tierra?

TORRES.   Sure. She's your momma too.

BERNABE.   Up yours! She's not my mother.

TORRES.   Bueno, your hot momma, then. But look how the ranchers treat her, hombre. They sell her whenever they feel like it—to the highest bidder! See those fields over there? I just bought 'em yesterday. I own the ground under your feet too. All the lots on this street. And I got more on the other side of the barrio. Check it out. But you know what, loco? I'll rent her to you. (*Laughs.*) Give me a few bucks, and I'll let you have her—for the night! (BERNABE *is genuinely puzzled. He finds* TORRES's *reasoning totally nonsensical.*)

BERNABE.   Say, Torres, you're even crazier than me! (*Laughs.*) ¡Ah, qué Torres!

TIO (*entering*). ¡Oye tú! Where you been?

BERNABE.   Right here.

TIO.   What are you up to, hombre? Why did you leave the bar? (*Spots* TORRES.) Oh, buenas noches, Señor Torres.

TORRES.   Buenas . . . (*Suspicious.*) What's up, Teodoro?

TIO (*nervous*). No, nothing, this burro . . . I don't know why I got into this! Eddie brought him here . . . to do him a favor . . . (*Barking at* BERNABE.) Let's go inside,

ándale! Your cousin already went up with the vieja. He said to get ready.

TORRES.   No, hombre! He's going in with Connie?

TIO.   Pos sí, if she lets him in.

TORRES (*smiles*). Sure she'll let him. She does what I tell her.

TIO.   My nephew's already talking her into it.

TORRES.   So you're going to get laid, eh Bernabé?

BERNABE (*getting scared*). I want another beer.

TIO.   There's no more. Go do your duty!

TORRES.   Don't rush him, hombre. This is an occasion. Come on in. So you're finally going to get married, eh loco?

TIO.   ¡Qué pinche vergüenza! (*Exits.*)

FOUR

Torres Club—interior. The upstairs hallway of a cheap hotel.
PRIMO *enters, his arm around* CONSUELO.

PRIMO.   Orale, Connie, gracias for doing me this favor, eh?

CONSUELO.   It's no favor, man. You gotta pay me.

PRIMO.   Simón, but the vato's muy especial, you know?

CONSUELO.   Who is this jerk?

PRIMO.   My cousin.

CONSUELO.   Who?

PRIMO.   Bernabé.

CONSUELO (*nonplussed*). You mean . . . el loquito del pueblo? Sorry, Eddie, I'm sorry, but no dice.

PRIMO.   ¿Por qué no?

CONSUELO.   Because, porque no. How do I know what he's gonna do? Because he's crazy, that's why!

PRIMO.   He's not that loco, chula. He just needs a little break.

CONSUELO.   Well, it's not me, man.

PRIMO.   Look, it's no big deal. I'm asking you to do the vato a favor. He's my primo—sure he's missing a few marbles, but so what? He's got everything else. Andale, chula—just for a little bit. I promised him—it's his birthday.

CONSUELO (*pause*). Give me fifteen bucks and he's on.

PRIMO.   Fifteen bolas? What are you—gold-plated down there? (CONNIE *starts to go.*) No, look, Connie—don't be that way. Besides, all I got are nine bills, see? Here. (*Gives her the money.*)

CONSUELO (*takes it reluctantly*). Bueno, okay. But just one turn on the merry-go-round and that's it. Where's the loco at?

PRIMO.   He's coming with el tío—they had a beer first.

CONSUELO.   Tío?

PRIMO.   Teodoro.

CONSUELO.   That winito's your tío?

PRIMO.   Simón, and also Bernabé's.

CONSUELO.   And is his mamá here too?

PRIMO.   Chale, what's with you?

CONSUELO. Naranjas, corazón. Okay, send him in, pues. (CONSUELO *exits into her room.*)

TIO (*offstage*). Guaro?

PRIMO. Orale, tío—up here.

TIO (*offstage*). Here comes Lover Boy . . . Drooling in his shorts! Is she ready?

PRIMO. And set to go.

TIO (*enters puffing*). Híjole, la chicharra, hombre! It took long enough to get up here. Where's the bride?

PRIMO. In her room.

TIO (*looking*). Ah, pos sí, I recognize the place.

PRIMO. Just like old times, eh tío?

TIO. Huy, what can I say, sobrino? I personally broke in this hotel. Every payday, I couldn't keep my nose out of here. They had some big fine things up here in those days.

PRIMO. And Bernabé?

TIO (*turning*). He was right behind . . . Adiós, where did he go? There he is! See? ¡Andale, oyes! Don't hide. Come on up.

BERNABE (*offstage*). For what?

TIO. For what? Pos—what do you think? It's payday. Are you scared?

BERNABE (*offstage*). NO!

PRIMO. All right, ese, the ruca's waiting for you.

BERNABE (*entering*). Where?

PRIMO. In there. It's la Connie, the one who was at the bar? La watchates? The fine buns and the big legs? (BERNABE *laughs.*) Simón qué yes, verdad? She's ready, she's willing, and she's able, carnal. So get in there. Go get it!

BERNABE (*playing dumb*). What?

PRIMO. You know, loco. (BERNABE *laughs lasciviously. He looks at his PRIMO and TIO, then hesitantly starts toward CONSUELO's room. He reaches the door and is about to go in, when he stops suddenly and turns grinning idiotically.*)

BERNABE (*backing off*). Chale.

PRIMO. Nel, primo—don't chicken out, man. She's all set. Andale!

BERNABE (*shaking his head*). No, she'll swallow me.

TIO. Swallow you!

BERNABE. La Luna. For being dirty.

PRIMO. That's bullshit, primo. Come on, you saw Connie. You liked what you saw, right?

BERNABE. Yeah.

PRIMO. Well then? Go see it all.

BERNABE. Not now.

PRIMO. Why not?

BERNABE. I don't feel like it.

TIO. You felt like it downstairs.

BERNABE (*turning*). I want another beer first.

TIO. Later—afterward.

PRIMO. You have to go in now, primo. She's waiting for you. Besides, I already paid her . . . twenty bucks. Okay?

BERNABE. I don't think so.

TIO. But didn't you hear, hombre. He already paid the vieja!

BERNABE. I don't give a shit. I don't want that vieja!

TIO. Bueno, if he's not going in . . . (*Pause.*) He's not going in. Take the idiot home, and that's it.

CONSUELO (*at her door*). Eddie? Oye, Eddie? ¿Qué pasó, pues?

PRIMO. Hold it a second.

CONSUELO. Hold it yourself! Tell him to hurry. (*She retreats into her room.*)

PRIMO. You see? She wants you to go in.

TIO. And to hurry.

PRIMO. Come on, ese. I know you want to.

TIO. Sure, he wants to. ¡Está buenota, hombre! I wouldn't hold back.

BERNABE. Then, you get in there.

TIO. Don't be an idiot! Qué caray, I would if I could, but I can't no more. She's more than I can handle. Here, have a drink—to give you strength. (*Gives him a swig of his beer.*)

PRIMO. Okay, pues, get in there, cuz!

TIO. Be a man, m'ijo. (BERNABE *starts to move toward CONSUELO's door again. Cautiously, he is about to enter, but he stops and beats a retreat.*)

BERNABE (*backing off again*). Chale, I can't!

TIO (*cursing*). ¡Me lleva la . . . que me trajo! This is a jackass without a rope, hombre.

PRIMO (*giving up*). Simón, let's go, pues.

BERNABE. Where we going?

PRIMO. Home to your chante.

BERNABE. Nel, I wanna booze it up.

TIO. We already boozed it up.

BERNABE. Just one.

TIO (*exasperated*). N'ombre! This fool don't want a puta, he wants a peda. Better take him home, Guaro. Before he gets drunk.

BERNABE. I'm not going to get drunk, oiga!

PRIMO. Let's go, Bernabé.

BERNABE. No! I wanna stay here.

TIO. Your madre's waiting for you.

BERNABE. ¡Me importa madre! They're waiting for me here too.

TIO (*shoving him toward the door*). Then, get in there!

BERNABE (*pause*). No . . . she'll swallow me.

PRIMO (*tries to pull him*). Let's go, ese.

BERNABE. No!

TIO. ¡Andale! Grab him! (PRIMO *and* TIO *grab* BERNABE.)

BERNABE (*resisting*). No! Nooo! I wanna drink! I wanna viejaaa! I want la tierraaa! (CONSUELO *comes out of her room in a nightgown.*)

CONSUELO. Oye, oye, what's happening, Eddie?

PRIMO.   Nothing. We're going.

CONSUELO.   ¿Qué pasó? Isn't he coming in?

PRIMO.   Chale.

TIO.   He's crazy. (CONSUELO *comes up to* BERNABE, *mockingly wanton, sultrily flaunting her body before his gaping eyes.*)

CONSUELO.   ¿Qué pasó, Bernabé? You don't want to come with me? You know me, ¿qué no? I'm Consuelo—la Connie. Come on, gimme a little hug. (BERNABE *retreats.*) Andale, hombre—don't back away! Eddie tells me you like las chavalonas. Is that true, eh? Mira—gimme your hand like this . . . and now we put it here. (*She wraps his arm around her.* BERNABE *opens his fist—the handful of earth falls to the floor.*) Like novios, see? Do you want to dance? I have a record player in my room. Come on, let's go to the baile . . . (*She takes him to the door of her room.*) ¿Y ustedes? What are you gawking at? Get lost! Can't you see we're going on our honeymoon? (CONSUELO *laughs and closes the door, pulling in* BERNABE *with her.* PRIMO *approaches the dirt on the floor.*)

TIO.   ¿Qué es eso? What did he drop?

PRIMO. Tierra . . . (*They look at each other.*) Come on, tío. I'll buy you a beer.

TIO.   Let's go. This idiot nephew's driving me crazy? (*They exit.*)

FIVE

CONSUELO's *room: darkness. A brief erotic silence, slowly punctuated by* CONSUELO's *moans and the pounding of* BERNABE's *heartbeat.*

CONSUELO (*in the dark*). Ay, papasito . . . Ay, ay, ¡AY!

BERNABE (*screaming*). ¡AYYY!

CONSUELO (*pause*). Bernabé?

BERNABE.   ¡Quítate! ¡AYYYY!

CONSUELO.   Shut up, hombre! ¿Qué tienes?

BERNABE.   No, mamá, yo no hice nadaaaa!

CONSUELO.   Are you going nuts on me?

BERNABE.   Mamá! Mamáááá! (*Strobe light effect, slow to fast.* BERNABE *is backing away from* CONSUELO—*or at least the* MADRE *dressed in* CONSUELO's *clothes. The effect is nightmarish.*)

MADRE (*as* CONSUELO). ¿Qué tienes, papasito?

BERNABE (*backing off*). No, nooooo!

MADRE.   Naranjas, corazón. Don't you want to be with me? I'm your girlfriend . . . tu novia. (*Changing into* MADRE.) ¡Pero también soy madre y te voy a pegar! ¡Por cochino! ¡Vente! ¡Vámonos pa' la casa! (*She grabs him by the hair.*)

BERNABE (*like a child*). No, mami, noooo! (MADRE *changes into* CONSUELO *and strokes* BERNABE's *head and face, calming him down.*)

MADRE (*as* CONSUELO). Pero, ¿por qué no, bonito? You know me, que no? I'm Consuelo, La Connie. Eddie tells

me you like las chavalonas. Don't you want me? Soy tu novia . . . (*Back to* MADRE.) ¡Y por eso te voy a pegar! Soy tu madre, y tengo derecho de castigarte mientras Dios me preste vida. You want la tierra to swallow you alive? Come with me!

BERNABE (*shoving her back*). No, noo, no quierooo! Tierraaaa! (BERNABE *runs out into the hallway. Lights up. Strobe effect disappears.* PRIMO, TORRES, *and* TIO *come running.*)

PRIMO.   What's the matter, primo?

TORRES.   ¡Oye, Connie! What the hell's going on, pues? (CONSUELO *comes out of her room, as herself.* BERNABE *screams.*)

CONSUELO.   Torres! Get this baboso out of here! ¡Sáquenlo!

PRIMO.   What happen, chula?

CONSUELO.   I don't know what happen. Está loco, ¿qué no ves?

BERNABE (*terrified*). ¡Yo no hice nada!

TORRES.   Did he go in at least?

PRIMO.   Sure he went in.

TIO.   Se metió bien contento.

CONSUELO.   I told you, Eddie! ¡Te dije!

PRIMO.   Come on, primo. Let's go home.

BERNABE (*cries out in horror*). No! Nooo! ¡Me pega! She'll hit me!

PRIMO.   Who'll hit you?

BERNABE (*points at* CONSUELO). ¡Mi 'amáááá!

TIO.   This isn't your mother, suato!

CONSUELO.   See what I mean. (BERNABE *screams.*)

TORRES (*to* CONSUELO). Don't talk to him, stupid! Keep your mouth shut!

CONSUELO.   You bastard. This is all your fault! You think I like to do this?

TORRES.   ¡Cállate el hocico!

CONSUELO.   And you keep the money!

TORRES.   Get into your room! (*He pushes her.*)

CONSUELO (*defiantly*). Tell them! Tell 'em how you use the girls! And for what? Your pinche drugs?

TORRES (*slapping her around*). I said shut your fucking mouth!

BERNABE (*reacting*). No, nooo! MAMA! (*Rushes* TORRES.)

PRIMO.   ¡Bernabé, cálmala!

TIO.   Settle down, hombre!

TORRES (BERNABE *on his back*). Get him out of here!

PRIMO.   We're trying, boss!

CONSUELO.   Kick his ass, Bernabé!

TORRES (*pushing* CONSUELO). I'm gonna get you!

BERNABE (*pounding on him*). No, ¡déjala! Leave her alone! (PRIMO *and* TIO *struggle to take* BERNABE *off* TORRES.)

PRIMO. Primo!

TIO.   Bernabé!

BERNABE.   She's mine! My woman is mine!

TORRES. ¡Quítenlo! Get him OFF OF ME! (*He falls.* CON-SUELO *laughs.* BERNABE *is hysterical, totally out of it.* PRIMO *and* TIO *succeed in pulling him off* TORRES.)

BERNABE. ¡Lo maté! ¡LO MATE! I KILLED TORRES! (BERNABE *runs out.* TIO *starts to run after him.* PRIMO *helps* TORRES *on his feet.* CONSUELO *is still laughing.*)

TIO (*calling*). Bernabé! Come back here, you idiot!

PRIMO. You okay, boss?

TORRES. ¿Pos, luego? Let me go.

TIO. ¡Oye, Guaro! The loco ran outside! What if he goes and tells his madre?

PRIMO. I don't understand what happened to him. What did you do?

CONSUELO. Don't ask me, man! It's not my fault if he thinks I'm his pinche madre!

TIO (*to* PRIMO). ¡Vámonos, hombre! We're gonna lose him!

PRIMO. Orale, let's go. Sorry, Torres. (*They exit.* CON-SUELO *and* TORRES *are left behind.* CONSUELO *looks at* TORRES *and starts laughing. A deep bitter laugh, not without a certain satisfaction. She exits into her room.*)

TORRES. Goddamn whore! (*He exits.*)

SIX

El llano: night. There is a full moon, unseen, but casting an eery light on the earth. BERNABE *is at his hole, pulling off the boards. Suddenly, from the sky comes music.*

BERNABE (*crying out*). ¡Tierraaa! I killed Torres! ¡Hijo 'e su tiznada madre! ¡LO MATE! (*Pause. He hears the danzón music.*) What's that? (*Stops. Fearfully looks at sky, sees moon.*) ¡La Luna! It's coming down! ¡Mamá, la lunaaa! (*Sobs like a child. Moonlight gathers into a spot focussed on him.* LA LUNA *enters, dressed like a Pachuco, 1942 style: Zoot suit, drapes, calcos, hat with feather, small chain, etc.*)

LUNA. Orale, pues, ese vato. No te escames. Soy yo, la Luna.

BERNABE (*wrapping himself into a ball*). ¡No, chale!

LUNA. Control, ese. Ain't you Chicano? You're a vato loco.

BERNABE (*looks up slowly*). I ain't loco.

LUNA. Oh, simón. I didn't mean it like that, carnal. Te estaba cabuliando. Watcha. If they don't like you the way you are, pos que tengan, ¡pa' que se mantengan! ¡Con safos, putos! Shine 'em on, ese. Inside you know who you are. Can you dig it?

BERNABE (*feeling better*). Simón.

LUNA. Pos a toda madre. (*Pause. Reaches into his pocket.*) Oye, like to do a little grifa? A good reefer will set you straight. You got any trolas? (*Finds match, lights joint for* BERNABE.) Alivian el esqueleto, carnal. Me and you are going to get bien locos tonight. Ahi te llevo. (*Grabs joint from* BERNABE.) No le aflojes. (BERNABE *gets joint again.*) Ese, you see them stars way up there?—some of

them got some fine asses . . . (BERNABE *laughs.*) Say, I saw you go into Torres Club tonight. How was it?

BERNABE (*guilty*). Okay.

LUNA. Simón, that Connie's a real mamasota, carnal. But tell me—a la bravota—why didn't you put it to her? Chicken? (BERNABE *throws the joint down.*) No, chale, don't tell me, pues. None of my beeswax. Here, no te agüites. (*Gives him back the joint.*) Oye, Bernabé, ¿sabes qué? I got a boner to pick with you, man. It's about my carnala.

BERNABE. Your carnala?

LUNA. Mi sister, loco. What you up to?

BERNABE. Nothing.

LUNA. Don't act pendejo, ese! I've been watching you get together almost every night. You dig me? She asked me to come down and see what's cooking. You just wanna get laid or what? She wants to make it forever, loco.

BERNABE. Forever?

LUNA. With you. Me la rayo. Watcha, let me call her. (*Calls.*) Oye, sister, come on! Somebody's waiting for you. (*Music accompanies the entrance of* LA TIERRA. *She emerges from the hole dressed as a soldadera [soldier woman of the Mexican Revolution, 1910] with a sombrero and cartridge belts.* BERNABE *is spellbound the moment he sees her. She stares at* BERNABE, *amazon and earth mother.*)

TIERRA. ¿Quién es?

LUNA. Pos, who? Your vato loco. Bernabé, this is my carnala. La Tierra.

TIERRA. Buenas noches, Bernabé. (BERNABE *makes a slight grunt, smiling idiotically.*) You don't know me? (BERNABE *is speechless and embarrassed.*)

LUNA. Orale, pues, carnal, say something. Don't tell me you're scared of her? (BERNABE *struggles to say something. His mind tries to form words. He ends up starting to laugh moronically, from helplessness.*)

TIERRA (*sharply*). No, hombre, don't laugh! Speak to me seriously. Soy la tierra. (BERNABE *stares at her. A sudden realization strikes him and turns into fear. He screams and runs.*)

LUNA. ¡Epale! Where you going, loco? (*Stops* BERNABE *with a wave of his arm.*) Cálmala—be cool! There's nothing to be scared of. (*Pulls him toward* TIERRA.) Look at my carnala, see how a toda madre she looks in the moonlight . . . She loves you, man. Verdad, sister?

TIERRA. If he is a man. (BERNABE *is caught in a strange spell. He and* LA TIERRA *look at each other for a long moment.* LA LUNA *gets restless.*)

LUNA. Bueno, le dijo la mula al freno. You know what? I'm going to take a little spin around the stars—check up on the latest chisme. Oye, Bernabé, watch it with my sister, eh? Llévensela suave, pues. (*Exits.*)

TIERRA (*softly*). What are you thinking, Bernabé?

BERNABE (*struggling to say something*). I killed Torres.

TIERRA (*pushing him down*). H'm, ¡qué pelado este! Weren't you thinking about me? Don't pride yourself. Torres isn't dead.

BERNABE. He's still alive?

TIERRA. Pos, luego. How were you going to kill him? With your bare hands? Right now, he's in his bar laughing at you!

BERNABE. ¿Por qué?

TIERRA. Because he knows I belong to him. Not to you.

BERNABE (*incensed*). Chale, you're mine!

TIERRA. And how am I yours, Bernabé? Where and when have you stood up for me? All your life you've worked in the fields like a dog—and for what? So others can get rich on your sweat, while other men lay claim to me? Torres says he owns me, Bernabé—what do you own? Nothing. (*Pause.* BERNABE's *head is down.*) Look at me, hombre! Soy la Tierra! Do you love me? Because if your love is true, then I want to be yours. (BERNABE *reaches out to embrace her.*) But not so fast, pelado! I'm not Consuelo, sabes? If you truly love me, you'll have to respect me for what I am, and then fight for me—¡como los machos! Don't you know anything? Many men have died just to have me. Are you capable of killing those who have me . . . and do not love me, Bernabé?

BERNABE. You want me to kill?

TIERRA. To set me free. For I was never meant to be the property of any man—not even you . . . though it is your destiny to lie with me. (*She extends her hand.* BERNABE *goes to her. She pulls him down, and they lay down. He is almost going to embrace her, when* LA LUNA *comes back.*)

LUNA. Orale, stop right there! (BERNABE *sits up.*) ¿Qué, pues, nuez? Didn't I tell you to watch it with my sister? What were you doing, eh?

BERNABE (*rises*). ¿Qué te importa, buey? (LA TIERRA *rises and stands to one side, observing silently but with strength.* BERNABE *seems more self-possessed.*)

LUNA. Oye, so bravo all of a sudden?

BERNABE. You'd better leave, Luna!

LUNA. I'd better not, carnal!

BERNABE. Get out of here!

LUNA. Look at him, will you? Muy machote. What did you do to him, sis?

BERNABE. ¡Lárgate! (*Pushes* LUNA.)

LUNA. Hey, man, watch the suit. I'm your camarada, remember? Almost your brother-in-law.

TIERRA (*with power*). Luna! Leave us in peace. He means me no harm.

LUNA. Pura madre, how do you know?

TIERRA. Because I know him. Since the very day of his birth, he has been innocent, and good. Others have laughed at him. But he has always come to my arms seeking my warmth. He loves me with an intensity most men cannot even imagine . . . for in his eyes I am woman . . . I am Madre . . .

LUNA. Simón—¡pura madre!

TIERRA. Yet I'm forever Virgin. So leave us alone!

LUNA. Nel, sister. Qué virgen ni que madre. I know what you two are up to. Are you going to get married or what? Is this a one night stand?

TIERRA. That's up to Bernabé.

LUNA. What do you say, loco? Is this forever?

BERNABE (*pause*). Simón.

LUNA. Pendejo.

TIERRA. Satisfied?

LUNA. Chale. You still need Jefe's blessing.

TIERRA. He'll grant it.

LUNA. Pos, you hope. First he's gotta meet Bernabé. You ready for Him, ese?

BERNABE. Who?

LUNA. El Mero Mero, loco. Su Papá. Mi Jefito. ¡EL SOL!

BERNABE. ¡¿Sol?!

LUNA (*turning*). He's coming—watcha. It's almost dawn. ¿Sabes qué, ese? You better let me do the talking first. Me and the Jefe get along real suave. I'll tell Him you're Chicano, my camarada.

TIERRA. No, Luna.

LUNA. What?

TIERRA. He has a voice. Let him speak for himself.

LUNA (*shrugging*). Orale, no hay pedo. But you know the Jefito.

TIERRA. You will have to face him, Bernabé. If you truly love me, then you should have no fear of my father. Speak to him with respect, but with courage. He has no patience with cowardly humans.

LUNA. ¡Al alba! Here he comes! Don't stare at his face too long, ese! He'll blind you! (LA TIERRA *and* LA LUNA *kneel before the place where the sun is rising. Indigena music: majestic flutes and drums.* EL SOL *rises in the guise of Tonatiuh, the Aztec Sun God. He speaks in a resounding voice.*)

SOL. Buenos días, mis hijos.

TIERRA. Buenos días, Papá.

LUNA. Buenos días, Jefe.

SOL. Luna! How goes my eternal war with the stars? ¿Cuidaste mi cielo por toda la noche?

LUNA. Simón, Jefe, the heavens are fine.

SOL. ¿Y tu hermana? Did you watch over her?

LUNA. Sí, señor. ¡Cómo no!

SOL. ¿Pues cómo? . . . ¡CALLATE!

TIERRA. ¿Apá?

SOL (*gently*). Sí, m'ija, ¿cómo estás?

TIERRA. Bien, Papá.

SOL. And all your humanity, that plague of miserable mortals you call your children? Do they still persist in their petty greed and hatred and fear of death?

TIERRA. Sí, Tata. (*To* BERNABE.) Go.

BERNABE. ¿Señor? (*Pause.*) ¿Señor de los cielos?

SOL. ¿Quién me llama?

BERNABE.   It's me, Señor. Down here.

SOL.   ¿Quién eres tú?

BERNABE.   Bernabé.

SOL.   ¿Qué? ¡LOOK AT ME!

BERNABE (*shielding his eyes*).   Bernabé . . . I come to tell you something, Señor . . . de mi amor . . .

SOL (*disdainfully*).   ¿Amor?

BERNABE.   Por la Tierra.

SOL.   ¡¿M'ija!?

BERNABE (*humbly*).   Con todo respeto, señor.

SOL (*pause*).   Many centuries have passed, Bernabé, since men remembered who is el padre de la tierra. En verdad, very few have ever had the courage to face me, como es debido. Why have you come?

BERNABE.   I am a man, Señor.

SOL.   ¿Y eso qué me importa a mí?

BERNABE.   I love her.

SOL (*scoffing majestically*).   Ha! Billions of men have loved her. Do you think you are the first? Look at her, Bernabé, this is la Tierra who has been all things to all men. Madre, prostituta, mujer. Aren't you afraid?

BERNABE (*bravely*).   No, Señor, of what?

SOL.   ¡De su PADRE, desgraciado! ¡¡¡EL SOL!!! (*There is a terrifying flash of light and thunder.* BERNABE *runs and hides.*) Look at him running like a coward! ¡MALHORA! I should kill you for what your kind has done to m'ija!

BERNABE.   It wasn't me, Señor!

TIERRA (*stepping forward*).   ¡Por favor, Tata! ¡Es inocente!

LUNA.   Es cierto, Jefe. The vato's a Chicano. He's never had any tierra!

SOL (*pause, calms down*).   What is your work, Bernabé?

BERNABE.   I work in the fields.

SOL.   You are dirt poor, then?

BERNABE.   Sí, Señor.

SOL.   Then, how do you intend to take care of my daughter? You have no money! You have no POWER!

BERNABE (*pause*).   Señor, I am nobody, that's true. In town people say I'm only a loco. But I know one thing, that the rich people are more locos than me. They sell la Tierra all the time, in little pedacitos here and there, but I know she should never be sold like that . . . because she doesn't belong to anyone. Like a woman should never be sold, ¿qué no? Eso es lo que pienso, Señor. If anybody has hurt la Tierra, it's not the pobres, it's the men with money and power. I can only love her.

LUNA (*sotto voce*).   ¡Orale, te aventates, ese! (EL SOL *silences* LUNA *with a powerful glance.*)

SOL.   Dices bien. (*Pause.*) Now I know who you are, Bernabé. Eres el último y el primero . . . The last of a great noble lineage of men I once knew in ancient times, and the first of a new raza cósmica that shall inherit the earth. Your face is a cosmic memory, Bernabé. It reminds me of an entire humanity, de tus mismos ojos, tu piel, tu sangre. They too loved la Tierra and honored su padre above all else. They too were my children. They pierced the human brain and penetrated the distant stars and found the hungry fire that eats of itself. They discovered what today only a loco can understand—that life is death, and that death is life. Que la vida no vale nada porque vale todo. That you are one, so you can be two, two so you can be four, and then eight, and then sixteen, and on and on until you are millions, billions!—only to return once again to the center and discover . . . nada, so you fill up the space with one again. ¿Me comprendes, Bernabé? What power was that?

BERNABE.   El poder del Sol, Señor?

SOL (*pauses*).   Tienes razón . . . and that's why if you unite with m'ija, you shall have that poder. And you shall be my Son! Tierra, do you love this man?

TIERRA.   Sí, Papá.

SOL.   Bernabé, ¿de veras quieres a la Tierra?

BERNABE.   Con todo el corazón.

SOL (*ironically*).   ¿Corazón? No, hijo, not with your corazón. You may love her with your body, your blood, your seed, but your heart belongs to me. ¿Estás listo para morir?

BERNABE.   ¡Morir!

SOL.   ¡Para vivir! (BERNABE *is momentarily stunned and confused. He looks at* LA LUNA *and* LA TIERRA. *They say nothing.*)

BERNABE.   Señor, I don't want to die.

SOL.   Hijo, I offer you the power of the Sun. You have been nothing, now you shall be everything. Yo soy el comienzo y el fin de todas las cosas. Believe in me and you shall never die. Will you give me your corazón?

BERNABE (*pause*).   Sí, Señor.

SOL.   ¡Que sea así! (*Drums and flutes.* BERNABE *is sacrificed.* LA TIERRA *and* LA LUNA *lay his body out.*)

SOL.   ¡Bernabé, levántate! (BERNABE *rises—a complete man.*) For here on you shall be un hombre nuevo and you shall help me to conquer the stars! (BERNABE *walks erect.*) Bernabé, la Tierra es virgen y tuya. Sean felices.

TIERRA.   ¡Bernabé! (BERNABE *and* LA TIERRA *embrace.*)

LUNA.   ¡Orale! Congratulations, loco—I mean, ese. ¡A toda madre!

SOL.   ¡SILENCIO PUES! (*Pause.*) The day is dying. The hour has come for me to go. Mis hijos, I leave you with my blessings. (*Blesses them.*) Luna, stand vigil over my cielo through the darkest night, and give light to your hermana, eh?

LUNA.   Sí, Jefe, like always.

SOL.   Bueno, me voy pues. Bernabé, Tierra, tengan hijos . . . muchos hijos. (*Starts to sink.*)

TIERRA.   Buenas noches, Papá.

LUNA.   Buenas noches, Jefe.

BERNABE.   Buenas noches, Señor.

SOL (*sinking fast*).   Buenas noches . . . Bernabé! (SOL *is gone. There is a silence.* LA TIERRA *shivers, then* BERNABE *and* LA LUNA.)

TIERRA. It's cold.

LUNA. Simón, the Jefito's gone. (*Looks up at the sky.*) Well, I better get up to my chante también. Orale, novios—what kind of moonlight would you like? Something muy romantic y de aquellas?

TIERRA. Never mind. Just leave.

LUNA. Mírala, mírala—just because you got married again! For the zillionth time.

BERNABE (*with a powerful calm*). Mira, hermano, the time for insults is over. If once I was a loco, now I am a man—and I belong to la Tierra, as she belongs to me. So, good night.

LUNA. Okay, 'ta bien, pues. I gotta get to work anyway. (*Looks up.*) Fat-assed stars! I bet you they're just itching to horn in on Jefe's territory. I better go keep 'em in line. Buenas noches, pues, y don't be afraid to get down and dirty, eh? ¡Orale! (LA LUNA *exits.* LA TIERRA *turns her back on* BERNABE.)

TIERRA. ¿Bernabé?

BERNABE. ¿Qué?

TIERRA. Will you love me—¿para siempre?

BERNABE. Siempre.

TIERRA. ¡Hasta la muerte? (*She turns. Her face is a death mask.*)

BERNABE. Hasta la muerte. (*They embrace.*)

SEVEN

BERNABE'*s house.* EL TIO *comes in quickly, looking over his shoulder.* MADRE *is at the door of her house.*

MADRE. Teodoro, ¿qué paso? Did you find m'ijo?

TIO. What are you doing in the street, hermanita? Get into the house, ándale!

MADRE. ¿Pa' qué? To worry even more?

TIO. ¡El sol está muy caliente!

MADRE. I don't care if it's hot! What happen with m'ijo? (*Pause.*) ¿Qué pasó, pues, hombre? Did they find him? Miserable wino, what good are you? Bernabé's your nephew, but nothing worries you, verdad? Did I tell you to go look in the pozo he made? (*Pause.*) You went, verdad? You know something! ¿Qué pasó, hombre? (*She looks down the street.*) Ay, Teodoro, some men are coming. Eduardo is with them! They're bringing a body. ¡Válgame Dios! (MADRE *starts to run forward.* TIO *stops her.*)

TIO. Stay here, hermanita!

MADRE (*starting to get hysterical*). NO, ¡déjame ir! ¡Déjame ir! It's m'ijo. You know it is, ¿verdad? ¿Qué pasó? ¿Qué pasó?

TIO. Está muerto.

MADRE. ¡Ay! (*Gasps. Can't get breath.*)

TIO. We found him—buried in the earth. (TORRES *and* PRIMO *bring in* BERNABE'*s body. They lay him down, covered with a canvas. Now* MADRE *releases a long, sorrowful cry as she leans over the body.*)

MADRE. M'ijo! M'IJITO!

PRIMO. It's all my fault, tío. Fue toda mi culpa.

TIO. No, hijo, don't blame yourself. You only wanted to help him. This was God's will. Fue por la voluntad de Dios. (*Drums and flutes. In the sky above and behind them,* BERNABE *and* LA TIERRA *appear in a cosmic embrace. He is naked, wearing only a loincloth. She is Coatlicue, Mother Earth, the Aztec Goddess of Life, Death, and Rebirth.*)

FOCUS QUESTIONS

1. In a short essay, describe *Bernabé's mito* style and show how it incorporates elements from the earlier *acto*.
2. Discuss the uses of allegory in the play.
3. Show how the images of womanhood address both the cultural and theatrical ends of the play.
4. In what specific ways is the Chicano experience reflected in the play.
5. Develop a character sketch of Bernabé in which you assess his cosmic nature and function.
6. Discuss the issues involved in the Bernabé/Torres conflict.
7. Describe and compare the language styles of any two characters.
8. Identify the themes of the play and comment on their timeliness.

OTHER ACTIVITIES

1. Locate documents that cover the historical Delano strike of the mid-1960s and briefly show how certain protest issues are reflected in the play.
2. Develop some set designs for the play and discuss your staging of Bernabé's communion with the earth.

BIBLIOGRAPHY

Bagby, Beth. "El Teatro Campesino: Interviews with Luis Valdez." *Tulane Drama Review* 11, no. 4 (1967): 70–80.

Broyles-Gonzalez, Yolanda. *El Teatro Campesino: Theater in the Chicano Movement.* Austin: University of Texas Press, 1994.

———. "Toward a Re-Vision of Chicano Theatre History: The Women of El Teatro Campesino." In *Making a Spectacle: Feminist Essays on Contemporary Women's Theatre,* edited by Lynda Hart. Ann Arbor: University of Michigan Press, 1989.

Frischmann, Donald H. "El Teatro Campesino y su mito *Bernabé:* un regreso a la madre tierra." *Aztlan* 12, no. 2 (Autumn 1981): 259–70.

Garza, Roberto J., ed. *Contemporary Chicano Theatre.* Indiana: University of Notre Dame Press, 1976.

Huerta, Jorge A., ed. *Necessary Theatre: Six Plays about the Chicano Experience.* Houston: Arte Publico Press, 1989.

———. "From Stereotypes to Archetypes: Chicano Theaters' Reflection of the Mexicano in the United States." In *Missions in Conflict: Essays on U.S.-Mexican Relations and Chicano Culture,* edited by Renata von Bardeleben, Dietrich Briesemeister, and Juan Bruce-Novoa. Tübingen: Gunter Narr Verlag, 1986: 75–84.

———, and John Harop. "The Agitprop Pilgrimage of Luis Valdez and El Teatro Campesino." *Theatre Quarterly* 5 (1975): 30–90.

Melville, Margarita B. "Female and Male in Chicano Theatre," in *Hispanic Theatre in the United States,* edited by Nicolas Kanellos. Houston: Arte Publico Press, 1984: 75–79.

Savran, David. *In Their Own Words: Contemporary American Playwrights.* New York: Theatre Communications Group, 1988.

Seller, Maxine Schwartz. *Ethnic Theater in the United States.* Westport, CT: Greenwood Press, 1983.

Shank, Theodore. *American Alternative Theater.* New York: Grove Press. 1982.

Sommers, Joseph, and Tomas Ybarra-Frauston, eds. *Modern Chicano Writers: A Collection of Critical Essays.* Englewood Cliffs, NJ: Prentice-Hall, 1979.

Valdez, Luis. *Actos.* San Juan Bautista, CA: Cucaracha Press, 1971.

RECOMMENDED VIDEOTAPES AND RECORDINGS

Luis Valdez and El Teatro Campesino. VHS. 26 min. Interview with the playwright. Distributed by Films for the Humanities and Sciences, Princeton, NJ.

Profile: Luis Valdez, the Making of a Mexican American Playwright. One sound cassette. (1987). National Public Radio.

THE CHICKENCOOP CHINAMAN
Frank Chin (1940-   )

Frank Chin, father of modern Asian American literature, pioneered in the development of Asian American culture, paving the way for the aesthetic approach.

—William Wei

Merwin Goldsmith (*left*) as the Lone Ranger, Sab Shimono as Kenji, Randall "Duk" Kim as Tam Lum, and Calvin Jung as Tonto in *The Chickencoop Chinaman,* presented by the American Place Theatre in 1972, under the direction of Jack Gelber. *Photo: Martha Holmes*

APPROACHING ASIAN-AMERICAN DRAMA

The saga of America's pluralistic society never ceases to generate controversy between storytellers and their listeners. It is as historical as the maiden voyage made by the English to a foreign shore already inhabited by Native Americans and as timely as the morning arrival of a young immigrant who seeks shelter from an oppressed homeland. The story has been rewritten countless times, partly to accommodate a glorified image of a bountiful America, many of whose citizens still lack equal rights and opportunities. The story will remain unfinished as long as the vision of democracy is undermined by racism and bigotry.

America, as the story points out, has been the most accessible haven for immigrants from every port. In any single century, four or five generations of a foreign-born culture have had ample opportunity to root themselves permanently into its New World heritage through assimilation or acculturation. But the story contains a large cast of protagonists and antagonists: those whose assimilation has been so complete that they have abandoned the cultural traditions of their countries of origin; and those whose militancy has helped them to preserve certain features of their cultural heritage instead of diving headlong into the melting pot that once symbolized America. Any possible compromise between the melting-pot assimilation and cultural separatism, desirable or not, has not come to pass.

Perhaps no immigrant group reflects this clash as dramatically as Asian Americans, whose outspoken literary artists—especially those who write for the stage—first began to be heard in America's cultural mainstream during the final quarter of the twentieth century. Descending from ancestors who initially emigrated from China, Japan, Korea, the Philippines and, more recently, from Laos, Cambodia, and Vietnam, they are American citizens of East Asian descent, whose protagonists ''hover 'between worlds,' suspended between countries of origin and adopted homelands, between marriage and divorce, between life and death, between war and peace.''[1] They have been lumped together as members of the Pan Asian community, despite the fact that their respective and illustrious ancestries as well as their individual American backgrounds are as varied and distinct from each other as the creative voices through which they speak.

While singling out one of these cultures as representative is difficult, it is not unreasonable to suppose that the experiences of one have some direct bearing on the rest. But if the issue is essentially one of identity, then it is important to recognize Frank Chin as an Asian-American writer who also happens to be a fifth-generation American of Chinese descent. But why Chin? Because his play, *The Chickencoop Chinaman,* was the first Asian-American work to confront crucial cultural issues that had long been repressed in the theatre and other performance media, and the first of its kind to be produced in the history of the legitimate American stage. While it has become a cliché to credit any single artist for opening certain doors and making things happen, the link between Chin's play—first produced at the American Place Theatre in New York City in 1972—and the Asian-American playwriting activity that flourished soon after its landmark production remains undisputed.

Chin's assertion that Asian Americans are as much a product of Asian culture as they are of American culture underscores the troubling dichotomy that permeates the society he represents: ''For us American born, both the Asian languages and the English language are foreign. We are a people without a native tongue. To whites, we're all foreigners, still learning English . . . And to Asians born to Asian culture—Asian by birth and experience and American by choice—our Chinese and Japanese is a fake.'' The problem with having ''no street tongue to flaunt and strut the way the blacks and chicanos do'' makes it ''dangerous to say anything, dangerous to talk because every time you open your mouth you run the risk of being corrected.''[2] These self-imposed restrictions in communicating on both social and political levels have merely reinforced the maligned image of the Asian American.

Chin's fixation on the relationship between language and identity and how it has been used to exclude people from their birthright fuels the polemical tone of his writing. His anger is an old one, stemming from the same isolationism that occurred not long after the first Chinese arrived in America to forge railroads that opened up the West and to pursue those same dreams of freedom sought by other immigrant groups. When the Chinese Exclusion Act of the 1880s prohibited the naturalization of the Chinese already living in America as well as the entry of women from China, it dealt a devastating blow to Chinese men and to Chinese-American women who would lose their citizenship if they married these men. For an immigrant population too fearful of deportation to protest the law, their only recourse would be to hide their indignation behind a collectively polite but passive demeanor until the dreaded Exclusion Act was repealed in 1943. By then, of course, racism had honed the Chinese-American image into a stereotype that was beyond repair.

Could Chin disregard the dreams he had wished upon as a child? Would they simply fade away? Was it not conceivable, therefore, that the Lone Ranger really wore a mask to hide his "slanty" eyes? Why should any Chinese-American child believe otherwise? Embracing this mythical, black-haired, masked symbol of law and order in the Old West, Chin is also proud to recall that one of his grandfathers worked for the Southern Pacific Railroad and that, years later, he himself "was hired with the first batch of blacks to go braking for the SP, in the 60's when the fair employment legislation went into effect."[3]

Chin's protagonist, Tam Lum, eulogizes those "Chinamans who knew they'd never be given passes to ride the rails they laid." Like Tam, Chin pays homage to the honorable achievements of his grandfather and other pioneers like him, those "Chinamans" who were too independent to be assimilated but whose children quietly succumbed to the white supremacy that isolated their alien communities into "Chinatowns" across America. This painful image of the once heroic and proud pioneer of the American West, which has been slowly reduced to a cardboard stereotype over decades of racist media misrepresentation, drives Chin's protagonist into lyrical tirades.

But off-stage, the playwright has been less vehement. "What are we?" asks Chin. "What holds us together? How do we define our culture, our work? What is the nature and content of Asian-American integrity? It isn't for the whites to sort out. It's for *us* to sort out. Asian-American artists have failed to assert any Asian-American integrity. It remains dependent on white racism. We've simply not addressed the question of what *is* Asian American."[4]

Perhaps this sorting out has actually begun to occur on professional stages not unlike the one from which Tam Lum spoke so candidly and eloquently in 1972. Since then, theatre companies expressly concerned with Asian-American themes—the Asian American Theatre Workshop, the East West Players, the Pan Asian Repertory, the Northwest Asian American Theatre Company, and the Canadian Artists Group—have emerged across America to address the need for collectivity. Whereas Chin once stood alone, there now exists a legitimate network that bonds Asian-American theatre artists with wider opportunities for writing, directing, and acting. The results have even filtered into mainstream popular entertainment, where racism once blurred the characteristics of the Asian-American culture and offensive stereotypes proliferated.

Certain Asian-American playwrights and **performance artists** have echoed Chin's sentiments in their work, while others have turned their cultural "otherness" to a creative advantage. Momoko Iko, R. A. Shiomi, Rosanna Yamagiwa Alfaro, Genny Lim, Ernest Abuba, Daryl Chin, Velina Houston, Dom Magwili, Philip Gotanda, Ping Chong, Jessica Hagedorn, Janice Tanaka, and David Henry Hwang have brought audiences closer to the complex intercultural issues at stake and have worked to restore a truthful image of the Asian American, despite their different points of view. That is why a retrospective glance at *The Chickencoop Chinaman* continues to refresh our sensibilities and shed light on the dilemmas confronting Asian-American artists who speak to us through their stage characters.

MAJOR WORKS

After *The Chickencoop Chinaman* premiered at the American Place Theatre in 1972, Chin's second play, *The Year of the Dragon,* was also produced there in 1974, then filmed for *Theatre in America* on Public Television where it was aired in 1975. *Gee, Pop!,* a real cartoon in two acts, was presented by the American Conservatory Theatre for the Plays-in-Progress Program in 1974. *Flood of Blood,* a play in one act, was published in *Seattle Review* in 1988.

As a film writer, Chin produced the documentary, *Chinaman's Chance: A Portrait of Changing Chinese America,* for WNET-TV. Chin is the author of a short-story collection, *The Chinaman Pacific & Frisco R. R. Co.,* and a novel, *Donald Duk.* He was awarded the prestigious Lannan Fellowship for Fiction in 1992.

THE ACTION

Tam Lum, a Chinese-American writer and filmmaker, arrives in Pittsburgh to interview Charley Popcorn, the father of his black ex-champion boxer-friend, Ovaltine Jack Dancer. Dancer is the subject for a documentary Tam is shooting. Prior to the interview, Tam visits his black friend Kenji and meets Robbie and his outspoken mother Lee, who hides her Chinese heritage. Tam, Kenji, and Lee argue over the racial circumstances that have shaped their lives and brought them together.

In a dream sequence, Tam confronts his boyhood idol, the Lone Ranger, who shoots him in the hand and tells him that "the West ain't big enough for the both of us!"

Tam finally meets Charley Popcorn, but finds out that the old man is not Dancer's father after all. In the meantime, one of Lee's former husbands, a Chinese American named Tom, has arrived to take her and Robbie back to San Francisco. Tam accuses Tom of projecting an "anti-Chinaman vision" that makes him view Lee as "white." But Lee has already decided to remain with Kenji. Tam refuses to let go of the "hard feelings" of anger and pride spawned by his heritage.

STRUCTURE AND LANGUAGE

The Chickencoop Chinaman is that rare first play whose unconventional style bursts with incisive language, biting humor, nonconformist characters, and enough socio-political targets to make its two acts swerve in their hyperactive unfolding. But Chin's stylistic risks effortlessly accommodate his daring stage venture and produce qualitative repercussions that bring the play's rich theatrical context into focus.

The work is both centered on and orchestrated by Tam Lum, a "multi-tongued word magician" so painfully in touch with his feelings that the actions that swirl within his imagination radiate a magnetic charge. He voices the soulful cry of the Asian American who balances the ancestral responsibility of one ancient culture with the contemporary reality of another, who is accused of "mispronouncing" his name—that it should be pronounced "Tom," who shifts uneasily between Eastern ancestry and Western acceptance, knowing that both lie beyond his reach. Tam is more than a mouthpiece for the playwright. His realistic portrait achieves a tragic dimension that is acutely heightened by his ironically comic view of the human condition.

The theme of dispossession propels the play, giving it the aura of a phantasmagorical journey launched by Tam's conception and descent from a "Limbo stage," where unwanted children are relegated to a final kitchen environment in which Tam recalls the consoling wisdom of his ancestral grandmother. The journey juxtaposes real and fantastic events to nurture his search for identity. No matter how often the fantasy flight attendant asks about his origin, her curiosity only fuels Tam's **stream of consciousness,** conspicuously enlivened by allusions to his "synthetic" birth: "Chinamen are made, not born, my dear. Out of junk-imports, lies, railroad scrap iron, dirty jokes, broken bottles, cigar smoke, Cosquilla Indian blood, wino spit, and lots of milk of magnesia." Haunted by a powerful iconography, Tam incarnates the play's outspoken ideology.

Tam's first stopover on the play's realistic level of action is a black ghetto in Pittsburgh where a Japanese-American buddy, the "BlackJap Kenji," has softened his own identity "with posters of black country, blues, and jazz musicians that clash with the few Japanese prints and art objects." The fact that both Tam and Kenji fluently speak black jargon reflects their own ghettoized childhood in the Chinatowns and Little Tokyos of America adjacent to black ghettos. Kenji's own identification with the black American culture reflects his hatred of "yellow-people," so that his apartment is less a haven than an outpost for the disenfranchised, two of whom happen to be Lee and her son Robbie.

While Lee reveals almost nothing about herself, including the fact that she tries to pass for white, her elusiveness does not prevent her from pursuing Tam, who is always ripe for confrontation and whose "gift of gab" ventilates the harsher underside of his life. But Lee's own story is bereft of happiness as well, most notably reflected by three unsuccessful marriages. The disclosure is not made by Lee, of course, but by Robbie, who feels comfortable with Tam and describes his three fathers to him: "A white one. A Chinese one. One was black. We talk with them on the phone. I liked the Chinese . . . Lee says he wasn't a man." Robbie's last remark, however innocently rendered, reveals a much darker subtext.

Chin has placed this insult to Chinese manhood on the lips of a young adolescent whose association with these three men still leaves him fatherless. As the product of a culturally dichotomized limbo not unlike the one Tam has known, Robbie was born to a mother who is "a one woman Minority of the Month Club," as Tam sarcastically puts it. While it is all too apparent that he wants a father and recognizes one in Tam, he can express this only by telling Tam that Lee's Chinese husband was "the nicest." What Robbie does not know is that Tam was once married to a white woman and is the father of a girl and a boy. "I want 'em to forget me," Tam later confides to Lee, when he decides to talk about his family.

Tam's contempt for the parent-child relationship—which he has demonstrated by turning his back on his own children because his "back's all that's good for them. My front's no good"—reflects a popular theme in Asian-American literature, one that underscores Chin's preoccupation with language and identity. For without a language to call his own, a person is no longer a person, the result of which is "the failure of Asian-American manhood to express itself in its simplest form: fathers and sons."[5]

This complex theme resounds through the play and is boldly highlighted in the Charley Popcorn subplot. It is ironic, for example, that Tam's documentary is supported by money "I should be usin for the child support," suggesting that this important venture is taking place at the expense of his own children's welfare. But when Tam discovers that Charley is "nobody's father, especially [Dancer's]," he urgently pleads with the old man: "He needs you to be his father, can't ya see? . . . You gotta be his father. Everybody knows you're his father . . . You can't turn your back on him." The powerful confrontation between Tam, who searches for a surrogate father, and Charley, who rejects a needy son, is analogous to the earlier one between Tam and Robbie and confirms the illusory nature of these father-son relationships, reducing them in Charley's words to "stories [Dancer] dreamed." Tam tries to strike Popcorn but misses, hits the floor, and comes up smiling: "My punch won't crack an egg, but I'll never fall down." His quick humor disguises all further embarrassment, assuring us that his survival mechanisms are still intact.

Perhaps no scene in *The Chickencoop Chinaman* proves more disturbing than Tam's encounter with the Lone Ranger. Occurring at the top of act 2 and counterpointing both the thematic concerns of the previous act and the emotional rhythms in the scenes that follow, the dramatic action epitomizes the disintegration of childhood illusion into the stuff of nightmares. The reunion with his masked idol, while pivotal to the action around it, is a surreal enactment of Tam's bitter enlightenment. Chin reinvents this icon of popular culture as an enemy who, in a pseudo-comical gunfight, betrays his most ardent fan. Although he once served as the mythical counterpart to a heroic Chinese grandfather who helped to civilize the West by building railroads, his deceptive double-talk convinces our protagonist that the "Lone Ranger ain't no Chinaman."

The scene is packed with irreverent humor and imagery, both of which address Chin's themes. One of the most powerful images alludes to Helen Keller, a personality who is parodied through seemingly vicious imitations quite early in the play when Kenji and Tam first meet. For Keller's tragedy—that she could not hear, see, or speak—is analogous to the experience of Asian Americans who are born without a language of their own, who therefore lack identity. In Tam's fantasy, the Lone Ranger denigrates her memory by getting "a kick watchin her bump into things" and then bequeaths her "curse" on Tam and Kenji: "Hear no evil, ya hear me? China boys, you be legendary obeyers of the law, legendary humble, legendary passive. Thank me now and I'll let ya get back to Chinatown preservin your culture!"

The final scene of the play is a fantasy interlude in which Tam finds himself alone in Kenji's kitchen, now his grandmother's, where "everything comes sniffin at you . . . sooner or later." In this comforting place, he hears the train in much the same way his "grandmother had an ear for trains." Acknowledging this real and honorable heritage and refusing to be an "honorary white," a label previously bestowed on him by the Lone Ranger, Tam acknowledges an era when the sound of a train signified a culture intact, before the potential for a true Chinese-American identity was shattered by the dreaded Exclusion Act. While his journey toward selfhood and quest for language and identity remain ongoing, this acknowledgment of the events of history gives him the strength to endure. With a humor that tempers the bittersweet outcome, Tam reminds us that his predicament can be resolved only when we openly share our history with one another.

THE CHICKENCOOP CHINAMAN-IN-PERFORMANCE

This first play by Frank Chin won top prize in a playwriting contest sponsored by the East West Players in Los Angeles. Although financial problems prevented the company from producing it, Chin's dream was realized when the script found its way to Wynn Handman, the artistic director of the American Place Theatre in New York City.

Opening on May 27, 1972, to a mixed critical press, the production confirmed Chin's unusual gifts. On the negative side, Julius Novick of *The New York Times* compared Chin's writing unfavorably to the angry playwriting voice of John Osborne. Writing for the same paper, however, Clive Barnes confessed that the playwright showed him "an ethnic attitude I had never previously encountered." Admiring the play's "cutting honesty," he thought Jack Gelber's direction "was both forceful and fluent [and] made the most of the play, isolating the special conflict of the hero and placing it against the background of his disillusionment." Barnes concluded that John Wulp's sets, Willa Kim's costumes, and Roger Morgan's lighting "maintained the American Place's reputation for excellence, and the acting was smooth and convincing."[6]

Calling *The Chickencoop Chinaman* "one of the most fascinating and original scripts ever offered at this seminal showcase of new writing talent," Emory Lewis complimented Chin for creating language that flowed "with a Joycean fecundity and delight." He also admired the set design, which "imaginatively divided the stage into comic strip frames [in which] everything is caricatured and bigger than life."[7]

William Wong welcomed the play's socio-political message for clarifying issues about Asian Americans that audiences "couldn't possibly learn from watching *The Flower Drum Song,* telecasts from the Great Wall of China or late-show re-runs of old Charlie Chan movies."[8]

Following its engagement at the American Place Theatre, a production of the work was mounted for one performance only at the Asian-American Writers' Conference at the Oakland Museum in California. *The Chickencoop Chinaman* was also produced by the East West Players during their 1975–1976 season, under the direction of Mako.

REFLECTIONS ON
THE CHICKENCOOP CHINAMAN

Wynn Handman is co-founder and artistic director of the
American Place Theatre in New York City.

The Chickencoop Chinaman was the final offering of our eighth season. The play exemplifies what the American Place Theatre has always been about: contemporary works by living American playwrights, alternative plays that would not be produced commercially. Our theatre has always had a very high multiethnic profile, for example, the early works of African-American playwrights Ron Milner, Phillip Hayes Dean, and Ed Bullins who, in the 1960s, was the cultural minister of the Black Panthers.

The Chickencoop Chinaman was immediately exciting, and I welcomed the opportunity to develop the work. We've always sought out the very best writers in America. Frank Chin impressed me at once as first-rate, with a tremendous sense of rhythm, with verve in his writing, and very strong feelings about the impact of American society on Asian Americans and vice versa. The history of the Chinese Americans who came in large numbers in the nineteenth century is evoked in *The Chickencoop Chinaman* with its dreams of the railroad.

I was immediately drawn to Frank's highly charged writing, even though the manuscript was the size of one of our New York City phone books. But it was not a viable script. There was an idea for a play in it and there was a lot of wonderful language, but it was sprawling and needed to be shaped and developed. It was originally called *The Chickencoop Chinaman's Pregnant Pause,* but we thought the title was better shortened.

Frank expresses himself brilliantly through his writing, but he is consumed by many passions which often overflow. You get rid of an epilogue and he supplies a prologue. You get rid of the prologue and something else comes along. While I didn't want to make a **well-made play** out of it, I did want to get something important that we could put on the stage. So we arranged for Frank to become a resident here, and we did extensive work over a period of many months. A script evolved that we were proud to put on the stage.

Fortunately we had a splendid actor for the lead, Randy Kim, who was *the* Frank Chin *persona* on the stage. Randy's talent is very large and it was thrilling to see how he grasped everything that Frank wrote. I didn't know about Randy Kim in advance, but once you're doing a play, you start investigating the possibilities of casting, both with casting directors whose profession is to find appropriate people to audition, plus actors you know, plus actors who respond to the Actors' Equity Union open calls. Somehow I

Continued

heard about Randy and when he came in he was obviously it. Then Sab Shimono was cast. Sally Kirkland played the white woman. The African-American actor Leonard Jackson was in it and Merwin Goldsmith, a Caucasian actor, played the Lone Ranger. We had an excellent cast and a good time with it.

Jack Gelber directed it. He is both a playwright and director, and he was a good choice because the sensibility of the play was one to which he could respond. As an experienced playwright, he could help this inexperienced playwright in shaping his play. He staged it on a set that had multilevels and different playing areas. There was a living room, a kitchen, a movie house. I especially remember the Lone Ranger sequence and the wonderful lighting that moved us from fantasy to reality.

More than half of our work—probably three-quarters of the plays we've done here—has gone through a process of development. That means that through a series of conferences, rehearsed readings, discussions, and more rehearsed readings, you gradually evolve a script that is ready for what we call full production. With both Frank's plays—the other was *The Year of the Dragon* which we produced a few seasons later—we went through a very similar process, just as many months, just as much of the good stuff that wasn't usable but was wonderful, but finally getting a script. In fact, our production of *The Year of the Dragon* was reproduced for national television, except that Randy Kim, who again was the lead, didn't choose to do it on television. It was questionable as to whether or not we would get it on because without Randy, Frank and I felt we were missing a lot. But we found an actor who could do it. It was the first play that took you inside an Asian-American home that ever played on American television.

Our production of *"Chickencoop"* was artistically rewarding. The large subscription audience was adventurous. This is the kind of work it would expect, since we're always doing unusual plays. I usually have some feeling for the percentage of the potential of the play I think was achieved, and I would give this production pretty high marks, somewhere between eighty-five and ninety percent.

Frank broke the ground. I hear from Asian-American writers and performance artists who often say, "You did Frank Chin!" like "He showed the way!" There's no doubt that he was the ground-breaker.

Notes

1. *Misha Berson, ed., "Introduction," in* BETWEEN WORLDS: CONTEMPORARY ASIAN-AMERICAN PLAYS *(Theatre Communications Group, 1990), ix.*
2. *"Backtalk,"* NEWS OF THE AMERICAN PLACE THEATRE *4, no. 4 (May 1972): 4.*
3. *Dorothy Ritsuko McDonald, "Introduction" in* TWO PLAYS BY FRANK CHIN *(Seattle: University of Washington Press, 1981), xi.*
4. *Telephone interview with Frank Chin, 26 July 1993.*
5. *"An Introduction to Chinese- and Japanese-American Literature" in* AIIIEEEEE!: AN ANTHOLOGY OF ASIAN-AMERICAN WRITERS, *eds. Frank Chin, Jeffrey Paul Chan, Lawson Fusao Inada, and Shawn Wong (New York: New American Library, 1991), 35.*
6. THE NEW YORK TIMES, *13 June 1972.*
7. THE RECORD, *13 June 1972.*
8. WALL STREET JOURNAL, *19 June 1972.*

THE CHICKENCOOP CHINAMAN
FRANK CHIN

CHARACTERS

Tam Lum, *a Chinese-American writer filmmaker with a gift of gab and an open mouth. A multi-tongued word magician losing his way to the spell who trips to Pittsburgh to conjure with his childhood friend and research a figure in his documentary movie.*

Hong Kong Dream Girl, *a dream monster from a popular American song of the twenties.*

Kenji, *a research dentist. Japanese American born and raised. Tam's childhood friend. Sullen, brooding. A zombie with taps on his shoes.*

Lee, *possible Eurasian or Chinese American passing for white. She's borne several kids in several racial combinations, but mothers only one, Robbie, her weird son.*

Robbie, *Lee's weird son.*

The Lone Ranger, *a legendary white racist with the funk of the West smouldering in his blood. In his senility, he still loves racistly, blesses racistly, shoots straight and is cuckoo with the notion that white folks are not white folks but just plain folks.*

Tonto, *a decrepit faithful Indian companion who's gone out of style.*

Charley Popcorn, *an ancient former boxing trainer and entrepreneur who runs a pornie movie house in Pittsburgh. Tam Lum has come to visit him.*

Tom, *a Chinese-American writer. One of Lee's former husbands.*

PLACE: The Oakland district of Pittsburgh, Pennsylvania
TIME: The late sixties

SETTINGS

ACT ONE SCENE 1: Tam's Hong Kong Dream Girl dream: screaming into Pittsburgh.
SCENE 2: Kenji's apartment. Early evening.
ACT TWO SCENE 1: Tam's dream Lone Ranger: the legendary radio childhood.
SCENE 2: Charley Popcorn's pornie house. Pittsburgh, night.
SCENE 3: Tam in Limbo.
SCENE 4: Kenji's apartment. Later that night.

ACT ONE
SCENE ONE

Curtain rises to Limbo stage. Black.

The sound of a screaming jet in flight runs for several seconds. In the dark a chuckle is heard, a mischievous but not sinister little laugh from TAM LUM. *Overriding his chuckle, the voice of* HONG KONG DREAM GIRL *as the stewardess and in-flight presence.*

HONG KONG DREAM GIRL (*as stewardess, voice-over in Limbo*). Ladies and Gentlemen, we are preparing to land in Pittsburgh. Please see that your seatbelts are securely fastened and your seat backs in the upright raised position and observe the no smoking sign. For your comfort and safety we ask that you remain seated and keep your seatbelts fastened until the plane has come to a complete stop. Thank you.

(*Overhead spot comes on. Upstage and high on a platform,* TAM *stands in a shaft of light. The rest of the stage is dark.*)

TAM.   She asked me if I thought she looked like she was born in Hong Kong. She looked all right to me except that I thought she was maybe fresh in from drill team practice.

(*Enter* GIRL *dressed as* TAM *describes. She struts and turns across the stage to the rhythm of brush and drums, from one pool of light to the next. She is Asian, beautiful, grinning, doll-like, and mechanical. A wind-up dream girl steppin' out.*)

TAM.   . . . because she was wearing high white boots with tassels and a satin dress that had no epaulets on it. And underneath one of them super no-knock, rust-proof, tit-stiffening bras, with the seams and rivets and buckles showing through. And she walked like she was on parade. And had a drill team Jackie Kennedy, nondescript bouffant hairdo. And hands! Hands just made to hold, not to speak of twirl a baton. Yessir, hands like greased smooth-bore cannons. So she asked if I thought she looked like she was born in Hong Kong.

GIRL.   Do you think I look like I was born in Hong Kong?

TAM.   "Sure you do, Honey," I said, thinking back to the days of high school assemblies and the girl with medals jingling on her satin and sequin chest. Twirling her baton! I especially remember her flaming baton number done in black light to the Ritual Fire Dance. She said, "You . . ."

GIRL.   You can tell I was born in Hong Kong, even though I've been here six years?

TAM.   . . . She asked. And I replied, "And there's a whole lot more where that came from!"

GIRL.   Where were you born?

TAM.   Chinamen are made, not born, my dear. Out of junk-imports, lies, railroad scrap iron, dirty jokes, broken bottles, cigar smoke, Cosquilla Indian blood, wino spit, and lots of milk of amnesia.

GIRL.   You sure have a way with the word, but I wish you'd do more than pay lip service to your Canton heritage.

(*Through the rest of the speech in this segment,* TAM *goes through voice and accent changes. From W.C. Fields to American Midwest, Bible Belt holy roller, etc. His own "normal" speech jumps between black and white rhythms and accents.*)

TAM.   My dear in the beginning there was the Word! Then there was me! And the Word was CHINAMAN. And there was me. I lipped the word as if it had little lips of its own. "Chinaman" said on a little kiss. I lived the Word! The Word is my heritage. Ah, but it has been many a teacake moon, many thousands of pardons for a dirty picture snapped in my raw youth now, that these lips have had a hankering for servicing some of my Canton heritage in the flesh. But I've never been able to get close enough. Now you, my Hong Kong flower, my sweet sloe-eyed beauty from the mysterious East, I can tell that your little fingers have twiddled many a chopstick. Your smooth-bore hands have the memory of gunpowder's invention in them and know how to shape a blast and I dare say, tickle out a shot. Let me lead your hands.

GIRL.   I can tell you are really Longtime Californ', and kind of slick too, but you were telling me of what you were made.

TAM.   I am the natural born ragmouth speaking the motherless bloody tongue. No real language of my own to make sense with, so out comes everybody else's trash that don't conceive. But the sound truth is that I AM THE NOTORIOUS ONE AND ONLY CHICKENCOOP CHINAMAN HIMSELF that talks in the dark heavy Midnight, the secret Chinatown Buck Buck Bagaw. I am the result of a pile of pork chop suey thrown up into the chickencoop in the dead of night and the riot of dark birds, night cocks and insomniac nympho hens running after strange food that followed. There was Mother Red built like a fighting cock and running like one too. Hellbent for feather, cocksure, running for pork chop suey in the dead of night. And DESTINY.

GIRL.   And then you were born?

TAM.   No, lass. Moonlight shone through the chinks of the coop. And seabreezes from the West brought the smell of the ships and the sewers. Moonlight caught prickly in her mad hen's eye and seabreeze in her feathers as she ran a dumb cluck in a bird gallop across the great dung prairie of an Oakland Chinatown Chickencoop. Following Mother Red was her Rhode Island featherbrains. Nickel and dime birds that even after being flat on their backs in Freudian analysis couldn't grunt out an egg between them. Promiscuous and criminal birds. Too lazy even to shape up a proper pecking order, they just grooved on running their fool heads off together, making chicken poetry after Mad Mother Red.

GIRL.   And then you were born?

TAM.   Meanwhile, back at the doghouse was a bird of a different feather. A mean critter with Red in its eyes, seen as it heard them clucks come loco around the corner.

GIRL.   And then you were born?

TAM.   No. Just at this moment coming through the fence was a troupe of Spanish Flamenco gypsy dwarves, Los Gitanos Cortos, taking a shortcut to their boxcar after a hard night's work dancing on the tops of Cadillacs and Lincolns in the T&D theatre parking lot. This crowd of shortstuff whiffed the pork chop and had visions of licking their trough clean. Like the mad dog, they ran full of wild Injuns. Blood whooping fast for to grab a quick bite.

GIRL.   And then you were born?

TAM (*as a Bible Belt preacher*). Born? No! Crashed! Not born. Stamped! Not born! Created! Not born. No more born than the heaven and earth. No more born than nylon or acrylic. For I am a Chinaman! A miracle synthetic! Drip dry and machine washable. For now, in one point of time and space, as never before and never after, in this one instant of eternity, was focused that terrific, that awesome power of the universe that marks a moment divine . . . For Mother Red and her herd of headless wonders! One mad hairy dog! And twelve little people in high heeled shoes, once and for all, blind and deaf and very dumb to the perpetration of righteous heinous love MET!

GIRL.   And then you were born?

(TAM *gives razzberry*.)

GIRL.   And you were born.

TAM.   Born. Born to talk to Chinaman sons of Chinamans, children of the dead. But enough of my sordid past. It's not right for a body to know his own origins, for it leaves the mother nothing secret to herself. I want to hear about you.

GIRL.   You sure have a way with words, but I'd like it better if you'd speak the mother tongue.

TAM.   I speak nothing but the mother tongues bein' born to none of my own, I talk the talk of orphans. But I got a tongue for you, baby. Any maybe you could handmake my bone China.

(TAM *and* GIRL *are in a single pool of light*. TAM *moves to put her hand on his fly and stuff one of his hands inside her shirt*. TAM *licks his lips and puckers up for a smooch, breathing heavy. She giggles and runs off. Blackout.*)

GIRL (*as stewardess, voice-over in black*). Ladies and Gentlemen, we have just landed in Pittsburgh. The time is now five forty-six, Eastern Standard Time. The temperature is 44 degrees. The weather is cloudy with a chance of snow.

CURTAIN

SCENE TWO

KENJI's *apartment. Night.*

Pittsburgh's black ghetto is called ''Oakland.'' It has the look of having been a high class, fashionable residential district at the turn of the century. The buildings are still solid, thick-walled . . . at least they seem that way on the outside. Inside the grand interiors have been lost after countless remodelings.

KENJI's *apartment is highceilinged. New diaphragm walls divide what was once a big room into three. The bathroom, complete with tub and sink, the living-dining room and entry area, and part of the kitchen are visible.*

The apartment has the look of having been recently moved into, while at the same time looking a long time settled. It is on the verge of having a style. A massive round table top is set low on the floor on cinder blocks. Wooden auditorium chairs. An overstuffed chair. A mattress and boxspring from a double bed serves as a couch. Tatami on the floor.

The walls are covered with posters of black country, blues and jazz musicians that clash with the few Japanese prints and art objects.

A cake with one piece cut from it is on the table. Sewing paraphernalia and curtain material are on the table.

The front door is open. Snow is seen falling outside through a window. The crash of cars coupling up from the railyard can be heard now and then.

TAM *and* KENJI *enter*. TAM *carries a small suitcase and an attaché case*. KENJI *carries a travelbag of suits*. TAM *puts his stuff down in the entryway*. KENJI *keeps the travelbag*. TAM *flexes, shakes his legs down, stretches and yawns, scanning the place* . . .

KENJI.   Well, man, this is it. My place . . . right in the heart of the black ghetto. Just like home.

TAM.   BlackJap Kenji! Mah brother! Whew, man, I thought for awhile you'd grown up, man. Twenty grand high class research dentist wit' his own lab, man, his own imported apes, twenty-three hunnerd miles from the childhood. Grownup, fat, middle-class! Ha. But here ya are, still livin in a slum, still my blackJap Kenji.

KENJI.   Who you callin ''grownup?''

TAM (*spying curtain stuff*). Yeah, Kenji's home in this Pittsburgh, with a woman and everything. Janet?

KENJI.   Naw man, that was . . . where was that?

TAM.   High school. I was going to ask you . . .

KENJI.   You okay?

TAM.   . . . Must be me. Them hours winging here sittin on my ass broke my momentum. I feel like I lost speed . . . It's even hard for me to talk . . . and if I can't talk to you, you know I . . . and I been doing a lotta talkin, Yeah . . . Mumbo Jumbo. Dancer sends his love.

TAM *flops in whatever's handy, leans back and closes his eyes* . . . KENJI *watches him*.

LEE (*sleepily from bedroom*). Robbie? Kenji?

(KENJI *responds to the voice by going to the bedroom and peeking in. He makes a quick survey of the apartment, looking into rooms, seeing who's where. He creeps up on* TAM, *brings his face down close and level with* TAM's *face and turns on Helen Keller . . .*)

KENJI (*as Helen Keller*). Moowahjeerffurher roar rungs!

(TAM *snaps awake, staring* KENJI *in the face, and deadpan says . . .*)

TAM (*as Helen Keller*). Moowahjeerffurher roar rungs?
KENJI (*as Helen Keller*). Moowahjeerffurher roar rungs.
TAM *and* KENJI (*continuing*). My dear friends!
TAM (*continuing*). Helen Keller! I'd know that voice anywhere!

(TAM *and* KENJI *exchange five.*)

KENJI (*as Helen Keller*). Aheeeha op eeehoooh too ooh wahyou oooh.
TAM (*as a Bible Belt preacher*). Yeah, talk to me, Helen! Hallelujah! I hear her talkin to me.

(TAM *jumps to his feet shuddering with fake religious fervor.* KENJI *supports with Hallelujahs and repetitions.*)

TAM.   Put your hands on the radio, children, feel the power of Helen Keller, children. Believe! And she, the Great White goddess, the mother of Charlie Chan, the Mumbler, the Squeaker, shall show you the way, children! Oh, yeah!
KENJI.   Hallelujah!
TAM.   Helen Keller overcame her handicaps without riot! She overcame her handicaps without looting! She overcame her handicaps without violence! And you Chinks and Japs can too. Oooh I feel the power, children. Feel so gooooood! I feeeeeel it!

(*Enter* ROBBIE *from the kitchen. He wears a bibbed apron. A professional apron, white, no frills.*)

LEE.   Tom? Tom? Kenji?
TAM (*as Helen Keller*). Yarr roar heh yelp wee ooh sub coawt unh ree-ssurch llee-dung toth enged roh dove fub earthed eff fecks.
KENJI (*as Helen Keller*). Your help will support research leading to the end of birth defects . . .
TAM.   Listen to the voice of the Great White Motha, come to show you the light, Chinks and Japs, I say Listen, Children! Whooo I feel the power!

(TAM *and* KENJI *exchange fives.* ROBBIE *is attracted to the action, comes and stands, makes himself available, grinning, looking from face to face, laughing.*)

TAM (*as Helen Keller*). nggg gah gallop nose weather bar hearth death facts sorrel lull heed new worm who whirl eye fees.

KENJI.   And help those born with birth defects lead normal lives.
TAM.   Believe!
KENJI.   I believe!
TAM.   I said, believe children!
KENJI *and* ROBBIE.   I believe!
TAM.   AH MEAN! BELIEVE!
KENJI *and* ROBBIE.   I believe!
TAM.   Hallelujah!

(TAM *and* KENJI *exchange five.* TAM *notices* ROBBIE, *glances at* KENJI, *grins, takes* ROBBIE's *hand, and sets it to give him five, and gives him five.* LEE *rushes angrily into the scene, too late to stop* ROBBIE *from returning five, and grabs her son.*)

LEE.   Kenji!
TAM.   Sister! Child!
KENJI.   For the sake of tomorrow's children.
TAM *and* KENJI (*as Helen Keller*). Thak ahhhnggkkk are are arf rung youuuu.
KENJI.   Thank you.

(TAM *and* KENJI *strut and exchange five, laughing and sparing.*)

KENJI.   Remember Helen Keller's telephone?
TAM.   It doesn't ring . . .
KENJI.   It just gets warm!

(TAM *less energetically, suddenly preoccupied, goes through the motions of exchanging five with* KENJI, *who wants to snuffle and spar.* ROBBIE *gets his five from* TAM *and stuffs himself into the scene sparring with* KENJI *while* TAM *catches his breath, and rubs his face.*)

LEE (*to* TAM). Leave my boy alone!
TAM.   Wha . . . ? What's happening? I got nothing but outtakes in my head.
LEE (*to* KENJI). I'm tired of you coming in like this! I'm tired of you putting my son down! Go get your nuts off beating up your own kid! Go on! Come here, Robbie.
ROBBIE.   I'm okay, Lee.
TAM.   How many kids you got?
LEE.   . . . What's it to you?
KENJI.   None.
TAM (*as Helen Keller*). Oh. Oh . . .
LEE.   Oh, you . . . Think you're funny?
KENJI.   Everything's cool.
LEE.   I've never seen anything so . . .
KENJI.   I said, everything's cool!
LEE.   You never shout at me. Why're you shouting?
KENJI.   Lee . . . Lee, this is my friend, Tam Lum. We used to call him "Tampax" . . .
LEE.   Oh, lovely.
KENJI.   . . . a long time ago. What's wrong?

LEE. I guess Kenji's told you about me. He tells all his friends.

TAM. No.

KENJI. Friends?

LEE. . . . that I'm pregnant and on my way to Africa.

TAM. No.

KENJI. How can you be pregnant? Who? What?

LEE. . . . and of course he told you the child isn't his.

TAM. No.

LEE. He didn't tell you the only reason he lets me stay here is that he thinks I'm crazy. He told you about my long distance phone calls.

(TAM *moves to say "no" again but* LEE *continues.*)

LEE. Robbie's waiting for you to shake his hand.

TAM. Hey, this is the wrong movie. I didn't mean to come into no situation.

LEE. That's right, run! I should've known. All afraid of the pretty girls? But oh so anxious to do the right thing—avoid trouble—save face. Look at you so stoic, and that dumb little smile. Do ya talk in giggles too? Are you going to shake my son's hand or not?

TAM. Wanna fuck?

LEE. Yeah.

TAM. Oh, wow, Kenji, you've really grown up!

KENJI. What's wrong, Lee?

LEE. I can't stand people who are rude to children.

KENJI. You're tired, babe.

LEE. I am tired.

TAM. I'm tired and dirty . . . filthy . . . hungry.

LEE. Not too tired to be polite to my son.

KENJI. Oh, hey, man, that's right. You need a bath, right?

TAM. Sure. Hey, kid . . .

LEE. His name is Robbie.

TAM. Hey, Robbie, gimme five!

(TAM *lifts his hand to slap with* ROBBIE, *but* LEE *stops them.*)

LEE. No, not that! It's sick of you to make fun of blacks . . . the way you walk . . . your talk . . . giving five. Who do you think you are?

(TAM *and* ROBBIE *shake hands,* TAM *turning to* LEE *saying . . .*)

TAM. You black?

LEE *and* ROBBIE. No.

TAM. I didn't think so.

LEE. I was married to a black for awhile.

TAM. You had to tell me, didn't ya? Couldn't let me guess. You gave up Janet for this girl, eh Kenji?

LEE. No, I'm not his girl. I'm his good deed.

KENJI. Here, drop your jacket, man.

TAM. I need some coffee. Coffee. I mean coffee! Gotta be bright for my man. Remember that night we were out with Ovaltine the Dancer? He sends ya his love, man. Where is that boy? he said. We're in his life story.

KENJI. Oh, hey . . . you gonna put it in the movie? I'm gonna be on T.V.?

TAM. Movie's gonna turn on two things man, double action, right? That title defense against Claude Dupree he did in his forties. His greatest fight, right? One. And Two how his daddy, Charley Popcorn, made him be that kind of fighter. You should see some of the stuff we shot, man.

KENJI. Yeah. You been on the case then.

TAM. Month in Oakland, our Oakland, shooting background and recreating the atmosphere of the Dupree fight, after a month with the Dancer, livin with him, man fifty hours of him blabbing his life out on quarter inch tape. And I got the rights to the film of that title defense against Dupree. But it's the Dancer's father, man, Charley Popcorn that's gonna make this movie go. Remember how Ovaltine the Dancer carried on about his mighty daddy? Well, he's here in Pittsburgh man, and we're gonna see him!

KENJI. Yeah!

(TAM *and* KENJI *exchange five.* TAM *grabs a handful of cake crumbs from the table during his speech.*)

TAM. We'll see this Popcorn later, ya know. No equipment on us, right? Nothin to scare him, sound him. Whoo. This child done been hisself up two days, seeing the last of the stuff we shot through the lab, and auditioning the tapes of his Popcorn stories. Now, I'm primed!

KENJI. Maybe you better grab some winks, man, or you won't have no juice to run on later, you know . . .

TAM. No, no, man. If I sleep now, I won't ever wake up. No, I came wired to meet Popcorn, just for a little bit, tonight, check out his pornie house as a possible location, right? And I'm gonna do it, like in that song, they say (TAM *and* KENJI):

SOMEWHERE OVER THE RAINBOW
BLUEBIRDS FLY
BIRDS FLY . . .

(TAM *and* KENJI *exchange five and laugh. Crumbs fall from* TAM'*s hand.*)

LEE. You're getting crumbs all over the floor. Why don't you hang up your clothes? I was making curtains there.

TAM. I put his . . .

KENJI. Oh . . .

LEE. Where do you think you are? This place is depressing enough without your mess . . . so dark and unhappy, and that awful noise outside night and day. What is that noise? It's worse today.

KENJI. Sounds like the end of World War 3.

TAM. It's the railroad, they're making up a train down in the yard.

LEE.   You're only saying that because you're Chinese.

(TAM *turns ugly a moment, ready to mess her up, then shrugs it off.*)

TAM.   I'll pick up the crumbs, okay? And I'll hang up the clothes. Just show me where . . .

LEE.   The closets are full.

KENJI.   Just leave your stuff, man. Go take your wash and I'll talk to Lee here, okay?

TAM.   Yeah.

(ROBBIE *shows* TAM *the way to the bathroom.*)

TAM.   Yeah, kid, tasty cake.

ROBBIE.   I'll have a piece cut for you when you're done.

(TAM *stalls in the bathroom waiting for* ROBBIE *to leave. Instead* ROBBIE *settles himself in the doorway.* TAM *finally begins stripping down to his shorts. He wears boxer type swimming trunks.*)

KENJI.   Why're you acting like this?

LEE.   How?

KENJI.   Either be nice to my friend or shut up.

ROBBIE.   You like kids. I can tell.

TAM.   Kenji . . . he your dad?

ROBBIE.   No. He hasn't been. You talk loud when you get mad, did you know that?

TAM.   You talk funny for a kid, did you know that?

ROBBIE.   I've been around. Kenji says you write movies and stuff. You don't look like you'd write kidstuff though.

TAM.   Kenji say I write kidstuff? I don't think my stuff is kidstuff.

ROBBIE.   That's what I mean. You don't write kidstuff. Maybe I'll be a writer and write movies . . . (TAM *and* ROBBIE) and stuff . . .

TAM.   Why don't you talk kidstuff? A man should be a kid when he's a kid. You don't wanna be old all your life.

ROBBIE.   Lee says a man should fight. But Lee isn't a man, is she?

TAM.   Well, people said I never talked like a kid either . . . used to give me quarters for my pearl-studded palaver like I was a kind of jukebox. Take it from me, kid. Talk like a kid while you're a kid, even if you have to fake it.

ROBBIE.   Kenji just tells me to shut up.

TAM.   I'm sure he has his reasons. Right, kid?

ROBBIE.   He doesn't like people to talk to him.

TAM.   You talk too much, kid. Cool it and just ask "Why?" and "How come?"

ROBBIE.   How come you're wearing swimming trunks?

TAM.   Funny you should ask me that. This is my secret suit! Whenever I see someone in distress I strip down to my secret suit, put up my dukes, and go swimming.

ROBBIE (*laughs*). Nobody tells me jokes like that.

TAM.   Maybe it's because nobody likes you! No. No. Forget I said that, kid. See, you talk like a little man long enough and I talk back at you like a man. But you can take it, right? You been around.

ROBBIE.   Nobody talks to me like a man. That isn't really your secret suit, is it. I mean, I'm not bothering you am I?

TAM.   Naw, it's something I picked up from an old dishwasher who was afraid of white old ladies peeking at him through the keyhole. True! I swear! You see, we had the kitchen in this old folks resthome thing. He thought all them old toothless goofy white ladies was all for peeking at his body, so he used to wear his underpants right in his bath. Crazy old dishwasher. Sometimes I'd wash his back, you know. But he was crazy about boxing.

ROBBIE.   I'd help my father in his bath too.

TAM.   Oh, you did? Must've been old, huh and . . . oh, I see, died and you and your mom, you came . . . Listen, I'm sorry . . .

ROBBIE.   I mean, if I had a father I'd help him like you helped yours.

TAM.   He wasn't my father. He was just a crazy old dishwasher.

ROBBIE.   But he took care of you.

TAM.   I took care of him. He couldn't get around outside of Chinatown without me. All he did for me was take me and Kenji to fights. He'd go anywhere to catch a fight. Otherwise he was crazy. He depended on my English, my bad Chinese, was what he was doing, like when I had to take him to the police to get a form filled out for the Immigration. Nothin serious. I didn't know that. He didn't know that, scared.

ROBBIE.   You dropped your soap.

TAM.   How old are you?

ROBBIE.   Eleven. Twelve. Almost twelve. You okay?

TAM.   When we got home he said he had to have a bath. He said I had to help him. I don't remember what kind of language he was using. I should though don't you think?

ROBBIE.   I don't know.

TAM.   Neither do I . . . You could see his veins like snakes swimming in rosewater.

ROBBIE.   You okay?

TAM.   You ever see real rosewater?

ROBBIE.   No.

TAM.   I helped him into his bath, and he died. It was just lights out. He finished it. Do you believe that, kid?

ROBBIE.   Yes.

TAM.   See what I mean? Now I tell it dry eyed, and I'm believed. I told it the same at the tub when they came, and they didn't believe me. Because I didn't cry. They got mad. They said I wouldn't get a quarter. I wasn't tellin a story . . . You know what I mean?

ROBBIE.   No.

TAM.   I mean, act your age, kid! Don't talk to me like a little man. I'm not your buddy. I'm an old dude who tells kids jokes, bosses 'em around gruffly, rough houses 'em, has a swell time, and forgets 'em, cuz that's what adults do. Now, do me a favor and get me my case, will ya? And tell your mother I know what trains sound like cuz I used to work on the railroad . . . No, don't. Just get my case, okay?

ROBBIE.   . . . and I'll cut you some cake.

(ROBBIE *goes to get case and cut a piece of cake in the kitchen.*)

LEE.   What were you two talking about in there?

ROBBIE.   Uhh . . . somebody he knew. A Chinese dishwasher who took baths wearing a swimsuit.

LEE.   Why don't you like being Chinese, Tam?

TAM.   I'm in the bath.

KENJI.   Goddamit, Lee, shut up.

LEE.   I said, why don't you like being Chinese, Tam? (*To* KENJI.) I know he's your childhood friend, but you're not children anymore.

(ROBBIE *returns to bathroom with* TAM'*s case and cake. He sets them inside and hangs around the doorway.*)

TAM.   What'd you say, Lee?

(KENJI *and* LEE *exchange glances.*)

KENJI.   Nothing, man. Be sure to wash under your arms.

ROBBIE.   You're Chinese, aren't you? I like Chinese people.

TAM.   Me too. They're nice and quiet aren't they?

ROBBIE.   One of my fathers was Chinese, like you. He was nice. The nicest.

TAM.   Fathers?

ROBBIE.   A white one. A Chinese one. One was black. We talk with them on the phone. I liked the Chinese . . . Lee says he wasn't a man.

TAM.   Whaddaya mean, Chinese like me and not a man? You some kind of racist midget trying to ride for half fare?

ROBBIE.   Should I have said that? Are you mad at me? I don't think you should have told me about the crazy old dishwasher, but I understand. I'm not mad at you.

TAM.   Listen, kid. Man to man. If I could be mad at you, I would. I'm not mad at you. But don't talk to me. Your idea of kid talk is just too strange for me.

ROBBIE.   Why?

TAM.   Ah, now! There's the kid . . . That's all, "Why?" "Why?" Say, "Why?" kid.

ROBBIE.   Why?

TAM.   You got it.

LEE.   What's he doing here anyway? Tell me again, please. I'm listening carefully this time.

KENJI.   Aww, Lee! I seeya. I hearya. You don't have to . . .

LEE.   Well, what is he doing here?

KENJI.   He's making some kind of documentary movie about Ovaltine Jack Dancer, an ex-champion of the light heavyweights. The Dancer's daddy lives here, and Tam's here to see him.

LEE.   That's boxing isn't it?

KENJI.   Yeah, and don't make anything of that! This could be Tam's big chance.

LEE.   Is this boxer Chinese? Of course not, he's black.

KENJI.   Yeah.

LEE.   I hate people making it on the backs of black people. I don't like your friend at all.

KENJI.   But you made it on your back under blacks, and that's okay, huh?

LEE.   That's not good grammar. I don't understand what you're saying. But I think you meant to be cruel. You've never been cruel to me before.

KENJI.   Listen, Lee.

LEE.   You're being cruel to me. You're going to scold me.

KENJI.   No, Lee . . . I was going to say I can see what you mean. But I think you're wrong too. About Tam, I mean. And me faking blackness.

LEE.   . . . Not you . . .

KENJI.   Yeah, me. I mean, Ovaltine Jack the Dancer was our hero, you know. We met him.

LEE.   Oh, a story. That's what I need right now, a story.

KENJI.   I'm explaining something. Maybe we act black, but it's not fake. Oakland was weirdness. No seasons. No snow. I was a kid missing the concentration camps . . . the country with just us, you know what I mean. Now it's blacks and Chinese all of a sudden. All changed. My folks, everybody . . .

LEE.   And you? The young prince returned from exile in the wilderness? Turned black! Presto change-o!

KENJI.   I changed! Yeah! Presto! School was all blacks and Mexicans. We were kids in school, and you either walked and talked right in the yard, or got the shit beat outa you every day, ya understand? But that Tam was always what you might say . . . "The Pacesetter." Whatever was happenin with hair, or the latest color, man . . . Sometimes he looked pretty exotic, you know, shades, high greasy hair, spitcurls, purple shiny shirt, with skull cufflinks and Frisko jeans worn like they was fallin off his ass. Me, I was the black one. "BlackJap Kenji" I used to be called and hated yellow-people. You look around and see where I'm livin, Lee, and it looks like I still do, Pittsburgh ain't exactly famous for no Chinatown or Li'l Tokyo, you know.

LEE.   "BlackJap"? I've always thought of you as just plain Kenji . . . a little sullen . . . a little shy.

KENJI.   I'm explaining something, okay?

LEE.   I was just commenting . . .

KENJI.   Okay?

LEE.   Okay.

KENJI.   Okay. When we were in college, we kidnapped Ovaltine. I mean, Tam did. Tricked him out of his hotel room, and we took him driving out of Oakland and all stood out by the car pissing in the bushes. And I remembered I'd been to New Orleans and, you know, stuck over on the colored side. And I had to piss, and didn't know which way to go. And this black dishwasher there, *saw my plight* so to speak, and took me out to the can and we took places at urinals right next to each other. I thought that was pretty friendly. And I wanted to tell Ovaltine, you know, but Ovaltine being black, might not understand a yellow man, standing next to him, pissing in the bushes, talking about the last memorable time he went pissing with a black man . . . He talked about pissing with the black dishwasher in New Orleans like it was him that did it.

LEE.   Sounds just like him.

KENJI.   You don't know him.

LEE.   Didn't that piss you off? What'd you do?

KENJI.   No, I wasn't pissed off. I was glad. I didn't have the guts to do it, you know. He took the risks.

LEE.   Ahh. But he's a charlatan, and you're for real.

TAM.   No, lass, I'm a charlatan, and he's for real.

LEE.   Have you been eavesdropping?

TAM.   No, I've been eavesdropping. Me and Robbie ran out of conversation. So since Kenji was tellin all my stories.

KENJI.   What's this thing of his about talkin in the bathroom anyway? Every time I go in there he comes to stand in the doorway. What is that?

LEE.   Didn't you do that as a boy?

TAM.   Where we come from boys who hung around watchin men in the pisser were considered a little funny that way, you know.

LEE.   It takes one to know one. *You know.*

KENJI.   Lee, what is this all about? Badmouthing my friend, someone you've never seen before, putting me down through him . . . I explained . . . !

LEE.   I never put you down!

KENJI.   The hell you didn't! I'm not imitating no black people. I'm no copycat. I know I live with 'em, I talk like 'em, I dress . . . maybe even eat what they eat and don't mess with, so what if I don't mess with other Orientals . . . Asians, whatever, blah blah blah. Hell, the way you been talkin to Tam, who's my brother, Lee, you make everything I do sound ugly, man, like I hate myself. And you got no right to say that about me.

LEE.   I never said that. I've never seen you like this before.

KENJI.   I've never been like this before. I'm with my friend, and in my house with my friend. I should be proud of my house with my friend in here, but you're making me ashamed. And I won't have it. You can mess around with this place anyway you want . . . put up curtains, I don't care. I like 'em. But you're just a guest here. You're not my woman or my lover or nothing but a guest. Now you act like one, you understand?

LEE.   I never put you down.

KENJI.   You put me down. Damn, you put me down! Bringin in this goddam tatami grassmat Japanese bullshit and knockin the legs off the table . . .

LEE.   I just thought . . .

KENJI.   You just thought like some little white bitch with the artbooks. I'm not Japanese! Tam ain't no Chinese! And don't give me any of that "If-you-don't-have-that-Oriental-culture,-baby,-all-you've-got-is-the-color-of-your-skin" bullshit. But we're not getting into no silk robes and walk around like fools for you!

LEE.   You're talking an awful lot!

TAM.   Oh, um . . .

KENJI.   Yeah, I am, huh. I must be happy.

LEE.   Tom's coming.

KENJI.   Never heard of him.

LEE.   My ex-husband.

KENJI.   Ex-husbands and kids. You have so many. White, yellow, black. What is this, Twenty Questions?

LEE.   If you'd stop interrupting . . .

KENJI.   I'm trying to avoid significant pauses. This conversation has got to have some flow, some pop, some rhythm, or I'm . . .

LEE.   He's Chinese . . . The Chinese husband I had, and he says he's coming to take me back to San Francisco with him. He wants my baby.

KENJI.   What baby? You been on the phone again with baby news?

LEE.   And I'm mad and I'm scared . . . and it isn't easy for me.

TAM.   Wow!

LEE.   He's a writer.

TAM.   What's he write, art books? Chinese cookbooks?

LEE.   He's writing a book called *Soul on Rice*.

KENJI *and* TAM.   SOUL ON RICE?

TAM.   He think that title up all by himself, or did you help?

LEE.   I'll tell ya how he thought it up . . .

TAM.   No! Don't tell me. Just tell me, is it white rice on brown rice? Must be a cookbook.

KENJI *and* TAM.   WILD RICE!

(TAM *and* KENJI *exchange five.* LEE *is laughing in spite of herself.*)

TAM.   Yeah, he didn't fulfill your lesbian fantasies. Or was it you found out you didn't like girls? So you left him for a black . . . but then, if he gave you this kid . . .

LEE.   It's not his!

KENJI.   It's not mine.

TAM.   All right, immaculate conception. But, for him to think so, you musta given him another chance . . . Lemme see your eyes.

(LEE *turns from* TAM.)

LEE.   I don't like being bossed.

TAM.   All these husbands and children, man. All colors and decorator combinations. A one woman Minority of the Month Club. Now to Africa, wow . . .

LEE.   You're supposed to be comforting me. This is serious.

TAM.   Whoowhee! Chinamans do make lousy fathers. I know. I have one.

LEE.   How can you laugh at a thing like that?

TAM.   I reminded you of your Chinese husband.

LEE.   Well, I . . .

TAM (*teasingly*). Huh? Come on, admit it.

LEE.   Tam.

TAM.   Huh? Yeah?

LEE.   Not exactly, maybe . . .

TAM.   We all look alike.

LEE.   Not exactly, but . . .

TAM.   It's okay. You remind me of somebody, too. So we're even. But that's okay. This trip's going to make me well. I'm going to see again, and talk and hear . . . And I got a solution to all your problems. Don't bother with no Twenty Questions, Ouija Board, I Ching or any of that. One: I'm splitting to take care of business. And two: If you don't want to see people, keep the door locked.

KENJI.   We'll go see Charley Popcorn, and Lee, if you don't wanta see Tom, keep the door locked. We'll be back soon, Tam's tired . . .

LEE.   Why do you have to go? Let Tam go.

TAM.   Yeah, I gotta see Charley Popcorn.

LEE.   And you and me and Robbie can stay home with the door locked.

KENJI.   But I want to see Charley Popcorn too. Father of a champion, man.

LEE.   Oh, he's Ovaltine Jack Dancer's father.

TAM.   The madman behind the badman! Come on, if you're gonna come on, man. Let's go someplace where we can talk and grab some eats before we see Popcorn.

LEE.   Aren't you going to eat here?

TAM.   I don't want to eat here!

LEE.   But Robbie's been cooking for all of us . . .

TAM.   Then you and him eat for all of us. I'm sorry. We hit it off wrong. Maybe under different circumstances . . . like in a dark alley.

LEE.   You wouldn't joke like that if you had kids of your own.

TAM.   I have two, Sarah and Jonah, named for Sarah and Jonah, remember, Kenji?

LEE.   Your wife was white of course.

KENJI.   What's color got to do with it? Right, Tam?

TAM.   Man, you got it all down, don't ya? Yes, she was white!

LEE.   I knew you hated being Chinese. You're all chicken! Not an ounce of guts in all of you put together! Instead of guts you have . . . all that you have is is . . . culture! Watery paintings, silk, all that grace and beauty arts and crafts crap! You're all very pretty, and all so intelligent. And . . . you couldn't even get one of your own girls, because they know . . .

TAM.   Know what?

LEE.   They know all about you, mama's boys and crybabies, not a man in all your males . . . so you go take advantage of some stupid white girl who's been to a museum, some scared little ninny with visions of jade and ancient art and being gently cared for.

TAM.   You're not talking about me.

KENJI.   Lee, you're not talking about Tam.

LEE.   I am talking about Tam. Tampax Lum, your friend. He's the worst kind. He knows he's no kind of man. Look at him, he's like those little vulnerable sea animals born with no shells of their own so he puts on the shells of the dead. You hear him when he talks? He's talking in so many goddam dialects and accents all mixed up at the same time, cracking wisecracks, lots of oh yeah, wisecracks, you might think he was a nightclub comic. What'sa wrong with your Chinatown acka-cent, huh?

KENJI.   Lee.

TAM.   I got tired of people correcting it. They were even telling me I was "mispronouncing" my name . . . kept telling me it was pronounced "Tom."

LEE.   See? More wisecracks. You're just saying that.

TAM.   Yeah, that's all I am. And they said I had rags in my mouth, which led to ragmouth, which ended up Tampax. But I hear something in your tongue . . . that funny red in the hair . . . You got the blood don't ya? You're Chinese, right? A breath of the blood?

(LEE *turns away.*)

TAM.   Did your Tom know? You were giving Chinamans a chance to smack up skin to skin . . . goin home to yellowness. No, I'm not puttin you down. I'm not arguing with you one bit. Bout nothin. You're right. Everything you say is right. I'm a good loser. I give up.

LEE.   Well, don't, can't you get mad? Can't you fight?

TAM.   For what? My country? The Alamo? And don't say my "soul." Anyway you're the wrong woman to ask me that. I'd like to hug you for askin though.

LEE.   Why don't you?

(TAM *spreads his arms, rises, seems about to move to embrace* LEE, *then shakes himself and sits and holds his head. He takes on some kind of white or European accent and says . . .*)

TAM.   "I've known many many women. But with you I'm afraid."

LEE.   Come on, I'm just one of the boys.

KENJI.   Good! Let's all go out by the car and piss in the bushes.

LEE.   Do you see your kids?

KENJI.   Well, I'm hungry . . .

TAM.   Do you see yours?

KENJI.   I'll give Robbie a hand.

LEE.   I can't. I want to but . . .

TAM.   I can't either. I don't want to. I want 'em to forget me.

LEE.   You can't mean that. They're your kids! You can't turn your back on them.

TAM.   My back's all that's good for them. My front's no good. Which one was Chinese? Your mother or your father? Grandmother? Grandfather . . . ? Hmmm? With me in their lives, they'd grow up to be like you.

LEE.   Don't you miss them? I miss my children. Robbie isn't enough. Sometimes I even miss their fathers.

TAM.   I mean, we grow up bustin our asses to be white anyway . . . "Don't wear green because it makes you look yellow, son." Now there's Confucius in America for you. "Don't be seen with no blacks, get good grades, lay low, an apple for the teacher, be good, suck up, talk proper, and be civilized." I couldn't be friends with Kenji in the open man until . . . I mean, it took us years after the war to finally not be scared of whitefolks mixing us up with Japs . . . When I went out, I told the folks I was goin to visit Mexicans and we didn't feature Mexicans and I was really running with BlackJap. BlackJap and Tampax, the Ragmouth—for my fancy yakity yak don't ya know. The Lone Ranger and Tonto of all those hot empty streets that got so hot in the summer, the concrete smelled like popcorn and you could smell the tires of parked cars baking. And what made the folks happiest was for some asshole, some white offthewall J.C. Penney's clerk type with his crispy suit to say I spoke English well.

LEE.   You're talking too fast for me. I can't . . .

TAM (*continuing through* LEE's *interruptions*). And praisin me for being "Americanized" and no juvenile delinquency. "The strong Chinese family . . . Chinese culture." And the folks just smiled. The reason there was no juvenile delinquency was because there was no kids! The laws didn't let our women in . . .

LEE.   What's this got to do with anything?

TAM.   . . . and our women born here lost their citizenship if they married a man from China. And all our men here, no women, stranded here burned all their diaries, their letters, everything with their names on it . . . threw the ashes into the sea . . . hopin that that much of themselves could find someplace friendly. I asked an old man if that was so. He told me it wasn't good for me to know such things, to let all that stuff die with the old.

LEE.   You taking me to school?

TAM.   He told me to forget it . . . to get along with "Americans." Well, they're all dead now. We laugh at 'em with the "Americans," talk about them saying "Buck buck bagaw" instead of "giddyup" to their horses and get along real nice here now, don't we?

LEE.   Oh, Tam, I don't know.

TAM.   I've given my folks white grandkids, right? I don't want 'em to be anything like me, or know me, or remember me. This guy they're calling "daddy" . . . I hear he's even a better writer than me.

KENJI.   Who said that? I'll kill him.

LEE.   Who said that?

TAM.   My mother, tellin me I was no good, to cheer me up. "Brabra," she said. She could never say, "Barbara." It was always "Brabra" like . . . (TAM *hefts imaginary boobs.*) You know there's a scientific relation between boobs and ambition. I'm not greedy for boobs. No ambition. I'm just gonna make this movie. Keep busy. Just do one thing right, right? That Ovaltine-Dupree fight! Damn! He was so happy Ovaltine the Dancer won. I bought into this movie to do it right, with money I should be usin for the child support. I even begged some up from the folks. Lots of home cooking and playing a goodboy listenin to his ma, for his "allowance."

LEE.   See? You do care.

TAM.   I even took a grubstake from you, eh, Kemo Sabay. You scared?

KENJI.   My silver bullets, your silver bullets, Masked Man.

TAM.   My kids might see it some day, and . . . And they'll see . . .

LEE.   You see, Tam? You can't turn your back on them. You don't mean it when you say you want them to forget you.

TAM.   I mean it. I mean, in case they don't forget. I should leave them something . . . I should have done some THING. One thing I've done alone, with all my heart. A gift. Not revenge. But they've already forgotten me. They got a new, ambitious, successful, go-for-bucks, superior white daddy.

LEE.   Tam, you bastard, you make me so pissed. You could be a wonderful father. No! No! I won't let Tom take this baby for his rich bitch mother again.

KENJI.   Huh?

LEE.   You won't make me see him. Don't talk about it. Don't even talk about it.

TAM (*interrupting*). I was talking about ambition! They say a man with an old lady with big tits is ambitious. The bigger the tits on his lady, the greater the ambition. "Brabra" didn't have any tits at all. She had depressions, like two bomb craters in the chest. And ma said, "Brabra" . . . NO, it was, "*Son,* Brabra must like writers, only Rex is successful." *I bet her tits are bigger now.* But ma seemed so pleased about it. That "I told you so" tone, as if she'd got her revenge on me, as if she'd known all my life I was no good and was just waiting to tell me . . . Kenji, stop me, I'm stealing your girl with cheap woo.

KENJI.   Sounds like pretty deluxe woo to me. I've been taking notes.

LEE.   I'm not his girl. I'm his guest. He says he won't touch white girls.

KENJI. Not me, too scary.

TAM. Man, Lee's not white.

KENJI. I didn't hear it from her.

TAM. She's chicken to say it. Help her out.

KENJI. Aww, man, if I'm going to go to all the trouble of mind to get a white girl, man, she's going to be all white. And tall. And giant, huge tits man. And blonde. The scariest kind of white girl there is, man, none of this working my way up for me. Blonde hairs all over her head. Tall . . . and tits, man like when I walk up to her and get my little nose stuck in her navel, man, and I look up at her belly, I feel like I'm on the road with you and see two Giant Orange stands across the road from each other.

TAM. Yeah, do it. You got ambition. No down in the cellar for Helen Keller for Kenji.

KENJI. I'm chicken.

TAM. If you were blonde and had these big tits, Kenji could . . .

KENJI. No, I'd chicken out. I'm chicken.

TAM. We're all chicken.

LEE. No one here but us chickens.

TAM. It's like that inspired wino sittin on the crapper in the T&D Theatre in old Oakland wrote on the wall (KENJI *listens with growing recognition*):

> "When Chickencoop Chinaman have wetdream far from home,
>> He cly Buck buck bagaw, squeezing off his bone."

TAM *and* KENJI. Longfellow.

LEE (*overlapping* TAM *and* KENJI). Buck buck bagaw?

(TAM *and* KENJI *pound up a rhythm on glasses, the tabletop, anything handy.* LEE *stamps her feet. They whinny, grunt, squeak, moan, come on like a screaming jungle at night full of animals.*)

KENJI. A fiery horse with the speed of light, a cloud of dust and a hearty . . .

ALL. BUCK BUCK BAGAW . . . THE CHICKENCOOP CHINAMAN!

(*All begin singing Buck Buck Bagaw to the* William Tell Overture *and pounding on things. The tune goes out of their voices and they're screaming noise, throwing in an occasional "Buck Buck Bagaw!" This isn't singing but a kind of vocal athletic event.*)

TAM. "If you don't have Chinese culture, baby, all you've got is the color of your skin."

ALL. BUCK BUCK BAGAW.

KENJI. "How do you tell Chinks from Japs?"

ALL. BUCK BUCK BAGAW.

(*The music becomes frantic, full of screams and whoops and lots of beating on things.* KENJI *grabs coins from his pockets and throws them at the wall. He stamps empty tin cans flat. He and* ROBBIE *howling and screaming take pots and pans*

out of the cupboard and beat on them awhile, get bored and throw them across the room, and get others. LEE *pounds on the table as hard as she can with her fists, beating up a rhythm, throwing the curtain material on the floor.* TAM *puts down the guitar and goes to the bathroom and turns on the shower taps, making the pipes shudder . . . and comes back to beat on cups, bottles, glasses with a spoon. All intermittently cry "Buck Buck Bagaw" and all answer with a cry of "Buck Buck Bagaw!"*)

TAM. Hey. Let's all go see Charley Popcorn at his pornie house! Give him a family.

ALL. BUCK BUCK BAGAW.

KENJI. We'll leave that Tom in the cold.

(*Enter* ROBBIE *from the kitchen.*)

ROBBIE. Dinner's ready.

ALL. BUCK BUCK BAGAW.

CURTAIN

ACT TWO
SCENE ONE

Blackout and fade-in spot on TAM *downstage center. Second spot on* KENJI *tuning a large old-fashioned radio.*

TAM. Did ya hear that . . . ? Listen, children, did I ever tellya, I ever tellya the Lone Ranger ain't a Chinaman? I ever tellya that? Don't blame me. That's what happens when you're a Chinaman boy in the kitchen, listening in the kitchen to the radio, for what's happenin in the other world, while grandmaw has an ear for nothing but ancient trains in the night, and talks pure Chinamouth you understood only by love and feel. She don't hear what a boy hears. She's for the Chinese Hour and chugablood red roving, livin to hear one train, once more. I heard JACK ARMSTRONG, ALL-AMERICAN BOY fight Japs, come outa the radio everyday into our kitchen to tell me everyday for years that ALL-AMERICAN BOYS are the best boys, the hee-rohs! the movie stars! that ALL-AMERICAN BOYS are white boys everyday, all their life long. And grandmaw heard thunder in the Sierra hundreds of miles away and listened for the Chinaman-known Iron Moonhunter, that train built by Chinamans who knew they'd never be given passes to ride the rails they laid. So of all American railroaders, only they sung no songs, told no jokes, drank no toasts to the ol' iron horse, but stole themselves some iron on the way, slowly stole up a pile of steel, children, and hid there in the granite face of the Sierra and builded themselves a wild engine to take them home. Every night, children, grandmaw listened in the kitchen, waiting, til the day she died. And I'd spin the dial looking for to hear ANYBODY, CHINESE AMERICAN BOY, ANYBODY, CHINESE AMERICAN BOY anywhere on the dial, doing anything grand on the air, anything at all. . . . I heard of the masked man. And I listened to him. And in the Sunday funnies he had black hair, and Chinatown was nothin but black hair, and for years, listen, years! I grew blind looking hard through the holes of his funnypaper mask for slanty eyes. Slanty eyes, boys! You see, I knew, children, I knew with all my heart's insight . . . shhh, listen, children . . . he wore that mask to hide his Asian eyes! And that made sense of me. I knew he wore a red shirt for good luck. I knew he rode a white horse named Silver cuz white be our color of death. Ha ha ha. And he was lucky Chinaman vengeance on the West . . . and silver bullets cuz death from a Chinaman is always expensive. Always classy. Always famous. I knew the Lone Ranger was the CHINESE AMERICAN BOY of the radio I'd looked for.

(*Music up: Rossini's* William Tell Overture. *Spot picks up* LONE RANGER *and* TONTO *on toy horses. The* RANGER *and* TONTO *are both old and decrepit.* RANGER *takes out a six-gun and struggles to take aim at* TAM's *hand.*)

TAM.   . . . And I tuned him in! And listened in the kitchen for the Ranger to bring me home (TAM *raises his right hand as if giving an oath.*) And I kept his secrets.

(RANGER *fires, says* . . .)

RANGER.   Kapow! Right in the hand . . .

(RANGER *rides off cackling and wheezing. Music down and out.*)

TAM (*narratively, still in reflection, points at his hand and says*). He shot me in the hand. (*Terrified and in pain.*) He shot me in the hand! (*Narratively.*) I shouted, and this old, old Indian in rotten buckskins . . .
RANGER.   Easy, big fella . . .

(TONTO *takes his bow and arrows, follows* TAM, *who moves toward* KENJI. TONTO *moves to a position behind* TAM *and the* RANGER . . .)

TAM.   . . . got behind his mouse, aimin his bow'n'arrow at me and shouted, ''Hey, who was that masked man?''
TONTO.   Hey! Who was that masked man?

(TAM *and* KENJI *turn toward* TONTO.)

TAM.   What masked man?
TONTO.   Louder!

(TAM *and* KENJI *turn toward* RANGER.)

TAM *and* KENJI.   That was a masked man?
TONTO.   Did you see that white horse?
TAM *and* KENJI (*to* TONTO). What white horse?
TONTO.   That white horse named Silver!
TAM *and* KENJI (*to* RANGER). Silver!

TONTO.   You see them bullets?

(TAM *and* KENJI *turn toward* TONTO.)

TAM.   What bullets?
TONTO.   Them *siiilver* bullets, gents!

(TAM *and* KENJI *turn toward* RANGER.)

KENJI.   Silver bullets! Yaaahhoooh! Hah ha ha. You was shot in the mitt with a silver bullet, ol compadre!
TAM (*to his hand*). Gahhhhhhk! (*To* TONTO.) Was he really wearin
TAM *and* KENJI.   a mask?
TONTO.   Ummmk.
KENJI (*whispers*). That means, ''Yes,'' you lucky dog.

(TONTO *draws back on his bow.*)

TONTO (*shouting*). HEY! Who was that MASKED MAN?
RANGER (*in the distance*). Tonto! What's holdin things up? It's near time for my injection.
TONTO (*sotto voce*). Come on China Boys, just answer the question. (*Shouting.*) Hey, who was that MASKED MAN?
TAM.   Blood!

(KENJI *claps a hand over* TAM's *mouth just as* TONTO *lets fly an arrow that sticks in the radio.*)

KENJI.   Why, that must be THE LONE RANGER!
TONTO.   . . . And?
TAM.   And?
TONTO.   . . . And don't you want to thank him? Hurry, man!
KENJI.   AND I WANTED TO THANK HIM.
TAM.   For shooting me in the hand?
TONTO *and* KENJI.   Shhh.
RANGER (*in the distance, shouting*). Come on big fella. (*In the distance.*) Hi yo Silver Awayyyy!
KENJI.   You lucky sonofabitch!

(*The* LONE RANGER *comes back on a staggering Silver, the* RANGER *stays mounted. He takes off and puts on his hat mechanically, breathlessly, compulsively muttering ''Hi yo Silver, Awayyy!'' perking up and listening for himself, then muttering the shout again.* TONTO *rushes over to him, rolls up the* RANGER's *sleeve, puts a tourniquet around his arm, fills a hypo and shoots the* RANGER *up.*)

TAM.   Why'd you shoot me in the hand?
RANGER *and* KENJI.   Kapow! Right in the hand.
RANGER.   Heh hah. (*Doing crazy gun tricks. His voice, and apparent age, abruptly change from the hero to various fans, to the old radio announcer.*) Nowhere in the pages of history can one find a greater/ Why that was the Lone Ranger/ Why! I wanted to thank him/ Hi yo Silver Awayyy! You hear that, Tonto? That cry . . . He's gone! Listen to them thundering hoofbeats. I wanted to thank him, Tonto. Hi yo Silver Awayy . . .

(KENJI *gallops and pat-a-cakes his butt around the radio chanting up the Lone Ranger music;* RANGER *runs down . . .*)

TONTO (*without accent*). Right, Kemo Sabay. Get off the horse now, Silver needs to rest a spell.
RANGER (*cringing*). You're not Tonto! Where's my Kemo Sabay? Where's my faithful Indian companion? Tonto!
TONTO (*faking accent*). Ummk, Kemo Sabay. You get off horse now.

(TAM *as* TONTO *takes on fake accent, gives a sneering, jeering, smartass climbing dirty laugh.* KENJI *grins happily.*)

RANGER.   There ya are, Tonto. Hi yo . . . Hi yo ssss . . . Hi yo what, Tonto?

(KENJI *shakes radio . . .*)

TAM.   *That* brought law and order to the early western United States?
RANGER.   A FIERY HORSE WITH THE SPEED OF LIGHT, A CLOUD OF DUST, AND A HEARTY HI YO SILVER!
ALL.   THE LONE RANGER!
RANGER.   GOD, I LOVE IT! *Nowhere in the pages of history can one find a greater champion of justice.* You China boys been lucky up to now, takin it easy, preservin your culture.
TAM *and* KENJI.   Huh?
RANGER.   . . . Some culture! Look at this shirt! A hero like me needs fast service, I said light starch, and look at this! This is what I tamed the West for? *You hear thundering hoofbeats? Anybody hear thundering hoofbeats?* You better do something about preservin your culture, boys, and light starch! *Hold it! Listen!*

(TAM *and* KENJI *get on their hands and knees and put an ear to the ground and listen for hoofbeats . . .*)

RANGER.   *Sounds like galloping out of the pages of history!* You hear? (*To* TAM *and* KENJI *on the floor at* RANGER'*s feet.*) Lookie that humility, Tonto. I admire it. (*Sits on* TAM'*s butt after dusting it off.*) You China Boys don't know what it's like ridin off into the distance all your life, and watchin your mouth. Watchin your mouth and ridin off into the distance. Riding off into the night toward the moon on your damned horse screamin away (KENJI *joins in.*) Hi Yo Silver, awayyyyyy! / Did you hear that cry? I didn't cotton to riding off into the distance one night screamin that Hi Yo Silver, awayyy / *Ya hear that? Shhh!*
TAM *and* KENJI.   NO!

(RANGER *spies microphone, rises, reaches into shirt and takes out a tattered script. He goes to the mike and tosses off pages as he reads.*)

RANGER.   It was a pie bakin shindig. And I sure had me a hankerin for some pie. But Tonto and the grateful town-folks what had gotten this function together for me by

way of thanks for doing somethin heroic had it all planned. How they'd all be in there *waiting* for me, you know, to *thank* me. And how they would all be in there together grinnin when they'd hear me too shy for pie gallop off and how they'd figger out who I was and how they'd say they wanted to thank me, just before I was off in the distance screamin at my horse! Easy, big fella. HI YO SILVER, AWAYYYY. *You hear that cry?* Well, tonight, I didn't feel like riding off into the distance!
TAM *and* KENJI.   No!

(*They pick up radio and shake it.*)

RANGER.   This time I wanted some pie. Ala mode too. And I was in love with a piece of local ass.
TAM *and* KENJI.   No!

(*They shake the radio.*)

RANGER.   Helen was her name too. White Old West translation of them three Chinee monkeys, Hear no Evil, See no Evil, Speak no Evil. Three in one compact model, boys. A blind girl. Stone blind. Deaf too, and dumb! Really give me a kick watchin her bump into things. You should have seen her pie!
TAM *and* KENJI.   Yeech!

(*They shake the radio, roll on the floor, pound the sides of their heads as if trying to get water out of their ears.*)

RANGER.   Made it by feel and smell, she did. I sure wanted me a piece of her pie! . . . And I got it / Huh? Was I a bad man, Tonto? Tell me, ol' compadre, Kemo Sabay, good ol' Tonto, was I bad for what I done?
TONTO.   Ummk.
KENJI.   That means, "Take it easy, Kemo Sabay."
RANGER.   I did ride off, didn't I, Tonto? And all the people was in there? And they . . . tell me what Helen . . . Helen What's hername said. I loved her, Tonto, cute as three monkeys. Heh. You hear that? LOVE!
TAM *and* KENJI.   Gak! Love!

(*They gallop around beating their butts.*)

RANGER.   She and me were kin in spirit. You hear that? Listen? *I think I hear the galloping hoofbeats of* / COME WITH US NOW AS ONCE AGAIN FROM OUT OF THE PAST / Tonto, tell me what she said again, I like to hear it.

(TAM *and* KENJI *collapse by radio and listen.*)

TONTO (*without accent*). Well Jeezis that was a long time ago, old timer. Let's see now, we were . . .
RANGER.   Not that way, Tonto. Be yourself. Kemo Sabay me.
TONTO (*fake accent, except when quoting*). She never speakum before. Folks heap surprised, Kemo Sabay, her say, "Hey, who was that masked man?"

(TAM *and* KENJI *exchange five.* TAM *winces in pain.*)

RANGER (*whispering in a reverie*). "Hey, who was that masked man?"

TONTO. Somebody sayum, "You see them silver bullets?"

(TAM *and* KENJI *as rolling train wheels* . . .)

RANGER. Hold it. Ya hear that in the distance? Hurry. Get to that part where she said . . .

TONTO. She say with tear in eye, "I wanted to thank him."

RANGER. I wanted to thank him . . .

TONTO. . . . and from far distance we hearum . . .

(TAM *and* KENJI *as whippoorwilling train whistle* . . .)

RANGER. Ya hear that . . . ?

TAM. . . . The Ranger said it were a train. I heard it come spooky, callin over the dark town. The Iron Moonhunter, grandmaw listened for til the day she died . . .

RANGER. You don't hear no train, China boys. Hear no evil, ya hear me? China boys, you be legendary obeyers of the law, legendary humble, legendary passive. Thank me now and I'll let ya get back to Chinatown preservin your culture!

TAM *and* KENJI. Culture.

TAM. You shot me in the hand.

RANGER. Thank me later boys. I hear ya breakin all kinds of law and order, rollin, vengeance after me . . . Me, Tonto! Chinamans with no songs, no jokes, no toasts, and no thanks. China Boys! No thanks for the masked man! Who was that masked man? I wanted to thank him. You think folks really give a hoot to see my eyes? You think I'd still be the Lone Ranger without this here mask? Now you wanta thank me?

TAM. Why'd you shoot me in the hand, old man? I ain't no bad guy.

RANGER. I curse ya honorary white!

TAM *and* KENJI. We don't wanta be honorary white.

RANGER. I'm the law, China Boys, it's a curse I'm a givin ya to thank me for, not a blessing. In your old age, as it were in your legendary childhood, in the name of Helen Keller, Pearl Buck, and Charlie Chan, kiss my ass, know thou that it be white, and go thou happy in honorary whiteness forever and ever, preservin your culture, AMEN.

TAM *and* KENJI. We don't wanta be honorary white.

RANGER. Don't move! Gettum up! Keep your asses off them long steel rails and short cross ties, stay off the track, don't be a followin me, stop chasin me, or you'll be like me, spendin your whole lifetime ridin outa your life into everybody's distance, runnin away from lookin for a train of sullen Chinamans, runaways from their place in the American dream, not thanking me . . . not thanking the masked man . . . the West ain't big enough for the both of us! But, say, ya speak good English, China Boy . . .

TAM. Thank you.

RANGER. He thanked me, Tonto. We can ride now, ol' compadre. Let's ride . . .

TAM. The masked man . . . I knew him better when I never knew him at all. The Lone Ranger ain't no Chinaman, children.

RANGER. Adios, compadres.

(*Music up on* RANGER*'s signal.* TONTO *and* RANGER *mount up and ride off.* KENJI *saunters, grins and waves after them.*)

KENJI. Adios, masked man. Adios! Adios!

RANGER. The Lone Ranger rides again! Hi Yo Silver Away.

TONTO. Get 'em up, Scout!

TAM. He deafened my ear for trains all my boyhood long . . .

CURTAIN

SCENE TWO

Porno movie house. Night.

CHARLEY POPCORN *is an old black man, dressed up conservatively flashy in a shiny suit cut a little out of date, pastel shirt, skinny tie, big cuff links, a diamond ring. A knit vest sweater, and incongruous aluminum hardhat and welder's goggles.*

Railroad crashing intermittently in background.

The theater is full of the juicy noises, moaning, whines, shrieks, grunts, creaks, bumps of the pornie soundtrack.

TAM *and* KENJI *in the lobby stare into the auditorium and look slowly from one end of the screen to the other, gaping.*

KENJI. She Chinese or Japanese?

(KENJI *wears a porkpie hat and shades, an old out-of-date jacket with leather patches, a good shirt with long collars, and a wide tie.* TAM *dressed dark, trim and slim. No hat. Cowboy boots.*)

POPCORN (*from inside theater*). Hey, you two queers, sit down and hold hands, and don't bother the perverts willya?

TAM. Charley Popcorn?

POPCORN (*entering lobby*). Quiet, man! People payin to hear the sucky fucky. Lotta my clientele is dirty word, sucky fucky sound freaks ya understand?

TAM. Customer's always right.

(POPCORN *is aloof, self-contained and a little shaky with age.* TAM *squirms, waiting for an opening for talk.*)

POPCORN. You want your money back or what?

(POPCORN *takes* TAM *and* KENJI *to office.*)

TAM. No, Mr. Popcorn, I'm Tam Lum. I phoned you from L.A. remember?

POPCORN.   Tam Lum?

TAM.   . . . about this documentary movie we're making on Ovaltine Jack Dancer . . . ?

POPCORN.   Tam Lum? What kind of name is that?

TAM.   Chinese.

POPCORN.   Sounds Chinese.

TAM.   It is Chinese, Mr. Popcorn.

POPCORN.   It is Chinese? Here, look at me, here. I be going blind. Eyes hurt, you understand. And I got a hurt in my head. One little bump and I die, ya see? These movies bad for my eyes. But I can't see a uhhh a (*Points at screen.*) vagina unless it's forty feet acrosst. You gonna put Ovaltine in a movie, huh? Why ya tellin me that? He's been in pictures before.

TAM.   No, this is a movie about Ovaltine. We're making a movie *about* his life.

POPCORN.   I'm half blind, boy, not half deaf, mind . . .

TAM.   Sorry, we're making this movie about Ovaltine Jack Dancer's life, and we're talking to all of his friends and relatives . . .

POPCORN.   "We"? Who's "we"?

TAM.   Condor Productions and me.

POPCORN.   I mean who's in charge?

TAM.   I am.

POPCORN.   Oh . . . You Chinese?

TAM.   I . . .

POPCORN.   That a Chinese company? from China?

TAM.   No, it's in L.A.

POPCORN.   American?

TAM.   Yeah.

POPCORN.   But you're Chinese.

TAM.   I . . .

POPCORN.   I don't want to do anything wrong, see? I used to be pretty slick! (*Chuckles reflectively.*)

TAM.   Yeah, I've heard a lot about you. Ovaltine has . . .

POPCORN.   Isn't it strange, you're Chinese.

TAM.   I'm a . . . I'm an American citizen.

POPCORN.   You don't talk like a Chinese, do ya? No, I don't think so . . .

TAM.   I was born here, Mr. Popcorn.

POPCORN.   The way you talked, why, I took you for colored over the phone. But "Lum"? Why would a Chinese talk like a colored man?

TAM.   Mr. Popcorn, I . . .

POPCORN.   You can talk like Mr. Charley too . . .

TAM.   I didn't know people still said "Mr. Charley." That's old where I come from.

POPCORN.   I am an old man. I'm too old to stand for jokes and signifying. You . . . Ovaltine know you're Chinese?

TAM.   Yeah. We're kind of old friends. Me and Kenji, when we were kids, a few years after the Dupree . . .

POPCORN.   Who?

TAM.   Kenji.

POPCORN.   Never heard of him. What's that, "Kenji"? Chinese too?

KENJI.   Japanese.

TAM.   No, Japanese. He's right here . . .

POPCORN.   Oh, Japanese, and you're . . .

TAM.   Chinese . . .

POPCORN.   You like music? I remember a cute little song about Chinese. American song. I still remember it:

> MY LITTLE HONG KING DREAM GIRL
> IN EVERY DREAM YOU SEEM, GIRL,
> TWO ALMOND EYES ARE SMILING,
> AND MY POOR HEART IS WHIRLING
> LIKE A BIG SAIL ROUND MY PIGTAIL . . .

You ever hear that before?

TAM.   No.

POPCORN.   Oh, before your time.

TAM.   About Ovaltine, Mr. Popcorn . . .

POPCORN.   You know Ovaltine likes music.

TAM (*fumbling*). Uh, yeah, as I was saying, I . . . we took Ovaltine for a ride, went out riding with Ovaltine when he was back in Oakland, uh California, where, you know, before we'd seen the Dupree fight? . . . and, we all got out of the short, the car, and under the stars, we stood next to the car, and on the road, you know, pissed all together into the bushes . . . (*Chuckles.* POPCORN *doesn't react* . . . TAM *and* KENJI *exchange looks.*) We were just kids then, but since then we say . . . it was the greatest . . . saw the Dancer come back and knock out Dupree in the 11th in Oakland, I guess he was our hero . . . He had fond memories of pissing on the, I mean, off the roadside with you . . .

POPCORN.   What?

TAM.   I guess that was the greatest piss we ever took in our lives, right Kenji?

KENJI.   Yeah, it was a dynamite piss, Mr. Popcorn.

POPCORN.   Why you talkin to me about pissin in bushes for? Why is it they want Chinese to make a picture on Ovaltine? I'm not sure about this. Ovaltine know you Chinese are doing a picture on him?

TAM.   I guess you don't feature Chinese too much, huh?

POPCORN.   "Feature"? I don't know. I don't like 'em though. You asked, and I'm tellin ya. I gotta watch out for the Dancer. He's pretty slick, but . . . (*Shakes his head.*) The only Chinese I ever talked to up close with face to face be waiters, I remember . . .

(TAM *moves to speak, but* KENJI *holds him back, saying* . . .)

KENJI.   Let 'em talk, man. It's just talk.

POPCORN.   They . . . they treated us worse 'n white men treated us. And those Chinese restaurants we went to wasn't fancy. Flies?

TAM.   How do you feel about being in a movie about your boy, Mr. Popcorn?

POPCORN.   You mean, you want me in the movie?

TAM.   Yeah, you gotta be.

POPCORN.   What kind o' money am I gonna get for this movie?

TAM.   You mean American or Chinese money?

POPCORN.   I mean Grants or Franklins?

TAM.   Well, this ain't no blockbuster, ya know.

POPCORN.   You mean no money?

TAM.   There'll be a legal dollar for signing the release, otherwise . . .

POPCORN.   No money!

TAM.   Ovaltine said you might like a print of the movie, when it's done. You know, somethin to remember him by.

POPCORN.   I think I better call him up.

TAM.   Don't you trust me? What do you think I'm doin' here?

KENJI.   Why don't we leave the man call up Ovaltine?

POPCORN.   I just wanta make sure, you know. This all makes me dizzy.

TAM.   You think I'm a practical joke or what?

KENJI.   You call up Ovaltine, and we'll be outside. We'll pop for the call.

TAM.   What're ya doin?

(KENJI *takes* TAM *out of* POPCORN'*s office*.)

KENJI.   You need some sleep, man.

TAM.   He's Ovaltine Jack Dancer's father?

KENJI.   What'd you expect, Joe Louis?

TAM.   You catch his Man from Mars costume, man? And the nice way he has with yellow people?

KENJI.   He's an old man.

TAM.   He's a bigot. He's nothin but a black white racist when it comes to yellow people.

KENJI.   He's an old man! He knows nothing about us. I mean, what would you do, you pick up the phone and someone's jabberin to you in Chinese, right? Whaddaya expect? And you meet the dude and he's black, and talkin Chinese. Wouldn't that shake you up?

TAM.   So ya want me to talk, "Ah-so, Misser Popcorn, Confucius say, Char-reeh Chan"?

KENJI.   You're over-reacting.

TAM.   Lee's right, man. This is a goddamned minstrel show . . . talk white to the blacks and black to the whites, is that what you're saying. Is that your formula for success in Pittsburgh?

KENJI.   Come on, man, you're not listening. Somebody you talked to on the phone soundin Chinese pops up black. Wouldn't that shake you up? Really. Be serious.

TAM.   You're saying I'm a bigot.

KENJI.   No, man, just listen . . . ! Listen.

TAM.   You think I'm a fool. I thought we were friends. Now I find you think I'm a fool.

KENJI.   This isn't you, man.

TAM.   I thought we were friends, man. I thought you were different. But you're not . . . you're nothin but a . . .

KENJI.   Jap dentist?

TAM.   Lee's right, you hate yourself. You hate your profession. You're in some kind of fog, man. It really hurt me, hearin you let alla Lee's badmouth on you bout fakin blackness for balls just slip by.

KENJI.   She was talkin 'bout you.

TAM.   Oh! I thought you had a reason, man. Cuz you always had reasons. Tell me, what's the reason for you runnin a refugee camp for the weird kid and his mother? And you not even sleeping with her. Ooh, and she likes to tell me too. Oh, I hate to see that. But I figure you got a reason. I wouldn't touch her myself.

KENJI.   Tam!

TAM.   I wouldn't let no bitch bleed me and thank me with badmouth, especially Lee! But you got reasons, right?

KENJI.   Right.

TAM.   Well what's your reason for thinkin I'm all for laughs?

KENJI.   I'm sorry if I lost my temper.

TAM (*cold*). I never noticed.

KENJI.   Hey, I'm on your side. You're tired, man.

TAM.   You're the one that's tired, man. Not me. I'm too fast for ya, right?

(*Enter* POPCORN.)

POPCORN.   Ovaltine says you're pretty slick, Mr. Lum, and I believe it. I remember his first fight . . . but let me say, first, we both businessmen, right? And maybe we can do some business. Maybe we could premiere that movie right here, invite folks, turn off the fuckshow for a night. Now with just a little money for a new paint job . . .

TAM.   Well, Ovaltine said you got him up to hittin the speedbag eight hundred times a minute for the Dupree fight.

POPCORN.   Aww, that Ovaltine, he likes to exaggerate, you know what I mean? He bullshits. We won that fight you know how? We bullshit Ovaltine about his age and strength, and he bullshit Dupree. Maybe I told him I timed his hittin the speedbag eight hundred times maybe even nine hundred times a round, but not in no one minute. Most he ever did in one minute, and nobody could keep this up more, I'm telling ya, is three hundred times. And when he could do that, every day, one time, maybe two times, I figured he was ready . . . You know, we had a Chinese used to come watch Ovaltine train for that fight.

TAM.   She was beautiful of course.

POPCORN.   Old Chinese gentleman. We nicknamed him the "Chinatown Kid." Ovaltine'd see him in the bleachers, and wave, say "Ho, Chinatown Kid," and he'd say, "Too moochie shi-yet." (*Chuckles*.) Reason he did that was one day I thought we'd let him in for free so I give him his dollar back, but he didn't understand, see. Me and Ovaltine didn't know that, and every time he stuck the dollar at us, we smiled and shook our heads and pointed inside, but he musta thought we were kickin him out. And he got this look on his face, and he held up his dollar, and we shook our heads, tellin him, you know, he was free. Then he said, I'll never forget it, "Too moochie shi-yet." And he walked away. I felt awful. I chased him down the street and held out my hand, and he gave me the dollar and I took him into the gym again. He had to pay. He would not be free. How bout our business proposition.

TAM. He wore a hat.

POPCORN. No. I don't remember no hat. But I liked to died, when he fierce, fierce! "Too moochie shi-yet!" like that. Then I could see his whole life, you understand?

TAM. A new hat, brushed.

POPCORN. I used to wonder how he ever got to find the gym, you know. No Chinese ever came by. I mean wherever we were training.

TAM. I took him by.

POPCORN. He was your daddy! Why didn't you come up with him?

TAM. No, he wasn't my father. He . . . He wore a hat.

POPCORN. No, no, I don't remember no hats. Maybe it wasn't the same gentleman.

KENJI. Maybe.

TAM. Man, nothing could keep him from boxin. He loved to be called that Chinatown Kid stuff too.

POPCORN. You know his name? Maybe, who knows? . . .

TAM. . . . No. I only heard it once . . . read it in a letter from the immigration. Isn't that strange? Not even at the funeral. I don't remember.

POPCORN. Oh, he passed . . .

TAM. Most of the old folks I knew never had names . . . I can't think of any. So he used to . . .

POPCORN. That don't make sense. What do Chinese call each other then? How can they talk?

TAM. I just called them "uncle," *Ah-bok Ah-sook,* like that. They were afraid of having names here. Afraid America would find 'em and deport 'em.

POPCORN. We called him "The Chinatown Kid."

TAM. I never thought about his name before . . . that's where he got that "Chinatown Kid" thing! Ha . . .

POPCORN. You shoulda come up the stairs with him to the gym.

TAM. Oh, man, he used to shout at me. He'd get scared.

POPCORN. I don't know nothin' 'bout that. I just know it's wrong to turn your back on your father however old you be.

TAM. He wasn't my father. He was . . . he was our dishwasher.

POPCORN. What's wrong with dishwashers?

TAM. Nothin wrong with dishwashers. Uh, listen. I think your story about him would be good in the movie, you know. "The Chinatown Kid," and the training for the Dupree fight . . . nice sidelight . . .

POPCORN. No, this old Chinese gentleman wasn't scared. He had dignity.

TAM. I said he wasn't chicken. But I should know if he was scared or not.

POPCORN. All right.

TAM. All right. Let's forget the old man for the time being. Let's not talk about him . . . but about the movie.

POPCORN. I don't think you should forget the old man.

TAM. You're doing this on purpose. I didn't mean it that way.

POPCORN. Well, that's none of my business I suppose. But I think maybe I respected him more than you . . . and colored people don't particularly favor Chinese, you know . . . I'm just tellin ya. You wouldn't want me to lie.

TAM. What do you know about it?

POPCORN. Maybe he was scared for you . . . It's none of my business.

TAM. No one respected him more than me.

POPCORN. That's none of my business. (*To* KENJI.) Oh, I was gonna tellya about Ovaltine's first fight, talkin of yellow Negroes . . . Now I'm not callin you no yellow Negroes, but it makes ya easier to think about, ya understand?

Long time ago, back in the depression days. Ovaltine was just a youngster then, and it was one of those out of doors matches. There was oil drum fires all around the ring. Coldsnap, you understand? Back in Ohio, coldsnap. Wouldya like some coffee or somethin, Mr. Lum?

TAM (*mumbles*). No, thanks.

POPCORN. Well, Ovaltine was fightin this big old yellow Negro man, older fella. A real tanker. He was yellow as a schoolbus, yellow as beer piss . . . This the kinda story you want me to tell?

KENJI. Was it a good fight?

POPCORN. Good fight?

TAM. We'll put it in the movie. You tellin it, and we seein it . . .

POPCORN. This old gentleman had a punch that wouldn't crack an egg.

TAM. Yeah, I see it.

POPCORN. Ovaltine stepped in and beat on him, hit him, jabs, right cross, left cross, uppercut, to the body, everywhere and it was like he was trying to knock down a haystack with his fists. The tanker just stood his self there and would not fall. Finally, after bout maybe twelve rounds, Ovaltine just wore his self out from all the dancin and prancin punchin and sockin and fell down in a faint. He done knocked hisself out. But I saw the talent, the natural timing, and the mean, I mean, smart, thinking mean, like a killer. That's how me and Ovaltine come to meet.

TAM (*snapping*). Hey!

POPCORN.   You like that?

TAM.   What do you mean, that's how you and Ovaltine came to meet?

POPCORN.   I never see'd that boy before. Soon's he got up from his faint, his sweat all froze on his body and hair too, he said, first thing, grinning like, ''I did enjoy the fight so very much.''

KENJI.   That's what he said after the Dupree fight.

POPCORN.   That's what he said after EVERY fight!

TAM.   Yeah, yeah. He said that after every fight, but he said you taught him to do that when he was a kid in Mississippi.

POPCORN.   Mississippi? What Mississippi? He was sixteen . . . seventeen when I ever first saw him. In Ohio that day!

TAM.   Hay, I don't know what's happenin between you and the Dancer, that's none of my business, but I read, and Ovaltine himself told me . . . You really Charley Popcorn?

POPCORN.   Forever!

TAM.   You ain't shittin me, you ain't signifying, you don't know what I'm talkin about?

(*Soundtrack: sucky fucky noises and music—a simple instrumental version of the ''Japanese Sandman.''*)

POPCORN.   How long's it been since you be sleepin, Mr. Lum?

TAM.   Do I sound tired? What're you talkin about?

KENJI.   He's been up two days listening to all the tapes he made with the Dancer, gettin ready to meet you, Mr. Popcorn.

POPCORN.   Me?

TAM.   You! I saw you as a bigger man, man, the way Ovaltine talked about watchin you strip off your shirt, and wash up out of a pan, outside the house. And how his eyes popped out when he was a kid, at your mighty back ripplin with muscles!

POPCORN.   Me?

TAM.   And the whiplash scars, how they made him cry, and how that made him sure, he'll be a fighter, a fighter down from his soul!

POPCORN.   Whiplash never touch *my* back! You're sleepin, young man. Dreamin!

TAM.   All right. This is the sheet on you. You're Charley Popcorn, Ovaltine Jack Dancer's Father.

POPCORN.   Huh?

TAM.   . . . uh lemme finish. Ovaltine when he was a little boy in Mississippi beat up on a white boy, and you told him you all would have to leave that part of the country, and then you told him bout the welts on your back, and gettin whipped. You and the family packed up in a car and Ovaltine remembers you and him pissin by the roadside next to the car with the ladies inside hiding their eyes.

You taught him ''psychology'' by tellin him, no matter how bad he ever got beat, or however he got beat, to always smile, stand up and say, loud, ''I did enjoy the fight so very much.''

POPCORN.   Where you hear all this shit, Mr. Lum?

TAM.   From his book, from his mouth, from his aunt, his wife . . .

POPCORN.   He wrote it in a BOOK??

TAM.   Why, what's wrong?

POPCORN.   I ain't nobody's father, especially his'n. I never been no Mississippi, or done none of that.

TAM.   You gotta be his father.

POPCORN.   I heard o' shotgun weddings but sheeeet . . . I'll show ya.

TAM.   Why should he lie? Maybe . . . accidents happen. Maybe it wasn't Mississippi. He was young, got it mixed up. And you, you know, wild oats . . .

POPCORN.   Wild oat! I'll show ya. Here! Here now! You look good now. (*Presenting his back.*) You see any kind of whip marks? Tell me, now, you see any kind of whiplash or dogbite on me?

TAM.   Well, you know . . .

POPCORN.   No, ''well, you know . . .'' Just ''no,'' you don't see none of that. (*Dresses, but holds his hardhat in his hands, adjusting insides.*) Ovaltine done bullshit you and the whole world, son. If you come all the way here to see Ovaltine's daddy, ha, you come for nothin! Ha! That Ovaltine, just can't leave go of me . . .

TAM.   But he *believes* you're his father! He really does.

POPCORN.   He believe that, he's crazy!

TAM.   Those stories, man! He . . . he drinks his coffee like you do, half milk, half coffee, a spoon of sugar . . .

POPCORN.   Yah, I drink it that way, but that don't make me his father. I never made him my son, so how can he make *me* his father? Coffee and condensed milk don't make seed, you understand.

TAM.   All he talks about is you.

POPCORN.   He do things to make me call him up, that's all. I don't know why. But I never heard of this whiplash and washin up trash.

TAM.   Well, why you, man? Why's he think you're his father, where'd all these stories come from? You're his father! You are, man! You are!

POPCORN.   That's dreamin, Mr. Lum. Those stories he dreamed, that's not me. That wasn't ever us, even when we were pardners. I always favored him and won't say a word to harm him ever. Let's just say when he started winning, and white people with money and ranches . . . You can't blame anybody if they don't want to live in a room and sometime in the back of an old station wagon no more. But you understand, prizefighting is a business, you gotta be a businessman, you see to be a good prizefighter. I was always a small businessman. A shopkeeper, no tycoon.

TAM.   What's this got to do with Ovaltine?

POPCORN.   A smart prizefighter, he got to be always thinking ahead, you see. I never knew how to make him champion of the world!

TAM.   What'd he do to you?

POPCORN.   I won't say nothin against the Dancer. He was champion of the world!

TAM.   . . . He couldn't've won the Dupree fight . . .

POPCORN.   He . . . that Dupree fight! What he say bout . . . No don't tell me. I'll tell you! He brought me back to train him. The night of the fight . . . I was in Cleveland in a bar, watchin the fight on TV. He fired me, ya see. He'd . . . just say, we'd had words.

TAM.   What about? What're you doin to Ovaltine?

POPCORN.   About nothin! I'm smalltime, penny ante slick, and that's good enough for me. I was in his way, that's all.

TAM (*standing up animated*).   Well, he's sorry, man. He's sorry! He needs you to be his father, can't ya see?

KENJI.   Take it easy, man.

TAM.   Jerk off! You gotta be his father. Everybody knows you're his father. You can forgive him. You're all the fight he has left! He's an ex-champ, an old forgotten man talkin more about you than his fights.

POPCORN.   What kind of shit you blowin at me? You're goofy! Fall down! Fall asleep, young man.

TAM.   You can't turn your back on him.

POPCORN.   Oh, you are a slick businessman. I see why Ovaltine favors you all right. So he needs a father for this show about him.

TAM.   Forget the movie, okay? And listen . . .

POPCORN.   Man, you shoulda knowed from those stories, that they was dreams! They was lies! All made up. Bullshit!

TAM.   Boys forget, don't you know that?

POPCORN.   Grease! Grease! Grease and bullshit!

(TAM *strikes at* POPCORN. POPCORN *easily shoves the punch away*.)

TAM (*to* POPCORN).   You gotta be his father.

KENJI (*restraining* TAM).   Cool it!

(TAM *elbows* KENJI *in the gut violently and shoves him away*.)

TAM (*to* KENJI).   You blew it!

(TAM *confronts* POPCORN *physically.* POPCORN *fends him off*.)

POPCORN.   You're so sleepy, you couldn't crack piecrust! Now, stop it, boy. Sit down, damn ya.

KENJI.   He didn't mean it.

POPCORN.   Sit down.

TAM.   Never! Fight, man, you can do it. Father of a champion . . .

POPCORN.   Why not sit down . . .

TAM.   Never, you gotta knock me down.

KENJI.   You're gonna fall down, man, come on.

(KENJI *takes* TAM'*s shoulders.* TAM *shrugs him off and swings on* POPCORN. POPCORN *steps away from the blow and* TAM *falls on his face, and doesn't move for a beat.* POPCORN *seems embarrassed, and tentatively moves to help* TAM *up but checks himself.* KENJI *is disgusted. He puts his hands in his pockets and looks down on* TAM. TAM *begins to laugh. He hits the floor with his fist and laughs. Rolling over onto his back he says . . .*)

TAM.   Never fall. I'm the Chickencoop Chinaman. My punch won't crack an egg, but I'll never fall down. That is why . . . That is why what, Kenji? Why is that?

KENJI.   This is why little men love to hear the call of their Chickencoop Chinaman cry, ''Buck Buck Bagaw.''

TAM.   Buck Buck Bagaw. (*Snorts and repeats the call a few times.*)

POPCORN.   We'll get you home after we close up here, Mr. Lum.

CURTAIN

SCENE THREE

(*Scene shifts to Limbo.* TAM *on* POPCORN'*s back.*)

TAM.   Foong. Wind. I knew the word for wind. I am the only noise of him left. Lawk sur, rain. We said it was Yit, gum yut yit, hot today or gum yut lahng, cold today. Windy, raining, hot or cold today. That's all we talked. Foong chur, lawk gun sur, yit, lahng, gum yut lahng, lawk gun sur, foong chur, gum yut yit . . .

The buck and cluck of this child, your Chickencoop Chinaman gushes furiously. Like sperm. Numerously. Chug and thud, to conceive! With only foong, lawk yur, yit, lahng I had long deep talks with a man I remember to this day, but with all the fine pronouns, synonyms, verbs, adjectives, adverbs, nouns of Barbara's language I'm told I talk good, she left me on my birthday with nothin, it's all talk. In the morning. Chur gun foong. I'd wondered why she'd made my birthday cake early, children. I'd said, ''Put on the coffee, okay?'' I saw her go out and must've thought she was going to put on the coffee for me. Then later I woke expecting to smell coffee burning, because she hadn't called me. And no one was home . . . My mother called and said she was proud I was taking it so well, and never asked if I was going to fight. IT'S TALK. ALL TALK. NOTHING I CAN'T TALK . . . BUCK BUCK BAGAW. BUCK BUCK BAGAW.

CURTAIN

SCENE FOUR

Scene shifts to KENJI's *apartment. Later that night.*

LEE *is taking the posters off the wall, rolling them up, putting rubber bands around them. She's between taking things apart and putting things together again into something else. She stands tiptoe on a cinder block she's removed from under the table, to remove the tacks holding the tops of the posters to the wall. She repositions the cinder block for each poster.*

Groceries are in various sized bags and cardboard boxes. Piled on the drainboard with the groceries are a Chinese round chopping block and a Chinese cleaver; a sharpening steel; a wok, a wok cover, and utensils (long-handled shaped spatula, spoon, strainer, bamboo scrub brush, extra long bamboo chopsticks); other kitchen utensils; tins of spices; packets, packages, and cans of Chinese and Japanese goods; and a gallon can of peanut oil.

The radio is on, blasting chicken rock and fifties tunes.

TOM, *a very neat, tidy, uptight hip Chinese American. Longish hair, round steel rim glasses. He speaks self-consciously, styling his voice like others style hair. A very cool, deep, intimate voice like an* FM *jock living with his eyes closed to adore his voice. He doesn't walk and gesture so much as move his body from pose to pose. He shies from touches, keeps his hands down, except when moving his hair out of his face. His face is deadpan, except for his premeditated spontaneous keyboard grin that comes up on the off-beat late for introductions and jokes.*

TOM *is warily keeping his distance from* LEE, *who ignores him.*

TOM *hangdog goes to the radio and tunes it in. Outside we hear many footsteps clumping up the stairs.* ROBBIE *appears out of the bedroom and runs toward the front door.*

ROBBIE.   They're back, Lee . . . I hear 'em.
TOM.   Robbie! Hey, Robbie! I didn't know you were here?
LEE.   Where else would he be but with me?
TOM.   Hey, Robbie, gimme five.
ROBBIE.   Hello, Tom. (*Tentatively gives five.*)
TOM.   You used to call me "Dad."

(*Outside we hear* TAM *struggling to lift* POPCORN *and carry him into the apartment.*)

LEE.   You better open the door, Robbie.

(ROBBIE *opens the door.*)

POPCORN.   You'll never do it, man.
TAM.   We built the fuckin railroad! Moved a whole Sierra Nevada over . . .
POPCORN.   Watch out for my head now. Put me down. You're gonna fall down and we'll both die!
TAM.   Never! Never!
POPCORN.   Put me down, put me down! I feel your bones crunchin up on each other.

(TAM *stumbles in carrying* POPCORN.)

TAM.   Never! (TAM *sees* TOM, LEE, *and* ROBBIE *staring . . .*) Ah, Scrooge! I am the ghost of Christmas Past! Ha ha ha ha.
ROBBIE.   Hi, Tam!

(TAM *ignores* ROBBIE *and moves toward* TOM *and does Alfonso Bedoya from* Treasure of the Sierra Madre.)

TAM.   Say, don't I know zhoo from sawmwheres?
POPCORN.   Put me down.
TAM.   I don't know how.
POPCORN.   I'm gonna throw up. Put me down.

(TAM *spies mattress and staggers toward it.* TOM *approaches* TAM *with his hand out.*)

TOM.   Kenji?

(TAM *flops with* POPCORN *down onto the couch and takes a pack of chewing gum out of his pocket. He unwraps a stick of gum, puts the gum in his mouth, starts chewing, and wads the foil wrapper up in one hand, rolling it around and around nervously.* TOM *offers his hand . . .* TAM *offers the pack of gum . . .*)

TOM.   Kenji?
TAM.   Gum?

(KENJI *appears in the doorway, wiping his feet. He scans the scene.*)

TOM.   Kenji?
TAM.   No, oh, you're . . .
TOM.   Tom.
TAM.   I knew she'd letya in. I wanted her to lock you out.
TOM.   You're being very familiar . . .
TAM.   That sounds English, Tom. (*Offers pack of gum again.*) You chew gum, Tom?
TOM.   No, thanks.
TAM.   No? Oh. How's *Soul on Rice* coming, Tom?
POPCORN.   SOUL ON RICE?
TOM.   My book.
TAM.   Tom's writing a book. Aren't ya, Tom?
POPCORN.   Book? I never heard of a Chinaman writing a book!
TAM (*to* POPCORN).   . . . . cookbook!
POPCORN.   Oh.
TOM.   It's not a cookbook.

(TAM *pops another stick of gum in his mouth and adds the foil wrapper to the wad he rolls in one hand.* KENJI *enters.*)

TAM (*cold, through a grin*).   I knew it wasn't a cookbook, Tom.
KENJI.   I'm Kenji. What's going on here, Lee? What're ya doin?
LEE.   I'm fixing this house up.

KENJI.   But that's my stuff.

LEE.   I said I'm cleaning. I'm tired of living out of trunks. It's not good for Robbie.

KENJI.   I thought you were going to Africa.

LEE.   Do you want me to leave?

KENJI.   I was going to let you stay here til you, you know, were ready to go to Africa.

LEE.   Well, I do have a ticket. I can go to Africa anytime. Anyway, the way you moped around here for months, how was I to know you knew how to talk at all? I never knew you were thinking of me. You never told me.

TOM.   Excuse me, this must be awkward . . .

KENJI.   You must be Tom.

TOM.   Go on ahead, brother. This is like watching a movie about me.

LEE.   You never told me. Why didn't you tell me, Kenji?

KENJI.   I'm the strong silent type.

LEE.   That would be cute if someone hadn't said that about Tom.

TOM.   Who said that about me, Lee?

TAM.   Your mother of course, Tom.

KENJI.   Hey, man! Cool it!

LEE.   That's right, your mother.

TOM (to TAM). And how did you know it was my mother?

TAM.   I'm the ghost of Christmas Past, Tom.

TOM.   Why do you keep repeating my name like that?

TAM.   One question at a time, Tom. Tell me, Tom, seriously, I gotta know . . . (To LEE.) Excuse me for interrupting . . . (To KENJI, answering a warning look.) I'm seriously interested, okay? Tom, are you really writing a book called Soul on Rice?

LEE.   He can't stand to be asked questions like that. You can't ask him direct questions like that. Don't look him in the eye.

TOM.   It's a book about Chinese-American identity.

TAM.   Oh. Thank you, Tom. You're wrong, Lee, he answered that beautifully. You answered that beautifully, Tom.

KENJI.   Hey, man! This is my house, okay?

TAM.   You talkin to me?

KENJI.   Okay?

TAM.   Okay.

KENJI.   Okay, man, why don't you crash.

TAM.   No, man. I wanta rundown slow. I'll just. I won't get in the way. I'll just listen.

LEE.   Oh, there'll be plenty to hear.

TAM.   Yeah, I can hardly wait.

TOM.   Who are you. I'd just like to know. Besides being the ghost of Christmas Past, that is, who are you?

TAM.   You don't know who I am?

(TAM rolls his wad of foil quickly. KENJI has seen this before and isn't in the mood for it.)

KENJI.   Hey, no jokes, man. Everyone's tired.

TOM (to TAM). No.

TAM.   You really don't recognize me?

KENJI.   Not now, man.

TOM.   No.

TAM.   Hold out your hand . . . (TOM holds out his hand. TAM drops the wad of foil gumwrappers in TOM's hand and says . . .) Here, this silver bullet should tell you who I am!

(TAM laughs and struts. LEE and POPCORN laugh.)

POPCORN.   That's a good one!

ROBBIE.   I don't get it. What's so funny.

KENJI.   It's an old joke, kid. Go to bed.

ROBBIE.   You're not my father. You can't tell me what to do.

LEE (softly, sorry he said that). Oh, Robbie . . .

KENJI.   In my house, you do what I say, okay?

ROBBIE (to TAM). Do you like blueberry pancakes?

KENJI.   Okay, Robbie?

TOM.   You still like pancakes, huh, Robbie?

KENJI.   Okay, Robbie?

ROBBIE.   I'll make you some in the morning.

TOM.   Well, if I'm . . .

ROBBIE.   I wasn't talking to you . . .

TAM.   You're hustling me, kid. I thought I told you . . .

KENJI.   Robbie . . .

LEE.   Stop badgering Robbie! Three grown men!

TAM.   Well, if you'd stop using him.

ROBBIE.   Will you ask Robbie to go to bed, Lee?

TAM.   Yeah! Hey, Kenji, let the kid . . .

KENJI (to TAM). Later for that!

LEE.   Are you angry with me, Kenji?

KENJI.   I don't wanta talk in front of the kid. He's a kid.

LEE.   Robbie's still my son.

KENJI.   Then you and Tom and Robbie all go out in . . .

LEE.   . . . by the car and piss in the bushes?

KENJI.   . . . out in the hall or somewhere else and talk. This is still my house.

LEE.   I didn't think you cared. Have you looked at this place?

KENJI.   I don't wanta talk in front of the kid!

LEE.   There's nothing to talk about. I told Tom I'm not pregnant.

TOM.   That doesn't matter. I want you.

LEE.   And we'd live together again.

TOM.   Yes.

LEE.   You and Robbie and me. Just like before.

TOM.   Yes, No! Not like before.

LEE.   And we'd have a baby. Another baby.

TOM.   I'd like that . . . if we could.

LEE. (turning sharply from TOM). Mama's boy! Listen to him, Robbie. I wouldn't want another of his children. His mother would only swoop in and take it away from him and me. No, not me. I wouldn't let him or her talk me into that again.

TOM. I think Kenji's right. Not in front of Robbie.

LEE. What do you care? He's not your son!

TAM. Ah! Whose son . . . ?

KENJI (*with a warning gesture*). Tam . . . !

TAM. Your house . . .

LEE. Oh, Tam. Be mean and funny! Why aren't you talking. Talk about your movie.

KENJI. Keep Tam out of this. Robbie go to bed.

LEE. You're so bossy all of a sudden. First you get talky, now you're bossy. What'd you do to him, Tam?

KENJI. Let him alone. Robbie, get your ass to bed or get it out of the house.

ROBBIE. You're not my father.

LEE. Robbie, I wish you'd stop saying that please! Let Robbie alone if he's not sleepy. What's happened to Tam? Why isn't he talking?

KENJI. You still here, Robbie?

(KENJI *stares* ROBBIE *down . . .*)

LEE. What's the matter, Tam, cat got your tongue?

TOM. Tam? That your name? Who are you?

LEE. Careful, Tom, Tam isn't what you'd expect.

TOM. What's that supposed to mean? What would I expect of you, Tam?

TAM. He's talkin to me, Kenji, can I talk back?

(ROBBIE *loses the stare-down with* KENJI.)

KENJI. Say, "Goodnight," Robbie.

ROBBIE. Goodnight. (*Exits.*)

TOM. 'Night, Robbie.

TAM. G'night, kid.

LEE. Tam just met me today, and he knows me better than you ever did, Tommy.

TOM. Oh, I see it. Lee does this all the time, brother. Games! She's put you through your paces and you don't care. Well, don't be blinded by her white beauty. You're not going to allow a white girl set you against a brother, are you? It's not worth it. I'm tellin you. I was married to Lee, can you dig it?

TAM. I don't see no white girl here. And I'm not hustling none of your ex-wives no matter what color.

LEE. Thanks a lot.

TAM. I'm not bragging, mindya. You're not the only woman I'm not hustling.

TOM. Now who's playing the fool?

TAM. Did I say you were playing the fool? I thought I called you straight out, "fool," fool!

TOM. I'm not prejudiced against Chinese like you. Just between you and me, brother, you have problems.

LEE. Oh, Tom the intellectual!

TAM. You Chinese? You don't talk like a Chinese.

TOM. Listen, you ever looked at yourself? You're willowy.

TAM. What're ya talkin about?

TOM. I'm telling you, for your own good, your peace of mind . . .

TAM. What? You got trouble with the language, Tom? What?

TOM. . . . you better be Chinese because Americans are hungup about homosexuality.

TAM. Huh? Lee, I think his mind just snapped!

TOM. It's true.

TAM. What're ya talking about. What's bein Chinese gotta do with "homosexuality"?

TOM. In American eyes we don't appear as he-men types.

TAM. Oh, we look like queers!

TOM. Yeah.

TAM. But if we read up on Chinese culture, building walls, writin with a brush, talk enough about gunpowder, paper money, Chairman Mao we can fool folks into thinking we're the way we are not because we're queer but because we're Chinese! "Willowy" huh? Me, I'm not going to go round sayin, "I'm not queer, boss, I'm Chinese!" (POP-CORN *laughs.*) No wonder she says you're not a man.

TOM. You're prejudiced against Chinese.

TAM. I said Lee says you're not a man!

TOM. You're prejudiced against Chinese!

TAM. Foreigners don't bother me, but ornamental Orientals like you make me sick.

TOM (*interrupting*). I don't know what you're trying to prove, brother. But you'd better face facts. You and me . . . we're both Chinese. Now maybe you don't like being Chinese and you're trying to prove you're something else. I used to be like that. I wondered why we didn't speak up more, then I saw we don't have to. We used to be kicked around, but that's history, brother. Today we have good jobs, good pay, and we're lucky. Americans are proud to say we send more of our kids to college than any other race. We're accepted. We worked hard for it. I've made my peace.

TAM. You sold your baby to be accepted by whites? Now you're at peace? That's too moochie shi-yet!

TOM. I didn't sell my baby.

TAM. Oh?

TOM. My mother didn't like Lee.

TAM. Oh. Why?

TOM. Why? Because she wasn't Chinese.

TAM. Your mother's not Chinese?

TOM. No, *Lee's* not Chinese!

TAM. Tom, you're beautiful. You wanted to be "accepted" by whites so much, you created one to accept you. You didn't know Lee's got a bucket of Chinese blood in her? At least a bucket?

TOM. She's white. Hey, I know! I was married to her. I know Chinese from white.

TAM. Gotcha scared, huh, Tom? How about that funny red in her hair, huh? Peroxide? She just peroxided her hair, Tom. You! Your whole soul, man, has been all washed out, treated, your nerves all taped up and packed away like mummies in the monster movies, man . . .

KENJI. Tam!

TAM (*speaking through*). doin the wicked work of nutty priests. Man, when they dig you up, they're gonna find petrified Cheerios, gobs of Aunt Jemima pancakes, a shiny can of Chun King chopped phooey.

TOM.   You're going to call me white. Well, I could call you black!

TAM.   Oh, did I turn Tom's feeings? Look at her. Go on up and get a good look, fella, and you tell me who's prejudiced against Chinese. You wanted a white girl so bad, so bad, you turned her white with your magic eyes. You got that anti-Chinaman vision.

TOM.   We're wonderful, I can call you "Chinaman" and insult you.

TAM.   Do you want to insult me?

TOM.   I can call you "Chinese American" and insult you, "Americanized Chinese" and insult you. "Chinese" and insult you, "American" "Chink" "Jap" "Japanese" "White" and insult you, "Black" and insult you. You're angry. I used to be angry like you. I understand, brother. But try to see me.

TAM.   What is this talk? *You* should be angry man, pissed off! about this family and Lee foolin you to come out here . . . not this, this smalltalk.

TOM.   Let's not lose our heads . . .

TAM.   Let's lose our heads! Let's panic, fly off the handle, go off half cocked. Let's act like animals!

KENJI (*taking* TAM *aside violently*). Tam, man, you're making trouble . . .

LEE.   What're you doing? I want to hear.

TAM.   Lee's terrific . . . putting us all through the hoops man. The ringmaster!

KENJI.   Keep Lee outa your mouth. What're you jumpin all over Tom for? He's a guest in my house.

TAM.   What's all this "my house" trash, man? Look, I've eased all the tensions here. Lee's not barking up pregnancy tales. Tom's not pissed off about anything personal. There's no situation! Just a dull party, with smalltalk, man.

KENJI.   Why do you talk so god damned much? I used to think it was funny, brave, man, the way you ripped everybody up with your tongue, showin 'em up for clowns and bullshit. Your tongue was fast and flashy with the sounds, man, savin your ass from this and that trouble, making people laugh, man, shooin in the girls . . . I used to know why you were mean and talkin all the time. I don't anymore, and you're still talkin the same crazy talk.

TAM.   You were my silent pardner. We used to run together.

KENJI.   It's not fun anymore. I never was the runner you were, never as crazy or . . . I don't even know why I admired you. You're vicious now. Vicious! Really . . . all over everybody, calling names . . .

TAM.   Is . . . think . . . I've lost my head. I've . . . I must be crazy, huh?

(LEE *laughs*).

KENJI.   I told you it's not funny, now, man. Nobody wants it anymore. You're too old to be badmouthing everything, everything like you do. Nobody's gonna run with that, man.

TAM.   Yeah, I'm a loner.

KENJI.   You wanta be a loner, you're a loner. You're a mean rogue, somewhere, out there, ya know what I mean?

TAM.   Like a mad elephant, blowin his nose alone in the dark.

KENJI.   It isn't funny.

LEE.   It is funny.

KENJI.   I'm tellin ya this. I loved you, man. And if you make a crack about that to Tom I'll take your face off!

TOM.   Can't we . . .

KENJI (*to* TOM). Now you be careful o' your mouth!

LEE.   Sit down, Kenji, you're scaring me!

TOM.   . . . Can't we be friends . . . act like friends at least?

TAM.   We should be friends, you know that? Easy, Kenji, I raised my hand before opening my mouth, huh? I know we should be friends. I know that. But I don't want to be your friend.

KENJI.   Who you talkin to?

TAM.   You have to ask?

KENJI.   Who you talkin to?

TAM.   Who you got? . . . (TAM *and* KENJI *stare down.*) Why couldn't we have just slapped hands and trotted out old radio shows, dead hit tunes and movies? I don't want to be your friend. I'm tired of you, man. Just one look, and I'm tired of you. I'm tired of everything . . .

KENJI.   Tired of talking?

TAM.   Really . . . really tired of talking, especially talking. But everytime I stop it's so goddamned awful!

POPCORN.   I never been alone with so many Chinese before. Ever! Uh. I never seen so many before without bein in a Chinese restaurant, you know what I mean? I don't mean you be foreigners ha! I know you're American . . . I been listenin, but it's late . . . (*Low nervous chuckle.*) I feel like you all lookin at me. You all be lookin at me? Did I say something wrong? I hurt anybody's feelings? Mr. Lum? Mr. Lum, I hurt your feelings?

LEE.   Who're you? Everyone's so polite around here.

POPCORN.   It's me, Charley Popcorn.

LEE.   Oh, I've been hearing about you, you're . . .

POPCORN.   No, I ain't no father of no Ovaltine Jack Dancer. I'm just a small businessman minding his own dirty movies.

LEE.   Oh, I'm sorry to hear that.

POPCORN.   I'm not. Maybe Mr. Lum is though, but he shouldn't be. It's Ovaltine that did him wrong, not me.

TAM.   Would you say you're not the Dancer's father on camera, Mr. Popcorn? Hold it! You know what that would do to him?

POPCORN.   . . . for one lousy dollar?

TAM. It's my movie, my worry not yours. Be a good movie though, wouldn't it? Make up some hokey connection between faking up a father, not knowing your past, and the killer instinct. But he's an old man now. Trusts me. I've failed all the old men that ever trusted me. Sold 'em out, watched 'em die, lost their names and been . . . been what, Kenji? What've I been for that?

KENJI. Don't ask me.

TAM. . . . You used to be like me, Tom? You've never been like me. You never knew better. I knew better. I must've known better. My whiteness runneth over and blackness . . . but people still send me back to the kitchen, you know what I mean?

TOM. You're oversensitive. You can't be oversensitive.

TAM. You're right. I can't be oversensitive. It's like havin too much taste. But that's me oversensitive. And I like it. I'm not going to dig up the Dancer, mock his birth, make a fool of him just to make a name for myself. That's the way it is with us Chinaman cooks! Dat's the code of the kitchen, children. Anybody hungry? (*Rises to go to kitchen.*)

POPCORN. What about the movie, Mr. Lum?

TAM. There won't be a word of fathers in it, Mr. Popcorn. You'll be part of a straight, professional, fight film. I won't need your money, Kenji.

KENJI. Okay.

(TAM *goes to the kitchen, finds a blue apron among the clutter of packing, and puts it on. He sets to work.*)

LEE. What's wrong? This is all so glum. I don't understand. What about your children, Tam? All your heart. What's happening here?

TAM. I haven't forgotten them. Jonah and Sarah. I'm in the kitchen. A cook. Ovaltine ever fry chicken for ya, Mr. Popcorn?

POPCORN. Yeah, ain't it awful what he do to chickens and grease?

TAM. The Chinatown Kid would've liked to have seen . . . How do I know what he would've liked. You speak Chinese, Tom?

TOM. Some Mandarin.

TAM. No, you couldn't talk to him either. Wrong dialect. It's in the hands, the food. There's conversation for you.

(TAM *works out with the cleaver on green onions . . . some fast chopping.*)

KENJI. You okay, Tam. You know what you're doing?

TAM. Don't worry about me, Dentist. You got your house, your lab. You're home. I'll cook for ya tonight . . . keep my mouth shut slicin greens and meat, and be gone tomorrow. Roguing like you say.

KENJI. No hard feelings.

TAM. Damn straight I have hard feelings. And I like 'em, they're mine! Thank you. (*Grinning.*) Hey, Dentist! I guess you and Lee and the kid'll be moving soon?

KENJI. Yeah, I'm going to be a father.

LEE. What're you talking about?

POPCORN. Sounds like she don't know she's pregnant.

LEE. I heard that, Charley Popcorn. What're you talking about?

POPCORN. You know, I'm having a wonderful time. I really am. Really opens my eyes.

KENJI. I just told Tom we're having a baby.

TOM. Were you talking to me. I didn't know people still did that.

LEE. Are we having a baby?

KENJI. Tell Tom.

TOM. Listen, I didn't mean to walk into any situation.

KENJI. That's right. You think that.

TOM. I'm a good loser.

LEE. Talk to me, Kenji. Not him.

KENJI. I don't know what to talk about, Lee. I don't have the gift of gab . . .

LEE. Sing a song.

KENJI. Lemme talk it.

LEE. Oh, Kenji, talk it then.

KENJI. Somewhere over the rainbow, bluebirds fly . . .

LEE. Not that one. One of your own . . .

KENJI.

> Gather round the fire boys, and
>   I'll tell you how I grew old.
> Seeking Helen Keller's smelly love like
>   other men seek gold.
> I rode with the Chickencoop Chinaman, who
>   was ornery and cruel,
> Notorious for spinnin a fast mean thread
>   offen life's wooden spool.

(*All pat-a-cake up a rhythm, give western hoots and yips and chew cake.*)

KENJI.

> Listen to this song from the Hollywood Confucius
>   says Dostoyevsky West
> Where the yellow highriders be damned and the
>   slantyeyed blind are blessed.
> I ride with a killer. I'm a goner. Doomed in my
>   lover's quest.
> For a long time seeing nothin but sand,
>   I've wanted to lose hope.
> But I'm STUBBORN, boys, rightly called yellow
>   Blackjap Kenji,
> Kenji, the Golden Goat.
> "Ride," he said. "Ride with me . . ."

(KENJI, LEE, *and* TOM *freeze, and fade into black. Spot up on* TAM *in the kitchen.*)

TAM. Ride with me . . . Everything comes sniffin at you in the kitchen sooner or later, children, grandmaw used to say. In the kitchen. Always in the kitchen. And listen!

Here comes Kenji's BlackJap song to sniff me up. A long song, from a long time ago, outa our Oakland.

Turn off them radios and listen in the kitchen!

My grandmaw told me, children, how when she was left alone to roll cigars all by herself, in the Old West when Chinamans was the only electricity and all the thunder in the mountains . . . in them awful old days of few mothers, few fathers, and rare songs . . . she used to leave a light on in the next room, and listen. And talkin to us—This is true!—sometimes she heard a train. A Chinaman borne, high steppin Iron Moonhunter, liftin eagles with its breath! ''Listen!'' she'd say.

And we'd listen in the kitchen.

She was on the air.

The house she said was like when her father came back from the granite face and was put in the next room, broken and frostbit on every finger and toe of him and his ears and nose, from the granite face, by Chinamans, nobodies' fathers, all night long running stolen horses, yelling for speed, for my grandmaw's ma. That's the truth!

Ya hear that cry?

From China Camp, Jacksonville, Westport, Placerville, a gallop and grandmaw's pa coming home.

And he died there, in the light of the next room, comfortable, comforting a little girl rolling counterfeit Spanish cigars.

Now and then, I feel them old days children, the way I feel the prowl of the dogs in the night and the bugs in the leaves and the thunder in the Sierra Nevadas however far they are. The way my grandmother had an ear for trains. Listen, children, I gotta go. Ride Buck Buck Bagaw with me . . . Listen in the kitchen for the Chickencoop Chinaman slowin on home.

CURTAIN

FOCUS QUESTIONS

1. Show how issues of multiethnicity are treated through characterization, dialogue, and action.
2. Discuss the origin of the father/son conflict and how it functions in the play.
3. How do the fantasy interludes enlighten the realistic scenes of the play?
4. Assess Tam Lum's growth of awareness from the first scene to the last.
5. Choose any three characters and briefly describe their contribution to the dramatic action. How do they mirror the play's themes?
6. In a short essay, discuss the impact of Tam's ancestral roots on his present condition. What is your prognosis?
7. With reference to Tam's use of language, defend him as a ''multi-tongued word magician.''
8. Compare *The Chickencoop Chinaman* with the more conventional portrait of the Asian-American experience as presented in the film *Flower Drum Song*.

OTHER ACTIVITIES

1. Discuss Chin's references to Asian-American stereotypes and show how they are now being redressed.
2. While researching your own production of the play, develop a list of aural and visual impressions that will enrich the play's fantasy interludes, yet serve as bridges to the realistic action. Suggest ways in which you might implement these effects in performance.

BIBLIOGRAPHY

Chin, Frank, and Jeffrey Paul Chan, Lawson Fusao Inada, Shawn Wong, eds. *AIIIEEEEE!: An Anthology of Asian-American Writers*. New York: New American Library, 1991.

Ellis, Donald, and Richard Schotter, eds. *News of The American Place Theatre* 4, no. 4 (May 1972).

MacDonald, Eric. *Theater at the Margins: Texts for a Poststructured Stage*. Ann Arbor: University of Michigan Press, 1993.

McDonald, Dorothy Ritsuko. ''Introduction'' to *Two Plays by Frank Chin*. Seattle: University of Washington Press, 1981.

Wei, William. *The Asian American Movement*. Philadelphia: Temple University Press, 1993.

RECOMMENDED VIDEOTAPE

Frank Chin, reading and conversation with Jeffrey Chan. VHS. 70 min. (1989). With selections from *The Chickencoop Chinaman*. San Francisco State University, American Poetry Archive.

THE TOOTH OF CRIME
SAM SHEPARD (1943–   )

[*The Tooth of Crime*] exhibits his theatrical inventiveness at its most brilliant
yet most uncapricious and coherent, and it reveals most powerfully his sense
of the reciprocities of art and life.

—RICHARD GILMAN

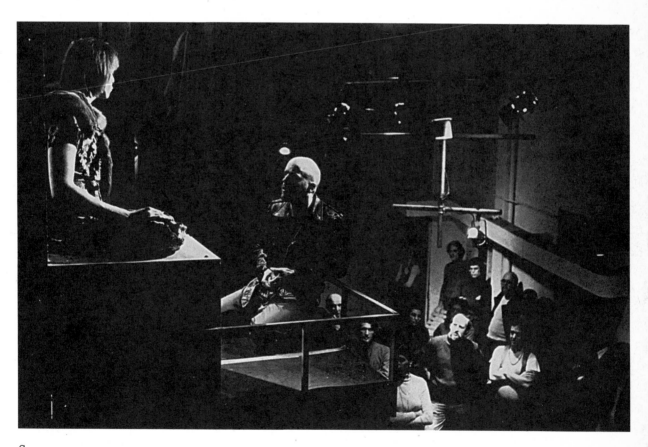

Stephen Borst (*left*) as Crow and Spalding Gray as Hoss in *The Tooth of Crime,* presented by the
Performance Group in 1973, under the direction of Richard Schechner. *Photo: Papers of Richard
Schechner. Theatre Collection. Department of Rare Books and Special Collections, Princeton University Libraries.*

APPROACHING NON-MAINSTREAM AMERICAN DRAMA

By mid-twentieth century, the American theatre was a commercially viable cultural institution among whose numerous artistic credentials was a durable stage literature. But the playwright's commercial success often hinged, as it still does, on that unpredictable journey from rehearsal page to live performance. Preparing a manuscript for both the director and actors, the playwright anticipated a Broadway opening that unveiled his work before a pleasure-seeking audience, including professional critics who publicly assessed its artistic merits. Prompted by certain expectations, not the least of which was the hope for a long-running engagement, the established hit-or-miss formula determined the fate of the play. Equally important was the publication of the script, a matter that ensured its availability to the public and enhanced its literary status. The frequency of future productions usually varied from one work to the next and was important for measuring the popularity of the play in performance.

Nor could the American theatre ignore the artistic upheaval from outside, especially when theatres abroad were responding to the revolutionary changes around them by the early fifties. The plays of Samuel Beckett, Eugene Ionesco, Arthur Adamov, Jean Genet, and other avant-garde writers throughout Europe were pointing to newer developments in contemporary stage performance. (See Prefaces to Beckett, p. 862, and Pinter, p. 822.) The impact resounded in New York, at a time when the dynamics of producing mainstream theatre on Broadway were shifting under increased artistic and financial pressures.

These forces culminated with astonishing results in the establishment of an Off-Broadway movement committed to presenting less conservative or non-mainstream forms of theatre at affordable prices. Audiences eager to support these adventurous enterprises promptly filled the intimate playhouses situated outside the commercial theatre district, such as the Circle-in-the-Square, the Phoenix Theatre, and the Cherry Lane. Fortunately the press stood close by, providing invaluable coverage that would assist their growth and popularity.

In time, the daring unconventionality of Off-Broadway, whose agenda included the works of American playwrights as well, grew less adventurous, so that by the early sixties, an altogether different vanguard also named for where it was situated—Off-Off-Broadway—assumed these responsibilities. Countless professionals joined the OOB movement, constructing their theatrical visions in loft spaces, church basements, cafés, and the backrooms of bars. While many of these enterprises fell quietly from sight, others like the Café Cino, Café La Mama, Judson Poets' Theatre, Performance Group, American Place Theatre, and the Open Theater generated their own unique style and influence.

In the meantime, the stirrings of a great cultural revolution surfaced across America with noteworthy consequences. Issues relating to civil rights, gender equality, employment vs. welfare, societal drop-outs, the drug culture, and the emergence of rock music with its violent undercurrents reflected a troubled and splintered society. Concerns were mostly social and confined to American shores, except for the timely political controversy surrounding the involvement in Vietnam that would cost American families many precious lives. Discovering theatre as a means of addressing their social and political commitments, whenever and wherever they felt the need to do so, artists sought alternative forms of expression.

Practitioners based in the less restrictive atmosphere of New York created an **alternative theatre** movement whose liberating spirit further fueled the OOB phenomenon. But outside of New York, the grassroots nature of alternative theatre led to a less centralized system, one that had been initially triggered by the growth of regional theatres across America in the mid-sixties. While recognition on Broadway remained a key factor in determining a stage artist's professional viability, the situation was beginning to change. Also significant were the theatre departments of colleges and universities, whose training programs expanded the professional horizons of their student-majors and heightened their audiences' appreciation of drama, because they delegated a part of their energy to non-mainstream theatre.

Then something of an event took place at St. Mark's in the Bowery, a church in the East Village of New York City. Encouraged by Ralph Cook, the founder of Theatre Genesis, an itinerant young actor who had recently settled in New York wrote two one-acts, *Cowboys* and *The Rock Garden,* which the company presented on October 10, 1964. Demonstrating a highly personal and unconventional set of playwriting rules, he had no need to contend with mainstream theatre tactics. Also absent was the commercial edge to publish-the-play or perish, which is why no copies of *Cowboys* have survived. Following the recommendation of a *Village Voice* review, audiences flocked to this intriguing double-bill, bringing acclaim to Theatre Genesis and to a first-time playwright named Sam Shepard.

What playgoers discovered was an artist instinctively prepared to explore the schizo-phrenic ethos of his own generation—its mythic past, pop-cultural present, and imagined future—through bold stage language and sharp character interaction. They would also discover a writer enthralled by the dynamic tensions between the old order and the new: a reverence for the America that was in conflict with what it had become. While a range of playwright-predecessors from Eugene O'Neill to Tennessee Williams and Edward Albee had already investigated the enigmatic American Dream, either by paying homage to its bright promise or wallowing cynically in its fading twilight, Shepard's grimly sardonic and wildly theatrical style celebrated its betrayal and death. But in the process of doing so, he uncovered a rich subtext of **themes:** the quest for individual and collective identity in a chaotic universe; the refusal to surrender the *self* to the mechanized forces outside; and survival, beyond its mere economic implications, in the wake of a shattered value system. No less urgent were his concerns for the American family, once an invincible stronghold, now reduced to pitching its tent in quicksand.

Among the diverse and contemporary cultural phenomena that have inspired Shepard's vision and shaped his dramatic style, perhaps none has exerted a heavier influence than jazz, rock and roll, and rock: *thematic* in its relation to the subject matter of certain works; *theatrical* in the incorporation of songs to evoke mood and enhance meaning; and *structural* in its effect on both nonverbal and spoken language. While music has been a deliberate focus in earlier plays, its repercussions have been set into eloquent motion in his later work, albeit abstractly, through staccato/legato speech rhythms, character counterpointings, and the solo/ensemble turns by eccentric characters prone to acting out, role playing, and expanding the limits of conventional stage performance.

Citing his "favorite playwright, [Bertolt] Brecht" for using music in meaningful ways, Shepard believed that music added "a whole different kind of perspective [in bringing] the audience to terms with an emotional reality."[1] But unlike his German predecessor, Shepard never simply affixed music to his work, either for political or "epic" purposes. (See Preface to Brecht, p. 737.) Rather he made it an integral part of a language system embedded in the anxieties of his own generation, a musically influenced code profoundly disturbing in its message but wryly seductive in its style.

There remained darker sides to Shepard's vocal music, ones that baffled critics who were determined to pigeonhole his sources. In the days before his professional theatre career, Shepard had accidentally discovered Samuel Beckett's *Waiting for Godot* and "read it with a very keen interest, but I didn't know anything about what it *was.*"[2] Whatever the attraction, Shepard's art, like Beckett's, became rooted in language and informed by music. More importantly, he was stylistically preoccupied with consciousness as subject matter. (See Preface to Beckett, p. 863.) The other influence was non-literary and discovered in Shepard's apparatus as an actor. It came from Joseph Chaikin whose unique methodology for the actors in his Open Theater included character transformations and improvisations, all of which inspired the playwright's versatile demonstration of stage voices in the characters he created.

MAJOR WORKS

Shepard's one-acts include the fantasy-comedy, *Chicago* (1965); *Icarus's Mother* (1965); *Red Cross* (1966); *Forensic and the Navigators* (1967); *Melodrama Play* (1967); *The Unseen Hand* (1969); *Cowboy Mouth* (a play with music written with Patti Smith, 1971); the apocalyptic play with music, *Back Bog Beast Bait* (1971); *Action* (1975); the monologue, *Killer's Head* (1975); "A Mysterious Overture" with music, *Suicide in B♭* (1976); and *Fool for Love* (1983). Full-lengths include *La Turista* (1967); the surreal two-act play with music, *Operation Sidewinder* (1970), which premiered in the more mainstream environment of the Vivian Beaumont Theatre at Lincoln Center; the "Two-act adventure show" with music, *Mad Dog Blues* (1971); *Geography of a Horse Dreamer* (1974); *Angel City* (1976), performed with music; *Seduced* (1978); *States of Shock* (1991); and *Simpatico* (1994). His cycle of so-called "family plays" is comprised of *Curse of the Starving Class* (1977), the Pulitzer Prize-winning *Buried Child* (1978), *True West* (1980), and *A Lie of the Mind* (1985).

Shepard wrote *The Tooth of Crime* (a Play with Music in Two Acts, 1972) while living in London from 1971 to 1975. The four years he spent there helped him sort through the personal disillusionment he experienced as an artist in America. Although the play is highly representative of his idiosyncratic canon, most especially those works that incorporate music into their dramatic structures, it succeeds beyond these technical merits by steering his fascination with language into newer directions. The overtly theatrical results have made this play an attractive and challenging choice for directors and actors as well as for audiences.

THE ACTION

A rock superstar (Hoss) feels threatened by the "gypsy movement" of younger stars who fearlessly compete with him for top-of-the-charts status. Hoss consults his staff, which includes a manager/girlfriend (Becky), a driver (Cheyenne), a private doctor (Doc), and an astrologer (Star-Man), the last of whom warns him that a gypsy killer is heading his way for the ultimate showdown. When the gypsy (Crow) appears and confronts Hoss in a new language he does not understand, Hoss begs him to "back the language up, man, I'm too old to follow the flash." They engage in fierce verbal combat until Hoss, who has hired his own referee to ensure his victory, loses the match. Hoss commits suicide to preserve his honor, as the usurper ascends the throne in triumph.

STRUCTURE AND LANGUAGE

Out of his artistic need to deal with the evanescence and futility of fame and to show, as Crow predicts, how power "shifts and sits till a bigger wind blows," Shepard wastes no time building his dramatic actions around two outspoken characters and two carefully interwoven themes: one of identity, the other of power and survival. Arrayed like a monarch in "rocker gear" in front of "an evil-looking black chair" that resembles "something like an Egyptian Pharaoh's throne," Hoss bemoans the tragic illusion "of the way things are" to hidden musical accompaniment: "I used to believe in rhythm and blues/ Always wore my blue suede shoes/ Now everything I do goes down in doubt."

Hoss was ''born to kill,'' and there is clever double meaning to his ''hits'' on his way to the top. But always having played the game according to the system has now made him ''respectable and safe,'' so that his ''touch is gone.'' His realization of this potentially fatal predicament, which frantically mounts during act 1, beckons loyal supporters from the old order who backed his reigning image as ''a true genius killer.'' While references to the worlds of big music, organized crime, and sports could once console him, they have become ''all zoned out.''

In sharp contrast stands his opponent, the considerably younger Crow who has achieved success outside of the system. A presence unseen but *felt* throughout act 1, he appears in act 2 and admits that he is ''lost at sea.'' But his shaky footing on Hoss' territory is merely deceptive. For unlike Hoss, Crow can ''switch to suit,'' thus shaping to his advantage the illusory and transient nature of the world—in this case, the musical charts he will inevitably conquer. His egocentric testament of faith is echoed with a haunting musical refrain: ''But I believe in my mask—The man I made up is me/ And I believe in my dance—And my destiny.'' Living for the moment and fearing no one, Crow assumes that image is everything.

Shepard has admitted that the roots of the play were aural, that the dialogue surfaced from ''a certain sound which [came] from the voice of this character, Hoss . . . and the whole kind of world that he was involved in;'' that Crow came ''from a yearning toward violence. A totally lethal human with no way or reason for tracing how he got that way. He just appeared. He spit words that became his weapons.''[3] What emerged on stage was a pair of universal forces or **archetypes:** on one hand, as ancient as two warring antagonists from storybook history; on the other, as familiar as two gunslingers exhumed from the mythic American West. Regardless of time or place, their eternal struggle engenders but one certainty: that age must submit to youth, the old must yield to the new; that the past must reconcile with the present, and the present with the future. But no matter how the cycle is manifested, there can be only one victor.

We become the innocent bystanders to a deadly showdown whose combatants are identified by two entirely different language codes for which no helpful clues exist. Resorting to ammunition that is purely verbal, Shepard demonstrates a contest between styles in which the conventional meanings of words, almost rendered useless, are carefully transformed, even reinvented, to define their speakers and serve the interests of the play. In effect, the playwright reflects the contemporary conflict between generations in which the younger one exercises power through a language of its own.

Hoss' style is the less jarring. It is filled with topical references that reflect an old-fashioned set of values and have become useless: ''Zip guns in the junk yard. Rock fights, dirt clods, bustin' windows. Vandals, juvies, West Side Story.'' Once having understood Hoss, we must shift our receptive modes for Crow, whose style is private, succinct, and assaultive: ''Razor, Leathers. Very razor.'' While their rapid-fire exchanges continually dislocate our bearings, they also heighten our internal responses to the events and draw us into the action. No longer mere bystanders, we are auditorily prepared to comprehend the central conflict of act 2 played out in a ritualized, coded, and poetic declamation reminiscent of the rap-style that would surface from a generation of black American music-artists more than a decade after Shepard wrote his play.

Serving several purposes, Shepard's dramatic landscapes, in this work as well as others, are richly strewn with the iconography of popular culture, a serious preoccupation that lends itself to the postmodern condition and is reflected in many exciting examples of art and literature. Concentrating totally on the power of language and expanding conventional meanings for characters like Hoss whose identity is inextricably linked to words, Shepard transforms the human voice into a phenomenon quite separate from the physical reality of his characters. His achievement might also be interpreted as ''a kind of allegorical conversation—or rather confrontation—between modernism and **postmodernism,**[4] in which Hoss' demise points to the death of modernism, while Crow's ascendancy sparks the beginning of a new or postmodern era.

From his position of power at the top of the charts, Hoss has never sat comfortably with success, at times shifting voices from his own to his father's, for example, to generate the need for questions: "(old) O.K. You're not so bad off. It's good to change. Good to feel your blood pump. (himself) But where to? Where am I going?" Having usurped Hoss' position, Crow cannot bother himself with questions, but simply accepts the new order he represents: "If I'm a fool then keep me blind/ I'd rather feel my way." He knows he will remain in power "till a bigger wind blows," perfectly at home with the transitory nature of the universe he has created.

THE TOOTH OF CRIME-IN-PERFORMANCE

Since his auspicious playwriting debut at Theatre Genesis in 1964, Shepard's several dozen works have received countless stagings in a variety of professional and non-professional settings: exclusively Off-Broadway, Off-Off Broadway, regional theatres, workshops, and the college/university environment. Most curious of all is that his status as a major dramatist of the twentieth century has been established without the support of Broadway or mainstream audiences. There are certain advantages to this. Foremost is the fact that no definitive productions of his work exist, which has prompted artists to establish their own insights into performing his plays. Furthermore, actors and directors working outside of the mainstream circuit have been instinctively drawn to Shepard's experimental aesthetic, which may not always hold our attention on the page, but comes boldly to life in performance.

The Tooth of Crime was commissioned by the Open Space Theatre in London, where it enjoyed its world premiere on July 17, 1972, under the direction of Charles Marowitz and Walter Donohue. Malcolm Storry created the role of Hoss, with David Schofield as Crow. The music was composed by Shepard himself and performed by Blunderpuss. Critic Irving Wardle noted that the "aggression of the music and the play are all of a piece in Charles Marowitz's production, which itself uses style as an instrument of assault."[5] There were also notable London productions at the Royal Court on June 5, 1974, directed by Jim Sharman; and at the Croydon Warehouse, presented by the Black Theatre Cooperative on September 15, 1983, under the direction of Charlie Hanson.

The first American production took place at the McCarter Theatre in Princeton, New Jersey, in November of 1972, under Louis Criss' direction. The brief engagement featured Frank Langella as Hoss and Mark Metcalf as Crow. T. E. Kalem called it "a striking play, and given here with the most commendable forcefulness."[6]

The play truly asserted itself as an important work in Shepard's growing canon when it was given its New York premiere by the Performance Group on March 7, 1973, under Richard Schechner's direction. In other highly adventurous productions at the Performing Garage, the Group explored the techniques of **environmental theatre,** in which the conventional agreements between performer and spectator were deliberately crossed to allow confrontation between both parties. Choosing *The Tooth of Crime* for an environmental staging, Schechner's company drew some of its most controversial responses ever, and from all corners, including the playwright's.

Rather than adhering to the author's script, Schechner wanted "to look at the play nakedly, approach its language not as a dialect but as a way into the heart of the play and a way to uncover things in the performers playing the roles."[7] Shepard responded by making it quite clear that his play was "very preconceived. I got exact diagrams and pictures in my head about how it should be done . . . It's like a kid brother that I wanna protect."[8] Nevertheless, Schechner proceeded with his and the Group members' discoveries to guide them, with changes in the script occurring as rehearsals progressed.

While it is understandable that the playwright might choose to take his director to task for not respecting "the form that vision takes place in,"[9] there is a good deal to be said about the environmentalist lens through which the Performance Group perceived Shepard's unconventional play. The plywood environment, designed by Jerry Rojo as a modular system of squares, rectangles, and polygons, was a centrally situated structure of more than thirty feet in diameter, with several towers rising twelve and sixteen feet. Windows were cut into different sides to expand the sightlines of spectators who perched themselves at specific corners of the environment, but needed to circulate from one space to another to follow the action.

On one hand, the environmentalist staging heightened the sense of participation audiences had when they attended rock concerts. But at the same time, the performance, according to Schechner, assumed the dimensions of a medieval pageant play: "the actual progression of events in space matched the awakening of consciousness on the part of the drama's protagonist, Hoss."[10] Critic Jeff Sweet commented on the impact of the Performance Group's imaginative efforts: "The danger of techniques such as this is that they tend to be employed to cover up lack of discipline and training on the part of the performers. Such was emphatically not the case in this production, however. Rather than camouflage, the staging proved to be a challenge to the company, and it met that challenge with gusto."[11]

The Performance Group presented 123 performances of *The Tooth of Crime* at the Performing Garage. The work received an Obie Award as distinguished play for that year, and the production later traveled to Paris. Featuring Spalding Gray as Hoss and Timothy Shelton as Crow, the cast included Elizabeth LeCompte and Joan MacIntosh. The production was also filmed for the Whitney Museum.

On February 14, 1983, exactly a decade after Schechner's Performance Group incarnated the play, *The Tooth of Crime* was produced for a five-week engagement at La Mama Annex in New York City. Directed by George Ferencz, with the collaborative efforts of Bill Stabile (scenery), Paul Mathiesen (lighting), David Kobernuss (sound), and Sally Lesser (costumes), the results adhered more closely to Shepard's intentions and succeeded in creating their own chilling effects. Critic Renfreu Neff called the production "definitive in its authenticity to Shepard's timeless equation between Fame and Death, and it succeeds in going beyond a theatrical context. Not since the Living Theatre's *Frankenstein* has a theatrepiece had such transcendant impact."[12]

REFLECTIONS ON THE TOOTH OF CRIME

George Ferencz is a resident director at La Mama.

I came to New York in 1970 from Cleveland, Ohio, and knew I wanted to be a stage director. Unfortunately you come to New York City and you want to be like certain people. Some of this is because, outside of New York, "good work" often depends on how much it looks like the New York production. This is supported by the scripts that used to come out of Sam French and the Dramatists Play Service. They not only give you the floor plans, but the lighting plot and everything else. The criteria were always how much it could be like a New York production.

When I came to New York, I wanted to be like certain directors—José Quintero, Marshall Mason—but it took a while for me to realize that in New York you had to create your own identity and indeed your own theatre. So in 1974 I started the Impossible

Continued

Ragtime Theatre. A lot of IRT was based on a very raw idea of rock-and-roll theatre. I was going to rock-and-roll concerts and still trying to stage **poetic realism.** I don't know why it took me so long to put the connection together and do theatre that used elements of rock and roll.

Live rock-and-roll performance has a forward lunge to it. What I enjoyed about rock-concert performances was the fact that, as opposed to looking at the sides of people's faces and profiles—which happens in naturalistic plays—and listening to this one-dimensional sort of reality, in rock and roll I could see their faces because it was performance-oriented. It was straight-on out. There was always more than one thing going on: there was a rich sexuality and the stage ignited with electricity. The mikes, the actual electric guitars, the lights, the costumes, the power of electricity all seemed much more alive, much more imaginative and exciting than what I saw in the theatre. I liked the use of microphones. I liked *hearing* the actors. I liked *seeing* the actors and the elements of performing. I liked that it *wasn't* naturalistic.

I directed *The Tooth of Crime* at La Mama in 1983, but my first experience with the play was at the summer festival of Sam Shepard plays at Columbia University in 1979, for which I was invited to be artistic director. We got a company of actors together and just enough money to do the rock-and-roll plays—*Cowboy Mouth, Melodrama Play, Mad Dog Blues,* and *Tooth.* We called the festival "Shep 'n Rep—Rock n' Roll Theatre." (Shepard's book of poetry—*Hawk Moon*—also contains some wonderful poems about the power of rock and roll.) Each actor would be in at least two of the shows. We did a concert version of *Cowboy Mouth.* What we had was an actress and an actor at two microphones. They never looked at each other. They simply performed the play out to the audience. So when we came to *The Tooth of Crime,* I also wanted to do it as if we were at a rock concert. But instead of using theatre lighting, I wanted to use eight follow-spots. It was something I'd once seen used at a Boontown Rats concert and I liked the idea of liquid lighting rather than conventional stage lighting.

I decided I would emphasize the music and treat not only the duel but the whole play as a rock concert. That was the key that allowed us to open the door with the actors, with the *performers.* The audition was to sing a rock-and-roll song, and we auditioned close to a thousand people. I was amazed at the response. An interesting sidenote, by the way, is that out of all those auditions, not one sang a Beatles song. But they sang everything else. I didn't want actors in the traditional sense. I wanted performers with attitude who could say, "This is the way it's done!" It was, as in rock and roll, a case of coming at the audience, a much more aggressive approach to the theatre than I had really been involved in or had ever seen.

Eventually I got a call from Arthur Storch to direct *The Tooth of Crime* at Syracuse Stage. Basically, that production, with some changes, came to La Mama. In fact, a few actors were in all three productions, most importantly Stephen Mellor, who played Crow. A lot of Crow was created by Stephen with makeup, the blemish on the side of his face, the long fingernail. We created a gangster out of Hoss. We used black and Hispanic actors. Our Becky Lou was Asian. In Syracuse we performed on a very large stage, so we were able to use cars. We had Hoss' car at stage right. On stage left, at the end of act 1 when Hoss is alone, we had a '56 Chevy with its back facing the audience, slowly advancing toward the audience. You could see the car's rear lights and on top of it was Crow. But at La Mama we introduced him with his long fingernail coming up through the grating.

It happened to be the tenth anniversary season at Syracuse Stage and they'd seldom done anything with music before. They were also near Syracuse University, but could hardly get the students to come. So they were hoping our show would bring them down the hill. On opening night, which was New Years Eve of 1982, almost a third of the subscription audience stood up and left shortly after the show started. They were throwing their programs at the stage and demanding their money back in the lobby, while the show was going on. I felt terrible and couldn't believe this was happening. We were very happy with the show, but began to wonder if we'd brought it to the wrong place, that the audience was not going to get it. The reviews came out and were just atrocious.

But the university students suddenly appeared in droves, creating a turnaround until the theatre was selling standing-room tickets at every performance. They also kept returning, dressing up like the stage characters and chanting in the aisles. They took it as a rock concert. In fact, it became such a controversial production in Syracuse, that we got an editorial from the newspaper discussing the purpose of art.

A year earlier I had become a resident director at La Mama. So I telephoned Ellen Stewart and told her we had a real hot show in Syracuse. By a happy coincidence, one of her productions had been cancelled at the La Mama Annex. So she flew up to Syracuse just in time to catch the final performance and decided she wanted the play. That's how we moved the production to La Mama and played for an extended run of six weeks.

We were constantly looking for ways to create tension in the production. Our stage designer, Bill Stabile, did a different type of set for La Mama, although the idea of the **raked stage** being on top of the band was the same in all three productions. The raked stage was so steep, it gave us an element of danger. For example, the actor playing the referee could skate very well. So I had him perform on roller skates on top of this raked stage. It looked simple, but was very complicated. The rubber matting on the rake was of a very special type, which meant that the actors also needed special shoes.

We started the show in the dark and we had something like two or three minutes of music before the stage lights came up, just to build tension in the audience. I realized something about the show when we were rehearsing it. It became very clear that *The Tooth of Crime* was basically like a Greek tragedy. The **unities** seemed to be observed, giving it the structure of a Greek tragedy. The use of microphones, not only when the actors sang their songs, but also when they spoke, also reflected the influence of Greek theatre.

The verbal combat wasn't sung. It was closer to what we now call rap. Once you had the rhythm set down, the rest depended on the words. The words came flowing out. Now when I look back at it, what we were doing was closer to rap, although we didn't realize it at the time. So there was this ever-present pulse against which the actors worked.

People ask what the play is about. It's very simple. It's about power. There's no question that Crow will win. The actor Ray Wise, who played Hoss and won an Obie for his performance, had a heightened, almost operatic performance sense. I had worked with Ray at the IRT, where he played Yank in *The Hairy Ape* and did several other O'Neill plays. Even for O'Neill you need that heightened sense, which Ray could capture very well. Consequently we had a lot of talk about Hoss' suicide. He didn't exactly know how to come to grips with the fact that this younger man was going to take over. In our discussion at the time he asked, "What else can I do except pull the trigger in my mouth?" He has tried

Continued

to learn Crow's style, but that doesn't really work for him. I felt the choices were very simple—either to put the gun this way in his mouth or to create an heir. That was the only way he could exist, the only way he could fight the younger man. But that he would not do.

Hoss does re-create his father in that monologue at the end of act 1. But Hoss is self-centered. He doesn't really have a sense of the power of having an heir, of what that implies. That having an heir is a way of combating Crow, that without one he is alone. He is the older man, and without that heir, there is no way he can beat Crow. He needs Becky Lou to help him. But the sado-masochistic elements of their relationship are an obstacle. On the other hand, she has an understanding of pain and of the world and of the high speed they're dealing with, and she deeply understands power. After Hoss' death, she goes right to the winner, she goes right to Crow.

Hoss' roots are much closer to the black experience than Crow's, whereas Crow can use any mask. He has no real relationship to the music as Hoss does. Hoss has an understanding, as he tells us during the battle, of where that music came from, that it came from the black experience. We were able to investigate this by casting several black actors in the production. With Crow, there was no concern for history. It was simply his mask, and this was his moment. Style was everything. Substance was not as important as style. It is tragic that style beats substance. Audiences have wondered about the message Shepard was sending. That style-over-content element has disturbed them. Yet that is what the playwright has been accused of himself. But I personally don't believe this. I believe that there is tremendous substance to the play.

There has always been some reaction to the play's datedness, which has something to do with the references to Keith Moon, Mick Jagger, and Bob Dylan. The language is filled with musicians' jargon, musicians' talk, and a hipness. And the thing about hipness is that it changes. Something like "suss the bounce" ["understand the situation"] was very hip in the sixties or early seventies, but has been replaced by new terms. It's musicians' talk, which is why it was very important to have a musical director who was a rock and roller, who had an appreciation and love for theatre, rather than your standard musical director.

That's where Bob Jewett was so helpful. He was our musical director from the start. He had a good sensibility about rock that he first brought to all four plays at the theatre festival at Columbia. So he traveled with us to Syracuse Stage, then to La Mama, and had to investigate the differences between rock a billy and Chicago blues and all these types of rock and roll. Even though Bob could not teach music in the traditional way, he understood the language. He understood what was being said on a whole other level, and that really helped us. The language is highly specific to musicians.

I believe that *The Tooth of Crime* is the best play written in English in the last twenty-five years. I don't know another play that has language like *Tooth*. The theatre is at its best when it has poetry to offer us. This play has poetry. What we want when we go to the theatre is poetry. Unfortunately what we get is prose. *The Tooth of Crime* is super-realism, heightened realism, fantasy-land.

I have a theory about *Tooth*. You have to look at *Cowboy Mouth,* which he wrote with Patti Smith, as well as *Tooth*. Patti's influences were from the French outlaw poets of the late nineteenth century. The title is suggested by symbolist Stéphane Mallarmé's poem

"Anguish," which includes the following: "But while there exists in your breast of stone/ A heart which the tooth of no crime can wound,/ I flee,/ In terror of dying while sleeping alone." It's generally believed that in *Cowboy Mouth* Patti wrote her own lines and Sam wrote his. This is just conjecture on my part, but from the language of *Tooth* I believe that Patti had a part in writing this as well. I can hear her voice at times. In fact, Sam might have written Hoss, and she might have written Crow. I'm just going out on a limb, but in terms of the writing and attitude, there's a lot of Patti Smith in Crow. They were together at the time in London when it was written, and in his other work her influence is pretty strong.

The Tooth of Crime led me to further work in terms of Shepard. That's when I moved into his jazz period as well as into my own. I left rock and roll behind and got involved with Max Roach. I directed *Suicide in Bb*, *Angel City*, and *Back Bog Beast Bait* at La Mama in 1984, using the jazz sensibility. Roach's original music won an Obie Award for this festival of plays which we entitled "Shepard Sets." I wouldn't say that my own evolution has followed Sam's, but I've always enjoyed meeting him through the page. In fact, when we did the festival at Columbia, he wrote us a very generous letter thanking us for what we were doing. Sam Shepard was a playwright who spoke to my heart, not to careerism, not to any other criteria, except to my heart. I would read his work and say, "I understand this person deeply and want to direct his work."

Notes

1. *Bonnie Marranca, ed.,* AMERICAN DREAMS: THE IMAGINATION OF SAM SHEPARD *(New York: PAJ Publications, 1981), 201–2.*
2. *Ibid., 191.*
3. *Ibid., 200.*
4. *Leonard Wilcox, ed.,* REREADING SHEPARD *(New York: St. Martin's Press, 1992), 564.*
5. THE TIMES, *18 July 1972.*
6. *T. E. Kalem,* TIME, *27 Nov. 1972.*
7. *Richard Schechner,* ENVIRONMENTAL THEATER *(New York: Hawthorne Books, 1973), 228–29.*
8. *Ibid., 235.*
9. *Schechner, "Drama, Script, Theatre, and Performance,"* THE DRAMA REVIEW *(September 1973): 11.*
10. *Ibid.*
11. *Jeff Sweet, "The 1972–73 Off-Off-Broadway Season," in* BEST PLAYS OF 1972–1973, *ed. Otis Guernsey (New York: Dodd, Mead & Company, 1973), 43.*
12. OTHER STAGES *(24 Feb. 1983).*

THE TOOTH OF CRIME
SAM SHEPARD

CHARACTERS

Hoss	Galactic Jack	Doc
Becky Lou	Referee	Crow
Star-Man	Cheyenne	

ACT ONE

SCENE: *A bare stage except for an evil-looking black chair with silver studs and a very high back, something like an Egyptian Pharaoh's throne but simple, centre stage. In the dark, heavy lurking Rock and Roll starts low and builds as the lights come up. The band should be hidden. The sound should be like "Heroin" by the Velvet Underground. When the lights are up full,* HOSS *enters in black rocker gear with silver studs and black kid gloves. He holds a microphone. He should look like a mean Rip Torn but a little younger. He takes the stage and sings "The Way Things Are." The words of the song should be understood so the band has to back off on volume when he starts singing.*

"The Way Things Are"
HOSS.

You may think every picture you see is a true history
   of the way things used to be or the way things are
While you're ridin' in your radio or walkin' through
   the late late show ain't it a drag to know you just
   don't know
you just don't know
So here's another illusion to add to your confusion
Of the way things are
Everybody's doin' time for everybody else's crime
   and
I can't swim for the waves in the ocean
All the heroes is dyin' like flies they say it's a sign
   a' the times
And everybody's walkin' asleep eyes open—eyes
   open

So here's another sleep-walkin' dream
A livin' talkin' show of the way things seem

I used to believe in rhythm and blues
Always wore my blue suede shoes
Now everything I do goes down in doubt

But sometimes in the blackest night I can see a little
   light
That's the only thing that keeps me rockin'—keeps
   me rockin'

So here's another fantasy
About the way things seem to be to me.

(*He finishes the song and throws down the microphone and yells off stage.*)

Becky Lou!

(BECKY *comes on in black rock and roll gear. She's very tall and blonde. She holds two black satchels, one in each hand. They should look like old country-doctor bags.*)

BECKY. Ready just about.
HOSS. Let's have a look at the gear.

(BECKY *sets the bags down on the floor and opens them. She pulls out a black velvet piece of cloth and lays it carefully on the floor then begins to take out pearl-handled revolvers, pistols, derringers and rifles with scopes, shotguns broken down. All the weapons should look really beautiful and clean. She sets them carefully on the velvet cloth.* HOSS *picks up the rifles and handles them like a pro, cocking them and looking down the barrel through the scope, checking out the chambers on the pistols and running his hands over them as though they were alive.*)

How's the Maserati?

BECKY.   Clean. Greased like a bullet. Cheyenne took it up to 180 on the Ventura Freeway then backed her right down. Said she didn't bark once.

HOSS.   Good. About time he stopped them quarter-mile orgasms. They were rippin' her up. Gotta let the gas flow in a machine like that. She's Italian. Likes a full-tilt feel.

BECKY.   Cheyenne's hungry for long distance now. Couldn't hold him back with nails. Got lead in his gas foot.

HOSS.   These look nice and blue. Did the Jeweler check 'em out?

BECKY.   Yeah, Hoss. Everything's taken care of.

HOSS.   Good. Now we can boogie.

BECKY.   What's the moon chart say?

HOSS.   Don't ask me! I hired a fucking star-man. A gazer. What the fuck's he been doin' up there.

BECKY.   I don't know. Last I knew it was the next first quarter moon. That's when he said things'd be right.

HOSS.   Get that fucker down here! I wanna see him. I gave him thirteen grand to get this chart in line. Tell him to get his ass down here!

BECKY.   O.K., O.K.

(*She exits,* HOSS *caresses the guns.*)

HOSS.   That fuckin' Scorpion's gonna crawl if this gets turned around now. Now is right. I can feel it's right. I need the points! Can't they see that! I'm winning in three fucking States! I'm controlling more borders than any a' them punk Markers. The El Camino Boys. Bunch a' fuckin' punks. GET THAT FUCKER DOWN HERE!!!

(STAR-MAN *enters with* BECKY. *He's dressed in silver but shouldn't look like Star Trek, more contemporary silver.*)

O.K., slick face, what's the scoop. Can we move now?

STAR-MAN.   Pretty risky, Hoss.

HOSS.   I knew it! I knew it! You fuckin' creep! Every time we get hot to trot you throw on the ice water. Whatsa matter now.

STAR-MAN.   Venus is entering Scorpio.

HOSS.   I don't give a shit if it's entering Brigitte Bardot. I'm ready for a kill!

STAR-MAN.   You'll blow it.

HOSS.   I'll blow it. What do you know. I've always moved on a sixth sense. I don't need you, meatball.

BECKY.   Hoss, you never went against the charts before.

HOSS.   Fuck before. This time I feel it. I can smell blood. It's right. The time is right! I'm fallin' behind. Maybe you don't understand that.

STAR-MAN.   Not true, Hoss. The El Caminos are about six points off the pace. Mojo Root Force is the only one close enough to even worry about.

HOSS.   Mojo? That fruit? What'd he knock over?

STAR-MAN.   Vegas, Hoss. He rolled the big one.

HOSS.   Vegas! He can't take Vegas, that's my mark! That's against the code!

STAR-MAN.   He took it.

HOSS.   I don't believe it.

BECKY.   We picked it up on the bleeper.

HOSS.   When? How come I'm the last to find out?

STAR-MAN.   We thought it'd rattle you too much.

HOSS.   When did it happen!

STAR-MAN.   This morning from what the teleprompters read.

HOSS.   I'm gonna get that chump. I'm gonna have him. He can't do that. He knew Vegas was on my ticket. He's trying to shake me. He thinks I'll just jump borders and try suburban shots. Well he's fuckin' crazy. I'm gonna roll him good.

BECKY.   You can't go against the code, Hoss. Once a Marker strikes and sets up colors, that's his turf. You can't strike claimed turf. They'll throw you out of the game.

HOSS.   *He* did it! He took my mark. It was on my ticket, goddamnit!

STAR-MAN.   He can just claim his wave system blew and he didn't find out till too late.

HOSS.   Well he's gonna find out now. I'll get a fleet together and wipe him out.

BECKY.   But, Hoss, you'll be forced to change class. You won't have solo rights no more. You'll be a gang man. A punk.

HOSS.   I don't care. I want that fuckin' gold record and nobody's gonna stop me. Nobody!

STAR-MAN.   You gotta hold steady, Hoss. This is a tender time. The wrong move'll throw you back a year or more. You can't afford that now. The charts are moving too fast. Every week there's a new star. You don't wanna be a flybynight mug in the crowd. You want something durable, something lasting. How're you gonna cop an immortal shot if you give up soloing and go into a gang war. They'll rip you up in a night. Sure you'll have a few moments of global glow, maybe even an interplanetary flash. But it won't last, Hoss, it won't last.

BECKY.   He's right, Hoss.

HOSS.   O.K., O.K. I'm just gettin' hungry that's all. I need a kill. I haven't had a kill for months now. You know what that's like. I gotta kill. It's my whole life. If I don't kill I get crazy. I start eating away at myself. It's not good. I was born to kill.

STAR-MAN.   Nobody knows that better than us, Hoss. But you gotta listen to management. That's what we're here for. To advise and direct. Without us you'd be just like a mad dog again. Can't you remember what that was like.

HOSS.   Yeah, yeah! Go away now. Go on! I wanna be alone with Becky.

STAR-MAN.   O.K. Just try and take it easy. I know you were wired for a big kill but your time is coming. Don't forget that.

HOSS. Yeah, all right. Beat it!

(STAR-MAN *exits leaving* HOSS *alone with* BECKY. *He looks around the stage dejected. He kicks at the guns and pulls off his gloves.*)

I'm too old fashioned. That's it. Gotta kick out the scruples. Go against the code. That's what they used to do. The big ones. Dylan, Jagger, Townsend. All them cats broke codes. Time can't change that.

BECKY. But they were playin' pussy, Hoss. They weren't killers . . . You're a killer, man. You're in the big time.

HOSS. So were they. My Pa told me what it was like. They were killers in their day too. Cold killers.

BECKY. Come on. You're talkin' treason against the game. You could get the slammer for less than that.

HOSS. Fuck 'em. I know my power. I can go on Gypsy Kill and still gain status. There's a whole underground movement going on. There's a lot of Gypsy Markers comin' up.

BECKY. Why do you wanna throw everything away. You were always suicidal like that. Right from the start.

HOSS. It's part of my nature.

BECKY. That's what we saved you from, your nature. Maybe you forgot that. When we first landed you, you were a complete beast of nature. A sideways killer. Then we molded and shaped you and sharpened you down to perfection because we saw in you a true genius killer. A killer to end them all. A killer's killer.

HOSS. Aw fuck off. I don't believe that shit no more. That stuff is for schoolies. Sure I'm good. I might even be great but I ain't no genius. Genius is something outside the game. The game can't contain a true genius. It's too small. The next genius is gonna be a Gypsy Killer. I can feel it. I know it's goin' down right now. We don't have the whole picture. We're too successful . . . We're insulated from what's really happening by our own fame.

BECKY. You're really trying to self-destruct aren't you? Whatsa matter, you can't take fame no more? You can't hold down the pressure circuits? Maybe you need a good lay or two.

HOSS. Your ass. I can handle the image like a fuckin' jockey. It's just that I don't trust the race no more. I dropped the blinkers.

BECKY. You're not gettin' buck fever are ya'?

HOSS. Get outa' here!

BECKY. Come on. Put it in fourth for a while, Hoss. Cruise it. You can afford to take it easy.

HOSS. GET THE FUCK OUTA' HERE!!!

BECKY. O.K., O.K. I'm your friend. Remember?

HOSS. Yeah, sure.

BECKY. I am. You're in a tough racket. The toughest. But now ain't the time to crack. You're knockin' at the door, Hoss. You gotta hold on. Once you get the gold then you can back off. But not now.

HOSS. I'm not backin' off. I'm just havin' a doubt dose.

BECKY. Maybe I should call a D.J. One a' the big ones. Then you could sit down with him and he could lay the charts out right in front of you. Show you exactly where you stand.

HOSS. That's a good idea. Good. Go get one. Get Galactic Jack and his Railroad Track. Tell him to bring his latest charts. Go on!

BECKY. O.K. I'll be back.

(*She exits.* HOSS *stalks around the stage building up his confidence.*)

HOSS. She's right! She's right goddamnit! I'm so fucking close. Knockin' at the door. I can't chicken out of it now. This is my last chance. I'm gettin' old. I can't do a Lee Marvin in the late sixties. I can't pull that number off. I've stomped too many heads. I'm past shitkicker class now. Past the rumble. I'm in the big time. Really big. It's now or never. Come on, Hoss, be a killer, man. Be a killer!

(*Music starts. He sings "Cold Killer."*)

"Cold Killer"
I'm a cold killer Mama—I got blood on my jeans
I got a Scorpion star hangin' over me
I got snakes in my pockets and a razor in my boot
You better watch it don't get you—It's faster'n you
    can shoot
I got the fastest action in East L.A.
I got the fastest action in San Berdoo
And if you don't believe it lemme shoot it to you

Now watch me slide into power glide—supercharged
    down the line
There ain't no way for you to hide from the killer's
    eye
My silver studs, my black kid gloves make you cry
    inside
But there ain't no way for you to hide from the
    killer's eye

I'm a cold killer Mama—and I've earned my tattoo
I got a Pachooko cross hangin' over you
I got whiplash magic and a rattlesnake tongue
My John the Conqueroot says I'm the cold gun

Now watch me slide into power glide supercharged
    down the line
There ain't no way for you to hide from the killer's
    eye
My silver studs, my black kid gloves make you cry
    inside
But there ain't no way for you to hide from the
    killer's eye.

(*The song ends.* BECKY *enters with* GALACTIC JACK *the disc jockey. He's white and dressed like a 42nd Street pimp, pink shirt, black tie, black patent leather shoes, white panama straw hat and a flash suit. He talks like Wolfman Jack and carries a bundle of huge charts.)*

Ah! The man. Galactic Jack and his Railroad Track.

GALACTIC JACK.   That's me, Jim. Heavy duty and on the whim. Back flappin', side trackin', finger poppin', reelin' rockin' with the tips on the picks in the great killer race. All tricks, no sale, no avail. It's in the can and on the lam. Grease it, daddyo!

(He holds out his hand palm up for HOSS *to give him five.* HOSS *holds back.)*

HOSS.   Back down, Jack. Just give it to me straight. Am I risin' or fallin'.

GALACTIC JACK.   A shootin' star, baby. High flyin' and no jivin'. You is off to number nine.

HOSS.   Show me what you got. Just lay it out on the floor.

BECKY.   Shall I get ya'll some drinks?

HOSS.   Yeah. Tequila Gold. What do you take, Jack?

GALACTIC JACK.   Not me, baby. I'm runnin' reds all down the spine. Feelin' fine and mixin's a crime.

BECKY.   Right.

(She exits. JACK *lays his chart on the floor.* HOSS *and* JACK *crouch down to get a close inspection.)*

GALACTIC JACK.   O.K. Here's the stand on the national band. The game's clean now. Solo is the word. Gang war is takin' a back seat. The Low Riders are outa' the picture and you is in, Jim. In like a stone winner.

HOSS.   Don't type it up, Jack. Just show me how it's movin'. I was ready to take Nevada clean and that meathead Mojo Root Force rolled Vegas.

GALACTIC JACK.   Yeah I heard that. Supposed to be on your ticket too. Bad news.

HOSS.   He can't get away with that can he?

GALACTIC JACK.   I can't dope them sheets, Hoss. You'll have to consult a Ref for the rules or go straight to the Keepers.

HOSS.   I can't go to the game Keepers. They'll ask for an itinerary and question past kills. I can't afford a penalty now. I need every point.

GALACTIC JACK.   Well lookee here. There's movement all around but no numero uno. That's what they're backin' their chips on you for, boy. The bookies got you two to one.

HOSS.   That close?

GALACTIC JACK.   All of 'em runnin' it down to you. There's Little Willard from the East in his formula Lotus. Fast machine. Doin' O.K. with a stainless steel Baretta.

HOSS.   Willard's solo now?

GALACTIC JACK.   Yeah but no threat. Just a front runner. Lots a' early speed but can't go the distance. Here's one outa Tupalo called Studie Willcock. Drivin' a hot Merc,

dual cams, Chrysler through and through. Fast but not deadly. He's offered four in a week and almost had Arkansas wrapped up but he's fadin' fast. You're it, Jim. You is the coldest on the circuit.

HOSS.   What about this mark? *(Pointing at the charts.)*

GALACTIC JACK.   Oh yeah, that's Grease Jam. Got a supercharged Mini Cooper. Takes the corners. Tried a hit on St. Paul and almost had Minnesota to its knees when he blew a head gasket. Some say he's even been offed by the El Caminos.

HOSS.   Those guys are pressin' it pretty hard. They're gonna get blown off sooner or later.

GALACTIC JACK.   No doubt. No need to pout. The course is clear. Maybe a few Gypsy Killers comin' into the picture but nothin' to fret your set.

HOSS.   Gypsies? Where? I knew it. I got a feeling.

GALACTIC JACK.   Just some side bets. They go anonymous 'cause a' the code. One slip and they is pissed. You can dig it. They's playin' with the king fire.

HOSS.   But they got a following right? They're growing in the poles?

GALACTIC JACK.   Hard to suss it yet, man. Some poles don't even mention their kills for fear of the Keepers comin' down on 'em. I could maybe sound some flies for ya'. See if I could whiff some sniff on that action.

HOSS.   Yeah, do.

GALACTIC JACK.   What's the keen to the Gypsy scene. These boys are losin' to the cruisin' baby.

HOSS.   They've got time on their side. Can't you see that. The youth's goin' to 'em. The kids are flocking to Gypsy Kills. It's a market opening up, Jack. I got a feeling. I know they're on their way in and we're going out. We're gettin' old, Jack.

GALACTIC JACK.   You just got the buggered blues, man. You been talkin' to the wrong visions. You gotta get a head set. Put yer ears on straight. Zoot yerself down, boy. These Gypsies is committin' suicide. We got the power. We got the game. If the Keepers whimsy it all they do is scratch 'em out. Simple. They're losers, man. The bookies don't even look past their left shoulder at a Gypsy Mark. They won't last, man. Believe me.

HOSS.   I don't know. There's power there. Full blown.

GALACTIC JACK.   They don't know the ropes, man. Rules is out. They're into slaughter straight off. Not a clean kill in the bunch.

HOSS.   But they got balls. They're on their own.

GALACTIC JACK.   So are you. Solo's the payolo.

HOSS.   But I'm inside and they're out. They could unseat us all.

GALACTIC JACK.   Not a King. The crown sticks where it fits and right now it looks about your size.

HOSS.   What if they turned the game against us. What if they started marking us!

GALACTIC JACK.   That's revolution, man.

HOSS.   You hit it.

GALACTIC JACK.   Old time shuffle. Don't stand a chance at this dance.

HOSS.   But that's how we started ain't it. We went up against the Dudes. Wiped 'em out.

GALACTIC JACK.   The Dudes weren't pros, man. You gotta see where you stand. I do believe you is tastin' fear. Runnin' scared. These Gypsies is just muckrakers. Second hand, one night stand. They ain't worth shit on shinola in your league. Dig yourself on the flip side. You're number one with a bullet and you ain't even got the needle in the groove.

HOSS.   We'll see. Somethin's goin' down big out there. The shit's gonna hit the fan before we can get to the bank.

GALACTIC JACK.   Take a deep knee bend, Hoss. It's just the pre-victory shakes. Tomorrow you'll have the gold in your hand. The bigee. Don't be shy, I tell no lie. Catch ya' on the re-bop. Say bye and keep the slide greased down.

HOSS.   Yeah. Thanks.

(JACK *collects his charts and exits.* HOSS *paces and talks to himself.*)

(*To himself.*) Come on, come on. Confidence, man. Confidence. Don't go on the skids now. Keep it together. Tighten down. Talk it out. Quit jumpin' at shadows. They got you goose bumped and they ain't even present. Put yourself in their place. They got nothin'. You got it all. All the chips. Come on dice! Come on dice! That's it. Roll 'em sweet. The sweet machine. Candy in the gas tank. Floor it. Now you got the wheel. Take it. Take it!

(BECKY *enters with the drink.* HOSS *catches himself.*)

BECKY.   What happened to Jack?

HOSS.   We ran the session.

BECKY.   Here's your drink.

HOSS.   Thanks. Listen, Becky, is Cheyenne ready to roll?

BECKY.   Yeah. He's hot. Why?

HOSS.   Maybe we could just do a cruise. No action. Just some scouting. I'm really feelin' cooped up in here. This place is drivin' me nuts.

BECKY.   Too dangerous, Hoss. We just got word that Eyes sussed somebody's marked you.

HOSS.   What! Marked *me?* Who?

BECKY.   One a' the Gypsies.

HOSS.   It's all comin' down like I said. I must be top gun then.

BECKY.   That's it.

HOSS.   They gotta be fools, man. A Gypsy's marked *me?*

BECKY.   That's the word from Eyes.

HOSS.   Where is he?

BECKY.   Vegas.

HOSS.   Vegas? Oh now I get it. Mojo. He's hired a Gypsy to off me clean. That's it. That fuckin' chicken shit. I'm gonna blast him good. Doesn't have the balls to come down to me. Gotta hire a Gypsy.

BECKY.   Might be just a renegade solo, Hoss. They're all lookin' to put you under. You're the main trigger. The word's out.

HOSS.   Don't you get it? The Root Force is slip-streamin' my time. Takin' my marks and hirin' amateurs to rub me out. It's a gang shot. They're workin' doubles. I gotta team up now. It's down to that. I gotta get ahold a' Little Willard. Get him on the line.

BECKY.   Hoss, don't fly off, man. You're safe here.

HOSS.   Safe! Safe and amputated from the neck down! I'm a Marker man, not a desk clerk. Get fucking Willard to the phone! And tell Cheyenne to come in here!

(BECKY *exits.*)

O.K. Now the picture brightens. I can play for high stakes now. I can draw to the straight, outside or in. I'm ready to take on any a' these flash heads. Vegas is mine, man. It belongs in my pocket. The West is mine. I could even take on the Keepers. That's it. I'll live outside the fucking law altogether. Outside the whole shot. That's it. Why didn't I think a' that before!

(CHEYENNE *enters in green velvet with silver boots and racing gloves.*)

CHEYENNE.   You want me, Hoss?

HOSS.   Yeah! Yeah I want you! You're my main man.

(*He gives* CHEYENNE *a bear hug.*)

Listen, Cheyenne, we done a lotta' marks in our time. Right?

CHEYENNE.   Yeah.

HOSS.   Good clean kills. Honest kills. But now the times are changin'. The race is deadly. Mojo Root Force is movin' in on turf marks and tryin' to put me out with a Gypsy.

CHEYENNE.   A Gypsy?

HOSS.   Yeah.

CHEYENNE.   They can't do that. It's against the code.

HOSS.   Fuck the code. Nobody's playin' by the rules no more. We been suckers to the code for too long now. Now we move outside. You remember Little Willard?

CHEYENNE.   East Coast. Drove a Galaxie. Into Remington over and unders.

HOSS.   Yeah. He's changed his style now. Got himself a Lotus Formula 2 and a Baretta.

CHEYENNE.   Sounds mean.

HOSS.   He is, man. And I trust him. He was right with me when we took off the Dudes. Becky's on the phone to him now. He's our man. Just him and us.

CHEYENNE.   But Root Force has probably got Vegas locked up, Hoss. It's gonna be hard penetration.

HOSS.   We rolled Phoenix didn't we?

CHEYENNE.   Yeah.

HOSS.   Tucson?

CHEYENNE.   Yeah.

HOSS.   San Berdoo?

CHEYENNE.   Yeah.

HOSS.   So Vegas ain't no Fort Knox.

CHEYENNE.   So it's back to the rumble?

HOSS.   Temporary. Just temporary. We can't sit back and let the good times roll when the game's breakin' down.

CHEYENNE.   I don't know. I love the game, Hoss. I ain't hot to go back to gang war.

HOSS.   We got to now! Otherwise we're down the tubes.

CHEYENNE.   What about the Keepers?

HOSS.   Fuck them too. We'll take 'em all on.

CHEYENNE.   The critics won't like it.

HOSS.   The critics! They're outside, man. They don't know what's goin' on.

CHEYENNE.   What about our reputation. We worked hard to get where we are. I'm not ready to throw that away. I want a taste a' that gold.

HOSS.   I'm surrounded by assholes! Can't you see what's happened to us. We ain't Markers no more. We ain't even Rockers. We're punk chumps cowering under the Keepers and the Refs and the critics and the public eye. We ain't free no more! Goddamnit! We ain't flyin' in the eye of contempt. We've become respectable and safe. Soft, mushy chewable ass lickers. What's happened to our killer heart. What's happened to our blind fucking courage! Cheyenne, we ain't got much time, man. We were warriors once.

CHEYENNE.   That was a long time ago.

HOSS.   Then you're backing down?

CHEYENNE.   No. I'm just playin' the game.

(CHEYENNE exits.)

HOSS.   God! Goddamnit! This is gettin' weird now. Solo ain't the word for it. It's gettin' lonely as an ocean in here. My driver's gone against me and my time's runnin' thin. Little Willard's my last chance. Him and me. He's runnin' without a driver, so can I. The two of us. Just the two of us. That's enough against the Root Force. He's East Coast though. Maybe he don't know the Western ropes. He could learn it. We'll cruise the action. He'll pick up the streets. Cheyenne knows the West though. Born and raised like me. Backyard schoolin'. Goddamn! Why's he have to go soft now! Why now!

(BECKY enters.)

You get Willard?

BECKY.   No.

HOSS.   How come! I need him bad. Keep tryin'!!

BECKY.   He's dead, Hoss. Shot himself in the mouth.

HOSS.   Who told you?

BECKY.   His Rep. They just found him in New Haven slumped over an intersection. They say his car was still runnin'.

HOSS.   Why'd he go and do that? He was in the top ten and risin'.

BECKY.   Couldn't take it I guess. Too vulnerable. They found a pound of Meth in the back seat.

HOSS.   Becky, I'm marked. What the fuck am I gonna do? I can't just sit here and wait for him to come.

BECKY.   Least you'll know he's comin'. If you go out cruisin' he's liable to strike anywhere, any time. A Gypsy's got the jump on you that way.

HOSS.   What if I busted into Vegas myself? Just me. They'd never expect somethin' like that. I could take off Mojo and split before they knew what happened.

BECKY.   You're dealin' with a pack now, man. It ain't one against one no more.

HOSS.   Well what am I gonna do!

BECKY.   Wait him out. Meet him on a singles match and bounce him hard. Challenge him.

HOSS.   What if he snipes me?

BECKY.   We got the watch out. We'll give him the usher routine. Say that you've been expecting him. That'll challenge his pride. Then fight him with shivs.

HOSS.   Shivs! I ain't used a blade for over ten years. I'm out of practice.

BECKY.   Practice up. I'll get you a set and a dummy.

HOSS.   O.K. And call in the Doc. I need a good shot.

BECKY.   Good.

(She exits. HOSS stalks the stage.)

HOSS.   Backed into a fucking box. I can't believe it. Things have changed that much. They don't even apprentice no more. Just mark for the big one. No respect no more. When I was that age I'd sell my leathers to get a crack at a good teacher. I would. And I had some a' the best. There's no sense of tradition in the game no more. There's no game. It's just back to how it was. Rolling night clubs, strip joints. Bustin' up poker games, Zip guns in the junk yard. Rock fights, dirt clods, bustin' windows. Vandals, juvies, West Side Story. Can't they see where they're goin'! Without a code it's just crime. No art involved. No technique, finesse. No sense of mastery. The touch is gone.

(BECKY enters with DOC who is dressed in red. BECKY has two knives and a dummy which she sets up centre stage right. HOSS sits in his chair. DOC has a syringe and a vial of dope and a rubber surgical hose. HOSS rolls his sleeve up and DOC goes about shooting him up.)

Oh, Doc, it's good to see ya'. I'm in need. I'm under the gun, Doc.

DOC.   Yeah. Things are tough now. This'll cool you out.

HOSS. Good. Doc, what do you think about Gypsy Kills. Do you think it's ethical?

DOC. Haven't thought too much about it actually. I suppose it was bound to happen. Once I remember this early Gypsy. I guess you'd call him a Gypsy now but at the time he was just a hard luck fella name a' Doc Carter. Little got to be known of the man on account a' the fact that he was ridin' a certain William F. Cody's shirttail all through the West, and, for that matter, half around the planet. Anyhow, ole Doc came to be known as the "Spirit Gun of the West" and a well-deserved title it was, too. That boy could shoot the hump off a buffalo on the backside of a nickel at a hundred paces. To this very day his saddle is settin' in some musty ole Wyoming museum decorated with a hundred silver coins. Each one shot through and through with his Colt .45. And all surroundin' this saddle is pictures tall as a man of this William F. Cody fella pallin' it up with the Indians. Ole Doc never got out from behind the shadow a' that Cody. But I suppose nowadays he'd just take over the whole show. Don't rightly know what made me think a' that. Just popped into my mind.

HOSS. Yeah. It's just funny finding myself on the other side.

BECKY. It ain't revolution, man. This Gypsy's a hired trigger from Mojo. He ain't a martyr.

HOSS. But he works outside the code.

BECKY. Fuck it. All you gotta worry about is gettin' him before he gets you.

HOSS. You were one of the ones who taught me the code. Now you can throw it away like that.

BECKY. It's back down to survival, Hoss. Temporary suspension. That's all.

HOSS. I don't think so. I think the whole system's gettin' shot to shit. I think the code's going down the tubes. These are gonna be the last days of honor. I can see it comin'.

DOC. There. That oughta' do you for a while.

HOSS. Thanks, Doc.

DOC. If you need any crystal later just call me down.

HOSS. Thanks, man.

(Doc *exits.*)

BECKY. You wanna try these out?

(*She offers the knives to* HOSS. *He goes limp and relaxed in the chair.*)

HOSS. Not now. Just come and sit with me for a while.

(BECKY *sits at his feet. He strokes her hair.*)

Becky?

BECKY. Yeah?

HOSS. You remember the El Monte Legion Stadium?

BECKY. Yeah.

HOSS. Ripple Wine?

BECKY. Yeah.

HOSS. The Coasters?

BECKY (*she sings a snatch*). "Take out the papers and the trash or you don't get no spendin' cash."

HOSS (*sings*). "Just tell your hoodlum friend outside. You ain't got time to take a ride."

BECKY. "Yackety yack."

HOSS. "Don't talk back."

(*They laugh.* HOSS *stops himself.*)

Don't let me go too soft.

BECKY. Why not. You've earned it.

HOSS. Earned it? I ain't earned nothin'. Everything just happened. Just fell like cards. I never made a choice.

BECKY. But you're here now. A hero. All those losers out there barkin' at the moon.

HOSS. But where am I goin'? The future's just like the past.

BECKY. You gotta believe, Hoss.

HOSS. In what?

BECKY. Power. That's all there is. The power of the machine. The killer Machine. That's what you live and die for. That's what you wake up for. Every breath you take you breathe the power. You live the power. You are the power.

HOSS. Then why do I feel so weak!

BECKY. The knife's gotta be pulled out before you can stab again. The gun's gotta be cocked. The energy's gotta be stored. You're just gettin' a trickle charge now. The ignition's gotta turn yet.

HOSS. Yeah. It's just hard to wait.

BECKY. It's harder for movers. You're a mover, Hoss. Some people, all they do is wait.

HOSS. Maybe I should take a ramble.

BECKY. Where to?

HOSS. Anywhere. Just to get out for a while.

BECKY. You carry your gun wherever you go.

HOSS. Listen, maybe I should go on the lam.

BECKY. Are you crazy?

HOSS. No, I'm serious. I'm gettin' too old for this. I need some peace.

BECKY. Do you know what it's like out there, outside the game? You wouldn't recognize it.

HOSS. What about New York? Second Avenue.

BECKY. What Second Avenue? There ain't no Second Avenue. They're all zoned out. You wouldn't stand a snowball's chance in hell of makin' it outside the game. You're too professional. It'd be like keepin' a wild animal as a pet then turnin' him back loose again. You couldn't cope, Hoss.

HOSS. I did it once. I was good on the streets. I was a true hustler.

BECKY.   The streets are controlled by the packs. They got it locked up. The packs are controlled by the gangs. The gangs and the Low Riders. They're controlled by cross syndicates. The next step is the Keepers.

HOSS.   What about the country. Ain't there any farmers left, ranchers, cowboys, open space? Nobody just livin' their life.

BECKY.   You ain't playin' with a full deck, Hoss. All that's gone. That's old time boogie. The only way to be an individual is in the game. You're it. You're on top. You're free.

HOSS.   What free! How free! I'm tearin' myself inside out from this fuckin' sport. That's free? That's being alive? Fuck it. I just wanna have some fun. I wanna be a fuck off again. I don't wanna compete no more.

BECKY.   And what about the kill? You don't need that?

HOSS.   I don't know, maybe not. Maybe I could live without it.

BECKY.   You're talkin' loser now, baby.

HOSS.   Maybe so. Maybe I am a loser. Maybe we're all fuckin' losers. I don't care no more.

BECKY.   What about the gold record. You don't need that?

HOSS.   I don't know! I just wanna back off for a while. I can't think straight. I need a change. A vacation or something.

BECKY.   Maybe so. I heard about a place, an island where they don't play the game. Everybody's on downers all day.

HOSS.   That sounds good. What about that. Maybe you could find out for me. All I need is a week or two. Just to rest and think things out.

BECKY.   I'll see what I can do.

HOSS.   Jesus. How'd I get like this?

BECKY.   It'll pass.

HOSS.   Sing me a song or somethin', would ya? Somethin' to cool me off.

BECKY.   O.K.

(*She sings.*)

"Becky's Song"
Lemme take you for a ride down the road
Lean back in the tuck and roll
The radio's broken and I got no beer
But I can ease your load

    Listen to the song that the V-8 sings
    Watch the rhythm of the line
    Isn't it some magic that the night-time brings
    Ain't the highway fine

Tell me where ya' wanna go just take yer pick
All I'm really doin' is cruisin'
Take ya' down to Baton Rouge—New Orleans
Pick us up a Louisiana trick

    Listen to the song that the V-8 sings
    Watch the rhythm of the line
    Isn't it some magic that the night-time brings
    Ain't the highway fine

You could tell me stories of your yesterdays
I could break out a few a' mine
Roll down the window and kiss the wind
Anyway ya' want to ease the time

    Listen to the song that the V-8 sings
    Watch the rhythm of the line
    Isn't it some magic that the night-time brings
    Ain't the highway fine

(*The song ends and* CHEYENNE *enters.*)

CHEYENNE.   Say, Hoss. We just got tapped that the Gypsy's made it through zone five. He's headed this way.

HOSS.   Already? What's he drivin'?

CHEYENNE.   You won't believe this. A '58 black Impala, fuel injected, bored and stroked, full blown Vet underneath.

HOSS.   I'm gonna like this dude. O.K. let him through.

CHEYENNE.   All the way?

HOSS.   Yeah. Stop him at the mote and sound him on a shiv duel.

CHEYENNE.   Shivs? You ain't in shape for blades, Hoss.

HOSS.   I can handle it. Walk on.

CHEYENNE.   O.K. (*He exits.*)

BECKY.   Good. He's finally comin'. This'll get ya' back on your feet, Hoss. Your waitin' time is over.

HOSS.   Go tell the Doc I want some snow.

BECKY.   You want the fit or snort?

HOSS.   Snort. Hurry up.

BECKY.   Right.

(BECKY *exits.* HOSS *picks up the knives and stalks the dummy. He circles it and talks to the dummy and himself. As he talks he stabs the dummy with sudden violent lunges then backs away again. Blood pours from the dummy onto the floor.*)

HOSS.   O.K. Gypsy King, where's your true heart. Let's get down now. Let's get down. You talk a good story. You got the true flash but where's yer heart. That's the whole secret. The heart of a Gypsy must be there!

(*He stabs the heart of the dummy then backs off.*)

Maybe not. Maybe yer colder than that. Maybe in the neck. Maybe it pumps from the neck down. Maybe there!

(*He stabs at the neck then backs off. Blood gushes out.*)

All right. All right. A secret's a secret. I can give you that much. But it comes from this end too. I'm your mystery. Figure me. Run me down to your experience. Go ahead. Make a move. Put me in a place. An inch is fatal. Just an inch. The wrong move'll leave you murdered. Come on. Lemme see it. Where's the action? That's not good enough for the back lot even. Here's one!

(*He makes a quick move and stabs the dummy in the stomach.*)

Now I get it. There ain't no heart to a Gypsy. Just bone. Just blind raging courage. Well that won't do you, boy. That won't take you the full length. Yer up against a pro, kid. A true champion Marker. Yer outclassed before the bell rings. Now you've stepped across the line, boy. No goin' back. Dead on yer feet. (*To himself.*) What am I gettin' so wired about? This kid is a punk. It ain't even a contest. He's still ridin' in the fifties. Beach Boys behind the eyeballs. A blonde boy. A fair head. Gang bangs, cheap wine and bonfires. I could take him in my sleep. I could. I could—

(BECKY *enters with* DOC. DOC *has a large sheet of foil with mounds of cocaine on it. He sets it down on the chair.*)

BECKY.   How's it goin'?

HOSS.   Something's lacking. I can't seem to get it up like the other kills. My heart's not in it.

DOC.   Have some a' this.

(*He holds out a rolled up hundred dollar bill.* HOSS *takes it and goes to the coke.*)

HOSS.   Yeah. Maybe that'll help.

(*He takes the bill and snorts the coke as he talks.*)

You know, I been thinkin'. What if the neutral field state failed. One time. Just once.

BECKY.   Like this time for instance?

HOSS.   Yeah. Like this time.

BECKY.   Then you're a gonner.

DOC.   It shouldn't fail, Hoss. You've been trained.

HOSS.   I know, but what if an emotional field came through stronger.

BECKY.   Like love or hate?

HOSS.   Not that gross, not that simple. Something subtle like the sound of his voice or a gesture or his timing. Something like that could throw me off.

BECKY.   You're really worried about this Gypsy.

HOSS.   Not worried. Intrigued. His style is copping my patterns. I can feel it already and he's not even here yet. He's got a presence. Maybe even star quality. His movements have an aura. Even his short. I mean nobody rides a '58 Impala to do battle with a star Marker.

BECKY.   He's just a fool.

DOC.   You gotta stay disengaged, Hoss. The other way is fatal.

HOSS.   Maybe not. Maybe there's an opening. A ground wire.

BECKY.   For what. He's come to knock you over, man.

HOSS.   O.K. but I can play in his key. Find his tuning. Jam a little before the big kill. I don't have to off him soon's he walks in the door.

DOC.   You'd be better off. He's probably got eyes to work that on you.

HOSS.   I don't think so. He's got more class than that. I can feel him coming. We might even be in the same stream. He's got respect.

BECKY.   Respect! He's a killer, man.

HOSS.   So am I. There's another code in focus here. An outside code. Once I knew this cat in High School who was a Creole. His name was Moose. He was real light skinned and big, curly blond hair, blue eyes. He could pass easy as a jock. Good musician. Tough in football but kinda dumb. Dumb in that way—that people put you down for in High School. Dumb in class. He passed as white until his sister started hangin' around with the black chicks. Then the white kids figured it out. He was black to them even though he looked white. He was a nigger, a coon, a jungle bunny. A Rock Town boy from that day on. We ran together, Moose and me and another cat from Canada who dressed and wore his hair like Elvis. They put him down too because he was too smart. His name was Cruise and he got straight A's without readin' none a' the books. Slept in a garage with his aunt. Built himself a cot right over an old Studebaker. His mother was killed by his father who drove skidders for a lumber company up near Vancouver. Got drunk and busted her in the head with a tire iron. The three of us had a brotherhood, a trust. Something unspoken. Then one day it came to the test. I was sorta' ridin' between 'em. I'd shift my personality from one to the other but they dug me 'cause I'd go crazy drunk all the time. We all went out to Bob's Big Boy in Pasadena to cruise the chicks and this time we got spotted by some jocks from our High School. Our own High School. There were eight of 'em, all crew cut and hot for blood. This was the old days ya' know. So they started in on Cruise 'cause he was the skinniest. Smackin' him around and pushin' him into the car. We was right in the parking lot there. Moose told 'em to ease off but they kept it up. They were really out to choose Moose. He was their mark. They wanted him bad. Girls and dates started gathering around until we was right in the center of a huge crowd a' kids. Then I saw it. This was a class war. These were rich white kids from Arcadia who got T-birds and deuce coups for Xmas from Mommy and Daddy. All them cardigan sweaters and chicks with ponytails and pedal pushers and bubble hairdo's. Soon as I saw that I flipped out. I found my strength. I started kickin' shit, man. Hard and fast. Three of 'em went down screamin' and holdin' their balls. Moose and Cruise went right into action. It was like John Wayne, Robert Mitchum, and Kirk Douglas all in one movie. Those chumps must a' swung on us three times and that was all she wrote. We had all eight of 'em bleedin' and cryin' for Ma right there in the parking lot at Bob's Big Boy. I'll never forget that. The courage we had. The look in all them rich kids' faces. The way they stepped aside just like they did for "Big John." The three of us had a silent pride. We just walked strong, straight into that fuckin' burger palace and ordered three cherry cokes with lemon and a order a' fries.

DOC.   Those were the old days.

HOSS.   Yeah. Look at me now. Impotent. Can't strike a kill unless the charts are right. Stuck in my image. Stuck in a mansion. Waiting. Waiting for a kid who's probably just like me. Just like I was then. A young blood. And I gotta off him. I gotta roll him or he'll roll me. We're fightin' ourselves. Just like turnin' the blade on ourselves. Suicide, man. Maybe Little Willard was right. Blow your fuckin' brains out. The whole thing's a joke. Stick a gun in your fuckin' mouth and pull the trigger. That's what it's all about. That's what we're doin'. He's my brother and I gotta kill him. He's gotta kill me. Jimmy Dean was right. Drive the fuckin' Spider till it stings ya' to death. Crack up your soul! Jackson Pollock! Duane Allman! Break it open! Pull the trigger! Trigger me! Trigger you! Drive it off the cliff! It's all an open highway. Long and clean and deadly beautiful. Deadly and lonesome as a jukebox.

DOC.   Come on, Becky, let's leave him alone.

HOSS.   Yeah. Right. Alone. That's me. Alone. That's us. All fucking alone. All of us. So don't go off in your private rooms with pity in mind. Your day is comin'. The mark'll come down to you one way or the other.

BECKY.   You better rest, Hoss.

HOSS.   Ya' know, you'd be O.K., Becky, if you had a self. So would I. Something to fall back on in a moment of doubt or terror or even surprise. Nothin' surprises me no more. I'm ready to take it all on. The whole shot. The big one. Look at the Doc. A slave. An educated slave. Look at me. A trained slave. We're all so pathetic it's downright pathetic. And confidence is just a hype to keep away the open-ended shakes. Ain't that the truth, Doc?

DOC.   I don't know.

HOSS.   Right. Right. "I don't know" is exactly right. Now beat it, both of ya' before I rip your fuckin' teeth out a' yer heads!! GO ON BEAT IT!!!

(BECKY and DOC exit. HOSS sits in his chair and stares out in front of him. He talks to himself, sometimes shifting voices from his own into an older man's.)

(Old.) All right, Hoss, this is me talkin'. Yer old Dad. Yer old fishin' buddy. We used to catch eels side by side down by the dump. The full moon lit up the stream and the junk. The rusty chrome flashin' across the marsh. The fireflies dancin' like a faraway city. They'd swallow the hook all the way down. You remember that? (Himself.) Yeah.

Sure. (Old.) O.K. You're not so bad off. It's good to change. Good to feel your blood pump. (Himself.) But where to? Where am I going? (Old.) It don't matter. The road's what counts. Just look at the road. Don't worry about where it's goin'. (Himself.) I feel so trapped. So fucking unsure. Everything's a mystery. I had it all in the palm of my hand. The gold, the silver. I knew. I was sure. How could it slip away like that? (Old.) It'll come back. (Himself.) But I'm not a true Marker no more. Not really. They're all countin' on me. The bookies, the agents, the Keepers. I'm a fucking industry. I even affect the stocks and bonds. (Old.) You're just a man, Hoss. Just a man. (Himself.) Yeah, maybe you're right. I'm just a man.

(CHEYENNE enters.)

CHEYENNE.   Hoss, He's here.

(HOSS stays seated, relaxed. He has an air of complete acceptance.)

HOSS.   Good. He's here. That's good. What's his name?

CHEYENNE.   He calls himself Crow.

HOSS.   Crow. That's a good name. Did you sound him on the duel?

CHEYENNE.   Yeah. He's game. He looks tougher than I thought, Hoss.

HOSS.   Tough. Tough? (He laughs.) Good. A tough Crow.

CHEYENNE.   What'll I tell him?

HOSS.   Tell him I like his style. Tell him I'm very tired right now and I'm gonna cop some z's. He can take a swim, have a sauna and a massage, some drinks, watch a movie, have a girl, dope, whatever he wants. Tell him to relax. I'll see him when I come to.

CHEYENNE.   O.K. You all right, Hoss?

HOSS.   Yeah. Just tired. Just a little tired.

CHEYENNE.   O.K.

HOSS.   Thanks, man.

CHEYENNE.   Sure.

(CHEYENNE exits. HOSS stays seated looking out.)

HOSS.   Maybe the night'll roll in. A New Mexico night. All gold and red and blue. That would be nice. A long slow New Mexico night. Put that in your dream, Hoss, and sleep tight. Tomorrow you live or die.

ACT TWO

(SCENE: The stage is the same. The lights come up on CROW. He looks just like Keith Richard. He wears high-heeled green rock and roll boots, tight greasy blue jeans, a tight yellow t-shirt, a green velvet coat, a shark tooth earring, a silver swastika hanging from his neck and a black eye-patch covering the left eye. He holds a short piece of silver chain in his hand and twirls it constantly, tossing it from hand to hand. He chews a stick of gum with violent chomps. He *exudes violent arrogance and cruises the stage with true contempt. Sometimes he stops to examine the guns on the floor, or check out the knives and the dummy. Finally he winds up sitting in* HOSS's *chair. A pause as he chews gum at the audience.* HOSS *enters dressed the same as in Act One.* CROW *doesn't move or behave any different than when he was alone. They just stare at each other for a while.*

HOSS.   My sleuth tells me you're drivin' a '58 Impala with a Vet underneath.

CROW.   Razor, Leathers. Very razor.

HOSS.   Did you rest up?

CROW.   Got the molar chomps. Eyes stitched. You can vision what's sittin'. Very razor to cop z's sussin' me to be on the far end of the spectrum.

HOSS.   It wasn't strategy man. I was really tired. You steal a lotta' energy from a distance.

CROW.   No shrewd from this end either. We both bow to bigger fields.

HOSS.   You wanna drink or somethin'?

CROW (*he laughs with a cackle*). Lush in sun time gotta smell of lettuce or turn of the century. Sure Leathers, squeeze on the grape vine one time.

HOSS.   White or red?

CROW.   Blood.

HOSS.   Be right back.

CROW.   No slaves in this crib?

HOSS.   They're all in the pool watchin' a movie.

CROW.   Very Greek.

HOSS.   Yeah. Just relax, I'll be right back.

(HOSS *exits.* CROW *gets up and walks around thinking out loud.*)

CROW.   Very razor. Polished. A gleam to the movements. Weighs out in the eighties from first to third. Keen on the left side even though he's born on the right. Maybe forced his hand to change. Butched some instincts down. Work them through his high range. Cut at the gait. Heel-toe action rhythms of New Orleans. Can't suss that particular. That's well covered. Meshing patterns. Easy mistakes here. Suss the bounce.

(CROW *tries to copy* HOSS's *walk. He goes back and forth across the stage practising different styles until he gets the exact one. It's important that he gets inside the feeling of* HOSS's *walk and not just the outer form.*)

Too heavy on the toe. Maybe work the shoulders down. Here's a mode. Three-four cut time copped from Keith Moon. Early. Very early. Now. Where's that pattern. Gotta be in the "Happy Jack" album. Right around there. Triplets. Six-eight. Here it comes. Battery. Double bass talk. Fresh Cream influence. Where's that? Which track. Yeah. The old Skip James tunes. Question there. Right there. (*Sings it.*) "I'm so glad, I'm so glad, I'm glad, I'm

glad, I'm glad." Yeah. Ancient. Inborn. Has to be a surgery. Grind down.

(*He hears* HOSS *coming and darts back to the chair and sits as though he'd never moved.* HOSS *enters with a bottle of red wine and two glasses. He hands one to* CROW *and then he pours himself one and sets the bottle down.*)

HOSS.   Ya know I had a feeling you were comin' this way. A sense. I was onto a Gypsy pattern early yesterday. Even conjured going that way myself.

CROW.   Cold, Leathers. Very icy. Back seat nights. Tuck and roll pillow time. You got fur on the skin in this trunk.

HOSS.   Yeah, yeah. I'm just gettin' bored I guess. I want out.

CROW.   I pattern a conflict to that line. The animal says no. The blood won't go the route. Re-do me right or wrong?

HOSS.   Right I guess. Can't you back the language up, man. I'm too old to follow the flash.

CROW.   Choose an argot Leathers. Singles or LPs. 45, 78, 33 1/3.

HOSS.   I musta' misfed my data somehow. I thought you were raw, unschooled. Ya' know? I mean, maybe the training's changed since my time. Look, I wanna just sound you for a while before we get down to the cut. O.K.? You don't know how lonely it's been. I can talk to Cheyenne but we mostly reminisce on old kills. Ya' know. I don't get new information. I'm starving for new food. Ya' know? That don't mean I won't be game to mark you when the time comes. I don't sleep standin' up. Ya' know what I mean? It's just that I wanna find out what's going on. None of us knows. I'm surrounded by boobs who're still playin' in the sixties. That's where I figured you were. Earlier. I figured you for Beach Boys in fact.

CROW.   That sand stayed on the beach with me. You can suss me in detail Leathers. What's your key?

HOSS.   This is really weird, me learnin' from you. I mean I can't believe myself admitting it. Ya' know? I thought I could teach you somethin'. I thought you were playin' to the inside. Choosin' me off just to get in the door. I mean I know you must be Mojo's trigger, right?

CROW.   De-rail Leathers. You're smokin' the track.

HOSS.   Eyes traced a Nevada route. It don't matter. If you ain't from the Root Force you're on the Killin' floor Jack. Anyway you cut it you're a corpse. So let's lay that one on the rack for now. Let's just suspend and stretch it out.

CROW.   We can breathe thin or thick. The air is your genius.

HOSS.   Good. Now, first I wanna find out how the Gypsy Killers feature the stars. Like me. How do I come off. Are we playin' to a packed house like the Keepers all say?

CROW (*he cackles*). Image shots are blown, man. No fuse to match the hole. Only power forces weigh the points in our match.

HOSS.   You mean we're just ignored? Nobody's payin' attention?

CROW.   We catch debris beams from your set. We scope it to our action then send it back to garbage game.

HOSS.   Listen chump, a lotta' cats take this game serious. There's a lotta' good Markers in this league.

CROW.   You chose ears against tongue Leathers. Not me, I can switch to suit. You wanna patter on my screen for a while?

HOSS.   Sorry. It's just hard to take. If it's true. I don't believe we could be that cut off. How did it happen? We're playing in a vacuum? All these years. All the kills and no one's watching?

CROW.   Watching takes a side seat. Outside. The Game hammered the outside.

HOSS.   And now you hammer us with fucking indifference! This is incredible. It's just like I thought. The Outside is the Inside now.

CROW (*he cackles*).   Harrison, Beatle did that ancient. It cuts a thinner slice with us. Roles fall to birth blood. We're star marked and playing inter-galactic modes. Some travel past earthbound and score on Venus, Neptune, Mars.

HOSS.   How do you get to fucking Neptune in a '58 Impala!

CROW.   How did you get to earth in a Maserati?

HOSS.   There! Why'd you slip just then? Why'd you suddenly talk like a person? You're into a wider scope than I thought. You're playin' my time Gypsy but it ain't gonna work. And get the fuck outa' my chair!!

(CROW *slides out of the chair and starts walking around, twirling his chain and chomping his gum. *HOSS* sits down. He sips his wine. Slowly through the dialogue *CROW* starts to get into *HOSS*'s walk until he's doing it perfect.*)

CROW.   Your tappets are knockin' rock-man. I sense an internal smokin' at the seams.

HOSS.   Yeah, so this is how you play the game. A style match. I'm beginning to suss the mode. Very deadly but no show. Time is still down to the mark, kid. How's your feel for shivs anyway?

CROW.   Breakdown lane. Side a' the road days.

HOSS.   Yeah, well that's the way it's gonna be. I ain't used a blade myself for over ten years. I reckon it's even longer for you. Maybe never.

(HOSS *begins to switch into a kind of Cowboy-Western image.*)

I reckon you ain't never even seen a knife. A pup like you. Up in Utah we'd use yer kind fer skunk bait and throw away the skunk.

CROW.   Throwin' to snake-eyes now Leathers.

HOSS.   So you gambled your measly grub stake for a showdown with the champ. Ain't that pathetic. I said that before and I'll say it again. Pathetic.

(CROW *is getting nervous. He feels he's losing the match. He tries to force himself into the walk. He chews more desperately and twirls the chain faster.*)

You young guns comin' up outa' prairie stock and readin' dime novels over breakfast. Drippin' hot chocolate down yer zipper. Pathetic.

CROW.   Time warps don't shift the purpose, just the style. You're clickin' door handles now. There'll be more paint on your side than mine.

HOSS.   We'd drag you through the street fer a nickel. Naw. Wouldn't even waste the horse. Just break yer legs and leave ya' fer dog meat.

CROW.   That's about all you'll get outa' second. Better shift it now Leathers.

(HOSS *shifts to 1920s gangster style.*)

HOSS.   You mugs expect to horn in on our district and not have to pay da' price? Da' bosses don't sell out dat cheap to small-time racketeers. You gotta tow da' line punk or you'll wind up just like Mugsy.

(CROW *begins to feel more confident now that he's got *HOSS* to switch.*)

CROW.   Good undertow. A riptide invisible moon shot. Very nice slide Leathers.

(HOSS *goes back to his own style.*)

HOSS.   Don't give me that. I had you hurtin'. You were down on one knee Crow Bait. I saw you shakin'.

CROW.   Fuel injected. Sometimes the skin deceives. Shows a power ripple. Misconstrued Leathers.

(CROW *is into *HOSS*'s walk now and does it perfect.*)

HOSS.   You were fish tailin' all over the track meathead! I had you tagged!

CROW.   Posi-traction rear end. No pit stops the whole route. Maybe you got a warp in your mirror.

HOSS.   There's no fuckin' warp. You were down!

CROW.   Sounds like a bad condenser. Points and plugs.

HOSS.   Suck ass! I had you clean! And stop walkin' like that! That's not the way you walk! That's the way I walk!

(CROW *stops still. They stare at each other for a second. *HOSS* rises slow.*)

All right. I can handle this action but we need a Ref. I ain't playin' unless we score.

CROW.   It's your turf.

HOSS.   Yeah, and it's stayin' that way. I'm gonna beat you Gypsy. I'm gonna whip you so bad you'll wish we *had* done the shivs. And then I'm gonna send you back with a mark on your forehead. Just a mark that won't never heal.

CROW. You're crossin' wires now Leathers. My send is to lay you cold. I'll play flat out to the myth but the blood runs when the time comes.

HOSS. We'll see. You're well padded Crow Bait but the layers'll peel like a skinned buck. I'm goin' to get a Ref now. You best use the time to work out. You ain't got your chops down. You're gonna need some sharpening up. When I get back it's head to head till one's dead.

(HOSS *exits. The band starts the music to* CROW's *song. He sings*.)

"Crow's Song"

CROW.

What he doesn't know—the four winds blow
Just the same for him as me
We're clutchin' at the straw and no one knows the
   law
That keeps us lost at sea

But I believe in my mask—The man I made up is me
And I believe in my dance—And my destiny

I coulda' gone the route—of beggin' for my life
Crawlin' on my hands and knees
But there ain't no Gods or saviors who'll give you
   flesh and blood
It's time to squeeze the trigger
But I believe in my mask—The man I made up is me
And I believe in my dance—And my destiny
The killer time—will leave us on the line
Before the cards are dealt
It's a blindman's bluff—without the stuff
To reason or to tell

But I believe in my mask—The man I made up is me
And I believe in my dance—And my destiny

(*The song ends.* HOSS *enters with the* REFEREE. *He's dressed just like an N.B.A. ref with black pants, striped shirt, sneakers, a whistle, baseball cap and a huge scoreboard which he sets up down right. He draws a big "H" on the top left side of the board and a big "C" on the other. He separates the letters with a line down the middle. As he goes about his business* HOSS *talks to* CROW.)

HOSS. I suppose you wouldn't know what's happened to my people? Becky. Cheyenne, Doc, Star-Man—they're all gone. So's my short.

CROW. Lotsa' force concentration in this spot Leathers. Could be they got bumped out to another sphere. They'll be back when the furnace cools.

HOSS. I don't fancy tap dancers Crow Bait. I like both feet on the ground. Nailed. Joe Frazier mode.

CROW. I vision you brought the rule, man.

HOSS. Yeah. He's gonna see that things stay clean. Points scored and lost on deviation from the neutral field state.

CROW. I'd say you already broke the mercury in round one.

HOSS. That don't count! We start when he's ready.

CROW. I can't cipher why you wanna play this course, Leathers. It's a long way from shivs.

HOSS. Just to prove I ain't outside.

CROW. To me or you?

(HOSS *considers for a second but shakes it off.*)

HOSS. I don't know how it is with you but for me it's like looking down a long pipe. All the time figurin' that to be the total picture. You take your eye away for a second and see you been gyped.

CROW. "Gyped"—coming from "Gypsy."

(*Through all this the* REF *puts himself through several yoga positions and regulated breathing exercises, cracks his knuckles, shakes his legs out like a track star and runs in place.*)

HOSS. I'm gonna have fun skinnin' you.

CROW. If narrow in the eye ball is your handicap then runnin' a gestalt match figures suicidal. Look, Leathers, may be best to run the blades and forget it.

HOSS. No! You ain't no better than me.

CROW. You smell loser, Leathers. This ain't your stompin' turf.

HOSS. We'll see.

CROW. It took me five seconds to suss your gait. I ran it down to Skip James via Ginger Baker. How long's it gonna take you to cop mine?

HOSS. I ain't a Warlock, I'm a Marker.

CROW. So stick to steel. Pistols. How 'bout the ancient chicken? Maserati against the Chevy. That's fair.

HOSS. I see you turnin' me in. I ain't stupid. I'm stickin' with this route Gypsy and that's what you want so can the horseshit. There's no Marker on the planet can out-kill me with no kinda' weapon or machine. You'd die with the flag still in the air. That's straight on. But too easy. I'm tired of easy marks. I'm drawin' to the flush. I'm gonna leave you paralyzed alive. Amputated from the neck down.

CROW. Just like you.

HOSS. We'll see.

(REF *wipes himself off with a towel and tests his whistle.*)

REF. All right. Let's get the show on the road. We all know the rules. When the bell rings, come out swingin'. When it rings again go to your corners. No bear hugs, rabbit punches, body pins or holdin' on. If a man goes down we give him five and that's it. After that you can kick the shit out of him. Ready? Let's have it!

(*An off-stage bell rings. The band starts slow, low-keyed lead guitar and bass music, it should be a lurking evil sound like the "Sister Morphine" cut on "Sticky Fingers."* HOSS *and* CROW *begin to move to the music, not really dancing but* feeling the power in their movements through the music. They each pick up microphones. They begin their assaults just talking the words in rhythmic patterns, sometimes going with the music, sometimes counterpointing it. As the round progresses the music builds with drums and piano coming in, maybe a rhythm guitar too. Their voices build so that sometimes they sing the words or shout. The words remain as intelligible as possible like a sort of talking opera.)

Round 1

CROW.   Pants down. The moon show. Ass out the window. Belt lash. Whip lash. Side slash to the kid with a lisp. The dumb kid. The loser. The runt. The mutt. The shame kid. Kid on his belly. Belly to the blacktop. Slide on the rooftop. Slide through the parkin' lot. Slide kid. Shame kid. Slide. Slide.

HOSS.   Never catch me with beer in my hand. Never caught me with my pecker out. Never get caught. Never once. Never, never. Fast on the hoof. Fast on the roof. Fast through the still night. Faster than the headlight. Fast to the move.

CROW.   Catch ya' outa' breath by the railroad track.

HOSS.   Never got caught!

CROW.   Catch ya' with yer pants down. Whip ya' with a belt. Whup ya' up one side and down to the other. Whup ya' all night long. Whup ya' to the train time. Leave ya' bleedin' and cryin'. Leave ya' cryin' for Ma. All through the night. All through the night long. Shame on the kid. Little dumb kid with a lisp in his mouth. Bleedin' up one side and down to the other.

HOSS.   No! Moved to a hard town. Moved in the midnight.

CROW.   Comin' in a wet dream. Pissin' on the pillow. Naked on a pillow. Naked in a bedroom. Naked in a bathroom. Beatin' meat to the face in a mirror. Beatin' it raw. Beatin' till the blood come. Pissin' blood on the floor. Hidin' dirty pictures. Hide 'em from his Ma. Hide 'em from Pa. Hide 'em from the teacher.

HOSS.   Never did happen! You got a high heel. Step to the lisp. Counter you, never me. Back steppin' Crow Bait. History don't cut it. History's in the pocket.

CROW.   The marks show clean through. Look to the guard. That's where it hides. Lurkin' like a wet hawk. Scuffle mark. Belt mark. Tune to the rumble. The first to run. The shame kid. The first on his heel. Shame on the shame kid. Never live it down. Never show his true face. Last in line. Never face a showdown. Never meet a face-off. Never make a clean break. Long line a' losers.

(All the other characters from Act One come on dressed in purple cheerleader outfits. Each has a pom-pom in one hand and a big card with the word ''Victory'' printed on it. They do a silent routine, mouthing the word ''Victory'' over and over and shaking their pom-poms. They move around the stage doing a shuffle step and stupid routines just like at the

football games. CROW and HOSS keep up the battle concentrating on each other. The REF bobs in and out between them, watching their moves closely like a fight ref.)

HOSS.   Missed the whole era. Never touched the back seat.

CROW.   Coughin' in the corner. Dyin' from phenmonia. Can't play after dinner. Lonely in a bedroom. Dyin' for attention. Starts to hit the small time. Knockin' over pay phones. Rollin' over Beethoven. Rockin' phenmonia. Be-boppin' to the Fat Man. Driving' to the small talk. Gotta make his big mark. Take a crack at the teacher. Find him in the can can. There he's doin' time time. Losin' like a wino. Got losin' on his mind. Got losin' all the time.

HOSS.   You can't do that!

(At some point the cheerleaders all come downstage in a line, turn their backs on the audience, take their pants down and bend over bare assed. When the bell rings marking the end of the round, they all turn around and show the reverse side of their cards which has the word ''Fight'' in big letters. Then they all hobble off with their pants around their ankles giggling like school kids.)

CROW.   In the slammer he's a useless. But he does his schoolin'. Tries to keep a blind face. Storin' up his hate cells. Thinks he's got it comin'. Bangin' out the street signs. Tryin' to do his time time. Turns into a candy-cock just to get a reprieve. Lost in the long sleeve. Couldn't get a back up. So he takes his lock up. Calls it bitter medicine. Makes a sour face. Gotta pay his dues back. Fakin' like a guru. Finally gets his big chance and sucks the warden's dinger. Gotta be a good boy. Put away the stinger. Put away the gun boy. I'll take away your time. Just gimme some head boy. Just get down on your knees. Gimme some blow boy. I'll give ya' back the key. I'll give ya' back the key boy! Just get down on my thing boy! Just get down! Get on down! Get on down! Get down! Get down! Get down! Come on!

(The bell rings. The music stops. The cheerleaders flash their cards and exit. REF goes to the scoreboard and without hesitation chalks up a big mark for CROW. CROW lies flat on his back and relaxes completely. He looks like he's dead. HOSS paces around nervous.)

HOSS.   What the fuck! What the fuck was that! (To the REF.) You call that fair? You're chalkin' that round up to him! On what fucking grounds!

CROW.   Good clean body punches. Nice left jab. Straight from the shoulder. Had you rocked on your heels two or three times. No doubt about it.

HOSS.   Are you kiddin' me! If flash and intensity is what you want I can give you plenty a' that. I thought we were shootin' honest pool. This kid's a fuckin' fish man. Nothin' but flash. No heart. Look at him. Wasted on his back and I'm still smokin'.

CROW (*looking at his watch*). Better get some rest. You got thirty seconds left.

HOSS.   I don't need rest. I'm ready to rock. It's him that's stroked out on the fuckin' floor, not me. Look at him. How can you give him the round when he's in that kinda' shape.

REF.   Good clean attack.

HOSS.   Clean! You call that clean? He was pickin' at a past that ain't even there. Fantasy marks. Like a dog scratchin' on ice. I can play that way if I was a liar. The reason I brought you into this match was to keep everything above the table. How can you give points to a liar.

REF.   I don't. I give 'em to the winner.

(*The bell rings.* CROW *jumps to his feet. The band strikes a note.* HOSS *steps in. He speaks to the band.*)

HOSS.   All right look. Can the music. This ain't Broadway. Let's get this down to the skinny.

REF.   What's going on! Play the round!

HOSS.   What'sa matter, Crowbait? Afraid to do it naked? Drop the echo stick and square me off.

CROW.   You should be past roots on this scale, Leathers. Very retrograde.

HOSS.   Don't gimme that. I wanna strip this down to what's necessary.

CROW (*laughing*). Necessity?

REF.   This is against the code. Either play this round or it's no match.

CROW.   We'll walk this dance so long as sounds can push round three. Certain muscles have gone green on me, Leathers. You can cipher.

(*The bell rings again.* HOSS *and* CROW *put down their mikes slowly and deliberately as though they both had knives and agreed instead to wrestle.* REF *moves around them. The band remains quiet.*)

Round Two

HOSS (*talking like an ancient delta blues singer*).   Chicago. Yeah, well I hear about all that kinda 'lectric machine gun music. All that kinda 'lectric shuffle, you dig? I hear you boys hook up in the toilet and play to da mirror all tru the night.

CROW (*nervously*). Yeah. Well, you know, twelve bars goes a long way.

HOSS (*growing physically older*). It come down a long way. It come down by every damn black back street you can move sideways through. 'Fore that even it was snakin' thru rubber plants. It had Cheetahs movin' to its rhythm. You dig?

CROW.   Yeah. Sure. It's a matter a' course.

(CROW *moves to get away from him as* HOSS *becomes a menacing ancient spirit. Like a voodoo man.*)

HOSS.   Yo' "yeah" is tryin' to shake a lie, boy. The radio's lost the jungle. You can't hear that space 'tween the radio and the jungle.

CROW.   It's in my blood. I got genius.

HOSS.   Fast fingers don't mean they hold magic. That's lost to you, dude. That's somethin' sunk on another continent and I don't mean Atlantis. You can dig where the true rhymes hold down. Yo' blood know that if nothin' else.

CROW.   Blood. Well listen, I need some spray on my callouses now and then, but it's not about endurance.

HOSS.   Ha! Yo lost dew claw. Extra weight. You ain't come inside the South. You ain't even opened the door. The brass band contain yo' world a million times over.

CROW.   Electricity brought it home. Without juice you'd be long forgot.

HOSS.   Who's doin' the rememberin'? The fields opened up red in Georgia, South Carolina. A moan lasted years back then. The grey and blue went down like a harvest and what was left?

CROW.   That scale hung itself short.

HOSS.   What was left was the clarinet, the bass drum, the trumpet. The fixin's for a salad. All hung gold and black in the pawnshop window. All them niggers with their hollers hangin' echoes from the fields. All the secret messages sent through a day a' blazin' work.

CROW.   I can't do nothing about that. I'm in a different time.

HOSS.   And what brought their heads up off the cement? Not no Abraham Lincoln. Not no Emancipation. Not no John Brown. It was the gold and black behind them windows. The music of somethin' inside that no boss man could touch.

CROW.   I touch down here, Leathers. Bring it to now.

HOSS.   You'd like a free ride on a black man's back.

CROW.   I got no guilt to conjure! Fence me with the present.

HOSS.   But you miss the origins, milk face. Little Brother Montegomery with the keyboard on his back. The turpintine circuit. Piano ringin' through the woods. Back then you get hung you couldn't play the blues. Back when the boogie wasn't named and every cat house had a professor. Hookers movin' to the ivory tinkle. Diplomats and sailors gettin' laid side by side to the blues. Gettin' laid so bad the U.S. Navy have to close down Storyville. That's how the move began. King Oliver got Chicago talkin' New Orleans, Ma Rainey, Blind Lemon Jefferson. They all come and got the gansters hoppin'.

CROW.   I'm a Rocker, not a hick!

HOSS.   You could use a little cow flop on yer shoes, boy. Yo' music's in yo' head. You a blind minstrel with a phoney shuffle. You got a wound gapin' 'tween the chords and the pickin'. Chuck Berry can't even mend you up. You doin' a pantomime in the eye of a hurricane. Ain't even got the sense to signal for help. You lost the barrelhouse, you lost the honkey-tonk. You lost your feelings in a suburban country club the first time they ask you to play ''Risin' River Blues'' for the debutante ball. You ripped your own self off and now all you got is yo' poison to call yo' gift. You a punk chump with a sequin nose and you'll need more'n a Les Paul Gibson to bring you home.

(REF *blows his whistle.*)

REF. Hold it, hold it, hold it!

(HOSS *snaps back to himself.*)

HOSS. What's wrong?
REF. I don't know. Somethin's funny. Somethin's outa whack here. We'll call this one a draw.
HOSS. A draw!
REF. I can't make heads or tails outa this.
HOSS. I had him cut over both eyes!
REF. We leave it. Let's get on with round 3.
HOSS. Look at him! He's unconscious standin' up.
REF. Play the round!

(*The bell rings.* CROW *jumps into action, dancing like Muhammad Ali.* HOSS *moves flatfooted trying to avoid him.* CROW *is now on the offensive. The music starts again.*)

Round 3.
CROW. So ya' wanna be a rocker. Study the moves. Jerry Lee Lewis. Buy some blue suede shoes. Move yer head like Rod Stewart. Put yer ass in a grind. Talkin' sock it to it, get the image in line. Get the image in line boy. The fantasy rhyme. It's all over the streets and you can't buy the time. You can't buy the bebop. You can't buy the slide. Got the fantasy blues and no place to hide.
HOSS. O.K., this time I stay solid. You ain't suckin' me into jive rhythms. I got my own. I got my patterns. Original. I'm my own man. Original. I stand solid. It's just a matter of time. I'll wear you to the bone.
CROW. Collectin' the South. Collectin' the blues. Flat busted in Chicago and payin' yer dues.
HOSS. Kick it out fish face! This time you bleed!

(REF *blows his whistle. The music stops.*)

REF (*to* HOSS). No clinches. This ain't a wrestlin' match.
HOSS. I was countering.
REF. Just keep daylight between ya'. Let's go.

(*The music starts again.* HOSS *goes back to the offense.*)

HOSS. (*to* REF). I was countering, man!
CROW. Ain't got his chops yet but listens to Hendricks. Ears in the stereo lappin' it up. Likes snortin' his horses too chicken to fix. Still gets a hard on but can't get it up.
HOSS. Backward tactics! I call a foul!

(REF *blows his whistle again.*)

REF. No stalls. Keep it movin'. Keep it movin'.

HOSS. I call a foul. He can't shift in midstream.
REF. Let's go, let's go.
HOSS. He can't do that!

(REF *blows his whistle again. The music comes up.*)

CROW. Can't get it sideways walkin' the dog. Tries trainin' his voice to sound like a frog. Sound like a Dylan, sound like a Jagger, sound like an earthquake all over the Fender. Wearin' a shag now, looks like a fag now. Can't get it together with chicks in the mag. Can't get it together for all of his tryin'. Can't get it together for fear that he's dyin'. Fear that he's crackin' busted in two. Busted in three parts. Busted in four. Busted and dyin' and cryin' for more. Busted and bleedin' all over the floor. All bleedin' and wasted and tryin' to score.

(REF *blows his whistle.*)

HOSS. What the fuck's wrong now?
REF. I'm gonna have to call that a T.K.O.
HOSS. Are you fuckin' crazy?
REF. That's the way I see it. The match is over.
HOSS. I ain't even started to make my move yet!
REF. Sorry.

(HOSS *lets loose a blood-curdling animal scream and runs to one of the pistols on the floor, picks it up and fires, emptying the gun into the* REF. REF *falls dead.* HOSS *should be out of control then snap himself back. He just stands there paralyzed and shaking.*)

CROW. Now the Keepers'll be knockin' down your hickory, Leathers.
HOSS. Fuck 'em. Let 'em come. I'm a Gypsy now. Just like you.
CROW. Just like me?
HOSS. Yeah. Outside the game.
CROW. And into a bigger one. You think you can cope?
HOSS. With the Gypsies? Why not. You could teach me. I could pick it up fast.
CROW. You wanna be like me now?
HOSS. Not exactly. Just help me into the style. I'll develop my own image. I'm an original man. A one and only. I just need some help.
CROW. But I beat you cold. I don't owe you nothin'.
HOSS. All right. Look. I'll set you up with a new short and some threads in exchange for some lessons.
CROW. No throw Leathers.
HOSS. I'll give ya' all my weapons and throw in some dope. How's that?
CROW. Can't hack it.
HOSS. All right, what do you want? Anything. It's all yours.

(CROW *pauses.*)

CROW.   O.K. This is what I want. All your turf from Phoenix to San Berdoo clear up to Napa Valley and back. The whole shot. That's what I want.

(HOSS *pauses for a while, stunned. Then a smile of recognition comes over him.*)

HOSS.   Now I get it. I should cut you in half right now. I shoulda' slit yer throat soon's you came through the door. You must be outa' yer fuckin' cake man! All my turf?! You know how long it's taken me to collect that ground. You know how many kills it's taken! I'm a fuckin' champion man. Not an amateur. All my turf! That's all I got.

CROW.   Yer throwin' away yer reputation, so why not give me yer turf. You got nothin' to lose. It won't do you no good once the Keepers suss this murder.

HOSS.   I still got power. The turf is my power. Without that I'm nothin'. I can survive without the image, but a Marker without no turf is just out to lunch.

CROW.   I thought you wanted to cop Gypsy style.

HOSS.   I do but I need my turf!

CROW.   The Gypsies float their ground, man. Nobody sets up colors.

HOSS.   *You* want it bad enough. What's a' matter with you. You movin' outa' Gypsy ranks?

CROW.   Razor Leathers.

HOSS.   Wait a minute. You tricked me. You wanna trade places with me? You had this planned right from the start.

CROW.   Very razor. An even trade. I give you my style and I take your turf.

HOSS.   That's easy for you and hard for me.

CROW.   You got no choice.

HOSS.   I could just move out like I am and keep everything. I could make it like that.

CROW.   Try it.

HOSS.   You got it all worked out don't ya, fish face? You run me through a few tricks, take everything I got and send me out to die like a chump. Well I ain't fallin' for it.

CROW.   Then what're you gonna do?

HOSS.   I'll think a' somethin'. What if we teamed up? Yeah! That's it! You, me and Cheyenne. We start a Gypsy pack.

CROW.   I'm a solo man. So are you. We'd do each other in. Who'd be the leader?

HOSS.   We don't need a leader. Cheyenne could be the leader.

CROW.   Not on my time. Rip that one up, Leathers.

HOSS.   How did this happen? This ain't the way it's supposed to happen. Why do you wanna be like me anyway. Look at me. Everything was going so good. I had everything at my finger-tips. Now I'm outa' control. I'm pulled and pushed around from one image to another. Nothin' takes a solid form. Nothin' sure and final. Where do I stand! Where the fuck do I stand!

CROW.   Alone, Leathers.

HOSS.   Yeah, well I guess I don't got your smarts. That's for sure. You played me just right. Sucked me right into it. There's nothin' to do but call ya'. All right. The turf's yours. The whole shot. Now show me how to be a man.

CROW.   A man's too hard, Leathers. Too many doors to that room. A Gypsy's easy. Here, chew on some sap.

(*He hands* HOSS *a stick of gum.* HOSS *chews it in a defeated way.*)

Bite down. Chew beyond yourself. That's what ya' wanna shoot for. Beyond. Walk like ya' got knives on yer heels. Talk like a fire. The eyes are important. First you gotta learn yer eyes. Now look here. Look in my eyes. Straight out.

(HOSS *stands close to* CROW's *face and looks in his eyes.* CROW *stares back.*)

No! Yer lookin' in. Back at yourself. You gotta look out. Straight into me and out the back a' my head. Like my eyes were tunnels goin' straight through to daylight. That's better. More. Cut me in half. Get mean. There's too much pity, man. Too much empathy. That's not the target. Use yer eyes like a weapon. Not defensive. Offensive. Always on the offense. You gotta get this down. You can paralyze a mark with a good set of eyes.

HOSS.   How's that?

CROW.   Better. Get down to it. Too much searchin'. I got no answers. Go beyond confidence. Beyond loathing. Just kill with the eyes. That's it. That's better. Now. How do you feel?

HOSS.   Paralyzed.

CROW.   That'll change. The power'll shift to the other side. Feel it?

HOSS.   No.

CROW.   It'll come. Just hang in there. Feel it now?

HOSS.   No. Can I blink now?

CROW.   Yeah. Give 'em a rest.

(HOSS *blinks his eyes and moves away.*)

It'll come. You gotta practice like a musician. You don't learn all yer licks in one session. Now try out yer walk. Start movin' to a different drummer man. Ginger Baker's burned down. Get into Danny Richmond, Sonny Murray, Tony Williams. One a' them cats. More Jazz licks. Check out Mongo Santamaria, he might get yer heels burnin'.

(HOSS *starts moving awkwardly around the stage.*)

HOSS.   I never heard a' them guys.

CROW.   O.K. pick one. Any one. Pick one ya' like.

HOSS.   Capaldi.

CROW.   Too clean man. Try out Ainsley Dunbar. Nice hot licks. Anyone that gets the knife goin'. You gotta slice blacktop man. Melt asphalt.

HOSS. Keith Moon.

CROW. Too much flash. Get off the cymbals. Stop flyin' around the kit. Get down to it. Get down.

HOSS. Buddy Miles.

CROW. Just loud, man. Blind strength but no touch.

HOSS. Let's go on to somethin' else.

CROW. O.K. Body moves. Do a few chick moves. Fluff up yer feathers. Side a' the head shots. Hand on the hip. Let the weight slide to one side. Straight leg and the opposite bent. Pull on yer basket.

(HOSS *tries to follow.* CROW *acts out all the gestures with a slick cool.*)

Spit out yer teeth. Ear pulls. Nose pulls. Pull out a booger. Slow scratches from shoulder to belly. Hitch up yer shirt. Sex man. Tighten your ass. Tighten one cheek and loosen the other. Play off yer thighs to yer calves. Get it all talkin' a language.

HOSS. Slow down! I ain't a fuckin' machine.

CROW. Yer gettin' it. Yer doin' O.K. It's comin'. Talk to yer blood. Get it together. Get it runnin' hot on the left side and cold on the right. Now split it. Now put it in halves. Get the top half churnin', the bottom relaxed. Control, Leathers. Ya' gotta learn control. Pull it together.

HOSS. I'm not prepared. I can't just plunge into this. I gotta have some preliminaries.

CROW. O.K. You're right. Tell ya' what. Sit down in the chair and relax. Just take it easy. Come on.

HOSS. Maybe I'm too old.

CROW. Come on, just sit yerself down.

(HOSS *sits in the chair.* CROW *paces around him.*)

We gotta break yer patterns down, Leathers. Too many bad habits. Re-program the tapes. Now just relax. Start breathin' deep and slow. Empty your head. Shift your attention to immediate sounds. The floor. The space around you. The sound of your heart. Keep away from fantasy. Shake off the image. No pictures just pure focus. How does it feel?

HOSS. I don't know. Different I guess.

CROW. Just ease down. Let everything go.

(BECKY *comes on down left facing the audience. She wears a black wig and is dressed like Anna Karina in "Alphaville." She caresses herself as though her hands were a man's, feeling her tits, her thighs, her waist. Sometimes when one hand seems to take too much advantage she seizes it with the other hand and pushes it away.* HOSS *seems to turn into a little boy.*)

HOSS. You won't let nobody hurt me will ya'?

CROW. Nobody's gonna hurt ya'.

HOSS. Where have I been. All this time. No memory. I was never there.

(BECKY *talks straight out to the audience. But directs it at* HOSS.)

BECKY. I never knew you were that kind of a guy. I thought you were nice. A nice guy. I never thought you'd be like the others. Why do you do that? You know I'm not that kind of a girl. Come on. I just wanna talk. I wanna have a conversation. Tell me about yourself. Come on. Don't do that. Can't we just talk or something. All right, I wanna go then. Take me home. Come on. Let's go get a Coke. Come on. I mean it. Don't do that! Don't!

(*Her hands pull off her sweater. The wig comes off with it. She's wearing a stiff white bra underneath. She struggles against her hands then lets them go then struggles again.*)

Can't we go back? I'm going to be late. Can't we just kiss? No! Don't! Come on. I don't wanna do this. I'm not that kind of a girl. Look, just keep your hands off! I mean it. I don't like it. I just wanna talk. Tell me something nice.

(*Her hands rip off her bra and feel her tits.*)

Just talk to me. Tell me about your car. What kind of an engine has it got? Come on. Don't! Do you go racing a lot? Don't you take it down to the strip. No! Don't do that! Has it got overhead lifters. I really like those fat tires. They're really boss. Cut it out! No! Stop it! Don't!

(*Her hands unzip her skirt and tear it off. One hand tries to get inside her panties while the other hand fights it off.*)

I don't go all the way. I can't. I've never ever gone this far before. I don't wanna go all the way. I'm not that kind of a girl. I'll get pregnant. Stop it! All right, just get away from me! Get away! I'm getting out. Let me outa' the car! Let me out! Don't! Let go of me! Let go! (*She starts screaming.*) Let me out! Let me out! Let me out! Let me out!

(*She picks up her clothes and runs off.*)

CROW. How is it now?

HOSS. I don't know. Trapped. Defeated. Shot down.

CROW. Just a wave. Time to scoop a Gypsy shot. Start with a clean screen. Are you blank now?

HOSS. I guess.

CROW. Good. Now vision him comin'. Walking towards you from a distance. Can't make out the face yet. Just feel his form. Get down his animal. Like a cat. Lethal and silent. Comin' from far off. Takin' his time. Pull him to ya'. Can you feel him?

HOSS. I think so. It's me. He's just like me only younger. More dangerous. Takes bigger chances. No doubt. No fear.

CROW. Keep him comin'. Pull him into ya'. Put on his gestures. Wear him like a suit a' clothes.

HOSS.   Yeah. It *is* me. Just like I always wanted to be.

(*The band starts playing the first two chords to "Slips Away." CHEYENNE, STAR-MAN, DOC and GALACTIC JACK come on dressed in white tuxedos with pink carnations in their lapels. They stand in a tight group and sing harmony notes to the music. They move in perfect choreographed movements like the old a capella bands. The music should build slowly with HOSS's voice until he stops talking and the SINGERS go right into the song.*)

Mean and tough and cool. Untouchable. A true killer. Don't take no shit from nobody. True to his heart. True to his voice. Everything's whole and unshakeable. His eyes cut through the jive. He knows his own fate. Beyond doubt. True courage in every move. Trusts every action to be what it is. Knows where he stands. Lives by a code. His own code. Knows something timeless. Unending trust in himself. No hesitation. Beyond pride or modesty. Speaks the truth without trying. Can't do anything false. Lived out his fantasies. Plunged into fear and come out the other side. Died a million deaths. Tortured and pampered. Holds no grudge. No blame. No guilt. Laughs with his whole being. Passed beyond tears. Beyond ache for the world. Pitiless. Indifferent and riding a state of grace. It ain't me! IT AIN'T ME! IT AIN'T ME! IT AIN'T ME!!

(*He collapses in a ball and holds himself tight. The FOUR GUYS sing.*)

"Slips Away"
FOUR GUYS.
I saw my face in yours—I took you for myself
I took you by mistake—for me
I learned your walk and talk—I learned your mouth
I learned the secrets in your eye

But now I find the feelin' slips away
What's with me night and day is gone

Where you left off and I begin
It took me time to break the line
And on your own is tough enough
Without the thread that we got broken

But now I find the feelin' slips away
What's with me night and day is gone

If we could signify from far away
Just close enough to get the touch
You'd find your face in mine
And all my faces tryin' to bring you back to me

But now I find the feelin' slips away
What's with me night and day is gone

(*Repeat chorus.*)

(*The song ends. The FOUR GUYS exit.*)

CROW.   Hey, Leathers. Come on man it's time to cope. Get ready to bop. The world's waitin'.

(HOSS *doesn't move.*)

Leathers, you gotta move out to it now. I taught ya' all I know. Now it's up to you. You got the power.

(HOSS *rises holding the gun in his hand.*)

HOSS.   In the palm a' my hand. I got the last say.
CROW.   That's it. Get ready to roll. You're gonna knock 'em dead.
HOSS.   Knock 'em dead.
CROW.   Yeah. What about it.
HOSS.   You know somethin' Crow? I really like you. I really have respect for you. You know who you are and you don't give a shit.
CROW.   Thanks, Leathers.
HOSS.   I just hope you never see yourself from the outside. Just a flash of what you're really like. A pitiful flash.
CROW.   Like you?
HOSS.   Like me.
CROW.   No chance, Leathers. The image is my survival kit.
HOSS.   Survival. Yeah. You'll last a long time Crow. A real long time. You're a master adapter. A visionary adapter.
CROW.   Switch to suit, Leathers, and mark to kill.
HOSS.   Tough as a blind man.
CROW.   Tough enough to beat the champ.
HOSS.   Yeah. You win all right. All this. Body and soul. All this invisible gold. All this collection of torture. It's all yours. You're the winner and I'm the loser. That's the way it stands. But I'm losin' big, Crow Bait. I'm losin' to the big power. All the way. I couldn't take my life in my hands while I was alive but now I can take it in death. I'm a born Marker Crow Bait. That's more than you'll ever be. Now stand back and watch some true style. The mark of a lifetime. A true gesture that won't never cheat on itself 'cause it's the last of its kind. It can't be taught or copied or stolen or sold. It's mine. An original. It's my life and my death in one clean shot.

(HOSS *turns his back to the audience. And puts the gun in his mouth. He raises one hand high in the air and pulls the trigger with the other. He falls in a heap. This gesture should not be in slow motion or use any jive theatrical gimmicks other than the actor's own courage on stage. To save the actor's face from powder burns an off-stage gun should be fired at the right moment. CROW stands silent for a while.*)

CROW.   Perfect, Leathers. Perfect. A genius mark. I gotta hand it to ya'. It took ya' long enough but you slid right home. (*He calls off stage.*) All right! Let's go!

(BECKY *and* CHEYENNE *enter, dressed like they were in Act One.*)

Becky, get some biceps to drag out these stiffs. Get the place lookin' a little decent. We're gonna have us a celebration.

BECKY.   I had a feeling you'd take him. Was it hard?

CROW.   Yeah. He was pretty tough. Went out in the old style. Clung right up to the drop.

BECKY.   He was a good Marker man. One a' the great ones.

CROW.   Not great enough.

BECKY.   I guess not.

(*She exits.* CROW *talks to* CHEYENNE *who eyes him.*)

CROW.   You eye me bitter wheel-boy. What's the skinny?

CHEYENNE.   I guess you want me to drive for you now.

CROW.   Maybe I hear you're the top handler in the gold circuit.

CHEYENNE.   You hear good.

CROW.   I cipher you turnin' sour through. Suicidal like the master. I don't fashion goin' down to a Kami-Kazi collision just after I knock the top.

CHEYENNE.   You're cuttin' me loose?

CROW.   That's it.

CHEYENNE.   You got big shoes to fill Gypsy. They'll be comin' for you next.

CROW.   Naw. That's fer lames. I'm throwin' the shoes away. I'm runnin' flat out to a new course.

CHEYENNE (*looking at* HOSS's *body*).   He was knockin' at the door. He was right up there. He came the long route. Not like you. He earned his style. He was a Marker. A true Marker.

CROW.   He was backed up by his own suction, man. Didn't answer to no name but loser. All that power goin' backwards. It's good he shut the oven. If he hadn't he'd be blowin' poison in non-directions. I did him a favor. Now the power shifts and sits till a bigger wind blows. Not in my life run but one to come. And all the ones after that. Changin' hands like a snake dance to heaven. This is my time Cowboy and I'm runnin' it up the middle. You best grab your ticket and leave the Maserati with the keys.

CHEYENNE.   Sure.

(*He reaches in his pocket and pulls out the keys to the car.*)

Good luck.

(*He throws the keys at* CROW's *feet and exits.* CROW *smiles, bends down slowly and picks up the keys. He tosses them in his hand. The band starts the music.* CROW *sings* ''Rollin' Down.'')

''Rollin' Down''

CROW.
Keep me rollin' down
Keep me rollin' down
Keep me in my state a' grace
Just keep me rollin' down
I've fooled the Devil's hand
I've fooled the Ace of Spades
I've called the bluff in God's own face
Now keep me from my fate

If I'm a fool then keep me blind
I'd rather feel my way
If I'm a tool for a bigger game
You better get down—you better get down and pray

Just keep me rollin' down
Keep me rollin' down
Keep me in my state a' grace
Just keep me rollin' down.

(*The song ends. The lights go to black.*)

FOCUS QUESTIONS

1. Select two songs from the play and show how the lyrics advance characterization, action, or theme.
2. In what specific ways do the assaultive elements of language and action impinge on the audience?
3. Analyze the dynamics of the Hoss/Crow relationship.
4. In a short essay, discuss the impact of popular culture on the environment of the play.
5. Develop a character sketch of Becky Lou, with emphasis on her function in the play.
6. Compare the language styles of Hoss and Crow.

OTHER ACTIVITIES

1. Select an excerpt from the second-act confrontation between Hoss and Crow. Block the physical action around circular patterns of movement and recite the dialogue in a heightened, staccato/legato, rap-like intonation.
2. Develop a scrapbook of pictorial impressions to establish the atmosphere (that is, auditorium, stage set, costumes, and props) for a production of *The Tooth of Crime*.
3. Using available documents, compare two productions of the play and evaluate their differences.
4. Adhering to Shepard's style, take the play's ending ''one scene further.'' Record the scene and discuss the choices you made.

BIBLIOGRAPHY

Auerbach, Doris. *Sam Shepard, Arthur Kopit and the Off-Broadway Theatre*. Boston: Twayne, 1982.

Baker-White, Robert. ''Rock/Poetry: Popular Theatricality in *The Tooth of Crime*.'' *The Journal of American Drama and Theatre* (Winter 1990): 66–87.

Cohn, Ruby. *New American Dramatists 1960–1980*. New York: Grove Press, 1982.

Falk, Florence. ''The Role of Performance in Sam Shepard's Plays.'' *Theatre Journal* 33(1981): 182–98.

Malkin, Jeanette. *Verbal Violence in Contemporary Drama: From Handke to Shepard*. Cambridge: Cambridge University Press, 1992.

Marranca, Bonnie, ed. *American Dreams: The Imagination of Sam Shepard*. New York: PAJ Publications, 1981.

Mottram, Ron. *Inner Landscapes: The Theatre of Sam Shepard*. Columbia: University of Missouri Press, 1984.

Orr, John. *Tragicomedy and Contemporary Culture*. Ann Arbor: University of Michigan Press, 1991.

Oumano, Ellen. *Sam Shepard: The Life and Work of an American Dreamer*. New York: St. Martin's Press, 1986.

Powe, Bruce. ''*The Tooth of Crime:* Sam Shepard's Way with Music.'' *Modern Drama* 24(March 1981): 13–25.

Rosen, Carol. *Sam Shepard*. New York: St. Martin's Press, 1993.

Schechner, Richard. *Environmental Théater*. New York: Hawthorn Books, 1973.

———. ''Drama, Script, Theatre, and Performance.'' *The Drama Review* 17(September 1973): 5–36.

Shewey, Don. *Sam Shepard*. New York: Dell, 1985.

Tucker, Martin. *Sam Shepard*. New York: The Continuum Publishing Co., 1992.

Wilcox, Leonard, ed. *Rereading Shepard: Contemporary Critical Essays on the Plays of Sam Shepard*. New York: St. Martin's Press, 1992.

———. ''Modernism vs. Postmodernism: Shepard's *The Tooth of Crime* and the Discourses of Popular Culture.'' *Modern Drama* 30(December 1987): 560–73.

RECOMMENDED RECORDING

A Critical Look at Sam Shepard. One sound cassette. (1983 ATA convention papers). Eastern Audio Associates.

DEATH AND THE KING'S HORSEMAN
WOLE SOYINKA (1934–   )

Rather than polarizing cultures, Soyinka gently draws parallels between them . . . [he] is a cultural relativist who uses the different literary and dramatic traditions in order to create a theatrical synthesis.

—ISHMAEL REED

Norman Matlock as Elesin in *Death and the King's Horseman*, presented by the Goodman Theatre in 1979, under the playwright's direction. *Photo: Janie Goldberg/Andrea Gronvall, Margie Korshak Associates, Inc.*

APPROACHING YORUBA TRAGEDY

Nigeria, on the west coast of Africa, has an oral history that traces its Hausa, Benin, and Yoruba ancestry back over two thousand years. Although the other two cultures were subsumed under the religion of Islam during the Middle Ages, the Yoruba religious traditions of the southwestern area bordering on the Atlantic Ocean have been preserved. Even when the British took over as the colonial power in 1906, their indirect rule allowed the Yoruba people to maintain autonomous kingship authority over their various tribes. This system solidified the community ritual practices celebrating their ancestors and pantheon of gods despite relentless efforts of missionaries to convert them to Christianity.

The elasticity of the Yoruba worldview has enabled the community to survive years of colonization. They believe that their behaviors must be adapted to their surroundings to maintain a natural affinity with the forests, animals, and the ocean. They also believe that their community exceeds the world of the living to include all ancestors, those living in the present, and those yet unborn. Finally, they believe that "all experiences flow into each other."[1] This sense of harmony with the environment and with community continuity has allowed the traditional Yoruba culture to keep pace with technology and the modern world as scientific discoveries and modes of thought introduced by Europeans have been integrated into their society. The god of lightning, Sango, for example, has become the god of electricity.

Such adaptability and eclecticism have had a profound effect on the Nigerian theatre. The oral histories record how funeral rites were transformed into traveling court masques, *egungun,* which celebrated ancestors by allowing them to *materialize* through the use of costumes. Other narratives refer to masked mummers, who danced and performed acrobatic tricks for the pleasure of the tribal kings. By the seventeenth century, they were enacting traditional stories. Yoruba masque theatre continued to develop throughout the eighteenth century into traveling spectacles that included narrative, song, dance, mime, and poetry. When European drama was introduced by 1880, Nigerians combined their own traditions with European models in folk operas that included dance, songs, and improvised dialogue. Akin to musical revues, these operas are still performed and provide social and political commentary on topical events. The most recent development, however, has been a Nigerian English-language drama with roots in realism initiated by Africa's most successful and prolific playwright, Wole Soyinka.

Born in Abeokuta, Soyinka was a product of a Yoruba heritage and a Christian upbringing. While he was completing an Anglican education at St. Peter's, the grammar school where his father was headmaster, his mother and grandparents acquainted him with the religious practices, myths, and folklore of his ancestors. Since 90 percent of Abeokuta's people spoke the Yoruba language, he was surrounded by Yoruba music and ritual as well as the imagery, proverbs, and wordplay of his native tongue. As he continued his studies through Government College and University College in Ibadan, Soyinka brought together the disparate cultural threads of his childhood.

This process of comparison and synthesis crystallized under the tutelage of G. Wilson Knight, his mentor at the University of Leeds. In addition to his immersion in European dramatic theory and literature, Soyinka participated in all aspects of university theatre. He graduated in 1957 with honors from the School of English, having written *The Swamp Dwellers* and *The Lion and the Jewel,* plays in which he drew on European theatrical traditions to explore Yoruba themes. Eventually he used his practical and intellectual training in his capacity as a reader for the Royal Court Theatre in London. By 1959, *The Swamp Dwellers* was given a small, experimental production.

The fruits of Soyinka's intellectual endeavor to cross-fertilize Yoruba cosmology with Western dramaturgy resulted in his constructing a poetics of Yoruba tragedy. Soyinka focused on a belief that Greeks and Yoruba people share: that no human being can escape fate. Since the Yoruba worldview connects the life-death cycle in its sense of community—the world of the departed ancestors, this earthbound world of the living, and the world of the unborn—Yoruba people are faced with the dramatic conflict between answering their own desires and fulfilling their destinies. In addition, every action they take is measured by how it will affect the needs of the community in terms of its past, present, and future. By depicting this subjugation of the individual, Soyinka envisioned his plays as cathartic rituals, like the plays performed at the festival of Dionysus, that would allow his audiences to experience the crisis empathically and thus be impelled to initiate revolutionary change.

Soyinka returned to Nigeria in 1959 to forge a new drama that would not only celebrate the poetic imagery, linguistic rhythms, and folk idioms of the Yoruba culture but also generate the community consciousness necessary for people to act on current social and political problems. As a professor at the University of Ibadan, he established a Department of Theatre Arts and founded the 1960 Masks and the Orisun Theatre Company to revitalize English-language theatre in his country. His plays, revues, and radio dramas were written for these companies before he was imprisoned for political activities in 1967. After his release and exile, he returned to become Professor of Comparative Literature and Dramatic Arts at the University of Ife in 1976 where he founded the Guerrilla Theatre Unit two years later.

Soyinka has been a significant force not only in Nigerian theatre and politics, but throughout the world. As the initiator of a new aesthetic, he has introduced performance and literary styles of Nigerian drama and has implemented a political agenda for African theatre that has had ramifications for the entire post-colonial continent. Using theatre to restore health to society by making powerful statements about social injustice, he has demonstrated a courageous, unflagging commitment to human rights that has placed him at the forefront of African *lettres*. His efforts to give Yoruba traditions universal resonance have also won him international acclaim as an author, intellectual, and theatre artist. In recognition of these many contributions, he was awarded the Nobel Prize for Literature in 1986.

MAJOR WORKS

Soyinka's work for the theatre, in excess of twenty stage and radio plays as well as **agit-prop, guerrilla theatre** pieces, and political revues, is divided into periods that correspond to Nigeria's recent history. In England during the final years of the colonial regime, he wrote about Nigeria in transition in *The Swamp Dwellers* (1957) and *The Lion and the Jewel* (1959). With the onslaught of independence and the threat of military dictatorship in the wake of colonialism, he wrote *The Trials of Brother Jero* (1960), *A Dance of Forests* (1960), *The Strong Breed* (1964), *The Road* (1965), and *Kongi's Harvest* (1965).

After spending two years in solitary confinement, he responded to the end of civil war in *Madmen and Specialists* (1970), written after his release. While in exile in Ghana, Great Britain, and the United States during the military dictatorship of Yakubu Gowon, Soyinka completed three plays: *Jero's Metamorphosis* (1973); *The Bacchae of Euripides* (1973), which was commissioned by the British National Theatre; and *Death and the King's Horseman* (1975). Since his return to Nigeria in 1975, Soyinka's plays have reflected his concerns about politics and social issues of the African nations at large. These are an adaptation of Bertolt Brecht's *Threepenny Opera, Opera Wonyosi* (1977); *The Biko Inquest* (1979); *A Play of Giants* (1981); and *Requiem for a Futurologist* (1983).

Wole Soyinka has been prolific in every genre of literature. In addition to his many plays, he has published four volumes of poetry, three autobiographical works, two novels, two collections of critical essays, and two film scripts. When he was awarded the Nobel Prize, however, *Death and the King's Horseman* garnered special attention.

THE ACTION

Elesin Oba, the King's Horseman, stops in the marketplace on his way to complete the ritual of willing his own death. As the women dress him in rich clothes, he notices a virgin and lusts after her. Although she is already betrothed, the women of the marketplace can deny Elesin nothing and agree to allow him to marry her that evening before he leaves this world. While this union is being consummated, the district officer, Simon Pilkings, sends his sergeant to arrest Elesin before he ''commits death.'' Prevented by the market women from interfering, the sergeant returns and reports that the ritual may generate a riot. Pilkings determines to quell any outbreaks of violence by preventing the ritual from taking place.

Olunde, the son of Elesin Oba, has returned from England to fulfill the traditional task of burying his father. Arriving too late to dissuade Pilkings from disrupting the ritual, he confronts his humiliated father in chains. He must now preserve the honor of his family and the integrity of his people by taking his father's place. Tragically both father and son die as a result of colonial intervention, although it remains unclear if their suicides have reestablished order for the Yoruba people or have been committed in vain.

STRUCTURE AND LANGUAGE

As a point of departure for any revolutionary change in Nigeria, Soyinka insists on ''a reinstatement of the values authentic to that society, modified only by the demands of the contemporary world.''[2] To facilitate this, he often sets his plays in historical moments during which these values have been tested. Thus *Death and the King's Horseman* focuses on an actual event that occurred during the British colonial period in 1945. Rather than depicting a clash of cultures, he shows how colonialism becomes a catalyst for the disruption of community integrity. Fictionalizing the well-known event, Soyinka explores how Elesin, one community leader, allows colonial intervention to support his more worldly desires, which weakens his resolve to die and join the king in the world of the ancestors. As a result, his son must die. This goes against the natural order, like the young shoot that ''has poured its sap into the parent stalk.'' Because of Elesin's lack of will, the Yoruba world is ''tilted from its groove,'' ''wrenched from its course,'' and sent ''tumbling in the void of strangers.'' This is the crisis facing post-colonial Nigeria. Through the play, Soyinka establishes the importance of individual sacrifice for the good of the community that once had allowed Yoruba culture to survive centuries of interference by invaders.

Soyinka uses a format similar to the traditional five-act structure for settings that alternate between the vibrant world of the village marketplace and the tawdry, imitative world of European colonials. In the first and third parts, the market is filled with men and women in brilliantly colored attire, who sing and dance to the accompaniment of live drums. They are at the center of their universe. This ''long-suffering home of Elesin's spirit'' is the site of life and death, where Elesin beds his new bride in a converted cloth stall covered in rich velvets and where he begins his dance of death to the poetry of the Praise-singer and the trance-inducing drum.

This intoxicating atmosphere is sharply contrasted with the second and fourth parts, which take place on the verandah of the Pilking's bungalow and in the decadent great hall of the Residency. A lonely tango accompanied by an old hand-cranked gramophone record and strains of the Viennese waltz mangled by the local police band expose a European culture bereft of any substance in its African context. Compared to the vitality and spectacle of the marketplace, the formalities of paying homage to the Prince of Wales are rendered superfluous. To outshine the other members of the British club costumed in various fancy dress from bygone eras, the Pilkings have usurped the exotic, native *egungun* costumes confiscated from cult leaders. Their desecration of the spiritual significance of these death-cult masques further underscores the vapidity of their colonial values and life-style.

The contrast between cultures is heightened through Soyinka's powerful handling of language as well: the rich poetic imagery and rhythmic speech patterns of the Praise-singer, Elesin, and the mother of the marketplace, Iyaloja, pitted against the direct colloquial, staccato prose of the colonials. Speaking of the uninterrupted Yoruba world, the Praise-singer conjures forth parallel lines of echoing images:

> In their time the great wars came and went, the little wars came and went; the white slavers came and went, they took away the heart of our race, they bore away the mind and muscle of our race. The city fell and was rebuilt; the city fell and our people trudged through mountain and forest to found a new home but . . . our world was never wrenched from its true course.

The dignity and pride intoned in these ancient recollections soar above the Resident's rigid manner and clichéd approach to preserving the British Empire:

> You realise how disastrous it would have been if things had erupted while His Highness was here . . . Nose to the ground Pilkings, nose to the ground. If we all let these little things slip past us where would the empire be, eh? Tell me that. Where would we all be?

Soyinka uses the Moslem sergeant Amusa's faltering English to comment further on Nigeria under colonial rule. Coming from a region where English is not the required language, Amusa remarks, "I tell you nobody go prove anyting tonight and anytime. Is ignorant and criminal to prove dat kin' prove." The young market women, who are required to use English as the official colonial language, make fun of him as one lower than the servants at the Residency, and they mock his employers by speaking in turn:

> You've kept the flag flying.
> We do our best for the old country.
> It's a pleasure to serve.
> Another whiskey old chap?
> You are indeed too too kind.
> Not at all sir. Where is that boy?
> Sergeant!

Thus they trick Amusa into snapping to attention and send him off as an unwelcome "eater of white left-overs."

Both worlds merge in the fifth and final part of the play. The setting is a prison "where the slaves were stored before being taken down to the coast." All along Elesin has been enslaved by his own human frailty, the "weight of longing on his earth-held limbs" that makes him yearn for rich clothes and one more night of sexual pleasure, rather than the strength to die. Near death, he transforms Pilking's intervention into a sign from the gods, committing "the awful treachery of relief" and allowing "the alien hand to pollute the source of his will." Soyinka has created an indelible visual metaphor for an Africa complicit in its enslavement to European advice and values. Rather than adhering to endemic and sustaining traditions, Africa has opted for a spiritual imprisonment.

Elesin's tragedy, emblematic of the stripping away of Africa's heritage, is expressed in Soyinka's handling of language and imagery in this finale. Once a grand manipulator of rhetoric, a trickster full of bravado, Elesin is reduced to a language as prosaic as that of the colonialists. Once he swore that he was ready for his destiny: "My rein is loosened./ I am master of my Fate. When the hour comes/ Watch me dance along the narrowing path/ Glazed by the soles of my great precursors." Now he can barely plead in self-defense: "My powers deserted me. My charms, my spells, even my voice lacked strength when I made to summon the powers that would lead me over the last measure of earth into the land of the fleshless.'' Once a great leader who was worthy of succulent meats, harvests of yams, palm wine, damask, and rich alari cloth, he is now one of the ''laggards who drag their feet in dung and vomit, whose lips are reeking of the left-overs of lesser men.'' Dishonored and disgraced for betraying his life's mission, he ends his life not in fulfillment of his destiny, but in despair over the loss of his son and at his own fallen state.

Death and the King's Horseman is an extended image of the loss of a future for Yoruba culture. Although Olunde, Elesin's son, has returned from England, signaling the triumph of Yoruba tradition over European education, his death marks the end of that ritual which most represents the continuity of the community. It is possible that Elesin's bride carries an unborn male child in her womb, yet there is no one left to teach him all the duties of a king's horseman, the oral tradition passed from father to son. This loss of a future embodies the dilemma facing Nigeria, which has molded itself along European lines, abandoned the richness of its native cultures, and replaced them with the emptiness of technocracy, the devastation of dictatorship, and the destruction of community viability in the face of materialistic gain. By contrasting the two worlds metaphorically and linguistically, Soyinka suggests that if Nigerians allow Yoruba culture to die and be supplanted by European models, their future will not be worth living.

DEATH AND THE KING'S HORSEMAN-IN-PERFORMANCE

Since its publication in 1975, *Death and the King's Horseman* has enjoyed accolades as a work of literary importance. Curiously, the play has been produced only five times, of which three have been directed by the playwright. The premiere was staged in December of 1976 in the new theatre of the University of Ife where Soyinka served on the faculty. Soyinka's additions to the well-known historical event on which the play was based had particular resonance for Nigerians who were still struggling for national identity after fifteen years of independence. Creating a communal ritual, Soyinka staged Elesin's dance from life to death with the King's chief attendant, played by Jimi Solanke, isolated on the wide, bare forestage, while the villagers sang antiphonally from the side balconies and the Praise-singer chanted his challenges and encouragements from his perch in the balcony. By physicalizing Elesin's psychic isolation in his journey through the transition between life and death, Soyinka underscored the human frailty behind Elesin's tragic hesitation. Ensuring the audience's engagement in the event and their empathic responses to the protagonist, Soyinka provided the necessary tools for the ritual catharsis to work its healing magic.

The U.S. premiere and second production of the play took place at the Goodman Theatre in Chicago in October 1979 under Soyinka's direction and featured Norman Matlock (Elesin Oba), Ben Halley, Jr. (Praise-singer), Celeste Heard (Iyaloja), Terry Alexander (Olunde), Jill Shellabarger (Jane Pilkings), and Alan Coates (Simon Pilkings). For this production, which traveled to the Kennedy Center in Washington, DC, in December of that year, some of the more complicated Arabic names and some of the traditional dances were rearranged to make the spirit of the play more accessible. Soyinka was applauded for his melding of the poetry, chorus, politics, and storytelling of native Yoruba folk opera with the European **well-made play** tradition. Billy Rowe praised the words and the music, claiming that ''they embrace the imagination and swing you into the midst of its make-believe to become a part of a living breathing reality.''[3] J. Linn Allen specifically noted the range of the play's dialogue ''from authoritative epic intensity to street sassiness to the antiseptic fatuity of the British middle class,'' as well as Soyinka's compassionate handling of all his characters, including the colonials who are seen from a biased, Afro-centric perspective.[4]

When artistic director Gregory Mosher invited the Nobel Prize-winning Soyinka to direct the play at the Vivian Beaumont in New York City in March 1987, no one was prepared for the hostile response from the press. The spectacle of the market vendors in their colorful costumes trooping down the theatre aisles, the overwhelming eerie quality of the *gbedu* drumming, and the symbolic dancing with whirling robes and circling steps were part of a seductive pageant designed to pull spectators into the performance. But New York critics refused to deal with the production on its own terms and judged the acting as uneven. Mosher later speculated that "Soyinka's unwillingness or, rather, lack of interest in presenting the play in Western terms became a kind of affront, and triggered denials of the production's validity."[5]

Although Toni Morrison was dissatisfied with the acting, she defended the play to hostile New York critics:

> Soyinka's play is powerful theater. And serious, and beautiful, and complex. But most of all, most of all, it is intelligent—it is about something. During intermission, several people kept saying (in various ways) "I want to go home and read this." Bad news perhaps for the production? But good news about the play. I had read *Death and the King's Horseman* some years ago and, after the performance at Lincoln Center, I read it again. I thought about it, remembered it, knew I wanted it done again, and again. I wondered how X would have directed it. How Y would have handled this role, or that. How the relentlessness of human behavior informs every gesture, no matter how playful. I wondered about spiritual excess and the will to be right. Well, those are the kinds of questions audiences are preoccupied with when they have seen something provocative, strong and beautiful . . . I am still haunted by the ideas in Soyinka's play, but I can't go back to watch the play of them. *Death and the King's Horseman* closed a week short of its intended run.[6]

Ironically, in the eight years that had transpired since the first U.S. production, Soyinka determined that he would direct the play for the Vivian Beaumont as he had written it. So he worked with a company and trained them to perform as Africans. Under the limited constraints of a five-week union rehearsal schedule, he helped the black performers understand an alien cultural background, hear the different patterns of speech, and undercut what he considered an over-romanticization of African spirituality and religion. Perhaps such limited rehearsals had proven insufficient to support his shift from universal themes to the African perspective of the play.

The British premiere of *Death and the King's Horseman* in December 1990 at the Royal Exchange Theatre in Manchester has been the most innovative. In a production designed by Anthony Ward, Phyllida Lloyd directed her cast through the nuances of the play while augmenting its concept of ritual tragedy.

As an alternative to Soyinka's naturalistic stage directions, the black actors and musicians danced, drummed, and clowned before the waiting patrons in the theatre's foyer ten minutes before curtain. Then they migrated to the auditorium to open the play. Taking seats, the audience joined those in the marketplace where Elesin Oba, played by George Harris, and the Praise-singer, played by Peter Badejo, were in the midst of their witty banter, poetry, and riddles in preparation for Elesin's obligatory suicidal dance. The atmosphere was enhanced by the stage setting which was "a huge sheet of batik, black margined, with a sun-yellow circle for the acting space, leaving all further specifications to music, mime, and the merest handful of props."[7]

This powerful opening scene contrasted sharply with the bumbling yet sympathetic caricatures of the Pilkings who, seen through the eyes of Africans, have unthinkingly desecrated sacred Yoruba practices. Their *faux-pas* in wearing *egungun* dress was convincingly captured by Simon Dormandy's and Nicola Redmond's portrayals and by Dhobi Oparei's enactment of Sergeant Amusa's horror at their blasphemy. This production offered an un-flinching glimpse at both England's colonizing agents and those colonized, and it captured the immediacy of a culture on the brink of being undermined. Staged in front of an audience devoid of pretenses about the colonial experience, the effects served the playwright's vision successfully.

REFLECTIONS ON
DEATH AND THE KING'S HORSEMAN

Norman Matlock created the role of Elesin Oba for the American premiere of
Death and the King's Horseman *at the Goodman Theatre in Chicago.*

When I went down to read for *Death and the King's Horseman,* I almost blew it. I had not gone down to get the book early because I'm a first-down reader. I don't have a problem reading anybody's script, so when I finally got down to the audition—late—I had com-pletely forgotten about it and not knowing anything about the play, I said, "Well, so what?" But, instead of letting me go up and read, the woman conducting the audition handed me the book and said, "Take this home and read it." So, being cooperative, I took it.

I was amazed. There was no way I could have auditioned with this script without having read it through. I did not know how to play the first scene until I saw the last. Some of the things are common, like a minister jumping up and down in church, a braggard, the entertainer. All of that is in there. But the why! Once I realized the man was working up to his death, then certain things started to happen.

One other thing, and it was weird. Like I said, I'm a first-down reader. I do it right the first time. But this time! I had to learn the script verbatim—and deliver it—before I knew what I was doing. This ran absolutely counter to anything I have ever done.

Soyinka did not want the East-West struggle, or the Western society confrontation with ancient society. He wrote the play to explore the complexity between Elesin and the Yoruba society—the old Yoruba society, before the advent of modernization.

Elesin, this particular man—and it helps the play—was an extrovert. I play him full of life and possibly more maniac at this time, because he hasn't got long to live. These are his last few hours, so everything starts getting compressed.

I was surprised to realize that for the first three weeks of rehearsal, I read the last scene wrong, because of certain aspects of the tides and the flow of the language. As I learned more about the language, the rhythms imposed themselves. But, I could not read the script and say, "Well, this is how I will say this and this." It is the first time I have ever encountered writing of this nature.

Onstage, I can see that the Africans are enjoying the hell out of it, while the Amer-icans are simply enjoying. They're getting only 50 percent, and that's to knock them over. It is the nature of the beast. Played with a certain verve, it's almost impossible to go wrong.

I was surprised to realize how fast I move, physically. During a performance, I was making an entrance at the last scene and went charging up the ramp, yelling and screaming, and I hit the wall. Something must have been off: I don't know what, but I hit with such force that it knocked the wind out of me and I hit the floor. The actor behind me fell to cover the accident, not knowing if I could bounce back up. I did get up. As I played the scene, I looked down and there was blood on the stage. Blood was dripping from my hand, from my leg, from my toe. I thought to myself, "It's effective." Add realism. But, if they think they're going to keep this in, they're crazy!

I expected the leg to stiffen and really hurt the show, but it didn't. I danced at a party until early the next morning; it must have helped. Which brings me to another point: Now, I'm no dancer. I had given up deep-knee bends and exercises like that long ago. Too painful. The choreographer of this show, Darlene Blackburn, worked wonders.

This role has me doing things I never imagined. The verve I mentioned has to be real. My mechanical abilities have to be well rested. I cannot go out there and fake it. There is no bullshitting with this one. What could I fake? I have to do the shouts and the howls. I have to do the leaps. The cast gets it across to the audience that this is a man of stature, of substance, and is held in reverence in his community. What he wants goes, in particular, this night. He is the Horseman of the King. He is the chief.

Excerpted from BLACK STARS, *March 1980.*

Notes

1. *Derek Wright,* WOLE SOYINKA REVISITED *(New York: Twayne Publishers, 1993), 3.*
2. *Soyinka,* MYTH, LITERATURE AND THE AFRICAN WORLD *(Cambridge: Cambridge University Press, 1979), x.*
3. AMSTERDAM NEWS, *15 Dec. 1979.*
4. THE READER, *19 Oct. 1979.*
5. *"Introduction,"* THE NEW THEATRE REVIEW 1, *no. 2 (Summer 1987): 1.*
6. *"More Thought on* Death and the King's Horseman," THE NEW THEATER REVIEW 1, *no. 2 (Summer 1987): 11.*
7. *Grevel Lindlop, "Into the Realm of the Ancestors,"* TIMES LITERARY SUPPLEMENT, *7 Dec. 1990.*

DEATH AND THE KING'S HORSEMAN
WOLE SOYINKA

AUTHOR'S NOTE

This play is based on events which took place in Oyo, ancient Yoruba city of Nigeria, in 1946. That year, the lives of Elesin (Olori Elesin), his son, and the Colonial District Officer intertwined with the disastrous results set out in the play. The changes I have made are in matters of detail, sequence and of course characterisation. The action has also been set back two or three years to while the war was still on, for minor reasons of dramaturgy.

The factual account still exists in the archives of the British Colonial Administration. It has already inspired a fine play in Yoruba (Oba Wàjà) by Duro Ladipo. It has also misbegotten a film by some German television company.

The bane of themes of this genre is that they are no sooner employed creatively than they acquire the facile tag of 'clash of cultures', a prejudicial label which, quite apart from its frequent misapplication, presupposes a potential equality *in every given situation* of the alien culture and the indigenous, on the actual soil of the latter. (In the area of misapplication, the overseas prize for illiteracy and mental conditioning undoubtedly goes to the blurb-writer for the American edition of my novel *Season of Anomy* who unblushingly declares that this work portrays the 'clash between old values and new ways, between western methods and African traditions'!) It is thanks to this kind of perverse mentality that I find it necessary to caution the would-be producer of this play against a sadly familiar reductionist tendency, and to direct his vision instead to the far more difficult and risky task of eliciting the play's threnodic essence.

One of the more obvious alternative structures of the play would be to make the District Officer the victim of a cruel dilemma. This is not to my taste and it is not by chance that I have avoided dialogue or situation which would encourage this. No attempt should be made in production to suggest it. The Colonial Factor is an incident, a catalytic incident merely. The confrontation in the play is largely metaphysical, contained in the human vehicle which is Elesin and the universe of the Yoruba mind—the world of the living, the dead and the unborn, and the numinous passage which links all: transition. *Death and the King's Horseman* can be fully realised only through an evocation of music from the abyss of transition.

W. S.

CHARACTERS

Praise-Singer	Sergeant Amusa	The Resident
Elesin, *Horseman of the King*	Joseph, *houseboy of the Pilkingses*	Aide-de-Camp
Iyaloja, *'Mother' of the market*	Bride	Olunde, *eldest son of Elesin*
Simon Pilkings, *District Officer*	H. R. H. The Prince	Drummers, Women, Young Girls,
Jane Pilkings, *his wife*		Dancers at the Ball

The play should run without an interval. For rapid scene changes,
one adjustable outline set is very appropriate.

Note to this edition

Certain Yoruba words which appear in italics in the text are
explained in a brief glossary on page 1044.

SCENE ONE

*A passage through a market in its closing stages. The stalls
are being emptied, mats folded. A few women pass through
on their way home, loaded with baskets. On a cloth-stand,
bolts of cloth are taken down, display pieces folded and piled
on a tray.* ELESIN OBA *enters along a passage before the
market, pursued by his drummers and praise-singers. He is
a man of enormous vitality, speaks, dances, and sings with
that infectious enjoyment of life which accompanies all his
actions.*

PRAISE-SINGER.   Elesin o! Elesin Oba! Howu! What tryst
is this the cockerel goes to keep with such haste that he
must leave his tail behind?

ELESIN (*slows down a bit, laughing*). A tryst where the cockerel needs no adornment.

PRAISE-SINGER.   O-oh, you hear that my companions?
That's the way the world goes. Because the man approaches a brand new bride he forgets the long faithful
mother of his children.

ELESIN.   When the horse sniffs the stable does he not strain
at the bridle? The market is the long-suffering home of
my spirit and the women are packing up to go. That Esu-
harrassed day slipped into the stewpot while we feasted.
We ate it up with the rest of the meat. I have neglected
my women.

PRAISE-SINGER.   We know all that. Still it's no reason for
shedding your tail on this day of all days. I know the
women will cover you in damask and *alari* but when the
wind blows cold from behind, that's when the fowl knows
his true friends.

ELESIN.   Olohun-iyo!

PRAISE-SINGER.   Are you sure there will be one like me on
the other side?

ELESIN.   Olohun-iyo!

PRAISE-SINGER.   Far be it for me to belittle the dwellers of
that place but, a man is either born to his art or he isn't.
And I don't know for certain that you'll meet my father,
so who is going to sing these deeds in accents that will
pierce the deafness of the ancient ones. I have prepared
by going—just tell me: Olohun-iyo, I need you on this
journey and I shall be behind you.

ELESIN.   You're like a jealous wife. Stay close to me, but
only on this side. My fame, my honour are legacies to the
living; stay behind and let the world sip its honey from
your lips.

PRAISE-SINGER.   Your name will be like the sweet berry a
child places under his tongue to sweeten the passage of
food. The world will never spit it out.

ELESIN.   Come then. This market is my roost. When I come
among the women I am a chicken with a hundred mothers.
I become a monarch whose palace is built with tenderness
and beauty.

PRAISE-SINGER.   They love to spoil you but beware. The
hands of women also weaken the unwary.

ELESIN.   This night I'll lay my head upon their lap and go
to sleep. This night I'll touch feet with their feet in a dance
that is no longer of this earth. But the smell of their flesh,
their sweat, the smell of indigo on their cloth, this is the
last air I wish to breathe as I go to meet my great
forebears.

PRAISE-SINGER.   In their time the world was never tilted
from its groove, it shall not be in yours.

ELESIN.   The gods have said No.

PRAISE-SINGER. In their time the great wars came and went, the little wars came and went; the white slavers came and went, they took away the heart of our race, they bore away the mind and muscle of our race. The city fell and was rebuilt; the city fell and our people trudged through mountain and forest to find a new home but— Elesin Oba do you hear me?

ELESIN. I hear your voice Olohun-iyo.

PRAISE-SINGER. Our world was never wrenched from its true course.

ELESIN. The gods have said No.

PRAISE-SINGER. There is only one home to the life of a river-mussel; there is only one home to the life of a tortoise; there is only one shell to the soul of man; there is only one world to the spirit of our race. If that world leaves its course and smashes on boulders of the great void, whose world will give us shelter?

ELESIN. It did not in the time of my forebears, it shall not in mine.

PRAISE-SINGER. The cockerel must not be seen without his feathers.

ELESIN. Nor will the Not-I bird be much longer without his nest.

PRAISE-SINGER (*stopped in his lyric stride*). The Not-I bird, Elesin?

ELESIN. I said, the Not-I bird.

PRAISE-SINGER. All respect to our elders but, is there really such a bird?

ELESIN. What! Could it be that he failed to knock on your door?

PRAISE-SINGER (*smiling*). Elesin's riddles are not merely the nut in the kernel that breaks human teeth; he also buries the kernel in hot embers and dares a man's fingers to draw it out.

ELESIN. I am sure he called on you, Olohun-iyo. Did you hide in the loft and push out the servant to tell him you were out?

ELESIN *executes a brief, half-taunting dance. The* DRUMMER *moves in and draws a rhythm out of his steps.* ELESIN *dances towards the market-place as he chants the story of the Not-I bird, his voice changing dexterously to mimic his characters. He performs like a born raconteur, infecting his retinue with his humour and energy. More* WOMEN *arrive during his recital, including* IYALOJA.

> Death came calling
> Who does not know his rasp of reeds?
> A twilight whisper in the leaves before
> The great araba falls? Did you hear it?
> Not I! swears the farmer. He snaps
> His fingers round his head, abandons
> A hard-worn harvest and begins
> A rapid dialogue with his legs.
>
> 'Not I,' shouts the fearless hunter, 'but—
> It's getting dark, and this night-lamp

> Has leaked out all its oil. I think
> It's best to go home and resume my hunt
> Another day.' But now he pauses, suddenly
> Lets out a wail: 'Oh foolish mouth, calling
> Down a curse on your own head! Your lamp
> Has leaked out all its oil, has it?
> Forwards or backwards now he dare not move.
> To search for leaves and make *etutu*
> On that spot? Or race home to the safety
> Of his hearth? Ten market-days have passed
> My friends, and still he's rooted there
> Rigid as the plinth of Orayan.
>
> The mouth of the courtesan barely
> Opened wide enough to take a ha'penny *robo*
> When she wailed: 'Not I.' All dressed she was
> To call upon my friend the Chief Tax Officer.
> But now she sends her go-between instead:
> 'Tell him I'm ill: my period has come suddenly
> But not—I hope—my time.'
>
> Why is the pupil crying?
> His hapless head was made to taste
> The knuckles of my friend the Mallam:
> 'If you were then reciting the Koran
> Would you have ears for idle noises
> Darkening the trees, you child of ill omen?'
> He shuts down school before its time
> Runs home and rings himself with amulets.
> And take my good kinsman Ifawomi.
> His hands were like a carver's, strong
> And true. I saw them
> Tremble like wet wings of a fowl.
> One day he cast his time-smoothed *opele*
> Across the divination board. And all because
> The suppliant looked him in the eye and asked,
> 'Did you hear that whisper in the leaves?'
> 'Not I,' was his reply; 'perhaps I'm growing deaf—
> Good-day.' And Ifa spoke no more that day
> The priest locked fast his doors,
> Sealed up his leaking roof—but wait!
> This sudden care was not for Fawomi
> But for Osanyin, a courier-bird of Ifa's
> Heart of wisdom. I did not know a kite
> Was hovering in the sky
> And Ifa now a twittering chicken in
> The brood of Fawomi the Mother Hen.
>
> Ah, but I must not forget my evening
> Courier from the abundant palm, whose groan
> Became Not I, as he constipated down
> A wayside bush. He wonders if Elegbara
> Has tricked his buttocks to discharge
> Against a sacred grove. Hear him
> Mutter spells to ward off penalties
> For an abomination he did not intend.
> If any here

Stumbles on a gourd of wine, fermenting
Near the road, and nearby hears a stream
Of spells issuing from a crouching form.
Brother to a *sigidi,* bring home my wine,
Tell my tapper I have ejected
Fear from home and farm. Assure him,
All is well.

PRAISE-SINGER.   In your time we do not doubt the peace
of farmstead and home, the peace of road and hearth, we
do not doubt the peace of the forest.

ELESIN.

There was fear in the forest too.
Not-I was lately heard even in the lair
Of beasts. The hyena cackled loud. Not I,
The civet twitched his fiery tail and glared:
Not I. Not-I became the answering-name
Of the restless bird, that little one
Whom Death found nesting in the leaves
When whisper of his coming ran
Before him on the wind. Not-I
Has long abandoned home. This same dawn
I heard him twitter in the gods' abode.
Ah, companions of this living world
What a thing this is, that even those
We call immortal
Should fear to die.

IYALOJA.

But you, husband of multitudes?

ELESIN.

I, when that Not-I bird perched
Upon my roof, bade him seek his nest again.
Safe, without care or fear. I unrolled
My welcome mat for him to see. Not-I
Flew happily away, you'll hear his voice
No more in this lifetime—You all know
What I am.

PRAISE-SINGER.

That rock which turns its open lodes
Into the path of lightning. A gay
Thoroughbred whose stride disdains
To falter though an adder reared
Suddenly in his path.

ELESIN.

My rein is loosened.
I am master of my Fate. When the hour comes
Watch me dance along the narrowing path
Glazed by the soles of my great precursors.
My soul is eager. I shall not turn aside.

WOMEN.

You will not delay?

ELESIN.

Where the storm pleases, and when, it directs
The giants of the forest. When friendship
summons
Is when the true comrade goes.

WOMEN.

Nothing will hold you back?

ELESIN.

Nothing. What! Has no one told you yet
I go to keep my friend and master company.
Who says the mouth does not believe in
'No, I have chewed all that before?' I say I
have.
The world is not a constant honey-pot.
Where I found little I made do with little.
Where there was plenty I gorged myself.
My master's hands and mine have always
Dipped together and, home or sacred feast,
The bowl was beaten bronze, the meats
So succulent our teeth accused us of neglect.
We shared the choicest of the season's
Harvest of yams. How my friend would read
Desire in my eyes before I knew the cause—
However rare, however precious, it was mine.

WOMEN.

The town, the very land was yours.

ELESIN.

The world was mine. Our joint hands
Raised housepots of trust that withstood
The siege of envy and the termites of time.
But the twilight hour brings bats and
rodents—
Shall I yield them cause to foul the rafters?

PRAISE-SINGER.

Elesin Oba! Are you not that man who
Looked out of doors that stormy day
The god of luck limped by, drenched
To the very lice that held
His rags together? You took pity upon
His sores and wished him fortune.
Fortune was footloose this dawn, he replied,
Till you trapped him in a heartfelt wish
That now returns to you. Elesin Oba!
I say you are that man who
Chanced upon the calabash of honour
You thought it was palm wine and
Drained its contents to the final drop.

ELESIN.

Life has an end. A life that will outlive
Fame and friendship begs another name.
What elder takes his tongue to his plate,
Licks it clean of every crumb? He will
encounter
Silence when he calls on children to fulfill
The smallest errand! Life is honour.
It ends when honour ends.

WOMEN.   We know you for a man of honour.

ELESIN.   Stop! Enough of that!

WOMEN (*puzzled, they whisper among themselves, turning mostly to* IYALOJA). What is it? Did we say something to give offence? Have we slighted him in some way?

ELESIN. Enough of that sound I say. Let me hear no more in that vein. I've heard enough.

IYALOJA. We must have said something wrong. (*Comes forward a little.*) Elesin Oba, we ask forgiveness before you speak.

ELESIN. I am bitterly offended.

IYALOJA. Our unworthiness has betrayed us. All we can do is ask your forgiveness. Correct us like a kind father.

ELESIN. This day of all days . . .

IYALOJA. It does not bear thinking. If we offend you now we have mortified the gods. We offend heaven itself. Father of us all, tell us where we went astray. (*She kneels, the other women follow.*)

ELESIN.

> Are you not ashamed? Even a tear-veiled
> Eye preserves its function of sight.
> Because my mind was raised to horizons
> Even the boldest man lowers his gaze
> In thinking of, must my body here
> Be taken for a vagrant's?

IYALOJA. Horseman of the King, I am more baffled than ever.

PRAISE-SINGER. The strictest father unbends his brow when the child is penitent, Elesin. When time is short, we do not spend it prolonging the riddle. Their shoulders are bowed with the weight of fear lest they have marred your day beyond repair. Speak now in plain words and let us pursue the ailment to the home of remedies.

ELESIN.

> Words are cheap. 'We know you for
> A man of honour.' Well tell me, is this how
> A man of honour should be seen?
> Are these not the same clothes in which
> I came among you a full half-hour ago?

He roars with laughter and the women, relieved, rise and rush into stalls to fetch rich clothes.

WOMEN. The gods are kind. A fault soon remedied is soon forgiven. Elesin Oba, even as we match our words with deed, let your heart forgive us completely.

ELESIN.

> You who are breath and giver of my being
> How shall I dare refuse you forgiveness
> Even if the offence was real.

IYALOJA (*dancing round him. Sings*).

> He forgives us. He forgives us.
> What a fearful thing it is when
> The voyager sets forth
> But a curse remains behind.

WOMEN.

> For a while we truly feared
> Our hands had wrenched the world adrift
> In emptiness.

IYALOJA.

> Richly, richly, robe him richly
> The cloth of honour is *alari*
> *Sanyan* is the band of friendship
> Boa-skin makes slippers of esteem.

WOMEN.

> For a while we truly feared
> Our hands had wrenched the world adrift
> In emptiness.

PRAISE-SINGER.

> He who must, must voyage forth
> The world will not roll backwards
> It is he who must, with one
> Great gesture overtake the world.

WOMEN.

> For a while we truly feared
> Our hands had wrenched the world
> In emptiness.

PRAISE-SINGER.

> The gourd you bear is not for shirking.
> The gourd is not for setting down
> At the first crossroad or wayside grove.
> Only one river may know its contents.

WOMEN.

> We shall all meet at the great market
> We shall all meet at the great market
> He who gives early takes the best bargains
> But we shall meet, and resume our banter.

ELESIN *stands resplendent in rich clothes, cap, shawl, etc. His sash is of a bright red alari cloth. The* WOMEN *dance round him. Suddenly, his attention is caught by an object off-stage.*

ELESIN.

> The world I know is good.

WOMEN.

> We know you'll leave it so.

ELESIN.

> The world I know is the bounty
> Of hives after bees have swarmed.
> No goodness teems with such open hands
> Even in the dreams of deities.

WOMEN.

> And we know you'll leave it so.

ELESIN.

> I was born to keep it so. A hive
> Is never known to wander. An anthill
> Does not desert its roots. We cannot see
> The still great womb of the world—

No man beholds his mother's womb—
Yet who denies it's there? Coiled
To the navel of the world is that
Endless cord that links us all
To the great origin. If I lose my way
The trailing cord will bring me to the roots.

WOMEN.

The world is in your hands.

The earlier distraction, a beautiful young girl, comes along the passage through which ELESIN *first made his entry.*

ELESIN.

I embrace it. And let me tell you, women—
I like this farewell that the world designed,
Unless my eyes deceive me, unless
We are already parted, the world and I,
And all that breeds desire is lodged
Among our tireless ancestors. Tell me friends,
Am I still earthed in that beloved market
Of my youth? Or could it be my will
Has outleapt the conscious act and I have
    come
Among the great departed?

PRAISE-SINGER.   Elesin Oba why do your eyes roll like a bush-rat who sees his fate like his father's spirit, mirrored in the eye of a snake? And all those questions! You're standing on the same earth you've always stood upon. This voice you hear is mine, Oluhun-iyo, not that of an acolyte in heaven.

ELESIN.

How can that be? In all my life
As Horseman of the King, the juiciest
Fruit on every tree was mine. I saw,
I touched, I wooed, rarely was the answer No.
The honour of my place, the veneration I
Received in the eye of man or woman
Prospered my suit and
Played havoc with my sleeping hours.
And they tell me my eyes were a hawk
In perpetual hunger. Split an iroko tree
In two, hide a woman's beauty in its
    heartwood
And seal it up again—Elesin, journeying by,
Would make his camp beside that tree
Of all the shades in the forest.

PRAISE-SINGER.   Who would deny your reputation, snake-on-the-loose in dark passages of the market! Bed-bug who wages war on the mat and receives the thanks of the vanquished! When caught with his bride's own sister he protested—but I was only prostrating myself to her as becomes a grateful in-law. Hunter who carries his powder-horn on the hips and fires crouching or standing! Warrior who never makes that excuse of the whining coward—but how can I go to battle without my trousers?—trouserless or shirtless it's all one to him. Oka-rearing-from-a-camouflage-of-leaves, before he strikes the victim is already prone! Once they told me, Howu, a stallion does not feed on the grass beneath him: he replied, true, but surely he can roll on it!

WOMEN.   Ba-a-a-ba O!

PRAISE-SINGER.   Ah, but listen yet. You know there is the leaf-knibbling grub and there is the cola-chewing beetle; the leaf-nibbling grub lives on the leaf, the cola-chewing beetle lives in the colanut. Don't we know what our man feeds on when we find him cocooned in a woman's wrapper?

ELESIN.

Enough, enough, you all have cause
To know me well. But, if you say this earth
Is still the same as gave birth to those songs,
Tell me who was that goddess through whose
    lips
I saw the ivory pebbles of Oya's river-bed.
Iyaloja, who is she? I saw her enter
Your stall; all your daughters I know well.
No, not even Ogun-of-the-farm toiling
Dawn till dusk on his tuber patch
Not even Ogun with the finest hoe he ever
Forged at the anvil could have shaped
That rise of buttocks, not though he had
The richest earth between his fingers.
Her wrapper was no disguise
For thighs whose ripples shamed the river's
Coils around the hills of Ilesi. Her eyes
Were new-laid eggs glowing in the dark.
Her skin . . .

IYALOJA.   Elesin Oba . . .

ELESIN.   What! Where do you all say I am?

IYALOJA.   Still among the living.

ELESIN.

And that radiance which so suddenly
Lit up this market I could boast
I knew so well?

IYALOJA.   Has one step already in her husband's home. She is betrothed.

ELESIN (*irritated*). Why do you tell me that?

IYALOJA *falls silent. The* WOMEN *shuffle uneasily.*

IYALOJA.   Not because we dare give you offence Elesin. Today is your day and the whole world is yours. Still, even those who leave town to make a new dwelling elsewhere like to be remembered by what they leave behind.

ELESIN.

Who does not seek to be remembered?
Memory is Master of Death, the chink
In his armour of conceit. I shall leave
That which makes my going the sheerest
Dream of an afternoon. Should voyagers

> Not travel light? Let the considerate traveller
> Shed, of his excessive load, all
> That may benefit the living.

WOMEN (*relieved*). Ah Elesin Oba, we knew you for a man of honour.

ELESIN.   Then honour me. I deserve a bed of honour to lie upon.

IYALOJA.   The best is yours. We know you for a man of honour. You are not one who eats and leaves nothing on his plate for children. Did you not say it yourself? Not one who blights the happiness of others for a moment's pleasure?

ELESIN.

> Who speaks of pleasure? O women, listen!
> Pleasure palls. Our acts should have meaning.
> The sap of the plantain never dries.
> You have seen the young shoot swelling
> Even as the parent stalks begins to wither.
> Women, let my going be likened to
> The twilight hour of the plantain.

WOMEN.   What does he mean Iyaloja? This language is the language of our elders, we do not fully grasp it.

IYALOJA.   I dare not understand you yet Elesin.

ELESIN.

> All you who stand before the spirit that dares
> The opening of the last door of passage,
> Dare to rid my going of regrets! My wish
> Transcends the blotting out of thought
> In one mere moment's tremor of the senses.
> Do me credit. And do me honour.
> I am girded for the route beyond
> Burdens of waste and longing.
> Then let me travel light. Let
> Seed that will not serve the stomach
> On the way remain behind. Let it take root
> In the earth of my choice, in this earth
> I leave behind.

IYALOJA (*turns to* WOMEN). The voice I hear is already touched by the waiting fingers of our departed. I dare not refuse.

WOMAN.   But Iyaloja . . .

IYALOJA.   The matter is no longer in our hands.

WOMAN.   But she is betrothed to your own son. Tell him.

IYALOJA.   My son's wish is mine. I did the asking for him, the loss can be remedied. But who will remedy the blight of closed hands on the day when all should be openness and light? Tell him, you say! You wish that I burden him with knowledge that will sour his wish and lay regrets on the last moments of his mind. You pray to him who is your intercessor to the world—don't set this world adrift in your own time; would you rather it was my hand whose sacrilege wrenched it loose?

WOMAN.   Not many men will brave the curse of a dispossessed husband.

IYALOJA.   Only the curses of the departed are to be feared. The claims of one whose foot is on the threshold of their abode surpasses even the claims of blood. It is impiety even to place hindrances in their ways.

ELESIN.

> What do my mothers say? Shall I step
> Burdened into the unknown?

IYALOJA.   Now we, but the very earth says No. The sap in the plantain does not dry. Let grain that will not feed the voyager at his passage drop here and take root as he steps beyond this earth and us. Oh you who fill the home from hearth to threshold with the voices of children, you who now bestride the hidden gulf and pause to draw the right foot across and into the resting-home of the great forebears, it is good that your loins be drained into the earth we know, that your last strength be ploughed back into the womb that gave you being.

PRAISE-SINGER.   Iyaloja, mother of multitudes in the teeming market of the world, how your wisdom transfigures you!

IYALOJA (*smiling broadly, completely reconciled*). Elesin, even at the narrow end of the passage I know you will look back and sigh a last regret for the flesh that flashed past your spirit in flight. You always had a restless eye. Your choice has my blessing. (*To the* WOMEN). Take the good news to our daughter and make her ready. (*Some* WOMEN *go off.*)

ELESIN.   Your eyes were clouded at first.

IYALOJA.   Not for long. It is those who stand at the gateway of the great change to whose cry we must pay heed. And then, think of this—it makes the mind tremble. The fruit of such a union is rare. It will be neither of this world nor of the next. Nor of the one behind us. As if the timelessness of the ancestor world and the unborn have joined spirits to wring an issue of the elusive being of passage . . . Elesin!

ELESIN.   I am here. What is it?

IYALOJA.   Did you hear all I said just now?

ELESIN.   Yes.

IYALOJA.   The living must eat and drink. When the moment comes, don't turn the food to rodents' droppings in their mouth. Don't let them taste the ashes of the world when they step out at dawn to breathe the morning dew.

ELESIN.   This doubt is unworthy of you Iyaloja.

IYALOJA.   Eating the awusa nut is not so difficult as drinking water afterwards.

ELESIN.

> The waters of the bitter stream are honey to a
>   man
> Whose tongue has savoured all.

IYALOJA.   No one knows when the ants desert their home; they leave the mound intact. The swallow is never seen to peck holes in its nest when it is time to move with the season. There are always throngs of humanity behind the

leave-taker. The rain should not come through the roof
for them, the wind must not blow through the walls at
night.

ELESIN.   I refuse to take offence.

IYALOJA.   You wish to travel light. Well, the earth is yours.
But be sure the seed you leave in it attracts no curse.

ELESIN.   You really mistake my person Iyaloja.

IYALOJA.   I said nothing. Now we must go prepare your
bridal chamber. Then these same hands will lay your
shrouds.

ELESIN (*exasperated*). Must you be so blunt? (*Recovers.*)
Well, weave your shrouds, but let the fingers of my bride
seal my eyelids with earth and wash my body.

IYALOJA.   Prepare yourself Elesin.

She gets up to leave. At that moment the WOMEN *return,
leading the* BRIDE. ELESIN's *face glows with pleasure. He
flicks the sleeves of his agbada with renewed confidence and
steps forward to meet the group. As the girl kneels before*
IYALOJA, *lights fade out on the scene.*

SCENE TWO

*The verandah of the District Officer's bungalow. A tango is
playing from an old hand-cranked gramophone and,
glimpsed through the wide windows and doors which open
onto the forestage verandah are the shapes of* SIMON PILK-
INGS *and his wife,* JANE, *tangoing in and out of shadows in
the living-room. They are wearing what is immediately apparent as some form of fancy-dress. The dance goes on for
some moments and then the figure of a 'Native Administration' POLICEMAN emerges and climbs up the steps onto the
verandah. He peeps through and observes the dancing
couple, reacting with what is obviously a long-standing bewilderment. He stiffens suddenly, his expression changes to
one of disbelief and horror. In his excitement he upsets a
flower-pot and attracts the attention of the couple. They stop
dancing.*

PILKINGS.   Is there anyone out there?

JANE.   I'll turn off the gramophone.

PILKINGS (*approaching the verandah*). I'm sure I heard
something fall over. (*The* CONSTABLE *retracts slowly,
open-mouthed as* PILKINGS *approaches the verandah.*) Oh
it's you Amusa. Why didn't you just knock instead of
knocking things over?

AMUSA (*stammers badly and points a shaky finger at his
dress*). Mista Pirinkin . . . Mista Pirinkin . . .

PILKINGS.   What is the matter with you?

JANE (*emerging*). Who is it dear? Oh, Amusa . . .

PILKINGS.   Yes it's Amusa, and acting most strangely.

AMUSA (*his attention now transferred to* MRS PILKINGS).
Mammadam . . . you too!

PILKINGS.   What the hell is the matter with you man!

JANE.   Your costume darling. Our fancy dress.

PILKINGS.   Oh hell, I'd forgotten all about that. (*Lifts the
face mask over his head showing his face. His* WIFE *follows suit.*)

JANE.   I think you've shocked his big pagan heart bless him.

PILKINGS.   Nonsense, he's a Moslem. Come on Amusa,
you don't believe in all that nonsense do you? I thought
you were a good Moslem.

AMUSA.   Mista Pirinkin, I beg you sir, what you think you
do with that dress? It belong to dead cult, not for human
being.

PILKINGS.   Oh Amusa, what a let down you are. I swear by
you at the club you know—thank God for Amusa, he
doesn't believe in any mumbo-jumbo. And now look at
you!

AMUSA.   Mista Pirinkin, I beg you, take it off. Is not good
for man like you to touch that cloth.

PILKINGS.   Well, I've got it on. And what's more Jane and
I have bet on it we're taking first prize at the ball. Now,
if you can just pull yourself together and tell me what you
wanted to see me about . . .

AMUSA.   Sir, I cannot talk this matter to you in that dress.
I no fit.

PILKINGS.   What's that rubbish again?

JANE.   He is dead earnest too Simon. I think you'll have to
handle this delicately.

PILKINGS.   Delicately my . . . ! Look here Amusa, I think
this little joke has gone far enough hm? Let's have some
sense. You seem to forget that you are a police officer in
the service of His Majesty's Government. I order you to
report your business at once or face disciplinary action.

AMUSA.   Sir, it is a matter of death. How can man talk
against death to person in uniform of death? Is like talking
against government to person in uniform of police. Please
sir, I go and come back.

PILKINGS (*roars*). Now! (AMUSA *switches his gaze to the
ceiling suddenly, remains mute.*)

JANE.   Oh Amusa, what is there to be scared of in the costume? You saw it confiscated last month from those
egungun men who were creating trouble in town. You
helped arrest the cult leaders yourself—if the juju didn't
harm you at the time how could it possibly harm you now?
And merely by looking at it?

AMUSA (*without looking down*). Madam, I arrest the ring-
leaders who make trouble but me I no touch *egungun*.
That *egungun* inself, I no touch. And I no abuse 'am. I
arrest ringleader but I treat *egungun* with respect.

PILKINGS.   It's hopeless. We'll merely end up missing the
best part of the ball. When they get this way there is
nothing you can do. It's simply hammering against a brick
wall. Write your report or whatever it is on that pad
Amusa and take yourself out of here. Come on Jane. We
only upset his delicate sensibilities by remaining here.

AMUSA *waits for them to leave, then writes in the notebook,
somewhat laboriously. Drumming from the direction of the*

town wells up. AMUSA *listens, makes a movement as if he wants to recall* PILKINGS *but changes his mind. Completes his note and goes. A few moments later* PILKINGS *emerges, picks up the pad and reads.*

Jane!

JANE (*from the bedroom*). Coming darling. Nearly ready.
PILKINGS. Never mind being ready, just listen to this.
JANE. What is it?
PILKINGS. Amusa's report. Listen. 'I have to report that it come to my information that one prominent chief, namely, the Elesin Oba, is to commit death tonight as a result of native custom. Because this is criminal offence I await further instruction at charge office. Sergeant Amusa.'

JANE *comes out onto the verandah while he is reading.*

JANE. Did I hear you say commit death?
PILKINGS. Obviously he means murder.
JANE. You mean a ritual murder?
PILKINGS. Must be. You think you've stamped it all out but it's always lurking under the surface somewhere.
JANE. Oh. Does it mean we are not getting to the ball at all?
PILKINGS. No-o. I'll have the man arrested. Everyone remotely involved. In any case there may be nothing to it. Just rumours.
JANE. Really? I thought you found Amusa's rumours generally reliable.
PILKINGS. That's true enough. But who knows what may have been giving him the scare lately. Look at his conduct tonight.
JANE (*laughing*). You have to admit he had his own peculiar logic. (*Deepens her voice.*) How can man talk against death to person in uniform of death? (*Laughs.*) Anyway, you can't go into the police station dressed like that.
PILKINGS. I'll send Joseph with instructions. Damn it, what a confounded nuisance!
JANE. But don't you think you should talk first to the man, Simon?
PILKINGS. Do you want to go to the ball or not?
JANE. Darling, why are you getting rattled? I was only trying to be intelligent. It seems hardly fair just to lock up a man—and a chief at that—simply on the er . . . what is the legal word again?—uncorroborated word of a sergeant.
PILKINGS. Well, that's easily decided. Joseph!
JOSEPH (*from within*). Yes master.
PILKINGS. You're quite right of course, I am getting rattled. Probably the effect of those bloody drums. Do you hear how they go on and on?
JANE. I wondered when you'd notice. Do you suppose it has something to do with this affair?
PILKINGS. Who knows? They always find an excuse for making a noise . . . (*Thoughtfully.*) Even so . . .

JANE. Yes Simon?
PILKINGS. It's different, Jane. I don't think I've heard this particular—sound—before. Something unsettling about it.
JANE. I thought all bush drumming sounded the same.
PILKINGS. Don't tease me now Jane. This may be serious.
JANE. I'm sorry. (*Gets up and throws her arms around his neck. Kisses him. The houseboy enters, retreats and knocks.*)
PILKINGS (*wearily*). Oh, come in Joseph! I don't know where you pick up all these elephantine notions of tact. Come over here.
JOSEPH. Sir?
PILKINGS. Joseph, are you a Christian or not?
JOSEPH. Yessir.
PILKINGS. Does seeing me in this outfit bother you?
JOSEPH. No sir, it has no power.
PILKINGS. Thank God for some sanity at last. Now Joseph, answer me on the honour of a Christian—what is supposed to be going on in town tonight?
JOSEPH. Tonight sir? You mean the chief who is going to kill himself?
PILKINGS. What?
JANE. What do you mean, kill himself?
PILKINGS. You do mean he is going to kill somebody don't you?
JOSEPH. No master. He will not kill anybody and no one will kill him. He will simply die.
JANE. But why Joseph?
JOSEPH. It is native law and custom. The King die last month. Tonight is his burial. But before they can bury him, the Elesin must die so as to accompany him to heaven.
PILKINGS. I seem to be fated to clash more often with that man than with any of the other chiefs.
JOSEPH. He is the King's Chief Horseman.
PILKINGS (*in a resigned way*). I know.
JANE. Simon, what's the matter?
PILKINGS. It would have to be him!
JANE. Who is he?
PILKINGS. Don't you remember? He's that chief with whom I had a scrap some three or four years ago. I helped his son get to a medical school in England, remember? He fought tooth and nail to prevent it.
JANE. Oh now I remember. He was that very sensitive young man. What was his name again?
PILKINGS. Olunde. Haven't replied to his last letter come to think of it. The old pagan wanted him to stay and carry on some family tradition or the other. Honestly I couldn't understand the fuss he made. I literally had to help the boy escape from close confinement and load him onto the next boat. A most intelligent boy, really bright.
JANE. I rather thought he was much too sensitive you know. The kind of person you feel should be a poet munching rose petals in Bloomsbury.

PILKINGS.   Well, he's going to make a first-class doctor. His mind is set on that. And as long as he wants my help he is welcome to it.

JANE (*after a pause*).   Simon.

PILKINGS.   Yes?

JANE.   This boy, he was the eldest son wasn't he?

PILKINGS.   I'm not sure. Who could tell with that old ram?

JANE.   Do you know, Joseph?

JOSEPH.   Oh yes madam. He was the eldest son. That's why Elesin cursed master good and proper. The eldest son is not supposed to travel away from the land.

JANE (*giggling*).   Is that true Simon? Did he really curse you good and proper?

PILKINGS.   By all accounts I should be dead by now.

JOSEPH.   Oh no, master is white man. And good Christian. Black man juju can't touch master.

JANE.   If he was his eldest, it means that he would be the Elesin to the next king. It's a family thing isn't it Joseph?

JOSEPH.   Yes madam. And if this Elesin had died before the King, his eldest son must take his place.

JANE.   That would explain why the old chief was so mad you took the boy away.

PILKINGS.   Well it makes me all the more happy I did.

JANE.   I wonder if he knew.

PILKINGS.   Who? Oh, you mean Olunde?

JANE.   Yes. Was that why he was so determined to get away? I wouldn't stay if I knew I was trapped in such a horrible custom.

PILKINGS (*thoughtfully*).   No, I don't think he knew. At least he gave no indication. But you couldn't really tell with him. He was rather close you know, quite unlike most of them. Didn't give much away, not even to me.

JANE.   Aren't they all rather close, Simon?

PILKINGS.   These natives here? Good gracious. They'll open their mouths and yap with you about their family secrets before you can stop them. Only the other day . . .

JANE.   But Simon, do they really give anything away? I mean, anything that really counts. This affair for instance, we didn't know they still practised that custom did we?

PILKINGS.   Ye-e-es, I suppose you're right there. Sly, devious bastards.

JOSEPH (*stiffly*).   Can I go now master? I have to clean the kitchen.

PILKINGS.   What? Oh, you can go. Forget you were still here.

JOSEPH *goes*.

JANE.   Simon, you really must watch your language. Bastard isn't just a simple swear-word in these parts, you know.

PILKINGS.   Look, just when did you become a social anthropologist, that's what I'd like to know.

JANE.   I'm not claiming to know anything. I just happen to have overheard quarrels among the servants. That's how I know they consider it a smear.

PILKINGS.   I thought the extended family system took care of all that. Elastic family, no bastards.

JANE (*shrugs*).   Have it your own way.

Awkward silence. The drumming increases in volume. JANE *gets up suddenly, restless.*

That drumming Simon, do you think it might really be connected with this ritual? It's been going on all evening.

PILKINGS.   Let's ask our native guide. Joseph! Just a minute Joseph. (JOSEPH *re-enters*.) What's the drumming about?

JOSEPH.   I don't know master.

PILKINGS.   What do you mean you don't know? It's only two years since your conversion. Don't tell me all that holy water nonsense also wiped out your tribal memory.

JOSEPH (*visibly shocked*).   Master!

JANE.   Now you've done it.

PILKINGS.   What have I done now?

JANE.   Never mind. Listen Joseph, just tell me this. Is that drumming connected with dying or anything of that nature?

JOSEPH.   Madam, this is what I am trying to say: I am not sure. It sounds like the death of a great chief and then, it sounds like the wedding of a great chief. It really mix me up.

PILKINGS.   Oh get back to the kitchen. A fat lot of help you are.

JOSEPH.   Yes master. (*Goes.*)

JANE.   Simon . . .

PILKINGS.   All right, all right. I'm in no mood for preaching.

JANE.   It isn't my preaching you have to worry about, it's the preaching of the missionaries who preceded you here. When they make converts they really convert them. Calling holy water nonsense to our Joseph is really like insulting the Virgin Mary before a Roman Catholic. He's going to hand in his notice tomorrow you mark my word.

PILKINGS.   Now you're being ridiculous.

JANE.   Am I? What are you willing to bet that tomorrow we are going to be without a steward-boy? Did you see his face?

PILKINGS.   I am more concerned about whether or not we will be one native chief short by tomorrow. Christ! Just listen to those drums. (*He strides up and down, undecided.*)

JANE (*getting up*).   I'll change and make up some supper.

PILKINGS.   What's that?

JANE.   Simon, it's obvious we have to miss this ball.

PILKINGS.   Nonsense. It's the first bit of real fun the European club has managed to organise for over a year, I'm damned if I'm going to miss it. And it is a rather special occasion. Doesn't happen every day.

JANE.   You know this business has to be stopped Simon. And you are the only man who can do it.

PILKINGS.   I don't have to stop anything. If they want to throw themselves off the top of a cliff or poison themselves for the sake of some barbaric custom what is that to me? If it were ritual murder or something like that I'd be duty-bound to do something. I can't keep an eye on all the potential suicides in this province. And as for that man—believe me it's good riddance.

JANE (*laughs*). I know you better than that Simon. You are going to have to do something to stop it—after you've finished blustering.

PILKINGS (*shouts after her*). And suppose after all it's only a wedding? I'd look a proper fool if I interrupted a chief on his honeymoon, wouldn't I? (*Resumes his angry stride, slows down.*) Ah well, who can tell what those chiefs actually do on their honeymoon anyway? (*He takes up the pad and scribbles rapidly on it.*) Joseph! Joseph! Joseph! (*Some moments later* JOSEPH *puts in a sulky appearance.*) Did you hear me call you? Why the hell didn't you answer?

JOSEPH.   I didn't hear master.

PILKINGS.   You didn't hear me! How come you are here then?

JOSEPH (*stubbornly*). I didn't hear master.

PILKINGS (*controls himself with an effort*). We'll talk about it in the morning. I want you to take this note directly to Sergeant Amusa. You'll find him at the charge office. Get on your bicycle and race there with it. I expect you back in twenty minutes exactly. Twenty minutes, is that clear?

JOSEPH.   Yes master (*Going.*)

PILKINGS.   Oh er . . . Joseph.

JOSEPH.   Yes master?

PILKINGS (*between gritted teeth*). Er . . . forget what I said just now. The holy water is not nonsense. *I* was talking nonsense.

JOSEPH.   Yes master (*Goes.*)

JANE (*pokes her head round the door*). Have you found him?

PILKINGS.   Found who?

JANE.   Joseph. Weren't you shouting for him?

PILKINGS.   Oh yes, he turned up finally.

JANE.   You sounded desperate. What was it all about?

PILKINGS.   Oh nothing. I just wanted to apologise to him. Assure him that the holy water isn't really nonsense.

JANE.   Oh? And how did he take it?

PILKINGS.   Who the hell gives a damn! I had a sudden vision of our Very Reverend Macfarlane drafting another letter of complaint to the Resident about my unchristian language towards his parishioners.

JANE.   Oh I think he's given up on you by now.

PILKINGS.   Don't be too sure. And anyway, I wanted to make sure Joseph didn't 'lose' my note on the way. He looked sufficiently full of the holy crusade to do some such thing.

JANE.   If you've finished exaggerating, come and have something to eat.

PILKINGS.   No, put it all away. We can still get to the ball.

JANE.   Simon . . .

PILKINGS.   Get your costume back on. Nothing to worry about. I've instructed Amusa to arrest the man and lock him up.

JANE.   But that station is hardly secure Simon. He'll soon get his friends to help him escape.

PILKINGS.   A-ah, that's where I have out-thought you. I'm not having him put in the station cell. Amusa will bring him right here and lock him up in my study. And he'll stay with him till we get back. No one will dare come here to incite him to anything.

JANE.   How clever of you darling. I'll get ready.

PILKINGS.   Hey.

JANE.   Yes darling.

PILKINGS.   I have a surprise for you. I was going to keep it until we actually got to the ball.

JANE.   What is it?

PILKINGS.   You know the Prince is on a tour of the colonies don't you? Well, he docked in the capital only this morning but he is already at the Residency. He is going to grace the ball with his presence later tonight.

JANE.   Simon! Not really.

PILKINGS.   Yes he is. He's been invited to give away the prizes and he has agreed. You must admit old Engleton is the best Club Secretary we ever had. Quick off the mark that lad.

JANE.   But how thrilling.

PILKINGS.   The other provincials are going to be damned envious.

JANE.   I wonder what he'll come as.

PILKINGS.   Oh I don't know. As a coat-of-arms perhaps. Anyway it won't be anything to touch this.

JANE.   Well that's lucky. If we are to be presented I won't have to start looking for a pair of gloves. It's all sewn on.

PILKINGS (*laughing*). Quite right. Trust a woman to think of that. Come on, let's get going.

JANE (*rushing off*). Won't be a second. (*Stops.*) Now I see why you've been so edgy all evening. I thought you weren't handling this affair with your usual brilliance—to begin with that is.

PILKINGS (*his mood is much improved*). Shut up woman and get your things on.

JANE.   All right boss, coming.

PILKINGS *suddenly begins to hum the tango to which they were dancing before. Starts to execute a few practice steps. Lights fade.*

SCENE THREE

A swelling, agitated hum of women's voices rises immediately in the background. The lights come on and we see the frontage of a converted cloth stall in the market. The floor leading up to the entrance is covered in rich velvets and woven cloth. The WOMEN *come on stage, borne backwards by the determined progress of Sergeant* AMUSA *and his two* CONSTABLES *who already have their batons out and use them as a pressure against the* WOMEN. *At the edge of the cloth-covered floor however the* WOMEN *take a determined stand and block all further progress of the* MEN. *They begin to tease them mercilessly.*

AMUSA.   I am tell you women for last time to commot my road. I am here on official business.

WOMAN.   Official business you white man's eunuch? Official business is taking place where you want to go and it's a business you wouldn't understand.

WOMAN (*makes a quick tug at the* CONSTABLE'S *baton*). That doesn't fool anyone you know. It's the one you carry under your government knickers that counts. (*She bends low as if to peep under the baggy shorts. The embarrassed* CONSTABLE *quickly puts his knees together. The* WOMEN *roar.*)

WOMAN.   You mean there is nothing there at all?

WOMAN.   Oh there was something. You know that hand-bell which the whiteman uses to summon his servants . . . ?

AMUSA (*he manages to preserve some dignity throughout*). I hope you women know that interfering with officer in execution of his duty is criminal offence.

WOMAN.   Interfere? He says we're interfering with him. You foolish man we're telling you there's nothing to interfere with.

AMUSA.   I am order you now to clear the road.

WOMAN.   What road? The one your father built?

WOMAN.   You are a policeman not so? Then you know what they call trespassing in court. Or—(*Pointing to the cloth-lined steps.*)—do you think that kind of road is built for every kind of feet.

WOMAN.   Go back and tell the white man who sent you to come himself.

AMUSA.   If I go I will come back with reinforcement. And we will all return carrying wapons.

WOMAN.   Oh, now I understand. Before they can put on those knickers the white man first cuts off their weapons.

WOMAN.   What a cheek! You mean you come here to show power to women and you don't even have a weapon.

AMUSA (*shouting above the laughter*). For the last time I warn you women to clear the road.

WOMAN.   To where?

AMUSA.   To that hut. I know he dey dere.

WOMAN.   Who?

AMUSA.   The chief who call himself Elesin Oba.

WOMAN.   You ignorant man. It is not he who calls himself Elesin Oba, it is his blood that says it. As it called out to his father before him and will to his son after him. And that is in spite of everything your white man can do.

WOMAN.   Is it not the same ocean that washes this land and the white man's land? Tell your white man he can

hide our son away as long as he likes. When the time comes for him, the same ocean will bring him back.

AMUSA.   The government say dat kin' ting must stop.

WOMAN.   Who will stop it? You? Tonight our husband and father will prove himself greater than the laws of strangers.

AMUSA.   I tell you nobody go prove anyting tonight or anytime. Is ignorant and criminal to prove dat kin' prove.

IYALOJA (*entering from the hut. She is accompanied by a group of young girls who have been attending the* BRIDE). What is it Amusa? Why do you come here to disturb the happiness of others.

AMUSA.   Madame Iyaloja, I glad you come. You know me, I no like trouble but duty is duty. I am here to arrest Elesin for criminal intent. Tell these women to stop obstructing me in the performance of my duty.

IYALOJA.   And you? What gives you the right to obstruct our leader of men in the performance of duty.

AMUSA.   What kin' duty be dat one Iyaloja.

IYALOJA.   What kin' duty? What kin' duty does a man have to his new bride?

AMUSA (*bewildered, looks at the women and at the entrance to the hut*). Iyaloja, is it wedding you call dis kin' ting?

IYALOJA.   You have wives haven't you? Whatever the white man has done to you he hasn't stopped you having wives. And if he has, at least he is married. If you don't know what a marriage is, go and ask him to tell you.

AMUSA.   This no to wedding.

IYALOJA.   And ask him at the same time what he would have done if anyone had come to disturb him on his wedding night.

AMUSA.   Iyaloja, I say dis no to wedding.

IYALOJA.   You want to look inside the bridal chamber? You want to see for yourself how a man cuts the virgin knot?

AMUSA.   Madam . . .

WOMAN.   Perhaps his wives are still waiting for him to learn.

AMUSA.   Iyaloja, make you tell dese women make den no insult me again. If I hear dat kin' insult once more . . .

GIRL (*pushing her way through*). You will do what?

GIRL.   He's out of his mind. It's our mothers you're talking to, do you know that? Not to any illiterate villager you can bully and terrorise. How dare you intrude here anyway?

GIRL.   What a cheek, what impertinence!

GIRL.   You've treated them too gently. Now let them see what it is to tamper with the mothers of this market.

GIRL.   Your betters dare not enter the market when the women say no!

GIRL.   Haven't you learnt that yet, you jester in khaki and starch?

IYALOJA.   Daughters . . .

GIRL.   No no Iyaloja, leave us to deal with him. He no longer knows his mother, we'll teach him.

With a sudden movement they snatch the batons of the two CONSTABLES. *They begin to hem them in.*

GIRL.   What next? We have your batons? What next? What are you going to do?

With equally swift movements they knock off their hats.

GIRL.   Move if you dare. We have your hats, what will you do about it? Didn't the white man teach you to take off your hats before women?

IYALOJA.   It's a wedding night. It's a night of joy for us. Peace . . .

GIRL.   Not for him. Who asked him here?

GIRL.   Does he dare to go to the Residency without an invitation?

GIRL.   Not even where the servants eat the left-overs.

GIRLS (*in turn. In an 'English' accent*). Well well it's Mister Amusa. Were you invited? (*Play-acting to one another. The older women encourage them with their titters.*)

—Your invitation card please?

—Who are you? Have we been introduced?

—And who did you say you were?

—Sorry, I didn't quite catch your name.

—May I take your hat?

—If you insist. May I take yours? (*Exchanging the PO-LICEMEN's hats.*)

—How very kind of you.

—Not at all. Won't you sit down?

—After you.

—Oh no.

—I insist.

—You're most gracious.

—And how do you find the place?

—The natives are all right.

—Friendly?

—Tractable.

—Not a teeny-weeny bit restless?

—Well, a teeny-weeny bit restless.

—One might even say, difficult?

—Indeed one might be tempted to say, difficult.

—But you do manage to cope?

—Yes indeed I do. I have a rather faithful ox called Amusa.

—He's loyal?

—Absolutely.

—Lay down his life for you what?

—Without a moment's thought.

—Had one like that once. Trust him with my life.

—Mostly of course they are liars.

—Never known a native to tell the truth.

—Does it get rather close around here?

—It's mild for this time of the year.

—But the rains may still come.

—They are late this year aren't they?

—They are keeping African time.

—Ha ha ha ha

—Ha ha ha ha

—The humidity is what gets me.

—It used to be whisky

—Ha ha ha ha

—Ha ha ha ha

—What's your handicap old chap?

—Is there racing by golly?

—Splendid golf course, you'll like it.

—I'm beginning to like it already.

—And a European club, exclusive.

—You've kept the flag flying.

—We do our best for the old country.

—It's a pleasure to serve.

—Another whisky old chap?

—You are indeed too too kind.

—Not at all sir. Where is that boy? (*With a sudden bellow.*) Sergeant!

AMUSA (*snaps to attention*). Yessir!

The WOMEN *collapse with laughter.*

GIRL.   Take your men out of here.

AMUSA (*realising the trick, he rages from loss of face*). I'm give you warning . . .

GIRL.   All right then. Off with his knickers! (*They surge slowly forward.*)

IYALOJA.   Daughters, please.

AMUSA (*squaring himself for defence*). The first woman wey touch me . . .

IYALOJA.   My children, I beg of you . . .

GIRL.   Then tell him to leave this market. This is the home of our mothers. We don't want the eater of white left-overs at the feast their hands have prepared.

IYALOJA.   You heard them Amusa. You had better go.

GIRL.   Now!

AMUSA (*commencing his retreat*). We dey go now, but make you no say we no warn you.

GIRLS.   Now!

GIRL.   Before we read the riot act—you should know all about that.

AMUSA.   Make we go. (*They depart, more precipitately.*)

The WOMEN *strike their palms across in the gesture of wonder.*

WOMEN.   Do they teach you all that at school?

WOMAN.   And to think I nearly kept Apinke away from the place.

WOMAN.   Did you hear them? Did you see how they mimicked the white man?

WOMAN.   The voices exactly. Hey, there are wonders in this world!

IYALOJA.   Well, our elders have said it: Dada may be weak, but he has a younger sibling who is truly fearless.

WOMAN.   The next time the white man shows his face in this market I will set Wuraola on his tail.

A WOMAN *bursts into song and dance of euphoria—'Tani l'awa o l'ogbeja? Kayi! A l'ogbeja. Omo Kekere l'ogbeja.'* The rest of the* WOMEN *join in, some placing the* GIRLS *on their back like infants, others dancing round them. The dance becomes general, mounting in excitement.* ELESIN *appears, in wrapper only. In his hands a white velvet cloth folded loosely as if it held some delicate object. He cries out.*

ELESIN.   Oh you mothers of beautiful brides! (*The dancing stops. They turn and see him, and the object in his hands.* IYALOJA *approaches and gently takes the cloth from him.*) Take it. It is no mere virgin stain, but the union of life and the seeds of passage. My vital flow, the last from this flesh is intermingled with the promise of future life. All is prepared. Listen! (*A steady drumbeat from the distance.*) Yes. It is nearly time. The King's dog has been killed. The King's favourite horse is about to follow his master. My brother chiefs know their task and perform it well. (*He listens again.*)

The BRIDE *emerges, stands shyly by the door. He turns to her.*

Our marriage is not yet wholly fulfilled. When earth and passage wed, the consummation is complete only when there are grains of earth on the eyelids of passage. Stay by me till then. My faithful drummers, do me your last service. This is where I have chosen to do my leave-taking, in this heart of life, this hive which contains the swarm of the world in its small compass. This is where I have known love and laughter away from the palace. Even the richest food cloys when eaten days on end; in the market, nothing ever cloys. Listen. (*They listen to the drums.*) They have begun to seek out the heart of the King's favourite horse. Soon it will ride in its bolt of raffia with the dog at its feet. Together they will ride on the shoulders of the King's grooms through the pulse centres of the town. They know it is here I shall await them. I have told them. (*His eyes appear to cloud. He passes his hand over them as if to clear his sight. He gives a faint smile.*) It promises well; just then I felt my spirit's eagerness. The kite makes for wide spaces and the wind creeps up behind its tail; can the kite say less than—thank you, the quicker the better? But wait a while my spirit. Wait. Wait for the coming of the courier of the King. Do you know friends, the horse is born to this one destiny, to bear the burden that is man upon its back. Except for this night, this night alone when the spotless stallion will ride in triumph on the back of man. In the time of my father I

witnessed the strange sight. Perhaps tonight also I shall see it for the last time. If they arrive before the drums beat for me, I shall tell him to let the Alafin know I follow swiftly. If they come after the drums have sounded, why then, all is well for I have gone ahead. Our spirits shall fall in step along the great passage. (*He listens to the drums. He seems again to be falling into a state of semihypnosis; his eyes scan the sky but it is in a kind of daze. His voice is a little breathless.*) The moon has fed, a glow from its full stomach fills the sky and air, but I cannot tell where is that gateway through which I must pass. My faithful friends, let our feet touch together this last time, lead me into the other market with sounds that cover my skin with down yet make my limbs strike earth like a thoroughbred. Dear mothers, let me dance into the passage even as I have lived beneath your roofs. (*He comes down progressively among them. They make way for him, the drummers playing. His dance is one of solemn, regal motions, each gesture of the body is made with a solemn finality. The* WOMEN *join him, their steps a somewhat more fluid version of his. Beneath the* PRAISE-SINGER'*s exhortations the* WOMEN *dirge 'Ale le le, awo mi lo'.*)

PRAISE-SINGER.
　　　　　Elesin Alafin, can you hear my voice?
ELESIN.
　　　　　Faintly, my friend, faintly.
PRAISE-SINGER.
　　　　　Elesin Alafin, can you hear my call?
ELESIN.
　　　　　Faintly my king, faintly.
PRAISE-SINGER.
　　　　　Is your memory sound Elesin?
　　　　　Shall my voice be a blade of grass and
　　　　　Tickle the armpit of the past?
ELESIN.
　　　　　My memory needs no prodding but
　　　　　What do you wish to say to me?
PRAISE-SINGER.
　　　　　Only what has been spoken. Only what
　　　　　　　concerns
　　　　　The dying wish of the father of all.
ELESIN.
　　　　　It is buried like seed-yam in my mind
　　　　　This is the season of quick rains, the harvest
　　　　　Is this moment due for gathering.
PRAISE-SINGER.
　　　　　If you cannot come, I said, swear
　　　　　You'll tell my favourite horse. I shall
　　　　　Ride on through the gates alone.
ELESIN.
　　　　　Elesin's message will be read
　　　　　Only when his loyal heart no longer beats.

*'Who says we haven't a defender? Silence! We have our defenders. Little children are our champions.'

PRAISE-SINGER.

> If you cannot come Elesin, tell my dog.
> I cannot stay the keeper too long
> At the gate.

ELESIN.

> A dog does not outrun the hand
> That feeds it meat. A horse that throws its
>   rider
> Slows down to a stop. Elesin Alafin
> Trust no beasts with messages between
> A king and his companion.

PRAISE-SINGER.

> If you get lost my dog will track
> The hidden path to me.

ELESIN.

> The seven-way crossroads confuses
> Only the stranger. The Horseman of the King
> Was born in the recesses of the house.

PRAISE-SINGER.

> I know the wickedness of men. If there is
> Weight on the loose end of your sash, such
>   weight
> As no mere man can shift; if your sash is
>   earthed
> By evil minds who mean to part us at the
>   last . . .

ELESIN.

> My sash is of the deep purple *alari;*
> It is no tethering-rope. The elephant
> Trails no tethering-rope; that king
> Is not yet crowned who will peg an elephant—
> Not even you my friend and King.

PRAISE-SINGER.

> And yet this fear will not depart from me
> The darkness of this new abode is deep—
> Will your human eyes suffice?

ELESIN.

> In a night which falls before our eyes
> However deep, we do not miss our way.

PRAISE-SINGER.

> Shall I now not acknowledge I have stood
> Where wonders met their end? The elephant
>   deserves
> Better than that we say 'I have caught
> A glimpse of something'. If we see the tamer
> Of the forest let us say plainly, we have seen
> An elephant.

ELESIN (*his voice is drowsy*).

> I have freed myself of earth and now
> It's getting dark. Strange voices guide my feet.

PRAISE-SINGER.

> The river is never so high that the eyes
> Of a fish are covered. The night is not so dark
> That the albino fails to find his way. A child

> Returning homewards craves no leading by the
>   hand.
> Gracefully does the mask regain his grove at
>   the end of the day . . .
> Gracefully. Gracefully does the mask dance
> Homeward at the end of the day, gracefully
>   . . .

ELESIN'*s trance appears to be deepening, his steps heavier.*

IYALOJA.

> It is the death of war that kills the valiant,
> Death of water is how the swimmer goes
> It is the death of markets that kills the trader
> And death of indecision takes the idle away
> The trade of the cutlass blunts its edge
> And the beautiful die the death of beauty.
> It takes an Elesin to die the death of
>   death . . .
> Only Elesin . . . dies the unknowable death
>   of death . . .
> Gracefully, gracefully does the horseman
>   regain
> The stables at the end of day, gracefully . . .

PRAISE-SINGER.   How shall I tell what my eyes have seen? The Horseman gallops on before the courier, how shall I tell what my eyes have seen? He says a dog may be confused by new scents of beings he never dreamt of, so he must precede the dog to heaven. He says a horse may stumble on strange boulders and be lamed, so he races on before the horse to heaven. It is best, he says, to trust no messenger who may falter at the outer gate; oh how shall I tell what my ears have heard? But do you hear me still Elesin, do you hear your faithful one?

ELESIN *in his motions appears to feel for a direction of sound, subtly, but he only sinks deeper into his trance-dance.*

Elesin Alafin, I no longer sense your flesh. The drums are changing now but you have gone far ahead of the world. It is not yet noon in heaven; let those who claim it is begin their own journey home. So why must you rush like an impatient bride: why do you race to desert your Olohun-iyo?

ELESIN *is now sunk fully deep in his trance, there is no longer sign of any awareness of his surroundings.*

Does the deep voice of *gbedu* cover you then, like the passage of royal elephants? Those drums that brook no rivals, have they blocked the passage to your ears that my voice passes into wind, a mere leaf floating in the night? Is your flesh lightened Elesin, is that lump of earth I slid between your slippers to keep you longer slowly sifting from your feet? Are the drums on the other side now tuning skin to skin with ours in *osugbo*? Are there sounds there I cannot hear, do footsteps surround you which pound the earth like *gbedu*, roll like thunder round the dome of the world? Is the darkness gathering in your head Elesin? Is there now a streak of light at the end of the passage, a light I dare not look upon? Does it reveal whose voices we often heard, whose touches we often felt, whose wisdoms come suddenly into the mind when the wisest have shaken their heads and murmured; It cannot be done? Elesin Alafin, don't think I do not know why your lips are heavy, why your limbs are drowsy as palm oil in the cold of harmattan. I would call you back but when the elephant heads for the jungle, the tail is too small a hand-hold for the hunter that would pull him back. The sun that heads for the sea no longer heeds the prayers of the farmer. When the river begins to taste the salt of the ocean, we no longer know what deity to call on, the river-god or Olokun. No arrow flies back to the string, the child does not return through the same passage that gave it birth. Elesin Oba, can you hear me at all? Your eyelids are glazed like a courtesan's, is it that you see the dark groom and master of life? And will you see my father? Will you tell him that I stayed with you to the last? Will my voice ring in your ears awhile, will you remember Olohun-iyo even if the music on the other side surpasses his mortal craft? But will they know you over there? Have they eyes to gauge your worth, have they the heart to love you, will they know what thoroughbred prances towards them in caparisons of honour? If they do not Elesin, if any there cuts your yam with a small knife, or pours you wine in a small calabash, turn back and return to welcoming hands. If the world were not greater than the wishes of Olohun-iyo, I would not let you go . . .

He appears to break down. ELESIN *dances on, completely in a trance. The dirge wells up louder and stronger.* ELESIN's *dance does not lose its elasticity but his gestures become, if possible, even more weighty. Lights fade slowly on the scene.*

SCENE FOUR

A Masque. The front side of the stage is part of a wide corridor around the great hall of the Residency extending beyond vision into the rear and wings. It is redolent of the tawdry decadence of a far-flung but key imperial frontier. The COUPLES *in a variety of fancy-dress are ranged around the walls, gazing in the same direction. The guest-of-honour is about to make an appearance. A portion of the local police brass band with its white* CONDUCTOR *is just visible. At last, the entrance of* ROYALTY. *The band plays 'Rule Britannia', badly, beginning long before he is visible. The couples bow and curtsey as he passes by them. Both he and his companions are dressed in seventeenth century European costume. Following behind are the* RESIDENT *and his* PARTNER *similarly attired. As they gain the end of the hall where the orchestra dais begins the music comes to an end. The* PRINCE *bows to the guests. The* BAND *strikes up a Viennese waltz*

and the PRINCE *formally opens the floor. Several bars later the* RESIDENT *and his companion follow suit. Others follow in appropriate pecking order. The orchestra's waltz rendition is not of the highest musical standard.*

Some time later the PRINCE *dances again into view and is settled into a corner by the* RESIDENT *who then proceeds to select* COUPLES *as they dance past for introduction, sometimes threading his way through the dancers to tap the lucky* COUPLE *on the shoulder. Desperate efforts from many to ensure that they are recognised in spite of perhaps, their costume. The ritual of introductions soon takes in* PILKINGS *and his* WIFE. *The* PRINCE *is quite fascinated by their costume and they demonstrate the adaptations they have made to it, pulling down the mask to demonstrate how the* egun-gun *normally appears, then showing the various press-button controls they have innovated for the face flaps, the sleeves, etc. They demonstrate the dance steps and the guttural sounds made by the* egungun, *harrass other dancers in the hall,* MRS PILKINGS *playing the 'restrainer' to* PILKINGS' *manic darts. Everyone is highly entertained, the Royal Party especially who lead the applause.*

At this point a liveried FOOTMAN *comes in with a note on a salver and is intercepted almost absent-mindedly by the* RESIDENT *who takes the note and reads it. After polite coughs he succeeds in excusing the* PILKINGS *from the* PRINCE *and takes them aside. The* PRINCE *considerately offers the* RESIDENT's WIFE *his hand and dancing is resumed.*

On their way out the RESIDENT *gives an order to his* AIDE-DE-CAMP. *They come into the side corridor where the* RESIDENT *hands the note to* PILKINGS.

RESIDENT.   As you see it says 'emergency' on the outside. I took the liberty of opening it because His Highness was obviously enjoying the entertainment. I didn't want to interrupt unless really necessary.

PILKINGS.   Yes, yes of course, sir.

RESIDENT.   Is it really as bad as it says? What's it all about?

PILKINGS.   Some strange custom they have, sir. It seems because the King is dead some important chief has to commit suicide.

RESIDENT.   The King? Isn't it the same one who died nearly a month ago?

PILKINGS.   Yes, sir.

RESIDENT.   Haven't they buried him yet?

PILKINGS.   They take their time about these things, sir. The preburial ceremonies last nearly thirty days. It seems tonight is the final night.

RESIDENT.   But what has it got to do with the market women? Why are they rioting? We've waived that troublesome tax haven't we?

PILKINGS.   We don't quite know that they are exactly rioting yet, sir. Sergeant Amusa is sometimes prone to exaggerations.

RESIDENT. He sounds desperate enough. That comes out even in his rather quaint grammar. Where is the man anyway? I asked my aide-de-camp to bring him here.

PILKINGS. They are probably looking in the wrong verandah. I'll fetch him myself.

RESIDENT. No no you stay here. Let your wife go and look for them. Do you mind my dear . . . ?

JANE. Certainly not, your Excellency. (*Goes.*)

RESIDENT. You should have kept me informed, Pilkings. You realise how disastrous it would have been if things had erupted while His Highness was here.

PILKINGS. I wasn't aware of the whole business until tonight, sir.

RESIDENT. Nose to the ground Pilkings, nose to the ground. If we all let these little things slip past us where would the empire be eh? Tell me that. Where would we all be?

PILKINGS (*low voice*). Sleeping peacefully at home I bet.

RESIDENT. What did you say, Pilkings?

PILKINGS. It won't happen again, sir.

RESIDENT. It mustn't, Pilkings. It mustn't. Where is that damned sergeant? I ought to get back to His Highness as quickly as possible and offer him some plausible explanation for my rather abrupt conduct. Can you think of one, Pilkings?

PILKINGS. You could tell him the truth, sir.

RESIDENT. I could? No no no no Pilkings, that would never do. What! Go and tell him there is a riot just two miles away from him? This is supposed to be a secure colony of His Majesty, Pilkings.

PILKINGS. Yes, sir.

RESIDENT. Ah, there they are. No, these are not our native police. Are these the ring-leaders of the riot?

PILKINGS. Sir, these are my police officers.

RESIDENT. Oh, I beg your pardon officers. You do look a little . . . I say, isn't there something missing in their uniform? I think they used to have some rather colourful sashes. If I remember rightly I recommended them myself in my young days in the service. A bit of colour always appeals to the natives, yes, I remember putting that in my report. Well well well, where are we? Make your report man.

PILKINGS (*moves close to* AMUSA, *between his teeth*). And let's have no more superstitious nonsense from you Amusa or I'll throw you in the guardroom for a month and feed you pork!

RESIDENT. What's that? What has pork to do with it?

PILKINGS. Sir, I was just warning him to be brief. I'm sure you are most anxious to hear his report.

RESIDENT. Yes yes yes of course. Come on man, speak up. Hey, didn't we give them some colourful fez hats with all those wavy things, yes, pink tassells . . .

PILKINGS. Sir, I think if he was permitted to make his report we might find that he lost his hat in the riot.

RESIDENT. Ah yes indeed. I'd better tell His Highness that. Lost his hat in the riot, ha ha. He'll probably say well, as long as he didn't lose his head. (*Chuckles to himself.*) Don't forget to send me a report first thing in the morning young Pilkings.

PILKINGS. No, sir.

RESIDENT. And whatever you do, don't let things get out of hand. Keep a cool head and—nose to the ground Pilkings. (*Wanders off in the general direction of the hall.*)

PILKINGS. Yes, sir.

AIDE-DE-CAMP. Would you be needing me, sir?

PILKINGS. No thanks, Bob. I think His Excellency's need of you is greater than ours.

AIDE-DE-CAMP. We have a detachment of soldiers from the capital, sir. They accompanied His Highness up here.

PILKINGS. I doubt if it will come to that but, thanks, I'll bear it in mind. Oh, could you send an orderly with my cloak.

AIDE-DE-CAMP. Very good, sir. (*Goes.*)

PILKINGS. Now, sergeant.

AMUSA. Sir . . . (*Makes an effort, stops dead. Eyes to the ceiling.*)

PILKINGS. Oh, not again.

AMUSA. I cannot against death to dead cult. This dress get power of dead.

PILKINGS. All right, let's go. You are relieved of all further duty Amusa. Report to me first thing in the morning.

JANE. Shall I come, Simon?

PILKINGS. No, there's no need for that. If I can get back later I will. Otherwise get Bob to bring you home.

JANE. Be careful Simon . . . I mean, be clever.

PILKINGS. Sure I will. You two, come with me. (*As he turns to go, the clock in the Residency begins to chime.* PILKINGS *looks at his watch then turns, horror-stricken, to stare at his* WIFE. *The same thought clearly occurs to her. He swallows hard. An* ORDERLY *brings his cloak.*) It's midnight. I had no idea it was that late.

JANE. But surely . . . they don't count the hours the way we do. The moon, or something . . .

PILKINGS. I am . . . not so sure.

He turns and breaks into a sudden run. The two CONSTABLES *follow, also at a run.* AMUSA, *who has kept his eyes on the ceiling throughout waits until the last of the footsteps has faded out of hearing. He salutes suddenly, but without once looking in the direction of the* WOMAN.

AMUSA. Goodnight, madam.

JANE. Oh. (*She hesitates.*) Amusa . . . (*He goes off without seeming to have heard.*) Poor Simon . . . (*A figure emerges from the shadows, a young black* MAN *dressed in a sober western suit. He peeps into the hall, trying to make out the figures of the dancers.*)

Who is that?

OLUNDE (*emerges into the light*). I didn't mean to startle you madam. I am looking for the District Officer.

JANE.   Wait a minute . . . don't I know you? Yes, you are Olunde, the young man who . . .

OLUNDE.   Mrs Pilkings! How fortunate. I came here to look for your husband.

JANE.   Olunde! Let's look at you. What a fine young man you've become. Grand but solemn. Good God, when did you return? Simon never said a word. But you do look well Olunde. Really!

OLUNDE.   You are . . . well, you look quite well yourself Mrs Pilkings. From what little I can see of you.

JANE.   Oh, this. It's caused quite a stir I assure you, and not all of it very pleasant. You are not shocked I hope?

OLUNDE.   Why should I be? But don't you find it rather hot in there? Your skin must find it difficult to breathe.

JANE.   Well, it is a little hot I must confess, but it's all in a good cause.

OLUNDE.   What cause Mrs Pilkings?

JANE.   All this. The ball. And His Highness being here in person and all that.

OLUNDE (*mildly*). And that is the good cause for which you desecrate an ancestral mask?

JANE.   Oh, so you are shocked after all. How disappointing.

OLUNDE.   No I am not shocked, Mrs Pilkings. You forget that I have now spent four years among your people. I discovered that you have no respect for what you do not understand.

JANE.   Oh. So you've returned with a chip on your shoulder. That's a pity Olunde. I am sorry.

An uncomfortable silence follows.

I take it then that you did not find your stay in England altogether edifying.

OLUNDE.   I don't say that. I found your people quite admirable in many ways, their conduct and courage in this war for instance.

JANE.   Ah yes, the war. Here of course it is all rather remote. From time to time we have a black-out drill just to remind us that there is a war on. And the rare convoy passes through on its way somewhere or on manoeuvres. Mind you there is the occasional bit of excitement like that ship that was blown up in the harbour.

OLUNDE.   Here? Do you mean through enemy action?

JANE.   Oh no, the war hasn't come that close. The captain did it himself. I don't quite understand it really. Simon tried to explain. The ship had to be blown up because it had become dangerous to the other ships, even to the city itself. Hundreds of the coastal population would have died.

OLUNDE.   Maybe it was loaded with ammunition and had caught fire. Or some of those lethal gases they've been experimenting on.

JANE.   Something like that. The captain blew himself up with it. Deliberately. Simon said someone had to remain on board to light the fuse.

OLUNDE.   It must have been a very short fuse.

JANE (*shrugs*). I don't know much about it. Only that there was no other way to save lives. No time to devise anything else. The captain took the decision and carried it out.

OLUNDE.   Yes . . . I quite believe it. I met men like that in England.

JANE.   Oh just look at me! Fancy welcoming you back with such morbid news. Stale too. It was at least six months ago.

OLUNDE.   I don't find it morbid at all. I find it rather inspiring. It is an affirmative commentary on life.

JANE.   What is?

OLUNDE.   That captain's self-sacrifice.

JANE.   Nonsense. Life should never be thrown deliberately away.

OLUNDE.   And the innocent people around the harbour?

JANE.   Oh, how does one know? The whole thing was probably exaggerated anyway.

OLUNDE.   That was a risk the captain couldn't take. But please Mrs Pilkings, do you think you could find your husband for me? I have to talk to him.

JANE.   Simon? (*As she recollects for the first time the full significance of* OLUNDE's *presence.*) Simon is . . . there is a little problem in town. He was sent for. But . . . when did you arrive? Does Simon know you're here?

OLUNDE (*suddenly earnest*). I need your help Mrs Pilkings. I've always found you somewhat more understanding than your husband. Please find him for me and when you do, you must help me talk to him.

JANE.   I'm afraid I don't quite . . . follow you. Have you seen my husband already?

OLUNDE.   I went to your house. Your houseboy told me you were here. (*He smiles.*) He even told me how I would recognise you and Mr Pilkings.

JANE.   Then you must know what my husband is trying to do for you.

OLUNDE.   For me?

JANE.   For you. For your people. And to think he didn't even know you were coming back! But how do you happen to be here? Only this evening we were talking about you. We thought you were still four thousand miles away.

OLUNDE.   I was sent a cable.

JANE.   A cable? Who did? Simon? The business of your father didn't begin till tonight.

OLUNDE.   A relation sent it weeks ago, and it said nothing about my father. All it said was, Our King is dead. But I knew I had to return home at once so as to bury my father. I understood that.

JANE.   Well, thank God you don't have to go through that agony. Simon is going to stop it.

OLUNDE.   That's why I want to see him. He's wasting his time. And since he has been so helpful to me I don't want him to incur the enmity of our people. Especially over nothing.

JANE (*sits down open-mouthed*). You . . . you Olunde!

OLUNDE.   Mrs Pilkings, I came home to bury my father. As soon as I heard the news I booked my passage home. In fact we were fortunate. We travelled in the same convoy as your Prince, so we had excellent protection.

JANE.   But you don't think your father is also entitled to whatever protection is available to him?

OLUNDE.   How can I make you understand? He *has* protection. No one can undertake what he does tonight without the deepest protection the mind can conceive. What can you offer him in place of his peace of mind, in place of the honour and veneration of his own people? What would you think of your Prince if he refused to accept the risk of losing his life on this voyage? This . . . showing-the-flag tour of colonial possessions.

JANE.   I see. So it isn't just medicine you studied in England.

OLUNDE.   Yet another error into which your people fall. You believe that everything which appears to make sense was learnt from you.

JANE.   Not so fast Olunde. You have learnt to argue I can tell that, but I never said you made sense. However clearly you try to put it, it is still a barbaric custom. It is even worse—it's feudal! The king dies and a chieftan must be buried with him. How feudalistic can you get!

OLUNDE (*waves his hand towards the background. The* PRINCE *is dancing past again—to a different step—and all the guests are bowing and curtseying as he passes*). And this? Even in the midst of a devastating war, look at that. What name would you give to that?

JANE.   Therapy, British style. The preservation of sanity in the midst of chaos.

OLUNDE.   Others would call it decadence. However, it doesn't really interest me. You white races know how to survive; I've seen proof of that. By all logical and natural laws this war should end with all the white races wiping out one another, wiping out their so-called civilisation for all time and reverting to a state of primitivism the like of which has so far only existed in your imagination when you thought of us. I thought all that at the beginning. Then I slowly realised that your greatest art is the art of survival. But at least have the humility to let others survive in their own way.

JANE.   Through ritual suicide?

OLUNDE.   Is that worse than mass suicide? Mrs Pilkings, what do you call what those young men are sent to do by their generals in this war? Of course you have also mastered the art of calling things by names which don't remotely describe them.

JANE.   You talk! You people with your long-winded, round-about way of making conversation.

OLUNDE.   Mrs Pilkings, whatever we do, we never suggest that a thing is the opposite of what it really is. In your newsreels I heard defeats, thorough, murderous defeats described as strategic victories. No wait, it wasn't just on your newsreels. Don't forget I was attached to hospitals all the time. Hordes of your wounded passed through those wards. I spoke to them. I spent long evenings by their bedsides while they spoke terrible truths of the realities of that war. I know now how history is made.

JANE.   But surely, in a war of this nature, for the morale of the nation you must expect . . .

OLUNDE.   That a disaster beyond human reckoning be spoken of as a triumph? No. I mean, is there no mourning in the home of the bereaved that such blasphemy is permitted?

JANE (*after a moment's pause*). Perhaps I can understand you now. The time we picked for you was not really one for seeing us at our best.

OLUNDE.   Don't think it was just the war. Before that even started I had plenty of time to study your people. I saw nothing, finally, that gave you the right to pass judgement on other peoples and their ways. Nothing at all.

JANE (*hesitantly*). Was it the . . . colour thing? I know there is some discrimination.

OLUNDE.   Don't make it so simple, Mrs Pilkings. You make it sound as if when I left, I took nothing at all with me.

JANE.   Yes . . . and to tell the truth, only this evening, Simon and I agreed that we never really knew what you left with.

OLUNDE.   Neither did I. But I found out over there. I am grateful to your country for that. And I will never give it up.

JANE.   Olunde, please . . . promise me something. Whatever you do, don't throw away what you have started to do. You want to be a doctor. My husband and I believe you will make an excellent one, sympathetic and competent. Don't let anything make you throw away your training.

OLUNDE (*genuinely surprised*). Of course not. What a strange idea. I intend to return and complete my training. Once the burial of my father is over.

JANE.   Oh, please . . .

OLUNDE.   Listen! Come outside. You can't hear anything against that music.

JANE.   What is it?

OLUNDE.   The drums. Can you hear the drums? Listen.

The drums come over, still distant but more distinct. There is a change of rhythm, it rises to a crescendo and then, suddenly, it is cut off. After a silence, a new beat begins, slow and resonant.

There it's all over.

JANE.   You mean he's . . .

OLUNDE.   Yes, Mrs Pilkings, my father is dead. His will-power has always been enormous; I know he is dead.

JANE (*screams*). How can you be so callous! So unfeeling! You announce your father's own death like a surgeon looking down on some strange . . . stranger's body! You're just a savage like all the rest.

AIDE-DE-CAMP (*rushing out*). Mrs Pilkings. Mrs Pilkings. (*She breaks down, sobbing.*) Are you all right, Mrs Pilkings?

OLUNDE.   She'll be all right. (*Turns to go.*)

AIDE-DE-CAMP.   Who are you? And who the hell asked your opinion?

OLUNDE.   You're quite right, nobody. (*Going.*)

AIDE-DE-CAMP.   What the hell! Did you hear me ask you who you were?

OLUNDE.   I have business to attend to.

AIDE-DE-CAMP.   I'll give you business in a moment you impudent nigger. Answer my question!

OLUNDE.   I have a funeral to arrange. Excuse me. (*Going.*)

AIDE-DE-CAMP.   I said stop! Orderly!

JANE.   No, no, don't do that. I'm all right. And for heaven's sake don't act so foolishly. He's a family friend.

AIDE-DE-CAMP.   Well he'd better learn to answer civil questions when he's asked them. These natives put a suit on and they get high opinions of themselves.

OLUNDE.   Can I go now?

JANE.   No no don't go. I must talk to you. I'm sorry about what I said.

OLUNDE.   It's nothing, Mrs Pilkings. And I'm really anxious to go. I couldn't see my father before, it's forbidden for me, his heir and successor to set eyes on him from the moment of the king's death. But now . . . I would like to touch his body while it is still warm.

JANE.   You will. I promise I shan't keep you long. Only, I couldn't possibly let you go like that. Bob, please excuse us.

AIDE-DE-CAMP.   If you're sure . . .

JANE.   Of course I'm sure. Something happened to upset me just then, but I'm all right now. Really.

The AIDE-DE-CAMP *goes, somewhat reluctantly.*

OLUNDE.   I mustn't stay long.

JANE.   Please, I promise not to keep you. It's just that . . . oh you saw yourself what happens to one in this place. The Resident's man thought he was being helpful, that's the way we all react. But I can't go in among that crowd just now and if I stay by myself somebody will come looking for me. Please, just say something for a few moments and then you can go. Just so I can recover myself.

OLUNDE.   What do you want me to say?

JANE.   Your calm acceptance for instance, can you explain that? It was so unnatural. I don't understand that at all. I feel a need to understand all I can.

OLUNDE.   But you explained it yourself. My medical training perhaps. I have seen death too often. And the soldiers who returned from the front, they died on our hands all the time.

JANE.   No. It has to be more than that. I feel it has to do with the many things we don't really grasp about your people. At least you can explain.

OLUNDE.   All these things are part of it. And anyway, my father has been dead in my mind for nearly a month. Ever since I learnt of the King's death. I've lived with my bereavement so long now that I cannot think of him alive. On that journey on the boat, I kept my mind on my duties as the one who must perform the rites over his body. I went through it all again and again in my mind as he himself had taught me. I didn't want to do anything wrong, something which might jeopardise the welfare of my people.

JANE.   But he had disowned you. When you left he swore publicly you were no longer his son.

OLUNDE.   I told you, he was a man of tremendous will. Sometimes that's another way of saying stubborn. But among our people, you don't disown a child just like that. Even if I had died before him I would still be buried like his eldest son. But it's time for me to go.

JANE.   Thank you. I feel calmer. Don't let me keep you from your duties.

OLUNDE.   Goodnight, Mrs Pilkings.

JANE.   Welcome home.

She holds out her hand. As he takes it footsteps are heard approaching the drive. A short while later a woman's sobbing is also heard.

PILKINGS (*off*). Keep them here till I get back. (*He strides into view, reacts at the sight of* OLUNDE *but turns to his* WIFE.) Thank goodness you're still here.

JANE.   Simon, what happened?

PILKINGS.   Later Jane, please. Is Bob still here?

JANE.   Yes, I think so. I'm sure he must be.

PILKINGS.   Try and get him out here as quickly as you can. Tell him it's urgent.

JANE.   Of course. Oh Simon, you remember . . .

PILKINGS.   Yes yes. I can see who it is. Get Bob out here. (*She runs off.*) At first I thought I was seeing a ghost.

OLUNDE.   Mr Pilkings, I appreciate what you tried to do. I want you to believe that. I can tell you it would have been a terrible calamity if you'd succeeded.

PILKINGS (*opens his mouth several times, shuts it*). You . . . said what?

OLUNDE.   A calamity for us, the entire people.

PILKINGS (*sighs*). I see. Hm.

OLUNDE.   And now I must go. I must see him before he turns cold.

PILKINGS.   Oh ah . . . em . . . but this is a shock to see you. I mean er thinking all this while you were in England and thanking God for that.

OLUNDE.   I came on the mail boat. We travelled in the Prince's convoy.

PILKINGS. Ah yes, a-ah, hm . . . er well . . .

OLUNDE. Goodnight. I can see you are shocked by the whole business. But you must know by now there are things you cannot understand—or help.

PILKINGS. Yes. Just a minute. There are armed policemen that way and they have instructions to let no one pass. I suggest you wait a little. I'll er . . . give you an escort.

OLUNDE. That's very kind of you. But do you think it could be quickly arranged.

PILKINGS. Of course. In fact, yes, what I'll do is send Bob over with some men to the er . . . place. You can go with them. Here he comes now. Excuse me a minute.

AIDE-DE-CAMP. Anything wrong sir?

PILKINGS (*takes him to one side*). Listen Bob, that cellar in the disused annexe of the Residency, you know, where the slaves were stored before being taken down to the coast . . .

AIDE-DE-CAMP. Oh yes, we use it as a storeroom for broken furniture.

PILKINGS. But it's still got the bars on it?

AIDE-DE-CAMP. Oh yes, they are quite intact.

PILKINGS. Get the keys please. I'll explain later. And I want a strong guard over the Residency tonight.

AIDE-DE-CAMP. We have that already. The detachment from the coast . . .

PILKINGS. No, I don't want them at the gates of the Residency. I want you to deploy them at the bottom of the hill, a long way from the main hall so they can deal with any situation long before the sound carries to the house.

AIDE-DE-CAMP. Yes of course.

PILKINGS. I don't want His Highness alarmed.

AIDE-DE-CAMP. You think the riot will spread here?

PILKINGS. It's unlikely but I don't want to take a chance. I made them believe I was going to lock the man up in my house, which was what I had planned to do in the first place. They are probably assailing it by now. I took a roundabout route here so I don't think there is any danger at all. At least not before dawn. Nobody is to leave the premises of course—the native employees I mean. They'll soon smell something is up and they can't keep their mouths shut.

AIDE-DE-CAMP. I'll give instructions at once.

PILKINGS. I'll take the prisoner down myself. Two policemen will stay with him throughout the night. Inside the cell.

AIDE-DE-CAMP. Right sir. (*Salutes and goes off at the double.*)

PILKINGS. Jane. Bob is coming back in a moment with a detachment. Until he gets back please stay with Olunde. (*He makes an extra warning gesture with his eyes.*)

OLUNDE. Please, Mr Pilkings . . .

PILKINGS. I hate to be stuffy old son, but we have a crisis on our hands. It has to do with your father's affair if you must know. And it happens also at a time when we have His Highness here. I am responsible for security so you'll

simply have to do as I say. I hope that's understood. (*Marches off quickly, in the direction from which he made his first appearance.*)

OLUNDE. What's going on? All this can't be just because he failed to stop my father killing himself.

JANE. I honestly don't know. Could it have sparked off a riot?

OLUNDE. No. If he'd succeeded that would be more likely to start the riot. Perhaps there were other factors involved. Was there a chieftancy dispute?

JANE. None that I know of.

ELESIN (*an animal bellow from off*). Leave me alone! Is it not enough that you have covered me in shame! White man, take your hand from my body!

OLUNDE *stands frozen to the spot.* JANE *understanding at last, tries to move him.*

JANE. Let's go in. It's getting chilly out here.

PILKINGS (*off*). Carry him.

ELESIN. Give me back the name you have taken away from me you ghost from the land of the nameless!

PILKINGS. Carry him! I can't have a disturbance here. Quickly! stuff up his mouth.

JANE. Oh God! Let's go in. Please Olunde.

OLUNDE *does not move.*

ELESIN. Take your albino's hand from me you . . .

Sounds of a struggle. His voice chokes as he is gagged.

OLUNDE (*quietly*). That was my father's voice.

JANE. Oh you poor orphan, what have you come home to?

There is a sudden explosion of rage from off-stage and powerful steps come running up the drive.

PILKINGS. You bloody fools, after him!

Immediately ELESIN, *in handcuffs, comes pounding in the direction of* JANE *and* OLUNDE, *followed some moments afterwards by* PILKINGS *and the* CONSTABLE. ELESIN *confronted by the seeming statue of his son, stops dead.* OLUNDE *stares above his head into the distance. The* CONSTABLES *try to grab him.* JANE *screams at them.*

JANE. Leave him alone! Simon, tell them to leave him alone.

PILKINGS. All right, stand aside you. (*Shrugs.*) Maybe just as well. It might help to calm him down.

For several moments they hold the same position. ELESIN *moves a step forward, almost as if he's still in doubt.*

ELESIN. Olunde? (*He moves his head, inspecting him from side to side.*) Olunde! (*He collapses slowly at* OLUNDE's *feet.*) Oh son, don't let the sight of your father turn you blind!

OLUNDE (*he moves for the first time since he heard his voice, brings his head slowly down to look on him*). I have no father, eater of left-overs.

He walks slowly down the way his father had run. Light fades out on ELESIN, *sobbing into the ground.*

SCENE FIVE

A wide iron-barred gate stretches almost the whole width of the cell in which ELESIN *is imprisoned. His wrists are encased in thick iron bracelets, chained together; he stands against the bars, looking out. Seated on the ground to one side on the outside is his recent* BRIDE, *her eyes bent perpetually to the ground. Figures of the two* GUARDS *can be seen deeper inside the cell, alert to every movement* ELESIN *makes.* PILKINGS *now in a police officer's uniform enters noiselessly, observes him a while. Then he coughs ostentatiously and approaches. Leans against the bars near a corner, his back to* ELESIN. *He is obviously trying to fall in mood with him. Some moments' silence.*

PILKINGS.   You seem fascinated by the moon.

ELESIN (*after a pause*). Yes, ghostly one. Your twin-brother up there engages my thoughts.

PILKINGS.   It is a beautiful night.

ELESIN.   Is that so?

PILKINGS.   The light on the leaves, the peace of the night . . .

ELESIN.   The night is not at peace, District Officer.

PILKINGS.   No? I would have said it was. You know, quiet . . .

ELESIN.   And does quiet mean peace for you?

PILKINGS.   Well, nearly the same thing. Naturally there is a subtle difference . . .

ELESIN.   The night is not at peace, ghostly one. The world is not at peace. You have shattered the peace of the world for ever. There is no sleep in the world tonight.

PILKINGS.   It is still a good bargain if the world should lose one night's sleep as the price of saving a man's life.

ELESIN.   You did not save my life, District Officer. You destroyed it.

PILKINGS.   Now come on . . .

ELESIN.   And not merely my life but the lives of many. The end of the night's work is not over. Neither this year nor the next will see it. If I wished you well, I would pray that you do not stay long enough on our land to see the disaster you have brought upon us.

PILKINGS.   Well, I did my duty as I saw it. I have no regrets.

ELESIN.   No. The regrets of life always come later.

Some moments' pause.

You are waiting for dawn, white man. I hear you saying to yourself: only so many hours until dawn and then the danger is over. All I must do is to keep him alive tonight. You don't quite understand it all but you know that tonight is when what ought to be must be brought about.

I shall ease your mind even more, ghostly one. It is not an entire night but a moment of the night, and that moment is past. The moon was my messenger and guide. When it reached a certain gateway in the sky, it touched that moment for which my whole life has been spent in blessings. Even I do not know the gateway. I have stood here and scanned the sky for a glimpse of that door but, I cannot see it. Human eyes are useless for a search of this nature. But in the house of *osugbo,* those who keep watch through the spirit recognised the moment, they sent word to me through the voice of our sacred drums to prepare myself. I heard them and I shed all thoughts of earth. I began to follow the moon to the abode of the gods . . . servant of the white king, that was when you entered my chosen place of departure on feet of desecration.

PILKINGS.   I'm sorry, but we all see our duty differently.

ELESIN.   I no longer blame you. You stole from me my first-born, sent him to your country so you could turn him into something in your own image. Did you plan it all beforehand? There are moments when it seems part of a larger plan. He who must follow my footsteps is taken from me, sent across the ocean. Then, in turn, I am stopped from fulfilling my destiny. Did you think it all out before, this plan to push our world from its course and sever the cord that links us to the great origin?

PILKINGS.   You don't really believe that. Anyway, if that was my intention with your son, I appear to have failed.

ELESIN.   You did not fail in the main, ghostly one. We know the roof covers the rafters, the cloth covers blemishes; who would have known that the white skin covered our future, preventing us from seeing the death our enemies had prepared for us. The world is set adrift and its inhabitants are lost. Around them, there is nothing but emptiness.

PILKINGS.   Your son does not take so gloomy a view.

ELESIN.   Are you dreaming now, white man? Were you not present at my reunion of shame? Did you not see when the world reversed itself and the father fell before his son, asking forgiveness?

PILKINGS.   That was in the heat of the moment. I spoke to him and . . . if you want to know, he wishes he could cut out his tongue for uttering the words he did.

ELESIN.   No. What he said must never be unsaid. The contempt of my own son rescued something of my shame at your hands. You have stopped me in my duty but I know now that I did give birth to a son. Once I mistrusted him for seeking the companionship of those my spirit knew as enemies of our race. Now I understand. One should seek to obtain the secrets of his enemies. He will avenge my shame, white one. His spirit will destroy you and yours.

PILKINGS.   That kind of talk is hardly called for. If you don't want my consolation . . .

ELESIN.   No white man, I do not want your consolation.

PILKINGS.   As you wish. Your son anyway, sends his consolation. He asks your forgiveness. When I asked him not to despise you his reply was: I cannot judge him, and if

I cannot judge him, I cannot despise him. He wants to come to you and say goodbye and to receive your blessing.

ELESIN.   Goodbye? Is he returning to your land?

PILKINGS.   Don't you think that's the most sensible thing for him to do? I advised him to leave at once, before dawn, and he agrees that is the right course of action.

ELESIN.   Yes, it is best. And even if I did not think so, I have lost the father's place of honour. My voice is broken.

PILKINGS.   Your son honours you. If he didn't he would not ask your blessing.

ELESIN.   No. Even a thoroughbred is not without pity for the turf he strikes with his hoof. When is he coming?

PILKINGS.   As soon as the town is a little quieter. I advised it.

ELESIN.   Yes, white man, I am sure you advised it. You advise all our lives although on the authority of what gods, I do not know.

PILKINGS (opens his mouth to reply, then appears to change his mind. Turns to go. Hesitates and stops again). Before I leave you, may I ask just one thing of you?

ELESIN.   I am listening.

PILKINGS.   I wish to ask you to search the quiet of your heart and tell me—do you not find great contradictions in the wisdom of your own race?

ELESIN.   Make yourself clear, white one.

PILKINGS.   I have lived among you long enough to learn a saying or two. One came to my mind tonight when I stepped into the market and saw what was going on. You were surrounded by those who egged you on with song and praises. I thought, are these not the same people who say: the elder grimly approaches heaven and you ask him to bear your greetings yonder; do you really think he makes the journey willingly? After that, I did not hesitate.

A pause. ELESIN sighs. Before he can speak a sound of running feet is heard.

JANE (off). Simon! Simon!

PILKINGS.   What on earth . . . ! (Runs off.)

ELESIN turns to his new WIFE, gazes on her for some moments.

ELESIN.   My young bride, did you hear the ghostly one? You sit and sob in your silent heart but say nothing to all this. First I blamed the white man, then I blamed my gods for deserting me. Now I feel I want to blame you for the mystery of the sapping of my will. But blame is a strange peace offering for a man to bring a world he has deeply wronged, and to its innocent dwellers. Oh little mother, I have taken countless women in my life but you were more than a desire of the flesh. I needed you as the abyss across which my body must be drawn, I filled it with earth and dropped my seed in it at the moment of preparedness for my crossing. You were the final gift of the living to their

emissary to the land of the ancestors, and perhaps your warmth and youth brought new insights of this world to me and turned my feet leaden on this side of the abyss. For I confess to you, daughter, my weakness came not merely from the abomination of the white man who came violently into my fading presence, there was also a weight of longing on my earth-held limbs. I would have shaken it off, already my foot had begun to lift but then, the white ghost entered and all was defiled.

Approaching voices of PILKINGS and his WIFE.

JANE.   Oh Simon, you will let her in won't you?

PILKINGS.   I really wish you'd stop interfering.

They come into view. JANE is in a dressing-gown. PILKINGS is holding a note to which he refers from time to time.

JANE.   Good gracious, I didn't initiate this. I was sleeping quietly, or trying to anyway, when the servant brought it. It's not my fault if one can't sleep undisturbed even in the Residency.

PILKINGS.   He'd have done the same thing if we were sleeping at home so don't sidetrack the issue. He knows he can get round you or he wouldn't send you the petition in the first place.

JANE.   Be fair Simon. After all he was thinking of your own interests. He is grateful you know, you seem to forget that. He feels he owes you something.

PILKINGS.   I just wish they'd leave this man alone tonight, that's all.

JANE.   Trust him Simon. He's pledged his word it will all go peacefully.

PILKINGS.   Yes, and that's the other thing. I don't like being threatened.

JANE.   Threatened? (Takes the note.) I didn't spot any threat.

PILKINGS.   It's there. Veiled, but it's there. The only way to prevent serious rioting tomorrow—what a cheek!

JANE.   I don't think he's threatening you Simon.

PILKINGS.   He's picked up the idiom all right. Wouldn't surprise me if he's been mixing with commies or anarchists over there. The phrasing sounds too good to be true. Damn! If only the Prince hadn't picked this time for his visit.

JANE.   Well, even so Simon, what have you got to lose? You don't want a riot on your hands, not with the Prince here.

PILKINGS (going up to ELESIN). Let's see what he has to say. Chief Elesin, there is yet another person who wants to see you. As she is not a next-of-kin I don't really feel obliged to let her in. But your son sent a note with her, so it's up to you.

ELESIN.   I know who that must be. So she found out your hiding-place. Well, it was not difficult. My stench of shame is so strong, it requires no hunter's dog to follow it.

PILKINGS.   If you don't want to see her, just say so and I'll send her packing.

ELESIN.   Why should I not want to see her? Let her come. I have no more holes in my rag of shame. All is laid bare.

PILKINGS.   I'll bring her in. (*Goes off.*)

JANE (*hesitates, then goes to* ELESIN). Please, try and understand. Everything my husband did was for the best.

ELESIN (*he gives her a long strange stare, as if he is trying to understand who she is*). You are the wife of the District Officer?

JANE.   Yes. My name, is Jane.

ELESIN.   That is my wife sitting down there. You notice how still and silent she sits? My business is with your husband.

PILKINGS *returns with* IYALOJA.

PILKINGS.   Here she is. Now first I want your word of honour that you will try nothing foolish.

ELESIN.   Honour? White one, did you say you wanted my word of honour?

PILKINGS.   I know you to be an honourable man. Give me your word of honour you will receive nothing from her.

ELESIN.   But I am sure you have searched her clothing as you would never dare touch your own mother. And there are these two lizards of yours who roll their eyes even when I scratch.

PILKINGS.   And I shall be sitting on that tree trunk watching even how you blink. Just the same I want your word that you will not let her pass anything to you.

ELESIN.   You have my honour already. It is locked up in that desk in which you will put away your report of this night's events. Even the honour of my people you have taken already; it is tied together with those papers of treachery which make you masters in this land.

PILKINGS.   All right. I am trying to make things easy but if you must bring in politics we'll have to do it the hard way. Madam, I want you to remain along this line and move no nearer to the cell door. Guards! (*They spring to attention.*) If she moves beyond this point, blow your whistle. Come on Jane. (*They go off.*)

IYALOJA.   How boldly the lizard struts before the pigeon when it was the eagle itself he promised us he would confront.

ELESIN.   I don't ask you to take pity on me Iyaloja. You have a message for me or you would not have come. Even if it is the curses of the world, I shall listen.

IYALOJA.   You made so bold with the servant of the white king who took your side against death. I must tell your brother chiefs when I return how bravely you waged war against him. Especially with words.

ELESIN.   I more than deserve your scorn.

IYALOJA (*with sudden anger*). I warned you, if you must leave a seed behind, be sure it is not tainted with the curses of the world. Who are you to open a new life when you dared not open the door to a new existence? I say who are you to make so bold? (*The* BRIDE *sobs and* IYALOJA *notices her. Her contempt noticeably increases as she turns back to* ELESIN.) Oh you self-vaunted stem of the plantain, how hollow it all proves. The pith is gone in the parent stem, so how will it prove with the new shoot? How will it go with that earth that bears it? Who are you to bring this abomination on us!

ELESIN.   My powers deserted me. My charms, my spells, even my voice lacked strength when I made to summon the powers that would lead me over the last measure of earth into the land of the fleshless. You saw it, Iyaloja. You saw me struggle to retrieve my will from the power of the stranger whose shadow fell across the doorway and left me floundering and blundering in a maze I had never before encountered. My senses were numbed when the touch of cold iron came upon my wrists. I could do nothing to save myself.

IYALOJA.   You have betrayed us. We fed you sweetmeats such as we hoped awaited you on the other side. But you said No, I must eat the world's left-overs. We said you were the hunter who brought the quarry down; to you belonged the vital portions of the game. No, you said, I am the hunter's dog and I shall eat the entrails of the game and the faeces of the hunter. We said you were the hunter returning home in triumph, a slain buffalo pressing down on his neck; you said wait, I first must turn up this cricket hole with my toes. We said yours was the doorway at which we first spy the tapper when he comes down from the tree, yours was the blessing of the twilight wine, the purl that brings night spirits out of doors to steal their portion before the light of day. We said yours was the body of wine whose burden shakes the tapper like a sudden gust on his perch. You said, No, I am content to lick the dregs from each calabash when the drinkers are done. We said, the dew on earth's surface was for you to wash your feet along the slopes of honour. You said No, I shall step in the vomit of cats and the droppings of mice; I shall fight them for the left-overs of the world.

ELESIN.   Enough Iyaloja, enough.

IYALOJA.   We called you leader and oh, how you led us on. What we have no intention of eating should not be held to the nose.

ELESIN.   Enough, enough. My shame is heavy enough.

IYALOJA.   Wait. I came with a burden.

ELESIN.   You have more than discharged it.

IYALOJA.   I wish I could pity you.

ELESIN.   I need neither pity nor the pity of the world. I need understanding. Even I need to understand. You were present at my defeat. You were part of the beginnings. You brought about the renewal of my tie to earth, you helped in the binding of the cord.

IYALOJA.   I gave you warning. The river which fills up before our eyes does not sweep us away in its flood.

ELESIN.   What were warnings beside the moist contact of living earth between my fingers? What were warnings beside the renewal of famished embers lodged eternally in the heart of man. But even that, even if it overwhelmed one with a thousandfold temptations to linger a little while, a man could overcome it. It is when the alien hand pollutes the source of will, when a stranger force of violence shatters the mind's calm resolution, this is when a man is made to commit the awful treachery of relief, commit in his thought the unspeakable blasphemy of seeing the hand of the gods in this alien rupture of his world. I know it was this thought that killed me, sapped my powers and turned me into an infant in the hands of unnamable strangers. I made to utter my spells anew but my tongue merely rattled in my mouth. I fingered hidden charms and the contact was damp; there was no spark left to sever the life-strings that should stretch from every fingertip. My will was squelched in the spittle of an alien race, and all because I had committed this blasphemy of thought—that there might be the hand of the gods in a stranger's intervention.

IYALOJA.   Explain it how you will, I hope it brings you peace of mind. The bush-rat fled his rightful cause, reached the market and set up a lamentation. 'Please save me!'—are these fitting words to hear from an ancestral mask? 'There's a wild beast at my heels' is not becoming language from a hunter.

ELESIN.   May the world forgive me.

IYALOJA.   I came with a burden I said. It approaches the gates which are so well guarded by those jackals whose spittle will from this day be on your food and drink. But first, tell me, you who were once Elesin Oba, tell me, you who know so well the cycle of the plantain: is it the parent shoot which withers to give sap to the younger or, does your wisdom see it running the other way?

ELESIN.   I don't see your meaning Iyaloja?

IYALOJA.   Did I ask you for a meaning? I asked a question. Whose trunk withers to give sap to the other? The parent shoot or the younger?

ELESIN.   The parent.

IYALOJA.   Ah. So you do know that. There are sights in this world which say different Elesin. There are some who choose to reverse the cycle of our being. Oh you emptied bark that the world once saluted for a pith-laden being, shall I tell you what the gods have claimed for you?

In her agitation she steps beyond the line indicated by PILK-INGS *and the air is rent by piercing whistles. The two* GUARDS *also leap forward and place safe-guarding hands on* ELESIN. IYALOJA *stops, astonished.* PILKINGS *comes racing in, followed by* JANE.

PILKINGS.   What is it? Did they try something?

GUARD.   She stepped beyond the line.

ELESIN (*in a broken voice*). Let her alone. She meant no harm.

IYALOJA.   Oh Elesin, see what you've become. Once you had no need to open your mouth in explanation because evil-smelling goats, itchy of hand and foot had lost their senses. And it was a brave man indeed who dared lay hands on you because Iyaloja stepped from one side of the earth onto another. Now look at the spectacle of your life. I grieve for you.

PILKINGS.   I think you'd better leave. I doubt you have done him much good by coming here. I shall make sure you are not allowed to see him again. In any case we are moving him to a different place before dawn, so don't bother to come back.

IYALOJA.   We foresaw that. Hence the burden I trudged here to lay beside your gates.

PILKINGS.   What was that you said?

IYALOJA.   Didn't our son explain? Ask that one. He knows what it is. At least we hope the man we once knew as Elesin remembers the lesser oaths he need not break.

PILKINGS.   Do you know what she is talking about?

ELESIN.   Go to the gates, ghostly one. Whatever you find there, bring it to me.

IYALOJA.   Not yet. It drags behind me on the slow, weary feet of women. Slow as it is Elesin, it has long overtaken you. It rides ahead of your laggard will.

PILKINGS.   What is she saying now? Christ! Must your people forever speak in riddles?

ELESIN.   It will come white man, it will come. Tell your men at the gates to let it through.

PILKINGS (*dubiously*). I'll have to see what it is.

IYALOJA.   You will. (*Passionately.*) But this is one oath he cannot shirk. White one, you have a king here, a visitor from your land. We know of his presence here. Tell me, were he to die would you leave his spirit roaming restlessly on the surface of earth? Would you bury him here among those you consider less than human? In your land have you no ceremonies of the dead?

PILKINGS.   Yes. But we don't make our chiefs commit suicide to keep him company.

IYALOJA.   Child, I have not come to help your understanding. (*Points to* ELESIN.) This is the man whose weakened understanding holds us in bondage to you. But ask him if you wish. He knows the meaning of a king's passage; he was not born yesterday. He knows the peril to the race when our dead father, who goes as intermediary, waits and waits and knows he is betrayed. He knows when the narrow gate was opened and he knows it will not stay for laggards who drag their feet in dung and vomit, whose lips are reeking of the left-overs of lesser men. He knows he has condemned our king to wander in the void of evil with beings who are enemies of life.

PILKINGS.   Yes er . . . but look here . . .

IYALOJA.   What we ask is little enough. Let him release our King so he can ride on homewards alone. The messenger is on his way on the backs of women. Let him send word through the heart that is folded up within the bolt. It is the least of all his oaths, it is the easiest fulfilled.

The AIDE-DE-CAMP *runs in.*

PILKINGS.   Bob?

AIDE-DE-CAMP.   Sir, there's a group of women chanting up the hill.

PILKINGS (*rounding on* IYALOJA). If you people want trouble . . .

JANE.   Simon, I think that's what Olunde referred to in his letter.

PILKINGS.   He knows damned well I can't have a crowd here! Damn it, I explained the delicacy of my position to him. I think it's about time I got him out of town. Bob, send a car and two or three soldiers to bring him in. I think the sooner he takes his leave of his father and gets out the better.

IYALOJA.   Save your labour white one. If it is the father of your prisoner you want, Olunde, he who until this night we knew as Elesin's son, he comes soon himself to take his leave. He has sent the women ahead, so let them in.

PILKINGS *remains undecided.*

AIDE-DE-CAMP.   What do we do about the invasion? We can still stop them far from here.

PILKINGS.   What do they look like?

AIDE-DE-CAMP.   They're not many. And they seem quite peaceful.

PILKINGS.   No men?

AIDE-DE-CAMP.   Mm, two or three at the most.

JANE.   Honestly, Simon, I'd trust Olunde. I don't think he'll deceive you about their intentions.

PILKINGS.   He'd better not. All right then, let them in Bob. Warn them to control themselves. Then hurry Olunde here. Make sure he brings his baggage because I'm not returning him into town.

AIDE-DE-CAMP.   Very good, sir. (*Goes.*)

PILKINGS (*to* IYALOJA). I hope you understand that if anything goes wrong it will be on your head. My men have orders to shoot at the first sign of trouble.

IYALOJA.   To prevent one death you will actually make other deaths? Ah, great is the wisdom of the white race. But have no fear. Your Prince will sleep peacefully. So at long last will ours. We will disturb you no further, servant of the white king. Just let Elesin fulfil his oath and we will retire home and pay homage to our King.

JANE.   I believe her Simon, don't you?

PILKINGS.   Maybe.

ELESIN.   Have no fear ghostly one. I have a message to send my King and then you have nothing more to fear.

IYALOJA.   Olunde would have done it. The chiefs asked him to speak the words but he said no, not while you lived.

ELESIN.   Even from the depths to which my spirit has sunk, I find some joy that this little has been left to me.

The WOMEN *enter, intoning the dirge 'Ale le le' and swaying from side to side. On their shoulders is borne a longish object roughly like a cylindrical bolt, covered in cloth. They set it down on the spot where* IYALOJA *had stood earlier, and form a semi-circle round it. The* PRAISE-SINGER *and* DRUMMER *stand on the inside of the semi-circle but the drum is not used at all. The* DRUMMER *intones under the* PRAISE-SINGER'*s invocations.*

PILKINGS (*as they enter*). What is *that?*

IYALOJA.   The burden you have made white one, but we bring it in peace.

PILKINGS.   I said *what* is it?

ELESIN.   White man, you must let me out. I have a duty to perform.

PILKINGS.   I most certainly will not.

ELESIN.   There lies the courier of my King. Let me out so I can perform what is demanded of me.

PILKINGS.   You'll do what you need to do from inside there or not at all. I've gone as far as I intend to with this business.

ELESIN.   The worshipper who lights a candle in your church to bear a message to his god bows his head and speaks in a whisper to the flame. Have I not seen it ghostly one? His voice does not ring out to the world. Mine are no words for anyone's ears. They are not words even for the bearers of this load. They are words I must speak secretly, even as my father whispered them in my ears and I in the ears of my first-born. I cannot shout them to the wind and the open night-sky.

JANE.   Simon . . .

PILKINGS.   Don't interfere. Please!

IYALOJA.   They have slain the favourite horse of the king and slain his dog. They have borne them from pulse to pulse centre of the land receiving prayers for their king. But the rider has chosen to stay behind. Is it too much to ask that he speak his heart to heart of the waiting courier? (PILKINGS *turns his back on her.*) So be it. Elesin Oba, you see how even the mere leavings are denied you. (*She gestures to the* PRAISE-SINGER.)

PRAISE-SINGER.   Elesin Oba! I call you by that name only this last time. Remember when I said, if you cannot come, tell my horse. (*Pause.*) What? I cannot hear you? I said, if you cannot come, whisper in the ears of my horse. Is your tongue severed from the roots? Elesin? I can hear no response. I said, if there are boulders you cannot climb, mount my horse's back, this spotless black stallion, he'll bring you over them. (*Pauses.*) Elesin Oba, once you had a tongue that darted like a drummer's stick. I said, if you get lost my dog will track a path to me. My memory fails me but I think you replied: My feet have found the path, Alafin.

The dirge rises and falls.

I said at the last, if evil hands hold you back, just tell my horse there is weight on the hem of your smock. I dare not wait too long.

The dirge rises and falls.

There lies the swiftest ever messenger of a king, so set me free with the errand of your heart. There lie the head and heart of the favourite of the gods, whisper in his ears. Oh my companion, if you had followed when you should, we would not say that the horse preceded its rider. If you had followed when it was time, we would not say the dog has raced beyond and left his master behind. If you had raised your will to cut the thread of life at the summons of the drums, we would not say your mere shadow fell across the gateway and took its owner's place at the banquet. But the hunter, laden with slain buffalo, stayed to root in the cricket's hole with his toes. What now is left? If there is a dearth of bats, the pigeon must serve us for the offering. Speak the words over your shadow which must now serve in your place.

ELESIN.   I cannot approach. Take off the cloth. I shall speak my message from heart to heart of silence.

IYALOJA (*moves forward and removes the covering*). Your courier Elesin, cast your eyes on the favoured companion of the King.

Rolled up in the mat, his head and feet showing at either end, is the body of OLUNDE.

There lies the honour of your household and of our race. Because he could not bear to let honour fly out of doors, he stopped it with his life. The son has proved the father Elesin, and there is nothing left in your mouth to gnash but infant gums.

PRAISE-SINGER.   Elesin, we placed the reins of the world in your hands yet you watched it plunge over the edge of the bitter precipice. You sat with folded arms while evil strangers tilted the world from its course and crashed it beyond the edge of emptiness—you muttered, there is little that one man can do, you left us floundering in a blind future. Your heir has taken the burden on himself. What the end will be, we are not gods to tell. But this young shoot has poured its sap into the parent stalk, and we know this is not the way of life. Our world is tumbling in the void of strangers, Elesin.

ELESIN *has stood rock-still, his knuckles taut on the bars, his eyes glued to the body of his son. The stillness seizes and paralyses everyone, including* PILKINGS *who has turned to look. Suddenly* ELESIN *flings one arm round his neck, once, and with the loop of the chain, strangles himself in a swift, decisive pull. The* GUARDS *rush forward to stop him but they are only in time to let his body down.* PILKINGS *has leapt to the door at the same time and struggles with the lock. He*

rushes within, fumbles with the handcuffs and unlocks them, raises the body to a sitting position while he tries to give resuscitation. The WOMEN *continue their dirge, unmoved by the sudden event.*

IYALOJA.   Why do you strain yourself? Why do you labour at tasks for which no one, not even the man lying there would give you thanks? He is gone at last into the passage but oh, how late it all is. His son will feast on the meat and throw him bones. The passage is clogged with droppings from the King's stallion; he will arrive all stained in dung.

PILKINGS (*in a tired voice*). Was this what you wanted?

IYALOJA.   No child, it is what you brought to be, you who play with strangers' lives, who even usurp the vestments of our dead, yet believe that the stain of death will not cling to you. The gods demanded only the old expired plantain but you cut down the sap-laden shoot to feed your pride. There is your board, filled to overflowing. Feast on it. (*She screams at him suddenly, seeing that* PILKINGS *is about to close* ELESIN's *staring eyes.*) Let him alone! However sunk he was in debt he is no pauper's carrion abandoned on the road. Since when have strangers donned clothes of indigo before the bereaved cries out his loss?

She turns to the BRIDE *who has remained motionless throughout.*

Child.

The girl takes up a little earth, walks calmly into the cell and closes ELESIN's *eyes. She then pours some earth over each eyelid and comes out again.*

Now forget the dead, forget even the living. Turn your mind only to the unborn.

She goes off, accompanied by the BRIDE. *The dirge rises in volume and the* WOMEN *continue their sway. Lights fade to a black-out.*

Glossary

alari	a rich, woven cloth, brightly coloured
egungun	ancestral masquerade
etutu	placatory rites or medicine
gbedu	a deep-timbred royal drum
opele	string of beads used in Ifa divination
osugbo	secret 'executive' cult of the Yoruba; its meeting place
robo	a delicacy made from crushed melon seeds, fried in tiny balls
sanyan	a richly valued woven cloth
sigidi	a squat, carved figure, endowed with the powers of an incubus

FOCUS QUESTIONS

1. In scene 1, Elesin boasts that he is ready to embark on the journey to the land of the ancestors. In a brief essay, show how ill-prepared he really is.
2. Compare Amusa's relationship to his employers with his treatment by the women of the marketplace.
3. Iyaloja and the Praise-singer have a great deal of power in their community. By analyzing their speeches, discuss the roles they play as community leaders.
4. Compare and contrast the symbolic actions of the leaders in the play: Elesin, the Prince of Wales, and the ship's captain to whom Olunde refers.
5. Discuss Olunde's perspective of European values during war-time in an effort to explain why he returns home to bury his father.
6. Soyinka wants to revitalize Yoruba culture through his plays. Explain how he accomplishes this by comparing the rituals of the marketplace with those of the colonialists' club.
7. Discuss why Simon and Jane Pilkings are both ill-suited to deal with the cultural differences they encounter in Nigeria. Note how neither Simon's attitude of *laissez-faire* nor Jane's compassionate tolerance is adequate.

OTHER ACTIVITIES

1. Select one of the European characters and one of the Yoruba characters in the play and write a monologue for each that depicts his or her attitude about the opposing culture.
2. Research pictures of Nigeria during the colonial period and create a scrapbook that suggests costumes and settings needed for a realistic production of the play.
3. Taking Elesin's story of the Not-I bird, write a boastful speech that includes all of the narrative elements but uses American idioms.

BIBLIOGRAPHY

Etherton, Michael. *The Development of African Drama*. New York: Africana Publishing Co., 1982.

Gibbs, James. *Critical Perspectives on Wole Soyinka*. Washington, DC: Three Continents Press, 1983.

———. *Wole Soyinka*. New York: Grove Press, 1986.

Jeyifo, Biodun. *The Truthful Lie: Essays in a Sociology of African Drama*. London: New Beacon Books, 1985.

Jones, Eldred Durosimi. *The Writing of Wole Soyinka*. Portsmouth, NH: Heinemann Educational Books, Inc., 1988.

Katrak, Ketu H. *Wole Soyinka and Modern Tragedy: A Study of Dramatic Theory and Practice*. Westport, CT: Greenwood Press, 1986.

King, Bruce, ed. *Post-Colonial English Drama*. New York: St. Martin's Press, 1993.

Maduakor, Obi. *Wole Soyinka: An Introduction to His Writing*. New York: Garland Publishing, Inc., 1987.

Maja-Pearce, Adewale, ed. *Wole Soyinka: An Appraisal*. Portsmouth, NH: Heinemann, 1994.

Moore, Gerald. *Wole Soyinka*. New York: Africana Publishing Co., 1971.

Peters, Jonathan A. *A Dance of Masks: Senghor, Achebe, Soyinka*. Washington, DC: Three Continents Press, 1978.

Wright, Derek. *Wole Soyinka Revisited*. New York: Twayne Publishers, 1993.

DOUBLE GOTHIC
MICHAEL KIRBY (1931–   )

In all of Michael Kirby's plays there are motifs of mystery—apparent political intrigues, assassinations, possible suicides, implied terrorist activities, gothic tales. No solution is presented . . . the real intrigue is the schematic structure which one attempts to grasp.

—THEODORE SHANK

Maria Myers (*left*) and Amy Heebner in *Double Gothic,* presented at the Performing Garage in 1978, under the playwright's direction. *Photo: Michael Kirby.*

APPROACHING STRUCTURALIST THEATRE

As photography developed and facilitated the reproduction of visual images, artists shifted their attention away from capturing what people saw to depicting emotions and dream states instead. This emphasis on the inner reality of human experience was a reaction against the tendency in the latter half of the nineteenth century to objectify human behavior. Painters experimented with different ways of seeing on a two-dimensional plane, rather than creating the illusion of three dimensionality. On the stage as well, playwrights began to question the recently established prominence of **naturalism** and **realism.** Their responses launched an **avant-garde** movement in art and performance.

One way for artists to counteract the omniscient relationship of the audience to what transpired on the realistic stage was to influence the audience's reception of a performance. The operas of Richard Wagner, for example, were intended to provide complete sensory experiences that enveloped audiences in sound and plunged them in darkness as they beheld the unfolding mythological spectacle. Symbolists Paul Fort and Aurélien-Marie Lugné Poë approximated dream states through the depiction of actions whose intelligibility was blurred by **scrims** and uninflected voices; futurists led by Filippo Tommaso Marinetti bombarded their audiences with insults, industrial noise, and instruments of technology; and **surrealists** like André Breton used chance, games, and juxtaposed narratives to elicit new meanings and perceptions from the viewer. In every case, artists were exploring truths about modern life that transcended appearances and highlighted underlying structures.

By the 1920s the traditional boundaries between visual arts, dance, and theatrical performance had already collapsed, as evidenced by the performance work of Wassily Kandinsky, Pablo Picasso, and Dada events staged by Tristan Tzara. This melding of artistic forms and the synthesis between art and technology were most evident in the performances staged by Oskar Schlemmer at the Bauhaus School in Germany. Costumed to look like mechanical objects or puppets, students moved across the floor using patterns that Schlemmer had originally envisioned on paper. These "dances" were investigations of how color, line, and pattern became transformed in space, performances that artist Xanti Schawinsky called "visual theatre, a realization of painting and constructions in motion, ideas in colour, form and space and their dramatic inter-action."[1] The theories and experiments of Bauhaus artists who had emigrated to the United States in the early 1930s would have a profound impact on art and performance in America.

These formal concerns with how art is made, how it is shaped by its materials, and how it is finally perceived, surfaced in post-World War II America. Artists' efforts to grapple with these aesthetic questions resulted in process painting, a form of abstract expressionism; chance music; experimental dance; and events known as "happenings." Using time and space like clay and paint, they created performances instead of objects. They structured the actions to be performed into intervals of time. They shaped the space and controlled the flow of movement through the performance environments by dividing their studios or galleries into rooms and corridors. Viewing the event from different angles, spectators received the visual and aural stimuli at varying intensities or, in some cases, were prevented from experiencing certain parts of the action. This ensured that patrons could witness a unique event as each of them processed what had transpired.

At the Judson Dance Group in New York, choreographers Simone Forti, Yvonne Rainer, Trisha Brown, and Steve Paxton responded to these same artistic concerns by using the patterns of everyday movements and gestures to avoid representation of emotional states or the enactment of narratives. Their challenge in developing a new dance aesthetic was, according to Rainer, to discover "how to move in the space between theatrical bloat with its burden of dramatic psychological 'meaning'—and—the imagery and atmospheric effects of the non-dramatic, non-verbal theatre (i.e., dancing and some 'happenings')—and—theatre of spectator participation and/or assault.''[2] Their approach to movement influenced other artists involved with the creation of happenings.

Among them was Michael Kirby, a former stage director whose personal disenchantment with the theatre resulted from his ''negative attitudes towards storytelling and fantasy, projection and empathy, mood and characterization.''[3] Sitting in the audience or performing new dance pieces and happenings, he was drawn to the works and often documented the performances of Robert Rauschenburg, Steve Paxton, Deborah Hay, Yvonne Rainer, Nam June Paik, Allan Kaprow, Red Grooms, Robert Whitman, Jim Dine, and Claes Oldenburg. In 1963, he began to stage his own happenings, performance art, dance theatre, and other avant-garde works in the United States, Italy, Korea, and Israel.

As founder of the Structuralist Workshop, Kirby developed a theatre interested in presenting plays which, although alogical, explored how ''the parts of a work related to each other, how they 'fit together' in the mind to form a particular configuration.''[4] These plays utilized discontinuous narratives that were experienced by spectators whose memories and expectations were engaged through the use of repeated phrases, gestures, or objects. He uncovered a new performance style in which elements of drama—humor, recognition, fulfillment of expectations or twists of the unexpected—could be achieved without manipulating the experiences for his audience through plot and characterization. Instead, the drama unfolded as his spectators became engaged in the structure through which lights, sound, color, movement, dialogue, and story fragments were assembled. These formal elements continued to characterize not only his work but also the performance pieces of Robert Wilson and Richard Foreman.

MAJOR WORKS

Kirby became a proponent of **structuralism** and a leading scholar of the avant-garde, elevating its importance in the study of contemporary theatre. To this end, he was editor of *The Drama Review* and published four books: *Happenings* (1965), *The Art of Time* (1969), *Futurist Performance* (1971), *The New Theatre: Performance Documentation* (1974). In addition to chronicling avant-garde performance since the early twentieth century, he became an internationally known creator of structuralist plays. From his earliest experimentation with performance as the enactment of the logic of games in *The First and Second Wilderness: A Civil War Game* (1963) for the Yam Festival, he staged performances similar to the happenings and events taking place in Manhattan studios and galleries. These included *Hand Happening* (1964), *Room 706* (1966), *The Chekov Machine* (1966), and *Expo Alogical* (1967).

Characterized by their use of mathematical configurations of scenic elements—such as film clips, slides, and dialogue fragments—and scenes with repetitive storylines often borrowed from popular genres like the folktale, the gothic novel, or science fiction, his playscripts were performed in Off-Off-Broadway theatres and artists' lofts and galleries. These included *There/This/Move* (1971), *Eight People* (1975), *Revolutionary Dance* (1975), *PhotoAnalysis* (1976), *Identity Control* (1977), *Incidents in Renaissance Venice* (1979), *The Alchemical Caligari* (1981), *Prisoners of the Invisible Kingdom* (1982), *First Signs of Decadence* (1989), *An Investigation of Unnatural Occurrences* (1993), *An Interrogation by Agents Unknown* (1993), *The Quadratic Rehearsals* (1995). Of these plays, *Double Gothic* (1978) has received the highest acclaim, winning the Villager Award for best scenography in 1979.

THE ACTION

A series of brief illuminated actions taken from the scenes to follow serve as **prologue.** Two similar and alternating stories now unravel and pass through each other. The storyline in each begins when the protagonist—a young woman stranded at night in an isolated place—is met by another woman who appears to be handicapped. They travel through the woods to an old house where they are greeted by the antagonist—an older woman who lives there. While the older woman shows the young woman her bedroom, the helper, who has been spying on them through what appears to be either a mirror or portrait, interrupts them. Left alone, the protagonist undresses for bed, unaware that her hostess is spying on her from another room. While she sleeps, the antagonist and her helper have a disagreement. One of them is jealous of their guest and intends to do her harm. In the end, the helper enters the protagonist's bedroom, awakening her and warning her that she should leave. Rather than heed this warning, the young woman takes a light and wanders through the house to investigate what kind of danger awaits her. The play ends with an epilogue of brief illuminated moments from both stories.

STRUCTURE AND LANGUAGE

The premise underlying the structure of *Double Gothic* was inspired by Vladimir Propp's study, *Morphology of the Folktale,* which asserts that all Russian fairy tales use a limited number of events organized in a fixed order. Determined to investigate this premise, Kirby has created two Gothic stories that progress through their six scenes in similar fashion. Although details of place, action, and character functions—heroine, antagonist, and helper—correspond, the stories stand independently and, in each, the innocent heroine is lured to a dark old house during a storm. She encounters ominous signs along the way—a suitcase that appears and disappears, the sound of glass breaking, a snake on the dark path, the distant scream of a woman—all of which **foreshadow** the peril awaiting her. In the mansion the presence of the snake in her bed, the undressed doll with hands and feet bound, the odd, almost fetishistic fascination of her hostess with her eyes or her hands and feet create a mounting tension that could be resolved only if she were killed or rescued. To our surprise, however, nothing happens to either heroine.

The sense of suspense is not only created by suggestive imagery, sound effects, and organ music, but is heightened by Kirby's reliance on repeated words and images. Furthermore, by alternating the stories, he "added the dynamic of anticipation. Once the spectator realized that the second story was a version of the first, certain elements could be expected . . . If anything was not perceived because of darkness, low vocal level, and intervening scrim walls, it could be assumed to be similar to what was perceived clearly in the corresponding close scene."[5]

The first structure presented to us is a prologue consisting of two mathematically constructed series of images and bits of dialogue from the first five pairs of scenes. Isolated by scrims and separated by blackouts, these brief flashforwards are grouped around their reference to feet: Heroine A holds up her shoe and says, "My shoe is broken;" Helper B feels the legs of a doll and remarks, "One of her shoes is missing;" and Antagonist B silently looks at a shoe. The second set refers to hands: feeling Heroine B's hand, Helper B asks, "Is that a wedding ring?" Heroine A takes off her gloves, and Antagonist A, examining her own hands, asks, "Are they long enough?" Other than the common theme of each line, there is no information that links them. There are resonances, however, when these phrases and visual images are echoed later in the action. The prologue ends with brief segments from scenes A–1 and B–1 which are presented twice, each with a bit more dia-logue. With the first full scene of each story, the audience sees and hears the opening for the third time and becomes conscious of the deliberate and formal use of repetition.

Recognition and memory are as important to the play as anticipation. Through the course of action, correspondences between the stories proliferate: the helpers, one blind and one mute, are not really handicapped; the heroines are given a warning, one to refrain from going outside and the other to refrain from going downstairs, without explanation; in both stories, the antagonists and helpers are voyeurs—in story A they peer through a painting and in story B they watch through a two-way mirror; and in each encounter with an antagonist, the telephone becomes a crucial indicator that the heroine may be in danger.

Further repetitions create intersections between the two stories when material pre-sented in one story appears to cross over into the other. In scene A–1, for example, the heroine has only one good high-heeled shoe, which she removes and leaves in the forest when she has to follow Helper A to the house. We see the shoe again in scene B–4 as Helper B enters with it and Antagonist B asks, ''Did you have to bring it here? . . . it has mud on it.'' Nothing can be deduced from its presence in Story B, despite the link made in the audience's mind, which adds to the play's eerie sense of foreboding. Similarly, the altered but mirrored intimation of a lesbian relationship—the Helper from story A and the Antagonist from story B are each dressed in tie and jacket—points to a possible reason for the jealousy expressed in scenes A–5 and B–5 and to a motive for violence awaiting each heroine. Nothing is certain, but merely suggested. As critic Noel Carroll has remarked, ''We have the feeling that a puzzle has fallen into place, but this is the function of structural clarity and interconnectedness rather than of the completion of the narrative.''[6]

By the sixth and final scene of each story, the differences between them have dis-appeared: the lines and actions are identical. As each heroine dismisses the helper's warning and attempts to find out what is happening, she traces the pattern of movement established by the preceding five scenes rather than moving toward a plot resolution, so that differing details of each story are no longer significant. *Double Gothic* ends formally, using a similar structure to its beginning: two distinct series of isolated images and phrases are taken from the first five scenes of each story. Now presented in reverse order, these brief glimpses or flashbacks from the play focus on accusatory pointing and women handing things to one another, images that trigger memories of these moments which run from the end of the play to the beginning. These are mere hints of motives seen in retrospect, although nothing has happened that needs to be explained. Closure occurs because there are no more possible patterns of movement through the five corridors.

Kirby's play hinges on how spectators piece together the patterns and fill in the perceptual gaps as they compare the actions and characters of the juxtaposed stories. Since there is no mystery to solve, recognition of how the play is systematically constructed is the point. *Double Gothic* finally illustrates that form is content and that the experience of engaging with its structures can be as rewarding as the triumph of good over evil.

DOUBLE GOTHIC-IN-PERFORMANCE

Under the playwright's meticulous direction, *Double Gothic* opened at the Envelope The-atre, an annex to the Performing Garage in New York City, in December 1978, and ran for eight weekends through February 1979. Kirby designed the production as well. The audi-ence, divided in half and seated facing opposite sides of a performance space that resembled a black box, viewed the progressing stories from behind translucent black scrims that dis-sected the box into five parallel corridors. Each corresponding scene was presented in reverse of the other: if, in a scene played close to you, the bed was on the right side, then, in the complementary scene played far away from you, the bed would be on the left side. Furthermore, the misty lighting effect accentuated the impression that the story that had begun closest to the audience was receding or becoming less comprehensible. Brooks McNamara recalled that "when the characters [were] in the corridors farthest away from you, you really [saw] fragments. The lights illuminate[d] the skin, light colored clothing and so on, but the rest of their bodies seem[ed] to trail off into the darkness."[7] According to Sally Sommer, who was fascinated by the visual play of images and the eerie detachment with which the performers calmly delivered their lines, the staging of the production was "complex and absolutely splendid" and provided "an intellectual lure to find the pattern [in Kirby's] cerebral game."[8]

Kirby's production was videotaped by Korean director Woo Ok Kim, who eventually directed two performances of the play in Seoul and would later recall some of his own experiences:

> The first performance was in May 1982 and the second one in May 1983. The venue both times was the hall of the Moonye Hoekwan built in 1981. We made a black box which was 7.2 metres long and 6 metres wide with five 1.2 metre compartments divided by 6 sheets of black scrim. Since scrim was not available at that time, we used fish nets instead. The general effect, however, was superb because of the rather wide holes in the net which were perfectly right to create the images in the play.
>
> The six actresses in my first production had a month of rehearsals to adjust to the acting style required for the play. We had only a two-week rehearsal period for the second production, in which the leading Korean actress, Keumji Kim, who had been used to a rather exaggerated performance style which the other actresses followed, was perplexed by the unusual acting style that I demanded. This was her first experimental play and she proved quite successful.
>
> General reactions to both productions were mixed. Those who had not been exposed to this kind of theatre were confused by the play's alternating stories. But those who were acquainted with art—paintings and sculpture in particular—were fascinated by the many beautiful images created in the different compartments of the black box. Korean critic, Sang Lee, wrote that my production "broadened our experience of theatre by employing film techniques of cutting and sequencing images." Another critic, Sang Chul Han, felt that works like *Double Gothic* helped us "decipher the characteristics and dispositions of the age we lived in."[9]

Performance artist, Cheryl Faver, directed *Double Gothic* at the Yale Cabaret in 1987. Unlike Kirby's production, which moved slowly and used abrupt cessations of musical sound effects, Faver approached the work as a unified whole whose actions flowed from start to finish. Knowing that the play revolved around the formal aspects of the gothic tale, she accentuated these stereotypical characteristics to enhance the inherent humor of the work. She emphasized the obligatory music, thunder claps, cricket chirps, hooting owls, croaking frogs, dog howls, and human cries—so typical of this genre—but employed poor quality sound effects to draw attention to them. The audience responded with the laughter of recognition at these familiar signifiers. But for those who fathomed the formulaic design, *Double Gothic* was "like metatheatre, an experience in how to see a production."[10]

REFLECTIONS ON DOUBLE GOTHIC

This review of Double Gothic *was written by Merle Ginsberg.*

Michael Kirby's *Double Gothic,* presented by the Structuralist Workshop at the Performing Garage, is not unlike a visit to an amusement park: an experience of extremes, of horror, laughter, and most of all, of a distancing from the actual experience. It is a dispensing with the "willing suspension of disbelief."

Kirby and his Structuralist Workshop have presented two pieces prior to this one, *PhotoAnalysis* and *Identity Control.* His theatre seems to be concerned with exposing the elements or structure of the theatrical experience. He seems to be looking for an intellectual response from his audience, rather than a traditional kind of involvement.

Double Gothic (a title which conjures up images of Heathcliff and Jane Eyre, each standing on their own moor against a grey sky, each with their own separate cloud lurking above them) uses the conventional elements of a Gothic horror: dim lights, murky music, sounds of rain and thunder, with the unconventional addition of an all-woman cast of six and a playing area of black scrims stretched across a black tent-like structure, giving the work a circus feeling, as the action switches abruptly from ring to ring.

The opening section of the piece comes at the audience like flashes of fear on the horror ride at Asbury Park: dim split-second *non-sequitur* scenes, expressions of panic and weirdness; a woman standing alone with a suitcase, holding her foot, exclaiming, "I've broken my shoe," or a woman in a wheelchair, saying suspiciously to another woman, "We'll just clean them off." Interspersed with all these scenes is the kind of music one associates with a tacky production of *Frankenstein* or *Dracula.*

I must admit I found these opening mini-scenes frightening. For one thing, they were so dimly lit that I felt like I was in the middle of nowhere and couldn't see anything, and secondly, they moved so rapidly through the scrimmed divisions of the playing area that I lost my sense of dimension and couldn't tell at all where the characters were speaking from. They came at the audience like ghosts in the night.

We found out in the course of the evening that these scenes were taken out of the actual "play," and that *Double Gothic* does actually move in the direction of most plays; it sets up a protagonist, an antagonist, and a woman, and there is exposition, action—but there are two plays, not quite mirrors of each other, but very similar, moving in front of our eyes and converging in their structural devices.

A woman has a distressing situation and accidentally (it seems) meets a strange woman who will bring her through a stormy night, an unknown road to the refuge of a house. The proprietor of the house, in both plays, is a somewhat older and mysteriously evil woman who, in some way, means to do indistinguishable harm. The two plays are fun-house mirror reflections of each other, and a showcase of all the effects of true Gothic horror.

Continued

The stars of the show are the scrims, the lights, the eerie music, the snakes, and the storms. The six actresses are more like non-actresses, using their own names, voices, and characteristics to involve (or alienate?) the audience in the structure of the event. If that was non-acting, it was surely some of the best non-acting I've ever seen.

At the amusement park, the spectator screams, gasps, laughs, fears, and then goes home. Is this exposing of the elements illuminating? Does the audience leave enriched, relieved, excited? Having been hit with a barrage of images and a look into the bare structure on which our traditional theatre is built, I wondered what I felt, what my reaction really was, and realized that reaction was just what Kirby had in mind.

From Merle Ginsberg, "From Terror to Laughter" in THE VILLAGER, *1 January 1979. Copyright © THE VILLAGER. Reprinted by permission.*

Notes

1. *Roselee Goldberg,* PERFORMANCE: LIVE ART 1909 TO THE PRESENT *(New York: Harry N. Abrams, 1979), 70.*
2. *Ibid., 91.*
3. *Kirby,* THE ART OF TIME *(New York: E. P. Dutton, 1969), 67.*
4. *Kirby,* A FORMALIST THEATRE *(Philadelphia: University of Pennsylvania Press, 1987), 21.*
5. *Ibid., 140.*
6. *"Twice-Told Tale," in* SOHO WEEKLY NEWS, *1 Jan. 1979.*
7. *"The Scenography of Michael Kirby," in* THEATRE DESIGN AND TECHNOLOGY *15, no. 4 (Winter 1979): 22.*
8. *"The Lure of Patterns,"* VILLAGE VOICE, *29 Jan. 1979.*
9. *Interview with Woo Ok Kim, September 1993.*
10. *Interview with Cheryl Faver, August 1993.*

DOUBLE GOTHIC

A Structuralist Play

Michael Kirby

When *Double Gothic* was presented at the Performing Garage, spectators sat on two opposite sides of the playing space. The two audiences were separated by a large, black, plastic-covered, box-like construction; they could not see each other. Each group of spectators faced a blank scrim wall. When lights went on behind the scrims, they could see into the box and watch the play.

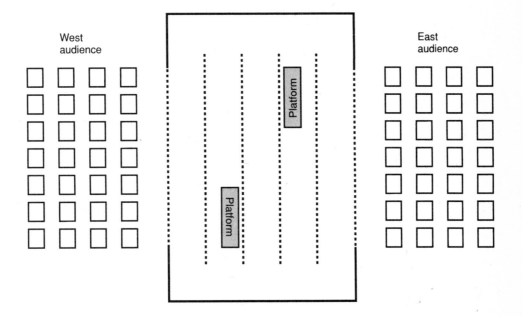

West audience

East audience

This arrangement is not necessary, however. Its purpose was to get as many spectators as possible as close as possible to the action. (The actors would not be speaking loudly.) *Double Gothic* may be done in a traditional proscenium arrangement with only one audience. If there are to be two audience groups, six walls of scrim are hung parallel to each other, creating five corridors about four feet wide. If a proscenium setup is used, only five walls of scrim will be necessary to create the five corridors.

Each corridor is lit by three hanging lights that cast their illumination straight down; all of the light is from above. When lights are turned on, the spectators can see through the scrim, sometimes looking through only one scrim and sometimes through as many as five scrims. All images are softened and blurred to varying degrees. (If all of the spectators watch the play from one side, the corridors might increase slightly in height, in a kind of step arrangement, as they move away from the audience.)

The space within the scrim curtains is empty except for two identical platforms, about six feet long and eighteen inches high, arranged symmetrically in two of the corridors. Actors will stand and sit upon these low platforms; when bedding is placed on them, the platforms will become beds.

We will number the corridors 1 through 5. If there is only one audience, corridor number 1 will be the one closest to them. Action in that corridor will be seen through only one scrim. Corridor 5 will be the one farthest away; action there will be seen through five scrims.

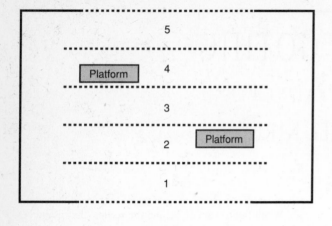

There are two similar, alternating stories in the play: Story A and Story B. Each is composed of six scenes. The first scene of the first story (scene A–1) will be presented in the corridor nearest the audience (or one of the audiences), corridor 1. The story will move, scene-by-scene and corridor-by-corridor, away from that audience (or toward the second of two audiences). The second story will begin at the opposite side of the playing area and progress, scene by scene, toward the corridor in which the first story began. The two stories will "pass through" each other, one getting progressively closer to the audience and one progressively farther away. The fifth scene of the second story (scene B–5) will be played in corridor 1, where the first story began. Scene 6 of each story will be played in the corridors with the low platforms that serve as beds.

[Since the characters were referred to by role type or character function in the script and had no real names, we used the names of the actresses when names were needed in the dialogue in the New York production; that usage has been preserved in this script. The actresses were Anne Fox, Amy Heebner, Brigitte Kueppers, Maria Myers, Marguerite Orlemans, and Ela Troyano. The names used in the dialogue do not need to be those that appear in this script. The names of whoever is acting the roles—or any other names—could be used.]

THE PLAY BEGINS

The lights go out. Loud recorded music is heard. It sounds somewhat like organ music: deep, sustained, droning sounds. For quite a while, there is only total darkness and the lugubrious music.

The music stops abruptly, and a light comes on. It hangs somewhere beyond the black scrim wall. We see a woman hobbling on one foot. "My shoe is broken," she says. Almost before she has finished, the light has gone out, and the music has returned.

Again the spectators sit in the dark listening to the music for quite a while. Suddenly the music stops again, and another light comes on at a different spot behind the scrim. In the cone of light under the hanging bulb, we see another woman. She points at something and says simply, "Your shoelace is untied." The light goes out, and the music comes on again.

Music and darkness continue to be interrupted by brief illuminated actions that appear for only a couple of seconds. There is no way of predicting where the next light will go on. Sometimes the actress who appears in the light—there are only women in the play—speaks; sometimes she merely performs a brief silent action. Some of the figures seem very dim, at a great distance away; others are clearer, but all are hazy.

Perhaps the spectator notices that the early actions and the spoken phrases relate to shoes, to feet. A woman holding a doll says, "One of her shoes is missing." A seated woman slowly takes off one of her stockings. A woman in a white laboratory coat stands looking at a high-heeled woman's shoe she holds in her hand. Later, as the intervals of darkness and music grow shorter and shorter, there are images of gloves, of hands. "Is that a wedding ring?" one of the women asks. The woman in the white lab coat takes off rubber gloves. A seated woman admires her finger nails and asks, "Are they long enough?"

For the first time, three lights come on simultaneously. They hang close to the spectators at equal intervals, lighting a narrow corridor behind the black scrim. The rear wall of the corridor, about four feet back, is another scrim. We cannot see behind it because the only light is between the two scrims. A scene begins and disappears. Another scene appears at a distance, and then is gone. The first scene begins again and continues for a little longer before the light goes out. The distant scene begins again and goes on a little longer before it is gone.

All of these brief images and scenes are moments from the play, done in exactly the same locations in which they will appear later in a more meaningful context. On page 1057, they are presented in chart form. The first column indicates the scene from which the image is taken. The second column gives the name of the character. The third column indicates the line of dialogue or the action. The fourth column shows the number of seconds of darkness preceding the illuminated image.

A–1	HEROINE A	"My shoe is broken."	21
B–1	HEROINE B	"Your shoelace is untied."	20
A–2	HEROINE A	(Steps on something.) "Oh!"	19
B–2	HELPER B	"One of her shoes is missing."	18
A–3	ANTAGONIST A	"We'll just clean them off."	17
B–3	HEROINE B	(Takes off socks.)	16
*B–4	ANTAGONIST B	(Looks at shoe.)	15
A–5	HELPER A	"No, no, don't do that!"	14
B–5	ANTAGONIST B	"My feet hurt."	13
A–1	HELPER A	"Oh, how stupid."	12
B–1	HELPER B	"Is that a wedding ring?"	11
A–2	HELPER A	(Puts on glove.)	10
B–2	HEROINE B	"Very soft with small ridges."	9
A–3	HEROINE A	(Takes off gloves.)	8
B–3	ANTAGONIST B	(Takes off gloves.)	7
A–4	ANTAGONIST A	"I said take off your gloves."	6
B–5	HELPER B	". . . you see what a refined sense of touch . . ."	5
A–5	ANTAGONIST A	"Are they long enough?"	4

The beginning of Scene A–1 to: "I had an accident."   3

The beginning of Scene B–1 to: "There's a star."   5

The beginning of Scene A–1 to: "Do you live around here?"   5

The beginning of Scene B–1 to: "Are you Ela?"   10

After another 10 seconds of darkness, the first scene begins.

SCENE A–1 (CORRIDOR 1)

Darkness. At some distance, a bell strikes eleven. A dog howls. Gradually a soft blue light comes on.

HEROINE A enters, limping. She wears a suit jacket and a skirt, driving gloves and high-heeled shoes. She carries a suitcase, which she puts down. There is the sound of a car passing rapidly and a white light, like headlights, flashes quickly over her. She turns and waves, but the car is gone.

HEROINE A takes off one shoe and examines it. The heel is broken. She takes off her jacket, puts the shoe on again and tries to walk. A dog howls. She stops, listens, puts the jacket back on. Again there is a car, a sudden light, and a futile wave.

*There is no mistake here. In fact, there is no A–4 because there will be no foot image in this scene.

She takes off the jacket, sits on the suitcase and takes off the shoe. There is the sound of a truck, already passing, and the flash of its headlights. HEROINE A waves and stands, turning to look after the truck.

A woman is standing at some distance, holding a lantern. HELPER A wears working-men's clothing: trousers, a shirt and necktie, a jacket, workboots, and a cap or hat. Her left arm is in a sling, the hand bandaged. The dog howls. HEROINE A puts on her jacket. Nobody speaks. HEROINE A moves her suitcase away from the newcomer, near the edge of the space.

HEROINE A (*finally*). Hello. I had an accident. I must have gone to sleep at the wheel. (*Laughs. Pause.*) Do you live around here? (*Pause.*) Is there a telephone?

HELPER A puts down the lantern and takes an envelope out of her pocket. She holds it out.

HEROINE A.   Is that for me? (*She steps toward* HELPER A, *limping because she has only one shoe.*) My shoe is broken. (*She holds it up.*) The heel came off. Is that for me?

(The suitcase, which is very close to the edge of the playing space, is taken off, hopefully unnoticed. If the person who takes it is seen, she might be recognized later as ANTAGONIST A.)

HEROINE A takes the letter, pausing questioningly as the exchange is made. HELPER A raises the lantern to provide light. HEROINE A is looking in her face.

HEROINE A.   I thought you were a man. Is this mine? Do you want me to read it? (HELPER A *nods slightly.* HEROINE A *opens the letter.*) My, the writing is small. (HEROINE A *rubs her eyes with one hand, takes out glasses and puts them on. A car passes. The dog howls.* HEROINE A *looks up.*) That's very nice. But how did this woman know I was here? Did she pass in a car? (*She takes off the glasses and puts them away.*) Can't you say something? (HELPER A *gestures in sign language.*) Oh, I see. Well, that's very nice. I accept the invitation. Under the circumstances. (*Laughs, takes off her glove, and holds out her hand to shake hands. One of* HELPER A's *hands is bandaged, and she has the lantern in the other.*) Oh. How stupid. (*She puts down her hand.*) Well, I'm pleased to meet you. (*She turns to get her suitcase.*) I suppose the car will be all right where it is. (*The suitcase is gone.* HEROINE A *looks around.*) My suitcase. It was right there. (*She points.*) I know I took it out of the car. Did you see it? It's gone. (*There is a flash of lightning and, several seconds later, the sound of thunder.*) Now there's going to be a storm. Of course. Perhaps we'd better go before the rain gets here. Is it far? (HELPER A *points.* HEROINE A *looks.*) I can't see anything. (HELPER A *leaves.* HEROINE A *starts after her, limping.*) Wait. This damned shoe! (*Takes off shoes*.) I'll try it without shoes. Don't go too fast. (*She exits. Lightning and thunder*.)

SCENE B–1 (CORRIDOR 5)

Darkness. A bell strikes the hour nearby. A light comes on slowly; HEROINE B steps into the light. She is dressed for traveling and carries a suitcase, a shoulder bag, and an umbrella. She stops, looks around, puts down the suitcase, holds out her hand, and looks up. A dog howls. HEROINE B sits on the suitcase, takes some overshoes out of her bag, and puts them on. There is a lightning flash and thunder. HEROINE B puts up the umbrella and paces. She holds out her hand again, looks up, collapses the umbrella.

HELPER B enters and stands at the edge of the space. She has a cane and wears gloves and dark glasses. There is a flash of lightning, then thunder. The dog howls. HEROINE B opens the umbrella, closes it.

HEROINE B. It's not raining, is it? (*She looks up*.) Perhaps it won't rain. There's a star. (*She points*.) Do you know what time it is? The train was late.

HELPER B. Are you Ela?

HEROINE B. Yes, I am. (*She fluffs her hair*.) You see? Just like the photograph. (*She steps toward* HELPER B *and holds out her hand*.) That's nice. I thought nobody had come to meet me. (HELPER B *does not move*.)

HELPER B. The doctor can't drive. I was the only one who could come. It's not far. (HEROINE B *makes a sound and puts her hand over her eye*.) What's the matter?

HEROINE B. I got something in my eye. (*Both hands stretch the skin near her eye*.)

HELPER B walks to HEROINE B and reaches out with the hand that is not on the cane, touching HEROINE B's hands and moving them away. HELPER B is blind.

HELPER B. Don't rub it. You'll make it worse.

She takes off her glove and runs her fingers over HEROINE B's face and down her neck.

HEROINE B. The doctor sent you?

HELPER B. Yes, of course. My name is Marguerite.

HELPER B holds out her hand. They shake hands.

HEROINE B. I'm pleased to meet you.

HELPER B (*still holding* HEROINE B's *hand*). Let me see your other hand. (*She runs her hand over* HEROINE B's *left hand and walks away quickly*.) Is that a wedding ring? You said you weren't married.

HEROINE B. The ring? It was given to me.

HELPER B (*pointing*). You're wearing something around your neck, too, aren't you?

There is a flash, thunder.

HEROINE B. Yes, I am.

HELPER B. Apparently you didn't read the instructions carefully. The agreement. Unless you do what you're told—what you're asked to do—you won't be allowed to remain with us.

HEROINE B. Yes, certainly I read the instructions. I had intended to remove all of my jewelry before I entered. (*She is taking off the chain around her neck and the rings. She opens her shoulder bag to put them away*.)

HELPER B. No, not in your purse. I think you had better check them in the station. You shouldn't have brought them.

HEROINE B. Check them?

HELPER B. There are lockers in the station. We can go that way. (*She taps the suitcase with her cane, points at it with the cane*.) Is this your bag?

HEROINE B. I'll take it. (HELPER B *has picked up the suitcase*.) Is it far to the hospital?

HELPER B. To the retreat. It's across the tracks and through the woods a way. (*She takes out a flashlight, turns it on, and holds it out to* HEROINE B.) Follow me.

HEROINE B. Wait. Your shoelace is untied. I'll do it. (*She ties the shoelace*.)

HELPER B. The doctor will be very happy to see you. She'll still be awake when we get there.

They exit. There is lightning and, soon after, thunder.

SCENE A–2 (CORRIDOR 2)

The sound of crickets, an owl, frogs; occasionally a dog howls. HELPER A enters with the lantern. She stops, turns abruptly, raises the lantern as if impatient. After a moment, she continues on, stops, and repeats the movement.

HEROINE A (*from offstage, unseen*). Wait! I can't . . . Wait!

HELPER A returns a little way and steps up on a low platform, hesitating as if surprised by something she sees on the platform. She raises the lamp and swings it three times as if signaling.

As HELPER A is stepping down from the platform, HEROINE A enters. She is looking through her purse, carrying her shoes and jacket. She is out of breath.

HEROINE A. Don't go so fast.

She can't find what she is looking for. HELPER A has turned to leave. HEROINE A moves quickly to her and touches her shoulder; HELPER A turns.

HEROINE A (*carefully, so that* HELPER A *can read her lips*). Please. Don't walk so fast.

Again HEROINE A starts to dig through her purse. HELPER A holds out the lantern to her.

HEROINE A (*turning*). What? I don't need . . . All right, I'll take it.

HEROINE A puts the lantern down on the platform, sits and starts hunting through her purse again. HEROINE A finds what she is looking for, takes it out, turns to show it to HELPER A: It is a pen. HELPER A is not there. She has disappeared. HEROINE A puts the pen back in her purse, stands and raises the lantern over her head, looking for HELPER A.

HEROINE A.   Damn it.

As she starts out, she steps on something with her bare foot and sucks in her breath sharply. She hops, looking at her foot. She sits again and starts digging through her purse. There is the sound of glass breaking. HEROINE A stops and listens. Again, there is the sound. HEROINE A takes a handkerchief out of her purse and ties it around her foot. She walks on it to test it, picks up her shoes, hits them together, and throws them away (offstage). HELPER A enters (if possible from the opposite side). HEROINE A turns and sees her.

HEROINE A.   Oh, there you are.

HEROINE A begins to search through her purse again. She finds the pen, shows it to HELPER A, continues to search. HELPER A steps up on the platform, catches HEROINE A's eye, and points. HEROINE A can't see what she's pointing at. HELPER A offers her hand to help HEROINE A up on the platform. HEROINE A looks at the hand, hesitates, takes HELPER A's hand, and steps up on the platform. HELPER A points again. HEROINE A looks.

HEROINE A.   Yes. That's the house. Is that the house? (*Points.*) The house? (HELPER A *nods.*) It's very dark. It's a very large house. Wait, I have a pen and paper. (*She digs in her purse again.*)

HELPER A steps down from the platform and holds her hand out to HEROINE A. HEROINE A has found the paper. She holds up the pen and paper.

HEROINE A.   There. For messages. I'll write messages to you.

HEROINE A starts to pick up the lantern and step down from the platform. She freezes, slowly pulls back, and points. HELPER A takes a glove out of her pocket, circles to the side of the platform, and holds out the glove to HEROINE A. HEROINE A takes the glove; HELPER A holds out her hand, and HEROINE A puts the glove on HELPER A's hand. HELPER A approaches the lantern carefully, makes a sudden lunge with the gloved hand, and holds something up: It is a snake. She smiles, examines the snake, and, in a friendly way, places it out of the way at the side.

HEROINE A climbs down from the platform and hands the lantern to HELPER A.

HEROINE A.   Here. You take the lantern. It's not far is it?

They exit.

SCENE B–2 (CORRIDOR 4)

There are night sounds: crickets, an owl, frogs, etc. Occasionally a dog howls. HELPER B enters, carrying the suitcase. She swings her cane quickly back and forth, then steps into the space she has ''cleared.'' She stops, listens, continues.

As HELPER B is leaving the space, HEROINE B enters with the flashlight. She stops and brushes at her face and arms.

HEROINE B.   Wait. What is this?
HELPER B.   Is something the matter?
HEROINE B.   There are long threads—like cobwebs. They're wet—damp.
HELPER B.   Don't pay any attention. It's nothing.
HEROINE B.   I can't see them, and I walk right into them.
HELPER B.   It bothers you not to see them?
HEROINE B.   No. It's all right. You must be getting tired of carrying that suitcase. I'll take it now. (*Crosses to suitcase.*) I want to put these boots away anyway. I don't think I need them anymore. (*Puts suitcase on platform, takes off one boot, see.*) Oh, look!
HELPER B.   What is it?
HEROINE B.   A doll. I wonder how it got here. Do many people use this path?

HELPER B walks to HEROINE B and runs her hand over the doll as HEROINE B holds it up. It is wearing a wedding dress.

HELPER B.   One of its shoes is missing.
HEROINE B.   That's all right. I can't leave it here. Perhaps I can find the shoe. (*She looks for the shoe.* HELPER B *exits.*) Something's wrong with the flashlight. It's getting dimmer.

HEROINE B turns and sees that HELPER B has disappeared. She looks around with the flashlight, crosses to the platform, brushes herself, sits, and takes off her overshoe. The faint scream of a woman is heard from the distance. HEROINE B stops, listens, starts to put the overshoes in the suitcase. The scream is heard again. HEROINE B scrambles up onto the platform, looking around. She listens, motionless. Then she puts the overshoes into the suitcase. HELPER B enters, carrying a lily.

HELPER B.   I brought you something.
HEROINE B.   Is that the house?

HELPER B walks to the platform, orients herself, and points with her cane in the direction HEROINE B is looking.

HELPER B.   Over there?
HEROINE B.   Yes. It seems quite dark. I can just see the outline against the sky. There are several turrets—pointed towers. Only one little window has a light in it. It looks as if it's built on the edge of a cliff.
HELPER B.   There are no other houses around here. Here, I brought you this. (*She holds out the lily.*)

HEROINE B (*pausing as she takes it*). It's very nice. Thank you.

HELPER B.   I know right where they grow. I don't care for them myself, though. This is my favorite. (*She holds out her closed hand.*) Close your eyes.

HEROINE B (*closing her eyes*). What is it?

HELPER B takes HEROINE B's hand, places it on her closed hand, and opens her hand.

HEROINE B (*feeling what's in the hand*). Oh, that's nice. Very soft with small ridges. Is it a large mushroom? The underside?

HELPER B (*starting off*). We'd better go. (*Stops.*) How is your eye?

HEROINE B.   It's much better, thank you. (*She climbs down from the platform, brushes at the cobwebs.*)

HELPER B.   Are you bringing the doll?

HEROINE B.   Here. You carry it. I'll take the suitcase. (*She hands HELPER B the doll.*)

HELPER B.   She's wearing a wedding dress.

HEROINE B.   It must be a special day today.

HEROINE B returns to get the flashlight, brushes herself off, picks up the suitcase, and stops, waiting for HELPER B. HELPER B leaves, then HEROINE B.

SCENE A–3 (CORRIDOR 3)

A chandelier with gas lamps. A chair. A suitcase. The sound of thunder, rain. HEROINE A enters slowly, taking off her gloves and looking around.

HEROINE A.   Listen to that rain. We got here just in time, didn't we? (*She sees the suitcase, points.*) My suitcase! Isn't that my suitcase? How did it get here?

ANTAGONIST A enters in a wheelchair, pushed by HELPER A. There is a blanket over her legs; she tugs at a silk scarf or handkerchief that she uses in gestures.

ANTAGONIST A.   Isn't this a surprise! Of course it's your suitcase, my dear. I merely sent someone to the car for it.

HEROINE A puts her glove back on, goes to the suitcase, lifts it.

HEROINE A.   I have another pair of shoes in here. And my slippers.

ANTAGONIST A.   Now we have to do something about those feet. (*She gestures with her scarf; HELPER A leaves.*) Sit down, my dear. Everything we have here is yours. Just make yourself at home.

HEROINE A (*sitting, taking off her gloves*). Is that gas? (*She points at the chandelier.*) It's very pretty.

ANTAGONIST A.   We have electricity, but this light is so much more flattering, don't you think? What do you think of my hair? Rather traditional, isn't it. Do you think my eyes need more makeup?

HEROINE A.   No, no, they're fine. You look very nice. (*She puts her gloves back on.*) Do you know . . . On my way here, I heard the sound of glass breaking—shattering. It was very clear.

ANTAGONIST A (*stopping*). In the house?

HEROINE A.   It must have been here. We were quite close. There's no place else.

ANTAGONIST A.   No, it couldn't have been here. It couldn't.

HEROINE A.   I wondered if you heard it.

ANTAGONIST A.   For the evening—for such a special occasion—I should be dressed more formally. Something more daring and exciting. (*She sees HELPER A enter with a pan of water, a sponge and a towel.*) Ah, here we are!

HEROINE A (*taking off her gloves*). That's all right. I can do it later. It was so strange, falling asleep at the wheel like that. I drive a lot, and that's never happened before. I just woke up—or whatever—and my car was off the road.

ANTAGONIST A says something in sign language to HELPER A. HELPER A puts the pan in front of HEROINE A and grips her ankle. HEROINE A calls out in pain.

ANTAGONIST A.   That's all right. We'll just clean them off.

HELPER A washes HEROINE A's feet. The sound of the rain and the thunder gets louder.

ANTAGONIST A.   It's amazing how much you are like someone I used to know many years ago. A young woman just like you. It seems like many, many years. There's a portrait of her in one of the bedrooms. You'll see it. (*HELPER A has finished washing; she starts to dry HEROINE A's feet with the towel.*) Here! I'll do that.

ANTAGONIST A reaches for the towel. HELPER A hands it to her, then pushes ANTAGONIST A's wheelchair close to HEROINE A so that ANTAGONIST A can dry her feet.

ANTAGONIST A (*as she dries*). You don't wear makeup, do you? You should. (*She touches HEROINE A's face and looks at her eyes.*) A little makeup around the eyes. My friend did. Tomorrow. We'll do that tomorrow. (*A telephone rings; HELPER A exits.*) There we are. All finished. Doesn't that feel better?

HEROINE A (*who has put on her gloves again*). Yes, it does. Thank you for taking me in like this. Anything could happen out there on the road. And the weather is so bad.

HELPER A enters with a telephone on a long cord and holds it so that ANTAGONIST A can speak into it. ANTAGONIST A tugs at her scarf and twists it. Her manner is now harsh and authoritative.

ANTAGONIST A.   Yes?   /   Yes.   /   Of course. I assume it's important.   /   That was stupid. Very stupid.   /   Yes.   /   You have until morning on this. I want it taken care of by morning.   /   I know that it's raining.

ANTAGONIST A gestures. HELPER A hangs up the phone and takes it away.

ANTAGONIST A.   I don't want you to go out of the house at night. Do you understand that? You're not to go out after dark.

HEROINE A.   I'm leaving tomorrow. And I'm much too tired to go out tonight. (*She takes off her gloves.*)

ANTAGONIST A.   I don't want you to leave the house after dark. Promise?

HEROINE A.   How did Brigitte hear the telephone? I thought she was deaf.

ANTAGONIST A.   What?

HEROINE A.   The telephone. When it rang . . . (*She stops;* HELPER A *is entering.*)

ANTAGONIST A.   Now, let's go to bed. We can talk in the morning. (*She says something in sign language to* HELPER A, *who starts to push the wheelchair off, then stops.*) Come along. Come along. (*The sound of the rain and the thunder grows loud again.* HEROINE A *stands, unconsciously putting on her gloves again.*) That's all right. Brigitte will bring your suitcase in a few minutes. Come along.

HELPER A wheels ANTAGONIST A out. Rain, thunder. HEROINE A follows them out.

SCENE B–3 (CORRIDOR 3)

One or two hanging lamps with shades. A chair, perhaps one that reclines like a dentist's chair. The sound of thunder, rain. The lights flicker. ANTAGONIST B enters, dressed in a man's suit with a tie, a laboratory coat and slippers. She wipes her hands on a cloth and looks up at the light.

ANTAGONIST B.   I'm afraid the storm is affecting the lights. We generate our own power here, you know. (*She is talking to someone offstage. Now she turns and points to the floor just offstage.*) Yes, yes. Just take off your shoes and leave them there with the others. We don't allow shoes in the main part of the house.

HELPER B passes through with HEROINE B's suitcase, shoulder bag, and umbrella. She wears slippers and does not have her cane. She leaves. HEROINE B enters without her shoes.

ANTAGONIST B.   There's a draft along the floor. We'll get you some slippers.

HEROINE B.   It was nice of you to wait up for me, doctor. It's such a long shot as it is.

ANTAGONIST B.   She may be here. She may be here. One or two of our people have lost their identities; many come under assumed names. We'll see in the morning. (*She twists the cloth and pats her face with it.*)

HEROINE B.   Her boyfriend—her fiance—lives near here, and I thought . . .

ANTAGONIST B.   Yes, yes, we'll see. Here is the key to your room. (*She holds it out.*) All of our rooms here are locked. Just like a hotel.

HEROINE B (*taking the key*). Thank you. (*She sees* HELPER B, *who has entered with a pair of slippers.*) Oh! You scared me.

ANTAGONIST B.   Yes, yes, these carpets absorb the sound. Here are some slippers for you. Why don't you sit over there? (*She points at the chair.*)

HEROINE B sits; ANTAGONIST B goes to HELPER B and takes the slippers from her one at a time. The sound of the rain and the thunder gets louder. Wiping her hands on the cloth, ANTAGONIST B crosses to HEROINE B, kneels, and lifts one of her feet.

ANTAGONIST B (*looking around*). This isn't the laboratory, although it might look like one. We work in different parts of the house—all through the house.

The lights flicker. HELPER B exits.

HEROINE B (*pointing*). I think the lights are going out.

ANTAGONIST B.   That's all right. We have plenty of candles. (*She puts a slipper on* HEROINE B's *foot.*) We generate our own electricity here, you know.

HEROINE B.   Well, it's quite far from town. Do you have a large staff?

ANTAGONIST B (*after wiping her hands again. She is holding* HEROINE B's *other foot*). You have very nice feet. The skin is very smooth. (*She runs her hand over* HEROINE B's *foot.*)

HEROINE B.   Yes, I suppose I do. (*Laughs.*)

ANTAGONIST B.   Don't laugh. Feet like that are very rare. Extremely rare.

HELPER B enters.

HELPER B.   It's locked.

ANTAGONIST B.   Of course it's locked. I've already given our friend the key. We'll come in a minute. (*She puts the other slipper on* HEROINE B *and stands.*) There. There's one important thing I must tell you. Do not go downstairs. Not that you will have any need to go there. (*She pats her face with the cloth and wipes her hands with it.*) All of the doors leading down are locked, of course. And there's no reason you should go down. But do not go down under any circumstances . . . even if someone should invite you.

HEROINE B.   Of course not. Who would invite me?

The telephone rings. Nobody moves. ANTAGONIST B catches HELPER B's eye and points offstage. HELPER B steps off and returns with the ringing phone. ANTAGONIST B lifts the receiver. The rain and thunder grow louder.

ANTAGONIST B.   Yes.   /   Yes, it is.   /   Who? /   Who is that?   /   Oh, yes, of course. (*She holds out the phone to* HEROINE B.) It's for you.

HEROINE B.   For me? (*She takes the phone, hesitating as the exchange is made.*) Hello. Hello. Hello. There's nobody there. Hello. (*Listens.*) I can hear someone breathing. (HELPER B *takes the phone.*)

ANTAGONIST B.   Did you tell someone you were coming here? Did you break our agreement?

HEROINE B.   No. Nobody knows that I'm here.

HELPER B.   How's your eye? Does it still hurt?

HEROINE B.   My eye?

HELPER B (*to* ANTAGONIST B). She got something in her eye. She was rubbing it, and I tried to stop her.

ANTAGONIST B.   Yes, your eye. Which one is it?

HELPER B.   The doctor specializes in eyes.

HEROINE B.   The right one. It's all right now. It's fine.

HEROINE B puts her hand over her eye. HELPER B exits with the phone.

ANTAGONIST B (*taking* HEROINE B'*s hand away.*) Let's have a look at it now. These things can be serious.

HEROINE B.   Do you see anything?

The sound of the rain has increased again.

ANTAGONIST B.   No. It's nice. Very nice.

The lights flicker. HEROINE B removes ANTAGONIST B's hands and steps away.

HEROINE B.   I don't think the lights will last much longer. Perhaps I should go to my room.

ANTAGONIST B.   Yes, perhaps we should. We have a lot to do tomorrow. (HELPER B *enters with a candelabra of candles.*) Ah, there we are! Now we don't need to worry about the lights going out.

HEROINE B.   One thing I've been meaning to ask . . . On the way here, I heard someone screaming. Could it have been one of your patients?

ANTAGONIST B.   Screaming? One of our guests? (*She is wiping her hands again.*)

HELPER B.   I didn't hear anything. I was with you.

ANTAGONIST B.   Our guests are not violent. We have no violent people here.

HELPER B.   Perhaps it was an owl. Or the wind through the trees.

ANTAGONIST B.   Yes, yes. You're not used to country like this. This isn't the city, you know. Well, let's be off to bed. After you. (HEROINE B *leaves.*) Do you have your key?

ANTAGONIST B exits after HEROINE B. After a moment, as the sound of the rain and thunder grows louder, HELPER B follows them.

HELPER B.   You've always shared with me. Why should it change? Why don't you watch? You can watch through the mirror. (HELPER B *steps suddenly toward* ANTAGONIST B *and reaches out to take her in her arms.*)

ANTAGONIST B.   No, don't hit me. I've had enough of that. (HELPER B *starts to pick up the clothes she has taken off.*) Everything. (*Pointing.*) Take everything.

HELPER B exits.

SCENE A–4 (CORRIDOR 4)

A pillow, a sheet and a blanket are on the platform, transforming it into a bed. There is a small table. Perhaps an empty picture frame hangs "on the wall."

ANTAGONIST A (*still unseen*). Go right in, my dear. This is your room.

HEROINE A enters, carrying an oil lamp with a shaded chimney. She stops in the center and looks around.

HEROINE A.   It's very nice. Snug.

HELPER A pushes ANTAGONIST A in her wheelchair into the room.

ANTAGONIST A.   It's the largest bedroom in the sanctuary. Larger than my own. They used to refer to it as the "Bridal Suite." Perhaps they still do.

ANTAGONIST A says something in sign language to HELPER A, who is bringing the suitcase into the room. HELPER A gives the room key to ANTAGONIST A (as usual, there is a brief hesitation as the exchange is made). HELPER A leaves the room.

HEROINE A (*holding the lamp up and pointing*). And this must be your friend—the woman you were telling me about. (ANTAGONIST A *doesn't answer.*) It is, isn't it? She does look like me! She really does. Especially around the eyes. If I wore my hair that way . . .

HEROINE A puts the lamp on the small table and, looking at the portrait, adjusts her hair. HELPER A appears on the other side of the portrait, in the next corridor. Her silhouette can be seen as she "looks through" the painting, watching HEROINE A.

ANTAGONIST A.   You're still wearing your gloves.

HEROINE A (*looking at her hands*). Oh, yes, I am. They're so comfortable, I forget about them.

ANTAGONIST A.   Take them off.

HEROINE A.   They're very light-weight. (*Pointing at the portrait.*) Do you ever see her now? How long ago was the picture made?

ANTAGONIST A.   I said take off your gloves. (*After a moment of hesitation,* HEROINE A *slowly takes off her gloves.*) Give them to me. (*She holds out her hand.*) I'd like to see them. (HEROINE A *gives the gloves to* ANTAGONIST A *one at a time; as she hands her the second glove,* ANTAGONIST A *takes her hand.*) Of course you don't use nail polish. Bright red would look very nice. On a special occasion like this. It would go well with your skin. (HEROINE A *bites her fingernails on the other hand.*) You're not married, are you? No, of course. not. I already asked. (*She puts the gloves into the hand she is holding.*) Don't let me stop you from getting ready for bed. I have to wait until Brigitte comes to get me.

HEROINE A puts the gloves on the table, bites her fingernail, takes off her jacket, folds it, and puts it on top of the gloves.

HEROINE A.   What time is it?

ANTAGONIST A.   It's very late. (*Pointing.*) You have a watch.

HEROINE A.   Oh, yes.

HEROINE A takes off the watch without looking at it and puts it with the jacket. She bites her fingernails. Then she walks quickly to the bed, turns back the covers, and freezes, drawing in her breath sharply. She backs away from the bed and points. HELPER A leaves the adjoining room.

ANTAGONIST A.   What is it?

HEROINE A goes to the table and puts on her gloves.

ANTAGONIST A.   What's the matter?

HEROINE A walks carefully to the bed. HELPER A enters. HEROINE A makes a sudden lunge, grabs something in the bed, and holds it up: It is a snake. She turns to ANTAGONIST A and HELPER A, then moves rapidly offstage.

ANTAGONIST A (*pointing*).   You fool! I know you did that. There are some things . . .

HEROINE A returns, slowly removes her gloves, shudders.

ANTAGONIST A.   I'm very sorry, my dear. I apologize. I don't know how it happened. They're really not dangerous. It must be the wet weather. They come inside occasionally in wet weather. Very rarely. What did you do with it?

HEROINE A (*who is biting her fingernail*).   I killed it.

ANTAGONIST A.   Oh, that's too bad. They wouldn't hurt you. People tend to despise them because . . . (*Trails off.*) Someone must have been playing a joke. They never come in the house.

HEROINE A goes to the bed, raises the covers, and searches thoroughly.

HEROINE A.   I'm just not used to living in the country. If you'll excuse me . . . (*She bites her fingernails.*)

ANTAGONIST A.   Put it out of your mind, my dear. You have nothing to worry about. (*Holds out the key.*) Here is the key to your room. After we leave, be sure you secure the door. (HEROINE A *takes the key.* ANTAGONIST A *says something in sign language to* HELPER A, *who wheels her to the door.*) Good night, my dear. You can sleep late in the morning. Nobody gets up in this house.

HELPER A and ANTAGONIST A exit. HEROINE A locks the door. She looks around the room, biting her fingernails. She goes to the table, picks up the lamp, and walks around the room, looking in the corners and behind things. ANTAGONIST A appears on the other side of the portrait and watches HEROINE A through it. As she does, HEROINE A stops as if she had seen something. She raises the lamp and stands looking at the portrait, biting her fingernail. Then, standing on one foot at a time, she takes off her slippers and drops them by the bed. She puts the lamp on the table and takes off her skirt and blouse. She bites her fingernails, then suddenly moves to the lamp and turns it out.

SCENE B–4 (CORRIDOR 2)

The platform has become a bed with a blanket, sheets and a pillow. A small table; on it is the lily in a vase. Perhaps an empty "mirror" frame hangs "on the wall."

HEROINE B (*entering, pushing back her hair*).   Well, the key works. Everything is fine.

ANTAGONIST B (*entering with a candelabra*).   Oh yes! You'll have everything you need. Let me show you.

HEROINE B (*trying to keep* ANTAGONIST B *from coming in*).   That's alright. I'm rather tired after riding that filthy little train. I'll find things. You can give me that. (*She reaches out and takes the candelabra.*)

ANTAGONIST B.   Tomorrow is Sunday. Everyone will be sleeping late.

HEROINE B.   That's fine. Just have someone call when you're ready for me.

ANTAGONIST B.   Ah, here's your suitcase with your toothbrush and your nightdress.

HELPER B (*entering with the suitcase*).   Excuse me. Where would you like me to put this?

HEROINE B (*pushing back her hair*).   That's alright. I'll take it.

HEROINE B reaches for the suitcase. HELPER B has pushed into the room and stops center. ANTAGONIST B follows her. HEROINE B runs her fingers through her hair nervously.

ANTAGONIST B. Yes, here we are. Put the suitcase over there. (*She points.* HELPER B *does not move.*) By the closet. Put it there.

HELPER B puts the suitcase down.

HELPER B. I made up the bed, and there are fresh towels in the bathroom down the hall. It's to the right as you go out.
HEROINE B (*crossing to the mirror and arranging her hair in it*). What a beautiful old mirror! It must be from the 18th century, at least.
ANTAGONIST B (*pointing at the lily*). I suppose you did that, too?
HELPER B. Did what?
ANTAGONIST B (*picking up the vase*). This. This . . . flower. This was your idea.
HELPER B. It's a lily.
ANTAGONIST B. Yes, the lily.
HEROINE B (*crossing to* ANTAGONIST B *and taking the vase*). It's a beautiful lily. (*Puts the lily back on the table.*) We picked it in the forest on the way here.

HELPER B exits, closing the door behind her.

ANTAGONIST B. A flower like that consumes the oxygen at night. It breathes, in a sense. It's very dangerous to sleep with one in the room.
HEROINE B (*running her hand through her hair*). I never heard that. I'm sure I won't have any difficulty sleeping tonight.

HEROINE B puts the candelabra on the table, goes to the bed, sees something, stops, and points.

HEROINE B. Oh, look!
ANTAGONIST B. What is it?
HEROINE B (*bending over the bed*). Isn't that cute! She's sleeping.

HELPER B appears in the next corridor and ''looks through'' the mirror. HEROINE B carefully lifts something from the bed and holds it up. It is the doll. Her clothes have been removed.

ANTAGONIST B. How strange. Let me see it. (*She reaches out;* HEROINE B *hands her the doll.* ANTAGONIST B *examines it, running her fingers over it.*)
HEROINE B. I found her. She was wearing clothes then. Now she's ready for bed.

ANTAGONIST B gives the doll back to HEROINE B, who puts it back in bed.

ANTAGONIST B. Are you going to sleep with her?
HEROINE B. Yes, of course. (*She takes a brush out of her shoulder bag and begins to brush her hair in the mirror.*) What time is breakfast in the morning? Does everyone eat together, or do you take the food to the rooms?

ANTAGONIST B. Tomorrow is Sunday, so breakfast will be later. (*She takes something out of her pocket.*) If you'll allow me. I just want to see something.
HEROINE B. What is it?

ANTAGONIST B puts a small container on the bed.

ANTAGONIST B (*taking* HEROINE B's *shoulder bag off*). First . . .

ANTAGONIST B puts the bag on the bed. She takes the brush from HEROINE B's hand, puts it on the bed, then picks up the container.

ANTAGONIST B. Eyelashes.
HEROINE B. Eyelashes?
ANTAGONIST B. Yes. Let's see.
HEROINE B. Why should I?
ANTAGONIST B. Why not? For me.

ANTAGONIST B puts false eyelashes on HEROINE B. They both look in the mirror.

ANTAGONIST B. Do you like them?

ANTAGONIST B takes off HEROINE B's jacket, folds it, and places it on the bed. She picks up the brush and begins to brush HEROINE B's hair.

ANTAGONIST B. May I? (HEROINE B *does not answer.* HELPER B *leaves the next room.*) How long will you be able to stay?
HEROINE B. I should be able to find out tomorrow, shouldn't I? She's either here or she's not here. Probably she's not.
ANTAGONIST B. That doesn't mean you can't stay longer. Treat it like a vacation . . .

HELPER B enters, holding a high-heeled shoe. Both ANTAGONIST B and HEROINE B see her and turn.

ANTAGONIST B. What do you want? (HELPER B *holds out the shoe.*) Did you have to bring it here? (*She goes to* HELPER B, *takes the shoe, and examines it.*) It has mud on it. Only one?
HELPER B (*nods*). It must be very difficult to walk in something like that.

ANTAGONIST B exits quickly with the shoe.

HELPER B. Is there anything I can do for you? Is there anything you need?
HEROINE B (*with doll*). No, everything's fine. My friend and I will take care of each other. (*She runs her hands through her hair.*)
HELPER B. Oh yes, your friend.

ANTAGONIST B appears on the other side of the mirror and stands, watching.

HEROINE B.   Thank you for getting her ready for bed. Thank you for the flower, too.

HELPER B.   I hope you sleep well. Good night. Don't forget to lock the door. (*She starts to leave, pauses.*) Do it now.

HELPER B leaves. HEROINE B goes to the door, locks it. She takes off one slipper and then the other. Looking into the mirror, she takes off her skirt and then her blouse, fluffs her hair, then goes to the candelabra and blows it out.

SCENE A–5 (CORRIDOR 5)

A small table with a mirror and a gas lamp on it. The sound of wind, rain, several dogs barking. ANTAGONIST A, wearing a robe, sits in her wheelchair, putting on long false fingernails. HELPER A enters, wearing a raincoat and overshoes. Her arm is neither bandaged nor in a sling. She takes off the raincoat.

ANTAGONIST A (*admiring fingernails*).   What do you think? Are they long enough? They look quite interesting, don't they? (*Pause. The Dogs bark.*) What's that noise? What's the matter with the dogs?

HELPER A.   They're back. Is she asleep? I thought you'd still be watching.

ANTAGONIST A.   Yes, they're back. Did they find anything?

HELPER A holds out something; ANTAGONIST A takes it, examines it, and hands it back. It is a pair of broken glasses.

ANTAGONIST A.   Put them on. (HELPER A *does.*) No, they're not hers.

HELPER A.   Are you sure? They look like hers.

ANTAGONIST A.   Perhaps these nails could be even longer. Do they make them longer?

HELPER A.   There were footprints under the window. If she wasn't cut on the broken glass, she was probably hurt when she jumped. It's a long way. But the rain makes it difficult for the dogs.

ANTAGONIST A.   They'll find her in the morning. She's probably hiding nearby, waiting for the storm to stop.

HELPER A.   You don't really care, do you?

ANTAGONIST A.   What do you mean by that?

HELPER A.   I mean you don't care about the old ones. That's over with. Forget it. It's the new ones you're excited about!

ANTAGONIST A (*pointing at* HELPER A).   You bitch! You tried to kill her, didn't you? You and your snakes!

HELPER A.   I tried to scare her. It wasn't poisonous.

ANTAGONIST A.   It was deadly. Do you think I'm a fool?

HELPER A.   Oh please! Why is everything changing? I don't want things to change.

ANTAGONIST A (*taking* HELPER A*'s wrist and holding up the hand*).   Look. Look at this. I pay to have her hand fixed, and this is the thanks I get. Don't you want to be like everyone else?

HELPER A (*sitting back*).   I do. I do. It's beautiful.

ANTAGONIST A.   Do you want the other one done? Perhaps we should send the doctor home?

HELPER A (*putting her hands in her armpits and rocking her body*).   No, no, don't do that!

ANTAGONIST A.   Then don't try to tell me what to do. I'd like to think you appreciated what I did for you. (HELPER A gets up, sits at the table, and examines her hand in the mirror.) Don't you think our new visitor is pretty? (ANTAGONIST A *extends her arm and snaps her fingers at* HELPER A.) I'm speaking to you. Don't you think that our new guest is attractive?

HELPER A.   You're not going in there tonight, are you?

ANTAGONIST A.   I might. I think I will. Do you want to watch? You can watch through the painting.

HELPER A.   Why don't you leave her alone? At least for tonight. I was the one who found her. I brought her here.

ANTAGONIST A.   You brought her to my house. She's in my house. And this is my room. (*Pointing to clothes.*) Get these things out of here. They're unsightly.

HELPER A.   What do you mean? Oh, please. I'm sorry.

ANTAGONIST A.   I mean I'd like this place cleaned up.

HELPER A (*taking the overshoes that* ANTAGONIST A *is holding out*).   Aren't you going to bed?

ANTAGONIST A.   I may be and I may not be. I have things to do. (*Pointing again.*) Everything. Everything.

HELPER A (*who has gathered her clothes*).   What are you going to do? I said I was sorry.

ANTAGONIST A.   Whatever it is won't need your help. I'll tell you about it in the morning. Good night. Sleep well.

HELPER A exits. ANTAGONIST A examines her fingernails.

SCENE B–5 (CORRIDOR 1)

A floor lamp. A small table with a mirror. The doll is on the table. There is a chair in front of the table. The sound of wind, rain. ANTAGONIST B, wearing a robe, is sitting, massaging her feet. HELPER B enters. She doesn't have her cane.

HELPER B.   It's raining very hard. Are you alone?

ANTAGONIST B.   Of course I'm alone. Who would be here?

HELPER B.   I thought I heard voices. What's the matter with you?

ANTAGONIST B.   My feet hurt.

HELPER B.   Do you want me to do that? (*Massages* ANTAGONIST B*'s feet.*) Are you ready for bed?

ANTAGONIST B.   I slept late this morning. There's no point in sleeping.

HELPER B.   I thought you'd be watching.

ANTAGONIST B.   You're the one who likes to watch. I like to do things. That's enough. You're tickling.

HELPER B.   No, I'm not. This is tickling. (*Tickles* ANTAGONIST B*'s foot.*)

ANTAGONIST B (*laughing and trying to pull her foot away*).   Oh, no. That's enough!

HELPER B (*dropping the foot and walking away*). Alright. That's enough. Do you see what a refined sense of touch a blind person has? (*Pointing at the doll.*) What's that?

ANTAGONIST B (*massaging her feet again*). What?

HELPER B.   Give it to me.

ANTAGONIST B.   Is that an order? (*She holds out the doll. There are cords tied to the wrists and ankles.*)

HELPER B (*taking the doll*). You've been in there, haven't you?

ANTAGONIST B.   Don't worry. She didn't wake up. There's nothing to be upset about.

HELPER B (*holding the cords and letting the doll hang alternately by its wrists and ankles*). You went downstairs while I was away, didn't you? I heard the screaming, too. I don't think I can trust you at all.

ANTAGONIST B.   You can't trust me? (*Pointing.*) It's you! You! Why did you bring me that shoe? Right in front of her! What is she going to think?

HELPER B.   She doesn't think anything. I just wanted you to know that I knew you'd been downstairs.

ANTAGONIST B.   Yes, I went down. That's my privilege. (*Stands, puts foot on chair.*)

HELPER B.   Then it's my turn, isn't it?

ANTAGONIST B.   That flower you gave her! How sweet! How touching! How sentimental!

HELPER B.   What about those eyelashes? ''May I?'' I saw that!

ANTAGONIST B (*slapping HELPER B*). You bitch!

There is a long pause. HELPER B has her hands over her face.

ANTAGONIST B.   Are you alright?

HELPER B.   My eye. My eye is hurt.

ANTAGONIST B (*taking HELPER B's hands away and looking at her eye*). No, no, it's alright. It's not hurt. (*She kisses it.*) It's going to be alright.

HELPER B starts to undress, taking off her shoes, her stockings, her blouse.

HELPER B.   If I can't trust you, there's nobody I can trust. Nobody.

ANTAGONIST B.   You can trust me. I'm sorry I hit you.

HELPER B.   Give me the doll. Please. I have an idea.

ANTAGONIST B.   What idea is that?

HELPER B.   An interesting idea.

ANTAGONIST B (*handing doll*). Tell me about it.

HELPER B.   I'd rather not. Some things are better—more beautiful—if they are completely private.

ANTAGONIST B.   What's happening to you. You're changing. Why don't you watch? You can watch through the mirror. (ANTAGONIST B *steps suddenly toward* HELPER B *and reaches out to take her in her arms.*)

HELPER B.   No, don't hit me. I've had enough of that. (*She starts to pick up the clothes she has taken off.*)

ANTAGONIST B.   Everything. (*Pointing.*) Take everything.

HELPER B exits.

SCENE A–6 (CORRIDOR 4)

HEROINE A is sleeping. HELPER A enters from the side opposite the door. She carries a light of some sort.

HEROINE A (*sitting up*). Who is it? Who's there?

HELPER A.   I'm sorry. Don't be afraid. It's me.

HEROINE A.   How did you get in here? What do you want?

HELPER A.   I came in through the other way. The wall. You can't stay here. You'll have to leave.

HEROINE A.   Where do you want me to go? Now? At night?

HELPER A.   You can't stay here. It's dangerous for you. It would be better in the woods.

HEROINE A.   What kind of danger? I don't understand you. I'm not going to run away, if that's what you mean. I want to find out what's going on here . . .

HELPER A.   Please. I can't talk now. I have to go.

HELPER A exits.

SCENE B–6 (CORRIDOR 2)

HEROINE B is sleeping. HELPER B enters from the side opposite the door. She carries a light of some sort.

HEROINE B (*sitting up*). Who is it? Who's there?

HELPER B.   I'm sorry. Don't be afraid. It's me.

HEROINE B.   How did you get in here? What do you want?

HELPER B.   I came in through the other way. The wall. You can't stay here. You'll have to leave.

HEROINE B.   Where do you want me to go? Now? At night?

HELPER B.   You can't stay here. It's dangerous for you. It would be better in the woods.

HEROINE B.   What kind of danger? I don't understand you. I'm not going to run away, if that's what you mean. I want to find out what's going on here.

HELPER B.   Please. I can't talk now. I have to go.

HELPER B exits.

THE ENDING

The loud, organ-like music swells in the darkness. For the first time, lights appear simultaneously in two different corridors. The two Heroines have lit the candelabra and the lamp with the glass chimney. Somewhat dim, these lamps are the only illumination. Holding the lamp and the candelabra, the two women begin to walk slowly through the corridors in their white slips, exploring the space. Lightning flashes. The music drones and rumbles. Vague blurs in the darkness, the women weave their way between the scrims. Now both of the women have disappeared. Nothing can be seen in the darkness. Only the loud surging music remains.

After a few moments, the music stops suddenly, and a single hanging light comes on briefly. In it we see the "crippled" woman standing and pointing, as we saw her do in the argument. "You tried to kill her," she says. The light goes out, and the music resumes. After about five seconds, the music and darkness are broken again by a single light at another spot. The "blind" woman is pointing, as she did not long ago. "What's that?" The lights go out.

As at the opening of the play, we see a series of images appearing briefly at unpredictable places. Now pointing recurs. The sequence is:

(Scene)	(Character)	(Line)	(Seconds of darkness before image)
A–5	ANTAGONIST A	"You tried to kill her."	10
B–5	HELPER B	"What's that?"	5
A–4	ANTAGONIST A	"You have a watch."	5
B–4	ANTAGONIST B	"You did that, too?"	6
A–3	ANTAGONIST A	"I don't want you leaving."	7
B–3	ANTAGONIST B	"There's a draft along the floor."	8
A–2	HELPER A	("The house.")	9
B–2	HELPER B	"Over there?"	10
A–1	HEROINE A	"My suitcase!"	11
B–1	HEROINE B	"There's a star."	12

(Now the people are handing something to someone else.)

A–5	ANTAGONIST A / HELPER A	"Put them on."	13
B–5	ANTAGONIST B / HELPER B	"You've been in there."	14
A–4	HEROINE A / ANTAGONIST A	"I'd like to see them."	15
B–4	ANTAGONIST B / HEROINE B	"It's a beautiful lily."	16
A–3	ANTAGONIST A / HELPER A	"I'll do that."	17
B–3	ANTAGONIST B / HEROINE B	"Here's the key . . ."	18
A–2	HELPER A / HEROINE A	"All right, I'll take it."	19
B–2	HELPER B / HEROINE B	"Look. I brought you this."	20
A–1	HELPER A / HEROINE A	"Is that for me?"	21
B–1	HELPER B / HEROINE B	(Handing flashlight.)	22

The intervals of darkness and music are quite long. The images revealed by the brief spots of illumination are from the first scenes of the play. The mute woman hands a piece of paper to the young woman whose car went off the road. The light goes out. The blind woman hands a flashlight to the young woman she came to meet. The light goes out. The music and darkness continue, but no more lights come on. Finally, the music fades; the house lights come on. *Double Gothic* is over.

FOCUS QUESTIONS

1. Discuss Kirby's use of expectation and memory to build tension and suspense in his play.
2. How do the play's prologue and epilogue augment the audience's experience of *Double Gothic?*
3. Discuss specific traits that help define and differentiate the three character functions for each story.

OTHER ACTIVITIES

1. Create a chart in which you list the similarities and enumerate the differences in the two narratives.
2. Construct the audience's experience of the two storylines; that is, connect the first half of A to the second half of B, and the first half of B to the second half of A. Discuss how the lack of coherence of your narratives shows how *Double Gothic* depends on structure rather than meaning.

BIBLIOGRAPHY

Carroll, Noel. "Twice-Told Tale." *Soho Weekly News,* 1 Jan. 1979.

Goldberg, Roselee. *Performance: Live Art 1909 to the Present.* New York: Harry N. Abrams, Inc., 1979.

Kirby, Michael. *The Art of Time: Essays on the Avant-Garde.* New York: E. P. Dutton and Co., Inc., 1969.

————. *A Formalist Theatre.* Philadelphia: University of Pennsylvania Press, 1987.

McNamara, Brooks. "The Scenography of Michael Kirby." *Theatre Design and Technology* 15, no. 4 (Winter 1979): 20–22.

Shank, Theodore. *American Alternative Theater.* New York: Grove Press, 1982.

Sommer, Sally R. "The Lure of Patterns." *The Village Voice,* 29 Jan. 1979.

STILL LIFE
EMILY MANN (1952–   )

Miss Mann has edited and dramatised her extraordinary material into a
continuous confessional and commentary in which the actors perform like an
instrumental trio, variously ignoring, embellishing or contradicting each
other's lines.

—MICHAEL RATCLIFFE

Timothy Near (*left*) as Nadine, Mary McDonnell as Cheryl, and John Spencer as Mark in *Still
Life*, presented by the Goodman Theatre in 1980, under the playwright's direction. *Photo: Janie
Goldberg/Andrea Gronvall, Margie Korshak Associates, Inc.*

APPROACHING THE DOCUMENTARY PLAY

"All the world's a stage," exclaims Jaques in *As You Like It,* while the eponymous Hamlet, Prince of Denmark, insists that the stage should hold a "mirror up to Nature." Shakespeare's metaphors pay tribute to the enduring power of the drama, including its reflection of who we are and how we live. Yet Hamlet's advice—that the stage should copy reality—betrays a surprisingly modern sensibility sharply suited to his youthful quest to uncover the truth.

But suppose Jaques twisted his metaphor and announced instead: "All the world's *on* stage." In fact, playwrights have grappled for centuries with the question of how to put real life on the stage. In the classical theatre, Aeschylus turned to Homer and Herodotus or others before them, no doubt, for background to his *dramatis personae* drawn from myth and history. Shakespeare, who reinvented the fabricated plots and characters from earlier literary masterpieces in his repertory of comedies and tragedies, populated his histories with real characters inspired by Raphael Holinshed, whose chronicles gave them the veneer of authenticity. In the modern era, Bernard Shaw felt no compunction in resorting to the original transcripts of at least one infamous trial in shaping his memorable portrait of the Maid in *Saint Joan.* By the same token, Arthur Miller investigated the extant documents of Salem to authenticate his dramatization of the notorious witch hunts at the heart of *The Crucible.* In every case, the audience must weigh the historical evidence that each playwright presents in order to assess these characters and actions.

Art imitating life acquired a new significance with the development of film. By the 1920s, Erwin Piscator incorporated newsreels to give his political plays a contemporary dimension. This unconventional, ambitious example was copied in the 1930s for the WPA's Living Newspaper productions, which brought up-to-the-minute news items to the American stage through slides, newsreels, the recorded voices of actual participants, and real-life dialogue spoken by actors. This final ingredient—hired actors—disqualified the ambitious theatre-cum-journalism format from the **documentary** genre, which would eventually find its most powerful expression in cinema and would be defined succinctly as the "reconstruction of reality, using real people and events in a socially-meaningful structure, and recorded at the time and place of their occurrence."[1]

Since World War II, the availability of photographic and film records, tape-recorded voices, and official transcripts of trials and meetings between political leaders has facilitated the literal reconstruction of events to trigger our prurient interests in hearing the dialogue of real people caught in crisis. Nevertheless, the art of transferring these transcripts to the stage is more easily said than accomplished, which is why the documentary play, according to Eric Bentley, "is a little trickier than it looks."[2] The playwright, above all, always risks succumbing to dull reportage when there are so many facts to consider. The overwhelming process of selecting, narrowing, and arranging the material becomes his most critical task, the moral value of his dramatization notwithstanding.

What emerges instead is **docudrama**—that troublesome mixture of fact (documentary) and fiction (drama)—whose form has never been adequately defined and whose blurred parameters elude traditions in reportage by tampering with reality. While the docudrama purports to dramatize actual events, it is often characterized by a certain poetic license that gives the illusion of authenticity, thus heightening its theatricality and audience appeal. Equally important, the popularity of docudrama has led artists to deal with the same subject matter from varying points of view, each version so radically different that no *single* truth seems to exist. The perception of reality is therefore determined by the viewer.

Prompted by the events of World War II, the German theatre of the 1960s responded eloquently to issues of moral responsibility and communal guilt. Working in a style derived from Piscator's, the playwrights developed a **theatre-of-fact** exemplified by *In the Matter of J. Robert Oppenheimer* by Heinar Kipphardt and *The Deputy* by Rolf Hochhuth. Their respective themes—the making of the atom bomb and a Pope's silent complicity in the slaughter of countless Jews—mixed documented fact with fabricated dialogue to produce an *interpretation* of the historical events under investigation. Thus Kipphardt and Hochhuth helped to legitimize the role of docudrama on the stage.

Other playwrights took this style one step further by adhering almost entirely to official transcripts, facing the challenging task of arranging their materials into a cohesive dramatic whole: Peter Weiss's *The Investigation* (the Auschwitz Trials) and *The Song of the Lusitanian Bogey* (the suppression of native Africans in Angola by the Portuguese), Donald Freed's *Inquest* (the Rosenberg Case), Eric Bentley's *Are You Now or Have You Ever Been* (the House Un-American Activities Committee hearings), and Emily Mann's *Execution of Justice* (the trial of Dan White for the murders of San Francisco Mayor George Moscone and City Supervisor Harvey Milk) come closest to exemplifying the documentary play. In their effort to construct a climate of reality from the lips of real-life characters played by actors, it is hardly coincidental that four of the five plays are confined to the courtroom.

On the other hand, source materials for the varieties of staged docudrama and documentary have expanded considerably in recent decades. Besides courtroom transcripts, which alone have generated an impressive body of stage literature, there are more personal and introspective examples drawn from private letters (Jerome Kilty's *Dear Liar*), diaries (Goodrich and Hackett's *Diary of Anne Frank*), memoirs (Patrick Garland's *Brief Lives*), biography (Samuel Gallu's *Give 'em Hell Harry!*), taped conversation-to-playtext (Wallace Shawn's *My Dinner with André*), and videotaped interviews (Anna Deavere Smith's *Fires in the Mirror*).

Furthermore subject matter is no longer impervious to the outside world. For the news media of the postmodern age have created a global village whose social and political turmoils are recorded on sight, hardening our more humanitarian instincts by making such events more commonplace while keeping us safely distanced from them. This obligation to document the harsher realities of our lives and to publicize the consequences, blemishes and all, has been facilitated by state-of-the-art technology: the capacity for photocopy and facsimile duplication and, most of all, the ubiquitously positioned film and video camera.

This tumultuous milieu has uncovered a more intimate *p.o.v.* (point of view) style of filmmaking—for example, the *talking-heads* approach to televised drama and journalism. It has also witnessed the development of a unique presentational format known as **performance art,** through which artists of every variety have generated original responses—whether verbal or not—to surviving in a world deprived of happy endings. Confrontational, confessional, strident, or conversational, the inner critical voices of performers like Spalding Gray, Eric Bogosian, Karen Finley, and Rachel Rosenthal have rendered stirring, intimate, and often radical reactions in league with the best of documentaries.

Confronting these complex issues from her dual perspective as a director and playwright, Emily Mann has recognized the vital significance of listening to people's stories: ''I hear the stories, then I let *you,* the audience, have the same experience I had as a listener. I don't actually reenact these stories, I let you hear them . . . When I put these stories on stage, the audience experiences a direct interaction which is in the moment.''[3]

In the moment not only suggests the timeliness of Mann's creative skill at transforming her documents into palpable stage works, but also reinforces the confrontational nature of her art, the split-second collision she achieves between performer and audience. It is a craft carefully sharpened by her experiences as a director, but nurtured by an uncompromising attitude toward exposition, that is, the essential information of the play which, she insists, ''has to be made theatrical, rather than expositional.'' While it must always seem to flow from the characters, the audience ''must experience the information in a visceral way so that they don't notice they are using their intellect; they must be sucked in by their emotions and love for story, and then they must use both intellect and feeling to sort out what they've learned.''[4]

As the daughter of a historian who once headed the American Jewish Committee's oral history project on Holocaust survivors, Mann discovered her interest in the documentary style during her college days when she came across some transcripts assembled by her father. The occasion moved her deeply and spurred her "quest with family documentary."[5] When she had the occasion to travel to Europe to study a friend's family history, she transcribed what would later evolve into *Annulla Allen*. This merely reinforced her interest in the documentary format, a "theater of testimony,"[6] as she would later call it, until her professional role as theatre director also included that of playwright.

Major Works

In addition to directing her own plays, Emily Mann has staged a range of classical and contemporary dramas and critically acclaimed performance pieces. Her first play, *Annulla Allen: An Autobiography* (1977, revised 1985), focused on a Holocaust survivor and established Mann's reputation as a documentary stylist. Her second, *Still Life* (1980), demonstrated through simple but powerful staging the complex and tragic repercussions of the Vietnam War. *Execution of Justice* premiered at the Actors Theatre of Louisville in 1984 before reaching New York two years later, when Mann became the first woman to direct her own work on the Broadway stage. Her next work, *Betsey Brown* (1989), was based on Ntozake Shange's novel of the same name and used a rhythm-and-blues operatic format. Mann returned to Broadway in 1995 as the director of *Having Our Say,* which she adapted from the oral history of Sara and Elizabeth Delany, recorded by Amy Hill Hearth.

Of all her works, *Still Life* forces the audience to confront a truly controversial episode in world history through its bold confessional tone and documentary style. Profound questions about human behavior and moral responsibility are raised but left unanswered, a necessary reality that enhances the play's objectivity as well as its universality.

The Action

Facing the audience from their seated positions at a long table, a man and two women deliver interwoven monologues independently of one another. Mark, the first to speak, has been emotionally scarred by his experiences as a Marine in Vietnam where "we were trained to kill." Painful repercussions of the war haunt every aspect of his shattered civilian life, particularly his relationship with Cheryl whom he married after returning home.

Cheryl speaks next. Turned into a casualty of the atrocities Mark has brought into their home, she lives each day in the shadow of his violence. Pregnant with their second child, she tolerates his abuse only because she does not want to "be alone for the rest of my life/ with two kids."

Nadine, the third character to speak, is Mark's mistress. Unlike Cheryl, she believes that Mark's "gonna make it." She has adopted a liberal stance that helps her to justify all of his actions in the war and at home. Nadine has never met Cheryl.

Structure and Language

Still Life opens with a Playwright's Note informing us that the play is a " 'documentary' because it is a distillation of interviews" conducted during the summer of 1978. The comment is not intended to soften our critical judgment of a work that is essentially Mann's, despite its sources. Instead she cautions us to assess the play through a different set of criteria: namely, how effectively the playwright has assembled her facts and how morally responsible her dramatization is.

Mann's approach matches the complexity of her subject—a war that marked a turning point in the lives of those who served, including the families that kept vigil. Most of all, the war symbolized a nation painfully divided and haunted by hostile criticism from the world outside. It marked an end to innocence, the result of nightmarish images that were documented in blood and televised nightly in homes across America. But it also marked the beginning of America's cynical stance and descent into violence, the result of a powerful denial of those same indelible images that had already penetrated the collective American conscience, but were tragically repressed in the process. *Still Life* cuts through these layers of denial like a scalpel.

Mann recognizes her own obsession "with violence in our country since I came of age in the 1960s"[7] and has admitted that her play is "a letter to my father who approved of the war in Vietnam, and who said if I had been a boy, he would have sent me to that war."[8] Composed in a straightforward manner, the play juxtaposes the responses of three people remembering traumatic events. Her objectivity as a documentary playwright firmly withstands the intrusion of any personal feelings she has about this war, but never isolates her from its repercussions, of responding personally to her father or publicly to an audience he partly represents. Suffice it to say that no war is quite like another. While politicians defend the fight, poets mourn the futility. Thus Mann uncovers arguments from both sides, letting the audience decide.

Her protagonists are ordinary people whose names have never made headlines; two of them have never met, in fact, but their simultaneous and contradictory perceptions expose the illusion of reality, the relativity of the truth. This philosophical premise is established early in the play, but underscores the internalized actions throughout. Cheryl talks about her husband's artistic fascination for decorative jars, one of which she found in the basement and contained "a naked picture of me in there,/ cut out to the form,/ tied to a stake with a string./ And there was all this broken glass,/ . . . Yeah, there was a razor blade in there/ and some old negatives of the blood stuff, I think." Although Cheryl interprets the jar as a symbol of his wish to kill her, Mann quietly shifts to Nadine's impression of the same artifact: "Those jars he makes are brilliant, humorous. He's preserving the war."

Still Life is filled with such eloquent and daring parallels through which Cheryl and Nadine view Mark from entirely different perspectives, so that our attempt to form a coherent impression of him becomes splintered. The effect is enhanced by Mann's seamless transitions which, like a hidden camera, move from one character to the next, supplanting one reality with another, one truth for another. When Nadine credits Mark's reference to himself as a "time-bomb," she projects his murdering instincts on the audience instead: "But so are you, aren't you?" By the end of the play, she is reconciled with the fact that Mark has become "a conscience for me./ Through him—I've come to understand the violence/ in myself . . . and in him, and in all of us." Instead of exonerating him, her words expose his endemic psychological disease.

Mann's skillful arrangement of personal testimony, her technique of pitting one character against the other—although they never actually confront each other face-to-face—and her building each anecdote to its own natural climax transform relentless verbiage into incisive storytelling. The presence of Mark's slides, which are ironically juxtaposed against what each character says, lifts the play from a courtroom-like atmosphere into the realm of psychological drama. Mark shows a slide of himself and R. J., a Vietnam buddy who was later killed in a Chicago robbery, and says, "We talked about everything./ We talked about how each of us lost our/ virginity, we talked about girls." Then Cheryl remarks, "My girlfriend across the street told me/ how babies were made when I was ten years old./ I just got sick. I hated it." We have no alternative but to dive into the wreckage of human lives damaged by drugs, crime, and domestic violence, with Vietnam always lurking as the sounding board for their kaleidoscopic outbursts.

Working with endless transcripts she had collected over long months of interviews with the original Cheryl, Nadine, and Mark, Mann was determined to find "a theatrical voice for each person, distilling each down to its own rhythm and poetry.''[9] Her counter-pointing of short sentences with intermittent **soliloquies** uncovers a verse-like format from beginning to end filled with the natural rhythms of **iambic pentameter,** suggesting the poetry of everyday speech. Mann's sensitivity to formulating these responses as though they were lyrics heightens the dramatic impact of her protagonists' one-sided conversations with an audience that sits in judgment.

Ultimately the evidence brought before us presents a visceral picture of the war as well as its devastating impact at home. Mark confesses an atrocity he committed at the front: ''I . . . killed three children, a mother and a father in cold blood.'' Nadine confesses something she has never told Mark: ''My husband's alcoholism has ruined us./ (Forty-five thousand dollars in debt.)/ I don't dare get angry anymore./ Can you imagine what would happen,/ if I got angry?/ My children . . .'' Cheryl confesses what she has suspected all along: ''I know [Mark] has other women. I don't know who they are./ At this point I don't really care./ I have a child to think about/ and just getting by every day.'' Each character harbors a private grief but is conjoined with the others by guilt and the instinct to survive, to ''come out on the other side.''

By asking us if the tragedy of Vietnam was the cause or the result of these characters' self-destructive natures, *Still Life* becomes a looking-glass in which Mark, Cheryl, and Nadine reflect aspects of ourselves. Their tragedies symbolize a universal loss of innocence, with Vietnam representing merely one of many possible catalysts that trigger our recognition of violence and point to our guilt. This shared humanity helps us reckon with these characters, until judging them becomes a futile task.

An allusion to the play's title, reserved until the final scene, reinforces Mann's concern with the subjective nature of truth and reality. Mark reveals that his unit ''got blown up'' and that he was sent fresh fruit and bread as ''a reward/ when you've had a heavy loss.'' Holding up the picture of ''an ordinary still-life'' for the audience to see, he says, ''I am still alive—my friends aren't./ It's a still-life.'' The words ''still-life,'' which share the same breath with ''still alive,'' resound like an echo, while we are left contemplating the conflicting image of a feigned reality versus the real thing. Mark's final words—''I didn't know what I was doing''—end the play, although a closing stage direction indicates that both women's eyes ''meet for the first time.'' Is Mark the victim or the perpetrator? We have gradually discovered that he is exactly what each woman feels at the moment she has talked about him. It is on this open-ended note that we must deliberate.

STILL LIFE-IN-PERFORMANCE

Under Emily Mann's direction, the world premiere of *Still Life* took place at the Goodman Studio Theatre in Chicago on October 21, 1980. The production, which featured John Spencer (Mark), Mary McDonnell (Cheryl), and Timothy Near (Nadine), moved to the American Place Theatre in New York where it opened in February 1981. The mixed critical reception was accompanied by controversy from every corner. On a positive note, Michael Feingold called the play ''a jagged and arresting chunk of shrapnel that is now lodged permanently in my brain'' and was quite impressed by the ''terrifying effect'' of the play-wright's arrangement of materials.[10] Robert Brustein complimented the play's ''serious effort to involve us with a searing contemporary issue,'' but felt that the ''single emotion one brings away is guilt—less over the war than over one's failure to sympathize with the sufferers.''[11] Later that season, *Still Life* swept the Obie Awards for best playwriting, best direction, and best production, and for all three actors as well.

Attracting west coast audiences at the Empty Space (1981), then at the Mark Taper Forum and the Eureka Theatre (1982), *Still Life* was also produced at Arena Stage in Washington, DC during the 1982–1983 season. While it was being performed across

America, its controversial reputation sparked enormous curiosity abroad: at the Zira Theatre in Tel Aviv (1982); and at the Market Theatre in Johannesburg (1983), where director Barney Simon gave the play a South African context by ''put[ting] 'No More Genocide' on at the end . . . [and] the names of everyone who had died in the resistance movement in the past ten years.''[12] The unanimously acclaimed production featured Wilson Dunster, Aletta Bezuidenhoret, and Fiona Ramsey.

When *Still Life* was mounted for the prestigious Edinburgh Fringe Festival in August 1984, the press simply bowed to the occasion. Writing for the *Glasgow Herald,* Mary Brennan remarked, ''They don't come any more powerful than this play,'' echoing the critical reactions of her colleagues. The production by the Vietnam Veterans' Company under Molly Fowler's direction won the Scotsman Fringe First Award and was invited to London. It continued to draw unanimous praise from West End critics and audiences alike. Featuring James Morrison (Mark), Deborah Carlisle (Cheryl), and Susan Barnes (Nadine), the play opened at the Donmar Warehouse in Covent Garden and continued its run at the Riverside Studios in Hammersmith through December 1984.

Mann has won the attention of international audiences whose wider experiences with the politics of war have prepared them for a play filled with the universal litany of recriminations and reveries. In a translation by Pierre Laville, *Still Life (Nature Morte)* was chosen by the Théâtre de la Bastille to be presented at the Avignon Theatre Festival in 1984 to reflect the festival's theme: ''The Living and the Artificial.'' Under Jean-Claude Fall's hyperrealistic staging, the characteristic *mise-en-scène* was transformed by a front stage framed by lighted palms and tropical beach. Sound effects included animals, radio-transmission noises, and rock music. The play was also produced for French television. Productions have taken place in Canada (1985) and in East Germany (1986) where it was presented in German under the title *Stilleben.*

REFLECTIONS ON STILL LIFE

Timothy Near originated the role of Nadine in the world premiere of Still Life.

In the late 1970s, I worked at the Guthrie Theatre for a year. John Spencer was an actor in the company as well. We were both in *Romeo and Juliet* and he played the Gentleman Caller for Emily Mann in *The Glass Menagerie.* So we were all in this world together, and I got to know John and Emily well. I believe she was doing the interviews with the real Mark, Cheryl, and Nadine for *Still Life* at that time. She hadn't begun to put it into play form. When we all got back to New York, she had me come in to audition, and we auditioned and auditioned and auditioned. John had already been cast, so he was playing Mark, I think, almost from the time that she had written it.

I seemed young to Emily, because Nadine was a little bit older than I was at the time, and so I think that was part of the reason for the endless reading. But eventually she decided that she would rather sacrifice the age and work with me. We all read before she made the final decisions, and it was exciting, doing those auditions, because when you are doing a play directly to the audience in front of you, it's very fresh each time.

One of the first things that we were all experimenting with was whether we wanted to look right into people's eyes or not. I think we all tried both, and I think that John and

Continued

Mary [McDonnell] did a lot of looking right into people's eyes. I think I did less. I found that when I would look at somebody for very long—unless they could take it—it became uncomfortable for them, and then it would make me uncomfortable. It didn't seem natural for me as an actress, because we don't do that to people. I find that when you're making speeches to great groups of people, you speak a little to one person, and then you move on so they don't feel like you're doing the whole thing right to them and they start to feel like they're in the hot seat. So this was certainly something different.

The whole idea is that three people have agreed to come in front of this audience and talk about their experience of how Vietnam affected them. That's the reality of it. The non-reality is that we don't seem to be there necessarily together. So we're all in each other's story, we're in each other's lives, and we feel each other very, very much, but we're not sharing the same space at that moment. Mark and Cheryl actually did acknowledge each other a little bit more. But Cheryl never acknowledged me. In her own life, and even in her psychological life, she didn't acknowledge Nadine's existence, so she never looked at me, and I never looked at her. But she and I were very, very aware of each other. There was a lot of electricity going on there. In fact, one time my hand slid over a little too much into her space, and I saw this ash tray start to come down on my hand, and I pulled it back.

Some of our production shots show John in the middle, but that's not how we did it. It was Mark and then Cheryl and then Nadine. That's how our table was set up. I was on the right. Cheryl was in the middle, and Mark was on the left, all facing the audience. And then there were a couple of times where I did look at Mark—behind Nadine's back, or in front leaning forward. But in a way that she really didn't, couldn't see. We found that the other way (with Mark in the middle) turned into kind of a competitive thing between the two women for him and put him in such a pressure position that all of the information about the war went down the tubes and it just became sort of a sexual battle.

The experience of performing *Still Life* was amazing for me. I felt like I really learned how to act, because I was working with two fine actors and with a director who is absolutely brilliant with actors. Emily comes to rehearsal so ready to give herself, that you automatically feel like you want to jump in and give yourself too. It's very free, and so you feel free to try anything! I remember Mary came in one day and rehearsed the whole show blindfolded, because she felt that Cheryl was blind in a lot of ways. Mary often worked with that imagery, as if she were wearing blinders.

Emily worked with each of us very differently. I think that Nadine was a very controlled woman, talking a lot about her liberation, but saying very little about herself. What was frustrating for me and Emily was that there seemed to be less personal material about Nadine than about the other two. So one time in Chicago, Emily told me to improvise. She let me see if I could find something personal about her—the place where I talk about my father. She let me improvise on the subject and we kept some of it, a monologue about her father. For that particular area of dialogue, she asked me not to memorize it, because for me, improvisation worked. Knowing that I had this one place in the play where I was going to just have to make it up every night kept me very fresh. Eventually Emily took what I said and mixed it with what Nadine had said, and it became part of the script. I mention this because it was how she dealt with my particular need to understand Nadine, to make Nadine more personal and to force me as an actress to keep the performance alive and fresh.

I remember how we smoked like fiends at that time, all four of us. The third time we did it—first in Chicago, then at the American Place, and then in L.A.—I was the first to stop smoking, so I always think of this as my stop-smoking play. We used to smoke during the performance, just as we had in rehearsals. Somehow the smoking seemed absolutely right. There's talk about alcoholism. And hadn't Mark been to AA? So that felt really right, because AA meetings—at least in those days—seemed to be filled with smoke, since everybody who'd stopped drinking was smoking and smoking and smoking. What was interesting for me as an actress, but having nothing to do with the script, is that I became much more vulnerable as Nadine when I quit smoking. I didn't have anything to hold on to, and it just made me a little bit more naked.

I felt that the West Coast production was my best time with this play. The first production was very raw, and we didn't quite know where we were going, and sometimes, of course, we'd get the lines totally messed up. The second time, it was hard for me to find it again, find the rawness. *Still Life* is so beautiful, so musical. But you can't just play *that* part of it, or it becomes very *hum de dum de dum* you know—too musical! You had to stay so aware, you had to hold on to your own tune or your own line of thought and your own passions, but play with the other two that often were varying a lot, because these two actors are so immediate and so present. The L.A. production, I kept what I had learned, but I found the rawness again.

I have a funny story about that, about messing up the lines. I was talking about having a C-section, and Cheryl was talking about opening the drawer and finding all these pictures that Mark had taken. I'm talking about how my lungs filled up with fluid, and so Mary as Cheryl says, ". . . and I opened the drawer . . ." And I said, ". . . and my lungs filled up with pictures." You know, Mary sat there for a minute, and we all just froze because it was so hysterical, and then I think she continued and said pictures as well. That's what could sometimes set us off and it took great concentration to continue.

At first Emily talked quite a bit about the real people, and then, as I recall, we actually became those people for her. Now I don't remember when that happened, but at some point we probably became more Mark, Cheryl, and Nadine than the real Mark, Cheryl, and Nadine. I don't think any of us ever felt like we were in competition in some way with trying to be who these people were or trying to be an imitation of who they were. Instead, we were very much encouraged to bring ourselves to this material. And of course my own sister, Holly [Near], had been doing an awful lot of Vietnam work and also feminist work at this time. So I used a lot of what we were all going through as women in the 70s to tap into Nadine's discovery of feminism and her excitement about that and her anger and all. We used the song, "No More Genocide," in the production. Mary and I always shared the same dressing room in New York City and we would both listen to a lot of Holly's music as preparation before we went on. And to Ferron—a Canadian musician and singer—who was part of the whole women's music movement.

Nadine was a difficult character to play. I had to realize that she wasn't as advanced in the feminist enlightenment as I was, and I had to put some of that in my back pocket. Why I think I did my best work in L.A. was that I finally realized she wasn't such a nice lady and I had to quit trying to make her all nice. She needed this man and she had a fairly

Continued

routine life in many ways. The danger that he offered and the excitement of that helped to fill out some real empty places in her life. I didn't have to try to smooth out all her edges and I didn't have to try to make her really understand Cheryl.

So I started to make some internal judgments about what a bad wife Cheryl must be, which I think is a really important thing to say to someone who is approaching that role. Try to make some negative judgments about Cheryl. Don't try to be all understanding or all good or all gracious. Nadine has a selfish side. I think it's something that you have to understand in order to be having an affair with a man who's abusing his wife. I also think in retrospect that women really seemed to reach out to Vietnam vets, although I actually don't know what that attraction is, exactly. But you know, the walking wounded, maybe because women felt oppressed and wounded themselves, and so they reached out to somebody who was wounded. Especially certain sophisticated, upper middle-class women.

Things that changed in production also affected our relation with the audience. In Chicago and New York, the audience was lit, and so we could really see them, and there was very little protection between us and them. From night to night, there was a sense of one of us feeling they don't like me, they hate me, or—God—they just love me or—you know. You really got to feel that people were taking sides. The lights seemed to make people very judgmental. Sometimes they'd walk out. We had walkouts usually when John started to talk about how he'd killed the mother and father of the three children. Then in L.A., Tom Lynch, who designed the set, and Emily decided to go with something a little more framed, and I actually think he made a frame. This time, the audience was not lit, and the lighting was more theatrical. As a result, the audience was given the privacy to have deeper feelings and to listen more. In any case, I don't think there were any walkouts in L.A., and I got the sense that a larger percent of people felt positive about the play, which is why the play worked the best in L.A. But I don't know if there was a best—I shouldn't say "worked the best"—but it worked differently.

We conducted talk sessions after the show, and Vietnam vets came and told us their stories. And that was good. But the time was so close. I mean, the Vietnam War was not long over. I'm sure if the play was done now, a lot more people who were affected by Vietnam would come out of the woodwork. But we did have people talk to us in every city we went to. We met vets and wives of vets and, you know, we eventually met Mark and Nadine. But not Cheryl. It happened at the American Place. I shook hands with Nadine. She and I were very different in size and she was probably five years older than I was and a very well put together, conservative-looking woman. It was hard for me to act her after I met her. I really had to go through a process where I said I was not trying to be her, because I couldn't. John was certainly more like Mark, and I think that Mary captured a kind of musicality that was very much like Cheryl, although we never met her. But I think Nadine and I were really different.

It took a little while to get over that, but then I did and gradually accepted who I was as Nadine and we certainly did try to give me a more conservative look than was really me. But ultimately, you have to bring your own experiences to this play, because you can't sit there night after night talking to the audience without bringing as much of yourself as possible to the piece, or it becomes a lie.

Another thing that's interesting is that I've met a few of the *Still Life* casts. There was the San Francisco *Still Life* cast who came down to see our production in L.A. and to say hello. Actually it was very disturbing to me to see somebody else playing Nadine, because it's like seeing somebody else be you! But it's also nice to talk to other actors, because we've all had that experience of going through this play. It was like meeting family!

Notes

1. Raymond L. Carroll, "Factual Television in America: An Analysis of Network Television Documentary Programs, 1948–1975" (Ph.D. diss., University of Wisconsin–Madison, 1978), 4.
2. THEATRE OF WAR (New York: Viking Press, 1972), 369.
3. Kathleen Betsko and Rachel Koenig, eds., INTERVIEWS WITH CONTEMPORARY WOMEN PLAYWRIGHTS (New York: Beech Tree/Morrow, 1987), 281.
4. Ibid., 277–78.
5. David Savran, ed., IN THEIR OWN WORDS: CONTEMPORARY AMERICAN PLAYWRIGHTS (New York: Theatre Communications Group, 1988), 151.
6. Betsko and Koenig, 297.
7. James Reston, Jr., ed., COMING TO TERMS: AMERICAN PLAYS AND THE VIETNAM WAR (New York: Theatre Communications Group, 1985), 215.
8. INTERVIEWS, 285.
9. IN THEIR OWN WORDS, 154.
10. VILLAGE VOICE, 25 Feb. 1981, p. 75.
11. NEW REPUBLIC, 28 March 1981.
12. IN THEIR OWN WORDS, 152.

STILL LIFE
Emily Mann

PLAYWRIGHT'S NOTE

Still Life is about three people I met in Minnesota during the summer of 1978. It is about violence in America. The Vietnam War is the backdrop to the violence at home. The play is dedicated to the casualties of the war—all of them.

The play is a "documentary" because it is a distillation of interviews I conducted during that summer. I chose the documentary style to insure that the reality of the people and events described could not be denied. Perhaps one could argue about the accuracy of the people's interpretations of events, but one cannot deny that these are actual people describing actual events as they saw and understood them.

The play is also a personal document. A specialist in the brain and its perceptions said to me after seeing *Still Life* that the play is constructed as a traumatic memory. Each character struggles with his traumatic memory of events and the play as a whole is my traumatic memory of their accounts. The characters speak directly to the audience so that the audience can hear what I heard, experience what I experienced.

I have been obsessed with violence in our country since I came of age in the 1960s. I have no answer to the questions I raise in the play, but I think the questions are worth asking. The play is a plea for examination and self-examination, an attempt at understanding our own violence and the hope that through understanding we can, as Nadine says, "Come out on the other side."

CHARACTERS

Mark, *an ex-marine, Vietnam veteran, husband, artist, lover, father*

Cheryl, *his wife, mother of his children*

Nadine, *his friend, artist, mother of three, divorcee, a woman with many jobs and many lives, 10–15 years older than Mark and Cheryl*

TIME: The present

PLACE

The setting is a long table with ashtrays, water glasses, Mark's pictures and slides upon it. Behind it is a large screen for slide projection. The look is of a conference room or perhaps a trial room.

The director may also choose to place each character in a separate area, i.e. Cheryl in her living room (couch), Mark in his studio (framing table), Nadine at home or at a cafe table.

PRODUCTION NOTES

The actors speak directly to the audience. The rhythms are of real people's speech, but may also at times have the sense of improvisation one finds with the best jazz musicians: the monologues should sometimes sound like extended riffs.

The play is written in three acts but this does not denote act breaks. Rather, the acts represent movements and the play should be performed without intermission. The ideal running time is one hour and 30 minutes.

ACT ONE

I

MARK *snaps on slide of* CHERYL: *young, fragile, thin, hair flowing, quintessentially innocent.*

MARK.
    This is a picture of my wife before.
    (*Lights up on* CHERYL. *Six months pregnant, heavy, rigid.*)
    This is her now.
    She's been through a lot.
    (*Snaps on photographic portrait of himself. Face gentle. Halo of light around head.*)
    This is a portrait Nadine made of me.
    (*Lights up on* NADINE.)
    This is Nadine.
    (*Lights out on* NADINE. *Snaps on slide of marine boot and leg just below the knee.*)
    This is a picture of my foot.
    I wanted a picture of it because if I ever lost it,
    I wanted to remember what it looked like.
    (He *laughs. Fade out.*)

II

CHERYL.
    If I thought about this too much I'd go crazy.
    So I don't think about it much.
    I'm not too good with the past.
    Now, Mark, he remembers.
    That's his problem.
    I don't know whether it's 1972 or 1981.
    Sometimes I think about divorce.
    God, I don't know.
    Divorce means a lot of nasty things
    like it's over.
    It says a lot like
    Oh yeah. I been there. I'm a divorcee. . . . Geez.
    You could go on forever about that thing.
    I gave up on it. No.
    You know, I wasn't willing to give up on it,
    and I should have,
    for my own damn good.

    You look:
    It's all over now,
    it's everywhere.
    There are so many men like him now.

    You don't have to look far to see how
    sucked in you can get.

    You got a fifty-fifty chance.

III

NADINE.

> When I first met Mark, it was the big stuff.
> Loss of ego, we shared everything.
>
> The first two hours I spent with him and what I
>   thought
> then is what I think now, and I know just about
>   everything
> there is to know, possibly.
>
> He told me about it *all* the first week I met him.
> We were discussing alcoholism.
> I'm very close to that myself.
> He said that one of his major projects
> was to face all the relationships he'd been in
> where he'd violated someone.
> His wife is one.
>
> He's so honest he doesn't hide anything.
>
> He told me he beat her very badly.
> He doesn't know if he can recover that relationship.
>
> I've met his wife.
> I don't know her.
> I sometimes even forget . . .
>
> He's the greatest man I've ever known.
> I'm still watching him.
>
> We're racing. It's very wild.
> No one's gaming.
> There are no expectations.
> You have a foundation for a lifelong relationship.
> He can't disappoint me.
>
> Men have been wonderful to me,
> but I've never been treated like this.
> All these—yes, all these men—
> businessmen, politicians, artists, patriarchs—none of
> them, no one has ever demonstrated this to me.
>
> He's beyond consideration.
> I have him under a microscope.
> I can't be fooled.
> I know what natural means.
> I know when somebody's studying.
> I've been around a long time.
> I'm forty-three years old.
> I'm not used to being treated like this.
>
> I don't know. I'm being honored, cherished, cared
>   about.
>
> Maybe this is how everybody's treated and I've
>   missed out.
> (*Laughs.*)

IV

MARK.

> My biggest question to myself all my life was
>
> How I would act under combat?
> That would be who I was as a man.
>
> I read my Hemingway.
> You know . . .
> The point is,
> you don't *need* to go through it.
>
> I would break both my son's legs
> before I let him go through it.

CHERYL.

> I'm telling you—
> if I thought about this, I'd go crazy.
> So I don't think about it.

MARK (*to* CHERYL).

> I know I did things to you, Cheryl.
> But you took it.
> I'm sorry.
> How many times can I say I'm sorry to you?
> (*To audience.*)
> I've, uh, I've, uh, hurt my wife.

NADINE.

> He is incredibly gentle. It's madness to be treated
>   this way. I don't need it. It's great without it.

CHERYL.

> He blames it all on the war . . . but I want to tell
>   you . . . don't let him.

MARK.

> My wife has come close to death a number of times,
>   but uh . . .

NADINE.

> Maybe he's in awe of me.

CHERYL.

> See, I read into things,
> and I don't know if you're supposed to, but I do.
> Maybe I'm too against his artist world,
> but Mark just gets into trouble
> when he's into that art world.

NADINE (*laughing*).

> Maybe he's this way to his mother.

CHERYL.

> One day I went into the basement to take my clothes
>   out of the washer,
> Jesus I have to clean out that basement,
> and I came across this jar . . .

NADINE.

> Especially from a guy who's done all these dastardly
>   deeds.

CHERYL.

> He had a naked picture of me in there,
> cut out to the form,
> tied to a stake with a string.

And there was all this broken glass,
and I know Mark.
Broken glass is a symbol of fire.
(*Thinking.*)
What else did he have at the bottom?

NADINE.

I accept everything he's done.

CHERYL.

Yeah, there was a razor blade in there
and some old negatives of the blood stuff, I think.
I mean, that was so violent.
That jar to me, scared me.
That jar to me said:
Mark wants to kill me.
Literally kill me for what I've done.
He's burning me at the stake like Joan of Arc.
It just blew my mind.

NADINE.

Those jars he makes are brilliant, humorous.
He's preserving the war.
I'm intrigued that people think he's violent.
I know all his stories.
He calls himself a time-bomb.
But so are you, aren't you?

MARK.

I don't know what it would be for women.
What war is for men.
I've thought about it. A lot.
I saw women brutalized in the war.
I look at what I've done to my wife.

CHERYL.

He keeps telling me: He's a murderer.
I gotta believe he can be a husband.

MARK.

The truth of it is, it's different
from what we've heard about war before.

NADINE.

He's just more angry than any of us.
He's been fighting for years.
Fighting the priests, fighting all of them.

MARK.

I don't want this to come off as a combat story.

CHERYL.

Well, a lot of things happened that I couldn't handle.

MARK.

It's a tragedy is what it is. It happened to a lot of
  people.

CHERYL.

But not too, you know, not anything
dangerous or anything like that—
just crazy things.

NADINE.

I guess all my friends are angry.

CHERYL.

But, uh, I don't know.
It's really hard for me to bring back those years.

NADINE.

Mark's just been demonstrating it, by picking up
  weapons,
leading a group of men.

CHERYL.

Really hard for me to bring back those years.

MARK.

My brother . . .
He has a whole bunch of doubts now,
thinking, "Well I wonder what I'd do
if I were in a fight."
And you don't NEED to go through that shit.
It's BULLSHIT.
It just chews people up.

NADINE.

Leading a whole group into group sex, vandalism,
  theft.
That's not uncommon in our culture.

MARK.

You go into a VFW hall, that's all men talk about.
Their trips on the war.

NADINE.

I don't know anyone who cares so much about his
  parents.
He's trying to save them.
Like he sent home this bone of a man he killed, from
  Nam.
It was this neat attempt to demand for them to listen,
about the war.

MARK.

I can't talk to these guys.
There's just no communication.
But we just . . . know.
We look and we know.

NADINE.

See, he's testing everyone all the time.
In very subtle ways.
He can't believe I'm not shocked.
I think that intrigues him.

CHERYL.

Oh. I don't know.
I want it suppressed as fast as possible.

NADINE.

He laughed at me once.
He'd just told a whole raft of stories.
He said: "Anyone who understands all this
  naughtiness
must have been pretty naughty themselves."
Which is a pretty simplistic way of saying we can all
  do it.

MARK.

> I thought:
> If I gave *you* the information,
> I couldn't wash my hands of the guilt,
> because I did things over there.
> We all did.

CHERYL.

> I would do anything to help suppress it.

MARK (*quietly to audience*).

> We all did.

V

NADINE.

> You know what war is for women?
> A friend of mine sent me this line:
> I'd rather go into battle three times than give birth
>   once.
> She said Medea said that.
> I stuck it on my refrigerator.
> I showed it to Mark. He laughed for days.

MARK.

> When Cheryl, uh, my wife and I first met,
> I'd just come back from Nam.
> I was so frightened of her.
> She had this long hair and she was really thin.
> I just thought she was really, uh,
> really American.

NADINE.

> Do you know I never talked with my husband
> about being pregnant?
> For nine months there was something going on down
>   there
> and we never mentioned it. Ever.

MARK.

> You know, it was like I couldn't talk to her.
> I didn't know how to respond.

NADINE.

> We completely ignored it.
> We were obsessed with names.
> We kept talking constantly about what we would
>   name it.
> I gained fifty pounds. It was sheer ignorance.
> I was a good Catholic girl
> and no one talked about such things.
> I never knew what that part of my body was doing.

CHERYL.

> It was my naivety.
> I was so naive to the whole thing, that his craziness
> had anything to do with where he'd been.
> I mean, I was naive to the whole world
> let alone somebody
> who had just come back from there.

NADINE.

> When the labor started, we merrily got in the car

and went to the hospital.

> They put me immediately into an operating room.
> I didn't even know what dilation meant.
> And I couldn't
> I could not dilate.

CHERYL.

> See, I'd hear a lot from his family.
> I worked for his father as a dental assistant.
> And it was all they talked about—Mark—so I had to
>   meet the guy.

NADINE.

> I was in agony, they knocked me out.

CHERYL.

> And I saw, I mean, I'd open a drawer and I'd see
> these pictures—

NADINE.

> My lungs filled up with fluid.

CHERYL.

> . . . dead men. Men hanging. Things like that.
> Pictures Mark had sent back.

MARK.

> Yeah. I kept sending everything back.

NADINE.

> They had to give me a tracheotomy.
> My trachea was too small.
> They went running out of the operating room to get
> the right equipment.
> Everyone thought I was going to die.

CHERYL.

> Once he sent back a bone of a man he killed. To his
>   mother.

MARK.

> To my brother, not my mother.

CHERYL.

> Boy, did that lady freak.

NADINE.

> My husband saw them burst out of the room in a
>   panic.
> He thought I was gone.

CHERYL.

> Now it doesn't take much for that lady to freak.
> Very hyper. I think I'd've gone nuts.
> I think I'd wanna take it
> and hit him over the head with it.
> You just don't do those things.
> WHAT THE HECK IS HAPPENING TO YOU? I'd
>   say.
> They never asked that though.
> I don't think they wanted to know
> and I think they were afraid to ask.

MARK.

> I know. I really wanted them to ask.

CHERYL.

> I think they felt the sooner forgotten, the better off
>   you'd be.

NADINE.
> I remember leaving my body.

MARK.
> I'll never forget that.

CHERYL.
> They didn't want to bring up a bad subject.

MARK.
> I came home from a war, walked in the door,
> they don't say anything.
> I asked for a cup of coffee,
> and my mother starts bitching at me about drinking
>> coffee.

NADINE.
> I looked down at myself on that operating table and
>> felt so free.

CHERYL.
> Your mother couldn't deal with it.

NADINE.
> They gave me a C-section.
> I don't remember anything else.

CHERYL.
> My memory's not as good as his.
> It's like I put bad things in one half
> and in time I erase them.

NADINE.
> I woke up in the hospital room with tubes in my
>> throat,
> stitches in my belly. I could barely breathe.
> My husband was there. He said: Have you seen the
>> baby?
> WHAT BABY, I said.
>
> Can you believe it?

CHERYL.
> That's why I say there's a lot of things, weird things,
> that happened to us, and I just generally put them
> under the title of weird things . . .
> and try to forget it.
> And to be specific, I'm real vague on a lot of things.

NADINE.
> I never knew they were in there
> and so I guess I didn't want them to come out.

CHERYL.
> I mean, my whole life has turned around since then.
> I mean, gosh, I got a kid and another one on the
>> way.
> And I'm thinking of climbing the social ladder.
> I've got to start thinking about schools for them,
> and I *mean* this, it's a completely
> different life,
> and I've had to . . .
> I've WANTED to change anyway.
>
> It's really hard to bring these things back out.

NADINE.
> For my second child, the same thing happened.
> By the third time around
> they had to drag me out of the car.
> I thought they were taking me to my death for sure.

MARK.
> Cheryl is amazing.
> Cheryl has always been like chief surgeon.
> When the shrapnel came out of my head,
> she would be the one to take it out.

CHERYL.
> It's no big deal.

NADINE.
> So when people ask me about the birth of my
>> children,
> I laugh.

MARK.
> Just like with Danny.
> She delivered Danny herself.

NADINE.
> My children were EXTRACTED from me.

CHERYL.
> It's no big deal. Just like pulling teeth.
> Once the head comes out, there's nothing to it.

VI

MARK.
> I want to tell you what a marine is.

NADINE.	CHERYL.
I have so much to do.	See, I got kids now.
Just to keep going.	
	I can't be looking into
Just to keep my kids going.	myself.
I don't sleep at all.	I've got to be looking *out*.
When my kids complain	
about supper.	For the next five years at
	least.
I just say:	
I know it's crappy food.	When I'm ready to look in,
Well, go upstairs	look out.
and throw it up.	
	God, don't get into the kid
I was in a cafe today.	routine. It'll do it to you
	every time.
	Because you're getting
	their best interests mixed
	up with *your* best interests.
	And they don't go together.
I heard the funniest	
comment:	They go together because it
	should be your best interest,
	and *then their* best interest.
	So what are you gonna do
	to them in the meantime?
She must be married.	
She spends so much money.	You're talking head-trips.

VII

MARK.

> There was this whole trip that we were really special.
> And our training was really hard,
> like this whole Spartan attitude.

CHERYL.

> The war is the base of all our problems.
> He gets crazy talking about it
> and you can't get him to stop
> no matter what he's doing to the people around him.

MARK.

> And there was this whole thing too
> I told Nadine about that really knocked me out.
> There was this whole ethic:
> You do not leave your man behind on the field.
> I love that.

CHERYL.

> Well, he's usually talking more than they can handle.

NADINE.

> You know, we had two months of foreplay.

MARK.

> I came to a point in there:
> Okay, you're here, there's no escape, you're going to
>   get taken,
> it's all right to commit suicide.
> And it was as rational as that.
>
> We came across a hit at night, we got ambushed,
> it was a black guy walking point, and you know,
> bang, bang, bang.
> You walk into it. It was a surprise.
>
> Well, they got this black guy.
> And they took his body and we found him about a
>   week later . . .

CHERYL.

> People start getting really uncomfortable,
> and you can see it in his eyes,
> the excitement.

NADINE.

> The first time I met Mark,
> I'd gone to his shop to buy supplies.
> I didn't think anything about him at first.
> (I've never been attracted to younger men.)
> But he seemed to know what he was doing.

CHERYL.

> It's almost like there's fire in his eyes.

MARK.

> And they had him tied to a palm tree,
> and his balls were in his mouth.
> They'd opened up his stomach and it had been
>   pulled out.
> And I knew . . .

NADINE.

> I saw some of his work.

MARK.

> Nobody was going to do that to me.

NADINE.

> Some of the blood photography I think.

MARK.

> Better for me to rationalize suicide
> because I didn't want . . .
> that.
> I don't know.

CHERYL.

> It bothers me because it's better left forgotten.
> It's just stirring up clear water.

NADINE.

> We talked and I left. But I felt strange.

MARK.

> R.J. was my best friend over there.
> He and I got into a whole weird trip.
> We found ourselves competing against one another,
> setting up ambushes,
> getting people on *kills* and things,
> being the best at it we could.

NADINE.

> All of a sudden, he came out of the shop and said:
> "You want a cup of tea?"
> I was in a hurry,
> (I'm always in a hurry)
> but I said, "Sure," and we went to a tea shop.
> (*Laughs.*)

MARK.

> R.J. is dead.
> He got killed in a bank robbery in Chicago.
> (He was one of the few friends of mine who survived
>   the war.)

NADINE.

> Two hours later, we got up from the table.
> I'm telling you, neither of us could stand up.
> We were gasping for breath.

MARK.

> See, I got all these people involved
> in a Far East smuggling scam when we got back,
> and then it all fell apart
> and we were waiting to get arrested.
>
> The smack got stashed in this car that was being held
> in a custody lot.
> Everyone was afraid to go get it.
> So I decided to get it.
> I did this whole trip Thanksgiving weekend.
> I crawled in there,
> stole the tires off the car
> that were loaded with the smack.
> I had R.J. help me.
> We were doing the war all over again.
> That was the last time I saw him alive.

NADINE.

> We had said it *all* in two hours.
> What I thought then is what I think now
> and I think I know everything there is to know.
>
> We must have looked pretty funny staggering out of
> there.

MARK.

> I heard from one guy on a regular basis, maybe once
> a year.
> He was green to Vietnam.
> We were getting into
> some real heavy contact that Christmas.
> It was late at night, the VC went to us
> while we were sleeping.
> They just threw grenades in on us.
> The explosion came, I threw this kid in a bush.
> All I did was grab him down,
> and he got a medical out of there.
> But he feels I saved his life.

NADINE.

> When we got out onto the street we said good-bye
> but we both knew that our whole lives had changed.

CHERYL.

> I know he has other women. I don't know who they
> are.
> At this point I don't really care.
> I have a child to think about
> and just getting by every day.

NADINE.

> We used to meet and talk.
> We'd meet in the plaza and talk.
> We'd go for rides in the car and talk.

CHERYL.

> See, lots of times people break up.
> And then the man goes on to the next one.
> And you hear the guy say:
> "Oh, my wife was crazy." Or something like that.
> "She couldn't take it."

NADINE.

> Sometimes we'd be driving,
> we'd have to stop the car and get our breaths.
> We were dizzy, we were gasping for breath,
> just from being together.

CHERYL.

> But the important question to ask is: WHY is she
> crazy?

MARK.

> So he wants to see me.
> I haven't been able to see him.

CHERYL.

> My brother is a prime example.
> He nearly killed his wife a number of times.
> She was a real high-strung person.
> She snapped.

The family keeps saying, oh, poor Marge, she was so
crazy.

MARK.

> He was only in the bush maybe five, six weeks,
> but it did something to him.
> He spent two years, he wrote me a letter,
> in a mental institution.
> I don't know.
>
> I knew he knew what I knew.

CHERYL.

> My brother's now got one little girl
> that SAW her little brother
> get shot in the head by his mother . . .

MARK.

> I know who's been there.
> And they know.

CHERYL.

> And then saw her mother come after her.

MARK.

> But in a sense we want to be as far away
> from each other as possible.
> It's become a *personal* thing. The guilt.
> There IS the guilt.
> It's getting off on having all that power every day.
> Because it was so nice.
> I mean, it was power . . .

NADINE.

> You know they're doing surveys now, medical
> research on this.

MARK.

> I had the power of life and death.

NADINE.

> They think something actually changes
> in the blood or the lungs when you feel this way.

CHERYL.

> I'm sorry. They were married too long
> for it just to have been Marge.

MARK.

> I'm sitting here now deep down thinking about
> it . . .

NADINE.

> You watch. Soon there'll be a science of love,
> and there should be.

CHERYL.

> When someone goes so-called crazy in a marriage,
> I always think:
> IT TAKES TWO.

MARK.

> It's like the best dope you've ever had,
> the best sex you've ever had.

NADINE.

> It was like dying,
> and it was the most beautiful feeling of my life.

CHERYL.

My brother's on to a new woman now.

MARK.

You never find anything better.
And that's not something
you're supposed to feel good about.

CHERYL.

If Mark and I split up, I pity the next one.

MARK.

I haven't told you what a marine is yet.

CHERYL.

Women should warn each other.

Pause.

NADINE.

Everything Mark did was justified.
We've all done it.
Murdered someone we loved, or ourselves.

MARK.

I mean, we were trained to do one thing.
That's the one thing about the marines.
We were trained to kill.

NADINE.

This is hard to say.
I have been in the jungle so long,
that even with intimates, I protect myself.
But I know that Mark felt good killing.
When he told me that I didn't bat an eye.
I understand.

CHERYL.

Look,
I think Mark and R. J. were close
only because they both got off on the war.
And I think they were the only two over there that
    did.
Doesn't it kill you when they get into this men-talk?
All men don't talk like that,
when they get together to reminisce.
They don't talk about getting laid and dope.
Imagine getting together with your best girlfriend
and talking about what it was like the night before in
    the sack.
That grosses me out.

NADINE.

I judge everyone so harshly
that it is pretty ironic
that I'm not moved by anything he tells me.
I'm not changed. I'm not shocked.
I'm not offended. And he must see that.

MARK.

I had the power of life and death.
I wrote home to my brother.
I wrote him, I told him.
I wrote:

I dug it. I enjoyed it.
I really enjoyed it.

NADINE.

I understand because I'm *convinced*
that I am even angrier than Mark.
I went off in a different direction, that's all.

CHERYL.

Now I don't think Mark and R. J. were rare.
I think the DEGREE is rare.
I mean men would not be going on fighting like this
for centuries if there wasn't something besides
having to do it for their country.
It has to be something like Mark says.
I mean he said it was like orgasm.
He said it was the best sex he ever had.
You know where he can take that remark.
But what better explanation can you want?
And believe me, that is Mark's definition of glory.
Orgasm is GLORY to Mark.

MARK.

I talked with R.J. about it.
He got into a hit once at about 8:30 at night.
And there was this "person" . . .
laying down, wounded,
holding onto a grenade.
(It was a high contact.)
He watched R.J. walk over and he just shot . . .
the person . . .
in the face.

He knew it.
As incredibly civilized as we are in this room, these
    things go on.

NADINE.

Until you know a lot of Catholics
you can't understand what hate means.
I mean I'm a . . . I was a Catholic.
And Catholics have every right to hate like they do.
It requires a whole lifetime
to undo what that training does to them.

MARK.

It's getting hard to talk.
Obviously, I need to tell it,
but I don't want to be seen as . . .
a monster.

NADINE.

Just start talking to Catholics
who allow themselves to talk.
It's unspeakable what's been done to Catholic
    youths.
Every aspect of their life from their table manners
to their sexuality. It's just terrible.

MARK.

I'm just moving through society now.

Pause.

VIII

NADINE.

I mean my definition of sophistication
is the inability to be surprised by anything.

MARK.

I look at my face in a mirror,
I look at my hand, and I cannot believe . . .
I did these things.

CHERYL.

Mark's hit me before.

MARK.

See, I see the war now through my wife.
She's a casualty too.
She doesn't get benefits for combat duties.
The war busted me up, I busted up my wife . . .

CHERYL.

He's hit me more than once.

MARK.

I mean I've hit my wife.

NADINE.

Have you ever been drunk for a long period of time?

MARK.

But I was always drunk.

NADINE.

Well, I have.

MARK.

We were always drunk.
It would boil out,
the anger,
when we were drunk.

NADINE.

I used to drink a lot
and did vicious things when I was drunk.
And until you're there,
you don't *know*.

MARK.

When I was sober, I found out what I'd done to her.
It was . . . I just couldn't stop.

CHERYL.

I was really into speed—oh, how many years ago?
I'm not good with the past.
I mean Mark knows dates and years.
God I don't know.

MARK.

It's like . . .
I feel terrible about it.
The last time it happened
it was about a year ago now.
I made up my mind to quit drinking
because drinking's what's brought it on.

CHERYL.

We got into some kind of argument about speed.
And he pushed me down the stairs.
He hit me a couple of times.

NADINE.

Yeah it's there and it takes years.
My husband I were
grooving on our fights.
I mean really creative.
And five years ago we got down to the count.
Where we were batting each other around.
Okay, I hit my husband. A lot.
See, I'm capable of it.

MARK.

I dropped out of AA.
I put the cork in the bottle myself.

NADINE.

Okay—I really was drunk, really mad.
And I beat him up and do you know what he said to
me?
He turned to me after he took it and he said:
I didn't know you cared that much.
It was the most incredible thing.
And he stood there and held his face
and took it
and turned around in a state of glory and said:
I didn't think you cared.
I'll never hit another person again.

CHERYL.

I went to the hospital
'cause my ribs . . .
I think, I don't know.
I don't remember it real clearly.
It had something to do with speed.
The fact that I wasn't, I was,
I wasn't rational.
No, I must have really tore into him.
I mean I can be nasty.
So anyway that was hard because I couldn't go to
work
for a couple of weeks.

NADINE.

And I see Mark.
The fact that he beat his wife.
I understand it.
I don't like it.
But I understand it.

MARK.

I've been sober so long now, it's terrifying.
See, I really got into photography while I was drunk.
Got involved in the art program at the U.
I mean I could be fine
and then the wrong thing would come up
and it would shut me off.

NADINE.

Don't distance yourself from Mark.

MARK.

I'd space out and start talking about the war.

See, most of these people
didn't have to deal with it.
They all dealt with the other side.

NADINE.

I was "anti-war," I marched, I was "non-violent."
(*Laughs.*)

MARK.

I brought some photos.
This is a picture of some people who at one point in
    time
were in my unit. That is,
they were there at the time the photo was taken.
Some of them are dead, some of them made it home,
(*Pause.*)
some of them are dead now.

NADINE.

But I'm capable of it.

MARK.

After I was there, I could never move with people
who were against the war in a real way.
It took a part of our life.
I knew what it was and they didn't.

NADINE.

We all are.

MARK.

They could get as pissed off as they wanted to
I didn't fight with them.
I didn't bitch with them.
I just shut up. Excuse me.
(*Looks at audience. Sees or thinks* HE *sees they're
    on the other side. Moment of murderous anger.*
    HE *shuts up and exits.*)

IX

CHERYL.

I'm scared knowing that I have to keep my mouth
    shut.
I don't know this for a fact, but I mean
I fantasize a lot.
I have to.
I've got nothing else to do.
See, I've got no real line of communication at all, on
    this issue.
If I ever told him I was scared for my life, he'd freak
    out.
If I ever said anything like that, how would he react?
Would he get angry?
What do you think? Do I want to take that chance?

I got too much to lose.
Before, you know, when we were just single
    together,
I had nothing to lose. I have a little boy here.
And if I ever caught Mark hurting me

or that little boy again, I'd kill him.
And I don't wanna be up for manslaughter.

Danny means more to me than Mark does.
Only because of what Mark does to me.
He doesn't realize it maybe, but he squelches me.

God, I'm scared.
I don't wanna be alone for the rest of my life
with two kids. And I can't rob my children of what
little father they could have.

NADINE.

I've always understood
how people could hurt each other
with weapons.

If you've been hurt to the quick,
and a weapon's around, WHAP.

I signed my divorce papers because
last time he came over, I knew if
there'd been a gun around, I'd've
killed him.

MARK *reenters.*

X

MARK.

I'm sorry.
I don't think you understand.
Sure, I was pissed off at myself that I let myself go.
Deep down inside I knew I could have stopped it.

I could just have said:
I won't do it.
Go back in the rear, just not go out,
let them put me in jail. I could have said:
"I got a toothache," gotten out of it.
They couldn't have forced me.
But it was this duty thing.
It was like:
YOU'RE UNDER ORDERS.
You have your orders, you have your job,
you've got to DO it.

Well, it was like crazy.
At night, you could do anything . . .
It was free-fire zones. It was dark, then
all of a sudden, everything would just burn loose.
It was beautiful. . . . You were given all this power
    to work outside the law.
We all dug it.

But I don't make any excuses for it.
I may even be trying to do that now.
I could have got out.
Everybody could've
If EVERYBODY had said *no,*
it couldn't have happened.

There were times we'd say:
let's pack up and go, let's quit.
But jokingly.
We knew we were there.
But I think I knew then
we could have got out of it.

NADINE.
Oh,
I'm worried about men.

MARK.
See, there was a point, definitely, when I was
genuinely interested in trying to win the war.
It was my own area.
I wanted to do the best I could.
I mean I could have played it really low-key.
I could have avoided things, I could have made sure
we didn't move where we could have contacts.

NADINE.
I worry about them a lot.

MARK.
And I watched the younger guys.
Maybe for six weeks there was nothing.
He'd drift in space wondering what he'd do under
fire.
It only takes once.
That's all it takes . . .
and then you dig it.

NADINE.
Men are stripped.

MARK.
It's shooting fireworks off, the Fourth of July.

NADINE.
We took away all their toys . . . their armor.

When I was younger, I'd see a man in uniform
and I'd think:
what a hunk.
Something would thrill in me.
Now we look at a man in uniform—
a Green Beret, a marine—
and we're embarrassed somehow.
We don't know who they are anymore.
What's a man? Where's the model?

All they had left was being Provider.
And now with the economics, they're losing it all.
My father is a farmer.
This year, my mother learned to plow.
I talked to my father on the phone the other night
and I said:
Hey, Dad, I hear Mom's learning how to plow.
Well, sure, he said.
She's been a farmer's wife for forty, fifty years.
Yes. But she's just learning to plow now.
And there was a silence

and then he said:
That's a feminist issue I'd rather not discuss
at the moment.

So. We don't want them to be the Provider,
because we want to do that ourselves.
We don't want them to be heroes,
and we don't want them to be knights in shining
armor, John Wayne—
so what's left for them to be, huh?

Oh, I'm worried about men.
They're not coming through.
(My husband)
How could I have ever gotten married?
They were programmed to fuck,
now they have to make love.
And they can't do it.
It all comes down to fucking versus loving.

We don't like them in the old way anymore.
And I don't think they like us, much.
Now that's a war, huh?

END OF ACT ONE

ACT TWO

I

MARK.
This is the photo I showed you.
Of some guys in my unit.

We were south-southwest of Danang—
we were in that whole triangle, not too far
from where My Lai was.
Near the mountains, near the coast.

Everybody knew about My Lai.
But it wasn't different from what was going on.
I mean, the grunts did it all the time.

This fellow up there, that's Michele.
He ended up in the nuthouse,
that's the fellow I pulled out of the bush.
This is the machine gunner.
The kid was so good
he handled the gun like spraying paint.
This kid was from down South.
Smart kid.
He got hit in the head, with grenade shrapnel.
He's alive, but he got rapped in the head.
That was the end of the war for him.

NADINE.
I don't know what it is with Mark.
I have a lot of charming friends
that are very quiet, like him—
but they don't have his power.

CHERYL.
        You know what Mark's power is:
        He's got an imagination that just doesn't quit.
NADINE.
        It got to be coincidental when we'd been somewhere
            together
        and someone said: You know your friend Mark,
        I liked the way he was so quiet.
MARK.
        There were no two ways about it . . .
CHERYL.
        He's got an imagination that, that embarrasses
            me . . .
MARK.
        People who were into it really got a chance to know.
CHERYL.
        Because I am conservative.
MARK.
        You knew that you were killing something.
        You actually knew it, you saw it, you had the body.
        You didn't take wounded. That was it.
        You just killed them.
        And they did the same to you.
NADINE (laughing).
        I told him his face is a dangerous weapon.
        He ought to be real responsible with it.
CHERYL.
        All his jars . . .
NADINE.
        I think we'd only known each other for a week and I
            said:
        You should really have a license for that face.
MARK.
        (That's my friend, that's R.J.)
        My friend R.J. used to carry a machete.
        I don't know why he never did it.
        But he always wanted to cut somebody's head off.
NADINE.
        You know why they went crazy out there?
        It's that totally negative religion.
        It makes you fit to kill.
        Those commandments . . .
MARK.
        He wanted to put it on a stick and put it in a village.
NADINE.
        Every one of them
        "Thou shalt not."
MARK.
        It was an abuse of the dead.
        We got very sacred about taking the dead.
NADINE.
        Take an infant and start him out on the whole world
            with
        THOU SHALT NOT . . .

and you're perpetually in a state of guilt
or a state of revolt.
MARK.
        There's a whole Buddhist ceremony.
        R.J., everybody—got pissed off.
        He wanted to let them know.
CHERYL.
        But he's got an imagination . . .
MARK.
        I never saw our guys rape women. I heard about it.
CHERYL.
        And it's usually sexually oriented somehow.
MARK.
        But you never took prisoners, so you'd have to get
        involved with them while they were dying
        or you'd wait until they were dead.
CHERYL.
        Everything Mark does is sexually orientated.
MARK.
        The Vietnamese got into that.
        There was this one instance I told you about
        where R.J. shot the person in the face . . .
        it was a woman.
CHERYL.
        I don't know why we got together.
MARK.
        The Vietnamese carried that body back.
        It took them all night long to work that body over.
CHERYL.
        When I think back on it, he was weird, off the war.
MARK.
        It was their spoils.
        They could do what they wanted.
NADINE.
        So you send these guys out there
        all their lives they've been listening
        to nuns and priests
        and they start learning to kill.
MARK (snaps on picture of him with medal. Full dress).
        This is a picture of my first Purple Heart.
NADINE.
        Sure Mark felt great. I understand that.
        His senses were finally alive.
CHERYL.
        His Purple Hearts never got to me.
        I was never impressed with the fighting man,
        I don't think.
MARK.
        A lot of people bullshitted that war
        for a lot of Purple Hearts.
        I heard about a guy who was in the rear
        who went to a whorehouse.
        He got cut up or something like that.
        And he didn't want to pay the woman

or something like that.
He ended up with a Purple Heart.

CHERYL.

Well, drugs helped, a lot.
We didn't have much in common.

MARK.

I don't know. We were out in the bush.
To me, a Purple Heart meant it was something you got
when you were wounded and you bled.
You were hurt during a contact.
I didn't feel anything getting it.
But I wanted a picture of it.

CHERYL.

I mean, I've got to get that basement cleaned out.

MARK.

Actually, I was pissed off about getting that medal.

CHERYL.

My little boy's getting curious.

MARK.

There were South Vietnamese who were sent out
with us, fought with us.

CHERYL.

He goes down and sees some of that crap down there
Mark's saved . . .

MARK.

They didn't really give a shit.

CHERYL.

Never throws anything away.

MARK.

If things got too hot you could always
count on them running.
Jackasses.

CHERYL.

Mark's a packrat . . .

MARK (*holds up a belt*).

I'm a packrat. I never throw anything away.
This belt is an artifact.
I took it off of somebody I killed.
It's an NVA belt.
I sent it home. I think it was kind of a trophy.

This is the man's blood.
That's a bullet hole.
This particular fellow had a belt of grenades
that were strapped to his belt.
See where the rust marks are?

CHERYL.

Everything he's done,
everything is sexually orientated in some way.
Whether it's nakedness or violence—it's all
sexually orientated.
And I don't know where this comes from.
(MARK *searches for more slides.*)
He can take those slides

and you know where he can put 'em.
Right up his butt.
I mean he's just,
he'll go down there
and dig up old slides.
I won't do that for him anymore.
I will not,
no way.

MARK.

Here's a picture of me . . .
(*Snaps on picture of him and some children.*)

CHERYL.

He asked if he can take pictures of Danny and I . . .

MARK.

And some kids. God I LOVED those kids.

CHERYL.

I think that's why I'm so against the artist world.
I just can't handle his work a lot of it.
It's because he's done that to me.

MARK.

Everybody hated them.
You couldn't trust 'em.

The VC would send the kids in with a flag.
I never saw this, I heard about it,
the kid would come in asking for C-rations,
try to be your friend, and they'd be maybe wired
with explosives or something
and the kid'd blow up.
There was a whole lot of weirdness . . .

CHERYL.

Mark's got this series of blood photographs.
He made me pose for them.
There's a kitchen knife sticking into me,
but all you can see is reddish-purplish blood.
It's about five feet high.
He had it hanging in the shop! In the street!
Boy, did I make him take it out of there.

MARK.

I really dug kids. I don't know why.
(*More pictures of kids.*)
I did a really bad number . . .
I went contrary, I think,
to everything I knew.
I'm not ready to talk about that yet.

CHERYL.

You just don't show people those things.

MARK.

These are some pictures of more or less dead bodies
and things.
(*Snaps on pictures of mass graves, people half blown
apart, gruesome pictures of this particular war.*)
I don't know if you want to see them.
(*Five slides. Last picture comes on of a man, eyes
toward us, the bones of his arm exposed, the flesh*

torn, eaten away. It is too horrible to look at.
MARK *looks at the audience, or hears them.*)
Oh, Jesus.
Yeah . . .
We have to be patient with each other.
(HE *snaps the pictures off.*)

CHERYL.

You know. I don't think . . .

MARK.

You know, I get panicky
if there's any element of control taken away from me.
(I don't like to be alone in the dark.
I'm scared of it. I'm not armed.)

I don't like fireworks.
If I can control them fine.
I don't like them when I can't control them.

I've had bad dreams
when my wife's had to bring me back out.
Nothing like jumping her, though.
I've heard about vets killing their wives in their sleep.
But this is personal—for me,
the gun was always the instrument, or a grenade.
I never grabbed somebody and slowly killed them.
I've never choked them to death or anything.
I've never beaten anybody up, well . . .

I never killed
with my bare hands.

Pause.

II

CHERYL.

You know, I don't think that
men ever really protected women
other than war time.

NADINE.

Listen, nobody can do it for you.
Now maybe if I weren't cunning and conniving and
manipulative and courageous,
maybe I wouldn't be able to say that.

MARK.

It's still an instinctive reaction to hit the ground.

NADINE.

I'll do anything as the times change to protect my
stake in life.

CHERYL.

And war's the only time man really goes out and
protects woman.

MARK.

You know—when I got back, I said I'd never work
again.
That's what I said constantly, that'd I'd never work
again, for anyone.

NADINE.

I have skills now.
I remember when I didn't have them.
I was still pretty mad, but I wasn't ready.

MARK.

I was MAD.
I figured I was *owed* a living.

NADINE.

I'm stepping out now, right?

CHERYL.

I know my mother protected my father all through
his life.
Held things from him, only because she knew it
would hurt him.

MARK.

And then I got in a position where I couldn't work
because after I got busted and went to prison, no
one would hire me.

I did the whole drug thing from a real
thought-out point of view.
I was really highly decorated, awards,
I was wounded twice.
I really looked good.

CHERYL.

That's where I get this blurting out when I'm drunk.
Because I'm like my mother—
That's the only time my mother would really let my
father know what's going on in this house.
(When he's not around seven days a week is when
she's had a couple.)
Otherwise she was protecting him all the time.
Excuse me. I'm going to get another drink.
(SHE *exits.*)

MARK.

I knew I could get away with a lot.
I knew I could probably walk down the streets
and kill somebody and I'd probably get off.
Simply because of the war.
I was convinced of it.

NADINE.

I could have ended my relationship
with my husband years ago.
I sometimes wonder why I didn't.
And I don't want to think it was because of the
support.

MARK.

I thought about killing people when I got back.

NADINE.

I've been pulling my own weight
for about eight years now.
Prior to that, I was doing a tremendous amount of
work
that in our society is not measurable.

CHERYL (*angry. Reenters*).
>My house is not my home.
>It's not mine.

NADINE.
>I kept a house.
>I raised my children.

CHERYL.
>Now, if it were mine I'd be busy at work.

NADINE.
>I was a model mother.

CHERYL.
>I'd be painting the walls,
>I would be wallpapering the bedroom.
>I would be making improvements.
>I would be . . . linoleum the floor.
>I can't do it.
>Because it's not mine.

MARK.
>I thought of killing people when I got back.
>I went to a party with a lady, Cheryl, you know,
>later we got married—
>She was into seeing people who were into LSD.
>And I had tried a little acid this night,
>but I wasn't too fucked-up.
>And we went to this party.

NADINE.
>I tried to explain to Mark
>that Cheryl may not always want from him what she
>>wants right now:
>looking for him to provide, looking for status.

CHERYL.
>And Mark will never be ready to have the
>>responsibility
>of his own home. Never. Never.

MARK.
>And there was this big guy.
>I was with a friend of mine who tried to rip him off,
>or something like that.
>He said, the big guy said:
>Get the fuck out of here
>or I'll take this fucking baseball bat
>and split your head wide open.

CHERYL.
>And I'm being stupid to ever want it from Mark.

MARK.
>I started to size up what my options were . . .

NADINE (*shaking her head*).
>Looking for him to provide, looking for status.

MARK.
>In a split second, I knew I could have him.
>He had a baseball bat,
>but there was one of these long glass coke bottles.
>I knew. . . . Okay, I grabbed that.
>I moved toward him, to stick it in his face.

>I mean, I killed him.
>I mean in my mind.
>I cut his throat and everything.

CHERYL.
>Because your own home means upkeep.
>Means, if there's a drip in the ceiling
>you gotta come home and take care of it.

NADINE.
>But between us, I can't understand why a woman her
>>age,
>an intelligent woman,
>who's lived through the sixties and the seventies,
>who's living now in a society where woman have
>>finally been given permission
>to drive and progress and do what they're entitled to
>>do
>. . . I mean, how can she think that way?

MARK.
>My wife saw this and grabbed me.
>I couldn't talk to anybody the rest of the night.
>I sat and retained the tension and said:
>"I want to kill him."
>They had to drive me home.
>It was only the third time I'd been out with my wife.

CHERYL.
>That fucking dog in the backyard
>—excuse my French—
>That dog is so bad. I mean,
>there are cow-pies like this out there.
>(*Demonstrates size.*)
>And when I was three months pregnant and alone
>>here—
>when Mark and I—
>when I finally got Mark to get out of here—
>I came back to live
>because I just could not go on living at my
>>girlfriend's,
>eating their food and not having any money and
>—and I came back here
>and I had to clean up that yard.

MARK.
>It wasn't till the next day that I really got shook by
>>it.
>My wife said,
>"Hey, cool your jets."
>She'd say, "Hey, don't do things like that.
>You're not over there anymore.
>Settle down, it's all right."

CHERYL.
>I threw up in that backyard picking up dog piles.
>That dog hasn't been bathed since I took her over to
>this doggie place and paid twenty dollars
>to have her bathed.
>And that was six months ago. That dog has flies.

You open the back door
and you always get one fly from the fricking dog.
She's like garbage. She . . , she . . .

MARK.

I think my wife's scared of me.
I really do.
She'd had this really straight upbringing.
Catholic.
Never had much . . . you know.
Her father was an alcoholic and her mother was too.
I came along and offered her
a certain amount of excitement.

CHERYL.

My backyard last year was so gorgeous.
I had flowers.
I had tomatoes.
I had a whole area garden.
That creeping vine stuff all over.
I had everything.
This year I could not do it with that dog back there.

MARK.

Just after I got back, I took her up to these races.
I had all this camera equipment.
I started running out on the field.
I started photographing these cars zipping by at
ninety miles an hour.

NADINE.

What's important to me is my work.
It's important to Mark too.

MARK.

She'd just gotten out of high school.
She was just, you know, *at that point*.
She was amazed at how I moved through space.

NADINE.

We talk for hours about our work.

MARK.

'Cuz I didn't take anybody with me.

NADINE.

We understand each other's work.

MARK.

I moved down everybody's throats verbally.
First of all it was a physical thing.
I was loud.
Then I'd do these trips to outthink people.

NADINE.

His jars are amazingly original. Artifacts of the war.
Very honest.

MARK.

I'd do these trips.

NADINE.

You should see the portrait Mark did of himself.

MARK.

I had a lot of power, drugs,
I was manipulating large sums of money.

NADINE.

He has a halo around his head.
(*Laughs.*)

MARK.

She became a real fan.

NADINE.

And the face of a devil.

CHERYL.

That dog grosses me out so bad.
That dog slimes all over the place.
My kid, I don't even let him out in the backyard.
He plays in the front.
That's why his bike's out front.
I'll take the chance of traffic before I'll let him out
to be slimed over by that dog.

NADINE.

She decided to have that child.

MARK.

Later on, it got into this whole thing.
We lived together and with this other couple.

NADINE.

It's madness.
Everyone was against it.

MARK.

It was a whole . . . I don't know whether I
directed it . . . but it became this *big* . . .
sexual thing . . . between us . . . between them . . .
between groups of other people . . .
It was really a fast kind of thing.
Because no one really gave a shit.

CHERYL.

Oh, shut up!

NADINE.

His theory is she's punishing him.

MARK.

I don't know why I was really into being a stud.

NADINE.

Now no man has ever been able to lead *me* into
sexual abuse.

MARK.

I wasn't that way before I left, so I don't know.
Maybe it was like I was trying to be like all the other
people.

NADINE.

See, she participated. She had the right to say no.

CHERYL.

That dog jumps the fence, takes off.
I have to pay twenty dollars
to get her out of the dog pound.
She is costin' me so damn much money that I hate
her.
She eats better than we do.
She eats better than we do.

NADINE.

    She must have thought it would be fun.

    And wow! That was that whole decade

    where a whole population of people that age thought

        that way.

CHERYL.

    My Danny is getting to the age where there's gotta

        be food.

    I mean he's three years old.

    He goes to the freezer he wants ice cream there.

    He goes in the icebox there's gotta be pop.

    I mean it's not like he's an infant anymore.

NADINE.

    Every foul thing I've ever done,

    I'm not uncomfortable about it.

    And I don't blame anyone in my life.

CHERYL.

    These things have to be there.

    And it's not there.

NADINE.

    I don't blame anyone.

    I'm sorry, maybe you have to be older

    to look back and say that.

CHERYL.

    But there's always a bag of dogfood in the place.

    Anyways I run out of dogfood,

    Mark sends me right up to the store.

    But I run out of milk I can always give him Kool-Aid

    for two or three days.

    Yeah—that's the way it is though.

    We haven't been to the grocery store in six months

    for anything over ten dollars worth of groceries at a

        time.

    There is no money.

III

MARK.

    You'd really become an animal out there.

    R.J. and I knew what we were doing.

    That's why a lot of other kids really got into trouble.

    They didn't know what they were doing.

    We knew it, we dug it, we knew

    we were very good.

IV

CHERYL.

    I'd turn off to him.

    Because I knew that it was hard for me to accept—

    you know what he . . . what happened and all that.

    And it was hard for me to live with, and him being

    drunk and *spreading* it around to others.

    (*To* MARK.)

How long has it been since anything like that

    happened?

MARK.

    Well, last July I hurt you.

CHERYL.

    Yeah, but Danny was what a year and half so

    everything was pretty . . .

MARK.

    He was exposed to it.

    My wife, uh, Cheryl, left one night.

CHERYL.

    Don't.

MARK.

    She left with, uh, she had a person come over and

    pick her up and take her away.

    I walked in on this.

    I was drunk. Danny was in her arms.

    I attacked this other man and . . .

    I did something to him.

    I don't know.

    What did I do to him?

    Something.

CHERYL.

    You smashed his car up with a sledge hammer.

MARK.

    I, uh, Dan saw all that.

CHERYL.

    He was only six months old though.

MARK.

    No. Dan I think he knows a lot more than we think.

    He saw me drunk and incapable of walking up the

        steps.

    Going to the bathroom

    half on the floor and half in the bowl.

    He's a sharp kid.

    Cheryl and I separated this spring.

    And he really knew what was going on.

NADINE.

    Christ, I hate this country.

    I hate all of it.

    I've never really said it before.

MARK.

    I come in and apologize when I think about the

        incidents

    that I've done in the past now that I'm sober,

    and I feel terribly guilty.

    I've exploited Cheryl as a person, sexually . . .

    it wasn't exactly rape, but . . .

CHERYL.

    I can't deal with *that* at all.

    But I find that if I can at least put it out of my mind

    it's easier.

    If I had to think about what he's done to me, I'd

    have been gone a long time ago.

NADINE.

> I have yet to be out of this country, by the way.
>
> And I'm criticizing it as if I think it's better
> everywhere else.

MARK.

> See, I wanted to get back into the society and
>
> I wanted to live so much life, but I couldn't.
>
> I was constantly experimenting.

CHERYL.

> It was awful . . .
>
> He'd pick fights with people on the streets.
>
> Just about anyone. It was like a rage.
>
> He'd just whomp on the guy.
>
> Not physically but he would become very obstinate,
> very mean and cruel. In bars, handling people . . .
>
> (*To* MARK.)
>
> You have to be *nice* to people to have them accept
> you.

MARK.

> I don't know.
>
> I was afraid.
>
> I thought people were . . . uh . . . I mean
>
> I was kind of paranoid.
>
> I thought everybody knew . . .
>
> I thought everybody knew what I did over there,
> and that they were against me.
>
> I was scared. I felt guilty and a sense of . . .

CHERYL.

> I can't talk to you.

NADINE.

> He's trying to judge himself.
>
> One time we were together after a
>
> long period of incredible, sharing times.
>
> I said: "You're so wonderful."
>
> And he started to cry.

MARK (*to* NADINE).

> I've done terrible things.

NADINE (*to* MARK).

> I know.
>
> (*Long pause.*)
>
> Christ, I hate this country.
>
> I can remember everything.
>
> Back to being two years old,
>
> and all these terrible things they taught us.
>
> I can't believe we obeyed them *all*.

MARK (*very quiet*).

> I had two cousins who went through Vietnam.
>
> One was a truck driver and got through it.
>
> My other cousin was in the army.
>
> His unit, about one hundred men were climbing up a
> hill.
>
> They were all killed except for him and another guy.
>
> And they were lying there.
>
> The VC were going around putting bullets

into people's heads.

> Making sure they were dead.
>
> And he had to lay there wounded faking he was
> dead.
>
> He and I never talked.
>
> Ever.
>
> Someone else communicated his story to me,
> and I know he knows my story.

> *Pause.*

V

CHERYL.

> I feel so sorry for Margie, my brother's wife.
>
> I told you about.
>
> You wonder why there's so much more lesbianism
> around now?
>
> Look at the men!
>
> You can see where that's turned a lot of women the
> other way.

NADINE.

> He possibly is overpowering.
>
> I don't know. She was proud to be his woman.
>
> So he said frog, and they all jumped.
>
> Well, that's terrific.
>
> It cost him a lot
>
> to have that power where he abused it.

CHERYL.

> Christ!
>
> Mark pushed me into that, once, too.
>
> We were doing this smack deal,
>
> he brought this woman into our room.
>
> He wanted me to play with her.
>
> He wanted me to get it on with her, too.
>
> It just blew my mind.
>
> I mean it just blew me away.

NADINE.

> I know, I know, I know . . .
>
> But I see when he talks about his wife,
>
> I feel encouraged that there are men that can be that
> way.
>
> He has never, ever said an unkind word about her.
>
> God, I mean it's incredibly civilized
>
> the way he talks about her.
>
> In fact, had he ever said anything foul about her,
> it would have grated on me.
>
> Maybe he just knows what I require.
>
> But I have yet to hear him say
>
> anything bad about anyone;
>
> even those terrible people he had to deal with
> in the jungle.

MARK.

> I saw my cousin at his dad's funeral last December.

CHERYL.
>Now it's so complex
>every time I look . . .
>Oh, God . . . every time I look
>at a piece of furniture,
>it reminds me of something.

MARK.
>Wherever we moved,
>we knew where the other was.
>Something radiates between us.

NADINE.
>I think he's quite superior.
>I really do.
>I think he's got it all figured out.

MARK.
>Our eyes will meet, but we can't touch.

NADINE.
>I think he's gonna make it.
>(*Nervous.*)
>I wonder how you perceive him.

MARK.
>There's no difference between this war and World
>>War II.
>I'm convinced of that.
>
>Maybe it was different in that it was the race thing.
>(*Admitting.*)
>We referred to them as zips, or dinks, or gooks.
>But I don't think I would have had any trouble
>>shooting anything.
>
>We weren't freaks out there.
>Guys in World War II cracked up, too.
>
>We're their children.
>
>I would like to play you a song.
>
>*Music: ''No More Genocide'' by Holly Near.* MARK
>>*turns on tape recorder.*

END OF ACT TWO

ACT THREE

I

MARK (*snaps on slide of him and R.J.*).
>This is a picture of me and R.J.
>We look like a couple of bad-asses.
>It was hot. Shit, I miss him.
>We were so close.
>We talked about everything.
>We talked about how each of us lost our
>virginity, we talked about girls.

CHERYL (*agitated*).
>My girlfriend across the street told me
>how babies were made when I was ten years old.
>I just got sick. I hated it.

MARK.
>We talked about fights, getting back on the streets,
>>drugs.

CHERYL.
>From that moment on,
>I had a model:
>I wanted kids . . .

MARK.
>We talked about getting laid . . .

CHERYL.
>But I didn't want the husband that went along with
>>it.
>I still feel that way.

MARK.
>We talked about how we would be inseparable
>when we came home.
>We never would have, even if he hadn't died.
>We knew too much about each other.

CHERYL.
>And this spooks me because I said this
>when I was ten years old.

MARK (*new slide*).
>This is the place, the Alamo.
>That's where the rocket came in and
>killed a man . . . uh . . .
>(*Indicates in the picture.*)
>We got hit one night.
>Some several people were sleeping, this fellow . . .
>(*Picture of him.*)
>A rocket came in and blew his head off.

NADINE.
>I said to Mark:
>''You're still pissed off because they let you go.
>Even assholes stopped their kids from going.
>Your good Catholic parents sent you to slaughter.''

MARK.
>It was near dawn.
>We moved his body out of there.
>We put his body on a rice-paddy dike.
>I watched him. He was dead and he was
>very close to me and I don't know.

NADINE.
>His parents pushed him into going.
>They believed all those terrible cliches.

MARK.
>I didn't want him to lay in that place where he died.
>I didn't want him laying in the mud.
>And I think I was talking to him.
>I was crying, I don't know.

NADINE.

> Do you know, to this day his father
> will not say the word Vietnam.

MARK.

> His dog came out and started . . .
> The dog was eating him.
> I just came out and fired at the dog.
> I got him killed.
> (*Snaps picture.*)
> Later, I took that picture.

NADINE.

> But his father talked to everyone but Mark about the
>> war.
> He's got his medals on his wall.

MARK.

> I don't know.
> It becomes a sacred place. It was "the Alamo."
> That's what we named it.
> I shot the dog because it was desecrating.
> The dog was eating our friend . . .
> I would have done anything, if I could have,
> if I could have kept flies off of him, even.

NADINE.

> His father's ashamed of himself.
> When you let your son go to war
> for all the wrong reasons,
> you can't face your son.

MARK (*crying*).

> I just wanted him . . .
> He coulda gone home the next day.
> The war was over for him.
> I wanted him to get home.

> *Pause.*

II

CHERYL.

> I want to go home.
> To the church, to my family.
> The sixties are over.

NADINE.

> The sixties . . .
> You know, a lot of us went through that whole
> decade pretending to ourselves we were pacifists.

MARK.

> I wanted to get home so bad.

CHERYL.

> Well, I mean I'm gonna have another kid.
> I'm gonna have to take him to the Cathedral to be
> baptized 'cuz our wedding wasn't blessed.
> It wasn't in a church.
> We had to get married and we had to do it fast.
> In South Dakota.
> In the clothes we'd been in for three days.

NADINE.

> As if we didn't know what violence was.

MARK.

> You know, the biggest thing I had to adjust to
> coming home was I didn't have my gun.

CHERYL.

> My dad had just died so I didn't really care.
> My dad and I were really close.
> He was the only one who mattered . . .

MARK.

> I mean, that gun was mine.

CHERYL.

> I don't know why I'm remembering all this
> all of a sudden . . .

MARK.

> I knew every part of it.

NADINE.

> God, we hated those vets.

MARK.

> The barrel burned out of it.
> You know, I had a new barrel put in,
> but I mean that gun was mine.
> I took that gun everywhere I went.
> I just couldn't live without that gun.

NADINE.

> All that nonsense about long hair, flowers and love.

CHERYL.

> I mean, my family just dug my father's hole
> and put him right in there.

NADINE.

> And the women were exempt!
> They were all supposed to be Mother Earths making
>> pots.

CHERYL.

> My brother's wife went nuts and shot her two-year-
> old son and killed him.
> I told you.
> I mean—all the things we did to him.
> He had to come and get me out of jail
> at three in the morning and he's not—
> he wasn't a strong man.
> So my father just jumped into that bottle
> and nobody could get him out of it.

NADINE.

> I think I knew then what I know now.

MARK.

> When I got on the plane coming home
> I was so happy. I didn't miss my gun then.
> It was my birthday.

NADINE.

> I don't know.

MARK.

> I turned twenty-one.
> I did my birthday coming home.

NADINE.

Oh, Jesus.

MARK.

I did my birthday across the dateline.

I was incredibly happy.

We hit Okinawa.

R.J. was there.

We saw all these guys who were just going over.

NADINE.

I only hope I would have done exactly what Mark
did.

MARK.

All these guys were asking us how it was.

We were really getting off on the fact

that we were done.

These guys were so green and fat.

We were brown, we were skinny.

We were animals.

NADINE.

I think he survived

because he became an animal.

I hope I would have wanted to live that bad.

CHERYL.

I used to stay up all night with my dad.

I was doing a lot of speed then

and I used to stay up all night with him and talk.

I'd be sewing or something like that at the kitchen
table

and he'd be sittin' there drinking and bitching.

MARK.

I don't know why I couldn't talk to my parents when
I got back.

NADINE.

We just can't face that in ourselves.

MARK.

I told my dad everything when I was over there.

CHERYL.

My dad was an intelligent, common-sense-type
man.

He had no college education, but judging
characters . . .

NADINE.

Oh, God.

CHERYL.

Oh, God.

MARK.

The only way I could cry was to write to my dad.

"God, Dad. I'm really scared. I'm really terrified."

CHERYL.

Oh, God. He could pick out people.

MARK.

When I sent somebody out and they got killed,

I could tell my dad.

CHERYL.

My dad told me: Stay away from Mark.

MARK.

I got into L.A. . . . , called:

"Hey, I'm back. I'm back."

My dad said: "Oh, great. We're so relieved.

I'm so happy." My mother cried, she was happy.

I said: "I'm going to buy a hamburger."

CHERYL.

He told me: Mark can't communicate, his style of
dress is weird, the war . . .

MARK.

I just got on this stool going round and round.

"Hey, I'm back."

No one wanted anything to do with me.

Fuckin' yellow ribbons.

I thought I was tired.

NADINE.

The problem now is knowing what to do with what
we know.

CHERYL.

My dad said:

I want you to forget him.

Just forget him.

Get out of this now, while you can.

MARK.

I waited around until 3 A.M.,

caught a flight, got out here.

6:30 in the morning.

Beautiful, beautiful day.

Got my stuff, threw it over my shoulder,

and started walking.

CHERYL.

I saw Mark occasionally, anyway.

Shortly after that, my dad had a stroke.

You know, my dad and I are identical.

MARK.

I walked in the door and set everything down.

I was home.

My dad looked at me, my mom looked at me.

I sat down. Said:

Could I have some coffee?

That's when my mother started raggin' on me

about drinking coffee.

The whole thing broke down.

NADINE.

Oh, God . . .

CHERYL.

My sister had a baby when she was seventeen.

They put her in a home, you know, the whole route.

Shortly after that, I was five years younger than her,

I was just starting to date.

MARK.

"Well," my mom said, "you better get some sleep.

I've got a lot to do."

I said: like I don't want to sleep.

I got incredibly drunk.

CHERYL.
    I remember—I'd come home from a date.
    The only time I saw my father was late at night.
    He would take a look at me and say:
    Well, I hope you learned from your sister
    that the only way to stay out of trouble
    is to keep your legs crossed.

MARK.
    My mom and dad had to go out that night.
    I thought, well, I'd sit down
    and talk with them at dinner.
    They were gone.

CHERYL.
    End of conversation.

MARK.
    We didn't see each other that day.
    We never really did see each other.

CHERYL.
    I mean, he got his point across . . .
    more or less.

MARK.
    I had no idea what was going on.
    This was 1970.
    My hair was short.
    I got really crazed out on junk and stuff.
    Then when I was totally avoiding going home
    somewhere in that I wanted to . . .
    I really wanted bad to . . .
    communicate with a woman.

NADINE.
    You know, all Mark did was—
    He brought the war back home
    and none of us could look at it.

MARK.
    I wanted to fuck my brains out.

CHERYL.
    God, I was naive.
    I was naive as they come.
    And to sit here and say that now knowing what I
        know
    and what I've been through
    just gives me the creeps.

MARK.
    No one wanted anything to do with me.

NADINE.
    We couldn't look at ourselves. We still can't.

CHERYL.
    Because I am so far from being naive.
    I mean, just the idea if I ever divorced Mark . . .
    I don't think I could ever find anyone who
    could handle my past.
    I mean, I have a hard time relating to it myself.

III

NADINE.
    Oh, God.
    I'm worried about us.
    I keep this quiet little knowledge with me every day.
    I don't tell my husband about it.
    I don't tell my kids,
    or Mark.
    Or anyone.
    But something has fallen apart.
    I'm having trouble being a mother.
    How can you believe in sending your children to
        special classes
    when you know it doesn't matter?
    Oh,
    I worry, I worry,
    I worry one of my daughters
    will be walking down the street
    and get raped or mugged by someone who is angry
        or hungry.
    I worry I have these three beautiful daughters (pieces
        of life)
    who I have devoted my whole life to,
    who I've put all my energy into—bringing up—
        raising—
    and then somebody up there goes crazy one day
    and pushes the "go" button and
    phew! bang, finished, the end.
    I worry that my daughters won't want to give birth
    because of my bad birthing experience.
    And I worry that they *will* want to give birth.

    I worry that—
    Well, one of my daughters does blame me
    for the divorce
    because I have protected them from knowing
    what kind of man their father really is.

    (I worry that I worry too much about all this
    and I worry that I really don't worry enough about it
        all.)
    I worry so much it makes me sick.

    I work eighteen hours a day just to pay the bills.
    This year, I work on the feminist caucus,
    I do my portraits, run my magazine, organize civic
        events.
    I hold two jobs and more.
    I invite my dear, sweet, ninety-one-year-old uncle
    to come die at my house.

    I go to recitals, shopping, graduation,
    I don't go through the ritual
    of getting undressed at night.
    I sleep with my shoes on.
    My husband's alcoholism has ruined us.

(Forty-five thousand dollars in debt.)

I don't dare get angry anymore.
Can you imagine what would happen,
if I got angry?
My children . . .
(*Can't go on.*)

MARK.

My wife means so much to me.
I don't want to jeopardize what she's giving to me.
I don't want to jeopardize her.

It's like the Marine Corps.
Cheryl is like a comrade. She's walking wounded
    now.
You don't leave a comrade on the field.

NADINE.

It's all out of control.

MARK.

Sometimes I think Nadine loses sight of things.
Sometimes, I think she's way ahead of me.

NADINE.

I don't know what I'm doing.

MARK.

I can't talk to you about Nadine.

NADINE.

Oh, men. I have to take care of them.
And they're all cripples.
It's so depressing.

MARK.

It's like I know that I'm carrying a time bomb
and there are times that I just don't know
if I'll go off.
I don't know that in the end
I won't destroy myself.

NADINE.

And yet, there's that little voice inside me
that reminds me that even though it's hopeless
I have little children that can't survive without me.

MARK.

Maybe because I just can't comprehend war.
War that's political enough in terms of
what you have and what you get out of it.

NADINE.

I guess I could possibly be the most
vulnerable person of all of us.
But I've also built up all these other devices
which will overrule that.

MARK.

I need to tell you what I did.
My wife knows it.
She's come through times
when I got to the very edge of suicide.
She's helped me through a couple of times
that without her help . . .

I'd be dead.
Now, I've been very honest with Nadine
except when she asked me about suicide.
I couldn't tell her that.

NADINE.

I couldn't even think about suicide.

IV
THE SPAGHETTI STORY

CHERYL.

I hate to cook.
Probably because he likes to cook.
I hate to cook.
I don't know how to cook,
and I hate it.

Mark does this spaghetti dinner once a year.
Has he ever told you about that?
Holy Christ!

MARK.

Excuse me.
(*Leaves.*)

CHERYL.

Every day before Thanksgiving
Mark does a spaghetti dinner, and this
is a traditional thing.
This is the one traditional bone Mark has in his
    body,
and I'd like to break it.

He has 20–45 people come to this thing.
He makes ravioli, lasagne, spaghetti, meatballs,
three different kinds of spaghetti sauce:
shrimp, plain, meat sauce.
Oh, he makes gnocchi! He makes his own noodles!
And it's good.
He's a damn good cook for Italian food.
But you can imagine what I go through
for three weeks for that party
to feed forty people.
Sit-down dinner.
He insists it's a sit-down dinner.

So here I am running around
with no time to cook with him.
I'm trying to get enough shit in my house
to feed forty people sit-down dinner.
We heated the porch last year
because we did not have enough room to seat forty
    people.
And I run around serving all these slobs,
and this is the first year he's really charged anyone.
And we lose on it every year.
I mean, we lose, first year we lost $300.
This dinner is a $500 deal.

I'm having a baby this November,
and if he thinks he's having
any kind of spaghetti dinner,
he can get his butt out of here.
I can't take it.

Pizzas! He makes homemade pizzas.
You should see my oven.
Oh my God! There's pizza-shit everywhere.
Baked on.
And when it's over with,
he just gets up and walks out.
He's just done.
The cleanup is no big deal to him.
He won't even help.
He rolls up the carpets for this dinner.
People get smashed!
He's got wine everywhere, red wine.
It has to be red so if it gets on my rugs,
my rugs are ruined and my couch is ruined.
I've just said it so many times I hate it.
He knows I hate it.

My brother brought over some speed
to get me through that night.
My brother, Jack, who is a capitalist—
intelligent—makes me sick.
Never got into drugs. Was too old.
Missed that whole scene.
But he now has speed occasionally
on his bad day, you know, drink, two drinks one
    night,
speed to get him through the day.
Business man.

He brought me some speed to get me through the
    night
'cause he knew what a basket case I'd be.

And then Mark goes and invites my family.
And they're the last people I want to see at this.
Sure, they love it.
I mean, they all sit around and they
stuff themselves to death.
I'm not kidding!
It is one big stuffing feast.

The first time, the first spaghetti dinner we had was
right after Danny was born.
Danny's baby book got torn up.
I had to start a whole new one.
Mark's crazy friends.
Drunk.
Broken dishes everywhere.
I'm not kidding.
It's just a disaster.

Spaghetti on the walls.
Spaghetti pots dropped in the kitchen.
Spaghetti all over the sink.

That's why I ask him.
I go: "Why?"
"It's traditional. I have to do this every year."
It was three years ago he started.
Tradition, my ass.

I'm telling you.
I mean, he wonders why I can't sleep with him
    sometimes.
Because I just work up such a hate for him inside
    that . . .
(MARK *reenters*.)
I'm a perfectionist.
My house has to be this way,
and before I go to sleep,
I'll pick up after him.
I'm constantly picking up after him.
Christ Almighty!
In the morning, if he comes in late,
he's read the newspaper
and there's newspaper all over the room.
He *throws* it when he's done with it.
I've broken toes on his shoes.
I broke *this* toe on his shoe.
He always leaves his shoes right out in walking
    space.
Every morning I trip on
either his tennis or his good shoes.
Whichever pair he doesn't have on.
He's so inconsiderate of other people.
He's so selfish, he's so self-centered.
And this is what I tell him.
I'm just tired of it.
He's so selfish.
Because this spaghetti dinner just ruins me.
Baby or no baby,
it just completely ruins me.
And he's showing off his,
his wonderful cooking that he does once a year.
And I suppose this is why I hate cooking.

V

MARK (*shows us slide of wounded children*).
This is a picture of some kids who were hurt.
I used to take care of them,
change their bandages and shit.
I loved these kids.

Oh, God . . .

VI

CHERYL.
> What am I gonna do? I mean,
> someday Danny's gonna have to see Mark
> for what he is.
> And that just scares the piss right out of me.

NADINE.
> How do you tell your children their father is an
> asshole?

CHERYL.
> I don't wanna be here when Mark tells Danny
> about the war.
> I don't trust him.

NADINE.
> How could I tell my children that their father is
> in town and hasn't called?

CHERYL.
> I don't trust what he's gonna tell the kid.
> And the way I wanna bring the kid up,
> you can't tell him anything.

NADINE.
> You can't tell your kids
> they can't have something they want
> because their father has squandered their money.

CHERYL.
> You're just better off not saying anything.

NADINE.
> What'm I going to do,
> tell them he's off somewhere getting drunk
> and has forgotten all about them?

CHERYL.
> I'm just, you know,
> when that sort of thing comes along,
> I live from day to day.

NADINE.
> The counselors tell me and my lawyers tell me
> that I should stop protecting them from him.
> But it's hard enough, don't you think?
> They hurt enough already.

CHERYL.
> Later on, you know—
> there might not be a war going on.
> I might not have to deal with that.
> And maybe someday I can explain to him.

NADINE.
> One time I told them he was in town
> because I couldn't find a way
> to cover up the fact that I knew.
> They were depressed for weeks.
> I have to protect them.

CHERYL (angry).
> See, why do I have to do all this????
> And I do.
> I find myself doing everything.
> Covering for him . . .

NADINE.
> I don't protect Mark.
> He doesn't need it.
> He judges himself all the time,
> he's devoted to his son.

CHERYL.
> Sure Mark plays with him.
> But when it comes to discipline,
> that kid's a little brat,
> I mean he is.
> And Mark's never around when it comes to
> discipline.

NADINE.
> He works hard at his shop. He is supporting his
> family.

CHERYL.
> He's never around.

NADINE.
> He is working his way back into society.
> He's beginning to believe in himself
> and do his work.

CHERYL.
> I'm past the sixties.
> I want to go back to the Church.
> And Mark just will not understand the importance of
> this for me.
> I mean, when there's no father around,
> the Church shows some order, you know.

NADINE.
> He told me he's discovering
> who he always thought he was.
> I think of him as an artist
> and a lifelong friend.

VII

MARK (holding the picture HE has framed of the children).
> I'm terrified . . .
> I have a son . . .
> There's another child on the way . . .
> I'm terrified for what I did now . . .

CHERYL.
> The war is the base of all our problems.

MARK.
> It's guilt . . .
> it's a dumb thing . . .
> it makes no sense logically . . .
> but I'm afraid there's this karma I built up
> of hurting . . .
> there are children involved . . .
> like it's all going to balance out
> at the expense of my kids.

CHERYL.
> I get so scared when he says that.
> I mean, I never did anything.

MARK.

There's no logic to it but it's there.
I try . . .
I'm really intense with my boy.

I think what we're beginning to see here is
that it was a different world I was in.
I'd like to be real academic about this . . .
closed case . . .
but this is an ongoing struggle.

NADINE.

Mark!

MARK.

I don't know.
I just don't know.
Sometimes I look at a news story.
I look at something someone goes to prison for here,
I think about it.
There's no difference.
It's just a different place.
This country had all these rules and regulations
and then all of a sudden they removed these things.

Then you came back and try to make your life
in that society where you had to deal with them.
You find that if you violate them,
which I found,
you go to jail,
which I did.
I sit back here sometimes and watch the news,
watch my mother,
watch my father.
My parents watch the news and say:
"Oh my God somebody did that!
Somebody went in there . . . and started
    shooting . . .
and killed all those people.
They ought to execute him."
I look at them.
I want to say,
"Hell, what the fuck,
why didn't you ever listen . . .
You want to hear what I did?"
It's real confusion.
I'm guilty and I'm not guilty.
I still want to tell my folks.
I need to tell them what I did.

VIII

CHERYL.

There was a time when a man would confess to me,
"I'm a jerk,"
at a private moment
and I would smile

sweetly
and try to comfort him.

Now I believe him.

IX
THE CONFESSION

MARK.

I . . . I killed three children, a mother and father in
    cold blood.
(*Crying.*)

CHERYL.

Don't.

MARK.

I killed three children, a mother and father . . .

Long pause.

NADINE.

Mark.

MARK.

I killed them with a pistol in front of a lot of people.

I demanded something from the parents and then
systematically destroyed them.
And that's . . .
that's the heaviest part of what I'm carrying around.
You know about it now, a few other people know
    about it,
my wife knows about it, Nadine knows about it,
and nobody else knows about it.
For the rest of my life . . .

I have a son . . .
He's going to die for what I've done.
This is what I'm carrying around;
that's what this logic is about with my children.

A friend hit a booby-trap.
And these people knew about it.
I knew they knew.
I knew that they were working with the VC
    infrastructure.
I demanded that they tell me.
They wouldn't say anything.
I just wanted them to confess before I killed them.
And they wouldn't.
So I killed their children
and then I killed them.

I was angry.
I was angry with all the power I had.
I couldn't beat them.
They beat me.
(*Crying.*)

I lost friends in my unit . . .
I did wrong.

People in the unit watched me kill them.
Some of them tried to stop me.
I don't know.
I can't. . . . Oh, God . . .

A certain amount of stink
went all the way back to the rear.
I almost got into a certain amount of trouble.

It was all rationalized,
that there was a logic behind it.
But they knew.
And everybody who knew had a part in it.
There was enough evidence,
but it wasn't a very good image to put out
in terms of . . .
the marines overseas, so nothing happened.

I have a child . . .
a child who passed through the age
that the little child was.
My son . . . my son
wouldn't know the difference between a VC and a
    marine.

The children were so little.

I suppose I could find a rationalization.

All that a person can do is try and find words
to try and excuse me,
but I know it's the same damn thing
as lining Jews up.
It's no different
than what the Nazis did.
It's the same thing.

I know that I'm not alone.
I know that other people did it, too.
More people went through more hell than I did . . .
but they didn't do this.

I don't know . . .
I don't know . . .
if it's a terrible flaw of *mine,*
then I guess deep down I'm just everything that's
    bad.

I guess there is a rationale that says
anyone who wants to live that bad
and gets in that situation . . .
(*Long pause.*)
but I should have done better.
I mean, I really strove to be good.
I had a whole set of values.
I had 'em and I didn't.
I don't know.

I want to come to the point
where I tell myself that I've punished myself
    enough.

In spite of it all,
I don't want to punish myself anymore.
I knew I would want to censor myself for you.

I didn't want you to say:
What kind of a nut, what kind of a bad person is he?
And yet, it's all right.
I'm not gonna lie.

My wife tries to censor me . . .
from people, from certain things.
I can't watch war shows.
I can't drive.
Certain things I can't deal with.
She has to deal with the situation,
us sitting around, a car backfires,
and I hit the deck.

She knows about the graveyards, and R.J. and the
    woman.
She lives with all this still hanging out.
I'm shell shocked.

X

NADINE.
    Well, I'm going to look forward to the rest of my
        life
    because of what I know.
    I can't wait to test myself.
    See, I guess I've known what it is to feel hopeless
    politically.
    And I've known what it is to plunge
    personally.
    But Mark has become a conscience for me.
    Through him—I've come to understand the violence
    in myself . . . and in him, and in all of us.
    And I think if we can stay aware of that,
    hold on to that knowledge,
    maybe we can protect ourselves
    and come out on the other side.
MARK (*mumbling*).
    I'm just a regular guy.
    A lot of guys saw worse.
NADINE.
    If anything I'm on a continuum now.
MARK.
    See, I didn't want to see people
    going through another era of
    being so ignorant of the fact that war kills people.
NADINE.
    And I don't know if it's cynicism or just experience,
    but I'm sure I'm never gonna plunge
    in the old way again.
    I'm not saying that trying to sound tough.
    I know about that. I know all about that.

MARK.

I feel protective of our children.

Once you're out there, you know there is no justice.

I don't want the children to die.

NADINE.

But I have no old expectations anymore.

And when you have none,

you're really free.

And you don't ever plunge.

What do you plunge for?

MARK.

It will happen again.

NADINE.

I'm just going to work so hard because of what I
know.

I do every day.

Did I tell you about not going to sleep at night
because I can't bear to stop thinking about it all?

I'm just going to be so busy for whatever's left.

(But I'm not mad at anyone.)

I don't blame anyone.

I've forgiven everyone.

God, I feel my house is in order at last.

MARK.

I DEDICATE . . . this evening to my friends . . .

I'd like a roll call for my friends who died.

NADINE.

There's one other thing.

When we all sit around together

with our friends

and we tell women

that no man can do it for you,

we all know it's true,

but I guess for some of us

it never works that way.

At this point in my life,

this curtain has dropped.

MARK.

Anderson, Robert.

NADINE.

And we see . . .

MARK.

Dafoe, Mark.

NADINE.

We need them—to be here, questioning themselves
and judging themselves—and us—like Mark.

MARK.

Dawson, Mark.

NADINE.

I love Mark.

MARK.

Fogel, Barry.

NADINE.

Well, . . . so . . .

The material has been turning over and over.

MARK.

Grant, Tommy.

NADINE.

Where is it at now?

MARK.

Gunther, Bobby.

NADINE.

You see.

MARK.

Heinz, Jerry.

NADINE.

What do you see, just a cast of characters?

MARK.

Jastrow, Alan.

Lawrence, Gordon.

Mullen, Clifford.

Roll call continues through CHERYL's *speech, ending with a
conscious decision on* MARK's *part to name R.J. among the
casualties of Vietnam.*

XI

CHERYL.

The men have it all.

MARK.

Nelson, Raymond.

CHERYL.

They've had it for the longest time.

MARK.

Nedelski, Michael.

CHERYL.

There's another thing I believe.

There's a lot more people

that are messed up because of the way we were
brought up.

MARK.

Nevin, Daniel.

CHERYL.

Not brought up, but the things we've been through
since we were brought up.

MARK.

O'Brien, Stephen.

CHERYL.

So I think our generation,

MARK.

Rodriguez, Daniel.

CHERYL.

the hippie generation, shortly before and after,

are gonna be the ones that suffer.

MARK.

Rogers, John.

CHERYL.

Because ninety percent of the men never straightened
out.

MARK.
>   Ryan, John.

CHERYL.
>   But what I also believe
>   is that for every woman that has her beliefs,
>   there's a man that matches.

MARK.
>   Sawyer, Steven.

CHERYL.
>   Whether you find him or not,
>   is, is like finding a needle in a haystack.
>   With our population,
>   *I mean,* that's the odds you have.

MARK.
>   Simon, Jimmy.

CHERYL.
>   And there's the Women's Libs.
>   And there's a man for them too.

MARK.
>   Skanolon, John.

CHERYL.
>   See, what we're doing is crossing.
>   We're meeting the men
>   that should be with the other ones.
>   And I truly believe that,
>   that there is an equal balance.
>   Even though our group is so fucked-up.
>   And we are.

MARK.
>   Spaulding, Henry.

CHERYL.
>   You'll look, you'll go in college campuses now
>   and it's completely back the way it was . . .
>   and it should stay there.

MARK.
>   Stanton, Ray.

CHERYL.
>   I don't wanna see that shit come back.
>   I didn't even get that involved in it.
>   I got involved in it in my own little niche.
>   But I didn't, you know, get into it
>   in the school matter.
>   I went two years and I had it up to here.

And sure I would like to have gone on to school,
>   but I was competing with Mark.
>   And I'm not,
>   I do not like competing with someone.

MARK.
>   Vechhio, Michael.

CHERYL.
>   I'm a happy-go-lucky person.
>   I used to be anyway, before I met Mark,
>   where you couldn't depress me on the worst day.
>   And I had a good day every day of my life.

MARK.
>   Walker,
>   *Pause.*

CHERYL.
>   And that is the way life was gonna be for me.

MARK.
>   R.J.
>   *Pause.*

XII

MARK *points to his photograph of two grapefruits, an orange, a broken egg, with a grenade in the center on a dark background. Also some fresh bread, a fly on the fruit. From far away it looks like an ordinary still life.*

MARK.
>   My unit got blown up.
>   It was a high contact.
>   We got hit very, very hard.
>   The Marine Corps sends you
>   this extra food, fresh fruit, bread,
>   a reward
>   when you've had a heavy loss.
>
>   What can I say?
>   I am still alive—my friends aren't.
>   It's a still life.
>   I didn't know what I was doing.

The WOMEN'*s eyes meet for the first time as lights
>   go down.*

END OF PLAY

FOCUS QUESTIONS

1. Defend *Still Life* as a documentary play.
2. Discuss the controversial issues of the play.
3. With reference to the traditional protagonist-antagonist dynamic, analyze the play's fluctuating relationships.
4. Noticing particular references to characters *outside* the action, what other combination of personalities would you seat at the table? Discuss your choices.
5. Develop a character sketch in which you suggest what will become of this character after the action of the play has transpired.
6. Write a short essay in which you assess the language of the play.
7. Assess Mann's creative contribution in composing *Still Life* and defend her role as playwright.

OTHER ACTIVITIES

1. Select any scene from the play and juxtapose the dialogue to suit your own feelings and speech rhythms. How do your alterations differ from Mann's version?
2. Research photographs for projection slides in your own production of the play and list the reasons for your selection.
3. Select any scene from the play and mobilize the actors on an entirely empty stage. Discuss your discoveries.

BIBLIOGRAPHY

Bennetts, Leslie. "When Reality Takes to the Stage." *The New York Times,* 9 March 1986, sec. 2, pp. 1, 4.

Betsko, Kathleen, and Rachel Koenig, eds. *Interviews with Contemporary Women Playwrights.* New York: Beech Tree/Morrow, 1987.

Kolin, Philip. "Emily Mann's *Still Life.*" *The Explicator* 48 (Fall 1989): 61–64.

Kolin, Philip and LaNelle Daniel. "Emily Mann: A Classified Bibliography." *Studies in American Drama, 1945–Present* (1989): 223–66.

Leipzig, Adam. "Political Theatre in America." *Theatre Communications* 5, no. 2 (Feb. 1983): 1–5.

Savran, David, ed. *In Their Own Words: Contemporary American Playwrights.* New York: Theatre Communications Group, 1988.

Shiff, Ellen. "Emily Mann." In *Contemporary Dramatists,* 4th ed., edited by D. L. Kirkpatrick, 342–43. Chicago: St. James Press, 1988.

RECOMMENDED VIDEOTAPE

Still Life. VHS. Two cassettes. 1989. A movement theatre adaptation. Boston Conservatory.

PAINTING CHURCHES
TINA HOWE (1937-   )

She brings the texture of painting and the lyricism of poetry to her writing for the theater.

—WENDY WASSERSTEIN

George N. Martin as Gardner, Marian Seldes as Fanny, and Elizabeth McGovern (*right*) as Mags in *Painting Churches,* presented at the Lamb's Theatre in 1983, under the direction of Carole Rothman. *Photo: © Martha Swope.*

APPROACHING FEMINIST PERSPECTIVES IN THE DRAMA

The visibility and accomplishments of contemporary women in the theatre are the long-awaited results of a difficult struggle. Sexual equality will endure as one of history's more problematical issues, mostly for its disquieting impact on the repression of women in the arts. Although the muses of creativity were envisioned as women, the truth remains that women's contribution to the development of Western performance was restricted for many centuries by religious and political sanctions.

It is not surprising, therefore, that the theatre, like most institutions, was a patriarchy. It was nurtured by religious customs practiced by the ancient Greeks, who granted priestly powers primarily to men. Women were kept off the stages of Europe until the theatre became secularized in the Renaissance. In England, actresses did not appear on the stage until the Restoration, decades after Shakespeare's women characters had been incarnated by men and nearly a century after their European counterparts had enacted women's roles. (See Preface to Behn, p. 390.)

Besides these societal factors, the development of Western drama was further influenced by its critics: most prominently in the classical Greek drama through the pithy observations of Aristotle. His playwriting models for tragedy were rooted in conflict and were built on the phallocentric characteristics of rising actions, climax, and denouement. For better or worse, Aristotle's criteria are still intact and continue to provide much of Western drama with durable designs for characterization, plot, and language. (to Euripides, p. 2.)

Prompted by a feminist movement in the mid-1960's America, issues of equality as well as difference were brought sharply into focus. The distinctions of gender became meaningful parameters for assessing the quality of artistic inspiration and creativity. Western drama no longer needed to deny the unlimited potential of the woman artist's *interior* life for exposing an emotional existence long hidden from view and reshaping the subject matter through her unique psychological perspective. But in the aftermath of this movement, the women writers who were canonized became the scapegoats of newly enlightened feminist critics who, after a scrutinous re-examination of their works, found their playwriting tactics overtly anti-feminist.

In an American society dominated by the artistic merits of men, the diverse but versatile achievements of women like Charlotte Barnes, Harriet Beecher Stowe, Anna Cora Mowatt, and Sidney Frances Bateman substantially embellished our nineteenth-century stage literature. When the formative years of the twentieth century had

evolved into a *modern* age, in which the woman suffrage movement underscored the social and material injustices faced by women, there arose both within and around the Bohemian colony of New York's Greenwich Village a powerful nucleus of women artists. Several of them expressed themselves through playwriting: Susan Glaspell, Alice Gerstenberg, Djuna Barnes, Edna St. Vincent Millay, Zoe Atkins, Zona Gale, Sophie Treadwell, and Rachel Crothers. Challenging the mores of society and redefining women's roles, these writers achieved success despite critical discomfort with their distinctly female point of view. For many of them, recognition on stage did not ensure publication of their works, however, and thus they were forgotten. Meanwhile, the unconventional and controversial Gertrude Stein gained notoriety at home and abroad.

The pioneering efforts of these artists allow us to approach the modern American drama of the post-Depression era with some satisfaction that, before mid-century, women were writing extensively for the New York stage. In addition to those from the Greenwich Village nucleus, these included Anne Nichols, Rose Francken, Anita Loos, Clare Boothe, Ruth Gordon, Fay Kanin, Mary Chase, and Lillian Hellman. In fact, the prolific

Hellman remained active into the second half of the century and would join a generation of contemporaries like Carson McCullers, Alice Childress, Jane Bowles, Lorraine Hansberry, and Jean Kerr. But the list pales considerably alongside that of their male colleagues whose works were produced under similar conditions. Of course, issues of sexual equality beyond the more visible profession of acting were never the concerns of Broadway, which inherited its mantle from the patriarchal Greek drama. As a commercial enterprise, it flourished quite well on the formulaic patterns of playwriting established by its leading male playwrights, although certain women playwrights would achieve critical acclaim by adhering to them.

The controversy is reflected by criticism leveled at Lillian Hellman, who willingly succumbed to patriarchal formulas by ignoring positive female protagonists as models for a so-called women's theatre. Her case reveals how the work of a particular female playwright may not always be distinguishable from that of her male counterpart's, a phenomenon that is the result of the way writers learn their craft from the works of those who preceded them. A woman playwright who wished to achieve success in mainstream theatre had been obliged to abide by the formulas established by men in her circle. This helps us account for Aphra Behn as well as Hellman, who had no alternative in their efforts to earn livings as playwrights except to follow the rules. By the same token, we cannot exclude the contributions of certain men playwrights, such as the classical Euripides, the modernist Ibsen, or the contemporary Tennessee Williams, whose female portraits have attempted to mirror the sexuality, passions, symbols, and language of women. Critical responses to such writers, whether male or female, are enlightened by the questions prompted by the feminist movement of how gender is represented in the arts.

Clearly a door was opened to women playwrights and to a new women's theatre, inspiring artistic changes that were not only quantitative but substantive as well. Often the content was political and the design anarchic, demonstrating the playwright's desire to challenge tired formulas from the past or abolish them forever. When the results were more conventional, the core still reflected some aspect of the female psyche, that is, of women at last writing out of their own experiences. Playwriting workshops in New York spawned feminist theatres across America almost overnight and encouraged women writers to celebrate their newly enlightened selfhoods through renewed dramatic styles, characters, themes, issues, and language. In fact, the first formal network to promote new plays by women was the Women's Theater Council established in 1972. (See Preface to Fornes, p. 1147.) Women playwrights who achieved prominence during this period include Megan Terry, Rochelle Owens, Rosalyn Drexler, Adrienne Kennedy, Maria Irene Fornes, Gretchen Cryer, Ntozake Shange, Beth Henley, Emily Mann, Marsha Norman, and Wendy Wasserstein. Their achievements represent a wide range of styles and themes and reflect, in almost every case, a **feminist aesthetic.**

High on the list of those more eloquent and imaginative stylists is Tina Howe. Revealing a unique theatrical vision that has flexibly served both mainstream and non-mainstream tastes, Howe has created a variety of stage landscapes that serve literal, metaphorical, and psychological ends—museum, restaurant, sandy beach, open road, domestic interior invaded by the forest—and filled them with eccentric characters who bear equally quirky names. By stretching the borders of realism to accommodate the absurdist dimensions of her settings, characters, and language, she has uncovered profound and bittersweet truths about our lives.

More importantly, the unconventional dynamics of Howe's dramatic art have appealed to women *and* men, transforming her deepest artistic yearnings—revealed through her perspectives as a woman—into universal stage images. While her strongest and most rounded characters are admittedly women—"I write about women because that's what I know best"[1]—her men emerge as notable allies to these women and their causes.

Our need to understand what is specifically feminist about Howe's work is encompassed by her vision of "what it means to be a woman artist, what it means to be a woman denied an outlet for her creativity, and the relationship between what is commonly thought of as 'art' and women's other creative activities.''[2] While her feminist voice is never strident or overtly political, it finds pleasure in being whimsically subversive on levels of theatricality and language, until it becomes tempered by deeper and more humanizing tones.

Howe's intense preoccupation with the theme of creativity, for example, resounds throughout her work, ranging from such familiar domestic preoccupations as childrearing and cooking to more exceptional ones like sculpturing and portrait-painting. Achieving a *mise-en-scène* whose exterior is deceptively playful, she develops her potent theme around sharp and sudden turns that lead both characters and audience to unexpected psychological depths.

MAJOR WORKS

Produced Off-Broadway, *The Nest* introduced Tina Howe to New York audiences in 1970. Howe herself directed a second full-length play, *Birth and After Birth,* in 1974. But her career as a playwright was solidly launched through different stage productions of three important works that became loosely connected through their similar themes: the less plotted comic entanglements that exposed the world of art in *Museum* (1976); the more desperate comic situations surrounding the elaborate creation and popular consumption of food in *The Art of Dining* (1979); and the surprisingly conventional but deeply moving *Painting Churches* (1983).

She achieved newer experimental heights when she brought her characters outdoors in search of love in the realistic beach locale of *Coastal Disturbances* (1986); then led them cross-country on a journey toward self-discovery in *Approaching Zanzibar* (1989). She undertook her most daring exploration of the human condition in the apocalyptic *One Shoe Off* (1993), produced at the Public Theater in New York City where her successes with *Museum* and *The Art of Dining* began.

Of all these works, *Painting Churches* has received the widest critical acclaim, largely for its unsentimental but affectionate portrait of a daughter's coming-of-age amid her aging parents' decline. The play earned Tina Howe the Rosamond Gilder Award for Outstanding Creative Achievement in the Theatre; an Obie Award for Distinguished Playwriting; a Rockefeller Playwright-in-Residence Award; the John Gassner Award for Outstanding New American Playwright; and the Outer Critics' Circle Award for Outstanding Off-Broadway Production.

THE ACTION

In their Boston townhouse, Fanny and Gardner Church frantically sort through a disarray of lifetime possessions, packing them for a permanent move to Cape Cod. Weakened by age and poor health, they nervously anticipate the arrival of their daughter Margaret (Mags), a successful New York artist, whose train is running late. When Mags finally appears, she reminds her mother of a promise once made: that she would let Mags paint their portrait ''just so long as you help us get out of here!'' The subject is momentarily brushed aside, while other more urgent concerns occupy their conversation.

Days later, boxes have been packed and removed from sight. Mags' portrait of her parents, who pose awkwardly in formal attire, sits on an easel, nearly completed. The finishing touches are made just prior to the beeping of a horn from the street, signaling the beginning of their leave-taking. Mags savors the moment in which her parents confront the portrait. Oblivious to her presence, Fanny and Gardner waltz dreamily around the empty living room in the glow of their daughter's latest masterpiece.

STRUCTURE AND LANGUAGE

On the surface, Howe explores a woman's uneasy reconciliation with eccentric, aristocratic parents and with traditions long since outgrown. But on a deeper level, she chronicles the protagonist's journey toward selfhood and the emergence of a genuine artist named Margaret Church. Thus *Painting Churches* provides a rare theatrical experience through its spare design, subtle psychological shadings, lush artistic metaphors, and wise but unpretentious insights on the dynamic union between art and life.

We might wonder at the parallels between the playwright's own experiences and Mags', since the play is an eloquent, undisguised cry from an artist's heart and "was very much a response to the death of [Howe's] parents."[3] But our concern for autobiographical allusion fades almost entirely against the play's more transcendent and universal landscape. That the work was conceived by a woman or that it deals with a female protagonist's quest for freedom pays homage to a feminist canon without limiting its scope.

Beneath a realistic structure so seamlessly unified by time, place, and action is a dense memory play that flexibly accommodates the steady flow of present action and past recollection. But Howe dispels any charge of realism by specifying in her description of the setting that the "light that pours through three soaring arched windows [of the living room] . . . transforms whatever it touches giving the room a distinct feeling of unreality." Light is dynamically incorporated into the atmosphere to give the play a "distinct character of its own," according to Heidi Landesman, designer of the original New York production, until it almost becomes "the fourth character."[4]

The surreal effect serves several functions: on a practical level, it softens and distances—rather like a faded photograph—the flamboyant, often dizzying interplay of three strong stage characters; but more symbolically, it facilitates Mags' psychological retreat into her childhood as well as her return to present time, where the finished portrait is suddenly bathed in "dreamy and dappled" light, as if to emblemize her newly found fulfillment as daughter and artist.

In a clever theatrical twist, the audience never views the finished portrait of Fanny and Gardner. Instead its "French Impressionistic" qualities are evoked through the subjects' confused and then amazed reactions, even though they have been too distracted with packing up their own lives to grasp the full import of Mags' discoveries, of her all-consuming need for their approval. These discoveries, incidentally, have made an impact on the portrait, so that it is Mags who is also revealed to us in an ironic and final self-disclosure. Just prior to painting her parents, Mags had remarked: "The great thing about being a portrait painter you see is, it's the *other* guy that's exposed; you're safely hidden behind the canvas and easel." The playwright has tricked Mags, producing instead a double portrait—not only of the artist's parents, but of Mags herself.

Each of the five scenes peels away facades, both physical and psychological, as the action moves from the box-cluttered atmosphere of act 1 to the final setting where "the room is completely empty except for Mags' backdrop." As the stage grows bare, matters of the heart build in intensity until Mags has reset the stage for her own final showdown with two formidable antagonists whose skill with words, challenged by their daughter's, constructs the fabric of the play.

Sporting her Lily Daché hats and displaying an amateurish knack for turning lamp shades into garish magic lanterns, Fanny is Mags' sharpest critic when she glances at the portrait: "Since when do I have purple skin?!" Spouting lines of verse to his confidant, a talking parrot named Toots, Gardner is kinder: "Good lighting effects!" While they disagree with their daughter's values on life and art, they are vital players in the generational conflict that will forge her victory, despite their criticism. The struggle, Mags soon learns, must rest in *her* hands.

Mags is finally reconciled with parents who once reprimanded her for oozing food between her teeth at the dinner table as if she were a ''tube of toothpaste,'' and who sent her to her room without dinner, where she proceeded to melt her countless crayons, night after night, into a ''colossal fruitcake, five feet tall.'' Fanny discovered the ''masterpiece'' and, thinking it ''a mountain of rotting garbage,'' blow-torched it to the ground. Mags proudly asserts her recollection of the incident, knowing what it meant even then: ''It *was* a monument of my cast-off dinners, only I hadn't built it with food . . . I found my own materials. I was languishing with hunger, but oh, dear Mother . . . I FOUND MY OWN MATERIALS!''

In the first of several epiphanies, Mags finds the voice to herald her accomplishment, the missing approval she has always craved from her parents, only to discover it must come from within. Final recognition of this is echoed from the perspective of her newly achieved selfhood, only seconds before she lets her parents view the portrait. She recalls one summer when she had been swimming with her father in an ocean full of phosphorus. Just when the phosphorus was about to desert them, she spotted its remnant brilliance on her father's leg: ''I grabbed it! . . . I remember wishing the moment would hold forever; that we could just be fixed there, laughing and iridescent . . . Even as I was reaching for you, you were gone. We'd never be like that again.''

Mags is powerless at retrieving the past. But her talents have helped her to preserve the present moment, no matter how illusory it may seem: she has captured the laughter and iridescence of two monumental Churches on canvas, as she finally understands them, thus bringing the titular wordplay full circle.

PAINTING CHURCHES-IN-PERFORMANCE

Scheduled for a limited engagement of four weeks, *Painting Churches* opened on January 25, 1983, at the South Street Theatre in New York City under the auspices of the Second Stage. T. E. Kalem called it ''a radiant, loving and zestfully humorous play about subjects that darken the mind with icy forebodings.''[5] The production, which was directed by Carole Rothman, re-opened at the Lamb's Theatre for an extended run of 206 performances on November 22, 1983, and featured Elizabeth McGovern (Mags), Marian Seldes (Fanny), and George N. Martin (Gardner). Critics noticed some production changes in its move to the Lamb's and were mixed in their responses. Frank Rich thought that the director ''gilded the Churches' farcical Act I packing maneuvers and their sad Act II breakdown into second childhood with added filigrees of physical business'' and concluded that the play required ''far fewer theatrical brush strokes, for it really is constructed with an Impressionist's precision.''[6] In contrast, Michael Feingold felt the production had ''undergone considerable improvement.''[7]

Douglas Watt praised McGovern for her ''exceedingly good account'' of Mags.[8] Seldes conveyed ''the destructiveness of Fanny Church quite beautifully through the seeming senility,'' wrote the critic for *Women's Wear Daily*.[9] Clive Barnes complimented Martin for ''bumbl[ing] magnificently in a portrait of genius in amiable decline.''[10]

The one-set show was a triumph of atmosphere, carefully designed by Heidi Landesman—in collaboration with lighting designer Frances Aronson and costumer Linda Fisher—to serve the play's lyrical content. The production was bathed in white, a favorite color of Impressionists, to offset the characters and props that were positioned within the proscenium frame of the intimate Lamb's Theatre. Arched doors and windows lined the elegant but tired living-room setting whose mural-like Colonial wallpaper had faded considerably and exposed the darker oval and square patches marking spots where pictures once hung.

Landesman supported Howe's call for ''unreality'' by texturing the walls and dappling the tinted glass windows with color. She achieved this by ''cover[ing] the floor with muslin, allowing it to spill over the edge of the stage. The floor cloth was evenly sprayed with a high-density foam and then painted.'' She covered the wallpaper ''with layers of tissue paper. The windows were also textured—acrylic sheet with dyed resin poured on to give the bubbly feeling of old glass.''[11] These luminous and reflective surfaces enhanced the different scenes as the source of light shifted to measure the progression of each day. The most magical moment of the play, when Fanny and Gardner waltz dreamily to Chopin, was created by a projector that filled the stage with the ''dreamy and dappled'' light spots indicated in Howe's original stage direction.

Painting Churches has been staged in theatres across America. Productions have also taken place in Canada, England, Italy, New Zealand, and Austria. A televised version, directed by Jack O'Brien, was presented for the American Playhouse series on July 6, 1988. It featured Donald Moffat, Sada Thompson, and Roxanne Hart as Mags. A filmed adaptation entitled *The Portrait,* directed by Arthur Penn, premiered in 1993 with Gregory Peck and Lauren Bacall as Gardner and Fanny Church and Cecilia Peck as Mags.

REFLECTIONS ON PAINTING CHURCHES

Elizabeth McGovern played Mags when Painting Churches *opened at the Lamb's Theatre in New York City.*

When I played Mags, I was much younger and less sure of myself as an actress. I have much more confidence now. It has taken me a long time to learn how to stand on stage and be heard with ease, how to make the choices that you make clear to an audience, and how to repeat those choices night after night. I learned a great deal during the run of *Painting Churches.* And by the end of it, I felt much stronger than I did at the beginning.

My way of preparing is not all that different from one part to the next. Yet I feel as though playing Shakespeare has taught me a lot about doing contemporary plays. To make a Shakespeare play clear to an audience, I have to be very clear about what my character wants so that the audience will understand because the words themselves are often completely obscure. But if it is staged in a way that the actors' *intentions* are clear, then the audience always gets it. That kind of discipline is good for contemporary plays too because I'm no longer happy until I've made every moment clear for myself. It makes me sharper.

In both classical and contemporary plays, I must open myself up to hear the music of each particular writer. Every playwright has a different music. The language in a Shakespeare play is farther away from the way we speak today than a contemporary writer. But everything is artifice. I mean, even when I do a much more "naturalistic" writer, it's never really like I would speak at a table. So there's a certain technique required for every writer.

Early in rehearsals, which lasted about four weeks, our director Carole Rothman sat us around a table where we created the world of the play by discussing the lives these people led and their moment to moment relationships. We raised all kinds of questions. The next step was to give our ideas some physical shape, that is, by expressing them through the way in which characters were physically positioned at each point in the play. Then we

Continued

repeated these different arrangements and adjusted decisions that were not good ones, trying to fill out the stage picture. We kept asking questions about each moment, always making sure that we were as clear as is humanly possible about what our characters wanted at any particular time.

Tina Howe was there during the course of rehearsals and worked very closely with our director. But she never got in the director's way in her relationship with the actors. She never came directly to us with a suggestion or an interpretation because this can become dangerous: you know, the director telling you one thing, the writer another. She was very supportive, as I recall, and if she had any feelings, she would tell the director, who would then speak to us. I think certain aspects of her play were sharpened in her work with Carole. There was lots of dialogue between them.

I think the important thing about Mags is not that she's a painter as much as the fact that she's a woman in need of the approval and recognition of her parents. Her vocation could probably have been any number of things. Probably the dynamic would be much the same if she were working as a nurse. It's easy for a writer to write about another artist because the mentality is similar. But the most important thing about the character of Mags in terms of the play itself is the need she had for her parents to recognize her. However, it is significant that during the course of the play she grows up and realizes that what she's looking for she can never get from outside herself. In that last act, rather than getting exactly what she's looking for, Mags is confronted by her mother who turns to her and says, "Grow up! We have our own problems. Do you think it's any easier for me? Where am I getting *my* approval?" Mags suddenly realizes that she's barking up the wrong tree.

Mags is so preoccupied with her own agenda that she doesn't see her parents as fallible and suffering human beings, full of weakness and loneliness. She's not unlike other characters I have played, including Ophelia. I prefer to think of it as the passage from innocence to experience. Nothing in life is static. The only absolute is death. Characters learn something in the course of any good play; they grow, they change. I think Mags grows up a bit before the play ends, whereas Ophelia falls apart.

The universal nature of the fact that we all need approval from our parents or from some substitute parental figure helps make *Painting Churches* so popular. Audiences recognize these characters, especially the imperfect way in which they love each other, as if to show that we cannot love each other perfectly. This is why Mags is so special to me. Otherwise there were no direct connections between Mags and myself at that time. Perhaps there was a great deal of Tina and her parents in the play, but this is not a matter for me to discuss.

During the actual run, there were special moments, always, that stood out, although these changed from one night to another. But mostly I remember the last night I played. I especially remember one of my own speeches: the one about the phosphorescence in the water. By this time, I had established such an affection for the other actors, and it was my final performance, and it all seemed so sad. All these things combined gave Mags' speech a resonance I'll never forget. I felt that everything I had been struggling with for so long actually clicked. It was a great personal moment for me.

Notes

1. *Betsko and Koenig,* INTERVIEWS WITH CONTEMPORARY WOMEN PLAYWRIGHTS *(New York: Beech Tree/Morrow, 1987), 231.*

2. *Judith Barlow, "The Art of Tina Howe," in* FEMININE FOCUS, *ed. Enoch Brater (New York: Oxford University Press, 1989), 249.*

3. *John L. DiGaetani,* A SEARCH FOR A POSTMODERN THEATER: INTERVIEWS WITH CONTEMPORARY PLAYWRIGHTS *(Westport, CT: Greenwood Press, 1991), 158.*

4. *Susan Lieberman, "Painting Churches,"* THEATRE CRAFTS *(May 1985): 18.*

5. TIME, *21 Feb. 1983.*

6. THE NEW YORK TIMES, *23 Nov. 1983.*

7. VILLAGE VOICE, *6 Dec. 1983.*

8. DAILY NEWS, *23 Nov. 1983.*

9. WOMEN'S WEAR DAILY, *23 Nov. 1983.*

10. NEW YORK POST, *23 Nov. 1983.*

11. *Lieberman, 44.*

PAINTING CHURCHES
Tina Howe

CHARACTERS

Fanny Sedgwick Church, *a Bostonian from a fine old family, in her sixties*

Gardner Church, *her husband, an eminent New England poet from a finer family, in his seventies*

Margaret Church (Mags), *their daughter, a painter, in her early thirties*

During the scene changes, the opening measures of the following Chopin waltzes are played:
As the house lights dim, the Waltz in A Minor, opus posthumous
Setting up Act I, Scene 2, the Waltz in E Minor, opus posthumous
Setting up Act I, Scene 3, the Waltz in E Major, opus posthumous
To close Act I, the final notes of the Waltz in B Minor, opus 69, #2
As the house lights dim for Act II, the Waltz in A flat Major, opus 64, #3
Setting up Act II, Scene 2, repeat the Waltz in A Minor, opus posthumous
To accompany the final moments of GARDNER's and FANNY's dance, the Waltz in D flat Major, opus 70, #3

ACT ONE
SCENE ONE

TIME: Several years ago.
PLACE: The living room of the Church's townhouse on Beacon Hill one week before everything will be moved to Cape Cod. Empty packing cartons line the room and all the furniture has been tagged with brightly colored markers. At first glance it looks like any discreet Boston interior, but on closer scrutiny one notices a certain flamboyance. Oddities from secondhand stores are mixed in with the fine old furniture, and exotic handmade curios vie with tasteful family objets d'art. What makes the room remarkable though is the play of light that pours through three soaring arched windows. At one hour it's hard edged and brilliant; the next, it's dappled and yielding. It transforms whatever it touches giving the room a distinct feeling of unreality. It's several years ago, a bright spring morning.

FANNY *is sitting on the sofa, wrapping a valuable old silver coffee service. She's wearing a worn bathrobe and fashionable hat. As she works, she makes a list of everything on a yellow legal pad.* GARDNER *can be heard typing in his study down the hall.*

FANNY (*she picks up a coffee pot*). God, this is good looking! I'd forgotten how handsome Mama's old silver was! It's probably worth a fortune. It certainly weighs enough! (*Calling out.*) GARRRRRRRRRRRRRRRRRRRDNERRRRRRRRRRRR? . . . Well, it should bring us a pretty penny, that's for sure. (*Wraps it, places it in a carton, and then picks up the tray that goes with it. She holds it up like a mirror and adjusts her hat. Louder in another register.*) OH, GARRRRRRRRRRRRRRRRRRRDNERRRRR? . . .
(*He continues typing.*)
FANNY (*she then reaches for a small box and opens it with reverence*). Grandma's Paul Revere teaspoons! . . . (*She*

takes out several and fondles them.) I don't care how desperate things get, these will never go! One has to maintain some standards! (*She writes on her list.*) ''Grandma's Paul Revere teaspoons, Cotuit!''' . . . WASN'T IT THE AMERICAN WING OF THE METROPOLITAN MUSEUM OF ART THAT WANTED GRANDMA'S PAUL REVERE TEASPOONS SO BADLY? . . . (*She looks at her reflection in the tray again.*) This is a very good looking hat, if I do say so. I was awfully smart to grab it up.

(*Silence.*)

DON'T YOU REMEMBER A DISTINGUISHED LOOKING MAN COMING TO THE HOUSE AND OFFERING US FIFTY THOUSAND DOLLARS FOR GRANDMA'S PAUL REVERE TEA SPOONS? . . . HE HAD ON THESE MARVELOUS SHOES! THEY WERE SO POINTED AT THE ENDS WE COULDN'T IMAGINE HOW HE EVER GOT THEM ON AND THEY WERE SHINED TO WITHIN AN INCH OF THEIR LIVES AND I REMEMBER HIM SAYING HE CAME FROM THE . . . AMERICAN WING OF THE METROPOLITAN MUSEUM OF ART! . . . HELLO? . . . GARDNER? . . . ARE YOU THERE!

(*The typing stops.*)

FANNY.   YOO-HOOOOOOO . . . (*Like a fog horn.*) GARRRRRRRRRRRDNERRRRRRR? . . .

GARDNER (*offstage; from his study*). YES DEAR . . . IS THAT YOU? . . .

FANNY.   OF COURSE IT'S ME! WHO ELSE COULD IT POSSIBLY BE? . . . DARLING, PLEASE COME HERE FOR A MINUTE.

(*The typing resumes.*)

FANNY.   FOR GOD'S SAKE, WILL YOU STOP THAT DREADFUL TYPING BEFORE YOU SEND ME STRAIGHT TO THE NUT HOUSE? . . . (*In a new register.*) GARRRRRRRRRRRRRDNERRRRRR? . . . (*He stops.*)

GARDNER (*offstage*). WHAT'S THAT? MAGS IS BACK FROM THE NUT HOUSE? . . .	FANNY. I SAID . . . Lord, I hate this yelling. . . . PLEASE . . . COME . . . HERE! (*Brief silence.*)
GARDNER (*offstage*). I'LL BE WITH YOU IN A MOMENT, I DIDN'T HEAR HER RING. (*Starts singing.*) ''Nothing could be finer than to be in Carolina.''	FANNY. It's a wonder I'm not in a strait jacket already. Actually, it might be rather nice for a change . . . peaceful. DARLING . . . I WANT TO SHOW YOU MY NEW HAT!

(*Silence.* GARDNER *enters, still singing. He's wearing mismatched tweeds and is holding a pack of papers which keep drifting to the floor.*)

GARDNER.   Oh, don't you look nice! Very attractive, very attractive!

FANNY.   But I'm still in my bathrobe.

GARDNER (*looking around the room, leaking more papers*). Well, where's Mags?

FANNY.   Darling, you're dropping your papers all over the floor.

GARDNER (*spies the silver tray*). I remember this! Aunt Alice gave it to us, didn't she? (*He picks it up.*) Good Lord, it's heavy. What's it made of? Lead?!

FANNY.   No, Aunt Alice did *not* give it to us. It was Mama's.

GARDNER.   Oh, yes . . .

(*He starts to exit with it.*)

FANNY.   Could I have it back, please?

GARDNER (*hands it to her, dropping more papers*). Oh, sure thing . . . Where's Mags? I thought you said she was here.

FANNY.   I didn't say Mags was here, I asked *you* to come here.

GARDNER (*papers spilling*).
Damned papers keep falling. . . .

FANNY.   I wanted to show you my new hat. I bought it in honor of Mags' visit. Isn't it marvelous?

GARDNER (*picking up the papers as more drop*).
Yes, yes, very nice . . .

FANNY.   Gardner, you're not even looking at it!

GARDNER.   Very becoming . . .

FANNY.   You don't think it's too bright, do you? I don't want to look like a traffic light. Guess how much it cost?

GARDNER (*a whole sheaf of papers slides to the floor; he dives for them*). OH, SHIT!

FANNY (*gets to them first*). It's alright, I've got them, I've got them. (*She hands them to him.*)

GARDNER.   You'd think they had wings on them. . . .

FANNY.   Here you go . . .   GARDNER.   . . . damned things won't hold still!

FANNY.   Gar? . . .

GARDNER   (*has become engrossed in one of the pages*). Mmmmm?

FANNY.   HELLO?

GARDNER (*startled*). What's that?

FANNY (*in a whisper*). My hat. Guess how much it cost.

GARDNER.   Oh, yes. Let's see . . . ten dollars?

FANNY.   Ten dollars . . . IS THAT ALL? . . .

GARDNER.   Twenty?

FANNY.   GARDNER, THIS HAPPENS TO BE A DESIGNER HAT! DESIGNER HATS START AT FIFTY DOLLARS . . . SEVENTY-FIVE!

GARDNER (*jumps*). Was that the door bell?

FANNY.   No, it wasn't the door bell. Though it's high time Mags were here. She was probably in a train wreck!

GARDNER (*looking through his papers*). I'm beginning to get fond of Wallace Stevens again.

FANNY. This damned move is going to kill me! Send me straight to my grave!

GARDNER (*reading from a page*).

> *"The mules that angels ride come slowly down*
> *The blazing passes, from beyond the sun.*
> *Descensions of their tinkling bells arrive.*
> *These muleteers are dainty of their way . . ."*

(*Pause.*) Don't you love that? "These muleteers are *dainty* of their way"!? . . .

FANNY. Gar, the hat. How much?

(GARDNER *sighs.*)

FANNY. Darling? . . .

GARDNER. Oh, yes. Let's see . . . fifty dollars? Seventy-five?

FANNY. It's French.

GARDNER. Three hundred!

FANNY (*triumphant*). No, eighty-five cents.

GARDNER. Eighty-five cents! . . . I thought you said . . .

FANNY. That's right . . . eighty . . . five . . . *cents!*

GARDNER. Well, you sure had me fooled!

FANNY. I found it at the thrift shop.

GARDNER. I thought it cost at least fifty dollars or seventy-five. You know, designer hats are very expensive!

FANNY. It was on the mark-down table. (*She takes it off and shows him the label.*) See that? Lily Daché! When I saw that label, I nearly keeled over right into the fur coats!

GARDNER (*handling it*). Well, what do you know, that's the same label that's in my bathrobe.

FANNY. Darling, Lily Daché designed hats, not men's bathrobes!

GARDNER. Yup . . . Lily Daché . . . same name . . .

FANNY. If you look again, I'm sure you'll see . . .

GARDNER. . . . same script, same color, same size. I'll show you.

(*He exits.*)

FANNY. Poor lamb can't keep anything straight anymore. (*Looks at herself in the tray again.*) God, this is a good-looking hat!

GARDNER (*returns with a nondescript plaid bathrobe. He points to the label*). See that? . . . What does it say?

FANNY (*refusing to look at it*). Lily Daché was a *hat* designer! She designed ladies' hats!

GARDNER. What . . . does . . . it . . . say?

FANNY. Gardner, you're being ridiculous.

GARDNER (*forcing it on her*). Read . . . the label!

FANNY. Lily Daché did *not* design this bathrobe, I don't care what the label says!

GARDNER. READ! (FANNY *reads it.*) ALL RIGHT, NOW WHAT DOES IT SAY? . . .

FANNY (*chagrined*). Lily DACHÉ

GARDNER. I told you!

FANNY. Wait a minute, let me look at that again. (*She does; then throws the robe at him in disgust.*) Gar, Lily DACHÉ never designed a bathrobe in her life! Someone obviously ripped the label off one of her hats and then sewed it into the robe.

GARDNER (*puts it on over his jacket*). It's damned good looking. I've always loved this robe. I think you gave it to me. . . . Well, I've got to get back to work.

(*He abruptly exits.*)

FANNY. Where did you get that robe anyway? . . . I didn't give it to you, did I? . . .

(*Silence.* GARDNER *resumes typing.*)

FANNY (*holding the tray up again and admiring herself*). You know, I think I *did* give it to him. I remember how excited I was when I found it at the thrift shop . . . fifty cents and never worn! *I* couldn't have sewn that label in to impress him, could I? . . . I can't be that far gone! . . . The poor lamb wouldn't even notice it, let alone understand its cachet. . . . Uuuuuuh, this damned tray is even heavier than the coffee pot. They must have been amazons in the old days! (*Writes on her pad.*) "Empire tray, Parke-Bernet Galleries," and good riddance! (*She wraps it and drops it into the carton with the coffee pot.*) Where *is* that wretched Mags? It would be just like her to get into a train wreck! She was supposed to be here hours ago. Well, if she doesn't show up soon, I'm going to drop dead of exhaustion. God, wouldn't that be wonderful? . . . Then they could just cart me off into storage with all the old chandeliers and china . . .

(*The door bell rings.*)

FANNY. IT'S MAGS, IT'S MAGS! (*A pause. Dashing out of the room, colliding into* GARDNER.) GOOD GOD, LOOK AT ME! I'M STILL IN MY BATHROBE!

GARDNER (*offstage*). COMING, COMING . . . I'VE GOT IT . . . COMING! (*Dashing into the room, colliding into* FANNY.) I'VE GOT IT . . . HOLD ON . . . COMING . . . COMING . . . . .

FANNY (*offstage*). MAGS IS HERE! IT'S MAGS. . . . SHE'S FINALLY HERE!

(GARDNER *exits to open the front door.* MAGS *comes staggering in carrying a suitcase and an enormous duffle bag. She wears wonderfully distinctive clothes and has very much her own look. She's extremely out of breath and too wrought up to drop her heavy bags.*)

MAGS. I'm sorry . . . I'm sorry I'm so late. . . . Everything went wrong! A passenger had a heart attack outside of New London and we had to stop. . . . It was terrifying! All these medics and policemen came swarming onto the train and the conductor kept running up and down the aisles telling everyone not to leave their seats under any circumstances. . . . Then the New London fire department came screeching down to the tracks, sirens blaring, lights whirling, and all these men in black rubber suits started pouring through the doors. . . . *That* took two hours. . . .

FANNY.   DARLING . . . DARLING . . . WHERE ARE YOU? . . .

MAGS.   *Then,* I couldn't get a cab at the station. There just weren't any! I must have circled the block fifteen times. Finally I just stepped out into the traffic with my thumb out, but no one would pick me up . . . so I walked. . . .

FANNY (*offstage*).   Damned zipper's stuck. . . .

GARDNER.   You walked all the way from the South Station?

MAGS.   Well actually, I ran. . . .

GARDNER.   You had poor Mum scared to death.

MAGS (*finally puts the bags down with a deep sigh*).   I'm sorry. . . . I'm really sorry. It was a nightmare.

FANNY (*reenters the room, her dress over her head. The zipper's stuck; she staggers around blindly*).   Damned zipper! Gar, will you please help me with this?

MAGS.   I sprinted all the way up Beacon Hill.

GARDNER (*opening his arms wide*).   Well, come here and let's get a look at you. (*He hugs her.*) Mags! . . .

MAGS (*squeezing him tight*).   Oh, Daddy . . . Daddy!

GARDNER.   My Mags!

MAGS.   I never thought I'd get here! . . . Oh, you look wonderful!

GARDNER.   Well, you don't look so bad yourself!

MAGS.   I love your hair. It's gotten so . . . white!

FANNY (*still lost in her dress, struggling with the zipper*).   This is *so* typical . . . just as Mags arrives, my zipper has to break! (FANNY *grunts and struggles.*)

MAGS (*waves at her*).   Hi, Mum. . . .

FANNY.   Just a minute, dear, my zipper's . . .

GARDNER (*picks up* MAG'S *bags*).   Well, sit down and take a load off your feet. . . .

MAGS.   I was so afraid I'd never make it. . . .

GARDNER (*staggering under the weight of her bags*).   What have you got in here? Lead weights?

MAGS.   I can't believe you're finally letting me do you.

FANNY (*flings her arms around* MAGS, *practically knocking her over*).   OH, DARLING . . . MY PRECIOUS MAGS, YOU'RE HERE AT LAST.

GARDNER (*lurching around in circles*).   Now let's see . . . where should I put these? . . .

FANNY.   I was sure your train had derailed and you were lying dead in some ditch!

MAGS (*pulls away from* FANNY *to come to* GARDNER'S *rescue*).   Daddy, please, let me . . . these are much too heavy.

FANNY (*finally noticing* MAGS).   GOOD LORD, WHAT HAVE YOU DONE TO YOUR HAIR?!

MAGS (*struggling to take the bags from* GARDNER).   Come on, give them to me . . . please? (*She sets them down by the sofa.*)

FANNY (*as her dress starts to slide off one shoulder*).   Oh, not again! . . . Gar, would you give me a hand and see what's wrong with this zipper. One minute it's stuck, the next it's falling to pieces.

(GARDNER *goes to her and starts fussing with it.*)

MAGS (*pacing*).   I don't know, it's been crazy all week. Monday, I forgot to keep an appointment I'd made with a new model. . . . Tuesday, I overslept and stood up my advanced painting students. . . . Wednesday, the day of my meeting with Max Zoll, I forgot to put on my underpants. . . .

FANNY.   GODDAMNIT, GAR, CAN'T YOU DO ANYTHING ABOUT THIS ZIPPER?!

MAGS.   I mean, there I was, racing down Broome Street in this gauzy Tibetan skirt when I tripped and fell right at his feet . . . SPLATTT! My skirt goes flying over my head and there I am . . . everything staring him in the face . . .

FANNY.   COME ON, GAR, USE A LITTLE MUSCLE!

MAGS (*laughing*).   Oh, well, all that matters is that I finally got here. . . . I mean . . . there you are. . . .

GARDNER (*struggling with the zipper*).   I can't see it, it's too small!

FANNY (*whirls away from* GARDNER, *pulling her dress off altogether*).   OH, FORGET IT! JUST FORGET IT! . . . The trolly's probably missing half its teeth, just like someone else I know. (*To* MAGS.) I grind my teeth in my sleep now, I've worn them all down to stubs. Look at that! (*She flings open her mouth and points.*) Nothing left but the gums!

GARDNER.   I never hear you grind your teeth. . . .

FANNY.   That's because I'm snoring so loud. How could you hear anything through all that racket? It even wakes me up. It's no wonder poor Daddy has to sleep downstairs.

MAGS (*looking around*).   Jeez, look at the place! So, you're finally doing it . . . selling the house and moving to Cotuit year round. I don't believe it. I just don't believe it!

GARDNER.   Well, how about a drink to celebrate Mags' arrival?

MAGS.   You've been here so long. Why move now?

FANNY.   Gardner, what are you wearing that bathrobe for? . . .

MAGS.   You can't move. I won't let you!

FANNY (*softly to* GARDNER).   Really, darling, you ought to pay more attention to your appearance.

MAGS.   You love this house. *I* love this house . . . this room . . . the light.

GARDNER.   So, Mags, how about a little . . . (*he drinks from an imaginary glass*) to wet your whistle?

FANNY.   We can't start drinking now, it isn't even noon yet!

MAGS.   I'm starving. I've got to get something to eat before I collapse!

(*She exits towards the kitchen.*)

FANNY. What *have* you done to your hair, dear? The color's so queer and all your nice curl is gone.

GARDNER. It looks to me as if she dyed it.

FANNY. Yes, that's it. You're absolutely right! It's a completely different color. She dyed it bright red!
(MAGS *can be heard thumping and thudding through the icebox.*)

FANNY. NOW MAGS, I DON'T WANT YOU FILLING UP ON SNACKS. . . . I'VE MADE A PERFECTLY BEAUTIFUL LEG OF LAMB FOR LUNCH! . . . HELLO? . . . DO YOU HEAR ME? . . . (*To* GARDNER.) No one in our family has *ever* had red hair, it's so common looking.

GARDNER. I like it. It brings out her eyes.

FANNY. WHY ON EARTH DID YOU DYE YOUR HAIR *RED*, OF ALL COLORS?! . . .

MAGS (*returns, eating Saltines out of the box*). I didn't dye my hair, I just added some highlight.

FANNY. I suppose that's what your arty friends in New York do . . . dye their hair all the colors of the rainbow!

GARDNER. Well, it's damned attractive if you ask me . . . damned attractive!
(MAGS *unzips her duffle bag and rummages around in it while eating the Saltines.*)

FANNY. Darling, I told you not to bring alot of stuff with you. We're trying to get rid of things.

MAGS (*pulls out a folding easel and starts setting it up*). AAAAAHHHHHH, here it is. Isn't it a beauty? I bought it just for you!

FANNY. Please don't get crumbs all over the floor. Crystal was just here yesterday. It was her last time before we move.

MAGS (*at her easel*). God, I can hardly wait! I can't believe you're finally letting me do you.

FANNY. ''*Do*'' us? . . . What *are* you talking about?

GARDNER (*reaching for the Saltines*). Hey, Mags, could I have a couple of those?

MAGS (*tosses him the box*). Sure! (*To* FANNY.) Your portrait.

GARDNER. Thanks. (*He starts munching on a handful.*)

FANNY. You're planning to paint our portrait now? While we're trying to move? . . .

GARDNER (*sputtering Saltines*). Mmmmm, I'd forgotten just how delicious Saltines are!

MAGS. It's a perfect opportunity. There'll be no distractions; you'll be completely at my mercy. Also, you promised.

FANNY. I did?

MAGS. Yes, you did.

FANNY. Well, I must have been off my rocker.

MAGS. No, you said, ''You can paint us, you can dip us in concrete, you can do anything you want with us, just so long as you help us get out of here!''

GARDNER (*offering the box of Saltines to* FANNY). You really ought to try some of these, Fan, they're absolutely delicious!

FANNY (*taking a few*). Why, thank you.

MAGS. I figure we'll pack in the morning and you'll pose in the afternoons. It'll be a nice diversion.

FANNY. These *are* good!

GARDNER. Here, dig in . . . take some more.

MAGS. I have some wonderful news . . . amazing news! I wanted to wait 'til I got here to tell you.
(*They eat their Saltines, passing the box back and forth as* MAGS *speaks.*)

MAGS. You'll die! Just fall over into the packing cartons and die! Are you ready? . . . BRACE YOURSELVES. . . . OK, HERE GOES . . . I'm being given a one woman show at one of the most important galleries in New York this fall. Me, Margaret Church, exhibited at Castelli's, 420 West Broadway . . . Can you believe it?! . . . MY PORTRAITS HANGING IN THE SAME ROOMS THAT HAVE SHOWN RAUSCHENBERG, JOHNS, WARHOL, KELLY, LICHTENSTEIN, STELLA, SERRA, ALL THE HEAVIES . . . It's incredible, beyond belief . . . I mean, at my age . . . Do you know how good you have to be to get in there? It's a miracle . . . an honest-to-God, star-spangled miracle!
(*Pause.*)

FANNY (*mouth full*). Oh, darling, that's wonderful. We're so happy for you!

GARDNER (*his mouth full*). No one deserves it more, no one deserves it more!

MAGS. Through some fluke, some of Castelli's people showed up at our last faculty show at Pratt and were knocked out. . . .

FANNY (*reaching for the box of Saltines*). More, more . . .

MAGS. They said they hadn't seen anyone handle light like me since the French Impressionists. They said I was this weird blend of Pierre Bonnard, Mary Cassat and David Hockney. . . .

GARDNER (*swallowing his own mouthful*). I told you they were good.

MAGS. Also, no one's doing portraits these days. They're considered passé. I'm so out of it, I'm in.

GARDNER. Well, you're loaded with talent and always have been.

FANNY. She gets it all from Mama, you know. Her miniature of Henry James is still one of the main attractions at the Atheneum. Of course no woman of breeding could be a professional artist in her day. It simply wasn't done. But talk about talent . . . that woman had talent to burn!

MAGS. I want to do one of you for the show.

FANNY. Oh, do Daddy, he's the famous one.

MAGS. No, I want to do you both. I've always wanted to do you and now I've finally got a good excuse.

FANNY. It's high time somebody painted Daddy again! I'm sick to death of that dreadful portrait of him in the National Gallery they keep reproducing. He looks like an undertaker!

GARDNER. Well, I think you should just do Mum. She's never looked handsomer.

FANNY.   Oh, come on, I'm a perfect fright and you know it.

MAGS.   I want to do you both. Side by side. In this room. Something really classy. You look so great. Mum with her crazy hats and everything and you with that face. If I could just get you to hold still long enough and actually pose.

GARDNER (*walking around, distracted*). Where are those papers I just had? God damnit, Fanny. . . .

MAGS.   I have the feeling it's either now or never.

GARDNER.   I can't hold on to anything around here. (*He exits to his study.*)

MAGS.   I've always wanted to do you. It would be such a challenge.

FANNY (*pulling MAGS next to her onto the sofa*). I'm so glad you're finally here, Mags. I'm very worried about Daddy.

MAGS.   Mummy, please. I just got here.

FANNY.   He's getting quite gaga.

MAGS.   Mummy! . . .

FANNY.   You haven't seen him in almost a year. Two weeks ago he walked through the front door of the Codman's house, kissed Emily on the cheek and settled down in the maid's room, thinking he was home!

MAGS.   Oh, come on, you're exaggerating.

FANNY.   He's as mad as a hatter and getting worse every day! It's this damned new book of his. He works on it around the clock. I've read some of it, and it doesn't make one word of sense, it's all at sixes and sevens. . . .

GARDNER (*poking his head back in the room, spies some of his papers on a table and grabs them*). Ahhh, here they are.

(*He exits.*)

FANNY (*voice lowered*). Ever since this dry spell with his poetry, he's been frantic, absolutely . . . frantic!

MAGS.   I hate it when you do this.

FANNY.   I'm just trying to get you to face the facts around here.

MAGS.   There's nothing wrong with him! He's just as sane as the next man. Even saner, if you ask me.

FANNY.   You know what he's doing now? You couldn't guess in a million years! . . . He's writing criticism! Daddy! (*She laughs.*) Can you believe it? The man doesn't have one analytic bone in his body. His mind is a complete jumble and always has been!

(*There's a loud crash from GARDNER's study.*)

GARDNER (*offstage*). SHIT!

MAGS.   He's abstracted. . . . That's the way he is.

FANNY.   He doesn't spend any time with me anymore. He just holes up in that filthy study with Toots. God, I hate that bird! Though actually they're quite cunning together. Daddy's teaching him Grey's Elegy. You ought to see them in there, Toots perched on top of Daddy's head, spouting out verse after verse . . . Daddy, tap-tap-tapping away on his typewriter. They're quite a pair.

GARDNER (*pokes his head back in*). Have you seen that Stevens' poem I was reading before?

FANNY (*long suffering*). NO, I HAVEN'T SEEN THAT STEVENS' POEM YOU WERE READING BEFORE! . . . Things are getting very tight around here, in case you haven't noticed. Daddy's last Pulitzer didn't even cover our real estate tax, and now that he's too doddery to give readings anymore, that income is gone. . . . (*Suddenly handing MAGS the sugar bowl she'd been wrapping.*) Mags, *do* take this sugar bowl. You can use it to serve tea to your students at that wretched art school of yours. . . .

MAGS.   It's called Pratt! The Pratt Institute.

FANNY.   Pratt, Splatt, whatever . . .

MAGS.   And I don't serve tea to my students, I teach them how to paint.

FANNY.   Well, I'm sure none of them has ever seen a sugar bowl as handsome as this before.

GARDNER (*reappearing again*). You're sure you haven't seen it? . . .

FANNY (*loud and angry*). YES, I'M SURE I HAVEN'T SEEN IT! I JUST TOLD YOU I HAVEN'T SEEN IT!

GARDNER (*retreating*). Right you are, right you are. (*He exits.*)

FANNY.   God!

(*Silence.*)

MAGS.   What do you have to yell at him like that for?

FANNY.   Because the poor thing's as deaf as an adder! (*MAGS sighs deeply; silence.*)

FANNY (*suddenly exuberant, leads her over to a lamp*). Come, I want to show you something.

MAGS (*looking at it*). What is it?

FANNY.   Something I made. (*MAGS is about to turn it on.*)

FANNY.   WAIT, DON'T TURN IT ON YET! It's got to be dark to get the full effect. (*She rushes to the windows and pulls down the shades.*)

MAGS.   What *are* you doing? . . .

FANNY.   Hold your horses a minute. You'll see. . . . (*As the room gets darker and darker.*) Poor me, you wouldn't believe the lengths I go to to amuse myself these days. . . .

MAGS (*touching the lamp shade*). What is this? It looks like a scene of some sort.

FANNY.   It's an invention I made . . . a kind of magic lantern.

MAGS.   Gee . . . it's amazing.

FANNY.   What I did was buy an old engraving of the Grand Canal. . . .

MAGS.   You *made* this?

FANNY.   . . . and then color it in with crayons. Next, I got out my sewing scissors and cut out all the street lamps and windows . . . anything that light would shine through. Then I pasted it over a plain lampshade, put the shade on this old horror of a lamp, turned on the switch and . . . (*She turns it on.*) . . . VOILA . . . VENICE TWINKLING AT DUSK! It's quite effective, don't you think? . . .

MAGS (*walking around it*). Jeeez . . .

FANNY.   And see, I poked out all the little lights on the gondolas with a straight pin.

MAGS.   Where on earth did you get the idea?

FANNY.   Well you know, idle minds . . . (FANNY *spins the shade, making the lights whirl.*)

MAGS. It's really amaz-ing. I mean, you could sell this in a store!

GARDNER (*enters*). HERE IT IS. IT WAS RIGHT ON TOP OF MY DESK THE WHOLE TIME. (*He crashes into a table.*) OOOOOWWWWW!

FANNY.   LOOK OUT, LOOK OUT!

MAGS (*rushes, over to him*). Oh, Daddy, are you all right!

FANNY. WATCH WHERE YOU'RE GOING, WATCH WHERE YOU'RE GOING!

GARDNER (*hopping up and down on one leg*). GOD-DAMNIT! . . . I HIT MY SHIN

FANNY.   I was just showing Mags my lamp. . . .

GARDNER (*limping over to it*). Oh, yes, isn't that something? Mum is awfully clever with that kind of thing. . . . It was all her idea. Buying the engraving, coloring it in, cutting out all those little dots.

FANNY.   Not "dots" . . . lights and windows, lights and windows!

GARDNER.   Right, right . . . lights and windows.

FANNY.   Well, we'd better get some light back in here before someone breaks their neck. (*She zaps the shades back up.*)

GARDNER (*puts his arm around* MAGS). Gee, it's good to have you back.

MAGS.   It's good to be back.

GARDNER.   And I like that new red hair of yours. It's very becoming.

MAGS.   But I told you, I hardly touched it. . . .

GARDNER.   Well, something's different. You've got a glow. So . . . how do you want us to pose for this grand portrait of yours? . . . (*He poses self-consciously.*)

MAGS.   Oh, Daddy, setting up a portrait takes a lot of time and thought. You've got to figure out the background, the lighting, what to wear, the sort of mood you want to . . .

FANNY.   OOOOH, LET'S DRESS UP, LET'S DRESS UP! (*She grabs a packing blanket, drapes it around herself and links arms with* GARDNER, *striking an elegant pose.*) This *is* going to be fun. She was absolutely right! Come on, Gar, look distinguished!

MAGS.   Mummy, please, it's not a game!

FANNY (*more and more excited*). You still have your tuxedo, don't you? And I'll wear my marvelous long black dress

that makes me look like that fascinating woman in the Sargent painting! (*She strikes the famous profile pose.*)

MAGS.   MUMMY?! . . .

FANNY.   I'm sorry, we'll behave, just tell us what to do. (*They settle down next to each other.*)

GARDNER.   That's right, you're the boss.

FANNY.   Yes, you're the boss.

MAGS.   But I'm not ready yet; I haven't set anything up.

FANNY.   Relax, darling, we just want to get the hang of it. . . .

(*They stare straight ahead, trying to look like suitable subjects, but they can't hold still. They keep making faces, lifting an eyebrow, dropping one corner of a mouth. It's not big contortions, just flickering changes; a half-smile here, a self-important frown there. They steal glances at each other every so often.*)

GARDNER.   How am I doing, Fan?

FANNY.   Brilliantly, absolutely brilliantly!

MAGS.   But you're making faces.

FANNY.   *I'm* not making faces. (*Turning to* GARDNER *and making a face.*) Are *you* making faces, Gar?

GARDNER (*instantly making one*). Certainly not! I'm the picture of restraint!

(*Without meaning to, they get sillier and sillier. They start giggling, then laughing.*)

MAGS (*can't help but join in*). You two are impossible . . . completely impossible! I was crazy to think I could ever pull this off! (*Laughing away.*) Look at you . . . just . . . look at you!

BLACKOUT

SCENE TWO

Two days later, around five in the afternoon. Half of the Church household has been dragged into the living room for packing. Overflowing cartons are everywhere. They're filled with pots and pans, dishes and glasses, and the entire contents of two linen closets. MAGS *has pulled a stepladder over to one of the windows. A pile of tablecloths and curtains is flung beneath it. Two side chairs have been placed nearby.*

MAGS (*has just pulled a large crimson tablecloth out of a carton. She unfurls it with one shimmering toss*). PER-FECT . . . PERFECT! . . .

FANNY (*seated on the sofa, clutches an old pair of galoshes to her chest*). Look at these old horrors; half the rubber is rotted away and the fasteners are falling to pieces. . . . GARDNER? . . . OH, GARRRRRRRRRDNERR-RRR? . . .

MAGS (*rippling out the tablecloth with shorter snapping motions*). Have you ever seen such a color? . . .

FANNY.   I'VE FOUND YOUR OLD SLEDDING GA-LOSHES IN WITH THE POTS AND PANS. DO YOU STILL WANT THEM?

MAGS.   It's like something out of a Rubens! . . . (*She slings it over a chair and then sits on a footstool to finish the Sara Lee banana cake she started. As she eats, she looks at the tablecloth making happy grunting sounds.*)

FANNY (*lovingly puts the galoshes on over her shoes and wiggles her feet*). God, these bring back memories! There were real snow storms in the old days. Not these pathetic little two inch droppings we have now. After a particularly heavy one, Daddy and I used to go sledding on the Common. This was way before you were born. . . . God, it was a hundred years ago! . . . Daddy would stop writing early, put on these galoshes and come looking for me, jingling the fasteners like castanets. It was a kind of mating call, almost. . . . (*She jingles them.*) The Common was always deserted after a storm; we had the whole place to ourselves. It was so romantic. . . . We'd haul the sled up Beacon Street, stop under the State House, and aim it straight down to the Park Street Church, which was much further away in those days. . . . Then Daddy would lie down on the sled, I'd lower myself on top of him, we'd rock back and forth a few times to gain momentum and then . . . WHOOOOOOOOOSSSSSSSHHHHH . . . down we'd plunge like a pair of eagles locked in a spasm of lovemaking. God, it was wonderful! . . . The city whizzing past us at ninety miles an hour . . . the cold . . . the darkness . . . Daddy's hair in my mouth . . . GAR . . . REMEMBER HOW WE USED TO GO SLEDDING IN THE OLD DAYS? . . . Sometimes he'd lie on top of me. That was fun. I liked that even more. (*In her foghorn voice.*) GARRRRRRRRRRDNERRRRRR? . . .

MAGS.   Didn't he say he was going out this afternoon?

FANNY.   Why, so he did! I completely forgot. (*She takes off the galoshes.*) I'm getting just as bad as him. (*She drops them into a different carton, wistful.*) Gar's galoshes, Cotuit.

(*A pause.*)

MAGS (*picks up the tablecloth again; holds it high over her head*). Isn't this fabulous? . . . (*She then wraps* FANNY *in it.*) It's the perfect backdrop. Look what it does to your skin.

FANNY.   Mags, what *are* you doing?

MAGS.   It makes you glow like a pomegranate. . . . (*She whips it off her.*) Now all I need is a hammer and nails. . . . (*She finds them.*) YES! (*She climbs up the stepladder and starts hammering a corner of the cloth into the moulding of one of the windows.*) This is going to look so great! I've never seen such a color!

FANNY.   Darling what is going on? . . .

MAGS.   Rembrandt, eat your heart out! You seventeenth-century Dutch has-been, you. (*She hammers more furiously.*)

FANNY.   MARGARET, THIS IS NOT A CONSTRUCTION SITE. . . . PLEASE . . . STOP IT. . . . YOO-HOOOOO . . . DO YOU HEAR ME? . . .

(GARDNER *suddenly appears, dressed in a raincoat.*)

GARDNER.   YES, DEAR, HERE I AM. I JUST STEPPED OUT FOR A WALK DOWN CHESTNUT STREET. BEAUTIFUL AFTERNOON, ABSOLUTELY BEAUTIFUL!

FANNY (*to* MAGS). YOU'RE GOING TO RUIN THE WALLS TO SAY NOTHING OF MAMA'S BEST TABLECLOTH. . . . MAGS, DO YOU HEAR ME? . . . YOO HOO! . . .

GARDNER.   WHY THAT LOOKS VERY NICE, MAGS, very nice indeed. . . .

FANNY.   DARLING, I MUST INSIST you stop that dreadful . . .

MAGS (*steps down; stands back and looks at it*). That's it. That's *it!*

FANNY (*to* GARDNER, *worried*). And where have *you* been? (MAGS *kisses her fingers at the backdrop and settles back into her banana cake.*)

GARDNER (*to* FANNY). You'll never guess who I ran into on Chestnut Street . . . Pate Baldwin!

(*He takes his coat off and drops it on the floor. He then sits in one of the posing chairs.*)

MAGS (*mouth full of cake*). Oh, Daddy, I'm nowhere near ready for you yet.

FANNY (*picks up his coat and hands it to him*). Darling, coats do *not* go on the floor.

GARDNER (*rises, but forgets where he's supposed to go*). He was in terrible shape. I hardly recognized him. Well, it's the Parkinson's disease. . . .

FANNY.   You mean, Hodgkin's disease. . . .

GARDNER.   Hodgkin's disease? . . .

MAGS (*leaves her cake and returns to the tablecloth*). Now to figure out exactly how to use the gorgeous light. . . .

FANNY.   Yes, Pate has Hodgkin's disease, not Parkinson's disease. Sammy Bishop has Parkinson's disease. In the closet . . . your coat goes . . . in the closet!

GARDNER.   You're absolutely right! Pate has Hodgkin's disease.

(*He stands motionless, the coat over his arm.*)

FANNY.   . . . and Goat Davis has Addison's disease.

GARDNER.   I always get them confused.

FANNY (*pointing towards the closet*). That way. . . .

(GARDNER *exits to the closet;* FANNY *calls after him.*) Grace Phelps has it too, I think. Or, it might be Hodgkin's, like Pate. I can't remember.

GARDNER (*returns with a hanger*). Doesn't the Goat have Parkinson's disease?

FANNY.   No, that's Sammy Bishop.

GARDNER.   God, I haven't seen the Goat in ages! (*The coat still over his arm; he hands* FANNY *the hanger.*)

FANNY.   He hasn't been well.

GARDNER.   Didn't Heppy . . . *die?!*

FANNY.   What are you giving me this for? . . . Oh, Heppy's been dead for years. She died on the same day as Luster Bright, don't you remember?

GARDNER.   I always liked her.

FANNY (*gives him back the hanger*). Here, I don't want this.

GARDNER.   She was awfully attractive.

FANNY.   Who?

GARDNER.   Heppy!

FANNY.   Oh, yes, Heppy had real charm.

MAGS (*keeps adjusting the tablecloth*). Better . . . better . . .

GARDNER.   . . . which is something the Goat is short on, if you ask me. He has Hodgkin's disease, doesn't he? (*Puts his raincoat back on and sits down.*)

FANNY.   Darling, what *are* you doing? I thought you wanted to hang up your coat!

GARDNER (*after a pause*). OH, YES, THAT'S RIGHT! (*He goes back to the closet; a pause.*)

FANNY.   Where were we?

GARDNER (*returns with yet another hanger*). Let's see. . . .

FANNY (*takes both hangers from him*). FOR GOD'S SAKE, GAR, PAY ATTENTION!

GARDNER.   It was something about the Goat. . . .

FANNY (*takes the coat from* GARDNER). HERE, LET ME DO IT! . . . (*Under her breath to* MAGS.) See what I mean about him? You don't know the half of it! (*She hangs it up in the closet.*) . . . . Not the half.

MAGS (*still tinkering with the backdrop*). Almost . . . almost . . .

GARDNER (*sitting back down on one of the posing chairs*). Oh, Fan, did I tell you, I ran into Pate Baldwin just now. I'm afraid he's not long for this world.

FANNY (*returning*). Well, it's that Hodgkin's disease. . . . (*She sits in the posing chair next to him.*)

GARDNER.   God, I'd hate to see him go. He's one of the great editors of our times. I couldn't have done it without him. He gave me everything, everything!

MAGS (*makes a final adjustment*). Yes, that's it! (*She stands back and gazes at them.*) You look wonderful! . . .

FANNY.   Isn't it getting to be . . . (*She taps at an imaginary watch on her wrist and drains an imaginary glass.*) Cocktail time?!

GARDNER (*looks at his watch*). On the button, on the button! (*He rises.*)

FANNY.   I'll have the usual, please. Do join us, Mags! Daddy bought some Dubonnet especially for you!

MAGS.   Hey. I was just getting some ideas.

GARDNER (*to* MAGS, *as he exits for the bar*). How about a little . . . *Dubonnet* to wet your whistle?

FANNY.   Oh, Mags, it's like old times having you back with us like this!

GARDNER (*offstage*). THE USUAL FOR YOU, FAN?

FANNY.   I wish we saw more of you. . . . PLEASE! . . . Isn't he darling? Have you ever known anyone more darling than Daddy? . . .

GARDNER (*offstage*). (Sings Jolson's "You Made Me Love You") MAGS, HOW ABOUT YOU? . . . A LITTLE . . . DUBONNET? . . .

FANNY.   Oh, *do* join us!   MAGS (*to* GARDNER). No, nothing, thanks.

FANNY.   Well, what do you think of your aged parents picking up and moving to Cotuit year round? Pretty crazy, eh what? . . . Nothing but the gulls, oysters and us!

GARDNER (*returns with* FANNY's *drink*). Here you go . . .

FANNY.   Why thank you, Gar. (*To* MAGS.) You sure you won't join us?

GARDNER (*lifts his glass towards* FANNY *and* MAGS). Cheers! (*GARDNER* and FANNY *take that first life-saving gulp.*)

FANNY.   Aaaaahhhhh!   GARDNER.   Hits the spot, hits the spot!

MAGS.   Well, I certainly can't do you like that!

FANNY.   Why not? I think we look very . . . *comme il faut!* (*She slouches into a rummy pose;* GARDNER *joins her.*) WAIT . . . I'VE GOT IT! I'VE GOT IT! (*She whispers excitedly to* GARDNER.)

MAGS.   Come on, let's not start this again!

GARDNER.   What's that? . . . Oh, yes . . . yes, yes . . . I know the one you mean. Yes, right, right . . . of course. (*A pause.*)

FANNY.   How's . . . *this?!* . . . (*FANNY grabs a large serving fork and they fly into an imitation of Grant Wood's American Gothic.*)

MAGS.   . . . and I wonder why it's taken me all these years to get you to pose for me. You just don't take me seriously! Poor old Mags and her ridiculous portraits . . .

FANNY.   Oh, darling, your portraits aren't *ridiculous!* They may not be all that one *hopes* for, but they're certainly not . . .

MAGS.   Remember how you behaved at my first group show in Soho? . . . Oh, come on, you remember. It was a real circus! Think back. . . . It was about six years ago. . . . Daddy had just been awarded some presidential medal of achievement and you insisted he wear it around his neck on a bright red ribbon, and you wore this . . . *huge* feathered hat to match! I'll never forget it! It was the size of a giant pizza with twenty-inch red turkey feathers shooting straight up into the air. . . . Oh, come on, you remember, don't you? . . .

FANNY (*leaping to her feet*). HOLD EVERYTHING! THIS IS IT! THIS IS REALLY IT! Forgive me for interrupting, Mags darling, it'll just take a minute. (*She whispers excitedly to* GARDNER.)

MAGS.   I had about eight portraits in the show, mostly of friends of mine, except for this old one I'd done of Mrs. Crowninshield.

GARDNER.   All right, all right . . . let's give it a whirl. (*A pause; then they mime Michelangelo's* Pieta *with* GARDNER *lying across* FANNY's *lap as the dead Christ.*)

MAGS (*depressed*). The *Pietà*. Terrific!

FANNY (*jabbing* GARDNER *in the ribs*). Hey, we're getting good at this.

GARDNER.   Of course it would help if we didn't have all these modern clothes on.

MAGS.   AS I WAS SAYING . . .

FANNY.   Sorry, Mags . . . sorry . . .

(*Huffing and creaking with the physical exertion of it all, they return to their seats.*)

MAGS.   . . . As soon as you stepped foot in the gallery you spotted it and cried out, "MY GOD, WHAT'S MILLICENT CROWNINSHIELD DOING HERE?" Everyone looked up what with Daddy's clanking medal and your amazing hat which I was sure would take off and start flying around the room. A crowd gathered. . . . Through some utter fluke, you latched on to *the* most important critic in the city, I mean . . . Mr. Modern Art himself, and you hauled him over to the painting, trumpeting out for all to hear. "THAT'S MILLICENT CROWNINSHIELD! I GREW UP WITH HER. SHE LIVES RIGHT DOWN THE STREET FROM US IN BOSTON. BUT IT'S A VERY POOR LIKENESS, IF YOU ASK ME! HER NOSE ISN'T NEARLY THAT LARGE AND SHE DOESN'T HAVE SOMETHING QUEER GROWING OUT OF HER CHIN! THE CROWNINSHIELDS ARE REALLY QUITE GOOD LOOKING, STUFFY, BUT GOOD LOOKING NONETHELESS!"

GARDNER (*suddenly jumps up, ablaze*). WAIT, WAIT . . . IF IT'S MICHELANGELO YOU WANT . . . I'm sorry, Mags . . . One more . . . just one more . . . please?

MAGS.   Sure, why not? Be my guest.

GARDNER.   *Fanny*, prepare yourself!

(*More whispering.*)

FANNY.   But I think *you* should be God.

GARDNER.   Me? . . . Really?

FANNY.   Yes, it's much more appropriate.

GARDNER.   Well, if you say so . . . (FANNY *and* GARDNER *ease down to the floor with some difficulty and lie on their sides,* FANNY *as Adam,* GARDNER *as God, their fingers inching closer and closer in the attitude of Michelangelo's* The Creation. *Finally they touch.*)

MAGS (*cheers, whistles, applauds*). THREE CHEERS . . . VERY GOOD . . . NICELY DONE, NICELY DONE!

(*They hold the pose a moment more, flushed with pleasure; then rise, dust themselves off and grope back to their chairs.*) So, there we were. . . .

FANNY.   Yes, *do* go on! . . .

MAGS.   . . . huddled around Millicent Crowninshield, when you whipped into your pocketbook and suddenly announced, "HOLD EVERYTHING! I'VE GOT A PHOTOGRAPH OF HER RIGHT HERE, THEN YOU CAN SEE WHAT SHE REALLY LOOKS LIKE!" . . . You then proceeded to crouch down to the floor and dump everything out of your bag, and I mean . . . *everything!*

. . . leaking packets of sequins and gummed stars, sea shells, odd pieces of fur, crochet hooks, a monarch butterfly embedded in plastic, dental floss, antique glass buttons, small jingling bells, lace . . . I thought I'd die! Just sink to the floor and quietly die! . . . You couldn't find it, you see. I mean, you spent the rest of the afternoon on your hands and knees crawling through this ocean of junk muttering, "It's *got* to be here somewhere; I know I had it with me!" . . . Then Daddy pulled me into the thick of it all and said, "By the way, have you met our daughter Mags yet? She's the one who did all these pictures . . . paintings . . . portraits . . . whatever you call them." (*She drops to her hands and knees and begins crawling out of the room.*) By this time, Mum had somehow crawled out of the gallery and was lost on another floor. She began calling for me . . . "YOO-HOO, MAGS . . . WHERE ARE YOU? . . . OH, MAGS, DARLING . . . HELLO? . . . ARE YOU THERE? . . ." (*She reenters and faces them.*) This was at my *first* show.

BLACKOUT

SCENE THREE

Twenty-four hours later. The impact of the impending move has struck with hurricane force. FANNY *has lugged all their clothing into the room and dumped it in various cartons. There are coats, jackets, shoes, skirts, suits, hats, sweaters, dresses, the works. She and* GARDNER *are seated on the sofa, going through it all.*

FANNY (*wearing a different hat and dress, holds up a ratty overcoat*). What about this gruesome old thing?

GARDNER (*is wearing several sweaters and vests, a Hawaiian holiday shirt, and a variety of scarves and ties around his neck. He holds up a pair of shoes*). God . . . remember these shoes? Pound gave them to me when he came back from Italy. I remember it vividly.

FANNY.   Do let me give it to the thrift shop! (*She stuffs the coat into the appropriate carton.*)

GARDNER.   He bought them for me in Rome. Said he couldn't resist; bought himself a pair too since we both wore the same size. God, I miss him! (*Pause.*) HEY, WHAT ARE YOU DOING WITH MY OVERCOAT?!

FANNY.   Darling, it's threadbare!

GARDNER.   But that's my overcoat! (*He grabs it out of the carton.*) I've been wearing it every day for the past thirty-five years!

FANNY.   That's just my point: It's had it.

GARDNER (*puts it on over everything else*). There's nothing wrong with this coat!

FANNY.   I trust you remember that the cottage is an eighth the size of this place and you simply won't have room for half this stuff! (*She holds up a sports jacket.*) This dreary old jacket, for instance. You've had it since Hector was a pup!

GARDNER (*grabs it and puts it on over his coat*). Oh, no you don't. . . .

FANNY.   . . . and this God-awful hat . . .

GARDNER.   Let me see that.

(*He stands next to her and they fall into a lovely tableau.*)

MAGS (*suddenly pops out from behind a wardrobe carton with a flash camera and takes a picture of them*). PERFECT!

| FANNY (*hands flying to her face*). GOOD GOD, WHAT WAS THAT? . . . | GARDNER (*hands flying to his heart*). JESUS CHRIST, I'VE BEEN SHOT! |

MAGS (*walks to the center of the room, advancing the film*). That was terrific. See if you can do it again.

FANNY.   What *are* you doing? . . .

GARDNER (*feeling his chest*). Is there blood?

FANNY.   I see lace everywhere. . . .

MAGS.   It's all right, I was just taking a picture of you. I often use a Polaroid at this stage.

FANNY (*rubbing her eyes*). Really, Mags, you might have given us some warning!

MAGS.   But that's the whole point: to catch you unawares!

GARDNER (*rubbing his eyes*). It's the damndest thing. . . . I see lace everywhere.

FANNY.   Yes, so do I. . . .

GARDNER.   It's rather nice, actually. It looks as if you're wearing a veil.

FANNY.   I *am* wearing a veil!

(*The camera spits out the photograph.*)

MAGS.   OH, GOODY, HERE COMES THE PICTURE!

FANNY (*grabs the partially developed print out of her hands*). Let me see, let me see . . .

GARDNER.   Yes, let's have a look.

(*They have another quiet moment together looking at the photograph.*)

MAGS (*tiptoes away from them and takes another picture*). YES!

| FANNY. NOT AGAIN! PLEASE, DARLING! | GARDNER. WHAT WAS THAT? . . . WHAT HAPPENED? . . . |

(*They stagger towards each other.*)

MAGS.   I'm sorry, I just couldn't resist. You looked so . . .

FANNY.   WHAT ARE YOU TRYING TO DO . . . *BLIND* US?!

GARDNER.   Really, Mags, enough is enough. . . .

(GARDNER *and* FANNY *keep stumbling about kiddingly.*)

FANNY.   Are you still there, Gar?

GARDNER.   Right as rain, right as rain!

MAGS.   I'm sorry; I didn't mean to scare you. It's just a photograph can show you things you weren't aware of. Here, have a look.

(*She gives them to* FANNY.) Well, I'm going out to the kitchen to get something to eat. Anybody want anything?

(*She exits.*)

FANNY (*looking at the photos, half-amused, half-horrified*). Oh, Gardner, have you ever? . . .

GARDNER (*looks at them and laughs*). Good grief . . .

MAGS (*offstage; from the kitchen*). IS IT ALL RIGHT IF I TAKE THE REST OF THIS TAPIOCA FROM LAST NIGHT?

FANNY.   IT'S ALL RIGHT WITH ME. How about you, Gar?

GARDNER.   Sure, go right ahead. I've never been that crazy about tapioca.

FANNY.   What are you talking about, tapioca is one of your favorites.

MAGS (*enters, slurping up the tapioca from a large bowl*). Mmmmmmmm . . .

FANNY.   Really, Mags, I've never seen anyone eat as much as you.

MAGS (*takes the photos back*). It's strange. I only do this when I come home.

FANNY.   What's the matter, don't I feed you enough?

GARDNER.   Gee, it's hot in here!

(*Starts taking off his coat.*)

FANNY.   God knows, you didn't eat anything as a child! I've never seen such a fussy eater. Gar, what *are* you doing?

GARDNER.   Taking off some of these clothes. It's hotter than Tofit in here!

(*Shedding clothes to the floor.*)

MAGS (*looking at her photos*). Yes, I like you looking at each other like that. . . .

FANNY (*to* GARDNER). Please watch where you're dropping things; I'm trying to keep some order around here.

GARDNER (*picks up what he dropped, dropping even more in the process*). Right, right. . . .

MAGS.   Now all I've got to do is figure out what you should wear.

FANNY.   Well, I'm going to wear my long black dress and you'd be a fool not to do Daddy in his tuxedo. He looks so distinguished in it, just like a banker!

MAGS.   I haven't really decided yet.

FANNY.   Just because you walk around looking like something the cat dragged in, doesn't mean Daddy and I want to, do we, Gar?

(GARDNER *is making a worse and worse tangle of his clothes.*)

FANNY.   HELLO? . . .

GARDNER (*looks up at* FANNY). Oh, yes, awfully attractive, awfully attractive!

FANNY (*to* MAGS). If you don't mind me saying so, I've never seen you looking so forlorn. You'll never catch a husband looking that way. Those peculiar clothes, that God-awful hair . . . Really, Mags, it's very distressing!

MAGS.   I don't think my hair's so bad, not that it's terrific or anything . . .

FANNY.   Well, I don't see other girls walking around like you. I mean, girls from your background. What would Lyman Wigglesworth think if he saw you in the street?

MAGS.   Lyman Wigglesworth?! . . . Uuuuuuughhhhhhh! (*She shudders.*)

FANNY.   Alright, then, that brilliant Cabot boy . . . what *is* his name?

GARDNER.   Sammy?

FANNY.   No, not Sammy. . . .

GARDNER.   Stephen.

FANNY.   Oh, for God's sake, Gardner.

GARDNER.   Stuart . . . Simon . . . Sinclair . . . Sumner! . . .

MAGS.   Spence!

FANNY.   SPENCE, THAT'S IT THAT'S IT! HIS NAME IS SPENCE!

GARDNER.   THAT'S IT . . . SPENCE! SPENCE CABOT!

FANNY.   Spence Cabot was first in his class at Harvard.

MAGS.   Mum, he has no facial hair.

FANNY.   He has his own law firm on Arlington Street.

MAGS.   Spence Cabot has six fingers on his right hand!

FANNY.   So, he isn't the best-looking thing in the world. Looks isn't everything. He can't help it if he has extra fingers. Have a little sympathy!

MAGS.   But the extra one has this weird nail on it that looks like a talon. . . . It's all black and . . . (*She shudders.*)

FANNY.   No one's perfect, darling. He has lovely handwriting and an absolutely saintly mother. Also, he's as rich as Croesus! He's a lot more promising than some of those creatures you've dragged home. What was the name of that dreadful Frenchman who smelled like sweaty socks? . . . Jean Duke of Scripto?

MAGS (*laughing*). Jean-Luc Zichot!

FANNY.   . . . and that peculiar little Oriental fellow with all the teeth! Really, Mags, he could have been put on display at the circus!

MAGS.   Oh, yes, Tsu Chin. He was strange, but very sexy. . . .

FANNY (*shudders*). He had such tiny . . . feet! Really, Mags, you've got to bear down. You're not getting any younger. Before you know it, all the nice young men will be taken and then where will you be? . . . All by yourself in that grim little apartment of yours with those peculiar clothes and that bright red hair . . .

MAGS.   MY HAIR IS NOT BRIGHT RED!

FANNY.   I only want what's best for you, you know that. You seem to go out of your way to look wanting. I don't understand it. . . . Gar, what *are* you putting your coat on for? . . . You look like some derelict out on the street. We don't wear coats in the house. (*She helps him out of it.*) That's the way. . . . I'll just put this in the carton along with everything else. . . . (*She drops it into the carton, then pauses.*) Isn't it about time for . . . *cocktails!*

GARDNER.   What's that?

(FANNY *taps her wrist and mimes drinking.*)

GARDNER (*looks at his watch*). Right you are right you are! (*Exits to the bar.*) THE USUAL? . . .

FANNY.   *Please!*

GARDNER (*offstage*). HOW ABOUT SOMETHING FOR YOU, MAGS?

MAGS.   SURE, WHY NOT? . . . LET 'ER RIP!

GARDNER (*offstage*). WHAT'S THAT? . . .

FANNY.   SHE SAID YES. SHE SAID YES!

MAGS.   I'LL HAVE SOME DUBONNET!

GARDNER (*poking his head back in*). How about a little Dubonnet?

FANNY.   That's just what she said. . . . She'd like some . . . Dubonnet!

GARDNER (*goes back to the bar and hums another Jolson tune*). GEE, IT'S GREAT HAVING YOU BACK LIKE THIS, MAGS. . . . IT'S JUST GREAT! (*More singing.*)

FANNY (*leaning closer to* MAGS). You have such *potential,* darling! It breaks my heart to see how you've let yourself go. If Lyman Wigglesworth . . .

MAGS.   Amazing as it may seem, I don't *care* about Lyman Wigglesworth!

FANNY.   From what I've heard, he's quite a lady killer!

MAGS.   But with whom! . . . Don't think I haven't heard about his fling with . . . Hopie Stonewall!

FANNY (*begins to laugh*). Oh, God, let's not get started on Hopie Stonewall again . . . ten feet tall with spots on her neck . . . (*To* GARDNER.) OH, DARLING, DO HURRY BACK! WE'RE TALKING ABOUT PATHETIC HOPIE STONEWALL!

MAGS.   It's not so much her incredible height and spotted skin; it's those tiny pointed teeth and the size eleven shoes!

FANNY.   I love it when you're like this! (MAGS *starts clomping around the room making tiny pointed teeth nibbling sounds.*)

FANNY.   GARDNER . . . YOU'RE MISSING EVERY-THING! (*Still laughing.*) Why is it Boston girls are always so . . . tall?

MAGS.   Hopie Stonewall isn't a Boston girl; she's a giraffe. (*She prances around the room with an imaginary dwarf-sized Lyman.*) She's perfect for Lyman Wigglesworth!

GARDNER (*returns with* FANNY'*s drink, which he hands her*). Now, where were we? . . .

FANNY (*trying not to laugh*). HOPIE STONEWALL! . . .

GARDNER.   Oh, yes, she's the very tall one, isn't she? (FANNIE *and* MAGS *burst into gales of laughter.*)

MAGS.   The only hope for us . . . ''Boston girls'' is to get as far away from our kind as possible.

FANNY.   She always asks after you, darling. She's very fond of you, you know.

MAGS.   Please, I don't want to hear!

FANNY.   Your old friends are *always* asking after you.

MAGS.   It's not so much how creepy they all are, as how much they remind me of myself!

FANNY.   But you're not "creepy," darling . . . just . . . shabby!

MAGS.   I mean, give me a few more inches and some brown splotches here and there, and Hopie and I could be sisters!

FANNY (*in a whisper to* GARDNER). Don't you love it when Mags is like this? I could listen to her forever!

MAGS.   I mean . . . look at me!

FANNY (*gasping*). Don't stop, don't stop!

MAGS.   Awkward . . . plain . . . I don't know how to dress, I don't know how to talk. When people find out Daddy's my father, they're always amazed. . . . "Gardner Church is YOUR father?! Aw come on, you're kidding?!"

FANNY (*in a whisper*). Isn't she divine? . . .

MAGS.   Sometimes I don't even tell them. I pretend I grew up in the midwest somewhere . . . farming people . . . we work with our hands.

GARDNER (*to* MAGS). Well, how about a little refill? . . .

MAGS.   No, no more thanks.

(*Pause.*)

FANNY.   What did you have to go and interrupt her for? She was just getting up a head of steam? . . .

MAGS (*walking over to her easel*). The great thing about being a portrait painter you see is, it's the *other* guy that's exposed; you're safely hidden behind the canvas and easel. (*Standing behind it.*) You can be as plain as a pitchfork, as inarticulate as mud, but it doesn't matter because you're completely concealed: your body, your face, your intentions. Just as you make your most intimate move, throw open your soul . . . they stretch and yawn, remembering the dog has to be let out at five. . . . To be so invisible while so enthralled . . . It takes your breath away!

GARDNER.   Well put, Mags. Awfully well put!

MAGS.   That's why I've always wanted to paint you, to see if I'm up to it. It's quite a risk. Remember what I went through as a child with my great masterpiece? . . .

FANNY.   You painted a masterpiece when you were a child? . . .

MAGS.   Well, it was a masterpiece to me.

FANNY.   I had no idea you were precocious as a child. Gardner, do you remember Mags painting a masterpiece as a child?

MAGS.   I didn't paint it. It was something I made!

FANNY.   Well, this is all news to me! Gar, *do* get me another drink! I haven't had this much fun in years! (*She hands him her glass and reaches for* MAGS'.) Come on, darling, join me. . . .

MAGS.   No, no more, thanks. I don't really like the taste.

FANNY.   Oh, come on, kick up your heels for once!

MAGS.   No, nothing . . . really.

FANNY.   Please? Pretty please? . . . To keep me company?!

MAGS (*hands* GARDNER *her glass*). Oh, all right, what the hell . . .

FANNY.   That's a good girl!

GARDNER (*exiting*). Coming right up, coming right up!

FANNY (*yelling after him*). DON'T GIVE ME TOO MUCH NOW. THE LAST ONE WAS AWFULLY STRONG . . . AND HURRY BACK SO YOU DON'T MISS ANYTHING! . . . Daddy's so cunning, I don't know what I'd do without him. If anything should happen to him, I'd just . . .

MAGS.   Mummy, nothing's going to happen to him! . . .

FANNY.   Well, wait 'til you're our age, it's no garden party. Now . . . where were we? . . .

MAGS.   My first masterpiece . . .

FANNY.   Oh, yes, but *do* wait 'til Daddy gets back so he can hear it too. . . . YOO-HOO . . . GARRRRRRD-NERRRRRR? . . . ARE YOU COMING? . . . (*Silence.*) Go and check on him, will you?

GARDNER (*enters with both drinks. He's very shaken*). I couldn't find the ice.

FANNY.   Well, *finally!*

GARDNER.   It just up and disappeared. . . . (*Hands* FANNY *her drink.*) There you go.

(FANNY *kisses her fingers and takes a hefty swig.*)

GARDNER.   Mags.

(*He hands* MAGS *her drink.*)

MAGS.   Thanks, Daddy.

GARDNER.   Sorry about the ice.

MAGS.   No problem, no problem.

(GARDNER *sits down; silence.*)

FANNY (*to* MAGS). Well, drink up, drink up! (MAGS *downs it in one gulp.*) GOOD GIRL! . . . Now, what's all this about a masterpiece? . . .

MAGS.   I did it during that winter you sent me away from the dinner table. I was about nine years old.

FANNY.   We sent you from the dinner table?

MAGS.   I was banished for six months.

FANNY.   You *were?* . . . How extraordinary!

MAGS.   Yes, it *was* rather extraordinary!

FANNY.   But why?

MAGS.   Because I played with my food.

FANNY.   You did?

MAGS.   I used to squirt it out between my front teeth.

FANNY.   Oh, I remember that! God, it used to drive me crazy, absolutely . . . crazy! (*Pause.*) "MARGARET, STOP THAT OOZING RIGHT THIS MINUTE, YOU ARE *NOT* A TUBE OF TOOTHPASTE!"

GARDNER.   Oh, yes . . .

FANNY.   It was perfectly disgusting!

GARDNER.   I remember. She used to lean over her plate and squirt it out in long runny ribbons. . . .

FANNY.   That's enough, dear.

GARDNER.   They were quite colorful, actually; decorative almost. She made the most intricate designs. They looked rather like small, moist Oriental rugs. . . .

FANNY (*to* MAGS). But why, darling? What on earth possessed you to do it?

MAGS. I couldn't swallow anything. My throat just closed up. I don't know, I must have been afraid of choking or something.

GARDNER. I remember one in particular. We'd had chicken fricassee and spinach. . . . She made the most extraordinary . . .

FANNY (to GARDNER). WILL YOU PLEASE SHUT UP?! (Pause.) Mags, what are you talking about? You never choked in your entire life! This is the most distressing conversation I've ever had. Don't you think it's distressing, Gar?

GARDNER. Well, that's not quite the word I'd use.

FANNY. What word would you use, then?

GARDNER. I don't know right off the bat, I'd have to think about it.

FANNY. THEN, THINK ABOUT IT!

(Silence.)

MAGS. I guess I was afraid of making a mess. I don't know; you were awfully strict about table manners. I was always afraid of losing control. What if I started to choke and began spitting up over everything? . . .

FANNY. Alright, dear, that's enough.

MAGS. No, I was really terrified about making a mess; you always got so mad whenever I spilled. If I just got rid of everything in neat little curlycues beforehand you see . . .

FANNY. I SAID: THAT'S ENOUGH!

(Silence.)

MAGS. I thought it was quite ingenious, but you didn't see it that way. You finally sent me from the table with, "When you're ready to eat like a human being, you can come back and join us!" . . . So, it was off to my room with a tray. But I couldn't seem to eat there either. I mean, it was so strange settling down to dinner in my bedroom. . . . So I just flushed everything down the toilet and sat on my bed listening to you: clinkity-clink, clatter clatter, slurp, slurp . . . but that got pretty boring after awhile, so I looked around for something to do. It was wintertime, because I noticed I'd left some crayons on top of my radiator and they'd melted down into these beautiful shimmering globs, like spilled jello, trembling and pulsing. . . . (overlapping.)

GARDNER (eyes closed). "This luscious and impeccable fruit of life
Falls, it appears, of its own weight to earth . . ."

MAGS. Naturally, I wanted to try it myself, so I grabbed a red one and pressed it down against the hissing lid. It oozed and bubbled like raspberry jam!

GARDNER. "When you were Eve, its acrid juice was sweet, Untasted, in its heavenly, orchard air . . ."

MAGS. I mean, that radiator was really hot! It took incredible will power not to let go, but I held on, whispering, "Mags, if you let go of this crayon, you'll be run over by a truck on Newberry Street, so help you God!" . . . So I

pressed down harder, my fingers steaming and blistering. . . .

FANNY. I had no idea about any of this, did you, Gar?

MAGS. Once I'd melted one, I was hooked! I finished off my entire supply in one night, mixing color over color until my head swam! . . . The heat, the smell, the brilliance that sank and rose . . . I'd never felt such exhilaration! . . . Every week I spent my allowance on crayons. I must have cleared out every box of Crayolas in the city!

GARDNER (gazing at MAGS). You know, I don't think I've ever seen you looking prettier! You're awfully attractive when you get going!

FANNY. Why, what a lovely thing to say.

MAGS. AFTER THREE MONTHS THAT RADIATOR WAS . . . SPECTACULAR! I MEAN, IT LOOKED LIKE SOME COLOSSAL FRUITCAKE, FIVE FEET TALL! . . .

FANNY. It sounds perfectly hideous.

MAGS. It was a knockout; shimmering with pinks and blues, lavenders and maroons, turquoise and golds, oranges and creams. . . . For every color, I imagined a taste . . . YELLOW: lemon curls dipped in sugar . . . RED: glazed cherries laced with rum . . . GREEN: tiny peppermint leaves veined with chocolate . . . PURPLE: . . .

FANNY. That's quite enough!

MAGS. And then the frosting . . . ahhhh, the frosting! A satiny mix of white and silver . . . I kept it hidden under blankets during the day. . . . My huge . . . (She starts laughing.) looming . . . teetering sweet . . .

FANNY. I ASKED YOU TO STOP! GARDNER, WILL YOU PLEASE GET HER TO STOP!

GARDNER. See here, Mags, Mum asked you to . . .

MAGS. I was so . . . hungry . . . losing weight every week. I looked like a scarecrow what with the bags under my eyes and bits of crayon wrapper leaking out of my clothes. It's a wonder you didn't notice. But finally you came to my rescue . . . if you could call what happened a rescue. It was more like a rout!

FANNY. Darling . . .   GARDNER. Now,   look,
Please!   young lady . . .

MAGS. The winter was almost over. . . . It was very late at night. . . . I must have been having a nightmare because suddenly you and Daddy were at my bed, shaking me. . . . I quickly glanced towards the radiator to see if it was covered. . . . It wasn't! It glittered and towered in the moonlight like some . . . gigantic Viennese pastry! You followed my gaze and saw it. Mummy screamed . . . "WHAT HAVE YOU GOT IN HERE? . . . MAGS, WHAT HAVE YOU BEEN DOING?" . . . She crept forward and touched it, and then jumped back. "IT'S FOOD!" she cried . . . "IT'S ALL THE FOOD SHE'S BEEN SPITTING OUT! OH, GARDNER, IT'S A MOUNTAIN OF ROTTING GARBAGE!"

FANNY (*softly*). Yes . . . it's coming back . . . it's coming back. . . .

MAGS. Daddy exited as usual; left the premises. He fainted, just keeled over onto the floor. . . .

GARDNER. Gosh, I don't remember any of this. . . .

MAGS. My heart stopped! I mean, I knew it was all over. My lovely creation didn't have a chance. Sure enough . . . out came the blow torch. Well, it couldn't have *really* been a blow torch, I mean, where would you have ever gotten a blow torch? . . . I just have this very strong memory of you standing over my bed, your hair streaming around your face, aiming this . . . flame thrower at my confection . . . my cake . . . my tart . . . my strudel . . . "IT'S GOT TO BE DESTROYED IMMEDIATELY! THE THING'S ALIVE WITH VERMIN! . . . JUST LOOK AT IT! . . . IT'S PRACTICALLY CRAWLING ACROSS THE ROOM!" . . . Of course in a sense you were right. It *was* a monument of my cast-off dinners, only I hadn't built it with food. . . . I found my own materials. I was languishing with hunger, but oh, dear Mother . . . I FOUND MY OWN MATERIALS! . . .

FANNY. Darling . . . *please?!*

MAGS. I tried to stop you, but you wouldn't listen. . . . OUT SHOT THE FLAME! . . . I remember these waves of wax rolling across the room and Daddy coming to, wondering what on earth was going on. . . . Well, what did you know about my abilities? . . . You see, I had . . . I mean, I *have* abilities. . . . (*Struggling to say it.*) I have abilities. I have . . . strong abilities. I have . . . very strong abilities. They are very strong . . . very very strong. . . .

(*She rises and runs out of the room, overcome as* FANNY *and* GARDNER *watch, speechless.*)

THE CURTAIN FALLS

ACT TWO

SCENE ONE

Three days later. Miracles have been accomplished. Almost all of the Churches' furniture has been moved out, and the cartons of dishes and clothing are gone. All that remains are odds and ends. MAGS's *tableau looms, impregnable.* FANNY *and* GARDNER *are dressed in their formal evening clothes, frozen in their pose. They hold absolutely still.* MAGS *stands at her easel, her hands covering her eyes.*

FANNY. All right, you can look now.

MAGS (*removes her hands*). Yes! . . . I told you you could trust me on the pose.

FANNY. Well, thank God you let us dress up. It makes all the difference. Now we really look like something.

MAGS (*starts to sketch them*). I'll say. . . .

(*A silence as she sketches.*)

GARDNER (*recites Yeats's "The Song of Wandering Aengus" in a wonderfully resonant voice as they pose*).
"I went out to the hazel wood,
Because a fire was in my head,
And cut and peeled a hazel wand,
And hooked a berry to a thread,
And when white moths were on the wing,
And moth-like stars were flickering out,
I dropped the berry in a stream
And caught a little silver trout.
When I had laid it on the floor
I went to blow the fire aflame,
But something rustled on the floor,
And someone called me by my name:

It had become a glimmering girl
With apple blossoms in her hair
Who called me by my name and ran
And faded through the brightening air.

Though I am old with wandering
Through hollow lands and hilly lands,
I will find out where she has gone,
And kiss her lips and take her hands;
And walk among long dappled grass,
And pluck till time and times are done,
The silver apples of the moon,
The golden apples of the sun."

FANNY. That's lovely, dear. Just lovely. Is it one of yours?

GARDNER. No, no, it's Yeats. I'm using it in my book.

FANNY. Well, you recited it beautifully, but then you've always recited beautifully. That's how you wooed me, in case you've forgotten. . . . You must have memorized every love poem in the English language! There was no stopping you when you got going . . . your Shakespeare, Byron, and Shelley . . . you were shameless . . . *shameless!*

GARDNER (*eyes closed*). "I will find out where she has gone, And kiss her lips and take her hands . . ."

FANNY. And then there was your own poetry to do battle with; your sonnets and quatrains. When you got going with them, there was nothing left of me! You could have had your pick of any girl in Boston! Why you chose me, I'll never understand. I had no looks to speak of and nothing much in the brains department. . . . Well, what did you know about women and the world? . . . What did any of us know? . . . (*Silence.*) GOD, MAGS, HOW LONG ARE WE SUPPOSED TO SIT LIKE THIS? . . . IT'S AGONY!

MAGS (*working away*). You're doing fine . . . just fine . . .

FANNY (*breaking her pose*). It's so . . . boring!

MAGS. Come on, don't move. You can have a break soon.

FANNY. I had no idea it would be so boring!

GARDNER. Gee, I'm enjoying it.

FANNY. You would! . . .

(*A pause.*)

GARDNER (*begins reciting more Yeats, almost singing it*).
  "He stood among a crowd at Drumahair;
  His heart hung all upon a silken dress,
  And he had known at last some tenderness,
  Before earth made of him her sleepy care;
  But when a man poured fish into a pile,
  It seemed they raised their little silver heads . . ."
FANNY.   Gar . . . PLEASE! (*She lurches out of her seat.*)
  God, I can't take this anymore!
MAGS (*keeps sketching* GARDNER). I know it's tedious at
  first, but it gets easier. . . .
FANNY.   It's like a Chinese water torture! . . . (*Crosses to*
  MAGS *and looks at* GARDNER *posing.*) Oh, darling, you
  look marvelous, absolutely marvelous! Why don't you
  just do Daddy!?
MAGS.   Because you look marvelous too. I want to do you
  both!
FANNY.   Please! . . . I have one foot in the grave and you
  know it! Also, we're way behind in our packing. There's
  still one room left which everyone seems to have for-
  gotten about!
GARDNER.   Which one is that?
FANNY.   You know perfectly well which one it is!
GARDNER.   I do? . . .
FANNY.   Yes, you do!
GARDNER.   Well, it's news to me.
FANNY.   I'll give you a hint. It's in . . . *that* direction. (*She
  points.*)
GARDNER.   The dining room?
FANNY.   No.
GARDNER.   The bedroom?
FANNY.   No.
GARDNER.   Mags' room?
FANNY.   No.
GARDNER.   The kitchen?
FANNY.   *Gar?!* . . .
GARDNER.   The guest room?
FANNY.   Your God-awful study!
GARDNER.   Oh, shit!
FANNY.   That's right, "Oh, shit!" It's books and papers up
  to the ceiling! If you ask me, we should just forget it's
  there and quietly tiptoe away. . . .
GARDNER.   My study! . . .
FANNY.   Let the new owners dispose of everything. . . .
GARDNER (*gets out of his posing chair*). Now, just one
  minute. . . .
FANNY.   You never look at half the stuff in there!
GARDNER.   I don't want you touching those books!
  They're mine!
FANNY.   Darling, we're moving to a cottage the size of a
  handkerchief! Where, pray tell, is there room for all your
  books?
GARDNER.   I don't know. We'll just have to make room!
MAGS (*sketching away*). RATS!

FANNY.   I don't know what we're doing fooling around
  with Mags like this when there's still so much to do. . . .
GARDNER (*sits back down, overwhelmed*). My study! . . .

FANNY.   You can stay with her if you'd like, but one of us
  has got to tackle those books!
  (*She exits to his study.*)
GARDNER.   I'm not up to this.
MAGS.   Oh, good, you're staying!
GARDNER.   There's a lifetime of work in there. . . .
MAGS.   Don't worry, I'll help. Mum and I will be able to
  pack everything up in no time.
GARDNER.   God. . . .
MAGS.   It won't be so bad. . . .
GARDNER.   I'm just not up to it.
MAGS.   We'll all pitch in. . . .
  (GARDNER *sighs, speechless. A silence as* FANNY *comes
  staggering in with an armload of books which she drops
  to the floor with a crash.*)
GARDNER.   WHAT WAS   MAGS.   GOOD GRIEF!
  THAT?! . . .
FANNY (*sheepish*). Sorry, sorry. . . .
  (*She exits for more.*)
GARDNER.   I don't know if I can take this. . . .
MAGS.   Moving is awful . . . I know. . . .
GARDNER (*settling back into his pose*). Ever since Mum
  began tearing the house apart, I've been having these
  dreams. . . . I'm a child again back at Sixteen Louisberg
  Square . . . and this stream of moving men is carrying
  furniture into our house . . . van after van of tables and
  chairs, sofas and loveseats, desks and bureaus . . . rugs,
  bathtubs, mirrors, chiming clocks, pianos, iceboxes, china
  cabinets . . . but what's amazing is that all of it is familiar. . . . (FANNY *comes in with another load which
  she drops on the floor. She exits for more.*) No matter how
  many items appear, I've seen every one of them before.
  Since my mother is standing in the midst of it directing
  traffic, I ask her where it's all coming from, but she
  doesn't hear me because of the racket . . . so finally I just
  scream out . . . "WHERE IS ALL THIS FURNITURE
  COMING FROM?" . . . Just as a moving man is carrying Toots into the room, she looks at me and says,
  "Why, from the land of Skye!" . . . The next thing I
  know, *people* are being carried in along with it. . . .
  (FANNY *enters with her next load; drops it and exits.*)
  People I've never seen before are sitting around our
  dining-room table. A group of foreigners is going through
  my books, chattering in a language I've never heard
  before. A man is playing a Chopin polonaise on Aunt
  Alice's piano. Several children are taking baths in our
  tubs from Cotuit. . . .
MAGS.   It sounds marvelous.
GARDNER.   Well, it isn't marvelous at all because all of
  these perfect strangers have taken over our things. . . .
  (FANNY *enters, hurls down another load and exits.*)

MAGS.   How odd. . . .

GARDNER.   Well, it *is* odd, but then something even odder happens. . . .

MAGS (*sketching away*). Tell me, tell me!

GARDNER.   Well, our beds are carried in. They're all made up with sheets and everything, but instead of all these strange people in them, *we're* in them! . . .

MAGS.   What's so odd about that? . . .

GARDNER.   Well, you and Mum are brought in, both sleeping like angels . . . Mum snoring away to beat the band. . . .

MAGS.   Yes . . .

(FANNY *enters with another load; lets it fall.*)

GARDNER.   But there's no one in mine. It's completely empty, never even been slept in! It's as if I were dead or had never even existed. . . . (FANNY *exits.*) "HEY . . . WAIT UP!" I yell to the moving men . . . "THAT'S MY BED YOU'VE GOT THERE!" But they don't stop; they don't even acknowledge me. . . . "HEY, COME BACK HERE . . . I WANT TO GET INTO MY BED!" I cry again and I start running after them . . . down the hall, through the dining room, past the library. . . . Finally I catch up to them and hurl myself right into the center of the pillow. Just as I'm about to land, the bed suddenly vanishes and I go crashing down to the floor like some insect that's been hit by a fly swatter!

FANNY (*staggers in with her final load; drops it with a crash and then collapses in her posing chair*). THAT'S IT FOR ME! I'M DEAD! (*Silence.*) Come on, Mags, how about you doing a little work around here.

MAGS.   That's all I've been doing! This is the first free moment you've given me!

FANNY.   You should see all the books in there . . . and papers! There are enough loose papers to sink a ship!

GARDNER.   Why is it we're moving, again? . . .

FANNY.   Because life is getting too complicated here.

GARDNER (*remembering*). Oh, yes . . .

FANNY.   And we can't afford it anymore.

GARDNER.   That's right, that's right. . . .

FANNY.   We don't have the . . . *income* we used to!

GARDNER.   Oh, yes . . . *income!*

FANNY (*assuming her pose again*). Of course we have our savings and various trust funds, but I wouldn't dream of touching those!

GARDNER.   No, no, you must never dip into capital!

FANNY.   I told Daddy I'd be perfectly happy to buy a gun and put a bullet through our heads so we could avoid all this, but he wouldn't hear of it!

MAGS (*sketching away*). No, I shouldn't think so.

(*Pause.*)

FANNY.   I've always admired people who kill themselves when they get to our stage of life. Well, no one can touch my Uncle Edmond in that department. . . .

MAGS.   I know, I know. . . .

FANNY.   The day before his seventieth birthday he climbed to the top of the Old North Church and hurled himself face down into Salem Street! They had to scrape him up with a spatula! God, he was a remarkable man . . . state senator, president of Harvard . . .

GARDNER (*rises and wanders over to his books*). Well, I guess I'm going to have to do something about all of these. . . .

FANNY.   Come on, Mags, help Daddy! Why don't you start bringing in his papers. . . .

(GARDNER *sits on the floor; picks up a book and soon is engrossed in it.* MAGS *keeps sketching, oblivious; silence.*)

FANNY (*to* MAGS). Darling? . . . HELLO? . . . God, you two are impossible! Just look at you . . . heads in the clouds! No one would ever know we've got to be out of here in two days. If it weren't for me, nothing would get done around here. . . . (*She starts stacking* GARDNER'*s books into piles.*) There! That's all the maroon ones!

GARDNER (*looks up*). What do you mean, *maroon* ones?! . . .

FANNY.   All your books that are maroon are in *this* pile . . . and your books that are green in *that* pile! . . . I'm trying to bring some order into your life for once. This will make unpacking so much easier.

GARDNER.   But my dear Fanny, it's not the color of a book that distinguishes it, but what's *inside* it!

FANNY.   This will be a great help, you'll see. Now what about this awful striped thing? (*She picks up a slim, aged volume.*) Can't it go? . . .

GARDNER.   No!

FANNY.   But it's as queer as Dick's hat band! There are no others like it.

GARDNER.   Open it and read. Go on . . . open it!

FANNY.   We'll get nowhere at this rate.

GARDNER.   I said . . . READ!

FANNY.   Really, Gar, I . . .

GARDNER.   Read the dedication!

FANNY (*opens and reads*). "To Gardner Church, you led the way. With gratitude and affection, Robert Frost."

(*She closes it and hands it to him.*)

GARDNER.   It was published the same year as my *Salem Gardens.*

FANNY (*picking up a very worn book*). Well, what about this dreadful thing? It's filthy. (*She blows off a cloud of dust.*)

GARDNER.   Please . . . *please?!*

FANNY (*looking through it*). It's all in French.

GARDNER (*snatching it away from her*). André Malraux gave me that! . . .

FANNY.   I'm just trying to help.

GARDNER.   It's a first edition of Baudelaire's *Fleurs du Mal.*

FANNY (*giving it back*). Well, pardon me for living!

GARDNER.   Why do you have to drag everything in here in the first place? . . .

FANNY.   Because there's no room in your study. You ought to see the mess in there! . . . WAKE UP, MAGS, ARE YOU GOING TO PITCH IN OR NOT?! . . .

GARDNER.   I'm not up to this.

FANNY.   Well, you'd better be unless you want to be left behind!

MAGS (*stops her sketching*). Alright, alright . . . I just hope you'll give me some more time later this evening.

FANNY (*to* MAGS). Since you're young and in the best shape, why don't you bring in the books and I'll cope with the papers. (*She exits to the study.*)

GARDNER.   Now just a minute. . . .

FANNY (*offstage*). WE NEED A STEAM SHOVEL FOR THIS!

MAGS.   OK, what do you want me to do?

GARDNER.   Look, I don't want you messing around with my . . .
(FANNY *enters with an armful of papers which she drops into an empty carton.*)

GARDNER.   HEY, WHAT'S GOING ON HERE?! . . .

FANNY.   I'm packing up your papers. COME ON, MAGS, LET'S GET CRACKING!
(*She exits for more papers.*)

GARDNER (*plucks several papers out of the carton*). What is this? . . .

MAGS (*exits into his study*). GOOD LORD, WHAT HAVE YOU DONE IN HERE?! . . .

GARDNER (*reading*). This is my manuscript.
(FANNY *enters with another batch which she tosses on top of the others.*)

GARDNER.   What *are* you doing?! . . .

FANNY.   Packing, darling . . . PACKING!
(*She exits for more.*)

GARDNER.   SEE HERE, YOU CAN'T MANHANDLE MY THINGS THIS WAY! (MAGS *enters, staggering under a load of books which she sets down on the floor.*) I PACK MY MANUSCRIPT! I KNOW WHERE EVERYTHING IS!

FANNY (*offstage*). IF IT WERE UP TO YOU, WE'D NEVER GET OUT OF HERE! WE'RE UNDER A TIME LIMIT, GARDNER. KITTY'S PICKING US UP IN TWO DAYS . . . TWO . . . DAYS!
(*She enters with a larger batch of papers and heads for the carton.*)

GARDNER (*grabbing* FANNY'*s wrist*). NOW, HOLD IT! . . . JUST . . . HOLD IT RIGHT THERE! . . .

FANNY.   OOOOOWWWWWWWW!

GARDNER.   *I* PACK MY THINGS! . . .

FANNY.   LET GO, YOU'RE HURTING ME!

GARDNER.   THAT'S MY MANUSCRIPT! GIVE IT TO ME!

FANNY (*lifting the papers high over her head*). I'M IN CHARGE OF THIS MOVE, GARDNER! WE'VE GOT TO GET CRACKING!

GARDNER.   I said . . . GIVE IT TO ME!

MAGS.   Come on, Mum, let him have it.
(*They struggle.*)

GARDNER (*finally wrenches the pages from her*). LET . . . ME . . . HAVE . . . IT! . . . THAT'S MORE LIKE IT! . . .

FANNY (*soft and weepy*). You see what he's like? . . . I try and help with his packing and what does he do? . . .

GARDNER (*rescues the rest of his papers from the carton*). YOU DON'T JUST THROW EVERYTHING INTO A BOX LIKE A PILE OF GARBAGE! THIS IS A BOOK, FANNY. SOMETHING I'VE BEEN WORKING ON FOR TWO YEARS! . . . (*Trying to assemble his papers, but only making things worse, dropping them all over the place.*) You show a little respect for my things. . . . You don't just throw them around every which way. . . . It's tricky trying to make sense of poetry; it's much easier to write the stuff . . . that is, if you've still got it in you. . . .

MAGS.   Here, let me help. . . . (*Taking some of the papers.*)

GARDNER.   Criticism is tough sledding. You can't just dash off a few images here, a few rhymes there. . . .

MAGS.   Do you have these pages numbered in any way?

FANNY (*returning to her posing chair*). HA!

GARDNER.   This is just the introduction.

MAGS.   I don't see any numbers on these.

GARDNER (*exiting to his study*). The important stuff is in my study . . .

FANNY (*to* MAGS). You don't know the half of it . . . *not the half.* . . .

GARDNER (*offstage; thumping around*). HAVE YOU SEEN THOSE YEATS POEMS I JUST HAD? . . .

MAGS (*reading over several pages*). What is this? . . . It doesn't make sense. It's just fragments . . . pieces of poems.

FANNY.   That's it, honey! That's his book. His great critical study! Now that he can't write his own poetry, he's trying to explain other people's. The only problem is, he can't get beyond typing them out. The poor lamb doesn't have the stamina to get beyond the opening stanzas, let alone trying to make sense of them.

GARDNER (*thundering back with more papers which keep falling*). GOD DAMNIT, FANNY, WHAT DID YOU DO IN THERE? I CAN'T FIND ANYTHING!

FANNY.   I just took the papers that were on your desk.

GARDNER.   Well, the entire beginning is gone.
(*He exits.*)

FANNY.   I'M TRYING TO HELP YOU, DARLING!

GARDNER (*returns with another armload*). SEE THAT? . . . NO SIGN OF CHAPTER ONE OR TWO. . . . (*He flings it all down on the floor.*)

FANNY.   Gardner . . . PLEASE?!

GARDNER (*kicking through the mess*). I TURN MY BACK FOR ONE MINUTE AND WHAT HAPPENS? . . . MY ENTIRE STUDY IS TORN APART!

(*He exits.*)

MAGS.   Oh, Daddy . . . don't . . . please . . . Daddy . . . please?!

GARDNER (*returns with a new batch of papers which he tosses up into the air*). THROWN OUT! . . . THE BEST PART IS THROWN OUT! . . . LOST. . . .

(*He starts to exit again.*)

MAGS (*reads one of the fragments to steady herself*).
"I have known the inexorable sadness of pencils,
Neat in their boxes, dolor of pad and paperweight,
All the misery of manilla folders and mucilage . . ."
They're beautiful . . . just beautiful.

GARDNER (*stops*). Hey, what's that you've got there?

FANNY.   It's your manuscript, darling. You see, it's right where you left it.

GARDNER (*to* MAGS). Read that again.

MAGS.
"I have known the inexorable sadness of pencils,
Neat in their boxes, dolor of pad and paperweight,
All the misery of manilla folders and mucilage . . ."

GARDNER.   Well, well, what do you know. . . .

FANNY (*hands him several random papers*). You see . . . no one lost anything. Everything's here, still in tack.

GARDNER (*reads*).
"I knew a woman, lovely in her bones,
When small birds sighed, she would sigh back at them;
Ah, when she moved, she moved more ways than one:
The shapes a bright container can contain! . . ."

FANNY (*hands him another*). And . . .

GARDNER (*reads*). Ahh . . . Frost . . .
"Some say the world will end in fire,
Some say ice.
From what I've tasted of desire
I hold with those who favor fire."

FANNY (*under her breath to* MAGS). He can't give up the words. It's the best he can do. (*Handing him another.*) Here you go, here's more.

GARDNER.
"Farm boys wild to couple
With anything with soft-wooded trees
With mounds of earth mounds
Of pinestraw will keep themselves off
Animals by legends of their own . . ."

MAGS (*eyes shut*). Oh, Daddy, I can't bear it . . . I . . .

FANNY.   Of course no one will ever publish this.

GARDNER.   Oh, here's a marvelous one. Listen to this!
"There came a Wind like a Bugle—
It quivered through the Grass
And a Green Chill upon the Heat

So ominous did pass
We barred the Windows and the Doors
As from an Emerald Ghost—

The Doom's electric Moccasin . . ."

SHIT, WHERE DID THE REST OF IT GO? . . .

FANNY.   Well, don't ask *me*.

GARDNER.   It just stopped in mid-air!

FANNY.   Then go look for the original.

GARDNER.   Good idea, good idea!

(*He exits to his study.*)

FANNY (*to* MAGS). He's incontinent now, too. He wets his pants, in case you haven't noticed. (*She starts laughing.*) You're not laughing. Don't you think it's funny? Daddy needs diapers. . . . I don't know about you, but I could use a drink! GAR . . . WILL YOU GET ME A SPLASH WHILE YOU'RE OUT THERE? . . .

MAGS.   STOP IT!

FANNY.   It means we can't go out anymore. I mean, what would people say? . . .

MAGS.   Stop it. Just stop it.

FANNY.   My poet laureate can't hold it in! (*She laughs harder.*)

MAGS.   That's enough . . . STOP IT . . . Mummy . . . I beg of you . . . *please stop it!*

GARDNER (*enters with a book and indeed a large stain has blossomed on his trousers. He plucks at his leg*). Here we go . . . I found it. . . .

FANNY (*pointing at it*). See that? See? . . . He just did it again! (*Goes off into a shower of laughter.*)

MAGS (*looks, turns away*). SHUT . . . UP! . . . (*Building to a howl.*) WILL YOU PLEASE JUST . . . SHUT . . . UP!

FANNY (*to* GARDNER). Hey, what about that drink?

GARDNER.   Oh, yes . . . sorry, sorry . . .

(*He heads towards the bar.*)

FANNY.   Never mind, I'll get it, I'll get it. (*She exits, convulsed; silence.*)

GARDNER.   Well, where were we? . . .

MAGS (*near tears*). Your poem.

GARDNER.   Oh, yes . . . the Dickinson. (*He shuts his eyes, reciting from memory, holding the book against his chest.*)
"There came a Wind like a Bugle—
It quivered through the Grass
And a Green Chill upon the Heat
So ominous did pass
We barred the Windows and the Doors
As from an Emerald Ghost—"

(*Opens the book and starts riffling through it.*) Let's see now, where's the rest? . . . (*He finally finds it.*) Ahhh, here we go! . . .

FANNY (*reenters; drink in hand*). I'm back! (*Takes one look at* GARDNER *and bursts out laughing again.*)

MAGS. I don't believe you! How you can laugh at him?! . . .

FANNY. I'm sorry, I wish I could stop, but there's really nothing else to do. Look at him . . . just . . . look at him! . . .

(*This is all simultaneous as* MAGS *gets angrier and angrier.*)

MAGS. It's so cruel. . . . You're so . . . incredibly cruel to him . . . I mean, YOUR DISDAIN REALLY TAKES MY BREATH AWAY! YOU'RE IN A CLASS BY YOURSELF WHEN IT COMES TO HUMILIA-TION! . . .

GARDNER (*reading*).

> "The Doom's electric Moccasin
> That very instant passed—
> On a strange Mob of panting Trees
> And Fences fled away
> And Rivers where the Houses ran
> Those looked that lived—that Day—
> The Bell within the steeple wild
> The flying tidings told—
> How much can come
> And much can go,
> And yet abide the World!"

(*He shuts the book with a bang, pauses and looks around the room, confused.*) Now, where was I? . . .

FANNY. Safe and sound in the middle of the living room with Mags and me.

GARDNER. But I was looking for something, wasn't I? . . .

FANNY. Your manuscript.

GARDNER. THAT'S RIGHT! MY MANUSCRIPT! My manuscript!

FANNY. And here it is all over the floor. See, you're standing on it.

GARDNER (*picks up a few pages and looks at them*). Why, so I am. . . .

FANNY. Now all we have to do is get it up off the floor and packed neatly into these cartons!

GARDNER. Yes, yes, that's right. Into the cartons.

FANNY (*kicks a carton over to him*). Here, you use this one and I'll start over here. . . . (*She starts dropping papers into a carton nearby.*) BOMBS AWAY! . . . Hey . . . this is fun! . . .

GARDNER (*picks up his own pile, lifts it high over his head and flings it down into the carton*). BOMBS AWAY . . . This *is* fun! . . .

FANNY. I told you! The whole thing is to figure out a system!

GARDNER. I don't know what I'd do without you, Fan. I thought I'd lost everything.

FANNY (*makes dive-bomber noises and machine-gun explosions as she wheels more and more papers into the carton*). TAKE THAT AND THAT AND THAT! . . .

GARDNER (*joins in the fun, outdoing her with dips, dives and blastings of his own*). BLAM BLAM BLAM BLAM! . . . ZZZZZZZZRAAAAAA FOOM! . . . BLATTY—DE—BLATTY—DE—BLATTY—DE—KABOOOOOOOOM! . . . WHAAAAAAA . . . DA—DAT—DAT—DAT—DAT . . . WHEEEEEEEE-AAAAAAAAAAAA . . . FOOOOOO . . .

(*THEY get louder and louder as papers fly every which way.*)

FANNY (*mimes getting hit with a bomb*). AEEEEEEIII-IIIIIIIII! YOU GOT ME RIGHT IN THE GIZZARD! (*She collapses on the floor and starts going through death throes, having an absolute ball.*)

GARDNER. TAKE THAT AND THAT AND THAT AND THAT . . . (*A series of explosions follow.*)

MAGS (*furious*). This is how you help him? . . . THIS IS HOW YOU PACK HIS THINGS? . . .

FANNY. I keep him company. I get involved . . . which is a hell of a lot more than you do!

MAGS (*wild with rage*). BUT YOU'RE MAKING A MOCKERY OF HIM. . . . YOU TREAT HIM LIKE A CHILD OR SOME DIM-WITTED SERVING BOY. HE'S JUST AN AMUSEMENT TO YOU! . . .

FANNY (*fatigue has finally overtaken her. She's calm almost serene*). . . . and to you who see him once a year, if that . . . What is he to *you*? . . . I mean, what do you give him from yourself that costs you something? . . . Hmmmmmm? . . . (*Imitating her.*) "Oh, hi Daddy, it's great to see you again. How have you been? . . . Gee, I love your hair. It's gotten so . . . *white!*" . . . What color do you expect it to get when he's this age? . . . I mean, if you care so much how he looks, why don't you come and see him once in a while? . . . But oh, no . . . you have your paintings to do and your shows to put on. You just come and see us when the whim strikes. (*Imitating her.*) "Hey, you know what would be really great? . . . To do a portrait of you! I've always wanted to paint you, you're such great subjects!" . . . *Paint* us?! . . . What about opening your eyes and really *seeing* us? . . . No-ticing what's going on around here for a change! It's all over for Daddy and me. This is it! "Finita la commedia!" . . . All I'm trying to do is exit with a little flourish; have some fun. . . . What's so terrible about that? . . . It can get pretty grim around here, in case you haven't noticed . . . Daddy, tap-tap-tapping out his nonsense all day; me traipsing around to the thrift shops trying to amuse myself . . . He never keeps me company anymore; never takes me out anywhere. . . . I'd put a bullet through my head in a minute, but then who'd look after him? . . . What do you think we're moving to the cottage for? . . . So I can watch him like a hawk and make sure he doesn't get lost. Do you think that's anything to look forward to? . . . Being Daddy's nursemaid out in the middle of nowhere? I'd much rather stay here in Boston with the few friends I have left, but you can't always do what you want in this world! "L'homme propose, Dieu dispose" . . . If you want to paint us so badly, you ought to paint us as we really are. There's your picture! . . . (*She points to* GARDNER *who's quietly playing with a paper glide.*) Daddy spread out on the floor with all his toys and me hovering over him to make sure he doesn't hurt himself! (*She goes over to him.*) YOO-HOO . . . GAR? . . . HELLO? . . .

GARDNER (*looks up at her*). Oh, hi there, Fan. What's up?

FANNY.   How's the packing coming? . . .

GARDNER.   Packing? . . .

FANNY.   Yes, you were packing your manuscript, remember?
   (*She lifts up a page and lets it fall into a carton.*)

GARDNER.   Oh, yes. . . .

FANNY.   Here's your picture, Mags. Face over this way . . . turn your easel over here . . . (*She lets a few more papers fall.*) Up, up . . . and away . . .

BLACKOUT

SCENE TWO

The last day. All the books and boxes are gone. The room is completely empty except for MAGS's *backdrop. Late afternoon light dapples the walls; it changes from pale peach to deeper violet. The finished portrait sits on the easel, covered with a cloth.* MAGS *is taking down the backdrop.*

FANNY (*offstage; to* GARDNER). DON'T FORGET TOOTS!

GARDNER (*offstage; from another part of the house*). WHAT'S THAT?

FANNY (*offstage*). I SAID: DON'T FORGET TOOTS! HIS CAGE IS SITTING IN THE MIDDLE OF YOUR STUDY! (*Silence.*)

FANNY (*offstage*). HELLO? . . . ARE YOU THERE? . . .   GARDNER (*offstage*). I'LL BE RIGHT WITH YOU; I'M JUST GETTING TOOTS!

GARDNER (*offstage*). WHAT'S THAT? I CAN'T HEAR YOU?

FANNY (*offstage*). I'M GOING THROUGH THE ROOMS ONE MORE TIME TO MAKE SURE WE DIDN'T FORGET ANYTHING. . . . KITTY'S PICKING US UP IN FIFTEEN MINUTES, SO PLEASE BE READY. . . . SHE'S DROPPING MAGS OFF AT THE STATION AND THEN IT'S OUT TO ROUTE 3 AND THE CAPE HIGHWAY. . . .

GARDNER (*enters, carrying* TOOTS *in his cage*). Well, this is it. The big moment has finally come, eh what, Toots? (*He sees* MAGS.) Oh, hi there, Mags, I didn't see you. . . .

MAGS.   Oh, hi Daddy, I'm just taking this down. . . . (*She does and walks over to* TOOTS.) Oh, Toots, I'll miss you. (*She makes little chattering noises into his cage.*)

GARDNER.   Come on, recite a little Grey's Elegy for Mags before we go.

MAGS.   Yes, Mum said he was really good at it now.

GARDNER.   Well, the whole thing is to keep at it every day. (*Slowly to* TOOTS.)
   "The curfew tolls the knell of parting day,
   The lowing herd wind slowly o'er the lea . . ."
Come on, show Mags your stuff!
   (*Slower.*)
   "The curfew tolls the knell of parting day,
   The lowing herd wind slowly o'er the lea."
   (*Silence;* GARDNER *makes little chattering sounds.*)
Come on, Toots, old boy. . . .

MAGS.   How does it go?

GARDNER (*to* MAGS).
   "The curfew tolls the knell of parting day,
   The lowing herd wind slowly o'er the lea . . ."

MAGS (*slowly to* TOOTS). "The curfew tolls for you and me,
   As quietly the herd winds down . . ."

GARDNER.   No, no, it's "The curfew tolls the knell of parting *day!* . . .

MAGS (*repeating after him*). "The curfew tolls the knell of parting day . . ."

GARDNER.   "The lowing herd wind slowly o'er the lea . . ."

MAGS (*with a deep breath*).
   "The curfew tolls at parting day,
   The herd low slowly down the lea . . . no, *knell!*
   They come winding down the *knell!* . . ."

GARDNER.   Listen, Mags . . . *listen!*
   (*A pause.*)

TOOTS (*loud and clear with* GARDNER's *inflection*).
   "The curfew tolls the knell of parting day,
   The lowing herd wind slowly o'er the lea,
   The ploughman homeward plods his weary way,
   And leaves the world to darkness and to me."

MAGS.   HE SAID IT. . . . HE SAID IT! . . . AND IN YOUR VOICE! . . . OH, DADDY, THAT'S AMAZING!

GARDNER.   Well, Toots is very smart, which is more than I can say for a lot of people I know. . . .

MAGS (*to* TOOTS). Polly want a cracker? Polly want a cracker?

GARDNER.   You can teach a parakeet to say anything; all you need is patience. . . .

MAGS.   But *poetry* . . . that's so hard. . . .

FANNY (*enters carrying a suitcase and* GARDNER's *typewriter in its case. She's dressed in her travelling suit, wearing a hat to match*). WELL, THERE YOU ARE! I THOUGHT YOU'D DIED!

MAGS (*to* FANNY). HE SAID IT! I FINALLY HEARD TOOTS RECITE GREY'S ELEGY. (*She makes silly clucking sounds into the cage.*)

FANNY.   Isn't it uncanny how much he sounds like Daddy? Sometimes when I'm alone here with him, I've actually thought he *was* Daddy and started talking to him. Oh, yes, Toots and I have had quite a few meaty conversations together!

(FANNY *wolf-whistles into the cage; then draws back.* GARDNER *covers the cage with a travelling cloth. Silence.*)

FANNY (*looking around the room*). God, the place looks so bare.

MAGS.   I still can't believe it . . . Cotuit, year round. I wonder if there'll be any phosphorus when you get there?

FANNY.   What on earth are you talking about? (*She carries the discarded backdrop out into the hall.*)

MAGS.   Remember that summer when the ocean was full of phosphorus?

GARDNER (*taking* TOOTS *out into the hall*). Oh, yes. . . .

MAGS.   It was a great mystery where it came from or why it settled in Cotuit. But one evening when Daddy and I were taking a swim, suddenly it was there!

GARDNER (*returns*). I remember.

MAGS.   I don't know where Mum was. . . .

FANNY (*reentering*). Probably doing the dishes!

MAGS (*to* GARDNER). As you dove into the water, this shower of silvery green sparks erupted all around you. It was incredible! I thought you were turning into a saint or something; but then you told me to jump in too and the same thing happened to me. . . .

GARDNER.   Oh, yes, I remember that . . . the water smelled all queer.

MAGS.   What *is* phosphorus, anyway?

GARDNER.   Chemicals, chemicals . . .

FANNY.   No, it isn't. Phosphorus is a green liquid inside insects. Fireflies have it. When you see sparks in the water it means insects are swimming around. . . .

GARDNER.   Where on earth did you get that idea? . . .

FANNY.   If you're bitten by one of them, it's fatal!

MAGS.   . . . and the next morning it was still there. . . .

GARDNER.   It was the damndest stuff to get off! We'd have to stay in the shower a good ten minutes. It comes from chemical waste, you see. . . .

MAGS.   Our bodies looked like mercury as we swam around. . . .

GARDNER.   It stained all the towels a strange yellow green.

MAGS.   I was in heaven, and so were you for that matter. You'd finished your day's poetry and would turn somersaults like some happy dolphin. . . .

FANNY.   Damned dishes . . . why didn't I see any of this?! . . .

MAGS.   I remember one night in particular. . . . We sensed the phosphorus was about to desert us; blow off to another town. We were chasing each other under water. At one point I lost you the brilliance was so intense . . . but finally your foot appeared . . . then your leg. I grabbed it! . . . I remember wishing the moment would hold forever; that we could just be fixed there, laughing and iridescent. . . . Then I began to get panicky because I knew

it would pass; it was passing already. You were slipping from my grasp. The summer was almost over. I'd be going back to art school; you'd be going back to Boston. . . . Even as I was reaching for you, you were gone. We'd never be like that again.

(*Silence.*)

FANNY (*spies* MAGS*'s portrait covered on the easel*). What's that over there? Don't tell me we forget something!

MAGS.   It's your portrait. I finished it.

FANNY.   You finished it? How on earth did you manage that?

MAGS.   I stayed up all night.

FANNY.   You did? . . . *I* didn't hear you, did you hear her, Gar? . . .

GARDNER.   Not a peep, not a peep!

MAGS.   Well, I wanted to get it done before you left. You know, see what you thought. It's not bad, considering . . . I mean, I did it almost completely from memory. The light was terrible and I was trying to be quiet so I wouldn't wake you. It was hardly an ideal situation. . . . I mean, you weren't the most cooperative models. . . . (*She suddenly panics and snatches the painting off the easel. She hugs it to her chest and starts dancing around the room with it.*) Oh, God, you're going to hate it! You're going to hate it! How did I ever get into this? . . . Listen, you don't really want to see it . . . it's nothing . . . just a few dabs here and there . . . It was awfully late when I finished it. The light was really impossible and my eyes were hurting like crazy. . . . Look, why don't we just go out to the sidewalk and wait for Kitty so she doesn't have to honk. . . .

GARDNER (*snatches the painting out from under her*). WOULD YOU JUST SHUT UP A MINUTE AND LET US SEE IT? . . .

MAGS (*laughing and crying*). But it's nothing, Daddy . . . really! . . . I've done better with my eyes closed! It was so late I could hardly see anything and then I spilled a whole bottle of thinner into my palette. . . .

GARDNER (*sets it down on the easel and stands back to look at it*). THERE!

MAGS (*dancing around them in a panic*). Listen, it's just a quick sketch. . . . It's still wet. . . . I didn't have enough time. . . . It takes at least forty hours to do a decent portrait. . . .

(*Suddenly it's very quiet as* FANNY *and* GARDNER *stand back to look at it.*)

MAGS (*more and more beside herself, keeps leaping around the room wrapping her arms around herself, making little whimpering sounds*). Please don't . . . no . . . don't . . . oh, please! . . . Come on, don't look. . . . Oh, God, don't . . . please . . .

(*An eternity passes as* FANNY *and* GARDNER *gaze at it.*)

GARDNER.   Well . . .

FANNY.   Well . . . (*More silence.*)

FANNY. I think it's per- GARDNER. Awfully
fectly dreadful. clever, awfully clever!

FANNY. What on earth did you do to my face? . . .

GARDNER. I particularly like Mum!

FANNY. Since when do I have purple skin?! . . .

MAGS. I told you it was nothing, just a silly . . .

GARDNER. She looks like a million dollars!

FANNY. AND WILL YOU LOOK AT MY HAIR . . . IT'S
BRIGHT ORANGE!

GARDNER (*views it from another angle*). It's really very
good!

FANNY (*pointing*). That doesn't look anything like me!

GARDNER. . . . first rate!

FANNY. Since when do I have purple skin and bright
orange hair?! . . .

MAGS (*trying to snatch it off the easel*). Listen, you don't
have to worry about my feelings . . . really . . . I . . .

GARDNER (*blocking her way*). NOT SO FAST . . .

FANNY. . . . and look at how I'm sitting! I've never sat
like that in my life!

GARDNER (*moving closer to it*). Yes, yes, it's awfully
clever. . . .

FANNY. I HAVE NO FEET!

GARDNER. The whole thing is quite remarkable!

FANNY. And what happened to my legs, pray tell? . . .
They just vanish below the knees! . . . At least my dress
is presentable. I've always loved that dress.

GARDNER. It sparkles somehow. . . .

FANNY (*to* GARDNER). Don't you think it's becoming?

GARDNER. Yes, very becoming, awfully becoming . . .

FANNY (*examining it at closer range*). Yes, she got the dress
very well, how it shows off what's left of my figure . . .
My smile is nice too.

GARDNER. Good and wide. . . .

FANNY. I love how the corners of my mouth turn up. . . .

GARDNER. It's very clever. . . .

FANNY. They're almost quivering. . . .

GARDNER. Good lighting effects!

FANNY. Actually, I look quite . . . *young,* don't you think?

GARDNER (*to* MAGS). You're awfully good with those
highlights.

FANNY (*looking at it from different angles*). And *you* look
darling! . . .

GARDNER. Well, I don't know about that. . . .

FANNY. No, you look absolutely darling. Good enough to
eat!

MAGS (*in a whisper*). They like it. . . . They like it!

(*A silence as* FANNY *and* GARDNER *keep gazing at it.*)

FANNY. You know what it is? The wispy brush strokes
make us look like a couple in a French Impressionist
painting.

GARDNER. Yes, I see what you mean. . . .

FANNY. . . . a Manet or Renoir . . .

GARDNER. It's very evocative.

FANNY. There's something about the light. . . . (*They
back up to survey it from a distance.*)

FANNY. You know those Renoir café scenes? . . .

GARDNER. She doesn't lay on the paint with a trowel; it's
just touches here and there. . . .

MAGS. They *like* it! . . .

FANNY. You know the one with the couple dancing? . . .
Not that we're dancing. There's just something similar in
the mood . . . a kind of gaiety, almost. . . . The man has
his back to you and he's swinging the woman
around. . . . OH, GAR, YOU'VE SEEN IT A MILLION
TIMES! IT'S HANGING IN THE MUSEUM OF FINE
ARTS! . . . They're dancing like this. . . .

(*She goes up to him and puts an arm on his shoulders.*)

MAGS. They like it. . . . They like it!

FANNY. She's got on this wonderful flowered dress with
ruffles at the neck and he's holding her like this. . . .
That's right . . . and she's got the most rhapsodic expression on her face. . . .

GARDNER (*getting into the spirit of it; takes* FANNY *in his
arms and slowly begins to dance around the room*). Oh,
yes . . . I know the one you mean. . . . They're in a sort
of haze . . . and isn't there a little band playing off to
one side? . . .

FANNY. Yes, that's it!

(*Kitty's horn honks outside.*)

MAGS (*is the only one who hears it*). There's Kitty! (*She is
torn and keeps looking towards the door, but finally gives
in to their stolen moment.*)

FANNY. . . . and there's a man in a dark suit playing the
violin and someone's conducting, I think . . . And aren't
Japanese lanterns strung up? . . .

(*They pick up speed, dipping and whirling around the
room. Strains of a far-away Chopin waltz are heard.*)

GARDNER. Oh, yes! There are all these little lights twinkling in the trees. . . .

FANNY. . . . and doesn't the woman have a hat on? . . .
a big red hat? . . .

GARDNER. . . . and lights all over the dancers, too.
Everything shimmers with this marvelous glow. Yes, yes
. . . I can see it perfectly! The whole thing is absolutely
extraordinary!

(*The lights become dreamy and dappled as they dance
around the room.* MAGS *watches them, moved to tears
as . . .*)

SLOWLY THE CURTAIN FALLS

FOCUS QUESTIONS

1. How do the differences between generations affect both the action and outcome of the play?
2. Develop a character sketch of Mags, paying close attention to her artistic expectations, first as a young adolescent, then as an adult.
3. Discuss the nature of Mags' physical and emotional cravings and show how they enlighten the play.
4. Show how setting, characterization, and language convey the important dimension of unreality.
5. Evaluate the comic elements in the play.
6. Describe the Fanny/Mags relationship with specific reference to dialogue and action.
7. In what specific ways does *Painting Churches* reflect a feminist aesthetic?
8. Howe once admitted that her play demanded three ''conversationalists.'' What does the playwright mean?

OTHER ACTIVITIES

1. Using your own designs as well as photos you have researched, suggest approaches to costuming the play.
2. Acquainting yourself with the original script, write a review of the movie version (*The Portrait*).

BIBLIOGRAPHY

Barlow, Judith E. ''An Interview with Tina Howe.'' *Studies in American Drama, 1945– Present* 4 (1989): 159–75.

———. ''The Art of Tina Howe.'' In *Feminine Focus,* edited by Enoch Brater. New York: Oxford University Press, 1989.

Betsko, Kathleen, and Rachel Koenig, eds. *Interviews with Contemporary Women Playwrights.* New York: Beech Tree/Morrow, 1987.

Brenson, Michael. ''Art Given a Role in Tina Howe's Play.'' *The New York Times,* 18 Feb. 1983, C3.

Brown, Janet. *Feminist Drama: Definition and Critical Analysis.* Metuchen NJ: Scarecrow, 1979.

DiGaetani, John L. *A Search for a Postmodern Theater: Interviews with Contemporary Playwrights.* Westport, CT: Greenwood Press, 1991.

Gilbert, Sandra M., and Susan Gubar. *The Madwoman in the Attic: The Woman Writer and the Nineteenth-Century Literary Imagination.* New Haven: Yale University Press, 1979.

Hart, Lynda, ed. *Making a Spectacle: Feminist Essays on Contemporary Women's Theatre.* Ann Arbor: University of Michigan Press, 1989.

Lamonte, Rose. ''Tina Howe's Secret Surrealism: Walking a Tightrope.'' *Modern Drama* 36 (1993).

Leahy, Mimi. ''Tina Howe: Writing a Totally WASP Play.'' *Other Stages,* 27 Jan. 1983, p. 3.

Lieberman, Susan. ''Painting Churches.'' *Theatre Crafts* (May 1985): 18, 44.

Wetzsteon, Ross. ''The Mad, Mad World of Tina Howe.'' *New York,* 28 Nov. 1983.

RECOMMENDED VIDEOTAPE

The Portrait. VHS. 89 min. 1993. An adaptation of *Painting Churches* starring Lauren Bacall, Gregory Peck, and Cecilia Peck. Directed by Arthur Penn. Turner Home Entertainment.

THE CONDUCT OF LIFE
MARIA IRENE FORNES (1930–   )

People requiring or giving instruction is a standard situation in Fornes's plays . . . These are not cerebral exercises or puzzles but the real questions, about . . . the conduct of life. There is much wit but no nonsense. No banalities. And no *non sequiturs.*

—SUSAN SONTAG

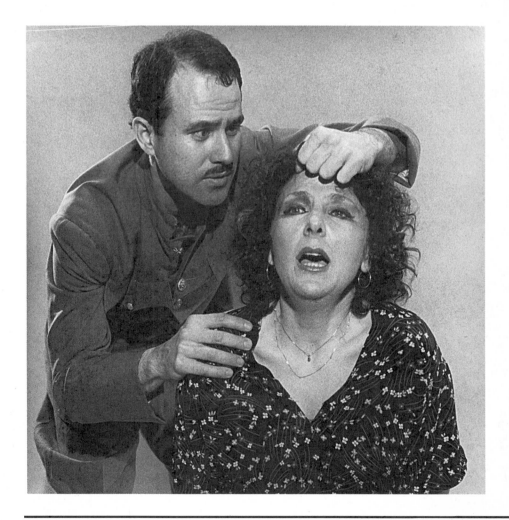

Pedro Garrido as Orlando and Crystal Field as Leticia in *The Conduct of Life,* presented by the Theater for the New City in 1985, under the playwright's direction. *Photo: © Martha Swope/ Photographer Carol Rosegg.*

APPROACHING EXPERIMENTAL THEATRE

Greenwich Village in New York City has been a gathering place for the avant-garde since the early decades of the twentieth century. Radical life-styles in response to Marxism, Freudian psychoanalysis, woman suffrage, and libertarianism permeated its narrow streets. This creative atmosphere generated by rebellion and experimentation during and after World War I nurtured such playwrights as Susan Glaspell, Rachel Crothers, e. e. cummings, and Eugene O'Neill whose plays were performed by theatre companies that dotted the district, most notably the Washington Square Players and Provincetown Players. (See Preface to O'Neill, p. 708.) When Kenneth Macgowan and Robert Edmond Jones championed European symbolists and expressionists in their newly founded *Theatre Arts Magazine,* the Greenwich Village theatre community rallied to their support throughout the 1920s.

Although the years of the Depression and World War II sent Village Bohemians under cover, a generation of beat poets emerged during the late 1940s, making lower Manhattan the center of artistic innovation once again. Artists of the Bauhaus School were teaching at the New School for Social Research on 12th Street, beat poets were reading their poems to jazzy drum accompaniment in the cafes along Macdougal and Bleecker Streets, and Abstract Expressionists were at home in the tenement studios of Little Italy. From the mid-1950s and into the 1960s, the Circle-in-the-Square, Greenwich Mews, and Cherry Lane Theatres produced the works of new American playwrights Adrienne Kennedy, Edward Albee, and LeRoi Jones (see Preface to Baraka, p. 878), as well as European absurdists like Fernando Arrabal, Eugene Ionesco, and Jean Genet. Thus the conventions of mainstream theatre continued to be challenged.

It was in the midst of this cauldron of creative activity, that Maria Irene Fornes found herself at the age of seventeen, two years after her family emigrated to New York from Havana, Cuba, in 1945. A high school dropout with very little formal training in English, she worked in an office by day before joining her Greenwich Village circles at night. She studied painting with Hans Hoffman and left for Paris where she spent three years as an artist. When she returned to New York in 1957, she worked as a textile designer.

In 1959, she shared an apartment with Susan Sontag and began writing. Her confidence grew under the nurturance and feedback of poet and novelist friends, although several kept insisting that her plays would never be taken seriously unless she studied the craft. Nevertheless, she was obsessed with an idea for a play and completed *Tango Palace* (1960) in nineteen days. Since then, Off-Off-Broadway theatres—specifically the Judson Poet's Theatre, The Open Theater, and Theater for the New City—have drawn wide audience response and critical appraisal for her unconventional dramas.

The self-taught Fornes developed her craft with little formal exposure to the theatre; she had read Ibsen's *Hedda Gabler* and recalls seeing Roger Blin's direction of Beckett's *Waiting for Godot* in Paris, as well as a production of *Endgame*. One evening she attended a performance of James Joyce's *Ulysses in Nighttown* in a tiny loft on West Houston Street in New York City. It was directed by Burgess Meredith and featured Zero Mostel as Leopold Bloom. Somehow this eclectic blend of dramatic styles inspired her to seize upon the powerful thematic premise of her playwriting: the human struggle to find ways to exist in the world.

Guided by trial and error, she invented writing games—like acting improvisations—to find "a kind of writing where the characters take over and they do what they do and you have nothing to do with it. All you do is write down what's happening."[1] Her unusual exploration of subtext, which was further influenced by her study of acting at the Actors Studio, led to the creation of autonomous characters and a unique mode of playwriting that drew part of its inspiration from **realism, symbolism, theatre of the absurd,** and **expressionism.** In spite of these discernible features, her work is not easily categorized.

Fornes' strong women characters have made feminists claim her as one of their own, although she has purposely eschewed any artistic agenda that classifies her work as political or feminist. Nevertheless, she does acknowledge writing from a personal universe, specifically from the aesthetic of a Hispanic woman whose characters speak of "their longing for enlightenment, and of their passions, or who make political or philosophical observations."[2] Her plays evolve through a unique creative consciousness in which her yearnings and passions, often buried, find their way to the surface and generate the characters in the play. Through them the text emerges.

Fornes has demonstrated her commitment to dramatic art by representing the rights of women and other Hispanic theatre artists. She helped to found the Women's Theatre Council and its antecedent, Theatre Strategy, an organization of women playwrights that sent experimental plays across America during the 1970s. She has implemented her own playwriting techniques for theatre labs at INTAR—specifically for Hispanic playwrights—led workshops, directed her own work, and inspired her fellow artists to investigate new approaches to writing and directing plays.

MAJOR WORKS

As playwright, director, teacher, translator, and adaptor of the work of other Hispanic playwrights, Fornes has been the recipient of six Obie Awards, the most important of which was bestowed in 1982 for Sustained Achievement in the Theatre. Her plays explore new directions but can be grouped stylistically as well as thematically. The early plays after *Tango Palace* are characterized by a formalized use of language and music, stage actions that mirror theatre games, and overt character types. These serio-comic works include *Promenade* (1965), a musical parable about political prisoners; *The Successful Life of 3* (1965), an exploration of the routines of behavior in a romantic triangle; *Vietnamese Wedding* (1967), a ceremony hosted by the characters and enacted by the audience; *Dr. Kheal* (1968), a classroom lecture; and *Molly's Dream* (1968), a musical presentation of a waitress' fantasies.

After a fallow period, Fornes continued her search for new theatrical forms, focusing this time on the darker and more secretive side of human behavior. *Fefu and Her Friends* (1977) was the first of several plays that centered around women who articulate their feelings. It was followed by *Evelyn Brown* (1980), *Mud* (1983), *Sarita* (1984), and *Abington Square* (1988), all of which dealt with the emotional reactions of women who are alienated through gender, race, or social class but, at the same time, must grapple with the dynamics of acquiring knowledge and power through their relationships with men.

Venturing beyond these women-centered plays, Fornes has explored the theme of disenfranchisement through characters who survive the threats of nuclear annihilation, military dictatorship, and ethnic cleansing. Her powerful treatments in *The Danube* (1983), a parable-love story set in an anti-nuclear context, and *Terra Incognito* (1992), an operatic work about the negative impact of imperialism, are exemplary. In one of her most controversial plays, *The Conduct of Life* (1985), Fornes intertwines the stories of three women around the vicissitudes of living under a totalitarian regime. The psychological exploration of their intense relationships amid political, social, and sexual domination both heightens and confirms the experimental aesthetic of this unique theatre artist.

THE ACTION

Orlando, an ambitious army lieutenant in an unnamed Latin American country, interrogates political prisoners. While brutalizing a homeless girl named Nena and making her his love slave, he ridicules his wife Leticia. In response to his neglect and her maid Olimpia's usurpation of her power in running her home, Leticia begins to educate herself. Eventually she takes a trip, making it feasible for Orlando to sneak Nena, who is ill, into the cellar of their house. Olimpia becomes the girl's protector, nursing her back to health and serving as her confidante. Returning home, Leticia is forced to tolerate her presence in the household.

As the three women form an empowering alliance, Orlando suffers under the watchful eyes of his military superiors and fears that his own tactics of torture will be turned against him. Lashing out at his wife because he suspects she is unfaithful, he interrogates her as he would one of his prisoners. Pushed to the brink by his violence, Leticia shoots him and places the revolver in Nena's hand.

STRUCTURE AND LANGUAGE

The Conduct of Life eludes the category of **well-made play,** despite its realistic environment populated with real characters. There is no explanation of character behaviors, no exposition to its rising actions and climax, and no denouement. The play ends abruptly with no clear sense of why its actions have transpired or what will become of its characters. Instead Fornes concentrates on the subjectivity of her characters and how each uses language to negotiate with the world. Relying on her own Hispanic sensibility to guide the play, she claims that "it is a very Spanish thing. We don't do our thinking reading, we do our thinking talking."[3] Similarly, Fornes' characters come to an understanding of how to conduct their lives by articulating their ambitions and fears.

In fleshing out characters whose strong visual presence is underscored by their simple yet unhalting disclosure of thoughts, Fornes uses her own sensations and experiences. Like an acting exercise, she asks subtextual questions: "What does the character want to say? What is the reality of what's happened? What is the need? What is it inside him that can be said to depict him?"[4] In approaching the creation of Orlando, for example, she needed to imagine the interior life of a sadist. Since she found none of these instincts within herself, Orlando's dialogue does not reflect his inner thoughts. Instead he uses language to rationalize, deceive himself, or take control of those around him.

In the play, when his boyhood friend Alejo reminds him that he once tortured Felo when they were young, Orlando denies the charge by exclaiming, "Boys play that way." This lack of self-understanding also distorts his perception of how he treated a prisoner who died during a recent interrogation. He laments that "things are bad and they are not going to improve. There is something malignant in the world. Destructiveness, aggressiveness. —Greed. People take what is not theirs." Incapable of seeing that he is describing himself, he places the blame on others, including his victims: "I didn't even touch this one and he died. He died of fear." Even when Nena recoils from him, he exclaims, "What I do to you is out of love. Out of want. It is a quiet feeling. It's a pleasure." Intending to calm her, he deludes himself instead.

In contrast to her portrait of Orlando, Fornes relies on her own interior life to shape the dialogue of her three women and shed light on their mutual struggle to establish identities in a patriarchy. Lacking sophistication as well as the skills to assert themselves in real society, they resort to simple and unschooled language to explain or combat their subjugation at the hands of Orlando and their world. Language allows them to talk their way to empowerment despite certain impediments. Olimpia is doubly handicapped by her servant-class status and a real speech defect, but learns how to use her coarse manner and unpleasant voice as a weapon. Thus Leticia has little choice but to give in to Olimpia's domestic demands, while Orlando's sharp reprimands collapse against her clever habit of spitting them back with equal force.

On the other hand, Nena is rendered nearly mute when Orlando takes control of her body. Her youth and naiveté have not prepared her for his conduct. Under Olimpia's motherly protection, however, the voice of this once frightened girl, struggling "to speak words as she whimpers,'' acquires the power to articulate dreams. When Nena fantasizes about her grandfather, she finally confronts the reality of Orlando's behavior and describes his brutality in detail. Although she blames herself at first, she has found a creed for conducting a new life: ''I should value the kindness that others bestow on me. And if someone should treat me unkindly, I should not blind myself with rage, but I should see them and receive them, since maybe they are in worse pain than me.'' Language helps Nena heal her emotional wounds and regain control of her life.

Leticia's predicament is the most complex of all, for her status as an uneducated woman is in conflict with her longing to acquire knowledge, to ''have others listen'' when she speaks, and to earn the respect of literate women. To compensate for this inadequacy, she develops a relationship with Mona, whose voice is never heard, but whose unseen presence gives Leticia an outlet for musing out loud until she has sorted through her destructive relationship with Orlando. Even when her conversation with Mona on the telephone is imaginary, Leticia can hear her own thoughts and draw her own conclusions. When she suspects that Orlando is keeping a woman in their home and admits that ''there's nothing I can do,'' she finally finds the courage to go to the cellar and investigate for herself. This internalized use of language has brought painful answers to difficult questions and a way to survive victimization.

The stark environment of the play emerges from these sharply drawn characters. Fornes has explained that there is a moment ''when the characters become crystallized, When that happens, I have an image in full color, technicolor . . . At some point I see a picture of the set with the characters in it.''[5] For this particular play, she has envisioned four horizontal planes whose structuring of the dramatic action becomes emblematic of life in a Latin-American military dictatorship. The two downstage planes, both living and dining-room areas, are the public places of the household, where the sparring matches between Orlando and Leticia as well as Olimpia's assertive demeanor achieve resonance. These planes also convey a social acceptability until the final scene, when they house the unspeakable.

Masking the truth about both household and society, these spaces serve as windows to the secretive, upstage planes on which the play's darker actions transpire. While Nena is initially terrorized in a nameless warehouse, she is eventually brought to Orlando's cellar situated on the other upstage plane. When Alejo announces the pending investigation of the death of Orlando's political prisoner, he enters this same cellar, now transformed into the site of Orlando's waning power, where the feared Orlando has become ''like an alligator, big mouth and no brains. Lots of teeth but no brains. All tongue.'' His brutal actions have been reduced to empty threats and self-deceptive rationalizations in a room where Alejo silently meddles in his affairs and Olimpia usurps his control over Nena. When Leticia has discovered Orlando's perverse love for the twelve-year-old Nena and his craving to torture the child, the stage action comes forward and remains on the downstage planes. It is here that Orlando's sadistic nature, his goal ''to achieve maximum power,'' and his role as pawn in a dictatorship merge and are exposed in a less darkly lit atmosphere, the consequences of which prompt his disintegration.

Orlando's demise and Leticia's enlightenment and release from his power are developed through a series of artistic strokes. Fornes asserts, ''The play is there as a lesson . . . You go to a museum to look at a painting and that painting teaches you something . . . a charge of some understanding, some knowledge that you have in your heart.''[6] Each of the play's nineteen short scenes captures a single dramatic moment in the lives of the characters, letting the audience piece together the moral tale unfolding before them. These visualized distillations of feelings from characters victimized by the social and political strictures imposed on them are sharpened by being held up for public scrutiny. But in this final distillation—when Orlando's interrogation of Leticia suddenly turns to physical torture and she ''goes to the telephone table, opens the drawer, takes a gun and shoots [him]''—Fornes forces the audience to feel compassion, but without offering any clear ideological paradigm. When the quietly imploring Leticia transfers the weapon into Nena's hands, Nena's terrified yet ''numb acceptance'' invites us to supply a conclusion from the knowledge within our own hearts. In a telephone interview on July 7, 1994, Fornes volunteered an alternate stage direction toward the end of the final scene: ''Leticia is disconcerted, then puts the revolver in Nena's hand, begging her to take responsibility for the shooting of Orlando.''

THE CONDUCT OF LIFE-IN-PERFORMANCE

Emerging from an earlier work entitled *No Time,* which was developed at the Padua Hills Theatre Festival during the summer of 1984, the script for *The Conduct of Life* evolved through an intense rehearsal process at Theater for the New City, where it premiered on February 21, 1985. Under Fornes' direction, Crystal Field (Leticia), Sheila Dabney (Nena), Alba Oms (Olimpia), Pedro Garrida (Orlando), and Hermann Lademann (Alejo) explored the playwright's tangled web of connections between ''dictatorship in the bedroom and in the country'' to sold out houses.[7] Several critics were bewildered by the play's style, particularly Fornes' use of brief **gestic** scenes separated by blackouts, ''much like dots with gaping spaces between them,'' which left the play open to private interpretation.[8]

But audiences were fascinated by the cumulative impact of images of subjugation and sadism, all of which gave the play a timeliness and feminist edge. Championing both playwright and play, Erika Munk offered a succinct rationale as to why *The Conduct of Life* won the Obie Award for Best New Play of the 1984–1985 season:

> Irene Fornes is America's truest poet of the theater. With *The Conduct of Life,* she takes on a subject so close to the bones of our times you'd think it unapproachable: the home life of a Latin American army captain who is a professional torturer and a domestic sadist. Fornes' freedom from psychological, naturalistic, and didactic conventions lets her explore what happens to this man, his wife, his young mistress, his childhood pal, and his servant without exploiting subject or audience. The events are as direct and mysterious as life, and as surprisingly funny. There's nothing goody-goody or hectoring about this most ethical play, and despite its surface simplicity I am still, 10 days after seeing it, finding new possibilities in the web of class, sex, and character she has woven.[9]

Fornes herself discovered new insights during the play's successful run at Theater for the New City and expanded Orlando's dialogue about his sadism for the published version.

Contrary to her usual custom, Fornes did not oversee the second production of the play, which was presented by the Organic Theater Company in Chicago on February 15, 1988, under Thomas Ricco's direction. The play was offered in repertory with an earlier work, *The Danube,* and the playwright inaugurated the special occasion by lecturing on her work and conducting a playwriting workshop for the company.

In October 1988, the play was presented by Union 212 at the Gate, a sixty-seat playhouse in the attic of a London pub in Notting Hill. Critics reacted in the same troubled way their American colleagues had, but were quick to acknowledge the play's undeniable power. Recommending the play to his readers, despite the acknowledgment of its grim subject matter, Andy Lavender wrote:

> There is no attempt at weedy psychoanalysis; no wasted rhetoric; no vague, well-meaning gestures . . . the facts of this particular domestic arrangement are laid out, stark and brutal—with the accompanying echoes of fear and gratuitous violence. The cast keep the screws turned, and the only real problem with Francesca Joseph's production is with the pacing . . . Otherwise her pitch at slightly stylized, disjointed realism hits the mark.[10]

Norma West (Leticia), Annabelle Lanyon (Nena), Joan Heal (Olimpia), Richard Lintern (Orlando), and Sean Fogarty (Alejo) sustained their chilling stage turns during the play's four-week engagement.

The Conduct of Life is one of Fornes' most popular plays, having been produced at the Pacific Theatre in Los Angeles (1988); the Rights of Reason Theatre in Providence, Rhode Island (1990); the Boston Playwrights Theatre (1992); and the Seven Stages Theatre in Atlanta, Georgia (1993).

REFLECTIONS ON THE CONDUCT OF LIFE

*Crystal Field is artistic director of Theater for the New City where
she created the role of Leticia.*

I had a leading role in *Promenade,* a musical performed at the Judson Memorial Church for which Irene wrote the book and lyrics. She not only wrote the lyrics *for* us, but *on* us. She actually interviewed me about my ideas on life and art and then wrote "The Cigarette Song," which became very famous. But the way she approached me for that song left an indelible impression. That's how I first met Irene.

As it happened, her way in the world was very much my way in the world. I eventually founded Theater for the New City with George Bartenieff around the same time Irene and several other writers founded Theatre Strategy. Her theatre had similar ideas and feelings to ours. So it wasn't hard for me to fall in love with her because she and I were kindred spirits. I also played in *Molly's Dream* at the New Dramatists, so I had a long relationship with her before Theater for the New City began. It simply continued.

As the years went by, I believe she did six plays for us, each one very different from the next, but all of them very much concerned with the position of women, all very romantic yet minimalist. I mean it's hard to be a romantic minimalist with a socio-political underpinning, but that's what I think Irene is. She can write about women better than any writer I've ever read. She's a true poet and hard to pin down. It's the kind of theatre we like to do as often as possible. That's what we have in common.

I'd been badgering Irene to write me a part. This is after six plays. But the more you ask Irene for something, the less likely you are to get it. She's a very independent "I"—and that's "E-Y-E" and "I" both. You've got to leave her alone. Our philosophy at Theater for the New City is to leave the artist alone. There's no censorship whatsoever. Once we commission a writer, the writer is king or queen here. If the writer wishes to fire the director, so be it. If the director wants the writer out of rehearsals, it's too bad. The writer has to be there. Whatever the writer wants, the writer gets. The writer has full range.

It took a year before *The Conduct of Life* arrived. I thought it was her best play. Of course, that doesn't mean that the others were not "as good"—in quotes. I just think there were certain things that seemed to gel completely in it. It was very serious, very dense. It had at least one humorous scene between my character and the maid, but generally speaking, it was a very serious play.

Continued

It didn't take long to put on. We had maybe four to six weeks of rehearsal. She not only wrote the play with me in mind, but had designed the program cover with my character on it. She picked my costume even unto the shoes. She gave me high heels for the part, but not the kind of high heels I would have really liked to wear to be the sexiest and most beautiful. They were thicker high heels but absolutely right for the character. So she really designed the character of Leticia for me.

The actress chosen for Nena—Sheila Dabney—was a very emotional person. She would often break down and we'd take her in our arms and hold her because of the emotional impact of the part. She was in her twenties but could play a younger age. The actress playing Olimpia did not have the same emotional relationship to the play. She was a servant and somewhat out of it. But I eventually shoot my husband. I'm used to playing deep emotional texts so it doesn't bother me. I'd say that in any part as emotional as Leticia was for me, at a certain point in rehearsals you walk a fine line between sanity and insanity.

But I come from a long line of mystics and we're used to swimming in that area. A character like Leticia is always difficult, but if you have done roles like this, you are not afraid of certain moments. They come about three-quarters of the way into the actual rehearsal where you are in this funny place. But I've been schooled in this sort of thing since childhood. You eventually come out of the other side of the character. Then the character lives in the play and you are no longer so important.

I like plays that have language. That used to be a prerequisite for what we called experimental drama which, of course, is no longer very experimental. The beauty of poetry and language has become watered down. The fact that Irene is a poet and that her words, although minimal, have tremendous ramifications and double and triple layers of meaning, was no problem for me either. You see, what's nice about not just being an actor but having a theatre or being part of the theatre is that it grounds you. Then the things that once seemed so incredibly exciting, enticing, and wild become very simply the world in which you navigate. Irene and I share that.

Irene just doesn't write plays in an ivory tower with no understanding of how they're ever going to get done. She's very practical when it comes to putting them on, so that a lot of things that go into making a really good play are not so bizarre. She doesn't have to reach very far either. That's the way really good stuff happens, when it doesn't become such a prize to have it. Irene has a great deal to do with every aspect of the production. There are directors who will hire a composer and say, "Help me out." But she doesn't do that. She says, "This is what I want." That's the way Irene is. She knows exactly what she wants completely from the beginning to the end of a production.

But then nothing is *found* with Irene. She has it all. I don't know when she goes through her own creative process, but she has it all decided before rehearsals begin. She also directs second to second. She worked with me on my character not just to create a reality. I had to have both humorous and tragic moments which were all laid out beforehand by Irene. Even the set was designed in her head way before it was built on our stage. Those physical planes were always there and we were only asked to be in the service of her vision, which we were very happy to do.

Now the gentleman playing Orlando wasn't so happy. That's because he was very new and very green. But he ended up being quite effective in his role, although he had to struggle. Whereas Sheila and I had no struggle because we knew Irene. In fact, Sheila had worked with Irene in capacities other than as an actress. She often assisted as stage manager to Irene's work. We had both developed great trust in her from previous pragmatic experience. Other people did not, which presented problems since Irene's got definite ideas before you approach the scene.

By the same token, one runs the risk of misinterpreting Irene's work by making it all too clear. My character lived with the fact that her husband kept this young girl locked up under their roof and was tormenting her and making love to her. So she finally takes her own lover to have some love in her life, for which her husband attacks her physically as well as emotionally. She kills him partially in self-defense. But in the final image, when Leticia passes the gun to Nena, perhaps she is telling Nena that we are women and must do something about our lives. We have to free ourselves from slavery. Nena had it literally, and I had it figuratively—through marriage.

The fact still remains that, no matter how tyrannical her husband was, he was a prey to his own time and to the position he had to take in the world. He was a torturer. That was his job. He was an interrogator under the suspicion of his superiors, and the play explores what happens to him emotionally. In a way Irene was as concerned with Orlando as she was with the women. In rehearsal she often spoke about Orlando's position and the effect of his work, how it filtered down to what he wanted to do, that men like Orlando were not their own masters, but were the flunkies for higher masters. He comes off as a villain, but not a complete one. He's a product of his time, his country, his society. There was a lot going on in Latin America that still goes on. Although it is never clear what country this is, the mentality of the authoritarian situation is ever-present. Yet we can't call her a political writer who writes against authoritarian governments. It's never as simple as any of these things with Irene.

Notes

1. David Savran, IN THEIR OWN WORDS: CONTEMPORARY AMERICAN PLAYWRIGHTS *(New York: Theatre Communications Group, 1988), 58.*
2. *Irene Fornes,* "Creative Danger," AMERICAN THEATRE *11, no. 5 (September 1985): 15.*
3. *Interview with Stephanie Harrington,* "Irene Fornes, Playwright: Alice and the Red Queen," VILLAGE VOICE, *21 April 1966.*
4. *Savran, 64.*
5. *Fornes,* "I Write the Messages that Come," DRAMA REVIEW *21, no. 4 (December 1977): 27.*
6. *Savran, 56.*
7. *Herbert Mitgang,* THE NEW YORK TIMES, *20 March 1985.*
8. *Sy Syna,* NEW YORK CITY TRIBUNE, *21 March 1985.*
9. VILLAGE VOICE, *26 March 1985.*
10. CITY LIMITS, *20 Oct. 1988.*

THE CONDUCT OF LIFE
Maria Irene Fornes

CHARACTERS

Orlando, *an army lieutenant at the start of the play. A lieutenant commander soon after*

Leticia, *his wife, ten years his elder*
Alejo, *a lieutenant commander. Their friend*

Nena, *a destitute girl of twelve*
Olimpia, *a servant*

A Latin American country. The present.

The floor is divided in four horizontal planes. Downstage is the livingroom, which is about ten feet deep. Center stage, eighteen inches high, is the diningroom, which is about ten feet deep. Further upstage, eighteen inches high, is a hallway which is about four feet deep. At each end of the hallway there is a door. The one to the right leads to the servants' quarters, the one to the left to the basement. Upstage, three feet lower than the hallway (same level as the livingroom), is the cellar, which is about sixteen feet deep. Most of the cellar is occupied by two platforms which are eight feet wide, eight feet deep, and three feet high. Upstage of the cellar are steps that lead up. Approximately ten feet above the cellar is another level, extending from the extreme left to the extreme right, which represents a warehouse. There is a door on the left of the warehouse. On the left and the right of the livingroom there are archways that lead to hallways or antechambers, the floors of these hallways are the same level as the diningroom. On the left and the right of the diningroom there is a second set of archways that lead to hallways or antechambers, the floors of which are the same level as the hallways. All along the edge of each level there is a step that leads to the next level. All floors and steps are black marble. In the livingroom there are two chairs. One is to the left, next to a table with a telephone. The other is to the right. In the diningroom there are a large green marble table and three chairs. On the cellar floor there is a mattress to the right and a chair to the left. In the warehouse there is a table and a chair to the left, and a chair and some boxes and crates to the right.

SCENE ONE

Orlando is doing jumping-jacks in the upper left corner of the diningroom in the dark. A light, slowly, comes up on him. He wears military breeches held by suspenders, and riding boots. He does jumping-jacks as long as it can be endured. He stops, the center area starts to become visible. There is a chair upstage of the table. There is a linen towel on the left side of the table. Orlando dries his face with the towel and sits as he puts the towel around his neck.

ORLANDO.   Thirty three and I'm still a lieutenant. In two years I'll receive a promotion or I'll leave the military. I promise I will not spend time feeling sorry for myself.— Instead I will study the situation and draw an effective plan of action. I must eliminate all obstacles.—I will make the acquaintance of people in high power. If I cannot achieve this on my own merit, I will marry a

woman in high circles. Leticia must not be an obstacle.—
Man must have an ideal, mine is to achieve maximum
power. That is my destiny.—No other interest will deter
me from this.—My sexual drive is detrimental to my
ideals. I must no longer be overwhelmed by sexual passion or I will be degraded beyond hope of recovery.
(*Lights fade to black.*)

Scene Two

*Alejo sits to the right of the diningroom table. Orlando
stands to Alejo's left. He is now a lieutenant commander. He
wears an army tunic, breeches, and boots. Leticia stands to
the left. She wears a dress that suggests 1940s fashion.*

LETICIA.   What! Me go hunting? Do you think I'm going
to shoot a deer, the most beautiful animal in the world?
Do you think I'm going to destroy a deer? On the contrary, I would run in the field and scream and wave my
arms like a mad woman and try to scare them away so the
hunters could not reach them. I'd run in front of the bullets and let the mad hunters kill me—stand in the way of
the bullets—stop the bullets with my body. I don't see
how anyone can shoot a deer.

ORLANDO (*to Alejo*). Do you understand that? You, who are
her friend, can you understand that? You don't think that
is madness? She's mad. Tell her that—she'll think it's
you who's mad. (*To Leticia.*) Hunting is a sport! A skill!
Don't talk about something you know nothing about.
Must you have an opinion about every damn thing! Can't
you keep your mouth shut when you don't know what
you're talking about? (*Orlando exits right.*)

LETICIA.   He told me that he didn't love me, and that his
sole relationship to me was simply a marital one. What
he means is that I am to keep this house, and he is to
provide for it. That's what he said. That explains why he
treats me the way he treats me. I never understood why
he did, but now it's clear. He doesn't love me. I thought
he loved me and that he stayed with me because he loved
me and that's why I didn't understand his behavior. But
now I know, because he told me that he sees me as a
person who runs the house. I never understood that because I would have never—if he had said, "Would you
marry me to run my house even if I don't love you." I
would have never—I would have never believed what I
was hearing. I would have never believed that these words
were coming out of his mouth. Because I loved him. (*Orlando has entered. Leticia sees him and exits left. Orlando
enters and sits center.*)

ORLANDO.   I didn't say any of that. I told her that she's
not my heir. That's what I said. I told her that she's not
in my will, and she will not receive a penny of my money
if I die. That's what I said. I didn't say anything about
running the house. I said she will not inherit a penny from

me because I didn't want to be humiliated. She is capable
of foolishness beyond anyone's imagination. Ask her
what she would do if she were rich and could do anything
she wants with her money. (*Leticia enters.*)

LETICIA.   I would distribute it among the poor.

ORLANDO.   She has no respect for money.

LETICIA.   That is not true. If I had money I would give it to
those who need it. I know what money is, what money
can do. It can feed people, it can put a roof over their
heads. Money can do that. It can clothe them. What do
you know about money? What does it mean to you? What
do you do with money? Buy rifles? To shoot deer?

ORLANDO.   You're foolish!—You're foolish! You're a
foolish woman! (*Orlando exits. He speaks from offstage.*)
Foolish. . . . Foolish. . . .

LETICIA.   He has no respect for me. He is insensitive. He
doesn't listen. You cannot reach him. He is deaf. He is an
animal. Nothing touches him except sensuality. He responds to food, to the flesh. To music sometimes, if it is
romantic. To the moon. He is romantic but he is not aware
of what you are feeling. I can't change him.—I'll tell you
why I asked you to come. Because I want something from
you.—I want you to educate me. I want to study. I want
to study so I am not an ignorant person. I want to go to
the university. I want to be knowledgeable. I'm tired of
being ignored. I want to study political science. Is political science what diplomats study? Is that what it is? You
have to teach me elemental things because I never finished
grammar school. I would have to study a great deal. A
great deal so I could enter the university. I would have to
go through all the subjects. I would like to be a woman
who speaks in a group and have others listen.

ALEJO.   Why do you want to worry about any of that?
What's the use? Do you think you can change anything?
Do you think anyone can change anything?

LETICIA.   Why not? (*Pause.*) Do you think I'm crazy?—He
can't help it.—Do you think I'm crazy?—Because I love
him? (*He looks away from her. Lights fade to black.*)

Scene Three

*Orlando enters the warehouse holding Nena close to him.
She wears a gray over-large uniform. She is barefoot. She
resists him. She is tearful and frightened. She pulls away and
runs to the right wall. He follows her.*

ORLANDO (*softly*). You called me a snake.

NENA.   No, I didn't. (*He tries to reach her. She pushes his
hands away from her.*) I was kidding.—I swear I was
kidding.

(*He grabs her and pushes her against the wall. He pushes
his pelvis against her. He moves to the chair dragging her
with him. She crawls to the left, pushes the table aside and
stands behind it. He walks around the table. She goes under*

it. He grabs her foot and pulls her out toward the downstage side. He opens his fly and pushes his pelvis against her. Lights fade to black.)

SCENE FOUR

Olimpia is wiping crumbs off the diningroom table. She wears a plain gray uniform. Leticia sits to the left of the table facing front. She wears a dressing gown. She writes in a notebook. There is some silverware on the table. Olimpia has a speech defect.

LETICIA.   Let's do this.

OLIMPIA.   O.K. (*She continues wiping the table.*)

LETICIA (*still writing*). What are you doing?

OLIMPIA.   I'm doing what I always do.

LETICIA.   Let's do this.

OLIMPIA (*in a mumble*). As soon as I finish doing this. You can't just ask me to do what you want me to do, and interrupt what I'm doing. I don't stop from the time I wake up in the morning to the time I go to sleep. You can't interrupt me whenever you want, not if you want me to get to the end of my work. I wake up at 5:30. I wash. I put on my clothes and make my bed. I go to the kitchen. I get the milk and the bread from outside and I put them on the counter. I open the icebox. I put one bottle in and take the butter out. I leave the other bottle on the counter. I shut the refrigerator door. I take the pan that I use for water and put water in it. I know how much. I put the pan on the stove, light the stove, cover it. I take the top off the milk and pour it in the milk pan except for a little. (*Indicating with her finger.*) Like this. For the cat. I put the pan on the stove, light the stove. I put coffee in the thing. I know how much. I light the oven and put bread in it. I come here, get the tablecloth and I lay it on the table. I shout "Breakfast." I get the napkins. I take the cups, the saucers, and the silver out and set the table. I go to the kitchen. I put the tray on the counter, put the butter on the tray. The water and the milk are getting hot. I pick up the cat's dish. I wash it. I pour the milk I left in the bottle in the milk dish. I put it on the floor for the cat. I shout "Breakfast." The water boils. I pour it in the thing. When the milk boils I turn off the gas and cover the milk. I get the bread from the oven. I slice it down the middle and butter it. Then I cut it in pieces (*indicating*) this big. I set a piece aside for me. I put the rest of the bread in the bread dish and shout "Breakfast." I pour the coffee in the coffee pot and the milk in the milk pitcher, except I leave (*indicating*) this much for me. I put them on the tray and bring them here. If you're not in the diningroom I call again "Breakfast." I go to the kitchen, I fill the milk pan with water and let it soak. I pour my coffee, sit at the counter and eat my breakfast. I go upstairs to make your bed and clean your bathroom. I come down here to meet you and figure out what you want for lunch and dinner. And try to get you to think quickly so I can run to the market and get it bought before all the fresh stuff is bought up. Then, I start the day.

LETICIA.   So?

OLIMPIA.   So I need a steam pot.

LETICIA.   What is a steam pot?

OLIMPIA.   A pressure cooker.

LETICIA.   And you want a steam pot? Don't you have enough pots?

OLIMPIA.   No.

LETICIA.   Why do you want a steam pot?

OLIMPIA.   It cooks faster.

LETICIA.   How much is it?

OLIMPIA.   Expensive.

LETICIA.   How much?

OLIMPIA.   Twenty.

LETICIA.   Too expensive. (*Olimpia throws the silver on the floor. Leticia turns her eyes up to the ceiling.*) Why do you want one more pot?

OLIMPIA.   I don't have a steam pot.

LETICIA.   A pressure cooker.

OLIMPIA.   A pressure cooker.

LETICIA.   You have too many pots. (*Olimpia goes to the kitchen and returns with an aluminum pan. She shows it to Leticia.*)

OLIMPIA.   Look at this. (*Leticia looks at it.*)

LETICIA.   What? (*Olimpia hits the pan against the back of a chair, breaking off a piece of the bottom.*)

OLIMPIA.   It's no good.

LETICIA.   All right! (*She takes money from her pocket and gives it to Olimpia.*) Here. Buy it!—What are we having for lunch?

OLIMPIA.   Fish.

LETICIA.   I don't like fish.—What else?

OLIMPIA.   Boiled plantains.

LETICIA.   Make something I like.

OLIMPIA.   Avocados. (*Leticia gives a look of resentment to Olimpia.*)

LETICIA.   Why can't you make something I like?

OLIMPIA.   Avocados.

LETICIA.   Something that needs cooking.

OLIMPIA.   Bread pudding.

LETICIA.   And for dinner?

OLIMPIA.   Pot roast.

LETICIA.   What else?

OLIMPIA.   Rice.

LETICIA.   What else?

OLIMPIA.   Salad.

LETICIA.   What kind?

OLIMPIA.   Avocado.

LETICIA.   Again. (*Olimpia looks at Leticia.*)

OLIMPIA.   You like avocados.

LETICIA.   Not again.—Tomatoes. (*Olimpia mumbles.*) What's wrong with tomatoes besides that you don't like them? (*Olimpia mumbles.*) Get some. (*Olimpia mumbles.*) What does that mean? (*Olimpia doesn't answer.*) Buy tomatoes.—What else?

OLIMPIA.   That's all.

LETICIA.   We need a green.

OLIMPIA.   Watercress.

LETICIA.   What else?

OLIMPIA.   Nothing.

LETICIA.   For dessert.

OLIMPIA.   Bread pudding.

LETICIA.   Again.

OLIMPIA.   Why not?

LETICIA.   Make a flan.

OLIMPIA.   No flan.

LETICIA.   Why not?

OLIMPIA.   No good.

LETICIA.   Why no good!—Buy some fruit then.

OLIMPIA.   What kind?

LETICIA.   Pineapple. (*Olimpia shakes her head.*) Why not? (*Olimpia shakes her head.*) Mango.

OLIMPIA.   No mango.

LETICIA.   Buy some fruit! That's all. Don't forget bread. (*Leticia hands Olimpia some bills. Olimpia holds it and waits for more. Leticia hands her one more bill. Lights fade to black.*)

SCENE FIVE

The warehouse table is propped against the door. The chair on the left faces right. The door is pushed and the table falls to the floor. Orlando enters. He wears an undershirt with short sleeves, breeches with suspenders and boots. He looks around the room for Nena. Believing she has escaped, he becomes still and downcast. He turns to the door and stands there for a moment. He takes a few steps to the right and stands there for a moment staring fixedly. He hears a sound from behind the boxes, walks to them and takes a box off. Nena is there. Her head is covered with a blanket. He pulls the blanket off. Nena is motionless and staring into space. He looks at her for a while, then walks to the chair and sits facing right staring into space. A few moments pass. Lights fade to black.

SCENE SIX

Leticia speaks on the telephone to Mona.

LETICIA.   Since they moved him to the new department he's different. (*Brief pause.*) He's distracted. I don't know where he goes in his mind. He doesn't listen to me. He worries. When I talk to him he doesn't listen. He's thinking about the job. He says he worries. What is there to worry about? Do you think there is anything to worry about? (*Brief pause.*) What meeting? (*Brief pause.*) Oh, sure. When is it? (*Brief pause.*) At what time? What do you mean I knew? No one told me.—I don't remember. Would you pick me up? (*Brief pause.*) At one? Isn't one early? (*Brief pause.*) Orlando may still be home at one. Sometimes he's here a little longer than usual. After lunch he sits and smokes. Don't you think one thirty will give us enough time? (*Brief pause.*) No. I can't leave while he's smoking . . . I'd rather not. I'd rather wait till he leaves. (*Brief pause.*) . . . One thirty, then. Thank you, Mona. (*Brief pause.*) See you then. Bye. (*Leticia puts down the receiver and walks to stage right area. Orlando's voice is heard offstage left. He and Alejo enter halfway through the following speech.*)

ORLANDO.   He made loud sounds not high-pitched like a horse. He sounded like a whale, like a wounded whale. He was pouring liquid from everywhere, his mouth, his nose, his eyes. He was not a horse but a sexual organ.—Helpless. A viscera.—Screaming. Making strange sounds. He collapsed on top of her. She wanted him off but he collapsed on top of her and stayed there on top of her. Like gum. He looked more like a whale than a horse. A seal. His muscles were soft. What does it feel like to be without shape like that. Without pride. She was indifferent. He stayed there for a while and then lifted himself off her and to the ground. (*Pause.*) He looked like a horse again.

LETICIA.   Alejo, how are you? (*Alejo kisses Leticia's hand.*)

ORLANDO (*as he walks to the livingroom. He sits left facing front*). Alejo is staying for dinner.

LETICIA.   Would you like some coffee?

ALEJO.   Yes, thank you.

LETICIA.   Would you like some coffee, Orlando?

ORLANDO.   Yes, thank you.

LETICIA (*in a loud voice towards the kitchen*). Olimpia . . .

OLIMPIA.   What?

LETICIA.   Coffee . . . (*Leticia sits to the right of the table. Alejo sits center.*)

ALEJO.   Have you heard?

LETICIA.   Yes, he's dead and I'm glad he's dead. An evil man. I knew he'd be killed. Who killed him?

ALEJO.   Someone who knew him.

LETICIA.   What is there to gain? So he's murdered. Someone else will do the job. Nothing will change. To destroy them all is to say we destroy us all.

ALEJO.   Do you think we're all rotten?

LETICIA.   Yes.

ORLANDO.   A bad germ?

LETICIA.   Yes.

ORLANDO.   In our hearts?

LETICIA.   Yes.—In our eyes.

ORLANDO.   You're silly.

LETICIA.   We're blind. We can't see beyond an arm's reach. We don't believe our life will last beyond the day. We only know what we have in our hand to put in our mouth, to put in our stomach, and to put in our pocket. We take care of our pocket, but not of our country. We take care of our stomachs but not of our hungry. We are primitive. We don't believe in the future. Each night when the sun goes down we think that's the end of life—so we have one last fling. We don't think we have a future. We don't think we have a country. Ask anybody, "Do you have a country?" They'll say, "Yes." Ask them, "What is your country?" They'll say, "My bed, my dinner plate." But, things can change. They can. I have changed. You have changed. He has changed.

ALEJO.   Look at me. I used to be an idealist. Now I don't have any feeling for anything. I used to be strong, healthy, I looked at the future with hope.

LETICIA.   Now you don't?

ALEJO.   Now I don't. I know what viciousness is.

ORLANDO.   What is viciousness?

ALEJO.   You.

ORLANDO.   Me?

ALEJO.   The way you tortured Felo.

ORLANDO.   I never tortured Felo.

ALEJO.   You did.

ORLANDO.   Boys play that way. You did too.

ALEJO.   I didn't.

ORLANDO.   He was repulsive to us.

ALEJO.   I never hurt him.

ORLANDO.   Well, you never stopped me.

ALEJO.   I didn't know how to stop you. I didn't know anyone could behave the way you did. It frightened me. It changed me. I became hopeless. (*Orlando walks to the diningroom.*)

ORLANDO.   You were always hopeless. (*He exits. Olimpia enters carrying three demi-tasse coffees on a tray. She places them on the table and exits.*)

ALEJO.   I am sexually impotent. I have no feelings. Things pass through me which resemble feelings but I know they are not. I'm impotent.

LETICIA.   Nonsense.

ALEJO.   It's not nonsense. How can you say it's nonsense?—How can one live in a world that festers the way ours does and take any pleasure in life? (*Lights fade to black.*)

SCENE SEVEN

Nena and Orlando stand against the wall in the warehouse. She is fully dressed. He is barebreasted. He pushes his pelvis against her gently. His lips touch her face as he speaks. The words are inaudible to the audience. On the table there is a tin plate with food and a tin cup with milk.

ORLANDO.   Look this way. I'm going to do something to you. (*She makes a move away from him.*) Don't do that. Don't move away. (*As he slides his hand along her side.*) I just want to put my hand here like this. (*He puts his lips*

on hers softly and speaks at the same time.*) Don't hold your lips so tight. Make them soft. Let them loose. So I can do this. (*She whimpers.*) Don't cry. I won't hurt you. This is all I'm going to do to you. Just hold your lips soft. Be nice. Be a nice girl. (*He pushes against her and reaches an orgasm. He remains motionless for a moment, them steps away from her still leaning his hand on the wall.*) Go eat. I brought you food. (*She goes to the table. He sits on the floor and watches her eat. She eats voraciously. She looks at the milk.*) Drink it. It's milk. It's good for you. (*She drinks the milk, then continues eating. Lights fade to black.*)

SCENE EIGHT

Leticia stands left of the diningroom table. She speaks words she has memorized. Olimpia sits to the left of the table. She holds a book close to her eyes. Her head moves from left to right along the written words as she mumbles the sound of imaginary words. She continues doing this through the rest of the scene.

LETICIA.   The impact of war is felt particularly in the economic realm. The destruction of property, private as well as public may paralyze the country. Foreign investment is virtually . . . (*To Olimpia.*) Is that right? (*Pause.*) Is that right!

OLIMPIA.   Wait a moment. (*She continues mumbling and moving her head.*)

LETICIA.   What for? (*Pause.*) You can't read. (*Pause.*) You can't read!

OLIMPIA.   Wait a moment. (*She continues mumbling and moving her head.*)

LETICIA (*slapping the book off Olimpia's hand*). Why are you pretending you can read? (*Olimpia slaps Leticia's hands. They slap each other's hands. Lights fade to black.*)

SCENE NINE

Orlando sits in the livingroom. He smokes. He faces front and is thoughtful. Leticia and Olimpia are in the diningroom. Leticia wears a hat and jacket. She tries to put a leather strap through the loops of a suitcase. There is a smaller piece of luggage on the floor.

LETICIA.   This strap is too wide. It doesn't fit through the loop. (*Orlando doesn't reply.*) Is this the right strap? Is this the strap that came with this suitcase? Did the strap that came with the suitcase break? If so, where is it? And when did it break? Why doesn't this strap fit the suitcase and how did it get here? Did you buy this strap, Orlando?

ORLANDO.   I may have.

LETICIA.   It doesn't fit.

ORLANDO.   Hm.

LETICIA.   It doesn't fit through the loops.

ORLANDO.   Just strap it outside the loops. (*Leticia stands. Olimpia tries to put the strap through the loop.*)

LETICIA.   No. You're supposed to put it through the loops. That's what the loops are for. What happened to the other strap?

ORLANDO.   It broke.

LETICIA.   How?

ORLANDO.   I used it for something.

LETICIA.   What! (*He looks at her.*) You should have gotten me one that fit. What did you use it for?—Look at that.

ORLANDO.   Strap it outside the loops.

LETICIA.   That wouldn't look right.

ORLANDO (*going to look at the suitcase*). Why do you need the straps?

LETICIA.   Because they come with it.

ORLANDO.   You don't need them.

LETICIA.   And travel like this?

ORLANDO.   Use another suitcase.

LETICIA.   What other suitcase. I don't have another. (*Orlando looks at his watch.*)

ORLANDO.   You're going to miss your plane.

LETICIA.   I'm not going. I'm not traveling like this.

ORLANDO.   Go without it. I'll send it to you.

LETICIA.   You'll get new luggage, repack it, and send it to me?—All right. (*She starts to exit left.*) It's nice to travel light. (*Off stage.*) Do I have everything?—Come, Olimpia.

(*Olimpia follows with the suitcases. Orlando takes the larger suitcase from Olimpia. She exits. Orlando goes up the hallway and exits through the left door. A moment later he enters holding Nena close to him. She is pale, dishevelled and has black circles around her eyes. She has a high fever and is almost unconscious. Her dress is torn and soiled. She is barefoot. He carries a new cotton dress on his arm. He takes her to a chair in the livingroom. He takes off the soiled dress and puts the new dress on her over a soiled slip.*)

ORLANDO.   That's nice. You look nice. (*Leticia's voice is heard. He hurriedly takes Nena out the door, closes it, and leans on it.*)

LETICIA (*off stage*). It would take but a second. You run to the garage and get the little suitcase and I'll take out the things I need. (*Leticia and Olimpia enter left. Olimpia exits right.*) Hurry. Hurry. It would take but a second. (*Seeing Orlando.*) Orlando, I came back because I couldn't leave without anything at all. I came to get a few things because I have a smaller suitcase where I can take a few things. (*She puts the suitcase on the table, opens it and takes out the things she mentions.*) A pair of shoes . . . (*Olimpia enters right with a small suitcase.*)

OLYMPIA.   Here.

LETICIA.	OLYMPIA.
A nightgown,	A robe,
a robe,	a dress,
underwear,	a nightgown,
a dress,	underwear,
a sweater.	a sweater,
	a pair of shoes.

(*Leticia closes the large suitcase. Olimpia closes the smaller suitcase.*)

LETICIA (*starting to exit*). Goodbye.

OLIMPIA (*following Leticia*). Goodbye.

ORLANDO.   Goodbye. (*Lights fade to black.*)

SCENE TEN

Nena is curled on the extreme right of the mattress. Orlando sits on the mattress using Nena as a back support. Alejo sits on the chair. He holds a green paper on his hand. Olimpia sweeps the floor.

ORLANDO.   Tell them to check him. See if there's a scratch on him. There's not a scratch on that body. Why the fuss! Who was he and who's making a fuss? Why is he so important.

ALEJO.   He was in deep. He knew names.

ORLANDO.   I was never told that. But it wouldn't have mattered if they had because he died before I touched him.

ALEJO.   You have to go to headquarters. They want you there.

ORLANDO.   He came in screaming and he wouldn't stop. I had to wait for him to stop screaming before I could even pose a question to him. He wouldn't stop. I had put the poker to his neck to see if he would stop. Just to see if he would shut up. He just opened his eyes wide and started shaking and screamed even louder and fell over dead. Maybe he took something. I didn't do anything to him. If I didn't get anything from him it's because he died before I could get to him. He died of fear, not from anything I did to him. Tell them to do an autopsy. I'm telling you the truth. That's the truth. Why the fuss.

ALEJO (*starting to put the paper in his pocket*). I'll tell them what you said.

ORLANDO.   Let me see that. (*Alejo takes it to him. Orlando looks at it and puts it back in Alejo's hands.*) O.K. so it's a trap. So what side are you on? (*Pause. Alejo says nothing.*) So what do they want? (*Pause.*) Who's going to question me? That's funny. That's very funny. They want to question me. They want to punch my eyes out? I knew something was wrong because they were getting nervous. Antonio was getting nervous. I went to him and I asked him if something was wrong. He said, no, nothing was wrong. But I could tell something was wrong. He looked at Velez and Velez looked back at him. They are stupid. They want to conceal something from me and they look at each other right in front of me, as if I'm blind, as if I can't tell that they are worried about something. As if there's something happening right in front of my nose but I'm blind and I can't see it. (*He grabs the paper from Alejo's hand.*) You understand? (*He goes up the steps.*)

OLIMPIA.   Like an alligator, big mouth and no brains. Lots of teeth but no brains. All tongue. (*Orlando enters through the left hallway door, and sits at the diningroom table. Alejo enters a few moments later. He stands to the right.*)

ORLANDO.   What kind of way is this to treat me?—After what I've done for them?—Is this a way to treat me?—I'll come up . . . as soon as I can—I haven't been well.—O.K. I'll come up. I get depressed because things are bad and they are not going to improve. There's something malignant in the world. Destructiveness, aggressiveness.—Greed. People take what is not theirs. There is greed. I am depressed, disillusioned . . . with life . . . with work . . . family. I don't see hope. (*He sits. He speaks more to himself than to Alejo.*) Some people get a cut in a finger and die. Because their veins are right next to their skin. There are people who, if you punch them in their stomach the skin around the stomach bursts and the bowels fall out. Other people, you cut them open and you don't see any veins. You can't find their intestines. There are people who don't even bleed. There are people who bleed like pigs. There are people who have the nerves right on their skins. You touch them and they scream. They have their vital organs close to the surface. You hit them and they burst an organ. I didn't even touch this one and he died. He died of fear. (*Lights fade to black.*)

SCENE ELEVEN

Nena, Alejo and Olimpia sit cross-legged on the mattress in the basement. Nena sits right, Alejo center, Olimpia left. Nena and Olimpia play pattycake. Orlando enters. He goes close to them.

ORLANDO.   What are you doing?

OLIMPIA.   I'm playing with her.

ORLANDO (*to Alejo*). What are you doing here? (*Alejo looks at Orlando as a reply. Orlando speaks sarcastically.*) They're playing pattycake. (*He goes near Nena.*) So? (*Short pause. Nena giggles.*) Stop laughing! (*Nena is frightened. Olimpia holds her.*)

OLIMPIA.   Why do you have to spoil everything. We were having a good time.

ORLANDO.   Shut up! (*Nena whimpers.*) Stop whimpering. I can't stand your whimpering. I can't stand it. (*Timidly, she tries to speak words as she whimpers.*) Speak up. I can't hear you! She's crazy! Take her to the crazy house!

OLIMPIA.   She's not crazy! She's a baby!

ORLANDO.   She's not a baby! She's crazy! You think she's a baby? She's older than you think. How old do you think she is—Don't tell me that.

OLIMPIA.   She's sick. Don't you see she's sick? Let her cry! (*To Nena.*) Cry!

ORLANDO.   You drive me crazy too with your . . . (*He imitates her speech defect. She punches him repeatedly.*)

OLIMPIA.   You drive me crazy! (*He pushes her off.*) You drive me crazy! You are a bastard! One day I'm going to kill you when you're asleep! I'm going to open you up and cut your entrails and feed them to the snakes. (*She tries to strangle him.*) I'm going to tear your heart out and feed it to the dogs! I'm going to cut your head open and have the cats eat your brain! (*Reaching for his fly.*) I'm going to cut your peepee and hang it on a tree and feed it to the birds!

ORLANDO.   Get off me! I'm getting rid of you too! (*He starts to exit.*) I can't stand you!

OLIMPIA.   Oh, yeah! I'm getting rid of you.

ORLANDO.   I can't stand you!

OLIMPIA.   I can't stand you!

ORLANDO.   Meddler! (*To Alejo.*) I can't stand you either.

OLIMPIA (*going to the stairs*). Tell the boss! Tell her! She won't get rid of me! She'll get rid of you! What good are you! Tell her! (*She goes to Nena.*) Don't pay any attention to him. He's a coward.—You're pretty. (*Orlando enters through the hallway left door. He sits center at the diningroom table and leans his head on it. Leticia enters. He turns to look at her.*)

LETICIA.   You didn't send it. (*Lights fade to black.*)

SCENE TWELVE

Leticia sits next to the phone. She speaks to Mona in her mind.

LETICIA.   I walk through the house and I know where he's made love to her I think I hear his voice making love to her. Saying the same things he says to me, the same words.—(*There is a pause.*) There is someone here. He keeps someone here in the house. (*Pause.*) I don't dare look. (*Pause.*) No, there's nothing I can do. I can't do anything. (*She walks to the hallway. She hears footsteps. She moves rapidly to left and hides behind a pillar. Olimpia enters from right. She takes a few steps down the hallway. She carries a plate of food. She sees Leticia and stops. She takes a few steps in various directions, then stops.*)

OLIMPIA.   Here kitty, kitty. (*Leticia walks to Olimpia, looks closely at the plate, then up to Olimpia.*)

LETICIA.   What is it?

OLIMPIA.   Food.

LETICIA.   Who is it for? (*Olimpia turns her eyes away and doesn't answer. Leticia decides to go to the cellar door. She stops halfway there.*) Who is it?

OLIMPIA.   A cat. (*Leticia opens the cellar door.*)

LETICIA.   It's not a cat. I'm going down. (*She opens the door to the cellar and starts to go down.*) I want to see who is there.

ORLANDO (*offstage from the cellar*). What is it you want? (*Lights fade to black.*)

SCENE THIRTEEN

Orlando leans back on the chair in the basement. His legs are outstretched. His eyes are bloodshot and leery. His tunic is open. Nena is curled on the floor. Orlando speaks quietly. He is deeply absorbed.

ORLANDO.   What I do to you is out of love. Out of want. It's not what you think. I wish you didn't have to be hurt. I don't do it out of hatred. It is not out of rage. It is love. It is a quiet feeling. It's a pleasure. It is quiet and it pierces my insides in the most internal way. It is my most private self. And this I give to you.—Don't be afraid.—It is a desire to destroy and to see things destroyed and to see the inside of them.—It's my nature. I must hide this from others. But I don't feel remorse. I was born this way and I must have this.—I need love. I wish you did not feel hurt and recoil from me. (*Lights fade to black.*)

SCENE FOURTEEN

Orlando sits to the right and Leticia sits to the left of the table.

LETICIA.   Don't make her scream. (*There is a pause.*)
ORLANDO.   You're crazy.
LETICIA.   Don't I give you enough?
ORLANDO (*he's calm*). Don't start.
LETICIA.   How long is she going to be here?
ORLANDO.   Not long.
LETICIA.   Don't make her cry. (*He looks at her.*) I can't stand it. (*Pause.*) Why do you make her scream?
ORLANDO.   I don't make her scream.
LETICIA.   She screams.
ORLANDO.   I can't help it. (*Pause.*)
LETICIA.   I tell you I can't stand it. I'm going to ask Mona to come and stay with me.
ORLANDO.   No.
LETICIA.   I want someone here with me.
ORLANDO.   I don't want her here.
LETICIA.   Why not?
ORLANDO.   I don't.
LETICIA.   I need someone here with me.
ORLANDO.   Not now.
LETICIA.   When?
ORLANDO.   Soon enough.—She's going to stay here for a while. She's going to work for us. She'll be a servant here.
LETICIA.   . . . No.
ORLANDO.   She's going to be a servant here. (*Lights fade to black.*)

SCENE FIFTEEN

Olimpia and Nena are sitting at the diningroom table. They are separating stones and other matter from dry beans.

NENA.   I used to clean beans when I was in the home. And also string beans. I also pressed clothes. The days were long. Some girls did hand sewing. They spent the day doing that. I didn't like it. When I did that, the day was even longer and there were times when I couldn't move even if I tried. And they said I couldn't go there anymore, that I had to stay in the yard. I didn't mind sitting in the yard looking at the birds. I went to the laundryroom and watched the women work. They let me go in and sit there. And they showed me how to press. I like to press because my mind wanders and I find satisfaction. I can iron all day. I like the way the wrinkles come out and things look nice. It's a miracle isn't it? I could earn a living pressing clothes. And I could find my grandpa and take care of him.
OLIMPIA.   Where is your grandpa?
NENA.   I don't know. (*They work a little in silence.*) He sleeps in the streets. Because he's too old to remember where he lives. He needs a person to take care of him. And I can take care of him. But I don't know where he is.—He doesn't know where I am.—He doesn't know who he is. He's too old. He doesn't know anything about himself. He only knows how to beg. And he knows that, only because he's hungry. He walks around and begs for food. He forgets to go home. He lives in the camp for the homeless and he has his own box. It's not an ugly box like the others. It is a real box. I used to live there with him. He took me with him when my mother died till they took me to the home. It is a big box. It's big enough for two. I could sleep in the front where it's cold. And he could sleep in the back where it's warmer. And he could lean on me. The floor is hard for him because he's skinny and it's hard on his poor bones. He could sleep on top of me if that would make him feel comfortable. I wouldn't mind. Except that he may pee on me because he pees in his pants. He doesn't know not to. He is incontinent. He can't hold it. His box was a little smelly. But that doesn't matter because I could clean it. All I would need is some soap. I could get plenty of water from the public faucet. And I could borrow a brush. You know how clean I could get it? As clean as new. You know what I would do? I would make holes in the floor so the pee would go down to the ground. And you know what else I would do?
OLIMPIA.   What?
NENA.   I would get straw and put it on the floor for him and for me and it would make it comfortable and clean and warm. How do you like that? Just as I did for my goat.
OLIMPIA.   You have a goat?
NENA.   . . . I did.

OLIMPIA.   What happened to him?

NENA.   He died. They killed him and ate him. Just like they did Christ.

OLIMPIA.   Nobody ate Christ.

NENA.   . . . I thought they did. My goat was eaten though.—In the home we had clean sheets. But that doesn't help. You can't sleep on clean sheets, not if there isn't someone watching over you while you sleep. And since my ma died there just wasn't anyone watching over me. Except you.—Aren't you? In the home they said guardian angels watch your sleep, but I didn't see any there. There weren't any. One day I heard my grandpa calling me and I went to look for him. And I didn't find him. I got tired and I slept in the street, and I was hungry and I was crying. And then he came to me and he spoke to me very softly so as not to scare me and he said he would give me something to eat and he said he would help me look for my grandpa. And he put me in the back of his van . . . And he took me to a place. And he hurt me. I fought with him but I stopped fighting—because I couldn't fight anymore and he did things to me. And he locked me in. And sometimes he brought me food and sometimes he didn't. And he did things to me. And he beat me. And he hung me on the wall. And I got sick. And sometimes he brought me medicine. And then he said he had to take me somewhere. And he brought me here. And I am glad to be here because you are here. I only wish my grandpa were here too. He doesn't beat me so much anymore.

OLIMPIA.   Why does he beat you? I hear him at night. He goes down the steps and I hear you cry. Why does he beat you?

NENA.   Because I'm dirty.

OLIMPIA.   You are not dirty.

NENA.   I am. That's why he beats me. The dirt won't go away from inside me.—He comes downstairs when I'm sleeping and I hear him coming and it frightens me. And he takes the covers off me and I don't move because I'm frightened and because I feel cold and I think I'm going to die. And he puts his hand on me and he recites poetry. And he is almost naked. He wears a robe but he leaves it open and he feels himself as he recites. He touches himself and he touches his stomach and his breasts and his behind. He puts his fingers in my parts and he keeps reciting. Then he turns me on my stomach and puts himself inside me. And he says I belong to him. (*There is a pause.*) I want to conduct each day of my life in the best possible way. I should value the things I have. And I should value all those who are near me. And I should value the kindness that others bestow upon me. And if someone should treat me unkindly, I should not blind myself with rage, but I should see them and receive them, since maybe they are in worse pain than me. (*Lights fade to black.*)

SCENE SIXTEEN

Leticia speaks on the telephone with Mona. She speaks rapidly.

LETICIA.   He is violent. He has become more so. I sense it. I feel it in him.—I understand his thoughts. I know what he thinks.—I raised him. I practically did. He was a boy when I met him. I saw him grow. I was the first woman he loved. That's how young he was. I have to look after him, make sure he doesn't get into trouble. He's not wise. He's trusting. They are changing him.—He tortures people. I know he does. He tells me he doesn't but I know he does. I know it. How could I not. Sometimes he comes from headquarters and his hands are shaking. Why should he shake? What do they do there?—He should transfer. Why do that? He says he doesn't do it himself. That the officers don't do it. He says that people are not being tortured. That that is questionable.—Everybody knows it. How could he not know it when everybody knows it. Sometimes you see blood in the streets. Haven't you seen it? Why do they leave the bodies in the streets,—how evil, to frighten people? They tear their fingernails off and their poor hands are bloody and destroyed. And they mangle their genitals and expose them and they tear their eyes out and you can see the empty eyesockets in the skull. How awful, Mona. He mustn't do it. I don't care if I don't have anything! What's money! I don't need a house as big as this! He's doing it for money! What other reason could he have! What other reason could he have!! He shouldn't do it. I cannot look at him without thinking of it. He's doing it. I know he's doing it.—Shhhh! I hear steps. I'll call you later. Bye, Mona. I'll talk to you. (*She hangs up the receiver. Lights fade to black.*)

SCENE SEVENTEEN

The livingroom. Olimpia sits to the right, Nena to the left.

OLIMPIA.   I don't wear high heels because they hurt my feet. I used to have a pair but they hurt my feet and also (*pointing to her calf*) here in my legs. So I don't wear them anymore even if they were pretty. Did you ever wear high heels? (*Nena shakes her head.*) Do you have ingrown nails? (*Nena looks at her questioningly.*) Nails that grow twisted into the flesh. (*Nena shakes her head.*) I don't either. Do you have sugar in the blood? (*Nena shakes her head.*) My mother had sugar in the blood and that's what she died of but she lived to be eighty six which is very old even if she had many things wrong with her. She had glaucoma and high blood pressure. (*Leticia enters and sits center at the table. Nena starts to get up. Olimpia signals her to be still. Leticia is not concerned with them.*)

LETICIA.   So, what are you talking about?

OLIMPIA.   Ingrown nails. (*Nena turns to Leticia to make sure she may remain seated there. Leticia is involved with her own thoughts. Nena turns front. Lights fade to black.*)

SCENE EIGHTEEN

Orlando is sleeping on the diningroom table. The telephone rings. He speaks as someone having a nightmare.

ORLANDO.   Ah! Ah! Ah! Get off me! Get off! I said get off! (*Leticia enters.*)

LETICIA (*going to him*). Orlando! What's the matter! What are you doing here!

ORLANDO.   Get off me! Ah! Ah! Ah! Get off me!

LETICIA.   Why are you sleeping here! On the table. (*Holding him close to her.*) Wake up.

ORLANDO.   Let go of me. (*He slaps her hands as she tries to reach him.*) Get away from me. (*He goes to the floor on his knees and staggers to the telephone.*) Yes. Yes, it's me—You did?—So?—It's true then.—What's the name?—Yes, sure.—Thanks.—Sure. (*He hangs up the receiver. He turns to look at Leticia. Lights fade to black.*)

SCENE NINETEEN

Two chairs are placed side by side facing front in the center of the living room. Leticia sits on the right. Orlando stands on the down left corner. Nena sits to the left of the dining room table facing front. She covers her face. Olimpia stands behind her, holding Nena and leaning her head on her.

ORLANDO.   Talk.

LETICIA.   I can't talk like this.

ORLANDO.   Why not?

LETICIA.   In front of everyone.

ORLANDO.   Why not?

LETICIA.   It is personal. I don't need the whole world to know.

ORLANDO.   Why not?

LETICIA.   Because it's private. My life is private.

ORLANDO.   Are you ashamed?

LETICIA.   Yes, I am ashamed.

ORLANDO.   What of . . . ? What of . . . ?—I want you to tell us—about your lover.

LETICIA.   I don't have a lover. (*He grabs her by the hair. Olimpia holds on to Nena and hides her face. Nena covers her face.*)

ORLANDO.   You have a lover.

LETICIA.   That's a lie.

ORLANDO (*moving closer to her*). It's not a lie. (*To Leticia.*) Come on tell us. (*He pulls harder.*) What's his name? (*She emits a sound of pain. He pulls harder, leans toward her and speaks in a low tone.*) What's his name?

LETICIA.   Albertico. (*He takes a moment to release her.*)

ORLANDO.   Tell us about it. (*There is silence. He pulls her hair.*)

LETICIA.   All right. (*He releases her.*)

ORLANDO.   What's his name?

LETICIA.   Albertico.

ORLANDO.   Go on. (*Pause.*) Sit up! (*She does.*) Albertico what?

LETICIA.   Estevez. (*Orlando sits next to her.*)

ORLANDO.   Go on. (*Silence.*) Where did you first meet him?

LETICIA.   At . . . I . . .

ORLANDO (*he grabs her by the hair*). In my office.

LETICIA.   Yes.

ORLANDO.   Don't lie.—When?

LETICIA.   You know when.

ORLANDO.   When! (*Silence.*) How did you meet him?

LETICIA.   You introduced him to me. (*He lets her go.*)

ORLANDO.   What else? (*Silence.*) Who is he!

LETICIA.   He's a lieutenant.

ORLANDO (*he stands*). When did you meet with him?

LETICIA.   Last week.

ORLANDO.   When!

LETICIA.   Last week.

ORLANDO.   When!

LETICIA.   Last week. I said last week.

ORLANDO.   Where did you meet him?

LETICIA.   . . . In a house of rendez-vous . . .

ORLANDO.   How did you arrange it?

LETICIA.   . . . I wrote to him . . . !

ORLANDO.   Did he approach you?

LETICIA.   No.

ORLANDO.   Did he!

LETICIA.   No.

ORLANDO (*he grabs her hair again*). He did! How!

LETICIA.   *I* approached him.

ORLANDO.   How!

LETICIA (*aggressively*). I looked at him! I looked at him! I looked at him! (*He lets her go.*)

ORLANDO.   When did you look at him?

LETICIA.   Please stop . . . !

ORLANDO.   Where! When!

LETICIA.   In your office!

ORLANDO.   When?

LETICIA.   I asked him to meet me!

ORLANDO.   What did he say?

LETICIA (*aggressively*). He walked away. He walked away! He walked away! I asked him to meet me.

ORLANDO.   What was he like?

LETICIA.   . . . Oh . . .

ORLANDO.   Was he tender? Was he tender to you!

(*She doesn't answer. He puts his hand inside her blouse. She lets out an excruciating scream. He lets her go and walks to the right of the diningroom. She goes to the telephone table, opens the drawer, takes a gun and shoots Orlando. Orlando falls dead. Nena runs to downstage of the table. Leticia is disconcerted, then puts the revolver in Nena's hand and steps away from her.*)

LETICIA.   Please . . .

(*Nena is in a state of terror and numb acceptance. She looks at the gun. Then, up. The lights fade.*)

END

FOCUS QUESTIONS

1. Olimpia's character does not undergo a transformation. How does she serve as a foil to the other characters so that their underlying natures can be revealed?
2. Both Orlando and Leticia reveal their conflicting and irreconcilable attitudes about life early in the play. Analyze these differences and discuss their relationship in terms of the inherent conflict.
3. Both Leticia and Nena are victimized in this play. In a brief essay, compare and contrast the nature of this victimization.
4. Discuss how Orlando falls prey to self-deception and how this leads to his downfall.
5. Alejo is depressed about the world in which he lives and yet does nothing about it. Discuss in what ways his presence is important to the play's themes.
6. Fornes contends with the question of how to conduct one's life in a military dictatorship. Note the various options available to her characters and discuss how the staging places the audience in the position of passing judgment on each of these choices.
7. Discuss the significance of Nena's elevated status to servant in Orlando's household and how this affects the play's outcome.

OTHER ACTIVITIES

1. Create an interior monologue for either Alejo or Olimpia which reveals his or her attitudes about the interrelationships between Orlando, Leticia, and Nena.
2. Improvise either a scene in which Orlando interrogates a political prisoner or one in which he justifies his tactics to his superior officers.
3. Research the psychological effects of rape on victims in an effort to comprehend the trauma that Nena is experiencing as a poor, ignorant twelve-year-old.

BIBLIOGRAPHY

Betsko, Kathleen, and Rachel Koenig. *Interviews with Contemporary Women Playwrights.* New York: Beechtree/Morrow Press, 1987.

Brater, Enoch, ed. *Feminine Focus: The New Women Playwrights.* New York: Oxford University Press, 1989.

Brater, Enoch, and Ruby Cohn, eds. *Around the Absurd: Essays on Modern and Postmodern Drama.* Ann Arbor: University of Michigan Press, 1990.

Chinoy, Helen Krich, and Linda Walsh Jenkins, eds. *Women in American Theatre.* New York: Theatre Communications Group, 1987.

Dolan, Jill. *The Feminist Spectator as Critic.* Ann Arbor: UMI Research Press, 1988.

Geis, Deborah R. "Wordscapes of the Body: Performative Language as Gestus in Maria Irene Fornes's Plays." *Theatre Journal* 42, no. 3 (October 1990): 291–307.

Hart, Lynda, ed. *Making a Spectacle: Feminist Essays on Contemporary Women's Theatre.* Ann Arbor: University of Michigan Press, 1989.

Keyssar, Helene. *Feminist Theatre.* New York: Grove Press, 1985.

Marranca, Bonnie. "The Real Life of Maria Irene Fornes." *Performing Arts Journal* 8, no. 1 (1984): 29–34.

Merrill, Lisa. "Maria Irene Fornes: Woman of Many Hats Has Just One Vision." *The Villager,* 6 June 1985, p. 9.

Savran, David. *In Their Own Words: Contemporary American Playwrights.* New York: Theatre Communications Group, 1988.

LARGO DESOLATO
Václav Havel (1936–   )

With the liquidation of the Communist system in Czechoslovakia, Havel's plays may begin to be more fully appreciated as searching visions of contemporary humanity under the pressure of any technocratic system rather than topical studies of the deformation of human identity under Communism.

—Jarka Burian

F. Murray Abraham (*center*) as Leopold, surrounded by David Margulies as First Chap and John Seitz as Second Chap in the film version of *Largo Desolato*, directed by Jiri Zizka.
Photo: Courtesy of The Wilma Theater.

APPROACHING SOCIO-POLITICAL DRAMA

Drama dating from antiquity has provided playwrights with an arena for addressing social and political upheavals. More recently, the popularity of socio-political drama has been demonstrated in **epic theatre,** the *actos* of El Teatro Campesino, the Black Arts movement, and feminist theatre, which have all used theatre as a political tool to address social inequities. (See Prefaces to Brecht, p. 736; Baraka, p. 878; Childress, p. 895; and Valdez, p. 920.) Inspired by moral responsibility and the humanitarian function of their craft, many writers have felt empowered to catch the pulse, heartbeat, and conscience of their respective times. Some have actually documented, however fictitiously, their own courageous participation in the making of history, no matter that the surrounding events have been marred by turmoil and repression or that the writers themselves have been targeted as enemies of the state. These works of art have consequently required an assessment of their historical contexts in order to be fully appreciated.

At mid-twentieth century, in the aftermath of two catastrophic wars waged across Europe and Asia, the relationship between art and politics produced some sweeping consequences. In contrast with the first war, World War II had generated deeper wounds— both spiritual and psychological—by exposing the machinations of several powerful leaders-turned-madmen. While some artists reacted conservatively to the encroaching malaise, others honed their frustrations into powerful literary documents that led to the establishment of an absurdist tradition. (See Prefaces to Pinter, p. 822, and Beckett, p. 862.) For the adventurous, the stage would remain as good a place as any to disentangle the ensnaring web of power, drawing distinctions once and for all between writers in a democracy who wanted to awaken consciousness versus those in a totalitarian government whose literary creations were considered acts of treason.

The quest of this latter group proved unusually challenging in the light of basic human rights and freedoms that had been usurped along the way. Fewer political systems wielded more control than Communism, whose ruthless suppression of individual liberties emerged from the Soviet Union under Stalin's rule before infiltrating different points of the globe after World War II. Artists behind the Iron Curtain, who had been swept up by the revolutionary charge to experiment with new forms of expression in the 1920s, were later strangled by the official sanctioning of socialist realism as the only viable aesthetic. Although the theatrical activity of Soviet-dominated Eastern Europe managed to overcome these political constraints by the end of the 1950s, the results on stage often failed to reach audiences beyond Communist borders.

By the 1960s, the Czech Republic was one of the few Soviet satellites where theatre companies were flourishing and whose experiments in stagecraft and playwriting were gaining international attention. The most prominent of these innovative practitioners was Josef Svoboda, whose eclectic scenic designs for the Prague National Theatre brought him acclaim as well as invitations to design for theatre and opera companies around the world. For reasons both practical and economical, Svoboda's emphasis on multimedia and minimalist stage designs incorporated new postwar technology that transformed the art of scenography until "the three-dimensionality on which [Adolph] Appia and [Edward Gordon] Craig had insisted came to seem as outmoded as nineteenth-century painted drops had to those earlier reformers."[1] Most of all, Svoboda's success brought notoriety to the Czech stage.

While technical advancements proliferated, less mainstream approaches to producing drama were nurtured in more intimate theatre spaces like Theatre on the Balustrade, headed by Jan Grossman between 1962 and 1969. Earning its reputation through an international repertory and visits to Europe and America, the studio was important for introducing— albeit fortuitously—the work of a young resident playwright named Václav Havel, whose fate as an artist in a bureaucratic society would prove emblematic of renewed repression in his country. When Soviet troops invaded the Czech Republic on August 20, 1968, and replaced its increasingly liberal regime with one of the most oppressive in Eastern Europe, censorship gradually eroded the intellectual life of a country in which the theatre once played a vital role. Not surprisingly, the careers of Havel and Grossman were abruptly halted.

Fortunately Grossman had recognized Havel's talent and defended it against those critics who initially thought the playwright was ''too rationalistic and precise to fulfill current ideas of dramatic narrative and psychology.'' The early plays in question were *The Garden Party* (1963) and *The Memorandum* (1965), both of which expressed Havel's concern for the mechanization of humanity. While the theme was a popular one among European playwrights, it was for Havel the central subject ''from which his technique derives and on which it is focused. At the beginning of [both plays], the audience is not dazzled by dramatic skills which elaborate on the subject; instead, there is mechanization itself, experienced as well as mediated by a manner which is technical and theoretical rather than dramatic.''[2] The difference between the first play and the second reflected Havel's development from outspoken propagandist to a craftsman of unusual subtlety who had wisely learned how to hide behind his story and characters. Since Grossman fostered experimental theatre in so much of the work he produced at the Balustrade, Havel's absurdist style and political leanings found a receptive home there.

While a tradition of the absurd was not a formal part of the Czech theatre agenda in the 1960s, its resonances were definitely ''in the air,'' according to Havel: ''I have the feeling that, if absurd theatre had not existed before me, I would have had to invent it.''[3] In fact, his characters and incidents would bear an uncanny resemblance to his own life, whether he would actually experience the nightmarish world he foreshadowed in these works, or incorporate its unsavory psychological repercussions into his writings to show how its absurdist elements were a nihilistic warning of things to come. The most obvious recourse was to merge politics with art, a decision over which he had little control. ''The idea that a writer is the conscience of his nation has its own logic,'' he later confirmed. ''This tradition has continued under totalitarian conditions, where it gains its own special coloring: the written word seems to have acquired a kind of heightened radioactivity— otherwise they wouldn't lock us up for it!''[4] No doubt he spoke for countless other writers who were experiencing the fate of political imprisonment.

Ironically it was not Havel's dramatic writing—already withdrawn from school and local and other public libraries by the early 1970s—but his involvement in the human rights movement that led in 1977 to the first of several arrests and prison sentences he would serve over the next decade or so. When his demonstrations persisted, he was arrested in 1979 on a charge of subversion and sentenced, this time, to five years. ''Prison seems to me a totalitarianism's test tube for the future. It is an atmosphere aimed at systematically breaking down one's personality,'' he remarked several years later.[5] Not only did the repercussions of this second incarceration seriously affect his writing, but the event itself caught the attention of literary circles and human rights activists throughout the world.

Their protests were so strong, in fact, that Czechoslovak authorities released Havel in 1983 when it was publicly disclosed that he had contracted pneumonia. He eventually resumed both his writing and human rights activism, this time under heavy surveillance by police who were no longer secretive about their invasive presence. But on January 16, 1989, Havel was arrested again for political demonstrations and, one month later, sentenced to nine months in prison.

In the meantime, the political world was in flux as one Communist regime after another succumbed to democratization in 1989. Of critical significance was the opening of East German borders to the west, which gave fresh impetus to the opponents of the Czech regime, where Communist leaders soon found themselves deprived of the support that had once come from their East German allies. Eventually eleven nations experienced nonviolent revolutions. The Czech Republic stood proudly among them in what began as an anti-Communist march of 30,000 students on November 17, 1989, but rapidly escalated to a demonstration in Wenceslas Square numbering more than 200,000 citizens. Before long, demonstrations spread to other cities, gripping the entire country in strikes. When a new federal government with a non-Communist majority was formed in December, Václav Havel, by far the Czech Republic's best-known opposition figure, was elected president on December 29, 1989. The people had chosen a playwright to lead them.

MAJOR WORKS

In 1960, Havel worked for Theatre on the Balustrade as a stagehand, before serving as literary adviser. Eventually he collaborated on playscripts and contributed revue sketches to the company. His first independent and full-length work, *The Garden Party,* was produced in 1963 and introduced the central theme that would inform all of his subsequent stage writing: the corrosive effects of bureaucracy on human identity. Less mechanistic in its dehumanized, absurdist treatment of power, his next play, *The Memorandum* (1965), satirized the mindlessness of authoritarian domination. Havel's unique theatrical premise involved the invention of an artificial language, thought to be a political coup, that winds up baffling its users by remaining untranslatable. The play received its American premiere at the New York Shakespeare Festival in 1968 in a production overseen by Havel himself and won the prestigious Obie Award. Havel's third play to be produced at the Theatre on the Balustrade was *The Increased Difficulty of Concentration* (1968). The title alludes to a scientist whose life is disorganized by family strife and a whimsical computer. The work was given its American premiere in 1970 by the Lincoln Center Repertory Theatre and earned the playwright a second Obie.

Following a ban on his work in 1969, Havel wrote *The Conspirators* (1971), which was circulated privately throughout the Czech Republic. Next came *The Beggar's Opera* (1972), Havel's music-free adaptation of John Gay's famous study of power and corruption, which was also circulated privately before its professional premiere in Trieste one year later. A television play, *Butterfly on the Aerial,* which was written in the sixties, was broadcast for the first time in 1975 on West German television, the year he completed two one-acts, *Audience* and *Private View.* These later one-acts circulated privately until their world premiere at Vienna's Burgtheater on October 7, 1976. Adding a third one-act, *Protest,* in 1978, Havel had all three works feature a character named Vanek who would inspire *Largo Desolato* (1984), a frankly autobiographical work in which the playwright examined what happens "when the personification of resistance finds himself at the end of his tether."[6]

Other Havel plays include *Mountain Hotel* (1976); *Mistake* (1983), a one-act written shortly after his release from prison and produced at the Stockholm Stadsteater in October of that same year, on a double-bill with *Catastrophe,* written and dedicated to Havel by fellow-playwright and friend, Samuel Beckett; *Temptation* (1985), a full-length that makes clever use of the Faust theme; and *Slum Clearance* (1987), Havel's most realistic play whose theme and action foreshadow the Czech liberation.

THE ACTION

Professor Leopold Nettles stares through the peep-hole of his apartment door, fearful that he is being pursued by "them" and will be taken "there," the consequence of having created an "intellectual disturbance of the peace" through his writings. In rapid succession, he is visited by Edward, who inquires after his health; Suzana—his roommate or wife—who keeps the apartment stocked with groceries; and two men named Sidney who enlist Leopold's support by encouraging him "to take the initiative." His mistress Lucy arrives and offers "mad passionate love" as a cure for his malaise.

Four secret policemen enter the apartment later that evening, two of whom abduct Lucy, while the others (First Chap and Second Chap) try to force Leopold into signing a paper that will "wipe this unpleasant business off the slate and give [him] one more chance." Their efforts prove futile. When they later inform him that his signature is no longer necessary and that his case has been adjourned "indefinitely for the time being," Leopold falls to his knees, begging for recognition and exclaiming tearfully that he "can't go on living like this."

STRUCTURE AND LANGUAGE

Surrounded by walls of books that portray entrapment and expose an intellect stretched to the breaking point, Havel's philosopher/protagonist is initially defined by a curious last name, Nettles, no doubt symbolic of entanglements incurred through earlier acts of political defiance. In response to the slow and stately orchestral music that underscores his cautious moves from sofa to peep-hole—the titular *largo desolato* is a musical term (slow and desolate) suggesting the brooding psychological despair underlying his predicament—Leopold Nettles directs his anti-heroic gestures toward actions that threaten to occur but never quite materialize. As the recipient of unscheduled visits from friends and enemies alike—intrusions that contribute to the play's jaunty pace, Leopold is a passive character, entirely acted upon. His intolerable personal and professional circumstances are intensified by the playwright's use of claustrophobic space and a fairly continuous time span.

Prompted by Havel's suggestive title, musical clues illuminate a merry-go-round of entrances and exits, including the various character interactions positioned in between. Pervasive themes of isolation and despair, echoed by the "impressive orchestral music" that the playwright offers as emotional backdrop to the stage action, are represented by a succession of moody, *legato*-like dispositions executed by Leopold. These are juxtaposed with an altogether different set of cadences sounded by the characters who enter his world, until the contrasts bring Leopold's infirmities to the surface.

Personifying the rhythmical motifs and refrains that enhance the play's verbally splintered, circular structure, these satellite characters invade Leopold's privacy and criticize his inertia, but have little real impact on changing him. Nevertheless, their assaultive comments are sharply orchestrated: the *staccato*-like solo turns executed by Edward, Suzana, and Lucy, each designed to shake Leopold from his malaise; the duet-like contrapuntal innuendoes of the two Sidneys and the two chaps who represent, in choric alternation, his good and bad angels respectively; and Bertram's blunt advice, delivered in aria-like fashion, which holds Leopold's attention but goes unheeded. Frustrated by demands from all sides and desperate to shed the responsibilities of public adulation and return to his simpler life, Leopold is caught between supporters and detractors who denounce him as "some hero" at the play's climactic crescendo.

Foremost is Leopold's acute state of equivocation, so central to the masked tensions that hover over the play that "[his] condition has some similarities to a hangover but it's not a hangover," so he tells Edward. While his self-diagnosis is sadly comical, it cannot relieve his growing uncertainty that the unnamed *they* "won't come today," a condition that would border on lunacy were it not for Havel's subtly absurdist subtext—quite deftly executed without forcing the audience to choose between tears or laughter—which propels Leopold's tragi-comic inaction and lightens the mood of his predicament.

His fate appears momentarily altered, however, when a female student named Marguerite pays a visit and, easily intoxicated by the rum Leopold serves her, offers him "mad passionate true love" to save him. Her seductive behavior, which echoes Lucy's, is interrupted by the return of the two chaps whose latest message—that Leopold's identity has been deemed irrelevant by the state—intensifies the play's uneasy coda: the permanence of his unresolved status. When Leopold is reduced to begging them to take him "there" once and for all, we encounter his one single action—or request—in the entire play. But his wish to collect the fragments of his self-identity at the cost of freedom ultimately proves futile and grandly ironic in its lack of fulfillment.

Havel's theatrical style, which effortlessly accommodates his protagonist's disintegration, pays homage to prominent literary predecessors in its unfolding: the interminable waiting—a predicament that strikes literal and symbolic overtones—recalls the themes of Beckett; the network of ambiguous relationships, intensified by the intrusion of menacing caretakers, suggests Pinter; the verbal dueling and repeated banalities parody Ionesco; while the notion of personal identity dissolving into the unknown celebrates Kafka.

Such allusive hints, all intended to enhance the darker tones of Havel's dramatic art, ultimately find their own reality in the dissident playwright—and prototype—himself. Denying all autobiographical underpinnings to a work that was written in a four-day period after his release from prison in 1983, Havel has admitted putting "a bit of [his] own instability into [Nettle's] instability" and caricaturing his own "postprison despair."[7] Thus his calculated allusions portray experiences reminiscent of his own, as if to prove, once and for all, that any life, including that of a political dissident, is capable of imitating art.

The results transform *Largo Desolato* into Havel's most revealing and self-critical stage work, and perhaps his most popular. Its issues not only reflect every artist's concern for preserving freedom and identity in a bureaucratized society, but also caution us against the perils of political upheaval in a universal context. If the play "has ambitions to be a human parable" in its investigation of corrupt anonymous powers heaped against society's powerless, it further succeeds in humanizing the portrait of a complex hero for our uneasy political times.[8]

LARGO DESOLATO-IN-PERFORMANCE

Smuggled out of Czechoslovakia in 1985 while Havel was still a political prisoner in his native country, *Largo Desolato* received its world premiere at the Akademie Theater in Vienna on April 13, 1985, in a translation by Joachim Bruss. The play was presented at the Nationaltheatret in Oslo during the following 1985–1986 season.

English-language productions quickly followed, the American premiere taking place at the Public Theater in New York City on March 25, 1986, under Richard Foreman's controversial direction. This time, production circumstances proved less favorable than the New York premieres of earlier Havel plays. Expressing disapproval, Frank Rich found fault with certain directorial liberties:

> Rather than stage the play in earnest, Mr. Foreman has tricked it up (and slowed it down) with studied Magritte-like *tableaux,* variously frenzied and catatonic performances, heavy-handed lighting effects and pauses as forbidding as Soviet tanks.[9]

Voicing a different view, Michael Feingold thought Foreman's "usual stage paraphernalia . . . fit astonishingly well."[10] The decidedly mixed press shortened the New York engagement.

Across the Atlantic, the English premiere took place at the New Vic in Bristol on October 13, 1986, in a translation by Tom Stoppard, the renowned English playwright to whom the play was also dedicated. Michael Coveney complimented director Claude Whatham for viewing the work "as a situation comedy with nightmare overtones and Jan Blake's ambiguous design of real and painted bookshelves [which] establishe[d] the central uneasy liaison between marginal English philosophical comedy and central European philosophical reality."[11] Stephen Smith thought John McEnery was "splendidly haggard" in his creation of Leopold Nettles.[12]

Shortly afterwards, on February 6, 1987, the play received its London premiere at the Orange Tree Theatre in a production that was ''beautifully acted throughout, and directed with great sensibility by Sam Walters.'' Writing for the *Daily Telegraph,* Edward Pearce concluded that it was ''unlikely we shall see a better play this year. Inconceivable that we shall see one which is more important.''[13]

Soon after Havel became president of Czechoslovakia, the timely reunion of two former artistic collaborators instantly lifted the pall of the past twenty years when Jan Grossman directed *Largo Desolato* at the Theatre on the Balustrade on October 12, 1990, in a Prague theatrical season that celebrated several of the playwright's works yet unseen by Czech audiences. Rather like a conductor who is sensitive to the musical nuances of his prize-winning pupil's most private composition, Grossman tricked the audience into attention from the moment the curtain ascended on actor Jiri Bartoska—portraying Leopold— who seemed caught on stage unprepared. When the curtain fell and ascended a second time, Leopold moved to recorded stage directions spoken by Havel himself. From the start, Grossman viewed the enterprise as a game, juxtaposing the elements of realism with a playful artificiality to heighten the work's thematic ambivalence.

A semicircular span of identical doors on the intimate proscenium stage of the Balustrade provided the desirable claustrophobic effect, further highlighting the play's erratic mixture of entrances and exists. Except for the central upstage door that led to the world outside, nothing in Leopold's apartment seemed certain: the interior locations of kitchen, bathroom, and bedroom were randomly designated behind doors that were used inconsistently, as if none of these locations could ever become permanently established. Spatial perspectives were thrown further out of kilter by the presence of a wide couch dominating the foreground, small piles of books used as chairs, and a stepladder leading to a vanished bookcase. The overt disorder of Ivo Zidek's stage set not only reflected the protagonist's internal confusion, but gradually served as an obstacle course to the rest of the characters, an ''adjunct to the basic situation of the play, which is on the border between the real and the unreal: it is a 'mental space' linked with the action, one from which the hero has been displaced.''[14]

Grossman's handling of comic scenes enlightened the play's ambiguous dramatic tone as well as its powerful absurdist subtext. From the simplest rings of the doorbell to Leopold's paranoic encounters with characters from the outside world, the director often explored the play's unique underside:

> The grotesqueness, which at first is merely comical, takes on monstrous proportions, conveys inexpressible anguish and alienation. Fear of the void, of the broken axis so often cited in the text—both seriously and ironically—reaches a peak in the scene with [Bertram] the orator, followed by the hallucinatory vision in which Leopold is attacked by all his visitors in illogical and wildly jumbled sequence until he finally collapses.[15]

Mindful of the historical realities that underscored the work and sensitive to the symbolic repercussions of Leopold's collapse, which was not indicated in Havel's stage directions, Grossman matched the playwright's socio-political concerns with equally vibrant theatrical metaphors. He thus paid homage to their country's ''inexpressible and inexplicable need to endure that absurdity and to strive constantly after meaning.''[15]

Back in America, the salute to Havel's political and literary status inspired two different productions of the play during 1990, both of which used Tom Stoppard's English translation. The first was a film directed by Jiri Zizka for WNET, which featured F. Murray Abraham who played Leopold with ''insinuating verve.''[16] The second highlighted the celebration of Yale Repertory Theatre's twenty-fifth anniversary season. The cast was headed by Jan Triska under Gitta Honegger's direction.

REFLECTIONS ON LARGO DESOLATO

Jiri Zizka is the Artistic Director of The Wilma Theater in Philadelphia. He directed the film version of Largo Desolato, *co-produced by The Wilma Theater and Great Performances (WNET) in New York and broadcast on National Public Television.*

At the end of 1989, when Czechoslovakia became the focus of the world media, I realized that there was a real lack of understanding about what was going on in Prague on a human level, apart from the informational tidbits on the evening news. I was searching for a play that would capture the central European tragicomedy of the Communist era that was rapidly coming to an end. For me, *Largo Desolato*—with its light, humorous touches, revealing absurdities, and sudden twists and turns of fate—was that play. As the blanket of the Velvet Revolution was spreading over the nation, it became clear that this period of socialism *without a human face* was on its last legs, hopefully never to come back. We started preparing to film *Largo Desolato* simultaneously with Václav Havel's rise to the Castle.

Largo Desolato is one of my favorite plays. Like any great play, it transcends the immediate political and personal situation that gave birth to it and becomes an insightful parable about the human condition. Havel's rootedness in the fabric of a dissident's life and his ability to invent a perfect form for that fabric—woven of thoughts, *double-entendres,* innuendos, echos, and déjà vus—gives the play a powerful charge.

Is our human identity decided on one fateful day, or in one fateful hour, or is it being fought for every moment of our life?

At what point does a man stop living his life and continue to play the role he invented for himself in the past?

Can we design our fate at all, or are we simply a creation of our immediate circumstances?

What is the price of commitment? When is it too high? And when does life without commitment become worthless?

Does responsibility destroy sensuality?

Do our public and private selves differ from each other? Do these two masks carry faces of good and evil?

Do absolute values like good and evil exist at all? Or are we, having dethroned God and replaced Him with Science, at the mercy of relative truths and relative sins?

Is what we say truthfully really true, or could the same words be true to one person and deceptive to another? Doesn't the meaning of what we say depend entirely on to whom and under what circumstances we say it?

These are some of the playful questions and paradoxes the play inspires. On one hand, *Largo Desolato* is a play about a known dissident; on the other, it aspires to be about any man searching for the key to the meaning of his existence. Many great personalities, like our protagonist Leopold Nettles, become isolated as they follow their vision with an eye on the rearview mirror, in which the undercover cops of doom are in hot pursuit.

In *Largo Desolato,* I was especially attracted to comic moments as they are juxtaposed with tragic ones. I was also intrigued by Havel's strong sense of form which becomes the content itself. It has a circular quality; or perhaps what we might call "spiral." The characters start in a certain place and then return to it, to the same word or phrase or idea. But this time they're a little bit higher on the spiral toward the play's climax. Although a character may use the same phrase, it has a completely different meaning because the context and circumstances surrounding the character have altered.

I knew that the film of this work was going to become an anti-film. After all, the play itself is based on incessant wordplay. In film, we try to use only as many words as are absolutely necessary and let the images tell the story. I did not want to hide the fact that it was a theater piece. I injected the titles—Scene One, Scene Two, etc.—into the action as a reminder that the work was based on a play. But more importantly, I wanted this device to be comically ironic, as if Professor Nettles thought of his life as a play that he helped to create, all the way up to the final bow. He was no longer capable of spontaneous action.

Throughout, Leopold is suffering from writer's block and the three women who are interested in him try to help, each awakening in him a different part of his identity. Suzana inspires commitment and stability; Lucy, a sensual and sexual excitement; Marguerite, the idealism of youth and spiritual rebirth. At one point, Leopold complains that his thoughts have started to go in circles, that he can't decide whether to use a pen or pencil. He discusses the effects of a writer's depression. Havel himself once admitted in an interview that he never was as badly off as Leopold Nettles or he could never have written this play with such ironic detachment. He wrote *Largo Desolato* in only four days—in a state of tremendous creative euphoria following his release from prison.

During the rehearsal period, I tried to go after characters' basic human needs as well as their comic dimensions. I didn't want us to decide whether these characters were good or bad. I wanted each actor to play both sides. It was the only way to bring the relativity of one's identity into the story.

Since Havel's writing is so intensely structured, many directors are tempted to stage his plays in a visually stunning but formalistic way. I think it's important to make his characters naturalistic and specifically human in order to breathe life into the brilliant structure.

We had extensive auditions and cast the play very carefully. Sally Kirkland, who played Suzana, was the only actor who had ever done a Havel play before. In fact, she had played the same role under Richard Foreman's direction at the Public Theater. F. Murray Abraham, whom I cast in the central role, had an immediate understanding of Leopold's duality. What I have always liked about Murray is that he's a genuinely funny actor. He knows that humor can enlighten an audience more than any statements. He understands it without pushing for it or resorting to gags. In films, he usually gets cast as a threatening character, like in *Amadeus* and *The Name of the Rose*. This role was great for him—he was playing Havel's stand-in, which is like playing Gandhi or some giant thinker-philosopher or poet-playwright. At the same time, he had the freedom to invent, since he knew that the play was not completely autobiographical and that he didn't have to follow somebody else's psychological pattern. Even with very little rehearsal time, he was able to layer the character to attain Leopold's cunning complexity.

My ultimate goal was to give the story a metaphoric universality. I didn't want the setting, for example, to look like a typical Prague apartment. We found an apartment in Brooklyn and then totally redesigned it. We created more space by removing one of the walls, painting the interior red, and refurnishing it completely. The results looked vaguely European, but also could have belonged to an American intellectual. The stairway,

Continued

Leopold's only connection to the outside, was located in a courthouse in Harlem. It looked like New York, Paris, and Prague combined. I chose it for its cool, mysterious quality.

I wanted the apartment to achieve a pressure-cooker or womb-like effect that acts upon the main character in a claustrophobic way, as if he's cooking in his own juices, a prisoner of his celebrity status and his paranoid thoughts.

Stylistically, I thought it was important to move the tragic and comic moments into close proximity and let them contrast with each other. I didn't want the film to be one-dimensional—heavy or serious. The little human touches were most important to me, not the big philosophical statements. So when the beautiful young student comes into Leopold's apartment, he cannot help but start to seduce her.

In his earlier works, Havel was writing in the style of the theatre of the absurd—for example, his comedy *The Memorandum* about an artificially created language called *ptydepe.* Absurd humor can be quite sophisticated. For such humor to resonate, the playwright needs an audience that is used to watching everyday absurdities in real life. This style is not prevalent in the American theatre; it essentially belongs to the European experience. Most of the absurdist writers thought of their work as naturalistic. After all, they were only reflecting the absurdity going on around them. European history, especially in the last hundred years, was a fertile ground for absurdity.

In American theatre, I think we tend to decide whether a play is a comedy or tragedy, mostly for marketing purposes. The only correct label for *Largo Desolato,* if one would be necessary, is a *play.* It would be impossible to put it into one category. Once Havel said that he didn't want his audience to have a unified opinion about any one of his plays. He intended his plays to be like a glass out of which each person takes what concerns him personally; at times, having a distinctly different impression of the same play from the person next to them.

For me, the real test of any absurdist play is the writer's ability to not bury the play's humanity under absurdist devices. Some absurdist plays become philosophical blueprints without a dramatic soul. In this play, I think, Havel has created a soul full of its own mystery and inexplicable contradictions.

I've had the opportunity of working with many different translations of Havel's plays. Tom Stoppard is particularly good at figuring out what this playwright wants and translating it into English through idioms rather than literally. I think his work is really an adaptation. For example, there is a brief exchange in which Leopold questions Lucy about life. She calls it depressing. Leopold asks why. She cites loneliness. And that's it. This quick exchange must have been difficult for Stoppard, because the original is longer. You see, the Czechs speak in a more flowery fashion. No doubt the literal English would have been out of rhythm and out of touch. It certainly would have sounded like a translation.

I do not know if Stoppard actually speaks Czech or if he has based his work on a literal translation. I know his parents were Czech. Regardless, he has a perfect ear for combining the sound, meaning, and absurdly comedic spirit of the original.

Take the protagonist's name, for example. If Stoppard were translating Chekhov, he probably wouldn't have translated a character's name. The reason he does so with Leopold Nettles is that the name is an essential part of the plot and tension. Two undercover agents enter Leopold's apartment. They ask him to consider changing his name. When he resists, they laugh at him, asking if he really thinks that Nettles is such a beautiful name that he couldn't bear to lose it. Of course, to the agents the idea of changing one's name is a matter of everyday life. The whole scene wouldn't have worked if the name remained Kopřiva.

By the way, *nettles* is a literal translation of *kopřiva,* a very unpleasant plant that burns your skin, sometimes used for making herb tea. In Czech, *Kopřiva* is a name that is both common—it has a definite peasant connotation—and humorously unusual.

The use of Beethoven's Ninth—the "Ode to Joy"—was my own invention. I chose it because it helped to establish Leopold's creative frustration. It is the kind of music that people listen to over and over again until it completely loses its meaning. It also has a circular progression that was visually complemented by a swirling old-fashioned record-player in the beginning and a vertiginous, spiral stairway in the end.

In the end, Leopold is no longer able to resist the pressure. He negotiates. His path leads him away from himself. This is further proof that the play is not an autobiographical work. Havel never took this route. He resisted, remained true to his own beliefs, feelings, and instincts. He ultimately came to represent this absolute moral attitude which can be best described by the title of one of his books: *Living in Truth.*

To intensify the script's spiral spirit, I wanted us to return to where we started: Leopold's listening to the "Ode to Joy." In the end, having left his apartment, his protective womb, for the first time, he runs after the undercover cops begging them to arrest him. All values are reversed. The abyss gapes open. Leopold collapses at the bottom of the stairwell. For the last time, the "Ode to Joy" echoes ironically through the empty corridors of his lost self. Until the last moment, Leopold Nettles will try desperately to figure out whose side he's on. The last notes that once brought him hope now belong to the snickering agents of doom.

Notes

1. *Oscar Brockett and Robert Findlay,* CENTURY OF INNOVATION *(Boston: Allyn & Bacon, 1991), 349.*
2. *"A Preface to Havel,"* TULANE DRAMA REVIEW *11 (Spring 1967): 118.*
3. *Václav Havel,* DISTURBING THE PEACE *(New York: Alfred Knopf, 1990), 54.*
4. *"Havel Discusses Writers and Politics,"* THE NEW YORK TIMES, *27 June 1990, sec. c, p. 7.*
5. *Samuel G. Freedman, "Portrait of a Playwright as an Enemy of the State,"* THE NEW YORK TIMES, *23 March 1986, sec. c, p. 36.*
6. *Havel,* DISTURBING THE PEACE, *66.*
7. *Ibid., 65.*
8. *Ibid.*
9. THE NEW YORK TIMES, *26 March 1986.*
10. VILLAGE VOICE, *1 Jan. 1986.*
11. FINANCIAL TIMES, *14 Oct. 1986.*
12. THE INDEPENDENT, *15 Oct. 1986.*
13. DAILY TELEGRAPH, *9 Feb. 1987.*
14. *Jana Patočková, "Largo Desolato: A Trap for the Audience,"* CZECH AND SLOVAK THEATER *(January 1991): 18.*
15. *Ibid., 18.*
16. *John J. O'Connor, "One by Havel and One About Havel,"* THE NEW YORK TIMES, *20 April 1990.*

LARGO DESOLATO

A PLAY IN SEVEN SCENES
VÁCLAV HAVEL
ENGLISH VERSION BY TOM STOPPARD

CHARACTERS

Professor Leopold Nettles	Second Sidney	Second Chap
Edward	Lucy	First Man
Suzana	Bertram	Second Man
First Sidney	First Chap	Marguerite

The whole play takes place in Leopold's and Suzana's living room. It is a spacious room and all the other rooms in the flat lead off it. On the left there is the front door of the flat. The door has a peep-hole. In the back wall, on the left, there is a glass-panelled door leading to a balcony. In the middle of the wall there is a glass-panelled door leading to the kitchen. To the right of that there is a small staircase leading to the door of Suzana's room. On the right hand side, opposite the front door, there is a door leading to the bathroom, and a further door leading to Leopold's room. Between the doors the walls are covered with bookcases and bookshelves. There is a hat-stand near the front door. In the right hand half of the room there is a sofa with a low table in front of it, and a few chairs. On the table there is a large bottle of rum and a glass which LEOPOLD keeps filling up throughout the play and from which he keeps sipping. This is an old and solidly bourgeois apartment but the furnishings indicate that the occupant is an intellectual. Impressive orchestral music is heard at the beginning and the end of the play and also during the intervals between the scenes.

SCENE ONE

As the music dies away the curtain rises slowly.

LEOPOLD *is alone on the stage. He is sitting on the sofa and staring at the front door. After a long pause he gets up and looks through the peep-hole. Then he puts his ear to the door and listens intently. After another long pause the curtain drops suddenly and at the same time the music returns.*

SCENE TWO

As the music dies away the curtain rises slowly.

LEOPOLD *is alone on the stage. He is sitting on the sofa and staring at the front door. After a long pause he gets up and looks through the peep-hole. Then he puts his ear to the door and listens intently. After another long pause the curtain drops suddenly and at the same time the music returns.*

SCENE THREE

As the music dies down the curtain rises slowly.

    LEOPOLD *is alone on the stage. He is sitting on the sofa and staring at the front door. After a long pause he gets up, goes to the door and looks through the peep-hole and then he puts his ear to the door and listens intently. He evidently hears something which makes him jump back. At the same moment the door bell rings.* LEOPOLD *hesitates for a moment and then cautiously approaches the door and looks through the peep-hole. That calms him and he opens the door.* EDWARD *enters.*

LEOPOLD. At last!

EDWARD. Has anything happened?

LEOPOLD. No—*

EDWARD. Were you worried?

LEOPOLD. I feel better when there's someone here. Come in—
(EDWARD *comes forward.* LEOPOLD *closes the door behind him.*)
What's it like outside?

EDWARD. Stifling—

LEOPOLD. Lots of people?

EDWARD. No more than usual—
(EDWARD *goes to the door leading to the balcony.*)

EDWARD. Do you mind if I open it a bit?

LEOPOLD. Go ahead—
(EDWARD *opens the balcony door wide.*)
What will you have?

EDWARD. Thanks, nothing for the moment—
(LEOPOLD *sits down on the sofa.* EDWARD *takes a chair. A short pause.*)
How did you sleep?

LEOPOLD. Essentially well. I would put it at six hours net. I woke up twice but only because I needed to pee—

EDWARD. No diarrhoea?

LEOPOLD. On the contrary—

EDWARD. How about dreams?

LEOPOLD. Nothing memorable, evidently. (*Pause.*) Do you mind if I close it now?

EDWARD. Leave it open for a while. (*Pause.*) So you're all right?

LEOPOLD. At first glance I would seem to have no reason to complain today. But in all honesty, I couldn't assert that I'm feeling up to the mark—

EDWARD. Nervous?

LEOPOLD. Well, I'm always nervous—

EDWARD. And the shakes you had yesterday? All gone?

LEOPOLD. I'm afraid not. In fact they're worse. It's almost as though I'd caught a chill. (*He pauses suddenly.*) Is that somebody coming?
(*They both listen quietly.*)

*Translator's footnote: the use of dashes rather than full stops at the end of speeches is Havel's punctuation.

EDWARD. Nothing. Everything's okay—

LEOPOLD. And on top of that I've got complications—a touch of vertigo, suggestion of an upset stomach, tingling in the joints, loss of appetite, and even the possibility of constipation—

EDWARD. You mean you didn't go this morning?

LEOPOLD. No—

EDWARD. Are you sure it isn't just a hangover?

LEOPOLD. My condition has some similarities to a hangover but it's not a hangover, in as much as I hardly touched a drop yesterday—

EDWARD. Well, perhaps there's something wrong with you.

LEOPOLD. No, I'm afraid not—

EDWARD. Well, that's something to be grateful for isn't it?

LEOPOLD. Is it? I'd rather be ill than well like this. If only I could be sure they won't come today—

EDWARD. They can't be coming now—

LEOPOLD. Do you think so? Surely they can come any time—
(*At that moment a key rattles in the lock.* LEOPOLD *is startled.* SUZANA *comes in through the front door carrying a full shopping bag.*)

SUZANA. Hello—
(LEOPOLD *and* EDWARD *get up.*)

LEOPOLD. Hello—let me—
(LEOPOLD *takes the bag from* SUZANA *and carries it into the kitchen.*)

SUZANA. How is he?

EDWARD. The same—
(LEOPOLD *returns from the kitchen.*)

LEOPOLD. Did you get any meat?

SUZANA. Liver—

LEOPOLD. You didn't!
(SUZANA *is going up the stairs to her room.* LEOPOLD *approaches her.*)
Suzy—
(*She stops halfway up the stairs and turns towards him.*)

SUZANA. Yes?

LEOPOLD. I was up by about eight today—I felt like doing something—I was thinking of making a few notes—I had a piece of paper all ready but nothing came—I wasn't feeling up to scratch again. Those shakes I had yesterday came back—so I did a bit of tidying up, wiped out the sink, took out the rubbish, dried my towel, cleaned my comb, made myself two soft boiled eggs for lunch—

SUZANA. What did you eat them with?

LEOPOLD. Well, with a teaspoon of course—

SUZANA. A silver one?

LEOPOLD. I don't know, it might have been—

SUZANA. How many times have I told you not to use the silver teaspoons for eggs—you can't get them clean properly—

LEOPOLD.   Oh yes, I'm sorry, I forgot. After lunch I tried to read a bit and then Edward here turned up . . .

SUZANA.   In other words, not a lot—

(*She goes up another step or two.*)

LEOPOLD.   Suzana—

(*She stops and turns towards him.*)

As you've managed to get some liver why don't we have a special supper. I'll make mustard sauce, open a bottle of decent wine—we'll ask Lucy as well, and I'm sure Edward would join us. I think it would be good for me to let my hair down, take my mind off things, reminisce a little . . .

SUZANA.   I'm sorry, Leopold, but I've got tickets for the cinema—

LEOPOLD.   How about after the cinema?

SUZANA.   That's too late for me—you know I've got to be up early—

(*SUZANA goes into her room. LEOPOLD stands for a moment looking after her awkwardly, then returns slowly to his place, and sits down. Another pause.*)

LEOPOLD.   Edward—

EDWARD.   Yes?

LEOPOLD.   Will you think of me?

EDWARD.   When?

LEOPOLD.   Well, when I'm there—

EDWARD.   You mustn't keep thinking about that all the time!

LEOPOLD.   I don't keep thinking about it all the time. It just came into my head. I'm sorry—

EDWARD.   Why don't you go for a walk once in a while?

LEOPOLD.   Are you mad? Go out?

EDWARD.   Why not?

LEOPOLD.   And be a nervous wreck the whole time, not knowing what's going on back here?

EDWARD.   Nothing's going on back here—

LEOPOLD.   I know, but how am I going to know that if I'm gadding about somewhere else? What if they came just then?

EDWARD.   They'd find you weren't at home. So what?

LEOPOLD.   I couldn't possibly—

(*At that moment the doorbell rings. LEOPOLD jumps up in confusion. EDWARD gets up as well. LEOPOLD goes to the peep-hole and looks through it and then turns towards EDWARD.*)

LEOPOLD (*whispering*). What did I tell you!

EDWARD (*whispering*). Is it them?

(*LEOPOLD nods. They pause, at a loss. The bell rings again.*)

LEOPOLD (*whispering*). Should I open the door?

EDWARD (*whispering*). Yes, you have to—

(*LEOPOLD hesitates a moment, then breathes in, goes to the door and opens it decisively. The newcomers are FIRST SIDNEY and SECOND SIDNEY.*)

FIRST SIDNEY.   Good afternoon, sir—

LEOPOLD.   Good afternoon—

SECOND SIDNEY.   Can we come in?

LEOPOLD.   Do . . .

(*FIRST SIDNEY and SECOND SIDNEY come forward a few paces. LEOPOLD closes the door behind them. They all remain standing and looking at each other somewhat at a loss.*)

FIRST SIDNEY.   You don't remember us?

LEOPOLD.   I can't place you at the moment—

FIRST SIDNEY.   We called on you once before, two years ago. You've obviously forgotten. I'm Sidney and he's also Sidney—

LEOPOLD.   How do you do—

SECOND SIDNEY.   We won't hold you up long—

LEOPOLD (*perplexed*). Well, do sit down—

(*They all sit down, LEOPOLD on the sofa, the others on the chairs.*)

FIRST SIDNEY.   Is it all right to smoke?

LEOPOLD.   Yes—certainly—

FIRST SIDNEY.   Actually, I don't smoke myself; I was asking for Sidney here, he smokes like a chimney—

(*SECOND SIDNEY is going through his pockets but can't find any cigarettes. LEOPOLD offers him one. SECOND SIDNEY takes one and lights it. There is an awkward pause.*)

Do you need any paper?

LEOPOLD.   Do you mean for writing on?

SECOND SIDNEY.   If you need any we can get you some—

LEOPOLD.   Really?

FIRST SIDNEY.   Seeing as we work in a paper mill—

LEOPOLD.   You do?

SECOND SIDNEY.   So no problem—

(*Pause. SUZANA comes out of her room and down the stairs.*)

LEOPOLD.   Suzana, these gentlemen are from the paper mill. It seems they've been here before—

SUZANA.   Good afternoon—

FIRST SIDNEY.   Good afternoon—

(*SUZANA beckons to EDWARD who gets up and goes with her to the kitchen. During the following scene both of them can be seen through the glass-panelled door taking out various foodstuffs from the shopping bag, putting them where they belong and, during all this time, either discussing something in a lively way or perhaps quarrelling. Pause.*)

Oh, by the way, we've got a lot of interesting stuff from the mill—minutes of meetings and so on—I'm sure you'd find it interesting—

LEOPOLD.   I'm sure I would—

SECOND SIDNEY.   We'll bring it you—

(*Pause.*)

FIRST SIDNEY.   We know everything—

LEOPOLD.   Every what thing?

FIRST SIDNEY.   About you—

LEOPOLD.   I see—

SECOND SIDNEY.   What Sidney is trying to say is, we're your fans. Not just us either—

LEOPOLD.   Thank you—

FIRST SIDNEY.   There's lots of people looking to you—

LEOPOLD.   Thank you—

SECOND SIDNEY.   We all believe that it will all turn out right for you in the end—

LEOPOLD.   Well, I'm not sure—

SECOND SIDNEY.   The main thing is that you mustn't weaken—we need you and we believe in you—you being the man you are—

LEOPOLD.   Thank you—

(*Pause.*)

FIRST SIDNEY.   We're not holding you up, are we?

LEOPOLD.   No—

FIRST SIDNEY.   Are you sure? Because if we are, you only have to say so and we'll push off—

LEOPOLD.   You're not holding me up—

(*Pause.*)

FIRST SIDNEY.   You know, I'm just an ordinary sort of bloke, a nobody, but I can spot a few things and I've got my own opinion and nobody can deny me that. And what I think is, there's a lot that could be done—certainly more than is being done at the moment—

LEOPOLD.   This is it—

SECOND SIDNEY.   Speaking for myself and Sidney here, we reckon—and this is partly why we're here—to our way of thinking not all the possibilities have been exhausted—I would venture to say that the most promising possibilities are still ahead of us. One has to take hold of the situation by the scruff of the neck—

LEOPOLD.   What possibilities in particular did you have in mind?

FIRST SIDNEY.   Well, that would require some discussion, of course—

LEOPOLD.   Well, at least tell me what direction we ought to be taking.

FIRST SIDNEY.   Different directions all at the same time. Surely no one knows that better than you! In short, it seems to us that it's time to take the initiative—something that would make them sit up.

LEOPOLD.   I'm not sure that present circumstances differ significantly from the circumstances that have prevailed up to now, but even so I'm not *a priori* against an initiative—

FIRST SIDNEY.   I'm glad we agree—who else but you could get things going again?

LEOPOLD.   Well as for *me*—

SECOND SIDNEY.   We realize that things are probably not easy for you at the moment. But the respect in which you're held puts you under an obligation—

LEOPOLD.   I know—

FIRST SIDNEY.   You'll know what's best to do, after all you're a philosopher and I'm an ordinary bloke, a nobody. It goes without saying we're not forcing you—we haven't got the right, and furthermore you can't be expected to do it for everybody, all on your own, but, that said, what we think is, don't get me wrong, I'll let you have it straight,—that said, we are of the opinion that you could be doing more than you are in your place—

LEOPOLD.   I'll think it over—

FIRST SIDNEY.   We're only saying this because we're your fans—and not just us—

LEOPOLD.   Thank you—

SECOND SIDNEY.   A lot of people are looking to you—

LEOPOLD.   Thank you—

FIRST SIDNEY.   The main thing is that you mustn't weaken—we believe in you and we need you—

LEOPOLD.   Thank you—

(*Pause.*)

SECOND SIDNEY.   We're not holding you up, are we?

LEOPOLD.   No—

SECOND SIDNEY.   Are you sure? Because if we are you only have to say so and we'll push off—

LEOPOLD.   You're not holding me up—

(*Pause.*)

SECOND SIDNEY.   One could certainly do more—you just have to get hold of the situation by the scruff of the neck—and who else but you is there to get things going again?

LEOPOLD.   Well, as for *me*—

FIRST SIDNEY.   We have faith in you—

SECOND SIDNEY.   And we need you—

LEOPOLD.   Thank you—

FIRST SIDNEY.   We're not holding you up, are we?

LEOPOLD.   No—

FIRST SIDNEY.   Are you really sure? Because if we are you only have to say so and we'll push off—

LEOPOLD.   You are not holding me up. Excuse me—

(LEOPOLD *gets up and walks to the balcony door, shuts it and returns to his seat.*)

SECOND SIDNEY.   The main thing is that you mustn't weaken—

LEOPOLD (*suddenly alert*). Just a moment—

FIRST SIDNEY.   What's up?

LEOPOLD.   I think somebody's coming—

SECOND SIDNEY.   I can't hear anything—

FIRST SIDNEY.   The respect in which you're held puts you under an obligation—

(*At that moment the doorbell rings. That startles* LEOPOLD *who gets up quickly, goes to the front door and looks through the peep-hole. He calms down and turns towards the* TWO SIDNEYS.)

LEOPOLD.   A friend of mine—

(LEOPOLD *opens the door and* LUCY *comes in.*)

LUCY.   Hello, Leo—

LEOPOLD.   Come in, Lucy—

(LEOPOLD *closes the door and leads* LUCY *to the table.*)

LUCY.   I see you've got company—

LEOPOLD.   They're friends from the paper mill—

LUCY.   Good afternoon—

FIRST SIDNEY.   Good afternoon, miss—

LEOPOLD.   Sit down—

(LUCY *sits down next to* LEOPOLD *on the sofa. There is a longer awkward pause.*)

Would you like some rum?

LUCY.   You know I don't drink rum—

(*Pause.*)

LEOPOLD.   How's life?

LUCY.   Depressing—

LEOPOLD.   Why's that?

LUCY.   Loneliness.

(*Pause.*)

LEOPOLD.   These gentlemen think it's time to take the initiative—

LUCY.   They've got something there.

(*Awkward pause.*)

Did I come at the wrong moment? You were obviously in the middle of discussing something—

LEOPOLD.   It's all right—

(*Awkward pause.*)

Have you had supper?

LUCY.   No—

LEOPOLD.   We're having liver. Would you like to stay?

LUCY.   That would be lovely—

(*Another awkward pause.* LUCY *takes a bottle of pills out of her handbag. She puts the bottle on the table.*)

I've brought you some vitamins—

LEOPOLD.   You never forget—

(*Awkward pause.*)

I'm told it's stifling today—

LUCY.   Stifling and humid—

(*Awkward pause.*)

LEOPOLD.   Edward opened the balcony door but I closed it again—I don't like draughts—

LUCY.   Is Edward here?

LEOPOLD.   Yes—

(*Awkward pause.* LEOPOLD *is becoming more and more nervous because both* FIRST *and* SECOND SIDNEY *are sitting there and not showing any signs of leaving. Several times he seems on the point of saying something but each time changes his mind. Finally he blurts out*—)

LEOPOLD.   Well, look how the evening's coming on—

(LUCY *bursts out laughing.* LEOPOLD *presses her hand. Awkward pause. Both* SIDNEYS *sitting there apparently dumbfounded.*)

I've still got a few things to do—

(LUCY *bursts out laughing despite herself.*)

LUCY.   What have you got to do?

(*She bursts out again and* LEOPOLD *kicks her under the table.*)

LEOPOLD (*stammering*).   Things—make some notes—some supper—

(*He relapses into a long stifling silence. Then* SUZANA *followed by* EDWARD, *enters from the kitchen.*)

SUZANA.   Lucy!

LUCY.   Suzy!

(LUCY *gets up at once and goes towards* SUZANA *and they embrace.*)

Darling! How's life?

SUZANA.   Never stops!

LUCY.   We must have a chat—I've got so much to tell you.

SUZANA.   Me too—but some other time, all right?—I'm in a rush.

LUCY.   Hey, are you leaving?

SUZANA.   I've got tickets for the cinema—

LUCY.   What a shame—I was so looking forward to seeing you!

(FIRST SIDNEY *suddenly thumps his knees and stands up.* SECOND SIDNEY *gets up as well.* LEOPOLD *starts getting up.*)

FIRST SIDNEY.   Well, we shall look in on you soon—

LEOPOLD.   Fine—

SECOND SIDNEY.   And we'll bring you that writing paper—

LEOPOLD.   Fine—

FIRST SIDNEY.   And also the stuff from the paper mill—

LEOPOLD.   Fine—

SECOND SIDNEY.   The main thing is—keep your chin up!

LEOPOLD.   Thank you—

FIRST SIDNEY.   When are you expecting them?

LEOPOLD.   All the time—

SECOND SIDNEY.   We're with you—stick with it! So long—

LEOPOLD.   So long—

LUCY.   So long—

(LEOPOLD *accompanies the* SIDNEYS *to the front door and opens the door for them. They go out.* LEOPOLD *closes the door behind them, and, completely spent, leans back against the door.*)

May I ask, who that was?

LEOPOLD.   I don't know. They wanted something from me. I'm not sure what. I'm sure they mean well—

SUZANA.   That sort of thing happens all the time round here—but I have to run. (*To* EDWARD.) Let's go! (*To* LUCY.) Bye for now—

LUCY.   Bye, Suzy—

EDWARD.   Bye—

(SUZANA *and* EDWARD *leave.* LUCY *and* LEOPOLD *are left alone.* LUCY *smiles at* LEOPOLD *for a moment, then takes hold of his hands, pulls him towards her and kisses him.*)

LUCY.   Do you love me?

LEOPOLD.   Mm.

LUCY.   Really?

LEOPOLD.   Really—

LUCY.   Well why don't you say so sometimes without being asked? You've never once!

LEOPOLD.   As you know, I avoid off-the-peg expressions—

LUCY.   The simple truth is, you're ashamed of loving me!

LEOPOLD. Phenomenology has taught me always to beware of the propositional statement that lies outside demonstrable experience. I prefer to say less than I feel rather than to risk saying more—

LUCY. You think loving me is not a demonstrable experience?

LEOPOLD. We may mean different things by the word love. Perhaps, though the difference may be small the word denotes, for me, something on a higher plane than for you—Just a minute!

(LEOPOLD *leaves* LUCY *to approach the front door and looks through the peep-hole.*)

LUCY. What is it?

LEOPOLD. I thought I heard someone coming—

LUCY. I can't hear anything—

(LEOPOLD *comes back from the door and turns towards her.*)

LEOPOLD. Forgive me, Lucy, but does our love have to consist solely in this endless examination of itself?

LUCY. What do you expect when you're so evasive all the time—

LEOPOLD. It's just that like all women you long for security and men look for something higher—

LUCY. Just my luck to keep picking lovers with a permanent crick in their neck—

LEOPOLD. Don't be disgusting!

LUCY. What do you mean?

LEOPOLD. Please don't use the word lover! At least don't apply it to me—

LUCY. Why?

LEOPOLD. It's disgusting—

LUCY. Why?

LEOPOLD. It turns man into nothing but an ever-naked prick—

LUCY (*laughing*). Oh, who's being disgusting now—

LEOPOLD. Why don't you sit down?

(LUCY *sits down on the sofa.*)

Can I get you anything?

LUCY. Is there any wine?

LEOPOLD. I'll get some—

(LEOPOLD *goes into the kitchen and after a moment returns with a bottle of wine, a bottle opener and two glasses. He opens the bottle, pours wine into both glasses, takes one and* LUCY *takes the other.*)

Well, cheers!

LUCY. Cheers!

(*They both take a drink.* LEOPOLD *sits down on the sofa next to her. Pause.*)

So tell me—

LEOPOLD. What?

LUCY. What did you do today?

LEOPOLD. I don't know—

LUCY. Did you write?

LEOPOLD. I wanted to but it wouldn't come. I wasn't feeling well—

LUCY. Did you have your depression again?

LEOPOLD. That was another thing—

LUCY. You won't get rid of it till you start writing. Everybody's waiting for your new piece—

LEOPOLD. That's just the trouble—

LUCY. But you had it all worked out—

LEOPOLD. What do you mean?

LUCY. Well, just what you were telling me—that love is actually a dimension of being—it gives fulfilment and meaning to existence—

LEOPOLD. I couldn't have made it sound like such a cliché—

LUCY. No doubt you put it better—

LEOPOLD. It's funny but when I run out of excuses for putting off writing and make up my mind to start, I stumble over the first banality—pencil or pen?—which paper?—and then this thing starts—

LUCY. What thing?

LEOPOLD. The cycle thing—

LUCY. What's that?

LEOPOLD. My thoughts just start going round in a loop—

LUCY. Hm—

LEOPOLD. Look, do we have to talk about me?

LUCY. You love to talk about yourself!

LEOPOLD. That's just what you think—

(LUCY *puts her head on* LEOPOLD's *shoulder. He embraces her but they both continue to look straight ahead, absorbed in thought. Pause.*)

LUCY. Leopold—

LEOPOLD. Yes—

LUCY. I can help you break out of that—

LEOPOLD. How?

LUCY. You need love—real love—mad passionate love—not that theoretical one, the one you write about—

LEOPOLD. I'm a bit old for that—

LUCY. You're not old, it's just that you've got an emotional block—but I'll unblock you—

(LUCY *embraces* LEOPOLD *and begins to kiss his face.* LEOPOLD *sits perplexed and remains quite passive. The curtain falls and the music returns.*)

SCENE FOUR

The music fades and the curtain rises slowly.

It is late in the evening. It is dark behind the balcony door. BERTRAM *is sitting on the sofa.* LEOPOLD, *who is standing in the background by the balcony door, wears a dressing gown with nothing underneath it, and he is rather dishevelled and seems to be cold.*

BERTRAM. How long is it since you went out?

LEOPOLD. I don't know—ages—

BERTRAM. You don't go out at all then?

LEOPOLD. No—

(*Pause.*)

BERTRAM.   How much do you drink?

LEOPOLD.   The same as everyone else—

BERTRAM.   Starting in the morning?

LEOPOLD.   As the case may be—

(*Pause.*)

BERTRAM.   How do you sleep?

LEOPOLD.   It varies—

BERTRAM.   Do you ever dream about them? Or dream that you're already there?

LEOPOLD.   Sometimes—

(*Pause.*)

BERTRAM.   Leopold—

LEOPOLD.   Yes?

BERTRAM.   You don't doubt, do you, that we all like you—

LEOPOLD.   I know—

LUCY (*off stage*). Leopold—

LEOPOLD (*calls out*). Just a minute—

(*Pause.* LEOPOLD *is trembling with cold and rubbing his arms.* BERTRAM *looks through the medicines lying on the table.*)

BERTRAM.   Vitamins?

LEOPOLD.   Yes—

BERTRAM.   Apart from vitamins are you on anything else?

LEOPOLD.   Not really—why do you ask?

BERTRAM.   There's some talk—

LEOPOLD.   What sort of talk?

BERTRAM.   Forget it—

(*Pause.*)

BERTRAM.   Quite a few people complain that you never answer letters—

LEOPOLD.   I was never much of a letter writer—

BERTRAM.   Well, there's no law about it . . . still, it's a pity that it lends support to the rumours—

LEOPOLD.   What rumours?

BERTRAM.   That you're no longer reliable, so—

LEOPOLD.   I reply to anything important—perhaps something got lost in the post somewhere—

(*Pause.*)

BERTRAM.   What did you think of that collection?

LEOPOLD.   What collection?

BERTRAM.   The stuff I lent you the other day—

LEOPOLD.   Ah yes—

BERTRAM.   Have you read it?

LEOPOLD.   To tell you the truth—

BERTRAM.   It's essential reading—

LEOPOLD.   I know—That's exactly why I couldn't just glance through it—There's a mood for everything—I can't just read anything any time—

(*Pause.*)

BERTRAM.   Leopold—

LEOPOLD.   Yes?

BERTRAM.   You don't doubt, do you, that we all like you?

LEOPOLD.   I know—

LUCY (*off stage*). Leopold—

LEOPOLD (*calls out*). Just a minute—

(*Pause.* LEOPOLD *is trembling with cold and rubbing his arms.*)

BERTRAM.   Leopold—

LEOPOLD.   Yes?

BERTRAM.   It goes without saying it's your own business—

LEOPOLD.   What is?

BERTRAM.   You don't have to account to me—

LEOPOLD.   What?

BERTRAM.   I'm asking as a friend—

LEOPOLD.   I know—

BERTRAM.   Is it true that you're seeing Lucy?

LEOPOLD.   It's not that simple—

BERTRAM.   And how are things between you and Suzana?

LEOPOLD.   We get along—

(*Pause.*)

BERTRAM.   Leopold—

LEOPOLD.   Yes?

BERTRAM.   You don't doubt, do you, that we all like you?

LEOPOLD.   I know—

(*Pause.*)

LUCY (*off stage*). Leopold—

LEOPOLD (*calls out*). Just a minute—

(*Pause.* LEOPOLD *is trembling with cold and is rubbing his arms*)

BERTRAM.   It's terrible of course to live with this nerve-racking uncertainty—we all understand that. None of us knows how we'd stand it ourselves. That's why so many people are concerned about you. You have to understand that—

LEOPOLD.   I do understand—

BERTRAM.   I'm not just speaking for myself—I'm really here on behalf of everyone—

LEOPOLD.   Who's everyone?

BERTRAM.   Your friends—

LEOPOLD.   Are you an emissary?

BERTRAM.   If you want to call it that—

LEOPOLD.   And what are you concerned about, specifically?

BERTRAM.   How shall I put it? I don't want to be hard on you or hurt you in any way but on the other hand I wouldn't be acting as your friend if I were to be less than frank—

LEOPOLD.   And what are you concerned about, specifically?

BERTRAM.   How should I put it? It's not simply a general issue, it's mostly about you personally—

LEOPOLD.   And what are you concerned about, specifically?

BERTRAM.   How should I put it? Simply, there's growing circumstantial evidence giving rise to certain speculations—

LEOPOLD.   What circumstantial evidence? What speculations?

BERTRAM.   Your friends—and I won't deny I include myself—we've all—for some time—and let's hope our fears are groundless—we've all—for some time—begun to question whether you might not crack under the strain—whether you'll be able to meet all the claims which, thanks to all you've done already—the claims which are made on you—that you'll be able to fulfil the expectations which—forgive me—are rightly expected of you—if you'll be, in short, up to your mission, which is to do justice to those great obligations, to the truth, to the world, to everyone for whom you set an example—set by your own work—forgive me—but quite simply we are beginning to be slightly afraid that you might let us down and in so doing bring upon yourself—forgive me—it would be bound to be so, given your sensitivity—bring upon yourself endless agony—

(*Short pause.*)

You're not angry, are you, that I'm speaking so openly?

LEOPOLD.   No—on the contrary—

(*Pause.*)

LUCY (*off stage*). Leopold—

LEOPOLD (*calls out*). Just a minute—

(*Pause.* LEOPOLD *is trembling with cold and is rubbing his arms.*)

BERTRAM.   It's terrible, of course, to live with this nerve-racking uncertainty. We all understand that. None of us knows how we'd stand it ourselves. That's why so many people are concerned about you. You have to understand that—

LEOPOLD.   I do understand—

BERTRAM.   The more they count on you the harder it would be for them if you failed to hold out in some way—

LEOPOLD.   People are calling on me all the time—not long ago a couple of lads from the paper mill showed up—typical workers—ordinary people—

BERTRAM.   That's certainly excellent, but, how should I put it?

LEOPOLD.   What?

BERTRAM.   How should I put it?

LEOPOLD.   How should you put what?

BERTRAM.   The question is whether a visit from a couple of paper-mill workers—excellent though it is in itself—is simply—or might become simply—forgive me—a kind of inaction in action—a leftover from a world which is no longer the case—whether you might not be playing the role in a mechanical, superficial way to reassure yourself that you are still the person to whom that role properly belonged. What is at stake here is that a gap should not open up between you and your role in society, so that your role, which was a true reflection of your personality, becomes a crutch to prop you up—circumstantial evidence of a supposed continuity of personality—but spurious, illusory, self-deceiving—by means of which you try to assure the world and yourself that you are still the person who you in fact no longer are—in short, that your role which grew naturally out of your attitudes and your work should not become a mere substitute, and that you don't attach to that role, which has long since kept going autonomously, on its own momentum, don't attach to it the sole and lasting proof of your moral existence, and thus let your entire human identity hang on a visit from a couple of know-nothing workers from the paper mill—

(*Short pause.*)

You're not angry, are you, that I'm speaking so openly?

LEOPOLD.   No—on the contrary—

(*Pause.*)

LUCY (*off stage*). Leopold—

LEOPOLD (*calls out*). Just a minute—

(*Pause.* LEOPOLD *is trembling with cold and rubbing his arms.*)

BERTRAM.   It's terrible of course to live with this nerve-racking uncertainty. We all understand that. None of us knows how we'd be able to stand it ourselves. That's why so many people are concerned about you. To have to understand that—

LEOPOLD.   I do understand—

BERTRAM.   You must believe me, too, that all I wish for is that we're worrying about nothing—

LEOPOLD.   I do believe you—

BERTRAM.   And even if this danger, which we your friends worry about, is infinitesimal, I have a duty—to you, to myself, to all of us—to confess those worries to you—

LEOPOLD.   I understand—

BERTRAM.   By all the things you did and have been doing up to now, you've earned our respect and our love, and in so doing you have suffered a great deal. Obviously you are not a superman, and the oppressive atmosphere in which you have had to live is bound to have left its mark. But all that said, I can't escape the awful feeling that lately something inside you has begun to collapse—as if an axis that has held you together has given way, as if the ground is collapsing under your feet—as if you've gone lame inside—that you are tending more and more to act the part of yourself instead of being yourself. Your personal life, that vital plank, is—don't be angry—in a mess, you're lacking a fixed point out of which everything inside you would grow and develop—you're losing the strength and perhaps even the will to put your affairs in order—you're erratic—you're letting yourself be tossed about by chance currents, you're sinking deeper and deeper into a void and you can't get a grip on things— you're just waiting for what is going to happen and so you're no longer the self-aware subject of your life, you're turning into its passive object—you're obviously at the mercy of great demons but they do not drive you in any direction, they merely drive about inside you— your existence seems to have become a cumbersome burden to you and you have really settled for listening helplessly to the passing of the time. What happened to your perspective on things? To your humour? Your industry and persistence? The pointedness of your observations? Your irony and self-irony? Your capacity for enthusiasm, for emotional involvement, for commitment, even for sacrifice?! I fear for you, Leopold—I fear for us! We need you! You have no idea how we need you, we need you the way you used to be! So I am asking you to swear that you won't give up—Don't weaken! Keep at it! Get a grip on yourself! Pull yourself together! Straighten up! Leopold—

LEOPOLD.   Yes?

BERTRAM.   You don't doubt, do you, that we all like you?

LEOPOLD.   I know—

BERTRAM.   So I beg you—be again that brilliant Leopold Nettles whom everybody held on high!

(*From Leopold's room* LUCY *emerges quietly, dressed only in a candlewick bedspread, naked underneath it.*)

LUCY.   Bertram—

(BERTRAM *is rather startled. He gets up quickly and looks at* LUCY *in astonishment.*)

BERTRAM.   Oh, Lucy—

LUCY.   Can't you see he's cold?

BERTRAM.   He never mentioned it—

LUCY.   Also, it's late—

BERTRAM.   Yes—of course—forgive me—I'm sorry—I didn't realize—I'm just going—

LEOPOLD.   You don't have to rush—stay the night if you like—

BERTRAM.   No—thank you—and so long—

LUCY.   So long—and don't be offended—

BERTRAM.   That's quite all right—it was presumptuous of me—so long—

LEOPOLD.   Cheerio and do come again some time!

BERTRAM.   Glad to—

(BERTRAM *goes out through the front door. Short pause.*)

LEOPOLD.   You didn't have to push him out like that—

LUCY.   He would have been sitting here all night—And I want you for myself—We get so little time—

LEOPOLD.   And it's not the best thing in the world that he saw you here—

LUCY.   Why?

LEOPOLD.   You know how much talk there'll be now—

LUCY.   So what? Or are you ashamed of me?

LEOPOLD.   It's not that—

LUCY.   Then why do you treat me like a stranger in front of other people?

LEOPOLD.   I don't, do I?

LUCY.   Yes you do! I can't remember you ever taking my hand in company—touching me—not even a fond glance—

LEOPOLD.   Hadn't we better go to bed?

LUCY.   No—

LEOPOLD.   Why?

LUCY.   Because I want to have a serious talk with you—

LEOPOLD.   About our relationship?

LUCY.   Yes—

LEOPOLD.   In that case at least fetch me a blanket—

(LUCY *goes to Leopold's room and returns in a moment with a blanket.* LEOPOLD *sits down comfortably on the sofa and wraps himself in the blanket. Short pause.*)

LUCY.   I knew it wasn't going to be easy for me—you know I had to make a few sacrifices—and what I am trying to say—reluctantly but I have to say it—look, I respect your idiosyncrasies—

LEOPOLD.   If you mean what happened—didn't happen—I mean in there—(*he points to his room*) then I've already explained that I haven't been feeling up to the mark today—

LUCY.   That's not what I meant—and if we're going to talk about it then there's other reasons behind it—

LEOPOLD.   Such as?

LUCY.   You're simply blocked—you're censoring yourself—you're afraid to give in to any emotion or experience—you're controlling, observing, watching yourself every minute—you're thinking about it, so in the end it's duty instead of pleasure, and then, of course, it doesn't work—but that's my problem—I wasn't going to talk about it now—

LEOPOLD.   About what, then?

LUCY.   Everything I've done for us I've done freely and willingly, I'm not complaining and I don't want anything in return—I only want you to admit what is true—

LEOPOLD.   What do you mean?

LUCY.   We're seeing each other—we're lovers—we love each other—

LEOPOLD.   Have I ever denied it?

LUCY.   Forgive me but you do everything you can to deny it, to make it invisible, to avoid acknowledging it, you behave as if it wasn't there—

LEOPOLD.   I'm possibly more reserved about some things than I should be, but—forgive me—you're partly to blame—

LUCY.   Me? How?

LEOPOLD.   You know—I'm really afraid of you—

LUCY.   Me?

LEOPOLD.   Your ceaseless effort to give a name to our relationship, to make your status somehow official, and the way you defend your territory while quietly but relentlessly trying to enlarge it—the way you have to discuss it endlessly—all that, quite naturally, makes me defensive. By my reserve, by wariness, perhaps even by a mild cynicism, I have been compensating for a subconscious fear of being manipulated, if not actually colonized—I reproach myself bitterly for my behaviour but I can't overcome it—

LUCY.   But I ask so little of you! You must see that I live only for you and through you and all I want is for you to admit to yourself that you love me!

LEOPOLD.   Hm—

LUCY.   And I believe you do love me! I don't believe that you are incapable of love! I don't believe that my love is incapable of awakening love even in you! I'm on your side. Without love no one is a complete person! We only achieve an identity through the person next to us!—isn't that how you put it in your *Ontology of the Human Self?!* You'll see that if you lose your ridiculous inhibitions you'll come alive again—and even your work will go better than you can imagine!

LEOPOLD.   I feel sorry for you, Lucy—

LUCY.   Why?

LEOPOLD.   You deserve someone better. I'm just worthless—

LUCY.   I don't like you talking about yourself like that—

LEOPOLD.   It's true, Lucy. I can't get rid of the awful feeling that lately something has begun to collapse inside me—as if some axis which was holding me together has broken, the ground collapsing under my feet, as if I'd gone lame inside—I sometimes have the feeling that I'm acting the part of myself instead of being myself. I'm lacking a fixed point out of which I can grow and develop. I'm erratic—I'm letting myself be tossed about by chance currents—I'm sinking deeper and deeper into a void and I can no longer get a grip on things. In truth I'm just waiting for this thing that's going to happen and am no longer the self-aware subject of my own life but becoming merely its passive object—I have a feeling sometimes that all I am doing is listening helplessly to the passing of the time. What happened to my perspective on things? My humour? My industry and persistence? The pointedness of my observations? My irony and self-irony? My capacity for enthusiasm, for emotional involvement, for commitment, even for sacrifice? The oppressive atmosphere in which I have been forced to live for so long is bound to have left its mark! Outwardly I go on acting my role as if nothing has happened but inside I'm no longer the person you all take me for. It's hard to admit it to myself, but if *I* can all the more reason for you to! It's a touching and beautiful thing that you don't lose hope of making me into someone better than I am but—don't be angry—it's an illusion. I've fallen apart, I'm paralyzed, I won't change and it would be best if they came for me and took me where I would no longer be the cause of unhappiness and disillusion—

(LUCY *gets up, upset, goes quickly to the balcony door. She opens it and goes out on to the balcony and stands looking out into the night with her back to the room. Soon it becomes clear that she is crying.* LEOPOLD *looks at her perplexed and after a while speaks to her.*)

Lucy—

(LUCY *doesn't react. Pause.*)

There, there, Lucy, what's the matter?

(LUCY *doesn't react. Pause.* LEOPOLD *gets up and approaches her slowly, still wrapped up in a blanket.*)

Are you crying, Lucy?

(*Pause.*)

Why are you crying?

(*Pause.*)

Don't cry!

(*Pause.*)

I didn't want to upset you—I didn't realize—

(*He has approached* LUCY *and touched her carefully on the shoulder.* LUCY *with a tear-stained face turns suddenly to him and cries out.*)

LUCY.   Don't touch me!

(LEOPOLD *steps back surprised.* LUCY *comes back into the room, wiping her eyes, sobbing quietly.*)

LEOPOLD.   What's the matter?

LUCY.   Leave me alone—

LEOPOLD.   There, there—what have I done now?

LUCY.   You're a worse case than I thought—

LEOPOLD.   How do you mean?

LUCY.   All this talk—it's nothing but excuses! You sang a different tune the first time you got me to stay with you! You said our relationship would give you back some of your lost integrity!—That it would renew your hope—that it would put you back together emotionally!—That it would open a door into a new life! You just say what suits you! No, Leopold, you're no broken wreck, you're an ordinary bullshit-artist—you've had enough of me and now you want to get shot of me—so now you paint a picture of your ruin to make me understand that there's nothing more I can expect from you and—on top of that—to make me feel sorry for you! You're ruined all right, but not in the way you say—it's your dishonesty that shows how ruined you are! And simpleton that I am, I believed that I could awaken love in you, that I'd give you back your zest for life, that I'd help you! You're beyond help! Serves me right—one great illusion less—

LEOPOLD.   You're being unfair, Lucy—I really am going through a crisis—even Bertram says so—

LUCY.   Please don't go on—there's no point. I'm going to get dressed—

LEOPOLD.   Don't be silly, Lucy! This is no way to part—

(LEOPOLD *tries to embrace her but she breaks free from him. At that moment the doorbell rings. It startles them both and they look at each other in confusion. Their quarrel is forgotten.* LEOPOLD *throws his blanket on the sofa, goes quickly to the front door and looks through the peep-hole. Then, completely rattled, turns to* LUCY.)

(*Whispering.*) It's them!

LUCY (*whispering*).   What are we going to do?

LEOPOLD (*whispering*).   I don't know—go in the bedroom—I'll let them in—

LUCY.   I'm staying here with you!

(*The doorbell rings again.* LEOPOLD *breathes in, smooths his hair, goes to the door and opens it decisively. The* FIRST CHAP *and* SECOND CHAP *enter.*)

FIRST CHAP. Good evening, Professor—

LEOPOLD. Good evening—

FIRST CHAP. I suppose you know who we are—

LEOPOLD. I suppose so—

SECOND CHAP. You thought we wouldn't come any more today, did you?

LEOPOLD. I realize you can come any time—

FIRST CHAP. We must apologize for the intrusion—you obviously had other plans for the evening—

(*The* TWO CHAPS *smile lecherously.*)

LEOPOLD. What plans I had is my own business—

SECOND CHAP. We possibly won't keep you long, it depends on you—

FIRST CHAP. It's a pleasure to meet you. According to our colleagues you're a sensible chap so with luck we'll soon come to an understanding—

LEOPOLD. I don't know what there is to understand. I've got my things ready, I just need time to get dressed—

SECOND CHAP. What's the hurry? It may not come to the worst—

FIRST CHAP. But we must ask the lady to kindly leave—

LUCY. I'm staying!

SECOND CHAP. No, you're leaving—

(LUCY *clings on to* LEOPOLD.)

LEOPOLD. My friend can't leave now—

FIRST CHAP. Why?

LEOPOLD. She's got nowhere to go—

SECOND CHAP. In that case we'll put her up for the night.

LEOPOLD. Oh no you won't!

FIRST CHAP. Watch!

(*The* FIRST CHAP *opens the front door and makes a gesture towards the corridor. The* FIRST MAN *and the* SECOND MAN *enter smartly. The* FIRST CHAP *points towards* LUCY. *The* FIRST *and* SECOND MAN *go to her and take her by the hands.* LUCY *struggles against them and* LEOPOLD *clasps her in his arms.*)

LUCY. You bastards!

LEOPOLD. Don't touch her!

(*The* FIRST *and* SECOND MAN *pull* LUCY *out of* LEOPOLD's *embrace and drag her towards the front door.* LEOPOLD *tries to prevent them but they push him roughly away.*)

LUCY (*shouting*). Help!

(FIRST *and* SECOND MAN *put their hands over Lucy's mouth and drag her out. The* FIRST CHAP *dismisses the men with a gesture and closes the door.*)

FIRST CHAP. Now that wasn't necessary was it?

(LEOPOLD *remains silent.*)

SECOND CHAP. You don't have to worry about your girlfriend, nobody's going to harm her. As soon as she comes to her senses we'll take her home. You don't think we'd let her run around the streets in a candlewick bedspread—

FIRST CHAP. We're not inhuman, you can be sure of that—

(LEOPOLD *closes the balcony door. He picks up his* blanket and wraps himself into it and sits down rebelliously on the sofa. Short pause.)

Do you mind if we sit down too?

(LEOPOLD *shrugs.* FIRST *and* SECOND CHAPS *sit down on chairs. Pause.*)

We're sorry about that little incident, but don't give it another thought. We're better off this way. And it wouldn't be very nice for you to have your girlfriend see this—

(*Pause.*)

SECOND CHAP. Miss Suzana isn't at home, then?

(LEOPOLD *shrugs.*)

FIRST CHAP. We know she's at the cinema—

(LEOPOLD *shrugs.*)

SECOND CHAP. Won't you talk to us?

(LEOPOLD *shrugs.*)

FIRST CHAP. What are you writing at the moment, may one ask?

LEOPOLD. What does it matter—

FIRST CHAP. No harm in asking—

(*Pause.*)

SECOND CHAP. When was the last time you went out?

LEOPOLD. I don't know—

FIRST CHAP. It was some time ago, wasn't it?

LEOPOLD. Hm—

(*Pause.* FIRST CHAP *looks through the medicines which are lying on the table.*)

FIRST CHAP. Vitamins?

LEOPOLD. Yes—

SECOND CHAP. Apart from vitamins are you on anything?

LEOPOLD. Not really—why?

FIRST CHAP. There's been some talk—

LEOPOLD. What sort of talk?

FIRST CHAP. Forget it—

(*Pause.*)

SECOND CHAP. How much do you drink?

LEOPOLD. The same as everyone else—

SECOND CHAP. Starting in the morning?

LEOPOLD. As the case may be—

(*Pause.*)

FIRST CHAP. Well look, Professor, we won't drag this out unnecessarily. We're here because we've been given the job of putting a proposition to you—

LEOPOLD. A proposition?

FIRST CHAP. Yes. As you know only too well, you're being threatened with something unpleasant which I personally wouldn't wish upon you and I don't suppose you are particularly looking forward to it yourself—

LEOPOLD. In a way it might be better than—

SECOND CHAP. Now, now, Professor, no blasphemy!

FIRST CHAP. As you've been told many times before, it's not our business to push these things to extremes—on the contrary we want to avoid confrontations, so that—if possible—thing don't come to the worst—

SECOND CHAP.   It's not in our interests—

FIRST CHAP.   And in some cases, when there is no better alternative, we even look for ways to achieve our object without having to go down every twist and turn of the path—

SECOND CHAP.   We always try to give people another chance—

FIRST CHAP.   And that's why we're here. We've been given the job of notifying you that under certain conditions this whole matter could be dropped—

LEOPOLD.   Dropped? How?

SECOND CHAP.   The whole thing would be declared null and void.

LEOPOLD.   Under what conditions?

FIRST CHAP.   As you know, what's coming to you is coming to you because under the name of Professor Leopold Nettles you put together a certain paper—

SECOND CHAP.   An essay, as you call it—

FIRST CHAP.   You never denied it and in effect therefore, you brought the whole thing upon yourself—by this act of nondenial, you unmasked the perpetrator—
(*Brief pause.*)

SECOND CHAP.   As a man of wide knowledge you must be aware that if the perpetrator isn't known one cannot proceed against him. This is known as the Principle of the Identity of the Perpetrator—

FIRST CHAP.   In a word, if you would sign, here and now, a short statement saying that you are not Professor Leopold Nettles, author of the paper in question, then the whole thing will be considered null and void and all previous decisions rescinded—

LEOPOLD.   If I understand you correctly you want me to declare that I am no longer me—

FIRST CHAP.   That's a way of putting it which might do for a philosopher but of course from a legal point of view it doesn't make sense. Obviously it is not a matter of you declaring that you are no longer you, but only declaring that you are not the same person who is the author of that thing—essentially it's a formality—

SECOND CHAP.   One name being like another name—

FIRST CHAP.   Or do you think that Nettles is such a beautiful name that you couldn't bear to lose it? You only have to look in the phone book to see how many equally nice names there are—

SECOND CHAP. ⎫
FIRST CHAP.   ⎬ And most of them even nicer—

LEOPOLD.   Do you mean that I have to change my name?

SECOND CHAP.   Not at all! You can have whatever name you like, that's entirely up to you—nobody—at least in this instance—could care less. The only thing which is important here is whether you are or are not the Nettles who wrote that paper—

FIRST CHAP.   If you insist on keeping your name for sentimental reasons then by all means keep it—

SECOND CHAP.   Though there's no denying that it would be neater if you were to decide otherwise—

FIRST CHAP.   It would be neater but it's not essential. After all there could be more than one Leopold Nettles—

SECOND CHAP.   There are three just in the phone book—

FIRST CHAP.   In other words, it is not so much a question of whether you are Nettles or Nichols but rather whether you are the Nettles who wrote the paper—

SECOND CHAP.   You have to admit it's a good offer—

LEOPOLD.   I don't understand what you'll achieve by it—or why, in that case, you're proposing it—as far as I know you never do anything without a reason—

FIRST CHAP.   Our interest is to wipe this unpleasant business off the slate and give you one more chance—

LEOPOLD.   What chance?

FIRST CHAP.   To keep out of trouble until the next time—

LEOPOLD.   I don't like it much—

FIRST CHAP.   Now look, whether you like it or not is your own affair. Nobody is forcing you to do anything, and nobody can force you. But I'm telling you man to man that you'd be making a mistake if you didn't go along with it—

SECOND CHAP.   It's a free gift!

FIRST CHAP.   No one will know a thing so long as you don't go prattling on about it, and even if it gets around everyone will understand why you did it—

SECOND CHAP.   They'd all do exactly the same—

FIRST CHAP.   Many of them have already done it—and what harm has it done them? None—

SECOND CHAP.   If you're hesitating then the only explanation I can think of is that you have no idea what's coming to you—
(*Pause.*)

LEOPOLD.   Would I have to do it right this minute?

FIRST CHAP.   It would be best of course—

LEOPOLD.   No,—this is definitely serious enough to require some reflection—

SECOND CHAP.   If you want to take the risk—

LEOPOLD.   What risk?

FIRST CHAP.   Look, we've been given the job of notifying you of what we have notified you. We don't make the decisions—

SECOND CHAP.   We're small fry—

FIRST CHAP.   And we can't be expected to know, of course, what the relevant authorities will make of this whole business—

SECOND CHAP.   All we can do is pass on your request for time to consider—

LEOPOLD.   But surely it can't make much difference to them whether it's going to be today or the day after tomorrow!

FIRST CHAP.   You must understand that their goodwill is not some kind of balloon which can be expanded indefinitely—

LEOPOLD.   I do understand—

(*Longer pause.* LEOPOLD *has been rattled by all this and furthermore he's evidently becoming cold again in spite of the fact that he is wrapped up in the blanket. After a while the* SECOND CHAP *suddenly says in a loud voice.*)

SECOND CHAP.   Don't be a fool, man! Here's a chance—with one stroke of the pen—to rid yourself of everything that's piled on your head, all the shit—a chance for a completely fresh start, it's once in a lifetime! What would I give for such a chance!

(*Short pause.* LEOPOLD *is openly trembling, either from nervousness or the cold.*)

LEOPOLD (*whispering*). Let's have a look—

(*The* SECOND CHAP *at once begins to go through all his pockets until finally in his back trouser pocket he finds a soiled piece of paper. He puts it on the table and straightens it out with the back of his hand. Then he gives it to* LEOPOLD *who holds it for a long time in his trembling hands and reads it carefully. After a while he slowly puts it back on the table and wraps himself up even more tightly in his blanket. Pause.*)

FIRST CHAP.   Well, what's it to be?

(*The curtain falls, the music returns.*)

SCENE FIVE

The music fades as the curtain rises.

LEOPOLD *is alone on stage. He paces the length of the room as a prisoner might pace his cell, back and forth between the front door and the bathroom door. When he reaches the front door for the third time he pauses and looks through the peep-hole. Then he puts his ear to the door and listens intently for a moment, and then continues walking. He paces back and forth twice more and then on reaching the door he pauses, reflects a moment, then goes to one of the bookcases and from behind some books he pulls out a wooden box. He takes it to the table, sits down on a chair and opens the box. It is full of various medicines.* LEOPOLD *starts going through them, then he considers a moment, hesitates, and prepares himself a dose from several of the medicines. He tosses the dose back into his mouth, takes a drink of rum and swallows the lot. He shuts the box, puts it back behind the books and continues to pace. When he comes to the bathroom door for the second time he pauses, considers a moment, and then goes into the bathroom leaving the door open. There is the sound of running water and* LEOPOLD *gasping. Evidently he is washing his face. After a while he re-enters, his face already dry, and closes the bathroom door and continues to pace. Reaching the front door for the third time he stops and looks through the peep-hole. He then puts his ear to the door, listening intently for a while, and then continues to pace. When he reaches the front door for the second time, he pauses, considers a moment, and then goes to the bookcase where his medicines are hidden and once more takes out his box. He takes it to the table, sits down on*

a chair and opens the box. He starts going through his medicines, considers a moment, hesitates, prepares himself another dose of various medicines, tosses the whole lot back into his mouth, takes a drink of rum and swallows the lot. He shuts the box, puts it back behind the books and continues to pace. When he reaches the bathroom door for the second time, he pauses, considers a moment and then goes into the bathroom leaving the door open. There is the sound of running water and* LEOPOLD *gasping. He is washing his face again. After a while he re-enters, his face already dry, closes the bathroom door and continues to pace. Reaching the front door for the third time he stops, considers a moment, looks through the peep-hole, steps quickly to the place where his medicines are hidden, takes out his box, takes out one bottle of medicine, empties it into his mouth and runs into the bathroom leaving the door open. There is the sound of running water and* LEOPOLD *gasping.* LEOPOLD *re-enters after a moment, closes the bathroom door and goes quickly to the front door. He puts his ear to the door, listens for a while and suddenly leaps back. At the same moment a key rattles in the lock and through the front door comes* SUZANA *carrying a full shopping bag.*

SUZANA.   Hello—

LEOPOLD.   Hello—

SUZANA.   Isn't Edward here?

LEOPOLD.   He hasn't come yet—

(LEOPOLD *takes the shopping bag from* SUZANA, *carries it into the kitchen and immediately returns.*)

Did you get any vegetables?

SUZANA.   A cauliflower—

LEOPOLD.   You didn't!

(SUZANA *goes up the little staircase to her room.* LEOPOLD *approaches the staircase, hesitating for a moment.*)

LEOPOLD.   Suzana—

(*She stops halfway up the staircase and turns towards him.*)

SUZANA.   Yes?

LEOPOLD.   They were here—

SUZANA (*surprised*). They were?

LEOPOLD.   Yes—

SUZANA.   When?

LEOPOLD.   During the night—

SUZANA.   And how come you're here?

LEOPOLD.   I'll explain—

SUZANA.   Did you promise them anything?

LEOPOLD.   No—

SUZANA.   You didn't get into trouble again in some way, did you?

LEOPOLD.   No—

SUZANA.   What happened, then?

LEOPOLD.   When you went out to the cinema with Edward, Lucy and I cooked ourselves that liver—

SUZANA.   Cooked it in what?

LEOPOLD.   In a frying pan—

SUZANA.   Which one?

LEOPOLD.   The new one—

SUZANA.   And you left it in a mess—

LEOPOLD.   We scrubbed it—

SUZANA.   With what?

LEOPOLD.   With washing powder—

SUZANA.   I might have known! You know very well you shouldn't use washing powder on it—

LEOPOLD.   It's all right, you can have a look—then we talked for a while and then Bertram turned up, apparently on behalf of several friends—he said they were concerned about me—that I was in a bad way—that my home life was in a mess—that I was erratic—that I wasn't doing anything—

SUZANA.   I've been telling you that for ages—

LEOPOLD.   When Bertram left, Lucy and I had a bit of a row—

SUZANA.   What about?

LEOPOLD.   It's complicated—basically she complains that I don't love her enough—that I'm evasive—that I don't make it clear in company that we belong to each other, and so on—and when I honestly tried to explain things to her she said I was making excuses—

SUZANA.   Well, does that surprise you?

LEOPOLD.   I don't know what she means but what am I supposed to do?

SUZANA.   Well, if you don't know—

LEOPOLD.   Before she could leave they came and then because she insisted on staying they called some men in and they dragged her away—

SUZANA.   Is she out yet?

LEOPOLD.   I don't know—perhaps—

SUZANA.   What do you mean, you don't know? Haven't you gone to see her?

LEOPOLD.   I can't possibly leave here! Not now!

SUZANA.   Of course. And what about them?

LEOPOLD.   Apparently I won't have to go there if I make a statement that I am not the author of that—if I say simply that I am somebody else—

SUZANA.   Somebody else! That would just suit them! Denounce yourself and spit on your own work!

LEOPOLD.   They are not asking me to make a value judgement, they only want a formal excuse to drop the whole thing—

SUZANA.   Tsss!

LEOPOLD.   They're obviously worried that once I get there it would only increase the respect in which I'm held—

SUZANA.   Whereas if you were to recant you'd lose it all! Obviously that would be much more to their liking! I hope you threw them out—

LEOPOLD.   I asked for time to consider—

SUZANA.   What?

LEOPOLD.   There's nothing to it, surely—

SUZANA.   Have you gone mad? What is there to consider? That's just showing them that they're half way to

breaking you—and now they'll increase the pressure! I knew as soon as I saw you that you'd got yourself into trouble! You wet!

LEOPOLD.   It's all very well for you to talk—

SUZANA.   If you can't take it you should never have got into it.

(SUZANA *turns abruptly and goes towards her room.*)

LEOPOLD.   Suzana—

SUZANA (*without looking at him*). Leave me alone—

(SUZANA *goes into her room.* LEOPOLD *nervously begins to pace his usual path. When he reaches the front door for the third time, he stops, goes to the spot where his medicines are hidden, quickly extracts his box, takes a pill out of a bottle, throws it into his mouth and swallows it. He puts the box back, then continues pacing and when he gets to the bathroom door he pauses, goes quickly to the front door, looks through the peep-hole and then runs into the bathroom leaving the door open. There is the sound of running water and* LEOPOLD's *gasping. Suddenly the doorbell rings. Water is still running,* LEOPOLD *is gasping and obviously does not hear the bell. After a while the bell rings again. The sound of running water stops, and after a moment* LEOPOLD *comes out of the bathroom, drying his wet hair with a towel. Drying his hair he continues to pace. When he reaches the front door for the third time he looks through the peep-hole. At that moment the bell rings again.* LEOPOLD *jumps, then he returns to the door and looks through the peep-hole. He calms down and looks through the door.* EDWARD *enters wearing a dinner jacket.*)

EDWARD.   At last!

LEOPOLD.   Has something happened?

EDWARD.   I rang three times—

LEOPOLD.   I was getting myself together—

EDWARD (*going to the balcony door*). Can I open it a bit?

LEOPOLD.   Go ahead.

(EDWARD *opens the balcony door wide.* LEOPOLD, *the towel round his neck, walks slowly round the room.* EDWARD *sits down on a chair.*)

EDWARD.   I'm relieved to find you here—

LEOPOLD.   You know, then?

EDWARD.   Lucy came to see me—

LEOPOLD.   So she's out—

EDWARD.   What did they want?

LEOPOLD.   To negotiate—

EDWARD.   Did you sign anything?

LEOPOLD.   I've asked for time to consider—

EDWARD.   When will they be back?

LEOPOLD.   They never say—

EDWARD.   You ought to go and see Lucy, she's having a bad time one way and another—

LEOPOLD.   I can't possibly leave here! Not now!

EDWARD.   Is Suzana at home?

LEOPOLD.   Yes—she was just asking for you—
(LEOPOLD *goes into the bathroom and after a while returns without the towel and with his hair combed.*)
Do you mind if I close it now?

EDWARD.   Leave it a while—
(LEOPOLD *returns to his place and sits down. Pause.*)

LEOPOLD.   That's a nice outfit you've got on—

EDWARD.   It's a dinner jacket—my uncle lent it to me—

LEOPOLD.   I know it's a dinner jacket—it's nice—

EDWARD.   You know my uncle—(*Pause.*) How did you sleep?

LEOPOLD.   Hardly at all—

EDWARD.   You couldn't get them out of your mind, could you?

LEOPOLD.   Well—
(*Pause.*)

EDWARD.   Did you go this morning?

LEOPOLD.   Yes—

EDWARD.   Well, that's something anyway—

LEOPOLD.   Not much of a thing, as it happens—
(*Pause.*)

EDWARD.   What did you eat?

LEOPOLD.   I wasn't hungry, I just ate a couple of onions and five almonds to calm myself down—

EDWARD.   And did it?

LEOPOLD.   Not really—
(*Pause.*)

EDWARD.   The main thing is that you're here—

LEOPOLD.   I'd rather be there than here like this! Why can't I get my life clear! It was wonderful when nobody was interested in me—when nobody expected anything from me, nobody urging me to do anything—I just browsed around the second-hand bookshops—studying the modern philosophers at my leisure—spending the nights making notes from their works—taking walks in the parks and meditating—why can't I change my name to Nichols, say, and forget everything and start a completely new life?

EDWARD.   Perhaps you need some of your pills—

LEOPOLD.   I splash water on my face—I don't want pills— I don't want to get dependent on them—
(*Pause.* LEOPOLD *becomes alert, and listening.*)

EDWARD.   Nothing—
(*At that moment the doorbell rings.* LEOPOLD *jumps up in confusion.* EDWARD *also gets up.* LEOPOLD *goes to the peep-hole and looks through it and leaps back from the door and runs across the room into the bathroom leaving the door open. Immediately there is the sound of running water.* EDWARD *is puzzled. He steps to the bathroom door. Short pause.*)
(*Whispering towards the bathroom.*) Leopold, come on—
(*Short pause and the sound of water.*)
(*Whispering towards the bathroom.*) Don't be silly, Leopold, face up to it!
(*Short pause and the sound of water.*)

(*Whispering towards the bathroom.*) I'll tell them you're not at home if you like but it would be better to get it over with—
(*Short pause and the sound of water. The bell rings again.* EDWARD *doesn't know what to do. Then he makes up his mind abruptly and goes decisively to the main door, to the front door, opens it wide and gazes with surprise.* FIRST SIDNEY *and* SECOND SIDNEY *enter each carrying a large suitcase. They put their suitcases down.*)

FIRST SIDNEY.   Good afternoon—

EDWARD.   Good afternoon—

FIRST SIDNEY.   Isn't the professor in?
(EDWARD *is puzzled. Finally he nods, slowly closes the door and goes into the bathroom leaving the door half open. There is a short pause. The sound of water stops suddenly and there is some incomprehensible whispering for quite a long time off stage.* FIRST SIDNEY *and* SECOND SIDNEY *stand motionless next to their suitcases. Finally* LEOPOLD *comes out of the bathroom with his hair wet but sleekly combed.* EDWARD *follows him, closing the bathroom door.*)

LEOPOLD.   Good afternoon—

SECOND SIDNEY.   Here we are, professor—

LEOPOLD.   Excellent—

FIRST SIDNEY.   We've got it—

LEOPOLD.   What?
(FIRST SIDNEY *and* SECOND SIDNEY *put their suitcases on the table and open them. Both suitcases are full of various documents.*)

FIRST SIDNEY (*pointing to his suitcase*). These are blank papers—these are normal office issue—these are for carbon copies—these are carbon papers—and here we have various envelopes and files and so on—

LEOPOLD.   Is that all for me?

FIRST SIDNEY.   Of course—

LEOPOLD.   How much do I owe you?

FIRST SIDNEY.   Do me a favour, professor, what do you take us for!

LEOPOLD.   Well, thank you very much—I think that should last me—

SECOND SIDNEY.   We're looking forward to what you'll be writing on these bits of paper—

FIRST SIDNEY (*pointing to the other suitcase*). Well, and this is the stuff from our plant—these are minutes of the board of management—these are minutes of meetings of all the paper-mill employees—these are specimens of factory correspondence—here we have various memos, internal regulations, information for the work-force, overtime summaries—and this is specially interesting, that's from the personnel department—personal records of employees—various complaints—returns— denunciations—

SECOND SIDNEY.   I think it'll make very nice reading for you—

FIRST SIDNEY.   Use it as you see fit—

SECOND SIDNEY.   If you can do anything with it, it will certainly be a bombshell—

FIRST SIDNEY.   Absolutely—

LEOPOLD.   Thank you so—

(FIRST SIDNEY *takes a sheaf of papers out of one of the suitcases and looks around.*)

FIRST SIDNEY.   Where do you want it?

LEOPOLD (*looking around*).   Where? Well, in this corner, here—

(LEOPOLD *points to the left-hand corner of the room, downstage.* FIRST SIDNEY *and* SECOND SIDNEY *start taking papers from the two suitcases and carrying them to the corner where they place them on the floor. After a while they are joined first by* LEOPOLD *and then by* EDWARD. *When the contents of both suitcases are in the corner,* SECOND SIDNEY *closes both of the now empty cases and carries them to the front door. Then* FIRST *and* SECOND SIDNEY *sit down at the table.* LEOPOLD *sits down on the sofa.* EDWARD *remains standing in the background. There is a long awkward pause.*)

LEOPOLD.   There's a lot of it—

SECOND SIDNEY.   For you we'd steal the whole paper mill if we had to—

LEOPOLD.   Thank you—

(*Awkward pause.*)

I wasn't expecting you so soon—

FIRST SIDNEY.   One must strike while the iron is hot, that's what me and Sidney always say—

LEOPOLD.   Very well put—

(*Awkward pause.*)

I don't know how I'm ever going to repay you—

SECOND SIDNEY.   What is there to repay? We've already told you that we're your fans—and not just us—

FIRST SIDNEY.   There's lots of people looking to you—

LEOPOLD.   Thank you—

(*Awkward pause.*)

I wasn't expecting you so soon—

SECOND SIDNEY.   One must strike while the iron is hot, that's what me and Sidney always say—

LEOPOLD.   Very well put—

(*Awkward pause.*)

I don't know how I'm ever going to repay you—

FIRST SIDNEY.   What is there to repay? We've already told you that we're your fans—and not just us—

SECOND SIDNEY.   There's lots of people looking to you—

(*Awkward pause.*)

LEOPOLD.   I don't know how I'll ever repay you—

SECOND SIDNEY.   What is there to repay? We've already told you that we're your fans—and not just us—

LEOPOLD.   Excuse me—

(LEOPOLD *gets up and goes to the balcony door and closes it and then returns to his seat.* SECOND SIDNEY *is feeling his pockets.* LEOPOLD *offers him a cigarette.*)

SECOND SIDNEY.   I've got some today—

(SECOND SIDNEY *finds his cigarettes at last and he lights one.*)

But could I ask you for something else—

LEOPOLD.   I'm at your disposal—

SECOND SIDNEY.   Would there be any chance of a glass of rum?

LEOPOLD.   Yes—of course—

SECOND SIDNEY.   Just to clarify—I'm a teetotaller—but I was asking for Sidney here—he drinks like a fish—

(LEOPOLD *gets up and goes to the kitchen and comes back at once with a glass. He pours rum from his bottle into the glass and hands it to* FIRST SIDNEY.)

FIRST SIDNEY.   Thanks! Cheers!

(FIRST SIDNEY *drinks the whole glass in one go and then burps, satisfied.* LEOPOLD *refills his glass.*)

FIRST SIDNEY.   Thanks! Cheers!

(FIRST SIDNEY *drinks the whole glass in one go and then burps, satisfied.* LEOPOLD *fills his glass again.*) Thanks! Cheers!

(FIRST SIDNEY *drinks the whole glass in one go and then burps, satisfied.* SUZANA *comes out of her room in a long evening dress and walks down the little staircase.*)

LEOPOLD.   Look, Suzana, these gentlemen have brought me all this paper and all sorts of interesting stuff—

SUZANA.   Where's it going to go?

LEOPOLD.   I'll find somewhere—that's a nice dress.

(SUZANA *makes a sign to* EDWARD *who accompanies her to the kitchen. During the rest of the scene both of them can be seen through the glass-panelled kitchen door taking out various foodstuffs from the shopping bag, putting them where they belong, and, during all this time either discussing something in a lively way or perhaps quarrelling.* LEOPOLD *notices that* FIRST SIDNEY's *glass is empty and fills it up again for him.*)

FIRST SIDNEY.   Thanks! Cheers!

(FIRST SIDNEY *drinks the whole glass in one go and then burps, satisfied.* LEOPOLD *refills the glass.*)

Thanks! Cheers!

(FIRST SIDNEY *drinks the whole glass in one go and then burps, satisfied.* LEOPOLD *refills the glass.*)

Thanks! Cheers!

(FIRST SIDNEY *drinks the whole glass in one go and then burps, satisfied.* LEOPOLD *refills the glass.* FIRST SIDNEY *takes the glass but when he is on the point of drinking it he puts it back on the table.*)

FIRST SIDNEY.   Someone has to be sensible—

(*Short pause.*)

SECOND SIDNEY.   We're not holding you up are we?

LEOPOLD.   No—

FIRST SIDNEY.   Are you sure? Because if we are you only have to say so and we'll push off—

LEOPOLD.   You're not holding me up—excuse me—

(LEOPOLD *gets up, goes to the place where his medicines are hidden, turns his back to the room so as not to be seen, pulls out his box, quickly takes out a pill, throws it into his mouth and swallows it and puts his box back and returns to his seat. Pause.*)

SECOND SIDNEY.   Have you thought about it yet?

LEOPOLD.   About what?

FIRST SIDNEY.   What we were talking about yesterday—that it's time for an initiative—

LEOPOLD.   Oh yes—I haven't got round to it yet—

SECOND SIDNEY.   Pity. You know, I'm an ordinary bloke, a nobody, but I can spot a few things and I've got my own opinion and nobody can deny me that. And what I think is, there's a lot that could be done—certainly more than is being done at the moment—

FIRST SIDNEY.   One just has to get hold of the situation by the—

SECOND SIDNEY.   Who else but you is there to get things going again?

(LEOPOLD *is starting to get nervous. He looks discreetly at his watch.*)

FIRST SIDNEY.   We're not holding you up are we?

LEOPOLD.   No—

SECOND SIDNEY.   Are you sure? Because if we are you only have to say so and we'll push off—

LEOPOLD.   You're not holding me up. Excuse me—

(LEOPOLD *gets up and goes into the bathroom, leaving the door open. There is the sound of running water and* LEOPOLD *gasping. The sound of water stops and shortly afterwards* LEOPOLD *returns to his seat.*)

FIRST SIDNEY.   That thing you wrote—even if we don't fully understand it—

SECOND SIDNEY.   We're ordinary people—

FIRST SIDNEY.   —and the fact that you're right behind it—

SECOND SIDNEY.   —regardless of the consequences—

FIRST SIDNEY.   —straight away leads one to hope that you will take the final step—

LEOPOLD.   What final step?

SECOND SIDNEY.   I'm not really good at explaining myself but let me put it like this—that whatever you're writing, you'll turn it into something that will have a practical effect—

FIRST SIDNEY.   To put it simply, that you'll come up with the pay-off to all your philosophizing—

LEOPOLD.   The trouble is that opinions differ about quite what the pay-off is—

SECOND SIDNEY.   You'll find it—

FIRST SIDNEY.   Who else but you is there to get things going again—

SECOND SIDNEY.   I'd say that's just what people are waiting for—

LEOPOLD.   What people?

FIRST SIDNEY.   Everybody—

LEOPOLD.   Isn't that a bit of an exaggeration?

SECOND SIDNEY.   Forgive me but you probably don't realize—

LEOPOLD.   What?

FIRST SIDNEY.   Your responsibility—

LEOPOLD.   For what?

SECOND SIDNEY.   For everything—

(LEOPOLD *is evidently nervous. He looks at his watch.*)

FIRST SIDNEY.   We're not holding you up?

LEOPOLD.   No—

FIRST SIDNEY.   ⎱ Are you sure? Because if we are you

SECOND SIDNEY. ⎰ only have to say so and we'll push off—

LEOPOLD.   You're not holding me up. Excuse me—

(LEOPOLD *gets up and goes to the kitchen and returns shortly with a small plate on which there are two onions and five almonds. He eats the lot during the following dialogue.*)

SECOND SIDNEY.   Sidney and I were giving it a bit of thought the other day—

FIRST SIDNEY.   And we got the following idea—

LEOPOLD.   What idea?

SECOND SIDNEY.   We think it's quite good—

LEOPOLD.   What idea?

FIRST SIDNEY.   This could be exactly the step that everyone is waiting for you to take—

LEOPOLD.   What?

SECOND SIDNEY.   That you should write a kind of declaration—

LEOPOLD.   What kind of declaration?

FIRST SIDNEY.   Quite simply a kind of general declaration covering all the basics—

SECOND SIDNEY.   It would have to be brief and easy to understand of course—

FIRST SIDNEY.   In other words you'd have to spend some time on it—

SECOND SIDNEY.   You've got plenty of paper now—

(LEOPOLD, *irritated, gets up, ambles round the room and then turns to the* TWO SIDNEYS.)

LEOPOLD.   Forgive me, gentlemen, but I'm not clear about—

(SUZANA, *followed by* EDWARD, *comes out of the kitchen.* LEOPOLD *looks at them in surprise.*)

(*To* SUZANA.) Are you leaving?

SUZANA.   Why?

LEOPOLD.   I thought that we might—since you got that cauliflower—since I need to calm down a bit—to examine everything calmly—to discuss—

SUZANA.   Forgive me, Leopold, but I've got tickets for a dance—I bought them ages ago—

LEOPOLD.   I see—I see—

SUZANA.   It's my first dance this year—

LEOPOLD.   I understand—I understand—

SUZANA. Not that I know what there is to discuss—I've already given you my opinion—

LEOPOLD. I know—I only thought—but it doesn't really matter—

SUZANA. Well, so long—

EDWARD. So long, Leopold—and get to bed soon—get some sleep—

(SUZANA and EDWARD *leave through the front door*. LEOPOLD *looks at them awkwardly as they leave. Pause*.)

FIRST SIDNEY. What aren't you clear about?

LEOPOLD (*turning round*). I beg your pardon?

SECOND SIDNEY. You were saying that you weren't clear about something—

LEOPOLD. Was I? Ah—yes—don't be angry, gentlemen, but I'm not really quite clear about—

FIRST SIDNEY. About what?

LEOPOLD. About what exactly you want from me—

(FIRST SIDNEY *drinks the glass of rum in one go and then gets up*. SECOND SIDNEY *gets up also. They both step nearer to* LEOPOLD.)

FIRST SIDNEY. Professor, you've obviously got us wrong—we don't want anything from you—

SECOND SIDNEY. We've only taken the liberty of giving you our opinion—

FIRST SIDNEY. It's the opinion of ordinary people—

SECOND SIDNEY. Of lots of ordinary people—

FIRST SIDNEY. We only wanted to offer a suggestion—

SECOND SIDNEY. We meant well—

FIRST SIDNEY. We can't help not being able to express ourselves exactly—

SECOND SIDNEY. We're not philosophers—

FIRST SIDNEY. We just thought you might be interested in our opinion—

SECOND SIDNEY. As representing the opinion of ordinary—

LEOPOLD. I'm not saying that I'm not interested in your opinion—

FIRST SIDNEY. Well, you seem to be implying that we're confusing you—

LEOPOLD. Really I'm not suggesting anything of the sort—

SECOND SIDNEY. You were saying that you weren't clear about what we want from you—

LEOPOLD. I don't exactly know what I was saying—

FIRST SIDNEY. But we know—

(At that moment the bathroom door opens. BERTRAM is standing in the doorway talking to LEOPOLD.)

BERTRAM. I don't want to be hard on you or hurt you in any way.

(At that moment the kitchen door opens. EDWARD is standing there speaking to LEOPOLD.)

EDWARD. Were you worried?

(At that moment the door of Suzana's room opens. SUZANA is standing there speaking to LEOPOLD.)

SUZANA. Are you sure you didn't get yourself into trouble again somehow?

BERTRAM. I'm not just speaking for myself.

EDWARD. Perhaps you should take some pills—

(At that moment the balcony door opens. LUCY is standing there in her bedspread and speaking to LEOPOLD.)

LUCY. You sang a different tune the first time you got me to stay here with you.

EDWARD. You ought to go and see Lucy.

FIRST SIDNEY. This could be what people are waiting for—

SECOND SIDNEY. You'll find a way—

SUZANA. What is there to consider, for goodness sake.

BERTRAM. And how are things between you and Suzana?

LUCY. You've had enough of me and now you want to get shot of me—

EDWARD. Did you sign anything?

FIRST SIDNEY. We've only taken the liberty of giving you our opinion—

SECOND SIDNEY. The opinion of ordinary people—

FIRST SIDNEY. Lots of ordinary people—

EDWARD. Some hero.

SUZANA. Some hero.

BERTRAM. Some hero.

LUCY. Some hero.

FIRST SIDNEY. You've had enough of me and now you want to get shot of me.

SECOND SIDNEY. Some hero.

FIRST SIDNEY. Did you sign anything?

LEOPOLD (*shouting*). GET OUT!

(*For a moment there is complete silence and then the doorbell rings*. LEOPOLD *runs into the bathroom*. BERTRAM *makes way for him and* LEOPOLD *disappears into the bathroom and immediately there is the sound of running water. All the people on stage disappear behind the doors through which they came*. FIRST *and* SECOND SIDNEY *disappear with their suitcases through the front door. They all go and all the doors except the bathroom door are closed. The only sound is running water and* LEOPOLD *gasping. The doorbell rings again. The curtain falls as the music begins to be heard*.)

SCENE SIX

The music fades as the curtain rises.

There is no one on the stage. The bathroom door is open. There is the sound of running water and of LEOPOLD *gasping. There is a short pause. Then the bell rings. The sound of water stops and* LEOPOLD *runs out of the bathroom. He was obviously having a shower. He is wet and is covered only by a towel wrapped round his waist. He runs to the main door, looks through the peep-hole, is taken aback, hesitates a moment and then opens the door*. MARGUERITE *enters*.

MARGUERITE. Good evening—

LEOPOLD (*a bit nonplussed*). Good evening—
 (*Short pause.*)
MARGUERITE.   Professor Nettles?
LEOPOLD.   Yes—
 (*Short pause.*)
MARGUERITE.   Sorry to disturb you—
LEOPOLD.   You're not disturbing me—
MARGUERITE.   I won't hold you up for long—
LEOPOLD.   I've got time—
 (*Short pause.*)
MARGUERITE.   My name's Marguerite. I'm a student of philosophy—
LEOPOLD.   At the university or a private student?
MARGUERITE.   Both—
 (MARGUERITE *walks to the middle of the room and looks round uncertainly.* LEOPOLD *closes the door. A short pause.*)
 Sit down—
MARGUERITE.   Thank you—
 (MARGUERITE *sits down shyly on the edge of the sofa.*)
LEOPOLD.   Would you like some rum?
MARGUERITE.   No—thank you—I'm not used to rum—
LEOPOLD.   One glass won't do you any harm—
 (LEOPOLD *pours some rum into the glass which has remained on the table.*)
MARGUERITE.   Well, thank you—
 (MARGUERITE *takes a very small sip and winces.*)
LEOPOLD.   Not bad is it?
MARGUERITE.   No—
 (*Awkward pause.*)
 You'll catch cold.
LEOPOLD.   Ah yes, of course—
 (LEOPOLD *goes quickly into the bathroom and comes back in a moment wearing a dressing gown under which he is naked. He sits down on the sofa next to* MARGUERITE *and smiles at her.* MARGUERITE *smiles back. There is a longer awkward pause.*)
MARGUERITE.   I know your work—
LEOPOLD.   Really? Which?
MARGUERITE.   *Phenomenology of Responsibility, Love and Nothingness, Ontology of the Human Self*—
LEOPOLD.   You've read all those?
MARGUERITE.   Several times—
LEOPOLD.   Well, I am impressed—
 (*Pause.*)
MARGUERITE.   I hear *Ontology of the Human Self* got you into trouble—
LEOPOLD.   It's because of that I'm supposed to go there—
MARGUERITE.   What—straight there? How come?
LEOPOLD.   Paragraph 511—intellectual hooliganism—
MARGUERITE.   That's awful!
LEOPOLD.   That's the sort of world we're living in—
MARGUERITE.   For such beautiful thoughts!
LEOPOLD.   Apparently someone didn't think they were so beautiful—

MARGUERITE.   And is it definite?
LEOPOLD.   I could get out of it by denying that I wrote it—
MARGUERITE.   Is that what they're offering you?
LEOPOLD.   Yes—
MARGUERITE.   They're disgusting!
 (*Pause.* MARGUERITE *takes a sip and winces.* LEOPOLD *promptly fills up her glass.*)
 Your essays have given me a great deal of—
LEOPOLD.   Yes? I'm so glad—
MARGUERITE.   It's because of them that I became interested in philosophy—
LEOPOLD.   Really?
MARGUERITE.   Somehow they opened my eyes—
LEOPOLD.   You're exaggerating—
MARGUERITE.   Really—
LEOPOLD.   Have another drink—
 (MARGUERITE *has a drink and winces.* LEOPOLD *promptly refills her glass. Awkward pause.*)
MARGUERITE.   Are you writing anything?
LEOPOLD.   I'm trying to—
MARGUERITE.   Could you tell me—excuse my curiosity— could you tell me what you're writing?
LEOPOLD.   I'm trying to think about love as a dimension of being—
MARGUERITE.   You touched on that a little in the second chapter of *Love and Nothingness*—
LEOPOLD.   That's right—
 (*Awkward pause.*)
MARGUERITE.   Professor—
LEOPOLD.   Yes, Marguerite?
MARGUERITE.   I wouldn't dare to trouble you—
LEOPOLD.   You're not troubling me at all! On the contrary—I'm very pleased to have met you—
MARGUERITE.   If it wasn't for the fact that I'm sure you're the only one who can help me—
LEOPOLD.   What's the matter?
MARGUERITE.   It's going to sound silly—
LEOPOLD.   You can tell me!
MARGUERITE.   I'm suddenly embarrassed—
LEOPOLD.   But why, there's no need—
 (MARGUERITE *has a drink and winces.* LEOPOLD *promptly refills her glass. Short pause.*)
MARGUERITE.   Where should I begin? I just don't know what to do—
LEOPOLD.   In your studies?
MARGUERITE.   In my life—
LEOPOLD.   In your life?
MARGUERITE.   I find everything so stifling—all those hopeless faces in the bus queues—the endless hue and cry in the streets—people twisted out of shape in their offices and everywhere else—the general misery of life—forgive me, I know it's silly, you don't even know me—but I didn't know anyone else I could turn to—
LEOPOLD.   I'm delighted that you should confide in me—

MARGUERITE.   I don't get on with my parents—they're middle class types who are always watching TV—I've no boyfriend—the other students seem terribly superficial—

LEOPOLD.   I know what you mean—

MARGUERITE.   You're not angry?

LEOPOLD.   Why do you make excuses for yourself all the time? What greater satisfaction could there be for a philosopher than to receive a visit from a reader in mid-crisis about the meaning of life?

MARGUERITE.   I know that you can't solve my problem for me—

LEOPOLD.   You're right in the sense that the meaning of life is not something which one can summarize or verbalize one way or the other and then hand over like a piece of information—it's not an object, it's more like an elusive spiritual state—and the more one needs it the more elusive it becomes—

MARGUERITE.   Yes, yes, that's exactly—

LEOPOLD.   On the other hand there is the fact—as I've already tried to show in *Ontology of the Human Self*—that there's a certain non-verbal, existential space in which—and only in which—one can get hold of something through experiencing the presence of another person—

MARGUERITE.   Forgive me, it's exactly that part—it's from chapter four—which made me decide to come and see you—

LEOPOLD.   There you are! But I wouldn't like to raise your hopes unduly, because the fact that I'm meditating on this subject doesn't automatically mean that I am myself capable of creating such a space—

MARGUERITE.   But you've been creating it for ages—by talking to me at all—by understanding me—forgive me, I'm probably a bit tipsy—

LEOPOLD.   Not at all! Drink up—

(MARGUERITE *takes a drink and winces.* LEOPOLD *promptly fills up her glass.*)

LEOPOLD.   I'll tell you something, Marguerite—honesty deserves honesty: if I am able to understand you then it is mainly because I'm in a similar or perhaps even worse situation than you—

MARGUERITE.   You? I can't believe it! You know so much—you've achieved so much—you're so wise—

LEOPOLD.   That guarantees nothing—

MARGUERITE.   I'm only a silly girl, but you—

LEOPOLD.   You're not silly—

MARGUERITE.   I am, I know it—

LEOPOLD.   You're clever, Marguerite—and not only that, you're beautiful—

MARGUERITE.   Me? Well, whatever next—

LEOPOLD.   I'll be quite frank with you, Marguerite: I'm in a very bad way—

MARGUERITE.   I know life has been hard on you but you seem so strong—

LEOPOLD.   Alas, that's only appearance. In reality I've had the feeling for some time now that something is collapsing inside me—as if an axis holding me together has started to break—the ground crumbling under my feet—I lack a fixed point from which everything inside me could grow and develop—I get the feeling sometimes that I'm not really doing anything except listening helplessly to the time going by. Gone is the perspective I once had—my humour—my industry and persistence—the pointedness of my observations—

MARGUERITE.   How beautifully you put it—

LEOPOLD.   You should have known me before! It's all gone, my irony, my self-irony, my capacity for enthusiasm, for emotional involvement, for commitment, even for sacrifice! This might disappoint you, Marguerite, but for a long time I haven't been the person that you obviously take me for! Basically I'm a tired, dried out, broken man—

MARGUERITE.   You mustn't speak like that, Professor! You're too hard on yourself! But even if it were all true the very fact that you are reflecting upon your situation shows that all is not lost—

LEOPOLD.   You're good to me, Marguerite! And please don't call me professor, it sounds so formal! Why aren't you drinking?

(MARGUERITE *has a drink and winces.* LEOPOLD *promptly fills up her glass. Short pause.*)

MARGUERITE.   So many people think so highly of you! Doesn't that alone give you strength?

LEOPOLD.   On the contrary! I often say to myself how wonderful it was when nobody was interested in me—when nobody expected anything from me and nobody was urging me to do things—I used to browse around the second-hand bookshops—studying modern philosophers at my leisure—spending the nights making notes from their works—taking walks in the parks and meditating—

MARGUERITE.   But it's thanks to all that that you are what you are today—

LEOPOLD.   That's true, but it's also true that I've taken upon myself a heavier burden that I'm able to bear—

MARGUERITE.   Leopold, I believe that you will win through!

LEOPOLD.   I have a feeling that my only way out is to accept a term there—somewhere far away from my nearest and dearest—and put my humble trust in a higher will, to give me the chance to atone for my guilt—to lose by apathy and regain my pride—and as a nameless cog in a giant machine to purify myself—thus and only thus—If I manage to drain the bitter cup with dignity—I can get back—perhaps—something of my lost human integrity—renew the hope inside me—reconstitute myself emotionally—open the door to a new life—

MARGUERITE (*shouts*). But Leopold!

LEOPOLD.   Yes?

MARGUERITE (*excitedly*). Don't you see that the punishment is deeply unjust and if you try—however honourably—to turn it into a purifying experience you'd just be agreeing with it and so prostrating yourself before it. And what's more, by giving it this so-called meaning you're hiding from yourself the fact that you're clinging to it as a kind of escape from your life, a way out of your problems. But however far they send you, punishment won't solve what you can't solve yourself! Don't you understand that you've done nothing and so there is nothing to atone! You're innocent!

LEOPOLD. Oh, Marguerite—why didn't I meet you before it was too late?

(LEOPOLD *takes hold of her hands and kisses them.* MARGUERITE *is embarrassed.* LEOPOLD *holds her hands. She drops her eyes. Long pause.*)

MARGUERITE (*whispering*). Leopold—

LEOPOLD. Yes—

MARGUERITE. Do you love anybody?

LEOPOLD. Ah, my dear girl, I really don't know if I'm capable of love—

MARGUERITE. Don't tell me that you've never felt anything towards a woman—

LEOPOLD. Nervousness—more with some, less with others—

MARGUERITE. You need love! Mad passionate true love! Didn't you yourself write in *Phenomenology of Responsibility* that a person who doesn't love doesn't exist? Only love will give you the strength to stand up to them!

LEOPOLD. That's easy for you to say, Marguerite, but where would one find it?

(MARGUERITE *takes a quick drink, winces and quietly blurts out.*)

MARGUERITE. With me!

LEOPOLD. What? You?

MARGUERITE (*excited*). Yes! You have given me back the meaning to my life, which is to give you the meaning back to yours! I'll save you!

(LEOPOLD *strokes her hair.*)

LEOPOLD. You're wonderful, Marguerite! But I can't allow you to throw your life away on someone as worthless as myself—

MARGUERITE. On the contrary I would be fulfilling my life!

LEOPOLD. Apart from the fact that I'm an old man—

MARGUERITE. That's nonsense! I've made up my mind—

LEOPOLD. If I'd known it would come to this I'd never have told you my problems—

MARGUERITE. Thank goodness you did! I'll give you back strength—courage—self-confidence—joy—appetite for life! I'll bring your failing heart back to life! I know you're capable of love! How else could you have written those things! I'll bring you back to life and at the same time back to philosophy!

(LEOPOLD *takes hold of* MARGUERITE's *arms and for a moment looks deeply into her eyes and then begins to kiss her rapidly over her face and neck.*)

MARGUERITE. Ah—Leopold—ah—I love you—I love your thoughts and your words—you awoke my love a long time ago without knowing it—without my knowing it— and now I'll awaken love in you!

(*At that moment the doorbell rings.* LEOPOLD *jumps up at once.*)

LEOPOLD (*whispering*). Quick—go out on the balcony!

MARGUERITE (*whispering*). Why?

LEOPOLD (*whispering*). They'll drag you off!

(LEOPOLD *takes her by the hand and hurries her to the balcony door. He opens the door and pushes her on to the balcony and closes the door. He runs into the bedroom leaving the door open. Pause. The doorbell rings again. Pause. Then* LEOPOLD, *grey-faced, emerges from the bedroom wearing a suit and an overcoat and carrying a small military valise. He goes to the front door. Opens it bravely.* FIRST CHAP *and* SECOND CHAP *enter.* LEOPOLD *closes the door behind them.*)

FIRST CHAP. On your own today?

LEOPOLD (*bravely*). Gentlemen! Do your duty! I'll get ready!

SECOND CHAP. What's the hurry? It may not come to the worst—

(*The* FIRST CHAP *goes to the balcony door, opens it and says:*)

FIRST CHAP. Come in, my little one—

(MARGUERITE *slowly enters the room.*)

LEOPOLD. Don't you dare touch her! If you drag her off, then—

SECOND CHAP. Then what?

LEOPOLD. Then—then—

FIRST CHAP. Don't you worry, there's no need for her to go anywhere. Today there'd be no point—

LEOPOLD. You're right. As you're obviously aware, I'm not going to sign that statement. I'd rather die than give up my own human identity—it's the only thing I've got!

SECOND CHAP. But Professor, why are you carrying on like that? You're not going anywhere—

LEOPOLD. Why not? I've told you quite clearly that I'm not going to sign anything! I'm not guilty!

FIRST CHAP. You don't have to sign anything! Your case has been adjourned indefinitely—

SECOND CHAP. Indefinitely for the time being.

FIRST CHAP. For the time being.

SECOND CHAP. Without signature!

LEOPOLD. What? Adjourned?

FIRST CHAP. That's right. Adjourned!

LEOPOLD. You mean no signature and no *there* either?

SECOND CHAP. For the time being, mind, for the time being—

LEOPOLD. I don't understand what it means—why don't you want my signature any more?

FIRST CHAP.   It would be just a formality. Who needs it? It's become pretty clear by now that in your case it would be superfluous—

LEOPOLD.   Are you trying to say that I am no longer me?

SECOND CHAP.   You said it, not me.

(*Short pause.* LEOPOLD *gazes at the* FIRST *and* SECOND CHAP *and then shouts.*)

LEOPOLD.   I don't want an adjournment! I want to go there!

(LEOPOLD *suddenly falls to his knees in front of the* CHAPS *and starts to sob.*)

I'm begging you—I beseech you—I can't go on living like this—

FIRST CHAP.   It seems you'll have to—

MARGUERITE (*calling to him*). Leopold get up! You're not going to beg them, are you!

LEOPOLD (*shouting at* MARGUERITE). Leave me alone! All of you leave me alone!

(LEOPOLD *collapses on the floor, banging his fists on it. The curtain falls and the music returns.*)

SCENE SEVEN

The music is fading and the curtain begins to rise slowly. LEOPOLD *is alone on the stage. He is sitting on the sofa staring at the front door. After a longer pause he gets up and goes to the door and looks through the peep-hole. Then he puts his ear to the door and listens intently. The lights start to come up in the auditorium and the music begins to be heard.* LEOPOLD *straightens up slowly, goes to the footlights and bows. At the same time all the other characters enter from the various doors and gather round* LEOPOLD *bowing. The curtain falls.*

END

FOCUS QUESTIONS

1. Briefly assess *Largo Desolato* within its historical context, highlighting the connections Havel has drawn between the real world and the one depicted in his play.
2. Show how language, characterization, and dramatic style enhance the themes of the play.
3. Develop a character sketch of the protagonist in which you carefully elaborate on his anti-heroic qualities.
4. In a short essay, defend *Largo Desolato* as a realistic work with absurdist elements or as an absurdist work with realistic elements.
5. Evaluate the comic elements in the play and show how they do or do not achieve tragic overtones.
6. With specific references to the text, show how theme and style are enlightened by the musical dimensions Havel has imposed on his play.
7. Discuss the significance of the play's final scene.

OTHER ACTIVITIES

1. Describe the color schemes and lighting designs you might employ for your own production of this play, and show why they would accommodate either an absurdist or realistic *mise-en-scène,* or perhaps both.
2. Read scene 6 aloud and describe ways in which you (as director) would handle Havel's sudden shift in dramatic tone.

BIBLIOGRAPHY

Freedman, Samuel G. ''Portrait of a Playwright As an Enemy of the State.'' *The New York Times,* 23 March 1986, sec. 2.

Havel, Václav. *Disturbing the Peace: A Conversation with Karel Hvizdala.* New York: Alfred Knopf, 1990.

Howe, Irving. ''One Can Stand Up to Lies.'' *The New York Times Book Review,* 17 June 1990.

''*Largo Desolato:* Václav Havel's New Work at the Akademietheater in Vienna.'' *Theater Heute* 6 (June, 1985).

Lordi, Karen E. '' 'Leave Me Alone!'—Chekhovian Echoes in Havel.'' *Theater* (Yale Publishing), 22, no. 3 (Summer/Fall 1991).

Patočhová, Jana. ''*Largo Desolato:* A Trap for the Audience.'' *Czech and Slovak Theatre* (January 1991).

Quinn, Michael L. ''*Largo Desolato* by Václav Havel.'' *Slavic and East European Performance* 12, no. 1 (Spring 1992).

Vladislav, Jan, ed. *Václav Havel or Living in Truth.* London: Faber and Faber, 1986.

Whipple, Tim D., ed. *After the Velvet Revolution: Václav Havel and the New Leaders of Czechoslovakia Speak Out.* Freedom House Press, 1990.

GLOSSARY

act A term designating the divisions of a play; a block of stage time that is sometimes divided into scenes to indicate other settings and actions.

acto A short satirical play developed by El Teatro Campesino to depict the plight of Mexican-American farmworkers in California.

aesthetic An artist's personally or culturally determined sense of what formal elements are appropriate for dramatic style.

aesthetic distance The acceptable physical and emotional space established between actor and audience.

agitprop Short for agitational propaganda; drama that delivers a specific political message and is designed to spur the audience to action.

agon A contest; suggests struggle or conflict; a formal debate or argument in classical Greek comedy.

Alexandrine verse The metrical verse format of neoclassical French tragedy; characterized by six accented beats to a line.

allegory A literary treatment in which stage characters are symbolic and function as personifications of ideas.

alternative theatre A term designating certain unconventional theatre styles in contrast with mainstream or commercial productions of plays.

analogous actions The paralleling of multiple plot structures in any single play.

antagonist A major character who is the protagonist's or hero's adversary; known as the villain in popular drama.

anti hero A protagonist who behaves passively or whose personality traits lack nobility.

apron The section of the stage that extends beyond the proscenium arch.

archetype A character who is the quintessential prototype for a person who shares the same traits, such as, the rebel, the villain, the womanizer, or the hero.

aside A dramatic convention in which a character talks to the audience without other characters hearing.

autos sacramentales Lyrical dialogues using symbolic stories to teach Catholic dogma; popular during Spain's Golden Age.

avant-garde A term often synonymous with "experimental," used to suggest the future direction of certain theatrical styles; in direct contrast with mainstream or commercial drama.

backdrop Sometimes called the cyclorama; a curtain-like panel positioned at the back of the stage that sets characters and props in relief and often lends a panoramic dimension to the dramatic action.

black comedy A theatrical style that uses the elements of comedy and farce to shock the audience into recognition about a social problem.

blank verse Stage dialogue patterned on unrhymed and loosely metered poetry.

blocking The performer's stage movements as set by the director to create effective stage pictures.

border A horizontal flat placed across the top of the stage to mask the lights that are hung above the stage.

bourgeois drama A popular dramatic style of the eighteenth century that focuses on merchant or middle-class characters and is characterized by sentimentality and the triumph of virtue over evil.

bowdlerization Taking its name from a nineteenth-century stage practitioner who served his own interests by tampering with established playtexts; a pejorative reference to inordinate textual changes that excise profane language or sexual references.

box set A set construction comprised of three flats and often a ceiling, creating the impression of an actual room.

Bunraku Japanese puppet theatre, which is characterized by a chanted narrative and by the presence of three puppeteers, dressed in black, who manipulate the nearly life-sized dolls in full view of the audience.

burlesque Originally an eighteenth- and nineteenth-century form of theatre once popular in England that was characterized by parodies of other plays or stories and the use of puns, jokes, and satirical music.

cabaret performance A popular form of entertainment in post-World War I Europe, in which song, dance, and innovative skits were staged in restaurants that served food and alcohol.

cadence The pattern of language created by the arrangement of stressed and unstressed syllables.

caesura In poetry, a break in the line.

canon In literature, those works recognized by experts which meet the artistic standards for the genre; all those works that are recognized as written by a specific author.

character A person in the play who speaks the playwright's dialogue or reacts to the events on stage.

chorus In the classical drama, a group of actors representing the voice of the community who speak and often move in unison to comment on the action.

chronicle play In the Elizabethan drama, a stage work that focuses on selected characters and events from English history.

claque The segment of the audience that reacts to a performance (or performer) in a vociferous and unruly manner; persons often hired by unscrupulous theatre managers to promote the success of any play or opera.

classicism In literature, a formal arrangement characterized by balance, proportion, and restraint—principles discussed in the works of Aristotle and Horace.

climax That part of the play that marks the height of the protagonist's crisis.

closet drama A drama enjoyed solely as a playreading experience, yet deemed unproducible for technical or literary reasons.

collective theatre The theatrical script that evolves out of the actors' improvisations, the designer's ideas, and the director's editorial eye, while the playwright serves as "recorder" of the performance piece during the rehearsal process.

comedia Any full-length play, whether serious or dramatic, that was popular during Spain's Golden Age.

comedy In the classical drama, a literary format that pays homage to the hero's triumph over calamity; rooted in ritual much like tragedy, except that renewal and rebirth are celebrated.

comedy of manners A term that describes the popular seventeenth-century satirical comedies of France and England; characterized by witty dialogue, sexual innuendo, and an emphasis on fashion and style.

comic relief In a serious play, a device in which the playwright introduces a humorous character or situation to offset the tragic circumstances of the stage action.

commedia dell'arte The popular performance style of the Italian Renaissance; improvisatory in format, performed in masks, and famous for its colorful and highly influential stock characters.

complication The rising and falling actions that fuel the plot and animate the characters; an important feature of Aristotle's design for tragedy.

confidant(e) A supporting character in whom the protagonist confides or shares background information relevant to the play's outcome.

conflict In Western drama, the problem or struggle shared by the characters, leading to the play's climax; an important feature of Aristotle's design for tragedy.

contaminatio A popular practice among Roman dramatists who merged the elements of two separate literary sources to fashion works of their own.

convention A device or practice that the audience agrees to accept even if it is unrealistic.

corrales Open courtyards surrounded by houses in which seventeenth-century Spanish plays were performed.

couplet Two successive poetic lines that rhyme and often signal the end of an act or scene.

cycles Short dramatic enactments inspired by the Bible which were performed in sequential order and eventually helped to fashion the English medieval drama; also known as Mysteries.

Dada The artistic movement developed after World War I that emphasized random and irrational expression as a way of attacking traditional artistic principles.

declamatory style Verbal delivery that is characterized by the emphasis on beautiful tones, rhetorical meaning and gesture, and clarity of speech rather than by the imitation of everyday speech.

decorum An expectation in the Renaissance that characters of distinct social strata will exhibit behaviors appropriate to their status and that the characters' social class will be appropriate for the type of play; for example, tragedy focuses on high characters, either royalty or mythological, heroic figures; comedy focuses on low characters, either the bourgeoisie or servants.

denouement The final outcome of the protagonist's fate, which usually follows the turning point.

deus ex machina Literally translated as "god from the machine;" a convention of Greek drama in which the god descended from a crane hovering above the stage to rescue the protagonist from danger; exemplified today by improbable endings in which the dramatic conflict is too easily resolved or the protagonist is released from harm's way in the "nick of time."

didacticism An emphasis on the instructional rather than entertainment value of the drama.

Dionysus The Greek god of wine and fertility, also known as Bacchus, in whose honor the Western tradition of drama began.

director The person in charge of all aspects of staging and interpreting the play.

director's theatre Productions in which the overall visual effects and interpretation of the script by the director take precedence over the play itself.

docudrama A stage work based on actual contemporary or historical characters or events which may incorporate real dialogue but may also be fictionalized.

documentary In the theatre, a work inspired by historical fact whose dialogue and actions are wholly derived from the recorded transcriptions of real-life participants in those events.

domestic drama A form of bourgeois drama that deals with family life.

double-entendre A literary device in which a character's witty wordplay may indicate one thing but imply something else, usually something risque.

downstage That area of the stage, behind the proscenium, nearest the audience.

dramatic irony A device that allows the audience to know more about certain characters and stage actions than the characters themselves know.

dramatis personae Literally, the cast of characters in the play.

dramaturgy The practice and study of how plays are created and structured.

drawing-room comedy A form of bourgeois drama popular in the early twentieth century which sets the action in an upper middle-class drawing room and its adjacent garden or balcony.

drop A large painted curtain that serves as the scenery.

Elizabethan drama The prolific body of stage work represented by verse dramatists like Shakespeare and Marlowe, and named after the ruling English monarch, Elizabeth I (1533–1603).

emblematic Refers to some object or situation that has a symbolic purpose.

ensemble The interdependent members of an acting company; the emphasis of group artistry versus solo performance.

entremeses See *interlude.*

environmental theatre A term that describes performances in which there is no separate stage or playing area and in which the actors play out their actions around audience members who share the same space.

epic theatre A term originated by Erwin Piscator and altered by Bertolt Brecht to differentiate their styles; demands an intellectual or objective audience response from theatre that relies on eliciting an emotional or subjective response; characterized by the use of projections of film and slides, narratives told directly to the audience, and stage effects that draw attention to the theatrical devices of the production.

epiphany A character's sudden awareness of what has been happening on stage or what the event really means.

episode In classical Greek drama, a scene of dramatic action.

eponymous character The protagonist after whom the play is named: for example, *Hamlet.*

existentialism A philosophical premise that emphasizes the isolation of human experience in a hostile or indifferent universe; stresses freedom of choice and responsibility for the consequences of the stage character's actions.

exodos The final scene that resolves a Greek tragedy and concludes with the chorus' departure from the stage.

exposition Background information that will impact on the events of the play and that is revealed to the audience through the dialogue.

expressionism A theatrical style characterized by distorted physical perspectives and jarring language codes in which the playwright imposes his or her own view of reality on the outside world or attempts to depict psychological states or nightmares reflecting a character's emotions.

farce A style of comedy that resorts to coarse wit, exaggerated incongruities, and the mechanical antics of sight gags to incite laughter.

feminist aesthetic A style of theatre that results from the need to address the specific political, social, and emotional concerns of women; often characterized by a conscious rejection of dramatic principles derived from the theories of Aristotle.

foil A character much like the protagonist who sets him or her off by serving as a basis for comparison.

folk drama Nationalistic plays that focus on the economic and personal struggles, physical and behavioral characteristics, and beliefs of unsophisticated, common people.

footlights Prior to the development of sophisticated electrical equipment, light sources positioned at the proscenium opening which illuminated the actors' faces from the floor.

foreshadowing A device in which the playwright suggests the final outcome early in the action, although the audience may not realize its function until the play's end.

forestage The stage apron or area that extends beyond the proscenium.

fourth wall The realistic convention in which an imaginary wall of the box set is all that separates the audience from the actors, so that the spectator serves as voyeur, cognizant of the action that transpires in the privacy of a room or office.

futurism An artistic movement in Italy in the early twentieth century which celebrated technology, machines, speed, light, and war, and assaulted audiences with abusive language, flying objects, and industrial noise.

genre A term that categorizes different literary works according to their formal elements or historic periods.

gestic A word used to describe language or situations that simultaneously convey the meaning of what is said or done while commenting on it.

Guerrilla theatre A term that refers to unpublicized political theatre performances since the 1960s that took place in the streets and dramatized oppressive social and governmental practices which impinged on the rights of the disenfranchised.

guild In the medieval drama, the organization of skilled artisans by trade; collectively responsible for producing the cycle of plays to be performed for the festival of Corpus Christi.

hana In Noh, the "flower" or freshness of the actor's performance, which gives it a quality of the unexpected and sustains audience interest.

hashigakari On the Noh stage, the bridgeway from which the *shite* or primary actor and doer enters and exits.

high comedy Intellectual rather than physical comedy relying on verbal jokes and wit rather than pratfalls; characteristic of the Restoration drama as well as the modern comedy of manners.

hyperrealism A late twentieth-century style in which the most minute details of everyday life, including bathroom rituals, are depicted on stage.

iambic pentameter A popular metrical verse pattern, featuring five accented beats to each line; characteristic of Shakespeare's work.

iconography A symbolic vocabulary of visual images through which playwrights reveal their dramatic purposes.

improvisation Spontaneous dialogue and actions, usually unscripted.

interlude A short play, usually comic, performed at court between other parts of an event or courses of a banquet.

intermezzi Short pieces of entertainment or skits that were performed between the acts.

irony An unexpected turn in the action or outcome of the play.

jeu-de-paume In seventeenth-century France, tennis courts that were transformed into theatre spaces.

jo-ha-kyu Literally means "introduction, development, and frenzy;" the aesthetic principle that determines how the types of Noh plays will be presented in the five-play cycle; refers to the progression of units of action in a Noh performance.

Kabuki The most popular and spectacular form of Japanese theatre, performed entirely by men in an unrealistic style; combines music, dance, and dramatic scenes to narrate stories often about honor and love.

katharsis The arousal of pity and terror that the audience experiences as redemptive after viewing tragedy.

kokata The child performer in Noh drama.

komos In classical Greek comedy, a dance and celebratory procession that signifies the restoration of order.

kusemai In Noh drama, the main narrative dance performed to an irregular drum beat.

kyogen A traditional genre of Japanese theatre which consists of short comic plays that poke fun at human foibles and serve as interludes between the five plays that constitute a Noh performance.

lazzi In the *commedia dell'arte,* stock bits of physical business or dialogue used to provoke laughter from the audience.

libretto The scripted verbal text for an opera.

little theatre movement During the end of the nineteenth century and early twentieth century in Europe and America, the development of small, independent community-based theatres which produced new or noncommercial plays to small audiences.

ludi Spectator games that constituted one aspect of the diverse Roman entertainments.

mansions In medieval drama, structures representing individual dwellings or locations placed around the playing area for the presentation of mysteries or morality plays.

masque A form of entertainment in which the performers, often courtiers, use pantomime, music, and dance to portray historical or mythological characters.

medieval drama The mysteries and moralities of the tenth through fifteenth centuries; evolved from church ritual and performed by guilds, with plots inspired by the Bible.

melodrama A term first coined in the eighteenth century for popular plays that used music to underscore the moral lesson of the action; by the nineteenth century, any play in which the hero or heroine is rewarded and the villain is punished after a series of sensational situations.

metatheatre A term that describes plays that call attention to their design and content and, in doing so, comment on the nature of theatre.

Middle Comedy A transitional style of ancient Greek comedy that dealt with domestic issues and everyday life and diminished the importance of the chorus.

miles gloriosus Literally the "braggart soldier;" a popular comic type from Roman comedy.

miracle play A type of medieval drama in which the Virgin Mary provided a solution to an otherwise hopeless situation.

mise-en-scène The arrangement of physical elements such as actors, props, set, and lighting to create the stage pictures for the drama.

mito A transitional performance style developed by El Teatro Campesino in which non-human characters and mythological figures explore narratives rooted in Mayan ritual.

monologue An uninterrupted speech by one character; a popular format in classical drama, less often used in realism.

monomane In Noh, the *shite's* ability to create believable representations of actions through slow, suggestive movements.

montage A cinematic device in which one shot overlaps with one or more other shots to create a single scenic impression.

moralities In the medieval drama, allegorical plays whose characters and themes demonstrate the triumph of good over evil.

motif A recurring element that contributes to the central theme of the play.

motivation A term from the Stanislavsky system of acting which refers to the dramatic justification for a character's actions.

mysteries Another name for the medieval cycle plays whose stories were drawn from the Bible.

naturalism A variation of realism which represents a "slice of life;" the audience observes how accumulation of details from the physical environment and a character's heredity determine his or her behaviors and personality; an influential literary style that emerged in the mid-nineteenth century.

neoclassicism A literary and artistic style of the Renaissance that revived the principles and standards set down by the ancient Greeks.

New Comedy A form of later Greek comedy dealing with the domestic problems of middle-class Athenians often characterized by reversals of fortune, mistaken or concealed identities, and thwarted lovers.

Noh Classical Japanese theatre dating from the fourteenth century that has its roots in Shintoism and Buddhism and is characterized by colorful costumes, masks, and carefully ordered and stylized movement.

okina The god plays in Noh.

Old Comedy Classical Greek comedy associated with Aristophanes in which the social and political conditions as well as selected public figures of Athens were satirized.

orchestra The circular performance space in Greek drama; also refers to the ground-floor seating area of most present-day theatres.

pageant wagons Constructed to transport players and stage sets from one town to the next when the medieval cycles expanded and could no longer be contained in the church; contributed to the secularization of drama.

parabasis In the Greek Old Comedy, a choral ode in which the playwright addressed the audience directly and which had no significant bearing on the dramatic action.

parodos The entrance to the orchestra of the ancient Greek theatre; the choral ode in which the chorus makes its entrance in the drama.

patio The pit area in Spain's Golden Age theatre.

performance art An avant-garde visual art form that depends on the blending of music, painting, dance, and drama.

persona Originally referred to the mask of clay worn by the actor; in the modern theatre, the public face or pose a character assumes in order to protect him or herself.

personification A literary device of the medieval morality play in which characters are the embodiment of universal qualities such as Good, Greed, and Gluttony.

pit The floor area in front of the stage where patrons stood to watch the performance.

plaudite The closing segment of Roman comedy in which a stage character sought audience approval and applause.

playwright's theatre A term that points to the visibility and popularity of playwrights, insofar as attracting audience support and approval; characteristic of the Elizabethan and Jacobean dramas.

plot The arrangement of the dramatic action into a cohesive storyline.

poetic realism A contemporary literary style whose characters and themes are tempered with expressive or heightened language and symbolic overtones.

poetry in the theatre The use of verse for expression on stage; characteristic of the classical Greek and the Elizabethan drama.

poetry of the theatre The use of prose to communicate the heightened emotional expression that is often the domain of verse on stage.

pole and chariot Giacomo Torelli's system for the simultaneous change of scenery; scenic flats attached to poles connected to chariots below the stage floor that are moved by running the chariots through a pulley system along tracks on the basement floor.

postmodernism In the drama, productions characterized by a disunified and layered structure of elements and the use of anachronistic "quotations" of costumes and props in order to make a contemporary statement.

prologue In the classical Greek drama, an introductory scene prior to the chorus' entrance; any introductory scene or speech that is not directly related to the main action.

prompter's box A small space at the center and foot of the stage; reserved for the person who follows the script and feeds forgotten lines to the actors.

proscenium Comes from the Greek *proskenion* or *proscenion;* in Greek drama, the forestage on which the leading actors spoke their lines; in modern drama, the arch that frames the stage picture and separates the stage from the auditorium.

prose drama The nonverse play whose language reflects the realistic speech of modern characters.

protagonist The central figure or hero of the drama.

raisonneur In French neoclassical drama, a character who presents the point of view closest to that of the playwright.

raked stage A playing area that inclines upstage; originally introduced to create the three-dimensional effects of prospective scene painting.

realism The literary style of the late nineteenth century that sought to depict the problems of everyday life of the bourgeoisie and lower classes.

Restoration The period in English history after 1660 when King Charles II was restored to the throne and the Puritans lost their power, thus enabling the theatres to reopen.

Restoration Drama A brief but lively era of the English stage (1660–1688) that introduced women in prominent stage roles and was renowned for witty comedies and boldly etched characters who mirrored the modish intrigues of their courtly audience.

revue Theatrical entertainment consisting of songs, dances, and skits which usually parody topical events or current social trends.

romanticism An episodic style of drama from the late eighteenth to the mid-nineteenth century that focused on exotic settings, individual emotions, and championed those outcasts from society who broke the rules.

rounds The earthen dug-outs that served the performance of medieval cycle plays, notably in Cornwall.

saragaku A form of Japanese masked, ritual dance that developed into Noh.

satire A literary form that aims at ridiculing negative aspects of human behavior or social conventions for the purpose of persuading the audience that there is need for change.

scaena frons The three-dimensional architectural facade that served as the background in the Roman theatre.

scenario An outline rather than a fully scripted text for any performance; the characteristic format of the *commedia dell'arte.*

scene Smaller units of stage time that indicate a change of characters, setting, or action; in consecutive order, constituting an entire act.

scrim A cloth curtain that can be painted to create the illusion of a solid wall or can be illuminated from behind to create a semi-transparent wall through which the action can be viewed.

sentimental comedy A bourgeois form developed in response to the bawdy humor of the Restoration in which characters, who are often in distress, are extolled for their virtues while their vices are diminished.

set A construction that serves to represent an actual or symbolic place in which the stage action transpires.

shimai The final dance performed by the *shite* in the Noh.

shite In Noh, the primary actor or doer who portrays the protagonist.

soggetti The written plot outlines or scenarios used in *commedia dell'arte.*

soliloquy A lengthy speech representing the private thoughts of the stage character.

stage left Designating the left side of the stage from the actor's point of view as he or she faces the audience.

stage right Designating the right side of the stage from the actor's point of view as he or she faces the audience.

stasimon In classical Greek drama, the choral odes that comment on the episodes which immediately precede them.

stations In the medieval drama, the physical locations where audiences gathered around scaffold stages or waited for traveling pageant wagons to view the short cycle plays performed on them.

stereopticon Also known as a magic lantern; a two-projector machine that allows visual images to focus and then dissolve.

stereotype A simplified and standard conception of the appearance and behavioral characteristics of people whose ethnicity, religion, and race differ from the audience.

stream of consciousness A device through which the playwright expresses the disordered and random internal responses of his characters; often the function of soliloquies.

structuralism In drama, a form of "new theatre" in which the structure is the content.

subplot A secondary storyline that is subordinate to the central one.

subtext A hidden level of meaning that surfaces slowly through character interaction and subtleties of language.

surrealism In drama, a style in which the irrationality of the emotions, particularly the subconscious as exhibited in dreams, is mirrored in the imagery and the stage actions.

symbolic nomenclature Affixing representative names to stage characters.

symbolism An artistic movement in late nineteenth- and early twentieth-century Europe in which poetic and spiritual matters were dramatized; characterized by non-realistic actions, atmospheric settings, and symbolic language used to capture a sense of subjective reality.

tableau A highly theatricalized but silent stage picture of characters seemingly frozen in time.

theatre-of-fact When the events on stage have been inspired by real characters and incidents from history; related to the documentary and the docudrama.

theatre of the absurd A style of the avant-garde drama in which language and action reflect the philosophical premise that humankind's condition on earth is hopeless and meaningless.

theme The central point or underlying message of the play.

thrust stage A performance space extending out to the audience so that patrons can be seated around three sides; similar to the Elizabethan stage.

tragedy In classical drama, a literary format that traces the downfall of a heroic, mythological, or aristocratic protagonist

and arouses pity and terror in the spectator.

tragicomedy A Renaissance term that describes plays centering on tragic themes or noble characters but ending happily; in twentieth-century drama, plays that contain both serious and comic elements.

tragic flaw A weakness in the protagonist that prompts his downfall and arouses our pity.

trilogy In the classical drama, the flexible three-play format that allowed the playwright to follow his protagonist or theme from one setting or action to another, but not within the same play.

trope A segment of chanted dialogue from the Christian mass; inspired fuller liturgical plays and led to the tradition of medieval drama.

unities Aristotle's rule that the play should tell a single story (action); that is should happen in a single day (time); and that it should occupy a single setting (place); hence the unities of action, time, and place.

upstage (n.) The area of the performance space farthest away from the audience; toward the rear of the stage; (v.) when an actor draws attention away from the central action either by doing too much business at the rear of the stage or by looking toward the rear of the stage while speaking.

vaudeville Originally a form of popular entertainment in eighteenth-century France which later developed into performances consisting of variety acts

with singers, dancers, acrobats, jugglers, ventriloquists, and animal trainers.

verisimilitude The expectation that the actions of the drama and the characters' behaviors will have the appearance of the truth and will be believable.

verse drama The play whose dialogue is comprised of poetry; demonstrates the use of poetry in the theatre.

waki In Noh, the second character or sideman who generally introduces the story and serves as confidant.

wakizure Those performers of Noh who serve as the companions to the sideman.

well-made play A manner of constructing a suspenseful dramatic plot which usually revolves around the unraveling of a secret through the presence of external objects, letters, or messages from strangers and is organized around a cause-and-effect structure.

wing and grove The traditional English method of changing scenery, in which painted flats slide on and off the stage through grooves in the floor and meet at the center to form shutters that create a background against which the dramatic action is played.

yugen In Noh, the ability of the *shite* to create a fragile and graceful quality that reveals the loneliness of old age and the mutability of life.

zanni The clown characters of the *commedia dell'arte* who play servant roles and are responsible for the acrobatics, juggling, and sight gags.

CREDITS